COLLINS

Compact Dictionary & Thesaurus

COLLINS

Compact Dictionary & Thesaurus

An Imprint of HarperCollins*Publishers*

Second edition 2008

www.collinsdictionaries.com

Collins is an imprint
of HarperCollins Publishers.

HarperCollins Publishers
10 East 53rd Street, New York, NY 10022

ISBN 978-0-06-137491-3

www.harpercollins.com

HarperCollins books may be purchased for educational, business, or sales promotional use. For information please write: Special Markets Department, HarperCollins Publishers, 10 East 53rd Street, New York, NY 10022.

Typeset by Interactive Sciences Limited, Gloucester, England

Printed and bound in the United States of America by RR Donnelley

CONTENTS

vi
Editorial Staff

vii
Foreword

ix–xii
Guide to the Text

xiii
Abbreviations used in this Dictionary & Thesaurus

1–686
Compact Dictionary & Thesaurus

1
Microsoft® Office – the basics and beyond

EDITORIAL STAFF

EDITORS

Frank Abate

Penny Hands

Emma McDade

Cormac McKeown

Anne Robertson

Jennifer Sagala

Elspeth Summers

Paige Weber

FOR THE PUBLISHERS

Morven Dooner

Elaine Higgleton

The Compact Dictionary & Thesaurus provides two kinds of language help, arranged on the same page for quick and easy look-up. In the top section of each page you will find a dictionary text which gives help with spellings and meanings, while the lower section of each page provides a matching thesaurus with a choice of synonyms. This layout is refreshingly clear and clutter-free, taking you straight to the information you want.

The dictionary text uses a clear and accessible defining style. Every definition is presented in everyday English. Where a word has more than one sense, the most common in today's language is given first. Other senses of a word—for example, historical and technical senses—are explained after its primary present-day meaning. The dictionary includes spelling help for all irregular forms of words and simple pronunciations for words that may be unfamiliar or confusing.

The thesaurus text is designed to help you find the right word for any occasion. The synonym lists are divided by sense, with the most useful synonym for each sense given first in capital letters. This layout enables you to see at once which sense of the word is being referred to, which is particularly helpful when an entry word has a number of different senses. It also gives you an idea of which synonym is the closest alternative to the word you have looked up.

The Microsoft® Supplement will help you get the most from your Microsoft software, by explaining clearly and concisely the most useful Microsoft programs: Word, Excel, Powerpoint, and Outlook. With step-by-step instructions and illustrative screenshots, this guide is simple and user-friendly.

This book is thus a uniquely helpful reference tool and an ideal companion for anyone who wants to increase their command of English.

USING THE DICTIONARY

Main Entry Words printed in colour bold type, eg

ab·bey

All main entry words, including abbreviations and combining forms, in one alphabetical sequence, eg

al·ge·bra
ALGOL
al·go·rithm

Variant Spellings shown in full, eg

an·eu·rysm, an·eu·rism

Pronunciations given in square brackets; the word is respelt as it is pronounced, with the stressed syllable in capital letters, eg

ca·chet [ka-SHAY]

Note: the symbol schwa (ə) is used to represent the neutral vowel sound typically occurring in unstressed syllables.

In some entries, the pronunciation is adequately shown by placing a mark (`) immediately after the syllable that carries the main stress, as in **mon·soon'**.

Center dots, as in **ab·sinthe** and **mol·lusk**, are used to indicate divisions between syllables.

Parts of Speech shown in italics, eg

a·blaze [ə-BLAYZ] *adjective*

When a word can be used as more than one part of speech, the change of part of speech is shown after an empty arrow, eg

mock [mok] *verb transitive* **1** make fun of, ridicule **2** mimic ▷ *verb intransitive* **3** scoff ▷ *noun* **4** act of mocking **5** laughing stock...

Parts of speech may be combined for some words, eg

an·y [EN-ee] *adjective, pronoun* **1** one indefinitely **2** some **3** every

Cross References shown in bold type, eg

lawyer *see* **law**

Irregular Parts or confusing forms of verb, nouns, adjectives, and adverbs shown in bold type, eg

be·gin [bi-GIN] *verb* **be·gan, be·gun, be·gin·ning**
col·o·ny [KOL-ə-nee] *noun, plural* **-nies**
hap·py *adjective* **-pi·er, -pi·est**

Meanings separated by sense numbers, eg

cas·u·al [KAZH-oo-əl] *adjective* **1** accidental **2** unforeseen **3** occasional **4** unconcerned **5** informal

Phrases and Idioms included immediately after the meanings of the main entry word, eg

salt [sawlt] *noun* ... *verb transitive*...
with a pinch of salt allowing for exaggeration **worth one's salt** efficient

Related Words shown in smaller bold type in the same paragraph as the main entry word, eg

ab·surd' *adjective* contrary to reason > **ab·surd'i·ty** *noun*

Note: where the meaning of a related word is not given, it may be understood from the main entry word, or from another related word.

Compounds shown in alphabetical order at the end of the paragraph, eg

hand *noun* ... **hand'stand** *noun* act of supporting body in upside-down position by hands alone
hand'writ·ing *noun* way person writes

USING THE THESAURUS

Main Entry Words printed in colour bold type, eg

abbey

All main entry words, including abbreviations and combining forms, in one alphabetical sequence, eg

abject
ablaze
able

Variant spellings shown in full, eg

amok *or* **amuck**

Parts of Speech	shown in italics, eg
	ablaze *adjective*
	When a word can be used as more than one part of speech, the change of part of speech is shown after an empty arrow, eg
	mock *verb* **1** LAUGH AT, deride, jeer ... ▷ *adjective* **3** IMITATION ...
	Parts of speech may be combined for some words, eg
	bat *noun*, *verb* HIT, bang,smack ...
Sense Numbers	shown in bold type, eg
	mock *verb* **1** LAUGH AT, deride, jeer ...
Key Synonyms	shown in small capitals, eg
	mock ... LAUGH AT
Cross References	shown in bold type, eg
	amuck *see* **amok**
Synonyms	separated by commas, eg
	mock *verb* **1** LAUGH AT, deride, jeer, make fun of, poke fun at, ridicule, scoff
Phrases and Idioms	included in entry, eg
	amok *or* **amuck** *adverb* ▷ **run amok**

ABBREVIATIONS USED IN THIS DICTIONARY & THESAURUS

abbrev	abbreviation
AD	anno Domini
Afr	Africa(n)
Amer	America(n)
approx	approximately
Aust	Australia(n)
BC	before Christ
Brit	British
Can	Canada, Canadian
chem	chemistry
comp	comparative
cu	cubic
dial	dialect
dim	diminutive
E	East
eg	for example
Eng	English
esp	especially
etc	et cetera
fem	feminine
foll	followed
Ger	German
Gr	Greek
hist	history
ie	that is
ind	indicative
It	Italian
k	kilogram(s)
km	kilometer(s)
l	liter(s)
Lat	Latin
lb	pound(s)
m	meter(s)
masc	masculine
math	mathematics
med	medicine
mm	millimeter(s)
mus	music
N	North
NZ	New Zealand
oft	often
orig	originally
pers	person
pert	pertaining
pl	plural
poss	possessive
pp	past participle
pres t	present tense
pr p	present participle
pt	past tense
®	trademark
RC	Roman Catholic
S	South
S Afr	South Africa(n)
Scot	Scottish
sing	singular
Sp	Spanish
sq	square
sup	superlative
US	United States
usu	usually
W	West

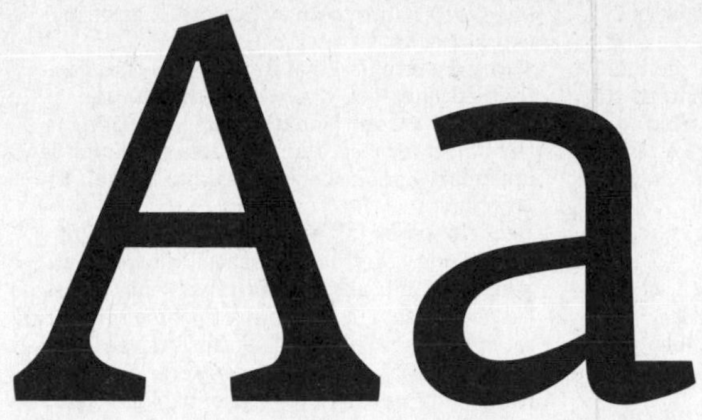

a *adjective* indefinite article, used before a noun being mentioned for the first time
aard•vark [AHRD-vahrk] *noun* S African mammal feeding on ants and termites
a•back [ə-BAK] *adverb* **taken aback** startled
ab•a•cus [AB-ə-kəs] *noun* **1** counting device of beads on wire frame **2** flat tablet at top of architectural column
ab•a•lo•ne [ab-ə-LOH-nee] *noun* edible shellfish, yielding mother-of-pearl
a•ban•don [ə-BAN-dən] *verb transitive* **1** desert **2** give up altogether ▷ *noun* **3** freedom from inhibitions, etc. > **a•ban'doned** *adjective* **1** deserted, forsaken **2** uninhibited **3** wicked
a•base [ə-BAYS] *verb transitive* **based, -bas•ing** humiliate, degrade > **a•base'ment** *noun*
a•bash [ə-BASH] *verb transitive* (*usually passive*) confuse, make ashamed > **a•bash'ment** *noun*
a•bate [ə-BAYT] *verb* **-bat•ed, -bat•ing** make or become less, diminish > **a•bate'ment** *noun*
ab•at•toir [AB-ə-twahr] *noun* slaughterhouse
ab•bey [AB-ee] *noun, plural* **-beys 1** dwelling place of community of monks or nuns **2** church of an abbey
ab•bot [AB-ət] *noun* head of abbey or monastery
ab•bre•vi•ate [ə-BREE-vee-ayt] *verb transitive* **-at•ed, -at•ing** shorten, abridge > **ab•bre•vi•a'tion** *noun* shortened form of word or phrase
ab•di•cate [AB-di-kayt] *verb* **-cat•ed, -cat•ing** formally give up (throne, etc.) > **ab•di•ca'tion** *noun*
ab•do•men [AB-də-mən] *noun* belly > **ab•dom'i•nal** *adjective*
ab•duct [ab-DUKT] *verb transitive* carry off, kidnap > **ab•duc'tion** *noun*
ab•er•ra•tion [ab-ə-RAY-shən] *noun* **1** deviation from what is normal **2** flaw **3** lapse > **ab•er•rant** [ə-BER-ənt] *adjective*
a•bet [ə-BET] *verb transitive* **-bet•ted, -bet•ting**

abandon *verb* **1** LEAVE, desert, forsake, strand **2** GIVE UP, relinquish, surrender, yield ▷ *noun* **3** WILDNESS, recklessness
abandonment *noun* LEAVING, dereliction, desertion, forsaking
abashed *adjective* EMBARRASSED, ashamed, chagrined, disconcerted, dismayed, humiliated, mortified, shamefaced, taken aback
abate *verb* DECREASE, decline, diminish, dwindle, fade, lessen, let up, moderate, relax, slacken, subside, weaken
abbey *noun* MONASTERY, convent, friary, nunnery, priory
abbreviate *verb* SHORTEN, abridge, compress, condense, contract, cut, reduce, summarize
abbreviation *noun* SHORTENING, abridgment, contraction, reduction, summary, synopsis
abdicate *verb* GIVE UP, abandon, quit, relinquish, renounce, resign, step down (*informal*)
abdication *noun* GIVING UP, abandonment, quitting, renunciation, resignation, retirement, surrender
abduct *verb* KIDNAP, carry off, seize, snatch (*slang*)
abduction *noun* KIDNAPING, carrying off, seizure
aberration *noun* ODDITY, abnormality, anomaly, defect, irregularity, lapse, peculiarity, quirk

assist, encourage, esp. in doing wrong > **a•bet'tor, a•bet'ter** *noun*
a•bey•ance [ə-BAY-əns] *noun* condition of not being in use or action
ab•hor' *verb transitive* **-horred, -hor•ring** dislike strongly, loathe > **ab•hor'rent** *adjective* hateful
a•bide [ə-BĪD] *verb transitive* **a•bode'** *or* **a•bid'ed, a•bid'ing** 1 endure, put up with ▷ *verb intransitive* **a•bode'** *or* **a•bid'ed, a•bid'ing** 2 (*obsolete*) stay, reside **abide by** obey
a•bil•i•ty [ə-BIL-i-tee] *noun, plural* **-ties** 1 competence, power 2 talent
ab•ject [AB-jekt] *adjective* 1 humiliated, wretched 2 despicable > **ab•ject'ness** *noun*
ab•jure [ab-JOOR] *verb transitive* **-jured, -jur•ing** give up by oath, renounce > **ab•ju•ra'tion** *noun*
a•blaze [ə-BLAYZ] *adjective* burning
a•ble [AY-bəl] *adjective* capable, competent > **a'bled** *adjective* having a range of physical powers as specified: *differently abled* > **a'bly** *adverb* > **a'ble-bod'ied** *adjective*
ab•lu•tion [ə-BLOO-shən] *noun* (*usually plural*) act of washing (oneself)
ab•ne•gate [AB-ni-gayt] *verb transitive* **-gat•ed, -gat•ing** give up, renounce > **ab•ne•ga'tion** *noun*
ab•nor•mal [ab-NOR-məl] *adjective* 1 irregular 2 not usual or typical 3 freakish, odd > **ab•nor•mal'i•ty** *noun, plural* **-ties** > **ab•nor'mal•ly** *adverb*
a•board [ə-BORD] *adverb* on board, on ship, train, or aircraft
a•bode [ə-BOHD] *noun* 1 home 2 dwelling 3 *pt./pp. of* **abide**
a•bol•ish [ə-BOL-ish] *verb transitive* do away with > **ab•o•li'tion** *noun* > **ab•o•li'tion•ist** *noun* one who wishes to do away with something, esp. slavery
a•bom•i•nate [ə-BOM-ə-nayt] *verb transitive* **-nat•ed, -nat•ing** detest > **a•bom'i•na•ble** *adjective* > **a•bom•i•na'tion** *noun* 1 loathing 2 the object loathed > **abominable snowman** large legendary apelike creature said to inhabit the Himalayas
ab•o•rig•i•nal [ab-ə-RIJ-ə-nl] *adjective* 1 (of people, etc.) original or earliest known in an area 2 of, relating to aborigines > **ab•o•rig'i•ne** [-ə-nee] *noun* 1 one of race of people inhabiting an area when European settlers arrived 2 original inhabitant of country, etc. 3 (**Ab•o•rig'i•ne**) one of a race of people originally inhabiting Australia
a•bort [ə-BORT] *verb* 1 (cause to) end prematurely (esp. pregnancy) ▷ *verb intransitive* 2 give birth to dead fetus 3 fail > **a•bor'tion** *noun* 1 operation to terminate pregnancy 2 something deformed > **a•bor'tion•ist** *noun* one who performs abortion, esp. illegally > **a•bor'tive** *adjective* unsuccessful
a•bound [ə-BOWND] *verb intransitive* 1 be plentiful 2 overflow > **a•bound'ing** *adjective*
a•bout [ə-BOWT] *adverb* 1 on all sides 2 nearly 3 up and down 4 out, on the move ▷ *preposition* 5 around 6 near 7 concerning 8 ready to > **about turn** reversal, complete change
a•bove [ə-BUV] *adverb* 1 higher up ▷ *preposition* 2 over 3 higher than, more than 4 beyond

abet *verb* HELP, aid, assist, connive at, support
abeyance *noun*
▷ **in abeyance** SHELVED, hanging fire, on ice (*informal*), pending, suspended
abhor *verb* HATE, abominate, detest, loathe, shrink from, shudder at
abhorrent *adjective* HATEFUL, abominable, disgusting, distasteful, hated, horrid, loathsome, offensive, repulsive, scuzzy (*slang*)
abide *verb* TOLERATE, accept, bear, endure, put up with, stand, suffer
abide by *verb* OBEY, agree to, comply with, conform to, follow, observe, submit to
abiding *adjective* EVERLASTING, continuing, enduring, lasting, permanent, persistent, unchanging
ability *noun* SKILL, aptitude, capability, competence, expertise, proficiency, talent
abject *adjective* 1 MISERABLE, deplorable, forlorn, hopeless, pitiable, wretched
2 SERVILE, cringing, degraded, fawning, groveling, submissive
ablaze *adjective* ON FIRE, aflame, alight, blazing, burning, fiery, flaming, ignited, lighted
able *adjective* CAPABLE, accomplished, competent, efficient, proficient, qualified, skillful
able-bodied *adjective* STRONG, fit, healthy, robust, sound, sturdy
abnormal *adjective* UNUSUAL, atypical, exceptional, extraordinary, irregular, odd, peculiar, strange, uncommon
abnormality *noun* ODDITY, deformity, exception, irregularity, peculiarity, singularity, strangeness
abode *noun* HOME, domicile, dwelling, habitat, habitation, house, lodging, pad (*slang, dated*), quarters, residence
abolish *verb* DO AWAY WITH, annul, cancel, destroy, eliminate, end, eradicate, put an end to, quash, rescind, revoke, stamp out
abolition *noun* ENDING, cancellation, destruction, elimination, end, extermination, termination, wiping out
abominable *adjective* TERRIBLE, despicable, detestable, disgusting, hateful, horrible, horrid, lousy (*slang*), repulsive, revolting, scuzzy (*slang*), vile
abort *verb* 1 TERMINATE (*a pregnancy*) miscarry
2 STOP, arrest, ax (*informal*), call off, check, end, fail, halt, terminate
abortion *noun* TERMINATION, deliberate miscarriage, miscarriage
abortive *adjective* FAILED, fruitless, futile, ineffectual, miscarried, unsuccessful, useless, vain
abound *verb* BE PLENTIFUL, flourish, proliferate, swarm, swell, teem, thrive
abounding *adjective* PLENTIFUL, abundant, bountiful, copious, full, profuse, prolific, rich
about *preposition* 1 REGARDING, as regards, concerning, dealing with, on, referring to, relating to
2 NEAR, adjacent to, beside, circa (*of a date*), close to, nearby
▷ *adverb* 3 NEARLY, almost, approaching, approximately, around, close to, more or less, roughly
above *preposition* OVER, beyond, exceeding, higher than, on top of, upon
above board *adjective* HONEST, fair, genuine, legitimate, square, straight

a•brade [ə-BRAYD] *verb transitive* **-brad•ed, -brad•ing** rub off, scrape away
a•bra•sion [ə-BRAY-zhən] *noun* 1 place scraped or worn by rubbing (e.g. on skin) 2 scraping, rubbing > **a•bra'sive** [-siv] *noun* 1 substance for grinding, polishing, etc. ▷ *adjective* 2 causing abrasion 3 grating > **a•bra'sive•ness** *noun* tendency to annoy
a•breast [ə-BREST] *adverb* 1 side by side 2 keeping up with
a•bridge [ə-BRIJ] *verb transitive* cut short, abbreviate > **a•bridg'ment** *noun*
a•broad [ə-BRAWD] *adverb* 1 to or in a foreign country 2 at large
ab•ro•gate [AB-rə-gayt] *verb transitive* cancel, repeal > **ab•ro•ga'tion** *noun*
ab•rupt [ə-BRUPT] *adjective* 1 sudden 2 blunt 3 hasty 4 steep
abs [ABZ] *plural noun* (*informal*) abdominal muscles
ab•scess [AB-ses] *noun* gathering of pus in any part of the body
ab•scis•sa [ab-SIS-ə] *noun, plural* **-sae** [-see] *math.* distance of point from the axis of coordinates
ab•scond [ab-SKOND] *verb intransitive* leave secretly, esp. having stolen something
ab•sent [AB-sənt] *adjective* 1 away 2 not attentive ▷ *verb transitive* [ab-SENT] 3 keep away > **ab'sence** *noun* > **ab•sen•tee'** *noun* one who stays away esp. habitually > **ab•sen•tee'ism** *noun* persistent absence from work, etc.
ab•sinthe [AB-sinth] *noun* potent aniseed-flavored liqueur
ab•so•lute [AB-sə-loot] *adjective* 1 complete 2 not limited, unconditional 3 pure: *absolute alcohol* ▷ *noun* > **ab'so•lute•ly** *adverb* 1 completely ▷ *interjection* [-LOOT-lee] 2 certainly
ab•solve [ab-ZOLV] *verb transitive* **-solved, -solv•ing** free from, pardon, acquit > **ab•so•lu'tion** [-sə-LOO-shən] *noun*
ab•sorb' *verb transitive* 1 suck up, drink in 2 engage, occupy (attention, etc.) 3 receive impact > **ab•sorb'ent** *adjective* > **ab•sorp'tion** *noun*
ab•stain [ab-STAYN] *verb intransitive* keep from, refrain from drinking alcohol, voting, etc. > **ab•sten'tion** *noun* > **ab'sti•nence** *noun*
ab•ste•mi•ous [ab-STEE-mee-əs] *adjective* sparing in food or esp. drink, temperate > **ab•ste'mi•ous•ness** *noun*
ab•stract [ab-STRAKT] *adjective* 1 existing only

DICTIONARY

a

THESAURUS

abrasion *noun* (*medical*) GRAZE, chafe, scrape, scratch, scuff, surface injury
abrasive *adjective* 1 UNPLEASANT, caustic, cutting, galling, grating, irritating, rough, sharp
2 ROUGH, chafing, grating, scraping, scratchy
abreast *adverb* 1 ALONGSIDE, beside, side by side
2 ▷ **abreast of** INFORMED ABOUT, acquainted with, au courant with (*French*), au fait with (*French*), conversant with, familiar with, in the picture about, in touch with, keeping one's finger on the pulse of, knowledgeable about, up to date with, up to speed with
abridge *verb* SHORTEN, abbreviate, condense, cut, decrease, reduce, summarize
abroad *adverb* OVERSEAS, in foreign lands, out of the country
abrupt *adjective* 1 SUDDEN, precipitate, quick, surprising, unexpected
2 CURT, brusque, gruff, impatient, rude, short, terse
abscond *verb* FLEE, clear out, disappear, escape, make off, run off, steal away
absence *noun* 1 NONATTENDANCE, absenteeism, truancy
2 LACK, deficiency, need, omission, unavailability, want
absent *adjective* 1 MISSING, away, elsewhere, gone, nonexistent, out, unavailable
2 ABSENT-MINDED, blank, distracted, inattentive, oblivious, preoccupied, vacant, vague
▷ *verb* 3 ▷ **absent oneself** STAY AWAY, keep away, play truant, withdraw
absent-minded *adjective* VAGUE, distracted, dreaming, forgetful, inattentive, preoccupied, unaware
absolute *adjective* 1 TOTAL, complete, outright, perfect, pure, sheer, thorough, utter
2 SUPREME, full, sovereign, unbounded, unconditional, unlimited, unrestricted
absolutely *adverb* TOTALLY, completely, entirely, fully, one hundred per cent, perfectly, utterly, wholly
absolution *noun* FORGIVENESS, deliverance, exculpation, exoneration, mercy, pardon, release
absolve *verb* FORGIVE, deliver, exculpate, excuse, let off, pardon, release, set free
absorb *verb* 1 SOAK UP, consume, digest, imbibe, incorporate, receive, suck up, take in
2 PREOCCUPY, captivate, engage, engross, fascinate, rivet
absorbed *adjective* 1 PREOCCUPIED, captivated, engrossed, fascinated, immersed, involved, lost, rapt, riveted, wrapped up
2 DIGESTED, assimilated, incorporated, received, soaked up
absorbent *adjective* PERMEABLE, porous, receptive, spongy
absorbing *adjective* FASCINATING, captivating, engrossing, gripping, interesting, intriguing, riveting, spellbinding
absorption *noun* 1 SOAKING UP, assimilation, consumption, digestion, incorporation, sucking up
2 CONCENTRATION, fascination, immersion, intentness, involvement, preoccupation
abstain *verb* REFRAIN, avoid, decline, deny (oneself), desist, fast, forbear, forgo, give up, keep from
abstemious *adjective* SELF-DENYING, ascetic, austere, frugal, moderate, sober, temperate
abstention *noun* REFUSAL, abstaining, abstinence, avoidance, forbearance, refraining, self-control, self-denial, self-restraint
abstinence *noun* SELF-DENIAL, abstemiousness, avoidance, forbearance, moderation, self-restraint, soberness, teetotalism, temperance
abstinent *adjective* SELF-DENYING, abstaining, abstemious, forbearing, moderate, self-controlled, sober, temperate
abstract *adjective* 1 THEORETICAL, abstruse, general, hypothetical, indefinite, notional, recondite
▷ *noun* 2 SUMMARY, abridgment, digest, epitome, outline, précis, résumé, synopsis

in the mind **2** not concrete **3** (of art) not representational ▷ *noun* [AB-strakt] **4** summary, abridgment ▷ *verb transitive* [ab-STRAKT] **5** draw from, remove **6** steal
> **ab•stract'ed** *adjective* preoccupied
> **ab•strac'tion** *noun*
ab•struse [ab-STROOS] *adjective* obscure, difficult to understand, profound
ab•surd' *adjective* contrary to reason
> **ab•surd'i•ty** *noun*
a•bun•dance [ə-BUN-dəns] *noun* great amount
> **a•bun'dant** *adjective* plentiful
a•buse [ə-BYOOZ] *verb transitive* **-bused, -bus•ing** **1** misuse **2** address rudely ▷ *noun* (ə-BYOOS)
> **a•bu'sive** [-siv] *adjective* > **a•bu'sive•ness** *noun*
a•but [ə-BUT] *verb intransitive* **-but•ted, -but•ting** adjoin, border on > **a•but'ment** *noun* support, esp. of bridge or arch
a•bys•mal [ə-BIZ-məl] *adjective* **1** immeasurable, very great **2** (*informal*) extremely bad > **a•bys'mal•ly** *adverb*
a•byss [ə-BIS] *noun* very deep gulf or pit
Ac *chemistry* actinium
a•cad•e•my [ə-KAD-ə-mee] *noun, plural* **-mies** **1** society to advance arts or sciences **2** institution for specialized training **3** secondary school
> **ac•a•dem•ic** [ak-ə-DEM-ik] *adjective* **1** of academy, university, etc. **2** theoretical
ac•cede [ak-SEED] *verb intransitive* **-ced•ed, -ced•ing** **1** agree, consent **2** attain (office, right, etc.)
ac•cel•er•ate [ak-SEL-ə-rayt] *verb* **-at•ed, -at•ing** (cause to) increase speed, hasten
> **ac•cel•er•a'tion** *noun* > **ac•cel'er•a•tor** *noun* mechanism to increase speed, esp. in automobile
ac•cent [AK-sent] *noun* **1** stress or pitch in speaking **2** mark to show such stress **3** local or national style of pronunciation **4** particular attention or emphasis ▷ *verb transitive*
ac•cen•tu•ate [ak-SEN-choo-ayt] *verb transitive* **-at•ed, -at•ing** stress, emphasize
ac•cept [ak-SEPT] *verb transitive* **1** take, receive **2** admit, believe **3** agree to > **ac•cept'a•ble** *adjective*
> **ac•cept'ance** *noun*
ac•cess [AK-ses] *noun* act, right, or means of entry > **ac•ces'si•ble** *adjective* easy to approach
ac•ces•sion [ak-SESH-ən] *noun* **1** attaining of

DICTIONARY • THESAURUS

▷ *verb* **3** SUMMARIZE, abbreviate, abridge, condense, digest, epitomize, outline, précis, shorten
4 REMOVE, detach, extract, isolate, separate, take away, take out, withdraw
abstraction *noun* **1** IDEA, concept, formula, generalization, hypothesis, notion, theorem, theory, thought
2 ABSENT-MINDEDNESS, absence, dreaminess, inattention, pensiveness, preoccupation, remoteness, woolgathering
abstruse *adjective* OBSCURE, arcane, complex, deep, enigmatic, esoteric, recondite, unfathomable, vague
absurd *adjective* RIDICULOUS, crazy (*informal*), farcical, foolish, idiotic, illogical, inane, incongruous, irrational, ludicrous, nonsensical, preposterous, senseless, silly, stupid, unreasonable
absurdity *noun* RIDICULOUSNESS, farce, folly, foolishness, incongruity, joke, nonsense, silliness, stupidity
abundance *noun* PLENTY, affluence, bounty, copiousness, exuberance, fullness, profusion
abundant *adjective* PLENTIFUL, ample, bountiful, copious, exuberant, filled, full, luxuriant, profuse, rich, teeming
abuse *noun* **1** ILL-TREATMENT, damage, exploitation, harm, hurt, injury, maltreatment, manhandling
2 INSULTS, blame, castigation, censure, defamation, derision, disparagement, invective, reproach, scolding, vilification
3 MISUSE, misapplication
▷ *verb* **4** ILL-TREAT, damage, exploit, harm, hurt, injure, maltreat, misuse, take advantage of
5 INSULT, castigate, curse, defame, disparage, malign, scold, vilify
abusive *adjective* **1** INSULTING, censorious, defamatory, disparaging, libelous, offensive, reproachful, rude, scathing
2 HARMFUL, brutal, cruel, destructive, hurtful, injurious, rough
abysmal *adjective* TERRIBLE, appalling, awful, bad, dire, dreadful
abyss *noun* PIT, chasm, crevasse, fissure, gorge, gulf, void
academic *adjective* **1** SCHOLARLY, bookish, erudite, highbrow, learned, literary, studious
2 HYPOTHETICAL, abstract, conjectural, impractical, notional, speculative, theoretical
▷ *noun* **3** SCHOLAR, academician, don, fellow, lecturer, master, professor, tutor
accede *verb* **1** AGREE, accept, acquiesce, admit, assent, comply, concede, concur, consent, endorse, grant
2 INHERIT, assume, attain, come to, enter upon, succeed, succeed to (*of an heir*)
accelerate *verb* SPEED UP, advance, expedite, further, hasten, hurry, quicken
acceleration *noun* SPEEDING UP, hastening, hurrying, quickening, stepping up (*informal*)
accent *noun* **1** PRONUNCIATION, articulation, brogue, enunciation, inflection, intonation, modulation, tone
2 EMPHASIS, beat, cadence, force, pitch, rhythm, stress, timbre
▷ *verb* **3** EMPHASIZE, accentuate, stress, underline, underscore
accentuate *verb* EMPHASIZE, accent, draw attention to, foreground, highlight, stress, underline, underscore
accept *verb* **1** RECEIVE, acquire, gain, get, obtain, secure, take
2 AGREE TO, admit, approve, believe, concur with, consent to, cooperate with, recognize
acceptable *adjective* SATISFACTORY, adequate, admissible, all right, fair, moderate, passable, tolerable
acceptance *noun* **1** ACCEPTING, acquiring, gaining, getting, obtaining, receipt, securing, taking
2 AGREEMENT, acknowledgment, acquiescence, admission, adoption, approval, assent, concurrence, consent, cooperation, recognition
accepted *adjective* AGREED, acknowledged, approved, common, conventional, customary, established, normal, recognized, traditional

office, right, etc. 2 increase, addition
ac•ces•so•ry [ak-SES-ə-ree] *noun, plural* **-ries** 1 additional or supplementary part of automobile, woman's dress, etc. 2 person inciting or assisting in crime ▷ *adjective* 3 contributory, assisting
ac•ci•dent [AK-si-dənt] *noun* 1 event happening by chance 2 misfortune or mishap, esp. causing injury 3 nonessential quality > **ac•ci•den'tal** *adjective*
ac•claim [ə-KLAYM] *verb transitive* 1 applaud, praise ▷ *noun* 2 applause > **ac•cla•ma'tion** *noun*
ac•cli•mate [AK-klə-mayt] *verb* **-mat•ed, -mat•ing** acclimatize
ac•cli•ma•tize [ə-KLĪ-mə-tīz] *verb* **-tized, -tiz•ing** accustom to new climate or environment > **ac•cli•ma•ti•za'tion** *noun*
ac•co•lade [AK-ə-layd] *noun* 1 praise, public approval 2 award, honor 3 token of award of knighthood, etc.
ac•com•mo•date [ə-KOM-ə-dayt] *verb transitive* **-dat•ed, -dat•ing** 1 supply, esp. with board and lodging 2 oblige 3 harmonize, adapt > **ac•com'mo•dat•ing** *adjective* obliging > **ac•com•mo•da'tions** *plural noun* lodgings
ac•com•pa•ny [ə-KUM-pə-nee] *verb transitive* **-nied, -ny•ing** 1 go with 2 supplement 3 occur with 4 provide a musical accompaniment > **ac•com'pa•ni•ment** *noun* that which accompanies, esp. in music, part that goes with solos, etc. > **ac•com'pa•nist** *noun*
ac•com•plice [ə-KOM-plis] *noun* one assisting another in criminal deed
ac•com•plish [ə-KOM-plish] *verb transitive* 1 carry out 2 finish > **ac•com'plished** *adjective* 1 complete, perfect 2 proficient > **ac•com'plish•ment** *noun* 1 completion 2 personal ability
ac•cord [ə-KORD] *noun* 1 agreement, harmony ▷ *verb* 2 (cause to) be in accord with ▷ *verb transitive* 3 grant > **ac•cord'ing•ly** *adverb* 1 as the circumstances suggest 2 therefore
ac•cor•di•on [ə-KOR-dee-ən] *noun* portable musical instrument with keys, metal reeds and a bellows
ac•cost [ə-KAWST] *verb intransitive* approach and

---

access *noun* ENTRANCE, admission, admittance, approach, entry, passage, path, road
accessibility *noun* 1 HANDINESS, availability, nearness, possibility, readiness
2 APPROACHABILITY, affability, cordiality, friendliness, informality
3 OPENNESS, susceptibility
accessible *adjective* 1 HANDY, achievable, at hand, attainable, available, near, nearby, obtainable, reachable
2 APPROACHABLE, affable, available, cordial, friendly, informal
3 OPEN, exposed, liable, susceptible, vulnerable, wide-open
accessory *noun* 1 ADDITION, accompaniment, adjunct, adornment, appendage, attachment, decoration, extra, supplement, trimming
2 ACCOMPLICE, abettor, assistant, associate, colleague, confederate, helper, partner
accident *noun* 1 MISFORTUNE, calamity, collision, crash, disaster, misadventure, mishap
2 CHANCE, fate, fluke, fortuity, fortune, hazard, luck
accidental *adjective* UNINTENTIONAL, casual, chance, fortuitous, haphazard, inadvertent, incidental, random, unexpected, unforeseen, unlooked-for, unplanned
accidentally *adverb* UNINTENTIONALLY, by accident, by chance, fortuitously, haphazardly, inadvertently, incidentally, randomly, unwittingly
acclaim *verb* 1 PRAISE, applaud, approve, celebrate, cheer, clap, commend, exalt, hail, honor, salute
▷ *noun* 2 PRAISE, acclamation, applause, approval, celebration, commendation, honor, kudos
acclamation *noun* PRAISE, acclaim, adulation, approval, ovation, plaudit, tribute
acclimatization *noun* ADAPTATION, adjustment, habituation, inurement, naturalization
acclimatize *verb* ADAPT, accommodate, accustom, adjust, get used to, habituate, inure, naturalize
accolade *noun* PRAISE, acclaim, applause, approval, commendation, compliment, ovation, recognition, tribute
accommodate *verb* 1 HOUSE, cater for, entertain, lodge, put up, shelter
2 HELP, aid, assist, oblige, serve
3 ADAPT, adjust, comply, conform, fit, harmonize, modify, reconcile, settle
accommodating *adjective* HELPFUL, considerate, cooperative, friendly, hospitable, kind, obliging, polite, unselfish, willing
accommodation *noun* HOUSING, board, house, lodging *or* lodgings, quarters, shelter
accompaniment *noun* 1 SUPPLEMENT, accessory, companion, complement
2 BACKING MUSIC, backing
accompany *verb* 1 GO WITH, attend, chaperon, conduct, convoy, escort, hold (someone's) hand
2 OCCUR WITH, belong to, come with, follow, go together with, supplement
accompanying *adjective* ADDITIONAL, associated, attached, attendant, complementary, related, supplementary
accomplice *noun* HELPER, abettor, accessory, ally, assistant, associate, collaborator, colleague, henchman, partner
accomplish *verb* DO, achieve, attain, bring about, carry out, complete, effect, execute, finish, fulfill, manage, perform, produce
accomplished *adjective* SKILLED, expert, gifted, masterly, polished, practiced, proficient, talented
accomplishment *noun* 1 COMPLETION, bringing about, carrying out, conclusion, execution, finishing, fulfillment, performance
2 ACHIEVEMENT, act, coup, deed, exploit, feat, stroke, triumph
accord *noun* 1 AGREEMENT, conformity, correspondence, harmony, rapport, sympathy, unison
▷ *verb* 2 FIT, agree, conform, correspond, harmonize, match, suit, tally
accordingly *adverb* 1 APPROPRIATELY, correspondingly, fitly, properly, suitably
2 CONSEQUENTLY, as a result, ergo, hence, in consequence, so, therefore, thus

DICTIONARY **a** THESAURUS

speak to, often aggressively
ac•count [ə-KOWNT] *noun* 1 report, description 2 importance, value 3 statement of moneys received, paid, or owed 4 person's money held in bank 5 credit available to person at store, etc. ▷ *verb transitive* 6 reckon 7 judge ▷ *verb intransitive* 8 give reason, answer (for) > **ac•count'a•ble** *adjective* responsible > **ac•count'an•cy** *noun* keeping, preparation of business accounts, financial records, etc. > **ac•count'ant** *noun* one practicing accountancy > **ac•count'ing** *noun* skill or practice of keeping and preparing business accounts ▷ *adjective*
ac•cred•it•ed [ə-KRED-i-tid] *adjective* authorized, officially recognized
ac•cre•tion [ə-KREE-shən] *noun* 1 growth 2 something added on
ac•crue [ə-KROO] *verb intransitive* **-crued, -cru•ing** 1 be added 2 result
ac•cu•mu•late [ə-KYOO-myə-layt] *verb* **-lat•ed, -lat•ing** 1 gather, become gathered in increasing quantity 2 collect > **ac•cu•mu•la'tion** *noun*
ac•cu•rate [AK-yər-it] *adjective* exact, correct, without errors > **ac'cu•ra•cy** *noun*
ac•curs•ed [ə-KUR-sid] *adjective* 1 under a curse 2 hateful, detestable
ac•cuse [ə-KYOOZ] *verb transitive* **-cused, -cus•ing** 1 charge with wrongdoing 2 blame > **ac•cu•sa•tion** [ak-yə-ZAY-shən] *noun* > **ac•cu'sa•tive** *noun* grammatical case indicating the direct object > **ac•cu'sa•to•ry** *adjective*
ac•cus•tom [ə-KUS-təm] *verb transitive* make used to, familiarize > **ac•cus'tomed** *adjective* 1 usual 2 used (to) 3 in the habit (of)
ace *noun* 1 the one at dice, cards, dominoes 2 *tennis* winning serve untouched by opponent 3 very successful fighter pilot ▷ *verb transitive* **aced, ac•ing** 4 score an ace 5 *golf* make hole in one 6 (*informal*) make grade of A
a•cer•bi•ty [ə-SUR-bi-tee] *noun* 1 severity, sharpness 2 sour tasting > **a•cerb'ic** *adjective*
ac•e•tate [AS-i-tayt] *noun* 1 salt or ester of acetic acid 2 synthetic textile fiber
a•ce•tic [ə-SEE-tik] *adjective* derived from or having the nature of vinegar
ac•e•tone [AS-i-tohn] *noun* colorless liquid used as a solvent
a•cet•y•lene [ə-SET-l-een] *noun* colorless, flammable gas used esp. in welding metals
ache [ayk] *noun* 1 continuous pain ▷ *verb intransitive* **ached, ach•ing** 2 to be in pain
a•chieve [ə-CHEEV] *verb transitive* **-chieved, -chiev•ing** 1 accomplish, perform successfully 2 gain > **a•chieve'ment** *noun* something

DICTIONARY • THESAURUS

according to *adverb* 1 AS STATED BY, as believed by, as maintained by, in the light of, on the authority of, on the report of
2 IN KEEPING WITH, after, after the manner of, consistent with, in accordance with, in compliance with, in line with, in the manner of
accost *verb* APPROACH, buttonhole, confront, greet, hail
account *noun* 1 DESCRIPTION, explanation, narrative, report, statement, story, tale, version
2 (*commerce*) STATEMENT, balance, bill, books, charge, invoice, reckoning, register, score, tally
3 IMPORTANCE, consequence, honor, note, significance, standing, value, worth
▷ *verb* 4 CONSIDER, count, estimate, judge, rate, reckon, regard, think, value
accountability *noun* RESPONSIBILITY, answerability, chargeability, culpability, liability
accountable *adjective* RESPONSIBLE, amenable, answerable, charged with, liable, obligated, obliged
accountant *noun* AUDITOR, bean counter (*informal*), book-keeper
account for *verb* EXPLAIN, answer for, clarify, clear up, elucidate, illuminate, justify, rationalize
accredited *adjective* AUTHORIZED, appointed, certified, empowered, endorsed, guaranteed, licensed, official, recognized
accrue *verb* INCREASE, accumulate, amass, arise, be added, build up, collect, enlarge, flow, follow, grow
accumulate *verb* COLLECT, accrue, amass, build up, gather, hoard, increase, pile up, store
accumulation *noun* COLLECTION, build-up, gathering, heap, hoard, increase, mass, pile, stack, stock, stockpile, store
accuracy *noun* EXACTNESS, accurateness, authenticity, carefulness, closeness, correctness, fidelity, precision, strictness, truthfulness, veracity
accurate *adjective* EXACT, authentic, close, correct, faithful, precise, scrupulous, strict, true, unerring
accurately *adverb* EXACTLY, authentically, closely, correctly, faithfully, precisely, scrupulously, strictly, to the letter, truly, unerringly
accursed *adjective* 1 CURSED, bewitched, condemned, damned, doomed, hopeless, ill-fated, ill-omened, jinxed, unfortunate, unlucky, wretched
2 HATEFUL, abominable, despicable, detestable, execrable, hellish, horrible, lousy (*slang*), scuzzy (*slang*)
accusation *noun* CHARGE, allegation, complaint, denunciation, incrimination, indictment, recrimination
accuse *verb* CHARGE, blame, censure, denounce, impeach, impute, incriminate, indict
accustom *verb* ADAPT, acclimatize, acquaint, discipline, exercise, familiarize, train
accustomed *adjective* 1 USUAL, common, conventional, customary, established, everyday, expected, habitual, normal, ordinary, regular, traditional
2 USED, acclimatized, acquainted, adapted, familiar, familiarized, given to, in the habit of, trained
ace *noun* 1 (*cards, dice, etc.*) ONE, single point
2 (*informal*) EXPERT, champion, master, star, virtuoso, wizard (*informal*)
ache *verb* 1 HURT, pain, pound, smart, suffer, throb, twinge
▷ *noun* 2 PAIN, hurt, pang, pounding, soreness, suffering, throbbing
achieve *verb* ATTAIN, accomplish, acquire, bring about, carry out, complete, do, execute, fulfill, gain, get, obtain, perform
achievement *noun* ACCOMPLISHMENT, act, deed,

accomplished
ac•id [AS-id] *adjective* 1 sharp, sour ▷ *noun* 2 sour substance 3 *chem.* one of a class of compounds that combine with bases (alkalis, oxides, etc.) to form salts > **a•cid'ic** *adjective* > **a•cid'i•fy** *verb transitive* **-fied, -fy•ing** > **a•cid'i•ty** *noun* > **a•cid'u•lous** *adjective* caustic > **acid rain** rain acidified by atmospheric pollution > **acid test** conclusive test of value
ac•knowl•edge [ak-NOL-ij] *verb transitive* **-edged, -edg•ing** 1 admit, own to knowing, recognize 2 say one has received > **ac•knowl'edg•ment** *noun*
ac•me [AK-mee] *noun* highest point
ac•ne [AK-nee] *noun* pimply skin disease
ac•o•lyte [AK-ə-līt] *noun* follower or attendant, esp. of priest
a•cous•tic [ə-KOO-stik] *adjective* pert. to sound and to hearing > **a•cous'tics** *noun* 1 science of sounds ▷ *plural noun* 2 features of room or building as regards sounds heard within it
ac•quaint [ə-KWAYNT] *verb transitive* 1 make familiar, inform > **ac•quaint'ance** *noun* 1 person known 2 personal knowledge
ac•qui•esce [ak-wee-ES] *verb intransitive* **-esced, -esc•ing** agree, consent without complaint > **ac•qui•es'cence** *noun*
ac•quire [ə-KWĪR] *verb transitive* **-quired, -quir•ing** gain, get > **ac•qui•si•tion** [ak-wə-ZISH-ən] *noun* 1 act of getting 2 material gain > **ac•quis'i•tive** *adjective* desirous of gaining
ac•quit [ə-KWIT] *verb transitive* **-quit•ted, -quit•ting** 1 declare innocent 2 settle, discharge, as a debt 3 behave (oneself) > **ac•quit'tal** *noun* declaration of innocence in court
a•cre [AY-kər] *noun* 1 measure of land, 43,560 square feet > **a•cres** 1 lands, estates 2 (*informal*) large area or plenty of > **a'cre•age** *noun* the extent of land in acres
ac•rid [AK-rid] *adjective* 1 pungent, sharp 2 irritating
ac•ri•mo•ny [AK-rə-moh-nee] *noun* bitterness of feeling or language > **ac•ri•mo'ni•ous** *adjective*
ac•ro•bat [AK-rə-bat] *noun* one skilled in gymnastic feats, esp. as entertainer in circus, etc. > **ac•ro•bat'ic** *adjective* > **ac•ro•bat'ics** *plural noun* activities requiring agility
ac•ro•nym [AK-rə-nim] *noun* word formed from initial letters of other words, such as NATO
a•crop•o•lis [ə-KROP-ə-lis] *noun* citadel, esp. in ancient Greece
a•cross [ə-KRAWS] *adverb, preposition* 1 crosswise 2 from side to side 3 on or to the other side 4 **get, put it across** explain, make (something) understood
a•cros•tic [ə-KRAW-stik] *noun* word puzzle (or verse) in which the first, middle, or last letters of each line spell a word or words
a•cryl•ic [ə-KRIL-ik] *noun* variety of synthetic materials, esp. paint and textiles
act [akt] *noun* 1 thing done, deed 2 doing 3

effort, exploit, feat, feather in one's cap, stroke
acid *adjective* 1 SOUR, acerbic, acrid, pungent, tart, vinegary
2 SHARP, biting, bitter, caustic, cutting, harsh, trenchant, vitriolic
acidity *noun* 1 SOURNESS, acerbity, pungency, tartness
2 SHARPNESS, bitterness, harshness
acknowledge *verb* 1 ACCEPT, admit, allow, concede, confess, declare, grant, own, profess, recognize, yield
2 GREET, address, hail, notice, recognize, salute
3 REPLY TO, answer, notice, react to, recognize, respond to, return
acknowledged *adjective* ACCEPTED, accredited, approved, confessed, declared, professed, recognized, returned
acknowledgment *noun* 1 ACCEPTANCE, admission, allowing, confession, declaration, profession, realization, yielding
2 GREETING, addressing, hail, hailing, notice, recognition, salutation, salute
3 APPRECIATION, answer, credit, gratitude, kudos, reaction, recognition, reply, response, return, thanks
acquaint *verb* TELL, disclose, divulge, enlighten, familiarize, inform, let (someone) know, notify, reveal
acquaintance *noun* 1 ASSOCIATE, colleague, contact
2 KNOWLEDGE, awareness, experience, familiarity, fellowship, relationship, understanding
acquainted with *adjective* FAMILIAR WITH, alive to, apprised of, au fait with (*French*), aware of, conscious of, experienced in, informed of, knowledgeable about, versed in
acquiesce *verb* AGREE, accede, accept, allow, approve, assent, comply, concur, conform, consent, give in, go along with, submit, yield
acquiescence *noun* AGREEMENT, acceptance, approval, assent, compliance, conformity, consent, giving in, obedience, submission, yielding
acquire *verb* GET, amass, attain, buy, collect, earn, gain, gather, obtain, receive, secure, win
acquisition *noun* 1 POSSESSION, buy, gain, prize, property, purchase
2 ACQUIRING, attainment, gaining, procurement
acquisitive *adjective* GREEDY, avaricious, avid, covetous, grabbing, grasping, predatory, rapacious
acquit *verb* 1 CLEAR, discharge, free, liberate, release, vindicate
2 BEHAVE, bear, comport, conduct, perform
acquittal *noun* CLEARANCE, absolution, deliverance, discharge, exoneration, liberation, release, relief, vindication
acrid *adjective* PUNGENT, bitter, caustic, harsh, sharp, vitriolic
acrimonious *adjective* BITTER, caustic, irascible, petulant, rancorous, spiteful, splenetic, testy
acrimony *noun* BITTERNESS, harshness, ill will, irascibility, rancor, virulence
act *noun* 1 DEED, accomplishment, achievement, action, exploit, feat, performance, undertaking
2 LAW, bill, decree, edict, enactment, measure, ordinance, resolution, statute
3 PERFORMANCE, routine, show, sketch, turn
4 PRETENSE, affectation, attitude, front, performance, pose, posture, show
▷ *verb* 5 DO, carry out, enact, execute, function, operate, perform, take effect, work
6 PERFORM, act out, impersonate, mimic, play,

law or decree **4** section of a play ▷ *verb* **5** perform, as in a play ▷ *verb intransitive* **6** exert force, work, as mechanism **7** behave > **act'ing** *noun* **1** performance of a part ▷ *adjective* **2** temporarily performing the duties of > **ac'tion** *noun* **1** operation **2** deed **3** gesture **4** expenditure of energy **5** battle **6** lawsuit > **ac'tion•a•ble** *adjective* subject to lawsuit > **ac'ti•vate** *verb transitive* **-vat•ed, -vat•ing** **1** to make active **2** make radioactive **3** make chemically active > **ac•ti•va'tion** *noun* > **ac'tive** *adjective* **1** moving, working **2** brisk, energetic > **ac'ti•vist** *noun* one who takes (direct) action to achieve political or social ends > **ac•tiv'i•ty** *noun* > **ac•tor, ac•tress** *noun* one who acts in a play, film, etc.

ac•tin•i•um [ak-TIN-ee-əm] *noun* radioactive element occurring as decay product of uranium

ac•tu•al [AK-choo-əl] *adjective* **1** existing in the present **2** real > **ac•tu•al'i•ty** *noun* > **ac'tu•al•ly** *adverb* really, indeed

ac•tu•ar•y [AK-choo-er-ee] *noun, plural* **-ar•ies** statistician who calculates insurance risks, premiums, etc. > **ac•tu•ar'i•al** *adjective*

ac•tu•ate [AK-choo-ayt] *verb transitive* **-at•ed, -at•ing** **1** activate **2** motivate > **ac'tu•a•tor** *noun* mechanism for controlling or moving something indirectly

a•cu•i•ty [ə-KYOO-i-tee] *noun* keenness, esp. in vision or thought

a•cu•men [ə-KYOO-mən] *noun* sharpness of wit, perception, penetration

ac•u•punc•ture [AK-yə-pungk-chər] *noun* medical treatment involving insertion of needles at various points on the body

a•cute [ə-KYOOT] *adjective* **1** keen, shrewd **2** sharp **3** severe **4** of angle, less than 90° ▷ *noun* **5** accent (´) over a letter to indicate the quality or length of its sound, as in café > **a•cute'ness** *noun*

ad•age [AD-ij] *noun* much used wise saying, proverb

a•da•gio [ə-DAH-joh] *adverb, noun, plural* **-gios** *mus.* leisurely, slow (passage)

ad•a•mant [AD-ə-mənt] *adjective* very hard, unyielding > **ad•a•man'tine** [-MAN-teen] *adjective*

Adam's apple [AD-əmz] projecting part at front of the throat, the thyroid cartilage

a•dapt [ə-DAPT] *verb transitive* **1** alter for new use **2** fit, modify **3** change > **a•dapt'a•ble** *adjective* > **ad•ap•ta'tion** *noun* > **a•dapt'er, a•dapt'or** *noun* device for connecting several electrical appliances to single socket

add *verb* **1** join **2** increase by **3** say further > **ad•di•tion** [ə-DISH-ən] *noun* > **ad•di'tion•al**

play the part of *or* take the part of, portray, represent

act for *verb* STAND IN FOR, cover for, deputize for, fill in for, replace, represent, substitute for, take the place of

acting *noun* **1** PERFORMANCE, characterization, impersonation, performing, playing, portrayal, stagecraft, theater
▷ *adjective* **2** TEMPORARY, interim, pro tem, provisional, substitute, surrogate

action *noun* **1** DEED, accomplishment, achievement, act, exploit, feat, performance
2 LAWSUIT, case, litigation, proceeding, prosecution, suit
3 ENERGY, activity, force, liveliness, spirit, vigor, vim, vitality
4 MOVEMENT, activity, functioning, motion, operation, process, working
5 BATTLE, clash, combat, conflict, contest, encounter, engagement, fight, skirmish, sortie

activate *verb* START, arouse, energize, galvanize, initiate, mobilize, move, rouse, set in motion, stir

active *adjective* **1** BUSY, bustling, hard-working, involved, occupied, on the go (*informal*), on the move, strenuous
2 ENERGETIC, alert, animated, industrious, lively, quick, sprightly, spry, vigorous
3 IN OPERATION, acting, at work, effectual, in action, in force, operative, working

activist *noun* MILITANT, organizer, partisan

activity *noun* **1** ACTION, animation, bustle, exercise, exertion, hustle, labor, motion, movement
2 PURSUIT, hobby, interest, pastime, project, scheme

actor *noun* PERFORMER, actress, player, Thespian

actress *noun* PERFORMER, actor, leading lady, player, starlet, Thespian

actual *adjective* DEFINITE, concrete, factual, physical, positive, real, substantial, tangible

actually *adverb* REALLY, as a matter of fact, indeed, in fact, in point of fact, in reality, in truth, literally, truly

act up *verb* (*informal*) MAKE A FUSS, have a fit, horse around, misbehave, raise Cain, raise hell

acumen *noun* JUDGMENT, astuteness, cleverness, ingenuity, insight, intelligence, perspicacity, shrewdness

acute *adjective* **1** SERIOUS, critical, crucial, dangerous, grave, important, severe, urgent
2 SHARP, excruciating, fierce, intense, piercing, powerful, severe, shooting, violent
3 PERCEPTIVE, astute, clever, insightful, keen, observant, sensitive, sharp, smart

acuteness *noun* **1** SERIOUSNESS, gravity, importance, severity, urgency
2 PERCEPTIVENESS, astuteness, cleverness, discrimination, insight, perspicacity, sharpness

adamant *adjective* DETERMINED, firm, fixed, obdurate, resolute, stubborn, unbending, uncompromising

adapt *verb* ADJUST, acclimatize, accommodate, alter, change, conform, convert, modify, remodel, tailor

adaptability *noun* FLEXIBILITY, changeability, resilience, versatility

adaptable *adjective* FLEXIBLE, adjustable, changeable, compliant, easy-going, plastic, pliant, resilient, versatile

adaptation *noun* **1** ACCLIMATIZATION, familiarization, naturalization
2 CONVERSION, adjustment, alteration, change, modification, transformation, variation, version

add *verb* **1** COUNT UP, add up, compute, reckon, total, tot up
2 INCLUDE, adjoin, affix, append, attach, augment, supplement

addendum *noun* ADDITION, appendage, appendix, attachment, extension, extra,

adjective > **ad'di•tive** *noun* something added, esp. to food
ad•den•dum [ə-DEN-dəm] *noun, plural* **-da** [-də] thing to be added
ad•der [AD-ər] *noun* small poisonous snake
ad•dict [AD-ikt] *noun* one who has become dependent on something, esp. drugs > **ad•dict'ed** *adjective* > **ad•dic'tion** *noun* > **ad•dic'tive** *adjective* causing addiction
ad•dle [AD-l] *verb* **-dled, -dling** make or become rotten, muddled
ad•dress [ə-DRES, AD-res] *noun* 1 direction on letter 2 place where one lives 3 *computing* number giving the location of a piece of stored information 4 speech ▷ *verb transitive* 5 mark destination, as on envelope 6 speak to 7 direct 8 dispatch > **address ball** *golf* adjust club before striking ball > **ad•dress•ee'** *noun* person addressed
ad•duce [ə-DOOS] *verb transitive* **-duced, -duc•ing** 1 offer as proof 2 cite > **ad•duc'i•ble** *adjective*
ad•e•noids [AD-n-oidz] *plural noun* tissue at back of nose and throat, sometimes obstructing breathing
a•dept [ə-DEPT] *adjective* 1 skilled ▷ *noun* [AD-ept] 2 expert
ad•e•quate [AD-i-kwit] *adjective* 1 sufficient, enough, suitable 2 not outstanding > **ad'e•qua•cy** *noun*
ad•here [ad-HEER] *verb intransitive* **-hered, -her•ing** 1 stick to 2 be firm in opinion, etc. > **ad•her'ent** *noun, adjective* > **ad•he'sion** [-HEE-zhən] *noun* > **ad•he'sive** [-siv] *adjective, noun*
ad hoc [ad-HOK] *adjective, adverb* 1 for a particular occasion only 2 improvised
a•dieu [ə-DYOO] *interjection* farewell ▷ *noun, plural* **a•dieus, a•dieux** [ə-DYOOZ] act of taking leave
ad in•fi•ni•tum [in-fə-NĪ-təm] *Lat.* endlessly
ad•i•pose [AD-ə-pohs] *adjective* of fat, fatty
ad•ja•cent [ə-JAY-sənt] *adjective* lying near, next (to)
ad•jec•tive [AJ-ik-tiv] *noun* word that modifies or limits a noun > **ad•jec•ti'val** [-TĪ-vəl] *adjective* of adjective
ad•join [ə-JOIN] *verb* 1 be next to 2 join > **ad•join'ing** *adjective* next to, near
ad•journ [ə-JURN] *verb* 1 postpone temporarily, as meeting 2 (*informal*) move elsewhere
ad•judge [ə-JUJ] *verb transitive* **-judged, -judg•ing** 1 declare 2 decide 3 award
ad•ju•di•cate [ə-JOO-di-kayt] *verb* **-cat•ed, -cat•ing** 1 try, judge 2 sit in judgment > **ad•ju•di•ca'tion** *noun*
ad•junct [AJ-ungkt] *adjective* 1 joined, added ▷ *noun* 2 person or thing added or subordinate
ad•jure [ə-JOOR] *verb transitive* **-jured, -jur•ing** beg, earnestly entreat > **ad•ju•ra•tion** [aj-ə-RAY-shən] *noun*
ad•just [ə-JUST] *verb transitive* 1 make suitable, adapt 2 alter slightly, regulate ▷ *verb intransitive* 3 adapt or conform to new conditions, etc. > **ad•just'a•ble** *adjective*
ad•ju•tant [AJ-ə-tənt] *noun* military officer who

DICTIONARY

a

THESAURUS

postscript, supplement
addict *noun* 1 JUNKIE (*informal*), fiend (*informal*), freak (*informal*)
2 FAN, adherent, buff (*informal*), devotee, enthusiast, follower, nut (*slang*)
addicted *adjective* HOOKED (*slang*), absorbed, accustomed, dedicated, dependent, devoted, habituated
addiction *noun* DEPENDENCE, craving, enslavement, habit, obsession
addition *noun* 1 INCLUSION, adding, amplification, attachment, augmentation, enlargement, extension, increasing
2 EXTRA, addendum, additive, appendage, appendix, extension, gain, increase, increment, supplement
3 COUNTING UP, adding up, computation, totaling, totting up
4 ▷ **in addition in addition to** AS WELL *or* AS WELL AS, additionally, also, besides, into the bargain, moreover, over and above, to boot, too
additional *adjective* EXTRA, added, fresh, further, new, other, spare, supplementary
address *noun* 1 LOCATION, abode, dwelling, home, house, residence, situation, whereabouts
2 SPEECH, discourse, dissertation, lecture, oration, sermon, talk
▷ *verb* 3 SPEAK TO, approach, greet, hail, talk to
4 ▷ **address (oneself) to** CONCENTRATE ON, apply (oneself) to, attend to, devote (oneself) to, engage in, focus on, take care of
add up *verb* COUNT UP, add, compute, count, reckon, total, tot up
adept *adjective* 1 SKILLFUL, able, accomplished, adroit, expert, practiced, proficient, skilled, versed
▷ *noun* 2 EXPERT, genius, hotshot (*informal*), master
adequacy *noun* SUFFICIENCY, capability, competence, fairness, suitability, tolerability
adequate *adjective* ENOUGH, competent, fair, satisfactory, sufficient, tolerable, up to scratch (*informal*)
adhere *verb* STICK, attach, cleave, cling, fasten, fix, glue, hold fast, paste
adherent *noun* SUPPORTER, admirer, devotee, disciple, fan, follower, upholder
adhesive *adjective* 1 STICKY, clinging, cohesive, gluey, glutinous, tenacious
▷ *noun* 2 GLUE, cement, gum, paste
adieu *noun* GOOD-BYE, farewell, leave-taking, parting, valediction
adjacent *adjective* NEXT, adjoining, beside, bordering, cheek by jowl, close, near, neighboring, next door, touching
adjoin *verb* CONNECT, border, join, link, touch
adjoining *adjective* CONNECTING, abutting, adjacent, bordering, neighboring, next door, touching
adjourn *verb* POSTPONE, defer, delay, discontinue, interrupt, put off, suspend
adjournment *noun* POSTPONEMENT, delay, discontinuation, interruption, putting off, recess, suspension
adjudicate *verb* JUDGE, adjudge, arbitrate, decide, determine, mediate, referee, settle, umpire
adjudication *noun* JUDGMENT, arbitration, conclusion, decision, finding, pronouncement, ruling, settlement, verdict
adjust *verb* ALTER, accustom, adapt, make conform, modify

assists superiors > **ad'ju•tan•cy** *noun* office, rank of adjutant

ad-lib *verb* **-libbed, -lib•bing** improvise and speak spontaneously > **ad lib** *noun* such speech, etc.

ad•min•is•ter [ad-MIN-ə-stər] *verb transitive* 1 manage, look after 2 dispense, as justice, etc. 3 apply > **ad•min•is•tra'tion** *noun* > **ad•min'is•tra•tive** *adjective*

ad•mi•ral [AD-mər-əl] *noun* naval officer of highest sea rank > **ad'mi•ral•ty** *noun law* court having jurisdiction over maritime matters

ad•mire [ad-MĪR] *verb transitive* **-mired, -mir•ing** 1 look on with wonder and pleasure 2 respect highly > **ad'mi•ra•ble** *adjective* > **ad'mi•ra•bly** *adverb* > **ad•mi•ra'tion** *noun* > **ad•mir'er** *noun* > **ad•mir'ing•ly** *adverb*

ad•mit [ad-MIT] *verb transitive* **-mit•ted, -mit•ting** 1 confess 2 accept as true 3 allow 4 let in > **ad•mis'si•ble** *adjective* > **ad•mis'sion** *noun* 1 permission to enter 2 entrance fee 3 confession > **ad•mit'tance** *noun* permission to enter > **ad•mit'ted•ly** *adverb*

ad•mix•ture [ad-MIKS-chər] *noun* 1 mixture 2 ingredient

ad•mon•ish [ad-MON-ish] *verb transitive* 1 reprove 2 advise 3 warn 4 exhort > **ad•mo•ni'tion** [-mə-NISH-ən] *noun* > **ad•mon'i•to•ry** *adjective*

ad nau•se•am [NAW-zee-əm] *Lat.* to a boring or disgusting extent

a•do [ə-DOO] *noun* fuss

a•do•be [ə-DOH-bee] *noun* sun-dried brick

ad•o•les•cence [ad-l-ES-ens] *noun* period of life just before maturity > **ad•o•les'cent** *noun* a youth ▷ *adjective*

a•dopt [ə-DOPT] *verb transitive* 1 take into relationship, esp. as one's child 2 take up, as principle, resolution > **a•dop'tion** *noun* > **a•dop'tive** *adjective* that which adopts or is adopted

a•dore [ə-DOR] *verb* **-dored, -dor•ing** 1 love intensely 2 worship > **a•dor'a•ble** *adjective* > **ad•o•ra'tion** *noun*

a•dorn [ə-DORN] *verb transitive* beautify, embellish, deck > **a•dorn'ment** *noun* ornament, decoration

ad•re•nal [ə-DREEN-l] *adjective* near the kidney > **adrenal glands** glands covering the top of the kidneys > **a•dren'a•line** [-DREN-l-in] *noun* 1 hormone secreted by adrenal glands 2 this substance used as drug

a•drift [ə-DRIFT] *adjective, adverb* 1 drifting free 2 (*informal*) detached 3 (*informal*) off course

a•droit [ə-DROIT] *adjective* 1 skillful, expert 2 clever > **a•droit'ness** *noun* dexterity

---

adjustable *adjective* ALTERABLE, adaptable, flexible, malleable, modifiable, movable

adjustment *noun* 1 ALTERATION, adaptation, modification, redress, regulation, tuning 2 ACCLIMATIZATION, orientation, settling in

ad-lib *verb* IMPROVISE, busk, extemporize, make up, speak off the cuff, wing it (*informal*)

administer *verb* 1 MANAGE, conduct, control, direct, govern, handle, oversee, run, supervise 2 GIVE, apply, dispense, impose, mete out, perform, provide

administration *noun* MANAGEMENT, application, conduct, control, direction, government, running, supervision

administrative *adjective* MANAGERIAL, directorial, executive, governmental, organizational, regulatory, supervisory

administrator *noun* MANAGER, bureaucrat, executive, official, organizer, supervisor

admirable *adjective* EXCELLENT, commendable, exquisite, fine, laudable, praiseworthy, wonderful, worthy

admiration *noun* REGARD, amazement, appreciation, approval, esteem, praise, respect, wonder

admire *verb* 1 RESPECT, appreciate, approve, esteem, look up to, praise, prize, think highly of, value 2 MARVEL AT, appreciate, delight in, take pleasure in, wonder at

admirer *noun* 1 SUITOR, beau, boyfriend, lover, sweetheart, wooer 2 FAN, devotee, disciple, enthusiast, follower, partisan, supporter

admissible *adjective* PERMISSIBLE, acceptable, allowable, passable, tolerable

admission *noun* 1 ENTRANCE, acceptance, access, admittance, entrée, entry, initiation, introduction 2 CONFESSION, acknowledgment, allowance, declaration, disclosure, divulgence, revelation

admit *verb* 1 CONFESS, acknowledge, declare, disclose, divulge, fess up (*informal*), own, reveal 2 ALLOW, agree, grant, let, permit, recognize 3 LET IN, accept, allow, give access, initiate, introduce, receive, take in

admonish *verb* REPRIMAND, berate, chide, rebuke, scold, slap on the wrist, tell off (*informal*)

adolescence *noun* 1 YOUTH, boyhood, girlhood, minority, teens 2 YOUTHFULNESS, childishness, immaturity

adolescent *adjective* 1 YOUNG, boyish, girlish, immature, juvenile, puerile, teenage, youthful ▷ *noun* 2 YOUTH, juvenile, minor, teenager, youngster

adopt *verb* 1 FOSTER, take in 2 CHOOSE, assume, espouse, follow, maintain, take up

adoption *noun* 1 FOSTERING, adopting, taking in 2 CHOICE, appropriation, assumption, embracing, endorsement, espousal, selection, taking up

adorable *adjective* LOVABLE, appealing, attractive, charming, cute, dear, delightful, fetching, pleasing

adore *verb* LOVE, admire, cherish, dote on, esteem, exalt, glorify, honor, idolize, put on a pedestal (*informal*), revere, worship

adoring *adjective* LOVING, admiring, affectionate, devoted, doting, fond

adorn *verb* DECORATE, array, embellish, festoon

adornment *noun* DECORATION, accessory, embellishment, festoon, frill, frippery, ornament, supplement, trimming

adrift *adjective* 1 DRIFTING, afloat, unanchored, unmoored 2 AIMLESS, directionless, goalless, purposeless ▷ *adverb* 3 WRONG, amiss, astray, off course

adroit *adjective* SKILLFUL, adept, clever, deft, dexterous, expert, masterful, neat, proficient,

ad•sorb [ad-SORB] *verb* (of gas, vapor) condense and form thin film on surface > **ad•sorb'ent** *adjective, noun* > **ad•sorp'tion** *noun*
ad•u•la•tion [aj-ə-LAY-shən] *noun* flattery > **ad'u•late** *verb transitive* **-lat•ed, -lat•ing** flatter > **ad'u•la•to•ry** *adjective*
a•dult [ə-DULT] *adjective* 1 grown-up, mature ▷ *noun* 2 grown-up person 3 full-grown animal or plant
a•dul•ter•ate [ə-DUL-tə-rayt] *verb transitive* **-at•ed, -at•ing** make impure by addition > **a•dul'ter•ant** *noun*
a•dul•ter•y [ə-DUL-tə-ree] *noun* sexual unfaithfulness of a husband or wife > **a•dul'ter•er, a•dul'ter•ess** *noun* > **a•dul'ter•ous** *adjective*
ad•vance [ad-VANS] *verb transitive* **-vanced, -vanc•ing** 1 bring forward 2 suggest 3 encourage 4 pay beforehand 5 *auto.* to time spark earlier in engine cycle ▷ *verb intransitive* **-vanced, -vanc•ing** 6 go forward 7 improve in position or value ▷ *noun* 8 movement forward 9 improvement 10 a loan ▷ *adjective* 11 ahead in time or position > **ad•vanc•es** *plural noun* personal approach(es) to gain favor, etc. > **ad•vanced'** *adjective* 1 at a late stage 2 not elementary 3 ahead of the times > **ad•vance'ment** *noun* promotion
ad•van•tage [ad-VAN-tij] *noun* 1 superiority 2 more favorable position or state 3 benefit > **ad•van•ta'geous** [-vən-TAY-jəs] *adjective*
ad•vent [AD-vent] *noun* 1 a coming, arrival 2 (**Ad•vent**) the four weeks before Christmas **the Advent** the coming of Christ > **Ad'vent•ist** *noun* one of number of Christian sects believing in imminent return of Christ
ad•ven•ti•tious [ad-vən-TISH-əs] *adjective* 1 added 2 accidental, casual
ad•ven•ture [ad-VEN-chər] *noun* 1 risk 2 bold exploit 3 remarkable happening 4 enterprise 5 commercial speculation > **ad•ven'tur•er, ad•ven'tur•ess** *noun* one who seeks adventures > **ad•ven'tur•ous** *adjective*
ad•verb [AD-vurb] *noun* word used with verb, adjective, or other adverb to modify meaning > **ad•ver'bi•al** *adjective*
ad•verse [ad-VURS] *adjective* 1 opposed to 2 hostile 3 unfavorable, bringing harm > **ad'ver•sar•y** *noun, plural* **-sar•ies** enemy > **ad•verse'ly** *adverb* > **ad•ver'si•ty** *noun* distress, misfortune
ad•ver•tise [AD-vər-tīz] *verb transitive* **-tised, -tis•ing** 1 publicize 2 make known 3 give notice of, esp. in newspapers, etc. ▷ *verb intransitive* **-tised, -tis•ing** make public request (for) > **ad•ver•tise'ment** *noun* > **ad'ver•tis•ing** *adjective, noun*
ad•vice [ad-VĪS] *noun* 1 opinion given 2 counsel 3 information 4 (formal) notification
ad•vise [ad-VĪZ] *verb transitive* **-vised, -vis•ing** 1 offer advice 2 recommend a line of conduct 3 give notice (of) > **ad•vis'a•ble** *adjective* expedient

DICTIONARY **a** THESAURUS

---

skilled
adulation *noun* WORSHIP, fawning, fulsome praise, servile flattery, sycophancy
adult *noun* 1 GROWN-UP, grown person *or* grown man grown woman grown-up person grown-up man grown-up woman, person of mature age ▷ *adjective* 2 FULLY GROWN, full grown, fully developed, grown-up, mature, of age, ripe
advance *verb* 1 PROGRESS, come forward, go on, hasten, make inroads, proceed, speed
2 BENEFIT, further, improve, prosper
3 SUGGEST, offer, present, proffer, put forward, submit
4 LEND, pay beforehand, supply on credit
▷ *noun* 5 PROGRESS, advancement, development, forward movement, headway, inroads, onward movement
6 IMPROVEMENT, breakthrough, gain, growth, progress, promotion, step
7 LOAN, credit, deposit, down payment, prepayment, retainer
8 ▷ **advances** OVERTURES, approach, approaches, moves, proposals, proposition
▷ *adjective* 9 PRIOR, beforehand, early, forward, in front
10 ▷ **in advance** BEFOREHAND, ahead, earlier, previously
advanced *adjective* FOREMOST, ahead, avant-garde, cutting-edge, forward, higher, leading, precocious, progressive
advancement *noun* PROMOTION, betterment, gain, improvement, preferment, progress, rise
advantage *noun* BENEFIT, ascendancy, dominance, good, help, lead, precedence, profit, superiority, sway
advantageous *adjective* 1 BENEFICIAL, convenient, expedient, helpful, of service, profitable, useful, valuable, worthwhile
2 SUPERIOR, dominant, dominating, favorable, win-win (*informal*)
adventure *noun* ESCAPADE, enterprise, experience, exploit, incident, occurrence, undertaking, venture
adventurer *noun* 1 MERCENARY, charlatan, fortune-hunter, gambler, opportunist, rogue, speculator
2 HERO, daredevil, heroine, knight-errant, traveler, voyager
adventurous *adjective* DARING, bold, daredevil, enterprising, intrepid, reckless
adversary *noun* OPPONENT, antagonist, competitor, contestant, enemy, foe, rival
adverse *adjective* UNFAVORABLE, contrary, detrimental, hostile, inopportune, negative, opposing
adversity *noun* HARDSHIP, affliction, bad luck, disaster, distress, hard times, misfortune, reverse, trouble
advertise *verb* PUBLICIZE, announce, inform, make known, notify, plug (*informal*), promote, tout
advertisement *noun* ad (*informal*), announcement, blurb, circular, commercial NOTICE, plug (*informal*), poster
advice *noun* GUIDANCE, counsel, help, opinion, recommendation, suggestion
advisability *noun* WISDOM, appropriateness, aptness, desirability, expediency, fitness, propriety, prudence, suitability
advisable *adjective* WISE, appropriate, desirable, expedient, fitting, politic, prudent, recommended, seemly, sensible
advise *verb* 1 RECOMMEND, admonish, caution, commend, counsel, prescribe, suggest, urge

> **ad•vised'** *adjective* considered, deliberate: *well-advised* > **ad•vis'ed•ly** [-zid-lee] *adverb* > **ad•vi'ser** *noun* > **ad•vi'so•ry** *adjective*
ad•vo•cate [AD-və-kit] *noun* 1 one who pleads the cause of another, esp. in court of law 2 attorney ▷ *verb transitive* [-kayt] 3 uphold, recommend > **ad'vo•ca•cy** [-kə-see] *noun*
ad•ware [AD-wair] *noun* 1 computer software that collects information about a user's interests in order to display relevant advertisements to that user 2 computer software that is given to a user with advertisements already embedded
ae•gis [EE-jis] *noun* sponsorship, protection (orig. shield of Zeus)
aer•ate [AIR-ayt] *verb transitive* **-at•ed, -at•ing** 1 charge liquid with gas, as effervescent drink 2 expose to air > **aer•a'tion** *noun* > **aer'a•tor** *noun* apparatus for charging liquid with gas
aer•i•al [AIR-ee-əl] *adjective* 1 of the air 2 operating in the air 3 pertaining to aircraft ▷ *noun* 4 part of radio, etc. receiving or sending radio waves
aer•ie, aer•y *noun see* **eyrie**
aero- *combining form* air or aircraft: *aerodynamics*
aer•o•bat•ics [air-ə-BAT-iks] *plural noun* stunt flying
aer•o•bics [air-OH-biks] *noun* exercise system designed to increase the amount of oxygen in the blood
aer•o•dy•nam•ics [air-oh-dī-NAM-iks] *noun* study of air flow, esp. around moving solid bodies
aer•o•naut [AIR-ə-nawt] *noun* pilot or navigator of lighter-than-air craft > **aer•o•nau'tics** *noun* science of air navigation and flying in general > **aer•o•nau'ti•cal** *adjective*
aer•o•sol [AIR-ə-sawl] *noun* (substance dispensed as fine spray from) pressurized can
aer•o•space [AIR-oh-spays] *noun* Earth's atmosphere and space beyond ▷ *adjective*
aes•thet•ic [es-THET-ik] *adjective* relating to principles of beauty, taste and art > **aes•thet'ics** *noun* study of art, taste, etc. > **aes•thete** [ES-theet] *noun* one who affects extravagant love of art
a•far [ə-FAHR] *adverb* from, at, or to, a great distance
af•fa•ble [AF-ə-bəl] *adjective* easy to speak to, polite and friendly > **af•fa•bil'i•ty** *noun*
af•fair [ə-FAIR] *noun* 1 thing done or attended to 2 business 3 happening 4 sexual liaison > **af•fairs** 1 personal or business interests 2 matters of public interest
af•fect [ə-FEKT] *verb transitive* 1 act on, influence 2 move feelings 3 make show of, make pretense 4 assume 5 have liking for > **affect** [AF-ekt] *noun psychology* emotion, feeling, desire > **af•fec•ta'tion** *noun* show, pretense > **af•fect'ed** *adjective* 1 making a pretense 2 moved 3 acted upon > **af•fect'ing** *adjective* moving the feelings > **af•fec'tion** *noun* fondness, love > **af•fec'tion•ate** *adjective*
af•fi•da•vit [af-i-DAY-vit] *noun* written statement under oath
af•fil•i•ate [ə-FIL-ee-ayt] *verb transitive* **-at•ed, -at•ing** 1 connect, attach, as society to federation, etc. 2 adopt ▷ *noun* [-ee-it] 3 affiliated organization
af•fin•i•ty [ə-FIN-i-tee] *noun, plural* **-ties** 1 natural liking 2 resemblance 3 relationship by marriage 4 chemical attraction
af•firm [ə-FURM] *verb* 1 assert positively, declare 2 maintain statement 3 make solemn declaration > **af•fir•ma'tion** *noun* > **af•firm'a•tive** *adjective* 1 asserting ▷ *noun* 2 word of assent
af•fix [ə-FIKS] *verb transitive* 1 fasten (to) 2 attach, append ▷ *noun* [AF-fiks] 3 addition, esp. to word, as suffix, prefix

---

2 NOTIFY, acquaint, apprise, inform, make known, report, tell, warn
adviser *noun* GUIDE, aide, confidant *or* confidante *feminine* consultant, counselor, helper, mentor, right-hand man
advisory *adjective* ADVISING, consultative, counseling, helping, recommending
advocate *verb* 1 RECOMMEND, advise, argue for, campaign for, champion, commend, encourage, promote, propose, support, uphold ▷ *noun* 2 SUPPORTER, campaigner, champion, counselor, defender, promoter, proponent, spokesman, upholder
3 (*law*) LAWYER, attorney, barrister, counsel
affable *adjective* FRIENDLY, amiable, amicable, approachable, congenial, cordial, courteous, genial, pleasant, sociable, urbane
affair *noun* 1 EVENT, activity, business, episode, happening, incident, matter, occurrence
2 RELATIONSHIP, amour, intrigue, liaison, romance
affect[1] *verb* 1 INFLUENCE, act on, alter, bear upon, change, concern, impinge upon, relate to
2 MOVE, disturb, overcome, perturb, stir, touch, upset
affect[2] *verb* PUT ON, adopt, aspire to, assume, contrive, feign, imitate, pretend, simulate
affectation *noun* PRETENSE, act, artificiality, assumed manners, façade, insincerity, pose, pretentiousness, show
affected *adjective* PRETENDED, artificial, contrived, feigned, insincere, mannered, phoney *or* phony (*informal*), put-on, unnatural
affecting *adjective* MOVING, pathetic, pitiful, poignant, sad, touching
affection *noun* FONDNESS, attachment, care, feeling, goodwill, kindness, liking, love, tenderness, warmth
affectionate *adjective* FOND, attached, caring, devoted, doting, friendly, kind, loving, tender, warm-hearted
affiliate *verb* JOIN, ally, amalgamate, associate, band together, combine, incorporate, link, unite
affinity *noun* 1 ATTRACTION, fondness, inclination, leaning, liking, partiality, rapport, sympathy
2 SIMILARITY, analogy, closeness, connection, correspondence, kinship, likeness, relationship, resemblance
affirm *verb* DECLARE, assert, certify, confirm, maintain, pronounce, state, swear, testify
affirmation *noun* DECLARATION, assertion, certification, confirmation, oath, pronouncement, statement, testimony
affirmative *adjective* AGREEING, approving, assenting, concurring, confirming, consenting, corroborative, favorable, positive

af•flict [ə-FLIKT] *verb transitive* 1 give pain or grief to, distress 2 trouble, vex > **af•flic'tion** *noun*
af•flu•ent [AF-loo-ənt] *adjective* 1 wealthy 2 abundant ▷ *noun* 3 tributary stream > **af'flu•ence** *noun* wealth, abundance
af•ford [ə-FORD] *verb transitive* 1 be able to buy 2 be able to spare the time, etc. 3 produce, yield, furnish
af•front [ə-FRUNT] *verb transitive* 1 insult openly ▷ *noun* 2 insult 3 offense
a•field [ə-FEELD] *adverb* 1 away from home 2 in or on the field
a•fire [ə-FĪR] *adverb* on fire
a•flame [ə-FLAYM] *adverb* burning
a•float [ə-FLOHT] *adverb* 1 floating 2 at sea 3 in circulation
a•foot [ə-FUUT] *adverb* 1 astir 2 on foot
a•fore [ə-FOR] *preposition, adverb* before, usually in compounds: *aforesaid; aforethought*
a•foul [ə-FOWL] *adjective, adverb* into difficulty (with)
a•fraid [ə-FRAYD] *adjective* 1 frightened 2 regretful
a•fresh [ə-FRESH] *adverb* again, anew
Af•ri•can [AF-ri-kən] *adjective* 1 belonging to Africa ▷ *noun* 2 native of Africa > **African-American** *noun* 1 American of African descent ▷ *adjective* 2 of African-Americans
Af•ri•kaans [af-ri-KAHNS] *noun* language used in S. Africa, derived from 17th cent. Dutch > **Af•ri•ka'ner** *noun* white native of S. Afr. with Afrikaans as mother tongue
aft *adverb* toward stern of ship or tail of aircraft
af•ter [AF-tər] *adverb* 1 later 2 behind ▷ *preposition* 3 behind 4 later than 5 on the model of 6 pursuing ▷ *conjunction* 7 at a later time than ▷ *adjective* 8 behind 9 later 10 nearer stern of ship or tail of aircraft
af'ter•birth [-burth] *noun* membrane expelled after a birth
af'ter•care [-kair] *noun* care, esp. medical, bestowed on person after period of treatment
af'ter•ef•fect [-ə-fekt] *noun* subsequent effect of deed, event, etc.
af'ter•glow [-gloh] *noun* 1 light after sunset 2 reflection of past emotion
af'ter•math *noun* result, consequence
af•ter•noon' *noun* time from noon to evening
af'ter•taste [-tayst] *noun* taste remaining or recurring after eating or drinking something
af'ter•thought [-thawt] *noun* idea occurring later
af'ter•ward [-wərd], **af'ter•wards** [-wərdz] *adverb* later
Ag *chem.* silver
a•gain [ə-GEN] *adverb* 1 once more 2 in addition 3 back, in return 4 besides
a•gainst [ə-GENST] *preposition* 1 in opposition to 2 in contact with 3 opposite 4 in readiness for
a•gape [ə-GAYP] *adjective, adverb* open-mouthed as in wonder, etc.
ag•ate [AG-it] *noun* colored, semiprecious, decorative form of quartz
age [ayj] *noun* 1 length of time person or thing has existed 2 time of life 3 period of history 4 maturity 5 long time ▷ *verb* **aged, ag•ing** 6 make or grow old > **aged** [AY-jid, ayjd] *adjective* 1 old ▷ *plural noun* [AY-jid] 2 old people > **aging** *noun, adjective* > **age'less** *adjective* not growing old, not showing signs of age > **age-old** *adjective* ancient
a•gen•da [ə-JEN-də] *noun* 1 things to be done 2 program of business meeting
a•gent [AY-jənt] *noun* 1 one authorized to carry

DICTIONARY

a

THESAURUS

afflict *verb* TORMENT, distress, grieve, harass, hurt, oppress, pain, plague, trouble
affliction *noun* SUFFERING, adversity, curse, disease, hardship, misfortune, ordeal, plague, scourge, torment, trial, trouble, woe
affluence *noun* WEALTH, abundance, fortune, opulence, plenty, prosperity, riches
affluent *adjective* WEALTHY, loaded (*slang*), moneyed, opulent, prosperous, rich, well-heeled (*informal*), well-off, well-to-do
afford *verb* 1 HAVE THE MONEY FOR, spare, bear, manage, stand, sustain
2 GIVE, offer, produce, provide, render, supply, yield
affordable *adjective* INEXPENSIVE, cheap, economical, low-cost, moderate, modest, reasonable
affront *noun* 1 INSULT, offense, outrage, provocation, slap in the face (*informal*), slight, slur
▷ *verb* 2 OFFEND, anger, annoy, displease, insult, outrage, provoke, slight
aflame *adjective* BURNING, ablaze, alight, blazing, fiery, flaming, lit, on fire
afoot *adverb* GOING ON, abroad, brewing, current, happening, in preparation, in progress, on the go (*informal*), up (*informal*)
afraid *adjective* 1 SCARED, apprehensive, cowardly, faint-hearted, fearful, frightened, nervous, wired (*slang*)
2 SORRY, regretful, unhappy
afresh *adverb* AGAIN, anew, newly, once again, once more, over again
after *adverb* FOLLOWING, afterwards, behind, below, later, subsequently, succeeding, thereafter
aftermath *noun* EFFECTS, aftereffects, consequences, end result, outcome, results, sequel, upshot, wake
again *adverb* 1 ONCE MORE, afresh, anew, another time
2 ALSO, besides, furthermore, in addition, moreover
against *preposition* 1 BESIDE, abutting, facing, in contact with, on, opposite to, touching, upon
2 OPPOSED TO, anti (*informal*), averse to, hostile to, in defiance of, in opposition to, resisting, versus
3 IN PREPARATION FOR, in anticipation of, in expectation of, in provision for
age *noun* 1 TIME, date, day *or* days, duration, epoch, era, generation, lifetime, period, span
2 OLD AGE, advancing years, decline, majority, maturity, senescence, senility, seniority
▷ *verb* 3 GROW OLD, decline, deteriorate, mature, mellow, ripen
aged *adjective* OLD, ancient, antiquated, antique, elderly, getting on, gray
agency *noun* 1 BUSINESS, bureau, department, office, organization
2 (*old-fashioned*) MEDIUM, activity, means, mechanism

on business or affairs for another **2** person or thing producing effect **3** cause **4** natural force > **a'gen•cy** *noun* **1** instrumentality **2** business, place of business, of agent
agent pro•vo•ca•teur [prə-vok-ə-TUR] *noun, plural* **agents pro•vo•ca•teur** Fr. police or secret service spy
ag•glu•ti•nate [ə-GLOOT-n-ayt] *verb transitive* **-nat•ed, -nat•ing** **1** unite with glue, etc. **2** form words into compounds ▷ *adjective* [-n-it] **3** united, as by glue > **ag•glu•ti•na'tion** *noun*
ag•gran•dize [ə-GRAN-dīz] *verb transitive* **-dized, -diz•ing** make greater in size, power, or rank > **ag•gran'dize•ment** [-diz-mənt] *noun*
ag•gra•vate [AG-rə-vayt] *verb transitive* **-vat•ed, -vat•ing** **1** make worse or more severe **2** (*informal*) annoy > **ag•gra•va'tion** *noun*
ag•gre•gate [AG-ri-gayt] *verb transitive* **-gat•ed, -gat•ing** **1** gather into mass ▷ *adjective* [-git] **2** gathered thus ▷ *noun* [-git] **3** mass, sum total **4** rock consisting of mixture of minerals **5** mixture of gravel, etc. for concrete > **ag•gre•ga'tion** *noun*
ag•gres•sion [ə-GRESH-ən] *noun* **1** unprovoked attack **2** hostile activity > **ag•gres'sive** *adjective* > **ag•gres'sive•ness** *noun* > **ag•gres'sor** *noun*
ag•grieve [ə-GREEV] *verb transitive* **-grieved, -griev•ing** pain, injure
a•ghast [ə-GAST] *adjective* struck, stupefied with horror or terror
ag•ile [AJ-əl] *adjective* **1** nimble **2** active **3** quick > **a•gil'i•ty** *noun*
ag•i•tate [AJ-i-tayt] *verb transitive* **-tat•ed, -tat•ing** **1** disturb, excite **2** to keep in motion, stir, shake up **3** trouble ▷ *verb intransitive* **-tat•ed, -tat•ing** **4** stir up public opinion (for or against) > **ag'i•ta•tor** *noun*
a•glow [ə-GLOH] *adjective* glowing
ag•nos•tic [ag-NOS-tik] *noun* **1** person who believes that it is impossible to know whether God exists ▷ *adjective* **2** of this theory > **ag•nos'ti•cism** *noun*
a•go [ə-goh] *adverb* in the past
a•gog [ə-GOG] *adjective, adverb* eager, astir
ag•o•ny [AG-ə-nee] *noun, plural* **-nies** extreme suffering of mind or body, violent struggle > **ag'o•nize** *verb intransitive* **-nized, -niz•ing** **1** suffer agony **2** worry greatly > **agony column** newspaper or magazine feature containing advertisements relating to personal problems, esp. to missing friends or relatives
ag•o•ra•pho•bi•a [ag-ər-ə-FOH-bee-ə] *noun* abnormal fear of open spaces
a•grar•i•an [ə-GRAIR-ee-ən] *adjective* of agriculture, land or its management
a•gree [ə-GREE] *verb* **-greed, -gree•ing** **1** be of same opinion **2** consent **3** harmonize **4** settle suit > **a•gree'a•ble** *adjective* **1** willing **2** pleasant

DICTIONARY • THESAURUS

agenda *noun* LIST, calendar, diary, plan, program, schedule, timetable
agent *noun* **1** REPRESENTATIVE, envoy, go-between, negotiator, rep (*informal*), surrogate
2 WORKER, author, doer, mover, operator, performer
3 FORCE, agency, cause, instrument, means, power, vehicle
aggravate *verb* **1** MAKE WORSE, exacerbate, exaggerate, increase, inflame, intensify, magnify, worsen
2 (*informal*) ANNOY, bother, get on one's nerves (*informal*), irritate, nettle, provoke
aggravation *noun* **1** WORSENING, exacerbation, exaggeration, heightening, increase, inflaming, intensification, magnification
2 (*informal*) ANNOYANCE, exasperation, gall, grief (*informal*), hassle (*informal*), irritation, provocation
aggregate *noun* **1** TOTAL, accumulation, amount, body, bulk, collection, combination, mass, pile, sum, whole
▷ *adjective* **2** TOTAL, accumulated, collected, combined, composite, cumulative, mixed
▷ *verb* **3** COMBINE, accumulate, amass, assemble, collect, heap, mix, pile
aggression *noun* **1** HOSTILITY, antagonism, belligerence, destructiveness, pugnacity
2 ATTACK, assault, injury, invasion, offensive, onslaught, raid
aggressive *adjective* **1** HOSTILE, belligerent, destructive, offensive, pugnacious, quarrelsome
2 FORCEFUL, assertive, bold, dynamic, energetic, enterprising, militant, pushy (*informal*), vigorous
aggressor *noun* ATTACKER, assailant, assaulter, invader
aggrieved *adjective* HURT, afflicted, distressed, disturbed, harmed, injured, unhappy, wronged
aghast *adjective* HORRIFIED, amazed, appalled, astonished, astounded, awestruck, confounded, shocked, startled, stunned
agile *adjective* **1** NIMBLE, active, brisk, lithe, quick, sprightly, spry, supple, swift
2 ACUTE, alert, bright (*informal*), clever, lively, quick-witted, sharp
agility *noun* NIMBLENESS, litheness, liveliness, quickness, suppleness, swiftness
agitate *verb* **1** UPSET, disconcert, distract, excite, fluster, perturb, trouble, unnerve, worry
2 STIR, beat, convulse, disturb, rouse, shake, toss
agitation *noun* **1** TURMOIL, clamor, commotion, confusion, disturbance, excitement, ferment, trouble, upheaval
2 TURBULENCE, convulsion, disturbance, shaking, stirring, tossing
agitator *noun* TROUBLEMAKER, agent provocateur, firebrand, instigator, rabble-rouser, revolutionary, stirrer (*informal*)
agog *adjective* EAGER, avid, curious, enthralled, enthusiastic, excited, expectant, impatient, in suspense, wired (*slang*)
agonize *verb* SUFFER, be distressed, be in agony, be in anguish, go through the mill, labor, strain, struggle, worry
agony *noun* SUFFERING, anguish, distress, misery, pain, throes, torment, torture
agree *verb* **1** CONSENT, assent, be of the same opinion, comply, concur, see eye to eye
2 GET ON *or* GET ON TOGETHER, coincide, conform, correspond, match, tally
agreeable *adjective* **1** PLEASANT, delightful, enjoyable, gratifying, likable *or* likeable, pleasing, satisfying, to one's taste
2 CONSENTING, amenable, approving, complying, concurring, in accord, onside (*informal*), sympathetic, well-disposed, willing

> **a•gree'ment** *noun* 1 concord 2 contract
ag•ri•cul•ture [AG-ri-kul-chər] *noun* art, practice of cultivating land > **ag•ri•cul'tur•al** *adjective*
a•gron•o•my [ə-GRON-ə-mee] *noun* the study of the management of the land and the scientific cultivation of crops > **a•gron'o•mist** *noun*
a•ground [ə-GROWND] *adverb* (of boat) touching bottom
a•head [ə-HED] *adverb* 1 in front 2 forward 3 in advance
a•hoy [ə-HOI] *interjection* shout used at sea for hailing
aid [ayd] *verb transitive* 1 to help ▷ *noun* 2 help, support, assistance
aide [ayd] *noun* person acting as an assistant
aide-de-camp [AYD-də-KAMP] *noun, plural* **aides-de-camp** [AYD-də-KAMP] military officer personally assisting superior
AIDS acquired immune deficiency syndrome
ail [ayl] *verb transitive* 1 trouble, afflict, disturb ▷ *verb intransitive* 2 be ill > **ail'ing** *adjective* sickly > **ail'ment** *noun* illness
ai•ler•on [AY-lə-ron] *noun* movable section of wing of aircraft that gives lateral control
aim [aym] *verb* 1 give direction to weapon, etc. 2 direct effort toward, try to ▷ *noun* 3 direction 4 object, purpose > **aim'less** *adjective* without purpose
ain't [aynt] (*not standard*) 1 am not 2 is not 3 are not 4 has not 5 have not
air *noun* 1 mixture of gases we breathe, the atmosphere 2 breeze 3 tune 4 manner ▷ *verb transitive* 5 expose to air to dry or ventilate > **airs** *plural noun* affected manners > **air'i•ly** *adverb* > **air'i•ness** *noun* > **air'ing** *verb* 1 time spent in the open air 2 exposure to public view 3 radio or TV broadcast > **air'less** *adjective* stuffy > **air'y** *adjective* **air•i•er, air•i•est** > **air'borne** *adjective* flying, in the air > **air'bag** *noun* safety device in car which inflates automatically in an accident to protect the driver or passenger > **air brake** 1 brake worked by compressed air 2 method of slowing down an aircraft > **air'brush** *noun* atomizer spraying paint by compressed air > **air'-con•di•tion** *verb transitive* maintain constant stream of clean fresh air in building at correct temperature > **air conditioner** *noun* > **air'craft** *noun* 1 collective name for flying machines 2 airplane > **aircraft carrier** warship with a long flat deck for the launching and landing of aircraft > **air cushion** pocket of air supporting hovercraft > **air'field** *noun* landing and takeoff area for aircraft > **air force** military organization of country for air warfare > **air gun** gun discharged by force of compressed air > **air'lift** *noun* transport of goods, etc. by aircraft > **air'line** *noun* company operating aircraft > **air'lock** *noun* 1 air bubble obstructing flow of liquid in pipe 2 airtight chamber > **air pocket** less dense air that causes airplane to drop suddenly > **air'port** *noun* station for civilian aircraft > **air pump** machine to extract or supply air > **air raid** attack by aircraft > **air shaft** passage for air into a mine, etc. > **air'ship** *noun* lighter-than-air flying machine with means of propulsion and steering > **air'sick•ness** *noun* nausea caused by motion of aircraft in flight > **air'speed** *noun* speed of aircraft relative to air > **air'strip** *noun* small airfield with only one runway > **air'tight** *adjective* not allowing passage of air > **air'way** *noun* regular aircraft route > **air'wor•thy** *adjective* fit for service in air > **air'wor•thi•ness** *noun*
air'plane [-playn] *noun* heavier-than-air

---

agreement *noun* 1 ASSENT, agreeing, compliance, concord, concurrence, consent, harmony, union, unison
2 CORRESPONDENCE, compatibility, conformity, congruity, consistency, similarity
3 CONTRACT, arrangement, bargain, covenant, deal (*informal*), pact, settlement, treaty, understanding
agricultural *adjective* FARMING, agrarian, country, rural, rustic
agriculture *noun* FARMING, cultivation, culture, husbandry, tillage
aground *adverb* BEACHED, ashore, foundered, grounded, high and dry, on the rocks, stranded, stuck
ahead *adverb* IN FRONT, at an advantage, at the head, before, cutting-edge, in advance, in the lead, leading, to the fore, winning
aid *noun* 1 HELP, assistance, benefit, encouragement, favor, promotion, relief, service, support
▷ *verb* 2 HELP, assist, encourage, favor, promote, serve, subsidize, support, sustain
aide *noun* ASSISTANT, attendant, helper, right-hand man, second, supporter
ailing *adjective* ILL, indisposed, infirm, poorly, sick, under the weather (*informal*), unwell, weak
ailment *noun* ILLNESS, affliction, complaint, disease, disorder, infirmity, malady, sickness
aim *verb* 1 INTEND, attempt, endeavor, mean, plan, point, propose, seek, set one's sights on, strive, try
▷ *noun* 2 INTENTION, ambition, aspiration, desire, goal, objective, plan, purpose, target
aimless *adjective* PURPOSELESS, directionless, pointless, random, stray
air *noun* 1 ATMOSPHERE, heavens, sky
2 WIND, breeze, draft, zephyr
3 MANNER, appearance, atmosphere, aura, demeanor, impression, look, mood
4 TUNE, aria, lay, melody, song
▷ *verb* 5 PUBLICIZE, circulate, display, exhibit, express, give vent to, make known, make public, reveal, voice
6 VENTILATE, aerate, expose, freshen
airborne *adjective* FLYING, floating, gliding, hovering, in flight, in the air, on the wing
airing *noun* 1 VENTILATION, aeration, drying, freshening
2 EXPOSURE, circulation, display, dissemination, expression, publicity, utterance, vent
airless *adjective* STUFFY, close, heavy, muggy, oppressive, stifling, suffocating, sultry
airs *plural noun* AFFECTATION, arrogance, haughtiness, hauteur, pomposity, pretensions, superciliousness
airy *adjective* 1 WELL-VENTILATED, fresh, light, open, spacious, uncluttered
2 LIGHT-HEARTED, blithe, cheerful, high-spirited, jaunty, lively, sprightly

flying machine
aisle [īl] *noun* passageway separating seating areas in church, theater, etc.
a•jar [ə-JAHR] *adverb* partly open
a•kim•bo [ə-KIM-boh] *adverb* with hands on hips and elbows outward
a•kin [ə-KIN] *adjective* 1 related by blood 2 alike, having like qualities
Al *chem.* aluminum
al•a•bas•ter [AL-ə-bas-tər] *noun* soft, white, semitransparent stone > **al•a•bas'trine** [-BAS-trin] *adjective* of, like this
à la carte [ah lə KAHRT] selected freely from the menu
a•lac•ri•ty [ə-LAK-ri-tee] *noun* quickness, briskness, readiness
à la mode [ah lə MOHD] 1 in fashion 2 topped with ice cream
a•larm [ə-LAHRM] *noun* 1 sudden fright 2 apprehension 3 notice of danger 4 bell, buzzer 5 call to arms ▷ *verb transitive* 6 frighten 7 warn of danger > **a•larm'ist** *noun* one given to prophesying danger or exciting alarm esp. needlessly
a•las [ə-LAS] *interjection* cry of grief, pity, or concern
al•ba•tross [AL-bə-traws] *noun* 1 large oceanic bird, of petrel family 2 someone or something thought to make accomplishment difficult
al•be•it [awl-BEE-it] *conjunction* although
al•bi•no [al-BĪ-noh] *noun, plural* **-nos** person or animal with white skin and hair, and pink eyes, due to lack of pigment > **al•bi•nism** [AL-bə-niz-əm] *noun*
al•bum [AL-bəm] *noun* 1 book of blank leaves, for photographs, stamps, autographs, etc. 2 one or more long-playing phonograph records or tape recordings
al•bu•men [al-BYOO-mən] *noun* egg white
al•bu•min [al-BYOO-mən] *noun* constituent of animal and vegetable matter, found nearly pure in white of egg
al•che•my [AL-kə-mee] *noun* medieval chemistry, esp. attempts to turn base metals into gold and find elixir of life > **al'che•mist** *noun*
al•co•hol [AL-kə-hawl] *noun* 1 intoxicating fermented liquor 2 class of organic chemical substances > **al•co•hol'ic** *adjective* 1 of alcohol ▷ *noun* 2 one addicted to alcoholic drink > **al'co•hol•ism** *noun* disease, alcohol poisoning
al•cove [AL-kohv] *noun* recessed section of a room
ale [ayl] *noun* fermented malt liquor, type of beer, orig. without hops
a•lert [ə-LURT] *adjective* 1 watchful 2 brisk, active ▷ *noun* 3 warning of sudden attack or surprise ▷ *verb transitive* 4 warn, esp. of danger 5 draw attention to > **a•lert'ness** *noun* **on the alert** watchful
al•fal•fa [al-FAL-fə] *noun* plant widely used as fodder
al•fres•co [al-FRES-koh] *adverb, adjective* in the open air
al•gae [AL-jee] *plural noun, sing* **-ga** [-gə] various water plants, including seaweed
al•ge•bra [AL-jə-brə] *noun* method of calculating, using symbols to represent quantities and to show relations between them, making a kind of abstract arithmetic > **al•ge•bra'ic** [-BRAY-ik] *adjective*
ALGOL, Algol [AL-gol] *computing* algorithmic oriented language
al•go•rithm [AL-gə-rith-əm] *noun* procedural model for complicated calculations
a•li•as [AY-lee-əs] *adverb* 1 otherwise known as ▷ *noun, plural* **-as•es** 2 assumed name
al•i•bi [AL-ə-bī] *noun* 1 plea of being somewhere else when crime was committed 2 (*informal*) excuse
a•li•en [AY-lee-ən] *adjective* 1 foreign 2 different in nature 3 repugnant (to) ▷ *noun* 4 foreigner > **a'li•en•a•ble** *adjective* able to be transferred to another owner > **a'li•en•ate** [-ə-nayt] *verb transitive* **-at•ed, -at•ing** 1 estrange 2 transfer > **a•li•en•a'tion** *noun*
a•light[1] [ə-LĪT] *verb intransitive* 1 get down 2 land, settle

---

aisle *noun* PASSAGEWAY, alley, corridor, gangway, lane, passage, path
alacrity *noun* EAGERNESS, alertness, enthusiasm, promptness, quickness, readiness, speed, willingness, zeal
alarm *noun* 1 FEAR, anxiety, apprehension, consternation, fright, nervousness, panic, scare, trepidation
2 DANGER SIGNAL, alarm bell, alert, bell, distress signal, hooter, siren, warning
▷ *verb* 3 FRIGHTEN, daunt, dismay, distress, give (someone) a fright (*informal*), panic, scare, startle, unnerve
alarming *adjective* FRIGHTENING, daunting, distressing, disturbing, scaring, shocking, startling, unnerving
alcoholic *noun* 1 DRUNKARD, dipsomaniac, drinker, drunk, inebriate, tippler, toper, wino (*informal*)
▷ *adjective* 2 INTOXICATING, brewed, distilled, fermented, hard, strong
alcove *noun* RECESS, bay, compartment, corner, cubbyhole, cubicle, niche, nook
alert *adjective* 1 WATCHFUL, attentive, awake, circumspect, heedful, observant, on guard, on one's toes, on the lookout, vigilant, wide-awake
▷ *noun* 2 WARNING, alarm, signal, siren
▷ *verb* 3 WARN, alarm, forewarn, inform, notify, signal
alertness *noun* WATCHFULNESS, attentiveness, heedfulness, liveliness, vigilance
alias *adverb* 1 ALSO KNOWN AS, also called, otherwise, otherwise known as
▷ *noun* 2 PSEUDONYM, assumed name, nom de guerre, nom de plume, pen name, stage name
alibi *noun* EXCUSE, defense, explanation, justification, plea, pretext, reason
alien *adjective* 1 FOREIGN, exotic, incongruous, strange, unfamiliar
▷ *noun* 2 FOREIGNER, newcomer, outsider, stranger
alienate *verb* SET AGAINST, disaffect, estrange, make unfriendly, shut out, turn away
alienation *noun* SETTING AGAINST, disaffection, estrangement, remoteness, separation, turning away
alight[1] *verb* 1 GET OFF, descend, disembark, dismount, get down

a•light² *adjective* lit up
a•lign [ə-LĪN] *verb transitive* bring into line or agreement
a•like [ə-LĪK] *adjective* 1 like, similar ▷ *adverb* 2 in the same way
al•i•men•ta•ry [al-ə-MEN-tə-ree] *adjective* of food > **alimentary canal** food passage in body
al•i•mo•ny [AL-ə-moh-nee] *noun* allowance paid under court order to separated or divorced spouse
a•live [ə-LĪV] *adjective* 1 living 2 active 3 aware 4 swarming
al•ka•li [AL-kə-lī] *noun, plural* **-lis** substance that combines with acid and neutralizes it, forming a salt > **al'ka•line** *adjective* > **al•ka•lin'i•ty** *noun*
all [awl] *adjective* 1 the whole of, every one of ▷ *adverb* 2 wholly, entirely ▷ *noun* 3 the whole 4 everything, everyone ▷ *pronoun* 5 everything, everyone > **all fours** hands and feet > **all in** exhausted > **all'-a•round'** *adjective* showing ability in many fields > **all right** 1 satisfactory 2 well, safe 3 pleasing 4 very well 5 beyond doubt
Al•lah [AH-lə] *noun* Muslim name for the Supreme Being
al•lay [ə-LAY] *verb transitive* lighten, relieve, calm, soothe
al•lege [ə-LEJ] *verb transitive* **-leged, -leg•ing** 1 state without or before proof 2 produce as argument > **al•le•ga•tion** [al-i-GAY-shən] *noun* > **al•leged'** *adjective* > **al•leg•ed•ly** *adverb*
al•le•giance [ə-LEE-jəns] *noun* 1 duty of a subject or citizen to sovereign or government 2 loyalty (to person or cause)
al•le•go•ry [AL-i-gor-ee] *noun, plural* **-ries** 1 story with a meaning other than literal one 2 description of one thing under image of another > **al•le•gor'i•cal** *adjective*
al•le•gret•to [al-i-GRET-oh] *adverb, adjective, noun mus.* lively (passage) but not so quick as allegro
al•le•gro [ə-LEG-roh] *adverb, adjective, noun mus.* fast (passage)
al•ler•gy [AL-ər-jee] *noun, plural* **-gies** abnormal sensitivity to some food or substance harmless to most people > **al'ler•gen** *noun* substance capable of inducing an allergy > **al•ler•gic** [ə-LUR-jik] *adjective* 1 having or caused by an allergy 2 (*informal*) having an aversion (to)
al•le•vi•ate [ə-LEE-vee-ayt] *verb transitive* **-at•ed, -at•ing** 1 ease, lessen, mitigate 2 make light > **al•le•vi•a'tion** *noun*
al•ley [AL-ee] *noun, plural* **-leys** 1 narrow street esp. through the middle of a block 2 walk, path 3 hardwood lane for bowling 4 building housing bowling lanes
al•li•ance [ə-LĪ-əns] *noun* 1 state of being allied 2 union between families by marriage, and states by treaty 3 confederation
al•li•ga•tor [AL-i-gay-tər] *noun* 1 animal of crocodile family 2 leather made from its hide
al•lit•er•a•tion [ə-lit-ə-RAY-shən] *noun* beginning of two or more words in close succession with same sound, e.g *Sing a Song of Sixpence* > **al•lit'er•a•tive** *adjective*
al•lo•cate [AL-ə-kayt] *verb transitive* **-cat•ed, -cat•ing** 1 assign as a share 2 designate > **al•lo•ca'tion** *noun*
al•lo•mor•phism [al-ə-MOR-fiz-əm] *noun* 1

DICTIONARY

a

THESAURUS

2 LAND, come down, come to rest, descend, light, perch, settle, touch down
alight² *adjective* 1 ON FIRE, ablaze, aflame, blazing, burning, fiery, flaming, lighted, lit
2 LIT UP, bright, brilliant, illuminated, shining
align *verb* 1 ALLY, affiliate, agree, associate, cooperate, join, side, sympathize
2 LINE UP, even up, order, range, regulate, straighten
alignment *noun* 1 ALLIANCE, affiliation, agreement, association, cooperation, sympathy, union
2 LINING UP, adjustment, arrangement, evening up, order, straightening up
alike *adjective* 1 SIMILAR, akin, analogous, corresponding, identical, of a piece, parallel, resembling, the same
▷ *adverb* 2 SIMILARLY, analogously, correspondingly, equally, evenly, identically, uniformly
alive *adjective* 1 LIVING, animate, breathing, in the land of the living (*informal*), subsisting
2 IN EXISTENCE, active, existing, extant, functioning, in force, operative
3 LIVELY, active, alert, animated, energetic, full of life, vital, vivacious
all *adjective* 1 THE WHOLE OF, every bit of, the complete, the entire, the sum of, the totality of, the total of
2 EVERY, each, each and every, every one of, every single
3 COMPLETE, entire, full, greatest, perfect, total, utter
▷ *adverb* 4 COMPLETELY, altogether, entirely, fully, totally, utterly, wholly
▷ *noun* 5 WHOLE AMOUNT, aggregate, entirety, everything, sum total, total, totality, utmost
allegation *noun* CLAIM, accusation, affirmation, assertion, charge, declaration, statement
allege *verb* CLAIM, affirm, assert, charge, declare, maintain, state
alleged *adjective* 1 STATED, affirmed, asserted, declared, described, designated
2 SUPPOSED, doubtful, dubious, ostensible, professed, purported, so-called, unproved
allegiance *noun* LOYALTY, constancy, devotion, faithfulness, fidelity, obedience
allegorical *adjective* SYMBOLIC, emblematic, figurative, symbolizing
allegory *noun* SYMBOL, fable, myth, parable, story, symbolism, tale
allergic *adjective* SENSITIVE, affected by, hypersensitive, susceptible
allergy *noun* SENSITIVITY, antipathy, hypersensitivity, susceptibility
alleviate *verb* EASE, allay, lessen, lighten, moderate, reduce, relieve, soothe
alley *noun* PASSAGE, alleyway, backstreet, lane, passageway, pathway, walk
alliance *noun* UNION, affiliation, agreement, association, coalition, combination, confederation, connection, federation, league, marriage, pact, partnership, treaty
allied *adjective* UNITED, affiliated, associated, combined, connected, in league, linked, related
allocate *verb* ASSIGN, allot, allow, apportion, budget, designate, earmark, mete, set aside, share out

variation of form without change in essential nature **2** variation of crystalline form of chemical compound > **al'lo•morph** *noun* > **al•lo•morph'ic** *adjective*

al•lop•a•thy [ə-LOP-ə-thee] *noun* **1** orthodox practice of medicine **2** opposite of homeopathy

al•lot [ə-LOT] *verb transitive* **-lot•ted, -lot•ting** **1** distribute as shares **2** give out > **al•lot'ment** *noun* **1** distribution **2** portion of land rented for cultivation **3** portion of land, pay, etc. allotted

al•low [ə-LOW] *verb transitive* **1** let happen **2** permit **3** acknowledge **4** set aside ▷ *verb intransitive* **5** (usu. with *for*) take into account > **al•low'a•ble** *adjective* > **al•low'ance** *noun* portion or amount allowed, esp. at regular times

al•loy [AL-oi] *noun* **1** mixture of two or more metals ▷ *verb transitive* **2** [ə-LOI] mix metals, debase

all right *see* **all**

all•spice [AWL-spīs] *noun* **1** berry of West Indian tree **2** the tree **3** aromatic spice prepared from its berries

al•lude [ə-LOOD] *verb intransitive* **-lud•ed, -lud•ing** **1** mention lightly, hint at, make indirect reference to **2** refer to > **al•lu'sion** [-LOO-zhən] *noun* > **al•lu'sive** [-siv] *adjective*

al•lure [ə-LOOR] *verb transitive* **-lured, -lur•ing** **1** entice, win over, fascinate ▷ *noun* **2** attractiveness > **al•lur'ing** *adjective* charming, seductive

al•lu•vi•al [ə-LOO-vee-əl] *adjective* deposited by rivers > **al•lu'vi•on** [-vee-ən] *noun* land formed by washed-up deposit > **al•lu'vi•um** [-vee-əm] *noun, plural* **-vi•a** [-vee-ə] water-borne matter deposited by rivers, floods, etc.

al•ly [ə-LĪ] *verb transitive* **-lied, -ly•ing** **1** join in relationship by treaty, marriage, or friendship, etc. ▷ *noun* [AL-ī] *plural* **-lies** **2** country or ruler bound to another by treaty **3** confederate

al•ma ma•ter [AL-mə MAH-tər] **1** one's school, college, or university **2** its song or hymn

al•ma•nac [AWL-mə-nak] *noun* yearly publication with detailed information on tides, events, etc.

al•might•y [awl-MĪ-tee] *adjective* **1** having all power, omnipotent **2** (*informal*) very great **The Almighty** God

al•mond [AH-mənd] *noun* **1** kernel of the fruit of a tree related to the peach **2** tree that bears it

al•most [AWL-mohst] *adverb* very nearly, all but

alms [ahmz] *plural noun* gifts to the poor

al•oe [AL-oh] *noun* genus of plants of medicinal value > **al•oes** bitter drug made from plant

a•loft [ə-LAWFT] *adverb* **1** on high **2** overhead **3** in ship's rigging

a•lone [ə-LOHN] *adjective* **1** single, solitary ▷ *adverb* **2** separately, only

a•long [ə-LAWNG] *adverb* **1** lengthwise **2** together (with) **3** forward ▷ *preposition* **4** over the length of > **a•long'side'** *adverb, preposition* beside

a•loof [ə-LOOF] *adverb* **1** withdrawn **2** at a distance **3** apart ▷ *adjective* **4** uninvolved > **a•loof'ness** *noun*

al•o•pe•ci•a [al-ə-PEESH-ə] *noun* baldness

a•loud [ə-LOWD] *adjective* **1** in a voice loud

DICTIONARY • THESAURUS

allocation *noun* ASSIGNMENT, allotment, allowance, lot, portion, quota, ration, share

allot *verb* ASSIGN, allocate, apportion, budget, designate, earmark, mete, set aside, share out

allotment *noun* **1** PLOT, kitchen garden, patch, tract
2 ASSIGNMENT, allocation, allowance, grant, portion, quota, ration, share, stint

all-out *adjective* TOTAL, complete, exhaustive, full, full-scale, maximum, thoroughgoing, undivided, unremitting, unrestrained

allow *verb* **1** PERMIT, approve, authorize, enable, endure, let, sanction, stand, suffer, tolerate
2 GIVE, allocate, allot, assign, grant, provide, set aside, spare
3 ACKNOWLEDGE, admit, concede, confess, grant, own

allowable *adjective* PERMISSIBLE, acceptable, admissible, all right, appropriate, suitable, tolerable

allowance *noun* **1** PORTION, allocation, amount, grant, lot, quota, ration, share, stint
2 CONCESSION, deduction, discount, rebate, reduction

allow for *verb* TAKE INTO ACCOUNT, consider, make allowances for, make concessions for, make provision for, plan for, provide for, take into consideration

alloy *noun* **1** MIXTURE, admixture, amalgam, blend, combination, composite, compound, hybrid
▷ *verb* **2** MIX, amalgamate, blend, combine, compound, fuse

all right *adjective* **1** SATISFACTORY, acceptable, adequate, average, fair, O.K. *or* okay (*informal*), standard, up to scratch (*informal*)
2 O.K. *or* OKAY (*informal*), healthy, safe, sound, unharmed, uninjured, well, whole

allude *verb* REFER, hint, imply, intimate, mention, suggest, touch upon

allure *noun* **1** ATTRACTIVENESS, appeal, attraction, charm, enchantment, enticement, glamour, lure, persuasion, seductiveness, temptation
▷ *verb* **2** ATTRACT, captivate, charm, enchant, entice, lure, persuade, seduce, tempt, win over

alluring *adjective* ATTRACTIVE, beguiling, captivating, come-hither, fetching, glamorous, seductive, tempting

allusion *noun* REFERENCE, casual remark, hint, implication, innuendo, insinuation, intimation, mention, suggestion

ally *noun* **1** PARTNER, accomplice, associate, collaborator, colleague, friend, helper, homeboy (*slang*), homegirl (*slang*)
▷ *verb* **2** UNITE, associate, collaborate, combine, join, join forces, unify

almighty *adjective* **1** ALL-POWERFUL, absolute, invincible, omnipotent, supreme, unlimited
2 (*informal*) GREAT, enormous, excessive, intense, loud, severe, terrible

almost *adverb* NEARLY, about, approximately, close to, just about, not quite, on the brink of, practically, virtually

alone *adjective* BY ONESELF, apart, detached, isolated, lonely, only, separate, single, solitary, unaccompanied

aloof *adjective* DISTANT, detached, haughty, remote, standoffish, supercilious, unapproachable, unfriendly

enough to be heard ▷ *adverb* 2 loudly 3 audibly
alp *noun* high mountain > **Alps** esp. mountains of Switzerland > **al•pine** [AL-pīn] *adjective* 1 of, growing on, high mountains 2 (**Al•pine**) of the Alps ▷ *noun* 3 mountain plant > **al•pin•ist** [AL-pə-nist] *noun* mountain climber > **al'pen•stock** [-pən-stok] *noun* iron-tipped staff used by climbers
al•pac•a [al-PAK-ə] *noun* 1 Peruvian llama 2 its wool 3 cloth made from this
al•pha•bet [AL-fə-bet] *noun* the set of letters used in writing a language > **al•pha•bet'i•cal** *adjective* in the standard order of the letters
al•pha male *noun* dominant male animal or person in a group
al-Qae•da [al-KAY-də, al-KĪ-də] *noun* militant Islamic organization believed to be behind various operations against Western interests
al•read•y [awl-RED-ee] *adverb* 1 before, previously 2 sooner than expected
al•so [AWL-soh] *adverb* 1 as well, too 2 besides, moreover
al•tar [AWL-tər] *noun* 1 raised place, stone, etc., on which sacrifices are offered 2 in Christian church, table on which priest consecrates the eucharist elements > **al'tar•cloth** *noun* > **al'tar•piece** *noun* > **al'tar rail** *noun*
altar boy *noun* acolyte
al•ter [AWL-tər] *verb* 1 change, make or become different 2 castrate, spay (animal) > **al'ter•a•ble** *adjective* > **al'ter•a•bly** *adverb* > **al•ter•a'tion** *noun*
al•ter•ca•tion [awl-tər-KAY-shən] *noun* dispute, wrangling, noisy controversy
al•ter e•go [AWL-tər EE-goh] 1 second self 2 close friend
al•ter•nate [AWL-tər-nayt] *verb* **-nat•ed, -nat•ing** occur or cause to occur by turns > **al'ter•nate** [-nit] *adjective, noun* (one) after the other, by turns > **al•ter•na•tive** [awl-TUR-nə-tiv] *noun* 1 one of two choices ▷ *adjective* 2 offering or expressing a choice > **al'ter•na•tor** *noun* electric generator for producing alternating current > **alternative medicine** treatment of disease by non-traditional methods such as homeopathy and acupuncture
al•though [awl-THOH] *conjunction* despite the fact that
al•tim•e•ter [al-TIM-i-tər] *noun* instrument for measuring height
al•ti•tude [AL-ti-tood] *noun* height, eminence, elevation, loftiness
al•to [AL-toh] *noun, plural* **-tos** *mus.* 1 male singing voice or instrument above tenor 2 contralto
al•to•geth•er [awl-tə-GETH-ər] *adverb* 1 entirely 2 on the whole 3 in total **in the altogether** nude
al•tru•ism [AL-troo-iz-əm] *noun* principle of living and acting for good of others > **al'tru•ist** *noun* > **al•tru•is'tic** *adjective*
a•lu•mi•num [ə-LOO-mə-nəm] *noun* light nonrusting metal resembling silver > **a•lu'mi•na** *noun* oxide of aluminum
a•lum•na [ə-LUM-nə] *noun, plural* **-nae** [-nee] girl or woman graduate of a particular school, college, or university
a•lum•nus [ə-LUM-nəs] *noun, plural* **-ni** [-nī] graduate of a particular school, college, or university
al•ways [AWL-wayz] *adverb* 1 at all times 2 forever
am *first person sing pres ind. of* **be**
Am *chem.* americium
A.M., a.m. ante meridiem: before noon
a•mal•gam [ə-MAL-gəm] *noun* 1 compound of mercury and another metal 2 soft, plastic mixture 3 combination of elements
a•mal•ga•mate [ə-MAL-gə-mayt] *verb* **-mat•ed, -mat•ing** mix, combine or cause to combine > **a•mal•ga•ma'tion** *noun*
a•man•u•en•sis [ə-man-yoo-EN-sis] *noun, plural* **-ses** [-seez] 1 one who writes from dictation 2 copyist, secretary

aloud *adverb* OUT LOUD, audibly, clearly, distinctly, intelligibly, plainly
already *adverb* BEFORE NOW, at present, before, by now, by then, even now, heretofore, just now, previously
also *adverb* TOO, additionally, and, as well, besides, further, furthermore, in addition, into the bargain, moreover, to boot
alter *verb* CHANGE, adapt, adjust, amend, convert, modify, reform, revise, transform, turn, vary
alteration *noun* CHANGE, adaptation, adjustment, amendment, conversion, difference, modification, reformation, revision, transformation, variation
alternate *verb* 1 CHANGE, act reciprocally, fluctuate, interchange, oscillate, rotate, substitute, take turns
▷ *adjective* 2 EVERY OTHER, alternating, every second, interchanging, rotating
alternative *noun* 1 CHOICE, option, other, preference, recourse, selection, substitute
▷ *adjective* 2 DIFFERENT, alternate, another, other, second, substitute
alternatively *adverb* OR, as an alternative, if not, instead, on the other hand, otherwise
although *conjunction* THOUGH, albeit, despite the fact that, even if, even though, notwithstanding, while
altogether *adverb* 1 COMPLETELY, absolutely, fully, perfectly, quite, thoroughly, totally, utterly, wholly
2 ON THE WHOLE, all in all, all things considered, as a whole, collectively, generally, in general
3 IN TOTAL, all told, everything included, in all, in sum, taken together
altruistic *adjective* SELFLESS, benevolent, charitable, generous, humanitarian, philanthropic, public-spirited, self-sacrificing, unselfish
always *adverb* CONTINUALLY, consistently, constantly, eternally, evermore, every time, forever, invariably, perpetually, repeatedly, twenty-four-seven (*slang*), without exception
amalgamate *verb* COMBINE, ally, blend, fuse, incorporate, integrate, merge, mingle, unite
amalgamation *noun* COMBINATION, blend, coalition, compound, fusion, joining, merger, mixture, union

a•mass [ə-MAS] *verb* collect in quantity
am•a•teur [AM-ə-chuur] *noun* 1 one who carries on an art, study, game, etc. for the love of it, not for money 2 unskilled practitioner > **am•a•teur'ish** *adjective* imperfect, untrained
am•a•to•ry [AM-ə-tor-ee] *adjective* relating to love
a•maze [ə-MAYZ] *verb transitive* **-mazed, -maz•ing** surprise greatly, astound > **a•maze'ment** *noun* > **amazing** *adjective*
Am•a•zon [AM-ə-zon] *noun* 1 female warrior of legend 2 tall, strong woman > **Am•a•zo'ni•an** [-ZOH-nee-ən] *adjective*
am•bas•sa•dor [am-BAS-ə-dər] *noun* senior diplomatic representative sent by one government to another > **am•bas•sa•do'ri•al** *adjective*
am•ber [AM-bər] *noun* 1 yellowish, translucent fossil resin ▷ *adjective* 2 made of, colored like amber
am•ber•gris [AM-bər-gris] *noun* waxy substance secreted by the sperm whale, used in making perfumes
am•bi•dex•trous [am-bi-DEK-strəs] *adjective* able to use both hands with equal ease > **am•bi•dex•ter'i•ty** *noun*
am•bi•ence, -ance [AM-bee-əns] *noun* atmosphere of a place
am•bi•ent [AM-bee-ənt] *adjective* surrounding
am•big•u•ous [am-BIG-yoo-əs] *adjective* 1 having more than one meaning 2 obscure > **am•bi•gu'ity** *noun*
am•bi•tion [am-BISH-ən] *noun* 1 desire for power, fame, honor 2 the object of that desire > **am•bi'tious** *adjective*
am•biv•a•lence [am-BIV-ə-ləns] *noun* simultaneous existence of two conflicting desires, opinions, etc. > **am•biv'a•lent** *adjective*
am•ble [AM-bəl] *verb intransitive* **-bled, -bling** 1 move along easily and gently 2 move at an easy pace ▷ *noun* 3 this movement or pace
am•bro•sia [am-BROH-*zhə*] *noun mythology* 1 food of the gods 2 anything smelling, tasting particularly good
am•bu•lance [AM-byə-ləns] *noun* conveyance for sick or injured
am•bush [AM-buush] *noun* 1 a lying in wait (for) ▷ *verb transitive* 2 waylay, attack from hiding, lie in wait for
a•mel•io•rate [ə-MEEL-yə-rayt] *verb* **-rat•ed, -rat•ing** make better, improve > **a•mel•io•ra'tion** *noun*
a•men [AY-MEN] *interjection* 1 surely 2 so let it be
a•me•na•ble [ə-MEE-nə-bəl] *adjective* 1 easy to be led or controlled 2 subject to, liable > **a•me'na•bly** *adverb*
a•mend [ə-MEND] *verb intransitive* 1 grow better ▷ *verb transitive* 2 correct 3 improve 4 alter in detail, as bill in legislature, etc. > **a•mend'ment** *noun* > **a•mends'** *plural noun* reparation
a•men•i•ty [ə-MEN-i-tee] *noun, plural* **-ties** useful or pleasant facility or service
A•mer•i•can [ə-MER-i-kən] *adjective* of, relating to, the North American continent or the United States of America
am•e•thyst [AM-ə-thist] *noun* 1 bluish-violet precious stone 2 its color
a•mi•a•ble [AY-mee-ə-bəl] *adjective* friendly, kindly > **a•mi•a•bil'i•ty** *noun*
am•i•ca•ble [AM-i-kə-bəl] *adjective* friendly > **am•i•ca•bil'i•ty** *noun*
a•mid [ə-MID], **a•midst** [ə-MIDST] *preposition* 1 in the middle of, among 2 during

DICTIONARY • THESAURUS

amass *verb* COLLECT, accumulate, assemble, compile, gather, hoard, pile up
amateur *noun* NONPROFESSIONAL, dabbler, dilettante, layman
amateurish *adjective* UNPROFESSIONAL, amateur, bungling, clumsy, crude, inexpert, unaccomplished
amaze *verb* ASTONISH, alarm, astound, bewilder, dumbfound, shock, stagger, startle, stun, surprise
amazement *noun* ASTONISHMENT, admiration, bewilderment, confusion, perplexity, shock, surprise, wonder
amazing *adjective* ASTONISHING, astounding, breathtaking, eye-opening, overwhelming, staggering, startling, stunning, surprising
ambassador *noun* REPRESENTATIVE, agent, consul, deputy, diplomat, envoy, legate, minister
ambiguity *noun* VAGUENESS, doubt, dubiousness, equivocation, obscurity, uncertainty
ambiguous *adjective* UNCLEAR, dubious, enigmatic, equivocal, inconclusive, indefinite, indeterminate, obscure, vague
ambition *noun* 1 ENTERPRISE, aspiration, desire, drive, eagerness, longing, striving, yearning, zeal
2 GOAL, aim, aspiration, desire, dream, hope, intent, objective, purpose, wish
ambitious *adjective* ENTERPRISING, aspiring, avid, eager, hopeful, intent, purposeful, striving, zealous
ambivalent *adjective* UNDECIDED, contradictory, doubtful, equivocal, in two minds, uncertain, wavering
amble *verb* STROLL, dawdle, meander, mosey (*informal*), ramble, saunter, walk, wander
ambush *noun* 1 TRAP, lying in wait, waylaying ▷ *verb* 2 TRAP, attack, bushwhack, ensnare, surprise, waylay
amenable *adjective* RECEPTIVE, able to be influenced, acquiescent, agreeable, open, persuadable, responsive, susceptible
amend *verb* CHANGE, alter, correct, fix, improve, mend, modify, reform, remedy, repair, revise
amendment *noun* 1 CHANGE, alteration, correction, emendation, improvement, modification, reform, remedy, repair, revision
2 ALTERATION, addendum, addition, attachment, clarification
amends *plural noun* COMPENSATION, atonement, recompense, redress, reparation, restitution, satisfaction
amenity *noun* FACILITY, advantage, comfort, convenience, service
amiable *adjective* PLEASANT, affable, agreeable, charming, congenial, engaging, friendly, genial, likable *or* likeable, lovable
amicable *adjective* FRIENDLY, amiable, civil, cordial, courteous, harmonious, neighborly, peaceful, sociable
amid *or* **amidst** *preposition* IN THE MIDDLE OF, among, amongst, in the midst of, in the thick

a•mid•ships [ə-MID-ships] *adverb* near, toward, middle of ship
a•mi•no acid [ə-MEE-noh] organic compound found in protein
a•miss [ə-MIS] *adjective* 1 wrong ▷ *adverb* 2 faultily, badly **take amiss** be offended (by)
am•i•ty [AM-i-tee] *noun* friendship
am•me•ter [AM-mee-tər] *noun* instrument for measuring electric current
am•mo•nia [ə-MOHN-yə] *noun* pungent alkaline gas containing hydrogen and nitrogen
am•mo•nite [AM-ə-nīt] *noun* whorled fossil shell like ram's horn
am•mu•ni•tion [am-yə-NISH-ən] *noun* 1 any projectiles (bullets, rockets, etc.) that can be discharged from a weapon 2 facts that can be used in an argument
am•ne•sia [am-NEE-*zh*ə] *noun* loss of memory
am•nes•ty [AM-nə-stee] *noun, plural* **-ties** 1 general pardon ▷ *verb transitive* **-tied, -ty•ing** 2 grant this
am•ni•ot•ic fluid [am-nee-OT-ik] fluid surrounding fetus in womb
a•moe•ba [ə-MEE-bə] *noun, plural* **-bas** microscopic single-celled animal found in ponds, etc. and able to change its shape
a•mok, a•muck [ə-MUK] *adverb* **run amok** rush about in murderous frenzy
a•mong [ə-MUNG], **a•mongst** [ə-MUNGST] *preposition* mixed with, in the midst of, of the number of, between
a•mor•al [ay-MOR-əl] *adjective* nonmoral, having no moral qualities > **a•mo•ral•i•ty** [ay-mə-RAL-i-tee] *noun*
am•o•rous [AM-ər-əs] *adjective* 1 inclined to love 2 in love > **am'o•rous•ness** *noun*
a•mor•phous [ə-MOR-fəs] *adjective* without distinct shape
am•or•tize [AM-ər-tīz] *verb transitive* pay off a debt by a sinking fund > **am'or•tiz•a•ble** *adjective*
a•mount [ə-MOWNT] *verb intransitive* 1 come, be equal (to) ▷ *noun* 2 quantity 3 sum total
a•mour [ə-MOOR] *noun* (illicit) love affair
am•pere [AM-peer] *noun* unit of electric current > **am•per•age** [AM-pə-rij] *noun* strength of current in amperes
am•per•sand [AM-pər-sand] *noun* the character (&), meaning *and*
am•phet•a•mine [am-FET-ə-meen] *noun* synthetic liquid used medicinally as stimulant, a dangerous drug if misused
am•phib•i•ous [am-FIB-ee-əs] *adjective* living or operating both on land and in water > **am•phib'i•an** *noun* 1 animal that lives first in water then on land 2 vehicle able to travel on land or water 3 aircraft that can alight on land or water
am•phi•the•a•ter [AM-fə-thee-ə-tər] *noun* 1 building with tiers of seats rising around an arena 2 room with gallery above from which one can observe surgical operations, etc.
am•pho•ra [AM-fər-ə] *noun, plural* **-rae** [-ree] two-handled vessel of ancient Greece and Rome
am•ple [AM-pəl] *adjective* 1 big enough 2 large, spacious > **am'ply** *adverb*
am•pli•fy [AM-plə-fī] *verb transitive* **-fied, -fy•ing** 1 increase 2 make bigger, louder, etc. > **am•pli•fi•ca'tion** *noun* > **am'pli•fi•er** *noun*
am•pli•tude [AM-pli-tood] *noun* 1 spaciousness, width 2 maximum departure from average of alternating current, etc. > **amplitude modulation** 1 modulation of amplitude of radio carrier wave 2 broadcasting system using this
am•pule [AM-pyool] *noun* container for hypodermic dose
am•pu•tate [AM-pyə-tayt] *verb intransitive* **-tat•ed, -tat•ing** cut off (limb, etc.) > **am•pu•ta'tion** *noun*
amuck *see* **amok**
am•u•let [AM-yə-lit] *noun* something carried or worn as a charm
a•muse [ə-MYOOZ] *verb transitive* **-mused, -mus•ing** divert 1 occupy pleasantly 2 cause to laugh or smile > **a•muse'ment** *noun* entertainment, pastime
an *adjective* form of **a** used before vowels, and

DICTIONARY **a** THESAURUS

of, surrounded by
amiss *adverb* 1 WRONGLY, erroneously, improperly, inappropriately, incorrectly, mistakenly, unsuitably
▷ *adjective* 2 WRONG, awry, faulty, incorrect, mistaken, untoward
3 ▷ **take (something) amiss** TAKE AS AN INSULT, take as offensive, take out of turn, take wrongly
ammunition *noun* MUNITIONS, armaments, explosives, powder, rounds, shells, shot
amnesty *noun* GENERAL PARDON, absolution, dispensation, forgiveness, immunity, remission, reprieve
amok *or* **amuck** *adverb*
▷ **run amok** GO MAD, go berserk, go into a frenzy, go insane, lose control, turn violent, go wild
among *or* **amongst** *preposition* 1 IN THE MIDST OF, amid, amidst, in the middle of, in the thick of, surrounded by, together with, with
2 IN THE GROUP OF, in the class of, in the company of, in the number of, out of
3 TO EACH OF, between
amorous *adjective* LOVING, erotic, impassioned, in love, lustful, passionate, tender
amount *noun* QUANTITY, expanse, extent, magnitude, mass, measure, number, supply, volume
amount to *verb* ADD UP TO, become, come to, develop into, equal, mean, total
ample *adjective* PLENTY, abundant, bountiful, copious, expansive, extensive, full, generous, lavish, plentiful, profuse
amplify *verb* 1 EXPLAIN, develop, elaborate, enlarge, expand, flesh out, go into detail
2 INCREASE, enlarge, expand, extend, heighten, intensify, magnify, strengthen, widen
amply *adverb* FULLY, abundantly, completely, copiously, generously, profusely, richly
amputate *verb* CUT OFF, curtail, lop, remove, separate, sever, truncate
amuck *see* **amok**
amuse *verb* ENTERTAIN, charm, cheer, delight, interest, please, tickle
amusement *noun* 1 ENTERTAINMENT, cheer, enjoyment, fun, merriment, mirth, pleasure
2 ENTERTAINMENT, diversion, game, hobby, joke, pastime, recreation, sport
amusing *adjective* FUNNY, comical, droll, enjoyable, entertaining, humorous, interesting, witty

sometimes before *h*: *an hour*

an•a•bol•ic ster•oid [an-ə-BOL-ik STEER-oid] any of various hormones used by athletes to encourage muscle growth

a•nach•ro•nism [ə-NAK-rə-niz-əm] *noun* 1 mistake of time, by which something is put in wrong historical period 2 something out-of-date

an•a•con•da [an-ə-KON-də] *noun* large semi-aquatic snake that kills by constriction

an•a•gram [AN-ə-gram] *noun* word or sentence made by reordering the letters of another word or sentence, such as *ant* from *tan*

anal *see* **anus**

an•al•ge•si•a [an-l-JEE-zee-ə] *noun* absence of pain > **an•al•ge'sic** *adjective, noun* (drug) relieving pain

a•na•log [AN-ə-log] *noun* 1 physical object or quantity used to measure or represent another quantity 2 something that is analogous to something else ▷ *adjective* 3 displaying information by means of a dial

a•nal•o•gy [ə-NAL-ə-jee] *noun, plural* **-gies** 1 agreement or likeness in certain respects 2 correspondence > **a•nal'o•gize** *verb* **-gized, -giz•ing** explain by analogy > **a•nal'o•gous** [-ə-gəs] *adjective* 1 similar 2 parallel

a•nal•y•sis [ə-NAL-ə-sis] *noun, plural* **-ses** [-seez] separation into elements or components > **an•a•lyze** [AN-l-īz] *verb transitive* **-lyzed, -lyz•ing** 1 examine critically 2 determine the constituent parts > **an•a•lyst** [AN-l-ist] *noun* 1 one skilled in analysis, esp. chemical analysis 2 psychoanalyst > **an•a•lyt•ic•al** [an-l-IT-i-kəl], **an•a•lyt•ic** [an-l-IT-ik] *adjective*

an•ar•chy [AN-ər-kee] *noun* 1 lawlessness 2 lack of government in a country 3 confusion > **an•ar•chic** [an-AHR-kik] *adjective* > **an'ar•chism** *noun* > **an'ar•chist** *noun* one who opposes all government

a•nath•e•ma [ə-NATH-ə-mə] *noun, plural* **-mas** 1 anything detested, hateful 2 ban of the church 3 curse > **a•nath'e•ma•tize** *verb transitive* **-tized, -tiz•ing**

a•nat•o•my [ə-NAT-ə-mee] *noun* 1 science of structure of the body 2 detailed analysis 3 the body > **an•a•tom'i•cal** *adjective*

an•ces•tor [AN-ses-tər] *noun* 1 person from whom another is descended 2 early type of later form or product > **an•ces'tral** *adjective* > **an'ces•try** *noun*

an•chor [ANG-kər] *noun* 1 heavy (usu. hooked) implement dropped on cable, chain, etc. to bottom of sea, etc. to secure vessel 2 *radio, tv* principal announcer in program of news, sports, etc. ▷ *verb transitive* 3 fasten by or as with anchor 4 perform as anchor > **an'chor•age** *noun* act of, place of anchoring

an•cho•rite [ANG-kə-rīt] *noun* hermit, recluse

an•cho•vy [AN-choh-vee] *noun, plural* **(-vies)** small fish of herring family

an•cient [AYN-shənt] *adjective* 1 belonging to former age 2 old 3 timeworn ▷ *noun* 4 one who lived in an earlier age > **ancient history** 1 history of ancient times 2 common knowledge

an•cil•lar•y [AN-sə-ler-ee] *adjective, noun, plural* **-ies** subordinate, subservient, auxiliary

and *conjunction* joins words, phrases, clauses, and sentences to introduce a consequence, etc.

an•dan•te [ahn-DAHN-tay] *adverb, noun mus.* moderately slow (passage)

and•i•ron [AND-ī-ərn] *noun* steel bar or bracket for supporting logs in a fireplace

an•drog•y•nous [an-DROJ-ə-nəs] *adjective* having characteristics of both male and female

an•ec•dote [AN-ik-doht] *noun* very short story dealing with single incident > **an'ec•do•tal** *adjective* > **an•ec•do'tal•ist** *noun* one given to recounting anecdotes

a•ne•mi•a [ə-NEE-mee-ə] *noun* deficiency in number of red blood cells > **a•ne'mic** *adjective* 1 suffering from anemia 2 pale, sickly

an•e•mom•e•ter [an-ə-MOM-i-tər] *noun* wind gauge

a•nem•o•ne [ə-NEM-ə-nee] *noun* flower related to buttercup **sea anemone** plantlike sea animal

an•er•oid [AN-ə-roid] *adjective* denoting a barometer that measures atmospheric pressure without use of mercury or other liquid

an•es•the•si•ol•o•gy [an-is-thee-zi-OL-ə-jee] *noun* branch of medicine dealing with anesthetics

an•es•thet•ic [an-əs-THET-ik] *noun, adjective* (drug) causing loss of sensation > **an•es•the•sia**

analogy *noun* SIMILARITY, comparison, correlation, correspondence, likeness, parallel, relation, resemblance

analysis *noun* EXAMINATION, breakdown, dissection, inquiry, investigation, perusal, scrutiny, sifting, test

analytic *or* **analytical** *adjective* RATIONAL, inquiring, inquisitive, investigative, logical, organized, problem-solving, systematic

analyze *verb* 1 EXAMINE, evaluate, investigate, research, test, work over
2 BREAK DOWN, dissect, divide, resolve, separate, think through

anarchic *adjective* LAWLESS, chaotic, disorganized, rebellious, riotous, ungoverned

anarchist *noun* REVOLUTIONARY, insurgent, nihilist, rebel, terrorist

anarchy *noun* LAWLESSNESS, chaos, confusion, disorder, disorganization, revolution, riot

anatomy *noun* 1 EXAMINATION, analysis, dissection, division, inquiry, investigation, study
2 STRUCTURE, build, composition, frame, framework, make-up

ancestor *noun* FOREFATHER, forebear, forerunner, precursor, predecessor

ancient *adjective* OLD, aged, antique, archaic, old-fashioned, primeval, primordial, timeworn

ancillary *adjective* SUPPLEMENTARY, additional, auxiliary, extra, secondary, subordinate, subsidiary, supporting

and *conjunction* ALSO, along with, as well as, furthermore, in addition to, including, moreover, plus, together with

anecdote *noun* STORY, reminiscence, short story, sketch, tale, urban legend, yarn

anemic *adjective* PALE, ashen, colorless, feeble, pallid, sickly, wan, weak

anesthetic *noun* 1 PAINKILLER, analgesic, anodyne, narcotic, opiate, sedative, soporific ▷ *adjective* 2 PAIN-KILLING, analgesic, anodyne, deadening, dulling, numbing, sedative, soporific

[-THEE-zhə] *noun* loss of sensation > **an•es•the•tist** [ə-NES-thi-tist] *noun* expert in use of anesthetics > **an•es'the•tize** *verb transitive* **-tized, -tiz•ing**

an•eu•rysm, an•eu•rism [AN-yə-riz-əm] *noun* swelling out of a part of an artery

a•new [ə-NOO] *adverb* afresh, again

an•gel [AYN-jəl] *noun* 1 divine messenger 2 ministering or attendant spirit 3 person with the qualities of such a spirit, as gentleness, purity, etc. > **an•gel'ic** *adjective*

An•ge•lus [AN-jə-ləs] *noun* 1 devotional service in R.C. Church in memory of the Incarnation, said at morning, noon and sunset 2 bell announcing the time for this service

an•ger [ANG-gər] *noun* 1 strong emotion excited by a real or supposed injury 2 wrath 3 rage ▷ *verb transitive* 4 excite to wrath 5 enrage > **an'gri•ly** *adverb* > **an'gry** *adjective* 1 full of anger 2 inflamed

an•gi•na [an-JĪ-nə], **an•gi•na pec•to•ris** [an-JĪ-nə PEK-tər-is] *noun* severe pain accompanying some heart diseases

an•gle[1] [ANG-gəl] *verb intransitive* **-gled, -gling** fish with hook and line > **an'gler** *noun*

angle[2] *noun* 1 meeting of two lines or surfaces 2 corner 3 point of view 4 (*informal*) devious motive ▷ *verb transitive* 5 bend at an angle

An•gli•can [ANG-gli-kən] *adjective, noun* (member) of the Church of England > **An'gli•can•ism** *noun*

An•gli•cize [ANG-glə-sīz] *verb transitive* **-cized, -ciz•ing** 1 express in English 2 turn into English form > **An'gli•cism** *noun* English idiom or peculiarity

Anglo- *combining form* 1 English: *Anglo-Scottish* 2 British: *Anglo-American*

an•glo•phil•ia [ang-glə-FIL-ee-ə] *noun* excessive admiration for English > **an'glo•phile** [-fīl] *noun*

An•glo•pho•bi•a [ang-glə-FOH-bee-ə] *noun* dislike of England, etc. > **an'glo•phobe** *noun*

an•go•ra [ang-GOR-ə] *noun* 1 variety of goat, cat, or rabbit with long silky hair 2 hair of the angora goat or rabbit 3 cloth made from this hair

an•gos•tu•ra bark [ang-gə-STOOR-ə] *noun* bitter bark of certain S American trees, used as flavoring in alcoholic drinks

angst [ankst] *noun* feeling of anxiety

ang•strom [ANG-strəm] *noun* unit of length for measuring wavelengths of electromagnetic radiation

an•guish [ANG-gwish] *noun* 1 great mental or bodily pain ▷ *verb* 2 suffer this pain 3 cause to suffer it

an•gu•lar [ANG-gyə-lər] *adjective* 1 (of people) bony, awkward 2 having angles 3 measured by an angle > **an•gu•lar'i•ty** *noun*

an•hy•drous [an-HĪ-drəs] *adjective* (of chemical substances) free from water

an•i•line [AN-l-in] *noun* product of coal tar or indigo that yields dyes

an•i•mal [AN-ə-məl] *noun* 1 living creature, having sensation and power of voluntary motion 2 beast ▷ *adjective* 3 of, pert. to animals 4 sensual > **an•i•mal•cule** [an-ə-MAL-kyool] *noun* very small animal, esp. one that cannot be seen by naked eye > **animal husbandry** branch of agriculture concerned with raising domestic animals

an•i•mate [AN-ə-mayt] *verb transitive* **-mat•ed, -mat•ing** 1 give life to 2 enliven 3 inspire 4 actuate 5 make cartoon film of > **an'i•mat•ed** *adjective* 1 lively 2 in form of cartoons > **an•i•ma'tion** *noun* 1 life, vigor 2 cartoon film

an•i•mism [AN-ə-miz-əm] *noun* primitive religion, belief that natural effects are due to spirits, that inanimate things have spirits > **an'i•mist** *noun*

an•i•mos•i•ty [an-ə-MOS-i-tee] *noun, plural* **-ties** hostility, enmity

an•i•mus [AN-ə-məs] *noun* 1 hatred 2 animosity

an•i•on [AN-ī-ən] *noun* ion with negative charge

an•ise [AN-is] *noun* plant with aromatic seeds, which are used for flavoring

an•i•seed [AN-ə-seed] *noun* the licorice-flavored seed of anise

an•kle [ANG-kəl] *noun* joint between foot and leg > **an•klet** [ANG-klit] *noun* 1 ankle-ornament 2 short sock reaching just above the ankle

---

angel *noun* 1 DIVINE MESSENGER, archangel, cherub, seraph
2 (*informal*) DEAR, beauty, darling, gem, jewel, paragon, saint, treasure

angelic *adjective* 1 PURE, adorable, beautiful, entrancing, lovely, saintly, virtuous
2 HEAVENLY, celestial, cherubic, ethereal, seraphic

anger *noun* 1 RAGE, annoyance, displeasure, exasperation, fury, ire, outrage, resentment, temper, wrath
▷ *verb* 2 MADDEN, annoy, displease, enrage, exasperate, gall, incense, infuriate, outrage, rile, vex

angle[1] *noun* 1 INTERSECTION, bend, corner, crook, edge, elbow, nook, point
2 POINT OF VIEW, approach, aspect, outlook, perspective, position, side, slant, standpoint, viewpoint

angle[2] *verb* FISH, cast

angry *adjective* FURIOUS, annoyed, cross, displeased, enraged, exasperated, incensed, infuriated, irate, mad, outraged, resentful

angst *noun* ANXIETY, apprehension, unease, worry

anguish *noun* SUFFERING, agony, distress, grief, heartache, misery, pain, sorrow, torment, woe

animal *noun* 1 CREATURE, beast, brute
2 (*applied to a person*) BRUTE, barbarian, beast, monster, savage, wild man
▷ *adjective* 3 PHYSICAL, bestial, bodily, brutish, carnal, gross, sensual

animate *verb* 1 ENLIVEN, energize, excite, fire, inspire, invigorate, kindle, move, stimulate
▷ *adjective* 2 LIVING, alive, alive and kicking, breathing, live, moving

animated *adjective* LIVELY, ebullient, energetic, enthusiastic, excited, passionate, spirited, vivacious, wired (*slang*)

animation *noun* LIVELINESS, ebullience, energy, enthusiasm, excitement, fervor, passion, spirit, verve, vivacity, zest

animosity *noun* HOSTILITY, acrimony, antipathy, bitterness, enmity, hatred, ill will, malevolence,

an•nals [AN-lz] *plural noun* historical records of events > **an'nal•ist** *noun*
an•neal [ə-NEEL] *verb transitive* 1 toughen (metal or glass) by heating and slow cooling 2 temper
an•ne•lid [AN-l-id] *noun* one of class of invertebrate animals, including the earthworm, etc.
an•nex [ə-NEKS] *verb transitive* 1 add, append, attach 2 take possession of (esp. territory) > **an•nex•a•tion** [an-ik-SAY-shən] *noun* > **annex** *noun* [AN-eks] 1 supplementary building 2 something added
an•ni•hi•late [ə-NĪ-ə-layt] *verb transitive* **-lat•ed, -lat•ing** reduce to nothing, destroy utterly > **an•ni•hi•la'tion** *noun*
an•ni•ver•sa•ry [an-ə-VUR-sə-ree] *noun* 1 yearly return of a date 2 celebration of this
an•no Dom•i•ni [AN-oh DOM-ə-nee] *Lat.* in the year of our Lord
an•no•tate [AN-ə-tayt] *verb transitive* **-tat•ed, -tat•ing** make notes upon, comment > **an•no•ta'tion** *noun*
an•nounce [ə-NOWNS] *verb transitive* **-nounced, -nounc•ing** make known, proclaim > **an•nounce'ment** *noun* > **an•nounc'er** *noun* broadcaster who announces items in program, introduces speakers, etc.
an•noy [ə-NOI] *verb transitive* 1 vex 2 make slightly angry 3 tease > **an•noy'ance** *noun*
an•nu•al [AN-yoo-əl] *adjective* 1 yearly 2 of, for a year ▷ *noun* 3 plant that completes its life cycle in a year 4 book published each year > **an'nu•al•ly** *adverb*
an•nu•i•ty [ə-NOO-i-tee] *noun, plural* **-ties** sum or grant paid every year > **an•nu'i•tant** [-tnt] *noun* holder of annuity
an•nul [ə-NUL] *verb transitive* **-nulled, -nul•ling** make void, cancel, abolish
an•nu•lar [AN-yə-lər] *adjective* ring-shaped > **an'nu•lat•ed** [-lay-tid] *adjective* formed in rings > **an'nu•let** [-lit] *noun* small ring or molding in shape of ring
An•nun•ci•a•tion [ə-nun-see-AY-shən] *noun* 1 angel's announcement of Incarnation to the Virgin Mary (**an•nun•ci•a•tion**) 2 announcing 3 announcement > **an•nun'ci•ate** *verb transitive* **-at•ed, -at•ing** proclaim, announce
an•ode [AN-ohd] *noun electricity* the positive electrode or terminal > **an•o•dize** [AN-ə-dīz] *verb transitive* cover (metal object) with protective film by using it as an anode in electrolysis
an•o•dyne [AN-ə-dīn] *adjective* 1 relieving pain, soothing ▷ *noun* 2 pain-relieving drug 3 something that soothes
a•noint [ə-NOINT] *verb transitive* 1 smear with oil or ointment 2 consecrate with oil > **a•noint'ment** *noun* 1 the Anointed 2 the Messiah
a•nom•a•lous [ə-NOM-ə-ləs] *adjective* irregular, abnormal > **a•nom'a•ly** *noun, plural* **-lies** 1 irregularity 2 deviation from rule
a•non [ə-NON] *adverb* (*obsolete*) 1 in a short time, soon 2 now and then
a•non•y•mous [ə-NON-ə-məs] *adjective* nameless, esp. without an author's name > **an•o•nym•i•ty** [an-ə-NIM-i-tee] *noun*
an•o•rak [AN-ə-rak] *noun* 1 lightweight, warm, waterproof, usu. hooded jacket 2 parka
an•o•rex•i•a ner•vo•sa [an-ə-REK-see-ə nur-VOH-sə] *noun* psychological disorder characterized by fear of becoming fat and refusal to eat
an•oth•er [ə-NUTH-ər] *pronoun, adjective* 1 one other 2 a different one 3 one more
an•ser•ine [AN-sə-rīn] *adjective* 1 of or like a goose 2 silly
an•swer [AN-sər] *verb* 1 reply (to) 2 solve 3 reply correctly 4 pay 5 meet 6 be accountable (for, to) 7 match 8 satisfy, suit ▷ *noun* 9 reply 10 solution > **an'swer•a•ble** *adjective* accountable

DICTIONARY • THESAURUS

malice, rancor, resentment
annals *plural noun* RECORDS, accounts, archives, chronicles, history
annex *verb* 1 SEIZE, acquire, appropriate, conquer, occupy, take over
2 JOIN, add, adjoin, attach, connect, fasten
annihilate *verb* DESTROY, abolish, decimate, eradicate, exterminate, extinguish, obliterate, wipe out
announce *verb* MAKE KNOWN, advertise, broadcast, declare, disclose, proclaim, report, reveal, tell
announcement *noun* STATEMENT, advertisement, broadcast, bulletin, communiqué, declaration, proclamation, report, revelation
announcer *noun* PRESENTER, broadcaster, commentator, master of ceremonies, newscaster, newsreader, reporter
annoy *verb* IRRITATE, anger, bother, displease, disturb, exasperate, get on one's nerves (*informal*), hassle (*informal*), madden, molest, pester, plague, trouble, vex
annoyance *noun* 1 IRRITATION, anger, bother, hassle (*informal*), nuisance, trouble
2 NUISANCE, bore, bother, drag (*informal*), pain (*informal*)
annoying *adjective* IRRITATING, disturbing, exasperating, maddening, troublesome
annual *adjective* YEARLY, once a year, yearlong
annually *adverb* YEARLY, by the year, once a year, per annum, per year
annul *verb* INVALIDATE, abolish, cancel, declare null and void *or* render null and void, negate, nullify, repeal, retract
anoint *verb* CONSECRATE, bless, hallow, sanctify
anomalous *adjective* UNUSUAL, abnormal, eccentric, exceptional, incongruous, inconsistent, irregular, odd, peculiar
anomaly *noun* IRREGULARITY, abnormality, eccentricity, exception, incongruity, inconsistency, oddity, peculiarity
anonymous *adjective* UNNAMED, incognito, nameless, unacknowledged, uncredited, unidentified, unknown, unsigned
answer *verb* 1 REPLY, explain, react, resolve, respond, retort, return, solve
▷ *noun* 2 REPLY, comeback, defense, explanation, reaction, rejoinder, response, retort, return, riposte, solution
answerable *adjective* (*usually with for or to*) RESPONSIBLE, accountable, amenable, chargeable, liable, subject, to blame
answer for *verb* BE RESPONSIBLE FOR, be accountable for, be answerable for, be chargeable for, be liable for, be to blame for

> **answering machine** apparatus for answering a telephone automatically and recording messages

ant *noun* small social insect, proverbial for industry > **ant'eat•er** *noun* animal that feeds on ants by means of a long, sticky tongue > **ant'hill** the mound raised by ants

an•tag•o•nist [an-TAG-ə-nist] *noun* opponent, adversary > **an•tag'o•nism** *noun* > **an•tag•o•nis'tic** *adjective* > **an•tag'o•nize** *verb transitive* **-nized, -niz•ing** arouse hostility in

Ant•arc•tic [ant-AHRK-tik] *adjective* 1 south polar ▷ *noun* 2 these regions

an•te [AN-tee] *noun* 1 player's stake in poker ▷ *verb transitive* **-ted, -te•ing** 2 (often with *up*) stake

ante- *prefix* before in time or position: *antedate; antechamber*

an•te•ced•ent [an-tə-SEED-nt] *adjective, noun* (thing) going before

an•te•di•lu•vi•an [an-tee-di-LOO-vee-ən] *adjective* 1 before the Flood 2 ancient

an•te•lope [AN-tl-ohp] *noun* deer-like ruminant animal, remarkable for grace and speed

ante me•rid•i•em [AN-tee mə-RID-ee-əm] *Lat.* before noon

an•ten•na [an-TEN-ə] *noun, plural* **-nae** [-nee] 1 insect's feeler 2 aerial

an•te•pe•nult [an-tee-PEE-nult] *noun* last syllable but two in a word > **an•te•pe•nul'ti•mate** *adjective, noun*

an•te•ri•or [an-TEER-ee-ər] *adjective* 1 to the front 2 before

an•them [AN-thəm] *noun* 1 song of loyalty, esp. to a country 2 Scripture passage set to music 3 piece of sacred music, originally sung in alternate parts by two choirs

an•ther [AN-thər] *noun* in flower, part at top of stamen containing pollen

an•thol•o•gy [an-THOL-ə-jee] *noun, plural* **-gies** collection of poems, literary extracts, etc. > **an•thol'o•gist** *noun* maker of such > **an•thol'o•gize** *verb transitive* **-gized, -giz•ing** compile or publish in an anthology

an•thra•cite [AN-thrə-sīt] *noun* hard coal burning slowly almost without flame or smoke

an•thrax [AN-thraks] *noun* 1 malignant disease in cattle, communicable to people 2 sore caused by this

an•thro•poid [AN-thrə-poid] *adjective* 1 like man ▷ *noun* 2 ape resembling human being

an•thro•pol•o•gy [an-thrə-POL-ə-jee] *noun* scientific study of origins, development of human race > **an•thro•po•log'i•cal** [-pə-LOJ-i-kəl] *adjective* > **an•thro•pol'o•gist** *noun*

an•thro•po•mor•phize [an-thrə-pə-MOR-fīz] *verb transitive* **-pized, -piz•ing** ascribe human attributes to God or an animal > **an•thro•po•mor'phic** *adjective*

anti- *prefix* 1 against, opposed to: *anti-war* 2 opposite to: *anticlimax* 3 counteracting: *antifreeze*

an•ti•bi•ot•ic [an-ti-bī-OT-ik] *noun* any of various chemical, fungal or synthetic substances, esp. penicillin, used against bacterial infection ▷ *adjective*

an•ti•bod•y [AN-ti-bod-ee] *noun* substance in, or introduced into, blood serum that counteracts the growth and harmful action of bacteria

an•tic•i•pate [an-TIS-ə-payt] *verb transitive* **-pat•ed, -pat•ing** 1 expect 2 take or consider beforehand 3 foresee 4 enjoy in advance > **an•tic•i•pa'tion** *noun* > **an•tic'i•pa•to•ry** [-pə-tor-ee] *adjective*

an•ti•cli•max [an-ti-KLĪ-maks] *noun* sudden descent to the trivial or ludicrous > **an•ti•cli•mac'tic** *adjective*

an•tics [AN-tiks] *plural noun* absurd or grotesque movements or acts

an•ti•cy•clone [an-tee-SĪ-klohn] *noun* system of winds moving around center of high barometric pressure

an•ti•dote [AN-ti-doht] *noun* counteracting remedy

an•ti•freeze [AN-ti-freez] *noun* liquid added to water to lower its freezing point, as in automobile radiators

an•ti•gen [AN-ti-jən] *noun* substance stimulating production of antibodies in the blood

an•ti•his•ta•mine [an-ti-HIS-tə-meen] *noun* drug used esp. to treat allergies

an•ti•mo•ny [AN-tə-moh-nee] *noun* brittle, bluish-white metal

an•tip•a•thy [an-TIP-ə-thee] *noun, plural* **-thies** dislike, aversion

an•ti•per•spi•rant [an-ti-PUR-spər-ənt] *noun* substance used to reduce sweating

an•ti•phon [AN-tə-fon] *noun* 1 composition in which verses, lines are sung alternately by two choirs 2 anthem > **an•tiph•o•nal** [an-TIF-ə-nl] *adjective*

an•tip•o•des [an-TIP-ə-deez] *plural noun* countries, peoples on opposite side of the globe (often refers to Aust. and N Zealand) > **an•tip•o•de'an** *adjective*

an•ti•pope [AN-ti-pohp] *noun* pope elected in opposition to the one regularly chosen

an•tique [an-TEEK] *noun* 1 relic of former times, usu. a piece of furniture, etc. that is

---

DICTIONARY

a

THESAURUS

antagonism *noun* HOSTILITY, antipathy, conflict, discord, dissension, friction, opposition, rivalry

antagonist *noun* OPPONENT, adversary, competitor, contender, enemy, foe, rival

antagonistic *adjective* HOSTILE, at odds, at variance, conflicting, incompatible, in dispute, opposed, unfriendly

antagonize *verb* ANNOY, anger, get on one's nerves (*informal*), hassle (*informal*), irritate, offend

anthem *noun* 1 HYMN, canticle, carol, chant, chorale, psalm
2 SONG OF PRAISE, paean

anthology *noun* COLLECTION, compendium, compilation, miscellany, selection, treasury

anticipate *verb* EXPECT, await, foresee, foretell, hope for, look forward to, predict, prepare for

anticipation *noun* EXPECTATION, expectancy, foresight, forethought, premonition, prescience

anticlimax *noun* DISAPPOINTMENT, bathos, comedown (*informal*), letdown

antics *plural noun* CLOWNING, escapades, horseplay, mischief, playfulness, pranks, tomfoolery, tricks

antidote *noun* CURE, countermeasure, remedy

antipathy *noun* HOSTILITY, aversion, bad blood, dislike, enmity, hatred, ill will

collected ▷ *adjective* 2 ancient 3 old-fashioned > **an•ti•quar'i•an** *noun* student or collector of old things > **an'ti•quat•ed** *adjective* out-of-date > **an•tiq•ui•ty** [an-TIK-wi-tee] *noun* 1 great age 2 former times

an•ti-Se•mit•ic [an-tee-sə-MIT-ik] *adjective* hostile or discriminating against Jews > **an•ti-Sem'i•tism** *noun* > **an•ti-Sem'ite** *noun*

an•ti•sep•tic [an-tə-SEPT-tik] *noun, adjective* (substance) preventing infection ▷ *adjective* free from infection

an•tith•e•sis [an-TITH-ə-sis] *noun, plural* **-ses** [-seez] 1 direct opposite 2 contrast 3 opposition of ideas > **an•ti•thet'i•cal** *adjective*

an•ti•tox•in [an-ti-TOK-sin] *noun* serum used to neutralize disease poisons

an•ti•trust [an-ti-TRUST] *adjective* (of laws) opposing business monopolies

an•ti•tus•sive [an-ti-TUS-iv] *noun, adjective* (substance) controlling or preventing coughing

an•ti•ven•in [an-tee-VEN-in] *noun* antitoxin to counteract specific venom, esp. of snake or spider

an•ti•vi•rus [an-tee-VĪ-rus] *adjective* relating to software designed to protect computer files from viruses

ant•ler [ANT-lər] *noun* branching horn of certain deer

an•to•nym [AN-tə-nim] *noun* word of opposite meaning to another, e.g. *cold* is an antonym of *hot*

a•nus [AY-nəs] *noun* the lower opening of the bowels > **a'nal** *adjective*

an'vil *noun* heavy iron block with steel face on which a blacksmith hammers metal into shape

anx•ious [ANGK-shəs] *adjective* 1 troubled, uneasy 2 concerned > **anx•i•e•ty** [ang-ZĪ-ə-tee] *noun*

an•y [EN-ee] *adjective, pronoun* 1 one indefinitely 2 some 3 every > **an'y•bod•y** *noun* > **an'y•how** *adverb* > **an'y•one** *noun* > **an'y•thing** *noun* > **an'y•way** *adverb* > **an'y•where** *adverb*

a•or•ta [ay-OR-tə] *noun* great artery rising from left ventricle of heart > **a•or'tal** *adjective*

a•pace [ə-PAYS] *adverb* swiftly

a•part [ə-PAHRT] *adverb* 1 separately, aside 2 in pieces

a•part•heid [ə-PAHRT-hayt] *noun* former official government policy of racial segregation in S Africa

a•part•ment [ə-PAHRT-mənt] *noun* room or suite of rooms in larger building used for dwelling

ap•a•thy [AP-ə-thee] *noun, plural* **-thies** 1 indifference 2 lack of emotion > **ap•a•thet'ic** *adjective*

ape [ayp] *noun* 1 tailless monkey such as the chimpanzee or gorilla 2 coarse, clumsy person 3 imitator ▷ *verb transitive* **aped, ap•ing** 4 imitate

a•pe•ri•od•ic [ay-peer-ee-OD-ik] *adjective* *electricity* having no natural period or frequency

a•pe•ri•tif [ə-per-i-TEEF] *noun* alcoholic appetizer

ap•er•ture [AP-ər-chər] *noun* opening, hole

a•pex [AY-peks] *noun, plural* **a•pex•es** 1 top, peak 2 vertex

a•pha•sia [ə-FAY-*zh*ə] *noun* dumbness, or loss of speech control, due to disease of the brain

a•phe•li•on [ə-FEE-lee-ən] *noun* point of planet's orbit farthest from the sun

a•phid [AY-fid] *noun* any of various sap-sucking insects

a•phis [AY-fis] *noun, plural* **a•phi•des** [AY-fi-deez] an aphid

aph•o•rism [AF-ə-riz-əm] *noun* maxim, pithy saying > **aph•o•ris'tic** [-RIS-tik] *adjective*

aph•ro•dis•i•ac [af-rə-DEE-zee-ak] *adjective* 1 exciting sexual desire ▷ *noun* 2 substance that so excites

a•pi•ar•y [AY-pee-er-ee] *noun, plural* **-ar•ies** place where bees are kept > **a'pi•a•rist** *noun* beekeeper > **a'pi•cul•ture** *noun*

a•piece [ə-PEES] *adverb* for each

a•plomb [ə-PLOM] *noun* self-possession, coolness, assurance

DICTIONARY • THESAURUS

antiquated *adjective* OBSOLETE, antique, archaic, dated, old-fashioned, out-of-date, passé

antique *noun* 1 PERIOD PIECE, bygone, heirloom, relic
▷ *adjective* 2 VINTAGE, antiquarian, classic, olden
3 OLD-FASHIONED, archaic, obsolete, outdated

antiquity *noun* 1 OLD AGE, age, ancientness, elderliness, oldness
2 DISTANT PAST, ancient times, olden days, time immemorial

antiseptic *adjective* 1 HYGIENIC, clean, germ-free, pure, sanitary, sterile, uncontaminated
▷ *noun* 2 DISINFECTANT, germicide, purifier

antisocial *adjective* 1 UNSOCIABLE, alienated, misanthropic, reserved, retiring, uncommunicative, unfriendly, withdrawn
2 DISRUPTIVE, antagonistic, belligerent, disorderly, hostile, menacing, rebellious, uncooperative

antithesis *noun* OPPOSITE, contrary, contrast, converse, inverse, reverse

anxiety *noun* UNEASINESS, angst, apprehension, concern, foreboding, misgiving, nervousness, tension, trepidation, worry

anxious *adjective* 1 UNEASY, apprehensive, concerned, fearful, in suspense, nervous, on tenterhooks, tense, troubled, wired (*slang*), worried
2 EAGER, desirous, impatient, intent, keen, yearning

apart *adverb* 1 TO PIECES, asunder, in bits, in pieces, to bits
2 SEPARATE, alone, aside, away, by oneself, isolated, to one side
3 ▷ **apart from** EXCEPT FOR, aside from, besides, but, excluding, not counting, other than, save

apartment *noun* ROOM, accommodation, flat, living quarters, penthouse, quarters, rooms, suite

apathetic *adjective* UNINTERESTED, cool, indifferent, passive, phlegmatic, unconcerned

apathy *noun* LACK OF INTEREST, coolness, indifference, inertia, nonchalance, passivity, torpor, unconcern

apex *noun* HIGHEST POINT, crest, crown, culmination, peak, pinnacle, point, summit, top

apiece *adverb* EACH, for each, from each, individually, respectively, separately, to each

aplomb *noun* SELF-POSSESSION, calmness, composure, confidence, level-headedness, poise,

a•poc•a•lypse [ə-POK-ə-lips] *noun* 1 prophetic revelation esp. of future of the world 2 (**A•poc•a•lypse**) revelation to St. John, recounted in last book of the New Testament > **a•poc•a•lyp'tic** *adjective*
a•poc•ry•pha [ə-POK-rə-fə] *plural noun* 1 religious writing of doubtful authenticity 2 (**A•poc•ry•pha**) collective name for 14 books originally in the Old Testament > **a•poc'ry•phal** *adjective* spurious
ap•o•gee [AP-ə-jee] *noun* 1 point farthest from Earth in orbit of moon or satellite 2 climax 3 highest point
a•pol•o•gy [ə-POL-ə-jee] *noun, plural* **-gies** 1 acknowledgment of offense and expression of regret 2 written or spoken defense 3 (with *for*) poor substitute > **a•pol•o•get'ic** *adjective* > **a•pol•o•get'ics** *noun* branch of theology charged with defense of Christianity > **a•pol'o•gist** *noun* > **a•pol'o•gize** *verb intransitive* **-gized, -giz•ing**
ap•o•plex•y [AP-ə-plek-see] *noun* 1 loss of sense and often paralysis caused by broken or blocked blood vessel in the brain 2 a stroke > **ap•o•plec'tic** *adjective*
a•pos•ta•sy [ə-POS-tə-see] *noun, plural* **-sies** abandonment of one's religious or other faith > **a•pos'tate** [-tayt] *noun, adjective*
a pos•te•ri•o•ri [ay po-steer-ee-OR-ī] *adjective* 1 denoting form of inductive reasoning that arrives at causes from effects 2 empirical
a•pos•tle [ə-POS-əl] *noun* 1 ardent supporter 2 leader of reform (**A•pos•tle**) 3 one sent to preach the Gospel, esp. one of the first disciples of Jesus 4 founder of Christian church in a country > **ap•os•tol'ic** *adjective*
a•pos•tro•phe [ə-POS-trə-fee] *noun* 1 a mark (') showing the omission of a letter or letters in a word 2 digression to appeal to someone dead or absent
ap•o•thegm [AP-ə-them] *noun* terse saying, maxim
a•poth•e•o•sis [ə-poth-ee-OH-sis] *noun, plural* **-ses** [-seez] deification, act of raising any person or thing into a god
ap•pall [ə-PAWL] *verb transitive* dismay, terrify > **ap•pall'ing** *adjective* (*informal*) dreadful, terrible
ap•pa•rat•us [ap-ə-RAT-əs] *noun* 1 equipment, tools, instruments, for performing any experiment, operation, etc. 2 means by which something operates
ap•par•el [ə-PAR-əl] *noun* 1 clothing ▷ *verb transitive* **-eled, -el•ing** 2 clothe
ap•par•ent [ə-PAR-ənt] *adjective* 1 seeming 2 obvious 3 acknowledged: *heir apparent*
ap•pa•ri•tion [ap-ə-RISH-ən] *noun* appearance, esp. of ghost
ap•peal [ə-PEEL] *verb intransitive* (with *to*) call upon, make earnest request 1 be attractive 2 refer to, have recourse to 3 apply to higher court ▷ *noun* 4 request, reference, supplication > **ap•peal'ing** *adjective* 1 making appeal 2 pleasant, attractive > **ap•pel'lant** [-PEL-ənt] *noun* one who appeals to higher court > **ap•pel'late** [-it] *adjective* of appeals
ap•pear [ə-PEER] *verb intransitive* 1 become visible or present 2 seem, be plain 3 be seen in public > **ap•pear'ance** *noun* 1 an appearing 2 aspect 3 pretense
ap•pease [ə-PEEZ] *verb transitive* **-peased, -peas•ing** pacify, quiet, allay, satisfy > **ap•pease'ment** *noun*
appellant *see* **appeal**
ap•pel•la•tion [ap-ə-LAY-shən] *noun* name

sang-froid, self-assurance, self-confidence
apocryphal *adjective* DUBIOUS, doubtful, legendary, mythical, questionable, unauthenticated, unsubstantiated
apologetic *adjective* REGRETFUL, contrite, penitent, remorseful, rueful, sorry
apologize *verb* SAY SORRY, ask forgiveness, beg pardon, express regret
apology *noun* 1 DEFENSE, acknowledgment, confession, excuse, explanation, justification, plea
2 ▷ **apology for** MOCKERY OF, caricature of, excuse for, imitation of, travesty of
apostle *noun* 1 EVANGELIST, herald, messenger, missionary, preacher
2 SUPPORTER, advocate, champion, pioneer, propagandist, proponent
apotheosis *noun* DEIFICATION, elevation, exaltation, glorification, idealization, idolization
appall *verb* HORRIFY, alarm, daunt, dishearten, dismay, frighten, outrage, shock, unnerve
appalling *adjective* HORRIFYING, alarming, awful, daunting, dreadful, fearful, frightful, horrible, shocking, terrifying
apparatus *noun* 1 EQUIPMENT, appliance, contraption (*informal*), device, gear, machinery, mechanism, tackle, tools
2 ORGANIZATION, bureaucracy, chain of command, hierarchy, network, setup (*informal*), structure, system
apparent *adjective* 1 OBVIOUS, discernible, distinct, evident, manifest, marked, unmistakable, visible
2 SEEMING, ostensible, outward, superficial
apparently *adverb* IT APPEARS THAT, it seems that, on the face of it, ostensibly, outwardly, seemingly, superficially
apparition *noun* GHOST, chimera, phantom, specter, spirit, wraith
appeal *verb* 1 PLEAD, ask, beg, call upon, entreat, pray, request
2 ATTRACT, allure, charm, entice, fascinate, interest, please, tempt
▷ *noun* 3 PLEA, application, entreaty, petition, prayer, request, supplication
4 ATTRACTION, allure, beauty, charm, fascination
appealing *adjective* ATTRACTIVE, alluring, charming, desirable, engaging, winsome
appear *verb* 1 COME INTO VIEW, be present, come out, come to light, crop up (*informal*), emerge, occur, show up (*informal*), surface, turn up
2 LOOK *or* LOOK LIKE look as if, occur, seem, strike one as
appearance *noun* 1 ARRIVAL, coming, emergence, introduction, presence
2 LOOK, demeanor, expression, figure, form, looks, manner, mien (*literary*)
3 IMPRESSION, front, guise, illusion, image, outward show, pretense, semblance
appease *verb* 1 PACIFY, calm, conciliate, de-stress, mollify, placate, quiet, satisfy, soothe

ap•pend [ə-PEND] *verb transitive* join on, add > **ap•pend'age** *noun*
ap•pen•di•ci•tis [ə-pen-də-SĪ-tis] *noun* inflammation of vermiform appendix
ap•pen•dix [ə-PEN-diks] *noun, plural* **-di•ces** [-də-seez] **1** subsidiary addition to book, etc. **2** *anatomy* projection, esp. the small worm-shaped part of the intestine
ap•per•cep•tion [ap-ər-SEP-shən] *noun* **1** perception **2** apprehension **3** the mind's perception of itself as a conscious agent
ap•per•tain [ap-ər-TAYN] *verb intransitive* belong, relate to, be appropriate
ap•pe•tite [AP-i-tīt] *noun* desire, inclination, esp. desire for food > **ap'pe•tiz•er** *noun* something stimulating to appetite > **ap'pe•tiz•ing** *adjective*
ap•plaud [ə-PLAWD] *verb transitive* **1** praise by handclapping **2** praise loudly > **ap•plause'** [-PLAWZ] *noun* loud approval
ap•ple [AP-əl] *noun* **1** round, firm, fleshy fruit **2** tree bearing it
ap•plet [AP-lət] *noun computing* computing program that runs within a page on the World Wide Web
ap•pli•ance [ə-PLĪ-əns] *noun* piece of equipment esp. electrical
ap•pli•qué [ap-li-KAY] *noun* **1** ornaments, embroidery, etc., secured to surface of material ▷ *verb transitive* **-quéd, -qué•ing 2** ornament thus
ap•ply [ə-PLĪ] *verb transitive* **-plied, -ply•ing 1** utilize, employ **2** lay or place on **3** administer, devote ▷ *verb intransitive* **-plied, -ply•ing 4** have reference (to) **5** make request (to) > **ap'pli•ca•ble** *adjective* relevant > **ap'pli•cant** *noun* > **ap•pli•ca'tion** *noun* **1** applying something for a particular use **2** relevance **3** request for a job, etc. **4** concentration, diligence > **applied** *adjective* (of skill, science, etc.) put to practical use
ap•point [ə-POINT] *verb transitive* **1** name, assign to a job or position **2** fix, settle **3** equip > **ap•point'ment** *noun* **1** engagement to meet **2** (selection for a) position > **ap•point'ments** equipment, furnishings
ap•por•tion [ə-POR-shən] *verb transitive* divide out in shares > **ap•por'tion•ment** *noun*
ap•po•site [AP-ə-zit] *adjective* suitable, apt > **ap'po•site•ness** *noun* > **ap•po•si'tion** [-ZISH-ən] *noun* **1** proximity **2** the placing of one word beside another that it describes
ap•praise [ə-PRAYZ] *verb transitive* **-praised, -prais•ing** set price on, estimate value of > **ap•prais'al** *noun* > **ap•prais'er** *noun*
ap•pre•ci•ate [ə-PREE-shee-ayt] *verb transitive* **-at•ed, -at•ing 1** value at true worth **2** be grateful for **3** understand **4** enjoy ▷ *verb*

DICTIONARY • THESAURUS

2 EASE, allay, alleviate, calm, relieve, soothe
appeasement *noun* **1** PACIFICATION, accommodation, compromise, concession, conciliation, mollification, placation
2 EASING, alleviation, lessening, relieving, soothing
appendage *noun* ATTACHMENT, accessory, addition, supplement
appendix *noun* SUPPLEMENT, addendum, addition, adjunct, appendage, postscript
appetite *noun* DESIRE, craving, demand, hunger, liking, longing, passion, relish, stomach, taste, yearning
appetizing *adjective* DELICIOUS, appealing, inviting, mouthwatering, palatable, succulent, tasty, tempting, yummy (*informal*)
applaud *verb* CLAP, acclaim, approve, cheer, commend, compliment, encourage, extol, praise
applause *noun* OVATION, accolade, approval, big hand, cheers, clapping, hand, praise
appliance *noun* DEVICE, apparatus, gadget, implement, instrument, machine, mechanism, tool
applicable *adjective* APPROPRIATE, apt, fitting, pertinent, relevant, suitable, useful
applicant *noun* CANDIDATE, claimant, inquirer
application *noun* **1** REQUEST, appeal, claim, inquiry, petition, requisition
2 EFFORT, commitment, dedication, diligence, hard work, industry, perseverance
apply *verb* **1** REQUEST, appeal, claim, inquire, petition, put in, requisition
2 USE, bring to bear, carry out, employ, exercise, exert, implement, practice, utilize
3 PUT ON, cover with, lay on, paint, place, smear, spread on
4 BE RELEVANT, be applicable, be appropriate, bear upon, be fitting, fit, pertain, refer, relate
5 ▷ **apply oneself** TRY, be diligent, buckle down (*informal*), commit oneself, concentrate, dedicate oneself, devote oneself, persevere, work hard
appoint *verb* **1** ASSIGN, choose, commission, delegate, elect, name, nominate, select
2 DECIDE, allot, arrange, assign, choose, designate, establish, fix, set
3 EQUIP, fit out, furnish, provide, supply
appointed *adjective* **1** ASSIGNED, chosen, delegated, elected, named, nominated, selected
2 DECIDED, allotted, arranged, assigned, chosen, designated, established, fixed, set
3 EQUIPPED, fitted out, furnished, provided, supplied
appointment *noun* **1** MEETING, arrangement, assignation, date, engagement, interview, rendezvous
2 SELECTION, assignment, choice, election, naming, nomination
3 JOB, assignment, office, place, position, post, situation
4 ▷ **appointments** FITTINGS, fixtures, furnishings, gear, outfit, paraphernalia, trappings
apportion *verb* DIVIDE, allocate, allot, assign, dispense, distribute, dole out, ration out, share
apportionment *noun* DIVISION, allocation, allotment, assignment, dispensing, distribution, doling out, rationing out, sharing
apposite *adjective* APPROPRIATE, applicable, apt, fitting, pertinent, relevant, suitable, to the point
appraisal *noun* ASSESSMENT, estimate, estimation, evaluation, judgment, opinion
appraise *verb* ASSESS, estimate, evaluate, gauge, judge, rate, review, value
appreciable *adjective* SIGNIFICANT, considerable, definite, discernible, evident, marked, noticeable, obvious, pronounced, substantial

intransitive **-at•ed, -at•ing** 5 rise in value > **ap•pre'ci•a•ble** [-shə-bəl] *adjective* 1 estimable 2 substantial > **ap•pre'ci•a•bly** *adverb* > **ap•pre•ci•a'tion** *noun* > **ap•pre'cia•tive** [-shə-tiv] *adjective* capable of expressing pleasurable recognition

ap•pre•hend [ap-ri-HEND] *verb transitive* 1 arrest, seize by authority 2 take hold of 3 recognize, understand 4 dread > **ap•pre•hen'si•ble** [-HEN-sə-bəl] *adjective* > **ap•pre•hen'sion** [-shən] *noun* 1 dread, anxiety 2 arrest 3 conception 4 ability to understand > **ap•pre•hen'sive** [-siv] *adjective* > **ap•pre•hen'sive•ly** *adverb*

ap•pren•tice [ə-PREN-tis] *noun* 1 person learning a trade under specified conditions 2 novice ▷ *verb transitive* **-ticed, -tic•ing** 3 bind, set to work, as apprentice > **ap•pren'tice•ship** *noun*

ap•prise [ə-PRĪZ] *verb transitive* **-prised, -pris•ing** inform

ap•proach [ə-PROHCH] *verb* 1 draw near (to) 2 set about 3 address request to 4 approximate to 5 make advances to ▷ *noun* 6 a drawing near 7 means of reaching or doing 8 approximation 9 (*often plural*) friendly or amatory overture(s) > **ap•proach'a•ble** *adjective*

ap•pro•ba•tion [ap-rə-BAY-shən] *noun* approval

ap•pro•pri•ate [ə-PROH-pree-ayt] *verb transitive* **-at•ed, -at•ing** 1 take for oneself 2 put aside for particular purpose ▷ *adjective* [-it] suitable, fitting > **ap•pro'pri•ate•ness** [-it-nis] *noun* > **ap•pro•pri•a'tion** *noun* 1 act of setting apart for purpose 2 legislative vote of money

ap•prove [ə-PROOV] *verb transitive* **-proved, -prov•ing** 1 think well of, commend 2 authorize, agree to > **ap•prov'al** *noun* > **ap•prov'ing•ly** *adverb*

ap•prox•i•mate [ə-PROK-sə-mit] *adjective* 1 very near, nearly correct 2 inexact, imprecise ▷ *verb transitive* [-mayt], **-mat•ed, -mat•ing** 3 bring close ▷ *verb intransitive* [-mayt], **-mat•ed, -mat•ing** 4 come near 5 be almost the same as > **ap•prox'i•mate•ly** *adverb*

ap•pur•te•nance [ə-PUR-tən-əns] *noun* 1 thing that appertains to 2 accessory

après-ski [ah-pray-SKEE] *noun* social activities after day's skiing

ap•ri•cot [AP-ri-kot] *noun* 1 orange-colored fruit related to the plum ▷ *adjective* 2 of the color of the fruit

A•pril fool [AY-prəl] butt of a joke or trick

DICTIONARY

a

THESAURUS

---

appreciate *verb* 1 VALUE, admire, enjoy, like, prize, rate highly, respect, treasure
2 BE AWARE OF, perceive, realize, recognize, sympathize with, take account of, understand
3 BE GRATEFUL FOR, be appreciative, be indebted, be obliged, be thankful for, give thanks for
4 INCREASE, enhance, gain, grow, improve, rise

appreciation *noun* 1 GRATITUDE, acknowledgment, gratefulness, indebtedness, obligation, thankfulness, thanks
2 AWARENESS, admiration, comprehension, enjoyment, perception, realization, recognition, sensitivity, sympathy, understanding
3 INCREASE, enhancement, gain, growth, improvement, rise

appreciative *adjective* 1 GRATEFUL, beholden, indebted, obliged, thankful
2 AWARE, admiring, enthusiastic, respectful, responsive, sensitive, sympathetic, understanding

apprehend *verb* 1 ARREST, capture, catch, seize, take prisoner
2 UNDERSTAND, comprehend, conceive, get the picture, grasp, perceive, realize, recognize

apprehension *noun* 1 ANXIETY, alarm, concern, dread, fear, foreboding, suspicion, trepidation, worry
2 ARREST, capture, catching, seizure, taking
3 AWARENESS, comprehension, grasp, perception, understanding

apprehensive *adjective* ANXIOUS, concerned, foreboding, nervous, uneasy, wired (*slang*), worried

apprentice *noun* TRAINEE, beginner, learner, novice, probationer, pupil, student

approach *verb* 1 MOVE TOWARDS, come close, come near, draw near, near, reach
2 MAKE A PROPOSAL TO, appeal to, apply to, make overtures to, sound out
3 SET ABOUT, begin work on, commence, embark on, enter upon, make a start, undertake
▷ *noun* 4 COMING, advance, arrival, drawing near, nearing
5 (*often plural*) PROPOSAL, advance, appeal, application, invitation, offer, overture, proposition
6 ACCESS, avenue, entrance, passage, road, way
7 WAY, manner, means, method, style, technique
8 LIKENESS, approximation, semblance

approachable *adjective* 1 FRIENDLY, affable, congenial, cordial, open, sociable
2 ACCESSIBLE, attainable, reachable

appropriate *adjective* 1 SUITABLE, apt, befitting, fitting, pertinent, relevant, to the point, well-suited
▷ *verb* 2 SEIZE, commandeer, confiscate, impound, take possession of, usurp
3 STEAL, embezzle, filch, misappropriate, pilfer, pocket
4 SET ASIDE, allocate, allot, apportion, assign, devote, earmark

approval *noun* 1 CONSENT, agreement, assent, authorization, blessing, endorsement, permission, recommendation, sanction
2 FAVOR, acclaim, admiration, applause, appreciation, esteem, good opinion, praise, respect

approve *verb* 1 FAVOR, admire, commend, have a good opinion of, like, praise, regard highly, respect
2 AGREE TO, allow, assent to, authorize, consent to, endorse, pass, permit, ratify, recommend, sanction

approximate *adjective* 1 CLOSE, near
2 ROUGH, estimated, inexact, loose
▷ *verb* 3 COME CLOSE, approach, border on, come near, reach, resemble, touch, verge on

approximately *adverb* ALMOST, about, around, circa (*of a date*), close to, in the region of, just about, more or less, nearly, roughly

approximation *noun* GUESS, conjecture, estimate, estimation, guesswork, rough calculation, rough idea

played on April Fools' Day, April 1

a pri•o•ri [ay-prī-OR-ī] *adjective* 1 denoting deductive reasoning from general principle to expected facts or effects 2 denoting knowledge gained independently of experience

a•pron [AY-prən] *noun* 1 cloth, piece of leather, etc., worn in front to protect clothes, or as part of costume 2 in theater, strip of stage before curtain 3 on airfield, paved area where aircraft stand, are refueled, etc. 4 any of a variety of things resembling these

ap•ro•pos [ap-rə-POH] *adverb* 1 to the purpose 2 with reference to ▷ *adjective* 3 apt, appropriate **apropos of** concerning

apse [aps] *noun* arched recess, esp. in a church

apt *adjective* 1 suitable 2 likely 3 prompt, quick-witted 4 dexterous > **ap•ti•tude** [AP-ti-tood] *noun* capacity, fitness > **apt'ly** *adverb* > **apt'ness** *noun*

aq•ua•ma•rine [ak-wə-mə-REEN] *noun* 1 precious stone, a transparent beryl ▷ *adjective* 2 greenish-blue, sea-colored

aq•ua•plane [AK-wə-playn] *noun* 1 plank or boat towed by fast motorboat and ridden by person standing on it ▷ *verb intransitive* **-planed, -plan•ing** 2 ride on aquaplane 3 (of automobile) be in contact with water on road, not with road surface > **aquaplaning** *noun*

a•quar•i•um [ə-KWAIR-ee-əm] *noun, plural* **-i•ums** tank or pond for keeping water animals or plants

a•quat•ic [ə-KWAT-ik] *adjective* living, growing, done in or on water > **a•quat'ics** *plural noun* water sports

aq•ua•vit [AH-kwə-veet] *noun* Scandinavian liquor usu. flavored with caraway seeds

aq•ue•duct [AK-wi-dukt] *noun* 1 artificial channel for water, esp. one like a bridge 2 conduit

a•que•ous [AY-kwee-əs] *adjective* of, like, containing water

aq•ui•fer [AK-wə-fər] *noun* geological formation containing or conveying ground water

aq•ui•line [AK-wə-līn] *adjective* 1 relating to eagle 2 hooked like an eagle's beak

Ar *chem.* argon

Ar•ab [AR-əb] *noun* 1 general term for inhabitants of Middle Eastern countries 2 Arabian horse > **Ar'a•bic** *noun* language of Arabs ▷ *adjective* > **Ar'ab•ist** *noun* specialist in Arabic language or in Arabic culture

ar•a•besque [ar-ə-BESK] *noun* 1 classical ballet position 2 fanciful painted or carved ornament of Arabian origin ▷ *adjective*

ar•a•ble [AR-ə-bəl] *adjective* suitable for plowing or planting crops

a•rach•nid [ə-RAK-nid] *noun* one of the Arachnida (spiders, scorpions, and mites) > **a•rach'noid** *adjective*

ar•bi•ter [AHR-bi-tər] *noun* judge, umpire > **ar•bi•trar'i•ly** [-TRER-ə-lee] *adverb* > **ar'bi•trar•y** *adjective* 1 not bound by rules, despotic 2 random > **ar'bi•trate** [-trayt] *verb* 1 decide dispute 2 submit to, settle by arbitration 3 act as an umpire > **ar•bi•tra'tion** *noun* hearing, settling of disputes, esp. industrial and legal, by impartial referee > **ar'bi•tra•tor** *noun*

ar•bor [AHR-bər] *noun* leafy glade, etc., sheltered by trees

ar•bo•re•al [ahr-BOR-ee-əl] *adjective* relating to trees > **ar•bo•re'tum** [-bə-REE-təm] *noun, plural* **-tums** place for cultivating specimens of trees > **ar•bor•i•cul•ture** [AHR-bər-i-kul-chər] *noun* forestry, cultivation of trees > **ar'bor•ist** *noun*

ar•bor vi•tae [ahr-bər VĪ-tee] a kind of evergreen conifer

arc [ahrk] *noun* 1 part of circumference of circle or similar curve 2 luminous electric discharge between two conductors > **arc lamp, arc light** light source in which an arc between two electrodes produces intense white illumination

ar•cade [ahr-KAYD] *noun* 1 row of arches on pillars 2 covered walk or avenue, esp. lined by shops

ar•cane [ahr-KAYN] *adjective* 1 mysterious 2 esoteric

arch¹ [ahrch] *noun* 1 curved structure in building, supporting itself over open space by pressure of stones one against the other 2 any similar structure 3 a curved shape 4 curved part of sole of the foot ▷ *verb* 5 form, make into, an arch > **arched** *adjective* > **arch'way** *noun*

arch² *adjective* 1 chief 2 experienced, expert 3 superior, knowing, coyly playful > **arch'ly** *adverb* > **arch'ness** *noun*

arch- *combining form* chief, principal: *archenemy*

ar•cha•ic [ahr-KAY-ik] *adjective* old, primitive > **ar•cha•ism** [AHR-kee-iz-əm] *noun* obsolete

DICTIONARY • THESAURUS

apron *noun* PINAFORE

apt *adjective* 1 INCLINED, disposed, given, liable, likely, of a mind, prone, ready
2 APPROPRIATE, fitting, pertinent, relevant, suitable, to the point
3 GIFTED, clever, quick, sharp, smart, talented

aptitude *noun* 1 TENDENCY, inclination, leaning, predilection, proclivity, propensity
2 GIFT, ability, capability, faculty, intelligence, proficiency, talent

arable *adjective* PRODUCTIVE, farmable, fertile, fruitful

arbiter *noun* 1 JUDGE, adjudicator, arbitrator, referee, umpire
2 AUTHORITY, controller, dictator, expert, governor, lord, master, pundit, ruler

arbitrary *adjective* RANDOM, capricious, chance, erratic, inconsistent, personal, subjective, whimsical

arbitrate *verb* SETTLE, adjudicate, decide, determine, judge, mediate, pass judgment, referee, umpire

arbitration *noun* SETTLEMENT, adjudication, decision, determination, judgment

arbitrator *noun* JUDGE, adjudicator, arbiter, referee, umpire

arc *noun* CURVE, arch, bend, bow, crescent, half-moon

arcade *noun* GALLERY, cloister, colonnade, portico

arcane *adjective* MYSTERIOUS, esoteric, hidden, occult, recondite, secret

arch¹ *noun* 1 CURVE, archway, dome, span, vault
2 CURVE, arc, bend, bow, hump, semicircle
▷ *verb* 3 CURVE, arc, bend, bow, bridge, span

arch² *adjective* PLAYFUL, frolicsome, mischievous, pert, roguish, saucy, sly, waggish

archaic *adjective* 1 OLD, ancient, antique,

word or phrase
arch•bish•op [ahrch-BISH-əp] *noun* chief bishop > **arch•bish'op•ric** *noun*
ar•che•ol•o•gy [ahr-kee-OL-ə-jee] *noun* study of ancient times from remains of art, implements, etc. > **ar•che•o•log'i•cal** *adjective* > **ar•che•ol'o•gist** *noun*
ar•cher•y [AHR-chə-ree] *noun* skill, sport of shooting with bow and arrow > **arch'er** *noun*
ar•che•type [AHR-ki-tīp] *noun* 1 prototype 2 perfect specimen > **ar•che•ty'pal** [-TĪ-pəl] *adjective*
ar•chi•pel•a•go [ahr-kə-PEL-ə-goh] *noun, plural* **-goes, -gos** 1 group of islands 2 sea with many small islands, esp. Aegean
ar•chi•tect [AHR-ki-tekt] *noun* 1 one qualified to design and supervise construction of buildings 2 contriver > **ar•chi•tec'tur•al** [-TEK-chər-əl] *adjective* > **ar'chi•tec•ture** *noun*
ar•chive [AHR-kīv] *noun* 1 (*often plural*) collection of records, documents, etc. about an institution, family, etc. 2 place where these are kept 3 *computing* data put on tape or disk for long-term storage ▷ *verb transitive* 4 store in an archive > **ar•chi'val** *adjective* > **ar'chi•vist** [-kə-vist] *noun*
Arc•tic [AHRK-tik] *adjective* 1 of northern polar regions 2 (**arc•tic**) very cold ▷ *noun* 3 region around north pole
ar•dent [AHR-dnt] *adjective* 1 fiery 2 passionate > **ar'dent•ly** *adverb* > **ar'dor** [-dər] *noun* 1 enthusiasm 2 zeal
ar•du•ous [AHR-joo-əs] *adjective* laborious, hard to accomplish, difficult, strenuous
are[1] [ahr] *pres ind. pl. of* **be**
are[2] [air] *noun* unit of measure, 100 square meters
ar•e•a [AIR-ee-ə] *noun* 1 extent, expanse of any surface 2 two-dimensional expanse enclosed by boundary (area of square, circle, etc.) 3 region 4 part, section 5 subject, field of activity
a•re•na [ə-REE-nə] *noun* 1 enclosure for sports events, etc. 2 space in middle of amphitheater or stadium 3 sphere, scene of conflict
ar•gon [AHR-gon] *noun* a gas, inert constituent of air
ar•go•sy [AHR-gə-see] *noun, plural* **-sies** *poet.* large richly-laden merchant ship
ar•got [AHR-goh] *noun* slang
ar•gue [AHR-gyoo] *verb intransitive* **-gued, -gu•ing** 1 quarrel, dispute 2 prove 3 offer reasons ▷ *verb transitive* **-gued, -gu•ing** 4 prove by reasoning 5 discuss > **ar'gu•a•ble** *adjective* > **ar'gu•ment** *noun* 1 quarrel 2 reasoning 3 discussion 4 theme > **ar•gu•men•ta'tion** *noun* > **ar•gu•men'ta•tive** *adjective*
a•ri•a [AHR-ee-ə] *noun* air or rhythmical song in cantata, opera, etc.
ar'id *adjective* 1 parched with heat, dry 2 dull > **a•rid•i•ty** [ə-RID-i-tee] *noun*
a•right [ə-RĪT] *adverb* rightly
a•rise [ə-RĪZ] *verb intransitive* **a•rose, a•ris•en** [ə-RIZ-ən], **a•ris•ing** 1 come about 2 get up 3 rise (up), ascend
ar•is•toc•ra•cy [ar-ə-STOK-rə-see] *noun, plural* **-cies** 1 government by the best in birth or fortune 2 nobility 3 upper classes > **a•ris•to•crat** [ə-RIS-tə-krat] *noun* > **a•ris•to•crat'ic** *adjective* 1 noble 2 elegant

bygone, olden (*archaic*), primitive
2 OLD-FASHIONED, antiquated, behind the times, obsolete, outmoded, out of date, passé
archetypal *adjective* 1 TYPICAL, classic, ideal, model, standard
2 ORIGINAL, prototypic *or* prototypical
archetype *noun* 1 STANDARD, model, paradigm, pattern, prime example
2 ORIGINAL, prototype
architect *noun* DESIGNER, master builder, planner
architecture *noun* 1 DESIGN, building, construction, planning
2 STRUCTURE, construction, design, framework, make-up, style
archive *noun* 1 RECORD OFFICE, museum, registry, repository
2 ▷ **archives** RECORDS, annals, chronicles, documents, papers, rolls
arctic *adjective* (*informal*) FREEZING, chilly, cold, frigid, frozen, glacial, icy
Arctic *adjective* POLAR, far-northern, hyperborean
ardent *adjective* 1 PASSIONATE, amorous, hot-blooded, impassioned, intense, lusty
2 ENTHUSIASTIC, avid, eager, keen, zealous
ardor *noun* 1 PASSION, fervor, intensity, spirit, vehemence, warmth
2 ENTHUSIASM, avidity, eagerness, keenness, zeal
arduous *adjective* DIFFICULT, exhausting, fatiguing, grueling, laborious, onerous, punishing, rigorous, strenuous, taxing, tiring
area *noun* 1 REGION, district, locality, neighborhood, zone
2 PART, portion, section, sector
3 FIELD, department, domain, province, realm, sphere, territory
arena *noun* 1 RING, amphitheater, bowl, enclosure, field, ground, stadium
2 SPHERE, area, domain, field, province, realm, sector, territory
argue *verb* 1 DISCUSS, assert, claim, debate, dispute, maintain, reason, remonstrate
2 QUARREL, bicker, disagree, dispute, fall out (*informal*), fight, squabble
argument *noun* 1 QUARREL, clash, controversy, disagreement, dispute, feud, fight, row, squabble
2 DISCUSSION, assertion, claim, debate, dispute, plea, questioning, remonstration
3 REASON, argumentation, case, defense, dialectic, ground *or* grounds, line of reasoning, logic, polemic, reasoning
argumentative *adjective* QUARRELSOME, belligerent, combative, contentious, contrary, disputatious, litigious, opinionated
arid *adjective* 1 DRY, barren, desert, parched, sterile, torrid, waterless
2 BORING, dreary, dry, dull, tedious, tiresome, uninspired, uninteresting
arise *verb* 1 HAPPEN, begin, emerge, ensue, follow, occur, result, start, stem
2 GET UP, get to one's feet, go up, rise, stand up, wake up
aristocracy *noun* UPPER CLASS, elite, gentry, nobility, patricians, peerage, ruling class
aristocrat *adjective* NOBLE, grandee, lady, lord, patrician, peer, peeress

a•rith•me•tic [ə-RITH-mə-tik] *noun* 1 science of numbers 2 art of reckoning by figures > **ar•ith•met'ic** *adjective* > **ar•ith•met'i•cal•ly** *adverb*
ark [ahrk] *noun* 1 Noah's vessel 2 (**Ark**) coffer containing scrolls of the Torah
arm[1] [ahrm] *noun* 1 limb extending from shoulder to wrist 2 anything projecting from main body, as branch of sea, supporting rail of chair, etc. > **arm'chair** *noun* > **arm'ful** *noun, plural* **-fuls** > **arm'hole** *noun* > **arm'pit** *noun* hollow under arm at shoulder > **arm-twisting** *noun* use of personal pressure to achieve a desired result
arm[2] *verb transitive* 1 supply with weapons, furnish 2 prepare bomb, etc. for use ▷ *verb intransitive* 3 take up arms ▷ *noun* 4 weapon 5 branch of army > **arms** 1 weapons 2 war, military exploits 3 official heraldic symbols > **ar'ma•ment** *noun*
ar•ma•da [ahr-MAH-də] *noun* large number of ships or aircraft
ar•ma•dil•lo [ahr-mə-DIL-oh] *noun, plural* **-los** small Amer. animal protected by bands of bony plates
ar•ma•ture [AHR-mə-chər] *noun* 1 revolving structure in electric motor, generator 2 framework used by a sculptor to support modeling clay, etc.
ar•mi•stice [AHR-mə-stis] *noun* truce, suspension of fighting
ar•mor [AHR-mər] *noun* 1 defensive covering or dress 2 plating of tanks, warships, etc. 3 armored fighting vehicles, as tanks > **ar'mor•y** *noun, plural* **-mor•ies**
ar•my [AHR-mee] *noun, plural* **-mies** 1 large body of soldiers armed for warfare and under military command 2 host 3 great number
a•ro•ma [ə-ROH-mə] *noun* 1 sweet smell 2 fragrance 3 peculiar charm > **ar•o•mat•ic** [ar-ə-MAT-ik] *adjective*
a•rose *pt. of* **arise**
a•round [ə-ROWND] *preposition* 1 on all sides of 2 somewhere in or near 3 approximately (of time) ▷ *adverb* 4 on every side 5 in a circle 6 here and there, nowhere in particular 7 (*informal*) present in or at some place
a•rouse [ə-ROWZ] *verb transitive* **-roused, -rous•ing** awaken, stimulate
ar•peg•gi•o [ahr-PEJ-ee-oh] *noun, plural* **-gi•os** *mus.* 1 notes sounded in quick succession, not together 2 chord so played
ar•raign [ə-RAYN] *verb transitive* accuse, indict, put on trial > **ar•raign'ment** *noun*
ar•range [ə-RAYNJ] *verb* **-ranged, -rang•ing** 1 set in order 2 make agreement 3 adjust 4 plan 5 adapt, as music 6 settle, as dispute > **ar•range'ment** *noun*
ar•rant [AR-ənt] *adjective* downright, notorious
ar•ras [AR-əs] *noun* tapestry
ar•ray [ə-RAY] *noun* 1 order, esp. military order 2 dress 3 imposing show, splendor ▷ *verb transitive* 4 set in order 5 dress, equip, adorn
ar•rears [ə-REERZ] *plural noun* amount unpaid or undone

DICTIONARY • THESAURUS

aristocratic *noun* UPPER-CLASS, blue-blooded, elite, gentlemanly, lordly, noble, patrician, titled
arm[1] *noun* UPPER LIMB, appendage, limb
arm[2] *verb* (*especially with weapons*) EQUIP, accouter, array, deck out, furnish, issue with, provide, supply
armada *noun* FLEET, flotilla, navy, squadron
armaments *plural noun* WEAPONS, ammunition, arms, guns, materiel, munitions, ordnance, weaponry
armed *adjective* CARRYING WEAPONS, equipped, fitted out, primed, protected
armistice *noun* TRUCE, ceasefire, peace, suspension of hostilities
armor *noun* PROTECTION, armor plate, covering, sheathing, shield
armored *adjective* PROTECTED, armor-plated, bombproof, bulletproof, ironclad, mailed, steel-plated
arms *plural noun* 1 WEAPONS, armaments, firearms, guns, instruments of war, ordnance, weaponry
2 HERALDRY, blazonry, crest, escutcheon, insignia
army *noun* 1 SOLDIERS, armed force, legions, military, military force, soldiery, troops
2 VAST NUMBER, array, horde, host, multitude, pack, swarm, throng
aroma *noun* SCENT, bouquet, fragrance, odor, perfume, redolence, savor, smell
aromatic *adjective* FRAGRANT, balmy, perfumed, pungent, redolent, savory, spicy, sweet-scented, sweet-smelling
around *preposition* 1 SURROUNDING, about, encircling, enclosing, encompassing, on all sides of, on every side of
2 APPROXIMATELY, about, circa (*used of a date*), roughly
▷ *adverb* 3 EVERYWHERE, about, all over, here and there, in all directions, on all sides, throughout, to and fro
4 NEAR, at hand, close, close at hand, nearby, nigh (*archaic* or *dialect*)
arouse *verb* 1 STIMULATE, excite, incite, instigate, provoke, spur, stir up, summon up, whip up
2 AWAKEN, rouse, waken, wake up
arrange *verb* 1 PLAN, construct, contrive, devise, fix up, organize, prepare
2 AGREE, adjust, come to terms, compromise, determine, settle
3 PUT IN ORDER, classify, group, line up, order, organize, position, sort
4 ADAPT, instrument, orchestrate, score
arrangement *noun* 1 (*often plural*) PLAN, organization, planning, preparation, provision, schedule
2 AGREEMENT, adjustment, compact, compromise, deal, settlement, terms
3 ORDER, alignment, classification, form, organization, structure, system
4 ADAPTATION, instrumentation, interpretation, orchestration, score, version
array *noun* 1 ARRANGEMENT, collection, display, exhibition, formation, line-up, parade, show, supply
2 (*poetic*) CLOTHING, apparel, attire, clothes, dress, finery, garments, regalia
▷ *verb* 3 ARRANGE, display, exhibit, group, parade, range, show
4 DRESS, adorn, attire, clothe, deck, decorate, festoon

ar•rest [ə-REST] *verb transitive* 1 detain by legal authority 2 stop 3 catch attention ▷ *noun* 4 seizure by warrant 5 making prisoner > **ar•rest'ing** *adjective* attracting attention, striking > **ar•rest'er** *noun* 1 person who arrests 2 mechanism to stop or slow moving object

ar•rive [ə-RĪV] *verb intransitive* **-rived, -riv•ing** 1 reach destination 2 (with *at*) reach, attain 3 (*informal*) succeed > **ar•ri'val** *noun*

ar•ro•gance [AR-ə-gəns] *noun* aggressive conceit > **ar'ro•gant** *adjective* 1 proud 2 overbearing

ar•ro•gate [AR-ə-gayt] *verb transitive* **-gat•ed, -gat•ing** seize or claim without right

ar•row [AR-oh] *noun* 1 pointed shaft shot from bow > **ar'row•head** *noun* 1 head of arrow 2 any triangular shape

ar•row•root [AR-oh-root] *noun* nutritious starch from W Indian plant, used as a food

ar•se•nal [AHR-sə-nl] *noun* 1 place for manufacture, storage weapons and ammunition 2 repertoire (of skills, skilled personnel, etc.)

ar•se•nic [AHR-sə-nik] *noun* 1 soft, gray, metallic element 2 its oxide, a powerful poison > **ar'se•nate** [-nayt] *noun* > **ar•sen'i•cal** *adjective*

ar•son [AHR-sən] *noun* crime of intentionally setting property on fire

art [ahrt] *noun* 1 skill 2 human skill as opposed to nature 3 creative skill in painting, poetry, music, etc. 4 any of the works produced thus 5 profession, craft 6 knack 7 contrivance, cunning, trick 8 system of rules > **arts** 1 certain branches of learning, languages, history, etc., as distinct from natural science 2 wiles > **art'ful** *adjective* wily > **art'ful•ly** *adverb* > **art'ist** *noun* 1 one who practices fine art, esp. painting 2 one who makes a fine art of a craft > **ar•tiste'** [-TEEST] *noun* professional entertainer, singer, dancer, etc. > **ar•tis'tic** *adjective* > **art'ist•ry** *noun* > **art'less** *adjective* natural, frank > **art'less•ness** *noun* > **art'y** *adjective* **art•i•er, art•i•est** ostentatiously artistic

ar•te•ri•o•scle•ro•sis [ahr-teer-ee-oh-sklə-ROH-sis] *noun* hardening of the arteries > **ar•te•ri•o•scle•rot'ic** *adjective*

ar•ter•y [AHR-tə-ree] *noun, plural* **-ter•ies** 1 one of the vessels carrying blood from heart 2 any main channel of communications > **ar•te'ri•al** [-TEER-ee-əl] *adjective* 1 pert. to an artery 2 (of a route) major

ar•te•sian [ahr-TEE-*zh*ən] *adjective* describes deep well in which water rises by internal pressure

ar•thri•tis [ahr-THRĪ-tis] *noun* painful inflammation of joint(s) > **ar•thrit'ic** [-THRIT-ik] *adjective, noun*

ar•thro•pod [AHR-thrə-pod] *noun* 1 invertebrate with jointed limbs and segmented body e.g. 2 insect, spider

ar•ti•choke [AHR-ti-chohk] *noun* thistle-like perennial, edible flower

ar•ti•cle [AHR-ti-kəl] *noun* 1 item, object 2 short written piece 3 paragraph, section 4 *grammar* any of the words *the, a,* or *an* 5 clause in a contract 6 rule, condition

ar•tic•u•late [ahr-TIK-yə-lit] *adjective* 1 able to express oneself fluently 2 jointed 3 of speech, clear, distinct ▷ *verb transitive* [-layt], **-lat•ed, -lat•ing** 4 joint 5 utter distinctly ▷ *verb intransitive* [-layt], **-lat•ed, -lat•ing** 6 speak > **ar•tic'u•late•ly** *adverb* > **ar•tic•u•la'tion** *noun*

ar•ti•fact [AHR-tə-fakt] *noun* something made by a person, esp. by hand

ar•ti•fice [AHR-tə-fis] *noun* contrivance, trick, cunning, skill > **ar•tif'i•cer** [-TIF-ə-sər] *noun*

arrest *verb* 1 CAPTURE, apprehend, catch, detain, seize, take prisoner
2 STOP, block, delay, end, inhibit, interrupt, obstruct, slow, suppress
3 GRIP, absorb, engage, engross, fascinate, hold, intrigue, occupy
▷ *noun* 4 CAPTURE, bust (*informal*), detention, seizure
5 STOPPING, blockage, delay, end, hindrance, interruption, obstruction, suppression

arresting *adjective* STRIKING, cool (*informal*), engaging, impressive, noticeable, outstanding, phat (*slang*), remarkable, stunning, surprising

arrival *noun* 1 COMING, advent, appearance, arriving, entrance, happening, occurrence, taking place
2 NEWCOMER, caller, entrant, incomer, visitor

arrive *verb* 1 COME, appear, enter, get to, reach, show up (*informal*), turn up
2 (*informal*) SUCCEED, become famous, make good, make it (*informal*), make the grade (*informal*)

arrogance *noun* CONCEIT, disdainfulness, haughtiness, high-handedness, insolence, pride, superciliousness, swagger

arrogant *adjective* CONCEITED, disdainful, haughty, high-handed, overbearing, proud, scornful, supercilious

arrow *noun* 1 DART, bolt, flight, quarrel, shaft (*archaic*)
2 POINTER, indicator

arsenal *noun* ARMORY, ammunition dump, arms depot, ordnance depot, stockpile, store, storehouse, supply

art *noun* SKILL, craft, expertise, ingenuity, mastery, virtuosity

artful *adjective* CUNNING, clever, crafty, shrewd, sly, smart, wily

article *noun* 1 PIECE, composition, discourse, essay, feature, item, paper, story, treatise
2 THING, commodity, item, object, piece, substance, unit
3 CLAUSE, item, paragraph, part, passage, point, portion, section

articulate *adjective* 1 EXPRESSIVE, clear, coherent, eloquent, fluent, lucid, well-spoken
▷ *verb* 2 EXPRESS, enunciate, pronounce, say, speak, state, talk, utter, voice

artifice *noun* 1 TRICK, contrivance, device, machination, maneuver, stratagem, subterfuge, tactic
2 CLEVERNESS, ingenuity, inventiveness, skill

artificial *adjective* 1 SYNTHETIC, man-made, manufactured, non-natural, plastic
2 FAKE, bogus, counterfeit, imitation, mock, sham, simulated
3 INSINCERE, affected, contrived, false, feigned, forced, phoney *or* phony (*informal*), unnatural

artillery *noun* BIG GUNS, battery, cannon, cannonry, gunnery, ordnance

artisan *noun* CRAFTSMAN, journeyman,

craftsperson > **ar•ti•fi'cial** [-FISH-əl] *adjective* 1 manufactured, synthetic 2 insincere > **ar•ti•fi'cial•ly** *adverb* > **artificial intelligence** ability of machines, esp. computers, to imitate intelligent human behavior > **artificial respiration** method of restarting person's breathing after it has stopped

ar•til•ler•y [ahr-TIL-ə-ree] *noun* 1 large guns on wheels 2 the troops that use them

ar•ti•san [AHR-tə-zən] *noun* craftsperson, skilled mechanic, manual worker

ar•tiste *see* **art**

Ar•y•an [AIR-ee-ən] *adjective* relating to Indo-European family of nations and languages

As *chem.* arsenic

as [az] *adverb, conjunction* 1 denoting: comparison 2 similarity 3 equality 4 identity 5 concurrence 6 reason

as•bes•tos [as-BES-təs] *noun* fibrous mineral that does not burn > **as•bes•to•sis** [as-be-STOH-sis] *noun* lung disease caused by inhalation of asbestos fiber

as•cend [ə-SEND] *verb intransitive* 1 climb, rise ▷ *verb transitive* 2 walk up, climb, mount > **as•cend'an•cy** *noun* control, dominance > **as•cend'ant** *adjective* rising > **as•cen'sion** [-shən] *noun* > **as•cent'** *noun* rise

as•cer•tain [as-ər-TAYN] *verb* get to know, find out, determine > **as•cer•tain'a•ble** *adjective*

as•cet•ic [ə-SET-ik] *noun* 1 one who practices severe self-denial ▷ *adjective* 2 rigidly abstinent, austere > **as•cet'i•cism** [-ə-siz-əm] *noun*

ASCII [ASS-kee] *noun* a code for transmitting data between computers

a•scor•bic acid [ə-SKOR-bik] vitamin C, present in green vegetables, citrus fruits, etc.

as•cribe [ə-SKRĪB] *verb transitive* **-cribed, -crib•ing** attribute, impute, assign > **a•scrib'a•ble** *adjective*

a•sep•tic [ə-SEP-tik] *adjective* germ-free > **a•sep'sis** *noun*

a•sex•u•al [ay-SEK-shoo-əl] *adjective* without sex

ash[1] *noun* dust or remains of anything burned > **ash•es** 1 ruins 2 remains after burning, esp. of a human body after cremation > **ash'en** *adjective* 1 like ashes 2 pale

ash[2] *noun* 1 deciduous timber tree 2 its wood > **ash'en** *adjective*

a•shamed [ə-SHAYMD] *adjective* affected with shame, abashed

a•shore [ə-SHOR] *adverb* on shore

Ash Wednesday first day of Lent

A•sian [AY-zhən] *adjective* 1 pert. to continent of Asia ▷ *noun* 2 native of Asia or descendant of one > **A•si•at'ic** [-zhee-AT-ik] *adjective*

a•side [ə-SĪD] *adverb* 1 to or on one side 2 privately ▷ *noun* 3 words spoken in an undertone not to be heard by some person present

as•i•nine [AS-ə-nīn] *adjective* of or like an ass, silly > **as•i•nin'i•ty** [-NIN-i-tee] *noun*

ask *verb transitive* 1 request, require, question, invite ▷ *verb intransitive* 2 make inquiry or request

a•skance [ə-SKANS] *adverb* 1 sideways, awry 2 with a side look or meaning **look askance** view with suspicion

a•skew [ə-SKYOO] *adverb* aside, awry

a•sleep [ə-SLEEP] *adjective, adverb* sleeping, at rest

asp *noun* small venomous snake

as•par•a•gus [ə-SPA-rə-gəs] *noun* plant whose young shoots are a table delicacy

as•pect [AS-pekt] *noun* look, view, appearance, expression

---

mechanic, skilled workman, technician

artistic *adjective* CREATIVE, aesthetic, beautiful, cultured, elegant, refined, sophisticated, stylish, tasteful

artistry *noun* SKILL, brilliance, craftsmanship, creativity, finesse, mastery, proficiency, virtuosity

artless *adjective* 1 STRAIGHTFORWARD, frank, guileless, open, plain
2 NATURAL, homely, plain, pure, simple, unadorned, unaffected, unpretentious

as *conjunction* 1 WHEN, at the time that, during the time that, just as, while
2 IN THE WAY THAT, in the manner that, like
3 WHAT, that which
4 SINCE, because, considering that, seeing that
5 FOR INSTANCE, like, such as
▷ *preposition* 6 BEING, in the character of, in the role of, under the name of

ascend *verb* MOVE UP, climb, go up, mount, scale

ascent *noun* 1 RISE, ascending, ascension, climb, mounting, rising, scaling, upward movement
2 UPWARD SLOPE, gradient, incline, ramp, rise, rising ground

ascertain *verb* FIND OUT, confirm, determine, discover, establish, learn

ascetic *noun* 1 MONK, abstainer, hermit, nun, recluse
▷ *adjective* 2 SELF-DENYING, abstinent, austere, celibate, frugal, puritanical, self-disciplined

ascribe *verb* ATTRIBUTE, assign, charge, credit, impute, put down, refer, set down

ashamed *adjective* EMBARRASSED, distressed, guilty, humiliated, mortified, remorseful, shamefaced, sheepish, sorry

ashen *adjective* PALE, colorless, gray, leaden, like death warmed over (*informal*), pallid, wan, white

ashore *adverb* ON LAND, aground, landwards, on dry land, on the beach, on the shore, shorewards, to the shore

aside *adverb* 1 TO ONE SIDE, apart, beside, on one side, out of the way, privately, separately, to the side
▷ *noun* 2 INTERPOLATION, parenthesis

asinine *adjective* STUPID, fatuous, foolish, idiotic, imbecilic, moronic (*offensive*), senseless

ask *verb* 1 INQUIRE, interrogate, query, question, quiz
2 REQUEST, appeal, beg, demand, plead, seek
3 INVITE, bid, summon

askew *adverb* 1 CROOKEDLY, aslant, awry, obliquely, off-center, to one side
▷ *adjective* 2 CROOKED, awry, cockeyed (*informal*), lopsided, oblique, off-center

asleep *adjective* SLEEPING, dormant, dozing, fast asleep, napping, slumbering, snoozing (*informal*), sound asleep

aspect *noun* 1 FEATURE, angle, facet, side
2 POSITION, outlook, point of view, prospect, scene, situation, view

as•pen [AS-pən] *noun* type of poplar tree
as•per•i•ty [ə-SPER-i-tee] *noun, plural* **-ties** 1 roughness 2 harshness 3 coldness
as•per•sion [ə-SPUR-zhən] *noun* **cast aspersions on** make derogatory remarks about
as•phalt [AS-fawlt] *noun* black, hard bituminous substance used for road surfaces, etc.
as•phyx•i•a [as-FIK-see-ə] *noun* suffocation > **as•phyx'i•ate** [-ayt] *verb* **-at•ed, -at•ing** > **as•phyx•i•a'tion** *noun*
as•pic [AS-pik] *noun* jelly used to coat or make a mold of meat, eggs, fish, etc.
as•pire [ə-SPĪR] *verb intransitive* **-pired, -pir•ing** 1 desire eagerly 2 aim at high things 3 rise to great height > **as•pi•rant** [AS-pər-ənt] *noun* 1 one who aspires 2 candidate > **as'pi•rate** [-pə-rayt] *verb transitive* pronounce with full breathing, as *h* > **as•pir'ing** *adjective*
as•pi•rin [AS-pər-in] *noun* (a tablet of) drug used to allay pain and fever
ass *noun* 1 quadruped of horse family 2 stupid person
as•sail [ə-SAYL] *verb transitive* attack, assault > **as•sail'a•ble** *adjective* > **as•sail'ant** *noun*
as•sas•sin [ə-SAS-in] *noun* 1 one who kills, esp. prominent person, by treacherous violence 2 murderer > **as•sas'si•nate** *verb transitive* **-nat•ed, -nat•ing** > **as•sas•si•na'tion** *noun*
as•sault [ə-SAWLT] *noun* 1 attack, esp. sudden ▷ *verb transitive* 2 attack
as•say [ə-SAY] *verb transitive* 1 test, esp. proportions of metals in alloy or ore ▷ *noun* [AS-ay] 2 analysis, esp. of metals 3 trial, test
as•sem•ble [ə-SEM-bəl] *verb* **-bled, -bling** 1 meet, bring together 2 collect 3 put together (of machinery, etc.) > **as•sem'blage** [-blij] *noun* > **as•sem'bly** *noun, plural* **-blies** 1 gathering, meeting 2 assembling > **assembly line** sequence of machines, workers in factory assembling product
as•sent [ə-SENT] *verb intransitive* 1 concur, agree ▷ *noun* 2 acquiescence, agreement, compliance
as•sert [ə-SURT] *verb transitive* declare strongly, insist upon > **as•ser'tion** *noun* > **as•sert'ive** *adjective* > **as•ser'tive•ly** *adverb*
as•sess [ə-SES] *verb transitive* 1 fix value 2 evaluate, estimate, esp. for taxation 3 fix amount (of tax or fine) 4 tax or fine > **as•sess'ment** *noun* > **as•ses'sor** *noun*
as•set [AS-et] *noun* valuable or useful person, thing > **as•sets** property available to pay debts, esp. of insolvent debtor
as•sid•u•ous [ə-SIJ-oo-əs] *adjective* persevering, attentive, diligent > **as•si•du•i•ty** [as-i-DOO-i-tee] *noun*
as•sign [ə-SĪN] *verb transitive* 1 appoint to job, etc. 2 allot, apportion, fix 3 ascribe 4 transfer > **as•sign'a•ble** *adjective* > **as•sig•na•tion** [as-ig-NAY-shən] *noun* 1 secret meeting 2

DICTIONARY **a** THESAURUS

---

3 APPEARANCE, air, attitude, bearing, condition, demeanor, expression, look, manner
asphyxiate *verb* SUFFOCATE, choke, smother, stifle, strangle, strangulate, throttle
aspiration *noun* AIM, ambition, desire, dream, goal, hope, objective, wish
aspire *verb* AIM, desire, dream, hope, long, seek, set one's heart on, wish
aspiring *adjective* HOPEFUL, ambitious, eager, longing, wannabe (*informal*), would-be
ass *noun* 1 DONKEY
2 FOOL, blockhead, dork (*slang*), halfwit, idiot, jackass, oaf, schmuck (*slang*)
assail *verb* ATTACK, assault, fall upon, set upon
assailant *noun* ATTACKER, aggressor, assailer, assaulter, invader
assassin *noun* MURDERER, executioner, hatchet man (*slang*), hit man (*slang*), killer, liquidator, slayer
assassinate *verb* MURDER, eliminate (*slang*), hit (*slang*), kill, liquidate, slay, take out (*slang*)
assault *noun* 1 ATTACK, charge, invasion, offensive, onslaught
▷ *verb* 2 ATTACK, beset, fall upon, set about, set upon, strike at
assemble *verb* 1 GATHER, amass, bring together, call together, collect, come together, congregate, meet, muster, rally
2 PUT TOGETHER, build up, connect, construct, fabricate, fit together, join, piece together, set up
assembly *noun* 1 GATHERING, collection, company, conference, congress, council, crowd, group, mass, meeting
2 PUTTING TOGETHER, building up, connecting, construction, piecing together, setting up
assent *noun* 1 AGREEMENT, acceptance, approval, compliance, concurrence, consent, permission, sanction
▷ *verb* 2 AGREE, allow, approve, consent, grant, permit
assert *verb* 1 STATE, affirm, declare, maintain, profess, pronounce, swear
2 INSIST UPON, claim, defend, press, put forward, stand up for, stress, uphold
3 ▷ **assert oneself** BE FORCEFUL, exert one's influence, make one's presence felt, put oneself forward, put one's foot down (*informal*)
assertion *noun* 1 STATEMENT, claim, declaration, pronouncement
2 INSISTENCE, maintenance, stressing
assertive *adjective* CONFIDENT, aggressive, domineering, emphatic, feisty (*informal*), forceful, insistent, positive, pushy (*informal*), strong-willed
assess *verb* 1 JUDGE, appraise, estimate, evaluate, rate, size up (*informal*), value, weigh
2 EVALUATE, fix, impose, levy, rate, tax, value
assessment *noun* 1 JUDGMENT, appraisal, estimate, evaluation, rating, valuation
2 EVALUATION, charge, fee, levy, rating, toll, valuation
asset *noun* 1 BENEFIT, advantage, aid, blessing, boon, feather in one's cap, help, resource, service
2 ▷ **assets** PROPERTY, capital, estate, funds, goods, money, possessions, resources, wealth
assiduous *adjective* DILIGENT, hard-working, indefatigable, industrious, persevering, persistent, unflagging
assign *verb* 1 SELECT, appoint, choose, delegate, designate, name, nominate
2 GIVE, allocate, allot, apportion, consign, distribute, give out, grant
3 ATTRIBUTE, accredit, ascribe, put down
assignation *noun* 1 SECRET MEETING,

appointment to meet > **as•sign'ment** *noun* 1 act of assigning 2 allotted duty

as•sim•i•late [ə-SIM-ə-layt] *verb transitive* **-lat•ed, -lat•ing** 1 learn and understand 2 make similar 3 absorb into the system > **as•sim•i•la'tion** *noun*

as•sist [ə-SIST] *verb* 1 give help 2 aid > **as•sis'tance** *noun* > **as•sis'tant** *noun* helper

as•so•ci•ate [ə-SOH-shee-ayt] *verb transitive* **-at•ed, -at•ing** 1 link, connect, esp. as ideas in mind 2 join ▷ *verb intransitive* **-at•ed, -at•ing** 3 formerly, keep company with 4 combine, unite ▷ *noun* [-it] 5 companion, partner 6 friend, ally 7 subordinate member of association ▷ *adjective* 8 affiliated > **as•so•ci•a'tion** *noun* society, club

as•sort [ə-SORT] *verb transitive* 1 classify, arrange ▷ *verb intransitive* 2 match, agree with, harmonize > **as•sort'ed** *adjective* mixed > **as•sort'ment** *noun*

as•suage [ə-SWAYJ] *verb transitive* **-suaged, -suag•ing** 1 soften, pacify 2 soothe

as•sume [ə-SOOM] *verb transitive* **-sumed, -sum•ing** 1 take for granted 2 pretend 3 take upon oneself 4 claim > **as•sump'tion** [-SUMP-shən] *noun*

as•sure [ə-SHOOR] *verb transitive* **-sured, -sur•ing** 1 tell positively, promise 2 make sure 3 insure against loss, esp. of life 4 affirm > **as•sured'** *adjective* sure > **as•sur'ed•ly** [-id-lee] *adverb*

as•ter•isk [AS-tə-risk] *noun* 1 star (*) used in printing ▷ *verb transitive* 2 mark thus

a•stern [ə-STURN] *adverb* 1 in, behind the stern 2 backward in direction

as•ter•oid [AS-tə-roid] *noun* 1 small planet ▷ *adjective* 2 star-shaped

asth•ma [AZ-mə] *noun* illness in which one has difficulty in breathing > **asth•mat'ic** *adjective, noun*

a•stig•ma•tism [ə-STIG-mə-tiz-əm] *noun* inability of lens (esp. of eye) to focus properly > **as•tig•mat•ic** [as-tig-MAT-ik] *adjective*

a•stir [ə-STUR] *adverb* 1 on the move 2 out of bed 3 in excitement

as•ton•ish [ə-STON-ish] *verb transitive* amaze, surprise > **as•ton'ish•ing** *adjective* > **as•ton'ish•ment** *noun*

as•tound [ə-STOWND] *verb transitive* 1 astonish greatly 2 stun with amazement > **as•tound'ing** *adjective* startling

as•tra•khan [AS-trə-kən] *noun* lambskin with curled wool

---

clandestine meeting, illicit meeting, rendezvous, tryst
2 SELECTION, appointment, assignment, choice, delegation, designation, nomination

assignment *noun* TASK, appointment, commission, duty, job, mission, position, post, responsibility

assimilate *verb* 1 LEARN, absorb, digest, incorporate, take in
2 ADJUST, adapt, blend in, mingle

assist *verb* HELP, abet, aid, cooperate, lend a helping hand, serve, support

assistance *noun* HELP, aid, backing, cooperation, helping hand, support

assistant *noun* HELPER, accomplice, aide, ally, colleague, right-hand man, second, supporter

associate *verb* 1 CONNECT, ally, combine, identify, join, link, lump together
2 MIX, accompany, consort, hobnob, mingle, socialize
▷ *noun* 3 PARTNER, collaborator, colleague, confederate, co-worker
4 FRIEND, ally, companion, comrade, homeboy (*slang*), homegirl (*slang*)

association *noun* 1 GROUP, alliance, band, club, coalition, federation, league, organization, society
2 CONNECTION, blend, combination, joining, juxtaposition, mixture, pairing, union

assorted *adjective* VARIOUS, different, diverse, miscellaneous, mixed, motley, sundry, varied

assortment *noun* VARIETY, array, choice, collection, jumble, medley, mixture, selection

assume *verb* 1 TAKE FOR GRANTED, believe, expect, fancy, imagine, infer, presume, suppose, surmise, think
2 TAKE ON, accept, enter upon, put on, shoulder, take over
3 PUT ON, adopt, affect, feign, imitate, impersonate, mimic, pretend to, simulate

assumed *adjective* 1 FALSE, bogus, counterfeit, fake, fictitious, made-up, make-believe
2 TAKEN FOR GRANTED, accepted, expected, hypothetical, presumed, presupposed, supposed, surmised

assumption *noun* 1 PRESUMPTION, belief, conjecture, guess, hypothesis, inference, supposition, surmise
2 TAKING ON, acceptance, acquisition, adoption, entering upon, putting on, shouldering, takeover, taking up
3 TAKING, acquisition, appropriation, seizure, takeover

assurance *noun* 1 ASSERTION, declaration, guarantee, oath, pledge, promise, statement, vow, word
2 CONFIDENCE, boldness, certainty, conviction, faith, nerve, poise, self-confidence

assure *verb* 1 PROMISE, certify, confirm, declare confidently, give one's word to, guarantee, pledge, swear, vow
2 CONVINCE, comfort, embolden, encourage, hearten, persuade, reassure
3 MAKE CERTAIN, clinch, complete, confirm, ensure, guarantee, make sure, seal, secure

assured *adjective* 1 CONFIDENT, certain, poised, positive, self-assured, self-confident, sure of oneself
2 CERTAIN, beyond doubt, confirmed, ensured, fixed, guaranteed, in the bag (*slang*), secure, settled, sure

astonish *verb* AMAZE, astound, bewilder, confound, daze, dumbfound, stagger, stun, surprise

astonishing *adjective* AMAZING, astounding, bewildering, breathtaking, brilliant, sensational (*informal*), staggering, stunning, surprising

astonishment *noun* AMAZEMENT, awe, bewilderment, confusion, consternation, surprise, wonder, wonderment

astounding *adjective* AMAZING, astonishing, bewildering, breathtaking, brilliant, cool (*informal*), impressive, phat (*slang*), sensational (*informal*), staggering, stunning, surprising

as•tral [AS-trəl] *adjective* of the stars or spirit world

a•stray [ə-STRAY] *adverb* off the right path, wanderingly

a•stride [ə-STRĪD] *adverb* with the legs apart, straddling

as•trin•gent [ə-STRIN-jənt] *adjective* 1 severe, harsh 2 sharp 3 constricting (body tissues, blood vessels, etc.) ▷ *noun* 4 astringent substance

as•trol•o•gy [ə-STROL-ə-jee] *noun* 1 foretelling of events by stars 2 medieval astronomy > **as•trol'o•ger** *noun* > **as•tro•log'i•cal** *adjective*

as•tro•naut [AS-trə-nawt] *noun* one trained for travel in space

as•tron•o•my [ə-STRON-ə-mee] *noun* scientific study of heavenly bodies > **as•tron'o•mer** *noun* > **as•tro•nom'i•cal** [-trə-NOM-i-kəl] *adjective* 1 very large 2 of astronomy > **astronomical unit** unit of distance used in astronomy equal to the mean distance between Earth and the sun

as•tro•phys•ics [as-troh-FIZ-iks] *noun* the science of the chemical and physical characteristics of heavenly bodies > **as•tro•phys'i•cist** *noun*

as•tute [ə-STOOT] *adjective* perceptive, shrewd > **as•tute'ly** *adverb* > **as•tute'ness** *noun*

a•sun•der [ə-SUN-dər] *adverb* 1 apart 2 in pieces

a•sy•lum [ə-SĪ-ləm] *noun* 1 refuge, sanctuary, place of safety 2 old name for hospital for mentally ill

a•sym•me•try [ay-SIM-i-tree] *noun* lack of symmetry > **a•sym•met'ric** [-sə-MET-rik] *adjective*

as•ymp•tote [AS-im-toht] *noun* straight line that continually approaches a curve, but never meets it

at *preposition, adverb* 1 denoting: location in space or time 2 rate 3 condition or state 4 amount 5 direction 6 cause

At *chem.* astatine

at•a•vism [AT-ə-viz-əm] *noun* appearance of ancestral, not parental, characteristics in human beings, animals or plants > **at•a•vis'tic** *adjective*

a•tax•i•a [ə-TAK-see-ə] *noun* lack of muscular coordination

ate [ayt] *pt. of* **eat**

at•el•ier [at-l-YAY] *noun* workshop, artist's studio

a•the•ism [AY-thee-iz-əm] *noun* belief that there is no God > **a'the•ist** *noun* > **a•the•is'tic** *adjective*

ath•lete [ATH-leet] *noun* 1 one trained for physical exercises, feats or contests of strength 2 one good at sports > **ath•let'ic** *adjective* > **ath•let'ics** *plural noun* sports such as running, jumping, throwing, etc. > **ath•let'i•cal•ly** *adverb*

a•thwart [ə-THWORT] *preposition* 1 across ▷ *adverb* 2 across, esp. obliquely

at•las [AT-ləs] *noun* volume of maps

at•mos•phere [AT-məs-feer] *noun* 1 mass of gas surrounding heavenly body, esp. Earth 2 prevailing tone or mood (of place, etc.) 3 unit of pressure in cgs system > **at•mos•pher'ic** [-FER-ik] *adjective* > **at•mos•pher'ics** *plural noun* 1 noises in radio reception due to electrical disturbance in the atmosphere 2 *politics* mood or atmosphere

at•oll [AT-awl] *noun* ring-shaped coral island enclosing lagoon

at•om [AT-əm] *noun* 1 smallest unit of matter that can enter into chemical combination 2 any very small particle > **a•tom•ic** [ə-TOM-ik] *adjective* of, arising from atoms > **at•o•mic•i•ty** [at-ə-MIS-i-tee] *noun* number of atoms in molecule of an element > **at'om•ize** *verb transitive* **-ized, -iz•ing** reduce to atoms or small particles > **at'om•iz•er** *noun* instrument for discharging liquids in a fine spray > **atom bomb** *or* **atomic bomb** one whose immense power derives from nuclear fission or fusion, nuclear bomb > **atomic energy** nuclear energy > **atomic number** the number of protons in the nucleus of an atom > **atomic reactor** *see also* **reactor** > **atomic weight** the weight of an atom of an element relative to that of carbon 12

a•tone [ə-TOHN] *verb intransitive* **-toned, -ton•ing** 1 make reparation, amends (for) 2 expiate 3 give satisfaction > **a•tone'ment** *noun*

a•ton•ic [ay-TON-ik] *adjective* unaccented

a•top [ə-TOP] *adverb* 1 at or on the top 2 above

a•tro•cious [ə-TROH-shəs] *adjective* 1 extremely

astray *adjective, adverb* OFF THE RIGHT TRACK, adrift, amiss, lost, off, off course, off the mark, off the subject

astute *adjective* INTELLIGENT, canny, clever, crafty, cunning, perceptive, sagacious, sharp, shrewd, subtle

asylum *noun* 1 REFUGE, harbor, haven, preserve, retreat, safety, sanctuary, shelter
2 (*old-fashioned*) MENTAL HOSPITAL, funny farm (*slang*), hospital, institution, madhouse (*informal*), psychiatric hospital, psychiatric ward

atheism *noun* NONBELIEF, disbelief, godlessness, heathenism, infidelity, irreligion, paganism, skepticism, unbelief

atheist *noun* NONBELIEVER, disbeliever, heathen, infidel, pagan, skeptic, unbeliever

athlete *noun* SPORTSPERSON, competitor, contestant, gymnast, player, runner, sportsman, sportswoman

athletic *adjective* FIT, active, energetic, muscular, powerful, strapping, strong, sturdy

athletics *plural noun* SPORTS, contests, exercises, gymnastics, races, track and field events

atmosphere *noun* 1 AIR, aerosphere, heavens, sky
2 FEELING, ambience, character, climate, environment, mood, spirit, surroundings, tone

atom *noun* PARTICLE, bit, dot, molecule, speck, spot, trace

atone *verb* (*usually with for*) MAKE AMENDS, compensate, do penance, make redress, make reparation, make up for, pay for, recompense, redress

atonement *noun* AMENDS, compensation, penance, recompense, redress, reparation, restitution

atrocious *adjective* 1 CRUEL, barbaric, brutal, fiendish, infernal, monstrous, savage, vicious, wicked
2 (*informal*) SHOCKING, appalling, detestable, grievous, horrible, horrifying, terrible

cruel or wicked 2 horrifying 3 very bad > **a•troc'i•ty** [-TROS-i-tee] *noun, plural* **-ties** wickedness

at•ro•phy [A-trə-fee] *noun* 1 wasting away, emaciation ▷ *verb intransitive* **-phied, -phy•ing** 2 waste away, become useless > **atrophied** *adjective*

at•tach [ə-TACH] *verb (mainly transitive)* 1 join, fasten 2 unite 3 be connected with 4 attribute 5 appoint 6 seize by law > **at•tached'** *adjective* (with *to*) fond of > **at•tach'ment** *noun*

at•ta•ché [a-ta-SHAY] *noun, plural* **-chés** specialist attached to diplomatic mission > **attaché case** small suitcase for papers

at•tack [ə-TAK] *verb transitive* 1 take action against (in war, etc.) 2 criticize 3 set about with vigor 4 affect adversely ▷ *noun* 5 attacking action 6 bout of sickness

at•tain [ə-TAYN] *verb transitive* 1 arrive at 2 reach, gain by effort, accomplish > **at•tain'a•ble** *adjective* > **at•tain'ment** *noun* esp. personal accomplishment

at•tain•der [ə-TAYN-dər] *noun hist.* loss of civil rights usu. through conviction of treason

at•tar [AT-ər] *noun* a fragrant oil made esp. from rose petals

at•tempt [ə-TEMPT] *verb transitive* 1 try, endeavor ▷ *noun* 2 trial, effort

at•tend [ə-TEND] *verb transitive* 1 be present at 2 accompany ▷ *verb intransitive* 3 (with *to*) take care of 4 give the mind (to), pay attention to > **at•tend'ance** *noun* 1 an attending 2 presence 3 persons attending > **at•tend•ee** [ə-ten-DEE] *noun* > **at•tend'ant** *noun, adjective* > **at•ten'tion** *noun* 1 notice 2 heed 3 act of attending 4 care 5 courtesy > **at•ten'tive** *adjective* > **at•ten'tive•ness** *noun*

at•ten•u•ate [ə-TEN-yoo-ayt] *verb* **-at•ed, -at•ing** 1 weaken or become weak 2 make or become thin > **at•ten'u•at•ed** *adjective* > **at•ten•u•a'tion** *noun* reduction of intensity > **at•ten'u•a•tor** *noun* device for attenuating, esp. for reducing the amplitude of an electrical signal

at•test [ə-TEST] *verb transitive* bear witness to, certify > **at•tes•ta•tion** [a-tes-TAY-shən] *noun* formal confirmation by oath, etc.

at•tic [AT-ik] *noun* space within roof where ceiling follows line of roof > **Attic** *adjective* 1 of Attica, Athens 2 (of literary or artistic style) pure, refined, elegant

at•tire [ə-TĪR] *verb transitive* **-tired, -tir•ing** 1 dress, array ▷ *noun* 2 dress, clothing

at•ti•tude [AT-i-tood] *noun* 1 mental view, opinion 2 posture, pose 3 disposition, behavior > **at•ti•tu'di•nize** *verb intransitive* **-nized, -niz•ing** assume affected attitudes

at•tor•ney [ə-TUR-nee] *noun, plural* **-neys** one legally appointed to act for another, esp. a lawyer > **attorney-at-law** *noun, plural* **-neys-at-law** a lawyer

at•tract [ə-TRAKT] *verb* 1 draw (attention, etc.) 2 arouse interest of 3 cause to come closer (as

DICTIONARY • THESAURUS

atrocity *noun* 1 CRUELTY, barbarity, brutality, fiendishness, horror, savagery, viciousness, wickedness
2 ACT OF CRUELTY, abomination, crime, evil, horror, outrage

attach *verb* 1 CONNECT, add, couple, fasten, fix, join, link, secure, stick, tie
2 PUT, ascribe, assign, associate, attribute, connect

attached *adjective* 1 SPOKEN FOR, accompanied, engaged, married, partnered
2 ▷ **attached to** FOND OF, affectionate towards, devoted to, full of regard for

attachment *noun* 1 FONDNESS, affection, affinity, attraction, liking, regard
2 ACCESSORY, accouterment, extension, extra, fitting, fixture, supplement

attack *verb* 1 ASSAULT, invade, raid, set upon, storm, strike *or* strike at
2 CRITICIZE, abuse, blame, censure, put down, vilify
▷ *noun* 3 ASSAULT, campaign, charge, foray, incursion, invasion, offensive, onslaught, raid, strike
4 CRITICISM, abuse, blame, censure, denigration, stick (*slang*), vilification
5 BOUT, convulsion, fit, paroxysm, seizure, spasm, stroke

attacker *noun* ASSAILANT, aggressor, assaulter, intruder, invader, raider

attain *verb* ACHIEVE, accomplish, acquire, complete, fulfill, gain, get, obtain, reach

attainment *noun* ACHIEVEMENT, accomplishment, completion, feat

attempt *verb* 1 TRY, endeavor, seek, strive, undertake, venture
▷ *noun* 2 TRY, bid, crack (*informal*), effort, go (*informal*), shot (*informal*), stab (*informal*), trial

attend *verb* 1 BE PRESENT, appear, frequent, go to, haunt, put in an appearance, show oneself, turn up, visit
2 LOOK AFTER, care for, mind, minister to, nurse, take care of, tend
3 PAY ATTENTION, hear, heed, listen, mark, note, observe, pay heed
4 ▷ **attend to** APPLY ONESELF TO, concentrate on, devote oneself to, get to work on, look after, occupy oneself with, see to, take care of

attendance *noun* 1 PRESENCE, appearance, attending, being there
2 TURNOUT, audience, crowd, gate, house, number present

attendant *noun* 1 ASSISTANT, aide, companion, escort, follower, guard, helper, servant
▷ *adjective* 2 ACCOMPANYING, accessory, associated, concomitant, consequent, related

attention *noun* 1 CONCENTRATION, deliberation, heed, intentness, mind, scrutiny, thinking, thought
2 NOTICE, awareness, consciousness, consideration, observation, recognition, regard
3 CARE, concern, looking after, ministration, treatment

attentive *adjective* 1 INTENT, alert, awake, careful, concentrating, heedful, mindful, observant, studious, watchful
2 CONSIDERATE, courteous, helpful, kind, obliging, polite, respectful, thoughtful

attic *noun* LOFT, garret

attire *noun* CLOTHES, apparel, costume, dress, garb, garments, outfit, robes, wear

attitude *noun* 1 DISPOSITION, approach, frame of mind, mood, opinion, outlook, perspective, point of view, position, stance

magnet, etc.) > **at•trac'tion** *noun* 1 power to attract 2 something offered so as to interest, please > **at•trac'tive** *adjective* > **at•trac'tive•ness** *noun*

at•trib•ute [ə-TRIB-yoot] *verb transitive* **-ut•ed, -ut•ing** 1 regard as belonging to or produced by ▷ *noun* 2 [A-trə-byoot] quality, property or characteristic of anything > **at•trib'ut•a•ble** *adjective* > **at•tri•bu'tion** *noun*

at•tri•tion [ə-TRISH-ən] *noun* 1 wearing away of strength, etc. 2 rubbing away, friction

at•tune [ə-TOON] *verb transitive* **-tuned, -tun•ing** 1 tune, harmonize 2 make accordant

Au *chem.* gold

au•burn [AW-bərn] *adjective* 1 reddish brown ▷ *noun* 2 this color

au cou•rant [oh koo-RAHN] 1 up-to-date 2 acquainted with

auc•tion [AWK-shən] *noun* public sale in which bidder offers increase of price over another and what is sold goes to one who bids highest ▷ *verb* > **auc•tion•eer'** *noun* > **auction bridge** card game **Dutch auction** one in which price starts high and is reduced until purchaser is found

au•da•cious [aw-DAY-shəs] *adjective* 1 bold 2 daring, impudent > **au•dac'i•ty** [-DAS-i-tee] *noun*

au•di•ble [AW-də-bəl] *adjective* able to be heard > **au'di•bly** *adverb*

au•di•ence [AW-dee-əns] *noun* 1 assembly of spectators or listeners 2 act of hearing 3 judicial hearing 4 formal interview

audio- *combining form* relating to sound or hearing

au•di•o•phile [AW-dee-ə-fīl] *noun* one who is enthusiastic about sound reproduction, esp. of music

au•di•o•vis•u•al [aw-dee-oh-VIZH-oo-əl] *adjective* (esp. of teaching aids) involving both sight and hearing

au•dit [AW-dit] *noun* 1 formal examination or settlement of financial accounts ▷ *verb transitive* 2 examine such accounts > **au'di•tor** *noun*

au•di•tion [aw-DISH-ən] *noun* 1 screen or other test of prospective performer 2 hearing ▷ *verb transitive* 3 conduct such a test > **au•di•to'ri•um** *noun, plural* **-ri•ums** 1 hall 2 place where audience sits > **au'di•to•ry** *adjective* pert. to sense of hearing

auf Wie•der•seh•en [owf VEE-dər-zay-ən] *Ger.* goodbye

au•ger [AW-gər] *noun* carpenter's tool for boring holes, large gimlet

aught [awt] *pronoun* (*obsolete*) anything whatever

aug•ment [awg-MENT] *verb* increase, enlarge > **aug•men•ta'tion** *noun* > **aug•ment'a•ble** *adjective* able to increase in force or size

au grat•in [oh GRAHT-n] cooked or baked to form light crust

au•gur [AW-gər] *noun* 1 among the Romans, soothsayer ▷ *verb* 2 be a sign of future events, foretell > **au'gu•ry** [-gyə-ree] *noun* 1 divination from omens, etc. 2 omen

au•gust [aw-GUST] *adjective* majestic, dignified > **au•gust'ly** *adverb*

auk [awk] *noun* northern web-footed seabird with short wings used only as paddles

aunt [ant] *noun* father's or mother's sister, uncle's wife

au pair [oh PAIR] *noun* young foreign person, usu. a girl, who receives free board and lodging and usu. an allowance in return for housework, etc.

au•ra [OR-ə] *noun, plural* **-ras** 1 quality, air, atmosphere considered distinctive of person or thing 2 medical symptom warning of impending epileptic seizure, etc.

au•ral [OR-əl] *adjective* of, by ear > **au'ral•ly** *adverb*

au•re•ole [OR-ee-ohl] *noun* 1 gold disk around head in sacred pictures 2 halo

au re•voir [oh rə-VWAHR] *Fr.* goodbye

au•ri•cle [OR-i-kəl] *noun* 1 outside ear 2 an upper cavity of heart > **au•ric•u•lar** [aw-RIK-yə-lər] *adjective* 1 of the auricle 2 aural

au•rif•er•ous [aw-RIF-ər-əs] *adjective* gold-bearing

au•ro•ra [aw-ROR-ə] *noun, plural* **-ras** 1 dawn 2 lights in the atmosphere seen radiating from regions of the poles > **aurora bo•re•al•is** [bor-ee-AL-is] the northern lights > **aurora aus•tra•lis** [aw-STRAY-lis] the southern lights

aus•cul•ta•tion [aw-skəl-TAY-shən] *noun* listening to sounds of heart and lungs with stethoscope

aus•pice [AW-spiss-siz] *plural noun* **under the auspices of** with the support and approval of

aus•pi•cious [aw-SPISH-əs] *adjective* of good

DICTIONARY

a

THESAURUS

2 POSITION, pose, posture, stance

attract *verb* APPEAL TO, allure, charm, draw, enchant, entice, lure, pull (*informal*), tempt

attraction *noun* APPEAL, allure, charm, enticement, fascination, lure, magnetism, pull (*informal*), temptation

attractive *adjective* APPEALING, alluring, charming, fair, fetching, good-looking, handsome, inviting, lovely, pleasant, pretty, tempting

attribute *verb* 1 ASCRIBE, assign, charge, credit, put down to, refer, set down to, trace to ▷ *noun* 2 QUALITY, aspect, character, characteristic, facet, feature, peculiarity, property, trait

attune *verb* ACCUSTOM, adapt, adjust, familiarize, harmonize, regulate

audacious *adjective* 1 DARING, bold, brave, courageous, fearless, intrepid, rash, reckless
2 CHEEKY, brazen, defiant, impertinent, impudent, insolent, presumptuous, shameless

audacity *noun* 1 DARING, boldness, bravery, courage, fearlessness, nerve, rashness, recklessness
2 CHEEK, chutzpah (*informal*), effrontery, impertinence, impudence, insolence, nerve

audible *adjective* CLEAR, detectable, discernible, distinct, hearable, perceptible

audience *noun* 1 SPECTATORS, assembly, crowd, gallery, gathering, listeners, onlookers, turnout, viewers
2 INTERVIEW, consultation, hearing, meeting, reception

aura *noun* AIR, ambience, atmosphere, feeling, mood, quality, tone

auspicious *adjective* FAVORABLE, bright, encouraging, felicitous, hopeful, promising

omen, favorable
aus•tere [aw-STEER] *adjective* 1 harsh, strict, severe 2 without luxury > **aus•tere'ly** *adverb* > **aus•ter•i•ty** [aw-STER-i-tee] *noun*
aus•tral [AW-strəl] *adjective* southern > **Austral** *adjective* Australian
Aus•tral•a•sian [aw-strə-LAY-zhən] *adjective, noun* (native or inhabitant) of Australasia (Australia, N Zealand and adjacent islands)
Aus•tral•ian [aw-STRAYL-yən] *noun, adjective* (native or inhabitant) of Australia
au•tar•chy [AW-tahr-kee] *noun, plural* **-chies** despotism, absolute power, dictatorship
au•then•tic [aw-THEN-tik] *adjective* 1 real, genuine, true 2 trustworthy > **au•then'ti•cal•ly** *adverb* > **au•then'ti•cate** [-ti-kayt] *verb transitive* 1 make valid, confirm 2 establish truth, authorship, etc. of > **au•then•tic'i•ty** *noun*
au•thor [AW-thər] *noun* 1 writer of book 2 originator, constructor
au•thor•i•ty [ə-THOR-i-tee] *noun, plural* **-ties** 1 legal power or right 2 delegated power 3 influence 4 permission 5 expert 6 body or board in control, esp. in pl. > **au•thor'i•ta•tive** [-tay-tiv] *adjective* > **au•thor'i•ta•tive•ly** *adverb* > **au•thor•i•za'tion** *noun* > **au'thor•ize** *verb transitive* **-ized, -iz•ing** 1 empower 2 permit, sanction
au•tis•tic [aw-TIS-tik] *adjective* withdrawn and divorced from reality > **au'tism** *noun* this condition
auto- *combining form* self-: *autobiography*
au•to [AW-toh] *noun* automobile
au•to•bi•og•ra•phy [aw-tə-bī-OG-rə-fee] *noun, plural* **-phies** life of person written by that person > **au•to•bi•o•graph'i•cal** *adjective*
au•toch•thon [aw-TOK-thən] *noun* 1 primitive or original inhabitant 2 native plant or animal > **au•toch'tho•nous** *adjective* indigenous, native
au•to•crat [AW-tə-krat] *noun* 1 absolute ruler 2 despotic person > **au•toc'ra•cy** [-TOK-rə-see] *noun, plural* **-cies** > **au•to•crat'ic** *adjective*
au•to•er•o•tism [aw-toh-ER-ə-tiz-əm] *noun* self-produced sexual arousal
au•to•gi•ro [aw-tə-JĪ-roh] *noun, plural* **-ros** aircraft like helicopter using horizontal airscrew for vertical ascent and descent
au•to•graph [AW-tə-graf] *noun* 1 a signature 2 one's own handwriting ▷ *verb transitive* 3 sign
au•to•in•tox•i•ca•tion [aw-toh-in-tok-si-KAY-shən] *noun* poisoning of tissues of the body as a result of the absorption of bodily waste
au•to•mate [AW-tə-mayt] *verb transitive* **-mat•ed, -mat•ing** 1 make manufacturing process, etc. 2 automatic > **au•to•ma'tion** *noun* use of automatic devices in industrial production
au•to•mat•ic [aw-tə-MAT-ik] *adjective* 1 operated or controlled mechanically 2 done without conscious thought ▷ *adjective, noun* 3 self-loading (weapon) > **au•to•mat'i•cal•ly** *adverb* > **au•tom'a•ton** *noun, plural* **-ta** [-tə] self-acting machine, esp. simulating a human being
au•to•mo•bile [aw-tə-mə-BEEL] *noun* motor car
au•ton•o•my [aw-TON-ə-mee] *noun, plural* **-mies** self-government > **au•ton'o•mous** *adjective*
au•top•sy [AW-top-see] *noun, plural* **-sies** postmortem examination to determine cause of death
au•to•sug•ges•tion [aw-toh-səg-JES-chən] *noun* process of influencing the mind (toward health, etc., conducted by oneself)
au•tumn [AW-təm] *noun, adjective* (typical of) the season after summer > **au•tum•nal** [aw-

---

austere *adjective* 1 STERN, forbidding, formal, serious, severe, solemn, strict
2 ASCETIC, abstemious, puritanical, self-disciplined, sober, solemn, strait-laced, strict
3 PLAIN, bleak, harsh, homely, simple, spare, Spartan, stark
austerity *noun* 1 STERNNESS, formality, inflexibility, rigor, seriousness, severity, solemnity, stiffness, strictness
2 ASCETICISM, puritanism, self-denial, self-discipline, sobriety
3 PLAINNESS, simplicity, starkness
authentic *adjective* GENUINE, actual, authoritative, bona fide, legitimate, pure, real, true-to-life, valid
authenticity *noun* GENUINENESS, accuracy, certainty, faithfulness, legitimacy, purity, truthfulness, validity
author *noun* 1 WRITER, composer, creator
2 CREATOR, architect, designer, father, founder, inventor, originator, producer
authoritarian *adjective* 1 STRICT, autocratic, dictatorial, doctrinaire, dogmatic, severe, tyrannical
▷ *noun* 2 DISCIPLINARIAN, absolutist, autocrat, despot, dictator, tyrant
authoritative *adjective* 1 RELIABLE, accurate, authentic, definitive, dependable, trustworthy, valid
2 COMMANDING, assertive, imperious, imposing, masterly, self-assured
authority *noun* 1 POWER, command, control, direction, influence, supremacy, sway, weight
2 (*usually plural*) POWERS THAT BE, administration, government, management, officialdom, police, the Establishment
3 EXPERT, connoisseur, judge, master, professional, specialist
authorization *noun* PERMISSION, a blank check, approval, leave, license, permit, warrant
authorize *verb* 1 EMPOWER, accredit, commission, enable, entitle, give authority
2 PERMIT, allow, approve, give authority for, license, sanction, warrant
autocracy *noun* DICTATORSHIP, absolutism, despotism, tyranny
autocrat *noun* DICTATOR, absolutist, despot, tyrant
autocratic *adjective* DICTATORIAL, absolute, all-powerful, despotic, domineering, imperious, tyrannical
automatic *adjective* 1 MECHANICAL, automated, mechanized, push-button, self-propelling
2 INVOLUNTARY, instinctive, mechanical, natural, reflex, spontaneous, unconscious, unwilled
autonomous *adjective* SELF-RULING, free, independent, self-determining, self-governing, sovereign
autonomy *noun* INDEPENDENCE, freedom, home rule, self-determination, self-government, self-rule, sovereignty

TUM-nl] *adjective* typical of the onset of winter
aux•il•ia•ry [awg-ZIL-yə-ree] *adjective* 1 helping, subsidiary ▷ *noun, plural* **-ries** 2 helper 3 something subsidiary, as troops 4 verb used to form tenses of others
a•vail [ə-VAYL] *verb* 1 be of use, advantage, value (to) ▷ *noun* 2 use or advantage: *to no avail* > **a•vail•a•bil'i•ty** *noun* > **a•vail'a•ble** *adjective* 1 obtainable 2 accessible **avail oneself of** make use of
av•a•lanche [AV-ə-lanch] *noun* 1 mass of snow, ice, sliding down mountain 2 a sudden overwhelming quantity of anything
a•vant-garde [ah-vahnt-GAHRD] *adjective* markedly experimental or in advance
av•a•rice [AV-ər-is] *noun* greed for wealth > **av•a•ri'cious** [-RISH-əs] *adjective*
a•vast [ə-VAST] *interjection nautical* stop
av•a•tar [AV-ə-tahr] *noun Hinduism* descent of god to Earth in bodily form
a•venge [ə-VENJ] *verb transitive* **-venged, -veng•ing** take vengeance on behalf of (person) or on account of (thing) > **a•veng'er** *noun*
av•e•nue [AV-ə-nyoo] *noun* 1 route 2 a way of approach, a channel
a•ver [ə-VUR] *verb transitive* **-verred, -ver•ring** affirm, assert
av•er•age [AV-rij] *noun* 1 the mean value or quantity of a number of values or quantities ▷ *adjective* 2 calculated as an average 3 medium, ordinary ▷ *verb transitive* **-aged, -ag•ing** 4 fix or calculate a mean ▷ *verb intransitive* **-aged, -ag•ing** 5 exist in or form a mean
a•verse [ə-VURS] *adjective* disinclined, unwilling > **a•ver'sion** [-*zhən*] *noun* 1 dislike 2 person or thing disliked
a•vert [ə-VURT] *verb transitive* 1 turn away 2 ward off
a•vi•ar•y [AY-vee-er-ee] *noun, plural* **-ar•ies** enclosure for birds > **a'vi•a•rist** *noun*
a•vi•a•tion [ay-vee-AY-shən] *noun* 1 art of flying aircraft 2 transport by aircraft > **a'vi•a•tor** *noun*
av•id [AV-id] *adjective* 1 keen, enthusiastic 2 greedy (for) > **a•vid'i•ty** *noun* > **av'id•ly** *adverb*
av•o•ca•do [av-ə-KAH-doh] *noun* 1 tropical tree 2 its green-skinned edible fruit, alligator pear
av•o•ca•tion [av-ə-KAY-shən] *noun* 1 vocation 2 employment, business
a•void [ə-VOID] *verb transitive* 1 keep away from 2 refrain from 3 not allow to happen > **a•void'a•ble** *adjective* > **a•void'ance** *noun*
av•oir•du•pois [av-ər-də-POIZ] *noun* system of weights used in many English-speaking countries based on pounds and ounces
a•vow [ə-VOW] *verb transitive* 1 declare 2 admit > **a•vow'a•ble** *adjective* > **a•vow'al** *noun* > **a•vowed'** *adjective* > **a•vow'ed•ly** *adverb*
a•vun•cu•lar [ə-VUNG-kyə-lər] *adjective* like or of an uncle esp. in manner
a•wait [ə-WAYT] *verb transitive* 1 wait or stay for 2 be in store for
a•wake [ə-WAYK] *verb* **a•wak•ing, a•woke,**

---

auxiliary *adjective* 1 SUPPLEMENTARY, back-up, emergency, fall-back, reserve, secondary, subsidiary, substitute
2 SUPPORTING, accessory, aiding, ancillary, assisting, helping
▷ *noun* 3 BACKUP, reserve
4 HELPER, assistant, associate, companion, subordinate, supporter
avail *verb* 1 BENEFIT, aid, assist, be of advantage, be useful, help, profit
▷ *noun* 2 BENEFIT, advantage, aid, good, help, profit, use
availability *noun* ACCESSIBILITY, attainability, handiness, readiness
available *adjective* ACCESSIBLE, at hand, at one's disposal, free, handy, on tap, ready, to hand
avalanche *noun* 1 SNOW-SLIDE, landslide, landslip
2 FLOOD, barrage, deluge, inundation, torrent
avant-garde *adjective* PROGRESSIVE, experimental, ground-breaking, innovative, pioneering, unconventional
avarice *noun* GREED, covetousness, meanness, miserliness, niggardliness, parsimony, stinginess
avaricious *adjective* GRASPING, covetous, greedy, mean, miserly, niggardly, parsimonious, stingy
avenge *verb* GET REVENGE FOR, get even for (*informal*), hit back, punish, repay, retaliate
avenue *noun* STREET, approach, boulevard, course, drive, passage, path, road, route, way
average *noun* 1 USUAL, mean, medium, midpoint, norm, normal, par, standard
2 ▷ **on average** USUALLY, as a rule, for the most part, generally, normally, typically
▷ *adjective* 3 USUAL, commonplace, fair, general, normal, ordinary, regular, standard, typical
4 MEAN, intermediate, median, medium, middle
▷ *verb* 5 MAKE ON AVERAGE, balance out to, be on average, do on average, even out to
averse *adjective* OPPOSED, disinclined, hostile, ill-disposed, loath, reluctant, unwilling
aversion *noun* HATRED, animosity, antipathy, disinclination, dislike, hostility, revulsion, unwillingness
avert *verb* 1 TURN AWAY, turn aside
2 WARD OFF, avoid, fend off, forestall, frustrate, preclude, prevent, stave off
aviator *noun* PILOT, aeronaut, airman, flyer
avid *adjective* 1 ENTHUSIASTIC, ardent, devoted, eager, fanatical, intense, keen, passionate, zealous
2 INSATIABLE, grasping, greedy, hungry, rapacious, ravenous, thirsty, voracious
avoid *verb* 1 REFRAIN FROM, dodge, duck *or* duck out of (*informal*), eschew, fight shy of, shirk
2 PREVENT, avert
3 KEEP AWAY FROM, bypass, dodge, elude, escape, evade, shun, steer clear of
avoidance *noun* EVASION, dodging, eluding, escape, keeping away, shunning, steering clear
avowed *adjective* 1 DECLARED, open, professed, self-proclaimed, sworn
2 CONFESSED, acknowledged, admitted
await *verb* 1 WAIT FOR, abide, anticipate, expect, look for, look forward to, stay for
2 BE IN STORE FOR, attend, be in readiness for, be prepared for, be ready for, wait for
awake *adjective* 1 NOT SLEEPING, aroused, awakened, aware, conscious, wakeful, wide-awake
2 ALERT, alive, attentive, aware, heedful, observant, on the lookout, vigilant, watchful
▷ *verb* 3 WAKE UP, awaken, rouse, wake

a•wok•en **1** emerge or rouse from sleep **2** become or cause to become alert > **a•wak'en•ing** *noun*

a•wak•en [ə-WAY-kən] *verb transitive* arouse (feelings, etc.) or cause to remember (memories, etc.)

a•ward [ə-WORD] *verb transitive* **1** to give formally (esp. a prize or punishment) ▷ *noun* **2** prize **3** judicial decision, amount awarded

a•ware [ə-WAIR] *adjective* informed, conscious > **a•ware'ness** *noun*

a•wash [ə-WOSH] *adverb* **1** level with the surface of water **2** filled or overflowing with water **awash in** marked by an abundance of

a•way [ə-WAY] *adverb* **1** absent, apart, at a distance, out of the way ▷ *adjective* **2** *sports.* played on opponent's grounds

awe [aw] *noun* dread mingled with reverence > **awe'some** [-səm] *adjective* > **awe'some•ly** *adverb* > **awe'some•ness** *noun* > **awe'struck** *adjective* filled with awe

aw•ful [AW-fəl] *adjective* **1** very bad, unpleasant **2** inspiring awe **3** (*informal*) very great > **aw'ful•ly** *adverb* **1** in an unpleasant way **2** (*informal*) very much

a•while [ə-HWĪL] *adverb* for a time

awk•ward [AWK-wərd] *adjective* **1** clumsy, ungainly **2** difficult **3** inconvenient **4** embarrassed > **awk'ward•ly** *adverb* > **awk'ward•ness** *noun*

awl *noun* pointed tool for marking or boring wood, leather, etc.

awn'ing *noun* (canvas, etc.) roof or shelter, to protect from weather

awoke *pt./pp. of* **awake**

a•wry [ə-RĪ] *adverb* **1** crookedly **2** amiss **3** at a slant ▷ *adjective* **4** crooked, distorted **5** wrong

ax, axe [aks] *noun* **1** tool with handle and heavy, sharp blade for chopping **2** (*informal*) dismissal from employment, etc. ▷ *verb transitive* **axed, ax•ing** **3** (*informal*) dismiss, dispense with

ax•iom [AK-see-əm] *noun* **1** received or accepted principle **2** self-evident truth > **ax•i•o•mat'ic** *adjective*

ax•is [AK-sis] *noun, plural* **ax•es** [AK-seez] **1** (imaginary) line around which a body spins **2** line or column about which parts are arranged > **ax'i•al** *adjective* > **ax'i•al•ly** *adverb*

Ax•is *noun* coalition of Germany, Italy and Japan, 1936—45

ax•le [AK-səl] *noun* shaft on which wheel turns

a•ya•tol•lah [ah-yə-TOH-lə] *adjective* one of a class of Islamic religious leaders

aye [ī] *adverb* **1** yes ▷ *noun* **2** affirmative answer or vote > **ayes** those voting for motion

a•zal•ea [ə-ZAYL-yə] *noun* any of group of shrubby plants of the rhododendron genus

az•i•muth [AZ-ə-məth] *noun* **1** vertical arc from zenith to horizon **2** angular distance of this from meridian

Az•tec [AZ-tek] *adjective, noun* (member) of people ruling Mexico before Spanish conquest

az•ure [AZH-ər] *noun* **1** sky-blue color **2** clear sky ▷ *adjective* **3** sky-blue

DICTIONARY • THESAURUS

---

4 ALERT, arouse, kindle, provoke, revive, stimulate, stir up

awaken *verb* **1** AWAKE, arouse, revive, rouse, wake **2** ALERT, kindle, provoke, stimulate, stir up

awakening *noun* WAKING UP, arousal, revival, rousing, stimulation, stirring up

award *verb* **1** GIVE, bestow, confer, endow, grant, hand out, present
▷ *noun* **2** PRIZE, decoration, gift, grant, trophy

aware *adjective* **1** ▷ **aware of** KNOWING ABOUT, acquainted with, conscious of, conversant with, familiar with, mindful of
2 INFORMED, enlightened, in the picture, knowledgeable

awareness *noun* KNOWLEDGE, consciousness, familiarity, perception, realization, recognition, understanding

away *adverb* **1** OFF, abroad, elsewhere, from here, from home, hence
2 AT A DISTANCE, apart, far, remote
3 ASIDE, out of the way, to one side
4 CONTINUOUSLY, incessantly, interminably, relentlessly, repeatedly, uninterruptedly, unremittingly
▷ *adjective* **5** NOT PRESENT, abroad, absent, elsewhere, gone, not at home, not here, out

awe *noun* **1** WONDER, admiration, amazement, astonishment, dread, fear, horror, respect, reverence, terror
▷ *verb* **2** IMPRESS, amaze, astonish, frighten, horrify, intimidate, stun, terrify

awesome *adjective* **1** AWE-INSPIRING, amazing, astonishing, breathtaking, cool (*informal*), formidable, impressive, intimidating, phat (*slang*), stunning
2 (*informal*) FIRST-CLASS, choice, elite, excellent, first-rate, hand-picked, superior, world-class

awful *adjective* **1** TERRIBLE, abysmal, appalling, deplorable, dreadful, frightful, ghastly, horrendous

awfully *adverb* **1** BADLY, disgracefully, dreadfully, reprehensibly, unforgivably, unpleasantly, woefully, wretchedly
2 (*informal*) VERY, dreadfully, exceedingly, exceptionally, extremely, greatly, immensely, terribly

awkward *adjective* **1** CLUMSY, gauche, gawky, inelegant, lumbering, uncoordinated, ungainly
2 UNMANAGEABLE, clunky (*informal*), cumbersome, difficult, inconvenient, troublesome, unwieldy
3 EMBARRASSING, delicate, difficult, ill at ease, inconvenient, uncomfortable

awkwardness *noun* **1** CLUMSINESS, gawkiness, inelegance, ungainliness
2 UNWIELDINESS, difficulty, inconvenience
3 EMBARRASSMENT, delicacy, difficulty, inconvenience

ax *noun* **1** HATCHET, adz, chopper
2 ▷ **the ax** (*informal*) DISMISSAL, termination, the boot (*slang*), the chop (*slang*)
▷ *verb* **3** (*informal*) CUT BACK, cancel, dismiss, dispense with, eliminate, fire (*informal*), get rid of, remove, sack (*informal*)

axiom *noun* PRINCIPLE, adage, aphorism, dictum, maxim, precept, truism

axiomatic *adjective* SELF-EVIDENT, accepted, assumed, certain, given, granted, manifest, understood

axis *noun* PIVOT, axle, center line, shaft, spindle

axle *noun* SHAFT, axis, pin, pivot, rod, spindle

Bb

B *chem.* boron
Ba *chem.* barium
bab•ble [BAB-əl] *verb* **-bled, -bling** 1 speak foolishly, incoherently, or childishly ▷ *noun* 2 foolish, confused talk > **bab'bler** *noun*
babe [bayb] *noun* 1 baby 2 guileless person
ba•bel [BAY-bəl] *noun* confused noise or scene, uproar
ba•boon [ba-BOON] *noun* large monkey of Africa and Asia
ba•by [BAY-bee] *noun, plural* **-bies** very young child, infant > **ba'by•ish** *adjective* > **ba'by-sit** *verb* **-sat, -sit•ting** > **ba'by-sit•ter** *noun* one who cares for children when parents are out
bac•ca•lau•re•ate [bak-ə-LOR-ee-it] *noun* 1 degree of bachelor 2 service held at college or university awarding degree 3 sermon delivered at this service
bac•ca•rat [BAH-kə-rah] *noun* gambling card game
bach•e•lor [BACH-lər] *noun* 1 unmarried man 2 holder of lowest four-year college or university degree
ba•cil•lus [bə-SIL-əs] *noun, plural* **-cil•li** [-SIL-ī] minute organism sometimes causing disease
back [bak] *noun* 1 hinder part of anything, e.g. human body 2 part opposite front 3 part or side of something farther away or less used 4 (position of) player in football and other games behind other (forward) players ▷ *adjective* 5 situated behind 6 earlier ▷ *adverb* 7 at, to the back 8 in, into the past 9 in return ▷ *verb intransitive* 10 move backward ▷ *verb transitive* 11 support 12 put wager on 13 provide with back or backing > **back'er** *noun* 1 one supporting another, esp. in contest or election campaign 2 one betting on horse, etc. in race > **back'ing** *noun* 1 support 2 material to protect the back of

---

babble *verb* 1 GABBLE, burble, chatter, jabber, prattle
2 GIBBER, gurgle
▷ *noun* 3 GABBLE, burble, drivel, gibberish
baby *noun* 1 INFANT, babe, babe in arms, child, newborn child
▷ *adjective* 2 SMALL, little, mini, miniature, minute, teeny-weeny, tiny, wee
babyish *adjective* CHILDISH, foolish, immature, infantile, juvenile, puerile, sissy, spoiled
back *noun* 1 REAR, end, far end, hind part, hindquarters, reverse, stern, tail end
2 ▷ **behind one's back** SECRETLY, covertly, deceitfully, sneakily, surreptitiously
▷ *verb* 3 MOVE BACK, back off, backtrack, go back, retire, retreat, reverse, turn tail, withdraw
4 SUPPORT, advocate, assist, champion, endorse, promote, sponsor
▷ *adjective* 5 REAR, end, hind, hindmost, posterior, tail
6 PREVIOUS, delayed, earlier, elapsed, former, overdue, past
backbiting *noun* SLANDER, bitchiness (*slang*), cattiness (*informal*), defamation, disparagement, gossip, malice, scandalmongering, spitefulness
backbone *noun* 1 (*medical*) SPINAL COLUMN, spine, vertebrae, vertebral column
2 STRENGTH OF CHARACTER, character, courage, determination, fortitude, grit, nerve, pluck, resolution

something > **back'ward, back'wards** *adverb* 1 to the rear 2 to the past 3 to worse state > **back'ward** *adjective* 1 directed toward the rear 2 (of a country, region or people) retarded in economic development 3 behind in education 4 reluctant, bashful > **back'ward•ness** *noun* > **back'bite** *verb transitive* **-bit, -bit•ten, -bit•ing** slander absent person > **back'bit•er** *noun* > **back'biting** *noun* > **back'bone** *noun* spinal column > **back'date** *verb transitive* **-dat•ed, -dat•ing** make effective from earlier date > **back'drop** *noun* painted cloth at back of stage > **back'fire** *verb intransitive* **-fired, -fir•ing** 1 ignite at wrong time, as fuel in cylinder of internal-combustion engine 2 (of plan, scheme, etc.) fail to work, esp. to the detriment of the instigator 3 ignite wrongly, as gas burner, etc. > **back'gam•mon** [-gam-ən] *noun* game played with counters and dice > **back'ground** *noun* 1 space behind chief figures of picture, etc. 2 past history of person > **back'hand** *noun* stroke with hand turned backward > **back'hand•ed** *adjective* (of compliment, etc.) with second, uncomplimentary meaning > **back'lash** *noun* sudden and adverse reaction > **back'log** *noun* accumulation of work, etc. to be dealt with > **back'pack** *noun* 1 type of knapsack ▷ *verb intransitive* **-packed, -pack•ing** 2 hike with this > **back'side** *noun* buttocks > **back'slash** *noun* backward-sloping diagonal mark (\) > **back'slide** *verb intransitive* **-slid, -slid** *or* **-slid•den, -slid•ing** fall back in faith or morals > **back'stab•bing** *noun* actions or remarks that betray trust and are likely to cause harm to a person > **back'stroke** *noun* swimming stroke performed on the back > **back'talk** *noun* impudent or insolent answer > **back'up** *noun* 1 a support or reinforcement 2 a reserve or substitute > **back up** *verb* 1 support 2 *computing* make a copy of (a data file), esp. as a security copy > **back'wash** *noun* 1 water thrown back by ship's propellers, etc. 2 a backward current 3 a reaction > **back'wa•ter** *noun* 1 still water fed by back flow of stream 2 backward or isolated place or condition > **back'woods'** *plural noun* 1 remote forest areas 2 remote or backward area

ba•con [BAY-kən] *noun* cured and smoked meat from side of pig

bac•te•ri•a [bak-TEER-ee-ə] *plural noun, sing* **-ri•um** microscopic organisms, some causing disease > **bac•te'ri•al** *adjective* > **bac•te•ri•cide** [-TEER-ə-sīd] *noun* substance that destroys bacteria > **bac•te•ri•ol'o•gist** [-OL-ə-jist] *noun* > **bac•te•ri•ol'o•gy** *noun* study of bacteria

bad *adjective* **worse, worst** 1 of poor quality 2 faulty 3 evil 4 immoral 5 offensive 6 severe 7 rotten, decayed > **bad'ly** *adverb* > **bad'ness** *noun* > **bad-mouth** *verb transitive* (*slang*) speak unfavourably about

bade [bad] *pt. of* **bid**

badge [baj] *noun* distinguishing emblem or sign

badg•er [BAJ-ər] *noun* 1 burrowing night animal, about the size of fox 2 its pelt or fur ▷ *verb transitive* 3 pester, worry

bad•i•nage [bad-n-AHZH] *noun* playful talk, banter

bad•min•ton [BAD-min-tn] *noun* game like tennis, played with rackets and shuttlecocks over high net

baf•fle [BAF-əl] *verb transitive* **-fled, -fling** check, frustrate, bewilder > **baffling** *adjective* > **baffle** *noun* device to regulate or divert flow of liquid, gas, sound waves, etc.

bag *noun* 1 sack, pouch 2 measure of quantity 3 woman's handbag 4 (*offensive*) unattractive woman ▷ *verb intransitive* **bagged, bag•ging** 5

DICTIONARY • THESAURUS

backbreaking *adjective* EXHAUSTING, arduous, crushing, grueling, hard, laborious, punishing, strenuous

back down *verb* GIVE IN, accede, admit defeat, back-pedal, concede, surrender, withdraw, yield

backer *noun* SUPPORTER, advocate, angel (*informal*), benefactor, patron, promoter, second, sponsor, subscriber

backfire *verb* FAIL, boomerang, disappoint, flop (*informal*), miscarry, rebound, recoil

background *noun* HISTORY, circumstances, culture, education, environment, grounding, tradition, upbringing

backing *noun* SUPPORT, aid, assistance, encouragement, endorsement, moral support, patronage, sponsorship

backlash *noun* REACTION, counteraction, recoil, repercussion, resistance, response, retaliation

backlog *noun* BUILD-UP, accumulation, excess, hoard, reserve, stock, supply

back out *verb* (*often with of*) WITHDRAW, abandon, cancel, excuse oneself, give up, go back on, quit, resign, retreat, wimp out (*slang*)

backslide *verb* RELAPSE, go astray, go wrong, lapse, revert, slip, stray, weaken

backslider *noun* RELAPSER, apostate, deserter, recidivist, recreant, renegade, turncoat

back up *verb* SUPPORT, aid, assist, bolster, confirm, corroborate, reinforce, second, stand by, substantiate

backward *adjective* SLOW, behind, dull, retarded, subnormal, underdeveloped, undeveloped

backwards *or* **backward** *adverb* TOWARDS THE REAR, behind, in reverse, rearward

bacteria *plural noun* MICROORGANISMS, bacilli, bugs (*slang*), germs, microbes, pathogens, viruses

bad *adjective* 1 INFERIOR, defective, faulty, imperfect, inadequate, lousy (*slang*), poor, substandard, unsatisfactory
2 HARMFUL, damaging, dangerous, deleterious, detrimental, hurtful, ruinous, unhealthy
3 EVIL, corrupt, criminal, immoral, mean, sinful, wicked, wrong
4 NAUGHTY, disobedient, mischievous, unruly
5 ROTTEN, decayed, moldy, putrid, rancid, sour, spoiled
6 UNFAVORABLE, adverse, distressing, gloomy, grim, troubled, unfortunate, unpleasant

badge *noun* MARK, brand, device, emblem, identification, insignia, sign, stamp, token

badger *verb* PESTER, bully, goad, harass, hound, importune, nag, plague, torment

badinage *noun* WORDPLAY, banter, mockery, pleasantry, repartee, teasing

badly *adverb* 1 POORLY, carelessly, imperfectly, inadequately, incorrectly, ineptly, wrongly
2 UNFAVORABLY, unfortunately, unsuccessfully
3 SEVERELY, deeply, desperately, exceedingly, extremely, greatly, intensely, seriously

bad-mouth *verb* (*slang*) CRITICIZE, abuse, deride,

swell out 6 bulge 7 sag ▷ *verb transitive* **bagged, bag•ging** 8 put in bag 9 kill as game, etc. > **bag'gy** *adjective* **-gi•er, -gi•est** loose, drooping > **bag lady** homeless woman who carries her possessions in shopping bags, etc. > **bag'man** *noun, plural* **-men** person who collects and distributes illicitly obtained money for another

bag•a•telle [bag-ə-TEL] *noun* 1 trifle 2 game like billiards

bag•gage [BAG-ij] *noun* 1 suitcases, etc., packed for journey 2 (*offensive*) woman

bag•pipe [BAG-pīp] *noun* (*often plural*) musical wind instrument, of windbag and pipes > **bag'pip•er** *noun*

bail[1] [bayl] *noun law* 1 security given for person's reappearance in court 2 one giving such security ▷ *verb transitive* 3 release, or obtain release of, on security 4 (*informal*) help a person, firm, etc. out of trouble

bail[2] *verb transitive* empty out water from boat > **bail out** 1 leave aircraft by parachute 2 give up on or abandon something

bail•iff [BAY-lif] *noun* minor court officer

bail•i•wick [BAY-li-wik] *noun* a person's domain or special area of competence

bait [bayt] *noun* 1 food to entice fish 2 any lure or enticement ▷ *verb transitive* 3 set a lure 4 annoy, persecute

baize [bayz] *noun* smooth woolen cloth

bake [bayk] *verb transitive* **baked, bak•ing** 1 cook or harden by dry heat ▷ *verb intransitive* **baked, bak•ing** 2 make bread, cakes, etc. 3 be scorched or tanned > **bak'er** *noun* > **bak'er•y** *noun* > **baking** *noun* > **baking powder** leavening agent containing sodium bicarbonate, etc. used in making baked goods

bal•a•cla•va [bal-ə-KLAH-və] *noun* close-fitting woolen helmet, covering head and neck

bal•a•lai•ka [bal-ə-LĪ-kə] *noun* Russian musical instrument, like guitar

bal•ance [BAL-əns] *noun* 1 pair of scales 2 equilibrium 3 surplus 4 sum due on an account 5 difference between two sums ▷ *verb transitive* **-anced, -anc•ing** 6 weigh 7 bring to equilibrium > **balance sheet** tabular statement of assets and liabilities > **balance wheel** regulating wheel of watch

bal•co•ny [BAL-kə-nee] *noun, plural* **-nies** 1 railed platform outside window 2 upper seats in theater

bald [bawld] *adjective* 1 hairless 2 plain 3 bare > **bald'ing** *adjective* becoming bald > **bald'ness** *noun*

bale [bayl] *noun* 1 bundle or package ▷ *verb transitive* **baled, bal•ing** 2 make into bundles or pack into cartons > **bal'er** *noun* machine that does this

ba•leen [bə-LEEN] *noun* whalebone

bale•ful [BAYL-fəl] *adjective* menacing > **bale'ful•ly** *adverb*

balk [bawk] *verb intransitive* 1 swerve, pull up 2 *baseball* commit a balk ▷ *verb transitive* 3 thwart, hinder 4 shirk ▷ *noun* 5 hindrance 6 rafter, beam 7 *baseball* illegal motion of pitcher before releasing ball to batter **balk at** 8 recoil 9 stop short

ball[1] [bawl] *noun* 1 anything round 2 globe, sphere, esp. as used in games 3 a ball as pitched 4 bullet ▷ *verb intransitive* 5 clog, gather into a mass > **ball bearings** hardened steel balls used to lessen friction on bearings > **ball'park** *noun* 1 stadium used for baseball games 2 (*informal*) approximate range ▷ *adjective* 3 (*informal*) approximate > **ball'point, ball'point pen** pen with tiny ball bearing as nib

ball[2] *noun* 1 formal social gathering for dancing 2 (*informal*) a very good time > **ball'room** *noun*

bal•lad [BAL-əd] *noun* 1 narrative poem 2 simple song

bal•lade [bə-LAHD] *noun* 1 short poem with refrain and envoi 2 piece of music

bal•last [BAL-əst] *noun* 1 heavy material put in ship to give steadiness 2 that which renders

---

insult, malign, mock, slander

baffle *verb* PUZZLE, bewilder, confound, confuse, flummox, mystify, nonplus, perplex, stump

bag *noun* 1 CONTAINER, receptacle, sac, sack ▷ *verb* 2 CATCH, acquire, capture, kill, land, shoot, trap

baggage *noun* LUGGAGE, accouterments, bags, belongings, equipment, gear, paraphernalia, suitcases, things

baggy *adjective* LOOSE, bulging, droopy, floppy, ill-fitting, oversize, roomy, sagging, slack

bail[1] *noun* (*law*) SECURITY, bond, guarantee, pledge, surety, warranty

bail out *verb* 1 HELP, aid, relieve, rescue, save (someone's) bacon (*informal*)
2 ESCAPE, quit, retreat, withdraw

bait *noun* 1 LURE, allurement, attraction, decoy, enticement, incentive, inducement, snare, temptation
▷ *verb* 2 TEASE, annoy, bother, harass, hassle (*informal*), hound, irritate, persecute, torment

baked *adjective* DRY, arid, desiccated, parched, scorched, seared, sun-baked, torrid

balance *noun* 1 STABILITY, composure, equanimity, poise, self-control, self-possession, steadiness
2 EQUILIBRIUM, correspondence, equity, equivalence, evenness, parity, symmetry
3 REMAINDER, difference, residue, rest, surplus
▷ *verb* 4 STABILIZE, level, match, parallel, steady
5 COMPARE, assess, consider, deliberate, estimate, evaluate, weigh
6 (*accounting*) CALCULATE, compute, settle, square, tally, total

balcony *noun* 1 TERRACE, veranda
2 UPPER CIRCLE, gallery, gods

bald *adjective* 1 HAIRLESS, baldheaded, depilated
2 PLAIN, blunt, direct, forthright, straightforward, unadorned, unvarnished

balderdash *noun* NONSENSE, claptrap (*informal*), drivel, garbage (*informal*), gibberish, hogwash, hot air (*informal*), rubbish

baldness *noun* 1 HAIRLESSNESS, alopecia (*pathology*), baldheadedness
2 PLAINNESS, austerity, bluntness, severity, simplicity

balk *verb* 1 RECOIL, evade, flinch, hesitate, jib, refuse, resist, shirk, shrink from
2 FOIL, check, counteract, defeat, frustrate, hinder, obstruct, prevent, thwart

ball *noun* SPHERE, drop, globe, globule, orb, pellet, spheroid

anything steady ▷ *verb transitive* 3 load with ballast, steady

bal•let [ba-LAY] *noun* theatrical presentation of dancing and miming to musical accompaniment > **bal•le•ri•na** [bal-ə-REE-nə] *noun*

bal•lis•tic [bə-LIS-tik] *adjective* moving as, or pertaining to motion of, a projectile > **bal•lis'tics** *noun* scientific study of ballistic motion

bal•loon [bə-LOON] *noun* 1 large bag filled with air or gas to make it rise in the air ▷ *verb intransitive* 2 puff out 3 increase rapidly > **bal•loon'ing** *noun* > **bal•loon'ist** *noun*

bal•lot [BAL-ət] *noun* 1 method of voting secretly, usually by marking ballot paper and putting it into box ▷ *verb intransitive* 2 vote or decide by ballot > **ballot box** box into which voting papers are dropped on completion

bal•ly•hoo [BAL-ee-hoo] *noun* 1 noisy confusion or uproar 2 flamboyant, exaggerated publicity or advertising

balm [bahm] *noun* 1 aromatic substance, healing or soothing ointment 2 anything soothing > **balm'y** *adjective* **balm•i•er, balm•i•est** 1 soothing 2 (of climate) mild 3 (of a person) foolish > **balm'i•ness** *noun*

ba•lo•ney [bə-LOW-nee] *noun* (*informal*) nonsense

bal•sa [BAWL-sə] *noun* American tree with light but strong wood

bal•sam [BAWL-səm] *noun* 1 resinous aromatic substance obtained from various trees and shrubs 2 soothing ointment > **bal•sam'ic** *adjective*

Baltimore oriole oriole of eastern N Amer.

bal•us•ter [BAL-ə-stər] *noun* short pillar used as support to rail of staircase, etc. > **bal'us•trade** [-strayd] *noun* row of short pillars topped by rail

bam•boo' *noun, plural* **-boos** large tropical treelike reed

bam•boo•zle [bam-BOO-zəl] *verb transitive* **-zled, -zling** mystify, hoodwink

ban *verb transitive* **banned, ban•ning** 1 prohibit, forbid, outlaw ▷ *noun* 2 prohibition 3 proclamation > **banns** *plural noun* proclamation of marriage

ba•nal [bə-NAL] *adjective* commonplace, trivial, trite > **ba•nal'i•ty** *noun*

ba•nan•a [bə-NAN-ə] *noun* 1 tropical treelike plant 2 its fruit

band¹ *noun* 1 strip used to bind 2 range of values, frequencies, etc., between two limits > **band•age** [BAN-dij] *noun* strip of cloth for binding wound

band² *noun* 1 company, group 2 company of musicians ▷ *verb* 3 bind together > **band'mas•ter** *noun* > **band'stand** *noun*

ban•dan•na [ban-DAN-ə] *noun* large decorated handkerchief

band•box [BAND-boks] *noun* 1 light box of cardboard for hats, etc. 2 theater or other public structure of small interior dimensions

ban•deau [ban-DOH] *noun, plural* **-deaux** [-DOHZ] 1 band, ribbon for the hair 2 narrow bra or top

ban'dit *noun* 1 outlaw 2 robber, brigand

ban•do•leer [ban-də-LEER] *noun* shoulder belt for cartridges

band•wag•on [BAND-wag-ən] *noun* **climb, jump, get on the bandwagon** join something that seems sure of success

ban•dy [BAN-dee] *verb transitive* **-died, -dy•ing** beat to and fro, toss from one to another > **ban'dy-leg•ged** [-leg-id] *adjective* bowlegged, having legs curving outward

bane [bayn] *noun* 1 poison 2 person or thing causing misery or distress > **bane'ful** *adjective*

bang¹ *noun* 1 sudden loud noise, explosion 2 heavy blow ▷ *verb transitive* 3 make loud noise 4 beat 5 strike violently, slam

bang² *noun* (*usually plural*) fringe of hair cut straight across forehead

ban•gle [BANG-gəl] *noun* ring worn on arm or leg

ban'ish *verb transitive* 1 condemn to exile 2 drive

DICTIONARY • THESAURUS

ballast *noun* COUNTERBALANCE, balance, counterweight, equilibrium, sandbag, stability, stabilizer, weight

balloon *verb* SWELL, billow, blow up, dilate, distend, expand, grow rapidly, inflate, puff out

ballot *noun* VOTE, election, poll, polling, voting

ballyhoo *noun* FUSS, babble, commotion, hubbub, hue and cry, hullabaloo, noise, racket, to-do

balm *noun* 1 OINTMENT, balsam, cream, embrocation, emollient, lotion, salve, unguent 2 COMFORT, anodyne, consolation, curative, palliative, restorative, solace

balmy *adjective* MILD, clement, pleasant, summery, temperate

baloney *noun* (*informal*) NONSENSE, claptrap (*informal*), crap (*slang*), drivel, garbage, hogwash, poppycock (*informal*), rubbish, stuff and nonsense, trash, tripe (*informal*)

bamboozle *verb* (*informal*) 1 CHEAT, con (*informal*), deceive, dupe, fool, hoodwink, swindle, trick 2 PUZZLE, baffle, befuddle, confound, confuse, mystify, perplex, stump

ban *verb* 1 PROHIBIT, banish, bar, block, boycott, disallow, disqualify, exclude, forbid, outlaw ▷ *noun* 2 PROHIBITION, boycott, disqualification, embargo, restriction, taboo

banal *adjective* UNORIGINAL, hackneyed, humdrum, mundane, pedestrian, stale, stereotyped, trite, unimaginative

band¹ *noun* 1 ENSEMBLE, combo, group, orchestra 2 GANG, body, company, group, party, posse (*informal*)

band² *noun* STRIP, belt, bond, chain, cord, ribbon, strap

bandage *noun* 1 DRESSING, compress, gauze, plaster ▷ *verb* 2 DRESS, bind, cover, swathe

bandit *noun* ROBBER, desperado, highwayman, marauder, outlaw, thief

bane *noun* PLAGUE, bête noire, curse, nuisance, pest, ruin, scourge, torment

bang *noun* 1 EXPLOSION, clang, clap, clash, pop, slam, thud, thump 2 BLOW, bump, cuff, knock, punch, smack, stroke, whack ▷ *verb* 3 HIT, belt (*informal*), clatter, knock, slam, strike, thump 4 EXPLODE, boom, clang, resound, thump, thunder

away 3 dismiss > **ban'ish•ment** *noun* exile
ban•is•ter [BAN-ə-stər] *noun* handrail held up by balusters
ban•jo [BAN-joh] *noun, plural* **-jos** musical instrument like guitar, with circular body > **ban'jo•ist** *noun*
bank[1] [bangk] *noun* 1 mound or ridge of earth 2 edge of river, lake, etc. 3 rising ground in sea ▷ *verb* 4 enclose with ridge 5 pile up 6 (of aircraft) tilt inward in turning
bank[2] *noun* 1 establishment for keeping, lending, exchanging, etc. money 2 any supply or store for future use, as a **blood bank** ▷ *verb transitive* 3 put in bank ▷ *verb intransitive* 4 keep with bank > **bank'er** *noun* > **bank'ing** *noun* > **bank teller** bank cashier > **bank'note** *noun* written promise of payment acceptable as money > **bank on** rely on
bank[3] *noun* arrangement of switches, keys, oars, etc. in a row or in tiers
bank•rupt [BANGK-rupt] *noun* 1 one who fails in business, insolvent debtor ▷ *adjective* 2 financially ruined 3 broken 4 destitute ▷ *verb transitive* 5 make, cause to be, bankrupt > **bank'rupt•cy** *noun*
ban•ner [BAN-ər] *noun* 1 long strip with slogan, etc. 2 placard 3 flag used as ensign
banns *noun see* **ban**
ban•quet [BANG-kwit] *noun* 1 feast ▷ *verb intransitive* 2 feast ▷ *verb transitive* 3 treat with feast
ban•quette [bang-KET] *noun* 1 upholstered bench usu. along a wall 2 raised firing step behind parapet
ban'shee *noun* (in Irish folklore) female spirit with a wail portending death
ban•tam [BAN-təm] *noun* 1 dwarf variety of domestic fowl 2 person of diminutive stature > **ban'tam•weight** *noun* boxer weighing no more than 118 pounds
ban•ter [BAN-tər] *verb transitive* 1 make fun of ▷ *noun* 2 light, teasing language
Ban•tu [BAN-too] *noun* 1 collective name for large group of related peoples in Africa 2 family of languages spoken by Bantu peoples
ban•yan [BAN-yən] *noun* Indian fig tree with spreading branches that take root
ba•o•bab [BAY-oh-bab] *noun* Afr. tree with thick trunk and angular branches
Bap'tist *noun* member of Protestant Christian denomination believing in necessity of baptism by immersion, esp. of adults > **baptist** *noun* one who baptizes
bap•tize [BAP-tīz] *verb transitive* **-tized, -tiz•ing** 1 immerse in, sprinkle with water ceremonially 2 christen > **bap'tism** [-tiz-əm] *noun* > **bap•tis'mal** [-TIZ-məl] *adjective* > **bap'tist•ry** *noun, plural* **-ries** place where baptism is performed
bar[1] [bahr] *noun* 1 rod or block of any substance 2 obstacle 3 bank of sand at mouth of river 4 rail in law court 5 body of lawyers 6 room or counter where drinks are served, esp. in hotel, etc. 7 unit of music ▷ *verb transitive* **barred, bar•ring** 8 fasten 9 obstruct 10 exclude ▷ *preposition* 11 except > **barring** *preposition* excepting > **bar code** arrangement of numbers and parallel lines on package, electronically scanned at checkout to give price, etc. > **bar'maid** *noun* > **bar'ten•der** *noun*
bar[2] *noun* unit of pressure
barb [bahrb] *noun* 1 sharp point curving backward behind main point of spear, fishhook, etc. 2 cutting remark > **barbed** *adjective* > **barbed wire** fencing wire with barbs at close intervals

---

▷ *adverb* 5 HARD, abruptly, headlong, noisily, suddenly
6 STRAIGHT, precisely, slap, smack
banish *verb* 1 EXPEL, deport, eject, evict, exile, outlaw
2 GET RID OF, ban, cast out, discard, dismiss, oust, remove
banishment *noun* EXPULSION, deportation, exile, expatriation, transportation
banisters *plural noun* RAILING, balusters, balustrade, handrail, rail
bank[1] *noun* 1 STOREHOUSE, depository, repository
2 STORE, accumulation, fund, hoard, reserve, reservoir, savings, stock, stockpile
▷ *verb* 3 SAVE, deposit, keep
bank[2] *noun* 1 MOUND, banking, embankment, heap, mass, pile, ridge
2 SIDE, brink, edge, margin, shore
▷ *verb* 3 PILE, amass, heap, mass, mound, stack
4 TILT, camber, cant, heel, incline, pitch, slant, slope, tip
bank[3] *noun* ROW, array, file, group, line, rank, sequence, series, succession
bankrupt *adjective* INSOLVENT, broke (*informal*), destitute, impoverished, in queer street, in the red, ruined, wiped out (*informal*)
bankruptcy *noun* INSOLVENCY, disaster, failure, liquidation, ruin
banner *noun* FLAG, colors, ensign, pennant, placard, standard, streamer
banquet *noun* FEAST, dinner, meal, repast, revel, treat
banter *verb* 1 JOKE, jest, kid (*informal*), rib (*informal*), taunt, tease
▷ *noun* 2 JOKING, badinage, jesting, kidding (*informal*), repartee, teasing, wordplay
baptism *noun* (*Christianity*) CHRISTENING, immersion, purification, sprinkling
baptize *verb* (*Christianity*) PURIFY, cleanse, immerse
bar *noun* 1 ROD, paling, palisade, pole, rail, shaft, stake, stick
2 OBSTACLE, barricade, barrier, block, deterrent, hindrance, impediment, obstruction, stop
3 PUBLIC HOUSE, canteen, counter, inn, saloon, tavern, watering hole (*facetious slang*)
▷ *verb* 4 FASTEN, barricade, bolt, latch, lock, secure
5 OBSTRUCT, hinder, prevent, restrain
6 EXCLUDE, ban, black, blackball, forbid, keep out, prohibit
Bar *noun*
▷ **the Bar** (*law*) BARRISTERS, body of lawyers, counsel, court, judgment, tribunal
barb *noun* 1 DIG, affront, cut, gibe, insult, sarcasm, scoff, sneer
2 POINT, bristle, prickle, prong, quill, spike, spur, thorn
barbarian *noun* 1 SAVAGE, brute, yahoo
2 LOUT, bigot, boor, philistine

bar•ba•rous [BAHR-bər-əs] *adjective* savage, brutal, uncivilized > **bar•bar'ian** [-BAIR-ee-ən] *noun* > **bar•bar'ic** *adjective* > **bar'ba•rism** *noun* > **bar•bar'i•ty** *noun*

bar•be•cue [BAHR-bi-kyoo] *noun* 1 food cooked outdoors over hot charcoal 2 fireplace, grill used for this ▷ *verb transitive* **-cued, cu•ing** 3 cook meat, etc. in this manner

bar•ber [BAHR-bər] *noun* 1 one whose job is to cut hair and shave beards ▷ *verb* **-bered, -ber•ing** 2 perform this service

bar•bi•tu•rate [bahr-BICH-ər-it] *noun* derivative of barbituric acid used as sedative drug

bar•ca•role [BAHR-kə-rohl] *noun* 1 gondolier's song 2 music imitative of this

bard [bahrd] *noun* 1 Celtic poet 2 wandering minstrel 3 poet **the Bard of Avon** Shakespeare

bare [bair] *adjective* **bar•er, bar•est** 1 uncovered 2 naked 3 plain 4 scanty ▷ *verb transitive* **bared, bar•ing** make bare > **bare'ly** *adverb* only just, scarcely > **bare'back, bare'backed** *adjective* on unsaddled horse > **bare'faced** *adjective* shameless

barf *verb* (*slang*) vomit

bar•gain [BAHR-gən] *noun* 1 something bought at price favorable to purchaser 2 contract, agreement ▷ *verb intransitive* 3 haggle, negotiate 4 make bargain

barge [bahrj] *noun* 1 flat-bottomed freight boat propelled by towing 2 roomy pleasure boat ▷ *verb intransitive* **barged, barg•ing** (*informal*) 3 interrupt 4 (*informal*) bump (into), push

bar•i•tone [BAR-i-tohn] *noun* 1 (singer with) second lowest adult male voice ▷ *adjective* 2 written for or possessing this vocal range

bar•i•um [BA-ree-əm] *noun* white metallic element

bark[1] [bahrk] *noun* 1 sharp loud cry of dog, etc. ▷ *verb* 2 make, utter with such sound > **bark'er** *noun* one who stands outside entrance to a circus, etc. calling out its attractions **bark up the wrong tree** 1 misdirect one's efforts 2 pursue a wrong course

bark[2] *noun* 1 outer layer of trunk, branches of tree ▷ *verb transitive* 2 strip bark from 3 rub off (skin), graze (shins, etc.)

bark[3] *noun* sailing ship, esp. large, three-masted one

bar•ley [BAHR-lee] *noun* grain used for food and making malt > **bar'ley•corn** *noun* a grain of barley **John Barleycorn** personification of intoxicating liquor

bar mitz•vah [bahr MITS-və] *noun* 1 Jewish boy at age 13 who participates in religious ceremony signifying entry into adulthood 2 the ceremony

barn [bahrn] *noun* building to store grain, hay, etc. > **barn dance** (party with) country music and dancing > **barn'yard** *noun* area adjoining barn > **barnyard humor** earthy or smutty humor

bar•na•cle [BAHR-nə-kəl] *noun* shellfish that adheres to rocks, logs, ships' bottoms, etc.

ba•rom•e•ter [bə-ROM-i-tər] *noun* instrument to measure pressure of atmosphere > **bar•o•met•ric** [bar-ə-ME-trik] *adjective* > **bar•o•graph** [BA-rə-graf] *noun* recording barometer

bar•on [BA-rən] *noun* 1 member of lowest rank of peerage in Great Britain 2 powerful businessman > **bar•o'ness** *noun* > **bar'o•ny** *noun* > **ba•ro'ni•al** [-ROH-nee-əl] *adjective*

bar•on•et [BA-rə-nit] *noun* lowest British hereditary title, below baron but above knight > **bar'o•net•cy** *noun*

ba•roque [bə-ROHK] *adjective* extravagantly ornamented, esp. in architecture and music > **baroque pearl** one irregularly shaped

bar•rack [BA-rək] *noun* (*usually plural*) 1 building for housing soldiers 2 bare, barnlike building ▷ *verb transitive* 3 house in barracks

bar•ra•cu•da [ba-rə-KOO-də] *noun* type of large, elongated, predatory fish, mostly tropical

bar•rage [bə-RAHZH] *noun* 1 heavy artillery fire 2 continuous and heavy delivery, esp. of questions, etc.

bar•rel [BA-rəl] *noun* 1 round wooden vessel, made of curved staves bound with hoops 2 its capacity 3 great amount or number 4 anything long and hollow, as tube of gun, etc. ▷ *verb* **-reled, -rel•ing** 5 put in barrel 6 move at high speed > **bar'rel•ful** *noun, plural* **-fuls** 1 as

DICTIONARY • THESAURUS

barbaric *adjective* 1 UNCIVILIZED, primitive, rude, wild
2 BRUTAL, barbarous, coarse, crude, cruel, fierce, inhuman, savage

barbarism *noun* SAVAGERY, coarseness, crudity

barbarous *adjective* 1 UNCIVILIZED, barbarian, brutish, primitive, rough, rude, savage, uncouth, wild
2 BRUTAL, barbaric, cruel, ferocious, heartless, inhuman, monstrous, ruthless, vicious

barbed *adjective* 1 CUTTING, critical, hostile, hurtful, nasty, pointed, scathing, unkind
2 SPIKED, hooked, jagged, prickly, spiny, thorny

bare *adjective* 1 NAKED, nude, stripped, unclad, unclothed, uncovered, undressed, without a stitch on (*informal*)
2 PLAIN, bald, basic, sheer, simple, stark, unembellished
3 SIMPLE, austere, homely, spare, spartan, unadorned, unembellished

barefaced *adjective* 1 OBVIOUS, blatant, flagrant, open, transparent, unconcealed
2 SHAMELESS, audacious, bold, brash, brazen, impudent, insolent

barely *adverb* ONLY JUST, almost, at a push, by the skin of one's teeth, hardly, just, scarcely

barf *verb* (*slang*) VOMIT, heave, puke (*slang*), retch, spew, throw up (*informal*), toss one's cookies (*slang*)
▷ *noun* VOMIT, puke, sick

bargain *noun* 1 AGREEMENT, arrangement, contract, pact, pledge, promise
2 GOOD BUY, purchase *or* cheap purchase, discount, giveaway, good deal, reduction, steal (*informal*)
▷ *verb* 3 NEGOTIATE, agree, contract, covenant, promise, stipulate, transact

barge *noun* CANAL BOAT, flatboat, lighter, narrow boat

bark[1] *noun*
▷ *verb* YAP, bay, growl, howl, snarl, woof, yelp

bark[2] *noun* COVERING, casing, cortex (*anatomy & botany*), crust, husk, rind, skin

barracks *plural noun* CAMP, billet, encampment,

much, as many, as a barrel can hold 2 large amount or number **over a barrel** helpless
bar•ren [BA-rən] *adjective* 1 unfruitful, sterile 2 unprofitable 3 dull > **bar'ren•ness** *noun*
bar•ri•cade [BA-ri-kayd] *noun* 1 improvised fortification, barrier ▷ *verb transitive* **-cad•ed, -cad•ing** 2 to protect by building barrier 3 block
bar•ri•er [BAR-ee-ər] *noun* fence, obstruction, obstacle, boundary > **barrier reef** coral reef lying parallel to shore
bar•row[1] [BA-roh] *noun* 1 small wheeled handcart 2 wheelbarrow
barrow[2] *noun* castrated male swine
barrow[3] *noun* burial mound of earth or stones
bar•ter [BAHR-tər] *verb* 1 trade by exchange of goods ▷ *noun* 2 trade by the exchange of goods
bar•y•on [BA-ree-on] *noun physics* elementary particle of matter
ba•salt [bə-SAWLT] *noun* dark-colored, hard, compact, igneous rock > **ba•sal'tic** *adjective*
base[1] [bays] *noun* 1 bottom, foundation 2 starting point 3 center of operations 4 fixed point 5 *chem.* compound that combines with an acid to form a salt 6 medium into which other substances are mixed ▷ *verb transitive* **based, bas•ing** 7 found, establish > **base'less** *adjective* > **base'ment** *noun* lowest floor of building, partly or entirely below ground
base[2] *adjective* **-er, -est** 1 low, mean 2 despicable > **base'ly** *adverb* > **base'ness** *noun*
base•ball [BAYS-bawl] *noun* 1 game played with bat and ball between teams of 9 (sometimes 10) players 2 the ball they use
ba•sen•ji [bə-SEN-jee] *noun* small African hunting dog that seldom barks
bash *verb* (*informal*) 1 strike violently ▷ *noun* 2 blow 3 attempt 4 festive party
bash•ful [BASH-fəl] *adjective* shy, modest > **bash'ful•ly** *adverb*
BASIC [BAY-sik] computer programing language that uses common English words
ba•sic [BAY-sik] *adjective* 1 relating to, serving as base 2 fundamental 3 necessary > **ba'si•cal•ly** *adverb*
ba•sil•i•ca [bə-SIL-i-kə] *noun* type of church with long hall and pillars
bas•i•lisk [BAS-ə-lisk] *noun* 1 legendary small fire-breathing dragon 2 type of tropical lizard related to iguanas
ba•sin [BAY-sən] *noun* 1 deep circular dish 2 harbor 3 land drained by river
basis [BAY-sis] *noun, plural* **-ses** [-seez] 1 foundation 2 principal constituent
bask *verb intransitive* lie in warmth and sunshine
bas•ket [BAS-kit] *noun* vessel made of woven cane, straw, etc. > **bas'ket•ry** [-ki-tree] > **bas'ket•ball** *noun* 1 ball game played by two teams of 5 players who score points by throwing ball through baskets suspended above ends of playing area 2 the ball they use
Basque [bask] *noun* 1 one of a people from W Pyrenees 2 their language
bas-re•lief [bah-ri-LEEF] *noun* sculpture with figures standing out slightly from background
bass[1] [bays] *noun* 1 lowest part in music 2 bass singer or voice ▷ *adjective*
bass[2] [bas] *noun* any of large variety of freshwater or seawater fishes
bas•set hound [BAS-it] *noun* type of smooth-haired short-legged dog
bas•soon [bə-SOON] *noun* woodwind instrument of low tone > **bas•soon'ist** *noun*
bas•tard [BAS-tərd] *noun* 1 child born of unmarried parents 2 (*slang*) person, esp. a man: *a lucky bastard* ▷ *adjective* 3 illegitimate 4 spurious
baste[1] [bayst] *verb transitive* **bast•ed, bast•ing** 1 moisten (meat) during cooking with hot fat 2 beat severely > **bast'er** *noun*

DICTIONARY

b

THESAURUS

garrison, quarters
barrage *noun* 1 TORRENT, burst, deluge, hail, mass, onslaught, plethora, stream
2 (*military*) BOMBARDMENT, battery, cannonade, fusillade, gunfire, salvo, shelling, volley
barren *adjective* 1 INFERTILE, childless, sterile
2 UNPRODUCTIVE, arid, desert, desolate, dry, empty, unfruitful, waste
barricade *noun* 1 BARRIER, blockade, bulwark, fence, obstruction, palisade, rampart, stockade
▷ *verb* 2 BAR, block, blockade, defend, fortify, obstruct, protect, shut in
barrier *noun* 1 BARRICADE, bar, blockade, boundary, fence, obstacle, obstruction, wall
2 HINDRANCE, difficulty, drawback, handicap, hurdle, obstacle, restriction, stumbling block
barter *verb* TRADE, bargain, drive a hard bargain, exchange, haggle, sell, swap, traffic
base[1] *noun* 1 BOTTOM, bed, foot, foundation, pedestal, rest, stand, support
2 BASIS, core, essence, heart, key, origin, root, source
3 CENTER, camp, headquarters, home, post, settlement, starting point, station
▷ *verb* 4 FOUND, build, construct, depend, derive, establish, ground, hinge
5 PLACE, locate, post, station
base[2] *adjective* 1 DISHONORABLE, contemptible, despicable, disreputable, evil, immoral, lousy (*slang*), scuzzy (*slang*), shameful, sordid, wicked
2 COUNTERFEIT, alloyed, debased, fake, forged, fraudulent, impure
baseless *adjective* UNFOUNDED, groundless, unconfirmed, uncorroborated, ungrounded, unjustified, unsubstantiated, unsupported
bash *verb* 1 (*informal*) HIT, belt (*informal*), smash, sock (*slang*), strike, wallop (*informal*)
bashful *adjective* SHY, blushing, coy, diffident, reserved, reticent, retiring, timid
basic *adjective* ESSENTIAL, elementary, fundamental, key, necessary, primary, vital
basically *adverb* ESSENTIALLY, at heart, fundamentally, inherently, in substance, intrinsically, mostly, primarily
basics *plural noun* ESSENTIALS, ABCs, brass tacks (*informal*), fundamentals, nitty-gritty (*informal*), nuts and bolts (*informal*), principles, rudiments
basis *noun* FOUNDATION, base, bottom, footing, ground, groundwork, support
bask *verb* LIE IN, laze, loll, lounge, relax, sunbathe, swim in
bass *adjective* DEEP, deep-toned, low, low-pitched, resonant, sonorous
bastard *noun* 1 (*informal, offensive*) ROGUE, miscreant, reprobate, scoundrel, villain, wretch
2 ILLEGITIMATE CHILD, love child, natural child

baste² *verb transitive* **bast•ed, bast•ing** sew loosely, tack

bas•ti•na•do [bas-tə-NAY-doh] *noun, plural* **-does** beating with stick, etc. esp. on soles of feet ▷ *verb transitive* **-doed, -do•ing**

bas•tion [BAS-chən] *noun* 1 projecting part of fortification, tower 2 strong defense or bulwark

bat¹ *noun* 1 any of various types of clubs used to hit ball in certain sports, e.g. baseball ▷ *verb* **bat•ted, bat•ting** 2 strike with bat or use bat in sport > **batting** *noun* performance with bat

bat² *noun* nocturnal mouselike flying animal

bat³ *verb transitive* **bat•ted, bat•ting** flutter (one's eyelids)

batch [bach] *noun* group or set of similar objects, esp. cakes, etc. baked together

bat•ed [BAY-tid] *adjective* **with bated breath** anxiously

bath *noun* 1 vessel or place to bathe in 2 water for bathing 3 act of bathing > **bath'house** *noun* building with dressing and washing facilities for bathers > **bath'room** *noun* room with toilet and washing facilities **take a bath** (*slang*) experience serious, esp. financial, losses in a venture

bathe [bayth] *verb* **bathed, bath'ing** 1 apply liquid 2 wash 3 immerse in water ▷ *noun* > **bath'er** *noun*

ba•thos [BAY-thos] *noun* ludicrous descent from the elevated to the ordinary in writing or speech

ba•tik [bə-TEEK] *noun* dyeing process using wax

ba•ton [bə-TON] *noun* stick, esp. of conductor, marshal, member of relay team

ba•tra•chi•an [bə-TRAY-kee-ən] *noun, adjective* (of) any amphibian, esp. frog or toad

bat•tal•ion [bə-TAL-yən] *noun* 1 military unit consisting of three or more companies 2 any large group

bat•ten¹ [BAT-n] *noun* 1 narrow piece of board, strip of wood ▷ *verb transitive* 2 (esp. with *down*) fasten, make secure

batten² *verb intransitive* (usu. with *on*) thrive, esp. at someone else's expense

bat•ter [BAT-ər] *verb transitive* 1 strike continuously ▷ *noun* 2 mixture of flour, eggs, liquid, used in cooking

bat•ter•y [BAT-ə-ree] *noun, plural* **-ter•ies** 1 connected group of electrical cells 2 any electrical cell 3 number of similar things occurring together 4 *law* assault by beating 5 number of guns 6 place where they are mounted 7 unit of artillery 8 *baseball* pitcher and catcher as a unit

bat•ting [BAT-ing] *noun* cotton or wool fiber as stuffing or lining

bat•tle [BAT-l] *noun* 1 fight between armies, combat ▷ *verb intransitive* **-tled, -tling** 2 fight, struggle > **battle-ax** *noun* (*slang*) sharp-tempered, domineering woman

bat•tle•ment [BAT-l-mənt] *noun* wall, parapet on fortification with openings for cannon

bat•tle•ship [BAT-l-ship] *noun* heavily armed and armored fighting ship of the largest and heaviest class

bat•ty [BAT-ee] *adjective* **-ti•er, -ti•est** (*informal*) crazy, silly

bau•ble [BAW-bəl] *noun* showy trinket

baud [bawd] *noun* unit of data transmission speed

baux•ite [BAWK-sīt] *noun* mineral yielding aluminum

bawd *noun* 1 prostitute 2 brothel keeper > **bawd'y** *adjective* **bawd•i•er, bawd•i•est** obscene, lewd

bawl *verb intransitive* 1 cry 2 shout ▷ *noun* 3 loud shout or cry > **bawl out** *verb transitive* (*informal*) reprimand severely

bay¹ *noun* 1 wide inlet of sea 2 space between two columns 3 recess > **bay window** window projecting from a wall

bay² *noun* 1 bark 2 cry of hounds in pursuit ▷ *verb* 3 bark (at) **at bay** cornered

bay³ *noun* laurel tree

bay⁴ *adjective* 1 reddish-brown ▷ *noun* 2 horse with body of this color and black mane

bay•o•net [BAY-ə-nit] *noun* 1 stabbing weapon fixed to rifle ▷ *verb transitive* **-net•ed, -net•ing** 2 stab with this

bay•ou [BĪ-oo] *noun, plural* **-ous** marshy inlet or outlet of lake, river, etc., usu. sluggish

DICTIONARY • THESAURUS

bastion *noun* STRONGHOLD, bulwark, citadel, defense, fortress, mainstay, prop, rock, support, tower of strength

bat *noun, verb* HIT, bang, smack, strike, swat, thump, wallop (*informal*), whack

batch *noun* GROUP, amount, assemblage, bunch, collection, crowd, lot, pack, quantity, set

bath *noun* 1 WASH, cleansing, douche, scrubbing, shower, soak, tub ▷ *verb* 2 WASH, bathe, clean, douse, scrub down, shower, soak

bathe *verb* 1 WASH, cleanse, rinse, soak 2 COVER, flood, immerse, steep, suffuse

baton *noun* STICK, club, crook, mace, rod, scepter, staff, truncheon, wand

batten¹ *verb* (*usually with down*) FASTEN, board up, clamp down, cover up, fix, nail down, secure, tighten

batter *verb* BEAT, buffet, clobber (*slang*), pelt, pound, pummel, thrash, wallop (*informal*)

battery *noun* ARTILLERY, cannon, cannonry, gun emplacements, guns

battle *noun* 1 FIGHT, action, attack, combat, encounter, engagement, hostilities, skirmish 2 CONFLICT, campaign, contest, crusade, dispute, struggle ▷ *verb* 3 STRUGGLE, argue, clamor, dispute, fight, lock horns, strive, war

battlefield *noun* BATTLEGROUND, combat zone, field, field of battle, front

battleship *noun* WARSHIP, gunboat, man-of-war

batty *adjective* CRAZY, absent-minded, bonkers (*informal*), daft (*informal*), eccentric, mad, odd, peculiar

bauble *noun* TRINKET, bagatelle, gewgaw, gimcrack, knick-knack, plaything, toy, trifle

baulk *see* **balk**

bawdy *adjective* RUDE, coarse, dirty, indecent, lascivious, lecherous, lewd, ribald, salacious, smutty

bawl *verb* 1 CRY, blubber, sob, wail, weep 2 SHOUT, bellow, call, clamor, howl, roar, yell

bay¹ *noun* 1 INLET, bight, cove, gulf, natural harbor, sound 2 *noun* RECESS, alcove, compartment, niche, nook, opening

ba•zaar [bə-ZAHR] *noun* 1 market (esp. in Orient) 2 sale of goods for charity
ba•zoo•ka [bə-ZOO-kə] *noun* antitank rocket launcher
be *verb, present sing 1st person* **am** *2nd person* **are** *3rd person* **is** *present plural* **are** *past singular 1st person* **was** *2nd person* **were** *3rd person* **was** *past plural* **were** *present participle* **being** *past participle* **been** 1 exist or live 2 pay a visit: *have you been to Spain?* 3 take place: *my birthday was last Monday* 4 used as a linking between the subject of a sentence and its complement: *John is a musician* 5 forms the progressive present tense: *the man is running* 6 forms the passive voice of all transitive verbs: *a good movie is being shown on television tonight*
Be *chem.* beryllium
beach [beech] *noun* 1 shore of sea ▷ *verb transitive* 2 run boat on shore > **beach'comb•er** [-koh-mər] *noun* 1 one who habitually searches shore debris for items of value 2 loafer spending days aimlessly on beach > **beach'head** *noun* 1 area on beach captured from enemy 2 base for operations 3 foothold
bea•con [BEE-kən] *noun* 1 signal fire 2 lighthouse, buoy 3 (radio) signal used for navigation
bead [beed] *noun* 1 little ball pierced for threading on string of necklace, rosary, etc. 2 drop of liquid 3 narrow molding ▷ *verb transitive* 4 string together or furnish with beads > **bead'ing** *noun* > **bead'y** *adjective* **bead•i•er, bead•i•est** small and bright
bea•gle [BEE-gəl] *noun* small hound
beak [beek] *noun* 1 projecting horny jaws of bird 2 anything pointed or projecting 3 (*slang*) nose
beak•er [BEE-kər] *noun* 1 large drinking cup 2 glass vessel used by chemists
beam [beem] *noun* 1 long squared piece of wood 2 ship's cross timber, side, or width 3 ray of light, etc. 4 broad smile 5 bar of a balance ▷ *verb transitive* 6 aim light, radio waves, etc. (to) ▷ *verb intransitive* 7 shine 8 smile benignly
bean [been] *noun* 1 any of various leguminous plants or their seeds 2 head **full of beans** (*informal*) lively > **bean sprout** edible sprout of newly germinated bean, esp. mung bean
bear[1] [bair] *verb transitive* **bore, borne** *or* **born, bear•ing** 1 carry 2 support 3 produce 4 endure 5 press (upon) > **bear'er** *noun*
bear[2] *noun* 1 heavy carnivorous quadruped 2 other bearlike animals, such as the koala > **bear'skin** *noun* tall fur helmet
beard [beerd] *noun* 1 hair on chin ▷ *verb transitive* 2 oppose boldly
bear•ing [BAIR-ing] *noun* 1 support or guide for mechanical part, esp. one reducing friction 2 relevance 3 behavior 4 direction 5 relative position
beast [beest] *noun* 1 animal 2 four-footed animal 3 brutal man > **beast'li•ness** *noun* > **beast'ly** *adjective*
beat [beet] *verb transitive* **beat, beat•en, beat•ing** 1 strike repeatedly 2 overcome 3 surpass 4 stir vigorously with striking action 5 flap (wings) 6 make, wear (path) ▷ *verb intransitive* **beat, beat•en, beat•ing** 7 throb 8 sail against wind ▷ *noun* 9 stroke 10 pulsation 11 appointed course 12 basic rhythmic unit in piece of music ▷ *adjective* (*slang*) 13 exhausted > **beat'er** *noun* 1 instrument for beating 2 one who rouses game for shooters
be•at•i•fy [bee-AT-ə-fī] *verb transitive* **-fied, -fy•ing** 1 make happy 2 *r.c. church* pronounce in eternal happiness (first step in canonization) > **be•a•tif•ic** [bee-ə-TIF-ik] *adjective* > **be•at•i•fi•ca'tion** *noun* > **be•at'i•tude** *noun* blessedness
beau [boh] *noun, plural* **beaux** [bohz] suitor

DICTIONARY

b

THESAURUS

bay[2] *verb* HOWL, bark, clamor, cry, growl, yelp
bazaar *noun* 1 FAIR, bring-and-buy, fête, sale of work
2 MARKET, exchange, marketplace
be *verb* EXIST, be alive, breathe, inhabit, live
beach *noun* SHORE, coast, sands, seashore, seaside, water's edge
beached *adjective* STRANDED, abandoned, aground, ashore, deserted, grounded, high and dry, marooned, wrecked
beacon *noun* SIGNAL, beam, bonfire, flare, lighthouse, sign, watchtower
bead *noun* DROP, blob, bubble, dot, droplet, globule, pellet, pill
beady *adjective* BRIGHT, gleaming, glinting, glittering, sharp, shining
beak *noun* BILL, mandible, neb (*archaic* or *dialect*), nib
beam *noun* 1 SMILE, grin
2 RAY, gleam, glimmer, glint, glow, shaft, streak, stream
3 RAFTER, girder, joist, plank, spar, support, timber
▷ *verb* 4 SMILE, grin
5 RADIATE, glare, gleam, glitter, glow, shine
6 SEND OUT, broadcast, emit, transmit
bear *verb* 1 SUPPORT, have, hold, maintain, possess, shoulder, sustain, uphold
2 CARRY, bring, convey, move, take, transport
3 PRODUCE, beget, breed, bring forth, engender, generate, give birth to, yield
4 TOLERATE, abide, allow, brook, endure, permit, put up with (*informal*), stomach, suffer
bearable *adjective* TOLERABLE, admissible, endurable, manageable, passable, sufferable, supportable, sustainable
bearer *noun* CARRIER, agent, conveyor, messenger, porter, runner, servant
bearing *noun* 1 (*usually with on or upon*) RELEVANCE, application, connection, import, pertinence, reference, relation, significance
2 MANNER, air, aspect, attitude, behavior, demeanor, deportment, posture
bearings *plural noun* POSITION, aim, course, direction, location, orientation, situation, track, way, whereabouts
bear out *verb* SUPPORT, confirm, corroborate, endorse, justify, prove, substantiate, uphold, vindicate
beast *noun* 1 ANIMAL, brute, creature
2 BRUTE, barbarian, fiend, monster, ogre, sadist, savage, swine
beastly *adjective* UNPLEASANT, awful, disagreeable, horrid, mean, nasty, rotten
beat *verb* 1 HIT, bang, batter, buffet, knock, pound, strike, thrash
2 FLAP, flutter
3 THROB, palpitate, pound, pulsate, quake,

Beau•fort scale [BOH-fərt] system of indicating wind strength (from 0, calm, to 17, hurricane)
beau•ty [BYOO-tee] *noun, plural* **-ties** 1 loveliness, grace 2 beautiful person or thing > **beau•ti•cian** [byoo-TISH-ən] *noun* one who gives treatment in beauty parlor > **beau'ti•ful** *adjective* > **beau'ti•fy** [-tə-fi] *verb transitive* **-fied, -fy•ing** > **beauty parlor** establishment offering hairdressing, manicure, etc.
bea•ver [BEE-vər] *noun* 1 amphibious rodent 2 its fur 3 exceptionally hard-working person
be•calmed [bi-KAHMD] *adjective* (of ship) motionless through lack of wind
became *pt. of* **become**
be•cause [bi-KAWZ] *adverb, conjunction* by reason of, since
beck [bek] *noun* **at someone's beck and call** subject to someone's slightest whim
beck•on [BEK-ən] *verb* summon or lure by silent signal
be•come [bi-KUM] *verb intransitive* **be•came, be•come, be•com•ing** 1 come to be ▷ *verb transitive* **be•came, be•come, be•com•ing** 2 suit > **becoming** *adjective* 1 suitable to 2 proper
bed *noun* 1 piece of furniture for sleeping on 2 garden plot 3 supporting structure 4 bottom of river 5 layer, stratum ▷ *verb transitive* **bed•ded, bed•ding** 6 lay in a bed 7 plant > **bedding** *noun* > **bed'bug** *noun* wingless bug infesting beds and sucking blood > **bed'pan** *noun* container used as toilet by bedridden person > **bed'rid•den** *adjective* confined to bed by age or sickness > **bed'rock** *noun* 1 solid rock beneath the surface soil 2 basic facts or principles > **bed'room** *noun* > **bed'spread** [-spred] *noun* cover for bed when not in use > **bed'stead** [-sted] *noun* framework of a bed
be•dev•il [bi-DEV-əl] *verb transitive* **-iled, -il•ing** 1 confuse 2 torment > **be•dev'il•ment** *noun*
bed•lam [BED-ləm] *noun* noisy confused scene
Bed•ou•in [BED-oo-in] *noun* 1 nomadic Arab of the desert 2 nomad
be•drag•gle [bi-DRAG-əl] *verb transitive* **-gled, -gling** dirty by trailing in wet or mud
bee *noun* insect that makes honey > **bee'hive** *noun* > **bee'line** *noun* shortest route > **bees'wax** *noun* wax secreted by bees **bee in one's bonnet** an obsession
beech *noun* 1 tree with smooth grayish bark and small nuts 2 its wood
beef *noun* 1 flesh of cattle raised and killed for eating 2 (*informal*) complaint ▷ *verb intransitive* (*informal*) 3 complain > **beef'y** *adjective* **beef•i•er, beef•i•est** fleshy, stolid > **beef'burg•er** *noun* hamburger
been *pp of* **be**
beep *noun* 1 short, loud sound of automobile horn, etc. ▷ *verb* 2 make this sound > **beep'er** *noun* small portable electronic signaling device
beer *noun* fermented alcoholic drink made from hops and malt > **beer'y** *adjective* **beer•i•er, beer•i•est** affected by, smelling of, beer
beet *noun* any of various plants with root used for food or extraction of sugar
bee•tle [BEET-l] *noun* class of insect with hard upper-wing cases closed over the back for protection > **bee'tle-browed** [browd] *adjective* with prominent brows
be•fall [bi-FAWL] *verb* **be•fell, be•fall•en, be•fall•ing** happen (to)
be•fit [bi-FIT] *verb transitive* **be•fit•ted, be•fit•ting** be suitable to
be•fog [bi-FOG] *verb transitive* **-fogged, -fog•ging**

---

thump, vibrate
4 DEFEAT, conquer, outdo, overcome, overwhelm, surpass, vanquish
▷ *noun* 5 THROB, palpitation, pulsation, pulse
6 ROUTE, circuit, course, path, rounds, way
7 RHYTHM, accent, cadence, meter, stress, time
beaten *adjective* 1 STIRRED, blended, foamy, frothy, mixed, whipped, whisked
2 DEFEATED, cowed, overcome, overwhelmed, thwarted, vanquished
beat up *verb* (*informal*) ASSAULT, attack, batter, beat the living daylights out of (*informal*), knock about *or* knock around, pound, pulverize, thrash
beau *noun* 1 (*old-fashioned*) BOYFRIEND, admirer, fiancé, lover, suitor, sweetheart
2 DANDY, coxcomb, fop, gallant, ladies' man
beautiful *adjective* ATTRACTIVE, charming, delightful, exquisite, fair, fine, gorgeous, handsome, lovely, pleasing
beautify *verb* MAKE BEAUTIFUL, adorn, decorate, embellish, festoon, garnish, glamorize, ornament
beauty *noun* 1 ATTRACTIVENESS, charm, comeliness, elegance, exquisiteness, glamor, grace, handsomeness, loveliness
2 BELLE, good-looker, lovely (*slang*), stunner (*informal*)
becalmed *adjective* STILL, motionless, settled, stranded, stuck
because *conjunction* SINCE, as, by reason of, in that, on account of, owing to, thanks to
beckon *verb* GESTURE, bid, gesticulate, motion, nod, signal, summon, wave at
become *verb* 1 COME TO BE, alter to, be transformed into, change into, develop into, grow into, mature into, ripen into
2 SUIT, embellish, enhance, fit, flatter, set off
becoming *adjective* 1 APPROPRIATE, compatible, fitting, in keeping, proper, seemly, suitable, worthy
2 FLATTERING, attractive, comely, enhancing, graceful, neat, pretty, tasteful
bed *noun* 1 BEDSTEAD, berth, bunk, cot, couch, divan
2 PLOT, area, border, garden, patch, row, strip
3 BOTTOM, base, foundation, groundwork
bedevil *verb* 1 TORMENT, afflict, distress, harass, plague, trouble, vex, worry
2 CONFUSE, confound
bedlam *noun* PANDEMONIUM, chaos, commotion, confusion, furor, tumult, turmoil, uproar
bedraggled *adjective* MESSY, dirty, disheveled, disordered, muddied, scuzzy (*slang*), unkempt, untidy
bedridden *adjective* CONFINED TO BED, confined, flat on one's back, incapacitated, laid up (*informal*)
bedrock *noun* 1 BOTTOM, bed, foundation, rock bottom, substratum, substructure
2 BASICS, basis, core, essentials, fundamentals, nuts and bolts (*informal*), roots
beefy *adjective* (*informal*) BRAWNY, bulky, hulking,

perplex, confuse
be•fore [bi-FOR] *preposition* 1 in front of 2 in presence of 3 in preference to 4 earlier than ▷ *adverb* 5 earlier 6 in front ▷ *conjunction* 7 sooner than > **be•fore'hand** *adverb* previously
be•foul [bi-FOWL] *verb transitive* make filthy
be•friend [bi-FREND] *verb transitive* make friend of
beg *verb transitive* **begged, beg•ging** 1 ask earnestly, beseech ▷ *verb intransitive* **begged, beg•ging** 2 ask for or live on charity > **beg•gar** [BEG-ər] *noun*
began *pt. of* **began**
be•get [bi-GET] *verb transitive* **be•got** *or* **be•gat, be•got•ten** *or* **be•got, be•get•ting** (*obsolete*) produce, generate
be•gin [bi-GIN] *verb* **be•gan, be•gun, be•gin•ning** 1 (cause to) start 2 initiate 3 originate > **be•gin'ner** *noun* novice
be•go•nia [bi-GOHN-yə] *noun* genus of tropical plant
be•got *pt./pp. of* **beget**
be•grudge [bi-GRUJ] *verb transitive* **-grudged, -grudg•ing** grudge, envy anyone the possession of
be•guile [bi-GĪL] *verb transitive* **-guiled, -guil•ing** 1 charm, fascinate 2 amuse 3 deceive > **beguiling** *adjective*
be•gun *pp. of* **begin**
be•half [bi-HAF] *noun* **on behalf of** in the interest of or for the benefit of
be•have [bi-HAYV] *verb intransitive* **-haved, -hav•ing** act, function in particular way > **be•hav•ior** [bi-HAYV-yər] *noun* conduct **behave oneself** conduct oneself well
be•head [bi-HED] *verb transitive* cut off head
be•held *pt./pp. of* **behold**
be•hest [bi-HEST] *noun* charge, command
be•hind [bi-HĪND] *preposition* 1 farther back or earlier than 2 in support of ▷ *adverb* 3 in the rear > **behind-the-scenes** kept or made in secret
be•hold [bi-HOHLD] *verb transitive* **be•held, be•hold•ing** watch, see > **be•hold'er** *noun*
be•hol•den [bi-HOHL-dən] *adjective* bound in gratitude
be•hoove [bi-HOOV] *verb intransitive* **-hooved, -hoov•ing** be necessary or fitting for
beige [bayzh] *noun* color of undyed woolen cloth
be•ing [BEE-ing] *noun* 1 existence 2 that which exists 3 creature 4 *pr. p. of* **be**
bel *noun* unit for comparing two power levels
be•la•bor [bi-LAY-bər] *verb transitive* 1 beat soundly 2 discuss (a subject) endlessly
be•lat•ed [bi-LAY-tid] *adjective* 1 late 2 too late
be•lay [bi-LAY] *verb transitive* fasten rope to peg, pin, etc.
belch *verb intransitive* 1 void gas by mouth ▷ *verb transitive* 2 eject violently 3 cast up ▷ *noun* 4 emission of gas, etc.
be•lea•guer [bi-LEE-gər] *verb transitive* besiege
bel•fry [BEL-free] *noun, plural* **-fries** bell tower
be•lie [bi-LĪ] *verb transitive* **-lied, -ly•ing** 1

muscular, stocky, strapping, sturdy, thickset
befall *verb* HAPPEN, chance, come to pass, fall, occur, take place, transpire (*informal*)
befitting *adjective* APPROPRIATE, apposite, becoming, fit, fitting, proper, right, seemly, suitable
before *preposition* 1 AHEAD OF, in advance of, in front of
2 EARLIER THAN, in advance of, prior to
3 IN THE PRESENCE OF, in front of
▷ *adverb* 4 PREVIOUSLY, ahead, earlier, formerly, in advance, sooner
5 IN FRONT, ahead
beforehand *adverb* IN ADVANCE, ahead of time, already, before, earlier, in anticipation, previously, sooner
befriend *verb* HELP, aid, assist, back, encourage, side with, stand by, support, welcome
beg *verb* 1 SCROUNGE, cadge, seek charity, solicit charity, sponge on
2 IMPLORE, beseech, entreat, petition, plead, request, solicit
beggar *noun* TRAMP, bag lady, bum (*informal*), down-and-out, pauper, vagrant
beggarly *adjective* POOR, destitute, impoverished, indigent, needy, poverty-stricken
begin *verb* 1 START, commence, embark on, initiate, instigate, institute, prepare, set about
2 HAPPEN, appear, arise, come into being, emerge, originate, start
beginner *noun* NOVICE, amateur, apprentice, learner, neophyte, rookie (*informal*), starter, trainee, tyro
beginning *noun* 1 START, birth, commencement, inauguration, inception, initiation, onset, opening, origin, outset
2 SEED, fount, germ, root
begrudge *verb* RESENT, be jealous, be reluctant, be stingy, envy, grudge
beguile *verb* 1 FOOL, cheat, deceive, delude, dupe, hoodwink, mislead, take for a ride (*informal*), trick
2 CHARM, amuse, distract, divert, engross, entertain, occupy
beguiling *adjective* CHARMING, alluring, attractive, bewitching, captivating, enchanting, enthralling, intriguing
behave *verb* 1 ACT, function, operate, perform, run, work
2 CONDUCT ONESELF PROPERLY, act correctly, keep one's nose clean, mind one's manners
behavior *noun* 1 CONDUCT, actions, bearing, demeanor, deportment, manner, manners, ways
2 ACTION, functioning, operation, performance
behind *preposition* 1 AFTER, at the back of, at the heels of, at the rear of, following, later than
2 CAUSING, at the bottom of, initiating, instigating, responsible for
3 SUPPORTING, backing, for, in agreement, on the side of
▷ *adverb* 4 AFTER, afterwards, following, in the wake *or* in the wake of, next, subsequently
5 OVERDUE, behindhand, in arrears, in debt
▷ *noun* 6 (*informal*) BOTTOM, butt, buttocks, posterior
behold *verb* LOOK AT, observe, perceive, regard, survey, view, watch, witness
beholden *adjective* INDEBTED, bound, grateful, obliged, owing, under obligation
being *noun* 1 EXISTENCE, life, reality
2 NATURE, entity, essence, soul, spirit, substance
3 CREATURE, human being, individual, living thing
belated *adjective* LATE, behindhand, behind

contradict 2 misrepresent

be•lieve [bi-LEEV] *verb transitive* **-lieved, -liev•ing** 1 regard as true or real ▷ *verb intransitive* **-lieved, -liev•ing** 2 have faith > **be•lief** *noun* > **be•liev'a•ble** *adjective* credible > **be•liev'er** *noun* esp. one of same religious faith

be•lit•tle [bi-LIT-l] *verb transitive* **-tled, -tling** regard, speak of, as having little worth or value > **be•lit'tler** *noun*

bell *noun* 1 hollow metal instrument giving ringing sound when struck 2 electrical device emitting ring or buzz as signal > **bell'hop** *noun* hotel employee who carries luggage, conducts guests to rooms, etc.

bel•la•don•na [bel-ə-DON-ə] *noun* deadly nightshade

belle [bel] *noun* beautiful woman, reigning beauty

bel•li•cose [BEL-i-kohs] *adjective* warlike

bel•lig•er•ent [bə-LIJ-ər-ənt] *adjective* 1 hostile, aggressive 2 making war ▷ *noun* 3 warring person or nation

bel•low [BEL-oh] *verb intransitive* 1 roar like bull 2 shout ▷ *noun* 3 roar of bull 4 any deep cry or shout

bel•lows [BEL-ohz] *plural noun* instrument for creating stream of air

bel•ly [BEL-ee] *noun, plural* **-lies** 1 part of body that contains intestines 2 stomach ▷ *verb* **-lied, -ly•ing** 3 swell out > **belly laugh** *noun* hearty laugh

be•long [bi-LAWNG] *verb intransitive* 1 be the property or attribute of 2 be a member or inhabitant of 3 have an allotted place 4 pertain to > **be•long'ings** *plural noun* personal possessions

be•lov•ed [bi-LUV-id or bi-LUVD] *adjective* 1 much loved ▷ *noun* 2 dear one

be•low [bi-LOH] *adverb* 1 beneath ▷ *preposition* 2 lower than

belt *noun* 1 band 2 girdle 3 zone or district ▷ *verb transitive* 4 surround, fasten with belt 5 mark with band 6 (*informal*) thrash

be•moan [bi-MOHN] *verb transitive* grieve over (loss, etc.)

be•muse [bi-MYOOZ] *verb* **-mused, -mus•ing** confuse, bewilder

bench *noun* 1 long seat 2 seat or body of judges, etc. ▷ *verb transitive* 3 provide with benches > **bench'mark** *noun* fixed point, criterion

bend *verb* **bent, bend•ing** 1 (cause to) form a curve ▷ *noun* 2 curve > **the bends** *plural noun* decompression sickness **bend over backward** exert oneself to the utmost

be•neath [bi-NEETH] *preposition* 1 under, lower than ▷ *adverb* 2 below

ben•e•dic•tion [ben-i-DIK-shən] *noun* invocation of divine blessing

ben•e•fit [BEN-ə-fit] *noun* 1 advantage, favor, profit, good 2 money paid by a government or

time, delayed, late in the day, overdue, tardy

belch *verb* 1 BURP (*informal*), hiccup
2 EMIT, discharge, disgorge, erupt, give off, spew forth, vent

beleaguered *adjective* 1 HARASSED, badgered, hassled (*informal*), persecuted, pestered, plagued, put upon, vexed
2 BESIEGED, assailed, beset, blockaded, hemmed in, surrounded

belief *noun* 1 TRUST, assurance, confidence, conviction, feeling, impression, judgment, notion, opinion
2 FAITH, credo, creed, doctrine, dogma, ideology, principles, tenet

believable *adjective* CREDIBLE, authentic, imaginable, likely, plausible, possible, probable, trustworthy

believe *verb* 1 ACCEPT, be certain of, be convinced of, credit, depend on, have faith in, rely on, swear by, trust
2 THINK, assume, gather, imagine, judge, presume, reckon, speculate, suppose

believer *noun* FOLLOWER, adherent, convert, devotee, disciple, supporter, upholder, zealot

belittle *verb* DISPARAGE, decry, denigrate, deprecate, deride, scoff at, scorn, sneer at

belligerent *adjective* 1 AGGRESSIVE, bellicose, combative, hostile, pugnacious, unfriendly, warlike, warring
▷ *noun* 2 FIGHTER, combatant, warring nation

bellow *noun*
▷ *verb* SHOUT, bawl, clamor, cry, howl, roar, scream, shriek, yell

belly *noun* 1 STOMACH, abdomen, gut, insides (*informal*), paunch, potbelly, tummy
▷ *verb* 2 SWELL OUT, billow, bulge, fill, spread, swell

bellyful *noun* SURFEIT, enough, excess, glut, plateful, plenty, satiety, too much

belonging *noun* RELATIONSHIP, acceptance, affinity, association, attachment, fellowship, inclusion, loyalty, rapport

belongings *plural noun* POSSESSIONS, accouterments, chattels, effects, gear, goods, paraphernalia, personal property, stuff, things

belong to *verb* 1 BE THE PROPERTY OF, be at the disposal of, be held by, be owned by
2 BE A MEMBER OF, be affiliated to, be allied to, be associated with, be included in

beloved *adjective* DEAR, admired, adored, darling, loved, pet, precious, prized, treasured, worshipped

below *preposition* 1 LESSER, inferior, subject, subordinate
2 LESS THAN, lower than
▷ *adverb* 3 LOWER, beneath, down, under, underneath

belt *noun* 1 WAISTBAND, band, cummerbund, girdle, girth, sash
2 (*geography*) ZONE, area, district, layer, region, stretch, strip, tract

bemoan *verb* LAMENT, bewail, deplore, grieve for, mourn, regret, rue, weep for

bemused *adjective* PUZZLED, at sea, bewildered, confused, flummoxed, muddled, nonplussed, perplexed

bench *noun* 1 SEAT, form, pew, settle, stall
2 WORKTABLE, board, counter, table, trestle table, workbench
3 ▷ **the bench** COURT, courtroom, judges, judiciary, magistrates, tribunal

benchmark *noun* REFERENCE POINT, criterion, gauge, level, measure, model, norm, par, standard, yardstick

bend *verb* 1 CURVE, arc, arch, bow, lean, turn, twist, veer

business, etc. to unemployed, etc. ▷ *verb* **-fit•ed, -fit•ing** 3 do good to 4 receive good
> **ben'e•fac•tor** *noun* 1 one who helps or does good to others 2 patron > **ben'e•fice** [-ə-fis] *noun* an ecclesiastical livelihood
> **be•nef'i•cence** *noun* > **be•nef'i•cent** *adjective* 1 doing good 2 kind > **ben•e•fi'cial** [-FISH-əl] *adjective* advantageous, helpful > **ben•e•fi'ci•ar•y** *noun, plural* **-ar•ies** > **benefit society** organization providing life insurance, sickness benefit, etc., to its members, and often also social activities

be•nev•o•lent [bə-NEV-ə-lənt] *adjective* kindly, charitable > **be•nev'o•lence** *noun*

be•night•ed [bi-NĪ-tid] *adjective* ignorant, uncultured

be•nign [bi-NĪN] *adjective* kindly, mild, favorable > **be•nign'ly** *adverb*

bent 1 *pt./pp. of* **bend** ▷ *adjective* 2 curved 3 resolved (on) 4 determined ▷ *noun* 5 inclination, personal propensity

be•numb [bi-NUM] *verb transitive* make numb, deaden

ben•zene [BEN-zeen] *noun* one of group of related flammable liquids used in chemistry and as solvents, cleaning agents, etc.

be•queath [bi-KWEETH] *verb transitive* leave property, etc. by will > **be•quest** [bi-KWEST] *noun* 1 bequeathing 2 legacy

be•rate [bi-RAYT] *verb transitive* **-rat•ed, -rat•ing** scold harshly

be•reave [bi-REEV] *verb transitive* **-reaved, -reft, -reav•ing** deprive of, esp. by death
> **be•reave'ment** *noun* loss, esp. by death

be•ret [bə-RAY] *noun* round, close-fitting hat

ber•i•ber•i [ber-ee-BER-ee] *noun* tropical disease caused by vitamin B deficiency

ber•ke•li•um [bər-KEE-lee-əm] *noun* artificial radioactive metallic element

ber•ry [BER-ee] *noun, plural* **-ries** 1 small juicy stoneless fruit ▷ *verb intransitive* **-ried, -ry•ing** 2 look for, pick, berries

ber•serk [bər-SURK] *adjective* frenzied

berth [burth] *noun* 1 ship's mooring place 2 place to sleep on ship or train ▷ *verb transitive* 3 to moor

ber•yl [BER-əl] *noun* variety of crystalline mineral including aquamarine and emerald

be•ryl•li•um [bə-RIL-ee-əm] *noun* strong brittle metallic element

be•seech [bi-SEECH] *verb transitive* **-sought** *or* **-seeched, -seech•ing** entreat, implore

be•set [bi-SET] *verb transitive* **-set, -set•ting** assail, surround with danger, problems

be•side [bi-SĪD] *adverb, preposition* 1 by the side of, near 2 distinct from > **be•sides'** *adverb, preposition* in addition (to)

be•siege [bi-SEEJ] *verb transitive* **-sieged, -sieg•ing** surround (with armed forces, etc.)

be•sot•ted [bi-SOT-id] *adjective* 1 drunk 2 foolish 3 infatuated

besought *pt./pp. of* **beseech**

be•speak [bi-SPEEK] *verb transitive* **-spoke, -spok•en, -speak•ing** engage beforehand

best *adjective, adverb* 1 *sup. of* **good** *or* **well** ▷ *verb transitive* 2 defeat > **best seller** 1 book or other product sold in great numbers 2 author of one

DICTIONARY

b

THESAURUS

▷ *noun* 2 CURVE, angle, arc, arch, bow, corner, loop, turn, twist

beneath *preposition* 1 UNDER, below, lower than, underneath
2 INFERIOR TO, below, less than
3 UNWORTHY OF, unbefitting
▷ *adverb* 4 UNDERNEATH, below, in a lower place

benefactor *noun* SUPPORTER, backer, donor, helper, patron, philanthropist, sponsor, well-wisher

beneficial *adjective* HELPFUL, advantageous, benign, favorable, profitable, useful, valuable, wholesome, win-win (*informal*)

beneficiary *noun* RECIPIENT, heir, inheritor, payee, receiver

benefit *noun* 1 HELP, advantage, aid, asset, assistance, favor, good, profit
▷ *verb* 2 HELP, aid, assist, avail, enhance, further, improve, profit

benevolent *adjective* KIND, altruistic, benign, caring, charitable, generous, philanthropic

benign *adjective* 1 KINDLY, amiable, friendly, genial, kind, obliging, sympathetic
2 (*medical*) HARMLESS, curable, remediable

bent *adjective* 1 CURVED, angled, arched, bowed, crooked, hunched, stooped, twisted
2 ▷ **bent on** DETERMINED TO, disposed to, fixed on, inclined to, insistent on, predisposed to, resolved on, set on
▷ *noun* 3 INCLINATION, ability, aptitude, leaning, penchant, preference, propensity, tendency

bequeath *verb* LEAVE, bestow, endow, entrust, give, grant, hand down, impart, pass on, will

bequest *noun* LEGACY, bestowal, endowment, estate, gift, inheritance, settlement

berate *verb* SCOLD, castigate, censure, chide, criticize, harangue, rebuke, reprimand, reprove, tell off (*informal*), upbraid

bereavement *noun* LOSS, affliction, death, deprivation, misfortune, tribulation

bereft *adjective* DEPRIVED, devoid, lacking, parted from, robbed of, wanting

berserk *adverb* CRAZY, amok, enraged, frantic, frenzied, mad, raging, wild

berth *noun* 1 BUNK, bed, billet, hammock
2 (*nautical*) ANCHORAGE, dock, harbor, haven, pier, port, quay, wharf
▷ *verb* 3 (*nautical*) ANCHOR, dock, drop anchor, land, moor, tie up

beseech *verb* BEG, ask, call upon, entreat, implore, plead, pray, solicit

beset *verb* PLAGUE, bedevil, harass, pester, trouble

beside *preposition* 1 NEXT TO, abreast of, adjacent to, alongside, at the side of, close to, near, nearby, neighboring
2 ▷ **beside oneself** DISTRAUGHT, apoplectic, at the end of one's tether, demented, desperate, frantic, frenzied, out of one's mind, unhinged

besides *adverb* 1 TOO, also, as well, further, furthermore, in addition, into the bargain, moreover, otherwise, what's more
▷ *preposition* 2 APART FROM, barring, excepting, excluding, in addition to, other than, over and above, without

besiege *verb* 1 SURROUND, blockade, encircle, hem in, lay siege to, shut in
2 HARASS, badger, harry, hassle (*informal*), hound, nag, pester, plague

besotted *adjective* INFATUATED, doting,

or more of these books
bes•tial [BES-chəl] *adjective* like a beast, brutish > **bes•ti•al'i•ty** [-chee-AL-i-tee] *noun*
be•stir [bi-STUR] *verb transitive* **-stirred, -stir•ring** rouse (oneself) to activity
be•stow [bi-STOH] *verb transitive* give, confer > **be•stow'al** *noun*
be•stride [bi-STRĪD] *verb transitive* **-strode** *or* **-strid, -strid•den** *or* **-strid, -strid•ing** sit or stand over with legs apart, mount horse
bet *verb* **bet** *or* **bet•ted, bet•ting** 1 agree to pay money, etc. if wrong (or win if right) in guessing result of contest, etc. ▷ *noun* 2 money risked in this way
be•tel [BEET-l] *noun* species of pepper > **betel nut** the nut of the betel palm
bête noire [bet NWAHR] *noun, plural* **bêtes noires** Fr. pet aversion
be•tide [bi-TĪD] *verb* **-tid•ed, -tid•ing** happen (to)
be•to•ken [bi-TOH-kən] *verb transitive* be a sign of
be•tray [bi-TRAY] *verb transitive* 1 be disloyal to, esp. by assisting an enemy 2 reveal, divulge 3 show signs of > **be•tray'al** *noun* > **be•tray'er** *noun*
be•troth [bi-TROHTH] *verb transitive* promise to marry > **be•troth'al** *noun* > **be•trothed'** *noun, adjective*
bet•ter [BET-ər] *adjective, adverb* 1 *comp. of* **good** *or* **well** ▷ *verb* 2 improve > **bet'ter•ment** *noun*
be•tween [bi-TWEEN] *preposition, adverb* 1 in the intermediate part in space or time 2 indicating reciprocal relation or comparison
be•twixt [bi-TWIKST] *preposition, adverb* (*obsolete*) between
bev•el [BEV-əl] *noun* 1 surface not at right angle to another 2 slant ▷ *verb* **-eled, -el•ing** 3 slope, slant 4 cut on slant > **bev'eled** *adjective* slanted
bev•er•age [BEV-rij] *noun* drink
bev•y [BEV-ee] *noun, plural* **bev•ies** flock or group
be•wail [bi-WAYL] *verb transitive* lament
be•ware [bi-WAIR] *verb intransitive* be on one's guard, take care
be•wil•der [bi-WIL-dər] *verb transitive* puzzle, confuse > **be•wil'der•ing** *adjective* > **be•wil'der•ment** *noun*
be•witch [bi-WICH] *verb transitive* 1 cast spell over 2 charm, fascinate > **be•witch'ing** *adjective*
be•yond [bee-OND] *adverb* 1 farther away 2 besides ▷ *preposition* 3 on the farther side of 4 later than 5 surpassing, out of reach of
Bh *chem.* bohrium
Bi *chem.* bismuth
bi•as [BĪ-əs] *noun, plural* **-as•es** 1 personal slant 2 inclination or preference 3 onesided inclination ▷ *verb transitive* **-ased, -as•ing** 4 influence, affect > **bi'ased** *adjective* prejudiced
bib *noun* 1 cloth put under child's chin to protect clothes when eating 2 part of apron or overalls above waist
Bi•ble [BĪ-bəl] *noun* the sacred writings of Christianity and Judaism > **bible** *noun* book or journal considered unchallengeably

DICTIONARY • THESAURUS

hypnotized, smitten, spellbound
best *adjective* 1 FINEST, foremost, leading, most excellent, outstanding, pre-eminent, principal, supreme, unsurpassed
▷ *adverb* 2 MOST HIGHLY, extremely, greatly, most deeply, most fully
▷ *noun* 3 FINEST, cream, crème de la crème (*French*), elite, flower, pick, prime, top
bestial *adjective* BRUTAL, barbaric, beastly, brutish, inhuman, savage, sordid
bestow *verb* PRESENT, award, commit, give, grant, hand out, impart, lavish
bet *noun* 1 GAMBLE, long shot, risk, speculation, stake, venture, wager
▷ *verb* 2 GAMBLE, chance, hazard, risk, speculate, stake, venture, wager
betoken *verb* INDICATE, bode, denote, promise, represent, signify, suggest
betray *verb* 1 BE DISLOYAL, be treacherous, be unfaithful, break one's promise, double-cross (*informal*), inform on *or* inform against, sell out (*informal*), stab in the back
2 GIVE AWAY, disclose, divulge, expose, let slip, reveal, uncover, unmask
betrayal *noun* 1 DISLOYALTY, back-stabbing (*informal*), deception, double-cross (*informal*), sell-out (*informal*), treachery, treason, trickery
2 GIVING AWAY, disclosure, divulgence, revelation
better *adjective* 1 SUPERIOR, excelling, finer, greater, higher-quality, more desirable, preferable, surpassing
2 WELL, cured, fully recovered, on the mend (*informal*), recovering, stronger
▷ *adverb* 3 IN A MORE EXCELLENT MANNER, in a superior way, more advantageously, more attractively, more competently, more effectively
4 TO A GREATER DEGREE, more completely, more thoroughly
▷ *verb* 5 IMPROVE, enhance, further, raise
between *preposition* AMIDST, among, betwixt, in the middle of, mid
beverage *noun* DRINK, liquid, liquor, refreshment
bevy *noun* GROUP, band, bunch (*informal*), collection, company, crowd, gathering, pack, troupe
bewail *verb* LAMENT, bemoan, cry over, deplore, grieve for, moan, mourn, regret
beware *verb* BE CAREFUL, be cautious, be wary, guard against, heed, look out, mind, take heed, watch out
bewilder *verb* CONFOUND, baffle, bemuse, confuse, flummox, mystify, nonplus, perplex, puzzle
bewildered *adjective* CONFUSED, at a loss, at sea, baffled, flummoxed, mystified, nonplussed, perplexed, puzzled
bewitch *verb* ENCHANT, beguile, captivate, charm, enrapture, entrance, fascinate, hypnotize
bewitched *adjective* ENCHANTED, charmed, entranced, fascinated, mesmerized, spellbound, under a spell
beyond *preposition* 1 PAST, above, apart from, at a distance, away from, over
2 EXCEEDING, out of reach of, superior to, surpassing
bias *noun* 1 PREJUDICE, favoritism, inclination, leaning, partiality, tendency
▷ *verb* 2 PREJUDICE, distort, influence, predispose, slant, sway, twist, warp, weight

authoritative > **Bib•li•cal** [BIB-li-kəl] *adjective*
bib•li•og•ra•phy [bib-lee-OG-rə-fee] *noun, plural* **-phies** 1 list of books on a subject 2 history and description of books > **bib•li•og'ra•pher** *noun*
bib•li•o•phile [BIB-lee-ə-fīl] *noun* lover, collector of books
bib•u•lous [BIB-yə-ləs] *adjective* given to drinking
bi•cam•er•al [bī-KAM-ər-əl] *adjective* (of a legislature) having two chambers
bi•car•bo•nate [bī-KAHR-bə-nit] *noun* chemical compound releasing carbon dioxide when mixed with acid
bi•cen•ten•ni•al [bī-sen-TEN-ee-əl] *noun* 1 two hundredth anniversary 2 its celebration ▷ *adjective* 3 relating to this
bi•ceps [BĪ-seps] *noun* two-headed muscle, esp. muscle of upper arm
bick•er [BIK-ər] *verb intransitive, noun* quarrel over petty things > **bick'er•ing** *noun*
bi•cy•cle [BĪ-si-kəl] *noun* vehicle with two wheels, one in front of other, pedaled by rider > **bi'cy•clist** *noun*
bid *verb transitive* **bade, bid** *or* **bid•den, bid•ding** 1 offer 2 say 3 command 4 invite ▷ *noun* 5 offer, esp. of price 6 try > **bid'der** *noun*
bide [bīd] *verb intransitive* **bid•ed, bid•ing** 1 remain 2 dwell ▷ *verb transitive* **bid•ed, bid•ing** 3 await > **bid'ing** *noun*
bi•det [bi-DAY] *noun* low basin for washing genital area
bi•en•ni•al [bī-EN-ee-əl] *adjective* 1 happening every two years 2 lasting two years ▷ *noun* 3 plant living two years > **bi•en'ni•um** [-əm] *noun* period of two years
bier [beer] *noun* 1 frame for bearing dead to grave 2 stand for holding dead 3 coffin and its stand
bi•fo•cal [bī-FOH-kəl] *adjective* having two different focal lengths > **bi•fo'cals** *plural noun* eyeglasses having bifocal lenses for near and distant vision
big *adjective* **big•ger, big•gest** of great or considerable size, height, number, power, etc. > **big cheese** (*informal*) important person > **big'head** *noun* (*informal*) conceit > **big'head'ed** *adjective* > **big shot** (*informal*) important or influential person > **big'-time** *adverb* (*informal*) very much, to a great extent
big•a•my [BIG-ə-mee] *noun, plural* **-mies** crime of marrying a person while one is still legally married to someone else > **big'a•mist** *noun*
bight [bīt] *noun* 1 curve or loop in rope 2 long curved shoreline or water bounded by it
big•ot [BIG-ət] *noun* person intolerant or not receptive to ideas of others (esp. on religion, race, etc.) > **big'ot•ed** *adjective* > **big'ot•ry** *noun*
bike [bīk] *noun* short for bicycle or motor bike
bi•ki•ni [bi-KEE-nee] *noun, plural* **-nis** woman's brief two-piece swimming costume
bi•lat•er•al [bī-LAT-ər-əl] *adjective* two-sided
bile [bīl] *noun* 1 fluid secreted by the liver 2 anger, ill temper > **bil•ious** [BIL-yəs] *adjective* nauseous, nauseating > **bil'ious•ness** *noun*
bilge [bilj] *noun* 1 bottom of ship's hull 2 dirty water collecting there 3 (*informal*) nonsense
bi•lin•gual [bī-LING-gwəl] *adjective* speaking, or written in, two languages > **bi•lin'gual•ism** *noun*
bill¹ *noun* 1 written account of charges 2 draft of legislative act 3 poster 4 commercial document 5 paper money ▷ *verb transitive* 6 present account of charges 7 announce by advertisement > **bill'able** *adjective* referring to time worked on behalf of a client and for which that client is to pay > **bill'ing** *noun* degree of importance (esp. in theater, etc.) > **bill'board** *noun* large panel for outdoor advertising
bill² *noun* 1 bird's beak ▷ *verb intransitive* 2 touch bills, as doves 3 caress affectionately
bil•let [BIL-it] *noun* 1 civilian quarters for troops 2 resting place ▷ *verb transitive* 3 quarter, as troops
bil•let-doux [bil-ee-DOO] *noun, plural* **billets-doux** [bil-ee-DOOZ] love letter

DICTIONARY **b** THESAURUS

---

biased *adjective* PREJUDICED, distorted, one-sided, partial, slanted, weighted
bicker *verb* QUARREL, argue, disagree, dispute, fight, squabble, wrangle
bid *verb* 1 OFFER, proffer, propose, submit, tender
2 SAY, call, greet, tell, wish
3 TELL, ask, command, direct, instruct, order, require
▷ *noun* 4 OFFER, advance, amount, price, proposal, sum, tender
5 ATTEMPT, crack (*informal*), effort, go (*informal*), stab (*informal*), try
bidding *noun* ORDER, beck and call, command, direction, instruction, request, summons
big *adjective* 1 LARGE, enormous, extensive, great, huge, immense, massive, substantial, supersize, vast
2 IMPORTANT, eminent, influential, leading, main, powerful, prominent, significant
3 GROWN-UP, adult, elder, grown, mature
4 GENEROUS, altruistic, benevolent, gracious, magnanimous, noble, unselfish
big cheese *noun* (*informal*) MANAGER, alpha male, boss (*informal*), bossman (*slang*), foreman, head honcho (*slang*), overseer, superintendent, supervisor
bighead *noun* (*informal*) BOASTER, braggart, know-all (*informal*)
bigheaded *adjective* BOASTFUL, arrogant, cocky, conceited, egotistic, immodest, overconfident, swollen-headed
bigot *noun* FANATIC, racist, sectarian, zealot
bigoted *adjective* INTOLERANT, biased, dogmatic, narrow-minded, opinionated, prejudiced, sectarian
bigotry *noun* INTOLERANCE, bias, discrimination, dogmatism, fanaticism, narrow-mindedness, prejudice, sectarianism
bill¹ *noun* 1 CHARGES, account, invoice, reckoning, score, statement, tally
2 PROPOSAL, measure, piece of legislation, projected law
3 ADVERTISEMENT, bulletin, circular, handbill, handout, leaflet, notice, placard, poster
4 LIST, agenda, card, catalog, inventory, listing, program, roster, schedule
▷ *verb* 5 CHARGE, debit, invoice
6 ADVERTISE, announce, give advance notice of, post
bill² *noun* BEAK, mandible, neb (*archaic* or *dialect*), nib

bil•liards [BIL-yərdz] *noun* game played on table with balls and cues
bil•lion [BIL-yən] *noun* thousand millions
bil•low [BIL-oh] *noun* 1 great swelling wave ▷ *verb intransitive* 2 surge 3 swell out
bi•month•ly [bī-MUNTH-lee] *adverb, adjective* 1 every two months 2 oft. twice a month
bin *noun* box, etc. used for storage
bi•na•ry [BĪ-nə-ree] *adjective* 1 composed of, characterized by, two 2 dual
bind [bīnd] *verb transitive* **bound, bind•ing** 1 tie fast 2 tie around, gird 3 tie together 4 oblige 5 seal 6 constrain 7 bandage 8 cohere 9 unite 10 put (book) into cover > **bind'er** *noun* one who, or that which binds > **bind'er•y** *noun, plural* **-er•ies** > **bind'ing** *noun* 1 cover of book 2 tape for hem, etc.
binge [binj] *noun (informal)* 1 excessive indulgence in eating or drinking 2 spree
bin•go [BING-goh] *noun* game of chance in which numbers drawn are matched with those on a card
bin•na•cle [BIN-ə-kəl] *noun* box holding ship's compass
bin•oc•u•lar [bə-NOK-yə-lər] *adjective* seeing with, made for, both eyes > **bin•oc'u•lars** *plural noun* telescope made for both eyes
bi•no•mi•al [bī-NOH-mee-əl] *adjective, noun* (denoting) algebraic expression consisting of two terms
bio- *combining form* life or living organisms: *biology*
bi•o•de•fense [bī-oh-di-FENS, bī-oh-DEE-fens] *noun* procedures used to defend against attacks involving biological weapons
bi•o•de•grad•a•ble [bī-oh-di-GRAY-də-bəl] *adjective* capable of decomposition by natural means
bi•o•di•ver•si•ty [bī-oh-dī-VURZ-ə-tee] *noun* existence of a wide variety of species in their natural environment
bi•og•ra•phy [bī-OG-rə-fee] *noun, plural* **-phies** story of one person's life > **bi•og'ra•pher** *noun* > **bi•o•graph'i•cal** *adjective*
bi•ol•o•gy [bī-OL-ə-jee] *noun* study of living organisms > **bi•o•log'i•cal** *adjective* > **bi•ol'o•gist** *noun*
bi•o•met•ric [bī-oh-MET-rik] *adjective* relating to digital scanning of physiological or behavioral traits of individuals for identification
bi•on•ics [bī-ON-iks] *noun* study of relation of biological and electronic processes > **bionic** *adjective* having physical functions controlled, augmented by electronic equipment
bi•op•sy [BĪ-op-see] *noun, plural* **-sies** examination of tissue removed surgically from a living body
bi•o•rhythm [BĪ-oh-rith-əm] *noun* cyclically recurring pattern of physiological states
bi•o•se•cu•ri•ty [bī-oh-si-KYOOR-i-tee] *noun* precautions taken to protect against the spread of harmful organisms and diseases
bi•o•ter•ror•ism [bī-oh-TER-ər-iz-əm] *noun* use of viruses, bacteria, etc by terrorists > **bi•o•ter'ror•ist** *noun*
bi•par•ti•san [bī-PAHR-tə-zən] *adjective* consisting of or supported by two political parties
bi•par•tite [bī-PAHR-tīt] *adjective* consisting of two parts, parties
bi•ped [BĪ-ped] *noun* two-footed animal
bi•plane [BĪ-playn] *noun* airplane with two pairs of wings
birch [burch] *noun* 1 tree with silvery bark 2 rod for punishment, made of birch twigs ▷ *verb transitive* 3 flog > **birch'en** *adjective*
bird [burd] *noun* 1 feathered animal ▷ *verb intransitive* 2 observe or identify wild birds as a hobby > **bird'brain** *noun* stupid person
bird•ie [BUR-dee] *noun, verb golf* (make) score of one under par for a hole
bi•ret•ta [bə-RET-ə] *noun* square cap with three or four ridges worn usu. by Catholic clergy
birth [burth] *noun* 1 bearing, or the being born, of offspring 2 parentage, origin > **birth control** limitation of childbearing usu. by artificial means > **birth'mark** *noun* blemish, usu. dark, formed on skin before birth > **birth'right** *noun* right one has by birth
bis•cuit [BIS-kit] *noun* quick bread made from spoonful of rolled dough
bi•sect [bī-SEKT] *verb transitive* divide into two equal parts
bi•sex•ual [bī-SEK-shoo-əl] *adjective* 1 sexually attracted to both men and women 2 of both sexes
bish•op [BISH-əp] *noun* 1 clergyman typically governing diocese 2 chess piece > **bish'op•ric** *noun* diocese or office of a bishop
bis•muth [BIZ-məth] *noun* reddish-white metal used in medicine, etc.
bi•son [BĪ-sən] *noun* 1 large wild ox 2 N Amer. buffalo
bis•tro [BIS-troh] *noun, plural* **-tros** small restaurant
bit[1] *noun* 1 fragment, piece 2 biting, cutting part of tool 3 mouthpiece of horse's bridle
bit[2] *pt./pp. of* **bite**

billet *verb* 1 QUARTER, accommodate, berth, station
▷ *noun* 2 QUARTERS, accommodation, barracks, lodging
billow *noun* 1 WAVE, breaker, crest, roller, surge, swell, tide
▷ *verb* 2 SURGE, balloon, belly, puff up, rise up, roll, swell
bind *verb* 1 SECURE, fasten, hitch, lash, strap, tie
2 OBLIGE, compel, constrain, engage, force, necessitate, require
▷ *noun (informal)* 3 NUISANCE, bore, drag (*informal*), pain in the neck (*informal*)
4 DIFFICULTY, dilemma, quandary, spot (*informal*)
binding *adjective* COMPULSORY, indissoluble, irrevocable, mandatory, necessary, obligatory, unalterable
binge *noun (informal)* BOUT, feast, fling, orgy, spree
biography *noun* LIFE STORY, account, curriculum vitae, CV, life, memoir, profile, record
birth *noun* 1 CHILDBIRTH, delivery, nativity, parturition
2 ANCESTRY, background, blood, breeding, lineage, parentage, pedigree, stock
bisect *verb* CUT IN TWO, cross, cut across, divide in two, halve, intersect, separate, split

bit[3] *noun computing* smallest unit of information

bitch [bich] *noun* 1 female dog, fox or wolf 2 (*offensive*) spiteful woman 3 (*informal*) complaint ▷ *verb intransitive* (*informal*) 4 complain > **bitch'y** *adjective* **bitch•i•er, bitch•i•est** > **bitch'i•ness** *noun*

bite [bīt] *verb transitive* **bit, bit•ten, bit•ing** 1 cut into esp. with teeth 2 grip 3 rise to bait 4 etch with acid ▷ *noun* 5 act of biting 6 wound so made 7 mouthful > **biting** *adjective* having power to bite

bit•ter [BIT-ər] *adjective* **-er, -est** 1 sharp, sour tasting 2 unpleasant 3 (of person) angry, resentful 4 sarcastic > **bit'ter•ly** *adverb* > **bit'ter•ness** *noun* > **bit'ters** *plural noun* essence of bitter usu. aromatic herbs > **bitter end** final extremity

bi•tu•men [bi-TOO-mən] *noun* viscous substance occurring in asphalt, tar, etc. > **bi•tu'mi•nous coal** coal yielding much bitumen on burning

bi•valve [BĪ-valv] *adjective* 1 having a double shell ▷ *noun* 2 mollusk with such shell

biv•ou•ac [BIV-oo-ak] *noun* 1 temporary encampment of soldiers, hikers, etc. ▷ *verb intransitive* **-acked, -ack•ing** 2 pass the night in temporary camp

bi•zarre [bi-ZAHR] *adjective* unusual, weird

Bk *chem.* berkelium

blab *verb* **blabbed, blab•bing** 1 reveal secrets 2 chatter idly ▷ *noun* 3 chatter > **blab•ber** *verb* **-bered, -ber•ing** blab

black [blak] *adjective* 1 of the darkest color 2 without light 3 dark 4 evil 5 somber 6 dishonorable ▷ *noun* 7 darkest color 8 black dye, clothing, etc. 9 (**Black**) person of dark-skinned race 10 African-American > **black'en** *verb* > **black'ing** *noun* substance used for blacking and cleaning leather, etc. > **black'ball** *verb transitive* vote against, exclude > **black'bird** *noun* common American black bird > **black'board** *noun* dark-colored surface for writing on with chalk > **black box** (*informal*) *name for* **flight recorder** > **black economy** illegally undeclared income > **black'head** *noun* dark, fatty plug blocking pore in skin > **black'list** *noun* 1 list of people, organizations considered suspicious, untrustworthy, etc. ▷ *verb transitive* 2 put on blacklist > **Black Ma•ri•a** [mə-RĪ-ə] police van for transporting prisoners > **black market** illegal buying and selling of goods > **black widow** highly poisonous N Amer. spider

black•guard [BLAG-ahrd] *noun* scoundrel

black•mail [BLAK-mayl] *verb transitive* 1 extort money from (a person) by threats ▷ *noun* 2 act of blackmailing 3 money extorted thus > **black'mail•er** *noun*

black•out [BLAK-owt] *noun* 1 complete failure of electricity supply 2 sudden turning off of all stagelights 3 state of temporary unconsciousness 4 obscuring of all lights as precaution against night air attack > **black out** *verb intransitive* lose consciousness, memory, or vision temporarily

black•smith [BLAK-smith] *noun* smith who works in iron

blad•der [BLAD-ər] *noun* membranous bag to contain liquid, esp. urinary bladder

blade [blayd] *noun* 1 edge, cutting part of knife or tool 2 leaf of grass, etc. 3 sword 4 (*obsolete*) dashing fellow 5 flat of oar

blame [blaym] *noun* 1 censure 2 culpability

---

bit[1] *noun* 1 PIECE, crumb, fragment, grain, morsel, part, scrap, speck
2 *noun* CURB, brake, check, restraint, snaffle

bitch *noun* 1 (*informal*) COMPLAINT, gripe (*informal*), grouse, grumble, objection, protest
▷ *verb* 2 (*informal*) COMPLAIN, bemoan, gripe (*informal*), grouse, grumble, lament, object

bitchy *adjective* (*informal*) SPITEFUL, backbiting, catty (*informal*), mean, nasty, snide, vindictive

bite *verb* 1 CUT, chew, gnaw, nip, pierce, pinch, snap, tear, wound
▷ *noun* 2 WOUND, nip, pinch, prick, smarting, sting, tooth marks
3 SNACK, food, light meal, morsel, mouthful, piece, refreshment, taste

biting *adjective* 1 PIERCING, bitter, cutting, harsh, penetrating, sharp
2 SARCASTIC, caustic, cutting, incisive, mordant, scathing, stinging, trenchant, vitriolic

bitter *adjective* 1 SOUR, acid, acrid, astringent, harsh, sharp, tart, unsweetened, vinegary
2 RESENTFUL, acrimonious, begrudging, hostile, sore, sour, sullen
3 FREEZING, biting, fierce, intense, severe, stinging

bitterness *noun* 1 SOURNESS, acerbity, acidity, sharpness, tartness
2 RESENTMENT, acrimony, animosity, asperity, grudge, hostility, rancor, sarcasm

bizarre *adjective* STRANGE, eccentric, extraordinary, fantastic, freakish, ludicrous, outlandish, peculiar, unusual, weird, zany

blab *verb* TELL, blurt out, disclose, divulge, give away, let slip, let the cat out of the bag, reveal, spill the beans (*informal*)

black *adjective* 1 DARK, dusky, ebony, jet, raven, sable, swarthy
2 HOPELESS, depressing, dismal, foreboding, gloomy, ominous, sad, somber
3 ANGRY, furious, hostile, menacing, resentful, sullen, threatening
4 WICKED, bad, evil, iniquitous, nefarious, villainous
▷ *verb* 5 BOYCOTT, ban, bar, blacklist

blacken *verb* 1 DARKEN, befoul, begrime, cloud, dirty, make black, smudge, soil
2 DISCREDIT, defame, denigrate, malign, slander, smear, smirch, vilify

blacklist *verb* EXCLUDE, ban, bar, boycott, debar, expel, reject, snub

black magic *noun* WITCHCRAFT, black art, diabolism, necromancy, sorcery, voodoo, wizardry

blackmail *noun* 1 THREAT, extortion, hush money (*slang*), intimidation, ransom
▷ *verb* 2 THREATEN, coerce, compel, demand, extort, hold to ransom, intimidate, squeeze

blackness *noun* DARKNESS, duskiness, gloom, murkiness, swarthiness

blackout *noun* 1 UNCONSCIOUSNESS, coma, faint, loss of consciousness, oblivion, swoon
2 NONCOMMUNICATION, censorship, radio silence, secrecy, suppression, withholding news

▷ *verb transitive* **blamed, blam•ing** 3 find fault with 4 censure > **blame'less** *adjective* > **blame'wor•thy** [-wur-*thee*] *adjective*

blanch *verb* 1 whiten, bleach, take color out of 2 (of foodstuffs) briefly boil or fry 3 turn pale

bland *adjective* **-er, -est** 1 devoid of distinctive characteristics 2 smooth in manner

blan'dish *verb transitive* 1 coax 2 flatter > **bland'ish•ment** *noun*

blank *adjective* 1 without marks or writing 2 empty 3 vacant, confused 4 (of verse) without rhyme ▷ *noun* 5 empty space 6 void 7 cartridge containing no bullet

blan•ket [BLANG-kit] *noun* 1 thick woven covering for bed, horse, etc. 2 concealing cover ▷ *verb transitive* 3 cover with blanket 4 cover, stifle

blare [blair] *verb* **blared, blar•ing** 1 sound loudly and harshly ▷ *noun* 2 such sound

blar•ney [BLAHR-nee] *noun* flattering talk

blasé [blah-ZAY] *adjective* 1 indifferent through familiarity 2 bored

blas•pheme [blas-FEEM] *verb* show contempt for God or sacred things, esp. in speech > **blas•phem'er** *noun* > **blas'phe•mous** [-fə-məs] *adjective* > **blas'phe•my** *noun*

blast *noun* 1 explosion 2 high-pressure wave of air coming from an explosion 3 current of air 4 gust of wind or air 5 loud sound 6 reprimand 7 (*slang*) riotous party ▷ *verb transitive* 8 blow up 9 remove, open, etc. by explosion 10 blight 11 ruin > **blast furnace** furnace for smelting ore, using blast of heated air

bla•tant [BLAYT-nt] *adjective* obvious > **bla'tan•cy** *noun*

blaze[1] [blayz] *noun* 1 strong fire or flame 2 brightness 3 outburst ▷ *verb intransitive* **blazed, blaz•ing** 4 burn strongly 5 be very angry

blaze[2] *verb* **blazed, blaz•ing** 1 (mark trees to) establish trail ▷ *noun* 2 mark on tree 3 white mark on horse's face

blaze[3] *verb transitive* **blazed, blaz•ing** proclaim

blaz•er [BLAY-zər] *noun* type of sports jacket

bla•zon [BLAY-zən] *verb transitive* make public, proclaim

bleach [bleech] *verb* 1 make or become white ▷ *noun* 2 bleaching substance

bleak [bleek] *adjective* **-er, -est** 1 cold and cheerless 2 exposed > **bleak'ly** *adverb* > **bleak'ness** *noun*

blear•y [BLEER-ee] *adjective* **blear•i•er, blear•i•est** (of the eyes) dimmed, as with tears, sleep

bleat [bleet] *verb* 1 cry, as sheep 2 say, speak, plaintively ▷ *noun* 3 sheep's cry

bleed *verb* **bled, bleed•ing** 1 lose blood 2 draw blood or liquid from 3 extort money from

bleep *noun* 1 short high-pitched sound e.g. from electronic device ▷ *verb transitive* 2 obscure sound e.g. of TV program by making bleep > **bleep•er** *noun* small portable radio receiver that makes a bleeping signal

blem'ish *noun* 1 defect 2 stain ▷ *verb transitive* 3 make (something) defective, dirty, etc. > **blem'ished** *adjective*

blend *verb transitive* 1 mix ▷ *noun* 2 mixture

DICTIONARY • THESAURUS

---

blame *verb* 1 HOLD RESPONSIBLE, accuse, censure, chide, condemn, criticize, find fault with, reproach
▷ *noun* 2 RESPONSIBILITY, accountability, culpability, fault, guilt, liability, onus

blameless *adjective* INNOCENT, above suspicion, clean, faultless, guiltless, immaculate, impeccable, irreproachable, perfect, unblemished, virtuous

blameworthy *adjective* REPREHENSIBLE, discreditable, disreputable, indefensible, inexcusable, iniquitous, reproachable, shameful

bland *adjective* DULL, boring, flat, humdrum, insipid, tasteless, unexciting, uninspiring, vapid

blank *adjective* 1 UNMARKED, bare, clean, clear, empty, plain, void, white
2 EXPRESSIONLESS, deadpan, empty, impassive, poker-faced (*informal*), vacant, vague
▷ *noun* 3 EMPTY SPACE, emptiness, gap, nothingness, space, vacancy, vacuum, void

blanket *noun* 1 COVER, coverlet, rug
2 COVERING, carpet, cloak, coat, layer, mantle, sheet
▷ *verb* 3 COVER, cloak, coat, conceal, hide, mask, obscure, suppress

blare *verb* SOUND OUT, blast, clamor, clang, resound, roar, scream, trumpet

blasé *adjective* INDIFFERENT, apathetic, lukewarm, nonchalant, offhand, unconcerned

blaspheme *verb* CURSE, abuse, damn, desecrate, execrate, profane, revile, swear

blasphemous *adjective* IRREVERENT, godless, impious, irreligious, profane, sacrilegious, ungodly

blasphemy *noun* IRREVERENCE, cursing, desecration, execration, impiety, profanity, sacrilege, swearing

blast *noun* 1 EXPLOSION, bang, burst, crash, detonation, discharge, eruption, outburst, salvo, volley
2 GUST, gale, squall, storm, strong breeze, tempest
3 BLARE, blow, clang, honk, peal, scream, toot, wail
▷ *verb* 4 BLOW UP, break up, burst, demolish, destroy, explode, put paid to, ruin, shatter

blatant *adjective* OBVIOUS, brazen, conspicuous, flagrant, glaring, obtrusive, ostentatious, overt

blaze[1] *noun* 1 FIRE, bonfire, conflagration, flames
2 GLARE, beam, brilliance, flare, flash, gleam, glitter, glow, light, radiance
▷ *verb* 3 BURN, fire, flame
4 SHINE, beam, flare, flash, glare, gleam, glow

bleach *verb* WHITEN, blanch, fade, grow pale, lighten, wash out

bleak *adjective* 1 EXPOSED, bare, barren, desolate, unsheltered, weather-beaten, windswept
2 DISMAL, cheerless, depressing, discouraging, dreary, gloomy, grim, hopeless, joyless, somber

bleary *adjective* DIM, blurred, blurry, foggy, fuzzy, hazy, indistinct, misty, murky

bleed *verb* 1 LOSE BLOOD, flow, gush, ooze, run, shed blood, spurt
2 DRAW BLOOD *or* TAKE BLOOD, extract, leech
3 (*informal*) EXTORT, drain, exhaust, fleece, milk, squeeze

blemish *noun* 1 MARK, blot, defect, disfigurement, fault, flaw, imperfection, smudge, stain, taint

> **blend'er** *noun* one who, that which blends, esp. electrical kitchen appliance for mixing food

bless *verb transitive* **blessed** *or* **blest, bless•ing** 1 consecrate 2 give thanks to 3 ask God's favor for 4 (*usually passive*) endow (with) 5 glorify 6 make happy > **bless'ed** [-id] *adjective* > **blessing** *noun* 1 (ceremony asking for) God's protection, aid 2 short prayer 3 approval 4 welcome event, benefit

blew *pt. of* **blow**

blight [blīt] *noun* 1 plant disease 2 harmful influence ▷ *verb transitive* 3 injure as with blight

blimp *noun* small, nonrigid airship used for observing

blind [blīnd] *adjective* 1 unable to see 2 heedless, random 3 dim 4 closed at one end 5 (*slang*) very drunk ▷ *verb transitive* 6 deprive of sight ▷ *noun* 7 something cutting off light 8 window screen 9 pretext 10 place of concealment for hunters > **blind'ly** *adverb* > **blind'ness** *noun* > **blind flying** navigation of aircraft by use of instruments alone > **blind'fold** *verb transitive* cover the eyes of so as to prevent vision ▷ *noun, adjective* > **blind•man's buff** game in which one player is blindfolded

blink [blingk] *verb intransitive* 1 wink 2 twinkle 3 shine intermittently ▷ *noun* 4 gleam > **blink'ers** *plural noun* leather flaps to prevent horse from seeing to the side **blink at** see, know about, but ignore **on the blink** (*informal*) not working (properly)

blip *noun* 1 repetitive sound or visible pulse, e.g. on radar screen ▷ *verb transitive* **blipped, blip•ping** 2 bleep

bliss *noun* perfect happiness > **bliss'ful** *adjective* > **bliss'ful•ly** *adverb*

blis•ter [BLIS-tər] *noun* 1 bubble on skin 2 surface swelling, e.g. on paint ▷ *verb* 3 form blisters (on) > **blis'ter•ing** *adjective* (of verbal attack) bitter > **blister pack** package for goods with hard, raised, transparent cover

blithe [blīth] *adjective* 1 happy, gay 2 heedless > **blithe'ly** *adverb* > **blithe'ness** *noun*

blitz [blits] *noun* sudden, concentrated attack > **blitz'krieg** [-kreeg] *noun* 1 sudden concentrated military attack 2 war conducted in this way

bliz•zard [BLIZ-ərd] *noun* blinding storm of wind and snow

bloat [bloht] *verb* 1 puff or swell out ▷ *noun* 2 distention of stomach of cow, etc. by gas > **bloat'ed** *adjective* swollen

blob *noun* 1 soft mass, esp. drop of liquid 2 shapeless form

bloc [blok] *noun* (political) grouping of people or countries

block [blok] *noun* 1 solid piece of wood, stone, etc. 2 *hist.* rectangular piece of wood on which people were beheaded 3 obstacle 4 stoppage 5 pulley with frame 6 group of buildings 7 urban area enclosed by intersecting streets ▷ *verb transitive* 8 obstruct, stop up 9 shape on block 10 sketch (in) > **block'age** *noun*

DICTIONARY **b** THESAURUS

▷ *verb* 2 STAIN, damage, disfigure, impair, injure, mar, mark, spoil, sully, taint, tarnish

blend *verb* 1 MIX, amalgamate, combine, compound, merge, mingle, unite
2 GO WELL, complement, fit, go with, harmonize, suit
▷ *noun* 3 MIXTURE, alloy, amalgamation, combination, compound, concoction, mix, synthesis, union

bless *verb* 1 SANCTIFY, anoint, consecrate, dedicate, exalt, hallow, ordain
2 GRANT, bestow, favor, give, grace, provide

blessed *adjective* HOLY, adored, beatified, divine, hallowed, revered, sacred, sanctified

blessing *noun* 1 BENEDICTION, benison, commendation, consecration, dedication, grace, invocation, thanksgiving
2 APPROVAL, backing, consent, favor, good wishes, leave, permission, sanction, support
3 BENEFIT, favor, gift, godsend, good fortune, help, kindness, service, windfall

blight *noun* 1 CURSE, affliction, bane, contamination, corruption, evil, plague, pollution, scourge, woe
2 DISEASE, canker, decay, fungus, infestation, mildew, pest, pestilence, rot
▷ *verb* 3 FRUSTRATE, crush, dash, disappoint, mar, ruin, spoil, undo, wreck

blind *adjective* 1 SIGHTLESS, eyeless, unseeing, unsighted, visionless
2 UNAWARE OF, careless, heedless, ignorant, inattentive, inconsiderate, indifferent, insensitive, oblivious, unconscious of
3 UNREASONING, indiscriminate, prejudiced
▷ *noun* 4 COVER, camouflage, cloak, façade, feint, front, mask, masquerade, screen, smoke screen

blindly *adverb* 1 THOUGHTLESSLY, carelessly, heedlessly, inconsiderately, recklessly, senselessly
2 AIMLESSLY, at random, indiscriminately, instinctively

blink *verb* 1 WINK, bat, flutter
2 FLICKER, flash, gleam, glimmer, shine, twinkle, wink
▷ *noun* 3 ▷ **on the blink** (*slang*) NOT WORKING *or* NOT WORKING PROPERLY, faulty, malfunctioning, out of action, out of order, playing up

bliss *noun* JOY, beatitude, blessedness, blissfulness, ecstasy, euphoria, felicity, gladness, happiness, heaven, nirvana, paradise, rapture

blissful *adjective* JOYFUL, ecstatic, elated, enraptured, euphoric, happy, heavenly (*informal*), rapturous

blister *noun* SORE, abscess, boil, carbuncle, cyst, pimple, pustule, swelling

blithe *adjective* HEEDLESS, careless, casual, indifferent, nonchalant, thoughtless, unconcerned, untroubled

blitz *noun* ATTACK, assault, blitzkrieg, bombardment, campaign, offensive, onslaught, raid, strike

blizzard *noun* SNOWSTORM, blast, gale, squall, storm, tempest

bloat *verb* PUFF UP, balloon, blow up, dilate, distend, enlarge, expand, inflate, swell

blob *noun* DROP, ball, bead, bubble, dab, droplet, globule, lump, mass

bloc *noun* GROUP, alliance, axis, coalition, faction, league, union

block *noun* 1 PIECE, bar, brick, chunk, hunk, ingot, lump, mass
2 OBSTRUCTION, bar, barrier, blockage, hindrance, impediment, jam, obstacle

obstruction > **block'head** *noun* fool, simpleton > **block letters** written capital letters
block•ade [blo-KAYD] *noun* physical prevention of access, esp. to port, etc. ▷ *verb transitive* **-ad•ed, -ad•ing**
blog [blawg] *noun* person's online journal (*also* **weblog**) > **blog'ger** *noun*
blonde, (*masc*) **blond** *adjective, noun* fair-haired (person)
blood [blud] *noun* **1** red fluid in veins **2** race **3** kindred **4** good parentage **5** temperament **6** passion ▷ *verb transitive* **7** initiate (into hunting, war, etc.) > **blood'less** *adjective* > **blood'y** *adjective* **-i•er, -i•est 1** covered in blood **2** slaughterous ▷ *adjective, adverb* **3** (*slang*) a common intensifier ▷ *verb* **4** make bloody > **blood bank** (institution managing) store of human blood preserved for transfusion > **blood'cur•dling** *adjective* horrifying > **blood'hound** *noun* breed of large hound noted for keen powers of scent > **blood'shed** *noun* slaughter, killing > **blood'shot** *adjective* inflamed (said of eyes) > **blood sport** sport in which animals are killed, e.g. fox hunting > **blood'suck•er** *noun* **1** parasite (e.g. mosquito) living on host's blood **2** parasitic person > **blood test** examination of sample of blood > **blood'thirst•y** *adjective* murderous, cruel > **blood transfusion** transfer of blood from one person into another
bloom *noun* **1** flower of plant **2** blossoming **3** prime, perfection **4** glow **5** powdery deposit on fruit ▷ *verb intransitive* **6** be in flower **7** flourish
bloom•er [BLOO-mər] *noun* (*informal*) **1** plant in bloom **2** person reaching full competence **3** person reaching puberty **4** ludicrous mistake
bloo•mers [BLOO-mərz] *plural noun* girls' or women's wide, baggy underpants
blos•som [BLOS-əm] *noun* **1** flower **2** flower bud ▷ *verb intransitive* **3** flower **4** develop
blot *noun* **1** spot, stain **2** disgrace ▷ *verb transitive* **-ted, -ting 3** spot, stain **4** obliterate **5** detract from **6** soak up ink, etc. from > **blot'ter** *noun* > **blotting paper** soft absorbent paper for soaking up ink
blotch [bloch] *noun* **1** dark spot on skin ▷ *verb transitive* **2** make spotted > **blotch'y** *adjective* **blotch•i•er, blotch•i•est**
blouse [blows] *noun* light, loose upper garment
blow[1] [bloh] *verb intransitive* **blew, blown, blow•ing 1** make a current of air **2** pant **3** emit sound ▷ *verb transitive* **blew, blown, blow•ing 4** drive air upon or into **5** drive by current of air **6** sound **7** spout (of whales) **8** fan **9** (*slang*) squander ▷ *noun* **10** blast **11** gale > **blow-dry** *verb transitive* **-dried, -dry•ing** style hair after washing using stream of hot air > **blow fly** fly that infects food, etc. > **blow'pipe** *noun* dart tube > **blow'out** *noun* **1** sudden puncture in tire **2** uncontrolled escape of oil, gas, from well **3** (*slang*) festive party > **blow up 1** explode **2** inflate **3** enlarge (photograph) **4** (*informal*) lose one's temper
blow[2] *noun* **1** stroke, knock **2** sudden misfortune, loss
blown *pp. of* **blow**[1]
blows•y [BLOW-zee] *adjective* **blows•i•er, blows•i•est 1** slovenly, sluttish **2** red-faced
blub•ber [BLUB-ər] *verb intransitive* **1** weep

DICTIONARY • THESAURUS

▷ *verb* **3** OBSTRUCT, choke, clog, close, plug, stem the flow, stop up
4 STOP, bar, check, halt, hinder, impede, obstruct, thwart
blockade *noun* STOPPAGE, barricade, barrier, block, hindrance, impediment, obstacle, obstruction, restriction, siege
blockage *noun* OBSTRUCTION, block, impediment, occlusion, stoppage
blockhead *noun* IDIOT, chump (*informal*), dork (*slang*), dunce, fool, nitwit, schmuck (*slang*), thickhead
blond *or* **blonde** *adjective* FAIR, fair-haired, fair-skinned, flaxen, golden-haired, light, tow-headed
blood *noun* **1** LIFEBLOOD, gore, vital fluid
2 FAMILY, ancestry, birth, descent, extraction, kinship, lineage, relations
bloodcurdling *adjective* TERRIFYING, appalling, chilling, dreadful, fearful, frightening, hair-raising, horrendous, horrifying, scaring, spine-chilling
bloodshed *noun* KILLING, blood bath, blood-letting, butchery, carnage, gore, massacre, murder, slaughter, slaying
bloodthirsty *adjective* CRUEL, barbarous, brutal, cut-throat, ferocious, gory, murderous, savage, vicious, warlike
bloody *adjective* **1** BLOODSTAINED, bleeding, blood-soaked, blood-spattered, gaping, raw
2 CRUEL, ferocious, fierce, sanguinary, savage
bloom *noun* **1** FLOWER, blossom, blossoming, bud, efflorescence, opening (*of flowers*)
2 PRIME, beauty, flourishing, freshness, glow, health, heyday, luster, radiance, vigor
▷ *verb* **3** BLOSSOM, blow, bud, burgeon, open, sprout
4 FLOURISH, develop, fare well, grow, prosper, succeed, thrive, wax
blossom *noun* **1** FLOWER, bloom, bud, floret, flowers
▷ *verb* **2** FLOWER, bloom, burgeon
3 GROW, bloom, develop, flourish, mature, progress, prosper, thrive
blot *noun* **1** SPOT, blotch, mark, patch, smear, smudge, speck, splodge
2 STAIN, blemish, defect, fault, flaw, scar, spot, taint
▷ *verb* **3** STAIN, disgrace, mark, smirch, smudge, spoil, spot, sully, tarnish
4 SOAK UP, absorb, dry, take up
5 ▷ **blot out a** OBLITERATE, darken, destroy, eclipse, efface, obscure, shadow **b** ERASE, cancel, expunge
blow[1] *verb* **1** CARRY, buffet, drive, fling, flutter, move, sweep, waft
2 EXHALE, breathe, pant, puff
3 PLAY, blare, mouth, pipe, sound, toot, trumpet, vibrate
blow[2] *noun* **1** KNOCK, bang, clout (*informal*), punch, smack, sock (*slang*), stroke, thump, wallop (*informal*), whack
2 SETBACK, bombshell, calamity, catastrophe, disappointment, disaster, misfortune, reverse, shock
blow out *verb* **1** PUT OUT, extinguish, snuff
2 BURST, erupt, explode, rupture, shatter

▷ *noun* 2 fat of whales 3 weeping
bludg•eon [BLUJ-ən] *noun* 1 short thick club ▷ *verb transitive* 2 strike with one 3 coerce (someone into)
blue [bloo] *adjective* **blu•er, blu•est** 1 of the color of sky or shades of that color 2 livid 3 depressed 4 indecent ▷ *noun* 5 the color 6 dye or pigment ▷ *verb transitive* **blued, blu•ing** 7 make blue 8 dip in blue liquid > **blues** *plural noun* (*informal*) 1 depression 2 song in slow tempo originating with Amer. Blacks, employed in jazz music > **blu'ish** *adjective* > **blue baby** baby born with bluish skin caused by heart defect > **blue blood** (person of) royal or aristocratic descent > **blue-col•lar** *adjective* denoting factory workers > **blue jeans** pants made usu. of blue denim > **blue-pen•cil** *verb transitive* **-ciled, -cil•ing** alter, delete parts of, esp. to censor > **blue'print** *noun* 1 copy of drawing 2 original plan > **blue state** US state with a majority of Democrat voters > **blue'stock•ing** *noun* scholarly, intellectual woman
bluff¹ *noun* 1 cliff, steep bank ▷ *adjective* **-er, -est** 2 hearty 3 blunt 4 steep 5 abrupt
bluff² *verb transitive* 1 deceive by pretense of strength ▷ *noun* 2 pretense
blu•ing [BLOO-ing] *noun* indigo powder used in laundering
blun•der [BLUN-dər] *noun* 1 clumsy mistake ▷ *verb intransitive* 2 make stupid mistake 3 act clumsily
blun•der•buss [BLUN-dər-bus] *noun* obsolete short gun with wide bore
blunt *adjective* **-er, -est** 1 not sharp 2 (of speech) abrupt ▷ *verb transitive* 3 make blunt > **blunt'ly** *adverb* > **blunt'ness** *noun*
blur *verb* **blurred, blur•ring** 1 make, become less distinct ▷ *noun* 2 something vague, indistinct > **blur'ry** *adjective* **-ri•er, -ri•est**
blurb *noun* statement advertising, recommending book, etc.
blurt *verb transitive* (usu. with *out*) utter suddenly or unadvisedly
blush *verb intransitive* 1 become red in face 2 be ashamed 3 redden ▷ *noun* 4 this effect
blus•ter [BLUS-tər] *verb intransitive, noun* (indulge in) noisy, aggressive behavior > **blus'ter•ing, blus'ter•y** *adjective* (of wind, etc.) noisy and gusty
bo•a [BOH-ə] *noun, plural* **bo•as** 1 large, nonvenomous snake, esp. boa constrictor 2 long scarf of fur or feathers
boar [bor] *noun* 1 male pig 2 wild pig
board [bord] *noun* 1 broad, flat piece of wood 2 sheet of rigid material for specific purpose 3 table 4 meals 5 group of people who administer company 6 governing body 7 thick, stiff paper ▷ *verb transitive* 8 cover with planks 9 supply food daily 10 enter ship, etc. ▷ *verb intransitive* 11 take daily meals > **boards** *plural noun* stage > **board'er** *noun* > **board•ing house** lodging house where meals may be had > **boarding school** school providing living accommodation for pupils > **board'room** *noun* room where board of company or governing body meets **above board** beyond suspicion **on board** aboard
boast [bohst] *verb intransitive* 1 speak too much

DICTIONARY

b

THESAURUS

blow up *verb* 1 EXPLODE, blast, blow sky-high, bomb, burst, detonate, rupture, shatter
2 INFLATE, bloat, distend, enlarge, expand, fill, puff up, pump up, swell
3 (*informal*) LOSE ONE'S TEMPER, become angry, erupt, fly off the handle (*informal*), hit the roof (*informal*), rage, see red (*informal*)
bludgeon *noun* 1 CLUB, cudgel, truncheon
▷ *verb* 2 CLUB, beat up, cudgel, knock down, strike
3 BULLY, bulldoze (*informal*), coerce, force, railroad (*informal*), steamroller
blue *adjective* 1 AZURE, cerulean, cobalt, cyan, navy, sapphire, sky-colored, ultramarine
2 DEPRESSED, dejected, despondent, downcast, low, melancholy, sad, unhappy
3 SMUTTY, indecent, lewd, obscene, risqué, X-rated (*informal*)
blueprint *noun* PLAN, design, draft, outline, pattern, pilot scheme, prototype, sketch
blues *plural noun* DEPRESSION, doldrums, dumps (*informal*), gloom, low spirits, melancholy, unhappiness
bluff¹ *noun* 1 PRECIPICE, bank, cliff, crag, escarpment, headland, peak, promontory, ridge
▷ *adjective* 2 HEARTY, blunt, blustering, genial, good-natured, open, outspoken, plain-spoken
bluff² *verb* 1 DECEIVE, con, delude, fake, feign, mislead, pretend, pull the wool over someone's eyes
▷ *noun* 2 DECEPTION, bluster, bravado, deceit, fraud, humbug, pretense, sham, subterfuge
blunder *noun* 1 MISTAKE, bloomer (*informal*), faux pas, foul-up (*slang*), indiscretion
2 ERROR, fault, inaccuracy, mistake, oversight, slip, slip-up (*informal*)
▷ *verb* 3 MAKE A MISTAKE, botch, bungle, err, foul up (*slang*), slip up (*informal*)
4 STUMBLE, bumble, flounder
blunt *adjective* 1 DULL, dulled, edgeless, pointless, rounded, unsharpened
2 FORTHRIGHT, bluff, brusque, frank, outspoken, plain-spoken, rude, straightforward, tactless
▷ *verb* 3 DULL, dampen, deaden, numb, soften, take the edge off, water down, weaken
blur *verb* 1 MAKE INDISTINCT, cloud, darken, make hazy, make vague, mask, obscure
▷ *noun* 2 INDISTINCTNESS, confusion, fog, haze, obscurity
blurt out *verb* EXCLAIM, disclose, let the cat out of the bag, reveal, spill the beans (*informal*), tell all, utter suddenly
blush *verb* 1 TURN RED, color, flush, go red *or* go red as a beetroot, redden, turn scarlet
▷ *noun* 2 REDDENING, color, flush, glow, pink tinge, rosiness, rosy tint, ruddiness
bluster *verb* 1 ROAR, bully, domineer, hector, rant, storm
▷ *noun* 2 HOT AIR (*informal*), bluff, bombast, bravado
blustery *adjective* GUSTY, boisterous, inclement, squally, stormy, tempestuous, violent, wild, windy
board *noun* 1 PLANK, panel, piece of timber, slat, timber
2 DIRECTORS, advisers, committee, conclave, council, panel, trustees
3 MEALS, daily meals, provisions, victuals

in praise of oneself, one's possessions ▷ *verb transitive* 2 brag of 3 have to show ▷ *noun* 4 something boasted (of) > **boast'er** *noun* > **boast'ful** *adjective*

boat [boht] *noun* 1 small open vessel 2 ship ▷ *verb intransitive* 3 sail about in boat > **boat'ing** *noun* > **boat'swain** [BOH-sən] *noun* ship's petty officer in charge of maintenance

bob *verb intransitive* **bobbed, bob•bing** 1 move up and down ▷ *verb transitive* **bobbed, bob•bing** 2 move jerkily 3 cut (women's) hair short ▷ *noun* 4 short, jerking motion 5 short hair style 6 weight on pendulum, etc. > **bobbed** *adjective*

bob•bin [BOB-in] *noun* cylinder on which thread is wound

bob•ble [BOB-əl] *baseball* ▷ *verb* **-bled, -bling** 1 fumble ▷ *noun* 2 fumbled ball

bob•cat [BOB-kat] *noun* N Amer. lynx

bob•o•link [BOB-ə-lingk] *noun* Amer. songbird

bode [bohd] *verb transitive* **bod•ed, bod•ing** be an omen of

bod•ice [BOD-is] *noun* upper part of woman's dress

bod•y [BOD-ee] *noun, plural* **bod•ies** 1 entire frame of person or animal 2 main part of such frame 3 corpse 4 main part of anything 5 substance 6 mass 7 person 8 number of persons united or organized 9 matter, opposed to spirit > **bod'i•ly** *adjective, adverb* > **bod'y•guard** *noun* escort to protect important person > **body stocking** undergarment covering body, oft. including arms and legs > **bod'y•work** *noun* 1 body of motor vehicle 2 repair of this

Boer [bor] *noun* a S Afr. of Dutch or Huguenot descent

bof•fo [BOF-oh] *adjective* (*slang*) 1 excellent 2 highly successful

bog *noun* wet, soft ground > **bog'gy** *adjective* **-gi•er, -gi•est** marshy > **bog down** stick as in a bog

bo•gey [BOH-gee] *noun* 1 evil or mischievous spirit 2 source of fear 3 *golf* one stroke over par on a hole > **bo'gey•man** *noun*

bog•gle [BOG-əl] *verb intransitive* **-gled, -gling** 1 be surprised 2 be baffled ▷ *verb transitive* **-gled, -gling** 3 overwhelm with wonder 4 bewilder

bo•gus [BOH-gəs] *adjective* sham, false

bo•he•mi•an [boh-HEE-mee-ən] *adjective* 1 unconventional ▷ *noun* 2 one who leads an unsettled life > **bo•he'mi•a** *noun* district, social circles of bohemians

boil[1] *verb intransitive* 1 change from liquid to gas, esp. by heating 2 become cooked by boiling 3 bubble 4 be agitated 5 seethe 6 (*informal*) be hot 7 (*informal*) be angry ▷ *verb transitive* 8 cause to boil 9 cook by boiling ▷ *noun* 10 boiling state > **boil'er** *noun* vessel for boiling > **boil'er•mak•er** *noun* 1 repairman, worker on boilers 2 whiskey with beer chaser > **boil•ing point** 1 temperature at which boiling occurs 2 point at which anger becomes uncontrollable

boil[2] *noun* inflamed suppurating swelling on skin

bois•ter•ous [BOI-stər-əs] *adjective* 1 wild 2 noisy 3 turbulent > **bois'ter•ous•ness** *noun*

bold [bohld] *adjective* **-er, -est** 1 daring, fearless 2 presumptuous 3 striking, prominent > **bold'ly** *adverb* > **bold'ness** *noun* > **bold'face** *noun printing* heavy-faced type

bole [bohl] *noun* trunk of a tree

bo•le•ro [bə-LAIR-oh] *noun, plural* **-ros** 1 Spanish dance 2 short loose jacket

boll [bohl] *noun* seed capsule of cotton, flax, etc. > **boll weevil** beetle infesting the cotton plant

Bol•she•vik [BOHL-shə-vik] *noun* violent revolutionary, esp. member of Russian group active in overthrow of czarist regime

bol•ster [BOHL-stər] *verb transitive* 1 support, uphold ▷ *noun* 2 long pillow 3 pad, support

bolt [bohlt] *noun* 1 bar or pin (esp. with thread for nut) 2 rush 3 discharge of lightning 4 roll of cloth ▷ *verb transitive* 5 fasten with bolt 6

▷ *verb* 4 GET ON, embark, enter, mount
5 LODGE, put up, quarter, room

boast *verb* 1 BRAG, blow one's own trumpet, crow, strut, swagger, talk big (*slang*), vaunt
2 POSSESS, be proud of, congratulate oneself on, exhibit, flatter oneself, pride oneself on, show off
▷ *noun* 3 BRAG, avowal

boastful *adjective* BRAGGING, cocky, conceited, crowing, egotistical, full of oneself, swaggering, swollen-headed, vaunting

bob *verb* DUCK, bounce, hop, nod, oscillate, wiggle, wobble

bode *verb* PORTEND, augur, be an omen of, forebode, foretell, predict, signify, threaten

bodily *adjective* PHYSICAL, actual, carnal, corporal, corporeal, material, substantial, tangible

body *noun* 1 PHYSIQUE, build, figure, form, frame, shape
2 TORSO, trunk
3 CORPSE, cadaver, carcass, dead body, remains, stiff (*slang*)
4 ORGANIZATION, association, band, bloc, collection, company, confederation, congress, corporation, society
5 MAIN PART, bulk, essence, mass, material, matter, substance

bog *noun* MARSH, fen, mire, morass, quagmire, slough, swamp, wetlands

bogey *noun* BUGBEAR, bête noire, bugaboo, nightmare

bogus *adjective* FAKE, artificial, counterfeit, false, forged, fraudulent, imitation, phoney *or* phony (*informal*), sham

bohemian *adjective* 1 UNCONVENTIONAL, alternative, artistic, arty (*informal*), left bank, nonconformist, offbeat, unorthodox
▷ *noun* 2 NONCONFORMIST, beatnik, dropout, hippie, iconoclast

boil[1] *verb* BUBBLE, effervesce, fizz, foam, froth, seethe

boil[2] *noun* PUSTULE, blister, carbuncle, gathering, swelling, tumor, ulcer

boisterous *adjective* UNRULY, disorderly, loud, noisy, riotous, rollicking, rowdy, unrestrained, vociferous, wild

bold *adjective* 1 FEARLESS, adventurous, audacious, brave, courageous, daring, enterprising, heroic, intrepid, valiant
2 IMPUDENT, barefaced, brazen, cheeky, confident, forward, insolent, rude, shameless

bolster *verb* SUPPORT, augment, boost, help, reinforce, shore up, strengthen

swallow hastily ▷ *verb intransitive* 7 rush away 8 break from control

bomb [bom] *noun* 1 explosive projectile 2 any explosive device 3 a failure ▷ *verb transitive* 4 attack with bombs **the bomb** nuclear bomb > **bom•bard'** *verb transitive* 1 shell 2 attack (verbally) > **bom•bar•dier'** [-bər-DEER] *noun* person in military aircraft who aims and releases bombs > **bom•bard'ment** *noun* > **bomb'er** *noun* 1 aircraft capable of carrying bombs 2 person using bombs illegally > **bomb'shell** *noun* 1 shell of bomb 2 surprise 3 (*informal*) very attractive woman

bom'bast *noun* 1 pompous language 2 pomposity > **bom•bas'tic** *adjective*

bo•na fide [BOH-nə fīd] *Lat.* 1 genuine(ly) 2 sincere(ly) > **bona fi•des** [FĪ-deez] good faith, sincerity

bo•nan•za [bə-NAN-zə] *noun* sudden good luck or wealth

bond *noun* 1 that which binds 2 link, union 3 written promise to pay money or carry out contract ▷ *verb transitive* 4 bind 5 store goods until duty is paid on them > **bond'ed** *adjective* 1 placed in bond 2 mortgaged > **bonds'man** [-mən] *noun law* one whose work is to enter into bonds as surety

bond•age [BON-dij] *noun* slavery

bone [bohn] *noun* 1 hard substance forming animal's skeleton 2 piece of this ▷ *verb transitive* **boned, bon•ing** 3 take out bone ▷ *verb intransitive* **boned, bon•ing** 4 (*informal*) (with *up*) study hard > **bone'less** *adjective* > **bon'y** *adjective* **bon•i•er, bon•i•est** > **bone'head** *noun* (*informal*) stupid person

bon•fire [BON-fīr] *noun* large outdoor fire

bon•go [BONG-goh] *noun, plural* **-gos, -goes** small drum, usu. one of a pair, played with the fingers

bon•net [BON-it] *noun* hat (usu. with strings)

bon•sai [BON-sī] *noun* (art of growing) dwarf trees, shrubs

bo•nus [BOH-nəs] *noun, plural* **-nus•es** extra (oft. unexpected) payment or gift

boob *noun* 1 fool 2 (*slang*) female breast

boo•by [BOO-bee] *noun, plural* **-bies** 1 fool 2 tropical marine bird > **booby hatch** (*informal*) insane asylum > **booby prize** mock prize for poor performance > **booby trap** 1 harmless-looking object that explodes when disturbed 2 form of practical joke

boog•ie-woog•ie [BUUG-ee-WUUG-ee] *noun* kind of jazz piano playing, emphasizing a rolling bass in syncopated eighth notes

book [buuk] *noun* 1 collection of sheets of paper bound together 2 literary work 3 main division of this ▷ *verb transitive* 4 reserve (table, ticket, etc.) 5 charge with legal offense 6 enter name in book 7 schedule engagements for > **book'ing** *noun* 1 scheduled performance for entertainer, etc. 2 reservation > **book'ie** *noun* (*informal*) bookmaker > **book'ish** *adjective* studious, fond of reading > **book'keep•ing** *noun* systematic recording of business transactions > **book'keep•er** *noun* > **book'let** *noun* > **book'mak•er** *noun* one whose work is taking bets (*also* **book'ie**) > **book'mark** *noun* 1 strip of some material put between the pages of a book to mark a place 2 *computers.* identifier put on a website that enables the user to return to it quickly and easily ▷ *verb transitive* 3 *computers.* identify and store a website so that one can return to it quickly and easily > **book'worm** *noun* great reader

boom¹ *noun* 1 sudden commercial activity 2 prosperity ▷ *verb intransitive* 3 become active, prosperous

boom² *verb intransitive, noun* (make) loud, deep sound

boom³ *noun* 1 long spar, as for stretching the bottom of a sail 2 barrier across harbor, river, etc. 3 pole carrying overhead microphone, etc.

boo•mer•ang [BOO-mə-rang] *noun* 1 curved wooden missile of Aust. Aborigines that returns to the thrower ▷ *verb intransitive* 2 recoil 3 return unexpectedly 4 backfire

boon *noun* something helpful, favor

boon•docks [BOON-doks] *plural noun* rural,

---

bolt *noun* 1 BAR, catch, fastener, latch, lock, sliding bar
2 PIN, peg, rivet, rod
▷ *verb* 3 RUN AWAY, abscond, dash, escape, flee, fly, make a break *or* make a break for it, run for it
4 LOCK, bar, fasten, latch, secure
5 GOBBLE, cram, devour, gorge, gulp, guzzle, stuff, swallow whole, wolf

bomb *noun* 1 EXPLOSIVE, device, grenade, mine, missile, projectile, rocket, shell, torpedo
▷ *verb* 2 BLOW UP, attack, blow sky-high, bombard, destroy, shell, strafe, torpedo

bombard *verb* 1 BOMB, assault, blitz, fire upon, open fire, pound, shell, strafe
2 ATTACK, assail, beset, besiege, harass, hound, pester

bombardment *noun* BOMBING, assault, attack, barrage, blitz, fusillade, shelling

bombastic *adjective* GRANDILOQUENT, grandiose, high-flown, inflated, pompous, verbose, wordy

bona fide *adjective* GENUINE, actual, authentic, honest, kosher (*informal*), legitimate, real, true

bond *noun* 1 FASTENING, chain, cord, fetter, ligature, manacle, shackle, tie
2 TIE, affiliation, affinity, attachment, connection, link, relation, union
3 AGREEMENT, contract, covenant, guarantee, obligation, pledge, promise, word
▷ *verb* 4 HOLD TOGETHER, bind, connect, fasten, fix together, glue, paste

bondage *noun* SLAVERY, captivity, confinement, enslavement, imprisonment, subjugation

bonus *noun* EXTRA, dividend, gift, icing on the cake, plus, premium, prize, reward

bony *adjective* THIN, emaciated, gaunt, lean, scrawny, skin and bone, skinny

book *noun* 1 WORK, publication, title, tome, tract, volume
2 NOTEBOOK, album, diary, exercise book, jotter, pad
▷ *verb* 3 RESERVE, arrange for, charter, engage, make reservations, organize, program, schedule
4 NOTE, enter, list, log, mark down, put down, record, register, write down

booklet *noun* BROCHURE, leaflet, pamphlet

boom *verb* 1 BANG, blast, crash, explode, resound, reverberate, roar, roll, rumble, thunder

backward area
boon•dog•gle [BOON-dog-əl] *noun, verb intransitive* **-gled, -gling** (do) work of no practical value performed merely to appear busy
boor *noun* rude person > **boor'ish** *adjective* > **boor'ish•ness** *noun*
boost *noun* 1 encouragement, help 2 upward push 3 increase ▷ *verb transitive* > **boost'er** *noun* person or thing that supports, increases power, etc.
boot *noun* 1 covering for the foot and ankle 2 (*informal*) kick ▷ *verb transitive* (*informal*) 3 kick 4 start up (a computer) > **boot'ed** *adjective*
booth *noun* 1 stall 2 cubicle
boot'leg *verb* **-legged, -leg•ging** make, carry, sell illicit goods, esp. alcohol ▷ *adjective* > **boot'leg•ger** *noun*
boo•ty [BOO-tee] *noun, plural* **-ties** plunder, spoil
booze [booz] *noun, verb intransitive* **boozed, booz•ing** (*informal*) 1 (consume) alcoholic drink 2 drinking spree > **booz'er** *noun* (*informal*) person fond of drinking
bo•rax [BOR-aks] *noun* white soluble substance, compound of boron > **bo•rac•ic** [bə-RAS-ik] *adjective*
bor•der [BOR-dər] *noun* 1 margin 2 frontier 3 limit 4 strip of garden ▷ *verb* 5 provide with border 6 adjoin
bore[1] [bor] *verb transitive* **bored, bor•ing** 1 pierce, making a hole ▷ *noun* 2 hole 3 caliber of gun > **bor'er** *noun* 1 instrument for making holes 2 insect that bores holes
bore[2] *verb transitive* **bored, bor•ing** 1 make weary by repetition, etc. ▷ *noun* 2 tiresome person or thing > **bore'dom** [-dəm] *noun*
bore[3] *pt. of* **bear**
borne, born *pp. of* **bear**
bo•ron [BOR-on] *noun* chemical element used in hardening steel, etc.
bor•ough [BUR-oh] *noun* political subdivision in some states
bor•row [BOR-oh] *verb transitive* 1 obtain on loan or trust 2 appropriate
bor'zoi *noun* breed of tall hound with long, silky coat
bos•om [BUUZ-əm] *noun* 1 human breast 2 seat of passions and feelings
boss[1] [baws] *noun* 1 person in charge of or employing others ▷ *verb transitive* 2 be in charge of 3 be domineering over > **boss'y** *adjective* **boss•i•er, boss•i•est** overbearing
boss[2] *noun* 1 knob or stud 2 raised ornament ▷ *verb transitive* 3 emboss
bo•sun [BOH-sən] *noun* boatswain
bot•a•ny [BOT-n-ee] *noun* study of plants > **bo•tan•ic•al** [bə-TAN-ik-əl] *adjective* > **bot'a•nist** *noun* > **botanical garden** garden for exhibition and study of plants
botch [boch] *verb transitive* spoil by clumsiness
both [bohth] *adjective, pronoun* 1 the two ▷ *adverb, conjunction* 2 as well
both•er [BOTH-ər] *verb transitive* 1 pester 2 perplex ▷ *verb intransitive, noun* 3 fuss, trouble
bot•tle [BOT-l] *noun* 1 vessel for holding liquid 2 its contents ▷ *verb transitive* **-tled, -tling** 3 put into bottle 4 restrain > **bot'tler** *noun* > **bot'tle•neck** *noun* 1 narrow outlet that impedes smooth flow of traffic or production of

2 FLOURISH, develop, expand, grow, increase, intensify, prosper, strengthen, swell, thrive
▷ *noun* 3 BANG, blast, burst, clap, crash, explosion, roar, rumble, thunder
4 EXPANSION, boost, development, growth, improvement, increase, jump, upsurge, upswing, upturn
boon *noun* BENEFIT, advantage, blessing, favor, gift, godsend, manna from heaven, windfall
boorish *adjective* LOUTISH, churlish, coarse, crude, oafish, uncivilized, uncouth, vulgar
boost *noun* 1 HELP, encouragement, praise, promotion
2 RISE, addition, expansion, improvement, increase, increment, jump
▷ *verb* 3 INCREASE, add to, amplify, develop, enlarge, expand, heighten, raise
4 ADVERTISE, encourage, foster, further, hype, plug (*informal*), praise, promote
boot *verb* KICK, drive, drop-kick, knock, punt, shove
booty *noun* PLUNDER, gains, haul, loot, prey, spoils, swag (*slang*), takings, winnings
border *noun* 1 FRONTIER, borderline, boundary, line, march
2 EDGE, bounds, brink, limits, margin, rim, verge
▷ *verb* 3 EDGE, bind, decorate, fringe, hem, rim, trim
bore[1] *verb* DRILL, burrow, gouge out, mine, penetrate, perforate, pierce, sink, tunnel
bore[2] *verb* 1 TIRE, be tedious, fatigue, jade, pall on, send to sleep, wear out, weary
▷ *noun* 2 NUISANCE, geek (*slang*), pain (*informal*)
▷ *noun* 3 PAIN (*informal*), yawn (*informal*)
bored *adjective* FED UP, listless, tired, uninterested, wearied
boredom *noun* TEDIUM, apathy, ennui, flatness, monotony, sameness, tediousness, weariness, world-weariness
boring *adjective* UNINTERESTING, dull, flat, humdrum, mind-numbing, monotonous, tedious, tiresome
borrow *verb* 1 TAKE ON LOAN, cadge, scrounge (*informal*), use temporarily
2 STEAL, adopt, copy, obtain, plagiarize, take, usurp
bosom *noun* 1 BREAST, bust, chest
▷ *adjective* 2 INTIMATE, boon, cherished, close, confidential, dear, very dear
boss[1] *noun* (*informal*) HEAD, alpha male, chief, director, employer, leader, manager, master, supervisor
boss[2] *noun* STUD, knob, point, protuberance, tip
boss around *verb* (*informal*) DOMINEER, bully, dominate, oppress, order, push around (*slang*)
bossy *adjective* DOMINEERING, arrogant, authoritarian, autocratic, dictatorial, hectoring, high-handed, imperious, overbearing, tyrannical
botch *verb* 1 SPOIL, blunder, bungle, foul up (*slang*), mar, mess up, screw up (*informal*)
▷ *noun* 2 MESS, blunder, bungle, failure
bother *verb* 1 TROUBLE, alarm, concern, disturb, harass, hassle (*informal*), inconvenience, pester, plague, worry
▷ *noun* 2 TROUBLE, difficulty, fuss, hassle (*informal*), inconvenience, irritation, nuisance,

goods **2** person who hampers flow of work, information, etc.
bot•tom [BOT-əm] *noun* **1** lowest part of anything **2** bed of sea, river, etc. **3** buttocks ▷ *verb transitive* **4** put bottom to **5** base (upon) **6** get to bottom of > **bot'tom•less** *adjective* > **bottom line** **1** last line of financial statement **2** crucial or deciding factor
bot•u•lism [BOCH-ə-liz-əm] *noun* kind of food poisoning
bou•clé [boo-KLAY] *noun* looped yarn giving knobby effect
bou•doir [BOO-dwahr] *noun* woman's bedroom, private sitting room
bough [rhymes with **cow**] *noun* branch of tree
bought *pt./pp. of* **buy**
boul•der [BOHL-dər] *noun* large weather-worn rounded stone
boul•e•vard [BUUL-ə-vahrd] *noun* broad street or promenade
bounce [bowns] *verb* **bounced, bounc•ing** **1** (cause to) rebound (repeatedly) on impact, as a ball ▷ *noun* **2** rebounding **3** quality in object causing this **4** (*informal*) vitality, vigor > **bounc'er** *noun* esp. one employed to evict undesirables (forcibly) > **bounc'ing** *adjective* vigorous, robust > **bounc'y** *adjective* **bounc•i•er, bounc•i•est** lively
bound[1] [bownd] *noun, verb transitive* limit > **bound'a•ry** *noun, plural* **-ries** > **bound'ed** *adjective* > **bound'less** *adjective*
bound[2] *verb intransitive, noun* spring, leap
bound[3] *adjective* on a specified course: *homeward bound*
bound[4] **1** *pt./pp. of* **bind** ▷ *adjective* **2** committed **3** certain **4** tied
boun•ty [BOWN-tee] *noun, plural* **-ties** **1** liberality **2** gift **3** premium > **boun'te•ous** [-tee-əs], **boun'ti•ful** *adjective* liberal, generous
bou•quet [boo-KAY] *noun* **1** bunch of flowers **2** perfume of wine **3** compliment
bour•bon [BUR-bən] *noun* whiskey made from corn, malt and rye
bour•geois [buur-ZHWAH] *noun, adjective* (*disparaging*) **1** middle class **2** smugly conventional (person) > **bourgeoisie** [buur-zhwah-ZEE] *noun* middle classes
bout [bowt] *noun* **1** contest, fight **2** period of time spent doing something
bou•tique [boo-TEEK] *noun* small shop, esp. one selling clothes
bo•vine [BOH-vīn] *adjective* **1** of cattle **2** oxlike **3** stolid, dull
bow[1] [boh] *noun* **1** weapon for shooting arrows **2** implement for playing violin, etc. **3** ornamental knot of ribbon, etc. **4** bend, bent line ▷ *verb* **5** bend > **bow'leg•ged** [-leg-id] *adjective* having legs curved outward > **bow window** one with outward curve
bow[2] [rhymes with **cow**] *verb intransitive* **1** bend body in respect, assent, etc. **2** submit ▷ *verb transitive* **3** bend downward **4** cause to stoop **5** crush ▷ *noun*
bow[3] [rhymes with **cow**] *noun* **1** fore end of ship **2** prow **3** rower nearest bow
bowd•ler•ize [BOHD-lə-rīz] *verb transitive* **-ized, -iz•ing** expurgate, censor
bow•el [BOW-əl] *noun* (*often plural*) **1** part of intestine (esp. with reference to defecation) **2** inside of anything
bow•er [BOW-ər] *noun* shady retreat, arbor
bowl[1] [bohl] *noun* **1** round vessel, deep basin **2** drinking cup **3** hollow
bowl[2] *noun* **1** wooden ball ▷ *verb* **2** roll or throw

DICTIONARY

b

THESAURUS

problem, worry
bottleneck *noun* HOLD-UP, block, blockage, congestion, impediment, jam, obstacle, obstruction
bottle up *verb* SUPPRESS, check, contain, curb, keep back, restrict, shut in, trap
bottom *noun* **1** LOWEST PART, base, bed, depths, floor, foot, foundation
2 UNDERSIDE, lower side, sole, underneath
3 BUTTOCKS, backside, behind (*informal*), posterior, rear, rump, seat, tush (*slang*)
▷ *adjective* **4** LOWEST, last
bottomless *adjective* UNLIMITED, boundless, deep, fathomless, immeasurable, inexhaustible, infinite, unfathomable
bounce *verb* **1** REBOUND, bob, bound, jump, leap, recoil, ricochet, spring
▷ *noun* **2** (*informal*) LIFE, dynamism, energy, go (*informal*), liveliness, vigor, vivacity, zip (*informal*)
3 SPRINGINESS, elasticity, give, recoil, resilience, spring
bound[1] *verb* LIMIT, confine, demarcate, encircle, enclose, hem in, restrain, restrict, surround
bound[2] *verb, noun* LEAP, bob, bounce, gambol, hurdle, jump, skip, spring, vault
bound[3] *adjective* **1** TIED, cased, fastened, fixed, pinioned, secured, tied up
2 CERTAIN, destined, doomed, fated, sure
3 OBLIGED, beholden, committed, compelled, constrained, duty-bound, forced, pledged, required
boundary *noun* LIMITS, barrier, border, borderline, brink, edge, extremity, fringe, frontier, margin
boundless *adjective* UNLIMITED, endless, immense, incalculable, inexhaustible, infinite, unconfined, untold, vast
bounds *plural noun* BOUNDARY, border, confine, edge, extremity, limit, rim, verge
bountiful *adjective* (*literary*) **1** PLENTIFUL, abundant, ample, bounteous, copious, exuberant, lavish, luxuriant, prolific
2 GENEROUS, liberal, magnanimous, open-handed, prodigal, unstinting
bounty *noun* (*literary*) **1** GENEROSITY, benevolence, charity, kindness, largesse *or* largess, liberality, philanthropy
2 REWARD, bonus, gift, present
bouquet *noun* **1** BUNCH OF FLOWERS, buttonhole, corsage, garland, nosegay, posy, spray, wreath
2 AROMA, fragrance, perfume, redolence, savor, scent
bourgeois *adjective* MIDDLE-CLASS, conventional, hidebound, materialistic, traditional
bout *noun* **1** PERIOD, fit, spell, stint, term, turn
2 FIGHT, boxing match, competition, contest, encounter, engagement, match, set-to, struggle
bow[2] *verb* **1** BEND, bob, droop, genuflect, nod, stoop
2 GIVE IN, acquiesce, comply, concede, defer, kowtow, relent, submit, succumb, surrender, yield

ball in various ways > **bowls** *plural noun* outdoor game played with such balls > **bowl'ing** *noun* indoor game, played usu. with large, heavy balls > **bowling green** place where bowls is played > **bowling alley** place where bowling is played

box[1] [boks] *noun* (wooden) container, usu. rectangular with lid 1 its contents 2 small enclosure 3 any boxlike cubicle, shelter or receptacle ▷ *verb transitive* 4 put in box 5 confine

box[2] *verb* 1 fight with fists, esp. with padded gloves on ▷ *verb transitive* 2 strike ▷ *noun* 3 blow > **box'er** *noun* 1 one who boxes 2 breed of pug-faced large dog

boy [boi] *noun* 1 male child 2 young man > **boy'hood** [-huud] *noun*

boy•cott [BOI-kot] *verb transitive* refuse to deal with or participate in ▷ *noun*

Br *chem.* bromine

bra [brah] *noun* brassiere

brace [brays] *noun* 1 tool for boring 2 clasp, clamp 3 pair, couple 4 strut, support ▷ *verb transitive* **braced, brac•ing** 5 steady (oneself) as before a blow 6 support, make firm > **brac•es** *plural noun* dental appliance worn to help straighten teeth > **bracing** *adjective* invigorating > **brace'let** *noun* ornament for the arm > **brace'lets** (*slang*) handcuffs

brack•et [BRAK-it] *noun* 1 support for shelf, etc. 2 group ▷ *verb transitive* 3 enclose in brackets 4 connect **brack•ets** *plural noun* marks **[ ]**, used to enclose words, etc.

brack•ish [BRAK-ish] *adjective* (of water) slightly salty

bract [brakt] *noun* small scalelike leaf

brad *noun* small nail

brag *verb intransitive* **bragged, brag•ging** 1 boast ▷ *noun* 2 boastful talk > **brag'gart** [-ərt] *noun*

Brah•man [BRAY-mən] *noun* breed of beef cattle

Brah•min [BRAH-min] *noun* 1 member of priestly Hindu caste 2 socially or intellectually aloof person

braid [brayd] *verb transitive* 1 interweave (hair, thread, etc.) 2 trim with braid ▷ *noun* 3 length of anything interwoven or plaited 4 ornamental tape

Braille [brayl] *noun* system of printing for blind, with raised dots instead of letters

brain [brayn] *noun* 1 mass of nerve tissue in head 2 intellect ▷ *verb transitive* 3 kill by hitting on head > **brain'less** *adjective* > **brain'y** *adjective* **brain•i•er, brain•i•est** > **brain'child** *noun* invention > **brain'storm** *noun* 1 sudden mental aberration 2 sudden clever idea ▷ *verb* 3 practice, subject to, brainstorming > **brain'storm•ing** *noun* technique for coming upon innovative ideas > **brain trust** group of experts without official status who advise government officials > **brain'wash** *verb transitive* change, distort a person's ideas or beliefs > **brain wave** electrical impulse in brain

braise [brayz] *verb transitive* **braised, brais•ing** cook slowly in covered pan

brake [brayk] *noun* 1 instrument for retarding motion of wheel on vehicle ▷ *verb transitive* **braked, brak•ing** 2 apply brake to

bram•ble [BRAM-bəl] *noun* prickly shrub > **bram'bly** *adjective* **-bli•er, -bli•est**

bran *noun* sifted husks of cereal grain

branch *noun* 1 limb of tree 2 offshoot or subsidiary part of something larger or primary ▷ *verb intransitive* 3 bear branches 4 diverge 5 spread > **branched** *adjective* > **branch'less** *adjective*

brand *noun* 1 trademark 2 class of goods 3 particular kind, sort 4 mark made by hot iron 5 burning piece of wood 6 sword 7 mark of disgrace ▷ *verb transitive* 8 burn with iron 9 mark 10 stigmatize > **brand-new** *adjective* absolutely new

bran'dish *verb transitive* flourish, wave (weapon, etc.)

bran•dy [BRAN-dee] *noun, plural* **-dies** 1 alcoholic liquor distilled from wine or fruit juice ▷ *verb transitive* **-died, -dy•ing** 2 flavor or preserve with brandy

brash *adjective* **-er, -est** bold, impudent

DICTIONARY • THESAURUS

▷ *noun* 3 BENDING, bob, genuflexion, kowtow, nod, obeisance

bow[3] *noun* (*nautical*) PROW, beak, fore, head, stem

bowels *plural noun* 1 GUTS, entrails, innards (*informal*), insides (*informal*), intestines, viscera, vitals
2 DEPTHS, belly, core, deep, hold, inside, interior

bowl[1] *noun* BASIN, dish, vessel

bowl[2] *verb* THROW, fling, hurl, pitch

box[1] *noun* 1 CONTAINER, carton, case, casket, chest, pack, package, receptacle, trunk
▷ *verb* 2 PACK, package, wrap

box[2] *verb* FIGHT, exchange blows, spar

boxer *noun* FIGHTER, prizefighter, pugilist, sparring partner

boy *noun* LAD, fellow, junior, schoolboy, stripling, youngster, youth

boycott *verb* EMBARGO, ban, bar, black, exclude, outlaw, prohibit, refuse, reject

boyfriend *noun* SWEETHEART, admirer, beau, date, lover, man, suitor

boyish *adjective* YOUTHFUL, adolescent, childish, immature, juvenile, puerile, young

brace *noun* 1 SUPPORT, bolster, bracket, buttress, prop, reinforcement, stay, strut, truss
▷ *verb* 2 SUPPORT, bolster, buttress, fortify, reinforce, steady, strengthen

bracing *adjective* REFRESHING, brisk, crisp, exhilarating, fresh, invigorating, stimulating

brag *verb* BOAST, blow one's own trumpet, bluster, crow, swagger, talk big (*slang*), vaunt

braggart *noun* BOASTER, bigmouth (*slang*), bragger, show-off (*informal*)

braid *verb* INTERWEAVE, entwine, interlace, intertwine, lace, plait, twine, weave

brainless *adjective* STUPID, foolish, idiotic, inane, mindless, senseless, thoughtless, witless

brains *plural noun* INTELLIGENCE, intellect, sense, understanding

brainy *adjective* (*informal*) INTELLIGENT, bright, brilliant, clever, smart

brake *noun* 1 CONTROL, check, constraint, curb, rein, restraint
▷ *verb* 2 SLOW, check, decelerate, halt, moderate, reduce speed, slacken, stop

branch *noun* 1 BOUGH, arm, limb, offshoot, shoot, spray, sprig
2 DIVISION, chapter, department, office, part, section, subdivision, subsection, wing

brass *noun* 1 alloy of copper and zinc 2 group of brass wind instruments forming part of orchestra or band 3 (*informal*) (military) officers ▷ *adjective* > **brass'y** *adjective* **brass•i•er, brass•i•est** 1 showy 2 harsh > **brass'i•ness** *noun*

bras•siere [brə-ZEER] *noun* woman's undergarment, supporting breasts, bra

brat *noun* contemptuous term for a child

bra•va•do [brə-VAH-doh] *noun* showy display of boldness

brave [brayv] *adjective* **brav•er, brav•est** 1 bold, courageous 2 splendid, fine ▷ *noun* 3 N Amer. Indian warrior ▷ *verb transitive* **braved, brav•ing** 4 defy, meet boldly > **brav'er•y** *noun, plural* **-er•ies**

bra•vo [BRAH-voh] *interjection* well done!

brawl *verb intransitive* fight noisily ▷ *noun* > **brawl'er** *noun*

brawn *noun* 1 muscle 2 strength > **brawn'y** *adjective* **brawn•i•er, brawn•i•est** muscular

bray *noun* 1 donkey's cry ▷ *verb intransitive* 2 utter this 3 give out harsh or loud sounds

braze [brayz] *verb transitive* **brazed, braz•ing** solder with alloy of brass or zinc

bra•zen [BRAY-zən] *adjective* 1 of, like brass 2 impudent, shameless ▷ *verb transitive* 3 (usu. with *out* or *through*) face, carry through with impudence > **bra'zen•ness** *noun* effrontery

bra•zier [BRAY-zhər] *noun* 1 pan for burning charcoal or coals 2 brassworker

breach [breech] *noun* 1 break, opening 2 breaking of rule, duty, etc. 3 quarrel ▷ *verb transitive* 4 make a gap in 5 break (rule, etc.)

bread [bred] *noun* 1 food made of flour or meal baked 2 food 3 (*slang*) money > **bread'fruit** *noun* breadlike fruit found in Pacific islands > **bread'win•ner** *noun* person who works to support family

breadth [bredth] *noun* 1 extent across, width 2 largeness of view, mind

break [brayk] *verb transitive* **broke, bro•ken, break•ing** 1 part by force 2 shatter 3 burst, destroy 4 fail to observe 5 disclose 6 interrupt 7 surpass 8 make bankrupt 9 relax 10 mitigate 11 accustom (horse) to being ridden 12 decipher (code) ▷ *verb intransitive* **broke, bro•ken, break•ing** 13 become broken, shattered, divided 14 open, appear 15 come suddenly 16 crack, give way 17 part, fall out 18 (of voice) change in tone, pitch ▷ *noun* 19 fracture 20 gap 21 opening 22 separation 23 interruption 24 respite 25 interval 26 (*informal*) opportunity 27 dawn 28 *pool* opening shot in a game 29 *boxing* separation after a clinch > **break'a•ble** *adjective* > **break'age** *noun* > **break'er** *noun* 1 person or device that breaks, for example an electrical circuit 2 wave beating on rocks or shore > **break dance** *noun* acrobatic dance style associated with hip-hop ▷ *verb intransitive* > **break'down** *noun* 1 collapse, as nervous breakdown 2 failure to function effectively 3 analysis > **break•fast** [BREK-fəst] *noun* first meal of the day > **break'-in** *noun* illegal entering of building, esp. by thieves > **break'neck** *adjective* dangerous > **break'through** *noun* important advance > **break'wa•ter** *noun*

DICTIONARY

b

THESAURUS

---

brand *noun* 1 LABEL, emblem, hallmark, logo, mark, marker, sign, stamp, symbol, trademark
2 KIND, cast, class, grade, make, quality, sort, species, type, variety
▷ *verb* 3 MARK, burn, burn in, label, scar, stamp
4 STIGMATIZE, censure, denounce, discredit, disgrace, expose, mark

brandish *verb* WAVE, display, exhibit, flaunt, flourish, parade, raise, shake, swing, wield

brash *adjective* BOLD, brazen, cocky, impertinent, impudent, insolent, pushy (*informal*), rude

bravado *noun* SWAGGER, bluster, boastfulness, boasting, bombast, swashbuckling, vaunting

brave *adjective* 1 COURAGEOUS, bold, daring, fearless, heroic, intrepid, plucky, resolute, valiant
▷ *verb* 2 CONFRONT, defy, endure, face, stand up to, suffer, tackle, withstand

bravery *noun* COURAGE, boldness, daring, fearlessness, fortitude, heroism, intrepidity, mettle, pluck, spirit, valor

brawl *noun* 1 FIGHT, affray (*law*), altercation, clash, dispute, fracas, fray, melee *or* mêlée, rumpus, scuffle, skirmish
▷ *verb* 2 FIGHT, scrap (*informal*), scuffle, tussle, wrestle

brawn *noun* MUSCLE, beef (*informal*), might, muscles, power, strength, vigor

brawny *adjective* MUSCULAR, beefy (*informal*), hefty (*informal*), lusty, powerful, strapping, strong, sturdy, well-built

brazen *adjective* BOLD, audacious, barefaced, brash, defiant, impudent, insolent, shameless, unabashed, unashamed

breach *noun* 1 NONOBSERVANCE, contravention, infraction, infringement, noncompliance, transgression, trespass, violation
2 CRACK, cleft, fissure, gap, opening, rift, rupture, split

bread *noun* 1 FOOD, fare, nourishment, sustenance
2 (*slang*) MONEY, cash, dough (*slang*)

breadth *noun* 1 WIDTH, broadness, latitude, span, spread, wideness
2 EXTENT, compass, expanse, range, scale, scope

break *verb* 1 SEPARATE, burst, crack, destroy, disintegrate, fracture, fragment, shatter, smash, snap, split, tear
2 DISOBEY, breach, contravene, disregard, infringe, renege on, transgress, violate
3 REVEAL, announce, disclose, divulge, impart, inform, let out, make public, proclaim, tell
4 STOP, abandon, cut, discontinue, give up, interrupt, pause, rest, suspend
5 WEAKEN, demoralize, dispirit, subdue, tame, undermine
6 (*a record, etc*) BEAT, better, exceed, excel, go beyond, outdo, outstrip, surpass, top
▷ *noun* 7 DIVISION, crack, fissure, fracture, gap, hole, opening, split, tear
8 REST, breather (*informal*), hiatus, interlude, intermission, interruption, interval, let-up (*informal*), lull, pause, respite
9 (*informal*) STROKE OF LUCK, advantage, chance, fortune, opening, opportunity

breakable *adjective* FRAGILE, brittle, crumbly, delicate, flimsy, frail, frangible, friable

breakdown *noun* COLLAPSE, disintegration, disruption, failure, mishap, stoppage

break down *verb* 1 COLLAPSE, come unstuck,

barrier to break force of waves
breast [brest] *noun* 1 human chest 2 milk-secreting gland on chest of human female 3 seat of the affections 4 any protuberance ▷ *verb transitive* 5 face, oppose 6 reach summit of > **breast'stroke** *noun* stroke in swimming
breath [breth] *noun* 1 air used by lungs 2 life 3 respiration 4 slight breeze > **breathe** [breeth] *verb intransitive* **breathed, breath•ing** 1 inhale and exhale air from lungs 2 live 3 pause, rest ▷ *verb transitive* **breathed, breath•ing** 4 inhale and exhale 5 utter softly, whisper > **breath'er** [-thər] *noun* short rest > **breath•less** [BRETH-lis] *adjective* > **breath'tak•ing** *adjective* causing awe or excitement
Breath•a•lyz•er [BRETH-ə-lī-zər] *noun* ® device that estimates amount of alcohol in breath
bred *pt./pp. of* **breed**
breech *noun* 1 buttocks 2 hinder part of anything, esp. gun > **breech'load•er** *noun*
breed *verb transitive* **bred, breed•ing** 1 generate, bring forth, give rise to 2 rear ▷ *verb intransitive* **bred, breed•ing** 3 be produced 4 be with young ▷ *noun* 5 offspring produced 6 race, kind > **breeding** *noun* 1 producing 2 manners 3 ancestry > **breeder reactor** nuclear reactor producing more fissionable material than it consumes
breeze [breez] *noun* gentle wind > **breez'i•ly** *adverb* > **breez'y** *adjective* **breez•i•er, breez•i•est** 1 windy 2 jovial, lively 3 casual **in a breeze** easily
breth•ren [BRETH-rən] (*obsolete*) *pl. of* **brother**
breve [breev] *noun* long musical note
bre•vi•ar•y [BREE-vee-er-ee] *noun, plural* **-ar•ies** book of daily prayers, hymns, etc.
brev•i•ty [BREV-i-tee] *noun* 1 conciseness of expression 2 short duration
brew [broo] *verb transitive* 1 prepare liquor, as beer from malt, etc. 2 make drink, as tea, by infusion 3 plot, contrive ▷ *verb intransitive* 4 be in preparation ▷ *noun* 5 beverage produced by brewing > **brew'er** *noun* > **brew'er•y** *noun*
bri•ar[1]**, br•ier** [BRĪ-ər] *noun* prickly shrub, esp. the wild rose
briar[2]**, brier** *noun* European shrub > **briar pipe** pipe made from its root
bribe [brīb] *noun* 1 anything offered or given to someone to gain favor, influence ▷ *verb transitive* **bribed, brib•ing** 2 influence by bribe > **brib'er•y** *noun, plural* **-er•ies**
bric-a-brac [BRIK-ə-brak] *noun* miscellaneous small objects, used for ornament
brick [brik] *noun* 1 oblong mass of hardened clay used in building 2 good-hearted person ▷ *verb transitive* 3 build, block, etc. with bricks
bride [brīd] *noun* woman about to be, or just, married > **brid'al** *adjective* of, relating to, a bride or wedding > **bride'groom** *noun* man about to

fail, seize up, stop, stop working
2 BE OVERCOME, crack up (*informal*), go to pieces
break-in *noun* BURGLARY, breaking and entering, robbery
break off *verb* 1 DETACH, divide, part, pull off, separate, sever, snap off, splinter
2 STOP, cease, desist, discontinue, end, finish, halt, pull the plug on, suspend, terminate
break out *verb* BEGIN, appear, arise, commence, emerge, happen, occur, set in, spring up, start
breakthrough *noun* DEVELOPMENT, advance, discovery, find, invention, leap, progress, quantum leap, step forward
break up *verb* 1 SEPARATE, dissolve, divide, divorce, part, scatter, sever, split
2 STOP, adjourn, disband, dismantle, end, suspend, terminate
breast *noun* BOSOM, bust, chest, front, teat, udder
breath *noun* RESPIRATION, breathing, exhalation, gasp, gulp, inhalation, pant, wheeze
breathe *verb* 1 INHALE AND EXHALE, draw in, gasp, gulp, pant, puff, respire, wheeze
2 WHISPER, murmur, sigh
breather *noun* (*informal*) REST, break, breathing space, halt, pause, recess, respite
breathless *adjective* 1 OUT OF BREATH, gasping, gulping, panting, short-winded, spent, wheezing
2 EXCITED, eager, on tenterhooks, open-mouthed, wired (*slang*), with bated breath
breathtaking *adjective* AMAZING, astonishing, awe-inspiring, cool (*informal*), exciting, impressive, magnificent, phat (*slang*), sensational, stunning (*informal*), thrilling
breed *verb* 1 REPRODUCE, bear, bring forth, hatch, multiply, procreate, produce, propagate
2 BRING UP, cultivate, develop, nourish, nurture, raise, rear
3 PRODUCE, arouse, bring about, cause, create, generate, give rise to, stir up
▷ *noun* 4 VARIETY, pedigree, race, species, stock, strain, type
5 KIND, brand, sort, stamp, type, variety
breeding *noun* 1 UPBRINGING, ancestry, cultivation, development, lineage, nurture, raising, rearing, reproduction, training
2 REFINEMENT, conduct, courtesy, cultivation, culture, polish, sophistication, urbanity
breeze *noun* 1 LIGHT WIND, air, breath of wind, current of air, draft, gust, waft, zephyr
▷ *verb* 2 MOVE BRISKLY, flit, glide, hurry, pass, sail, sweep
breezy *adjective* 1 WINDY, airy, blowy, blustery, fresh, gusty, squally
2 CAREFREE, blithe, casual, easy-going, free and easy, jaunty, light-hearted, lively, sprightly
brevity *noun* 1 SHORTNESS, briefness, impermanence, transience, transitoriness
2 CONCISENESS, crispness, curtness, economy, pithiness, succinctness, terseness
brew *verb* 1 MAKE (*beer*) boil, ferment, infuse (*tea*) soak, steep, stew
2 DEVELOP, foment, form, gather, start, stir up
▷ *noun* 3 DRINK, beverage, blend, concoction, infusion, liquor, mixture, preparation
bribe *verb* 1 BUY OFF, corrupt, grease the palm of *or* grease the hand of (*slang*), pay off (*informal*), reward, suborn
▷ *noun* 2 INDUCEMENT, allurement, backhander (*slang*), enticement, kickback, pay-off (*informal*), sweetener (*slang*)
bribery *noun* BUYING OFF, corruption, inducement, palm-greasing (*slang*), payola (*informal*)
bric-a-brac *noun* KNICK-KNACKS, baubles, curios,

be, or just, married > **brides'maid** *noun*
bridge[1] [brij] *noun* 1 structure for crossing river, etc. 2 something joining or supporting other parts 3 raised narrow platform on ship 4 upper part of nose 5 part of violin supporting strings ▷ *verb transitive* **bridged, bridg•ing** 6 make bridge over, span
bridge[2] *noun* card game
bri•dle [BRĪD-l] *noun* 1 headgear of horse harness 2 curb ▷ *verb* **-dled, -dling** 3 *verb transitive* 4 put on bridle 5 restrain ▷ *verb intransitive* 6 show resentment > **bridle path** path suitable for riding horses
brief [breef] *adjective* **-er, -est** 1 short in duration 2 concise 3 scanty ▷ *noun* 4 summary of case for judge or lawyer's use 5 papal letter 6 instructions ▷ *verb transitive* 7 give instructions, information > **briefs** ▷ *plural noun* 1 underpants 2 panties > **brief'ly** *adverb* > **brief'case** *noun* hand case for carrying papers > **brief•ing book** one prepared to provide (participant) information on meeting, etc.
brier *see* **briar**
brig *noun* 1 two-masted, square-rigged ship 2 (*informal*) ship's jail, guardhouse
bri•gade [bri-GAYD] *noun* 1 subdivision of army 2 organized band > **brig•a•dier' gen•er•al** [-ə-DEER] one-star general
brig•an•tine [BRIG-ən-teen] *noun* two-masted vessel, with square-rigged foremast and fore-and-aft mainmast
bright [brīt] *adjective* **-er, -est** 1 shining 2 full of light 3 cheerful 4 clever > **bright'en** *verb*
bril•liant [BRIL-yənt] *adjective* 1 shining 2 sparkling 3 splendid 4 very intelligent or clever 5 distinguished > **bril'liance** *noun*
brim *noun* margin, edge, esp. of river, cup, hat > **brim•ful** *adjective* > **brim'less** *adjective* > **brim'ming** *adjective* 1 to the brim 2 until it can hold no more
brim•stone [BRIM-stohn] *noun* sulfur
brin•dled [BRIN-dld] *adjective* brownish with streaks of other color > **brin'dle** *noun* 1 this color 2 a brindled animal
brine [brīn] *noun* salt water > **brin'y** *adjective* **brin•i•er, brin•i•est** 1 very salty ▷ *noun* (*informal*) 2 the sea
bring *verb transitive* **brought, bring•ing** 1 fetch 2 carry with one 3 cause to come
brink [bringk] *noun* 1 edge of steep place 2 verge, margin > **brink'man•ship** *noun* technique of attempting to gain advantage through maneuvering dangerous situation to limit of tolerance
bri•quette [bri-KET] *noun* block of compressed coal dust
brisk *adjective* **-er, -est** active, vigorous > **brisk'ly** *adverb* > **brisk'ness** *noun*
bris•ket [BRIS-kit] *noun* cut of meat from breast of animal

DICTIONARY

b

THESAURUS

---

ornaments, trinkets
bridal *adjective* MATRIMONIAL, conjugal, connubial, marital, marriage, nuptial, wedding
bridge[1] *noun* 1 ARCH, flyover, overpass, span, viaduct
▷ *verb* 2 CONNECT, join, link, span
bridle *noun* 1 CURB, check, control, rein, restraint
▷ *verb* 2 GET ANGRY, be indignant, bristle, draw (oneself) up, get one's back up, raise one's hackles, rear up
brief *adjective* 1 SHORT, ephemeral, fleeting, momentary, quick, short-lived, swift, transitory
▷ *noun* 2 SUMMARY, abridgment, abstract, digest, epitome, outline, précis, sketch, synopsis
▷ *verb* 3 INFORM, advise, explain, fill in (*informal*), instruct, keep posted, prepare, prime, put (someone) in the picture (*informal*)
briefing *noun* INSTRUCTIONS, conference, directions, guidance, information, preparation, priming, rundown
briefly *adverb* SHORTLY, concisely, hastily, hurriedly, in a nutshell, in brief, momentarily, quickly
brigade *noun* GROUP, band, company, corps, force, organization, outfit, squad, team, troop, unit
bright *adjective* 1 SHINING, brilliant, dazzling, gleaming, glowing, luminous, lustrous, radiant, shimmering, vivid
2 INTELLIGENT, astute, aware, clever, inventive, quick-witted, sharp, smart, wide-awake
3 SUNNY, clear, cloudless, fair, limpid, lucid, pleasant, translucent, transparent, unclouded
brighten *verb* MAKE BRIGHTER, gleam, glow, illuminate, lighten, light up, shine
brightness *noun* 1 SHINE, brilliance, glare, incandescence, intensity, light, luminosity, radiance, vividness
2 INTELLIGENCE, acuity, cleverness, quickness, sharpness, smartness
brilliance *noun* 1 BRIGHTNESS, dazzle, intensity, luminosity, luster, radiance, sparkle, vividness
2 TALENT, cleverness, distinction, excellence, genius, greatness, inventiveness, wisdom
3 SPLENDOR, éclat, glamour, grandeur, illustriousness, magnificence
brilliant *adjective* 1 SHINING, bright, dazzling, glittering, intense, luminous, radiant, sparkling, vivid
2 SPLENDID, celebrated, famous, glorious, illustrious, magnificent, notable, outstanding, superb
3 INTELLIGENT, clever, expert, gifted, intellectual, inventive, masterly, penetrating, profound, talented
brim *noun* 1 RIM, border, brink, edge, lip, margin, skirt, verge
▷ *verb* 2 BE FULL, fill, fill up, hold no more, overflow, run over, spill, well over
bring *verb* 1 TAKE, bear, carry, conduct, convey, deliver, escort, fetch, guide, lead, transfer, transport
2 CAUSE, contribute to, create, effect, inflict, occasion, produce, result in, wreak
bring about *verb* CAUSE, accomplish, achieve, create, effect, generate, give rise to, make happen, produce
bring off *verb* ACCOMPLISH, achieve, carry off, execute, perform, pull off, succeed
bring up *verb* 1 REAR, breed, develop, educate, form, nurture, raise, support, teach, train
2 MENTION, allude to, broach, introduce, move, propose, put forward, raise
brink *noun* EDGE, border, boundary, brim, fringe, frontier, limit, lip, margin, rim, skirt, threshold,

bris•tle [BRIS-əl] *noun* 1 short stiff hair ▷ *verb intransitive* **-tled, -tling** 2 stand erect 3 show temper > **bris'tly** *adjective* **-tli•er, -tli•est**
brit•tle [BRIT-l] *adjective* 1 easily broken, fragile 2 curt, irritable > **brit'tle•ness** *noun*
broach [brohch] *verb transitive* 1 pierce (cask) 2 open, begin
broad [brawd] *adjective* **-er, -est** 1 wide, spacious, open 2 plain, obvious 3 coarse 4 general 5 tolerant 6 (of pronunciation) dialectal > **broad'en** *verb transitive* > **broad'ly** *adverb* > **broad'ness** *noun* > **broad'cast** *verb transitive* **-cast** *or* **-cast•ed, -cast•ing** 1 transmit by radio or television 2 make widely known 3 scatter, as seed ▷ *noun* 4 radio or TV program > **broad'cast•er** *noun* > **broad'loom** *noun, adjective* (carpet) woven on wide loom > **broad'-mind•ed** [-MĪN-did] *adjective* 1 tolerant 2 generous > **broad'side** *noun* 1 discharge of all guns on one side 2 strong (verbal) attack
bro•cade [broh-KAYD] *noun* rich woven fabric with raised design
broc•co•li [BROK-ə-lee] *noun* type of cabbage
bro•chette [broh-SHET] *noun* 1 small spit 2 skewer
bro•chure [broh-SHUUR] *noun* pamphlet, booklet
brogue [brohg] *noun* 1 stout shoe 2 dialect, esp. Irish accent
broil *verb transitive* 1 cook over hot coals 2 grill ▷ *verb intransitive* 3 be heated
broke 1 *see* **break** ▷ *adjective* 2 (*informal*) penniless
bro•ker [BROH-kər] *noun* 1 one employed to buy and sell for others 2 dealer > **bro'ker•age** *noun* 1 business of broker 2 payment to broker
bro•mide [BROH-mīd] *noun* 1 chemical compound used in medicine and photography 2 hackneyed, commonplace statement > **bro•mid'ic** [-MID-ik] *adjective* lacking in originality
bro•mine [BROH-meen] *noun* liquid element used in production of chemicals
bron•chus [BRONG-kəs] *noun, plural* **-chi** [-kee] branch of windpipe > **bron'chi•al** *adjective* > **bron•chi'tis** [-KĪ-tis] *noun* inflammation of bronchi
bron•co [BRONG-koh] *noun, plural* **-cos** N Amer. half-tamed horse
bron•to•sau•rus [bron-tə-SOR-əs] *noun* very large herbivorous dinosaur
bronze [bronz] *noun* 1 alloy of copper and tin ▷ *adjective* 2 made of, or colored like, bronze ▷ *verb transitive* **bronzed, bronz•ing** 3 give appearance of bronze to
brooch [brohch] *noun* ornamental pin or fastening
brood *noun* 1 family of young, esp. of birds 2 tribe, race ▷ *verb* 3 sit, as hen on eggs 4 meditate, fret over > **brood'y** *adjective* **brood•i•er, brood•i•est** moody, sullen
brook[1] [bruuk] *noun* small stream
brook[2] *verb transitive* put up with, endure, tolerate
broom *noun* 1 brush for sweeping 2 yellow-flowered shrub > **broom'stick** *noun* handle of broom
broth [brawth] *noun* 1 thick soup 2 stock

DICTIONARY • THESAURUS

verge
brisk *adjective* LIVELY, active, bustling, busy, energetic, quick, sprightly, spry, vigorous
briskly *adverb* QUICKLY, actively, apace, efficiently, energetically, promptly, rapidly, readily, smartly
bristle *noun* 1 HAIR, barb, prickle, spine, stubble, thorn, whisker
▷ *verb* 2 STAND UP, rise, stand on end
3 BE ANGRY, bridle, flare up, rage, see red, seethe
bristly *adjective* HAIRY, prickly, rough, stubbly
brittle *adjective* FRAGILE, breakable, crisp, crumbling, crumbly, delicate, frail, frangible, friable
broach *verb* 1 BRING UP, introduce, mention, open up, propose, raise the subject, speak of, suggest, talk of, touch on
2 OPEN, crack, draw off, pierce, puncture, start, tap, uncork
broad *adjective* 1 WIDE, ample, expansive, extensive, generous, large, roomy, spacious, vast, voluminous, widespread
2 GENERAL, all-embracing, comprehensive, encyclopedic, inclusive, sweeping, wide, wide-ranging
broadcast *noun* 1 TRANSMISSION, program, show, telecast
▷ *verb* 2 TRANSMIT, air, beam, cable, put on the air, radio, relay, show, televise
3 MAKE PUBLIC, advertise, announce, circulate, proclaim, publish, report, spread
broaden *verb* EXPAND, develop, enlarge, extend, increase, spread, stretch, supplement, swell, widen
broad-minded *adjective* TOLERANT, free-thinking, indulgent, liberal, open-minded, permissive, unbiased, unbigoted, unprejudiced
broadside *noun* ATTACK, assault, battering, bombardment, censure, criticism, denunciation, diatribe
brochure *noun* BOOKLET, advertisement, circular, folder, handbill, hand-out, leaflet, mailshot, pamphlet
broke *adjective* (*informal*) PENNILESS, bankrupt, bust (*informal*), down and out, down on one's luck (*informal*), impoverished, insolvent, in the red, ruined, short
broken *adjective* 1 SMASHED, burst, fractured, fragmented, ruptured, separated, severed, shattered
2 INTERRUPTED, discontinuous, erratic, fragmentary, incomplete, intermittent, spasmodic
3 NOT WORKING, defective, imperfect, kaput (*informal*), on the blink (*slang*), out of order
4 IMPERFECT, disjointed, halting, hesitating, stammering
brokenhearted *adjective* HEARTBROKEN, desolate, devastated, disconsolate, grief-stricken, inconsolable, miserable, sorrowful, wretched
broker *noun* DEALER, agent, factor, go-between, intermediary, middleman, negotiator
bronze *adjective* REDDISH-BROWN, brownish, chestnut, copper, rust, tan
brood *noun* 1 OFFSPRING, clutch, family, issue, litter, progeny
▷ *verb* 2 THINK UPON, agonize, dwell upon,

broth•el [BROTH-əl] *noun* house of prostitution
broth•er [BRUTH-ər] *noun* 1 son of same parents 2 one closely united with another > **broth'er•hood** [-huud] *noun* 1 relationship 2 fraternity, company > **broth'er•ly** *adjective* > **broth'er-in-law** *noun* 1 brother of husband or wife 2 husband of sister
brought *pt./pp. of* **bring**
brow *noun* 1 ridge over eyes 2 forehead 3 eyebrow 4 edge of hill > **brow'beat** *verb transitive* **-beat, -beat•en, -beat•ing** bully
brown *adjective* **-er, -est** 1 of dark color inclining to red or yellow ▷ *noun* 2 the color ▷ *verb* 3 make, become brown > **browned off** (*slang*) 1 angry 2 fed up
Brown•ie [BROW-nee] *noun* 1 Girl Scout 7 to 10 years old 2 (**brown•ie**) 3 small, nutted square of chocolate cake > **Brownie point** notional mark to one's credit for being seen to do the right thing
browse [browz] *verb intransitive* **browsed, brows•ing** 1 look through (book, articles for sale, etc.) in a casual manner 2 feed on shoots and leaves 3 *computing* read hypertext, esp. on the Internet > **brows'er** *noun computers.* software package that enables a user to read hypertext, esp. on the Internet
bruise [brooz] *verb transitive* **bruised, bruis•ing** 1 injure without breaking skin ▷ *noun* 2 contusion, discoloration caused by blow > **bruis'er** *noun* (*informal*) strong, tough person
brunch *noun* (*informal*) breakfast and lunch combined
bru•nette [broo-NET] *noun* 1 person of dark complexion and hair ▷ *adjective* 2 dark brown
brunt *noun* 1 shock of attack, chief stress 2 first blow
brush *noun* 1 device with bristles, hairs, wires, etc. used for cleaning, painting, etc. 2 act, instance of brushing 3 brief contact 4 skirmish, fight 5 bushy tail, bushy haircut 6 dense growth of bushes, shrubs, etc. 7 (carbon) device taking electric current from moving to stationary parts of generator, etc. ▷ *verb* 8 apply, remove, clean, with brush 9 touch, discuss lightly > **brush'off** *noun* (*informal*) 1 dismissal 2 refusal 3 snub 4 rebuff > **brush'fire** *noun* fire in area of bushes, shrubs, etc. > **brush'wood** *noun* 1 broken-off branches 2 land covered with scrub
brusque [brusk] *adjective* rough in manner, curt, blunt
brute [broot] *noun* 1 any animal except man 2 crude, vicious person ▷ *adjective* 3 animal 4 sensual, stupid 5 physical > **bru'tal** *adjective* > **bru•tal'i•ty** *noun* > **bru'tal•ize** *verb transitive* **-ized, -iz•ing** > **brut'ish** *adjective* bestial, gross
Btu British thermal unit
bub•ble [BUB-əl] *noun* 1 hollow globe of liquid, blown out with air 2 something insubstantial, not serious 3 transparent dome ▷ *verb intransitive* **-bled, -bling** 4 rise in bubbles 5 make gurgling sound
bu•bon•ic plague [byoo-BON-ik playg] *noun* acute infectious disease characterized by swellings and fever
buc•ca•neer [buk-ə-NEER] *noun* 1 pirate 2 unscrupulous adventurer > **buc•ca•neer'ing** *noun*
buck [buk] *noun* 1 male deer, or other male animal 2 act of bucking 3 (*slang*) dollar ▷ *verb* 4 of horse, attempt to throw rider by jumping upward, etc. 5 resist, oppose (something) > **buck'shot** *noun* lead shot in shotgun shell > **buck•teeth** *plural noun* projecting upper teeth **pass the buck** shift blame or responsibility to another person
buck•et [BUK-it] *noun* 1 vessel, round with arched handle, for water, etc. 2 anything

DICTIONARY **b** THESAURUS

mope, mull over, muse, ponder, ruminate
brook¹ *noun* STREAM, beck, rill, rivulet, watercourse
brother *noun* 1 SIBLING, blood brother, kin, kinsman, relation, relative
2 MONK, cleric, friar
brotherhood *noun* 1 FELLOWSHIP, brotherliness, camaraderie, companionship, comradeship, friendliness, kinship
2 ASSOCIATION, alliance, community, fraternity, guild, league, order, society, union
brotherly *adjective* KIND, affectionate, altruistic, amicable, benevolent, cordial, fraternal, friendly, neighborly, philanthropic, sympathetic
browbeat *verb* BULLY, badger, coerce, dragoon, hector, intimidate, ride roughshod over, threaten, tyrannize
brown *adjective* 1 BRUNETTE, auburn, bay, bronze, chestnut, chocolate, coffee, dun, hazel, sunburned, tan, tanned, tawny, umber
▷ *verb* 2 FRY, cook, grill, sauté, seal, sear
browse *verb* 1 SKIM, dip into, examine cursorily, flip through, glance at, leaf through, look round, look through, peruse, scan, survey
2 GRAZE, chow down (*slang*), eat, feed, nibble
bruise *verb* 1 DISCOLOR, damage, injure, mar, mark, pound
▷ *noun* 2 DISCOLORATION, black mark, blemish, contusion, injury, mark, swelling
brunt *noun* FULL FORCE, burden, force, impact, pressure, shock, strain, stress, thrust, violence
brush¹ *noun* 1 BROOM, besom, sweeper
2 ENCOUNTER, clash, conflict, confrontation, skirmish, tussle
▷ *verb* 3 CLEAN, buff, paint, polish, sweep, wash
4 TOUCH, flick, glance, graze, kiss, scrape, stroke, sweep
brush² *noun* SHRUBS, brushwood, bushes, copse, scrub, thicket, undergrowth
brush off *verb* (*slang*) IGNORE, blow off (*slang*), disdain, dismiss, disregard, reject, repudiate, scorn, snub, spurn
brush up *verb* REVISE, bone up (*informal*), cram, go over, polish up, read up, refresh one's memory, relearn, study
brusque *adjective* CURT, abrupt, discourteous, gruff, impolite, sharp, short, surly, terse
brutal *adjective* 1 CRUEL, bloodthirsty, heartless, inhuman, ruthless, savage, uncivilized, vicious
2 HARSH, callous, gruff, impolite, insensitive, rough, rude, severe
brutality *noun* CRUELTY, atrocity, barbarism, bloodthirstiness, ferocity, inhumanity, ruthlessness, savagery, viciousness
brute *noun* 1 SAVAGE, barbarian, beast, devil, fiend, monster, sadist, swine
2 ANIMAL, beast, creature, wild animal
▷ *adjective* 3 MINDLESS, bodily, carnal, fleshly,

resembling this > **buck'et•ful** *noun, plural* **-fuls** > **bucket seat** seat with back shaped to occupier's figure
buck•le [BUK-əl] *noun* 1 metal clasp for fastening belt, strap, etc. ▷ *verb transitive* **-led, -ling** 2 fasten with buckle ▷ *verb intransitive* **-led, -ling** 3 warp, bend > **buckle down** start work
bu•col•ic [byoo-KOL-ik] *adjective* rustic
bud *noun* 1 shoot or sprout on plant containing unopened leaf, flower, etc. ▷ *verb intransitive* **bud•ded, bud•ding** 2 begin to grow ▷ *verb transitive* **bud•ded, bud•ding** 3 to graft
Bud•dhism [BOO-diz-əm] *noun* religion founded in India by Buddha > **Bud'dhist** *adjective, noun*
bud•dy [BUD-ee] *noun, plural* **-dies** (*informal*) pal, chum
budge [buj] *verb intransitive* **budged, budg•ing** move, stir
budg•et [BUJ-it] *noun* 1 annual financial statement 2 plan of systematic spending ▷ *verb intransitive* 3 prepare financial statement 4 plan financially
buff[1] *noun* 1 light yellow color 2 bare skin 3 polishing pad ▷ *verb transitive* 4 polish
buff[2] *noun* (*informal*) expert on some subject
buf•fa•lo [BUF-ə-loh] *noun, plural* **-los, -loes** any of several species of large oxen
buff•er [BUF-ər] *noun* 1 contrivance to lessen shock of concussion 2 person, country that shields another against annoyance, etc.
buf•fet[1] [BUF-it] *noun* 1 blow, slap 2 misfortune ▷ *verb transitive* 3 strike with blows 4 contend against > **buf'fet•ing** *noun*
buf•fet[2] [bə-FAY] *noun* 1 refreshment bar 2 meal at which guests serve themselves 3 sideboard
buf•foon [bə-FOON] *noun* 1 clown 2 fool > **buf•foon'er•y** *noun* clowning
bug *noun* 1 any small insect 2 (*informal*) disease, infection 3 concealed listening device ▷ *verb transitive* **bugged, bug•ging** 4 install secret microphone, etc. 5 (*informal*) annoy
bug•a•boo [BUG-ə-boo] *noun, plural* **-boos** something that causes fear or worry
bug•bear [BUG-bair] *noun* 1 object of needless terror 2 nuisance
bug•ger [BUG-ər] *noun* 1 (*vulgar*) sodomite 2 (*informal*) worthless person 3 (*informal*) lad
bu•gle [BYOO-gəl] *noun* instrument like trumpet > **bu'gler** *noun*
build [bild] *verb* **built, build•ing** 1 make, construct, by putting together parts or materials ▷ *noun* 2 make, form 3 physique > **build'ing** *noun*
bulb *noun* 1 modified leaf bud emitting roots from base, e.g. onion 2 anything resembling this 3 globe surrounding filament of electric light ▷ *verb intransitive* 4 form bulbs > **bul'bous** *adjective*
bulge [bulj] *noun* 1 swelling, protuberance 2 temporary increase ▷ *verb intransitive* **bulged, bulg•ing** 3 swell out > **bulg'i•ness** *noun*
bu•li•mi•a [byoo-LEE-mee-ə] *noun* disorder characterized by compulsive overeating followed by self-induced vomiting > **bu•li'mic** [byoo-LEE-mik] *adjective, noun*
bulk *noun* 1 size 2 volume 3 greater part 4 cargo ▷ *verb intransitive* 5 be of weight or importance > **bulk'i•ness** *noun* > **bulk'y** *adjective* **bulk•i•er, bulk•i•est**
bulk•head [BULK-hed] *noun* partition in

instinctive, physical, senseless, unthinking
bubble *noun* 1 AIR BALL, bead, blister, blob, drop, droplet, globule
▷ *verb* 2 FOAM, boil, effervesce, fizz, froth, percolate, seethe, sparkle
3 GURGLE, babble, burble, murmur, ripple, trickle
bubbly *adjective* 1 LIVELY, animated, bouncy, elated, excited, happy, merry, sparky, wired (*slang*)
2 FROTHY, carbonated, effervescent, fizzy, foamy, sparkling
buccaneer *noun* PIRATE, corsair, freebooter, privateer, sea-rover
buckle *noun* 1 FASTENER, catch, clasp, clip, hasp
▷ *verb* 2 FASTEN, clasp, close, hook, secure
3 DISTORT, bend, bulge, cave in, collapse, contort, crumple, fold, twist, warp
bud *noun* 1 SHOOT, embryo, germ, sprout
▷ *verb* 2 DEVELOP, burgeon, burst forth, grow, shoot, sprout
budding *adjective* DEVELOPING, beginning, burgeoning, embryonic, fledgling, growing, incipient, nascent, potential, promising
budge *verb* MOVE, dislodge, push, shift, stir
budget *noun* 1 ALLOWANCE, allocation, cost, finances, funds, means, resources
▷ *verb* 2 PLAN, allocate, apportion, cost, estimate, ration
buff[1] *adjective* 1 YELLOWISH-BROWN, sandy, straw, tan, yellowish
▷ *verb* 2 POLISH, brush, burnish, rub, shine, smooth
buff[2] *noun* (*informal*) EXPERT, addict, admirer, aficionado, connoisseur, devotee, enthusiast, fan
buffer *noun* SAFEGUARD, bulwark, bumper, cushion, fender, intermediary, screen, shield, shock absorber
buffet[1] *noun* SNACK BAR, brasserie, café, cafeteria, refreshment counter, sideboard
buffet[2] *verb* BATTER, beat, bump, knock, pound, pummel, strike, thump, wallop (*informal*)
buffoon *noun* CLOWN, comedian, comic, fool, harlequin, jester, joker, wag
bug *noun* 1 (*informal*) ILLNESS, disease, infection, virus
2 FAULT, defect, error, flaw, glitch, gremlin
▷ *verb* 3 (*informal*) ANNOY, bother, disturb, get on one's nerves (*informal*), hassle (*informal*), irritate, pester, vex
4 TAP, eavesdrop, listen in, spy
bugbear *noun* PET HATE, bane, bête noire, bogey, dread, horror, nightmare
build *verb* 1 CONSTRUCT, assemble, erect, fabricate, form, make, put up, raise
▷ *noun* 2 PHYSIQUE, body, figure, form, frame, shape, structure
building *noun* STRUCTURE, domicile, dwelling, edifice, house
build-up *noun* INCREASE, accumulation, development, enlargement, escalation, expansion, gain, growth
bulbous *adjective* BULGING, bloated, convex,

interior of ship

bull[1] [buul] *noun* 1 male of cattle 2 male of various other animals > **bull'dog** *noun* thickset breed of dog > **bull'doze** [-dohz] *verb* **-dozed, -doz•ing** > **bull'doz•er** *noun* powerful tractor with blade for excavating, etc. > **bul'lock** [-lək] *noun* castrated bull > **bull's'-eye** *noun, plural* **-eyes** middle part of target

bull[2] *noun* papal edict

bull[3] *noun* (*slang*) 1 nonsense ▷ *verb* 2 talk nonsense (to)

bul•let [BUUL-it] *noun* projectile discharged from rifle, pistol, etc.

bul•le•tin [BUUL-i-tn] *noun* official report

bul•lion [BUUL-yən] *noun* gold or silver in mass

bul•ly [BUUL-ee] *noun, plural* **-lies** 1 one who hurts, persecutes, or intimidates weaker people ▷ *verb transitive* **-lied, -ly•ing** 2 intimidate, overawe 3 ill-treat ▷ *adjective, interjection* 4 first-rate

bul•rush [BUUL-rush] *noun* tall reedlike marsh plant with brown velvety spike

bul•wark [BUUL-wərk] *noun* 1 rampart 2 any defense or means of security 3 raised side of ship 4 breakwater

bum *noun* 1 loafer, scrounger ▷ *verb transitive* **bummed, bum•ming** (*informal*) 2 get by scrounging ▷ *adjective* (*slang*) 3 worthless 4 inferior 5 disabled

bum•ble [BUM-bəl] *verb* **-bled, -bling** perform clumsily > **bum'bler** *noun*

bum•ble•bee [BUM-bəl-bee] *noun* large bee

bump *noun* 1 heavy blow, dull in sound 2 swelling caused by blow 3 protuberance 4 sudden movement ▷ *verb transitive* 5 strike or push against > **bump'er** *noun* 1 horizontal bar at front and rear of automobile to protect against damage 2 full glass ▷ *adjective* 3 full, abundant > **bump off** (*slang*) murder

bump•kin [BUMP-kin] *noun* rustic

bump•tious [BUMP-shəs] *adjective* offensively self-assertive

bun *noun* 1 small, round bread or cake 2 round knot of hair 3 (*slang*) enough liquor to make one drunk

bunch *noun* 1 number of things tied or growing together 2 cluster 3 tuft, knot 4 group, party ▷ *verb transitive* 5 put together in bunch ▷ *verb intransitive* 6 gather together

bun•dle [BUN-dl] *noun* 1 package 2 number of things tied together 3 (*slang*) lot of money ▷ *verb transitive* **-dled, -dling** 4 tie in bundle 5 send (off) without ceremony

bung *noun* 1 stopper for cask 2 large cork ▷ *verb transitive* 3 stop up, seal, close > **bung'hole** *noun*

bun•ga•low [BUNG-gə-loh] *noun* one-storied house

bun•gle [BUNG-gəl] *verb transitive* **-gled, -gling** 1 do badly from lack of skill, botch ▷ *verb intransitive* **-gled, -gling** 2 act clumsily, awkwardly ▷ *noun* 3 blunder, muddle > **bun'gler** *noun*

bun•ion [BUN-yən] *noun* inflamed swelling on foot or toe

bunk[1] [bungk] *noun* 1 narrow, shelflike bed ▷ *verb intransitive* 2 stay the night (with) > **bunk bed** one of pair of beds constructed one above the other

---

rounded, swelling, swollen

bulge *noun* 1 SWELLING, bump, hump, lump, projection, protrusion, protuberance
2 INCREASE, boost, intensification, rise, surge
▷ *verb* 3 SWELL OUT, dilate, distend, expand, project, protrude, puff out, stick out

bulk *noun* 1 SIZE, dimensions, immensity, largeness, magnitude, substance, volume, weight
2 MAIN PART, better part, body, lion's share, majority, mass, most, nearly all, preponderance

bulky *adjective* LARGE, big, cumbersome, heavy, hulking, massive, substantial, unwieldy, voluminous, weighty

bulldoze *verb* DEMOLISH, flatten, level, raze

bullet *noun* PROJECTILE, ball, missile, pellet, shot, slug

bulletin *noun* ANNOUNCEMENT, account, communication, communiqué, dispatch, message, news flash, notification, report, statement

bully *noun* 1 PERSECUTOR, browbeater, bully boy, coercer, intimidator, oppressor, ruffian, tormentor, tough
▷ *verb* 2 PERSECUTE, browbeat, coerce, domineer, hector, intimidate, oppress, push around (*slang*), terrorize, tyrannize

bulwark *noun* 1 FORTIFICATION, bastion, buttress, defense, embankment, partition, rampart
2 DEFENSE, buffer, guard, mainstay, safeguard, security, support

bumbling *adjective* CLUMSY, awkward, blundering, bungling, incompetent, inefficient, inept, maladroit, muddled

bump *verb* 1 KNOCK, bang, collide *or* collide with, crash, hit, slam, smash into, strike
2 JERK, bounce, jolt, rattle, shake
▷ *noun* 3 KNOCK, bang, blow, collision, crash, impact, jolt, thud, thump
4 LUMP, bulge, contusion, hump, nodule, protuberance, swelling

bumper *adjective* EXCEPTIONAL, abundant, bountiful, excellent, jumbo (*informal*), massive, whopping (*informal*)

bumpkin *noun* YOKEL, country bumpkin, hick (*informal*), hillbilly, peasant, redneck (*slang*), rustic

bumptious *adjective* COCKY, arrogant, brash, conceited, forward, full of oneself, overconfident, pushy (*informal*), self-assertive

bumpy *adjective* ROUGH, bouncy, choppy, jarring, jerky, jolting, rutted, uneven

bunch *noun* 1 NUMBER, assortment, batch, bundle, clump, cluster, collection, heap, lot, mass, pile
2 GROUP, band, crowd, flock, gang, gathering, party, team
▷ *verb* 3 GROUP, assemble, bundle, cluster, collect, huddle, mass, pack

bundle *noun* 1 BUNCH, assortment, batch, collection, group, heap, mass, pile, stack
▷ *verb* 2 (*with out, off, into, etc.*) PUSH, hurry, hustle, rush, shove, throw, thrust

bundle up *verb* WRAP UP, swathe

bungle *verb* MESS UP, blow (*slang*), blunder, botch, foul up, make a mess of, muff, ruin, spoil

bungling *adjective* INCOMPETENT, blundering,

DICTIONARY **b** THESAURUS

bunk[2] *noun* bunkum
bun•ker [BUNG-kər] *noun* 1 large storage container for oil, coal, etc. 2 sandy hollow on golf course 3 (military) underground defensive position
bun•ko [BUNG-koh] *noun, plural* **-kos** swindling scheme or game
bun•kum [BUNG-kəm] *noun* nonsense
bun•ny [BUN-ee] *noun, plural* **-nies** (*informal*) rabbit
Bun•sen burner [BUN-sən] gas burner, producing great heat, used for chemical experiments
bun'ting[1] *noun* material for flags
bunting[2] *noun* bird with short, stout bill
bu•oy [BOO-ee] *noun* 1 floating marker anchored in sea 2 lifebuoy ▷ *verb transitive* 3 mark with buoy 4 keep from sinking 5 support > **buoy•an•cy** [BOI-ən-see] *noun* > **buoy'ant** *adjective*
bur•ble [BUR-bəl] *verb intransitive* **-bled, -bling** 1 gurgle, as stream or baby 2 talk idly
bur•den [BUR-dn] *noun* 1 load 2 weight, cargo 3 anything difficult to bear ▷ *verb transitive* 4 load, encumber > **burd'en•some** [-səm] *adjective*
bu•reau [BYUUR-oh] *noun, plural* **-reaus, -reaux** [-rohz] 1 office 2 government department > **bu•reauc•ra•cy** [byuu-ROK-rə-see] *noun, plural* **-cies** 1 government by officials 2 body of officials > **bu•reau•crat** [BYUUR-ə-krat] *noun*
bur•geon [BUR-jən] *verb intransitive* 1 bud 2 develop rapidly
burg•er [BUR-gər] *noun* hamburger
bur•gess [BUR-jis] *noun* member of colonial Maryland or Virginia legislature
bur•glar [BUR-glər] *noun* one who enters building to commit theft > **bur'gla•ry** [-glə-ree] *noun* > **bur'gle** [-gəl] *verb transitive* **-gled, -gling**
Bur•gun•dy [BUR-gən-dee] *noun, plural* **-dies** 1 red or white wine produced in Burgundy, France 2 (**bur•gun•dy**) similar wine made elsewhere > **bur•gun•dy** *adjective* dark-purplish red
bur'lap *noun* coarse canvas
bur•lesque [bər-LESK] *noun* 1 (artistic) caricature 2 ludicrous imitation 3 provocative and humorous stage show ▷ *verb transitive* **-lesqued, -lesqu•ing** 4 caricature
bur•ly [BUR-lee] *adjective* **-li•er, -li•est** sturdy, stout, robust
burn *verb transitive* **burned** *or* **burnt, burn•ing** 1 destroy or injure by fire 2 record data on (a CD) ▷ *verb intransitive* **burned** *or* **burnt, burn•ing** 3 be or feel hot 4 be consumed by fire ▷ *noun* 5 injury, mark caused by fire
bur'nish *verb transitive* 1 make bright by rubbing 2 polish ▷ *noun* 3 gloss, luster
burp *verb* (*informal*) belch (esp. of baby) ▷ *noun*
burr[1] *noun* soft trilling sound given to letter *r* in some dialects
burr[2] *noun* rough edge left after cutting, drilling, etc.
burr[3] *noun* head of plant with prickles or hooks
bur•ro [BUR-oh] *noun, plural* **-ros** small donkey
bur•row [BUR-oh] *noun* 1 hole dug by rabbit, etc. ▷ *verb transitive* 2 make holes in ground 3 bore 4 conceal oneself
bur•sar [BUR-sər] *noun* official managing finances of college, monastery, etc.
burst *verb intransitive* **burst, burst•ing** 1 fly asunder 2 break into pieces 3 rend 4 break

clumsy, inept, maladroit
bunk[2] *or* **bunkum** *noun* (*informal*) NONSENSE, balderdash, baloney (*informal*), garbage (*informal*), hogwash, hot air (*informal*), moonshine, poppycock (*informal*), rubbish, stuff and nonsense, twaddle
buoy *noun* 1 MARKER, beacon, float, guide, signal
▷ *verb* 2 ▷ **buoy up** ENCOURAGE, boost, cheer, cheer up, hearten, keep afloat, lift, raise, support, sustain
buoyancy *noun* 1 LIGHTNESS, weightlessness
2 CHEERFULNESS, animation, bounce (*informal*), good humor, high spirits, liveliness
buoyant *adjective* 1 FLOATING, afloat, light, weightless
2 CHEERFUL, carefree, chirpy (*informal*), happy, jaunty, light-hearted, upbeat (*informal*)
burden *noun* 1 LOAD, encumbrance, weight
2 TROUBLE, affliction, millstone, onus, responsibility, strain, weight, worry
▷ *verb* 3 WEIGH DOWN, bother, handicap, load, oppress, saddle with, tax, worry
bureau *noun* 1 OFFICE, agency, branch, department, division, service
2 DESK, writing desk
bureaucracy *noun* 1 GOVERNMENT, administration, authorities, civil service, corridors of power, officials, the system
2 RED TAPE, officialdom, regulations
bureaucrat *noun* OFFICIAL, administrator, civil servant, functionary, mandarin, officer, public servant
burglar *noun* HOUSEBREAKER, cat burglar, filcher, pilferer, robber, sneak thief, thief
burglary *noun* BREAKING AND ENTERING, break-in, housebreaking, larceny, robbery, stealing, theft, thieving
burial *noun* INTERMENT, entombment, exequies, funeral, obsequies
buried *adjective* 1 INTERRED, entombed, laid to rest
2 HIDDEN, concealed, private, sequestered, tucked away
burlesque *noun* 1 PARODY, caricature, mockery, satire, spoof (*informal*), travesty
▷ *verb* 2 SATIRIZE, ape, caricature, exaggerate, imitate, lampoon, make a monkey out of, make fun of, mock, parody, ridicule, spoof (*informal*), travesty
burly *adjective* BRAWNY, beefy (*informal*), big, bulky, hefty, hulking, stocky, stout, sturdy, thickset, well-built
burn *verb* 1 BE ON FIRE, be ablaze, blaze, flame, flare, glow, go up in flames, smoke
2 SET ON FIRE, char, ignite, incinerate, kindle, light, parch, scorch, sear, singe, toast
3 BE PASSIONATE, be angry, be aroused, be inflamed, fume, seethe, simmer, smolder
burning *adjective* 1 INTENSE, ardent, eager, fervent, impassioned, passionate, vehement
2 CRUCIAL, acute, compelling, critical, essential, important, pressing, significant, urgent, vital
3 BLAZING, fiery, flaming, flashing, gleaming, glowing, illuminated, scorching, smoldering
burnish *verb* POLISH, brighten, buff, furbish,

suddenly into some expression of feeling ▷ *verb transitive* **burst, burst•ing** 5 shatter, break violently ▷ *noun* 6 bursting 7 explosion 8 outbreak 9 spurt

bur•y [BER-ee] *verb transitive* **bur•ied, bur•y•ing** 1 put underground 2 inter 3 conceal > **bur'i•al** *noun, adjective*

bus *noun* 1 large motor vehicle for passengers ▷ *verb* 2 travel or transport by bus 3 work as busboy > **bus'man's holiday** vacation spent in an activity closely resembling one's work

bus•boy [BUS-boi] *noun* waiter's helper in public dining room

bush [buush] *noun* 1 shrub 2 woodland, thicket 3 uncleared country, backwoods, interior > **bushed** *adjective* (*informal*) tired out > **bush'y** *adjective* **bush•i•er, bush•i•est** shaggy > **bush jacket** shirtlike jacket with patch pockets

bush•el [BUUSH-əl] *noun* dry measure of eight gallons

busi•ness [BIZ-nis] *noun* 1 profession, occupation 2 commercial or industrial establishment 3 commerce, trade 4 responsibility, affair, matter 5 work > **business casual** style of casual clothing worn by businesspeople at work

bust¹ *noun* 1 sculpture of head and shoulders of human body 2 woman's breasts

bust² *verb* (*informal*) 1 burst 2 make, become bankrupt ▷ *verb transitive* (*slang*) 3 raid 4 arrest ▷ *adjective* (*informal*) 5 broken 6 bankrupt ▷ *noun* 7 (*slang*) police raid or arrest 8 (*informal*) punch

bus•tle¹ [BUS-əl] *verb intransitive* **-tled, -tling** 1 be noisily busy, active ▷ *noun* 2 fuss, commotion

bustle² *noun hist.* pad worn by ladies to support back of the skirt

bus•y [BIZ-ee] *adjective* **bus•i•er, bus•i•est** 1 actively employed 2 full of activity ▷ *verb transitive* **bus•ied, bus•y•ing** 3 occupy > **bus'y•bod•y** *noun, plural* **-bod•ies** meddler

but *preposition, conjunction* 1 without 2 except 3 only 4 yet 5 still 6 besides

bu•tane [BYOO-tayn] *noun* gas used for fuel

butch [buuch] *adjective, noun* (*slang*) markedly or aggressively masculine (person)

butch•er [BUUCH-ər] *noun* 1 one who kills, dresses animals for food, or sells meat 2 bloody, savage man ▷ *verb transitive* 3 slaughter, murder 4 spoil work > **butch'er•y** *noun*

but•ler [BUT-lər] *noun* chief male servant

butt¹ *noun* 1 the thick end 2 target 3 object of ridicule 4 bottom or unused end of anything

DICTIONARY

b

THESAURUS

glaze, rub up, shine, smooth

burrow *noun* 1 HOLE, den, lair, retreat, shelter, tunnel
▷ *verb* 2 DIG, delve, excavate, hollow out, scoop out, tunnel

burst *verb* 1 EXPLODE, blow up, break, crack, puncture, rupture, shatter, split, tear apart
2 RUSH, barge, break, break out, erupt, gush forth, run, spout
▷ *noun* 3 EXPLOSION, bang, blast, blowout, break, crack, discharge, rupture, split
4 RUSH, gush, gust, outbreak, outburst, outpouring, spate, spurt, surge, torrent
▷ *adjective* 5 RUPTURED, flat, punctured, rent, split

bury *verb* 1 INTER, consign to the grave, entomb, inhume, lay to rest
2 EMBED, engulf, submerge
3 HIDE, conceal, cover, enshroud, secrete, stow away

bush *noun* 1 SHRUB, hedge, plant, shrubbery, thicket
2 ▷ **the bush** THE WILD, backwoods, brush, scrub, scrubland, woodland

bushy *adjective* THICK, bristling, fluffy, fuzzy, luxuriant, rough, shaggy, unruly

busily *adverb* ACTIVELY, assiduously, briskly, diligently, energetically, industriously, purposefully, speedily, strenuously

business *noun* 1 TRADE, bargaining, commerce, dealings, industry, manufacturing, selling, transaction
2 ESTABLISHMENT, company, concern, corporation, enterprise, firm, organization, venture
3 PROFESSION, career, employment, function, job, line, occupation, trade, vocation, work
4 CONCERN, affair, assignment, duty, problem, responsibility, task

businesslike *adjective* EFFICIENT, methodical, orderly, organized, practical, professional, systematic, thorough, well-ordered

businessman *noun* EXECUTIVE, capitalist, employer, entrepreneur, financier, industrialist, merchant, tradesman, tycoon

bust¹ *noun* BOSOM, breast, chest, front, torso

bust² (*informal*) *verb* 1 BREAK, burst, fracture, rupture
2 ARREST, catch, raid, search
▷ *adjective* 3 ▷ **go bust** GO BANKRUPT, become insolvent, be ruined, fail

bustle¹ *verb* 1 HURRY, fuss, hasten, rush, scamper, scurry, scuttle
▷ *noun* 2 ACTIVITY, ado, commotion, excitement, flurry, fuss, hurly-burly, stir, to-do

bustling *adjective* BUSY, active, buzzing, crowded, full, humming, lively, swarming, teeming

busy *adjective* 1 OCCUPIED, active, employed, engaged, hard at work, industrious, on duty, rushed off one's feet, working
2 LIVELY, energetic, exacting, full, hectic, hustling
▷ *verb* 3 OCCUPY, absorb, employ, engage, engross, immerse, interest

busybody *noun* NOSY ROSY (*United States informal*), gossip, meddler, snooper, stirrer (*informal*), troublemaker

but *conjunction* 1 HOWEVER, further, moreover, nevertheless, on the contrary, on the other hand, still, yet
▷ *preposition* 2 EXCEPT, bar, barring, excepting, excluding, notwithstanding, save, with the exception of
▷ *adverb* 3 ONLY, just, merely, simply, singly, solely

butcher *noun* 1 MURDERER, destroyer, killer, slaughterer, slayer
▷ *verb* 2 SLAUGHTER, carve, clean, cut, cut up, dress, joint, prepare
3 KILL, assassinate, cut down, destroy, exterminate, liquidate, massacre, put to the sword, slaughter, slay

▷ *verb* 5 lie, be placed end on to
butt² *verb* 1 strike with head 2 push ▷ *noun* 3 blow with head, as of sheep **butt in** interfere, meddle > **butt•in'sky** *noun, plural* **-skies** (*slang*) meddler
but•ter [BUT-ər] *noun* 1 fatty substance got from cream by churning ▷ *verb transitive* 2 spread with or as if with butter 3 flatter
but•ter•fly [BUT-ər-flī] *noun, plural* **-flies** 1 insect with large wings 2 inconstant person 3 stroke in swimming ▷ *verb transitive* **-flied, -fly•ing** 4 split (foodstuff) into shape resembling butterfly
but•ter•milk [BUT-ər-milk] *noun* milk that remains after churning
but•tock [BUT-ək] *noun* (*usually plural*) rump, protruding hinder part
but•ton [BUT-n] *noun* 1 knob, stud for fastening dress 2 knob that operates doorbell, machine, etc. ▷ *verb transitive* 3 fasten with buttons > **but'ton•hole** *noun* 1 slit in garment to pass button through as fastening ▷ *verb transitive* **-holed, -hol•ing** 2 detain (unwilling) person in conversation
but•tress [BU-tris] *noun* 1 structure to support wall 2 prop ▷ *verb transitive*
bux•om [BUK-səm] *adjective* 1 full of health, plump, gay 2 large-breasted
buy [bī] *verb transitive* **bought, buy•ing** 1 get by payment, purchase 2 bribe > **buy'er** *noun*
buzz *verb intransitive* 1 make humming sound ▷ *noun* 2 humming sound of bees 3 (*informal*) telephone call > **buzz'er** *noun* any apparatus that makes buzzing sound > **buzz word** (*informal*) word, oft. orig. jargon, that becomes fashionable
buz•zard [BUZ-ərd] *noun* bird of prey of hawk family
by [bī] *preposition* 1 near 2 along 3 across 4 past 5 during 6 not later than 7 through use or agency of 8 in units of ▷ *adverb* 9 near 10 away, aside 11 past **by and by** soon, in the future **by and large** 12 on the whole 13 speaking generally > **come by** obtain
bye [bī] *noun sports* in early round of a tournament, a situation in which player, team not paired with opponent advances to next round without playing
by•gone [BĪ-gawn] *adjective* 1 past, former ▷ *noun* (*often plural*) 2 past occurrence
by-law [BĪ-law] *noun* law, regulation made by an organization
by•line [BĪ-līn] *noun* printed line identifying author of news story, article, etc.
by•pass [BĪ-pas] *noun* 1 road for diversion of traffic from crowded centers 2 secondary channel carrying fluid around a part and back to the main stream ▷ *verb transitive*
by•play [BĪ-play] *noun* diversion, action apart from main action of play
byte [bīt] *noun computing* sequence of bits processed as single unit of information
by•word [BĪ-wurd] *noun* a well-known name, saying

DICTIONARY • THESAURUS

butt¹ *noun* 1 END, haft, handle, hilt, shaft, shank, stock
2 STUB, cigarette end, leftover, tip
3 (*informal*) BUTTOCKS, behind (*informal*), bottom, derrière (*French*) (*euphemistic*), rump (*informal*), tush (*slang*)
4 TARGET, dupe, laughing stock, victim
butt³ *verb*
▷ *noun* 1 (*with or of the head or horns*) KNOCK, bump, poke, prod, push, ram, shove, thrust
▷ *verb* 2 ▷ **butt in** INTERFERE, chip in (*informal*), cut in, interrupt, intrude, meddle, put one's oar in, stick one's nose in
butt⁴ *noun* CASK, barrel
buttonhole *verb* DETAIN, accost, bore, catch, grab, importune, take aside, waylay
buttress *noun* 1 SUPPORT, brace, mainstay, prop, reinforcement, stanchion, strut
▷ *verb* 2 SUPPORT, back up, bolster, prop up, reinforce, shore up, strengthen, sustain, uphold
buxom *adjective* PLUMP, ample, bosomy, busty, curvaceous, healthy, voluptuous, well-rounded
buy *verb* 1 PURCHASE, acquire, get, invest in, obtain, pay for, procure, shop for
▷ *noun* 2 PURCHASE, acquisition, bargain, deal
by *preposition* 1 VIA, by way of, over
2 THROUGH, through the agency of
3 NEAR, along, beside, close to, next to, past
▷ *adverb* 4 NEAR, at hand, close, handy, in reach
5 PAST, aside, away, to one side
bygone *adjective* PAST, antiquated, extinct, forgotten, former, lost, of old, olden
bypass *verb* GO ROUND, avoid, circumvent, depart from, detour round, deviate from, get round, give a wide berth to, pass round
bystander *noun* ONLOOKER, eyewitness, looker-on, observer, passer-by, spectator, viewer, watcher, witness
byword *noun* SAYING, adage, maxim, motto, precept, proverb, slogan

Cc

C 1 *chem.* Carbon 2 Celsius
Ca *chem.* calcium
cab *noun* 1 taxi 2 driver's enclosed compartment on locomotive, truck, etc. > **cab'driv•er** *noun* > **cab'stand** *noun* place where taxis may wait to be hired
ca•bal [kə-BAL] *noun* 1 small group of intriguers 2 secret plot
cab•a•ret [kab-ə-RAY] *noun* night club
cab•bage [KAB-ij] *noun* green vegetable with usu. round head of leaves
ca•ber [KAY-bər] *noun* pole tossed as trial of strength at Scottish games
cab•in [KAB-in] *noun* 1 hut, shed 2 small room esp. in ship > **cabin cruiser** power boat with cabin, bunks, etc.
cab•i•net [KAB-ə-nit] *noun* 1 piece of furniture with drawers or shelves 2 outer case of television, radio, etc. 3 body of advisers to head of state > **cab'i•net•mak•er** *noun* artisan who makes fine furniture
ca•ble [KAY-bəl] *noun* 1 strong rope 2 wire or bundle of wires conveying electric power, telegraph signals, etc. 3 message sent by this 4 cable TV ▷ *verb* **-bled, -bling** 5 telegraph by cable > **ca'ble•gram** *noun* cabled message > **cable TV** TV service conveyed by cable to subscribers
ca•boo•dle [kə-BOOD-l] *noun* (*informal*) **the whole caboodle** the whole lot
ca•boose [kə-BOOS] *noun* (usu. last) car of freight train, for use by train crew
ca•ca•o [kə-KAH-oh] *noun* tropical tree from the seeds of which chocolate and cocoa are made
cache [kash] *noun* 1 secret hiding place 2 store of food, arms, etc.
ca•chet [ka-SHAY] *noun* 1 mark, stamp 2 mark of authenticity 3 prestige, distinction
cack•le [KAK-əl] *verb intransitive* **-led, -ling** 1 make chattering noise, as hen ▷ *noun* 2 cackling noise or laughter 3 empty chatter
ca•coph•o•ny [kə-KOF-ə-nee] *noun, plural* **-nies** 1 disagreeable sound 2 discord of sounds > **ca•coph'o•nous** *adjective*
cac•tus [KAK-təs] *noun, plural* **-ti** [-tī] spiny succulent plant
cad *noun* dishonorable, ungentlemanly person
ca•dav•er [kə-DAV-ər] *noun* corpse > **ca•dav'er•ous** *adjective* 1 corpselike 2 sickly-looking 3 gaunt
cad•die [KAD-ee] *noun* person hired to carry

---

cab *noun* TAXI, hackney carriage, minicab, taxicab
cabal *noun* 1 CLIQUE, caucus, conclave, faction, league, party, set
2 PLOT, conspiracy, intrigue, machination, scheme
cabin *noun* 1 ROOM, berth, compartment, quarters
2 HUT, chalet, cottage, lodge, shack, shanty, shed
cabinet *noun* CUPBOARD, case, chiffonier, closet, commode, dresser, escritoire, locker
Cabinet *noun* COUNCIL, administration, assembly, counselors, ministry
caddish *adjective* UNGENTLEMANLY, despicable, ill-bred, lousy (*slang*), low, scuzzy (*slang*),

golfer's clubs, find the ball, etc.

ca•dence [KAYD-ns] *noun* fall or modulation of voice in music, speech, or verse

ca•den•za [kə-DEN-zə] *noun mus.* elaborate passage for solo instrument or singer

ca•det [kə-DET] *noun* youth in training, esp. for officer status in armed forces

cadge [kaj] *verb* **cadged, cadg•ing** get (food, money, etc.) by begging > **cadg'er** *noun* sponger

cad•mi•um [KAD-mee-əm] *noun* metallic element

ca•dre [KAD-ree] *noun* nucleus or framework, esp. skeleton of military unit

Cae•sar•e•an section [si-ZAIR-ee-ən] surgical incision through abdominal wall to deliver a baby

café [ka-FAY] *noun* 1 small or inexpensive restaurant serving light refreshments 2 bar > **caf•e•te•ri•a** [kaf-ə-TEE-ree-ə] *noun* restaurant designed for self-service

caf•feine [ka-FEEN] *noun* stimulating alkaloid found in tea and coffee plants

caf•tan [KAF-tan] *noun* 1 long coatlike Eastern garment 2 imitation of it, esp. as woman's long, loose dress with sleeves

cage [kayj] *noun* 1 enclosure, box with bars or wires, esp. for keeping animals or birds 2 place of confinement 3 enclosed platform of elevator, esp. in mine ▷ *verb transitive* **caged, cag•ing** 4 put in cage, confine > **cag'ey** *adjective* **cag•i•er, cag•i•est** wary, shrewd

ca•hoots [kə-HOOTS] *plural noun* (*slang*) partnership, as **in cahoots with**

cairn [kairn] *noun* heap of stones, esp. as monument or landmark

cais•son [KAY-son] *noun* 1 chamber for working under water 2 apparatus for lifting vessel out of the water 3 ammunition wagon > **caisson disease** the bends

ca•jole [kə-JOHL] *verb transitive* **-joled, -jol•ing** persuade by flattery, wheedle > **ca•jol'er** *noun*

cake [kayk] *noun* 1 baked, sweetened, bread-like food 2 compact mass ▷ *verb* **caked, cak•ing** 3 make into a cake 4 harden (as of mud)

cal•a•boose [KAL-ə-boos] *noun* (*informal*) jail

cal•a•mine [KAL-ə-mīn] *noun* pink powder used medicinally in soothing ointment

ca•lam•i•ty [kə-LAM-i-tee] *noun, plural* **-ties** 1 great misfortune 2 deep distress, disaster > **ca•lam'i•tous** *adjective*

cal•ci•um [KAL-see-əm] *noun* metallic element, the basis of lime > **cal•car'e•ous** [-KAIR-ee-əs] *adjective* containing lime > **cal'ci•fy** *verb* **-fied, -fy•ing** convert, be converted, to lime

cal•cu•late [KAL-kyə-layt] *verb transitive* **-lat•ed, -lat•ing** 1 estimate 2 compute ▷ *verb intransitive* **-lat•ed, -lat•ing** 3 make reckonings > **cal'cu•lat•ing** *adjective* 1 able to perform calculations 2 shrewd, designing, scheming > **cal'cu•la•tor** *noun* electronic or mechanical device for making calculations > **cal'cu•lus** *noun, plural* **-li** [-lī] 1 branch of mathematics 2 stone in body

cal•en•dar [KAL-ən-dər] *noun* 1 table of months and days in the year 2 list of events, documents 3 register

calf[1] [kaf] *noun, plural* **calves** [kavz] 1 young of cow and of other animals 2 leather made of calf's skin > **calve** [kav] *verb intransitive* **calved, calv•ing** give birth to calf

calf[2] *noun, plural* **calves** fleshy back part of leg below knee

cal•i•ber [KAL-ə-bər] *noun* 1 size of bore of gun 2 capacity, character > **cal'i•brate** [-brayt] *verb transitive* **-brat•ed, -brat•ing** mark scale of measuring instrument, etc. > **cal•i•bra'tion** *noun*

cal•i•co [KAL-i-koh] *noun, plural* **-coes, -cos** printed cotton fabric

cal•i•per [KAL-ə-pər] *noun* 1 instrument for measuring diameters 2 thickness, esp. of tree, paper

cal•is•then•ics [kal-əs-THEN-iks] *plural noun* light gymnastic exercises

call [kawl] *verb transitive* 1 speak loudly to attract attention 2 summon 3 (oft. with *up*) telephone 4 name ▷ *verb intransitive* 5 shout 6 pay visit ▷ *noun* 7 shout 8 animal's cry 9 visit 10 inner urge, summons, as to be minister, etc. 11 need, demand > **call'ing** *noun* vocation, profession > **call box** outdoor telephone for

---

unmannerly

café *noun* SNACK BAR, brasserie, cafeteria, coffee bar, coffee shop, lunchroom, restaurant, tearoom

cage *noun* ENCLOSURE, pen, pound

cagey *adjective* (*informal*) WARY, careful, cautious, chary, discreet, guarded, noncommittal, shrewd, wily

cajole *verb* PERSUADE, brown-nose (*slang*), coax, flatter, seduce, sweet-talk (*informal*), wheedle

cake *noun* 1 BLOCK, bar, cube, loaf, lump, mass, slab
▷ *verb* 2 ENCRUST, bake, coagulate, congeal, solidify

calamitous *adjective* DISASTROUS, cataclysmic, catastrophic, deadly, devastating, dire, fatal, ruinous, tragic

calamity *noun* DISASTER, cataclysm, catastrophe, misadventure, misfortune, mishap, ruin, tragedy, tribulation

calculate *verb* 1 WORK OUT, compute, count, determine, enumerate, estimate, figure, reckon
2 PLAN, aim, design, intend

calculated *adjective* DELIBERATE, considered, intended, intentional, planned, premeditated, purposeful

calculating *adjective* SCHEMING, crafty, cunning, devious, Machiavellian, manipulative, sharp, shrewd, sly

calculation *noun* 1 WORKING OUT, answer, computation, estimate, forecast, judgment, reckoning, result
2 PLANNING, contrivance, deliberation, discretion, foresight, forethought, precaution

caliber *noun* 1 WORTH, ability, capacity, distinction, merit, quality, stature, talent
2 DIAMETER, bore, gauge, measure

call *verb* 1 NAME, christen, describe as, designate, dub, entitle, label, style, term
2 CRY, arouse, hail, rouse, shout, yell
3 PHONE, telephone
4 SUMMON, assemble, convene, gather, muster, rally
▷ *noun* 5 CRY, hail, scream, shout, signal, whoop, yell
6 SUMMONS, appeal, command, demand,

calling police or fire department > **call girl** prostitute who accepts appointments by telephone > **call up** 1 summon to serve in army 2 imagine

cal•lig•ra•phy [kə-LIG-rə-fee] *noun* handwriting, penmanship > **cal•li•graph'ic** *adjective*

cal•lous [KAL-əs] *adjective* hardened, unfeeling > **cal'lous•ness** *noun*

cal•low [KAL-oh] *adjective* 1 inexperienced 2 immature

cal•lus [KAL-əs] *noun, plural* **-lus•es** area of thick, hardened skin

calm [kahm] *adjective* **-er, -est** 1 still, quiet, tranquil ▷ *noun* 2 stillness 3 tranquility 4 absence of wind ▷ *verb* 5 become, make, still or quiet > **calm'ly** *adverb*

cal•o•rie [KAL-ə-ree] *noun* 1 unit of heat 2 unit of energy obtained from foods > **cal•o•rif'ic** *adjective* heat-making > **cal•o•rim'e•ter** *noun*

cal•u•met [KAL-yə-met] *noun* 1 tobacco pipe of N Amer. Indians 2 peace pipe

cal•um•ny [KAL-əm-nee] *noun, plural* **-nies** slander, false accusation > **ca•lum'ni•ate** *verb transitive* **-at•ed, -at•ing** > **ca•lum•ni•a'tion** *noun*

ca•lyp•so [kə-LIP-soh] *noun, plural* **-sos** (West Indies) improvised song on topical subject

ca•lyx [KAY-liks] *noun, plural* **-lyx•es** covering of bud

cam [kam] *noun* device to change rotary to reciprocating motion > **cam'shaft** *noun* in motor vehicles, rotating shaft to which cams are fixed to lift valves

ca•ma•ra•de•rie [kah-mə-RAH-də-ree] *noun* spirit of comradeship, trust

cam•ber [KAM-bər] *noun* 1 convexity on upper surface of road, bridge, etc. 2 curvature of aircraft wing 3 setting of motor vehicle wheels closer together at bottom than at top

cam•bric [KAYM-brik] *noun* fine white linen or cotton cloth

cam•cord•er [KAM-kor-dər] *noun* combined portable video camera and recorder

came *pt. of* **come**

cam•el [KAM-əl] *noun* animal of Asia and Africa, with humped back, used as beast of burden

cam•e•o [KAM-ee-oh] *noun, plural* **-e•os** 1 medallion, brooch, etc. with profile head or design carved in relief 2 single brief scene or appearance in film, etc. by well-known performer

cam•er•a [KAM-ər-ə] *noun* apparatus used to make photographs > **cam'er•a•man** *noun* photographer, esp. for TV or film > **camera ob•scu•ra** [ob-SKYUUR-ə] darkened chamber in which views of external objects are shown on sheet by means of lenses > **camera phone** cell phone that includes a camera **in camera** (of legal proceedings, etc.) conducted in private

cam•i•sole [KAM-ə-sohl] *noun* woman's short sleeveless undergarment

cam•ou•flage [KAM-ə-flahzh] *noun* disguise, means of deceiving enemy observation, e.g. by paint, screen ▷ *verb transitive* **-flaged, -flag•ing** disguise

camp [kamp] *noun* 1 (place for) tents of hikers, army, etc. 2 cabins, etc. for temporary accommodation 3 group supporting political party, etc. ▷ *adjective* 4 (*informal*) consciously artificial ▷ *verb intransitive* 5 form or lodge in a camp

cam•paign [kam-PAYN] *noun* 1 series of coordinated activities for some purpose, e.g. political or military campaign ▷ *verb intransitive* 2 serve in campaign > **cam•paign'er** *noun*

cam•pa•nol•o•gy [kam-pə-NOL-ə-jee] *noun* art of ringing bells musically

cam•phor [KAM fər] *noun* solid essential oil with aromatic taste and smell > **cam'phor•at•ed** *adjective*

cam•pus [KAM-pəs] *noun, plural* **-pus•es** grounds of college or university

can[1] [kan] *verb intransitive, past tense* **could** 1 be able 2 have the power 3 be allowed

can[2] *noun* 1 container, usu. metal, for liquids, foods ▷ *verb* **canned, can•ning** 2 put in can 3 prepare (food) for canning > **canned** *adjective* 1 preserved in jar or can 2 (of music, TV or radio programs, etc.) previously recorded > **can'ner•y** *noun, plural* **-ner•ies** factory where food is canned

Can•a•da Day [KAN-ə-də] July 1st, anniversary of establishment of Confederation in 1867

Canada goose large grayish-brown N Amer. goose

Ca•na•di•an [kə-NAY-dee-ən] *noun, adjective*

DICTIONARY

C

THESAURUS

invitation, notice, order, plea, request
7 NEED, cause, excuse, grounds, justification, occasion, reason

call for *verb* 1 REQUIRE, demand, entail, involve, necessitate, need, occasion, suggest
2 FETCH, collect, pick up

calling *noun* PROFESSION, career, life's work, mission, trade, vocation

call on *verb* VISIT, drop in on, look in on, look up, see

callous *adjective* HEARTLESS, cold, hard-boiled, hardened, hardhearted, insensitive, uncaring, unfeeling

callow *adjective* INEXPERIENCED, green, guileless, immature, naive, raw, unsophisticated

calm *adjective* 1 COOL, collected, composed, dispassionate, relaxed, sedate, self-possessed, unemotional
2 STILL, balmy, mild, quiet, serene, smooth, tranquil, windless
▷ *noun* 3 PEACEFULNESS, hush, peace, quiet, repose, serenity, stillness
▷ *verb* 4 QUIETEN, de-stress, hush, mollify, placate, relax, soothe

calmness *noun* 1 COOLNESS, composure, cool (*slang*), equanimity, impassivity, poise, sang-froid, self-possession
2 PEACEFULNESS, calm, hush, quiet, repose, restfulness, serenity, stillness, tranquillity

camouflage *noun* 1 DISGUISE, blind, cloak, concealment, cover, mask, masquerade, screen, subterfuge
▷ *verb* 2 DISGUISE, cloak, conceal, cover, hide, mask, obfuscate, obscure, screen, veil

camp *noun* 1 CAMP SITE, bivouac, camping ground, encampment, tents
▷ *adjective* 2 (*informal*) EFFEMINATE, affected, artificial, mannered, ostentatious, posturing

campaign *noun* OPERATION, attack, crusade, drive, expedition, movement, offensive, push

(native) of Canada

ca•nal [kə-NAL] *noun* 1 artificial watercourse 2 duct in body > **can•al•ize** [KAN-l-īz] *verb transitive* **-ized, -iz•ing** 1 convert into canal 2 direct (thoughts, energies, etc.) into one channel

can•a•pé [KAN-ə-pay] *noun* small piece of toast, etc. with cheese, etc. topping

ca•nar•y [kə-NAIR-ee] *noun, plural* **-nar•ies** yellow singing bird

ca•nas•ta [kə-NAS-tə] *noun* card game played with two packs

can•can [KAN-kan] *noun* high-kicking (orig. French music-hall) dance

can•cel [KAN-səl] *verb transitive* **-celed, -cel•ing** 1 cross out 2 annul 3 invalidate 4 call off > **can•cel•la'tion** *noun*

can•cer [KAN-sər] *noun* malignant growth or tumor > **can'cer•ous** *adjective*

can•de•la [kan-DEE-lə] *noun* basic unit of luminous intensity

can•did [KAN-did] *adjective* frank, open, impartial > **can'did•ly** *adverb* > **can'dor** [-dər] *noun* frankness

can•di•date [KAN-di-dayt] *noun* 1 one who seeks office, employment, etc. 2 person taking examination or test > **can'di•da•cy** [-də-see] *noun, plural* **-cies**

can•dle [KAN-dl] *noun* 1 stick of wax with wick 2 light > **can•de•la'brum** [-AH-brəm] *plural* **-bra** [-brə] *noun* large, branched candle holder > **can'dle•pow•er** *noun* unit for measuring light **can't hold a candle to** compare unfavorably with

can•dy [KAN-dee] *noun, plural* **-dies** 1 crystallized sugar 2 confectionery in general ▹ *verb* **-died, -dy•ing** 3 preserve with sugar 4 become encrusted with sugar

cane [kayn] *noun* 1 stem of small palm or large grass 2 walking stick ▹ *verb transitive* **caned, can•ing** 3 beat with cane

ca•nine [KAY-nīn] *adjective* like, pert. to, dog > **canine tooth** one of four sharp, pointed teeth, two in each jaw

can•is•ter [KAN-ə-stər] *noun* container, oft. of metal, for storing dry food

can•ker [KANG-kər] *noun* 1 spreading sore 2 thing that eats away, destroys, corrupts > **canker sore** painful ulcer esp. in mouth

can•na•bis [KAN-ə-bis] *noun* 1 hemp plant 2 drug derived from this 3 marijuana 4 hashish

can•nel•lo•ni [kan-l-OH-nee] *noun* tubular pieces of pasta filled with meat, etc.

can•ni•bal [KAN-ə-bəl] *noun* 1 one who eats human flesh ▹ *adjective* 2 relating to this practice > **can'ni•bal•ism** *noun* > **can'ni•bal•ize** *verb transitive* **-ized, -iz•ing** use parts from one machine, etc. to repair another

can•non [KAN-ən] *noun, plural* **-nons** *or* **-non** large gun > **can'non•ball** *noun*

can•not [KAN-ot] *negative form of* **can**[1]

can•ny [KAN-ee] *adjective* **-ni•er, -ni•est** 1 shrewd 2 cautious 3 crafty > **can'ni•ly** *adverb*

ca•noe [kə-NOO] *noun, plural* **-noes** very light boat propelled with paddle or paddles > **ca•noe'ist** *noun*

can•on[1] [KAN-ən] *noun* 1 law or rule, esp. of church 2 standard 3 body of books accepted as genuine 4 list of saints > **can•on•i•za'tion** *noun* > **can'on•ize** *verb transitive* **-ized, -iz•ing** enroll in list of saints

canon[2] *noun* church dignitary, member of cathedral or collegiate chapter or staff > **ca•non'i•cal** *adjective* > **ca•non'i•cals** *plural noun* canonical vestments

can•o•py [KAN-ə-pee] *noun, plural* **-pies** 1 covering over throne, bed, etc. 2 any overhanging shelter ▹ *verb transitive* **-pied, -py•ing** 3 cover with canopy

cant[1] [kant] *noun* 1 hypocritical speech 2 whining 3 language of a sect 4 technical jargon 5 slang, esp. of thieves

cant[2] *verb* **cant•ed, cant•ing** 1 tilt, slope 2 bevel

can•ta•loupe [KAN-tl-ohp] *noun* variety of muskmelon

can•tan•ker•ous [kan-TANG-kər-əs] *adjective* ill-natured, quarrelsome

can•ta•ta [kən-TAH-tə] *noun* choral work like, but shorter than, oratorio

can•teen [kan-TEEN] *noun* 1 flask for carrying water 2 place in factory, school, etc. where light meals are provided 3 post exchange

can•ter [KAN-tər] *noun* 1 easy gallop ▹ *verb* 2 move at, make to canter

canal *noun* WATERWAY, channel, conduit, duct, passage, watercourse

cancel *verb* 1 CALL OFF, abolish, abort, annul, delete, do away with, eliminate, erase, expunge, obliterate, repeal, revoke
2 ▹ **cancel out** MAKE UP FOR, balance out, compensate for, counterbalance, neutralize, nullify, offset

cancellation *noun* ABANDONMENT, abolition, annulment, deletion, elimination, repeal, revocation

cancer *noun* GROWTH, corruption, malignancy, pestilence, sickness, tumor

candid *adjective* HONEST, blunt, forthright, frank, open, outspoken, plain, straightforward, truthful

candidate *noun* CONTENDER, applicant, claimant, competitor, contestant, entrant, nominee, runner

candor *noun* HONESTY, directness, forthrightness, frankness, openness, outspokenness, straightforwardness, truthfulness

canker *noun* DISEASE, bane, blight, cancer, corruption, infection, rot, scourge, sore, ulcer

cannon *noun* GUN, big gun, field gun, mortar

canny *adjective* SHREWD, astute, careful, cautious, clever, judicious, prudent, wise

canon *noun* 1 RULE, criterion, dictate, formula, precept, principle, regulation, standard, statute, yardstick
2 LIST, catalog, roll

canopy *noun* AWNING, covering, shade, sunshade

cant[1] *noun* 1 HYPOCRISY, humbug, insincerity, lip service, pretense, pretentiousness, sanctimoniousness
2 JARGON, argot, lingo, patter, slang, vernacular

cant[2] *verb* TILT, angle, bevel, incline, rise, slant, slope

cantankerous *adjective* BAD-TEMPERED, choleric, contrary, disagreeable, grumpy, irascible, irritable, testy, waspish

can•ti•le•ver *noun* 1 beam, girder, etc. fixed at one end only ▷ *verb intransitive* 2 project like a cantilever ▷ *verb transitive* 3 build to project in this manner

can•to [KAN-toh] *noun, plural* **-tos** division of a poem

can•ton [KAN-tn] *noun* division of country, esp. Swiss federal state

can•ton•ment [kan-TON-mənt] *noun* quarters for troops

can•tor [KAN-tər] *noun* chief singer of liturgy in synagogue

can•vas [KAN-vəs] *noun* 1 coarse cloth used for sails, painting on, etc. 2 sails of ship 3 picture

can•vass [KAN-vəs] *verb transitive* 1 solicit votes, contributions, etc. 2 discuss, examine ▷ *noun* 3 solicitation

can•yon [KAN-yən] *noun* deep gorge

cap [kap] *noun* 1 covering for head 2 lid, top, or other covering ▷ *verb transitive* **capped, cap•ping** 3 put a limit on 4 outdo 5 seal (a well)

ca•pa•ble [KAY-pə-bəl] *adjective* 1 able, gifted 2 competent 3 having the capacity, power > **ca•pa•bil'i•ty** *noun*

ca•pac•i•ty [kə-PAS-i-tee] *noun, plural* **-ties** 1 power of holding or grasping 2 room 3 volume 4 character 5 ability, power of mind > **ca•pa'cious** [-PAY-shəs] *adjective* roomy > **ca•pac'i•tance** *noun* (measure of) ability of system to store electric charge > **ca•pac'i•tor** *noun*

cape[1] [kayp] *noun* covering for shoulders

cape[2] *noun* point of land running into sea, headland > **Cape Cod** common type of cottage in Mass. and elsewhere in Northeast

ca•per[1] [KAY-pər] *noun* 1 skip 2 frolic 3 escapade ▷ *verb intransitive* 4 skip, dance

caper[2] *noun* pickled flower bud of Sicilian shrub

cap•il•lar•y [KAP-ə-ler-ee] *adjective* 1 hairlike ▷ *noun, plural* **-lar•ies** 2 tube with very small bore, esp. small blood vessel

cap•i•tal [KAP-i-tl] *noun* 1 chief town 2 money, stock, funds 3 large-sized letter 4 headpiece of column ▷ *adjective* 5 involving or punishable by death 6 serious 7 chief 8 leading 9 excellent > **cap'i•tal•ism** *noun* economic system based on private ownership of industry > **cap'i•tal•ist** *noun* 1 owner of capital 2 supporter of capitalism ▷ *adjective* 3 run by, possessing, capital, as capitalist state > **cap'i•tal•ize** *verb* **-ized, -iz•ing** 1 convert into capital 2 (with *on*) turn to advantage

Cap•i•tol [KAP-i-tl] *noun* 1 building in which US Congress meets 2 (**cap•i•tol**) a state legislature building

ca•pit•u•late [kə-PICH-ə-layt] *verb intransitive* **-lat•ed, -lat•ing** surrender on terms, give in > **ca•pit•u•la'tion** *noun*

ca•pon [KAY-pon] *noun* castrated male fowl fattened for eating > **ca'pon•ize** *verb transitive* **-ized, -iz•ing**

cap•puc•ci•no [kap-ə-CHEE-noh] *noun* espresso coffee with steamed milk

ca•price [kə-PREES] *noun* whim, freak > **ca•pri'cious** [-PRISH-əs] *adjective*

cap•size [KAP-sīz] *verb transitive* **-sized, -siz•ing** 1 (of boat) upset ▷ *verb intransitive* **-sized, -siz•ing** 2 be overturned

cap•stan [KAP-stən] *noun* machine to wind cable, esp. to hoist anchor

cap•sule [KAP-səl] *noun* 1 gelatin case for dose of medicine or drug 2 any small enclosed area or container 3 seed vessel of plant > **cap'sul•ize** *verb transitive* **-ized, -iz•ing** 1 enclose in a capsule 2 put (news or information) in concise form

cap•tain [KAP-tən] *noun* 1 commander of ship

DICTIONARY

C

THESAURUS

---

canter *noun* 1 JOG, amble, dogtrot, lope ▷ *verb* 2 JOG, amble, lope

canvass *verb* 1 CAMPAIGN, electioneer, solicit, solicit votes
2 POLL, examine, inspect, investigate, scrutinize, study
▷ *noun* 3 POLL, examination, investigation, scrutiny, survey, tally

cap *verb* BEAT, better, crown, eclipse, exceed, outdo, outstrip, surpass, top, transcend

capability *noun* ABILITY, capacity, competence, means, potential, power, proficiency, qualification *or* qualifications, wherewithal

capable *adjective* ABLE, accomplished, competent, efficient, gifted, proficient, qualified, talented

capacious *adjective* SPACIOUS, broad, commodious, expansive, extensive, roomy, sizable *or* sizeable, substantial, vast, voluminous, wide

capacity *noun* 1 SIZE, amplitude, compass, dimensions, extent, magnitude, range, room, scope, space, volume
2 ABILITY, aptitude, aptness, capability, competence, facility, genius, gift
3 FUNCTION, office, position, post, province, role, sphere

cape[2] *noun* HEADLAND, head, peninsula, point, promontory

caper[1] *noun* 1 ESCAPADE, antic, high jinks, jape, lark (*informal*), mischief, practical joke, prank, stunt
▷ *verb* 2 DANCE, bound, cavort, frolic, gambol, jump, skip, spring, trip

capital *noun* 1 MONEY, assets, cash, finances, funds, investment *or* investments, means, principal, resources, wealth, wherewithal
▷ *adjective* 2 PRINCIPAL, cardinal, major, prime, vital
3 (*old-fashioned*) FIRST-RATE, excellent, fine, splendid, sterling, superb

capitalism *noun* PRIVATE ENTERPRISE, free enterprise, laissez faire *or* laisser faire, private ownership

capitalize on *verb* TAKE ADVANTAGE OF, benefit from, cash in on (*informal*), exploit, gain from, make the most of, profit from

capitulate *verb* GIVE IN, come to terms, give up, relent, submit, succumb, surrender, yield

caprice *noun* WHIM, fad, fancy, fickleness, impulse, inconstancy, notion, whimsy

capricious *adjective* UNPREDICTABLE, changeful, erratic, fickle, fitful, impulsive, inconsistent, inconstant, mercurial, variable, wayward, whimsical

capsize *verb* OVERTURN, invert, keel over, tip over, turn over, turn turtle, upset

capsule *noun* 1 PILL, lozenge, tablet
2 (*botany*) POD, case, receptacle, seed case, sheath, shell, vessel

or company of soldiers 2 leader, chief ▷ *verb transitive* 3 be captain of
cap•tion [KAP-shən] *noun* heading, title of article, picture, etc.
cap•tious [KAP-shəs] *adjective* 1 ready to find fault 2 critical 3 peevish > **cap'tious•ness** *noun*
cap•tive [KAP-tiv] *noun* 1 prisoner ▷ *adjective* 2 taken, imprisoned > **cap'ti•vate** *verb transitive* **-vat•ed, -vat•ing** fascinate > **cap'ti•vat•ing** *adjective* delightful > **cap•tiv'i•ty** *noun*
cap•ture [KAP-chər] *verb transitive* **-tured, -tur•ing** 1 seize, make prisoner ▷ *noun* 2 seizure, taking > **cap'tor** *noun*
car [kahr] *noun* 1 automobile 2 passenger compartment, as in cable car 3 vehicle running on rails > **car park** area, building where vehicles may be left for a time
ca•rafe [kə-RAF] *noun* glass water bottle for the table, decanter
car•a•mel [KAR-ə-məl] *noun* 1 burned sugar or syrup for cooking 2 type of confectionery > **car'a•mel•ize** *verb* **-ized, -iz•ing** 1 change (sugar, etc.) into caramel 2 become caramel
car•at [KAR-ət] *noun* 1 small weight used for gold, diamonds, etc. 2 proportional measure of twenty-fourths used to state fineness of gold
car•a•van [KAR-ə-van] *noun* company of merchants traveling together for safety in the East
car•a•way [KAR-ə-way] *noun* plant whose seeds are used as a spice in bread, etc.
carb [kahrb] *noun short for* **carbohydrate**
car•bide [KAHR-bīd] *noun* compound of carbon with an element, esp. calcium carbide
car•bine [KAHR-been] *noun* light rifle
car•bo•hy•drate [kahr-boh-HĪ-drayt] *noun* any of large group of compounds containing carbon, hydrogen and oxygen, esp. sugars and starches as components of food
car•bol•ic ac•id [kahr-BOL-ik] disinfectant derived from coal tar
car•bon [KAHR-bən] *noun* nonmetallic element, substance of pure charcoal, found in all organic matter > **car'bon•ate** *noun* salt of carbonic acid > **car•bon'ic** *adjective* > **car'bon•ize** *verb transitive* **-ized, -iz•ing** > **carbonic acid** 1 carbon dioxide 2 compound formed by carbon dioxide and water > **carbon dioxide** colorless gas exhaled in respiration of animals > **carbon paper** paper coated with a dark, waxy pigment, used for duplicating written or typed matter, producing carbon copy
car•bo•run•dum [kahr-bə-RUN-dəm] *noun* artificial silicate of carbon
car•bun•cle [KAHR-bung-kəl] *noun* inflamed ulcer, boil or tumor
car•bu•re•tor [KAHR-bə-ray-tər] *noun* device for vaporizing and mixing gasoline with air in internal combustion engine
car•cass [KAHR-kəs] *noun* 1 dead animal body 2 skeleton
car•cin•o•gen [kahr-SIN-ə-jən] *noun* substance producing cancer
car•ci•no•ma [kahr-sə-NOH-mə] *noun, plural* **-mas** a cancer
card[1] [kahrd] *noun* 1 thick, stiff paper 2 piece of this giving identification, etc. 3 greeting card 4 one of the 48 or 52 playing cards making up a pack 5 (*informal*) a character, eccentric ▷ *plural noun* 6 any card game > **card'board** *noun* thin, stiff board made of paper pulp > **card'hold•er** *noun* person who owns a credit or debit card
card[2] *noun* 1 instrument for combing wool, etc. ▷ *verb transitive* 2 comb
car•di•ac [KAHR-dee-ak] *adjective* 1 pert. to the heart ▷ *noun* 2 person with heart disease > **car'di•o•graph** [-ə-graf] *noun* instrument that records movements of the heart > **car'di•o•gram** *noun* graph of such
car•di•gan [KAHR-di-gən] *noun* knitted sweater opening in front
car•di•nal [KAHR-dn-l] *adjective* 1 chief, principal ▷ *noun* 2 highest rank, next to the Pope in Cath. church 3 N Amer. finch, male of which is bright red in summer > **cardinal numbers** 1, 2, 3, etc. > **cardinal points** N, S, E, W
care [kair] *verb intransitive* **cared, car•ing** 1 be anxious 2 have regard or liking (for) 3 look after 4 be disposed to ▷ *noun* 5 attention 6 pains, heed 7 charge, protection 8 anxiety 9 caution > **care'free** *adjective* > **care'ful** *adjective*

captain *noun* LEADER, boss (*informal*), chief, commander, head, master, skipper
captivate *verb* CHARM, allure, attract, beguile, bewitch, enchant, enrapture, enthrall, entrance, fascinate, infatuate, mesmerize
captive *noun* 1 PRISONER, convict, detainee, hostage, internee, prisoner of war, slave ▷ *adjective* 2 CONFINED, caged, enslaved, ensnared, imprisoned, incarcerated, locked up, penned, restricted, subjugated
captivity *noun* CONFINEMENT, bondage, custody, detention, imprisonment, incarceration, internment, slavery
capture *verb* 1 CATCH, apprehend, arrest, bag, collar (*informal*), secure, seize, take, take prisoner ▷ *noun* 2 CATCHING, apprehension, arrest, imprisonment, seizure, taking, taking captive, trapping
car *noun* 1 VEHICLE, auto, automobile, clunker (*informal*), jalopy (*informal*), machine, motor, motorcar, wheels (*informal*) 2 CARRIAGE *or* RAILWAY CARRIAGE, buffet car, cable car, coach, dining car, sleeping car, van
carcass *noun* BODY, cadaver (*medical*), corpse, dead body, framework, hulk, remains, shell, skeleton
cardinal *adjective* PRINCIPAL, capital, central, chief, essential, first, fundamental, key, leading, main, paramount, primary
care *verb* 1 BE CONCERNED, be bothered, be interested, mind ▷ *noun* 2 CAUTION, attention, carefulness, consideration, forethought, heed, management, pains, prudence, vigilance, watchfulness 3 PROTECTION, charge, control, custody, guardianship, keeping, management, supervision 4 WORRY, anxiety, concern, disquiet, perplexity, pressure, responsibility, stress, trouble
career *noun* 1 OCCUPATION, calling, employment, life's work, livelihood, pursuit, vocation ▷ *verb* 2 RUSH, barrel *or* barrel along (*informal*), bolt, dash, hurtle, race, speed, tear
care for *verb* 1 LOOK AFTER, attend, foster, mind,

> **care'less** *adjective* > **care'tak•er** *noun* 1 person in charge of premises ▷ *adjective* 2 temporary, interim

ca•reen [kə-REEN] *verb transitive* 1 cause ship to list 2 lay ship over on its side for cleaning and repair ▷ *verb intransitive* 3 keel over 4 sway dangerously

ca•reer [kə-REER] *noun* 1 course through life 2 profession 3 rapid motion ▷ *verb intransitive* 4 run or move at full speed

ca•ress [kə-RES] *verb transitive* 1 fondle, embrace, treat with affection ▷ *noun* 2 act or expression of affection

car•et [KAR-it] *noun* mark (ʎ) showing where to insert something omitted

car•go [KAHR-goh] *noun, plural* **-goes** load, freight, carried by ship, plane, etc.

car•i•bou [KAR-ə-boo] *noun* N Amer. reindeer

car•i•ca•ture [KAR-i-kə-chər] *noun* 1 likeness exaggerated or distorted to appear ridiculous ▷ *verb transitive* **-tured, -tur•ing** 2 portray in this way > **car'i•ca•tur•ist** *noun*

car•ies [KAIR-eez] *noun* tooth decay

car•il•lon [KAR-ə-lon] *noun* 1 set of bells usu. hung in tower and played by set of keys, pedals, etc. 2 tune so played

car•min•a•tive [kahr-MIN-ə-tiv] *noun* 1 medicine to remedy flatulence ▷ *adjective* 2 acting as this

car•mine [KAHR-min] *noun* 1 brilliant red color (prepared from cochineal) ▷ *adjective* 2 of this color

car•nage [KAHR-nij] *noun* slaughter

car•nal [KAHR-nl] *adjective* 1 fleshly, sensual 2 worldly

car•na•tion [kahr-NAY-shən] *noun* 1 cultivated flower 2 flesh color

car•ni•val [KAHR-nə-vəl] *noun* 1 festive occasion 2 traveling fair 3 show or display for amusement

car•niv•o•rous [kahr-NIV-ər-əs] *adjective* flesh-eating > **car'ni•vore** [-nə-vor] *noun*

car•ob [KAR-əb] *noun* Mediterranean tree with edible pods

car•ol [KAR-əl] *noun* 1 song or hymn of joy or praise (esp. Christmas carol) ▷ *verb intransitive* **-oled, -ol•ing** 2 sing (carols)

car•om [KAR-əm] *noun* 1 billiard stroke, hitting both object balls with one's own ▷ *verb intransitive* 2 make this stroke 3 rebound, collide

ca•rouse [kə-ROWZ] *verb intransitive* **-roused, -rous•ing** have merry drinking spree ▷ *noun* > **ca•rous'er** *noun*

car•ou•sel [kar-ə-SEL] *noun* merry-go-round

carp[1] [kahrp] *noun* freshwater fish

carp[2] *verb intransitive* complain about small faults or errors > **carp'ing** *adjective*

car•pen•ter [KAHR-pən-tər] *noun* worker in timber as in building, etc. > **car'pen•try** [-tree] *noun* this art

car•pet [KAHR-pit] *noun* 1 heavy fabric for covering floor ▷ *verb transitive* 2 cover floor > **car'pet•bag** *noun* traveling bag > **car'pet•bag•ger** *noun* political adventurer **on the carpet** called up for censure

car•riage [KA-rij] *noun* 1 bearing, conduct 2 horse-drawn vehicle 3 act, cost, of carrying

car•ri•on [KA-ree-ən] *noun* rotting dead flesh

car•rot [KA-rət] *noun* 1 plant with orange-red edible root 2 inducement > **car'rot-top** *noun* person with red hair

car•ry [KA-ree] *verb transitive* **-ried, -ry•ing** 1 convey, transport 2 capture, win 3 effect 4 behave ▷ *verb intransitive* **-ried, -ry•ing** 5 (of projectile, sound) reach ▷ *noun* 6 range > **car'ri•er** *noun* 1 one that carries goods 2 immune person who communicates a disease to

DICTIONARY

C

THESAURUS

minister to, nurse, protect, provide for, tend, watch over

2 LIKE, be fond of, desire, enjoy, love, prize, take to, want

carefree *adjective* UNTROUBLED, blithe, breezy, cheerful, easy-going, halcyon, happy-go-lucky, light-hearted

careful *adjective* 1 CAUTIOUS, chary, circumspect, discreet, prudent, scrupulous, thoughtful, thrifty

2 THOROUGH, conscientious, meticulous, painstaking, particular, precise

careless *adjective* 1 SLAPDASH, cavalier, inaccurate, irresponsible, lackadaisical, neglectful, offhand, slipshod, sloppy (*informal*)

2 NEGLIGENT, absent-minded, forgetful, hasty, remiss, thoughtless, unthinking

3 NONCHALANT, artless, casual, unstudied

carelessness *noun* NEGLIGENCE, indiscretion, irresponsibility, laxity, neglect, omission, slackness, sloppiness (*informal*), thoughtlessness

caress *verb* 1 STROKE, cuddle, embrace, fondle, hug, kiss, make out (*informal*), neck (*informal*), nuzzle, pet

▷ *noun* 2 STROKE, cuddle, embrace, fondling, hug, kiss, pat

caretaker *noun* WARDEN, concierge, curator, custodian, janitor, keeper, porter, superintendent, watchman

cargo *noun* LOAD, baggage, consignment, contents, freight, goods, merchandise, shipment

caricature *noun* 1 PARODY, burlesque, cartoon, distortion, farce, lampoon, satire, travesty

▷ *verb* 2 PARODY, burlesque, distort, lampoon, mimic, mock, ridicule, satirize

carnage *noun* SLAUGHTER, blood bath, bloodshed, butchery, havoc, holocaust, massacre, mass murder, murder, shambles

carnal *adjective* SEXUAL, erotic, fleshly, lascivious, lewd, libidinous, lustful, sensual

carnival *noun* FESTIVAL, celebration, fair, fête, fiesta, gala, holiday, jamboree, jubilee, merrymaking, revelry

carol *noun* SONG, chorus, ditty, hymn, lay

carp *verb* FIND FAULT, cavil, complain, criticize, pick holes, quibble, reproach

carpenter *noun* JOINER, cabinet-maker, woodworker

carriage *noun* 1 VEHICLE, cab, coach, conveyance

2 BEARING, air, behavior, comportment, conduct, demeanor, deportment, gait, manner, posture

carry *verb* 1 TRANSPORT, bear, bring, conduct, convey, fetch, haul, lug, move, relay, take, transfer

2 WIN, accomplish, capture, effect, gain, secure

others **3** aircraft carrier **4** kind of pigeon
> **carry on** **1** continue **2** (*informal*) fuss unnecessarily

cart [kahrt] *noun* **1** open (two-wheeled) vehicle, esp. pulled by horse ▷ *verb transitive* **2** convey in cart **3** carry with effort > **cart'er** *noun* > **cart'horse** *noun* > **cart'wheel** *noun* **1** large, spoked wheel **2** sideways somersault > **cart'wright** *noun* maker of carts

carte blanche [kahrt blanch] *noun, plural* **cartes blanches** [kahrts blanch] complete discretion or authority

car•tel [kahr-TEL] *noun* **1** commercial combination for the purpose of fixing prices, output, etc. **2** alliance of political parties, etc. to further common aims

Car•te•sian [kahr-TEE-*zh*ən] *adjective* **1** pert. to the French philosopher René Descartes (1596—1650) or his system of coordinates ▷ *noun* **2** an adherent of his philosophy

car•ti•lage [KAHR-tl-ij] *noun* **1** firm elastic tissue in the body **2** gristle > **car•ti•lag'i•nous** *adjective*

car•tog•ra•phy [kahr-TOG-rə-fee] *noun* map making > **car•tog'ra•pher** *noun*

car•ton [KAHR-tn] *noun* cardboard or plastic container

car•toon [kahr-TOON] *noun* **1** drawing, esp. humorous or satirical **2** sequence of drawings telling story **3** animated cartoon

car•tridge [KAHR-trij] *noun* **1** case containing charge for gun **2** container for film, magnetic tape, etc. **3** unit in head of phonograph pickup

carve [kahrv] *verb transitive* **carved, carv•ing** **1** cut **2** hew **3** sculpture **4** engrave **5** cut in pieces or slices (meat) > **carv'er** *noun*

car•y•at•id [kar-ee-AT-id] *noun* supporting column in shape of female figure

cas•cade [kas-KAYD] *noun* **1** waterfall **2** anything resembling this ▷ *verb intransitive* **-cad•ed, -cad•ing** **3** fall in cascades

case[1] [kays] *noun* **1** instance **2** event, circumstance **3** question at issue **4** state of affairs, condition **5** arguments supporting particular action, etc. **6** *med.* patient under treatment **7** law suit **8** grounds for suit **9** grammatical relation of words in sentence

case[2] *noun* **1** box, sheath, covering **2** receptacle **3** box and contents ▷ *verb transitive* **cased, cas•ing** **4** put in a case > **case'hard•en** *verb transitive* **1** harden by carbonizing the surface of (esp. iron) by converting into steel **2** make hard, callous

case•ment [KAYS-mənt] *noun* window opening on hinges

cash [kash] *noun* **1** money, bills and coin ▷ *verb transitive* **2** turn into or exchange for money > **cash•ier** [ka-SHEER] *noun* one in charge of receiving and paying of money > **cash dispenser** computerized device outside a bank for supplying cash > **cash register** till that records amount of money put in

cash•ier [ka-SHEER] *verb transitive* dismiss from office or service

cash•mere [KAZH-meer] *noun* **1** fine soft fabric **2** yarn made from goat's wool

ca•si•no [kə-SEE-noh] *noun, plural* **-nos** **1** building, institution for gambling **2** type of card game

cask [kask] *noun* **1** barrel **2** container for wine

cas•ket [KAS-kit] *noun* **1** small case for jewels, etc. **2** coffin

Cas•san•dra [kə-SAN-drə] *noun* prophet of misfortune or disaster

cas•se•role [KAS-ə-rohl] *noun* **1** fireproof cooking and serving dish **2** food cooked in this

cas•sette [kə-SET] *noun* plastic container for film, magnetic tape, etc.

cas•sock [KAS-ək] *noun* long tunic worn by clergymen

cast [kast] *verb* **1** throw or fling **2** shed **3** throw down **4** deposit (a vote) **5** allot, as parts in play **6** mold, as metal ▷ *noun* **7** throw **8** distance thrown **9** squint **10** mold **11** that which is shed or ejected **12** set of actors **13** type or quality > **cast'ing** *noun* > **cast'a•way** *noun*

carry on *verb* **1** CONTINUE, endure, keep going, last, maintain, perpetuate, persevere, persist

carry out *verb* PERFORM, accomplish, achieve, carry through, effect, execute, fulfill, implement, realize

carton *noun* BOX, case, container, pack, package, packet

cartoon *noun* **1** DRAWING, caricature, comic strip, lampoon, parody, satire, sketch
2 ANIMATION, animated cartoon, animated film

cartridge *noun* **1** SHELL, charge, round
2 CONTAINER, capsule, case, cassette, cylinder, magazine

carve *verb* CUT, chip, chisel, engrave, etch, hew, mold, sculpt, slice, whittle

cascade *noun* **1** WATERFALL, avalanche, cataract, deluge, downpour, falls, flood, fountain, outpouring, shower, torrent
▷ *verb* **2** FLOW, descend, fall, flood, gush, overflow, pitch, plunge, pour, spill, surge, teem, tumble

case[1] *noun* **1** INSTANCE, example, illustration, occasion, occurrence, specimen
2 SITUATION, circumstance *or* circumstances, condition, context, contingency, event, position, state
3 (*law*) LAWSUIT, action, dispute, proceedings, suit, trial

case[2] *noun* **1** CONTAINER, box, canister, carton, casket, chest, crate, holder, receptacle, suitcase, tray
2 COVERING, capsule, casing, envelope, jacket, sheath, shell, wrapper

cash *noun* MONEY, coinage, currency, dough (*slang*), funds, notes, ready money, silver

cashier[1] *noun* TELLER, bank clerk, banker, bursar, clerk, purser, treasurer

cashier[2] *verb* DISMISS, discard, discharge, drum out, expel, give the boot to (*slang*)

casket *noun* BOX, case, chest, coffer, jewel box

cast *noun* **1** ACTORS, characters, company, dramatis personae, players, troupe
2 TYPE, complexion, manner, stamp, style
▷ *verb* **3** CHOOSE, allot, appoint, assign, name, pick, select
4 GIVE OUT, bestow, deposit, diffuse, distribute, emit, radiate, scatter, shed, spread
5 FORM, found, model, mold, set, shape
6 THROW, fling, hurl, launch, pitch, sling, thrust, toss

shipwrecked person > **cast-iron** *adjective* 1 made of a hard but brittle type of iron 2 definite, unchallengeable

cas•ta•nets [kas-tə-NETS] *plural noun* (in Spanish dancing) two small curved pieces of wood, etc. clicked together in hand

caste [kast] *noun* 1 section of society in India 2 social rank

cast•er [KAS-tər] *noun* 1 container for salt, etc. with perforated top 2 small swiveled wheel on table leg, etc.

cas•ti•gate [KAS-ti-gayt] *verb transitive* **-gat•ed, -gat•ing** 1 punish, rebuke severely, correct 2 chastise > **cas'ti•ga•tor** *noun*

cas•tle [KAS-əl] *noun* 1 fortress 2 mansion 3 chess piece **castle in the air** pipe dream

cas•tor oil [KAS-tər] vegetable medicinal oil

cas•trate [KAS-trayt] *verb transitive* **-trat•ed, -trat•ing** 1 remove testicles, deprive of power of generation 2 deprive of vigor > **cas•tra'tion** *noun*

cas•tra•to [ka-STRAH-toh] *noun, plural* **-ti** [-tee] singer castrated in boyhood to preserve soprano or alto voice

cas•u•al [KAZH-oo-əl] *adjective* 1 accidental 2 unforeseen 3 occasional 4 unconcerned 5 informal > **cas'u•al•ty** *noun, plural* **-ties** 1 person killed or injured in accident, war, etc. 2 thing lost, destroyed, in accident, etc.

cas•u•ist [KAZH-oo-ist] *noun* 1 one who studies and solves moral problems 2 quibbler > **cas'u•ist•ry** *noun*

cat [kat] *noun* any of various feline animals, including, e.g. small domesticated furred animal, and lions, tigers, etc. > **cat'ty** *adjective* **-ti•er, -ti•est** spiteful > **cat'call** *noun* derisive cry > **cat'fish** *noun* mainly freshwater fish with catlike whiskers > **cat'kin** *noun* drooping flower spike > **cat'nap** *verb intransitive, noun* doze > **cat's'-eye** *noun, plural* **-eyes** glass reflector set in road to reflect beams from automobile headlights > **cat'walk** *noun* narrow, raised path or plank

ca•tab•o•lism [kə-TAB-ə-liz-əm] *noun* breaking down of complex molecules, destructive metabolism

cat•a•clysm [KAT-ə-kliz-əm] *noun* (disastrous) upheaval; deluge > **cat•a•clys'mic** *adjective*

cat•a•comb [KAT-ə-kohm] *noun* underground gallery for burial > **cat•a•combs** series of underground tunnels and caves

cat•a•lep•sy [KAT-l-ep-see] *noun* condition of unconsciousness with rigidity of muscles > **cat•a•lep'tic** *adjective*

cat•a•log [KAT-l-awg] *noun* 1 descriptive list ▷ *verb transitive* 2 make such list of 3 enter in catalog

cat•a•lyst [KAT-l-ist] *noun* 1 substance causing or assisting a chemical reaction without taking part in it 2 person or thing that precipitates event or change > **cat'a•lyze** [-l-īz] *verb transitive* **-lyzed, -lyz•ing** > **ca•tal'y•sis** *noun* > **cat•a•lyt'ic** *adjective* > **catalytic converter** type of antipollution device for automotive exhaust system

cat•a•ma•ran [kat-ə-mə-RAN] *noun* 1 type of sailing boat with twin hulls 2 raft of logs

cat•a•pult [KAT-ə-pult] *noun* 1 small forked stick with elastic sling used for throwing stones 2 *hist.* engine of war for hurling arrows, stones, etc. 3 launching device ▷ *verb transitive*

cat•a•ract [KAT-ə-rakt] *noun* 1 waterfall 2 downpour 3 disease of eye

ca•tas•tro•phe [kə-TAS-trə-fee] *noun* 1 great disaster, calamity 2 culmination of a tragedy > **cat•a•stroph'ic** *adjective*

catch [kach] *verb transitive* **caught, catch•ing** 1 take hold of, seize, understand 2 hear 3 contract (disease) 4 be in time for 5 surprise, detect ▷ *verb intransitive* **caught, catch•ing** 6 be contagious 7 get entangled 8 begin to burn ▷ *noun* 9 seizure 10 thing that holds, stops, etc. 11 what is caught 12 (*informal*) snag,

caste *noun* CLASS, estate, grade, order, rank, social order, status, stratum

castigate *verb* REPRIMAND, berate, censure, chastise, criticize, lambast *or* lambaste, rebuke, scold

cast-iron *adjective* CERTAIN, copper-bottomed, definite, established, fixed, guaranteed, settled

castle *noun* FORTRESS, chateau, citadel, keep, palace, stronghold, tower

cast-off *adjective* 1 UNWANTED, discarded, rejected, scrapped, surplus to requirements, unneeded, useless
▷ *noun* 2 REJECT, discard, failure, outcast, second

castrate *verb* NEUTER, emasculate, geld

casual *adjective* 1 CARELESS, blasé, cursory, lackadaisical, nonchalant, offhand, relaxed, unconcerned
2 OCCASIONAL, accidental, chance, incidental, irregular, random, unexpected
3 INFORMAL, non-dressy, sporty

casualty *noun* VICTIM, death, fatality, loss, sufferer, wounded

cat *noun* FELINE, kitty (*informal*), puss (*informal*), pussy (*informal*), tabby

catacombs *plural noun* VAULT, crypt, tomb

catalog *noun* 1 LIST, directory, gazetteer, index, inventory, record, register, roll, roster, schedule
▷ *verb* 2 LIST, accession, alphabetize, classify, file, index, inventory, register, tabulate

catapult *noun* 1 SLING, slingshot (*United States*)
▷ *verb* 2 SHOOT, heave, hurl, pitch, plunge, propel

catastrophe *noun* DISASTER, adversity, calamity, cataclysm, fiasco, misfortune, tragedy, trouble

catcall *noun* JEER, boo, gibe, hiss, raspberry, whistle

catch *verb* 1 SEIZE, clutch, get, grab, grasp, grip, lay hold of, snatch, take
2 CAPTURE, apprehend, arrest, ensnare, entrap, snare
3 DISCOVER, catch in the act, detect, expose, find out, surprise, take unawares, unmask
4 CONTRACT, develop, get, go down with, incur, succumb to, suffer from
5 MAKE OUT, comprehend, discern, get, grasp, hear, perceive, recognize, sense, take in
▷ *noun* 6 FASTENER, bolt, clasp, clip, latch
7 DRAWBACK, disadvantage, fly in the ointment, hitch, snag, stumbling block, trap, trick

catching *adjective* INFECTIOUS, communicable, contagious, transferable, transmittable

catch on *verb* UNDERSTAND, comprehend, find out, get the picture, grasp, see, see through

disadvantage 13 form of musical composition 14 thing, person worth catching, esp. as spouse > **catch'er** *noun* > **catching** *adjective* > **catch'y** *adjective* **catch•i•er, catch•i•est** 1 pleasant, memorable 2 tricky > **catch'word** *noun* popular phrase or idea > **catch 22** inescapable dilemma > **catch•ment area** 1 drainage basin, area in which rainfall collects to form the supply of river, etc. 2 area from which people are allocated to a particular social service agency, hospital, etc. > **catch-as-catch-can** *adjective* using any method that can be applied

cat•e•chize [KAT-i-kīz] *verb transitive* **-chized, -chiz•ing** 1 instruct by question and answer 2 question > **cat'e•chism** *noun* 1 such instruction > **cat'e•chist** *noun*

cat•e•go•ry [KAT-i-gohr-ee] *noun, plural* **-ries** class, order, division > **cat•e•gor'i•cal** *adjective* 1 positive 2 of category > **cat•e•gor'i•cal•ly** *adverb* > **cat'e•go•rize** *verb transitive* **-ized, -iz•ing**

ca•ter [KAY-tər] *verb intransitive* provide what is required or desired, esp. food, etc. > **ca'ter•er** *noun*

cat•er•pil•lar [KAT-ə-pil-ər] *noun* hairy grub of moth or butterfly

cat•er•waul [KAT-ər-wawl] *verb intransitive* 1 wail, howl 2 argue noisily

ca•the•dral [kə-THEE-drəl] *noun* 1 principal church of diocese ▷ *adjective* 2 pert. to, containing cathedral

cath•ode [KATH-ohd] *noun* negative electrode > **cathode rays** stream of electrons

cath•o•lic [KATH-lik] *adjective* 1 universal 2 including whole body of Christians 3 (**Cath•o•lic**) relating to Catholic Church ▷ *noun* **C-** 4 adherent of Catholic Church > **Ca•thol•i•cism** [kə-THOL-ə-siz-əm] *noun* > **cath•o•lic•i•ty** [kath-ə-LIS-i-tee] *noun*

CAT scan [kat skan] computerized axial tomography (*also* **CT scan**)

cat•tle [KAT-l] *plural noun* beasts of pasture, esp. steers, cows > **cat'tle•man** *noun* > **cattle guard** heavy grid over ditch in road to prevent passage of livestock

Cau•ca•sian [kaw-KAY-zhən] *adjective, noun* (of, pert. to) light-complexioned racial group of mankind > **Cau'ca•soid** [-kə-soid] *adjective, noun*

cau•cus [KAW-kəs] *noun* group, meeting, esp. of members of political party, with power to decide policy, etc.

caught *pt./pp. of* **catch**

caul•dron [KAWL-drən] *noun* large pot used for boiling

cau•li•flower [KAW-li-flow-ər] *noun* variety of cabbage with edible white flowering head

caulk [kawk] *verb transitive* stop up cracks (orig. of ship) with waterproof filler > **caulk'er** *noun* > **caulk'ing** *noun* > **caulking compound** filler used in caulking

cause [kawz] *noun* 1 that which produces an effect 2 reason, origin 3 motive, purpose 4 charity, movement 5 lawsuit ▷ *verb transitive* **caused, caus•ing** 6 bring about, make happen > **caus'al** *adjective* > **cau•sal'i•ty** *noun* > **cau•sa'tion** *noun* > **cause'less** *adjective* groundless

cause cé•lè•bre [kawz sə-LEB-rə] *noun, plural* **causes cé•lè•bres** [kawz sə-LEB-rəz] great controversy e.g. famous legal case

cause•way [KAWZ-way] *noun* 1 raised way over marsh, etc. 2 highway

caus•tic [KAW-stik] *adjective* 1 burning 2 bitter, severe ▷ *noun* 3 corrosive substance > **caus'ti•cal•ly** *adverb*

cau•ter•ize [KAW-tə-rīz] *verb transitive* **-ized, -iz•ing** burn with caustic or hot iron > **cau•ter•i•za'tion** *noun*

cau•tion [KAW-shən] *noun* 1 heedfulness, care 2 warning ▷ *verb transitive* 3 warn > **cau'tion•ary** *adjective* containing warning or precept > **cau'tious** *adjective*

cav•al•cade [KAV-əl-kayd] *noun* 1 column or procession of riders 2 series

cav•a•lier [kav-ə-LEER] *adjective* 1 careless, disdainful ▷ *noun* 2 courtly gentleman 3 (*obsolete*) horseman

cav•al•ry [KAV-əl-ree] *noun, plural* **-ries** mounted troops

cave [kayv] *noun* 1 hollow place in the earth 2

catchword *noun* SLOGAN, byword, motto, password, watchword

catchy *adjective* MEMORABLE, captivating, haunting, popular

categorical *adjective* ABSOLUTE, downright, emphatic, explicit, express, positive, unambiguous, unconditional, unequivocal, unqualified, unreserved

category *noun* CLASS, classification, department, division, grade, grouping, heading, section, sort, type

cater *verb* PROVIDE, furnish, outfit, purvey, supply

cattle *plural noun* cows, beasts, bovines, livestock, stock

catty *adjective* SPITEFUL, backbiting, bitchy (*informal*), malevolent, malicious, rancorous, shrewish, snide, venomous

cause *noun* 1 ORIGIN, agent, beginning, creator, genesis, mainspring, maker, producer, root, source, spring
2 REASON, basis, grounds, incentive, inducement, justification, motivation, motive, purpose
3 AIM, belief, conviction, enterprise, ideal, movement, principle
▷ *verb* 4 PRODUCE, bring about, create, generate, give rise to, incite, induce, lead to, result in

caustic *adjective* 1 BURNING, acrid, astringent, biting, corroding, corrosive, mordant, vitriolic
2 SARCASTIC, acrimonious, cutting, pungent, scathing, stinging, trenchant, virulent, vitriolic

caution *noun* 1 CARE, alertness, carefulness, circumspection, deliberation, discretion, forethought, heed, prudence, vigilance, watchfulness
2 WARNING, admonition, advice, counsel, injunction
▷ *verb* 3 WARN, admonish, advise, tip off, urge

cautious *adjective* CAREFUL, cagey (*informal*), chary, circumspect, guarded, judicious, prudent, tentative, wary

cavalcade *noun* PARADE, array, march-past, procession, spectacle, train

cavalier *adjective* HAUGHTY, arrogant, disdainful, lofty, lordly, offhand, scornful, supercilious

cavalry *noun* HORSEMEN, horse, mounted troops

cave *noun* HOLLOW, cavern, cavity, den, grotto

den > **cav•ern** [KAV-ərn] *noun* deep cave > **cav'ern•ous** *adjective* > **cav'i•ty** *noun, plural* **-ties** hollow > **cave'man** *noun* prehistoric cave dweller > **cave in** 1 fall inward 2 submit 3 give in
cav•i•ar [KAV-ee-ahr] *noun* salted sturgeon roe
cav•il [KAV-əl] *verb intransitive* **-iled, -il•ing** find fault without sufficient reason, make trifling objections > **cav'il•ing** *noun* > **cav'il•er** *noun*
cav•i•ta•tion [kav-i-TAY-shən] *noun* rapid formation of cavities or bubbles > **cav'i•tate** *verb intransitive* **-tat•ed, -tat•ing** undergo cavitation
ca•vort [kə-VORT] *verb intransitive* prance, frisk
caw [kaw] *noun* 1 crow's cry ▷ *verb intransitive* 2 cry so
cay•enne pepper [kī-EN] *noun* pungent red pepper
Cd *chem.* cadmium
CD 1 compact disk 2 certificate of deposit > **CD-R** compact disk recordable > **CD-ROM** compact disk storing digitized read-only data > **CD-RW** compact disk read-write
cease [sees] *verb* **ceased, ceas•ing** bring or come to an end > **cease'less** *adjective*
ce•dar [SEE-dər] *noun* 1 large evergreen tree 2 its wood
cede [seed] *verb transitive* **ced•ed, ced•ing** yield, give up, transfer, esp. of territory
ce•dil•la [si-DIL-ə] *noun* hooklike mark placed under a letter *c* to show the sound of *s*
ceil•ing [SEE-ling] *noun* 1 inner, upper surface of a room 2 maximum price, wage, etc. 3 *aviation* lower level of clouds 4 limit of height to which aircraft can climb
cel•e•brate [SEL-ə-brayt] *verb* **-brat•ed, -brat•ing** 1 rejoice or have festivities to mark (happy day, event, etc.) ▷ *verb transitive* 2 observe (birthday, etc.) 3 perform (religious ceremony, etc.) 4 praise publicly > **cel'e•brant** *noun* > **celebrated** *adjective* famous > **cel•e•bra'tion** *noun* > **ce•leb'ri•ty** *noun, plural* **-ties** 1 famous person 2 fame
ce•ler•i•ty [sə-LER-i-tee] *noun* swiftness
cel•er•y [SEL-ə-ree] *noun* vegetable with long juicy edible stalks
ce•les•tial [sə-LES-chəl] *adjective* 1 heavenly, divine 2 of the sky
cel•i•ba•cy [SEL-ə-bə-see] *noun* sexual abstinence > **cel'i•bate** [-bit] *noun, adjective*
cell [sel] *noun* 1 small room, esp. in prison 2 small cavity 3 minute, basic unit of living matter 4 device converting chemical energy into electrical energy 5 small local group operating as nucleus of larger political or religious organization 6 *short for* **cell phone** > **cel•lu•lar** [SEL-yə-lər] *adjective* > **cell phone, cellular phone** ; portable telephone operating by radio communication via a network of transmitters each serving a small area
cel•lar [SEL-ər] *noun* 1 underground room or story 2 stock of wine 3 wine cellar
cel•lo [CHEL-oh] *noun, plural* **-los** stringed instrument of violin family
cel•lo•phane [SEL-ə-fayn] *noun* transparent wrapping
cel•lu•loid [SEL-yə-loid] *noun* 1 synthetic plastic substance with wide range of uses 2 motion-picture film
cel•lu•lose [SEL-yə-lohs] *noun* 1 substance of vegetable cell wall 2 group of carbohydrates
Cel•si•us [SEL-see-əs] *adjective, noun* (of) scale of temperature from 0° (melting point of ice) to 100° (boiling point of water)
Celt•ic [KEL-tik, SEL-] *noun* 1 branch of language including Gaelic and Welsh ▷ *adjective* 2 of, or relating to the Celtic peoples or languages
ce•ment [si-MENT] *noun* 1 fine mortar 2 adhesive, glue ▷ *verb transitive* 3 unite with cement 4 join firmly
cem•e•ter•y [SEM-i-ter-ee] *noun, plural* **-ter•ies** burial ground
cen•o•taph [SEN-ə-taf] *noun* monument to one buried elsewhere
cen•ser [SEN-sər] *noun* pan in which incense is burned
cen•sor [SEN-sər] *noun* one authorized to examine films, books, etc. and suppress all or part if considered morally or otherwise

DICTIONARY **C** THESAURUS

cavern *noun* CAVE, hollow, pothole
cavernous *adjective* DEEP, hollow, sunken, yawning
cavity *noun* HOLLOW, crater, dent, gap, hole, pit
cease *verb* STOP, break off, conclude, discontinue, end, finish, halt, leave off, refrain, terminate
ceaseless *adjective* CONTINUAL, constant, endless, eternal, everlasting, incessant, interminable, never-ending, nonstop, perpetual, twenty-four-seven (*slang*), unremitting
cede *verb* SURRENDER, concede, hand over, make over, relinquish, renounce, resign, transfer, yield
celebrate *verb* 1 REJOICE, commemorate, drink to, keep, kill the fatted calf, observe, put the flags out, toast
2 PERFORM, bless, honor, solemnize
celebrated *adjective* WELL-KNOWN, acclaimed, distinguished, eminent, famous, illustrious, notable, popular, prominent, renowned
celebration *noun* 1 PARTY, festival, festivity, gala, jubilee, merrymaking, red-letter day, revelry
2 PERFORMANCE, anniversary, commemoration, honoring, observance, remembrance, solemnization
celebrity *noun* 1 PERSONALITY, big name, big shot (*informal*), dignitary, luminary, star, superstar, V.I.P.
2 FAME, distinction, notability, prestige, prominence, renown, reputation, repute, stardom
celestial *adjective* HEAVENLY, angelic, astral, divine, ethereal, spiritual, sublime, supernatural
celibacy *noun* CHASTITY, continence, purity, virginity
cell *noun* 1 ROOM, cavity, chamber, compartment, cubicle, dungeon, stall
2 UNIT, caucus, core, coterie, group, nucleus
cement *noun* 1 MORTAR, adhesive, glue, gum, paste, plaster, sealant
▷ *verb* 2 STICK TOGETHER, attach, bind, bond, combine, glue, join, plaster, seal, unite, weld
cemetery *noun* GRAVEYARD, burial ground, churchyard, God's acre, necropolis
censor *verb* CUT, blue-pencil, bowdlerize,

unacceptable ▷ *verb transitive* > **cen•so•ri•al** [sen-SOHR-ee-əl] *adjective* of censor > **cen•so'ri•ous** *adjective* faultfinding > **cen'sor•ship** *noun*
cen•sure [SEN-shər] *noun* 1 blame 2 harsh criticism ▷ *verb transitive* **-sured, -sur•ing** 3 blame 4 criticize harshly
cen•sus [SEN-səs] *noun, plural* **-sus•es** official counting of people, things, etc.
cent [sent] *noun* hundredth part of dollar, etc.
cen•taur [SEN-tor] *noun* mythical creature, half man, half horse
cen•ten•ar•y [sen-TEN-ə-ree] *noun, adjective* centennial > **cen•te•nar•i•an** [sen-tn-AIR-ee-ən] *noun* person a hundred years old
cen•ten•ni•al [sen-TEN-ee-əl] *adjective* 1 lasting, happening every hundred years ▷ *noun* 2 100 years 3 celebration of hundredth anniversary
cen•ter [SEN-tər] *noun* 1 midpoint 2 pivot, axis 3 point to or from which things move or are drawn 4 place for specific organization or activity > **cen'tral** [-trəl] *adjective* > **cen•tral'i•ty** *noun* > **cen'tral•ize** *verb transitive* **-ized, -iz•ing** 1 bring to a center 2 concentrate under one control > **cen'tral•ly** *adverb* > **cen•trif'.u•gal** [-TRIF-yə-gəl] *adjective* tending away from center > **cen•trip'e•tal** [-TRIP-i-tl] *adjective* tending toward center > **central heating** method of heating building from one central source > **central processing unit** *computing* part of a computer that performs logical and arithmetical operations
cen•ti•grade [SEN-ti-grayd] *adjective* 1 another name for Celsius 2 having one hundred degrees
cen•ti•me•ter [SEN-tə-mee-tər] *noun* hundredth part of meter
cen•ti•pede [SEN-tə-peed] *noun* small segmented animal with many legs
cen•tu•ry [SEN-chə-ree] *noun, plural* **-ries** 1 100 years 2 any set of 100
CEO chief executive officer
ce•ram•ic [sə-RAM-ik] *noun* 1 hard brittle material of baked clay 2 object made of this ▷ *adjective* 3 made of ceramic > **ce•ram'ics** ▷ *plural noun* art of producing ceramic objects
ce•re•al [SEER-ee-əl] *noun* 1 any edible grain, such as wheat, rice, etc. 2 (breakfast) food made from grain ▷ *adjective*
ce•re•bral [sə-REE-brəl] *adjective* pert. to brain or intellect
cer•e•mo•ny [SER-ə-moh-nee] *noun, plural* **-nies** 1 formal observance 2 sacred rite 3 courteous act > **cer•e•mo'ni•al** *adjective, noun* > **cer•e•mo'ni•ous** *adjective*
ce•rise [sə-REES] *noun, adjective* clear, pinkish red
cer•tain [SUR-tn] *adjective* 1 sure 2 settled, inevitable 3 some, one 4 of moderate (quantity, degree, etc.) > **cer'tain•ly** *adverb* > **cer'tain•ty** *noun, plural* **-ties** > **cer'ti•tude** *noun* confidence
cer•ti•fy [SUR-tə-fī] *verb transitive* **-fied, -fy•ing** 1 declare formally 2 endorse, guarantee 3 declare legally insane > **cer•tif'i•cate** [-kit] *noun* 1 written declaration ▷ *verb transitive* [-kayt], **-cat•ed, -cat•ing** 2 give written declaration > **cer•ti•fi•ca'tion** *noun*
ce•ru•le•an [sə-ROO-lee-ən] *adjective* 1 sky blue 2 deep blue
cer•vix [SUR-viks] *noun, plural* **-vix•es** neck, esp. of womb > **cer'vi•cal** *adjective*
ces•sa•tion [se-SAY-shən] *noun* ceasing or stopping, pause
ces•sion [SESH-ən] *noun* yielding up
cess•pit [SES-pit] *noun* pit for receiving sewage or other refuse
cess•pool [SES-pool] *noun* 1 catch basin in which sewage collects 2 filthy place 3 place of moral filth
Cf *chem.* californium
cf. compare
CFC chlorofluorocarbon
cgs units metric system of units based on *centimeter, gram, second*

expurgate
censorious *adjective* CRITICAL, captious, carping, cavilling, condemnatory, disapproving, disparaging, fault-finding, hypercritical, scathing, severe
censure *noun* 1 DISAPPROVAL, blame, condemnation, criticism, obloquy, rebuke, reprimand, reproach, reproof, stick (*slang*) ▷ *verb* 2 CRITICIZE, blame, castigate, condemn, denounce, rap over the knuckles, rebuke, reprimand, reproach, scold, slap on the wrist
center *noun* 1 MIDDLE, core, focus, heart, hub, kernel, midpoint, nucleus, pivot ▷ *verb* 2 FOCUS, cluster, concentrate, converge, revolve
central *adjective* 1 MIDDLE, inner, interior, mean, median, mid 2 MAIN, chief, essential, focal, fundamental, key, primary, principal
centralize *verb* UNIFY, concentrate, condense, incorporate, rationalize, streamline
ceremonial *adjective* 1 RITUAL, formal, liturgical, ritualistic, solemn, stately ▷ *noun* 2 RITUAL, ceremony, formality, rite, solemnity
ceremonious *adjective* FORMAL, civil, courteous, deferential, dignified, punctilious, solemn, stately, stiff
ceremony *noun* 1 RITUAL, commemoration, function, observance, parade, rite, service, show, solemnities 2 FORMALITY, ceremonial, decorum, etiquette, niceties, pomp, propriety, protocol
certain *adjective* 1 SURE, assured, confident, convinced, positive, satisfied 2 KNOWN, conclusive, incontrovertible, irrefutable, true, undeniable, unequivocal 3 INEVITABLE, bound, definite, destined, fated, inescapable, sure 4 FIXED, decided, definite, established, settled
certainly *adverb* DEFINITELY, assuredly, indisputably, indubitably, surely, truly, undeniably, undoubtedly, without doubt
certainty *noun* 1 SURENESS, assurance, confidence, conviction, faith, positiveness, trust, validity 2 FACT, reality, sure thing (*informal*), truth
certificate *noun* DOCUMENT, authorization, credential *or* credentials, diploma, license, testimonial, voucher, warrant
certify *verb* CONFIRM, assure, attest, authenticate, declare, guarantee, testify,

chad *noun* small pieces removed during the punching of holes in punch cards, printer paper, etc.
chafe [chayf] *verb transitive* **chafed, chaf•ing** 1 make sore or worn by rubbing 2 make warm by rubbing 3 vex, irritate
chaff *noun* 1 husks of corn 2 worthless matter 3 banter ▷ *verb* 4 tease good-naturedly
cha•grin [shə-GRIN] *noun* 1 vexation, disappointment ▷ *verb transitive* 2 embarrass 3 annoy 4 disappoint
chain [chayn] *noun* 1 series of connected links or rings 2 thing that binds 3 connected series of things or events 4 surveyor's measure ▷ *verb transitive* 5 fasten with a chain 6 confine 7 restrain
chair *noun* 1 movable seat, with back, for one person 2 seat of authority 3 professorship ▷ *verb transitive* 4 preside over 5 carry in triumph > **chair'lift** *noun* series of chairs fixed to cable for conveying people (esp. skiers) up mountain > **chair'per•son, chair'wom•an, chair'man** *noun* one who presides over meeting > **chair'man•ship** *noun*
chaise [shayz] *noun* light horse-drawn carriage > **chaise longue** [lawng] sofa
chal•ced•o•ny [kal-SED-n-ee] *noun* whitish, bluish-white variety of quartz
cha•let [sha-LAY] *noun* 1 Swiss wooden house 2 house in this style
chal•ice [CHAL-is] *noun* 1 cup or bowl 2 communion cup
chalk [chawk] *noun* 1 white substance, carbonate of lime 2 crayon ▷ *verb* 3 rub, draw, mark with chalk > **chalk'y** *adjective* **chalk•i•er, chalk•i•est**
chal•lenge [CHAL-inj] *verb transitive* **-lenged, -leng•ing** 1 call to fight or account 2 dispute 3 stimulate 4 object to 5 claim ▷ *noun* > **chal'lenged** *adjective* disabled as specified: *physically challenged; mentally challenged* > **chal'leng•er** *noun* > **chal'leng•ing** *adjective* difficult but stimulating
cham•ber [CHAYM-bər] *noun* 1 room for assembly 2 assembly, body of legislators 3 compartment 4 cavity 5 (*obsolete*) room 6 chamber pot > **cham•bers** 1 office of lawyer or judge 2 lodgings > **cham'ber•lain** [-lin] *noun* official at court of a monarch having charge of domestic and ceremonial affairs > **cham'ber•maid** *noun* female servant with care of bedrooms > **chamber music** music for performance by a few instruments > **chamber pot** vessel for urine
cha•me•le•on [kə-MEEL-yən] *noun* small lizard famous for its power of changing color
cham•fer [CHAM-fər] *verb transitive* 1 groove 2 bevel 3 flute ▷ *noun* 4 groove
cham•ois [SHAM-ee] *noun* 1 goatlike mountain antelope 2 a soft pliable leather
champ[1] *verb* 1 munch (food) noisily, as horse 2 be nervous, impatient
champ[2] *noun short for* **champion**
cham•pagne [sham-PAYN] *noun* 1 light, sparkling white wine from Champagne region of France 2 similar wine made elsewhere
cham•pi•on [CHAM-pee-ən] *noun* 1 one that excels all others 2 defender of a cause 3 one who fights for another 4 hero ▷ *verb transitive* 5 fight for, maintain > **cham'pi•on•ship** *noun*
chance [chans] *noun* 1 unpredictable course of events 2 fortune, luck 3 opportunity 4 possibility 5 risk 6 probability ▷ *verb transitive* **chanced, chanc•ing** 7 risk ▷ *verb intransitive* **chanced, chanc•ing** 8 happen ▷ *adjective* 9 casual, unexpected > **chanc'y** *adjective* **chanc•i•er, chanc•i•est** risky
chan•cel [CHAN-səl] *noun* part of a church where altar is
chan•cel•lor [CHAN-sə-lər] *noun* 1 high officer of state 2 head of university, state educational system
chan•cer•y [CHAN-sə-ree] *noun, plural* **-ies** court of equity
chan•de•lier [shan-dl-EER] *noun* hanging frame with branches for holding lights
change [chaynj] *verb* **changed, chang•ing** 1 alter, make or become different 2 put on

DICTIONARY

C

THESAURUS

validate, verify
chafe *verb* 1 RUB, abrade, rasp, scrape, scratch
2 BE ANNOYED, be impatient, fret, fume, rage, worry
chaff[1] *noun* WASTE, dregs, husks, refuse, remains, rubbish, trash
chaff[2] *verb* TEASE, mock, rib (*informal*), ridicule, scoff, taunt
chain *noun* 1 LINK, bond, coupling, fetter, manacle, shackle
2 SERIES, progression, sequence, set, string, succession, train
▷ *verb* 3 BIND, confine, enslave, fetter, handcuff, manacle, restrain, shackle, tether
chairman *noun* DIRECTOR, chairperson, chairwoman, master of ceremonies, president, speaker, spokesman
challenge *noun* 1 TEST, confrontation, provocation, question, trial, ultimatum
▷ *verb* 2 TEST, confront, defy, dispute, object to, question, tackle, throw down the gauntlet
chamber *noun* 1 ROOM, apartment, bedroom, compartment, cubicle, enclosure, hall
2 COUNCIL, assembly, legislative body, legislature
champion *noun* 1 WINNER, conqueror, hero, title holder, victor
2 DEFENDER, backer, guardian, patron, protector, upholder
▷ *verb* 3 SUPPORT, advocate, back, commend, defend, encourage, espouse, fight for, promote, uphold
chance *noun* 1 PROBABILITY, likelihood, odds, possibility, prospect
2 OPPORTUNITY, occasion, opening, time
3 LUCK, accident, coincidence, destiny, fate, fortune, providence
4 RISK, gamble, hazard, jeopardy, speculation, uncertainty
▷ *verb* 5 RISK, endanger, gamble, hazard, jeopardize, stake, try, venture, wager
chancy *adjective* (*slang*) DANGEROUS, difficult, hazardous, perilous, risky
change *noun* 1 ALTERATION, difference, innovation, metamorphosis, modification, mutation, revolution, transformation, transition
2 VARIETY, break (*informal*), departure, diversion,

(different clothes, fresh coverings) ▷ *verb transitive* 3 put or give for another 4 exchange, interchange ▷ *noun* 5 alteration, variation 6 variety 7 conversion of money 8 small money, coins 9 balance received on payment
> **change'a•ble** *adjective* > **change'less** *adjective*
> **change'ling** *noun* child exchanged for another

chan•nel [CHAN-l] *noun* 1 bed of stream 2 strait 3 deeper part of strait, bay, harbor 4 groove 5 means of passing or conveying 6 band of radio frequencies 7 TV broadcasting station ▷ *verb transitive* 8 groove, furrow 9 guide, convey

chant *noun* 1 simple song or melody 2 rhythmic or repetitious slogan ▷ *verb* 3 sing or utter chant 4 speak monotonously or repetitiously

chan•tey [SHAN-tee] *noun* sailor's song with chorus

chan•ti•cleer [CHAN-tə-kleer] *noun* rooster

cha•os [KAY-os] *noun* 1 disorder, confusion 2 state of universe before Creation > **cha•ot'ic** *adjective* > **cha•ot'i•cal•ly** *adverb*

chap[1] *verb* **chapped, chap•ping** of skin, become dry, raw and cracked, esp. by exposure to cold and wind > **chapped** *adjective*

chap[2] *noun* (*informal*) fellow, man

chap•el [CHAP-əl] *noun* 1 private church 2 subordinate place of worship 3 division of church with its own altar 4 place of worship used by a nonconforming Christian group 5 print shop

chap•er•on, chaperone [SHAP-ə-rohn] *noun* 1 one who attends young unmarried woman in public as protector ▷ *verb transitive* **-oned, -on•ing** 2 attend in this way

chap•lain [CHAP-lin] *noun* clergyman attached to chapel, regiment, warship, institution, etc.
> **chap'lain•cy** *noun* office or term of chaplain

chaps *plural noun* cowboy's leggings of thick leather

chap•ter [CHAP-tər] *noun* 1 division of book 2 section, heading 3 assembly of clergy, bishop's council, etc. 4 organized branch of society, fraternity

char [chahr] *verb transitive* **charred, char•ring** scorch, burn to charcoal > **charred** *adjective*

char•ac•ter [KAR-ik-tər] *noun* 1 nature 2 total of qualities making up individuality 3 moral qualities 4 reputation of possessing them 5 statement of qualities of person 6 an eccentric 7 personality in play or novel 8 letter, sign, or any distinctive mark 9 essential feature
> **char•ac•ter•is'tic** *adjective, noun*
> **char•ac•ter•is'ti•cal•ly** *adverb* > **char'ac•ter•ize** *verb transitive* **-ized, -iz•ing** 1 mark out, distinguish 2 describe by peculiar qualities

char•ade [shə-RAYD] *noun* 1 absurd act 2 travesty > **char•ades** word-guessing parlor game with syllables of word acted

char•coal [CHAHR-kohl] *noun* 1 black residue of wood, bones, etc., produced by smothered burning 2 charred wood

charge [chahrj] *verb transitive* **charged, charg•ing** 1 ask as price 2 bring accusation against 3 lay task on 4 command 5 attack 6 deliver

novelty, variation
3 EXCHANGE, conversion, interchange, substitution, swap, trade
▷ *verb* 4 ALTER, convert, modify, mutate, reform, reorganize, restyle, shift, transform, vary
5 EXCHANGE, barter, convert, interchange, replace, substitute, swap, trade

changeable *adjective* VARIABLE, erratic, fickle, inconstant, irregular, mobile, mutable, protean, shifting, unsettled, unstable, volatile, wavering

channel *noun* 1 ROUTE, approach, artery, avenue, course, means, medium, path, way
2 PASSAGE, canal, conduit, duct, furrow, groove, gutter, route, strait
▷ *verb* 3 DIRECT, conduct, convey, guide, transmit

chant *verb* 1 SING, carol, chorus, descant, intone, recite, warble
▷ *noun* 2 SONG, carol, chorus, melody, psalm

chaos *noun* DISORDER, anarchy, bedlam, confusion, disorganization, lawlessness, mayhem, pandemonium, tumult

chaotic *adjective* DISORDERED, anarchic, confused, deranged, disorganized, lawless, riotous, topsy-turvy, tumultuous, uncontrolled

chap[2] *noun* (*informal*) FELLOW, character, guy (*informal*), individual, man, person

chaperone *noun* 1 ESCORT, companion
▷ *verb* 2 ESCORT, accompany, attend, protect, safeguard, shepherd, watch over

chapter *noun* SECTION, clause, division, episode, part, period, phase, stage, topic

character *noun* 1 NATURE, attributes, caliber, complexion, disposition, personality, quality, temperament, type
2 REPUTATION, honor, integrity, rectitude, strength, uprightness
3 ROLE, part, persona, portrayal
4 ECCENTRIC, card (*informal*), oddball (*informal*), original
5 SYMBOL, device, figure, hieroglyph, letter, mark, rune, sign

characteristic *noun* 1 FEATURE, attribute, faculty, idiosyncrasy, mark, peculiarity, property, quality, quirk, trait
▷ *adjective* 2 TYPICAL, distinctive, distinguishing, idiosyncratic, individual, peculiar, representative, singular, special, symbolic, symptomatic

characterize *verb* IDENTIFY, brand, distinguish, indicate, mark, represent, stamp, typify

charade *noun* PRETENSE, fake, farce, pantomime, parody, travesty

charge *verb* 1 ACCUSE, arraign, blame, impeach, incriminate, indict
2 RUSH, assail, assault, attack, stampede, storm
3 FILL, load
4 COMMAND, bid, commit, demand, entrust, instruct, order, require
▷ *noun* 5 PRICE, amount, cost, expenditure, expense, outlay, payment, rate, toll
6 ACCUSATION, allegation, imputation, indictment
7 RUSH, assault, attack, onset, onslaught, sortie, stampede
8 CARE, custody, duty, office, responsibility, safekeeping, trust
9 WARD
10 INSTRUCTION, command, demand, direction, injunction, mandate, order, precept

injunction 7 fill with electricity 8 fill, load ▷ *verb intransitive* **charged, charg•ing** 9 make onrush, attack ▷ *noun* 10 cost, price 11 accusation 12 attack, onrush 13 command, exhortation 14 accumulation of electricity > **charg•es** expenses > **charge'a•ble** *adjective* > **charg'er** *noun* 1 strong, fast battle horse 2 that which charges, esp. electrically

char•i•ot [CHAR-ee-ət] *noun* two-wheeled vehicle used in ancient fighting > **char•i•ot•eer'** *noun*

cha•ris•ma [kə-RIZ-mə] *noun* special power of person to inspire fascination, loyalty, etc. > **char•is•mat•ic** [kar-iz-MAT-ik] *adjective*

char•i•ty [CHAR-i-tee] *noun, plural* **-ties** 1 the giving of help, money, etc. to those in need 2 organization for doing this 3 the money, etc. given 4 love, kindness 5 disposition to think kindly of others > **char'i•ta•ble** *adjective*

char•la•tan [SHAHR-lə-tn] *noun* quack, impostor

charm [chahrm] *noun* 1 attractiveness 2 anything that fascinates 3 amulet 4 magic spell ▷ *verb transitive* 5 bewitch 6 delight, attract > **charmed** *adjective* > **charm'ing** *adjective*

char•nel house [CHAHR-nl] *noun* vault for bones of the dead

chart [chahrt] *noun* 1 map of sea 2 diagram or tabulated statement ▷ *verb transitive* 3 map 4 represent on chart

char•ter [CHAHR-tər] *noun* 1 document granting privileges, etc. ▷ *verb transitive* 2 let or hire 3 establish by charter

char•wom•an [CHAHR-wuum-ən] *noun* woman paid to clean office, house, etc.

char•y [CHAIR-ee] *adjective* **char•i•er, char•i•est** cautious, sparing > **char'i•ly** *adverb* > **char'i•ness** *noun* caution

chase[1] [chays] *verb transitive* **chased, chas•ing** 1 hunt, pursue 2 drive from, away, into, etc. ▷ *noun* 3 pursuit, hunting 4 the hunted 5 hunting ground > **chas'er** *noun* drink of beer, soda, etc., taken after straight whiskey

chase[2] *verb transitive* **chased, chas•ing** ornament, engrave (metal) > **chas'er** *noun* > **chas'ing** *noun*

chasm [KAZ-əm] *noun* 1 deep cleft, fissure 2 abyss

chas•sis [CHAS-ee] *noun, plural* **chassis** [-eez] frame, wheels and machinery of motor vehicle on which body is supported

chaste [chayst] *adjective* 1 virginal 2 pure 3 modest 4 virtuous > **chas•ti•ty** [CHAS-ti-tee] *noun*

chas•ten [CHAY-sən] *verb transitive* 1 correct by punishment 2 restrain, subdue > **chas'tened** *adjective* > **chas•tise** [chas-TĪZ] *verb transitive* **-tised, -tis•ing** inflict punishment on

chas•u•ble [CHAZ-yə-bəl] *noun* priest's long sleeveless outer vestment

chat *verb intransitive* **chat•ted, chat•ting** 1 talk idly, or familiarly ▷ *noun* 2 familiar idle talk > **chat'bot** *noun* computer program in the form of a virtual e-mail correspondent > **chat'room** *noun* site on the Internet where users have group discussions by e-mail

châ•teau [shat-TOH] *noun, plural* **-teaus** *or* **-teaux** [-TOHZ] (esp. in France) castle, country house

chat•tel [CHAT-l] *noun* any movable property

chat•ter [CHAT-ər] *verb intransitive* 1 talk idly or rapidly 2 rattle teeth ▷ *noun* 3 idle talk > **chat'ter•er** *noun* > **chat'terbox** *noun* one who chatters incessantly

charisma *noun* CHARM, allure, attraction, lure, magnetism, personality

charismatic *adjective* CHARMING, alluring, attractive, enticing, influential, magnetic

charitable *adjective* 1 TOLERANT, considerate, favorable, forgiving, humane, indulgent, kindly, lenient, magnanimous, sympathetic, understanding
2 GENEROUS, beneficent, benevolent, bountiful, kind, lavish, liberal, philanthropic

charity *noun* 1 DONATIONS, assistance, benefaction, contributions, endowment, fund, gift, hand-out, help, largesse *or* largess, philanthropy, relief
2 KINDNESS, altruism, benevolence, compassion, fellow feeling, generosity, goodwill, humanity, indulgence

charlatan *noun* FRAUD, cheat, con man (*informal*), fake, impostor, phoney *or* phony (*informal*), pretender, quack, sham, swindler

charm *noun* 1 ATTRACTION, allure, appeal, fascination, magnetism
2 SPELL, enchantment, magic, sorcery
3 TALISMAN, amulet, fetish, trinket
▷ *verb* 4 ATTRACT, allure, beguile, bewitch, captivate, delight, enchant, enrapture, entrance, fascinate, mesmerize, win over

charming *adjective* ATTRACTIVE, appealing, captivating, cute, delightful, fetching, likable *or* likeable, pleasing, seductive, winsome

chart *noun* 1 TABLE, blueprint, diagram, graph, map, plan, road map
▷ *verb* 2 PLOT, delineate, draft, map out, outline, shape, sketch

charter *noun* 1 DOCUMENT, contract, deed, license, permit, prerogative
▷ *verb* 2 HIRE, commission, employ, lease, rent
3 AUTHORIZE, sanction

chase[1] *verb* 1 PURSUE, course, follow, hunt, run after, stalk, track
2 DRIVE AWAY, drive, expel, hound, put to flight
▷ *noun* 3 PURSUIT, hunt, hunting, race

chasm *noun* GULF, abyss, crater, crevasse, fissure, gap, gorge, ravine

chaste *adjective* PURE, immaculate, innocent, modest, simple, unaffected, undefiled, virtuous

chasten *verb* SUBDUE, chastise, correct, discipline, humble, humiliate, put in one's place, tame

chastise *verb* 1 SCOLD, berate, castigate, censure, correct, discipline, upbraid
2 (*old-fashioned*) BEAT, flog, lash, lick (*informal*), punish, scourge, whip

chastity *noun* PURITY, celibacy, continence, innocence, maidenhood, modesty, virginity, virtue

chat *noun* 1 TALK, chatter, conversation, gossip, heart-to-heart, natter, tête-à-tête
▷ *verb* 2 TALK, chatter, chew the fat (*slang*), gossip, jaw (*slang*), natter

chatter *noun* 1 PRATTLE, babble, blather, chat, gab (*informal*), gossip
▷ *verb* 2 PRATTLE, babble, blather, chat, chew the fat (*slang*), gab (*informal*), gossip, schmooze

chauf•feur [SHOH-fər] *noun* 1 paid driver of automobile ▷ *verb transitive* 2 perform this work
chau•vin•ism [SHOH-və-niz-əm] *noun* aggressive patriotism **male chauvinism** smug sense of male superiority over women > **chau'vin•ist** *noun*
cheap [cheep] *adjective* **-er, -est** 1 low in price 2 inexpensive 3 easily obtained 4 of little value or estimation 5 mean, inferior > **cheap'en** *verb transitive*
cheat [cheet] *verb transitive* 1 deceive, defraud, swindle, impose upon ▷ *verb intransitive* 2 practice deceit to gain advantage 3 (oft. followed by *on*) be sexually unfaithful > **cheat, cheat'er** *noun* one who cheats > **cheat'ers** *plural noun* (*slang*) eyeglasses
check [chek] *verb transitive* 1 stop 2 restrain 3 hinder 4 repress 5 control 6 examine for accuracy, quality, etc. ▷ *noun* 7 repulse 8 stoppage 9 restraint 10 brief examination for correctness or accuracy 11 pattern of squares on fabric 12 threat to king at chess 13 written order to banker to pay money from one's account 14 printed slip of paper used for this > **check'book** *noun* book of checks > **check'mate** *noun* 1 *chess* final winning move 2 any overthrow, defeat ▷ *verb transitive* **-mat•ed, -mat•ing** 3 *chess* make game-ending move 4 defeat > **check'out** *noun* counter in supermarket where customers pay > **check'up** *noun* examination (esp. medical) to see if all is in order
checked [chekt] *adjective* having pattern of small squares
check•er [CHEK-ər] *noun* 1 marking as on checkerboard 2 playing piece in game of checkers ▷ *verb transitive* 3 mark in squares 4 variegate > **check'ered** *adjective* 1 marked in squares 2 uneven, varied > **check'ers** *noun* game played on checkered board of 64 squares with flat round playing pieces > **check'er•board** *noun*
Ched•dar [CHED-ər] *noun* smooth hard cheese
cheek *noun* 1 side of face below eye 2 impudence 3 buttock ▷ *verb transitive* (*informal*) 4 address impudently **cheek by jowl** in close intimacy
cheep *verb intransitive, noun* (utter) high-pitched cry, as of young bird
cheer *verb transitive* 1 comfort 2 gladden 3 encourage by shouts ▷ *verb intransitive* 4 shout applause ▷ *noun* 5 shout of approval 6 happiness, good spirits 7 mood > **cheer'ful** *adjective* > **cheer'i•ly** *adverb* > **cheer'less** *adjective*
cheese [cheez] *noun* curd of milk coagulated, separated from the whey and pressed > **chees'y** *adjective* **chees•i•er, chees•i•est** 1 suggesting cheese in aroma, etc. 2 (*slang*) cheap, shabby > **cheese'cake** *noun* 1 cake made with cottage or cream cheese and oft. with fruit mixture 2 (*informal*) photograph of shapely, scantily clad woman > **cheese'cloth** *noun* loosely woven cotton cloth
chee•tah [CHEE-tə] *noun* large, swift, spotted feline animal
chef [shef] *noun* head cook, esp. in restaurant
chef-d'oeu•vre [shay-DUR-vr] *Fr.* masterpiece
chem•is•try [KEM-ə-stree] *noun* 1 science concerned with properties of substances and their combinations and reactions 2 interaction of one personality with another > **chem'i•cal** *noun, adjective* > **chem'ist** *noun* one trained in chemistry > **chemical peeling** cosmetic process in which a chemical substance is applied to the face and peeled away to remove dead skin cells
che•mo•ther•a•py [kee-moh-THER-ə-pee] *noun* treatment of disease by chemical means
che•nille [shə-NEEL] *noun* soft yarn, fabric of silk, wool, etc.
cher'ish *verb transitive* 1 treat with affection 2 (*slang*)

cheap *adjective* 1 INEXPENSIVE, bargain, cut-price, economical, keen, low-cost, low-priced, reasonable, reduced
2 INFERIOR, common, poor, second-rate, shoddy, tatty, tawdry, two a penny, worthless
cheapen *verb* DEGRADE, belittle, debase, demean, denigrate, depreciate, devalue, discredit, disparage, lower
cheat *verb* 1 DECEIVE, beguile, con (*informal*), defraud, double-cross (*informal*), dupe, fleece, fool, mislead, rip off (*slang*), swindle, trick
▷ *noun* 2 DECEIVER, charlatan, con man (*informal*), double-crosser (*informal*), shark, sharper, swindler, trickster
3 DECEPTION, deceit, fraud, rip-off (*slang*), scam (*slang*), swindle, trickery
check *verb* 1 EXAMINE, inquire into, inspect, investigate, look at, make sure, monitor, research, scrutinize, study, test, vet
2 STOP, delay, halt, hinder, impede, inhibit, limit, obstruct, restrain, retard
▷ *noun* 3 EXAMINATION, inspection, investigation, once-over (*informal*), research, scrutiny, test
4 STOPPAGE, constraint, control, curb, damper, hindrance, impediment, limitation, obstacle, obstruction, restraint
cheeky *adjective* IMPUDENT, audacious, disrespectful, forward, impertinent, insolent, insulting, pert, saucy
cheer *verb* 1 APPLAUD, acclaim, clap, hail
2 CHEER UP, brighten, buoy up, comfort, encourage, gladden, hearten, uplift
▷ *noun* 3 APPLAUSE, acclamation, ovation, plaudits
cheerful *adjective* HAPPY, buoyant, cheery, chirpy (*informal*), enthusiastic, jaunty, jolly, light-hearted, merry, optimistic, upbeat (*informal*)
cheerfulness *noun* HAPPINESS, buoyancy, exuberance, gaiety, geniality, good cheer, good humor, high spirits, jauntiness, light-heartedness
cheerless *adjective* GLOOMY, bleak, desolate, dismal, drab, dreary, forlorn, miserable, somber, woeful
cheer up *verb* 1 COMFORT, encourage, enliven, gladden, hearten
2 TAKE HEART, buck up (*informal*), perk up, rally
cheery *adjective* CHEERFUL, breezy, carefree, chirpy (*informal*), genial, good-humored, happy, jovial, upbeat (*informal*)
chemist *noun* PHARMACIST, apothecary (*obsolete*), dispenser
cherish *verb* 1 CLING TO, cleave to, encourage, entertain, foster, harbor, hold dear, nurture,

protect **3** foster
che•root [shə-ROOT] *noun* cigar with both ends open
cher•ry [CHER-ee] *noun* **1** small red fruit with stone **2** tree bearing it ▷ *adjective* **3** ruddy, bright red
cher•ub [CHER-əb] *noun* **cher•u•bim, cher•ubs** **1** winged creature with human face **2** angel > **che•ru•bic** [chə-ROO-bik] *adjective*
cher•vil [CHUR-vil] *noun* an herb
chess *noun* game of skill played by two with 32 pieces on checkered board of 64 squares > **chess'board** *noun* > **chess'man** *noun, plural* **-men** piece used in chess
chest *noun* **1** upper part of trunk of body **2** large, strong box > **chest of drawers** piece of furniture containing drawers
chest•nut [CHES-nut] *noun* **1** large reddish-brown nut growing in prickly husk **2** tree bearing it **3** horse of chestnut color **4** old joke ▷ *adjective* **5** reddish-brown
chev•ron [SHEV-rən] *noun military* V-shaped band of braid worn on sleeve to designate rank
chew [choo] *verb* grind with teeth ▷ *noun* > **chew'y** *adjective* **chew•i•er, chew•i•est** firm, sticky when chewed
chi•an•ti [kee-AHN-tee] *noun* dry red Italian wine
chic [sheek] *adjective* **-er, -est** stylish, elegant ▷ *noun*
chi•can•er•y [shi-KAY-nə-ree] *noun, plural* **-er•ies** **1** quibbling **2** trick, artifice
chick [chik], **chick•en** [CHIK-ən] *noun* **1** young of birds, esp. of hen **2** (*slang, often offensive*) **3** girl, young woman > **chicken feed** trifling amount of money > **chick'en•heart•ed** *adjective* cowardly > **chick'en•pox** *noun* infectious disease, esp. of children > **chick'pea** *noun* **1** legume bearing pods containing pealike seeds **2** seed of this plant
chic•o•ry [CHIK-ə-ree] *noun* **1** salad plant **2** ground root of the plant used with, or instead of, coffee
chide [chīd] *verb transitive* **chid•ed** *or* **chid, chid•ed** *or* **chid chid•den, chid•ing** scold, reprove, censure
chief [cheef] *noun* **1** head or principal person ▷ *adjective* **2** principal, foremost, leading > **chief'ly** *adverb* > **chief'tain** [-tən] *noun* leader, chief of clan or tribe
chif•fon [shi-FON] *noun* thin gauzy material
chi•gnon [SHEEN-yon] *noun* roll, knot, of hair worn at back of head
chi•hua•hua [chi-WAH-wah] *noun* breed of tiny dog, orig. from Mexico
chil•blain [CHIL-blayn] *noun* inflamed sore on hands, legs, etc., due to cold
child [chīld] *noun, plural* **chil•dren** [CHIL-drən] **1** young human being **2** offspring > **child'ish** *adjective* **1** of or like a child **2** silly **3** trifling > **child'ish•ly** *adverb* > **child'less** *adjective* > **child'like** *adjective* **1** of or like a child **2** innocent **3** frank **4** docile > **child'birth** *noun* > **child'hood** *noun* period between birth and puberty > **child's play** very easy task
chil•i [CHIL-ee] *noun, plural* **chil•ies** **1** small red hot-tasting seed pod **2** plant producing it **3** > **chili con carne** [kon KAHR-nee] Mexican-style dish of chilies or chili powder, ground beef, onions, etc.
chill *noun* **1** coldness **2** cold with shivering **3** anything that damps, discourages ▷ *verb* **4** make, become cold (esp. food, drink) > **chill'i•ness** *noun* > **chill'y** *adjective* **chill•i•er, chill•i•est** > **chill out** (*slang*) **1** relax, calm down **2** spend time in trivial occupations **3** keep company (with) > **chill pill** imaginary medicinal pill with a calming effect
chime [chīm] *noun* **1** sound of bell **2** harmonious, ringing sound ▷ *verb intransitive* **chimed, chim•ing** **3** ring harmoniously **4** agree ▷ *verb transitive* **chimed, chim•ing** **5** strike (bells) > **chime in** break into a conversation to express an opinion
chi•me•ra [ki-MEER-ə] *noun* **1** fabled monster, made up of parts of various animals **2** wild fancy > **chi•mer'i•cal** [-MER-i-kəl] *adjective* fanciful

DICTIONARY

C

THESAURUS

prize, sustain, treasure
2 CARE FOR, comfort, hold dear, love, nurse, shelter, support
chest *noun* BOX, case, casket, coffer, crate, strongbox, trunk
chew *verb* BITE, champ, chomp, crunch, gnaw, grind, masticate, munch
chewy *adjective* TOUGH, as tough as old boots, leathery
chic *adjective* STYLISH, cool (*informal*), elegant, fashionable, phat (*slang*), smart, trendy (*informal*)
chide *verb* (*old-fashioned*) SCOLD, admonish, berate, censure, criticize, lecture, rebuke, reprimand, reproach, reprove, tell off (*informal*)
chief *noun* **1** HEAD, alpha male, boss (*informal*), captain, commander, director, governor, leader, manager, master, principal, ruler
▷ *adjective* **2** PRIMARY, cutting-edge, foremost, highest, key, leading, main, predominant, pre-eminent, premier, prime, principal, supreme, uppermost
chiefly *adverb* **1** ESPECIALLY, above all, essentially, primarily, principally
2 MAINLY, in general, in the main, largely, mostly, on the whole, predominantly, usually
child *noun* YOUNGSTER, babe, baby, juvenile, kid (*informal*), minor, offspring, toddler, tot
childbirth *noun* CHILD-BEARING, confinement, delivery, labor, lying-in, parturition, travail
childhood *noun* YOUTH, boyhood *or* girlhood, immaturity, infancy, minority, schooldays
childish *adjective* IMMATURE, boyish *or* girlish, foolish, infantile, juvenile, puerile, young
childlike *adjective* INNOCENT, artless, guileless, ingenuous, naive, simple, trusting
chill *noun* **1** COLD, bite, coldness, coolness, crispness, frigidity, nip, rawness, sharpness
▷ *verb* **2** COOL, freeze, refrigerate
3 DISHEARTEN, dampen, deject, depress, discourage, dismay
▷ *adjective* **4** COLD, biting, bleak, chilly, freezing, frigid, raw, sharp, wintry
chilly *adjective* **1** COOL, brisk, crisp, drafty, fresh, nippy, penetrating, sharp
2 UNFRIENDLY, frigid, hostile, unresponsive, unsympathetic, unwelcoming
chime *verb*
▷ *noun* RING, clang, jingle, peal, sound, tinkle,

chim•ney [CHIM-nee] *noun, plural* **-neys** 1 a passage for smoke 2 narrow vertical cleft in rock
chim•pan•zee [chim-pan-ZEE] *noun* gregarious, intelligent ape of Africa
chin *noun* part of face below mouth
chi•na [CHĪ-nə] *noun* 1 fine earthenware, porcelain 2 cups, saucers, etc. collectively
chin•chil•la [chin-CHIL-ə] *noun* 1 S Amer. rodent with soft, gray fur 2 its fur
chine [chīn] *noun* 1 backbone 2 cut of meat including backbone 3 ridge or crest of land 4 intersection of bottom and side of boat
chink[1] [chingk] *noun* cleft, crack
chink[2] *noun* 1 light metallic sound ▷ *verb* 2 (cause to) make this sound
chintz [chints] *noun* cotton cloth printed in colored designs
chip *noun* 1 splinter 2 place where piece has been broken off 3 tiny wafer of silicon forming integrated circuit in computer, etc. ▷ *verb* **chipped, chip•ping** 4 *verb transitive* 5 chop into small pieces 6 break small pieces from 7 shape by cutting off pieces ▷ *verb intransitive* 8 break off > **chip in** 1 contribute 2 butt in > **chip'set** *noun* 1 circuit in a computer that controls many of its data transfer functions 2 the main processing circuitry on many video cards
chip•munk [CHIP-mungk] *noun* small, striped N Amer. squirrel
chi•rop•o•dist [ki-ROP-ə-dist] *noun* one who treats disorders of feet > **chi•rop'o•dy** *noun*
chi•ro•prac•tor [KĪ-rə-prak-tər] *noun* one skilled in treating bodily disorders by manipulation, massage, etc. > **chi•ro•prac'tic** *noun*
chirp [churp] *noun* 1 short, sharp cry of bird ▷ *verb intransitive* 2 make this sound > **chirp'y** *adjective* **chirp•i•er, chirp•i•est** (*informal*) happy
chis•el [CHIZ-əl] *noun* 1 cutting tool, usu. bar of steel with edge across main axis ▷ *verb transitive* **-eled, -el•ing** 2 cut, carve with chisel 3 (*slang*) cheat
chit[1] *noun* 1 signed note for money owed 2 informal receipt
chit[2] *noun* child, esp. young girl
chiv•al•ry [SHIV-əl-ree] *noun* 1 bravery and courtesy 2 medieval system of knighthood > **chiv'al•rous** *adjective*
chive [chīv] *noun* herb with mild onion flavor
chlo•rine [KLOR-een] *noun* nonmetallic element, yellowish-green poison gas, used as disinfectant > **chlo'rate** [-ayt] *noun* salt of chloric acid > **chlo'ric** *adjective* > **chlo'ride** *noun* 1 compound of chlorine 2 bleaching agent > **chlo•ri•nate** [KLOR-ə-nayt] *verb transitive* **-nat•ed, -nat•ing** 1 disinfect 2 purify with chlorine
chlo•ro•fluo•ro•car•bon [klor-ə-fluur-ə-KAHR-bən] *noun* (*also* **CFC**) any of various gaseous compounds of carbon, hydrogen, chlorine, and fluorine, used in refrigerators and aerosol propellants, some of which break down the ozone in the atmosphere
chlo•ro•form [KLOR-ə-form] *noun* 1 volatile liquid formerly used as anesthetic ▷ *verb transitive* 2 render insensible with it
chlo•ro•phyll [KLOR-ə-fil] *noun* green coloring matter in plants
chock [chok] *noun* block or wedge to prevent heavy object from rolling or sliding > **chock'-full** *adjective* packed full
choc•o•late [CHAWK-lit] *noun* 1 paste from ground cacao seeds 2 candy, drink made from this ▷ *adjective* 3 dark brown
choice [chois] *noun* 1 act or power of choosing 2 alternative 3 thing or person chosen ▷ *adjective* 4 select, fine, worthy of being chosen
choir [kwīr] *noun* 1 company of singers, esp. in church 2 part of church set aside for them
choke [chohk] *verb transitive* **choked, chok•ing** 1 hinder, stop the breathing of 2 smother, stifle 3 obstruct ▷ *verb intransitive* **choked, chok•ing** 4 suffer choking ▷ *noun* 5 act, noise of choking 6 device in carburetor to increase richness of fuel-air mixture
chol•er [KOL-ər] *noun* bile, anger > **chol'er•ic** *adjective* irritable
chol•er•a [KOL-ər-ə] *noun* deadly infectious disease marked by vomiting and diarrhea
cho•les•ter•ol [kə-LES-tə-rawl] *noun* substance found in animal tissue and fat
chomp *verb* chew noisily
choose [chooz] *verb transitive* **chose, cho•sen, choos•ing** 1 pick out, select 2 take by preference ▷ *verb intransitive* **chose, cho•sen, choos•ing** 3 decide, think fit > **choos'y** *adjective* **choos•i•er, choos•i•est** fussy
chop *verb transitive* **chopped, chop•ping** 1 cut with blow 2 hack ▷ *noun* 3 hewing blow 4 slice of meat containing rib or other bone > **chop'per** *noun* 1 short axe 2 (*informal*) helicopter > **chop'py** *adjective* **-pi•er, -pi•est** (of

toll
china *noun* POTTERY, ceramics, crockery, porcelain, service, tableware, ware
chink *noun* OPENING, aperture, cleft, crack, cranny, crevice, fissure, gap
chip *noun* 1 SCRATCH, fragment, nick, notch, shard, shaving, sliver, wafer
▷ *verb* 2 NICK, chisel, damage, gash, whittle
chirp *verb* CHIRRUP, cheep, peep, pipe, tweet, twitter, warble
chivalrous *adjective* COURTEOUS, bold, brave, courageous, gallant, gentlemanly, honorable, valiant
chivalry *noun* COURTESY, courage, gallantry, gentlemanliness, knight-errantry, knighthood, politeness
choice *noun* 1 OPTION, alternative, pick, preference, say
2 SELECTION, range, variety
▷ *adjective* 3 BEST, elite, excellent, exclusive, prime, rare, select
choke *verb* 1 STRANGLE, asphyxiate, gag, overpower, smother, stifle, suffocate, suppress, throttle
2 BLOCK, bar, bung, clog, congest, constrict, obstruct, stop
choose *verb* PICK, adopt, designate, elect, opt for, prefer, select, settle upon
choosy *adjective* FUSSY, discriminating, faddy, fastidious, finicky, particular, picky (*informal*), selective
chop *verb* CUT, cleave, fell, hack, hew, lop, sever

sea) having short, broken waves
chops *plural noun* jaw, mouth
chop•sticks [CHOP-stiks] *plural noun* implements used by Chinese and others for eating food
cho•ral [KOR-əl] *adjective* of, for, sung by, a choir
cho•rale [kə-RAL] *noun* slow, stately hymn tune
chord [kord] *noun* 1 emotional response, esp. of sympathy 2 simultaneous sounding of musical notes 3 straight line joining ends of arc
chore [chor] *noun* 1 (unpleasant) task 2 odd job
cho•re•og•ra•phy [kor-ee-OG-rə-fee] *noun* 1 art of arranging dances, esp. ballet 2 art, notation of ballet dancing > **cho•re•og'ra•pher** *noun* > **cho•re•o•graph'ic** *adjective*
chor•tle [CHOR-tl] *verb intransitive* **-tled, -tling** chuckle happily ▷ *noun*
cho•rus [KOR-əs] *noun* 1 group of singers 2 combination of voices singing together 3 refrain ▷ *verb transitive* **-rused, -rus•ing** 4 sing or say together > **chor'is•ter** *noun*
chose *pt. of* **choose** > **cho'sen** *pp. of* **choose**
chow[1] (*informal*) ▷ *noun* 1 food ▷ *verb intransitive* 2 (oft. with *down*) eat heartily > **chow'hound** *noun* (*slang*) glutton
chow[2] *noun* thick-coated dog with curled tail, orig. from China
chow•der [CHOW-dər] *noun* 1 thick soup of seafood, vegetables, etc. 2 soup resembling it, such as corn chowder
Christ [krīst] *noun* Jesus of Nazareth, regarded by Christians as the Messiah
Chris•tian [KRIS-chən] *noun* 1 follower of Christ ▷ *adjective* 2 following Christ 3 relating to Christ or his religion > **chris'ten** [-ən] *verb transitive* baptize, give name to > **Chris'ten•dom** [-ən-dəm] *noun* all the Christian world > **Chris•ti•an'i•ty** [-chee-AN-i-tee] *noun* religion of Christ > **Christian name** name given at baptism > **Christian Science** religious system founded by Mary Baker Eddy
Christ•mas [KRIS-məs] *noun* festival of birth of Christ
chro•mat•ic [kroh-MAT-ik] *adjective* 1 of color 2 *mus.* of scale proceeding by semitones
chro•ma•tin [KROH-mə-tin] *noun* part of protoplasmic substance in nucleus of cells that takes color in staining tests
chrome [krohm], **chro'mi•um** [-mee-əm] *noun* metal used in alloys and for plating
chro•mo•some [KROH-mə-sohm] *noun* microscopic gene-carrying body in the tissue of a cell
Chron. Chronicles
chron•ic [KRON-ik] *adjective* 1 lasting a long time 2 habitual
chron•i•cle [KRON-i-kəl] *noun* 1 record of events in order of time 2 account ▷ *verb transitive* **-cled, -cling** 3 record > **chron'i•cler** *noun*
chro•nol•o•gy [krə-NOL-ə-jee] *noun, plural* **-gies** 1 determination of sequence of past events 2 arrangement in order of occurrence 3 account of events, reference work arranged in order of time > **chron•o•log•i•cal** [kron-l-OJ-i-kəl] *adjective* arranged in order of time
chro•nom•e•ter [krə-NOM-i-tər] *noun* 1 instrument for measuring time exactly 2 watch
chrys•a•lis [KRIS-ə-lis] *noun, plural* **chry•sal•i•des** [kri-SAL-i-deez] 1 resting state of insect between grub and butterfly, etc. 2 case enclosing it
chry•san•the•mum [kri-SAN-thə-məm] *noun* garden flower of various colors
chub•by [CHUB-ee] *adjective* **-bi•er, -bi•est** plump
chuck[1] [chuk] *verb transitive* (*informal*) 1 throw 2 pat affectionately (under chin) 3 give up, reject
chuck[2] *noun* 1 cut of beef 2 device for gripping, adjusting bit in power drill, etc.
chuck•le [CHUK-əl] *verb intransitive* **-led, -ling** 1 laugh softly ▷ *noun* 2 such laugh
chuk•ker [CHUK-ər] *noun* period of play in game of polo
chum *noun* (*informal*) close friend > **chum'my** *adjective* **-mi•er, -mi•est**
chunk [chungk] *noun* thick, solid piece > **chunk'y** *adjective* **chunk•i•er, chunk•i•est**
church *noun* 1 building for Christian worship 2 (**Church**) whole body or sect of Christians 3 clergy > **church'ward•en** *noun* 1 officer who represents interests of Anglican parish 2 long clay pipe > **church'yard** *noun*
churl *noun* 1 rustic 2 rude, boorish person > **churl'ish** *adjective* > **churl'ish•ness** *noun*
churn *noun* 1 vessel for making butter ▷ *verb* 2 shake up, stir (liquid) violently 3 make (butter) in churn 4 (of a stockbroker) trade (stocks) excessively to increase commissions
chute [shoot] *noun* 1 slide for sending down parcels, coal, etc. 2 channel 3 narrow passageway, e.g. for spraying, counting cattle, sheep, etc. 4 (*informal*) *short for* **parachute**
chut•ney [CHUT-nee] *noun* condiment of fruit, spices, etc.
chutz•pah [HUUT-spə] *noun* 1 shameless audacity 2 gall
ci•ca•da [si-KAY-də] *noun* cricketlike insect

chore *noun* TASK, burden, duty, errand, job
chortle *verb, noun* CHUCKLE, cackle, crow, guffaw
chorus *noun* 1 CHOIR, choristers, ensemble, singers, vocalists
2 REFRAIN, burden, response, strain
3 UNISON, accord, concert, harmony
christen *verb* 1 BAPTIZE
2 NAME, call, designate, dub, style, term, title
Christmas *noun* FESTIVE SEASON, Noel, Xmas, Yule, Yuletide
chronicle *noun* 1 RECORD, blog (*informal*), account, annals, diary, history, journal, narrative, register, story, weblog
▷ *verb* 2 RECORD, enter, narrate, put on record, recount, register, relate, report, set down, tell
chubby *adjective* PLUMP, buxom, flabby, portly, rotund, round, stout, tubby
chuckle *verb* LAUGH, chortle, crow, exult, giggle, snigger, titter
chum *noun* (*informal*) FRIEND, companion, comrade, crony, homeboy (*slang*), homegirl (*slang*), pal (*informal*)
chunk *noun* PIECE, block, dollop (*informal*), hunk, lump, mass, nugget, portion, slab
churlish *adjective* RUDE, brusque, harsh, ill-tempered, impolite, sullen, surly, uncivil
churn *verb* STIR UP, agitate, beat, convulse, swirl, toss

cic•a•trix [SIK-ə-triks] *noun* scar of healed wound

cic•e•ro•ne [sis-ə-ROH-nee] *noun* guide for sightseers

ci•der [SĪ-dər] *noun* drink made from apples **hard cider** cider after fermentation **soft cider** cider before fermentation

ci•gar [si-GAHR] *noun* roll of tobacco leaves for smoking > **cig•a•rette** [sig-ə-RET] *noun* finely cut tobacco rolled in paper for smoking

ci•lan•tro [si-LAN-troh, -LAHN-] *noun* coriander

cinch [sinch] *noun* (*informal*) 1 easy task, certainty 2 strong girth used on saddle

cin•der [SIN-dər] *noun* remains of burned coal

cin•e•ma [SIN-ə-mə] *noun* 1 building used for showing of motion pictures 2 these generally or collectively

cin•na•mon [SIN-ə-mən] *noun* 1 spice got from bark of Asian tree 2 the tree ▷ *adjective* 3 light-brown color

ci•pher [SĪ-fər] *noun* 1 secret writing 2 arithmetical symbol 3 person of no importance 4 monogram ▷ *verb transitive* 5 write in cipher

cir•ca [SUR-kə] *Lat.* about, approximately

cir•cle [SUR-kəl] *noun* 1 perfectly round figure 2 ring 3 *theater* balcony or tier of seats above main level of auditorium 4 group, society with common interest 5 class of society ▷ *verb transitive* **-cled, -cling** 6 surround ▷ *verb intransitive* **-cled, -cling** 7 move in circle > **cir'cu•lar** [-kyə-lər] *adjective* 1 round 2 in a circle ▷ *noun* 3 letter, etc. intended for wide distribution > **cir'cu•late** [-kyə-layt] *verb intransitive* **-lat•ed, -lat•ing** 1 move around 2 pass from hand to hand or place to place ▷ *verb transitive* **-lat•ed, -lat•ing** 3 send around > **cir•cu•la'tion** *noun* 1 flow of blood from, and back to, heart 2 act of moving around 3 extent of sale of newspaper, etc. > **cir'cu•la•to•ry** *adjective*

cir•cuit [SUR-kit] *noun* 1 complete round or course 2 area 3 path of electric current 4 round of visitation, esp. of judges 5 series of sporting events 6 district > **cir•cu•i•tous** [sər-KYOO-i-təs] *adjective* roundabout, indirect > **cir'cuit•ry** *noun* electrical circuit(s)

cir•cum•cise [SUR-kəm-sīz] *verb transitive* **-cised, -cis•ing** cut off foreskin of (penis) > **cir•cum•ci'sion** [-SIZH-ən] *noun*

cir•cum•fer•ence [sər-KUM-fər-əns] *noun* boundary line, esp. of circle

cir•cum•flex [SUR-kəm-fleks] *noun* accent (ˆ) over vowel to indicate length of its sound

cir•cum•lo•cu•tion [sur-kəm-loh-KYOO-shən] *noun* roundabout speech

cir•cum•nav•i•gate [sur-kəm-NAV-i-gayt] *verb transitive* **-gat•ed, -gat•ing** sail or fly right around

cir•cum•scribe [SUR-kəm-skrīb] *verb transitive* **-scribed, -scrib•ing** confine, bound, limit, hamper

cir•cum•spect [SUR-kəm-spekt] *adjective* watchful, cautious, prudent > **cir•cum•spec'tion** *noun*

cir•cum•stance [SUR-kəm-stans] *noun* 1 detail 2 event 3 matter of fact > **cir•cum•stan•ces** 1 state of affairs 2 condition in life, esp. financial 3 surroundings or things accompanying an action > **cir•cum•stan'tial** *adjective* 1 depending on detail or circumstances 2 detailed, minute 3 incidental

cir•cum•vent [sur-kəm-VENT] *verb transitive* outwit, evade, get round > **cir•cum•ven'tion** *noun*

cir•cus [SUR-kəs] *noun, plural* **-cus•es** 1 (performance of) traveling group of acrobats, clowns, performing animals, etc. 2 circular structure for public shows

cir•rho•sis [si-ROH-sis] *noun* any of various chronic progressive diseases of liver > **cir•rhot'ic** [-ROT-ik] *adjective*

cir•rus [SIR-əs] *noun, plural* **cirrus** high wispy cloud

cis•tern [SIS-tərn] *noun* water tank, esp. for rain water

cit•a•del [SIT-ə-dl] *noun* fortress in, near, or commanding a city

cite [sīt] *verb transitive* **cit•ed, cit•ing** 1 quote 2 bring forward as proof > **ci•ta•tion** [sī-TAY-shən] *noun* 1 quoting 2 commendation for bravery, etc.

cit•i•zen [SIT-ə-zən] *noun* 1 native, naturalized member of state, nation, etc. 2 inhabitant of city > **cit'i•zen•ship** *noun*

cit•ron [SI-trən] *noun* 1 fruit like a lemon 2 the tree > **cit'ric** *adjective* of the acid of lemon or

DICTIONARY • THESAURUS

cinema *noun* FILMS, big screen (*informal*), flicks (*slang*), motion pictures, movies, pictures

cipher *noun* 1 CODE, cryptograph
2 NOBODY, nonentity

circle *noun* 1 RING, disc, globe, orb, sphere
2 GROUP, clique, club, company, coterie, set, society
▷ *verb* 3 GO ROUND, circumnavigate, circumscribe, encircle, enclose, envelop, ring, surround

circuit *noun* COURSE, journey, lap, orbit, revolution, route, tour, track

circuitous *adjective* INDIRECT, labyrinthine, meandering, oblique, rambling, roundabout, tortuous, winding

circular *adjective* 1 ROUND, ring-shaped, rotund, spherical
2 ORBITAL, circuitous, cyclical
▷ *noun* 3 ADVERTISEMENT, notice

circulate *verb* 1 SPREAD, broadcast, disseminate, distribute, issue, make known, promulgate, publicize, publish
2 FLOW, gyrate, radiate, revolve, rotate

circulation *noun* 1 BLOODSTREAM
2 FLOW, circling, motion, rotation
3 DISTRIBUTION, currency, dissemination, spread, transmission

circumference *noun* BOUNDARY, border, edge, extremity, limits, outline, perimeter, periphery, rim

circumstance *noun* EVENT, accident, condition, contingency, happening, incident, occurrence, particular, respect, situation

circumstances *plural noun* SITUATION, means, position, state, state of affairs, station, status

cistern *noun* TANK, basin, reservoir, sink, vat

citadel *noun* FORTRESS, bastion, fortification, keep, stronghold, tower

cite *verb* QUOTE, adduce, advance, allude to, enumerate, extract, mention, name, specify

citron > **cit•rus fruit** citrons, lemons, limes, oranges, etc.
cit•y [SIT-ee] *noun, plural* **cit•ies** a large town
civ•et [SIV-it] *noun* strong, musky perfume > **civet cat** catlike animal producing it
civ•ic [SIV-ik] *adjective* pert. to city or citizen > **civ'ics** *noun* study of the responsibilities and rights of citizenship
civ•il [SIV-əl] *adjective* 1 relating to citizens of state 2 not military 3 refined, polite 4 *law* not criminal > **ci•vil•ian** [si-VIL-yən] *noun* nonmilitary person > **ci•vil'i•ty** *noun, plural* **-ties** > **civ'il•ly** *adverb* > **civil service** service responsible for the public administration of the government of a city, state, or country
civ•i•lize [SIV-ə-līz] *verb transitive* **-lized, -liz•ing** 1 bring out of barbarism 2 refine > **civ•i•li•za'tion** *noun*
Cl *chem.* chlorine
clack [klak] *noun* sound, as of two pieces of wood striking together ▷ *verb*
clad *pt./pp. of* **clothe**
clad•ding [KLAD-ing] *noun* metal bonded to inner core of another metal, as protection against corrosion
claim [klaym] *verb transitive* 1 demand as right 2 assert 3 call for ▷ *noun* 4 demand for thing supposed due 5 right 6 thing claimed 7 plot of mining land marked out by stakes as required by law > **claim'ant** [-mənt] *noun*
clair•voy•ance [klair-VOI-əns] *noun* power of seeing things not present to senses, second sight > **clair•voy'ant** *noun, adjective*
clam [klam] *noun* edible mollusk
clam•ber [KLAM-bər] *verb intransitive* to climb with difficulty or awkwardly
clam•my [KLAM-ee] *adjective* **-mi•er, -mi•est** moist and sticky > **clam'mi•ness** *noun*
clam•or [KLAM-ər] *noun* 1 loud shouting, outcry, noise ▷ *verb intransitive* 2 shout, call noisily (for) > **clam'or•ous** *adjective*
clamp [klamp] *noun* 1 tool for holding or compressing ▷ *verb transitive* 2 fasten, strengthen with or as with clamp
clan [klan] *noun* 1 tribe or collection of families under chief and of common ancestry 2 faction, group > **clan'nish** *adjective*
clan•des•tine [klan-DES-tin] *adjective* 1 secret 2 sly
clang [klang] *verb* 1 (cause to) make loud ringing sound ▷ *noun* 2 loud ringing sound
clank [klangk] *noun* 1 short sound as of pieces of metal struck together ▷ *verb* 2 cause, move with, such sound
clap[1] [klap] *verb* **clapped, clap•ping** 1 (cause to) strike with noise 2 strike (hands) together 3 applaud ▷ *verb transitive* 4 pat 5 place or put quickly ▷ *noun* 6 hard, explosive sound 7 slap > **clap'per** *noun* > **clap'trap** *noun* empty words
clap[2] *noun* (*slang*) gonorrhea
clar•et [KLAR-it] *noun* 1 a dry dark red wine of Bordeaux 2 similar wine made elsewhere
clar•i•fy [KLAR-ə-fī] *verb* **-fied, -fy•ing** make or become clear, pure, or more easily understood > **clar•i•fi•ca'tion** *noun* > **clar'i•ty** *noun* clearness
clar•i•net [klar-ə-NET] *noun* woodwind musical instrument
clar•i•on [KLAR-ee-ən] *noun* 1 clear-sounding trumpet 2 rousing sound
clash [klash] *noun* 1 loud noise, as of weapons striking 2 conflict, collision ▷ *verb intransitive* 3 make clash 4 come into conflict 5 (of events) coincide 6 (of colors) look ugly together ▷ *verb transitive* 7 strike together to make clash
clasp [klasp] *noun* 1 hook or other means of fastening 2 embrace ▷ *verb transitive* 3 fasten 4

citizen *noun* INHABITANT, denizen, dweller, resident, subject, townsman
city *noun* TOWN, conurbation, metropolis, municipality
civic *adjective* PUBLIC, communal, local, municipal
civil *adjective* 1 CIVIC, domestic, municipal, political
2 POLITE, affable, courteous, obliging, refined, urbane, well-mannered
civilization *noun* 1 CULTURE, advancement, cultivation, development, education, enlightenment, progress, refinement, sophistication
2 SOCIETY, community, nation, people, polity
civilize *verb* CULTIVATE, educate, enlighten, refine, sophisticate, tame
civilized *adjective* CULTURED, educated, enlightened, humane, polite, sophisticated, tolerant, urbane
claim *verb* 1 ASSERT, allege, challenge, insist, maintain, profess, uphold
2 DEMAND, ask, call for, insist, need, require ▷ *noun* 3 ASSERTION, affirmation, allegation, pretension, privilege, protestation
4 DEMAND, application, call, petition, request, requirement
5 RIGHT, title
clairvoyant *noun* 1 PSYCHIC, diviner, fortune-teller, visionary ▷ *adjective* 2 PSYCHIC, extrasensory, second-sighted, telepathic, visionary
clamber *verb* CLIMB, claw, scale, scrabble, scramble, shin
clammy *adjective* MOIST, close, damp, dank, sticky, sweaty
clamor *noun* NOISE, commotion, din, hubbub, outcry, racket, shouting, uproar
clamp *noun* 1 VICE, bracket, fastener, grip, press ▷ *verb* 2 FASTEN, brace, fix, make fast, secure
clan *noun* FAMILY, brotherhood, faction, fraternity, group, society, tribe
clandestine *adjective* SECRET, cloak-and-dagger, concealed, covert, furtive, private, stealthy, surreptitious, underground
clap *verb* APPLAUD, acclaim, cheer
clarification *noun* EXPLANATION, elucidation, exposition, illumination, interpretation, simplification
clarify *verb* EXPLAIN, clear up, elucidate, illuminate, interpret, make plain, simplify, throw light on *or* shed light on
clarity *noun* CLEARNESS, definition, limpidity, lucidity, precision, simplicity, transparency
clash *verb* 1 CONFLICT, cross swords, feud, grapple, lock horns, quarrel, war, wrangle
2 CRASH, bang, clang, clank, clatter, jangle, jar, rattle ▷ *noun* 3 CONFLICT, brush, collision, confrontation, difference of opinion,

embrace, grasp

class [klas] *noun* 1 any division, order, kind, sort 2 rank 3 group of school pupils, etc. taught together 4 division by merit 5 quality 6 (*informal*) excellence or elegance ▷ *verb transitive* 7 assign to proper division > **clas'si•fy** [-ə-fī] *verb transitive* **-fied, -fy•ing** 1 arrange methodically in classes > **clas•si•fi•ca'tion** *noun* > **clas•si•fied** *adjective* 1 arranged in classes 2 secret 3 (of advertisements) arranged under headings in newspapers, etc. > **class'room** *noun* room in a school where lessons take place > **class'y** *adjective* **class•i•er, class•i•est** (*informal*) stylish, elegant

clas•sic [KLAS-ik] *adjective* 1 of first rank 2 of highest rank generally, but esp. of art 3 refined 4 typical 5 famous ▷ *noun* 6 (literary) work of recognized excellence > **clas•sics** 1 ancient Latin and Greek literature > **clas'si•cal** *adjective* 1 of Greek and Roman literature, art, culture 2 of classic quality 3 *mus.* of established standards of form, complexity, etc. > **clas'si•cism** *noun* > **clas'si•cist** *noun*

clat•ter [KLAT-ər] *noun* 1 rattling noise 2 noisy conversation ▷ *verb* 3 (cause to) make clatter

clause [klawz] *noun* 1 part of sentence, containing verb 2 article in formal document as treaty, contract, etc.

claus•tro•pho•bia [klaw-strə-FOH-bee-ə] *noun* abnormal fear of confined spaces

clav•i•chord [KLAV-i-kord] *noun* musical instrument with keyboard, forerunner of piano

clav•i•cle [KLAV-i-kəl] *noun* collarbone

claw [klaw] *noun* 1 sharp hooked nail of bird or beast 2 foot of bird of prey 3 clawlike article ▷ *verb transitive* 4 tear with claws 5 grip

clay [klay] *noun* 1 fine-grained earth, plastic when wet, hardening when baked 2 earth

clean [kleen] *adjective* **-er, -est** 1 free from dirt, stain, or defilement 2 pure 3 guiltless 4 trim, shapely ▷ *adverb* **-er, -est** 5 so as to leave no dirt 6 entirely ▷ *verb transitive* 7 free from dirt > **clean•li•ness** [KLEN-lee-nis] *noun* > **clean•ly** [KLEEN-lee] *adverb, adjective* **-li•er, -li•est** clean > **cleanse** [klenz] *verb transitive* **cleansed, cleans•ing** make clean **come clean** (*informal*) confess

clear [kleer] *adjective* **-er, -est** 1 pure, undimmed, bright 2 free from cloud 3 transparent 4 plain, distinct 5 without defect or drawback 6 unimpeded ▷ *adverb* **-er, -est** 7 brightly 8 wholly, quite ▷ *verb transitive* 9 make clear 10 acquit 11 pass over or through 12 make as profit 13 free from obstruction, debt, difficulty ▷ *verb intransitive* 14 become clear,

DICTIONARY • THESAURUS

disagreement, fight, showdown (*informal*)

clasp *noun* 1 FASTENING, brooch, buckle, catch, clip, fastener, grip, hook, pin
2 GRASP, embrace, grip, hold, hug
▷ *verb* 3 GRASP, clutch, embrace, grip, hold, hug, press, seize, squeeze
4 FASTEN, connect

class *noun* 1 GROUP, category, division, genre, kind, set, sort, type
▷ *verb* 2 CLASSIFY, brand, categorize, designate, grade, group, label, rank, rate

classic *adjective* 1 DEFINITIVE, archetypal, exemplary, ideal, model, quintessential, standard
2 TYPICAL, characteristic, regular, standard, time-honored, usual
3 BEST, consummate, finest, first-rate, masterly, world-class
4 LASTING, abiding, ageless, deathless, enduring, immortal, undying
▷ *noun* 5 STANDARD, exemplar, masterpiece, model, paradigm, prototype
6 comical (*informal*) HILARIOUS, hysterical, ludicrous, uproarious

classical *adjective* PURE, elegant, harmonious, refined, restrained, symmetrical, understated, well-proportioned

classification *noun* CATEGORIZATION, analysis, arrangement, grading, sorting, taxonomy

classify *verb* CATEGORIZE, arrange, catalog, grade, pigeonhole, rank, sort, systematize, tabulate

classy *adjective* (*informal*) HIGH-CLASS, elegant, exclusive, ritzy, stylish, superior, swanky, top-drawer, up-market

clause *noun* SECTION, article, chapter, condition, paragraph, part, passage

claw *noun* 1 NAIL, pincer, talon, tentacle
▷ *verb* 2 SCRATCH, dig, lacerate, maul, rip, scrape, tear

clean *adjective* 1 PURE, flawless, fresh, immaculate, impeccable, spotless, unblemished, unsullied
2 HYGIENIC, antiseptic, decontaminated, purified, sterile, sterilized, uncontaminated, unpolluted
3 MORAL, chaste, decent, good, honorable, innocent, pure, respectable, upright, virtuous
4 COMPLETE, conclusive, decisive, entire, final, perfect, thorough, total, unimpaired, whole
▷ *verb* 5 CLEANSE, disinfect, launder, purge, purify, rinse, sanitize, scour, scrub, wash

cleanse *verb* CLEAN, absolve, clear, purge, purify, rinse, scour, scrub, wash

cleanser *noun* DETERGENT, disinfectant, purifier, scourer, soap, solvent

clear *adjective* 1 CERTAIN, convinced, decided, definite, positive, resolved, satisfied, sure
2 OBVIOUS, apparent, blatant, comprehensible, conspicuous, distinct, evident, manifest, palpable, plain, pronounced, recognizable, unmistakable
3 TRANSPARENT, crystalline, glassy, limpid, pellucid, see-through, translucent
4 BRIGHT, cloudless, fair, fine, light, luminous, shining, sunny, unclouded
5 UNOBSTRUCTED, empty, free, open, smooth, unhindered, unimpeded
6 UNBLEMISHED, clean, immaculate, innocent, pure, untarnished
▷ *verb* 7 UNBLOCK, disentangle, extricate, free, loosen, open, rid, unload
8 PASS OVER, jump, leap, miss, vault
9 BRIGHTEN, break up, lighten
10 CLEAN, cleanse, erase, purify, refine, sweep away, tidy *or* tidy up, wipe
11 ABSOLVE, acquit, excuse, exonerate, justify, vindicate
12 GAIN, acquire, earn, make, reap, secure

clear-cut *adjective* STRAIGHTFORWARD, black-and-white, cut-and-dried (*informal*), definite, explicit, plain, precise, specific, unambiguous,

bright, free, transparent > **clear'ance** *noun* 1 making clear 2 removal of obstructions, surplus stock, etc. 3 certificate that ship has been cleared at custom house 4 space for moving part, vehicle, to pass within, through or past something > **clear'ing** *noun* land cleared of trees > **clear'ly** *adverb* > **clear'head•ed** [-hed-id] *adjective* discerning

cleat [kleet] *noun* 1 wedge 2 piece of wood or iron with two projecting ends round which ropes are made fast 3 (on shoes) projecting piece to furnish a grip > **cleats** shoes equipped with cleats

cleave[1] [kleev] *verb transitive* **cleft, cleaved** *or* **clove; cleft, cleaved** *or* **clo•ven; cleav•ing** 1 split asunder ▹ *verb intransitive* 2 crack, part asunder > **cleav'age** *noun* 1 space between a woman's breasts, as revealed by a low-cut dress, top, etc. 2 division, split > **cleav'er** *noun* butcher's heavy knife with a square blade

cleave[2] *verb intransitive* **cleaved, cleav•ing** 1 stick, adhere 2 be loyal

clef *noun mus.* mark showing pitch of music on staff

cleft *noun* 1 crack, fissure, chasm 2 opening made by cleaving 3 *pt./pp. of* **cleave[1]**

clem•ent [KLEM-ənt] *adjective* 1 merciful 2 gentle 3 mild > **clem'en•cy** *noun*

clench *verb transitive* 1 set firmly together 2 grasp, close (fist)

cler•gy [KLUR-jee] *noun* body of ordained ministers in a religion > **cler'gy•man** *noun*

cler•ic [KLER-ik] *noun* member of clergy

cler•i•cal [KLER-i-kəl] *adjective* 1 of clergy 2 of, connected with, office work

clerk [klurk] *noun* 1 employee who keeps files, etc. in an office 2 officer in charge of records, correspondence, etc. of court, government department, etc. 3 sales or service employee

clev•er [KLEV-ər] *adjective* 1 quick to understand 2 able, skillful, adroit > **clev'er•ly** *adverb* > **clev'er•ness** *noun*

cli•ché [klee-SHAY] *noun, plural* **-chés** stereotyped hackneyed phrase

click[1] [klik] *noun* 1 short, sharp sound, as of latch in door 2 catch ▹ *verb intransitive* 3 make this sound ▹ *verb* 4 (usu. foll by *on*) *computers.* press and release (button on a mouse) > **click'able** *adjective* (of a website) having links that can be accessed by clicking a computer mouse > **click through** navigate around (a website) using links provided to move onto different pages

click[2] *verb intransitive* 1 (*slang*) be a success 2 (*informal*) become clear 3 (*informal*) strike up friendship

cli•ent [KLĪ-ənt] *noun* 1 customer 2 one who employs professional person 3 *computers.* program or work station that requests data from a server > **cli•en•tele'** [-ən-TEL] *noun* body of clients

cliff [klif] *noun* steep rock face > **cliff'hang•er** *noun* tense situation

cli•mate [KLĪ-mit] *noun* 1 condition of region with regard to weather 2 prevailing feeling, atmosphere > **cli•mat'ic** *adjective* of climate

cli•max [KLĪ-maks] *noun* 1 highest point, culmination 2 point of greatest excitement, tension in story, etc. > **cli•mac'tic** *adjective*

climb [klīm] *verb* 1 go up or ascend 2 progress with difficulty 3 creep up, mount 4 slope upwards

clinch [klinch] *verb transitive* 1 clench 2 settle, conclude (an agreement) ▹ *verb intransitive* (in boxing) hold opponent close with arm or arms 3 (*slang*) embrace, esp. passionately ▹ *noun* 4 clinching 5 (*slang*) embrace > **clinch'er** *noun* (*informal*) something decisive

cling *verb intransitive* **clung, cling•ing** 1 adhere 2 be firmly attached to 3 be dependent

clin•ic [KLIN-ik] *noun* 1 hospital facility for examination, treatment of outpatients 2 medical training session with hospital patients as subjects > **clin'i•cal** *adjective* 1 relating to clinic, care of sick, etc. 2 objective, unemotional 3 bare, plain > **clinical thermometer** used for taking body temperature

clink[1] [klingk] *noun* 1 sharp metallic sound ▹ *verb* 2 (cause to) make this sound

clink[2] *noun* (*slang*) prison

clink•er [KLING-kər] *noun* 1 fused coal residues from fire or furnace 2 hard brick

clip[1] *verb transitive* **clipped, clip•ping** 1 cut with scissors 2 cut short 3 (*slang*) cheat ▹ *noun* 4

DICTIONARY

C

THESAURUS

unequivocal

clearly *adverb* OBVIOUSLY, beyond doubt, distinctly, evidently, markedly, openly, overtly, undeniably, undoubtedly

clergy *noun* PRIESTHOOD, churchmen, clergymen, clerics, holy orders, ministry, the cloth

clergyman *noun* MINISTER, chaplain, cleric, man of God, man of the cloth, padre, parson, pastor, priest, vicar

clever *adjective* INTELLIGENT, bright, gifted, ingenious, knowledgeable, quick-witted, resourceful, shrewd, smart, talented

cleverness *noun* INTELLIGENCE, ability, brains, ingenuity, quick wits, resourcefulness, shrewdness, smartness

cliché *noun* PLATITUDE, banality, commonplace, hackneyed phrase, stereotype, truism

client *noun* CUSTOMER, applicant, buyer, consumer, patient, patron, shopper

clientele *noun* CUSTOMERS, business, clients, following, market, patronage, regulars, trade

cliff *noun* ROCK FACE, bluff, crag, escarpment, overhang, precipice, scar, scarp

climactic *adjective* CRUCIAL, critical, decisive, paramount, peak

climate *noun* WEATHER, temperature

climax *noun* CULMINATION, height, highlight, high point, peak, summit, top, zenith

climb *verb* ASCEND, clamber, mount, rise, scale, shin up, soar, top

climb down *verb* 1 DESCEND, dismount 2 BACK DOWN, eat one's words, retract, retreat

clinch *verb* SETTLE, conclude, confirm, decide, determine, seal, secure, set the seal on, sew up (*informal*)

cling *verb* STICK, adhere, clasp, clutch, embrace, grasp, grip, hug

clinical *adjective* UNEMOTIONAL, analytic, cold, detached, dispassionate, impersonal, objective, scientific

clip[1] *verb* 1 TRIM, crop, curtail, cut, pare, prune,

(*informal*) sharp blow > **clip'per** *noun*
clip² *noun* device for gripping or holding together, esp. hair, clothing, etc.
clip•per [KLIP-ər] *noun* fast commercial sailing ship
clique [kleek] *noun* 1 small exclusive set 2 faction, group of people > **cli'quish** *adjective* > **cli'quish•ness** *noun*
clit•o•ris [KLIT-ər-is] *noun* small erectile part of female genitals
cloak [klohk] *noun* 1 loose outer garment 2 disguise, pretext ▷ *verb transitive* 3 cover with cloak 4 disguise, conceal
clob•ber [KLOB-ər] *verb transitive* (*informal*) 1 beat, batter 2 defeat utterly
clock [klok] *noun* 1 instrument for measuring time 2 device with dial for recording or measuring > **clock'wise** *adverb, adjective* 1 in the direction that the hands of a clock rotate > **clock'work** *noun* mechanism similar to that of a clock, as in a windup toy > **clock in, clock on** *verb* record arrival on an automatic time recorder > **clock out, clock off** *verb* record departure on an automatic time recorder
clod [klod] *noun* 1 lump of earth 2 blockhead > **clod'dish** *adjective*
clog [klog] *verb transitive* **clogged, clog•ging** 1 hamper, impede, choke up ▷ *noun* 2 obstruction, impediment 3 wooden-soled shoe
cloi•son•né [kloi-zə-NAY] *noun* enamel decoration in compartments formed by small strips of metal ▷ *adjective*
clois•ter [KLOI-stər] *noun* 1 covered pillared arcade 2 monastery or convent > **clois'tered** *adjective* confined, secluded, sheltered
clone [klohn] *noun* 1 group of organisms, cells of same genetic constitution as another, derived by asexual reproduction, as graft of plant, etc. 2 person closely resembling another in appearance, behavior, etc. ▷ *verb* **cloned, clon•ing**
clop [klop] *verb intransitive* **clopped, clop•ping** move, sound, as horse's hooves
close¹ [klohs] *adjective* **clos•er, clos•est** 1 adjacent, near 2 compact 3 crowded 4 affectionate, intimate 5 almost equal 6 careful, searching 7 confined 8 secret 9 unventilated, stifling 10 reticent 11 niggardly 12 strict, restricted ▷ *adverb* 13 nearly 14 tightly > **close'ly** *adverb* > **close'fist'ed** *adjective* 1 mean 2 avaricious > **close'up** *noun* close view, esp. portion of motion picture
close² [klohz] *verb transitive* **closed, clos•ing** 1 shut 2 stop up 3 prevent access to 4 finish ▷ *verb intransitive* **closed, clos•ing** 5 come together 6 grapple ▷ *noun* 7 end > **closed season** when it is illegal to kill certain kinds of game and fish > **closed shop** place of work in which all workers must belong to a union
clos•et [KLOZ-it] *noun* 1 small room, etc. for storing clothing 2 small private room ▷ *verb transitive* 3 shut up in private room, esp. for conference > **clos'et•ful** *noun, plural* **-fuls**
clo•sure [KLOH-zhər] *noun* 1 act of closing 2 (sense of contentment experienced after) resolution of a significant event or relationship in a person's life 3 cloture
clot [klot] *noun* 1 mass or lump 2 *med.* coagulated mass of blood ▷ *verb* **clot•ted, clot•ting** 3 form into lumps 4 coagulate
cloth [klawth] *noun* 1 woven fabric > **clothes** [klohthz] *plural noun* 1 dress 2 bed coverings > **clothe** [klohth] *verb transitive* **clothed** *or* **clad, cloth•ing** put clothes on > **clo•thier** [KLOHTH-yər] *noun* > **cloth•ing** [KLOH-thing] *noun*
clo•ture [KLOH-chər] *noun* ending of debate by majority vote or other authority
cloud [klowd] *noun* 1 condensed water vapor floating in air 2 state of gloom 3 multitude ▷ *verb transitive* 4 overshadow, dim, darken ▷ *verb intransitive* 5 become cloudy > **cloud'less** *adjective* > **cloud'y** *adjective* **cloud•i•er, cloud•i•est**

DICTIONARY • THESAURUS

shear, shorten, snip
▷ *noun, verb* 2 (*informal*) SMACK, clout (*informal*), cuff, knock, punch, strike, thump, wallop (*informal*), whack
clip² *verb* ATTACH, fasten, fix, hold, pin, staple
clique *noun* GROUP, cabal, circle, coterie, faction, gang, set
cloak *noun* 1 CAPE, coat, mantle, wrap
▷ *verb* 2 COVER, camouflage, conceal, disguise, hide, mask, obscure, screen, veil
clog *verb* OBSTRUCT, block, congest, hinder, impede, jam
close¹ *adjective* 1 NEAR, adjacent, adjoining, at hand, cheek by jowl, handy, impending, nearby, neighboring, nigh
2 INTIMATE, attached, confidential, dear, devoted, familiar, inseparable, loving
3 CAREFUL, detailed, intense, minute, painstaking, rigorous, thorough
4 COMPACT, congested, crowded, dense, impenetrable, jam-packed, packed, tight
5 STIFLING, airless, heavy, humid, muggy, oppressive, stuffy, suffocating, sweltering
6 SECRETIVE, private, reticent, secret, taciturn, uncommunicative
7 MEAN, miserly, stingy
close² *verb* 1 SHUT, bar, block, lock, plug, seal, secure, stop up
2 END, cease, complete, conclude, finish, shut down, terminate, wind up
3 CONNECT, come together, couple, fuse, join, unite
▷ *noun* 4 END, completion, conclusion, culmination, denouement, ending, finale, finish
closed *adjective* 1 SHUT, fastened, locked, out of service, sealed
2 EXCLUSIVE, restricted
3 FINISHED, concluded, decided, ended, over, resolved, settled, terminated
cloth *noun* FABRIC, material, textiles
clothe *verb* DRESS, array, attire, cover, drape, equip, fit out, garb, robe, swathe
clothes *plural noun* CLOTHING, apparel, attire, costume, dress, garb, garments, gear (*informal*), outfit, wardrobe, wear
clothing *noun* CLOTHES, apparel, attire, costume, dress, garb, garments, gear (*informal*), outfit, wardrobe, wear
cloud *noun* 1 MIST, gloom, haze, murk, vapor
▷ *verb* 2 OBSCURE, becloud, darken, dim, eclipse, obfuscate, overshadow, shade, shadow, veil
3 CONFUSE, disorient, distort, impair, muddle, muddy the waters

clout [klowt] *noun (informal)* 1 blow 2 influence, power ▷ *verb transitive* 3 strike
clove¹ [klohv] *noun* 1 dried flower bud of tropical tree, used as spice 2 one of small bulbs making up compound bulb
clove² *pt. of* **cleave¹** > **clo'ven** *pp. of* **cleave¹**
clo•ver [KLOH-vər] *noun* low-growing forage plant **be in clover** be in luxury
clown [klown] *noun* 1 comic entertainer in circus 2 jester, fool
cloy [kloi] *verb transitive* weary by sweetness, sameness, etc.
club [klub] *noun* 1 thick stick 2 bat, stick used in some games 3 association for pursuance of common interest 4 building used by such association 5 one of the suits at cards ▷ *verb* **clubbed, club•bing** 6 strike with club 7 combine for a common object > **club foot** deformed foot
cluck [kluk] *verb intransitive, noun* (make) noise of hen
clue [kloo] *noun* indication, esp. of solution of mystery or puzzle **not have a clue** be ignorant or incompetent
clump¹ [klump] *noun* 1 cluster of trees or plants 2 compact mass
clump² *verb intransitive* walk, tread heavily ▷ *noun*
clum•sy [KLUM-zee] *adjective* **-si•er, -si•est** 1 awkward, unwieldy, ungainly 2 badly made or arranged > **clum'si•ly** *adverb* > **clum'si•ness** *noun*
clung *pt./pp. of* **cling**
clunk [klungk] *noun* (sound of) blow or something falling
clus•ter [KLUS-tər] *noun* 1 group, bunch ▷ *verb* 2 gather, grow in cluster
clutch¹ [kluch] *verb* 1 grasp eagerly 2 snatch (at) ▷ *noun* 3 grasp, tight grip 4 device enabling two rotating shafts to be connected and disconnected at will
clutch² *noun* 1 set of eggs hatched at one time 2 brood of chickens
clut•ter [KLUT-ər] *verb* 1 strew 2 crowd together in disorder ▷ *noun* 3 disordered, obstructive mass of objects
Cm *chem.* curium
Co *chem.* cobalt
coach [kohch] *noun* 1 large four-wheeled carriage 2 railway carriage 3 class of airline travel 4 tutor, instructor ▷ *verb transitive* 5 instruct > **coach class** class of air travel that is cheaper than first class
co•ag•u•late [koh-AG-yə-layt] *verb* **-lat•ed, -lat•ing** 1 curdle, clot, form into a mass 2 congeal, solidify > **co•ag•u•la'tion** *noun*
coal [kohl] *noun* 1 mineral consisting of carbonized vegetable matter, used as fuel 2 glowing ember ▷ *verb* 3 supply with or take in coal > **coal'field** *noun* area in which coal is found
co•a•lesce [koh-ə-LES] *verb intransitive* **-lesced, -lesc•ing** unite, merge > **co•a•les'cence** *noun*
co•a•li•tion [koh-ə-LISH-ən] *noun* alliance, esp. of political parties
coarse [kors] *adjective* **coars•er, coars•est** 1 rough, harsh 2 unrefined 3 indecent > **coarse'ness** *noun*
coast [kohst] *noun* 1 seashore ▷ *verb* 2 move under momentum 3 proceed without making much effort 4 sail by the coast > **coast'er** *noun* 1 small ship 2 that which, one who, coasts 3 small table mat for glasses, etc.
coat [koht] *noun* 1 sleeved outer garment 2 animal's fur or feathers 3 covering layer ▷ *verb transitive* 4 cover with layer 5 clothe > **coat of arms** armorial bearings
coax [kohks] *verb transitive* wheedle, cajole, persuade, force gently

cloudy *adjective* 1 DULL, dim, gloomy, leaden, louring *or* lowering, overcast, somber, sunless 2 OPAQUE, muddy, murky
clout *(informal) noun* 1 INFLUENCE, authority, power, prestige, pull, weight ▷ *verb* 2 HIT, clobber (*slang*), punch, sock (*slang*), strike, thump, wallop (*informal*)
clown *noun* 1 COMEDIAN, buffoon, comic, fool, harlequin, jester, joker, prankster ▷ *verb* 2 PLAY THE FOOL, act the fool, jest, mess about
club *noun* 1 ASSOCIATION, company, fraternity, group, guild, lodge, set, society, union 2 STICK, bat, bludgeon, cudgel, truncheon ▷ *verb* 3 BEAT, bash, batter, bludgeon, hammer, pummel, strike
clue *noun* INDICATION, evidence, hint, lead, pointer, sign, suggestion, suspicion, trace
clueless *adjective* STUPID, dim, dull, half-witted, simple, slow, thick, unintelligent, witless
clump *noun* 1 CLUSTER, bunch, bundle, group, mass ▷ *verb* 2 STOMP, lumber, plod, thud, thump, tramp
clumsy *adjective* AWKWARD, bumbling, gauche, gawky, lumbering, maladroit, ponderous, uncoordinated, ungainly, unwieldy
cluster *noun* 1 GATHERING, assemblage, batch, bunch, clump, collection, group, knot ▷ *verb* 2 GATHER, assemble, bunch, collect, flock, group
clutch¹ *verb* SEIZE, catch, clasp, cling to, embrace, grab, grasp, grip, snatch
clutches *plural noun* POWER, claws, control, custody, grasp, grip, hands, keeping, possession, sway
clutter *verb* 1 LITTER, scatter, strew ▷ *noun* 2 UNTIDINESS, confusion, disarray, disorder, jumble, litter, mess, muddle
coach *noun* 1 BUS, car, carriage, charabanc, vehicle 2 INSTRUCTOR, handler, teacher, trainer, tutor ▷ *verb* 3 INSTRUCT, drill, exercise, prepare, train, tutor
coalesce *verb* BLEND, amalgamate, combine, fuse, incorporate, integrate, merge, mix, unite
coalition *noun* ALLIANCE, amalgamation, association, bloc, combination, confederation, conjunction, fusion, merger, union
coarse *adjective* 1 ROUGH, crude, homespun, impure, unfinished, unpolished, unprocessed, unpurified, unrefined 2 VULGAR, earthy, improper, indecent, indelicate, ribald, rude, smutty
coarseness *noun* 1 ROUGHNESS, crudity, unevenness 2 VULGARITY, bawdiness, crudity, earthiness, indelicacy, ribaldry, smut, uncouthness
coast *noun* 1 SHORE, beach, border, coastline, seaboard, seaside

co•ax•i•al [koh-AK-see-əl] *adjective* having the same axis > **co•ax'i•al•ly** *adverb*
co•balt [KOH-bawlt] *noun* 1 metallic element 2 blue pigment from it
cob•ble [KOB-əl] *verb transitive* **-bled, -bling** 1 patch roughly 2 mend shoes ▷ *noun* 3 round stone > **cob'bler** *noun* shoe mender
co•bra [KOH-brə] *noun* venomous, hooded snake of Asia and Africa
cob'web *noun* spider's web
co•caine [koh-KAYN] *noun* addictive narcotic drug used medicinally as anesthetic
coch•i•neal [koch-ə-NEEL] *noun* scarlet dye from Mexican insect
cock [kok] *noun* 1 male bird, esp. of domestic fowl 2 tap for liquids 3 hammer of gun 4 its position drawn back ▷ *verb transitive* 5 draw back (gun hammer) to firing position 6 raise, turn in alert or jaunty manner > **cock'eyed** [-īd] *adjective* 1 crosseyed 2 with a squint 3 askew > **cock'fight** *noun* staged fight between roosters
cock•a•trice [KOK-ə-tris] *noun* fabulous animal similar to basilisk
cock•chaf•er [KOK-chay-fər] *noun* large, flying beetle
cock•le [KOK-əl] *noun* shellfish
Cock•ney [KOK-nee] *noun, plural* **-neys** 1 native of East End of London 2 urban dialect of London or its East End
cock•pit [KOK-pit] *noun* 1 pilot's seat, compartment in small aircraft 2 driver's seat in racing car 3 orig. enclosure for cockfighting
cock•roach [KOK-rohch] *noun* kind of insect, household pest
cock•tail [KOK-tayl] *noun* short drink of whiskey, gin, etc. with flavorings, etc.
cock•y [KOK-ee] *adjective* **cock•i•er, cock•i•est** conceited, pert > **cock'i•ness** *noun*
co•coa [KOH-koh] *noun* 1 powder made from seed of cacao (tropical) tree 2 drink made from the powder
co•co•nut [KOH-kə-nut] *noun* 1 tropical palm 2 very large, hard nut from this palm
co•coon [kə-KOON] *noun* 1 sheath of insect in chrysalis stage 2 any protective covering
co•da [KOH-də] *noun mus.* final part of musical composition
cod•dle [KOD-l] *verb transitive* **-dled, -dling** 1 overprotect, pamper 2 cook (eggs) lightly
code [kohd] *noun* 1 system of letters, symbols and rules for their association to transmit messages secretly or briefly 2 scheme of conduct 3 collection of laws > **cod'i•fy** [KOD-] *verb transitive* **-fied, - fy•ing** > **cod•i•fi•ca'tion** *noun*
co•deine [KOH-deen] *noun* alkaline sedative, analgesic drug
co•de•pend•ent [koh-di-PEND-dənt] *adjective* of a relationship involving an addict ▷ *noun* > **co•de•pen'den•cy** *noun*
co•dex [KOH-deks] *noun, plural* **-di•ces** [-də-seez] ancient manuscript volume, esp. of Bible, etc.
codg•er [KOJ-ər] *noun* (*informal*) man, esp. old
cod•i•cil [KOD-ə-səl] *noun* addition to will
co•ed•u•ca•tion•al [koh-ej-ə-KAY-shə-nl] *adjective* of education of boys and girls together in mixed classes > **co-ed** [koh-ed] *noun* (female student at) coeducational school ▷ *adjective*
co•ef•fi•cient [koh-ə-FISH-ənt] *noun math.* numerical or constant factor
co•erce [koh-URS] *verb transitive* **-erced, -erc•ing** compel, force > **co•er'cion** [-UR-shən] *noun* forcible compulsion or restraint
co•ex•ist [koh-ig-ZIST] *verb intransitive* exist together > **co•ex•ist'ence** *noun*
cof•fee [KAW-fee] *noun* 1 seeds of tropical shrub 2 drink made from roasting and grinding these
cof•fer [KAW-fər] *noun* 1 chest for valuables 2 treasury, funds
cof•fer•dam [KAW-fər-dam] *noun* watertight structure enabling construction work to be done underwater
cof•fin [KAW-fin] *noun* box for corpse
cog [kog] *noun* 1 one of series of teeth on rim of wheel 2 person, thing forming small part of big process, organization, etc.
co•gent [KOH-jənt] *adjective* convincing, compelling, persuasive > **co'gen•cy** *noun*
cog•i•tate [KOJ-i-tayt] *verb intransitive* **-tat•ed, -tat•ing** think, reflect, ponder
co•gnac [KOHN-yak] *noun* French brandy
cog•nate [KOG-nayt] *adjective* of same stock, related, kindred
cog•ni•tion [kog-NISH-ən] *noun* act or faculty of knowing > **cog'ni•tive** *adjective*
cog•ni•zance [KOG-nə-zəns] *noun* knowledge, perception > **cog'ni•zant** *adjective*
co•gno•scen•ti [kon-yə-SHEN-tee] *plural noun* people with knowledge in particular field, esp. arts
co•hab•it [koh-HAB-it] *verb intransitive* live together as husband and wife
co•here [koh-HEER] *verb intransitive* **-hered, -her•ing** stick together, be consistent > **co•her'ence** *noun* > **co•her'ent** *adjective* 1 capable of logical speech, thought 2 connected, making sense 3 sticking together > **co•he'sion** [-HEE-zhən] *noun* cohering > **co•he'sive** *adjective*
co•hort [KOH-hort] *noun* 1 troop 2 associate
coif•feur [kwah-FUUR] *noun* hairdresser
coif•fure [kwah-FYUUR] *noun* hairstyle

▷ *verb* 2 CRUISE, drift, freewheel, glide, sail, taxi
coat *noun* 1 FUR, fleece, hair, hide, pelt, skin, wool
2 LAYER, coating, covering, overlay
▷ *verb* 3 COVER, apply, plaster, smear, spread
coax *verb* PERSUADE, allure, cajole, entice, prevail upon, sweet-talk (*informal*), talk into, wheedle
cocktail *noun* MIXTURE, blend, combination, mix
cocky *adjective* OVERCONFIDENT, arrogant, brash, cocksure, conceited, egotistical, full of oneself, swaggering, vain
code *noun* 1 CIPHER, cryptograph
2 PRINCIPLES, canon, convention, custom, ethics, etiquette, manners, maxim, regulations, rules, system
cogent *adjective* CONVINCING, compelling, effective, forceful, influential, potent, powerful, strong, weighty
cogitate *verb* THINK, consider, contemplate, deliberate, meditate, mull over, muse, ponder, reflect, ruminate
coherent *adjective* 1 CONSISTENT, logical, lucid, meaningful, orderly, organized, rational, reasoned, systematic
2 INTELLIGIBLE, articulate, comprehensible

coil [koil] *verb transitive* 1 lay in rings 2 twist into winding shape ▷ *verb intransitive* 3 twist, take up a winding shape or spiral ▷ *noun* 4 series of rings 5 device in vehicle, etc. to transform low-voltage direct current to higher voltage for ignition purposes 6 contraceptive device inserted in womb
coin [koin] *noun* 1 piece of money 2 money ▷ *verb transitive* 3 make into money, stamp 4 invent > **coin'age** *noun* 1 coining 2 coins collectively **coin money** (*informal*) make money rapidly
co•in•cide [koh-in-SĪD] *verb intransitive* **-cid•ed, -cid•ing** 1 happen together 2 agree exactly > **co•in'ci•dence** [-si-dəns] *noun* > **co•in'ci•dent** *adjective* coinciding > **co•in•ci•den'tal** *adjective*
co•i•tus [KOH-i-təs], **co•i•tion** [koh-ISH-ən] *noun* sexual intercourse
coke[1] [kohk] *noun* residue left from distillation of coal, used as fuel
coke[2] *noun* (*slang*) cocaine
Col. Colossians
co•la [KOH-lə] *noun* 1 tropical tree 2 its nut, used to flavor drink
col•an•der [KUL-ən-dər] *noun* culinary strainer perforated with small holes
cold [kohld] *adjective* **-er, -est** 1 lacking heat 2 indifferent, unmoved, apathetic 3 dispiriting 4 reserved or unfriendly 5 (of colors) giving an impression of coldness ▷ *noun* 6 lack of heat 7 illness, marked by runny nose, etc. > **cold'ly** *adverb* > **cold'-blood•ed** *adjective* 1 lacking pity, mercy 2 having body temperature that varies with that of the surroundings > **cold chisel** toughened steel chisel > **cold feet** fear > **cold storage** method of preserving perishable foods, etc. by keeping them at artificially reduced temperature > **cold turkey** (*slang*) abrupt halt in use of addictive drug, etc. > **cold war** economic, diplomatic but nonmilitary hostility
cole•slaw [KOHL-slaw] *noun* salad dish based on shredded cabbage
col•ic [KOL-ik] *noun* severe pains in the intestines > **co•li•tis** [kə-LĪ-tis] *noun* inflammation of the colon
col•lab•o•rate [kə-LAB-ə-rayt] *verb intransitive* **-rat•ed, -rat•ing** work with another on a project > **col•lab'o•ra•tor** *noun* one who works with another, esp. one who aids an enemy in occupation of his own country
col•lage [kə-LAHZH] *noun* (artistic) composition of bits and pieces stuck together on background
col•lapse [kə-LAPS] *verb intransitive* **-lapsed, -laps•ing** 1 fall 2 give way 3 lose strength, fail ▷ *noun* 4 act of collapsing 5 breakdown > **col•laps'i•ble** *adjective*
col•lar [KOL-ər] *noun* 1 band, part of garment, worn round neck 2 (*informal*) police arrest ▷ *verb transitive* 3 seize by collar 4 (*informal*) capture, seize > **col'lar•bone** *noun* bone from shoulder to breastbone
col•late [kə-LAYT] *verb transitive* **-lat•ed, -lat•ing** 1 compare carefully 2 place in order (as printed sheets for binding) > **col•la'tion** *noun* 1 collating 2 light meal
col•lat•er•al [kə-LAT-ər-əl] *noun* 1 security pledged for repayment of loan ▷ *adjective* 2 accompanying 3 side by side 4 of same stock but different line 5 subordinate > **collateral damage** unintentional civilian casualties or damage to civilian property caused by military action
col•league [KOL-eeg] *noun* associate, companion in office or employment, fellow worker
col•lect [kə-LEKT] *verb transitive* 1 gather, bring together ▷ *verb intransitive* 2 come together 3 (*informal*) receive money > **col•lect'ed** *adjective* 1 calm 2 gathered > **col•lec'tion** *noun* > **col•lect'ive** *noun* factory, farm, etc., run on principles of

DICTIONARY

C

THESAURUS

---

coil *verb* WIND, curl, loop, snake, spiral, twine, twist, wreathe, writhe
coin *noun* 1 MONEY, cash, change, copper, silver, specie
▷ *verb* 2 INVENT, create, fabricate, forge, make up, mint, mold, originate
coincide *verb* 1 OCCUR SIMULTANEOUSLY, be concurrent, coexist, synchronize
2 AGREE, accord, concur, correspond, harmonize, match, square, tally
coincidence *noun* 1 CHANCE, accident, fluke, happy accident, luck, stroke of luck
2 COINCIDING, concurrence, conjunction, correlation, correspondence
coincidental *adjective* CHANCE, accidental, casual, fluky (*informal*), fortuitous, unintentional, unplanned
cold *adjective* 1 CHILLY, arctic, bleak, cool, freezing, frigid, frosty, frozen, icy, wintry
2 UNFRIENDLY, aloof, distant, frigid, indifferent, reserved, standoffish
▷ *noun* 3 COLDNESS, chill, frigidity, frostiness, iciness
cold-blooded *adjective* CALLOUS, dispassionate, heartless, ruthless, steely, stony-hearted, unemotional, unfeeling
collaborate *verb* 1 WORK TOGETHER, cooperate, join forces, participate, play ball (*informal*), team up
2 CONSPIRE, collude, cooperate, fraternize
collaboration *noun* TEAMWORK, alliance, association, cooperation, partnership
collaborator *noun* 1 CO-WORKER, associate, colleague, confederate, partner, team-mate
2 TRAITOR, fraternizer, quisling, turncoat
collapse *verb* 1 FALL DOWN, cave in, crumple, fall, fall apart at the seams, give way, subside
2 FAIL, come to nothing, fold, founder, go belly-up (*informal*)
▷ *noun* 3 FALLING DOWN, cave-in, disintegration, falling apart, ruin, subsidence
4 FAILURE, downfall, flop, slump
5 FAINT, breakdown, exhaustion, prostration
collar *verb* (*informal*) SEIZE, apprehend, arrest, capture, catch, grab, nail (*informal*)
colleague *noun* FELLOW WORKER, ally, assistant, associate, collaborator, comrade, helper, partner, team-mate, workmate
collect *verb* 1 ASSEMBLE, cluster, congregate, convene, converge, flock together, rally
2 GATHER, accumulate, amass, assemble, heap, hoard, save, stockpile
collected *adjective* CALM, composed, cool, poised, self-possessed, serene, unperturbed, unruffled
collection *noun* 1 ACCUMULATION, anthology, compilation, heap, hoard, mass, pile, set,

collectivism ▷ *adjective* > **col•lec'tiv•ism** *noun* theory that a government should own all means of production

col•lege [KOL-ij] *noun* **1** place of higher education **2** society of scholars **3** association > **col•le•giate** [kə-LEE-jit] *adjective* > **col•le•gian** *noun* student

col•lide [kə-LĪD] *verb intransitive* **-lid•ed, -lid•ing** **1** strike or dash together **2** come into conflict > **col•li'sion** [-LIZH-ən] *noun* colliding

col•lo•di•on [kə-LOH-dee-ən] *noun* chemical solution used in photography and medicine

col•loid [KOL-oid] *noun* suspension of particles in a solution

col•lo•qui•al [kə-LOH-kwee-əl] *adjective* pert. to or used in informal conversation > **col•lo'qui•al•ism** *noun* > **col•lo•quy** [KOL-ə-kwee] *noun, plural* **-quies** **1** conversation **2** dialogue

col•lu•sion [kə-LOO-*zh*ən] *noun* secret agreement for a fraudulent purpose, esp. in legal proceedings > **col•lu'sive** [-siv] *adjective*

co•logne [kə-LOHN] *noun* perfumed liquid

co•lon[1] [KOH-lən] *noun* mark (:) indicating break in a sentence

colon[2] *noun* part of large intestine from cecum to rectum

colo•nel [KUR-nl] *noun* commander of regiment or battalion

col•on•nade [kol-ə-NAYD] *noun* row of columns

col•o•ny [KOL-ə-nee] *noun, plural* **-nies** **1** body of people who settle in new country but remain subject to parent country **2** country so settled **3** distinctive group living together > **co•lo•ni•al** [kə-LOH-nee-əl] *adjective* of colony > **col'o•nist** *noun* > **col•o•ni•za'tion** *noun* > **col'o•nize** *verb transitive* **-nized, -niz•ing**

col•or [KUL-ər] *noun* **1** hue, tint **2** complexion **3** paint **4** pigment **5** semblance, pretext **6** timbre, quality **7** mood ▷ *verb transitive* **8** stain, dye, paint, give color to **9** disguise **10** influence or distort ▷ *verb intransitive* **11** become colored **12** blush > **col•ors** *plural noun* **1** flag **2** distinguishing symbol > **col•or•a'tion** *noun* > **col'or•ful** *adjective* **1** with bright or varied colors **2** distinctive

co•los•sus [kə-LOS-əs] *noun, plural* **-los•si** [-LOS-ī] **1** huge statue **2** something, somebody very large > **co•los'sal** *adjective* huge, gigantic

colt [kohlt] *noun* young male horse

col•umn [KOL-əm] *noun* **1** long vertical cylinder, pillar **2** support **3** division of page **4** body of troops > **co•lum•nar** [kə-LUM-nər] *adjective* > **col'um•nist** *noun* journalist writing regular feature for newspaper

com-, con- *prefix* together, jointly: *commingle*

co•ma [KOH-mə] *noun* state of unconsciousness > **co'ma•tose** [-tohs] *adjective*

comb [kohm] *noun* **1** toothed instrument for tidying, arranging, ornamenting hair **2** rooster's crest **3** mass of honey cells ▷ *verb transitive* **4** use comb on **5** search with great care > **comb'-over** *noun* hairstyle in which long hairs from the side of the head are swept over the scalp to cover a bald patch

com•bat [KOM-bat] *noun* **1** fight or struggle ▷ *verb transitive* [kəm-BAT] **2** fight, contest > **com•bat•ant** [kəm-BAT-nt] *noun* > **combat boot** heavy army boot > **com•bat'ive** *adjective*

com•bine [kəm-BĪN] *verb* **1** join together **2** ally ▷ *noun* [KOM-bīn] trust, syndicate, esp. of businesses, trade organizations, etc. > **com•bi•na•tion** [kom-bə-NAY-shən] *noun* > **com'bine** *noun* machine to harvest and thresh grain in one operation

com•bus•tion [kəm-BUS-chən] *noun* process of burning > **com•bus'ti•ble** *adjective*

come [kum] *verb intransitive* **came, come,**

---

stockpile, store
2 GROUP, assembly, assortment, cluster, company, crowd
3 CONTRIBUTION, alms, offering, offertory

collective *adjective* COMBINED, aggregate, composite, corporate, cumulative, joint, shared, unified, united

collide *verb* **1** CRASH, clash, come into collision, meet head-on
2 CONFLICT, clash

collision *noun* **1** CRASH, accident, bump, impact, pile-up (*informal*), smash
2 CONFLICT, clash, confrontation, encounter, opposition, skirmish

colloquial *adjective* INFORMAL, conversational, demotic, everyday, familiar, idiomatic, vernacular

colony *noun* SETTLEMENT, community, dependency, dominion, outpost, possession, province, satellite state, territory

color *noun* **1** HUE, colorant, dye, paint, pigment, shade, tint
▷ *verb* **2** PAINT, dye, stain, tinge, tint
3 BLUSH, flush, redden

colorful *adjective* **1** BRIGHT, brilliant, multicolored, psychedelic, variegated
2 INTERESTING, distinctive, graphic, lively, picturesque, rich, vivid

colorless *adjective* **1** DRAB, achromatic, anemic, ashen, bleached, faded, wan, washed out
2 UNINTERESTING, characterless, dreary, dull, insipid, lackluster, vapid

colossal *adjective* HUGE, enormous, gigantic, immense, mammoth, massive, monumental, prodigious, vast

column *noun* **1** PILLAR, obelisk, post, shaft, support, upright
2 LINE, cavalcade, file, procession, rank, row

coma *noun* UNCONSCIOUSNESS, oblivion, stupor, trance

comb *verb* **1** UNTANGLE, arrange, dress, groom
2 SEARCH, forage, hunt, rake, ransack, rummage, scour, sift

combat *noun* **1** FIGHT, action, battle, conflict, contest, encounter, engagement, skirmish, struggle, war, warfare
▷ *verb* **2** FIGHT, defy, do battle with, oppose, resist, withstand

combatant *noun* FIGHTER, adversary, antagonist, enemy, opponent, soldier, warrior

combination *noun* **1** MIXTURE, amalgamation, blend, coalescence, composite, connection, mix
2 ASSOCIATION, alliance, coalition, confederation, consortium, federation, syndicate, union

combine *verb* JOIN TOGETHER, amalgamate, blend, connect, integrate, link, merge, mix, pool, unite

com•ing 1 approach, arrive, move toward 2 reach 3 happen to 4 occur 5 be available 6 originate (from) 7 become 8 turn out to be > **come'back** *noun* (*informal*) 1 return to active life after retirement 2 retort > **come'down** *noun* 1 setback 2 descent in social status

com•e•dy [KOM-i-dee] *noun, plural* **-dies** 1 dramatic or other work of light, amusing character 2 humor > **co•me•di•an** [kə-MEE-dee-ən] *noun* 1 entertainer who tells jokes, etc. 2 actor in comedy

come•ly [KUM-lee] *adjective* fair, pretty, good-looking > **come'li•ness** *noun*

co•mes•ti•bles [kə-MES-tə-bəlz] *noun* food

com•et [KOM-it] *noun* luminous heavenly body consisting of diffuse head, nucleus and long tail

com•fort [KUM-fərt] *noun* 1 well-being 2 ease 3 consolation 4 means of consolation or satisfaction ▷ *verb transitive* 5 soothe 6 cheer, gladden, console > **com•fort•a•ble** [KUMF-tə-bəl] *adjective* 1 free from pain, etc. 2 (*informal*) financially secure > **com'fort•a•bly** *adverb* > **com'fort•er** *noun* 1 one who comforts 2 woolen scarf 3 quilt > **comfort food** food that makes the eater feel better emotionally

com•ic [KOM-ik] *adjective* 1 relating to comedy 2 funny, laughable ▷ *noun* 3 comedian 4 magazine consisting of strip cartoons > **com'i•cal** *adjective*

com•ma [KOM-ə] *noun* punctuation mark (,) separating parts of sentence

com•mand [kə-MAND] *verb transitive* 1 order 2 rule 3 compel 4 have in one's power 5 overlook, dominate ▷ *verb intransitive* 6 exercise rule ▷ *noun* 7 order 8 power of controlling, ruling, dominating, overlooking 9 knowledge, mastery 10 post of one commanding 11 district commanded, jurisdiction > **com'man•dant** [KOM-ən-dant] *noun* > **com•man•deer'** *verb transitive* seize for military use, appropriate > **com•mand'er** *noun* > **com•mand'ing** *adjective* 1 in command 2 with air of authority > **com•mand'ment** *noun*

com•man•do [kə-MAN-doh] *noun, plural* **-dos** (member of) special military unit trained for airborne, amphibious attack

com•mem•o•rate [kə-MEM-ə-rayt] *verb transitive* **-rat•ed, -rat•ing** 1 celebrate, keep in memory by ceremony 2 be a memorial of > **com•mem•o•ra'tion** *noun* > **com•mem'o•ra•tive** *adjective*

com•mence [kə-MENS] *verb* **-menced, -menc•ing** begin > **com•mence'ment** *noun* 1 beginning 2 graduation of students

DICTIONARY

C

THESAURUS

come *verb* 1 MOVE TOWARDS, advance, approach, draw near, near
2 ARRIVE, appear, enter, materialize, reach, show up (*informal*), turn up (*informal*)
3 HAPPEN, fall, occur, take place
4 RESULT, arise, emanate, emerge, flow, issue, originate
5 REACH, extend
6 BE AVAILABLE, be made, be offered, be on offer, be produced

come about *verb* HAPPEN, arise, befall, come to pass, occur, result, take place, transpire (*informal*)

come across *verb* FIND, bump into (*informal*), chance upon, discover, encounter, meet, notice, stumble upon, unearth

comeback *noun* 1 (*informal*) RETURN, rally, rebound, recovery, resurgence, revival, triumph
2 RESPONSE, rejoinder, reply, retaliation, retort, riposte

come back *verb* RETURN, reappear, recur, re-enter

comedian *noun* COMIC, card (*informal*), clown, funny man, humorist, jester, joker, wag, wit

comedown *noun* 1 DECLINE, deflation, demotion, reverse
2 (*informal*) DISAPPOINTMENT, anticlimax, blow, humiliation, letdown

comedy *noun* HUMOR, farce, fun, hilarity, jesting, joking, light entertainment

comfort *noun* 1 LUXURY, cosiness, ease, opulence, snugness, wellbeing
2 RELIEF, compensation, consolation, help, succor, support
▷ *verb* 3 CONSOLE, commiserate with, hearten, reassure, soothe

comfortable *adjective* 1 RELAXING, agreeable, convenient, cozy, homely, homey, pleasant, restful, snug
2 HAPPY, at ease, at home, contented, gratified, relaxed, serene
3 (*informal*) WELL-OFF, affluent, in clover (*informal*), prosperous, well-to-do

comforting *adjective* CONSOLING, cheering, consolatory, encouraging, heart-warming, reassuring, soothing

comic *adjective* 1 FUNNY, amusing, comical, droll, farcical, humorous, jocular, witty
▷ *noun* 2 COMEDIAN, buffoon, clown, funny man, humorist, jester, wag, wit

comical *adjective* FUNNY, amusing, comic, droll, farcical, hilarious, humorous, priceless, side-splitting

coming *adjective* 1 APPROACHING, at hand, forthcoming, imminent, impending, in store, near, nigh
▷ *noun* 2 ARRIVAL, advent, approach

command *verb* 1 ORDER, bid, charge, compel, demand, direct, require
2 HAVE AUTHORITY OVER, control, dominate, govern, handle, head, lead, manage, rule, supervise
▷ *noun* 3 ORDER, commandment, decree, demand, directive, instruction, requirement, ultimatum
4 AUTHORITY, charge, control, government, management, mastery, power, rule, supervision

commandeer *verb* SEIZE, appropriate, confiscate, requisition, sequester, sequestrate

commander *noun* OFFICER, alpha male, boss (*informal*), captain, chief, commanding officer, head, leader, ruler

commanding *adjective* CONTROLLING, advantageous, decisive, dominant, dominating, superior

commemorate *verb* REMEMBER, celebrate, honor, immortalize, pay tribute to, salute

commemoration *noun* REMEMBRANCE, ceremony, honoring, memorial service, tribute

commence *verb* BEGIN, embark on, enter upon, initiate, open, originate, start

com•mend [kə-MEND] *verb transitive* 1 praise 2 commit, entrust > **com•mend'a•ble** *adjective* > **com•men•da'tion** *noun*
com•men•su•rate [kə-MEN-sər-it] *adjective* 1 equal in size or length of time 2 in proportion, adequate
com•ment [KOM-ent] *noun* 1 remark, criticism 2 gossip 3 note, explanation ▷ *verb intransitive* 4 remark, note 5 annotate, criticize > **com'men•tar•y** *noun, plural* **-tar•ies** 1 explanatory notes or comments 2 spoken accompaniment to film, etc. > **com'men•ta•tor** *noun* author, speaker of commentary
com•merce [KOM-ərs] *noun* 1 buying and selling 2 dealings 3 trade > **com•mer•cial** [kə-MUR-shəl] *adjective* 1 of, concerning, business, trade, profit, etc. ▷ *noun* 2 advertisement on radio or TV
com•mis•er•ate [kə-MIZ-ə-rayt] *verb transitive* **-at•ed, -at•ing** pity, condole, sympathize with
com•mis•sion [kə-MISH-ən] *noun* 1 something entrusted to be done 2 delegated authority 3 body entrusted with some special duty 4 payment by percentage for doing something 5 warrant, esp. presidential warrant, giving authority 6 document appointing person to officer's rank 7 doing, committing ▷ *verb transitive* 8 charge with duty or task 9 *military* confer a rank 10 give order for > **com•mis'sion•er** *noun* 1 one empowered to act by commission or warrant 2 member of commission or government board 3 administrative head of professional sport
com•mit [kə-MIT] *verb transitive* **-mit•ted, -mit•ting** 1 entrust, give in charge 2 perpetrate, be guilty of 3 pledge, promise 4 compromise, entangle 5 place in prison or mental institution > **com•mit'ment** *noun*
com•mit•tee [kə-MIT-ee] *noun* body appointed, elected for special business usu. from larger body
com•mode [kə-MOHD] *noun* 1 chest of drawers 2 toilet
com•mo•di•ous [kə-MOH-dee-əs] *adjective* roomy
com•mod•i•ty [kə-MOD-i-tee] *noun, plural* **-ties** 1 article of trade 2 anything useful
com•mon [KOM-ən] *adjective* 1 shared by or belonging to all, or to several 2 public, general 3 ordinary, usual, frequent 4 inferior 5 vulgar ▷ *noun* 6 land belonging to community > **com•mons** 1 ordinary people 2 (**Com•mons**) lower house of British parliament > **com'mon•ly** *adverb* > **Common Market** *former name for* **European Union** > **com'mon•place** *adjective* 1 ordinary, everyday ▷ *noun* 2 trite remark 3 anything occurring frequently > **common sense** sound, practical understanding > **com'mon•wealth** *noun* 1 republic 2 state of the US 3 federation of self-governing countries
com•mo•tion [kə-MOH-shən] *noun* stir, disturbance, tumult
com•mune[1] [kə-MYOON] *verb intransitive* **-muned, -mun•ing** converse together intimately > **com•mun'ion** *noun* 1 sharing of thoughts, feelings, etc. 2 fellowship 3 body with common faith 4 (**Com•mun'ion**) participation in sacrament of the Lord's Supper 5 (**Com•mun'ion**) that sacrament, Eucharist
com•mune[2] [KOM-yoon] *noun* group of

DICTIONARY • THESAURUS

commend *verb* PRAISE, acclaim, applaud, approve, compliment, extol, recommend, speak highly of
commendable *adjective* PRAISEWORTHY, admirable, creditable, deserving, estimable, exemplary, laudable, meritorious, worthy
commendation *noun* PRAISE, acclaim, acclamation, approbation, approval, credit, encouragement, good opinion, kudos, panegyric, recommendation
comment *noun* 1 REMARK, observation, statement
2 NOTE, annotation, commentary, explanation, exposition, illustration
▷ *verb* 3 REMARK, mention, note, observe, point out, say, utter
4 ANNOTATE, elucidate, explain, interpret
commentary *noun* 1 NARRATION, description, voice-over
2 NOTES, analysis, critique, explanation, review, treatise
commentator *noun* 1 REPORTER, special correspondent, sportscaster
2 CRITIC, annotator, interpreter
commerce *noun* TRADE, business, dealing, exchange, traffic
commercial *adjective* 1 MERCANTILE, trading
2 MATERIALISTIC, mercenary, profit-making
▷ *noun* 3 ADVERTISEMENT, ad (*informal*), announcement, plug (*informal*)
commiserate *verb* SYMPATHIZE, console, feel for, pity
commission *noun* 1 DUTY, errand, mandate, mission, task
2 FEE, cut, percentage, rake-off (*slang*), royalties
3 COMMITTEE, board, commissioners, delegation, deputation, representatives
▷ *verb* 4 APPOINT, authorize, contract, delegate, depute, empower, engage, nominate, order, select
commit *verb* 1 DO, carry out, enact, execute, perform, perpetrate
2 PUT IN CUSTODY, confine, imprison
commitment *noun* 1 DEDICATION, devotion, involvement, loyalty
2 RESPONSIBILITY, duty, engagement, liability, obligation, tie
common *adjective* 1 AVERAGE, commonplace, conventional, customary, everyday, familiar, frequent, habitual, ordinary, regular, routine, standard, stock, usual
2 POPULAR, accepted, general, prevailing, prevalent, universal, widespread
3 COLLECTIVE, communal, popular, public, social
4 VULGAR, coarse, inferior, plebeian
commonplace *adjective* 1 EVERYDAY, banal, common, humdrum, mundane, obvious, ordinary, widespread
▷ *noun* 2 CLICHÉ, banality, platitude, truism
common sense *noun* GOOD SENSE, horse sense, level-headedness, native intelligence, prudence, sound judgment, wit
commotion *noun* DISTURBANCE, disorder, excitement, furor, fuss, hue and cry, rumpus, tumult, turmoil, upheaval, uproar
communal *adjective* PUBLIC, collective, general,

families, individuals living together and sharing property, responsibility, etc.
> **com•mu•nal** [kə-MYOON-l] *adjective* for common use

com•mu•ni•cate [kə-MYOO-ni-kayt] *verb transitive* **-cat•ed, -cat•ing** 1 impart, convey 2 reveal ▷ *verb intransitive* **-cat•ed, -cat•ing** 3 give or exchange information 4 have connecting passage, door 5 receive Communion
> **com•mu'ni•ca•ble** *adjective* > **com•mu'ni•cant** *noun* one who receives Communion
> **com•mu•ni•ca'tion** *noun* 1 act of giving, esp. information 2 information, message 3 (*usually plural*) passage (road, railway, etc.), or means of exchanging messages (radio, mail, etc.) between places > **com•mu•ni•ca'tions** connections between military base and front
> **com•mu'ni•ca•tive** *adjective* free with information

com•mu•ni•qué [kə-myoo-ni-KAY] *noun* official announcement

com•mu•nism [KOM-yə-niz-əm] *noun* doctrine that all goods, means of production, etc., should be property of community > **com'mu•nist** *noun, adjective*

com•mu•ni•ty [kə-MYOO-ni-tee] *noun, plural* **-ties** 1 body of people with something in common, e.g. neighborhood, religion, etc. 2 society, the public 3 joint ownership 4 similarity, agreement

com•mute [kə-MYOOT] *verb intransitive* **-mut•ed, -mut•ing** 1 travel daily some distance to work ▷ *verb transitive* **-mut•ed, -mut•ing** 2 exchange 3 change (punishment, etc.) into something less severe 4 change (payment, etc.) into another form ▷ *noun* 5 journey made by commuting
> **com•mu•ta•tion** [kom-yə-TAY-shən] *noun*
> **com'mu•ta•tor** *noun* device to change alternating electric current into direct current
> **com•mut'er** *noun* one who daily travels some distance to work

com•pact[1] [kəm-PAKT] *adjective* 1 neatly arranged or packed 2 solid, concentrated 3 terse ▷ *verb* 4 make, become compact 5 compress > **com•pact'ness** *noun* > **com•pact disk** [KOM-pakt] small disk on which sound is recorded as series of metallic pits enclosed in polyvinyl chloride and played back by optical scanning by laser

com•pact[2] [KOM-pakt] *noun* small case to hold face powder, powder puff and mirror

com•pact[3] [KOM-pakt] *noun* agreement, covenant, treaty, contract

com•pan•ion[1] [kəm-PAN-yən] *noun* 1 chum, fellow, comrade, associate 2 person employed to live with another > **com•pan'ion•a•ble** *adjective*

companion[2] *noun* 1 raised cover over staircase from deck to cabin of ship 2 deck skylight
> **com•pan'ion•way** *noun* staircase from deck to cabin

com•pa•ny [KUM-pə-nee] *noun, plural* **-nies** 1 gathering of persons 2 companionship, fellowship 3 guests 4 business firm 5 division of regiment under captain 6 crew of ship 7 actors in play

com•pare [kəm-PAIR] *verb transitive* **-pared, -par•ing** 1 notice or point out likenesses and differences of things 2 liken 3 make comparative and superlative of adjective or adverb ▷ *verb intransitive* 4 be like 5 compete with > **com•pa•ra•bil•i•ty** [kom-pər-ə-BIL-i-tee] *noun* > **com'pa•ra•ble** *adjective* > **com•par'a•tive** *adjective* 1 that may be compared 2 not absolute 3 relative, partial 4 *grammar* denoting form of adjective, adverb, indicating "more" ▷ *noun*
> **com•par'a•tive•ly** *adverb* > **com•par'i•son** *noun* act of comparing

DICTIONARY

C

THESAURUS

joint, shared

commune[2] *noun* COMMUNITY, collective, cooperative, kibbutz

commune with *verb* CONTEMPLATE, meditate on, muse on, ponder, reflect on

communicate *verb* MAKE KNOWN, convey, declare, disclose, impart, inform, pass on, proclaim, transmit

communication *noun* 1 PASSING ON, contact, conversation, correspondence, dissemination, link, transmission
2 MESSAGE, announcement, disclosure, dispatch, information, news, report, statement, word

communicative *adjective* TALKATIVE, chatty, expansive, forthcoming, frank, informative, loquacious, open, outgoing, voluble

communism *noun* SOCIALISM, Bolshevism, collectivism, Marxism, state socialism

communist *noun* SOCIALIST, Bolshevik, collectivist, Marxist, Red (*informal*)

community *noun* SOCIETY, brotherhood, commonwealth, company, general public, people, populace, public, residents, state

commuter *noun* DAILY TRAVELER, straphanger (*informal*), suburbanite

compact[1] *adjective* 1 CLOSELY PACKED, compressed, condensed, dense, pressed together, solid, thick
2 BRIEF, compendious, concise, succinct, terse, to the point
▷ *verb* 3 PACK CLOSELY, compress, condense, cram, stuff, tamp

compact[3] *noun* AGREEMENT, arrangement, bargain, bond, contract, covenant, deal, pact, treaty, understanding

companion[1] *noun* 1 FRIEND, accomplice, ally, associate, colleague, comrade, consort, homeboy (*slang*), homegirl (*slang*), mate (*informal*), partner
2 ESCORT, aide, assistant, attendant, chaperon, squire

companionship *noun* FELLOWSHIP, camaraderie, company, comradeship, conviviality, esprit de corps, friendship, rapport, togetherness

company *noun* 1 BUSINESS, association, concern, corporation, establishment, firm, house, partnership, syndicate
2 GROUP, assembly, band, collection, community, crowd, gathering, party, set
3 GUESTS, callers, party, visitors

comparable *adjective* 1 ON A PAR, a match for, as good as, commensurate, equal, equivalent, in a class with, on a level playing field (*informal*), proportionate, tantamount
2 SIMILAR, akin, alike, analogous, cognate, corresponding, cut from the same cloth, of a piece, related

comparative *adjective* RELATIVE, by comparison,

com•part•ment [kəm-PAHRT-mənt] *noun* 1 division or part divided off 2 section
com•pass [KUM-pəs] *noun* 1 instrument for showing the north 2 instrument for drawing circles 3 circumference, measurement around 4 space, area 5 scope, reach ▷ *verb transitive* 6 surround 7 comprehend 8 attain, accomplish
com•pas•sion [kəm-PASH-ən] *noun* pity, sympathy > **com•pas'sion•ate** [-it] *adjective*
com•pat•i•ble [kəm-PAT-ə-bəl] *adjective* 1 capable of harmonious existence 2 consistent, agreeing with > **com•pat•i•bil'i•ty** *adverb*
com•pa•tri•ot [kəm-PAY-tree-ət] *noun* fellow countryman ▷ *adjective*
com•pel [kəm-PEL] *verb transitive* **-pelled, -pel•ling** 1 force, oblige 2 bring about by force
com•pen•di•um [kəm-PEN-dee-əm] *noun, plural* **-di•ums** abridgment, summary > **com•pen'di•ous** *adjective* brief but inclusive
com•pen•sate [KOM-pən-sayt] *verb transitive* **-sat•ed, -sat•ing** 1 make up for 2 recompense suitably 3 reward > **com•pen•sa'tion** *noun*
com•pete [kəm-PEET] *verb intransitive* **-pet•ed, -pet•ing** (oft. with *with*) strive in rivalry, contend for, vie with > **com•pe•ti•tion** [kom-pi-TISH-ən] *noun* > **com•pet'i•tive** [kəm-] *adjective* > **com•pet'i•tor** *noun*
com•pe•tent [KOM-pi-tənt] *adjective* 1 able, skillful 2 properly qualified 3 proper, due, legitimate 4 suitable, sufficient > **com'pe•tence** *noun* efficiency
com•pile [kəm-PĪL] *verb transitive* **-piled, -pil•ing** 1 make up (e.g. book) from various sources or materials 2 gather, put together > **com•pi•la•tion** [kom-pə-LAY-shən] *noun* > **com•pil'er** *noun*
com•pla•cent [kəm-PLAY-sənt] *adjective* 1 self-satisfied 2 pleased or gratified > **com•pla'cen•cy** *noun*
com•plain [kəm-PLAYN] *verb intransitive* 1 grumble 2 bring charge, make known a grievance 3 (with *of*) make known that one is suffering from > **com•plaint'** *noun* 1 statement of a wrong, grievance 2 ailment, illness > **com•plain'ant** *noun*
com•ple•ment [KOM-plə-mənt] *noun* 1

qualified
compare *verb* 1 WEIGH, balance, contrast, juxtapose, set against
2 (*usually with with*) BE ON A PAR WITH, approach, bear comparison, be in the same class as, be the equal of, compete with, equal, hold a candle to, match
3 ▷ **compare to** LIKEN TO, correlate to, equate to, identify with, mention in the same breath as, parallel, resemble
comparison *noun* 1 CONTRAST, distinction, juxtaposition
2 SIMILARITY, analogy, comparability, correlation, likeness, resemblance
compartment *noun* SECTION, alcove, bay, berth, booth, carriage, cubbyhole, cubicle, locker, niche, pigeonhole
compass *noun* RANGE, area, boundary, circumference, extent, field, limit, reach, realm, scope
compassion *noun* SYMPATHY, condolence, fellow feeling, humanity, kindness, mercy, pity, sorrow, tender-heartedness, tenderness, understanding
compassionate *adjective* SYMPATHETIC, benevolent, charitable, humane, humanitarian, kind-hearted, merciful, pitying, tender-hearted, understanding
compatibility *noun* HARMONY, affinity, agreement, concord, empathy, like-mindedness, rapport, sympathy
compatible *adjective* HARMONIOUS, adaptable, congruous, consistent, in harmony, in keeping, suitable
compel *verb* FORCE, coerce, constrain, dragoon, impel, make, oblige, railroad (*informal*)
compelling *adjective* 1 FASCINATING, enchanting, enthralling, gripping, hypnotic, irresistible, mesmeric, spellbinding
2 PRESSING, binding, coercive, imperative, overriding, peremptory, unavoidable, urgent
3 CONVINCING, cogent, conclusive, forceful, irrefutable, powerful, telling, weighty
compensate *verb* 1 RECOMPENSE, atone, make amends, make good, refund, reimburse, remunerate, repay
2 CANCEL *or* CANCEL OUT, balance, counteract, counterbalance, make up for, offset, redress
compensation *noun* RECOMPENSE, amends, atonement, damages, reimbursement, remuneration, reparation, restitution, satisfaction
compete *verb* CONTEND, be in the running, challenge, contest, fight, strive, struggle, vie
competence *noun* ABILITY, capability, capacity, expertise, fitness, proficiency, skill, suitability
competent *adjective* ABLE, adequate, capable, fit, proficient, qualified, suitable
competition *noun* 1 RIVALRY, opposition, strife, struggle
2 CONTEST, championship, event, head-to-head, puzzle, quiz, tournament
3 OPPOSITION, challengers, field, rivals
competitive *adjective* 1 CUT-THROAT, aggressive, antagonistic, at odds, dog-eat-dog, opposing, rival
2 AMBITIOUS, combative
competitor *noun* CONTESTANT, adversary, antagonist, challenger, opponent, rival
compilation *noun* COLLECTION, accumulation, anthology, assemblage, assortment, treasury
compile *verb* PUT TOGETHER, accumulate, amass, collect, cull, garner, gather, marshal, organize
complacency *noun* SELF-SATISFACTION, contentment, satisfaction, smugness
complacent *adjective* SELF-SATISFIED, contented, pleased with oneself, resting on one's laurels, satisfied, serene, smug, unconcerned
complain *verb* FIND FAULT, bemoan, bewail, carp, deplore, groan, grouse, grumble, lament, moan, whine
complaint *noun* 1 CRITICISM, charge, grievance, gripe (*informal*), grouse, grumble, lament, moan, protest
2 ILLNESS, affliction, ailment, disease, disorder, malady, sickness, upset
complement *noun* 1 COMPLETION, companion, consummation, counterpart, finishing touch, rounding-off, supplement
2 TOTAL, aggregate, capacity, entirety, quota, totality, wholeness

something making up a whole 2 full allowance, equipment, etc. ▷ *verb transitive* 3 add to, make complete > **com•ple•men'ta•ry** *adjective*

com•plete [kəm-PLEET] *adjective* 1 full, perfect 2 finished, ended 3 entire 4 thorough ▷ *verb transitive* **-plet•ed, -plet•ing** 5 make whole, perfect 6 finish > **com•plete'ly** *adverb* > **com•ple'tion** *noun*

com•plex [kəm-PLEKS] *adjective* 1 intricate, compound, involved ▷ *noun* [KOM-pleks] 2 complicated whole 3 group of related buildings 4 psychological abnormality, obsession > **com•plex'i•ty** *noun*

com•plex•ion [kəm-PLEK-shən] *noun* 1 look, color, of skin, esp. of face, appearance 2 aspect, character 3 disposition

compliant *see* **comply**

com•pli•cate [KOM-pli-kayt] *verb transitive* **-cat•ed, -cat•ing** 1 make intricate, involved, difficult 2 mix up > **com•pli•ca'tion** *noun*

com•plic•i•ty [kəm-PLIS-i-tee] *noun, plural* **-ties** partnership in wrongdoing

com•pli•ment [KOM-plə-mənt] *noun* 1 expression of regard, praise 2 flattering speech ▷ *verb transitive* 3 praise, congratulate > **com•pli•ments** *plural noun* expression of courtesy, formal greetings > **com•pli•men'ta•ry** *adjective* 1 expressing praise 2 free of charge

com•ply [kəm-PLĪ] *verb intransitive* **-plied, -ply•ing** consent, yield, do as asked > **com•pli'ance** *noun* > **com•pli'ant** *adjective*

com•po•nent [kəm-POH-nənt] *noun* 1 part, element, constituent of whole ▷ *adjective* 2 composing, making up

com•port [kəm-PORT] *verb* 1 agree 2 behave

com•pose [kəm-POHZ] *verb transitive* **-posed, -pos•ing** 1 arrange, put in order 2 write, invent 3 make up 4 calm 5 settle, adjust > **com•posed'** *adjective* calm > **com•pos'er** *noun* one who composes, esp. music > **com•po•site** [kəm-POZ-it] *adjective* made up of distinct parts > **com•po•si•tion** [kom-pə-ZISH-ən] *noun* > **com•pos•i•tor** [kəm-POZ-i-tər] *noun* typesetter, one who arranges type for printing > **com•po•sure** [kəm-POH-zhər] *noun* calmness

---

▷ *verb* 3 COMPLETE, cap (*informal*), crown, round off, set off

complementary *adjective* COMPLETING, companion, corresponding, interdependent, interrelating, matched, reciprocal

complete *adjective* 1 TOTAL, absolute, consummate, outright, perfect, thorough, thoroughgoing, utter
2 FINISHED, accomplished, achieved, concluded, ended
3 ENTIRE, all, faultless, full, intact, plenary, unbroken, whole
▷ *verb* 4 FINISH, close, conclude, crown, end, finalize, round off, settle, wind up (*informal*), wrap up (*informal*)

completely *adverb* TOTALLY, absolutely, altogether, entirely, every inch, fully, hook, line and sinker, in full, lock, stock and barrel, one hundred per cent, perfectly, thoroughly, utterly, wholly

completion *noun* FINISHING, bitter end, close, conclusion, culmination, end, fruition, fulfillment

complex *adjective* 1 COMPOUND, composite, heterogeneous, manifold, multifarious, multiple
2 COMPLICATED, convoluted, elaborate, intricate, involved, labyrinthine, tangled, tortuous
▷ *noun* 3 STRUCTURE, aggregate, composite, network, organization, scheme, system
4 OBSESSION, fixation, fixed idea, idée fixe (*French*), phobia, preoccupation

complexion *noun* 1 SKIN, color, coloring, hue, pigmentation, skin tone
2 NATURE, appearance, aspect, character, guise, light, look, make-up

complexity *noun* COMPLICATION, elaboration, entanglement, intricacy, involvement, ramification

complicate *verb* MAKE DIFFICULT, confuse, entangle, involve, muddle, ravel

complicated *adjective* 1 DIFFICULT, involved, perplexing, problematic, puzzling, troublesome
2 INVOLVED, complex, convoluted, elaborate, intricate, labyrinthine

complication *noun* 1 COMPLEXITY, confusion, entanglement, intricacy, web
2 PROBLEM, difficulty, drawback, embarrassment, obstacle, snag

compliment *noun* 1 PRAISE, bouquet, commendation, congratulations, eulogy, flattery, honor, tribute
▷ *verb* 2 PRAISE, brown-nose (*slang*), commend, congratulate, extol, flatter, pay tribute to, salute, speak highly of

complimentary *adjective* 1 FLATTERING, appreciative, approving, commendatory, congratulatory, laudatory
2 FREE, courtesy, donated, gratis, gratuitous, honorary, on the house

compliments *plural noun* GREETINGS, good wishes, regards, remembrances, respects, salutation

comply *verb* OBEY, abide by, acquiesce, adhere to, conform to, follow, observe, submit, toe the line

component *noun* 1 PART, constituent, element, ingredient, item, piece, unit
▷ *adjective* 2 CONSTITUENT, inherent, intrinsic

compose *verb* 1 PUT TOGETHER, build, comprise, constitute, construct, fashion, form, make, make up
2 CREATE, contrive, devise, invent, produce, write
3 CALM, collect, control, pacify, placate, quiet, soothe
4 ARRANGE, adjust

composed *adjective* CALM, at ease, collected, cool, level-headed, poised, relaxed, sedate, self-possessed, serene, unflappable

composition *noun* 1 CREATION, compilation, fashioning, formation, formulation, making, production, putting together
2 DESIGN, arrangement, configuration, formation, layout, make-up, organization, structure
3 ESSAY, exercise, literary work, opus, piece, treatise, work

composure *noun* CALMNESS, aplomb, equanimity, poise, sang-froid, self-assurance,

com•pos men•tis [KOM-pəs MEN-tis] *Lat.* of sound mind
com•post [KOM-pohst] *noun* fertilizing mixture of decayed vegetable matter for soil
com•pote [KOM-poht] *noun* fruit stewed or preserved in syrup
com•pound[1] [KOM-pownd] *noun* 1 mixture, joining 2 substance, word, made up of parts ▷ *adjective* 3 not simple 4 composite, mixed ▷ *verb transitive* [kəm-POWND] 5 mix, make up, put together 6 intensify, make worse 7 compromise, settle debt by partial payment
com•pound[2] [KOM-pownd] *noun* (fenced or walled) enclosure containing houses, etc.
com•pre•hend [kom-pri-HEND] *verb transitive* 1 understand, take in 2 include, comprise > **com•pre•hen'si•ble** *adjective* > **com•pre•hen'sion** *noun* > **com•pre•hen'sive** *adjective* 1 wide, full 2 taking in much
com•press [kəm-PRES] *verb transitive* 1 squeeze together 2 make smaller in size, bulk ▷ *noun* [KOM-pres] pad of cloth applied to wound, inflamed part, etc. > **com•press'i•ble** *adjective* > **com•pres•sion** [kəm-PRESH-ən] *noun* in internal combustion engine, squeezing of explosive charge before ignition, to give additional force > **com•pres'sor** *noun* esp. machine to compress air, gas
com•prise [kəm-PRĪZ] *verb transitive* **-prised, -pris•ing** include, contain
com•pro•mise [KOM-prə-mīz] *noun* 1 meeting halfway, coming to terms by giving up part of claim 2 middle course ▷ *verb* **-mised, -mis•ing** 3 settle (dispute) by making concessions ▷ *verb transitive* 4 expose to risk or suspicion
comp•trol•ler [kən-TROH-lər] *noun* controller (in some titles)
com•pul•sion [kəm-PUL-shən] *noun* 1 act of compelling 2 irresistible impulse > **com•pul'sive** *adjective* > **com•pul'so•ri•ly** [-sə-rə-lee] *adverb* > **com•pul'so•ry** *adjective* not optional
com•punc•tion [kəm-PUNGK-shən] *noun* regret for wrongdoing
com•pute [kəm-PYOOT] *verb transitive* **-put•ed, -put•ing** reckon, calculate, esp. using computer > **com•pu•ta•tion** [kom-pyə-TAY-shən] *noun* reckoning, estimate > **com•put'er** *noun* electronic device for storing, retrieving information and performing calculations > **com•put'er•ize** *verb* **-ized, -iz•ing** equip with, perform by computer
com•rade [KOM-rad] *noun* chum, companion, friend > **com'radeship** *noun* > **com'rade•ly** *adjective*
con[1] [kon] *verb* **conned, con•ning** (*informal*) 1 swindle, defraud 2 cajole
con[2] *verb transitive* **conned, con•ning** direct steering (of ship)
con- *prefix see* **com-**
con•cat•e•nate [kon-KAT-n-ayt] *verb transitive* **-nat•ed, -nat•ing** link together > **con•cat•e•na'tion** *noun* connected chain (as of circumstances)
con•cave [kon-KAYV] *adjective* hollow, rounded inward > **con•cav'i•ty** *noun*
con•ceal [kən-SEEL] *verb transitive* hide, keep secret
con•cede [kən-SEED] *verb transitive* **-ced•ed, -ced•ing** 1 admit, admit truth of 2 grant, allow, yield
con•ceit [kən-SEET] *noun* 1 vanity, overweening opinion of oneself 2 far-fetched comparison

DICTIONARY • THESAURUS

---

self-possession, serenity
compound[1] *noun* 1 COMBINATION, alloy, amalgam, blend, composite, fusion, medley, mixture, synthesis
▷ *verb* 2 COMBINE, amalgamate, blend, intermingle, mix, synthesize, unite
3 INTENSIFY, add to, aggravate, augment, complicate, exacerbate, heighten, magnify, worsen
▷ *adjective* 4 COMPLEX, composite, intricate, multiple
comprehend *verb* UNDERSTAND, apprehend, conceive, fathom, grasp, know, make out, perceive, see, take in
comprehensible *adjective* UNDERSTANDABLE, clear, coherent, conceivable, explicit, intelligible, plain
comprehension *noun* UNDERSTANDING, conception, discernment, grasp, intelligence, perception, realization
comprehensive *adjective* BROAD, all-embracing, all-inclusive, blanket, complete, encyclopedic, exhaustive, full, inclusive, thorough
compress *verb* SQUEEZE, abbreviate, concentrate, condense, contract, crush, press, shorten, squash
comprise *verb* 1 BE COMPOSED OF, consist of, contain, embrace, encompass, include, take in
2 MAKE UP, compose, constitute, form
compromise *noun* 1 GIVE-AND-TAKE, accommodation, adjustment, agreement, concession, settlement, trade-off
▷ *verb* 2 MEET HALFWAY, adjust, agree, concede, give and take, go fifty-fifty (*informal*), settle, strike a balance
3 DISHONOR, discredit, embarrass, expose, jeopardize, prejudice, weaken
compulsion *noun* 1 URGE, drive, necessity, need, obsession, preoccupation
2 FORCE, coercion, constraint, demand, duress, obligation, pressure, urgency
compulsive *adjective* IRRESISTIBLE, compelling, driving, neurotic, obsessive, overwhelming, uncontrollable, urgent
compulsory *adjective* OBLIGATORY, binding, de rigueur (*French*), forced, imperative, mandatory, required, requisite
compute *verb* CALCULATE, add up, count, enumerate, figure out, reckon, tally, total
comrade *noun* COMPANION, ally, associate, colleague, co-worker, fellow, friend, homeboy (*slang*), homegirl (*slang*), partner
con (*informal*) *noun* 1 SWINDLE, deception, fraud, scam (*slang*), sting (*informal*), trick
▷ *verb* 2 SWINDLE, cheat, deceive, defraud, double-cross (*informal*), dupe, hoodwink, rip off (*slang*), trick
concave *adjective* HOLLOW, indented
conceal *verb* HIDE, bury, camouflage, cover, disguise, mask, obscure, screen
concede *verb* 1 ADMIT, accept, acknowledge, allow, confess, grant, own
2 GIVE UP, cede, hand over, relinquish, surrender, yield

> **con•ceit'ed** *adjective*

con•ceive [kən-SEEV] *verb* **-ceived, -ceiv•ing** 1 think of, imagine 2 believe 3 form in the mind 4 become pregnant > **con•ceiv'a•ble** *adjective*

con•cen•trate [KON-sən-trayt] *verb transitive* **-trat•ed, -trat•ing** 1 focus (one's efforts, etc.) 2 increase in strength 3 reduce to small space ▷ *verb intransitive* **-trat•ed, -trat•ing** 4 devote all attention 5 come together ▷ *noun* 6 concentrated material or solution > **con•cen•tra'tion** *noun* > **concentration camp** prison camp, esp. one in Nazi Germany

con•cen•tric [kən-SEN-trik] *adjective* having the same center

con•cept [KON-sept] *noun* 1 abstract idea 2 mental expression > **con•cep•tu•al** [kən-SEP-choo-əl] *adjective*

con•cep•tion [kən-SEP-shən] *noun* 1 idea, notion 2 act of conceiving

con•cern [kən-SURN] *verb transitive* 1 relate, apply to 2 interest, affect, trouble 3 (with *in* or *with*) involve (oneself) ▷ *noun* 4 affair 5 regard, worry 6 importance 7 business, enterprise > **con•cerned'** *adjective* 1 connected with 2 interested 3 worried 4 involved > **con•cern'ing** *preposition* respecting, about

con•cert [KON-surt] *noun* 1 musical entertainment 2 harmony, agreement ▷ *verb transitive* [kən-SURT] 3 arrange, plan together > **con•cert'ed** *adjective* 1 mutually arranged, planned 2 determined > **con•cer•ti•na** [kon-sər-TEE-nə] *noun* musical instrument with bellows and keys > **con•cer•to** [kən-CHER-toh] *noun, plural* **-tos** musical composition for solo instrument and orchestra

con•ces•sion [kən-SESH-ən] *noun* 1 act of conceding 2 thing conceded 3 grant 4 special privilege

conch [kongk] *noun* seashell > **con•chol•o•gy** [kong-KOL-ə-jee] *noun* study, collection of shells and shellfish

con•cierge [kon-see-AIRZH] *noun* in France esp., caretaker, doorkeeper

con•cil•i•ate [kən-SIL-ee-ayt] *verb transitive* **-at•ed, -at•ing** pacify, win over from hostility > **con•cil'i•a•tor** *noun* > **con•cil'i•a•to•ry** *adjective*

con•cise [kən-SĪS] *adjective* brief, terse > **con•cise'ly** *adverb* > **con•cise'ness** *noun*

con•clave [KON-klayv] *noun* 1 private meeting 2 assembly for election of a pope

con•clude [kən-KLOOD] *verb transitive* **-clud•ed, -clud•ing** 1 end, finish 2 deduce 3 settle ▷ *verb intransitive* **-clud•ed, -clud•ing** 4 come to

---

conceit *noun* 1 SELF-IMPORTANCE, arrogance, egotism, narcissism, pride, swagger, vanity

conceited *adjective* SELF-IMPORTANT, arrogant, bigheaded (*informal*), cocky, egotistical, full of oneself, immodest, narcissistic, too big for one's boots *or* too big for one's breeches, vain

conceivable *adjective* IMAGINABLE, believable, credible, possible, thinkable

conceive *verb* 1 IMAGINE, believe, comprehend, envisage, fancy, suppose, think, understand
2 THINK UP, contrive, create, design, devise, formulate
3 BECOME PREGNANT, become impregnated

concentrate *verb* 1 FOCUS ONE'S ATTENTION ON, be engrossed in, put one's mind to, rack one's brains
2 FOCUS, bring to bear, center, cluster, converge
3 GATHER, accumulate, cluster, collect, congregate, huddle

concentrated *adjective* 1 INTENSE, all-out (*informal*), deep, hard, intensive
2 CONDENSED, boiled down, evaporated, reduced, rich, thickened, undiluted

concentration *noun* 1 SINGLE-MINDEDNESS, absorption, application, heed
2 FOCUSING, bringing to bear, centralization, centring, consolidation, convergence, intensification
3 CONVERGENCE, accumulation, aggregation, cluster, collection, horde, mass

concept *noun* IDEA, abstraction, conception, conceptualization, hypothesis, image, notion, theory, view

conception *noun* 1 IDEA, concept, design, image, notion, plan
2 IMPREGNATION, fertilization, germination, insemination

concern *noun* 1 WORRY, anxiety, apprehension, burden, care, disquiet, distress
2 IMPORTANCE, bearing, interest, relevance
3 BUSINESS, affair, interest, job, responsibility, task
4 BUSINESS, company, corporation, enterprise, establishment, firm, organization
▷ *verb* 5 WORRY, bother, disquiet, distress, disturb, make anxious, perturb, trouble
6 BE RELEVANT TO, affect, apply to, bear on, interest, involve, pertain to, regard, touch

concerned *adjective* 1 INVOLVED, active, implicated, interested, mixed up, privy to
2 WORRIED, anxious, bothered, distressed, disturbed, troubled, uneasy, upset

concerning *preposition* REGARDING, about, apropos of, as regards, on the subject of, re, relating to, respecting, touching, with reference to

concession *noun* 1 GRANT, adjustment, allowance, boon, compromise, indulgence, permit, privilege, sop
2 CONCEDING, acknowledgment, admission, assent, confession, surrender, yielding

conciliate *verb* PACIFY, appease, clear the air, mediate, mollify, placate, reconcile, soothe, win over

conciliation *noun* PACIFICATION, appeasement, mollification, placation, reconciliation, soothing

conciliatory *adjective* PACIFYING, appeasing, mollifying, pacific, peaceable, placatory

concise *adjective* BRIEF, compendious, condensed, laconic, pithy, short, succinct, terse

conclude *verb* 1 DECIDE, assume, deduce, gather, infer, judge, surmise, work out
2 END, cease, close, complete, finish, round off, terminate, wind up
3 ACCOMPLISH, bring about, carry out, effect, pull off

end 5 decide > **con•clu'sion** [-KLOO-zhən] *noun* > **con•clu'sive** *adjective* decisive, convincing
con•coct [kən-KOKT] *verb transitive* 1 make mixture, prepare with various ingredients 2 make up 3 contrive, plan > **con•coc'tion** *noun*
con•com•i•tant [kon-KOM-i-tənt] *adjective* accompanying
con•cord [KON-kord] *noun* 1 agreement 2 harmony ▷ *verb intransitive* [kən-KORD] 3 agree > **con•cord'ance** [-əns] *noun* 1 agreement 2 index to words of book (esp. Bible)
con•course [KON-kors] *noun* 1 crowd 2 large, open place in public area 3 boulevard
con•crete [KON-kreet] *noun* 1 mixture of sand, cement, etc., used in building ▷ *adjective* 2 made of concrete 3 particular, specific 4 perceptible, actual 5 solid > **con•crete'ly** *adverb*
con•cu•bine [KONG-kyə-bīn] *noun* 1 woman living with man as his wife, but not married to him 2 mistress > **con•cu•bi•nage** [kon-KYOO-bə-nij] *noun*
con•cu•pis•cence [kon-KYOO-pi-səns] *noun* lust
con•cur [kən-KUR] *verb intransitive* **-curred, -cur•ring** 1 agree, express agreement 2 happen together 3 coincide > **con•cur'rence** *noun* > **con•cur'rent** *adjective* > **con•cur'rent•ly** *adverb* at the same time
con•cus•sion [kən-KUSH-ən] *noun* 1 brain injury 2 physical shock
con•demn [kən-DEM] *verb transitive* 1 blame 2 find guilty 3 doom 4 find, declare unfit for use > **con•dem•na•tion** [kon-dem-NAY-shən] *noun* > **con•dem'na•to•ry** *adjective*
con•dense [kən-DENS] *verb transitive* **-densed, -dens•ing** 1 concentrate, make more solid 2 turn from gas into liquid 3 pack into few words ▷ *verb intransitive* **-densed, -dens•ing** 4 turn from gas to liquid > **con•den•sa•tion** [kon-den-SAY-shən] *noun* > **con•dens'er** *noun* 1 *electricity* apparatus for storing electrical energy, a capacitor 2 apparatus for reducing gas to liquid form 3 a lens or mirror for focusing light
con•de•scend [kon-də-SEND] *verb intransitive* 1 treat graciously one regarded as inferior 2 do something below one's dignity > **con•de•scend'ing** *adjective* > **con•de•scen'sion** *noun*
con•di•ment [KON-də-mənt] *noun* sauce, seasoning for food
con•di•tion [kən-DISH-ən] *noun* 1 state or circumstances of anything 2 thing on which statement or happening or existing depends 3 stipulation, prerequisite 4 health, physical fitness 5 rank ▷ *verb transitive* 6 accustom 7 regulate 8 make fit, healthy 9 be essential to happening or existence of 10 stipulate > **con•di'tion•al** *adjective* 1 dependent on circumstances or events ▷ *noun grammar* 2 form of verbs
con•do [KON-doh] *noun, plural* **-dos** condominium (building)
con•dole [kən-DOHL] *verb intransitive* **-doled, -dol•ing** 1 grieve with, offer sympathy 2 commiserate with > **con•do'lence** *noun*
con•dom [KON-dəm] *noun* sheathlike usu. rubber contraceptive device worn by man
con•do•min•i•um [kon-də-MIN-ee-əm] *noun* 1 joint rule by two or more countries 2 building with apartments, offices, etc.

DICTIONARY • THESAURUS

conclusion *noun* 1 DECISION, conviction, deduction, inference, judgment, opinion, verdict
2 END, bitter end, close, completion, ending, finale, finish, result, termination
3 OUTCOME, consequence, culmination, end result, result, upshot
conclusive *adjective* DECISIVE, clinching, convincing, definite, final, irrefutable, ultimate, unanswerable
concoct *verb* MAKE UP, brew, contrive, devise, formulate, hatch, invent, prepare, think up
concoction *noun* MIXTURE, blend, brew, combination, compound, creation, preparation
concrete *adjective* 1 SPECIFIC, definite, explicit
2 REAL, actual, factual, material, sensible, substantial, tangible
concur *verb* AGREE, acquiesce, assent, consent
condemn *verb* 1 DISAPPROVE, blame, censure, damn, denounce, reproach, reprove, upbraid
2 SENTENCE, convict, damn, doom, pass sentence on
condemnation *noun* 1 DISAPPROVAL, blame, censure, denunciation, reproach, reproof, stricture
2 SENTENCE, conviction, damnation, doom, judgment
condensation *noun* 1 DISTILLATION, liquefaction, precipitate, precipitation
2 ABRIDGMENT, contraction, digest, précis, synopsis
3 CONCENTRATION, compression, consolidation, crystallization, curtailment, reduction
condense *verb* 1 ABRIDGE, abbreviate, compress, concentrate, epitomize, shorten, summarize
2 CONCENTRATE, boil down, reduce, thicken
condensed *adjective* 1 ABRIDGED, compressed, concentrated, shortened, shrunken, slimmed-down, summarized
2 CONCENTRATED, boiled down, reduced, thickened
condescend *verb* 1 PATRONIZE, talk down to
2 LOWER ONESELF, bend, deign, humble oneself *or* demean oneself, see fit, stoop
condescending *adjective* PATRONIZING, disdainful, lofty, lordly, snobbish, snooty (*informal*), supercilious, superior
condition *noun* 1 STATE, circumstances, lie of the land, position, shape, situation, state of affairs
2 REQUIREMENT, limitation, prerequisite, proviso, qualification, restriction, rider, stipulation, terms
3 HEALTH, fettle, fitness, kilter, order, shape, state of health, trim
4 AILMENT, complaint, infirmity, malady, problem, weakness
▷ *verb* 5 ACCUSTOM, adapt, equip, prepare, ready, tone up, train, work out
conditional *adjective* DEPENDENT, contingent, limited, provisional, qualified, subject to, with reservations
conditions *plural noun* CIRCUMSTANCES, environment, milieu, situation, surroundings, way of life

3 individually owned
con•done [kən-DOHN] *verb transitive* **-doned, don•ing** overlook, forgive, treat as not existing
con•duce [kən-DOOS] *verb intransitive* **-duced, -duc•ing** 1 help, promote 2 tend toward > **con•du'cive** *adjective*
con•duct [KON-dukt] *noun* 1 behavior 2 management ▷ *verb transitive* [kən-DUKT] 3 escort, guide 4 lead, direct 5 manage 6 transmit (heat, electricity) > **con•duc'tion** *noun* > **con•duc'tive** *adjective* > **con•duc•tiv'i•ty** *noun* > **con•duc'tor** *noun* 1 employee on bus, train, etc. who collects fares 2 director of orchestra 3 one who leads, guides 4 substance capable of transmitting heat, electricity, etc.
con•du•it [KON-doo-it] *noun* channel or pipe for conveying water, electric cables, etc.
cone [kohn] *noun* 1 solid figure with circular base, tapering to a point 2 fruit of pine, fir, etc. > **con•ic** [KON-ik], **con'i•cal** *adjective*
con•fab•u•late [kən-FAB-yə-layt] *verb intransitive* **-lat•ed, -lat•ing** chat > **con•fab** [KON-fab] *noun* (*informal*) shortened form of confabulation > **con•fab•u•la'tion** *noun* confidential conversation
con•fec•tion [kən-FEK-shən] *noun* 1 prepared delicacy, esp. something sweet 2 candy > **con•fec'tion•er** *noun* dealer in candies, fancy cakes, etc. > **con•fec'tion•er•y** *noun* 1 confectioner's shop 2 things confectioner sells
con•fed•er•ate [kən-FED-ər-it] *noun* 1 ally 2 accomplice ▷ *verb* [-ə-rayt], **-at•ed, -at•ing** 3 unite > **con•fed'er•a•cy** *noun* > **con•fed•er•a'tion** *noun* alliance of political units
con•fer [kən-FUR] *verb transitive* **-ferred, -fer•ring** 1 grant, give 2 bestow 3 award ▷ *verb intransitive* **-ferred, -fer•ring** 4 talk with, take advice > **con•fer•ence** [KON-fər-əns] *noun* meeting for consultation or deliberation
con•fess [kən-FES] *verb transitive* 1 admit, own 2 (of priest) hear sins of ▷ *verb intransitive* 3 acknowledge 4 declare one's sins orally to priest > **con•fes'sion** [-FESH-ən] *noun* > **con•fes'sion•al** *noun* confessor's stall > **con•fes'sor** *noun* priest who hears confessions
con•fet•ti [kən-FET-ee] *noun* small bits of colored paper for throwing at weddings
con•fide [kən-FĪD] *verb intransitive* **-fid•ed, -fid•ing** 1 (with *in*) tell secrets, trust ▷ *verb transitive* **-fid•ed, -fid•ing** 2 entrust > **con•fi•dant(e)** [KON-fi-dant] *noun* one entrusted with secrets > **con'fi•dence** *noun* 1 trust 2 boldness, assurance 3 intimacy 4 something confided, secret > **con'fi•dent** *adjective* > **con•fi•den'tial** [-shəl] *adjective* 1 private 2 secret 3 entrusted with another's confidences > **con'fi•dent•ly** *adverb* > **confidence game** con game, swindle in which victim entrusts money, etc. to thief, believed honest
con•fig•u•ra•tion [kən-fig-yə-RAY-shən] *noun* shape, aspect, conformation, arrangement
con•fine [kən-FĪN] *verb transitive* **-fined, fin•ing** 1 keep within bounds 2 keep in house, bed, etc. 3 shut up, imprison > **con•fines** [KON-fīnz] *plural noun* boundaries, limits > **confine'ment** *noun* 1 esp. childbirth 2 imprisonment
con•firm [kən-FURM] *verb transitive* 1 make sure, verify 2 strengthen, settle 3 make valid, ratify 4 administer confirmation to > **con•fir•ma•tion** [kon-fər-MAY-shən] *noun* 1 making strong,

DICTIONARY

C

THESAURUS

condone *verb* OVERLOOK, excuse, forgive, let pass, look the other way, make allowance for, pardon, turn a blind eye to
conduct *noun* 1 BEHAVIOR, attitude, bearing, demeanor, deportment, manners, ways
2 MANAGEMENT, administration, control, direction, guidance, handling, organization, running, supervision
▷ *verb* 3 CARRY OUT, administer, control, direct, handle, manage, organize, preside over, run, supervise
4 BEHAVE, acquit, act, carry, comport, deport
5 ACCOMPANY, convey, escort, guide, lead, steer, usher
confederacy *noun* UNION, alliance, coalition, confederation, federation, league
confer *verb* 1 DISCUSS, consult, converse, deliberate, discourse, talk
2 GRANT, accord, award, bestow, give, hand out, present
conference *noun* MEETING, colloquium, congress, consultation, convention, discussion, forum, seminar, symposium
confess *verb* 1 ADMIT, acknowledge, come clean (*informal*), concede, confide, disclose, divulge, fess up (*informal*), own up
2 DECLARE, affirm, assert, confirm, profess, reveal
confession *noun* ADMISSION, acknowledgment, disclosure, exposure, revelation, unbosoming
confidant *or* **confidante** *noun* CLOSE FRIEND, alter ego, bosom friend, crony, familiar, intimate
confide *verb* 1 TELL, admit, confess, disclose, divulge, impart, reveal, whisper
2 (*formal*) ENTRUST, commend, commit, consign
confidence *noun* 1 TRUST, belief, credence, dependence, faith, reliance
2 SELF-ASSURANCE, aplomb, assurance, boldness, courage, firmness, nerve, self-possession
3 ▷ **in confidence** IN SECRECY, between you and me *or* between you and me and the gatepost, confidentially, privately
confident *adjective* 1 CERTAIN, convinced, counting on, positive, satisfied, secure, sure
2 SELF-ASSURED, assured, bold, dauntless, fearless, self-reliant
confidential *adjective* SECRET, classified, hush-hush (*informal*), intimate, off the record, private, privy
confidentially *adverb* IN SECRET, behind closed doors, between ourselves, in camera, in confidence, personally, privately, sub rosa
confine *verb* RESTRICT, cage, enclose, hem in, hold back, imprison, incarcerate, intern, keep, limit, shut up
confinement *noun* IMPRISONMENT, custody, detention, incarceration, internment
confines *plural noun* LIMITS, boundaries, bounds, circumference, edge, precincts
confirm *verb* 1 PROVE, authenticate, bear out, corroborate, endorse, ratify, substantiate, validate, verify
2 STRENGTHEN, buttress, establish, fix, fortify, reinforce
confirmation *noun* 1 PROOF, authentication,

certain 2 Christian rite administered to confirm vows made at baptism 3 Jewish ceremony to admit boys, girls to adult status > **con•firm'a•to•ry** *adjective* 1 tending to confirm or establish 2 corroborative > **con•firmed'** *adjective* (of habit, etc.) long-established

con•fis•cate [KON-fə-skayt] *verb transitive* **-cat•ed, -cat•ing** seize by authority > **con•fis•ca'tion** *noun* > **con•fis•ca•to•ry** [kən-FIS-kə-tor-ee] *adjective*

con•fla•gra•tion [kon-flə-GRAY-shən] *noun* great destructive fire

con•flict [KON-flikt] *noun* 1 struggle, trial of strength 2 disagreement ▷ *verb intransitive* [kən-FLIKT] 3 be at odds with, be inconsistent with 4 clash

con•flu•ence [KON-floo-əns] *noun* 1 union of streams 2 meeting place > **con'flu•ent** *adjective*

con•form [kən-FORM] *verb* 1 comply with accepted standards, conventions, etc. 2 adapt to rule, pattern, custom, etc. > **con•for•ma•tion** [kon-for-MAY-shən] *noun* structure, adaptation > **con•form'ist** *noun* one who conforms, esp. excessively > **con•form'i•ty** *noun* compliance

con•found [kon-FOWND] *verb transitive* 1 baffle, perplex 2 confuse 3 defeat > **con•found'ed** *adjective* (*old-fashioned*) damned

con•front [kən-FRUNT] *verb transitive* 1 face 2 bring face to face with > **con•fron•ta•tion** [kon-frən-TAY-shən] *noun*

con•fuse [kən-FYOOZ] *verb transitive* **-fused, -fus•ing** 1 bewilder 2 jumble 3 make unclear 4 mistake (one thing) for another 5 disconcert > **con•fu'sion** *noun*

con•geal [kən-JEEL] *verb* solidify by cooling or freezing

con•gen•ial [kən-JEEN-yəl] *adjective* 1 pleasant, to one's liking 2 of similar disposition, tastes, etc. > **con•ge•ni•al'i•ty** *noun*

con•gen•i•tal [kən-JEN-i-tl] *adjective* 1 existing at birth 2 dating from birth

con•ge•ries [KON-jə-reez] *noun* (*functioning as singular or plural*) collection or mass of small bodies, conglomeration

con•gest [kən-JEST] *verb* overcrowd or clog > **con•ges'tion** *noun* abnormal accumulation, overcrowding > **con•gest'ed** *adjective*

con•glom•er•ate [kən-GLOM-ər-it] *noun* 1 thing, substance (esp. rock) composed of mixture of other, smaller elements or pieces 2 business organization comprising many companies ▷ *verb* [-ə-rayt], **-at•ed, -at•ing** 3 gather together ▷ *adjective* > **con•glom•er•a'tion** *noun*

con•grat•u•late [kən-GRACH-ə-layt] *verb transitive* **-lat•ed, -lat•ing** express pleasure at good fortune, success, etc. > **con•grat•u•la'tion** *noun* > **con•grat'u•la•to•ry** *adjective*

con•gre•gate [KONG-gri-gayt] *verb* **-gat•ed, -gat•ing** 1 assemble 2 collect, flock together

---

corroboration, evidence, substantiation, testimony, validation, verification
2 SANCTION, acceptance, agreement, approval, assent, endorsement, ratification

confirmed *adjective* LONG-ESTABLISHED, chronic, dyed-in-the-wool, habitual, hardened, ingrained, inveterate, seasoned

confiscate *verb* SEIZE, appropriate, commandeer, impound, sequester, sequestrate

confiscation *noun* SEIZURE, appropriation, forfeiture, impounding, sequestration, takeover

conflict *noun* 1 OPPOSITION, antagonism, difference, disagreement, discord, dissension, friction, hostility, strife
2 BATTLE, clash, combat, contest, encounter, fight, strife, war
▷ *verb* 3 BE INCOMPATIBLE, be at variance, clash, collide, differ, disagree, interfere

conflicting *adjective* INCOMPATIBLE, antagonistic, clashing, contradictory, contrary, discordant, inconsistent, opposing, paradoxical

conform *verb* 1 COMPLY, adapt, adjust, fall in with, follow, obey, toe the line
2 AGREE, accord, correspond, harmonize, match, suit, tally

conformist *noun* TRADITIONALIST, stick-in-the-mud (*informal*), yes man

conformity *noun* COMPLIANCE, conventionality, observance, orthodoxy, traditionalism

confound *verb* BEWILDER, astound, baffle, confuse, dumbfound, flummox, mystify, nonplus, perplex

confront *verb* FACE, accost, challenge, defy, encounter, oppose, stand up to, tackle

confrontation *noun* CONFLICT, contest, encounter, fight, head-to-head, showdown (*informal*)

confuse *verb* 1 MIX UP, disarrange, disorder, jumble, mingle, muddle, ravel
2 BEWILDER, baffle, bemuse, faze, flummox, mystify, nonplus, perplex, puzzle
3 DISCONCERT, discompose, disorient, fluster, rattle (*informal*), throw off balance, unnerve, upset

confused *adjective* 1 BEWILDERED, at sea, baffled, disorientated, flummoxed, muddled, nonplussed, perplexed, puzzled, taken aback
2 DISORDERED, chaotic, disorganized, in disarray, jumbled, mixed up, topsy-turvy, untidy

confusing *adjective* BEWILDERING, baffling, contradictory, disconcerting, misleading, perplexing, puzzling, unclear

confusion *noun* 1 BEWILDERMENT, disorientation, mystification, perplexity, puzzlement
2 DISORDER, chaos, commotion, jumble, mess, muddle, shambles, turmoil, untidiness, upheaval

congenial *adjective* 1 PLEASANT, affable, agreeable, companionable, favorable, friendly, genial, kindly
2 COMPATIBLE, kindred, like-minded, sympathetic, well-suited

congenital *adjective* INBORN, immanent, inbred, inherent, innate, natural

congested *adjective* 1 OVERCROWDED, crowded, teeming
2 CLOGGED, blocked-up, crammed, jammed, overfilled, overflowing, packed, stuffed

congestion *noun* 1 OVERCROWDING, crowding
2 CLOGGING, bottleneck, jam, surfeit

congratulate *verb* COMPLIMENT, pat on the back, wish joy to

congratulations *plural noun*
▷ *interjection* GOOD WISHES, best wishes, compliments, felicitations, greetings

> **con•gre•ga'tion** *noun* assembly, esp. for worship > **con•gre•ga'tion•al** *adjective* > **con•gre•ga'tion•al•ism** *noun* form of Protestant church organization in which local churches are self-governing

con•gress [KONG-gris] *noun* 1 meeting 2 sexual intercourse 3 formal assembly for discussion 4 legislative body > **con•gres•sion•al** [kən-GRESH-ə-nl] *adjective* > **con'gress•man** *noun* member of US House of Representatives

con•gru•ent [KONG-groo-ənt] *adjective* 1 suitable, accordant 2 fitting together, esp. triangles > **con'gru•ence** *noun* > **con•gru'i•ty** *noun* > **con'gru•ous** *adjective*

conic *see* **cone**

con•i•fer [KON-ə-fər] *noun* cone-bearing tree, as fir, pine, etc. > **co•nif•er•ous** [koh-NIF-ər-əs] *adjective*

con•jec•ture [kən-JEK-chər] *noun* 1 guess, guesswork ▷ *verb* **-tured, -tur•ing** 2 guess, surmise > **con•jec'tur•al** *adjective*

con•join•ed twins [kən-JOIND twinz] *plural noun the technical name for* **Siamese twins**

con•ju•gal [KON-jə-gəl] *adjective* 1 relating to marriage 2 between married persons > **con•ju•gal'i•ty** *noun*

con•ju•gate [KON-jə-gayt] *verb* **-gat•ed, -gat•ing** inflect verb in its various forms (past, present, etc.) > **con•ju•ga'tion** *noun*

con•junc•tion [kən-JUNGK-shən] *noun* 1 union 2 simultaneous happening 3 part of speech joining words, phrases, etc. > **con•junc'tive** *adjective*

con•junc•ti•va [kon-jungk-TĪ-və] *noun* mucous membrane lining eyelid > **con•junc•ti•vi•tis** [kən-jungk-tə-VĪ-tis] *noun* inflammation of this

con•jure [KON-jər] *verb* **-jured, -jur•ing** 1 produce magic effects 2 perform tricks by sleight of hand, etc. 3 invoke devils 4 [kən-JUUR] implore earnestly > **con•jur•a•tion** [kon-jə-RAY-shən] *noun* > **con'jur•er** *noun*

conk [kongk] *verb transitive* (*informal*) strike (esp. on head) > **conk out** *verb intransitive* (*informal*) 1 break down, stall 2 faint 3 fall asleep

con•nect [kə-NEKT] *verb* 1 join together, unite 2 associate in the mind > **con•nec'tion** *noun* 1 association 2 train, etc. timed to enable passengers to transfer from another 3 family relation 4 social, commercial, etc. relationship > **con•nec'tive** *adjective* > **con•nec•ti'vi•ty** *noun* 1 state of being or being able to be connected 2 state of being connected to the Internet 3 capacity of a machine to be connected to other machines > **connecting rod** part of engine that transfers motion from piston to crankshaft

con•ning tower [KON-ing] raised observation tower containing the periscope on a submarine

con•nive [kə-NĪV] *verb intransitive* **-nived, -niv•ing** 1 plot, conspire 2 assent, refrain from preventing or forbidding > **con•niv'ance** *noun*

con•nois•seur [kon-ə-SUR] *noun* 1 critical expert in matters of taste, esp. fine arts 2 competent judge

con•note [kə-NOHT] *verb transitive* **-not•ed, -not•ing** imply, mean in addition to primary meaning > **con•no•ta•tion** [kon-ə-TAY-shən] *noun*

con•nu•bi•al [kə-NOO-bee-əl] *adjective* of marriage

con•quer [KONG-kər] *verb transitive* 1 win by force of arms, overcome 2 defeat ▷ *verb intransitive* 3 be victorious > **con'quer•or** *noun* > **con•quest** [KON-kwest] *noun*

con•san•guin•i•ty [kon-sang-GWIN-i-tee] *noun* kinship > **con•san•guin'e•ous** *adjective*

con•science [KON-shəns] *noun* sense of right or wrong governing person's words and actions > **con•sci•en'tious** [-shee-EN-shəs] *adjective* 1 scrupulous 2 obedient to the dictates of

DICTIONARY

C

THESAURUS

congregate *verb* COME TOGETHER, assemble, collect, convene, converge, flock, gather, mass, meet

congregation *noun* ASSEMBLY, brethren, crowd, fellowship, flock, multitude, throng

congress *noun* MEETING, assembly, caucus, conclave, conference, convention, council, legislature, parliament

conjecture *noun* 1 GUESS, hypothesis, shot in the dark, speculation, supposition, surmise, theory
▷ *verb* 2 GUESS, hypothesize, imagine, speculate, suppose, surmise, theorize

conjugal *adjective* MARITAL, bridal, connubial, married, matrimonial, nuptial, wedded

conjure *verb* PERFORM TRICKS, juggle

conjurer *or* **conjuror** *noun* MAGICIAN, illusionist, sorcerer, wizard

conjure up *verb* BRING TO MIND, contrive, create, evoke, produce as if by magic, recall, recollect

connect *verb* LINK, affix, attach, couple, fasten, join, unite

connected *adjective* LINKED, affiliated, akin, allied, associated, combined, coupled, joined, related, united

connection *noun* 1 ASSOCIATION, affinity, bond, liaison, link, relationship, relevance, tie-in
2 LINK, alliance, association, attachment, coupling, fastening, junction, tie, union
3 CONTACT, acquaintance, ally, associate, friend, homeboy (*slang*), homegirl (*slang*), sponsor

connivance *noun* COLLUSION, abetting, complicity, conspiring, tacit consent

connive *verb* 1 CONSPIRE, collude, cook up (*informal*), intrigue, plot, scheme
2 ▷ **connive at** TURN A BLIND EYE TO, abet, disregard, let pass, look the other way, overlook, wink at

connoisseur *noun* EXPERT, aficionado, appreciator, authority, buff (*informal*), devotee, judge

conquer *verb* 1 DEFEAT, beat, crush, get the better of, master, overcome, overpower, overthrow, quell, subjugate, vanquish
2 SEIZE, acquire, annex, obtain, occupy, overrun, win

conqueror *noun* WINNER, conquistador, defeater, master, subjugator, vanquisher, victor

conquest *noun* 1 DEFEAT, mastery, overthrow, rout, triumph, victory
2 TAKEOVER, annexation, coup, invasion, occupation, subjugation

conscience *noun* PRINCIPLES, moral sense, scruples, sense of right and wrong, still small voice

conscientious *adjective* THOROUGH, careful,

conscience > **con•sci•en'tious•ly** *adverb* > **conscientious objector** one who refuses military service on moral or religious grounds

con•scious [KON-shəs] *adjective* 1 aware 2 awake to one's surroundings and identity 3 deliberate, intentional > **con'scious•ly** *adverb* > **con'scious•ness** *noun* being conscious

con•script [KON-skript] *noun* 1 one compulsorily enlisted for military service ▷ *verb transitive* [kən-SKRIPT] 2 enrol (someone) for compulsory military service > **con•scrip'tion** *noun*

con•se•crate [KON-si-krayt] *verb transitive* **-crat•ed, -crat•ing** make sacred > **con•se•cra'tion** *noun*

con•sec•u•tive [kən-SEK-yə-tiv] *adjective* in unbroken succession

con•sen•sus [kən-SEN-səs] *noun* widespread agreement, unanimity

con•sent [kən-SENT] *verb intransitive* 1 agree to, comply ▷ *noun* 2 acquiescence 3 permission 4 agreement

con•se•quence [KON-si-kwens] *noun* 1 result, effect, outcome 2 that which naturally follows 3 significance, importance > **con'se•quent** *adjective* > **con•se•quen'tial** *adjective* important > **con'se•quent•ly** *adverb* therefore, as a result

con•serv•a•to•ry [kən-SUR-və-tor-ee] *noun, plural* **-ries** 1 school for teaching music or painting, etc. 2 greenhouse

con•serve [kən-SURV] *verb transitive* **-served, -serv•ing** 1 keep from change or decay 2 preserve 3 maintain ▷ *noun* [KON-surv] 4 jam, preserved fruit, etc. > **con•ser•va•tion** [kon-sər-VAY-shən] *noun* protection, careful management of natural resources and environment > **con•ser•va'tion•ist** *noun, adjective* > **con•serv'a•tive** *adjective* 1 tending or wishing to conserve 2 moderate ▷ *noun* 3 *politics* one who desires to preserve institutions of country against change and innovation 4 one opposed to hasty changes or innovations > **con•serv'a•tism** *noun*

con•sid•er [kən-SID-ər] *verb transitive* 1 think over 2 examine 3 make allowance for 4 be of opinion that 5 discuss > **con•sid'er•a•ble** *adjective* 1 important 2 somewhat large > **con•sid'er•ate** [-it] *adjective* thoughtful for others' feelings, careful > **con•sid'er•ate•ly** *adverb* > **con•sid•er•a'tion** *noun* 1 deliberation 2 point of importance 3 thoughtfulness 4 bribe, recompense

con•sign [kən-SĪN] *verb transitive* 1 commit, hand over 2 entrust to carrier > **con•sign•ee** [kon-sī-NEE], **con•sign'or** *noun* > **con•sign'ment** *noun* goods consigned

con•sist [kən-SIST] *verb intransitive* 1 be composed of 2 (with *in*) have as basis 3 agree with, be compatible > **con•sist'en•cy** *noun* 1 agreement 2 harmony 3 degree of firmness > **con•sist'ent** *adjective* 1 unchanging, constant 2 agreeing (with)

---

diligent, exact, faithful, meticulous, painstaking, particular, punctilious

conscious *adjective* 1 AWARE, alert, alive to, awake, responsive, sensible, sentient
2 DELIBERATE, calculated, intentional, knowing, premeditated, self-conscious, studied, willful

consciousness *noun* AWARENESS, apprehension, knowledge, realization, recognition, sensibility

consecrate *verb* SANCTIFY, dedicate, devote, hallow, ordain, set apart, venerate

consecutive *adjective* SUCCESSIVE, in sequence, in turn, running, sequential, succeeding, uninterrupted

consensus *noun* AGREEMENT, assent, common consent, concord, general agreement, harmony, unanimity, unity

consent *noun* 1 AGREEMENT, acquiescence, approval, assent, compliance, go-ahead (*informal*), O.K. *or* okay (*informal*), permission, sanction
▷ *verb* 2 AGREE, acquiesce, allow, approve, assent, concur, permit

consequence *noun* 1 RESULT, effect, end result, issue, outcome, repercussion, sequel, upshot
2 IMPORTANCE, account, concern, import, moment, significance, value, weight

consequent *adjective* FOLLOWING, ensuing, resultant, resulting, subsequent, successive

consequently *adverb* AS A RESULT, accordingly, ergo, hence, subsequently, therefore, thus

conservation *noun* PROTECTION, guardianship, husbandry, maintenance, preservation, safeguarding, safekeeping, saving, upkeep

conservative *adjective* 1 TRADITIONAL, cautious, conventional, die-hard, hidebound, reactionary, sober
▷ *noun* 2 TRADITIONALIST, reactionary, stick-in-the-mud (*informal*)

conserve *verb* PROTECT, hoard, husband, keep, nurse, preserve, save, store up, take care of, use sparingly

consider *verb* 1 THINK, believe, deem, hold to be, judge, rate, regard as
2 THINK ABOUT, cogitate, contemplate, deliberate, meditate, ponder, reflect, ruminate, turn over in one's mind, weigh
3 BEAR IN MIND, keep in view, make allowance for, reckon with, remember, respect, take into account

considerable *adjective* LARGE, appreciable, goodly, great, marked, noticeable, plentiful, sizable *or* sizeable, substantial, supersize

considerably *adverb* GREATLY, appreciably, markedly, noticeably, remarkably, significantly, substantially, very much

considerate *adjective* THOUGHTFUL, attentive, concerned, kindly, mindful, obliging, patient, tactful, unselfish

consideration *noun* 1 THOUGHT, analysis, deliberation, discussion, examination, reflection, review, scrutiny
2 FACTOR, concern, issue, point
3 THOUGHTFULNESS, concern, considerateness, kindness, respect, tact
4 PAYMENT, fee, recompense, remuneration, reward, tip

considering *preposition* TAKING INTO ACCOUNT, in the light of, in view of

consignment *noun* SHIPMENT, batch, delivery, goods

consist *verb* 1 ▷ **consist of** BE MADE UP OF, amount to, be composed of, comprise, contain, embody, include, incorporate, involve
2 ▷ **consist in** LIE IN, be expressed by, be found

con•sis•to•ry [kən-SIS-tə-ree] *noun, plural* **-ries** ecclesiastical court or council, esp. of pope and cardinals

con•sole[1] [kən-SOHL] *verb transitive* **-soled, -sol•ing** comfort, cheer in distress > **con•so•la•tion** [kon-sə-LAY-shən] *noun*

con•sole[2] [KON-sohl] *noun* 1 bracket supporting shelf 2 keyboard, stops, etc., of organ 3 cabinet for TV, radio, etc.

con•sol•i•date [kən-SOL-i-dayt] *verb transitive* **-dat•ed, -dat•ing** 1 combine into connected whole 2 make firm, secure > **con•sol•i•da'tion** *noun*

con•som•mé [kon-sə-MAY] *noun* clear meat soup

con•so•nant [KON-sə-nənt] *noun* 1 sound making a syllable only with vowel 2 non-vowel ▷ *adjective* 3 agreeing with, in accord > **con'so•nance** *noun*

con•sort [kən-SORT] *verb intransitive* 1 associate, keep company with ▷ *noun* [KON-sort] 2 husband, wife, esp. of ruler 3 ship sailing with another > **con•sor'ti•um** [-SOR-shee-əm] *noun, plural* **-ti•a** [-shee-ə] *noun* association of banks, companies, etc.

con•spic•u•ous [kən-SPIK-yoo-əs] *adjective* 1 striking, noticeable, outstanding 2 prominent 3 eminent

con•spire [kən-SPĪR] *verb intransitive* **-spired, -spir•ing** 1 combine for evil purpose 2 plot, devise > **con•spir'a•cy** [-SPIR-ə-see] *noun, plural* **-cies** > **con•spir'a•tor** *noun* > **con•spir•a•to'ri•al** *adjective*

con•stant [KON-stənt] *adjective* 1 fixed, unchanging 2 steadfast 3 always duly happening or continuing ▷ *noun* 4 quantity that does not vary > **con'stan•cy** *noun* 1 steadfastness 2 loyalty

con•stel•la•tion [kon-stə-LAY-shən] *noun* group of stars

con•ster•na•tion [kon-stər-NAY-shən] *noun* alarm, dismay, panic > **con'ster•nate** *verb* **-nat•ed, -nat•ing**

con•sti•pa•tion [kon-stə-PAY-shən] *noun* difficulty in emptying bowels > **con'sti•pate** *verb transitive* **-pat•ed, -pat•ing** affect with this disorder

con•stit•u•ent [kən-STICH-oo-ənt] *adjective* 1 going toward making up whole 2 having power to make, alter constitution of a government ▷ *noun* 3 component part 4 element 5 voter > **con•stit'u•en•cy** *noun* body of constituents, supporters

con•sti•tute [KON-sti-toot] *verb transitive* **-tut•ed, -tut•ing** 1 compose, set up, establish, form 2 make into, found, give form to > **con•sti•tu'tion** *noun* 1 structure, composition 2 health 3 character, disposition 4 principles on which country, state is governed > **con•sti•tu'tion•al** *adjective* 1 pert. to constitution 2 in harmony with political constitution ▷ *noun* 3 walk taken for health's sake

con•strain [kən-STRAYN] *verb transitive* 1 force, compel > **con•straint'** *noun* 1 compulsion 2 restraint 3 embarrassment, tension

DICTIONARY

C

THESAURUS

in *or* be contained in, inhere in, reside in

consistency *noun* 1 TEXTURE, compactness, density, firmness, thickness, viscosity 2 CONSTANCY, evenness, regularity, steadfastness, steadiness, uniformity

consistent *adjective* 1 UNCHANGING, constant, dependable, persistent, regular, steady, true to type, undeviating 2 AGREEING, coherent, compatible, congruous, consonant, harmonious, logical

consolation *noun* COMFORT, cheer, encouragement, help, relief, solace, succor, support

console *verb* COMFORT, calm, cheer, encourage, express sympathy for, soothe

consolidate *verb* 1 STRENGTHEN, fortify, reinforce, secure, stabilize 2 COMBINE, amalgamate, federate, fuse, join, unite

consort *verb* 1 ASSOCIATE, fraternize, go around with, hang about with *or* hang around with hang out with, keep company, mix ▷ *noun* 2 SPOUSE, companion, husband, partner, wife

conspicuous *adjective* 1 OBVIOUS, blatant, clear, evident, noticeable, patent, salient 2 NOTEWORTHY, illustrious, notable, outstanding, prominent, remarkable, salient, signal, striking

conspiracy *noun* PLOT, collusion, intrigue, machination, scheme, treason

conspirator *noun* PLOTTER, conspirer, intriguer, schemer, traitor

conspire *verb* 1 PLOT, contrive, intrigue, machinate, maneuver, plan, scheme 2 WORK TOGETHER, combine, concur, contribute, cooperate, tend

constant *adjective* 1 CONTINUOUS, ceaseless, incessant, interminable, nonstop, perpetual, sustained, twenty-four-seven (*slang*), unrelenting 2 UNCHANGING, even, fixed, invariable, permanent, stable, steady, uniform, unvarying 3 FAITHFUL, devoted, loyal, stalwart, staunch, true, trustworthy, trusty

constantly *adverb* CONTINUOUSLY, all the time, always, continually, endlessly, incessantly, interminably, invariably, nonstop, perpetually, twenty-four-seven (*slang*)

consternation *noun* DISMAY, alarm, anxiety, distress, dread, fear, trepidation

constituent *noun* 1 VOTER, elector 2 COMPONENT, element, factor, ingredient, part, unit ▷ *adjective* 3 COMPONENT, basic, elemental, essential, integral

constitute *verb* MAKE UP, compose, comprise, establish, form, found, set up

constitution *noun* 1 HEALTH, build, character, disposition, physique 2 STRUCTURE, composition, form, make-up, nature

constitutional *adjective* 1 STATUTORY, chartered, vested ▷ *noun* 2 WALK, airing, stroll, turn

constrain *verb* 1 FORCE, bind, coerce, compel, impel, necessitate, oblige, pressurize 2 RESTRICT, check, confine, constrict, curb, restrain, straiten

constraint *noun* 1 RESTRICTION, check, curb,

con•stric•tion [kən-STRIK-shən] *noun* compression, squeezing together > **con•strict'** *verb transitive* > **con•stric'tive** *adjective* > **con•stric'tor** *noun* 1 that which constricts 2 *see also* **boa**
con•struct [kən-STRUKT] *verb transitive* 1 make, build, form 2 put together 3 compose > **con•struct** [KON-strukt] *noun* > **con•struc'tion** *noun* > **con•struc'tive** *adjective* 1 serving to improve 2 positive
con•strue [kən-STROO] *verb transitive* **-strued, -stru•ing** 1 interpret 2 deduce 3 analyze grammatically
con•sul [KON-səl] *noun* 1 official appointed by a government to represent it in a foreign country 2 in ancient Rome, one of the chief magistrates > **con'su•lar** *adjective* > **con'su•late** [-lit] *noun*
con•sult [kən-SULT] *verb* seek counsel, advice, information from > **con•sult'ant** *noun* specialist, expert > **con•sul•ta•tion** [kon-səl-TAY-shən] *noun* 1 consulting 2 appointment to seek professional advice, esp. of doctor, lawyer > **con•sul•ta•tive** [kən-SUL-tə-tiv] *adjective* 1 having privilege of consulting, but not of voting 2 advisory
con•sume [kən-SOOM] *verb transitive* **-sumed, -sum•ing** 1 eat or drink 2 engross, possess 3 use up 4 destroy > **con•sum'er** *noun* 1 buyer or user of commodity 2 one who consumes > **con•sump'tion** [-SUMP-shən] *noun* 1 using up 2 destruction 3 (*old-fashioned*) pulmonary tuberculosis > **con•sump'tive** *adjective, noun*
con•sum•mate [KON-sə-mayt] *verb transitive* **-mat•ed, -mat•ing** 1 perfect 2 fulfill 3 complete (esp. marriage by sexual intercourse) ▷ *adjective* [kən-SUM-it] 4 of greatest perfection or completeness > **con•sum'mate•ly** *adverb* > **con•sum•ma'tion** *noun*
con•tact [KON-takt] *noun* 1 touching 2 being in touch 3 junction of two or more electrical conductors 4 useful acquaintance ▷ *verb transitive* > **contact lens** lens fitting over eyeball to correct defect of vision
con•ta•gion [kən-TAY-jən] *noun* 1 passing on of disease by touch, contact 2 contagious disease 3 harmful physical or moral influence > **con•ta'gious** *adjective* communicable by contact, catching
con•tain [kən-TAYN] *verb transitive* 1 hold 2 have room for 3 include, comprise 4 restrain (oneself) > **con•tain'er** *noun* 1 box, etc. for holding 2 large cargo-carrying standard-sized receptacle for various modes of transport
con•tam•i•nate [kən-TAM-ə-nayt] *verb transitive* **-nat•ed, -nat•ing** 1 stain, pollute, infect 2 make radioactive > **con•tam•i•na'tion** *noun* pollution
con•tem•plate [KON-təm-playt] *verb transitive* **-plat•ed, -plat•ing** 1 reflect, meditate on 2 gaze upon 3 intend > **con•tem•pla'tion** *noun* 1 thoughtful consideration 2 spiritual meditation > **con•tem•pla•tive** [kən-TEM-plə-tiv] *adjective, noun*
con•tem•po•rar•y [kən-TEM-pə-rer-ee] *adjective* 1 existing or lasting at same time 2 of same age 3 modern ▷ *noun, plural* **-rar•ies** 4 one

deterrent, hindrance, limitation, rein
2 FORCE, coercion, compulsion, necessity, pressure, restraint
construct *verb* BUILD, assemble, compose, create, fashion, form, make, manufacture, put together, shape
construction *noun* 1 BUILDING, composition, creation, edifice
2 INTERPRETATION, explanation, inference, reading, rendering
constructive *adjective* HELPFUL, positive, practical, productive, useful, valuable
consult *verb* ASK, compare notes, confer, pick (someone's) brains, question, refer to, take counsel, turn to
consultant *noun* SPECIALIST, adviser, authority
consultation *noun* SEMINAR, appointment, conference, council, deliberation, dialogue, discussion, examination, hearing, interview, meeting, session
consume *verb* 1 EAT, chow down (*slang*), devour, eat up, gobble *or* gobble up, put away, swallow
2 USE UP, absorb, dissipate, exhaust, expend, spend, squander, waste
3 DESTROY, annihilate, demolish, devastate, lay waste, ravage
4 (*often passive*) OBSESS, absorb, dominate, eat up, engross, monopolize, preoccupy
consumer *noun* BUYER, customer, purchaser, shopper, user
consummate *verb* 1 COMPLETE, accomplish, conclude, crown, end, finish, fulfill
▷ *adjective* 2 SKILLED, accomplished, matchless, perfect, polished, practiced, superb, supreme
3 COMPLETE, absolute, conspicuous, extreme, supreme, total, utter
consumption *noun* 1 USING UP, depletion, diminution, dissipation, exhaustion, expenditure, loss, waste
2 (*old-fashioned*) TUBERCULOSIS, T.B.
contact *noun* 1 COMMUNICATION, association, connection
2 TOUCH, contiguity
3 ACQUAINTANCE, connection
▷ *verb* 4 GET IN TOUCH WITH *or* BE IN TOUCH WITH, approach, call, communicate with, reach, speak to, write to
contagious *adjective* INFECTIOUS, catching, communicable, spreading, transmissible
contain *verb* 1 HOLD, accommodate, enclose, have capacity for, incorporate, seat
2 INCLUDE, comprehend, comprise, consist of, embody, embrace, involve
3 RESTRAIN, control, curb, hold back, hold in, keep a tight rein on, repress, stifle
container *noun* HOLDER, receptacle, repository, vessel
contaminate *verb* POLLUTE, adulterate, befoul, corrupt, defile, infect, stain, taint, tarnish
contamination *noun* POLLUTION, contagion, corruption, defilement, impurity, infection, poisoning, taint
contemplate *verb* 1 THINK ABOUT, consider, deliberate, meditate, muse over, ponder, reflect upon, ruminate *or* ruminate upon
2 CONSIDER, envisage, expect, foresee, intend, plan, think of
3 LOOK AT, examine, eye up, gaze at, inspect, regard, stare at, study, survey, view
contemporary *adjective* 1 COEXISTING,

existing at same time as another
> **con•tem•po•ra'ne•ous** [-RAY-nee-əs] *adjective*
con•tempt [kən-TEMPT] *noun* 1 feeling that something is worthless, despicable, etc. 2 expression of this feeling 3 state of being despised, disregarded 4 willful disrespect of authority
con•tend [kən-TEND] *verb intransitive* 1 strive, fight 2 dispute ▷ *verb transitive* 3 maintain (that) > **con•ten'tion** *noun* 1 strife 2 debate 3 subject matter of dispute > **con•ten'tious** *adjective* 1 quarrelsome 2 causing dispute
con•tent[1] [KON-tent] *noun* 1 that contained 2 holding capacity > **con•tents** 1 that contained 2 index of topics in book
con•tent[2] [kən-TENT] *adjective* 1 satisfied 2 willing (to) ▷ *verb transitive* 3 satisfy ▷ *noun* 4 satisfaction > **con•tent'ed** *adjective*
con•ter•mi•nous [kən-TUR-mə-nəs] *adjective* 1 of the same extent (in time, etc.) 2 meeting along a common boundary 3 meeting end to end
con•test [KON-test] *noun* 1 competition 2 conflict ▷ *verb transitive* [kən-TEST] 3 dispute, debate 4 fight or compete for > **con•test'a•ble** *adjective* > **con•test'ant** *noun*
con•text [KON-tekst] *noun* 1 words coming before, after a word or passage 2 conditions and circumstances of event, fact, etc.
> **con•tex•tu•al** [kən-TEKS-choo-əl] *adjective*
con•tig•u•ous [kən-TIG-yoo-əs] *adjective* touching, near > **con•ti•gu'i•ty** *noun*
con•ti•nent[1] [KON-tə-nənt] *noun* large continuous mass of land > **con•ti•nen'tal** *adjective*
continent[2] *adjective* 1 able to control one's urination and defecation 2 sexually chaste > **con'ti•nence** *noun*
con•tin•gent [kən-TIN-jənt] *adjective* 1 depending (on) 2 possible 3 accidental ▷ *noun* 4 group (of troops, supporters, etc.) 5 part of or representative of a larger group > **con•tin'gen•cy** *noun*
con•tin•ue [kən-TIN-yoo] *verb* **-ued, -u•ing** 1 remain, keep in existence 2 carry on, last, go on 3 resume 4 prolong > **con•tin'u•al** *adjective* > **con•tin•u•a'tion** *noun* 1 extension, extra part 2 resumption 3 constant succession, prolongation > **con•ti•nu'i•ty** *noun* 1 logical sequence 2 state of being continuous > **con•tin'u•ous** *adjective*
con•tort [kən-TORT] *verb transitive* twist out of normal shape > **con•tor'tion** *noun* > **con•tor'tion•ist** *noun* one who contorts own body to entertain
con•tour [KON-tuur] *noun* 1 outline, shape, esp. of mountains, coast, etc. 2 (*also* **contour line**) line on map drawn through places of

DICTIONARY

C

THESAURUS

concurrent, contemporaneous
2 MODERN, à la mode, current, newfangled, present, present-day, recent, up-to-date
▷ *noun* 3 PEER, fellow
contempt *noun* SCORN, derision, disdain, disregard, disrespect, mockery, neglect, slight
contemptible *adjective* DESPICABLE, detestable, ignominious, lousy (*slang*), measly, paltry, pitiful, scuzzy (*slang*), shameful, worthless
contemptuous *adjective* SCORNFUL, arrogant, condescending, derisive, disdainful, haughty, sneering, supercilious, withering
contend *verb* 1 COMPETE, clash, contest, fight, jostle, strive, struggle, vie
2 ARGUE, affirm, allege, assert, dispute, hold, maintain
content[1] *noun* 1 MEANING, essence, gist, significance, substance
2 AMOUNT, capacity, load, measure, size, volume
content[2] *adjective* 1 SATISFIED, agreeable, at ease, comfortable, contented, fulfilled, willing to accept
▷ *verb* 2 SATISFY, appease, humor, indulge, mollify, placate, please
▷ *noun* 3 SATISFACTION, comfort, contentment, ease, gratification, peace of mind, pleasure
contented *adjective* SATISFIED, comfortable, content, glad, gratified, happy, pleased, serene, thankful
contentious *adjective* ARGUMENTATIVE, bickering, captious, cavilling, disputatious, quarrelsome, querulous, wrangling
contentment *noun* SATISFACTION, comfort, content, ease, equanimity, fulfillment, happiness, peace, pleasure, serenity
contents *plural noun* CONSTITUENTS, elements, ingredients, load
contest *noun* 1 COMPETITION, game, match, tournament, trial
2 STRUGGLE, battle, combat, conflict, controversy, dispute, fight
▷ *verb* 3 DISPUTE, argue, call in question *or* call into question, challenge, debate, doubt, object to, oppose, question
4 COMPETE, contend, fight, strive, vie
contestant *noun* COMPETITOR, candidate, contender, entrant, participant, player
context *noun* 1 CIRCUMSTANCES, ambience, conditions, situation
2 FRAME OF REFERENCE, background, connection, framework, relation
contingency *noun* POSSIBILITY, accident, chance, emergency, event, eventuality, happening, incident
continual *adjective* CONSTANT, frequent, incessant, interminable, recurrent, regular, repeated, twenty-four-seven (*slang*), unremitting
continually *adverb* CONSTANTLY, all the time, always, forever, incessantly, interminably, nonstop, persistently, repeatedly, twenty-four-seven (*slang*)
continuation *noun* 1 CONTINUING, perpetuation, prolongation, resumption
2 ADDITION, extension, furtherance, postscript, sequel, supplement
continue *verb* 1 REMAIN, abide, carry on, endure, last, live on, persist, stay, survive
2 KEEP ON, carry on, go on, maintain, persevere, persist in, stick at, sustain
3 RESUME, carry on, pick up where one left off, proceed, recommence, return to, take up
continuing *adjective* LASTING, enduring, in progress, ongoing, sustained
continuity *noun* SEQUENCE, cohesion, connection, flow, progression, succession
continuous *adjective* CONSTANT, extended, prolonged, twenty-four-seven (*slang*), unbroken, unceasing, undivided, uninterrupted

same height
con·tra- *prefix* against or contrasting: *contradistinction; contrapuntal*
con·tra·band [KON-trə-band] *noun* 1 smuggled goods 2 illegal traffic in such goods ▷ *adjective* 3 prohibited by law
con·tra·cep·tion [kon-trə-SEP-shən] *noun* prevention of conception usu. by artificial means, birth control > **con·tra·cep'tive** *adjective, noun*
con·tract [kən-TRAKT] *verb* 1 make or become smaller, shorter 2 enter into agreement 3 agree upon ▷ *verb transitive* 4 incur, become affected by ▷ *noun* [KON-trakt] bargain, agreement 5 formal document recording agreement 6 agreement enforceable by law > **con·tract'ed** *adjective* drawn together > **con·trac·tile** [kən-TRAK-tl] *adjective* tending to contract > **con·trac'tion** *noun* > **con'trac·tor** *noun* one making contract, esp. builder > **con·trac'tu·al** [-choo-əl] *adjective*
con·tra·dict [kon-trə-DIKT] *verb transitive* 1 deny 2 be at variance or inconsistent with > **con·tra·dic'tion** *noun* > **con·tra·dic'to·ry** *adjective*
con·tral·to [kən-TRAL-toh] *noun, plural* **-tos** lowest of female voices
con·trap·tion [kən-TRAP-shən] *noun* 1 gadget 2 device 3 construction, device often overelaborate or eccentric
con·tra·pun·tal [kon-trə-PUN-tl] *adjective mus.* pert. to counterpoint
con·trar·y [KON-trer-ee] *adjective* 1 opposed 2 opposite, other 3 [kən-TRAIR-ee] perverse, obstinate ▷ *noun* 4 something the exact opposite of another ▷ *adverb* 5 in opposition > **con'trar·i·ness** *noun*
con·trast [kən-TRAST] *verb transitive* 1 bring out differences 2 set in opposition for comparison ▷ *verb intransitive* 3 show great difference ▷ *noun* [KON-trast] 4 striking difference 5 *tv* sharpness of image
con·tra·vene [kon-trə-VEEN] *verb transitive* **-vened, -ven·ing** 1 transgress, infringe 2 conflict with 3 contradict > **con·tra·ven'tion** *noun*
con·tre·temps [KON-trə-tahn] *noun* unexpected and embarrassing event or mishap
con·trib·ute [kən-TRIB-yoot] *verb* **-ut·ed, -ut·ing** 1 give, pay to common fund 2 help to occur 3 write for the press > **con·tri·bu·tion** [kon-trə-BYOO-shən] *noun* > **con·trib'u·tive** *adjective* > **con·trib'u·tor** *noun* 1 one who writes articles for newspapers, etc. 2 one who donates > **con·trib'u·to·ry** *adjective* 1 partly responsible 2 giving to pension fund, etc.
con·trite [kən-TRĪT] *adjective* remorseful for wrongdoing, penitent > **con·trite'ly** *adverb* > **con·tri'tion** [-TRISH-ən] *noun*
con·trive [kən-TRĪV] *verb transitive* **-trived, -triv·ing** 1 manage 2 devise, invent, design > **con·triv'ance** *noun* artifice or device > **con·trived'** *adjective* obviously planned, artificial
con·trol [kən-TROHL] *verb transitive* **-trolled, -trol·ling** 1 command, dominate 2 regulate 3

DICTIONARY • THESAURUS

contraband *noun* 1 SMUGGLING, black-marketing, bootlegging, trafficking ▷ *adjective* 2 SMUGGLED, banned, bootleg, forbidden, hot (*informal*), illegal, illicit, prohibited, unlawful
contract *noun* 1 AGREEMENT, arrangement, bargain, commitment, covenant, pact, settlement ▷ *verb* 2 AGREE, bargain, come to terms, commit oneself, covenant, negotiate, pledge 3 SHORTEN, abbreviate, curtail, diminish, dwindle, lessen, narrow, reduce, shrink, shrivel 4 CATCH, acquire, be afflicted with, develop, get, go down with, incur
contraction *noun* SHORTENING, abbreviation, compression, narrowing, reduction, shrinkage, shriveling, tightening
contradict *verb* DENY, be at variance with, belie, challenge, controvert, fly in the face of, negate, rebut
contradiction *noun* DENIAL, conflict, contravention, incongruity, inconsistency, negation, opposite
contradictory *adjective* INCONSISTENT, conflicting, contrary, incompatible, opposed, opposite, paradoxical
contraption *noun* (*informal*) DEVICE, apparatus, contrivance, gadget, instrument, mechanism
contrary *noun* 1 OPPOSITE, antithesis, converse, reverse ▷ *adjective* 2 OPPOSED, adverse, clashing, contradictory, counter, discordant, hostile, inconsistent, opposite, paradoxical 3 PERVERSE, awkward, cantankerous, difficult, disobliging, intractable, obstinate, unaccommodating
contrast *noun* 1 DIFFERENCE, comparison, disparity, dissimilarity, distinction, divergence, foil, opposition ▷ *verb* 2 DIFFERENTIATE, compare, differ, distinguish, oppose, set in opposition, set off
contribute *verb* 1 GIVE, add, bestow, chip in (*informal*), donate, provide, subscribe, supply 2 ▷ **contribute to** BE PARTLY RESPONSIBLE FOR, be conducive to, be instrumental in, help, lead to, tend to
contribution *noun* GIFT, addition, donation, grant, input, offering, subscription
contributor *noun* GIVER, donor, patron, subscriber, supporter
contrite *adjective* SORRY, chastened, conscience-stricken, humble, penitent, regretful, remorseful, repentant, sorrowful
contrivance *noun* 1 DEVICE, apparatus, appliance, contraption, gadget, implement, instrument, invention, machine, mechanism 2 PLAN, intrigue, machination, plot, ruse, scheme, stratagem, trick
contrive *verb* 1 BRING ABOUT, arrange, effect, manage, maneuver, plan, plot, scheme, succeed 2 DEVISE, concoct, construct, create, design, fabricate, improvise, invent, manufacture
contrived *adjective* FORCED, artificial, elaborate, labored, overdone, planned, strained, unnatural
control *noun* 1 POWER, authority, charge, command, guidance, management, oversight, supervision, supremacy 2 RESTRAINT, brake, check, curb, limitation, regulation ▷ *verb* 3 HAVE POWER OVER, administer,

direct, check, test ▷ *noun* 4 power to direct or determine 5 curb, check 6 standard of comparison in experiment > **con•trols** system of instruments to control automobile, aircraft, etc. > **con•trol'la•ble** *adjective* > **con•trol'ler** *noun* 1 one who controls 2 official controlling expenditure > **control tower** tower in airport from which takeoffs and landings are directed

con•tro•ver•sy [KON-trə-vur-see] *noun, plural* **-sies** dispute, debate, esp. over public issues > **con•tro•ver'sial** *adjective* > **con'tro•vert** *verb transitive* 1 deny 2 argue > **con•tro•vert'i•ble** *adjective*

con•tu•ma•cy [KON-tuu-mə-see] *noun, plural* **-cies** stubborn disobedience > **con•tu•ma'cious** [-MAY-shəs] *adjective*

con•tu•me•ly [kon-TUU-mə-lee] *noun, plural* **-lies** insulting language or treatment > **con•tu•me'li•ous** [-MEE-lee-əs] *adjective* abusive, insolent

con•tu•sion [kən-TOO-zhən] *noun* bruise

co•nun•drum [kə-NUN-drəm] *noun* riddle, esp. with punning answer

con•ur•ba•tion [kon-ər-BAY-shən] *noun* densely populated urban sprawl formed by spreading of towns

con•va•lesce [kon-və-LES] *verb intransitive* **-lesced, -lesc•ing** recover health after illness, operation, etc. > **con•va•les'cence** *noun* > **con•va•les'cent** *adjective, noun*

con•vec•tion [kən-VEK-shən] *noun* transmission, esp. of heat, by currents in liquids or gases > **con•vec'tor** *noun* > **con•vec'tive** *adjective*

con•vene [kən-VEEN] *verb transitive* **-vened, -ven•ing** call together, assemble, convoke > **con•ven'tion** *noun* 1 assembly 2 treaty, agreement 3 rule 4 practice based on agreement 5 accepted usage > **con•ven'tion•al** *adjective* 1 (slavishly) observing customs of society 2 customary 3 (of weapons, war, etc.) not nuclear

con•ven•ient [kən-VEEN-yənt] *adjective* 1 handy 2 favorable to needs, comfort 3 well adapted to one's purpose > **con•ven'ience** *noun* 1 ease, comfort, suitability ▷ *adjective* 2 (of food) quick to prepare

con•vent [KON-vent] *noun* 1 religious community, esp. of nuns 2 their building

con•verge [kən-VURJ] *verb intransitive* **-verged, -verg•ing** approach, tend to meet > **con•ver'gence, con•ver'gen•cy** *noun* > **con•ver'gent** *adjective*

con•ver•sant [kən-VUR-sənt] *adjective* acquainted, familiar (with), versed in

conversation *see* **converse**[1]

con•verse[1] [kən-VURS] *verb intransitive* **-versed, -vers•ing** talk (with) > **con•ver•sa'tion** *noun* > **con•ver•sa'tion•al** *adjective*

con•verse[2] [KON-vurs] *adjective* 1 opposite, turned around, reversed ▷ *noun* 2 the opposite, contrary

con•vert [kən-VURT] *verb transitive* 1 apply to another purpose 2 change 3 transform 4 cause to adopt (another) religion, opinion 5 *football* make a conversion ▷ *noun* [KON-vurt] 6 converted person > **con•ver'sion** [-zhən] *noun* 1 change of state 2 unauthorized appropriation 3 change of opinion, religion, or party 4 *football* extra point scored after a touchdown > **con•vert'er** *noun* 1 one who, that which converts 2 electrical device for changing alternating current into direct current 3 vessel in which molten metal is refined

DICTIONARY

C

THESAURUS

command, direct, govern, handle, have charge of, manage, manipulate, supervise
4 RESTRAIN, check, constrain, contain, curb, hold back, limit, repress, subdue

controls *plural noun* INSTRUMENTS, console, control panel, dash, dashboard, dials

controversial *adjective* DISPUTED, at issue, contentious, debatable, disputable, open to question, under discussion

controversy *noun* ARGUMENT, altercation, debate, dispute, quarrel, row, squabble, wrangling

convalescence *noun* RECOVERY, improvement, recuperation, rehabilitation, return to health

convalescent *adjective* RECOVERING, getting better, improving, mending, on the mend, recuperating

convene *verb* GATHER, assemble, bring together, call, come together, congregate, convoke, meet, summon

convenience *noun* 1 AVAILABILITY, accessibility, advantage, appropriateness, benefit, fitness, suitability, usefulness, utility
2 APPLIANCE, amenity, comfort, facility, help, labor-saving device

convenient *adjective* 1 USEFUL, appropriate, fit, handy, helpful, labor-saving, serviceable, suitable, timely
2 NEARBY, accessible, at hand, available, close at hand, handy, just round the corner, within reach

convention *noun* 1 CUSTOM, code, etiquette, practice, propriety, protocol, tradition, usage
2 AGREEMENT, bargain, contract, pact, protocol, treaty
3 ASSEMBLY, conference, congress, convocation, council, meeting

conventional *adjective* 1 ORDINARY, accepted, customary, normal, orthodox, regular, standard, traditional, usual
2 UNORIGINAL, banal, hackneyed, prosaic, routine, stereotyped

converge *verb* COME TOGETHER, coincide, combine, gather, join, meet, merge

conversation *noun* TALK, chat, conference, dialogue, discourse, discussion, gossip, tête-à-tête

converse[1] *verb* TALK, chat, chew the fat (*slang*), commune, confer, discourse, exchange views

converse[2] *noun* 1 OPPOSITE, antithesis, contrary, obverse, other side of the coin, reverse ▷ *adjective* 2 OPPOSITE, contrary, counter, reverse, reversed, transposed

conversion *noun* 1 CHANGE, metamorphosis, transformation
2 ADAPTATION, alteration, modification, reconstruction, remodeling, reorganization

convert *verb* 1 CHANGE, alter, transform, transpose, turn
2 ADAPT, apply, customize, modify, remodel, reorganize, restyle, revise
3 REFORM, convince, proselytize

> **con•vert'i•ble** *noun* car with folding roof ▷ *adjective*

con•vex [kon-VEKS] *adjective* **1** curved outward **2** of a rounded form > **con•vex'i•ty** *noun*

con•vey [kən-VAY] *verb transitive* **1** carry, transport **2** impart, communicate **3** *law* make over, transfer > **con•vey'ance** *noun* **1** carrying **2** vehicle **3** act by which title to property is transferred > **con•vey'or belt** continuous moving belt for transporting things, esp. in factory

con•vict [kən-VIKT] *verb transitive* **1** prove or declare guilty ▷ *noun* [KON-vikt] **2** person found guilty of crime **3** criminal serving prison sentence > **con•vic'tion** *noun* **1** verdict of guilty **2** being convinced, firm belief, state of being sure

con•vince [kən-VINS] *verb transitive* **-vinced, -vinc•ing** firmly persuade, satisfy by evidence or argument > **con•vinc'ing** *adjective* capable of compelling belief, effective

con•viv•i•al [kən-VIV-ee-əl] *adjective* sociable, festive, jovial > **con•viv•i•al'i•ty** *noun*

con•voke [kən-VOHK] *verb transitive* **-voked, -vok•ing** call together > **con•vo•ca•tion** [kon-və-KAY-shən] *noun* calling together, assembly, esp. of clergy, college faculty, etc.

con•vo•lute [KON-və-loot] *verb transitive* **-lut•ed, -lut•ing** twist, coil, tangle > **con'vo•lut•ed** *adjective* > **con•vo•lu'tion** *noun*

con•voy [KON-voi] *noun* **1** party (of ships, troops, trucks, etc.) traveling together for protection ▷ *verb transitive* **2** escort for protection

con•vulse [kən-VULS] *verb transitive* **-vulsed, -vuls•ing** **1** shake violently **2** affect with violent involuntary contractions of muscles > **con•vul'sion** *noun* violent upheaval > **con•vul'sions** **1** spasms **2** fits of laughter or hysteria > **con•vul'sive** *adjective*

coo [koo] *noun* cry of doves ▷ *verb intransitive* **cooed, coo•ing** make such cry

cook [kuuk] *verb transitive* **1** prepare (food) for table, esp. by heat **2** (*informal*) falsify (accounts, etc.) ▷ *verb intransitive* **3** undergo cooking **4** act as cook ▷ *noun* **5** one who prepares food for table > **cook'er** *noun* cooking apparatus > **cook'ie** *noun* small cake made from sweet dough > **cook'out** *noun* (party featuring) meal cooked and served outdoors > **cook up** (*informal*) **1** invent, plan **2** prepare (meal)

cool [kool] *adjective* **1** moderately cold **2** unexcited, calm **3** lacking friendliness or interest **4** (*informal*) calmly insolent **5** (*informal*) sophisticated, elegant ▷ *verb* **6** make, become cool ▷ *noun* **7** cool time, place, etc. **8** (*informal*) calmness, composure > **cool'ant** *noun* fluid used for cooling tool, machinery, etc. > **cool'er** *noun* **1** vessel in which liquids are cooled **2** iced drink usu. with wine or whiskey base **3** (*slang*) jail **cool one's heels** be kept waiting, esp. because of deliberate discourtesy

coon [koon] *noun* raccoon

coop [koop] *noun* **1** cage or pen for pigeons, etc. ▷ *verb transitive* **2** shut up in a coop **3** confine

co-op [KOH-op] *noun* **1** cooperative enterprise **2** apartment or business run by one

coop•er [KOO-pər] *noun* one who makes casks

co•op•er•ate [koh-OP-ə-rayt] *verb intransitive* **-at•ed, -at•ing** work together > **co•op•er•a'tion** *noun* > **co•op'er•a•tive** *adjective* **1** willing to cooperate **2** (of an enterprise) owned collectively and managed for joint economic benefit ▷ *noun* **3** cooperative organization

co•opt [koh-OPT] *verb transitive* **1** preempt, appropriate as one's own **2** elect by votes of existing members

co•or•di•nate [koh-OR-dn-ayt] *verb transitive* **-nat•ed, -nat•ing** **1** bring into order as parts of whole **2** place in same rank **3** put into harmony ▷ *noun* [-it] **4** *math.* any of set of numbers defining location of point ▷ *adjective* **5** equal in degree, status, etc. > **co•or•di•na'tion** *noun*

coot [koot] *noun* **1** small black water fowl **2** (*informal*) silly (old) person

▷ *noun* **4** NEOPHYTE, disciple, proselyte

convex *adjective* ROUNDED, bulging, gibbous, protuberant

convey *verb* **1** COMMUNICATE, disclose, impart, make known, relate, reveal, tell
2 CARRY, bear, bring, conduct, fetch, guide, move, send, transport

convict *verb* **1** FIND GUILTY, condemn, imprison, pronounce guilty, sentence
▷ *noun* **2** PRISONER, criminal, culprit, felon, jailbird, lag (*slang*), perp (*informal*)

conviction *noun* **1** BELIEF, creed, faith, opinion, persuasion, principle, tenet, view
2 CONFIDENCE, assurance, certainty, certitude, firmness, reliance

convince *verb* PERSUADE, assure, bring round, prevail upon, satisfy, sway, win over

convincing *adjective* PERSUASIVE, cogent, conclusive, credible, impressive, plausible, powerful, telling

convulse *verb* SHAKE, agitate, churn up, derange, disorder, disturb, twist, work

convulsion *noun* SPASM, contraction, cramp, fit, paroxysm, seizure

cool *adjective* **1** COLD, chilled, chilly, nippy, refreshing
2 CALM, collected, composed, relaxed, sedate, self-controlled, self-possessed, unemotional, unruffled
3 UNFRIENDLY, aloof, distant, indifferent, lukewarm, offhand, standoffish, unenthusiastic, unwelcoming
4 (*informal*) FASHIONABLE, hip, phat (*slang*), trendy (*informal*)
▷ *verb* **5** CHILL, cool off, freeze, lose heat, refrigerate
▷ *noun* **6** (*slang*) CALMNESS, composure, control, poise, self-control, self-discipline, self-possession, temper

cooperate *verb* WORK TOGETHER, collaborate, combine, conspire, coordinate, join forces, pool resources, pull together

cooperation *noun* TEAMWORK, collaboration, combined effort, esprit de corps, give-and-take, unity

cooperative *adjective* **1** HELPFUL, accommodating, obliging, onside (*informal*), responsive, supportive
2 SHARED, collective, combined, joint

coordinate *verb* BRING TOGETHER, harmonize, integrate, match, organize, synchronize, systematize

cop [kop] *verb transitive* **copped, cop•ping** (*slang*) 1 catch ▷ *noun* 2 (*informal*) policeman **cop a plea** (*slang*) plead guilty in return for light sentence
cope [kohp] *verb intransitive* **coped, cop•ing** deal successfully (with)
Co•per•ni•can [koh-PUR-ni-kən] *adjective* pert. to Copernicus, Polish astronomer (1473—1543), or to his system
cop•ing [KOH-ping] *noun* top course of wall, usu. sloping to throw off rain
co•pi•ous [KOH-pee-əs] *adjective* 1 abundant 2 plentiful 3 full, ample
cop•per[1] [KOP-ər] *noun* 1 reddish-brown malleable ductile metal 2 bronze money, coin ▷ *verb transitive* 3 cover with copper > **copper beech** tree with reddish leaves > **cop'per•plate** [-playt] *noun* 1 plate of copper for engraving, etching 2 print from this 3 copybook writing 4 first-class handwriting
copper[2] *noun* (*slang*) policeman
co•pra [KOH-prə] *noun* dried coconut kernels
copse [kops] *noun* a wood of small trees
cop•u•la [KOP-yə-lə] *noun, plural* **-las** 1 word, esp. verb acting as connecting link in sentence 2 connection, tie
cop•u•late [KOP-yə-layt] *verb intransitive* **-lat•ed, -lat•ing** unite sexually > **cop•u•la'tion** *noun*
cop•y [KOP-ee] *noun, plural* **cop•ies** 1 imitation 2 single specimen of book 3 matter for printing ▷ *verb transitive* **cop•ied, cop•y•ing** 4 make copy of 5 imitate 6 transcribe 7 follow an example > **cop'y•right** *noun* 1 legal exclusive right to print and publish book, article, work of art, etc. ▷ *verb transitive* 2 protect by copyright > **cop'y•writ•er** *noun* one who writes advertisements
co•quette [koh-KET] *noun* woman who flirts > **co•quet•ry** [KOH-ki-tree] *noun* > **co•quet'tish** *adjective*
Cor. Corinthians
cor•al [KOR-əl] *noun* 1 hard substance made by sea polyps and forming growths, islands, reefs 2 ornament of coral ▷ *adjective* 3 made of coral 4 of deep pink color
cord [kord] *noun* 1 thin rope or thick string 2 rib on cloth 3 ribbed fabric ▷ *verb transitive* 4 fasten with cord > **cord'age** *noun*
cor•date [KOR-dayt] *adjective* heart-shaped
cor•dial [KOR-jəl] *adjective* 1 hearty, sincere, warm ▷ *noun* 2 sweet, fruit flavored alcoholic drink 3 liqueur > **cor•di•al•i•ty** [kor-jee-AL-i-tee] *noun* warmth
cord•ite [KOR-dīt] *noun* explosive compound
cor•don [KOR-dn] *noun* 1 chain of troops or police 2 fruit tree grown as single stem ▷ *verb transitive* 3 form cordon around
cor•don bleu [kor-DAWN BLUU] *adjective* (esp. of food preparation) of highest standard
cor•du•roy [KOR-də-roi] *noun* cotton fabric with velvety, ribbed surface
core [kor] *noun* 1 horny seed case of apple and other fruits 2 central or innermost part of anything ▷ *verb transitive* **cored, cor•ing** 3 take out the core
co•re•spond•ent [koh-ri-SPON-dənt] *noun* one cited in divorce case, alleged to have committed adultery with the respondent
cor•gi [KOR-gee] *noun* short-legged sturdy dog
co•ri•an•der [KOR-ee-an-dər] *noun* plant grown for its aromatic seeds and leaves
Co•rin•thi•an [kə-RIN-thee-ən] *adjective* 1 of Corinth 2 of Corinthian order of architecture, ornate Greek > **Co•rin•thi•ans** books in New Testament
cork [kork] *noun* 1 bark of an evergreen Mediterranean oak tree 2 piece of it or other material, esp. used as stopper for bottle, etc. ▷ *verb transitive* 3 stop up with cork > **cork'age** *noun* charge for opening wine bottles in restaurant > **cork'er** *noun* (*slang*) something, someone outstanding > **cork'screw** *noun* tool for pulling out corks
corn[1] [korn] *noun* 1 (kernels of) sweet corn, corn on the cob 2 (*informal*) oversentimental, trite quality in play, film, etc. ▷ *verb transitive* 3 preserve (meat) with salt or brine > **corn'y** *adjective* **corn•i•er, corn•i•est** (*informal*) trite, oversentimental, hackneyed > **corn•cob** *noun* ear of sweet corn > **corn'flour** *noun* finely ground corn > **corn'flow•er** *noun* blue flower, oft. growing in grainfields
corn[2] *noun* painful horny growth on foot or toe
cor•ne•a [KOR-nee-ə] *noun* transparent membrane covering front of eye
cor•ner [KOR-nər] *noun* 1 part of room where two sides meet 2 remote or humble place 3 point where two walls, streets, etc. meet 4 angle, projection 5 *business* buying up of whole existing stock of commodity, shares ▷ *verb transitive* 6 drive into position of difficulty, or leaving no escape 7 establish monopoly ▷ *verb intransitive* 8 turn around corner > **cor'ner•stone** *noun* indispensable part, basis > **corner kick** *soccer* free kick from corner of field

DICTIONARY

C

THESAURUS

cope *verb* 1 MANAGE, carry on, get by (*informal*), hold one's own, make the grade, struggle through, survive
2 ▷ **cope with** DEAL WITH, contend with, grapple with, handle, struggle with, weather, wrestle with
copious *adjective* ABUNDANT, ample, bountiful, extensive, full, lavish, plentiful, profuse
copy *noun* 1 REPRODUCTION, counterfeit, duplicate, facsimile, forgery, imitation, likeness, model, replica
▷ *verb* 2 REPRODUCE, counterfeit, duplicate, replicate, transcribe
3 IMITATE, ape, emulate, follow, mimic, mirror, repeat
cord *noun* ROPE, line, string, twine
cordial *adjective* WARM, affable, agreeable, cheerful, congenial, friendly, genial, hearty, sociable
cordon *noun* 1 CHAIN, barrier, line, ring
▷ *verb* 2 ▷ **cordon off** SURROUND, close off, encircle, enclose, fence off, isolate, picket, separate
core *noun* CENTER, crux, essence, gist, heart, kernel, nub, nucleus, pith
corner *noun* 1 ANGLE, bend, crook, joint
2 SPACE, hideaway, hideout, nook, retreat
▷ *verb* 3 TRAP, run to earth
4 (*a market*) MONOPOLIZE, dominate, engross, hog (*slang*)
corny *adjective* (*slang*) UNORIGINAL, banal, dull, hackneyed, old-fashioned, old hat, stale,

cor•net [kor-NET] *noun* trumpet with valves
cor•nice [KOR-nis] *noun* 1 projection near top of wall 2 ornamental, carved molding below ceiling
cor•nu•co•pia [kor-nə-KOH-pee-ə] *noun* symbol of plenty, consisting of goat's horn, overflowing with fruit and flowers
co•rol•la [kə-ROL-ə] *noun* flower's inner envelope of petals
cor•ol•lar•y [KOR-ə-ler-ee] *noun, plural* **-lar•ies** 1 inference from a preceding statement 2 deduction 3 result
co•ro•na [kə-ROH-nə] *noun, plural* **-nas** 1 halo around heavenly body 2 flat projecting part of cornice 3 top or crown
cor•o•nar•y [KOR-ə-ner-ee] *adjective* 1 of blood vessels surrounding heart ▷ *noun, plural* **-nar•ies** 2 coronary thrombosis > **coronary thrombosis** disease of the heart
cor•o•na•tion [kor-ə-NAY-shən] *noun* ceremony of crowning a sovereign
cor•o•ner [KOR-ə-nər] *noun* officer who holds inquests on bodies of persons supposed killed by violence, accident, etc.
cor•o•net [KOR-ə-net] *noun* small crown
cor•po•ral[1] [KOR-pər-əl] *adjective* 1 of the body 2 material, not spiritual > **corporal punishment** (flogging, etc.) of physical nature
corporal[2] *noun* noncommissioned officer below sergeant
cor•po•ra•tion [kor-pə-RAY-shən] *noun* 1 association, body of persons legally authorized to act as an individual 2 authorities of town or city > **cor'po•rate** [-rit] *adjective*
cor•po•re•al [kor-POR-ee-əl] *adjective* 1 of the body, material 2 tangible
corps [kor] *noun, plural* **corps** [korz] 1 military force, body of troops 2 any organized body of persons
corpse [korps] *noun* dead body
cor•pu•lent [KOR-pyə-lənt] *adjective* fat > **cor'pu•lence** *noun*
cor•pus [KOR-pəs] *noun* 1 collection or body of works, esp. by single author 2 main part or body of something
cor•pus•cle [KOR-pə-səl] *noun* minute organism or particle, esp. red and white corpuscles of blood
cor•ral [kə-RAL] *noun* enclosure for cattle, or for defense ▷ *verb transitive* **-raled, -ral•ing**
cor•rect [kə-REKT] *verb transitive* 1 set right 2 indicate errors in 3 rebuke, punish 4 counteract, rectify ▷ *adjective* 5 right, exact, accurate 6 in accordance with facts or standards > **cor•rec'tion** *noun* > **cor•rec'tive** *noun, adjective*
cor•re•late [KOR-ə-layt] *verb transitive* **-lat•ed, -lat•ing** 1 bring into reciprocal relation ▷ *noun* [-lit] 2 either of two things or words necessarily implying the other > **cor•re•la'tion** *noun* > **cor•rel•a•tive** [kə-REL-ə-tiv] *adjective, noun*
cor•re•spond [kor-ə-SPOND] *verb intransitive* 1 be in agreement, be consistent with 2 be similar (to) 3 exchange letters > **cor•re•spond'ence** *noun* 1 agreement, corresponding 2 similarity 3 exchange of letters 4 letters received > **cor•re•spond'ent** *noun* 1 writer of letters 2 one employed by newspaper, etc. to report on particular topic, country, etc.
cor•ri•dor [KOR-i-dər] *noun* 1 passage in building, etc. 2 strip of territory (or air route) not under control of country through which it passes 3 densely populated area incl. two or more major cities
cor•ri•gen•dum [kor-i-JEN-dəm] *noun, plural* **-da** [-də] thing to be corrected
cor•rob•o•rate [kə-ROB-ə-rayt] *verb transitive* **-rat•ed, -rat•ing** confirm, support (statement, etc.) > **cor•rob•o•ra'tion** *noun* > **cor•rob'o•ra•tive** *adjective*
cor•rode [kə-ROHD] *verb transitive* **-rod•ed, -rod•ing** eat, wear away, eat into (by chemical

DICTIONARY • THESAURUS

stereotyped, trite
corporation *noun* 1 BUSINESS, association, corporate body, society
2 TOWN COUNCIL, civic authorities, council, municipal authorities
corps *noun* TEAM, band, company, detachment, division, regiment, squadron, troop, unit
corpse *noun* BODY, cadaver, carcass, remains, stiff (*slang*)
correct *adjective* 1 TRUE, accurate, exact, faultless, flawless, O.K. *or* okay (*informal*), precise, right
2 PROPER, acceptable, appropriate, fitting, kosher (*informal*), O.K. *or* okay (*informal*), seemly, standard
▷ *verb* 3 RECTIFY, adjust, amend, cure, emend, redress, reform, remedy, right
4 PUNISH, admonish, chasten, chastise, chide, discipline, rebuke, reprimand, reprove
correction *noun* 1 RECTIFICATION, adjustment, alteration, amendment, emendation, improvement, modification
2 PUNISHMENT, admonition, castigation, chastisement, discipline, reformation, reproof
correctly *adverb* RIGHTLY, accurately, perfectly, precisely, properly, right
correctness *noun* 1 TRUTH, accuracy, exactitude, exactness, faultlessness, fidelity, preciseness, precision, regularity
2 DECORUM, civility, good breeding, propriety, seemliness
correspond *verb* 1 BE CONSISTENT, accord, agree, conform, fit, harmonize, match, square, tally
2 COMMUNICATE, exchange letters, keep in touch, write
correspondence *noun* 1 LETTERS, communication, mail, post, writing
2 RELATION, agreement, coincidence, comparison, conformity, correlation, harmony, match, similarity
correspondent *noun* 1 LETTER WRITER, pen friend *or* pen pal
2 REPORTER, contributor, journalist
corresponding *adjective* RELATED, analogous, answering, complementary, equivalent, matching, reciprocal, similar
corridor *noun* PASSAGE, aisle, alley, hallway, passageway
corroborate *verb* SUPPORT, authenticate, back up, bear out, confirm, endorse, ratify, substantiate, validate
corrode *verb* EAT AWAY, consume, corrupt, erode, gnaw, oxidize, rust, wear away

action, disease, etc.) > **cor•ro'sion** [-ROH-zhən] *noun* > **cor•ro'sive** *adjective*

cor•ru•gate [KOR-ə-gayt] *verb* **-gat•ed, -gat•ing** wrinkle, bend into wavy ridges

cor•rupt [kə-RUPT] *adjective* 1 lacking integrity 2 open to, or involving, bribery 3 wicked 4 spoiled by mistakes, altered for the worse (of words, literary passages, etc.) ▷ *verb transitive* 5 make evil, pervert 6 bribe 7 make rotten > **cor•rupt'i•ble** *adjective* > **cor•rup'tion** *noun*

cor•sage [kor-SAHZH] *noun* (flower, spray, worn on) bodice of woman's dress

cor•sair [KOR-sair] *noun* pirate (ship)

cor•set [KOR-sit] *noun* close-fitting undergarment stiffened to give support or shape to the body

cor•tege [kor-TEZH] *noun* formal (funeral) procession

cor•tex [KOR-teks] *noun, plural* **-ti•ces** [-tə-seez] *anatomy* 1 outer layer 2 bark 3 sheath > **cor'ti•cal** *adjective*

cor•ti•sone [KOR-tə-zohn] *noun* synthetic hormone used in the treatment of a variety of diseases

cor•vette [kor-VET] *noun* lightly armed warship for escort and antisubmarine duties

co•sine [KOH-sīn] *noun* in a right triangle, the ratio of a side adjacent to a given angle and the hypotenuse

cos•met•ic [koz-MET-ik] *noun* 1 preparation to beautify or improve skin, hair, etc. ▷ *adjective* 2 designed to improve appearance only

cos•mic [KOZ-mik] *adjective* 1 relating to the universe 2 of the vastness of the universe > **cos•mog'ra•pher** *noun* > **cos•mog'ra•phy** *noun* description or mapping of the universe > **cos•mo•log•i•cal** [koz-mə-LOJ-i-kəl] *adjective* > **cos•mol'o•gy** *noun* the science or study of the universe

cosmic rays high-energy electromagnetic rays from space

cos•mo•naut [KOZ-mə-nawt] *noun* the Russian name for an astronaut

cos•mo•pol•i•tan [koz-mə-POL-i-tn] *noun* 1 person who has lived and traveled in many countries ▷ *adjective* 2 familiar with many countries 3 sophisticated 4 free from national prejudice

cos•mos[1] [KOZ-məs] *noun* the world or universe considered as an ordered system

cosmos[2] *noun, plural* **-mos** plant cultivated for brightly colored flowers

cos•sack [KOS-ak] *noun* member of people in SE Russia

cost [kawst] *noun* 1 price 2 cost price 3 expenditure of time, labor, etc. ▷ *verb transitive* **cost, cost•ing** 4 have as price 5 entail payment, or loss, or sacrifice of > **costs** *plural noun* expenses of lawsuit > **costing** *noun* system of calculating cost of production, sale > **cost'li•ness** *noun* > **cost'ly** *adjective* **-li•er, -li•est** 1 valuable 2 expensive > **cost price** price at which article is bought by one intending to resell it

cos•tal [KOS-tl] *adjective* pert. to side of body or ribs

cos•tume [KOS-toom] *noun* 1 style of dress of particular place or time, or for particular activity 2 theatrical clothes > **cos'tum•er** *noun* dealer in costumes > **costume jewelry** inexpensive jewelry

cot [kot] *noun* narrow, usu. collapsible bed

cote [koht] *noun* shelter, shed for animals or birds: *dovecote*

co•te•rie [KOH-tə-ree] *noun* 1 exclusive group of people with common interests 2 social clique

coterminous *see* **conterminous**

cot•tage [KOT-ij] *noun* small house > **cottage cheese** mild, soft cheese > **cottage industry** industry in which workers work in their own homes

cot•ter [KOT-ər] *noun* pin, wedge, etc. to prevent relative motion of two parts of machine, etc.

cot•ton [KOT-n] *noun* 1 plant 2 white downy fibrous covering of its seeds 3 thread or cloth made of this **cotton (on) to** begin to like, understand (idea, person, etc.)

cot•y•le•don [kot-l-EED-n] *noun* primary leaf of plant embryos

couch [kowch] *noun* 1 piece of furniture for sitting or reclining on by day, sofa ▷ *verb transitive* 2 put into (words), phrase 3 cause to

DICTIONARY

C

THESAURUS

corrosive *adjective* CORRODING, caustic, consuming, erosive, virulent, vitriolic, wasting, wearing

corrupt *adjective* 1 DISHONEST, bent (*slang*), bribable, crooked (*informal*), fraudulent, unprincipled, unscrupulous, venal
2 DEPRAVED, debased, degenerate, dissolute, profligate, vicious
3 DISTORTED, altered, doctored, falsified
▷ *verb* 4 BRIBE, buy off, entice, fix (*informal*), grease (someone's) palm (*slang*), lure, suborn
5 DEPRAVE, debauch, pervert, subvert
6 DISTORT, doctor, tamper with

corruption *noun* 1 DISHONESTY, bribery, extortion, fraud, shady dealings (*informal*), unscrupulousness, venality
2 DEPRAVITY, decadence, evil, immorality, perversion, vice, wickedness
3 DISTORTION, doctoring, falsification

corset *noun* GIRDLE, belt, bodice

cosmetic *adjective* BEAUTIFYING, nonessential, superficial, surface

cosmic *adjective* UNIVERSAL, stellar

cosmopolitan *adjective* 1 SOPHISTICATED, broad-minded, catholic, open-minded, universal, urbane, well-traveled, worldly-wise
▷ *noun* 2 MAN OF THE WORLD *or* WOMAN OF THE WORLD, jet-setter, sophisticate

cost *noun* 1 PRICE, amount, charge, damage (*informal*), expense, outlay, payment, worth
2 LOSS, damage, detriment, expense, harm, hurt, injury, penalty, sacrifice, suffering
▷ *verb* 3 SELL AT, come to, command a price of, set (someone) back (*informal*)
4 LOSE, do disservice to, harm, hurt, injure

costly *adjective* 1 EXPENSIVE, dear, exorbitant, extortionate, highly-priced, steep (*informal*), stiff
2 DAMAGING, catastrophic, deleterious, disastrous, harmful, loss-making, ruinous

costs *plural noun* EXPENSES, budget, outgoings, overheads

costume *noun* OUTFIT, apparel, attire, clothing,

lie down > **couch potato** (*informal*) lazy person whose only hobby is watching television **on the couch** under psychiatric treatment
cou•gar [KOO-gər] *noun* mountain lion
cough [kawf] *verb intransitive* 1 expel air from lungs with sudden effort and noise, often to remove obstruction ▷ *noun* 2 act of coughing
could *pt. of* **can**[1]
cou•lomb [KOO-lom] *noun* unit of quantity of electricity
coun•cil [KOWN-səl] *noun* 1 deliberative or administrative body 2 one of its meetings 3 local governing authority of town, etc. > **coun'ci•lor** *noun* member of council
coun•sel [KOWN-səl] *noun* 1 advice, deliberation or debate 2 lawyer or lawyers 3 plan, policy ▷ *verb transitive* 4 advise, recommend > **coun'se•lor** *noun* 1 adviser 2 lawyer **keep one's counsel** keep a secret
count[1] [kownt] *verb transitive* 1 reckon, calculate, number 2 include 3 consider to be ▷ *verb intransitive* 4 be reckoned in 5 depend (on) 6 be of importance ▷ *noun* 7 reckoning 8 total number reached by counting 9 item in list of charges or indictment 10 act of counting > **count'less** *adjective* too many to be counted
count[2] *noun* European nobleman of rank corresponding to that of British earl
coun•te•nance [KOWN-tn-əns] *noun* 1 face, its expression 2 support, approval ▷ *verb transitive* **-nanced, -nanc•ing** 3 give support, approve
count•er[1] [KOWN-tər] *noun* 1 horizontal surface in bank, store, etc., on which business is transacted 2 work surface in kitchen 3 disk, token used for counting or scoring, esp. in board games > **coun'ter•top** flat upper surface of counter, display case, etc.
coun•ter[2] *adverb* 1 in opposite direction 2 contrary ▷ *verb intransitive* 3 oppose, contradict 4 *fencing* parry ▷ *noun* 5 parry
counter- *prefix* 1 opposite, against: *counterattack* 2 complementary, corresponding: *counterpart*
coun•ter•act [kown-tər-AKT] *verb transitive* neutralize or hinder
coun•ter•at•tack [KOWN-tər-ə-tak] *verb, noun* attack after enemy's advance
coun•ter•bal•ance [KOWN-tər-bal-əns] *noun* weight balancing or neutralizing another ▷ *verb transitive* **-anced, anc•ing**
coun•ter•feit [KOWN-tər-fit] *adjective* 1 sham, forged ▷ *noun* 2 imitation, forgery ▷ *verb transitive* 3 imitate with intent to deceive 4 forge
coun•ter•mand [kown-tər-MAND] *verb transitive* cancel (previous order)
coun•ter•part [KOWN-tər-pahrt] *noun* 1 thing so like another as to be mistaken for it 2 something complementary to or correlative of another
coun•ter•point [KOWN-tər-point] *noun* 1 melody added as accompaniment to given melody 2 art of so adding melodies
coun•ter•sign [KOWN-tər-sīn] *verb transitive* 1 sign document already signed by another 2 ratify ▷ *noun military* 3 secret sign
coun•ter•sink [KOWN-tər-singk] *verb* **-sunk, -sink•ing** enlarge upper part of hole (drilled in wood, etc.) to take head of screw, bolt, etc. below surface
count'ess *noun* wife or widow of count or earl
coun•try [KUN-tree] *noun, plural* **-tries** 1 region, district 2 territory of nation 3 land of birth, residence, etc. 4 rural districts as opposed to city 5 nation > **coun'tri•fied** [-fīd] *adjective*

DICTIONARY • THESAURUS

dress, ensemble, garb, livery, uniform
cottage *noun* CABIN, chalet, hut, lodge, shack
cough *noun* 1 FROG IN ONE'S THROAT *or* TICKLE IN ONE'S THROAT, bark, hack
▷ *verb* 2 CLEAR ONE'S THROAT, bark, hack
council *noun* GOVERNING BODY, assembly, board, cabinet, committee, conference, congress, convention, panel, parliament
counsel *noun* 1 ADVICE, direction, guidance, information, recommendation, suggestion, warning
2 LEGAL ADVISER, advocate, attorney, barrister, lawyer
▷ *verb* 3 ADVISE, advocate, exhort, instruct, recommend, urge, warn
count *verb* 1 ADD *or* ADD UP, calculate, compute, enumerate, number, reckon, tally, tot up
2 MATTER, be important, carry weight, rate, signify, tell, weigh
3 CONSIDER, deem, judge, look upon, rate, regard, think
4 TAKE INTO ACCOUNT *or* TAKE INTO CONSIDERATION, include, number among
▷ *noun* 5 CALCULATION, computation, enumeration, numbering, poll, reckoning, sum, tally
counter[2] *verb* 1 RETALIATE, answer, hit back, meet, oppose, parry, resist, respond, ward off
▷ *adverb* 2 OPPOSITE TO, against, at variance with, contrariwise, conversely, in defiance of, versus
counteract *verb* ACT AGAINST, foil, frustrate, negate, neutralize, offset, resist, thwart
counterbalance *verb* OFFSET, balance, compensate, make up for, set off
counterfeit *adjective* 1 FAKE, bogus, false, forged, imitation, phoney *or* phony (*informal*), sham, simulated
▷ *noun* 2 FAKE, copy, forgery, fraud, imitation, phoney *or* phony (*informal*), reproduction, sham
▷ *verb* 3 FAKE, copy, fabricate, feign, forge, imitate, impersonate, pretend, sham, simulate
countermand *verb* CANCEL, annul, override, repeal, rescind, retract, reverse, revoke
counterpart *noun* OPPOSITE NUMBER, complement, equal, fellow, match, mate, supplement, tally, twin
countless *adjective* INNUMERABLE, endless, immeasurable, incalculable, infinite, legion, limitless, myriad, numberless, uncountable, untold
count on, count upon *verb* DEPEND ON, bank on, believe in, lean on, pin one's faith on, reckon on, rely on, take for granted, take on trust, trust
country *noun* 1 NATION, commonwealth, kingdom, people, realm, state
2 TERRITORY, land, region, terrain
3 PEOPLE, citizens, community, inhabitants, nation, populace, public, society
4 COUNTRYSIDE, backwoods, farmland, green belt, outback (*Austral & New Zealand*), provinces,

rural in manner or appearance > **coun'try•man** *noun* 1 rustic 2 compatriot > **country music** popular music based on Amer. folk music > **coun'try•side** *noun* 1 rural district 2 its inhabitants
coun•ty [KOWN-tee] *noun, plural* **-ties** division of a state
coup [koo] *noun, plural* **coups** [kooz] 1 successful stroke, move or gamble 2 coup d'état > **coup d'é•tat** [koo-day-TAH] sudden, violent seizure of government
cou•ple [KUP-əl] *noun* 1 two, pair 2 husband and wife 3 any two persons ▷ *verb transitive* **-pled, -pling** 4 connect, fasten together 5 associate, connect in the mind ▷ *verb intransitive* **-pled, -pling** 6 join, associate > **cou'plet** *noun* two lines of verse, esp. rhyming and of equal length > **cou'pling** *noun* connection
cou•pon [KOO-pon] *noun* 1 ticket or voucher entitling holder to discount, gift, etc. 2 detachable slip used as order form
cour•age [KUR-ij] *noun* bravery, boldness > **cou•ra•geous** [kə-RAY-jəs] *adjective*
cour•i•er [KUUR-ee-ər] *noun* express messenger
course [kors] *noun* 1 movement in space or time 2 direction of movement 3 successive development, sequence 4 line of conduct or action 5 series of lessons, exercises, etc. 6 any of successive parts of meal 7 continuous line of masonry at particular level in building 8 area where golf is played 9 track or ground on which a race is run ▷ *verb transitive* **coursed, cours•ing** 10 hunt ▷ *verb intransitive* **coursed, cours•ing** 11 run swiftly, gallop about 12 (of blood) circulate
court [kort] *noun* 1 space enclosed by buildings, yard 2 area marked off or enclosed for playing various games 3 retinue and establishment of sovereign 4 body with judicial powers, place where it meets, one of its sittings 5 attention, homage, flattery ▷ *verb transitive* 6 woo, try to win or attract 7 seek, invite > **cour•ti•er** [KOR-tee-ər] *noun* one who frequents royal court > **court'li•ness** *noun* > **court'ly** *adjective* **-li•er, -li•est** 1 ceremoniously polite 2 characteristic of a court > **court martial** *noun, plural* **courts martial** court of naval or military officers for trying naval or military offenses > **court'yard** *noun* paved space enclosed by buildings or walls
cour•te•san [KOR-tə-zən] *noun* 1 court mistress 2 high-class prostitute
cour•te•sy [KUR-tə-see] *noun, plural* **-sies** 1 politeness, good manners 2 act of civility > **cour'te•ous** *adjective* polite
court•ship [KORT-ship] *noun* wooing
cous•in [KUZ-ən] *noun* son or daughter of uncle or aunt
cove [kohv] *noun* small inlet of coast, sheltered bay
cov•en [KUV-ən] *noun* gathering of witches
cov•e•nant [KUV-ə-nənt] *noun* 1 contract, mutual agreement 2 compact ▷ *verb* 3 agree to a covenant
cov•er [KUV-ər] *verb transitive* 1 place or spread over 2 extend, spread 3 bring upon (oneself) 4 screen, protect 5 travel over 6 include 7 be

DICTIONARY

C

THESAURUS

sticks (*informal*)
countryside *noun* COUNTRY, farmland, green belt, outback (*Austral & New Zealand*), outdoors, sticks (*informal*)
count up *verb* ADD, reckon up, sum, tally, total
county *noun* PROVINCE, shire
coup *noun* MASTERSTROKE, accomplishment, action, deed, exploit, feat, maneuver, stunt
couple *noun* 1 PAIR, brace, duo, two, twosome ▷ *verb* 2 LINK, connect, hitch, join, marry, pair, unite, wed, yoke
coupon *noun* SLIP, card, certificate, ticket, token, voucher
courage *noun* BRAVERY, daring, fearlessness, gallantry, heroism, mettle, nerve, pluck, resolution, valor
courageous *adjective* BRAVE, bold, daring, fearless, gallant, gritty, intrepid, lion-hearted, stouthearted, valiant
courier *noun* 1 GUIDE, representative
2 MESSENGER, bearer, carrier, envoy, runner
course *noun* 1 CLASSES, curriculum, lectures, program, schedule
2 PROGRESSION, development, flow, movement, order, progress, sequence, unfolding
3 ROUTE, direction, line, passage, path, road, track, trajectory, way
4 RACECOURSE, cinder track, circuit
5 PROCEDURE, behavior, conduct, manner, method, mode, plan, policy, program
6 PERIOD, duration, lapse, passage, passing, sweep, term, time
7 ▷ **of course** NATURALLY, certainly, definitely, indubitably, needless to say, obviously, undoubtedly, without a doubt
▷ *verb* 8 RUN, flow, gush, race, speed, stream, surge
9 HUNT, chase, follow, pursue, stalk
court *noun* 1 LAW COURT, bar, bench, tribunal
2 COURTYARD, cloister, piazza, plaza, quad (*informal*), quadrangle, square, yard
3 PALACE, hall, manor
4 ROYAL HOUSEHOLD, attendants, cortege, entourage, retinue, suite, train
▷ *verb* 5 WOO, date, go with *or* go out with, run after, serenade, set one's cap at, take out, walk out with
6 CULTIVATE, brown-nose (*slang*), curry favor with, fawn upon, flatter, pander to, seek, solicit
7 INVITE, attract, bring about, incite, prompt, provoke, seek
courteous *adjective* POLITE, affable, attentive, civil, gallant, gracious, refined, respectful, urbane, well-mannered
courtesy *noun* 1 POLITENESS, affability, civility, courteousness, gallantry, good manners, graciousness, urbanity
2 FAVOR, benevolence, indulgence, kindness
courtier *noun* ATTENDANT, follower, squire
courtly *adjective* CEREMONIOUS, chivalrous, dignified, elegant, formal, gallant, polished, refined, stately, urbane
courtyard *noun* YARD, enclosure, quad, quadrangle
cove *noun* BAY, anchorage, inlet, sound
covenant *noun* 1 PROMISE, agreement, arrangement, commitment, contract, pact, pledge
▷ *verb* 2 PROMISE, agree, contract, pledge, stipulate, undertake

sufficient **8** point a gun at ▷ *noun* **9** lid, wrapper, envelope, binding, screen, anything that covers > **cov'er•age** *noun* amount, extent covered > **cov'er•let** *noun* bedspread > **cover girl** attractive model whose picture appears on magazine cover

co•vert [KOH-vərt] *adjective* **1** secret, veiled, concealed, sly ▷ *noun* [KUV-ərt] **2** thicket, place sheltering game

cov•et [KUV-it] *verb transitive* long to possess, esp. what belongs to another > **cov'et•ous** *adjective* greedy

cov•ey [KUV-ee] *noun, plural* **-eys** brood of partridges or quail

cow[1] [kow] *noun* **1** mature female of cattle and of certain other mammals, such as the elephant or seal > **cow'boy** *noun* **1** ranch hand in charge of cattle on western plains of US **2** (*informal*) reckless driver, etc.

cow[2] *verb transitive* frighten into submission, overawe, subdue

cow•ard [KOW-ərd] *noun* one who lacks courage, shrinks from danger > **cow'ard•ice** [-dis] *noun* > **cow'ard•ly** *adjective*

cow•er [KOW-ər] *verb intransitive* crouch, shrink in fear

cowl [kowl] *noun* **1** monk's hooded cloak **2** its hood **3** cowling

cowl•ing [KOW-ling] *noun* covering for aircraft engine

cow•rie [KOW-ree] *noun* brightly colored sea shell

cox•swain [KOK-sən] *noun* steersman of boat > **cox** *verb* (*informal*) act as coxswain

coy [koi] *adjective* **-er, -est** (pretending to be) shy, modest > **coy'ness** *noun*

coy•o•te [kī-OH-tee] *noun* N Amer. prairie wolf

co•zy [KOH-zee] *adjective* **-zi•er, -zi•est** **1** snug, comfortable, sheltered **2** suggesting conspiratorial intimacy > **co'zi•ly** *adverb* > **co'zi•ness** *noun*

CPU *computers.* central processing unit

Cr *chem.* chromium

crab [krab] *noun* **1** edible crustacean with ten legs, noted for sidelong and backward walk **2** type of louse ▷ *verb intransitive* **crabbed, crab•bing** **3** catch crabs **4** move sideways > **crab•bed** [KRAB-id] *adjective* of handwriting, hard to read > **crab'by** *adjective* **-bi•er, -bi•est** irritable

crack [krak] *verb transitive* **1** break, split partially **2** break with sharp noise **3** cause to make sharp noise, as of whip, rifle, etc. **4** break down, yield **5** (*informal*) tell (joke) **6** solve, decipher ▷ *verb intransitive* **7** make sharp noise **8** split, fissure **9** of the voice, lose clearness when changing from boy's to man's ▷ *noun* **10** sharp explosive noise **11** split, fissure **12** flaw **13** (*informal*) joke, esp. sarcastic **14** chat **15** (*slang*) pure, highly addictive form of cocaine ▷ *adjective* **16** (*informal*) special, smart, of great reputation for skill or fashion > **crack'er** *noun* **1** thin dry biscuit **2** (**Crack'er**) (*slang, offensive*) native or inhabitant of Georgia > **crack'le** [-əl] *noun* **1** sound of repeated small cracks ▷ *verb intransitive* **-led, -ling** **2** make this sound > **crack'ling** *noun* **1** crackle **2** crisp skin of roast pork, etc.

cra•dle [KRAYD-l] *noun* **1** infant's bed (on

DICTIONARY • THESAURUS

cover *verb* **1** CLOTHE, dress, envelop, put on, wrap
2 OVERLAY, coat, daub, encase, envelop
3 SUBMERGE, engulf, flood, overrun, wash over
4 CONCEAL, cloak, disguise, enshroud, hide, mask, obscure, shroud, veil
5 TRAVEL OVER, cross, pass through *or* pass over, traverse
6 PROTECT, defend, guard, shield
7 REPORT, describe, investigate, narrate, relate, tell of, write up
▷ *noun* **8** COVERING, canopy, case, coating, envelope, jacket, lid, top, wrapper
9 DISGUISE, façade, front, mask, pretext, screen, smoke screen, veil
10 PROTECTION, camouflage, concealment, defense, guard, shelter, shield
11 INSURANCE, compensation, indemnity, protection, reimbursement

covering *adjective* **1** EXPLANATORY, accompanying, descriptive, introductory
▷ *noun* **2** COVER, blanket, casing, coating, layer, wrapping

cover-up *noun* CONCEALMENT, complicity, conspiracy, front, smoke screen, whitewash (*informal*)

cover up *verb* CONCEAL, draw a veil over, hide, hush up, suppress, sweep under the carpet, whitewash (*informal*)

covet *verb* LONG FOR, aspire to, crave, desire, envy, lust after, set one's heart on, yearn for

covetous *adjective* ENVIOUS, acquisitive, avaricious, close-fisted, grasping, greedy, jealous, rapacious, yearning

coward *noun* WIMP (*informal*), chicken (*slang*), scaredy-cat (*informal*), yellow-belly (*slang*)

cowardice *noun* FAINT-HEARTEDNESS, fearfulness, spinelessness, weakness

cowardly *adjective* FAINT-HEARTED, chicken (*slang*), craven, fearful, scared, soft, spineless, timorous, weak, yellow (*informal*)

cowboy *noun* COWHAND, cattleman, drover, gaucho, herdsman, rancher, stockman

cower *verb* CRINGE, draw back, flinch, grovel, quail, shrink, tremble

coy *adjective* SHY, bashful, demure, modest, reserved, retiring, shrinking, timid

cozy *adjective* SNUG, comfortable, comfy (*informal*), homely, homey, intimate, sheltered, tucked up, warm

crack *verb* **1** BREAK, burst, cleave, fracture, snap, splinter, split
2 SNAP, burst, crash, detonate, explode, pop, ring
3 GIVE IN, break down, collapse, give way, go to pieces, lose control, succumb, yield
4 (*informal*) HIT, clip (*informal*), clout (*informal*), cuff, slap, smack, whack
5 SOLVE, decipher, fathom, get the answer to, work out
▷ *noun* **6** SNAP, burst, clap, crash, explosion, pop, report
7 BREAK, chink, cleft, cranny, crevice, fissure, fracture, gap, rift
8 (*informal*) BLOW, clip (*informal*), clout (*informal*), cuff, slap, smack, whack
9 (*informal*) JOKE, dig, funny remark, gag (*informal*), jibe, quip, wisecrack (*informal*),

rockers) **2** earliest resting place or home **3** supporting framework ▷ *verb transitive* **-dled, -dling** **4** hold or rock as in a cradle **5** cherish

craft[1] [kraft] *noun* **1** skill, ability, esp. manual ability **2** cunning **3** skilled trade **4** members of a trade > **craft'i•ly** *adverb* > **craft'y** *adjective* **craft•i•er, craft•i•est** cunning, shrewd > **crafts'man** *noun* > **crafts'man•ship** *noun*

craft[2] *noun* **1** vessel **2** ship

crag [krag] *noun* steep rugged rock > **crag'gy** *adjective* **-gi•er, -gi•est** rugged

cram [kram] *verb transitive* **crammed, cram•ming** **1** fill quite full **2** stuff, force **3** pack tightly ▷ *verb intransitive* **4** feed to excess **5** prepare quickly for examination

cramp [kramp] *noun* **1** painful muscular contraction **2** clamp for holding masonry, wood, etc. together ▷ *verb transitive* **3** restrict or hamper **4** hem in, keep within too narrow limits

cram•pon [KRAM-pon] *noun* spike in shoe for mountain climbing esp. on ice

crane [krayn] *noun* **1** wading bird with long legs, neck, and bill **2** machine for moving heavy weights ▷ *verb intransitive* **craned, cran•ing** **3** stretch neck to see

cra•ni•um [KRAY-nee-əm] *noun* skull > **cra'ni•al** *adjective*

crank [krangk] *noun* **1** arm at right angles to axis, for turning main shaft, changing reciprocal into rotary motion, etc. **2** (*informal*) eccentric person, faddist ▷ *verb* **3** start (engine) by turning crank > **crank'y** *adjective* **crank•i•er, crank•i•est** **1** bad-tempered **2** eccentric > **crank'shaft** *noun* principal shaft of engine

cran•ny [KRAN-ee] *noun, plural* **-nies** small opening, chink > **cran'nied** *adjective*

crap [krap] *noun* gambling game played with two dice (*also* **craps**)

crape [krayp] *noun* crepe, esp. when used for mourning clothes

crash [krash] *verb* (cause to) make loud noise **1** (cause to) fall with crash ▷ *verb intransitive* **2** break, smash **3** collapse, fail, esp. financially **4** cause (aircraft) to hit land or water **5** collide with (another car, etc.) **6** move noisily or violently ▷ *verb intransitive* **7** (of computer system or program) fail suddenly because of malfunction ▷ *noun* **8** loud, violent fall or impact **9** collision, esp. between vehicles **10** sudden, uncontrolled descent of aircraft to land **11** sudden collapse or downfall, esp. of economy **12** bankruptcy ▷ *adjective* **13** requiring, using, great effort to achieve results quickly > **crash helmet** helmet worn by motorcyclists, etc. to protect head

crass [kras] *adjective* **-er, -est** **1** grossly stupid **2** insensitive > **crass'ness** *noun*

crate [krayt] *noun* large (usu. wooden) container for packing goods

cra•ter [KRAY-tər] *noun* **1** mouth of volcano **2** bowl-shaped cavity, esp. one made by explosion of large shell, bomb, mine, etc.

cra•vat [krə-VAT] *noun* man's neckband or scarf

crave [krayv] *verb* **craved, crav•ing** **1** have very strong desire for, long for ▷ *verb transitive* **2** ask humbly **3** beg > **craving** *noun*

cra•ven [KRAY-vən] *adjective* **1** cowardly, abject, spineless ▷ *noun* **2** coward > **cra'ven•ness** *noun*

craw [kraw] *noun* **1** bird's or animal's stomach **2** bird's crop

crawl [krawl] *verb intransitive* **1** move on belly or

witticism

crackdown *noun* SUPPRESSION, clampdown, crushing, repression

cracked *adjective* BROKEN, chipped, damaged, defective, faulty, flawed, imperfect, split

cradle *noun* **1** CRIB, bassinet, cot
2 BIRTHPLACE, beginning, fount, fountainhead, origin, source, spring, wellspring
▷ *verb* **3** HOLD, lull, nestle, nurse, rock, support

craft[1] *noun* **1** OCCUPATION, business, employment, handicraft, pursuit, trade, vocation, work
2 SKILL, ability, aptitude, art, artistry, expertise, ingenuity, know-how (*informal*), technique, workmanship

craft[2] *noun* VESSEL, aircraft, boat, plane, ship, spacecraft

craftsman *noun* SKILLED WORKER, artisan, maker, master, smith, technician, wright

craftsmanship *noun* WORKMANSHIP, artistry, expertise, mastery, technique

crafty *adjective* CUNNING, artful, calculating, devious, sharp, shrewd, sly, subtle, wily

crag *noun* ROCK, bluff, peak, pinnacle, tor

cram *verb* **1** STUFF, compress, force, jam, pack in, press, shove, squeeze
2 OVEREAT, glut, gorge, satiate, stuff
3 STUDY, bone up (*informal*), review

cramp *noun* **1** SPASM, ache, contraction, convulsion, pain, pang, stitch, twinge
▷ *verb* **2** RESTRICT, constrain, hamper, handicap, hinder, impede, inhibit, obstruct

cramped *adjective* CLOSED IN, confined, congested, crowded, hemmed in, overcrowded, packed, uncomfortable

cranny *noun* CREVICE, chink, cleft, crack, fissure, gap, hole, opening

crash *noun* **1** COLLISION, accident, bump, pile-up (*informal*), smash, wreck
2 SMASH, bang, boom, clang, clash, clatter, din, racket, thunder
3 COLLAPSE, debacle, depression, downfall, failure, ruin
▷ *verb* **4** COLLIDE, bump *or* bump into, crash-land (*an aircraft*) drive into, have an accident, hit, plow into, wreck
5 COLLAPSE, be ruined, fail, fold, fold up, go belly up (*informal*), go bust (*informal*), go to the wall, go under
6 HURTLE, fall headlong, give way, lurch, overbalance, plunge, topple

crass *adjective* INSENSITIVE, boorish, gross, indelicate, oafish, stupid, unrefined, witless

crate *noun* CONTAINER, box, case, packing case, tea chest

crater *noun* HOLLOW, depression, dip

crave *verb* **1** LONG FOR, desire, hanker after, hope for, lust after, want, yearn for
2 BEG, ask, beseech, entreat, implore, petition, plead for, pray for, seek, solicit, supplicate

craving *noun* LONGING, appetite, desire, hankering, hope, hunger, thirst, yearning, yen (*informal*)

crawl *verb* **1** CREEP, advance slowly, inch, slither, on hands and knees 2 move very slowly 3 ingratiate oneself, cringe 4 swim with crawl stroke 5 be overrun (with) ▷ *noun* 6 crawling motion 7 very slow walk 8 racing stroke at swimming

cray•fish [KRAY-fish] *noun* edible freshwater crustacean like lobster (*also* **craw'fish**)

cray•on [KRAY-on] *noun* stick or pencil of colored chalk, wax, etc.

craze [krayz] *noun* 1 short-lived current fashion 2 strong desire or passion, mania 3 madness > **crazed** *adjective* 1 demented 2 (of porcelain) having fine cracks > **cra'zy** *adjective* **-zi•er, -zi•est** 1 insane 2 very foolish 3 madly eager (for) > **crazy quilt** 1 patchwork quilt of irregular patches 2 jumble

creak [kreek] *noun* 1 harsh grating noise ▷ *verb intransitive* 2 make creaking sound

cream [kreem] *noun* 1 fatty part of milk 2 various foods, dishes, resembling cream 3 cosmetic, etc. with creamlike consistency 4 yellowish-white color 5 best part of anything ▷ *verb transitive* 6 take cream from 7 take best part from 8 beat to creamy consistency > **cream'y** *adjective* **cream•i•er, cream•i•est**

crease [krees] *noun* 1 line made by folding 2 wrinkle 3 *ice hockey* marked rectangular area in front of goal cage 4 superficial bullet wound ▷ *verb* **creased, creas•ing** 5 make, develop creases

cre•ate [kree-AYT] *verb transitive* **-at•ed, -at•ing** 1 bring into being 2 give rise to 3 make ▷ *verb intransitive* **-at•ed, -at•ing** 4 (*informal*) make a fuss > **cre•a'tion** *noun* > **cre•a'tive** *adjective* > **cre•a'tor** *noun*

crea•ture [KREE-chər] *noun* 1 living being 2 thing created 3 dependent, tool (of another) > **creature comforts** bodily comforts

crèche [kresh] *noun* representation of the Nativity scene

cre•dence [KREED-ns] *noun* 1 belief, credit 2 small table for bread and wine of the Eucharist

cre•den•tials [kri-DEN-shəlz] *plural noun* 1 testimonials 2 letters of introduction, esp. those given to ambassador

cred•i•ble [KRED-ə-bəl] *adjective* 1 worthy of belief 2 trustworthy > **cred•i•bil'i•ty** *noun*

cred•it [KRED-it] *noun* 1 commendation, approval 2 source, cause, of honor 3 belief, trust 4 good name 5 influence, honor or power based on trust of others 6 system of allowing customers to take goods for later payment 7 money at one's disposal in bank, etc. 8 side of ledger on which such sums are entered 9 reputation for financial reliability ▷ *verb transitive* 10 attribute, believe that person has 11 believe 12 put on credit side of account > **cred•its** *plural noun* list of those responsible for

DICTIONARY • THESAURUS

worm one's way, wriggle, writhe
2 GROVEL, brown-nose (*slang*), creep, fawn, humble oneself, kiss ass (*slang*), toady
3 BE FULL OF, be overrun (*slang*), swarm, teem

craze *noun* FAD, enthusiasm, fashion, infatuation, mania, rage, trend, vogue

crazy *adjective* 1 RIDICULOUS, absurd, foolish, idiotic, ill-conceived, ludicrous, nonsensical, preposterous, senseless
2 FANATICAL, devoted, enthusiastic, infatuated, mad, passionate, wild (*informal*)
3 INSANE, crazed, demented, deranged, mad, nuts (*slang*), out of one's mind, unbalanced

creak *verb* SQUEAK, grate, grind, groan, scrape, scratch, screech

cream *noun* 1 LOTION, cosmetic, emulsion, essence, liniment, oil, ointment, paste, salve, unguent
2 BEST, crème de la crème (*French*), elite, flower, pick, prime
▷ *adjective* 3 OFF-WHITE, yellowish-white

creamy *adjective* SMOOTH, buttery, milky, rich, soft, velvety

crease *noun* 1 LINE, corrugation, fold, groove, ridge, wrinkle
▷ *verb* 2 WRINKLE, corrugate, crumple, double up, fold, rumple, screw up

create *verb* 1 MAKE, compose, devise, formulate, invent, originate, produce, spawn
2 CAUSE, bring about, lead to, occasion
3 APPOINT, constitute, establish, install, invest, make, set up

creation *noun* 1 MAKING, conception, formation, generation, genesis, procreation
2 SETTING UP, development, establishment, formation, foundation, inception, institution, production
3 INVENTION, achievement, brainchild (*informal*), concoction, handiwork, magnum opus, pièce de résistance (*French*), production
4 UNIVERSE, cosmos, nature, world

creative *adjective* IMAGINATIVE, artistic, clever, gifted, ingenious, inspired, inventive, original, visionary

creativity *noun* IMAGINATION, cleverness, ingenuity, inspiration, inventiveness, originality

creator *noun* MAKER, architect, author, designer, father, inventor, originator, prime mover

creature *noun* 1 LIVING THING, animal, beast, being, brute
2 PERSON, human being, individual, man, mortal, soul, woman

credentials *plural noun* CERTIFICATION, authorization, document, license, papers, passport, reference *or* references, testimonial

credibility *noun* BELIEVABILITY, integrity, plausibility, reliability, trustworthiness

credible *adjective* 1 BELIEVABLE, conceivable, imaginable, likely, plausible, possible, probable, reasonable, thinkable
2 RELIABLE, dependable, honest, sincere, trustworthy, trusty

credit *noun* 1 PRAISE, acclaim, acknowledgment, approval, commendation, honor, kudos, recognition, tribute
2 SOURCE OF SATISFACTION *or* SOURCE OF PRIDE, feather in one's cap, honor
3 PRESTIGE, esteem, good name, influence, position, regard, reputation, repute, standing, status
4 BELIEF, confidence, credence, faith, reliance, trust
5 ▷ **on credit** ON ACCOUNT, by deferred payment, by installments, on the card
▷ *verb* 6 BELIEVE, accept, have faith in, rely on, trust
7 ▷ **credit with** ATTRIBUTE TO, ascribe to, assign to, impute to

production of film, etc. > **cred'it•a•ble** *adjective* bringing honor > **cred'i•tor** *noun* one to whom debt is due

cred•u•lous [KREJ-ə-ləs] *adjective* too easy of belief, easily deceived or imposed on, gullible > **cre•du•li•ty** [krə-DOO-li-tee] *noun*

creed [kreed] *noun* 1 formal statement of religious beliefs 2 statement, system of beliefs or principles

creek [kreek] *noun* narrow inlet on seacoast

creel [kreel] *noun* angler's fishing basket

creep [kreep] *verb intransitive* **crept, creep•ing** 1 make way along ground, as snake 2 move with stealthy, slow movements 3 crawl 4 act in servile way 5 of skin or flesh, feel shrinking, shivering sensation, due to fear or repugnance ▷ *noun* 6 creeping 7 (*slang*) repulsive person > **creeps** feeling of fear or repugnance > **creep'er** *noun* creeping or climbing plant, such as ivy > **creep'y** *adjective* **creep•i•er, creep•i•est** (*informal*) 1 uncanny, unpleasant 2 causing flesh to creep

cre•ma•tion [kri-MAY-shən] *noun* burning as means of disposing of corpses > **cre•mate** [KREE-mayt] *verb transitive* **-mat•ed, -mat•ing** > **cre•ma•to•ri•um** [kree-mə-TOR-ee-əm] *noun* place for cremation

cre•ole [KREE-ohl] *noun* 1 hybrid language 2 (**Cre•ole**) native born W Indian, Latin American, of European descent

cre•o•sote [KREE-ə-soht] *noun* 1 oily antiseptic liquid distilled from coal or wood tar, used for preserving wood ▷ *verb transitive* **-sot•ed, -sot•ing** 2 coat or impregnate with creosote

crepe [krayp] *noun* 1 fabric with crimped surface 2 crape 3 thin, light pancake > **crepe rubber** rough-surfaced rubber used for soles of shoes

crept *pt./pp. of* **creep**

cre•scen•do [kri-SHEN-doh] *noun* gradual increase of loudness, esp. in music ▷ *adjective, adverb*

cres•cent [KRES-ənt] *noun* (shape of) moon as seen in first or last quarter 1 any figure of this shape 2 curved portion of a street

crest [krest] *noun* 1 comb or tuft on bird's or animal's head 2 plume on top of helmet 3 top of mountain, ridge, wave, etc. 4 badge above shield of coat of arms, also used separately on seal, plate, etc. ▷ *verb intransitive* 5 crown ▷ *verb transitive* 6 reach top of > **crest'fall•en** *adjective* cast down by failure, dejected

cre•ta•ceous [kri-TAY-shəs] *adjective* chalky

cre•tin [KREET-n] *noun* 1 (*offensive*) stupid or mentally defective person 2 (*obsolete*) person afflicted with deficiency in thyroid gland causing physical and mental retardation

cre•vasse [kri-VAS] *noun* deep open chasm, esp. in glacier

crev•ice [KREV-is] *noun* cleft, fissure, chink

crew [kroo] *noun* 1 ship's, boat's or aircraft's company, excluding passengers 2 (*informal*) gang or set ▷ *verb* 3 serve as crew > **crew cut** closely cropped haircut

crew•el [KROO-əl] *noun* fine worsted yarn, used in needlework and embroidery

crib [krib] *noun* 1 child's cot 2 barred rack used for fodder 3 plagiarism 4 translation used by students, sometimes illicitly ▷ *verb transitive* **cribbed, crib•bing** 5 confine in small space 6 copy unfairly

crib•bage [KRIB-ij] *noun* card game for two, three, or four players

crick [krik] *noun* spasm or cramp in muscles, esp. in neck

crick•et[1] [KRIK-it] *noun* chirping insect

cricket[2] *noun* outdoor game played with bats, ball and wickets by teams of eleven a side > **crick'et•er** *noun*

crime [krīm] *noun* 1 violation of law (usu. a serious offense) 2 wicked or forbidden act 3 (*informal*) something to be regretted > **crim•i•nal** [KRIM-ə-nl] *adjective, noun* > **crim•i•nal'i•ty** *noun*

DICTIONARY

C

THESAURUS

creditable *adjective* PRAISEWORTHY, admirable, commendable, honorable, laudable, reputable, respectable, worthy

credulity *noun* GULLIBILITY, blind faith, credulousness, naivety

creed *noun* BELIEF, articles of faith, catechism, credo, doctrine, dogma, principles

creek *noun* STREAM, bayou, brook, rivulet, runnel, tributary, watercourse

creep *verb* 1 SNEAK, approach unnoticed, skulk, slink, steal, tiptoe
2 CRAWL, glide, slither, squirm, wriggle, writhe
▷ *noun* 3 (*slang*) BROWN-NOSER (*slang*), crawler (*slang*), scuzzbucket (*slang*), sneak, sycophant, toady
4 (*slang*) JERK, loser, lowlife, pervert, scumbag (*slang*), scuzzbucket (*slang*)

creeper *noun* CLIMBING PLANT, rambler, runner, trailing plant, vine

creeps *plural noun* ▷ **give one the creeps** (*informal*) DISGUST, frighten, make one's hair stand on end, make one squirm, repel, repulse, scare

creepy *adjective* (*informal*) DISTURBING, eerie, frightening, hair-raising, macabre, menacing, scary (*informal*), sinister

crescent *noun* MENISCUS, new moon, sickle

crest *noun* 1 TOP, apex, crown, highest point, peak, pinnacle, ridge, summit
2 TUFT, comb, crown, mane, plume
3 EMBLEM, badge, bearings, device, insignia, symbol

crestfallen *adjective* DISAPPOINTED, dejected, depressed, despondent, discouraged, disheartened, downcast, downhearted

crevice *noun* GAP, chink, cleft, crack, cranny, fissure, hole, opening, slit

crew *noun* 1 COMPANY *or* SHIP'S COMPANY, hands, complement *or* ship's complement
2 TEAM, corps, gang, posse, squad
3 (*informal*) CROWD, band, bunch (*informal*), gang, horde, mob, pack, set

crib *noun* 1 CRADLE, bassinet, bed, cot
2 MANGER, rack, stall
▷ *verb* 3 (*informal*) COPY, cheat, pirate, plagiarize, purloin, steal

crime *noun* 1 OFFENSE, felony, misdeed, misdemeanor, transgression, trespass, unlawful act, violation
2 LAWBREAKING, corruption, illegality, misconduct, vice, wrongdoing

criminal *noun* 1 LAWBREAKER, convict, crook (*informal*), culprit, felon, offender, perp (*informal*), sinner, villain
▷ *adjective* 2 UNLAWFUL, corrupt, crooked

> **crim•i•nol'o•gy** *noun* study of crime and criminals
crimp [krimp] *verb transitive* 1 pinch into tiny parallel pleats 2 wrinkle
crim•son [KRIM-zən] *adjective, noun* (of) rich deep red
cringe [krinj] *verb intransitive* **cringed, cring•ing** 1 shrink, cower 2 behave obsequiously
crin•kle [KRING-kəl] *verb, noun* **-kled, -kling** wrinkle
crin•o•line [KRIN-l-in] *noun* hooped petticoat or skirt of stiff material
crip•ple [KRIP-əl] *noun* 1 (*offensive*) one not having normal use of limbs, disabled or deformed person ▷ *verb transitive* **-pled, -pling** 2 maim, disable, impair 3 weaken, lessen efficiency of
cri•sis [KRĪ-sis] *noun, plural* **-ses** [-seez] 1 turning point or decisive moment, esp. in illness 2 time of acute danger or difficulty
crisp [krisp] *adjective* **-er, -est** 1 brittle but firm 2 brisk, decided 3 clear-cut 4 fresh, invigorating 5 crackling 6 of hair, curly ▷ *noun* 7 dessert of fruit baked with a crunchy mixture > **crisp'er** *noun* refrigerator compartment for storing salads, etc.
cri•te•ri•on [krī-TEER-ee-ən] *noun, plural* **-ri•a** [-ree-ə] standard of judgment
crit•i•cal [KRIT-i-kəl] *adjective* 1 faultfinding 2 discerning 3 skilled in or given to judging 4 of great importance, crucial, decisive > **crit'ic** *noun* 1 one who passes judgment 2 writer expert in judging works of literature, art, etc. > **crit'i•cism** *noun* > **crit'i•cize** *verb transitive* **-cized, ciz•ing**
> **cri•tique** [kri-TEEK] *noun* critical essay, carefully written criticism
croak [krohk] *verb* 1 utter deep hoarse cry, as raven, frog 2 talk dismally ▷ *verb intransitive* 3 (*slang*) die ▷ *noun* 4 deep hoarse cry
cro•chet [kroh-SHAY] *noun* 1 kind of handicraft like knitting, done with small hooked needle ▷ *verb* 2 do, make such work
crock [krok] *noun* 1 earthenware jar or pot 2 broken piece of earthenware > **crock'er•y** *noun* earthenware dishes, utensils, etc.
croc•o•dile [KROK-ə-dīl] *noun* large amphibious reptile > **crocodile tears** insincere grief
crois•sant [krwah-SAHN] *noun* buttery, crescent-shaped roll of leavened dough or puff pastry
crone [krohn] *noun* witchlike old woman
cro•ny [KROH-nee] *noun, plural* **-nies** intimate friend
crook [kruuk] *noun* 1 hooked staff 2 any hook, bend, sharp turn 3 (*informal*) swindler, criminal > **crook'ed** *adjective* 1 bent, twisted 2 deformed 3 dishonest
croon [kroon] *verb* hum, sing in soft, low tone > **croon'er** *noun*
crop [krop] *noun* 1 produce of cultivation of any plant or plants 2 harvest 3 pouch in bird's gullet 4 stock of whip 5 hunting whip 6 short haircut ▷ *verb* **cropped, crop•ping** 7 cut short 8 raise, produce or occupy land with crop 9 (of animals) bite, eat down 10 poll or clip > **crop'-dust•ing** *noun* spreading fungicide, etc. on crops from aircraft > **crop-top** *noun* short T-shirt or vest that reveals the wearer's midriff

(*informal*), illegal, illicit, immoral, lawless, wicked, wrong
3 DISGRACEFUL, deplorable, foolish, preposterous, ridiculous, scandalous, senseless
cringe *verb* SHRINK, cower, draw back, flinch, recoil, shy, wince
cripple *verb* 1 DISABLE, hamstring, incapacitate, lame, maim, paralyze, weaken
2 DAMAGE, destroy, impair, put out of action, put paid to, ruin, spoil
crippled *adjective* DISABLED, challenged, handicapped, incapacitated, laid up (*informal*), lame, paralyzed
crisis *noun* 1 CRITICAL POINT, climax, crunch (*informal*), crux, culmination, height, moment of truth, turning point
2 EMERGENCY, deep water, dire straits, meltdown (*informal*), panic stations (*informal*), plight, predicament, trouble
crisp *adjective* 1 CRUNCHY, brittle, crispy, crumbly, firm, fresh
2 CLEAN, neat, smart, spruce, tidy, trim, well-groomed, well-pressed
3 BRACING, brisk, fresh, invigorating, refreshing
criterion *noun* STANDARD, bench mark, gauge, measure, principle, rule, test, touchstone, yardstick
critic *noun* 1 JUDGE, analyst, authority, commentator, connoisseur, expert, pundit, reviewer
2 FAULT-FINDER, attacker, detractor, knocker (*informal*)
critical *adjective* 1 CRUCIAL, all-important, decisive, pivotal, precarious, pressing, serious, urgent, vital
2 DISPARAGING, captious, censorious, derogatory, disapproving, fault-finding, nagging, nit-picking (*informal*), scathing
3 ANALYTICAL, discerning, discriminating, fastidious, judicious, penetrating, perceptive
criticism *noun* 1 FAULT-FINDING, bad press, censure, character assassination, disapproval, disparagement, flak (*informal*), stick (*slang*)
2 ANALYSIS, appraisal, appreciation, assessment, comment, commentary, critique, evaluation, judgment
criticize *verb* FIND FAULT WITH, carp, censure, condemn, disapprove of, disparage, knock (*informal*), put down
croak *verb* SQUAWK, caw, grunt, utter huskily *or* speak huskily, wheeze
crook *noun* CRIMINAL, cheat, racketeer, robber, rogue, perp (*informal*), shark, swindler, thief, villain
crooked *adjective* 1 BENT, curved, deformed, distorted, hooked, irregular, misshapen, out of shape, twisted, warped, zigzag
2 AT AN ANGLE, askew, awry, lopsided, off-center, slanting, squint, uneven
3 DISHONEST, bent (*slang*), corrupt, criminal, fraudulent, illegal, shady (*informal*), underhand, unlawful
croon *verb* SING, hum, purr, warble
crop *noun* 1 PRODUCE, fruits, gathering, harvest, reaping, vintage, yield
▷ *verb* 2 CUT, clip, lop, pare, prune, shear, snip, trim
3 GRAZE, browse, nibble

> **crop up** (*informal*) happen unexpectedly
cro•quet [kroh-KAY] *noun* lawn game played with balls, wooden mallets and hoops
cro•quette [kroh-KET] *noun* breaded, fried ball of minced meat, fish, etc.
cro•sier [KROH-zhər] *noun* bishop's or abbot's staff
cross [kraws] *noun* **1** structure or symbol of two intersecting lines or pieces (at right angles) **2** such a structure of wood as means of execution by tying or nailing victim to it **3** symbol of Christian faith **4** any thing or mark in the shape of cross **5** misfortune, annoyance, affliction **6** intermixture of breeds, hybrid ▷ *verb* **7** move or go across (something) **8** intersect **9** meet and pass ▷ *verb transitive* **10** mark with lines across **11** (with *out*) delete **12** place or put in form of cross **13** make sign of cross on or over **14** modify breed of animals or plants by intermixture **15** thwart **16** oppose ▷ *adjective* **17** out of temper, angry **18** peevish, perverse **19** transverse **20** intersecting **21** contrary **22** adverse > **cross'ing** *noun* **1** intersection of roads, rails, etc. **2** part of street where pedestrians are expected to cross > **cross'ly** *adverb* > **cross'wise** *adverb, adjective* > **cross'bow** [-boh] *noun* bow fixed across wooden shoulder stock > **cross'breed** *noun* breed produced from parents of different breeds > **cross-country** *adjective, noun* (long race) held over open ground > **cross'-ex•am'ine** *verb transitive* examine witness already examined by other side > **cross'-eyed** *adjective* having eye(s) turning inward > **cross'-fer•ti•li•za•tion** *noun* fertilization of one plant by pollen of another > **cross'-grained'** *adjective* having fibers running diagonally, etc. **1** perverse > **cross'-ref'er•ence** *noun* reference within text to another part of text > **cross section** **1** transverse section **2** group of people fully representative of a nation, community, etc. > **cross'word puzzle** puzzle built up of intersecting words, of which some letters are common, the words being indicated by clues
crotch [kroch] *noun* **1** angle between legs, genital area **2** fork
crotch•et [KROCH-it] *noun* musical note, equal to half the length of a minim
crotch•et•y [KROCH-i-tee] *adjective* **1** peevish **2** irritable
crouch [krowch] *verb intransitive* **1** bend low **2** huddle down close to ground **3** stoop servilely, cringe ▷ *noun*
croup [kroop] *noun* throat disease of children, with cough
crou•pi•er [KROO-pee-ər] *noun* person dealing cards, collecting money, etc. at gambling table
crow[1] [kroh] *noun* large black scavenging bird > **crow's'-foot** *noun* wrinkle at corner of eye > **crow's'-nest** *noun* lookout platform high on ship's mast
crow[2] *verb intransitive* **1** utter rooster's cry **2** boast one's happiness or superiority ▷ *noun* **3** rooster's cry
crow•bar [KROH-bahr] *noun* iron or steel bar, usu. wedge-shaped, for levering
crowd [krowd] *noun* **1** throng, mass ▷ *verb intransitive* **2** flock together ▷ *verb transitive* **3** cram, force, thrust, pack **4** fill with people **crowd out** exclude by excess already in
crown [krown] *noun* **1** monarch's headdress **2** wreath for head **3** monarch **4** monarchy **5** royal power **6** various foreign coins **7** top of head **8** summit, top **9** completion or perfection of thing ▷ *verb transitive* **10** put crown on **11** confer title **12** occur as culmination of series of events **13** (*informal*) hit on head > **crown prince** heir to throne
cru•cial [KROO-shəl] *adjective* **1** decisive, critical **2** (*informal*) very important
cru•ci•ble [KROO-sə-bəl] *noun* small

DICTIONARY

C

THESAURUS

crop up *verb* HAPPEN, appear, arise, emerge, occur, spring up, turn up
cross *verb* **1** GO ACROSS, bridge, cut across, extend over, move across, pass over, span, traverse
2 INTERSECT, crisscross, intertwine
3 OPPOSE, block, impede, interfere, obstruct, resist
4 INTERBREED, blend, crossbreed, cross-fertilize, cross-pollinate, hybridize, intercross, mix, mongrelize
▷ *noun* **5** CRUCIFIX, rood
6 CROSSROADS, crossing, intersection, junction
7 MIXTURE, amalgam, blend, combination
8 TROUBLE, affliction, burden, grief, load, misfortune, trial, tribulation, woe, worry
▷ *adjective* **9** ANGRY, annoyed, grumpy, ill-tempered, in a bad mood, irascible, put out, short
10 TRANSVERSE, crosswise, diagonal, intersecting, oblique
cross-examine *verb* QUESTION, grill (*informal*), interrogate, pump, quiz
cross out, cross off *verb* STRIKE OFF *or* STRIKE OUT, blue-pencil, cancel, delete, eliminate, score off *or* score out
crouch *verb* BEND DOWN, bow, duck, hunch, kneel, squat, stoop
crow *verb* GLOAT, blow one's own trumpet, boast, brag, exult, strut, swagger, triumph
crowd *noun* **1** MULTITUDE, army, horde, host, mass, mob, pack, swarm, throng
2 GROUP, bunch (*informal*), circle, clique, lot, set
3 AUDIENCE, attendance, gate, house, spectators
▷ *verb* **4** FLOCK, congregate, gather, mass, stream, surge, swarm, throng
5 SQUEEZE, bundle, congest, cram, pack, pile
crowded *adjective* PACKED, busy, congested, cramped, full, jam-packed, swarming, teeming
crown *noun* **1** CORONET, circlet, diadem, tiara
2 LAUREL WREATH, garland, honor, laurels, prize, trophy, wreath
3 HIGH POINT, apex, crest, pinnacle, summit, tip, top
▷ *verb* **4** HONOR, adorn, dignify, festoon
5 CAP, be the climax of *or* be the culmination of, complete, finish, perfect, put the finishing touch to, round off, top
6 (*slang*) STRIKE, belt (*informal*), box, hit over the head, punch
Crown *noun* **1** MONARCHY, royalty, sovereignty
2 MONARCH, emperor *or* empress, king *or* queen, ruler, sovereign
crucial *adjective* **1** VITAL, essential, high-priority, important, momentous, pressing, urgent
2 CRITICAL, central, decisive, pivotal

melting pot

cru•ci•fy [KROO-sə-fī] *verb transitive* **-fied, -fy•ing** 1 put to death on cross 2 treat cruelly 3 (*informal*) ridicule > **cru'ci•fix** [-fiks] *noun* 1 cross 2 image of (Christ on the) Cross > **cru•ci•fix'ion** *noun*

crude [krood] *adjective* **crud•er, crud•est** 1 lacking taste, vulgar 2 in natural or raw state, unrefined 3 rough, unfinished > **cru'di•ty** *noun, plural* **-ties**

cru•el [KROO-əl] *adjective* **-er, -est** 1 delighting in others' pain 2 causing pain or suffering > **cru'el•ly** *adverb* > **cru'el•ty** *noun, plural* **-ties**

cru•et [KROO-it] *noun* 1 small container for salt, pepper, vinegar, oil, etc. 2 stand holding such containers

cruise [krooz] *verb intransitive* **cruised, cruis•ing** 1 travel about in a ship for pleasure, etc. 2 (of vehicle, aircraft) travel at safe, average speed ▷ *noun* 3 cruising voyage > **cruis'er** *noun* 1 ship that cruises 2 warship lighter and faster than battleship > **cruise missile** subsonic missile guided throughout its flight

crumb [krum] *noun* 1 small particle, fragment, esp. of bread ▷ *verb transitive* 2 reduce to, break into, cover with crumbs

crum•ble [KRUM-bəl] *verb* **-bled, -bling** 1 break into small fragments, disintegrate, crush 2 perish, decay ▷ *verb intransitive* 3 fall apart or away > **crum'bly** *adjective* **-bli•er, -bli•est**

crum•my [KRUM-ee] *adjective* **-mi•er, -mi•est** (*slang*) inferior, contemptible

crum•ple [KRUM-pəl] *verb* **-pled, -pling** 1 (cause to) collapse 2 make or become crushed, wrinkled, creased

crunch [krunch] *noun* 1 sound made by chewing crisp food, treading on gravel, hard snow, etc. 2 (*informal*) critical moment or situation ▷ *verb* 3 make crunching sound

cru•sade [kroo-SAYD] *noun* 1 medieval Christian war to recover Holy Land 2 campaign against something believed to be evil 3 concerted action to further a cause ▷ *verb intransitive* **-sad•ed, -sad•ing** > **cru•sad'er** *noun*

crush[1] [krush] *verb transitive* 1 compress so as to break, bruise, crumple 2 break to small pieces 3 defeat utterly, overthrow ▷ *noun* 4 act of crushing 5 crowd of people, etc.

crush[2] *noun* (*informal*) infatuation

crust [krust] *noun* 1 hard outer part of bread 2 similar hard outer casing on anything ▷ *verb* 3 cover with, form, crust > **crust'i•ly** *adverb* > **crust'y** *adjective* **crust•i•er, crust•i•est** 1 having, or like, crust 2 harsh, surly 3 rude

crus•ta•cean [kru-STAY-shən] *noun* hard-shelled animal, e.g. crab, lobster ▷ *adjective*

crutch [kruch] *noun* 1 staff with crosspiece to go under armpit of lame person, device resembling this 2 support 3 groin, crotch

crux [kruks] *noun, plural* **-es** 1 that on which a decision turns 2 anything that puzzles very much

cry [krī] *verb intransitive* **cried, cry•ing** 1 weep 2 wail 3 utter call 4 shout 5 clamor or beg (for) ▷ *verb transitive* **cried, cry•ing** 6 utter loudly, proclaim ▷ *noun* 7 loud utterance 8 scream, wail, shout 9 call of animal 10 fit of weeping 11 watchword

cry•o•gen•ics [krī-ə-JEN-iks] *noun* branch of physics concerned with phenomena at very low temperatures > **cry•o•gen'ic** *adjective*

crypt [kript] *noun* vault, esp. under church

DICTIONARY • THESAURUS

crucify *verb* EXECUTE, persecute, torment, torture

crude *adjective* 1 PRIMITIVE, clumsy, makeshift, rough, rough-and-ready, rudimentary, unpolished
2 VULGAR, coarse, dirty, gross, indecent, obscene, off-color, scuzzy (*slang*), smutty, tasteless, uncouth
3 UNREFINED, natural, raw, unprocessed

crudely *adverb* VULGARLY, bluntly, coarsely, impolitely, roughly, rudely, tastelessly

crudity *noun* 1 ROUGHNESS, clumsiness, crudeness
2 VULGARITY, coarseness, impropriety, indecency, indelicacy, obscenity, smuttiness

cruel *adjective* 1 BRUTAL, barbarous, callous, hard-hearted, heartless, inhumane, malevolent, sadistic, spiteful, unkind, vicious
2 MERCILESS, pitiless, ruthless, unrelenting

cruelly *adverb* 1 BRUTALLY, barbarously, callously, heartlessly, in cold blood, mercilessly, pitilessly, sadistically, spitefully
2 BITTERLY, deeply, fearfully, grievously, monstrously, severely

cruelty *noun* BRUTALITY, barbarity, callousness, depravity, fiendishness, inhumanity, mercilessness, ruthlessness, spitefulness

cruise *noun* 1 SAIL, boat trip, sea trip, voyage
▷ *verb* 2 SAIL, coast, voyage
3 TRAVEL ALONG, coast, drift, keep a steady pace

crumb *noun* BIT, fragment, grain, morsel, scrap, shred, soupçon (*French*)

crumble *verb* 1 DISINTEGRATE, collapse, decay, degenerate, deteriorate, fall apart, go to pieces, go to rack and ruin, tumble down
2 CRUSH, fragment, granulate, grind, pound, powder, pulverize

crummy *adjective* (*informal*) 1 DESPICABLE, contemptible, lousy (*slang*), mean, scuzzy (*slang*)
2 INFERIOR, deficient, inadequate, lousy (*slang*), of poor quality, poor, substandard
3 UNWELL, below par, off color, under the weather (*informal*)

crumple *verb* 1 CRUSH, crease, rumple, screw up, scrumple, wrinkle
2 COLLAPSE, break down, cave in, fall, give way, go to pieces

crunch *verb* 1 CHOMP, champ, chew noisily, grind, munch
▷ *noun* 2 (*informal*) CRITICAL POINT, crisis, crux, emergency, moment of truth, test

crusade *noun* CAMPAIGN, cause, drive, movement, push

crush[1] *verb* 1 SQUASH, break, compress, press, pulverize, squeeze
2 OVERCOME, conquer, overpower, overwhelm, put down, quell, stamp out, subdue
3 HUMILIATE, abash, mortify, put down (*slang*), quash, shame
▷ *noun* 4 CROWD, huddle, jam

crust *noun* LAYER, coating, covering, shell, skin, surface

crusty *adjective* 1 CRISPY, hard
2 IRRITABLE, cantankerous, cross, gruff, prickly,

> **cryp'tic** *adjective* secret, mysterious > **cryp'ti•cal•ly** *adverb* > **cryp'to•gram** *noun* piece of writing in code > **cryp•tog'ra•phy** *noun* art of writing, decoding ciphers

crys•tal [KRIS-tl] *noun* 1 clear transparent mineral 2 very clear glass 3 cut-glass ware 4 characteristic form assumed by many substances, with definite internal structure and external shape of symmetrically arranged plane surfaces > **crys'tal•line** [-tl-in] *adjective* > **crys•tal•li•za'tion** *noun* > **crys'tal•lize** *verb* **-lized, -liz•ing** 1 form into crystals 2 become definite

Cs *chem.* cesium

Cu *chem.* copper

cub [kub] *noun* 1 young of fox and other animals 2 cub scout ▷ *verb* **cubbed, cub•bing** 3 bring forth cubs > **cub scout** member of junior division of the Boy Scouts

cub•by•hole [KUB-ee-hohl] *noun* 1 small, enclosed space or room 2 pigeonhole

cube [kyoob] *noun* 1 regular solid figure contained by six equal square sides 2 cube-shaped block 3 product obtained by multiplying number by itself twice ▷ *verb transitive* **cubed, cub•ing** 4 multiply thus > **cu'bic** *adjective* > **cub'ism** *noun* style of art in which objects are presented as assemblage of geometrical shapes > **cub'ist** *noun, adjective*

cu•bi•cle [KYOO-bi-kəl] *noun* partially or totally enclosed section of room, as in study hall

cu•bit [KYOO-bit] *noun* old measure of length, about 18 inches

cuck•old [KUK-əld] *noun* man whose wife has committed adultery ▷ *verb transitive*

cuck•oo [KOO-koo] *noun, plural* **-oos** 1 migratory bird that deposits its eggs in the nests of other birds 2 its call ▷ *adjective* (*slang*) 3 crazy ▷ *verb intransitive* **-ooed, -oo•ing**

cu•cum•ber [KYOO-kum-bər] *noun* 1 plant with long fleshy green fruit 2 the fruit, used in salad

cud [kud] *noun* food that ruminant animal brings back into mouth to chew again **chew the cud** reflect, meditate

cud•dle [KUD-l] *verb transitive* **-dled, -dling** 1 hug ▷ *verb intransitive* **-dled, -dling** 2 lie close and snug, nestle ▷ *noun*

cudg•el [KUJ-əl] *noun* 1 short thick stick ▷ *verb transitive* **-eled, -el•ing** 2 beat with cudgel

cue[1] [kyoo] *noun* 1 last words of actor's speech, etc. as signal to another to act or speak 2 signal, hint, example for action

cue[2] *noun* long tapering rod used in pool, billiards, etc.

cuff[1] [kuf] *noun* 1 ending of sleeve 2 wristband **off the cuff** (*informal*) without preparation

cuff[2] *verb transitive* 1 strike with open hand ▷ *noun* 2 blow with hand

cui•sine [kwi-ZEEN] *noun* 1 style of cooking 2 menu, food offered by restaurant, etc.

cul-de-sac [KUL-də-SAK] *noun, plural* **culs-** [kulz-] 1 street, lane open only at one end 2 blind alley

cu•li•nar•y [KYOO-lə-ner-ee] *adjective* of, for, suitable for, cooking or kitchen

cull [kul] *verb transitive* 1 gather, select 2 take out selected animals from herd ▷ *noun* 3 something culled

cul•mi•nate [KUL-mə-nayt] *verb intransitive* **-nat•ed, -nat•ing** 1 reach highest point 2 come to climax, to a head > **cul•mi•na'tion** *noun*

cul•pa•ble [KUL-pə-bəl] *adjective* blameworthy > **cul•pa•bil'i•ty** *noun*

cul•prit [KUL-prit] *noun* one guilty of usu. minor offense

cult [kult] *noun* 1 system of religious worship 2 pursuit of, devotion to, some person, thing, or activity > **cult'ism** *noun* practices of a religious cult > **cult'ist** *noun*

cul•ti•vate [KUL-tə-vayt] *verb transitive* **-vat•ed, -vat•ing** 1 till and prepare (soil) to raise crops 2 develop, improve, refine 3 devote attention to, cherish 4 practice 5 foster > **cul•ti•va'tion** *noun*

cul•ture [KUL-chər] *noun* 1 state of manners, taste, and intellectual development at a time or place 2 cultivating 3 artificial rearing 4 set of bacteria so reared > **cul'tur•al** *adjective* > **cul'tured** *adjective* refined, showing culture > **cultured**

---

short-tempered, testy

cry *verb* 1 WEEP, blubber, shed tears, snivel, sob
2 SHOUT, bawl, bellow, call out, exclaim, howl, roar, scream, shriek, yell
▷ *noun* 3 WEEPING, blubbering, snivelling, sob, sobbing, weep
4 SHOUT, bellow, call, exclamation, howl, roar, scream, screech, shriek, yell
5 APPEAL, plea

cub *noun* YOUNG, offspring, whelp

cuckoo *adjective* (*slang*) INSANE, bonkers (*informal*), crazy, daft (*informal*), foolish, idiotic, nuts (*slang*), out of one's mind, stupid

cuddle *verb* HUG, bill and coo, cosset, embrace, fondle, pet, snuggle

cudgel *noun* CLUB, baton, bludgeon, stick, truncheon

cue *noun* SIGNAL, catchword, hint, key, prompting, reminder, sign, suggestion

cul-de-sac *noun* DEAD END, blind alley

culminate *verb* END UP, climax, close, come to a climax, come to a head, conclude, finish, wind up

culmination *noun* CLIMAX, acme, conclusion, consummation, finale, peak, pinnacle, zenith

culpable *adjective* BLAMEWORTHY, at fault, found wanting, guilty, in the wrong, to blame, wrong

culprit *noun* OFFENDER, criminal, evildoer, felon, guilty party, miscreant, perp (*informal*), transgressor, wrongdoer

cult *noun* 1 SECT, clique, faction, religion, school
2 DEVOTION, idolization, worship

cultivate *verb* 1 FARM, plant, plow, tend, till, work
2 DEVELOP, foster, improve, promote, refine
3 COURT, dance attendance upon, run after, seek out

cultivation *noun* 1 FARMING, gardening, husbandry, planting, plowing, tillage
2 DEVELOPMENT, encouragement, fostering, furtherance, nurture, patronage, promotion, support

cultural *adjective* ARTISTIC, civilizing, edifying, educational, enlightening, enriching, humane, liberal

culture *noun* 1 CIVILIZATION, customs, lifestyle, mores, society, way of life
2 REFINEMENT, education, enlightenment, good

pearl pearl artificially induced to grow in oyster shell
cul•vert [KUL-vərt] *noun* tunneled drain for passage of water under road, railroad, etc.
cum•ber•some [KUM-bər-səm] *adjective* awkward, unwieldy
cu•mu•la•tive [KYOO-myə-lə-tiv] *adjective* 1 becoming greater by successive additions 2 representing the sum of many items
cu•mu•lus [KYOO-myə-ləs] *noun, plural* **-li** [-lī] cloud shaped in rounded white woolly masses
cu•ne•i•form [kyoo-NEE-ə-form] *adjective* wedge-shaped, esp. of ancient Babylonian writing
cun•ning [KUN-ing] *adjective* 1 crafty, sly 2 ingenious 3 cute ▷ *noun* 4 skill in deceit or evasion 5 skill, ingenuity
cup [kup] *noun* 1 small drinking vessel with handle at one side 2 any small drinking vessel 3 contents of cup 4 various cup-shaped formations, cavities, sockets, etc. 5 cup-shaped trophy as prize 6 portion or lot 7 iced drink of wine and other ingredients ▷ *verb transitive* **cupped, cup•ping** 8 shape as cup (hands, etc.) > **cup•ful** *noun, plural* **-fuls** > **cup•board** [KUB-ərd] *noun* piece of furniture, recess in room, with door, for storage
Cu•pid [KYOO-pid] *noun* god of love
cu•pid•i•ty [kyoo-PID-i-tee] *noun* 1 greed for possessions 2 covetousness
cu•po•la [KYOO-pə-lə] *noun* dome
cu•pre•ous [KYOO-pree-əs] *adjective* of, containing, copper
cur [kur] *noun* 1 dog of mixed breed 2 surly, contemptible, or mean person
cu•ra•re [kyuu-RAHR-ee] *noun* poisonous resin of S Amer. tree, now used as muscle relaxant in medicine
cu•rate [KYUUR-it] *noun* parish priest > **cu'ra•cy** *noun* office or term of office of curate
cur•a•tive [KYUUR-ə-tiv] *adjective* tending to cure disease ▷ *noun*
cu•ra•tor [kyuur-AY-tər] *noun* person in charge, esp. of museum, library, etc.
curb [kurb] *noun* 1 check, restraint 2 chain or strap passing under horse's lower jaw and giving powerful control with reins 3 edging, esp. of stone or concrete, along street, path, etc. ▷ *verb transitive* 4 restrain 5 apply curb to
curd [kurd] *noun* 1 coagulated milk > **cur•dle** [KUR-dl] *verb* **-dled, -dling** 1 turn into curd, coagulate
cure [kyuur] *verb transitive* **cured, cur•ing** 1 heal, restore to health 2 remedy 3 preserve (fish, skins, etc.) ▷ *noun* 4 remedy 5 course of medical treatment 6 successful treatment, restoration to health > **cur'a•ble** *adjective*
cu•rette [kyuu-RET] *noun* surgical instrument for removing dead tissue, etc. from some body cavities > **cu•ret•tage** [kyuur-i-TAHZH] *noun*
cur•few [KUR-fyoo] *noun* 1 official regulation restricting or prohibiting movement of people, esp. at night 2 time set as deadline by such regulation
cu•rie [KYUUR-ee] *noun* standard unit of radium emanation
cu•ri•o [KYUUR-ee-oh] *noun, plural* **-ri•os** rare or curious thing of the kind sought for collections
cu•ri•ous [KYUUR-ee-əs] *adjective* 1 eager to know, inquisitive 2 prying 3 puzzling, strange, odd > **cu•ri•os'i•ty** *noun, plural* **-ties** 1 eagerness to know 2 inquisitiveness 3 strange or rare thing
cu•ri•um [KYUUR-ee-əm] *noun* element produced from plutonium
curl [kurl] *verb intransitive* 1 take spiral or curved shape or path ▷ *verb transitive* 2 bend into spiral or curved shape ▷ *noun* 3 spiral lock of hair 4 spiral, curved state, form or motion > **curl'ing** *noun* target game played with large rounded stones on ice > **curl'y** *adjective* **curl•i•er, curl•i•est**
cur•mudg•eon [kər-MUJ-ən] *noun* surly or miserly person
cur•rent [KUR-ənt] *adjective* 1 of immediate present, going on 2 up-to-date, not yet superseded 3 in circulation or general use ▷ *noun* 4 body of water or air in motion 5 tendency, drift 6 transmission of electricity through conductor > **cur'ren•cy** *noun* 1 money in use 2 state of being in use 3 time during

taste, sophistication, urbanity
3 FARMING, cultivation, husbandry
cultured *adjective* REFINED, educated, enlightened, highbrow, sophisticated, urbane, well-informed, well-read
culvert *noun* DRAIN, channel, conduit, gutter, watercourse
cumbersome *adjective* AWKWARD, bulky, burdensome, heavy, unmanageable, unwieldy, weighty
cunning *adjective* 1 CRAFTY, artful, devious, Machiavellian, sharp, shifty, sly, wily
2 SKILLFUL, imaginative, ingenious
▷ *noun* 3 CRAFTINESS, artfulness, deviousness, guile, slyness, trickery
4 SKILL, artifice, cleverness, ingenuity, subtlety
cup *noun* 1 MUG, beaker, bowl, chalice, goblet, teacup
2 TROPHY
cupboard *noun* CABINET, press
curb *noun* 1 RESTRAINT, brake, bridle, check, control, deterrent, limitation, rein
▷ *verb* 2 RESTRAIN, check, control, hinder, impede, inhibit, restrict, retard, suppress
cure *verb* 1 MAKE BETTER, correct, ease, heal, mend, relieve, remedy, restore
2 PRESERVE, dry, pickle, salt, smoke
▷ *noun* 3 REMEDY, antidote, medicine, nostrum, panacea, treatment
curiosity *noun* 1 INQUISITIVENESS, interest, nosiness (*informal*), prying, snooping (*informal*)
2 ODDITY, freak, novelty, phenomenon, rarity, sight, spectacle, wonder
curious *adjective* 1 INQUIRING, inquisitive, interested, questioning, searching
2 INQUISITIVE, meddling, nosy (*informal*), prying
3 UNUSUAL, bizarre, extraordinary, mysterious, novel, odd, peculiar, rare, strange, unexpected
curl *verb* 1 TWIRL, bend, coil, curve, loop, spiral, turn, twist, wind
▷ *noun* 2 TWIST, coil, kink, ringlet, spiral, whorl
curly *adjective* CURLING, crinkly, curled, frizzy, fuzzy, wavy, winding
currency *noun* 1 MONEY, coinage, coins, notes
2 ACCEPTANCE, circulation, exposure, popularity, prevalence, vogue

which thing is current
cur•ric•u•lum [kə-RIK-yə-ləm] *noun, plural* **-la** [-lə] specified course of study
cur•ry[1] [KUR-ee] *noun, plural* **-ries** 1 highly-flavored, pungent condiment 2 meat, etc. dish flavored with curry ▷ *verb transitive* **-ried, -ry•ing** 3 prepare, flavor dish with curry
curry[2] *verb transitive* **-ried, -ry•ing** 1 groom (horse) with comb 2 dress (leather) **curry favor** try to win favor unworthily, ingratiate oneself
curse [kurs] *noun* 1 profane or obscene expression of anger, etc. 2 utterance expressing extreme ill will toward some person or thing 3 affliction, misfortune, scourge ▷ *verb* **cursed, curs•ing** 4 utter curse, swear (at) 5 afflict > **curs•ed** [KUR-sid] *adjective* 1 hateful 2 wicked 3 deserving of, or under, a curse
cur•sive [KUR-siv] *adjective, noun* (written in) running script, with letters joined
cur•so•ry [KUR-sə-ree] *adjective* rapid, hasty, not detailed, superficial > **cur'so•ri•ly** *adverb*
curt [kurt] *adjective* **-er, -est** short, rudely brief, abrupt > **curt'ness** *noun*
cur•tail [kər-TAYL] *verb transitive* cut short, diminish
cur•tain [KUR-tn] *noun* 1 hanging drapery at window, etc. 2 cloth hung as screen 3 screen separating audience and stage in theater 4 end to act or scene, etc. ▷ *verb transitive* 5 provide, cover with curtain > **cur•tains** *plural noun* (*slang*) death > **curtain call** return to stage by performers to acknowledge applause
curt•sy [KURT-see] *noun, plural* **-sies** woman's bow or respectful gesture made by bending knees and lowering body ▷ *verb intransitive* **-sied, sy•ing**
curve [kurv] *noun* 1 line of which no part is straight 2 bent line or part ▷ *verb* 3 bend into curve > **cur•va'ceous** [-VAY-shəs] *adjective* shapely > **cur'va•ture** [-və-chər] *noun* 1 a bending 2 bent shape
cush•ion [KUUSH-ən] *noun* 1 bag filled with soft stuffing or air, to support or ease body 2 any soft pad or support 3 resilient rim of pool table ▷ *verb transitive* 4 provide, protect with cushion 5 lessen effects of
cush•y *adjective* **cush•i•er, cush•i•est** (*informal*) easy
cusp [kusp] *noun* 1 pointed end, esp. of tooth 2 *astrology* point marking the beginning of a house or sign > **cus'pid** *noun* pointed tooth
cus•pi•dor [KUS-pi-dor] *noun* spittoon
cus•tard [KUS-tərd] *noun* dessert made of eggs, sugar and milk
cus•to•dy [KUS-tə-dee] *noun, plural* **-dies** safekeeping, guardianship, imprisonment > **cus•to'di•an** *noun* keeper, caretaker
cus•tom [KUS-təm] *noun* 1 habit 2 practice 3 fashion, usage 4 business patronage 5 tax > **cus•toms** 1 duties levied on imports 2 government department that collects these 3 area in airport, etc. where customs officials examine baggage for dutiable goods > **cus•tom•ar'i•ly** *adverb* > **cus'tom•ar•y** *adjective* usual, habitual > **cus'tom•er** *noun* 1 one who enters store to buy, esp. regularly 2 purchaser
cut [kut] *verb transitive* **cut, cut•ting** 1 sever, penetrate, wound, divide, or separate with

DICTIONARY

C

THESAURUS

current *adjective* 1 PRESENT, contemporary, cool (*informal*), fashionable, in fashion, in vogue, phat (*slang*), present-day, trendy (*informal*), up-to-date
2 PREVALENT, accepted, common, customary, in circulation, popular, topical, widespread
▷ *noun* 3 FLOW, course, draft, jet, progression, river, stream, tide, undertow
4 MOOD, atmosphere, feeling, tendency, trend, undercurrent
curse *verb* 1 SWEAR, blaspheme, cuss (*informal*), take the Lord's name in vain
2 DAMN, anathematize, excommunicate
▷ *noun* 3 OATH, blasphemy, expletive, obscenity, swearing, swearword
4 DENUNCIATION, anathema, ban, excommunication, hoodoo (*informal*), jinx
5 AFFLICTION, bane, hardship, plague, scourge, torment, trouble
cursed *adjective* DAMNED, accursed, bedevilled, doomed, ill-fated
curt *adjective* SHORT, abrupt, blunt, brief, brusque, gruff, monosyllabic, succinct, terse
curtail *verb* CUT SHORT, cut back, decrease, diminish, dock, lessen, reduce, shorten, truncate
curtain *noun* HANGING, drape
curve *noun* 1 BEND, arc, curvature, loop, trajectory, turn
▷ *verb* 2 BEND, arc, arch, coil, hook, spiral, swerve, turn, twist, wind
curved *adjective* BENT, arched, bowed, rounded, serpentine, sinuous, twisted
cushion *noun* 1 PILLOW, beanbag, bolster, hassock, headrest, pad
▷ *verb* 2 SOFTEN, dampen, deaden, muffle, stifle, suppress
custody *noun* 1 SAFEKEEPING, care, charge, keeping, protection, supervision
2 IMPRISONMENT, confinement, detention, incarceration
custom *noun* 1 TRADITION, convention, policy, practice, ritual, rule, usage
2 HABIT, practice, procedure, routine, way, wont
3 CUSTOMERS, patronage, trade
customary *adjective* USUAL, accepted, accustomed, common, conventional, established, normal, ordinary, routine, traditional
customer *noun* CLIENT, buyer, consumer, patron, purchaser, regular (*informal*), shopper
customs *plural noun* DUTY, import charges, tariff, tax, toll
cut *verb* 1 PENETRATE, chop, pierce, score, sever, slash, slice, slit, wound
2 DIVIDE, bisect, dissect, slice, split
3 TRIM, clip, hew, lop, mow, pare, prune, shave, snip
4 ABRIDGE, abbreviate, condense, curtail, delete, shorten
5 REDUCE, contract, cut back, decrease, diminish, lower, slash, slim *or* slim down
6 SHAPE, carve, chisel, engrave, fashion, form, sculpt, whittle
7 HURT, insult, put down, snub, sting, wound
▷ *noun* 8 INCISION, gash, laceration, nick, slash, slit, stroke, wound
9 REDUCTION, cutback, decrease, fall, lowering, saving

pressure of edge or edged instrument **2** pare, detach, trim, or shape by cutting **3** divide **4** intersect **5** reduce, decrease **6** abridge **7** (*informal*) ignore (person) **8** strike (with whip, etc.) **9** (*informal*) deliberately stay away from ▷ *noun* **10** act of cutting **11** stroke **12** blow, wound (of knife, whip, etc.) **13** reduction, decrease **14** fashion, shape **15** incision **16** engraving **17** piece cut off **18** division **19** excavation (for road, canal, etc.) through high ground **20** (*informal*) share, esp. of profits > **cut'ter** *noun* **1** one who, that which, cuts **2** ship's boat for carrying stores, etc. **3** small armed government boat > **cut'ting** *noun* **1** act of cutting, thing cut off or out **2** shoot, twig of plant ▷ *adjective* **3** sarcastic, unkind > **cut'ting edge** *noun* **1** the leading position in any field ▷ *adjective* **2** leading > **cut'throat** *adjective* **1** merciless ▷ *noun* **2** murderer **cut dead** refuse to recognize an acquaintance

cu•ta•ne•ous [kyoo-TAY-nee-əs] *adjective* of skin

cute [kyoot] *adjective* **cut•er, cut•est** appealing, attractive, pretty

cu•ti•cle [KYOO-ti-kəl] *noun* dead skin, esp. at base of fingernail

cut•lass [KUT-ləs] *noun* short broad-bladed sword

cut•ler•y [KUT-lə-ree] *noun* knives, forks, spoons, etc.

cut•let [KUT-lit] *noun* small piece of meat broiled or fried

cy•a•nide [SĪ-ə-nīd] *noun* extremely poisonous chemical compound

cy•a•no•sis [sī-ə-NOH-sis] *noun* blueness of the skin > **cy•a•not'ic** *adjective*

cyber- [SĪ-bər] *combining form* indicating computers: *cyberspace*

cy•ber•net•ics [sī-bər-NET-iks] *noun* comparative study of control mechanisms of electronic and biological systems

cy•ber•space [SĪ-bər-spays] *noun* hypothetical environment containing all the data stored in computers

cy•ber•squat•ting [SĪ-bər-skwot-ing] *noun* registering an Internet domain name belonging to another person in the hope of selling it to them for a profit > **cy'ber•squat•ter** *noun*

cy•cle [SĪ-kəl] *noun* **1** recurrent series or period **2** rotation of events **3** complete series or period **4** development following course of stages **5** series of poems, etc. **6** bicycle ▷ *verb intransitive* **-cled, -cling 7** move in cycles **8** ride bicycle > **cy'clist** *noun* bicycle rider

cy•clone [SĪ-klohn] *noun* **1** system of winds moving around center of low pressure **2** circular storm > **cy•clon'ic** [-KLON-ik] *adjective*

cy•clo•tron [SĪ-klə-tron] *noun* powerful apparatus that accelerates the circular movement of subatomic particles in a magnetic field, used for work in nuclear disintegration

cyg•net [SIG-nit] *noun* young swan

cyl•in•der [SIL-in-dər] *noun* **1** roller-shaped solid or hollow body, of uniform diameter **2** piston chamber of engine > **cy•lin'dri•cal** *adjective*

cym•bal [SIM-bəl] *noun* one of pair of two brass plates struck together to produce ringing or clashing sound in music

cyn•ic [SIN-ik] *noun* one who expects, believes, the worst about people, their motives, or outcome of events > **cyn'i•cal** *adjective* > **cyn'i•cism** *noun* being cynical

cy•no•sure [SĪN-nə-shuur] *noun* center of attraction

cyst [sist] *noun* sac containing liquid secretion or pus > **cys'tic** *adjective* **1** of cysts **2** of the bladder > **cys•ti'tis** *noun* inflammation of bladder

Czar [zahr] *noun hist* emperor of Russia > **Cza•ri•na** [zah-REE-nə] *noun* wife of Czar

10 (*informal*) SHARE, percentage, piece, portion, section, slice
11 STYLE, fashion, look, shape

cutback *noun* REDUCTION, cut, decrease, economy, lessening, retrenchment

cut down *verb* **1** FELL, hew, level, lop **2** REDUCE, decrease, lessen, lower

cute *adjective* APPEALING, attractive, charming, delightful, engaging, lovable, sweet, winning, winsome

cut in *verb* INTERRUPT, break in, butt in, intervene, intrude

cut off *verb* **1** SEPARATE, isolate, sever **2** INTERRUPT, disconnect, intercept

cut out *verb* STOP, cease, give up, refrain from

cutthroat *adjective* **1** COMPETITIVE, dog-eat-dog, fierce, relentless, ruthless, unprincipled ▷ *noun* **2** MURDERER, assassin, butcher, executioner, hit man (*slang*), killer

cutting *adjective* HURTFUL, acrimonious, barbed, bitter, caustic, malicious, sarcastic, scathing, vitriolic, wounding

cycle *noun* ERA, circle, period, phase, revolution, rotation

cynic *noun* SKEPTIC, doubter, misanthrope, misanthropist, pessimist, scoffer

cynical *adjective* SKEPTICAL, contemptuous, derisive, distrustful, misanthropic, mocking, pessimistic, scoffing, scornful, unbelieving

cynicism *noun* SKEPTICISM, disbelief, doubt, misanthropy, pessimism

Dd

D *chem.* deuterium
dab *verb transitive* **dabbed, dab•bing** 1 apply with momentary pressure, esp. anything wet and soft 2 strike feebly ▷ *noun* 3 smear 4 slight blow or tap 5 small mass
dab•ble [DAB-əl] *verb intransitive* **-bled, -bling** 1 splash about 2 be desultory student or amateur (in) > **dab'bler** *noun*
dac•tyl [DAK-til] *noun* metrical foot of one long followed by two short syllables
dad•dy [DAD-ee] *noun, plural* **-dies** (*informal*) father
da•do [DAY-doh] *noun, plural* **-dos** lower part of room wall when lined or painted separately
dag•ger [DAG-ər] *noun* short, edged stabbing weapon
da•guerre•o•type [də-GAIR-ə-tīp] *noun* 1 early photographic process 2 photograph by it
dahl•ia [DAL-yə] *noun* garden plant of various colors
dai•ly [DAY-lee] *adjective* 1 done, occurring, published every day ▷ *adverb* 2 every day ▷ *noun, plural* **-lies** 3 daily newspaper
dain•ty [DAYN-tee] *adjective* **daint•i•er, daint•i•est** 1 delicate 2 elegant, choice 3 pretty and neat 4 fastidious ▷ *noun, plural* **-ties** 5 delicacy > **dain'ti•ly** *adverb* > **dain'ti•ness** *noun*
dair•y [DAIR-ee] *noun, plural* **-ries** place for processing milk and its products > **dair'y•ing** *noun*
da•is [DAY-is] *noun* raised platform, usually at end of hall
dai•sy [DAY-zee] *noun, plural* **-sies** flower with yellow center and white petals
Da•lai La•ma [DAH-lī-LAH-mə] *noun* head of Buddhist hierarchy in Tibet
dale [dayl] *noun* valley
dal•ly [DAL-ee] *verb intransitive* **-lied, -ly•ing** 1 trifle, spend time in idleness or amusement 2 loiter > **dal'li•ance** *noun*
Dal•ma•tian [dal-MAY-shən] *noun* large dog, white with black spots
dam¹ *noun* 1 barrier to hold back flow of waters 2 water so collected ▷ *verb transitive* **dammed, dam'ming** 3 hold with or as with dam
dam² *noun* female parent (used of animals)
dam•age [DAM-ij] *noun* 1 injury, harm, loss ▷ *verb transitive* **-maged, -mag•ing** 2 harm

---

dab *verb* 1 PAT, daub, stipple, tap, touch ▷ *noun* 2 SPOT, bit, drop, pat, smudge, speck 3 PAT, flick, stroke, tap, touch
dabble *verb* 1 PLAY AT, dip into, potter, tinker, trifle *or* trifle with 2 SPLASH, dip
daft *adjective* (*informal*) 1 FOOLISH, absurd, asinine, bonkers (*informal*), crackpot (*informal*), crazy, idiotic, silly, stupid, witless 2 CRAZY, bonkers (*slang*), demented, deranged, insane, nuts (*slang*), touched, unhinged
dagger *noun* KNIFE, bayonet, dirk, stiletto
daily *adjective* 1 EVERYDAY, diurnal, quotidian ▷ *adverb* 2 EVERY DAY, day by day, once a day
dainty *adjective* DELICATE, charming, elegant, exquisite, fine, graceful, neat, petite, pretty
dam *noun* 1 BARRIER, barrage, embankment, obstruction, wall ▷ *verb* 2 BLOCK UP, barricade, hold back, obstruct, restrict

> **dam•ag•es** *plural noun* sum claimed or adjudged in compensation for injury
dam•ask [DAM-əsk] *noun* 1 figured woven material of silk or linen, esp. white table linen with design shown up by light 2 color of damask rose, velvety red
dame [daym] *noun* 1 (*obsolete*) lady 2 (*slang*) woman
damn [dam] *verb transitive* **damned, damn•ing** 1 condemn to hell 2 be the ruin of 3 give hostile reception to ▷ *verb intransitive* **damned, damn•ing** 4 curse ▷ *interjection* 5 expression of annoyance, impatience, etc. > **dam'na•ble** *adjective* 1 deserving damnation 2 hateful, annoying > **dam•na'tion** *noun*
damp *adjective* 1 moist 2 slightly moist ▷ *noun* 3 diffused moisture 4 in coal mines, dangerous gas ▷ *verb transitive* 5 make damp 6 (often with *down*) deaden, discourage > **damp'en** *verb* 1 make, become damp ▷ *verb transitive* 2 stifle, deaden > **damp'er** *noun* 1 anything that discourages or depresses 2 plate in a flue to control draft
Dan. Daniel
dance [dans] *verb intransitive* **danced, danc•ing** 1 move with measured rhythmic steps, usu. to music 2 be in lively movement 3 bob up and down ▷ *verb transitive* **danced, danc•ing** 4 perform (dance) 5 cause to dance ▷ *noun* 6 lively, rhythmical movement 7 arrangement of such movements 8 tune for them 9 social gathering for the purpose of dancing > **danc'er** *noun* > **dan•seuse** [dahn-SUUZ] *noun* female battle dancer
dan•de•li•on [DAN-dl-ī-ən] *noun* yellow-flowered wild plant
dan•der [DAN-dər] *noun* (*informal*) temper, fighting spirit
dan•druff [DAN-drəf] *noun* dead skin in small scales on the scalp, in hair
dan•dy [DAN-dee] *noun, plural* **-dies** 1 man excessively concerned with smartness of dress ▷ *adjective* 2 (*informal*) excellent
dan•ger [DAYN-jər] *noun* 1 liability or exposure to harm 2 risk, peril > **dan'ger•ous** *adjective*
dan•gle [DANG-gəl] *verb* **-gled, -gling** 1 hang loosely and swaying 2 hold suspended 3 tempt with
dank [dangk] *adjective* **-er, -est** unpleasantly damp and chilly > **dank'ness** *noun*
dap•per [DAP-ər] *adjective* neat and precise, esp. in dress, spruce
dap•ple [DAP-əl] *verb* **-pled, -pling** mark with spots > **dappled** *adjective* 1 spotted 2 mottled 3 variegated > **dapple-gray** *adjective* (of horse) gray marked with darker spots
dare [dair] *verb transitive* **dared, dar•ing** 1 venture, have courage (to) 2 challenge ▷ *noun* 3 challenge > **daring** *adjective* 1 bold ▷ *noun* 2 adventurous courage > **dare'dev•il** *adjective, noun* reckless (person)
dark [dahrk] *adjective* **-er, -est** 1 without light 2 gloomy 3 deep in tint 4 dim, secret 5 unenlightened 6 wicked ▷ *noun* 7 absence of

DICTIONARY • THESAURUS

damage *verb* 1 HARM, hurt, impair, injure, ruin, spoil, weaken, wreck
▷ *noun* 2 HARM, destruction, detriment, devastation, hurt, injury, loss, suffering
3 (*informal*) COST, bill, charge, expense
damages *plural noun* (*law*) COMPENSATION, fine, reimbursement, reparation, satisfaction
damaging *adjective* HARMFUL, deleterious, detrimental, disadvantageous, hurtful, injurious, ruinous
dame *noun* NOBLEWOMAN, baroness, dowager, grande dame (*French*), lady, peeress
damn *verb* 1 CONDEMN, blast, censure, criticize, denounce, put down
2 SENTENCE, condemn, doom
damnation *noun* CONDEMNATION, anathema, damning, denunciation, doom
damned *adjective* 1 DOOMED, accursed, condemned, lost
2 (*slang*) DETESTABLE, confounded, hateful, infernal, loathsome
damp *adjective* 1 MOIST, clammy, dank, dewy, drizzly, humid, soggy, sopping, wet
▷ *noun* 2 MOISTURE, dampness, dankness, drizzle
▷ *verb* 3 MOISTEN, dampen, wet
4 ▷ **damp down** REDUCE, allay, check, curb, diminish, inhibit, pour cold water on, stifle
dampen *verb* 1 REDUCE, check, dull, lessen, moderate, restrain, stifle
2 MOISTEN, make damp, spray, wet
damper *noun* DISCOURAGEMENT, cold water (*informal*), hindrance, restraint, wet blanket (*informal*)
dance *verb* 1 PRANCE, hop, jig, skip, sway, trip, whirl
▷ *noun* 2 BALL, disco, discotheque, hop (*informal, dated*), social
dancer *noun* BALLERINA, Terpsichorean
danger *noun* PERIL, hazard, jeopardy, menace, pitfall, risk, threat, vulnerability
dangerous *adjective* PERILOUS, breakneck, chancy (*informal*), hazardous, insecure, precarious, risky, unsafe, vulnerable
dangerously *adverb* PERILOUSLY, alarmingly, hazardously, precariously, recklessly, riskily, unsafely
dangle *verb* 1 HANG, flap, hang down, sway, swing, trail
2 WAVE, brandish, flaunt, flourish
dapper *adjective* NEAT, smart, soigné *or* soignée, spruce, spry, trim, well-groomed, well turned out
dare *verb* 1 RISK, hazard, make bold, presume, venture
2 CHALLENGE, defy, goad, provoke, taunt, throw down the gauntlet
▷ *noun* 3 CHALLENGE, provocation, taunt
daredevil *noun* 1 ADVENTURER, desperado, exhibitionist, show-off (*informal*), stunt man
▷ *adjective* 2 DARING, adventurous, audacious, bold, death-defying, reckless
daring *adjective* 1 BRAVE, adventurous, audacious, bold, daredevil, fearless, intrepid, reckless, venturesome
▷ *noun* 2 BRAVERY, audacity, boldness, courage, fearlessness, nerve (*informal*), pluck, temerity
dark *adjective* 1 DIM, dingy, murky, shadowy, shady, sunless, unlit
2 BLACK, dark-skinned, dusky, ebony, sable, swarthy
3 GLOOMY, bleak, dismal, grim, morose,

light or color or knowledge > **dark'en** *verb* > **dark'ness** *noun* > **dark horse** somebody, something, esp. competitor in race, about whom little is known > **dark'room** *noun* darkened room for processing film

dar•ling [DAHR-ling] *adjective, noun* much loved or very lovable (person)

darn¹ [dahrn] *verb transitive* 1 mend by filling (hole) with yarn ▷ *noun* 2 place so mended > **darn'ing** *noun*

darn² *interjection* mild expletive

dart [dahrt] *noun* 1 small light pointed missile 2 darting motion 3 small seam or intake in garment ▷ *verb transitive* 4 cast, throw rapidly (dart glance, etc.) ▷ *verb intransitive* 5 go rapidly or abruptly > **darts** *plural noun* indoor game played with numbered target and miniature darts

dash *verb transitive* 1 smash, throw, thrust, send with violence 2 cast down 3 tinge, flavor, mix ▷ *verb intransitive* 4 move, go with great speed or violence ▷ *noun* 5 rush 6 vigor 7 smartness 8 small quantity, tinge 9 stroke (—) between words > **dash'ing** *adjective* spirited, showy > **dash'board** *noun* in car, etc., instrument panel in front of driver

da•shi•ki [də-SHEE-kee] *noun, plural* **-kis** loose pullover garment, orig. African

das•tard [DAS-tərd] *noun* (*obsolete*) contemptible, sneaking coward > **das'tard•ly** *adjective*

da•ta [DAY-tə] *noun* 1 information consisting of observations, measurements, or facts 2 numbers, digits, etc., stored by a computer > **database** *noun* systematized collection of data that can be manipulated by data-processing system for specific purpose > **data processing** handling of data by computer

date¹ [dayt] *noun* 1 day of the month 2 statement on document of its time of writing 3 time of occurrence 4 period of work of art, etc. 5 engagement, appointment ▷ *verb transitive* **dat•ed, dat•ing** 6 mark with date 7 refer to date 8 reveal age of 9 (*informal*) accompany on social outing ▷ *verb intransitive* **dat•ed, dat•ing** 10 exist (from) 11 betray time or period of origin, become old-fashioned > **date'less** *adjective* 1 without date 2 immemorial

date² *noun* 1 sweet, single-stone fruit of palm 2 the palm

da•tive [DAY-tiv] *noun* case indicating indirect object, etc.

da•tum *noun, plural* **da•ta** single piece of information in the form of a fact or statistic

daub [dawb] *verb transitive* 1 coat, plaster, paint coarsely or roughly ▷ *noun* 2 crude picture 3 smear > **daub'er** *noun*

daugh•ter [DAW-tər] *noun* one's female child > **daugh'ter-in-law** *noun, plural* **daugh'ters-in-law** son's wife

daunt [dawnt] *verb transitive* frighten, esp. into giving up purpose > **daunt'less** *adjective* intrepid, fearless

dav•en•port [DAV-ən-port] *noun* 1 small writing table with drawers 2 large couch or settee

Da•vy Jones's locker [DAY-vee JOHN-ziz] bottom of sea, considered as sailors' grave

daw•dle [DAWD-l] *verb intransitive* **-dled, -dling** idle, waste time, loiter > **daw'dler** *noun*

dawn *noun* 1 first light, daybreak 2 first gleam or beginning of anything ▷ *verb intransitive* 3

DICTIONARY

d

THESAURUS

mournful, sad, somber
4 EVIL, foul, infernal, sinister, vile, wicked
5 SECRET, concealed, hidden, mysterious
▷ *noun* 6 DARKNESS, dimness, dusk, gloom, murk, obscurity, semi-darkness
7 NIGHT, evening, nightfall, night-time, twilight

darken *verb* MAKE DARK, blacken, dim, obscure, overshadow

darkness *noun* DARK, blackness, duskiness, gloom, murk, nightfall, shade, shadows

darling *noun* 1 BELOVED, dear, dearest, love, sweetheart, truelove
▷ *adjective* 2 BELOVED, adored, cherished, dear, precious, treasured

darn *verb* 1 MEND, cobble up, patch, repair, sew up, stitch
▷ *noun* 2 MEND, invisible repair, patch, reinforcement

dart *verb* DASH, fly, race, run, rush, shoot, spring, sprint, tear

dash *verb* 1 RUSH, bolt, fly, hurry, race, run, speed, sprint, tear
2 THROW, cast, fling, hurl, slam, sling
3 CRASH, break, destroy, shatter, smash, splinter
4 FRUSTRATE, blight, foil, ruin, spoil, thwart, undo
▷ *noun* 5 RUSH, dart, race, run, sortie, sprint, spurt
6 LITTLE, bit, drop, hint, pinch, soupçon (*French*), sprinkling, tinge, touch
7 STYLE, brio, élan, flair, flourish, panache, spirit, verve

dashing *adjective* 1 BOLD, debonair, gallant, lively, spirited, swashbuckling
2 STYLISH, elegant, flamboyant, jaunty, showy, smart, sporty

data *noun* INFORMATION, details, facts, figures, statistics

date *noun* 1 TIME, age, epoch, era, period, stage
2 APPOINTMENT, assignation, engagement, meeting, rendezvous, tryst
3 PARTNER, escort, friend
▷ *verb* 4 PUT A DATE ON, assign a date to, fix the period of
5 BECOME OLD-FASHIONED, be dated, show one's age
6 ▷ **date from date back to** COME FROM, bear a date of, belong to, exist from, originate in

dated *adjective* OLD-FASHIONED, obsolete, old hat, outdated, outmoded, out of date, passé, unfashionable

daub *verb* SMEAR, coat, cover, paint, plaster, slap on (*informal*)

daunting *adjective* INTIMIDATING, alarming, demoralizing, disconcerting, discouraging, disheartening, frightening, unnerving

dauntless *adjective* FEARLESS, bold, doughty, gallant, indomitable, intrepid, resolute, stouthearted, undaunted, unflinching

dawdle *verb* WASTE TIME, dally, delay, drag one's feet *or* drag one's heels, hang about, idle, loaf, loiter, trail

dawn *noun* 1 DAYBREAK, aurora (*poetic*), cockcrow,

begin to grow light 4 appear, begin 5 (begin to) be understood
day *noun* 1 period of 24 hours 2 time when sun is above horizon 3 point or unit of time 4 daylight 5 part of day occupied by certain activity, time period 6 special or designated day > **day'break** *noun* dawn > **day-care center** place providing daytime care, meals, etc. for preschool children, etc. > **day'dream** *noun* idle fancy ▷ *verb intransitive* > **day'light** *noun* 1 natural light 2 dawn > **day'lights** consciousness, wits > **daylight saving** in summer, time set one hour ahead of local standard time, giving extra daylight in evenings > **day'time** *noun* time between sunrise and sunset
daze [dayz] *verb transitive* **dazed, daz•ing** 1 stupefy, stun, bewilder ▷ *noun* 2 stupefied or bewildered state
daz•zle [DAZ-əl] *verb transitive* **-zled, -zling** 1 blind, confuse or overpower with brightness, light, brilliant display or prospects ▷ *noun* 2 brightness that dazzles the vision
Db *chem.* dubnium
D-day [DEE-day] day selected for start of something, orig. the Allied invasion of Europe on June 6th 1944
de- *prefix* 1 (indicating) removal: *dethrone* 2 (indicating) reversal: *declassify* 3 (indicating) departure: *decamp*
dea•con [DEE-kən] *noun* 1 in hierarchical churches, member of the clergy next below priest 2 in other churches, one who superintends secular affairs > **dea'con•ess** *noun feminine*
dead [ded] *adjective* **-er, -est** 1 no longer alive 2 obsolete 3 numb, without sensation 4 no longer functioning, extinguished 5 lacking luster or movement or vigor 6 sure, complete ▷ *adverb* 7 utterly **the dead** dead person or persons > **dead'en** *verb transitive* > **dead'ly** *adjective* **-li•er, -li•est** 1 fatal 2 deathlike ▷ *adverb* 3 as if dead > **dead'beat** *noun* (*informal*) 1 one who avoids payment of debts 2 lazy, useless person > **dead'head** *noun* 1 log sticking out of water as hindrance to navigation 2 boring person 3 train, aircraft, etc. operating empty, as when returning to terminal > **dead heat** race in which competitors finish exactly even > **dead letter** 1 rule no longer observed 2 letter that post office cannot deliver > **dead'line** *noun* limit of time allowed > **dead'lock** *noun* standstill > **dead'pan** *adjective* expressionless > **dead reckoning** calculation of ship's position from log and compass, when observations cannot be taken > **dead set** 1 absolutely 2 resolute attack **dead of night** time of greatest stillness and darkness
deaf [def] *adjective* **-er, -est** 1 wholly or partly without hearing 2 unwilling to listen > **deaf'en** *verb transitive* make deaf
deal [deel] *verb transitive* **dealt, deal'ing** 1 distribute, give out 2 inflict ▷ *verb intransitive* **dealt, deal'ing** 3 act 4 treat 5 do business

DICTIONARY • THESAURUS

crack of dawn, daylight, morning, sunrise, sunup
2 BEGINNING, advent, birth, emergence, genesis, origin, rise, start
▷ *verb* 3 GROW LIGHT, break, brighten, lighten
4 BEGIN, appear, develop, emerge, originate, rise, unfold
5 ▷ **dawn on, dawn upon** HIT, become apparent, come into one's head, come to mind, occur, register (*informal*), strike
day *noun* 1 TWENTY-FOUR HOURS, daylight, daytime
2 POINT IN TIME, date, time
3 TIME, age, epoch, era, heyday, period, zenith
daybreak *noun* DAWN, break of day, cockcrow, crack of dawn, first light, morning, sunrise, sunup
daydream *noun* 1 FANTASY, dream, fancy, imagining, pipe dream, reverie, wish
▷ *verb* 2 FANTASIZE, dream, envision, fancy, imagine, muse
daylight *noun* SUNLIGHT, light of day, sunshine
daze *verb* 1 STUN, benumb, numb, paralyze, shock, stupefy
▷ *noun* 2 SHOCK, bewilderment, confusion, distraction, stupor, trance, trancelike state
dazed *adjective* SHOCKED, bewildered, confused, disorientated, dizzy, muddled, punch-drunk, staggered, stunned
dazzle *verb* 1 IMPRESS, amaze, astonish, bowl over (*informal*), overpower, overwhelm, take one's breath away
2 BLIND, bedazzle, blur, confuse, daze
▷ *noun* 3 SPLENDOR, brilliance, glitter, magnificence, razzmatazz (*slang*), sparkle
dazzling *adjective* SPLENDID, brilliant, glittering, glorious, scintillating, sensational (*informal*), sparkling, stunning, virtuoso
dead *adjective* 1 DECEASED, defunct, departed, extinct, late, passed away, perished
2 NOT WORKING, inactive, inoperative, stagnant, unemployed, useless
3 NUMB, inert, paralyzed
4 TOTAL, absolute, complete, outright, thorough, unqualified, utter
5 (*informal*) EXHAUSTED, spent, tired, worn out
6 BORING, dull, flat, uninteresting
▷ *noun* 7 MIDDLE, depth, midst
deaden *verb* REDUCE, alleviate, blunt, cushion, diminish, dull, lessen, muffle, smother, stifle, suppress, weaken
deadline *noun* TIME LIMIT, cutoff point, limit, target date
deadlock *noun* 1 DRAW, dead heat, tie
2 IMPASSE, gridlock, stalemate, standoff, standstill
deadlocked *adjective* 1 EVEN, equal, level, neck and neck, on a level playing field (*informal*)
2 GRIDLOCKED, at an impasse, at a standstill
deadly *adjective* 1 LETHAL, dangerous, death-dealing, deathly, fatal, malignant, mortal
deadpan *adjective* EXPRESSIONLESS, blank, impassive, inexpressive, inscrutable, poker-faced, straight-faced
deaf *adjective* 1 HARD OF HEARING, stone deaf, without hearing
2 OBLIVIOUS, indifferent, unconcerned, unhearing, unmoved
deafen *verb* MAKE DEAF, din, drown out, split the eardrums *or* burst the eardrums
deafening *adjective* EAR-PIERCING, booming, ear-splitting, overpowering, piercing, resounding, ringing, thunderous
deal *noun* 1 AGREEMENT, arrangement, bargain,

(with, in) ▷ *noun* 6 agreement 7 treatment 8 share 9 business transaction > **deal'er** *noun* 1 one who deals (esp. cards) 2 trader > **deal'ings** *plural noun* transactions or relations with others > **deal with** handle, act toward (someone)

dean [deen] *noun* 1 university or college official 2 head of cathedral chapter

dear [deer] *adjective* 1 beloved 2 precious 3 costly, expensive ▷ *noun* 4 beloved one ▷ *adverb* 5 at a high price > **dear'ly** *adverb*

dearth [durth] *noun* scarcity

death [deth] *noun* 1 dying 2 end of life 3 end, extinction 4 annihilation 5 (**Death**) personification of death, as skeleton > **death'less** *adjective* immortal > **death'ly** *adjective, adverb* like death > **death mask** cast of person's face taken after death > **death'watch** *noun* vigil at dying person's bedside

de•ba•cle [day-BAH-kəl] *noun* utter collapse, rout, disaster

de•bar [di-BAHR] *verb transitive* **-barred, -bar'ring** 1 shut out from 2 stop 3 prohibit 4 preclude

de•bark [di-BAHRK] *verb* disembark

de•base [di-BASE] *verb transitive* **-based, -bas•ing** 1 lower in value, quality or character 2 adulterate coinage > **de•base'ment** *noun*

de•bate [di-BAYT] *verb* **-bat•ed, -bat•ing** 1 argue, discuss, esp. in a formal assembly 2 consider ▷ *noun* 3 discussion 4 controversy > **de•bat'a•ble** *adjective*

de•bauch [di-BAWCH] *verb transitive* 1 lead into a life of depraved self-indulgence ▷ *noun* 2 bout of sensual indulgence > **de•bauch•ee** [deb-aw-CHEE] *noun* dissipated person > **de•bauch'er•y** *noun*

de•ben•ture [di-BEN-chər] *noun* bond of company or corporation

de•bil•i•ty [di-BIL-i-tee] *noun, plural* **-ties** 1 feebleness, esp. of health 2 languor > **de•bil'i•tate** *verb transitive* weaken, enervate

deb•it [DEB-it] *noun accounting* 1 entry in account of sum owed 2 side of ledger in which such sums are entered ▷ *verb transitive* 3 charge, enter as due

deb•o•nair [deb-ə-NAIR] *adjective* suave, genial

de•brief [dee-BREEF] *verb* of soldier, etc., report to superior on result of mission

de•bris [də-BREE] *noun* fragments, rubbish

debt [det] *noun* 1 what is owed 2 state of owing > **debt'or** *noun*

de•bug [dee-BUG] *verb transitive* **-bugged, -bugging** 1 (*informal*) find and remove defects in (computer program) 2 remove concealed microphones from (room or telephone)

de•bunk [di-BUNGK] *verb transitive* expose falseness, pretentiousness of, esp. by ridicule

de•but [day-BYOO] *noun* first appearance in public > **deb•u•tante** [DEB-yuu-tahnt] *noun* young woman making official debut into society

deca- *combining form* ten: *decagon*

dec•ade [DEK-ayd] *noun* 1 period of ten years 2 set of ten

dec•a•dent [DEK-ə-dənt] *adjective* 1 declining, deteriorating 2 morally corrupt > **dec'a•dence** *noun*

de•caf•fein•at•ed [dee-KAF-ə-nay-tid] *adjective* (of coffee) with the caffeine removed

dec•a•gon [DEK-ə-gon] *noun* figure of 10 angles

dec•a•he•dron [dek-ə-HEE-drən] *noun* solid of 10 faces

contract, pact, transaction, understanding
2 AMOUNT, degree, extent, portion, quantity, share
▷ *verb* 3 SELL, bargain, buy and sell, do business, negotiate, stock, trade, traffic

dealer *noun* TRADER, merchant, purveyor, supplier, tradesman, wholesaler

deal out *verb* DISTRIBUTE, allot, apportion, assign, dispense, dole out, give, mete out, share

deal with *verb* 1 HANDLE, attend to, cope with, get to grips with, manage, see to, take care of, treat
2 BE CONCERNED WITH, consider

dear *noun* 1 BELOVED, angel, darling, loved one, precious, treasure
▷ *adjective* 2 BELOVED, cherished, close, favorite, intimate, precious, prized, treasured
3 EXPENSIVE, at a premium, costly, high-priced, overpriced, pricey (*informal*)

dearly *adverb* 1 VERY MUCH, extremely, greatly, profoundly
2 AT GREAT COST, at a high price

dearth *noun* SCARCITY, deficiency, inadequacy, insufficiency, lack, paucity, poverty, shortage, want

death *noun* 1 DYING, demise, departure, end, exit, passing
2 DESTRUCTION, downfall, extinction, finish, ruin, undoing

deathly *adjective* DEATHLIKE, ghastly, grim, pale, pallid, wan

debacle *noun* DISASTER, catastrophe, collapse, defeat, fiasco, reversal, rout

debase *verb* DEGRADE, cheapen, devalue, lower, reduce

debatable *adjective* DOUBTFUL, arguable, controversial, dubious, moot, problematical, questionable, uncertain

debate *noun* 1 DISCUSSION, argument, contention, controversy, dispute
▷ *verb* 2 DISCUSS, argue, dispute, question
3 CONSIDER, deliberate, ponder, reflect, ruminate, weigh

debauchery *noun* DEPRAVITY, dissipation, dissoluteness, excess, indulgence, intemperance, lewdness, overindulgence

debonair *adjective* ELEGANT, charming, courteous, dashing, refined, smooth, suave, urbane, well-bred

debrief *verb* INTERROGATE, cross-examine, examine, probe, question, quiz

debris *noun* REMAINS, bits, detritus, fragments, rubble, ruins, waste, wreckage

debt *noun* 1 DEBIT, commitment, liability, obligation
2 ▷ **in debt** OWING, in arrears, in the red (*informal*), liable

debtor *noun* BORROWER, mortgagor

debunk *verb* EXPOSE, cut down to size, deflate, disparage, mock, ridicule, show up

debut *noun* INTRODUCTION, beginning, bow, coming out, entrance, first appearance, initiation, presentation

decadence *noun* DEGENERATION, corruption, decay, decline, deterioration, dissipation, dissolution

de•cal•ci•fy [dee-KAL-si-fī] *verb transitive* **-fied, -fy•ing** deprive of lime, as bones or teeth
Dec•a•logue [DEK-ə-lawg] *noun* the Ten Commandments
de•camp [di-KAMP] *verb intransitive* make off, break camp, abscond
de•cant [di-KANT] *verb transitive* pour off (liquid, as wine) to leave sediment > **de•cant'er** *noun* stoppered bottle for wine or whiskey
de•cap•i•tate [di-KAP-i-tayt] *verb transitive* behead > **de•cap•i•ta'tion** *noun*
de•cath•lon [di-KATH-lon] *noun* athletic contest with ten events
de•cay [di-KAY] *verb* 1 rot, decompose 2 fall off, decline ▷ *noun* 3 rotting 4 a falling away, break up
de•cease [di-SEES] *noun* 1 death ▷ *verb intransitive* **-ceased, -ceas•ing** 2 die > **deceased** *adjective* 1 dead ▷ *noun* 2 person lately dead
de•ceive [di-SEEV] *verb transitive* **-ceived, -ceiv•ing** mislead, delude, cheat > **de•ceit'** *noun* 1 fraud 2 duplicity > **de•ceit'ful** *adjective*
de•cel•er•ate [dee-SEL-ə-rayt] *verb intransitive* **-at•ed, -at•ing** slow down
de•cen•ni•al [di-SEN-ee-əl] *adjective* of period of ten years
de•cent [DEE-sənt] *adjective* 1 respectable 2 fitting, seemly 3 not obscene 4 adequate 5 (*informal*) kind > **de'cen•cy** *noun*
de•cen•tral•ize [dee-SEN-trə-līz] *verb transitive* **-ized, -iz•ing** divide (government, organization) among local centers
de•cep•tion [di-SEP-shən] *noun* 1 deceiving 2 illusion 3 fraud 4 trick > **de•cep'tive** *adjective* 1 misleading 2 apt to mislead
deci- *combining form* one tenth: *decimetre*
dec•i•bel [DES-ə-bəl] *noun* unit for measuring intensity of a sound
de•cide [di-SĪD] *verb transitive* **-cid•ed, -cid•ing** 1 settle, determine, bring to resolution 2 give judgment ▷ *verb intransitive* **-cid•ed, -cid•ing** 3 come to a decision, conclusion > **de•cid'ed** *adjective* 1 unmistakable 2 settled 3 resolute > **de•cid'ed•ly** *adverb* certainly, undoubtedly > **de•cis'ion** [-SIZH-ən] *noun* > **de•ci'sive** *adjective* > **de•ci'sive•ness** *noun*
de•cid•u•ous [di-SIJ-oo-əs] *adjective* 1 of trees, losing leaves annually 2 of antlers, teeth, etc. being shed at the end of a period of growth
dec•i•mal [DES-ə-məl] *adjective* 1 relating to tenths 2 proceeding by tens ▷ *noun* 3 decimal fraction > **decimal system** system of weights and measures, or coinage, in which value of each denomination is ten times the one below it
dec•i•mate [DES-ə-mayt] *verb transitive* **-mat•ed, -mat•ing** destroy or kill a tenth of, large proportion of > **dec•i•ma'tion** *noun*
de•ci•pher [di-SĪ-fər] *verb transitive* 1 make out meaning of 2 decode > **de•ci'pher•a•ble** *adjective*
deck [dek] *noun* 1 platform or floor, esp. one covering whole or part of ship's hull 2 cassette deck 3 pack of playing cards 4 (*slang*) small packet of a narcotic ▷ *verb transitive* 5 array, decorate > **deck chair** folding chair made of canvas suspended in wooden frame
de•claim [di-KLAYM] *verb* 1 speak dramatically,

decadent *adjective* DEGENERATE, corrupt, decaying, declining, dissolute, immoral, self-indulgent
decapitate *verb* BEHEAD, execute, guillotine
decay *verb* 1 DECLINE, crumble, deteriorate, disintegrate, dwindle, shrivel, wane, waste away, wither
2 ROT, corrode, decompose, perish, putrefy
▷ *noun* 3 DECLINE, collapse, degeneration, deterioration, fading, failing, wasting, withering
4 ROT, caries, decomposition, gangrene, putrefaction
decease *noun* (*formal*) DEATH, demise, departure, dying, release
deceased *adjective* DEAD, defunct, departed, expired, former, late, lifeless
deceit *noun* DISHONESTY, back-stabbing (*informal*), cheating, chicanery, deception, fraud, lying, pretense, treachery, trickery
deceitful *adjective* DISHONEST, deceptive, down and dirty (*informal*), false, fraudulent, sneaky, treacherous, two-faced, untrustworthy
deceive *verb* DUPE (*informal*), cheat, con (*informal*), fool, hoodwink, mislead, swindle, trick
deceiver *noun* LIAR, cheat, con man (*informal*), double-dealer, fraud, impostor, swindler
decency *noun* RESPECTABILITY, civility, correctness, courtesy, decorum, etiquette, modesty, propriety
decent *adjective* 1 REASONABLE, adequate, ample, fair, passable, satisfactory, sufficient, tolerable
2 RESPECTABLE, chaste, decorous, modest, proper, pure
3 PROPER, appropriate, becoming, befitting, fitting, seemly, suitable
4 (*informal*) KIND, accommodating, courteous, friendly, generous, gracious, helpful, obliging, thoughtful
deception *noun* 1 TRICKERY, cunning, deceit, fraud, guile, legerdemain, treachery
2 TRICK, bluff, decoy, hoax, illusion, lie, ruse, subterfuge
deceptive *adjective* MISLEADING, ambiguous, deceitful, dishonest, false, fraudulent, illusory, unreliable
decide *verb* REACH A DECISION *or* COME TO A DECISION, adjudge, adjudicate, choose, conclude, determine, make up one's mind, resolve
decidedly *adverb* DEFINITELY, clearly, distinctly, downright, positively, unequivocally, unmistakably
decimate *verb* DEVASTATE, ravage, wreak havoc on
decipher *verb* FIGURE OUT (*informal*), crack, decode, deduce, interpret, make out, read, solve
decision *noun* 1 JUDGMENT, arbitration, conclusion, finding, resolution, ruling, sentence, verdict
2 DECISIVENESS, determination, firmness, purpose, resolution, resolve, strength of mind *or* strength of will
decisive *adjective* 1 INFLUENTIAL, conclusive, critical, crucial, fateful, momentous, significant
2 RESOLUTE, decided, determined, firm, forceful, incisive, strong-minded, trenchant
deck *verb* DECORATE, adorn, array, beautify, clothe, dress, embellish, festoon
declaim *verb* 1 ORATE, harangue, hold forth, lecture, proclaim, rant, recite, speak

rhetorically or passionately **2** protest loudly > **dec•la•ma•tion** [dek-lə-MAY-shən] *noun* > **de•clam'a•to•ry** *adjective*

de•clare [di-KLAIR] *verb transitive* **-clared, -clar•ing 1** announce formally **2** state emphatically **3** show **4** name (as liable to customs duty) ▷ *verb intransitive* **-clared, -clar•ing 5** take sides (for) **6** *bridge* bid (a suit or no trump) > **dec•la•ra•tion** [dek-lə-RAY-shən] *noun* > **de•clar'a•tive** *adjective* > **de•clar'er** *noun bridge* person who plays the contract

de•cline [di-KLĪN] *verb* **-clined, -clin•ing 1** refuse **2** slope, bend or sink downward **3** deteriorate gradually **4** grow smaller, diminish **5** list the case endings of nouns, pronouns, adjectives ▷ *noun* **6** gradual deterioration **7** movement downward **8** diminution **9** downward slope > **de•clen'sion** *noun* **1** in grammar, set of nouns, pronouns, etc. **2** falling off **3** declining > **de•clin'a•ble** *adjective* > **dec•li•na'tion** *noun* **1** sloping away, deviation **2** angle

de•cliv•i•ty [di-KLIV-i-tee] *noun* downward slope

de•code [dee-KOHD] *verb transitive* **-cod•ed, -cod•ing** put in intelligible terms a message in code or secret alphabet

dé•colle•té [day-kol-TAY] *adjective* (of women's garment) having a low-cut neckline > **dé•colle•tage'** [-TAHZH] *noun* low-cut neckline

de•com•mis•sion [dee-kə-MISH-ən] *verb transitive* **1** dismantle (nuclear reactor, industrial plant) sufficiently to abandon safely **2** remove (ship) from service

de•com•pose [dee-kəm-POHZ] *verb* **-posed, -pos•ing 1** separate into elements **2** rot > **de•com•po•si•tion** [dee-kom-pə-ZISH-ən] *noun* decay

de•com•press [dee-kəm-PRES] *verb transitive* **1** free from pressure **2** return to condition of normal atmospheric pressure > **de•com•pres'sion** *noun*

de•con•ges•tant [dee-kən-JES-tənt] *adjective, noun* (drug) relieving (esp. nasal) congestion

de•con•struct•ed [dee-kən-STRUKT-əd] *adjective* having no formal structure

de•con•tam•i•nate [dee-kən-TAM-ə-nayt] *verb transitive* **-nat•ed, -nat•ing** free from contamination e.g. from poisons, radioactive substances

de•con•trol [dee-kən-TROHL] *verb transitive* **-trolled, -trol•ling** release from government control

dé•cor [day-KOR] *noun* **1** decorative scheme of a room, etc. **2** stage decoration, scenery

dec•o•rate [DEK-ə-rayt] *verb transitive* **-rat•ed, -rat•ing 1** beautify by additions **2** select paint, furniture, etc. for room, apartment, etc. **3** award (medal, etc.) > **dec•o•ra'tion** *noun* > **dec'o•ra•tive** [-rə-tiv] *adjective*

de•co•rum [di-KOR-əm] *noun* seemly behavior, propriety, decency > **dec•o•rous** [DEK-ə-rəs] *adjective*

de•coy [DEE-koi] *noun* **1** something used to entrap others or to distract their attention **2** bait, lure ▷ *verb* [di-KOI] **3** lure, be lured as with decoy

de•crease [di-KREES] *verb* **-creased, -creas•ing 1** diminish, lessen ▷ *noun* [DEE-krees] **2** lessening

de•cree [di-KREE] *noun* **1** order having the force of law **2** edict ▷ *verb* **-creed, -cree•ing 3** determine judicially **4** order

dec•re•ment [DEK-rə-mənt] *noun* **1** act or state

DICTIONARY **d** THESAURUS

---

2 ▷ **declaim against** PROTEST AGAINST, attack, decry, denounce, inveigh, rail

declaration *noun* **1** STATEMENT, acknowledgment, affirmation, assertion, avowal, disclosure, protestation, revelation, testimony
2 ANNOUNCEMENT, edict, notification, proclamation, profession, pronouncement

declare *verb* **1** STATE, affirm, announce, assert, claim, maintain, proclaim, profess, pronounce, swear, utter
2 MAKE KNOWN, confess, disclose, reveal, show

decline *verb* **1** LESSEN, decrease, diminish, dwindle, ebb, fade, fall off, shrink, sink, wane
2 DETERIORATE, decay, degenerate, droop, languish, pine, weaken, worsen
3 REFUSE, abstain, avoid, reject, say 'no', turn down
▷ *noun* **4** LESSENING, downturn, drop, dwindling, falling off, recession, slump
5 DETERIORATION, decay, degeneration, failing, weakening, worsening

decode *verb* DECIPHER, crack, decrypt, interpret, solve, unscramble, work out

decompose *verb* ROT, break up, crumble, decay, fall apart, fester, putrefy

decor *noun* DECORATION, color scheme, furnishing style, ornamentation

decorate *verb* **1** ADORN, beautify, embellish, festoon, grace, ornament, trim
2 RENOVATE, color, do up (*informal*), furbish, paint, paper, wallpaper
3 PIN A MEDAL ON, cite, confer an honor on *or* confer an honor upon

decoration *noun* **1** ADORNMENT, beautification, elaboration, embellishment, enrichment, ornamentation, trimming
2 ORNAMENT, bauble, frill, garnish, trimmings
3 MEDAL, award, badge, ribbon, star

decorative *adjective* ORNAMENTAL, beautifying, fancy, nonfunctional, pretty

decorous *adjective* PROPER, becoming, correct, decent, dignified, fitting, polite, seemly, well-behaved

decorum *noun* PROPRIETY, decency, dignity, etiquette, good manners, politeness, protocol, respectability

decoy *noun* **1** LURE, bait, enticement, inducement, pretense, trap
▷ *verb* **2** LURE, deceive, ensnare, entice, entrap, seduce, tempt

decrease *verb* **1** LESSEN, cut down, decline, diminish, drop, dwindle, lower, reduce, shrink, subside
▷ *noun* **2** LESSENING, contraction, cutback, decline, dwindling, falling off, loss, reduction, subsidence

decree *noun* **1** LAW, act, command, edict, order, proclamation, ruling, statute
▷ *verb* **2** ORDER, command, demand, ordain, prescribe, proclaim, pronounce, rule

of decreasing 2 quantity lost by decrease
de•crep•it [di-KREP-it] *adjective* 1 old and feeble 2 broken down, worn out > **de•crep'i•tude** *noun*
de•cry [di-KRĪ] *verb transitive* **-cried, -cry•ing** disparage
ded•i•cate [DED-i-kayt] *verb transitive* **-cat•ed, -cat•ing** 1 commit wholly to special purpose or cause 2 inscribe or address (book, etc.) 3 devote to God's service > **ded•i•ca'tion** *noun* > **ded'i•ca•to•ry** [-kə-tor-ee] *adjective*
de•duce [di-DOOS] *verb transitive* **-duced, -duc•ing** draw as conclusion from facts > **de•duct** [di-DUKT] *verb transitive* take away, subtract > **de•duct'i•ble** *adjective* > **de•duc'tion** *noun* 1 deducting 2 amount subtracted 3 conclusion deduced 4 inference from general to particular > **de•duc'tive** *adjective*
deed *noun* 1 action or fact 2 exploit 3 legal document
deem *verb transitive* judge, consider, regard
deep *adjective* **-er, -est** 1 extending far down, in or back 2 at, of given depth 3 profound 4 heartfelt 5 hard to fathom 6 cunning 7 engrossed, immersed 8 of color, dark and rich 9 of sound, low and full ▷ *noun* 10 deep place 11 the sea ▷ *adverb* 12 far down, etc. > **deep'en** *verb transitive* > **deep'ly** *adverb* > **deep freeze** condition or period of suspended activity
deer *noun, plural* **deer** family of ruminant animals typically with antlers in male > **deer'stalk•er** *noun* 1 one who stalks deer 2 kind of cloth hat with visor in front and behind
de•face [di-FAYS] *verb transitive* **-faced, -fac•ing** 1 spoil or mar surface 2 disfigure > **de•face'ment** *noun*
de fac•to [day FAK-toh] *Lat.* existing in fact, whether legally recognized or not
de•fal•ca•tion [dee-fal-KAY-shən] *noun* 1 misappropriation of money held by trustee, etc. 2 the money taken > **de•fal•cate** [di-FAL-kayt] *verb intransitive* **-cat•ed, -cat•ing**
de•fame [di-FAYM] *verb transitive* **-famed, -fam•ing** speak ill of, dishonor by slander or rumor > **def•a•ma•tion** [def-ə-MAY-shən] *noun* > **de•fam'a•to•ry** *adjective*
de•fault [di-FAWLT] *noun* 1 failure, neglect to act, appear or pay 2 *computers* instruction to a computer to select a particular option unless the user specifies otherwise ▷ *verb* 3 fail (to pay) > **de•fault'er** *noun* one who defaults
de•feat [di-FEET] *verb transitive* 1 overcome, vanquish 2 thwart ▷ *noun* 3 overthrow 4 lost battle or encounter 5 frustration > **de•feat'ism** *noun* attitude tending to accept defeat > **de•feat'ist** *noun, adjective*
def•e•cate [DEF-i-kayt] *verb transitive* **-cat•ed, -cat•ing** 1 empty the bowels 2 clear of impurities > **def•e•ca'tion** *noun*
de•fect [DEE-fekt] *noun* 1 lack, blemish, failing ▷ *verb intransitive* [di-FEKT] 2 desert one's country, cause, etc., esp. to join opponents > **de•fec'tion** *noun* abandonment of duty or

DICTIONARY • THESAURUS

decrepit *adjective* 1 WEAK, aged, doddering, feeble, frail, infirm
2 WORN-OUT, battered, beat-up (*informal*), broken-down, dilapidated, ramshackle, rickety, run-down, tumbledown, weather-beaten
decry *verb* CONDEMN, belittle, criticize, denigrate, denounce, discredit, disparage, put down, run down
dedicate *verb* 1 DEVOTE, commit, give over to, pledge, surrender
2 INSCRIBE, address
dedicated *adjective* DEVOTED, committed, enthusiastic, purposeful, single-minded, wholehearted, zealous
dedication *noun* 1 DEVOTION, adherence, allegiance, commitment, faithfulness, loyalty, single-mindedness, wholeheartedness
2 INSCRIPTION, address, message
deduce *verb* CONCLUDE, draw, gather, glean, infer, reason, take to mean, understand
deduct *verb* SUBTRACT, decrease by, knock off (*informal*), reduce by, remove, take away, take off
deduction *noun* 1 SUBTRACTION, decrease, diminution, discount, reduction, withdrawal
2 CONCLUSION, assumption, finding, inference, reasoning, result
deed *noun* 1 ACTION, achievement, act, exploit, fact, feat, performance
2 (*law*) DOCUMENT, contract, title
deep *adjective* 1 WIDE, bottomless, broad, far, profound, unfathomable, yawning
2 MYSTERIOUS, abstract, abstruse, arcane, esoteric, hidden, obscure, recondite, secret
3 INTENSE, extreme, grave, great, profound, serious (*informal*), unqualified
4 ABSORBED, engrossed, immersed, lost, preoccupied, rapt
5 DARK, intense, rich, strong, vivid
6 LOW, bass, booming, low-pitched, resonant, sonorous
▷ *noun* 7 ▷ **the deep** (*poetic*) OCEAN, briny (*informal*), high seas, main, sea
deepen *verb* INTENSIFY, grow, increase, magnify, reinforce, strengthen
deeply *adverb* 1 THOROUGHLY, completely, gravely, profoundly, seriously, severely, to the core, to the heart, to the quick
2 INTENSELY, acutely, affectingly, distressingly, feelingly, mournfully, movingly, passionately, sadly
deface *verb* VANDALIZE, damage, deform, disfigure, mar, mutilate, spoil, tarnish
de facto *adverb* 1 IN FACT, actually, in effect, in reality, really
▷ *adjective* 2 ACTUAL, existing, real
defame *verb* SLANDER, bad-mouth (*slang*), cast aspersions on, denigrate, discredit, disparage, knock (*informal*), libel, malign, smear
default *noun* 1 FAILURE, deficiency, dereliction, evasion, lapse, neglect, nonpayment, omission
▷ *verb* 2 FAIL, dodge, evade, neglect
defeat *verb* 1 BEAT, conquer, crush, master, overwhelm, rout, trounce, vanquish, wipe the floor with (*informal*)
2 FRUSTRATE, baffle, balk, confound, foil, get the better of, ruin, thwart
▷ *noun* 3 CONQUEST, beating, overthrow, rout
4 FRUSTRATION, failure, rebuff, reverse, setback, thwarting
defeatist *noun* 1 PESSIMIST, prophet of doom, quitter
▷ *adjective* 2 PESSIMISTIC
defect *noun* 1 IMPERFECTION, blemish, blotch, error, failing, fault, flaw, spot, taint

allegiance > **de•fec'tive** *adjective* 1 incomplete 2 faulty
de•fend [di-FEND] *verb transitive* 1 protect, ward off attack 2 support by argument, evidence 3 (try to) maintain (title, etc.) against challenger > **de•fense'** *noun* > **de•fend'ant** *noun* person accused in court > **de•fend'er** *noun* > **de•fen'si•ble** *adjective* > **de•fen'sive** *adjective* 1 serving for defense ▷ *noun* 2 position or attitude of defense
de•fer[1] [di-FUR] *verb transitive* **-ferred, -fer•ring** put off, postpone > **de•fer'ment, de•fer'ral** *noun*
de•fer[2] *verb intransitive* **-ferred, -fer•ring** submit to opinion or judgment of another > **def'er•ence** *noun* respectful submission to views, etc. of another > **def•er•en'tial** [-shəl] *adjective*
defiance, defiant *see* **defy**
de•fi•cient [di-FISH-ənt] *adjective* lacking or falling short in something, insufficient > **de•fi'cien•cy** *noun* > **def•i•cit** [DEF-ə-sit] *noun* 1 amount by which sum of money is too small 2 lack, shortage
de•file[1] [di-FĪL] *verb transitive* **-filed, -fil•ing** 1 make dirty, pollute, soil 2 sully 3 desecrate
de•file[2] *noun* 1 narrow pass or valley ▷ *verb intransitive* **-filed, -fil•ing** 2 march in file
de•fine [di-FĪN] *verb transitive* **-fined, -fin•ing** 1 state contents or meaning of 2 show clearly the form 3 lay down clearly, fix 4 mark out > **de•fin'a•ble** *adjective* > **def•i•ni'tion** [-NISH-ən] *noun* > **def'i•nite** [-nit] *adjective* 1 exact, defined 2 clear, specific 3 certain, sure > **de•fin'i•tive** *adjective* conclusive, to be looked on as final
de•flate [di-FLAYT] *verb* **-flat•ed, -flat•ing** 1 (cause to) collapse by release of gas from 2 take away (person's) self-esteem 3 *economics* cause deflation > **de•fla'tion** *noun* 1 deflating 2 *economics* reduction of economic and industrial activity > **de•fla'tion•ar•y** *adjective*
de•flect [di-FLEKT] *verb* (cause to) turn from straight course > **de•flec'tion** *noun*
de•flow•er [di-FLOW-ər] *verb transitive* deprive of virginity, innocence, etc. > **def•lo•ra'tion** *noun*
de•fo•li•ate [dee-FOH-lee-ayt] *verb* **-at•ed, -at•ing** (cause to) lose leaves, esp. by action of chemicals > **defo'li•ant** *noun* > **de•fo•li•a'tion** *noun*
de•form [di FORM] *verb transitive* 1 spoil shape of 2 make ugly 3 disfigure > **de•formed'**

▷ *verb* 2 DESERT, abandon, change sides, go over, rebel, revolt, walk out on (*informal*)
defection *noun* DESERTION, apostasy, rebellion
defective *adjective* FAULTY, broken, deficient, flawed, imperfect, not working, on the blink (*slang*), out of order
defector *noun* DESERTER, apostate, renegade, turncoat
defend *verb* 1 PROTECT, cover, guard, keep safe, preserve, safeguard, screen, shelter, shield
2 SUPPORT, champion, endorse, justify, speak up for, stand up for, stick up for (*informal*), uphold, vindicate
defendant *noun* THE ACCUSED, defense, offender, prisoner at the bar, respondent
defender *noun* 1 PROTECTOR, bodyguard, escort, guard
2 SUPPORTER, advocate, champion, sponsor
defense *noun* 1 PROTECTION, cover, guard, immunity, resistance, safeguard, security, shelter
2 SHIELD, barricade, bulwark, buttress, fortification, rampart
3 ARGUMENT, excuse, explanation, justification, plea, vindication
4 (*law*) PLEA, alibi, denial, rebuttal, testimony
defenseless *adjective* HELPLESS, exposed, naked, powerless, unarmed, unguarded, unprotected, vulnerable, wide open
defensive *adjective* ON GUARD, on the defensive, protective, uptight (*informal*), watchful
defer[1] *verb* POSTPONE, delay, hold over, procrastinate, put off, put on ice, shelve, suspend
defer[2] *verb* COMPLY, accede, bow, capitulate, give in, give way to, submit, yield
deference *noun* RESPECT, attention, civility, consideration, courtesy, honor, politeness, regard, reverence
deferential *adjective* RESPECTFUL, ingratiating, obedient, obeisant, obsequious, polite, reverential, submissive
defiance *noun* RESISTANCE, confrontation, contempt, disobedience, disregard, insolence, insubordination, opposition, rebelliousness
defiant *adjective* RESISTING, audacious, bold, daring, disobedient, insolent, insubordinate, mutinous, provocative, rebellious
deficiency *noun* 1 LACK, absence, dearth, deficit, scarcity, shortage
2 FAILING, defect, demerit, fault, flaw, frailty, imperfection, shortcoming, weakness
deficient *adjective* 1 LACKING, inadequate, insufficient, meager, scant, scarce, short, skimpy, wanting
2 UNSATISFACTORY, defective, faulty, flawed, impaired, imperfect, incomplete, inferior, lousy (*slang*), weak
deficit *noun* SHORTFALL, arrears, deficiency, loss, shortage
define *verb* 1 DESCRIBE, characterize, designate, explain, expound, interpret, specify, spell out
2 MARK OUT, bound, circumscribe, delineate, demarcate, limit, outline
definite *adjective* 1 CLEAR, black-and-white, cut-and-dried (*informal*), exact, fixed, marked, particular, precise, specific
2 CERTAIN, assured, decided, guaranteed, positive, settled, sure
definitely *adverb* CERTAINLY, absolutely, categorically, clearly, positively, surely, undeniably, unmistakably, unquestionably, without doubt
definition *noun* 1 EXPLANATION, clarification, elucidation, exposition, statement of meaning
2 SHARPNESS, clarity, contrast, distinctness, focus, precision
definitive *adjective* 1 FINAL, absolute, complete, conclusive, decisive
2 AUTHORITATIVE, exhaustive, perfect, reliable, ultimate
deflate *verb* 1 COLLAPSE, empty, exhaust, flatten, puncture, shrink
2 HUMILIATE, chasten, disconcert, dispirit, humble, mortify, put down (*slang*), squash
3 (*economics*) REDUCE, depress, devalue, diminish
deflect *verb* TURN ASIDE, bend, deviate, diverge, glance off, ricochet, swerve, veer

adjective > **de•form'i•ty** *noun, plural* **-ties**
de•fraud [di-FRAWD] *verb transitive* cheat, swindle
de•fray [di-FRAY] *verb transitive* provide money for (expenses, etc.)
de•frock [dee-FROK] *verb transitive* deprive (priest, minister) of ecclesiastical status
de•frost [di-FRAWST] *verb* 1 make, become free of frost, ice 2 thaw
deft *adjective* **-er, -est** skillful, adroit > **deft'ly** *adverb* > **deft'ness** *noun*
de•funct [di-FUNGKT] *adjective* dead, obsolete
de•fuse [dee-FYOOZ] *verb transitive* **-fused, -fus•ing** 1 remove fuse of bomb, etc. 2 remove tension (from situation, etc.)
de•fy [di-FĪ] *verb transitive* **-fied, -fy•ing** 1 challenge, resist successfully 2 disregard > **de•fi'ance** *noun* resistance > **de•fi'ant** *adjective* 1 openly and aggressively hostile 2 insolent
de•gauss [dee-GOWS] *verb transitive* neutralize magnetic field (of ship's hull, electronic apparatus, etc.)
de•gen•er•ate [di-JEN-ə-rayt] *verb intransitive* **-rat•ed, -rat•ing** 1 deteriorate to lower mental, moral, or physical level ▷ *adjective* [-rit] 2 fallen away in quality ▷ *noun* [-rit] 3 degenerate person > **de•gen'er•a•cy** *noun*
de•grade [di-GRAYD] *verb transitive* **-grad•ed, -grad•ing** 1 dishonor 2 debase 3 reduce to lower rank ▷ *verb intransitive* **-grad•ed, -grad•ing** 4 decompose chemically > **de•grad'a•ble** *adjective* capable of chemical, biological decomposition > **de•grad'ed** *adjective* shamed, humiliated > **deg•ra•da'tion** *noun*
de•gree [di-GREE] *noun* 1 step, stage in process, scale, relative rank, order, condition, manner, way 2 academic title conferred by university or college 3 unit of measurement of temperature or angle **third degree** severe, lengthy examination, esp. of accused person by police, to extract information, confession
de•hu•mid•i•fy [dee-hyoo-MID-ə-fī] *verb transitive* **-fied, -fy•ing** extract moisture from
de•hy•drate [dee-HĪ-drayt] *verb transitive* **-drat•ed, -drat•ing** remove moisture from > **de•hy•dra'tion** *noun*
de-ice [dee-ĪS] *verb transitive* **-iced, -ic•ing** to dislodge ice from (e.g. windshield) or prevent its forming
de•i•fy [DEE-ə-fī] *verb transitive* **-fied, -fy•ing** 1 make god of 2 treat, worship as god > **de•i•fi•ca'tion** *noun*
deign [dayn] *verb transitive* 1 condescend, stoop 2 think fit
de•ism [DEE-iz-əm] *noun* belief in god but not in revelation > **de'ist** *noun* > **de•i•ty** [DEE-i-tee] *noun, plural* **-ties** 1 divine status or attributes 2 a god
dé•jà vu [DAY-*zhah* VOO] Fr. experience of perceiving new situation as if it had occurred before
de•ject [di-JEKT] *verb transitive* dishearten, cast down, depress > **de•ject'ed** *adjective* > **de•jec'tion** *noun*
de ju•re [di JUUR-ee] *Lat.* in law, by right
de•lay [di-LAY] *verb transitive* 1 postpone, hold back ▷ *verb intransitive* 2 be tardy, linger ▷ *noun* 3 act or instance of delaying 4 interval of time between events
de•lec•ta•ble [di-LEK-tə-bəl] *adjective* delightful delicious > **de•lec•ta•tion** [dee-lek-TAY-shən] *noun* pleasure
del•e•gate [DEL-i-git] *noun* 1 person chosen to represent another ▷ *verb transitive* [-gayt], **-gat•ed, -gat•ing** 2 send as deputy 3 commit (authority, business, etc.) to a deputy

DICTIONARY • THESAURUS

deflection *noun* DEVIATION, bend, divergence, swerve
deform *verb* 1 DISTORT, buckle, contort, gnarl, mangle, misshape, twist, warp
2 DISFIGURE, deface, maim, mar, mutilate, ruin, spoil
deformity *noun* ABNORMALITY, defect, disfigurement, malformation
defraud *verb* CHEAT, con (*informal*), embezzle, fleece, pilfer, rip off (*slang*), swindle, trick
deft *adjective* SKILLFUL, adept, adroit, agile, dexterous, expert, neat, nimble, proficient
defunct *adjective* 1 DEAD, deceased, departed, extinct, gone
2 OBSOLETE, bygone, expired, inoperative, invalid, nonexistent, out of commission
defy *verb* RESIST, brave, confront, disregard, flout, scorn, slight, spurn
degenerate *adjective* 1 DEPRAVED, corrupt, debauched, decadent, dissolute, immoral, low, perverted
▷ *verb* 2 WORSEN, decay, decline, decrease, deteriorate, fall off, lapse, sink, slip
degradation *noun* 1 DISGRACE, discredit, dishonor, humiliation, ignominy, mortification, shame
2 DETERIORATION, decline, degeneration, demotion, downgrading
degrade *verb* 1 DISGRACE, debase, demean, discredit, dishonor, humble, humiliate, shame
2 DEMOTE, downgrade, lower
degrading *adjective* DEMEANING, dishonorable, humiliating, shameful, undignified, unworthy
degree *noun* STAGE, grade, notch, point, rung, step, unit
deity *noun* GOD, divinity, goddess, godhead, idol, immortal, supreme being
dejected *adjective* DOWNHEARTED, crestfallen, depressed, despondent, disconsolate, disheartened, downcast, glum, miserable, sad
dejection *noun* LOW SPIRITS, depression, despair, despondency, doldrums, downheartedness, gloom, melancholy, sadness, sorrow, unhappiness
de jure *adverb* LEGALLY, by right, rightfully
delay *verb* 1 PUT OFF, defer, hold over, postpone, procrastinate, shelve, suspend
2 HOLD UP, bog down, detain, hinder, hold back, impede, obstruct, set back, slow up
▷ *noun* 3 PUTTING OFF, deferment, postponement, procrastination, suspension
4 HOLD-UP, hindrance, impediment, interruption, interval, setback, stoppage, wait
delegate *noun* 1 REPRESENTATIVE, agent, ambassador, commissioner, deputy, envoy, legate
▷ *verb* 2 ENTRUST, assign, consign, devolve, give, hand over, pass on, transfer
3 APPOINT, accredit, authorize, commission, depute, designate, empower, mandate

> **del•e•ga'tion** *noun*
de•lete [di-LEET] *verb transitive* **-let•ed, -let•ing** remove, cancel, erase > **de•le'tion** *noun*
del•e•te•ri•ous [del-i-TEER-ee-əs] *adjective* harmful, injurious
de•lib•er•ate [di-LIB-ər-it] *adjective* 1 intentional 2 well considered 3 without haste, slow ▷ *verb* [-rayt] **-rat•ed, -rat•ing** 4 consider, debate > **de•lib•er•a'tion** *noun*
del•i•cate [DEL-i-kit] *adjective* 1 exquisite 2 not robust, fragile 3 sensitive 4 requiring tact 5 deft > **del'i•ca•cy** *noun*
del•i•ca•tes•sen [del-i-kə-TES-ən] *noun* 1 store selling ready-to-eat foods 2 the food sold
de•li•cious [di-LISH-əs] *adjective* delightful, pleasing to senses, esp. taste
de•light [di-LĪT] *verb transitive* 1 please greatly ▷ *verb intransitive* 2 take great pleasure (in) ▷ *noun* 3 great pleasure > **de•light'ful** *adjective* charming
de•lin•e•ate [di-LIN-ee-ayt] *verb transitive* **-at•ed, -at•ing** 1 portray by drawing or description 2 represent accurately > **de•lin•e•a'tion** *noun*
de•lin•quent [di-LING-kwənt] *noun* someone, esp. young person, guilty of delinquency ▷ *adjective* > **de•lin'quen•cy** *noun, plural* **-cies** (minor) offense or misdeed
del•i•quesce [del-i-KWES] *verb intransitive* **-quesced, -quesc•ing** become liquid > **del•i•ques'cence** *noun* > **del•i•ques'cent** *adjective*
de•lir•i•um [di-LEER-ee-əm] *noun* 1 disorder of the mind, esp. in feverish illness 2 violent excitement > **de•lir'i•ous** *adjective* 1 raving 2 light-headed, wildly excited
de•liv•er [di-LIV-ər] *verb transitive* 1 carry (goods, etc.) to destination 2 hand over 3 release 4 give birth or assist in birth (of) 5 utter or present (speech, etc.) > **de•liv'er•ance** *noun* rescue > **de•liv'er•y** *noun*
Del•phic [DEL-fik] *adjective* pert. to Delphi or to the oracle of Apollo
del•ta [DEL-tə] *noun* 1 alluvial tract where river at mouth breaks into streams 2 fourth letter in the Greek alphabet 3 shape of this letter
de•lude [di-LOOD] *verb transitive* **-lud•ed, -lud•ing** 1 deceive 2 mislead > **de•lu'sion** [-zhən] *noun*

---

delegation *noun* 1 DEPUTATION, commission, contingent, embassy, envoys, legation, mission 2 DEVOLUTION, assignment, commissioning, committal
delete *verb* REMOVE, cancel, cross out, efface, erase, expunge, obliterate, rub out, strike out
deliberate *adjective* 1 INTENTIONAL, calculated, conscious, planned, prearranged, premeditated, purposeful, willful
2 UNHURRIED, careful, cautious, circumspect, measured, methodical, ponderous, slow, thoughtful
▷ *verb* 3 CONSIDER, cogitate, consult, debate, discuss, meditate, ponder, reflect, think, weigh
deliberately *adverb* INTENTIONALLY, by design, calculatingly, consciously, in cold blood, knowingly, on purpose, willfully, wittingly
deliberation *noun* 1 CONSIDERATION, calculation, circumspection, forethought, meditation, reflection, thought
2 DISCUSSION, conference, consultation, debate
delicacy *noun* 1 FINENESS, accuracy, daintiness, elegance, exquisiteness, lightness, precision, subtlety
2 FRAGILITY, flimsiness, frailty, slenderness, tenderness, weakness
3 TREAT, dainty, luxury, savory, tidbit
4 FASTIDIOUSNESS, discrimination, finesse, purity, refinement, sensibility, taste
5 SENSITIVITY, sensitiveness, tact
delicate *adjective* 1 FINE, deft, elegant, exquisite, graceful, precise, skilled, subtle
2 SUBTLE, choice, dainty, delicious, fine, savory, tender, yummy (*informal*)
3 FRAGILE, flimsy, frail, slender, slight, tender, weak
4 CONSIDERATE, diplomatic, discreet, sensitive, tactful
delicately *adverb* 1 FINELY, daintily, deftly, elegantly, exquisitely, gracefully, precisely, skillfully, subtly
2 TACTFULLY, diplomatically, sensitively
delicious *adjective* DELECTABLE, appetizing, choice, dainty, mouthwatering, savory, tasty, toothsome, yummy (*informal*)
delight *noun* 1 PLEASURE, ecstasy, enjoyment, gladness, glee, happiness, joy, rapture
▷ *verb* 2 PLEASE, amuse, charm, cheer, enchant, gratify, thrill
3 ▷ **delight in** TAKE PLEASURE IN, appreciate, enjoy, feast on, like, love, relish, revel in, savor
delighted *adjective* PLEASED, ecstatic, elated, enchanted, happy, joyous, jubilant, overjoyed, thrilled
delightful *adjective* PLEASANT, agreeable, charming, delectable, enchanting, enjoyable, pleasurable, rapturous, thrilling
delinquent *noun* CRIMINAL, culprit, lawbreaker, miscreant, offender, villain, wrongdoer
delirious *adjective* 1 MAD, crazy, demented, deranged, incoherent, insane, raving, unhinged
2 ECSTATIC, beside oneself, carried away, excited, frantic, frenzied, hysterical, wild, wired (*slang*)
delirium *noun* 1 MADNESS, derangement, hallucination, insanity, raving
2 FRENZY, ecstasy, fever, hysteria, passion
deliver *verb* 1 CARRY, bear, bring, cart, convey, distribute, transport
2 HAND OVER, commit, give up, grant, make over, relinquish, surrender, transfer, turn over, yield
3 GIVE, announce, declare, present, read, utter
4 RELEASE, emancipate, free, liberate, loose, ransom, rescue, save
5 STRIKE, administer, aim, deal, direct, give, inflict, launch
deliverance *noun* RELEASE, emancipation, escape, liberation, ransom, redemption, rescue, salvation
delivery *noun* 1 HANDING OVER, consignment, conveyance, dispatch, distribution, surrender, transfer, transmission
2 SPEECH, articulation, elocution, enunciation, intonation, utterance
3 CHILDBIRTH, confinement, labor, parturition
delude *verb* DECEIVE, beguile, dupe, fool, hoodwink, kid (*informal*), mislead, trick
deluge *noun* 1 FLOOD, cataclysm, downpour,

del•uge [DEL-yooj] *noun* 1 flood, great flow, rush, downpour, cloudburst ▷ *verb transitive* **-uged, -ug•ing** 2 flood, overwhelm
deluxe [də-LUKS] *adjective* 1 rich, sumptuous 2 superior in quality
delve [delv] *verb* **delved, delv•ing** 1 (with *into*) search intensively 2 dig
de•mag•net•ize [dee-MAG-ni-tīz] *verb transitive* **-tized, -tiz•ing** deprive of magnetic polarity
dem•a•gogue [DEM-ə-gog] *noun* mob leader or agitator > **dem•a•gog'ic** [-GOJ-ik] *adjective* > **dem'a•go•gy** [-goh-jee] *noun*
de•mand [di-MAND] *verb transitive* 1 ask as giving an order 2 ask as by right 3 call for as due, right or necessary ▷ *noun* 4 urgent request, claim, requirement 5 call for (specific commodity) > **de•mand'ing** *adjective* requiring great skill, patience, etc.
de•mar•cate [di-MAHR-kayt] *verb transitive* **-cat•ed, -cat•ing** mark boundaries or limits of > **de•mar•ca'tion** *noun*
de•mean [di-MEEN] *verb transitive* degrade, lower, humiliate
de•mean•or [di-MEEN-ər] *noun* conduct, bearing, behavior
de•men•ted [di-MEN-tid] *adjective* 1 mad, crazy 2 beside oneself > **de•men'tia** [-shə] *noun* form of insanity
de•mer•it [di-MER-it] *noun* 1 bad mark 2 undesirable quality
demi- *combining form* half: *demigod*
de•mil•i•ta•rize [dee-MIL-i-tə-rīz] *verb transitive* **-rized, -riz•ing** prohibit military presence or function in (an area)
dem•i•monde [DEM-ee-mond] *noun* 1 class of women of doubtful reputation 2 group behaving with doubtful legality, etc.
de•mise [di-MĪZ] *noun* 1 death 2 conveyance by will or bequest 3 transfer of sovereignty on death or abdication
dem•i•urge [DEM-ee-urj] *noun* name given in some philosophies (esp. Platonic) to the creator of the world and man
dem•o [DEM-oh] *noun* (*informal*) *short for* **demonstration**
de•mo•bi•lize [dee-MOH-bə-līz] *verb transitive* **-lized, -liz•ing** 1 disband (troops) 2 discharge (soldier)
de•moc•ra•cy [di-MOK-rə-see] *noun, plural* **-cies** 1 government by the people or their elected representatives 2 country so governed > **dem•o•crat** [DEM-ə-krat] *noun* advocate of democracy > **dem•o•crat'ic** *adjective* 1 connected with democracy 2 favoring popular rights > **de•moc'ra•tize** *verb transitive* **-tized, -tiz•ing**
de•mog•ra•phy [di-MOG-rə-fee] *noun* study of population statistics, as births, deaths, diseases > **dem•o•graph•ic** [dem-ə-GRAF-ik] *adjective*
de•mol•ish [di-MOL-ish] *verb transitive* 1 knock to pieces 2 destroy utterly, raze > **dem•o•li•tion** [dem-ə-LISH-ən] *noun*
de•mon [DEE-mən] *noun* 1 devil, evil spirit 2 very cruel or malignant person 3 person very good at or devoted to a given activity > **de•mo•ni•ac** [di-MOH-nee-ak] *noun* one possessed with a devil > **de•mo•ni•a•cal** [dee-mə-NĪ-ə-kəl] *adjective* > **de•mon•ic** [di-MON-ik] *adjective* of the nature of a devil > **de•mon•ol'o•gy** [dee-] *noun* study of demons
dem•on•strate [DEM-ən-strayt] *verb transitive* **-strat•ed, -strat•ing** 1 show by reasoning, prove 2 describe, explain by specimens or experiments ▷ *verb intransitive* **-strat•ed, -strat•ing** 3 make exhibition of support, protest, etc. by public

DICTIONARY • THESAURUS

inundation, overflowing, spate, torrent
2 RUSH, avalanche, barrage, flood, spate, torrent
▷ *verb* 3 FLOOD, douse, drench, drown, inundate, soak, submerge, swamp
4 OVERWHELM, engulf, inundate, overload, overrun, swamp
delusion *noun* MISCONCEPTION, error, fallacy, false impression, fancy, hallucination, illusion, misapprehension, mistake
deluxe *adjective* LUXURIOUS, costly, exclusive, expensive, grand, opulent, select, special, splendid, superior
delve *verb* RESEARCH, burrow, explore, ferret out, forage, investigate, look into, probe, rummage, search
demagogue *noun* AGITATOR, firebrand, rabble-rouser
demand *verb* 1 REQUEST, ask, challenge, inquire, interrogate, question
2 REQUIRE, call for, cry out for, entail, involve, necessitate, need, want
3 CLAIM, exact, expect, insist on, order
▷ *noun* 4 REQUEST, inquiry, order, question, requisition
5 NEED, call, claim, market, requirement, want
demanding *adjective* DIFFICULT, challenging, exacting, hard, high-maintenance, taxing, tough, trying, wearing
demarcation *noun* DELIMITATION, differentiation, distinction, division, separation
demean *verb* LOWER, abase, debase, degrade, descend, humble, stoop
demeanor *noun* BEHAVIOR, air, bearing, carriage, comportment, conduct, deportment, manner
demented *adjective* MAD, crazed, crazy, deranged, frenzied, insane, maniacal, unbalanced, unhinged
demise *noun* 1 FAILURE, collapse, downfall, end, fall, ruin
2 (*euphemistic*) DEATH, decease, departure
democracy *noun* SELF-GOVERNMENT, commonwealth, republic
democratic *adjective* SELF-GOVERNING, autonomous, egalitarian, popular, populist, representative
demolish *verb* 1 KNOCK DOWN, bulldoze, destroy, dismantle, flatten, level, raze, tear down
2 DEFEAT, annihilate, destroy, overthrow, overturn, undo, wreck
demolition *noun* KNOCKING DOWN, bulldozing, destruction, explosion, levelling, razing, tearing down, wrecking
demon *noun* 1 EVIL SPIRIT, devil, fiend, ghoul, goblin, malignant spirit
2 WIZARD, ace (*informal*), fiend, master
demonic *or* **demoniac, demoniacal** *adjective* 1 DEVILISH, diabolic, diabolical, fiendish, hellish, infernal, satanic
2 FRENZIED, crazed, frantic, frenetic, furious, hectic, maniacal, manic
demonstrable *adjective* PROVABLE, evident, irrefutable, obvious, palpable, self-evident,

parade, demonstration 4 make show of armed force > **de•mon•stra•ble** [di-MON-strə-bəl] *adjective* > **dem•on•stra'tion** *noun* 1 making clear, proving by evidence 2 exhibition and description 3 organized public expression of opinion 4 display of armed force > **de•mon'stra•tive** *adjective* 1 expressing feelings, emotions easily and unreservedly 2 pointing out 3 conclusive > **dem'on•stra•tor** *noun* 1 one who demonstrates equipment, products, etc. 2 one who takes part in a public demonstration

de•mor•al•ize [di-MOR-ə-līz] *verb transitive* **-ized, -iz•ing** 1 deprive of courage and discipline 2 undermine morally > **de•mor•al•i•za'tion** *noun*

de•mote [di-MOHT] *verb transitive* **-mot•ed, -mot•ing** reduce in status or rank > **de•mo'tion** *noun*

de•mur [di-MUR] *verb intransitive* **-murred, -mur•ring** make difficulties, object > **de•mur'ral** *noun* 1 raising of objection 2 objection raised > **de•mur'rer** *noun*

de•mure [di-MYUUR] *adjective* **-mur•er, -mur•est** reserved, quiet > **de•mure'ly** *adverb*

den *noun* 1 cave or hole of wild beast 2 lair 3 small room, esp. study 4 site, haunt

de•na•tion•a•lize [dee-NASH-ə-nl-īz] *verb transitive* **-lized, -liz•ing** return (an industry) from public to private ownership

de•na•ture [dee-NAY-chər] *verb transitive* **-tured, -tur•ing** deprive of essential qualities, adulterate > **denatured alcohol** alcohol made undrinkable

den•gue [DENG-gee] *noun* an infectious tropical fever

denial *see* **deny**

de•nier [DEN-yər] *noun* unit of weight of silk and synthetic yarn

den•i•grate [DEN-i-grayt] *verb transitive* **-grat•ed, -grat•ing** belittle or disparage character of

den•im [DEN-əm] *noun* strong twilled cotton fabric for trousers, overalls, etc. > **den•ims** garment made of this

den•i•zen [DEN-ə-zən] *noun* inhabitant

de•nom•i•nate [di-NOM-ə-nayt] *verb transitive* **-nat•ed, -nat•ing** give name to > **de•nom•i•na'tion** *noun* 1 distinctly named church or sect 2 name, esp. of class or group > **de•nom•i•na'tion•al** *adjective* > **de•nom'i•na•tor** *noun arithmetic* divisor in fraction

de•note [di-NOHT] *verb transitive* **-not•ed, -not•ing** 1 stand for, be the name of 2 mark, indicate, show > **de•no•ta•tion** [dee-noh-TAY-shən] *noun* esp. explicit meaning of word or phrase

de•noue•ment [day-noo-MAHN] *noun* 1 unraveling of dramatic plot 2 final solution of mystery

de•nounce [di-NOWNS] *verb transitive* **-nounced, -nounc•ing** 1 speak violently against 2 accuse 3 terminate (treaty) > **de•nun•ci•a'tion** *noun* denouncing

dense [dens] *adjective* **dens•er, dens•est** 1 thick, compact 2 stupid > **den'si•ty** *noun, plural* **-ties** mass per unit of volume

dent *noun* 1 hollow or mark left by blow or pressure ▷ *verb transitive* 2 make dent in 3 mark with dent

den•tal [DEN-tl] *adjective* 1 of, pert. to teeth or dentistry 2 pronounced by applying tongue to teeth > **den'ti•frice** [-fris] *noun* powder, paste, or wash for cleaning teeth > **den'tist** *noun* one skilled in care, repair of teeth > **den'tis•try** *noun* art of dentist > **den•ti'tion** *noun* 1 teething 2 arrangement of teeth > **den'ture** [-chər] *noun* (*usually plural*) set of false teeth > **dental floss** soft thread, oft. waxed, for cleaning between teeth

den•tine [DEN-teen] *noun* the hard bonelike part of a tooth

de•nude [di-NOOD] *verb transitive* **-nud•ed, -nud•ing** 1 strip, make bare 2 expose (rock) by erosion of plants, soil, etc.

denunciation *see* **denounce**

de•ny [di-NĪ] *verb transitive* **-nied, -ny•ing** 1 declare untrue 2 contradict 3 reject, disown 4 refuse to give 5 refuse 6 (*reflexive*) abstain from

DICTIONARY

d

THESAURUS

unmistakable, verifiable

demonstrate *verb* 1 PROVE, display, exhibit, indicate, manifest, show, testify to
2 SHOW HOW, describe, explain, illustrate, make clear, teach
3 MARCH, parade, picket, protest, rally

demonstration *noun* 1 MARCH, mass lobby, parade, picket, protest, rally, sit-in
2 EXPLANATION, description, exposition, presentation, test, trial
3 PROOF, confirmation, display, evidence, exhibition, expression, illustration, testimony

demoralize *verb* DISHEARTEN, deject, depress, discourage, dispirit, undermine, unnerve, weaken

demote *verb* DOWNGRADE, degrade, kick downstairs (*slang*), lower in rank, relegate

demur *verb* 1 OBJECT, balk, dispute, hesitate, protest, refuse, take exception, waver
▷ *noun* 2 OBJECTION, compunction, dissent, hesitation, misgiving, protest, qualm

demure *adjective* SHY, diffident, modest, reserved, reticent, retiring, sedate, unassuming

den *noun* 1 LAIR, cave, cavern, haunt, hideout, hole, shelter
2 (*chiefly United States*) STUDY, cubbyhole, hideaway, living room, retreat, sanctuary, sanctum

denial *noun* 1 NEGATION, contradiction, dissent, renunciation, repudiation, retraction
2 REFUSAL, prohibition, rebuff, rejection, repulse, veto

denigrate *verb* DISPARAGE, bad-mouth (*slang*), belittle, knock (*informal*), malign, run down, slander, vilify

denomination *noun* 1 RELIGIOUS GROUP, belief, creed, persuasion, school, sect
2 UNIT, grade, size, value

denote *verb* INDICATE, betoken, designate, express, imply, mark, mean, show, signify

denounce *verb* CONDEMN, accuse, attack, censure, denunciate, revile, stigmatize, vilify

dense *adjective* 1 THICK, close-knit, compact, condensed, heavy, impenetrable, opaque, solid
2 STUPID, dull, obtuse, slow-witted, stolid, thick

density *noun* TIGHTNESS, bulk, compactness, consistency, denseness, impenetrability, mass, solidity, thickness

> **de•ni'a•ble** *adjective* > **de•ni'al** *noun*
de•o•dor•ize [dee-OH-də-rīz] *verb transitive* **-ized, -iz•ing** rid of smell or mask smell of > **de•o'dor•ant** *noun* > **de•o'dor•iz•er** *noun*
de•ox•i•dize [dee-OK-si-dīz] *verb transitive* **-dized, -diz•ing** deprive of oxygen
de•part [di-PAHRT] *verb intransitive* 1 go away 2 start out, set forth 3 deviate, vary 4 die > **de•par'ture** [-chər] *noun*
de•part•ment [di-PAHRT-mənt] *noun* 1 division 2 branch 3 province > **de•part•men'tal** *adjective*
de•pend [di-PEND] *verb intransitive* (usu. with *on*) 1 rely entirely 2 live 3 be contingent, await settlement or decision > **de•pend'a•ble** *adjective* reliable > **de•pend'ent** *noun* 1 one for whose maintenance another is responsible ▷ *adjective* 2 depending on > **de•pend'ence** *noun* > **de•pend'en•cy** *noun* 1 dependence 2 subject territory
de•pict [di-PIKT] *verb transitive* 1 give picture of 2 describe in words > **de•pic'tion** *noun*
de•pil•a•to•ry [di-PIL-ə-tor-ee] *noun, plural* **-ries** substance that removes unwanted hair ▷ *adjective*
de•plete [di-PLEET] *verb transitive* **-plet•ed, -plet•ing** 1 empty 2 reduce 3 exhaust > **de•ple'tion** *noun*
de•plore [di-PLOR] *verb transitive* **-plored, -plor•ing** 1 lament, regret 2 deprecate, complain of > **de•plor'a•ble** *adjective* 1 lamentable 2 disgraceful
de•ploy [di-PLOI] *verb* 1 of troops, ships, aircraft, (cause to) adopt battle formation 2 arrange > **de•ploy'ment** *noun*
de•po•nent [di-POH-nənt] *adjective* 1 of verb, having passive form but active meaning ▷ *noun* 2 deponent verb 3 one who makes statement under oath
de•pop•u•late [di-POP-yə-layt] *verb* **-lat•ed, -lat•ing** (cause to) be reduced in population > **de•pop•u•la'tion** *noun*
de•port [di-PORT] *verb transitive* expel from foreign country, banish > **de•por•ta'tion** [dee-] *noun*
de•port•ment [di-PORT-mənt] *noun* behavior, conduct, bearing > **de•port'** *verb* behave, carry (oneself)
de•pose [di-POHZ] *verb transitive* **-posed, -pos•ing** 1 remove from office, esp. of ruler ▷ *verb intransitive* **-posed, -pos•ing** 2 make statement under oath, give evidence > **de•pos'al** *noun* removal from office
de•pos•it [di-POZ-it] *verb transitive* 1 set down, esp. carefully 2 give into safekeeping, esp. in bank 3 let fall (as sediment) ▷ *noun* 4 thing deposited 5 money given in part payment or as security 6 sediment > **dep•o•si•tion** [dep-ə-ZISH-ən] *noun* 1 statement written and attested 2 act of deposing or depositing > **de•pos'i•tor** *noun* > **de•pos'i•to•ry** *noun, plural* **-ries** place for safekeeping
dep•ot [DEE-poh] *noun* 1 storehouse 2 building for storage and servicing of buses,

DICTIONARY • THESAURUS

dent *noun* 1 HOLLOW, chip, crater, depression, dimple, dip, impression, indentation, pit ▷ *verb* 2 MAKE A DENT IN, gouge, hollow, press in, push in
deny *verb* 1 CONTRADICT, disagree with, disprove, rebuff, rebut, refute
2 REFUSE, begrudge, disallow, forbid, reject, turn down, withhold
3 RENOUNCE, disclaim, disown, recant, repudiate, retract
depart *verb* 1 LEAVE, absent (oneself), disappear, exit, go, go away, quit, retire, retreat, withdraw
2 DEVIATE, differ, digress, diverge, stray, swerve, turn aside, vary, veer
department *noun* SECTION, branch, bureau, division, office, station, subdivision, unit
departure *noun* 1 LEAVING, exit, exodus, going, going away, leave-taking, removal, retirement, withdrawal
2 DIVERGENCE, deviation, digression, variation
3 SHIFT, change, difference, innovation, novelty, whole new ball game (*informal*)
depend *verb* 1 TRUST IN, bank on, count on, lean on, reckon on, rely upon, turn to
2 BE DETERMINED BY, be based on, be contingent on, be subject to, be subordinate to, hang on, hinge on, rest on, revolve around
dependable *adjective* RELIABLE, faithful, reputable, responsible, staunch, steady, sure, trustworthy, trusty, unfailing
dependant *noun* RELATIVE, child, minor, protégé, subordinate
dependent *adjective* 1 RELYING ON, defenseless, helpless, reliant, vulnerable, weak
2 ▷ **dependent on, dependent upon** DETERMINED BY, conditional on, contingent on, depending on, influenced by, subject to
depict *verb* 1 DRAW, delineate, illustrate, outline, paint, picture, portray, sketch
2 DESCRIBE, characterize, narrate, outline, represent
depiction *noun* REPRESENTATION, delineation, description, picture, portrayal, sketch
deplete *verb* USE UP, consume, drain, empty, exhaust, expend, impoverish, lessen, reduce
deplorable *adjective* 1 REGRETTABLE, grievous, lamentable, pitiable, sad, unfortunate, wretched
2 DISGRACEFUL, dishonorable, reprehensible, scandalous, shameful
deplore *verb* DISAPPROVE OF, abhor, censure, condemn, denounce, object to, take a dim view of
deploy *verb* POSITION, arrange, set out, station, use, utilize
deployment *noun* POSITION, arrangement, organization, spread, stationing, use, utilization
deport *verb* 1 EXPEL, banish, exile, expatriate, extradite, oust
2 ▷ **deport oneself** BEHAVE, acquit oneself, act, bear oneself, carry oneself, comport oneself, conduct oneself, hold oneself
depose *verb* 1 REMOVE FROM OFFICE, demote, dethrone, dismiss, displace, oust
2 (*law*) TESTIFY, avouch, declare, make a deposition
deposit *verb* 1 PUT, drop, lay, locate, place
2 STORE, bank, consign, entrust, lodge ▷ *noun* 3 DOWN PAYMENT, installment, part payment, pledge, retainer, security, stake
4 SEDIMENT, accumulation, dregs, lees, precipitate, silt
depot *noun* 1 STOREHOUSE, depository,

trains, etc. 3 railroad, bus station

de•prave [di-PRAYV] *verb transitive* **-praved, -prav•ing** make bad, corrupt, pervert > **de•prav'i•ty** *noun, plural* **-ties** wickedness, viciousness

dep•re•cate [DEP-ri-kayt] *verb transitive* **-cat•ed, -cat•ing** 1 express disapproval of 2 advise against > **dep•re•ca'tion** *noun* > **dep're•ca•to•ry** *adjective*

de•pre•ci•ate [di-PREE-shee-ayt] *verb transitive* **-at•ed, -at•ing** 1 lower price, value or purchasing power of 2 belittle ▷ *verb intransitive* **-at•ed, -at•ing** 3 fall in value > **de•pre•ci•a'tion** *noun*

dep•re•da•tion [dep-ri-DAY-shən] *noun* plundering, pillage > **dep're•date** *verb transitive* **-dat•ed, -dat•ing** plunder, despoil

de•press [di-PRES] *verb transitive* 1 affect with low spirits 2 lower, in level or activity > **de•pres'sion** [-PRESH-ən] *noun* 1 hollow 2 low spirits, dejection, despondency 3 poor condition of business, slump > **de•pres'sant** *adjective, noun*

de•prive [di-PRĪV] *verb transitive* **-prived, -priv•ing** strip, dispossess > **dep•ri•va•tion** [dep-rə-VAY-shən] *noun* > **deprived** *adjective* lacking adequate food, care, amenities, etc.

depth *noun* 1 (degree of) deepness 2 deep place, abyss 3 intensity (of color, feeling) 4 profundity (of mind) > **depth charge** bomb for use against submarines

de•pute [di-PYOOT], **-put•ed, -put•ing,** ▷ *verb transitive* 1 allot 2 appoint as an agent or substitute > **dep•u•ta•tion** [dep-yə-TAY-shən] *noun* persons sent to speak for others > **dep'u•tize** *verb intransitive* **-tized, -tiz•ing** 1 act for another ▷ *verb transitive* 2 depute > **dep'u•ty** *noun, plural* **-ties** 1 assistant 2 substitute, delegate

de•rail [dee-RAYL] *verb* (cause to) go off the rails, as train, etc. > **de•rail'ment** *noun*

de•rail•leur [di-RAY-lər] *noun* gear-changing mechanism for bicycles

de•range [di-RAYNJ] *verb transitive* **-ranged, -rang•ing** 1 put out of place, out of order 2 upset 3 make insane > **de•range'ment** *noun*

der•by [DUR-bee] *noun* 1 horserace, esp. Kentucky Derby, held at Churchill Downs, Kentucky 2 contest between teams of skaters, etc. 3 man's low-crowned stiff felt hat

de•reg•u•late [dee-REG-yə-layt] *verb transitive* **-lat•ed, -lat•ing** remove regulations or controls from

der•e•lict [DER-ə-likt] *adjective* 1 abandoned, forsaken 2 falling into ruins, dilapidated ▷ *noun* 3 social outcast, vagrant 4 abandoned property, ship, etc. > **der•e•lic'tion** *noun* 1 neglect (of duty) 2 abandoning

de•ride [di-RĪD] *verb transitive* **-rid•ed, -rid•ing** speak of or treat with contempt, ridicule > **de•ri'sion** [-RIZH-ən] *noun* ridicule > **de•ri'sive** [-RĪ-siv] *adjective*

DICTIONARY **d** THESAURUS

---

repository, warehouse
2 BUS STATION, garage, terminus

depraved *adjective* CORRUPT, degenerate, dissolute, evil, immoral, sinful, vicious, vile, wicked

depravity *noun* CORRUPTION, debauchery, evil, immorality, sinfulness, vice, wickedness

depreciate *verb* 1 DEVALUE, decrease, deflate, lessen, lose value, lower, reduce
2 DISPARAGE, belittle, denigrate, deride, detract, run down, scorn, sneer at

depreciation *noun* 1 DEVALUATION, deflation, depression, drop, fall, slump
2 DISPARAGEMENT, belittlement, denigration, deprecation, detraction

depress *verb* 1 SADDEN, deject, discourage, dishearten, dispirit, make despondent, oppress, weigh down
2 LOWER, cheapen, depreciate, devalue, diminish, downgrade, lessen, reduce
3 PRESS DOWN, flatten, level, lower, push down

depressed *adjective* 1 LOW-SPIRITED, blue, dejected, despondent, discouraged, dispirited, downcast, downhearted, fed up, sad, unhappy
2 POVERTY-STRICKEN, deprived, disadvantaged, needy, poor, run-down
3 LOWERED, cheapened, depreciated, devalued, weakened
4 SUNKEN, concave, hollow, indented, recessed

depressing *adjective* BLEAK, discouraging, disheartening, dismal, dispiriting, gloomy, harrowing, sad, saddening

depression *noun* 1 LOW SPIRITS, dejection, despair, despondency, downheartedness, dumps (*informal*), gloominess, melancholy, sadness, the blues
2 RECESSION, economic decline, hard times *or* bad times, inactivity, slump, stagnation
3 HOLLOW, bowl, cavity, dent, dimple, dip, indentation, pit, valley

deprivation *noun* 1 WITHHOLDING, denial, dispossession, expropriation, removal, withdrawal
2 WANT, destitution, distress, hardship, need, privation

deprive *verb* WITHHOLD, bereave, despoil, dispossess, rob, strip

deprived *adjective* POOR, bereft, destitute, disadvantaged, down at heel, in need, lacking, needy

depth *noun* 1 DEEPNESS, drop, extent, measure
2 INSIGHT, astuteness, discernment, penetration, profoundness, profundity, sagacity, wisdom

deputation *noun* DELEGATION, commission, embassy, envoys, legation

deputize *verb* STAND IN FOR, act for, take the place of, understudy

deputy *noun* SUBSTITUTE, delegate, legate, lieutenant, number two, proxy, representative, second-in-command, surrogate

deranged *adjective* MAD, crazed, crazy, demented, distracted, insane, irrational, unbalanced, unhinged

derelict *adjective* 1 ABANDONED, deserted, dilapidated, discarded, forsaken, neglected, ruined
▷ *noun* 2 TRAMP, bag lady, down-and-out, outcast, vagrant

deride *verb* MOCK, disdain, disparage, insult, jeer, ridicule, scoff, scorn, sneer, taunt

derisory *adjective* RIDICULOUS, contemptible, insulting, laughable, lousy (*slang*), ludicrous, outrageous, preposterous

de ri•gueur [də ri-GUR] Fr. required by etiquette, fashion or custom
de•rive [di-RĪV] *verb transitive* **-rived, -riv•ing** 1 deduce, get from 2 show origin of ▷ *verb intransitive* 3 issue, be descended (from) > **der•i•va•tion** [der-ə-VAY-shən] *noun* > **de•riv•a•tive** [di-RIV-ə-tiv] *adjective, noun*
der•ma•ti•tis [dur-mə-TĪ-tis] *noun* inflammation of skin
der•ma•tol•o•gy [dur-mə-TOL-ə-jee] *noun* science of skin > **der•ma•tol'o•gist** *noun* physician specializing in skin diseases
de•rog•a•to•ry [di-ROG-ə-tor-ee] *adjective* disparaging, belittling, intentionally offensive > **der•o•gate** [DER-ə-gayt] *verb transitive* **-gat•ed, -gat•ing** 1 disparage ▷ *verb intransitive* **-gat•ed, -gat•ing** 2 detract
der•rick [DER-ik] *noun* 1 hoisting machine 2 framework over oil well, etc.
der•ring-do [DER-ing DOO] *noun* (act of) spirited bravery, boldness
der•rin•ger [DER-in-jər] *noun* short-barreled pocket pistol
der•vish [DUR-vish] *noun* member of Muslim ascetic order, noted for frenzied, whirling dance
des•cant [DES-kant] *noun* 1 *mus.* decorative variation sung as accompaniment to basic melody ▷ *verb intransitive* [des-KANT] 2 *mus.* sing or play a descant 3 talk about in detail 4 dwell (on) at length
de•scend [di-SEND] *verb intransitive* 1 come or go down 2 slope down 3 stoop, condescend 4 spring from (ancestor, etc.) 5 pass to heir, be transmitted 6 swoop on or attack ▷ *verb transitive* 7 go or come down > **de•scend'ant** *noun* person descended from an ancestor > **de•scent'** *noun*
de•scribe [di-SKRĪB] *verb transitive* **-scribed, -scrib•ing** 1 give detailed account of 2 pronounce or label 3 trace out (geometric figure, etc.) > **de•scrip'tion** [-SKRIP-shən] *noun* 1 detailed account 2 marking out 3 kind, sort, species > **de•scrip'tive** *adjective*
de•scry [di-SKRĪ] *verb transitive* **-scried, -scry•ing** make out, catch sight of, esp. at a distance espy
des•e•crate [DES-i-krayt] *verb transitive* **-crat•ed, -crat•ing** 1 violate sanctity of 2 profane 3 convert to evil use > **des•e•cra'tion** *noun*
des•ert[1] [DEZ-ərt] *noun* 1 uninhabited and barren region ▷ *adjective* 2 barren, uninhabited, desolate
de•sert[2] [di-ZURT] *verb transitive* 1 abandon, forsake, leave ▷ *verb intransitive* 2 run away from service, esp. of soldiers, sailors, etc. > **de•sert'er** *noun* > **de•ser'tion** *noun*
de•sert[3] [di-ZURT] *noun* (*usually plural*) 1 what is due as reward or punishment 2 merit, virtue
de•serve [di-ZURV] *verb transitive* **-served, -serv•ing** 1 show oneself worthy of 2 have by conduct a claim to > **de•serv'ed•ly** *adverb* > **de•serv'ing** *adjective* worthy (of reward, etc.)
deshabille *noun see* **dishabille**
des•ic•cate [DES-i-kayt] *verb* **-cat•ed, -cat•ing** 1 dry 2 dry up
de•sid•er•a•tum [di-sid-ə-RAH-təm] *noun, plural* **-ta** [-tə] something lacked and wanted
de•sign [di-ZĪN] *verb transitive* 1 make working drawings for 2 sketch 3 plan out 4 intend, select for ▷ *noun* 5 outline sketch 6 working plan 7 art of making decorative patterns, etc. 8 project, purpose, mental plan > **de•sign'ed•ly** *adverb* on purpose > **de•sign'er** *noun* esp. one who

DICTIONARY • THESAURUS

derivation *noun* ORIGIN, beginning, foundation, root, source
derive from *verb* COME FROM, arise from, emanate from, flow from, issue from, originate from, proceed from, spring from, stem from
derogatory *adjective* DISPARAGING, belittling, defamatory, offensive, slighting, uncomplimentary, unfavorable, unflattering
descend *verb* 1 MOVE DOWN, drop, fall, go down, plummet, plunge, sink, subside, tumble
2 SLOPE, dip, incline, slant
3 LOWER ONESELF, degenerate, deteriorate, stoop
4 ▷ **be descended** ORIGINATE, be handed down, be passed down, derive, issue, proceed, spring
5 ▷ **descend on** ATTACK, arrive, invade, raid, swoop
descent *noun* 1 COMING DOWN, drop, fall, plunge, swoop
2 SLOPE, declivity, dip, drop, incline, slant
3 ANCESTRY, extraction, family tree, genealogy, lineage, origin, parentage
4 DECLINE, degeneration, deterioration
describe *verb* 1 RELATE, depict, explain, express, narrate, portray, recount, report, tell
2 TRACE, delineate, draw, mark out, outline
description *noun* 1 ACCOUNT, depiction, explanation, narrative, portrayal, report, representation, sketch
2 KIND, brand, category, class, order, sort, type, variety
descriptive *adjective* GRAPHIC, detailed, explanatory, expressive, illustrative, pictorial, picturesque, vivid
desert[1] *noun* WILDERNESS, solitude, waste, wasteland, wilds
desert[2] *verb* ABANDON, abscond, forsake, jilt, leave, leave stranded, maroon, quit, strand, walk out on (*informal*)
deserted *adjective* ABANDONED, derelict, desolate, empty, forsaken, neglected, unoccupied, vacant
deserter *noun* DEFECTOR, absconder, escapee, fugitive, renegade, runaway, traitor, truant
desertion *noun* ABANDONMENT, absconding, apostasy, betrayal, defection, dereliction, escape, evasion, flight, relinquishment
deserve *verb* MERIT, be entitled to, be worthy of, earn, justify, rate, warrant
deserved *adjective* WELL-EARNED, due, earned, fitting, justified, merited, proper, rightful, warranted
deserving *adjective* WORTHY, commendable, estimable, laudable, meritorious, praiseworthy, righteous
design *verb* 1 PLAN, draft, draw, outline, sketch, trace
2 CREATE, conceive, fabricate, fashion, invent, originate, think up
3 INTEND, aim, mean, plan, propose, purpose
▷ *noun* 4 PLAN, blueprint, draft, drawing, model, outline, scheme, sketch
5 ARRANGEMENT, construction, form, organization, pattern, shape, style
6 INTENTION, aim, end, goal, object, objective, purpose, target

draws designs for manufacturers or selects typefaces, etc. for books, etc. > **de•sign'ing** *adjective* crafty, scheming
des•ig•nate [DEZ-ig-nayt] *verb transitive* **-nat•ed, -nat•ing** 1 name, pick out, appoint to office ▷ *adjective* [-nit] 2 appointed but not yet installed > **des•ig•na'tion** *noun* name, appellation
de•sire [di-ZĪR] *verb transitive* **-sired, -sir•ing** 1 wish, long for 2 ask for, entreat ▷ *noun* 3 longing, craving 4 expressed wish, request 5 sexual appetite 6 something wished for or requested > **de•sir'a•ble** *adjective* worth desiring > **de•sir'ous** *adjective* filled with desire
de•sist [di-ZIST] *verb intransitive* cease, stop
desk *noun* 1 table or other piece of furniture designed for reading or writing 2 counter 3 editorial section of newspaper, etc. covering specific subject 4 section of State Department having responsibility for particular operations
des•o•late [DES-ə-lit] *adjective* 1 uninhabited 2 neglected, barren, ruinous 3 solitary 4 dreary, dismal, forlorn ▷ *verb transitive* [-layt], **-lat•ed, -lat•ing** 5 depopulate, lay waste 6 overwhelm with grief > **des•o•la'tion** *noun*
de•spair [di-SPAIR] *verb intransitive* 1 lose hope ▷ *noun* 2 loss of all hope 3 cause of this 4 despondency
despatch *see* **dispatch**
des•pe•rate [DES-pər-it] *adjective* 1 reckless from despair 2 difficult or dangerous 3 frantic 4 hopelessly bad 5 leaving no room for hope > **des•per•a'do** [-pə-RAH-doh] *noun, plural* **-dos** reckless, lawless person > **des'per•ate•ly** *adverb* > **des•per•a'tion** *noun*
de•spise [di-SPĪZ] *verb transitive* **-spised, -spis•ing** look down on as contemptible, inferior > **des•pi•ca•ble** [des-PI-kə-bəl] *adjective* base, contemptible, vile
de•spite [di-SPĪT] *preposition* in spite of
de•spoil [di-SPOIL] *verb transitive* plunder, rob, strip of > **de•spo•li•a•tion** [di-spoh-lee-AY-shən] *noun*
de•spond•ent [di-SPON-dənt] *adjective* dejected, depressed > **de•spond'en•cy** *noun*
des•pot [DES-pət] *noun* tyrant, oppressor > **des•pot•ic** [di-SPOT-ik] *adjective* > **des'pot•ism** *noun* autocratic government, tyranny
des•sert [di-ZURT] *noun* course of pastry, fruit, etc. served at end of meal
des•ti•na•tion [des-tə-NAY-shən] *noun* 1 place a person or thing is bound for 2 goal 3 purpose

DICTIONARY

d

THESAURUS

designate *verb* 1 NAME, call, dub, entitle, label, style, term
2 APPOINT, assign, choose, delegate, depute, nominate, select
designation *noun* NAME, description, label, mark, title
designer *noun* CREATOR, architect, deviser, inventor, originator, planner
desirable *adjective* 1 WORTHWHILE, advantageous, advisable, beneficial, good, preferable, profitable, win-win (*informal*)
2 ATTRACTIVE, adorable, alluring, fetching, glamorous, seductive, sexy (*informal*)
desire *verb* 1 WANT, crave, hanker after, hope for, long for, set one's heart on, thirst for, wish for, yearn for
▷ *noun* 2 WISH, aspiration, craving, hankering, hope, longing, thirst, want
3 LUST, appetite, libido, passion
desist *verb* STOP, break off, cease, discontinue, end, forbear, leave off, pause, refrain from
desolate *adjective* 1 UNINHABITED, bare, barren, bleak, dreary, godforsaken, solitary, wild
2 MISERABLE, dejected, despondent, disconsolate, downcast, forlorn, gloomy, wretched
▷ *verb* 3 LAY WASTE, depopulate, despoil, destroy, devastate, lay low, pillage, plunder, ravage, ruin
4 DEJECT, depress, discourage, dishearten, dismay, distress, grieve
desolation *noun* 1 RUIN, destruction, devastation, havoc
2 BLEAKNESS, barrenness, isolation, solitude
3 MISERY, anguish, dejection, despair, distress, gloom, sadness, woe, wretchedness
despair *noun* 1 DESPONDENCY, anguish, dejection, depression, desperation, gloom, hopelessness, misery, wretchedness
▷ *verb* 2 LOSE HOPE, give up, lose heart
despairing *adjective* HOPELESS, dejected, desperate, despondent, disconsolate, frantic, grief-stricken, inconsolable, miserable, wretched
despatch *see* **dispatch**
desperado *noun* CRIMINAL, bandit, lawbreaker, outlaw, villain
desperate *adjective* 1 RECKLESS, audacious, daring, frantic, furious, risky
2 GRAVE, drastic, extreme, urgent
desperately *adverb* 1 GRAVELY, badly, dangerously, perilously, seriously, severely
2 HOPELESSLY, appallingly, fearfully, frightfully, shockingly
desperation *noun* 1 RECKLESSNESS, foolhardiness, frenzy, impetuosity, madness, rashness
2 MISERY, agony, anguish, despair, hopelessness, trouble, unhappiness, worry
despicable *adjective* CONTEMPTIBLE, detestable, disgraceful, hateful, lousy (*slang*), mean, scuzzy (*slang*), shameful, sordid, vile, worthless, wretched
despise *verb* LOOK DOWN ON, abhor, detest, loathe, revile, scorn
despite *preposition* IN SPITE OF, against, even with, in the face of, in the teeth of, notwithstanding, regardless of, undeterred by
despondency *noun* DEJECTION, depression, despair, desperation, gloom, low spirits, melancholy, misery, sadness
despondent *adjective* DEJECTED, depressed, disconsolate, disheartened, dispirited, downhearted, glum, in despair, sad, sorrowful
despot *noun* TYRANT, autocrat, dictator, oppressor
despotic *adjective* TYRANNICAL, authoritarian, autocratic, dictatorial, domineering, imperious, oppressive
despotism *noun* TYRANNY, autocracy, dictatorship, oppression, totalitarianism
destination *noun* JOURNEY'S END, haven, resting-place, station, stop, terminus
destined *adjective* FATED, bound, certain, doomed, intended, meant, predestined

des•tine [DES-tin] *verb transitive* **-tined, -tin•ing** 1 ordain or fix beforehand 2 set apart, devote
des•ti•ny [DES-tə-nee] *noun, plural* **-nies** 1 course of events or person's fate 2 the power that foreordains
des•ti•tute [DES-ti-toot] *adjective* 1 in absolute want 2 in great need, devoid (of) 3 penniless > **des•ti•tu'tion** *noun*
de-stress [dee-STRES] *verb* to become or cause to become less anxious
de•stroy [di-STROI] *verb transitive* 1 ruin 2 pull to pieces 3 undo 4 put an end to 5 demolish 6 annihilate > **de•stroy'er** *noun* 1 one who destroys 2 small, swift, heavily armed warship > **de•struct** [di-STRUKT] *verb* 1 destroy (one's own missile, etc.) for safety 2 be destroyed > **de•struct'i•ble** *adjective* > **de•struc'tion** *noun* 1 ruin, overthrow 2 death > **de•struc'tive** *adjective* 1 destroying 2 negative, not constructive
des•ue•tude [DES-wi-tood] *noun* disuse, discontinuance
des•ul•to•ry [DES-əl-tor-ee] *adjective* 1 passing, changing fitfully from one thing to another 2 aimless 3 unmethodical
de•tach [di-TACH] *verb transitive* unfasten, disconnect, separate > **de•tach'a•ble** *adjective* > **de•tached'** *adjective* 1 standing apart, isolated 2 impersonal, disinterested > **de•tach'ment** *noun* 1 aloofness 2 detaching 3 a body of troops detached for special duty
de•tail [di-TAYL, DEE-tayl] *noun* 1 particular 2 small or unimportant part 3 treatment of anything item by item 4 party or personnel assigned for duty in military unit ▷ *verb transitive* 5 relate in full 6 appoint for duty
de•tain [di-TAYN] *verb transitive* 1 keep under restraint 2 hinder 3 keep waiting > **de•ten'tion** *noun* 1 confinement 2 arrest 3 detaining
de•tect [di-TEKT] *verb transitive* find out or discover existence, presence, nature or identity of > **de•tec'tion** *noun* > **de•tec'tive** *noun* 1 police officer or private agent employed in detecting crime ▷ *adjective* 2 employed in detection > **de•tec'tor** *noun* esp. mechanical sensing device or device for detecting radio signals, etc.
dé•tente [day-TAHNT] *noun* lessening of tension in political or international affairs
detention *noun see* **detain**
de•ter [di-TUR] *verb transitive* **-terred, -ter•ring** 1 discourage, frighten 2 hinder, prevent > **de•ter'rent** *adjective, noun*
de•ter•gent [di-TUR-jənt] *noun* 1 cleansing, purifying substance ▷ *adjective* 2 having cleansing power
de•te•ri•o•rate [di-TEER-ee-ə-rayt] *verb* **-rat•ed, -rat•ing** become or make worse > **de•te•ri•o•ra'tion** *noun*
de•ter•mine [di-TUR-min] *verb transitive* **-mined, -min•ing** 1 make up one's mind, decide 2 fix as known 3 bring to a decision 4 be deciding factor in 5 *law* end ▷ *verb intransitive* **-mined, -min•ing** 6 come to an end 7 come to a decision > **de•ter'mi•nant** *adjective, noun* > **de•ter'mi•nate** [-nit] *adjective* fixed in scope or nature > **de•ter•mi•na'tion** *noun* 1 determining

DICTIONARY • THESAURUS

destiny *noun* FATE, doom, fortune, karma, kismet, lot, portion
destitute *adjective* PENNILESS, down and out, down on one's luck (*informal*), impoverished, indigent, insolvent, moneyless, penurious, poor, poverty-stricken
destroy *verb* RUIN, annihilate, crush, demolish, devastate, eradicate, shatter, wipe out, wreck
destruction *noun* RUIN, annihilation, demolition, devastation, eradication, extermination, havoc, slaughter, wreckage
destructive *adjective* DAMAGING, calamitous, catastrophic, deadly, devastating, fatal, harmful, lethal, ruinous
detach *verb* SEPARATE, cut off, disconnect, disengage, divide, remove, sever, tear off, unfasten
detached *adjective* 1 SEPARATE, disconnected, discrete, unconnected
2 UNINVOLVED, disinterested, dispassionate, impartial, impersonal, neutral, objective, reserved, unbiased
detachment *noun* 1 INDIFFERENCE, aloofness, coolness, nonchalance, remoteness, unconcern
2 IMPARTIALITY, fairness, neutrality, objectivity
3 (*military*) UNIT, body, force, party, patrol, squad, task force
detail *noun* 1 POINT, aspect, component, element, fact, factor, feature, particular, respect
2 FINE POINT, nicety, particular, triviality
3 (*military*) PARTY, assignment, body, detachment, duty, fatigue, force, squad
▷ *verb* 4 LIST, catalog, enumerate, itemize, recite, recount, rehearse, relate, tabulate
5 APPOINT, allocate, assign, charge, commission, delegate, send
detailed *adjective* COMPREHENSIVE, blow-by-blow, exhaustive, full, intricate, minute, particular, thorough
detain *verb* 1 DELAY, check, hinder, hold up, impede, keep back, retard, slow up *or* slow down
2 HOLD, arrest, confine, intern, restrain
detect *verb* 1 NOTICE, ascertain, identify, note, observe, perceive, recognize, spot
2 DISCOVER, find, track down, uncover, unmask
detective *noun* INVESTIGATOR, cop (*slang*), gumshoe (*slang*), private eye, private investigator, sleuth (*informal*)
detention *noun* IMPRISONMENT, confinement, custody, incarceration, quarantine
deter *verb* DISCOURAGE, dissuade, frighten, inhibit from, intimidate, prevent, put off, stop, talk out of
detergent *noun* CLEANER, cleanser
deteriorate *verb* DECLINE, degenerate, go downhill (*informal*), lower, slump, worsen
determination *noun* TENACITY, dedication, doggedness, fortitude, perseverance, persistence, resolve, single-mindedness, steadfastness, willpower
determine *verb* 1 SETTLE, conclude, decide, end, finish, ordain, regulate
2 FIND OUT, ascertain, detect, discover, learn, verify, work out
3 DECIDE, choose, elect, make up one's mind, resolve
determined *adjective* RESOLUTE, dogged, firm, intent, persevering, persistent, single-minded, steadfast, tenacious, unwavering

2 firm or resolute conduct or purpose 3 resolve > **determined** *adjective* resolute > **de•ter'min•ism** *noun* theory that human action is settled by forces independent of human will

de•test [di-TEST] *verb transitive* hate, loathe > **de•test'a•ble** *adjective* > **de•tes•ta•tion** [dee-te-STAY-shən] *noun*

de•throne [dee-THROHN] *verb transitive* **-throned, -thron•ing** remove from throne, depose

det•o•nate [DET-n-ayt] *verb* of bomb, mine, explosives, etc., (cause to) explode > **det•o•na'tion** *noun* > **det'o•na•tor** *noun* mechanical, electrical device, or small amount of explosive, used to set off main explosive charge

de•tour [DEE-tuur] *noun* 1 course that leaves main route to rejoin it later 2 roundabout way ▷ *verb intransitive*

de•tox [DEE-toks] (*informal*) ▷ *noun* 1 treatment to rid the body of poisonous substances ▷ *verb* [dee-TOKS] 2 undergo or subject to such treatment

de•tract [di-TRAKT] *verb* take away (a part) from, diminish > **de•trac'tor** *noun*

det•ri•ment [DE-trə-mənt] *noun* harm done, loss, damage > **det•ri•men'tal** *adjective* damaging, injurious

de•tri•tus [di-TRĪ-təs] *noun* 1 worn-down matter such as gravel, or rock debris 2 debris

de trop [də TROH] Fr. not wanted, superfluous

deuce [doos] *noun* 1 two 2 playing card with two spots 3 *tennis* forty all 4 in exclamatory phrases, the devil

Deut. Deuteronomy

deu•te•ri•um [doo-TEER-ee-əm] *noun* isotope of hydrogen twice as heavy as the normal gas

de•val•ue [dee-VAL-yoo], **-ued, -u•ing,** ▷ *verb* 1 (of currency) reduce or be reduced in value 2 reduce the value or worth of > **de•val•u•a'tion** *noun*

dev•as•tate [DEV-ə-stayt] *verb transitive* **-tat•ed, -tat•ing** 1 lay waste 2 ravage 3 (*informal*) overwhelm > **dev•as•ta'tion** *noun*

de•vel•op [di-VEL-əp] *verb transitive* 1 bring to maturity 2 elaborate 3 bring forth, bring out 4 evolve 5 treat photographic plate or film to bring out image 6 improve value or change use of (land) by building, etc. ▷ *verb intransitive* 7 grow to maturer state > **de•vel'op•er** *noun* 1 one who develops land 2 chemical for developing film > **de•vel'op•ment** *noun*

de•vi•ate [DEE-vee-ayt] *verb intransitive* **-at•ed, -at•ing** leave the way, turn aside, diverge > **de'vi•ant** *noun, adjective* (person) deviating from normal esp. in sexual practices > **de•vi•a'tion** *noun* > **de'vi•ous** *adjective* 1 deceitful, underhanded 2 roundabout, rambling 3 erring

de•vice [di-VĪS] *noun* 1 contrivance, invention 2 apparatus 3 stratagem 4 scheme, plot 5 heraldic or emblematic figure or design

dev•il [DEV-əl] *noun* 1 personified spirit of evil 2 superhuman evil being 3 person of great wickedness, cruelty, etc. 4 (*informal*) fellow 5 (*informal*) something difficult or annoying 6 energy, dash, unconquerable spirit 7 (*informal*) rogue, rascal ▷ *verb transitive* **-iled, -il•ing** 8 prepare (eggs, etc.) with spicy seasoning > **dev'il•ish** *adjective* 1 like, of the devil 2 evil ▷ *adverb* 3 (*informal*) very, extremely > **dev'il•try** *noun, plural* **-tries** 1 wickedness 2 wild and reckless mischief, revelry, high spirits > **dev'il-may-care'** *adjective* happy-go-lucky > **devil's advocate** 1 one who advocates opposing, unpopular view, usu. for sake of argument 2 *Catholic Church* one appointed to state disqualifications of person who has been proposed for sainthood

deterrent *noun* DISCOURAGEMENT, check, curb, disincentive, hindrance, impediment, obstacle, restraint

detest *verb* HATE, abhor, abominate, despise, dislike intensely, loathe, recoil from

detonate *verb* EXPLODE, blast, blow up, discharge, set off, trigger

detour *noun* DIVERSION, bypass, circuitous route or indirect route, roundabout way

detract *verb* LESSEN, devaluate, diminish, lower, reduce, take away from

detriment *noun* DAMAGE, disadvantage, disservice, harm, hurt, impairment, injury, loss

detrimental *adjective* DAMAGING, adverse, deleterious, destructive, disadvantageous, harmful, prejudicial, unfavorable

devastate *verb* DESTROY, demolish, lay waste, level, ravage, raze, ruin, sack, wreck

devastating *adjective* OVERWHELMING, cutting, overpowering, savage, trenchant, vitriolic, withering

devastation *noun* DESTRUCTION, demolition, desolation, havoc, ruin

develop *verb* 1 ADVANCE, evolve, flourish, grow, mature, progress, prosper, ripen
2 FORM, breed, establish, generate, invent, originate
3 EXPAND, amplify, augment, broaden, elaborate, enlarge, unfold, work out

development *noun* 1 GROWTH, advance, evolution, expansion, improvement, increase, progress, spread
2 EVENT, happening, incident, occurrence, result, turn of events, upshot

deviant *adjective* 1 PERVERTED, kinky (*slang*), sick (*informal*), twisted, warped
▷ *noun* 2 PERVERT, freak, misfit

deviate *verb* DIFFER, depart, diverge, stray, swerve, veer, wander

deviation *noun* DEPARTURE, digression, discrepancy, disparity, divergence, inconsistency, irregularity, shift, variation

device *noun* 1 GADGET, apparatus, appliance, contraption, implement, instrument, machine, tool
2 PLOY, gambit, maneuver, plan, scheme, stratagem, trick, wile

devil *noun* 1 ▷ **the Devil** SATAN, Beelzebub, Evil One, Lucifer, Mephistopheles, Prince of Darkness
2 BRUTE, beast, demon, fiend, monster, ogre, terror
3 SCAMP, rascal, rogue, scoundrel
4 PERSON, beggar, creature, thing, wretch

devilish *adjective* FIENDISH, atrocious, damnable, detestable, diabolical, hellish, infernal, satanic, wicked

devious *adjective see* **deviate**
de•vise [di-VĪZ] *verb transitive* **-vised, -vis•ing** 1 plan, contrive 2 invent 3 plot 4 leave by will
de•void [di-VOID] *adjective* (usu. with *of*) empty, lacking, free from
de•volve [di-VOLV] *verb intransitive* **-volved, -volv•ing** 1 pass or fall (to, upon) ▷ *verb transitive* 2 throw (duty, etc.) on to another
> **dev•o•lu•tion** [dev-ə-LOO-shən] *noun* devolving, esp. transfer of authority from central to regional government
de•vote [di-VOHT] *verb transitive* **-vot•ed, -vot•ing** set apart, give up exclusively (to person, purpose, etc.) > **devoted** *adjective* loving, attached > **dev•o•tee** [dev-ə-TEE] *noun* 1 ardent enthusiast 2 zealous worshiper > **de•vo'tion** *noun* 1 deep affection, loyalty 2 dedication 3 religious earnestness > **de•vo'tions** prayers, religious exercises > **de•vo'tion•al** *adjective*
de•vour [di-VOWR] *verb transitive* 1 eat greedily 2 consume, destroy 3 read, gaze at eagerly
de•vout [di-VOWT] *adjective* 1 earnestly religious, pious 2 sincere, heartfelt
dew [doo] *noun* 1 moisture from air deposited as small drops on cool surface between nightfall and morning 2 any beaded moisture ▷ *verb transitive* 3 wet with or as with dew > **dew'y** *adjective* **dew•i•er, dew•i•est** > **dew'claw** *noun* partly developed inner toe of dogs > **dew'lap** *noun* fold of loose skin hanging from neck
dex•ter•i•ty [dek-STER-i-tee] *noun* manual skill, neatness, deftness, adroitness
> **dex'ter•ous** *adjective* showing dexterity, skillful
dex•trose [DEK-strohs] *noun* white, soluble, sweet-tasting crystalline solid, occurring naturally in fruit, honey, animal tissue
dia- *prefix* through
di•a•be•tes [dī-ə-BEE-tis] *noun* various disorders characterized by excretion of abnormal amount of urine in which body fails to store and utilize glucose > **di•a•bet'ic** *noun, adjective*
di•a•bol•ic [dī-ə-BOL-ik], **di•a•bol'i•cal** *adjective* 1 devilish 2 (*informal*) very bad
> **di•a•bol'i•cal•ly** *adverb*
di•a•crit•ic [dī-ə-KRIT-ik] *noun* sign above letter or character indicating special phonetic value, etc. > **di•a•crit'i•cal** *adjective* 1 of a diacritic 2 showing a distinction
di•a•dem [DĪ-ə-dem] *noun* a crown
di•ag•no•sis [dī-əg-NOH-sis] *noun, plural* **-ses** [-seez] identification of disease from symptoms
> **di'ag•nose** [-nohz] *verb transitive* **-nosed, -nos•ing** > **di•ag•nos'tic** [-NOS-tik] *adjective*
di•ag•o•nal [dī-AG-ə-nl] *adjective* 1 from corner to corner 2 oblique ▷ *noun* 3 line from corner to corner > **di•ag'o•nal•ly** *adverb*
di•a•gram [DĪ-ə-gram] *noun* drawing, figure in lines, to illustrate something being expounded
> **di•a•gram•mat'i•cal•ly** *adverb*
di•al [DĪ-əl] *noun* 1 face of clock, etc. 2 plate marked with graduations on which a pointer moves (as on a meter, radio, scale, etc.) 3 numbered disk on front of telephone ▷ *verb transitive* 4 operate telephone 5 indicate on dial
di•a•lect [DĪ-ə-lekt] *noun* 1 characteristic speech of region 2 local variety of a language
> **di•a•lec'tal** *adjective*
di•a•lec•tic [dī-ə-LEK-tik] *noun* art of arguing
> **di•a•lec'ti•cal** *adjective* > **di•a•lec•ti'cian** [-TISH-ən] *noun* 1 logician 2 reasoner
di•a•logue [DĪ-ə-lawg] *noun* 1 conversation between two or more (persons) 2 representation of such conversation in drama, novel, etc. 3 discussion between representatives of two governments, etc.
di•al•y•sis [dī-AL-ə-sis] *noun, plural* **-ses** [-seez] *med.* filtering of blood through membrane to remove waste products

devious *adjective* 1 SLY, calculating, deceitful, dishonest, double-dealing, insincere, scheming, surreptitious, underhand, wily
2 INDIRECT, circuitous, rambling, roundabout
devise *verb* WORK OUT, conceive, construct, contrive, design, dream up, formulate, invent, think up
devoid *adjective* LACKING, bereft, deficient, destitute, empty, free from, wanting, without
devote *verb* DEDICATE, allot, apply, assign, commit, give, pledge, reserve, set apart
devoted *adjective* DEDICATED, ardent, committed, constant, devout, faithful, loyal, staunch, steadfast, true
devotee *noun* ENTHUSIAST, adherent, admirer, aficionado, buff (*informal*), disciple, fan, fanatic, follower, supporter
devotion *noun* 1 DEDICATION, adherence, allegiance, commitment, constancy, faithfulness, fidelity, loyalty
2 LOVE, affection, attachment, fondness, passion
3 DEVOUTNESS, godliness, holiness, piety, reverence, spirituality
4 ▷ **devotions** PRAYERS, church service, divine office, religious observance
devour *verb* 1 EAT, chow down (*slang*), consume, gobble, gulp, guzzle, polish off (*informal*), swallow, wolf
2 DESTROY, annihilate, consume, ravage, waste, wipe out
3 ENJOY, read compulsively *or* read voraciously, take in
devout *adjective* RELIGIOUS, godly, holy, orthodox, pious, prayerful, pure, reverent, saintly
dexterity *noun* 1 SKILL, adroitness, deftness, expertise, finesse, nimbleness, proficiency, touch
2 CLEVERNESS, ability, aptitude, ingenuity
diabolical *adjective* (*informal*) DREADFUL, abysmal, appalling, atrocious, hellish, outrageous, shocking, terrible
diagnose *verb* IDENTIFY, analyze, determine, distinguish, interpret, pinpoint, pronounce, recognize
diagnosis *noun* 1 EXAMINATION, analysis, investigation, scrutiny
2 OPINION, conclusion, interpretation, pronouncement
diagonal *adjective* SLANTING, angled, cross, crossways, crosswise, oblique
diagonally *adverb* ASLANT, at an angle, cornerwise, crosswise, obliquely
diagram *noun* PLAN, chart, drawing, figure, graph, representation, sketch
dialect *noun* LANGUAGE, brogue, idiom, jargon, patois, provincialism, speech, vernacular
dialogue *noun* CONVERSATION, communication,

di•am•e•ter [dī-AM-i-tər] *noun* 1 (length of) straight line from side to side of figure or body (esp. circle) through center 2 thickness > **di•a•met'ri•cal** *adjective* opposite > **di•a•met'ri•cal•ly** *adverb*
di•a•mond [DĪ-mənd] *noun* 1 very hard and brilliant precious stone, also used in industry 2 rhomboid figure 3 suit at cards 4 playing field in baseball > **diamond jubilee** sixtieth anniversary of an event > **diamond wedding** sixtieth anniversary of a wedding
di•a•pa•son [dī-ə-PAY-zən] *noun* 1 fundamental organ stop 2 compass of voice or instrument
dia•per [DĪ-pər] *noun* 1 garment of absorbent material to absorb an infant's excrement ▷ *verb transitive* 2 put a diaper on
di•aph•a•nous [dī-AF-ə-nəs] *adjective* transparent
di•a•pho•ret•ic [dī-ə-fə-RET-ik] *noun* drug promoting perspiration ▷ *adjective*
di•a•phragm [DĪ-ə-fram] *noun* 1 muscular partition dividing two cavities of body, midriff 2 plate or disk wholly or partly closing tube or opening 3 any thin dividing or covering membrane
di•ar•rhe•a [dī-ə-REE-ə] *noun* excessive looseness of the bowels
di•a•ry [DĪ-ə-ree] *noun, plural* **-ries** 1 daily record of events or thoughts 2 book for this 3 book for noting appointments, memoranda, etc. > **di'a•rist** *noun* writer of diary
di•as•to•le [dī-AS-tl-ee] *noun* dilatation of the chambers of the heart
di•a•ther•my [DĪ-ə-thur-mee] *noun* heating of body tissues with electric current for medical or surgical purposes
di•a•tom [DĪ-ə-tom] *noun* one of order of microscopic algae > **di•a•tom'ic** *adjective* of two atoms
di•a•ton•ic [dī-ə-TON-ik] *adjective mus.* 1 pert. to regular major and minor scales 2 (of melody) composed in such a scale
di•a•tribe [DĪ-ə-trīb] *noun* violently bitter verbal attack, invective, denunciation
dice [dīs] *noun, plural* **dice** 1 small cube each of whose sides has a different number of spots (1 to 6), used in games of chance ▷ *verb intransitive* **diced, dic•ing** 2 gamble with dice ▷ *verb transitive* **diced, dic•ing** 3 *cookery* cut vegetables into small cubes > **dic'er** *noun* > **dic'ey** *adjective* **dic•i•er, dic•i•est** (*informal*) dangerous, risky
di•chot•o•my [dī-KOT-ə-mee] *noun, plural* **-mies** division into two parts
dic•tate [DIK-tayt] *verb* **-tat•ed, -tat•ing** 1 say or read for another to transcribe 2 prescribe, lay down 3 impose (as terms) ▷ *noun* 4 bidding > **dic•ta'tion** *noun* > **dic'ta•tor** *noun* absolute ruler > **dic•ta•to'ri•al** *adjective* 1 despotic 2 overbearing > **dic•ta'tor•ship** *noun*
dic•tion [DIK-shən] *noun* 1 choice and use of words 2 enunciation
dic•tion•ar•y [DIK-shə-ner-ee] *noun, plural* **-ar•ies** 1 book setting forth, alphabetically, words of language with meanings, etc. 2 reference book with items in alphabetical order
dic•tum [DIK-təm] *noun, plural* **-ta** [-tə] pronouncement, saying, maxim
did *pt. of* **do**
di•dac•tic [dī-DAK-tik] *adjective* 1 designed to instruct 2 (of people) opinionated, dictatorial
die[1] [dī] *verb intransitive* **died, dy•ing** 1 cease to live 2 come to an end 3 stop functioning 4 (*informal*) be nearly overcome (with laughter, etc.) 5 (*informal*) look forward (to) > **die'hard** *noun* one who resists (reform, etc.) to the end
die[2] *see* **dice**
die[3] *noun* 1 shaped block of hard material to form metal in forge, press, etc. 2 tool for cutting thread on pipe, etc.
di•e•lec•tric [dī-i-LEK-trik] *noun* 1 substance through or across which electric induction takes place 2 nonconductor 3 insulator
di•er•e•sis [dī-ER-ə-sis] *noun, plural* **-ses** [-seez] mark (¨) placed over vowel to show that it is sounded separately from preceding one, for example in *Noël*
die•sel [DEE-zəl] *adjective* 1 pert. to internal-combustion engine using oil as fuel ▷ *noun* 2 this engine 3 vehicle powered by it
di•et[1] [DĪ-it] *noun* 1 restricted or regulated course of feeding 2 kind of food lived on 3 food ▷ *verb intransitive* 4 follow a dietary

---

conference, discourse, discussion
diary *noun* JOURNAL, appointment book, blog (*informal*), chronicle, daily record, engagement book, Filofax®, weblog
dictate *verb* 1 SPEAK, read out, say, utter
2 ORDER, command, decree, demand, direct, impose, lay down the law, pronounce
▷ *noun* 3 COMMAND, decree, demand, direction, edict, fiat, injunction, order
4 PRINCIPLE, code, law, rule
dictator *noun* ABSOLUTE RULER, autocrat, despot, oppressor, tyrant
dictatorial *adjective* 1 ABSOLUTE, arbitrary, autocratic, despotic, totalitarian, tyrannical, unlimited, unrestricted
2 DOMINEERING, authoritarian, bossy (*informal*), imperious, oppressive, overbearing
dictatorship *noun* ABSOLUTE RULE, absolutism, authoritarianism, autocracy, despotism, totalitarianism, tyranny
diction *noun* PRONUNCIATION, articulation, delivery, elocution, enunciation, fluency, inflection, intonation, speech
dictionary *noun* WORDBOOK, glossary, lexicon, vocabulary
die *verb* 1 PASS AWAY, breathe one's last, croak (*slang*), expire, give up the ghost, kick the bucket (*slang*), perish, snuff it (*slang*)
2 DWINDLE, decay, decline, fade, sink, subside, wane, wilt, wither
3 STOP, break down, fade out *or* fade away, fail, fizzle out, halt, lose power, peter out, run down
4 ▷ **be dying** LONG, ache, be eager, desire, hunger, pine for, yearn
die-hard *noun* REACTIONARY, fanatic, old fogey, stick-in-the-mud (*informal*)
diet[1] *noun* 1 FOOD, fare, nourishment, nutriment, provisions, rations, sustenance, victuals
2 REGIME, abstinence, fast, regimen
▷ *verb* 3 SLIM, abstain, eat sparingly, fast, lose weight
diet[2] *noun* COUNCIL, chamber, congress, convention, legislature, meeting, parliament

regimen, as to lose weight > **di'e•ta•ry** *adjective* 1 relating to diet ▷ *noun* 2 a regulated diet > **di•e•tet'ic** *adjective* > **di•e•tet'ics** *noun* science of diet > **di•e•ti'tian** [-TISH-ən] *noun* one skilled in dietetics > **dietary fiber** fibrous substances in fruit and vegetables, consumption of which aids digestion

diet[2] *noun* 1 parliament of some countries 2 formal assembly

dif•fer [DIF-ər] *verb intransitive* 1 be unlike 2 disagree > **dif'fer•ence** *noun* 1 unlikeness 2 degree or point of unlikeness 3 disagreement 4 remainder left after subtraction > **dif'fer•ent** *adjective* unlike

dif•fer•en•tial [dif-ə-REN-shəl] *adjective* 1 varying with circumstances 2 special 3 *math.* pert. to an infinitesimal change in variable quantity 4 *physics* relating to difference between sets of motions acting in the same direction or between pressures, etc. ▷ *noun* 5 *math.* infinitesimal difference between two consecutive states of variable quantity 6 mechanism in automobile, etc. permitting back wheels to revolve at different speeds when rounding corner 7 difference between rates of pay for different types of labor > **dif•fer•en'ti•ate** [-shee-ayt] *verb transitive* **-at•ed, -at•ing** 1 serve to distinguish between, make different ▷ *verb intransitive* **-at•ed, -at•ing** 2 discriminate > **dif•fer•en•ti•a'tion** *noun* > **differential calculus** method of calculating relative rate of change for continuously varying quantities

dif•fi•cult [DIF-i-kult] *adjective* 1 requiring effort, skill, etc. to do or understand, not easy 2 obscure > **dif'fi•cul•ty** *noun, plural* **-ties** 1 being difficult 2 difficult task, problem 3 embarrassment 4 hindrance 5 obscurity 6 trouble

dif•fi•dent [DIF-i-dənt] *adjective* lacking confidence, timid, shy > **dif'fi•dence** *noun* shyness

dif•fract [di-FRAKT] *verb intransitive* break up, esp. of rays of light, sound waves > **dif•frac'tion** [-FRAK-shən] *noun* deflection of ray of light, electromagnetic wave caused by an obstacle

dif•fuse [di-FYOOZ] *verb transitive* **-fused, -fus•ing** 1 spread abroad ▷ *adjective* [-FYOOS] 2 widely spread 3 loose, verbose, wordy > **dif•fuse'ly** *adverb* 1 loosely 2 wordily > **dif•fu'sion** [-zhən] *noun* > **dif•fu'sive** *adjective*

dig *verb intransitive* **dug, dig•ging** 1 work with spade 2 search, investigate ▷ *verb transitive* **dug, dig•ging** 3 turn up with spade 4 hollow out, make hole in 5 excavate 6 thrust into 7 discover by searching 8 (*slang*) understand ▷ *noun* 9 archaeological excavation 10 thrust 11 gibe, taunt > **dig'ger** *noun*

di•gest [di-JEST] *verb transitive* 1 prepare (food) in stomach, etc. for assimilation 2 bring into handy form by sorting, tabulating, summarizing 3 reflect on 4 absorb ▷ *verb intransitive* 5 of food, undergo digestion ▷ *noun* [DĪ-jest] 6 methodical summary, of laws, research, etc. 7 magazine containing condensed version of articles, etc. already published elsewhere > **di•gest'i•ble** *adjective* > **di•ges'tion** *noun* digesting

dig•it [DIJ-it] *noun* 1 finger or toe 2 any of the numbers 0 to 9 > **dig'it•al** *adjective* 1 of, resembling digits 2 performed with fingers 3

DICTIONARY • THESAURUS

differ *verb* 1 BE DISSIMILAR, contradict, contrast, depart from, diverge, run counter to, stand apart, vary
2 DISAGREE, clash, contend, debate, demur, dispute, dissent, oppose, take exception, take issue

difference *noun* 1 DISSIMILARITY, alteration, change, contrast, discrepancy, disparity, diversity, variation, variety
2 DISAGREEMENT, argument, clash, conflict, contretemps, debate, dispute, quarrel
3 REMAINDER, balance, rest, result

different *adjective* 1 UNLIKE, altered, changed, contrasting, disparate, dissimilar, divergent, inconsistent, opposed
2 VARIOUS, assorted, diverse, miscellaneous, sundry, varied
3 UNUSUAL, atypical, distinctive, extraordinary, peculiar, singular, special, strange, uncommon

differentiate *verb* 1 DISTINGUISH, contrast, discriminate, make a distinction, mark off, separate, set off *or* set apart, tell apart
2 MAKE DIFFERENT, adapt, alter, change, convert, modify, transform

difficult *adjective* 1 HARD, arduous, demanding, formidable, laborious, onerous, strenuous, uphill
2 PROBLEMATICAL, abstruse, baffling, complex, complicated, intricate, involved, knotty, obscure
3 HARD TO PLEASE, demanding, fastidious, fussy, high-maintenance, perverse, refractory, unaccommodating

difficulty *noun* 1 LABORIOUSNESS, arduousness, awkwardness, hardship, strain, strenuousness, tribulation
2 PREDICAMENT, dilemma, embarrassment, hot water (*informal*), jam (*informal*), mess, plight, quandary, trouble
3 PROBLEM, complication, hindrance, hurdle, impediment, obstacle, pitfall, snag, stumbling block

diffidence *noun* SHYNESS, bashfulness, hesitancy, insecurity, modesty, reserve, self-consciousness, timidity

diffident *adjective* SHY, bashful, doubtful, hesitant, insecure, modest, reserved, self-conscious, timid, unassertive, unassuming

dig *verb* 1 EXCAVATE, burrow, delve, hollow out, mine, quarry, scoop, tunnel
2 INVESTIGATE, delve, dig down, go into, probe, research, search
3 (*with out* or *up*) FIND, discover, expose, uncover, unearth, uproot
4 POKE, drive, jab, prod, punch, thrust
▷ *noun* 5 POKE, jab, prod, punch, thrust
6 CUTTING REMARK, barb, gibe, insult, jeer, sneer, taunt, wisecrack (*informal*)

digest *verb* 1 INGEST, absorb, assimilate, dissolve, incorporate
2 TAKE IN, absorb, consider, contemplate, grasp, study, understand
▷ *noun* 3 SUMMARY, abridgment, abstract, epitome, précis, résumé, synopsis

digestion *noun* INGESTION, absorption, assimilation, conversion, incorporation, transformation

displaying information (time, etc.) by numbers rather than by pointer on dial 4 of, relating to device that can write, read, or store information represented in numerical form > **digital recording** sound recording process that converts audio signals into pulses corresponding to voltage level > **digital television** television in which the picture is transmitted in digital form and then decoded > **dig'it•ized** *adjective* recorded or stored in digital form

dig•i•tal•is [dij-i-TAL-is] *noun* drug made from foxglove

dig•ni•ty [DIG-ni-tee] *noun, plural* **-ties** 1 stateliness, gravity 2 worthiness, excellence, repute 3 honorable office or title > **dig'ni•fy** *verb transitive* **-fied, -fy•ing** give dignity to > **dignified** *adjective* stately, majestic > **dig'ni•ta•ry** [-ter-ee] *noun, plural* **-tar•ies** holder of high office

di•gress [di-GRES] *verb intransitive* turn from main course, esp. to deviate from subject in speaking or writing > **di•gres'sion** *noun*

di•he•dral [dī-HEE-drəl] *adjective* having two plane faces or sides

dike [dīk] *noun* 1 embankment to prevent flooding 2 ditch

di•lap•i•dat•ed [di-LAP-i-day-tid] *adjective* 1 in ruins 2 decayed

dil•a•ta•tion [dil-ə-TAY-shən] *noun* widening of body aperture for medical treatment, for example for curettage

di•late [dī-LAYT] *verb transitive* **-lat•ed, -lat•ing** 1 widen, expand ▷ *verb intransitive* **-lat•ed, -lat•ing** 2 expand 3 talk or write at length (on) > **di•la'tion** *noun*

dil•a•to•ry [DIL-ə-tor-ee] *adjective* tardy, slow, belated > **dil'a•to•ri•ness** *noun* delay

di•lem•ma [di-LEM-ə] *noun* 1 position in fact or argument offering choice only between unwelcome alternatives 2 predicament

dil•et•tante [DIL-i-tahnt] *noun* 1 person with taste and knowledge of fine arts as pastime 2 dabbler ▷ *adjective* 3 amateur, desultory > **dil'et•tant•ism** *noun*

dil•i•gent [DIL-i-jənt] *adjective* unremitting in effort, industrious, hardworking > **dil'i•gence** *noun*

di•lute [di-LOOT] *verb transitive* **-lut•ed, -lut•ing** 1 reduce (liquid) in strength, esp. by adding water 2 thin 3 reduce in force, effect, etc. ▷ *adjective* 4 weakened thus > **di•lu'tion** *noun*

dim *adjective* **dim•mer, dim•mest** 1 indistinct, faint, not bright 2 mentally dull 3 unfavorable ▷ *verb* **dimmed, dim•ming** 4 make, grow dim > **dim'ly** *adverb* > **dim'mer** *noun* device for dimming electric lights > **dim'ness** *noun*

dime [dīm] *noun* 10-cent piece, coin of US and Canada

di•men•sion [di-MEN-shən] *noun* 1 measurement, size 2 aspect **fourth dimension** 1 *physics* time 2 supernatural, fictional dimension additional to those of length, breadth, thickness

di•min'ish *verb* lessen > **dim•i•nu•tion** [dim-ə-NOO-shən] *noun* > **di•min•u•tive** [di-MIN-yə-tiv] *adjective* 1 very small ▷ *noun* 2 derivative word, affix implying smallness

di•min•u•en•do [di-min-yoo-EN-doh] *adjective, adverb mus.* of sound, dying away

dim•ple [DIM-pəl] *noun* 1 small hollow in surface of skin, esp. of cheek 2 any small hollow ▷ *verb* **-pled, -pling** 3 mark with, show dimples

din *noun* 1 continuous roar of confused noises ▷ *verb transitive* **dinned, din•ning** 2 repeat to weariness, ram (fact, opinion, etc.) into

dine [dīn] *verb intransitive* **dined, din•ing** 1 eat esp. dinner ▷ *verb transitive* **dined, din•ing** 2 give dinner to > **din'er** *noun* 1 one who dines 2

DICTIONARY

d

THESAURUS

dignified *adjective* DISTINGUISHED, formal, grave, imposing, noble, reserved, solemn, stately

dignitary *noun* PUBLIC FIGURE, high-up (*informal*), notable, personage, pillar of society, V.I.P., worthy

dignity *noun* 1 DECORUM, courtliness, grandeur, gravity, loftiness, majesty, nobility, solemnity, stateliness
2 HONOR, eminence, importance, rank, respectability, standing, status
3 SELF-IMPORTANCE, pride, self-esteem, self-respect

digress *verb* WANDER, depart, deviate, diverge, drift, get off the point *or* get off the subject, go off at a tangent, ramble, stray

digression *noun* DEPARTURE, aside, detour, deviation, divergence, diversion, straying, wandering

dilapidated *adjective* RUINED, broken-down, crumbling, decrepit, in ruins, ramshackle, rickety, run-down, tumbledown

dilate *verb* ENLARGE, broaden, expand, puff out, stretch, swell, widen

dilatory *adjective* TIME-WASTING, delaying, lingering, procrastinating, slow, sluggish, tardy, tarrying

dilemma *noun* PREDICAMENT, difficulty, mess, plight, problem, puzzle, quandary, spot (*informal*)

dilettante *noun* AMATEUR, aesthete, dabbler, trifler

diligence *noun* APPLICATION, attention, care, industry, laboriousness, perseverance

diligent *adjective* HARD-WORKING, assiduous, attentive, careful, conscientious, industrious, painstaking, persistent, studious, tireless

dilute *verb* 1 WATER DOWN, adulterate, cut, make thinner, thin *or* thin out, weaken
2 REDUCE, attenuate, decrease, diffuse, diminish, lessen, mitigate, temper, weaken

dim *adjective* 1 POORLY LIT, cloudy, dark, gray, overcast, shadowy, tenebrous
2 UNCLEAR, bleary, blurred, faint, fuzzy, ill-defined, indistinct, obscured, shadowy
3 ▷ **take a dim view** DISAPPROVE, be displeased, be skeptical, look askance, reject, suspect, take exception, view with disfavor
▷ *verb* 4 DULL, blur, cloud, darken, fade, obscure

dimension *noun* (*often plural*) MEASUREMENT, amplitude, bulk, capacity, extent, proportions, size, volume

diminish *verb* 1 DECREASE, curtail, cut, lessen, lower, reduce, shrink
2 DWINDLE, decline, die out, recede, subside, wane

diminutive *adjective* SMALL, little, mini, miniature, minute, petite, tiny, undersized

din *noun* 1 NOISE, clamor, clatter, commotion, crash, pandemonium, racket, row, uproar

informal usu. cheap restaurant > **dining room** room where meals are eaten
din•ghy [DING-gee] *noun, plural* **-ghies** 1 small open boat 2 inflatable life raft
din•go [DING-goh] *noun, plural* **-goes** Aust. wild dog
din•gy [DIN-jee] *adjective* **-gi•er, -gi•est** dirty-looking, shabby > **din'gi•ness** *noun*
din•ner [DIN-ər] *noun* 1 chief meal of the day 2 official banquet
di•no•saur [DĪ-nə-sor] *noun* extinct reptile, often of gigantic size
dint *noun* force, power **by dint of** by means of
di•o•cese [DĪ-ə-sis] *noun* ecclesiastical district under jurisdiction of bishop > **di•oc•e•san** [dī-OS-ə-sən] *adjective* having jurisdiction over diocese
di•ode [DĪ-ohd] *noun electronics* device for converting alternating current to direct current
di•op•ter [dī-OP-tər] *noun* unit for measuring refractive power of lens
di•o•ram•a [dī-ə-RAM-ə] *noun* miniature three-dimensional scene, esp. as museum exhibit
di•ox•ide [dī-OK-sīd] *noun* oxide with two parts of oxygen to one of the other constituents
di•ox•in [dī-OK-sin] *noun* extremely toxic byproduct of the manufacture of certain herbicides and bactericides
dip *verb transitive* **dipped, dip•ping** 1 put partly or for a moment into liquid 2 immerse, involve 3 lower and raise again 4 take up in ladle, bucket, etc. ▷ *verb intransitive* **dipped, dip•ping** 5 plunge partially or temporarily 6 go down, sink 7 slope downward ▷ *noun* 8 act of dipping 9 brief swim 10 liquid chemical in which livestock are immersed to treat insect pests, etc. 11 downward slope 12 hollow 13 creamy mixture in which cracker, etc. is dipped before being eaten > **dip into** glance at (book, etc.)
diph•the•ri•a [dif-THEER-ee-ə] *noun* infectious disease of throat with membranous growth
diph•thong [DIF-thawng] *noun* union of two vowel sounds in single compound sound
di•plo•ma [di-PLOH-mə] *noun, plural* **-mas** 1 document vouching for person's proficiency 2 title to degree, honor, etc.
di•plo•ma•cy [di-PLOH-mə-see] *noun* 1 management of international relations 2 skill in negotiation 3 tactful, adroit dealing > **dip•lo•mat** [DIP-lə-mat] *noun* one engaged in official diplomacy > **dip•lo•mat'ic** *adjective* > **di•plo'ma•tist** *noun* tactful person
di•plo•pi•a [di-PLOH-pee-ə] *noun* double vision
di•po•lar [dī-POH-lər] *adjective* having two poles
di•pole [DĪ-pohl] *noun* type of radio and television antenna
dip•per [DIP-ər] *noun* ladle, bucket, scoop
dip•so•ma•ni•a [dip-sə-MAY-nee-ə] *noun* uncontrollable craving for alcohol > **dip•so•ma'ni•ac** *noun* victim of this
dip•tych [DIP-tik] *noun* 1 ancient tablet hinged in the middle, folding together like a book 2 painting, carving on two hinged panels
dire [dīr] *adjective* **dir•er, dir•est** 1 terrible 2 urgent
di•rect [di-REKT] *verb transitive* 1 control, manage, order 2 point out the way 3 aim, point, turn 4 address (letter, etc.) 5 supervise actors, etc. in play or film ▷ *adjective* 6 frank, straightforward 7 straight 8 going straight to the point 9 immediate 10 lineal > **di•rec'tion** *noun* 1 directing 2 aim, course of movement 3 address, instruction > **di•rec'tive** *adjective, noun* > **di•rec'tor** *noun* 1 one who directs, esp. a film 2

▷ *verb* 2 ▷ **din (something) into (someone)** INSTILL, drum into, go on at, hammer into, inculcate, instruct, teach
dine *verb* EAT, banquet, chow down (*slang*), feast, lunch, sup
dingy *adjective* DULL, dark, dim, drab, dreary, gloomy, murky, obscure, somber
dinner *noun* MEAL, banquet, feast, main meal, repast, spread (*informal*)
dip *verb* 1 PLUNGE, bathe, douse, duck, dunk, immerse
2 SLOPE, decline, descend, drop *or* drop down, fall, lower, sink, subside
▷ *noun* 3 PLUNGE, douche, drenching, ducking, immersion, soaking
4 BATHE, dive, plunge, swim
5 HOLLOW, basin, concavity, depression, hole, incline, slope
6 DROP, decline, fall, lowering, sag, slip, slump
dip into *verb* SAMPLE, browse, glance at, peruse, skim
diplomacy *noun* 1 STATESMANSHIP, international negotiation, statecraft
2 TACT, artfulness, craft, delicacy, discretion, finesse, savoir-faire, skill, subtlety
diplomat *noun* NEGOTIATOR, conciliator, go-between, mediator, moderator, politician, tactician
diplomatic *adjective* TACTFUL, adept, discreet, polite, politic, prudent, sensitive, subtle
dire *adjective* 1 DISASTROUS, awful, calamitous, catastrophic, horrible, ruinous, terrible, woeful
2 DESPERATE, critical, crucial, drastic, extreme, now or never, pressing, urgent
3 GRIM, dismal, dreadful, fearful, gloomy, ominous, portentous
direct *adjective* 1 STRAIGHT, nonstop, not crooked, shortest, through, unbroken, uninterrupted
2 IMMEDIATE, face-to-face, first-hand, head-on, personal
3 HONEST, candid, frank, open, plain-spoken, straight, straightforward, upfront (*informal*)
4 EXPLICIT, absolute, blunt, categorical, downright, express, plain, point-blank, unambiguous, unequivocal
▷ *verb* 5 CONTROL, conduct, guide, handle, lead, manage, oversee, run, supervise
6 ORDER, bid, charge, command, demand, dictate, instruct
7 GUIDE, indicate, lead, point in the direction of, point the way, show
8 ADDRESS, label, mail, route, send
9 AIM, focus, level, point, train
direction *noun* 1 WAY, aim, bearing, course, line, path, road, route, track
2 MANAGEMENT, administration, charge, command, control, guidance, leadership, order, supervision
directions *plural noun* INSTRUCTIONS, briefing, guidance, guidelines, plan, recommendation, regulations
directive *noun* ORDER, command, decree, edict,

member of board of directors of company > **di•rec'to•rate** [-tər-it] *noun* 1 body of directors 2 office of director > **di•rec'to•ry** *noun, plural* **-ries** 1 book of names, addresses, streets, etc. 2 *computers* area of a disk containing the names and locations of the files it currently holds > **direction finder** radio receiver that determines the direction of incoming waves

dirge [durj] *noun* song of mourning

dir•i•gi•ble [DIR-i-jə-bəl] *adjective* 1 steerable ▷ *noun* 2 airship

dirt [durt] *noun* 1 filth 2 soil, earth 3 obscene material 4 contamination > **dirt'i•ness** *noun* > **dirt'y** *adjective* **-i•er, -i•est** 1 unclean, filthy 2 obscene 3 unfair 4 dishonest

dis- *prefix* 1 (indicating) reversal: *disconnect* 2 (indicating) negation or lack: *dissimilar; disgrace* 3 (indicating) removal or release: *disembowel*

dis•a•ble [dis-AY-bəl] *verb transitive* **-bled, -bling** make ineffective, unfit, or incapable > **dis•a'bled** *adjective* lacking a physical power, such as the ability to walk > **dis•a•bil'i•ty** *noun, plural* **-ties** 1 incapacity 2 drawback

dis•a•buse [dis-ə-BYOOZ] *verb transitive* **-bused, -bus•ing** 1 undeceive, disillusion 2 free from error

dis•ad•van•tage [dis-əd-VAN-tij] *noun* 1 drawback 2 hindrance 3 detriment ▷ *verb transitive* **-taged, -tag•ing** 4 handicap > **disadvantaged** *adjective* deprived, discriminated against, underprivileged > **dis•ad•van•ta•geous** [-TAY-jəs] *adjective*

dis•af•fect•ed [dis-ə-FEK-tid] *adjective* ill-disposed, alienated, estranged > **dis•af•fec'tion** *noun*

dis•a•gree [dis-ə-GREE] *verb intransitive* **-greed, -gree•ing** 1 be at variance 2 conflict 3 (of food, etc.) have bad effect on > **dis•a•gree'ment** *noun* 1 difference of opinion 2 discord 3 discrepancy > **dis•a•gree'a•ble** *adjective* unpleasant

dis•al•low [dis-ə-LOW] *verb transitive* reject as untrue or invalid

dis•ap•pear [dis-ə-PEER] *verb intransitive* 1 vanish 2 cease to exist 3 be lost > **dis•ap•pear'ance** *noun*

dis•ap•point [dis-ə-POINT] *verb transitive* fail to fulfill (hope), frustrate > **dis•ap•point'ment** *noun*

---

injunction, instruction, mandate, regulation, ruling

directly *adverb* 1 STRAIGHT, by the shortest route, exactly, in a beeline, precisely, unswervingly, without deviation
2 HONESTLY, openly, plainly, point-blank, straightforwardly, truthfully, unequivocally
3 AT ONCE, as soon as possible, forthwith, immediately, promptly, right away, straightaway

director *noun* CONTROLLER, administrator, chief, executive, governor, head, leader, manager, supervisor

dirge *noun* LAMENT, dead march, elegy, funeral song, requiem, threnody

dirt *noun* 1 FILTH, dust, grime, impurity, muck, mud
2 SOIL, clay, earth, loam
3 OBSCENITY, indecency, pornography, sleaze, smut

dirty *adjective* 1 FILTHY, foul, grimy, grubby, messy, mucky, muddy, polluted, scuzzy (*slang*), soiled, unclean
2 DISHONEST, crooked, fraudulent, illegal, lowdown (*slang*), scuzzy (*slang*), treacherous, unfair, unscrupulous, unsporting
3 OBSCENE, blue, indecent, pornographic, salacious, scuzzy (*slang*), sleazy, smutty, X-rated
4 (*look*) ANGRY, annoyed, bitter, choked, indignant, offended, resentful, scorching
▷ *verb* 5 SOIL, blacken, defile, foul, muddy, pollute, smirch, spoil, stain

disability *noun* 1 HANDICAP, affliction, ailment, complaint, defect, disorder, impairment, infirmity, malady
2 INCAPACITY, inability, unfitness

disable *verb* 1 HANDICAP, cripple, damage, enfeeble, immobilize, impair, incapacitate, paralyze
2 DISQUALIFY, invalidate, render incapable *or* declare incapable

disabled *adjective* HANDICAPPED, challenged (*informal*), crippled, incapacitated, infirm, lame, paralyzed, weakened

disadvantage *noun* 1 HARM, damage, detriment, disservice, hurt, injury, loss, prejudice
2 DRAWBACK, downside, handicap, inconvenience, nuisance, snag, trouble

disagree *verb* 1 DIFFER *or* DIFFER IN OPINION, argue, clash, cross swords, dispute, dissent, object, quarrel, take issue with
2 CONFLICT, be dissimilar, contradict, counter, differ, diverge, run counter to, vary
3 MAKE ILL, bother, discomfort, distress, hurt, nauseate, sicken, trouble, upset

disagreeable *adjective* 1 NASTY, disgusting, displeasing, distasteful, objectionable, obnoxious, offensive, repugnant, repulsive, scuzzy (*slang*), unpleasant
2 RUDE, bad-tempered, churlish, difficult, disobliging, irritable, surly, unpleasant

disagreement *noun* 1 INCOMPATIBILITY, difference, discrepancy, disparity, dissimilarity, divergence, incongruity, variance
2 ARGUMENT, altercation, clash, conflict, dispute, dissent, quarrel, row, squabble

disallow *verb* REJECT, disavow, dismiss, disown, rebuff, refuse, repudiate

disappear *verb* 1 VANISH, evanesce, fade away, pass, recede
2 CEASE, die out, dissolve, evaporate, leave no trace, melt away, pass away, perish

disappearance *noun* VANISHING, departure, eclipse, evanescence, evaporation, going, melting, passing

disappoint *verb* LET DOWN, disenchant, disgruntle, dishearten, disillusion, dismay, dissatisfy, fail

disappointed *adjective* LET DOWN, cast down, despondent, discouraged, disenchanted, disgruntled, dissatisfied, downhearted, frustrated

disappointing *adjective* UNSATISFACTORY, depressing, disconcerting, discouraging, inadequate, insufficient, lousy (*slang*), sad, sorry

disappointment *noun* 1 FRUSTRATION, chagrin, discontent, discouragement, disenchantment,

dis•ap•prove' *verb intransitive* (foll by *of*) consider wrong or bad > **dis•ap•prov'al** *noun*

dis•arm [dis-AHRM] *verb* 1 deprive of arms or weapons 2 reduce country's war weapons 3 win over > **dis•ar'ma•ment** *noun* > **dis•arm'ing** *adjective* removing hostility, suspicion

dis•ar•range *verb transitive* throw into disorder

dis•ar•ray [dis-ə-RAY] *verb transitive* 1 throw into disorder, derange ▷ *noun* 2 disorderliness, esp. of clothing

dis•as•ter [di-ZAS-tər] *noun* calamity, sudden or great misfortune > **dis•as'trous** *adjective* calamitous

dis•band' *verb* (cause to) cease to function as a group

dis•bar [dis-BAHR] *verb transitive* **-barred, -bar•ring** *law* expel from the bar

dis•be•lieve' *verb transitive* 1 reject as false ▷ *verb intransitive* 2 (foll by *in*) have no faith (in) > **dis•be•lief'** *noun*

dis•burse [dis-BURS] *verb transitive* **-bursed, -burs•ing** pay out (money) > **dis•burse'ment** *noun*

disc *see* **disk** > **disc jockey** person who introduces and plays pop records on a radio program or at a disco

dis•card [di-SKAHRD] *verb transitive* 1 reject 2 give up 3 cast off, dismiss

dis•cern [di-SURN] *verb transitive* 1 make out 2 distinguish > **dis•cern'i•ble** *adjective* > **dis•cern'ing** *adjective* 1 discriminating 2 penetrating > **dis•cern'ment** *noun* insight

dis•charge [dis-CHAHRJ] *verb transitive* **-charged, -charg•ing** 1 release 2 dismiss 3 emit 4 perform (duties), fulfill (obligations) 5 let go 6 fire off 7 unload 8 pay ▷ *noun* [DIS-chahrj] 9 discharging 10 being discharged 11 release 12 matter emitted 13 document certifying release, payment, etc.

dis•ci•ple [di-SĪ-pəl] *noun* follower, one who takes another as teacher and model

dis•ci•pline [DIS-ə-plin] *noun* 1 training that produces orderliness, obedience, self-control 2 result of such training in order, conduct, etc. 3 system of rules, etc. ▷ *verb transitive* **-plined, -plin•ing** 4 train 5 punish > **dis•ci•pli•nar'i•an** *noun* one who enforces rigid discipline > **dis'ci•pli•nar•y** *adjective*

dis•claim [dis-KLAYM] *verb transitive* deny, renounce > **dis•claim'er** *noun* repudiation, denial

dis•close [di-SKLOHZ] *verb transitive* **-closed, -clos•ing** 1 allow to be seen 2 make known > **dis•clo'sure** [-*zhər*] *noun* revelation

dis•col•or [dis-KUL-ər] *verb transitive* alter color of, stain > **dis•col•or•a'tion** *noun*

disillusionment, dissatisfaction, regret
2 LETDOWN, blow, calamity, choker (*informal*), misfortune, setback

disapproval *noun* DISPLEASURE, censure, condemnation, criticism, denunciation, dissatisfaction, objection, reproach

disapprove *verb* CONDEMN, deplore, dislike, find unacceptable, frown on, look down one's nose at (*informal*), object to, reject, take a dim view of, take exception to

disarm *verb* 1 RENDER DEFENSELESS, disable
2 WIN OVER, persuade, set at ease
3 DEMILITARIZE, deactivate, demobilize, disband

disarmament *noun* ARMS REDUCTION, arms limitation, de-escalation, demilitarization, demobilization

disarming *adjective* CHARMING, irresistible, likable *or* likeable, persuasive, winning

disarrange *verb* DISORDER, confuse, disorganize, disturb, jumble *or* jumble up, mess *or* mess up, scatter, shake *or* shake up, shuffle

disarray *noun* 1 CONFUSION, disorder, disorganization, disunity, indiscipline, unruliness
2 UNTIDINESS, chaos, clutter, jumble, mess, muddle, shambles

disaster *noun* CATASTROPHE, adversity, calamity, cataclysm, misfortune, ruin, tragedy, trouble

disastrous *adjective* TERRIBLE, calamitous, cataclysmic, catastrophic, devastating, fatal, ruinous, tragic

disbelief *noun* SKEPTICISM, distrust, doubt, dubiety, incredulity, mistrust, unbelief

discard *verb* GET RID OF, abandon, cast aside, dispense with, dispose of, drop, dump (*informal*), jettison, reject, throw away *or* throw out

discharge *verb* 1 RELEASE, allow to go, clear, free, liberate, pardon, set free
2 DISMISS, cashier, discard, expel, fire (*informal*), oust, remove, sack (*informal*)
3 FIRE, detonate, explode, let loose (*informal*), let off, set off, shoot
4 POUR FORTH, dispense, emit, exude, give off, leak, ooze, release
5 CARRY OUT, accomplish, do, execute, fulfill, observe, perform
6 PAY, clear, honor, meet, relieve, satisfy, settle, square up
▷ *noun* 7 RELEASE, acquittal, clearance, liberation, pardon
8 DISMISSAL, demobilization, ejection
9 FIRING, blast, burst, detonation, explosion, report, salvo, shot, volley
10 EMISSION, excretion, ooze, pus, secretion, seepage, suppuration

disciple *noun* FOLLOWER, adherent, apostle, devotee, pupil, student, supporter

disciplinarian *noun* AUTHORITARIAN, despot, martinet, stickler, taskmaster, tyrant

discipline *noun* 1 TRAINING, drill, exercise, method, practice, regimen, regulation
2 PUNISHMENT, castigation, chastisement, correction
3 SELF-CONTROL, conduct, control, orderliness, regulation, restraint, strictness
4 FIELD OF STUDY, area, branch of knowledge, course, curriculum, speciality, subject
▷ *verb* 5 TRAIN, bring up, drill, educate, exercise, prepare
6 PUNISH, bring to book, castigate, chasten, chastise, correct, penalize, reprimand, reprove

disclose *verb* 1 MAKE KNOWN, broadcast, communicate, confess, divulge, let slip, publish, relate, reveal
2 SHOW, bring to light, expose, lay bare, reveal, uncover, unveil

disclosure *noun* REVELATION, acknowledgment, admission, announcement, confession, declaration, divulgence, leak, publication

discolor *verb* STAIN, fade, mark, soil, streak,

dis•com•fit [dis-KUM-fit] *verb transitive* embarrass, disconcert, baffle > **dis•com'fi•ture** [-fi-chər] *noun*
dis•com•pose' *verb transitive* disturb, upset > **dis•com•po'sure** *noun*
dis•con•cert [dis-kən-SURT] *verb transitive* ruffle, confuse, upset, embarrass
dis•con•nect' *verb transitive* 1 undo or break the connection between (two things) 2 stop the supply of electricity or gas of ▷ *noun* 3 lack of a connection
dis•con•so•late [dis-KON-sə-lit] *adjective* unhappy, downcast, forlorn
dis•con•tent' *noun* lack of contentment > **dis•con•tent'ed** *adjective* > **dis•con•tent'ment** *noun*
dis•con•tin'ue *verb* come or bring to an end > **dis•con•ti'nu•ous** *adjective* characterized by interruptions > **dis•con•ti•nu'i•ty** *noun*
dis•cord [DIS-kord] *noun* 1 strife 2 difference, dissension 3 disagreement of sounds > **dis•cord'ant** *adjective*
dis•co•theque [DIS-kə-tek] *noun* club, etc. for dancing to recorded music
dis•count [dis-KOWNT] *verb transitive* 1 consider as possibility but reject as unsuitable, inappropriate, etc. 2 deduct (amount, percentage) from usual price 3 sell at reduced price ▷ *noun* [DIS-kownt] 4 amount deducted from price, expressed as cash amount or percentage
dis•coun•te•nance [dis-KOWN-tn-əns] *verb transitive* **-nanced, -nanc•ing** 1 abash 2 discourage 3 frown upon
dis•cour•age [di-SKUR-ij] *verb transitive* **-aged, -ag•ing** 1 reduce confidence of 2 deter 3 show disapproval of
dis•course [DIS-kors] *noun* 1 conversation 2 speech, treatise, sermon ▷ *verb intransitive* [dis-KORS], **-coursed, -cours•ing** 3 speak, converse, lecture
dis•cour'te•sy *noun* showing bad manners > **dis•cour'teous•ly** *adverb*
dis•cov•er [di-SKUV-ər] *verb transitive* (be the first to) find out, light upon; make known > **dis•cov'er•a•ble** *adjective* > **dis•cov'er•er** *noun* > **dis•cov'er•y** *noun, plural* **-er•ies**
dis•cred•it [dis-KRED-it] *verb transitive* 1 damage

DICTIONARY
d
THESAURUS

tarnish, tinge
discomfort *noun* 1 PAIN, ache, hurt, irritation, malaise, soreness
2 UNEASINESS, annoyance, distress, hardship, irritation, nuisance, trouble
disconcert *verb* DISTURB, faze, fluster, perturb, rattle (*informal*), take aback, unsettle, upset
disconcerting *adjective* DISTURBING, alarming, awkward, bewildering, confusing, distracting, embarrassing, perplexing, upsetting
disconnect *verb* CUT OFF, detach, disengage, divide, part, separate, sever, take apart, uncouple
disconnected *adjective* ILLOGICAL, confused, disjointed, incoherent, jumbled, mixed-up, rambling, unintelligible
disconsolate *adjective* INCONSOLABLE, crushed, dejected, desolate, forlorn, grief-stricken, heartbroken, miserable, wretched
discontent *noun* DISSATISFACTION, displeasure, envy, regret, restlessness, uneasiness, unhappiness
discontented *adjective* DISSATISFIED, disaffected, disgruntled, displeased, exasperated, fed up, unhappy, vexed
discontinue *verb* STOP, abandon, break off, cease, drop, end, give up, quit, suspend, terminate
discord *noun* 1 DISAGREEMENT, conflict, dissension, disunity, division, friction, incompatibility, strife
2 DISHARMONY, cacophony, din, dissonance, harshness, jarring, racket, tumult
discordant *adjective* 1 DISAGREEING, at odds, clashing, conflicting, contradictory, contrary, different, incompatible
2 INHARMONIOUS, cacophonous, dissonant, grating, harsh, jarring, shrill, strident
discount *verb* 1 LEAVE OUT, brush off (*slang*), disbelieve, disregard, ignore, overlook, pass over
2 DEDUCT, lower, mark down, reduce, take off
▷ *noun* 3 DEDUCTION, concession, cut, rebate, reduction
discourage *verb* 1 DISHEARTEN, dampen, deject, demoralize, depress, dispirit, intimidate, overawe, put a damper on
2 PUT OFF, deter, dissuade, inhibit, prevent, talk out of
discouraged *adjective* PUT OFF, crestfallen, deterred, disheartened, dismayed, dispirited, downcast, down in the mouth, glum
discouragement *noun* 1 LOSS OF CONFIDENCE, dejection, depression, despair, despondency, disappointment, dismay, downheartedness
2 DETERRENT, damper, disincentive, hindrance, impediment, obstacle, opposition, setback
discouraging *adjective* DISHEARTENING, dampening, daunting, depressing, disappointing, dispiriting, unfavorable
discourse *noun* 1 CONVERSATION, chat, communication, dialogue, discussion, seminar, speech, talk
2 SPEECH, dissertation, essay, homily, lecture, oration, sermon, treatise
▷ *verb* 3 HOLD FORTH, expatiate, speak, talk
discourteous *adjective* RUDE, bad-mannered, boorish, disrespectful, ill-mannered, impolite, insolent, offhand, ungentlemanly, ungracious
discourtesy *noun* 1 RUDENESS, bad manners, disrespectfulness, impertinence, impoliteness, incivility, insolence
2 INSULT, affront, cold shoulder, kick in the teeth (*slang*), rebuff, slight, snub
discover *verb* 1 FIND, come across, come upon, dig up, locate, turn up, uncover, unearth
2 FIND OUT, ascertain, detect, learn, notice, perceive, realize, recognize, uncover
discovery *noun* 1 FINDING, detection, disclosure, exploration, location, revelation, uncovering
2 BREAKTHROUGH, find, innovation, invention, secret
discredit *verb* 1 DISGRACE, bring into disrepute, defame, dishonor, disparage, slander, smear, vilify
2 DOUBT, challenge, deny, disbelieve, discount, dispute, distrust, mistrust, question
▷ *noun* 3 DISGRACE, dishonor, disrepute, ignominy, ill-repute, scandal, shame, stigma

reputation of 2 cast doubt on 3 reject as untrue ▷ *noun* 4 disgrace 5 doubt > **dis•cred'it•a•ble** *adjective*
dis•creet [di-SKREET] *adjective* prudent, circumspect > **dis•creet'ness** *noun*
dis•crep•an•cy [di-SKREP-ən-see] *noun, plural* **-cies** conflict, variation, as between figures > **dis•crep'ant** *adjective*
dis•crete [di-SKREET] *adjective* separate, disunited, discontinuous
dis•cre•tion [di-SKRESH-ən] *noun* 1 quality of being discreet 2 prudence 3 freedom to act as one chooses > **dis•cre'tion•ar•y** *adjective*
dis•crim•i•nate [di-SKRIM-ə-nayt] *verb intransitive* **-nat•ed, -nat•ing** 1 single out for special favor or disfavor 2 distinguish between 3 be discerning > **dis•crim•i•na'tion** *noun*
dis•cur•sive [di-SKUR-siv] *adjective* passing from subject to subject, rambling
dis•cus [DIS-kəs] *noun* disk-shaped object thrown in athletic competition
dis•cuss [di-SKUS] *verb transitive* 1 exchange opinions about 2 debate > **dis•cus'sion** *noun*
dis•dain [dis-DAYN] *noun* 1 scorn, contempt ▷ *verb transitive* 2 scorn > **dis•dain'ful** *adjective*
dis•ease [di-ZEEZ] *noun* 1 illness 2 disorder of health
dis•em•bark' *verb* get off a ship, aircraft, or bus > **dis•em•bar•ka'tion** *noun*
dis•em•bod•ied [dis-em-BOD-eed] *adjective* (of spirit) released from bodily form
dis•em•bow•el [dis-em-BOW-əl] *verb transitive* take out entrails of
dis•en•chant•ed [dis-en-CHAN-tid] *adjective* disillusioned
dis•en•gage' *verb* release from a connection > **dis•en•gage'ment** *noun*
dis•en•tan'gle *verb* release from entanglement or confusion
dis•es•tab'lish *verb transitive* remove state support from (a church etc.) > **dis•es•tab'lish•ment** *noun*
dis•fa'vor *noun* disapproval or dislike
dis•fig•ure [dis-FIG-yər] *verb transitive* **-ured, -ur•ing** mar appearance of > **dis•fig•ur•a'tion** *noun* > **dis•fig'ure•ment** *noun* blemish, defect
dis•gorge [dis-GORJ] *verb transitive* **-gorged, -gorg•ing** 1 vomit 2 give up
dis•grace [dis-GRAYS] *noun* 1 shame, loss of reputation, dishonor ▷ *verb transitive* **-graced, -grac•ing** 2 bring shame or discredit upon > **dis•grace'ful** *adjective* shameful
dis•grun•tled [dis-GRUN-tld] *adjective* 1 vexed 2 put out
dis•guise [dis-GĪZ] *verb transitive* **-guised, -guis•ing** 1 change appearance of, make

DICTIONARY • THESAURUS

---

discreditable *adjective* DISGRACEFUL, dishonorable, ignominious, reprehensible, scandalous, shameful, unworthy
discreet *adjective* TACTFUL, careful, cautious, circumspect, considerate, diplomatic, guarded, judicious, prudent, wary
discrepancy *noun* DISAGREEMENT, conflict, contradiction, difference, disparity, divergence, incongruity, inconsistency, variation
discretion *noun* 1 TACT, carefulness, caution, consideration, diplomacy, judiciousness, prudence, wariness
2 CHOICE, inclination, pleasure, preference, volition, will
discriminate *verb* 1 SHOW PREJUDICE, favor, show bias, single out, treat as inferior, treat differently, victimize
2 DIFFERENTIATE, distinguish, draw a distinction, segregate, separate, tell the difference
discriminating *adjective* DISCERNING, cultivated, fastidious, particular, refined, selective, tasteful
discrimination *noun* 1 PREJUDICE, bias, bigotry, favoritism, intolerance, unfairness
2 DISCERNMENT, judgment, perception, refinement, subtlety, taste
discuss *verb* TALK ABOUT, argue, confer, consider, converse, debate, deliberate, examine
discussion *noun* TALK, analysis, argument, conference, consultation, conversation, debate, deliberation, dialogue, discourse, exchange
disdain *noun* 1 CONTEMPT, arrogance, derision, haughtiness, scorn, superciliousness
▷ *verb* 2 SCORN, deride, disregard, look down on, reject, slight, sneer at, spurn
disdainful *adjective* CONTEMPTUOUS, aloof, arrogant, derisive, haughty, proud, scornful, sneering, supercilious, superior
disease *noun* ILLNESS, affliction, ailment, complaint, condition, disorder, infection, infirmity, malady, sickness
diseased *adjective* SICK, ailing, infected, rotten, sickly, unhealthy, unsound, unwell, unwholesome
disembark *verb* LAND, alight, arrive, get off, go ashore, step out of
disenchanted *adjective* DISILLUSIONED, cynical, disappointed, indifferent, jaundiced, let down, sick of, soured
disenchantment *noun* DISILLUSIONMENT, disappointment, disillusion, rude awakening
disengage *verb* RELEASE, disentangle, extricate, free, loosen, set free, unloose, untie
disentangle *verb* UNTANGLE, disconnect, disengage, extricate, free, loose, unravel
disfavor *noun* DISAPPROVAL, disapprobation, dislike, displeasure
disfigure *verb* DAMAGE, blemish, deface, deform, distort, mar, mutilate, scar
disgorge *verb* VOMIT, discharge, eject, empty, expel
disgrace *noun* 1 SHAME, degradation, dishonor, disrepute, ignominy, infamy, odium, opprobrium
2 STAIN, blemish, blot, reproach, scandal, slur, stigma
▷ *verb* 3 BRING SHAME UPON, degrade, discredit, dishonor, humiliate, shame, sully, taint
disgraceful *adjective* SHAMEFUL, contemptible, detestable, dishonorable, disreputable, ignominious, lousy (*slang*), scandalous, shocking, unworthy
disgruntled *adjective* DISCONTENTED, annoyed, displeased, dissatisfied, grumpy, irritated, peeved, put out, vexed
disguise *verb* 1 HIDE, camouflage, cloak, conceal, cover, mask, screen, shroud, veil
2 MISREPRESENT, fake, falsify
▷ *noun* 3 COSTUME, camouflage, cover, mask, screen, veil

unrecognizable **2** conceal, cloak **3** misrepresent ▷ *noun* **4** false appearance **5** device to conceal identity
dis•gust' *noun* **1** violent distaste, loathing, repugnance ▷ *verb transitive* **2** affect with loathing
dish *noun* **1** shallow vessel for food **2** portion or variety of food **3** contents of dish **4** (*slang*) attractive person > **dish out** (*informal*) **1** put in dish **2** serve up **3** dispense (money, abuse, etc.)
dis•ha•bille [dis-ə-BEEL] *noun* state of being partly or carelessly dressed
dis•har'mo•ny *noun* lack of agreement, discord
dis•heart'en *verb transitive* weaken or destroy the hope, courage, or enthusiasm of
di•shev•eled [di-SHEV-əld] *adjective* **1** with disordered hair **2** ruffled, untidy, unkempt
dis•hon'est *adjective* not honest or fair > **dis•hon'est•ly** *adverb* > **dis•hon'es•ty** *noun*
dis•hon'or *verb transitive* **1** treat with disrespect **2** refuse to cash (a check) ▷ *noun* **3** lack of respect **4** state of shame or disgrace **5** something that causes a loss of honor > **dis•hon'or•a•ble** *adjective* > **dis•hon'or•a•bly** *adverb*
dis•il•lu•sion [dis-i-LOO-zhən] *verb transitive* destroy ideals, illusions, or false ideas of ▷ *noun*
dis•in•fect•ant [dis-in-FEK-tənt] *noun* substance that prevents or removes infection > **dis•in•fect'** *verb transitive*
dis•in•for•ma•tion [dis-in-fər-MAY-shən] *noun* false information intended to deceive or mislead
dis•in•gen•u•ous [dis-in-JEN-yoo-əs] *adjective* not sincere or frank
dis•in•her•it [dis-in-HE-rit] *verb transitive* to deprive of inheritance
dis•in•te•grate [dis-IN-tə-grayt] *verb* **-grat•ed, -grat•ing** break up, fall to pieces > **dis•in•te•gra'tion** *noun*
dis•in•ter' *verb transitive* **-ter•ring, -terred** **1** dig up **2** reveal, make known
dis•in•ter•est [dis-IN-trist] *noun* freedom from bias or involvement > **dis•in'ter•est•ed** *adjective*
dis•joint' *verb transitive* **1** put out of joint **2** break the natural order or logical arrangement of > **dis•joint'ed** *adjective* **1** (of discourse) incoherent **2** disconnected
disk *noun* **1** thin, flat, circular object like a coin **2** *computing* storage device, consisting of a disk coated with a magnetic layer, used to record and retrieve data **3** a phonograph record > **disk drive** *computing* controller and mechanism for reading and writing data on computer disks > **disk harrow** harrow that cuts the soil with inclined disks > **disk jockey, disc jockey** person who introduces and plays pop records on a radio program or at a disco
dis•lo•cate [DIS-loh-kayt] *verb transitive* **-cat•ed, -cat•ing** **1** put out of joint (e.g. dislocate shoulder) **2** disrupt, displace > **dis•lo•ca'tion** *noun*
dis•lodge [dis-LOJ] *verb transitive* **-lodged,**

DICTIONARY

d

THESAURUS

4 FAÇADE, deception, dissimulation, front, pretense, semblance, trickery, veneer
disguised *adjective* IN DISGUISE, camouflaged, covert, fake, false, feigned, incognito, masked, undercover
disgust *noun* **1** LOATHING, abhorrence, aversion, dislike, distaste, hatred, nausea, repugnance, repulsion, revulsion
▷ *verb* **2** SICKEN, displease, nauseate, offend, put off, repel, revolt
disgusted *adjective* SICKENED, appalled, nauseated, offended, repulsed, scandalized
disgusting *adjective* SICKENING, foul, gross, loathsome, nauseating, offensive, repellent, repugnant, revolting
dish *noun* **1** BOWL, plate, platter, salver **2** FOOD, fare, recipe
dishearten *verb* DISCOURAGE, cast down, deject, depress, deter, dismay, dispirit, put a damper on
disheveled *adjective* UNTIDY, bedraggled, disordered, messy, ruffled, rumpled, tousled, uncombed, unkempt
dishonest *adjective* DECEITFUL, bent (*slang*), cheating, corrupt, crooked (*informal*), disreputable, double-dealing, false, lying, treacherous
dishonesty *noun* DECEIT, cheating, chicanery, corruption, fraud, treachery, trickery, unscrupulousness
dishonor *verb* **1** SHAME, debase, debauch, defame, degrade, discredit, disgrace, sully
▷ *noun* **2** SHAME, discredit, disgrace, disrepute, ignominy, infamy, obloquy, reproach, scandal **3** INSULT, abuse, affront, discourtesy, indignity, offense, outrage, sacrilege, slight
dishonorable *adjective* **1** SHAMEFUL, contemptible, despicable, discreditable, disgraceful, ignominious, infamous, lousy (*slang*), scandalous, scuzzy (*slang*)
2 UNTRUSTWORTHY, corrupt, disreputable, shameless, treacherous, unprincipled, unscrupulous
disillusioned *adjective* DISENCHANTED, disabused, disappointed, enlightened, undeceived
disinclination *noun* RELUCTANCE, aversion, dislike, hesitance, objection, opposition, repugnance, resistance, unwillingness
disinclined *adjective* RELUCTANT, averse, hesitating, loath, not in the mood, opposed, resistant, unwilling
disinfect *verb* STERILIZE, clean, cleanse, decontaminate, deodorize, fumigate, purify, sanitize
disinfectant *noun* ANTISEPTIC, germicide, sterilizer
disinherit *verb* (*law*) CUT OFF, disown, dispossess, oust, repudiate
disintegrate *verb* BREAK UP, break apart, crumble, fall apart, go to pieces, separate, shatter, splinter
disinterest *noun* IMPARTIALITY, detachment, fairness, neutrality
disinterested *adjective* IMPARTIAL, detached, dispassionate, even-handed, impersonal, neutral, objective, unbiased, unprejudiced
disjointed *adjective* INCOHERENT, confused, disconnected, disordered, rambling
dislike *verb* **1** BE AVERSE TO, despise, detest, disapprove, hate, loathe, not be able to bear *or* not be able to abide, not be able to stand, object to, take a dim view of
▷ *noun* **2** AVERSION, animosity, antipathy, disapproval, disinclination, displeasure, distaste, enmity, hostility, repugnance

-lodg•ing drive out or remove from hiding place or previous position
dis•loy'al *adjective* not loyal, deserting one's allegiance > **dis•loy'al•ty** *noun*
dis•mal [DIZ-məl] *adjective* 1 depressing 2 depressed 3 cheerless, dreary, gloomy > **dis'mal•ly** *adverb*
dis•man•tle [dis-MAN-tl] *verb transitive* **-tled, -tling** take apart > **dis•man'tle•ment** *noun*
dis•may' *verb transitive* 1 dishearten, daunt ▷ *noun* 2 consternation, horrified amazement 3 apprehension
dis•mem•ber [dis-MEM-bər] *verb transitive* 1 tear or cut limb from limb 2 divide, partition > **dis•mem'ber•ment** *noun*
dis•miss' *verb transitive* 1 remove from employment 2 send away 3 reject > **dis•miss'al** *noun*
dis•mount' *verb* get off a horse or bicycle
dis•o•bey [dis-ə-BAY] *verb* refuse or fail to obey > **dis•o•be'di•ence** [-BEE-dee-əns] *noun*
dis•o•blige [dis-ə-BLĪJ] *verb transitive* **-bliged, -blig•ing** disregard the wishes, preferences of
dis•or•der [dis-OR-dər] *noun* 1 disarray, confusion, disturbance 2 upset of health, ailment ▷ *verb transitive* 3 upset order of 4 disturb health of > **dis•or'der•ly** *adjective* 1 untidy 2 unruly
dis•or'gan•ize *verb transitive* disrupt the arrangement or system of > **dis•or•gan•i•za'tion** *noun*
dis•o•ri•ent [dis-OR-ee-ənt] *verb transitive* cause to lose one's bearings, confuse
dis•own [dis-OHN] *verb transitive* refuse to acknowledge
dis•par•age [di-SPAR-ij] *verb transitive* **-aged, -ag•ing** 1 speak slightingly of 2 belittle > **dis•par'age•ment** *noun*
dis•pa•rate [DIS-pər-it] *adjective* essentially different, unrelated > **dis•par'i•ty** *noun, plural* **-ties** 1 inequality 2 incongruity
dis•pas•sion•ate [dis-PASH-ə-nit] *adjective* 1 unswayed by passion 2 calm, impartial
dis•patch [di-SPACH] *verb transitive* 1 send off to destination or on an errand 2 send off 3 finish off, get done with speed 4 (*informal*) eat up 5 kill ▷ *noun* 6 sending off 7 efficient speed 8 official message, report
dis•pel [di-SPEL] *verb transitive* **-pelled, -pel•ling** clear, drive away, scatter
dis•pense [di-SPENS] *verb transitive* **-pensed, -pens•ing** 1 deal out 2 make up (medicine) 3 administer (justice) 4 grant exemption from > **dis•pen'sa•ble** *adjective* > **dis•pen'sa•ry** *noun, plural* **-ries** place where medical aid is given > **dis•pen•sa'tion** *noun* 1 act of dispensing 2

DICTIONARY • THESAURUS

dislodge *verb* DISPLACE, disturb, extricate, force out, knock loose, oust, remove, uproot
disloyal *adjective* TREACHEROUS, faithless, false, subversive, traitorous, two-faced, unfaithful, untrustworthy
disloyalty *noun* TREACHERY, back-stabbing (*informal*), breach of trust, deceitfulness, double-dealing, falseness, inconstancy, infidelity, treason, unfaithfulness
dismal *adjective* GLOOMY, bleak, cheerless, dark, depressing, discouraging, dreary, forlorn, somber, wretched
dismantle *verb* TAKE APART, demolish, disassemble, strip, take to pieces
dismay *verb* 1 ALARM, appall, distress, frighten, horrify, paralyze, scare, terrify, unnerve
2 DISAPPOINT, daunt, discourage, dishearten, disillusion, dispirit, put off
▷ *noun* 3 ALARM, anxiety, apprehension, consternation, dread, fear, horror, trepidation
4 DISAPPOINTMENT, chagrin, discouragement, disillusionment
dismember *verb* CUT INTO PIECES, amputate, dissect, mutilate, sever
dismiss *verb* 1 SACK (*informal*), ax (*informal*), cashier, discharge, fire (*informal*), give notice to, give (someone) their marching orders, lay off, remove
2 LET GO, disperse, dissolve, free, release, send away
3 PUT OUT OF ONE'S MIND, banish, discard, dispel, disregard, lay aside, reject, set aside
dismissal *noun* THE SACK (*informal*), expulsion, marching orders (*informal*), notice, removal, the boot (*slang*)
disobedience *noun* DEFIANCE, indiscipline, insubordination, mutiny, noncompliance, nonobservance, recalcitrance, revolt, unruliness, waywardness
disobedient *adjective* DEFIANT, contrary, disorderly, insubordinate, intractable, naughty, refractory, undisciplined, unruly, wayward
disobey *verb* REFUSE TO OBEY, contravene, defy, disregard, flout, ignore, infringe, rebel, violate
disorder *noun* 1 UNTIDINESS, chaos, clutter, confusion, disarray, jumble, mess, muddle, shambles
2 DISTURBANCE, commotion, riot, turmoil, unrest, unruliness, uproar
3 ILLNESS, affliction, ailment, complaint, disease, malady, sickness
disorderly *adjective* 1 UNTIDY, chaotic, confused, disorganized, jumbled, messy
2 UNRULY, disruptive, indisciplined, lawless, riotous, rowdy, tumultuous, turbulent, ungovernable
disorganized *adjective* MUDDLED, chaotic, confused, disordered, haphazard, jumbled, unsystematic
disown *verb* DENY, cast off, disavow, disclaim, reject, renounce, repudiate
disparage *verb* RUN DOWN, belittle, denigrate, deprecate, deride, malign, put down, ridicule, slander, vilify
dispassionate *adjective* 1 UNEMOTIONAL, calm, collected, composed, cool, imperturbable, serene, unruffled
2 OBJECTIVE, detached, disinterested, fair, impartial, impersonal, neutral, unbiased, unprejudiced
dispatch *or* **despatch** *verb* 1 SEND, consign, dismiss, hasten
2 CARRY OUT, discharge, dispose of, finish, perform, settle
3 MURDER, assassinate, execute, kill, slaughter, slay
▷ *noun* 4 MESSAGE, account, bulletin, communication, communiqué, news, report, story
dispel *verb* DRIVE AWAY, banish, chase away,

license or exemption 3 provision of nature or providence > **dis•pens'er** *noun* **dispense with** 1 do away with 2 manage without
dis•perse [di-SPURS] *verb transitive* **-persed, -pers•ing** scatter > **dispersed** *adjective* 1 scattered 2 placed here and there > **dis•per'sal, dis•per'sion** [-zhən] *noun*
dis•pir•it•ed [di-SPIR-i-tid] *adjective* dejected, disheartened > **dis•pir'it•ing** *adjective*
dis•place [dis-PLAYS] *verb transitive* **-placed, -plac•ing** 1 move from its place 2 remove from office 3 take place of > **dis•place'ment** *noun* 1 displacing 2 weight of liquid displaced by a solid in it
dis•play [di-SPLAY] *verb transitive* 1 spread out for show 2 show, expose to view ▷ *noun* 3 displaying 4 parade 5 show, exhibition 6 ostentation
dis•please [dis-PLEEZ] *verb* **-pleased, pleas•ing** 1 offend 2 annoy > **dis•pleas'ure** [-PLEZH-ər] *noun* anger, vexation
dis•port [di-SPORT] *verb reflexive* gambol, amuse oneself, frolic
dis•pose [di-SPOHZ] *verb transitive* **-posed, -pos•ing** 1 arrange 2 distribute 3 incline 4 adjust ▷ *verb intransitive* **-posed, -pos•ing** 5 determine > **dis•pos'a•ble** *adjective* designed to be thrown away after use > **dis•pos'al** *noun* > **dis•po•si•tion** [dis-pə-ZISH-ən] *noun* 1 inclination 2 temperament 3 arrangement 4 plan **dispose of** 1 sell, get rid of 2 have authority over, deal with
dis•pos•sess [dis-pə-ZES] *verb transitive* cause to give up possession (of)
dis•pro•por'tion *noun* lack of proportion or equality > **dis•pro•por'tion•ate** *adjective*
dis•prove' *verb transitive* show (an assertion or claim) to be incorrect
dis•pute [di-SPYOOT] *verb intransitive* **-put•ed, -put•ing** 1 debate, discuss ▷ *verb transitive* **-put•ed, -put•ing** 2 call in question 3 debate, argue 4 oppose, contest > **dis•put'a•ble** *adjective* > **dis•pu'tant** *noun* > **dis•pu•ta'tious** *adjective* 1 argumentative 2 quarrelsome
dis•qual•i•fy [dis-KWOL-ə-fī] *verb transitive* **-fied, -fy•ing** make ineligible, unfit for some special purpose
dis•qui•et [dis-KWĪ-it] *noun* 1 anxiety, uneasiness ▷ *verb transitive* 2 cause (someone) to feel this
dis•qui•si•tion [dis-kwə-ZISH-ən] *noun* learned or elaborate treatise, discourse or essay

DICTIONARY **d** THESAURUS

dismiss, disperse, eliminate, expel
dispense *verb* 1 DISTRIBUTE, allocate, allot, apportion, assign, deal out, dole out, share
2 PREPARE, measure, mix, supply
3 ADMINISTER, apply, carry out, discharge, enforce, execute, implement, operate
4 ▷ **dispense with a** DO AWAY WITH, abolish, brush aside, cancel, dispose of, get rid of **b** DO WITHOUT, abstain from, forgo, give up, relinquish
disperse *verb* 1 SCATTER, broadcast, diffuse, disseminate, distribute, spread, strew
2 BREAK UP, disband, dissolve, scatter, separate
dispirited *adjective* DISHEARTENED, crestfallen, dejected, depressed, despondent, discouraged, downcast, gloomy, glum, sad
displace *verb* 1 MOVE, disturb, misplace, shift, transpose
2 REPLACE, oust, succeed, supersede, supplant, take the place of
display *verb* 1 SHOW, demonstrate, disclose, exhibit, expose, manifest, present, reveal
2 SHOW OFF, flaunt, flourish, parade, vaunt
▷ *noun* 3 EXHIBITION, array, demonstration, presentation, revelation, show
4 SHOW, flourish, ostentation, pageant, parade, pomp, spectacle
displease *verb* ANNOY, anger, irk, irritate, offend, pique, put out, upset, vex
displeasure *noun* ANNOYANCE, anger, disapproval, dissatisfaction, distaste, indignation, irritation, resentment
disposable *adjective* 1 THROWAWAY, biodegradable, nonreturnable
2 AVAILABLE, consumable, expendable
disposal *noun* 1 THROWING AWAY, discarding, dumping (*informal*), ejection, jettisoning, removal, riddance, scrapping
2 ▷ **at one's disposal** AVAILABLE, at one's service, consumable, expendable, free for use
dispose *verb* ARRANGE, array, distribute, group, marshal, order, place, put
dispose of *verb* 1 GET RID OF, destroy, discard, dump (*informal*), jettison, scrap, throw out *or* throw away, unload
2 DEAL WITH, decide, determine, end, finish with, settle
disposition *noun* 1 CHARACTER, constitution, make-up, nature, spirit, temper, temperament
2 TENDENCY, bent, bias, habit, inclination, leaning, proclivity, propensity
3 ARRANGEMENT, classification, distribution, grouping, ordering, organization, placement
disproportion *noun* INEQUALITY, asymmetry, discrepancy, disparity, imbalance, lopsidedness, unevenness
disproportionate *adjective* UNEQUAL, excessive, inordinate, out of proportion, unbalanced, uneven, unreasonable
disprove *verb* PROVE FALSE, contradict, discredit, expose, give the lie to, invalidate, negate, rebut, refute
dispute *noun* 1 DISAGREEMENT, altercation, argument, conflict, feud, quarrel
2 ARGUMENT, contention, controversy, debate, discussion, dissension
▷ *verb* 3 DOUBT, challenge, contest, contradict, deny, impugn, question, rebut
4 ARGUE, clash, cross swords, debate, quarrel, squabble
disqualification *noun* BAN, elimination, exclusion, ineligibility, rejection
disqualified *adjective* INELIGIBLE, debarred, eliminated, knocked out, out of the running
disqualify *verb* BAN, debar, declare ineligible, preclude, prohibit, rule out
disquiet *noun* 1 UNEASINESS, alarm, anxiety, concern, disturbance, foreboding, nervousness, trepidation, worry
▷ *verb* 2 MAKE UNEASY, bother, concern, disturb, perturb, trouble, unsettle, upset, worry
disregard *verb* 1 IGNORE, brush aside *or* brush away, discount, make light of, neglect, overlook, pass over, pay no heed to, turn a blind eye to

dis•re•pute' *noun* loss or lack of good reputation > **dis•rep'u•ta•ble** *adjective* having or causing a bad reputation
dis•re•spect' *noun* lack of respect > **dis•re•spect'ful** *adjective*
dis•rupt' *verb transitive* 1 interrupt 2 throw into turmoil or disorder > **dis•rup'tion** *noun* > **dis•rup'tive** *adjective*
dis•sat'is•fied *adjective* not pleased or contented > **dis•sat•is•fac'tion** *noun*
dis•sect [di-SEKT] *verb transitive* 1 cut up (body, organism) for detailed examination 2 examine or criticize in detail > **dis•sec'tion** *noun*
dis•sem•ble [di-SEM-bəl] *verb* **-bled, -bling** 1 conceal, disguise (feelings, etc.) 2 act the hypocrite > **dis•sem'bler** *noun*
dis•sem•i•nate [di-SEM-ə-nayt] *verb transitive* **-nat•ed, -nat•ing** spread abroad, scatter > **dis•sem•i•na'tion** *noun*
dis•sent [di-SENT] *verb intransitive* 1 differ in opinion 2 express such difference 3 disagree with doctrine, etc. of established church, etc. ▷ *noun* 4 such disagreement > **dis•sent'er** *noun*
dis•ser•ta•tion [dis-ər-TAY-shən] *noun* 1 written thesis 2 formal discourse
dis•serv•ice [dis-SUR-vis] *noun* ill turn, wrong, injury
dis•si•dent [DIS-i-dənt] *noun, adjective* (one) not in agreement, esp. with government > **dis'si•dence** *noun* 1 dissent 2 disagreement
dis•sim'i•lar *adjective* not alike, different > **dis•sim•i•lar'i•ty** *noun*
dis•sim•u•late [di-SIM-yə-layt] *verb* **-lat•ed, -lat•ing** 1 pretend not to have 2 practice deceit > **dis•sim•u•la'tion** *noun*
dis•si•pate [DIS-ə-payt] *verb transitive* **-pat•ed, -pat•ing** 1 scatter 2 waste, squander > **dis'si•pat•ed** *adjective* 1 indulging in pleasure without restraint, dissolute 2 scattered, wasted > **dis•si•pa'tion** *noun* 1 scattering 2 frivolous, dissolute way of life
dis•so•ci•ate [di-SOH-shee-ayt] *verb* **-at•ed, -at•ing** 1 separate, sever 2 disconnect
dis•so•lute [DIS-ə-loot] *adjective* lacking restraint, esp. lax in morals
dis•so•lu•tion [dis-ə-LOO-shən] *noun* 1 breakup 2 termination of legislature, meeting or legal relationship 3 destruction 4 death
dis•solve [di-ZOLV] *verb transitive* **-solved, -solv•ing** 1 absorb or melt in fluid 2 break up, put an end to, annul ▷ *verb intransitive* **-solved, -solv•ing** 3 melt in fluid 4 disappear, vanish 5 break up, scatter > **dis•sol•u•ble** [di-SOL-yə-bəl] *adjective* capable of being dissolved
dis•so•nant [DIS-ə-nənt] *adjective* jarring, discordant > **dis'so•nance** *noun*
dis•suade [di-SWAYD] *verb transitive* **-suad•ed, -suad•ing** advise to refrain, persuade not to

DICTIONARY • THESAURUS

▷ *noun* 2 INATTENTION, contempt, disdain, disrespect, indifference, neglect, negligence, oversight
disrepair *noun* DILAPIDATION, collapse, decay, deterioration, ruination
disreputable *adjective* DISCREDITABLE, dishonorable, ignominious, infamous, louche, notorious, scandalous, shady (*informal*), shameful
disrepute *noun* DISCREDIT, disgrace, dishonor, ignominy, ill repute, infamy, obloquy, shame, unpopularity
disrespect *noun* CONTEMPT, cheek, impertinence, impoliteness, impudence, insolence, irreverence, lack of respect, rudeness
disrespectful *adjective* CONTEMPTUOUS, cheeky, discourteous, impertinent, impolite, impudent, insolent, insulting, irreverent, rude
disrupt *verb* 1 DISTURB, confuse, disorder, disorganize, spoil, upset
2 INTERRUPT, break up *or* break into, interfere with, intrude, obstruct, unsettle, upset
disruption *noun* DISTURBANCE, interference, interruption, stoppage
disruptive *adjective* DISTURBING, disorderly, distracting, troublesome, unruly, unsettling, upsetting
dissatisfaction *noun* DISCONTENT, annoyance, chagrin, disappointment, displeasure, frustration, irritation, resentment, unhappiness
dissatisfied *adjective* DISCONTENTED, disappointed, disgruntled, displeased, fed up, frustrated, unhappy, unsatisfied
dissect *verb* 1 CUT UP *or* CUT APART, anatomize, dismember, lay open
2 ANALYZE, break down, explore, inspect, investigate, research, scrutinize, study
disseminate *verb* SPREAD, broadcast, circulate, disperse, distribute, publicize, scatter
dissension *noun* DISAGREEMENT, conflict, discord, dispute, dissent, friction, quarrel, row, strife
dissent *verb* 1 DISAGREE, differ, object, protest, refuse, withhold assent *or* withhold approval
▷ *noun* 2 DISAGREEMENT, discord, dissension, objection, opposition, refusal, resistance
dissenter *noun* OBJECTOR, dissident, nonconformist
dissertation *noun* THESIS, critique, discourse, disquisition, essay, exposition, treatise
disservice *noun* BAD TURN, harm, injury, injustice, unkindness, wrong
dissident *adjective* 1 DISSENTING, disagreeing, discordant, heterodox, nonconformist
▷ *noun* 2 PROTESTER, agitator, dissenter, rebel
dissimilar *adjective* DIFFERENT, disparate, divergent, diverse, heterogeneous, unlike, unrelated, various
dissipate *verb* 1 SQUANDER, consume, deplete, expend, fritter away, run through, spend, waste
2 DISPERSE, disappear, dispel, dissolve, drive away, evaporate, scatter, vanish
dissipation *noun* 1 DISPERSAL, disappearance, disintegration, dissolution, scattering, vanishing
2 DEBAUCHERY, dissoluteness, excess, extravagance, indulgence, intemperance, prodigality, profligacy, wantonness, waste
dissociate *verb* 1 BREAK AWAY, break off, part company, quit
2 SEPARATE, detach, disconnect, distance, divorce, isolate, segregate, set apart
dissolute *adjective* IMMORAL, debauched, degenerate, depraved, dissipated, profligate, rakish, wanton, wild
dissolution *noun* 1 BREAKING UP, disintegration, division, parting, separation
2 ADJOURNMENT, discontinuation, end, finish, suspension, termination

> **dis•sua'sion** [-zhən] *noun* > **dis•sua'sive** *adjective*
dis•taff [DIS-taf] *noun* cleft stick to hold wool, etc., for spinning > **distaff side** 1 maternal side 2 female line
dis•tance [DIS-təns] *noun* 1 amount of space between two things 2 remoteness 3 aloofness, reserve ▷ *verb transitive* **-tanced, -tanc•ing** 4 hold or place at distance > **dis'tant** *adjective* 1 far off, remote 2 haughty, cold
dis•taste [dis-TAYST] *noun* 1 dislike of food or drink 2 aversion, disgust > **dis•taste'ful** *adjective* unpleasant, displeasing to feelings > **dis•taste'ful•ness** *noun*
dis•tem•per [dis-TEM-pər] *noun* 1 disease of dogs 2 method of painting on plaster without oil 3 paint used for this ▷ *verb transitive* 4 paint with distemper
dis•tend [di-STEND] *verb* swell out by pressure from within, inflate > **dis•ten'sion** *noun*
dis•tich [DIS-tik] *noun* couplet
dis•till [di-STIL] *verb transitive* 1 vaporize and recondense a liquid 2 purify, separate, concentrate liquids by this method 3 extract quality of ▷ *verb intransitive* 4 trickle down > **dis•til•late** [DIS-tə-lit] *noun* distilled liquid, esp. as fuel for some engines > **dis•till'er** *noun* one who distills, esp. manufacturer of whiskey
dis•tinct [di-STINGKT] *adjective* 1 clear, easily seen 2 definite 3 separate, different > **dis•tinc'tion** *noun* 1 point of difference 2 act of distinguishing 3 eminence, repute, high honor, high quality > **dis•tinc'tive** *adjective* characteristic > **dis•tinct'ly** *adverb*
dis•tin•guish [di-STING-gwish] *verb transitive* 1 make difference in 2 recognize, make out 3 honor 4 (*usually reflexive*) make prominent or honored 5 classify ▷ *verb intransitive* (usu with *between* or *among*) 6 draw distinction, grasp difference > **dis•tin'guish•a•ble** *adjective* > **dis•tin'guished** *adjective* 1 dignified 2 famous, eminent
dis•tort [di-STORT] *verb transitive* 1 put out of shape, deform 2 misrepresent 3 garble, falsify > **dis•tor'tion** *noun*
dis•tract [di-STRAKT] *verb transitive* 1 draw attention of (someone) away from work, etc. 2 divert 3 perplex, bewilder, drive mad > **dis•trac'tion** *noun*
dis•traught [di-STRAWT] *adjective* 1 bewildered, crazed with grief 2 frantic, distracted
dis•tress [di-STRES] *noun* 1 severe trouble, mental pain 2 severe pressure of hunger,

DICTIONARY **d** THESAURUS

---

dissolve *verb* 1 MELT, deliquesce, fuse, liquefy, soften, thaw
2 END, break up, discontinue, suspend, terminate, wind up
dissuade *verb* DETER, advise against, discourage, put off, remonstrate, talk out of, warn
distance *noun* 1 SPACE, extent, gap, interval, length, range, span, stretch
2 RESERVE, aloofness, coldness, coolness, remoteness, restraint, stiffness
3 ▷ **in the distance** FAR OFF, afar, far away, on the horizon, yonder
▷ *verb* 4 ▷ **distance oneself** SEPARATE ONESELF, be distanced from, dissociate oneself
distant *adjective* 1 FAR-OFF, abroad, far, faraway, far-flung, outlying, out-of-the-way, remote
2 APART, dispersed, distinct, scattered, separate
3 RESERVED, aloof, cool, reticent, standoffish, unapproachable, unfriendly, withdrawn
distaste *noun* DISLIKE, aversion, disgust, horror, loathing, odium, repugnance, revulsion
distasteful *adjective* UNPLEASANT, disagreeable, objectionable, offensive, repugnant, repulsive, scuzzy (*slang*), uninviting, unpalatable, unsavory
distill *verb* EXTRACT, condense, purify, refine
distinct *adjective* 1 DIFFERENT, detached, discrete, individual, separate, unconnected
2 DEFINITE, clear, decided, evident, marked, noticeable, obvious, palpable, unmistakable, well-defined
distinction *noun* 1 DIFFERENTIATION, discernment, discrimination, perception, separation
2 FEATURE, characteristic, distinctiveness, individuality, mark, particularity, peculiarity, quality
3 DIFFERENCE, contrast, differential, division, separation
4 EXCELLENCE, eminence, fame, greatness, honor, importance, merit, prominence, repute
distinctive *adjective* CHARACTERISTIC, idiosyncratic, individual, original, peculiar, singular, special, typical, unique
distinctly *adverb* DEFINITELY, clearly, decidedly, markedly, noticeably, obviously, patently, plainly, unmistakably
distinguish *verb* 1 DIFFERENTIATE, ascertain, decide, determine, discriminate, judge, tell apart, tell the difference
2 CHARACTERIZE, categorize, classify, mark, separate, set apart, single out
3 MAKE OUT, discern, know, perceive, pick out, recognize, see, tell
distinguished *adjective* EMINENT, acclaimed, celebrated, famed, famous, illustrious, noted, renowned, well-known
distort *verb* 1 MISREPRESENT, bias, color, falsify, pervert, slant, twist
2 DEFORM, bend, buckle, contort, disfigure, misshape, twist, warp
distortion *noun* 1 MISREPRESENTATION, bias, falsification, perversion, slant
2 DEFORMITY, bend, buckle, contortion, crookedness, malformation, twist, warp
distract *verb* 1 DIVERT, draw away, sidetrack, turn aside
2 AMUSE, beguile, engross, entertain, occupy
distracted *adjective* AGITATED, at sea, flustered, harassed, in a flap (*informal*), perplexed, puzzled, troubled
distraction *noun* 1 DIVERSION, disturbance, interference, interruption
2 ENTERTAINMENT, amusement, diversion, pastime, recreation
3 AGITATION, bewilderment, commotion, confusion, discord, disorder, disturbance
distraught *adjective* FRANTIC, agitated, beside oneself, desperate, distracted, distressed, out of one's mind, overwrought, worked-up
distress *noun* 1 WORRY, grief, heartache, misery, pain, sorrow, suffering, torment, wretchedness
2 NEED, adversity, difficulties, hardship, misfortune, poverty, privation, trouble
▷ *verb* 3 UPSET, disturb, grieve, harass, sadden,

fatigue or want ▷ *verb transitive* 3 afflict, give mental pain > **dis•tress'ful** *adjective*
dis•trib•ute [di-STRIB-yoot] *verb transitive* **-ut•ed, -ut•ing** 1 deal out, dispense 2 spread, dispose at intervals 3 classify > **dis•tri•bu'tion** *noun* > **dis•trib'u•tive** *adjective* > **dis•trib'u•tor** *noun* rotary switch distributing electricity in automotive engine
dis•trict [DIS-trikt] *noun* 1 region, locality 2 portion of territory
dis•trust' *verb transitive* 1 regard as untrustworthy ▷ *noun* 2 feeling of suspicion or doubt > **dis•trust'ful** *adjective*
dis•turb' *verb transitive* trouble, agitate, unsettle, derange > **dis•turb'ance** *noun*
dis•use [dis-YOOS] *noun* state of being no longer used > **dis•used'** [-YOOZD] *adjective*
ditch [dich] *noun* 1 long narrow hollow dug in ground for drainage, etc. ▷ *verb* 2 make, repair ditches 3 run car, etc. into ditch ▷ *verb transitive* 4 (*slang*) abandon, discard
dith•er [DITH-ər] *verb intransitive* 1 be uncertain or indecisive ▷ *noun* 2 this state
dith•y•ramb [DITH-ə-ram] *noun* ancient Greek hymn sung in honor of Dionysus
dit•to [DIT-oh] *noun, plural* **-tos** same, aforesaid (used to avoid repetition in lists, etc.)
dit•ty [DIT-ee] *noun, plural* **-ties** simple song
di•u•ret•ic [dī-ə-RET-ik] *adjective* 1 increasing the discharge of urine ▷ *noun* 2 substance with this property
di•ur•nal [dī-UR-nəl] *adjective* 1 daily 2 in or of daytime 3 taking a day
di•va•lent [dī-VAY-lənt] *adjective* capable of combining with two atoms of hydrogen or their equivalent
di•van' *noun* bed, couch without back or head
dive [dīv] *verb intransitive* **dived** *or* **dove, div•ing** 1 plunge under surface of water 2 descend suddenly 3 disappear 4 go deep down into 5 reach quickly ▷ *noun* 6 act of diving 7 (*slang*) disreputable bar, club, etc. > **div'er** *noun* one who descends into deep water > **dive bomber** aircraft that attacks after diving steeply
di•verge [di-VURJ] *verb intransitive* **-verged, -verg•ing** 1 get farther apart 2 separate > **di•ver'gence** *noun* > **di•ver'gent** *adjective*
di•vers [DĪ-vərz] *adjective* (*obsolete*) some, various
di•verse [di-VURS] *adjective* different, varied > **di•ver'si•ty** *noun, plural* **-ties** 1 quality of being different or varied 2 range of difference > **di•ver'si•fy** *verb transitive* **-fied, -fy•ing** 1 make diverse or varied 2 give variety to > **di•ver•si•fi•ca'tion** *noun*
di•vert [di-VURT] *verb transitive* 1 turn aside, ward off 2 amuse, entertain > **di•ver'sion** [-*zhən*] *noun* 1 a diverting 2 official detour for traffic

DICTIONARY • THESAURUS

---

torment, trouble, worry
distressed *adjective* 1 UPSET, agitated, distracted, distraught, tormented, troubled, worried, wretched
2 POVERTY-STRICKEN, destitute, down at heel, indigent, needy, poor, straitened
distressing *adjective* UPSETTING, disturbing, harrowing, heart-breaking, painful, sad, worrying
distribute *verb* 1 HAND OUT, circulate, convey, deliver, pass round
2 SHARE, allocate, allot, apportion, deal, dispense, dole out
distribution *noun* 1 DELIVERY, dealing, handling, mailing, transportation
2 SHARING, allocation, allotment, apportionment, division
3 CLASSIFICATION, arrangement, grouping, organization, placement
district *noun* AREA, locale, locality, neighborhood, parish, quarter, region, sector, vicinity
distrust *verb* 1 SUSPECT, be suspicious of, be wary of, disbelieve, doubt, mistrust, question, smell a rat (*informal*)
▷ *noun* 2 SUSPICION, disbelief, doubt, misgiving, mistrust, question, skepticism, wariness
disturb *verb* 1 INTERRUPT, bother, butt in on, disrupt, interfere with, intrude on, pester
2 UPSET, alarm, distress, fluster, harass, perturb, trouble, unnerve, unsettle, worry
3 MUDDLE, disarrange, disorder
disturbance *noun* 1 INTERRUPTION, annoyance, bother, distraction, intrusion
2 DISORDER, brawl, commotion, fracas, fray, rumpus
disturbed *adjective* 1 (*psychiatry*) UNBALANCED, disordered, maladjusted, neurotic, troubled, upset
2 WORRIED, anxious, apprehensive, bothered, concerned, nervous, troubled, uneasy, upset, wired (*slang*)
disturbing *adjective* WORRYING, alarming, disconcerting, distressing, frightening, harrowing, startling, unsettling, upsetting
disuse *noun* NEGLECT, abandonment, decay, idleness
ditch *noun* 1 CHANNEL, drain, dyke, furrow, gully, moat, trench, watercourse
▷ *verb* 2 (*slang*) GET RID OF, abandon, discard, dispose of, drop, dump (*informal*), jettison, scrap, throw out *or* throw overboard
dither *verb* 1 VACILLATE, hesitate, hum and haw, shillyshally (*informal*), teeter, waver
▷ *noun* 2 FLUTTER, flap (*informal*), fluster, tizzy (*informal*)
dive *verb* 1 PLUNGE, descend, dip, drop, duck, nose-dive, plummet, swoop
▷ *noun* 2 PLUNGE, jump, leap, lunge, nose dive, spring
diverge *verb* 1 SEPARATE, branch, divide, fork, part, split, spread
2 DEVIATE, depart, digress, meander, stray, turn aside, wander
diverse *adjective* 1 VARIOUS, assorted, manifold, miscellaneous, of every description, several, sundry, varied
2 DIFFERENT, discrete, disparate, dissimilar, distinct, divergent, separate, unlike, varying
diversify *verb* VARY, branch out, change, expand, have a finger in every pie, spread out
diversion *noun* 1 PASTIME, amusement, distraction, entertainment, game, recreation, relaxation, sport
diversity *noun* DIFFERENCE, distinctiveness, diverseness, heterogeneity, multiplicity, range, variety
divert *verb* 1 REDIRECT, avert, deflect, switch,

when main route is closed 3 amusement

di•vest' *verb transitive* 1 unclothe,strip 2 dispossess, deprive 3 sell off

di•vide [di-VĪD] *verb transitive* **-vid•ed, -vid•ing** 1 make into two or more parts, split up, separate 2 distribute, share 3 diverge in opinion 4 classify ▷ *verb intransitive* **-vid•ed, -vid•ing** 5 become separated 6 part into two groups for voting, etc. ▷ *noun* 7 division esp. between adjacent drainage areas > **div'i•dend** *noun* 1 share of profits, of money divided among shareholders, etc. 2 number to be divided by another > **di•vid'ers** *plural noun* pair of compasses

di•vine [di-VĪN] *adjective* **-vin•er, -vin•est** 1 of, pert. to, proceeding from, God 2 sacred 3 heavenly ▷ *noun* 4 theologian 5 clergyman ▷ *verb* **-vined, -vin•ing** guess 6 predict, foresee, tell by inspiration or magic > **div•i•na•tion** [div-ə-NAY-shən] *noun* divining > **di•vine'ly** *adverb* > **di•vin'er** *noun* > **di•vin'i•ty** *noun* 1 quality of being divine 2 god 3 theology > **divining rod** (forked) stick, etc. said to move when held over ground where water is present

di•vi•sion [di-VIZH-ən] *noun* 1 act of dividing 2 part of whole 3 barrier 4 section 5 difference in opinion, etc. 6 *math.* method of finding how many times one number is contained in another 7 army unit 8 separation, disunion > **di•vis'i•ble** *adjective* capable of division > **di•vi'sive** [-VĪ-siv] *adjective* causing disagreement > **di•vi'sor** [-VĪ-zər] *noun math.* number that divides dividend

di•vorce [di-VORS] *noun* 1 legal dissolution of marriage 2 complete separation, disunion ▷ *verb transitive* **-vorced, -vorc•ing** 3 dissolve marriage 4 separate 5 sunder > **di•vor•cee'** [-SAY] *noun*

div•ot [DIV-ət] *noun* piece of turf

di•vulge [di-VULJ] *verb transitive* **-vulged, -vulg•ing** reveal, let out (secret)

Dix•ie [DIK-see] *noun* southern states of the US

diz•zy [DIZ-ee] *adjective* **-zi•er, -zi•est** 1 feeling dazed, unsteady, as if about to fall 2 causing or fit to cause dizziness, as speed, etc. 3 (*informal*) silly ▷ *verb transitive* **-zied, -zy•ing** 4 make dizzy > **diz'zi•ly** *adverb* > **diz'zi•ness** *noun*

DJ *noun* 1 disc jockey ▷ *verb* **DJ'd, DJ'•ing** 2 act as DJ

DNA *noun* deoxyribonucleic acid, the main constituent of the chromosomes of all organisms

do[1] [doo] *verb transitive* **did, done, do•ing** 1 perform, effect, transact, bring about, finish 2 work at 3 work out, solve 4 suit 5 cover (distance) 6 provide, prepare 7 (*informal*) cheat, trick 8 frustrate 9 look after ▷ *verb intransitive* 10 act 11 manage 12 work 13 fare 14 serve, suffice 15 happen ▷ *verb auxiliary* 16 makes negative and interrogative sentences and expresses emphasis ▷ *noun* (*informal*) 17 celebration, festivity **do away with** destroy > **do up** 1 fasten 2 renovate > **do with** 1 need 2 make use of > **do without** deny oneself

do[2] [doh] *noun* first sol-fa note

doc•ile [DOS-əl] *adjective* willing to obey,

DICTIONARY

d

THESAURUS

turn aside
2 DISTRACT, draw away from *or* lead away from, lead astray, sidetrack
3 ENTERTAIN, amuse, beguile, delight, gratify, regale

diverting *adjective* ENTERTAINING, amusing, beguiling, enjoyable, fun, humorous, pleasant

divide *verb* 1 SEPARATE, bisect, cut *or* cut up, part, partition, segregate, split
2 SHARE, allocate, allot, deal out, dispense, distribute
3 CAUSE TO DISAGREE, break up, come between, estrange, split

dividend *noun* BONUS, cut (*informal*), divvy (*informal*), extra, gain, plus, portion, share, surplus

divine *adjective* 1 HEAVENLY, angelic, celestial, godlike, holy, spiritual, superhuman, supernatural
2 SACRED, consecrated, holy, religious, sanctified, spiritual
3 (*informal*) WONDERFUL, beautiful, excellent, glorious, marvelous, perfect, splendid, superlative
▷ *verb* 4 INFER, apprehend, deduce, discern, guess, perceive, suppose, surmise

divinity *noun* 1 THEOLOGY, religion, religious studies
2 GOD *or* GODDESS, deity, guardian spirit, spirit
3 GODLINESS, deity, divine nature, holiness, sanctity

divisible *adjective* DIVIDABLE, separable, splittable

division *noun* 1 SEPARATION, cutting up, dividing, partition, splitting up
2 SHARING, allotment, apportionment, distribution
3 PART, branch, category, class, department, group, section
4 DISAGREEMENT, difference of opinion, discord, rupture, split, variance

divorce *noun* 1 SEPARATION, annulment, dissolution, split-up
▷ *verb* 2 SEPARATE, disconnect, dissociate, dissolve (*marriage*), divide, part, sever, split up

divulge *verb* MAKE KNOWN, confess, declare, disclose, let slip, proclaim, reveal, tell

dizzy *adjective* 1 GIDDY, faint, light-headed, off balance, reeling, shaky, swimming, wobbly, woozy (*informal*)
2 CONFUSED, at sea, befuddled, bemused, bewildered, dazed, dazzled, muddled

do *verb* 1 PERFORM, accomplish, achieve, carry out, complete, execute
2 BE ADEQUATE, be sufficient, cut the mustard, pass muster, satisfy, suffice
3 GET READY, arrange, fix, look after, prepare, see to
4 SOLVE, decipher, decode, figure out, puzzle out, resolve, work out
5 CAUSE, bring about, create, effect, produce

do away with *verb* 1 KILL, exterminate, murder, slay
2 GET RID OF, abolish, discard, discontinue, eliminate, put an end to, put paid to, remove

docile *adjective* SUBMISSIVE, amenable, biddable, compliant, manageable, obedient, pliant

docility *noun* SUBMISSIVENESS, compliance, manageability, meekness, obedience

dock[1] *noun* 1 WHARF, harbor, pier, quay, waterfront

submissive
dock[1] [dok] *noun* 1 artificial enclosure near harbor for loading or repairing ships 2 platform for loading and unloading trucks ▷ *verb* 3 of vessel, put or go into dock 4 (of spacecraft) link or be linked together in space > **dock'er** *noun* longshoreman > **dock'yard** *noun* enclosure with docks, for building or repairing ships
dock[2] *noun* 1 solid part of animal's tail 2 cut end, stump ▷ *verb transitive* 3 cut short, esp. tail 4 curtail, deduct (an amount) from
dock[3] *noun* enclosure in criminal court for prisoner
dock•et [DOK-it] *noun* 1 agenda 2 list of court cases to be heard ▷ *verb transitive* 3 place on docket
doc•tor [DOK-tər] *noun* 1 medical practitioner 2 one holding university's highest degree in any faculty ▷ *verb transitive* 3 treat medically 4 repair, mend 5 falsify (accounts, etc.) > **doc'tor•al** [-əl] *adjective* > **doc'tor•ate** [-it] *noun*
doc•trine [DOK-trin] *noun* 1 what is taught 2 teaching of church, school, or person 3 belief, opinion, dogma > **doc•tri•naire'** [-trə-NAIR] *adjective* stubbornly insistent on applying theory without regard for circumstances ▷ *noun* > **doc'tri•nal** *adjective*
doc•u•ment [DOK-yə-mənt] *noun* 1 piece of paper, etc. providing information or evidence ▷ *verb transitive* 2 furnish with proofs, illustrations, certificates > **doc•u•men'ta•ry** *adjective, noun, plural* **-ries** (of) type of film, TV program dealing with real life, not fiction > **doc•u•men•ta'tion** *noun*
dod•der [DOD-ər] *verb intransitive* totter or tremble, as with age
dodge [doj] *verb* **dodged, dodging** 1 avoid or attempt to avoid (blow, discovery, etc.) as by moving quickly 2 evade questions by cleverness ▷ *noun* 3 trick, artifice 4 ingenious method 5 act of dodging > **dodg'er** *noun* 1 shifty person 2 evader
do•do [DOH-doh] *noun, plural* **-dos** 1 large extinct bird 2 person with old-fashioned ideas
doe [doh] *noun* female of deer, hare, rabbit
Doe [doh] *noun* **John Doe** 1 unknown or unidentified male person **Jane Doe** 2 unknown or unidentified female person
does [duz] *third pers. sing, pres ind. active of* **do**
doff [dof] *verb transitive* 1 take off (hat, clothing) 2 discard, lay aside
dog [dawg] *noun* 1 domesticated carnivorous four-legged mammal 2 person (in contempt, abuse or playfully) 3 name given to various mechanical contrivances for gripping, holding 4 device with tooth that penetrates or grips object and detains it 5 andiron or firedog 6 (*slang*) ugly person 7 (*slang*) thing of extremely poor quality 8 (*informal*) a fellow ▷ *verb transitive* **dogged, dog•ging** 9 follow steadily or closely > **dog'ged** [-gid] *adjective* persistent, resolute, tenacious > **dog'gy** *adjective* **-gi•er, -gi•est** > **dog days** 1 hot season of the rising of Dog Star 2 period of inactivity > **dog'-ear** *noun* 1 turned-down corner of page in book ▷ *verb transitive* 2 turn down corners of pages > **dog'-eat-dog'** *noun* action based on complete cynicism, ruthless competition > **dog'fight** *noun* 1 skirmish between fighter planes 2 savage contest characterized by disregard of rules > **doggy bag** bag in which diner may take leftovers (ostensibly for dog) > **dog'house** *noun* kennel **in the doghouse** (*informal*) in disfavor > **dog'leg** *noun* sharp bend or angle > **dog's age** quite a long time **Dog Star** star Sirius **go to the dogs** degenerate
doge [dohj] *noun* formerly, chief magistrate in Venice
dog•ger•el [DAW-gər-əl] *noun* slipshod, unpoetic or trivial verse
do•gie [DOH-gee] *noun* motherless calf
dog•ma [DAWG-mə] *noun, plural* **-mas** 1 article of belief, esp. one laid down authoritatively by church 2 body of beliefs > **dog•mat'ic** *adjective* 1 asserting opinions with arrogance 2 relating to dogma > **dog•mat'i•cal•ly** *adverb* > **dog'ma•tism** *noun* arrogant assertion of opinion
doi•ly [DOI-lee] *noun, plural* **-lies** small cloth, paper, piece of lace to place under cake or dish.
Dol•by [DOHL-bee] *noun* ® system used in tape recording to reduce unwanted noise

DICTIONARY • THESAURUS

▷ *verb* 2 MOOR, anchor, berth, drop anchor, land, put in, tie up
3 (*of a spacecraft*) LINK UP, couple, hook up, join, rendezvous, unite
dock[2] *verb* 1 DEDUCT, decrease, diminish, lessen, reduce, subtract, withhold
2 CUT OFF, clip, crop, curtail, cut short, shorten
doctor *noun* 1 G.P., general practitioner, medic (*informal*), medical practitioner, physician
▷ *verb* 2 CHANGE, alter, disguise, falsify, misrepresent, pervert, tamper with
3 ADD TO, adulterate, cut, dilute, mix with, spike, water down
doctrinaire *adjective* DOGMATIC, biased, fanatical, inflexible, insistent, opinionated, rigid
doctrine *noun* TEACHING, article of faith, belief, conviction, creed, dogma, opinion, precept, principle, tenet
document *noun* 1 PAPER, certificate, record, report
▷ *verb* 2 SUPPORT, authenticate, certify, corroborate, detail, substantiate, validate, verify
dodge *verb* 1 DUCK, dart, sidestep, swerve, turn aside
2 EVADE, avoid, elude, get out of, shirk
dog *noun* 1 HOUND, canine, cur, man's best friend, pooch (*slang*)
2 ▷ **go to the dogs** (*informal*) GO TO RUIN, degenerate, deteriorate, go down the drain, go to pot
▷ *verb* 3 TROUBLE, follow, haunt, hound, plague, pursue, stalk, track, trail
dogged *adjective* DETERMINED, indefatigable, obstinate, persistent, resolute, steadfast, stubborn, tenacious, unflagging, unshakable
dogma *noun* DOCTRINE, belief, credo, creed, opinion, teachings
dogmatic *adjective* OPINIONATED, arrogant, assertive, doctrinaire, emphatic, obdurate, overbearing
doldrums *noun* ▷ **the doldrums** INACTIVITY, depression, dumps (*informal*), gloom, listlessness, malaise

dol•ce [DOHL-chay] *adjective music* sweet
dol•drums [DOHL-drəmz] *plural noun* 1 state of depression, dumps 2 region of light winds and calms near the equator
dole [dohl] *noun* 1 charitable allotment, gift ▷ *verb transitive* **doled, dol•ing** 2 (usu. with *out*) deal out sparingly
dole•ful [DOHL-fəl] *adjective* dreary, mournful > **dole'ful•ly** *adverb*
doll [dol] *noun* 1 child's toy image of human being 2 (*slang*) attractive person ▷ *verb* 3 dress (up) in latest fashion or smartly
dol•lar [DOL-ər] *noun* standard monetary unit of many countries, esp. US and Canada
dol•lop [DOL-əp] *noun* (*informal*) 1 semisolid lump 2 unmeasured amount, a dash
dol•ly [DOL-ee] *noun, plural* **-lies** 1 doll 2 wheeled support for film, TV camera 3 platform on wheels for moving heavy objects 4 various metal devices used as aids in hammering, riveting
dol•men [DOHL-mən] *noun* 1 prehistoric monument 2 stone table
do•lo•mite [DOH-lə-mīt] *noun* a type of limestone
do•lor [DOH-lər] *noun* grief, sadness, distress > **dol'or•ous** [DOL-] *adjective*
dol•phin [DOL-fin] *noun* sea mammal, smaller than whale, with beaklike snout
dolt [dohlt] *noun* stupid fellow > **dolt'ish** *adjective*
do•main [doh-MAYN] *noun* 1 lands held or ruled over 2 sphere, field of influence 3 province 4 *computers* group of computers with the same name on the Internet
dome [dohm] *noun* 1 a rounded vault forming a roof 2 something of this shape
Domes•day Book [DOOMZ-day] record of survey of England in 1086
do•mes•tic [də-MES-tik] *adjective* 1 of, in the home 2 homeloving 3 (of animals) tamed, kept by man 4 of, in one's own country, not foreign ▷ *noun* 5 household servant
> **do•mes'ti•cate** [-kayt] *verb transitive* **-cat•ed, -cat•ing** 1 tame (animals) 2 accustom to home life 3 adapt to an environment
> **do•mes•tic•i•ty** [doh-me-STIS-i-tee] *noun*
dom•i•cile [DOM-ə-sīl] *noun* person's regular place of abode > **dom'i•ciled** *adjective* living
dom•i•nate [DOM-ə-nayt] *verb transitive* **-nat•ed, -nat•ing** 1 rule, control, sway 2 of heights, overlook ▷ *verb intransitive* 3 control, be the most powerful or influential member or part of something > **dom'i•nant** *adjective* > **dom•i•na'tion** *noun* > **dom•i•neer'** *verb* act imperiously, tyrannize
Do•min•i•can [də-MIN-i-kən] *noun* 1 priest or nun of the order of St. Dominic ▷ *adjective* 2 pert. to this order
do•min•ion [də-MIN-yən] *noun* 1 sovereignty, rule 2 territory of government
dom•i•noes [DOM-ə-nohz] *noun* game played with 28 oblong flat pieces marked on one side with 0 to 6 spots on each half of the face > **dom•i•no** *noun* 1 one of these pieces 2 cloak with eye mask for masquerading
don[1] *verb transitive* **donned, don•ning** put on (clothes)
don[2] *noun* 1 in English universities, fellow or tutor of college 2 Spanish title, Sir 3 in Mafia, head of a family or syndicate
do•nate [DOH-nayt] *verb transitive* **-nat•ed, -nat•ing** give > **do•na'tion** *noun* gift to fund > **do•nor** [DOH-nər] *noun* > **donor card** card specifying organs that may be used for transplant after cardholder's death
done *pp. of* **do**
don•key [DONG-kee] *noun, plural* **-keys** 1 ass 2 stupid or obstinate person > **donkey engine** auxiliary engine > **don'key•work** *noun* drudgery
donned *pt./pp. of* **don**
doo•dle [DOOD-l] *verb intransitive* **-dled, -dling** scribble absentmindedly ▷ *noun*
doom *noun* 1 fate, destiny 2 ruin 3 judicial sentence, condemnation 4 the Last Judgment

DICTIONARY **d** THESAURUS

---

dole *verb* ▷ **dole out** GIVE OUT, allocate, allot, apportion, assign, dispense, distribute, hand out
dollop *noun* LUMP, helping, portion, scoop, serving
dolt *noun* IDIOT, ass, blockhead, chump (*informal*), dope (*informal*), dork (*slang*), dunce, fool, oaf, schmuck (*slang*)
domestic *adjective* 1 HOME, family, household, private
2 HOME-LOVING, domesticated, homely, housewifely, stay-at-home
3 DOMESTICATED, house-trained, pet, tame, trained
4 NATIVE, indigenous, internal
▷ *noun* 5 SERVANT, charwoman, daily, help, maid
dominant *adjective* 1 CONTROLLING, assertive, authoritative, commanding, governing, ruling, superior, supreme
2 MAIN, chief, predominant, pre-eminent, primary, principal, prominent
dominate *verb* 1 CONTROL, direct, govern, have the whip hand over, monopolize, rule, tyrannize
2 TOWER ABOVE, loom over, overlook, stand head and shoulders above, stand over, survey
domination *noun* CONTROL, ascendancy, authority, command, influence, power, rule, superiority, supremacy
domineering *adjective* OVERBEARING, arrogant, authoritarian, bossy (*informal*), dictatorial, high-handed, imperious, oppressive, tyrannical
dominion *noun* 1 CONTROL, authority, command, jurisdiction, power, rule, sovereignty, supremacy
2 KINGDOM, country, domain, empire, realm, territory
don *verb* PUT ON, clothe oneself in, dress in, get into, pull on, slip on *or* slip into
donate *verb* GIVE, contribute, make a gift of, present, subscribe
donation *noun* CONTRIBUTION, gift, grant, hand-out, offering, present, subscription
donor *noun* GIVER, benefactor, contributor, donator, philanthropist
doom *noun* 1 DESTRUCTION, catastrophe, downfall, fate, fortune, lot, ruin
▷ *verb* 2 CONDEMN, consign, damn, destine, sentence
doomed *adjective* CONDEMNED, bewitched, cursed, fated, hopeless, ill-fated, ill-omened, luckless, star-crossed
door *noun* OPENING, doorway, entrance, entry,

▷ *verb transitive* 5 sentence, condemn 6 destine to destruction or suffering > **dooms'day** *noun* the day of the Last Judgment
door [dor] *noun* hinged or sliding barrier to close any entrance > **door'way** *noun* entrance with or without door
dope [dohp] *noun* 1 kind of varnish 2 (*slang*) drug, esp. illegal, narcotic drug 3 (*informal*) information 4 (*informal*) stupid person ▷ *verb transitive* **doped, dop•ing** 5 drug (esp. of racehorses) > **dop•ey** [DOH-pee] *adjective* **dop•i•er, dop•i•est** (*informal*) 1 foolish 2 drugged 3 half-asleep
Dop•pler effect [DOP-lər] shift in frequency of sound, light, other waves when emitting source moves closer or farther from the observer
Dor•ic [DOR-ik] *noun* 1 dialect of Dorians 2 style of Greek architecture 3 rustic dialect ▷ *adjective* > **Do•ri•an** [DOR-ee-ən] *adjective, noun* (member) of early Greek race
dork [dork] *noun* 1 (*vulgar slang*) penis 2 (*slang*) stupid or clumsy person > **dorky** [DOR-kee] *adjective* **dork•i•er, dork•i•est**
dor•mant [DOR-mənt] *adjective* 1 not active, in state of suspension 2 sleeping > **dor'man•cy** *noun*
dor•mer [DOR-mər] *noun* 1 upright window set in sloping roof 2 such a projecting structure
dor•mi•to•ry [DOR-mi-tor-ee] *noun, plural* **-ries** sleeping room with many beds **dormitory suburb** suburb whose inhabitants commute to work
dor•mouse [DOR-mows] *noun* small hibernating mouselike rodent
dor•sal [DOR-səl] *adjective* of, on back
do•ry [DOR-ee] *noun, plural* **-ries** flat-bottomed boat with high bow and flaring sides
dose [dohs] *noun* 1 amount (of drug, etc.) administered at one time 2 (*informal*) instance or period of something unpleasant, esp. disease ▷ *verb transitive* **dosed, dos•ing** 3 give doses to > **dos'age** *noun*
dos•si•er [DOS-ee-ay] *noun* set of papers on some particular subject or event
dot *noun* 1 small spot, mark ▷ *verb transitive* **dot•ted, dot•ting** 2 mark with dot(s) 3 sprinkle > **dot'ty** *adjective* **-ti•er, -ti•est** (*informal*) 1 eccentric 2 crazy 3 (with *about*) (*informal*) extremely fond of > **dot'com, dot-com** *noun* company that conducts most of its business on the Internet
dote [doht] *verb intransitive* **dot•ed, dot•ing** 1 (with *on* or *upon*) be passionately fond of 2 be silly or weak-minded > **dot'age** [-ij] *noun* senility > **do'tard** [-tərd] *noun* > **dot'ing** *adjective* blindly affectionate
dotty *see* **dot**
dou•ble [DUB-əl] *adjective* 1 of two parts, layers, etc., folded 2 twice as much or many 3 of two kinds 4 designed for two users 5 ambiguous 6 deceitful ▷ *adverb* 7 twice 8 to twice the amount or extent 9 in a pair ▷ *noun* 10 person or thing exactly like, or mistakable for, another 11 quantity twice as much as another 12 sharp turn 13 running pace ▷ *verb* **-bled, -bling** 14 make, become double 15 increase twofold 16 fold in two 17 turn sharply 18 get around, sail around > **dou'bly** *adverb* > **double agent** spy employed simultaneously by two opposing sides > **double bass** largest and lowest-toned instrument in violin form > **dou'ble-cross'** *verb* betray, swindle a colleague > **dou'ble-cross'er** *noun* > **dou'ble-deal'ing** *noun* artifice, duplicity > **double Dutch** (*slang*) incomprehensible talk, gibberish > **double dutch** form of the game of jump rope > **double glazing** two panes of glass in a window to insulate against cold, sound, etc. > **dou'ble•head'er** *noun sports* two games played consecutively on same day in same stadium > **dou'ble-quick'** *adjective, adverb* very fast > **double take** delayed reaction to a remark, situation, etc. > **dou'ble-talk** *noun, verb transitive* (engage in) intentionally garbled speech
dou•ble en•ten•dre [DUB-əl ahn-TAHN-drə] *noun, plural* **-dres** [-drəz] word or phrase with two meanings, one usu. indelicate

exit
dope *noun* 1 (*slang*) DRUG, narcotic, opiate 2 (*informal*) IDIOT, dimwit (*informal*), doofus (*slang*), dork (*slang*), dunce, dweeb (*slang*), fool, nitwit (*informal*), schmuck (*slang*) ▷ *verb* 3 DRUG, anesthetize, knock out, narcotize, sedate, stupefy
dork *noun* (*slang*), doofus (*slang*), dope (*slang*), dunce, dweeb (*slang*), fool, geek (*slang*) IDIOT, nerd
dormant *adjective* INACTIVE, asleep, hibernating, inert, inoperative, latent, sleeping, slumbering, suspended
dose *noun* QUANTITY, dosage, draft, measure, portion, potion, prescription
dot *noun* 1 SPOT, fleck, jot, mark, point, speck, speckle 2 ▷ **on the dot** ON TIME, exactly, on the button (*informal*), precisely, promptly, punctually, to the minute ▷ *verb* 3 SPOT, dab, dabble, fleck, speckle, sprinkle, stipple, stud
dotage *noun* SENILITY, decrepitude, feebleness, imbecility, old age, second childhood, weakness
dote on, dote upon *verb* ADORE, admire, hold dear, idolize, lavish affection on, prize, treasure
doting *adjective* ADORING, devoted, fond, foolish, indulgent, lovesick
double *adjective* 1 TWICE, coupled, dual, duplicate, in pairs, paired, twin, twofold ▷ *verb* 2 MULTIPLY, duplicate, enlarge, grow, increase, magnify ▷ *noun* 3 TWIN, clone, dead ringer (*slang*), Doppelgänger, duplicate, lookalike, replica, spitting image (*informal*) 4 ▷ **at the double, on the double** QUICKLY, at full speed, briskly, immediately, posthaste, without delay
double-cross *verb* BETRAY, cheat, defraud, hoodwink, mislead, swindle, trick, two-time (*informal*)
doubt *noun* 1 UNCERTAINTY, hesitancy, hesitation, indecision, irresolution, lack of conviction, suspense 2 SUSPICION, apprehension, distrust, misgiving, mistrust, qualm, skepticism ▷ *verb* 3 BE UNCERTAIN, be dubious, demur, fluctuate, hesitate, scruple, vacillate, waver 4 SUSPECT, discredit, distrust, fear, lack confidence in, mistrust, query, question

dou•blet [DUB-lit] *noun* close-fitting body garment formerly worn by men
dou•bloon [du-BLOON] *noun* ancient Spanish gold coin
doubt [dowt] *verb transitive* 1 hesitate to believe 2 call in question 3 suspect ▷ *verb intransitive* 4 be wavering or uncertain in belief or opinion ▷ *noun* 5 uncertainty, wavering in belief 6 state of affairs giving cause for uncertainty > **doubt'ful** *adjective* > **doubt'less** *adverb*
douche [doosh] *noun* 1 jet or spray of water applied to (part of) body 2 device for douching ▷ *verb transitive* **douched, douch•ing** 3 give douche to
dough [doh] *noun* 1 flour or meal kneaded with water 2 (*slang*) money > **dough'nut** *noun* sweetened and fried, usu. ring-shaped, piece of dough
dough•ty [DOW-tee] *adjective* **-ti•er, -ti•est** valiant > **dough'ti•ness** *noun* boldness
dour [duur] *adjective* grim, stubborn, severe
douse [dows] *verb transitive* **doused, dous•ing** 1 thrust into water 2 extinguish (light)
dove [duv] *noun* 1 bird of pigeon family 2 person opposed to war > **dove'cote** [-koht] *noun* house for doves > **dove'tail** *noun* 1 joint made with fan-shaped tenon ▷ *verb* 2 fit closely, neatly, firmly together
dow•a•ger [DOW-ə-jər] *noun* 1 widow with title or property derived from deceased husband 2 dignified elderly woman, esp. with wealth or social prominence
dow•dy [DOW-dee] *adjective* **-di•er, -di•est** 1 unattractively or shabbily dressed ▷ *noun* 2 woman so dressed
dow•el [DOW-əl] *noun* wooden, metal peg, esp. joining two adjacent parts
dow•er [DOW-ər] *noun* 1 widow's share for life of husband's estate ▷ *verb transitive* 2 endow > **dow'ry** *noun* 1 property wife brings to husband at marriage 2 any endowment
down¹ *adverb* 1 to, in, or toward, lower position 2 below the horizon 3 (of payment) on the spot, immediate ▷ *preposition* 4 from higher to lower part of 5 at lower part of 6 along ▷ *adjective* 7 depressed, miserable ▷ *verb transitive* 8 knock, pull, push down 9 (*informal*) drink, esp. quickly > **down'ward** *adjective, adverb* > **down'wards** *adverb* > **down'cast** *adjective* 1 dejected 2 looking down > **down'er** *noun* (*slang*) 1 barbiturate, tranquillizer, or narcotic 2 state of depression > **down'load** *verb transitive* transfer (data) from the memory of one computer to that of another ▷ *noun* data obtained in this way > **down'pour** *noun* heavy rainfall > **down'right** *adjective* 1 plain, straightforward ▷ *adverb* 2 quite, thoroughly > **down•stage** *adjective, adverb* at, to front of stage > **down'-and-out'** finished, defeated **down in the mouth** dejected, discouraged **down East** New England, esp. the state of Maine > **down under** Australia and New Zealand
down² *noun* 1 soft underfeathers, hair or fiber 2 fluff > **down'y** *adjective* **down•i•er, down•i•est**
Down syndrome genetic disorder characterized by degree of mental and physical retardation
dowry *see* **dower**
dowse [dowz] *verb* **dowsed, dows•ing** use divining rod > **dows'er** *noun* water diviner
dox•ol•o•gy [dok-SOL-ə-jee] *noun* short hymn of praise to God
doy•en [doi-EN] *noun* senior member of a body or profession > **doyenne** *noun feminine*
doze [dohz] *verb intransitive* **dozed, doz•ing** 1

DICTIONARY **d** THESAURUS

doubtful *adjective* 1 UNLIKELY, debatable, dubious, equivocal, improbable, problematic *or* problematical, questionable, unclear
2 UNSURE, distrustful, hesitating, in two minds (*informal*), skeptical, suspicious, tentative, uncertain, unconvinced, wavering
doubtless *adverb* 1 CERTAINLY, assuredly, indisputably, of course, surely, undoubtedly, unquestionably, without doubt
2 PROBABLY, apparently, most likely, ostensibly, presumably, seemingly, supposedly
dour *adjective* GLOOMY, dismal, dreary, forbidding, grim, morose, sour, sullen, unfriendly
dowdy *adjective* FRUMPY, dingy, drab, dumpy (*informal*), frowzy, homely (*United States*), shabby, unfashionable
do without *verb* MANAGE WITHOUT, abstain from, dispense with, forgo, get along without, give up, kick (*informal*)
down *adjective* 1 DEPRESSED, dejected, disheartened, downcast, low, miserable, sad, unhappy
▷ *verb* 2 (*informal*) SWALLOW, drain, drink *or* drink down, gulp, put away, toss off
▷ *noun* 3 ▷ **have a down on, be down on** (*informal*) BE ANTAGONISTIC TO *or* BE HOSTILE TO, bear a grudge towards, be prejudiced against, be set against, have it in for (*slang*)
down-and-out *noun* 1 TRAMP, bag lady, beggar, derelict, pauper, vagabond, vagrant
▷ *adjective* 2 DESTITUTE, derelict, down on one's luck (*informal*), impoverished, penniless, short, without two pennies to rub together (*informal*)
downcast *adjective* DEJECTED, crestfallen, depressed, despondent, disappointed, disconsolate, discouraged, disheartened, dismayed, dispirited
downer *noun* (*informal*) MOANER, killjoy, pessimist, prophet of doom, sourpuss (*informal*), spoilsport, wet blanket (*informal*)
downfall *noun* RUIN, collapse, destruction, disgrace, fall, overthrow, undoing
downgrade *verb* DEMOTE, degrade, humble, lower in rank *or* reduce in rank, take down a peg (*informal*)
downhearted *adjective* DEJECTED, crestfallen, depressed, despondent, discouraged, disheartened, dispirited, downcast, sad, unhappy
downpour *noun* RAINSTORM, cloudburst, deluge, flood, inundation, torrential rain
downright *adjective* COMPLETE, absolute, out-and-out, outright, plain, thoroughgoing, total, undisguised, unqualified, utter
down-to-earth *adjective* SENSIBLE, matter-of-fact, no-nonsense, plain-spoken, practical, realistic, sane, unsentimental
downtrodden *adjective* OPPRESSED, exploited, helpless, subjugated, subservient, tyrannized
downward *adjective* DESCENDING, declining, earthward, heading down, sliding, slipping

sleep drowsily, be half-asleep ▷ *noun* 2 nap
doz•en [DUZ-ən] *noun* (set of) twelve
drab *adjective* 1 dull, monotonous 2 of a dingy brown color ▷ *noun* 3 mud color 4 slut, prostitute
drach•ma [DRAK-mə] *noun, plural* **-mas** former monetary unit of Greece
Dra•co•ni•an [dray-KOH-nee-ən] *adjective* 1 like the laws of Draco 2 (**dra•co•ni•an**) very harsh, cruel
draft[1] *noun* 1 design, sketch 2 preliminary plan or layout for work to be executed 3 rough copy of document 4 order for money 5 current of air between apertures in room, etc. 6 act or action of drawing 7 act or action of drinking 8 amount drunk at once 9 inhaling 10 depth of ship in water ▷ *verb transitive* 11 make sketch, plan, or rough design of 12 make rough copy (of writing, etc.) ▷ *adjective* 13 of beer, etc., for drawing 14 drawn > **draft'y** *adjective* **draft•i•er, draft•i•est** full of air currents > **draft horse** horse for vehicles carrying heavy loads > **drafts'man** *noun, plural* **-men** one who makes drawings, plans, etc. > **drafts'man•ship** *noun*
draft[2] *verb transitive* 1 select for compulsory military service 2 select (professional athlete) by draft 3 compel (person) to serve
drag *verb transitive* **dragged, drag•ging** 1 pull along with difficulty or friction 2 trail, go heavily 3 sweep with net or grapnels 4 protract 5 *computers* move (an image) on screen by use of the mouse ▷ *verb intransitive* **dragged, drag•ging** 6 lag, trail 7 be tediously protracted ▷ *noun* 8 check on progress 9 checked motion 10 sledge, net, grapnel, rake 11 (*slang*) influence 12 (*slang*) tedious person or thing 13 (*slang*) women's clothes worn by (transvestite) man > **drag'ster** *noun* 1 automobile designed, modified for drag racing 2 driver of such a car > **drag'net** *noun* 1 fishing net to be dragged along sea floor 2 comprehensive search, esp. by police for criminal, etc. > **drag race** automobile race where cars are timed over measured distance
drag•on [DRAG-ən] *noun* 1 mythical fire-breathing monster, like winged crocodile 2 type of large lizard > **drag'on•fly** *noun, plural* **-flies** long-bodied insect with gauzy wings
dra•goon [drə-GOON] *noun* 1 formerly, cavalryman of certain regiments ▷ *verb transitive* 2 oppress 3 coerce
drain [drayn] *verb transitive* 1 draw off (liquid) by pipes, ditches, etc. 2 dry 3 drink to dregs 4 empty, exhaust ▷ *verb intransitive* 5 flow off or away 6 become rid of liquid ▷ *noun* 7 channel for removing liquid 8 sewer 9 depletion, strain > **drain'age** [-ij] *noun*
drake [drayk] *noun* male duck
dram *noun* 1 small draft of strong drink 2 unit of weight, one eighth of fluid ounce, one sixteenth of avoirdupois ounce
dra•ma [DRAH-mə] *noun* 1 stage play 2 art or literature of plays 3 playlike series of events > **dra•mat•ic** [drə-MAT-ik] *adjective* 1 pert. to drama 2 suitable for stage representation 3 with force and vividness of drama 4 striking 5 tense 6 exciting > **dram'a•tist** *noun* writer of plays > **dram•a•ti•za'tion** *noun* > **dram'a•tize** *verb transitive* **-tized, -tiz•ing** adapt story, novel for acting
dram•a•tur•gy [DRAM-ə-tur-jee] *noun* the technique of writing and producing plays > **dram'a•tur•gist** *noun* playwright
drape [drayp] *verb transitive* **draped, drap•ing** 1 cover, adorn with cloth 2 arrange in graceful folds > **dra•per•y** [DRAY-pə-ree] *noun, plural* **-per•ies** covering, curtain, etc. of cloth
dras•tic [DRAS-tik] *adjective* 1 extreme, forceful 2 severe
draw *verb transitive* **drew, drawn, draw•ing** 1 pull, pull along, haul 2 inhale 3 entice 4 delineate, portray with pencil, etc. 5 frame,

THESAURUS • DICTIONARY

doze *verb* 1 NAP, nod off (*informal*), sleep, slumber, snooze (*informal*)
▷ *noun* 2 NAP, catnap, forty winks (*informal*), shuteye (*slang*), siesta, snooze (*informal*)
drab *adjective* DULL, dingy, dismal, dreary, flat, gloomy, shabby, somber
draft[1] *noun* 1 OUTLINE, abstract, plan, rough, sketch, version
2 ORDER, bill of exchange, check, postal order
▷ *verb* 3 OUTLINE, compose, design, draw, draw up, formulate, plan, sketch
draft[2] *noun* 1 BREEZE, current, flow, movement, puff
2 DRINK, cup, dose, potion, quantity
drag *verb* 1 PULL, draw, haul, lug, tow, trail, tug
2 ▷ **drag on, drag out** LAST, draw out, extend, keep going, lengthen, persist, prolong, protract, spin out, stretch out
▷ *noun* 3 (*informal*) NUISANCE, annoyance, bore, bother, downer (*informal*), pain (*informal*), pest
dragoon *verb* FORCE, browbeat, bully, coerce, compel, constrain, drive, impel, intimidate, railroad (*informal*)
drain *noun* 1 PIPE, channel, conduit, culvert, ditch, duct, sewer, sink, trench
2 REDUCTION, depletion, drag, exhaustion, sap, strain, withdrawal
▷ *verb* 3 REMOVE, bleed, draw off, dry, empty, pump off *or* pump out, tap, withdraw
4 FLOW OUT, effuse, exude, leak, ooze, seep, trickle, well out
5 DRINK UP, finish, gulp down, quaff, swallow
6 EXHAUST, consume, deplete, dissipate, empty, sap, strain, use up
drama *noun* 1 PLAY, dramatization, show, stage show
2 THEATER, acting, dramaturgy, stagecraft
3 EXCITEMENT, crisis, histrionics, scene, spectacle, turmoil
dramatic *adjective* 1 THEATRICAL, dramaturgical, Thespian
2 POWERFUL, expressive, impressive, moving, striking, vivid
3 EXCITING, breathtaking, climactic, electrifying, melodramatic, sensational, suspenseful, tense, thrilling
dramatist *noun* PLAYWRIGHT, dramaturge, screenwriter, scriptwriter
dramatize *verb* EXAGGERATE, lay it on *or* lay it on thick (*slang*), overdo, overstate, play to the gallery
drape *verb* COVER, cloak, fold, swathe, wrap
drastic *adjective* EXTREME, desperate, dire, forceful, harsh, radical, severe, strong

compose, draft, write **6** attract **7** bring (upon, out, etc.) **8** get by lot **9** of ship, require (depth of water) **10** take from (well, barrel, etc.) **11** receive (money) **12** bend (bow) ▷ *verb intransitive* **drew, drawn, draw•ing 13** pull, shrink **14** attract **15** make, admit current of air **16** make pictures with pencil, etc. **17** finish game in tie **18** write orders for money **19** come, approach (near) ▷ *noun* **20** act of drawing **21** casting of lots **22** unfinished game, tie > **draw'er** *noun* **1** one who or that which draws **2** sliding box in table or chest > **draw'ers** undergarment for the lower body > **draw'ing** *noun* **1** art of depicting in line **2** sketch so done **3** action of verb > **draw'back** *noun* **1** anything that takes away from satisfaction **2** snag > **draw'bridge** *noun* hinged bridge to pull up > **drawing room** living room, sitting room > **draw near** approach > **draw out** lengthen > **draw up 1** arrange **2** come to a halt

drawl *verb* **1** speak slowly ▷ *noun* **2** such speech

drawn *pp. of* **draw**

dread [dred] *verb transitive* **1** fear greatly ▷ *noun* **2** awe, terror ▷ *adjective* **3** feared, awful > **dread'ful** *adjective* disagreeable, shocking or bad > **dread'locks** *plural noun* Rastafarian hair style of long matted or tightly curled strands > **dread'nought** *noun* large battleship

dream [dreem] *noun* **1** vision during sleep **2** fancy, reverie, aspiration **3** very pleasant idea, person, thing ▷ *verb intransitive* **dreamed** *or* **dreamt, dream•ing 4** have dreams ▷ *verb transitive* **dreamed** *or* **dreamt, dream•ing 5** see, imagine in dreams **6** think of as possible > **dream'y** *adjective* **dream•i•er, dream•i•est 1** given to daydreams, impractical, vague **2** (*informal*) wonderful

drear•y [DREER-ee] *adjective* **drear•i•er, drear•i•est** dismal, dull > **drear'i•ly** *adverb* > **drear'i•ness** *noun* gloom

dredge[1] [drej] *verb* **dredged, dredg•ing 1** bring up mud, etc., from sea bottom **2** deepen channel by dredge **3** search for, produce obscure, remote, unlikely material ▷ *noun* **4** form of scoop or grab > **dredg'er** *noun* ship for dredging

dredge[2] *verb transitive* sprinkle with flour, etc. > **dredg'er** *noun*

dregs [dregz] *plural noun* **1** sediment, grounds **2** worthless part

drench *verb transitive* **1** wet thoroughly, soak **2** make (an animal) take dose of medicine ▷ *noun* **3** soaking **4** dose for animal

dress *verb transitive* **1** clothe **2** array for show **3** trim, smooth, prepare surface of **4** prepare (food) for market or table **5** put dressing on (wound) **6** align (troops) ▷ *verb intransitive* **7** put on one's clothes **8** form in proper line ▷ *noun* **9** one-piece garment for woman **10** clothing **11** clothing for ceremonial evening wear > **dress'er** *noun* **1** one who dresses, esp. actors or actresses **2** chest of drawers, oft. with mirror > **dress'ing** *noun* something applied to something else, as sauce to food, ointment to wound, manure to land, etc. > **dress'y** *adjective* **dress•i•er, dress•i•est 1** stylish **2** fond of dress > **dress circle** usu. first gallery in theater > **dressing down** (*informal*) scolding > **dressing gown** coat-

DICTIONARY **d** THESAURUS

---

draw *verb* **1** SKETCH, depict, design, map out, mark out, outline, paint, portray, trace
2 PULL, drag, haul, tow, tug
3 TAKE OUT, extract, pull out
4 ATTRACT, allure, elicit, entice, evoke, induce, influence, invite, persuade
5 DEDUCE, derive, infer, make, take
▷ *noun* **6** (*informal*) ATTRACTION, enticement, lure, pull (*informal*)
7 TIE, dead heat, deadlock, gridlock, impasse, stalemate

drawback *noun* DISADVANTAGE, deficiency, difficulty, downside, flaw, handicap, hitch, snag, stumbling block

drawing *noun* PICTURE, cartoon, depiction, illustration, outline, portrayal, representation, sketch, study

drawn *adjective* TENSE, haggard, pinched, stressed, tired, worn

draw on *verb* MAKE USE OF, employ, exploit, extract, fall back on, have recourse to, rely on, take from, use

draw out *verb* EXTEND, drag out, lengthen, make longer, prolong, protract, spin out, stretch, string out

draw up *verb* **1** DRAFT, compose, formulate, frame, prepare, write out
2 HALT, bring to a stop, pull up, stop

dread *verb* **1** FEAR, cringe at, have cold feet (*informal*), quail, shrink from, shudder, tremble
▷ *noun* **2** FEAR, alarm, apprehension, dismay, fright, horror, terror, trepidation

dreadful *adjective* TERRIBLE, abysmal, appalling, atrocious, awful, fearful, frightful, hideous, horrible, shocking

dream *noun* **1** VISION, delusion, hallucination, illusion, imagination, trance
2 DAYDREAM, fantasy, pipe dream
3 AMBITION, aim, aspiration, desire, goal, hope, wish
4 DELIGHT, beauty, gem, joy, marvel, pleasure, treasure
▷ *verb* **5** HAVE DREAMS, conjure up, envisage, fancy, hallucinate, imagine, think, visualize
6 DAYDREAM, build castles in the air *or* build castles in Spain, fantasize, stargaze

dreamer *noun* IDEALIST, daydreamer, escapist, fantasist, utopian, visionary, Walter Mitty

dreamy *adjective* **1** VAGUE, absent, abstracted, daydreaming, faraway, pensive, preoccupied, with one's head in the clouds
2 IMPRACTICAL, airy-fairy, fanciful, imaginary, quixotic, speculative

dreary *adjective* DULL, boring, drab, humdrum, monotonous, tedious, tiresome, uneventful, wearisome

dregs *plural noun* **1** SEDIMENT, deposit, dross, grounds, lees, residue, residuum, scum, waste
2 SCUM, good-for-nothings, rabble, riffraff

drench *verb* SOAK, drown, flood, inundate, saturate, souse, steep, swamp, wet

dress *noun* **1** FROCK, gown, outfit, robe
2 CLOTHING, apparel, attire, clothes, costume, garb, garments, togs
▷ *verb* **3** PUT ON, attire, change, clothe, don, garb, robe, slip on *or* slip into
4 BANDAGE, bind up, plaster, treat
5 ARRANGE, adjust, align, get ready, prepare,

shaped garment worn over pyjamas or nightdress > **dressing room** room used for changing clothes, esp. backstage in a theater > **dressing table** piece of bedroom furniture with a mirror and drawers > **dress'mak•er** *noun*

dres•sage [drə-SAHZH] *noun* method of training horse in special maneuvers to show obedience

drew *pt. of* **draw**

drib•ble [DRIB-əl] *verb* **-bled, -bling** 1 flow in drops, trickle 2 run at the mouth 3 *basketball* work ball forward with short bounces 4 *soccer* work ball forward with short kicks ▷ *noun* 5 trickle, drop > **drib'let** *noun* small portion or installment

drift *verb intransitive* 1 be carried as by current of air, water 2 move aimlessly or passively ▷ *noun* 3 process of being driven by current 4 slow current or course 5 deviation from course 6 tendency 7 speaker's, writer's meaning 8 wind-heaped mass of snow, sand, etc. 9 material driven or carried by water > **drift'er** *noun* 1 one who, that which drifts 2 (*informal*) aimless person with no fixed job, etc. > **drift'wood** [-wuud] *noun* wood washed ashore by sea

drill[1] *noun* 1 boring tool or machine 2 exercise of soldiers or others in handling of arms and maneuvers 3 repeated routine in teaching ▷ *verb transitive* 4 bore, pierce hole 5 exercise in military and other routine ▷ *verb intransitive* 6 practice routine

drill[2] *noun* 1 machine for sowing seed 2 small furrow for seed 3 row of plants ▷ *verb transitive* 4 sow seed in drills or furrows

drill[3] *noun* coarsely woven twilled fabric

drink [dringk] *verb* **drank, drunk, drink•ing** 1 swallow liquid 2 absorb 3 take intoxicating liquor, esp. to excess ▷ *noun* 4 liquid for drinking 5 portion of this 6 act of drinking 7 intoxicating liquor 8 excessive use of it > **drink'a•ble** *adjective* **drink to** *or* **drink the health of** express good wishes, etc. by drinking a toast to

drip *verb* **dripped, drip•ping** 1 fall or let fall in drops ▷ *noun* 2 act of dripping 3 drop 4 *med.* intravenous administration of solution 5 (*slang*) dull, insipid person > **dripping** *noun* 1 melted fat that drips from roasting meat ▷ *adjective* 2 very wet > **drip-dry** [-drī] *adjective* (of fabric) drying free of creases if hung up while wet

drive [drīv] *verb transitive* **drove, driv•en, driv•ing** 1 urge in some direction 2 make move and steer (vehicle, animal, etc.) 3 urge, impel 4 fix by blows, as nail 5 chase 6 convey in vehicle 7 hit a ball with force as in golf, baseball ▷ *verb intransitive* **drove, driv•en, driv•ing** 8 keep machine, animal, going 9 steer it 10 be conveyed in vehicle 11 rush, dash, drift fast ▷ *noun* 12 act, action of driving 13 journey in vehicle 14 private road leading to house 15 capacity for getting things done 16 united effort, campaign 17 energy 18 forceful stroke in golf, baseball > **driv'er** *noun* 1 one that drives 2 golf club > **drive time** time in the morning or evening when people drive to and from work

driv•el [DRIV-əl] *verb intransitive* 1 run at the mouth or nose 2 talk nonsense ▷ *noun* 3 silly nonsense

driz•zle [DRIZ-əl] *verb intransitive* **-zled, -zling** 1 rain in fine drops ▷ *noun* 2 fine, light rain

drogue [drohg] *noun* 1 any funnel-like device, esp. of canvas, used as sea anchor 2 small parachute 3 wind indicator 4 windsock towed behind target aircraft 5 funnel-shaped device on end of refueling hose of tanker aircraft to receive probe of aircraft being refueled

droll [drohl] *adjective* **-er, -est** funny, odd,

DICTIONARY • THESAURUS

straighten

dressmaker *noun* SEAMSTRESS, couturier, tailor

dribble *verb* 1 RUN, drip, drop, fall in drops, leak, ooze, seep, trickle
2 DROOL, drivel, slaver, slobber

drift *verb* 1 FLOAT, be carried along, coast, go *or* go aimlessly, meander, stray, waft, wander
2 PILE UP, accumulate, amass, bank up, drive, gather
▷ *noun* 3 PILE, accumulation, bank, heap, mass, mound
4 MEANING, direction, gist, import, intention, purport, significance, tendency, thrust

drifter *noun* WANDERER, beachcomber, bum (*informal*), hobo, itinerant, rolling stone, vagrant

drill *noun* 1 BORING TOOL, bit, borer, gimlet
2 TRAINING, discipline, exercise, instruction, practice, preparation, repetition
▷ *verb* 3 BORE, penetrate, perforate, pierce, puncture, sink in
4 TRAIN, coach, discipline, exercise, instruct, practice, rehearse, teach

drink *verb* 1 SWALLOW, gulp, guzzle, imbibe, quaff, sip, suck, sup
2 BOOZE (*informal*), hit the bottle (*informal*), tipple, tope
▷ *noun* 3 BEVERAGE, liquid, potion, refreshment
4 ALCOHOL, booze (*informal*), hooch *or* hootch, liquor, spirits, the bottle (*informal*)
5 GLASS, cup, draft

drip *verb* 1 DROP, dribble, exude, plop, splash, sprinkle, trickle
▷ *noun* 2 DROP, dribble, leak, trickle
3 (*informal*) WEAKLING, mama's boy (*informal*)

drive *verb* 1 OPERATE, direct, guide, handle, manage, motor, ride, steer, travel
2 GOAD, coerce, constrain, force, press, prod, prompt, spur
3 PUSH, herd, hurl, impel, propel, send, urge
4 PUSH, hammer, ram, thrust
▷ *noun* 5 RUN, excursion, jaunt, journey, outing, ride, spin (*informal*), trip
6 CAMPAIGN, action, appeal, crusade, effort, push (*informal*)
7 INITIATIVE, ambition, energy, enterprise, get-up-and-go (*informal*), motivation, vigor, zip (*informal*)

drivel *noun* 1 NONSENSE, garbage (*informal*), gibberish, hogwash, hot air (*informal*), poppycock (*informal*), rubbish, trash
▷ *verb* 2 BABBLE, blether, gab (*informal*), prate, ramble

driving *adjective* FORCEFUL, compelling, dynamic, energetic, sweeping, vigorous, violent

drizzle *noun* 1 FINE RAIN, mist
▷ *verb* 2 RAIN, shower, spot with rain *or* spit with rain, spray, sprinkle

droll *adjective* AMUSING, comical, entertaining,

comical > **droll'ness** *noun* > **drol'ly** *adverb*
drone [drohn] *noun* 1 male of honey bee 2 lazy idler 3 deep humming 4 bass pipe of bagpipe 5 its note ▷ *verb* **droned, dron•ing** 6 hum 7 talk in monotonous tone
drool *verb intransitive* to slaver, drivel
droop *verb intransitive* 1 hang down 2 wilt, flag ▷ *verb transitive* 3 let hang down ▷ *noun* 4 drooping condition > **droop'y** *adjective* **droop•i•er, droop•i•est**
drop *noun* 1 globule of liquid 2 very small quantity 3 fall, descent 4 distance through which thing falls 5 thing that falls, as gallows platform ▷ *verb transitive* **dropped, drop•ping** 6 let fall 7 let fall in drops 8 utter casually 9 set down, unload 10 discontinue ▷ *verb intransitive* **dropped, drop•ping** 11 fall 12 fall in drops 13 lapse 14 come or go casually > **drop'let** *noun* > **drop'pings** *plural noun* dung of birds, rabbits, etc. > **drop'out** *noun* person who fails to complete course of study or one who rejects conventional society
dross [draws] *noun* 1 scum of molten metal 2 impurity, refuse 3 anything of little or no value
drought [drowt] *noun* long spell of dry weather
drove[1] [drohv] *pt. of* **drive**
drove[2] *noun* herd, flock, crowd, esp. in motion > **drov'er** *noun* driver of cattle
drown *verb* 1 die or be killed by immersion in liquid 2 get rid of as by submerging in liquid 3 make sound inaudible by louder sound
drow•sy [DROW-zee] *adjective* **-si•er, -si•est** 1 half-asleep 2 lulling 3 dull > **drowse** *verb intransitive* > **drow'si•ly** *adverb* > **drow'si•ness** *noun*
drub *verb transitive* **drubbed, drub•bing** thrash, beat > **drubbing** *noun* beating
drudge [druj] *verb intransitive* 1 work at menial or distasteful tasks, slave ▷ *noun* 2 one who drudges, hack > **drudg'er•y** *noun, plural* **-er•ies**
drug *noun* 1 medical substance 2 narcotic 3 merchandise that is unsalable because of overproduction ▷ *verb transitive* **drugged, drug•ging** 4 mix drugs with 5 administer drug to, esp. one inducing unconsciousness > **drug'store** *noun* pharmacy where wide variety of goods is available > **drug•gist** *noun*
dru•id [DROO-id] *noun* (**Dru•id**) member of ancient order of Celtic priests
drum *noun* 1 percussion instrument of skin stretched over round hollow frame, played by beating with sticks 2 various things shaped like drum 3 part of ear ▷ *verb* **drummed, drum•ming** 4 play drum 5 tap, thump continuously > **drum'mer** *noun* 1 one who plays drum 2 traveling salesman > **drum'head** *noun* part of drum that is struck > **drumhead court-martial** summary one held at war front > **drum major** leader of military band > **drum'stick** *noun* 1 stick for beating drum 2 lower joint of cooked fowl's leg > **drum out** expel from military service, etc.
drunk [drungk] *adjective* **-er, -est** 1 overcome by strong drink 2 under influence of strong emotion > **drunk'ard** [-ərd] *noun* one given to excessive drinking > **drunk'en** *adjective* 1 drunk 2 caused by, showing intoxication

DICTIONARY

d

THESAURUS

funny, humorous, jocular, waggish, whimsical
drone[1] *verb* 1 HUM, buzz, purr, thrum, vibrate, whirr
2 ▷ **drone on** SPEAK MONOTONOUSLY, be boring, chant, intone, spout, talk interminably
▷ *noun* 3 HUM, buzz, murmuring, purr, thrum, vibration, whirring
drool *verb* 1 DRIBBLE, drivel, salivate, slaver, slobber, water at the mouth
2 ▷ **drool over** GLOAT OVER, dote on, gush, make much of, rave about (*informal*)
droop *verb* SAG, bend, dangle, drop, fall down, hang *or* hang down, sink
drop *verb* 1 FALL, decline, descend, diminish, plummet, plunge, sink, tumble
2 DRIP, dribble, fall in drops, trickle
3 DISCONTINUE, ax (*informal*), give up, kick (*informal*), quit, relinquish
▷ *noun* 4 DROPLET, bead, bubble, drip, globule, pearl, tear
5 DASH, mouthful, shot (*informal*), sip, spot, swig (*informal*), trace, trickle
6 DECREASE, cut, decline, deterioration, downturn, fall-off, lowering, reduction, slump
7 FALL, descent, plunge
drop off *verb* 1 SET DOWN, deliver, leave, let off
2 (*informal*) FALL ASLEEP, doze *or* doze off, have forty winks (*informal*), nod *or* nod off, snooze (*informal*)
3 DECREASE, decline, diminish, dwindle, fall off, lessen, slacken
drop out *verb* LEAVE, abandon, fall by the wayside, give up, quit, stop, withdraw
drought *noun* DRY SPELL, aridity, dehydration, dryness
drove *noun* HERD, collection, company, crowd, flock, horde, mob, multitude, swarm, throng
drown *verb* 1 DRENCH, deluge, engulf, flood, go under, immerse, inundate, sink, submerge, swamp
2 OVERPOWER, deaden, muffle, obliterate, overcome, overwhelm, stifle, swallow up, wipe out
drowsy *adjective* SLEEPY, dopey (*slang*), dozy, half asleep, heavy, lethargic, somnolent, tired, torpid
drudge *noun* MENIAL, factotum, servant, slave, toiler, worker
drudgery *noun* MENIAL LABOR, donkey-work, grind (*informal*), hard work, labor, slog, toil
drug *noun* 1 MEDICATION, medicament, medicine, physic, poison, remedy
2 DOPE (*slang*), narcotic, opiate, stimulant
▷ *verb* 3 DOSE, administer a drug, dope (*slang*), medicate, treat
4 KNOCK OUT, anesthetize, deaden, numb, poison, stupefy
drum *verb* 1 BEAT, pulsate, rap, reverberate, tap, tattoo, throb
2 ▷ **drum into** DRIVE HOME, din into, hammer away, harp on, instill into, reiterate
drunk *adjective* 1 INTOXICATED, drunken, inebriated, plastered (*slang*), tipsy, under the influence (*informal*)
▷ *noun* 2 DRUNKARD, alcoholic, boozer (*informal*), inebriate, lush (*slang*), wino (*informal*)
drunkard *noun* DRINKER, alcoholic, dipsomaniac, drunk, lush (*slang*), tippler, wino (*informal*)

> **drunk'en•ness** *noun*

dry [drī] *adjective* **dri•er, dri•est** 1 without moisture 2 rainless 3 not yielding milk, or other liquid 4 cold, unfriendly 5 caustically witty 6 having prohibition of alcoholic drink 7 uninteresting 8 needing effort to study 9 lacking sweetness (as wines) ▷ *verb* **dried, dry•ing** 10 remove water, moisture 11 become dry 12 evaporate > **dri'ly** *adverb* > **dry'ness** *noun* > **dry'er** *noun* 1 person or thing that dries 2 apparatus for removing moisture > **dry battery** electric battery without liquid > **dry'-clean** *verb* clean clothes with solvent other than water > **dry'-clean•er** *noun* > **dry ice** solid carbon dioxide > **dry'point** 1 needle for engraving without acid 2 engraving so made > **dry rot** fungoid decay in wood > **dry run** practice, rehearsal in simulated conditions

dry•ad [DRĪ-əd] *noun* wood nymph

du•al [DOO-əl] *adjective* 1 twofold 2 of two, double, forming pair > **du'al•ism** *noun* recognition of two independent powers or principles, e.g. good and evil, mind and matter > **du•al'i•ty** *noun*

dub *verb transitive* **dubbed, dub•bing** 1 give title to 2 confer knighthood on 3 provide film with soundtrack not in original language 4 smear with grease, dubbin > **dub'bin, dub'bing** *noun* grease for making leather supple

du•bi•ous [DOO-bee-əs] *adjective* 1 causing doubt, not clear or decided 2 of suspect character > **du•bi'e•ty** [-BĪ-i-tee] *noun, plural* **-ties** uncertainty, doubt

du•cal [DOO-kəl] *adjective* of, like a duke

duch•ess [DUCH-is] *noun* duke's wife or widow

duch•y [DUCH-ee] *noun, plural* **duch•ies** territory of duke, dukedom

duck[1] [duk] *noun* 1 common swimming bird ▷ *verb* 2 plunge (someone) under water 3 bob down > **duck'ling** *noun* > **duck'billed platypus** *see* **platypus**

duck[2] *noun* strong linen or cotton fabric > **ducks** trousers of it

duct [dukt] *noun* channel, tube > **duc•tile** [DUK-tl] *adjective* 1 capable of being drawn into wire 2 flexible and tough 3 easily led > **duc•til'i•ty** *noun* > **duct'less** *adjective* (of glands) secreting directly certain substances essential to health

dud *noun* 1 futile, worthless person or thing 2 shell that fails to explode ▷ *adjective* 3 worthless

dude [dood] *noun* 1 city man, esp. Easterner in the West 2 (*slang*) fellow > **dude ranch** ranch operating as vacation resort

dudg•eon [DUJ-ən] *noun* anger, indignation, resentment

duds [dudz] *plural noun* (*informal*) clothes

due [doo] *adjective* 1 owing 2 proper to be given, inflicted, etc. 3 adequate, fitting 4 under engagement to arrive, be present 5 timed for ▷ *adverb* (with points of compass) exactly ▷ *noun* 6 person's right 7 (*usually plural*) charge, fee, etc. > **du'ly** *adverb* 1 properly 2 fitly 3 rightly 4 punctually **due to** 1 attributable to 2 caused by

du•el [DOO-əl] *noun* 1 arranged fight with deadly weapons, between two persons 2 keen two-sided contest ▷ *verb intransitive* **-eled, -el•ing** 3 fight in duel > **du'el•ist** *noun*

du•en•na [doo-EN-ə] *noun* in Spain or Portugal, elderly governess, guardian, chaperone

du•et [doo-ET] *noun* piece of music for two performers

duff *noun* (*slang*) buttocks

duf•fel [DUF-əl] *noun* 1 coarse woolen cloth 2 coat of this

duff•er [DUF-ər] *noun* (*informal*) 1 stupid inefficient person 2 inept golfer

dug[1] *pt./pp. of* **dig**

dug[2] *noun* udder, teat of animal

dug•out [DUG-owt] *noun* 1 covered excavation to provide shelter for troops, etc. 2 canoe of hollowed-out tree 3 *baseball* roofed structure with bench for players when not on the field

duke [dook] *noun* 1 in Great Britain, peer of rank next below prince 2 ruler of duchy > **duch'ess** *noun feminine* > **duke'dom** [-dəm] *noun*

dukes [dooks] *plural noun* (*slang*) fists

DICTIONARY • THESAURUS

---

drunkenness *noun* INTOXICATION, alcoholism, bibulousness, dipsomania, inebriation, insobriety, intemperance

dry *adjective* 1 DEHYDRATED, arid, barren, desiccated, dried up, parched, thirsty
2 DULL, boring, dreary, monotonous, plain, tedious, tiresome, uninteresting
3 SARCASTIC, deadpan, droll, low-key, sly
▷ *verb* 4 DEHYDRATE, dehumidify, desiccate, drain, make dry, parch, sear

dry out, dry up *verb* BECOME DRY, harden, shrivel up, wilt, wither, wizen

dual *adjective* TWOFOLD, binary, double, duplex, duplicate, matched, paired, twin

dubious *adjective* 1 SUSPECT, fishy (*informal*), questionable, suspicious, unreliable, untrustworthy
2 UNSURE, doubtful, hesitant, skeptical, uncertain, unconvinced, undecided, wavering

duck *verb* 1 BOB, bend, bow, crouch, dodge, drop, lower, stoop
2 PLUNGE, dip, dive, douse, dunk, immerse, souse, submerge, wet
3 (*informal*) DODGE, avoid, escape, evade, shirk, shun, sidestep

dud (*informal*) *noun* 1 FAILURE, flop (*informal*), washout (*informal*)
▷ *adjective* 2 USELESS, broken, failed, inoperative, worthless

dudgeon *noun* ▷ **in high dudgeon** INDIGNANT, angry, choked, fuming, offended, resentful, ticked off (*informal*), vexed

due *adjective* 1 EXPECTED, scheduled
2 PAYABLE, in arrears, outstanding, owed, owing, unpaid
3 FITTING, appropriate, deserved, justified, merited, proper, rightful, suitable, well-earned
▷ *noun* 4 RIGHT *or* RIGHTS, deserts, merits, privilege
▷ *adverb* 5 DIRECTLY, dead, exactly, straight, undeviatingly

duel *noun* 1 SINGLE COMBAT, affair of honor
2 CONTEST, clash, competition, encounter, engagement, fight, head-to-head, rivalry
▷ *verb* 3 FIGHT, clash, compete, contend, contest, lock horns, rival, struggle, vie with

dues *plural noun* MEMBERSHIP FEE, charge, charges, contribution, fee, levy

dul•cet [DUL-sit] *adjective* (of sounds) sweet, melodious

dul•ci•mer [DUL-sə-mər] *noun* stringed instrument played with light hammers, ancestor of piano

dull *adjective* **-er, -est** 1 stupid 2 insensible 3 sluggish 4 tedious 5 lacking liveliness or variety 6 gloomy, overcast ▷ *verb* 7 make or become dull > **dull'ard** [-ərd] *noun*

duly *see* **due**

dumb [dum] *adjective* **-er, -est** 1 incapable of speech 2 silent 3 (*informal*) stupid > **dumb'ly** *adverb* > **dumb'ness** *noun* > **dumb'bell** *noun* 1 weight for exercises 2 dolt > **dumb•found'** *verb transitive* confound into silence

dumb down *verb transitive* make less intellectually demanding or sophisticated > **dumb show** gestures without speech

dum'dum *noun* soft-nosed bullet that expands on impact

dum•my [DUM-ee] *noun, plural* **-mies** 1 tailor's, dressmaker's model 2 imitation object 3 *cards* hand exposed on table and played by partner ▷ *adjective* 4 sham, bogus **dummy up** (*informal*) to keep silent

dump *verb transitive* 1 throw down in mass 2 deposit 3 unload 4 send (low-priced goods) for sale abroad ▷ *noun* 5 place where garbage is dumped 6 (*informal*) dirty, unpleasant place 7 temporary depot of stores or munitions > **dumps** low spirits, dejection > **dump'ling** *noun* 1 small round mass of boiled or steamed dough 2 dessert of fruit wrapped in dough and baked > **dump truck** truck for hauling and dumping sand, stone, etc. > **dump'y** *adjective* **dump•i•er, dump•i•est** short, stout

dun[1] *verb transitive* **dunned, dun•ning** 1 persistently demand payment of debts ▷ *noun* 2 one who duns 3 urgent request for payment

dun[2] *adjective* 1 of dull grayish brown ▷ *noun* 2 this color 3 dun horse

dunce [duns] *noun* slow learner, stupid pupil

dune [doon] *noun* sandhill on coast or desert

dung *noun* 1 excrement of animals 2 manure ▷ *verb transitive* 3 fertilize or spread with manure

dun•ga•ree [dung-gə-REE] *noun* blue denim > **dun•ga•rees** work clothes, etc. of this material

dun•geon [DUN-jən] *noun* 1 underground cell or vault for prisoners 2 formerly, tower or keep of castle

dunk [dungk] *verb transitive* 1 dip bread, etc. in liquid before eating it 2 submerge > **dunk shot** *basketball* shot made by jumping high to thrust ball through basket

dun•nage [DUN-ij] *noun* padding, loose material for packing cargo

du•o [DOO-oh] *noun, plural* **du•os** pair of performers, etc.

du•o•dec•i•mal [doo-ə-DES-ə-məl] *adjective* 1 computed by twelves 2 twelfth

du•o•dec•i•mo [doo-ə-DES-ə-moh] *noun, plural* **-mos** 1 size of book in which each sheet is folded into 12 leaves before cutting 2 book of this size ▷ *adjective* 3 of this size

du•o•de•num [doo-ə-DEE-nəm] *noun* upper part of small intestine > **du•o•de'nal** *adjective*

dupe [doop] *noun* 1 victim of delusion or sharp practice ▷ *verb transitive* **duped, dup•ing** 2 deceive for advantage, impose upon

du•plex [DOO-pleks] *adjective* 1 twofold ▷ *noun* 2 apartment with rooms on two floors 3 two-family house

du•pli•cate [DOO-pli-kayt] *verb transitive* **-cat•ed, -cat•ing** 1 make exact copy of 2 double ▷ *adjective* [-kit] 3 double 4 exactly the same as something else ▷ *noun* 5 exact copy > **du'pli•ca•tor** *noun* machine for making copies (of typewritten matter, etc.) > **du•plic'i•ty** [-PLIS-i-tee] *noun, plural* **-ties** deceitfulness, double-dealing, bad faith

dull *adjective* 1 BORING, dreary, dumpy (*informal*), flat, frowzy, homely (*United States*), humdrum, monotonous, plain, tedious, uninteresting
2 STUPID, dense, dim-witted (*informal*), slow, thick, unintelligent
3 CLOUDY, dim, dismal, gloomy, leaden, overcast
4 LIFELESS, apathetic, blank, indifferent, listless, passionless, unresponsive
5 BLUNT, blunted, unsharpened
▷ *verb* 6 RELIEVE, allay, alleviate, blunt, lessen, moderate, soften, take the edge off

duly *adverb* 1 PROPERLY, accordingly, appropriately, befittingly, correctly, decorously, deservedly, fittingly, rightfully, suitably
2 ON TIME, at the proper time, punctually

dumb *adjective* 1 MUTE, mum, silent, soundless, speechless, tongue-tied, voiceless, wordless
2 (*informal*) STUPID, asinine, dense, dim-witted (*informal*), dull, foolish, thick, unintelligent

dumbfounded *adjective* AMAZED, astonished, astounded, flabbergasted (*informal*), lost for words, nonplussed, overwhelmed, speechless, staggered, stunned

dummy *noun* 1 MODEL, figure, form, manikin, mannequin
2 COPY, counterfeit, duplicate, imitation, sham, substitute
3 (*slang*) FOOL, blockhead, dork (*slang*), dunce, idiot, nitwit (*informal*), oaf, schmuck (*slang*), simpleton
▷ *adjective* 4 IMITATION, artificial, bogus, fake, false, mock, phoney *or* phony (*informal*), sham, simulated

dump *verb* 1 DROP, deposit, fling down, let fall, throw down
2 GET RID OF, dispose of, ditch (*slang*), empty out, jettison, scrap, throw away *or* throw out, tip, unload
▷ *noun* 3 RUBBISH TIP, junkyard, refuse heap, rubbish heap, tip
4 (*informal*) PIGSTY, hovel, mess, slum

dumpy *adjective* (*informal*) DOWDY, frowzy, frumpy, homely (*United States*), unfashionable

dunce *noun* SIMPLETON, blockhead, dunderhead, ignoramus, moron (*offensive*), thickhead

dungeon *noun* PRISON, cage, cell, oubliette, vault

duplicate *adjective* 1 IDENTICAL, corresponding, matched, matching, twin, twofold
▷ *noun* 2 COPY, carbon copy, clone, double, facsimile, photocopy, replica, reproduction
▷ *verb* 3 COPY, clone, double, repeat, replicate, reproduce

du•ra•ble [DUUR-ə-bəl] *adjective* lasting, resisting wear > **du•ra•bil'i•ty** *noun*
du•ra•tion [duu-RAY-shən] *noun* time thing lasts
du•ress [duu-RES] *noun* compulsion by use of force or threats
dur•ing [DUUR-ing] *preposition* throughout, in the time of, in the course of
dusk *noun* 1 darker stage of twilight 2 partial darkness > **dusk'y** *adjective* **dusk•i•er, dusk•i•est** 1 dark 2 dark-colored
dust *noun* 1 fine particles, powder of earth or other matter, lying on surface or blown along by wind 2 ashes of the dead ▷ *verb transitive* 3 sprinkle with powder, fertilizer, etc. 4 rid of dust > **dust'er** *noun* 1 cloth for removing dust 2 housecoat > **dust'y** *adjective* **dust•i•er, dust•i•est** covered with dust > **dust'bowl** [-bohl] *noun* area in which dust storms have carried away the top soil
Dutch [duch] *adjective* pert. to the Netherlands, its inhabitants, its language > **Dutch courage** drunken bravado > **Dutch treat** one where each person pays own share
du•ty [DOO-tee] *noun, plural* **-ties** 1 moral or legal obligation 2 that which is due 3 tax on goods 4 military service 5 one's proper employment > **du'te•ous** *adjective* > **du'ti•a•ble** *adjective* liable to customs duty > **du•ti•ful** *adjective*
du•vet [doo-VAY] *noun* quilt filled with down or artificial fiber
DVD Digital Versatile *or* Video Disk
dwarf [dworf] *noun, plural* **dwarfs** *or* **dwarves** [dworvz] 1 very undersized person 2 mythological, small, manlike creature ▷ *adjective* 3 unusually small, stunted ▷ *verb transitive* 4 make seem small by contrast 5 make stunted
dwell *verb intransitive* **dwelt** *or* **dwelled, dwell•ing** 1 live, make one's abode (in) 2 fix one's attention, write or speak at length (on) > **dweller** *noun* > **dwell'ing** *noun* house
dwin•dle [DWIN-dl] *verb intransitive* **-dled, -dling** grow less, waste away, decline
Dy *chem.* dysprosium
dye [dī] *verb transitive* **dyed, dye•ing** 1 impregnate (cloth, etc.) with coloring matter 2 color thus ▷ *noun* 3 coloring matter in solution or that can be dissolved for dyeing 4 tinge, color > **dy'er** *noun*
dyke[1] [dīk] *noun* wall built to prevent flooding
dyke[2] *noun* (*slang, often offensive*) lesbian
dy•nam•ics [dī-NAM-iks] *noun* 1 branch of physics dealing with force as producing or affecting motion ▷ *plural noun* 2 forces that produce change in a system > **dy•nam'ic** *adjective* 1 of, relating to motive force, force in operation 2 energetic and forceful > **dy•nam'i•cal•ly** *adverb*
dy•na•mite [DĪ-nə-mīt] *noun* 1 high explosive mixture ▷ *verb transitive* **-mit•ed, -mit•ing** 2 blow up with this ▷ *adjective* 3 (*informal*) topnotch
dy•na•mo [DĪ-nə-moh] *noun, plural* **-mos** machine to convert mechanical into electrical energy, generator of electricity > **dy•na•mom'e•ter** *noun* instrument to measure energy expended
dy•nas•ty [DĪ-nə-stee] *noun, plural* **-ties** line, family, succession of hereditary rulers > **dy'nast** *noun* ruler > **dy•nas'tic** *adjective* of dynasty
dyne [dīn] *noun* cgs unit of force
dys•en•ter•y [DIS-ən-ter-ee] *noun* infection of intestine causing severe diarrhea
dys•func•tion [dis-FUNGK-shən] *noun* abnormal, impaired functioning, esp. of bodily organ
dys•lex•ia [dis-LEK-see-ə] *noun* impaired ability to read, caused by condition of the brain

---

durability *noun* DURABLENESS, constancy, endurance, imperishability, permanence, persistence
durable *adjective* LONG-LASTING, dependable, enduring, hard-wearing, persistent, reliable, resistant, strong, sturdy, tough
duration *noun* LENGTH, extent, period, span, spell, stretch, term, time
duress *noun* PRESSURE, coercion, compulsion, constraint, threat
dusk *noun* TWILIGHT, dark, evening, eventide, gloaming (*Scottish poetic*), nightfall, sundown, sunset
dusky *adjective* 1 DARK, dark-complexioned, sable, swarthy
2 DIM, cloudy, gloomy, murky, obscure, shadowy, shady, tenebrous, twilit
dust *noun* 1 GRIME, grit, particles, powder
▷ *verb* 2 SPRINKLE, cover, dredge, powder, scatter, sift, spray, spread
dusty *adjective* DIRTY, grubby, scuzzy (*slang*), sooty, unclean, unswept
dutiful *adjective* CONSCIENTIOUS, devoted, obedient, respectful, reverential, submissive
duty *noun* 1 RESPONSIBILITY, assignment, function, job, obligation, role, task, work
2 LOYALTY, allegiance, deference, obedience, respect, reverence
3 TAX, excise, levy, tariff, toll
4 ▷ **on duty** AT WORK, busy, engaged, on active service
dwarf *verb* 1 TOWER ABOVE *or* TOWER OVER, diminish, dominate, overshadow
▷ *adjective* 2 MINIATURE, baby, bonsai, diminutive, small, tiny, undersized
▷ *noun* 3 MIDGET, Lilliputian, pygmy *or* pigmy, Tom Thumb
dweeb *noun* (*slang*) DOOFUS (*slang*), dope (*slang*), dunce, fool, geek (*slang*), idiot, nerd
dwell *verb* LIVE, abide, inhabit, lodge, reside
dwelling *noun* HOME, abode, domicile, habitation, house, lodging, pad (*slang*), quarters, residence
dwindle *verb* LESSEN, decline, decrease, die away, diminish, fade, peter out, shrink, subside, taper off, wane
dye *noun* 1 COLOR, colorant, coloring, pigment, stain, tinge, tint
▷ *verb* 2 COLOR, pigment, stain, tinge, tint
dying *adjective* EXPIRING, at death's door, failing, in extremis (*Latin*), moribund, not long for this world
dynamic *adjective* ENERGETIC, forceful, go-ahead, go-getting (*informal*), high-powered, lively, powerful, vital
dynasty *noun* EMPIRE, government, house,

> **dys•lex'ic** *adjective, noun*

dys•pep•sia [dis-PEP-see-ə] *noun* indigestion

> **dys•pep'tic** *adjective, noun*

dys•tro•phy [DIS-trə-fee] *noun* wasting of body tissues, esp. muscles

regime, rule, sovereignty

Ee

e- *prefix* electronic: *e-mail; e-tail*
each [eech] *adjective, pronoun* every one taken separately
ea•ger [EE-gər] *adjective* 1 having a strong wish (for something) 2 keen, impatient > **ea'ger•ness** *noun*
ea•gle [EE-gəl] *noun* 1 large bird with keen sight that preys on small birds and animals 2 *golf* score of two strokes under par for a hole > **ea•glet** [EE-glit] *noun* young eagle
ear[1] [eer] *noun* 1 organ of hearing, esp. external part of it 2 sense of hearing 3 sensitiveness to sounds 4 attention > **ear'ache** *noun* acute pain in ear > **ear'mark** *verb transitive* assign, reserve for definite purpose > **ear'phone** *noun* receiver for radio, etc. held to or put in ear > **ear'ring** *noun* ornament for lobe of the ear > **ear'shot** *noun* hearing distance
ear[2] *noun* spike, head of corn
earl [url] *noun* British nobleman ranking next below marquis
ear•ly [UR-lee] *adjective, adverb* **-li•er, -li•est** 1 before expected or usual time 2 in first part, near or nearer beginning of some portion of time
earn [urn] *verb transitive* 1 obtain by work or merit 2 gain > **earn'ings** *plural noun*
ear•nest[1] [UR-nist] *adjective* serious, ardent, sincere **in earnest** serious, determined
earnest[2] *noun* 1 money paid over in token to bind bargain, pledge 2 token, foretaste
earth [urth] *noun* 1 (**Earth**) planet or world we

DICTIONARY • THESAURUS

each *adjective* 1 EVERY
▷ *pronoun* 2 EVERY ONE, each and every one, each one, one and all
▷ *adverb* 3 APIECE, for each, individually, per capita, per head, per person, respectively, to each
eager *adjective* KEEN, agog, anxious, athirst, avid, enthusiastic, fervent, gung ho (*slang*), hungry, impatient, longing
eagerness *noun* KEENNESS, ardor, enthusiasm, fervor, hunger, impatience, thirst, yearning, zeal
ear *noun* SENSITIVITY, appreciation, discrimination, perception, taste
early *adjective* 1 PREMATURE, advanced, forward, untimely
2 PRIMITIVE, primeval, primordial, undeveloped, young
▷ *adverb* 3 TOO SOON, ahead of time, beforehand, in advance, in good time, prematurely
earmark *verb* SET ASIDE, allocate, designate, flag, label, mark out, reserve
earn *verb* 1 MAKE, bring in, collect, gain, get, gross, net, receive
2 DESERVE, acquire, attain, be entitled to, be worthy of, merit, rate, warrant, win
earnest *adjective* 1 SERIOUS, grave, intent, resolute, resolved, sincere, solemn, thoughtful
▷ *noun* 2 ▷ **in earnest** SERIOUSLY, sincerely, truthfully
earnings *plural noun* INCOME, pay, proceeds, profits, receipts, remuneration, salary, takings, wages
earth *noun* 1 WORLD, globe, orb, planet, sphere
2 SOIL, clay, dirt, ground, land, turf

live on **2** ground, dry land **3** mold, soil, mineral > **earth'en** *adjective* made of clay or earth > **earth'ly** *adjective* possible, feasible > **earth'y** *adjective* **earth•i•er, earth•i•est 1** of earth **2** uninhibited **3** vulgar > **earth'en•ware** *noun* (vessels of) baked clay > **earth'quake** *noun* convulsion of Earth's surface

ease [eez] *noun* **1** comfort **2** freedom from constraint, annoyance, awkwardness, pain or trouble **3** idleness ▷ *verb* **eased, eas•ing 4** reduce burden **5** give bodily or mental ease to **6** slacken **7** (cause to) move carefully or gradually **8** relieve of pain > **ease'ment** *noun law* right of way, etc., over another's land > **eas'i•ly** *adverb* > **eas'y** *adjective* **eas•i•er, eas•i•est 1** not difficult **2** free from pain, care, constraint or anxiety **3** compliant **4** characterized by low demand **5** fitting loosely **6** (*informal*) having no preference for any particular course of action > **easy-going** *adjective* **1** not fussy **2** indolent

ea•sel [EE-zəl] *noun* frame to support picture, etc.

east [eest] *noun* **1** part of horizon where sun rises **2** (**East**) eastern lands, Orient ▷ *adjective* **3** on, in, or near, east **4** coming from east ▷ *adverb* **5** from, or to, east > **east'er•ly** *adjective, adverb* from, or to, east > **east'ern** *adjective* of, dwelling in, east > **east'ern•er** *noun* > **east'ward** *adjective, adverb, noun* > **east'ward, east'wards** *adverb*

Eas•ter [EE-stər] *noun* annual festival of the resurrection of Christ

easy *see* **ease**

eat [eet] *verb* **ate, eat•en, eat•ing 1** chew and swallow **2** consume, destroy **3** gnaw **4** wear away

eaves [eevz] *plural noun* overhanging edges of roof > **eaves'drop** *verb* **-dropped, -drop•ping** listen secretly > **eaves'drop•per** *noun*

ebb *verb intransitive* **1** flow back **2** decay ▷ *noun* **3** flowing back of tide **4** decline, decay **at a low ebb** in a state of weakness

eb•on•y [EB-ə-nee] *noun* **-on•ies 1** hard black wood ▷ *adjective* **2** made of, black as ebony

e-book [EE-buuk] *noun* **1** book in the form of a file that can be downloaded to a computer via the Internet ▷ *verb transitive* **2** book (tickets, etc.) through the Internet

e•bul•lient [i-BUUL-yənt] *adjective* **1** exuberant **2** boiling > **e•bul'lience** *noun* > **eb•ul•li•tion** [eb-ə-LISH-ən] *noun* **1** boiling **2** effervescence **3** outburst

ec•cen•tric [ik-SEN-trik] *adjective* **1** odd, unconventional **2** irregular **3** not placed, or not having axis placed, centrally **4** not circular (in orbit) ▷ *noun* **5** odd, unconventional person **6** mechanical device to change circular into to-and-fro movement > **ec•cen•tric'i•ty** *noun*

Eccles. Ecclesiastes

ec•cle•si•as•tic [i-klee-zee-AS-tik] *noun* **1** clergyman ▷ *adjective* **2** of, relating to the Christian Church > **ec•cle•si•as'ti•cal** *adjective*

ech•e•lon [ESH-ə-lon] *noun* **1** level, grade, of responsibility or command **2** formation of troops, planes, etc. in parallel divisions each slightly to left or right of the one in front

ech•o [EK-oh] *noun, plural* **ech•oes 1** repetition of sounds by reflection **2** close imitation ▷ *verb transitive* **ech•oed, ech•o•ing 3** repeat as echo, send back the sound of **4** imitate closely ▷ *verb intransitive* **ech•oed, ech•o•ing 5** resound **6** be

DICTIONARY

e

THESAURUS

earthenware *noun* CROCKERY, ceramics, pots, pottery, terracotta

earthly *adjective* **1** WORLDLY, human, material, mortal, secular, temporal

earthy *adjective* CRUDE, bawdy, coarse, raunchy (*slang*), ribald, robust, uninhibited, unsophisticated

ease *noun* **1** EASINESS, effortlessness, facility, readiness, simplicity
2 CONTENT, comfort, happiness, peace, peace of mind, quiet, serenity, tranquillity
3 REST, leisure, relaxation, repose, restfulness
▷ *verb* **4** RELIEVE, alleviate, calm, comfort, lessen, lighten, relax, soothe
5 MOVE CAREFULLY, edge, inch, maneuver, slide, slip

easily *adverb* WITHOUT DIFFICULTY, comfortably, effortlessly, readily, smoothly, with ease, with one hand tied behind one's back

easy *adjective* **1** NOT DIFFICULT, a piece of cake (*informal*), child's play (*informal*), effortless, no trouble, painless, plain sailing, simple, straightforward, uncomplicated, undemanding
2 CAREFREE, comfortable, leisurely, peaceful, quiet, relaxed, serene, tranquil, untroubled
3 TOLERANT, easy-going, indulgent, lenient, mild, permissive, unoppressive

easy-going *adjective* RELAXED, carefree, casual, easy, even-tempered, happy-go-lucky, laid-back (*informal*), nonchalant, placid, tolerant, undemanding

eat *verb* **1** CONSUME, chew, devour, gobble, ingest, munch, scoff (*slang*), swallow
2 HAVE A MEAL, chow down (*slang*), dine, feed, take nourishment
3 DESTROY, corrode, decay, dissolve, erode, rot, waste away, wear away

eavesdrop *verb* LISTEN IN, monitor, overhear, snoop (*informal*), spy

ebb *verb* **1** FLOW BACK, go out, recede, retire, retreat, subside, wane, withdraw
2 DECLINE, decrease, diminish, dwindle, fade away, fall away, flag, lessen, peter out
▷ *noun* **3** FLOWING BACK, going out, low tide, low water, retreat, subsidence, wane, withdrawal

eccentric *adjective* **1** ODD, freakish, idiosyncratic, irregular, outlandish, peculiar, quirky, strange, unconventional
▷ *noun* **2** CRANK (*informal*), character (*informal*), nonconformist, oddball (*informal*), weirdo *or* weirdie (*informal*)

eccentricity *noun* ODDITY, abnormality, caprice, capriciousness, foible, idiosyncrasy, irregularity, peculiarity, quirk

ecclesiastic *noun* **1** CLERGYMAN, churchman, cleric, holy man, man of the cloth, minister, parson, pastor, priest
▷ *adjective* **2** *also* **ecclesiastical** CLERICAL, divine, holy, pastoral, priestly, religious, spiritual

echo *noun* **1** REPETITION, answer, reverberation
2 COPY, imitation, mirror image, parallel, reflection, reiteration, reproduction
▷ *verb* **3** REPEAT, resound, reverberate
4 COPY, ape, imitate, mirror, parallel, recall,

repeated > **echo sounding** system of ascertaining depth of water by measuring time required to receive an echo from sea bottom or submerged object

éclair [ee-KLAIR] *noun* finger-shaped, chocolate-frosted cake filled with whipped cream or custard

éclat [ay-KLAH] *noun* splendor, renown, acclamation

e•clec•tic [i-KLEK-tik] *adjective* 1 selecting 2 borrowing one's philosophy from various sources 3 catholic in views or taste ▷ *noun* > **e•clec'ti•cism** *noun*

e•clipse [i-KLIPS] *noun* 1 blotting out of sun, moon, etc. by another heavenly body 2 obscurity ▷ *verb transitive* **-clipsed, -clips•ing** 3 obscure, hide 4 surpass > **e•clip'tic** *adjective* 1 of eclipse ▷ *noun* 2 apparent path of sun

e•col•o•gy [i-KOL-ə-jee] *noun* science of plants and animals in relation to their environment > **ec•o•log'i•cal** *adjective* > **e•col'o•gist** *noun* specialist in or advocate of ecological studies

e-com•merce *noun* business transactions conducted on the Internet

e•con•o•my [i-KON-ə-mee] *noun, plural* **-mies** 1 careful management of resources to avoid unnecessary expenditure or waste 2 sparing, restrained or efficient use 3 system of interrelationship of money, industry and employment in a country > **ec•o•nom'ic** *adjective* 1 of economics 2 profitable 3 economical > **ec•o•nom'i•cal** *adjective* 1 not wasteful of money, time, effort, etc. 2 frugal > **ec•o•nom'ics** *noun* 1 study of economies of nations 2 financial aspects > **e•con'o•mist** *noun* specialist in economics > **e•con'o•mize** *verb* **-mized, -miz•ing** limit or reduce expense, waste, etc.

ec•ru [EK-roo] *noun, adjective* (of) color of unbleached linen

ec•sta•sy [EK-stə-see] *noun, plural* **-sies** 1 exalted state of feeling, mystic trance 2 frenzy 3 (**Ec•sta•sy**) (*slang*) powerful drug that can produce hallucinations > **ec•stat•ic** [ik-STAT-ik] *adjective* > **ec•stat'i•cal•ly** *adverb*

ec•u•men•i•cal [ek-yuu-MEN-i-kəl] *adjective* 1 of the Christian Church throughout the world, esp. with regard to its unity 2 interdenominational 3 universal > **ec•u•men'i•cism** *noun*

ec•ze•ma [EK-sə-mə] *noun* skin disease

ed•dy [ED-ee] *noun, plural* **-dies** 1 small whirl in water, smoke, etc. ▷ *verb intransitive* **-died, -dy•ing** 2 move in whirls

e•del•weiss [AY-dəl-vīs] *noun* white-flowered alpine plant

e•de•ma [i-DEE-mə] *noun* 1 an abnormal excess of fluid in tissues, organs 2 swelling due to this

E•den [EE-dən] *noun* 1 garden in which Adam and Eve were placed at the Creation 2 any delightful, happy place or condition

edge [ej] *noun* 1 border, boundary 2 cutting side of blade 3 sharpness 4 advantage 5 acrimony, bitterness ▷ *verb transitive* **edged, edg•ing** 6 sharpen, give edge or border to 7 move gradually ▷ *verb intransitive* **edged, edg•ing** 8 advance sideways or gradually > **edge'ways, edge'wise** *adverb* > **edg'ing** *noun* > **edg'y** *adjective* **edg•i•er, edg•i•est** irritable, sharp or keen in temper **on edge** 1 nervous, irritable 2 excited

ed•i•ble [ED-ə-bəl] *adjective* eatable, fit for eating

e•dict [EE-dikt] *noun* order proclaimed by authority, decree

ed•i•fice [ED-ə-fis] *noun* building, esp. big one

ed•i•fy [ED-ə-fī] *verb transitive* **-fied, -fy•ing** improve morally, instruct > **ed•i•fi•ca'tion** *noun* improvement of the mind or morals

ed'it *verb transitive* prepare book, film, tape, etc. for publication or broadcast > **e•di•tion** [i-DISH-ən] *noun* 1 form in which something is

---

reflect, resemble

eclipse *noun* 1 OBSCURING, darkening, dimming, extinction, shading
▷ *verb* 2 SURPASS, exceed, excel, outdo, outshine, put in the shade (*informal*), transcend

economic *adjective* 1 FINANCIAL, commercial, industrial
2 PROFITABLE, money-making, productive, profit-making, remunerative, viable
3 *also* **economical**

economical *adjective* 1 THRIFTY, careful, frugal, prudent, scrimping, sparing
2 COST-EFFECTIVE, efficient, money-saving, sparing, time-saving
3 INEXPENSIVE, cheap, low-priced, modest, reasonable

economize *verb* CUT BACK, be economical, be frugal, draw in one's horns, retrench, save, scrimp, tighten one's belt

economy *noun* THRIFT, frugality, husbandry, parsimony, prudence, restraint

ecstasy *noun* RAPTURE, bliss, delight, elation, euphoria, fervor, joy, seventh heaven

ecstatic *adjective* RAPTUROUS, blissful, elated, enraptured, entranced, euphoric, in seventh heaven, joyous, on cloud nine (*informal*), overjoyed

eddy *noun* 1 SWIRL, counter-current, counterflow, undertow, vortex, whirlpool
▷ *verb* 2 SWIRL, whirl

edge *noun* 1 BORDER, boundary, brink, fringe, limit, outline, perimeter, rim, side, verge
2 SHARPNESS, bite, effectiveness, force, incisiveness, keenness, point
3 ADVANTAGE, ascendancy, dominance, lead, superiority, upper hand
4 ▷ **on edge** NERVOUS, apprehensive, edgy, ill at ease, impatient, irritable, keyed up, on tenterhooks, tense, wired (*slang*)
▷ *verb* 5 BORDER, fringe, hem
6 INCH, creep, ease, sidle, steal

edgy *adjective* NERVOUS, anxious, ill at ease, irritable, keyed up, on edge, on tenterhooks, restive, tense, wired (*slang*)

edible *adjective* EATABLE, digestible, fit to eat, good, harmless, palatable, wholesome

edict *noun* DECREE, act, command, injunction, law, order, proclamation, ruling

edifice *noun* BUILDING, construction, erection, house, structure

edify *verb* INSTRUCT, educate, enlighten, guide, improve, inform, nurture, school, teach

edit *verb* REVISE, adapt, condense, correct, emend, polish, rewrite

published 2 number of copies of new publication printed at one time > **ed•i•to'ri•al** *adjective* 1 of editor ▷ *noun* 2 article stating opinion of newspaper, etc.
ed•u•cate [EJ-uu-kayt] *verb transitive* **-cat•ed, -cat•ing** 1 provide schooling for 2 teach 3 train mentally and morally 4 train 5 improve, develop > **ed•u•ca'tion** *noun* > **ed•u•ca'tion•al** *adjective* > **ed'u•ca•tive** *adjective* > **ed'u•ca•tor** *noun*
e•duce [i-DOOS] *verb transitive* **-duced, -duc•ing** 1 bring out, elicit, develop 2 infer, deduce
ee•rie [EER-ee] *adjective* **-ri•er, -ri•est** 1 weird, uncanny 2 causing superstitious fear
ef•face [i-FAYS] *verb transitive* **-faced, -fac•ing** wipe or rub out > **ef•face'a•ble** *adjective*
ef•fect [i-FEKT] *noun* 1 result, consequence 2 efficacy 3 impression 4 condition of being operative ▷ *verb transitive* 5 bring about, accomplish > **ef•fects** *plural noun* 1 movable property 2 lighting, sounds, etc. to accompany film, broadcast, etc. > **ef•fec'tive** *adjective* 1 having power to produce effects 2 in effect, operative 3 serviceable 4 powerful 5 striking > **ef•fec'tive•ly** *adverb* > **ef•fec'tu•al** [-choo-əl] *adjective* 1 successful in producing desired effect 2 satisfactory 3 efficacious > **ef•fec'tu•ate** [-choo-ayt] *verb transitive* **-at•ed, -at•ing** bring about, effect
ef•fem•i•nate [i-FEM-ə-nit] *adjective* womanish, unmanly > **ef•fem'i•na•cy** *noun*
ef•fer•ent [EF-ər-ənt] *adjective* conveying outward or away
ef•fer•vesce [ef-ər-VES] *verb intransitive* **-vesced, -vesc•ing** 1 give off bubbles 2 be in high spirits > **ef•fer•ves'cent** *adjective*
ef•fete [i-FEET] *adjective* worn out, feeble
ef•fi•ca•cious [ef-i-KAY-shəs] *adjective* 1 producing or sure to produce desired effect 2 effective 3 powerful 4 adequate > **ef'fi•ca•cy** [-kə-see] *noun, plural* **-cies** 1 potency 2 force 3 efficiency
ef•fi•cient [i-FISH-ənt] *adjective* capable, competent, producing effect > **ef•fi'cien•cy** *noun, plural* **-cies**
ef•fi•gy [EF-i-jee] *noun, plural* **-gies** image, likeness
ef•flo•resce [ef-lə-RES] *verb intransitive* **-resced, -res•cing** burst into flower > **ef•flo•res'cence** *noun*
ef•flu•ent [EF-loo-ənt] *noun* 1 liquid discharged as waste 2 stream flowing from larger stream, lake, etc. ▷ *adjective* 3 flowing out > **ef•flu•vi•um** [i-FLOO-vee-əm] *noun, plural* **-vi•a** something flowing out invisibly, esp. affecting lungs or sense of smell
ef•fort [EF-ərt] *noun* exertion, endeavor, attempt or something achieved > **ef'fort•less** *adjective*
ef•fron•ter•y [i-FRUN-tə-ree] *noun, plural* **-ter•ies** brazen impudence
ef•ful•gent [i-FUL-jənt] *adjective* radiant, shining brightly > **ef•ful'gence** *noun*
ef•fu•sion [i-FYOO-zhən] *noun* (unrestrained) outpouring > **ef•fuse** [i-FYOOZ] *verb* **fused,**

DICTIONARY e THESAURUS

edition *noun* VERSION, copy, impression, issue, number, printing, program (*tv, radio*), volume
educate *verb* TEACH, civilize, develop, discipline, enlighten, improve, inform, instruct, school, train, tutor
educated *adjective* 1 TAUGHT, coached, informed, instructed, nurtured, schooled, tutored
2 CULTURED, civilized, cultivated, enlightened, knowledgeable, learned, refined, sophisticated
education *noun* TEACHING, development, discipline, enlightenment, instruction, nurture, schooling, training, tuition
educational *adjective* INSTRUCTIVE, cultural, edifying, educative, enlightening, improving, informative
eerie *adjective* FRIGHTENING, creepy (*informal*), ghostly, mysterious, scary (*informal*), spooky (*informal*), strange, uncanny, unearthly, weird
efface *verb* OBLITERATE, blot out, cancel, delete, destroy, eradicate, erase, expunge, rub out, wipe out
effect *noun* 1 RESULT, conclusion, consequence, end result, event, outcome, upshot
2 OPERATION, action, enforcement, execution, force, implementation
3 IMPRESSION, essence, impact, sense, significance, tenor
▷ *verb* 4 BRING ABOUT, accomplish, achieve, complete, execute, fulfill, perform, produce
effective *adjective* 1 EFFICIENT, active, adequate, capable, competent, productive, serviceable, useful
2 IN OPERATION, active, current, in effect, in force, operative
3 POWERFUL, cogent, compelling, convincing, forceful, impressive, persuasive, telling
effects *plural noun* BELONGINGS, gear, goods, paraphernalia, possessions, property, things
effeminate *adjective* WOMANLY, camp (*informal*), feminine, sissy, soft, tender, unmanly, weak, womanish
effervescent *adjective* 1 BUBBLING, carbonated, fizzy, foaming, frothy, sparkling
2 LIVELY, animated, bubbly, ebullient, enthusiastic, exuberant, irrepressible, vivacious
effete *adjective* DECADENT, dissipated, enfeebled, feeble, ineffectual, spoiled, weak
efficacious *adjective* EFFECTIVE, adequate, efficient, operative, potent, powerful, productive, successful, useful
efficiency *noun* COMPETENCE, adeptness, capability, economy, effectiveness, power, productivity, proficiency
efficient *adjective* COMPETENT, businesslike, capable, economic, effective, organized, productive, proficient, well-organized, workmanlike
effigy *noun* LIKENESS, dummy, figure, guy, icon, idol, image, picture, portrait, representation, statue
effluent *noun* WASTE, effluvium, pollutant, sewage
effort *noun* 1 EXERTION, application, elbow grease (*facetious*), endeavor, energy, pains, struggle, toil, trouble, work
2 ATTEMPT, endeavor, essay, go (*informal*), shot (*informal*), stab (*informal*), try
effortless *adjective* EASY, painless, plain sailing, simple, smooth, uncomplicated, undemanding
effrontery *noun* INSOLENCE, arrogance, audacity, brazenness, cheek (*informal*), impertinence, impudence, nerve, presumption, temerity

-fus•ing 1 pour out, shed 2 radiate > **ef•fu'sive** [-siv] *adjective* gushing, demonstrative
e.g. for example
e•gal•i•tar•i•an [i-gal-i-TAIR-ee-ən] *adjective* 1 believing that all people should be equal 2 promoting this ideal ▷ *noun*
egg[1] *noun* oval or round object produced by female of bird, etc., from which young emerge, esp. egg of domestic hen, used as food > **egg'plant** *noun* 1 egg-shaped dark purple fruit 2 plant bearing it
egg[2] *verb transitive* **egg on** 1 encourage, urge 2 incite
e•go [EE-goh] *noun, plural* **e•gos** 1 the self 2 the conscious thinking subject 3 one's image of oneself 4 morale > **e'go•ism** *noun* 1 systematic selfishness 2 theory that bases morality on self-interest > **e'go•tism** *noun* 1 selfishness 2 self-conceit > **e'go•tist, eg'o•ist** *noun* > **e•go•tis'tic, e•go•is'tic** *adjective* > **e•go•cen'tric** *adjective* 1 self-centered 2 egoistic 3 centered in the ego
e•gre•gious [i-GREE-jəs] *adjective* 1 outstandingly bad, blatant 2 absurdly obvious, esp. of mistake, etc.
e•gress [EE-gres] *noun* 1 way out 2 departure
e•gret [EE-grit] *noun* one of several white herons
ei•der [Ī-dər] *noun* 1 any of several northern sea ducks 2 eiderdown > **ei'der•down** *noun* 1 its breast feathers 2 quilt (stuffed with feathers)
eight [ayt] *noun* 1 cardinal number one above seven 2 crew of eight-oared shell ▷ *adjective* > **eight•een'** *adjective, noun* eight more than ten > **eight•eenth'** *adjective, noun* > **eighth** [ayth] *adjective, noun* ordinal number > **eight'i•eth** *adjective, noun* > **eight'y** *adjective, noun, plural* **eight•ies** ten times eight **figure eight** 1 a skating figure 2 any figure shaped as 8
ei•ther [EE-thər] *adjective, pronoun* 1 one or the other 2 one of two 3 each ▷ *adverb, conjunction* 4 bringing in first of alternatives or strengthening an added negation
e•jac•u•late [i-JAK-yə-layt] *verb* **-lat•ed, -lat•ing** 1 eject (semen) 2 exclaim, utter suddenly > **e•jac•u•la'tion** *noun*
e•ject [i-JEKT] *verb transitive* 1 throw out 2 expel, drive out > **e•jec'tion** *noun*
eke out [eek] *verb transitive* 1 make (supply) last, esp. by frugal use 2 supply deficiencies of 3 make with difficulty (a living, etc.)
e•lab•o•rate [i-LAB-ər-it] *adjective* 1 carefully worked out, detailed 2 complicated ▷ *verb intransitive* [-ayt], **-rat•ed, -rat•ing** 3 expand (upon) ▷ *verb transitive* [-ayt], **-rat•ed, -rat•ing** 4 work out in detail 5 take pains with
élan [ay-LAHN] *noun* 1 dash 2 ardor 3 impetuosity > **élan vi•tal** [vee-TAL] esp. in Bergsonian philosophy, the creative force within an organism that is responsible for growth, change, etc.
e•lapse [i-LAPS] *verb intransitive* **-lapsed, -laps•ing** of time, pass
e•las•tic [i-LAS-tik] *adjective* 1 resuming normal shape after distortion, springy 2 flexible ▷ *noun* 3 tape, fabric, containing interwoven strands of flexible rubber, etc. > **e•las'ti•cized** [-sīzd] *adjective* > **e•las•tic'i•ty** *noun*
e•la•tion [i-LAY-shən] *noun* 1 high spirits 2 pride > **e•late** [i-LAYT] *verb transitive* **-lat•ed, -lat•ing** 1 (*usually passive*) be elated, etc. 2 raise the spirits of 3 make happy 4 exhilarate
el•bow [EL-boh] *noun* 1 joint between fore and upper parts of arm (esp. outer part of it) 2 part of sleeve covering this 3 something resembling this, esp. angular pipe fitting ▷ *verb transitive* 4 shove, strike with elbow > **elbow grease** hard work > **elbow room** *noun* sufficient room
eld•er[1] [EL-dər] *adjective* 1 older, senior 2 *comp. of* **old** ▷ *noun* 3 person of greater age 4 old person 5 official of certain churches > **el'der•ly** *adjective* growing old > **eld'est** *adjective* 1 oldest 2 *sup. of* **old**
el•der[2] *noun* white-flowered tree or shrub
El Do•ra•do [el də-RAH-doh] *noun* fictitious country rich in gold

DICTIONARY • THESAURUS

effusive *adjective* DEMONSTRATIVE, ebullient, expansive, exuberant, gushing, lavish, unreserved, unrestrained
egg on *verb* ENCOURAGE, exhort, goad, incite, prod, prompt, push, spur, urge
egocentric *adjective* SELF-CENTERED, egoistic, egoistical, egotistic, egotistical, selfish
egotism *or* **egoism** *noun* SELF-CENTEREDNESS, conceitedness, narcissism, self-absorption, self-esteem, self-importance, self-interest, selfishness, vanity
egotist *or* **egoist** *noun* EGOMANIAC, bighead (*informal*), boaster, braggart, narcissist
egotistic *or* **egotistical, egoistic, egoistical** *adjective* SELF-CENTERED, boasting, conceited, egocentric, full of oneself, narcissistic, self-absorbed, self-important, vain
egress *noun* (*formal*) EXIT, departure, exodus, way out, withdrawal
eject *verb* THROW OUT, banish, drive out, evict, expel, oust, remove, turn out
ejection *noun* EXPULSION, banishment, deportation, eviction, exile, removal
eke out *verb* BE SPARING WITH, economize on, husband, stretch out
elaborate *adjective* 1 DETAILED, intricate, minute, painstaking, precise, studied, thorough 2 COMPLICATED, complex, fancy, fussy, involved, ornamented, ornate
▷ *verb* 3 EXPAND *or* EXPAND UPON, add detail, amplify, develop, embellish, enlarge, flesh out
elapse *verb* PASS, glide by, go by, lapse, roll by, slip away
elastic *adjective* 1 STRETCHY, plastic, pliable, pliant, resilient, rubbery, springy, supple, tensile 2 ADAPTABLE, accommodating, adjustable, compliant, flexible, supple, tolerant, variable, yielding
elated *adjective* JOYFUL, delighted, ecstatic, euphoric, exhilarated, gleeful, jubilant, overjoyed
elation *noun* JOY, bliss, delight, ecstasy, euphoria, exhilaration, glee, high spirits, jubilation, rapture
elbow *noun* 1 JOINT, angle
▷ *verb* 2 PUSH, jostle, knock, nudge, shove
elbow room *noun* SCOPE, freedom, latitude, leeway, play, room, space
elder *adjective* 1 OLDER, first-born, senior
▷ *noun* 2 OLDER PERSON, senior

e-learn•ing [EE-lurn-ing] *noun* Internet-based teaching system
e•lect [i-LEKT] *verb transitive* 1 choose by vote 2 choose ▷ *adjective* 3 appointed but not yet in office 4 chosen, select, choice > **e•lec'tion** *noun* choosing, esp. by voting > **e•lec•tion•eer'** *verb intransitive* work in political campaign > **e•lec'tive** *adjective* appointed, filled, or chosen by election > **e•lec'tor** *noun* one who elects > **e•lec'tor•al** *adjective* > **electoral college** body of electors chosen by voters to elect President and Vice President > **e•lec'tor•ate** *noun* body of persons entitled to vote
e•lec•tric•i•ty [i-lek-TRIS-i-tee] *noun* 1 form of energy associated with stationary or moving electrons or other charged particles 2 electric current or charge 3 science dealing with electricity > **e•lec'tric** *adjective* 1 derived from, produced by, producing, transmitting or powered by electricity 2 excited, emotionally charged > **e•lec'tri•cal** *adjective* > **e•lec•tri'cian** *noun* one trained in installation, etc. of electrical wiring and devices > **e•lec•tri•fi•ca'tion** *noun* > **e•lec'tri•fy** *verb transitive* **-fied, -fy•ing** > **electric chair** chair in which criminals sentenced to death are electrocuted > **electric organ** *mus.* organ in which sound is produced by electric devices instead of wind
electro- *combining form* operated by or caused by electricity: *electrocute*
e•lec•tro•car•di•o•graph [i-lek-troh-KAHR-dee-ə-graf] *noun* instrument for recording electrical activity of heart > **e•lec•tro•car'di•o•gram** *noun* tracing produced by this
e•lec•tro•cute [i-LEK-trə-kyoot] *verb transitive* **-cut•ed, -cut•ing** execute, kill by electricity > **e•lec•tro•cu'tion** *noun*
e•lec•trode [i-LEK-trohd] *noun* conductor by which electric current enters or leaves battery, vacuum tube, etc.
e•lec•tro•en•ceph•a•lo•graph [i-lek-troh-en-SEF-ə-lə-graf] *noun* instrument for recording electrical activity of brain > **e•lec•tro•en•ceph'a•lo•gram** *noun* tracing produced by this
e•lec•tro•lyte [i-LEK-trə-līt] *noun* solution, molten substance that conducts electricity > **e•lec•tro•lyt'ic** [-LIT-ik] *adjective*
e•lec•tro•lyze [i-LEK-trə-līz] *verb transitive* **-lyzed, -lyz•ing** decompose by electricity > **e•lec•trol'y•sis** [-TROL-ə-sis] *noun*
e•lec•tro•mag•net [i-lek-troh-MAG-nit] *noun* magnet containing coil of wire through which electric current is passed > **e•lec•tro•mag•net'ic** *adjective*
e•lec•tron [i-LEK-tron] *noun* one of fundamental particles of matter identified with unit of charge of negative electricity and essential component of the atom > **e•lec•tron'ic** *adjective* 1 of electrons or electronics 2 using devices, such as semiconductors, transistors or vacuum tubes, dependent on action of electrons > **electronic mail** *see* **e-mail** > **e•lec•tron'ics** *noun* 1 technology concerned with development of electronic devices and circuits 2 science of behavior and control of electrons > **electron volt** unit of energy used in nuclear physics
e•lec•tro•plate [i-LEK-trə-playt] *verb transitive* **-plat•ed, -plat•ing** 1 coat with silver, etc. by electrolysis ▷ *noun* 2 articles electroplated
el•e•gant [EL-ə-gənt] *adjective* 1 graceful, tasteful 2 refined > **el'e•gance** *noun*
el•e•gy [EL-ə-jee] *noun, plural* **-gies** lament for the dead in poem or song > **el•e•gi•ac** [el-ə-JI-ək] *adjective* 1 suited to elegies 2 plaintive
el•e•ment [EL-ə-mənt] *noun* 1 substance that cannot be separated into other substances by ordinary chemical techniques 2 component part 3 small amount, trace 4 heating wire in electric kettle, stove, etc. 5 proper abode or sphere > **el•e•ments** 1 powers of atmosphere 2 rudiments, first principles > **el•e•men'tal** *adjective* 1 fundamental 2 of powers of nature > **el•e•men'ta•ry** *adjective* rudimentary, simple
el•e•phant [EL-ə-fənt] *noun* huge four-footed, thick-skinned animal with ivory tusks and long trunk > **el•e•phan•ti'a•sis** *noun* disease with hardening of skin and enlargement of legs, etc. > **el•e•phan'tine** [-FAN-teen] *adjective* unwieldy, clumsy, heavily big
el•e•vate [EL-ə-vayt] *verb transitive* **-vat•ed, -vat•ing** raise, lift up, exalt > **el•e•va'tion** *noun* 1 raising 2 height, esp. above sea level 3 angle above horizon, as of gun 4 drawing of one side

DICTIONARY

e

THESAURUS

elect *verb* CHOOSE, appoint, determine, opt for, pick, prefer, select, settle on, vote
election *noun* VOTING, appointment, choice, judgment, preference, selection, vote
elector *noun* VOTER, constituent, selector
electric *adjective* CHARGED, dynamic, exciting, rousing, stimulating, stirring, tense, thrilling
electrify *verb* STARTLE, astound, excite, galvanize, invigorate, jolt, shock, stir, thrill
elegance *noun* STYLE, dignity, exquisiteness, grace, gracefulness, grandeur, luxury, refinement, taste
elegant *adjective* STYLISH, chic, delicate, exquisite, fine, graceful, handsome, polished, refined, tasteful
element *noun* 1 COMPONENT, constituent, factor, ingredient, part, section, subdivision, unit
2 ▷ **be in one's element** BE IN ONE'S NATURAL ENVIRONMENT, be in one's domain, be in one's field, be in one's habitat, be in one's medium, be in one's milieu, be in one's sphere, feel at home
elementary *adjective* SIMPLE, clear, easy, plain, rudimentary, straightforward, uncomplicated
elements *plural noun* 1 BASICS, essentials, foundations, fundamentals, nuts and bolts (*informal*), principles, rudiments
2 WEATHER CONDITIONS, atmospheric conditions, powers of nature
elevate *verb* 1 RAISE, heighten, hoist, lift, lift up, uplift
2 PROMOTE, advance, aggrandize, exalt, prefer, upgrade
elevated *adjective* HIGH-MINDED, dignified, exalted, grand, high-flown, inflated, lofty, noble, sublime
elevation *noun* 1 PROMOTION, advancement, aggrandizement, exaltation, preferment, upgrading
2 ALTITUDE, height

of building, etc. > **el'e•va•tor** *noun* cage raised and lowered in vertical shaft to transport people, etc.
e•lev•en [i-LEV-ən] *noun* 1 number next above 10 2 team of 11 persons ▷ *adjective* > **e•lev'en•fold** *adjective, adverb* > **e•lev'enth** *adjective* the ordinal number > **eleventh hour** latest possible time
elf *noun, plural* **elves** 1 fairy 2 woodland sprite > **elf'in** *adjective* roguish, mischievous
e•lic•it [i-LIS-it] *verb transitive* 1 draw out, evoke 2 bring to light
e•lide [i-LĪD] *verb transitive* **e•lid•ed, e•lid•ing** omit in pronunciation a vowel or syllable > **e•li•sion** [i-LIZH-ən] *noun*
el•i•gi•ble [EL-ə-jə-bəl] *adjective* 1 fit or 2 qualified to be chosen 3 suitable, desirable > **el•i•gi•bil'i•ty** *noun*
e•lim•i•nate [i-LIM-ə-nayt] *verb transitive* **-nat•ed, -nat•ing** remove, get rid of, set aside > **e•lim•i•na'tion** *noun*
elision *see* **elide**
e•lite [i-LEET] *noun* 1 choice or select body 2 the pick or best part of society 3 typewriter type size (12 letters to inch) ▷ *adjective* > **e•lit'ism** *noun* > **e•lit'ist** *noun*
e•lix•ir [i-LIK-sər] *noun* 1 preparation sought by alchemists to change base metals into gold, or to prolong life 2 panacea
elk *noun* large deer
el•lipse [i-LIPS] *noun* oval > **el•lip'ti•cal** *adjective*
el•lip•sis [i-LIP-sis] *noun, plural* **-ses** [-seez] 1 omission of parts of word or sentence 2 mark (. . .) indicating this
el•o•cu•tion [el-ə-KYOO-shən] *noun* art of public speaking, voice management > **el•o•cu'tion•ist** *noun* teacher of this
e•lon•gate [i-LAWNG-gayt] *verb transitive* **-gat•ed, -gat•ing** lengthen, extend, prolong > **e•lon•ga'tion** *noun*
e•lope [i-LOHP] *verb intransitive* **-loped, -lop•ing** 1 run away from home with lover 2 do this with intention of marrying > **e•lope'ment** *noun*
el•o•quence [EL-ə-kwəns] *noun* fluent, powerful use of language > **el'o•quent** *adjective*
else [els] *adverb* 1 besides, instead 2 otherwise > **else•where** *adverb* in or to some other place
e•lu•ci•date [i-LOO-si-dayt] *verb transitive* **-dat•ed, -dat•ing** throw light upon, explain > **e•lu•ci•da'tion** *noun*
e•lude [i-LOOD] *verb transitive* **-lud•ed, -lud•ing** 1 escape, slip away from, dodge 2 baffle > **e•lu'sion** *noun* 1 act of eluding 2 evasion > **e•lu'sive** *adjective* difficult to catch hold of, deceptive > **e•lu'sive•ness** *noun*
elves, elvish *see* **elf**
em *noun printing* the square of any size of type
em- *prefix see* **en-**
e•ma•ci•ate [i-MAY-see-ayt] *verb* **-at•ed, -at•ing** make or become abnormally thin > **e•ma•ci•a'tion** *noun*
e-mail, e•mail *noun* 1 (*also* **electronic mail**) sending of messages between computer terminals or other electronic devices ▷ *verb* 2 communicate in this way
em•a•nate [EM-ə-nayt] *verb intransitive* **-nat•ed, -nat•ing** issue, proceed from, originate > **em•a•na'tion** *noun*
e•man•ci•pate [i-MAN-sə-payt] *verb transitive* **-pat•ed, -pat•ing** set free > **e•man•ci•pa'tion** *noun* 1 act of setting free, esp. from social, legal restraint 2 state of being set free > **e•man'ci•pa•tor** *noun*
e•mas•cu•late [i-MAS–kyə-layt] *verb transitive* **-lat•ed, -lat•ing** 1 castrate 2 enfeeble, weaken > **e•mas•cu•la'tion** *noun*
em•balm [em-BAHM] *verb transitive* preserve corpse from decay by use of chemicals, herbs, etc. > **em•balm'er** *noun*
em•bank•ment [em-BANGK-mənt] *noun* artificial mound carrying road, railway, or serving to dam water

elicit *verb* 1 BRING ABOUT, bring forth, bring out, bring to light, call forth, cause, derive, evolve, give rise to
2 OBTAIN, draw out, evoke, exact, extort, extract, wrest
eligible *adjective* QUALIFIED, acceptable, appropriate, desirable, fit, preferable, proper, suitable, worthy
eliminate *verb* GET RID OF, cut out, dispose of, do away with, eradicate, exterminate, remove, stamp out, take out
elite *noun* BEST, aristocracy, cream, crème de la crème (*French*), flower, nobility, pick, upper class
elitist *adjective* SNOBBISH, exclusive, selective
elixir *noun* PANACEA, nostrum
elocution *noun* DICTION, articulation, declamation, delivery, enunciation, oratory, pronunciation, speech, speechmaking
elongate *verb* MAKE LONGER, draw out, extend, lengthen, prolong, protract, stretch
elope *verb* RUN AWAY, abscond, bolt, decamp, disappear, escape, leave, run off, slip away, steal away
eloquence *noun* EXPRESSIVENESS, expression, fluency, forcefulness, oratory, persuasiveness, rhetoric, way with words
eloquent *adjective* 1 SILVER-TONGUED, articulate, fluent, forceful, moving, persuasive, stirring, well-expressed
2 EXPRESSIVE, meaningful, suggestive, telling, vivid
elsewhere *adverb* IN ANOTHER PLACE *or* TO ANOTHER PLACE, abroad, away, hence (*archaic*), not here, somewhere else
elucidate *verb* CLARIFY, clear up, explain, explicate, expound, illuminate, illustrate, make plain, shed light on *or* throw light on, spell out
elude *verb* 1 ESCAPE, avoid, dodge, duck (*informal*), evade, flee, get away from, outrun
2 BAFFLE, be beyond (someone), confound, escape, foil, frustrate, puzzle, stump, thwart
elusive *adjective* 1 DIFFICULT TO CATCH, shifty, slippery, tricky
2 INDEFINABLE, fleeting, intangible, subtle, transient, transitory
emaciated *adjective* SKELETAL, cadaverous, gaunt, haggard, lean, pinched, scrawny, thin, undernourished, wasted
emanate *verb* FLOW, arise, come forth, derive, emerge, issue, originate, proceed, spring, stem
emancipate *verb* FREE, deliver, liberate, release, set free, unchain, unfetter
emancipation *noun* FREEDOM, deliverance, liberation, liberty, release

em•bar•go [em-BAHR-goh] *noun, plural* **-goes** 1 order stopping movement of ships 2 suspension of commerce 3 ban ▷ *verb transitive* **-goed, -go•ing** put under embargo
em•bark [em-BAHRK] *verb* 1 put, go, on board ship, aircraft, etc. 2 (with *on* or *upon*) commence new project, venture, etc. > **em•bar•ka'tion** *noun*
em•bar•rass [em-BAR-əs] *verb transitive* 1 perplex, disconcert 2 abash 3 confuse 4 encumber > **em•bar'rass•ment** *noun*
em•bas•sy [EM-bə-see] *noun, plural* **-sies** 1 office, work or official residence of ambassador 2 deputation
em•bed' *verb transitive* **-bed•ded, -bed•ding** fix fast in something solid
em•bel'lish *verb transitive* adorn, enrich > **em•bel'lish•ment** *noun*
em•ber [EM-bər] *noun* glowing cinder > **em•bers** red-hot ashes
em•bez•zle [em-BEZ-əl] *verb transitive* **-zled, -zling** divert fraudulently, misappropriate (money in trust, etc.) > **em•bez'zle•ment** *noun* > **em•bez'zler** *noun*
em•bit•ter [em-BIT-ər] *verb transitive* make bitter > **em•bit'ter•ment** *noun*
em•bla•zon [em-BLAY-zən] *verb transitive* adorn richly, esp. heraldically
em•blem [EM-bləm] *noun* 1 symbol 2 badge, device > **em•ble•mat'ic** *adjective*
em•bod•y [em-BOD-ee] *verb transitive* **-bod•ied, -bod•y•ing** 1 give body, concrete expression to 2 represent, include, be expression of > **em•bod'i•ment** *noun*
em•bo•lism [EM-bə-liz-əm] *noun med.* obstruction of artery by blood clot or air bubble
em•boss [em-BAWS] *verb transitive* mold, stamp or carve in relief
em•brace [em-BRAYS] *verb transitive* **-braced, -brac•ing** 1 clasp in arms, hug 2 seize, avail oneself of, accept 3 comprise ▷ *noun*
em•bra•sure [em-BRAY-zhər] *noun* 1 opening in wall for cannon 2 beveling of wall at sides of window
em•bro•ca•tion [em-brə-KAY-shən] *noun* lotion for rubbing limbs, etc. to relieve pain > **em'bro•cate** *verb transitive* **-cat•ed, -cat•ing** apply lotion, etc.
em•broi•der [em-BROI-dər] *verb transitive* 1 ornament with needlework 2 embellish, exaggerate (story) > **em•broi'der•y** *noun*
em•broil' *verb transitive* 1 bring into confusion 2 involve in hostility > **em•broil'ment** *noun*
em•bry•o [EM-bree-oh] *noun, plural* **-os** 1 unborn or undeveloped offspring, germ 2 undeveloped thing > **em•bry•ol'o•gist** *noun* > **em•bry•ol'o•gy** *noun* > **em•bry•on'ic** *adjective*
e•mend [i-MEND] *verb transitive* remove errors from, correct > **e•men•da'tion** *noun*
em•er•ald [EM-ər-əld] *noun* 1 bright green precious stone ▷ *adjective* 2 of the color of emerald
e•merge [i-MURJ] *verb intransitive* **-merged, -merg•ing** 1 come up, out 2 rise to notice 3 come into view 4 come out on inquiry

DICTIONARY **e** THESAURUS

embalm *verb* PRESERVE, mummify
embargo *noun* 1 BAN, bar, boycott, interdiction, prohibition, restraint, restriction, stoppage ▷ *verb* 2 BAN, bar, block, boycott, prohibit, restrict, stop
embark *verb* 1 GO ABOARD, board ship, take ship 2 ▷ **embark on, embark upon** BEGIN, commence, enter, launch, plunge into, set about, set out, start, take up
embarrass *verb* SHAME, discomfit, disconcert, distress, fluster, humiliate, mortify, show up (*informal*)
embarrassed *adjective* ASHAMED, awkward, blushing, discomfited, disconcerted, humiliated, mortified, red-faced, self-conscious, sheepish
embarrassing *adjective* HUMILIATING, awkward, compromising, discomfiting, disconcerting, mortifying, sensitive, shameful, toe-curling (*informal*), uncomfortable
embarrassment *noun* 1 SHAME, awkwardness, bashfulness, distress, humiliation, mortification, self-consciousness, showing up (*informal*)
2 PREDICAMENT, bind (*informal*), difficulty, mess, pickle (*informal*), scrape (*informal*)
embellish *verb* DECORATE, adorn, beautify, elaborate, embroider, enhance, enrich, festoon, ornament
embellishment *noun* DECORATION, adornment, elaboration, embroidery, enhancement, enrichment, exaggeration, ornament, ornamentation
embezzle *verb* MISAPPROPRIATE, appropriate, filch, misuse, peculate, pilfer, purloin, rip off (*slang*), steal
embezzlement *noun* MISAPPROPRIATION, appropriation, filching, fraud, misuse, peculation, pilfering, stealing, theft
embittered *adjective* RESENTFUL, angry, bitter, disaffected, disillusioned, rancorous, soured, with a chip on one's shoulder (*informal*)
emblem *noun* SYMBOL, badge, crest, image, insignia, mark, sign, token
embodiment *noun* PERSONIFICATION, epitome, example, exemplar, expression, incarnation, representation, symbol
embody *verb* 1 PERSONIFY, exemplify, manifest, represent, stand for, symbolize, typify
2 INCORPORATE, collect, combine, comprise, contain, include
embolden *verb* ENCOURAGE, fire, inflame, invigorate, rouse, stimulate, stir, strengthen
embrace *verb* 1 HUG, clasp, cuddle, envelop, hold, seize, squeeze, take in one's arms *or* hold in one's arms
2 ACCEPT, adopt, espouse, seize, take on board, take up, welcome
3 INCLUDE, comprehend, comprise, contain, cover, encompass, involve, take in
▷ *noun* 4 HUG, clasp, clinch (*slang*), cuddle, squeeze
embroil *verb* INVOLVE, enmesh, ensnare, entangle, implicate, incriminate, mire, mix up
embryo *noun* GERM, beginning, nucleus, root, rudiment
emend *verb* REVISE, amend, correct, edit, improve, rectify
emendation *noun* REVISION, amendment, correction, editing, improvement, rectification
emerge *verb* 1 COME INTO VIEW, appear, arise, come forth, emanate, issue, rise, spring up,

> **e•mer'gence** *noun* > **e•mer'gent** *adjective*

e•mer•gen•cy [i-MUR-jən-see] *noun, plural* **-cies** 1 sudden unforeseen thing or event needing prompt action 2 difficult situation 3 exigency, crisis

e•mer•i•tus [i-MER-i-təs] *adjective* retired, honorably discharged but retaining one's title (e.g. professor) on honorary basis

em•er•y [EM-ər-ee] *noun* hard mineral used for polishing > **emery board** cardboard coated with powdered emery

e•met•ic [i-MET-ik] *noun, adjective* (medicine or agent) causing vomiting

em•i•grate [EM-i-grayt] *verb intransitive* **-grat•ed, -grat•ing** go and settle in another country > **em'i•grant** [-grənt] *noun* > **em•i•gra'tion** *noun*

é•mi•gré [EM-i-gray] *noun, plural* **-grés** emigrant, esp. one forced to leave native land for political reasons

em•i•nent [EM-ə-nənt] *adjective* distinguished, notable > **em'i•nence** *noun* 1 distinction 2 height 3 rank 4 fame 5 rising ground 6 (**Em'i•nence**) title of cardinal > **em'i•nent•ly** *adverb* > **é•mi•nence grise** [ay-mee-nahns GREEZ] *Fr.* person wielding unofficial power, oft. surreptitiously

em•is•sar•y [EM-ə-ser-ee] *noun, plural* **-sar•ies** agent, representative (esp. of government) sent on mission

e•mit [i-MIT] *verb transitive* **-mit•ted, -mit•ting** give out, put forth > **e•mis'sion** *noun* > **e•mit'ter** *noun*

e•mol•lient [i-MOL-yənt] *adjective* 1 softening, soothing ▷ *noun* 2 ointment or other softening application

e•mol•u•ment [i-MOL-yə-mənt] *noun* salary, pay, profit from work

e•mot•i•con [i-MOH-ti-kon] *noun* series of keyed characters, used esp. in e-mail, to indicate an emotion

e•mo•tion [i-MOH-shən] *noun* mental agitation, excited state of feeling, as joy, fear, etc. > **e•mo'tion•al** *adjective* 1 given to emotion 2 appealing to the emotions > **e•mo'tive** *adjective* tending to arouse emotion

em•pa•thy [EM-pə-thee] *noun* power of understanding, imaginatively entering into, another's feelings

em•per•or [EM-pər-ər] *noun* ruler of an empire > **em'press** [-pris] *noun feminine*

em•pha•sis [EM-fə-sis] *noun, plural* **-ses** [-seez] 1 importance attached 2 stress on words 3 vigor of speech, expression > **em'pha•size** *verb transitive* **-sized, -siz•ing** > **em•phat'ic** [-FAT-ik] *adjective* 1 forceful, decided 2 stressed

em•pire [EM-pīr] *noun* large territory, esp. aggregate of territories or peoples under supreme ruler, supreme control

em•pir•i•cal [em-PIR-i-kəl] *adjective* relying on experiment or experience, not on theory > **em•pir'i•cal•ly** *adverb* > **em•pir'i•cist** [-ə-sist] *noun* one who relies solely on experience and observation > **em•pir'i•cism** *noun*

em•place•ment [em-PLAYS-mənt] *noun* 1 putting in position 2 gun platform

em•ploy [em-PLOI] *verb transitive* 1 provide work for (a person) in return for money, hire 2 keep busy 3 use > **em•ploy•ee'** *noun* > **em•ploy'er** *noun* > **em•ploy'ment** *noun* 1 an employing, being

---

surface
2 BECOME APPARENT, become known, come out, come out in the wash, come to light, crop up, transpire

emergence *noun* COMING, advent, appearance, arrival, development, materialization, rise

emergency *noun* CRISIS, danger, difficulty, extremity, necessity, plight, predicament, quandary, scrape (*informal*)

emigrate *verb* MOVE ABROAD, migrate, move

emigration *noun* DEPARTURE, exodus, migration

eminence *noun* PROMINENCE, distinction, esteem, fame, greatness, importance, note, prestige, renown, repute

eminent *adjective* PROMINENT, celebrated, distinguished, esteemed, famous, high-ranking, illustrious, noted, renowned, well-known

emission *noun* GIVING OFF *or* GIVING OUT, discharge, ejaculation, ejection, exhalation, radiation, shedding, transmission

emit *verb* GIVE OFF, cast out, discharge, eject, emanate, exude, radiate, send out, transmit

emotion *noun* FEELING, ardor, excitement, fervor, passion, sensation, sentiment, vehemence, warmth

emotional *adjective* 1 SENSITIVE, demonstrative, excitable, hot-blooded, passionate, sentimental, temperamental
2 MOVING, affecting, emotive, heart-warming, poignant, sentimental, stirring, touching

emotive *adjective* SENSITIVE, controversial, delicate, touchy

emphasis *noun* STRESS, accent, attention, force, importance, priority, prominence, significance, weight

emphasize *verb* STRESS, accentuate, dwell on, give priority to, highlight, lay stress on, play up, press home, underline

emphatic *adjective* FORCEFUL, categorical, definite, insistent, positive, pronounced, resounding, unequivocal, unmistakable, vigorous

empire *noun* KINGDOM, commonwealth, domain, realm

empirical *adjective* FIRST-HAND, experiential, experimental, observed, practical, pragmatic

employ *verb* 1 HIRE, commission, engage, enlist, retain, take on
2 KEEP BUSY, engage, fill, make use of, occupy, take up, use up
3 USE, apply, bring to bear, exercise, exert, make use of, ply, put to use, utilize
▷ *noun* 4 ▷ **in the employ of** IN THE SERVICE OF, employed by, engaged by, hired by

employed *adjective* WORKING, active, busy, engaged, in a job, in employment, in work, occupied

employee *noun* WORKER, hand, job-holder, staff member, wage-earner, workman

employer *noun* BOSS (*informal*), company, firm, owner, patron, proprietor

employment *noun* 1 TAKING ON, engagement, enlistment, hire, retaining
2 USE, application, exercise, exertion, utilization
3 JOB, line, occupation, profession, trade,

employed **2** work, trade **3** occupation
em•po•ri•um [em-POHR-ee-əm] *noun, plural* **-ri•ums 1** large store, esp. one carrying general merchandise **2** center of commerce
em•pow•er [em-POW-ər] *verb transitive* enable, authorize > **em•pow•er•ment** *noun*
empress *see* **emperor**
emp•ty [EM-tee] *adjective* **-ti•er, -ti•est 1** containing nothing **2** unoccupied **3** senseless **4** vain, foolish ▷ *verb* **-tied, -ty•ing 5** make, become devoid of content **6** discharge (contents) into > **emp'ties** *plural noun* empty boxes, bottles, etc. > **emp'ti•ness** *noun*
EMT *noun* emergency medical technician
e•mu [EE-myoo] *noun* large Aust. flightless bird like ostrich
em•u•late [EM-yə-layt] *verb transitive* **-lat•ed, -lat•ing 1** strive to equal or excel **2** imitate > **em•u•la'tion** *noun* **1** rivalry **2** competition > **em'u•la•tive** *adjective* > **em'u•la•tor** *noun*
e•mul•sion [i-MUL-shən] *noun* **1** light-sensitive coating of film **2** milky liquid with oily or resinous particles in suspension **3** paint, etc. in this form > **e•mul'si•fi•er** *noun* > **e•mul'si•fy** *verb transitive* **-fied, -fy•ing**
en *noun printing* unit of measurement, half an em
en-, em- *prefix* put in, into, or on: *enrage*
en•a•ble [en-AY-bəl] *verb transitive* **-bled, -bling** make able, authorize, empower, supply with means (to do something)
en•act [en-AKT] *verb intransitive* **1** make law **2** act part > **en•act'ment** *noun*
e•nam•el [i-NAM-əl] *noun* **1** glasslike coating applied to metal, etc. to preserve surface **2** coating of teeth **3** any hard outer coating ▷ *verb transitive* **-eled, -el•ing**
e•nam•or [i-NAM-ər] *verb transitive* **1** inspire with love **2** charm **3** bewitch
en•camp [en-KAMP] *verb* set up (in) camp > **en•camp'ment** *noun* camp
en•cap•su•late [en-KAP-sə-layt] *verb transitive* **-lat•ed, -lat•ing 1** enclose in capsule **2** put in concise or abridged form > **en•cap•su•la'tion** *noun*
en•ceph•a•lo•gram [en-SEF-ə-lə-gram] *noun* X-ray photograph of brain
en•chant' *verb transitive* bewitch, delight > **en•chant'er** *noun* > **en•chant'ress** *noun feminine* > **en•chant'ment** *noun*
en•chi•la•da [en-chə-LAH-də] *noun* rolled tortilla filled with sauce of meat, etc.
en•cir•cle [en-SUR-kəl] *verb transitive* **-cled, -cling 1** surround **2** enfold **3** go around so as to surround
en•clave [EN-klayv] *noun* **1** portion of territory entirely surrounded by foreign land **2** distinct area or group isolated within larger one
en•close [en-KLOHZ] *verb transitive* **-closed, -clos•ing 1** shut in **2** surround **3** envelop **4** place in with something else (in letter, etc.) > **en•clo'sure** [-zhər] *noun*
en•co•mi•um [en-KOH-mee-əm] *noun* **-mi•ums 1** formal praise **2** eulogy > **en•co'mi•ast** *noun* one who composes encomiums
en•com•pass [en-KUM-pəs] *verb transitive* surround, encircle, contain
en•core [ONG-kor] *interjection* **1** again, once more ▷ *noun* **2** call for repetition of song, etc. **3** the repetition
en•coun•ter [en-KOWN-tər] *verb transitive* **1** meet unexpectedly **2** meet in conflict **3** be faced with (difficulty, etc.) ▷ *noun*
en•cour•age [en-KUR-ij] *verb transitive* **-aged,**

vocation, work
emporium *noun* (*old-fashioned*) SHOP, bazaar, market, mart, store, warehouse
empower *verb* ENABLE, allow, authorize, commission, delegate, entitle, license, permit, qualify, sanction, warrant
emptiness *noun* **1** BARENESS, blankness, desolation, vacancy, vacuum, void, waste
2 PURPOSELESSNESS, banality, futility, hollowness, inanity, meaninglessness, senselessness, vanity, worthlessness
3 INSINCERITY, cheapness, hollowness, idleness
empty *adjective* **1** BARE, blank, clear, deserted, desolate, hollow, unfurnished, uninhabited, unoccupied, vacant, void
2 PURPOSELESS, banal, fruitless, futile, hollow, inane, meaningless, senseless, vain, worthless
3 INSINCERE, cheap, hollow, idle
▷ *verb* **4** EVACUATE, clear, drain, exhaust, pour out, unload, vacate, void
empty-headed *adjective* SCATTERBRAINED, brainless, dizzy (*informal*), featherbrained, harebrained, silly, vacuous
emulate *verb* IMITATE, compete with, copy, echo, follow, mimic, rival
enable *verb* ALLOW, authorize, empower, entitle, license, permit, qualify, sanction, warrant
enact *verb* **1** ESTABLISH, authorize, command, decree, legislate, ordain, order, proclaim, sanction
2 PERFORM, act out, depict, play, play the part of, portray, represent
enamored *adjective* IN LOVE, captivated, charmed, enraptured, fond, infatuated, smitten, taken
encampment *noun* CAMP, base, bivouac, camping ground, campsite, cantonment, quarters, tents
encapsulate *verb* SUM UP, abridge, compress, condense, digest, epitomize, précis, summarize
enchant *verb* FASCINATE, beguile, bewitch, captivate, charm, delight, enrapture, enthrall, ravish, spellbind
enchanter *noun* SORCERER, conjurer, magician, magus, necromancer, warlock, witch, wizard
enchanting *adjective* FASCINATING, alluring, attractive, bewitching, captivating, charming, delightful, entrancing, lovely, pleasant
enclose *verb* **1** SURROUND, bound, encase, encircle, fence, hem in, shut in, wall in
2 SEND WITH, include, insert, put in
encompass *verb* **1** SURROUND, circle, encircle, enclose, envelop, ring
2 INCLUDE, admit, comprise, contain, cover, embrace, hold, incorporate, take in
encounter *verb* **1** MEET, bump into (*informal*), chance upon, come upon, confront, experience, face, run across
▷ *noun* **2** MEETING, brush, confrontation, rendezvous
3 BATTLE, clash, conflict, contest, head-to-head, run-in (*informal*)

-ag•ing 1 hearten, animate, inspire with hope 2 embolden > **en•cour'age•ment** *noun*

en•croach [en-KROHCH] *verb intransitive* 1 intrude (on) as usurper 2 trespass > **en•croach'ment** *noun*

en•crust [en-KRUST] *verb* incrust > **en•crus•ta'tion** *noun*

en•cum•ber [en-KUM-bər] *verb transitive* 1 hamper 2 burden > **en•cum'brance** *noun* impediment, burden

en•cyc•li•cal [en-SIK-li-kəl] *adjective* 1 sent to many persons or places ▷ *noun* 2 circular letter, esp. papal letter to all Catholic bishops

en•cy•clo•pe•dia [en-sī-klə-PEE-dee-ə] *noun* book, set of books of information on all subjects, or on every branch of subject, usu. arranged alphabetically > **en•cy•clo•pe'dic** *adjective*

end *noun* 1 limit 2 extremity 3 conclusion, finishing 4 fragment 5 latter part 6 death 7 event, issue 8 purpose, aim 9 *football* one of two linemen stationed farthest from the center ▷ *verb* 10 put an end to 11 come to an end, finish > **end'ing** *noun* > **end'less** *adjective* > **end'pa•pers** *plural noun* blank pages at beginning and end of book

en•dear [en-DEER] *verb transitive* to make dear or beloved > **en•dear'ing** *adjective* > **en•dear'ment** *noun* 1 loving word 2 tender affection

en•deav•or [en-DEV-ər] *verb intransitive* 1 try, strive after ▷ *noun* 2 attempt, effort

en•dem•ic [en-DEM-ik] *adjective* 1 found only among a particular people or in a particular place ▷ *noun* 2 endemic disease

en•dive [EN-dīv] *noun* curly-leaved plant used in salad

endo- *combining form* within: *endocrine*

en•do•car•di•um [en-doh-KAHR-dee-əm] *noun* lining membrane of the heart > **en•do•car•di'tis** [-dī-tis] *noun* inflammation of this

en•do•crine [EN-də-krin] *adjective* of those glands (thyroid, pituitary, etc.) that secrete hormones directly into bloodstream > **en•do•cri•nol'o•gy** *noun* science dealing with endocrine glands

en•dorse [en-DORS] *verb transitive* **-dorsed, -dors•ing** 1 sanction 2 confirm 3 write (esp. sign name) on back of > **en•dorse'ment** *noun*

en•dow' *verb transitive* 1 provide permanent income for 2 furnish (with) > **en•dow'ment** *noun*

en•dure [en-DUUR] *verb* **-dured, -dur•ing** 1 undergo 2 tolerate, bear 3 last > **en•dur'a•ble** *adjective* > **en•dur'ance** *noun* act or power of enduring

en•e•ma [EN-ə-mə] *noun* medicine, liquid injected into rectum

en•e•my [EN-ə-mee] *noun, plural* **-mies** 1 hostile person 2 opponent 3 armed foe 4 hostile force

en•er•gy [EN-ər-jee] *noun, plural* **-gies** 1 vigor,

DICTIONARY • THESAURUS

---

encourage *verb* 1 INSPIRE, buoy up, cheer, comfort, console, embolden, hearten, reassure 2 SPUR, advocate, egg on, foster, promote, prompt, support, urge

encouragement *noun* INSPIRATION, cheer, incitement, promotion, reassurance, stimulation, stimulus, support

encouraging *adjective* PROMISING, bright, cheerful, comforting, good, heartening, hopeful, reassuring, rosy

encroach *verb* INTRUDE, impinge, infringe, invade, make inroads, overstep, trespass, usurp

encumber *verb* BURDEN, hamper, handicap, hinder, impede, inconvenience, obstruct, saddle, weigh down

end *noun* 1 EXTREMITY, boundary, edge, extent, extreme, limit, point, terminus, tip
2 FINISH, cessation, close, closure, ending, expiration, expiry, stop, termination
3 CONCLUSION, culmination, denouement, ending, finale, resolution
4 REMNANT, butt, fragment, leftover, oddment, remainder, scrap, stub
5 DESTRUCTION, death, demise, doom, extermination, extinction, ruin
6 PURPOSE, aim, goal, intention, object, objective, point, reason
▷ *verb* 7 FINISH, cease, close, conclude, culminate, stop, terminate, wind up

endanger *verb* PUT AT RISK, compromise, imperil, jeopardize, put in danger, risk, threaten

endearing *adjective* ATTRACTIVE, captivating, charming, cute, engaging, lovable, sweet, winning

endearment *noun* LOVING WORD, sweet nothing

endeavor *verb* 1 TRY, aim, aspire, attempt, labor, make an effort, strive, struggle, take pains ▷ *noun* 2 EFFORT, attempt, enterprise, trial, try, undertaking, venture

ending *noun* FINISH, cessation, close, completion, conclusion, culmination, denouement, end, finale

endless *adjective* ETERNAL, boundless, continual, everlasting, incessant, infinite, interminable, unlimited

endorse *verb* 1 APPROVE, advocate, authorize, back, champion, promote, ratify, recommend, support
2 SIGN, countersign

endorsement *noun* 1 APPROVAL, advocacy, approbation, authorization, backing, favor, ratification, recommendation, seal of approval, support
2 SIGNATURE, countersignature

endow *verb* PROVIDE, award, bequeath, bestow, confer, donate, finance, fund, give

endowment *noun* PROVISION, award, benefaction, bequest, donation, gift, grant, legacy

endurable *adjective* BEARABLE, acceptable, sufferable, sustainable, tolerable

endurance *noun* 1 STAYING POWER, fortitude, patience, perseverance, persistence, resolution, stamina, strength, tenacity, toleration
2 PERMANENCE, continuity, durability, duration, longevity, stability

endure *verb* 1 BEAR, cope with, experience, stand, suffer, sustain, undergo, withstand
2 LAST, continue, live on, persist, remain, stand, stay, survive

enduring *adjective* LONG-LASTING, abiding, continuing, lasting, perennial, persistent, steadfast, unfaltering, unwavering

enemy *noun* FOE, adversary, antagonist, competitor, opponent, rival, the opposition, the other side

force, activity 2 source(s) of power, as oil, coal, etc. 3 capacity of machine, battery, etc. for work or output of power > **en•er•get'ic** *adjective* > **en'er•gize -gized, -giz•ing** *verb transitive* give vigor to

en•er•vate [EN-ər-vayt] *verb transitive* **-vat•ed, -vat•ing** weaken, deprive of vigor > **en•er•va'tion** *noun* lassitude, weakness

en•fee•ble [en-FEE-bəl] *verb transitive* **-bled, -bling** weaken, debilitate

en•fi•lade [EN-fi-layd] *noun* fire from artillery, sweeping line from end to end

en•force [en-FORS] *verb transitive* **-forced, -for•cing** 1 compel obedience to 2 impose (action) upon 3 drive home > **en•force'a•ble** *adjective*

en•fran•chise [en-FRAN-chīz] *verb transitive* **-chised, -chis•ing** 1 give right of voting to 2 give legislative representation to 3 set free > **en•fran'chise•ment** [-chiz-mənt] *noun*

en•gage [en-GAYJ] *verb transitive* **-gaged, -gag•ing** 1 employ 2 reserve, hire 3 bind by contract or promise 4 order 5 pledge oneself 6 betroth 7 undertake 8 attract 9 occupy 10 bring into conflict 11 interlock ▷ *verb intransitive* **-gaged, -gag•ing** 12 employ oneself (in) 13 promise 14 begin to fight > **en•gaged'** *adjective* 1 betrothed 2 in use 3 occupied, busy > **en•gage'ment** *noun* > **engaging** *adjective* charming

en•gen•der [en-JEN-dər] *verb transitive* 1 give rise to 2 beget 3 rouse

en•gine [EN-jin] *noun* 1 any machine to convert energy into mechanical work, as steam or gasoline engine 2 railroad locomotive 3 fire engine > **en•gi•neer'** *noun* 1 one who is in charge of engines, machinery, etc. or construction work (e.g. roads, bridges) 2 one who originates, organizes something 3 one trained and skilled in engineering ▷ *verb transitive* 4 construct as engineer 5 contrive > **en•gi•neer'ing** *noun*

Eng•lish [ING-glish] *noun* 1 the language of the US, Britain, most parts of the British Commonwealth and certain other countries 2 the people of England ▷ *adjective* 3 relating to England

engrain *verb transitive see* **ingrain**

en•grave [en-GRAYV] *verb transitive* **-graved, -grav•ing** 1 cut in lines on metal for printing 2 carve, incise 3 impress deeply > **en•grav'er** *noun* > **en•grav'ing** *noun* copy of picture printed from engraved plate

en•gross [en-GROHS] *verb transitive* 1 absorb (attention) 2 occupy wholly 3 write out in large letters or in legal form 4 monopolize

en•gulf' *verb transitive* swallow up

en•hance [en-HANS] *verb transitive* **-hanced, -hanc•ing** heighten, intensify, increase value or attractiveness > **en•hance'ment** *noun*

e•nig•ma [ə-NIG-mə] *noun, plural* **-mas** 1 puzzling thing or person 2 riddle > **en•ig•mat'ic** *adjective*

en•join' *verb transitive* 1 command 2 impose, prescribe

en•joy [en-JOI] *verb transitive* 1 delight in 2 take pleasure in 3 have use or benefit of ▷ *verb reflexive* 4 be happy > **en•joy'a•ble** *adjective*

en•large [en-LAHRJ] *verb transitive* **-larged, -larg•ing** 1 make bigger 2 reproduce on larger

DICTIONARY

e

THESAURUS

energetic *adjective* VIGOROUS, active, animated, dynamic, forceful, indefatigable, lively, strenuous, tireless

energy *noun* VIGOR, drive, forcefulness, get-up-and-go (*informal*), liveliness, pep, stamina, verve, vitality

enforce *verb* IMPOSE, administer, apply, carry out, execute, implement, insist on, prosecute, put into effect

engage *verb* 1 PARTICIPATE, embark on, enter into, join, set about, take part, undertake
2 OCCUPY, absorb, engross, grip, involve, preoccupy
3 CAPTIVATE, arrest, catch, fix, gain
4 EMPLOY, appoint, enlist, enroll, hire, retain, take on
5 (*military*) BEGIN BATTLE WITH, assail, attack, encounter, fall on, join battle with, meet, take on
6 SET GOING, activate, apply, bring into operation, energize, switch on

engaged *adjective* 1 BETROTHED (*archaic*), affianced, pledged, promised, spoken for
2 OCCUPIED, busy, employed, in use, tied up, unavailable

engagement *noun* 1 APPOINTMENT, arrangement, commitment, date, meeting
2 BETROTHAL, troth (*archaic*)
3 BATTLE, action, combat, conflict, encounter, fight

engaging *adjective* CHARMING, agreeable, attractive, fetching (*informal*), likable *or* likeable, pleasing, winning, winsome

engender *verb* PRODUCE, breed, cause, create, generate, give rise to, induce, instigate, lead to

engine *noun* MACHINE, mechanism, motor

engineer *verb* BRING ABOUT, contrive, create, devise, effect, mastermind, plan, plot, scheme

engrave *verb* 1 CARVE, chisel, cut, etch, inscribe
2 FIX, embed, impress, imprint, ingrain, lodge

engraving *noun* CARVING, etching, inscription, plate, woodcut

engross *verb* ABSORB, engage, immerse, involve, occupy, preoccupy

engrossed *adjective* ABSORBED, caught up, enthralled, fascinated, gripped, immersed, lost, preoccupied, rapt, riveted

engulf *verb* IMMERSE, envelop, inundate, overrun, overwhelm, submerge, swallow up, swamp

enhance *verb* IMPROVE, add to, boost, heighten, increase, lift, reinforce, strengthen, swell

enigma *noun* MYSTERY, conundrum, problem, puzzle, riddle, teaser

enigmatic *adjective* MYSTERIOUS, ambiguous, cryptic, equivocal, inscrutable, obscure, puzzling, unfathomable

enjoy *verb* 1 TAKE PLEASURE IN *or* TAKE PLEASURE FROM, appreciate, be entertained by, be pleased with, delight in, like, relish
2 HAVE, be blessed with *or* be favored with, experience, have the benefit of, own, possess, reap the benefits of, use

enjoyable *adjective* PLEASURABLE, agreeable, delightful, entertaining, gratifying, pleasant, satisfying, to one's liking

scale, as photograph ▷ *verb intransitive* **-larged, -larg•ing** 3 grow bigger 4 talk, write about, in greater detail > **en•large'a•ble** *adjective* > **en•large'ment** *noun* > **en•larg'er** *noun* optical instrument for enlarging photographs

en•light•en [en-LĪ-tən] *verb transitive* 1 give information to 2 instruct, inform, shed light on > **en•light'en•ment** *noun*

en•list' *verb* engage as soldier or helper > **en•list'ment** *noun*

en•liv•en [en-LĪ-vən] *verb transitive* brighten, make more lively, animate

en masse [ahn MAS] *adverb* 1 in a group, body 2 all together

en•mesh' *verb transitive* entangle

en•mi•ty [EN-mi-tee] *noun, plural* **-ties** ill will, hostility

en•no•ble [en-NOH-bəl] *verb transitive* **-bled, -bling** make noble, elevate > **en•no'ble•ment** *noun*

en•nui [ahn-WEE] *noun* boredom

e•nor•mous [i-NOR-məs] *adjective* very big, vast > **e•nor'mi•ty** *noun* 1 a gross offense 2 great wickedness 3 (*informal*) great size

e•nough [i-NUF] *adjective* 1 as much or as many as need be 2 sufficient ▷ *noun* 3 sufficient quantity ▷ *adverb* 4 (just) sufficiently

enquire *see* **inquire**

en•rap•ture [en-RAP-chər] *verb transitive* **-tured, -tur•ing** 1 delight excessively 2 charm

en•rich' *verb transitive* 1 make rich 2 add to > **en•rich'ment** *noun*

en•roll [en-ROHL] *verb transitive* 1 write name of on roll or list 2 engage, enlist, take in as member 3 enter, record ▷ *verb intransitive* 4 become member > **en•roll'ment** *noun*

en route [ahn ROOT] *Fr.* on the way

en•sconce [en-SKONS] *verb transitive* **-sconced, -sconc•ing** 1 place snugly 2 establish in safety

en•sem•ble [ahn-SAHM-bəl] *noun* 1 whole 2 all parts taken together 3 woman's complete outfit 4 company of actors, dancers, etc. 5 *mus.* group of soloists performing together 6 *mus.* concerted passage 7 general effect

en•shrine [en-SHRĪN] *verb transitive* **-shrined, -shrin•ing** set in shrine, preserve with great care and sacred affection

en•sign [EN-sin] *noun* 1 naval or military flag 2 badge 3 (in the US Navy or Coast Guard) lowest commissioned officer

ensilage *see* **silage**

en•slave [en-SLAYV] *verb transitive* **-slaved, -slav•ing** make into slave > **en•slave'ment** *noun* bondage

en•snare [en-SNAIR] *verb transitive* **-snared, -snar•ing** 1 capture in snare or trap 2 trick into false position 3 entangle

en•sue [en-SOO] *verb intransitive* **-sued, -su•ing** follow, happen after

en•sure [en-SHUUR] *verb transitive* **-sured, -sur•ing** 1 make safe or sure 2 make certain to happen 3 secure

en•tail [en-TAYL] *verb transitive* 1 involve as result, necessitate 2 *law* restrict ownership of

enjoyment *noun* PLEASURE, amusement, delectation, delight, entertainment, fun, gratification, happiness, joy, relish

enlarge *verb* 1 INCREASE, add to, amplify, broaden, expand, extend, grow, magnify, swell, widen
2 ▷ **enlarge on** EXPAND ON, descant on, develop, elaborate on, expatiate on, give further details about

enlighten *verb* INFORM, advise, cause to understand, counsel, edify, educate, instruct, make aware, teach

enlightened *adjective* INFORMED, aware, civilized, cultivated, educated, knowledgeable, open-minded, reasonable, sophisticated

enlightenment *noun* UNDERSTANDING, awareness, comprehension, education, insight, instruction, knowledge, learning, wisdom

enlist *verb* 1 JOIN UP, enroll, enter *or* enter into, join, muster, register, sign up, volunteer
2 OBTAIN, engage, procure, recruit

enliven *verb* CHEER UP, animate, excite, inspire, invigorate, pep up, rouse, spark, stimulate, vitalize

enmity *noun* HOSTILITY, acrimony, animosity, bad blood, bitterness, hatred, ill will, malice

ennoble *verb* DIGNIFY, aggrandize, elevate, enhance, exalt, glorify, honor, magnify, raise

enormity *noun* 1 WICKEDNESS, atrocity, depravity, monstrousness, outrageousness, vileness, villainy
2 ATROCITY, abomination, crime, disgrace, evil, horror, monstrosity, outrage
3 (*informal*) HUGENESS, greatness, immensity, magnitude, vastness

enormous *adjective* HUGE, colossal, gigantic, gross, immense, mammoth, massive, mountainous, tremendous, vast

enough *adjective* 1 SUFFICIENT, abundant, adequate, ample, plenty
▷ *noun* 2 SUFFICIENCY, abundance, adequacy, ample supply, plenty, right amount
▷ *adverb* 3 SUFFICIENTLY, abundantly, adequately, amply, reasonably, satisfactorily, tolerably

enquire *see* **inquire**

enquiry *see* **inquiry**

enrage *verb* ANGER, exasperate, incense, inflame, infuriate, madden

enrich *verb* 1 ENHANCE, augment, develop, improve, refine, supplement
2 MAKE RICH, make wealthy

enroll *verb* ENLIST, accept, admit, join up, recruit, register, sign up *or* sign on, take on

enrollment *noun* ENLISTMENT, acceptance, admission, engagement, matriculation, recruitment, registration

en route *adverb* ON THE WAY *or* ALONG THE WAY, in transit, on the road

ensemble *noun* 1 WHOLE, aggregate, collection, entirety, set, sum, total, totality
2 OUTFIT, costume, get-up (*informal*), suit
3 GROUP, band, cast, chorus, company, troupe

ensign *noun* FLAG, banner, colors, jack, pennant, pennon, standard, streamer

ensue *verb* FOLLOW, arise, come next, derive, flow, issue, proceed, result, stem

ensure *verb* 1 MAKE CERTAIN, certify, confirm, effect, guarantee, make sure, secure, warrant
2 PROTECT, guard, make safe, safeguard, secure

entail *verb* INVOLVE, bring about, call for, demand, give rise to, necessitate, occasion, require

property to designated line of heirs > **en•tail'ment** *noun*

en•tan•gle [en-TANG-gəl] *verb transitive* **-gled, -gling** 1 ensnare 2 perplex > **en•tan'gle•ment** *noun*

en•tente [ahn-TAHNT] *noun* friendly understanding between nations

en•ter [EN-tər] *verb transitive* 1 go, come into 2 penetrate 3 join 4 write in, register ▷ *verb intransitive* 5 go, come in, join, begin > **en'trance** [-trəns] *noun* 1 going, coming in 2 door, passage to enter 3 right to enter 4 fee paid for this > **en'trant** *noun* one who enters, esp. contest > **en'try** *noun, plural* **-tries** 1 entrance 2 entering 3 item entered, e.g. in account, list

en•ter•ic [en-TER-ik] *adjective* of or relating to the intestines > **en•ter•i'tis** *noun* inflammation of intestines

en•ter•prise [EN-tər-prīz] *noun* 1 bold or difficult undertaking 2 bold spirit 3 force of character in launching out 4 business, company > **en'ter•pris•ing** *adjective*

en•ter•tain [en-tər-TAYN] *verb transitive* 1 amuse, divert 2 receive as guest 3 maintain 4 consider favorable, take into consideration > **en•ter•tain'er** *noun*

en•thrall [en-THRAWL] *verb transitive* captivate, thrill, hold spellbound

en•thu•si•asm [en-THOO-zee-az-əm] *noun* ardent eagerness, zeal > **en•thuse'** *verb* (cause to) show enthusiasm > **en•thu'si•ast** *noun* ardent supporter of > **en•thu•si•as'tic** *adjective*

en•tice [en-TĪS] *verb transitive* **-ticed, -tic•ing** allure, attract, inveigle, tempt > **en•tic'ing** *adjective* alluring

en•tire [en-TĪR] *adjective* whole, complete, unbroken > **en•tire'ly** *adverb* > **en•tire'ty** *noun, plural* **-ties**

en•ti•tle [en-TĪ-təl] *verb intransitive* **-tled, -tling** 1 give claim to 2 qualify 3 give title to

en•ti•ty [EN-ti-tee] *noun, plural* **-ties** 1 thing's being or existence 2 reality 3 thing having real existence

en•to•mol•o•gy [en-tə-MOL-ə-jee] *noun* study of insects > **en•to•mol'o•gist** *noun*

en•tou•rage [ahn-tuu-RAHZH] *noun* 1 associates, retinue 2 surroundings

en•trails [EN-traylz] *plural noun* 1 bowels, intestines 2 inner parts

en•trance[1] *noun see* **enter**

en•trance[2] [en-TRANS] *verb transitive* **-tranced, -tranc•ing** 1 delight 2 throw into a trance

en•treat [en-TREET] *verb transitive* 1 ask earnestly 2 beg, implore > **en•treat'y** *noun, plural* **-treat•ies** earnest request

en•trée [AHN-tray] *noun* 1 main course of meal

---

entangle *verb* 1 TANGLE, catch, embroil, enmesh, ensnare, entrap, implicate, snag, snare, trap
2 MIX UP, complicate, confuse, jumble, muddle, perplex, puzzle

enter *verb* 1 COME IN *or* COME INTO, arrive, go in *or* go into, make an entrance, pass into, penetrate, pierce
2 JOIN, commence, embark upon, enlist, enroll, set out on, start, take up
3 RECORD, inscribe, list, log, note, register, set down, take down

enterprise *noun* 1 FIRM, business, company, concern, establishment, operation
2 UNDERTAKING, adventure, effort, endeavor, operation, plan, program, project, venture
3 INITIATIVE, adventurousness, boldness, daring, drive, energy, enthusiasm, resourcefulness

enterprising *adjective* RESOURCEFUL, adventurous, bold, daring, energetic, enthusiastic, go-ahead, intrepid, spirited

entertain *verb* 1 AMUSE, charm, cheer, delight, please, regale
2 SHOW HOSPITALITY TO, accommodate, be host to, harbor, have company, lodge, put up, treat
3 CONSIDER, conceive, contemplate, imagine, keep in mind, think about

entertaining *adjective* ENJOYABLE, amusing, cheering, diverting, funny, humorous, interesting, pleasant, pleasurable

entertainment *noun* ENJOYMENT, amusement, fun, leisure activity, pastime, pleasure, recreation, sport, treat

enthrall *verb* FASCINATE, captivate, charm, enchant, enrapture, entrance, grip, mesmerize

enthusiasm *noun* KEENNESS, eagerness, fervor, interest, passion, relish, zeal, zest

enthusiast *noun* LOVER, aficionado, buff (*informal*), devotee, fan, fanatic, follower, supporter

enthusiastic *adjective* KEEN, avid, eager, fervent, gung ho (*slang*), passionate, vigorous, wholehearted, zealous

entice *verb* ATTRACT, allure, cajole, coax, lead on, lure, persuade, seduce, tempt

entire *adjective* WHOLE, complete, full, gross, total

entirely *adverb* COMPLETELY, absolutely, altogether, fully, in every respect, thoroughly, totally, utterly, wholly

entitle *verb* 1 GIVE THE RIGHT TO, allow, authorize, empower, enable, license, permit
2 CALL, christen, dub, label, name, term, title

entity *noun* THING, being, creature, individual, object, organism, substance

entourage *noun* RETINUE, associates, attendants, company, court, escort, followers, staff, train

entrails *plural noun* INTESTINES, bowels, guts, innards (*informal*), insides (*informal*), offal, viscera

entrance[1] *noun* 1 WAY IN, access, door, doorway, entry, gate, opening, passage
2 APPEARANCE, arrival, coming in, entry, introduction
3 ADMISSION, access, admittance, entrée, entry, permission to enter

entrance[2] *verb* 1 ENCHANT, bewitch, captivate, charm, delight, enrapture, enthrall, fascinate
2 MESMERIZE, hypnotize, put in a trance

entrant *noun* COMPETITOR, candidate, contestant, entry, participant, player

entreaty *noun* PLEA, appeal, earnest request, exhortation, petition, prayer, request, supplication

entrenched *adjective* FIXED, deep-rooted, deep-seated, ineradicable, ingrained, rooted, set, unshakable, well-established

entrepreneur *noun* BUSINESSMAN *or* BUSINESSWOMAN, impresario, industrialist, magnate, tycoon

2 right of access, admission

en•trench' *verb transitive* 1 establish in fortified position with trenches 2 establish firmly

en•tre•pre•neur [ahn-trə-prə-NUR] *noun* person who attempts to profit by risk and initiative

en•tro•py [EN-trə-pee] *noun* 1 unavailability of the heat energy of a system for mechanical work 2 measurement of this

en•trust' *verb transitive* 1 commit, charge with 2 put into care or protection of

en•twine [en-TWĪN] *verb transitive* **-twined, -twin•ing** 1 interweave 2 wreathe with 3 embrace

e•nu•mer•ate [i-NOO-mə-rayt] *verb transitive* **-at•ed, -at•ing** 1 mention one by one 2 count > **e•nu•mer•a'tion** *noun* > **e•nu'mer•a•tor** *noun*

e•nun•ci•ate [i-NUN-see-ayt] *verb transitive* **-at•ed, -at•ing** 1 state clearly 2 proclaim 3 pronounce > **e•nun•ci•a'tion** *noun*

en•vel•op [en-VEL-əp] *verb transitive* 1 wrap up, enclose, surround 2 encircle > **en•vel'op•ment** *noun*

en•vel•ope [EN-və-lohp] *noun* 1 folded, gummed cover of letter 2 covering, wrapper

en•ven•om [en-VEN-əm] *verb transitive* 1 put poison, venom in 2 embitter

en•vi•ron [en-VĪ-rən] *verb transitive* surround > **en•vi'ron•ment** *noun* 1 surroundings 2 conditions of life or growth > **en•vi•ron•men'tal** *adjective* > **en•vi•ron•men'tal•ist** *noun* ecologist > **en•vi'rons** *plural noun* districts around (town, etc.), outskirts

en•vis•age [en-VIZ-ij] *verb transitive* **-aged, -ag•ing** 1 conceive of as possibility 2 visualize

en•voy [EN-voi] *noun* 1 messenger, representative 2 diplomatic agent of rank below ambassador

en•vy [EN-vee] *noun, plural* **-vies** 1 bitter contemplation of another's good fortune 2 object of this feeling ▷ *verb transitive* **-vied, -vy•ing** grudge another's good fortune, success or qualities 3 feel envy of > **en'vi•a•ble** *adjective* arousing envy > **en'vi•ous** *adjective* full of envy

en•zyme [EN-zīm] *noun* any of group of complex proteins produced by living cells and acting as catalysts in biochemical reactions

e•on [EE-ən] *noun* age, very long period of time

ep•au•lette [EP-ə-let] *noun* shoulder ornament on uniform

Eph. Ephesians

e•phem•er•al [i-FEM-ər-əl] *adjective* short-lived, transient > **e•phem'er•a** [i-FEM-ər-ə] *plural noun* items designed to last only for a short time, such as programmes or posters

epi-, eph- (*or before a vowel*) **ep-** *prefix* upon, during: *epitaph; ephemeral; epoch*

ep•ic [EP-ik] *noun* 1 long poem or story telling of achievements of hero or heroes 2 film, etc. about heroic deeds ▷ *adjective* 3 of, like, an epic 4 impressive, grand

ep•i•cene [EP-i-seen] *adjective* 1 common to both sexes 2 effeminate 3 weak ▷ *noun* 4 epicene person or thing

ep•i•cen•ter [EP-i-sen-tər] *noun* focus of earthquake

ep•i•cure [EP-i-kyuur] *noun* one delighting in eating and drinking > **ep•i•cu•re'an** *adjective* 1 of Epicurus, who taught that pleasure, in the shape of practice of virtue, was highest good 2 given to refined sensuous enjoyment ▷ *noun* 3 such person or philosopher > **ep•i•cu•re'an•ism** *noun*

ep•i•dem•ic [ep-i-DEM-ik] *adjective* (esp. of disease) prevalent and spreading rapidly; widespread ▷ *noun*

ep•i•der•mis [ep-i-DUR-mis] *noun* outer skin

ep•i•du•ral [ep-i-DUUR-əl] *noun, adjective* (of) spinal anesthetic used esp. for relief of pain during childbirth

ep•i•glot'tis *noun, plural* **-tis•es** cartilage that covers opening of larynx in swallowing > **ep•i•glot'tal** [-GLOT-əl] *adjective*

ep•i•gone [EP-i-gohn] *noun* imitative follower

ep'i•gram *noun* concise, witty poem or saying > **ep•i•gram•mat'ic** [-grə-MAT-ik] *adjective*

---

entrust *verb* GIVE CUSTODY OF, assign, commit, confide, delegate, deliver, hand over, turn over

entry *noun* 1 WAY IN, access, door, doorway, entrance, gate, opening, passage
2 COMING IN, appearance, entering, entrance, initiation, introduction
3 ADMISSION, access, entrance, entrée, permission to enter
4 RECORD, account, item, listing, note

entwine *verb* TWIST, interlace, interweave, knit, plait, twine, weave, wind

enumerate *verb* LIST, cite, itemize, mention, name, quote, recite, recount, relate, spell out

enunciate *verb* 1 PRONOUNCE, articulate, enounce, say, sound, speak, utter, vocalize, voice
2 STATE, declare, proclaim, promulgate, pronounce, propound, publish

envelop *verb* ENCLOSE, cloak, cover, encase, encircle, engulf, shroud, surround, wrap

envelope *noun* WRAPPING, case, casing, cover, covering, jacket, wrapper

enviable *adjective* DESIRABLE, advantageous, favored, fortunate, lucky, privileged, to die for (*informal*), win-win (*informal*)

envious *adjective* COVETOUS, green with envy, grudging, jealous, resentful

environment *noun* SURROUNDINGS, atmosphere, background, conditions, habitat, medium, setting, situation

environmental *adjective* ECOLOGICAL, green

environmentalist *noun* CONSERVATIONIST, ecologist, green

environs *plural noun* SURROUNDING AREA, district, locality, neighborhood, outskirts, precincts, suburbs, vicinity

envisage *verb* 1 IMAGINE, conceive *or* conceive of, conceptualize, contemplate, fancy, picture, think up, visualize
2 FORESEE, anticipate, envision, predict, see

envoy *noun* MESSENGER, agent, ambassador, courier, delegate, diplomat, emissary, intermediary, representative

envy *noun* 1 COVETOUSNESS, enviousness, jealousy, resentfulness, resentment
▷ *verb* 2 COVET, be envious *or* be envious of, begrudge, be jealous *or* be jealous of, grudge, resent

ephemeral *adjective* BRIEF, fleeting, momentary, passing, short-lived, temporary, transient, transitory

> **ep•i•gram'ma•tist** [-GRAM-ə-tist] *noun*
ep•i•graph [EP-i-graf] *noun* inscription
ep•i•lep•sy [EP-ə-lep-see] *noun* disorder of nervous system causing convulsions > **ep•i•lep'tic** *noun* 1 sufferer from this ▷ *adjective* 2 of, subject to, this
ep•i•logue [EP-ə-lawg] *noun* short speech or poem at end, esp. of play
E•piph•a•ny [i-PIF-ə-nee] *noun, plural* **-nies** 1 festival of the announcement of Christ to the Magi, celebrated January 6 2 (**e•piph•a•ny**) sudden intuitive perception or insight
e•pis•co•pal [i-PIS-kə-pəl] *adjective* 1 of bishop 2 ruled by bishops > **e•pis'co•pa•cy** [-pə-see] *noun* government by body of bishops > **E•pis•co•pa'li•an** [-PAYL-yən] *adjective, noun* (member, adherent) of Episcopalian church > **e•pis'co•pate** [-kə-pit] *noun* 1 bishop's office, see, or duration of office 2 body of bishops
ep•i•sode [EP-ə-sohd] *noun* 1 incident 2 section of (serialized) book, TV program, etc. > **ep•i•sod'ic** [-SOD-ik] *adjective*
e•pis•te•mol•o•gy [i-pis-tə-MOL-ə-jee] *noun* study of source, nature and limitations of knowledge > **e•pis•te•mo•log'i•cal** *adjective*
e•pis•tle [i-PIS-əl] *noun* 1 letter, esp. of apostle 2 poem in letter form > **e•pis'to•lar•y** [-tə-ler-ee] *adjective*
e•pi•taph [EP-i-taf] *noun* memorial inscription on tomb
ep•i•thet [EP-ə-thet] *noun* additional, descriptive word or name
e•pit•o•me [i-PIT-ə-mee] *noun* 1 embodiment, typical example 2 summary > **e•pit'o•mize** [-ə-mīz] *verb transitive* **-mized, -miz•ing** typify
ep•och [EP-ək] *noun* 1 beginning of period 2 period, era, esp. one of notable events > **ep'o•chal** [-ə-kəl] *adjective*
eq•ua•ble [EK-wə-bəl] *adjective* 1 even-tempered, placid 2 uniform, not easily disturbed > **eq'ua•bly** *adverb* > **eq•ua•bil'i•ty** *noun*
e•qual [EE-kwəl] *adjective* 1 the same in number, size, merit, etc. 2 identical 3 fit or qualified 4 evenly balanced ▷ *noun* 5 one equal to another ▷ *verb transitive* 6 be equal to > **e•qual•i•ty** [i-KWOL-i-tee] *noun, plural* **-ties** 1 state of being equal 2 uniformity > **e'qual•ize** *verb* **-ized, -iz•ing** make, become, equal > **e'qual•ly** *adverb* > **equal opportunity** nondiscrimination as to sex, race, etc. in employment, pay, etc.
e•qua•nim•i•ty [ee-kwə-NIM-i-tee] *noun* calmness, composure, steadiness
e•quate [i-KWAYT] *verb transitive* **-quat•ed, -quat•ing** 1 make equal 2 bring to a common standard > **e•qua'tion** [-zhən] *noun* 1 equating of two mathematical expressions 2 balancing
e•qua•tor [i-KWAY-tər] *noun* imaginary circle around Earth equidistant from the poles > **e•qua•to•ri•al** [ee-kwə-TOR-ee-əl] *adjective*
e•ques•tri•an [i-KWES-tree-ən] *adjective* 1 of, skilled in, horseback riding 2 mounted on horse ▷ *noun* 3 rider
equi- *combining form* equal, at equal: *equidistant*
e•qui•an•gu•lar [ee-kwee-ANG-gyə-lər] *adjective* having equal angles
e•qui•lat•er•al [ee-kwə-LAT-ər-əl] *adjective* having equal sides
e•qui•lib•ri•um [ee-kwə-LIB-ree-əm] *noun* state of steadiness, equipoise or stability
e•quine [EE-kwīn] *adjective* of, like a horse
e•qui•nox [EE-kwə-noks] *noun* 1 time when sun crosses equator and day and night are equal 2 either point at which sun crosses equator
e•quip [i-KWIP] *verb transitive* **-quipped, -quip•ping** supply, fit out, array > **e•quip'ment** *noun*
eq•ui•poise [EK-wə-poiz] *noun* 1 perfect

---

epidemic *noun* SPREAD, contagion, growth, outbreak, plague, rash, upsurge, wave
epigram *noun* WITTICISM, aphorism, bon mot, quip
epilogue *noun* CONCLUSION, coda, concluding speech, postscript
episode *noun* 1 EVENT, adventure, affair, escapade, experience, happening, incident, matter, occurrence
2 PART, chapter, installment, passage, scene, section
epistle *noun* LETTER, communication, message, missive, note
epitaph *noun* MONUMENT, inscription
epithet *noun* NAME, appellation, description, designation, moniker *or* monicker (*slang*), nickname, sobriquet, tag, title
epitome *noun* PERSONIFICATION, archetype, embodiment, essence, quintessence, representation, type, typical example
epitomize *verb* TYPIFY, embody, exemplify, illustrate, personify, represent, symbolize
epoch *noun* ERA, age, date, period, time
equable *adjective* EVEN-TEMPERED, calm, composed, easy-going, imperturbable, level-headed, placid, serene, unflappable (*informal*)
equal *adjective* 1 IDENTICAL, alike, corresponding, equivalent, the same, uniform
2 REGULAR, symmetrical, uniform, unvarying
3 EVEN, balanced, evenly matched, fifty-fifty (*informal*)
4 FAIR, egalitarian, even handed, impartial, just, on a level playing field (*informal*), unbiased
5 ▷ **equal to** CAPABLE OF, competent to, fit for, good enough for, ready for, strong enough, suitable for, up to
▷ *noun* 6 MATCH, counterpart, equivalent, rival, twin
▷ *verb* 7 MATCH, amount to, be tantamount to, correspond to, equate, level, parallel, tie with
equality *noun* 1 SAMENESS, balance, correspondence, equivalence, evenness, identity, likeness, similarity, uniformity
2 FAIRNESS, egalitarianism, equal opportunity, parity
equalize *verb* MAKE EQUAL, balance, equal, even up, level, match, regularize, smooth, square, standardize
equate *verb* MAKE EQUAL *or* BE EQUAL, be commensurate, compare, correspond with *or* correspond to, liken, mention in the same breath, parallel
equation *noun* EQUATING, comparison, correspondence, parallel
equilibrium *noun* STABILITY, balance, equipoise, evenness, rest, steadiness, symmetry
equip *verb* SUPPLY, arm, array, fit out, furnish, provide, stock

balance **2** counterpoise **3** equanimity

eq•ui•ty [EK-wə-tee] *noun, plural* **-ties** **1** fairness **2** use of principles of justice to supplement law **3** system of law so made > **eq'ui•ta•ble** *adjective* fair, reasonable, just

e•quiv•a•lent [i-KWIV-ə-lənt] *adjective* **1** equal in value **2** having the same meaning or result **3** tantamount **4** corresponding > **e•quiv'a•lence** *noun* > **e•quiv'a•len•cy** *noun*

e•quiv•o•cal [i-KWIV-ə-kəl] *adjective* **1** of double or doubtful meaning **2** questionable **3** liable to suspicion > **e•quiv'o•cate** *verb intransitive* **-cat•ed, -cat•ing** use equivocal words to mislead > **e•quiv•o•ca'tion** *noun*

Er *chem.* erbium

e•ra [EER-ə] *noun* **1** system of time in which years are numbered from particular event **2** time of the event **3** memorable date, period

e•rad•i•cate [i-RAD-i-kayt] *verb transitive* **-cat•ed, -cat•ing** **1** wipe out, exterminate **2** root out > **e•rad'i•ca•ble** *adjective* > **e•rad•i•ca'tion** *noun*

e•rase [i-RAYS] *verb transitive* **-rased, -ras•ing** **1** rub out **2** remove, e.g. recording from magnetic tape > **e•ra'ser** *noun* > **e•ra'sure** [-shər] *noun*

ere [air] *preposition, conjunction poet.* **1** before **2** sooner than

e•rect [i-REKT] *adjective* **1** upright ▷ *verb transitive* **2** set up **3** build > **e•rec'tile** [-tl] *adjective* > **e•rec'tion** *noun* esp. an erect penis > **e•rect'or** *noun*

erg [urg] *noun* cgs unit of work or energy

er•go•nom•ics [ur-gə-NOM-iks] *noun* study of relationship between workers and their environment

er•got [UR-gət] *noun* **1** disease of grain **2** diseased seed used as drug > **er'got•ism** *noun* disease caused by eating ergot-infested grain

er•mine [UR-min] *noun* **1** weasel in northern regions, esp. in winter **2** its white winter fur

e•rode [i-ROHD] *verb transitive* **-rod•ed, -rod•ing** **1** wear away **2** eat into > **e•ro'sion** [-*zh*ən] *noun*

e•rog•e•nous [i-ROJ-ə-nəs] *adjective* sensitive to sexual stimulation

e•rot•ic [i-ROT-ik] *adjective* relating to, or treating of, sexual pleasure > **e•rot'i•ca** [-ə-kə] *noun* sexual literature or art > **e•rot'i•cism** [-ə-sizm] *noun*

err [er] *verb intransitive* **1** make mistakes **2** be wrong **3** sin > **er•rat•ic** [i-RAT-ik] *adjective* irregular in movement, conduct, etc. > **er•rat'i•cal•ly** *adverb* > **er•ra•tum** [i-RAH-təm] *noun, plural* **-ta** [-tə] printing mistake noted for correction > **er•ro•ne•ous** [i-ROH-nee-əs] *adjective* mistaken, wrong > **er'ror** *noun* **1** mistake **2** wrong opinion **3** sin

er•rand [ER-ənd] *noun* **1** short journey for simple business **2** the business, mission of messenger **3** purpose

er•rant [ER-ənt] *adjective* **1** wandering in search of adventure **2** erring > **er'ran•cy** *noun, plural* **-cies** erring state or conduct > **er'rant•ry** *noun, plural* **-ries** state or conduct of knight errant

erst•while [URST-hwīl] *adjective* of times past, former

er•u•dite [ER-yə-dīt] *adjective* learned > **er•u•di'tion** [-DISH-ən] *noun* learning

e•rupt [i-RUPT] *verb intransitive* burst out > **e•rup'tion** *noun* **1** bursting out, esp. volcanic outbreak **2** rash on the skin

er•y•sip•e•las [er-ə-SIP-ə-ləs] *noun* acute skin infection

Es *chem.* einsteinium

es•ca•late [ES-kə-layt] *verb* **-lat•ed, -lat•ing**

DICTIONARY • THESAURUS

equipment *noun* TOOLS, accouterments, apparatus, gear, paraphernalia, stuff, supplies, tackle

equitable *adjective* FAIR, even-handed, honest, impartial, just, proper, reasonable, unbiased

equivalence *noun* EQUALITY, correspondence, evenness, likeness, parity, sameness, similarity

equivalent *noun* **1** EQUAL, counterpart, match, opposite number, parallel, twin ▷ *adjective* **2** EQUAL, alike, commensurate, comparable, corresponding, interchangeable, of a piece, on a level playing field (*informal*), same, similar, tantamount

equivocal *adjective* AMBIGUOUS, evasive, indefinite, indeterminate, misleading, oblique, obscure, uncertain, vague

era *noun* AGE, date, day *or* days, epoch, generation, period, time

eradicate *verb* WIPE OUT, annihilate, destroy, eliminate, erase, exterminate, extinguish, obliterate, remove, root out

erase *verb* WIPE OUT, blot, cancel, delete, expunge, obliterate, remove, rub out

erect *verb* **1** BUILD, construct, put up, raise **2** FOUND, create, establish, form, initiate, institute, organize, set up ▷ *adjective* **3** UPRIGHT, elevated, perpendicular, pricked-up, stiff, straight, vertical

erode *verb* WEAR DOWN *or* WEAR AWAY, abrade, consume, corrode, destroy, deteriorate, disintegrate, eat away, grind down

erosion *noun* DETERIORATION, abrasion, attrition, destruction, disintegration, eating away, grinding down, wearing down *or* wearing away

erotic *adjective* SEXUAL, amatory, carnal, lustful, seductive, sensual, sexy (*informal*), voluptuous

err *verb* MAKE A MISTAKE, blunder, go wrong, miscalculate, misjudge, mistake, slip up (*informal*)

errand *noun* JOB, charge, commission, message, mission, task

erratic *adjective* UNPREDICTABLE, changeable, inconsistent, irregular, uneven, unreliable, unstable, variable, wayward

erroneous *adjective* INCORRECT, fallacious, false, faulty, flawed, invalid, mistaken, unsound, wrong

error *noun* MISTAKE, bloomer (*informal*), blunder, miscalculation, oversight, slip, solecism

erstwhile *adjective* FORMER, bygone, late, old, once, one-time, past, previous, sometime

erudite *adjective* LEARNED, cultivated, cultured, educated, knowledgeable, scholarly, well-educated, well-read

erupt *verb* **1** EXPLODE, belch forth, blow up, burst out, gush, pour forth, spew forth *or* spew out, spout, throw off **2** (*medical*) BREAK OUT, appear

eruption *noun* **1** EXPLOSION, discharge, ejection, flare-up, outbreak, outburst **2** (*medical*) INFLAMMATION, outbreak, rash

increase, be increased, in extent, intensity, etc.
es•ca•la•tor [ES-kə-lay-tər] *noun* moving staircase
es•cape [i-SKAYP] *verb intransitive* **-caped, -cap•ing** 1 get free 2 get off safely 3 go unpunished 4 find way out ▷ *verb transitive* **-caped, -cap•ing** 5 elude 6 be forgotten by ▷ *noun* 7 escaping > **es'ca•pade** *noun* wild (mischievous) adventure > **es•cap'ism** [-KAYP-izm] *noun* taking refuge in fantasy to avoid facing disagreeable facts
es•carp•ment [i-SKAHRP-mənt] *noun* steep hillside
es•cha•tol•o•gy [es-kə-TOL-ə-jee] *noun* study of death, judgment and last things > **es•cha•to•log'i•cal** *adjective*
es•chew [es-CHOO] *verb transitive* avoid, abstain from, shun
es•cort [ES-kort] *noun* 1 armed guard for traveler, etc. 2 person or persons accompanying another > **es•cort'** *verb transitive*
es•cri•toire [es-kri-TWAHR] *noun* writing desk
es•cut•cheon [i-SKUCH-ən] *noun* 1 shield with coat of arms 2 ornamental plate around keyhole, etc.
Es•ki•mo [ES-kə-moh] *noun, plural* **-mos** 1 member of the aboriginal race inhabiting N Canada, Greenland, Alaska, and E Siberia 2 their language. Note that many of the peoples traditionally called **Eskimos** prefer to call themselves **Inuit**
e•so•phag•us [i-SOF ə gəs] *noun, plural* **-gi** [-jī] canal from mouth to stomach; gullet > **e•soph•a•ge'al** [-JEE-əl] *adjective*
es•o•ter•ic [es-ə-TER-ik] *adjective* 1 abstruse, obscure 2 secret 3 restricted to initiates
ESP extrasensory perception
es•pal•ier [i-SPAL-yər] *noun* 1 shrub, (fruit) tree trained to grow flat, as against wall, etc. 2 trellis for this
es•pe•cial [i-SPESH-əl] *adjective* 1 preeminent, more than ordinary 2 particular > **es•pe'cial•ly** *adverb*
Es•pe•ran•to [es-pə-RAHN-toh] *noun* artificial language designed for universal use
es•pi•o•nage [ES-pee-ə-nahzh] *noun* 1 spying 2 use of secret agents
es•pla•nade [ES-plə-nahd] *noun* level space, esp. one used as public promenade
es•pouse [i-SPOWZ] *verb transitive* **-poused, -pous•ing** 1 support, embrace (cause, etc.) 2 marry > **es•pous'al** *noun*
es•pres•so [e-SPRES-oh] *noun* 1 strong coffee made by forcing steam through ground coffee beans 2 cup of espresso
es•prit [e-SPREE] *noun* 1 spirit 2 animation > **esprit de corps** [də kor] attachment, loyalty to the society, etc., one belongs to
es•py [i-SPĪ] *verb transitive* **-pied, -py•ing** catch sight of
es•quire [ES-kwīr] *noun* 1 gentleman's courtesy title used on letters 2 formerly, a squire
es'say *noun* 1 prose composition 2 short treatise 3 attempt > **es•say'** *verb transitive* **-sayed, -say'ing** 1 try, attempt 2 test > **es'say•ist** *noun*
es•sence [ES-əns] *noun* 1 all that makes thing what it is 2 existence, being 3 entity, reality 4 extract got by distillation > **es•sen•tial** [ə-SEN-shəl] *adjective* 1 necessary, indispensable 2 inherent 3 of, constituting essence of thing ▷ *noun* 4 indispensable element 5 chief point
es•tab•lish [i-STAB-lish] *verb transitive* 1 make secure 2 set up 3 settle 4 prove > **es•tab'lish•ment** *noun* 1 establishing 2 permanent organized body 3 place of business together with its employees, equipment, etc. 4 household 5 public institution > **established church** church officially recognized as national institution > **the Establishment** *noun* group, class of people holding authority within a

DICTIONARY

e

THESAURUS

escalate *verb* INCREASE, expand, extend, grow, heighten, intensify, mount, rise
escapade *noun* ADVENTURE, antic, caper, prank, scrape (*informal*), stunt
escape *verb* 1 GET AWAY, abscond, bolt, break free *or* break out, flee, fly, make one's getaway, run away *or* run off, slip away
2 AVOID, dodge, duck, elude, evade, pass, shun, slip
3 LEAK, emanate, exude, flow, gush, issue, pour forth, seep
▷ *noun* 4 GETAWAY, break, break-out, flight
5 AVOIDANCE, circumvention, evasion
6 RELAXATION, distraction, diversion, pastime, recreation
7 LEAK, emanation, emission, seepage
escort *noun* 1 GUARD, bodyguard, convoy, cortege, entourage, retinue, train
2 COMPANION, attendant, beau, chaperon, guide, partner
▷ *verb* 3 ACCOMPANY, chaperone, conduct, guide, lead, partner, shepherd, usher
especial *adjective* (*formal*) EXCEPTIONAL, noteworthy, outstanding, principal, special, uncommon, unusual
especially *adverb* EXCEPTIONALLY, conspicuously, markedly, notably, outstandingly, remarkably, specially, strikingly, uncommonly, unusually
espionage *noun* SPYING, counter-intelligence, intelligence, surveillance, undercover work
espousal *noun* SUPPORT, adoption, advocacy, backing, championing, championship, defense, embracing, promotion, taking up
espouse *verb* SUPPORT, adopt, advocate, back, champion, embrace, promote, stand up for, take up, uphold
essay *noun* 1 COMPOSITION, article, discourse, dissertation, paper, piece, tract, treatise
▷ *verb* 2 (*formal*) ATTEMPT, aim, endeavor, try, undertake
essence *noun* 1 FUNDAMENTAL NATURE, being, core, heart, nature, quintessence, soul, spirit, substance
2 CONCENTRATE, distillate, extract, spirits, tincture
essential *adjective* 1 VITAL, crucial, important, indispensable, necessary, needed, requisite
2 FUNDAMENTAL, basic, cardinal, elementary, innate, intrinsic, main, principal
▷ *noun* 3 PREREQUISITE, basic, fundamental, must, necessity, rudiment, sine qua non (*Latin*)
establish *verb* 1 CREATE, constitute, form, found, ground, inaugurate, institute, settle, set up
2 PROVE, authenticate, certify, confirm, corroborate, demonstrate, substantiate, verify
establishment *noun* 1 CREATION, formation,

profession, society, etc.
es•tate [i-STAYT] *noun* 1 landed property 2 person's property 3 deceased person's property 4 class as part of nation 5 rank, state, condition of life
es•teem [i-STEEM] *verb transitive* 1 think highly of 2 consider ▷ *noun* 3 favorable opinion, regard, respect
es•ter [ES-tər] *noun chem.* organic compound produced by reaction between acid and alcohol
es•ti•mate [ES-tə-mayt] *verb transitive* **-mat•ed, -mat•ing** 1 form approximate idea of (amounts, measurements, etc.) 2 form opinion of 3 quote probable price for ▷ *noun* [-mit] 4 approximate judgment of amounts, etc. 5 amount, etc., arrived at 6 opinion 7 price quoted by contractor > **es'ti•ma•ble** *adjective* worthy of regard > **es•ti•ma'tion** *noun* opinion, judgment
es•ti•vate [ES-tə-vayt] *verb intransitive* **-vat•ed, -vat•ing** spend the summer
es•trange [i-STRAYNJ] *verb transitive* **-tranged, -trang•ing** 1 lose affection of 2 alienate > **es•trange'ment** *noun*
es•tro•gen [ES-trə-jən] *noun* hormone in females esp. controlling changes, cycles, in reproductive organs > **es•tro•gen'ic** *adjective*
es•tu•ar•y [ES-choo-er-ee] *noun, plural* **-ar•ies** tidal mouth of river, inlet
e-tail *noun* selling of goods via the Internet
etc. et cetera
et cet•er•a [et SET-ər-ə] 1 and the rest, and others 2 or the like > **etceteras** *plural noun* miscellaneous extra things or people
etch [ech] *verb transitive* 1 make engraving by eating away surface of metal plate with acids, etc. 2 imprint vividly > **etch'er** *noun* > **etch'ing** *noun*
e•ter•nal [i-TUR-nəl] *adjective* 1 without beginning or end 2 everlasting 3 changeless > **e•ter'ni•ty** *noun, plural* **-ties**
e•ther [EE-thər] *noun* 1 colorless volatile liquid used as anesthetic 2 intangible fluid formerly supposed to fill all space 3 the clear sky, region above clouds > **e•the•re•al** [i-THEER-ee-əl] *adjective* 1 light, airy 2 heavenly, spirit-like
eth•i•cal [ETH-i-kəl] *adjective* relating to morals > **eth'i•cal•ly** *adverb* > **eth'ics** *noun* 1 science of morals 2 moral principles, rules of conduct
eth•nic [ETH-nik] *adjective* of race or relating to classification of humans into social, cultural, etc., groups > **eth•nog'ra•phy** [-NOG-rə-fee] *noun* description of human races > **eth•nol'o•gy** *noun* study of human races > **ethnic cleansing** expulsion or extermination of other ethnic groups by the dominant ethnic group in an area
e•thos [EE-thos] *noun* distinctive character, spirit, etc. of people, culture, etc.
eth•yl [ETH-əl] *noun* of, consisting of, or containing the hydrocarbon group C_2H_5 > **eth'y•lene** [-leen] *noun* poisonous gas used as anesthetic and fuel
e•ti•ol•o•gy [ee-tee-OL-ə-jee] *noun, plural* **-gies** study of causes, esp. inquiry into origin of disease > **e•ti•o•log'i•cal** *adjective*
et•i•quette [ET-i-kit] *noun* conventional code of conduct or behavior
é•tude [AY-tood] *noun* short musical composition, study, intended often as technical exercise
et•y•mol•o•gy [et-ə-MOL-ə-jee] *noun* 1 tracing, account of, formation of word's origin, development 2 study of this > **et•y•mo•log'i•cal** *adjective* > **et•y•mol'o•gist** *noun*

foundation, founding, inauguration, installation, institution, organization, setting up
2 ORGANIZATION, business, company, concern, corporation, enterprise, firm, institution, outfit (*informal*)
3 ▷ **the Establishment** THE AUTHORITIES, ruling class, the powers that be, the system
estate *noun* 1 LANDS, area, domain, holdings, manor, property
2 (*law*) PROPERTY, assets, belongings, effects, fortune, goods, possessions, wealth
esteem *noun* 1 RESPECT, admiration, credit, estimation, good opinion, honor, kudos, regard, reverence, veneration
▷ *verb* 2 RESPECT, admire, love, prize, regard highly, revere, think highly of, treasure, value
3 CONSIDER, believe, deem, estimate, judge, reckon, regard, think, view
estimate *verb* 1 CALCULATE ROUGHLY, assess, evaluate, gauge, guess, judge, number, reckon, value
2 FORM AN OPINION, believe, conjecture, consider, judge, rank, rate, reckon, surmise
▷ *noun* 3 APPROXIMATE CALCULATION, assessment, ballpark figure (*informal*), guess, guesstimate (*informal*), judgment, valuation
4 OPINION, appraisal, assessment, belief, estimation, judgment
estimation *noun* OPINION, appraisal, appreciation, assessment, belief, consideration, considered opinion, judgment, view
estuary *noun* INLET, creek, firth, fjord, mouth
et cetera *adverb* 1 AND SO ON, and so forth
▷ *noun* 2 AND THE REST, and others, and the like, et al.
etch *verb* CUT, carve, eat into, engrave, impress, imprint, inscribe, stamp
etching *noun* PRINT, carving, engraving, impression, imprint, inscription
eternal *adjective* 1 EVERLASTING, endless, immortal, infinite, never-ending, perpetual, timeless, unceasing, unending
2 PERMANENT, deathless, enduring, immutable, imperishable, indestructible, lasting, unchanging
eternity *noun* 1 INFINITY, ages, endlessness, immortality, perpetuity, timelessness
2 (*theology*) THE AFTERLIFE, heaven, paradise, the hereafter, the next world
ethical *adjective* MORAL, conscientious, fair, good, honorable, just, principled, proper, right, upright, virtuous
ethics *plural noun* MORAL CODE, conscience, morality, moral philosophy, moral values, principles, rules of conduct, standards
ethnic *adjective* CULTURAL, folk, indigenous, national, native, racial, traditional
etiquette *noun* GOOD BEHAVIOR *or* PROPER BEHAVIOR, civility, courtesy, decorum, formalities, manners, politeness, propriety, protocol

eu-, ev- *combining form* well: *eugenic; euphony; evangelist*
Eu *chem.* europium
eu•ca•lyp•tus [yoo-kə-LIP-təs] *noun* mostly Aust. genus of tree, the gum tree, yielding timber and oil, used medicinally from leaves
Eu•cha•rist [YOO-kə-rist] *noun* **1** Christian sacrament of the Lord's Supper **2** the consecrated elements **3** (**eu•cha•rist**) thanksgiving
eu•gen•ic [yoo-JEN-ik] *adjective* relating to, or tending toward, production of fine offspring > **eu•gen'ics** *noun* this science
eu•lo•gy [YOO-lə-jee] *noun, plural* **-gies** **1** speech or writing in praise of person esp. dead person **2** praise > **eu'lo•gist** *noun* > **eu'lo•gize** [-jīz] *verb transitive* **-gized, -giz•ing**
eu•nuch [YOO-nək] *noun* castrated man, esp. formerly one employed in harem
eu•phe•mism [YOO-fə-miz-əm] *noun* **1** substitution of mild term for offensive or hurtful one **2** instance of this > **eu•phe•mis'tic** *adjective* > **eu•phe•mis'ti•cal•ly** *adverb*
eu•pho•ny [YOO-fə-nee] *noun, plural* **-nies** pleasantness of sound > **eu•phon'ic** [-FON-ik] *adjective* > **eu•pho'ni•ous** [-FOH-nee-əs] *adjective* pleasing to ear
eu•pho•ria [yoo-FOR-ee-ə] *noun* sense of well-being or elation > **eu•phor'ic** *adjective*
eu•phu•ism [YOO-fyoo-iz-əm] *noun* affected high-flown manner of writing, esp. in imitation of Lyly's *Euphues* (1580) > **eu•phu•is'tic** *adjective*
Eu•ra•sian [yuu-RAY-*zh*ən] *adjective* **1** of mixed European and Asiatic descent **2** of Europe and Asia ▷ *noun* **3** one of this descent
eu•re•ka [yuu-REE-kə] *interjection* exclamation of triumph at finding something
eu•ro *noun, plural* **eu'ros** unit of the single currency of the European Union
Euro- *combining form* Europe or European: *Euroland*
Eu•ro•land *noun* (*also* **Eurozone**) the countries within the European Union that have adopted the euro
Eu•ro•pe•an [yuur-ə-PEE-ən] *noun, adjective* (native) of Europe > **European Union** (*also* **EU**) economic and political association of a number of European nations
Eu•sta•chian tube [yoo-STAY-shən] passage leading from pharynx to middle ear
eu•tha•na•sia [yoo-thə-NAY-*zh*ə] *noun* **1** gentle, painless death **2** putting to death in this way, esp. to relieve suffering
e•vac•u•ate [i-VAK-yoo-ayt] *verb transitive* **-at•ed, -at•ing** **1** empty **2** withdraw from **3** discharge > **e•vac•u•a'tion** *noun* > **e•vac•u•ee'** *noun* person moved from dangerous area esp. in time of war
e•vade [i-VAYD] *verb transitive* **-vad•ed, -vad•ing** **1** avoid, escape from **2** elude > **e•va'sion** [-*zh*ən] *noun* **1** subterfuge **2** excuse **3** equivocation > **e•va'sive** *adjective* elusive, not straightforward
e•val•u•ate [i-VAL-yoo-ayt] *verb transitive* **-at•ed, -at•ing** find or judge value of > **e•val•u•a'tion** *noun*
ev•a•nesce [ev-ə-NES] *verb intransitive* **-nesced, -nesc•ing** fade away > **ev•a•nes'cence** *noun* > **ev•a•nes'cent** *adjective* fleeting, transient
e•van•gel•i•cal [ee-van-JEL-i-kəl] *adjective* **1** of, or according to, gospel teaching **2** of Protestant sect that stresses salvation by faith ▷ *noun* **3** member of evangelical sect > **e•van'ge•lism** *noun* > **e•van'ge•list** *noun* **1** writer of one of the four gospels **2** ardent, zealous preacher of the gospel **3** revivalist > **e•van'ge•lize** *verb transitive* **-lized, -liz•ing** **1** preach gospel to **2** convert
e•vap•o•rate [i-VAP-ə-rayt] *verb intransitive* **-rat•ed, -rat•ing** **1** turn into, pass off in, vapor ▷ *verb transitive* **-rat•ed, -rat•ing** **2** turn into vapor > **e•vap•o•ra'tion** *noun*
evasion *see* **evade**
eve [eev] *noun* **1** evening before (holiday, etc.) **2** time just before (event, etc.)
e•ven [EE vən] *adjective* **1** flat, smooth **2** uniform in quality, equal in amount, balanced **3** divisible by two **4** impartial ▷ *verb transitive* **5** make even **6** smooth **7** equalize ▷ *adverb* **8** equally **9** simply **10** notwithstanding **11** (used to express emphasis)
eve•ning [EEV-ning] *noun* **1** the close of day or early part of night **2** decline, end
e•vent [i-VENT] *noun* **1** happening **2** notable

DICTIONARY

e

THESAURUS

euphoria *noun* ELATION, ecstasy, exaltation, exhilaration, intoxication, joy, jubilation, rapture
evacuate *verb* CLEAR, abandon, desert, forsake, leave, move out, pull out, quit, vacate, withdraw
evade *verb* **1** AVOID, dodge, duck, elude, escape, get away from, sidestep, steer clear of
2 AVOID ANSWERING, equivocate, fend off, fudge, hedge, parry
evaluate *verb* ASSESS, appraise, calculate, estimate, gauge, judge, rate, reckon, size up (*informal*), weigh
evaporate *verb* **1** DRY UP, dehydrate, desiccate, dry, vaporize
2 DISAPPEAR, dematerialize, dissolve, fade away, melt away, vanish
evasion *noun* **1** AVOIDANCE, dodging, escape
2 DECEPTION, equivocation, evasiveness, prevarication
evasive *adjective* DECEPTIVE, cagey (*informal*), equivocating, indirect, oblique, prevaricating, shifty, slippery
eve *noun* **1** NIGHT BEFORE, day before, vigil
2 BRINK, edge, point, threshold, verge
even *adjective* **1** LEVEL, flat, horizontal, parallel, smooth, steady, straight, true, uniform
2 REGULAR, constant, smooth, steady, unbroken, uniform, uninterrupted, unvarying, unwavering
3 EQUAL, comparable, fifty-fifty (*informal*), identical, level, like, matching, neck and neck, on a level playing field (*informal*), on a par, similar, tied
4 CALM, composed, cool, even-tempered, imperturbable, placid, unruffled, well-balanced
5 ▷ **get even, get even with** PAY BACK, give tit for tat, reciprocate, repay, requite, retaliate
evening *noun* DUSK, twilight
event *noun* **1** INCIDENT, affair, business, circumstance, episode, experience, happening, occasion, occurrence
2 COMPETITION, bout, contest, game, tournament
even-tempered *adjective* CALM, composed, cool, imperturbable, level-headed, placid, tranquil,

occurrence 3 issue, result 4 any one contest in series in sports program > **e•vent'ful** *adjective* full of exciting events > **e•ven'tu•al** [-choo-əl] *adjective* 1 resulting in the end 2 ultimate 3 final > **e•ven•tu•al'i•ty** [-AL-i-tee] *noun* possible event > **e•ven'tu•ate** *verb intransitive* **-at•ed, -at•ing** 1 turn out 2 happen 3 end

ev•er [EV-ər] *adverb* 1 always 2 constantly 3 at any time > **ev'er•green** *noun, adjective* (tree or shrub) bearing foliage throughout year > **ev•er•more'** *adverb* > **ev'er•net** *noun* hypothetical form of the Internet that is continuously accessible

eve•ry [EV-ree] *adjective* 1 each of all 2 all possible > **eve'ry•body** *pronoun* > **eve'ry•day** *adjective* usual, ordinary > **eve'ry•one** *pronoun* > **eve'ry•thing** *pronoun, noun* > **eve'ry•where** *adverb* in all places

e•vict [i-VIKT] *verb transitive* expel by legal process, turn out > **e•vic'tion** [-shən] *noun*

ev•i•dent [EV-i-dənt] *adjective* plain, obvious > **ev'i•dence** *noun* 1 ground of belief 2 sign, indication 3 testimony ▷ *verb transitive* **-denced, -denc•ing** indicate, prove > **ev•i•den'tial** *adjective* > **ev'i•dent•ly** *adverb* **in evidence** conspicuous

e•vil [EE-vəl] *adjective* 1 bad, harmful ▷ *noun* 2 what is bad or harmful 3 sin > **e'vil•ly** *adverb* > **e'vil•do•er** *noun* sinner

e•vince [i-VINS] *verb transitive* **-vinced, -vinc•ing** show, indicate

e•voke [i-VOHK] *verb transitive* **-voked, -vok•ing** 1 draw forth 2 call to mind > **ev•o•ca•tion** [ev-ə-KAY-shən] *noun* > **e•voc•a•tive** [i-VOK-ə-tiv] *adjective*

e•volve [i-VOLV] *verb* **-volved, -volv•ing** 1 develop or cause to develop gradually ▷ *verb intransitive* 2 undergo slow changes in process of growth > **ev•o•lu•tion** [ev-ə-LOO-shən] *noun* 1 evolving 2 development of species from earlier forms > **ev•o•lu'tion•ar•y** *adjective* > **ev•o•lu'tion•ist** *noun* one who supports theory of evolution

ewe [yoo] *noun* female sheep

ew•er [YOO-ər] *noun* pitcher with wide spout

Ex. Exodus

ex-, e-, ef- *prefix* out from, from, out of, formerly: *exclaim; evade; effusive; exodus*

ex•ac•er•bate [ig-ZAS-ər-bayt] *verb transitive* **-bat•ed, -bat•ing** aggravate, embitter, make worse > **ex•ac•er•ba'tion** *noun*

ex•act [ig-ZAKT] *adjective* 1 precise, accurate, strictly correct ▷ *verb transitive* 2 demand, extort 3 insist upon 4 enforce > **ex•act'ing** *adjective* making rigorous or excessive demands > **ex•ac'tion** *noun* 1 act of exacting 2 that which is exacted, as excessive work, etc. 3 oppressive demand > **ex•act'ly** *adverb* > **ex•act'ness** *noun* 1 accuracy 2 precision

unexcitable, unruffled

eventful *adjective* EXCITING, active, busy, dramatic, full, lively, memorable, remarkable

eventual *adjective* FINAL, concluding, overall, ultimate

eventuality *noun* POSSIBILITY, case, chance, contingency, event, likelihood, probability

eventually *adverb* IN THE END, after all, at the end of the day, finally, one day, some time, ultimately, when all is said and done

ever *adverb* 1 AT ANY TIME, at all, at any period, at any point, by any chance, in any case, on any occasion
2 ALWAYS, at all times, constantly, continually, evermore, for ever, perpetually, twenty-four-seven (*slang*)

everlasting *adjective* ETERNAL, endless, immortal, indestructible, never-ending, perpetual, timeless, undying

evermore *adverb* FOR EVER, always, eternally, ever, to the end of time

every *adjective* EACH, all, each one

everybody *pronoun* EVERYONE, all and sundry, each one, each person, every person, one and all, the whole world

everyday *adjective* COMMON, customary, mundane, ordinary, routine, stock, usual, workaday

everyone *pronoun* EVERYBODY, all and sundry, each one, each person, every person, one and all, the whole world

everything *pronoun* ALL, each thing, the lot, the whole lot

everywhere *adverb* TO EVERY PLACE *or* IN EVERY PLACE, all around, all over, far and wide *or* far and near, high and low, in every nook and cranny, the world over, ubiquitously

evict *verb* EXPEL, boot out (*informal*), eject, kick out (*informal*), oust, remove, throw out, turn out

evidence *noun* 1 PROOF, confirmation, corroboration, demonstration, grounds, indication, sign, substantiation, testimony ▷ *verb* 2 SHOW, demonstrate, display, exhibit, indicate, prove, reveal, signify, witness

evident *adjective* OBVIOUS, apparent, clear, manifest, noticeable, perceptible, plain, unmistakable, visible

evidently *adverb* 1 OBVIOUSLY, clearly, manifestly, plainly, undoubtedly, unmistakably, without question
2 APPARENTLY, ostensibly, outwardly, seemingly, to all appearances

evil *noun* 1 WICKEDNESS, badness, depravity, malignity, sin, vice, villainy, wrongdoing
2 HARM, affliction, disaster, hurt, ill, injury, mischief, misfortune, suffering, woe
▷ *adjective* 3 WICKED, bad, depraved, immoral, malevolent, malicious, sinful, villainous
4 HARMFUL, calamitous, catastrophic, destructive, dire, disastrous, pernicious, ruinous
5 OFFENSIVE, foul, noxious, pestilential, unpleasant, vile

evoke *verb* RECALL, arouse, awaken, call, give rise to, induce, rekindle, stir up, summon up

evolution *noun* DEVELOPMENT, expansion, growth, increase, maturation, progress, unfolding, working out

evolve *verb* DEVELOP, expand, grow, increase, mature, progress, unfold, work out

exact *adjective* 1 ACCURATE, correct, definite, faultless, precise, right, specific, true, unerring ▷ *verb* 2 DEMAND, claim, command, compel, extort, extract, force

exacting *adjective* DEMANDING, difficult, hard, harsh, rigorous, severe, strict, stringent, taxing, tough

exactly *adverb* 1 PRECISELY, accurately, correctly, explicitly, faithfully, scrupulously, truthfully,

ex•ag•ger•ate [ig-ZAJ-ə-rayt] *verb transitive* **-at•ed, -at•ing** 1 magnify beyond truth, overstate 2 enlarge 3 overestimate > **ex•ag•ger•a'tion** *noun*
ex•alt [ig-ZAWLT] *verb transitive* 1 raise up 2 praise 3 make noble, dignify > **ex•al•ta•tion** [eg-zawl-TAY-shən] *noun* 1 an exalting 2 elevation in rank, dignity or position 3 rapture
ex•am•ine [ig-ZAM-in] *verb transitive* **-ined, -in•ing** 1 investigate 2 look at closely 3 ask questions of 4 test knowledge or proficiency of 5 inquire into > **ex•am•i•na'tion** *noun* > **ex•am'in•er** *noun*
ex•am•ple [ig-ZAM-pəl] *noun* 1 thing illustrating general rule 2 specimen 3 model 4 warning, precedent, instance
ex•as•per•ate [ig-ZAS-pə-rayt] *verb transitive* **-at•ed, -at•ing** 1 irritate, enrage 2 intensify, make worse > **ex•as•per•a'tion** *noun*
ex•ca•vate [EKS-kə-vayt] *verb transitive* **-vat•ed, -vat•ing** 1 hollow out 2 make hole by digging 3 unearth > **ex•ca•va'tion** *noun*
ex•ceed [ik-SEED] *verb transitive* 1 be greater than 2 do more than authorized 3 go beyond 4 surpass > **ex•ceed'ing•ly** *adverb* 1 very 2 greatly
ex•cel [ik-SEL] *verb transitive* **-celled, -cel•ling** 1 surpass, be better than ▷ *verb intransitive* **-celled, -cel•ling** 2 be very good, preeminent > **ex'cel•lence** *noun* > **ex'cel•len•cy** *noun* title borne by certain high officials > **ex'cel•lent** *adjective* very good
ex•cept [ik-SEPT] *preposition* 1 not including 2 but ▷ *verb transitive* 3 leave or take out 4 exclude > **ex•cept'ing** *preposition* not including > **ex•cep'tion** *noun* 1 thing excepted, not included in a rule 2 objection > **ex•cep'tion•a•ble** *adjective* open to objection > **ex•cep'tion•al** *adjective* not ordinary, esp. much above average
ex•cerpt [EK-surpt] *noun* quoted or extracted passage from book, etc. > **ex•cerpt'** *verb transitive* extract, quote (passage from book, etc.)
ex•cess [EK-ses] *noun* 1 an exceeding 2 amount by which thing exceeds 3 too great amount 4 intemperance or immoderate conduct > **ex•ces'sive** [-siv] *adjective*
ex•change [iks-CHAYNJ] *verb transitive* **-changed,**

DICTIONARY

e

THESAURUS

unerringly
2 IN EVERY RESPECT, absolutely, indeed, precisely, quite, specifically, to the letter
exactness *noun* PRECISION, accuracy, correctness, exactitude, rigorousness, scrupulousness, strictness, veracity
exaggerate *verb* OVERSTATE, amplify, embellish, embroider, enlarge, overemphasize, overestimate
exaggeration *noun* OVERSTATEMENT, amplification, embellishment, enlargement, hyperbole, overemphasis, overestimation
exalt *verb* 1 PRAISE, acclaim, extol, glorify, idolize, set on a pedestal, worship
2 RAISE, advance, elevate, ennoble, honor, promote, upgrade
exaltation *noun* 1 PRAISE, acclaim, glorification, idolization, reverence, tribute, worship
2 RISE, advancement, elevation, ennoblement, promotion, upgrading
exalted *adjective* HIGH-RANKING, dignified, eminent, grand, honored, lofty, prestigious
examination *noun* 1 INSPECTION, analysis, exploration, interrogation, investigation, research, scrutiny, study, test
2 QUESTIONING, inquiry, inquisition, probe, quiz, test
examine *verb* 1 INSPECT, analyze, explore, investigate, peruse, scrutinize, study, survey
2 QUESTION, cross-examine, grill (*informal*), inquire, interrogate, quiz, test
example *noun* 1 SPECIMEN, case, illustration, instance, sample
2 MODEL, archetype, ideal, paradigm, paragon, prototype, standard
3 WARNING, caution, lesson
exasperate *verb* IRRITATE, anger, annoy, enrage, incense, inflame, infuriate, madden, pique
exasperation *noun* IRRITATION, anger, annoyance, fury, pique, provocation, rage, wrath
excavate *verb* DIG OUT, burrow, delve, dig up, mine, quarry, tunnel, uncover, unearth
exceed *verb* 1 SURPASS, beat, better, cap (*informal*), eclipse, outdo, outstrip, overtake, pass, top
2 GO OVER THE LIMIT OF, go over the top, overstep
exceedingly *adverb* EXTREMELY, enormously, exceptionally, extraordinarily, hugely, superlatively, surpassingly, unusually, very
excel *verb* 1 BE SUPERIOR, beat, eclipse, outdo, outshine, surpass, transcend
2 ▷ **excel in, excel at** BE GOOD AT, be proficient in, be skillful at, be talented at, shine at, show talent in
excellence *noun* HIGH QUALITY, distinction, eminence, goodness, greatness, merit, pre-eminence, superiority, supremacy
excellent *adjective* OUTSTANDING, brilliant, exquisite, fine, first-class, first-rate, good, great, superb, superlative, world-class
except *preposition* 1 *also* **except for** APART FROM, barring, besides, but, excepting, excluding, omitting, other than, saving, with the exception of
▷ *verb* 2 EXCLUDE, leave out, omit, pass over
exception *noun* 1 SPECIAL CASE, anomaly, deviation, freak, inconsistency, irregularity, oddity, peculiarity
2 EXCLUSION, leaving out, omission, passing over
exceptional *adjective* 1 SPECIAL, abnormal, atypical, extraordinary, irregular, odd, peculiar, strange, unusual
2 REMARKABLE, excellent, extraordinary, marvelous, outstanding, phenomenal, prodigious, special, superior
excerpt *noun* EXTRACT, fragment, part, passage, piece, quotation, section, selection
excess *noun* 1 SURFEIT, glut, overload, superabundance, superfluity, surplus, too much
2 OVERINDULGENCE, debauchery, dissipation, dissoluteness, extravagance, intemperance, prodigality
excessive *adjective* IMMODERATE, disproportionate, exaggerated, extreme, inordinate, overmuch, superfluous, too much, undue, unfair, unreasonable

-chang•ing 1 give (something) in return for something else 2 barter ▷ *noun* 3 giving one thing and receiving another 4 giving or receiving currency of one country for that of another 5 thing given for another 6 building where merchants, dealers meet for business 7 central telephone office > **ex•change'a•ble** *adjective*

ex•cheq•uer [eks-CHEK-ər] *noun* 1 treasury, e.g. of a government 2 (*informal*) personal funds

ex•cise¹ [EK-sīz] *noun* tax levied on domestic goods during manufacture or before sale

ex•cise² [ik-SĪZ] *verb transitive* **-cised, -cis•ing** cut out, cut away > **ex•ci•sion** [ek-SIZH-ən] *noun*

ex•cite [ik-SĪT] *verb transitive* **-cit•ed, -cit•ing** 1 arouse to strong emotion, stimulate 2 rouse up, set in motion 3 *electricity* energize to produce electric activity or a magnetic field > **ex•cit'a•ble** *adjective* > **ex•ci•ta•tion** [ek-si-TAY-shən] *noun* > **ex•cite'ment** *noun* > **ex•cit'ing** *adjective* 1 thrilling 2 rousing to action

ex•claim [ik-SKLAYM] *verb* speak suddenly, cry out > **ex•cla•ma•tion** [ek-sklə-MAY-shən] *noun* > **ex•clam•a•to•ry** [ik-SKLAM-ə-tor-ee] *adjective*

ex•clude [ik-SKLOOD] *verb transitive* **-clud•ed, -clud•ing** 1 shut out 2 debar from 3 reject, not consider > **ex•clu'sion** [-zhən] *noun* > **ex•clu'sive** *adjective* 1 excluding 2 inclined to keep out (from society, etc.) 3 sole, only 4 select ▷ *noun* 5 something exclusive, esp. story appearing only in one newspaper > **ex•clu'sive•ly** *adverb*

ex•com•mu•ni•cate [eks-kə-MYOO-ni-kayt] *verb transitive* **-cat•ed, -cat•ing** to cut off from the sacraments of the Church > **ex•com•mu•ni•ca'tion** *noun*

ex•cre•ment [EKS-krə-mənt] *noun* 1 waste matter from body, esp. from bowels 2 dung > **ex•cre•ta** [ik-SKREE-tə] *noun* excrement > **ex•crete'** *verb intransitive* **-cret•ed, -cret•ing** discharge from the system > **ex•cre'tion** *noun* > **ex'cre•to•ry** *adjective*

ex•cres•cent [ik-SKRES-ənt] *adjective* 1 growing out of 2 redundant > **ex•cres'cence** *noun* unnatural outgrowth

ex•cru•ci•ate [ik-SKROO-shee-ayt] *verb transitive* **-at•ed, -at•ing** torment acutely, torture in body or mind

ex•cul•pate [EK-skul-payt] *verb transitive* **-pat•ed, -pat•ing** free from blame, acquit > **ex•cul•pa'tion** *noun* > **ex•cul'pa•to•ry** *adjective*

ex•cur•sion [ik-SKUR-zhən] *noun* 1 journey, ramble, trip for pleasure 2 digression

ex•cuse [ik-SKYOOZ] *verb transitive* **-cused, -cus•ing** 1 forgive, overlook 2 try to clear from blame 3 gain exemption 4 set free, remit ▷ *noun* [-SKYOOS] 5 that which serves to excuse 6 apology > **ex•cus•a•ble** [ik-SKYOO-zə-bəl] *adjective*

ex•e•cra•ble [EK-si-krə-bəl] *adjective* abominable, hatefully bad

ex•e•cute [EK-si-kyoot] *verb transitive* **-cut•ed, -cut•ing** 1 inflict capital punishment on, kill 2 carry out, perform 3 make, produce 4 sign (document) > **ex•e•cu'tion** *noun* > **ex•e•cu'tion•er** *noun* one employed to execute criminals > **ex•ec'u•tive** *noun* 1 person in administrative

DICTIONARY • THESAURUS

---

exchange *verb* 1 INTERCHANGE, barter, change, convert into, swap, switch, trade
▷ *noun* 2 INTERCHANGE, barter, quid pro quo, reciprocity, substitution, swap, switch, tit for tat, trade

excitable *adjective* NERVOUS, emotional, highly strung, hot-headed, mercurial, quick-tempered, temperamental, volatile, wired (*slang*)

excite *verb* AROUSE, animate, galvanize, inflame, inspire, provoke, rouse, stir up, thrill

excitement *noun* AGITATION, action, activity, animation, commotion, furor, passion, thrill

exciting *adjective* STIMULATING, dramatic, electrifying, exhilarating, rousing, sensational, stirring, thrilling

exclaim *verb* CRY OUT, call out, declare, proclaim, shout, utter, yell

exclamation *noun* CRY, call, interjection, outcry, shout, utterance, yell

exclude *verb* 1 KEEP OUT, ban, bar, boycott, disallow, forbid, prohibit, refuse, shut out
2 LEAVE OUT, count out, eliminate, ignore, omit, pass over, reject, rule out, set aside

exclusion *noun* 1 BAN, bar, boycott, disqualification, embargo, prohibition, veto
2 ELIMINATION, omission, rejection

exclusive *adjective* 1 SOLE, absolute, complete, entire, full, total, undivided, whole
2 LIMITED, confined, peculiar, restricted, unique
3 SELECT, chic, cliquish, cool (*informal*), fashionable, phat (*slang*), restricted, snobbish, up-market

excommunicate *verb* EXPEL, anathematize, ban, banish, cast out, denounce, exclude, repudiate

excruciating *adjective* AGONIZING, harrowing, insufferable, intense, piercing, severe, unbearable, violent

exculpate *verb* ABSOLVE, acquit, clear, discharge, excuse, exonerate, pardon, vindicate

excursion *noun* TRIP, day trip, expedition, jaunt, journey, outing, pleasure trip, ramble, tour

excusable *adjective* FORGIVABLE, allowable, defensible, justifiable, pardonable, permissible, understandable, warrantable

excuse *noun* 1 JUSTIFICATION, apology, defense, explanation, grounds, mitigation, plea, reason, vindication
▷ *verb* 2 JUSTIFY, apologize for, defend, explain, mitigate, vindicate
3 FORGIVE, acquit, exculpate, exonerate, make allowances for, overlook, pardon, tolerate, turn a blind eye to
4 FREE, absolve, discharge, exempt, let off, release, relieve, spare

execute *verb* 1 PUT TO DEATH, behead, electrocute, guillotine, hang, kill, shoot
2 CARRY OUT, accomplish, administer, discharge, effect, enact, implement, perform, prosecute

execution *noun* 1 CARRYING OUT, accomplishment, administration, enactment, enforcement, implementation, operation, performance, prosecution
2 KILLING, capital punishment, hanging

executioner *noun* 1 HANGMAN, headsman
2 KILLER, assassin, exterminator, hit man (*slang*), liquidator, murderer, slayer

executive *noun* 1 ADMINISTRATOR, director, manager, official
2 ADMINISTRATION, directorate, directors,

position **2** executive body **3** executive branch of government ▷ *adjective* **4** carrying into effect, esp. of branch of government executing laws > **ex•ec•u•tor** [ig-ZEK-yə-tər] *noun* person appointed to carry out provisions of a will > **ex•ec•u•trix** *noun feminine*

ex•e•ge•sis [ek-si-JEE-sis] *noun, plural* **-ses** [-seez] explanation, esp. of Scripture > **ex'e•gete** [-jeet] *noun* one skilled in exegesis

ex•em•plar [ig-ZEM-plər] *noun* model type > **ex•em'pla•ry** [-plə-ree] *adjective* **1** fit to be imitated, serving as example **2** commendable **3** typical

ex•em•pli•fy [ig-ZEM-plə-fī] *verb transitive* **-fied, -fy•ing** **1** serve as example of **2** illustrate **3** exhibit **4** make attested copy of > **ex•em•pli•fi•ca'tion** *noun*

ex•empt [ig-ZEMPT] *verb transitive* **1** free from **2** excuse ▷ *adjective* **3** freed from, not liable for **4** not affected by > **ex•emp'tion** *noun*

ex•e•quies [EK-si-kweez] *plural noun* funeral rites or procession

ex•er•cise [EK-sər-sīz] *verb transitive* **-cised, -cis•ing** **1** use, employ **2** give exercise to **3** carry out, discharge **4** trouble, harass ▷ *verb intransitive* **-cised, -cis•ing** **5** take exercise ▷ *noun* **6** use of limbs for health **7** practice for training **8** task for training **9** lesson **10** employment **11** use (of limbs, mind, etc.)

ex•ert [ig-ZURT] *verb transitive* **1** apply (oneself) diligently, make effort **2** bring to bear > **ex•er'tion** *noun* effort, physical activity

ex•fo•li•ate [eks-FOH-lee-ayt] *verb* wash (the body) with a granular cosmetic to remove dead cells from the skin's surface

ex•hale [eks-HAYL] *verb* **-haled, -hal•ing** **1** breathe out **2** give, pass off as vapor

ex•haust [ig-ZAWST] *verb transitive* **1** tire out **2** use up **3** empty **4** draw off **5** treat, discuss thoroughly ▷ *noun* **6** used steam or fluid from engine **7** waste gases from internal combustion engine **8** passage for, or coming out of this > **ex•haust'i•ble** *adjective* > **ex•haus'tion** [-chən] *noun* **1** state of extreme fatigue **2** limit of endurance > **ex•haus'tive** *adjective* **1** thorough **2** comprehensive

ex•hib•it [ig-ZIB-it] *verb transitive* **1** show, display **2** manifest **3** show publicly (often in competition) ▷ *noun* **4** thing shown, esp. in competition or as evidence in court > **ex•hi•bi•tion** [ek-sə-BISH-ən] *noun* **1** display, act of displaying **2** public show (of works of art, etc.) > **ex•hi•bi'tion•ist** *noun* one with compulsive desire to draw attention to self or to expose genitals publicly > **ex•hib'i•tor** *noun* one who exhibits, esp. in show

ex•hil•a•rate [ig-ZIL-ə-rayt] *verb transitive* **-rat•ed, -rat•ing** enliven, gladden > **ex•hil•a•ra'tion** *noun* high spirits, enlivenment

ex•hort [ig-ZORT] *verb transitive* urge, admonish earnestly > **ex•hor•ta•tion** [eg-zor-TAY-shən] *noun* > **ex•hort'er** *noun*

ex•hume [ig-ZOOM] *verb transitive* **-humed, -hum•ing** unearth what has been buried, disinter > **ex•hu•ma•tion** [eks-hyuu-MAY-shən] *noun*

ex•i•gent [EK-si-jənt] *adjective* **1** exacting **2** urgent, pressing > **ex'i•gen•cy** *noun, plural* **-cies** **1**

DICTIONARY **e** THESAURUS

---

government, hierarchy, leadership, management
▷ *adjective* **3** ADMINISTRATIVE, controlling, decision-making, directing, governing, managerial

exemplary *adjective* **1** IDEAL, admirable, commendable, excellent, fine, good, model, praiseworthy
2 WARNING, cautionary

exemplify *verb* SHOW, demonstrate, display, embody, exhibit, illustrate, represent, serve as an example of

exempt *adjective* **1** IMMUNE, excepted, excused, free, not liable, released, spared
▷ *verb* **2** GRANT IMMUNITY, absolve, discharge, excuse, free, let off, release, relieve, spare

exemption *noun* IMMUNITY, absolution, discharge, dispensation, exception, exoneration, freedom, release

exercise *noun* **1** EXERTION, activity, effort, labor, toil, training, work, work-out
2 TASK, drill, lesson, practice, problem
3 USE, application, discharge, fulfillment, implementation, practice, utilization
▷ *verb* **4** PUT TO USE, apply, bring to bear, employ, exert, use, utilize
5 TRAIN, practice, work out

exert *verb* **1** USE, apply, bring to bear, employ, exercise, make use of, utilize, wield
2 ▷ **exert oneself** MAKE AN EFFORT, apply oneself, do one's best, endeavor, labor, strain, strive, struggle, toil, work

exertion *noun* EFFORT, elbow grease (*facetious*), endeavor, exercise, industry, strain, struggle, toil

exhaust *verb* **1** TIRE OUT, debilitate, drain, enervate, enfeeble, fatigue, sap, weaken, wear out
2 USE UP, consume, deplete, dissipate, expend, run through, spend, squander, waste

exhausted *adjective* **1** WORN OUT, debilitated, done in (*informal*), drained, fatigued, spent, tired out
2 USED UP, consumed, depleted, dissipated, expended, finished, spent, squandered, wasted

exhausting *adjective* TIRING, backbreaking, debilitating, grueling, laborious, punishing, sapping, strenuous, taxing

exhaustion *noun* **1** TIREDNESS, debilitation, fatigue, weariness
2 DEPLETION, consumption, emptying, using up

exhaustive *adjective* THOROUGH, all-embracing, complete, comprehensive, extensive, full-scale, in-depth, intensive

exhibit *verb* DISPLAY, demonstrate, express, indicate, manifest, parade, put on view, reveal, show

exhibition *noun* DISPLAY, demonstration, exposition, performance, presentation, representation, show, spectacle

exhilarating *adjective* EXCITING, breathtaking, enlivening, invigorating, stimulating, thrilling

exhort *verb* URGE, advise, beseech, call upon, entreat, persuade, press, spur

exhume *verb* DIG UP, disentomb, disinter, unearth

exigency *noun* NEED, constraint, demand, necessity, requirement

pressing need **2** emergency
ex•ig•u•ous [ig-ZIG-yoo-əs] *adjective* scanty, meager
ex•ile [EG-zīl] *noun* **1** banishment, expulsion from one's own country **2** long absence abroad **3** one banished or permanently living away from own home or country ▷ *verb transitive* **-iled, -il•ing 4** banish, expel
ex•ist [ig-ZIST] *verb intransitive* be, have being, live > **ex•ist'ence** *noun* > **ex•ist'ent** *adjective*
ex•is•ten•tial•ism [eg-zi-STEN-shə-liz-əm] *noun* philosophy stressing importance of personal responsibility and the free agency of the individual in a seemingly meaningless universe
ex•it [EG-zit] *noun* **1** way out **2** going out **3** death **4** actor's departure from stage ▷ *verb intransitive* **5** go out > **exit strategy** *noun* plan for freeing oneself from an undesirable situation
ex li•bris [eks LEE-bris] *Lat.* from the library of
ex•o•crine [EK-sə-krin] *adjective* of gland (e.g. salivary, sweat) secreting its products through ducts
ex•o•dus [EK-sə-dəs] *noun* **1** departure, esp. of crowd **2** (**Ex•o•dus**) second book of Old Testament **the Exodus** departure of Israelites from Egypt
ex of•fi•ci•o [eks ə-FISH-ee-oh] *Lat.* by right of position or office
ex•on•er•ate [ig-ZON-ə-rayt] *verb transitive* **-at•ed, -at•ing 1** free, declare free, from blame **2** exculpate **3** acquit > **ex•on•er•a'tion** *noun*
ex•or•bi•tant [ig-ZOR-bi-tənt] *adjective* very excessive, inordinate, immoderate > **ex•or'bi•tance** *noun*
ex•or•cise [EK-sor-sīz] *verb transitive* **-cised, -cis•ing 1** cast out (evil spirits) by invocation **2** free person of evil spirits > **ex'or•cism** *noun* > **ex'or•cist** *noun*
ex•ot•ic [ig-ZOT-ik] *adjective* **1** brought in from abroad, foreign **2** rare, unusual, having strange or bizarre allure ▷ *noun* **3** exotic plant, etc. > **ex•ot'i•ca** [-i-kə] *plural noun* (collection of) exotic objects > **ex•ot'i•cism** *noun* > **exotic dancer** stripper
ex•pand [ik-SPAND] *verb* increase, spread out, dilate, develop > **ex•pand'a•ble, ex•pand'i•ble** *adjective* > **ex•panse'** *noun* **1** wide space **2** open stretch of land > **ex•pan'si•ble** *adjective* > **ex•pan'sion** *noun* > **ex•pan'sive** *adjective* **1** wide **2** extensive **3** friendly, talkative
ex•pa•ti•ate [ik-SPAY-shee-ayt] *verb intransitive* **-at•ed, -at•ing 1** speak or write at great length (on) **2** enlarge (upon) > **ex•pa•ti•a'tion** *noun*
ex•pa•tri•ate [eks-PAY-tree-ayt] *verb transitive* **-at•ed, -at•ing 1** banish **2** exile **3** withdraw (oneself) from one's native land ▷ *adjective, noun* (-tree-it) > **ex•pa•tri•a'tion** *noun*
ex•pect [ik-SPEKT] *verb transitive* **1** regard as probable **2** look forward to **3** await, hope > **ex•pect'an•cy** *noun* **1** state or act of expecting **2** that which is expected **3** hope > **ex•pect'ant** *adjective* looking or waiting for, esp. for birth of child > **ex•pect'ant•ly** *adverb* > **ex•pec•ta•tion** [ek-spek-TAY-shən] *noun* **1** act or state of

DICTIONARY • THESAURUS

exile *noun* **1** BANISHMENT, deportation, expatriation, expulsion
2 EXPATRIATE, deportee, émigré, outcast, refugee
▷ *verb* **3** BANISH, deport, drive out, eject, expatriate, expel
exist *verb* **1** BE, be present, endure, live, occur, survive
2 SURVIVE, eke out a living, get along *or* get by, keep one's head above water, stay alive, subsist
existence *noun* BEING, actuality, life, subsistence
existent *adjective* IN EXISTENCE, alive, existing, extant, living, present, standing, surviving
exit *noun* **1** WAY OUT, door, gate, outlet
2 DEPARTURE, exodus, farewell, going, good-bye, leave-taking, retreat, withdrawal
▷ *verb* **3** DEPART, go away, go offstage (*theater*), go out, leave, make tracks, retire, retreat, take one's leave, withdraw
exodus *noun* DEPARTURE, evacuation, exit, flight, going out, leaving, migration, retreat, withdrawal
exonerate *verb* CLEAR, absolve, acquit, discharge, exculpate, excuse, justify, pardon, vindicate
exorbitant *adjective* EXCESSIVE, extortionate, extravagant, immoderate, inordinate, outrageous, preposterous, unreasonable
exorcise *verb* DRIVE OUT, cast out, deliver *or* deliver from, expel, purify
exotic *adjective* **1** UNUSUAL, colorful, fascinating, glamorous, mysterious, strange, striking, unfamiliar
2 FOREIGN, alien, external, imported, naturalized
expand *verb* **1** INCREASE, amplify, broaden, develop, enlarge, extend, grow, magnify, swell, widen
2 SPREAD *or* SPREAD OUT, diffuse, stretch *or* stretch out, unfold, unfurl, unravel, unroll
3 ▷ **expand on** GO INTO DETAIL ABOUT, amplify, develop, elaborate on, embellish, enlarge on, expatiate on, expound on, flesh out
expanse *noun* AREA, breadth, extent, range, space, stretch, sweep, tract
expansion *noun* INCREASE, amplification, development, enlargement, growth, magnification, opening out, spread
expansive *adjective* **1** WIDE, broad, extensive, far-reaching, voluminous, wide-ranging, widespread
2 TALKATIVE, affable, communicative, effusive, friendly, loquacious, open, outgoing, sociable, unreserved
expatriate *adjective* **1** EXILED, banished, emigrant, émigré
▷ *noun* **2** EXILE, emigrant, émigré, refugee
expect *verb* **1** THINK, assume, believe, imagine, presume, reckon, suppose, surmise, trust
2 LOOK FORWARD TO, anticipate, await, contemplate, envisage, hope for, predict, watch for
3 REQUIRE, call for, demand, insist on, want
expectant *adjective* **1** EXPECTING, anticipating, apprehensive, eager, hopeful, in suspense, ready, watchful
2 PREGNANT, expecting (*informal*), gravid
expectation *noun* **1** PROBABILITY, assumption, belief, conjecture, forecast, likelihood, presumption, supposition
2 ANTICIPATION, apprehension, expectancy, hope, promise, suspense

expecting 2 prospect of future good 3 what is expected 4 promise 5 value of something expected > **ex•pec•ta•tions** prospect of fortune or profit esp. by inheritance

ex•pec•to•rate [ik-SPEK-tə-rayt] *verb* **-rat•ed, -rat•ing** spit out (phlegm, etc.) > **ex•pec•to•ra'tion** *noun*

ex•pe•di•ent [ik-SPEE-dee-ənt] *adjective* 1 fitting, advisable 2 politic 3 suitable 4 convenient ▷ *noun* 5 something suitable, useful, esp. in emergency > **ex•pe'di•en•cy** *noun*

ex•pe•dite [EK-spi-dīt] *verb transitive* 1 help on, hasten 2 dispatch > **ex•pe•di'tion** [-DISH-ən] *noun* 1 journey for definite (often scientific or military) purpose 2 people, equipment engaged in expedition 3 excursion 4 promptness > **ex•pe•di'tion•ar•y** *adjective* > **ex•pe•di'tious** *adjective* prompt, speedy

ex•pel [ik-SPEL] *verb transitive* **-pelled, -pel•ling** 1 drive, cast out 2 exclude 3 discharge > **ex•pul'sion** *noun*

ex•pend [ik-SPEND] *verb transitive* 1 spend, pay out 2 use up > **ex•pend'a•ble** *adjective* likely, or meant, to be used up or destroyed > **ex•pend'i•ture** [-i-chər] *noun* > **ex•pense'** *noun* 1 cost 2 (cause of) spending > **ex•pense's** charges, outlay incurred > **ex•pen'sive** *adjective*

ex•pe•ri•ence [ik-SPEER-ee-əns] *noun* 1 observation of facts as source of knowledge 2 being affected consciously by event 3 the event 4 knowledge, skill, gained from life, by contact with facts and events ▷ *verb transitive* **-enced, -enc•ing** 5 undergo, suffer, meet with > **experienced** *adjective* skilled, expert, capable > **ex•pe•ri•en•tial** [ik-speer-ee-EN-shəl] *adjective*

ex•per•i•ment [ik-SPER-ə-mənt] *noun* 1 test, trial, something done in the hope that it may succeed, or to test hypothesis, principle, etc. ▷ *verb intransitive* 2 conduct experiment > **ex•per•i•men'tal** *adjective*

ex•pert [EK-spurt] *noun* 1 one skillful, knowledgeable, in something 2 authority ▷ *adjective* 3 practiced, skillful > **ex•per•tise** [ek-spər-TEEZ] *noun* 1 expertness 2 know-how

ex•pi•ate [EK-spee-ayt] *verb transitive* **-at•ed, -at•ing** 1 pay penalty for 2 make amends for > **ex•pi•a'tion** *noun* > **ex'pi•a•to•ry** [-ə-tor-ee] *adjective*

ex•pire [ik-SPĪR] *verb intransitive* **-pired, -pir•ing** 1 come to an end 2 give out breath 3 die ▷ *verb transitive* 4 breathe out > **ex•pi•ra•tion** *noun*

ex•plain [ik-SPLAYN] *verb transitive* 1 make clear, intelligible 2 interpret 3 elucidate 4 give details of 5 account for > **ex•pla•na•tion** [ek-splə-NAY-shən] *noun* > **ex•plan'a•to•ry** *adjective*

ex•ple•tive [EK-spli-tiv] *noun* 1 exclamation 2 exclamatory oath ▷ *adjective* 3 serving only to fill out sentence, etc.

ex•pli•ca•ble [EK-splik-ə-bəl] *adjective* explainable > **ex'pli•cate** *verb transitive* **-cat•ed, -cat•ing** develop, explain > **ex'pli•ca•to•ry** *adjective*

ex•plic•it [ik-SPLIS-it] *adjective* 1 stated in detail 2 stated, not merely implied 3 outspoken 4

DICTIONARY e THESAURUS

expediency *noun* SUITABILITY, advisability, benefit, convenience, pragmatism, profitability, prudence, usefulness, utility

expedient *noun* 1 MEANS, contrivance, device, makeshift, measure, method, resort, scheme, stopgap
▷ *adjective* 2 ADVANTAGEOUS, appropriate, beneficial, convenient, effective, helpful, opportune, practical, suitable, useful, win-win (*informal*)

expedition *noun* JOURNEY, excursion, mission, quest, safari, tour, trek, voyage

expel *verb* 1 DRIVE OUT, belch, cast out, discharge, eject, remove, spew
2 DISMISS, ban, banish, chuck out (*slang*), drum out, evict, exclude, exile, throw out

expend *verb* SPEND, consume, dissipate, exhaust, go through, pay out, use *or* use up

expendable *adjective* DISPENSABLE, inessential, nonessential, replaceable, unimportant, unnecessary

expenditure *noun* SPENDING, consumption, cost, expense, outgoings, outlay, output, payment

expense *noun* COST, charge, expenditure, loss, outlay, payment, spending

expensive *adjective* DEAR, costly, exorbitant, extravagant, high-priced, lavish, overpriced, steep (*informal*), stiff

experience *noun* 1 KNOWLEDGE, contact, exposure, familiarity, involvement, participation, practice, training
2 EVENT, adventure, affair, encounter, episode, happening, incident, occurrence
▷ *verb* 3 UNDERGO, encounter, endure, face, feel, go through, live through, sample, taste

experienced *adjective* KNOWLEDGEABLE, accomplished, expert, practiced, seasoned, tested, tried, veteran, well-versed

experiment *noun* 1 TEST, examination, experimentation, investigation, procedure, proof, research, trial, trial run
▷ *verb* 2 TEST, examine, investigate, put to the test, research, sample, try, verify

experimental *adjective* TEST, exploratory, pilot, preliminary, probationary, provisional, speculative, tentative, trial, trial-and-error

expert *noun* 1 MASTER, authority, connoisseur, past master, professional, specialist, virtuoso
▷ *adjective* 2 SKILLFUL, adept, adroit, experienced, masterly, practiced, professional, proficient, qualified, virtuoso

expertise *noun* SKILL, adroitness, command, facility, judgment, know-how (*informal*), knowledge, mastery, proficiency

expire *verb* 1 FINISH, cease, close, come to an end, conclude, end, lapse, run out, stop, terminate
2 BREATHE OUT, emit, exhale, expel
3 DIE, depart, kick the bucket (*informal*), pass away *or* pass on, perish

explain *verb* 1 MAKE CLEAR *or* MAKE PLAIN, clarify, clear up, define, describe, elucidate, expound, resolve, teach
2 ACCOUNT FOR, excuse, give a reason for, justify

explanation *noun* 1 REASON, account, answer, excuse, justification, motive, vindication
2 DESCRIPTION, clarification, definition, elucidation, illustration, interpretation

explanatory *adjective* DESCRIPTIVE, illustrative, interpretive

explicit *adjective* CLEAR, categorical, definite, frank, precise, specific, straightforward, clear, plain **5** unequivocal

ex•plode [ik-SPLOHD] *verb intransitive* **-plod•ed, -plod•ing** **1** go off with bang **2** burst violently **3** (of population) increase rapidly ▷ *verb transitive* **-plod•ed, -plod•ing** **4** make explode **5** discredit, expose (a theory, etc.) > **ex•plo'sion** [-zhən] *noun* > **ex•plo'sive** *adjective, noun*

ex•ploit [EK-sploit] *noun* **1** brilliant feat, deed ▷ *verb transitive* [ik-SPLOIT] **2** turn to advantage **3** make use of for one's own ends > **ex•ploi•ta'tion** [ek-] *noun*

ex•plore [ik-SPLOHR] *verb transitive* **-plored, -plor•ing** **1** investigate **2** examine **3** scrutinize **4** examine (country, etc.) by going through it > **ex•plo•ra•tion** [ek-splə-RAY-shən] *noun* > **ex•plor•a•to•ry** [ik-SPLOR-ə-tor-ee] *adjective* > **ex•plor'er** *noun*

explosion *see* **explode**

exponent *see* **expound**

ex•port [ik-SPORT] *verb transitive* send (goods) out of the country ▷ *noun, adjective* [EK-sport] > **ex•por•ta'tion** [-TAY-shən] *noun* > **ex•port'er** *noun*

ex•pose [ik-SPOHZ] *verb transitive* **-posed, -pos•ing** **1** exhibit **2** disclose, reveal **3** lay open (to) **4** leave unprotected **5** expose photographic plate or film to light > **ex•po•sure** [-zhər] *noun*

ex•po•sé [ek-spoh-ZAY] *noun* newspaper article, etc., disclosing scandal, crime, etc.

exposition *see* **expound**

ex•pos•tu•late [ik-SPOS-chə-layt] *verb intransitive* **-lat•ed, -lat•ing** **1** remonstrate **2** reason with (in a kindly manner) > **ex•pos•tu•la'tion** *noun*

ex•pound [ik-SPOWND] *verb transitive* explain, interpret > **ex•po•nent** [ik-SPOH-nənt] *noun* **1** one who expounds or promotes (idea, cause, etc.) **2** performer, executant **3** *math.* small, raised number showing the power of a factor > **ex•po•nen•tial** [ek-spə-NEN-shəl] *adjective* > **ex•po•si'tion** [-ZISH-ən] *noun* **1** explanation, description **2** exhibition of goods, etc. > **ex•pos•i•tor** [ik-SPOZ-i-tər] *noun* one who explains, interpreter > **ex•pos'i•to•ry** *adjective* explanatory

ex•press [ik-SPRES] *verb transitive* **1** put into words **2** make known or understood by words, behavior, etc. **3** squeeze out ▷ *adjective* **4** definitely stated **5** specially designed **6** clear **7** positive **8** speedy **9** of train, fast and making few stops ▷ *adverb* **10** by express **11** with speed ▷ *noun* **12** express train **13** rapid parcel delivery service > **ex•press'i•ble** *adjective* > **ex•pres'sion** [-shən] *noun* **1** expressing **2** word, phrase **3** look, aspect **4** feeling **5** utterance > **ex•pres'sion•ism** *noun* theory that art depends on expression of artist's creative self, not on mere reproduction > **ex•pres'sive** *adjective* > **ex•press'ly** *adverb* > **ex•pres'sive•ness** *noun*

ex•pro•pri•ate [eks-PROH-pree-ayt] *verb transitive* **-at•ed, -at•ing** **1** dispossess **2** take out of owner's hands > **ex•pro•pri•a'tion** *noun*

expulsion *see* **expel**

unambiguous

explode *verb* **1** BLOW UP, burst, detonate, discharge, erupt, go off, set off, shatter
2 DISPROVE, debunk, discredit, give the lie to, invalidate, refute, repudiate

exploit *verb* **1** TAKE ADVANTAGE OF, abuse, manipulate, milk, misuse, play on *or* play upon
2 MAKE THE BEST USE OF, capitalize on, cash in on (*informal*), profit by *or* profit from, use, utilize
▷ *noun* **3** FEAT, accomplishment, achievement, adventure, attainment, deed, escapade, stunt

exploitation *noun* MISUSE, abuse, manipulation

exploration *noun* **1** INVESTIGATION, analysis, examination, inquiry, inspection, research, scrutiny, search
2 EXPEDITION, reconnaissance, survey, tour, travel, trip

exploratory *adjective* INVESTIGATIVE, experimental, fact-finding, probing, searching

explore *verb* **1** INVESTIGATE, examine, inquire into, inspect, look into, probe, research, search
2 TRAVEL, reconnoiter, scout, survey, tour

explosion *noun* **1** BANG, blast, burst, clap, crack, detonation, discharge, report
2 OUTBURST, eruption, fit, outbreak

explosive *adjective* **1** UNSTABLE, volatile
2 VIOLENT, fiery, stormy, touchy, vehement

exponent *noun* **1** ADVOCATE, backer, champion, defender, promoter, proponent, supporter, upholder
2 PERFORMER, player

expose *verb* **1** UNCOVER, display, exhibit, present, reveal, show, unveil
2 MAKE VULNERABLE, endanger, imperil, jeopardize, lay open, leave open, subject

exposed *adjective* **1** UNCONCEALED, bare, on display, on show, on view, revealed, uncovered
2 UNSHELTERED, open, unprotected
3 VULNERABLE, in peril, laid bare, susceptible, wide open

exposure *noun* PUBLICITY, display, exhibition, presentation, revelation, showing, uncovering, unveiling

expound *verb* EXPLAIN, describe, elucidate, interpret, set forth, spell out, unfold

express *verb* **1** STATE, articulate, communicate, declare, phrase, put into words, say, utter, voice, word
2 SHOW, convey, exhibit, indicate, intimate, make known, represent, reveal, signify, stand for, symbolize
▷ *adjective* **3** EXPLICIT, categorical, clear, definite, distinct, plain, unambiguous
4 SPECIFIC, clear-cut, especial, particular, singular, special
5 FAST, direct, high-speed, nonstop, rapid, speedy, swift

expression *noun* **1** STATEMENT, announcement, communication, declaration, utterance
2 INDICATION, demonstration, exhibition, manifestation, representation, show, sign, symbol, token
3 LOOK, air, appearance, aspect, countenance, face
4 PHRASE, idiom, locution, remark, term, turn of phrase, word

expressive *adjective* VIVID, eloquent, moving, poignant, striking, telling

expressly *adverb* **1** DEFINITELY, categorically, clearly, distinctly, explicitly, in no uncertain terms, plainly, unambiguously
2 SPECIFICALLY, especially, particularly, specially

ex•punge [ik-SPUNJ] *verb transitive* **-punged, -pung•ing** strike out, erase
ex•pur•gate [EK-spər-gayt] *verb transitive* **-gat•ed, -gat•ing** remove objectionable parts (from book, etc.), purge > **ex•pur•ga'tion** *noun*
ex•quis•ite [EK-skwiz-it] *adjective* 1 of extreme beauty or delicacy 2 keen, acute 3 keenly sensitive > **ex•quis'ite•ly** *adverb*
ex•tant [EK-stənt] *adjective* still existing
ex•tem•po•re [ik-STEM-pə-ree] *adjective, adverb* without previous thought or preparation > **ex•tem•po•ra'ne•ous** *adjective* > **ex•tem'po•rize** *verb transitive* **-rized, -riz•ing** 1 speak without preparation 2 devise for the occasion
ex•tend [ik-STEND] *verb transitive* 1 stretch out, lengthen 2 prolong in duration 3 widen in area, scope 4 accord, grant ▷ *verb intransitive* 5 reach 6 cover area 7 have range or scope 8 become larger or wider > **ex•tend'i•ble** *or* **ex•tend'a•ble, ex•ten'si•ble** *adjective* > **ex•ten•sile** [ik-STEN-səl] *adjective* that can be extended > **ex•ten'sion** *noun* 1 stretching out, prolongation or enlargement 2 expansion 3 continuation, additional part, as of telephone, etc. > **ex•ten'sive** *adjective* wide, large, comprehensive > **ex•ten'sor** *noun* straightening muscle > **ex•tent'** *noun* 1 space or degree to which thing is extended 2 size 3 compass 4 volume
ex•ten•u•ate [ik-STEN-yoo-ayt] *verb transitive* **-at•ed, -at•ing** 1 make less blameworthy, lessen 2 mitigate > **ex•ten•u•a'tion** *noun*
ex•te•ri•or [ik-STEER-ee-ər] *noun* 1 the outside 2 outward appearance ▷ *adjective* 3 outer, outward, external
ex•ter•mi•nate [ik-STUR-mə-nayt] *verb transitive* **-nat•ed, -nat•ing** destroy utterly, annihilate, root out, eliminate > **ex•ter•mi•na'tion** *noun* > **ex•ter'mi•na•tor** *noun* destroyer
ex•ter•nal [ik-STUR-nəl] *adjective* outside, outward > **ex•ter•nal•ly** *adverb*
ex•tinct [ik-STINGKT] *adjective* 1 having died out or come to an end 2 no longer existing 3 quenched, no longer burning > **ex•tinc'tion** *noun*
ex•tin•guish [ik-STING-gwish] *verb transitive* 1 put out, quench 2 wipe out > **ex•tin'guish•er** *noun* device, esp. spraying liquid or foam, used to put out fires
ex•tir•pate [EK-stər-payt] *verb transitive* **-pat•ed, -pat•ing** root out, destroy utterly > **ex•tir•pa'tion** *noun* > **ex'tir•pa•tor** *noun*
ex•tol [ik-STOHL] *verb transitive* **-tolled, -tol•ling** praise highly
ex•tort [ik-STORT] *verb transitive* 1 get by force or threats 2 wring out 3 exact > **ex•tor'tion** *noun*
ex•tra [EK-strə] *adjective* 1 additional 2 larger, better, than usual ▷ *adverb* 3 additionally 4 more than usually ▷ *noun* 5 extra thing 6 something charged as additional 7 *films* actor hired for crowd scenes
extra- *prefix* outside or beyond an area or scope: *extradition; extramural; extraterritorial*
ex•tract [ik-STRAKT] *verb transitive* 1 take out, esp. by force 2 obtain against person's will 3 get by pressure, distillation, etc. 4 deduce, derive 5 copy out, quote ▷ *noun* [EK-strakt] 6 passage from book, film, etc. 7 matter got by

DICTIONARY

e

THESAURUS

expulsion *noun* EJECTION, banishment, dismissal, eviction, exclusion, removal
exquisite *adjective* 1 BEAUTIFUL, attractive, charming, comely, lovely, pleasing, striking 2 FINE, beautiful, dainty, delicate, elegant, lovely, precious 3 INTENSE, acute, keen, sharp
extempore *adverb, adjective* IMPROMPTU, ad lib, freely, improvised, offhand, off the cuff (*informal*), spontaneously, unpremeditated, unprepared
extend *verb* 1 MAKE LONGER, drag out, draw out, lengthen, prolong, spin out, spread out, stretch 2 LAST, carry on, continue, go on 3 WIDEN, add to, augment, broaden, enhance, enlarge, expand, increase, supplement 4 OFFER, confer, impart, present, proffer
extension *noun* 1 ANNEX, addition, appendage, appendix, supplement 2 LENGTHENING, broadening, development, enlargement, expansion, increase, spread, widening
extensive *adjective* WIDE, broad, far-flung, far-reaching, large-scale, pervasive, spacious, vast, voluminous, widespread
extent *noun* SIZE, amount, area, breadth, expanse, length, stretch, volume, width
extenuating *adjective* MITIGATING, justifying, moderating, qualifying
exterior *noun* 1 OUTSIDE, coating, covering, façade, face, shell, skin, surface ▷ *adjective* 2 OUTSIDE, external, outer, outermost, outward, surface
exterminate *verb* DESTROY, abolish, annihilate, eliminate, eradicate
external *adjective* 1 OUTER, exterior, outermost, outside, outward, surface 2 OUTSIDE, alien, extrinsic, foreign
extinct *adjective* DEAD, defunct, gone, lost, vanished
extinction *noun* DYING OUT, abolition, annihilation, destruction, eradication, extermination, obliteration, oblivion
extinguish *verb* 1 PUT OUT, blow out, douse, quench, smother, snuff out, stifle 2 DESTROY, annihilate, eliminate, end, eradicate, exterminate, remove, wipe out
extol *verb* PRAISE, acclaim, commend, eulogize, exalt, glorify, sing the praises of
extort *verb* FORCE, blackmail, bully, coerce, extract, squeeze
extortionate *adjective* EXORBITANT, excessive, extravagant, inflated, outrageous, preposterous, sky-high, unreasonable
extra *adjective* 1 ADDITIONAL, added, ancillary, auxiliary, further, more, supplementary 2 SURPLUS, excess, leftover, redundant, spare, superfluous, unused ▷ *noun* 3 ADDITION, accessory, attachment, bonus, extension, supplement ▷ *adverb* 4 EXCEPTIONALLY, especially, extraordinarily, extremely, particularly, remarkably, uncommonly, unusually
extract *verb* 1 PULL OUT, draw, pluck out, pull, remove, take out, uproot, withdraw 2 DERIVE, draw, elicit, glean, obtain ▷ *noun* 3 PASSAGE, citation, clipping, cutting, excerpt, quotation, selection

distillation **8** concentrated solution
> **ex•trac'tion** *noun* **1** extracting, esp. of tooth **2** ancestry

ex•tra•di•tion [ek-strə-DISH-ən] *noun* delivery, under treaty, of foreign fugitive from justice to authorities concerned > **ex'tra•dite** [-dīt] *verb transitive* **-dit•ed, -dit•ing** give or obtain such delivery

ex•tra•mur•al [ek-strə-MYUUR-əl] *adjective* **1** connected with but outside normal courses, etc. of college or school **2** situated outside walls or boundaries of a place

ex•tra•ne•ous [ik-STRAY-nee-əs] *adjective* **1** not essential **2** irrelevant **3** added from without, not belonging

ex•tra•or•di•na•ry [ik-STROR-dn-er-ee] *adjective* **1** out of the usual course **2** additional **3** unusual, surprising, exceptional

ex•trap•o•late [ik-STRAP-ə-layt] *verb transitive* **-lat•ed, -lat•ing 1** infer something not known from known facts **2** *math.* estimate a value beyond known values

ex•tra•sen•so•ry [ek-strə-SEN-sə-ree] *adjective* of perception apparently gained without use of known senses

ex•tra•ter•res•tri•al [ek-strə-tə-RES-tree-əl] *adjective* of, or from outside Earth's atmosphere

ex•trav•a•gant [ik-STRAV-ə-gənt] *adjective* **1** wasteful **2** exorbitant **3** wild, absurd
> **ex•trav'a•gance** *noun* > **ex•trav'a•gant•ly** *adverb*
> **ex•trav•a•gan'za** [-GAN-zə] *noun* elaborate, lavish, entertainment, display, etc.

extravert *see* **extrovert**

ex•treme [ik-STREEM] *adjective* **-trem•er, -trem•est 1** of high or highest degree **2** severe **3** going beyond moderation **4** at the end **5** outermost ▷ *noun* **6** utmost degree **7** thing at one end or the other, first and last of series
> **ex•trem'ist** *noun* advocate of extreme measures
> **ex•trem'i•ty** [-TREM-i-tee] *noun, plural* **-ties** farthest point > **ex•trem'i•ties 1** hands and feet **2** utmost distress **3** extreme measures
> **extreme sport** any of various sports with a high risk of injury or death

ex•tri•cate [EK-stri-kayt] *verb transitive* **-cat•ed, -cat•ing** disentangle, unravel, set free
> **ex•tri•ca'tion** *noun*

ex•trin•sic [ik-STRIN-sik] *adjective* accessory, not belonging, not intrinsic > **ex•trin'si•cal•ly** *adverb*

ex•tro•vert [EK-strə-vurt] *noun* one who is interested in other people and things rather than own feelings > **ex•tro•ver'sion** [-VUR-zhən] *noun*

ex•trude [ik-STROOD] *verb transitive* **-trud•ed, -trud•ing 1** squeeze, force out **2** (esp. of molten metal or plastic, etc.) shape by squeezing through suitable nozzle or die

ex•u•ber•ant [ig-ZOO-bər-ənt] *adjective* **1** high-spirited, vivacious **2** prolific, abundant, luxurious > **ex•u'ber•ance** *noun*

ex•ude [ig-ZOOD] *verb intransitive* **-ud•ed, -ud•ing 1** ooze out ▷ *verb transitive* **-ud•ed, -ud•ing 2** give off (moisture)

ex•ult [ig-ZULT] *verb intransitive* rejoice, triumph
> **exult'an•cy** *noun* > **ex•ult'ant** *adjective* triumphant > **ex•ul•ta•tion** [eg-zul-TAY-shən] *noun*

ex•urb [EKS-urb] *noun* residential area outside the suburbs of a city

eye [ī] *noun* **1** organ of sight **2** look, glance **3** attention **4** aperture **5** view **6** judgment **7** watch, vigilance **8** thing, mark resembling eye **9** slit in needle for thread ▷ *verb transitive* **eyed, ey•ing 10** look at **11** observe > **eye'less** *adjective*
> **eye'ball** *noun* ball of eye > **eye'brow** *noun* crescent of hair above eye > **eye'glass** *noun* **1** glass to assist sight **2** monocle > **eye'lash** *noun* hair fringing eyelid > **eye'let** *noun* small hole for rope, etc. to pass through > **eye'lid** *noun* lid or cover of eye > **eye'o•pen•er** *noun* **1** surprising news **2** revealing statement > **eye shadow**

DICTIONARY • THESAURUS

4 ESSENCE, concentrate, distillation, juice

extraneous *adjective* IRRELEVANT, beside the point, immaterial, inappropriate, off the subject, unconnected, unrelated

extraordinary *adjective* UNUSUAL, amazing, exceptional, fantastic, outstanding, phenomenal, remarkable, strange, uncommon

extravagance *noun* **1** WASTE, lavishness, overspending, prodigality, profligacy, squandering, wastefulness
2 EXCESS, exaggeration, outrageousness, preposterousness, wildness

extravagant *adjective* **1** WASTEFUL, lavish, prodigal, profligate, spendthrift
2 EXCESSIVE, outrageous, over the top (*slang*), preposterous, reckless, unreasonable

extreme *adjective* **1** MAXIMUM, acute, great, highest, intense, severe, supreme, ultimate, utmost
2 SEVERE, drastic, harsh, radical, rigid, strict, uncompromising
3 EXCESSIVE, fanatical, immoderate, radical
4 FARTHEST, far-off, most distant, outermost, remotest
▷ *noun* **5** LIMIT, boundary, edge, end, extremity, pole

extremely *adverb* VERY, awfully (*informal*), exceedingly, exceptionally, extraordinarily, severely, terribly, uncommonly, unusually

extremist *noun* FANATIC, die-hard, radical, zealot

extremity *noun* **1** LIMIT, border, boundary, edge, extreme, frontier, pinnacle, tip
2 CRISIS, adversity, dire straits, disaster, emergency, exigency, trouble
3 ▷ **extremities** HANDS AND FEET, fingers and toes, limbs

extricate *verb* FREE, disengage, disentangle, get out, release, remove, rescue, wriggle out of

extrovert *adjective* OUTGOING, exuberant, gregarious, sociable

exuberance *noun* **1** HIGH SPIRITS, cheerfulness, ebullience, enthusiasm, liveliness, spirit, vitality, vivacity, zest
2 LUXURIANCE, abundance, copiousness, lavishness, profusion

exuberant *adjective* **1** HIGH-SPIRITED, animated, cheerful, ebullient, energetic, enthusiastic, lively, spirited, vivacious
2 LUXURIANT, abundant, copious, lavish, plentiful, profuse

exult *verb* BE JOYFUL, be overjoyed, celebrate, jump for joy, rejoice

eye *noun* **1** EYEBALL, optic (*informal*)

colored cosmetic put on around the eyes > **eye'sore** *noun* 1 ugly object 2 thing that annoys one to see > **eye'tooth** *noun* canine tooth > **eye'wash** *noun* (*informal*) deceptive talk, etc., nonsense > **eye'wit•ness** *noun* one who actually sees something and can give firsthand account of it

ey•rie [AIR-ee] *noun* 1 nest of bird of prey, esp. eagle 2 high dwelling place

e-zine [EE-zeen] *noun* magazine available only in electronic form

2 APPRECIATION, discernment, discrimination, judgment, perception, recognition, taste ▷ *verb* 3 LOOK AT, check out (*informal*), contemplate, inspect, study, survey, view, watch

eyesight *noun* VISION, perception, sight

eyesore *noun* MESS, blemish, blot, disfigurement, horror, monstrosity, sight (*informal*)

eyewitness *noun* OBSERVER, bystander, onlooker, passer-by, spectator, viewer, witness

Ff

F *chem.* fluorine
fa [fah] *noun* fourth sol-fa note
fa•ble [FAY-bəl] *noun* 1 short story with moral, esp. one with animals as characters 2 tale 3 legend 4 fiction or lie ▷ *verb transitive* 5 invent, tell fables about > **fab'u•list** *noun* writer of fables > **fab'u•lous** [-yə-ləs] *adjective* 1 amazing 2 (*informal*) extremely good 3 told of in fables 4 unhistorical
fab•ric [FAB-rik] *noun* 1 cloth 2 texture 3 frame, structure > **fab'ri•cate** *verb transitive* **-cat•ed, -cat•ing** 1 build 2 frame 3 construct 4 invent (lie, etc.) 5 forge (document) > **fab•ri•ca'tion** *noun*
fa•cade [fə-SAHD] *noun* 1 front of building 2 outward appearance
face [fays] *noun* 1 front of head 2 distorted expression 3 outward appearance 4 front, upper surface, or chief side of anything 5 dial of a clock, etc. 6 dignity ▷ *verb transitive* **faced, fac•ing** 7 look or front toward 8 meet (boldly) 9 give a covering surface ▷ *verb intransitive* **faced, fac•ing** 10 turn > **fac•et** [FAS-it] *noun* 1 one side of many-sided body, esp. cut gem 2 one aspect > **fa•cial** [FAY-shəl] *adjective* 1 pert. to face ▷ *noun* 2 cosmetic treatment for face

DICTIONARY • THESAURUS

fable *noun* 1 STORY, allegory, legend, myth, parable, tale
2 FICTION, fabrication, fantasy, fish story (*informal*), invention, tall tale (*informal*), urban legend, yarn (*informal*)
fabric *noun* 1 CLOTH, material, stuff, textile, web
2 FRAMEWORK, constitution, construction, foundations, make-up, organization, structure
fabricate *verb* 1 MAKE UP, concoct, devise, fake, falsify, feign, forge, invent, trump up
2 BUILD, assemble, construct, erect, form, make, manufacture, shape
fabrication *noun* 1 FORGERY, concoction, fake, falsehood, fiction, invention, lie, myth
2 CONSTRUCTION, assembly, building, erection, manufacture, production
fabulous *adjective* 1 (*informal*) WONDERFUL, brilliant, fantastic (*informal*), marvelous, out-of-this-world (*informal*), sensational (*informal*), spectacular, superb
2 ASTOUNDING, amazing, breathtaking, inconceivable, incredible, phenomenal, unbelievable
3 LEGENDARY, apocryphal, fantastic, fictitious, imaginary, invented, made-up, mythical, unreal
façade *noun* APPEARANCE, exterior, face, front, guise, mask, pretense, semblance, show
face *noun* 1 COUNTENANCE, features, mug (*slang*), visage
2 EXPRESSION, appearance, aspect, look
3 SCOWL, frown, grimace, pout, smirk
4 FAÇADE, appearance, display, exterior, front, mask, show
5 SIDE, exterior, front, outside, surface
6 SELF-RESPECT, authority, dignity, honor, image, prestige, reputation, standing, status
▷ *verb* 7 MEET, brave, come up against, confront, deal with, encounter, experience, oppose, tackle
8 LOOK ONTO, be opposite, front onto, overlook
9 COAT, clad, cover, dress, finish
faceless *adjective* IMPERSONAL, anonymous, remote

> **fac'ings** *plural noun* lining for decoration or reinforcement, sewn on collar, cuff, etc. > **face'less** *adjective* 1 without a face 2 anonymous > **face'lift•ing** *noun* operation to tighten skin of face to remove wrinkles > **face recognition** ability of a computer to scan, store, and recognize human faces
fa•ce•tious [fə-SEE-shəs] *adjective* 1 (sarcastically) witty 2 humorous, given to jesting, esp. at inappropriate time
facia *noun see* **fascia**
fac•ile [FAS-il] *adjective* 1 easy 2 working easily 3 easygoing 4 superficial, silly > **fa•cil'i•tate** *verb transitive* make easy, help > **fa•cil'i•ta•tor** *noun* > **fa•cil'i•ty** *noun, plural* **-ties** easiness, dexterity > **fa•cil'i•ties** 1 good conditions 2 means, equipment for doing something
fac•sim•i•le [fak-SIM-ə-lee] *noun* an exact copy
fact [fakt] *noun* 1 thing known to be true 2 deed 3 reality > **fac'tu•al** [-choo-əl] *adjective*
fac•tion [FAK-shən] *noun* 1 (dissenting) minority group within larger body 2 dissension > **fac'tious** *adjective* of or producing factions
fac•ti•tious [fak-TISH-əs] *adjective* 1 artificial 2 specially made up 3 unreal
fac•tor [FAK-tər] *noun* 1 something contributing to a result 2 one of numbers that multiplied together give a given number 3 agent, dealer 4 business that provides money to finance commerce > **fac•to'tum** [-TOH-təm] *noun* one performing all types of work
fac•to•ry [FAK-tə-ree] *noun* building in which things are manufactured
fac•ul•ty [FAK-əl-tee] *noun, plural* **-ties** 1 inherent power 2 power of the mind 3 ability, aptitude 4 staff of school, college or university 5 department of university
fad *noun* 1 short-lived fashion 2 whim > **fad'dish** *adjective* > **fad'dism** *noun* > **fad'dist** *noun*
fade [fayd] *verb intransitive* **fad•ed, fad•ing** 1 lose color, strength 2 wither 3 grow dim 4 disappear gradually ▷ *verb transitive* **fad•ed, fad•ing** 5 cause to fade > **fade'-in, fade'-out** *noun* 1 *radio* variation in strength of signals 2 *tv, film* gradual appearance and disappearance of picture
fag *noun* (*slang, offensive*) *short for* **faggot** (sense 2)
fag•got [FAG-ət] *noun* 1 bundle of sticks for fuel, etc. 2 (*slang, offensive*) male homosexual
Fahr•en•heit [FAR-ən-hīt] *adjective* measured by thermometric scale with freezing point of water 32°, boiling point 212°
fa•ience [FAY-ahns] *noun* glazed earthenware or china
fail [fayl] *verb intransitive* 1 be unsuccessful 2 stop operating or working 3 be below the required standard 4 be insufficient 5 run short 6 be wanting when in need 7 lose power 8 die away 9 become bankrupt ▷ *verb transitive* 10 disappoint, give no help to 11 neglect, forget to do 12 judge (student) to be below required standard > **fail'ing** *noun* 1 deficiency 2 fault ▷ *preposition* 3 in default of > **fail'ure** *noun* > **fail'-safe** *adjective* of device ensuring safety or remedy

DICTIONARY **f** THESAURUS

---

facet *noun* ASPECT, angle, face, part, phase, plane, side, slant, surface
facetious *adjective* FUNNY, amusing, comical, droll, flippant, frivolous, humorous, jocular, playful, tongue in cheek
face up to *verb* ACCEPT, acknowledge, come to terms with, confront, cope with, deal with, meet head-on, tackle
facile *adjective* SUPERFICIAL, cursory, glib, hasty, shallow, slick
facilitate *verb* PROMOTE, expedite, forward, further, help, make easy, pave the way for, speed up
facility *noun* 1 SKILL, ability, adroitness, dexterity, ease, efficiency, effortlessness, fluency, proficiency
2 (*often plural*) EQUIPMENT, advantage, aid, amenity, appliance, convenience, means, opportunity, resource
facsimile *noun* COPY, carbon copy, duplicate, fax, photocopy, print, replica, reproduction, transcript
fact *noun* 1 EVENT, act, deed, fait accompli (*French*), happening, incident, occurrence, performance
2 TRUTH, certainty, reality
faction *noun* 1 GROUP, bloc, cabal, clique, contingent, coterie, gang, party, set, splinter group
2 DISSENSION, conflict, disagreement, discord, disunity, division, infighting, rebellion
factor *noun* ELEMENT, aspect, cause, component, consideration, influence, item, part
factory *noun* WORKS, mill, plant
factual *adjective* TRUE, authentic, correct, exact, genuine, precise, real, true-to-life
faculties *plural noun* POWERS, capabilities, intelligence, reason, senses, wits
faculty *noun* 1 ABILITY, aptitude, capacity, facility, power, propensity, skill
2 DEPARTMENT, school
fad *noun* CRAZE, fashion, mania, rage, trend, vogue, whim
fade *verb* 1 PALE, bleach, discolor, lose color, wash out
2 DWINDLE, decline, die away, disappear, dissolve, melt away, vanish, wane
faded *adjective* DISCOLORED, bleached, dull, indistinct, pale, washed out
fading *adjective* DECLINING, decreasing, disappearing, dying, on the decline, vanishing
fail *verb* 1 BE UNSUCCESSFUL, bite the dust, break down, come to grief, come unstuck, fall, fizzle out (*informal*), flop (*informal*), founder, miscarry, misfire
2 DISAPPOINT, abandon, desert, forget, forsake, let down, neglect, omit
3 GIVE OUT, conk out (*informal*), cut out, die, peter out, stop working
4 GO BANKRUPT, become insolvent, close down, fold (*informal*), go broke (*informal*), go bust (*informal*), go into receivership, go out of business, go to the wall, go under
▷ *noun* 5 ▷ **without fail** REGULARLY, conscientiously, constantly, dependably, like clockwork, punctually, religiously, twenty-four-seven (*slang*), without exception
failing *noun* 1 WEAKNESS, blemish, defect, deficiency, drawback, fault, flaw, imperfection, shortcoming
▷ *preposition* 2 IN THE ABSENCE OF, in default of, lacking

of malfunction in machine, weapon, etc. **without fail** 1 in spite of every difficulty 2 certainly

faint [faynt] *adjective* **-er, -est** 1 feeble, dim, pale 2 weak 3 dizzy, about to lose consciousness ▷ *verb intransitive* 4 lose consciousness temporarily

fair[1] *adjective* **-er, -est** 1 just, impartial 2 according to rules, legitimate 3 blond 4 beautiful 5 ample 6 of moderate quality or amount 7 unblemished 8 plausible 9 middling 10 (of weather) favorable ▷ *adverb* 11 honestly > **fair'ing** *noun aviation* streamlined structure, or any part so shaped that it provides streamlined form > **fair'ly** *adverb* > **fair'ness** *noun* > **fair'way** *noun* 1 *golf* trimmed turf between tee and green 2 navigable channel

fair[2] *noun* 1 traveling entertainment with sideshows, amusements, etc. 2 large exhibition of farm, commercial or industrial products 3 periodical market often with amusements > **fair'ground** *noun*

fair•y [FAIR-ee] *noun, plural* **fair•ies** 1 imaginary small creature with powers of magic 2 (*slang, offensive*) male homosexual ▷ *adjective* 3 of fairies 4 like fairy, beautiful and delicate, imaginary > **fair'y•land** *noun* > **fair'y-tale** *adjective* of or like fairy tale > **fairy tale** story of imaginary beings and happenings, esp. as told to children

fait ac•com•pli [fay ta-kawn-PLEE] *noun, plural* **faits accomplis** [fe za-kawn-PLEE] Fr. something already done that cannot be altered

faith [fayth] *noun* 1 trust 2 belief 3 belief without proof 4 religion 5 promise 6 loyalty, constancy > **faith'ful** *adjective* constant, true > **faith'ful•ly** *adverb* > **faith'less** *adjective*

fa•ji•tas [fa-HEE-taz] *plural noun* Mexican dish of soft tortillas wrapped around fried strips of meat or vegetables

fake [fayk] *verb transitive* **faked, fak•ing** 1 conceal defects of by artifice 2 touch up 3 counterfeit ▷ *noun* 4 fraudulent object, person, act ▷ *adjective* > **fak'er** *noun* 1 one who deals in fakes 2 swindler

fa•kir [fə-KEER] *noun* 1 member of Islamic religious order 2 Hindu ascetic

fa•la•fel [fə-LAH-fəl] *noun* seasoned croquette of flour or ground chickpeas

fal•con [FAL-kən] *noun* small bird of prey, esp. trained in hawking for sport > **fal'con•er** *noun* one who keeps, trains, or hunts with falcons > **fal'con•ry** *noun* hawking

fall [fawl] *verb intransitive* **fell, fall•en** 1 drop,

DICTIONARY • THESAURUS

failure *noun* 1 DEFEAT, breakdown, collapse, downfall, fiasco, lack of success, miscarriage, overthrow
2 LOSER, dead duck (*slang*), disappointment, dud (*informal*), flop (*informal*), nonstarter, washout (*informal*)
3 BANKRUPTCY, crash, downfall, insolvency, liquidation, ruin

faint *adjective* 1 DIM, distant, faded, indistinct, low, muted, soft, subdued, vague
2 SLIGHT, feeble, remote, unenthusiastic, weak
3 DIZZY, exhausted, giddy, light-headed, muzzy, weak, woozy (*informal*)
▷ *verb* 4 PASS OUT, black out, collapse, keel over (*informal*), lose consciousness, swoon (*literary*)
▷ *noun* 5 BLACKOUT, collapse, swoon (*literary*), unconsciousness

faintly *adverb* 1 SOFTLY, feebly, in a whisper, indistinctly, weakly
2 SLIGHTLY, a little, dimly, somewhat

fair[1] *adjective* 1 UNBIASED, above board, equitable, even-handed, honest, impartial, just, lawful, legitimate, proper, unprejudiced
2 LIGHT, blond, blonde, fair-haired, flaxen-haired, towheaded
3 RESPECTABLE, adequate, average, decent, moderate, O.K. *or* okay (*informal*), passable, reasonable, satisfactory, tolerable
4 BEAUTIFUL, bonny, comely, handsome, lovely, pretty
5 FINE, bright, clear, cloudless, dry, sunny, unclouded

fair[2] *noun* CARNIVAL, bazaar, festival, fête, gala, show

fairly *adverb* 1 MODERATELY, adequately, pretty well, quite, rather, reasonably, somewhat, tolerably
2 DESERVEDLY, equitably, honestly, impartially, justly, objectively, properly, without fear or favor
3 POSITIVELY, absolutely, really

fairness *noun* IMPARTIALITY, decency, disinterestedness, equitableness, equity, justice, legitimacy, rightfulness

fairy *noun* SPRITE, brownie, elf, imp, leprechaun, peri, pixie, Robin Goodfellow

fairy tale, fairy story *noun* 1 FOLK TALE, romance
2 LIE, cock-and-bull story (*informal*), fabrication, fiction, invention, tall tale (*informal*), untruth

faith *noun* 1 CONFIDENCE, assurance, conviction, credence, credit, dependence, reliance, trust
2 RELIGION, belief, church, communion, creed, denomination, dogma, persuasion
3 ALLEGIANCE, constancy, faithfulness, fidelity, loyalty

faithful *adjective* 1 LOYAL, constant, dependable, devoted, reliable, staunch, steadfast, true, trusty
2 ACCURATE, close, exact, precise, strict, true

faithless *adjective* DISLOYAL, false, fickle, inconstant, traitorous, treacherous, unfaithful, unreliable

fake *verb* 1 FORGE, copy, counterfeit, fabricate, feign, pretend, put on, sham, simulate
▷ *noun* 2 IMPOSTOR, charlatan, copy, forgery, fraud, hoax, imitation, reproduction, sham
▷ *adjective* 3 ARTIFICIAL, counterfeit, false, forged, imitation, mock, phoney *or* phony (*informal*), sham

fall *verb* 1 DESCEND, cascade, collapse, dive, drop, plummet, plunge, sink, subside, tumble
2 DECREASE, decline, diminish, drop, dwindle, go down, lessen, slump, subside
3 BE OVERTHROWN, capitulate, pass into enemy hands, succumb, surrender
4 DIE, be killed, meet one's end, perish
5 OCCUR, befall, chance, come about, come to pass, happen, take place
6 SLOPE, fall away, incline
7 LAPSE, err, go astray, offend, sin, transgress, trespass
▷ *noun* 8 DESCENT, dive, drop, nose dive, plummet, plunge, slip, tumble

come down freely 2 become lower 3 decrease 4 hang down 5 come to the ground, cease to stand 6 perish 7 collapse 8 be captured 9 revert 10 lapse 11 be uttered 12 become 13 happen ▷ *noun* 14 falling 15 amount that falls 16 amount of descent 17 decrease 18 collapse, ruin 19 drop 20 (*often plural*) cascade 21 cadence 22 yielding to temptation 23 autumn > **fall'out** *noun* 1 radioactive particles spread as result of nuclear explosion 2 incidental effect or outcome > **fall for** 1 (*informal*) fall in love with 2 (*informal*) be taken in by

fal•la•cy [FAL-ə-see] *noun, plural* **-cies** 1 incorrect, misleading opinion or argument 2 flaw in logic 3 illusion > **fal•la•cious** [fə-LAY-shəs] *adjective* > **fal•li•bil'i•ty** *noun* > **fal'li•ble** *adjective* liable to error

fallen *pp. of* **fall**

Fal•lo•pi•an tube [fə-LOH-pee-ən] either of a pair of tubes through which egg cells pass from ovary to womb

fal•low¹ [FAL-oh] *adjective* 1 plowed and harrowed but left without crop 2 uncultivated 3 neglected

fallow² *adjective* brown or reddish yellow > **fallow deer** deer of this color

false [fawls] *adjective* **fals•er, fals•est** 1 wrong, erroneous 2 deceptive 3 faithless 4 sham, artificial > **false'ly** *adverb* > **false'ness** *noun* faithlessness > **fal•si•fi•ca'tion** *noun* > **fal'si•fy** *verb transitive* **-fied, -fy•ing** 1 alter fraudulently 2 misrepresent > **fal'si•ty** *noun, plural* **-ties** > **false'hood** *noun* lie

fal•set•to [fawl-SET-oh] *noun, plural* **-tos** forced voice above natural range

Fal•staff•i•an [fawl-STAF-ee-ən] *adjective* 1 like Shakespeare's Falstaff 2 fat 3 convivial 4 boasting

fal•ter [FAWL-tər] *verb intransitive* 1 hesitate 2 waver 3 stumble > **fal'ter•ing•ly** *adverb*

fame [faym] *noun* 1 reputation 2 renown > **famed** *adjective* > **fa'mous** *adjective* 1 widely known 2 excellent

fa•mil•i•ar [fə-MIL-yər] *adjective* 1 well-known 2 frequent, customary 3 intimate 4 closely acquainted 5 unceremonious 6 impertinent, too friendly ▷ *noun* 7 familiar friend 8 familiar demon > **fa•mil•i•ar'•i•ty** *noun, plural* **-ties** > **fa•mil'iar•ize** *verb transitive* **-ized, -iz•ing**

fam•i•ly [FAM-ə-lee] *noun, plural* **-lies** 1 group of parents and children, or near relatives 2 person's children 3 all descendants of common ancestor 4 household 5 group of allied objects > **fa•mil•ial** [fə-MIL-yəl] *adjective* > **family leave** unpaid work leave for family reasons

fam•ine [FAM-in] *noun* 1 extreme scarcity of food 2 starvation > **fam'ished** *adjective* very hungry

famous *see* **fame**

fan¹ *noun* 1 instrument for producing current of air, esp. for ventilating or cooling 2 folding object of paper, etc., used, esp. formerly, for cooling the face 3 outspread feathers of a bird's tail ▷ *verb* **fanned, fan•ning** 4 spread out like fan ▷ *verb transitive* 5 blow or cool with fan > **fan'light** *noun* (fan-shaped) window over door

fan² *noun* (*informal*) 1 devoted admirer 2 an enthusiast, particularly of a sport, etc.

fa•nat•ic [fə-NAT-ik] *adjective* 1 filled with abnormal enthusiasm, esp. in religion ▷ *noun* 2

DICTIONARY **f** THESAURUS

---

9 DECREASE, cut, decline, dip, drop, lessening, lowering, reduction, slump
10 COLLAPSE, capitulation, defeat, destruction, downfall, overthrow, ruin
11 LAPSE, sin, transgression

fallacy *noun* ERROR, delusion, falsehood, flaw, misapprehension, misconception, mistake, untruth

fallible *adjective* IMPERFECT, erring, frail, ignorant, uncertain, weak

fall out *verb* ARGUE, clash, come to blows, differ, disagree, fight, quarrel, squabble

fallow *adjective* UNCULTIVATED, dormant, idle, inactive, resting, unplanted, unused

false *adjective* 1 INCORRECT, erroneous, faulty, inaccurate, inexact, invalid, mistaken, wrong
2 UNTRUE, lying, unreliable, unsound, untruthful
3 ARTIFICIAL, bogus, counterfeit, fake, forged, imitation, sham, simulated
4 DECEPTIVE, deceitful, fallacious, fraudulent, hypocritical, misleading, trumped up

falsehood *noun* 1 UNTRUTHFULNESS, deceit, deception, dishonesty, dissimulation, mendacity
2 LIE, fabrication, fib, fiction, story, untruth

falsify *verb* FORGE, alter, counterfeit, distort, doctor, fake, misrepresent, tamper with

falter *verb* HESITATE, stammer, stumble, stutter, totter, vacillate, waver

faltering *adjective* HESITANT, broken, irresolute, stammering, tentative, timid, uncertain, weak

fame *noun* PROMINENCE, celebrity, glory, honor, kudos, renown, reputation, repute, stardom

familiar *adjective* 1 WELL-KNOWN, accustomed, common, customary, frequent, ordinary, recognizable, routine
2 FRIENDLY, amicable, close, easy, intimate, relaxed
3 DISRESPECTFUL, bold, forward, impudent, intrusive, presumptuous

familiarity *noun* 1 ACQUAINTANCE, awareness, experience, grasp, understanding
2 FRIENDLINESS, ease, informality, intimacy, openness, sociability
3 DISRESPECT, boldness, forwardness, presumption

familiarize *verb* ACCUSTOM, habituate, instruct, inure, school, season, train

family *noun* 1 RELATIONS, folk (*informal*), household, kin, kith and kin, one's nearest and dearest, one's own flesh and blood, relatives
2 CLAN, dynasty, house, race, tribe
3 GROUP, class, genre, network, subdivision, system

famine *noun* HUNGER, dearth, scarcity, starvation

famished *adjective* STARVING, ravenous, voracious

famous *adjective* WELL-KNOWN, acclaimed, celebrated, distinguished, eminent, illustrious, legendary, noted, prominent, renowned

fan¹ *noun* 1 BLOWER, air conditioner, ventilator ▷ *verb* 2 BLOW, air-condition, cool, refresh, ventilate

fan² *noun* SUPPORTER, admirer, aficionado, buff (*informal*), devotee, enthusiast, follower, lover

fanatic *noun* EXTREMIST, activist, bigot,

fanatic person > **fa•nat'i•cal** *adjective* > **fa•nat'i•cism** *noun*
fan•cy [FAN-see] *adjective* **-ci•er, -ci•est** 1 ornamental, not plain 2 of whimsical or arbitrary kind ▷ *noun, plural* **-cies** 3 whim, caprice 4 liking, inclination 5 imagination 6 mental image ▷ *verb transitive* **-cied, -cy•ing** 7 imagine 8 be inclined to believe 9 (*informal*) have a liking for > **fan'ci•er** *noun* one with liking and expert knowledge (respecting some specific thing) > **fan'ci•ful** *adjective* > **fan'ci•ful•ly** *adverb*
fan•dan•go [fan-DANG-goh] *noun, plural* **-goes** 1 lively Spanish dance with castanets 2 music for this dance
fan•fare [FAN-fair] *noun* 1 a flourish of trumpets or bugles 2 ostentatious display
fang *noun* 1 snake's poison tooth 2 long, pointed tooth
fan•tail [FAN-tayl] *noun* 1 (kind of bird with) fan-shaped tail 2 projecting part of ship's stern
fan•ta•sy [FAN-tə-see] *noun, plural* **-sies** 1 power of imagination, esp. extravagant 2 mental image 3 fanciful invention or design > **fan•ta'sia** [-TAY-*zh*ə] *noun* fanciful musical composition > **fan'ta•size** *verb* **-sized, -siz•ing** > **fan•tas'tic** *adjective* 1 quaint, grotesque, extremely fanciful, wild 2 (*informal*) very good 3 (*informal*) very large > **fan•tas'ti•cal•ly** *adverb*
FAQ *internet.* frequently asked question *or* questions
far [fahr] *adverb* **far•ther** *or* **fur•ther, far•thest** *or* **fur•thest** 1 at or to a great distance, or advanced point 2 at or to a remote time 3 by very much ▷ *adjective* 4 distant 5 more distant > **far'-fetched'** *adjective* incredible
far•ad [FA-rəd] *noun* unit of electrical capacity
farce [fahrs] *noun* 1 comedy of boisterous humor 2 absurd and futile proceeding > **far'ci•cal** *adjective* ludicrous
fare [fair] *noun* 1 charge for passenger's transport 2 passenger 3 food ▷ *verb intransitive* **fared, far•ing** 4 get on 5 happen 6 travel, progress > **fare•well'** *interjection* 1 goodbye ▷ *noun* 2 leave-taking
far•i•na•ceous [far-ə-NAY-shəs] *adjective* 1 mealy, starchy 2 made of flour or meal
farm [fahrm] *noun* 1 tract of land for cultivation or rearing livestock 2 unit of land, water, for growing or rearing a particular crop, animal, etc. ▷ *verb* 3 cultivate (land) 4 rear livestock (on farm) > **farm'er** *noun* > **farm'house** *noun* > **farm'yard** *noun* > **farm out** 1 send (work) to be done by others 2 put into care of others
far•o [FAIR-oh] *noun* card game
far•ra•go [fə-RAH-goh] *noun, plural* **-gos** medley, hodgepodge
far•row [FA-roh] *noun* 1 litter of pigs ▷ *verb* 2 produce this
fart [fahrt] *noun* (*vulgar*) (audible) emission of gas from anus ▷ *verb intransitive*
far•ther [FAHR-*th*ər] *adverb, adjective* 1 further 2 *comp. of* **far** > **far'thest** *adverb, adjective* 1 furthest 2 *sup. of* **far**
fas•ces [FAS-eez] *plural noun* 1 bundle of rods bound together around ax, forming Roman badge of authority 2 emblem of Italian fascists
fas•cia [FAY-shə] *noun, plural* **-cias** 1 *architecture* long flat surface between moldings under eaves 2 face of wood or stone in a building
fas•ci•nate [FAS-ə-nayt] *verb transitive* **-nat•ed, -nat•ing** 1 attract and delight by arousing

DICTIONARY • THESAURUS

militant, zealot
fanatical *adjective* PASSIONATE, bigoted, extreme, fervent, frenzied, immoderate, obsessive, overenthusiastic, wild, zealous
fanciful *adjective* UNREAL, imaginary, mythical, romantic, visionary, whimsical, wild
fancy *adjective* 1 ELABORATE, baroque, decorative, embellished, extravagant, intricate, ornamental, ornate
▷ *noun* 2 WHIM, caprice, desire, humor, idea, impulse, inclination, notion, thought, urge
3 DELUSION, chimera, daydream, dream, fantasy, vision
▷ *verb* 4 SUPPOSE, believe, conjecture, imagine, reckon, think, think likely
5 WISH FOR, crave, desire, hanker after, hope for, long for, thirst for, yearn for
fantasize *verb* DAYDREAM, dream, envision, imagine
fantastic *adjective* 1 (*informal*) EXCELLENT, awesome (*slang*), first-rate, marvelous, sensational (*informal*), superb, wonderful
2 STRANGE, fanciful, grotesque, outlandish
3 UNREALISTIC, extravagant, far-fetched, ludicrous, ridiculous, wild
4 IMPLAUSIBLE, absurd, cock-and-bull (*informal*), incredible, preposterous, unlikely
fantasy *noun* 1 IMAGINATION, creativity, fancy, invention, originality
2 DAYDREAM, dream, flight of fancy, illusion, mirage, pipe dream, reverie, vision
far *adverb* 1 A LONG WAY, afar, a good way, a great distance, deep, miles
2 MUCH, considerably, decidedly, extremely, greatly, incomparably, very much
▷ *adjective* 3 REMOTE, distant, faraway, far-flung, far-off, outlying, out-of-the-way
farce *noun* 1 COMEDY, buffoonery, burlesque, satire, slapstick
2 MOCKERY, joke, nonsense, parody, sham, travesty
farcical *adjective* LUDICROUS, absurd, comic, derisory, laughable, nonsensical, preposterous, ridiculous, risible
fare *noun* 1 CHARGE, price, ticket money
2 FOOD, provisions, rations, sustenance, victuals
▷ *verb* 3 GET ON, do, get along, make out, manage, prosper
farewell *noun* GOOD-BYE, adieu, departure, leave-taking, parting, sendoff (*informal*), valediction
far-fetched *adjective* UNCONVINCING, cock-and-bull (*informal*), fantastic, implausible, incredible, preposterous, unbelievable, unlikely, unrealistic
farm *noun* 1 SMALLHOLDING, farmstead, grange, homestead, plantation, ranch
▷ *verb* 2 CULTIVATE, plant, work
fascinate *verb* INTRIGUE, absorb, beguile, captivate, engross, enthrall, entrance, hold spellbound, rivet, transfix
fascinating *adjective* GRIPPING, alluring, captivating, compelling, engaging, engrossing, enticing, intriguing, irresistible, riveting

interest and curiosity **2** render motionless, as with a fixed stare > **fas•ci•na'tion** *noun*
fas•cism [FASH-iz-əm] *noun* **1** authoritarian political system opposed to democracy and liberalism **2** behavior (esp. by those in authority) supposedly typical of this system > **fas'cist** *adjective, noun* > **fa•scis•tic** [fə-SHIS-tik] *adjective*
fash•ion [FASH-ən] *noun* **1** (latest) style, esp. of dress, etc. **2** manner, mode **3** form, type ▷ *verb transitive* **4** shape, make > **fash'ion•a•ble** *adjective* > **fash'ion•a•bly** *adverb*
fast[1] *adjective* **-er, -est 1** (capable of) moving quickly **2** permitting, providing, rapid progress **3** ahead of true time **4** firm, steady **5** permanent ▷ *adverb* **6** rapidly **7** tightly > **fast'ness** *noun* **1** fast state **2** fortress, stronghold > **fast'back** *noun* car with back forming continuous slope from roof to rear > **fast casual** style of fast food that is healthier and fresher than traditional fast food > **fast food** food, esp. hamburgers, etc., prepared and served very quickly
fast[2] *verb intransitive* **fast•ed, fast•ing** go without food, or some kinds of food ▷ *noun* > **fasting** *noun*
fas•ten [FAS-ən] *verb transitive* **1** attach, fix, secure ▷ *verb intransitive* **2** become joined **3** seize (upon)
fas•tid•i•ous [fa-STID-ee-əs] *adjective* **1** hard to please **2** discriminating **3** particular
fat *noun* **1** oily animal substance **2** fat part ▷ *adjective* **fat•ter, fat•test 3** having too much fat **4** containing fat, greasy **5** profitable **6** fertile > **fat'ten** *verb transitive* **1** feed (animals) for slaughter ▷ *verb intransitive* **2** become fat > **fat'ness** *noun* > **fat'ty** *adjective* **-ti•er, -i•est 1** containing fat ▷ *noun, plural* **-ties 2** (*informal*) fat person > **fat'head** *noun* (*slang*) dolt, fool > **fat farm** resort for helping people lose weight
fate [fayt] *noun* **1** power supposed to predetermine events **2** goddess of destiny **3** destiny **4** person's appointed lot or condition **5** death or destruction ▷ *verb transitive* **fat•ed, fat•ing 6** preordain > **fa'tal** *adjective* **1** deadly, ending in death **2** destructive **3** disastrous **4** inevitable > **fa'tal•ism** *noun* **1** belief that everything is predetermined **2** submission to fate > **fa'tal•ist** *noun* > **fa•tal•is'tic** *adjective* > **fa•tal'i•ty** *noun, plural* **-ties 1** accident resulting in death **2** person killed in war, accident > **fa'tal•ly** *adverb* > **fate'ful** *adjective* fraught with destiny, prophetic
fa•ther [FAH-*th*ər] *noun* **1** male parent **2** forefather, ancestor **3** (**Fa•ther**) God **4** originator, early leader **5** priest, confessor **6** oldest member of a society ▷ *verb transitive* **7** beget **8** originate **9** pass as father or author of **10** act as father to > **fa'ther•hood** *noun* > **fa'ther•less** *adjective* > **fa'ther•ly** *adjective* > **fa•ther-in-law** *noun* husband's or wife's father
fath•om [FATH-əm] *noun* **1** measure of six feet of water ▷ *verb transitive* **2** sound (water) **3** get to bottom of, understand > **fath'om•a•ble** *adjective* > **fath'om•less** *adjective* too deep to fathom
fa•tigue [fə-TEEG] *noun* **1** weariness **2** toil **3**

DICTIONARY f THESAURUS

fascination *noun* ATTRACTION, allure, charm, enchantment, lure, magic, magnetism, pull
fashion *noun* **1** STYLE, craze, custom, fad, look, mode, rage, trend, vogue
2 METHOD, manner, mode, style, way
▷ *verb* **3** MAKE, construct, create, forge, form, manufacture, mold, shape
fashionable *adjective* POPULAR, à la mode, chic, cool (*informal*), in (*informal*), in vogue, modern, phat (*slang*), stylish, trendy (*informal*), up-to-date, with it (*informal*)
fast[1] *adjective* **1** QUICK, brisk, fleet, flying, hasty, rapid, speedy, swift
2 FIXED, close, fastened, firm, immovable, secure, sound, steadfast, tight
3 DISSIPATED, dissolute, extravagant, loose, profligate, reckless, self-indulgent, wanton, wild
▷ *adverb* **4** QUICKLY, hastily, hurriedly, in haste, like lightning, rapidly, speedily, swiftly
5 SOUNDLY, deeply, firmly, fixedly, securely, tightly
fast[2] *verb* **1** GO HUNGRY, abstain, deny oneself, go without food
▷ *noun* **2** FASTING, abstinence
fasten *verb* FIX, affix, attach, bind, connect, join, link, secure, tie
fat *adjective* **1** OVERWEIGHT, corpulent, heavy, obese, plump, portly, rotund, stout, tubby
2 FATTY, adipose, greasy, oily, oleaginous
▷ *noun* **3** FATNESS, blubber, bulk, corpulence, flab, flesh, lard (*slang*), obesity, paunch, spare tire (*informal*)
fatal *adjective* **1** LETHAL, deadly, final, incurable, killing, malignant, mortal, terminal
2 RUINOUS, baleful, baneful, calamitous, catastrophic, disastrous
fatality *noun* DEATH, casualty, loss, mortality
fate *noun* **1** DESTINY, chance, divine will, fortune, kismet, nemesis, predestination, providence
2 FORTUNE, horoscope, lot, portion, stars
fated *adjective* DESTINED, doomed, foreordained, inescapable, inevitable, predestined, preordained, sure, written
fateful *adjective* **1** CRUCIAL, critical, decisive, important, portentous, significant
2 DISASTROUS, deadly, destructive, fatal, lethal, ominous, ruinous
father *noun* **1** DAD (*informal*), daddy (*informal*), old man (*informal*), pa (*informal*), papa (*old-fashioned informal*), parent, pater (*old-fashioned informal, chiefly Brit*), pop (*informal*), sire
2 FOREFATHER, ancestor, forebear, predecessor, progenitor
3 FOUNDER, architect, author, creator, inventor, maker, originator, prime mover
4 PRIEST, padre (*informal*), pastor
▷ *verb* **5** SIRE, beget, get, procreate
fatherland *noun* HOMELAND, motherland, native land
fatherly *adjective* PATERNAL, affectionate, benevolent, benign, kindly, patriarchal, protective, supportive
fathom *verb* UNDERSTAND, comprehend, get to the bottom of, grasp, interpret
fatigue *noun* **1** TIREDNESS, heaviness, languor, lethargy, listlessness
▷ *verb* **2** TIRE, drain, exhaust, take it out of (*informal*), weaken, wear out, weary

weakness of metals, etc., subjected to stress **4** soldier's nonmilitary duty ▷ *verb transitive* **-tigued, -tigu•ing 5** weary > **fa•tigues** *plural noun* clothing worn for such duty

fat•u•ous [FACH-oo-əs] *adjective* very silly, idiotic > **fat'u•ous•ness** *noun*

fau•cet [FAW-sit] *noun* **1** device for controlling flow of liquid **2** tap

fault [fawlt] *noun* **1** defect **2** flaw **3** misdeed **4** blame, culpability **5** blunder **6** mistake **7** *tennis* ball wrongly served **8** *geology* break in strata ▷ *verb* **9** find fault in **10** (cause to) undergo or commit fault > **fault'i•ly** *adverb* > **fault'less** *adjective* > **fault'y** *adjective* **fault•i•er, fault•i•est**

faun [fawn] *noun* mythological woodland being with tail and horns

fau•na [FAW-nə] *noun, plural* **-nas** *or* **-nae** [-nee] animals of region or period collectively

faux pas [foh-PAH] *noun, plural* **faux pas** [-PAHZ] social blunder or indiscretion

fa•vor [FAY-vər] *noun* **1** goodwill **2** approval **3** special kindness **4** partiality ▷ *verb transitive* **5** regard or treat with favor **6** oblige **7** treat with partiality **8** aid **9** support **10** resemble > **fa•vors** *plural noun* **1** sexual intimacy granted by woman **2** small party gift for a guest > **fa'vor•a•ble** *adjective* > **fa'vor•ite** [-it] *noun* **1** favored person or thing **2** horse, team, etc. expected to win race (or game) ▷ *adjective* **3** chosen, preferred > **fa'vor•it•ism** *noun* practice of showing undue preference

fawn[1] *noun* **1** young deer ▷ *adjective* **2** light yellowish brown

fawn[2] *verb intransitive* **1** of person, cringe, court favor servilely **2** esp. of dog, show affection by wagging tail and groveling

fax [faks] *noun* **1** facsimile ▷ *verb transitive* **2** transmit facsimile of (printed matter, etc.) electronically

faze [fayz] *verb transitive* **fazed, faz•ing 1** fluster **2** daunt

Fe *chem.* iron

fear [feer] *noun* **1** dread, alarm, anxiety, unpleasant emotion caused by coming evil or danger ▷ *verb intransitive* **2** have this feeling, be afraid ▷ *verb transitive* **3** regard with fear **4** hesitate, shrink from **5** revere > **fear'ful** *adjective*

DICTIONARY • THESAURUS

fatten *verb* **1** GROW FAT, expand, gain weight, put on weight, spread, swell, thicken
2 (*often with up*) FEED UP, build up, feed, nourish, overfeed, stuff

fatty *adjective* GREASY, adipose, fat, oily, oleaginous, rich

fatuous *adjective* FOOLISH, brainless, idiotic, inane, ludicrous, mindless, moronic (*offensive*), silly, stupid, witless

fault *noun* **1** FLAW, blemish, defect, deficiency, failing, imperfection, shortcoming, weakness, weak point
2 MISTAKE, blunder, error, indiscretion, lapse, oversight, slip
3 RESPONSIBILITY, accountability, culpability, liability
4 ▷ **at fault** GUILTY, answerable, blamable, culpable, in the wrong, responsible, to blame
5 ▷ **find fault with** CRITICIZE, carp at, complain, pick holes in, pull to pieces, quibble, take to task
6 ▷ **to a fault** EXCESSIVELY, immoderately, in the extreme, overmuch, unduly
▷ *verb* **7** CRITICIZE, blame, censure, find fault with, hold (someone) responsible, impugn

faultless *adjective* FLAWLESS, correct, exemplary, foolproof, impeccable, model, perfect, unblemished

faulty *adjective* DEFECTIVE, broken, damaged, flawed, impaired, imperfect, incorrect, malfunctioning, out of order, unsound

favor *noun* **1** APPROVAL, approbation, backing, good opinion, goodwill, patronage, support
2 GOOD TURN, benefit, boon, courtesy, indulgence, kindness, service
▷ *verb* **3** SIDE WITH, indulge, reward, smile upon
4 ADVOCATE, approve, champion, commend, encourage, incline towards, prefer, support

favorable *adjective* **1** ADVANTAGEOUS, auspicious, beneficial, encouraging, helpful, opportune, promising, propitious, suitable, win-win (*informal*)
2 POSITIVE, affirmative, agreeable, approving, encouraging, enthusiastic, reassuring, sympathetic

favorably *adverb* **1** ADVANTAGEOUSLY, auspiciously, conveniently, fortunately, opportunely, profitably, to one's advantage, well
2 POSITIVELY, approvingly, enthusiastically, helpfully, with approval

favorite *adjective* **1** PREFERRED, best-loved, choice, dearest, esteemed, favored
▷ *noun* **2** DARLING, beloved, blue-eyed boy (*informal*), idol, pet, teacher's pet, the apple of one's eye

fawn[1] *verb* (*often with on or upon*) CURRY FAVOR, brown-nose (*slang*), crawl, creep, cringe, dance attendance, flatter, grovel, ingratiate oneself, kiss ass (*slang*), kowtow, pander to

fawn[2] *adjective* BEIGE, buff, grayish-brown, neutral

fawning *adjective* OBSEQUIOUS, crawling, cringing, deferential, flattering, grovelling, servile, sycophantic

fear *noun* **1** ALARM, apprehensiveness, dread, fright, horror, panic, terror, trepidation
2 BUGBEAR, bête noire, bogey, horror, nightmare, specter
▷ *verb* **3** BE AFRAID, dread, shake in one's shoes, shudder at, take fright, tremble at
4 ▷ **fear for** WORRY ABOUT, be anxious about, feel concern for

fearful *adjective* **1** SCARED, afraid, alarmed, frightened, jumpy, nervous, timid, timorous, uneasy, wired (*slang*)
2 FRIGHTFUL, awful, dire, dreadful, gruesome, hair-raising, horrendous, horrific, terrible

> **fear'ful•ly** *adverb* > **fear'less** *adjective* intrepid > **fear'some** *adjective* terrifying
fea•si•ble [FEE-zə-bəl] *adjective* 1 able to be done 2 likely > **fea•si•bil'i•ty** *noun*
feast [feest] *noun* 1 banquet, lavish meal 2 religious anniversary 3 something very pleasant, sumptuous ▷ *verb intransitive* 4 partake of banquet, fare sumptuously ▷ *verb transitive* 5 regale with feast 6 provide delight for
feat [feet] *noun* 1 notable deed 2 surprising or striking trick
feath•er [FETH-ər] *noun* 1 one of the barbed shafts that form covering of birds 2 anything resembling this ▷ *verb transitive* 3 provide, line with feathers ▷ *verb intransitive* 4 grow feathers ▷ *verb* 5 turn (oar, propeller) edgewise > **feath'er•y** *adjective* > **feath'er•weight** *noun* 1 very light person (esp. boxer) or thing 2 (*informal*) person of small consequence or ability **feather one's nest** enrich oneself **in fine feather** in good form
fea•ture [FEE-chər] *noun* 1 (*usually plural*) part of face 2 characteristic or notable part of anything 3 main or special item ▷ *verb transitive* **-tured, -tur•ing** 4 portray 5 present in leading role in a film 6 give prominence to ▷ *verb intransitive* **-tured, -tur•ing** 7 be prominent (in) > **fea'ture•less** *adjective* without striking features
fe•brile [FEE-brəl] *adjective* 1 of fever 2 feverish
fe•ces [FEE-seez] *plural noun* excrement, waste matter > **fe'cal** [-kəl] *adjective*
feck•less [FEK-lis] *adjective* spiritless, weak, irresponsible > **feck'less•ness** *noun*
fec•u•lent [FEK-yə-lənt] *adjective* full of sediment, turbid, foul > **fec'u•lence** *noun*
fe•cund [FEE-kund] *adjective* fertile, fruitful, fertilizing > **fe'cun•date** *verb transitive* **-dat•ed, -dat•ing** fertilize, impregnate > **fe•cun•di•ty** [fi-KUN-di-tee] *noun*
fed *pt./pp. of* **feed** > **fed up** bored, dissatisfied
fed•er•al [FED-ər-əl] *adjective* of, or like, the government of countries that are united but retain internal independence of the separate states > **fed'er•al•ism** *noun* > **fed'er•ate** [-ə-rayt] *verb* **-at•ed, -at•ing** form into, become, a federation > **fed•er•a'tion** *noun* 1 league 2 federal union
fee *noun* payment for professional and other services
fee•ble [FEE-bəl] *adjective* **-bler, -blest** 1 weak 2 lacking strength or effectiveness, insipid > **fee'bly** *adverb*
feed *verb* **fed, feed•ing** 1 give food to 2 supply, support 3 take food ▷ *noun* 4 feeding 5 fodder, pasturage 6 allowance of fodder 7 material supplied to machine 8 part of machine taking in material > **feed'er** *noun* one who or that which feeds > **feed'back** *noun* 1 return of part of output of electrical circuit or loudspeakers 2 information received in response to inquiry, etc. > **feed'lot** *noun* area, building where cattle are fattened for market
feel *verb* **felt, feel•ing** 1 perceive, examine by touch 2 experience 3 proceed, find (one's way) cautiously 4 be sensitive to 5 show emotion (for) 6 believe, consider ▷ *noun* 7 act or instance of feeling 8 quality or impression of something perceived by feeling 9 sense of

DICTIONARY

f

THESAURUS

---

fearfully *adverb* 1 NERVOUSLY, apprehensively, diffidently, timidly, timorously, uneasily
2 VERY, awfully, exceedingly, excessively, frightfully, terribly, tremendously
fearless *adjective* BRAVE, bold, courageous, dauntless, indomitable, intrepid, plucky, unafraid, undaunted, valiant
fearsome *adjective* TERRIFYING, awe-inspiring, daunting, formidable, frightening, horrifying, menacing, unnerving
feasible *adjective* POSSIBLE, achievable, attainable, likely, practicable, reasonable, viable, workable
feast *noun* 1 BANQUET, dinner, repast, spread (*informal*), treat
2 FESTIVAL, celebration, fête, holiday, holy day, red-letter day, saint's day
3 TREAT, delight, enjoyment, gratification, pleasure
▷ *verb* 4 EAT ONE'S FILL, gorge, gormandize, indulge, overindulge, pig out (*slang*), wine and dine
feat *noun* ACCOMPLISHMENT, achievement, act, attainment, deed, exploit, performance
feathers *plural noun* PLUMAGE, down, plumes
feature *noun* 1 ASPECT, characteristic, facet, factor, hallmark, peculiarity, property, quality, trait
2 HIGHLIGHT, attraction, main item, speciality
3 ARTICLE, column, item, piece, report, story
▷ *verb* 4 SPOTLIGHT, emphasize, foreground, give prominence to, play up, present, star
features *plural noun* FACE, countenance, lineaments, physiognomy
feckless *adjective* IRRESPONSIBLE, good-for-nothing, hopeless, incompetent, ineffectual, shiftless, worthless
federation *noun* UNION, alliance, amalgamation, association, coalition, combination, league, syndicate
fed up *adjective* DISSATISFIED, bored, depressed, discontented, down in the mouth, glum, sick and tired (*informal*), tired
fee *noun* CHARGE, bill, payment, remuneration, toll
feeble *adjective* 1 WEAK, debilitated, doddering, effete, frail, infirm, puny, sickly, weedy (*informal*)
2 UNCONVINCING, flimsy, inadequate, insufficient, lame, lousy (*slang*), paltry, pathetic, poor, tame, thin
feebleness *noun* WEAKNESS, effeteness, frailty, infirmity, languor, lassitude, sickliness
feed *verb* 1 CATER FOR, nourish, provide for, provision, supply, sustain, victual, wine and dine
2 (*sometimes with on*) EAT, chow down (*slang*), devour, exist on, live on, partake of
▷ *noun* 3 FOOD, fodder, pasturage, provender
4 (*informal*) MEAL, feast, repast, spread (*informal*)
feel *verb* 1 TOUCH, caress, finger, fondle, handle, manipulate, paw, stroke
2 EXPERIENCE, be aware of, notice, observe, perceive
3 SENSE, be convinced, intuit
4 BELIEVE, consider, deem, hold, judge, think
▷ *noun* 5 TEXTURE, finish, surface, touch
6 IMPRESSION, air, ambience, atmosphere, feeling, quality, sense

touch > **feel'er** *noun* 1 special organ of touch in some animals 2 proposal put forward to test others' opinions 3 that which feels > **feel'ing** *noun* 1 sense of touch 2 ability to feel 3 physical sensation 4 emotion 5 sympathy, tenderness 6 conviction or opinion not solely based on reason ▷ *adjective* 7 sensitive, sympathetic, heartfelt > **feel'ings** susceptibilities **feel like** have an inclination for

feet *see* **foot feet of clay** hidden flaw in person's character

feign [fayn] *verb* pretend, sham

feint [faynt] *noun* 1 sham attack or blow meant to deceive opponent 2 semblance, pretense ▷ *verb intransitive* 3 make feint

feist•y [FĪ-stee] *adjective* **feist•i•er, feist•i•est** 1 spirited, spunky, plucky 2 ill-tempered > **feist'i•ness** *noun*

feld•spar [FELD-spahr] *noun* crystalline mineral found in granite, etc.

fe•lic•i•ty [fi-LIS-i-tee] *noun, plural* **-ties** 1 great happiness, bliss 2 appropriateness of wording > **fe•lic'i•tate** *verb transitive* **-tat•ed, -tat•ing** congratulate > **fe•lic•i•ta'tions** *plural noun* congratulations > **fe•lic'i•tous** *adjective* 1 apt, well-chosen 2 happy

fe•line [FEE-līn] *adjective* 1 of cats 2 catlike

fell[1] *pt. of* **fall**

fell[2] *verb transitive* 1 knock down 2 cut down (tree)

fell[3] *adjective* fierce, terrible

fell[4] *noun* skin or hide with hair

fel•low [FEL-oh] *noun* 1 (*informal*) man, boy 2 person 3 comrade, associate 4 counterpart 5 like thing 6 member (of society) 7 student granted university fellowship ▷ *adjective* 8 of the same class, associated > **fel'low•ship** *noun* 1 fraternity 2 friendship 3 (in university, etc.) research post or special scholarship

fel•on [FEL-ən] *noun* one guilty of felony > **fe•lo•ni•ous** [fə-LOH-nee-əs] *adjective* > **fel'o•ny** *noun, plural* **-nies** serious crime

felt[1] *pt./pp. of* **feel**

felt[2] *noun* 1 soft, matted fabric made by bonding fibers chemically and by pressure 2 thing made of this ▷ *verb transitive* 3 make into, or cover with, felt ▷ *verb intransitive* 4 become matted like felt > **felt'-tip pen** pen with writing point made of pressed fibers

fe•male [FEE-mayl] *adjective* 1 of sex that bears offspring 2 relating to this sex ▷ *noun* 3 one of this sex

fem•i•nine [FEM-ə-nin] *adjective* 1 of women 2 womanly 3 class or type of grammatical inflection in some languages > **fem'i•nism** *noun* advocacy of equal rights for women > **fem'i•nist** *noun, adjective* > **fem•i•nin'i•ty** *noun*

femme fa•tale [FAHM fat-TAHL] *noun, plural* **femmes fa•tales** Fr. alluring woman who leads men into dangerous situations by her charm

fem•o•ral [FEM-ər-əl] *adjective* of the thigh

fe•mur [FEE-mər] *noun* thigh bone

fen *noun* tract of marshy land, swamp

fence [fens] *noun* 1 structure of wire, wood, etc. enclosing an area 2 (machinery) guard, guide 3 (*slang*) dealer in stolen property ▷ *verb* **fenced, fenc•ing** 4 erect fence 5 enclose 6 fight (as sport) with swords 7 avoid question, etc. 8 (*slang*) deal in stolen property > **fencing** *noun* art of swordplay

fend *verb transitive* 1 ward off, repel ▷ *verb intransitive* 2 provide (for oneself, etc.) > **fend'er** *noun* 1 low metal frame in front of fireplace 2 name for various protective devices 3 frame 4 edge 5 buffer 6 mudguard of car > **fender bender** (*informal*) collision between automobiles causing minor damage

fen•es•tra•tion [fen-ə-STRAY-shən] *noun* 1 arrangement of windows in a building 2 (in medicine) perforation in a structure 3 operation to create this

feng shui [FUNG SHWAY] *noun* Chinese art of deciding the best design or position of a grave, building, furniture, etc., in order to bring good luck

fe•ral[1] [FER-əl] *adjective* wild, uncultivated

feral[2] *adjective* 1 funereal, gloomy 2 causing death

fer•ment [FUR-ment] *noun* 1 leaven, substance causing thing to ferment 2 excitement, tumult ▷ *verb* [fər-MENT] 3 (cause to) undergo chemical change with effervescence, liberation of heat and alteration of properties, e.g. process set up in dough by yeast 4 (cause to) become excited > **fer•men•ta'tion** [fur-] *noun*

fern [furn] *noun* plant with feathery fronds

feeler *noun* 1 ANTENNA, tentacle, whisker
2 APPROACH, advance, probe

feeling *noun* 1 EMOTION, ardor, fervor, intensity, passion, sentiment, warmth
2 IMPRESSION, hunch, idea, inkling, notion, presentiment, sense, suspicion
3 OPINION, inclination, instinct, point of view, view
4 SYMPATHY, compassion, concern, empathy, pity, sensibility, sensitivity, understanding
5 SENSE OF TOUCH, perception, sensation
6 ATMOSPHERE, air, ambience, aura, feel, mood, quality

fell *verb* CUT DOWN, cut, demolish, hew, knock down, level

fellow *noun* 1 MAN, chap (*informal*), character, guy (*informal*), individual, person
2 ASSOCIATE, colleague, companion, comrade, partner, peer

fellowship *noun* 1 CAMARADERIE, brotherhood, companionship, sociability
2 SOCIETY, association, brotherhood, club, fraternity, guild, league, order

feminine *adjective* WOMANLY, delicate, gentle, ladylike, soft, tender

femme fatale
▷ *noun* SEDUCTRESS, enchantress, siren, succubus, vamp (*informal*)

fen *noun* MARSH, bog, morass, quagmire, slough, swamp

fence *noun* 1 BARRIER, barricade, defense, hedge, palisade, railings, rampart, wall
▷ *verb* 2 (*often with in or off*) ENCLOSE, bound, confine, encircle, pen, protect, surround
3 EVADE, dodge, equivocate, parry

ferment *noun* COMMOTION, disruption, excitement, frenzy, furor, stir, tumult, turmoil, unrest, uproar

fe•ro•cious [fə-ROH-shəs] *adjective* fierce, savage, cruel > **fe•roc'i•ty** [-ROS-i-tee] *noun*
fer•ret [FER-it] *noun* 1 tamed animal like weasel, used to catch rabbits, rats, etc. ▷ *verb transitive* 2 drive out with ferrets 3 search out ▷ *verb intransitive* 4 search about, rummage
fer•ric [FER-ik], **fer•rous** [FER-əs] *adjective* pert. to, containing, iron > **fer•ru•gi•nous** [fə-ROO-jə-nəs] *adjective* 1 containing iron 2 reddish-brown > **fer•ro•con'crete** *noun* reinforced concrete (strengthened by framework of metal)
Fer•ris wheel [FER-is] in amusement park, large, vertical wheel with seats for riding
fer•rule [FER-əl] *noun* metal cap to strengthen end of stick, etc.
fer•ry [FER-ee] *noun, plural* **-ries** 1 boat, etc. for transporting people, vehicles, across body of water, esp. as repeated or regular service ▷ *verb* **-ried, -ry•ing** 2 carry, travel, by ferry 3 deliver (airplanes, etc.) by air
fer•tile [FUR-tl] *adjective* 1 (capable of) producing offspring, bearing crops, etc. 2 fruitful, producing abundantly 3 inventive > **fer•til•i•ty** [fər-TIL-i-tee] *noun* > **fer•ti•li•za'tion** *noun* > **fer'ti•lize** *verb transitive* **-lized, -liz•ing** make fertile > **fer'ti•liz•er** *noun*
fer•vent [FUR-vənt], **fer•vid** [-vid] *adjective* ardent, vehement, intense > **fer'ven•cy** *noun* > **fer'vent•ly** *adverb* > **fer'vor** [-vər] *noun*
fes•cue [FES-kyoo] *noun* grass for pasture or lawns, with stiff narrow leaves
fes•tal [FES-tl] *adjective* 1 of feast or holiday 2 merry
fes•ter [FES-tər] *verb* 1 (cause to) form pus ▷ *verb intransitive* 2 rankle 3 become embittered
fes•ti•val [FES-tə-vəl] *noun* 1 day, period set aside for celebration, esp. of religious feast 2 organized series of events, performances, etc. usu. in one place > **fes•tive** [-tiv] *adjective* 1 joyous, merry 2 of feast > **fes•tiv'i•ty** *noun* 1 gaiety, mirth 2 rejoicing > **fes•tiv'i•ties** celebrations
fe•stoon' *noun* 1 chain of flowers, ribbons, etc. hung in curve between two points ▷ *verb transitive* 2 form, adorn with festoons
fetch [fech] *verb transitive* 1 go and bring 2 draw forth 3 be sold for 4 attract ▷ *noun* 5 act of fetching > **fetch'ing** *adjective* attractive
fete [fayt] *noun, plural* **fetes** 1 gala, bazaar, etc., esp. one held out of doors 2 festival, holiday, celebration ▷ *verb transitive* **fet•ed, fet•ing** 3 feast 4 honor with festive entertainment
fet'id *adjective* stinking
fet'ish *noun* 1 (inanimate) object believed to have magical powers 2 excessive attention to something 3 object, activity, to which excessive devotion is paid 4 form of behaviour in which sexual pleasure is derived from looking at or handling an inanimate object > **fet'ish•ism** *noun* > **fet'ish•ist** *noun*
fet•lock [FET-lok] *noun* projection behind and above horse's hoof, or tuft of hair on this
fet•ter [FET-ər] *noun* 1 chain or shackle for feet 2 check, restraint ▷ *verb transitive* 3 chain up 4 restrain, hamper > **fet•ters** *plural noun* captivity
fet•tle [FET-l] *noun* condition, state of health
fe•tus [FEE-təs] *noun, plural* **-tus•es** fully developed young in womb or egg > **fe•tal** [FEET-l] *adjective*
feud [fyood] *noun* 1 bitter, lasting, mutual hostility, esp. between two families or tribes 2 vendetta ▷ *verb intransitive* 3 carry on feud
feu•dal [FYOOD-l] *adjective* of, like, medieval social and economic system based on holding land from superior in return for service > **feu'dal•ism** *noun*
fe•ver [FEE-vər] *noun* 1 condition of illness with high body temperature 2 intense nervous excitement > **fe'vered, fe'ver•ish** *adjective* 1 having fever 2 accompanied by, caused by, fever

DICTIONARY **f** THESAURUS

ferocious *adjective* 1 FIERCE, predatory, rapacious, ravening, savage, violent, wild
2 CRUEL, barbaric, bloodthirsty, brutal, ruthless, vicious
ferocity *noun* SAVAGERY, bloodthirstiness, brutality, cruelty, fierceness, viciousness, wildness
ferret out *verb* TRACK DOWN, dig up, discover, elicit, root out, search out, trace, unearth
ferry *noun* 1 FERRY BOAT, packet, packet boat
▷ *verb* 2 CARRY, chauffeur, convey, run, ship, shuttle, transport
fertile *adjective* RICH, abundant, fecund, fruitful, luxuriant, plentiful, productive, prolific, teeming
fertility *noun* FRUITFULNESS, abundance, fecundity, luxuriance, productiveness, richness
fertilizer *noun* COMPOST, dressing, dung, manure
fervent *or* **fervid** *adjective* ARDENT, devout, earnest, enthusiastic, heartfelt, impassioned, intense, vehement
fervor *noun* INTENSITY, ardor, enthusiasm, excitement, passion, vehemence, warmth, zeal
fester *verb* 1 DECAY, putrefy, suppurate, ulcerate
2 INTENSIFY, aggravate, smolder
festival *noun* 1 CELEBRATION, carnival, entertainment, fête, gala, jubilee
2 HOLY DAY, anniversary, commemoration, feast, fête, fiesta, holiday, red-letter day, saint's day
festive *adjective* CELEBRATORY, cheery, convivial, happy, jovial, joyful, joyous, jubilant, merry
festivity *noun* (*often plural*) CELEBRATION, entertainment, festival, party
festoon *verb* DECORATE, array, deck, drape, garland, hang, swathe, wreathe
fetch *verb* 1 BRING, carry, convey, deliver, get, go for, obtain, retrieve, transport
2 SELL FOR, bring in, earn, go for, make, realize, yield
fetching *adjective* ATTRACTIVE, alluring, captivating, charming, cute, enticing, winsome
fetish *noun* 1 FIXATION, mania, obsession, thing (*informal*)
2 TALISMAN, amulet
feud *noun* 1 HOSTILITY, argument, conflict, disagreement, enmity, quarrel, rivalry, row, vendetta
▷ *verb* 2 QUARREL, bicker, clash, contend, dispute, fall out, row, squabble, war
fever *noun* EXCITEMENT, agitation, delirium, ferment, fervor, frenzy, restlessness
feverish *adjective* 1 HOT, febrile, fevered, flushed, inflamed, pyretic (*medical*)
2 EXCITED, agitated, frantic, frenetic, frenzied,

3 in a state of restless excitement > **fe'ver•ish•ly** *adverb* > **fever pitch** 1 very fast pace 2 intense excitement

few [fyoo] *adjective* **-er, -est** 1 not many ▷ *noun* 2 small number > **quite a few** several

fey [fay] *adjective* 1 supernatural, unreal 2 enchanted

fez *noun, plural* **fez•zes** red, brimless, orig. Turkish tasseled cap

fi•anc•é [fee-ahn-SAY] *noun* man engaged to be married > **fi•anc•ée** *noun feminine*

fi•as•co [fee-AS-koh] *noun, plural* **-cos** breakdown, total failure

fi•at [FEE-aht] *noun* 1 decree 2 official permission

fib *noun* 1 trivial lie, falsehood ▷ *verb intransitive* **fibbed, fib•bing** 2 tell fib > **fib'ber** *noun*

fi•ber [FĪ-bər] *noun* 1 filament forming part of animal or plant tissue 2 substance that can be spun (e.g. wool, cotton) > **fi'brous** *adjective* made of fiber > **fi'ber•board** *noun* building material of compressed plant fibers > **fi'ber•glass** *noun* material made of fine glass fibers > **fiber optics** use of bundles of long transparent glass fibers in transmitting light

fib•u•la [FIB-yə-lə] *noun* slender outer bone of lower leg > **fib'u•lar** *adjective*

fick•le [FIK-əl] *adjective* changeable, inconstant > **fick'le•ness** *noun*

fic•tion [FIK-shən] *noun* 1 prose, literary works of the imagination 2 invented statement or story > **fic'tion•al** *adjective* > **fic•ti'tious** [-TISH-əs] *adjective* 1 not genuine, false 2 imaginary 3 assumed

fid•dle [FID-l] *noun* 1 violin ▷ *verb intransitive* **-dled, -dling** 2 play fiddle 3 make idle movements, fidget, trifle > **fid'dle•sticks** *interjection* nonsense

Fi•de•i De•fen•sor [FEE-de-ee de-FEN-sor] *Lat.* defender of the faith

fi•del•i•ty [fi-DEL-i-tee] *noun, plural* **-ties** 1 (conjugal) faithfulness 2 quality of sound reproduction

fidg•et [FIJ-it] *verb intransitive* 1 move restlessly 2 be uneasy ▷ *noun* 3 (*often plural*) nervous restlessness, restless mood 4 one who fidgets > **fidg'et•y** *adjective*

fi•du•ci•ar•y [fi-DOO-shee-er-ee] *adjective* 1 held, given in trust 2 relating to trustee ▷ *noun* 3 trustee

fief [feef] *noun hist.* land held of a superior in return for service > **fief'dom** [-dəm] *noun* 1 estate of a feudal lord 2 (*informal*) organization, etc. owned by, controlled by one person

field [feeld] *noun* 1 area of (farming) land 2 enclosed piece of land 3 tract of land rich in specified product (e.g. gold field) 4 players in a game or sport collectively 5 all competitors but the favorite 6 battlefield 7 area over which electric, gravitational, magnetic force can be exerted 8 sphere of knowledge 9 range, area of operation ▷ *verb baseball* 10 stop and return ball 11 send player, team, on to field > **field'er** *noun* > **field day** 1 day of outdoor activities 2 important occasion > **field events** throwing and jumping events in athletics > **field glasses** binoculars > **field hockey** hockey played on field, as distinct from ice hockey > **field marshal** (in some countries) army officer of highest rank > **field'work** *noun* research, practical work, conducted away from the classroom, laboratory, etc. > **field of view** area covered in telescope, camera, etc.

fiend [feend] *noun* 1 demon, devil 2 wicked

DICTIONARY • THESAURUS

overwrought, restless, wired (*slang*)

few *adjective* NOT MANY, meager, negligible, rare, scanty, scarcely any, sparse, sporadic

fiasco *noun* DEBACLE, catastrophe, disaster, failure, mess, washout (*informal*)

fib *noun* LIE, fiction, story, untruth, white lie

fiber *noun* 1 THREAD, filament, pile, strand, texture, wisp
2 ESSENCE, nature, quality, spirit, substance
3 ▷ **moral fiber** STRENGTH OF CHARACTER, resolution, stamina, strength, toughness

fickle *adjective* CHANGEABLE, capricious, faithless, inconstant, irresolute, temperamental, unfaithful, variable, volatile

fiction *noun* 1 TALE, fantasy, legend, myth, novel, romance, story, yarn (*informal*)
2 LIE, cock and bull story (*informal*), fabrication, falsehood, invention, tall tale (*informal*), untruth, urban legend

fictional *adjective* IMAGINARY, invented, legendary, made-up, nonexistent, unreal

fictitious *adjective* FALSE, bogus, fabricated, imaginary, invented, made-up, make-believe, mythical, untrue

fiddle *verb* 1 FIDGET, finger, interfere with, mess about *or* mess around, play, tamper with, tinker
▷ *noun* 2 VIOLIN
3 ▷ **fit as a fiddle** HEALTHY, blooming, hale and hearty, in fine fettle, in good form, in good shape, in rude health, in the pink, sound, strong

fiddling *adjective* TRIVIAL, futile, insignificant, pettifogging, petty, trifling

fidelity *noun* 1 LOYALTY, allegiance, constancy, dependability, devotion, faithfulness, staunchness, trustworthiness
2 ACCURACY, closeness, correspondence, exactness, faithfulness, precision, scrupulousness

fidget *verb* 1 MOVE RESTLESSLY, fiddle (*informal*), fret, squirm, twitch
▷ *noun* 2 ▷ **the fidgets** RESTLESSNESS, fidgetiness, jitters (*informal*), nervousness, unease, uneasiness

fidgety *adjective* RESTLESS, antsy (*slang*), impatient, jittery (*informal*), jumpy, nervous, on edge, restive, twitchy (*informal*), uneasy, wired (*slang*)

field *noun* 1 MEADOW, grassland, green, lea (*poetic*), pasture
2 COMPETITORS, applicants, candidates, competition, contestants, entrants, possibilities, runners
3 SPECIALITY, area, department, discipline, domain, line, province, territory
▷ *verb* 4 RETRIEVE, catch, pick up, return, stop
5 DEAL WITH, deflect, handle, turn aside

fiend *noun* 1 DEMON, devil, evil spirit
2 BRUTE, barbarian, beast, ghoul, monster, ogre, savage
3 (*informal*) ENTHUSIAST, addict, fanatic, freak (*informal*), maniac

person 3 person very fond of or addicted to something: *fresh-air fiend; drug fiend* > **fiend'ish** *adjective* wicked, difficult, unpleasant

fierce [feers] *adjective* **fierc•er, fierc•est** 1 savage, wild, violent 2 rough 3 severe 4 intense > **fierce'ly** *adverb* > **fierce'ness** *noun*

fier•y [FĪ-ə-ree] *adjective* **fier•i•er, fier•i•est** 1 consisting of fire 2 blazing, glowing, flashing 3 irritable 4 spirited > **fier'i•ness** *noun*

fi•es•ta [fee-ES-tə] *noun* (religious) celebration, carnival

fife [fīf] *noun* 1 high-pitched flute ▷ *verb* **fifed, fif•ing** 2 play on fife > **fif'er** *noun*

fifteen, fifth, fifty *see* **five**

fig *noun* 1 soft, pear-shaped fruit 2 tree bearing it

fight [fīt] *verb* **fought, fight•ing** 1 contend with in battle or in single combat 2 maintain against opponent 3 settle by combat ▷ *noun* > **fight'er** *noun* 1 one who fights 2 prizefighter 3 aircraft designed for destroying other aircraft

fig•ment [FIG-mənt] *noun* invention, purely imaginary thing

fig•ure [FIG-yər] *noun* 1 numerical symbol 2 amount, number 3 form, shape 4 bodily shape 5 appearance, esp. conspicuous appearance 6 space enclosed by lines, or surfaces 7 diagram, illustration 8 likeness 9 image 10 pattern, movement in dancing, skating, etc. 11 abnormal form of expression for effect in speech, e.g. metaphor ▷ *verb transitive* **-ured, -ur•ing** 12 calculate, estimate 13 represent by picture or diagram 14 ornament ▷ *verb intransitive* **-ured, -ur•ing** 15 (oft. with *in*) show, appear, be conspicuous, be included > **fig'ur•a•tive** *adjective* 1 metaphorical 2 full of figures of speech > **fig'ur•a•tive•ly** *adverb* > **fig•ur•ine'** [-REEN] *noun* statuette > **fig'ure•head** *noun* 1 nominal leader 2 ornamental figure under bowsprit of ship

fil•a•ment [FIL-ə-mənt] *noun* 1 fine wire in electric light bulb and vacuum tube that is heated by electric current 2 threadlike body

filch *verb transitive* steal, pilfer

file[1] [fīl] *noun* 1 box, folder, clip, etc. holding papers for reference 2 papers so kept 3 information about specific person, subject 4 orderly line, as of soldiers, one behind the other 5 *computers* organized collection of related material ▷ *verb transitive* **filed, fil•ing** 6 arrange (papers, etc.) and put them away for reference 7 transmit (e.g. tax return) 8 *law* place on records of a court 9 bring suit in law court ▷ *verb intransitive* **filed, fil•ing** 10 march in file > **filing** *noun* **single file** single line of people one behind the other

file[2] *noun* 1 roughened tool for smoothing or shaping ▷ *verb transitive* **filed, fil•ing** 2 apply file to, smooth, polish > **filing** *noun* 1 action of using file 2 scrap of metal removed by file

filet *see* **fillet**

fil•i•al [FIL-ee-əl] *adjective* of, befitting, son or daughter

fil•i•bus•ter [FIL-ə-bus-tər] *noun* process of obstructing legislation by using delaying tactics ▷ *verb intransitive*

fil•i•gree [FIL i gree] *noun* fine tracery or openwork of metal, usu. gold or silver wire

fill *verb transitive* 1 make full 2 occupy completely 3 hold, discharge duties of 4 stop

f DICTIONARY THESAURUS

fiendish *adjective* WICKED, cruel, devilish, diabolical, hellish, infernal, malignant, monstrous, satanic, unspeakable

fierce *adjective* 1 WILD, brutal, cruel, dangerous, ferocious, fiery, menacing, savage, vicious
2 STRONG, furious, howling, inclement, powerful, raging, stormy, tempestuous, violent
3 INTENSE, cut-throat, keen, relentless, strong

fiercely *adverb* FEROCIOUSLY, furiously, passionately, savagely, tempestuously, tigerishly, tooth and nail, viciously, with no holds barred

fiery *adjective* 1 BURNING, ablaze, afire, aflame, blazing, flaming, on fire
2 EXCITABLE, fierce, hot-headed, impetuous, irascible, irritable, passionate

fight *verb* 1 BATTLE, box, clash, combat, do battle, grapple, spar, struggle, tussle, wrestle
2 OPPOSE, contest, defy, dispute, make a stand against, resist, stand up to, withstand
3 ENGAGE IN, carry on, conduct, prosecute, wage
▷ *noun* 4 CONFLICT, battle, clash, contest, dispute, duel, encounter, struggle, tussle
5 RESISTANCE, belligerence, militancy, pluck, spirit

fighter *noun* 1 SOLDIER, fighting man, man-at-arms, warrior
2 BOXER, prize fighter, pugilist

fight off *verb* REPEL, beat off, keep at bay *or* hold at bay, repress, repulse, resist, stave off, ward off

figure *noun* 1 NUMBER, character, digit, numeral, symbol
2 AMOUNT, cost, price, sum, total, value
3 SHAPE, body, build, frame, physique, proportions
4 DIAGRAM, design, drawing, illustration, pattern, representation, sketch
5 CHARACTER, big name, celebrity, dignitary, personality
▷ *verb* 6 CALCULATE, compute, count, reckon, tally, tot up, work out
7 (*usually with in*) FEATURE, act, appear, be featured, contribute to, play a part

figurehead *noun* FRONT MAN, mouthpiece, puppet, titular head *or* nominal head

figure out *verb* 1 CALCULATE, compute, reckon, work out
2 UNDERSTAND, comprehend, decipher, fathom, make out, see

filch *verb* STEAL, embezzle, misappropriate, pilfer, pinch (*informal*), take, thieve, walk off with

file[1] *noun* 1 FOLDER, case, data, documents, dossier, information, portfolio
2 LINE, column, queue, row
▷ *verb* 3 REGISTER, document, enter, pigeonhole, put in place, record
4 MARCH, parade, troop

file[2] *verb* SMOOTH, abrade, polish, rasp, rub, scrape, shape

fill *verb* 1 STUFF, cram, crowd, glut, pack, stock, supply, swell
2 SATURATE, charge, imbue, impregnate, pervade, suffuse
3 PLUG, block, bung, close, cork, seal, stop
4 PERFORM, carry out, discharge, execute, fulfill, hold, occupy

up **5** satisfy **6** fulfill ▷ *verb intransitive* **7** become full ▷ *noun* **8** full supply **9** as much as desired **10** soil, etc., to bring area of ground up to required level > **fill'ing** *noun* > **filling station** business selling oil, gasoline, etc. **fill the bill** (*informal*) supply all that is wanted

fil•let [fi-LAY] *noun* **1** boneless slice of meat, fish **2** narrow strip ▷ *verb transitive* **filleted, filleting 3** cut into fillets, bone

fil•lip [FIL-əp] *noun* **1** stimulus **2** sudden release of finger bent against thumb **3** snap so produced

fil•ly [FIL-ee] *noun, plural* **-lies 1** young female horse **2** (*informal*) girl, young woman

film *noun* **1** sequence of images projected on screen, creating illusion of movement **2** story, etc. presented thus, and shown in movie theater or on TV **3** sensitized celluloid roll used in photography, cinematography **4** thin skin or layer **5** dimness on eyes **6** slight haze ▷ *adjective* **7** connected with movies ▷ *verb transitive* **8** photograph with movie camera **9** make movie of (scene, story, etc.) ▷ *verb* **10** cover, become covered, with film > **film'y** *adjective* **film•i•er, film•i•est 1** membranous **2** gauzy > **film star** popular movie actor or actress

fil•ter [FIL-tər] *noun* **1** cloth or other material, or a device, permitting fluid to pass but retaining solid particles **2** anything performing similar function ▷ *verb transitive* **3** act as filter, or as if passing through filter ▷ *verb intransitive* **4** pass slowly (through) > **fil•trate** [FIL-trayt] *noun* filtered gas or liquid > **fil•tra'tion** *noun*

filth *noun* **1** disgusting dirt **2** pollution **3** obscenity > **filth'i•ly** *adverb* > **filth'i•ness** *noun* > **filth'y** *adjective* **filth•i•er, filth•i•est 1** unclean **2** foul

fin *noun* **1** propelling or steering organ of fish **2** vertical tailplane of an airplane **3** (*slang*) five-dollar bill

fi•nal [FĪN-l] *adjective* **1** at the end **2** conclusive ▷ *noun* **3** game, heat, examination, etc., coming at end of series or school term > **fi•na•le** [fi-NAL-ee] *noun* **1** closing part of musical composition, opera, etc. **2** termination > **fi•nal•i•ty** [fī-NAL-i-tee] *noun* > **fi'na•lize** *verb* **-lized, -liz•ing** > **fi'nal•ly** *adverb*

fi•nance [fi-NANS] *noun* **1** management of money ▷ *verb transitive* **-nanced, nanc•ing 2** find capital for > **fi•nanc•es** *plural noun* money resources > **fi•nan'cial** [-shəl] *adjective* of finance > **fin•an•cier'** [-SEER] *noun*

finch *noun* one of family of small songbirds

find [fīnd] *verb transitive* **found, find•ing 1** come across **2** light upon, obtain **3** recognize **4** experience, discover **5** discover by searching **6** ascertain **7** supply (as funds) **8** *law* give a verdict ▷ *noun* **9** finding **10** (valuable) thing found > **find'er** *noun* > **finding** *noun* judicial verdict

fine¹ [fīn] *adjective* **fin•er, fin•est 1** choice, of high quality **2** delicate, subtle **3** pure **4** in

DICTIONARY • THESAURUS

▷ *noun* **5** ▷ **one's fill** SUFFICIENT, all one wants, ample, enough, plenty

filler *noun* PADDING, makeweight, stopgap

fill in *verb* **1** INFORM, acquaint, apprise, bring up to date, give the facts *or* give the background **2** REPLACE, deputize, represent, stand in, sub, substitute, take the place of

filling *noun* **1** STUFFING, contents, filler, inside, insides, padding, wadding ▷ *adjective* **2** SATISFYING, ample, heavy, square, substantial

fill out *verb* COMPLETE, answer, fill in, fill up

film *noun* **1** MOVIE, flick (*slang*), motion picture **2** LAYER, coating, covering, dusting, membrane, skin, tissue ▷ *verb* **3** PHOTOGRAPH, shoot, take, video, videotape

filter *noun* **1** SIEVE, gauze, membrane, mesh, riddle, strainer ▷ *verb* **2** PURIFY, clarify, filtrate, refine, screen, sieve, sift, strain, winnow **3** TRICKLE, dribble, escape, exude, leak, ooze, penetrate, percolate, seep

filth *noun* **1** DIRT, excrement, grime, muck, refuse, sewage, slime, sludge, squalor **2** OBSCENITY, impurity, indecency, pornography, smut, vulgarity

filthy *adjective* **1** DIRTY, foul, polluted, putrid, slimy, squalid, unclean **2** MUDDY, begrimed, blackened, grimy, grubby, scuzzy (*slang*) **3** OBSCENE, corrupt, depraved, impure, indecent, lewd, licentious, pornographic, smutty, X-rated

final *adjective* **1** LAST, closing, concluding, latest, terminal, ultimate **2** DEFINITIVE, absolute, conclusive, decided, definite, incontrovertible, irrevocable, settled

finale *noun* ENDING, climax, close, conclusion, culmination, denouement, epilogue

finalize *verb* COMPLETE, clinch, conclude, decide, settle, tie up, wind up, work out, wrap up (*informal*)

finally *adverb* **1** EVENTUALLY, at last, at length, at long last, in the end, lastly, ultimately **2** IN CONCLUSION, in summary, to conclude

finance *noun* **1** ECONOMICS, accounts, banking, business, commerce, investment, money ▷ *verb* **2** FUND, back, bankroll, guarantee, pay for, subsidize, support, underwrite

finances *plural noun* RESOURCES, affairs, assets, capital, cash, funds, money, wherewithal

financial *adjective* ECONOMIC, fiscal, monetary, pecuniary

find *verb* **1** DISCOVER, come across, encounter, hit upon, locate, meet, recognize, spot, uncover **2** PERCEIVE, detect, discover, learn, note, notice, observe, realize ▷ *noun* **3** DISCOVERY, acquisition, asset, bargain, catch, good buy

find out *verb* **1** LEARN, detect, discover, note, observe, perceive, realize **2** DETECT, catch, disclose, expose, reveal, uncover, unmask

fine¹ *adjective* **1** EXCELLENT, accomplished, exceptional, exquisite, first-rate, magnificent, masterly, outstanding, splendid, superior **2** SUNNY, balmy, bright, clear, clement, cloudless, dry, fair, pleasant **3** SATISFACTORY, acceptable, all right, convenient, good, O.K. *or* okay (*informal*), suitable **4** DELICATE, dainty, elegant, expensive, exquisite, fragile, quality **5** SUBTLE, abstruse, acute, hairsplitting, minute, nice, precise, sharp

small particles **5** slender **6** excellent **7** handsome **8** showy **9** (*informal*) healthy, at ease, comfortable **10** free of rain ▷ *verb transitive* **fined, fin•ing 11** make clear or pure **12** refine **13** thin > **fine'ly** *adverb* > **fine'ness** *noun* > **fin'er•y** *noun, plural* **-er•ies** showy dress > **fi•nesse** [fi-NES] *noun* elegant, skillful management > **fine art** art produced for its aesthetic value > **fine-tune** *verb transitive* make fine adjustments to for optimum performance

fine² *noun* **1** sum fixed as penalty ▷ *verb transitive* **fined, fin•ing 2** punish by fine **in fine 1** in conclusion **2** in brief

fin•ger [FING-gər] *noun* **1** one of the jointed branches of the hand **2** various things like this ▷ *verb transitive* **3** touch or handle with fingers **4** (*slang*) inform against (a criminal) > **fin'ger•ing** *noun* **1** manner or act of touching **2** choice of fingers, as in playing musical instrument **3** indication of this > **fin'ger•board** *noun* part of violin, etc. against which fingers are placed > **fin'ger•print** *noun* impression of tip of finger, esp. as used for identifying criminals

fin•i•al [FIN-ee-əl] *noun* ornament at apex of gable, spire, furniture, etc.

fin•ick•y [FIN-i-kee] *adjective* **-ick•i•er, -ick•i•est 1** fastidious, fussy **2** too fine

fin'is *Lat.* end, esp. of book

fin'ish *verb* (*mainly transitive*) **1** bring, come to an end, conclude **2** complete **3** perfect **4** kill ▷ *noun* **5** end **6** way in which thing is finished of furniture: *oak finish* **7** final appearance

fi•nite [FĪ-nīt] *adjective* bounded, limited

fiord *see* **fjord**

fir [fur] *noun* **1** kind of coniferous resinous tree **2** its wood

fire [fīr] *noun* **1** state of burning, combustion, flame, glow **2** mass of burning fuel **3** destructive burning, conflagration **4** burning fuel for heating a room, etc. **5** ardor, keenness, spirit **6** shooting of firearms ▷ *verb transitive* **fired, fir•ing 7** discharge (firearm) **8** propel from firearm **9** (*informal*) dismiss from employment **10** bake **11** make burn **12** supply with fuel **13** inspire **14** explode ▷ *verb intransitive* **fired, fir•ing 15** discharge firearm **16** begin to burn **17** become excited > **fire'arm** *noun* gun, rifle, pistol, etc. > **fire'brand** *noun* **1** burning piece of wood **2** energetic (troublesome) person > **fire'break** [-brayk] *noun* strip of cleared land to arrest progress of forest or grass fire > **fire'bug** *noun* (*informal*) person who practices arson > **fire department** organized body of personnel and equipment to put out fires and rescue those in danger > **fire drill** rehearsal of procedures for escape from fire > **fire engine** vehicle with apparatus for extinguishing fires > **fire escape** means, esp. metal stairs, for escaping from burning buildings > **fire'fight•er** *noun* **1** member of fire department **2** person employed to fight forest fires > **fire'fly** *noun, plural* **-flies** insect giving off phosphorescent glow > **fire'guard** *noun* protective grating in front of fire > **fire irons** tongs, poker and shovel > **fire'man** *noun, plural* **fire'men 1** firefighter **2** stoker **3** assistant to locomotive driver > **fire'place** *noun* recess in room for fire > **fire house** building housing fire department equipment and personnel > **fire'work** *noun* device to give spectacular effects by explosions and colored sparks > **fire'works 1** show of fireworks **2** outburst of temper, anger > **firing squad** group of soldiers ordered to execute an offender by shooting

fir•kin [FUR-kin] *noun* small cask

firm [furm] *adjective* **-er, -est 1** solid, fixed, stable **2** steadfast **3** resolute **4** settled ▷ *verb* **5**

DICTIONARY

---

f

THESAURUS

6 SLENDER, diaphanous, flimsy, gauzy, gossamer, light, sheer, thin

fine² *noun* **1** PENALTY, damages, forfeit, punishment
▷ *verb* **2** PENALIZE, punish

finery *noun* SPLENDOR, frippery, gear (*informal*), glad rags (*informal*), ornaments, showiness, Sunday best, trappings, trinkets

finesse *noun* SKILL, adeptness, adroitness, craft, delicacy, diplomacy, discretion, savoir-faire, sophistication, subtlety, tact

finger *verb* TOUCH, feel, fiddle with (*informal*), handle, manipulate, maul, paw (*informal*), toy with

finish *verb* **1** STOP, cease, close, complete, conclude, end, round off, terminate, wind up, wrap up (*informal*)
2 CONSUME, devour, dispose of, eat, empty, exhaust, use up
3 DESTROY, bring down, defeat, dispose of, exterminate, overcome, put an end to, put paid to, rout, ruin
4 PERFECT, polish, refine
5 COAT, gild, lacquer, polish, stain, texture, veneer, wax
▷ *noun* **6** END, cessation, close, completion, conclusion, culmination, denouement, finale, run-in
7 DEFEAT, annihilation, curtains (*informal*), death, end, end of the road, ruin
8 SURFACE, luster, patina, polish, shine, smoothness, texture

finished *adjective* **1** POLISHED, accomplished, perfected, professional, refined
2 OVER, closed, complete, done, ended, finalized, through
3 SPENT, done, drained, empty, exhausted, used up
4 RUINED, defeated, done for (*informal*), doomed, lost, through, undone, wiped out

finite *adjective* LIMITED, bounded, circumscribed, delimited, demarcated, restricted

fire *noun* **1** FLAMES, blaze, combustion, conflagration, inferno
2 BOMBARDMENT, barrage, cannonade, flak, fusillade, hail, salvo, shelling, sniping, volley
3 PASSION, ardor, eagerness, enthusiasm, excitement, fervor, intensity, sparkle, spirit, verve, vigor
▷ *verb* **4** SHOOT, detonate, discharge, explode, let off, pull the trigger, set off, shell
5 INSPIRE, animate, enliven, excite, galvanize, impassion, inflame, rouse, stir
6 DISMISS, cashier, discharge, make redundant, sack (*informal*), show the door

firebrand *noun* RABBLE-ROUSER, agitator, demagogue, incendiary, instigator, tub-thumper

fireworks *plural noun* **1** PYROTECHNICS, illuminations
2 RAGE, hysterics, row, storm, trouble, uproar

make, become firm ▷ *noun* 6 commercial enterprise 7 partnership

fir•ma•ment [FUR-mə-mənt] *noun* expanse of sky, heavens

first [furst] *adjective* 1 earliest in time or order 2 foremost in rank or position 3 most excellent 4 highest, chief ▷ *noun* 5 beginning 6 first occurrence of something 7 *baseball* first base ▷ *adverb* 8 before others in time, order, etc. > **first'ly** *adverb* > **first aid** help given to injured person before arrival of doctor > **first-hand** *adjective* obtained directly from the first source > **first mate, first officer** officer of merchant vessel immediately below captain > **first-rate** *adjective* of highest class or quality > **first-strike** *adjective* (of a nuclear missile) for use in an opening attack to destroy enemy nuclear weapons

fis•cal [FIS-kəl] *adjective* of (government) finances

fish *noun, plural* **fish** *or* **fish•es** 1 vertebrate cold-blooded animal with gills, living in water 2 its flesh as food ▷ *verb* 3 (attempt to) catch fish 4 search (for) 5 try to get information indirectly > **fish'er** *noun* > **fish'er•y** *noun, plural* **-er•ies** 1 business of fishing 2 fishing ground > **fish'y** *adjective* **fish•i•er, fish•i•est** 1 of, like, or full of fish 2 dubious, open to suspicion 3 unsafe > **fish'er•man** *noun, plural* **-men** one who catches fish for a living or for pleasure > **fish'plate** *noun* piece of metal holding wooden beams, etc. together > **fish stick** small piece of fish covered in breadcrumbs

fis•sure [FISH-ər] *noun* cleft, split, cleavage > **fis'sile** [-əl] *adjective* 1 capable of splitting 2 tending to split > **fis•sion** [FISH-ən] *noun* 1 splitting 2 reproduction by division of living cells with two parts, each of which becomes complete organism 3 splitting of atomic nucleus with release of large amount of energy > **fis'sio•n•able** *adjective* capable of undergoing nuclear fission > **fis•sip•a•rous** [fi-SIP-ər-əs] *adjective* reproducing by fission

fist *noun* clenched hand > **fist'i•cuffs** *plural noun* fighting

fis•tu•la [FIS-chuu-lə] *noun, plural* **-las** pipelike ulcer

fit[1] *verb transitive* **fit•ted** *or* **fit, fit•ting** 1 be suited to 2 be properly adjusted to 3 arrange, adjust, apply, insert 4 supply, furnish ▷ *verb intransitive* **fit•ted** *or* **fit, fit•ting** 5 be correctly adjusted or adapted 6 be of right size ▷ *adjective* **fit•ter, fit•test** 7 well-suited, worthy 8 qualified 9 proper, becoming 10 ready 11 in good condition or health ▷ *noun* 12 way anything fits, its style 13 adjustment > **fit'ly** *adverb* > **fit'ment** *noun* piece of equipment > **fit'ness** *noun* > **fitter** *noun* 1 one who, that which, makes fit 2 one who supervises making and fitting of garments 3 mechanic skilled in fitting up metal work > **fitting** *adjective* 1 appropriate, suitable 2 proper ▷ *noun* 3 fixture 4 apparatus 5 action of fitting

fit[2] *noun* 1 seizure with convulsions, spasms, loss of consciousness, etc., as of epilepsy, hysteria, etc. 2 sudden passing attack of illness 3 passing state, mood > **fit'ful** *adjective* spasmodic, capricious > **fit'ful•ly** *adverb*

five [fīv] *adjective, noun* cardinal number after four > **fifth** *adjective, noun* ordinal number

---

firm[1] *adjective* 1 HARD, dense, inflexible, rigid, set, solid, solidified, stiff, unyielding
2 SECURE, embedded, fast, fixed, immovable, rooted, stable, steady, tight, unshakable
3 DEFINITE, adamant, inflexible, resolute, resolved, set on, unbending, unshakable, unyielding

firm[2] *noun* COMPANY, association, business, concern, conglomerate, corporation, enterprise, organization, partnership

firmly *adverb* 1 SECURELY, immovably, like a rock, steadily, tightly, unflinchingly, unshakably
2 RESOLUTELY, staunchly, steadfastly, unchangeably, unwaveringly

firmness *noun* 1 HARDNESS, inelasticity, inflexibility, resistance, rigidity, solidity, stiffness
2 RESOLVE, constancy, inflexibility, resolution, staunchness, steadfastness

first *adjective* 1 FOREMOST, chief, cutting-edge, head, highest, leading, pre-eminent, prime, principal, ruling
2 EARLIEST, initial, introductory, maiden, opening, original, premier, primordial
3 ELEMENTARY, basic, cardinal, fundamental, key, primary, rudimentary
▷ *adverb* 4 BEFOREHAND, at the beginning, at the outset, firstly, initially, in the first place, to begin with, to start with
▷ *noun* 5 ▷ **from the first** FROM THE START, from the beginning, from the commencement, from the inception, from the introduction, from the outset, from the starting point

first-rate *adjective* EXCELLENT, crack (*slang*), elite, exceptional, first class, outstanding, superb, superlative, top-notch (*informal*), world-class

fishy *adjective* 1 (*informal*) SUSPICIOUS, dubious, funny (*informal*), implausible, odd, questionable, suspect, unlikely
2 FISHLIKE, piscatorial, piscatory, piscine

fissure *noun* CRACK, breach, cleft, crevice, fault, fracture, opening, rift, rupture, split

fit[1] *verb* 1 MATCH, accord, belong, conform, correspond, meet, suit, tally
2 PREPARE, arm, equip, fit out, provide
3 ADAPT, adjust, alter, arrange, customize, modify, shape
▷ *adjective* 4 APPROPRIATE, apt, becoming, correct, fitting, proper, right, seemly, suitable
5 HEALTHY, able-bodied, hale, in good shape, robust, strapping, trim, well

fit[2] *noun* 1 SEIZURE, attack, bout, convulsion, paroxysm, spasm
2 OUTBREAK, bout, burst, outburst, spell

fitful *adjective* IRREGULAR, broken, desultory, disturbed, inconstant, intermittent, spasmodic, sporadic, uneven

fitness *noun* 1 APPROPRIATENESS, aptness, competence, eligibility, propriety, readiness, suitability
2 HEALTH, good condition, good health, robustness, strength, vigor

fitting *adjective* 1 APPROPRIATE, apposite, becoming, correct, decent, proper, right, seemly, suitable
▷ *noun* 2 ACCESSORY, attachment, component,

> **fifth'ly** *adverb* > **fif'teen** *adjective, noun* ten plus five > **fif'teenth** *adjective, noun* > **fif'ti•eth** *adjective, noun* > **fif'ty** *adjective, noun, plural* **-ties** five tens > **fifth column** organization spying for enemy within country at war

527 *noun* non-profit US political organization that is exempt from taxes

fix [fiks] *verb transitive* 1 fasten, make firm or stable 2 set, establish 3 appoint, assign, determine 4 make fast 5 repair 6 (*informal*) influence the outcome of unfairly or by deception 7 bribe 8 (*slang*) treat someone vengefully ▷ *verb intransitive* 9 become firm or solidified 10 determine ▷ *noun* 11 difficult situation 12 position of ship, aircraft ascertained by radar, observation, etc. 13 (*slang*) dose of narcotic drug > **fix•a'tion** *noun* 1 act of fixing 2 preoccupation, obsession 3 situation of being set in some way of acting or thinking > **fix'a•tive** *adjective* capable of, or tending to fix ▷ *noun* > **fix'ed•ly** [-sid-lee] *adverb* intently > **fix'ture** [-chər] *noun* 1 thing fixed in position 2 thing attached to house 3 sporting event that takes place regularly 4 person long-established in a place > **fix up** arrange **fix (someone) up** attend to person's needs, esp. arrange date

fizz *verb intransitive* 1 hiss, splutter ▷ *noun* 2 hissing noise 3 effervescent liquid such as champagne > **fiz'zle** [-əl] *verb intransitive* **-zled, -zling** 1 splutter weakly ▷ *noun* 2 fizzling noise 3 fiasco **fizzle out** (*informal*) come to nothing, fail

fjord [fyord] *noun* (esp. in Norway) long, narrow inlet of sea

flab•ber•gast [FLAB-ər-gast] *verb transitive* overwhelm with astonishment

flab•by [FLAB-ee] *adjective* **-bi•er, -bi•est** 1 hanging loose, limp 2 out of condition, too fat 3 feeble 4 yielding > **flab** *noun* (*informal*) unsightly fat on the body > **flab'bi•ness** *noun*

flac•cid [FLAK-sid] *adjective* flabby, lacking firmness > **flac•cid'i•ty** *noun*

flag¹ *noun* 1 banner, piece of bunting attached to staff or halyard as standard or signal ▷ *verb transitive* **flagged, flag•ging** 2 inform by flag signals > **Flag Day** June 14 > **flag'ship** *noun* 1 admiral's ship 2 most important ship of fleet > **flag'staff** *noun* pole for flag

flag² *noun* 1 flat slab of stone ▷ *verb transitive* **flagged, flag•ging** 2 pave with flags > **flags** *plural noun* pavement of flags > **flag'stone** *noun*

flag³ *verb intransitive* **flagged, flag•ging** 1 droop, fade 2 lose vigor

flag•el•late [FLAJ-ə-layt] *verb transitive* **-lat•ed, -lat•ing** scourge, flog > **flag'el•lant** [-lənt] *noun* one who scourges self, esp. in religious penance > **flag•el•la'tion** *noun* > **flag'el•la•tor** *noun*

flag•eo•let [flaj-ə-LET] *noun* small flutelike instrument

flag•on [FLAG-ən] *noun* large bottle of wine, etc.

fla•grant [FLAY-grənt] *adjective* glaring, scandalous, blatant > **fla'gran•cy** *noun*

flail [flayl] *noun* 1 instrument for threshing grain by hand ▷ *verb* 2 beat with, move as, flail

flair *noun* 1 natural ability 2 elegance

flak *noun* 1 antiaircraft fire 2 (*informal*) adverse criticism

flake [flayk] *noun* 1 small, thin piece, esp. particle of snow 2 piece chipped off ▷ *verb* **flaked, flak•ing** 3 (cause to) peel off in flakes > **flak'y** *adjective* **flak•i•er, flak•i•est** 1 of or like flakes 2 (*slang*) eccentric > **flake out** (*informal*) collapse, sleep from exhaustion

flam•boy•ant [flam-BOI-ənt] *adjective* 1 florid,

DICTIONARY **f** THESAURUS

part, piece, unit

fix *verb* 1 PLACE, embed, establish, implant, install, locate, plant, position, set
2 FASTEN, attach, bind, connect, link, secure, stick, tie
3 DECIDE, agree on, arrange, arrive at, determine, establish, set, settle, specify
4 REPAIR, correct, mend, patch up, put to rights, see to
5 FOCUS, direct
6 (*informal*) MANIPULATE, influence, rig
▷ *noun* 7 (*informal*) PREDICAMENT, difficulty, dilemma, embarrassment, mess, pickle (*informal*), plight, quandary

fixation *noun* PREOCCUPATION, complex, hang-up (*informal*), idée fixe (*French*), infatuation, mania, obsession, thing (*informal*)

fixed *adjective* 1 PERMANENT, established, immovable, rigid, rooted, secure, set
2 INTENT, resolute, steady, unwavering
3 AGREED, arranged, decided, definite, established, planned, resolved, settled

fix up *verb* 1 ARRANGE, agree on, fix, organize, plan, settle, sort out
2 (*often with with*) PROVIDE, arrange for, bring about, lay on

fizz *verb* BUBBLE, effervesce, fizzle, froth, hiss, sparkle, sputter

fizzy *adjective* BUBBLY, bubbling, carbonated, effervescent, gassy, sparkling

flabbergasted *adjective* ASTONISHED, amazed, astounded, dumbfounded, lost for words, overwhelmed, speechless, staggered, stunned

flabby *adjective* LIMP, baggy, drooping, flaccid, floppy, loose, pendulous, sagging

flag¹ *noun* 1 BANNER, colors, ensign, pennant, pennon, standard, streamer
▷ *verb* 2 MARK, indicate, label, note
3 (*sometimes with down*) HAIL, signal, warn, wave

flag² *verb* WEAKEN, abate, droop, fade, languish, peter out, sag, wane, weary, wilt

flagging *adjective* FADING, declining, deteriorating, faltering, waning, weakening, wilting

flagrant *adjective* OUTRAGEOUS, barefaced, blatant, brazen, glaring, heinous, scandalous, shameless

flagstone *noun* PAVING STONE, block, flag, slab

flail *verb* THRASH, beat, thresh, windmill

flair *noun* 1 ABILITY, aptitude, faculty, feel, genius, gift, knack, mastery, talent
2 STYLE, chic, dash, discernment, elegance, panache, stylishness, taste

flake *noun* 1 WAFER, layer, peeling, scale, shaving, sliver
▷ *verb* 2 BLISTER, chip, peel *or* peel off

flake out *verb* COLLAPSE, faint, keel over, pass out

flamboyant *adjective* 1 EXTRAVAGANT, dashing, elaborate, florid, ornate, ostentatious, showy, swashbuckling, theatrical
2 COLORFUL, brilliant, dazzling, glamorous,

gorgeous, showy **2** exuberant, ostentatious
flame [flaym] *noun* **1** burning gas, esp. above fire **2** visible burning **3** passion, esp. love **4** (*informal*) sweetheart **5** (*informal*) an abusive message sent by e-mail ▷ *verb* **flamed, flam•ing 6** give out flames, blaze **7** shine **8** burst out **9** (*informal*) to send an abusive message by e-mail
fla•men•co [flə-MENG-koh] *noun, plural* **-cos 1** Spanish dance to guitar **2** music for this
fla•min•go [flə-MING-goh] *noun, plural* **-gos** *or* **-goes** large pink to scarlet bird with long neck and legs
flam•ma•ble [FLAM-ə-bəl] *adjective* liable to catch fire,inflammable
flan *noun* **1** open sweet dessert with caramel topping **2** tartlike pastry
flange [flanj] *noun* **1** projecting flat rim, collar, or rib ▷ *verb* **flanged, flang•ing 2** provide with or take form of flange
flank [flangk] *noun* **1** part of side between hips and ribs **2** side of anything, e.g. body of troops ▷ *verb transitive* **3** guard or strengthen on flank **4** attack or take in flank **5** be at, move along either side of
flan•nel [FLAN-l] *noun* soft woolen fabric for clothing, esp. trousers > **flan'nel•mouth** *noun* person of slow, thick speech or deceptively smooth speech
flap *verb* **flapped, flap•ping 1** move (wings, arms, etc.) as bird flying **2** (cause to) sway **3** strike with flat object **4** (*slang*) be agitated, flustered ▷ *noun* **5** act of flapping **6** broad piece of anything hanging from hinge or loosely from one side **7** movable part of aircraft wing **8** (*informal*) state of excitement or panic > **flap'pa•ble** *adjective* (*informal*) easily confused, esp. under stress
flare [flair] *verb intransitive* **flared, flar•ing 1** blaze with unsteady flame **2** (*informal*) (with *up*) burst suddenly into anger **3** spread outward, as bottom of skirt ▷ *noun* **4** instance of flaring **5** signal light
flash *noun* **1** sudden burst of light or flame **2** sudden short blaze **3** very short time **4** brief news item **5** display ▷ *verb intransitive* **6** break into sudden flame **7** gleam **8** burst into view **9** move very fast **10** appear suddenly **11** (*slang*) expose oneself indecently ▷ *verb transitive* **12** cause to gleam **13** emit (light, etc.) suddenly > **flash'er** *noun* **1** thing that flashes **2** (*slang*) one who indecently exposes self > **flash'back** *noun* break in continuity of book, play or film, to introduce what has taken place previously > **flash'y** *adjective* **flash•i•er, flash•i•est** showy, sham > **flash point 1** temperature at which a vapor ignites **2** point at which violence or anger breaks out
flask *noun* **1** long-necked bottle for scientific use **2** metal or glass pocket bottle
flat[1] *adjective* **flat•ter, flat•test 1** level **2** spread out **3** at full length **4** smooth **5** downright **6** dull, lifeless **7** *mus.* below true pitch **8** (of vehicle tire) deflated, punctured ▷ *noun* **9** what is flat **10** *mus.* note half tone below natural pitch > **flat'ly** *adverb* > **flat'ness** *noun* > **flat'ten** *verb transitive* > **flat feet** feet with abnormally flattened arches > **flat'foot** *noun, plural* **-foots** (*slang*) police officer > **flat race** horse race over level ground with no jumps > **flat rate** the same price in all cases **flat out** at, with maximum speed or effort
flat[2] *noun* apartment
flat•ter [FLAT-ər] *verb transitive* **1** fawn on **2** praise insincerely **3** inspire unfounded belief **4**

DICTIONARY • THESAURUS

glitzy (*slang*)
flame *noun* **1** FIRE, blaze, brightness, light
2 (*informal*) SWEETHEART, beau, boyfriend, girlfriend, heart-throb (*Brit*), lover
▷ *verb* **3** BURN, blaze, flare, flash, glare, glow, shine
flaming *adjective* BURNING, ablaze, blazing, fiery, glowing, raging, red-hot
flank *noun* **1** SIDE, hip, loin, thigh
2 WING, side
flap *verb* **1** FLUTTER, beat, flail, shake, thrash, vibrate, wag, wave
▷ *noun* **2** FLUTTER, beating, shaking, swinging, swish, waving
flare *verb* **1** BLAZE, burn up, flicker, glare
2 WIDEN, broaden, spread out
▷ *noun* **3** FLAME, blaze, burst, flash, flicker, glare
flare up *verb* LOSE ONE'S TEMPER, blow one's top (*informal*), boil over, explode, fly off the handle (*informal*), throw a tantrum
flash *noun* **1** BLAZE, burst, dazzle, flare, flicker, gleam, shimmer, spark, streak
2 MOMENT, instant, jiffy (*informal*), second, split second, trice, twinkling of an eye
▷ *verb* **3** BLAZE, flare, flicker, glare, gleam, shimmer, sparkle, twinkle
4 SPEED, dart, dash, fly, race, shoot, streak, whistle, zoom
5 SHOW, display, exhibit, expose, flaunt, flourish
flashy *adjective* SHOWY, flamboyant, garish, gaudy, glitzy (*slang*), jazzy (*informal*), ostentatious, snazzy (*informal*)
flat[1] *adjective* **1** EVEN, horizontal, level, levelled, low, smooth
2 DULL, boring, dead, lackluster, lifeless, monotonous, tedious, tiresome, uninteresting
3 ABSOLUTE, categorical, downright, explicit, out-and-out, positive, unequivocal, unqualified
4 PUNCTURED, blown out, burst, collapsed, deflated, empty
▷ *adverb* **5** COMPLETELY, absolutely, categorically, exactly, point blank, precisely, utterly
6 ▷ **flat out** AT FULL SPEED, all out, at full tilt, for all one is worth
flat[2] *noun* APARTMENT, rooms
flatly *adverb* ABSOLUTELY, categorically, completely, positively, unhesitatingly
flatness *noun* **1** EVENNESS, smoothness, uniformity
2 DULLNESS, monotony, tedium
flatten *verb* LEVEL, compress, even out, iron out, raze, smooth off, squash, trample
flatter *verb* **1** PRAISE, brown-nose (*slang*), butter up, compliment, pander to, sweet-talk (*informal*), wheedle
2 SUIT, become, do something for, enhance, set off, show to advantage
flattering *adjective* **1** BECOMING, effective, enhancing, kind, well-chosen
2 INGRATIATING, adulatory, complimentary, fawning, fulsome, laudatory

gratify (senses) 5 represent too favorably > **flat'ter•er** *noun* > **flat'ter•y** *noun, plural* **-ter•ies**
flat•u•lent [FLACH-ə-lənt] *adjective* 1 suffering from, generating (excess) gases in intestines 2 pretentious > **flat'u•lence** *noun* 1 flatulent condition 2 verbosity, emptiness
flaunt [flawnt] *verb* 1 show off 2 wave proudly
flautist *noun see* **flute**
fla•vor [FLAY-vər] *noun* 1 mixed sensation of smell and taste 2 distinctive taste, savor 3 undefinable characteristic, quality of anything ▷ *verb transitive* 4 give flavor to 5 season > **fla'vor•ing** *noun* > **fla'vor•ful** *adjective*
flaw *noun* 1 crack 2 defect, blemish ▷ *verb transitive* 3 make flaw in > **flaw'less** *adjective* perfect
flax [flaks] *noun* 1 plant grown for its textile fiber and seeds 2 its fibers, spun into linen thread > **flax'en** *adjective* 1 of flax 2 light yellow or straw-colored
flay *verb transitive* 1 strip skin off 2 criticize severely
flea [flee] *noun* small, wingless, jumping, blood-sucking insect > **flea'bag** *noun* (*slang*) 1 worthless racehorse, unkempt dog, etc. 2 shabby hotel, etc. > **flea'bite** *noun* 1 insect's bite 2 trifling injury 3 trifle > **flea'-bit•ten** *adjective* 1 bitten by flea 2 mean, worthless 3 scruffy > **flea market** market, usu. held outdoors, for used articles, cheap goods
fleck [flek] *noun* 1 small mark, streak, or particle ▷ *verb transitive* 2 mark with flecks
fled *pt./pp. of* **flee**
fledged [flejd] *adjective* 1 (of birds) able to fly 2 experienced, trained > **fledg'ling** *noun* 1 young bird 2 inexperienced person
flee *verb* **fled, flee•ing** run away from
fleece [flees] *noun* 1 sheep's wool ▷ *verb transitive* **fleeced, fleec•ing** 2 rob > **fleec'y** *adjective* **fleec•i•er, fleec•i•est** resembling wool
fleet[1] *noun* 1 number of warships organized as unit 2 number of ships, automobiles, etc. operating together
fleet[2] *adjective* **-er, -est** swift, nimble > **fleet'ing** *adjective* passing, transient > **fleet'ing•ly** *adverb*
flesh *noun* 1 soft part, muscular substance, between skin and bone 2 in plants, pulp 3 fat 4 person's family > **flesh'ly** *adjective* **-li•er, -li•est** carnal, material > **flesh'y** *adjective* **flesh•i•er, flesh•i•est** plump, pulpy > **flesh'pots** *plural noun* (places catering to) self-indulgent living **in the flesh** in person, actually present
fleur-de-lis [flur-dl-EE] *noun, plural* **fleurs-de-lis** [-dl-EEZ] heraldic lily with three petals
flew *pt. of* **fly**
flex [fleks] *noun* 1 act of flexing ▷ *verb* 2 bend, be bent > **flex•i•bil'i•ty** *noun* > **flex'i•ble** *adjective* 1 easily bent 2 manageable 3 adaptable > **flex'time** *noun* system permitting variation in starting and finishing times of work, providing agreed total time is worked over a specified period
flib•ber•ti•gib•bet [FLIB-ər-tee-jib-it] *noun* flighty, chattering person
flick [flik] *verb transitive* 1 strike lightly, jerk ▷ *noun* 2 light blow 3 jerk 4 (*slang*) motion picture
flick•er [FLIK-ər] *verb intransitive* 1 burn, shine, unsteadily 2 waver, quiver ▷ *noun* 3 unsteady light or movement
flight [flīt] *noun* 1 act or manner of flying through air 2 number flying together, as birds 3 journey in aircraft 4 air force unit of command 5 power of flying 6 swift movement or passage 7 sally 8 distance flown 9 stairs between two landings 10 running away > **flight recorder** electronic device in aircraft storing information about its flight
flight•y [FLĪ-tee] *adjective* **flight•i•er, flight•i•est** frivolous, erratic
flim•sy [FLIM-zee] *adjective* **-si•er, -si•est** 1 frail,

DICTIONARY **f** THESAURUS

---

flattery *noun* OBSEQUIOUSNESS, adulation, blandishment, fawning, servility, sweet-talk (*informal*), sycophancy
flaunt *verb* SHOW OFF, brandish, display, exhibit, flash about, flourish, parade, sport (*informal*)
flavor *noun* 1 TASTE, aroma, flavoring, piquancy, relish, savor, seasoning, smack, tang, zest 2 QUALITY, character, essence, feel, feeling, style, tinge, tone ▷ *verb* 3 SEASON, ginger up, imbue, infuse, leaven, spice
flaw *noun* WEAKNESS, blemish, chink in one's armor, defect, failing, fault, imperfection, weak spot
flawed *adjective* DAMAGED, blemished, defective, erroneous, faulty, imperfect, unsound
flawless *adjective* PERFECT, faultless, impeccable, spotless, unblemished, unsullied
flee *verb* RUN AWAY, bolt, depart, escape, fly, make one's getaway, take flight, take off (*informal*), take to one's heels, turn tail
fleet *noun* NAVY, armada, flotilla, task force
fleeting *adjective* MOMENTARY, brief, ephemeral, passing, short-lived, temporary, transient, transitory
flesh *noun* 1 MEAT, brawn, fat, tissue, weight 2 HUMAN NATURE, carnality, flesh and blood 3 ▷ **one's own flesh and blood** FAMILY, blood, kin, kinsfolk, kith and kin, relations, relatives
flexibility *noun* ADAPTABILITY, adjustability, elasticity, give (*informal*), pliability, pliancy, resilience, springiness
flexible *adjective* 1 PLIABLE, elastic, lithe, plastic, pliant, springy, stretchy, supple 2 ADAPTABLE, adjustable, discretionary, open, variable
flick *verb* 1 STRIKE, dab, flip, hit, tap, touch 2 ▷ **flick through** BROWSE, flip through, glance at, skim, skip, thumb
flicker *verb* 1 TWINKLE, flare, flash, glimmer, gutter, shimmer, sparkle 2 FLUTTER, quiver, vibrate, waver ▷ *noun* 3 GLIMMER, flare, flash, gleam, spark 4 TRACE, breath, glimmer, iota, spark
flight[1] *noun* 1 JOURNEY, trip, voyage 2 AVIATION, aeronautics, flying 3 FLOCK, cloud, formation, squadron, swarm, unit
flight[2] *noun* ESCAPE, departure, exit, exodus, fleeing, getaway, retreat, running away
flimsy *adjective* 1 FRAGILE, delicate, frail, insubstantial, makeshift, rickety, shaky 2 THIN, gauzy, gossamer, light, sheer, transparent

weak, thin 2 easily destroyed > **flim'si•ness** *noun*
flinch *verb intransitive* shrink, draw back, wince
fling *verb* **flung, fling•ing** (*mainly transitive*) 1 throw, send, move, with force ▷ *noun* 2 throw 3 hasty attempt 4 spell of indulgence 5 vigorous dance
flint *noun* 1 hard steel-gray stone 2 piece of this 3 hard substance used (as flint) for striking fire > **flint'y** *adjective* **flint•i•er, flint•i•est** 1 like or consisting of flint 2 hard, cruel
flip *verb* **flipped, flip•ping** 1 throw or flick lightly 2 turn over 3 (*slang*) react with astonishment, become irrational ▷ *noun* 4 instance, act, of flipping 5 drink with beaten egg > **flip'pan•cy** *noun, plural* **-cies** > **flip'pant** *adjective* treating serious things lightly > **flip'per** *noun* limb, fin for swimming > **flip'pers** fin-shaped rubber devices worn on feet to help in swimming
flirt [flurt] *verb intransitive* 1 toy, play with another's affections 2 trifle, toy (with) ▷ *noun* 3 person who flirts > **flir•ta'tion** [-TAY-shən] *noun* > **flir•ta'tious** *adjective*
flit *verb intransitive* **flit•ted, flit•ting** 1 pass lightly and rapidly 2 dart 3 (*informal*) go away hastily
flitch [flich] *noun* side of bacon
float [floht] *verb intransitive* 1 rest, drift on surface of liquid 2 be suspended freely 3 move aimlessly ▷ *verb transitive* 4 of liquid, support, bear alone 5 in commerce, get (company) started 6 obtain loan ▷ *noun* 7 light object used to help someone or something float 8 motor vehicle carrying tableau, etc., in parade 9 uncollected checks, etc. in process of transfer between banks, etc. > **flo•ta'tion** *noun* act of floating, esp. floating of business venture
floc•cu•late [FLOK-yə-layt] *verb transitive* **-lat•ed, -lat•ing** form into masses of particles > **floc'cu•lant** [-lənt] *noun* chemical for accomplishing this
floc•cu•lent [FLOK-yə-lənt] *adjective* like tufts of wool
flock[1] [flok] *noun* 1 number of animals of one kind together 2 body of people 3 religious congregation ▷ *verb intransitive* 4 gather in a crowd
flock[2] *noun* 1 lock, tuft of wool, etc. 2 wool refuse for stuffing cushions, etc.
floe [floh] *noun* sheet of floating ice
flog *verb transitive* **flogged, flog•ging** 1 beat with whip, stick, etc. 2 (*slang*) sell, esp. vigorously
flood [flud] *noun* 1 inundation, overflow of water 2 rising of tide 3 outpouring 4 flowing water ▷ *verb transitive* 5 inundate 6 cover, fill with water 7 arrive, move, etc. in great numbers > **flood'gate** *noun* gate, sluice for letting water in or out > **flood'light** *noun* broad, intense beam of artificial light > **flood'lit** *adjective* > **flood tide** the rising tide
floor [flor] *noun* 1 lower surface of room 2 set of rooms on one level, story 3 flat space 4 (right to speak in) meeting or legislative chamber 5 lower limit ▷ *verb transitive* 6 supply with floor 7 knock down 8 confound > **floor'ing** *noun* material for floors > **floor show** entertainment in nightclub, etc.
flop *verb intransitive* **flopped, flop•ping** 1 bend, fall, collapse loosely, carelessly 2 fall flat on floor, on water, etc. 3 (*informal*) go to sleep 4 (*informal*) fail ▷ *noun* 5 flopping movement or sound 6 (*informal*) failure > **flop'pi•ness** *noun* > **flop'py** *adjective* **-pi•er, -pi•est** limp, unsteady > **flop'house** *noun* run-down rooming house

3 UNCONVINCING, feeble, implausible, inadequate, lousy (*slang*), pathetic, poor, unsatisfactory, weak
flinch *verb* RECOIL, cower, cringe, draw back, quail, shirk, shrink, shy away, wince
fling *verb* 1 THROW, cast, catapult, heave, hurl, propel, sling, toss
▷ *noun* 2 BINGE (*informal*), bash, good time, party, spree
flip *verb, noun* TOSS, flick, snap, spin, throw
flippancy *noun* FRIVOLITY, impertinence, irreverence, levity, pertness, sauciness
flippant *adjective* FRIVOLOUS, cheeky, disrespectful, glib, impertinent, irreverent, offhand, superficial
flirt *verb* 1 LEAD ON, hit on (*slang*), make advances, make eyes at, philander
2 (*usually with with*) TOY WITH, consider, dabble in, entertain, expose oneself to, give a thought to, play with, trifle with
▷ *noun* 3 TEASE, coquette, heart-breaker, hussy, philanderer
flirtatious *adjective* TEASING, amorous, come-hither, coquettish, coy, enticing, flirty, provocative, sportive
float *verb* 1 BE BUOYANT, hang, hover
2 GLIDE, bob, drift, move gently, sail, slide, slip along
3 LAUNCH, get going, promote, set up
floating *adjective* 1 BUOYANT, afloat, buoyed up, sailing, swimming
2 FLUCTUATING, free, movable, unattached, variable, wandering
flock *noun* 1 HERD, colony, drove, flight, gaggle, skein
2 CROWD, collection, company, congregation, gathering, group, herd, host, mass
▷ *verb* 3 GATHER, collect, congregate, converge, crowd, herd, huddle, mass, throng
flog *verb* BEAT, flagellate, flay, lash, scourge, thrash, trounce, whack, whip
flood *noun* 1 DELUGE, downpour, inundation, overflow, spate, tide, torrent
2 ABUNDANCE, flow, glut, profusion, rush, stream, torrent
▷ *verb* 3 IMMERSE, drown, inundate, overflow, pour over, submerge, swamp
4 ENGULF, overwhelm, surge, swarm, sweep
5 OVERSUPPLY, choke, fill, glut, saturate
floor *noun* 1 TIER, level, stage, story
▷ *verb* 2 KNOCK DOWN, deck (*slang*), prostrate
3 (*informal*) BEWILDER, baffle, confound, defeat, disconcert, dumbfound, perplex, puzzle, stump, throw (*informal*)
flop *verb* 1 FALL, collapse, dangle, droop, drop, sag, slump
2 (*informal*) FAIL, come unstuck, fall flat, fold (*informal*), founder, go belly-up (*slang*), misfire
▷ *noun* 3 (*informal*) FAILURE, debacle, disaster, fiasco, nonstarter, washout (*informal*)
floppy *adjective* DROOPY, baggy, flaccid, limp, loose, pendulous, sagging, soft

> **floppy disk** *computing* flexible magnetic disk that stores information

flo•ra [FLOR-ə] *noun* 1 plants of a region 2 list of them > **flor'al** *adjective* of flowers > **flo•res'cence** [-əns] *noun* state or time of flowering > **flo•ret** [FLOR-it] *noun* small flower forming part of composite flower > **flo'ri•cul•ture** *noun* cultivation of flowers > **flo•ri•cul'tur•ist** *noun* > **flo'rist** *noun* dealer in flowers

flor•id *adjective* 1 with red, flushed complexion 2 ornate

floss [flaws] *noun* 1 mass of fine, silky fibers 2 fluff > **floss'y** *adjective* **floss•i•er, floss•i•est** 1 light and downy 2 excessively fancy

flotation *see* **float**

flo•til•la [floh-TIL-ə] *noun* fleet of small vessels, esp. naval vessels

flot•sam [FLOT-səm] *noun* 1 floating wreckage 2 discarded waste objects 3 penniless population of city, etc.

flounce[1] [flowns] *verb intransitive* **flounced, flounc•ing** 1 go, move abruptly and impatiently ▷ *noun* 2 fling, jerk of body or limb

flounce[2] *noun* ornamental gathered strip on woman's garment

floun•der[1] [FLOWN-dər] *verb intransitive* 1 plunge and struggle, esp. in water or mud 2 proceed in bungling, hesitating manner ▷ *noun* 3 act of floundering

flounder[2] *noun* type of flatfish

flour [FLOW-ər] *noun* 1 powder prepared by sifting and grinding wheat, etc. 2 fine soft powder ▷ *verb transitive* 3 sprinkle with flour

flour•ish [FLUR-ish] *verb intransitive* 1 thrive 2 be in the prime ▷ *verb transitive* 3 brandish, display 4 wave about ▷ *noun* 5 ornamental curve 6 showy gesture in speech, etc. 7 waving of hand, weapon, etc. 8 fanfare (of trumpets)

flout [flowt] *verb transitive* 1 show contempt for, mock 2 defy

flow [floh] *verb intransitive* 1 glide along as stream 2 circulate, as the blood 3 move easily 4 move in waves 5 hang loose 6 be present in abundance ▷ *noun* 7 act, instance of flowing 8 quantity that flows 9 rise of tide 10 ample supply > **flow chart** diagram showing sequence of operations in industrial, etc. process

flow•er [FLOW-ər] *noun* 1 colored (not green) part of plant from which fruit is developed 2 bloom, blossom 3 ornamentation 4 choicest part, pick ▷ *verb intransitive* 5 produce flowers 6 bloom 7 come to prime condition ▷ *verb transitive* 8 ornament with flowers > **flow'er•et** *noun* small flower > **flow'er•y** *adjective* **-er•i•er, -er•i•est** 1 abounding in flowers 2 full of fine words, ornamented with figures of speech > **flower girl** 1 girl selling flowers 2 young girl designated to attend bride at wedding ceremony

flown *pp. of* **fly**

flu *noun short for* **influenza**

fluc•tu•ate [FLUK-choo-ayt] *verb* **-at•ed, -at•ing** vary, rise and fall, undulate > **fluc•tu•a'tion** *noun*

flue [floo] *noun* passage or pipe for smoke or hot air, chimney

flu•ent [FLOO-ənt] *adjective* 1 speaking, writing a given language easily and well 2 easy, graceful

fluff *noun* 1 soft, feathery stuff 2 down 3 (*informal*) mistake 4 (*informal*) anything insubstantial ▷ *verb* 5 make or become soft, light 6 (*informal*) make mistake > **fluff'y** *adjective* **fluff•i•er, fluff•i•est**

flu•id [FLOO-id] *adjective* 1 flowing easily, not solid ▷ *noun* 2 gas or liquid > **flu•id'i•ty** *noun* > **fluid ounce** one sixteenth of a pint

fluke[1] [flook] *noun* flat triangular point of anchor > **flukes** whale's tail

fluke[2] *noun* stroke of luck, accident > **fluk'y** *adjective* **fluk•i•er, fluk•i•est** 1 uncertain 2 got by luck

DICTIONARY

f

THESAURUS

---

floral *adjective* FLOWERY, flower-patterned

florid *adjective* 1 FLUSHED, blowsy, high-colored, rubicund, ruddy
2 FLOWERY, baroque, flamboyant, fussy, high-flown, ornate, overelaborate

flotsam *noun* DEBRIS, detritus, jetsam, junk, odds and ends, wreckage

flounder *verb* FUMBLE, grope, struggle, stumble, thrash, toss

flourish *verb* 1 PROSPER, bloom, blossom, boom, flower, grow, increase, succeed, thrive
2 WAVE, brandish, display, flaunt, shake, wield
▷ *noun* 3 WAVE, display, fanfare, parade, show
4 ORNAMENTATION, curlicue, decoration, embellishment, plume, sweep

flourishing *adjective* SUCCESSFUL, blooming, going places, in the pink, luxuriant, prospering, rampant, thriving

flout *verb* DEFY, laugh in the face of, mock, scoff at, scorn, sneer at, spurn

flow *verb* 1 RUN, circulate, course, move, roll
2 POUR, cascade, flood, gush, rush, stream, surge, sweep
3 RESULT, arise, emanate, emerge, issue, proceed, spring
▷ *noun* 4 TIDE, course, current, drift, flood, flux, outpouring, spate, stream

flower *noun* 1 BLOOM, blossom, efflorescence
2 ELITE, best, cream crème de la crème (*French*), pick
▷ *verb* 3 BLOSSOM, bloom, flourish, mature, open, unfold

flowery *adjective* ORNATE, baroque, embellished, fancy, florid, high-flown

flowing *adjective* 1 STREAMING, falling, gushing, rolling, rushing, smooth, sweeping
2 FLUENT, continuous, easy, smooth, unbroken, uninterrupted

fluctuate *verb* CHANGE, alternate, oscillate, seesaw, shift, swing, vary, veer, waver

fluency *noun* EASE, articulateness, assurance, command, control, facility, glibness, readiness, slickness, smoothness

fluent *adjective* SMOOTH, articulate, easy, effortless, flowing, natural, voluble, well-versed

fluff *noun* FUZZ, down, nap, pile

fluffy *adjective* SOFT, downy, feathery, fleecy, fuzzy

fluid *noun* 1 LIQUID, liquor, solution
▷ *adjective* 2 LIQUID, flowing, liquefied, melted, molten, runny, watery

fluke *noun* LUCKY BREAK, accident, chance, coincidence, quirk of fate, serendipity, stroke of luck

fluke[3] *noun* 1 type of flatfish 2 parasitic worm
flume [floom] *noun* narrow (artificial) channel for water
flum•mer•y [FLUM-ə-ree] *noun, plural* **-mer•ies** 1 nonsense, idle talk, humbug 2 dish of milk, flour, eggs, etc.
flum•mox [FLUM-əks] *verb transitive* (*informal*) bewilder, perplex
flung *pt./pp. of* **fling**
flun•ky [FLUNG-kee] *noun, plural* **-kies** 1 servant, esp. liveried manservant 2 assistant doing menial work 3 servile person
fluo•res•cence [fluu-RES-əns] *noun* emission of light or other radiation from substance when bombarded by particles (electrons, etc. or other radiation, as in fluorescent lamp) > **fluo•res'cent** *adjective*
fluor•ide [FLUUR-īd] *noun* salt containing fluorine, esp. as added to domestic water supply as protection against tooth decay > **fluor'i•date** *verb transitive* **-dat•ed, -dat•ing** treat with fluoride > **fluor•i•da'tion** *noun* > **fluor'ine** [-een] *noun* nonmetallic element, yellowish gas
flur•ry [FLUR-ee] *noun, plural* **-ries** 1 squall, gust 2 bustle, commotion 3 fluttering (as of snowflakes) ▷ *verb transitive* **-ried, -ry•ing** 4 agitate, bewilder, fluster
flush[1] *verb intransitive* 1 blush 2 of skin, redden 3 flow suddenly or violently 4 be excited ▷ *verb transitive* 5 send water through (a toilet or pipe) so as to clean it 6 excite ▷ *noun* 7 reddening, blush 8 rush of water 9 excitement 10 elation 11 glow of color 12 freshness, vigor ▷ *adjective* 13 full, in flood 14 well supplied 15 level with surrounding surface
flush[2] *verb* (cause to) leave cover and take flight
flush[3] *noun* set of cards all of one suit
flus•ter [FLUS-tər] *verb* make or become nervous, agitated ▷ *noun*
flute [floot] *noun* 1 wind instrument of tube with holes stopped by fingers or keys and blowhole in side 2 groove, channel ▷ *verb intransitive* **flut•ed, flut•ing** 3 play on flute ▷ *verb transitive* **flut•ed, flut•ing** 4 make grooves in > **flut'ist, flaut'ist** [FLOWT-] *noun* flute player
flut•ter [FLUT-ər] *verb* 1 flap (as wings) rapidly without flight or in short flights 2 quiver 3 be or make excited, agitated ▷ *noun* 4 flapping movement 5 nervous agitation
flu•vi•al [FLOO-vee-əl] *adjective* of rivers
flux [fluks] *noun* 1 discharge 2 constant succession of changes 3 substance mixed with metal to clean, aid adhesion in soldering, etc. 4 measure of strength in magnetic field
fly[1] [flī] *verb* **flew, flown, fly•ing** 1 move through air on wings or in aircraft 2 pass quickly (through air) 3 float loosely 4 spring, rush 5 flee, run away ▷ *verb transitive* 6 operate aircraft 7 cause to fly 8 set flying ▷ *verb intransitive* 9 run from ▷ *noun* 10 (zipper or buttons fastening) opening in trousers 11 flap in garment or tent 12 flying > **flying** *adjective* hurried, brief > **fly'fish** *verb* fish with artificial fly as lure > **flying boat** airplane fitted with floats instead of landing wheels > **flying buttress** *architecture* arched or slanting structure attached at only one point to a mass of masonry > **flying colors** conspicuous success > **flying fish** fish with winglike fins used for gliding above the sea > **flying saucer** unidentified (disk-shaped) flying object, supposedly from outer space > **flying squad** special detachment of police, etc., ready to act quickly > **fly'leaf** *noun, plural* **-leaves** blank leaf at beginning or end of book > **fly'o•ver** *noun* formation of aircraft in flight for observation from ground > **fly'wheel** *noun* heavy wheel regulating speed of machine
fly[2] *noun, plural* **flies** two-winged insect, esp. common housefly > **fly'catch•er** *noun* small insect-eating songbird
Fm *chem.* fermium
foal [fohl] *noun* 1 young of horse, ass, etc. ▷ *verb* 2 bear (foal)
foam [fohm] *noun* 1 collection of small bubbles on liquid 2 froth of saliva or sweat 3 light cellular solid used for insulation, packing, etc. ▷ *verb* (cause to) produce foam 4 be very angry > **foam'y** *adjective* **foam•i•er, foam•i•est**
fob *noun* 1 short watch chain 2 small pocket in waistband of trousers or vest
fob off *verb* **fobbed, fob•bing** 1 ignore, dismiss someone or something in offhand (insulting) manner 2 dispose of
foci *pl. of* **focus**
fo•cus [FOH-kəs] *noun, plural* **-cus•es** *or* **-ci** [-sī] 1 point at which rays meet after being reflected or

DICTIONARY • THESAURUS

flurry *noun* 1 COMMOTION, ado, bustle, disturbance, excitement, flutter, fuss, stir
2 GUST, squall
flush[1] *verb* 1 BLUSH, color, glow, go red, redden
2 RINSE OUT, cleanse, flood, hose down, wash out
▷ *noun* 3 BLUSH, color, glow, redness, rosiness
flush[2] *adjective* 1 LEVEL, even, flat, square, true
2 (*informal*) WEALTHY, in the money (*informal*), moneyed, rich, well-heeled (*informal*), well-off
flushed *adjective* BLUSHING, crimson, embarrassed, glowing, hot, red, rosy, ruddy
fluster *verb* 1 UPSET, agitate, bother, confuse, disturb, perturb, rattle (*informal*), ruffle, unnerve
▷ *noun* 2 TURMOIL, disturbance, dither, flap (*informal*), flurry, flutter, furor
flutter *verb* 1 BEAT, flap, palpitate, quiver, ripple, tremble, vibrate, waver
▷ *noun* 2 VIBRATION, palpitation, quiver, shiver, shudder, tremble, tremor, twitching
3 AGITATION, commotion, confusion, dither, excitement, fluster
fly *verb* 1 TAKE WING, flit, flutter, hover, sail, soar, wing
2 PILOT, control, maneuver, operate
3 DISPLAY, flap, float, flutter, show, wave
4 PASS, elapse, flit, glide, pass swiftly, roll on, run its course, slip away
5 RUSH, career, dart, dash, hurry, race, shoot, speed, sprint, tear
6 FLEE, escape, get away, run for it, skedaddle (*informal*), take to one's heels
flying *adjective* HURRIED, brief, fleeting, hasty, rushed, short-lived, transitory
foam *noun* 1 FROTH, bubbles, head, lather, spray, spume, suds
▷ *verb* 2 BUBBLE, boil, effervesce, fizz, froth, lather
focus *noun* 1 CENTER, focal point, heart, hub, target

refracted **2** state of optical image when it is clearly defined **3** state of instrument producing such image **4** point of convergence **5** point on which interest, activity is centered ▷ *verb transitive* **-cused, -cus•ing** **6** bring to focus, adjust **7** concentrate ▷ *verb intransitive* **-cused, -cus•ing** **8** come to focus **9** converge > **fo'cal** [-kəl] *adjective* of, at focus

fod•der [FOD-ər] *noun* bulk food for livestock

foe [foh] *noun* enemy

fog *noun* **1** thick mist **2** dense watery vapor in lower atmosphere **3** cloud of anything reducing visibility **4** stupor ▷ *verb transitive* **fogged, fog•ging** **5** cover in fog **6** puzzle > **fog'gy** *adjective* **-gi•er, -gi•est** > **fog'horn** *noun* instrument to warn ships in fog

fo•gy [FOH-gee] *noun, plural* **-gies** old-fashioned person

foi•ble [FOI-bəl] *noun* minor weakness, idiosyncrasy

foil[1] *verb transitive* **1** baffle, defeat, frustrate ▷ *noun* **2** blunt sword, with button on point for fencing

foil[2] *noun* **1** metal in thin sheet **2** anything or person that sets off another to advantage

foist *verb transitive* (usu. with *on* or *upon*) sell, pass off inferior or unwanted thing as valuable

fold[1] [fohld] *verb transitive* **1** double up, bend part of **2** interlace (arms) **3** wrap up **4** clasp (in arms) **5** *cookery* mix gently ▷ *verb intransitive* **6** become folded **7** admit of being folded **8** (*informal*) fail ▷ *noun* **9** folding **10** coil **11** winding **12** line made by folding **13** crease **14** foldlike geological formation > **fold'er** *noun* binder, file for loose papers

fold[2] *noun* **1** enclosure for sheep **2** body of believers, church

fo•li•age [FOH-lee-ij] *noun* leaves collectively, leafage > **fo•li•a'ceous** [-AY-shəs] *adjective* of or like leaf > **fo'li•ate** [-it] *adjective* leaflike, having leaves

fo•li•o [FOH-lee-oh] *noun, plural* **-li•os** **1** sheet of paper folded in half to make two leaves of book **2** book of largest common size made up of such sheets **3** page numbered on one side only **4** page number

folk [fohk] *noun* **1** people in general **2** family, relatives **3** race of people > **folk dance** traditional country dance > **folk'lore** *noun* tradition, customs, beliefs popularly held > **folk song** music originating among a people

fol•li•cle [FOL-i-kəl] *noun* **1** small cavity, sac **2** seed vessel

fol•low [FOL-oh] *verb* **1** go or come after ▷ *verb transitive* **2** accompany, attend on **3** keep to (path, etc.) **4** take as guide, conform to **5** engage in **6** have a keen interest in **7** be consequent on **8** grasp meaning of ▷ *verb intransitive* **9** come next **10** result > **fol'low•er** *noun* disciple, supporter > **fol'low•ing** *adjective* **1** about to be mentioned ▷ *noun* **2** body of supporters > **fol'low-through** *noun* in ball games, continuation of stroke after impact with ball > **fol'low-up** *noun* something done to reinforce initial action

fol•ly [FOL-ee] *noun, plural* **-lies** **1** foolishness **2** foolish action, idea, etc. **3** useless, extravagant structure

fo•ment [foh-MENT] *verb transitive* **1** foster, stir up **2** bathe with warm lotions

fond *adjective* **-er, -est** tender, loving > **fond'ly** *adverb* > **fond'ness** *noun* **fond of** having liking for

fon•dant [FON-dənt] *noun* **1** soft sugar mixture for candies **2** candy made of this

fon•dle [FON-dl] *verb transitive* **-dled, -dling** caress

▷ *verb* **2** CONCENTRATE, aim, center, direct, fix, pinpoint, spotlight, zoom in

foe *noun* ENEMY, adversary, antagonist, opponent, rival

fog *noun* MIST, gloom, miasma, murk, smog

foggy *adjective* MISTY, cloudy, dim, hazy, indistinct, murky, smoggy, vaporous

foil[1] *verb* THWART, balk, counter, defeat, disappoint, frustrate, nullify, stop

foil[2] *noun* CONTRAST, antithesis, complement

foist *verb* IMPOSE, fob off, palm off, pass off, sneak in, unload

fold *verb* **1** BEND, crease, double over
2 (*informal*) GO BANKRUPT, collapse, crash, fail, go bust (*informal*), go to the wall, go under, shut down
▷ *noun* **3** CREASE, bend, furrow, overlap, pleat, wrinkle

folder *noun* FILE, binder, envelope, portfolio

folk *noun* PEOPLE, clan, family, kin, kindred, race, tribe

follow *verb* **1** COME AFTER, come next, succeed, supersede, supplant, take the place of
2 PURSUE, chase, dog, hound, hunt, shadow, stalk, track, trail
3 ACCOMPANY, attend, escort, tag along
4 OBEY, be guided by, conform, heed, observe
5 UNDERSTAND, appreciate, catch on (*informal*), comprehend, fathom, grasp, realize, take in
6 RESULT, arise, develop, ensue, flow, issue, proceed, spring
7 BE INTERESTED IN, cultivate, keep abreast of, support

follower *noun* SUPPORTER, adherent, apostle, devotee, disciple, fan, pupil

following *adjective* **1** NEXT, consequent, ensuing, later, subsequent, succeeding, successive
▷ *noun* **2** SUPPORTERS, clientele, coterie, entourage, fans, retinue, suite, train

folly *noun* FOOLISHNESS, imprudence, indiscretion, lunacy, madness, nonsense, rashness, stupidity

fond *adjective* **1** LOVING, adoring, affectionate, amorous, caring, devoted, doting, indulgent, tender, warm
2 FOOLISH, deluded, delusive, empty, naive, overoptimistic, vain
3 ▷ **fond of** KEEN ON, addicted to, attached to, enamored of, having a soft spot for, hooked on, into (*informal*), partial to

fondle *verb* CARESS, cuddle, dandle, pat, pet, stroke

fondly *adverb* **1** LOVINGLY, affectionately, dearly, indulgently, possessively, tenderly, with affection
2 FOOLISHLY, credulously, naively, stupidly, vainly

fondness *noun* **1** LIKING, attachment, fancy, love, partiality, penchant, soft spot, taste, weakness

fon•due [fon-DOO] *noun* Swiss dish of cheese and seasonings into which pieces of bread, etc. are dipped
font *noun* 1 bowl for baptismal water usu. on pedestal 2 productive source 3 assortment of printing type of one size
fon•ta•nel [fon-tn-EL] *noun* soft, membraneous gap between bones of baby's skull
food *noun* 1 solid nourishment 2 what one eats 3 mental or spiritual nourishment > **food additive** natural or synthetic substance added to commercially processed food as preservative or to add color, flavor, etc. > **food group** any category into which a food may be placed according to its nutritional content > **food processor** electric kitchen appliance for automatic chopping, blending, etc. of foodstuffs > **food'stuff** *noun* food
fool *noun* 1 silly, empty-headed person 2 dupe 3 simpleton 4 *hist.* jester, clown ▷ *verb transitive* 5 delude 6 dupe ▷ *verb intransitive* 7 act as fool > **fool'er•y** *noun, plural* **-er•ies** 1 habitual folly 2 act of playing the fool 3 absurdity > **fool'har•di•ness** *noun* > **fool'har•dy** *adjective* **-di•er, -di•est** foolishly adventurous > **fool'ish** *adjective* ill-considered, silly, stupid > **fool'proof** *adjective* proof against failure > **fool's cap** jester's or dunce's cap > **fools'cap** *noun* inexpensive paper, esp. legal-size (formerly with fool's cap as watermark)
foot [fuut] *noun, plural* **feet** 1 lowest part of leg, from ankle down 2 lowest part of anything, base, stand 3 end of bed, etc. 4 measure of twelve inches 5 division of line of verse ▷ *verb (usually transitive)* 6 dance **foot it** (*informal*) walk **foot the bill** pay the entire cost > **foot'age** *noun* 1 length in feet 2 length, extent, of film used > **foot'ing** *noun* 1 basis, foundation 2 firm standing, relations, conditions > **foot'ings** (concrete) foundations for walls of buildings > **foot-and-mouth disease** infectious viral disease in sheep, cattle, etc. > **foot'ball** *noun* 1 game played with inflated oval ball 2 the ball > **foot'ball pool** form of gambling on results of football games > **foot brake** brake operated by pressure on foot pedal > **foot fault** *tennis* fault of overstepping baseline while serving > **foot'hold** *noun* 1 place affording secure grip for the foot 2 secure position from which progress may be made > **foot'lights** *plural noun* lights across front of stage > **foot'loose** *adjective* free of any ties > **foot'note** *noun* note of reference or explanation printed at foot of page > **foot-pound** *noun* unit of measurement of work in fps system > **foot'print** *noun* mark left by foot **playing foot'sie** flirting or sharing a surreptitious intimacy > **foot'slog** *verb intransitive* **-slogged, slogging** walk, go on foot > **foot'slog•ger** *noun*
fop *noun* man excessively concerned with fashion > **fop'per•y** *noun, plural* **-per•ies** > **fop'pish** *adjective*
for *preposition* 1 intended to reach, directed or belonging to 2 because of 3 instead of 4 toward 5 on account of 6 in favor of 7 respecting 8 during 9 in search of 10 in payment of 11 in the character of 12 in spite of ▷ *conjunction* 13 because **in for it** (*informal*) liable for punishment or blame
for- *prefix* from, away, against: *forswear; forbid*
for•age [FOR-ij] *noun* 1 food for cattle and horses ▷ *verb intransitive* **-aged, -ag•ing** 2 collect forage 3 make roving search
for'ay *noun* 1 raid, inroad ▷ *verb intransitive* 2 make one
for•bear [for-BAIR] *verb* **-bore, -borne, -bear•ing** cease or refrain (from doing something) > **for•bear'ance** *noun* self-control, patience
for•bid [fər-BID] *verb transitive* **-bade** *or* **-bad, -bid** *or* **-bid•den, -bid** *or* **-bid•ding** 1 prohibit 2 refuse to allow > **forbidding** *adjective* uninviting, threatening
force [fors] *noun* 1 strength, power 2

DICTIONARY • THESAURUS

2 DEVOTION, affection, attachment, kindness, love, tenderness
food *noun* NOURISHMENT, cuisine, diet, fare, grub (*slang*), nutrition, rations, refreshment
fool *noun* 1 SIMPLETON, blockhead, dork (*slang*), dunce, halfwit, idiot, ignoramus, imbecile (*informal*), schmuck (*slang*)
2 DUPE, fall guy (*informal*), laughing stock, mug (*Brit slang*), stooge (*slang*), sucker (*slang*)
3 CLOWN, buffoon, harlequin, jester
▷ *verb* 4 DECEIVE, beguile, con (*informal*), delude, dupe, hoodwink, mislead, take in, trick
foolhardy *adjective* RASH, hot-headed, impetuous, imprudent, irresponsible, reckless
foolish *adjective* UNWISE, absurd, ill-judged, imprudent, injudicious, senseless, silly
foolishly *adverb* UNWISELY, idiotically, ill-advisedly, imprudently, injudiciously, mistakenly, stupidly
foolishness *noun* STUPIDITY, absurdity, folly, imprudence, indiscretion, irresponsibility, silliness, weakness
foolproof *adjective* INFALLIBLE, certain, guaranteed, safe, sure-fire (*informal*), unassailable, unbreakable
footing *noun* 1 BASIS, foundation, groundwork
2 RELATIONSHIP, grade, position, rank, standing, status
footstep *noun* STEP, footfall, tread
forage *verb* 1 SEARCH, cast about, explore, hunt, rummage, scour, seek
▷ *noun* 2 (*cattle, etc.*) FODDER, feed, food, provender
foray *noun* RAID, incursion, inroad, invasion, sally, sortie, swoop
forbear *verb* REFRAIN, abstain, cease, desist, hold back, keep from, restrain oneself, stop
forbearance *noun* PATIENCE, long-suffering, moderation, resignation, restraint, self-control, temperance, tolerance
forbearing *adjective* PATIENT, forgiving, indulgent, lenient, long-suffering, merciful, moderate, tolerant
forbid *verb* PROHIBIT, ban, disallow, exclude, outlaw, preclude, rule out, veto
forbidden *adjective* PROHIBITED, banned, outlawed, out of bounds, proscribed, taboo, vetoed
forbidding *adjective* THREATENING, daunting, frightening, hostile, menacing, ominous, sinister, unfriendly
force *noun* 1 POWER, energy, impulse, might, momentum, pressure, strength, vigor
2 COMPULSION, arm-twisting (*informal*), coercion,

compulsion 3 that which tends to produce a change in a physical system 4 mental or moral strength 5 body of troops, police, etc. 6 group of people organized for particular task or duty 7 effectiveness, operative state 8 violence ▷ *verb transitive* **forced, forc•ing** 9 constrain, compel 10 produce by effort, strength 11 break open 12 urge, strain 13 drive 14 hasten maturity of > **forced** *adjective* 1 accomplished by great effort 2 compulsory 3 unnatural 4 strained 5 excessive > **force'ful** *adjective* powerful, persuasive > **for'ci•ble** *adjective* 1 done by force 2 efficacious, compelling, impressive 3 strong > **for'ci•bly** *adverb*

for•ceps [FOR-səps] *plural noun* surgical pincers

ford *noun* shallow place where river may be crossed ▷ *verb transitive* > **ford'a•ble** *adjective*

fore[1] [for] *adjective* 1 in front ▷ *noun* 2 front part

fore[2] *interjection* golfer's warning

fore- *prefix* 1 before in time or rank: *forefather* 2 at the front: *forecourt*

fore-and-aft [FOR-ənd-AFT] *adjective* placed in line from bow to stern of ship

fore•arm [FOR-ahrm] *noun* 1 arm between wrist and elbow ▷ *verb transitive* [for-AHRM] 2 arm beforehand

fore•bear [FOR-bair] *noun* ancestor

fore•bode [for-BOHD] *verb transitive* **-bod•ed, -bod•ing** indicate in advance > **foreboding** *noun* anticipation of evil

fore•cast [FOR-kast] *verb transitive* 1 estimate beforehand (esp. weather) 2 prophesy ▷ *noun* 3 prediction

fore•castle [FOHK-səl] *noun* 1 forward raised part of ship 2 sailors' quarters

fore•close [for-KLOHZ] *verb transitive* **-closed, -clos•ing** 1 take away power of redeeming (mortgage) 2 prevent, shut out, bar > **fore•clo'sure** [-*zhər*] *noun*

fore•court [FOR-kort] *noun* 1 courtyard, open space, in front of building 2 *tennis* part of court between service line and net

fore•fa•ther [FOR-fah-*thər*] *noun* ancestor

fore•fin•ger [FOR-fing-gər] *noun* finger next to thumb, index finger

foregather *see* **forgather**

fore•go [for-GOH] *verb transitive* **-went, -gone, -go•ing** precede in time, place > **foregoing** *adjective* going before, preceding > **foregone** *adjective* 1 determined beforehand 2 preceding > **foregone conclusion** result that might have been foreseen

fore•ground [FOR-grownd] *noun* part of view, esp. in picture, nearest observer

fore•hand [FOR-hand] *adjective* of stroke in racquet games made with inner side of wrist leading

fore•head [FOR-id] *noun* part of face above eyebrows and between temples

for•eign [FOR-in] *adjective* 1 not of, or in, one's own country 2 relating to, or connected with other countries 3 irrelevant 4 coming from outside 5 unfamiliar, strange > **for'eign•er** *noun*

fore•man [FOR-mən] *noun, plural* **-men** 1 one in charge of work 2 leader of jury

fore•mast [FOR-mast] *noun* mast nearest bow

fore•most [FOR-mohst] *adjective, adverb* first in time, place, importance, etc.

fore•noon [FOR-noon] *noun* morning

fo•ren•sic [fə-REN-sik] *adjective* of courts of law > **forensic medicine** application of medical knowledge in legal matters

fore•play [FOR-play] *noun* sexual stimulation before intercourse

fore•run•ner [FOR-run-ər] *noun* one that goes before, precursor

fore•see [for-SEE] *verb transitive* **-saw, -seen, -see•ing** see beforehand

fore•shad•ow [for-SHAD-oh] *verb transitive* show, suggest beforehand, be a type of

fore•short•en [for-SHOR-tn] *verb transitive* 1 draw (object) so that it appears shortened 2 make shorter

f DICTIONARY THESAURUS

constraint, duress, pressure, violence
3 INTENSITY, emphasis, fierceness, vehemence, vigor
4 ARMY, host, legion, patrol, regiment, squad, troop, unit
5 ▷ **in force** a VALID, binding, current, effective, in operation, operative, working b IN GREAT NUMBERS, all together, in full strength
▷ *verb* 6 COMPEL, coerce, constrain, dragoon, drive, impel, make, oblige, press, pressurize
7 BREAK OPEN, blast, prise, wrench, wrest
8 PUSH, propel, thrust

forced *adjective* 1 COMPULSORY, conscripted, enforced, involuntary, mandatory, obligatory
2 FALSE, affected, artificial, contrived, insincere, labored, stiff, strained, unnatural, wooden

forceful *adjective* POWERFUL, cogent, compelling, convincing, dynamic, effective, persuasive

forcible *adjective* 1 VIOLENT, aggressive, armed, coercive, compulsory
2 STRONG, compelling, energetic, forceful, potent, powerful, weighty

forebear *noun* ANCESTOR, father, forefather, forerunner, predecessor

foreboding *noun* DREAD, anxiety, apprehension, apprehensiveness, chill, fear, misgiving, premonition, presentiment

forecast *verb* 1 PREDICT, anticipate, augur, divine, foresee, foretell, prophesy
▷ *noun* 2 PREDICTION, conjecture, guess, prognosis, prophecy

forefather *noun* ANCESTOR, father, forebear, forerunner, predecessor

forefront *noun* LEAD, center, fore, foreground, front, prominence, spearhead, vanguard

foregoing *adjective* PRECEDING, above, antecedent, anterior, former, previous, prior

foreign *adjective* ALIEN, exotic, external, imported, remote, strange, unfamiliar, unknown

foreigner *noun* ALIEN, immigrant, incomer, stranger

foremost *adjective* LEADING, chief, cutting-edge, highest, paramount, pre-eminent, primary, prime, principal, supreme

forerunner *noun* PRECURSOR, envoy, harbinger, herald, prototype

foresee *verb* ANTICIPATE, envisage, forecast, foretell, predict, prophesy

foreshadow *verb* PREDICT, augur, forebode, indicate, portend, prefigure, presage, promise, signal

fore•sight [FOR-sīt] *noun* 1 foreseeing 2 care for future
fore•skin [FOR-skin] *noun* skin that covers end of penis
for•est [FOR-ist] *noun* 1 area with heavy growth of trees and plants 2 these trees 3 something resembling forest ▷ *verb transitive* 4 plant, create forest (in an area) > **for'est•er** *noun* one skilled in forestry > **for'est•ry** *noun* study, management of forest planting and maintenance
fore•stall [for-STAWL] *verb transitive* 1 anticipate 2 prevent, guard against in advance
fore•taste [FOR-tayst] *noun* 1 anticipation 2 taste beforehand
fore•tell [for-TEL] *verb transitive* **-told, -tel•ling** prophesy
fore•thought [FOR-thawt] *noun* thoughtful consideration of future events
for•ev•er [for-EV-ər] *adverb* 1 always 2 eternally 3 (*informal*) for a long time
fore•warn [for-WORN] *verb transitive* warn, caution in advance
forewent *see* **forego**
fore•word [FOR-wurd] *noun* preface
for•feit [FOR-fit] *noun* 1 thing lost by crime or fault 2 penalty, fine ▷ *adjective* 3 lost by crime or fault ▷ *verb transitive* 4 lose by penalty > **for'fei•ture** [-fi-chər] *noun*
for•gath•er [for-GATH-ər] *verb intransitive* meet together, assemble, associate
forge[1] [forj] *noun* 1 place where metal is worked, smithy 2 furnace, workshop for melting or refining metal ▷ *verb transitive* **forged, forg•ing** 3 shape (metal) by heating in fire and hammering 4 make, shape, invent 5 make a fraudulent imitation of thing 6 counterfeit > **forg'er** *noun* > **for'ger•y** *noun, plural* **-ger•ies** 1 forged artwork, document, currency, etc. 2 the making of it
forge[2] *verb intransitive* **forged, forg•ing** advance steadily
for•get [fər-GET] *verb transitive* **-got, -got•ten** *or* **-got, -get•ting** lose memory of, neglect, overlook > **for•get'ful** *adjective* liable to forget
for•give [fər-GIV] *verb* **-gave, -giv•en, -giv•ing** 1 cease to blame or hold resentment against 2 pardon > **for•give'ness** *noun*
for•go [for-GOH] *verb transitive* **-went, -gone, -go•ing** 1 go without 2 give up
forgot, forgotten *see* **forget**
fork *noun* 1 pronged instrument for eating food 2 pronged tool for digging or lifting 3 division into branches 4 point of this division 5 one of the branches ▷ *verb intransitive* 6 branch ▷ *verb transitive* 7 dig, lift, throw, with fork 8 make fork-shaped > **fork out** (*informal*) pay (reluctantly)
for•lorn' *adjective* 1 forsaken 2 desperate > **forlorn hope** anything undertaken with little hope of success
form *noun* 1 shape, visible appearance 2 visible person or animal 3 structure 4 nature 5 species, kind 6 regularly drawn up document, esp. printed one with blanks for particulars 7 condition, good condition 8 customary way of

DICTIONARY • THESAURUS

---

foresight *noun* ANTICIPATION, far-sightedness, forethought, precaution, preparedness, prescience, prudence
foretell *verb* PREDICT, forecast, forewarn, presage, prognosticate, prophesy
forethought *noun* ANTICIPATION, far-sightedness, foresight, precaution, providence, provision, prudence
forever *adverb* 1 EVERMORE, always, for all time, for keeps, in perpetuity, till Doomsday, till the cows come home (*informal*)
2 CONSTANTLY, all the time, continually, endlessly, eternally, incessantly, interminably, perpetually, twenty-four-seven (*slang*), unremittingly
forewarn *verb* CAUTION, advise, alert, apprise, give fair warning, put on guard, tip off
forfeit *noun* 1 PENALTY, damages, fine, forfeiture, loss
▷ *verb* 2 LOSE, be deprived of, be stripped of, give up, relinquish, renounce, say good-bye to, surrender
forge *verb* 1 CREATE, construct, devise, fashion, form, frame, make, mold, shape, work
2 FALSIFY, copy, counterfeit, fake, feign, imitate
forgery *noun* 1 FRAUDULENCE, coining, counterfeiting, falsification, fraudulent imitation
2 FAKE, counterfeit, falsification, imitation, phoney *or* phony (*informal*), sham
forget *verb* NEGLECT, leave behind, lose sight of, omit, overlook
forgetful *adjective* ABSENT-MINDED, careless, inattentive, neglectful, oblivious, unmindful, vague
forgive *verb* EXCUSE, absolve, acquit, condone, exonerate, let bygones be bygones, let off (*informal*), pardon
forgiveness *noun* PARDON, absolution, acquittal, amnesty, exoneration, mercy, remission
forgiving *adjective* MERCIFUL, clement, compassionate, forbearing, lenient, magnanimous, soft-hearted, tolerant
forgo *verb* GIVE UP, abandon, do without, relinquish, renounce, resign, surrender, waive, yield
forgotten *adjective* LEFT BEHIND, bygone, lost, omitted, past, past recall, unremembered
fork *verb* BRANCH, bifurcate, diverge, divide, part, split
forked *adjective* BRANCHING, angled, bifurcate *or* bifurcated, branched, divided, pronged, split, zigzag
forlorn *adjective* MISERABLE, disconsolate, down in the dumps (*informal*), helpless, hopeless, pathetic, pitiful, unhappy, woebegone, wretched
form *noun* 1 SHAPE, appearance, configuration, formation, pattern, structure
2 TYPE, kind, sort, style, variety
3 CONDITION, fettle, fitness, health, shape, trim
4 PROCEDURE, convention, custom, etiquette, protocol
5 DOCUMENT, application, paper, sheet
6 CLASS, grade, rank
▷ *verb* 7 MAKE, build, construct, create, fashion, forge, mold, produce, shape
8 ARRANGE, combine, draw up, organize
9 TAKE SHAPE, appear, become visible, come into being, crystallize, grow, materialize, rise
10 DEVELOP, acquire, contract, cultivate, pick up

doing things **9** set order of words **10** *printing* frame for type ▷ *verb transitive* **11** shape, mold, arrange, organize **12** train, shape in the mind, conceive **13** go to make up, make part of ▷ *verb intransitive* **14** come into existence or shape > **for•ma'tion** *noun* **1** forming **2** thing formed **3** structure, shape, arrangement **4** military order > **form'a•tive** *adjective* **1** of, relating to, development **2** serving or tending to form **3** used in forming > **form'less** *adjective*

for•mal [FOR-məl] *adjective* **1** ceremonial, according to rule **2** of outward form or routine **3** of, for, formal occasions **4** according to rule that does not matter **5** precise **6** stiff ▷ *noun* **7** formal dance > **for'mal•ism** *noun* **1** quality of being formal **2** exclusive concern for form, structure, technique in an activity > **for•mal'i•ty** *noun, plural* **-ties** **1** observance required by custom or etiquette **2** condition or quality of being formal **3** conformity to custom **4** conventionality, mere form **5** in art, precision, stiffness, as opposed to originality

for•mal•de•hyde [for-MAL-də-hīd] *noun* colorless, poisonous, pungent gas, used in making antiseptics and in chemistry > **for'ma•lin** [-mə-lin] *noun* solution of formaldehyde in water, used as disinfectant, preservative, etc.

for'mat *noun* **1** size and shape of book **2** organization of TV show, etc.

for•mer [FOR-mər] *adjective* **1** earlier in time **2** of past times **3** first named ▷ *pronoun* **4** first named thing or person or fact > **for'mer•ly** *adverb* previously

for•mi•da•ble [FOR-mi-də-bəl] *adjective* **1** to be feared **2** overwhelming, terrible, redoubtable **3** likely to be difficult, serious > **for'mi•da•bly** *adverb*

for•mu•la [FOR-myə-lə] *noun, plural* **-las** *or* **-lae** [-lee] **1** set form of words setting forth principle, method or rule for doing, producing something **2** substance so prepared **3** specific category of racing car **4** recipe **5** group of numbers, letters, or symbols expressing a scientific or mathematical rule > **for'mu•late** [-layt] *verb transitive* **-lat•ed, -lat•ing** **1** reduce to, express in formula, or in definite form **2** devise > **for•mu•la'tion** *noun*

for•ni•ca•tion [for-ni-KAY-shən] *noun* sexual intercourse outside marriage > **for'ni•cate** *verb intransitive* **-cat•ed, -cat•ing**

for•sake [for-SAYK] *verb transitive* **-sook, -sak•en, -sak•ing** **1** abandon, desert **2** give up

for•sooth' *adverb* (*obsolete*) in truth

for•swear [for-SWAIR] *verb transitive* **-swore, -sworn, -swear•ing** **1** renounce, deny **2** *verb reflexive* perjure

for•syth•i•a [for-SITH-ee-ə] *noun* widely cultivated shrub with yellow flowers

fort *noun* fortified place, stronghold

forte[1] [fort] *noun* one's strong point, that in which one excels

for•te[2] [FOR-tay] *adverb mus.* loudly > **for•tis'si•mo** *adverb mus.* very loudly

forth *adverb* onward, into view > **forth•com'ing** *adjective* **1** about to come **2** ready when wanted **3** willing to talk, communicative > **forth•with'** *adverb* at once, immediately

forth•right [FORTH-rīt] *adjective* **1** direct **2** outspoken

fortieth *see* **four**

for•ti•fy [FOR-tə-fī] *verb transitive* **-fied, -fy•ing** **1**

DICTIONARY **f** THESAURUS

11 CONSTITUTE, compose, comprise, make up

formal *adjective* **1** OFFICIAL, ceremonial, ritualistic, solemn
2 CONVENTIONAL, affected, correct, precise, stiff, unbending

formality *noun* **1** CONVENTION, custom, procedure, red tape, rite, ritual
2 CORRECTNESS, decorum, etiquette, protocol

format *noun* STYLE, appearance, arrangement, construction, form, layout, look, make-up, plan, type

formation *noun* **1** ESTABLISHMENT, constitution, development, forming, generation, genesis, manufacture, production
2 PATTERN, arrangement, configuration, design, grouping, structure

formative *adjective* DEVELOPMENTAL, influential

former *adjective* PREVIOUS, earlier, erstwhile, one-time, prior

formerly *adverb* PREVIOUSLY, at one time, before, lately, once

formidable *adjective* **1** INTIMIDATING, daunting, dismaying, fearful, frightful, menacing, terrifying, threatening
2 IMPRESSIVE, awesome, cool (*informal*), great, mighty, phat (*slang*), powerful, redoubtable, terrific (*informal*), tremendous

formula *noun* METHOD, blueprint, precept, principle, procedure, recipe, rule

formulate *verb* **1** DEFINE, detail, express, frame, give form to, set down, specify, systematize
2 DEVISE, develop, forge, invent, map out, originate, plan, work out

forsake *verb* **1** DESERT, abandon, disown, leave in the lurch, strand
2 GIVE UP, forgo, relinquish, renounce, set aside, surrender, yield

forsaken *adjective* DESERTED, abandoned, disowned, forlorn, left in the lurch, marooned, outcast, stranded

fort *noun* **1** FORTRESS, blockhouse, camp, castle, citadel, fortification, garrison, stronghold
2 ▷ **hold the fort** STAND IN, carry on, keep things on an even keel, take over the reins

forte *noun* SPECIALITY, gift, métier, strength, strong point, talent

forth *adverb* FORWARD, ahead, away, onward, out, outward

forthcoming *adjective* **1** APPROACHING, coming, expected, future, imminent, impending, prospective, upcoming
2 ACCESSIBLE, at hand, available, in evidence, obtainable, on tap (*informal*), ready
3 COMMUNICATIVE, chatty, expansive, free, informative, open, sociable, talkative, unreserved

forthright *adjective* OUTSPOKEN, blunt, candid, direct, frank, open, plain-spoken, straightforward, upfront (*informal*)

forthwith *adverb* AT ONCE, directly, immediately, instantly, quickly, right away, straightaway, without delay

fortification *noun* **1** DEFENSE, bastion, fastness, fort, fortress, protection, stronghold

strengthen 2 provide with defensive works
> **for•ti•fi•ca'tion** *noun*
for•ti•tude [FOR-ti-tood] *noun* courage in adversity or pain, endurance
fort•night [FORT-nīt] *noun* two weeks
> **fort'night•ly** *adverb*
FORTRAN [FOR-tran] *computing* a programming language for mathematical and scientific purposes
for•tress [FOR-tris] *noun* large fort or fortified town
for•tu•i•tous [for-TOO-i-təs] *adjective* accidental, by chance > **for•tu'i•tous•ly** *adverb*
for•tune [FOR-chən] *noun* 1 good luck, prosperity 2 wealth 3 stock of wealth 4 chance, luck > **for'tu•nate** [-nit] *adjective* > **for'tu•nate•ly** *adverb* > **fortune hunter** person seeking fortune, esp. by marriage > **fortuneteller** *noun* one who predicts a person's future
forty *see* **four**
fo•rum [FOR-əm] *noun* (place or medium for) meeting, assembly for open discussion or debate
for•ward [FOR-wərd] *adjective* 1 lying in front of 2 onward 3 presumptuous, impudent 4 advanced, progressive 5 relating to the future ▷ *noun* 6 player placed in forward position in various team games, e.g. basketball ▷ *adverb* 7 toward the future 8 toward the front, to the front, into view 9 at, in fore part of ship 10 onward, so as to make progress ▷ *verb transitive* 11 help forward 12 send, dispatch > **for'ward•ly** *adverb* pertly > **for'ward•ness** *noun* > **for'wards** [-wərdz] *adverb* > **forward slash** forward-sloping diagonal mark (/)
forwent *see* **forgo**
fos•sil [FOS-əl] *noun* 1 remnant or impression of animal or plant, esp. prehistoric one, preserved in earth 2 (*informal*) person, idea, etc. that is outdated and incapable of change > **fos'sil•ize** *verb* **-ized, -iz•ing** 1 turn into fossil 2 petrify
fos•ter [FAW-stər] *verb transitive* 1 promote growth or development of 2 bring up child, esp. not one's own ▷ *adjective* 3 of or involved in fostering a child: *foster parents*
fought *pt./pp. of* **fight**
foul [fowl] *adjective* **-er, -est** 1 loathsome, offensive 2 stinking 3 dirty 4 unfair 5 wet, rough 6 obscene, disgustingly abusive 7 charged with harmful matter, clogged, choked ▷ *noun* 8 act of unfair play 9 the breaking of a rule ▷ *adverb* 10 unfairly ▷ *verb* (*mainly transitive*) 11 make, become foul 12 jam 13 collide with > **foul'ly** *adverb*
found[1] [fownd] *pt./pp. of* **find**
found[2] *verb transitive* 1 establish, institute 2 lay base of 3 base, ground > **foun•da'tion** *noun* 1 basis 2 base, lowest part of building 3 founding 4 endowed institution, etc. > **found'er** *noun* > **foundation stone** one of stones forming foundation of building, esp. stone laid with public ceremony
found[3] *verb transitive* 1 melt and run into mold 2 cast > **found'er** *noun* > **found'ry** *noun, plural* **-ries** 1 place for casting 2 art of this
found•er [FOWN-dər] *verb intransitive* 1 collapse 2 sink 3 become stuck as in mud, etc.
found•ling [FOWND-ling] *noun* deserted infant
fount [fownt] *noun* fountain

DICTIONARY • THESAURUS

2 STRENGTHENING, reinforcement
fortify *verb* STRENGTHEN, augment, buttress, protect, reinforce, shore up, support
fortitude *noun* COURAGE, backbone, bravery, fearlessness, grit, perseverance, resolution, strength, valor
fortress *noun* CASTLE, citadel, fastness, fort, redoubt, stronghold
fortunate *adjective* 1 LUCKY, favored, in luck, successful, well-off
2 FAVORABLE, advantageous, convenient, expedient, felicitous, fortuitous, helpful, opportune, providential, timely, win-win (*informal*)
fortunately *adverb* LUCKILY, by a happy chance, by good luck, happily, providentially
fortune *noun* 1 WEALTH, affluence, opulence, possessions, property, prosperity, riches, treasure
2 LUCK, chance, destiny, fate, kismet, providence
3 ▷ **fortunes** DESTINY, adventures, experiences, history, lot, success
forward *adjective* 1 LEADING, advance, first, foremost, front, head
2 PRESUMPTUOUS, bold, brash, brazen, cheeky, familiar, impertinent, impudent, pushy (*informal*)
3 WELL-DEVELOPED, advanced, precocious, premature
▷ *adverb* 4 AHEAD, forth, on, onward
▷ *verb* 5 PROMOTE, advance, assist, expedite, further, hasten, hurry
6 SEND, dispatch, post, send on
foster *verb* 1 PROMOTE, cultivate, encourage, feed, nurture, stimulate, support, uphold
2 BRING UP, mother, nurse, raise, rear, take care of
foul *adjective* 1 DIRTY, fetid, filthy, funky (*slang*), malodorous, nauseating, putrid, repulsive, scuzzy (*slang*), squalid, stinking, unclean
2 OBSCENE, abusive, blue, coarse, indecent, lewd, profane, scurrilous, vulgar
3 OFFENSIVE, abhorrent, despicable, detestable, disgraceful, lousy (*slang*), scandalous, scuzzy (*slang*), shameful, wicked
4 UNFAIR, crooked, dishonest, fraudulent, shady (*informal*), underhand, unscrupulous
▷ *verb* 5 POLLUTE, besmirch, contaminate, defile, dirty, stain, sully, taint
found *verb* ESTABLISH, constitute, create, inaugurate, institute, organize, originate, set up, start
foundation *noun* 1 GROUNDWORK, base, basis, bedrock, bottom, footing, substructure, underpinning
2 SETTING UP, endowment, establishment, inauguration, institution, organization, settlement
founder[1] *noun* INITIATOR, architect, author, beginner, father, inventor, originator
founder[2] *verb* 1 SINK, be lost, go down, go to the bottom, submerge
2 FAIL, break down, collapse, come to grief, come unstuck, fall through, miscarry, misfire
3 STUMBLE, lurch, sprawl, stagger, trip
foundling *noun* STRAY, orphan, outcast, waif

foun•tain [FOWN-tn] *noun* 1 jet of water, esp. ornamental one 2 spring 3 source > **foun'tain•head** [-hed] *noun* source > **fountain pen** pen with ink reservoir

four [for] *noun, adjective* cardinal number next after three > **fourth** *adjective* the ordinal number > **fourth'ly** *adverb* > **for'ti•eth** *adjective* > **for'ty** *adjective, noun, plural* **-ties** four tens > **four'teen'** *noun, adjective* four plus ten > **four•teenth'** *adjective* > **four-stroke** *adjective* describing an internal-combustion engine firing once every four strokes of piston > **four'post•er** *noun* bed with four posts for curtains, etc. > **four'some** *noun* 1 group of four people 2 game or dance for four people > **four'square** *adjective* firm, steady **on all fours** on hands and knees > **401K** employer-run savings plan for retirement

fowl *noun* 1 domestic rooster or hen 2 bird, its flesh ▷ *verb intransitive* 3 hunt wild birds > **fowling piece** shotgun for fowling

fox [foks] *noun* 1 red bushy-tailed animal 2 its fur 3 cunning person ▷ *verb transitive* 4 perplex 5 discolor (paper) with brown spots 6 mislead ▷ *verb intransitive* 7 act craftily 8 sham > **fox'y** *adjective* **fox•i•er, fox•i•est** 1 foxlike 2 (*slang*) sexually appealing 3 attractive > **fox'hole** *noun* in war, small trench giving protection > **fox'hound** *noun* dog bred for hunting foxes > **fox terrier** small dog now mainly kept as a pet > **fox'trot** *noun* (music for) ballroom dance ▷ *verb*

foy•er [FOI-ər] *noun* 1 entrance hall in theaters, hotels, etc. 2 vestibule

Fr *chem.* francium

fra•cas [FRAY-kəs] *noun* 1 noisy quarrel 2 uproar, brawl

frac•tion [FRAK-shən] *noun* 1 numerical quantity not an integer 2 fragment, piece > **frac'tion•al** *adjective* 1 constituting a fraction 2 forming but a small part 3 insignificant

frac•tious [FRAK-shəs] *adjective* unruly, irritable

frac•ture [FRAK-chər] *noun* 1 breakage, part broken 2 breaking of bone 3 breach, rupture ▷ *verb* **-tured, -tur•ing** 4 break

frag•ile [FRAJ-əl] *adjective* 1 breakable 2 frail 3 delicate > **fra•gil'i•ty** *noun*

frag•ment [FRAG-mənt] *noun* 1 piece broken off 2 small portion, incomplete part ▷ *verb* (-MENT) > **frag'men•tar•y** [-te-ree] *adjective*

fra•grant [FRAY-grənt] *adjective* sweet-smelling > **fra'grance** *noun* scent

frail [frayl] *adjective* **-er, -est** 1 fragile, delicate 2 infirm 3 in weak health 4 morally weak > **frail'ly** *adverb* > **frail'ty** *noun, plural* **-ties**

frame [fraym] *noun* 1 that in which thing is set, as square of wood around picture, etc. 2 structure 3 build of body 4 constitution 5 mood 6 individual exposure on strip of film ▷ *verb transitive* 7 put together, make 8 adapt 9 put into words 10 put into frame 11 bring false charge against > **frame-up** *noun* (*informal*) plot, manufactured evidence > **frame'work** *noun* 1 structure into which completing parts can be fitted 2 supporting work

franc [frangk] *noun* monetary unit of Switzerland and (formerly) France

fran•chise [FRAN-chīz] *noun* 1 right of voting 2 citizenship 3 privilege or right, esp. right to sell certain goods ▷ *verb* **-chised, -chis•ing**

fran•gi•pane [FRAN-jə-payn] *noun* 1 type of pastry cake 2 its filling

fran•gi•pan•i [fran-jə-PAN-ee] *noun* 1 tropical American shrub 2 perfume made of its flower

frank [frangk] *adjective* **-er, -est** 1 candid, outspoken 2 sincere ▷ *noun* 3 official mark on letter either canceling stamp or ensuring delivery without stamp ▷ *verb transitive* 4 mark letter thus > **frank'ly** *adverb* candidly > **frank'ness** *noun*

---

fountain *noun* 1 JET, font, fount, reservoir, spout, spray, spring, well
2 SOURCE, cause, derivation, fount, fountainhead, origin, wellspring

foyer *noun* ENTRANCE HALL, antechamber, anteroom, lobby, reception area, vestibule

fracas *noun* BRAWL, affray (*law*), disturbance, melee *or* mêlée, riot, rumpus, scuffle, skirmish

fraction *noun* PIECE, part, percentage, portion, section, segment, share, slice

fractious *adjective* IRRITABLE, captious, cross, petulant, querulous, refractory, testy, tetchy, touchy

fracture *noun* 1 BREAK, cleft, crack, fissure, opening, rift, rupture, split
▷ *verb* 2 BREAK, crack, rupture, splinter, split

fragile *adjective* DELICATE, breakable, brittle, dainty, fine, flimsy, frail, frangible, weak

fragment *noun* 1 PIECE, bit, chip, particle, portion, scrap, shred, sliver
▷ *verb* 2 BREAK, break up, come apart, come to pieces, crumble, disintegrate, shatter, splinter, split up

fragmentary *adjective* INCOMPLETE, bitty, broken, disconnected, incoherent, partial, piecemeal, scattered, scrappy, sketchy

fragrance *noun* SCENT, aroma, balm, bouquet, fragrancy, perfume, redolence, smell, sweet odor

fragrant *adjective* PERFUMED, aromatic, balmy, odorous, redolent, sweet-scented, sweet-smelling

frail *adjective* WEAK, delicate, feeble, flimsy, fragile, infirm, insubstantial, puny, vulnerable

frailty *noun* FEEBLENESS, fallibility, frailness, infirmity, susceptibility, weakness

frame *noun* 1 CASING, construction, framework, shell, structure
2 PHYSIQUE, anatomy, body, build, carcass
3 ▷ **frame of mind** MOOD, attitude, disposition, humor, outlook, state, temper
▷ *verb* 4 CONSTRUCT, assemble, build, make, manufacture, put together
5 DRAFT, compose, devise, draw up, formulate, map out, sketch
6 MOUNT, case, enclose, surround

framework *noun* STRUCTURE, foundation, frame, groundwork, plan, shell, skeleton, the bare bones

frank *adjective* HONEST, blunt, candid, direct, forthright, open, outspoken, plain-spoken, sincere, straightforward, truthful

frankly *adverb* 1 HONESTLY, candidly, in truth, to be honest
2 OPENLY, bluntly, directly, freely, plainly, without reserve

frankness *noun* OUTSPOKENNESS, bluntness, candor, forthrightness, openness, plain speaking, truthfulness

frank•furt•er [FRANGK-fər-tər] *noun* smoked sausage, hot dog
frank•in•cense [FRANG-kin-sens] *noun* aromatic gum resin burned as incense
fran•tic [FRAN-tik] *adjective* **1** distracted with rage, grief, joy, etc. **2** frenzied > **fran'ti•cal•ly** *adverb*
fra•ter•nal [frə-TUR-nl] *adjective* of brother, brotherly > **fra•ter'nal•ly** *adverb* > **fra•ter'ni•ty** *noun, plural* **-ties** **1** brotherliness **2** brotherhood **3** college society > **frat•er•ni•za'tion** *noun* > **frat'er•nize** *verb intransitive* **-nized, -niz•ing** to associate, make friends > **frat•ri•cid'al** [-SĪD-əl] *adjective* > **frat'ri•cide** *noun* killing, killer of brother or sister
fraud [frawd] *noun* **1** criminal deception **2** swindle, imposture > **fraud•u•lence** [FRAW-jə-ləns] *noun* > **fraud'u•lent** *adjective*
fraught [frawt] *adjective* filled (with), involving
fray[1] *noun* **1** fight **2** noisy quarrel
fray[2] *verb* **1** wear through by rubbing **2** make, become ragged at edge
fraz•zle [FRAZ-əl] (*informal*) ▷ *verb* **-zled, -zling** **1** make or become exhausted **2** make or become irritated ▷ *noun* **3** exhausted state
freak [freek] *noun* abnormal person, animal, thing ▷ *adjective* > **freak'ish** *adjective* > **freak'y** *adjective* **freak•i•er, freak•i•est** > **freak out** (*slang*) (cause to) hallucinate, be wildly excited, etc.
freck•le [FREK-əl] *noun* **1** light brown spot on skin, esp. caused by sun **2** any small spot ▷ *verb* **-led, -ling** **3** bring, come out in freckles
free *adjective* **fre•er, fre•est** **1** able to act at will, not under compulsion or restraint **2** not restricted or affected by **3** not subject to cost or tax **4** independent **5** not exact or literal **6** generous **7** not in use **8** (of person) not occupied, having no appointment **9** loose, not fixed ▷ *verb transitive* **freed, free•ing** set at liberty **10** remove (obstacles, pain, etc.) **11** rid (of) > **free'dom** *noun* > **free'ly** *adverb* > **free-for-all** *noun* brawl > **free'hand** *adjective* drawn without guiding instruments > **free'lance** [-lans] *adjective, noun* (of) self-employed, unattached person > **Free•ma•son** [-may-sən] *noun* member of secret fraternity for mutual help > **freemasonry** *noun* **1** principles of Freemasons **2** fellowship, secret brotherhood > **free'-range** *adjective* (of livestock and poultry) kept, produced in natural, nonintensive conditions > **free space** region that has no gravitational and electromagnetic fields > **free speech** right to express opinions publicly > **free-swinging** *adjective* recklessly daring > **free•think'er** *noun* skeptic who forms own opinions, esp. in religion > **free trade** international trade free of protective tariffs > **free'way** *noun* express highway
freeze [freez] *verb* **froze, fro•zen, freez•ing** **1** change (by reduction of temperature) from liquid to solid, as water to ice ▷ *verb transitive* **2** preserve (food, etc.) by extreme cold, as in freezer **3** fix (prices, etc.) ▷ *verb intransitive* **4** feel very cold **5** become rigid as with fear **6** stop > **freez'er** *noun* insulated cabinet for long-term storage of perishable foodstuffs > **frozen** *adjective* of assets, etc., unrealizable > **freezing point** temperature at which liquid becomes solid
freight [frayt] *noun* **1** commercial transport (esp. by rail, ship) **2** cost of this **3** goods so carried ▷ *verb transitive* **4** send as or by freight > **freight'er** *noun*

DICTIONARY • THESAURUS

frantic *adjective* **1** FURIOUS, at the end of one's tether, berserk, beside oneself, distracted, distraught, wild
2 HECTIC, desperate, fraught (*informal*), frenetic, frenzied
fraternity *noun* **1** CLUB, association, brotherhood, circle, company, guild, league, union
2 COMPANIONSHIP, brotherhood, camaraderie, fellowship, kinship
fraternize *verb* ASSOCIATE, consort, cooperate, hobnob, keep company, mingle, mix, socialize
fraud *noun* **1** DECEPTION, back-stabbing (*informal*), chicanery, deceit, double-dealing, duplicity, sharp practice, swindling, treachery, trickery
2 IMPOSTOR, charlatan, fake, fraudster, hoaxer, phoney *or* phony (*informal*), pretender, swindler
fraudulent *adjective* DECEITFUL, crooked (*informal*), dishonest, double-dealing, duplicitous, sham, swindling, treacherous
fray *verb* WEAR THIN, chafe, rub, wear
freak *noun* **1** ODDITY, aberration, anomaly, malformation, monstrosity, weirdo *or* weirdie (*informal*)
2 ENTHUSIAST, addict, aficionado, buff (*informal*), devotee, fan, fanatic, fiend (*informal*), nut (*slang*)
▷ *adjective* **3** ABNORMAL, exceptional, unparalleled, unusual
free *adjective* **1** FOR NOTHING, complimentary, for free (*informal*), free of charge, gratis, gratuitous, on the house, unpaid, without charge
2 AT LIBERTY, at large, footloose, independent, liberated, loose, on the loose, unfettered
3 ALLOWED, able, clear, permitted, unimpeded, unrestricted
4 AVAILABLE, empty, idle, spare, unemployed, unoccupied, unused, vacant
5 GENEROUS, lavish, liberal, unsparing, unstinting
▷ *verb* **6** RELEASE, deliver, let out, liberate, loose, set free, turn loose, unchain, untie
7 EXTRICATE, cut loose, disengage, disentangle, rescue
freedom *noun* **1** LIBERTY, deliverance, emancipation, independence, release
2 OPPORTUNITY, a blank check, carte blanche, discretion, free rein, latitude, license
free-for-all *noun* FIGHT, brawl, fracas, melee *or* mêlée, riot, row, scrimmage
freely *adverb* **1** WILLINGLY, of one's own accord, of one's own free will, spontaneously, voluntarily, without prompting
2 OPENLY, candidly, frankly, plainly, unreservedly, without reserve
3 ABUNDANTLY, amply, copiously, extravagantly, lavishly, liberally, unstintingly
freeze *verb* **1** CHILL, harden, ice over *or* ice up, stiffen
2 SUSPEND, fix, hold up, inhibit, peg, stop
freezing *adjective* ICY, arctic, biting, bitter, chill, frosty, glacial, raw, wintry
freight *noun* **1** TRANSPORTATION, carriage, conveyance, shipment
2 CARGO, burden, consignment, goods, load,

French *noun* 1 language spoken by people of France ▷ *adjective* 2 of, or pertaining to France > **French dressing** salad dressing > **French fries** deep-fried strips of potato > **French horn** musical wind instrument > **French leave** unauthorized leave > **French window** window extended to floor level and used as door

fre•net•ic [frə-NET-ik] *adjective* frenzied

fren•zy [FREN-zee] *noun, plural* **-zies** 1 violent mental derangement 2 wild excitement > **fren'zied** *adjective*

fre•quent [FREE-kwənt] *adjective* 1 happening often 2 common 3 numerous ▷ *verb transitive* [fri-KWENT] 4 go often to > **fre'quen•cy** *noun, plural* **-cies** 1 rate of occurrence 2 in radio, etc. cycles per second of alternating current > **fre•quen'ta•tive** [fri-KWEN-tə-tiv] *adjective* expressing repetition

fres•co [FRES-koh] *noun, plural* **-coes** 1 method of painting in water color on plaster of wall before it dries 2 painting done thus

fresh *adjective* **-er, -est** 1 not stale 2 new 3 additional 4 different 5 recent 6 inexperienced 7 pure 8 not pickled, frozen, etc. 9 not faded or dimmed 10 not tired 11 of wind, strong 12 (*informal*) impudent 13 forward > **fresh'en** *verb* > **fresh'et** *noun* 1 rush of water at river mouth 2 flood of river water > **fresh'ly** *adverb* > **fresh'man** *noun, plural* **-men** first-year high school or college student

fret[1] *verb* **fret•ted, fret•ting** 1 be irritated, worry ▷ *noun* 2 irritation > **fret'ful** *adjective* irritable, (easily) upset

fret[2] *noun* 1 repetitive geometrical pattern 2 small bar on fingerboard of guitar, etc. ▷ *verb transitive* **fret•ted, fret•ting** 3 ornament with carved pattern > **fret saw** saw with narrow blade and fine teeth, used for fretwork > **fret'work** *noun* carved or open woodwork in ornamental patterns and devices

Freud•i•an [FROI-dee-ən] *adjective* pert. to Austrian psychologist Sigmund Freud, or his theories

fri•a•ble [FRĪ-ə-bəl] *adjective* easily crumbled > **fri•a•bil'i•ty** *noun*

fri•ar [FRĪ-ər] *noun* member of mendicant religious order > **fri'ar•y** *noun* house of friars

fric•as•see [frik-ə-SEE] *noun* 1 dish of pieces of chicken or meat, fried or stewed and served with rich sauce ▷ *verb transitive* **-seed, -see•ing** 2 cook thus

fric•tion [FRIK-shən] *noun* 1 rubbing 2 resistance met with by body moving over another 3 clash of wills, etc., disagreement > **fric'tion•al** *adjective*

fried *pt./pp. of* **fry**

friend [frend] *noun* 1 one well known to another and regarded with affection and loyalty 2 intimate associate 3 supporter 4 (**Friend**) Quaker > **friend'less** *adjective* > **friend'li•ness** *noun* > **friend'ly** *adjective* **-li•er, -li•est** 1 having disposition of a friend, kind 2 favorable > **friend'ship** *noun* > **friendly fire** *military* shooting or bombing that injures or kills comrades or allies

frieze [freez] *noun* ornamental band, strip (on wall)

frig•ate [FRIG-it] *noun* 1 old (sailing) warship corresponding to modern cruiser 2 fast warship equipped for escort and antisubmarine duties

fright [frīt] *noun* 1 sudden fear 2 shock 3 alarm 4 grotesque or ludicrous person or thing

DICTIONARY **f** THESAURUS

---

merchandise, payload

French *adjective* GALLIC

frenzied *adjective* FURIOUS, distracted, feverish, frantic, frenetic, rabid, uncontrolled, wild

frenzy *noun* FURY, derangement, hysteria, paroxysm, passion, rage, seizure

frequent *adjective* 1 COMMON, customary, everyday, familiar, habitual, persistent, recurrent, repeated, usual
▷ *verb* 2 VISIT, attend, be found at, hang out at (*informal*), haunt, patronize

frequently *adverb* OFTEN, commonly, habitually, many times, much, not infrequently, repeatedly

fresh *adjective* 1 NEW, different, modern, novel, original, recent, up-to-date
2 ADDITIONAL, added, auxiliary, extra, further, more, other, supplementary
3 INVIGORATING, bracing, brisk, clean, cool, crisp, pure, refreshing, unpolluted
4 LIVELY, alert, energetic, keen, refreshed, sprightly, spry, vigorous
5 NATURAL, unprocessed
6 (*informal*) CHEEKY, disrespectful, familiar, forward, impudent, insolent, presumptuous

freshen *verb* REFRESH, enliven, freshen up, liven up, restore, revitalize

freshness *noun* 1 NOVELTY, inventiveness, newness, originality
2 CLEANNESS, brightness, clearness, glow, shine, sparkle, vigor, wholesomeness

fret *verb* WORRY, agonize, brood, grieve, lose sleep over, upset oneself *or* distress oneself

fretful *adjective* IRRITABLE, crotchety, edgy, fractious, querulous, short-tempered, testy, touchy, uneasy

friction *noun* 1 RUBBING, abrasion, chafing, grating, rasping, resistance, scraping
2 HOSTILITY, animosity, bad blood, conflict, disagreement, discord, dissension, resentment

friend *noun* 1 COMPANION, buddy (*informal*), chum (*informal*), comrade, homeboy (*slang*), homegirl (*slang*), pal (*informal*), playmate
2 SUPPORTER, ally, associate, patron, well-wisher

friendliness *noun* KINDLINESS, affability, amiability, congeniality, conviviality, geniality, neighborliness, sociability, warmth

friendly *adjective* SOCIABLE, affectionate, amicable, buddy-buddy (*informal*), close, familiar, helpful, intimate, neighborly, on good terms, pally (*informal*), sympathetic, welcoming

friendship *noun* GOODWILL, affection, amity, attachment, concord, familiarity, friendliness, harmony, intimacy

fright *noun* FEAR, alarm, consternation, dread, horror, panic, scare, shock, trepidation

> **fright'en** *verb transitive* cause fear, fright in > **fright'ful** *adjective* 1 terrible, calamitous 2 shocking 3 (*informal*) very great, very large > **fright'ful•ly** *adverb* (*informal*) 1 terribly 2 very

frig•id [FRIJ-id] *adjective* 1 formal, dull 2 (sexually) unfeeling 3 cold > **fri•gid'i•ty** *noun* > **frig'id•ly** *adverb*

frill *noun* 1 fluted strip of fabric gathered at one edge 2 ruff of hair, feathers around neck of dog, bird, etc. 3 fringe 4 unnecessary words, politeness 5 superfluous thing 6 adornment ▷ *verb transitive* 7 make into, decorate with frill

fringe [frinj] *noun* 1 ornamental edge of hanging threads, tassels, etc. 2 anything like this 3 edge, limit ▷ *verb transitive* **fringed, fring•ing** 4 adorn with, serve as, fringe > **fringe benefit** benefit provided in addition to pay

frip•per•y [FRIP-ə-ree] *noun, plural* **-per•ies** 1 finery 2 trivia

fris•bee [FRIZ-bee] *noun* ® disk-shaped object for throwing and catching as a sport or pastime

frisk *verb intransitive* 1 move, leap, playfully ▷ *verb transitive* 2 wave briskly 3 search (person) for concealed weapons, etc. ▷ *noun* > **frisk'y** *adjective* **frisk•i•er, frisk•i•est**

frit•ter[1] [FRIT-ər] *verb transitive* waste **fritter away** throw away, waste

fritter[2] *noun* small deep-fried cake of batter oft. containing corn

friv•o•lous [FRI-ə-ləs] *adjective* 1 not serious, unimportant 2 flippant > **fri•vol'i•ty** *noun*

frizz *verb transitive* 1 curl into small crisp curls ▷ *noun* 2 frizzed hair > **friz'zy** *adjective* **-zi•er, -zi•est**

fro [froh] *adverb* away: *to and fro*

frock [frok] *noun* 1 woman's dress 2 various similar garments ▷ *verb transitive* 3 dress with frock 4 invest with office of priest

frog[1] *noun* tailless amphibious animal developed from tadpole > **frog'man** *noun, plural* **-men** swimmer equipped for swimming, working, underwater

frog[2] *noun* 1 ornamental coat fastening of button and loop 2 (military) attachment to belt to carry sword

frol•ic [FROL-ik] *noun* 1 merrymaking ▷ *verb intransitive* **-icked, -ick•ing** 2 behave playfully > **frol'ic•some** *adjective*

from [frum] *preposition* expressing point of departure, source, distance, cause, change of state, etc.

frond *noun* plant organ consisting of stem and foliage, usually with fruit forms, esp. in ferns

front [frunt] *noun* 1 fore part 2 position directly before or ahead 3 battle line or area 4 *meteorology* dividing line between two air masses of different characteristics 5 outward aspect, bearing 6 (*informal*) something serving as a respectable cover for another, usu. criminal, activity 7 field of activity 8 group with common goal ▷ *verb* 9 look, face 10 (*informal*) be a cover for ▷ *adjective* 11 of, at, the front > **front'age** [-ij] *noun* 1 front of building 2 property line along street, lake, etc. > **fron'tal** [-əl] *adjective* > **fron'tier** [-TEER] *noun* part of country that borders on another > **fron'tis•piece** *noun* illustration facing title page of book

frost [frawst] *noun* 1 frozen dew or mist 2 act or state of freezing 3 weather in which temperature falls below point at which water turns to ice ▷ *verb* 4 cover, be covered with frost or something similar in appearance 5 give slightly roughened surface > **frost'i•ly** *adverb* > **frost'y** *adjective* **frost•i•er, frost•i•est** 1 accompanied by frost 2 chilly 3 cold 4 unfriendly > **frost'bite** *noun* destruction by cold

DICTIONARY • THESAURUS

frighten *verb* SCARE, alarm, intimidate, petrify, shock, startle, terrify, terrorize, unnerve

frightened *adjective* AFRAID, alarmed, petrified, scared, scared stiff, startled, terrified, terrorized, terror-stricken

frightening *adjective* TERRIFYING, alarming, fearful, fearsome, horrifying, menacing, scary (*informal*), shocking, unnerving

frightful *adjective* TERRIFYING, alarming, awful, dreadful, fearful, ghastly, horrendous, horrible, terrible, traumatic

frigid *adjective* 1 COLD, arctic, frosty, frozen, glacial, icy, wintry
2 FORBIDDING, aloof, austere, formal, unapproachable, unfeeling, unresponsive

frills *plural noun* TRIMMINGS, additions, bells and whistles, embellishments, extras, frippery, fuss, ornamentation, ostentation

fringe *noun* 1 BORDER, edging, hem, trimming
2 EDGE, borderline, limits, margin, outskirts, perimeter, periphery
▷ *adjective* 3 UNOFFICIAL, unconventional, unorthodox

frisk *verb* 1 FROLIC, caper, cavort, gambol, jump, play, prance, skip, trip
2 SEARCH, check, inspect, run over, shake down (*United States slang*)

frisky *adjective* LIVELY, coltish, frolicsome, high-spirited, kittenish, playful, sportive

fritter away *verb* WASTE, dissipate, idle away, misspend, run through, spend like water, squander

frivolity *noun* FUN, flippancy, frivolousness, gaiety, levity, light-heartedness, silliness, superficiality, triviality

frivolous *adjective* 1 FLIPPANT, childish, foolish, idle, juvenile, puerile, silly, superficial
2 TRIVIAL, minor, petty, shallow, trifling, unimportant

frolic *verb* 1 PLAY, caper, cavort, frisk, gambol, lark, make merry, romp, sport
▷ *noun* 2 REVEL, antic, game, lark, romp, spree

frolicsome *adjective* PLAYFUL, coltish, frisky, kittenish, lively, merry, sportive

front *noun* 1 EXTERIOR, façade, face, foreground, frontage
2 FOREFRONT, front line, head, lead, vanguard
3 DISGUISE, blind, cover, cover-up, façade, mask, pretext, show
▷ *adjective* 4 FIRST, cutting edge, foremost, head, lead, leading, topmost
▷ *verb* 5 FACE ONTO, look over *or* look into, overlook

frontier *noun* BOUNDARY, borderline, edge, limit, perimeter, verge

frost *noun* HOARFROST, freeze, rime

frosty *adjective* 1 COLD, chilly, frozen, icy, wintry
2 UNFRIENDLY, discouraging, frigid, standoffish, unenthusiastic, unwelcoming

of tissue, esp. of fingers, ears, etc.
froth [frawth] *noun* 1 collection of small bubbles, foam 2 scum 3 idle talk ▷ *verb* 4 (cause to) foam > **froth'i•ly** *adverb* > **froth'y** *adjective* **froth•i•er, froth•i•est**
frown *verb intransitive* wrinkle brows ▷ *noun*
frowz•y [FROW-zee] *adjective* **frowz•i•er, frowz•i•est** dirty, unkempt
froze *pt. of* **freeze** > **frozen** *pp. of* **freeze**
fruc•ti•fy [FRUK-tə-fī] *verb* **-fied, -fy•ing** (cause to) bear fruit
fru•gal [FROO-gəl] *adjective* 1 sparing 2 thrifty, economical 3 meager > **fru•gal'i•ty** *noun*
fruit [froot] *noun* 1 seed and its envelope, esp. edible one 2 vegetable product 3 (*usually plural*) result, benefit ▷ *verb intransitive* 4 bear fruit > **fruit'ful** [-fəl] *adjective* > **fru•i•tion** [froo-ISH-ən] *noun* 1 enjoyment 2 realization of hopes > **fruit'less** *adjective* > **fruit'y** *adjective* **fruit•i•er, fruit•i•est**
frump *noun* dowdy woman > **frump'ish** *adjective* > **frump'y** *adjective* **frump•i•er, frump•i•est**
frus•trate [FRUS-trayt] *verb transitive* **-trat•ed, -trat•ing** 1 thwart, balk 2 baffle, disappoint > **frus•tra'tion** *noun*
fry[1] [frī] *verb* **fried, fry•ing** 1 cook with fat 2 be cooked thus 3 (*slang*) be executed by electrocution
fry[2] *noun, plural* **fry** young of fish **small fry** young or insignificant beings
fuch•sia [FYOO-shə] *noun* ornamental shrub with purple-red flowers
fud•dle [FUD-l] *verb* **-dled, -dling** 1 (cause to) be intoxicated, confused ▷ *noun* 2 this state
fudge[1] [fuj] *noun* soft, variously flavored candy
fudge[2] *verb transitive* **fudged, fudg•ing** 1 make, do carelessly or dishonestly 2 fake
fuel [FYOO-əl] *noun* 1 material for burning as source of heat or power 2 something that nourishes ▷ *verb transitive* 3 provide with fuel
fu•gi•tive [FYOO-ji-tiv] *noun* 1 one who flees, esp. from arrest or pursuit ▷ *adjective* 2 fleeing, elusive
fugue [fyoog] *noun* musical composition in which themes are repeated in different parts
Füh•rer [FYUUR-ər] *noun Ger.* leader: title used by Hitler as Nazi dictator
ful•crum [FUUL-krəm] *noun, plural* **-crums** point on which a lever is placed for support
ful•fill [fuul-FIL] *verb intransitive* 1 satisfy 2 carry out 3 obey 4 satisfy (desire, etc.) > **ful•fill'ment** *noun*
full [fuul] *adjective* **-er, -est** 1 containing as much as possible 2 abundant 3 complete 4 ample 5 plump 6 (of garment) of ample cut ▷ *adverb* 7 very 8 quite 9 exactly > **ful'ly** *adverb* > **full'ness** *noun* > **ful•some** [FUUL-səm] *adjective* excessive > **full•blown'** [-BLOHN] *adjective* fully developed
ful•mi•nate [FUL-mə-nayt] *verb intransitive*

DICTIONARY

f

THESAURUS

froth *noun* 1 FOAM, bubbles, effervescence, head, lather, scum, spume, suds
▷ *verb* 2 FIZZ, bubble over, come to a head, effervesce, foam, lather
frothy *adjective* FOAMY, foaming, sudsy
frown *verb* 1 SCOWL, glare, glower, knit one's brows, look daggers, lour *or* lower
2 ▷ **frown on** DISAPPROVE OF, discourage, dislike, look askance at, take a dim view of
frozen *adjective* ICY, arctic, chilled, frigid, frosted, icebound, ice-cold, ice-covered, numb
frugal *adjective* THRIFTY, abstemious, careful, economical, niggardly, parsimonious, prudent, sparing
fruit *noun* 1 PRODUCE, crop, harvest, product, yield
2 RESULT, advantage, benefit, consequence, effect, end result, outcome, profit, return, reward
fruitful *adjective* USEFUL, advantageous, beneficial, effective, productive, profitable, rewarding, successful, win-win (*informal*), worthwhile
fruition *noun* MATURITY, attainment, completion, fulfillment, materialization, perfection, realization, ripeness
fruitless *adjective* USELESS, futile, ineffectual, pointless, profitless, unavailing, unproductive, unprofitable, unsuccessful, vain
frustrate *verb* THWART, balk, block, check, counter, defeat, disappoint, foil, forestall, nullify, stymie
frustrated *adjective* DISAPPOINTED, discouraged, disheartened, embittered, resentful
frustration *noun* 1 OBSTRUCTION, blocking, circumvention, foiling, thwarting
2 ANNOYANCE, disappointment, dissatisfaction, grievance, irritation, resentment, vexation
fuel *noun* INCITEMENT, ammunition, provocation
fugitive *noun* 1 RUNAWAY, deserter, escapee, refugee
▷ *adjective* 2 MOMENTARY, brief, ephemeral, fleeting, passing, short-lived, temporary, transient, transitory
fulfill *verb* 1 ACHIEVE, accomplish, carry out, complete, perform, realize, satisfy
2 COMPLY WITH, answer, conform to, fill, meet, obey, observe
fulfillment *noun* ACHIEVEMENT, accomplishment, attainment, completion, consummation, implementation, realization
full *adjective* 1 SATURATED, brimming, complete, filled, loaded, replete, satiated, stocked
2 PLENTIFUL, abundant, adequate, ample, comprehensive, exhaustive, extensive, generous
3 RICH, clear, deep, distinct, loud, resonant, rounded
4 PLUMP, buxom, curvaceous, rounded, voluptuous
5 LOOSE, baggy, capacious, large, puffy, voluminous
▷ *noun* 6 ▷ **in full** COMPLETELY, in its entirety, in total, without exception
full-blooded *adjective* VIGOROUS, hearty, lusty, red-blooded, virile
fullness *noun* 1 PLENTY, abundance, copiousness, fill, profusion, satiety, saturation, sufficiency
2 RICHNESS, clearness, loudness, resonance, strength
full-scale *adjective* MAJOR, all-out, comprehensive, exhaustive, in-depth, sweeping, thorough, thoroughgoing, wide-ranging
fully *adverb* TOTALLY, altogether, completely, entirely, in all respects, one hundred per cent, perfectly, thoroughly, utterly, wholly

-nat•ed, -nat•ing 1 (esp. with *against*) criticize harshly ▷ *noun* 2 chemical compound exploding readily > **ful•mi•na'tion** *noun*

fulsome *see* **full**

fum•ble [FUM-bəl] *verb* **-bled, -bling** 1 grope about 2 handle awkwardly 3 in football, etc., drop (ball) ▷ *noun* 4 awkward attempt

fume [fyoom] *verb intransitive* 1 be angry 2 emit smoke or vapor ▷ *noun* 3 smoke 4 vapor > **fu'mi•gate** *verb transitive* **-gat•ed, -gat•ing** apply fumes or smoke to, esp. for disinfection > **fu'mi•ga•tor** *noun*

fun *noun* anything enjoyable, amusing, etc. > **fun'ni•ly** *adverb* > **fun'ny** *adjective* **-ni•er, -ni•est** 1 comical 2 odd 3 difficult to explain

func•tion [FUNGK-shən] *noun* 1 work a thing is designed to do 2 (large) social event 3 duty 4 profession 5 *math.* quantity whose value depends on varying value of another ▷ *verb intransitive* 6 operate, work > **func'tion•al** *adjective* 1 having a special purpose 2 practical, necessary 3 capable of operating > **func'tion•ar•y** *noun, plural* **-ar•ies** official

fund *noun* 1 stock or sum of money 2 supply, store ▷ *verb transitive* 3 (in financial, business dealings) provide or obtain funds in various ways > **funds** *plural noun* money resources

fun•da•men•tal [fun-də-MEN-tl] *adjective* 1 of, affecting, or serving as, the base 2 essential, primary ▷ *noun* 3 basic rule or fact > **fun'da•ment** [-mənt] *noun* 1 buttocks 2 foundation > **fun•da•men'tal•ism** *noun* > **fun•da•men'tal•ist** *noun* one laying stress on belief in literal and verbal inspiration of Bible and other traditional creeds

fu•ner•al [FYOO-nər-əl] *noun* (ceremony associated with) burial or cremation of dead > **fu•ne're•al** [-NEE-ree-əl] *adjective* 1 like a funeral 2 dark 3 gloomy

fun•gi•ble [FUN-jə-bəl] *adjective* (of assets) freely exchangeable

fun•gus [FUNG-gəs] *noun, plural* **-gi** [-jī] **-gus•es** plant without leaves, flowers, or roots, as mushroom, mold > **fun'gal** *adjective* > **fun'gous** *adjective* > **fun'gi•cide** [-jə-sīd] *noun* fungus destroyer

fu•nic•u•lar [fyoo-NIK-yə-lər] *noun* cable railway on mountainside with two counterbalanced cars

funk [fungk] *noun* style of dance music with strong beat > **funk'y** *adjective* **funk•i•er, funk•i•est** 1 (of music) having a strong beat 2 (*slang*) unconventional 3 (*slang*) fetid

fun•nel [FUN-l] *noun* 1 cone-shaped vessel or tube 2 chimney of locomotive or ship 3 ventilating shaft ▷ *verb* **-neled, -nel•ing** 4 (cause to) move as through funnel 5 concentrate, focus

funny *see* **fun**

fur *noun* 1 soft hair of animal 2 garment, etc. 3 of dressed skins with such hair 4 furlike coating ▷ *verb transitive* **furred, fur•ring** 5 cover with fur > **fur'ri•er** *noun* 1 dealer in furs 2 repairer, dresser of furs > **fur'ry** *adjective* **-ri•er, -ri•est** of, like fur

fur'bish *verb transitive* clean up

fu•ri•ous [FYUUR-ee-əs] *adjective* 1 extremely angry 2 violent > **fu'ri•ous•ly** *adverb*

furl *verb transitive* roll up and bind (sail, umbrella, etc.)

fur•long [FUR-lawng] *noun* eighth of mile

fur•lough [FUR-loh] *noun* leave of absence, esp. to soldier

fur•nace [FUR-nis] *noun* 1 apparatus for applying great heat to metals 2 closed fireplace for heating boiler, etc. 3 hot place

---

fulsome *adjective* INSINCERE, excessive, extravagant, immoderate, inordinate, sycophantic, unctuous

fumble *verb* GROPE, feel around, flounder, scrabble

fume *verb* RAGE, get hot under the collar (*informal*), rant, see red (*informal*), seethe, smolder, storm

fumes *plural noun* SMOKE, exhaust, gas, pollution, smog, vapor

fumigate *verb* DISINFECT, clean out *or* clean up, cleanse, purify, sanitize, sterilize

fuming *adjective* ANGRY, enraged, in a rage, incensed, on the warpath (*informal*), raging, seething, up in arms

fun *noun* 1 ENJOYMENT, amusement, entertainment, jollity, merriment, mirth, pleasure, recreation, sport
2 ▷ **make fun of** MOCK, lampoon, laugh at, parody, poke fun at, ridicule, satirize
▷ *adjective* 3 ENJOYABLE, amusing, convivial, diverting, entertaining, lively, witty

function *noun* 1 PURPOSE, business, duty, job, mission, raison d'être (*French*), responsibility, role, task
2 RECEPTION, affair, gathering, social occasion
▷ *verb* 3 WORK, act, behave, do duty, go, operate, perform, run

functional *adjective* 1 PRACTICAL, hard-wearing, serviceable, useful, utilitarian
2 WORKING, operative

fund *noun* 1 RESERVE, kitty, pool, stock, store, supply
▷ *verb* 2 FINANCE, pay for, subsidize, support

fundamental *adjective* 1 ESSENTIAL, basic, cardinal, central, elementary, key, primary, principal, rudimentary, underlying
▷ *noun* 2 PRINCIPLE, axiom, cornerstone, law, rudiment, rule

fundamentally *adverb* ESSENTIALLY, at bottom, at heart, basically, intrinsically, primarily, radically

funds *plural noun* MONEY, capital, cash, finance, ready money, resources, savings, the wherewithal

funeral *noun* BURIAL, cremation, inhumation, interment, obsequies

funnel *verb* CHANNEL, conduct, convey, direct, filter, move, pass, pour

funny *adjective* 1 HUMOROUS, amusing, comic, comical, droll, entertaining, hilarious, riotous, side-splitting, witty
2 PECULIAR, curious, mysterious, odd, queer, strange, suspicious, unusual, weird

furious *adjective* 1 ANGRY, beside oneself, enraged, fuming, incensed, infuriated, livid (*informal*), raging, up in arms
2 VIOLENT, fierce, intense, savage, turbulent, unrestrained, vehement

fur'nish *verb transitive* 1 fit up house with furniture 2 equip 3 supply, yield > **fur'ni•ture** [-chər] *noun* movable contents of a house or room
fu•ror [FYUUR-or] *noun* 1 public outburst, esp. of protest 2 sudden enthusiasm
fur•row [FUR-oh] *noun* 1 trench as made by plow 2 groove ▷ *verb transitive* 3 make furrows in
fur•ther [FUR-thər] *adverb* 1 more 2 in addition 3 at or to a greater distance or extent ▷ *adjective* 4 additional 5 more distant 6 *comp. of* **far** ▷ *verb transitive* 7 help forward 8 promote > **fur'ther•ance** *noun* > **fur'ther•more** *adverb* besides > **fur'thest** *adjective sup. of* **far** ▷ *adverb* > **fur'ther•most** *adjective*
fur•tive [FUR-tiv] *adjective* stealthy, sly, secret > **fur'tive•ly** *adverb*
fu•ry [FYUUR-ee] *noun, plural* **-ries** 1 wild rage, violent anger 2 violence of storm, etc. 3 usu. snake-haired avenging deity
fuse [fyooz] *verb* **fused, fus•ing** 1 blend by melting 2 melt with heat 3 amalgamate ▷ *noun* 4 (*also* **fuze**) soft wire, with low melting point, used as safety device in electrical systems 5 device (orig. combustible cord) for igniting bomb, etc. > **fu'si•ble** [-zə-bəl] *adjective* > **fu•sion** [FYOO-zhən] *noun* 1 melting 2 state of being melted 3 union of things, as atomic nuclei, as if melted together
fu•se•lage [FYOO-sə-lahzh] *noun* body of aircraft
fu•sil•lade [FYOO-sə-layd] *noun* continuous discharge of firearms
fuss *noun* 1 needless bustle or concern 2 complaint 3 objection ▷ *verb intransitive* 4 make fuss > **fuss'i•ly** *adverb* > **fuss'i•ness** *noun* > **fuss'y** *adjective* **fuss•i•er, fuss•i•est** 1 particular 2 hard to please 3 overmeticulous 4 overelaborate
fus•tian [FUS-chən] *noun* 1 thick cotton cloth 2 inflated language
fus•ty [FUS-tee] *adjective* **-ti•er, -ti•est** 1 moldy 2 smelling of damp 3 old-fashioned > **fus'ti•ness** *noun*
fu•tile [FYOOT-l] *adjective* useless, ineffectual, trifling > **fu•til'i•ty** *noun, plural* **-ties**
fu•ton [FOO-ton] *noun* Japanese padded quilt, laid on floor as bed
fu•ture [FYOO-chər] *noun* 1 time to come 2 what will happen 3 tense of verb indicating this 4 likelihood of development ▷ *adjective* 5 that will be 6 of, relating to, time to come > **fu'tur•ism** *noun* movement in art marked by revolt against tradition > **fu'tur•ist** *noun, adjective* > **fu•tur•ist'ic** *adjective* ultramodern > **fu•tu'ri•ty** [-TUUR-i-tee] *noun, plural* **-ties** future time
fuze *see* **fuse**
fuzz *noun* 1 fluff 2 fluffy or frizzed hair 3 blur 4 (*slang*) police (officer) > **fuzz'y** *adjective* **fuzz•i•er, fuzz•i•est** 1 fluffy, frizzy 2 blurred, indistinct

DICTIONARY

f

THESAURUS

furnish *verb* 1 DECORATE, equip, fit out, stock 2 SUPPLY, give, grant, hand out, offer, present, provide
furniture *noun* HOUSEHOLD GOODS, appliances, fittings, furnishings, goods, possessions, things (*informal*)
furor *noun* DISTURBANCE, commotion, hullabaloo, outcry, stir, to-do, uproar
furrow *noun* 1 GROOVE, channel, crease, hollow, line, rut, seam, trench, wrinkle
▷ *verb* 2 WRINKLE, corrugate, crease, draw together, knit
further *adverb* 1 IN ADDITION, additionally, also, besides, furthermore, into the bargain, moreover, to boot
▷ *adjective* 2 ADDITIONAL, extra, fresh, more, new, other, supplementary
▷ *verb* 3 PROMOTE, advance, assist, encourage, forward, help, lend support to, work for
furthermore *adverb* BESIDES, additionally, as well, further, in addition, into the bargain, moreover, to boot, too
furthest *adjective* MOST DISTANT, extreme, farthest, furthermost, outmost, remotest, ultimate
furtive *adjective* SLY, clandestine, conspiratorial, secretive, sneaky, stealthy, surreptitious, underhand, under-the-table
fury *noun* 1 ANGER, frenzy, impetuosity, madness, passion, rage, wrath
2 VIOLENCE, ferocity, fierceness, force, intensity, savagery, severity, vehemence
fuss *noun* 1 BOTHER, ado, commotion, excitement, palaver, stir, to-do
2 ARGUMENT, complaint, furor, objection, row, squabble, trouble
▷ *verb* 3 WORRY, fidget, fret, get worked up, take pains
fussy *adjective* 1 HARD TO PLEASE, choosy (*informal*), difficult, fastidious, finicky, high-maintenance, nit-picking (*informal*), particular, picky (*informal*)
2 OVERELABORATE, busy, cluttered, overworked, rococo
fusty *adjective* STALE, airless, damp, mildewed, moldering, musty, stuffy
futile *adjective* USELESS, fruitless, ineffectual, unavailing, unprofitable, unsuccessful, vain, worthless
futility *noun* USELESSNESS, emptiness, hollowness, ineffectiveness
future *noun* 1 HEREAFTER, time to come
2 OUTLOOK, expectation, prospect
▷ *adjective* 3 FORTHCOMING, approaching, coming, fated, impending, later, subsequent, to come
fuzzy *adjective* 1 FLUFFY, downy, frizzy, woolly
2 INDISTINCT, bleary, blurred, distorted, ill-defined, obscure, out of focus, unclear, vague

Gg

Ga *chem.* gallium

gab•ar•dine, gab•er•dine [GAB-ər-deen] *noun* 1 fine twill cloth like serge 2 *hist.* loose outer garment worn by Orthodox Jews

gab•ble [GAB-əl] *verb* **-bled, -bling** 1 talk, utter inarticulately or too fast ▷ *noun* 2 such talk > **gab** *noun, verb* **gabbed, gab•bing** (*informal*) talk, chatter > **gab'by** *adjective* **-bi•er, -bi•est** (*informal*) talkative **gift of the gab** eloquence, loquacity

ga•ble [GAY-bəl] *noun* triangular upper part of wall at end of ridged roof

gad *verb intransitive* **gad•ded, gad•ding gad about, around** go around in search of pleasure > **gad'a•bout** *noun* pleasure seeker

gad•fly [GAD-flī] *noun, plural* **-flies** 1 cattle-biting fly 2 worrying person

gadg•et [GAJ-it] *noun* 1 small mechanical device 2 object valued for its novelty or ingenuity > **gadg'et•ry** *noun*

Gael [gayl] *noun* one who speaks Gaelic > **Gael'ic** *noun* 1 language of Ireland and Scottish Highlands ▷ *adjective* 2 of Gaels, their language or customs

gaff *noun* 1 stick with iron hook for landing fish 2 spar for top of fore-and-aft sail ▷ *verb transitive* 3 seize (fish) with gaff

gaffe [gaf] *noun* 1 blunder 2 tactless remark

gaf•fer [GAF-ər] *noun* 1 (*informal*) old man 2 senior electrician on a TV or movie set

gag[1] *verb* **gagged, gag•ging** 1 stop up (person's mouth) with cloth, etc. 2 retch, choke ▷ *noun* 3 cloth, etc. put into, tied across mouth

gag[2] *noun* joke, funny story

ga•ga [GAH-gah] *adjective* (*informal*) 1 foolishly enthusiastic 2 infatuated

gage[1] [gayj] *noun* 1 pledge, thing given as security 2 challenge, or something symbolizing one

gage[2] *see* **gauge**

gag•gle [GAG-əl] *noun* 1 flock of geese 2 (*informal*) disorderly crowd

gaiety *see* **gay**

gain [gayn] *verb transitive* 1 obtain, secure 2 obtain as profit 3 win 4 earn 5 reach ▷ *verb intransitive* 6 increase, improve 7 get nearer 8 (of watch, clock) operate too fast ▷ *noun* 9

gabble *verb* 1 PRATTLE, babble, blabber, gibber, gush, jabber, spout
▷ *noun* 2 GIBBERISH, babble, blabber, chatter, drivel, prattle, twaddle

gadabout *noun* PLEASURE-SEEKER, gallivanter, rambler, rover, wanderer

gadget *noun* DEVICE, appliance, contraption (*informal*), contrivance, gizmo (*slang*), instrument, invention, thing, tool

gaffe *noun* BLUNDER, bloomer (*informal*), faux pas, indiscretion, lapse, mistake, slip, solecism

gag[1] *verb* 1 SUPPRESS, curb, muffle, muzzle, quiet, silence, stifle, stop up
2 RETCH, barf (*slang*), heave, puke (*slang*), spew, throw up (*informal*), toss one's cookies (*slang*), vomit

gag[2] *noun* JOKE, crack (*slang*), funny (*informal*), hoax, jest, wisecrack (*informal*), witticism

gaiety *noun* 1 CHEERFULNESS, blitheness, exhilaration, glee, high spirits, jollity, light-heartedness, merriment, mirth
2 MERRYMAKING, conviviality, festivity, fun,

profit 10 increase, improvement > **gain'ful•ly** *adverb* 1 profitably 2 for a wage, salary
gain•say [GAYN-say] *verb transitive* **-said, -say•ing** deny, contradict
gait [gayt] *noun* 1 manner of walking 2 pace
Gal. Galatians
ga•la [GAY-lə] *noun* 1 festive occasion 2 celebration 3 special entertainment ▷ *adjective* 4 festive 5 showy
gal•ax•y [GAL-ək-see] *noun, plural* **-ax•ies** 1 system of stars bound by gravitational forces 2 splendid gathering, esp. of famous people > **ga•lac•tic** [gə-LAK-tik] *adjective*
gale [gayl] *noun* 1 strong wind 2 (*informal*) loud outburst, esp. of laughter
gall¹ [gawl] *noun* (*informal*) 1 impudence 2 bitterness > **gall'blad•der** *noun* sac attached to liver, reservoir for bile > **gall'stone** *noun* hard secretion in gallbladder or ducts leading from it
gall² *noun* 1 painful swelling, esp. on horse 2 sore caused by chafing ▷ *verb transitive* 3 make sore by rubbing 4 vex, irritate
gall³ *noun* abnormal growth or excrescence on trees, etc.
gal•lant [GAL-ənt] *adjective* 1 fine, stately, brave 2 [gə-LANT] chivalrous, very attentive to women ▷ *noun* 3 [gə-LANT] lover, suitor 4 dashing, fashionable young man > **gal'lant•ly** *adverb* > **gal'lant•ry** *noun, plural* **-ries**
gal•le•on [GAL-ee-ən] *noun* large, high-built sailing ship of war
gal•ler•y [GAL-ə-ree] *noun, plural* **-ler•ies** 1 covered walk with side openings, colonnade 2 platform or projecting upper floor in theater, etc. 3 group of spectators 4 long, narrow platform on outside of building 5 room or rooms for special purposes, e.g. showing works of art 6 passage in wall, open to interior of building
gal•ley [GAL-ee] *noun, plural* **-leys** 1 one-decked vessel with sails and oars, usu. rowed by slaves or criminals 2 kitchen of ship or aircraft 3 printer's tray for composed type > **galley proof** printer's proof before being made up into pages > **galley slave** 1 one condemned to row in galley 2 drudge
Gal•lic [GAL-ik] *adjective* 1 of ancient Gaul 2 French > **Gal'li•cism** *noun* French word or idiom
gal•li•um [GAL-ee-əm] *noun* soft, gray metal of great fusibility
gal•li•vant [GAL-ə-vant] *verb intransitive* gad about
gal•lon [GAL-ən] *noun* liquid measure of four quarts (3.7853 liters)
gal•lop [GAL-əp] *verb* 1 go, ride at gallop 2 move fast ▷ *noun* 3 horse's fastest pace with all four feet off ground together in each stride 4 ride at this pace > **gal'lop•ing** *adjective* 1 at a gallop 2 speedy, swift
gal•lows [GAL-ohz] *noun* structure, usu. of two upright beams and crossbar, esp. for hanging criminals
Gal•lup poll [GAL-əp] *noun* method of finding out public opinion by questioning a cross section of the population
ga•loot [gə-LOOT] *noun* (*informal*) silly, clumsy person
ga•lore [gə-LOR] *adverb* in plenty
ga•losh•es [gə-LOSH-əz] *plural noun* waterproof overshoes
gal•van•ic [gal-VAN-ik] *adjective* 1 of, producing, concerning electric current, esp. when produced chemically 2 (*informal*) resembling effect of electric shock, startling > **gal'va•nize** [-və-nīz] *verb transitive* **-nized, -niz•ing** 1 stimulate to action 2 excite, startle 3 cover (iron, etc.) with protective zinc coating
gam'bit *noun* 1 *chess* opening involving sacrifice of a piece 2 any opening maneuver, comment, etc. intended to secure an advantage
gam•ble [GAM-bəl] *verb intransitive* **-bled, -bling** 1 play games of chance to win money 2 act on

DICTIONARY

g

THESAURUS

jollification, revelry
gaily *adverb* 1 CHEERFULLY, blithely, gleefully, happily, joyfully, light-heartedly, merrily 2 COLORFULLY, brightly, brilliantly, flamboyantly, flashily, gaudily, showily
gain *verb* 1 OBTAIN, acquire, attain, capture, collect, gather, get, land, pick up, secure, win 2 REACH, arrive at, attain, come to, get to 3 ▷ **gain on** GET NEARER, approach, catch up with, close, narrow the gap, overtake ▷ *noun* 4 PROFIT, advantage, benefit, dividend, return, yield 5 INCREASE, advance, growth, improvement, progress, rise
gainful *adjective* PROFITABLE, advantageous, beneficial, fruitful, lucrative, productive, remunerative, rewarding, useful, win-win (*informal*), worthwhile
gains *plural noun* PROFITS, earnings, prize, proceeds, revenue, takings, winnings
gainsay *verb* CONTRADICT, contravene, controvert, deny, disagree with, dispute, rebut, retract
gait *noun* WALK, bearing, carriage, pace, step, stride, tread
gala *noun* FESTIVAL, carnival, celebration, festivity, fête, jamboree, pageant
gale *noun* 1 STORM, blast, cyclone, hurricane, squall, tempest, tornado, typhoon 2 OUTBURST, burst, eruption, explosion, fit, howl, outbreak, peal, shout, shriek
gall¹ *noun* 1 (*informal*) IMPUDENCE, brazenness, cheek (*informal*), chutzpah (*informal*), effrontery, impertinence, insolence, nerve (*informal*) 2 BITTERNESS, acrimony, animosity, bile, hostility, rancor
gall² *verb* 1 SCRAPE, abrade, chafe, irritate 2 ANNOY, exasperate, irk, irritate, provoke, rankle, vex
gallant *adjective* 1 BRAVE, bold, courageous, heroic, honorable, intrepid, manly, noble, valiant 2 CHIVALROUS, attentive, courteous, gentlemanly, gracious, noble, polite
gallantry *noun* 1 BRAVERY, boldness, courage, heroism, intrepidity, manliness, spirit, valor 2 ATTENTIVENESS, chivalry, courteousness, courtesy, gentlemanliness, graciousness, nobility, politeness
galling *adjective* ANNOYING, bitter, exasperating, irksome, irritating, provoking, vexatious
gallivant *verb* WANDER, gad about, ramble, roam, rove
gallop *verb* RUN, bolt, career, dash, hurry, race,

expectation of something ▷ *noun* 3 risky undertaking 4 bet, wager > **gam'bler** *noun*

gam•bol [GAM-bəl] *verb intransitive* **-boled, -bol•ing** 1 skip, jump playfully ▷ *noun* 2 frolic

game[1] [gaym] *noun* 1 diversion, pastime 2 jest 3 contest for amusement 4 scheme, strategy 5 animals or birds hunted 6 their flesh ▷ *adjective* **gam•er, gam•est** 7 brave 8 willing > **game'ster** *noun* gambler > **game'cock** *noun* rooster bred for fighting > **game'keep•er** *noun* person employed to breed game, prevent poaching

game[2] *adjective* lame, crippled (leg)

gam•ete [GAM-eet] *noun biology* a sexual cell that unites with another for reproduction or the formation of a new individual

gam•ma [GAM-ə] *noun* third letter of the Greek alphabet > **gamma ray** a very penetrative electromagnetic ray

gam•mon [GAM-ən] *noun* 1 cured or smoked ham 2 lower end of side of bacon

gam•ut [GAM-ət] *noun* whole range or scale (orig. of musical notes)

gan•der [GAN-dər] *noun* 1 male goose 2 (*slang*) a quick look

gang *noun* 1 (criminal) group 2 organized group of persons working together ▷ *verb intransitive* 3 (esp. with *together*) form gang > **gang up** *verb intransitive* form an alliance (against)

gang'ling *adjective* lanky, awkward in movement

gan•gli•on [GANG-glee-ən] *noun, plural* **-gli•a** [-glee-ə] nerve nucleus

gang•plank [GANG-plangk] *noun* portable bridge for boarding or leaving vessel

gan•grene [GANG-green] *noun* death or decay of body tissue as a result of disease or injury > **gan'gre•nous** [-grə-nəs] *adjective*

gang•sta rap [GANG-sta] *noun* a style of rap music featuring lyrics that are anti-authority and often derogatory to women

gang•ster [GANG-stər] *noun* 1 member of criminal gang 2 notorious or hardened criminal

gang'way *noun* 1 bridge from ship to shore 2 anything similar ▷ *interjection* 3 make way!

gan•try [GAN-tree] *noun, plural* **-tries** 1 structure to support crane, railway signals, etc. 2 framework beside rocket on launching pad

gap *noun* 1 breach, opening, interval 2 cleft 3 empty space

gape [gayp] *verb intransitive* **gaped, gap•ing** 1 stare in wonder 2 open mouth wide, as in yawning 3 be, become wide open

ga•rage [gə-RAHZH] *noun* 1 (part of) building to house automobiles 2 refueling and repair center for them ▷ *verb transitive* **-raged, -rag•ing** 3 leave automobile in garage

garb [gahrb] *noun* 1 dress 2 fashion of dress ▷ *verb transitive* 3 dress, clothe

gar•bage [GAHR-bij] *noun* 1 rubbish 2 refuse > **garbage can** large, usu. cylindrical container for household rubbish

gar•ble [GAHR-bəl] *verb transitive* **-bled, -bling** jumble or distort (story, account, etc.)

gar•den [GAHR-dn] *noun* 1 ground for growing flowers, fruit, or vegetables ▷ *verb intransitive* 2 cultivate garden > **gar•den•er** [GAHRD-nər] *noun* > **gar•den•ing** [GAHRD-ning] *noun*

gar•de•nia [gahr-DEE-nyə] *noun* (sub)tropical shrub, with fragrant white or yellow flowers

gar•gan•tu•an [gahr-GAN-choo-ən] *adjective* immense, enormous, huge

gar•gle [GAHR-gəl] *verb intransitive* **-gled, -gling** 1 wash throat with liquid kept moving by the breath ▷ *verb transitive* **-gled, -gling** 2 wash (throat) thus ▷ *noun* 3 gargling 4 preparation for this purpose

gar•goyle [GAHR-goil] *noun* carved (grotesque) face on waterspout, esp. on Gothic church

gar•ish [GAIR-ish] *adjective* 1 showy 2 gaudy

gar•land [GAHR-lənd] *noun* 1 wreath of flowers worn or hung as decoration ▷ *verb transitive* 2 decorate with garlands

gar•lic [GAHR-lik] *noun* (bulb of) plant with strong smell and taste, used in cooking and

---

rush, speed, sprint

galore *adverb* IN ABUNDANCE, all over the place, aplenty, everywhere, in great quantity, in great numbers, in profusion, to spare

galvanize *verb* STIMULATE, electrify, excite, inspire, invigorate, jolt, provoke, spur, stir

gamble *verb* 1 BET, game, play, wager
2 RISK, chance, hazard, speculate, stick one's neck out (*informal*), take a chance
▷ *noun* 3 RISK, chance, leap in the dark, lottery, speculation, uncertainty, venture
4 BET, wager

gambol *verb* 1 FROLIC, caper, cavort, frisk, hop, jump, prance, skip
▷ *noun* 2 FROLIC, caper, hop, jump, prance, skip

game[1] *noun* 1 PASTIME, amusement, distraction, diversion, entertainment, lark, recreation, sport
2 MATCH, competition, contest, event, head-to-head, meeting, tournament
3 WILD ANIMALS, prey, quarry
4 SCHEME, design, plan, plot, ploy, stratagem, tactic, trick
▷ *adjective* 5 BRAVE, courageous, gallant, gritty, intrepid, persistent, plucky, spirited
6 WILLING, desirous, eager, interested, keen, prepared, ready

gamut *noun* RANGE, area, catalog, compass, field, scale, scope, series, sweep

gang *noun* GROUP, band, clique, club, company, coterie, crowd, mob, pack, squad, team

gangling *adjective* TALL, angular, awkward, lanky, rangy, rawboned, spindly

gangster *noun* RACKETEER, crook (*informal*), hood (*slang*), hoodlum, mobster (*slang*)

gap *noun* 1 OPENING, break, chink, cleft, crack, hole, space
2 INTERVAL, breathing space, hiatus, interlude, intermission, interruption, lacuna, lull, pause, respite
3 DIFFERENCE, disagreement, disparity, divergence, inconsistency

gape *verb* 1 STARE, gawk, goggle, wonder
2 OPEN, crack, split, yawn

gaping *adjective* WIDE, broad, cavernous, great, open, vast, wide open, yawning

garbage *noun* RUBBISH, litter, refuse, trash, waste

garbled *adjective* JUMBLED, confused, distorted, double-Dutch, incomprehensible, mixed up, unintelligible

seasoning
gar•ment [GAHR-mənt] *noun* article of clothing > **gar•ments** clothes
gar•ner [GAHR-nər] *verb transitive* store up, collect, as if in granary
gar•net [GAHR-nit] *noun* red semiprecious stone
gar•nish [GAHR-nish] *verb transitive* 1 adorn, decorate (esp. food) ▷ *noun* 2 material for this
gar•ret [GAR-it] *noun* small (usu. wretched) room on top floor, attic
gar•ri•son [GAR-ə-sən] *noun* 1 troops stationed in town, fort, etc. 2 fortified place ▷ *verb transitive* 3 furnish or occupy with garrison
gar•rote [gə-ROHT] *noun* 1 capital punishment by strangling 2 apparatus for this ▷ *verb transitive* **-rot•ed, -rot•ing** 3 execute, kill thus > **gar•rot'er** *noun*
gar•ru•lous [GAR-ə-ləs] *adjective* (frivolously) talkative > **gar•ru•li•ty** [gə-ROO-li-tee] *noun* loquacity
gar•ter [GAHR-tər] *noun* band worn around leg to hold up sock or stocking > **garter snake** type of harmless snake
gas *noun, plural* **-es** 1 airlike substance, esp. one that does not liquefy or solidify at ordinary temperatures 2 fossil fuel in form of gas, used for heating or lighting 3 gaseous anesthetic 4 poisonous or irritant substance dispersed through atmosphere in warfare, etc. 5 gasoline 6 automobile accelerator 7 (*slang*) idle, boastful talk ▷ *verb* **gassed, gas•sing** 8 project gas over 9 poison with gas 10 fill with gas 11 (*slang*) talk idly, boastfully > **gas'e•ous** [-ee-əs] *adjective* of, like gas > **gass'y** *adjective* **-si•er, -si•est** filled with gas > **gas'bag** *noun* (*slang*) person who talks idly > **gas mask** mask with chemical filter to guard against poisoning by gas
gash *noun* 1 gaping wound, slash ▷ *verb transitive* 2 cut deeply
gas•ket [GAS-kit] *noun* rubber, neoprene, etc. used as seal between metal faces, esp. in engines
gas•o•hol [GAS-ə-hawl] *noun* mixture of gasoline and ethyl alcohol used as fuel for automobiles
gas•o•line [gas-ə-LEEN] *noun* refined petroleum used in automobiles, etc.
gasp *verb intransitive* 1 catch breath with open mouth, as in exhaustion or surprise ▷ *noun* 2 convulsive catching of breath
gas•tric [GAS-trik] *adjective* of stomach > **gas•tro•nom'i•cal** [-trə-NOM-ə-kəl] *adjective* > **gas•tron•o•my** [ga-STRON-ə-mee] *noun* art of good eating
gas•tro•en•ter•i•tis [gas-troh-en-tə-RĪ-tis] *noun* inflammation of stomach and intestines
gas•tro•pod [GAS-trə-pod] *noun* mollusk, e.g. snail, with disklike organ of locomotion on ventral surface
gate [gayt] *noun* 1 opening in wall, fence, etc. 2 barrier for closing it 3 sluice 4 any entrance or way out 5 (entrance money paid by) those attending sports event > **gate'-crash•er** *noun* (*informal*) person who enters sports event, social function, etc. uninvited
gath•er [GATH-ər] *verb* (cause to) assemble 1 increase gradually 2 draw together ▷ *verb transitive* 3 collect 4 learn, understand 5 draw material into small tucks or folds > **gath'er•ing** *noun* assembly
gauche [gohsh] *adjective* tactless, blundering > **gau'che•rie** *noun* awkwardness, clumsiness
gau•cho [GOW-choh] *noun, plural* **-chos** cowboy of S Amer. pampas
gaud [gawd] *noun* showy ornament > **gaud'i•ly** *adverb* > **gaud'iness** *noun* > **gaud'y** *adjective* **gaud•i•er, gaud•i•est** showy in tasteless way
gauge, gage [gayj] *noun* 1 standard measure, as of diameter of wire, thickness of sheet metal, etc. 2 distance between rails of railway 3 capacity, extent 4 instrument for measuring such things as wire, rainfall, height of water in boiler, etc. ▷ *verb transitive* **gauged, gaug•ing** 5 measure 6 estimate
gaunt [gawnt] *adjective* **-er, -est** extremely lean, haggard
gaunt•let [GAWNT-lit] *noun* 1 armored glove 2

DICTIONARY g THESAURUS

garish *adjective* GAUDY, brash, brassy, flashy, loud, showy, tacky (*informal*), tasteless, vulgar
garland *noun* 1 WREATH, bays, chaplet, crown, festoon, honors, laurels
▷ *verb* 2 ADORN, crown, deck, festoon, wreathe
garments *plural noun* CLOTHES, apparel, attire, clothing, costume, dress, garb, gear (*slang*), outfit, uniform
garner *verb* COLLECT, accumulate, amass, gather, hoard, save, stockpile, store, stow away
garnish *verb* 1 DECORATE, adorn, embellish, enhance, ornament, set off, trim
▷ *noun* 2 DECORATION, adornment, embellishment, enhancement, ornamentation, trimming
garrison *noun* 1 TROOPS, armed force, command, detachment, unit
2 FORT, base, camp, encampment, fortification, fortress, post, station, stronghold
▷ *verb* 3 STATION, assign, position, post, put on duty
garrulous *adjective* TALKATIVE, chatty, gossiping, loquacious, prattling, verbose, voluble
gash *verb* 1 CUT, gouge, lacerate, slash, slit, split, tear, wound
▷ *noun* 2 CUT, gouge, incision, laceration, slash, slit, split, tear, wound
gasp *verb* 1 GULP, blow, catch one's breath, choke, pant, puff
▷ *noun* 2 GULP, exclamation, pant, puff, sharp intake of breath
gate *noun* BARRIER, door, entrance, exit, gateway, opening, passage, portal
gather *verb* 1 ASSEMBLE, accumulate, amass, collect, garner, mass, muster, stockpile
2 LEARN, assume, conclude, deduce, hear, infer, surmise, understand
3 PICK, cull, garner, glean, harvest, pluck, reap, select
4 INTENSIFY, deepen, expand, grow, heighten, increase, rise, swell, thicken
5 FOLD, pleat, tuck
gathering *noun* ASSEMBLY, company, conclave, congress, convention, crowd, group, meeting
gauche *adjective* AWKWARD, clumsy, ill-mannered, inelegant, tactless, unsophisticated
gaudy *adjective* GARISH, bright, flashy, loud, showy, tacky (*informal*), tasteless, vulgar

glove covering part of arm **3** **run the gauntlet** formerly, run as punishment between two lines of men striking at runner with sticks, etc. **4** be exposed to criticism or unpleasant treatment **5** undergo ordeal **throw down the gauntlet** offer challenge

gauss [gows] *noun* unit of density of magnetic field

gauze [gawz] *noun* **1** thin transparent fabric of silk, wire, etc. **2** this as surgical dressing

gave *pt. of* **give**

gav•el [GAV-əl] *noun* mallet of presiding officer or auctioneer

ga•votte [gə-VOT] *noun* **1** lively dance **2** music for it

gawk *verb intransitive* stare stupidly > **gawk'y** *adjective* **gawk•i•er, gawk•i•est** clumsy, awkward

gay *adjective* **-er, -est** **1** homosexual **2** merry **3** lively **4** cheerful **5** bright **6** lighthearted **7** showy **8** given to pleasure ▷ *noun* **9** homosexual > **gai'e•ty** *noun, plural* **-ties** > **gai'ly** *adverb*

gaze [gayz] *verb intransitive* **gazed, gaz•ing** look fixedly ▷ *noun*

ga•ze•bo [gə-ZEE-boh] *noun* summerhouse, small roofed structure, with extensive view

ga•zelle [gə-ZEL] *noun* small graceful antelope

ga•zette [gə-ZET] *noun* name for newspaper > **gaz•et•teer'** *noun* geographical dictionary

ga•zil•lion [gə-ZIL-yən] *noun* (*informal*) extremely large unspecified number

Gd *chem.* gadolinium

Ge *chem.* germanium

gear [geer] *noun* **1** set of wheels working together, esp. by engaging cogs **2** connection by which engine, motor, etc. is brought into work **3** arrangement by which driving wheel of cycle, automobile, etc. performs more or fewer revolutions relative to pedals, pistons, etc. **4** equipment **5** clothing **6** goods, utensils **7** apparatus, tackle, tools **8** rigging **9** harness ▷ *verb transitive* **10** adapt (one thing) so as to conform with another **11** provide with gear **12** put in gear > **gear'box** *noun* case protecting gearing of bicycle, automobile, etc. **in gear** connected up and ready for work **out of gear** disconnected

geek *noun* (*informal*) boring, unattractive person

geese [gees] *pl. of* **goose**

gee•zer [GEE-zər] *noun* (*slang*) (old, eccentric) man

ge•fil•te fish [gə-FIL-tə] in Jewish cookery, a dish of various freshwater fish chopped and blended with eggs, matzo meal, etc.

Gei•ger count•er [GĪ-gər] *noun* instrument for detecting radioactivity, cosmic radiation and charged atomic particles

gei•sha [GAY-shə] *noun* in Japan, professional female entertainer and companion for men

gel [jel] *noun* **1** jelly-like substance ▷ *verb intransitive* **gelled, gel•ling** **2** form a gel **3** jell

gel•a•tin [JEL-ə-tn] *noun* **1** substance prepared from animal bones, etc., producing edible jelly **2** anything resembling this > **ge•lat•i•nous** [jə-LAT-n-əs] *adjective* like gelatin or jelly

geld *verb transitive* castrate > **geld'ing** *noun* castrated horse

gel•id [JEL-id] *adjective* very cold

gem [jem] *noun* **1** precious stone, esp. when cut and polished **2** treasure ▷ *verb transitive* **gemmed, gem•ming** **3** adorn with gems

Gen. Genesis

gen•darme [ZHAHN-dahrm] *noun* policeman in France

gen•der [JEN-dər] *noun* **1** sex, male or female **2** grammatical classification of nouns, according to sex (actual or attributed)

gene [jeen] *noun* biological factor determining inherited characteristics

ge•ne•al•o•gy [jee-nee-AL-ə-jee] *noun, plural* **-gies** **1** account of descent from ancestors **2** pedigree **3** study of pedigrees > **ge•ne•a•log'i•cal** [-LOJ-ə-kəl] *adjective*

genera *pl. of* **genus**

gen•er•al [JEN-ər-əl] *adjective* **1** common, widespread **2** not particular or specific **3** applicable to all or most **4** usual, prevalent **5**

gauge *verb* **1** MEASURE, ascertain, calculate, check, compute, count, determine, weigh
2 JUDGE, adjudge, appraise, assess, estimate, evaluate, guess, rate, reckon, value
▷ *noun* **3** INDICATOR, criterion, guide, guideline, measure, meter, standard, test, touchstone, yardstick

gaunt *adjective* EMACIATED, angular, anorexic, bony, cadaverous, lean, pinched, scrawny, skeletal, skinny, spare

gawky *adjective* AWKWARD, clumsy, gauche, loutish, lumbering, maladroit, ungainly

gay *adjective* **1** HOMOSEXUAL, bent (*informal, derogatory*), lesbian, queer (*informal, derogatory*)
2 CAREFREE, blithe, cheerful, jovial, lighthearted, lively, merry, sparkling
3 COLORFUL, bright, brilliant, flamboyant, flashy, rich, showy, vivid
▷ *noun* **4** HOMOSEXUAL, lesbian

gaze *verb* **1** STARE, gape, look, regard, view, watch, wonder
▷ *noun* **2** STARE, fixed look, look

gazette *noun* NEWSPAPER, journal, news-sheet, paper, periodical

gear *noun* **1** COG, cogwheel, gearwheel
2 MECHANISM, cogs, machinery, works
3 EQUIPMENT, accouterments, apparatus, instruments, paraphernalia, supplies, tackle, tools
4 CLOTHING, clothes, costume, dress, garments, outfit, togs, wear
▷ *verb* **5** EQUIP, adapt, adjust, fit

geek *noun* (*slang*) BORE, anorak (*informal*), dork (*slang*), drip (*informal*), obsessive, trainspotter (*informal*), wonk (*informal*)

gelatinous *adjective* JELLY-LIKE, gluey, glutinous, gummy, sticky, viscous

gelid *adjective* COLD, arctic, chilly, freezing, frigid, frosty, frozen, glacial, ice-cold, icy

gem *noun* **1** PRECIOUS STONE, jewel, stone
2 PRIZE, jewel, masterpiece, pearl, treasure

general *adjective* **1** COMMON, accepted, broad, extensive, popular, prevalent, public, universal, widespread
2 IMPRECISE, approximate, ill-defined, indefinite, inexact, loose, unspecific, vague
3 UNIVERSAL, across-the-board, blanket, collective, comprehensive, indiscriminate,

miscellaneous **6** dealing with main element only **7** vague, indefinite ▷ *noun* **8** army officer of rank above colonel > **gen•er•al'i•ty** *noun, plural* **-ties 1** general principle **2** vague statement **3** indefiniteness > **gen•er•al•i•za'tion** *noun* **1** general conclusion from particular instance **2** inference > **gen'er•al•ize** *verb transitive* **-ized, -iz•ing 1** reduce to general laws ▷ *verb intransitive* **-ized, -iz•ing 2** draw general conclusions > **general practitioner** physician with practice not restricted to particular branch of medicine

gen•er•ate [JEN-ə-rayt] *verb transitive* **-at•ed, -at•ing 1** bring into being **2** produce > **gen•er•a'tion** *noun* **1** bringing into being **2** all persons born about same time **3** average time between two such generations (about 30 years) > **gen'er•a•tor** *noun* **1** apparatus for producing (steam, electricity, etc.) **2** begetter

ge•ner•ic [ji-NER-ik] *adjective* belonging to, characteristic of class or genus > **ge•ner'i•cal•ly** *adverb* > **generic drug** one sold without brand name

gen•er•ous [JEN-ər-əs] *adjective* **1** liberal, free in giving **2** abundant > **gen•er•os'i•ty** *noun, plural* **-ties**

gen•e•sis [JEN-ə-sis] *noun, plural* **-ses** [-seez] **1** origin **2** mode of formation **3** (**Gen•e•sis**) first book of Bible

ge•net•ics [jə-NET-iks] *noun* scientific study of heredity and variation in organisms > **ge•net'ic** *adjective* > **ge•net'i•cist** *noun* > **genetic engineering** deliberate modification of heredity characteristics by treatment of DNA to transfer selected genes

gen•ial [JEEN-yəl] *adjective* **1** cheerful, warm in behavior **2** mild, conducive to growth > **ge•ni•al'i•ty** *noun*

ge•nie [JEE-nee] *noun* in fairy tales, servant appearing by, and working, magic

gen•i•tal [JEN-i-tl] *adjective* relating to sexual organs or reproduction > **gen'i•tals** *plural noun* the sexual organs

gen•i•tive [JEN-i-tiv] *adjective, noun* possessive (case)

gen•ius [JEEN-yəs] *noun* **1** (person with) exceptional power or ability, esp. of mind **2** distinctive spirit or nature (of nation, etc.)

gen•o•cide [JEN-ə-sīd] *noun* murder of a nationality or ethnic group

gen•re [ZHAHN-rə] *noun* **1** kind **2** sort **3** style **4** painting of homely scene

gen•teel [jen-TEEL] *adjective* **1** well-bred **2** stylish **3** affectedly proper

gen•tile [JEN-tīl] *adjective, noun* non-Jewish (person)

gen•tle [JEN-tl] *adjective* **-tler, -tlest 1** mild, quiet, not rough or severe **2** soft and soothing **3** courteous **4** moderate **5** gradual **6** wellborn > **gen•til'i•ty** *noun* respectability, (pretentious) politeness > **gen'tle•ness** *noun* **1** quality of being gentle **2** tenderness > **gent'ly** *adverb* > **gen•tri•fi•ca'tion** *noun* buying of properties in run-down urban neighborhoods by affluent people, thus increasing property values but displacing less affluent residents and owners of small businesses > **gent'ry** *noun* wellborn people > **gen'tle•man** *noun* **1** well-bred man **2** man of good social position **3** man (used as a mark of politeness) > **gen'tle•man•ly** *adjective* > **gentlemen's agreement 1** agreement binding by honor but not valid in law **2** unwritten law in private club, etc. to discriminate against members of certain groups > **gen'tri•fy** *verb* **-fied, -fy•ing** change by gentrification,

DICTIONARY

g

THESAURUS

miscellaneous, sweeping, total

generally *adverb* **1** USUALLY, as a rule, by and large, customarily, normally, on the whole, ordinarily, typically
2 COMMONLY, extensively, popularly, publicly, universally, widely

generate *verb* PRODUCE, breed, cause, create, engender, give rise to, make, propagate

generation *noun* **1** PRODUCTION, creation, formation, genesis, propagation, reproduction
2 AGE GROUP, breed, crop
3 AGE, epoch, era, period, time

generic *adjective* COLLECTIVE, blanket, common, comprehensive, general, inclusive, universal, wide

generosity *noun* **1** CHARITY, beneficence, bounty, kindness, largesse *or* largess, liberality, munificence, open-handedness
2 UNSELFISHNESS, goodness, high-mindedness, magnanimity, nobleness

generous *adjective* **1** CHARITABLE, beneficent, bountiful, hospitable, kind, lavish, liberal, open-handed, unstinting
2 UNSELFISH, big-hearted, good, high-minded, lofty, magnanimous, noble
3 PLENTIFUL, abundant, ample, copious, full, lavish, liberal, rich, unstinting

genesis *noun* BEGINNING, birth, creation, formation, inception, origin, start

genial *adjective* CHEERFUL, affable, agreeable, amiable, congenial, friendly, good-natured, jovial, pleasant, warm

geniality *noun* CHEERFULNESS, affability, agreeableness, amiability, conviviality, cordiality, friendliness, good cheer, joviality, warmth

genius *noun* **1** MASTER, brainbox, expert, hotshot (*informal*), maestro, mastermind, savant, virtuoso, whiz (*informal*)
2 BRILLIANCE, ability, aptitude, bent, capacity, flair, gift, knack, talent

genre *noun* TYPE, category, class, group, kind, sort, species, style

genteel *adjective* REFINED, courteous, cultured, elegant, gentlemanly, ladylike, polite, respectable, urbane, well-mannered

gentle *adjective* **1** SWEET-TEMPERED, compassionate, humane, kindly, meek, mild, placid, tender
2 MODERATE, light, mild, muted, slight, soft, soothing
3 GRADUAL, easy, imperceptible, light, mild, moderate, slight, slow
4 TAME, biddable, broken, docile, manageable, placid, tractable

gentlemanly *adjective* POLITE, civil, courteous, gallant, genteel, honorable, refined, urbane, well-mannered

gentleness *noun* TENDERNESS, compassion, kindness, mildness, softness, sweetness

gentry *noun* NOBILITY, aristocracy, elite, upper class, upper crust (*informal*)

undergo this change

gen•u•flect [JEN-yə-flekt] *verb intransitive* bend knee, esp. in worship > **gen•u•flec'tion** *noun*

gen•u•ine [JEN-yoo-in] *adjective* 1 real, true, not sham, authentic 2 sincere 3 pure

ge•nus [JEE-nəs] *noun, plural* **gen•e•ra** [JEN-ər-ə] class, order, group (esp. of insects, animals, etc.) with common characteristics usu. comprising several species

ge•o•cen•tric [jee-oh-SEN-trik] *adjective astronomy* 1 measured, seen from Earth 2 having Earth as center

ge•ode [JEE-ohd] *noun* 1 cavity lined with crystals 2 stone containing this

ge•o•des•ic [jee-ə-DES-ik] *adjective* of geometry of curved surfaces > **geodesic dome** light but strong hemispherical construction formed from set of polygons

ge•og•ra•phy [jee-OG-rə-fee] *noun, plural* **-phies** science of Earth's form, physical features, climate, population, etc. > **ge•og'ra•pher** *noun*

ge•ol•o•gy [jee-OL-ə-jee] *noun* science of Earth's crust, rocks, strata, etc. > **ge•o•log'ic•al** *adjective*

ge•om•e•try [jee-OM-i-tree] *noun* science of properties and relations of lines, surfaces, etc. > **ge•o•met'ric** *adjective*

ge•o•phys•ics [jee-oh-FIZ-iks] *noun* science dealing with physics of Earth > **ge•o•phys'i•cal** *adjective*

ge•o•sta•tion•ar•y [jee-oh-STAY-shə-ner-ee] *adjective* (of satellite) in orbit around Earth so satellite remains over same point on surface

ger•bil [JUR-bəl] *noun* burrowing, desert rodent of Asia and Africa

ger•i•at•rics [jer-ee-A-triks] *noun* branch of medicine dealing with old age and its diseases > **ger•i•at'ric** *adjective* 1 old ▷ *noun* 2 (*slang*) old person

germ [jurm] *noun* 1 microbe, esp. causing disease 2 elementary thing 3 rudiment of new organism, of animal or plant > **ger'mi•cide** [-mə-sīd] *noun* substance for destroying disease germs

Ger•man [JUR-mən] *noun, adjective* (language or native) of Germany > **German measles** rubella, mild disease with symptoms like measles

german *adjective* 1 of the same parents 2 closely akin: *brother-german*

ger•mane [jər-MAYN] *adjective* relevant, pertinent

ger•mi•nate [JUR-mə-nayt] *verb* **-nat•ed, -nat•ing** (cause to) sprout or begin to grow

ger•ry•man•der [JER-i-man-dər] *verb transitive* manipulate election districts so as to favor one side

ger•und [JER-ənd] *noun* noun formed from verb: *living*

ges•ta•tion [je-STAY-shən] *noun* 1 carrying of young in womb between conception and birth 2 this period

ges•tic•u•late [je-STIK-yə-layt] *verb intransitive* use expressive movements of hands and arms when speaking

ges•ture [JES-chər] *noun* 1 movement to convey meaning 2 indication of state of mind ▷ *verb intransitive* **-tured, -tur•ing** 3 make such a movement

get *verb transitive* **got, got** *or* **got•ten, get•ting** 1 obtain, procure 2 contract 3 catch 4 earn 5 cause to go or come 6 bring into position or state 7 induce 8 engender 9 be in possession of, have (to do) 10 (*informal*) understand ▷ *verb intransitive* **got, got** *or* **got•ten, get•ting** 11 succeed in coming or going 12 reach, attain 13 become > **get'a•way** *noun* escape > **get across** be understood > **get at** 1 gain access to 2 annoy 3 criticize 4 influence

gey•ser [GĪ-zər] *noun* hot spring throwing up spout of water from time to time

ghast•ly [GAST-lee] *adjective* **-li•er, -li•est** (*informal*) 1 unpleasant 2 deathlike, pallid 3

DICTIONARY • THESAURUS

---

genuine *adjective* 1 AUTHENTIC, actual, bona fide, legitimate, real, the real McCoy, true, veritable
2 SINCERE, candid, earnest, frank, heartfelt, honest, unaffected, unfeigned

germ *noun* 1 MICROBE, bacterium, bug (*informal*), microorganism, virus
2 BEGINNING, embryo, origin, root, rudiment, seed, source, spark

germane *adjective* RELEVANT, apposite, appropriate, apropos, connected, fitting, material, pertinent, related, to the point *or* to the purpose

germinate *verb* SPROUT, bud, develop, generate, grow, originate, shoot, swell, vegetate

gesticulate *verb* SIGNAL, gesture, indicate, make a sign, motion, sign, wave

gesture *noun* 1 SIGNAL, action, gesticulation, indication, motion, sign
▷ *verb* 2 SIGNAL, gesticulate, indicate, motion, sign, wave

get *verb* 1 OBTAIN, acquire, attain, fetch, gain, land, net, pick up, procure, receive, secure, win
2 CONTRACT, catch, come down with, fall victim to, take
3 CAPTURE, grab, lay hold of, seize, take
4 BECOME, come to be, grow, turn
5 UNDERSTAND, catch, comprehend, fathom, follow, perceive, see, take in, work out
6 PERSUADE, convince, induce, influence, prevail upon
7 (*informal*) ANNOY, bug (*informal*), gall, irritate, upset, vex

get across *verb* 1 CROSS, ford, negotiate, pass over, traverse
2 COMMUNICATE, bring home to, convey, impart, make clear *or* make understood, put over, transmit

get along *verb* BE FRIENDLY, agree, be compatible, click (*slang*), concur, hit it off (*informal*)

get at *verb* 1 GAIN ACCESS TO, acquire, attain, come to grips with, get hold of, reach
2 IMPLY, hint, intend, lead up to, mean, suggest
3 CRITICIZE, attack, blame, find fault with, nag, pick on

getaway *noun* ESCAPE, break, break-out, flight

get by *verb* MANAGE, cope, exist, fare, get along, keep one's head above water, make both ends meet, survive

get off *verb* LEAVE, alight, depart, descend, disembark, dismount, escape, exit

get on *verb* BOARD, ascend, climb, embark, mount

get over *verb* RECOVER FROM, come round, get

horrible ▷ *adverb* 4 horribly
gher•kin [GUR-kin] *noun* small cucumber used in pickling
ghet•to [GET-oh] *noun, plural* **-tos** densely populated (esp. by one racial or ethnic group) slum area > **ghet'to-blast•er** *noun* (*informal*) large portable cassette or CD player and radio
ghost [gohst] *noun* 1 spirit, dead person appearing again 2 specter 3 semblance 4 faint trace 5 one who writes work to appear under another's name, ghostwriter ▷ *verb* 6 (*also* **ghost'write**) write another's work, speeches, etc. > **ghost'ly** *adjective*
ghoul [gool] *noun* 1 malevolent spirit 2 person with morbid interests 3 fiend > **ghoul'ish** *adjective* 1 of or like ghoul 2 horrible
gi•ant [JĪ-ənt] *noun* 1 mythical being of superhuman size 2 very tall person, plant, etc. ▷ *adjective* 3 huge > **gi•gan'tic** *adjective* enormous, huge
gib•ber [JIB-ər] *verb intransitive* make meaningless sounds with mouth, jabber, chatter > **gib'ber•ish** *noun* meaningless speech or words
gib•bet [JIB-it] *noun* 1 gallows 2 post with arm on which executed criminal was hung 3 death by hanging ▷ *verb transitive* 4 hang on gibbet 5 hold up to scorn
gib•bon [GIB-ən] *noun* type of ape
gibe [jīb] *verb* **gibed, gib•ing** 1 utter taunts 2 mock 3 jeer ▷ *noun* 4 insulting remark
gib•lets [JIB-lits] *plural noun* internal edible parts of fowl, such as liver, gizzard, etc.
gid•dy [GID-ee] *adjective* **-di•er, -di•est** 1 dizzy, feeling as if about to fall 2 liable to cause this feeling 3 flighty, frivolous > **gid'di•ness** *noun*
gift *noun* 1 thing given, present 2 faculty, power ▷ *verb transitive* 3 present (with) 4 endow, bestow > **gift'ed** *adjective* talented
gig *noun* 1 light, two-wheeled carriage 2 (*informal*) single booking of musicians to play at club, etc.
giga- *prefix* 1 denoting 10^9: *gigavolt* 2 *computing* denoting 2^{30}: *gigabyte*
gigantic *see* **giant**
gig•gle [GIG-əl] *verb intransitive* **-gled, -gling** 1 laugh nervously, foolishly ▷ *noun* 2 such a laugh
gig•o•lo [JIG-ə-loh] *noun, plural* **-los** man kept, paid, by (older) woman to be her escort, lover
gild *verb transitive* **gilded** *or* **gilt, gild•ing** 1 put thin layer of gold on 2 make falsely attractive > **gilt** *adjective* 1 gilded ▷ *noun* 2 thin layer of gold put on
gill [jil] *noun* liquid measure, quarter of pint
gills [gillz] *plural noun* breathing organs in fish and other water creatures
gim•bals [JIM-bəlz] *plural noun* pivoted rings, for keeping things, e.g. compass, horizontal at sea or in space
gim•let [GIM-lit] *noun* 1 boring tool, usu. with screw point 2 drink of vodka or gin with lime juice
gim•mick [GIM-ik] *noun* clever device, stratagem, etc., esp. one designed to attract attention or publicity
gimp *noun* 1 narrow fabric or braid used as edging or trimming 2 (*slang*) a limp 3 (*slang*) person who limps
gin¹ [jin] *noun* alcoholic liquor flavored with juniper berries
gin² *noun* 1 primitive engine in which vertical shaft is turned to drive horizontal beam in a circle 2 machine for separating cotton from seeds
gin•ger [JIN-jər] *noun* 1 plant with pungent spicy root used in cooking, etc. 2 the root 3 (*informal*) spirit, mettle 4 light reddish-yellow color ▷ *verb transitive* 5 stimulate > **gin'ger•y** *adjective* 1 of, like ginger 2 spicy 3 high-spirited 4 reddish > **ginger ale, ginger beer** ginger-flavored soft drink > **gin'ger•bread** *noun* cake, cookie flavored with ginger
gin•ger•ly [JIN-jər-lee] *adverb* cautiously, warily, reluctantly
ging•ham [GING-əm] *noun* cotton cloth, usu. checked, woven from dyed yarn
gink•go [GING-koh] *noun, plural* **-goes** large

DICTIONARY

g

THESAURUS

better, mend, pull through, rally, revive, survive
ghastly *adjective* HORRIBLE, dreadful, frightful, gruesome, hideous, horrendous, loathsome, shocking, terrible, terrifying
ghost *noun* 1 SPIRIT, apparition, phantom, poltergeist, soul, specter, spook (*informal*), wraith 2 TRACE, glimmer, hint, possibility, semblance, shadow, suggestion
ghostly *adjective* SUPERNATURAL, eerie, ghostlike, phantom, spectral, spooky (*informal*), unearthly, wraithlike
ghoulish *adjective* MACABRE, disgusting, grisly, gruesome, morbid, sick (*informal*), unwholesome
giant *noun* 1 OGRE, colossus, monster, titan ▷ *adjective* 2 HUGE, colossal, enormous, gargantuan, gigantic, immense, mammoth, titanic, vast
gibberish *noun* NONSENSE, babble, drivel, gobbledygook (*informal*), mumbo jumbo, twaddle
gibe *or* **jibe** *verb* 1 TAUNT, jeer, make fun of, mock, poke fun at, ridicule, scoff, scorn, sneer ▷ *noun* 2 TAUNT, barb, crack (*slang*), dig, jeer, sarcasm, scoffing, sneer
giddiness *noun* DIZZINESS, faintness, light-headedness, vertigo
giddy *adjective* DIZZY, dizzying, faint, light-headed, reeling, unsteady, vertiginous
gift *noun* 1 DONATION, bequest, bonus, contribution, grant, hand-out, legacy, offering, present
2 TALENT, ability, capability, capacity, flair, genius, knack, power
gifted *adjective* TALENTED, able, accomplished, brilliant, capable, clever, expert, ingenious, masterly, skilled
gigantic *adjective* ENORMOUS, colossal, giant, huge, immense, mammoth, stupendous, titanic, tremendous
giggle *verb*
▷ *noun* LAUGH, cackle, chortle, chuckle, snigger, titter, twitter
gild *verb* EMBELLISH, adorn, beautify, brighten, coat, dress up, embroider, enhance, ornament
gimmick *noun* STUNT, contrivance, device, dodge, ploy, scheme
gingerly *adverb* CAUTIOUSLY, carefully, charily, circumspectly, hesitantly, reluctantly, suspiciously, timidly, warily

Chinese shade tree
gin•seng [JIN-seng] *noun* (root of) plant believed to have tonic and energy-giving properties
gi•raffe [jə-RAF] *noun* Afr. ruminant animal, with spotted coat and very long neck and legs
gird [gurd] *verb transitive* **gird•ed** *or* **girt, gird•ing** 1 put belt around 2 fasten clothes thus 3 equip with, or belt on, a sword 4 prepare (oneself) 5 encircle > **gird'er** *noun* large beam, esp. of steel
gir•dle [GURD-l] *noun* 1 corset 2 waistband 3 anything that surrounds, encircles ▷ *verb transitive* **-dled, -dling** 4 surround, encircle 5 remove bark (of tree) from a band around it
girl [gurl] *noun* 1 female child 2 young (formerly, an unmarried) woman > **girl'hood** [-huud] *noun*
girt *pt./pp. of* **gird**
girth [gurth] *noun* 1 measurement around thing 2 leather or cloth band put around horse to hold saddle, etc. ▷ *verb transitive* 3 surround, secure, with girth 4 girdle
gist [jist] *noun* substance, main point (of remarks, etc.)
give [giv] *verb transitive* **gave, giv•en, giv•ing** 1 bestow, confer ownership of, make present of 2 deliver 3 impart 4 assign 5 yield, supply 6 utter 7 emit 8 be host of (party, etc.) 9 make over 10 cause to have ▷ *verb intransitive* **gave, giv•en, giv•ing** 11 yield, give way, move ▷ *noun* 12 yielding, elasticity > **give'a•way** *noun* 1 act of giving something away 2 what is given away 3 telltale sign > **give up** 1 acknowledge defeat 2 abandon
giz•zard [GIZ-ərd] *noun* part of bird's stomach
gla•brous [GLAY-brəs] *adjective* 1 smooth 2 without hairs or any unevenness
gla•cier [GLAY-shər] *noun* river of ice, slow-moving mass of ice formed by accumulated snow in mountain valleys > **gla'cial** *adjective* 1 of ice, or of glaciers 2 very cold > **gla•ci•a'tion** *noun*
glad *adjective* **-der, -dest** 1 pleased 2 happy, joyous 3 giving joy > **glad'den** *verb transitive* make glad > **glad'ly** *adverb* > **glad rags** (*informal*) dressy clothes for party, etc.
glade [glayd] *noun* clear, grassy space in wood or forest
glad•i•a•tor [GLAD-ee-ay-tər] *noun* trained fighter in ancient Roman arena
glam•our [GLAM-ər] *noun* alluring charm, fascination > **glam'or•ize** *verb transitive* **-ized, -iz•ing** make appear glamorous > **glam'or•ous** *adjective*
glance [glans] *verb intransitive* **glanced, glanc•ing** 1 look rapidly or briefly 2 allude, touch 3 glide off something struck 4 pass quickly ▷ *noun* 5 brief look 6 flash 7 gleam 8 sudden (deflected) blow
gland *noun* one of various small organs controlling different bodily functions by chemical means > **glan•du•lar** [GLAN-jə-lər] *adjective*
glare [glair] *verb intransitive* **glared, glar•ing** 1 look fiercely 2 shine brightly, intensely 3 be conspicuous ▷ *noun*
glass *noun* 1 hard transparent substance made by fusing sand, soda, potash, etc. 2 things made of it 3 tumbler 4 its contents 5 lens 6 mirror 7 spyglass > **glass•es** eyeglasses > **glass'i•ness** *noun* > **glass'y** *adjective* **glass•i•er,**

DICTIONARY • THESAURUS

gird *verb* SURROUND, encircle, enclose, encompass, enfold, hem in, ring
girdle *noun* 1 BELT, band, cummerbund, sash, waistband
▷ *verb* 2 SURROUND, bound, encircle, enclose, encompass, gird, ring
girl *noun* FEMALE CHILD, damsel (*archaic*), daughter, lass, maid (*archaic*), maiden (*archaic*), miss
girth *noun* CIRCUMFERENCE, bulk, measure, size
gist *noun* POINT, core, essence, force, idea, meaning, sense, significance, substance
give *verb* 1 PRESENT, award, contribute, deliver, donate, grant, hand over *or* hand out, provide, supply
2 ANNOUNCE, communicate, issue, notify, pronounce, transmit, utter
3 CONCEDE, grant, hand over, relinquish, surrender, yield
4 PRODUCE, cause, engender, make, occasion
give away *verb* REVEAL, betray, disclose, divulge, expose, leak, let out, let slip, uncover
give in *verb* ADMIT DEFEAT, capitulate, collapse, concede, quit, submit, succumb, surrender, yield
give off *verb* EMIT, discharge, exude, produce, release, send out, throw out
give out *verb* EMIT, discharge, exude, produce, release, send out, throw out
give up *verb* ABANDON, call it a day *or* call it a night, cease, desist, leave off, quit, relinquish, renounce, stop, surrender
glad *adjective* 1 HAPPY, contented, delighted, gratified, joyful, overjoyed, pleased
2 PLEASING, cheerful, cheering, gratifying, pleasant
gladden *verb* PLEASE, cheer, delight, gratify, hearten
gladly *adverb* HAPPILY, cheerfully, freely, gleefully, readily, willingly, with pleasure
gladness *noun* HAPPINESS, cheerfulness, delight, gaiety, glee, high spirits, joy, mirth, pleasure
glamorous *adjective* ELEGANT, attractive, dazzling, exciting, fascinating, glittering, glossy, prestigious, smart
glamour *noun* CHARM, allure, appeal, attraction, beauty, enchantment, fascination, prestige
glance *verb* 1 LOOK, glimpse, peek, peep, scan, view
2 GLEAM, flash, glimmer, glint, glisten, glitter, reflect, shimmer, shine, twinkle
▷ *noun* 3 LOOK, glimpse, peek, peep, view
glare *verb* 1 SCOWL, frown, glower, look daggers, lour *or* lower
2 DAZZLE, blaze, flame, flare
▷ *noun* 3 SCOWL, black look, dirty look, frown, glower, lour *or* lower
4 DAZZLE, blaze, brilliance, flame, glow
glaring *adjective* 1 CONSPICUOUS, blatant, flagrant, gross, manifest, obvious, outrageous, unconcealed
2 DAZZLING, blazing, bright, garish, glowing
glassy *adjective* 1 TRANSPARENT, clear, glossy, shiny, slippery, smooth
2 EXPRESSIONLESS, blank, cold, dull, empty,

glass•i•est 1 like glass 2 expressionless > **glass wool** insulating fabric of spun glass
glau•co•ma [glow-KOH-mə] *noun* eye disease
glaze [glayz] *verb transitive* **glazed, glaz•ing** 1 furnish with glass 2 cover with glassy substance ▷ *verb intransitive* **glazed, glaz•ing** 3 become glassy ▷ *noun* 4 transparent coating 5 substance used for this 6 glossy surface > **gla•zier** [GLAY-*zh*ər] *noun* one who glazes windows
gleam [gleem] *noun* 1 slight or passing beam of light 2 faint or momentary show ▷ *verb intransitive* 3 give out gleams
glean [gleen] *verb* 1 pick up (facts, etc.) 2 gather, pick up, orig. after reapers in grainfields > **glean'er** *noun*
glee *noun* mirth, merriment 2 musical composition for three or more voices > **glee'ful** *adjective* > **glee club** chorus organized for singing choral music
glen *noun* narrow valley, usu. wooded and with a stream
glib *adjective* **-ber, -best** 1 fluent but insincere or superficial 2 plausible > **glib'ness** *noun*
glide [glīd] *verb intransitive* **glid•ed, glid•ing** 1 pass smoothly and continuously 2 of airplane, move without use of engines ▷ *noun* 3 smooth, silent movement 4 *mus.* sounds made in passing from tone to tone > **glid'er** *noun* 1 aircraft without engine that moves through the action of gravity and air currents 2 porch swing > **glid'ing** *noun* sport of flying gliders
glim•mer [GLIM-ər] *verb intransitive* shine faintly, flicker ▷ *noun* > **glim'mer•ing** *noun* 1 faint gleam of light 2 faint idea, notion
glimpse [glimps] *noun* 1 brief or incomplete view ▷ *verb transitive* **glimpsed, glimps•ing** 2 catch glimpse of
glint *verb* 1 flash, glance, glitter 2 reflect ▷ *noun*
glis•ten [GLIS-ən] *verb intransitive* gleam by reflecting light
glitch [glich] *noun* small problem that stops something from working properly
glit•ter [GLIT-ər] *verb intransitive* 1 shine with bright quivering light, sparkle 2 be showy ▷ *noun* 3 luster 4 sparkle
gloam•ing [GLOH-ming] *noun* evening twilight
gloat [gloht] *verb intransitive* regard, dwell on with smugness or malicious satisfaction
glob *noun* soft lump or mass
globe [glohb] *noun* 1 sphere with map of Earth or stars 2 heavenly sphere, esp. Earth 3 ball, sphere > **glob'al** *adjective* 1 of globe 2 relating to whole world > **glob•al•i•za'tion** [gloh-bəl-ī-ZAY-shən] *noun* broadening the scope, application, influence, or effect of something to the entire world > **glob'u•lar** [-yə-lər] *adjective* globe-shaped > **glob'ule** [-yool] *noun* 1 small round particle 2 drop > **glob'u•lin** *noun* kind of simple protein > **global warming** increase in overall temperature worldwide believed to be caused by pollutants > **globe'trot•ter** *noun* (habitual) world traveler
glock•en•spiel [GLOK-ən-speel] *noun* percussion instrument of metal bars struck with hammers
gloom *noun* 1 darkness 2 melancholy, depression > **gloom'y** *adjective* **gloom•i•er, gloom•i•est**

DICTIONARY

g

THESAURUS

---

fixed, glazed, lifeless, vacant
glaze *verb* 1 COAT, enamel, gloss, lacquer, polish, varnish
▷ *noun* 2 COAT, enamel, finish, gloss, lacquer, luster, patina, polish, shine, varnish
gleam *noun* 1 GLOW, beam, flash, glimmer, ray, sparkle
2 TRACE, flicker, glimmer, hint, inkling, suggestion
▷ *verb* 3 SHINE, flash, glimmer, glint, glisten, glitter, glow, shimmer, sparkle
glee *noun* DELIGHT, elation, exhilaration, exuberance, exultation, joy, merriment, triumph
gleeful *adjective* DELIGHTED, elated, exuberant, exultant, joyful, jubilant, overjoyed, triumphant
glib *adjective* SMOOTH, easy, fluent, insincere, plausible, quick, ready, slick, suave, voluble
glide *verb* SLIDE, coast, drift, float, flow, roll, run, sail, skate, slip
glimmer *verb* 1 FLICKER, blink, gleam, glisten, glitter, glow, shimmer, shine, sparkle, twinkle
▷ *noun* 2 GLEAM, blink, flicker, glow, ray, shimmer, sparkle, twinkle
3 TRACE, flicker, gleam, hint, inkling, suggestion
glimpse *noun* 1 LOOK, glance, peek, peep, sight, sighting
▷ *verb* 2 CATCH SIGHT OF, espy, sight, spot, spy, view
glint *verb* 1 GLEAM, flash, glimmer, glitter, shine, sparkle, twinkle
▷ *noun* 2 GLEAM, flash, glimmer, glitter, shine, sparkle, twinkle, twinkling
glisten *verb* GLEAM, flash, glance, glare, glimmer, glint, glitter, shimmer, shine, sparkle, twinkle
glitch *noun* PROBLEM, blip, difficulty, gremlin, hitch, interruption, malfunction, snag
glitter *verb* 1 SHINE, flash, glare, gleam, glimmer, glint, glisten, shimmer, sparkle, twinkle
▷ *noun* 2 SHINE, brightness, flash, glare, gleam, radiance, sheen, shimmer, sparkle
3 GLAMOUR, display, gaudiness, pageantry, show, showiness, splendor, tinsel
gloat *verb* RELISH, brag, crow, drool, exult, glory, revel in, rub it in (*informal*), triumph
global *adjective* 1 WORLDWIDE, international, planetary, universal, world
2 COMPREHENSIVE, all-inclusive, exhaustive, general, total, unlimited
globe *noun* SPHERE, ball, earth, orb, planet, world
globule *noun* DROPLET, bead, bubble, drop, particle, pearl, pellet
gloom *noun* 1 DARKNESS, blackness, dark, dusk, murk, obscurity, shade, shadow, twilight
2 DEPRESSION, dejection, despondency, low spirits, melancholy, sorrow, unhappiness, woe
gloomy *adjective* 1 DARK, black, dim, dismal, dreary, dull, gray, murky, somber
2 DEPRESSING, bad, cheerless, disheartening, dispiriting, dreary, sad, somber
3 MISERABLE, crestfallen, dejected, dispirited, downcast, downhearted, glum, melancholy,

glo•ry [GLOR-ee] *noun* 1 renown, honorable fame 2 splendor 3 exalted or prosperous state 4 heavenly bliss ▷ *verb intransitive* **-ried, -ry•ing** 5 take pride (in) > **glor'i•fy** *verb transitive* **-fied, -fy•ing** 1 make glorious 2 invest with glory > **glo'ri•ous** *adjective* 1 illustrious 2 splendid 3 excellent 4 delightful

gloss[1] *noun* 1 surface shine, luster ▷ *verb transitive* 2 put gloss on 3 (esp. with *over*) (try to) cover up, pass over (fault, error) > **gloss'i•ness** *noun* > **gloss'y** *adjective* **gloss•i•er, gloss•i•est** 1 smooth, shiny ▷ *noun* 2 photograph printed on shiny paper

gloss[2] *noun* 1 marginal interpretation of word 2 comment, explanation ▷ *verb transitive* 3 interpret 4 comment 5 explain away > **glos'sa•ry** *noun, plural* **-ries** dictionary, vocabulary of special words

glot'tis *noun* human vocal apparatus, larynx > **glot'tal** [GLOT-l] *adjective*

glove [gluv] *noun* 1 covering for the hand ▷ *verb transitive* **gloved, glov•ing** 2 cover with, or as with glove > **glove compartment** storage area in dashboard of automobile **the gloves** boxing gloves

glow [gloh] *verb intransitive* 1 give out light and heat without flames 2 shine 3 experience well-being or satisfaction 4 be or look hot 5 burn with emotion ▷ *noun* 6 shining heat 7 warmth of color 8 feeling of well-being 9 ardor > **glow•worm** [GLOH-wurm] *noun* female insect giving out green light

glow•er [GLOW-ər] *verb intransitive* scowl

glu•cose [GLOO-kohs] *noun* type of sugar found in fruit, etc.

glue [gloo] *noun* 1 any natural or synthetic adhesive 2 any sticky substance ▷ *verb transitive* **glued, glu•ing** 3 fasten (as if) with glue > **glue sniffing** practice of inhaling fumes of glue for intoxicating or hallucinatory effects

glum *adjective* **glum•mer, glum•mest** sullen, moody, gloomy

glut *noun* 1 surfeit, excessive amount ▷ *verb transitive* **glut•ted, glut•ting** 2 feed, gratify to the full or to excess 3 overstock

glu•ten [GLOOT-n] *noun* protein present in cereal grain > **glu'ti•nous** *adjective* sticky, gluey

glut•ton [GLUT-n] *noun* 1 greedy person 2 one with great liking or capacity for something, esp. food and drink > **glut'ton•ous** *adjective* like glutton, greedy > **glut'ton•y** *noun*

glyc•er•in [GLIS-ər-in] *noun* colorless sweet liquid with wide application in chemistry and industry

GM genetically modified

GMO genetically modified organism

gnarled [nahrld] *adjective* knobbly, rugged, twisted

gnash [nash] *verb* grind (teeth) together as in anger or pain

gnat [nat] *noun* small, biting, two-winged fly

gnaw [naw] *verb* 1 bite or chew steadily 2 (esp. with *at*) cause distress to

gneiss [nīs] *noun* coarse-grained metamorphic rock

gnome [nohm] *noun* 1 legendary creature like small old man 2 international financier > **gnom'ish** *adjective*

gno•mic [NOH-mik] *adjective* of or like an aphorism

gnos•tic [NOS-tik] *adjective* of, relating to knowledge, esp. spiritual knowledge

gnu [noo] *noun* S Afr. antelope somewhat like ox

go [goh] *verb intransitive* **went, gone, go•ing** 1 move along, make way 2 be moving 3 depart 4 function 5 make specified sound 6 fail, give

morose, pessimistic, sad

glorify *verb* 1 ENHANCE, aggrandize, dignify, elevate, ennoble, magnify
2 WORSHIP, adore, bless, exalt, honor, idolize, pay homage to, revere, venerate
3 PRAISE, celebrate, eulogize, extol, sing the praises of *or* sound the praises of

glorious *adjective* 1 FAMOUS, celebrated, distinguished, eminent, honored, illustrious, magnificent, majestic, renowned
2 SPLENDID, beautiful, brilliant, dazzling, gorgeous, shining, superb
3 DELIGHTFUL, excellent, fine, gorgeous, marvelous, wonderful

glory *noun* 1 HONOR, dignity, distinction, eminence, fame, kudos, praise, prestige, renown
2 SPLENDOR, grandeur, greatness, magnificence, majesty, nobility, pageantry, pomp
▷ *verb* 3 TRIUMPH, boast, exult, pride oneself, relish, revel, take delight

gloss[1] *noun* SHINE, brightness, gleam, luster, patina, polish, sheen, veneer

gloss[2] *noun* 1 COMMENT, annotation, commentary, elucidation, explanation, footnote, interpretation, note, translation
▷ *verb* 2 INTERPRET, annotate, comment, elucidate, explain, translate

glossy *adjective* SHINY, bright, glassy, glazed, lustrous, polished, shining, silky

glow *verb* 1 SHINE, brighten, burn, gleam, glimmer, redden, smolder
▷ *noun* 2 LIGHT, burning, gleam, glimmer, luminosity, phosphorescence
3 RADIANCE, brightness, brilliance, effulgence, splendor, vividness

glower *verb* 1 SCOWL, frown, give a dirty look, glare, look daggers, lour *or* lower
▷ *noun* 2 SCOWL, black look, dirty look, frown, glare, lour *or* lower

glowing *adjective* 1 BRIGHT, aglow, flaming, luminous, radiant
2 COMPLIMENTARY, adulatory, ecstatic, enthusiastic, laudatory, rave (*informal*), rhapsodic

glue *noun* 1 ADHESIVE, cement, gum, paste
▷ *verb* 2 STICK, affix, cement, fix, gum, paste, seal

glum *adjective* GLOOMY, crestfallen, dejected, doleful, low, morose, pessimistic, sullen

glut *noun* 1 SURFEIT, excess, oversupply, plethora, saturation, superfluity, surplus
▷ *verb* 2 SATURATE, choke, clog, deluge, flood, inundate, overload, oversupply

glutton *noun* GOURMAND, pig (*informal*)

gluttonous *adjective* GREEDY, gormandizing, insatiable, piggish, ravenous, voracious

gluttony *noun* GREED, gormandizing, greediness, voracity

gnarled *adjective* TWISTED, contorted, knotted, knotty, rough, rugged, weather-beaten, wrinkled

way, break down **7** elapse **8** be kept, put **9** be able to be put **10** result **11** contribute to result **12** tend to **13** be accepted, have force **14** become ▷ *noun* **15** going **16** energy, vigor **17** attempt **18** turn > **go-go dancer** dancer, usu. scantily dressed, who performs rhythmic and oft. erotic modern dance routines, esp. in nightclub

goad [gohd] *noun* **1** spiked stick for driving cattle **2** anything that urges to action **3** incentive ▷ *verb transitive* **4** urge on **5** torment

goal [gohl] *noun* **1** end of race **2** object of effort **3** posts through which ball is to be driven in various games **4** the score so made

goat [goht] *noun* four-footed animal with long hair, horns and beard > **goat•ee'** *noun* beard like goat's **get someone's goat** (*informal*) annoy (someone)

gob *noun* **1** lump **2** (*slang*) sailor > **gob•ble** [GOB-əl] *verb transitive* **-bled, -bling** eat hastily, noisily or greedily

gob•ble *noun* **1** throaty, gurgling cry of male turkey ▷ *verb intransitive* **-bled, -bling 2** make such a noise

gob•ble•dy•gook, -de•gook [GOB-əl-dee-guuk] *noun* pretentious, usu. incomprehensible language, esp. as used by officials

gob•let [GOB-lit] *noun* drinking cup

gob'lin *noun folklore* small, usu. malevolent being

god *noun* **1** superhuman being worshipped as having supernatural power **2** object of worship, idol **3** (**God**) in monotheistic religions, the Supreme Being, creator and ruler of universe > **god'dess** *noun feminine* > **god'like** *adjective* > **god'li•ness** *noun* > **god'ly** *adjective* **-li•er, -li•est** devout, pious > **god'child** *noun* child for whom a person stands as godparent > **god'father** *noun* > **god'mother** *noun* > **god'parent** *noun* sponsor at baptism > **God-fearing** *adjective* religious, good > **god'for•sak•en** [-fər-say-ken] *adjective* hopeless, dismal > **God'head** *noun* divine nature or deity > **god'send** *noun* something unexpected but welcome

gog•gle [GOG-əl] *verb intransitive* **-gled, -gling 1** (of eyes) bulge **2** stare ▷ *plural noun* **3** protective eyeglasses

goi•ter [GOI-tər] *noun* neck swelling due to enlargement of thyroid gland

go-kart, go-cart *see* **kart**

gold [gohld] *noun* **1** yellow precious metal **2** coins of this **3** wealth **4** beautiful or precious thing **5** color of gold ▷ *adjective* **6** of, like gold > **gold'en** *adjective* > **gold digger** (*informal*) woman skillful in extracting money from men > **golden mean** middle way between extremes > **gold'en•rod** *noun* tall plant with golden flower spikes > **golden rule** important principle > **golden wedding** fiftieth wedding anniversary > **gold'field** *noun* place where gold deposits are known to exist > **gold'finch** *noun* bird with yellow feathers > **gold'fish** *noun* any of various ornamental pond or aquarium fish > **gold standard** financial arrangement whereby currencies of countries accepting it are expressed in fixed terms of gold

golf *noun* **1** outdoor game in which small hard ball is struck with clubs into a succession of holes ▷ *verb intransitive* **2** play this game

go•nad [GOH-nad] *noun* gland producing gametes

gon•do•la [GON-dl-ə] *noun* Venetian canal boat > **gon•do•lier'** *noun* rower of gondola

gone [gawn] *pp. of* **go**

gong *noun* **1** metal plate with turned rim that resounds as bell when struck with soft mallet **2** anything used thus

gon•or•rhea [gon-ə-REE-ə] *noun* a venereal disease

good [guud] *adjective* **bet•ter, best 1** commendable **2** right **3** proper **4** excellent **5** beneficial **6** well-behaved **7** virtuous **8** kind

DICTIONARY

g

THESAURUS

---

gnaw *verb* BITE, chew, munch, nibble

go *verb* **1** MOVE, advance, journey, make for, pass, proceed, set off, travel
2 LEAVE, depart, make tracks, move out, slope off, withdraw
3 FUNCTION, move, operate, perform, run, work
4 CONTRIBUTE, lead to, serve, tend, work towards
5 HARMONIZE, agree, blend, chime, complement, correspond, fit, match, suit
6 ELAPSE, expire, flow, lapse, pass, slip away
▷ *noun* 7 ATTEMPT, bid, crack (*informal*), effort, shot (*informal*), try, turn
8 (*informal*) ENERGY, drive, force, life, spirit, verve, vigor, vitality, vivacity

goad *verb* 1 PROVOKE, drive, egg on, exhort, incite, prod, prompt, spur
▷ *noun* 2 PROVOCATION, impetus, incentive, incitement, irritation, spur, stimulus, urge

goal *noun* AIM, ambition, end, intention, object, objective, purpose, target

gobble *verb* DEVOUR, bolt, cram, gorge, gulp, guzzle, stuff, swallow, wolf

go-between *noun* INTERMEDIARY, agent, broker, dealer, mediator, medium, middleman

godforsaken *adjective* DESOLATE, abandoned, bleak, deserted, dismal, dreary, forlorn, gloomy, lonely, remote, wretched

godlike *adjective* DIVINE, celestial, heavenly, superhuman, transcendent

godly *adjective* DEVOUT, god-fearing, good, holy, pious, religious, righteous, saintly

godsend *noun* BLESSING, boon, manna, stroke of luck, windfall

go for *verb* 1 FAVOR, admire, be attracted to, be fond of, choose, like, prefer
2 ATTACK, assail, assault, launch oneself at, rush upon, set about *or* set upon, spring upon

golden *adjective* 1 YELLOW, blond *or* blonde, flaxen
2 SUCCESSFUL, flourishing, glorious, halcyon, happy, prosperous, rich
3 PROMISING, excellent, favorable, opportune

gone *adjective* 1 FINISHED, elapsed, ended, over, past
2 MISSING, absent, astray, away, lacking, lost, vanished

good *adjective* 1 PLEASING, acceptable, admirable, excellent, fine, first-class, first-rate, great, satisfactory, splendid, superior
2 PRAISEWORTHY, admirable, ethical, honest, honorable, moral, righteous, trustworthy, upright, virtuous, worthy
3 EXPERT, able, accomplished, adept, adroit,

9 safe 10 adequate 11 sound 12 valid ▷ *noun* 13 benefit 14 well-being 15 profit > **goods** 1 property 2 wares > **good'ly** *adjective* large, considerable > **good'ness** *noun* > **good will** 1 kindly feeling, heartiness 2 value of a business in reputation, etc. over and above its tangible assets

good-bye [guud-BĪ] *interjection, noun* form of address on parting

goof *noun* (*informal*) 1 mistake 2 stupid person ▷ *verb intransitive* 3 make mistake > **goof'y** *adjective* **goof•i•er, goof•i•est** silly

goo•gle [GOO-gəl] *verb transitive* 1 search for (something) on the Internet using a search engine 2 check (someone's credentials) by entering that person's name into an Internet search engine

goon *noun* (*slang*) 1 stupid, awkward fellow 2 (*informal*) hired thug, hoodlum

goose [goos] *noun, plural* **geese** 1 web-footed bird 2 its flesh 3 simpleton > **goose flesh** bristling of skin due to cold, fright > **goose step** formal parade step

go•pher [GOH-fər] *noun* various species of Amer. burrowing rodents > **gopher ball** *baseball* (*slang*) pitched ball hit for home run

gore¹ [gor] *noun* (dried) blood from wound > **gor'y** *adjective* **gor•i•er, gor•i•est**

gore² *verb transitive* **gored, gor•ing** pierce with horns

gore³ *noun* 1 triangular piece inserted to shape garment ▷ *verb transitive* **gored, gor•ing** 2 shape thus

gorge [gorj] *noun* 1 ravine 2 disgust, resentment ▷ *verb intransitive* **gorged, gorg•ing** 3 feed greedily

gor•geous [GOR-jəs] *adjective* 1 splendid, showy, dazzling 2 (*informal*) extremely pleasing

gor•gon [GOR-gən] *noun* 1 terrifying or repulsive woman 2 (**Gor•gon**) in Greek mythology, any of three sisters whose appearance turned any viewer to stone

go•ril•la [gə-RIL-ə] *noun* largest anthropoid ape, found in Afr.

gor•mand•ize [GOR-mən-dīz] *verb transitive* **-ized, -iz•ing** eat hurriedly or like a glutton

gory *see* **gore¹**

gos'hawk *noun* large hawk

gos•ling [GOZ-ling] *noun* young goose

gos•pel [GOS-pəl] *noun* 1 unquestionable truth 2 (**Gos•pel**) any of first four books of New Testament

gos•sa•mer [GOS-ə-mər] *noun* 1 filmy substance like spider's web 2 thin gauze or silk fabric

gos•sip [GOS-əp] *noun* 1 idle (malicious) talk

DICTIONARY • THESAURUS

clever, competent, proficient, skilled, talented
4 BENEFICIAL, advantageous, convenient, favorable, fitting, helpful, profitable, suitable, useful, wholesome, win-win (*informal*)
5 KIND, altruistic, benevolent, charitable, friendly, humane, kind-hearted, kindly, merciful, obliging
6 VALID, authentic, bona fide, genuine, legitimate, proper, real, true
7 WELL-BEHAVED, dutiful, obedient, orderly, polite, well-mannered
8 FULL, adequate, ample, complete, considerable, extensive, large, substantial, sufficient
▷ *noun* 9 BENEFIT, advantage, gain, interest, profit, use, usefulness, welfare, wellbeing
10 VIRTUE, excellence, goodness, merit, morality, rectitude, right, righteousness, worth
11 ▷ **for good** PERMANENTLY, finally, for ever, irrevocably, once and for all

good-bye *noun* FAREWELL, adieu, leave-taking, parting

good-for-nothing *noun* 1 IDLER, couch potato (*slang*), slacker (*informal*), waster, wastrel
▷ *adjective* 2 WORTHLESS, feckless, idle, irresponsible, useless

goodly *adjective* CONSIDERABLE, ample, large, significant, sizable *or* sizeable, substantial, tidy (*informal*)

goodness *noun* 1 EXCELLENCE, merit, quality, superiority, value, worth
2 KINDNESS, benevolence, friendliness, generosity, goodwill, humaneness, kind-heartedness, kindliness, mercy
3 VIRTUE, honesty, honor, integrity, merit, morality, probity, rectitude, righteousness, uprightness
4 BENEFIT, advantage, salubriousness, wholesomeness

goods *plural noun* 1 PROPERTY, belongings, chattels, effects, gear, paraphernalia, possessions, things, trappings
2 MERCHANDISE, commodities, stock, stuff, wares

goodwill *noun* FRIENDLINESS, amity, benevolence, friendship, heartiness, kindliness

go off *verb* 1 EXPLODE, blow up, detonate, fire
2 LEAVE, decamp, depart, go away, move out, part, quit, slope off

go out *verb* 1 LEAVE, depart, exit
2 BE EXTINGUISHED, die out, expire, fade out

go over *verb* EXAMINE, inspect, rehearse, reiterate, review, revise, study, work over

gore¹ *noun* BLOOD, bloodshed, butchery, carnage, slaughter

gore² *verb* PIERCE, impale, transfix, wound

gorge¹ *noun* 1 RAVINE, canyon, chasm, cleft, defile, fissure, pass
▷ *verb* 2 OVEREAT, cram, devour, feed, glut, gobble, gulp, guzzle, stuff, wolf

gorgeous *adjective* 1 BEAUTIFUL, dazzling, elegant, magnificent, ravishing, splendid, stunning (*informal*), sumptuous, superb
2 (*informal*) PLEASING, delightful, enjoyable, exquisite, fine, glorious, good, lovely

gory *adjective* BLOODTHIRSTY, blood-soaked, bloodstained, bloody, murderous, sanguinary

gospel *noun* 1 TRUTH, certainty, fact, the last word
2 DOCTRINE, credo, creed, message, news, revelation, tidings

gossip *noun* 1 IDLE TALK, blether, chitchat, hearsay, scandal, small talk, tittle-tattle
2 BUSYBODY, chatterbox (*informal*), chatterer, gossipmonger, scandalmonger, tattler, telltale
▷ *verb* 3 CHAT, blether, chew the fat (*slang*), gabble, jaw (*slang*), prate, prattle, tattle

go through *verb* 1 SUFFER, bear, brave, endure, experience, tolerate, undergo, withstand
2 EXAMINE, check, explore, forage, hunt,

about other persons, esp. regardless of fact 2 one who talks thus ▷ *verb intransitive* **-siped, -sip•ing** 3 engage in gossip 4 chatter
got *see* **get**
Goth•ic [GOTH-ik] *adjective* 1 *architecture* of the pointed arch style common in Europe from twelfth to sixteenth century 2 of Goths 3 barbarous 4 gloomy 5 grotesque 6 (of type) German black letter
gouge [gowj] *verb transitive* **gouged, goug•ing** 1 scoop out 2 force out 3 extort from 4 overcharge ▷ *noun* 5 chisel with curved cutting edge
gou•lash [GOO-lahsh] *noun* stew of meat and vegetables seasoned with paprika, etc.
gourd [gord] *noun* 1 trailing or climbing plant 2 its large fleshy fruit 3 its rind as vessel
gour•mand [guur-MAHND] *noun* glutton
gour•met [guur-MAY] *noun* 1 connoisseur of wine, food 2 epicure
gout [gowt] *noun* disease with inflammation, esp. of joints
gov [guv] Internet domain name for a US governmental organization
gov•ern [GUV-ərn] *verb transitive* 1 rule, direct, guide, control 2 decide or determine 3 be followed by (grammatical case, etc.) > **gov'ern•a•ble** *adjective* > **gov'ern•ess** *noun* woman teacher in private household > **gov'ern•ment** *noun* 1 exercise of political authority in directing a people, country, etc. 2 system by which community is ruled 3 body of people in charge of government of country 4 executive power 5 control 6 direction 7 exercise of authority > **gov'ern•or** *noun* 1 one who governs, esp. one invested with supreme authority in a state, etc. 2 chief administrator of an institution 3 member of committee responsible for an organization or institution 4 regulator for speed of engine
gown *noun* 1 loose flowing outer garment 2 woman's (long) dress 3 official robe, as in university, etc.
GPS Global Positioning System: a satellite-based navigation system
grab *verb transitive* **grabbed, grab•bing** 1 grasp suddenly 2 snatch ▷ *noun* 3 sudden clutch 4 quick attempt to seize 5 device or implement for clutching
grace [grays] *noun* 1 charm, elegance 2 accomplishment 3 goodwill, favor 4 sense of propriety 5 postponement granted 6 short thanksgiving before or after meal ▷ *verb transitive* **graced, grac•ing** 7 add grace to, honor > **grace'ful** *adjective* > **grace'less** *adjective* shameless, depraved > **gra'cious** [-shəs] *adjective* 1 favorable 2 kind 3 pleasing 4 indulgent, beneficent, condescending > **grace note** *mus.* melodic ornament
grade [grayd] *noun* 1 step, stage 2 degree of rank, etc. 3 class 4 mark, rating 5 slope ▷ *verb transitive* **grad•ed, grad•ing** 6 arrange in classes 7 assign grade to 8 level ground, move earth with grader > **gra•da'tion** *noun* 1 series of degrees or steps 2 each of them 3 arrangement in steps 4 in painting, gradual passing from one shade, etc. to another > **grad'er** *noun* esp. machine with wide blade used in road making **make the grade** succeed
gra•di•ent [GRAY-dee-ənt] *noun* (degree of) slope
grad•u•al [GRAJ-oo-əl] *adjective* 1 taking place by degrees 2 slow and steady 3 not steep > **grad'u•al•ly** *adverb*
grad•u•ate [GRAJ-oo-ayt] *verb intransitive* **-at•ed, -at•ing** 1 receive diploma or degree on completing course of study ▷ *verb transitive* **-at•ed, -at•ing** 2 divide into degrees 3 mark, arrange according to scale ▷ *noun* [-it] 4 holder of diploma or degree > **grad•u•a'tion** *noun*
graf•fi•ti [grə-FEE-tee] *plural noun* words or drawings scribbled or sprayed on walls etc.
graft[1] *noun* 1 shoot of plant set in stalk of another 2 the process 3 surgical transplant of

DICTIONARY

g

THESAURUS

look, search
gouge *verb* 1 SCOOP, chisel, claw, cut, dig *or* dig out, hollow *or* hollow out
▷ *noun* 2 GASH, cut, furrow, groove, hollow, scoop, scratch, trench
gourmet *noun* CONNOISSEUR, bon vivant (*French*), epicure, foodie (*informal*), gastronome
govern *verb* 1 RULE, administer, command, control, direct, guide, handle, lead, manage, order
2 RESTRAIN, check, control, curb, discipline, hold in check, master, regulate, subdue, tame
government *noun* 1 RULE, administration, authority, governance, sovereignty, statecraft
2 EXECUTIVE, administration, ministry, powers-that-be, regime
governor *noun* LEADER, administrator, chief, commander, controller, director, executive, head, manager, ruler
gown *noun* DRESS, costume, frock, garb, garment, habit, robe
grab *verb* SNATCH, capture, catch, catch hold of *or* take hold of, clutch, grasp, grip, pluck, seize, snap up
grace *noun* 1 ELEGANCE, attractiveness, beauty, charm, comeliness, ease, gracefulness, poise, polish, refinement, tastefulness
2 GOODWILL, benefaction, benevolence, favor, generosity, goodness, kindliness, kindness
3 MANNERS, consideration, decency, decorum, etiquette, propriety, tact
4 INDULGENCE, mercy, pardon, reprieve
5 PRAYER, benediction, blessing, thanks, thanksgiving
▷ *verb* 6 HONOR, adorn, decorate, dignify, embellish, enhance, enrich, favor, ornament, set off
graceful *adjective* ELEGANT, beautiful, charming, comely, easy, pleasing, tasteful
gracious *adjective* KIND, charitable, civil, considerate, cordial, courteous, friendly, polite, well-mannered
grade *noun* 1 LEVEL, category, class, degree, echelon, group, rank, stage
▷ *verb* 2 CLASSIFY, arrange, class, group, order, range, rank, rate, sort
gradient *noun* SLOPE, bank, declivity, grade, hill, incline, rise
gradual *adjective* STEADY, gentle, graduated, piecemeal, progressive, regular, slow, unhurried
gradually *adverb* STEADILY, by degrees, gently, little by little, progressively, slowly, step by step,

skin, tissue ▷ *verb transitive* 4 insert (shoot) in another stalk 5 transplant (living tissue in surgery)

graft² *noun* (*informal*) 1 self-advancement, profit by unfair means, esp. through official or political privilege 2 bribe 3 swindle

grail [grayl] *noun* cup or dish used by Christ at the Last Supper (*also* **Holy Grail**)

grain [grayn] *noun* 1 seed, fruit of cereal plant 2 wheat and allied plants 3 small hard particle 4 unit of weight, 0.0648 gram 5 texture 6 arrangement of fibers 7 any very small amount 8 natural temperament or disposition

gram *noun* unit of weight (equivalent to 0.035 ounce) in metric system, one thousandth of a kilogram

gram•mar [GRAM-ər] *noun* 1 science of structure and usage of language 2 book on this 3 correct use of words > **gram•mar•i•an** [grə-MAIR-ee-ən] *noun* > **gram•mat'i•cal** *adjective* according to grammar > **grammar school** elementary school

gra•na•ry [GRAY-nə-ree] *noun, plural* **-ries** 1 storehouse for grain 2 rich grain-growing region

grand *adjective* **-er, -est** 1 imposing 2 magnificent 3 majestic 4 noble 5 splendid 6 eminent 7 lofty 8 chief, of chief importance 9 final (total) > **gran•deur** [GRAN-jər] *noun* 1 nobility 2 magnificence 3 dignity > **gran•dil'o•quence** *noun* > **gran•dil'o•quent** *adjective* pompous in speech > **gran'di•ose** [-dee-ohs] *adjective* 1 imposing 2 affectedly grand 3 striking > **grand'child** *noun* child of one's child > **grand'daugh•ter** *noun* female grandchild > **grand'fa•ther** *noun* male grandparent > **grand'moth•er** *noun* female grandparent > **grand'par•ent** *noun* parent of one's parent > **grand piano** large harp-shaped piano with horizontal strings > **grand'son** *noun* male grandchild > **grand'stand** *noun* structure with tiered seats for spectators

grange [graynj] *noun* farm with its farmhouse and farm buildings

gran•ite [GRAN-it] *noun* hard crystalline igneous rock > **gran'ite•like** *adjective*

gran•ny [GRAN-ee] *noun, plural* **-nies** (*informal*) grandmother

gra•no•la [grə-NOH-lə] *noun* mixture of rolled oats, brown sugar, nuts, and fruit, eaten with milk

grant *verb transitive* 1 consent to fulfill (request) 2 permit 3 bestow 4 admit ▷ *noun* 5 sum of money provided by government or other source for specific purpose, as education 6 gift 7 allowance, concession

gran•ule [GRAN-yool] *noun* 1 small grain 2 small particle > **gran'u•lar** [-yə-lər] *adjective* of or like grains

grape [grayp] *noun* fruit of vine > **grape'shot** *noun* bullets scattering when fired > **grape'vine** [-vīn] *noun* 1 grape-bearing vine 2 (*informal*) unofficial means of conveying information

grape•fruit [GRAYP-froot] *noun* subtropical citrus fruit

graph [graf] *noun* 1 drawing depicting relation of different numbers, quantities, etc. ▷ *verb transitive* 2 represent by graph

graph•ic [GRAF-ik] *adjective* 1 vividly descriptive 2 of, in, relating to, writing, drawing, painting, etc. > **graphics** *plural noun* diagrams, graphs, etc., esp. as used on a TV programme or computer screen > **graph'i•cal•ly** *adverb* > **graph'ite** [-īt] *noun* form of carbon (used in pencils) > **graph•ol'o•gy** *noun* study of handwriting

grap•nel [GRAP-nl] *noun* 1 hooked iron instrument for seizing anything 2 small anchor with several flukes

grap•ple [GRAP-əl] *verb* **-pled, -pling** 1 come to grips with, wrestle 2 cope or contend ▷ *noun* 3 grappling 4 grapnel

grasp *verb* (try, struggle to) seize hold 1 understand ▷ *noun* 2 act of grasping 3 grip 4

---

unhurriedly

graduate *verb* 1 MARK OFF, calibrate, grade, measure out, proportion, regulate
2 CLASSIFY, arrange, grade, group, order, rank, sort

graft *noun* 1 SHOOT, bud, implant, scion, splice, sprout
▷ *verb* 2 TRANSPLANT, affix, implant, ingraft, insert, join, splice

grain *noun* 1 CEREALS, corn
2 SEED, grist, kernel
3 BIT, fragment, granule, modicum, morsel, particle, piece, scrap, speck, trace
4 TEXTURE, fiber, nap, pattern, surface, weave
5 INCLINATION, character, disposition, humor, make-up, temper

grand *adjective* 1 IMPRESSIVE, dignified, grandiose, great, imposing, large, magnificent, regal, splendid, stately, sublime
2 EXCELLENT, cool (*informal*), fine, first-class, great (*informal*), outstanding, phat (*slang*), splendid, wonderful

grandeur *noun* SPLENDOR, dignity, magnificence, majesty, nobility, pomp, stateliness, sublimity

grandiose *adjective* 1 PRETENTIOUS, affected, bombastic, extravagant, flamboyant, high-flown, ostentatious, pompous, showy
2 IMPOSING, grand, impressive, lofty, magnificent, majestic, monumental, stately

grant *verb* 1 CONSENT TO, accede to, agree to, allow, permit
2 GIVE, allocate, allot, assign, award, donate, hand out, present
3 ADMIT, acknowledge, concede
▷ *noun* 4 AWARD, allowance, donation, endowment, gift, hand-out, present, subsidy

granule *noun* GRAIN, atom, crumb, fragment, molecule, particle, scrap, speck

graphic *adjective* 1 VIVID, clear, detailed, explicit, expressive, lively, lucid, striking
2 PICTORIAL, diagrammatic, visual

grapple *verb* 1 GRIP, clutch, grab, grasp, seize, wrestle
2 DEAL WITH, address oneself to, confront, get to grips with, struggle, tackle, take on

grasp *verb* 1 GRIP, catch, clasp, clinch, clutch, grab, grapple, hold, lay hold of *or* take hold of, seize, snatch
2 UNDERSTAND, catch on, catch the drift of *or* get the drift of, comprehend, get, realize, see, take in

comprehension > **grasp'ing** *adjective* greedy, avaricious

grass *noun* 1 common type of plant with jointed stems and long narrow leaves (including cereals, bamboo, etc.) 2 such plants grown as lawn 3 pasture 4 (*slang*) marijuana ▷ *verb transitive* 5 cover with grass > **grass'hop•per** *noun* jumping, chirping insect > **grass roots** 1 ordinary people 2 fundamentals > **grass-roots** *adjective* coming from ordinary people, the rank and file

grate[1] [grayt] *noun* framework of metal bars for holding fuel in fireplace > **grat'ing** *noun* framework of parallel or latticed bars covering opening

grate[2] *verb transitive* **grat•ed, grat•ing** 1 rub into small bits on rough surface ▷ *verb intransitive* **grat•ed, grat•ing** 2 rub with harsh noise 3 have irritating effect > **grat'er** *noun* utensil with rough surface for reducing substance to small particles > **grating** *adjective* 1 harsh 2 irritating

grate•ful [GRAYT-fəl] *adjective* 1 thankful 2 appreciative 3 pleasing > **grat•i•tude** [GRAT-ə-tood] *noun* sense of being thankful for favor

grat•i•fy [GRAT-ə-fī] *verb transitive* **-fied, -fy•ing** 1 satisfy 2 please 3 indulge > **grat•i•fi•ca'tion** *noun*

gratin *see* **au gratin**

grat'is *adverb, adjective* free, for nothing

gra•tu•i•tous [grə-TOO-i-təs] *adjective* 1 given free 2 uncalled for > **gra•tu'i•tous•ly** *adverb* > **gra•tu'i•ty** *noun, plural* **-ties** a tip

grave[1] [grayv] *noun* 1 hole dug to bury corpse 2 death > **grave'stone** *noun* monument on grave > **grave'yard** *noun*

grave[2] *adjective* **grav•er, grav•est** 1 serious, weighty 2 dignified, solemn 3 plain, dark in color 4 deep in note > **grave'ly** *adverb*

grave[3] *noun* accent (`) over vowel to indicate special sound quality

grav•el [GRAV-əl] *noun* 1 small stones 2 coarse sand ▷ *verb transitive* **-eled, -el•ing** 3 cover with gravel > **grav'el•ly** *adjective*

grav•en [GRAY-vən] *adjective* carved, engraved

grav•i•tate [GRAV-i-tayt] *verb intransitive* **-tat•ed, -tat•ing** 1 move by gravity 2 tend (toward) center of attraction 3 sink, settle down > **grav•i•ta'tion** *noun*

grav•i•ty [GRAV-i-tee] *noun, plural* **-ties** 1 force of attraction of one body for another, esp. of objects to Earth 2 heaviness 3 importance 4 seriousness 5 staidness

gra•vy [GRAY-vee] *noun, plural* **-vies** 1 juices from meat in cooking 2 sauce for food made from these 3 thing of value obtained unexpectedly

gray *adjective* 1 between black and white, as ashes or lead 2 clouded 3 dismal 4 turning white 5 aged 6 intermediate, indeterminate ▷ *noun* 7 gray color 8 gray or white horse

graze[1] [grayz] *verb* **grazed, graz•ing** feed on grass, pasture

graze[2] *verb transitive* **grazed, graz•ing** 1 touch lightly in passing, scratch, scrape ▷ *noun* 2 grazing 3 abrasion

grease [grees] *noun* 1 soft melted fat of animals 2 thick oil as lubricant ▷ *verb transitive* **greased, greas•ing** 3 apply grease to > **greas'i•ness** *noun* > **greas'y** *adjective* **greas•i•er, greas•i•est** > **grease gun** appliance for injecting grease into machinery > **grease monkey** (*informal*) mechanic > **grease'paint** *noun* theatrical makeup

great [grayt] *adjective* **-er, -est** 1 large, big 2 important 3 preeminent, distinguished 4 (*informal*) excellent > **great-** *prefix* one generation

DICTIONARY

g

THESAURUS

▷ *noun* 3 GRIP, clasp, clutches, embrace, hold, possession, tenure
4 CONTROL, power, reach, scope
5 UNDERSTANDING, awareness, comprehension, grip, knowledge, mastery

grasping *adjective* GREEDY, acquisitive, avaricious, covetous, rapacious

grate *verb* 1 SHRED, mince, pulverize, triturate
2 SCRAPE, creak, grind, rasp, rub, scratch
3 ANNOY, exasperate, get on one's nerves (*informal*), irritate, jar, rankle, set one's teeth on edge

grateful *adjective* THANKFUL, appreciative, beholden, indebted, obliged

gratification *noun* SATISFACTION, delight, enjoyment, fulfillment, indulgence, pleasure, relish, reward, thrill

gratify *verb* PLEASE, delight, give pleasure, gladden, humor, requite, satisfy

grating[1] *adjective* IRRITATING, annoying, discordant, displeasing, harsh, jarring, offensive, raucous, strident, unpleasant

grating[2] *noun* GRILLE, grate, grid, gridiron, lattice, trellis

gratitude *noun* THANKFULNESS, appreciation, gratefulness, indebtedness, obligation, recognition, thanks

gratuitous *adjective* 1 FREE, complimentary, gratis, spontaneous, unasked-for, unpaid, unrewarded, voluntary
2 UNJUSTIFIED, baseless, causeless, groundless, needless, superfluous, uncalled-for, unmerited, unnecessary, unwarranted, wanton

gratuity *noun* TIP, bonus, donation, gift, largesse *or* largess, reward

grave[1] *noun* BURYING PLACE, crypt, mausoleum, pit, sepulcher, tomb, vault

grave[2] *adjective* 1 SOLEMN, dignified, dour, earnest, serious, sober, somber, unsmiling
2 IMPORTANT, acute, critical, dangerous, pressing, serious, severe, threatening, urgent

graveyard *noun* CEMETERY, burial ground, charnel house, churchyard, necropolis

gravity *noun* 1 IMPORTANCE, acuteness, momentousness, perilousness, seriousness, severity, significance, urgency, weightiness
2 SOLEMNITY, dignity, earnestness, gravitas, seriousness, sobriety

gray *adjective* 1 PALE, ashen, pallid, wan
2 DISMAL, dark, depressing, dim, drab, dreary, dull, gloomy
3 CHARACTERLESS, anonymous, colorless, dull

graze[1] *verb* FEED, browse, crop, pasture

graze[2] *verb* 1 TOUCH, brush, glance off, rub, scrape, shave, skim
2 SCRATCH, abrade, chafe, scrape, skin
▷ *noun* 3 SCRATCH, abrasion, scrape

greasy *adjective* FATTY, oily, oleaginous, slimy, slippery

great *adjective* 1 LARGE, big, enormous, gigantic, huge, immense, prodigious, supersize, vast, voluminous

older or younger than: *great-grandfather* > **great'ly** *adverb* > **great'ness** *noun* > **Great Dane** breed of very large dog

Gre•cian [GREE-shən] *adjective* of (ancient) Greece

greed *noun* excessive consumption of, desire for, food, wealth > **greed'y** *adjective* **greed•i•er, greed•i•est** 1 gluttonous 2 eagerly desirous 3 voracious 4 covetous > **greed'i•ly** *adverb*

Greek *noun* 1 native language of Greece ▷ *adjective* 2 of Greece or Greek

green *adjective* **-er, -est** 1 of color between blue and yellow 2 grass-colored 3 emerald 4 unripe 5 inexperienced 6 gullible 7 envious ▷ *noun* 8 color 9 area of grass, esp. in golf, for putting > **greens** green vegetables > **green'er•y** vegetation > **green belt** area of farms, open country around a community > **green'horn** *noun* 1 inexperienced person 2 (*slang*) recent immigrant, newcomer > **green'house** *noun, plural* **-hous•es** [-how-ziz] (usu.) glass house for rearing plants > **greenhouse effect** rise in the temperature of the earth caused by heat absorbed from the sun being unable to leave the atmosphere > **green'room** *noun* room for actors, TV performers, when offstage > **green thumb** talent for gardening

greet *verb transitive* 1 meet with expressions of welcome 2 accost, salute 3 receive > **greet'ing** *noun*

gre•gar•i•ous [gri-GAIR-ee-əs] *adjective* 1 fond of company, sociable 2 living in flocks > **gre•gar'i•ous•ness** *noun*

grem'lin *noun* imaginary being blamed for mechanical and other troubles

gre•nade [gri-NAYD] *noun* explosive shell or bomb, thrown by hand or shot from rifle

gren•a•dine [gren-ə-DEEN] *noun* syrup made from pomegranate juice, for sweetening and coloring drinks

grew *pt. of* **grow**

grey•hound [GRAY-hownd] *noun* swift slender dog used in racing

grid *noun* 1 network of horizontal and vertical lines, bars, etc. 2 any interconnecting system of links 3 regional network of electricity supply

grid•dle [GRID-l] *noun* frying pan, flat iron plate for cooking > **grid'dle•cake** *noun* pancake

grid•i•ron [GRID-ī-ərn] *noun* 1 frame of metal bars for grilling 2 (field of play for) football

grid•lock [GRID-lok] *noun* 1 situation where traffic is not moving 2 point in a dispute at which no agreement can be reached > **grid'locked** *adjective*

grief [greef] *noun* deep sorrow > **griev•ance** [GREE-vəns] *noun* real or imaginary ground of complaint > **grieve** *verb intransitive* **grieved, griev•ing** 1 feel grief ▷ *verb transitive* **grieved, griev•ing** 2 cause grief to > **griev'ous** *adjective* 1 painful, oppressive 2 very serious

grif•fin, grif•fon [GRIF-in] *noun* fabulous monster with eagle's head and wings and lion's body

grill *noun* 1 grated utensil for broiling meat, etc. 2 food cooked on grill 3 grillroom ▷ *verb* 4 cook (food) on grill 5 subject to severe questioning > **grill'ing** *noun* severe cross-examination > **grill'room** *noun* restaurant specializing in grilled food

grille [gril] *noun* grating, crosswork of bars over opening

grim *adjective* **grim•mer, grim•mest** 1 stern 2 of stern or forbidding aspect, relentless 3 joyless

grim•ace [GRIM-əs] *noun* 1 wry face ▷ *verb*

DICTIONARY • THESAURUS

2 IMPORTANT, critical, crucial, momentous, serious, significant
3 FAMOUS, eminent, illustrious, noteworthy, outstanding, prominent, remarkable, renowned
4 (*informal*) EXCELLENT, fantastic (*informal*), fine, marvelous, superb, terrific (*informal*), tremendous (*informal*), wonderful

greatly *adverb* VERY MUCH, considerably, enormously, exceedingly, hugely, immensely, remarkably, tremendously, vastly

greatness *noun* 1 IMMENSITY, enormity, hugeness, magnitude, prodigiousness, size, vastness
2 IMPORTANCE, gravity, momentousness, seriousness, significance, urgency, weight
3 FAME, celebrity, distinction, eminence, glory, grandeur, illustriousness, kudos, note, renown

greed *or* **greediness** *noun* 1 GLUTTONY, edacity, esurience, gormandizing, hunger, voracity
2 AVARICE, acquisitiveness, avidity, covetousness, craving, desire, longing, selfishness

greedy *adjective* 1 GLUTTONOUS, gormandizing, hungry, insatiable, piggish, ravenous, voracious
2 GRASPING, acquisitive, avaricious, avid, covetous, craving, desirous, rapacious, selfish

green *adjective* 1 LEAFY, grassy, verdant
2 ECOLOGICAL, conservationist, environment-friendly, non-polluting, ozone-friendly
3 IMMATURE, gullible, inexperienced, naive, new, raw, untrained, wet behind the ears (*informal*)
4 JEALOUS, covetous, envious, grudging, resentful
▷ *noun* 5 LAWN, common, sward, turf

greet *verb* WELCOME, accost, address, compliment, hail, meet, receive, salute

greeting *noun* WELCOME, address, reception, salutation, salute

gregarious *adjective* OUTGOING, affable, companionable, convivial, cordial, friendly, sociable, social

gridlock *noun* STANDSTILL, deadlock, impasse, stalemate

grief *noun* SADNESS, anguish, distress, heartache, misery, regret, remorse, sorrow, suffering, woe

grievance *noun* COMPLAINT, ax to grind, gripe (*informal*), injury, injustice

grieve *verb* 1 MOURN, complain, deplore, lament, regret, rue, suffer, weep
2 SADDEN, afflict, distress, hurt, injure, pain, wound

grievous *adjective* 1 PAINFUL, dreadful, grave, harmful, severe
2 DEPLORABLE, atrocious, dreadful, monstrous, offensive, outrageous, shameful, shocking

grim *adjective* FORBIDDING, formidable, harsh, merciless, ruthless, severe, sinister, stern, terrible

grimace *noun* 1 SCOWL, face, frown, sneer
▷ *verb* 2 SCOWL, frown, lour *or* lower, make a

intransitive **-aced, -ac•ing** 2 make wry face
grime [grīm] *noun* 1 ingrained dirt, soot ▷ *verb transitive* **grimed, grim•ing** 2 soil 3 dirty 4 blacken > **grim'y** *adjective* **grim•i•er, grim•i•est**
grin *verb intransitive* **grinned, grin•ning** 1 show teeth, as in laughter ▷ *noun* 2 grinning smile
grind [grīnd] *verb transitive* **ground, grind•ing** 1 crush to powder 2 oppress 3 make sharp, smooth 4 grate ▷ *verb intransitive* **ground, grind•ing** 5 perform action of grinding 6 (*informal*) (with *away*) work (esp. study) hard 7 grate ▷ *noun* (*informal*) 8 hard work, excessively diligent student 9 action of grinding
grin•go [GRING-goh] *noun, plural* **-gos** in Mexico, contemptuous name for foreigner, esp. American or Englishman
grip *noun* 1 firm hold, grasp 2 grasping power 3 mastery 4 handle 5 suitcase or traveling bag ▷ *verb transitive* **gripped, grip•ping** 6 grasp or hold tightly 7 hold interest or attention of
gripe [grīp] *verb intransitive* **griped, grip•ing** (*informal*) 1 complain (persistently) ▷ *noun* 2 (*informal*) complaint > **gripes** intestinal pain
gris•ly [GRIZ-lee] *adjective* **-li•er, -li•est** grim, causing terror, ghastly
grist *noun* grain to be ground **grist for one's mill** something that can be turned to advantage
gris•tle [GRIS-əl] *noun* cartilage, tough flexible tissue
grit *noun* 1 rough particles of sand 2 coarse sandstone 3 courage ▷ *verb transitive* **grit•ted, grit•ting** 4 clench, grind (teeth) > **grits** *plural noun* hominy, etc. coarsely ground and cooked as breakfast food > **grit'ty** *adjective* **-ti•er, -ti•est**
griz•zle [GRIZ-əl] *verb* **-zled, -zling** make, become gray > **griz'zly** large Amer. bear (*also* **grizzly bear**)
groan [grohn] *verb intransitive* 1 make low, deep sound of grief or pain 2 be in pain or overburdened ▷ *noun*
groats [grohts] *plural noun* hulled grain or kernels of oats, wheat, etc. broken into fragments
gro•cer [GROH-sər] *noun* dealer in foodstuffs > **gro'cer•ies** *plural noun* commodities sold by a grocer > **gro'cer•y** *noun, plural* **-cer•ies** trade, premises of grocer
grog•gy [GROG-ee] *adjective* **-gi•er, -gi•est** (*informal*) unsteady, shaky, weak
groin *noun* 1 fold where legs meet abdomen 2 euphemism for genitals
groom *noun* 1 person caring for horses 2 bridegroom ▷ *verb transitive* 3 tend or look after 4 brush or clean (esp. horse) 5 train (someone for something) > **well-groomed** *adjective* neat, smart
groove [groov] *noun* 1 narrow channel, hollow, esp. cut by tool 2 rut, routine ▷ *verb transitive* **grooved, groov•ing** 3 cut groove in > **groov'y** *adjective* **groov•i•er, groov•i•est** (*slang*) attractive, exciting
grope [grohp] *verb intransitive* **groped, grop•ing** feel about, search blindly
gros•beak [GROHS-beek] *noun* finch with large powerful bill
gross [grohs] *adjective* **-er, -est** 1 very fat 2 total, not net 3 coarse 4 indecent 5 flagrant 6 thick, rank ▷ *noun* 7 twelve dozen > **gross out** (*slang*) disgust, sicken
gro•tesque [groh-TESK] *adjective* (horribly) distorted 1 absurd ▷ *noun* 2 grotesque person, thing
grot•to [GROT-oh] *noun, plural* **-toes** small picturesque cave
grouch [growch] *noun* (*informal*) 1 persistent grumbler 2 discontented mood ▷ *verb intransitive*

---

face *or* make faces, sneer
grime *noun* DIRT, filth, grease, smut, soot
grimy *adjective* DIRTY, filthy, foul, grubby, scuzzy (*slang*), soiled, sooty, unclean
grind *verb* 1 CRUSH, abrade, granulate, grate, mill, pound, powder, pulverize, triturate
2 SMOOTH, polish, sand, sharpen, whet
3 SCRAPE, gnash, grate
▷ *noun* 4 (*informal*) HARD WORK, chore, drudgery, labor, sweat (*informal*), toil
grip *noun* 1 CLASP, hold
2 CONTROL, clutches, domination, influence, possession, power
3 UNDERSTANDING, command, comprehension, grasp, mastery
▷ *verb* 4 GRASP, clasp, clutch, hold, seize, take hold of
5 ENGROSS, absorb, enthrall, entrance, fascinate, hold, mesmerize, rivet
gripping *adjective* FASCINATING, compelling, engrossing, enthralling, entrancing, exciting, riveting, spellbinding, thrilling
grisly *adjective* GRUESOME, appalling, awful, dreadful, ghastly, horrible, macabre, shocking, terrifying
grit *noun* 1 GRAVEL, dust, pebbles, sand
2 COURAGE, backbone, determination, fortitude, guts (*informal*), perseverance, resolution, spirit, tenacity
▷ *verb* 3 GRIND, clench, gnash, grate
gritty *adjective* 1 ROUGH, dusty, granular, gravelly, rasping, sandy
2 COURAGEOUS, brave, determined, dogged, plucky, resolute, spirited, steadfast, tenacious
groan *noun* 1 MOAN, cry, sigh, whine
▷ *verb* 2 MOAN, cry, sigh, whine
groggy *adjective* DIZZY, confused, dazed, faint, shaky, unsteady, weak, wobbly
groom *noun* 1 STABLEMAN, stableboy
▷ *verb* 2 SMARTEN UP, clean, preen, primp, spruce up, tidy
3 RUB DOWN, brush, clean, curry, tend
4 TRAIN, coach, drill, educate, make ready, nurture, prepare, prime, ready
groove *noun* INDENTATION, channel, cut, flute, furrow, hollow, rut, trench, trough
grope *verb* FEEL, cast about, fish, flounder, forage, fumble, scrabble, search
gross *adjective* 1 FAT, corpulent, hulking, obese, overweight
2 TOTAL, aggregate, before deductions, before tax, entire, whole
3 VULGAR, coarse, crude, indelicate, obscene, offensive
4 BLATANT, flagrant, grievous, heinous, rank, sheer, unmitigated, utter
▷ *verb* 5 EARN, bring in, make, rake in (*informal*), take
grotesque *adjective* UNNATURAL, bizarre, deformed, distorted, fantastic, freakish,

3 grumble, be peevish
ground[1] [grownd] *noun* 1 surface of Earth 2 soil, earth 3 reason, motive 4 coating to work on with paint 5 background, main surface worked on in painting, embroidery, etc. 6 special area 7 bottom of sea ▷ *verb transitive* 8 establish 9 instruct (in elements) 10 place on ground ▷ *verb intransitive* 11 run ashore 12 strike ground > **grounds** *plural noun* 1 dregs 2 land around house and belonging to it > **ground'ed** *adjective* 1 of aircraft or pilot, unable or not permitted to fly 2 (*informal*) of child, punished by restriction of activities > **ground'ing** *noun* basic general knowledge of a subject > **ground'less** *adjective* without reason > **ground'speed** *noun* aircraft's speed in relation to ground
ground[2] *pt./pp. of* **grind**
group [groop] *noun* 1 number of persons or things near together, or placed or classified together 2 small musical band of players or singers 3 class 4 two or more figures forming one artistic design ▷ *verb* 5 place, fall into group
grouse[1] [grows] *noun, plural* **grouse** 1 game bird 2 its flesh
grouse[2] *verb intransitive* **groused, grous•ing** 1 grumble, complain ▷ *noun* 2 complaint > **grous'er** *noun* grumbler
grout [growt] *noun* 1 thin fluid mortar ▷ *verb transitive* 2 fill up with grout
grove [grohv] *noun* small group of trees
grov•el [GRUV-əl] *verb intransitive* **-eled, -el•ing** 1 abase oneself 2 lie or crawl facedown
grow [groh] *verb intransitive* **grew, grown, grow•ing** 1 develop naturally 2 increase in size, height, etc. 3 be produced 4 become by degrees ▷ *verb transitive* **grew, grown, grow•ing** 5 produce by cultivation > **growth** *noun* 1 growing 2 increase 3 what has grown or is growing > **grown-up** *adjective* > **grownup** *noun* adult
growl *verb intransitive* 1 make low guttural sound of anger 2 rumble 3 murmur, complain ▷ *noun*
grub *verb* **grubbed, grub•bing** 1 dig superficially 2 root up 3 dig, rummage 4 plod 5 drudge ▷ *noun* 6 larva of insect 7 (*slang*) food > **grub'by** *adjective* **-bi•er, -bi•est** dirty
grudge [gruj] *verb transitive* **grudged, grudg•ing** 1 be unwilling to give, allow ▷ *noun* 2 ill will
gru•el [GROO-əl] *noun* food of cereal boiled in milk or water > **gru'el•ing** *adjective, noun* exhausting, severe (experience)
grue•some [GROO-səm] *adjective* fearful, horrible, grisly > **grue'some•ness** *noun*
gruff *adjective* **-er, -est** rough in manner or voice, surly > **gruff'ness** *noun*
grum•ble [GRUM-bəl] *verb intransitive* **-bled, -bling** 1 complain 2 rumble, murmur 3 make growling sounds ▷ *noun* 4 complaint 5 low

DICTIONARY • THESAURUS

outlandish, preposterous, strange
ground *noun* 1 EARTH, dry land, land, soil, terra firma, terrain, turf
2 STADIUM, arena, field, park, pitch
3 (*often plural*) LAND, estate, fields, gardens, terrain, territory
4 (*usually plural*) DREGS, deposit, lees, sediment
5 ▷ **grounds** REASON, basis, cause, excuse, foundation, justification, motive, occasion, pretext, rationale
▷ *verb* 6 BASE, establish, fix, found, set, settle
7 INSTRUCT, acquaint with, familiarize with, initiate, teach, train, tutor
groundless *adjective* UNJUSTIFIED, baseless, empty, idle, uncalled-for, unfounded, unwarranted
groundwork *noun* PRELIMINARIES, foundation, fundamentals, preparation, spadework, underpinnings
group *noun* 1 SET, band, bunch, cluster, collection, crowd, gang, pack, party
▷ *verb* 2 ARRANGE, bracket, class, classify, marshal, order, sort
grouse *verb* 1 COMPLAIN, bellyache (*slang*), carp, gripe (*informal*), grumble, moan, whine
▷ *noun* 2 COMPLAINT, grievance, gripe (*informal*), grouch (*informal*), grumble, moan, objection, protest
grove *noun* WOOD, coppice, copse, covert, plantation, spinney, thicket
grovel *verb* HUMBLE ONESELF, abase oneself, bow and scrape, brown-nose (*slang*), crawl, creep, cringe, demean oneself, fawn, kiss ass (*slang*), kowtow, toady
grow *verb* 1 INCREASE, develop, enlarge, expand, get bigger, multiply, spread, stretch, swell
2 ORIGINATE, arise, issue, spring, stem
3 IMPROVE, advance, flourish, progress, prosper, succeed, thrive
4 BECOME, come to be, get, turn
5 CULTIVATE, breed, farm, nurture, produce, propagate, raise
grown-up *adjective* 1 MATURE, adult, fully-grown, of age
▷ *noun* 2 ADULT, man, woman
growth *noun* 1 INCREASE, development, enlargement, expansion, multiplication, proliferation, stretching
2 IMPROVEMENT, advance, expansion, progress, prosperity, rise, success
3 (*medical*) TUMOR, lump
grub *noun* 1 LARVA, caterpillar, maggot
2 (*slang*) FOOD, rations, sustenance, victuals
▷ *verb* 3 DIG UP, burrow, pull up, root (*informal*)
4 SEARCH, ferret, forage, hunt, rummage, scour, uncover, unearth
grubby *adjective* DIRTY, filthy, grimy, messy, mucky, scuzzy (*slang*), seedy, shabby, sordid, squalid, unwashed
grudge *verb* 1 RESENT, begrudge, complain, covet, envy, mind
▷ *noun* 2 RESENTMENT, animosity, antipathy, bitterness, dislike, enmity, grievance, rancor
grueling *adjective* EXHAUSTING, arduous, backbreaking, demanding, laborious, punishing, severe, strenuous, taxing, tiring
gruesome *adjective* HORRIFIC, ghastly, grim, grisly, horrible, macabre, shocking, terrible
gruff *adjective* 1 SURLY, bad-tempered, brusque, churlish, grumpy, rough, rude, sullen, ungracious
2 HOARSE, croaking, guttural, harsh, husky, low, rasping, rough, throaty
grumble *verb* 1 COMPLAIN, bleat, carp, gripe (*informal*), grouch (*informal*), grouse, moan, whine
2 RUMBLE, growl, gurgle, murmur, mutter, roar

growl

grump•y [GRUM-pee] *adjective* **grump•i•er, grump•i•est** ill-tempered, surly > **grump'i•ness** *noun*

grunge [grunj] *noun* 1 style of rock music with a fuzzy guitar sound 2 deliberately untidy and uncoordinated fashion style

grunt *verb intransitive* 1 make sound characteristic of pig ▷ *noun* 2 pig's sound 3 gruff noise

G-string [JEE-string] *noun* 1 very small covering for genitals 2 *mus.* string tuned to G

gua•no [GWAH-noh] *noun* manure of seabird

guar•an•tee [gar-ən-TEE] *noun* 1 formal assurance (esp. in writing) that product, etc. will meet certain standards, last for given time, etc. ▷ *verb transitive* **-teed, -tee'ing** 2 give guarantee of, for something 3 secure (against risk, etc.) > **guar'an•tor** *noun* one who guarantees > **guar'an•ty** *noun, plural* **-ties**

guard [gahrd] *verb transitive* 1 protect, defend ▷ *verb intransitive* 2 be careful, take precautions (against) ▷ *noun* 3 person, group that protects, supervises, keeps watch 4 sentry 5 soldiers protecting anything 6 official in charge of train 7 protection 8 screen for enclosing anything dangerous 9 protector 10 posture of defense > **guard'i•an** [-ee-ən] *noun* 1 keeper, protector 2 person having custody of infant, etc. > **guard'i•an•ship** *noun* care > **guard'house** *noun* place for stationing those on guard or for prisoners

gua•va [GWAH-və] *noun* tropical tree with fruit used to make jelly

Guern•sey [GURN-zee] *noun, plural* **-seys** breed of cattle

guer•ril•la [gə-RIL-ə] *noun* member of irregular armed force, esp. fighting established force, government, etc. ▷ *adjective*

guess [ges] *verb transitive* 1 estimate without calculation 2 conjecture, suppose 3 consider, think ▷ *verb intransitive* 4 form conjectures ▷ *noun*

guest [gest] *noun* 1 one entertained at another's house 2 one living in hotel > **guest'house** *noun* small house for guests, separate from main house

guff *noun* (*informal*) 1 silly talk 2 insolent talk

guf•faw [gə-FAW] *noun* 1 crude noisy laugh ▷ *verb intransitive* 2 laugh in this way

guide [gīd] *noun* 1 one who shows the way 2 adviser 3 book of instruction or information 4 contrivance for directing motion ▷ *verb transitive* **guid•ed, guid•ing** 5 lead, act as guide to 6 arrange > **guid'ance** [-əns] *noun* > **guided missile** missile whose flight path is controlled by radio signals or programmed homing mechanism

guild [gild] *noun* 1 organization, club 2 society for mutual help, or with common object 3 *hist.* society of merchants or tradesmen

guile [gīl] *noun* cunning, deceit > **guile'ful** *adjective* > **guile'less** *adjective* sincere, straightforward

guil•lo•tine [GIL-ə-teen] *noun* 1 machine for beheading ▷ *verb transitive* **-tined, -tin•ing** 2 behead

guilt [gilt] *noun* 1 fact, state of having done wrong 2 responsibility for criminal or moral

---

▷ *noun* 3 COMPLAINT, grievance, gripe (*informal*), grouch (*informal*), grouse, moan, objection, protest

4 RUMBLE, growl, gurgle, murmur, muttering, roar

grumpy *adjective* IRRITABLE, cantankerous, crotchety, ill-tempered, peevish, sulky, sullen, surly, testy

guarantee *noun* 1 ASSURANCE, bond, certainty, pledge, promise, security, surety, warranty, word of honor

▷ *verb* 2 MAKE CERTAIN, assure, certify, ensure, pledge, promise, secure, vouch for, warrant

guard *verb* 1 WATCH OVER, defend, mind, preserve, protect, safeguard, secure, shield

▷ *noun* 2 PROTECTOR, custodian, defender, lookout, picket, sentinel, sentry, warden, watch, watchman

3 PROTECTION, buffer, defense, safeguard, screen, security, shield

4 ▷ **off guard** UNPREPARED, napping, unready, unwary

5 ▷ **on guard** PREPARED, alert, cautious, circumspect, on the alert, on the lookout, ready, vigilant, wary, watchful

guarded *adjective* CAUTIOUS, cagey (*informal*), careful, circumspect, noncommittal, prudent, reserved, reticent, suspicious, wary

guardian *noun* KEEPER, champion, curator, custodian, defender, guard, protector, warden

guerrilla *noun* FREEDOM FIGHTER, partisan, underground fighter

guess *verb* 1 ESTIMATE, conjecture, hypothesize, predict, speculate, work out

2 SUPPOSE, believe, conjecture, fancy, imagine, judge, reckon, suspect, think

▷ *noun* 3 PREDICTION, conjecture, hypothesis, shot in the dark, speculation, supposition, theory

guesswork *noun* SPECULATION, conjecture, estimation, supposition, surmise, theory

guest *noun* VISITOR, boarder, caller, company, lodger, visitant

guidance *noun* ADVICE, counseling, direction, help, instruction, leadership, management, teaching

guide *noun* 1 ESCORT, adviser, conductor, counselor, leader, mentor, teacher, usher

2 MODEL, example, ideal, inspiration, paradigm, standard

3 POINTER, beacon, guiding light, landmark, lodestar, marker, sign, signpost

4 GUIDEBOOK, Baedeker, catalog, directory, handbook, instructions, key, manual

▷ *verb* 5 LEAD, accompany, conduct, direct, escort, shepherd, show the way, usher

6 STEER, command, control, direct, handle, manage, maneuver

7 SUPERVISE, advise, counsel, influence, instruct, oversee, superintend, teach, train

guild *noun* SOCIETY, association, brotherhood, club, company, corporation, fellowship, fraternity, league, lodge, order, organization, union

guile *noun* CUNNING, artifice, cleverness, craft, deceit, slyness, trickery, wiliness

guilt *noun* 1 CULPABILITY, blame, guiltiness, misconduct, responsibility, sinfulness, offense > **guilt'less** *adjective* innocent > **guilt'y** *adjective* **guilt•i•er, guilt•i•est** having committed an offense

guin•ea pig [GIN-ee] *noun* 1 rodent originating in S Amer. 2 (*informal*) person used in experiments

guise [gīz] *noun* external appearance, esp. one assumed

gui•tar [gi-TAHR] *noun* usu. six-stringed instrument played by plucking or strumming > **gui•tar'ist** *noun*

gulch *noun* 1 ravine 2 gully

gulf *noun* 1 large inlet of the sea 2 chasm 3 large gap

gull[1] *noun* long-winged web-footed seabird

gull[2] *noun* 1 dupe, fool ▷ *verb transitive* 2 dupe, cheat > **gul•li•bil'i•ty** *noun* > **gul'li•ble** *adjective* easily imposed on, credulous

gul•let [GUL-it] *noun* food passage from mouth to stomach

gul•ly [GUL-ee] *noun, plural* **-lies** channel or ravine worn by water

gulp *verb transitive* 1 swallow eagerly ▷ *verb intransitive* 2 gasp, choke ▷ *noun*

gum[1] *noun* 1 firm flesh in which teeth are set ▷ *verb transitive* **gummed, gum•ming** 2 chew with the gums

gum[2] *noun* 1 sticky substance issuing from certain trees 2 an adhesive 3 chewing gum 4 gum tree, eucalyptus ▷ *verb transitive* **gummed, gum•ming** 5 stick with gum > **gum'my** *adjective* **-mi•er, -mi•est** > **gum'shoe** *noun* 1 shoe of rubber 2 (*slang*) detective > **gum tree** any species of eucalyptus **gum up the works** (*slang*) impede progress

gump•tion [GUM-shən] *noun* 1 resourcefulness 2 shrewdness, sense

gun *noun* 1 weapon with metal tube from which missiles are discharged by explosion 2 cannon, pistol, etc. ▷ *verb* **gunned, gun•ning** 3 shoot 4 pursue, as with gun 5 race engine (of car) > **gun'ner** *noun* > **gun'ner•y** *noun* use or science of large guns > **gun'boat** *noun* small warship > **gun dog** (breed of) dog used to retrieve, etc. game > **gun'man** *noun* armed criminal > **gun'met•al** *noun* alloy of copper and tin or zinc, formerly used for guns > **gun'pow•der** *noun* explosive mixture of saltpeter, sulfur, charcoal > **gun'shot** *noun* 1 shot or range of gun ▷ *adjective* 2 caused by missile from gun > **gun'wale, gun'nel** [GUN-l] *noun* upper edge of ship's side

gunk [gungk] *noun* (*informal*) any sticky, oily matter

gun•ny [GUN-ee] *noun, plural* **-nies** strong, coarse sacking made from jute

gup•py [GUP-ee] *noun, plural* **-pies** small colorful aquarium fish

gur•gle [GUR-gəl] *noun* 1 bubbling noise ▷ *verb intransitive* **-gled, -gling** 2 utter, flow with gurgle

gur•ney [GUR-nee] *noun, plural* **-neys** wheeled bed

gu•ru [GUUR-oo] *noun* a spiritual teacher, esp. in India

gush *verb intransitive* 1 flow out suddenly and copiously, spurt ▷ *noun* 2 sudden and copious flow 3 effusiveness > **gush'er** *noun* 1 gushing person 2 oil well

gus•set [GUS-it] *noun* triangle or diamond-shaped piece of material let into garment > **gus'set•ed** *adjective*

gust *noun* 1 sudden blast of wind 2 burst of rain, anger, passion, etc. > **gust'y** *adjective* **gust•i•er, gust•i•est**

gus•to [GUS-toh] *noun* enjoyment, zest

gut *noun* 1 (*often plural*) entrails, intestines 2 material made from guts of animals, e.g. for violin strings, etc. ▷ *verb transitive* **gut•ted, gut•ting** 3 remove guts from (fish, etc.) 4 remove, destroy contents of (house) > **guts** *plural noun* (*informal*) 1 essential, fundamental part 2 courage > **guts'y** *adjective* **guts•i•er, guts•i•est** (*informal*) 1 courageous 2 vigorous

---

wickedness, wrongdoing
2 REMORSE, contrition, guilty conscience, regret, self-reproach, shame, stigma

guiltless *adjective* INNOCENT, blameless, clean (*slang*), irreproachable, pure, sinless, spotless, squeaky-clean, untainted

guilty *adjective* 1 RESPONSIBLE, at fault, blameworthy, culpable, reprehensible, sinful, to blame, wrong
2 REMORSEFUL, ashamed, conscience-stricken, contrite, regretful, rueful, shamefaced, sheepish, sorry

guise *noun* FORM, appearance, aspect, demeanor, disguise, mode, pretense, semblance, shape

gulf *noun* 1 BAY, bight, sea inlet
2 CHASM, abyss, gap, opening, rift, separation, split, void

gullibility *noun* CREDULITY, innocence, naivety, simplicity

gullible *adjective* NAIVE, born yesterday, credulous, innocent, simple, trusting, unsuspecting, wet behind the ears (*informal*)

gully *noun* CHANNEL, ditch, gutter, watercourse

gulp *verb* 1 SWALLOW, devour, gobble, guzzle, quaff, swig (*informal*), swill, wolf
2 GASP, choke, swallow
▷ *noun* 3 SWALLOW, draft, mouthful, swig (*informal*)

gum *noun* 1 GLUE, adhesive, cement, paste, resin
▷ *verb* 2 STICK, affix, cement, glue, paste

gun *noun* FIREARM, handgun, piece (*slang*), pistol, revolver, rifle, saturday night special (*slang*)

gunman *noun* TERRORIST, bandit, gunslinger (*slang*), killer

gurgle *verb* 1 MURMUR, babble, bubble, lap, plash, purl, ripple, splash
▷ *noun* 2 MURMUR, babble, purl, ripple

guru *noun* TEACHER, authority, leader, master, mentor, sage, Svengali, tutor

gush *verb* 1 FLOW, cascade, flood, pour, run, rush, spout, spurt, stream
2 ENTHUSE, babble, chatter, effervesce, effuse, overstate, spout
▷ *noun* 3 STREAM, cascade, flood, flow, jet, rush, spout, spurt, torrent

gust *noun* 1 BLAST, blow, breeze, puff, rush, squall
▷ *verb* 2 BLOW, blast, squall

gusto *noun* RELISH, delight, enjoyment, enthusiasm, fervor, pleasure, verve, zeal

gut *noun* 1 (*informal*) PAUNCH, belly, potbelly, spare tire (*slang*)

gut•ter [GUT-ər] *noun* 1 shallow trough for carrying off water from roof or side of street ▷ *verb transitive* 2 make channels in ▷ *verb intransitive* 3 flow in streams 4 of candle, melt away by wax forming channels and running down > **gutter press** journalism that relies on sensationalism > **gut'ter•snipe** [-snīp] *noun* neglected slum child

gut•tur•al [GUT-ər-əl] *adjective* 1 of, relating to, or produced in, the throat ▷ *noun* 2 guttural sound or letter

guy[1] [gī] *noun* 1 (*informal*) person (usu. male) ▷ *verb transitive* **guyed, guy•ing** 2 make fun of 3 ridicule **wise guy** (*informal, usually disparaging*) clever person

guy[2] *noun* 1 rope, chain, etc. to steady, secure something, e.g. tent ▷ *verb transitive* **guyed, guy•ing** 2 keep in position by guy

guz•zle [GUZ-əl] *verb* **-zled, -zling** eat or drink greedily ▷ *noun*

gym [jim] *noun* *short for* **gymnasium** or **gymnastics**

gym•kha•na [jim-KAH-nə] *noun* 1 competition or display of horse riding or gymnastics 2 place for this

gym•na•si•um [jim-NAY-zee-əm] *noun* place equipped for muscular exercises, athletic training > **gym'nast** *noun* expert in gymnastics > **gym•nas'tics** *plural noun* muscular exercises, with or without apparatus, e.g. parallel bars

gy•ne•col•o•gy [gī-ni-KOL-ə-jee] *noun* branch of medicine dealing with functions and diseases of women > **gy•ne•col'o•gist** *noun*

gyp•sum [JIP-səm] *noun* crystalline sulfate of lime, a source of plaster

Gyp•sy [JIP-see] *noun, plural* **-sies** one of a wandering people originally from NW India, Romany

gy•rate [JĪ-rayt] *verb intransitive* **-rat•ed, -rat•ing** move in circle, spirally, revolve > **gy•ra'tion** *noun*

gy•ro•com•pass [JĪ-roh-kum-pəs] *noun* compass using gyroscope

gy•ro•scope [JĪ-rə-skohp] *noun* disk or wheel so mounted as to be able to rotate about any axis, esp. to keep disk (with compass, etc.) level despite movement of ship, etc. > **gy•ro•scop'ic** [-SKOP-ik] *adjective*

gy•ro•sta•bi•liz•er [jī-rə-STAY-bə-lī-zər] *noun* gyroscopic device to prevent rolling of ship or airplane

---

2 ▷ **guts** **a** INTESTINES, belly, bowels, entrails, innards (*informal*), insides (*informal*), stomach, viscera **b** (*informal*) COURAGE, audacity, backbone, daring, mettle, nerve, pluck, spirit ▷ *verb* 3 DISEMBOWEL, clean 4 RAVAGE, clean out, despoil, empty ▷ *adjective* 5 (*reaction*) INSTINCTIVE, basic, heartfelt, intuitive, involuntary, natural, spontaneous, unthinking, visceral

gutsy *adjective* BRAVE, bold, courageous, determined, gritty, indomitable, plucky, resolute, spirited

gutter *noun* DRAIN, channel, conduit, ditch, sluice, trench, trough

guttural *adjective* THROATY, deep, gravelly, gruff, hoarse, husky, rasping, rough, thick

guy *noun* (*informal*) MAN, chap, dude (*slang*), fellow, lad, person

guzzle *verb* DEVOUR, bolt, cram, drink, gobble, stuff (oneself), swill, wolf

Gypsy *noun* TRAVELER, Bohemian, nomad, rambler, roamer, Romany, rover, wanderer

Hh

H *chem.* hydrogen
ha•be•as cor•pus [HAY-bee-əs KOR-pəs] *noun* writ issued to produce prisoner in court
hab•er•dash•er [HAB-ər-dash-ər] *noun* dealer in articles of dress, ribbons, pins, needles, etc. > **hab'er•dash•er•y** *noun, plural* **-er•ies**
hab'it *noun* 1 settled tendency or practice 2 constitution 3 customary apparel esp. of nun or monk 4 woman's riding dress > **ha•bit•u•al** [hə-BICH-oo-əl] *adjective* 1 formed or acquired by habit 2 usual, customary > **ha•bit'u•ate** [-ayt] *verb transitive* **-at•ed, -at•ing** accustom > **ha•bit•u•a'tion** *noun* > **ha•bit'u•é** [-oo-ay] *noun* constant visitor
hab•it•a•ble [HAB-i-tə-bəl] *adjective* fit to live in > **hab'i•tat** *noun* natural home (of animal, etc.) > **hab•i•ta'tion** [-TAY-shən] *noun* dwelling place
ha•ci•en•da [hah-see-EN-də] *noun, plural* **-das** ranch or large estate in Sp. Amer.
hack[1] [hak] *verb transitive* 1 cut, chop (at) violently 2 (*informal*) utter harsh, dry cough 3 (*slang*) deal or cope with ▷ *noun* > **hack'er** *noun* (*slang*) person who through personal computer breaks into computer system of company or government **hack around** (*slang*) pass time idly
hack[2] *noun* 1 drudge, esp. writer of inferior literary works 2 cabdriver > **hack'work** *noun* dull, repetitive work
hack•le [HAK-əl] *noun* neck feathers of rooster, etc. > **hack•les** hairs on back of neck of dog and other animals that are raised in anger
hack•ney [HAK-nee] *noun, plural* **-neys** harness horse, carriage, coach kept for hire
hack•neyed [HAK-need] *adjective* (of words, etc.) stale, trite because of overuse
hack•saw [HAK-saw] *noun* handsaw for cutting metal
had *pt./pp. of* **have**
Ha•des [HAY-deez] *noun Greek myth* underworld home of the dead
haft *noun* 1 handle (of knife, etc.) ▷ *verb transitive* 2 fit with one
hag *noun* 1 ugly old woman 2 witch
hag•gard [HAG-ərd] *adjective* 1 wild-looking 2 anxious, careworn
hag'gis *noun* Scottish dish made from sheep's heart, lungs, liver, chopped with oatmeal, suet, onion, etc., and boiled in the stomach

habit *noun* 1 MANNERISM, custom, practice, proclivity, propensity, quirk, tendency, way 2 ADDICTION, dependence
habitation *noun* 1 DWELLING, abode, domicile, home, house, living quarters, lodging, quarters, residence 2 OCCUPANCY, inhabitance, occupation, tenancy
habitual *adjective* CUSTOMARY, accustomed, familiar, normal, regular, routine, standard, traditional, usual
hack[1] *verb* CUT, chop, hew, lacerate, mangle, mutilate, slash
hack[2] *noun* 1 SCRIBBLER, literary hack, penny-a-liner 2 HORSE, crock, nag
hackneyed *adjective* UNORIGINAL, clichéd, commonplace, overworked, stale, stereotyped, stock, threadbare, tired, trite
hag *noun* WITCH, crone, harridan
haggard *adjective* GAUNT, careworn, drawn,

hag•gle [HAG-əl] *verb intransitive* **-gled, -gling** bargain, wrangle over price ▷ *noun*

hag•i•ol•o•gy [hag-ee-OL-ə-jee] *noun, plural* **-gies** literature of the lives of saints > **hag•i•og'ra•pher** [-rə-fər] *noun* > **hag•i•og'ra•phy** *noun, plural* **-phies** writing of this

hail¹ [hayl] *noun* (shower of) pellets of ice 1 intense shower, barrage ▷ *verb* 2 pour down as shower of hail > **hail'stone** *noun*

hail² *verb transitive* 1 greet (esp. enthusiastically) 2 acclaim, acknowledge 3 call ▷ *verb intransitive* 4 come (from)

hair *noun* 1 filament growing from skin of animal, as covering of person's head 2 such filaments collectively > **hair'i•ness** *noun* > **hair'y** *adjective* **hair•i•er, hair•i•est** > **hair'do** [-doo] *noun, plural* **-dos** way of styling hair > **hair'dress•er** *noun* one who attends to and cuts hair, esp. women's hair > **hair'line** *adjective, noun* 1 very fine (line) 2 lower edge of human hair e.g. on forehead > **hair'pin** *noun* pin for keeping hair in place > **hairpin bend** U-shaped turn in road > **hair'split•ting** *noun* making of overly fine distinctions > **hair'spring** *noun* very fine, delicate spring in timepiece > **hair trigger** trigger operated by light touch > **hair-trigger** *adjective* easily set off: *a hair-trigger temper*

hal•cy•on [HAL-see-ən] *noun* bird fabled to calm the sea and to breed on floating nest > **halcyon days** time of peace and happiness

hale [hayl] *adjective* **hal•er, hal•est** robust, healthy: *hale and hearty*

half [haf] *noun, plural* **halves** [havz] 1 either of two equal parts of thing ▷ *adjective* 2 forming half ▷ *adverb* 3 to the extent of half > **half'back** *noun football* one of two players lining up on each side of fullback > **half-baked** *adjective* 1 underdone 2 (*informal*) immature, silly > **half-breed** *noun* (*offensive*) person with parents of different races > **half'-broth•er** *noun* brother by one parent only > **half-cocked** *adjective* ill-prepared > **half-heart•ed** *adjective* unenthusiastic > **half'-life** *noun, plural* **-lives** time taken for half the atoms in radioactive material to decay > **half nel'son** hold in wrestling > **half'-sis•ter** *noun* sister by one parent only > **half'time** *noun sports* rest period between two halves of a game > **half'tone** *noun* illustration printed by photoengraving from plate, showing lights and shadows by means of minute dots > **half vol•ley** *sport* striking of a ball the moment it bounces > **half'wit** *noun* 1 feeble-minded person 2 stupid person

hal•i•but [HAL-ə-bət] *noun* large edible flatfish

hal•i•to•sis [hal-i-TOH-sis] *noun* bad-smelling breath

hall [hawl] *noun* (entrance) passage; large room or building belonging to particular group or used for particular purpose esp. public assembly

hal•le•lu•jah [hal-ə-LOO-yə] *noun, interjection* exclamation of praise to God

hall•mark [HAWL-mahrk] *noun* 1 mark used to indicate standard of tested gold and silver 2 mark of excellence 3 distinguishing feature

hal•low [HAL-oh] *verb transitive* make, or honor as holy > **Hal•low•een** [hal-ə-WEEN] *noun* the evening of Oct 31st, the day before All Saints' Day

hal•lu•ci•nate [hə-LOO-sə-nayt] *verb intransitive* **-nat•ed, -nat•ing** suffer illusions > **hal•lu•ci•na'tion** *noun* illusion > **hal•lu'ci•na•to•ry** *adjective* > **hal•lu'ci•no•gen** [-jən] *noun* drug inducing hallucinations

ha•lo [HAY-loh] *noun, plural* **-los, -loes** 1 circle of light around moon, sun, etc. 2 disk of light around saint's head in picture 3 ideal glory attaching to person ▷ *verb transitive* **-loed, -lo•ing**

DICTIONARY **h** THESAURUS

---

emaciated, pinched, thin, wan

haggle *verb* BARGAIN, barter, beat down

hail¹ *noun* 1 BOMBARDMENT, barrage, downpour, rain, shower, storm, volley
▷ *verb* 2 RAIN DOWN ON, batter, beat down upon, bombard, pelt, rain, shower

hail² *verb* 1 GREET, acclaim, acknowledge, applaud, cheer, honor, salute, welcome
2 FLAG DOWN, signal to, wave down
3 ▷ **hail from** COME FROM, be a native of, be born in, originate in

hair *noun* LOCKS, head of hair, mane, mop, shock, tresses

hairdresser *noun* STYLIST, barber, coiffeur *or* coiffeuse

hair-raising *adjective* FRIGHTENING, alarming, bloodcurdling, horrifying, scary, shocking, spine-chilling, terrifying

hairstyle *noun* HAIRCUT, coiffure, cut, hairdo, style

hairy *adjective* SHAGGY, bushy, furry, hirsute, stubbly, unshaven, woolly

halcyon *adjective* 1 PEACEFUL, calm, gentle, quiet, serene, tranquil, undisturbed
2 (*days*) HAPPY, carefree, flourishing, golden, palmy, prosperous

hale *adjective* HEALTHY, able-bodied, fit, flourishing, in the pink, robust, sound, strong, vigorous, well

half *noun* 1 EQUAL PART, fifty per cent, hemisphere, portion, section
▷ *adjective* 2 PARTIAL, halved, limited, moderate
▷ *adverb* 3 PARTIALLY, in part, partly

half-baked *adjective* ILL-JUDGED, ill-conceived, impractical, poorly planned, short-sighted, unformed, unthought out *or* unthought through

half-hearted *adjective* UNENTHUSIASTIC, apathetic, indifferent, lackluster, listless, lukewarm, perfunctory, tame

halfway *adverb* 1 MIDWAY, to the middle *or* in the middle
▷ *adjective* 2 MIDWAY, central, equidistant, intermediate, mid, middle

halfwit *noun* FOOL, airhead (*slang*), dork (*slang*), dunderhead, idiot, imbecile (*informal*), moron (*offensive*), schmuck (*slang*), simpleton

hall *noun* 1 ENTRANCE HALL, corridor, entry, foyer, hallway, lobby, passage, passageway, vestibule
2 MEETING PLACE, assembly room, auditorium, chamber, concert hall

hallmark *noun* 1 SEAL, device, endorsement, mark, sign, stamp, symbol
2 INDICATION, sure sign, telltale sign

hallucination *noun* ILLUSION, apparition, delusion, dream, fantasy, figment of the imagination, mirage, vision

halo *noun* RING OF LIGHT, aura, corona, nimbus,

4 surround with halo
halt[1] [hawlt] *noun* 1 interruption or end to progress, etc. (esp. as command to stop marching) ▷ *verb* 2 (cause to) stop
halt[2] *verb intransitive* falter, fail > **halt'ing** *adjective* hesitant, lame
hal•ter [HAWL-tər] *noun* 1 rope or strap with headgear to fasten horses or cattle 2 low-cut dress style with strap passing behind neck ▷ *verb transitive* 3 put halter on, fasten with one
halve [hav] *verb transitive* **halved, halv•ing** 1 cut in half 2 reduce to half 3 share
hal•yard [HAL-yərd] *noun* rope for raising sail, signal flags, etc.
ham *noun* 1 meat (esp. salted or smoked) from thigh of pig 2 actor adopting exaggerated, unconvincing style 3 amateur radio enthusiast 4 **ham it up** overact > **ham'string** *noun* 1 tendon at back of knee ▷ *verb transitive* **-strung, -string•ing** 2 cripple by cutting this 3 render useless 4 thwart
ham•burg•er [HAM-burg-gər] *noun* broiled, fried patty of ground beef, esp. served in bread roll
ham•let [HAM-lit] *noun* small village
ham•mer [HAM-ər] *noun* 1 tool usu. with heavy head at end of handle, for beating, driving nails, etc. 2 machine for same purposes 3 contrivance for exploding charge of gun 4 auctioneer's mallet 5 heavy metal ball on wire thrown in sports ▷ *verb* 6 strike with, or as with, hammer > **ham'mer•head** [-hed] *noun* shark with wide, flattened head > **ham'mer•toe** *noun* deformed toe > **hammer out** solve problem by painstaking work
ham•mock [HAM-ək] *noun* bed of canvas, etc., hung on cords
ham•per[1] [HAM-pər] *noun* 1 large covered basket, such as for laundry 2 large parcel, box, etc. of food, wines, etc., esp. one sent as gift
ham•per[2] *verb transitive* impede, obstruct movements of
ham•ster [HAM-stər] *noun* type of rodent, sometimes kept as pet
ham'strung *adjective* 1 crippled, thwarted 2 *see* **ham**
hand *noun* 1 extremity of arm beyond wrist 2 side, quarter, direction 3 style of writing 4 cards dealt to player 5 measure of four inches 6 manual worker 7 sailor 8 help, aid 9 pointer on dial 10 applause ▷ *verb transitive* 11 pass 12 deliver 13 hold out > **hand'ful** *noun, plural* **-fuls** 1 small amount or number 2 (*informal*) person, thing causing problems > **hand'i•ly** *adverb* > **hand'i•ness** *noun* 1 dexterity 2 state of being near, available > **hand'y** *adjective* **hand•i•er, hand•i•est** 1 convenient 2 clever with the hands > **hand'bag** *noun* 1 woman's bag for personal articles 2 bag for carrying in hand > **hand'bill** *noun* small printed notice > **hand'book** *noun* small reference or instruction book > **hand'held** *adjective* 1 able to be held in the hand ▷ *noun* 2 computer that can be held in the hand > **hand'cuff** *noun* 1 fetter for wrist, usu. joined in pair ▷ *verb transitive* 2 secure thus > **hand'i•craft** *noun* manual occupation or skill > **hand'i•work** *noun* thing done by particular person > **hand•ker•chief** [HANG-kər-chif] *noun* small square of fabric carried in pocket for wiping nose, etc. > **hand'out** *noun* 1 (*informal*) money, food, etc. given free 2 pamphlet giving news, information, etc. > **hands-on** *adjective* involving practical experience of equipment > **hand'stand** *noun* act of supporting body in upside-down position by hands alone > **hand'writ•ing** *noun* way person writes > **hand'y•man** *noun* 1 one employed to do various tasks 2 one skilled in odd jobs **hand in glove** very intimate
hand•i•cap [HAN-dee-kap] *noun* 1 something

DICTIONARY • THESAURUS

radiance
halt[1] *verb* 1 STOP, break off, cease, come to an end, desist, rest, stand still, wait
2 END, block, bring to an end, check, curb, cut short, nip in the bud, terminate
▷ *noun* 3 STOP, close, end, pause, standstill, stoppage
halting *adjective* FALTERING, awkward, hesitant, labored, stammering, stumbling, stuttering
halve *verb* BISECT, cut in half, divide equally, share equally, split in two
hammer *verb* 1 HIT, bang, beat, drive, knock, strike, tap
2 (*informal*) DEFEAT, beat, drub, run rings around (*informal*), thrash, trounce, wipe the floor with (*informal*)
hamper *verb* HINDER, frustrate, hamstring, handicap, impede, interfere with, obstruct, prevent, restrict
hand *noun* 1 PALM, fist, mitt (*slang*), paw (*informal*)
2 HIRED MAN, artisan, craftsman, employee, laborer, operative, worker, workman
3 PENMANSHIP, calligraphy, handwriting, script
4 OVATION, clap, round of applause
5 ▷ **at hand, on hand** NEARBY, at one's fingertips, available, close, handy, near, ready, within reach
▷ *verb* 6 PASS, deliver, hand over
handbook *noun* GUIDEBOOK, Baedeker, guide, instruction book, manual
handcuff *verb* SHACKLE, fetter, manacle
handcuffs *plural noun* SHACKLES, cuffs (*informal*), fetters, manacles
handful *noun* FEW, small number, smattering, sprinkling
handicap *noun* 1 DISADVANTAGE, barrier, drawback, hindrance, impediment, limitation, obstacle, restriction, stumbling block
2 ADVANTAGE, head start
3 DISABILITY, defect, impairment
▷ *verb* 4 RESTRICT, burden, encumber, hamper, hamstring, hinder, hold back, impede, limit
handicraft *noun* CRAFTSMANSHIP, art, craft, handiwork, skill, workmanship
handiwork *noun* CREATION, achievement, design, invention, product, production
handle *noun* 1 GRIP, haft, hilt, stock
▷ *verb* 2 HOLD, feel, finger, grasp, pick up, touch
3 CONTROL, direct, guide, manage, maneuver, manipulate
4 DEAL WITH, cope with, manage
hand-out *noun* 1 CHARITY, alms
2 LEAFLET, bulletin, circular, literature (*informal*), mailshot, press release
handsome *adjective* 1 GOOD-LOOKING, attractive,

that hampers or hinders **2** race, contest in which chances are equalized by weights carried, golf strokes, etc. **3** condition so imposed **4** any physical disability ▷ *verb transitive* **-capped, -cap•ping 5** hamper **6** impose handicap on **7** attempt to predict winner of race, game > **handicapped** (*dated*) physically or mentally disabled

han•dle [HAN-dl] *noun* **1** part of thing to hold it by ▷ *verb intransitive* **-dled, -dling 2** touch, feel with hands **3** manage **4** deal with **5** trade > **han'dle•bars** *plural noun* curved metal bars used to steer bicycle, motorbike, etc. > **handlebar mustache** one resembling handlebar

hand•some [HAN-səm] *adjective* **1** of fine appearance **2** generous **3** ample

hang *verb transitive* **hung** *or* **hanged, hang•ing 1** suspend **2** kill by suspension by neck **3** attach, set up (wallpaper, doors, etc.) ▷ *verb intransitive* **hung** *or* **hanged, hang•ing 4** be suspended, cling > **hang'er** *noun* frame on which clothes, etc. can be hung > **hang'dog** *adjective* sullen, dejected > **hang glider** glider like large kite, with pilot hanging in frame below > **hang gliding** *noun* > **hang'man** *noun* executioner > **hang'o•ver** *noun* aftereffects of too much drinking > **hang out** (*informal*) reside, frequent > **hang-up** *noun* (*slang*) **1** persistent emotional problem **2** preoccupation

hang•ar [HANG-ər] *noun* large shed for aircraft

hank [hangk] *noun* coil, skein, length, esp. as measure of yarn

hank•er [HANG-kər] *verb intransitive* (oft. with *after* or *for*) crave

han•ky-pan•ky [HANG-kee-PANG-kee] *noun* (*informal*) **1** trickery **2** illicit sexual relations

han•som [HAN-səm] *noun* two-wheeled horse-drawn cab for two to ride inside with driver mounted up behind

hap•haz•ard [hap-HAZ-ərd] *adjective* random, careless

hap•less [HAP-lis] *adjective* unlucky

hap•pen [HAP-ən] *verb intransitive* **1** come about, occur **2** chance to do > **hap'pen•ing** *noun* occurrence, event

hap•py *adjective* **-pi•er, -pi•est 1** glad, content **2** lucky, fortunate **3** apt > **hap'pi•ly** *adverb* > **hap'pi•ness** *noun* > **hap'py-go-luck'y** *adjective* casual, lighthearted

ha•ra-ki•ri [HAHR-ə-KEER-ee] *noun* in Japan, ritual suicide by disemboweling

ha•rangue [hə-RANG] *noun* **1** vehement speech **2** tirade ▷ *verb* **-rangued, -rangu•ing**

ha•rass [hə-RAS] *verb transitive* worry, trouble, torment > **ha•rass'ment** *noun*

har•bin•ger [HAHR-bin-jər] *noun* **1** one who announces another's approach **2** forerunner, herald

har•bor [HAHR-bər] *noun* **1** shelter for ships **2** shelter ▷ *verb* **3** give shelter, protection to **4** maintain (secretly) esp. grudge, etc.

hard [hahrd] *adjective* **-er, -est 1** firm, resisting pressure **2** solid **3** difficult to understand **4** harsh, unfeeling **5** difficult to bear **6** practical,

comely, elegant, gorgeous, personable, well-proportioned
2 LARGE, abundant, ample, considerable, generous, liberal, plentiful, sizable *or* sizeable

handwriting *noun* PENMANSHIP, calligraphy, hand, scrawl, script

handy *adjective* **1** AVAILABLE, accessible, at hand, at one's fingertips, close, convenient, nearby, on hand, within reach
2 USEFUL, convenient, easy to use, helpful, manageable, neat, practical, serviceable, user-friendly
3 SKILLFUL, adept, adroit, deft, dexterous, expert, proficient, skilled

hang *verb* **1** SUSPEND, dangle, droop
2 EXECUTE, lynch, string up (*informal*)
▷ *noun* **3** ▷ **get the hang of** GRASP, comprehend, understand

hang back *verb* HESITATE, be reluctant, demur, hold back, recoil

hangdog *adjective* GUILTY, cowed, cringing, defeated, downcast, furtive, shamefaced, wretched

hangover *noun* AFTEREFFECTS, crapulence, morning after (*informal*)

hang-up *noun* PREOCCUPATION, block, difficulty, inhibition, obsession, problem, thing (*informal*)

hank *noun* COIL, length, loop, piece, roll, skein

hanker *verb* (*with for* or *after*) DESIRE, crave, hunger, itch, long, lust, pine, thirst, yearn

haphazard *adjective* DISORGANIZED, aimless, casual, hit or miss (*informal*), indiscriminate, random, slapdash

happen *verb* **1** OCCUR, come about, come to pass, develop, result, take place, transpire (*informal*)
2 CHANCE, turn out

happening *noun* EVENT, affair, episode, experience, incident, occurrence, proceeding

happily *adverb* **1** WILLINGLY, freely, gladly, with pleasure
2 JOYFULLY, blithely, cheerfully, gaily, gleefully, joyously, merrily
3 LUCKILY, fortunately, opportunely, providentially

happiness *noun* JOY, bliss, cheerfulness, contentment, delight, ecstasy, elation, jubilation, pleasure, satisfaction

happy *adjective* **1** JOYFUL, blissful, cheerful, content, delighted, ecstatic, elated, glad, jubilant, merry, overjoyed, pleased, thrilled
2 FORTUNATE, advantageous, auspicious, favorable, lucky, timely, win-win (*informal*)

happy-go-lucky *adjective* CAREFREE, blithe, easy-going, light-hearted, nonchalant, unconcerned, untroubled

harangue *verb* **1** RANT, address, declaim, exhort, hold forth, lecture, spout (*informal*)
▷ *noun* **2** SPEECH, address, declamation, diatribe, exhortation, tirade

harass *verb* ANNOY, bother, harry, hassle (*informal*), hound, persecute, pester, plague, trouble, vex

harassed *adjective* WORRIED, careworn, distraught, hassled (*informal*), strained, tormented, troubled, under pressure, vexed

harassment *noun* TROUBLE, annoyance, bother, hassle (*informal*), irritation, nuisance, persecution, pestering

harbor *noun* **1** PORT, anchorage, haven
▷ *verb* **2** SHELTER, hide, protect, provide refuge, shield
3 MAINTAIN, cling to, entertain, foster, hold,

shrewd **7** heavy **8** strenuous **9** of water, not making lather well with soap **10** of drugs, highly addictive ▷ *adverb* **11** vigorously **12** with difficulty **13** close > **hard'en** *verb* > **hard'ly** *adverb* **1** unkindly, harshly **2** scarcely, not quite **3** only just > **hard'ship** *noun* **1** bad luck **2** severe toil, suffering **3** instance of this > **hard'ball** *noun* **1** baseball **2** (*informal*) forceful or ruthless methods of achieving a goal > **hard-boiled** *adjective* **1** boiled so long as to be hard **2** (*informal*) of person, unemotional, unsentimental > **hard copy** **1** computer output printed on paper **2** original paper document > **hard disk** *computers.* rigid data-storage disk in a sealed container

hard drive mechanism on a computer that handles the reading, writing, and storage of data on a hard disk > **hard-hat** *noun* (*informal*) construction worker > **hard'head'ed** *adjective* shrewd > **hard-pressed** *adjective* heavily burdened > **hard'ware** *noun* **1** tools, implements **2** necessary (parts of) machinery **3** *computing* mechanical and electronic parts > **hard'wood** *noun* wood from deciduous trees > **hard of hearing** rather deaf **hard up** very short of money

har•dy [HAHR-dee] *adjective* **-di•er, -di•est** **1** robust, vigorous **2** bold **3** of plants, able to grow in the open all the year round > **har'di•hood** [-huud] *noun* extreme boldness, audacity > **hard'i•ly** *adverb* > **har'di•ness** *noun*

hare [hair] *noun* animal like large rabbit, with longer legs and ears, noted for speed > **hare'brained** *adjective* rash, wild > **hare'lip** *noun* fissure of upper lip

har•em [HAIR-əm] *noun* **1** women's part of Muslim dwelling **2** one man's wives and concubines

hark [hahrk] *verb intransitive* listen > **hark back** return to previous subject of discussion

har•le•quin [HAHR-lə-kwin] *noun* stock comic character, esp. masked clown in diamond-patterned costume > **har•le•quin•ade'** [-NAYD] *noun* **1** scene in pantomime **2** buffoonery

har•lot [HAHR-lət] *noun* whore, prostitute > **har'lot•ry** *noun*

harm [hahrm] *noun* **1** damage, injury ▷ *verb transitive* **2** cause harm to > **harm'ful** *adjective* > **harm'less** *adjective* unable or unlikely to hurt

har•mo•ny [HAHR-mə-nee] *noun, plural* **-nies** **1** agreement **2** concord **3** peace **4** combination of notes to make chords **5** melodious sound > **har•mon'ic** *adjective* **1** of harmony ▷ *noun* **2** tone or note whose frequency is a multiple of its pitch > **har•mon'ics** *noun* science of musical sounds > **har•mon'i•ca** *noun* various musical instruments, but esp. mouth organ > **har•mo'ni•ous** *adjective* > **har'mo•nize** [-mə-nīz] *verb transitive* **-nized, -niz•ing** **1** bring into harmony **2** cause to agree **3** reconcile ▷ *verb intransitive* **-nized, -niz•ing** **4** be in harmony

har•ness [HAHR-nis] *noun* **1** equipment for attaching horse to cart, plow, etc. **2** any such equipment ▷ *verb transitive* **3** put on, in harness **4** utilize energy or power of (waterfall, etc.)

harp [hahrp] *noun* **1** musical instrument of strings played by hand ▷ *verb intransitive* **2** play on harp **3** dwell (on) persistently > **harp'ist** *noun*

nurse, nurture, retain

hard *adjective* **1** SOLID, firm, inflexible, rigid, rocklike, stiff, strong, tough, unyielding
2 STRENUOUS, arduous, backbreaking, exacting, exhausting, laborious, rigorous, tough
3 DIFFICULT, complicated, intricate, involved, knotty, perplexing, puzzling, thorny
4 UNFEELING, callous, cold, cruel, hardhearted, pitiless, stern, unkind, unsympathetic
5 PAINFUL, disagreeable, distressing, grievous, intolerable, unpleasant
▷ *adverb* **6** ENERGETICALLY, fiercely, forcefully, forcibly, heavily, intensely, powerfully, severely, sharply, strongly, vigorously, violently, with all one's might, with might and main
7 DILIGENTLY, doggedly, industriously, persistently, steadily, untiringly

hard-boiled, hard-bitten *adjective* TOUGH, cynical, hard-nosed (*informal*), matter-of-fact, practical, realistic, unsentimental

harden *verb* **1** SOLIDIFY, anneal, bake, cake, freeze, set, stiffen
2 ACCUSTOM, habituate, inure, season, train

hardened *adjective* **1** HABITUAL, chronic, incorrigible, inveterate, shameless
2 ACCUSTOMED, habituated, inured, seasoned, toughened

hard-headed *adjective* SENSIBLE, level-headed, practical, pragmatic, realistic, shrewd, tough, unsentimental

hardhearted *adjective* UNSYMPATHETIC, callous, cold, hard, heartless, insensitive, uncaring, unfeeling

hardiness *noun* RESILIENCE, resolution, robustness, ruggedness, sturdiness, toughness

hardly *adverb* BARELY, just, only just, scarcely, with difficulty

hardship *noun* SUFFERING, adversity, difficulty, misfortune, need, privation, tribulation

hard up *adjective* POOR, broke (*informal*), impecunious, impoverished, on the breadline, out of pocket, penniless, short, strapped for cash (*informal*)

hardy *adjective* STRONG, robust, rugged, sound, stout, sturdy, tough

harm *verb* **1** INJURE, abuse, damage, hurt, ill-treat, maltreat, ruin, spoil, wound
▷ *noun* **2** INJURY, abuse, damage, hurt, ill, loss, mischief, misfortune

harmful *adjective* DESTRUCTIVE, damaging, deleterious, detrimental, hurtful, injurious, noxious, pernicious

harmless *adjective* INNOCUOUS, gentle, innocent, inoffensive, nontoxic, safe, unobjectionable

harmonious *adjective* **1** MELODIOUS, agreeable, concordant, consonant, dulcet, mellifluous, musical, sweet-sounding, tuneful
2 FRIENDLY, agreeable, amicable, compatible, congenial, cordial, sympathetic

harmonize *verb* BLEND, chime with, cohere, coordinate, correspond, match, tally, tone in with

harmony *noun* **1** AGREEMENT, accord, amicability, compatibility, concord, cooperation, friendship, peace, rapport, sympathy
2 TUNEFULNESS, euphony, melody, tune, unison

harness *noun* **1** EQUIPMENT, gear, tack, tackle
▷ *verb* **2** EXPLOIT, channel, control, employ,

> **harp'si•chord** [-si-kord] *noun* stringed instrument like piano
har•poon [hahr-POON] *noun* 1 barbed spear with rope attached for catching whales ▷ *verb transitive* 2 catch, kill with this > **har•poon'er** *noun* > **harpoon gun** gun for firing harpoon in whaling
Har•py [HAHR-pee] *noun, plural* **-pies** 1 monster with body of woman and wings and claws of bird 2 (**har•py**) cruel, grasping person
har•ri•dan [HAHR-i-dn] *noun* shrewish old woman, hag
har•row [HAR-oh] *noun* 1 implement for smoothing, leveling or stirring up soil ▷ *verb transitive* 2 draw harrow over 3 distress greatly > **har'row•ing** *adjective* 1 heartrending 2 distressful
har•ry [HAR-ee] *verb transitive* **-ried, -ry•ing** 1 harass 2 ravage
harsh [hahrsh] *adjective* **-er, -est** 1 rough, discordant 2 severe 3 unfeeling > **harsh•ness** *noun*
har•um-scar•um [HAIR-əm-SKAIR-əm] *adjective* 1 reckless, wild 2 disorganized
har•vest [HAHR-vist] *noun* (season for) gathering in grain 1 gathering 2 crop 3 product of action ▷ *verb transitive* 4 reap and gather in
has [haz] *third person sing pres indicative of* **have**
hash *noun* 1 dish of hashed meat, etc. 2 (*informal*) *short for* **hashish** 3 mess, jumble ▷ *verb transitive* 4 cut up small, chop 5 mix up
hash•ish [hash-EESH] *noun* resinous extract of Indian hemp, esp. used as hallucinogen
hasp *noun* 1 clasp passing over a staple for fastening door, etc. ▷ *verb transitive* 2 fasten, secure with hasp
has•sle [HAS-əl] *noun* (*informal*) 1 quarrel 2 a lot of bother, trouble ▷ *verb* **-sled, -sling**
has•sock [HAS-ək] *noun* 1 cushion used as footstool, ottoman 2 tuft of grass
haste [hayst] *noun* 1 speed, quickness, hurry ▷ *verb intransitive* **hast•ed, hast•ing** 2 hasten > **has•ten** [HAY-sən] *verb* **hast•ed, hast•ing** (cause to) hurry, increase speed > **hast'i•ly** *adverb* > **hast'y** *adjective* **hast•i•er, hast•i•est**
hat *noun* head covering, usu. with brim > **hat'ter** *noun* dealer in, maker of hats > **hat trick** any three successive achievements, esp. in sports
hatch[1] [hach] *verb* 1 of young, esp. of birds, (cause to) emerge from egg 2 contrive, devise > **hatch'er•y** *noun, plural* **-er•ies**
hatch[2] *noun* 1 hatchway 2 trapdoor over it 3 lower half of divided door > **hatch'back** *noun* automobile with single lifting door in rear > **hatch'way** *noun* opening in deck of ship, etc.
hatch[3] *verb transitive* 1 engrave or draw lines on for shading 2 shade with parallel lines
hatch•et [HACH-it] *noun* small ax > **hatchet job** malicious verbal attack > **hatchet man** 1 person carrying out unpleasant assignments for another 2 professional assassin **bury the hatchet** make peace
hate [hayt] *verb transitive* **hat•ed, hat•ing** 1 dislike strongly 2 bear malice toward ▷ *noun* 3 this feeling 4 that which is hated > **hate'ful** *adjective* detestable > **ha•tred** [HAY-trid] *noun* extreme dislike, active ill will
haugh•ty [HAW-tee] *adjective* **-ti•er, -ti•est** proud, arrogant > **haugh'ti•ness** *noun*
haul [hawl] *verb transitive* 1 pull, drag with effort ▷ *verb intransitive* 2 of wind, shift in direction ▷ *noun* 3 hauling 4 what is hauled 5 catch of fish 6 acquisition 7 distance (to be) covered > **haul•age** [HAW-lij] *noun* 1 carrying of loads 2 charge for this > **haul'er** *noun* firm, person that transports goods by road
haunch [hawnch] *noun* 1 human hip or fleshy

---

mobilize, utilize
harrowing *adjective* DISTRESSING, agonizing, disturbing, heart-rending, nerve-racking, painful, terrifying, tormenting, traumatic
harry *verb* PESTER, badger, bother, chivvy, harass, hassle (*informal*), molest, plague
harsh *adjective* 1 RAUCOUS, discordant, dissonant, grating, guttural, rasping, rough, strident
2 SEVERE, austere, cruel, draconian, drastic, pitiless, punitive, ruthless, stern
harshly *adverb* SEVERELY, brutally, cruelly, roughly, sternly, strictly
harshness *noun* SEVERITY, asperity, austerity, brutality, rigor, roughness, sternness
harvest *noun* 1 CROP, produce, yield
▷ *verb* 2 GATHER, mow, pick, pluck, reap
hassle *noun* 1 ARGUMENT, bickering, disagreement, dispute, fight, quarrel, row, squabble
2 TROUBLE, bother, difficulty, grief (*informal*), inconvenience, problem
▷ *verb* 3 BOTHER, annoy, badger, bug (*informal*), harass, hound, pester
haste *noun* 1 SPEED, alacrity, quickness, rapidity, swiftness, urgency, velocity
2 RUSH, hurry, hustle, impetuosity
hasten *verb* RUSH, dash, fly, hurry *or* hurry up, make haste, race, scurry, speed
hastily *adverb* 1 SPEEDILY, promptly, quickly, rapidly
2 HURRIEDLY, impetuously, precipitately, rashly
hasty *adjective* 1 SPEEDY, brisk, hurried, prompt, rapid, swift, urgent
2 IMPETUOUS, impulsive, precipitate, rash, thoughtless
hatch *verb* 1 INCUBATE, breed, bring forth, brood
2 DEVISE, conceive, concoct, contrive, cook up (*informal*), design, dream up (*informal*), think up
hate *verb* 1 DETEST, abhor, despise, dislike, loathe, recoil from
2 BE UNWILLING, be loath, be reluctant, be sorry, dislike, feel disinclined, shrink from
▷ *noun* 3 DISLIKE, animosity, antipathy, aversion, detestation, enmity, hatred, hostility, loathing
hateful *adjective* DESPICABLE, abhorrent, detestable, horrible, loathsome, lousy (*slang*), obnoxious, odious, offensive, repellent, repugnant, repulsive, scuzzy (*slang*)
hatred *noun* DISLIKE, animosity, antipathy, aversion, detestation, enmity, hate, repugnance, revulsion
haughty *adjective* PROUD, arrogant, conceited, contemptuous, disdainful, imperious, scornful, snooty (*informal*), stuck-up (*informal*), supercilious
haul *verb* 1 DRAG, draw, heave, lug, pull, tug
▷ *noun* 2 GAIN, booty, catch, harvest, loot, spoils, takings, yield

hindquarter of animal 2 leg and loin of animal as food

haunt [hawnt] *verb transitive* 1 visit regularly 2 visit in form of ghost 3 recur to ▷ *noun* 4 esp. place frequently visited > **haunt'ed** *adjective* 1 frequented by ghosts 2 worried

hau•teur [hoh-TUR] *noun* 1 haughty spirit 2 arrogance

have [hav] *verb transitive* **had, hav•ing** 1 hold, possess 2 be possessed, affected with 3 be obliged (to do) 4 cheat, outwit 5 engage in, obtain 6 contain 7 allow 8 cause to be done 9 give birth to 10 used to form past tenses (with a past participle): *we have looked; she had done enough*

ha•ven [HAY-vən] *noun* place of safety

hav•er•sack [HAV-ər-sak] *noun* canvas bag for provisions, etc. carried on back or shoulder when hiking, etc.

hav•oc [HAV-ək] *noun* 1 devastation, ruin 2 (*informal*) confusion, chaos

hawk[1] *noun* 1 bird of prey smaller than eagle 2 supporter, advocate, of warlike policies ▷ *verb intransitive* 3 hunt with hawks 4 attack like hawk

hawk[2] *verb transitive* offer (goods) for sale, as in street > **hawk'er** *noun*

hawk[3] *verb intransitive* clear throat noisily

haw•ser [HAW-zər] *noun* large rope or cable

hay *noun* grass mown and dried > **hay'cock** *noun* conical pile of hay for drying > **hay fever** allergic reaction to pollen, dust, etc. > **hay'stack** *noun* large pile of hay > **hay'wire** *adjective* 1 crazy 2 disorganized

haz•ard [HAZ-ərd] *noun* 1 chance 2 risk, danger ▷ *verb transitive* 3 expose to risk 4 run risk of > **haz'ard•ous** *adjective* risky

haze [hayz] *noun* 1 mist, often due to heat 2 obscurity > **ha'zy** *adjective* **-zi•er, -zi•est** 1 misty 2 obscured 3 vague

ha•zel [HAY-zəl] *noun* 1 bush or small tree bearing nuts 2 yellowish-brown color of the nuts ▷ *adjective* 3 light brown

He *chem.* helium

he [hee] *pronoun* 1 third person masculine pronoun 2 person, animal already referred to ▷ *combining form* 3 male: *he-goat*

head [hed] *noun* 1 upper part of person's or animal's body, containing mouth, sense organs and brain 2 upper part of anything 3 chief of organization, school, etc. 4 chief part 5 aptitude, capacity 6 crisis 7 leader 8 title 9 headland 10 person, animal considered as unit 11 white froth on beer, etc. 12 (*informal*) headache 13 (*slang*) addict, habitual user of drug ▷ *adjective* 14 chief, principal 15 of wind, contrary ▷ *verb transitive* 16 be at the top, head of 17 lead, direct 18 provide with head 19 hit (ball) with head ▷ *verb intransitive* 20 make for 21 form a head > **head'er** *noun* 1 headfirst plunge 2 brick laid with end in face of wall 3 action of striking ball with head > **head'ing** *noun* title > **heads** *adverb* (*informal*) with obverse side (of coin) uppermost > **head'y** *adjective* **head•i•er, head•i•est** apt to intoxicate or excite > **head'ache** [-ayk] *noun* 1 continuous pain in

---

haunt *verb* 1 PLAGUE, obsess, possess, prey on, recur, stay with, torment, trouble, weigh on ▷ *noun* 2 MEETING PLACE, hangout (*informal*), rendezvous, stamping ground

haunted *adjective* 1 POSSESSED, cursed, eerie, ghostly, jinxed, spooky (*informal*)
2 PREOCCUPIED, obsessed, plagued, tormented, troubled, worried

haunting *adjective* POIGNANT, evocative, nostalgic, persistent, unforgettable

have *verb* 1 POSSESS, hold, keep, obtain, own, retain
2 RECEIVE, accept, acquire, gain, get, obtain, procure, secure, take
3 EXPERIENCE, endure, enjoy, feel, meet with, suffer, sustain, undergo
4 GIVE BIRTH TO, bear, beget, bring forth, deliver
5 ▷ **have to** BE OBLIGED, be bound, be compelled, be forced, have got to, must, ought, should

haven *noun* SANCTUARY, asylum, refuge, retreat, sanctum, shelter

havoc *noun* DISORDER, chaos, confusion, disruption, mayhem, shambles

haywire *adjective* TOPSY-TURVY, chaotic, confused, disordered, disorganized, mixed up, out of order, shambolic (*informal*)

hazard *noun* 1 DANGER, jeopardy, peril, pitfall, risk, threat
▷ *verb* 2 JEOPARDIZE, endanger, expose, imperil, risk, threaten
3 (*a guess*) CONJECTURE, advance, offer, presume, throw out, venture, volunteer

hazardous *adjective* DANGEROUS, difficult, insecure, perilous, precarious, risky, unsafe

haze *noun* MIST, cloud, fog, obscurity, vapor

hazy *adjective* 1 MISTY, cloudy, dim, dull, foggy, overcast
2 VAGUE, fuzzy, ill-defined, indefinite, indistinct, muddled, nebulous, uncertain, unclear

head *noun* 1 SKULL, crown, noodle (*slang*), nut (*slang*), pate
2 LEADER, alpha male, boss (*informal*), captain, chief, commander, director, manager, master, principal, supervisor
3 TOP, crest, crown, peak, pinnacle, summit, tip
4 BRAIN, brains (*informal*), intellect, intelligence, mind, thought, understanding
5 ▷ **go to one's head** EXCITE, intoxicate, make conceited, puff up
6 ▷ **head over heels** UNCONTROLLABLY, completely, intensely, thoroughly, utterly, wholeheartedly
▷ *adjective* 7 CHIEF, arch, first, leading, main, pre-eminent, premier, prime, principal, supreme
▷ *verb* 8 LEAD, be first *or* go first, cap, crown, lead the way, precede, top
9 CONTROL, be in charge of, command, direct, govern, guide, lead, manage, run
10 MAKE FOR, aim, go to, make a beeline for, point, set off for, set out, start towards, steer, turn

headache *noun* 1 MIGRAINE, neuralgia
2 PROBLEM, bane, bother, inconvenience, nuisance, trouble, vexation, worry

heading *noun* TITLE, caption, headline, name, rubric

headlong *adverb*

head **2** worrying circumstance > **head'board** *noun* vertical board at head of bed > **head'land** [-lənd] *noun* promontory > **head'light** *noun* powerful lamp carried on front of locomotive, motor vehicle, etc. > **head'line** *noun* news summary, in large type in newspaper > **head'long** *adverb* head foremost, in rush > **head'quar•ters** *plural noun* **1** residence of commander-in-chief **2** center of operations > **head'stone** *noun* gravestone > **head'strong** *adjective* self-willed > **head'way** *noun* advance, progress

heal [heel] *verb* make or become well > **health** [helth] *noun* **1** soundness of body **2** condition of body **3** toast drunk in person's honor > **health'i•ly** *adverb* > **health'y** *adjective* **health•i•er, health•i•est** **1** of strong constitution **2** of or producing good health, well-being, etc. **3** vigorous > **health food** vegetarian food, organically grown, eaten for dietary value

heap [heep] *noun* **1** pile of things lying one on another **2** great quantity ▷ *verb transitive* **3** pile, load with

hear [heer] *verb* **heard** [hurd], **hear•ing** **1** perceive by ear **2** listen to **3** *law* try (case) **4** heed **5** perceive sound **6** learn > **hear'ing** *noun* **1** ability to hear **2** earshot **3** judicial examination > **hear'say** *noun* rumor ▷ *adjective*

heark•en [HAHR-kən] *verb intransitive* listen

hearse [hurs] *noun* funeral carriage for coffin

heart [hahrt] *noun* **1** organ that makes blood circulate **2** seat of emotions and affections **3** mind, soul, courage **4** central part **5** playing card marked with figure of heart **6** one of these marks > **heart'en** *verb* make, become cheerful > **heart'i•ly** *adverb* > **heart'less** [-lis] *adjective* unfeeling > **heart'y** *adjective* **heart•i•er, heart•i•est** **1** friendly **2** vigorous **3** in good health **4** satisfying the appetite > **heart attack** sudden severe malfunction of heart > **heart'burn** *noun* pain in upper intestine > **heart'rend•ing** *adjective* **1** overwhelming with grief **2** agonizing > **heart'throb** *noun* object of infatuation > **heart'-to-heart'** *adjective* frank, sincere **by heart** by memory

hearth [hahrth] *noun* **1** floor of fireplace **2** part of room where fire is made **3** home

heat [heet] *noun* **1** hotness **2** sensation of this **3** hot weather or climate **4** warmth of feeling, anger, etc. **5** sexual excitement caused by readiness to mate in female animals **6** one of

DICTIONARY

h

THESAURUS

▷ *adjective* **1** HEADFIRST, head-on
▷ *adverb* **2** HASTILY, heedlessly, helter-skelter, hurriedly, pell-mell, precipitately, rashly, thoughtlessly
▷ *adjective* **3** HASTY, breakneck, dangerous, impetuous, impulsive, inconsiderate, precipitate, reckless, thoughtless

headstrong *adjective* OBSTINATE, foolhardy, heedless, impulsive, perverse, pig-headed, self-willed, stubborn, unruly, willful

headway *noun* PROGRESS, advance, improvement, progression, way

heady *adjective* **1** INEBRIATING, intoxicating, potent, strong
2 EXCITING, exhilarating, intoxicating, stimulating, thrilling

heal *verb* CURE, make well, mend, regenerate, remedy, restore, treat

health *noun* **1** WELLBEING, fitness, good condition, healthiness, robustness, soundness, strength, vigor
2 CONDITION, constitution, fettle, shape, state

healthy *adjective* **1** WELL, active, fit, hale and hearty, in fine fettle, in good shape (*informal*), in the pink, robust, strong
2 WHOLESOME, beneficial, hygienic, invigorating, nourishing, nutritious, salubrious, salutary

heap *noun* **1** PILE, accumulation, collection, hoard, lot, mass, mound, stack
2 (*often plural*) A LOT, great deal, lots (*informal*), mass, plenty, pot *or* pots (*informal*), stack *or* stacks, tons
▷ *verb* **3** PILE, accumulate, amass, collect, gather, hoard, stack
4 CONFER, assign, bestow, load, shower upon

hear *verb* **1** LISTEN TO, catch, overhear
2 LEARN, ascertain, discover, find out, gather, get wind of (*informal*), pick up
3 (*law*) TRY, examine, investigate, judge

hearing *noun* INQUIRY, industrial tribunal, investigation, review, trial

hearsay *noun* RUMOR, gossip, idle talk, report, talk, tittle-tattle, word of mouth

heart *noun* **1** NATURE, character, disposition, soul, temperament
2 BRAVERY, courage, fortitude, pluck, purpose, resolution, spirit, will
3 CENTER, core, hub, middle, nucleus, quintessence
4 ▷ **by heart** BY MEMORY, by rote, off pat, parrot-fashion (*informal*), pat, word for word

heartache *noun* SORROW, agony, anguish, despair, distress, grief, heartbreak, pain, remorse, suffering, torment, torture

heartbreak *noun* GRIEF, anguish, desolation, despair, misery, pain, sorrow, suffering

heartbreaking *adjective* TRAGIC, agonizing, distressing, harrowing, heart-rending, pitiful, poignant, sad

heartbroken *adjective* MISERABLE, brokenhearted, crushed, desolate, despondent, disconsolate, dispirited, heartsick

heartfelt *adjective* SINCERE, deep, devout, earnest, genuine, honest, profound, unfeigned, wholehearted

heartily *adverb* ENTHUSIASTICALLY, eagerly, earnestly, resolutely, vigorously, zealously

heartless *adjective* CRUEL, callous, cold, hard, hardhearted, merciless, pitiless, uncaring, unfeeling

heart-rending *adjective* MOVING, affecting, distressing, harrowing, heartbreaking, poignant, sad, tragic

hearty *adjective* **1** FRIENDLY, back-slapping, ebullient, effusive, enthusiastic, genial, jovial, warm
2 SUBSTANTIAL, ample, filling, nourishing, sizable *or* sizeable, solid, square

heat *verb* **1** WARM UP, make hot, reheat
▷ *noun* **2** HOTNESS, high temperature, warmth
3 INTENSITY, excitement, fervor, fury, passion, vehemence

many races, etc. to decide persons to compete in finals ▷ *verb* 7 make, become hot > **heat'ed** *adjective* esp. angry

heath [heeth] *noun* 1 tract of wasteland 2 low-growing evergreen shrub

hea•then [HEE-*th*ən] *adjective* 1 not adhering to a religious system 2 pagan 3 barbarous 4 unenlightened ▷ *noun* 5 heathen person > **hea'then•ish** *adjective* 1 of or like heathen 2 rough 3 barbarous

heath•er [HE*th*-ər] *noun* shrub growing on heaths and mountains

heave [heev] *verb transitive* **heaved, heav•ing** 1 lift with effort 2 throw (something heavy) 3 utter (sigh) ▷ *verb intransitive* **heaved, heav•ing** 4 swell, rise 5 vomit ▷ *noun*

heav•en [HEV-ən] *noun* 1 abode of God 2 place of bliss 3 (*also plural*) sky > **heav'en•ly** *adjective* 1 lovely, delightful, divine 2 beautiful 3 of or like heaven

heav•y [HEV-ee] *adjective* **heav•i•er, heav•i•est** 1 weighty, striking, falling with force 2 dense 3 sluggish 4 difficult, severe 5 sorrowful 6 serious 7 dull 8 (*slang*) serious, excellent > **heav'i•ly** *adverb* > **heav'i•ness** *noun* > **heavy industry** basic, large-scale industry producing metal, machinery, etc. > **heavy metal** rock music with strong beat and amplified instrumental effects > **heavy water** deuterium oxide, water in which normal hydrogen content has been replaced by deuterium

Heb. Hebrews

He•brew [HEE-broo] *noun* 1 member of an ancient Semitic people 2 their language 3 its modern form, used in Israel

heck•le [HEK-əl] *verb* **-led, -ling** interrupt or try to annoy (speaker) by questions, taunts, etc.

hect-, hecto- *combining form* one hundred: *hectoliter; hectometer*

hec•tare [HEK-tahr] *noun* one hundred ares (10,000 square meters, 2.471 acres)

hec•tic [HEK-tik] *adjective* rushed, busy

hec•tor [HEK-tər] *verb* 1 bully, bluster ▷ *noun* 2 bully

hedge [hej] *noun* 1 fence of bushes ▷ *verb transitive* **hedged, hedg•ing** 2 surround with hedge 3 obstruct 4 hem in 5 bet on both sides ▷ *verb intransitive* **hedged, hedg•ing** 6 make hedge 7 be evasive 8 secure against loss > **hedge'hog** *noun* small animal covered with spines

he•don•ism [HEED-n-iz-əm] *noun* doctrine that pleasure is the chief good > **he'don•ist** *noun*

heed *verb transitive* take notice of, care for > **heed'ful** *adjective* > **heed'less** *adjective* careless

heel¹ *noun* 1 hinder part of foot 2 part of shoe supporting this 3 undesirable person ▷ *verb transitive* 4 supply with heel 5 touch ground with heel ▷ *verb intransitive* 6 of dog, follow at one's heels

heel² *verb* 1 of ship, (cause to) lean to one side ▷ *noun* 2 heeling, list

heft•y [HEF-tee] *adjective* **heft•i•er, heft•i•est** 1 bulky 2 weighty 3 strong

he•gem•o•ny [hi-JEM-ə-nee] *noun, plural* **-nies** leadership, political domination

heif•er [HEF-ər] *noun* young cow

height [hīt] *noun* 1 measure from base to top 2 quality of being high 3 elevation 4 highest degree 5 (*often plural*) area of high ground 6

DICTIONARY • THESAURUS

heated *adjective* ANGRY, excited, fierce, frenzied, furious, impassioned, intense, passionate, stormy, vehement

heathen *noun* 1 UNBELIEVER, infidel, pagan
▷ *adjective* 2 PAGAN, godless, idolatrous, irreligious

heave *verb* 1 LIFT, drag *or* drag up, haul *or* haul up, hoist, pull *or* pull up, raise, tug
2 THROW, cast, fling, hurl, pitch, send, sling, toss
3 SIGH, groan, puff
4 VOMIT, barf (*slang*), gag, retch, spew, throw up (*informal*)

heaven *noun* 1 PARADISE, bliss, Elysium *or* Elysian fields (*Greek myth*), hereafter, life everlasting, next world, nirvana (*buddhism, hinduism*), Zion (*Christianity*)
2 HAPPINESS, bliss, ecstasy, paradise, rapture, seventh heaven, utopia
3 ▷ **the heavens** SKY, ether, firmament

heavenly *adjective* 1 BEAUTIFUL, blissful, delightful, divine (*informal*), exquisite, lovely, ravishing, sublime, wonderful
2 CELESTIAL, angelic, blessed, divine, holy, immortal

heavily *adverb* 1 PONDEROUSLY, awkwardly, clumsily, weightily
2 DENSELY, closely, compactly, thickly
3 CONSIDERABLY, a great deal, copiously, excessively, to excess, very much

heaviness *noun* WEIGHT, gravity, heftiness, ponderousness

heavy *adjective* 1 WEIGHTY, bulky, hefty, massive, ponderous
2 CONSIDERABLE, abundant, copious, excessive, large, profuse

heckle *verb* JEER, boo, disrupt, interrupt, shout down, taunt

hectic *adjective* FRANTIC, animated, chaotic, feverish, frenetic, heated, turbulent

hedge *noun* 1 BARRIER, boundary, screen, windbreak
▷ *verb* 2 DODGE, duck, equivocate, evade, prevaricate, sidestep, temporize
3 INSURE, cover, guard, protect, safeguard, shield

heed *noun* 1 CARE, attention, caution, mind, notice, regard, respect, thought
▷ *verb* 2 PAY ATTENTION TO, bear in mind, consider, follow, listen to, note, obey, observe, take notice of

heedless *adjective* CARELESS, foolhardy, inattentive, oblivious, thoughtless, unmindful

heel *noun* (*slang*) SWINE, louse, rat, scumbag, scuzzbucket (*slang*), skunk

heel over *verb* LEAN OVER, keel over, list, tilt

hefty *adjective* STRONG, big, burly, hulking, massive, muscular, robust, strapping

height *noun* 1 ALTITUDE, elevation, highness, loftiness, stature, tallness
2 PEAK, apex, crest, crown, pinnacle, summit, top, zenith
3 CULMINATION, climax, limit, maximum, ultimate

heights extremes: *dizzy heights of success* > **height'en** *verb transitive* 1 make higher 2 intensify
hei•nous [HAY-nəs] *adjective* atrocious, extremely wicked, detestable
heir [air] *noun* person entitled to inherit property or rank > **heir'ess** *noun feminine* > **heir'loom** *noun* thing that has been in family for generations
held *pt./pp. of* **hold**
hel•i•cal [HEL-i-kəl] *adjective* spiral
hel•i•cop•ter [HEL-i-kop-tər] *noun* aircraft made to rise vertically by pull of rotating blades turning horizontally > **hel'i•port** *noun* airport for helicopters
helio- *combining form* sun: *heliograph*
he•li•o•graph [HEE-lee-ə-graf] *noun* signaling apparatus employing a mirror to reflect sun's rays
he•li•o•ther•a•py [hee-lee-oh-THER-ə-pee] *noun* therapeutic use of sunlight
he•li•o•trope [HEE-lee-ə-trohp] *noun* 1 plant with purple flowers 2 color of the flowers > **he•li•o•trop'ic** [-TROP-ik] *adjective* growing, turning toward source of light
he•li•um [HEE-lee-əm] *noun* very light, nonflammable gaseous element
he•lix [HEE-liks] *noun* spiral
hell *noun* 1 abode of the damned 2 abode of the dead generally 3 place or state of wickedness, or misery, or torture > **hell'ish** *adjective*
Hel•len•ic [he-LEN-ik] *adjective* pert. to inhabitants of Greece
hel•lo [he-LOH] *interjection* expression of greeting or surprise
helm *noun* tiller, wheel for turning ship's rudder
hel•met [HEL-mit] *noun* defensive or protective covering for head
help *verb transitive* 1 aid, assist 2 support 3 succor 4 remedy, prevent ▷ *noun* 5 assistance or support > **help'ful** *adjective* > **help'ing** *noun* single portion of food taken at a meal > **help'less** [-lis] *adjective* 1 useless, incompetent 2 unaided 3 unable to help > **help'mate, help'meet** *noun* 1 helpful companion 2 husband or wife
hel•ter-skel•ter [HEL-tər-SKEL-tər] *adverb, adjective, noun* (in) hurry and confusion
hem *noun* 1 border of cloth, esp. one made by turning over edge and sewing it down ▷ *verb transitive* **hemmed, hem•ming** 2 sew thus 3 confine, shut in > **hem'stitch** *noun* ornamental stitch ▷ *verb transitive*
hemi- *combining form* half: *hemisphere*
hem•i•ple•gi•a [hem-i-PLEE-jə] *noun* paralysis of one side of body > **hem•i•ple'gic** *adjective, noun*
hem•i•sphere [HEM-i-sfeer] *noun* 1 half sphere 2 half of celestial sphere 3 half of Earth > **hem•i•spher'i•cal** [-sfe-rə-kəl] *adjective*
hem•lock [HEM-lok] *noun* 1 poisonous plant 2 poison extracted from it 3 evergreen of pine family
hemo-, hema- *combining form* blood: *hemophilia*
he•mo•glo•bin [HEE-mə-gloh-bin] *noun* coloring and oxygen-bearing matter of red blood corpuscles
he•mo•phil•i•a [hee-mə-FIL-ee-ə] *noun* hereditary tendency to intensive bleeding as blood fails to clot > **he•mo•phil'i•ac** *noun*
hem•or•rhage [HEM-ər-ij] *noun* 1 profuse bleeding ▷ *verb intransitive* **-rhaged, -rhag•ing** 2 bleed profusely 3 lose assets, esp. in large amounts
hem•or•rhoids [HEM-ə-roidz] *plural noun* swollen veins in rectum (*also* **piles**)
hemp *noun* 1 Indian plant 2 its fiber used for rope, etc. 3 any of several narcotic drugs made from varieties of hemp > **hemp'en** [-pən] *adjective* made of hemp or rope
hen *noun* female of domestic fowl and others > **hen'peck** *verb transitive* (of a woman) harass (a man, esp. husband) by nagging
hence [hens] *adverb* 1 from this point 2 for this reason > **hence•for'ward, hence'forth** *adverb* from now onward
hench•man [HENCH-mən] *noun* 1 trusty follower 2 unscrupulous supporter

---

heighten *verb* INTENSIFY, add to, amplify, enhance, improve, increase, magnify, sharpen, strengthen
heir *noun* SUCCESSOR, beneficiary, heiress *feminine* inheritor, next in line
hell *noun* 1 UNDERWORLD, abyss, fire and brimstone, Hades (*Greek myth*), hellfire, inferno, nether world
2 TORMENT, agony, anguish, misery, nightmare, ordeal, suffering, wretchedness
hellish *adjective* DEVILISH, damnable, diabolical, fiendish, infernal
hello *interjection* WELCOME, good afternoon, good evening, good morning, greetings
helm *noun* 1 TILLER, rudder, wheel
2 ▷ **at the helm** IN CHARGE, at the wheel, in command, in control, in the driving seat
help *verb* 1 AID, abet, assist, cooperate, lend a hand, succor, support
2 IMPROVE, alleviate, ameliorate, ease, facilitate, mitigate, relieve
3 REFRAIN FROM, avoid, keep from, prevent, resist
▷ *noun* 4 ASSISTANCE, advice, aid, cooperation, guidance, helping hand, support
helper *noun* ASSISTANT, adjutant, aide, ally, attendant, collaborator, helpmate, mate, partner, right-hand man, second, supporter
helpful *adjective* 1 USEFUL, advantageous, beneficial, constructive, practical, profitable, timely, win-win (*informal*)
2 COOPERATIVE, accommodating, considerate, friendly, kind, neighborly, supportive, sympathetic
helping *noun* PORTION, dollop (*informal*), piece, plateful, ration, serving
helpless *adjective* WEAK, challenged, disabled, impotent, incapable, infirm, paralyzed, powerless
helter-skelter *adjective* 1 HAPHAZARD, confused, disordered, hit-or-miss, jumbled, muddled, random, topsy-turvy
▷ *adverb* 2 CARELESSLY, anyhow, hastily, headlong, hurriedly, pell-mell, rashly, recklessly, wildly
hem *noun* 1 EDGE, border, fringe, margin, trimming
▷ *verb* 2 ▷ **hem in** SURROUND, beset, circumscribe, confine, enclose, restrict, shut in
hence *conjunction* THEREFORE, ergo, for this

hen•na [HEN-ə] *noun* 1 flowering shrub 2 reddish dye made from it
hen•o•the•ism [HEN-ə-thee-iz-əm] *noun* belief in one god (of several) as special god of one's family, tribe, etc.
hen•ry [HEN-ree] *noun, plural* **-ries** SI unit of electrical inductance
he•pat•ic [hi-PAT-ik] *adjective* pert. to the liver > **hep•a•ti•tis** [hep-ə-TĪ-tis] *noun* inflammation of the liver
hepta- *combining form* seven: *heptagon*
hep•ta•gon [HEP-tə-gon] *noun* figure with seven angles > **hep•tag'o•nal** *adjective*
her [hur] *adjective objective and possessive case of* **she** > **hers** *pronoun of* **her** > **her•self** *pronoun emphatic form of* **she**
her•ald [HER-əld] *noun* 1 messenger, envoy 2 officer who makes royal proclamations, arranges ceremonies, etc. ▷ *verb transitive* 3 announce 4 proclaim approach of > **he•ral•dic** [hi-RAL-dik] *adjective* > **her'ald•ry** *noun* study of (right to have) heraldic bearings
herb [urb] *noun* 1 plant with soft stem that dies down after flowering 2 plant of which parts are used in cookery or medicine > **her•ba•ceous** [hur-BAY-shəs] *adjective* 1 of, like herbs 2 perennially flowering > **herb•al** [HUR-bəl] *adjective* 1 of herbs ▷ *noun* 2 book on herbs > **herb'al•ist** *noun* 1 writer on herbs 2 collector, dealer in medicinal herbs > **herb'i•cide** [-sīd] *noun* chemical that destroys plants > **her•biv'o•rous** [-ə-rəs] *adjective* feeding on plants
Her•cu•les [HUR-kyə-leez] *noun* mythical hero noted for strength > **her•cu•le'an** [-kyə-LEE-ən] *adjective* 1 requiring great strength, courage 2 hard to perform
herd [hurd] *noun* 1 company of animals, usu. of same species, feeding or traveling together ▷ *verb* 2 crowd together ▷ *verb transitive* 3 tend (herd) > **herds•man** [HURDZ-mən] *noun*
here [heer] *adverb* 1 in this place 2 at or to this point > **here•after** *adverb* 1 in time to come ▷ *noun* 2 future existence after death > **here•to•fore'** [-tə-FOR] *adverb* before
he•red•i•ty [hə-RED-i-tee] *noun* tendency of organism to transmit its nature to its descendants > **he•red'i•tar•y** [-ter-ee] *adjective* 1 descending by inheritance 2 holding office by inheritance 3 that can be transmitted from one generation to another
her•e•sy [HER-ə-see] *noun, plural* **-sies** [-seez] opinion contrary to orthodox opinion or belief > **her'e•tic** *noun* one holding opinions contrary to orthodox faith > **he•ret'i•cal** [-kəl] *adjective*
her•it•age [HER-i-tij] *noun* 1 what may be or is inherited 2 anything from past, esp. owned or handed down by tradition > **her'it•a•ble** *adjective* that can be inherited
her•maph•ro•dite [hur-MAF-rə-dīt] *noun* person, animal with characteristics or reproductive organs of both sexes
her•met•ic [hur-MET-ik] *adjective* sealed so as to be airtight > **her•met'i•cal•ly** *adverb*
her•mit [HUR-mit] *noun* one living in solitude, esp. from religious motives > **her'mit•age** [-tij] *noun* this person's abode
her•ni•a [HUR-nee-ə] *noun* projection of (part of) organ through lining encasing it
he•ro [HEER-oh] *noun, plural* **-roes** 1 one greatly regarded for achievements or qualities 2 principal character in poem, play, story 3 illustrious warrior 4 demigod > **her•o•ine** [HER-oh-in] *noun feminine* > **he•ro'ic** [hi-ROH-ik] *adjective* 1 of, like hero 2 courageous, daring > **he•ro'i•cal•ly** *adverb* > **he•ro'ics** *plural noun* extravagant behavior > **her'o•ism** *noun* 1 qualities of hero 2 courage, boldness > **hero sandwich** large sandwich of meats, etc. on loaf of Italian bread > **hero worship** 1 admiration of heroes or of great men 2 excessive admiration of others
her•o•in [HER-oh-in] *noun* white crystalline derivative of morphine, a highly addictive narcotic
her•on [HER-ən] *noun* long-legged wading bird
her•pes [HUR-peez] *noun* any of several diseases, including shingles and cold sores
her'ring *noun* important food fish of northern hemisphere
hertz [hurts] *noun, plural* **hertz** SI unit of frequency
hes•i•tate [HEZ-i-tayt] *verb intransitive* **-tat•ed, -tat•ing** 1 hold back 2 feel, or show indecision

reason, on that account, thus
henchman *noun* ATTENDANT, associate, bodyguard, follower, minder (*slang*), right-hand man, sidekick (*slang*), subordinate, supporter
henpecked *adjective* BULLIED, browbeaten, dominated, meek, subjugated, timid
herald *noun* 1 MESSENGER, crier 2 FORERUNNER, harbinger, indication, omen, precursor, sign, signal, token ▷ *verb* 3 INDICATE, foretoken, portend, presage, promise, show, usher in
herd *noun* 1 MULTITUDE, collection, crowd, drove, flock, horde, mass, mob, swarm, throng ▷ *verb* 2 CONGREGATE, assemble, collect, flock, gather, huddle, muster, rally
hereafter *adverb* 1 IN FUTURE, from now on, hence, henceforth, henceforward ▷ *noun* 2 AFTERLIFE, life after death, next world
hereditary *adjective* 1 GENETIC, inborn, inbred, inheritable, transmissible 2 INHERITED, ancestral, traditional
heredity *noun* GENETICS, constitution, genetic make-up, inheritance
heresy *noun* DISSIDENCE, apostasy, heterodoxy, iconoclasm, unorthodoxy
heretic *noun* DISSIDENT, apostate, dissenter, nonconformist, renegade, revisionist
heretical *adjective* UNORTHODOX, heterodox, iconoclastic, idolatrous, impious, revisionist
heritage *noun* INHERITANCE, bequest, birthright, endowment, legacy, tradition
hermit *noun* RECLUSE, anchorite, eremite, loner (*informal*), monk
hero *noun* 1 IDOL, champion, conqueror, star, superstar, victor 2 LEADING MAN, protagonist
heroic *adjective* COURAGEOUS, brave, daring, fearless, gallant, intrepid, lion-hearted, valiant
heroine *noun* LEADING LADY, diva, prima donna, protagonist
heroism *noun* BRAVERY, courage, courageousness, fearlessness, gallantry,

3 be reluctant > **hes'i•tan•cy** [-tən-see] *noun* > **hes•i•ta'tion** *noun* 1 wavering 2 doubt 3 stammering > **hes'i•tant** *adjective* undecided, pausing
hetero- *combining form* other or different: *heterosexual*
het•er•o•dox [HET-ər-ə-doks] *adjective* not orthodox > **het'er•o•dox•y** *noun, plural* **-dox•ies**
het•er•o•ge•ne•ous [het-ər-ə-JEE-nee-əs] *adjective* composed of diverse elements > **het•er•o•ge•ne'i•ty** [-jə-NEE-i-tee] *noun*
het•er•o•sex•u•al [het-ər-ə-SEK-shoo-əl] *noun* person sexually attracted to members of the opposite sex
heu•ris•tic [hyuu-RIS-tik] *adjective* serving to find out or to stimulate investigation
hew [hyoo] *verb* **hewed, hewed** *or* **hewn, hew•ing** chop, cut with axe > **hew'er** *noun*
hex [heks] *noun* 1 magic spell ▷ *verb* 2 bewitch
hex-, hexa- *combining form* six: *hexagon*
hex•a•gon [HEK-sə-gon] *noun* figure with six angles > **hex•ag'o•nal** *adjective*
hex•am•e•ter [hek-SAM-i-tər] *noun* line of verse of six feet
hey•day [HAY-day] *noun* bloom, prime
Hf *chem.* hafnium
Hg *chem.* mercury
hi•a•tus [hī-AY-təs] *noun, plural* **-tus•es** break or gap where something is missing
hi•ber•nate [HĪ-bər-nayt] *verb intransitive* **-nat•ed, -nat•ing** pass the winter, esp. in a torpid state > **hi•ber•na'tion** *noun*
hi•bis•cus [hī-BIS-kəs] *noun* flowering (sub)tropical shrub
hic•cup [HIK-up] *noun* 1 spasm of the breathing organs with an abrupt cough-like sound ▷ *verb intransitive* **-cupped, -cup•ping** 2 have this
hick [hik] *adjective* (*informal*) 1 rustic 2 unsophisticated ▷ *noun* 3 person, place like this
hick•o•ry [HIK-ə-ree] *noun, plural* **-o•ries** 1 N Amer. nut-bearing tree 2 its tough wood
hide[1] [hīd] *verb transitive* **hid, hid•den** *or* **hid, hid•ing** 1 put, keep out of sight 2 conceal, keep secret ▷ *verb intransitive* **hid, hid•den** *or* **hid, hid•ing** 3 conceal oneself > **hide'out** *noun* hiding place
hide[2] *noun* skin of animal > **hid'ing** *noun* (*slang*) thrashing > **hide'bound** *adjective* 1 restricted, esp. by petty rules, etc. 2 narrow-minded
hid•e•ous [HID-ee-əs] *adjective* repulsive, revolting
hi•er•ar•chy [HĪ-ə-rahr-kee] *noun, plural* **-chies** system of persons or things arranged in graded order > **hi•er•ar'chi•cal** *adjective*
hi•er•o•glyph•ic [hī-ər-ə-GLIF-ik] *adjective* 1 of a system of picture writing, as used in ancient Egypt ▷ *noun* 2 symbol representing object, concept or sound 3 symbol, picture, difficult to decipher > **hi'er•o•glyph** *noun*
hi-fi [HĪ-FĪ] *adjective* 1 *short for* **high-fidelity** ▷ *noun* 2 high-fidelity equipment
high [hī] *adjective* **-er, -est** 1 tall, lofty 2 far up 3 of roads, main 4 of meat, tainted 5 of sound, acute in pitch 6 expensive 7 of great importance, quality, or rank 8 (*informal*) in state of euphoria, esp. induced by alcohol or drugs ▷ *adverb* 9 far up 10 strongly, to a great extent 11 at, to a high pitch 12 at a high rate > **high'ly** *adverb* > **high'ness** *noun* 1 quality of being high 2 (**High'ness**) 3 title of prince and princess > **high'brow** *noun* 1 intellectual, esp. intellectual snob ▷ *adjective* 2 intellectual 3 difficult 4 serious > **high'-fi•del'i•ty** *adjective* of high-quality sound-reproducing equipment > **high-flown** *adjective* extravagant, bombastic > **high'-hand'ed** *adjective* domineering, dogmatic

DICTIONARY h THESAURUS

intrepidity, spirit, valor
hesitant *adjective* UNCERTAIN, diffident, doubtful, half-hearted, halting, irresolute, reluctant, unsure, vacillating, wavering
hesitate *verb* 1 WAVER, delay, dither, doubt, hum and haw, pause, vacillate, wait
2 BE RELUCTANT, balk, be unwilling, demur, hang back, scruple, shrink from, think twice
hesitation *noun* 1 INDECISION, delay, doubt, hesitancy, irresolution, uncertainty, vacillation
2 RELUCTANCE, misgiving *or* misgivings, qualm *or* qualms, scruple *or* scruples, unwillingness
hew *verb* 1 CUT, ax, chop, hack, lop, split
2 CARVE, fashion, form, make, model, sculpt, sculpture, shape, smooth
heyday *noun* PRIME, bloom, pink, prime of life, salad days
hiatus *noun* PAUSE, break, discontinuity, gap, interruption, interval, respite, space
hidden *adjective* CONCEALED, clandestine, covert, latent, secret, under wraps, unseen, veiled
hide[1] *verb* 1 CONCEAL, secrete, stash (*informal*)
2 GO INTO HIDING, go to ground, go underground, hole up, lie low, take cover
3 DISGUISE, camouflage, cloak, conceal, cover, mask, obscure, shroud, veil
4 SUPPRESS, draw a veil over, hush up, keep dark, keep secret, keep under one's hat, withhold
hide[2] *noun* SKIN, pelt
hidebound *adjective* CONVENTIONAL, narrow-minded, rigid, set in one's ways, strait-laced, ultraconservative
hideous *adjective* UGLY, ghastly, grim, grisly, grotesque, gruesome, monstrous, repulsive, revolting, scuzzy (*slang*), unsightly
hideout *noun* HIDEAWAY, den, hiding place, lair, shelter
hierarchy *noun* GRADING, pecking order, ranking
high *adjective* 1 TALL, elevated, lofty, soaring, steep, towering
2 EXTREME, excessive, extraordinary, great, intensified, sharp, strong
3 IMPORTANT, arch, chief, eminent, exalted, powerful, superior
4 (*informal*) INTOXICATED, stoned (*slang*), tripping (*informal*)
5 HIGH-PITCHED, acute, penetrating, piercing, piping, sharp, shrill, strident
▷ *adverb* 6 ALOFT, at great height, far up, way up
highbrow *noun* 1 INTELLECTUAL, aesthete, egghead (*informal*), scholar
▷ *adjective* 2 INTELLECTUAL, bookish, cultivated, cultured, sophisticated
high-flown *adjective* EXTRAVAGANT, elaborate, exaggerated, florid, grandiose, inflated, lofty, overblown, pretentious
high-handed *adjective* DICTATORIAL, despotic, domineering, imperious, oppressive, overbearing, tyrannical, willful

> **high'land** [-lənd] *noun* relatively high ground > **High'land** *adjective* of, from the highlands of Scotland > **high'light** *noun* 1 lightest or brightest area in painting, photograph, etc. 2 outstanding feature ▷ *verb transitive* 3 bring into prominence > **high-main'tenance** *adjective* 1 (of equipment) requiring regular maintenance to keep it in working order 2 (*informal*) (of a person) requiring a high level of care and attention > **high'-rise** *adjective, noun* (of) building that has many stories and elevators > **high'-sound'ing** *adjective* pompous, imposing > **high-strung** *adjective* excitable, nervous > **high-tech** *same as* **hi-tech** > **high time** latest possible time > **high'way** *noun* main road > **highway robbery** (*informal*) exorbitant fee or charge > **high'way•man** [-mən] *noun* (formerly) robber on road, esp. mounted

hi•jack [HĪ-jak] *verb transitive* 1 divert or wrongfully take command of a vehicle (esp. aircraft) or its contents or passengers 2 rob > **hi'jack•er** *noun*

hike [hīk] *verb intransitive* **hiked, hik•ing** 1 walk a long way (for pleasure) in country ▷ *verb transitive* **hiked, hik•ing** 2 pull (up), hitch ▷ *noun* > **hik'er** *noun*

hi•lar•i•ty [hi-LAR-i-tee] *noun* cheerfulness, gaiety > **hi•lar'i•ous** *adjective*

hill *noun* 1 natural elevation, small mountain 2 mound > **hill'ock** [-ək] *noun* little hill > **hill'y** *adjective* **hill•i•er, hill•i•est** > **hill'bil•ly** *noun, plural* **-lies** (*offensive*) unsophisticated country person

hilt *noun* handle of sword, etc **up to the hilt** completely

him *pronoun objective case of pronoun* **he** > **him•self'** *pronoun emphatic form of* **he**

hind[1] [hīnd] *noun* female of deer

hind[2] *adjective* at the back, posterior (*also* **hind•er**) [HĪN-dər]

hin•der [HIN-dər] *verb transitive* obstruct, impede, delay > **hin'drance** [-drəns] *noun*

Hin•di [HIN-dee] *noun* language of N central India > **Hin'du** [-doo] *noun* person who adheres to Hinduism > **Hin'du•ism** *noun* the dominant religion of India

hinge [hinj] *noun* 1 movable joint, as that on which door hangs ▷ *verb transitive* **hinged, hing•ing** 2 attach with, or as with, hinge ▷ *verb intransitive* **hinged, hing•ing** 3 turn, depend on

hint *noun* 1 slight indication or suggestion ▷ *verb* 2 give hint of

hin•ter•land [HIN-tər-land] *noun* district lying behind coast, or near city, port, etc.

hip *noun* 1 either side of body below waist and above thigh 2 angle formed where sloping sides of roof meet 3 fruit of rose, esp. wild

hip-hop [HIP-hop] *noun* pop-culture movement involving rap music, graffiti, and break dancing

hip•pie [HIP-ee] *noun* (formerly) (young) person whose behavior, dress, etc. implies rejection of conventional values

hip•po•pot•a•mus [hip-ə-POT-ə-məs] *noun, plural* **-mus•es** *or* **-mi** [-mī] large Afr. animal living in and near rivers

hire [hīr] *verb transitive* **hired, hir•ing** 1 obtain temporary use of by payment 2 engage for wage ▷ *noun* 3 hiring or being hired 4 payment for use of thing > **hire'ling** *noun* one who works for wages

hir•sute [HUR-soot] *adjective* hairy

his [hiz] *pronoun, adjective* belonging to him

His•pan•ic [hi-SPAN-ik] *adjective* 1 relating to Spain or to Spanish-speaking Central and S. America ▷ *noun* 2 Spanish-speaking person 3 U.S. resident of Hispanic descent

his'pid *adjective* 1 rough with bristles or minute spines 2 bristly, shaggy

hiss *verb intransitive* 1 make sharp sound of letter S, esp. in disapproval ▷ *verb transitive* 2 express disapproval, deride thus ▷ *noun*

his•ta•mine [HIS-tə-meen] *noun* substance released by body tissues, sometimes creating

highlight *noun* 1 FEATURE, climax, focal point, focus, high point, high spot, peak ▷ *verb* 2 EMPHASIZE, accent, accentuate, bring to the fore, show up, spotlight, stress, underline

highly *adverb* EXTREMELY, exceptionally, greatly, immensely, tremendously, vastly, very, very much

highly strung *adjective* NERVOUS, edgy, excitable, neurotic, sensitive, stressed, temperamental, tense, twitchy (*informal*), wired (*slang*)

hijack *verb* SEIZE, commandeer, expropriate, take over

hike *noun* 1 WALK, march, ramble, tramp, trek ▷ *verb* 2 WALK, back-pack, ramble, tramp 3 ▷ **hike up** RAISE, hitch up, jack up, lift, pull up

hilarious *adjective* FUNNY, amusing, comical, entertaining, humorous, rollicking, side-splitting, uproarious

hilarity *noun* LAUGHTER, amusement, exhilaration, glee, high spirits, jollity, merriment, mirth

hill *noun* MOUNT, fell, height, hillock, hilltop, knoll, mound, tor

hillock *noun* MOUND, hummock, knoll

hilly *adjective* MOUNTAINOUS, rolling, undulating

hilt *noun* HANDLE, grip, haft, handgrip

hinder *verb* OBSTRUCT, block, check, delay, encumber, frustrate, hamper, handicap, hold up *or* hold back, impede, interrupt, stop

hindmost *adjective* LAST, final, furthest, furthest behind, rearmost, trailing

hindrance *noun* OBSTACLE, barrier, deterrent, difficulty, drawback, handicap, hitch, impediment, obstruction, restriction, snag, stumbling block

hinge *verb* DEPEND, be contingent, hang, pivot, rest, revolve around, turn

hint *noun* 1 INDICATION, allusion, clue, implication, innuendo, insinuation, intimation, suggestion
2 ADVICE, help, pointer, suggestion, tip
3 TRACE, dash, suggestion, suspicion, tinge, touch, undertone
▷ *verb* 4 SUGGEST, imply, indicate, insinuate, intimate

hippie *noun* BOHEMIAN, beatnik, dropout

hire *verb* 1 EMPLOY, appoint, commission, engage, sign up, take on
2 RENT, charter, engage, lease, let
▷ *noun* 3 RENTAL, charge, cost, fee, price, rent

hiss *noun* 1 SIBILATION, buzz, hissing
2 CATCALL, boo, jeer
▷ *verb* 3 WHISTLE, sibilate, wheeze, whirr, whiz

allergic reactions
his•tol•o•gy [hi-STOL-ə-jee] *noun* science that treats of minute structure of organic tissues
his•to•ry [HIS-tə-ree] *noun, plural* **-ries** 1 record of past events 2 study of these 3 past events 4 train of events, public or private 5 course of life or existence 6 systematic account of phenomena > **his•to'ri•an** *noun* writer of history > **his•tor'ic** *adjective* noted in history > **his•tor'i•cal** *adjective* 1 of, based on, history 2 belonging to past > **his•tor•ic'i•ty** [-tə-RIS-i-tee] *noun* historical authenticity > **his•to•ri•og'ra•pher** *noun* 1 official historian 2 one who studies historical method > **his•to•ri•og'ra•phy** *noun* methods of historical research
his•tri•on•ic [his-tree-ON-ik] *adjective* excessively theatrical, insincere, artificial in manner > **his•tri•on'ics** *noun* behavior like this
hit *verb transitive* **hit, hit•ting** 1 strike with blow or missile 2 affect injuriously 3 find ▷ *verb intransitive* **hit, hit•ting** 4 strike 5 light (upon) ▷ *noun* 6 blow 7 success 8 *computers.* single visit to a website or single result of a search > **hit'ter** *noun* > **hit man** (*slang*) hired assassin **hit it off** (*informal*) get along with (person) > **hit or miss** haphazard(ly) **hit the hay** (*informal*) go to bed **hit the road** (*informal*) 1 proceed on journey 2 depart
hitch [hich] *verb transitive* 1 fasten with loop, etc. 2 raise, move with jerk ▷ *verb intransitive* 3 be caught or fastened ▷ *noun* 4 difficulty 5 knot, fastening 6 jerk > **hitch'hike** *verb intransitive* **-hiked, -hik•ing** travel by begging free rides
hi-tech *noun* 1 technology requiring sophisticated scientific equipment and engineering techniques 2 interior design using features of industrial equipment ▷ *adjective*
hith•er [HITH-ər] *adverb* to or toward this place > **hith'er•to** *adverb* up to now or to this time
hive [hīv] *noun* 1 structure in which bees live or are housed 2 any place swarming with busy occupants ▷ *verb* **hived, hiv•ing** 3 gather, place bees, in hive
hives [hīvz] *plural noun* eruptive skin disease
HMO Health Maintenance Organization: an organization that provides health care to voluntarily enrolled clients in a particular U.S. geographic area
Ho *chem.* holmium
hoard [hord] *noun* 1 stock, store, esp. hidden away ▷ *verb transitive* 2 amass and hide away 3 store
hoarse [hors] *adjective* **hoars•er, hoars•est** rough, harsh sounding, husky
hoar•y [HOR-ee] *adjective* **hoar•i•er, hoar•i•est** 1 gray with age 2 grayish-white 3 of great antiquity 4 venerable > **hoar'frost** *noun* frozen dew
hoax [hohks] *noun* 1 practical joke 2 deceptive trick ▷ *verb transitive* 3 play trick on 4 deceive > **hoax'er** *noun*
hob *noun* 1 projection or shelf at side or back of fireplace, used for keeping food warm 2 tool for cutting gear teeth, etc. > **hob'nail** [-nayl] *noun* large-headed nail for boot soles
hob•ble [HOB-əl] *verb intransitive* **-bled, -bling** 1 walk lamely ▷ *verb transitive* **-bled, -bling** 2 tie legs together (of horse, etc.) 3 impede, hamper ▷ *noun* 4 straps or ropes put on an animal's legs to prevent it from straying 5 limping gait
hob•by [HOB-ee] *noun, plural* **-bies** favorite occupation as pastime > **hob'by•horse** *noun* 1 toy horse 2 favorite topic, preoccupation
hob'gob•lin *noun* mischievous fairy
hob'nob *verb intransitive* **-nobbed, -nob•bing** associate, be familiar (with)
ho•bo [HOH-boh] *noun, plural* **-boes** shiftless,

DICTIONARY **h** THESAURUS

4 JEER, boo, deride, hoot, mock
historic *adjective* SIGNIFICANT, epoch-making, extraordinary, famous, ground-breaking, momentous, notable, outstanding, remarkable
historical *adjective* FACTUAL, actual, attested, authentic, documented, real
history *noun* 1 CHRONICLE, account, annals, narrative, recital, record, story
2 THE PAST, antiquity, olden days, yesterday, yesteryear
hit *verb* 1 STRIKE, bang, beat, clout (*informal*), knock, slap, smack, thump, wallop (*informal*), whack
2 COLLIDE WITH, bang into, bump, clash with, crash against, run into, smash into
3 REACH, accomplish, achieve, arrive at, attain, gain
4 AFFECT, damage, devastate, impact on, influence, leave a mark on, overwhelm, touch
5 ▷ **hit it off** (*informal*) GET ON *or* GET ON WELL, be on good terms, click (*slang*), get on like a house on fire (*informal*)
▷ *noun* 6 STROKE, belt (*informal*), blow, clout (*informal*), knock, rap, slap, smack, wallop (*informal*)
7 SUCCESS, sensation, smash (*informal*), triumph, winner
hit-and-miss *adjective* HAPHAZARD, aimless, casual, disorganized, indiscriminate, random, undirected, uneven
hitch *noun* 1 PROBLEM, catch, difficulty, drawback, hindrance, hold-up, impediment, obstacle, snag
▷ *verb* 2 FASTEN, attach, connect, couple, harness, join, tether, tie
3 (*informal*) HITCHHIKE, thumb a lift
4 ▷ **hitch up** PULL UP, jerk, tug, yank
hitherto *adverb* PREVIOUSLY, heretofore, so far, thus far, until now
hit on *verb* THINK UP, arrive at, discover, invent, light upon, strike upon, stumble on
hoard *noun* 1 STORE, accumulation, cache, fund, pile, reserve, stockpile, supply, treasure-trove
▷ *verb* 2 SAVE, accumulate, amass, collect, gather, lay up, put by, stash away (*informal*), stockpile, store
hoarse *adjective* RAUCOUS, croaky, grating, gravelly, gruff, guttural, husky, rasping, rough, throaty
hoax *noun* 1 TRICK, con (*informal*), deception, fraud, practical joke, prank, spoof (*informal*), swindle
▷ *verb* 2 DECEIVE, con (*slang*), dupe, fool, hoodwink, swindle, trick
hobby *noun* PASTIME, diversion, activity *or* leisure activity, leisure pursuit, relaxation
hobnob *verb* SOCIALIZE, associate, consort, fraternize, hang about, hang out (*informal*), keep

wandering person
hock [hok] *noun* 1 backward-pointing joint on leg of horse, etc., corresponding to human ankle ▷ *verb transitive* 2 disable by cutting tendons of hock, hamstring
hock•ey [HOK-ee] *noun* 1 team game played on a field with ball and curved sticks 2 ice hockey
ho•cus-po•cus [HOH-kəs-POH-kəs] *noun* 1 trickery 2 mystifying jargon
hod *noun* small trough on a pole for carrying mortar, bricks, etc.
hoe [hoh] *noun* tool for weeding, breaking ground, etc. ▷ *verb transitive* **hoed, hoe•ing**
hog [hawg] *noun* 1 pig, esp. castrated male for fattening 2 greedy, dirty person ▷ *verb transitive* **hogged, hog•ging** (*informal*) 3 eat, use (something) selfishly > **hogs•head** [HAWGZ-hed] *noun* 1 large cask 2 liquid measure of 63 to 140 gallons (238 to 530 liters) > **hog'tie** *verb transitive* **-tied, -ty•ing** 1 hobble 2 hamper > **hog'wash** *noun* 1 nonsense 2 pig food
ho•gan [HOH-gən] *noun* Navajo Indian dwelling of earth, branches, etc.
hoi pol•loi [HOI pə-LOI] *noun* 1 the common mass of people 2 the masses
hoist *verb transitive* raise aloft, raise with tackle, etc.
ho•key•po•key [HO-kee-PO-kee] *noun* kind of playful dance or its music
hold[1] [hohld] *verb transitive* **held, hold•ing** 1 keep fast, grasp 2 support in or with hands, etc. 3 maintain in position 4 have capacity for 5 own, occupy 6 carry on 7 detain 8 celebrate 9 keep back 10 believe ▷ *verb intransitive* **held, hold•ing** 11 cling 12 not to give away 13 abide (by) 14 keep (to) 15 last, proceed, be in force 16 occur ▷ *noun* 17 grasp 18 influence > **hold'ing** *noun* (*often plural*) property, as land or stocks and bonds > **hold'up** *noun* 1 armed robbery 2 delay
hold[2] *noun* space in ship or aircraft for cargo
hole [hohl] *noun* 1 hollow place, cavity 2 perforation 3 opening 4 (*informal*) unattractive place 5 (*informal*) difficult situation ▷ *verb* **holed, hol•ing** 6 make holes in 7 go into a hole 8 drive into a hole
hol'i•day *noun* day or other period of rest from work, etc., esp. spent away from home
hol•low [HOL-oh] *adjective* **-er, -est** 1 having a cavity, not solid 2 empty 3 false 4 insincere 5 not full-toned ▷ *noun* 6 cavity, hole, valley ▷ *verb transitive* 7 make hollow, make hole in 8 excavate
hol•ly [HOL-ee] *noun, plural* **-lies** [-leez] evergreen shrub usu. with prickly leaves and red berries
hol•o•caust [HOL-ə-kawst] *noun* 1 great destruction of life, esp. by fire 2 (**Hol•o•caust**) 3 mass slaughter of Jews in Nazi concentration camps during World War II
hol•o•gram [HOL-ə-gram] *noun* a three-dimensional photographic image
hol•o•graph [HOL-ə-graf] *noun* document wholly written by the signer
ho•log•ra•phy [hə-LOG-rə-fee] *noun* science of using lasers to produce a photographic record that can reproduce a three-dimensional image
hol•ster [HOHL-stər] *noun* case for pistol, hung from belt, etc.
ho•ly [HOH-lee] *adjective* **-li•er, -li•est** 1 belonging, devoted to God 2 free from sin 3 divine 4 consecrated > **ho'li•ness** *noun* 1 sanctity 2 (**Ho'li•ness**) 3 Pope's title > **holy day** day of religious festival > **Holy Communion** service of the Eucharist > **Holy Week** that before Easter Sunday
hom•age [HOM-ij] *noun* 1 tribute, respect, reverence 2 formal acknowledgment of

---

company, mingle, mix
hoist *verb* 1 RAISE, elevate, erect, heave, lift ▷ *noun* 2 LIFT, crane, elevator, winch
hold *verb* 1 OWN, have, keep, maintain, occupy, possess, retain
2 GRASP, clasp, cling, clutch, cradle, embrace, enfold, grip
3 RESTRAIN, confine, detain, impound, imprison
4 CONSIDER, assume, believe, deem, judge, presume, reckon, regard, think
5 CONVENE, call, conduct, preside over, run
6 ACCOMMODATE, contain, have a capacity for, seat, take
▷ *noun* 7 GRIP, clasp, grasp
8 FOOTHOLD, footing, support
9 CONTROL, influence, mastery
holder *noun* 1 OWNER, bearer, keeper, possessor, proprietor
2 CASE, container, cover
hold forth *verb* SPEAK, declaim, discourse, go on, lecture, preach, spiel (*informal*), spout (*informal*)
hold-up *noun* 1 DELAY, bottleneck, hitch, setback, snag, stoppage, traffic jam, wait
2 ROBBERY, mugging (*informal*), stick-up (*slang*), theft
hold up *verb* 1 DELAY, detain, hinder, retard, set back, slow down, stop
2 SUPPORT, prop, shore up, sustain
3 ROB, mug (*informal*), waylay
hold with *verb* APPROVE OF, agree to *or* agree with, be in favor of, countenance, subscribe to, support
hole *noun* 1 OPENING, aperture, breach, crack, fissure, gap, orifice, perforation, puncture, tear, vent
2 CAVITY, cave, cavern, chamber, hollow, pit
3 BURROW, den, earth, lair, shelter
4 (*informal*) HOVEL, dive (*slang*), dump (*informal*), slum
holiday *noun* 1 VACATION, break, leave, recess, time off
2 FESTIVAL, celebration, feast, fête, gala
holiness *noun* DIVINITY, godliness, piety, purity, righteousness, sacredness, saintliness, sanctity, spirituality
hollow *adjective* 1 EMPTY, unfilled, vacant, void
2 DEEP, dull, low, muted, reverberant
3 WORTHLESS, fruitless, futile, meaningless, pointless, useless, vain
▷ *noun* 4 CAVITY, basin, bowl, crater, depression, hole, pit, trough
5 VALLEY, dale, dell, dingle, glen
▷ *verb* 6 SCOOP, dig, excavate, gouge
holocaust *noun* GENOCIDE, annihilation, conflagration, destruction, devastation, massacre
holy *adjective* 1 DEVOUT, god-fearing, godly, pious, pure, religious, righteous, saintly, virtuous
2 SACRED, blessed, consecrated, hallowed,

allegiance
home [hohm] *noun* 1 dwelling place 2 residence 3 native place 4 institution for the elderly, infirm, etc. ▷ *adjective* 5 of, connected with, home 6 native ▷ *adverb* 7 to, at one's home 8 to the point ▷ *verb* **homed, hom•ing** 9 direct or be directed onto a point or target **bring home to** impress deeply upon **home free** sure of success > **home'less** *adjective* > **home'ly** *adjective* **-li•er, -li•est** 1 unpretentious 2 warm and domesticated 3 plain > **home'ward** [-wərd] *adjective, adverb* > **home'wards** *adverb* > **home'boy** *noun* (*slang*) close friend > **home-brew** *noun* alcoholic drink made at home, esp. beer > **home fries** boiled potatoes, sliced and fried in butter, etc. > **home'land** *noun* country from which a person's ancestors came > **homeland security** domestic governmental actions intended to protect against terrorist attacks > **home page** *internet.* introductory information about a website with links to the information or services provided > **home'room** *noun* 1 classroom in a school used by a particular group of students as a base 2 group of students who use the same classroom as a base in school > **home'sick** *adjective* depressed by absence from home > **home'spun** *adjective* 1 domestic 2 simple ▷ *noun* 3 cloth made of homespun yarn > **home'stead** [-sted] *noun* house with outbuildings, esp. on farm > **home'stead•er** *noun* > **home'work** *noun* school work done usu. at home
ho•me•op•athy [hoh-mee-OP-ə-thee] *noun* treatment of disease by small doses of what would produce symptoms in healthy person > **ho•me•o•path'ic** *adjective*
hom•i•cide [HOM-ə-sīd] *noun* 1 killing of human being 2 killer > **hom•i•cid'al** *adjective*
hom•i•ly [HOM-ə-lee] *noun, plural* **-lies** [-leez] 1 sermon 2 religious discourse > **hom•i•let'ic** *adjective* of sermons > **hom•i•let'ics** *noun* art of preaching
Ho•mo [HOH-moh] *noun* genus to which modern man belongs
homo- *combining form* same, like: *homophone; homosexual*
ho•mo•ge•ne•ous [hoh-mə-JEE-nee-əs] *adjective* 1 formed of uniform parts 2 similar, uniform 3 of the same nature > **ho•mo•ge•ne'i•ty** *noun* > **ho•mog•e•nize** [hə-MOJ-ə-nīz] *verb transitive* **-nized, -niz•ing** 1 break up fat globules in milk and cream to distribute them evenly 2 make uniform or similar
ho•mol•o•gous [hə-MOL-ə-gəs] *adjective* having the same relation, relative position, etc. > **ho•mo•logue** [HOH-mə-lawg] *noun* homologous thing
hom•o•nym [HOM-ə-nim] *noun* word of same form as another, but of different sense
ho•mo•sex•u•al [hoh-mə-SEK-shoo-əl] *noun* person sexually attracted to members of the same sex ▷ *adjective* > **ho•mo•sex•u•al'i•ty** *noun* > **ho•mo•pho'bi•a** [-PHOH-bee-ə] *noun* hate or fear of homosexuals and homosexuality
hone [hohn] *noun* 1 whetstone for sharpening razors, etc. ▷ *verb transitive* **honed, hon•ing** 2 sharpen on one
hon•est [ON-ist] *adjective* 1 not cheating, lying, stealing, etc. 2 genuine 3 without pretension > **hon'est•y** *noun* quality of being honest
hon•ey [HUN-ee] *noun, plural* **-eys** sweet fluid made by bees > **hon'ey•comb** [-kohm] *noun* 1 wax structure in hexagonal cells in which bees place honey, eggs, etc. ▷ *verb transitive* 2 fill with cells or perforations > **hon'ey•dew** [-doo] *noun* 1 sweet sticky substance found on plants 2 type of sweet melon > **hon'ey•moon** *noun* 1 holiday taken by newly wedded couple 2 any new

DICTIONARY **h** THESAURUS

sacrosanct, sanctified, venerable
homage *noun* RESPECT, adoration, adulation, deference, devotion, honor, reverence, worship
home *noun* 1 HOUSE, abode, domicile, dwelling, habitation, pad (*slang, dated*), residence
2 BIRTHPLACE, home town
3 ▷ **at home a** IN, available, present **b** AT EASE, comfortable, familiar, relaxed
4 ▷ **bring home to** MAKE CLEAR, drive home, emphasize, impress upon, press home
▷ *adjective* 5 DOMESTIC, familiar, internal, local, native
homeboy, home girl *noun* (*slang*) FRIEND, buddy (*informal*), chum (*informal*), comrade, crony, pal (*informal*)
homeland *noun* NATIVE LAND, country of origin, fatherland, mother country, motherland
homeless *adjective* 1 DESTITUTE, displaced, dispossessed, down-and-out, down on one's luck (*informal*)
▷ *noun* 2 ▷ **the homeless** VAGRANTS, squatters
homely *adjective* (*United States*) DOWDY, dumpy (*informal*), frowzy, frumpy, ugly, unattractive, unfashionable
homespun *adjective* UNSOPHISTICATED, coarse, dumpy (*informal*), homely (*United States*), home-made, plain, rough
homey *adjective* COMFORTABLE, cozy, friendly, homespun, modest, ordinary, plain, simple, welcoming
homicidal *adjective* MURDEROUS, deadly, lethal, maniacal, mortal
homicide *noun* 1 MURDER, bloodshed, killing, manslaughter, slaying
2 MURDERER, killer, slayer
homily *noun* SERMON, address, discourse, lecture, preaching
homogeneity *noun* UNIFORMITY, consistency, correspondence, sameness, similarity
homogeneous *adjective* UNIFORM, akin, alike, analogous, comparable, consistent, identical, similar, unvarying
hone *verb* SHARPEN, edge, file, grind, point, polish, whet
honest *adjective* 1 TRUSTWORTHY, ethical, honorable, law-abiding, reputable, scrupulous, truthful, upright, virtuous
2 OPEN, candid, direct, forthright, frank, plain, sincere, upfront (*informal*)
honestly *adverb* 1 ETHICALLY, by fair means, cleanly, honorably, lawfully, legally
2 FRANKLY, candidly, in all sincerity, plainly, straight *or* straight out, to one's face, truthfully
honesty *noun* 1 INTEGRITY, honor, incorruptibility, morality, probity, rectitude, scrupulousness, trustworthiness, truthfulness, uprightness, virtue
2 FRANKNESS, bluntness, candor, openness,

relationship with initial period of harmony ▷ *verb intransitive* 3 spend one's honeymoon

honk [hongk] *noun* 1 call of goose 2 any sound like this, esp. sound of automobile horn ▷ *verb intransitive* 3 make this sound ▷ *verb transitive* 4 cause (automobile horn) to sound

hon•or [ON-ər] *noun* 1 personal integrity 2 renown 3 reputation 4 sense of what is right or due 5 chastity 6 high rank or position 7 source, cause of honor 8 pleasure, privilege ▷ *verb transitive* 9 respect highly 10 confer honor on 11 accept or pay (bill, etc.) when due > **hon•ors** *plural noun* 1 mark of respect 2 distinction in examination > **hon'or•a•ble** *adjective* > **hon•o•rar'i•um** *noun, plural* **-rar•i•a** a fee > **hon'or•ar•y** *adjective* 1 conferred for the sake of honor only 2 holding position without pay or usual requirements 3 giving services without pay > **hon•or•if'ic** *adjective* 1 conferring, indicating honor ▷ *noun* 2 in certain languages, form used to show respect, esp. in direct address

hood[1] [huud] *noun* 1 covering for head and neck, often part of cloak or gown 2 hoodlike thing, as covering of engine compartment of automobile, etc. > **hood'ed** *adjective* covered with or shaped like a hood > **hood'wink** *verb transitive* deceive

hood[2] *noun* (*slang*) hoodlum

hood•lum [HUUD-ləm] *noun* 1 gangster 2 street ruffian

hoo'doo *noun* cause of bad luck

hoof [huuf] *noun, plural* **hoofs** *or* **hooves** horny casing of foot of horse, etc. **on the hoof** (of livestock) alive

hoo-ha [HOO-hah] *noun* 1 uproar ▷ *interjection* 2 exclamation expressing excitement or surprise

hook [huuk] *noun* 1 bent piece of metal, etc., for catching hold, hanging up, etc. 2 something resembling hook in shape or function 3 curved cutting tool 4 enticement 5 *boxing* blow delivered with elbow bent ▷ *verb transitive* 6 grasp, catch, hold, as with hook 7 fasten with hook 8 *golf* drive (ball) widely to the left (of right-handed golfer, and vice versa) > **hooked** *adjective* 1 shaped like hook 2 caught 3 (*informal*) addicted to 4 (*slang*) married > **hook'er** *noun* (*slang*) prostitute > **hook'up** *noun* linking of radio, television stations > **hook'worm** [-wurm] *noun* parasitic worm infesting humans and animals

hook•ah [HUUK-ə] *noun* oriental pipe in which smoke is drawn through cooling water and long tube

hoo•li•gan [HOO-li-gən] *noun* 1 violent, irresponsible (young) person 2 ruffian > **hoo'li•gan•ism** *noun*

hoop *noun* 1 rigid circular band of metal, wood, etc. such a band used for binding barrel, etc., for use as a toy, or for jumping through as in circus acts ▷ *verb transitive* 2 bind with hoops 3 encircle **put through the hoops** (*informal*) subject to ordeal or test

hoop•la [HOOP-lah] *noun* (*informal*) 1 excitement 2 hullabaloo

hoot *noun* 1 owl's cry or similar sound 2 cry of disapproval or derision 3 (*slang*) funny person or thing ▷ *verb intransitive* 4 utter hoot (esp. in derision) ▷ *verb transitive* 5 assail (someone) with derisive cries 6 drive (someone) away by hooting

hop[1] *verb intransitive* **hopped, hop•ping** 1 spring on one foot 2 (*informal*) move quickly ▷ *noun* 3 leap, skip 4 one stage of journey > **hop'scotch** [-skoch] *noun* children's game of hopping in pattern drawn on ground

hop[2] *noun* climbing plant with bitter cones used to flavor beer, etc. > **hops** the cones

hope [hohp] *noun* 1 expectation of something desired 2 thing that gives, or object of, this feeling ▷ *verb* **hoped, hop•ing** 3 feel hope (for) > **hope'ful** *adjective* > **hope'less** *adjective* **young**

---

outspokenness, sincerity, straightforwardness

honor *noun* 1 GLORY, credit, dignity, distinction, fame, kudos, prestige, renown, reputation
2 TRIBUTE, accolade, commendation, homage, praise, recognition
3 FAIRNESS, decency, goodness, honesty, integrity, morality, probity, rectitude
4 PRIVILEGE, compliment, credit, pleasure
▷ *verb* 5 RESPECT, adore, appreciate, esteem, prize, value
6 FULFILL, be true to, carry out, discharge, keep, live up to, observe
7 ACCLAIM, commemorate, commend, decorate, praise
8 ACCEPT, acknowledge, pass, pay, take

honorable *adjective* RESPECTED, creditable, estimable, reputable, respectable, virtuous

honorary *adjective* NOMINAL, complimentary, in name only *or* in title only, titular, unofficial, unpaid

hoodwink *verb* DECEIVE, con (*informal*), delude, dupe, fool, mislead, swindle, trick

hook *noun* 1 FASTENER, catch, clasp, link, peg
▷ *verb* 2 FASTEN, clasp, fix, secure
3 CATCH, ensnare, entrap, snare, trap

hooked *adjective* 1 BENT, aquiline, curved, hook-shaped
2 ADDICTED, devoted, enamored, obsessed, taken, turned on (*slang*)

hooligan *noun* DELINQUENT, lager lout, ruffian, vandal

hooliganism *noun* DELINQUENCY, disorder, loutishness, rowdiness, vandalism, violence

hoop *noun* RING, band, circlet, girdle, loop, wheel

hoot *noun* 1 CRY, call, toot
2 CATCALL, boo, hiss, jeer
▷ *verb* 3 JEER, boo, hiss, howl down

hop *verb* 1 JUMP, bound, caper, leap, skip, spring, trip, vault
▷ *noun* 2 JUMP, bounce, bound, leap, skip, spring, step, vault

hope *verb* 1 DESIRE, aspire, cross one's fingers, long, look forward to, set one's heart on
▷ *noun* 2 DESIRE, ambition, assumption, dream, expectation, longing

hopeful *adjective* 1 OPTIMISTIC, buoyant, confident, expectant, looking forward to, sanguine
2 PROMISING, auspicious, bright, encouraging, heartening, reassuring, rosy

hopefully *adverb* OPTIMISTICALLY, confidently, expectantly

hopeless *adjective* POINTLESS, futile, impossible,

hopeful promising boy or girl
hop•per [HOP-ər] *noun* 1 one who hops 2 device for feeding material into mill or machine or grain into truck, etc. > **hopper car** railroad freight car, usu. open at top and containing one or more hoppers, for transport and discharge of grain, etc.
horde [hord] *noun* large crowd (esp. moving together)
ho•ri•zon [hə-RĪ-zən] *noun* 1 boundary of part of Earth seen from any given point 2 lines where Earth and sky seem to meet 3 boundary of mental outlook > **hor•i•zon•tal** [hor-ə-ZON-tl] *adjective* parallel with horizon, level
hor•mone [HOR-mohn] *noun* 1 substance secreted by certain glands that stimulates organs of the body 2 synthetic substance with same effect
horn *noun* 1 hard projection on heads of certain animals, e.g. cattle 2 substance of it 3 various things made of, or resembling it 4 *music* wind instrument orig. made of a horn 5 device (esp. in car) emitting sound as alarm, warning, etc. > **horned** *adjective* having horns > **horn'y** *adjective* **horn•i•er, horn•i•est** 1 hornlike 2 (*slang*) lustful > **horn'pipe** *noun* lively dance, esp. associated with sailors
hor•net [HOR-nit] *noun* large insect of wasp family **hornet's nest** much opposition, animosity
hor•o•scope [HOR-ə-skohp] *noun* 1 observation of, or scheme showing disposition of planets, etc. at given moment, esp. birth, by which character and abilities of individual are predicted 2 telling of person's fortune by this method
hor•ren•dous [haw-REN-dəs] *adjective* horrific
hor•ror [HOR-ər] *noun* 1 terror 2 loathing, fear of 3 its cause > **hor'ri•ble** *adjective* exciting horror, hideous, shocking > **hor'ri•bly** *adverb* > **hor'rid** *adjective* 1 unpleasant, repulsive 2 (*informal*) unkind > **hor'ri•fy** *verb transitive* **-fied, -fy•ing** move to horror > **hor•rif'ic** *adjective* particularly horrible
hors d'oeu•vre [or-DURV] *noun, plural* **-vres** [-DURVZ] small appetizer served before main meal
horse [hors] *noun* 1 four-legged animal used for riding and work 2 cavalry 3 vaulting horse 4 frame for support 5 (*slang*) heroin ▷ *verb transitive* **horsed, hors•ing** 6 provide with horse or horses > **hors'y** *adjective* **hors•i•er, hors•i•est** 1 having to do with horses 2 devoted to horses or horse racing > **horse'fly** *noun, plural* **-flies** large bloodsucking fly > **horse laugh** harsh boisterous laugh usu. expressing derision > **horse'man** [-mən], **horse'wom•an** *noun* rider on horse > **horse'play** *noun* rough, boisterous play > **horse'pow•er** *noun* unit of power of engine, etc., 550 foot-pounds per second > **horse'shoe** [-shoo] *noun* 1 protective U-shaped piece of iron nailed to horse's hoof 2 thing so shaped > **horse around** (*slang*) play roughly, boisterously
hor•ti•cul•ture [HOR-ti-kul-chər] *noun* art or science of gardening > **hor•ti•cul'tur•al** *adjective*
Hos. Hosea
ho•san•na [hoh-ZAN-ə] *noun, plural* **-nas** cry of praise, adoration
hose [hohz] *noun* 1 flexible tube for conveying liquid or gas 2 stockings ▷ *verb transitive* **hosed, hos•ing** 3 water with hose > **ho'sier•y** *noun* stockings or socks
hos•pice [HOS-pis] *noun* 1 traveler's house of rest kept by religious order 2 residence for care of terminally ill
hos•pi•tal [HOS-pi-tl] *noun* institution for care of sick > **hos•pi•tal•i•za'tion** *noun* > **hos'pi•tal•ize** *verb transitive* **-ized, -iz•ing** to place for care in a hospital
hos•pi•tal•i•ty [hos-pi-TAL-i-tee] *noun, plural* **-ties** friendly and liberal reception of strangers or guests > **hos'pi•ta•ble** *adjective* welcoming, kindly
host[1] [hohst] *noun* 1 one who entertains another 2 master of ceremonies of show 3 animal, plant on which parasite lives 4 *computers.* computer that provides data or connectivity to others on a network ▷ *verb transitive* 5 act as a host > **-ess** *noun feminine*
host[2] *noun* large number

DICTIONARY **h** THESAURUS

no-win, unattainable, useless, vain
horde *noun* CROWD, band, drove, gang, host, mob, multitude, pack, swarm, throng
horizon *noun* SKYLINE, vista
horizontal *adjective* LEVEL, flat, parallel
horrible *adjective* 1 TERRIFYING, appalling, dreadful, frightful, ghastly, grim, grisly, gruesome, hideous, repulsive, revolting, shocking
2 UNPLEASANT, awful, cruel, disagreeable, dreadful, horrid, lousy (*slang*), mean, nasty, scuzzy (*slang*), terrible
horrid *adjective* 1 UNPLEASANT, awful, disagreeable, dreadful, horrible, terrible
2 UNKIND, beastly (*informal*), cruel, mean, nasty
horrific *adjective* TERRIFYING, appalling, awful, dreadful, frightful, ghastly, grisly, horrendous, horrifying, shocking
horrify *verb* 1 TERRIFY, alarm, frighten, intimidate, make one's hair stand on end, petrify, scare
2 SHOCK, appall, dismay, outrage, sicken
horror *noun* 1 TERROR, alarm, consternation, dread, fear, fright, panic
2 HATRED, aversion, detestation, disgust, loathing, odium, repugnance, revulsion
horse *noun* NAG, colt, filly, mare, mount, stallion, steed (*archaic* or *literary*)
horseman *noun* RIDER, cavalier, cavalryman, dragoon, equestrian
horseplay *noun* BUFFOONERY, clowning, fooling around, high jinks, pranks, romping, rough-and-tumble, skylarking (*informal*)
hospitable *adjective* WELCOMING, cordial, friendly, generous, gracious, kind, liberal, sociable
hospitality *noun* WELCOME, conviviality, cordiality, friendliness, neighborliness, sociability, warmth
host[1] *noun* 1 MASTER OF CEREMONIES, entertainer, innkeeper, landlord *or* landlady, proprietor
2 PRESENTER, anchorman *or* anchorwoman
▷ *verb* 3 PRESENT, front (*informal*), introduce
host[2] *noun* MULTITUDE, army, array, drove, horde, legion, myriad, swarm, throng

Host *noun* consecrated bread of the Eucharist
hos•tage [HOS-tij] *noun* person taken or given as pledge or security
hos•tel [HOS-tl] *noun* building providing accommodation at low cost for particular category of people, as students, or the homeless
hos•tile [HOS-tl] *adjective* 1 opposed, antagonistic 2 warlike 3 of an enemy 4 unfriendly > **hos•til'i•ty** *noun* enmity > **hos•til'i•ties** *plural noun* acts of warfare
hot *adjective* **hot•ter, hot•test** 1 of high temperature, very warm, giving or feeling heat 2 angry 3 severe 4 recent, new 5 much favored 6 spicy 7 (*slang*) good, quick, smart, lucky, successful 8 (*slang*) stolen > **hot'ly** *adverb* > **hot'ness** *noun* > **hot air** (*informal*) boastful, empty talk > **hot'bed** *noun* 1 bed of earth heated by manure and grass for young plants 2 any place encouraging growth 3 center of activity > **hot'-blood•ed** [-blud-id] *adjective* passionate, excitable > **hot dog** frankfurter (in split bread roll) > **hot'foot** [-fuut] *verb, adverb* (go) quickly > **hot'head** [-hed] *noun* hasty, intemperate person > **hot'house** *noun* 1 forcing house for plants 2 heated building for cultivating tropical plants in cold or temperate climates > **hot line** direct communication link between heads of governments, etc. > **hot pants** 1 extremely brief and close-fitting pants for women 2 (*slang*) strong sexual desire > **hot'plate** *noun* 1 heated plate on electric cooker 2 portable device for keeping food warm
ho•tel [hoh-TEL] *noun* commercial establishment providing lodging
hound [hownd] *noun* 1 hunting dog ▷ *verb transitive* 2 chase, urge, pursue
hour [owr] *noun* 1 twenty-fourth part of day 2 sixty minutes 3 time of day 4 appointed time > **hours** 1 fixed periods for work, prayers, etc. 2 book of prayers > **hour'ly** *adverb* 1 every hour 2 frequently ▷ *adjective* 3 frequent 4 happening every hour > **hour'glass** *noun* instrument using dropping sand or mercury to indicate passage of an hour
hou•ri [HUUR-ee] *noun, plural* **-ris** beautiful virgin provided in the Muslim paradise
house [hows] *noun, plural* **hous•es** [HOW-ziz] 1 building for human habitation 2 building for other specified purpose 3 legislative or other assembly 4 family 5 business firm 6 theater audience, performance ▷ *verb transitive* [howz] **housed, hous•ing** 7 give or receive shelter, lodging or storage 8 cover or contain > **housing** *noun* 1 (providing of) houses 2 part or structure designed to cover, protect, contain > **house'boat** *noun* boat for living in on river, etc. > **house'break•er** [-brayk-ər] *noun* burglar > **house'coat** *noun* woman's long loose garment for casual wear at home > **house'hold** *noun* inmates of house collectively > **house'hold•er** *noun* 1 occupier of house as own dwelling 2 head of household > **house'-hus•band** *noun* man who runs a household > **house'keep•er** *noun* person managing affairs of household > **house'keep•ing** *noun* running household > **house'warm•ing** *noun* party to celebrate entry into new house > **house'wife** *noun* woman who runs a household
hov•el [HUV-əl] *noun* mean dwelling
hov•er [HUV-ər] *verb intransitive* 1 hang in the air (of bird, etc.) 2 loiter 3 be in state of indecision > **hov'er•craft** *noun* type of craft that can travel over land and sea on a cushion of air
how *adverb* 1 in what way 2 by what means 3 in what condition 4 to what degree 5 (in direct or dependent question) > **how•ev'er**

DICTIONARY • THESAURUS

hostage *noun* PRISONER, captive, pawn
hostile *adjective* 1 OPPOSED, antagonistic, belligerent, contrary, ill-disposed, rancorous
2 UNFRIENDLY, adverse, inhospitable, unsympathetic, unwelcoming
hostilities *plural noun* WARFARE, conflict, fighting, war
hostility *noun* OPPOSITION, animosity, antipathy, enmity, hatred, ill will, malice, resentment, unfriendliness
hot *adjective* 1 HEATED, boiling, roasting, scalding, scorching, searing, steaming, sultry, sweltering, torrid, warm
2 SPICY, biting, peppery, piquant, pungent, sharp
3 FIERCE, fiery, intense, passionate, raging, stormy, violent
4 RECENT, fresh, just out, latest, new, up to the minute
5 POPULAR, approved, favored, in demand, in vogue, sought-after
hot air *noun* EMPTY TALK, bombast, claptrap (*informal*), guff (*slang*), verbiage, wind
hot-blooded *adjective* PASSIONATE, ardent, excitable, fiery, impulsive, spirited, temperamental, wild
hot-headed *adjective* RASH, fiery, foolhardy, hasty, hot-tempered, impetuous, quick-tempered, reckless, volatile
hot water *noun* (*usually preceded by in*) (*informal*) PREDICAMENT, dilemma, fix (*informal*), jam (*informal*), mess, scrape (*informal*), spot (*informal*), tight spot
hound *verb* HARASS, badger, goad, harry, impel, persecute, pester, provoke
house *noun* 1 HOME, abode, domicile, dwelling, habitation, homestead, pad (*slang, dated*), residence
2 FAMILY, household
3 DYNASTY, clan, tribe
4 FIRM, business, company, organization, outfit (*informal*)
5 ASSEMBLY, Commons, legislative body, parliament
6 ▷ **on the house** FREE, for nothing, gratis
▷ *verb* 7 ACCOMMODATE, billet, harbor, lodge, put up, quarter, take in
8 CONTAIN, cover, keep, protect, sheathe, shelter, store
household *noun* FAMILY, home, house
householder *noun* OCCUPANT, homeowner, resident, tenant
housing *noun* 1 ACCOMMODATION, dwellings, homes, houses
2 CASE, casing, container, cover, covering, enclosure, sheath
hovel *noun* HUT, cabin, den, hole, shack, shanty, shed
hover *verb* 1 FLOAT, drift, flutter, fly, hang
2 LINGER, hang about

conjunction 1 nevertheless ▷ *adverb* 2 in whatever way, degree 3 all the same
how•dah [HOW-də] *noun* (canopied) seat on elephant's back
how•itz•er [HOW-it-sər] *noun* short gun firing shells at high elevation
howl *verb intransitive* 1 utter long loud cry ▷ *noun* 2 such cry > **howl'er** *noun* 1 one that howls 2 embarrassing mistake
hoy•den [HOID-n] *noun* wild, boisterous girl, tomboy
Hs *chem.* hassium
HTML *computing* hypertext markup language: text description language that is used on the World Wide Web
hub *noun* 1 middle part of wheel, from which spokes radiate 2 central point of activity
hub'bub *noun* 1 confused noise of many voices 2 uproar
huck•ster [HUK-stər] *noun* 1 retailer, peddler 2 person using aggressive or questionable methods of selling ▷ *verb transitive* 3 sell goods thus
hud•dle [HUD-l] *noun* 1 crowded mass 2 (*informal*) impromptu conference, esp. of offensive football team during game ▷ *verb* **-dled, -dling** 3 heap, crowd together 4 hunch 5 confer
hue [hyoo] *noun* color, complexion
hue and cry 1 public uproar, outcry 2 loud outcry usually in pursuit of wrongdoer
huff *noun* 1 passing mood of anger ▷ *verb* 2 make or become angry, resentful ▷ *verb intransitive* 3 blow, puff heavily > **huff'i•ly** *adverb* > **huff'y** *adjective* **huff•i•er, huff•i•est**
hug *verb transitive* **hugged, hug•ging** 1 clasp tightly in the arms 2 cling 3 keep close to ▷ *noun* 4 fond embrace
huge [hyooj] *adjective* very big > **huge'ly** *adverb* very much
hu•la [HOO-lə] *noun* native dance of Hawaii
hulk *noun* body of abandoned vessel; large, unwieldy thing > **hulk'ing** *adjective* unwieldy, bulky
hull *noun* 1 frame, body of ship 2 calyx of strawberry, raspberry, or similar fruit 3 shell, husk ▷ *verb transitive* 4 remove shell, hull
hul•la•ba•loo [HUL-ə-bə-loo] *noun, plural* **-loos** uproar, clamor, row
hum *verb intransitive* **hummed, hum•ming** 1 make low continuous sound as bee 2 be very active ▷ *verb transitive* **hummed, hum•ming** 3 sing with closed lips ▷ *noun* 4 humming sound 5 smell 6 great activity 7 in radio, disturbance affecting reception > **hum'ming•bird** *noun* very small bird whose wings make humming noise
hu•man [HYOO-mən] *adjective* 1 of people 2 relating to, characteristic of, people's nature > **hu•mane'** [-MAYN] *adjective* 1 benevolent, kind 2 merciful > **hu'man•ism** *noun* 1 belief in human effort rather than religion 2 interest in human welfare and affairs 3 classical literary culture > **hu'man•ist** *noun* > **hu•man•i•tar'i•an** *noun* philanthropist ▷ *adjective* > **hu•man'i•ty** *noun, plural* **-ties** [-teez] 1 human nature 2 human race 3 kindliness > **hu•man'i•ties** study of literature, philosophy, the arts > **hu'man•ize** *verb transitive* **-ized, -iz•ing** 1 make human 2 civilize > **hu'man•ly** *adverb* > **hu'man•kind** [-kīnd] *noun* human race as a whole
hum•ble [HUM-bəl] *adjective* **-bler, -blest** 1 lowly, modest ▷ *verb transitive* **-bled, -bling** 2 bring low, abase, humiliate > **hum'bly** *adverb*
hum'bug *noun* 1 impostor 2 sham, nonsense, deception ▷ *verb transitive* **-bugged, -bug•ging** 3

DICTIONARY **h** THESAURUS

---

3 WAVER, dither, fluctuate, oscillate, vacillate
however *adverb* NEVERTHELESS, after all, anyhow, but, nonetheless, notwithstanding, still, though, yet
howl *noun* 1 CRY, bawl, bay, clamor, groan, roar, scream, shriek, wail
▷ *verb* 2 CRY, bawl, bellow, roar, scream, shriek, wail, weep, yell
hub *noun* CENTER, core, focal point, focus, heart, middle, nerve center
huddle *verb* 1 CROWD, cluster, converge, flock, gather, press, throng
2 CURL UP, crouch, hunch up
▷ *noun* 3 (*informal*) CONFERENCE, discussion, meeting, powwow
hue *noun* COLOR, dye, shade, tinge, tint, tone
hug *verb* 1 CLASP, cuddle, embrace, enfold, hold close, squeeze, take in one's arms
▷ *noun* 2 EMBRACE, bear hug, clasp, clinch (*slang*), squeeze
huge *adjective* LARGE, colossal, enormous, gigantic, immense, mammoth, massive, monumental, supersize, tremendous, vast
hulk *noun* 1 WRECK, frame, hull, shell, shipwreck
2 OAF, lout, lubber, lump (*informal*)
hull *noun* FRAME, body, casing, covering, framework
hum *verb* 1 MURMUR, buzz, drone, purr, throb, thrum, vibrate, whir
2 BE BUSY, bustle, buzz, pulsate, pulse, stir
human *adjective* 1 MORTAL, manlike
▷ *noun* 2 HUMAN BEING, creature, individual, man *or* woman, mortal, person, soul
humane *adjective* KIND, benign, compassionate, forgiving, good-natured, merciful, sympathetic, tender, understanding
humanitarian *adjective* 1 COMPASSIONATE, altruistic, benevolent, charitable, humane, philanthropic, public-spirited
▷ *noun* 2 PHILANTHROPIST, altruist, benefactor, Good Samaritan
humanity *noun* 1 HUMAN RACE, Homo sapiens, humankind, man, mankind, people
2 HUMAN NATURE, mortality
3 SYMPATHY, charity, compassion, fellow feeling, kind-heartedness, kindness, mercy, philanthropy
humanize *verb* CIVILIZE, educate, enlighten, improve, soften, tame
humble *adjective* 1 MODEST, meek, self-effacing, unassuming, unostentatious, unpretentious
2 LOWLY, mean, modest, obscure, ordinary, plebeian, poor, simple, undistinguished
▷ *verb* 3 HUMILIATE, chasten, crush, disgrace, put (someone) in their place, subdue, take down a peg (*informal*)
humbug *noun* 1 FRAUD, charlatan, con man (*informal*), faker, impostor, phoney *or* phony (*informal*), swindler, trickster

deceive **4** defraud

hum•ding•er [HUM-DING-ər] *noun* (*informal*) excellent person or thing

hum'drum *adjective* commonplace, dull, monotonous

hu•mer•us [HYOO-mər-əs] *noun, plural* **-mer•i** [-mə-rī] long bone of upper arm

hu•mid [HYOO-mid] *adjective* moist, damp > **hu•mid'i•fi•er** *noun* device for increasing amount of water vapor in air in room, etc. > **hu•mid'i•fy** *verb transitive* **-fied, -fy•ing** > **hu•mid'i•ty** *noun*

hu•mil•i•ate [hyoo-MIL-ee-ayt] *verb transitive* **-at•ed, -at•ing** lower dignity of, abase, mortify

hu•mil•i•ty [hyoo-MIL-i-tee] *noun* **1** state of being humble **2** meekness

hum•mock [HUM-ək] *noun* **1** low knoll, hillock **2** ridge of ice

hum•mus [HEW-mus] *noun* creamy dip of Middle East origin, made from puréed chickpeas

hu•mor [HYOO-mər] *noun* **1** faculty of saying or perceiving what excites amusement **2** state of mind, mood **3** temperament **4** (*obsolete*) one of four chief fluids of body ▷ *verb transitive* **5** gratify, indulge > **hu'mor•ist** *noun* person who acts, speaks, writes humorously > **hu'mor•ous** *adjective* **1** funny **2** amusing

hump *noun* **1** normal or deforming lump, esp. on back **2** hillock ▷ *verb transitive* **3** make hump-shaped **4** (*informal*) exert (oneself), hurry **5** (*slang*) carry or heave > **hump'back** *noun* person with hump > **hump'backed** *adjective* having a hump

hu•mus [HYOO-məs] *noun* decayed vegetable and animal mold

hunch *noun* (*informal*) **1** intuition or premonition **2** hump ▷ *verb transitive* **3** thrust, bend into hump > **hunch'back** *noun* humpback

hun•dred [HUN-drid] *noun, adjective* cardinal number, ten times ten > **hun'dredth** [-dridth] *adjective* the ordinal number > **hun'dred•fold** *adjective, adverb* > **hun'dred•weight** *noun* weight of 100 lbs (45.359 kg)

hung **1** *pt./pp. of* **hang** ▷ *adjective* **2** (of jury, etc.) unable to decide **3** not having majority > **hung'o'ver** *adjective* (*informal*) experiencing a hangover **hung up** (*informal*) **1** delayed **2** stymied **3** baffled **hung up on** (*slang*) obsessed by

hun•ger [HUNG-gər] *noun* **1** discomfort, exhaustion from lack of food **2** strong desire ▷ *verb intransitive* > **hun'gri•ly** *adverb* > **hun'gry** *adjective* **-gri•er, -gri•est** having keen appetite > **hunger strike** refusal of all food, as a protest

hunk [hungk] *noun* **1** thick piece **2** (*slang*) attractive man with excellent physique

hunt *verb* **1** seek out to kill or capture for sport or food **2** search (for) ▷ *noun* **3** chase, search **4** track of country hunted over **5** (party organized for) hunting **6** pack of hounds **7** hunting club > **hunt'er** *noun* **1** one who hunts **2** horse, dog bred for hunting > **hunt'ress** *noun feminine*

hur•dle [HUR-dl] *noun* **1** portable frame of bars for temporary fences or for jumping over **2** obstacle ▷ *verb intransitive* **-dled, -dling** **3** race over hurdles > **hurdles** *noun* a race over hurdles > **hurd'ler** *noun*

hurl *verb transitive* throw violently > **hurl•y-burl•y** [HUR-lee-BUR-lee] *noun, plural* **-burl•ies** loud

2 NONSENSE, baloney (*informal*), cant, claptrap (*informal*), hypocrisy, quackery, rubbish
3 KILLJOY, scrooge (*informal*), spoilsport, wet blanket (*informal*)

humdrum *adjective* DULL, banal, boring, dreary, monotonous, mundane, ordinary, tedious, tiresome, uneventful

humid *adjective* DAMP, clammy, dank, moist, muggy, steamy, sticky, sultry, wet

humidity *noun* DAMP, clamminess, dampness, dankness, moistness, moisture, mugginess, wetness

humiliate *verb* EMBARRASS, bring low, chasten, crush, degrade, humble, mortify, put down, put (someone) in their place, shame

humiliating *adjective* EMBARRASSING, crushing, degrading, humbling, ignominious, mortifying, shaming

humiliation *noun* EMBARRASSMENT, degradation, disgrace, dishonor, humbling, ignominy, indignity, loss of face, mortification, put-down, shame

humility *noun* MODESTY, humbleness, lowliness, meekness, submissiveness, unpretentiousness

humor *noun* **1** FUNNINESS, amusement, comedy, drollery, facetiousness, fun, jocularity, ludicrousness
2 JOKING, comedy, farce, jesting, pleasantry, wisecracks (*informal*), wit, witticisms
3 MOOD, disposition, frame of mind, spirits, temper
▷ *verb* **4** INDULGE, accommodate, flatter, go along with, gratify, mollify, pander to

humorist *noun* COMEDIAN, card (*informal*), comic, funny man, jester, joker, wag, wit

humorous *adjective* FUNNY, amusing, comic, comical, droll, entertaining, jocular, playful, waggish, witty

hump *noun* **1** LUMP, bulge, bump, mound, projection, protrusion, protuberance, swelling

hunch *noun* **1** FEELING, idea, impression, inkling, intuition, premonition, presentiment, suspicion
▷ *verb* **2** DRAW IN, arch, bend, curve

hunger *noun* **1** FAMINE, starvation
2 APPETITE, emptiness, hungriness, ravenousness
3 DESIRE, ache, appetite, craving, itch, lust, thirst, yearning
▷ *verb* **4** WANT, ache, crave, desire, hanker, itch, long, thirst, wish, yearn

hungry *adjective* **1** EMPTY, famished, ravenous, starved, starving, voracious
2 EAGER, athirst, avid, covetous, craving, desirous, greedy, keen, yearning

hunk *noun* LUMP, block, chunk, mass, nugget, piece, slab, wedge

hunt *verb* **1** STALK, chase, hound, pursue, track, trail
2 SEARCH, ferret about, forage, look, scour, seek
▷ *noun* **3** SEARCH, chase, hunting, investigation, pursuit, quest

hurdle *noun* **1** FENCE, barricade, barrier
2 OBSTACLE, barrier, difficulty, handicap, hazard, hindrance, impediment, obstruction, stumbling block

confusion
hur•rah [hə-RAH], **hur•ray** [-RAY] *interjection* exclamation of joy or applause **last hurrah** final occasion of achievement
hur•ri•cane [HUR-i-kayn] *noun* very strong, potentially destructive wind or storm > **hurricane lamp** lamp with glass chimney around flame
hur•ry [HUR-ee] *verb* **-ried, -ry•ing** 1 (cause to) move or act in great haste ▷ *noun, plural* **-ries** 2 undue haste 3 eagerness > **hur'ried•ly** *adverb*
hurt *verb transitive* **hurt, hurt•ing** 1 injure, damage, give pain to, wound feelings of 2 distress ▷ *verb intransitive* **hurt, hurt•ing** (*informal*) 3 feel pain ▷ *noun* 4 wound, injury, harm > **hurt'ful** *adjective*
hur•tle [HUR-tl] *verb intransitive* **-tled, -tling** 1 move rapidly 2 rush violently 3 whirl
hus•band [HUZ-bənd] *noun* 1 married man ▷ *verb transitive* 2 economize 3 use to best advantage > **hus'ban•dry** [-dree] *noun* 1 farming 2 economy
hush *verb* 1 make or be silent ▷ *noun* 2 stillness 3 quietness > **hush-hush** *adjective* (*informal*) secret > **hush up** 1 suppress rumors, information 2 make secret
husk *noun* 1 dry covering of certain seeds and fruits 2 worthless outside part ▷ *verb transitive* 3 remove husk from > **husk'y** *adjective* **husk•i•er, husk•i•est** 1 rough in tone 2 hoarse 3 dry as husk, dry in the throat 4 of, full of, husks 5 big and strong
husk•y [HUS-kee] *noun, plural* **husk•ies** Arctic sledge dog with thick hair and curled tail
hus•sy [HUS-ee] *noun, plural* **-sies** 1 brazen or immoral woman 2 impudent girl or woman
hus•tings [HUS-tingz] *plural noun* 1 any place from which political campaign speeches are made 2 political campaigning
hus•tle [HUS-əl] *verb* **-tled, -tling** 1 push about, jostle, hurry ▷ *verb intransitive* 2 (*slang*) solicit clients esp. for prostitution ▷ *noun* > **hus•tler** [HUS-lər] 1 industrious person 2 (*slang*) prostitute
hut *noun* any small house or shelter, usu. of wood or metal
hutch [huch] *noun* boxlike pen for rabbits, etc.
hy•brid [HĪ-brid] *noun* 1 offspring of two plants or animals of different species 2 mongrel ▷ *adjective* 3 crossbred > **hy'brid•ism** *noun* > **hy'brid•ize** *verb* **-ized, -iz•ing** 1 make hybrid 2 crossbreed
hy•dra [HĪ-drə] *noun, plural* **-dras** [-drəz] fabulous many-headed water serpent 1 any persistent problem 2 freshwater polyp > **hy'dra-head•ed** *adjective* hard to understand, root out
hy•dran•gea [hī-DRAYN-jə] *noun* ornamental shrub with pink, blue, or white flowers
hy•drant [HĪ-drənt] *noun* water pipe with nozzle for hose
hy•drau•lic [hī-DRAW-lik] *adjective* concerned with, operated by, pressure transmitted through liquid in pipe > **hy•drau'lics** *noun* science of mechanical properties of liquid in motion
hydro- *combining form* 1 water: *hydroelectric* 2 presence of hydrogen: *hydrocarbon*
hy•dro•car•bon [hī-drə-KAHR-bən] *noun* compound of hydrogen and carbon
hy•dro•chlor•ic ac•id [hī-drə-KLOR-ik] strong colorless acid used in many industrial and laboratory processes
hy•dro•dy•nam•ics [hī-droh-dī-NAM-iks] *noun* science of the motions of system wholly or partly fluid
hy•dro•e•lec•tric [hī-droh-i-LEK-trik] *adjective* pert. to generation of electricity by use of water
hy•dro•foil [HĪ-drə-foil] *noun* fast, light vessel with hull raised out of water at speed by action of vanes in water
hy•dro•gen [HĪ-drə-jən] *noun* colorless gas that combines with oxygen to form water > **hydrogen bomb** atom bomb of enormous power in which hydrogen nuclei are converted into helium nuclei > **hydrogen peroxide** colorless liquid used as antiseptic and bleach
hy•drog•ra•phy [hī-DROG-rə-fee] *noun* description of waters of the earth > **hy•dro•graph'ic** *adjective*

DICTIONARY **h** THESAURUS

hurl *verb* THROW, cast, fling, heave, launch, let fly, pitch, propel, sling, toss
hurricane *noun* STORM, cyclone, gale, tempest, tornado, twister, typhoon
hurried *adjective* HASTY, brief, cursory, perfunctory, quick, rushed, short, speedy, swift
hurry *verb* 1 RUSH, dash, fly, get a move on (*informal*), make haste, scoot, scurry, step on it (*informal*)
▷ *noun* 2 URGENCY, flurry, haste, quickness, rush, speed
hurt *verb* 1 HARM, bruise, damage, disable, impair, injure, mar, spoil, wound
2 ACHE, be sore, be tender, burn, smart, sting, throb
3 SADDEN, annoy, distress, grieve, pain, upset, wound
▷ *noun* 4 DISTRESS, discomfort, pain, pang, soreness, suffering
▷ *adjective* 5 INJURED, bruised, cut, damaged, harmed, scarred, wounded
6 OFFENDED, aggrieved, crushed, wounded
hurtful *adjective* UNKIND, cruel, cutting, damaging, destructive, malicious, nasty, spiteful, upsetting, wounding
hurtle *verb* RUSH, charge, crash, fly, plunge, race, shoot, speed, stampede, tear
husband *noun* 1 PARTNER, better half (*humorous*), mate, spouse
▷ *verb* 2 ECONOMIZE, budget, conserve, hoard, save, store
husbandry *noun* 1 FARMING, agriculture, cultivation, tillage
2 THRIFT, economy, frugality
hush *verb* 1 QUIETEN, mute, muzzle, shush, silence
▷ *noun* 2 QUIET, calm, peace, silence, stillness, tranquillity
hush-hush *adjective* SECRET, classified, confidential, restricted, top-secret, under wraps
husky *adjective* 1 HOARSE, croaky, gruff, guttural, harsh, raucous, rough, throaty
2 MUSCULAR, burly, hefty, powerful, rugged, stocky, strapping, thickset
hustle *verb* JOSTLE, elbow, force, jog, push, shove
hut *noun* SHED, cabin, den, hovel, lean-to, shanty, shelter
hybrid *noun* CROSSBREED, amalgam, composite,

hy•drol•y•sis [hī-DROL-ə-sis] *noun* decomposition of chemical compound reacting with water
hy•drom•e•ter [hī-DROM-i-tər] *noun* device for measuring relative density of liquid
hy•dro•pho•bi•a [hī-drə-FOH-bee-ə] *noun* **1** aversion to water, esp. as symptom of rabies **2** rabies
hy•dro•plane [HĪ-drə-playn] *noun* **1** light skimming motorboat **2** seaplane **3** vane controlling motion of submarine, etc.
hy•dro•pon•ics [hī-drə-PON-iks] *noun* science of cultivating plants in water without using soil
hy•dro•ther•a•py [hī-drə-THER-ə-pee] *noun med.* treatment of disease by external application of water
hy•drous [HĪ-drəs] *adjective* containing water
hy•e•na [hī-EE-nə] *noun* wild animal related to dog
hy•giene [HĪ-jeen] *noun* **1** principles and practice of health and cleanliness **2** study of these principles > **hy•gi•en•ic** [hī-jee-EN-ik] *adjective* > **hy•gien'ist** [-JEE-nist] *noun*
hy•grom•e•ter [hī-GROM-i-tər] *noun* instrument for measuring humidity of air
hy•gro•scop•ic [hī-grə-SKOP-ik] *adjective* readily absorbing moisture from the atmosphere
hy•men [HĪ-mən] *noun* **1** membrane partly covering vagina of virgin **2** (**Hy•men**) Greek god of marriage
hymn [him] *noun* **1** song of praise, esp. to God ▷ *verb transitive* **2** praise in song > **hym•nal** [HIM-nl] *adjective* **1** of hymns ▷ *noun* **2** book of hymns (*also* **hymn book**)
hype[1] [hīp] *noun* (*slang*) **1** hypodermic syringe **2** drug addict
hype[2] *noun* (*informal*) **1** deception, racket **2** intensive publicity ▷ *verb* **hyped, hyp•ing 3** (*informal*) promote (a product) using intensive publicity
hyper- *combining form* over, above, excessively: *hyperactive*
hy•per•bo•la [hī-PUR-bə-lə] *noun* curve produced when cone is cut by plane making larger angle with the base than the side makes
hy•per•bo•le [hī-PUR-bə-lee] *noun* rhetorical exaggeration > **hy•per•bol'ic** *adjective*
hy•per•bo•re•an [hī-pər-BOR-ee-ən] *adjective, noun* (inhabitant) of extreme north
hy•per•crit•i•cal [hī-pər-KRIT-i-kəl] *adjective* too critical
hy•per•link [HĪ-pər-lingk] *computing noun* **1** link from a hypertext file that gives users instant access to related material in another file ▷ *verb transitive* **2** link (files) in this way
hy•per•sen•si•tive [hī-pər-SEN-si-tiv] *adjective* unduly vulnerable emotionally or physically
hy•per•ten•sion [hī-pər-TEN-shən] *noun* abnormally high blood pressure
hy•per•text [HĪ-pər-tekst] *noun* computer software and hardware that allows users to store and view text and move between related items easily
hy•phen [HĪ-fən] *noun* short line (-) indicating that two words or syllables are to be connected > **hy•phen•ate** [-nayt] *verb transitive* **-at•ed, -at•ing** join by a hyphen
hyp•no•sis [HIP-noh-sis] *noun, plural* **-ses** [-seez] induced state like deep sleep in which subject acts on external suggestion > **hyp•not'ic** *adjective* **1** of hypnosis or of the person or thing producing it **2** like something that induces hypnosis > **hyp•no•tism** [HIP-nə-tiz-əm] *noun* > **hyp'no•tist** *noun* > **hyp•no•tize** *verb transitive* **-tized, -tiz•ing 1** affect with hypnosis **2** affect in way resembling hypnotic state
hy•po [HĪ-poh] *noun* short for hyposulfite (sodium thiosulfate), used as fixer in developing photographs
hypo-, hyph-, hyp- *combining forms* under, below, less: *hypothermia*
hy•po•al•ler•gen•ic [hī-poh-al-ər-JEN-ik] *adjective* (of cosmetics, etc.) not likely to cause allergic reaction
hy•po•chon•dri•a [hī-pə-KON-dree-ə] *noun* morbid depression, without cause, about one's own health > **hy•po•chon'dri•ac** *adjective, noun*
hy•poc•ri•sy [hi-POK-rə-see] *noun, plural* **-sies** [-seez] assuming of false appearance of virtue; insincerity > **hyp•o•crite** [HIP-ə-krit] *noun* > **hyp•o•crit'i•cal** *adjective*
hy•po•der•mic [hī-pə-DUR-mik] *adjective* **1** introduced, injected beneath the skin ▷ *noun* **2** hypodermic syringe or needle
hy•po•gas•tric [hī-pə-GAS-trik] *adjective* relating to, situated in, lower part of abdomen
hy•pot•e•nuse [hī-POT-n-oos] *noun* side of a right triangle opposite the right angle
hy•po•ther•mi•a [hī-pə-THUR-mee-ə] *noun* condition of having body temperature reduced to dangerously low level
hy•poth•e•sis [hī-POTH-ə-sis] *noun, plural* **-ses** [-seez] suggested explanation of something; assumption as basis of reasoning > **hy•po•thet'i•cal** *adjective* > **hy•poth'e•size** [-POTH-ə-sīz] *verb* **-sized, -siz•ing**
hypso- *combining form* height: *hypsometry*
hyp•sog•ra•phy [hip-SOG-rə-fee] *noun* branch of geography dealing with altitudes
hyp•som•e•ter [hip-SOM-i-tər] *noun* instrument for measuring altitudes

compound, cross, half-breed, mixture, mongrel
hygiene *noun* CLEANLINESS, sanitation
hygienic *adjective* CLEAN, aseptic, disinfected, germ-free, healthy, pure, sanitary, sterile
hymn *noun* ANTHEM, carol, chant, paean, psalm
hype *noun* PUBLICITY, ballyhoo (*informal*), brouhaha, plugging (*informal*), promotion, razzmatazz (*slang*)
hypnotic *adjective* MESMERIC, mesmerizing, sleep-inducing, soothing, soporific, spellbinding
hypnotize *verb* MESMERIZE, put in a trance, put to sleep
hypocrisy *noun* INSINCERITY, cant, deceitfulness, deception, duplicity, pretense
hypocrite *noun* FRAUD, charlatan, deceiver, impostor, phoney *or* phony (*informal*), pretender
hypocritical *adjective* INSINCERE, canting, deceitful, duplicitous, false, fraudulent, phoney *or* phony (*informal*), sanctimonious, two-faced
hypothesis *noun* ASSUMPTION, postulate, premise, proposition, supposition, theory, thesis
hypothetical *adjective* THEORETICAL, academic, assumed, conjectural, imaginary, putative, speculative, supposed

> **hyp•som'e•try** [-tree] *noun* science of measuring altitudes
hys•ter•ec•to•my [his-tə-REK-tə-mee] *noun, plural* **-mies** surgical operation for removing the uterus
hys•ter•e•sis [his-tə-REE-sis] *noun physics* lag or delay in changes in variable property of a system
hys•te•ri•a [hi-STER-ee-ə] *noun* **1** mental disorder with emotional outbursts **2** any frenzied emotional state **3** fit of crying or laughing > **hys•ter'i•cal** *adjective* > **hys•ter'ics** *plural noun* **1** fits of hysteria **2** (*informal*) uncontrollable laughter
Hz hertz

DICTIONARY **h** THESAURUS

hysteria *noun* FRENZY, agitation, delirium, hysterics, madness, panic
hysterical *adjective* **1** FRENZIED, crazed, distracted, distraught, frantic, overwrought, raving
2 (*informal*) HILARIOUS, comical, side-splitting, uproarious

Ii

I *chem.* iodine
I *pronoun* the pronoun of the first person singular
i•amb [Ī-amb] *noun* metrical foot of short and long syllable > **i•am'bic** *adjective*
i•bex [Ī-beks] *noun, plural* **-bex•es** wild goat with large horns
ibid. [IB-id] (referring to a book, page, or passage already mentioned) in the same place
i•bis [Ī-bis] *noun* storklike bird
ice [īs] *noun* 1 frozen water 2 frozen dessert made of sweetened water and fruit flavoring ▷ *verb* **iced, ic•ing** 3 cover, become covered with ice 4 cool with ice 5 cover with icing > **i'ci•cle** [-sə-kəl] *noun* tapering spike of ice hanging where water has dripped > **i'ci•ly** *adverb* in icy manner > **i'ci•ness** *noun* > **i'cing** *noun* mixture of sugar and water, etc. used to decorate cakes > **i'cy** *adjective* **i•ci•er, i•ci•est** 1 covered with ice 2 cold 3 chilling > **ice'berg** [-burg] *noun* large floating mass of ice > **ice cream** sweetened frozen dessert made from cream, eggs, etc. > **ice floe** [-floh] sheet of floating ice > **ice hockey** team game played on ice with puck
ich•thy•ol•o•gy [ik-thee-OL-ə-jee] *noun* scientific study of fish
icicle *see* **ice**
i•con [Ī-kon] *noun* 1 image, representation, esp. of religious figure 2 graphic representing a function, activated by clicking on > **i•con'o•clast** *noun* 1 one who attacks established principles, etc. 2 breaker of icons > **i•con•o•clas'tic** *adjective* > **i•co•nog'ra•phy** *noun* 1 icons collectively 2 study of icons
id *noun psychoanalysis* the mind's instinctive energies
i•de•a [ī-DEE-ə] *noun* 1 notion in the mind 2 conception 3 vague belief 4 plan, aim > **i•de'al** *noun* 1 conception of something that is perfect 2 perfect person or thing ▷ *adjective* 3 perfect 4 visionary 5 existing only in idea > **i•de'al•ism** *noun* 1 tendency to seek perfection in everything 2 philosophy that mind is the only reality > **i•de'al•ist** *noun* 1 one who holds doctrine of idealism 2 one who strives after the ideal 3 impractical person > **i•de•al•is'tic** *adjective* > **i•de'al•ize** *verb transitive* **-ized, -iz•ing**

DICTIONARY • THESAURUS

icy *adjective* 1 COLD, biting, bitter, chill, chilly, freezing, frosty, ice-cold, raw
2 SLIPPERY, glassy, slippy (*informal/dialect*)
3 UNFRIENDLY, aloof, cold, distant, frigid, frosty, unwelcoming
idea *noun* 1 THOUGHT, concept, impression, perception
2 BELIEF, conviction, notion, opinion, teaching, view
3 PLAN, aim, intention, object, objective, purpose
ideal *adjective* 1 PERFECT, archetypal, classic, complete, consummate, model, quintessential, supreme
▷ *noun* 2 MODEL, last word, paradigm, paragon, pattern, perfection, prototype, standard
idealist *noun* ROMANTIC, dreamer, Utopian, visionary
idealistic *adjective* PERFECTIONIST, impracticable, optimistic, romantic, starry-eyed, Utopian, visionary
idealize *verb* ROMANTICIZE, apotheosize, ennoble,

portray as ideal
i•dem [Ī-dem] *Lat.* the same
i•den•ti•ty [ī-DEN-ti-tee] *noun, plural* **-ties** 1 individuality 2 being the same, exactly alike > **i•den'ti•cal** *adjective* very same > **i•den'ti•fi•a•ble** *adjective* > **i•den'ti•fy** *verb* **-fied, -fy•ing** 1 establish identity of 2 associate (oneself) with 3 treat as identical > **identity theft** crime of setting up and using bank accounts and credit facilities in another person's name without that person's knowledge
id•e•o•graph [ID-ee-ə-graf] *noun* picture, symbol, figure, etc., suggesting an object without naming it (*also* **id'e•o•gram**)
i•de•ol•o•gy [ī-dee-OL-ə-jee] *noun, plural* **-gies** body of ideas, beliefs of group, nation, etc. > **i•de•o•log'i•cal** *adjective* > **i'de•o•logue** [-lawg] *noun* zealous advocate of an ideology
ides [īdz] *noun* (in the Ancient Roman calendar) the 15th of March, May, July, or October, or the 13th of other months
idiocy *see* **idiot**
id•i•om [ID-ee-əm] *noun* 1 way of expression natural or peculiar to a language or group 2 characteristic style of expression > **id•i•o•mat'ic** *adjective* 1 using idioms 2 colloquial
id•i•o•syn•cra•sy [id-ee-ə-SING-krə-see] *noun* peculiarity of mind, temper, or disposition in a person > **id•i•o•syn•crat'ic** [-oh-sing-KRAT-ik] *adjective*
id•i•ot [ID-ee-ət] *noun* foolish, senseless person > **id'i•o•cy** [-ə-see] *noun* > **id•i•ot'ic** *adjective* utterly senseless or stupid
i•dle [ĪD-l] *adjective* **-dler, -dlest** 1 unemployed 2 lazy 3 useless, vain, groundless ▷ *verb intransitive* **-dled, -dling** 4 be idle 5 (of engine) run slowly with gears disengaged ▷ *verb transitive* 6 (esp. with *away*) waste > **i'dle•ness** *noun* > **i'dler** *noun* > **i'dly** *adverb*
i•dol [ĪD-l] *noun* 1 image of deity as object of worship 2 object of excessive devotion > **i•dol'a•ter** *noun* worshiper of idols > **i•dol'a•trous** [-trəs] *adjective* > **i•dol'a•try** *noun* > **i'dol•ize** *verb transitive* **-ized, -iz•ing** 1 love or venerate to excess 2 make an idol of
i•dyll [ĪD-l] *noun* short descriptive poem of picturesque or charming scene or episode, esp. of rustic life > **i•dyl•lic** [ī-DIL-ik] *adjective* 1 of, like, idyll 2 delightful
i.e. that is to say
if *conjunction* 1 on condition or supposition that 2 whether 3 although ▷ *noun* 4 uncertainty or doubt: *no ifs, ands, or buts* > **if'fy** [-ee] *adjective* **-fi•er, -fi•est** (*informal*) dubious
ig'loo *noun* dome-shaped Inuit house of snow and ice
ig•ne•ous [IG-nee-əs] *adjective* esp. of rocks, formed as molten rock cools and hardens
ig•nite [ig-NĪT] *verb* **-nit•ed, -nit•ing** (cause to) burn > **ig•ni'tion** [-NISH-ən] *noun* 1 act of kindling or setting on fire 2 in internal combustion engine, means of firing explosive mixture, usu. electric spark
ig•no•ble [ig-NOH-bəl] *adjective* 1 mean, base 2 of low birth > **ig•no'bly** *adverb*
ig•no•min•y [IG-nə-min-ee] *noun, plural* **-min•ies** 1 dishonor, disgrace 2 shameful act > **ig•no•min'i•ous** [-ee-əs] *adjective*
ig•nore [ig-NOR] *verb transitive* **-nored, -nor•ing** disregard, leave out of account > **ig•no•ra'mus**

DICTIONARY

THESAURUS

exalt, glorify, magnify, put on a pedestal, worship
ideally *adverb* IN A PERFECT WORLD, all things being equal, if one had one's way
identical *adjective* ALIKE, duplicate, indistinguishable, interchangeable, matching, twin
identification *noun* 1 RECOGNITION, naming, pinpointing
2 EMPATHY, association, connection, fellow feeling, involvement, rapport, relationship, sympathy
identify *verb* 1 RECOGNIZE, diagnose, make out, name, pick out, pinpoint, place, point out, put one's finger on (*informal*), spot
2 ▷ **identify with** RELATE TO, associate with, empathize with, feel for, respond to
identity *noun* 1 EXISTENCE, individuality, personality, self
2 SAMENESS, correspondence, unity
idiocy *noun* FOOLISHNESS, asininity, fatuousness, imbecility, inanity, insanity, lunacy, senselessness
idiom *noun* 1 PHRASE, expression, turn of phrase
2 LANGUAGE, jargon, parlance, style, vernacular
idiosyncrasy *noun* PECULIARITY, characteristic, eccentricity, mannerism, oddity, quirk, trick
idiot *noun* FOOL, chump, cretin (*offensive*), dork (*slang*), dunderhead, halfwit, imbecile, moron (*offensive*), schmuck (*slang*), simpleton
idiotic *adjective* FOOLISH, asinine, bonkers (*informal*), crazy, daft (*informal*), foolhardy, harebrained, insane, moronic (*offensive*), senseless, stupid
idle *adjective* 1 INACTIVE, redundant, unemployed, unoccupied, unused, vacant
2 LAZY, good-for-nothing, indolent, lackadaisical, shiftless, slothful, sluggish
3 USELESS, fruitless, futile, groundless, ineffective, pointless, unavailing, unsuccessful, vain, worthless
▷ *verb* 4 (*often with away*) LAZE, dally, dawdle, kill time, loaf, loiter, lounge, potter
idleness *noun* 1 INACTIVITY, inaction, leisure, time on one's hands, unemployment
2 LAZINESS, inertia, shiftlessness, sloth, sluggishness, torpor
idol *noun* 1 GRAVEN IMAGE, deity, god
2 HERO, beloved, darling, favorite, pet, pin-up (*slang*)
idolatry *noun* ADORATION, adulation, exaltation, glorification
idolize *verb* WORSHIP, adore, dote upon, exalt, glorify, hero-worship, look up to, love, revere, venerate
idyllic *adjective* IDEALIZED, charming, halcyon, heavenly, ideal, picturesque, unspoiled
if *conjunction* PROVIDED, assuming, on condition that, providing, supposing
ignite *verb* 1 CATCH FIRE, burn, burst into flames, flare up, inflame, take fire
2 SET FIRE TO, kindle, light, set alight, torch
ignominious *adjective* HUMILIATING, discreditable, disgraceful, dishonorable, indecorous, inglorious, shameful, sorry, undignified

[-RA-məs] *noun, plural* **-mus•es** ignorant person > **ig'no•rance** [-rəns] *noun* lack of knowledge > **ig'no•rant** *adjective* 1 lacking knowledge 2 uneducated 3 unaware

i•gua•na [i-GWAH-nə] *noun* large tropical American lizard

il- *prefix same as* **in-**[1] *or* **in-**[2]

il•e•um [IL-ee-əm] *noun* lower part of small intestine > **il'e•ac** *adjective*

ilk *noun* sort, kind **of that ilk** of the same type or class

ill *adjective* 1 not in good health 2 bad, evil 3 faulty 4 unfavorable ▷ *noun* 5 evil, harm 6 mild disease ▷ *adverb* 7 badly 8 hardly, with difficulty > **ill'ness** *noun* > **ill'-ad•vised'** *adjective* 1 imprudent 2 injudicious > **ill'-fat'ed** [-FAY-tid] *adjective* unfortunate > **ill'-fa'vored** [-FAY-vərd] *adjective* 1 ugly, deformed 2 offensive > **ill'-got•ten** *adjective* obtained dishonestly > **ill'-man'nered** *adjective* boorish, uncivil > **ill-timed** *adjective* inopportune > **ill-treat** *verb transitive* treat cruelly > **ill will** unkind feeling, hostility

il•le'gal *adjective* against the law > **il•le'gal•ly** *adverb* > **il•le•gal'i•ty** *noun, plural* **-ties**

il•leg'i•ble *adjective* unable to be read or deciphered > **il•leg•i•bil'i•ty** *noun*

il•le•git•i•mate [il-i-JIT-ə-mit] *adjective* 1 born out of wedlock 2 unlawful 3 not regular ▷ *noun* 4 bastard

il•lic•it [i-LIS-it] *adjective* 1 illegal 2 prohibited, forbidden

il•lit•er•ate [i-LIT-ər-it] *adjective* 1 not literate 2 unable to read or write ▷ *noun* 3 illiterate person > **il•lit'er•a•cy** *noun*

il•log'i•cal *adjective* 1 unreasonable 2 not logical

il•lu•mi•nate [i-LOO-mə-nayt] *verb transitive* **-nat•ed, -nat•ing** 1 light up 2 clarify 3 decorate with lights 4 decorate with gold and colors > **il•lu•mi•na'tion** *noun* > **il•lu'mine** *verb transitive* **-mined, -min•ing** illuminate

il•lu•sion [i-LOO-zhən] *noun* deceptive appearance or belief > **il•lu'sion•ist** *noun* conjurer > **il•lu'so•ry** [-LOO-sə-ree] *adjective* deceptive

il•lus•trate [IL-ə-strayt] *verb transitive* **-trat•ed, -trat•ing** 1 provide with pictures or examples 2 exemplify > **il•lus•tra'tion** *noun* 1 picture,

ignominy *noun* DISGRACE, discredit, dishonor, disrepute, humiliation, infamy, obloquy, shame, stigma

ignorance *noun* UNAWARENESS, inexperience, innocence, unconsciousness, unfamiliarity

ignorant *adjective* 1 UNINFORMED, benighted, inexperienced, innocent, oblivious, unaware, unconscious, unenlightened, uninitiated, unwitting
2 UNEDUCATED, illiterate
3 INSENSITIVE, crass, half-baked (*informal*), rude

ignore *verb* OVERLOOK, blow off (*slang*), discount, disregard, neglect, pass over, reject, take no notice of, turn a blind eye to

ill *adjective* 1 UNWELL, ailing, diseased, indisposed, infirm, off-color, sick, under the weather (*informal*), unhealthy
2 HARMFUL, bad, damaging, deleterious, detrimental, evil, foul, injurious, unfortunate
▷ *noun* 3 HARM, affliction, hardship, hurt, injury, misery, misfortune, trouble, unpleasantness, woe
▷ *adverb* 4 BADLY, inauspiciously, poorly, unfavorably, unfortunately, unluckily
5 HARDLY, barely, by no means, scantily

ill-advised *adjective* MISGUIDED, foolhardy, ill-considered, ill-judged, imprudent, incautious, injudicious, rash, reckless, thoughtless, unwise

ill-disposed *adjective* UNFRIENDLY, antagonistic, disobliging, hostile, inimical, uncooperative, unwelcoming

illegal *adjective* UNLAWFUL, banned, criminal, felonious, forbidden, illicit, outlawed, prohibited, unauthorized, unlicensed

illegality *noun* CRIME, felony, illegitimacy, lawlessness, wrong

illegible *adjective* INDECIPHERABLE, obscure, scrawled, unreadable

illegitimate *adjective* 1 UNLAWFUL, illegal, illicit, improper, unauthorized
2 BORN OUT OF WEDLOCK, bastard

ill-fated *adjective* DOOMED, hapless, ill-omened, ill-starred, luckless, star-crossed, unfortunate, unhappy, unlucky

illicit *adjective* 1 ILLEGAL, criminal, felonious, illegitimate, prohibited, unauthorized, unlawful, unlicensed
2 FORBIDDEN, clandestine, furtive, guilty, immoral, improper

illiterate *adjective* UNEDUCATED, ignorant, uncultured, untaught, untutored

ill-mannered *adjective* RUDE, badly behaved, boorish, churlish, discourteous, impolite, insolent, loutish, uncouth

illness *noun* DISEASE, affliction, ailment, disorder, infirmity, malady, sickness

illogical *adjective* IRRATIONAL, absurd, inconsistent, invalid, meaningless, senseless, unreasonable, unscientific, unsound

ill-treat *verb* ABUSE, damage, harm, injure, maltreat, mishandle, misuse, oppress

illuminate *verb* 1 LIGHT UP, brighten
2 EXPLAIN, clarify, clear up, elucidate, enlighten, interpret, make clear, shed light on

illuminating *adjective* INFORMATIVE, enlightening, explanatory, helpful, instructive, revealing

illumination *noun* 1 LIGHT, brightness, lighting, radiance
2 ENLIGHTENMENT, clarification, insight, revelation

illusion *noun* 1 FANTASY, chimera, daydream, figment of the imagination, hallucination, mirage, will-o'-the-wisp
2 MISCONCEPTION, deception, delusion, error, fallacy, misapprehension

illusory *adjective* UNREAL, chimerical, deceptive, delusive, fallacious, false, hallucinatory, mistaken, sham

illustrate *verb* DEMONSTRATE, bring home, elucidate, emphasize, explain, point up, show

illustrated *adjective* PICTORIAL, decorated, graphic

illustration *noun* 1 EXAMPLE, case, instance, specimen
2 PICTURE, decoration, figure, plate, sketch

illustrious *adjective* FAMOUS, celebrated, distinguished, eminent, glorious, great, notable,

diagram 2 example 3 act of illustrating > **il·lus'tra·tive** *adjective* providing explanation
il·lus·tri·ous [i-LUS-tree-əs] *adjective* 1 famous 2 distinguished 3 exalted
IM *see* **instant messaging**
im- *prefix same as* **in-[1]** *or* **in-[2]**
im·age [IM-ij] *noun* 1 representation or likeness of person or thing 2 optical counterpart, as in mirror 3 double, copy 4 general impression 5 mental picture created by words, esp. in literature ▷ *verb transitive* **-aged, -mag·ing** 6 make image of 7 reflect > **im'age·ry** *noun* images collectively, esp. in literature
im·ag·ine [i-MAJ-in] *verb transitive* 1 picture to oneself 2 think 3 conjecture > **im·ag'i·na·ble** *adjective* > **im·ag'i·nar·y** *adjective* existing only in fancy > **im·ag·i·na'tion** *noun* 1 faculty of making mental images of things not present 2 fancy 3 resourcefulness > **im·ag'i·na·tive** *adjective*
i·mam [i-MAHM] *noun* Islamic minister or priest
im·bal·ance [im-BAL-əns] *noun* lack of balance, proportion
im·be·cile [IM-bə-sil] *noun* 1 idiot ▷ *adjective* 2 idiotic > **im·be·cil'i·ty** *noun*
im·bibe [im-BĪB] *verb transitive* **-bibed, -bib·ing** 1 drink in 2 absorb ▷ *verb intransitive* **-bibed, -bib·ing** 3 drink
im·bri·cate [IM-brə-kit] *adjective* lying over each other in regular order, like tiles or shingles on roof > **im·bri·ca'tion** *noun*
im·bro·glio [im-BROHL-yoh] *noun, plural* **-glios** 1 disagreement 2 complicated situation, plot
im·bue [im-BYOO] *verb transitive* **-bued, -bu·ing** 1 inspire 2 saturate
im·i·tate [IM-i-tayt] *verb transitive* **-tat·ed, -tat·ing** 1 take as model 2 mimic, copy > **im'i·ta·ble** *adjective* > **im·i·ta'tion** *noun* 1 act of imitating 2 copy of original 3 likeness 4 counterfeit > **im'i·ta·tive** *adjective* > **im'i·ta·tor** *noun*
im·mac·u·late [im-AK-yə-lit] *adjective* 1 spotless 2 pure 3 unsullied
im·ma·nent [IM-mə-nənt] *adjective* abiding in, inherent > **im'ma·nence** *noun*
im·ma·te·ri·al [im-ə-TEER-ee-əl] *adjective* 1 unimportant, trifling 2 not consisting of matter 3 spiritual
im·ma·ture' *adjective* 1 not fully developed 2 lacking wisdom or stability because of youth > **im·ma·tu'ri·ty** *noun*
im·me·di·ate [i-MEE-dee-it] *adjective* 1 occurring at once 2 direct, not separated by others > **im·me'di·a·cy** *noun*
im·me·mo·ri·al [im-ə-MOR-ee-əl] *adjective*

DICTIONARY THESAURUS

---

prominent, renowned
ill will *noun* HOSTILITY, animosity, bad blood, dislike, enmity, hatred, malice, rancor, resentment, venom
image *noun* 1 REPRESENTATION, effigy, figure, icon, idol, likeness, picture, portrait, statue
2 REPLICA, counterpart, ringer *or* dead ringer (*slang*), Doppelgänger, double, facsimile, spitting image (*informal*)
3 CONCEPT, idea, impression, mental picture, perception
imaginable *adjective* POSSIBLE, believable, comprehensible, conceivable, credible, likely, plausible
imaginary *adjective* FICTIONAL, fictitious, hypothetical, illusory, imagined, invented, made-up, nonexistent, unreal
imagination *noun* 1 CREATIVITY, enterprise, ingenuity, invention, inventiveness, originality, resourcefulness, vision
2 UNREALITY, illusion, supposition
imaginative *adjective* CREATIVE, clever, enterprising, ingenious, inspired, inventive, original
imagine *verb* 1 ENVISAGE, conceive, conceptualize, conjure up, picture, plan, think of, think up, visualize
2 BELIEVE, assume, conjecture, fancy, guess (*informal*), infer, suppose, surmise, suspect, take it, think
imbecile *noun* 1 IDIOT, chump, cretin (*offensive*), dork (*slang*), fool, halfwit, moron (*offensive*), schmuck (*slang*), thickhead
▷ *adjective* 2 STUPID, asinine, fatuous, feeble-minded, foolish, idiotic, moronic (*offensive*), thick, witless
imbibe *verb* 1 DRINK, consume, knock back (*informal*), quaff, sink (*informal*), swallow, swig (*informal*)
2 (*literary*) ABSORB, acquire, assimilate, gain, gather, ingest, receive, take in
imbroglio *noun* COMPLICATION, embarrassment, entanglement, involvement, misunderstanding, quandary
imitate *verb* COPY, ape, echo, emulate, follow, mimic, mirror, repeat, simulate
imitation *noun* 1 MIMICRY, counterfeiting, duplication, likeness, resemblance, simulation
2 REPLICA, fake, forgery, impersonation, impression, reproduction, sham, substitution
▷ *adjective* 3 ARTIFICIAL, dummy, ersatz, man-made, mock, phoney *or* phony (*informal*), reproduction, sham, simulated, synthetic
imitative *adjective* DERIVATIVE, copycat (*informal*), mimetic, parrot-like, second-hand, simulated, unoriginal
imitator *noun* IMPERSONATOR, copier, copycat (*informal*), impressionist, mimic, parrot
immaculate *adjective* 1 CLEAN, neat, spick-and-span, spotless, spruce, squeaky-clean
2 FLAWLESS, above reproach, faultless, impeccable, perfect, unblemished, unexceptionable, untarnished
immaterial *adjective* IRRELEVANT, extraneous, inconsequential, inessential, insignificant, of no importance, trivial, unimportant
immature *adjective* 1 YOUNG, adolescent, undeveloped, unformed, unripe
2 CHILDISH, callow, inexperienced, infantile, juvenile, puerile
immaturity *noun* 1 UNRIPENESS, greenness, imperfection, rawness, unpreparedness
2 CHILDISHNESS, callowness, inexperience, puerility
immediate *adjective* 1 INSTANT, instantaneous
2 NEAREST, close, direct, near, next
immediately *adverb* AT ONCE, directly, forthwith, instantly, now, promptly, right away, straight away, this instant, without delay

beyond memory
im•mense [i-MENS] *adjective* huge, vast > **im•men'si•ty** *noun* vastness
im•merse [i-MURS] *verb transitive* **-mersed, -mers•ing** 1 dip, plunge, into liquid 2 involve 3 engross > **im•mer'sion** [-zhən] *noun* immersing > **immersion heater** *noun* electric appliance for heating liquid in which it is immersed
im•mi•grate [IM-i-grayt] *verb intransitive* **-grat•ed, -grat•ing** come into country as settler > **im'mi•grant** [-grənt] *noun, adjective* > **im•mi•gra'tion** *noun*
im•mi•nent [IM-ə-nənt] *adjective* 1 liable to happen soon 2 close at hand > **im'mi•nence** *noun*
im•mo'bile *adjective* 1 not moving 2 unable to move > **im•mo•bil'i•ty** *noun* > **im•mo'bi•lize** *verb transitive* make unable to move or work
im•mod'er•ate *adjective* excessive or unreasonable
im•mod'est *adjective* 1 behaving in an indecent or improper manner 2 behaving in a boastful or conceited manner > **im•mod'es•ty** *noun*
im•mo•late [IM-ə-layt] *verb transitive* **-lat•ed, -lat•ing** kill, sacrifice > **im•mo•la'tion** *noun*
im•mor•al [i-MOR-əl] *adjective* 1 corrupt 2 promiscuous 3 indecent 4 unethical > **im•mo•ral'i•ty** *noun, plural* **-ties**
im•mor•tal [i-MOR-tl] *adjective* 1 deathless 2 famed for all time ▷ *noun* 3 immortal being 4 god 5 one whose fame will last > **im•mor•tal'i•ty** *noun* > **im•mor'tal•ize** *verb transitive* **-ized, -iz•ing**
im•mov'a•ble *adjective* 1 unable to be moved 2 unwilling to change one's opinions or beliefs 3 not affected by feeling, emotionless
im•mune [i-MYOON] *adjective* 1 proof (against a disease, etc.) 2 secure, exempt > **im•mu'ni•ty** *noun* 1 state of being immune 2 freedom from prosecution, etc. > **im•mu•ni•za'tion** *noun* process of making immune to disease > **im'mu•nize** *verb transitive* **-nized, -niz•ing** make immune > **im•mu•nol'o•gy** *noun* branch of biology concerned with study of immunity
im•mu•ta•ble [i-MYOO-tə-bəl] *adjective* unchangeable
imp *noun* 1 little devil 2 mischievous child
im•pact [IM-pakt] *noun* 1 collision 2 profound effect > **impact** [im-PAKT] *verb transitive* drive, press
im•pair' *verb transitive* weaken, damage > **im•pair'ment** *noun*
im•pal•a [im-PAL-ə] *noun, plural* **-pal•as** antelope of Africa
im•pale [im-PAYL] *verb transitive* **-paled, -pal•ing** 1 pierce with sharp instrument 2 make helpless as if pierced through
im•part [im-PAHRT] *verb transitive* 1 communicate (information, etc.) 2 give
im•par•tial [im-PAHR-shəl] *adjective* 1 not

DICTIONARY • THESAURUS

immense *adjective* HUGE, colossal, enormous, extensive, gigantic, great, massive, monumental, stupendous, tremendous, vast
immensity *noun* SIZE, bulk, enormity, expanse, extent, greatness, hugeness, magnitude, vastness
immerse *verb* 1 PLUNGE, bathe, dip, douse, duck, dunk, sink, submerge
2 ENGROSS, absorb, busy, engage, involve, occupy, take up
immersion *noun* 1 DIPPING, dousing, ducking, dunking, plunging, submerging
2 INVOLVEMENT, absorption, concentration, preoccupation
immigrant *noun* SETTLER, incomer, newcomer
imminent *adjective* NEAR, at hand, close, coming, forthcoming, gathering, impending, in the pipeline, looming
immobile *adjective* STATIONARY, at a standstill, at rest, fixed, immovable, motionless, rigid, rooted, static, still, stock-still, unmoving
immobility *noun* STILLNESS, fixity, inertness, motionlessness, stability, steadiness
immobilize *verb* PARALYZE, bring to a standstill, cripple, disable, freeze, halt, stop, transfix
immoderate *adjective* EXCESSIVE, exaggerated, exorbitant, extravagant, extreme, inordinate, over the top (*slang*), undue, unjustified, unreasonable
immoral *adjective* WICKED, bad, corrupt, debauched, depraved, dissolute, indecent, sinful, unethical, unprincipled, wrong
immorality *noun* WICKEDNESS, corruption, debauchery, depravity, dissoluteness, sin, vice, wrong
immortal *adjective* 1 ETERNAL, deathless, enduring, everlasting, imperishable, lasting, perennial, undying
▷ *noun* 2 GOD, goddess
3 GREAT, genius, hero
immortality *noun* 1 ETERNITY, everlasting life, perpetuity
2 FAME, celebrity, glory, greatness, renown
immortalize *verb* COMMEMORATE, celebrate, exalt, glorify
immovable *adjective* 1 FIXED, firm, immutable, jammed, secure, set, stable, stationary, stuck
2 INFLEXIBLE, adamant, obdurate, resolute, steadfast, unshakable, unwavering, unyielding
immune *adjective* EXEMPT, clear, free, invulnerable, proof *or* proof against, protected, resistant, safe, unaffected
immunity *noun* 1 EXEMPTION, amnesty, freedom, indemnity, invulnerability, license, release
2 RESISTANCE, immunization, protection
immunize *verb* VACCINATE, inoculate, protect, safeguard
imp *noun* 1 DEMON, devil, sprite
2 RASCAL, brat, minx, rogue, scamp
impact *noun* 1 COLLISION, blow, bump, contact, crash, jolt, knock, smash, stroke, thump
2 EFFECT, consequences, impression, influence, repercussions, significance
▷ *verb* 3 HIT, clash, collide, crash, crush, strike
impair *verb* WORSEN, blunt, damage, decrease, diminish, harm, hinder, injure, lessen, reduce, undermine, weaken
impaired *adjective* DAMAGED, defective, faulty, flawed, imperfect, unsound
impart *verb* 1 COMMUNICATE, convey, disclose, divulge, make known, pass on, relate, reveal, tell
2 GIVE, accord, afford, bestow, confer, grant, lend, yield
impartial *adjective* NEUTRAL, detached,

biased or prejudiced 2 fair > **im•par•ti•al'i•ty** *noun*
im•passe [IM-pas] *noun* 1 deadlock 2 place, situation, from which there is no outlet
im•pas•sioned [im-PASH-ənd] *adjective* deeply moved, ardent
im•pas•sive [im-PAS-iv] *adjective* 1 showing no emotion 2 calm > **im•pas•siv'i•ty** *noun*
im•pa'tient *adjective* 1 irritable at any delay or difficulty 2 restless (to have or do something) > **im•pa'tience** *noun*
im•peach [im-PEECH] *verb transitive* 1 charge with crime 2 call to account 3 *law* challenge credibility of (a witness) > **im•peach'a•ble** *adjective*
im•pec•ca•ble [im-PEK-ə-bəl] *adjective* without flaw or error
im•pe•cu•ni•ous [im-pi-KYOO-nee-əs] *adjective* poor > **im•pe•cu'ni•ous•ness** *noun* > **im•pe•cu•ni•os'i•ty** *noun*
im•pede [im-PEED] *verb transitive* **-ped•ed, -ped•ing** hinder > **im•ped'ance** *noun electricity* measure of opposition offered to flow of alternating current > **im•ped'i•ment** [-PED-ə-mənt] *noun* 1 obstruction 2 defect
im•pel' *verb transitive* **-pelled, -pel•ling** 1 induce, incite 2 drive, force > **im•pel'ler** *noun*
im•pend' *verb intransitive* 1 threaten 2 be imminent 3 hang over > **im•pend'ing** *adjective*
im•per•a•tive [im-PER-ə-tiv] *adjective* 1 necessary 2 peremptory 3 expressing command ▷ *noun* 4 imperative mood
im•per•cep'ti•ble *adjective* too slight or gradual to be noticed
im•per'fect *adjective* 1 having faults or mistakes 2 not complete 3 *grammar* denoting a tense of verbs describing continuous, incomplete, or repeated past actions ▷ *noun* 4 *grammar* imperfect tense > **im•per•fec'tion** *noun*
im•pe•ri•al [im-PEER-ee-əl] *adjective* 1 of empire, or emperor 2 majestic > **im•pe'ri•al•ism** *noun* extension of empire 1 belief in colonial empire > **im•pe'ri•al•ist** *noun*
im•per•il [im-PER-əl] *verb transitive* **-iled, -il•ing** bring into peril, endanger
im•pe•ri•ous [im-PEER-ee-əs] *adjective* 1 domineering 2 haughty 3 dictatorial > **im•pe'ri•ous•ness** *noun*
im•per•son•al [im-PUR-sə-nl] *adjective* 1 objective, having no personal significance 2 devoid of human warmth, personality, etc. 3 (of verb) without personal subject > **im•per•son•al'i•ty** *noun*
im•per•son•ate [im-PUR-sə-nayt] *verb transitive* **-at•ed, -at•ing** 1 pretend to be (another person) 2 play the part of > **im•per•son•a'tion** *noun*
im•per•ti•nent [im-PUR-tn-ənt] *adjective* insolent, rude > **im•per'ti•nence** *noun*
im•per•turb•a•ble [im-pər-TUR-bə-bəl] *adjective* calm, not excitable

---

disinterested, equitable, even-handed, fair, just, objective, open-minded, unbiased, unprejudiced
impartiality *noun* NEUTRALITY, detachment, disinterestedness, dispassion, equity, even-handedness, fairness, objectivity, open-mindedness
impassable *adjective* BLOCKED, closed, impenetrable, obstructed
impasse *noun* DEADLOCK, dead end, gridlock, stalemate, standoff, standstill
impassioned *adjective* INTENSE, animated, fervent, fiery, heated, inspired, passionate, rousing, stirring
impatience *noun* 1 HASTE, impetuosity, intolerance, rashness
2 RESTLESSNESS, agitation, anxiety, eagerness, edginess, fretfulness, nervousness, uneasiness
impatient *adjective* 1 HASTY, demanding, hot-tempered, impetuous, intolerant
2 RESTLESS, eager, edgy, fretful, straining at the leash
impeach *verb* CHARGE, accuse, arraign, indict
impeccable *adjective* FAULTLESS, blameless, flawless, immaculate, irreproachable, perfect, unblemished, unimpeachable
impecunious *adjective* POOR, broke (*informal*), destitute, down and out, down on one's luck (*informal*), indigent, insolvent, penniless, poverty-stricken
impede *verb* HINDER, block, check, disrupt, hamper, hold up, obstruct, slow *or* slow down, thwart
impediment *noun* OBSTACLE, barrier, difficulty, encumbrance, hindrance, obstruction, snag, stumbling block
impel *verb* FORCE, compel, constrain, drive, induce, oblige, push, require
impending *adjective* LOOMING, approaching, coming, forthcoming, gathering, imminent, in the pipeline, near, upcoming
impenetrable *adjective* 1 SOLID, dense, impassable, impermeable, impervious, inviolable, thick
2 INCOMPREHENSIBLE, arcane, enigmatic, inscrutable, mysterious, obscure, unfathomable, unintelligible
imperative *adjective* URGENT, crucial, essential, pressing, vital
imperceptible *adjective* UNDETECTABLE, faint, indiscernible, microscopic, minute, slight, small, subtle, tiny
imperfect *adjective* FLAWED, damaged, defective, faulty, impaired, incomplete, limited, unfinished
imperfection *noun* FAULT, blemish, defect, deficiency, failing, flaw, frailty, shortcoming, taint, weakness
imperial *adjective* ROYAL, kingly, majestic, princely, queenly, regal, sovereign
imperil *verb* ENDANGER, expose, jeopardize, risk
impersonal *adjective* REMOTE, aloof, cold, detached, dispassionate, formal, inhuman, neutral
impersonate *verb* IMITATE, ape, do (*informal*), masquerade as, mimic, pass oneself off as, pose as (*informal*)
impersonation *noun* IMITATION, caricature, impression, mimicry, parody
impertinence *noun* RUDENESS, brazenness, cheek (*informal*), disrespect, effrontery, front, impudence, insolence, nerve (*informal*), presumption
impertinent *adjective* RUDE, brazen, cheeky (*informal*), disrespectful, impolite, impudent, insolent, presumptuous
imperturbable *adjective* CALM, collected,

im•per•vi•ous [im-PUR-vee-əs] *adjective* 1 not affording passage 2 impenetrable (to feeling, argument, etc.)
im•pe•ti•go [im-pi-TĪ-goh] *noun* contagious skin disease
im•pet•u•ous [im-PECH-oo-əs] *adjective* likely to act without consideration, rash
> **im•pet•u•os'i•ty** *noun*
im•pe•tus [IM-pi-təs] *noun* 1 force with which body moves 2 impulse
im•pinge [im-PINJ] *verb intransitive* **pinged, -ping•ing** 1 encroach (upon) 2 collide (with)
> **im•pinge'ment** *noun*
im•pi•ous [IM-pee-əs] *adjective* irreverent, profane, wicked > **im•pi'e•ty** [-PĪ-i-tee] *noun*
im•plac•a•ble [im-PLAK-ə-bəl] *adjective* 1 not to be appeased 2 unyielding > **im•plac•a•bil'i•ty** *noun*
im•plant' *verb transitive* insert, fix > **im'plant** *noun* 1 *dentistry* artificial tooth implanted permanently in jaw 2 implanted breast enhancement
im•ple•ment [IM-plə-mənt] *noun* 1 tool, instrument, utensil ▷ *verb transitive* [-ment] 2 carry out (instructions, etc.) 3 put into effect
im•pli•cate [IM-pli-kayt] *verb transitive* **-cat•ed, -cat•ing** 1 involve, include 2 entangle 3 imply
> **im•pli•ca'tion** *noun* something implied
> **im•plic'it** [-PLIS-it] *adjective* 1 implied but not expressed 2 absolute and unreserved
im•plore [im-PLOR] *verb transitive* **-plored, -plor•ing** entreat earnestly
im•ply [im-PLĪ] *verb transitive* **-plied, -ply•ing** 1 indicate by hint, suggest 2 mean
im•po•lite' *adjective* showing bad manners
im•port' *verb transitive* 1 bring in, introduce (esp. goods from foreign country) 2 imply > **im'port** *noun* 1 thing imported 2 meaning 3 importance > **im•port'er** *noun*
im•por•tant [im-POR-tnt] *adjective* 1 of great consequence 2 momentous 3 pompous
> **im•por'tance** *noun*
im•por•tune [im-por-TOON] *verb transitive* **-tuned, -tun•ing** request, demand persistently
> **im•por'tu•nate** [-POR-chə-nit] *adjective* persistent > **im•por•tu'ni•ty** *noun*
im•pose [im-POHZ] *verb transitive* **-posed, -pos•ing** 1 levy (tax, duty, etc., upon) ▷ *verb intransitive* **-posed, -pos•ing** 2 take advantage (of), practice deceit on > **im•pos'ing** *adjective* impressive > **im•po•si'tion** *noun* 1 that which is imposed 2 tax 3 burden 4 deception

DICTIONARY • THESAURUS

composed, cool, nerveless, self-possessed, serene, unexcitable, unflappable (*informal*), unruffled
impervious *adjective* 1 SEALED, impassable, impenetrable, impermeable, resistant
2 UNAFFECTED, immune, invulnerable, proof against, unmoved, untouched
impetuosity *noun* HASTE, impulsiveness, precipitateness, rashness
impetuous *adjective* RASH, hasty, impulsive, precipitate, unthinking
impetus *noun* 1 INCENTIVE, catalyst, goad, impulse, motivation, push, spur, stimulus
2 FORCE, energy, momentum, power
impinge *verb* 1 ENCROACH, infringe, invade, obtrude, trespass, violate
2 AFFECT, bear upon, have a bearing on, impact, influence, relate to, touch
impious *adjective* SACRILEGIOUS, blasphemous, godless, irreligious, irreverent, profane, sinful, ungodly, unholy, wicked
impish *adjective* MISCHIEVOUS, devilish, puckish, rascally, roguish, sportive, waggish
implacable *adjective* UNYIELDING, inflexible, intractable, merciless, pitiless, unbending, uncompromising, unforgiving
implant *verb* 1 INSTILL, inculcate, infuse
2 INSERT, fix, graft
implement *verb* 1 CARRY OUT, bring about, complete, effect, enforce, execute, fulfill, perform, realize
▷ *noun* 2 TOOL, apparatus, appliance, device, gadget, instrument, utensil
implicate *verb* INCRIMINATE, associate, embroil, entangle, include, inculpate, involve
implication *noun* SUGGESTION, inference, innuendo, meaning, overtone, presumption, significance
implicit *adjective* 1 IMPLIED, inferred, latent, tacit, taken for granted, undeclared, understood, unspoken
2 ABSOLUTE, constant, firm, fixed, full, steadfast, unqualified, unreserved, wholehearted
implied *adjective* UNSPOKEN, hinted at, implicit, indirect, suggested, tacit, undeclared, unexpressed, unstated
implore *verb* BEG, beseech, entreat, importune, plead with, pray
imply *verb* 1 HINT, insinuate, intimate, signify, suggest
2 ENTAIL, indicate, involve, mean, point to, presuppose
impolite *adjective* BAD-MANNERED, discourteous, disrespectful, ill-mannered, insolent, loutish, rude, uncouth
impoliteness *noun* BAD MANNERS, boorishness, churlishness, discourtesy, disrespect, insolence, rudeness
import *verb* 1 BRING IN, introduce
▷ *noun* 2 MEANING, drift, gist, implication, intention, sense, significance, thrust
3 IMPORTANCE, consequence, magnitude, moment, significance, substance, weight
importance *noun* 1 SIGNIFICANCE, concern, consequence, import, interest, moment, substance, usefulness, value, weight
2 PRESTIGE, distinction, eminence, esteem, influence, prominence, standing, status
important *adjective* 1 SIGNIFICANT, far-reaching, momentous, seminal, serious, substantial, urgent, weighty
2 POWERFUL, eminent, high-ranking, influential, noteworthy, pre-eminent, prominent
importunate *adjective* PERSISTENT, demanding, dogged, insistent, pressing, urgent
impose *verb* 1 ESTABLISH, decree, fix, institute, introduce, levy, ordain
2 INFLICT, appoint, enforce, saddle (someone) with
imposing *adjective* IMPRESSIVE, commanding, dignified, grand, majestic, stately, striking
imposition *noun* 1 APPLICATION, introduction,

> im'post *noun* duty, tax on imports
im•pos•si•ble [im-POS-ə-bəl] *adjective* 1 incapable of being done or experienced 2 absurd 3 unreasonable > **im•pos•si•bil'i•ty** *noun, plural* **-ties**
im•pos•tor [im-POS-tər] *noun* deceiver, one who assumes false identity
im•po•tent [IM-pə-tənt] *adjective* 1 powerless 2 (of males) incapable of sexual intercourse > **im'po•tence** *noun*
im•pound [im-POWND] *verb transitive* 1 take legal possession of and, often, place in a pound (automobile, animal, etc.) 2 confiscate
im•pov•er•ish [im-POV-ər-ish] *verb transitive* make poor or weak > **im•pov'er•ish•ment** *noun*
im•prac'ti•ca•ble *adjective* incapable of being put into practice
im•prac'ti•cal *adjective* not sensible
im•pre•ca•tion [im-pri-KAY-shən] *noun* 1 invoking of evil 2 curse > **im'pre•cate** *verb transitive* **-cat•ed, -cat•ing**
im•preg•na•ble [im-PREG-nə-bəl] *adjective* 1 proof against attack 2 unassailable 3 unable to be broken into > **im•preg•na•bil'i•ty** *noun*
im•preg•nate [im-PREG-nayt] *verb transitive* **-nat•ed, -nat•ing** 1 saturate, infuse 2 make pregnant > **im•preg•na'tion** *noun*
im•pre•sa•ri•o [im-prə-SAHR-ee-oh] *noun, plural* **-ri•os** 1 organizer of public entertainment 2 manager of opera, ballet, etc.
im•press'[1] *verb transitive* 1 affect deeply, usu. favorably 2 imprint, stamp 3 fix ▷ *noun* [IM-pres] 4 act of impressing 5 mark impressed > **im•pres'sion** *noun* 1 effect produced, esp. on mind 2 notion, belief 3 imprint 4 a printing 5 total of copies printed at once 6 printed copy > **im•pres'sion•a•ble** *adjective* susceptible to external influences > **im•pres'sion•ism** *noun* art style that renders general effect without detail > **im•pres'sion•ist** *noun* > **im•pres'sive** *adjective* making deep impression
im•press'[2] *verb transitive* press into service
im•pri•ma•tur [im-pri-MAH-tər] *noun* 1 license to print book, etc. 2 sanction, approval
im'print *noun* 1 mark made by pressure 2 characteristic mark ▷ *verb transitive* [im-PRINT] 3 produce mark 4 stamp 5 fix in mind
im•pris•on [im-PRIZ-ən] *verb transitive* put in prison > **im•pris'on•ment** *noun*
im•prob'a•ble *adjective* not likely to be true or to happen > **im•prob•a•bil'i•ty** *noun, plural* **-ties**
im•promp•tu [im-PROMP-too] *adverb, adjective* 1

DICTIONARY | THESAURUS

levying
2 INTRUSION, liberty, presumption
impossibility *noun* HOPELESSNESS, impracticability, inability
impossible *adjective* 1 UNATTAINABLE, impracticable, inconceivable, out of the question, unachievable, unobtainable, unthinkable
2 ABSURD, ludicrous, outrageous, preposterous, unreasonable
impostor *noun* IMPERSONATOR, charlatan, deceiver, fake, fraud, phoney *or* phony (*informal*), pretender, sham, trickster
impotence *noun* POWERLESSNESS, feebleness, frailty, helplessness, inability, incapacity, incompetence, ineffectiveness, paralysis, uselessness, weakness
impotent *adjective* POWERLESS, feeble, frail, helpless, incapable, incapacitated, incompetent, ineffective, paralyzed, weak
impoverish *verb* 1 BANKRUPT, beggar, break, ruin
2 DIMINISH, deplete, drain, exhaust, reduce, sap, use up, wear out
impoverished *adjective* POOR, bankrupt, destitute, impecunious, needy, penurious, poverty-stricken
impracticable *adjective* UNFEASIBLE, impossible, out of the question, unachievable, unattainable, unworkable
impractical *adjective* 1 UNWORKABLE, impossible, impracticable, inoperable, nonviable, unrealistic, wild
2 IDEALISTIC, romantic, starry-eyed, unrealistic
imprecise *adjective* INDEFINITE, equivocal, hazy, ill-defined, indeterminate, inexact, inexplicit, loose, rough, vague, woolly
impregnable *adjective* INVULNERABLE, impenetrable, indestructible, invincible, secure, unassailable, unbeatable, unconquerable
impregnate *verb* 1 SATURATE, infuse, permeate, soak, steep, suffuse
2 FERTILIZE, inseminate, make pregnant
impress' *verb* 1 EXCITE, affect, inspire, make an impression, move, stir, strike, touch
2 STRESS, bring home to, emphasize, fix, inculcate, instill into
3 IMPRINT, emboss, engrave, indent, mark, print, stamp
impression *noun* 1 EFFECT, feeling, impact, influence, reaction
2 IDEA, belief, conviction, feeling, hunch, notion, sense, suspicion
3 MARK, dent, hollow, imprint, indentation, outline, stamp
4 IMITATION, impersonation, parody
impressionable *adjective* SUGGESTIBLE, gullible, ingenuous, open, receptive, responsive, sensitive, susceptible, vulnerable
impressive *adjective* GRAND, awesome, cool (*informal*), dramatic, exciting, moving, phat (*slang*), powerful, stirring, striking
imprint *noun* 1 MARK, impression, indentation, sign, stamp
▷ *verb* 2 FIX, engrave, etch, impress, print, stamp
imprison *verb* JAIL, confine, detain, incarcerate, intern, lock up, put away, send down (*informal*)
imprisoned *adjective* JAILED, behind bars, captive, confined, incarcerated, in jail, inside (*slang*), locked up, under lock and key
imprisonment *noun* CUSTODY, confinement, detention, incarceration
improbability *noun* DOUBT, dubiety, uncertainty, unlikelihood
improbable *adjective* DOUBTFUL, dubious, fanciful, far-fetched, implausible, questionable, unconvincing, unlikely, weak
impromptu *adjective* UNPREPARED, ad-lib, extemporaneous, improvised, offhand, off the cuff (*informal*), spontaneous, unrehearsed, unscripted

on the spur of the moment 2 unrehearsed
im•prop'er *adjective* 1 indecent 2 incorrect or irregular > **improper fraction** fraction in which the numerator is larger than the denominator, as in 5/3
im•pro•pri'e•ty *noun, plural* **-ties** unsuitable or slightly improper behavior
im•prove [im-PROOV] *verb* **-proved, -prov•ing** make or become better in quality, standard, value, etc. > **im•prove'ment** *noun*
im•prov•i•dent [im-PROV-i-dənt] *adjective* 1 thriftless 2 negligent 3 imprudent > **im•prov'i•dence** *noun*
im•pro•vise [IM-prə-vīz] *verb* **-vised, -vis•ing** 1 make use of materials at hand 2 compose, utter without preparation > **im•prov•i•sa'tion** [-ZAY-shən] *noun*
im•pu•dent [IM-pyə-dənt] *adjective* disrespectful, impertinent > **im'pu•dence** *noun*
im•pugn [im-PYOON] *verb transitive* **-pugned, -pugn•ing** call in question, challenge as false
im•pulse [IM-puls] *noun* 1 sudden inclination to act 2 sudden application of force 3 motion caused by it 4 stimulation of nerve moving muscle > **im•pul'sion** *noun* impulse, usu. in its first sense > **im•pul'sive** *adjective* given to acting without reflection, rash
im•pu•ni•ty [im-PYOO-ni-tee] *noun* freedom, exemption from injurious consequences or punishment
im•pure' *adjective* 1 having dirty or unwanted substances mixed in 2 immoral, obscene > **im•pu'ri•ty** *noun, plural* **-ties**
im•pute [im-PYOOT] *verb transitive* **-put•ed, -put•ing** ascribe, attribute to > **im•pu•ta'tion** *noun* 1 that which is imputed as a charge or fault 2 reproach, censure
in *preposition* 1 expresses inclusion within limits of space, time, circumstance, sphere, etc. ▷ *adverb* 2 in or into some state, place, etc. 3 (*informal*) in vogue, etc. ▷ *adjective* 4 (*informal*) fashionable
In *chem.* indium
in-¹, il-, im-, ir- *prefix* 1 not, non: *incredible* 2 lack of: *inexperience*
in-², il-, im-, ir- *prefix* in, into, towards, within, on: *infiltrate*
in•a•bil'i•ty *noun* lack of means or skill to do something
in•ac'cu•rate *adjective* not correct > **in•ac'cu•ra•cy** *noun, plural* **-cies**
in•ad'e•quate *adjective* 1 not enough 2 not good enough > **in•ad'e•qua•cy** *noun, plural* **-cies**
in•ad•vert•ent [in-əd-VUR-tnt] *adjective* 1 not attentive 2 negligent 3 unintentional > **in•ad•vert'ence** *noun*
in•ane [i-NAYN] *adjective* foolish, silly, vacant > **in•a•ni'tion** [-NISH-ən] *noun* 1 exhaustion 2

improper *adjective* 1 INDECENT, risqué, smutty, suggestive, unbecoming, unseemly, untoward, vulgar
2 UNWARRANTED, inappropriate, out of place, uncalled-for, unfit, unsuitable
impropriety *noun* INDECENCY, bad taste, incongruity, vulgarity
improve *verb* 1 ENHANCE, advance, better, correct, help, rectify, touch up, upgrade
2 PROGRESS, develop, make strides, pick up, rally, rise
improvement *noun* 1 ENHANCEMENT, advancement, betterment
2 PROGRESS, development, rally, recovery
improvident *adjective* IMPRUDENT, careless, negligent, prodigal, profligate, reckless, short-sighted, spendthrift, thoughtless, wasteful
improvisation *noun* 1 SPONTANEITY, ad-libbing, extemporizing, invention
2 MAKESHIFT, ad-lib, expedient
improvise *verb* 1 EXTEMPORIZE, ad-lib, invent, play it by ear (*informal*), speak off the cuff (*informal*), wing it (*informal*)
2 CONCOCT, contrive, devise, throw together
imprudent *adjective* UNWISE, careless, foolhardy, ill-advised, ill-considered, ill-judged, injudicious, irresponsible, rash, reckless
impudence *noun* BOLDNESS, audacity, brazenness, cheek (*informal*), effrontery, impertinence, insolence, nerve (*informal*), presumption, shamelessness
impudent *adjective* BOLD, audacious, brazen, cheeky (*informal*), impertinent, insolent, pert, presumptuous, rude, shameless
impulse *noun* URGE, caprice, feeling, inclination, notion, whim, wish
impulsive *adjective* INSTINCTIVE, devil-may-care, hasty, impetuous, intuitive, passionate, precipitate, rash, spontaneous
impunity *noun* SECURITY, dispensation, exemption, freedom, immunity, liberty, license, permission
impure *adjective* 1 UNREFINED, adulterated, debased, mixed
2 CONTAMINATED, defiled, dirty, infected, polluted, tainted
3 IMMORAL, corrupt, indecent, lascivious, lewd, licentious, obscene, unchaste
impurity *noun* CONTAMINATION, defilement, dirtiness, infection, pollution, taint
imputation *noun* BLAME, accusation, aspersion, censure, insinuation, reproach, slander, slur
inability *noun* INCAPABILITY, disability, disqualification, impotence, inadequacy, incapacity, incompetence, ineptitude, powerlessness
inaccessible *adjective* OUT OF REACH, impassable, out of the way, remote, unapproachable, unattainable, unreachable
inaccuracy *noun* ERROR, defect, erratum, fault, lapse, mistake
inaccurate *adjective* INCORRECT, defective, erroneous, faulty, imprecise, mistaken, out, unreliable, unsound, wrong
inactive *adjective* UNUSED, dormant, idle, inoperative, unemployed, unoccupied
inactivity *noun* IMMOBILITY, dormancy, hibernation, inaction, passivity, unemployment
inadequacy *noun* 1 SHORTAGE, dearth, insufficiency, meagerness, paucity, poverty, scantiness
2 INCOMPETENCE, deficiency, inability, incapacity, ineffectiveness
3 SHORTCOMING, defect, failing, imperfection, weakness
inadequate *adjective* 1 INSUFFICIENT, meager, scant, sketchy, sparse
2 INCOMPETENT, deficient, faulty, found

silliness > **in•an'i•ty** *noun*
in•an•i•mate [in-AN-ə-mit] *adjective* 1 lacking qualities of living beings 2 appearing dead 3 lacking vitality
in•ap•pro'pri•ate *adjective* not suitable
in•as•much as [in-əz-MUCH] *conjunction* because or in so far as
in•au•gu•rate [in-AW-gyə-rayt] *verb transitive* **-rat•ed, -rat•ing** 1 begin, initiate the use of, esp. with ceremony 2 admit to office > **in•au'gu•ral** *adjective* > **in•au•gu•ra'tion** *noun* 1 act of inaugurating 2 ceremony to celebrate the initiation or admittance of
in•aus•pi•cious [in-aw-SPISH-əs] *adjective* 1 not auspicious 2 unlucky 3 unfavorable > **in•aus•pi'cious•ly** *adverb*
in•board [IN-bord] *adjective* inside hull or bulwarks
in'born *adjective* 1 existing from birth 2 inherent
in'breed *verb transitive* **-bred, -breed•ing** breed from union of closely related individuals > **in'bred** *adjective* 1 produced as result of inbreeding 2 inborn, ingrained
in•cal•cu•la•ble [in-KAL-kyə-lə-bəl] *adjective* 1 beyond calculation 2 very great
in cam•er•a [KAM-ə-rə] in secret or private session
in•can•des•cent [in-kən-DES-ənt] *adjective* 1 glowing with heat, shining 2 of artificial light, produced by glowing filament > **in•can•des'cence** *noun*
in•can•ta•tion [in-kan-TAY-shən] *noun* magic spell or formula, charm
in•ca'pa•ble *adjective* 1 (foll by *of*) unable (to do something) 2 incompetent
in•ca•pac•i•tate [in-kə-PAS-i-tayt] *verb transitive* **-tat•ed, -tat•ing** 1 disable 2 make unfit 3 disqualify > **in•ca•pac'i•ty** *noun*
in•car•cer•ate [in-KAHR-sə-rayt] *verb transitive* **-at•ed, -at•ing** imprison > **in•car•cer•a'tion** *noun*
in•car•nate [in-KAR-nayt] *verb transitive* **-nat•ed, -nat•ing** 1 embody in flesh, esp. in human form ▷ *adjective* [-nit] 2 embodied in flesh, in human form 3 typified > **in•car•na'tion** *noun*
in•cen•di•ar•y [in-SEN-dee-er-ee] *adjective* 1 of malicious setting on fire of property 2 creating strife, violence, etc. 3 designed to cause fires ▷ *noun* 4 arsonist 5 agitator 6 bomb, etc. filled with inflammatory substance
in•cense[1] [in-SENS] *verb transitive* **-censed, -cens•ing** enrage
in•cense[2] [IN-sens] *noun* 1 gum, spice giving perfume when burned 2 its smoke ▷ *verb transitive* **-censed, -cens•ing** 3 burn incense to 4

---

wanting, incapable, lousy (*slang*), not up to scratch (*informal*), unqualified
inadmissible *adjective* UNACCEPTABLE, inappropriate, irrelevant, unallowable
inadvertently *adverb* UNINTENTIONALLY, accidentally, by accident, by mistake, involuntarily, mistakenly, unwittingly
inadvisable *adjective* UNWISE, ill-advised, impolitic, imprudent, inexpedient, injudicious
inane *adjective* SENSELESS, empty, fatuous, frivolous, futile, idiotic, mindless, silly, stupid, vacuous
inanimate *adjective* LIFELESS, cold, dead, defunct, extinct, inert
inapplicable *adjective* IRRELEVANT, inappropriate, unsuitable
inappropriate *adjective* UNSUITABLE, improper, incongruous, out of place, unbecoming, unbefitting, unfitting, unseemly, untimely
inarticulate *adjective* FALTERING, halting, hesitant, poorly spoken
inattention *noun* NEGLECT, absent-mindedness, carelessness, daydreaming, inattentiveness, preoccupation, thoughtlessness
inattentive *adjective* PREOCCUPIED, careless, distracted, dreamy, negligent, unobservant, vague
inaudible *adjective* INDISTINCT, low, mumbling, out of earshot, stifled, unheard
inaugural *adjective* FIRST, initial, introductory, maiden, opening
inaugurate *verb* 1 LAUNCH, begin, commence, get under way, initiate, institute, introduce, set in motion
2 INVEST, induct, install
inauguration *noun* 1 LAUNCH, initiation, institution, opening, setting up
2 INVESTITURE, induction, installation
inauspicious *adjective* UNPROMISING, bad, discouraging, ill-omened, ominous, unfavorable, unfortunate, unlucky, unpropitious
inborn *adjective* NATURAL, congenital, hereditary, inbred, ingrained, inherent, innate, instinctive, intuitive, native
inbred *adjective* INNATE, constitutional, deep-seated, ingrained, inherent, native, natural
incalculable *adjective* COUNTLESS, boundless, infinite, innumerable, limitless, numberless, untold, vast
incantation *noun* CHANT, charm, formula, invocation, spell
incapable *adjective* 1 INCOMPETENT, feeble, inadequate, ineffective, inept, inexpert, insufficient, lousy (*slang*), unfit, unqualified, weak
2 UNABLE, helpless, impotent, powerless
incapacitate *verb* DISABLE, cripple, immobilize, lay up (*informal*), paralyze, put out of action (*informal*)
incapacitated *adjective* INDISPOSED, hors de combat (*French*), immobilized, laid up (*informal*), out of action (*informal*), unfit
incapacity *noun* INABILITY, impotence, inadequacy, incapability, incompetency, ineffectiveness, powerlessness, unfitness, weakness
incarcerate *verb* IMPRISON, confine, detain, impound, intern, jail, lock up, throw in jail
incarceration *noun* IMPRISONMENT, captivity, confinement, detention, internment
incarnate *adjective* PERSONIFIED, embodied, typified
incarnation *noun* EMBODIMENT, epitome, manifestation, personification, type
incense[1] *verb* ANGER, enrage, inflame, infuriate, irritate, madden, make one's hackles rise, rile (*informal*)
incensed *adjective* ANGRY, enraged, fuming, furious, indignant, infuriated, irate, maddened, steamed up (*slang*), up in arms

perfume with it
in•cen•tive [in-SEN-tiv] *noun* 1 something that arouses to effort or action 2 stimulus
in•cep•tion [in-SEP-shən] *noun* beginning > **in•cep'tive** [-tiv] *adjective*
in•ces•sant [in-SES-ənt] *adjective* unceasing
in•cest [IN-sest] *noun* sexual intercourse between two people too closely related to marry > **in•ces'tu•ous** [-SES-choo-əs] *adjective*
inch *noun* 1 one twelfth of foot, or 2.54 centimeters ▷ *verb* 2 move very slowly
in•cho•ate [in-KOH-it] *adjective* 1 just begun 2 undeveloped
in•ci•dent [IN-si-dənt] *noun* 1 event, occurrence ▷ *adjective* 2 naturally attaching to 3 striking, falling (upon) > **in'ci•dence** *noun* 1 degree, extent or frequency of occurrence 2 a falling on, or affecting > **in•ci•den'tal** *adjective* occurring as a minor part or an inevitable accompaniment or by chance > **in•ci•den'tal•ly** *adverb* 1 by chance 2 by the way > **in•ci•den'tals** *plural noun* accompanying items
in•cin•er•ate [in-SIN-ə-rayt] *verb transitive* **-at•ed, -at•ing** 1 burn up completely 2 reduce to ashes > **in•cin'er•a•tor** *noun*
in•cip•i•ent [in-SIP-ee-ənt] *adjective* beginning
in•cise [in-SĪZ] *verb transitive* **-cised, -cis•ing** 1 cut into 2 engrave > **in•ci'sion** [in-SIZH-ən] *noun* > **in•ci'sive** *adjective* 1 keen or biting (of remark, etc.) 2 sharp > **in•ci'sor** *noun* cutting tooth
in•cite [in-SĪT] *verb transitive* **-cit•ed, -cit•ing** urge, stir up > **in•cite'ment** *noun*
in•clem•ent [in-KLEM-ənt] *adjective* of weather, stormy, severe, cold > **in•clem'en•cy** *noun*
in•cline [in-KLĪN] *verb* **-clined, -clin•ing** 1 lean, slope 2 (cause to) be disposed 3 bend or lower (the head, etc.) ▷ *noun* [IN-klīn] 4 slope > **in•cli•na'tion** *noun* 1 liking, tendency or preference 2 sloping surface 3 degree of deviation
in•clude [in-KLOOD] *verb transitive* **-clud•ed, -clud•ing** 1 have as (part of) contents 2 comprise 3 add in 4 take in > **in•clu'sion** [-*zhən*] *noun* > **in•clu'sive** *adjective* including (everything)
in•cog•ni•to [in-kog-NEE-toh] *adverb, adjective* 1 under assumed identity ▷ *noun, plural* **-tos** 2 assumed identity
in•co•her•ent [in-koh-HEER-ənt] *adjective* 1 lacking clarity, disorganized 2 inarticulate > **in•co•her'ence** *noun*
in•come [IN-kum] *noun* 1 amount of money, esp. annual, from salary, investments, etc. 2 receipts > **income tax** personal, corporate tax levied on annual income
in•com•ing [IN-kum-ing] *adjective* 1 coming in 2 about to come into office 3 next
in•com•mode [in-kə-MOHD] *verb transitive* **-mod•ed, -mod•ing** 1 trouble, inconvenience 2 disturb > **in•com•mo'di•ous** *adjective* 1 cramped

incentive *noun* ENCOURAGEMENT, bait, carrot (*informal*), enticement, inducement, lure, motivation, spur, stimulus
inception *noun* BEGINNING, birth, commencement, dawn, initiation, origin, outset, start
incessant *adjective* ENDLESS, ceaseless, constant, continual, eternal, interminable, never-ending, nonstop, perpetual, twenty-four-seven (*slang*), unceasing, unending
incessantly *adverb* ENDLESSLY, ceaselessly, constantly, continually, eternally, interminably, nonstop, perpetually, persistently, twenty-four-seven (*slang*)
incident *noun* 1 HAPPENING, adventure, episode, event, fact, matter, occasion, occurrence 2 DISTURBANCE, clash, commotion, confrontation, contretemps, scene
incidental *adjective* SECONDARY, ancillary, minor, nonessential, occasional, subordinate, subsidiary
incidentally *adverb* PARENTHETICALLY, by the bye, by the way, in passing
incinerate *verb* BURN UP, carbonize, char, cremate, reduce to ashes
incipient *adjective* BEGINNING, commencing, developing, embryonic, inchoate, nascent, starting
incision *noun* CUT, gash, notch, opening, slash, slit
incisive *adjective* PENETRATING, acute, keen, perspicacious, piercing, trenchant
incite *verb* PROVOKE, encourage, foment, inflame, instigate, spur, stimulate, stir up, urge, whip up
incitement *noun* PROVOCATION, agitation, encouragement, impetus, instigation, prompting, spur, stimulus
incivility *noun* RUDENESS, bad manners, boorishness, discourteousness, discourtesy, disrespect, ill-breeding, impoliteness
inclement *adjective* STORMY, foul, harsh, intemperate, rough, severe, tempestuous
inclination *noun* 1 TENDENCY, disposition, liking, partiality, penchant, predilection, predisposition, proclivity, proneness, propensity 2 SLOPE, angle, gradient, incline, pitch, slant, tilt
incline *verb* 1 PREDISPOSE, influence, persuade, prejudice, sway 2 SLOPE, lean, slant, tilt, tip, veer ▷ *noun* 3 SLOPE, ascent, descent, dip, grade, gradient, rise
inclined *adjective* DISPOSED, apt, given, liable, likely, minded, predisposed, prone, willing
include *verb* 1 CONTAIN, comprise, cover, embrace, encompass, incorporate, involve, subsume, take in 2 INTRODUCE, add, enter, insert
inclusion *noun* ADDITION, incorporation, insertion
inclusive *adjective* COMPREHENSIVE, across-the-board, all-embracing, blanket, general, global, sweeping, umbrella
incognito *adjective* IN DISGUISE, disguised, under an assumed name, unknown, unrecognized
incoherence *noun* UNINTELLIGIBILITY, disjointedness, inarticulateness
incoherent *adjective* UNINTELLIGIBLE, confused, disjointed, disordered, inarticulate, inconsistent, jumbled, muddled, rambling, stammering, stuttering
income *noun* REVENUE, earnings, pay, proceeds, profits, receipts, salary, takings, wages
incoming *adjective* ARRIVING, approaching, entering, homeward, landing, new, returning

2 inconvenient
in•com•mu•ni•ca•do [in-kə-MYOO-ni-kah-doh] *adjective, adverb* deprived (by force or by choice) of communication with others
in•com'pa•ra•ble *adjective* beyond comparison, unequalled
in•com•pat'i•ble *adjective* inconsistent or conflicting > **in•com•pat•i•bil'i•ty** *noun*
in•com'pe•tent *adjective* not having the necessary ability or skill to do something > **in•com'pe•tence** *noun*
in•con•gru•ous [in-KONG-groo-əs] *adjective* 1 not appropriate 2 inconsistent, absurd > **in•con•gru'i•ty** *noun*
in•con•se•quen•tial [in-kon-si-KWEN-shəl] *adjective* 1 illogical 2 irrelevant, trivial
in•con•sid'er•ate *adjective* not considering other people
in•con•sist'ent *adjective* 1 changeable in behavior or mood 2 containing contradictory elements 3 not in accordance > **in•con•sist'en•cy** *noun, plural* **-cies**
in•con•tro•vert•i•ble [in-kon-trə-VUR-tə-bəl] *adjective* 1 undeniable 2 indisputable
in•con•ven'ience *noun* 1 trouble or difficulty ▷ *verb* 2 cause trouble or difficulty to > **in•con•ven'ient** *adjective*
in•cor•po•rate [in-KOR-pə-rayt] *verb transitive* **-rat•ed, -rat•ing** 1 include 2 unite into one body 3 form into corporation
in•cor•ri•gi•ble [in-KOR-i-jə-bəl] *adjective* 1 beyond correction or reform 2 firmly rooted
in•crease [in-KREES] *verb* **-creased, -creas•ing** 1 make or become greater in size, number, etc. ▷ *noun* [IN-krees] 2 growth, enlargement, profit > **in•creas'ing•ly** *adverb* more and more
in•cred•i•ble [in-KRED-ə-bəl] *adjective* 1 unbelievable 2 (*informal*) marvelous, amazing
in•cred•u•lous [in-KREJ-ə-ləs] *adjective* unbelieving > **in•cre•du'li•ty** [-krə-DOO-lə-tee] *noun*

---

incomparable *adjective* UNEQUALED, beyond compare, inimitable, matchless, peerless, superlative, supreme, transcendent, unmatched, unparalleled, unrivaled
incompatible *adjective* INCONSISTENT, conflicting, contradictory, incongruous, mismatched, unsuited
incompetence *noun* INEPTITUDE, inability, inadequacy, incapability, incapacity, ineffectiveness, unfitness, uselessness
incompetent *adjective* INEPT, bungling, floundering, incapable, ineffectual, inexpert, unfit, useless
incomplete *adjective* UNFINISHED, deficient, fragmentary, imperfect, partial, wanting
incomprehensible *adjective* UNINTELLIGIBLE, baffling, beyond one's grasp, impenetrable, obscure, opaque, perplexing, puzzling, unfathomable
inconceivable *adjective* UNIMAGINABLE, beyond belief, incomprehensible, incredible, mind-boggling (*informal*), out of the question, unbelievable, unheard-of, unthinkable
inconclusive *adjective* INDECISIVE, ambiguous, indeterminate, open, unconvincing, undecided, up in the air (*informal*), vague
incongruity *noun* INAPPROPRIATENESS, conflict, discrepancy, disparity, incompatibility, inconsistency, unsuitability
incongruous *adjective* INAPPROPRIATE, discordant, improper, incompatible, out of keeping, out of place, unbecoming, unsuitable
inconsiderable *adjective* INSIGNIFICANT, inconsequential, minor, negligible, slight, small, trifling, trivial, unimportant
inconsiderate *adjective* SELFISH, indelicate, insensitive, rude, tactless, thoughtless, unkind, unthinking
inconsistency *noun* 1 INCOMPATIBILITY, disagreement, discrepancy, disparity, divergence, incongruity, variance 2 UNRELIABILITY, fickleness, instability, unpredictability, unsteadiness
inconsistent *adjective* 1 INCOMPATIBLE, at odds, conflicting, contradictory, discordant, incongruous, irreconcilable, out of step 2 CHANGEABLE, capricious, erratic, fickle, unpredictable, unstable, unsteady, variable
inconsolable *adjective* HEARTBROKEN, brokenhearted, desolate, despairing
inconspicuous *adjective* UNOBTRUSIVE, camouflaged, hidden, insignificant, ordinary, plain, unassuming, unnoticeable, unostentatious
incontrovertible *adjective* INDISPUTABLE, certain, established, incontestable, indubitable, irrefutable, positive, sure, undeniable, unquestionable
inconvenience *noun* 1 TROUBLE, awkwardness, bother, difficulty, disadvantage, disruption, disturbance, fuss, hindrance, nuisance ▷ *verb* 2 TROUBLE, bother, discommode, disrupt, disturb, put out, upset
inconvenient *adjective* TROUBLESOME, awkward, bothersome, disadvantageous, disturbing, inopportune, unsuitable, untimely
incorporate *verb* INCLUDE, absorb, assimilate, blend, combine, integrate, merge, subsume
incorrect *adjective* FALSE, erroneous, faulty, flawed, inaccurate, mistaken, untrue, wrong
incorrigible *adjective* INCURABLE, hardened, hopeless, intractable, inveterate, irredeemable, unreformed
incorruptible *adjective* 1 HONEST, above suspicion, straight, trustworthy, upright 2 IMPERISHABLE, everlasting, undecaying
increase *verb* 1 GROW, advance, boost, develop, enlarge, escalate, expand, extend, multiply, raise, spread, swell ▷ *noun* 2 GROWTH, development, enlargement, escalation, expansion, extension, gain, increment, rise, upturn
increasingly *adverb* PROGRESSIVELY, more and more
incredible *adjective* 1 IMPLAUSIBLE, beyond belief, far-fetched, improbable, inconceivable, preposterous, unbelievable, unimaginable, unthinkable 2 (*informal*) AMAZING, astonishing, astounding, extraordinary, prodigious, sensational (*informal*), wonderful
incredulity *noun* DISBELIEF, distrust, doubt, skepticism
incredulous *adjective* DISBELIEVING, distrustful,

in•cre•ment [IN-krə-mənt] *noun* increase, esp. one of a series > **in•cre•men'tal** *adjective*
in•crim•i•nate [in-KRIM-ə-nayt] *verb transitive* **-nat•ed, -nat•ing** 1 imply guilt of 2 accuse of crime > **in•crim'i•na•to•ry** *adjective*
in•crust [in-KRUST] *verb* cover with or form a crust or hard covering
in•cu•bate [IN-kyə-bayt] *verb transitive* **-bat•ed, -bat•ing** 1 provide (eggs, embryos, bacteria, etc.) with heat or other favorable condition for development ▷ *verb intransitive* 2 develop in this way > **in•cu•ba'tion** *noun* > **in'cu•ba•tor** *noun* apparatus for artificially hatching eggs, for rearing premature babies
in•cu•bus [IN-kyə-bəs] *noun, plural* **-bi** [-bī] 1 nightmare or obsession 2 orig. demon believed to afflict sleeping person
in•cul•cate [in-KUL-kayt] *verb transitive* **-cat•ed, -cat•ing** impress on the mind > **in•cul•ca'tion** *noun*
in•cum•bent [in-KUM-bənt] *adjective* 1 lying, resting (on) ▷ *noun* 2 holder of office, esp. elective office in government > **in•cum'ben•cy** *noun* 1 obligation 2 office or tenure of incumbent **it is incumbent on** it is the duty of
in•cur [in-KUR] *verb transitive* **-curred, -cur•ring** fall into, bring upon oneself > **in•cur'sion** [-*zhən*] *noun* invasion, penetration
in•cur'a•ble *adjective* 1 not able to be cured 2 not willing or able to change > **in•cur'a•bly** *adverb*
in•debt•ed [in-DET-id] *adjective* 1 owing gratitude for help, favors, etc. 2 owing money > **in•debt'ed•ness** *noun*
in•de'cent *adjective* 1 morally or sexually offensive 2 unsuitable or unseemly > **in•de'cen•cy** *noun*
in•de•ci'sive *adjective* unable to make decisions > **in•de•cis'ion** *noun*
in•deed' *adverb* 1 in truth 2 really 3 in fact 4 certainly ▷ *interjection* 5 denoting surprise, doubt, etc.
in•de•fat•i•ga•ble [in-di-FAT-i-gə-bəl] *adjective* untiring > **in•de•fat'i•ga•bly** *adverb*
in•de•fen•si•ble [in-di-FEN-sə-bəl] *adjective* not justifiable or defensible
in•def'i•nite *adjective* 1 without exact limits 2 vague, unclear > **indefinite article** *grammar* the word *a* or *an*
in•del•i•ble [in-DEL-ə-bəl] *adjective* 1 that cannot be blotted out, effaced or erased 2 producing such a mark > **in•del'i•bly** *adverb*
in•del•i•cate [in-DEL-i-kit] *adjective* coarse, embarrassing, tasteless
in•dem•ni•ty [in-DEM-ni-tee] *noun, plural* **-ties** 1 compensation 2 security against loss > **in•dem•ni•fi•ca'tion** *noun* > **in•dem'ni•fy** [-fī] *verb transitive* **-fied, -fy•ing** 1 give indemnity to 2 compensate
in•dent' *verb* 1 set in (from margin, etc.) 2 make notches in ▷ *noun* [IN-dent] 3 indentation 4 notch > **in•den•ta'tion** *noun* > **in•den'ture** *noun* 1 contract, esp. one binding apprentice to master 2 indentation ▷ *verb transitive* **-tured, -tur•ing** 3 bind by indenture
in•de•pend•ent [in-di-PEN-dənt] *adjective* 1 not subject to others 2 self-reliant 3 free 4 valid in itself 5 politically of no party > **in•de•pend'ence** *noun* 1 being independent 2 self-reliance 3 self-support
in•de•scrib•a•ble [in-di-SKRĪ-bə-bəl] *adjective* 1 beyond description 2 too intense, etc. for words

doubtful, dubious, skeptical, suspicious, unbelieving, unconvinced
increment *noun* INCREASE, accrual, addition, advancement, augmentation, enlargement, gain, step up, supplement
incriminate *verb* IMPLICATE, accuse, blame, charge, impeach, inculpate, involve
incumbent *adjective* OBLIGATORY, binding, compulsory, mandatory, necessary
incur *verb* EARN, arouse, bring *or* bring upon oneself, draw, expose oneself to, gain, meet with, provoke
incurable *adjective* FATAL, inoperable, irremediable, terminal
indebted *adjective* GRATEFUL, beholden, in debt, obligated, obliged, under an obligation
indecency *noun* OBSCENITY, immodesty, impropriety, impurity, indelicacy, lewdness, licentiousness, pornography, vulgarity
indecent *adjective* 1 LEWD, crude, dirty, filthy, immodest, improper, impure, licentious, pornographic, salacious, scuzzy (*slang*), X-rated 2 UNBECOMING, in bad taste, indecorous, unseemly, vulgar
indecipherable *adjective* ILLEGIBLE, indistinguishable, unintelligible, unreadable
indecision *noun* HESITATION, dithering, doubt, indecisiveness, uncertainty, vacillation, wavering
indecisive *adjective* HESITATING, dithering, faltering, in two minds (*informal*), tentative, uncertain, undecided, vacillating, wavering
indeed *adverb* REALLY, actually, certainly, in truth, truly, undoubtedly
indefensible *adjective* UNFORGIVABLE, inexcusable, unjustifiable, unpardonable, untenable, unwarrantable, wrong
indefinable *adjective* INEXPRESSIBLE, impalpable, indescribable
indefinite *adjective* UNCLEAR, doubtful, equivocal, ill-defined, imprecise, indeterminate, inexact, uncertain, unfixed, vague
indefinitely *adverb* ENDLESSLY, ad infinitum, continually, forever
indelible *adjective* PERMANENT, enduring, indestructible, ineradicable, ingrained, lasting
indelicate *adjective* OFFENSIVE, coarse, crude, embarrassing, immodest, off-color, risqué, rude, suggestive, tasteless, vulgar
indemnify *verb* 1 INSURE, guarantee, protect, secure, underwrite
2 COMPENSATE, reimburse, remunerate, repair, repay
indemnity *noun* 1 INSURANCE, guarantee, protection, security
2 COMPENSATION, redress, reimbursement, remuneration, reparation, restitution
independence *noun* FREEDOM, autonomy, liberty, self-reliance, self-rule, self-sufficiency, sovereignty
independent *adjective* 1 FREE, liberated, separate, unconstrained, uncontrolled
2 SELF-GOVERNING, autonomous, nonaligned, self-determining, sovereign

> **in•de•scrib'a•bly** *adverb*
in•de•ter•mi•nate [in-di-TUR-mə-nit] *adjective* 1 uncertain 2 inconclusive 3 incalculable
in•dex [IN-deks] *noun, plural* **-dex•es, -di•ces** [-də-seez] 1 alphabetical list of references, usu. at end of book 2 pointer, indicator 3 *math.* exponent 4 *economics* quantity indicating relative level of wages, prices, etc. compared with date established as standard ▷ *verb transitive* 5 provide book with index 6 insert in index 7 adjust wages, prices, etc. to reflect change in some economic indicator
In•di•an [IN-dee-ən] *noun* 1 native of India 2 (*often offensive*) person descended from indigenous peoples of N America ▷ *adjective*
in•di•cate [IN-di-kayt] *verb transitive* **-cat•ed, -cat•ing** 1 point out 2 state briefly 3 signify > **in•di•ca'tion** *noun* 1 sign 2 token 3 explanation > **in•dic'a•tive** *adjective* 1 pointing to 2 *grammar* stating fact > **in'di•ca•tor** *noun* 1 one who, that which, indicates 2 on vehicle, light showing driver's intention to turn
in•dict [in-DĪT] *verb transitive* accuse, esp. by legal process > **in•dict'ment** [-mənt] *noun*
in•dif•fer•ent [in-DIF-ər-ənt] *adjective* 1 uninterested 2 unimportant 3 neither good nor bad 4 inferior 5 neutral > **in•dif'fer•ence** *noun*
in•dig•e•nous [in-DIJ-ə-nəs] *adjective* born in or natural to a country
in•di•gent [IN-di-jənt] *adjective* poor, needy > **in'di•gence** *noun* poverty
in•di•ges•tion [in-di-JES-chən] *noun* (discomfort, pain caused by) difficulty in digesting food > **in•di•gest'i•ble** *adjective*
in•dig•nant [in-DIG-nənt] *adjective* 1 moved by anger and scorn 2 angered by sense of injury or injustice > **in•dig•na'tion** *noun* > **in•dig'ni•ty** *noun* humiliation, insult, slight
in•di•go [IN-də-goh] *noun, plural* **-gos** 1 blue dye obtained from plant 2 the plant ▷ *adjective* 3 deep blue
in•di•rect' *adjective* 1 done or caused by someone or something else 2 not by a straight route
in•dis•creet' *adjective* incautious or tactless in revealing secrets > **in•dis•cre'tion** *noun*
in•dis•crim•i•nate [in-di-SKRIM-ə-nit] *adjective* 1 lacking discrimination 2 jumbled
in•dis•pen•sa•ble [in-di-SPEN-sə-bəl] *adjective* 1 necessary 2 essential
in•dis•po•si•tion [in-dis-pə-ZISH-ən] *noun* 1 sickness 2 disinclination > **in•dis•posed'** [-POHZD] *adjective* 1 unwell, not fit 2 disinclined
in•dis•sol•u•ble [in-di-SOL-yə-bəl] *adjective* permanent
in•di•um [IN-dee-əm] *noun* soft silver-white metallic element
in•di•vid•u•al [in-də-VIJ-oo-əl] *adjective* 1 single 2 characteristic of single person or thing 3

DICTIONARY • THESAURUS

---

3 SELF-SUFFICIENT, liberated, self-contained, self-reliant, self-supporting
independently *adverb* SEPARATELY, alone, autonomously, by oneself, individually, on one's own, solo, unaided
indescribable *adjective* UNUTTERABLE, beyond description, beyond words, indefinable, inexpressible
indestructible *adjective* PERMANENT, enduring, everlasting, immortal, imperishable, incorruptible, indelible, indissoluble, lasting, unbreakable
indeterminate *adjective* UNCERTAIN, imprecise, indefinite, inexact, undefined, unfixed, unspecified, unstipulated, vague
indicate *verb* 1 SIGNIFY, betoken, denote, imply, manifest, point to, reveal, suggest
2 POINT OUT, designate, specify
3 SHOW, display, express, read, record, register
indication *noun* SIGN, clue, evidence, hint, inkling, intimation, manifestation, mark, suggestion, symptom
indicative *adjective* SUGGESTIVE, pointing to, significant, symptomatic
indicator *noun* SIGN, gauge, guide, mark, meter, pointer, signal, symbol
indict *verb* CHARGE, accuse, arraign, impeach, prosecute, summon
indictment *noun* CHARGE, accusation, allegation, impeachment, prosecution, summons
indifference *noun* DISREGARD, aloofness, apathy, coldness, coolness, detachment, inattention, negligence, nonchalance, unconcern
indifferent *adjective* 1 UNCONCERNED, aloof, callous, cold, cool, detached, impervious, inattentive, uninterested, unmoved, unsympathetic
2 MEDIOCRE, moderate, ordinary, passable, so-so (*informal*), undistinguished
indigestion *noun* HEARTBURN, dyspepsia, upset stomach
indignant *adjective* RESENTFUL, angry, disgruntled, exasperated, incensed, irate, peeved (*informal*), riled, scornful, ticked off (*informal*), up in arms (*informal*)
indignation *noun* RESENTMENT, anger, exasperation, pique, rage, scorn, umbrage
indignity *noun* HUMILIATION, affront, dishonor, disrespect, injury, insult, opprobrium, slight, snub
indirect *adjective* 1 CIRCUITOUS, long-drawn-out, meandering, oblique, rambling, roundabout, tortuous, wandering
2 INCIDENTAL, secondary, subsidiary, unintended
indiscreet *adjective* TACTLESS, impolitic, imprudent, incautious, injudicious, naive, rash, reckless, unwise
indiscretion *noun* MISTAKE, error, faux pas, folly, foolishness, gaffe, lapse, slip
indiscriminate *adjective* RANDOM, careless, desultory, general, uncritical, undiscriminating, unsystematic, wholesale
indispensable *adjective* ESSENTIAL, crucial, imperative, key, necessary, needed, requisite, vital
indisposed *adjective* ILL, ailing, sick, under the weather, unwell
indisposition *noun* ILLNESS, ailment, ill health, sickness
indisputable *adjective* UNDENIABLE, beyond doubt, certain, incontestable, incontrovertible, indubitable, irrefutable, unquestionable
indistinct *adjective* UNCLEAR, blurred, faint, fuzzy, hazy, ill-defined, indeterminate, shadowy, undefined, vague

distinctive ▷ *noun* **4** single person or thing > **in•di•vid'u•al•ism** *noun* principle of asserting one's independence > **in•di•vid'u•al•ist** *noun* > **in•di•vid•u•al'i•ty** *noun* **1** distinctive character **2** personality > **in•di•vid'u•al•ize** *verb transitive* **-ized, -iz•ing** make (or treat as) individual > **in•di•vid'u•al•ly** *adverb* singly

in•doc•tri•nate [in-DOK-trə-nayt] *verb transitive* **-nat•ed, -nat•ing** implant beliefs in the mind of

in•do•lent [IN-dl-ənt] *adjective* lazy > **in'do•lence** *noun*

in•dom•i•ta•ble [in-DOM-i-tə-bəl] *adjective* unyielding

in•door [IN-dor] *adjective* **1** within doors **2** under cover > **in•doors** [in-DORZ] *adverb*

in•du•bi•ta•ble [in-DOO-bi-tə-bəl] *adjective* **1** beyond doubt **2** certain > **in•du'bi•ta•bly** *adverb*

in•duce [in-DOOS] *verb transitive* **-duced, -duc•ing** **1** persuade **2** bring on **3** cause **4** produce by induction > **in•duce'ment** *noun* incentive, attraction

in•duct [in-DUKT] *verb transitive* install in office > **in•duc'tion** *noun* **1** an inducting **2** general inference from particular instances **3** production of electric or magnetic state in body by its being near (not touching) electrified or magnetized body > **in•duc'tance** [-təns] *noun* > **in•duc'tive** *adjective*

in•dulge [in-DULJ] *verb transitive* **-dulged, -dulg•ing** **1** gratify **2** give free course to **3** pamper **4** spoil > **in•dul'gence** [-jəns] *noun* **1** an indulging **2** extravagance **3** something granted as a favor or privilege **4** *r.c. church* remission of temporal punishment due after absolution > **in•dul'gent** [-jənt] *adjective*

in•dus•try [IN-də-stree] *noun* **1** manufacture, processing, etc. of goods **2** branch of this **3** diligence **4** habitual hard work > **in•dus'tri•al** *adjective* of industries, trades > **in•dus'tri•al•ize** *verb transitive* **-ized, -iz•ing** > **in•dus'tri•ous** [-tree-əs] *adjective* diligent

in•e•bri•ate [in-EE-bree-ayt] *verb transitive* **-at•ed, -at•ing** **1** make drunk **2** intoxicate ▷ *adjective* [-bree-it] **3** drunken ▷ *noun* **4** habitual drunkard > **in•e•bri•a'tion** *noun* drunkenness

in•ed•i•ble [in-ED-ə-bəl] *adjective* **1** not eatable **2** unfit for food

in•ed•u•ca•ble [in-EJ-uu-kə-bəl] *adjective* incapable of being educated, e.g. through mental disability

in•ef•fa•ble [in-EF-ə-bəl] *adjective* **1** too great or sacred for words **2** unutterable > **in•ef•fa•bil'i•ty** *noun*

in•ef•fi'cient *adjective* unable to perform a task or function to the best advantage > **in•ef•fi'cien•cy** *noun*

in•el•i•gi•ble [in-EL-i-jə-bəl] *adjective* not fit or qualified (for something) > **in•el•i•gi•bil'i•ty** *noun*

DICTIONARY • THESAURUS

individual *adjective* **1** PERSONAL, characteristic, distinctive, exclusive, idiosyncratic, own, particular, peculiar, singular, special, specific, unique
▷ *noun* **2** PERSON, being, character, creature, soul, unit

individualist *noun* MAVERICK, freethinker, independent, loner, lone wolf, nonconformist, original

individuality *noun* DISTINCTIVENESS, character, originality, personality, separateness, singularity, uniqueness

individually *adverb* SEPARATELY, apart, independently, one at a time, one by one, singly

indoctrinate *verb* TRAIN, brainwash, drill, ground, imbue, initiate, instruct, school, teach

indoctrination *noun* TRAINING, brainwashing, drilling, grounding, inculcation, instruction, schooling

indolent *adjective* LAZY, idle, inactive, inert, languid, lethargic, listless, slothful, sluggish, workshy

indomitable *adjective* INVINCIBLE, bold, resolute, staunch, steadfast, unbeatable, unconquerable, unflinching, unyielding

indubitable *adjective* CERTAIN, incontestable, incontrovertible, indisputable, irrefutable, obvious, sure, undeniable, unquestionable

induce *verb* **1** PERSUADE, convince, encourage, incite, influence, instigate, prevail upon, prompt, talk into
2 CAUSE, bring about, effect, engender, generate, give rise to, lead to, occasion, produce

inducement *noun* INCENTIVE, attraction, bait, carrot (*informal*), encouragement, incitement, lure, reward

indulge *verb* **1** GRATIFY, feed, give way to, pander to, satisfy, yield to
2 SPOIL, cosset, give in to, go along with, humor, pamper

indulgence *noun* **1** GRATIFICATION, appeasement, fulfillment, satiation, satisfaction
2 LUXURY, extravagance, favor, privilege, treat
3 TOLERANCE, forbearance, patience, understanding

indulgent *adjective* LENIENT, compliant, easy-going, forbearing, kindly, liberal, permissive, tolerant, understanding

industrialist *noun* CAPITALIST, big businessman, captain of industry, magnate, manufacturer, tycoon

industrious *adjective* HARD-WORKING, busy, conscientious, diligent, energetic, persistent, purposeful, tireless, zealous

industry *noun* **1** BUSINESS, commerce, manufacturing, production, trade
2 EFFORT, activity, application, diligence, labor, tirelessness, toil, zeal

inebriated *adjective* DRUNK, crocked (*slang*), intoxicated, paralytic (*informal*), plastered (*slang*), three sheets to the wind (*slang*), tipsy, under the influence (*informal*)

ineffective *adjective* USELESS, fruitless, futile, idle, impotent, inefficient, unavailing, unproductive, vain, worthless

ineffectual *adjective* WEAK, feeble, impotent, inadequate, incompetent, ineffective, inept, lousy (*slang*)

inefficiency *noun* INCOMPETENCE, carelessness, disorganization, muddle, slackness, sloppiness

inefficient *adjective* INCOMPETENT, disorganized, ineffectual, inept, wasteful, weak

ineligible *adjective* UNQUALIFIED, disqualified, ruled out, unacceptable, unfit, unsuitable

in•ept' *adjective* 1 absurd 2 out of place 3 clumsy > **in•ept'i•tude** *noun*
in•ert [in-URT] *adjective* 1 without power of action or resistance 2 slow, sluggish 3 chemically unreactive > **in•er'tia** [-UR-shə] *noun* 1 inactivity 2 property by which matter continues in its existing state of rest or motion in straight line, unless that state is changed by external force
in•es•ti•ma•ble [in-ES-tə-mə-bəl] *adjective* too good, too great, to be estimated
in•ev•i•ta•ble [in-EV-i-tə-bəl] *adjective* 1 unavoidable 2 sure to happen > **in•ev•i•ta•bil'i•ty** *noun*
in•ex•o•ra•ble [in-EK-sər-ə-bəl] *adjective* relentless > **in•ex'o•ra•bly** *adverb*
in•ex•pe'ri•enced *adjective* having no knowledge or experience of a particular situation, activity, etc. > **in•ex•pe'ri•ence** *noun*
in•ex•pli•ca•ble [in-EK-spli-kə-bəl] *adjective* impossible to explain
in ex•tre•mis [eks-TREE-mis] *Lat.* at the point of death
in•fal•li•ble [in-FAL-ə-bəl] *adjective* 1 unerring 2 not liable to fail 3 certain, sure > **in•fal•li•bil'i•ty** *noun*
in•fa•mous [IN-fə-məs] *adjective* 1 notorious 2 shocking > **in'fa•my** [-mee] *noun, plural* **-mies**
in•fant [IN-fənt] *noun* very young child > **in'fan•cy** *noun* > **in•fan'ti•cide** [-FAN-tə-sīd] *noun* 1 murder of newborn child 2 person guilty of this > **in'fan•tile** [-fən-tīl] *adjective* childish
in•fan•try [IN-fən-tree] *noun, plural* **-tries** foot soldiers
in•fat•u•ate [in-FACH-oo-ayt] *verb transitive* **-at•ed, -at•ing** inspire with folly or foolish passion > **in•fat'u•at•ed** *adjective* foolishly enamored > **in•fat•u•a'tion** *noun*
in•fect [in-FEKT] *verb transitive* 1 affect (with disease) 2 contaminate > **in•fec'tion** [-shən] *noun* > **in•fec'tious** [-shəs] *adjective* catching, spreading, pestilential
in•fer [in-FUR] *verb transitive* **-ferred, -fer•ring** deduce, conclude > **in'fer•ence** [-fər-əns] *noun* > **in•fer•en'tial** [-fər-EN-shəl] *adjective* deduced
in•fe•ri•or [in-FEER-ee-ər] *adjective* 1 of poor quality 2 lower ▷ *noun* 3 one lower (in rank, etc.) > **in•fe•ri•or'i•ty** *noun* > **inferiority complex** *psychoanalysis* intense sense of inferiority

DICTIONARY

THESAURUS

inept *adjective* INCOMPETENT, bumbling, bungling, clumsy, inexpert, maladroit
ineptitude *noun* INCOMPETENCE, clumsiness, inexpertness, unfitness
inequality *noun* DISPARITY, bias, difference, disproportion, diversity, irregularity, prejudice, unevenness
inequitable *adjective* UNFAIR, biased, discriminatory, one-sided, partial, partisan, preferential, prejudiced, unjust
inert *adjective* INACTIVE, dead, dormant, immobile, lifeless, motionless, static, still, unreactive, unresponsive
inertia *noun* INACTIVITY, apathy, immobility, lethargy, listlessness, passivity, sloth, unresponsiveness
inescapable *adjective* UNAVOIDABLE, certain, destined, fated, ineluctable, inevitable, inexorable, sure
inestimable *adjective* INCALCULABLE, immeasurable, invaluable, precious, priceless, prodigious
inevitable *adjective* UNAVOIDABLE, assured, certain, destined, fixed, ineluctable, inescapable, inexorable, sure
inevitably *adverb* UNAVOIDABLY, as a result, automatically, certainly, necessarily, of necessity, perforce, surely, willy-nilly
inexcusable *adjective* UNFORGIVABLE, indefensible, outrageous, unjustifiable, unpardonable, unwarrantable
inexorable *adjective* UNRELENTING, inescapable, relentless, remorseless, unbending, unyielding
inexpensive *adjective* CHEAP, bargain, budget, economical, modest, reasonable
inexperience *noun* UNFAMILIARITY, callowness, greenness, ignorance, newness, rawness
inexperienced *adjective* IMMATURE, callow, green, new, raw, unpracticed, untried, unversed
inexpert *adjective* AMATEURISH, bungling, clumsy, inept, maladroit, unpracticed, unprofessional, unskilled
inexplicable *adjective* UNACCOUNTABLE, baffling, enigmatic, incomprehensible, insoluble, mysterious, mystifying, strange, unfathomable, unintelligible
inextricably *adverb* INSEPARABLY, indissolubly, indistinguishably, intricately, irretrievably, totally
infallibility *noun* PERFECTION, impeccability, omniscience, supremacy, unerringness
infallible *adjective* FOOLPROOF, certain, dependable, reliable, sure, sure-fire (*informal*), trustworthy, unbeatable, unfailing
infamous *adjective* NOTORIOUS, disreputable, ignominious, ill-famed
infancy *noun* BEGINNINGS, cradle, dawn, inception, origins, outset, start
infant *noun* BABY, babe, child, minor, toddler, tot
infantile *adjective* CHILDISH, babyish, immature, puerile
infatuate *verb* OBSESS, besot, bewitch, captivate, enchant, enrapture, fascinate
infatuated *adjective* OBSESSED, besotted, bewitched, captivated, carried away, enamored, enraptured, fascinated, possessed, smitten (*informal*), spellbound
infatuation *noun* OBSESSION, crush (*informal*), fixation, madness, passion, thing (*informal*)
infect *verb* CONTAMINATE, affect, blight, corrupt, defile, poison, pollute, taint
infection *noun* CONTAMINATION, contagion, corruption, defilement, poison, pollution, virus
infectious *adjective* CATCHING, communicable, contagious, spreading, transmittable, virulent
infer *verb* DEDUCE, conclude, derive, gather, presume, surmise, understand
inference *noun* DEDUCTION, assumption, conclusion, presumption, reading, surmise
inferior *adjective* 1 LOWER, lesser, menial, minor, secondary, subordinate, subsidiary ▷ *noun* 2 UNDERLING, junior, menial, subordinate
inferiority *noun* 1 INADEQUACY, deficiency, imperfection, insignificance, mediocrity, shoddiness, worthlessness

in•fer•nal [in-FUR-nl] *adjective* 1 devilish 2 hellish 3 (*informal*) irritating, confounded
in•fer•no [in-FUR-noh] *noun* 1 region of hell 2 great destructive fire
in•fer'tile *adjective* 1 unable to produce offspring 2 (of soil) barren, not productive > **in•fer•tile** *noun*
in•fest' *verb transitive* inhabit or overrun in dangerously or unpleasantly large numbers > **in•fes•ta'tion** *noun*
in•fi•del•i•ty [in-fi-DEL-i-tee] *noun* 1 unfaithfulness 2 religious disbelief 3 disloyalty 4 treachery > **in'fi•del** [-dl] *noun* unbeliever ▷ *adjective*
in•fil•trate [in-FIL-trayt] *verb* **-trat•ed, -trat•ing** 1 trickle through 2 cause to pass through pores 3 gain access surreptitiously > **in•fil•tra'tion** *noun*
in•fi•nite [IN-fə-nit] *adjective* boundless > **in'fi•nite•ly** *adverb* exceedingly > **in•fin•i•tes'i•mal** [-TES-ə-məl] *adjective* extremely, infinitely small > **in•fin'i•ty** *noun* unlimited and endless extent
in•fin•i•tive [in-FIN-i-tiv] *adjective grammar* 1 in form expressing notion of verb without limitation of tense, person, or number ▷ *noun* 2 verb in this form 3 the form
in•firm [in-FURM] *adjective* 1 physically weak 2 mentally weak 3 irresolute > **in•fir'ma•ry** [-mə-ree] *noun* 1 hospital 2 dispensary > **in•fir'mi•ty** *noun, plural* **-ties**
in•flame [in-FLAYM] *verb* **-flamed, -flam•ing** 1 rouse to anger, excitement 2 cause inflammation in 3 become inflamed > **in•flam•ma•bil'i•ty** *noun* > **in•flam'ma•ble** *adjective* 1 easily set on fire 2 excitable > **in•flam•ma'tion** *noun* infection of part of the body, with pain, heat, swelling, and redness
in•flate [in-FLAYT] *verb* **-flat•ed, -flat•ing** 1 blow up with air, gas 2 swell 3 cause economic inflation 4 raise price, esp. artificially > **in•fla'tion** *noun* increase in prices and fall in value of money > **in•fla'tion•ar•y** *adjective*
in•flect [in-FLEKT] *verb transitive* 1 modify (words) to show grammatical relationships 2 bend inward > **in•flec'tion** *noun* 1 modification of word 2 modulation of voice
in•flex•i•ble [in-FLEK-sə-bəl] *adjective* 1 incapable of being bent 2 stern > **in•flex•i•bil'i•ty** *noun*
in•flict [in-FLIKT] *verb transitive* impose, deliver forcibly > **in•flic'tion** *noun* 1 inflicting 2 punishment
in•flu•ence [IN-floo-əns] *noun* 1 effect of one person or thing on another 2 power of person or thing having an effect 3 thing, person exercising this ▷ *verb transitive* **-enced, -enc•ing** 4 sway 5 induce 6 affect > **in•flu•en'tial** *adjective*
in•flu•en•za [in-floo-EN-zə] *noun* contagious feverish respiratory virus disease
in•flux [IN-fluks] *noun* 1 a flowing in 2 inflow
in•form' *verb transitive* 1 tell 2 animate ▷ *verb*

---

2 SUBSERVIENCE, abasement, lowliness, subordination
infernal *adjective* DEVILISH, accursed, damnable, damned, diabolical, fiendish, hellish, satanic
infertile *adjective* BARREN, sterile, unfruitful, unproductive
infertility *noun* STERILITY, barrenness, infecundity, unproductiveness
infest *verb* OVERRUN, beset, invade, penetrate, permeate, ravage, swarm, throng
infested *adjective* OVERRUN, alive, crawling, ravaged, ridden, swarming, teeming
infiltrate *verb* PENETRATE, filter through, insinuate oneself, make inroads *or* make inroads into, percolate, permeate, pervade, sneak in (*informal*)
infinite *adjective* NEVER-ENDING, boundless, eternal, everlasting, illimitable, immeasurable, inexhaustible, limitless, measureless, unbounded
infinitesimal *adjective* MICROSCOPIC, insignificant, minuscule, minute, negligible, teeny, tiny, unnoticeable
infinity *noun* ETERNITY, boundlessness, endlessness, immensity, vastness
infirm *adjective* FRAIL, ailing, debilitated, decrepit, doddering, enfeebled, failing, feeble, weak
infirmity *noun* FRAILTY, decrepitude, ill health, sickliness, vulnerability
inflame *verb* ENRAGE, anger, arouse, excite, incense, infuriate, madden, provoke, rouse, stimulate
inflamed *adjective* SORE, fevered, hot, infected, red, swollen
inflammable *adjective* FLAMMABLE, combustible, incendiary
inflammation *noun* SORENESS, painfulness, rash, redness, tenderness
inflammatory *adjective* PROVOCATIVE, explosive, fiery, intemperate, like a red rag to a bull, rabble-rousing
inflate *verb* EXPAND, bloat, blow up, dilate, distend, enlarge, increase, puff up *or* puff out, pump up, swell
inflated *adjective* EXAGGERATED, ostentatious, overblown, swollen
inflation *noun* EXPANSION, enlargement, escalation, extension, increase, rise, spread, swelling
inflexibility *noun* OBSTINACY, intransigence, obduracy
inflexible *adjective* 1 OBSTINATE, implacable, intractable, obdurate, resolute, set in one's ways, steadfast, stubborn, unbending, uncompromising
2 INELASTIC, hard, rigid, stiff, taut
inflict *verb* IMPOSE, administer, apply, deliver, levy, mete out *or* deal out, visit, wreak
infliction *noun* IMPOSITION, administration, perpetration, wreaking
influence *noun* 1 EFFECT, authority, control, domination, magnetism, pressure, weight
2 POWER, clout (*informal*), hold, importance, leverage, prestige, pull (*informal*)
▷ *verb* 3 AFFECT, control, direct, guide, manipulate, sway
influential *adjective* IMPORTANT, authoritative, instrumental, leading, potent, powerful, significant, telling, weighty
influx *noun* ARRIVAL, incursion, inrush, inundation, invasion, rush

intransitive 3 give information (about) > **in•form'ant** [-ənt] *noun* one who tells > **in•for•ma'tion** *noun* what is told, knowledge > **in•form'a•tive** *adjective* > **in•fo•mer'cial** [in-foh-MUR-shəl] *noun* TV commercial advertising something in an informative way > **information superhighway** worldwide network of computers sharing information at high speed > **information technology** use of computers and electronic technology to store and communicate information

in•for'mal *adjective* 1 relaxed and friendly 2 appropriate for everyday life or use > **in•for•mal'i•ty** *noun*

infraction *noun see* **infringe**

in•fra•red [in-frə-RED] *adjective* denoting rays below red end of visible spectrum

in•fra•struc•ture [IN-frə-struk-chər] *noun* basic structure or fixed capital items of an organization or economic system

in•fre'quent *adjective* not happening often

in•fringe [in-FRINJ] *verb transitive* **-fringed, -fring•ing** transgress, break > **in•fringe'ment** *noun* > **in•frac'tion** *noun* 1 breach 2 violation

in•fu•ri•ate [in-FYUUR-ee-ayt] *verb transitive* **-at•ed, -at•ing** enrage

in•fuse [in-FYOOZ] *verb* **-fused, -fus•ing** 1 soak to extract flavor, etc. 2 instill, charge > **in•fu'sion** [-FYOO-zhən] *noun* 1 an infusing 2 liquid extract obtained

in•gen•ious [in-JEEN-yəs] *adjective* 1 clever at contriving 2 cleverly contrived > **in•ge•nu'i•ty** [-jə-NOO-ə-tee] *noun*

in•gé•nue [AN-zhə-noo] *noun* 1 artless girl or young woman 2 actress playing such a part

in•gen•u•ous [in-JEN-yoo-əs] *adjective* 1 frank 2 naive, innocent > **in•gen'u•ous•ness** *noun*

in•ges•tion [in-JES-chən] *noun* act of introducing food into the body

in•got [ING-gət] *noun* brick of cast metal, esp. gold

in•grain [in-GRAYN] *verb transitive* implant deeply > **in•grained'** *adjective* 1 deep-rooted 2 inveterate

in•gra•ti•ate [in-GRAY-shee-ayt] *verb reflexive* get (oneself) into favor > **in•gra'ti•at•ing•ly** *adverb*

in•grat'i•tude *noun* lack of gratitude or thanks

in•gre•di•ent [in-GREE-dee-ənt] *noun* component part of a mixture

in'gress *noun* entry, means, right of entrance

in•hab'it *verb transitive* dwell in > **in•hab'it•a•ble** *adjective* > **in•hab'it•ant** [-i-tənt] *noun*

in•hale [in-HAYL] *verb* **-haled, -hal•ing** breathe in (air, etc.) > **in•ha•la'tion** *noun* esp. medical preparation for inhaling > **in•ha'ler** *noun* 1 person who inhales 2 (*also* **in'ha•la•tor**) device producing, and assisting inhalation of therapeutic vapors

in•here [in-HEER] *verb intransitive* **-hered, -her•ing** 1 of qualities, exist (in) 2 of rights, be vested (in person) > **in•her'ent** [-HEER-ənt] *adjective* existing as an inseparable part

in•her'it *verb transitive* 1 receive as heir 2 derive from parents ▷ *verb intransitive* 3 succeed as heir > **in•her'it•ance** [-əns] *noun*

---

inform *verb* 1 TELL, advise, communicate, enlighten, instruct, notify, teach, tip off 2 INCRIMINATE, betray, blow the whistle on (*informal*), denounce, inculpate, squeal (*slang*)

informal *adjective* RELAXED, casual, colloquial, cozy, easy, familiar, homey, natural, simple, unofficial

informality *noun* FAMILIARITY, casualness, ease, naturalness, relaxation, simplicity

information *noun* FACTS, data, intelligence, knowledge, message, news, notice, report

informative *adjective* INSTRUCTIVE, chatty, communicative, edifying, educational, enlightening, forthcoming, illuminating, revealing

informed *adjective* KNOWLEDGEABLE, enlightened, erudite, expert, familiar, in the picture, learned, up to date, versed, well-read

informer *noun* BETRAYER, accuser, Judas, sneak, stool pigeon

infrequent *adjective* OCCASIONAL, few and far between, once in a blue moon, rare, sporadic, uncommon, unusual

infringe *verb* BREAK, contravene, disobey, transgress, violate

infringement *noun* CONTRAVENTION, breach, infraction, transgression, trespass, violation

infuriate *verb* ENRAGE, anger, exasperate, incense, irritate, madden, provoke, rile

infuriating *adjective* ANNOYING, exasperating, galling, irritating, maddening, mortifying, provoking, vexatious

ingenious *adjective* CREATIVE, bright, brilliant, clever, crafty, inventive, original, resourceful, shrewd

ingenuity *noun* ORIGINALITY, cleverness, flair, genius, gift, inventiveness, resourcefulness, sharpness, shrewdness

ingenuous *adjective* NAIVE, artless, guileless, honest, innocent, open, plain, simple, sincere, trusting, unsophisticated

inglorious *adjective* DISHONORABLE, discreditable, disgraceful, disreputable, ignoble, ignominious, infamous, shameful, unheroic

ingratiate *verb* PANDER TO, brown-nose (*slang*), crawl, curry favor, fawn, flatter, grovel, insinuate oneself, kiss ass (*slang*), toady

ingratiating *adjective* SYCOPHANTIC, crawling, fawning, flattering, humble, obsequious, servile, toadying, unctuous

ingratitude *noun* UNGRATEFULNESS, thanklessness

ingredient *noun* COMPONENT, constituent, element, part

inhabit *verb* LIVE, abide, dwell, occupy, populate, reside

inhabitant *noun* DWELLER, citizen, denizen, inmate, native, occupant, occupier, resident, tenant

inhabited *adjective* POPULATED, colonized, developed, occupied, peopled, settled, tenanted

inhale *verb* BREATHE IN, draw in, gasp, respire, suck in

inherent *adjective* INNATE, essential, hereditary, inborn, inbred, inbuilt, ingrained, inherited, intrinsic, native, natural

inherit *verb* BE LEFT, come into, fall heir to, succeed to

inheritance *noun* LEGACY, bequest, birthright, heritage, patrimony

in•hib'it *verb transitive* 1 restrain (impulse, desire, etc.) 2 hinder (action) 3 forbid > **in•hi•bi'tion** *noun* 1 repression of emotion, instinct 2 a stopping or retarding > **in•hib'i•to•ry** *adjective*

in•hos•pi'ta•ble *adjective* 1 not welcoming, unfriendly 2 difficult to live in, harsh

in•hu•man [in-HYOO-mən] *adjective* 1 cruel, brutal 2 not human > **in•hu•man'i•ty** *noun*

in•im•i•cal [i-NIM-i-kəl] *adjective* 1 unfavorable (to) 2 unfriendly 3 hostile

in•im•i•ta•ble [i-NIM-i-tə-bəl] *adjective* defying imitation > **in•im'i•ta•bly** *adverb*

in•iq•ui•ty [i-NIK-wi-tee] *noun, plural* **-ties** 1 gross injustice 2 wickedness, sin > **in•iq'ui•tous** *adjective* unfair, sinful, unjust

in•i•tial [i-NISH-əl] *adjective* 1 of, occurring at the beginning ▷ *noun* 2 initial letter, esp. of person's name ▷ *verb transitive* **-tialed, -tial•ing** 3 mark, sign with one's initials

in•i•ti•ate [i-NISH-ee-ayt] *verb transitive* **-at•ed, -at•ing** 1 originate 2 begin 3 admit into closed society 4 instruct in elements (of) ▷ *noun* [-ee-it] 5 initiated person > **in•i•ti•a'tion** *noun* > **in•i'ti•a•tive** *noun* 1 first step, lead 2 ability to act independently ▷ *adjective* 3 originating

in•ject [in-JEKT] *verb transitive* introduce (esp. fluid, medicine, etc. with syringe) > **in•jec'tion** *noun*

in•junc•tion [in-JUNGK-shən] *noun* 1 judicial order to restrain 2 authoritative order

in•ju•ry [IN-jə-ree] *noun, plural* **-ries** 1 physical damage or harm 2 wrong > **in•jure** [IN-jər] *verb transitive* **-jured, -jur•ing** do harm or damage to > **in•ju'ri•ous** [-JUU-ree-əs] *adjective*

in•jus•tice [in-JUS-tis] *noun* 1 want of justice 2 wrong 3 injury 4 unjust act

ink *noun* 1 fluid used for writing or printing ▷ *verb transitive* 2 mark with ink 3 cover, smear with it

ink•ling [INGK-ling] *noun* hint, slight knowledge or suspicion

inlaid *see* **inlay**

in'land *noun* 1 interior of country ▷ *adjective* [IN-lənd] 2 in this 3 away from the sea 4 within a country ▷ *adverb* [IN-land] 5 in or toward the inland

in'-law *noun* relative by marriage esp. mother-in-law and father-in-law

in'lay *verb transitive* **-laid, -lay•ing** 1 embed 2 decorate with inset pattern ▷ *noun* 3 inlaid piece or pattern

in'let *noun* 1 entrance 2 small arm of sea, lake, etc. 3 piece inserted

in lo•co pa•ren•tis [LOH-koh pə-REN-tis] *Lat.* in place of a parent

DICTIONARY • THESAURUS

inhibit *verb* RESTRAIN, check, constrain, curb, discourage, frustrate, hinder, hold back *or* hold in, impede, obstruct

inhibited *adjective* SHY, constrained, guarded, repressed, reserved, reticent, self-conscious, subdued

inhibition *noun* SHYNESS, block, hang-up (*informal*), reserve, restraint, reticence, self-consciousness

inhospitable *adjective* 1 UNWELCOMING, cool, uncongenial, unfriendly, unreceptive, unsociable, xenophobic
2 BLEAK, barren, desolate, forbidding, godforsaken, hostile

inhuman *adjective* CRUEL, barbaric, brutal, cold-blooded, heartless, merciless, pitiless, ruthless, savage, unfeeling

inhumane *adjective* CRUEL, brutal, heartless, pitiless, unfeeling, unkind, unsympathetic

inhumanity *noun* CRUELTY, atrocity, barbarism, brutality, heartlessness, pitilessness, ruthlessness, unkindness

inimical *adjective* HOSTILE, adverse, antagonistic, ill-disposed, opposed, unfavorable, unfriendly, unwelcoming

inimitable *adjective* UNIQUE, consummate, incomparable, matchless, peerless, unparalleled, unrivaled

iniquitous *adjective* WICKED, criminal, evil, immoral, reprehensible, sinful, unjust

iniquity *noun* WICKEDNESS, abomination, evil, injustice, sin, wrong

initial *adjective* FIRST, beginning, incipient, introductory, opening, primary

initially *adverb* AT FIRST, at the beginning *or* in the beginning, first, firstly, originally, primarily

initiate *verb* 1 BEGIN, commence, get under way, kick off (*informal*), launch, open, originate, set in motion, start
2 INDUCT, indoctrinate, introduce, invest
3 INSTRUCT, acquaint with, coach, familiarize with, teach, train
▷ *noun* 4 NOVICE, beginner, convert, entrant, learner, member, probationer

initiation *noun* INTRODUCTION, debut, enrollment, entrance, inauguration, induction, installation, investiture

initiative *noun* 1 FIRST STEP, advantage, first move, lead
2 RESOURCEFULNESS, ambition, drive, dynamism, enterprise, get-up-and-go (*informal*), leadership

inject *verb* 1 VACCINATE, inoculate
2 INTRODUCE, bring in, infuse, insert, instill

injection *noun* 1 VACCINATION, inoculation, shot (*informal*)
2 INTRODUCTION, dose, infusion, insertion

injudicious *adjective* UNWISE, foolish, ill-advised, ill-judged, impolitic, imprudent, incautious, inexpedient, rash, unthinking

injunction *noun* ORDER, command, exhortation, instruction, mandate, precept, ruling

injure *verb* HURT, damage, harm, impair, ruin, spoil, undermine, wound

injured *adjective* HURT, broken, challenged, damaged, disabled, undermined, weakened, wounded

injury *noun* HARM, damage, detriment, disservice, hurt, ill, trauma (*pathology*), wound, wrong

injustice *noun* UNFAIRNESS, bias, discrimination, inequality, inequity, iniquity, oppression, partisanship, prejudice, wrong

inkling *noun* SUSPICION, clue, conception, hint, idea, indication, intimation, notion, suggestion, whisper

inland *adjective* INTERIOR, domestic, internal, upcountry

inlet *noun* BAY, bight, creek, firth *or* frith (*Scottish*), fjord, passage

in•mate [IN-mayt] *noun* occupant, esp. of prison, hospital, etc.
in•most [IN-mohst] *adjective* 1 most inward, deepest 2 most secret
inn *noun* 1 restaurant or tavern 2 country hotel > **inn'keep•er** *noun*
in•nards [IN-ərdz] *plural noun* internal organs or working parts
in•nate [i-NAYT] *adjective* 1 inborn 2 inherent
in•ner [IN-ər] *adjective* lying within > **in'ner•most** *adjective* > **inner tube** rubber air tube of pneumatic tire
in'ning *noun sports* 1 side's turn at bat 2 spell, turn
in•no•cent [IN-ə-sənt] *adjective* 1 pure 2 guiltless 3 harmless ▷ *noun* 4 innocent person, esp. young child > **in•'no•cence** *noun*
in•noc•u•ous [i-NOK-yoo-əs] *adjective* harmless
in•no•vate [IN-ə-vayt] *verb transitive* **-vat•ed, -vat•ing** introduce changes, new things > **in•no•va'tion** *noun*
in•nu•en•do [in-yoo-EN-doh] *noun, plural* **-dos** 1 allusive remark, hint 2 indirect accusation
in•nu•mer•a•ble [i-NOO-mər-ə-bəl] *adjective* 1 countless 2 very numerous
in•oc•u•late [i-NOK-yə-layt] *verb transitive* **-lat•ed, -lat•ing** immunize by injecting vaccine > **in•oc•u•la'tion** *noun*
in•of•fen'sive *adjective* causing no harm
in•op•er•a•ble [in-OP-ər-ə-bəl] *adjective* 1 unworkable 2 *med.* that cannot be operated on > **in•op'er•a•tive** *adjective* 1 not operative 2 ineffective
in•op•por•tune [in-op-ər-TOON] *adjective* badly timed
in•or•di•nate [in-OR-dn-it] *adjective* excessive
in•or•gan•ic [in-or-GAN-ik] *adjective* 1 not having structure or characteristics of living organisms 2 of substances without carbon
in•pa•tient [IN-pay-shənt] *noun* patient who stays in hospital
in•put [IN-puut] *noun* 1 act of putting in 2 that which is put in, as resource needed for industrial production, etc. 3 data, etc. fed into a computer
in•quest [IN-kwest] *noun* 1 legal or judicial inquiry presided over by a coroner 2 detailed inquiry or discussion
in•quire [in-KWĪR] *verb intransitive* **-quired, -quir•ing** seek information > **in•quir'er** *noun* > **in•quir'y** *noun, plural* **-quir•ies** 1 question 2 investigation
in•qui•si•tion [in-kwə-ZISH-ən] *noun* 1 searching investigation, official inquiry 2 (**In•qui•si•tion**) *hist.* organization within the Catholic Church for suppressing heresy > **in•quis'i•tor** [-KWIZ-ə-tər] *noun*
in•quis•i•tive [in-KWIZ-i-tiv] *adjective* 1 curious 2 prying
in•road [IN-rohd] *noun* 1 incursion 2 encroachment
in•sane [in-SAYN] *adjective* 1 mentally deranged

DICTIONARY • THESAURUS

inmost, innermost *adjective* DEEPEST, basic, central, essential, intimate, personal, private, secret
innate *adjective* INBORN, congenital, constitutional, essential, inbred, ingrained, inherent, instinctive, intuitive, native, natural
inner *adjective* 1 INSIDE, central, interior, internal, inward, middle
2 PRIVATE, hidden, intimate, personal, repressed, secret, unrevealed
innkeeper *noun* PROPRIETOR, host *or* hostess, hotelier, landlord *or* landlady, owner
innocence *noun* 1 GUILTLESSNESS, blamelessness, clean hands, incorruptibility, probity, purity, uprightness, virtue
2 HARMLESSNESS, innocuousness, inoffensiveness
3 INEXPERIENCE, artlessness, credulousness, gullibility, ingenuousness, naivety, simplicity, unworldliness
innocent *adjective* 1 NOT GUILTY, blameless, guiltless, honest, in the clear, uninvolved
2 HARMLESS, innocuous, inoffensive, unobjectionable, well-intentioned, well-meant
3 NAIVE, artless, childlike, credulous, gullible, ingenuous, open, simple, unworldly
innovation *noun* MODERNIZATION, alteration, change, departure, introduction, newness, novelty, variation
innuendo *noun* INSINUATION, aspersion, hint, implication, imputation, intimation, overtone, suggestion, whisper
innumerable *adjective* COUNTLESS, beyond number, incalculable, infinite, multitudinous, myriad, numberless, numerous, unnumbered, untold
inoffensive *adjective* HARMLESS, innocent, innocuous, mild, quiet, retiring, unobjectionable, unobtrusive
inoperative *adjective* OUT OF ACTION, broken, defective, ineffective, invalid, null and void, out of order, out of service, useless
inopportune *adjective* INCONVENIENT, ill-chosen, ill-timed, inappropriate, unfavorable, unfortunate, unpropitious, unseasonable, unsuitable, untimely
inordinate *adjective* EXCESSIVE, disproportionate, extravagant, immoderate, intemperate, preposterous, unconscionable, undue, unreasonable, unwarranted
inorganic *adjective* ARTIFICIAL, chemical, man-made
inquest *noun* INQUIRY, inquisition, investigation, probe
inquire *verb* 1 INVESTIGATE, examine, explore, look into, make inquiries, probe, research
2 *also* **enquire** ASK, query, question
inquiry *noun* 1 INVESTIGATION, examination, exploration, inquest, interrogation, probe, research, study, survey
2 *also* **enquiry** QUESTION, query
inquisition *noun* INVESTIGATION, cross-examination, examination, grilling (*informal*), inquest, inquiry, questioning, third degree (*informal*)
inquisitive *adjective* CURIOUS, inquiring, nosy (*informal*), probing, prying, questioning
insane *adjective* 1 MAD, crazed, crazy, demented, deranged, mentally ill, out of one's mind, unhinged
2 STUPID, bonkers (*informal*), daft (*informal*), foolish, idiotic, impractical, irrational, irresponsible, preposterous, senseless

2 crazy, senseless > **in•sane'ly** *adverb* 1 like a lunatic, madly 2 excessively > **in•san'i•ty** *noun*
in•san'i•tar•y *adjective* dirty or unhealthy
in•sa•tia•ble [in-SAY-shə-bəl] *adjective* incapable of being satisfied
in•scribe [in-SKRĪB] *verb transitive* **-scribed, -scrib•ing** 1 write, engrave (in or on something) 2 mark 3 dedicate 4 trace (figure) within another > **in•scrip'tion** *noun* 1 inscribing 2 words inscribed on monument, etc.
in•scru•ta•ble [in-SKROO-tə-bəl] *adjective* 1 mysterious, impenetrable 2 affording no explanation > **in•scru•ta•bil'i•ty** *noun*
in•sect [IN-sekt] *noun* small invertebrate animal with six legs, usu. segmented body and two or four wings > **in•sec'ti•cide** [-sīd] *noun* preparation for killing insects > **in•sec•tiv'o•rous** *adjective* insect-eating
in•se•cure [in-si-KYUUR] *adjective* 1 not safe or firm 2 anxious, not confident
in•sem•i•nate [in-SEM-ə-nayt] *verb transitive* **-nat•ed, -nat•ing** implant semen into **artificial insemination** impregnation of the female by artificial means
in•sen•sate [in-SEN-sayt] *adjective* 1 without sensation, unconscious 2 unfeeling
in•sen•si•ble [in-SEN-sə-bəl] *adjective* 1 unconscious 2 without feeling 3 not aware 4 not perceptible > **in•sen'si•bly** *adverb* imperceptibly
in•sen'si•tive *adjective* unaware of or ignoring other people's feelings > **in•sen•si•tiv'i•ty** *noun*
in•sert [in-SURT] *verb transitive* 1 introduce 2 place or put (in, into, between) ▷ *noun* [IN-surt] 3 something inserted > **in•ser'tion** [-shən] *noun*
in'set *noun* something extra inserted esp. as decoration > **in•set'** *verb transitive* **-set, -set•ting**
in•shore [IN-shor] *adjective* 1 near shore ▷ *adverb* 2 toward shore
in•side [IN-sīd] *noun* 1 inner side, surface, or part 2 inner circle of influence 3 (*slang*) confidential information ▷ *adjective* 4 of, in, or on, inside ▷ *adverb* [in-SĪD] 5 in or into the inside 6 (*slang*) in prison ▷ *preposition* 7 within, on inner side > **in•sides** *plural, noun* (*informal*) internal parts of body
in•sid•i•ous [in-SID-ee-əs] *adjective* 1 stealthy, treacherous 2 unseen but deadly
in•sight [IN-sīt] *noun* deep understanding
in•sig•ni•a [in-SIG-nee-ə] *noun, plural* **-ni•as, -ni•a** badge or emblem of honor or office
in•sig•nif'i•cant *adjective* not important > **in•sig•nif'i•cance** *noun*
in•sin•cere' *adjective* showing false feelings, not genuine > **in•sin•cer'i•ty** *noun, plural* **-ties**
in•sin•u•ate [in-SIN-yoo-ayt] *verb transitive* **-at•ed, -at•ing** 1 hint 2 work oneself into favor 3 introduce gradually or subtly > **in•sin•u•a'tion** *noun*
in•sip'id *adjective* dull, tasteless, spiritless
in•sist' *verb intransitive* 1 demand persistently 2 maintain 3 emphasize > **in•sist'ence** *noun*

DICTIONARY • THESAURUS

insanitary *adjective* UNHEALTHY, dirty, disease-ridden, filthy, infested, insalubrious, polluted, scuzzy (*slang*), unclean, unhygienic
insanity *noun* 1 MADNESS, delirium, dementia, mental disorder, mental illness
2 STUPIDITY, folly, irresponsibility, lunacy, senselessness
insatiable *adjective* UNQUENCHABLE, greedy, intemperate, rapacious, ravenous, voracious
inscribe *verb* CARVE, cut, engrave, etch, impress, imprint
inscription *noun* ENGRAVING, dedication, legend, words
inscrutable *adjective* 1 ENIGMATIC, blank, deadpan, impenetrable, poker-faced (*informal*)
2 MYSTERIOUS, hidden, incomprehensible, inexplicable, unexplainable, unfathomable, unintelligible
insecure *adjective* 1 ANXIOUS, afraid, uncertain, unsure
2 UNSAFE, defenseless, exposed, unguarded, unprotected, vulnerable, wide-open
insecurity *noun* ANXIETY, fear, uncertainty, worry
insensible *adjective* UNAWARE, impervious, oblivious, unaffected, unconscious, unmindful
insensitive *adjective* UNFEELING, callous, hardened, indifferent, thick-skinned, tough, uncaring, unconcerned
inseparable *adjective* 1 INDIVISIBLE, indissoluble
2 DEVOTED, bosom, close, intimate
insert *verb* ENTER, embed, implant, introduce, place, put, stick in
insertion *noun* INCLUSION, addition, implant, interpolation, introduction, supplement
inside *adjective* 1 INNER, interior, internal, inward
2 CONFIDENTIAL, classified, exclusive, internal, private, restricted, secret
▷ *adverb* 3 INDOORS, under cover, within
▷ *noun* 4 INTERIOR, contents
5 **insides** (*informal*) STOMACH, belly, bowels, entrails, guts, innards (*informal*), viscera, vitals
insidious *adjective* STEALTHY, deceptive, sly, smooth, sneaking, subtle, surreptitious
insight *noun* UNDERSTANDING, awareness, comprehension, discernment, judgment, observation, penetration, perception, perspicacity, vision
insignia *noun* BADGE, crest, emblem, symbol
insignificance *noun* UNIMPORTANCE, inconsequence, irrelevance, meaninglessness, pettiness, triviality, worthlessness
insignificant *adjective* UNIMPORTANT, inconsequential, irrelevant, meaningless, minor, nondescript, paltry, petty, trifling, trivial
insincere *adjective* DECEITFUL, dishonest, disingenuous, duplicitous, false, hollow, hypocritical, lying, two-faced, untruthful
insincerity *noun* DECEITFULNESS, dishonesty, dissimulation, duplicity, hypocrisy, pretense, untruthfulness
insinuate *verb* 1 IMPLY, allude, hint, indicate, intimate, suggest
2 INGRATIATE, curry favor, get in with, worm one's way in *or* work one's way in
insinuation *noun* IMPLICATION, allusion, aspersion, hint, innuendo, slur, suggestion
insipid *adjective* 1 BLAND, anemic, characterless, colorless, prosaic, uninteresting, vapid, wishy-washy (*informal*)
2 TASTELESS, bland, flavorless, unappetizing, watery
insist *verb* 1 DEMAND, lay down the law, put

> **in•sist'ent** *adjective*
in si•tu [SĪ-too] *Lat.* in its original place or position
in•so•lent [IN-sə-lənt] *adjective* arrogantly impudent > **in'so•lence** *noun*
in•sol'vent *adjective* unable to pay one's debts > **in•sol'ven•cy** *noun*
in•som•ni•a [in-SOM-nee-ə] *noun* sleeplessness > **in•som'ni•ac** [-nee-ak] *adjective, noun*
in•so•much [in-sə-MUCH] *adverb* to such an extent
in•sou•ci•ant [in-SOO-see-ənt] *adjective* indifferent, careless, unconcerned > **in•sou'ci•ance** *noun*
in•spect [in-SPEKT] *verb transitive* examine closely or officially > **in•spec'tion** *noun* > **in•spec'tor** *noun* 1 one who inspects 2 high-ranking police or fire officer
in•spire [in-SPĪR] *verb transitive* **-spired, -spir•ing** 1 animate, invigorate 2 arouse, create feeling, thought 3 give rise to 4 breathe in, inhale > **in•spi•ra'tion** *noun* 1 good idea 2 creative influence or stimulus
in•stall [in-STAWL] *verb transitive* 1 have (apparatus) put in 2 establish 3 place (person in office, etc.) with ceremony > **in•stal•la'tion** *noun* 1 act of installing 2 that which is installed
in•stall•ment [in-STAWL-mənt] *noun* 1 payment of part of debt 2 any of parts of a whole delivered in succession
in•stance [IN-stəns] *noun* 1 example 2 particular case 3 request ▷ *verb transitive* **-stanced, -stanc•ing** 4 cite
in•stant [IN-stənt] *noun* 1 moment, point of time ▷ *adjective* 2 immediate 3 urgent 4 (of foods) requiring little preparation > **in•stan•ta'ne•ous** *adjective* happening in an instant > **in•stan'ter** *adverb* at once > **in'stant•ly** *adverb* at once > **instant messaging** online facility that allows the instant exchange of written messages between people using different computers or cell phones
in•stead [in-STED] *adverb* 1 in place (of) 2 as a substitute
in'step *noun* top of foot between toes and ankle
in•sti•gate [IN-sti-gayt] *verb transitive* **-gat•ed, -gat•ing** 1 incite, urge 2 bring about

DICTIONARY

THESAURUS

one's foot down (*informal*), require
2 ASSERT, aver, claim, maintain, reiterate, repeat, swear, vow
insistence *noun* PERSISTENCE, emphasis, importunity, stress
insistent *adjective* PERSISTENT, dogged, emphatic, importunate, incessant, persevering, unrelenting, urgent
insolence *noun* RUDENESS, boldness, cheek (*informal*), disrespect, effrontery, impertinence, impudence
insolent *adjective* RUDE, bold, contemptuous, impertinent, impudent, insubordinate, insulting
insoluble *adjective* INEXPLICABLE, baffling, impenetrable, indecipherable, mysterious, unaccountable, unfathomable, unsolvable
insolvency *noun* BANKRUPTCY, failure, liquidation, ruin
insolvent *adjective* BANKRUPT, broke (*informal*), failed, gone bust (*informal*), gone to the wall, in receivership, ruined
insomnia *noun* SLEEPLESSNESS, wakefulness
inspect *verb* EXAMINE, check, go over *or* go through, investigate, look over, scrutinize, survey, vet
inspection *noun* EXAMINATION, check, checkup, investigation, once-over (*informal*), review, scrutiny, search, survey
inspector *noun* EXAMINER, censor, investigator, overseer, scrutinizer, superintendent, supervisor
inspiration *noun* 1 INFLUENCE, muse, spur, stimulus
2 REVELATION, creativity, illumination, insight
inspire *verb* 1 STIMULATE, animate, encourage, enliven, galvanize, influence, spur
2 AROUSE, enkindle, excite, give rise to, produce
inspired *adjective* 1 BRILLIANT, cool (*informal*), dazzling, impressive, memorable, outstanding, phat (*slang*), superlative, thrilling, wonderful
2 UPLIFTED, elated, enthused, exhilarated, stimulated
inspiring *adjective* UPLIFTING, exciting, exhilarating, heartening, moving, rousing, stimulating, stirring
instability *noun* UNPREDICTABILITY, changeableness, fickleness, fluctuation, impermanence, inconstancy, insecurity, unsteadiness, variability, volatility, wavering
install *verb* 1 SET UP, fix, lay, lodge, place, position, put in, station
2 INDUCT, establish, inaugurate, institute, introduce, invest
3 SETTLE, ensconce, position
installation *noun* 1 SETTING UP, establishment, fitting, installment, placing, positioning
2 INDUCTION, inauguration, investiture
3 EQUIPMENT, machinery, plant, system
installment *noun* PORTION, chapter, division, episode, part, repayment, section
instance *noun* 1 EXAMPLE, case, illustration, occasion, occurrence, situation
▷ *verb* 2 QUOTE, adduce, cite, mention, name, specify
instant *noun* 1 SECOND, flash, jiffy (*informal*), moment, split second, trice, twinkling of an eye (*informal*)
2 JUNCTURE, moment, occasion, point, time
▷ *adjective* 3 IMMEDIATE, direct, instantaneous, on-the-spot, prompt, quick, split-second
4 PRECOOKED, convenience, fast, ready-mixed
instantaneous *adjective* IMMEDIATE, direct, instant, on-the-spot, prompt
instantaneously *adverb* IMMEDIATELY, at once, instantly, in the twinkling of an eye (*informal*), on the spot, promptly, straight away
instantly *adverb* IMMEDIATELY, at once, directly, instantaneously, now, right away, straight away, this minute
instead *adverb* 1 RATHER, alternatively, in lieu, in preference, on second thoughts, preferably
2 **instead of** IN PLACE OF, in lieu of, rather than
instigate *verb* PROVOKE, bring about, incite, influence, initiate, prompt, set off, start, stimulate, trigger

> **in•sti•ga'tion** *noun*
in•still' *verb transitive* 1 implant 2 inculcate
> **in•still'ment** *noun*
in•stinct [IN-stingkt] *noun* 1 inborn impulse or propensity 2 unconscious skill 3 intuition
> **in•stinc'tive** *adjective*
in•sti•tute [IN-sti-toot] *verb transitive* **-tut•ed, -tut•ing** 1 establish, found 2 appoint 3 set in motion ▷ *noun* 4 society for promoting some public goal, esp. scientific 5 its building
> **in•sti•tu'tion** *noun* 1 an instituting 2 establishment for care or education, hospital, college, etc. 3 an established custom or law 4 (*informal*) a well-established person
> **in•sti•tu'tion•al** *adjective* 1 of institutions 2 routine > **in•sti•tu'tion•al•ize** *verb transitive* **-ized, -iz•ing** 1 place in an institution esp. for care of mentally ill 2 make or become an institution
in•struct [in-STRUKT] *verb transitive* 1 teach 2 inform 3 order 4 brief (jury, lawyer)
> **in•struc'tion** *noun* 1 teaching 2 order
> **in•struc'tions** directions > **in•struc'tive** *adjective* 1 informative 2 useful
in•stru•ment [IN-strə-mənt] *noun* 1 tool, implement, means, person, thing used to make, do, measure, etc. 2 mechanism for producing musical sound 3 legal document
> **in•stru•men'tal** *adjective* 1 acting as instrument or means 2 helpful 3 belonging to, produced by musical instruments
> **in•stru•men'tal•ist** *noun* player of musical instrument > **in•stru•men•tal'i•ty** *noun, plural* **-ties** agency, means > **in•stru•men•ta'tion** *noun* arrangement of music for instruments
in•sub•or•di•nate [in-sə-BOR-dn-it] *adjective* 1 not submissive 2 mutinous, rebellious
> **in•sub•or•di•na'tion** *noun*
in•su•lar [IN-sə-lər] *adjective* 1 of an island 2 remote, detached 3 narrow-minded or prejudiced > **in•su•lar'i•ty** *noun*
in•su•late [IN-sə-layt] *verb transitive* **-lat•ed, -lat•ing** 1 prevent or reduce transfer of electricity, heat, sound, etc. 2 isolate, detach
> **in•su•la'tion** *noun*
in•su•lin [IN-sə-lin] *noun* pancreatic hormone, used in treating diabetes
in•sult' *verb transitive* 1 behave rudely to 2 offend ▷ *noun* [IN-sult] 3 offensive remark 4 affront > **in•sult'ing** *adjective*
in•su•per•a•ble [in-SOO-pər-ə-bəl] *adjective* 1 that cannot be overcome or surmounted 2 unconquerable
in•sure [in-SHUUR] *verb* **-sured, -sur•ing** 1

DICTIONARY • THESAURUS

instigation *noun* PROMPTING, behest, bidding, encouragement, incentive, incitement, urging
instigator *noun* RINGLEADER, agitator, leader, motivator, prime mover, troublemaker
instill *verb* INTRODUCE, engender, imbue, implant, inculcate, infuse, insinuate
instinct *noun* INTUITION, faculty, gift, impulse, knack, predisposition, proclivity, talent, tendency
instinctive *adjective* INBORN, automatic, inherent, innate, intuitive, involuntary, natural, reflex, spontaneous, unpremeditated, visceral
instinctively *adverb* INTUITIVELY, automatically, by instinct, involuntarily, naturally, without thinking
institute *noun* 1 SOCIETY, academy, association, college, foundation, guild, institution, school
▷ *verb* 2 ESTABLISH, fix, found, initiate, introduce, launch, organize, originate, pioneer, set up, start
institution *noun* 1 ESTABLISHMENT, academy, college, foundation, institute, school, society
2 CUSTOM, convention, law, practice, ritual, rule, tradition
institutional *adjective* CONVENTIONAL, accepted, established, formal, orthodox
instruct *verb* 1 ORDER, bid, charge, command, direct, enjoin, tell
2 TEACH, coach, drill, educate, ground, school, train, tutor
instruction *noun* 1 TEACHING, coaching, education, grounding, guidance, lesson *or* lessons, schooling, training, tuition
2 ORDER, command, demand, directive, injunction, mandate, ruling
instructions *plural noun* ORDERS, advice, directions, guidance, information, key, recommendations, rules
instructive *adjective* INFORMATIVE, edifying, educational, enlightening, helpful, illuminating, revealing, useful
instructor *noun* TEACHER, adviser, coach, demonstrator, guide, mentor, trainer, tutor
instrument *noun* 1 TOOL, apparatus, appliance, contraption (*informal*), device, gadget, implement, mechanism
2 MEANS, agency, agent, mechanism, medium, organ, vehicle
instrumental *adjective* ACTIVE, contributory, helpful, influential, involved, useful
insubordinate *adjective* DISOBEDIENT, defiant, disorderly, mutinous, rebellious, recalcitrant, refractory, undisciplined, ungovernable, unruly
insubordination *noun* DISOBEDIENCE, defiance, indiscipline, insurrection, mutiny, rebellion, recalcitrance, revolt
insubstantial *adjective* FLIMSY, feeble, frail, poor, slight, tenuous, thin, weak
insufferable *adjective* UNBEARABLE, detestable, dreadful, impossible, insupportable, intolerable, unendurable
insufficient *adjective* INADEQUATE, deficient, incapable, lacking, scant, short
insular *adjective* NARROW-MINDED, blinkered, circumscribed, inward-looking, limited, narrow, parochial, petty, provincial
insulate *verb* ISOLATE, close off, cocoon, cushion, cut off, protect, sequester, shield
insult *verb* 1 OFFEND, abuse, affront, call names, put down, slander, slight, snub
▷ *noun* 2 ABUSE, affront, aspersion, insolence, offense, put-down, slap in the face (*informal*), slight, snub
insulting *adjective* OFFENSIVE, abusive, contemptuous, degrading, disparaging, insolent, rude, scurrilous
insuperable *adjective* INSURMOUNTABLE, impassable, invincible, unconquerable
insupportable *adjective* 1 INTOLERABLE, insufferable, unbearable, unendurable
2 UNJUSTIFIABLE, indefensible, untenable

contract for payment in event of loss, death, etc., by payment of premiums 2 make such contract about 3 make safe (against) > **in•sur'a•ble** *adjective* > **in•sur'ance** *noun* > **in•sur'er** *noun* 1 insurance policy 2 contract of insurance

in•sur•gent [in-SUR-jənt] *adjective* 1 in revolt ▷ *noun* 2 rebel > **in•sur'gence, in•sur•rec'tion** *noun* revolt

in•tact [in-TAKT] *adjective* 1 untouched 2 uninjured

in•tagl•io [in-TAL-yoh] *noun, plural* **-tagl•ios** 1 engraved design 2 gem so cut

in•take [IN-tayk] *noun* 1 what is taken in 2 quantity taken in 3 opening for taking in 4 in car, air passage into carburetor

in•tan'gi•ble *adjective* not clear or definite enough to be seen or felt easily

in•te•ger [IN-ti-jər] *noun* 1 whole number 2 whole of anything

in•te•gral [IN-ti-grəl] *adjective* constituting an essential part of a whole > **in'te•grate** *verb transitive* **-grat•ed, -grat•ing** 1 combine into one whole 2 unify diverse elements (of community, etc.) > **in•te•gra'tion** *noun* > **integral calculus** branch of mathematics of changing quantities that calculates total effects of the change > **integrated circuit** tiny electronic circuit

in•teg•ri•ty [in-TEG-ri-tee] *noun* 1 honesty 2 original perfect state

in•teg•u•ment [in-TEG-yə-mənt] *noun* natural covering, skin, rind, husk

in•tel•lect [IN-tl-ekt] *noun* power of thinking and reasoning > **in•tel•lec'tu•al** *adjective* 1 of, appealing to intellect 2 having good intellect ▷ *noun* 3 one endowed with intellect and attracted to intellectual things

in•tel•li•gent [in-TEL-i-jənt] *adjective* 1 having, showing good intellect 2 quick at understanding 3 informed > **in•tel'li•gence** *noun* 1 quickness of understanding 2 mental power or ability 3 intellect 4 information, news, esp. military information > **in•tel•li•gent'si•a** [-JENT-see-ə] *noun* intellectual or cultured classes > **in•tel'li•gi•ble** [-jə-bəl] *adjective* understandable

in•tem•per•ate [in-TEM-pər-it] *adjective* 1 drinking alcohol to excess 2 immoderate 3 unrestrained > **in•tem'per•ance** [-əns] *noun*

in•tend' *verb transitive* propose, mean (to do, say, etc.) > **in•tend'ed** *adjective* 1 planned, future ▷ *noun* 2 (*informal*) proposed spouse

in•tense [in-TENS] *adjective* 1 very strong or acute 2 emotional > **in•ten•si•fi•ca'tion** *noun* > **in•ten'si•fy** *verb* **-fied, -fy•ing** 1 make or become stronger 2 increase > **in•ten'si•ty** *noun* 1 intense quality 2 strength > **in•ten'sive** *adjective* characterized by intensity or emphasis on specified factor

in•tent' *noun* 1 purpose ▷ *adjective* 2 concentrating (on) 3 resolved, bent 4 preoccupied, absorbed > **in•ten'tion** *noun*

insurance *noun* PROTECTION, assurance, cover, guarantee, indemnity, safeguard, security, warranty

insure *verb* PROTECT, assure, cover, guarantee, indemnify, underwrite, warrant

insurgent *noun* 1 REBEL, insurrectionist, mutineer, revolutionary, rioter ▷ *adjective* 2 REBELLIOUS, disobedient, insubordinate, mutinous, revolting, revolutionary, riotous, seditious

insurmountable *adjective* INSUPERABLE, hopeless, impassable, impossible, invincible, overwhelming, unconquerable

insurrection *noun* REBELLION, coup, insurgency, mutiny, revolt, revolution, riot, uprising

intact *adjective* UNDAMAGED, complete, entire, perfect, sound, unbroken, unharmed, unimpaired, unscathed, whole

integral *adjective* ESSENTIAL, basic, component, constituent, fundamental, indispensable, intrinsic, necessary

integrate *verb* COMBINE, amalgamate, assimilate, blend, fuse, incorporate, join, merge, unite

integration *noun* ASSIMILATION, amalgamation, blending, combining, fusing, incorporation, mixing, unification

integrity *noun* 1 HONESTY, goodness, honor, incorruptibility, principle, probity, purity, rectitude, uprightness, virtue
2 UNITY, coherence, cohesion, completeness, soundness, wholeness

intellect *noun* INTELLIGENCE, brains (*informal*), judgment, mind, reason, sense, understanding

intellectual *adjective* 1 SCHOLARLY, bookish, cerebral, highbrow, intelligent, studious, thoughtful ▷ *noun* 2 THINKER, academic, egghead (*informal*), highbrow

intelligence *noun* 1 UNDERSTANDING, acumen, brain power, brains (*informal*), cleverness, comprehension, intellect, perception, sense
2 INFORMATION, data, facts, findings, knowledge, news, notification, report

intelligent *adjective* CLEVER, brainy (*informal*), bright, enlightened, perspicacious, quick-witted, sharp, smart, well-informed

intelligentsia *noun* INTELLECTUALS, highbrows, literati

intelligible *adjective* UNDERSTANDABLE, clear, comprehensible, distinct, lucid, open, plain

intemperate *adjective* EXCESSIVE, extreme, immoderate, profligate, self-indulgent, unbridled, unrestrained, wild

intend *verb* PLAN, aim, have in mind *or* have in view, mean, propose, purpose

intense *adjective* 1 EXTREME, acute, deep, excessive, fierce, great, powerful, profound, severe
2 PASSIONATE, ardent, fanatical, fervent, fierce, heightened, impassioned, vehement

intensify *verb* INCREASE, add to, aggravate, deepen, escalate, heighten, magnify, redouble, reinforce, sharpen, strengthen

intensity *noun* FORCE, ardor, emotion, fanaticism, fervor, fierceness, passion, strength, vehemence, vigor

intensive *adjective* CONCENTRATED, comprehensive, demanding, exhaustive, in-depth, thorough, thoroughgoing

intent *noun* 1 INTENTION, aim, design, end, goal, meaning, object, objective, plan, purpose ▷ *adjective* 2 ATTENTIVE, absorbed, determined, eager, engrossed, preoccupied, rapt, resolved,

purpose, aim > **in•ten'tion•al** *adjective*
in•ter [in-TUR] *verb transitive* **-terred, -ter•ring** bury > **in•ter'ment** *noun*
inter- *prefix* between, among, mutually: *interglacial; interrelation*
in•ter•act [in-tər-AKT] *verb intransitive* act on each other > **in•ter•ac'tion** *noun*
in•ter•cede [in-tər-SEED] *verb intransitive* **-ced•ed, -ced•ing** 1 plead in favor of 2 mediate > **in•ter•ces'sion** *noun*
in•ter•cept [in-tər-SEPT] *verb transitive* 1 cut off 2 seize, stop in transit > **in•ter•cep'tion** *noun* > **in•ter•cept'or, in•ter•cept'er** *noun* 1 one who, that which intercepts 2 fast fighter plane, missile, etc.
in•ter•change [in-tər-CHAYNJ] *verb* **-changed, -chang•ing** 1 (cause to) exchange places ▷ *noun* [IN-tər-chaynj] 2 interchanging 3 highway intersection > **in•ter•change'a•ble** *adjective* able to be exchanged in position or use
in•ter•con•ti•nen•tal [in-tər-kon-tn-EN-təl] *adjective* 1 connecting continents 2 (of missile) able to reach one continent from another
in•ter•course [IN-tər-kors] *noun* 1 mutual dealings 2 communication 3 sexual joining of two people 4 copulation
in•ter•dict [IN-tər-dikt] *noun* 1 in Catholic church, decree restraining faithful from receiving certain sacraments 2 formal prohibition > **in•ter•dict'** *verb transitive* 1 prohibit, forbid 2 restrain > **in•ter•dic'tion** *noun*
in•ter•est [IN-tər-ist] *noun* 1 concern, curiosity 2 thing exciting this 3 sum paid for use of borrowed money 4 legal concern 5 right, advantage, share ▷ *verb transitive* 6 excite, cause to feel interest > **in'ter•est•ing** *adjective*
in•ter•face [IN-tər-fays] *noun* area, surface, boundary linking two systems
in•ter•fere [in-tər-FEER] *verb intransitive* **-fered, -fer•ing** 1 meddle, intervene 2 clash > **in•ter•fer'ence** *noun* 1 act of interfering 2 *radio* interruption of reception by atmospherics or by unwanted signals
in•ter•fer•on [in-tər-FEER-on] *noun* a cellular protein that stops development of an invading virus
in•ter•im [IN-tər-əm] *noun* 1 meantime ▷ *adjective* 2 temporary, intervening
in•te•ri•or [in-TEER-ee-ər] *adjective* 1 inner 2 inland 3 indoors ▷ *noun* 4 inside 5 inland region
in•ter•ject [in-tər-JEKT] *verb transitive* interpose (remark, etc.) > **in•ter•jec'tion** *noun* 1 exclamation 2 interjected remark
in•ter•lard [in-tər-LAHRD] *verb* intersperse
in•ter•loc•u•tor [in-tər-LOK-yə-tər] *noun* 1 one who takes part in conversation 2 middle man in line of minstrel performers > **in•ter•loc'u•to•ry** *adjective* of a court decree, issued before the final decision in an action
in•ter•lop•er [IN-tər-lohp-ər] *noun* 1 one intruding upon another's affairs 2 intruder
in•ter•lude [IN-tər-lood] *noun* 1 interval (in play, etc.) 2 something filling an interval
in•ter•mar•ry [in-tər-MAR-ee] *verb intransitive* **-ried, -ry•ing** 1 (of families, races, religions) become linked by marriage 2 marry within one's family > **in•ter•mar'riage** *noun*
in•ter•me•di•ate [in-tər-MEE-dee-it] *adjective* 1 coming between 2 interposed > **in•ter•me'di•ar•y** *noun*
in•ter•mez•zo [in-tər-MET-soh] *noun, plural* **-zos**

DICTIONARY • THESAURUS

steadfast, watchful
intention *noun* PURPOSE, aim, design, end, goal, idea, object, objective, point, target
intentional *adjective* DELIBERATE, calculated, intended, meant, planned, premeditated, willful
intentionally *adverb* DELIBERATELY, designedly, on purpose, willfully
inter *verb* BURY, entomb, lay to rest
intercede *verb* MEDIATE, arbitrate, intervene, plead
intercept *verb* SEIZE, block, catch, cut off, head off, interrupt, obstruct, stop
interchange *verb* 1 SWITCH, alternate, exchange, reciprocate, swap
▷ *noun* 2 JUNCTION, intersection
interchangeable *adjective* IDENTICAL, equivalent, exchangeable, reciprocal, synonymous
intercourse *noun* 1 COMMUNICATION, commerce, contact, dealings
2 SEXUAL INTERCOURSE, carnal knowledge, coitus, copulation, sex
interest *noun* 1 CURIOSITY, attention, concern, notice, regard
2 HOBBY, activity, diversion, pastime, preoccupation, pursuit
3 ADVANTAGE, benefit, good, profit
4 STAKE, claim, investment, right, share
▷ *verb* 5 INTRIGUE, attract, catch one's eye, divert, engross, fascinate
interested *adjective* 1 CURIOUS, attracted, drawn, excited, fascinated, keen
2 INVOLVED, concerned, implicated
interesting *adjective* INTRIGUING, absorbing, appealing, attractive, compelling, engaging, engrossing, gripping, stimulating, thought-provoking
interface *noun* CONNECTION, border, boundary, frontier, link
interfere *verb* 1 INTRUDE, butt in, intervene, meddle, stick one's oar in (*informal*), tamper
2 (*often with with*) CONFLICT, clash, hamper, handicap, hinder, impede, inhibit, obstruct
interference *noun* 1 INTRUSION, intervention, meddling, prying
2 CONFLICT, clashing, collision, obstruction, opposition
interim *adjective* TEMPORARY, acting, caretaker, improvised, makeshift, provisional, stopgap
interior *noun* 1 INSIDE, center, core, heart
▷ *adjective* 2 INSIDE, inner, internal, inward
3 MENTAL, hidden, inner, intimate, personal, private, secret, spiritual
interloper *noun* TRESPASSER, gate-crasher (*informal*), intruder, meddler
interlude *noun* INTERVAL, break, breathing space, delay, hiatus, intermission, pause, respite, rest, spell, stoppage
intermediary *noun* MEDIATOR, agent, broker, go-between, middleman
intermediate *adjective* MIDDLE, halfway, in-between (*informal*), intervening, mid, midway, transitional
interment *noun* BURIAL, funeral

short performance between acts of play or opera

in•ter•mi•na•ble [in-TUR-mə-nə-bəl] *adjective* endless > **in•ter'mi•na•bly** *adverb*

in•ter•mis•sion [in-tər-MISH-ən] *noun* short interval between parts of a concert, play, etc. > **in•ter•mit'tent** *adjective* occurring at intervals

in•tern[1] [in-TURN] *verb transitive* confine to special area or camp > **in•tern'ment** *noun* > **in•tern•ee'** *noun*

in•tern[2]**, in•terne** [IN-turn] *noun* 1 recent medical school graduate residing in hospital and working under supervision as member of staff 2 trainee in occupation or profession > **in'tern•ship** *noun*

in•ter•nal [in-TUR-nl] *adjective* 1 inward 2 interior 3 within (a country, organization) > **internal combustion** process of exploding mixture of air and fuel within engine cylinder

in•ter•na•tion•al [in-tər-NASH-ə-nl] *adjective* 1 of relations between nations ▷ *noun* 2 labor union, etc. with units, members, in more than one country

in•ter•ne•cine [in-tər-NEE-seen] *adjective* 1 mutually destructive 2 deadly

In•ter•net, in•ter•net [IN-tər-net] *noun* large international public access computer network

in•ter•po•late [in-TUR-pə-layt] *verb transitive* **-lat•ed, -lat•ing** 1 insert new (esp. misleading) matter (in book, etc.) 2 interject (remark) 3 *math.* estimate a value between known values > **in•ter•po•la'tion** *noun*

in•ter•pose [in-tər-POHZ] *verb transitive* **-posed, -pos•ing** 1 insert 2 say as interruption 3 put in the way ▷ *verb intransitive* **-posed, -pos•ing** 4 intervene 5 obstruct > **in•ter•po•si'tion** [-pə-ZISH-ən] *noun*

in•ter•pret [in-TUR-prit] *verb* 1 explain 2 translate, esp. orally 3 *art* render, represent > **in•ter•pre•ta'tion** *noun*

in•ter•reg•num [in-tər-REG-nəm] *noun, plural* **-nums** 1 interval between reigns 2 gap in continuity

in•ter•ro•gate [in-TER-ə-gayt] *verb transitive* **-gat•ed, -gat•ing** question, esp. closely or officially > **in•ter•ro•ga'tion** *noun* > **in•ter•rog'a•tive** *adjective* 1 questioning ▷ *noun* 2 word used in asking question > **in•ter•rog'a•to•ry** *adjective* 1 of inquiry ▷ *noun* 2 question, set of questions

in•ter•rupt [in-tə-RUPT] *verb* 1 break in (upon) 2 stop the course of 3 block > **in•ter•rup'tion** *noun*

in•ter•sect [in-tər-SEKT] *verb transitive* 1 divide by passing across or through ▷ *verb intransitive* 2 meet and cross > **in•ter•sec'tion** *noun* point where lines, roads cross

in•ter•sperse [in-tər-SPURS] *verb transitive* **-spersed, -spers•ing** sprinkle (something with or something among or in)

in•ter•stel•lar [in-tər-STEL-ər] *adjective* (of the space) between stars

in•ter•stice [in-TUR-stis] *noun, plural* **-stic•es** [-stə-seez] chink, gap, crevice > **in•ter•sti'tial** [-STISH-əl] *adjective*

in•ter•val [IN-tər-vəl] *noun* 1 intervening time or space 2 pause, break 3 short period between parts of play, concert, etc. 4 difference (of pitch)

in•ter•vene [in-tər-VEEN] *verb intransitive* **-vened, -ven•ing** 1 come into a situation in order to change it 2 be, come between or among 3 occur in meantime 4 interpose > **in•ter•ven'tion** *noun*

in•tes•tate [in-TES-tayt] *adjective* 1 not having made a will ▷ *noun* 2 person dying intestate > **in•tes'ta•cy** [-tə-see] *noun*

in•tes•tine [in-TES-tin] *noun* (*usually plural*) lower part of alimentary canal between stomach

interminable *adjective* ENDLESS, ceaseless, everlasting, infinite, long-drawn-out, long-winded, never-ending, perpetual, protracted

intermingle *verb* MIX, blend, combine, fuse, interlace, intermix, interweave, merge

intermission *noun* INTERVAL, break, interlude, pause, recess, respite, rest, stoppage

intermittent *adjective* PERIODIC, broken, fitful, irregular, occasional, spasmodic, sporadic

intern[1] *verb* IMPRISON, confine, detain, hold, hold in custody

internal *adjective* 1 INNER, inside, interior 2 DOMESTIC, civic, home, in-house, intramural

international *adjective* UNIVERSAL, cosmopolitan, global, intercontinental, worldwide

Internet *noun* INFORMATION SUPERHIGHWAY, cyberspace, the net (*informal*), the web (*informal*), World Wide Web

interpose *verb* INTERRUPT, insert, interject, put one's oar in

interpret *verb* EXPLAIN, construe, decipher, decode, elucidate, make sense of, render, translate

interpretation *noun* EXPLANATION, analysis, clarification, elucidation, exposition, portrayal, rendition, translation, version

interpreter *noun* TRANSLATOR, commentator

interrogate *verb* QUESTION, cross-examine, examine, grill (*informal*), investigate, pump, quiz

interrogation *noun* QUESTIONING, cross-examination, examination, grilling (*informal*), inquiry, inquisition, third degree (*informal*)

interrupt *verb* 1 INTRUDE, barge in (*informal*), break in, butt in, disturb, heckle, interfere *or* interfere with 2 SUSPEND, break off, cut short, delay, discontinue, hold up, lay aside, stop

interruption *noun* STOPPAGE, break, disruption, disturbance, hitch, intrusion, pause, suspension

intersection *noun* JUNCTION, crossing, crossroads, interchange

interval *noun* BREAK, delay, gap, interlude, intermission, pause, respite, rest, space, spell

intervene *verb* 1 INVOLVE ONESELF, arbitrate, intercede, interfere, intrude, lend a hand, mediate, step in (*informal*) 2 HAPPEN, befall, come to pass, ensue, occur, take place

intervention *noun* MEDIATION, agency, interference, intrusion

interview *noun* 1 MEETING, audience, conference, consultation, dialogue, press conference, talk ▷ *verb* 2 QUESTION, examine, interrogate, talk to

interviewer *noun* QUESTIONER, examiner, interrogator, investigator, reporter

intestines *plural noun* GUTS, bowels, entrails,

and anus > **in•tes'ti•nal** *adjective* of bowels

in•ti•mate[1] [IN-tə-mit] *adjective* 1 closely acquainted, familiar 2 private 3 extensive 4 having sexual relations (with) ▷ *noun* 5 intimate friend > **in'ti•ma•cy** [-mə-see] *noun*

in•ti•mate[2] [IN-tə-mayt] *verb transitive* **-mat•ed, -mat•ing** 1 imply 2 announce > **in•ti•ma'tion** *noun* notice

in•tim•i•date [in-TIM-i-dayt] *verb transitive* **-dat•ed, -dat•ing** 1 frighten into submission 2 deter by threats > **in•tim•i•da'tion** *noun*

in•to [IN-too] *preposition* 1 expresses motion to a point within 2 indicates change of state 3 indicates coming up against, encountering 4 indicates arithmetical division

in•tol'er•a•ble *adjective* more than can be endured

in•tone [in-TOHN] *verb transitive* **-toned, -ton•ing** 1 chant 2 recite in monotone > **in•to•na'tion** *noun* 1 modulation of voice 2 intoning 3 accent

in•tox•i•cate [in-TOK-si-kayt] *verb transitive* **-cat•ed, -cat•ing** 1 make drunk 2 excite to excess > **in•tox'i•cant** [-kənt] *adjective, noun* intoxicating (liquor)

intr. intransitive

intra- *prefix* within: *intravenous*

in•trac•ta•ble [in-TRAK-tə-bəl] *adjective* 1 difficult to influence 2 hard to control

in•tra•net [IN-trə-net] *noun computing* local network that makes use of Internet technology

in•tran•si•gent [in-TRAN-si-jənt] *adjective* uncompromising, obstinate

in•tra•u•ter•ine [in-trə-YOO-tər-in] *adjective* within the womb

in•tra•ve•nous [in-trə-VEE-nəs] *adjective* into a vein

in•trep'id *adjective* fearless, undaunted > **in•tre•pid'i•ty** *noun*

in•tri•cate [IN-tri-kit] *adjective* involved, puzzlingly entangled > **in'tri•ca•cy** *noun, plural* **-cies**

in•trigue [in-TREEG] *noun* 1 underhanded plot 2 secret love affair ▷ *verb intransitive* **-trigued, -tri•guing** 3 carry on intrigue ▷ *verb transitive* 4 interest, puzzle

in•trin•sic [in-TRIN-sik] *adjective* inherent, essential > **in•trin'si•cal•ly** *adverb*

intro- *prefix* into, within: *introduce; introvert*

in•tro•duce [in-trə-DOOS] *verb transitive* **-duced,**

innards (*informal*), insides (*informal*), viscera

intimacy *noun* FAMILIARITY, closeness, confidentiality

intimate[1] *adjective* 1 CLOSE, bosom, buddy-buddy (*informal*), confidential, dear, near, thick (*informal*)
2 PERSONAL, confidential, private, secret
3 DETAILED, deep, exhaustive, first-hand, immediate, in-depth, profound, thorough
4 SNUG, comfy (*informal*), cozy, friendly, homey, warm
▷ *noun* 5 FRIEND, close friend, confidant *or* confidante, *feminine* companion *or* constant companion, crony, homeboy (*slang*), homegirl (*slang*), soul mate

intimate[2] *verb* 1 SUGGEST, hint, imply, indicate, insinuate
2 ANNOUNCE, communicate, declare, make known, state

intimately *adverb* 1 CONFIDINGLY, affectionately, confidentially, familiarly, personally, tenderly, warmly
2 IN DETAIL, fully, inside out, thoroughly, very well

intimation *noun* 1 HINT, allusion, indication, inkling, insinuation, reminder, suggestion, warning
2 ANNOUNCEMENT, communication, declaration, notice

intimidate *verb* FRIGHTEN, browbeat, bully, coerce, daunt, overawe, scare, subdue, terrorize, threaten

intimidation *noun* BULLYING, arm-twisting (*informal*), browbeating, coercion, menaces, pressure, terrorization, threat *or* threats

intolerable *adjective* UNBEARABLE, excruciating, impossible, insufferable, insupportable, painful, unendurable

intolerance *noun* NARROW-MINDEDNESS, bigotry, chauvinism, discrimination, dogmatism, fanaticism, illiberality, prejudice

intolerant *adjective* NARROW-MINDED, bigoted, chauvinistic, dictatorial, dogmatic, fanatical, illiberal, prejudiced, small-minded

intone *verb* RECITE, chant

intoxicated *adjective* 1 DRUNK, drunken, inebriated, paralytic (*informal*), plastered (*slang*), tipsy, under the influence (*informal*)
2 EUPHORIC, dizzy, elated, enraptured, excited, exhilarated, high (*informal*), wired (*slang*)

intoxicating *adjective* 1 ALCOHOLIC, strong
2 EXCITING, exhilarating, heady, thrilling

intoxication *noun* 1 DRUNKENNESS, inebriation, insobriety, tipsiness
2 EXCITEMENT, delirium, elation, euphoria, exhilaration

intransigent *adjective* UNCOMPROMISING, hardline, intractable, obdurate, obstinate, stiff-necked, stubborn, unbending, unyielding

intrepid *adjective* FEARLESS, audacious, bold, brave, courageous, daring, gallant, plucky, stouthearted, valiant

intricacy *noun* COMPLEXITY, complication, convolutions, elaborateness

intricate *adjective* COMPLICATED, complex, convoluted, elaborate, fancy, involved, labyrinthine, tangled, tortuous

intrigue *verb* 1 INTEREST, attract, fascinate, rivet, titillate
2 PLOT, connive, conspire, machinate, maneuver, scheme
▷ *noun* 3 PLOT, chicanery, collusion, conspiracy, machination, maneuver, scheme, stratagem, wile
4 AFFAIR, amour, intimacy, liaison, romance

intriguing *adjective* INTERESTING, beguiling, compelling, diverting, exciting, fascinating, tantalizing, titillating

intrinsic *adjective* INBORN, basic, built-in, congenital, constitutional, essential, fundamental, inbred, inherent, native, natural

introduce *verb* 1 PRESENT, acquaint, familiarize, make known
2 BRING IN, establish, found, initiate, institute, launch, pioneer, set up, start
3 BRING UP, advance, air, broach, moot, put forward, submit

-duc•ing 1 make acquainted 2 present 3 bring in 4 bring forward 5 bring into practice 6 insert > **in•tro•duc'tion** *noun* 1 an introducing 2 presentation of one person to another 3 preliminary section or treatment > **in•tro•duc'to•ry** *adjective* preliminary

in•tro•spec•tion *noun* [in-trə-SPEK-shən] examination of one's own thoughts > **in•tro•spec'tive** *adjective*

in•tro•vert [IN-trə-vurt] *noun psychoanalysis* one who looks inward rather than at the external world > **in•tro•ver'sion** [-*zhən*] *noun* > **in'tro•vert•ed** *adjective*

in•trude [in-TROOD] *verb* **-trud•ed, -trud•ing** thrust (oneself) in uninvited > **in•tru'sion** [-*zhən*] *noun* > **in•tru'sive** *adjective*

in•tu•i•tion [in-too-ISH-ən] *noun* 1 immediate mental apprehension without reasoning 2 immediate insight > **in•tu'it** *verb* > **in•tu'i•tive** *adjective*

In•u•it [IN-oo-it] *noun* one of race of indigenous people of Alaska, N Canada, and Greenland ▷ *adjective*

in•un•date [IN-ən-dayt] *verb transitive* **-dat•ed, -dat•ing** 1 flood 2 overwhelm > **in•un•da'tion** *noun*

in•ure [in-YUUR] *verb transitive* **-ured, -ur•ing** accustom, esp. to hardship, danger, etc.

in•vade [in-VAYD] *verb transitive* **-vad•ed, -vad•ing** 1 enter by force with hostile intent 2 overrun 3 pervade > **in•va'sion** [-*zhən*] *noun*

in•va•lid[1] [IN-və-lid] *noun* 1 one suffering from chronic ill health ▷ *adjective* 2 ill, suffering from sickness or injury ▷ *verb* 3 become an invalid 4 retire from active service because of illness, etc.

in•val•id[2] [in-VAL-id] *adjective* not valid

in•val•u•a•ble [in-VAL-yoo-ə-bəl] *adjective* priceless

invasion *see* **invade**

in•veigh [in-VAY] *verb intransitive* speak violently (against) > **in•vec'tive** *noun* abusive speech or writing, vituperation

in•vei•gle [in-VAY-gəl] *verb transitive* **-gled, -gling** entice, seduce, wheedle

in•vent' *verb transitive* 1 devise, originate 2 fabricate (falsehoods, etc.) > **in•ven'tion** *noun* 1 that which is invented 2 ability to invent 3 contrivance 4 deceit 5 lie > **in•vent'ive** *adjective* 1 resourceful 2 creative > **in•ven'tor** *noun*

in•ven•to•ry [IN-vən-tor-ee] *noun, plural* **-ries** 1 detailed list of goods, etc. ▷ *verb transitive* **-ried, -ry•ing** 2 make list of

in•vert [in-VURT] *verb transitive* 1 turn upside

---

4 INSERT, add, inject, put in, throw in (*informal*)

introduction *noun* 1 LAUNCH, establishment, inauguration, institution, pioneering
2 OPENING, foreword, intro (*informal*), lead-in, preamble, preface, prelude, prologue

introductory *adjective* PRELIMINARY, first, inaugural, initial, opening, preparatory

introspective *adjective* INWARD-LOOKING, brooding, contemplative, introverted, meditative, pensive

introverted *adjective* INTROSPECTIVE, inner-directed, inward-looking, self-contained, withdrawn

intrude *verb* INTERFERE, butt in, encroach, infringe, interrupt, meddle, push in, trespass

intruder *noun* TRESPASSER, gate-crasher (*informal*), infiltrator, interloper, invader, prowler

intrusion *noun* INVASION, encroachment, infringement, interference, interruption, trespass, violation

intrusive *adjective* INTERFERING, impertinent, importunate, meddlesome, nosy (*informal*), presumptuous, pushy (*informal*), uncalled-for, unwanted

intuition *noun* INSTINCT, hunch, insight, perception, presentiment, sixth sense

intuitive *adjective* INSTINCTIVE, innate, spontaneous, untaught

inundate *verb* FLOOD, drown, engulf, immerse, overflow, overrun, overwhelm, submerge, swamp

invade *verb* 1 ATTACK, assault, burst in, descend upon, encroach, infringe, make inroads, occupy, raid, violate
2 INFEST, overrun, permeate, pervade, swarm over

invader *noun* ATTACKER, aggressor, plunderer, raider, trespasser

invalid[1] *adjective* 1 DISABLED, ailing, bedridden, challenged, frail, ill, infirm, sick
▷ *noun* 2 PATIENT, convalescent, valetudinarian

invalid[2] *adjective* NULL AND VOID, fallacious, false, illogical, inoperative, irrational, unfounded, unsound, void, worthless

invalidate *verb* NULLIFY, annul, cancel, overthrow, undermine, undo

invaluable *adjective* PRECIOUS, inestimable, priceless, valuable, worth one's weight in gold *or* worth its weight in gold

invariably *adverb* CONSISTENTLY, always, customarily, day in, day out, habitually, perpetually, regularly, unfailingly, without exception

invasion *noun* 1 ATTACK, assault, campaign, foray, incursion, inroad, offensive, onslaught, raid
2 INTRUSION, breach, encroachment, infraction, infringement, usurpation, violation

invective *noun* ABUSE, censure, denunciation, diatribe, tirade, tongue-lashing, vilification, vituperation

invent *verb* 1 CREATE, coin, conceive, design, devise, discover, formulate, improvise, originate, think up
2 MAKE UP, concoct, cook up (*informal*), fabricate, feign, forge, manufacture, trump up

invention *noun* 1 CREATION, brainchild (*informal*), contraption, contrivance, design, device, discovery, gadget, instrument
2 CREATIVITY, genius, imagination, ingenuity, inventiveness, originality, resourcefulness
3 FICTION, fabrication, falsehood, fantasy, forgery, lie, untruth, yarn

inventive *adjective* CREATIVE, fertile, imaginative, ingenious, innovative, inspired, original, resourceful

inventor *noun* CREATOR, architect, author, coiner, designer, maker, originator

inventory *noun* LIST, account, catalog, file, record, register, roll, roster

inverse *adjective* OPPOSITE, contrary, converse, reverse, reversed, transposed

down **2** reverse position, relations of > **in•verse'** *adjective* **1** inverted **2** opposite ▷ *noun* > **in•verse'ly** *adverb* > **in•ver'sion** [-zhən] *noun*

in•ver•te•brate [in-VUR-tə-brit] *noun* **1** animal having no vertebral column ▷ *adjective* **2** spineless

in•vest' *verb transitive* **1** lay out (money, time, effort, etc.) for profit or advantage **2** install **3** endow **4** *poet.* cover as with garment > **in•ves'ti•ture** [-chər] *noun* formal installation of person in office or rank > **in•vest'ment** *noun* **1** investing **2** money invested **3** stocks, bonds, etc. bought

in•ves•ti•gate [in-VES-ti-gayt] *verb* **1** inquire into **2** examine > **in•ves•ti•ga'tion** *noun*

in•vet•er•ate [in-VET-ər-it] *adjective* **1** deep-rooted **2** long established, confirmed

in•vid•i•ous [in-VID-ee-əs] *adjective* likely to cause ill will or envy

in•vig•or•ate [in-VIG-ə-rayt] *verb transitive* **-at•ed, -at•ing** give vigor to, strengthen

in•vin•ci•ble [in-VIN-sə-bəl] *adjective* unconquerable > **in•vin•ci•bil'i•ty** *noun*

in•vi•o•la•ble [in-VĪ-ə-lə-bəl] *adjective* **1** not to be profaned **2** sacred **3** unalterable > **in•vi'o•late** [-ə-lit] *adjective* **1** unhurt **2** unprofaned **3** unbroken

in•vis'i•ble *adjective* not able to be seen > **in•vis•i•bil'i•ty** *noun*

in•vite [in-VĪT] *verb transitive* **-vit•ed, -vit•ing** **1** request the company of **2** ask courteously **3** ask for **4** attract, call forth ▷ *noun* [IN-vīt] **5** (*informal*) an invitation > **in•vi•ta'tion** *noun*

in•voice [IN-vois] *noun* **1** itemized bill for goods or services sold ▷ *verb transitive* **-voiced, -voic•ing** **2** make or present an invoice

in•voke [in-VOHK] *verb transitive* **-voked, -vok•ing** **1** call on **2** appeal to **3** ask earnestly for **4** summon > **in•vo•ca'tion** *noun*

in•vol•un•tar•y [in-VOL-ən-ter-ee] *adjective* **1** not done willingly **2** unintentional **3** instinctive

in•vo•lute [IN-və-loot] *adjective* **1** complex **2** coiled spirally **3** (*also* **in•vo•lut'ed**) rolled inward

in•volve [in-VOLV] *verb transitive* **-volved, -volv•ing** **1** include **2** entail **3** implicate (person) **4** concern **5** entangle > **involved** *adjective* **1** complicated **2** concerned (in)

in•vul'ner•a•ble *adjective* not able to be wounded or harmed

in•ward [IN-wərd] *adjective* **1** internal **2** situated within **3** spiritual, mental ▷ *adverb* (*also* **in'wards**) **4** toward the inside **5** into the mind > **in'ward•ly** *adverb* **1** in the mind **2** internally

i•o•dine [Ī-ə-dīn] *noun* nonmetallic element found in seaweed and used in antiseptic solution, photography, etc. > **i'o•dize** *verb transitive* **-dized, -diz•ing** treat or react with iodine

i•on [Ī-ən] *noun* electrically charged atom or

DICTIONARY • THESAURUS

invert *verb* OVERTURN, reverse, transpose, upset, upturn

invest *verb* **1** SPEND, advance, devote, lay out, put in, sink
2 EMPOWER, authorize, charge, license, sanction, vest

investigate *verb* EXAMINE, explore, go into, inquire into, inspect, look into, probe, research, study

investigation *noun* EXAMINATION, exploration, inquest, inquiry, inspection, probe, review, search, study, survey

investigator *noun* EXAMINER, gumshoe (*slang*), inquirer, detective *or* private detective, private eye (*informal*), researcher, sleuth

investiture *noun* INSTALLATION, enthronement, inauguration, induction, ordination

investment *noun* **1** TRANSACTION, speculation, venture
2 STAKE, ante (*informal*), contribution

inveterate *adjective* LONG-STANDING, chronic, confirmed, deep-seated, dyed-in-the-wool, entrenched, habitual, hardened, incorrigible, incurable

invidious *adjective* UNDESIRABLE, hateful

invigorate *verb* REFRESH, energize, enliven, exhilarate, fortify, galvanize, liven up, revitalize, stimulate

invincible *adjective* UNBEATABLE, impregnable, indestructible, indomitable, insuperable, invulnerable, unassailable, unconquerable

inviolable *adjective* SACROSANCT, hallowed, holy, inalienable, sacred, unalterable

inviolate *adjective* INTACT, entire, pure, unbroken, undefiled, unhurt, unpolluted, unsullied, untouched, whole

invisible *adjective* UNSEEN, imperceptible, indiscernible

invitation *noun* REQUEST, call, invite (*informal*), summons

invite *verb* **1** REQUEST, ask, beg, bid, summon
2 ENCOURAGE, ask for (*informal*), attract, court, entice, provoke, tempt, welcome

inviting *adjective* TEMPTING, alluring, appealing, attractive, enticing, mouthwatering, seductive, welcoming

invocation *noun* APPEAL, entreaty, petition, prayer, supplication

invoke *verb* **1** CALL UPON, appeal to, beg, beseech, entreat, implore, petition, pray, supplicate
2 APPLY, implement, initiate, put into effect, resort to, use

involuntary *adjective* UNINTENTIONAL, automatic, instinctive, reflex, spontaneous, unconscious, uncontrolled, unthinking

involve *verb* **1** ENTAIL, imply, mean, necessitate, presuppose, require
2 CONCERN, affect, draw in, implicate, touch

involved *adjective* **1** COMPLICATED, complex, confusing, convoluted, elaborate, intricate, labyrinthine, tangled, tortuous
2 CONCERNED, caught *or* caught up, implicated, mixed up in *or* mixed up with, participating, taking part

involvement *noun* CONNECTION, association, commitment, interest, participation

invulnerable *adjective* SAFE, impenetrable, indestructible, insusceptible, invincible, proof against, secure, unassailable

inward *adjective* **1** INCOMING, entering, inbound, ingoing
2 INTERNAL, inner, inside, interior
3 PRIVATE, confidential, hidden, inmost,

group of atoms > **i•on'ic** *adjective* > **i•on•i•za'tion** *noun* > **i'on•ize** *verb transitive* **-ized, -iz•ing** change into ions > **i•on'o•sphere** *noun* region of atmosphere about 50 to 250 miles (80 to 400 km) above Earth

I•on•ic [ī-ON-ik] *adjective architecture* distinguished by scroll-like decoration on columns

i•o•ta [ī-OH-tə] *noun* 1 the Greek letter *i* 2 (usu. with *not*) very small amount

IP ad•dress *noun* Internet protocol address: numeric code that identifies all computers that are connected to the Internet

iPod [Ī-pod] *noun* ® small portable digital audio player capable of storing thousands of tracks downloaded from the Internet or transferred from CDs

ip•so fac•to [IP-soh FAK-toh] *Lat.* by that very fact

Ir *chem.* iridium

ir- *prefix same as* **in-¹** *or* **in-²**

ire [īr] *noun* anger, wrath > **i•ras•ci•ble** [i-RAS-ə-bəl] *adjective* hot-tempered > **i•ras'ci•bly** *adverb* > **i•rate** [ī-RAYT] *adjective* angry

ir•i•des•cent [ir-i-DES-ənt] *adjective* exhibiting changing colors like those of the rainbow > **ir•i•des'cence** *noun*

i•rid•i•um [i-RID-ee-əm] *noun* very hard, corrosion-resistant metallic element

i•ris [Ī-ris] *noun* 1 circular membrane of eye containing pupil 2 plant with sword-shaped leaves and showy flowers

irk [urk] *verb transitive* irritate, vex > **irk'some** [-sum] *adjective* tiresome

i•ron [Ī-ərn] *noun* 1 metallic element, much used for tools, etc., and the raw material of steel 2 tool, etc., of this metal 3 appliance used, when heated, to smooth cloth 4 metal-headed golf club ▷ *adjective* 5 of, like, iron 6 inflexible, unyielding 7 robust ▷ *verb* 8 smooth, cover, fetter, etc., with iron or an iron > **i•rons** *plural, noun* fetters > **i'ron•clad** *adjective* protected with or as with iron > **iron curtain** any barrier that separates communities or ideologies > **iron lung** apparatus for administering artificial respiration

i•ro•ny [Ī-rə-nee] *noun, plural* **-nies** 1 (usu. humorous or mildly sarcastic) use of words to mean the opposite of what is said 2 event, situation opposite of that expected > **i•ron'ic** *adjective* of, using, irony

ir•ra•di•ate [i-RAY-dee-ayt] *verb transitive* **-at•ed, -at•ing** 1 treat by irradiation 2 shine upon, throw light upon, light up > **ir•ra•di•a'tion** *noun* impregnation by X-rays, light rays

ir•ra'tion•al *adjective* not based on or not using logical reasoning

ir•re•fran•gi•ble [ir-i-FRAN-jə-bəl] *adjective* 1 inviolable 2 in optics, not susceptible to refraction

ir•ref•u•ta•ble [i-REF-yə-tə-bəl] *adjective* that cannot be refuted, disproved

ir•reg'u•lar *adjective* 1 not regular or even 2 not conforming to accepted practice 3 (of a word) not following the typical pattern of formation in a language > **ir•reg•u•lar'i•ty** *noun, plural* **-ties**

ir•rel'e•vant *adjective* not connected with the matter in hand > **ir•rel'e•vance** *noun*

ir•rep•a•ra•ble [i-REP-ər-ə-bəl] *adjective* not able to be repaired or remedied

ir•re•place'a•ble *adjective* impossible to replace

ir•re•sist'i•ble *adjective* too attractive or strong to resist

ir•res'o•lute *adjective* unable to make decisions

ir•re•spec•tive [ir-i-SPEK-tiv] *adjective* without taking account (of)

ir•re•spon'si•ble *adjective* not showing or not done with due care for the consequences of

DICTIONARY

innermost, personal, secret

inwardly *adverb* PRIVATELY, at heart, deep down, inside, secretly

irate *adjective* ANGRY, annoyed, cross, enraged, furious, incensed, indignant, infuriated, livid

irksome *adjective* IRRITATING, annoying, bothersome, disagreeable, exasperating, tiresome, troublesome, trying, vexing, wearisome

iron *adjective* 1 FERROUS, chalybeate, ferric
2 INFLEXIBLE, adamant, hard, implacable, indomitable, rigid, steely, strong, tough, unbending, unyielding

ironic *adjective* 1 SARCASTIC, double-edged, mocking, sardonic, satirical, with tongue in cheek, wry
2 PARADOXICAL, incongruous

iron out *verb* SETTLE, clear up, get rid of, put right, reconcile, resolve, smooth over, sort out, straighten out

irony *noun* 1 SARCASM, mockery, satire
2 PARADOX, incongruity

irrational *adjective* ILLOGICAL, absurd, crazy, nonsensical, preposterous, unreasonable

irrefutable *adjective* UNDENIABLE, certain, incontestable, incontrovertible, indisputable, indubitable, sure, unquestionable

irregular *adjective* 1 VARIABLE, erratic, fitful, haphazard, occasional, random, spasmodic, sporadic, unsystematic
2 UNCONVENTIONAL, abnormal, exceptional, extraordinary, peculiar, unofficial, unorthodox, unusual
3 UNEVEN, asymmetrical, bumpy, crooked, jagged, lopsided, ragged, rough

irregularity *noun* 1 UNCERTAINTY, desultoriness, disorganization, haphazardness
2 ABNORMALITY, anomaly, oddity, peculiarity, unorthodoxy
3 UNEVENNESS, asymmetry, bumpiness, jaggedness, lopsidedness, raggedness, roughness

irrelevant *adjective* UNCONNECTED, beside the point, extraneous, immaterial, impertinent, inapplicable, inappropriate, neither here nor there, unrelated

irreparable *adjective* BEYOND REPAIR, incurable, irremediable, irretrievable, irreversible

irrepressible *adjective* EBULLIENT, boisterous, buoyant, effervescent, unstoppable

irreproachable *adjective* BLAMELESS, beyond reproach, faultless, impeccable, innocent, perfect, pure, unimpeachable

irresistible *adjective* OVERWHELMING, compelling, compulsive, overpowering, urgent

irresponsible *adjective* IMMATURE, careless, reckless, scatterbrained, shiftless, thoughtless, unreliable, untrustworthy

THESAURUS

one's actions or attitudes
ir•rev•o•ca•ble [i-REV-ə-kə-bəl] *adjective* not able to be changed, undone, altered
ir•ri•gate [IR-i-gayt] *verb transitive* **-gat•ed, -gat•ing** water by artificial channels, pipes, etc. > **ir•ri•ga'tion** *noun*
ir•ri•tate [IR-i-tayt] *verb transitive* **-tat•ed, -tat•ing** 1 annoy 2 inflame 3 stimulate > **ir'ri•ta•ble** *adjective* easily annoyed > **ir'ri•tant** *adjective, noun* (person or thing) causing irritation > **ir•ri•ta'tion** *noun*
Is. Isaiah
is [iz] *third person singular, present indicative of* **be**
Is•lam [iz-LAHM] *noun* Muslim faith or world > **Is•lam'ic** *adjective*
is•land [Ī-lənd] *noun* 1 piece of land surrounded by water 2 raised area for pedestrians in middle of road
isle [īl] *noun* island > **is•let** [Ī-lit] *noun* little island
i•so•bar [Ī-sə-bahr] *noun* line on map connecting places of equal mean barometric pressure
i•so•late [Ī-sə-layt] *verb transitive* **-lat•ed, -lat•ing** place apart or alone > **i•so•la'tion** *noun* > **i•so•la'tion•ism** *noun* policy of not participating in international affairs
i•so•mer [Ī-sə-mər] *noun* substance with same molecules as another but different atomic arrangement > **i•so•mer'ic** *adjective*
i•so•met•ric [ī-sə-ME-trik] *adjective* 1 having equal dimensions 2 relating to muscular contraction without movement > **i•so•met'rics** *plural noun* system of isometric exercises
i•sos•ce•les [ī-SOS-ə-leez] *adjective* of triangle, having two sides equal
i•so•therm [Ī-sə-thurm] *noun* line on map connecting points of equal mean temperature
i•so•tope [Ī-sə-tohp] *noun* atom of element having a different nuclear mass and atomic weight from other atoms in same element > **i•so•top'ic** *adjective*
ISP Internet service provider: business providing its customers with connection to the Internet
is•sue [ISH-oo] *noun* 1 sending or giving out officially or publicly 2 number or amount so given out 3 discharge 4 offspring, children 5 topic of discussion 6 question, dispute 7 outcome, result ▷ *verb intransitive* **-sued, -su•ing** 8 go out 9 result in 10 arise (from) ▷ *verb transitive* **-sued, -su•ing** 11 emit, give out, send out 12 distribute, publish
isth•mus [IS-məs] *noun* neck of land between two seas
it *pronoun* neuter pronoun of the third person > **its** *adjective* belonging to it > **it's** 1 it is 2 it has > **it•self'** *pronoun* *emphatic form of* **it**
i•tal•ic [i-TAL-ik] *adjective* of type, sloping > **i•tal'ics** *plural noun* this type, now used for emphasis, etc. > **i•tal'i•cize** [-sīz] *verb transitive* put in italics
itch [ich] *verb intransitive, noun* (feel) irritation in the skin > **itch'y** *adjective* **itch•i•er, itch•i•est**
i•tem [Ī-təm] *noun* 1 single thing in list, collection, etc. 2 piece of information 3 entry in account, etc. > **i'tem•ize** *verb transitive* **-ized, -iz•ing**
it•er•ate [IT-ə-rayt] *verb transitive* **-at•ed, -at•ing** repeat > **it•er•a'tion** *noun* > **it'er•a•tive** *adjective*
i•tin•er•ant [ī-TIN-ər-ənt] *adjective* 1 traveling from place to place 2 working for a short time in various places 3 traveling on circuit

irreverent *adjective* DISRESPECTFUL, cheeky (*informal*), flippant, iconoclastic, impertinent, impudent, mocking, tongue-in-cheek
irreversible *adjective* IRREVOCABLE, final, incurable, irreparable, unalterable
irrevocable *adjective* FIXED, fated, immutable, irreversible, predestined, predetermined, settled, unalterable
irrigate *verb* WATER, flood, inundate, moisten, wet
irritability *noun* BAD TEMPER, ill humor, impatience, irascibility, prickliness, testiness, tetchiness, touchiness
irritable *adjective* BAD-TEMPERED, cantankerous, crotchety, ill-tempered, irascible, oversensitive, prickly, testy, tetchy, touchy
irritate *verb* 1 ANNOY, anger, bother, exasperate, get on one's nerves (*informal*), infuriate, needle (*informal*), nettle, rankle with, try one's patience
2 RUB, chafe, inflame, pain
irritated *adjective* ANNOYED, angry, bothered, cross, exasperated, nettled, piqued, put out, vexed
irritating *adjective* ANNOYING, disturbing, infuriating, irksome, maddening, nagging, troublesome, trying
irritation *noun* 1 ANNOYANCE, anger, displeasure, exasperation, indignation, resentment, testiness, vexation
2 NUISANCE, drag (*informal*), irritant, pain in the neck (*informal*), thorn in one's flesh
island *noun* ISLE, atoll, cay *or* key, islet
isolate *verb* SEPARATE, cut off, detach, disconnect, insulate, segregate, set apart
isolated *adjective* REMOTE, hidden, lonely, off the beaten track, outlying, out-of-the-way, secluded
isolation *noun* SEPARATION, detachment, remoteness, seclusion, segregation, solitude
issue *noun* 1 TOPIC, bone of contention, matter, point, problem, question, subject
2 OUTCOME, consequence, effect, end result, result, upshot
3 EDITION, copy, number, printing
4 CHILDREN, descendants, heirs, offspring, progeny
5 **take issue** DISAGREE, challenge, dispute, object, oppose, raise an objection, take exception
▷ *verb* 6 PUBLISH, announce, broadcast, circulate, deliver, distribute, give out, put out, release
isthmus *noun* STRIP, spit
itch *noun* 1 IRRITATION, itchiness, prickling, tingling
2 DESIRE, craving, hankering, hunger, longing, lust, passion, yearning, yen (*informal*)
▷ *verb* 3 PRICKLE, irritate, tickle, tingle
4 LONG, ache, crave, hanker, hunger, lust, pine, yearn
itchy *adjective* IMPATIENT, eager, edgy, fidgety, restive, restless, unsettled
item *noun* 1 DETAIL, article, component, entry, matter, particular, point, thing
2 REPORT, account, article, bulletin, dispatch,

> **i•tin'er•ar•y** *noun, plural* **-ar•ies** 1 record, line of travel 2 route 3 guidebook
i•vo•ry [ī-və-ree] *noun, plural* **-ries** hard white substance of the tusks of elephants, etc. > **ivory tower** seclusion, remoteness
i•vy [ī-vee] *noun, plural* **-vies** climbing evergreen plant > **i'vied** *adjective* covered with ivy

feature, note, notice, paragraph, piece
itinerant *adjective* WANDERING, migratory, nomadic, peripatetic, roaming, roving, traveling, vagrant
itinerary *noun* SCHEDULE, program, route, timetable

jab *verb transitive* **jabbed, jab•bing** 1 poke roughly 2 thrust, stab abruptly ▷ *noun* 3 poke 4 punch

jab•ber [JAB-ər] *verb* 1 chatter 2 utter, talk rapidly, incoherently > **Jab'ber•wock•y** *noun* nonsense, esp. in verse

jack [jak] *noun* 1 fellow, man 2 (*informal*) sailor 3 male of some animals 4 device for lifting heavy weight, esp. automobile 5 playing card with picture of soldier or servant 6 socket and plug connection for electrical equipment 7 small flag, esp. national, at sea ▷ *verb transitive* (usu. with *up*) lift (an object) with a jack > **jack-of-all-trades** *plural* **jacks** person adept at many kinds of work

jack•al [JAK-əl] *noun* wild, gregarious animal of Asia and Africa closely allied to dog

jack•ass [JAK-as] *noun* 1 male donkey 2 blockhead

jack•et [JAK-it] *noun* 1 outer garment, short coat 2 outer casing, cover

jack•knife [JAK-nīf] *noun, plural* **-knives** 1 clasp knife 2 dive with sharp bend at waist in midair ▷ *verb* **-knifed, -knif•ing** bend sharply, e.g. an articulated truck forming a sharp angle with its trailer

jack•pot [JAK-pot] *noun* 1 large prize 2 accumulated stakes, as in poker

jac•quard [JAK-ahrd] *noun* fabric in which design is incorporated into the weave

Ja•cuz•zi [jə-KOO-zee] *noun* ® 1 device that swirls water in a bath 2 bath with this device

jade[1] [jayd] *noun* 1 ornamental semiprecious stone, usu. dark green 2 this color

jade[2] *noun* 1 sorry or worn-out horse 2 disreputable woman > **jad'ed** *adjective* tired and unenthusiastic

jag *noun* 1 sharp or ragged projection 2 spree > **jag'ged** [-id] *adjective*

jag•uar [JAG-wahr] *noun* large S Amer. spotted cat

jail [jayl] *noun* 1 building for confinement of criminals or suspects ▷ *verb transitive* 2 send to, confine in prison > **jail'bait** [-bayt] *noun* (*slang*) underage girl with whom sexual intercourse is considered a crime > **jail'er** *noun* > **jail'bird** *noun* hardened criminal

ja•lop•y [jə-LOP-ee] *noun, plural* **-lop•ies** (*informal*) old car

jam *verb transitive* **jammed, jam•ming** 1 pack

DICTIONARY • THESAURUS

jab *verb, noun* POKE, dig, lunge, nudge, prod, punch, stab, tap, thrust

jabber *verb* CHATTER, babble, blather, gabble, mumble, ramble, yap (*informal*)

jacket *noun* COVERING, case, casing, coat, sheath, skin, wrapper, wrapping

jackpot *noun* PRIZE, award, bonanza, reward, winnings

jack up *verb* RAISE, elevate, hoist, lift, lift up

jaded *adjective* TIRED, exhausted, fatigued, spent, weary

jagged *adjective* UNEVEN, barbed, craggy, indented, ragged, serrated, spiked, toothed

jail *noun* 1 PRISON, penitentiary, reformatory, slammer (*slang*) ▷ *verb* 2 IMPRISON, confine, detain, incarcerate, lock up, send down

jailer *noun* GUARD, keeper, warden

together **2** (cause to) stick together and become unworkable **3** apply fiercely **4** squeeze **5** *radio* block (another station) with impulses of equal wavelength ▷ *noun* **6** fruit preserved by boiling with sugar **7** crush **8** delay of traffic **9** awkward situation > **jam-packed** *adjective* filled to capacity > **jam session** (improvised) jazz session
jamb [jam] *noun* side post of arch, door, etc.
jam•bo•ree [jam-bə-REE] *noun* **1** large gathering or rally of scouts **2** spree, celebration
jan•gle [JANG-gəl] *verb* **-gled, -gling** **1** (cause to) sound harshly, as bell **2** (of nerves) irritate ▷ *noun* **3** harsh sound
jan•i•tor [JAN-i-tər] *noun* custodian, cleaner
jar[1] [jahr] *noun* **1** round vessel of glass, earthenware, etc. **2** (*informal*) drink of beer, whiskey, etc.
jar[2] *verb* **jarred, jar•ring** **1** (cause to) vibrate suddenly, violently **2** have disturbing, painful effect on ▷ *noun* **3** jarring sound **4** shock, etc.
jar•gon [JAHR-gən] *noun* **1** specialized language concerned with particular subject **2** pretentious or nonsensical language
jas•per [JAS-pər] *noun* red, yellow, dark green or brown quartz
jaun•dice [JAWN-dis] *noun* **1** disease marked by yellowness of skin **2** bitterness, ill humor **3** prejudice ▷ *verb* **-diced, -dic•ing** **4** make, become prejudiced, bitter, etc.
jaunt [jawnt] *noun* **1** short pleasure trip ▷ *verb intransitive* **2** make one
jaun•ty [JAWN-tee] *adjective* **-ti•er, -ti•est** **1** sprightly **2** brisk **3** smart, trim > **jaun'ti•ly** *adverb*
Java [JAH-və] *noun* ® computer programming language that is widely used on the Internet
jave•lin [JAV-lin] *noun* spear, esp. for throwing in sporting events
jaw *noun* **1** one of bones in which teeth are set ▷ *verb intransitive* **2** (*slang*) talk lengthily > **jaws** *plural noun* **1** mouth **2** narrow opening of a gorge or valley **3** gripping part of vise, etc.
jay *noun* noisy bird of brilliant plumage > **jay'walk•er** *noun* careless pedestrian > **jay'walk** *verb intransitive*
jazz *noun* syncopated music and dance > **jazz'y** *adjective* **-jazz•i•er, jazz•i•est** flashy, showy > **jazz up** **1** play as jazz **2** make more lively, appealing
jeal•ous [JEL-əs] *adjective* **1** distrustful of the faithfulness (of) **2** envious **3** suspiciously watchful
jeans [jeenz] *plural noun* casual trousers, esp. of denim
jeer *verb* **1** scoff, deride ▷ *noun* **2** scoff, taunt, gibe
Je•ho•vah [ji-HO-və] *noun* God
je•june [ji-JOON] *adjective* **1** simple, naive **2** meager
jell *verb* **1** congeal **2** assume definite form
jel•ly [JEL-ee] *noun, plural* **-lies** **1** semitransparent food made with gelatin, becoming softly stiff as it cools **2** anything of the consistency of this > **jel'ly•fish** *noun* jellylike small sea animal
jeop•ard•y [JEP-ər-dee] *noun* danger > **jeop'ard•ize** *verb transitive* **-ized, -iz•ing** endanger
Jer. Jeremiah
jerk [jurk] *noun* **1** sharp, abruptly stopped movement **2** twitch **3** sharp pull **4** (*slang*) stupid person, inconsequential person ▷ *verb* **5** move or throw with a jerk > **jerk'i•ly** *adverb* > **jerk'y** *adjective* **jerk•i•er, jerk•i•est** uneven, spasmodic
jer•sey [JUR-zee] *noun, plural* **-seys** **1** knitted sweater **2** machine-knitted fabric **3** (**Jer•sey**)

---

jam *verb* **1** PACK, cram, force, press, ram, squeeze, stuff, wedge
2 CROWD, crush, throng
3 CONGEST, block, clog, obstruct, stall, stick
▷ *noun* **4** PREDICAMENT, deep water, fix (*informal*), hot water, pickle (*informal*), tight spot, trouble
jamboree *noun* FESTIVAL, carnival, celebration, festivity, fête, revelry, spree
jangle *verb* RATTLE, chime, clank, clash, clatter, jingle, vibrate
janitor *noun* CARETAKER, concierge, custodian, doorkeeper, porter
jar[1] *noun* POT, container, crock, jug, pitcher, urn, vase
jar[2] *verb* **1** JOLT, bump, convulse, rattle, rock, shake, vibrate
2 IRRITATE, annoy, get on one's nerves (*informal*), grate, irk, nettle, offend
▷ *noun* **3** JOLT, bump, convulsion, shock, vibration
jargon *noun* PARLANCE, argot, idiom, usage
jaundiced *adjective* **1** CYNICAL, skeptical
2 BITTER, envious, hostile, jealous, resentful, spiteful, suspicious
jaunt *noun* OUTING, airing, excursion, expedition, ramble, stroll, tour, trip
jaunty *adjective* SPRIGHTLY, buoyant, carefree, high-spirited, lively, perky, self-confident, sparky
jaw *verb* TALK, chat, chatter, chew the fat (*slang*), gossip, spout
jaws *plural noun* OPENING, entrance, mouth
jazz up *verb* ENLIVEN, animate, enhance, improve
jazzy *adjective* FLASHY, fancy, gaudy, snazzy (*informal*)
jealous *adjective* **1** ENVIOUS, covetous, desirous, green, grudging, resentful
2 WARY, mistrustful, protective, suspicious, vigilant, watchful
jealousy *noun* ENVY, covetousness, mistrust, possessiveness, resentment, spite, suspicion
jeans *plural noun* DENIMS, Levis ®
jeer *verb* **1** SCOFF, barrack, deride, gibe, heckle, mock, ridicule, taunt
▷ *noun* **2** TAUNT, abuse, boo, catcall, derision, gibe, ridicule
jell *verb* **1** SOLIDIFY, congeal, harden, set, thicken
2 TAKE SHAPE, come together, crystallize, materialize
jeopardize *verb* ENDANGER, chance, expose, gamble, imperil, risk, stake, venture
jeopardy *noun* DANGER, insecurity, peril, risk, vulnerability
jerk *verb, noun* TUG, jolt, lurch, pull, thrust, twitch, wrench, yank
jerky *adjective* BUMPY, convulsive, jolting, jumpy,

breed of cow
jest *noun, verb intransitive* joke > **jest'er** *noun hist.* professional clown at court
Jes•u•it [JEZH-oo-it] *noun* member of Society of Jesus, order founded by Ignatius Loyola in 1534 > **Jes•u•it'i•cal** *adjective* 1 of Jesuits 2 (**jes•u•it'i•cal**) crafty, using overly subtle reasoning
jet[1] *noun* 1 stream of liquid, gas, etc., esp. shot from small hole 2 the small hole 3 spout, nozzle 4 aircraft driven by jet propulsion ▷ *verb* **jet•ted, -jet•ting** 5 throw out 6 shoot forth > **jet-black** *adjective* deep black > **jet lag** fatigue caused by crossing time zones in jet aircraft > **jet propulsion** propulsion by thrust provided by jet of gas or liquid > **jet ski** small self-propelled vehicle resembling a scooter, which skims across water on a flat keel
jet[2] *noun* hard black mineral capable of brilliant polish
jet•sam [JET-səm] *noun* goods thrown out to lighten ship and later washed ashore > **jet'ti•son** [-tə-sən] *verb transitive* 1 abandon 2 throw overboard
jet•ty [JET-ee] *noun* **-ties** small pier, wharf
Jew [joo] *noun* 1 one of Hebrew ancestry 2 one who practices Judaism > **Jew'ish** *adjective* > **Jew'ry** *noun* the Jews > **jew's harp** *noun* small musical instrument held between teeth and played by finger
jew•el [JOO-əl] *noun* 1 precious stone 2 ornament containing one 3 precious thing > **jew'el•er** *noun* dealer in jewels > **jew'el•ry** *noun*
jib *noun* 1 triangular sail set forward of mast 2 projecting arm of crane or derrick
jibe *see* **gibe**
jif•fy [JIF-ee] *noun, plural* **-fies** (*informal*) very short period of time
jig *noun* 1 lively dance 2 music for it 3 small mechanical device 4 guide for cutting, etc. 5 *angling* any of various lures ▷ *verb intransitive* **jigged, jig•ging** 6 dance jig 7 make jerky up-and-down movements > **jig'saw** *noun* machine-mounted saw for cutting curves, etc. > **jigsaw puzzle** picture stuck on board and cut into interlocking pieces with jigsaw
jig•ger [JIG-ər] *noun* small glass holding and pouring measure of whiskey, etc.
jig•gle [JIG-əl] *verb* **-gled, -gling** move (up and down, etc.) with short jerky movements
jilt *verb transitive* cast off (lover)
jim•my [JIM-ee] *noun, plural* **-mies** 1 short steel crowbar ▷ *verb transitive* **-mied, -my•ing** 2 force open with a jimmy, etc.
jin•gle [JING-gəl] *noun* 1 mixed metallic noise, as of shaken chain 2 catchy, rhythmic verse, song, etc. ▷ *verb* **-gled, -gling** 3 (cause to) make jingling sound
jin•go•ism [JING-goh-iz-əm] *noun* chauvinism > **jin•go•is'tic** *adjective*
jinks [jingks] *plural noun* **high jinks** boisterous merrymaking
jinx [jingks] *noun* 1 force, person, thing bringing bad luck ▷ *verb* 2 be or put a jinx on
jit•ters [JIT-ərz] *plural noun* worried nervousness, anxiety > **jit'ter•y** *adjective* **-ter•i•er, -ter•i•est** nervous
jiujitsu *noun see* **jujitsu**
jive [jīv] *noun* 1 (dance performed to) swing music, esp. of 1950's ▷ *verb* **jived, jiv•ing** 2 play, dance to, swing music 3 (*slang*) tease 4 fool
job *noun* 1 piece of work, task 2 position, office 3 (*informal*) difficult task 4 (*slang*) a crime, esp. robbery > **job'ber** *noun* wholesale merchant > **job'less** [-lis] *adjective, plural noun* unemployed (people)
jock•ey [JOK-ee] *noun, plural* **-eys** 1 professional rider in horse races ▷ *verb* **-eyed, -ey•ing** 2 (esp. with *for*) maneuver
jo•cose [joh-KOHS] *adjective* waggish, humorous > **jo•cos'i•ty** [-KOS-i-tee] *noun* > **joc'u•lar** [-yə-lər] *adjective* 1 joking 2 given to joking > **joc•u•lar'i•ty** *noun*
joc•und [JOK-ənd] *adjective* merry, cheerful

DICTIONARY • THESAURUS

shaky, spasmodic, twitchy
jest *noun* 1 JOKE, bon mot, crack (*slang*), jape, pleasantry, prank, quip, wisecrack (*informal*), witticism
▷ *verb* 2 JOKE, kid (*informal*), mock, quip, tease
jester *noun* CLOWN, buffoon, fool, harlequin
jet[1] *noun* 1 STREAM, flow, fountain, gush, spout, spray, spring
2 NOZZLE, atomizer, sprayer, sprinkler
▷ *verb* 3 FLY, soar, zoom
jet[2] *adjective* BLACK, coal-black, ebony, inky, pitch-black, raven, sable
jettison *verb* ABANDON, discard, dump, eject, expel, scrap, throw overboard, unload
jetty *noun* PIER, breakwater, dock, groyne, mole, quay, wharf
jewel *noun* 1 GEMSTONE, ornament, rock (*slang*), sparkler (*informal*)
2 RARITY, collector's item, find, gem, pearl, treasure, wonder
jewelry *noun* JEWELS, finery, gems, ornaments, regalia, treasure, trinkets
jib *verb* REFUSE, balk, recoil, retreat, shrink, stop short
jibe *see* **gibe**
jiffy *noun* (*slang*) INSTANT, blink of an eye (*informal*), flash, heartbeat (*informal*), second, two shakes of a lamb's tail (*slang*)
jig *verb* SKIP, bob, bounce, caper, prance, wiggle
jingle *noun* 1 RATTLE, clang, clink, reverberation, ringing, tinkle
2 SONG, chorus, ditty, melody, tune
▷ *verb* 3 RING, chime, clatter, clink, jangle, rattle, tinkle
jinx *noun* 1 CURSE, evil eye (*informal*), hex (*informal*), hoodoo (*informal*), nemesis
▷ *verb* 2 CURSE, bewitch, hex (*informal*)
jitters *plural noun* NERVES, anxiety, butterflies *or* butterflies in one's stomach (*informal*), cold feet (*informal*), fidgets, nervousness, the shakes (*informal*)
jittery *adjective* NERVOUS, agitated, anxious, fidgety, jumpy, shaky, trembling, twitchy (*informal*), wired (*slang*)
job *noun* 1 TASK, assignment, chore, duty, enterprise, errand, undertaking, venture
2 OCCUPATION, business, calling, career, employment, livelihood, profession, vocation
jobless *adjective* UNEMPLOYED, idle, inactive, out of work, unoccupied
jocular *adjective* HUMOROUS, amusing, droll, facetious, funny, joking, jovial, playful, sportive,

> **jo•cun•di•ty** [joh-KUN-di-tee] *noun, plural* **-ties**
jodh•purs [JOD-pərz] *plural noun* tight-legged riding breeches
jog *verb intransitive* **jogged, jog•ging** 1 run slowly or move at trot, esp. for physical exercise ▷ *verb transitive* **jogged, jog•ging** 2 jar, nudge 3 remind, stimulate ▷ *noun* 4 jogging > **jog'ger** *noun* > **jogging** *noun*
jog•gle [JOG-əl] *verb* **-gled, -gling** 1 move to and fro in jerks 2 shake
John [jon] *noun* 1 name 2 (**john**) (*slang*) toilet 3 (*slang*) prostitute's customer
joie de vi•vre [zhwad VEE-vrə] Fr. enjoyment of life, ebullience
join *verb transitive* 1 put together, fasten, unite 2 become a member (of) ▷ *verb intransitive* 3 become united, connected 4 (with *up*) enlist 5 take part (in) ▷ *noun* 6 joining 7 place of joining, seam > **join'er** *noun* 1 maker of finished woodwork 2 one who joins
joint *noun* 1 arrangement by which two things fit together, rigidly or loosely 2 place of this 3 (*slang*) house, place, etc. 4 (*slang*) disreputable bar or nightclub 5 (*slang*) marijuana cigarette ▷ *adjective* 6 common 7 shared by two or more ▷ *verb transitive* 8 connect by joints 9 divide at the joints > **joint'ly** *adverb* **out of joint** 1 dislocated 2 disorganized
joist *noun* one of the parallel beams stretched from wall to wall on which to fix floor or ceiling
joke [johk] *noun* 1 thing said or done to cause laughter 2 something not in earnest, or ridiculous ▷ *verb intransitive* **joked, jok•ing** 3 make jokes > **jok'er** *noun* 1 one who jokes 2 (*informal*) fellow 3 extra card in pack, counting as highest card in some games
jol•ly [JOL-ee] *adjective* **-li•er, -li•est** 1 jovial 2 festive, merry ▷ *verb transitive* **-lied, -ly•ing** 3 (esp. with *along*) (try to) make person, occasion, etc. happier
jolt [johlt] *noun* 1 sudden jerk 2 bump 3 shock 4 (*informal*) a strong drink ▷ *verb* 5 move, shake with jolts
joss [jos] *noun* Chinese idol > **joss house** Chinese temple > **joss stick** stick of Chinese incense
jos•tle [JOS-əl] *verb* **-tled, -tling** knock or push against
jot *noun* 1 small amount, whit ▷ *verb transitive* **jot•ted, jot•ting** 2 write briefly 3 make note of > **jot'ting** *noun* 1 quick note 2 memorandum
joule [jool] *noun electricity* unit of work or energy
jour•nal [JUR-nl] *noun* 1 daily newspaper or other periodical 2 daily record 3 logbook 4 part of axle or shaft resting on the bearings > **jour•nal•ese'** [-EEZ] *noun* 1 journalist's jargon 2 style full of clichés > **jour'nal•ism** *noun* editing, writing in periodicals
jour•ney [JUR-nee] *noun, plural* **-neys** 1 going to a place, excursion 2 distance traveled ▷ *verb intransitive* **-neyed, -ney•ing** 3 travel
joust [jowst] *noun hist.* 1 encounter with lances between two mounted knights ▷ *verb intransitive* 2 engage in joust
jo•vi•al [JOH-vee-əl] *adjective* convivial, merry, gay > **jo•vi•al'i•ty** *noun*
jowl *noun* 1 cheek, jaw 2 outside of throat when prominent
joy [joi] *noun* 1 gladness, pleasure, delight 2 cause of this > **joy'ful** [-fuul] *adjective* > **joy'less** [-lis] *adjective* > **joy'ride** *noun* (high-speed) automobile trip > **joy'stick** *noun* (*informal*)

DICTIONARY **j** THESAURUS

---

teasing, waggish
jog *verb* 1 NUDGE, prod, push, shake, stir 2 RUN, canter, lope, trot
John Doe *noun* (*informal*) MAN IN THE STREET, average guy, average person, know-nothing (*slang*)
joie de vivre
▷ *noun* ENTHUSIASM, ebullience, enjoyment, gusto, relish, zest
join *verb* 1 CONNECT, add, append, attach, combine, couple, fasten, link, unite 2 ENROLL, enlist, enter, sign up
joint *adjective* 1 SHARED, collective, combined, communal, cooperative, joined, mutual, united ▷ *noun* 2 JUNCTION, connection, hinge, intersection, nexus, node ▷ *verb* 3 DIVIDE, carve, cut up, dissect, segment, sever
jointly *adverb* COLLECTIVELY, as one, in common, in conjunction, in league, in partnership, mutually, together
joke *noun* 1 JEST, gag (*informal*), jape, prank, pun, quip, wisecrack (*informal*), witticism 2 CLOWN, buffoon, laughing stock ▷ *verb* 3 JEST, banter, kid (*informal*), mock, play the fool, quip, taunt, tease
joker *noun* COMEDIAN, buffoon, clown, comic, humorist, jester, prankster, trickster, wag, wit
jolly *adjective* HAPPY, cheerful, chirpy (*informal*), genial, jovial, merry, playful, sprightly, upbeat (*informal*)
jolt *noun* 1 JERK, bump, jar, jog, jump, lurch, shake, start 2 SURPRISE, blow, bolt from the blue, bombshell, setback, shock ▷ *verb* 3 JERK, jar, jog, jostle, knock, push, shake, shove 4 SURPRISE, discompose, disturb, perturb, stagger, startle, stun
jostle *verb* PUSH, bump, elbow, hustle, jog, jolt, shake, shove
jot *verb* 1 NOTE DOWN, list, record, scribble ▷ *noun* 2 BIT, fraction, grain, morsel, scrap, speck
journal *noun* 1 NEWSPAPER, daily, gazette, magazine, monthly, periodical, weekly 2 DIARY, blog (*informal*), chronicle, log, record, weblog
journalist *noun* REPORTER, broadcaster, columnist, commentator, correspondent, hack, newsman *or* newswoman, pressman
journey *noun* 1 TRIP, excursion, expedition, odyssey, pilgrimage, tour, trek, voyage ▷ *verb* 2 TRAVEL, go, proceed, roam, rove, tour, traverse, trek, voyage, wander
jovial *adjective* CHEERFUL, animated, cheery, convivial, happy, jolly, merry, mirthful
joy *noun* DELIGHT, bliss, ecstasy, elation, gaiety, glee, pleasure, rapture, satisfaction
joyful *adjective* DELIGHTED, elated, enraptured, glad, gratified, happy, jubilant, merry, pleased
joyless *adjective* UNHAPPY, cheerless, depressed, dismal, dreary, gloomy, miserable, sad
joyous *adjective* JOYFUL, festive, merry, rapturous

control stick of aircraft or computer device

ju•bi•lant [JOO-bə-lənt] *adjective* exultant > **ju•bi•la'tion** *noun*

ju•bi•lee [JOO-bə-lee] *noun* time of rejoicing, esp. 25th (silver) or 50th (golden) anniversary

Jud. Judges

Ju•da•ic [joo-DAY-ik] *adjective* Jewish > **Ju'da•ism** *noun*

judge [juj] *noun* **1** officer appointed to try cases in law courts **2** one who decides in a dispute, contest, etc. **3** one able to form a reliable opinion, arbiter **4** umpire **5** in Jewish history, ruler ▷ *verb intransitive* **judged, judg•ing 6** act as judge ▷ *verb transitive* **judged, judg•ing 7** act as judge of **8** try, estimate **9** decide > **judg'ment** *noun* **1** faculty of judging **2** sentence of court **3** opinion **4** misfortune regarded as sign of divine displeasure

ju•di•ca•ture [JOO-di-kə-chər] *noun* **1** administration of justice **2** body of judges > **ju•di'cial** [-DISH-əl] *adjective* **1** of or by a court or judge **2** proper to a judge **3** discriminating > **ju•di'ci•ar•y** [-shee-er-ee] *noun, plural* **-ar•ies** system of courts and judges > **ju•di'cious** [-shəs] *adjective* well-judged, sensible, prudent

ju•do [JOO-doh] *noun* modern sport derived from jujitsu

jug *noun* **1** vessel for liquids, with handle and small spout **2** its contents **3** (*slang*) prison ▷ *verb transitive* **jugged, jug•ging 4** stew (esp. hare) in jug

jug•ger•naut [JUG-ər-nawt] *noun* large overpowering, destructive force

jug•gle [JUG-əl] *verb* **-gled, -gling 1** throw and catch (several objects) so most are in the air simultaneously **2** manage, manipulate (accounts, etc.) to deceive ▷ *noun* > **jug'gler** *noun*

jug•u•lar vein [JUG-yə-lər] one of three large veins of the neck returning blood from the head

juice [joos] *noun* **1** liquid part of vegetable, fruit, or meat **2** (*slang*) electric current **3** (*slang*) fuel used to run engine **4** vigor, vitality > **juic'y** *adjective* **juic•i•er, juic•i•est 1** succulent **2** scandalous, improper

ju•jit•su [joo-JIT-soo] *noun* the Japanese art of wrestling and self-defense

ju•jube [JOO-joo-bee] *noun* **1** lozenge of gelatin, sugar, etc. **2** a fruit

ju•lep [JOO-lip] *noun* **1** sweet drink **2** medicated drink

Jul•ian [JOOL-yən] *adjective* of Julius Caesar > **Julian calendar** calendar as adjusted by Julius Caesar in 46 B.C., in which the year was made to consist of 365 days, 6 hours, instead of 365 days

ju•li•enne [joo-lee-EN] *noun* **1** kind of clear soup ▷ *adjective* **2** of food, cut into thin strips or small pieces ▷ *verb transitive* **3** to cut into thin strips

jum•ble [JUM-bəl] *verb transitive* **-bled, -bling 1** mingle, mix in confusion ▷ *noun* **2** confused heap, muddle

jum•bo [JUM-boh] *noun* (*informal*) **1** elephant **2** anything very large

jump *verb* **1** (cause to) spring, leap (over) **2** move hastily **3** pass or skip (over) ▷ *verb intransitive* **4** move hastily **5** rise steeply **6** parachute from aircraft **7** start, jerk (with astonishment, etc.) **8** of faulty film, etc., make abrupt movements ▷ *verb transitive* **9** come off (tracks, rails, etc.) **10** attack without warning ▷ *noun* **11** act of jumping **12** obstacle to be jumped **13** distance, height jumped **14** sudden nervous jerk or start **15** sudden rise in prices > **jump'er** *noun* **1** one who, that which jumps **2** sleeveless dress **3** electric cable to connect discharged car battery to external battery to aid starting of engine > **jump'y** *adjective* **jump•i•er, jump•i•est** nervous > **jump'suit** *noun* one-piece

DICTIONARY • THESAURUS

---

jubilant *adjective* OVERJOYED, elated, enraptured, euphoric, exuberant, exultant, thrilled, triumphant

jubilation *noun* JOY, celebration, ecstasy, elation, excitement, exultation, festivity, triumph

jubilee *noun* CELEBRATION, festival, festivity, holiday

judge *noun* **1** REFEREE, adjudicator, arbiter, arbitrator, moderator, umpire
2 CRITIC, arbiter, assessor, authority, connoisseur, expert
3 MAGISTRATE, justice
▷ *verb* **4** ARBITRATE, adjudicate, decide, mediate, referee, umpire
5 CONSIDER, appraise, assess, esteem, estimate, evaluate, rate, value

judgment *noun* **1** SENSE, acumen, discernment, discrimination, prudence, shrewdness, understanding, wisdom
2 VERDICT, arbitration, decision, decree, finding, ruling, sentence
3 OPINION, appraisal, assessment, belief, diagnosis, estimate, finding, valuation, view

judicial *adjective* LEGAL, official

judicious *adjective* SENSIBLE, astute, careful, discriminating, enlightened, prudent, shrewd, thoughtful, well-judged, wise

jug *noun* CONTAINER, carafe, crock, ewer, jar, pitcher, urn, vessel

juggle *verb* MANIPULATE, alter, change, maneuver, modify

juice *noun* LIQUID, extract, fluid, liquor, nectar, sap

juicy *adjective* **1** MOIST, lush, succulent
2 INTERESTING, colorful, provocative, racy, risqué, sensational, spicy (*informal*), suggestive, vivid

jumble *noun* **1** MUDDLE, clutter, confusion, disarray, disorder, mess, mishmash, mixture
▷ *verb* **2** MIX, confuse, disorder, disorganize, mistake, muddle, shuffle

jumbo *adjective* GIANT, gigantic, huge, immense, large, oversized, supersize

jump *verb* **1** LEAP, bounce, bound, hop, hurdle, skip, spring, vault
2 RECOIL, flinch, jerk, start, wince
3 MISS, avoid, evade, omit, skip
4 INCREASE, advance, ascend, escalate, rise, surge
▷ *noun* **5** LEAP, bound, hop, skip, spring, vault
6 INTERRUPTION, break, gap, hiatus, lacuna, space
7 RISE, advance, increase, increment, upsurge, upturn

jumped-up *adjective* CONCEITED, arrogant, insolent, overbearing, pompous, presumptuous

jumpy *adjective* NERVOUS, agitated, anxious, apprehensive, fidgety, jittery (*informal*), on edge,

garment of trousers and top
junc•tion [JUNGK-shən] *noun* 1 railroad station, etc. where lines, routes join 2 place of joining 3 joining
junc•ture [JUNGK-chər] *noun* state of affairs
jun•gle [JUNG-gəl] *noun* 1 tangled vegetation of equatorial forest 2 land covered with it 3 tangled mass 4 condition of intense competition, struggle for survival
jun•ior [JOON-yər] *adjective* 1 younger 2 of lower standing ▷ *noun* 3 junior person
ju•ni•per [JOON-ə-pər] *noun* evergreen shrub with berries yielding oil of juniper, used for medicine and gin making
junk[1] [jungk] *noun* 1 discarded, useless objects 2 (*informal*) nonsense 3 (*slang*) narcotic drug esp. heroin > **junk'ie** *noun, plural* **-junk•ies** (*informal*) drug addict > **junk food** food, oft. of low nutritional value, eaten in addition to or instead of regular meals > **junk mail** unsolicited mail advertising goods or services
junk[2] *noun* Chinese sailing vessel
jun•ket [JUNG-kit] *noun* 1 curdled milk flavored and sweetened 2 pleasure trip esp. one paid for by others ▷ *verb intransitive* 3 go on a junket
jun•ta [HUUN-tə] *noun* group of military officers holding power in a country
Ju•pi•ter [JOO-pi-tər] *noun* 1 Roman chief of gods 2 largest of the planets
ju•ris•dic•tion [juur-is-DIK-shən] *noun* 1 administration of justice 2 authority 3 territory covered by it > **ju•ris•pru'dence** [-PROO-dəns] *noun* science of, skill in, law > **ju'rist** *noun* one skilled in law
ju•ry [JUUR-ee] *noun, plural* **-ries** 1 body of persons sworn to render verdict in court of law 2 body of judges of competition > **ju'ror** *noun* member of jury
just *adjective* 1 fair 2 upright, honest 3 proper, right, equitable ▷ *adverb* 4 exactly 5 barely 6 at this instant 7 merely, only 8 really > **jus'tice** *noun* 1 quality of being just 2 fairness 3 judicial proceedings 4 judge, magistrate > **jus'ti•fy** *verb transitive* **-fied, -fy•ing** 1 prove right, true or innocent 2 vindicate 3 excuse > **jus'ti•fi•a•ble** *adjective*
jut *verb intransitive* **jut•ted, jut•ting** 1 project, stick out ▷ *noun* 2 projection
jute [joot] *noun* fiber of certain plants, used for rope, canvas, etc.
ju•ve•nile [JOO-və-nl] *adjective* 1 young 2 of, for young children 3 immature ▷ *noun* 4 young person, child, male actor > **ju•ve•nil'i•a** *plural noun* works produced in author's youth > **juvenile court** court dealing with young offenders or children in need of care > **juvenile delinquent** young person guilty of some offense, antisocial behavior, etc.
jux•ta•pose [JUK-stə-pohz] *verb transitive* **-posed, -pos•ing** put side by side > **jux•ta•po•si'tion** *noun* contiguity, being side by side

restless, tense, wired (*slang*)
junction *noun* CONNECTION, coupling, linking, union
juncture *noun* MOMENT, occasion, point, time
junior *adjective* MINOR, inferior, lesser, lower, secondary, subordinate, younger
junk[1] *noun* RUBBISH, clutter, debris, litter, odds and ends, refuse, scrap, trash, waste
jurisdiction *noun* 1 AUTHORITY, command, control, influence, power, rule
2 RANGE, area, bounds, compass, field, province, scope, sphere
just *adverb* 1 EXACTLY, absolutely, completely, entirely, perfectly, precisely
2 RECENTLY, hardly, lately, only now, scarcely
3 MERELY, by the skin of one's teeth, only, simply, solely
▷ *adjective* 4 FAIR, conscientious, equitable, fair-minded, good, honest, upright, virtuous
5 PROPER, appropriate, apt, deserved, due, fitting, justified, merited, rightful
justice *noun* 1 FAIRNESS, equity, honesty, integrity, law, legality, legitimacy, right
2 JUDGE, magistrate
justifiable *adjective* REASONABLE, acceptable, defensible, excusable, legitimate, sensible, understandable, valid, warrantable
justification *noun* 1 EXPLANATION, defense, excuse, rationalization, vindication
2 REASON, basis, grounds, warrant
justify *verb* EXPLAIN, defend, exculpate, excuse, exonerate, support, uphold, vindicate, warrant
justly *adverb* PROPERLY, correctly, equitably, fairly, lawfully
jut *verb* STICK OUT, bulge, extend, overhang, poke, project, protrude
juvenile *adjective* 1 YOUNG, babyish, callow, childish, immature, inexperienced, infantile, puerile, youthful
▷ *noun* 2 CHILD, adolescent, boy, girl, infant, minor, youth
juxtaposition *noun* PROXIMITY, adjacency, closeness, contact, nearness, propinquity, vicinity

Kk

K 1 Kelvin 2 *chem.* potassium
ka•bob [kə-BOB], **ke•bab** [kə-BAB] *noun* dish of small pieces of meat, tomatoes, etc. grilled on skewers
kale [kayl] *noun* type of cabbage
ka•lei•do•scope [kə-LĪ-də-skohp] *noun* 1 optical toy for producing changing symmetrical patterns by multiple reflections of colored glass chips, etc., in inclined mirrors enclosed in tube 2 any complex, frequently changing pattern > **ka•lei•do•scop'ic** [-SKOP-ik] *adjective* swiftly changing
ka•mi•ka•ze [kah-mi-KAH-zə] *noun* suicidal attack, esp. as in World War II, by Japanese pilots
kan•ga•roo [kang-gə-ROO] *noun, plural* **-roos** Aust. marsupial with very strongly developed hind legs for jumping > **kangaroo court** irregular, illegal court
ka•pok [KAY-pok] *noun* 1 tropical tree 2 fiber from its seed pods used to stuff cushions, etc.
ka•put [kah-PUUT] *adjective* (*slang*) ruined, out of order, no good
ka•ra•te [kə-RAH-tee] *noun* Japanese system of unarmed combat using feet, hands, elbows, etc. as weapons in a variety of ways
kar•ma [KAHR-mə] *noun Buddhism, Hinduism* one's actions seen as affecting fate for next reincarnation
kart [kahrt] *noun* miniature low-powered racing car (*also* **go-kart**)
kay•ak [KĪ-ak] *noun* 1 Inuit canoe made of sealskins stretched over frame 2 any canoe of this design
ka•zoo [kə-ZOO] *noun, plural* **-zoos** cigar-shaped musical instrument producing nasal sound
kbyte *computing* kilobyte
kebab, kebob *see* kabob
ked•ger•ee [KEJ-ə-ree] *noun* East Indian dish of fish cooked with rice, eggs, etc.
keel *noun* lowest longitudinal support on which ship is built > **keel'haul** *verb transitive* 1 formerly, punish by hauling under keel of ship 2 rebuke severely > **keel over** 1 turn upside down 2 collapse suddenly
keen[1] *adjective* **-er, -est** 1 sharp 2 acute 3 eager 4 shrewd, strong > **keen'ly** *adverb* > **keen'ness** *noun*
keen[2] *noun* 1 funeral lament ▷ *verb intransitive* 2 wail over the dead
keep *verb* **kept, keep•ing** 1 retain possession of, not lose 2 store 3 cause to continue 4 take

---

kamikaze *adjective* SELF-DESTRUCTIVE, foolhardy, suicidal
keel over *verb* COLLAPSE, black out (*informal*), faint, pass out
keen[1] *adjective* 1 EAGER, ardent, avid, enthusiastic, impassioned, intense, zealous 2 SHARP, cutting, incisive, razor-like 3 ASTUTE, canny, clever, perceptive, quick, shrewd, wise
keenness *noun* EAGERNESS, ardor, enthusiasm, fervor, intensity, passion, zeal, zest
keep *verb* 1 RETAIN, conserve, control, hold, maintain, possess, preserve 2 STORE, carry, deposit, hold, place, stack, stock 3 LOOK AFTER, care for, guard, maintain, manage, mind, protect, tend, watch over

charge of **5** maintain, detain **6** provide upkeep **7** reserve **8** remain good **9** remain **10** continue ▷ *noun* **11** living or support **12** charge or care **13** central tower of castle, stronghold > **keep'er** *noun* > **keep'ing** *noun* **1** harmony, agreement **2** care, charge, possession > **keep'sake** *noun* thing treasured for sake of giver

keg *noun* small barrel usu. holding 5 to 10 gallons (19 to 38 liters)

kelp *noun* **1** large seaweed **2** its ashes, yielding iodine

Kel'vin *adjective* **1** of thermometric scale starting at absolute zero (-273.15° Celsius) ▷ *noun* **2** SI unit of temperature

ken *noun* **1** range of knowledge ▷ *verb transitive* **kenned** *or* **kent, ken•ning** **2** *Scot* know

ken•do [KEN-doh] *noun* Japanese sport of fencing, using bamboo staves

ken•nel [KEN-l] *noun* **1** house, shelter for dog **2** (*often plural*) place for breeding, boarding dogs ▷ *verb transitive* **-neled, -nel•ing** **3** put into kennel

kept *pt./pp. of* **keep**

ker•chief [KUR-chif] *noun* **1** square scarf used as head covering **2** handkerchief

ker•nel [KUR-nl] *noun* **1** inner seed of nut or fruit stone **2** central, essential part

ker•o•sene [KER-ə-seen] *noun* fuel distilled from petroleum or coal and shale

ketch [kech] *noun* two-masted sailing vessel

ketch•up [KECH-əp] *noun* condiment of vinegar, tomatoes, etc.

ket•tle [KET-l] *noun* metal vessel with spout and handle, esp. for boiling water > **ket'tle•drum** *noun* musical instrument made of membrane stretched over copper, brass, etc. hemisphere **a fine kettle of fish** awkward situation, mess

key [kee] *noun* **1** instrument for operating lock, winding clock, etc. **2** something providing control, explanation, means of achieving an end, etc. **3** *mus.* set of related notes **4** operating lever of typewriter, piano, computer, etc. **5** mode of thought ▷ *verb transitive* **6** (*also* **key in**) enter (text) using a keyboard **7** provide symbols on map, etc. to assist identification of positions on it ▷ *adjective* **8** vital **9** most important > **key'board** [-bord] *noun* set of keys on piano, computer, etc. > **key'hole** *noun* **1** hole for inserting key into lock **2** any shape resembling this > **key'note** [-noht] *noun* **1** dominant idea **2** basic note of musical key > **key'pad** *noun* small keyboard with push buttons > **key'stone** *noun* central stone of arch that locks all in position

khak•i [KAK-ee] *adjective* **1** dull yellowish-brown ▷ *noun, plural* **khakis** **2** khaki cloth **3** (*usually plural*) military uniform

Khmer [kmair] *noun* member of a people of Cambodia

Ki. Kings

kib•ble [KIB-əl] *verb transitive* **-bled, -bling** **1** grind into small pieces ▷ *noun* **2** dry dog food prepared in this way

kib•butz [ki-BUUTS] *noun* in Israel, Jewish communal agricultural settlement > **kib•butz'nik** *noun* member of kibbutz

ki•bosh [KĪ-bosh] *noun* (*informal*) nonsense **to put the kibosh on** **1** silence **2** check **3** defeat

kick [kik] *verb intransitive* **1** strike out with foot **2** score with a kick **3** be recalcitrant **4** recoil ▷ *verb transitive* **5** strike or hit with foot **6** (*slang*) free oneself of (drug habit, etc.) ▷ *noun* **7** foot blow **8** recoil **9** excitement, thrill > **kick'back** *noun* **1** strong reaction **2** money paid illegally for favors done, etc. > **kick off** *verb* **1** start game of football **2** begin (discussion, etc.) > **kick-start** *verb* start motorcycle engine, etc. by pedal that is kicked downward

kid *noun* **1** young goat **2** leather of its skin **3** (*informal*) child ▷ *verb* **kid•ded, kid•ding** **4** (of a goat) give birth **5** (*informal*) tease, deceive **6** (*informal*) behave, speak in fun

kid'nap *verb transitive* **-napped, -nap•ping** seize and hold for ransom > **kid'nap•per** *noun*

kid•ney [KID-nee] *noun, plural* **-neys** **1** either of the pair of organs that secrete urine **2** animal kidney used as food **3** nature, kind > **kidney bean** common bean, kidney-shaped at maturity

---

4 SUPPORT, feed, maintain, provide for, subsidize, sustain
5 DETAIN, delay, hinder, hold back, keep back, obstruct, prevent, restrain
▷ *noun* **6** BOARD, food, living, maintenance
7 TOWER, castle

keeper *noun* GUARDIAN, attendant, caretaker, curator, custodian, guard, preserver, steward, warden

keeping *noun* **1** CARE, charge, custody, guardianship, possession, protection, safekeeping
2 in keeping with IN AGREEMENT WITH, in accord with, in balance with, in compliance with, in conformity with, in correspondence with, in harmony with, in observance with

keepsake *noun* SOUVENIR, memento, relic, reminder, symbol, token

keep up *verb* MAINTAIN, continue, keep pace, preserve, sustain

keg *noun* BARREL, cask, drum, vat

kernel *noun* ESSENCE, core, germ, gist, nub, pith, substance

key *noun* **1** OPENER, latchkey
2 ANSWER, explanation, solution
▷ *adjective* **3** ESSENTIAL, crucial, cutting-edge, decisive, fundamental, important, leading, main, major, pivotal, principal

key in *verb* TYPE, enter, input, keyboard

keynote *noun* HEART, center, core, essence, gist, substance, theme

kick *verb* **1** BOOT, punt
2 (*informal*) GIVE UP, abandon, desist from, leave off, quit, stop
▷ *noun* **3** (*informal*) THRILL, buzz (*slang*), pleasure, stimulation

kick off *verb* BEGIN, commence, get the show on the road, initiate, open, start

kick out *verb* DISMISS, eject, evict, expel, get rid of, remove, sack (*informal*)

kid *noun* **1** (*informal*) CHILD, baby, infant, minor, teenager, tot, youngster, youth
▷ *verb* **2** TEASE, delude, fool, hoax, jest, joke, pretend, trick

kidnap *verb* ABDUCT, capture, hijack, hold to ransom, seize

kill *verb transitive* 1 deprive of life 2 destroy 3 neutralize 4 pass (time) 5 weaken or dilute 6 (*informal*) tire, exhaust 7 (*informal*) cause to suffer pain 8 (*informal*) quash, defeat, veto ▷ *noun* 9 act of killing 10 animals, etc. killed in hunt 11 enemy troops, aircraft, etc. killed or destroyed in combat > **kill'er** *noun* one who, that which, kills > **kill'ing** *adjective* (*informal*) 1 very tiring 2 very funny ▷ *noun* 3 sudden success, esp. on stock market

kiln *noun* furnace, oven

kil•o [KEE-loh] *noun short for* **kilogram**

kilo- *combining form* one thousand: *kiloliter; kilometer*

kil•o•byte [KIL-ə-bīt] *noun computing* 1 1,024 bytes 2 (loosely) one thousand bytes

kil•o•gram [KIL-ə-gram] *noun* weight of one thousand grams

kil•o•hertz [KIL-ə-hurts] *noun* one thousand cycles per second

kil•o•watt [KIL-ə-wot] *noun electricity* one thousand watts

kilt *noun* short, usu. tartan, skirt, deeply pleated, worn orig. by Scottish Highlanders > **kilt'ed** *adjective*

ki•mo•no [kə-MOH-nə] *noun, plural* **-nos** 1 loose, wide-sleeved Japanese robe, fastened with sash 2 woman's garment like this

kin *noun* family, relatives ▷ *adjective* related by blood > **kin'dred** [-drid] *noun* 1 relationship 2 relatives ▷ *adjective* 3 similar 4 related > **kin'folk** [-fohk] *noun* > **kin'ship** *noun*

kind [kīnd] *noun* 1 genus, sort, class ▷ *adjective* **-er, -est** 2 sympathetic, considerate 3 good, benevolent 4 gentle > **kind'li•ness** *noun* > **kind'ly** *adjective* **-li•er, -li•est** kind, genial ▷ *adverb* > **kind'ness** *noun* > **kind'heart•ed** *adjective* **in kind** 1 (of payment) in goods rather than money 2 with something similar

kin•der•gar•ten [KIN-dər-gahr-tn] *noun* class, school for children of about four to six years old

kin•dle [KIN-dl] *verb transitive* **-dled, -dling** 1 set on fire 2 inspire, excite ▷ *verb intransitive* **-dled, -dling** 3 catch fire > **kind'ling** *noun* small wood to kindle fires

ki•net•ic [ki-NET-ik] *adjective* of motion in relation to force > **ki•net'ics** *noun* the branch of mechanics concerned with the study of bodies in motion

king *noun* 1 male sovereign ruler of independent country 2 monarch 3 piece in game of chess 4 playing card with picture of a king 5 *checkers* two pieces on top of one another, allowed freedom of movement > **king'ly** *adjective* **-li•er, -li•est** 1 royal 2 appropriate to a king > **king'dom** [-dəm] *noun* 1 country ruled by king 2 realm 3 sphere > **king'fish** *noun* 1 any of several types of fish 2 (*informal*) person in position of authority > **king'pin** *noun* 1 swivel pin 2 central or front pin in bowling 3 (*informal*) chief thing or person > **king-size, king-sized** *adjective* (*informal*) 1 large 2 larger than standard size

kink [kingk] *noun* 1 tight twist in rope, wire, hair, etc. 2 crick, as of neck 3 (*informal*) eccentricity ▷ *verb* 4 make, become kinked 5 put, make kink in 6 twist > **kink'y** *adjective* **kink•i•er, kink•i•est** 1 full of kinks 2 (*informal*) eccentric, esp. given to deviant (sexual) practices

ki•osk [KEE-osk] *noun* small, sometimes movable booth selling soft drinks, cigarettes, newspapers, etc.

kip•per [KIP-ər] *verb transitive* 1 cure (fish) by splitting open, rubbing with salt, and drying or smoking ▷ *noun* 2 kippered fish

kirsch [keersh] *noun* brandy made from cherries

DICTIONARY • THESAURUS

kill *verb* 1 SLAY, assassinate, butcher, destroy, execute, exterminate, liquidate, massacre, murder, slaughter
2 SUPPRESS, extinguish, halt, quash, quell, scotch, smother, stifle, stop

killer *noun* ASSASSIN, butcher, cut-throat, executioner, exterminator, gunman, hit man (*slang*), murderer, slayer

killing *noun* 1 SLAUGHTER, bloodshed, carnage, extermination, homicide, manslaughter, massacre, murder, slaying
2 (*informal*) BONANZA, cleanup (*informal*), coup, gain, profit, success, windfall

killjoy *noun* SPOILSPORT, dampener, wet blanket (*informal*)

kin *noun* FAMILY, kindred, kinsfolk, relations, relatives

kind *adjective* 1 CONSIDERATE, benign, charitable, compassionate, courteous, friendly, generous, humane, kindly, obliging, philanthropic, tender-hearted
▷ *noun* 2 CLASS, brand, breed, family, set, sort, species, variety

kind-hearted *adjective* SYMPATHETIC, altruistic, compassionate, considerate, generous, good-natured, helpful, humane, kind, tender-hearted

kindle *verb* 1 SET FIRE TO, ignite, inflame, light
2 AROUSE, awaken, induce, inspire, provoke, rouse, stimulate, stir

kindliness *noun* KINDNESS, amiability, benevolence, charity, compassion, friendliness, gentleness, humanity, kind-heartedness

kindly *adjective* 1 GOOD-NATURED, benevolent, benign, compassionate, helpful, kind, pleasant, sympathetic, warm
▷ *adverb* 2 POLITELY, agreeably, cordially, graciously, tenderly, thoughtfully

kindness *noun* GOODWILL, benevolence, charity, compassion, generosity, humanity, kindliness, philanthropy, understanding

kindred *adjective* 1 SIMILAR, akin, corresponding, like, matching, related
▷ *noun* 2 FAMILY, kin, kinsfolk, relations, relatives

king *noun* RULER, emperor, monarch, sovereign

kingdom *noun* COUNTRY, nation, realm, state, territory

kink *noun* 1 TWIST, bend, coil, wrinkle
2 QUIRK, eccentricity, fetish, foible, idiosyncrasy, vagary, whim

kinky *adjective* 1 (*slang*) WEIRD, eccentric, odd, outlandish, peculiar, queer, quirky, strange
2 TWISTED, coiled, curled, tangled

kinship *noun* 1 RELATION, consanguinity, kin, ties of blood
2 SIMILARITY, affinity, association, connection, correspondence, relationship

kiosk *noun* BOOTH, bookstall, counter, newsstand, stall, stand

kis•met [KIZ-mit] *noun* fate, destiny
kiss *noun* 1 touch or caress with lips 2 light touch ▷ *verb* > **kiss'er** *noun* 1 one who kisses 2 (*slang*) mouth or face > **kissing kin** relative(s) familiar enough to greet with polite kiss > **kiss of death** apparently friendly ruinous act
kit *noun* 1 outfit, equipment 2 personal effects, esp. of traveler 3 set of pieces of equipment sold ready to be assembled > **kit bag** small bag for holding soldier's or traveler's kit
kitch•en [KICH-ən] *noun* room used for cooking > **kitch•en•ette'** *noun* small compact kitchen > **kitchen garden** garden for raising vegetables, herbs, etc. > **kitchen sink** 1 sink in kitchen 2 final item imaginable
kite [kīt] *noun* 1 light papered frame flown in wind 2 large hawk 3 check drawn against nonexistent funds ▷ *verb transitive* **kit•ed, kit•ing** 4 use check in this way 5 cash or pass such a check
kith *noun* **kith and kin** friends and relatives
kitsch [kich] *noun* vulgarized, pretentious art, literature, etc., usu. with popular, sentimental appeal
kit•ten [KIT-n] *noun* young cat
kit•ty [KIT-ee] *noun, plural* **-ties** 1 *short for* **kitten** 2 in some card games, pool of money 3 communal fund
ki•wi [KEE-wee] *noun, plural* **-wis** 1 any N.Z. flightless bird of the genus *Apteryx* 2 (*informal*) New Zealander > **kiwi fruit** fuzzy fruit of Asian climbing plant, the Chinese gooseberry
klax•on [KLAK-sən] *noun* powerful electric horn, used as warning signal
klep•to•ma•ni•a [klep-tə-MAY-nee-ə] *noun* compulsive tendency to steal for the sake of theft > **klep•to•ma'ni•ac** *noun*
knack [nak] *noun* 1 acquired facility or dexterity 2 trick 3 habit
knap•sack [NAP-sak] *noun* soldier's or traveler's bag to strap to the back, rucksack
knave [nayv] *noun* 1 jack at cards 2 (*obsolete*) rogue > **knav'er•y** *noun* villainy > **knav'ish** *adjective*
knead [need] *verb transitive* 1 work (flour) into dough 2 work, massage
knee [nee] *noun* 1 joint between thigh and lower leg 2 part of garment covering knee ▷ *verb transitive* **kneed, knee•ing** strike, push with knee > **knee'cap** *noun* bone in front of knee
kneel [neel] *verb intransitive* **knelt** *or* **kneeled, kneel•ing** fall, rest on knees
knell [nel] *noun* 1 sound of a bell, esp. at funeral or death 2 portent of doom
knew *pt. of* **know**
knick•ers [NIK-ərz] *plural noun* loose-fitting short trousers gathered in at knee
knick-knack [NIK-nak] *noun* small ornament or toy
knife [nīf] *noun, plural* **knives** 1 cutting blade, esp. one in handle, used as implement or weapon ▷ *verb transitive* **knifed, knif•ing** 2 cut or stab with knife > **knife edge** critical, possibly dangerous situation
knight [nīt] *noun Brit* 1 man of rank below baronet, having right to prefix *Sir* to his name 2 member of medieval order of chivalry 3 champion 4 piece in chess ▷ *verb transitive* 5 confer knighthood on > **knight'hood** [-huud] *noun*
knish *noun* turnover filled with potato, meat, etc. and fried or baked
knit [nit] *verb* **knit'ted** *or* **knit, knit•ting** 1 form (garment, etc.) by putting together series of loops in wool or other yarn 2 draw together 3 unite > **knit'ting** *noun* 1 knitted work 2 act of knitting
knob [nob] *noun* rounded lump, esp. at end or on surface of anything > **knob•by** *adjective* **-bi•er, -bi•est**
knock [nok] *verb transitive* 1 strike, hit 2 (*informal*) disparage 3 rap audibly 4 (of engine) make metallic noise, ping ▷ *noun* 5 blow, rap > **knock'er** *noun* 1 metal appliance for knocking on door 2 who or what knocks > **knock-kneed** *adjective* having incurved legs **knocked out** exhausted, tired, worn out > **knock off** 1 (*informal*) cease work 2 (*informal*) copy, plagiarize 3 (*slang*) kill 4 (*slang*) steal > **knock out** (*informal*) 1 render (opponent) unconscious 2 overwhelm, amaze 3 make (something) hurriedly > **knock'out** *noun* 1 blow, etc. that renders unconscious 2 (*informal*) person or thing overwhelmingly attractive > **knock up**

kiss *verb* 1 OSCULATE, neck (*informal*), peck (*informal*)
2 BRUSH, glance, graze, scrape, touch
▷ *noun* 3 OSCULATION, peck (*informal*), smacker (*slang*), smooch (*slang*)
kit *noun* EQUIPMENT, apparatus, gear, paraphernalia, tackle, tools
knack *noun* SKILL, ability, aptitude, capacity, expertise, facility, gift, propensity, talent, trick
knave *noun* ROGUE, rascal, scoundrel, villain
knead *verb* SQUEEZE, form, manipulate, massage, mold, press, rub, shape, work
kneel *verb* GENUFLECT, get on one's knees *or* get down on one's knees, stoop
knell *noun* RINGING, chime, peal, sound, toll
knick-knack *noun* TRINKET, bagatelle, bauble, bric-a-brac, plaything, trifle
knife *noun* 1 BLADE, cutter
▷ *verb* 2 CUT, lacerate, pierce, slash, stab, wound
knit *verb* 1 JOIN, bind, fasten, intertwine, link, tie, unite, weave
2 WRINKLE, crease, furrow, knot, pucker
knob *noun* LUMP, bump, hump, knot, projection, protrusion, stud
knock *verb* 1 HIT, belt (*informal*), cuff, punch, rap, smack, strike, thump
2 (*informal*) CRITICIZE, abuse, belittle, censure, condemn, denigrate, deprecate, disparage, find fault, run down
▷ *noun* 3 BLOW, clip, clout (*informal*), cuff, rap, slap, smack, thump
4 SETBACK, defeat, failure, rebuff, rejection, reversal
knock down *verb* DEMOLISH, destroy, fell, level, raze
knock off *verb* 1 STOP WORK, clock off, clock out, finish
2 STEAL, pinch, rob, thieve
knockout *noun* 1 KILLER BLOW, coup de grâce (*French*), KO *or* K.O. (*slang*)
2 SUCCESS, hit, sensation, smash, smash hit, triumph, winner

(*slang*) make pregnant
knoll [nohl] *noun* small rounded hill, mound
knot [not] *noun* 1 fastening of strands by looping and pulling tight 2 cluster 3 small closely knit group 4 tie, bond 5 hard lump, esp. of wood where branch joins or has joined in 6 unit of speed used by ships, equal to one nautical mile per hour 7 difficulty ▷ *verb transitive* **knot•ted, knot•ting** 8 tie with knot, in knots > **knot'ty** *adjective* **-ti•er, -ti•est** 1 full of knots 2 puzzling, difficult > **knot'hole** [-hohl] *noun* hole in wood where knot has been
know [noh] *verb transitive* **knew, known, know•ing** 1 be aware of, have information about, be acquainted with, recognize, have experience, understand ▷ *verb intransitive* **knew, known, know•ing** 2 have information or understanding > **know'ing** *adjective* cunning, shrewd > **know'ing•ly** *adverb* 1 shrewdly 2 deliberately > **knowl•edge** [NOL-ij] *noun* 1 knowing 2 what one knows 3 learning > **knowl'edge•a•ble** *adjective* intelligent, well-informed > **know-how** *noun* practical knowledge, experience, aptitude **in the know** informed
knuck•le [nuk-əl] *noun* 1 bone at finger joint 2 knee joint of calf or pig ▷ *verb transitive* **-led, -ling** strike with knuckles > **knuckle ball** *baseball* pitch delivered by holding ball by thumb and first joints or tips of first two or three fingers > **knuckle-dust•er** *noun* metal appliances worn on knuckles to add force to blow, brass knuckles > **knuckle down** get down (to work) > **knuckle under** yield, submit
knurled [nurld] *adjective* 1 serrated 2 gnarled
ko•a•la [koh-AH-lə] *noun* marsupial Aust. animal, native bear
kohl *noun* powdered antimony used orig. in Eastern countries for darkening the eyelids
kohl•ra•bi [kohl-RAH-bee] *noun, plural* **-bies** type of cabbage with edible stem
ko•peck [KOH-pek] *noun* monetary unit of Russia and Belarus, one hundredth of ruble
Ko•ran [kə-RAN] *noun* sacred book of Muslims
ko•sher [KOH-shər] *adjective* 1 permitted, clean, good, as of food, etc., conforming to the Jewish dietary law 2 (*informal*) legitimate, authentic ▷ *noun* 3 (*informal*) kosher food ▷ *verb transitive* 4 make (food, etc.) kosher
kow•tow *noun* 1 former Chinese custom of touching ground with head in respect 2 submission ▷ *verb intransitive* 3 (esp. with *to*) prostrate oneself 4 be obsequious, fawn on
Kr *chem.* krypton
Krem'lin *noun* central government of Russia and, formerly, the Soviet Union
krill [kril] *noun, plural* **krill** small shrimplike marine animal
kryp•ton [KRIP-ton] *noun* rare gaseous element, present in atmosphere
ku•dos [KOO-dohz] *noun* 1 honor 2 acclaim
ku•du [KOO-doo] *noun* Afr. antelope with spiral horns
ku•lak [kuu-LAHK] *noun* independent well-to-do Russian peasant of Czarist times
kum•quat [KUM-kwot] *noun* 1 small Chinese tree 2 its round orange fruit
kung fu [kung foo] Chinese martial art combining techniques of judo and karate
Kwan•zaa [KWAHN-zə, -zah] *noun* African-American festival held from December 26 through January 1

DICTIONARY • THESAURUS

knot *noun* 1 CONNECTION, bond, joint, ligature, loop, tie
2 CLUSTER, bunch, clump, collection
▷ *verb* 3 TIE, bind, loop, secure, tether
know *verb* 1 REALIZE, comprehend, feel certain, notice, perceive, recognize, see, understand
2 BE ACQUAINTED WITH, be familiar with, have dealings with, have knowledge of, recognize
know-how *noun* CAPABILITY, ability, aptitude, expertise, ingenuity, knack, knowledge, savoir-faire, skill, talent
knowing *adjective* MEANINGFUL, expressive, significant
knowingly *adverb* DELIBERATELY, consciously, intentionally, on purpose, purposely, willfully, wittingly
knowledge *noun* 1 LEARNING, education, enlightenment, erudition, instruction, intelligence, scholarship, wisdom
2 ACQUAINTANCE, cognizance, familiarity, intimacy
knowledgeable *adjective* 1 WELL-INFORMED, au fait (*French*), aware, clued-up (*informal*), cognizant, conversant, experienced, familiar, in the know (*informal*)
2 INTELLIGENT, educated, erudite, learned, scholarly
known *adjective* FAMOUS, acknowledged, avowed, celebrated, noted, recognized, well-known
knuckle under *verb* GIVE WAY, accede, acquiesce, capitulate, cave in (*informal*), give in, submit, succumb, surrender, yield
kudos *noun* PRAISE, acclaim, applause, credit, laudation, plaudits, recognition

Ll

la *see* **lah**
La *chem.* lanthanum
la•bel [LAY-bəl] *noun* 1 slip of paper, metal, etc., fixed to object to give information about it 2 brief, descriptive phrase or term ▷ *verb transitive* **-beled, -bel•ing**
la•bi•al [LAY-bee-əl] *adjective* 1 of the lips 2 pronounced with the lips ▷ *noun* 3 labial consonant
la•bor [LAY-bər] *noun* 1 exertion of body or mind 2 task 3 workers collectively 4 effort, pain, of childbirth or time taken for this ▷ *verb intransitive* 5 work hard 6 strive 7 maintain normal motion with difficulty 8 (esp. of ship) be tossed heavily ▷ *verb transitive* 9 elaborate 10 stress to excess > **la'bored** *adjective* uttered, done, with difficulty > **la'bor•er** *noun* one who labors, esp. person doing manual work for wages > **la•bo•ri•ous** [lə-BOR-ee-əs] *adjective* tedious
lab•o•ra•to•ry [LAB-rə-tor-ee] *noun* place for scientific investigations or for manufacture of chemicals
lab•ra•dor [LAB-rə-dor] *noun* breed of large, smooth-coated retriever dog
lab•y•rinth [LAB-ə-rinth] *noun* 1 network of tortuous passages, maze 2 inexplicable difficulty 3 perplexity > **lab•y•rin'thine** [-RIN-thin] *adjective*
lace [lays] *noun* 1 fine patterned openwork fabric 2 cord, usu. one of pair, to draw edges together, e.g. to tighten shoes, etc. 3 ornamental braid ▷ *verb transitive* **laced, lac•ing** 4 fasten with laces 5 flavor with whiskey, etc. > **lac'y** *adjective* **lac•i•er, lac•i•est** fine, like lace
lac•er•ate [LAS-ə-rayt] *verb transitive* **-at•ed, -at•ing** 1 tear, mangle 2 distress > **lac•er•a'tion** *noun*
lach•ry•mal [LAK-rə-məl] *adjective* of tears > **lach'ry•ma•to•ry** [-mə-tor-ee] *adjective* causing tears or inflammation of eyes > **lach'ry•mose**

DICTIONARY

THESAURUS

label *noun* 1 TAG, marker, sticker, ticket ▷ *verb* 2 MARK, stamp, tag
labor *noun* 1 WORK, industry, toil
2 WORKERS, employees, hands, laborers, workforce
3 CHILDBIRTH, delivery, parturition
▷ *verb* 4 WORK, endeavor, slave, strive, struggle, sweat (*informal*), toil
5 (*usually with under*) BE DISADVANTAGED, be a victim of, be burdened by, suffer
6 OVEREMPHASIZE, dwell on, elaborate, overdo, strain
labored *adjective* FORCED, awkward, difficult, heavy, stiff, strained
laborer *noun* WORKER, blue-collar worker, drudge, hand, manual worker
laborious *adjective* HARD, arduous, backbreaking, exhausting, onerous, strenuous, tiring, tough, wearisome
labyrinth *noun* MAZE, intricacy, jungle, tangle
lace *noun* 1 NETTING, filigree, openwork
2 CORD, bootlace, shoelace, string, tie
▷ *verb* 3 FASTEN, bind, do up, thread, tie
4 MIX IN, add to, fortify, spike
lacerate *verb* TEAR, claw, cut, gash, mangle, rip, slash, wound
laceration *noun* CUT, gash, rent, rip, slash, tear, wound

[-mohs] *adjective* tearful

lack [lak] *noun* 1 deficiency, need ▷ *verb transitive* 2 need, be short of > **lack'lus•ter** *adjective* lacking brilliance or vitality

lack•a•dai•si•cal [lak-ə-DAY-zi-kəl] *adjective* 1 languid, listless 2 lazy, careless

lack•ey [LAK-ee] *noun, plural* **-eys** 1 servile follower 2 footman ▷ *verb* **-eyed, -ey•ing** 3 be, or play, the lackey 4 wait upon

la•con•ic [lə-KON-ik] *adjective* 1 using, expressed in few words 2 brief, terse 3 offhand, not caring > **la•con'i•cal•ly** *adverb*

lac•quer [LAK-ər] *noun* 1 hard varnish ▷ *verb transitive* 2 coat with this

la•crosse [lə-KRAWS] *noun* ball game played with long-handled racket, or crosse

lac•tic [LAK-tik] *adjective* of milk > **lac'tate** *verb intransitive* **-tat•ed, -tat•ing** secrete milk > **lac•ta'tion** *noun* > **lac'tose** [-tohs] *noun* white crystalline substance occurring in milk

la•cu•na [lə-KYOO-nə] *noun, plural* **-nae** [-nee] gap, missing part, esp. in document or series

lad *noun* boy, young fellow

lad•der [LAD-ər] *noun* 1 frame of two poles connected by crossbars called rungs, used for climbing 2 flaw in stockings, caused by running of torn stitch

lade [layd] *verb transitive* **lad•ed, lad•ed** *or* **lad•en, lad•ing** 1 load 2 ship 3 burden, weigh down > **lad'ing** *noun* cargo, freight

la•dle [LAYD-l] *noun* 1 spoon with long handle for large bowl ▷ *verb transitive* **-dled, -dling** 2 serve out liquid with a ladle

la•dy [LAY-dee] *noun, plural* **-dies** 1 female counterpart of gentleman 2 polite term for a woman 3 title of some women of rank > **la'dy•like** *adjective* 1 gracious 2 well-mannered **Our Lady** the Virgin Mary > **la'dy•fin•ger** *noun* small sponge cake in shape of finger > **lady-of-the-night** *noun, plural* **ladies-** prostitute

lag[1] *verb intransitive* **lagged, lag•ging** 1 go too slowly, fall behind ▷ *noun* 2 lagging, interval of time between events > **lag'gard** [-ərd] *noun* one who lags > **lagging** *adjective* loitering, slow

lag[2] *verb transitive* **lagged, lag•ging** wrap boiler, pipes, etc. with insulating material > **lagging** *noun* this material

la•ger [LAH-gər] *noun* 1 a light-bodied type of beer ▷ *verb transitive* 2 age (beer) by storing in tanks

la•goon [lə-GOON] *noun* saltwater lake, enclosed by atoll, or separated by sandbank from sea

lah, la *noun* sixth sol-fa note

la•ic [LAY-ik] *adjective* secular, lay > **la'i•cize** [-sīz] *verb transitive* **-cized, -ciz•ing** render secular or lay

laid [layd] *pt./pp. of* **lay** > **laid-back** *adjective* (*informal*) relaxed

lain [layn] *pp. of* **lie**

lair *noun* resting place, den of animal

lais•sez faire [les-ay FAIR] *noun* 1 principle of nonintervention, esp. by government in commercial affairs 2 indifference

la•i•ty [LAY-i-tee] *noun* lay worshipers, the people as opposed to clergy

lake [layk] *noun* expanse of inland water

lam *noun* (*slang*) 1 hasty escape ▷ *verb intransitive* **lammed, lam•ming** (*slang*) 2 run away fast 3 escape **on the lam** (*slang*) 4 escaping 5 hiding esp. from police

Lam. Lamentations

la•ma [LAH-mə] *noun* Buddhist priest in Tibet or Mongolia > **la'ma•ser•y** *noun* monastery of lamas

lamb [lam] *noun* 1 young of the sheep 2 its meat 3 innocent or helpless creature ▷ *verb intransitive* (of sheep) 4 give birth to lamb > **lamb'like** *adjective* meek, gentle

lam•baste [lam-BAYST] *verb transitive* **-bast•ed, -bast•ing** beat, reprimand

lam•bent [LAM-bənt] *adjective* 1 (of flame) flickering softly 2 glowing

lame [laym] *adjective* **lam•er, lam•est** 1 crippled in a limb, esp. leg 2 limping 3 (of excuse, etc.) unconvincing ▷ *verb transitive* **lamed, lam•ing** 4 cripple > **lame duck** 1 official serving out term of office while waiting for elected successor to assume office 2 disabled, weak person or thing

la•mé [la-MAY] *noun, adjective* (fabric) interwoven with gold or silver thread

la•ment [lə-MENT] *verb* 1 feel, express sorrow

DICTIONARY • THESAURUS

lack *noun* 1 SHORTAGE, absence, dearth, deficiency, need, scarcity, want ▷ *verb* 2 NEED, be deficient in, be short of, be without, miss, require, want

lackadaisical *adjective* 1 LETHARGIC, apathetic, dull, half-hearted, indifferent, languid, listless 2 LAZY, abstracted, dreamy, idle, indolent, inert

lackey *noun* 1 HANGER-ON, brown-noser (*slang*), flatterer, minion, sycophant, toady, yes man 2 MANSERVANT, attendant, flunky, footman, valet

lackluster *adjective* FLAT, drab, dull, leaden, lifeless, muted, prosaic, uninspired, vapid

laconic *adjective* TERSE, brief, concise, curt, monosyllabic, pithy, short, succinct

lad *noun* BOY, fellow, guy (*informal*), juvenile, kid (*informal*), youngster, youth

laden *adjective* LOADED, burdened, charged, encumbered, full, weighed down

lady *noun* 1 GENTLEWOMAN, dame 2 WOMAN, female

ladylike *adjective* REFINED, elegant, genteel, modest, polite, proper, respectable, sophisticated, well-bred

lag *verb* HANG BACK, dawdle, delay, linger, loiter, straggle, tarry, trail

laggard *noun* STRAGGLER, dawdler, idler, loiterer, slowpoke (*informal*), sluggard, snail

laid-back *adjective* RELAXED, casual, easy-going, free and easy, unflappable (*informal*), unhurried

lair *noun* NEST, burrow, den, earth, hole

laissez faire *noun* NONINTERVENTION, free enterprise, free trade

lake *noun* POND, basin, lagoon, mere, pool, reservoir, tarn

lame *adjective* 1 DISABLED, challenged, crippled, game, handicapped, hobbling, limping 2 UNCONVINCING, feeble, flimsy, inadequate, lousy (*slang*), pathetic, poor, thin, unsatisfactory, weak

lament *verb* 1 COMPLAIN, bemoan, bewail, deplore, grieve, mourn, regret, sorrow, wail, weep ▷ *noun* 2 COMPLAINT, lamentation,

(for) ▷ *noun* 2 passionate expression of grief 3 song of grief > **lam'en•ta•ble** [LAM-] *adjective* deplorable > **lam•en•ta'tion** *noun*

lam•i•na [LAM-ə-nə] *noun, plural* **-nas** thin plate, scale, flake > **lam'i•nate** [-nayt] *verb* **-nat•ed, -nat•ing** 1 make (sheet of material) by bonding together two or more thin sheets 2 split, beat, form into thin sheets 3 cover with thin sheet of material ▷ *noun* [-nit] 4 laminated sheet > **lam•i•na'tion** *noun*

lamp *noun* 1 any of various 2 appliances (esp. electrical) that produce light, heat, radiation, etc. 3 formerly, vessel holding oil burned by wick for lighting > **lamp'black** *noun* pigment made from soot > **lamp'light** *noun* > **lamp'post** *noun* post supporting lamp in street

lam•poon' *noun* 1 satire ridiculing person, literary work, etc. ▷ *verb transitive* 2 satirize, ridicule > **lam•poon'ist** *noun*

lam•prey [LAM-pree] *noun, plural* **-preys** fish like an eel with a round sucking mouth

lance [lans] *noun* 1 horseman's spear ▷ *verb transitive* **lanced, lanc•ing** 2 pierce with lance or lancet > **lan'ce•o•late** [-see-ə-layt] *adjective* lance-shaped, tapering > **lanc'er** *noun* formerly, cavalry soldier armed with lance > **lan'cet** [-sit] *noun* pointed two-edged surgical knife

land *noun* 1 solid part of Earth's surface 2 ground, soil 3 country 4 property consisting of land ▷ *verb intransitive* 5 come to land, disembark 6 bring an aircraft from air to land or water 7 alight, step down 8 arrive on ground ▷ *verb transitive* 9 bring to land 10 come or bring to some point or condition 11 (*informal*) obtain 12 catch > **lands** *plural noun* estates > **land'ed** *adjective* possessing, consisting of lands > **land'ing** *noun* 1 act of landing 2 platform between flights of stairs > **land'fall** *noun* ship's approach to land at end of voyage > **land'locked** *adjective* enclosed by land > **land'lord, land'la•dy** *noun* 1 person who lets land or houses, etc. 2 owner of apartment house, etc. > **land'lub•ber** *noun* person ignorant of the sea and ships > **land'mark** *noun* 1 boundary mark, conspicuous object, as guide for direction, etc. 2 event, decision, etc. considered as important stage in development of something > **land'scape** *noun* 1 piece of inland scenery 2 picture of it 3 prospect ▷ *verb* **-scaped, -scap•ing** 4 create, arrange, garden, park, etc. > **landscape gardener** *noun* person who designs gardens or parks so that they look attractive > **land'slide** *noun* 1 falling of soil, rock, etc. down mountainside 2 overwhelming electoral victory

lane [layn] *noun* 1 narrow road or street 2 specified route followed by shipping or aircraft 3 area of road for one stream of traffic

lan•guage [LANG-gwij] *noun* 1 system of sounds, symbols, etc. for communicating thought 2 specialized vocabulary used by a particular group 3 style of speech or expression 4 system of words and symbols for computer programming

lan•guish [LANG-gwish] *verb intransitive* 1 be or become weak or faint 2 be in depressing or painful conditions 3 droop, pine > **lan'guid** *adjective* 1 lacking energy, interest 2 spiritless, dull > **lan'guor** [-gər] *noun* 1 want of energy or interest 2 faintness 3 tender mood 4 softness of atmosphere > **lan'guor•ous** *adjective*

lank [langk] *adjective* 1 lean and tall 2 straight and limp > **lank'y** *adjective* **lank•i•er, lank•i•est**

lan•o•lin [LAN-l-in] *noun* grease from wool used in ointments, etc.

lan•tern [LAN-tərn] *noun* 1 transparent case for lamp or candle 2 erection on dome or roof to let out smoke, admit light

lan•tha•num [LAN-thə-nəm] *noun* silvery-white ductile metallic element

lan•yard [LAN-yərd] *noun* 1 short cord for securing knife or whistle 2 short nautical rope 3 cord for firing cannon

lap[1] *noun* 1 the part between waist and knees of a person when sitting 2 protected place or

---

moan, wailing
3 DIRGE, elegy, requiem, threnody

lamentable *adjective* REGRETTABLE, deplorable, distressing, grievous, mournful, tragic, unfortunate, woeful

lampoon *noun* 1 SATIRE, burlesque, caricature, parody, spoof (*informal*)
▷ *verb* 2 RIDICULE, caricature, make fun of, mock, parody, satirize

land *noun* 1 GROUND, dry land, earth, terra firma
2 SOIL, dirt, ground, loam
3 COUNTRYSIDE, farmland
4 PROPERTY, estate, grounds, realty
5 COUNTRY, district, nation, province, region, territory, tract
▷ *verb* 6 ARRIVE, alight, come to rest, disembark, dock, touch down
7 END UP, turn up, wind up
8 (*informal*) OBTAIN, acquire, gain, get, secure, win

landlord *noun* 1 INNKEEPER, host, hotelier
2 OWNER, freeholder, lessor, proprietor

landmark *noun* 1 FEATURE, monument
2 MILESTONE, turning point, watershed

landscape *noun* SCENERY, countryside, outlook, panorama, prospect, scene, view, vista

landslide *noun* 1 ROCKFALL, avalanche, landslip
▷ *adjective* 2 OVERWHELMING, conclusive, decisive, runaway

lane *noun* ROAD, alley, footpath, passageway, path, pathway, street, way

language *noun* 1 SPEECH, communication, discourse, expression, parlance, talk
2 TONGUE, dialect, patois, vernacular

languid *adjective* 1 LAZY, indifferent, lackadaisical, languorous, listless, unenthusiastic
2 LETHARGIC, dull, heavy, sluggish, torpid

languish *verb* 1 WEAKEN, decline, droop, fade, fail, faint, flag, wilt, wither
2 (*often with for*) PINE, desire, hanker, hunger, long, yearn
3 BE NEGLECTED, be abandoned, rot, suffer, waste away

lank *adjective* 1 LIMP, lifeless, straggling
2 THIN, emaciated, gaunt, lean, scrawny, skinny, slender, slim, spare

lanky *adjective* GANGLING, angular, bony, gaunt, rangy, spare, tall

lap[1] *noun* CIRCUIT, circle, loop, orbit, tour

lap[2] *verb* 1 RIPPLE, gurgle, plash, purl, splash, swish, wash

environment: *the lap of luxury* 3 single circuit of racetrack, track 4 stage or part of journey 5 single turn of wound thread, etc. ▷ *verb transitive* **lapped, lap•ping** 6 enfold, wrap around 7 overtake opponent to be one or more circuits ahead > **lap dog** *noun* small pet dog > **lap'top** *adjective* 1 (of a computer) small and light enough to be held on the user's lap ▷ *noun* 2 such a computer

lap² *verb transitive* **lapped, lap•ping** 1 drink by scooping up with tongue 2 (of waves, etc.) beat softly

la•pel [lə-PEL] *noun* part of front of a jacket or coat folded back toward shoulders

lap•i•dar•y [LAP-i-der-ee] *adjective* 1 of stones 2 engraved on stone 3 exhibiting extreme refinement 4 concise and dignified ▷ *noun, plural* **-dar-ies** 5 cutter, engraver of stones

lap•is laz•u•li [LAP-is LAZ-uu-lee] bright blue stone or pigment

lapse [laps] *noun* 1 fall (in standard, condition, virtue, etc.) 2 slip 3 mistake 4 passing (of time, etc.) ▷ *verb intransitive* **lapsed, laps•ing** 5 fall away 6 end, esp. through disuse

lar•board [LAHR-bord] *noun, adjective* old term for port (side of ship)

lar•ce•ny [LAHR-sə-nee] *noun, plural* **-nies** theft

lard [lahrd] *noun* 1 prepared pig fat ▷ *verb transitive* 2 insert strips of bacon in (meat) 3 intersperse, decorate (speech with strange words, etc.)

lar•der [LAHR-dər] *noun* storeroom for food

large [lahrj] *adjective* **larg•er, larg•est** 1 broad in range or area 2 great in size, number, etc. 3 liberal 4 generous ▷ *adverb* 5 in a big way > **large'ly** *adverb* > **lar•gess', lar•gesse'** *noun* 1 bounty 2 gift 3 donation **at large** 1 free, not confined 2 in general 3 fully

lar•go [LAHR-goh] *adverb mus.* slow and dignified

lar•i•at [LAR-ee-ət] *noun* lasso

lark¹ [lahrk] *noun* small brown songbird, skylark

lark² *noun* 1 frolic, spree ▷ *verb intransitive* 2 indulge in lark

lar•va [LAHR-və] *noun, plural* **-vae** [-vee] insect in immature but active stage > **lar'val** *adjective*

lar•ynx [LAR-ingks] *noun, plural* **-es** part of throat containing vocal cords > **lar•yn•gi'tis** [-jī-tis] *noun* inflammation of this

la•sa•gne [lə-ZAHN-yə] *noun* 1 pasta formed in wide, flat sheets 2 baked dish of this with meat, cheese, tomato sauce, etc.

las•civ•i•ous [lə-SIV-ee-əs] *adjective* lustful

la•ser [LAY-zər] *noun* device for concentrating electromagnetic radiation or light of mixed frequencies into an intense, narrow, concentrated beam

lash¹ *noun* 1 stroke with whip 2 flexible part of whip 3 eyelash ▷ *verb transitive* 4 strike with whip, thong, etc. 5 dash against (as waves) 6 attack verbally, ridicule 7 flick, wave sharply to and fro ▷ *verb intransitive* 8 (with *out*) hit, kick

lash² *verb transitive* fasten or bind tightly with cord, etc.

las•si•tude [LAS-i-tood] *noun* weariness

las•so [LAS-oh] *noun, plural* **-sos** *or* **-soes** rope with noose for catching cattle, etc. ▷ *verb transitive* **-soed, -so•ing**

last¹ *adjective, adverb* 1 after all others, coming at the end 2 most recent(ly) ▷ *adjective* 3 only remaining 4 *sup. of* **late** ▷ *noun* 5 last person or thing > **last'ly** *adverb* finally

last² *verb intransitive* continue, hold out, remain alive or unexhausted, endure

last³ *noun* model of foot on which shoes are made, repaired

latch [lach] *noun* 1 fastening for door, consisting of bar, catch for it, and lever to lift it 2 small lock with spring action ▷ *verb transitive* 3 fasten with latch > **latch'key** [-kee] *noun*

late [layt] *adjective* **lat•er** *or* **lat•ter, lat•est** *or* **last** 1 coming after the appointed time 2 delayed 3

THESAURUS • DICTIONARY

2 DRINK, lick, sip, sup

lapse *noun* 1 MISTAKE, error, failing, fault, indiscretion, negligence, omission, oversight, slip
2 INTERVAL, break, breathing space, gap, intermission, interruption, lull, pause
3 DROP, decline, deterioration, fall
▷ *verb* 4 DROP, decline, degenerate, deteriorate, fall, sink, slide, slip
5 END, expire, run out, stop, terminate

lapsed *adjective* OUT OF DATE, discontinued, ended, expired, finished, invalid, run out

large *adjective* 1 BIG, considerable, enormous, gigantic, great, huge, immense, massive, monumental, sizable *or* sizeable, substantial, supersize, vast
2 ▷ **at large a** FREE, at liberty, on the loose, on the run, unconfined **b** IN GENERAL, as a whole, chiefly, generally, in the main, mainly **c** AT LENGTH, exhaustively, greatly, in full detail

largely *adverb* MAINLY, as a rule, by and large, chiefly, generally, mostly, predominantly, primarily, principally, to a great extent

large-scale *adjective* WIDE-RANGING, broad, extensive, far-reaching, global, sweeping, vast, wholesale, wide

lark *noun* 1 PRANK, caper, escapade, fun, game, jape, mischief
▷ *verb* 2 ▷ **lark about** PLAY, caper, cavort, have fun, make mischief

lash¹ *noun* 1 BLOW, hit, stripe, stroke, swipe (*informal*)
▷ *verb* 2 WHIP, beat, birch, flog, scourge, thrash
3 POUND, beat, buffet, dash, drum, hammer, smack, strike
4 SCOLD, attack, blast, censure, criticize, put down, upbraid

lash² *verb* FASTEN, bind, make fast, secure, strap, tie

lass *noun* GIRL, damsel, maid, maiden, young woman

last¹ *adjective* 1 HINDMOST, at the end, rearmost
2 MOST RECENT, latest
3 FINAL, closing, concluding, terminal, ultimate
▷ *adverb* 4 IN THE REAR, after, behind, bringing up the rear, in the end *or* at the end

last² *verb* CONTINUE, abide, carry on, endure, keep on, persist, remain, stand up, survive

lasting *adjective* CONTINUING, abiding, durable, enduring, long-standing, long-term, perennial, permanent

latch *noun* 1 FASTENING, bar, bolt, catch, hasp, hook, lock
▷ *verb* 2 FASTEN, bar, bolt, make fast, secure

that was recently but now is not 4 recently dead 5 recent in date 6 of late stage of development ▷ *adverb* **lat•er, lat•est** 7 after proper time 8 recently 9 at, till late hour > **late'ly** *adverb* not long since

la•tent [LAYT-nt] *adjective* 1 existing but not developed 2 hidden

lat•er•al [LAT-ər-əl] *adjective* of, at, from the side > **lat'er•al•ly** *adverb*

la•tex [LAY-teks] *noun* sap or fluid of plants, esp. of rubber tree

lath *noun, plural* **laths** [lathz] thin strip of wood, or wire mesh > **lath'ing** *noun*

lathe [layth] *noun* machine for turning object while it is being shaped

lath•er [LATH-ər] *noun* 1 froth of soap and water 2 frothy sweat ▷ *verb* 3 make frothy 4 (*informal*) beat

Lat•in [LAT-n] *noun* 1 language of ancient Romans ▷ *adjective* 2 of ancient Romans, of, in their language 3 denoting people speaking a language descended from Latin esp. Spanish > **La•ti•no** [lə-TEE-noh] *noun, plural* **-nos** person of Central or S Amer. descent

lat•i•tude [LAT-i-tood] *noun* 1 angular distance on meridian reckoned N or S from equator 2 deviation from a standard 3 freedom from restriction 4 scope > **lat•i•tudes** regions

la•trine [lə-TREEN] *noun* in army, etc., toilet

lat•ter [LAT-ər] *adjective* 1 second of two 2 later 3 more recent > **lat'ter•ly** *adverb*

lat•tice [LAT-is] *noun* 1 structure of strips of wood, metal, etc. crossing with spaces between 2 window, gate, so made > **lat'ticed** *adjective*

laud [lawd] *noun* hymn, song, of praise ▷ *verb transitive* > **laud'a•ble** *adjective* praiseworthy > **laud'a•bly** *adverb* > **laud'a•to•ry** [-tor-ee] *adjective* expressing, containing, praise

lau•da•num [LAWD-n-əm] *noun* tincture of opium

laugh [laf] *verb intransitive* make sounds instinctively expressing amusement, merriment, or scorn ▷ *noun* > **laugh'a•ble** *adjective* ludicrous > **laugh'a•bly** *adverb* > **laugh'ter** *noun* > **laughing gas** nitrous oxide as anesthetic > **laughing stock** object of general derision

launch[1] [lawnch] *verb transitive* 1 set afloat 2 set in motion 3 start 4 propel (missile, spacecraft) into space 5 hurl, send ▷ *verb intransitive* 6 enter on course > **launch'er** *noun* installation, vehicle, device for launching rockets, missiles, etc.

launch[2] *noun* large engine-driven boat

laun•dry [LAWN-dree] *noun, plural* **-dries** 1 place for washing clothes, esp. as a business 2 clothes, etc. for washing > **laun'der** *verb transitive* wash and iron > **laun•der•ette'** *noun* self-service laundry with coin-operated washing, drying machines

lau•re•ate [LOR-ee-ət] *adjective* 1 crowned with laurels ▷ *noun* 2 person honored for achievements **poet laureate** poet honored as most eminent of country or region

lau•rel [LOR-əl] *noun* glossy-leaved shrub, bay tree > **lau•rels** its leaves, emblem of victory or merit

la•va [LAH-və] *noun* molten matter thrown out by volcanoes, solidifying as it cools

lav•a•to•ry [LAV-ə-tor-ee] *noun* **-ries** 1 washroom 2 toilet

lave [layv] *verb transitive* **laved, lav•ing** wash, bathe

lav•en•der [LAV-ən-dər] *noun* 1 shrub with fragrant flowers 2 color of the flowers, pale lilac

lav'ish *adjective* 1 giving or spending profusely 2 very, too abundant ▷ *verb transitive* 3 spend,

DICTIONARY | THESAURUS

---

late *adjective* 1 OVERDUE, behind, behindhand, belated, delayed, last-minute, tardy
2 RECENT, advanced, fresh, modern, new
3 DEAD, deceased, defunct, departed, former, past
▷ *adverb* 4 BELATEDLY, at the last minute, behindhand, behind time, dilatorily, tardily

lately *adverb* RECENTLY, in recent times, just now, latterly, not long ago, of late

lateness *noun* DELAY, belatedness, tardiness

latent *adjective* HIDDEN, concealed, dormant, invisible, potential, undeveloped, unrealized

later *adverb* AFTERWARDS, after, by and by, in a while, in time, later on, subsequently, thereafter

lateral *adjective* SIDEWAYS, edgeways, flanking

latest *adjective* UP-TO-DATE, cool (*informal*), current, fashionable, modern, most recent, newest, phat (*slang*), up-to-the-minute

lather *noun* 1 FROTH, bubbles, foam, soapsuds, suds
▷ *verb* 2 FROTH, foam, soap

latitude *noun* SCOPE, elbowroom, freedom, laxity, leeway, liberty, license, play

latter *adjective* LAST-MENTIONED, closing, concluding, last, second

latterly *adverb* RECENTLY, lately, of late

lattice *noun* GRID, grating, grille, trellis

laudable *adjective* PRAISEWORTHY, admirable, commendable, creditable, excellent, meritorious, of note, worthy

laugh *verb* 1 CHUCKLE, be in stitches, chortle, giggle, guffaw, snigger, split one's sides, titter
▷ *noun* 2 CHUCKLE, chortle, giggle, guffaw, snigger, titter
3 (*informal*) JOKE, hoot (*informal*), lark, scream (*informal*)

laughable *adjective* RIDICULOUS, absurd, derisory, farcical, ludicrous, nonsensical, preposterous, risible

laughing stock *noun* FIGURE OF FUN, butt, target, victim

laugh off *verb* DISREGARD, brush aside, dismiss, ignore, minimize, pooh-pooh, shrug off

laughter *noun* AMUSEMENT, glee, hilarity, merriment, mirth

launch *verb* 1 PROPEL, discharge, dispatch, fire, project, send off, set in motion
2 BEGIN, commence, embark upon, inaugurate, initiate, instigate, introduce, open, start

laurels *plural noun* GLORY, credit, distinction, fame, honor, kudos, praise, prestige, recognition, renown

lavatory *noun* TOILET, bathroom, latrine, powder room, convenience *or* public convenience, washroom, water closet, W.C.

lavish *adjective* 1 PLENTIFUL, abundant, copious, profuse, prolific
2 GENEROUS, bountiful, free, liberal,

bestow, profusely

law *noun* 1 rule binding on community 2 system of such rules 3 legal science 4 knowledge, administration of it 5 (*informal*) (member of) police force 6 general principle deduced from facts 7 invariable sequence of events in nature > **law'ful** [-fəl] *adjective* allowed by law > **law'ful•ly** *adverb* > **law'less** [-lis] *adjective* 1 ignoring laws 2 violent > **law'yer** *noun* professional expert in law > **law'-a•bid•ing** [-bīd-ing] *adjective* 1 obedient to laws 2 well-behaved > **law'giv•er** *noun* one who makes laws > **law'suit** [-soot] *noun* prosecution of claim in court

lawn[1] *noun* stretch of carefully tended turf in garden, etc. > **lawn tennis** tennis played on grass court

lawn[2] *noun* fine linen

lawyer *see* **law**

lax [laks] *adjective* 1 not strict 2 lacking precision 3 loose, slack > **lax'a•tive** *adjective* having loosening effect on bowels ▷ *noun* > **lax'i•ty, lax'ness** *noun* 1 slackness 2 looseness of (moral) standards

lay[1] *pt. of* **lie**[1]

lay[2] *verb transitive* **laid, lay•ing** deposit, set, cause to lie > **lay'er** *noun* 1 single thickness of some substance, as stratum or coating on surface 2 laying hen 3 shoot of plant pegged down or partly covered with soil or plastic to encourage root growth ▷ *verb transitive* 4 propagate plants by making layers > **lay'down** *noun* in bridge, unbeatable hand held by declarer who plays with all cards exposed to view > **lay'out** *noun* arrangement, esp. of matter for printing > **lay off** dismiss employees during slack period > **lay'off** *noun* > **lay on** 1 provide, supply 2 apply 3 strike **lay on hands** of healer, place hands on person to be cured > **lay out** 1 display 2 expend 3 prepare for burial 4 plan copy for printing, etc. 5 (*slang*) knock out 6 (*slang*) criticize severely **lay waste** devastate

lay[3] *noun* minstrel's song

lay[4] *adjective* 1 not clerical or professional 2 of, or done, by persons not clergymen > **lay'man, lay'per•son** *noun* ordinary person

lay•ette [lay-ET] *noun* clothes, etc. for newborn child

laz•ar [LAZ-ər] *noun* leper

la•zy [LAY-zee] *adjective* **-zi•er, -zi•est** averse to work, indolent > **laze** *verb intransitive* **lazed, laz•ing** indulge in laziness > **la'zi•ly** *adverb* > **la'zi•ness** *noun*

lead[1] [leed] *verb transitive* **led, lead•ing** 1 guide, conduct 2 persuade 3 direct 4 conduct people

munificent, open-handed, unstinting
3 EXTRAVAGANT, exaggerated, excessive, immoderate, prodigal, unrestrained, wasteful, wild
▷ *verb* 4 SPEND, deluge, dissipate, expend, heap, pour, shower, squander, waste

law *noun* 1 CONSTITUTION, charter, code
2 RULE, act, command, commandment, decree, edict, order, ordinance, regulation, statute
3 PRINCIPLE, axiom, canon, precept

law-abiding *adjective* OBEDIENT, compliant, dutiful, good, honest, honorable, lawful, orderly, peaceable

law-breaker *noun* CRIMINAL, convict, crook (*informal*), culprit, delinquent, felon, miscreant, offender, perp (*informal*), villain, wrongdoer

lawful *adjective* LEGAL, authorized, constitutional, legalized, legitimate, licit, permissible, rightful, valid, warranted

lawless *adjective* DISORDERLY, anarchic, chaotic, rebellious, riotous, unruly, wild

lawlessness *noun* ANARCHY, chaos, disorder, mob rule

lawsuit *noun* CASE, action, dispute, industrial tribunal, litigation, proceedings, prosecution, suit, trial

lawyer *noun* LEGAL ADVISER, advocate, attorney, barrister (*chiefly Brit*), counsel, counselor

lax *adjective* SLACK, careless, casual, lenient, negligent, overindulgent, remiss, slapdash, slipshod

lay[1] *verb* 1 PLACE, deposit, leave, plant, put, set, set down, spread
2 ARRANGE, organize, position, set out
3 PRODUCE, bear, deposit
4 PUT FORWARD, advance, bring forward, lodge, offer, present, submit
5 ATTRIBUTE, allocate, allot, ascribe, assign, impute
6 DEVISE, concoct, contrive, design, hatch, plan, plot, prepare, work out
7 BET, gamble, give odds, hazard, risk, stake, wager

lay[2] *adjective* 1 NONCLERICAL, secular
2 NONSPECIALIST, amateur, inexpert, nonprofessional

layer *noun* TIER, row, seam, stratum, thickness

layman *noun* AMATEUR, lay person, nonprofessional, outsider

layoff *noun* DISMISSAL, discharge, unemployment

lay off *verb* DISMISS, discharge, let go, pay off

lay on *verb* PROVIDE, cater *or* cater for, furnish, give, purvey, supply

layout *noun* ARRANGEMENT, design, formation, outline, plan

lay out *verb* 1 ARRANGE, design, display, exhibit, plan, spread out
2 (*informal*) SPEND, disburse, expend, fork out (*slang*), invest, pay, shell out (*informal*)
3 (*informal*) KNOCK OUT, knock for six (*informal*), knock unconscious, KO *or* K.O. (*slang*)

laziness *noun* IDLENESS, inactivity, indolence, slackness, sloth, sluggishness

lazy *adjective* 1 IDLE, inactive, indolent, inert, slack, slothful, slow, workshy
2 LETHARGIC, drowsy, languid, languorous, sleepy, slow-moving, sluggish, somnolent, torpid

lead *verb* 1 GUIDE, conduct, escort, pilot, precede, show the way, steer, usher
2 PERSUADE, cause, dispose, draw, incline, induce, influence, prevail, prompt
3 COMMAND, direct, govern, head, manage, preside over, supervise
4 BE AHEAD *or* BE AHEAD OF, blaze a trail, come first, exceed, excel, outdo, outstrip, surpass, transcend
5 LIVE, experience, have, pass, spend, undergo
6 RESULT IN, bring on, cause, contribute, produce
▷ *noun* 7 FIRST PLACE, precedence, primacy,

▷ *verb intransitive* **led, lead•ing** 5 be, go, play first 6 result 7 give access to ▷ *noun* 8 leading 9 that which leads or is used to lead 10 example 11 front or principal place, role, etc. 12 cable bringing current to electric instrument > **lead'er** *noun* 1 one who leads 2 most important or prominent article in newspaper (*also* **leading article**) > **lead'er•ship** *noun* > **leading question** question worded to prompt answer desired > **lead time** time between design of product and its production

lead² [led] *noun* 1 soft heavy gray metal 2 plummet, used for sounding depths of water 3 graphite ▷ *verb transitive* **-ed, -ing** 4 cover, weight or space with lead > **lead'en** *adjective* 1 of, like lead 2 heavy 3 dull **go over like a lead balloon** (*slang*) fail to arouse interest or support

leaf [leef] *noun, plural* **leaves** 1 organ of photosynthesis in plants, consisting of a flat, usu. green blade on stem 2 two pages of book, etc. 3 thin sheet 4 flap, movable part of table, etc. ▷ *verb transitive* 5 turn through (pages, etc.) cursorily > **leaf'less** [-lis] *adjective* > **leaf'let** [-lit] *noun* 1 small leaf 2 single sheet, often folded, of printed matter for distribution as e.g. notice or advertisement > **leaf'y** *adjective* **leaf•i•er, leaf•i•est**

league¹ [leeg] *noun* 1 agreement for mutual help 2 parties to it 3 federation of teams, etc. 4 (*informal*) class, level ▷ *verb intransitive* **leagued, lea•guing** 5 unite in a league 6 combine in an association > **lea'guer** *noun* member of league

league² *noun* (*obsolete*) measure of distance, about three miles

leak [leek] *noun* 1 hole, defect, that allows escape or entrance of liquid, gas, radiation, etc. 2 disclosure ▷ *verb intransitive* 3 let fluid, etc. in or out 4 (of fluid, etc.) find its way through leak ▷ *verb transitive* 5 let escape ▷ *verb* (allow to) become known little by little > **leak'age** [-ij] *noun* 1 leaking 2 gradual escape or loss > **leak'y** *adjective* **leak•i•er, leak•i•est**

lean¹ [leen] *adjective* **-er, -est** 1 lacking fat 2 thin 3 meager 4 (of mixture of fuel and air) with too little fuel ▷ *noun* 5 lean part of meat, mainly muscular tissue

lean² *verb* **leaned, lean•ing** 1 rest against 2 bend, incline 3 tend (toward) 4 depend, rely (on) > **leaning** *noun* tendency > **lean-to** *noun, plural* **-tos** shed built against tree or post

leap [leep] *verb* **leaped** *or* **leapt, leap•ing** 1 spring, jump 2 spring over ▷ *noun* 3 jump > **leap'frog** *noun* game in which player vaults over another bending down > **leap year** year with February 29th as extra day, occurring every fourth year

learn [lurn] *verb* **learned** *or* **learnt, learn•ing** 1 gain skill, knowledge by study, practice or teaching 2 gain knowledge 3 be taught 4 find out > **learn'ed** [LUR-nid] *adjective* 1 erudite, deeply read 2 showing much learning > **learn'er**

DICTIONARY | THESAURUS

priority, supremacy, vanguard
8 ADVANTAGE, edge, margin, start
9 EXAMPLE, direction, guidance, leadership, model
10 CLUE, hint, indication, suggestion
11 LEADING ROLE, principal, protagonist, title role
▷ *adjective* 12 MAIN, chief, cutting-edge, first, foremost, head, leading, premier, primary, prime, principal

leader *noun* PRINCIPAL, alpha male, boss (*informal*), captain, chief, chieftain, commander, director, guide, head, ringleader, ruler

leadership *noun* 1 GUIDANCE, direction, domination, management, running, superintendency
2 AUTHORITY, command, control, influence, initiative, pre-eminence, supremacy

leading *adjective* MAIN, chief, cutting-edge, dominant, first, foremost, greatest, highest, primary, principal

lead on *verb* ENTICE, beguile, deceive, draw on, lure, seduce, string along (*informal*), tempt

lead up to *verb* INTRODUCE, pave the way, prepare for

leaf *noun* 1 FROND, blade
2 PAGE, folio, sheet
▷ *verb* 3 ▷ **leaf through** BROWSE, flip, glance, riffle, skim, thumb *or* thumb through

leaflet *noun* BOOKLET, brochure, circular, pamphlet

leafy *adjective* GREEN, bosky (*literary*), shaded, shady, verdant

league *noun* 1 ASSOCIATION, alliance, coalition, confederation, consortium, federation, fraternity, group, guild, partnership, union
2 CLASS, category, level

leak *noun* 1 HOLE, aperture, chink, crack, crevice, fissure, opening, puncture
2 DRIP, leakage, percolation, seepage
3 DISCLOSURE, divulgence
▷ *verb* 4 DRIP, escape, exude, ooze, pass, percolate, seep, spill, trickle
5 DISCLOSE, divulge, give away, let slip, make known, make public, pass on, reveal, tell

leaky *adjective* PUNCTURED, cracked, holey, leaking, perforated, porous, split

lean¹ *verb* 1 REST, be supported, prop, recline, repose
2 BEND, heel, incline, slant, slope, tilt, tip
3 TEND, be disposed to, be prone to, favor, prefer
4 ▷ **lean on** DEPEND ON, count on, have faith in, rely on, trust

lean² *adjective* 1 SLIM, angular, bony, gaunt, rangy, skinny, slender, spare, thin, wiry
2 UNPRODUCTIVE, barren, meager, poor, scanty, unfruitful

leaning *noun* TENDENCY, bent, bias, disposition, inclination, partiality, penchant, predilection, proclivity, propensity

leap *verb* 1 JUMP, bounce, bound, hop, skip, spring
▷ *noun* 2 JUMP, bound, spring, vault
3 INCREASE, escalation, rise, surge, upsurge, upswing

learn *verb* 1 MASTER, grasp, pick up
2 MEMORIZE, commit to memory, get off pat, learn by heart
3 DISCOVER, ascertain, detect, discern, find out, gather, hear, understand

learned *adjective* SCHOLARLY, academic, erudite, highbrow, intellectual, versed, well-informed, well-read

learner *noun* BEGINNER, apprentice, neophyte,

noun > **learn'ing** *noun* knowledge acquired by study

lease [lees] *noun* 1 contract by which land or property is rented for stated time by owner to tenant ▷ *verb transitive* **leased, leas•ing** 2 let, rent by, take on lease

leash [leesh] *noun* 1 thong for holding a dog 2 curb ▷ *verb transitive* 3 hold on leash 4 restrain

least [leest] *adjective* 1 smallest 2 *sup. of* **little** ▷ *noun* 3 smallest one ▷ *adverb* 4 in smallest degree

leath•er [LETH-ər] *noun* prepared skin of animal > **leath'er•y** *adjective* like leather, tough

leave[1] [leev] *verb* **left, leav•ing** 1 go away from 2 deposit 3 allow to remain 4 depart from 5 entrust 6 bequeath 7 go away, set out

leave[2] *noun* 1 permission 2 permission to be absent from work, duty 3 period of such absence 4 formal parting

leav•en [LEV-ən] *noun* 1 yeast 2 any transforming influence ▷ *verb transitive* 3 raise with leaven 4 influence 5 modify

lech•er [LECH-ər] *noun* man given to lewdness > **lech'er•ous** *adjective* 1 lewd 2 provoking lust 3 lascivious > **lech'er•ous•ly** *adverb* > **lech'er•ous•ness** *noun* > **lech'er•y** *noun, plural* **-er•ies**

lec•tern [LEK-tərn] *noun* 1 reading desk, esp. in church 2 stand with slanted top to hold book, notes, etc.

lec•ture [LEK-chər] *noun* 1 instructive discourse 2 speech of reproof ▷ *verb intransitive* **-tured, -tur•ing** 3 deliver discourse ▷ *verb transitive* **-tured, -tur•ing** 4 reprove > **lec'tur•er** *noun*

ledge [lej] *noun* 1 narrow shelf sticking out from wall, cliff, etc. 2 ridge, rock below surface of sea

ledg•er [LEJ-ər] *noun* 1 book of debit and credit accounts, chief account book of firm 2 flat stone > **ledger line** *mus.* short line, above or below stave

lee *noun* 1 shelter 2 side of anything, esp. ship, away from wind > **lee'ward** [-wərd] *adjective, noun* 1 (on) lee side ▷ *adverb* 2 toward this side > **lee'way** *noun* 1 leeward drift of ship 2 room for free movement within limits

leech *noun* species of bloodsucking worm

leek *noun* plant like onion with long bulb and thick stem

leer *verb intransitive* 1 glance with malign, sly, or lascivious expression ▷ *noun* 2 such glance

lees [leez] *plural noun* 1 sediment of wine, etc. 2 dregs

left[1] *adjective* 1 denotes the side that faces west when the front faces north 2 opposite to the right ▷ *noun* 3 the left hand or part 4 *politics* reforming or radical party (*also* **left wing**) ▷ *adverb* 5 on or toward the left > **left'ist** *noun, adjective* (person) of the political left

left[2] *pt./pp. of* **leave**

leg *noun* 1 one of limbs on which person or animal walks, runs, stands 2 part of garment covering leg 3 anything that supports, as leg of table 4 stage of journey > **leg'gings** *plural noun* covering of leather or other material for legs > **leg'gy** *adjective* **-gi•er, -gi•est** 1 long-legged 2 (of plants) straggling > **leg'warm•er** *noun* one of pair of long knitted footless socks worn over tights when exercising

leg•a•cy [LEG-ə-see] *noun, plural* **-cies** 1 anything left by will, bequest 2 thing handed down to successor

---

novice, tyro

learning *noun* KNOWLEDGE, culture, education, erudition, information, lore, scholarship, study, wisdom

lease *verb* HIRE, charter, let, loan, rent

leash *noun* LEAD, rein, tether

least *adjective* SMALLEST, fewest, lowest, meanest, minimum, poorest, slightest, tiniest

leathery *adjective* TOUGH, hard, rough

leave[1] *verb* 1 DEPART, decamp, disappear, exit, go away, make tracks, move, pull out, quit, retire, slope off, withdraw
2 FORGET, leave behind, mislay
3 CAUSE, deposit, generate, produce, result in
4 GIVE UP, abandon, drop, relinquish, renounce, surrender
5 ENTRUST, allot, assign, cede, commit, consign, give over, refer
6 BEQUEATH, hand down, will

leave[2] *noun* 1 PERMISSION, allowance, authorization, concession, consent, dispensation, freedom, liberty, sanction
2 HOLIDAY, furlough, leave of absence, sabbatical, time off, vacation
3 PARTING, adieu, departure, farewell, good-bye, leave-taking, retirement, withdrawal

leave out *verb* OMIT, blow off (*slang*), cast aside, disregard, exclude, ignore, neglect, overlook, reject

lecherous *adjective* LUSTFUL, lascivious, lewd, libidinous, licentious, prurient, salacious

lecture *noun* 1 TALK, address, discourse, instruction, lesson, speech
2 REBUKE, reprimand, reproof, scolding, talking-to (*informal*), telling off (*informal*)
▷ *verb* 3 TALK, address, discourse, expound, hold forth, speak, spout, teach
4 SCOLD, admonish, berate, castigate, censure, reprimand, reprove, tell off (*informal*)

ledge *noun* SHELF, mantle, projection, ridge, sill, step

leer *noun*
▷ *verb* GRIN, gloat, goggle, ogle, smirk, squint, stare

lees *plural noun* SEDIMENT, deposit, dregs, grounds

leeway *noun* ROOM, elbowroom, latitude, margin, play, scope, space

left *adjective* 1 LEFT-HAND, larboard (*nautical*), port, sinistral
2 (*of politics*) SOCIALIST, leftist, left-wing, radical

leftover *noun* REMNANT, oddment, scrap

left-wing *adjective* SOCIALIST, communist, radical, red (*informal*)

leg *noun* 1 LIMB, lower limb, member, pin (*informal*), stump (*informal*)
2 SUPPORT, brace, prop, upright
3 STAGE, lap, part, portion, section, segment, stretch
4 ▷ **pull someone's leg** (*informal*) TEASE, fool, kid (*informal*), make fun of, trick

legacy *noun* BEQUEST, estate, gift, heirloom, inheritance

le•gal [LEE-gəl] *adjective* of, appointed or permitted by, or based on, law > **le•gal'i•ty** *noun* > **le'gal•ize** *verb transitive* **-ized, -iz•ing** make legal
leg•ate [LEG-it] *noun* ambassador, esp. papal > **le•ga'tion** *noun* 1 diplomatic minister and staff 2 headquarters for these
leg•a•tee [leg-ə-TEE] *noun* recipient of legacy
le•ga•to [lə-GAH-toh] *adverb mus.* smoothly
leg•end [LEJ-ənd] *noun* 1 traditional story or myth 2 traditional literature 3 famous, renowned, person or event 4 inscription > **leg'end•ar•y** *adjective*
leg•er•de•main [lej-ər-də-MAYN] *noun* juggling, conjuring, sleight of hand, trickery
leg•i•ble [LEJ-ə-bəl] *adjective* easily read > **leg•i•bil'i•ty** *noun*
le•gion [LEE-jən] *noun* 1 body of infantry in Roman army 2 various modern military bodies 3 association of veterans 4 large number > **le'gion•ar•y** *adjective, noun* > **le•gion•naires' disease** [-NAIRZ] serious bacterial disease similar to pneumonia
leg•is•la•tor [LEJ-is-lay-tər] *noun* maker of laws > **leg'is•late** *verb intransitive* **-lat•ed, -lat•ing** make laws > **leg•is•la'tion** *noun* 1 act of legislating 2 law or laws that are made > **leg'is•la•tive** *adjective* > **leg'is•la•ture** [-chər] *noun* body that makes laws of a country or state
le•git•i•mate [lə-JIT-ə-mit] *adjective* 1 born in wedlock 2 lawful, regular 3 fairly deduced > **le•git'i•ma•cy** [-mə-see] *noun* > **le•git'i•mize** *verb transitive* **-mized, -miz•ing** make legitimate
le•gu•mi•nous [li-GYOO-mə-nəs] *adjective* (of plants) pod-bearing > **leg•ume** [LEG-yoom] *noun* leguminous plant
lei [lay] *noun* garland of flowers
lei•sure [LEE-zhər] *noun* 1 freedom from occupation 2 spare time > **lei'sure•ly** *adjective* 1 deliberate, unhurried ▷ *adverb* 2 slowly > **lei'sured** *adjective* with plenty of spare time
leit•mo•tif [LĪT-moh-teef] *noun mus.* recurring theme associated with some person, situation, thought
lem•ming [LEM-ing] *noun* rodent of northern regions
lem•on [LEM-ən] *noun* 1 pale yellow acid fruit 2 tree bearing it 3 its color 4 (*informal*) useless or defective person or thing > **lem•on•ade'** [-AYD] *noun* drink made from lemon juice
le•mur [LEE-mər] *noun* nocturnal animal like monkey
lend *verb transitive* **lent, lend•ing** 1 give temporary use of 2 let out for hire or interest 3 give, bestow **lends itself to** is suitable for
length [lengkth] *noun* 1 quality of being long 2 measurement from end to end 3 duration 4 extent 5 piece of a certain length > **length'en** *verb* 1 make, become, longer 2 draw out > **length'i•ly** *adverb* > **length'wise** *adjective, adverb* > **length'y** *adjective* **length•i•er, length•i•est** (over)long **at length** 1 in full detail 2 at last
le•ni•ent [LEE-nee-ənt] *adjective* mild, tolerant, not strict > **le'ni•en•cy** *noun*
len•i•ty [LEN-i-tee] *noun, plural* **-ties** 1 mercy

DICTIONARY

THESAURUS

legal *adjective* 1 LEGITIMATE, allowed, authorized, constitutional, lawful, licit, permissible, sanctioned, valid
2 JUDICIAL, forensic, juridical
legality *noun* LEGITIMACY, lawfulness, rightfulness, validity
legalize *verb* ALLOW, approve, authorize, decriminalize, legitimate, legitimize, license, permit, sanction, validate
legation *noun* DELEGATION, consulate, embassy, representation
legend *noun* 1 MYTH, fable, fiction, folk tale, saga, story, tale
2 CELEBRITY, luminary, megastar (*informal*), phenomenon, prodigy
3 INSCRIPTION, caption, motto
legendary *adjective* 1 MYTHICAL, apocryphal, fabled, fabulous, fictitious, romantic, traditional
2 FAMOUS, celebrated, famed, illustrious, immortal, renowned, well-known
legibility *noun* CLARITY, neatness, readability
legible *adjective* CLEAR, decipherable, distinct, easy to read, neat, readable
legion *noun* 1 ARMY, brigade, company, division, force, troop
2 MULTITUDE, drove, horde, host, mass, myriad, number, throng
legislation *noun* 1 LAWMAKING, enactment, prescription, regulation
2 LAW, act, bill, charter, measure, regulation, ruling, statute
legislative *adjective* LAW-MAKING, judicial, law-giving
legislator *noun* LAWMAKER, lawgiver
legislature *noun* PARLIAMENT, assembly, chamber, congress, senate
legitimate *adjective* 1 LEGAL, authentic, authorized, genuine, kosher (*informal*), lawful, licit, rightful
2 REASONABLE, admissible, correct, justifiable, logical, sensible, valid, warranted, well-founded
▷ *verb* 3 AUTHORIZE, legalize, legitimize, permit, pronounce lawful, sanction
legitimize *verb* LEGALIZE, authorize, permit, sanction
leisure *noun* SPARE TIME, ease, freedom, free time, liberty, recreation, relaxation, rest
leisurely *adjective* UNHURRIED, comfortable, easy, gentle, lazy, relaxed, slow
lend *verb* 1 LOAN, advance
2 ADD, bestow, confer, give, grant, impart, provide, supply
3 ▷ **lend itself to** SUIT, be appropriate, be serviceable
length *noun* 1 (*of linear extent*) DISTANCE, extent, longitude, measure, reach, span
2 (*of time*) DURATION, period, space, span, stretch, term
3 PIECE, measure, portion, section, segment
4 ▷ **at length a** IN DETAIL, completely, fully, in depth, thoroughly, to the full **b** FOR A LONG TIME, for ages, for hours, interminably **c** AT LAST, at long last, eventually, finally, in the end
lengthen *verb* EXTEND, continue, draw out, elongate, expand, increase, prolong, protract, spin out, stretch
lengthy *adjective* LONG, drawn-out, extended, interminable, long-drawn-out, long-winded, prolonged, protracted, tedious
leniency *noun* TOLERANCE, clemency, compassion, forbearance, indulgence,

2 clemency
lens [lenz] *noun, plural* **-es** piece of glass or similar material with one or both sides curved, used to converge or diverge light rays in cameras, eyeglasses, telescopes, etc.
lent *pt./pp. of* **lend**
Lent *noun* period of fasting from Ash Wednesday to Easter > **Lent'en** *adjective* of, in, or suitable to Lent
len'til *noun* edible seed of leguminous plant > **len•tic'u•lar** *adjective* like lentil
len•to [LEN-toh] *adverb mus.* slowly
le•o•nine [LEE-ə-nīn] *adjective* like a lion
leop•ard [LEP-ərd] *noun* large, spotted, carnivorous animal of cat family, like panther
le•o•tard [LEE-ə-tahrd] *noun* tight-fitting garment covering most of body, worn by acrobats, dancers, etc.
lep•er [LEP-ər] *noun* 1 one suffering from leprosy 2 person ignored or despised > **lep'ro•sy** [-rə-see] *noun* disease attacking nerves and skin resulting in loss of feeling in affected parts > **lep'rous** [-rəs] *adjective*
lep•re•chaun [LEP-rə-kawn] *noun* mischievous elf of Irish folklore
les•bi•an [LEZ-bee-ən] *noun* a homosexual woman > **les'bi•an•ism** *noun*
lese maj•es•ty [LEEZ] *noun* 1 treason 2 taking of liberties
le•sion [LEE-*zh*ən] *noun* injury, injurious change in texture or action of an organ of the body
less *adjective* 1 *comp. of* **little** 2 not so much ▷ *noun* 3 smaller part, quantity 4 a lesser amount ▷ *adverb* 5 to a smaller extent or degree ▷ *preposition* 6 after deducting, minus > **less'en** *verb transitive* 1 diminish 2 reduce > **less'er** *adjective* 1 less 2 smaller 3 minor
les•see [le-SEE] *noun* one to whom lease is granted
les•son [LES-ən] *noun* 1 installment of course of instruction 2 content of this 3 experience that teaches 4 portion of Scripture read in church
les•sor [LES-or] *noun* grantor of a lease
lest *conjunction* 1 in order that not 2 for fear that
let[1] *verb transitive* **let, let•ting** 1 allow, enable, cause 2 allow to escape 3 grant use of for rent, lease ▷ *verb intransitive* **let, let•ting** 4 be leased ▷ *verb auxiliary* 5 used to express a proposal, command, threat, assumption
let[2] *noun* 1 in law, obstacle or hindrance 2 in tennis, etc., minor infringement, esp. obstruction of ball by net on service, requiring replaying of point
le•thal [LEE-thəl] *adjective* deadly
leth•ar•gy [LETH-ər-jee] *noun, plural* **-gies** 1 apathy, want of energy or interest 2 unnatural drowsiness > **le•thar'gic** *adjective* > **le•thar'gi•cal•ly** *adverb*
let•ter [LET-ər] *noun* 1 alphabetical symbol 2 written message 3 strict meaning, interpretation ▷ *verb transitive* 4 mark with, in, letters > **let•ters** *plural noun* literature, knowledge of books > **let'tered** *adjective* learned > **let'ter•press** *noun* 1 process of printing from raised type 2 matter printed in this way
let•tuce [LET-is] *noun* plant grown for use in salad
leu•co•cyte [LOO-kə-sīt] *noun* one of white blood corpuscles
leu•ke•mi•a [loo-KEE-mee-ə] *noun* a progressive blood disease
Lev. Leviticus
lev'ee[1] *noun hist.* 1 reception held by sovereign on rising 2 reception in someone's honor
levee[2] *noun* river embankment, natural or artificial
lev•el [LEV-əl] *adjective* 1 horizontal 2 even in

DICTIONARY • THESAURUS

mercy, moderation, pity, quarter
lenient *adjective* TOLERANT, compassionate, forbearing, forgiving, indulgent, kind, merciful, sparing
lesbian *adjective* HOMOSEXUAL, gay, sapphic
less *adjective* 1 SMALLER, shorter ▷ *preposition* 2 MINUS, excepting, lacking, subtracting, without
lessen *verb* REDUCE, contract, decrease, diminish, ease, lower, minimize, narrow, shrink
lesser *adjective* MINOR, inferior, less important, lower, secondary
lesson *noun* 1 CLASS, coaching, instruction, period, schooling, teaching, tutoring
2 EXAMPLE, deterrent, message, moral
let[1] *verb* 1 ALLOW, authorize, entitle, give permission, give the go-ahead, permit, sanction, tolerate
2 LEASE, hire, rent
let[2] *noun* HINDRANCE, constraint, impediment, interference, obstacle, obstruction, prohibition, restriction
letdown *noun* DISAPPOINTMENT, anticlimax, blow, comedown (*informal*), setback, washout (*informal*)
let down *verb* DISAPPOINT, disenchant, disillusion, dissatisfy, fail, fall short, leave in the lurch, leave stranded
lethal *adjective* DEADLY, dangerous, destructive, devastating, fatal, mortal, murderous, virulent
lethargic *adjective* SLUGGISH, apathetic, drowsy, dull, languid, listless, sleepy, slothful
lethargy *noun* SLUGGISHNESS, apathy, drowsiness, inertia, languor, lassitude, listlessness, sleepiness, sloth
let off *verb* 1 FIRE, detonate, discharge, explode
2 EMIT, exude, give off, leak, release
3 EXCUSE, absolve, discharge, exempt, exonerate, forgive, pardon, release, spare
let on *verb* REVEAL, admit, disclose, divulge, give away, let the cat out of the bag (*informal*), make known, say
let out *verb* 1 EMIT, give vent to, produce
2 RELEASE, discharge, free, let go, liberate
letter *noun* 1 CHARACTER, sign, symbol
2 MESSAGE, communication, dispatch, epistle, line, missive, note
let-up *noun* LESSENING, break, breathing space, interval, lull, pause, remission, respite, slackening
let up *verb* STOP, abate, decrease, diminish, ease *or* ease up, moderate, relax, slacken, subside
level *adjective* 1 HORIZONTAL, flat
2 EVEN, consistent, plain, smooth, uniform
3 EQUAL, balanced, commensurate, comparable, equivalent, even, neck and neck, on a level playing field (*informal*), on a par, proportionate ▷ *verb* 4 FLATTEN, even off *or* even out,

surface 3 consistent in style, quality, etc. ▷ *noun* 4 horizontal line or surface 5 instrument for showing, testing horizontal plane 6 position on scale 7 standard, grade 8 horizontal passage in mine ▷ *verb* **-eled, -el•ing** 9 make level 10 bring to same level 11 knock down 12 aim (gun, or, *fig* accusation, etc.) 13 (*informal*) (esp. with *with*) be honest, frank > **le'vel•head'ed** [-HED-id] *adjective* not apt to be carried away by emotion

lev•er [LEV-ər] *noun* 1 rigid bar pivoted about a fulcrum to transfer a force with mechanical advantage 2 handle pressed, pulled, etc. 3 to operate something ▷ *verb transitive* 4 pry, move, with lever > **lev'er•age** [-ij] *noun* 1 action, power of lever 2 influence 3 power to accomplish something 4 advantage

le•vi•a•than [lə-VĪ-ə-thən] *noun* 1 sea monster 2 anything huge or formidable

lev•i•ta•tion [lev-i-TAY-shən] *noun* the power of raising a solid body into the air supernaturally > **lev'i•tate** *verb* **-tat•ed, -tat•ing** (cause to) do this

lev•i•ty [LEV-i-tee] *noun, plural* **-ties** 1 inclination to make a joke of serious matters, frivolity 2 facetiousness

lev•y [LEV-ee] *verb transitive* **lev•ied, lev•y•ing** 1 impose (tax) 2 raise (troops) ▷ *noun, plural* **lev•ies** 3 imposition or collection of taxes 4 enrolling of troops 5 amount, number levied

lewd [lood] *adjective* **-er, -est** 1 lustful 2 indecent > **lewd'ly** *adverb* > **lewd'ness** *noun*

lex•i•con [LEK-si-kon] *noun* dictionary > **lex•i•cog'ra•pher** [-rə-fər] *noun* writer of dictionaries > **lex•i•cog'ra•phy** *noun*

Li *chem.* lithium

li•a•ble [LĪ-ə-bəl] *adjective* 1 answerable 2 exposed (to) 3 subject (to) 4 likely (to) > **li•a•bil'i•ty** *noun* 1 state of being liable, obligation 2 hindrance, disadvantage 3 (*plural* **-ties**) debts

li•ai•son [lee-AY-zon] *noun* 1 union 2 connection 3 intimacy, esp. secret 4 person who keeps others in touch with one another

li•ar [LĪ-ər] *noun* one who tells lies

li•ba•tion [lī-BAY-shən] *noun* 1 drink poured as offering to the gods 2 (*facetious*) 3 drink of whiskey

li•bel [LĪ-bəl] *noun* 1 published statement falsely damaging person's reputation ▷ *verb transitive* **-beled, -bel•ing** 2 defame falsely > **li'bel•ous** *adjective* defamatory

lib•er•al [LIB-ər-əl] *adjective* 1 of political party favoring democratic reforms or favoring individual freedom 2 generous 3 tolerant 4 abundant 5 (of education) designed to develop general cultural interests ▷ *noun* 6 one who has liberal ideas or opinions > **lib'er•al•ism** *noun* > **lib•er•al'i•ty** *noun, plural* **-ties** munificence > **lib'er•al•ize** *verb transitive* **-ized, -iz•ing**

lib•er•ate [LIB-ə-rayt] *verb transitive* **-at•ed, -at•ing** set free > **lib•er•a'tion** *noun*

DICTIONARY | THESAURUS

---

plane, smooth

5 EQUALIZE, balance, even up

6 RAZE, bulldoze, demolish, destroy, devastate, flatten, knock down, pull down, tear down

7 DIRECT, aim, focus, point, train

▷ *noun* 8 POSITION, achievement, degree, grade, rank, stage, standard, standing, status

9 ▷ **on the level** (*informal*) HONEST, above board, fair, genuine, square, straight

level-headed *adjective* STEADY, balanced, calm, collected, composed, cool, sensible, unflappable (*informal*)

lever *noun* 1 HANDLE, bar

▷ *verb* 2 PRISE, force

leverage *noun* INFLUENCE, authority, clout (*informal*), pull (*informal*), weight

levity *noun* LIGHT-HEARTEDNESS, facetiousness, flippancy, frivolity, silliness, skittishness, triviality

levy *verb* 1 IMPOSE, charge, collect, demand, exact

2 CONSCRIPT, call up, mobilize, muster, raise

▷ *noun* 3 IMPOSITION, assessment, collection, exaction, gathering

4 TAX, duty, excise, fee, tariff, toll

lewd *adjective* INDECENT, bawdy, lascivious, libidinous, licentious, lustful, obscene, pornographic, smutty, wanton, X-rated

lewdness *noun* INDECENCY, bawdiness, carnality, debauchery, depravity, lasciviousness, lechery, licentiousness, obscenity, pornography, wantonness

liability *noun* 1 RESPONSIBILITY, accountability, answerability, culpability

2 DEBT, debit, obligation

3 DISADVANTAGE, burden, drawback, encumbrance, handicap, hindrance, inconvenience, millstone, nuisance

liable *adjective* 1 RESPONSIBLE, accountable, answerable, obligated

2 VULNERABLE, exposed, open, subject, susceptible

3 LIKELY, apt, disposed, inclined, prone, tending

liaise *verb* LINK, communicate, keep contact, mediate

liaison *noun* 1 COMMUNICATION, connection, contact, hook-up, interchange

2 AFFAIR, amour, entanglement, intrigue, love affair, romance

liar *noun* FALSIFIER, fabricator, fibber, perjurer

libel *noun* 1 DEFAMATION, aspersion, calumny, denigration, smear

▷ *verb* 2 DEFAME, blacken, malign, revile, slur, smear, vilify

libelous *adjective* DEFAMATORY, derogatory, false, injurious, malicious, scurrilous, untrue

liberal *adjective* 1 PROGRESSIVE, libertarian, radical, reformist

2 GENEROUS, beneficent, bountiful, charitable, kind, open-handed, open-hearted, unstinting

3 TOLERANT, broad-minded, indulgent, permissive

4 ABUNDANT, ample, bountiful, copious, handsome, lavish, munificent, plentiful, profuse, rich

liberality *noun* 1 GENEROSITY, beneficence, benevolence, bounty, charity, kindness, largesse *or* largess, munificence, philanthropy

2 TOLERATION, broad-mindedness, latitude, liberalism, libertarianism, permissiveness

liberalize *verb* RELAX, ease, loosen, moderate, modify, slacken, soften

liberate *verb* FREE, deliver, emancipate, let loose, let out, release, rescue, set free

lib•er•tar•i•an [lib-ər-TAIR-ee-ən] *noun* believer in freedom of thought, etc., or in free will ▷ *adjective*
lib•er•tine [LIB-ər-teen] *noun* 1 morally dissolute person ▷ *adjective* 2 dissolute
lib•er•ty [LIB-ər-tee] *noun* 1 freedom 2 (*plural* **-ties**) rights, privileges **at liberty** 3 free 4 having the right 5 out of work **take liberties (with)** be presumptuous
li•bi•do [li-BEE-doh] *noun, plural* **-dos** 1 life force 2 emotional craving, esp. of sexual origin > **li•bid'i•nous** *adjective* lustful
li•brar•y [LĪ-brer-ee] *noun, plural* **-brar•ies** 1 room, building where books are kept 2 collection of books, phonograph records, etc. 3 reading, writing room in house > **li•brar'i•an** *noun* keeper of library
li•bret•to [li-BRET-oh] *noun, plural* **-tos** *or* **-ti** [-tee] words of an opera > **li•bret'tist** *noun*
lice *noun see* **louse**
li•cense [LĪ-səns] *noun* 1 (document, certificate, giving) leave, permission 2 excessive liberty 3 dissoluteness 4 writer's, artist's intentional transgression of rules of art (*also* **poetic license**) ▷ *verb transitive* **-censed, -cens•ing** 5 grant license to > **li•cen•see'** *noun* holder of license
li•cen•tious [lī-SEN-shəs] *adjective* 1 dissolute 2 sexually immoral
li•chen [LĪ-kən] *noun* small flowerless plants forming crust on rocks, trees, etc.
lick [lik] *verb transitive* 1 pass the tongue over 2 touch lightly 3 (*informal*) defeat 4 (*informal*) flog, beat ▷ *noun* 5 act of licking 6 small amount (esp. of work, etc.) 7 block or natural deposit of salt or other chemical licked by cattle, etc. > **lick'ing** *noun* 1 beating 2 defeat
lic•o•rice [LIK-ər-ish] *noun* 1 black substance used in medicine and as a candy 2 plant, its root from which it is obtained
lid *noun* 1 movable cover 2 cover of the eye 3 (*slang*) hat
lie[1] [lī] *verb intransitive* **lay, lain, ly•ing** 1 be horizontal, at rest 2 be situated 3 remain, be in certain state or position 4 exist, be found 5 recline ▷ *noun* 6 manner, direction, position in which thing lies 7 of a golf ball, its position relative to difficulty of hitting it
lie[2] *verb intransitive* **lied, ly•ing** 1 make false statement knowingly ▷ *noun* 2 deliberate falsehood > **li'ar** [-ər] *noun* **white lie** untruth said without evil intent **give the lie to** disprove
lien [leen] *noun* right to hold another's property until claim is met
lieu [loo] *noun* place **in lieu of** instead of
lieu•ten•ant [loo-TEN-ənt] *noun* 1 deputy 2 (in the Army and Marine Corps) rank below captain 3 (in the Navy) rank below lieutenant commander 4 police, fire department officer
life [līf] *noun, plural* **lives** 1 active principle of existence of animals and plants, animate existence 2 time of its lasting 3 history of such existence 4 way of living 5 vigor, vivacity > **life'less** [-lis] *adjective* 1 dead 2 inert 3 dull > **life'long** *adjective* lasting a lifetime > **life belt, life jacket** buoyant device to keep afloat person in danger of drowning > **life coach** person whose job it is to improve the quality of his or her clients' lives, by offering advice on professional and personal matters > **life style** particular attitudes, habits, etc. of person or group > **life-support** *adjective* of equipment or treatment necessary to keep a person alive > **life'time** *noun* length of time person, animal, or object lives or functions

DICTIONARY • THESAURUS

liberation *noun* DELIVERANCE, emancipation, freedom, freeing, liberty, release
liberator *noun* DELIVERER, emancipator, freer, redeemer, rescuer, savior
libertine *noun* REPROBATE, debauchee, lecher, profligate, rake, roué, sensualist, voluptuary, womanizer
liberty *noun* 1 FREEDOM, autonomy, emancipation, immunity, independence, liberation, release, self-determination, sovereignty
2 IMPERTINENCE, impropriety, impudence, insolence, presumption
3 ▷ **at liberty** FREE, on the loose, unrestricted
libidinous *adjective* LUSTFUL, carnal, debauched, lascivious, lecherous, sensual, wanton
license *noun* 1 CERTIFICATE, charter, permit, warrant
2 PERMISSION, authority, authorization, blank check, carte blanche, dispensation, entitlement, exemption, immunity, leave, liberty, right
3 LATITUDE, freedom, independence, leeway, liberty
4 LAXITY, excess, immoderation, indulgence, irresponsibility
license *verb* PERMIT, accredit, allow, authorize, certify, empower, sanction, warrant
licentious *adjective* PROMISCUOUS, abandoned, debauched, dissolute, immoral, lascivious, lustful, sensual, wanton
lick *verb* 1 TASTE, lap, tongue
2 (*of a flame*) FLICKER, dart, flick, play over, ripple, touch
3 (*slang*) BEAT, defeat, master, outdo, outstrip, overcome, rout, trounce, vanquish
▷ *noun* 4 DAB, bit, stroke, touch
5 (*informal*) PACE, clip (*informal*), rate, speed
lie[1] *verb* 1 FALSIFY, dissimulate, equivocate, fabricate, fib, prevaricate, tell untruths
▷ *noun* 2 FALSEHOOD, deceit, fabrication, fib, fiction, invention, prevarication, untruth
lie[2] *verb* 1 RECLINE, loll, lounge, repose, rest, sprawl, stretch out
2 BE SITUATED, be, be placed, exist, remain
life *noun* 1 BEING, sentience, vitality
2 EXISTENCE, being, lifetime, span, time
3 BIOGRAPHY, autobiography, confessions, history, life story, memoirs, story
4 BEHAVIOR, conduct, life style, way of life
5 LIVELINESS, animation, energy, high spirits, spirit, verve, vigor, vitality, vivacity, zest
lifeless *adjective* 1 DEAD, deceased, defunct, extinct, inanimate
2 DULL, colorless, flat, lackluster, lethargic, listless, sluggish, wooden
3 UNCONSCIOUS, comatose, dead to the world (*informal*), insensible
lifelike *adjective* REALISTIC, authentic, exact, faithful, natural, true-to-life, vivid
lifelong *adjective* LONG-STANDING, enduring, lasting, long-lasting, perennial, persistent
lifetime *noun* EXISTENCE, career, day *or* days,

lift *verb transitive* 1 raise in position, status, mood, volume, etc. 2 take up and remove 3 exalt spiritually 4 (*informal*) steal ▷ *verb intransitive* 5 rise ▷ *noun* 6 raising apparatus 7 ride in car, etc., as passenger 8 force of air acting at right angles on aircraft wing, so lifting it 9 (*informal*) feeling of cheerfulness, uplift
lig•a•ment [LIG-ə-mənt] *noun* band of tissue joining bones > **lig'a•ture** [-chər] *noun* 1 anything that binds 2 thread for tying up blood vessels or for removing tumors
light[1] [līt] *adjective* **-er, -est** 1 of, or bearing, little weight 2 not severe 3 gentle 4 easy, requiring little effort 5 trivial 6 (of industry) producing small, usu. consumer goods, using light machinery ▷ *adverb* 7 in light manner ▷ *verb intransitive* **light•ed** *or* **lit, light•ing** 8 alight (from vehicle, etc.) 9 come by chance (upon) > **light'en** *verb transitive* **light•ed** *or* **lit, light•ing** reduce, remove (load, etc.) > **lights** *plural noun* lungs of animals as food > **light'head'ed** *adjective* 1 dizzy, inclined to faint 2 delirious > **light'heart'ed** *adjective* carefree > **light'weight** *noun, adjective* 1 (person) of little weight or importance 2 boxer weighing between 126 and 135 pounds (56.7 to 61 kg)
light[2] *noun* 1 electromagnetic radiation by which things are visible 2 source of this, lamp 3 window 4 light part of anything 5 means or act of setting fire to 6 understanding ▷ *adjective* **-er, -est** 7 bright 8 pale, not dark ▷ *verb* **light•ed** *or* **lit, light•ing** 9 set burning 10 give light to 11 take fire 12 brighten > **lights** *plural noun* traffic lights > **light'en** *verb transitive* make light > **light'ing** *noun* apparatus for supplying artificial light > **light'ning** *noun* visible discharge of electricity in atmosphere > **light'house** *noun* tower with a light to guide ships > **light-year** *noun astronomy* distance light travels in one year, about six trillion miles
light•er [LĪ-tər] *noun* 1 device for lighting cigarettes, etc. 2 flat-bottomed boat for unloading ships
like[1] [līk] *adjective* 1 resembling 2 similar 3 characteristic of ▷ *adverb* 4 in the manner of ▷ *pronoun* 5 similar thing > **like'li•hood** [-huud] *noun* probability > **like'ly** *adjective* **-li•er, -li•est** 1 probable 2 hopeful, promising ▷ *adverb* 3 probably > **lik'en** *verb transitive* compare > **like'ness** *noun* 1 resemblance 2 portrait > **like'wise** *adverb*

span, time
lift *verb* 1 RAISE, draw up, elevate, hoist, pick up, uplift, upraise
2 REVOKE, annul, cancel, countermand, end, remove, rescind, stop, terminate
3 DISAPPEAR, be dispelled, disperse, dissipate, vanish
▷ *noun* 4 RIDE, drive, run
5 BOOST, encouragement, pick-me-up, shot in the arm (*informal*)
light[1] *noun* 1 BRIGHTNESS, brilliance, glare, gleam, glint, glow, illumination, luminosity, radiance, shine
2 LAMP, beacon, candle, flare, lantern, taper, torch
3 ASPECT, angle, context, interpretation, point of view, slant, vantage point, viewpoint
4 MATCH, flame, lighter
▷ *adjective* 5 BRIGHT, brilliant, illuminated, luminous, lustrous, shining, well-lit
6 PALE, bleached, blond, faded, fair, pastel
▷ *verb* 7 IGNITE, inflame, kindle
8 ILLUMINATE, brighten, light up
light[2] *adjective* 1 INSUBSTANTIAL, airy, buoyant, flimsy, portable, slight, underweight
2 WEAK, faint, gentle, indistinct, mild, moderate, slight, soft
3 INSIGNIFICANT, inconsequential, inconsiderable, scanty, slight, small, trifling, trivial
4 NIMBLE, agile, graceful, lithe, sprightly, sylphlike
5 LIGHT-HEARTED, amusing, entertaining, frivolous, funny, humorous, witty
6 DIGESTIBLE, frugal, modest
▷ *verb* 7 SETTLE, alight, land, perch
8 ▷ **light on, light upon** COME ACROSS, chance upon, discover, encounter, find, happen upon, hit upon, stumble on
lighten[1] *verb* BRIGHTEN, become light, illuminate, irradiate, light up
lighten[2] *verb* 1 EASE, allay, alleviate, ameliorate, assuage, lessen, mitigate, reduce, relieve
2 CHEER, brighten, buoy up, lift, perk up, revive
light-headed *adjective* FAINT, dizzy, giddy, hazy, vertiginous, woozy (*informal*)
light-hearted *adjective* CAREFREE, blithe, cheerful, happy-go-lucky, jolly, jovial, playful, upbeat (*informal*)
lightly *adverb* 1 GENTLY, delicately, faintly, slightly, softly
2 MODERATELY, sparingly, sparsely, thinly
3 EASILY, effortlessly, readily, simply
4 CARELESSLY, breezily, flippantly, frivolously, heedlessly, thoughtlessly
lightweight *adjective* UNIMPORTANT, inconsequential, insignificant, paltry, petty, slight, trifling, trivial, worthless
likable *or* **likeable** *adjective* ATTRACTIVE, agreeable, amiable, appealing, charming, engaging, nice, pleasant, sympathetic
like[1] *adjective* SIMILAR, akin, alike, analogous, corresponding, equivalent, identical, parallel, same
like[2] *verb* 1 ENJOY, be fond of, be keen on, be partial to, delight in, go for, love, relish, revel in
2 ADMIRE, appreciate, approve, cherish, esteem, hold dear, prize, take to
3 WISH, care to, choose, desire, fancy, feel inclined, prefer, want
4 (*informal*) BE ATTRACTED TO, be captivated by, be turned on by (*informal*), lust after, take a liking to, take to
likelihood *noun* PROBABILITY, chance, possibility, prospect
likely *adjective* 1 INCLINED, apt, disposed, liable, prone, tending
2 PROBABLE, anticipated, expected, odds-on, on the cards, to be expected
3 PLAUSIBLE, believable, credible, feasible, possible, reasonable
4 PROMISING, hopeful, up-and-coming
liken *verb* COMPARE, equate, match, parallel, relate, set beside
likeness *noun* 1 RESEMBLANCE, affinity, correspondence, similarity

in like manner
like² *verb transitive* **liked, lik•ing** find agreeable, enjoy, love > **lik'a•ble** *adjective* > **liking** *noun* 1 fondness 2 inclination, taste
li•lac [LĪ-lək] *noun* 1 shrub bearing purple or white flowers 2 pale reddish purple ▷ *adjective* 3 of this color
Lil•li•pu•tian [lil-i-PYOO-shən] *adjective* 1 diminutive ▷ *noun* 2 very small person
lilt *verb* 1 sing merrily 2 move lightly ▷ *noun* 3 rhythmical effect in music, swing > **lilt'ing** *adjective*
lil•y [LIL-ee] *noun, plural* **lil•ies** bulbous flowering plant > **lil•y-white** *adjective* 1 white 2 pure, above reproach 3 of an organization or community, forbidding admission to blacks
limb¹ [lim] *noun* 1 arm or leg 2 wing 3 branch of tree
limb² *noun* 1 edge of sun or moon 2 edge of sextant
lim•ber¹ [LIM-bər] *noun* detachable front of gun carriage
lim•ber² *adjective* pliant, lithe > **limber up** loosen stiff muscles by exercises
lim•bo¹ [LIM-boh] *noun, plural* **-bos** 1 supposed region intermediate between heaven and hell for the unbaptized 2 intermediate, indeterminate place or state
lim•bo² *noun, plural* **-bos** West Indian dance in which dancers pass under a bar
lime¹ [līm] *noun* 1 any of certain calcium compounds used in making fertilizer, cement ▷ *verb transitive* **limed, lim•ing** 2 treat (land) with lime > **lime'light** *noun* 1 formerly, intense white light obtained by heating lime 2 glare of publicity > **lime'stone** *noun* sedimentary rock used in building
lime² *noun* small acid fruit like lemon
lim•er•ick [LIM-ər-ik] *noun* self-contained, nonsensical, humorous verse of five lines
lim'it *noun* 1 utmost extent or duration 2 boundary ▷ *verb transitive* 3 restrict, restrain, bound > **lim•i•ta'tion** *noun* > **lim'it•less** *adjective*
lim•ou•sine [LIM-ə-zeen] *noun* large, luxurious car
limp¹ *adjective* **-er, -est** without firmness or stiffness > **limp'ly** *adverb*
limp² *verb intransitive* 1 walk lamely ▷ *noun* 2 limping gait
lim'pid *adjective* 1 clear 2 translucent > **lim•pid'i•ty** *noun*
linch'pin *noun* 1 pin to hold wheel on its axle 2 essential person or thing
line [līn] *noun* 1 long narrow mark 2 stroke made with pen, etc. 3 continuous length without breadth 4 row 5 series, course 6 telephone connection 7 progeny 8 province of activity 9 shipping company 10 railroad track 11 any class of goods 12 cord 13 string 14 wire 15 advice, guidance ▷ *verb transitive* **lined, lin•ing** 16 cover inside 17 mark with lines 18 bring into line 19 be, form border, edge > **lin'e•age** [-ee-ij] *noun* descent from, descendants of an ancestor > **lin'e•al** *adjective* 1 of lines 2 in direct line of descent > **lin'e•a•ment** *noun* feature of face > **lin'e•ar** *adjective* of, in lines > **lin•er** [LĪN-ər] *noun* large ship or aircraft of passenger line > **line dancing** form of social dancing performed by rows of people to popular music > **lines'man** [-mən] *noun sports* official who helps referee, umpire **get a line on** obtain all relevant information about
lin•en [LIN-ən] *adjective* 1 made of flax ▷ *noun* 2 cloth made of flax 3 linen articles collectively 4 sheets, tablecloths, etc., or shirts (orig. made of linen)
lin•ger [LING-gər] *verb intransitive* 1 delay, loiter 2 remain long

DICTIONARY • THESAURUS

2 PORTRAIT, depiction, effigy, image, picture, representation
likewise *adverb* SIMILARLY, in like manner, in the same way
liking *noun* FONDNESS, affection, inclination, love, partiality, penchant, preference, soft spot, taste, weakness
limb *noun* 1 PART, appendage, arm, extremity, leg, member, wing
2 BRANCH, bough, offshoot, projection, spur
limelight *noun* PUBLICITY, attention, celebrity, fame, prominence, public eye, recognition, stardom, the spotlight
limit *noun* 1 BREAKING POINT, deadline, end, ultimate
2 BOUNDARY, border, edge, frontier, perimeter
▷ *verb* 3 RESTRICT, bound, check, circumscribe, confine, curb, ration, restrain
limitation *noun* RESTRICTION, check, condition, constraint, control, curb, qualification, reservation, restraint
limited *adjective* RESTRICTED, bounded, checked, circumscribed, confined, constrained, controlled, curbed, finite
limitless *adjective* INFINITE, boundless, countless, endless, inexhaustible, unbounded, unlimited, untold, vast
limp¹ *adjective* FLOPPY, drooping, flabby, flaccid, pliable, slack, soft
limp² *verb* 1 HOBBLE, falter, hop, shamble, shuffle
▷ *noun* 2 LAMENESS, hobble
line¹ *noun* 1 STROKE, band, groove, mark, score, scratch, streak, stripe
2 WRINKLE, crease, crow's foot, furrow, mark
3 BOUNDARY, border, borderline, edge, frontier, limit
4 STRING, cable, cord, rope, thread, wire
5 TRAJECTORY, course, direction, path, route, track
6 JOB, area, business, calling, employment, field, occupation, profession, specialization, trade
7 ROW, column, file, procession, queue, rank
8 ▷ **in line for** DUE FOR, in the running for
▷ *verb* 9 MARK, crease, furrow, rule, score
10 BORDER, bound, edge, fringe
lineaments *plural noun* FEATURES, countenance, face, physiognomy
lined *adjective* 1 RULED, feint
2 WRINKLED, furrowed, wizened, worn
lines *plural noun* WORDS, part, script
line-up *noun* ARRANGEMENT, array, row, selection, team
linger *verb* 1 STAY, hang around, loiter, remain, stop, tarry, wait
2 DELAY, dally, dawdle, drag one's feet *or* drag one's heels, idle, take one's time

lin•ge•rie [LAHN-zhə-ree] *noun* women's underwear or nightwear
lin•go [LING-goh] *noun* (*informal*) language, speech esp. applied to jargon and slang
lin•gua fran•ca [LING-gwə FRANG-kə] *noun, plural* **-fran•cas** language used for communication between people of different mother tongues
lin•gual [LING-gwəl] *adjective* 1 of the tongue or language ▷ *noun* 2 sound made by the tongue, as *d, l, t* > **lin'guist** *noun* 1 one skilled in languages or language study > **lin•guis'tic** *adjective* of languages or their study > **lin•guis'tics** *noun* study, science of language
lin•i•ment [LIN-ə-mənt] *noun* lotion for rubbing on limbs, etc. for relieving pain
lin•ing [LĪ-ning] *noun* covering for the inside of garment, etc.
link [lingk] *noun* 1 ring of a chain 2 connection 3 measure, one hundredth part of surveyor's chain ▷ *verb transitive* 4 join with, as with, link 5 intertwine ▷ *verb intransitive* 6 be so joined > **link'age** [-ij] *noun*
links [lingks] *plural noun* golf course, esp. one by the sea
li•no•le•um [li-NOH-lee-əm] *noun* floor covering of burlap or canvas with smooth, hard, decorative coating of powdered cork, etc.
lin'seed *noun* seed of flax plant
lint *noun* 1 tiny shreds of yarn 2 bits of thread 3 soft material for dressing wounds
lin•tel [LIN-tl] *noun* top piece of door or window
li•on [LĪ-ən] *noun* large animal of cat family > **li'on•ess** *noun feminine* > **li'on•ize** *verb transitive* **-ized, -iz•ing** treat as celebrity > **li'on•heart•ed** *adjective* exceptionally brave
lip *noun* 1 upper or lower edge of the mouth 2 edge or margin 3 (*slang*) impudence > **lip gloss** cosmetic to give lips sheen > **lip'read•ing** *noun* method of understanding spoken words by interpreting movements of speaker's lips > **lip service** insincere tribute or respect > **lip'stick** *noun* cosmetic preparation, usu. in stick form, for coloring lips
lip•o•suc•tion [LIP-oh-suk-shən, LĪP-oh-] *noun* cosmetic operation removing fat from the body by suction
li•queur [li-KUR] *noun* alcoholic liquor flavored and sweetened
liq•uid [LIK-wid] *adjective* 1 fluid, not solid or gaseous 2 flowing smoothly 3 (of assets) in form of money or easily converted into money ▷ *noun* 4 substance in liquid form > **liq'ue•fy** [-wə-fī] *verb* **-fied, -fy•ing** make or become liquid > **li•quid'i•ty** *noun* state of being able to meet financial obligations > **liquid air, liquefied gas** air, gas reduced to liquid state on application of increased pressure at low temperature
liq•ui•date [LIK-wi-dayt] *verb transitive* **-dat•ed, -dat•ing** 1 pay (debt) 2 arrange affairs of, and dissolve (company) 3 wipe out, kill > **liq•ui•da'tion** *noun* 1 process of clearing up financial affairs 2 state of being bankrupt > **liq'ui•da•tor** *noun* official appointed to liquidate business
liq•uor [LIK-ər] *noun* liquid, esp. an alcoholic one
li•ra [LEER-ə] *noun, plural* **-ras** monetary unit of Turkey and (formerly) Italy
lisle [līl] *noun* fine hard-twisted cotton thread
lisp *verb* 1 speech defect in which *s* and *z* are pronounced *th* 2 speak falteringly ▷ *noun*
lis•some [LIS-əm] *adjective* supple, agile
list¹ *noun* 1 inventory, register 2 catalog 3 edge of cloth, selvage ▷ *verb transitive* 4 place on list > **lists** *plural noun* field for combat
list² *verb intransitive* 1 (of ship) lean to one side ▷ *noun* 2 inclination of ship
lis•ten [LIS-ən] *verb intransitive* try to hear, attend to > **lis'ten•er** *noun*
list•less [LIST-lis] *adjective* indifferent, languid
lit *pt./pp. of* **light**
lit•a•ny [LIT-n-ee] *noun, plural* **-nies** 1 prayer with responses from congregation 2 tedious account
li•ter [LEE-tər] *noun* measure of volume of fluid, one cubic decimeter, about 1.05 quarts
lit•er•al [LIT-ər-əl] *adjective* 1 according to sense of actual words, not figurative 2 exact in wording 3 of letters
lit•er•ate [LIT-ər-it] *adjective* 1 able to read and

DICTIONARY

THESAURUS

link *noun* 1 COMPONENT, constituent, element, member, part, piece
2 CONNECTION, affinity, association, attachment, bond, relationship, tie-up
▷ *verb* 3 FASTEN, attach, bind, connect, couple, join, tie, unite
4 ASSOCIATE, bracket, connect, identify, relate
lip *noun* 1 EDGE, brim, brink, margin, rim
2 (*slang*) IMPUDENCE, backchat (*informal*), cheek (*informal*), effrontery, impertinence, insolence
liquid *noun* 1 FLUID, juice, solution
▷ *adjective* 2 FLUID, aqueous, flowing, melted, molten, running, runny
3 (*assets*) CONVERTIBLE, negotiable
liquidate *verb* 1 PAY, clear, discharge, honor, pay off, settle, square
2 DISSOLVE, abolish, annul, cancel, terminate
3 KILL, destroy, dispatch, eliminate, exterminate, get rid of, murder, wipe out (*informal*)
liquor *noun* 1 ALCOHOL, booze (*informal*), drink, hard stuff (*informal*), spirits, strong drink
2 JUICE, broth, extract, liquid, stock
list¹ *noun* 1 REGISTER, catalog, directory, index, inventory, record, roll, series, tally
▷ *verb* 2 TABULATE, catalog, enter, enumerate, itemize, record, register
list² *verb* 1 LEAN, careen, heel over, incline, tilt, tip
▷ *noun* 2 TILT, cant, leaning, slant
listen *verb* 1 HEAR, attend, lend an ear, prick up one's ears
2 PAY ATTENTION, heed, mind, obey, observe, take notice
listless *adjective* LANGUID, apathetic, indifferent, indolent, lethargic, sluggish
literacy *noun* EDUCATION, knowledge, learning
literal *adjective* 1 EXACT, accurate, close, faithful, strict, verbatim, word for word
2 ACTUAL, bona fide, genuine, plain, real, simple, true, unvarnished
literally *adverb* STRICTLY, actually, exactly, faithfully, precisely, really, to the letter, truly, verbatim, word for word

write 2 educated ▷ *noun* 3 literate person > **lit'er•a•cy** *noun* > **lit•e•ra'ti** [-RAH-tee] *plural noun* scholarly, literary people

lit•er•a•ture [LIT-ər-ə-chər] *noun* books and writings of a country, period or subject > **lit'er•ar•y** *adjective* of or learned in literature

lithe [līth] *adjective* **lith•er, lith•est** supple, pliant > **lithe'some** [-səm] *adjective* lissome, supple

lith•i•um [LITH-ee-əm] *noun* 1 one of the lightest alkaline metallic elements 2 this substance used in treatment of depression, etc.

li•thog•ra•phy [li-THOG-rə-fee] *noun* method of printing from metal or stone block using the antipathy of grease and water > **lith'o•graph** *noun* 1 print so produced ▷ *verb transitive* 2 print thus > **li•thog'ra•pher** *noun*

lit•i•gant [LIT-i-gənt] *noun, adjective* (person) conducting a lawsuit > **lit•i•ga'tion** *noun* lawsuit

lit•i•gate [LIT-i-gayt] *verb transitive* **-gat•ed, -gat•ing** 1 contest in law ▷ *verb intransitive* **-gat•ed, -gat•ing** 2 carry on a lawsuit > **li•ti'gious** [-jəs] *adjective* 1 given to engaging in lawsuits 2 disputatious > **li•ti'gious•ness** *noun*

lit•mus [LIT-məs] *noun* blue dye turned red by acids and restored to blue by alkali > **litmus paper** paper impregnated with litmus > **litmus test** 1 use of litmus paper to test acidity or alkalinity of a solution 2 any crucial test based on only one factor

lit•ter [LIT-ər] *noun* 1 untidy refuse 2 odds and ends 3 young of animal produced at one birth 4 straw, etc. as bedding for animals 5 portable couch 6 kind of stretcher for wounded ▷ *verb transitive* 7 strew with litter 8 bring forth

lit•tle [LIT-l] *adjective* 1 small, not much ▷ *noun* 2 small quantity ▷ *adverb* 3 slightly

lit•to•ral [LIT-ər-əl] *adjective* 1 pert. to the shore of sea, lake, ocean ▷ *noun* 2 littoral region

lit•ur•gy [LIT-ər-jee] *noun, plural* **-gies** prescribed form of public worship > **li•tur'gi•cal** *adjective*

live[1] [liv] *verb* **lived, liv•ing** 1 have life 2 pass one's life 3 continue in life 4 continue, last 5 dwell 6 feed > **liv'a•ble** *adjective* 1 suitable for living in 2 tolerable > **living** *noun* 1 action of being in life 2 people now alive 3 way of life 4 means of living 5 church benefice

live[2] [līv] *adjective* 1 living, alive, active, vital 2 flaming 3 (of transmission line, etc.) carrying electric current 4 (of broadcast) transmitted during the actual performance > **live'ly** *adjective* **-li•er, -li•est** brisk, active, vivid > **live'li•ness** *noun* > **liv'en** *verb transitive* (esp. with *up*) make (more) lively > **live'stock** *noun* domestic animals > **live wire** 1 wire carrying electric current 2 able, very energetic person

live•li•hood [LĪV-lee-huud] *noun* 1 means of living 2 subsistence, support

live•long [LIV-lawng] *adjective* of a period of time, lasting throughout, esp. as though forever

liv•er [LIV-ər] *noun* 1 organ secreting bile 2 animal liver as food > **liv'er•ish** *adjective* 1 unwell, as from liver upset 2 cross, touchy, irritable

liv•er•y [LIV-ə-ree] *noun, plural* **-er•ies** 1 distinctive dress of person or group, esp. servant(s) 2 care, feeding of horses 3 a livery stable > **livery stable** where horses are kept at a charge or hired out

liv'id *adjective* 1 of a bluish pale color 2 discolored, as by bruising 3 of reddish color

---

literary *adjective* WELL-READ, bookish, erudite, formal, learned, scholarly

literate *adjective* EDUCATED, informed, knowledgeable

literature *noun* WRITINGS, letters, lore

lithe *adjective* SUPPLE, flexible, limber, lissom *or* lissome, loose-limbed, pliable

litigant *noun* CLAIMANT, party, plaintiff

litigate *verb* SUE, go to court, press charges, prosecute

litigation *noun* LAWSUIT, action, case, prosecution

litter *noun* 1 RUBBISH, debris, detritus, garbage, muck, refuse, trash
2 BROOD, offspring, progeny, young
▷ *verb* 3 CLUTTER, derange, disarrange, disorder, mess up
4 SCATTER, strew

little *adjective* 1 SMALL, diminutive, miniature, minute, petite, short, tiny, wee
2 YOUNG, babyish, immature, infant, junior, undeveloped
▷ *adverb* 3 HARDLY, barely
4 RARELY, hardly ever, not often, scarcely, seldom
▷ *noun* 5 BIT, fragment, hint, particle, speck, spot, touch, trace

live[1] *verb* 1 EXIST, be, be alive, breathe
2 PERSIST, last, prevail
3 DWELL, abide, inhabit, lodge, occupy, reside, settle
4 SURVIVE, endure, get along, make ends meet, subsist, support oneself
5 THRIVE, flourish, prosper

live[2] *adjective* 1 LIVING, alive, animate, breathing
2 TOPICAL, burning, controversial, current, hot, pertinent, pressing, prevalent
3 BURNING, active, alight, blazing, glowing, hot, ignited, smoldering

livelihood *noun* OCCUPATION, bread and butter (*informal*), employment, job, living, work

liveliness *noun* ENERGY, animation, boisterousness, dynamism, spirit, sprightliness, vitality, vivacity

lively *adjective* 1 VIGOROUS, active, agile, alert, brisk, energetic, keen, perky, quick, sprightly
2 ANIMATED, cheerful, chirpy (*informal*), sparky, spirited, upbeat (*informal*), vivacious
3 VIVID, bright, colorful, exciting, forceful, invigorating, refreshing, stimulating

liven up *verb* STIR, animate, brighten, buck up (*informal*), enliven, perk up, rouse

liverish *adjective* 1 SICK, bilious, queasy
2 IRRITABLE, crotchety, crusty, disagreeable, grumpy, ill-humored, irascible, splenetic, tetchy

livery *noun* COSTUME, attire, clothing, dress, garb, regalia, suit, uniform

livid *adjective* 1 (*informal*) ANGRY, beside oneself, enraged, fuming, furious, incensed, indignant, infuriated, outraged
2 DISCOLORED, black-and-blue, bruised, contused, purple

living *adjective* 1 ALIVE, active, breathing, existing

4 (*informal*) angry, furious
liz•ard [LIZ-ərd] *noun* four-footed reptile
Lk. Luke
lla•ma [LAH-mə] *noun* woolly-haired animal used as beast of burden in S Amer.
load [lohd] *noun* 1 burden 2 amount usu. carried at once 3 actual load carried by vehicle 4 resistance against which engine has to work 5 amount of electrical energy drawn from a source ▷ *verb transitive* 6 put load on or into 7 charge (gun) 8 weigh down > **load'ed** *adjective* 1 carrying a load 2 (of dice) dishonestly weighted 3 biased 4 (of question) containing hidden trap or implication 5 (*slang*) wealthy 6 (*slang*) drunk
loadstar, -stone *noun see* **lode**
loaf[1] [lohf] *noun, plural* **loaves** 1 mass of bread as baked 2 shaped mass of food
loaf[2] *verb intransitive* idle, loiter > **loaf'er** *noun* idler
loam [lohm] *noun* fertile soil
loan [lohn] *noun* 1 act of lending 2 thing lent 3 money borrowed at interest 4 permission to use ▷ *verb transitive* 5 grant loan of
loath, loth [lohth] *adjective* unwilling, reluctant (to) > **loathe** [lohth] *verb transitive* **loathed, loath•ing** hate, abhor > **loathing** [LOHTH-ing] *noun* 1 disgust 2 repulsion > **loath•some** [LOHTH-səm] *adjective* disgusting
lob *noun* **lobbed, lob•bing** 1 in tennis, artillery, etc., ball, shell, sent high in air ▷ *verb* 2 hit, fire, thus
lob•by [LOB-ee] *noun, plural* **-bies** 1 corridor into which rooms open 2 passage or room adjacent to legislative chamber 3 group of people who try to influence members of legislature > **lob'by•ing** *noun* activity of this group > **lob'by•ist** *noun*
lobe [lohb] *noun* 1 any rounded projection 2 subdivision of body organ 3 soft, hanging part of ear > **lobed** *adjective* > **lo•bot•o•my** [lə-BOT-ə-mee] *noun, plural* **-mies** surgical incision into lobe of organ, esp. brain
lob•ster [LOB-stər] *noun* shellfish with long tail and claws, turning red when boiled
lo•cal [LOH-kəl] *adjective* 1 of, existing in particular place 2 confined to a definite spot, district or part of the body 3 of place 4 (of train) making many stops ▷ *noun* 5 person belonging to a district 6 local branch of labor union 7 local train > **lo•cale** [loh-KAL] *noun* scene of event > **lo•cal'i•ty** *noun* 1 place, situation 2 district > **lo'cal•ize** *verb transitive* **-ized, -iz•ing** assign, restrict to definite place > **local anesthetic** one that produces insensibility in one part of body
lo•cate [loh-KAYT] *verb transitive* **-cat•ed, -cat•ing** 1 attribute to a place 2 find the place of 3 situate > **lo•ca'tion** *noun* 1 placing 2 situation 3 site of film production away from studio
lock[1] [lok] *noun* 1 appliance for fastening door, lid, etc. 2 mechanism for firing gun 3 enclosure in river or canal for moving boats from one level to another 4 air lock 5 appliance to check the motion of a mechanism 6 interlocking 7 block, jam ▷ *verb transitive* 8 fasten, make secure with lock 9 place in locked container 10 join firmly 11 cause to become immovable 12 embrace closely ▷ *verb intransitive* 13 become fixed or united 14 become immovable > **lock'er** *noun* small closet with lock > **lock'down** *noun* security measure in which those inside a building are required to remain confined in it for a time > **lock'jaw** *noun* tetanus > **lock'out** *noun* exclusion of workmen by employers as means of coercion > **lock'smith** *noun* one who makes and mends locks > **lock'up**

DICTIONARY

THESAURUS

2 CURRENT, active, contemporary, extant, in use ▷ *noun* 3 EXISTENCE, being, existing, life, subsistence
4 LIFE STYLE, way of life
load *noun* 1 CARGO, consignment, freight, shipment
2 BURDEN, albatross, encumbrance, millstone, onus, trouble, weight, worry
▷ *verb* 3 FILL, cram, freight, heap, pack, pile, stack, stuff
4 BURDEN, encumber, oppress, saddle with, weigh down, worry
5 (*a firearm*) MAKE READY, charge, prime
loaded *adjective* 1 WEIGHTED, biased, distorted
2 TRICKY, artful, insidious, manipulative, prejudicial
3 (*slang*) RICH, affluent, flush (*informal*), moneyed, wealthy, well-heeled (*informal*), well off, well-to-do
loaf[1] *noun* 1 LUMP, block, cake, cube, slab
loaf[2] *verb* IDLE, laze, lie around, loiter, lounge around, take it easy
loan *noun* 1 ADVANCE, credit
▷ *verb* 2 LEND, advance, let out
loath *or* **loth** *adjective* UNWILLING, averse, disinclined, opposed, reluctant
loathe *verb* HATE, abhor, abominate, despise, detest, dislike
loathing *noun* HATRED, abhorrence, antipathy, aversion, detestation, disgust, repugnance, repulsion, revulsion
loathsome *adjective* HATEFUL, abhorrent, detestable, disgusting, nauseating, obnoxious, odious, offensive, repugnant, repulsive, revolting, scuzzy (*slang*), vile
lobby *noun* 1 CORRIDOR, entrance hall, foyer, hallway, passage, porch, vestibule
2 PRESSURE GROUP
▷ *verb* 3 CAMPAIGN, influence, persuade, press, pressure, promote, push, urge
local *adjective* 1 REGIONAL, provincial
2 RESTRICTED, confined, limited
▷ *noun* 3 RESIDENT, inhabitant, native
locality *noun* 1 NEIGHBORHOOD, area, district, neck of the woods (*informal*), region, vicinity
2 SITE, locale, location, place, position, scene, setting, spot
localize *verb* RESTRICT, circumscribe, confine, contain, delimit, limit
locate *verb* 1 FIND, come across, detect, discover, pin down, pinpoint, track down, unearth
2 PLACE, establish, fix, put, seat, set, settle, situate
location *noun* POSITION, locale, place, point, site, situation, spot, venue
lock[1] *noun* 1 FASTENING, bolt, clasp, padlock
▷ *verb* 2 FASTEN, bolt, close, seal, secure, shut
3 UNITE, clench, engage, entangle, entwine,

noun prison
lock² *noun* tress of hair
lock•et [LOK-it] *noun* small hinged pendant for portrait, etc.
lo•co•mo•tive [loh-kə-MOH-tiv] *noun* 1 engine for pulling train on railway tracks ▷ *adjective* 2 having power of moving from place to place > **lo•co•mo'tion** *noun* action, power of moving
lo•cus [LOH-kəs] *noun, plural* **-ci** [-sī] 1 exact place or locality 2 curve made by all points satisfying certain mathematical condition, or by point, line or surface moving under such condition
lo•cust [LOH-kəst] *noun* 1 destructive winged insect 2 N Amer. tree 3 wood of this tree
lo•cu•tion [loh-KYOO-shən] *noun* 1 a phrase 2 speech 3 mode or style of speaking
lode [lohd] *noun* vein of ore > **lode'star** *noun* 1 star that shows the way 2 any guide on which attention is fixed 3 Polaris > **lode'stone** *noun* magnetic iron ore
lodge [loj] *noun* 1 house, cabin used seasonally or occasionally, e.g. for hunting, skiing 2 gatekeeper's house 3 meeting place of branch of certain fraternal organizations 4 the branch ▷ *verb transitive* **lodged, lodg•ing** 5 house 6 deposit 7 bring (a charge, etc.) against someone ▷ *verb intransitive* **lodged, lodg•ing** 8 live in another's house at fixed rent 9 come to rest (in, on) > **lodg'er** *noun* > **lodgings** *plural noun* rented room(s) in another person's house
loft [lawft] *noun* 1 space between top story and roof 2 upper story of warehouse, factory, etc. typically with large unpartitioned space 3 gallery in church, etc. ▷ *verb transitive* 4 send (golf ball, etc.) high > **loft building** building in which all stories have large unobstructed space once used for manufacturing but now usu. are converted to residences > **loft'i•ly** *adverb* haughtily > **loft'i•ness** *noun* > **loft'y** *adjective* **loft•i•er, loft•i•est** 1 of great height 2 elevated 3 haughty
log¹ [lawg] *noun* 1 portion of felled tree stripped of branches 2 detailed record of voyages, time traveled, etc., of ship, aircraft, etc. 3 apparatus used formerly for measuring ship's speed ▷ *verb transitive* **logged, log•ging** 4 keep a record of 5 travel (specified distance, time) > **log'ging** *noun* cutting and transporting logs to river > **log in, log out** *verb* gain entrance to *or* leave a computer system by keying in a special command
log² *noun* logarithm
log•a•rithm [LAW-gə-rith-əm] *noun* one of series of arithmetical functions tabulated for use in calculation
log•ger•head [LAW-gər-hed] *noun* **at loggerheads** quarreling, disputing
log•ic [LOJ-ik] *noun* 1 art or philosophy of reasoning 2 reasoned thought or argument 3 coherence of various facts, events, etc. > **log'i•cal** *adjective* 1 of logic 2 according to reason 3 reasonable 4 apt to reason correctly > **lo•gi•cian** [loh-JISH-ən] *noun*
lo•gis•tics [loh-JIS-tiks] *noun* 1 the transport, housing and feeding of troops 2 organization of any project, operation > **lo•gis'ti•cal** *adjective*
lo•go [LOH-goh] *noun, plural* **-gos** company emblem or similar device
loin *noun* 1 part of body between ribs and hip 2 cut of meat from this > **loins** hips and lower abdomen > **loin'cloth** *noun* garment covering loins only
loi•ter [LOI-tər] *verb intransitive* 1 dawdle, hang about 2 idle > **loi'ter•er** *noun*
loll [lol] *verb intransitive* 1 sit, lie lazily 2 hang out ▷ *verb transitive* 3 allow to hang out
lone [lohn] *adjective* solitary > **lone'ly** *adjective* **-li•er, -li•est** 1 sad because alone 2 unfrequented 3 solitary, alone > **lone'li•ness**

join, link
4 EMBRACE, clasp, clutch, encircle, enclose, grasp, hug, press
lock² *noun* STRAND, curl, ringlet, tress, tuft
lockup *noun* PRISON, cell, jail
lock up *verb* IMPRISON, cage, confine, detain, incarcerate, jail, put behind bars, shut up
lodge *noun* 1 CABIN, chalet, cottage, gatehouse, hut, shelter
2 SOCIETY, branch, chapter, club, group
▷ *verb* 3 STAY, board, room
4 STICK, come to rest, imbed, implant
5 REGISTER, file, put on record, submit
lodger *noun* TENANT, boarder, paying guest, resident
lodging *noun* (*often plural*) ACCOMMODATION, abode, apartments, quarters, residence, rooms, shelter
lofty *adjective* 1 HIGH, elevated, raised, soaring, towering
2 NOBLE, dignified, distinguished, elevated, exalted, grand, illustrious, renowned
3 HAUGHTY, arrogant, condescending, disdainful, patronizing, proud, supercilious
log *noun* 1 STUMP, block, chunk, trunk
2 RECORD, account, journal, logbook
▷ *verb* 3 CHOP, cut, fell, hew
4 RECORD, chart, note, register, set down
loggerheads *plural noun*
▷ **at loggerheads** QUARRELING, at daggers drawn, at each other's throats, at odds, feuding, in dispute, opposed
logic *noun* REASON, good sense, sense
logical *adjective* 1 RATIONAL, clear, cogent, coherent, consistent, sound, valid, well-organized
2 REASONABLE, plausible, sensible, wise
loiter *verb* LINGER, dally, dawdle, dilly-dally (*informal*), hang about *or* hang around, idle, loaf, skulk
loll *verb* 1 LOUNGE, loaf, recline, relax, slouch, slump, sprawl
2 DROOP, dangle, drop, flap, flop, hang, sag
lone *adjective* SOLITARY, one, only, single, sole, unaccompanied
loneliness *noun* SOLITUDE, desolation, isolation, seclusion
lonely *adjective* 1 ABANDONED, destitute, forlorn, forsaken, friendless, lonesome
2 SOLITARY, alone, apart, companionless, isolated, lone, single, withdrawn
3 REMOTE, deserted, desolate, godforsaken, isolated, out-of-the-way, secluded, unfrequented, uninhabited

noun > **lon'er** *noun* one who prefers to be alone > **lone'some** [-səm] *adjective*
long¹ [lawng] *adjective* **-er, -est** 1 having length, esp. great length, in space or time 2 extensive 3 protracted ▷ *adverb* 4 for a long time > **long'hand** *noun* writing in which words are written out in full by hand rather than on typewriter, etc. > **long'-play'ing** *adjective* (of record) lasting for 10 to 30 minutes because of its fine grooves > **long-range** *adjective* 1 of the future 2 able to travel long distances without refueling 3 (of weapons) designed to hit distant target > **long shot** competitor, undertaking, bet, etc. with small chance of success > **long ton** 2240 lbs. > **long'-wind'ed** *adjective* tediously loquacious
long² *verb intransitive* have keen desire, yearn (for) > **long'ing** *noun* yearning
lon•gev•i•ty [lon-JEV-i-tee] *noun* 1 long existence or life 2 length of existence or life 3 tenure
lon•gi•tude [LON-ji-tood] *noun* distance east or west from prime meridian > **lon•gi•tu'di•nal** *adjective* 1 of length or longitude 2 lengthwise
long•shore•man [LAWNG-SHOR-mən] *noun* dock laborer
look [luuk] *verb intransitive* 1 direct, use eyes 2 face 3 seem 4 search (for) 5 hope (for) 6 (with *after*) take care of ▷ *noun* 7 looking 8 view 9 search > **looks** appearance **good looks** beauty > **look'a•like** *noun* person who is double of another > **look'out** *noun* 1 guard 2 place for watching 3 watchman 4 object of worry, concern > **look after** tend **look down on** despise
loom¹ *noun* 1 machine for weaving 2 middle part of oar
loom² *verb intransitive* 1 appear dimly 2 seem ominously close 3 assume great importance
loon¹ *noun* American fish-eating diving bird
loon² *noun* stupid, foolish person > **loon'y** *adjective* **loon•i•er, loon•i•est** crazy, foolish ▷ *noun, plural* **-nies** lunatic, crazy person > **loony bin** (*informal*) mental hospital or ward
loop *noun* 1 figure made by curved line crossing itself 2 similar rounded shape in cord or rope, etc. crossed on itself 3 contraceptive coil 4 aerial maneuver in which aircraft describes complete circle ▷ *verb* 5 form loop
loop•hole [LOOP-hohl] *noun* 1 means of evading rule without infringing it 2 vertical slit in building wall, esp. for defense
loose [loos] *adjective* **loos•er, loos•est** 1 not tight, fastened, fixed, or tense 2 slack 3 vague 4 dissolute ▷ *verb transitive* **loosed, loos•ing** 5 free 6 unfasten 7 slacken ▷ *verb intransitive* **loosed, loos•ing** 8 (with *off*) shoot, let fly > **loose'ly** *adverb* > **loos'en** *verb transitive* make loose > **loose'ness** *noun* **on the loose** 1 free 2

DICTIONARY

THESAURUS

loner *noun* INDIVIDUALIST, lone wolf, maverick, outsider, recluse
lonesome *adjective* LONELY, companionless, desolate, dreary, forlorn, friendless, gloomy
long¹ *adjective* 1 ELONGATED, expanded, extended, extensive, far-reaching, lengthy, spread out, stretched
2 PROLONGED, interminable, lengthy, lingering, long-drawn-out, protracted, sustained
long² *verb* DESIRE, crave, hanker, itch, lust, pine, want, wish, yearn
longing *noun* DESIRE, ambition, aspiration, craving, hope, itch, thirst, urge, wish, yearning, yen (*informal*)
long-lived *adjective* LONG-LASTING, enduring
long shot *noun* OUTSIDER, dark horse
long-standing *adjective* ESTABLISHED, abiding, enduring, fixed, long-established, long-lasting, time-honored
long-suffering *adjective* UNCOMPLAINING, easy-going, forbearing, forgiving, patient, resigned, stoical, tolerant
long-winded *adjective* RAMBLING, lengthy, long-drawn-out, prolix, prolonged, repetitious, tedious, tiresome, verbose, wordy
look *verb* 1 SEE, contemplate, examine, eye, gaze, glance, observe, scan, study, survey, view, watch
2 SEEM, appear, look like, strike one as
3 FACE, front, overlook
4 HOPE, anticipate, await, expect, reckon on
5 SEARCH, forage, hunt, seek
▷ *noun* 6 VIEW, examination, gaze, glance, glimpse, inspection, observation, peek, sight
7 APPEARANCE, air, aspect, bearing, countenance, demeanor, expression, manner, semblance
look after *verb* TAKE CARE OF, attend to, care for, guard, keep an eye on, mind, nurse, protect, supervise, take charge of, tend
look down on *verb* DISDAIN, contemn, despise, scorn, sneer, spurn
look forward to *verb* ANTICIPATE, await, expect, hope for, long for, look for, wait for
lookout *noun* 1 VIGIL, guard, readiness, watch
2 WATCHMAN, guard, sentinel, sentry
3 WATCHTOWER, observation post, observatory, post
look out *verb* BE CAREFUL, beware, keep an eye out, pay attention, watch out
look up *verb* 1 RESEARCH, find, hunt for, search for, seek out, track down
2 IMPROVE, get better, perk up, pick up, progress, shape up (*informal*)
3 VISIT, call on, drop in on (*informal*), look in on
4 ▷ **look up to** RESPECT, admire, defer to, esteem, honor, revere
loom *verb* APPEAR, bulk, emerge, hover, impend, menace, take shape, threaten
loop *noun* 1 CURVE, circle, coil, curl, ring, spiral, twirl, twist, whorl
▷ *verb* 2 TWIST, coil, curl, knot, roll, spiral, turn, wind round
loophole *noun* LET-OUT, escape, excuse
loose *adjective* 1 UNTIED, free, insecure, unattached, unbound, unfastened, unfettered, unrestricted
2 SLACK, easy, relaxed, sloppy
3 VAGUE, ill-defined, imprecise, inaccurate, indistinct, inexact, rambling, random
4 PROMISCUOUS, abandoned, debauched, dissipated, dissolute, fast, immoral, profligate
▷ *verb* 5 FREE, detach, disconnect, liberate, release, set free, unfasten, unleash, untie
loosen *verb* 1 UNTIE, detach, separate, undo, unloose
2 FREE, liberate, release, set free
3 ▷ **loosen up** RELAX, de-stress, ease up *or* ease

on a spree
loot *noun, verb transitive* plunder
lop[1] *verb transitive* **lopped, lop•ping** 1 cut away twigs and branches 2 chop off
lop[2] *verb intransitive* **lopped, lop•ping** hang limply > **lop'-eared** *adjective* having drooping ears > **lop'sid•ed** *adjective* 1 with one side lower than the other 2 badly balanced
lope [lohp] *verb intransitive* **loped, lop•ing** run with long, easy strides
lo•qua•cious [loh-KWAY-shəs] *adjective* talkative > **lo•quac'i•ty** [-KWAS-ə-tee] *noun*
lord *noun* 1 British nobleman, peer of the realm 2 feudal superior 3 one ruling others 4 owner 5 (**Lord**) God ▷ *verb intransitive* 6 domineer > **lord'li•ness** *noun* > **lord'ly** *adjective* **-li•er, -li•est** 1 imperious, proud 2 fit for a lord > **lord'ship** *noun* 1 rule, ownership 2 domain 3 title of some noblemen
lore [lor] *noun* 1 learning 2 body of facts and traditions
lor•gnette [lorn-YET] *noun* pair of eyeglasses mounted on long handle
lorn *adjective* (*poetic*) 1 abandoned 2 desolate
lose [looz] *verb transitive* **lost, los•ing** 1 be deprived of, fail to retain or use 2 let slip 3 fail to get 4 (of clock, etc.) run slow (by specified amount) 5 be defeated in ▷ *verb intransitive* **lost, los•ing** 6 suffer loss > **loss** [laws] *noun* 1 a losing 2 what is lost 3 harm or damage resulting from losing > **lost** *adjective* 1 unable to be found 2 unable to find one's way 3 bewildered 4 not won 5 not utilized
lot *noun* 1 great number 2 collection 3 large quantity 4 share 5 fate 6 destiny 7 item at auction 8 one of a set of objects used to decide something by chance, as in **to cast lots** 9 area of land ▷ *adverb* 10 a great deal > **lots** *plural noun* great numbers or quantity
loth *see* **loath**
lo•tion [LOH-shən] *noun* liquid for washing to reduce itching, etc., improving skin, etc.
lot•ter•y [LOT-ə-ree] *noun, plural* **-ter•ies** 1 method of raising funds by selling tickets and prizes by chance 2 any gamble
lot•to [LOT-oh] *noun* game of chance like bingo
lo•tus [LOH-təs] *noun, plural* **-tus•es** 1 legendary plant whose fruits induce forgetfulness when eaten 2 Egyptian water lily > **lotus position** seated cross-legged position used in yoga, etc.
loud [lowd] *adjective* **-er, -est** 1 strongly audible 2 noisy 3 obtrusive > **loud'ly** *adverb* > **loud'speak•er** *noun* instrument for converting electrical signals into sound audible at a distance
lounge [lownj] *verb intransitive* **lounged, loung•ing** 1 sit, lie, walk, or stand in a relaxed manner ▷ *noun* 2 general waiting, relaxing area in airport, hotel, etc. 3 bar > **loung'er** *noun* loafer
louse [lows] *noun, plural* **lice** a parasitic insect > **lous'y** *adjective* **lous•i•er, lous•i•est** (*informal*) 1 nasty, unpleasant 2 (*slang*) (too) generously provided, thickly populated (with) 3 bad, poor 4 having lice
lout [lowt] *noun* crude, oafish person

DICTIONARY • THESAURUS

off, go easy (*informal*), let up, soften
loot *noun* 1 PLUNDER, booty, goods, haul, prize, spoils, swag (*slang*)
▷ *verb* 2 PLUNDER, despoil, pillage, raid, ransack, ravage, rifle, rob, sack
lopsided *adjective* CROOKED, askew, asymmetrical, awry, cockeyed, disproportionate, squint, unbalanced, uneven, warped
lord *noun* 1 MASTER, commander, governor, leader, liege, overlord, ruler, superior
2 NOBLEMAN, earl, noble, peer, viscount
3 ▷ **Our Lord, the Lord** Christ, God, Jehovah JESUS CHRIST, the Almighty
▷ *verb* 4 ▷ **lord it over** ORDER AROUND, boss around (*informal*), domineer, pull rank, put on airs, swagger
lordly *adjective* PROUD, arrogant, condescending, disdainful, domineering, haughty, high-handed, imperious, lofty, overbearing
lore *noun* TRADITIONS, beliefs, doctrine, sayings, teaching, wisdom
lose *verb* 1 MISLAY, be deprived of, drop, forget, misplace
2 FORFEIT, miss, pass up (*informal*), yield
3 BE DEFEATED, come to grief, lose out
loser *noun* 1 FAILURE, also-ran, dud (*informal*), flop (*informal*)
2 NERD, dork (*slang*), drip (*informal*), dweeb (*slang*), geek (*slang*)
loss *noun* 1 DEFEAT, failure, forfeiture, mislaying, squandering, waste
2 DAMAGE, cost, destruction, harm, hurt, injury, ruin
3 (*sometimes plural*) DEFICIT, debit, debt, deficiency, depletion
4 ▷ **at a loss** CONFUSED, at one's wits' end, baffled, bewildered, helpless, nonplussed, perplexed, puzzled, stumped
lost *adjective* 1 MISSING, disappeared, mislaid, misplaced, vanished, wayward
2 OFF-COURSE, adrift, astray, at sea, disoriented, off-track
lot *noun* 1 COLLECTION, assortment, batch, bunch (*informal*), consignment, crowd, group, quantity, set
2 DESTINY, accident, chance, doom, fate, fortune
3 ▷ **a lot, lots** PLENTY, abundance, a great deal, heap *or* heaps, masses (*informal*), piles (*informal*), scores, stack *or* stacks
loth *see* **loath**
lotion *noun* CREAM, balm, embrocation, liniment, salve, solution
lottery *noun* 1 RAFFLE, drawing, sweepstakes
2 GAMBLE, chance, hazard, risk, toss-up (*informal*)
loud *adjective* 1 NOISY, blaring, booming, clamorous, deafening, ear-splitting, forte (*music*), resounding, thundering, tumultuous, vociferous
2 GARISH, brash, flamboyant, flashy, gaudy, glaring, lurid, showy
loudly *adverb* NOISILY, deafeningly, fortissimo (*music*), lustily, shrilly, uproariously, vehemently, vigorously, vociferously
lounge *verb* RELAX, laze, lie about, loaf, loiter, loll, sprawl, take it easy
lousy *adjective* (*informal*) CRUMMY, awful, crappy (*slang*), inadequate, inferior, shabby, shoddy, terrible
lout *noun* OAF, boor, dolt, lummox (*informal*)

> **lout'ish** *adjective*
lou•ver [LOO-vər] *noun* 1 one of a set of boards or slats set parallel and slanted to admit air but not rain or sunlight 2 ventilating structure of these
love [luv] *noun* 1 warm affection 2 benevolence 3 charity 4 sexual passion 5 sweetheart 6 *tennis etc* score of zero ▷ *verb transitive* **loved, lov•ing** 7 admire passionately 8 delight in ▷ *verb intransitive* **loved, lov•ing** 9 be in love > **lov'a•ble** *adjective* > **love'less** [-lis] *adjective* > **love'lorn** *adjective* forsaken by, pining for a lover > **love'li•ness** *noun* > **love'ly** *adjective* **-li•er, -li•est** beautiful, delightful > **loving** *adjective* 1 affectionate 2 tender > **lov'ing•ly** *adverb* > **loving cup** 1 bowl formerly passed around at banquet 2 large cup given as prize **make love** (to) have sexual intercourse (with)
low¹ [loh] *adjective* **-er, -est** 1 not tall, high or elevated 2 humble 3 commonplace 4 coarse, vulgar 5 dejected 6 ill 7 not loud 8 moderate 9 cheap > **low'er** *verb transitive* 1 cause, allow to descend 2 move down 3 diminish, degrade ▷ *adjective* 4 below in position or rank 5 at an early stage, period of development > **low'li•ness** *noun* > **low'ly** *adjective* **-li•er, -li•est** modest, humble > **low'brow** *noun* person with no intellectual or cultural interests ▷ *adjective* > **low'down** *noun* (*informal*) 1 inside information ▷ *adjective* 2 mean, shabby, dishonorable > **low frequency** 1 in electricity any frequency of alternating current from about 30 to 300 kilohertz 2 frequency within audible range > **low-key** [-kee] *adjective* subdued, restrained, not intense > **low'land** *noun* low-lying land > **low-ten•sion** *adjective* carrying, operating at low voltage
low² *verb intransitive* 1 of cattle, utter their cry, bellow ▷ *noun* 2 cry of cattle, bellow
low•er [LOW-ər] *verb intransitive* 1 look gloomy or threatening, as sky 2 scowl ▷ *noun* 3 scowl, frown
loy•al [LOI-əl] *adjective* faithful, true to allegiance > **loy'al•ly** *adverb* > **loy'al•ty** *noun*
loz•enge [LOZ-inj] *noun* 1 small candy or tablet of medicine 2 rhombus, diamond figure
Lr *chem.* lawrencium
LSD lysergic acid diethylamide (hallucinogenic drug)
Lu *chem.* lutetium
lub•ber [LUB-ər] *noun* 1 clumsy fellow 2 unskilled seaman
lu•bri•cate [LOO-bri-kayt] *verb transitive* **-cat•ed, -cat•ing** 1 oil, grease 2 make slippery > **lu'bri•cant** [-kənt] *noun* substance used for this > **lu•bri•ca'tion** [-KAY-shən] *noun* > **lu•bric'i•ty** [-BRIS-i-tee] *noun, plural* **-ties** 1 slipperiness, smoothness 2 lewdness
lu•cid [LOO-sid] *adjective* 1 clear 2 easily understood 3 sane > **lu•cid'i•ty** *noun*
Lu•ci•fer [LOO-sə-fər] *noun* Satan
luck [luk] *noun* 1 fortune, good or bad 2 good

DICTIONARY | THESAURUS

lovable *or* **loveable** *adjective* ENDEARING, adorable, amiable, charming, cute, delightful, enchanting, likable *or* likeable, lovely, sweet
love *verb* 1 ADORE, cherish, dote on, hold dear, idolize, prize, treasure, worship
2 ENJOY, appreciate, delight in, like, relish, savor, take pleasure in
▷ *noun* 3 PASSION, adoration, affection, ardor, attachment, devotion, infatuation, tenderness, warmth
4 LIKING, devotion, enjoyment, fondness, inclination, partiality, relish, soft spot, taste, weakness
5 BELOVED, darling, dear, dearest, lover, sweetheart, truelove
6 ▷ **in love** ENAMORED, besotted, charmed, enraptured, infatuated, smitten
love affair *noun* ROMANCE, affair, amour, intrigue, liaison, relationship
lovely *adjective* 1 ATTRACTIVE, adorable, beautiful, charming, comely, exquisite, graceful, handsome, pretty
2 ENJOYABLE, agreeable, delightful, engaging, nice, pleasant, pleasing
lover *noun* SWEETHEART, admirer, beloved, boyfriend *or* girlfriend, flame (*informal*), mistress, suitor
loving *adjective* AFFECTIONATE, amorous, dear, devoted, doting, fond, tender, warm-hearted
low¹ *adjective* 1 SMALL, little, short, squat, stunted
2 INFERIOR, deficient, inadequate, lousy (*slang*), poor, second-rate, shoddy
3 COARSE, common, crude, disreputable, rough, rude, undignified, vulgar
4 DEJECTED, depressed, despondent, disheartened, downcast, down in the dumps (*informal*), fed up, gloomy, glum, miserable
5 ILL, debilitated, frail, stricken, weak
6 QUIET, gentle, hushed, muffled, muted, soft, subdued, whispered
lowdown *noun* (*informal*) INFORMATION, info (*informal*), inside story, intelligence
lower¹ *adjective* 1 MINOR, inferior, junior, lesser, secondary, second-class, smaller, subordinate
2 REDUCED, curtailed, decreased, diminished, lessened
▷ *verb* 3 DROP, depress, fall, let down, sink, submerge, take down
4 LESSEN, cut, decrease, diminish, minimize, prune, reduce, slash
low-key *adjective* SUBDUED, muted, quiet, restrained, toned down, understated
lowly *adjective* HUMBLE, meek, mild, modest, unassuming
low-spirited *adjective* DEPRESSED, dejected, despondent, dismal, down, down-hearted, fed up, low, miserable, sad
loyal *adjective* FAITHFUL, constant, dependable, devoted, dutiful, staunch, steadfast, true, trustworthy, trusty, unwavering
loyalty *noun* FAITHFULNESS, allegiance, constancy, dependability, devotion, fidelity, staunchness, steadfastness, trustworthiness
lubricate *verb* OIL, grease, smear
lucid *adjective* 1 CLEAR, comprehensible, explicit, intelligible, transparent
2 TRANSLUCENT, clear, crystalline, diaphanous, glassy, limpid, pellucid, transparent
3 CLEAR-HEADED, all there, compos mentis (*Latin*), in one's right mind, rational, sane
luck *noun* 1 FORTUNE, accident, chance, destiny, fate
2 GOOD FORTUNE, advantage, blessing, godsend,

fortune 3 chance > **luck'i•ly** *adverb* fortunately > **luck'less** *adjective* having bad luck > **luck'y** *adjective* **luck•i•er, luck•i•est** having good luck
lu•cre [LOO-kər] *noun* money, wealth > **lu'cra•tive** [-krə-tiv] *adjective* very profitable **filthy lucre** (*informal*) money
lu•di•crous [LOO-di-krəs] *adjective* absurd, laughable, ridiculous
lug[1] *verb transitive* **lugged, lug•ging** 1 drag with effort ▷ *verb intransitive* 2 pull hard
lug[2] *noun* 1 projection, tag serving as handle or support 2 (*slang*) fellow, blockhead
lug•gage [LUG-ij] *noun* traveler's suitcases and other baggage
lu•gu•bri•ous [luu-GOO-bree-əs] *adjective* mournful, doleful, gloomy > **lu•gu'bri•ous•ly** *adverb*
luke•warm [look-worm] *adjective* 1 moderately warm, tepid 2 indifferent
lull *verb transitive* 1 soothe, sing to sleep 2 make quiet ▷ *verb intransitive* 3 become quiet, subside ▷ *noun* 4 brief time of quiet in storm, etc. > **lull'a•by** *noun, plural* **-bies** lulling song, esp. for children
lum•bar [LUM-bahr] *adjective* relating to body between lower ribs and hips > **lum•ba'go** [-BAY-goh] *noun* rheumatism in lower part of the back
lum•ber [LUM-bər] *noun* 1 sawn timber 2 disused articles, useless rubbish ▷ *verb intransitive* 3 move heavily ▷ *verb transitive* 4 convert (a number of trees) into lumber 5 burden with something unpleasant > **lum'ber•jack** *noun* logger
lu•men [LOO-mən] *noun, plural* **-mi•na** [-mə-nə] SI unit of luminous flux
lu•mi•nous [LOO-mə-nəs] *adjective* 1 bright 2 shedding light 3 glowing 4 lucid > **lu'mi•nar•y** [-ner-ee] *noun* 1 learned person 2 prominent person 3 heavenly body giving light > **lu•mi•nes'cence** [-NES-əns] *noun* emission of light at low temperatures by process (e.g. chemical) not involving burning > **lu•mi•nos'i•ty** *noun*
lump *noun* 1 shapeless piece or mass 2 swelling 3 large sum ▷ *verb transitive* 4 throw together in one mass or sum ▷ *verb intransitive* 5 move heavily > **lump'ish** *adjective* 1 clumsy 2 stupid > **lump'y** *adjective* **lump•i•er, lump•i•est** 1 full of lumps 2 uneven **lump it** (*informal*) 3 put up with 4 accept and endure
lu•nar [LOO-nər] *adjective* relating to the moon
lu•na•tic [LOO-nə-tik] *adjective* 1 insane ▷ *noun* 2 insane person > **lu'na•cy** *noun, plural* **-cies** > **lunatic fringe** extreme, radical section of group, etc.
lunch *noun* 1 meal taken in the middle of the day ▷ *verb* 2 eat, entertain at lunch > **lunch'eon** [-ən] *noun* a lunch
lung *noun* one of the two organs of respiration in vertebrates > **lung'fish** *noun* type of fish with air-breathing lung
lunge [lunj] *verb intransitive* **lunged, lung•ing** 1 thrust with sword, etc. ▷ *noun* 2 such thrust 3 sudden movement of body, plunge
lu•pine[1] [LOO-pin] *noun* leguminous plant with tall spikes of flowers
lu•pine[2] [LOO-pīn] *adjective* like a wolf
lu•pus [LOO-pəs] *noun* skin disease
lurch *noun* 1 sudden roll to one side ▷ *verb intransitive* 2 stagger **leave in the lurch** leave in difficulties
lure [luur] *noun* 1 something that entices 2 bait 3 power to attract ▷ *verb transitive* **lured, lur•ing** 4 entice 5 attract
lu•rid [LUUR-id] *adjective* 1 vivid in shocking detail, sensational 2 pale, wan 3 lit with

prosperity, serendipity, success, windfall
luckily *adverb* FORTUNATELY, favorably, happily, opportunely, propitiously, providentially
luckless *adjective* ILL-FATED, cursed, doomed, hapless, hopeless, jinxed, unfortunate, unlucky
lucky *adjective* FORTUNATE, advantageous, blessed, charmed, favored, serendipitous, successful, win-win (*informal*)
lucrative *adjective* PROFITABLE, advantageous, fruitful, productive, remunerative, well-paid
lucre *noun* MONEY, gain, mammon, pelf, profit, riches, spoils, wealth
ludicrous *adjective* RIDICULOUS, absurd, crazy, farcical, laughable, nonsensical, outlandish, preposterous, silly
luggage *noun* BAGGAGE, bags, cases, gear, impedimenta, paraphernalia, suitcases, things
lugubrious *adjective* GLOOMY, doleful, melancholy, mournful, sad, serious, somber, sorrowful, woebegone
lukewarm *adjective* 1 TEPID, warm
2 HALF-HEARTED, apathetic, cool, indifferent, unenthusiastic, unresponsive
lull *verb* 1 CALM, allay, pacify, quell, soothe, subdue, tranquilize
▷ *noun* 2 RESPITE, calm, hush, let-up (*informal*), pause, quiet, silence
lumber *verb* PLOD, clump, shamble, shuffle, stump, trudge, trundle, waddle
lumbering *adjective* AWKWARD, clumsy, heavy, hulking, ponderous, ungainly
luminous *adjective* BRIGHT, glowing, illuminated, luminescent, lustrous, radiant, shining
lump[1] *noun* 1 PIECE, ball, chunk, hunk, mass, nugget
2 SWELLING, bulge, bump, growth, hump, protrusion, tumor
▷ *verb* 3 GROUP, collect, combine, conglomerate, consolidate, mass, pool
lumpy *adjective* BUMPY, knobbly, uneven
lunacy *noun* 1 INSANITY, dementia, derangement, madness, mania, psychosis
2 FOOLISHNESS, absurdity, craziness, folly, foolhardiness, madness, stupidity
lunatic *adjective* 1 IRRATIONAL, bonkers (*informal*), crackbrained (*informal*), crackpot (*informal*), crazy, daft, deranged, insane, mad
▷ *noun* 2 MADMAN, maniac, nutcase (*slang*), psychopath
lunge *noun* 1 THRUST, charge, jab, pounce, spring, swing
▷ *verb* 2 POUNCE, charge, dive, leap, plunge, thrust
lurch *verb* 1 TILT, heave, heel, lean, list, pitch, rock, roll
2 STAGGER, reel, stumble, sway, totter, weave
lure *verb* 1 TEMPT, allure, attract, draw, ensnare, entice, invite, seduce
▷ *noun* 2 TEMPTATION, allurement, attraction,

unnatural glare
lurk *verb intransitive* lie hidden > **lurk'ing** *adjective* (of suspicion) not definite
lus•cious [LUSH-əs] *adjective* 1 sweet, juicy 2 extremely pleasurable or attractive
lush[1] *adjective* **-er, -est** (of grass, etc.) luxuriant and juicy, fresh
lush[2] *noun (slang)* 1 heavy drinker 2 alcoholic
lust *noun* 1 strong desire for sexual gratification 2 any strong desire ▷ *verb intransitive* 3 have passionate desire > **lust'ful** [-fəl] *adjective* > **lust'i•ly** *adverb* > **lust'y** *adjective* **lust•i•er, lust•i•est** vigorous, healthy
lus•ter [LUST-ər] *noun* 1 gloss, sheen 2 splendor 3 renown 4 glory 5 glossy material 6 metallic pottery glaze > **lus'trous** [-trəs] *adjective* shining, luminous
lute [loot] *noun* old stringed musical instrument played with the fingers > **lu'te•nist** *noun*
lux [luks] *noun, plural* **lu•ces** [LOO-seez] SI unit of illumination
lux•u•ry [LUK-shə-ree] *noun, plural* **-ries** 1 possession and use of costly, choice things for enjoyment 2 enjoyable but not necessary thing 3 comfortable surroundings > **lux•u•ri•ance** [lug-ZHUUR-ee-əns] *noun* abundance, proliferation > **lux•u'ri•ant** *adjective* 1 growing thickly 2 abundant > **lux•u'ri•ate** [-ayt] *verb intransitive* **-at•ed, -at•ing** 1 indulge in luxury 2 flourish profusely 3 take delight (in) > **lux•u'ri•ous** *adjective* 1 fond of luxury 2 self-indulgent 3 sumptuous
ly•ce•um [lī-SEE-əm] *noun* 1 institution for popular education e.g. concerts, lectures 2 public building for this purpose
lye [lī] *noun* water made alkaline with wood ashes, etc. for washing
lying *pr. p. of* **lie**
lymph [limf] *noun* colorless bodily fluid, mainly of white blood cells > **lym•phat'ic** *adjective* 1 of lymph 2 flabby, sluggish ▷ *noun* 3 vessel in the body conveying lymph
lynch [linch] *verb transitive* put to death without trial > **lynch law** procedure of self-appointed court trying and punishing esp. executing accused
lynx [lingks] *noun* animal of cat family
lyre [līr] *noun* instrument like harp > **lyr•ic** [LIR-ik], **lyr'i•cal** *adjective* 1 of short personal poems expressing emotion 2 of lyre 3 meant to be sung > **ly•ric** *noun* lyric poem > **ly•rics** writer of lyrics 2 lyric poet **wax lyrical** express great enthusiasm

DICTIONARY | THESAURUS

---

bait, carrot (*informal*), enticement, incentive, inducement
lurid *adjective* 1 SENSATIONAL, graphic, melodramatic, shocking, vivid
2 GLARING, intense
lurk *verb* HIDE, conceal oneself, lie in wait, prowl, skulk, slink, sneak
luscious *adjective* DELICIOUS, appetizing, juicy, mouth-watering, palatable, succulent, sweet, toothsome, yummy (*informal*)
lush *adjective* 1 ABUNDANT, dense, flourishing, green, rank, verdant
2 LUXURIOUS, elaborate, extravagant, grand, lavish, opulent, ornate, palatial, plush (*informal*), sumptuous
lust *noun* 1 LECHERY, lasciviousness, lewdness, sensuality
2 APPETITE, craving, desire, greed, longing, passion, thirst
▷ *verb* 3 DESIRE, covet, crave, hunger for *or* hunger after, want, yearn
luster *noun* 1 SPARKLE, gleam, glint, glitter, gloss, glow, sheen, shimmer, shine
2 GLORY, distinction, fame, honor, kudos, prestige, renown
lusty *adjective* VIGOROUS, energetic, healthy, hearty, powerful, robust, strong, sturdy, virile
luxurious *adjective* SUMPTUOUS, comfortable, expensive, lavish, magnificent, opulent, plush (*informal*), rich, splendid
luxury *noun* 1 OPULENCE, affluence, hedonism, richness, splendor, sumptuousness
2 EXTRAVAGANCE, extra, frill, indulgence, treat
lying *noun* 1 DISHONESTY, deceit, mendacity, perjury, untruthfulness
▷ *adjective* 2 DECEITFUL, dishonest, false, mendacious, perfidious, treacherous, two-faced, untruthful
lyrical *adjective* ENTHUSIASTIC, effusive, impassioned, inspired, poetic, rhapsodic

Mm

ma•ca•bre [mə-KAH-brə] *adjective* gruesome, ghastly
mac•ad•am [mə-KAD-əm] *noun* **1** road surface made of pressed layers of small broken stones **2** this stone
mac•a•roon [mak-ə-ROON] *noun* small cookie made of egg whites, almond paste, etc.
ma•caw [mə-KAW] *noun* kind of parrot
mace [mays] *noun* spice made of the husk of the nutmeg
Mace [mays] *noun* ® liquid causing tears and nausea, used as spray for riot control
mac•er•ate [MAS-ə-rayt] *verb transitive* **-at•ed, -at•ing 1** soften by soaking **2** cause to waste away
mach [mahk]**, mach number** *noun* the ratio of the air speed of an aircraft to the velocity of sound under given conditions
ma•chet•e [mə-SHET-ee] *noun* broad, heavy knife used for cutting or as a weapon
Mach•i•a•vel•li•an [mak-ee-ə-VEL-ə-ən] *adjective* politically unprincipled, crafty, perfidious, subtle
mach•i•na•tion [mak-ə-NAY-shən] *noun* (*usually plural*) plotting, intrigue
ma•chine [mə-SHEEN] *noun* **1** apparatus combining action of several parts to apply mechanical force **2** controlling organization **3** mechanical appliance **4** vehicle ▷ *verb transitive* **-chined, -chin•ing 5** sew, print, shape, etc. with machine > **ma•chin'er•y** *noun, plural* **-er•ies 1** parts of machine collectively **2** machines > **ma•chin'ist** *noun* one who makes or operates machines
ma•chis•mo [mah-CHEEZ-moh] *noun* strong or exaggerated masculine pride or masculinity > **ma'cho** [-choh] *adjective* **1** denoting or exhibiting such pride in masculinity ▷ *noun, plural* **-chos 2** person exhibiting this
mack•er•el [MAK-ər-əl] *noun* edible sea fish with blue and silver stripes
mac•ra•mé [MAK-rə-may] *noun* ornamental webbing of knotted cord
mac•ro•bi•ot•ics [mak-roh-bī-OT-iks] *noun* (*with sing v.*) dietary system advocating grain and vegetables grown without chemical additives > **mac•ro•bi•ot'ic** *adjective, noun* (relating to the diet of) person practicing macrobiotics
mac•ro•cosm [MAK-rə-koz-əm] *noun* **1** the universe **2** any large, complete system
mad *adjective* **-der, -dest 1** suffering from mental disease, insane **2** wildly foolish **3** very

DICTIONARY • THESAURUS

macabre *adjective* GRUESOME, dreadful, eerie, frightening, ghastly, ghostly, ghoulish, grim, grisly, morbid
machiavellian *adjective* SCHEMING, astute, crafty, cunning, cynical, double-dealing, opportunist, sly, underhand, unscrupulous
machine *noun* **1** APPLIANCE, apparatus, contraption, contrivance, device, engine, instrument, mechanism, tool **2** SYSTEM, machinery, organization, setup (*informal*), structure
machinery *noun* EQUIPMENT, apparatus, gear, instruments, tackle, tools
macho *adjective* MANLY, chauvinist, masculine, virile
mad *adjective* **1** INSANE, crazy (*informal*),

enthusiastic (about) 4 excited 5 furious, angry > **mad'den** *verb transitive* make mad > **mad'ly** *adverb* > **mad'man** *noun* > **mad'ness** *noun* 1 insanity 2 folly

mad•am [MAD-əm] *noun* 1 polite form of address to a woman 2 woman in charge of house 3 woman in charge of house of prostitution

made *pt./pp. of* **make**

Ma•don•na [mə-DON-ə] *noun* 1 the Virgin Mary 2 picture or statue of her

mad•ri•gal [MAD-ri-gəl] *noun* 1 unaccompanied part song 2 short love poem or song

mael•strom [MAYL-strəm] *noun* 1 great whirlpool 2 turmoil

ma•es•to•so [mī-STOH-soh] *adverb mus.* grandly, in majestic manner

maes•tro [MĪ-stroh] *noun* 1 outstanding musician, conductor 2 man regarded as master of any art

Ma•fi•a [MAH-fee-ə] *noun* international secret organization engaging in crime, orig. Italian

mag•a•zine [mag-ə-ZEEN] *noun* 1 periodical publication with stories and articles by different writers 2 appliance for supplying cartridges automatically to gun 3 storehouse for explosives or arms

ma•gen•ta [mə-JEN-tə] *adjective, noun* (of) purplish-red color

mag•got [MAG-ət] *noun* grub, larva of certain flies > **mag'got•y** *adjective* infested with maggots

Ma•gi [MAY-jī] *plural noun* 1 priests of ancient Persia 2 the wise men from the East at the Nativity

mag•ic [MAJ-ik] *noun* 1 art of supposedly invoking supernatural powers to influence events, etc. 2 any mysterious agency or power 3 witchcraft, conjuring ▷ *adjective* > **mag'i•cal** *adjective* > **ma•gi'cian** *noun* one skilled in magic, wizard, conjurer, enchanter

mag•is•trate [MAJ-ə-strayt] *noun* 1 civil officer administering law 2 justice of the peace > **mag•is•te'ri•al** [-STEER-ee-əl] *adjective* 1 of, referring to magistrate 2 authoritative 3 weighty > **mag'is•tra•cy** [-strə-see] *noun, plural* **-cies** 1 office of magistrate 2 magistrates collectively

mag•ma [MAG-mə] *noun* 1 paste, suspension 2 molten rock inside Earth's crust

mag•nan•i•mous [mag-NAN-ə-məs] *adjective* noble, generous, not petty > **mag•na•nim'i•ty** *noun*

mag•nate [MAG-nayt] *noun* influential or wealthy person

mag•ne•si•um [mag-NEE-zee-əm] *noun* metallic element > **mag•ne'sia** [-zhə] *noun* white powder compound of this used in medicine

mag•net [MAG-nit] *noun* 1 piece of iron, steel having properties of attracting iron, steel and pointing north and south when suspended 2 lodestone > **mag•net'ic** *adjective* 1 with properties of magnet 2 exerting powerful attraction > **mag•net'i•cal•ly** *adverb* > **mag'net•ism** [-ni-tiz-əm] *noun* 1 magnetic phenomena 2 science of this 3 personal charm

DICTIONARY

m

THESAURUS

demented, deranged, non compos mentis (*Latin*), nuts (*slang*), of unsound mind, out of one's mind, psychotic, raving, unhinged, unstable
2 FOOLISH, absurd, asinine, bonkers (*informal*), daft (*informal*), foolhardy, irrational, nonsensical, preposterous, senseless, wild
3 ANGRY, berserk, enraged, furious, incensed, livid (*informal*), wild
4 ENTHUSIASTIC, ardent, avid, crazy (*informal*), fanatical, impassioned, infatuated, wild
5 FRENZIED, excited, frenetic, uncontrolled, unrestrained, wild, wired (*slang*)
6 ▷ **like mad** (*informal*) ENERGETICALLY, enthusiastically, excitedly, furiously, rapidly, speedily, violently, wildly

madden *verb* INFURIATE, annoy, derange, drive one crazy, enrage, incense, inflame, irritate, upset

madly *adverb* 1 INSANELY, crazily, deliriously, distractedly, frantically, frenziedly, hysterically
2 FOOLISHLY, absurdly, irrationally, ludicrously, senselessly, wildly
3 ENERGETICALLY, excitedly, furiously, like mad (*informal*), recklessly, speedily, wildly
4 (*informal*) PASSIONATELY, desperately, devotedly, intensely, to distraction

madman, madwoman *noun* LUNATIC, maniac, nutcase (*slang*), psycho (*slang*), psychopath

madness *noun* 1 INSANITY, aberration, craziness, delusion, dementia, derangement, distraction, lunacy, mania, mental illness, psychopathy, psychosis
2 FOOLISHNESS, absurdity, daftness (*informal*), folly, foolhardiness, idiocy, nonsense, preposterousness, wildness

maelstrom *noun* 1 WHIRLPOOL, vortex
2 TURMOIL, chaos, confusion, disorder, tumult, upheaval

maestro *noun* MASTER, expert, genius, virtuoso

magazine *noun* 1 JOURNAL, pamphlet, periodical
2 STOREHOUSE, arsenal, depot, store, warehouse

magic *noun* 1 SORCERY, black art, enchantment, necromancy, witchcraft, wizardry
2 CONJURING, illusion, legerdemain, prestidigitation, sleight of hand, trickery
3 CHARM, allurement, enchantment, fascination, glamour, magnetism, power
▷ *adjective* 4 *also* **magical** MIRACULOUS, bewitching, charming, enchanting, entrancing, fascinating, marvelous, spellbinding

magician *noun* SORCERER, conjurer, enchanter *or* enchantress, illusionist, necromancer, warlock, witch, wizard

magisterial *adjective* AUTHORITATIVE, commanding, lordly, masterful

magistrate *noun* JUDGE, J.P., justice, justice of the peace

magnanimity *noun* GENEROSITY, benevolence, big-heartedness, largesse *or* largess, nobility, selflessness, unselfishness

magnanimous *adjective* GENEROUS, big-hearted, bountiful, charitable, kind, noble, selfless, unselfish

magnate *noun* TYCOON, baron, captain of industry, mogul, plutocrat

magnetic *adjective* ATTRACTIVE, captivating, charismatic, charming, fascinating, hypnotic, irresistible, mesmerizing, seductive

or power of attracting others > **mag'net•ize** *verb transitive* **-ized, -iz•ing** 1 make into a magnet 2 attract as if by magnet 3 fascinate > **mag•ne'to** [-NEE-toh] *noun, plural* **-tos** apparatus for ignition in internal combustion engine
mag•nif•i•cent [mag-NIF-ə-sənt] *adjective* 1 splendid 2 stately, imposing 3 excellent > **mag•nif'i•cence** *noun*
mag•ni•fy [MAG-nə-fī] *verb* **-fied, -fy•ing** 1 increase apparent size of, as with lens 2 exaggerate 3 make greater > **mag•ni•fi•ca'tion** [-KAY-shən] *noun*
mag•nil•o•quent [mag-NIL-ə-kwənt] *adjective* 1 speaking pompously 2 grandiose > **mag•nil'o•quence** *noun*
mag•ni•tude [MAG-ni-tood] *noun* 1 importance 2 greatness, size
mag•num [MAG-nəm] *noun* large wine bottle (approx. 1.6 quarts, 1.5 liters)
mag•pie [MAG-pī] *noun* 1 black-and-white bird 2 incessantly talkative person
ma•ha•ra•jah [mah-hə-RAH-jə] *noun* former title of some Indian princes
ma•ha•ri•shi [mah-hə-REE-shee] *noun* Hindu religious teacher or mystic
ma•hat•ma [mə-HAHT-mə] *noun Hinduism* 1 man of saintly life with supernatural powers 2 one endowed with great wisdom and power
mahl•stick [MAHL-stik] *noun* light stick with ball at one end, held in other hand to support working hand while painting
maid•en [MAYD-n] *noun* 1 (*literary*) young unmarried woman ▷ *adjective* 2 unmarried 3 of, suited to maiden 4 first 5 having blank record > **maid** *noun* 1 woman servant 2 (*literary*) young unmarried woman > **maid'en•ly** *adjective* modest > **maid'en•hair** *noun* fern with delicate stalks and fronds > **maid'en•head** *noun* virginity > **maiden name** woman's surname before marriage
mail[1] [mayl] *noun* 1 letters, etc. transported and delivered by the post office 2 letters, etc. conveyed at one time 3 the postal system 4 train, ship, etc. carrying mail 5 *same as* **e-mail.** ▷ *verb transitive* 6 send by mail > **mail'box** *noun* (on a computer) the directory in which e-mail messages are stored
mail[2] *noun* armor of interlaced rings or overlapping plates > **mailed** *adjective* covered with mail
maim [maym] *verb transitive* cripple, mutilate
main [mayn] *adjective* 1 chief, principal, leading ▷ *noun* 2 principal pipe, line carrying water, gas, etc. 3 chief part 4 strength, power 5 (*obsolete*) open sea > **main'ly** *adverb* for the most part, chiefly > **main'frame** *computing* ▷ *adjective* 1 denoting a high-speed general-purpose computer ▷ *noun* 2 such a computer > **main'land** *noun* stretch of land that forms main part of a country > **main'mast** *noun* chief mast in ship > **main'sail** *noun* lowest sail of mainmast > **main'spring** *noun* 1 chief spring of watch or clock 2 chief cause or motive > **main'stay** *noun* 1 rope from mainmast 2 chief support
main•tain [mayn-TAYN] *verb transitive* 1 carry on 2 preserve 3 support 4 sustain 5 keep up 6 keep supplied 7 affirm 8 support by argument 9 defend > **main'te•nance** [-tə-nəns] *noun* 1 maintaining 2 means of support 3 upkeep of buildings, etc. 4 provision of money for separated or divorced spouse

magnetism *noun* CHARM, allure, appeal, attraction, charisma, drawing power, magic, pull, seductiveness
magnification *noun* INCREASE, amplification, enhancement, enlargement, expansion, heightening, intensification
magnificence *noun* SPLENDOR, brilliance, glory, grandeur, majesty, nobility, opulence, stateliness, sumptuousness
magnificent *adjective* 1 SPLENDID, cool (*informal*), glorious, gorgeous, imposing, impressive, majestic, regal, sublime, sumptuous
2 EXCELLENT, brilliant, fine, outstanding, phat (*slang*), splendid, superb
magnify *verb* 1 ENLARGE, amplify, blow up (*informal*), boost, dilate, expand, heighten, increase, intensify
2 OVERSTATE, exaggerate, inflate, overemphasize, overplay
magnitude *noun* 1 IMPORTANCE, consequence, greatness, moment, note, significance, weight
2 SIZE, amount, amplitude, extent, mass, quantity, volume
maid *noun* 1 GIRL, damsel, lass, maiden, wench
2 SERVANT, housemaid, maidservant, serving-maid
maiden *noun* 1 GIRL, damsel, lass, maid, virgin, wench
▷ *adjective* 2 UNMARRIED, unwed
3 FIRST, inaugural, initial, introductory
maidenly *adjective* MODEST, chaste, decent, decorous, demure, pure, virginal
mail *noun* 1 LETTERS, correspondence, junk mail, post
2 POSTAL SERVICE, collection, delivery, post office
▷ *verb* 3 POST, dispatch, forward, send, transmit
maim *verb* CRIPPLE, disable, hurt, injure, mutilate, wound
main *adjective* 1 CHIEF, central, essential, foremost, head, leading, pre-eminent, primary, principal
▷ *noun* 2 CONDUIT, cable, channel, duct, line, pipe
3 ▷ **in the main** ON THE WHOLE, for the most part, generally, in general, mainly, mostly
mainly *adverb* CHIEFLY, for the most part, in the main, largely, mostly, on the whole, predominantly, primarily, principally
mainstay *noun* PILLAR, anchor, backbone, bulwark, buttress, lynchpin, prop
mainstream *adjective* CONVENTIONAL, accepted, current, established, general, orthodox, prevailing, received
maintain *verb* 1 KEEP UP, carry on, continue, perpetuate, preserve, prolong, retain, sustain
2 SUPPORT, care for, look after, provide for, supply, take care of
3 ASSERT, avow, claim, contend, declare, insist, profess, state
maintenance *noun* 1 CONTINUATION, carrying-on, perpetuation, prolongation
2 UPKEEP, care, conservation, keeping, nurture, preservation, repairs
3 ALLOWANCE, alimony, keep, support

maî•tre d'hô•tel [may-tər doh-TEL] *noun, plural* **maî•tres** [-tərz] headwaiter, owner, or manager of hotel
maize [mayz] *noun* primitive corn with kernels of various colors, Indian corn
maj•es•ty [MAJ-ə-stee] *noun* 1 stateliness 2 sovereignty 3 grandeur > **ma•jes'tic** [mə-] *adjective* 1 splendid 2 regal > **ma•jes'ti•cal•ly** *adverb*
ma•jor [MAY-jər] *noun* 1 military officer ranking next above captain 2 scale in music 3 principal field of study at college 4 person engaged in this ▷ *adjective* 5 greater in number, quality, extent 6 significant, serious > **ma•jor'i•ty** *noun* 1 greater number 2 larger party voting together 3 more than half of votes cast in election 4 coming of age 5 rank of major > **major-do•mo** [-DOH-moh] *noun, plural* **-mos** male servant in charge of large household
make [mayk] *verb* **made, mak•ing** 1 construct 2 produce 3 create 4 establish 5 appoint 6 amount to 7 cause to do something 8 accomplish 9 reach 10 earn 11 tend 12 contribute ▷ *noun* 13 brand, type, or style > **mak•ing** *noun* creation > **mak•ings** necessary requirements or qualities **make allowance for** take mitigating circumstance into consideration > **make'shift** *noun* temporary expedient > **make'up** *noun* 1 cosmetics 2 characteristics 3 layout > **make up** 1 compose 2 compile 3 complete 4 compensate 5 apply cosmetics 6 invent **on the make** 7 (*informal*) intent on gain 8 (*slang*) seeking sexual relations
mal- *combining form* ill, badly: *malformation; malevolent*
ma•lac•ca [mə-LAK-ə] *noun* brown cane used for walking stick
mal•a•droit [mal-ə-DROIT] *adjective* clumsy, awkward
mal•a•dy [MAL-ə-dee] *noun, plural* **-dies** disease
ma•laise [ma-LAYZ] *noun* vague, unlocated feeling of bodily discomfort
mal•a•prop•ism [MAL-ə-prop-iz-əm] *noun* ludicrous misuse of word
ma•lar•i•a [mə-LAIR-ee-ə] *noun* infectious disease caused by parasite transmitted by bite of some mosquitoes > **ma•lar'i•al** *adjective*
mal•con•tent [mal-kən-TENT] *adjective* 1 actively discontented ▷ *noun* 2 malcontent person
male [mayl] *adjective* 1 of sex producing gametes that fertilize female gametes 2 of men or male

DICTIONARY

m

THESAURUS

majestic *adjective* GRAND, grandiose, impressive, magnificent, monumental, regal, splendid, stately, sublime, superb
majesty *noun* GRANDEUR, glory, magnificence, nobility, pomp, splendor, stateliness
major *adjective* 1 MAIN, bigger, chief, greater, higher, leading, senior, supreme
2 IMPORTANT, critical, crucial, great, notable, outstanding, serious, significant
majority *noun* 1 PREPONDERANCE, best part, bulk, greater number, mass, most
2 ADULTHOOD, manhood *or* womanhood, maturity, seniority
make *verb* 1 CREATE, assemble, build, construct, fashion, form, manufacture, produce, put together, synthesize
2 PRODUCE, accomplish, bring about, cause, create, effect, generate, give rise to, lead to
3 FORCE, cause, compel, constrain, drive, impel, induce, oblige, prevail upon, require
4 AMOUNT TO, add up to, compose, constitute, form
5 PERFORM, carry out, do, effect, execute
6 EARN, clear, gain, get, net, obtain, win
7 ▷ **make it** (*informal*) SUCCEED, arrive (*informal*), get on, prosper
▷ *noun* 8 BRAND, kind, model, sort, style, type, variety
make-believe *noun* FANTASY, imagination, play-acting, pretense, unreality
make for *verb* HEAD FOR, aim for, be bound for, head towards
make off *verb* 1 FLEE, bolt, clear out (*informal*), run away *or* run off, take to one's heels
2 ▷ **make off with** STEAL, abduct, carry off, filch, kidnap, pinch (*informal*), run away with *or* run off with
make out *verb* 1 SEE, detect, discern, discover, distinguish, perceive, recognize
2 UNDERSTAND, comprehend, decipher, fathom, follow, grasp, work out
3 WRITE OUT, complete, draw up, fill in *or* fill out
4 PRETEND, assert, claim, let on, make as if *or* make as though
5 FARE, get on, manage
maker *noun* MANUFACTURER, builder, constructor, producer
makeshift *adjective* TEMPORARY, expedient, provisional, stopgap, substitute
make-up *noun* 1 COSMETICS, face (*informal*), greasepaint (*theatre*), paint (*informal*), powder
2 STRUCTURE, arrangement, assembly, composition, configuration, constitution, construction, format, organization
3 NATURE, character, constitution, disposition, temperament
make up *verb* 1 FORM, compose, comprise, constitute
2 INVENT, coin, compose, concoct, construct, create, devise, dream up, formulate, frame, originate
3 COMPLETE, fill, supply
4 SETTLE, bury the hatchet, call it quits, reconcile
5 ▷ **make up for** COMPENSATE FOR, atone for, balance, make amends for, offset, recompense
making *noun* CREATION, assembly, building, composition, construction, fabrication, manufacture, production
makings *plural noun* BEGINNINGS, capacity, ingredients, potential
maladjusted *adjective* DISTURBED, alienated, neurotic, unstable
maladministration *noun* MISMANAGEMENT, corruption, dishonesty, incompetence, inefficiency, malpractice, misrule
maladroit *adjective* CLUMSY, awkward, inept, inexpert, unskillful
malady *noun* DISEASE, affliction, ailment, complaint, disorder, illness, infirmity, sickness
malaise *noun* UNEASE, anxiety, depression, disquiet, melancholy
malcontent *noun* TROUBLEMAKER, agitator,

animals 3 of machine part, made to fit inside corresponding recessed female part ▷ *noun* 4 male person or animal
mal•e•dic•tion [mal-i-DIK-shən] *noun* curse
mal•e•fac•tor [MAL-ə-fak-tər] *noun* criminal
ma•lev•o•lent [mə-LEV-ə-lənt] *adjective* full of ill will > **ma•lev'o•lence** *noun*
mal•fea•sance [mal-FEE-zəns] *noun* 1 illegal action 2 official misconduct
mal•ice [MAL-is] *noun* 1 ill will 2 spite > **ma•li•cious** [mə-LISH-əs] *adjective* 1 intending evil or unkindness 2 spiteful 3 moved by hatred
ma•lign [mə-LĪn] *adjective* 1 evil in influence or effect ▷ *verb transitive* 2 slander, misrepresent > **ma•lig'nan•cy** [-LIG-nən-see] *noun* > **ma•lig'nant** *adjective* 1 feeling extreme ill will 2 (of disease) resistant to therapy 3 tending to produce death > **ma•lig'ni•ty** *noun* malignant disposition
ma•lin•ger [mə-LING-gər] *verb intransitive* feign illness to escape duty > **ma•lin'ger•er** *noun*
mall [mawl] *noun* 1 level, shaded walk 2 street, shopping area closed to vehicles
mal•le•a•ble [MAL-ee-ə-bəl] *adjective* 1 capable of being hammered into shape 2 adaptable
mal•let [MAL-it] *noun* (wooden, etc.) hammer; croquet or polo stick
mal•nu•tri•tion [mal-noo-TRISH-ən] *noun* inadequate nutrition
mal•o•dor•ous [mal-OH-dər-əs] *adjective* evil-smelling
mal•prac•tice [mal-PRAK-tis] *noun* immoral, careless illegal or unethical conduct
malt [mawlt] *noun* 1 grain used for brewing or distilling ▷ *verb transitive* 2 make into malt
mal•ware [MAL-wair] *noun* computer program designed to damage or disrupt a system
mam•bo [MAHM-boh] *noun, plural* **-bos** Latin Amer. dance like rumba
mam•mal [MAM-əl] *noun* animal of type that suckles its young > **mam•ma'li•an** [-MAY-lee-ən] *adjective*
mam•ma•ry [MAM-er-ee] *adjective* of, relating to breast or milk-producing gland
mam•mon [MAM-ən] *noun* 1 wealth regarded as source of evil 2 (**Mam•mon**) false god of covetousness
mam•moth [MAM-əth] *noun* 1 extinct animal like an elephant ▷ *adjective* 2 colossal
man *noun, plural* **men** 1 human being 2 person 3 human race 4 adult male 5 manservant 6 piece used in chess, etc. ▷ *verb transitive* **manned, man•ning** 7 supply (ship, artillery, etc.) with necessary crew 8 fortify > **man'ful** *adjective* brave, vigorous > **man'li•ness** *noun* > **man'ly** *adjective* **-li•er, -li•est** > **man'nish** *adjective* like a man > **man'han•dle** *verb transitive* **-dled, -dling** treat roughly > **man'hole** *noun* opening through which person can pass to a drain, sewer, etc. > **man'hood** [-huud] *noun* > **man'kind'** [-KĪND] *noun* human beings in general > **man'pow•er**

mischief-maker, rebel, stirrer (*informal*)
male *adjective* MASCULINE, manly, virile
malefactor *noun* WRONGDOER, criminal, delinquent, evildoer, miscreant, offender, villain
malevolence *noun* MALICE, hate, hatred, ill will, rancor, spite, vindictiveness
malevolent *adjective* SPITEFUL, hostile, ill-natured, malicious, malign, vengeful, vindictive
malformation *noun* DEFORMITY, distortion, misshapenness
malformed *adjective* MISSHAPEN, abnormal, crooked, deformed, distorted, irregular, twisted
malfunction *verb* 1 BREAK DOWN, fail, go wrong ▷ *noun* 2 FAULT, breakdown, defect, failure, flaw, glitch
malice *noun* ILL WILL, animosity, enmity, evil intent, hate, hatred, malevolence, spite, vindictiveness
malicious *adjective* SPITEFUL, ill-disposed, ill-natured, malevolent, rancorous, resentful, vengeful
malign *verb* 1 DISPARAGE, abuse, defame, denigrate, libel, run down, slander, smear, vilify ▷ *adjective* 2 EVIL, bad, destructive, harmful, hostile, injurious, malevolent, malignant, pernicious, wicked
malignant *adjective* 1 HARMFUL, destructive, hostile, hurtful, malevolent, malign, pernicious, spiteful
2 (*medical*) UNCONTROLLABLE, cancerous, dangerous, deadly, fatal, irremediable
malleable *adjective* 1 WORKABLE, ductile, plastic, soft, tensile
2 MANAGEABLE, adaptable, biddable, compliant, impressionable, pliable, tractable
malodorous *adjective* SMELLY, fetid, funky (*slang*), mephitic, nauseating, noisome, offensive, putrid, reeking, stinking
malpractice *noun* MISCONDUCT, abuse, dereliction, mismanagement, negligence
maltreat *verb* ABUSE, bully, harm, hurt, ill-treat, injure, mistreat
mammoth *adjective* COLOSSAL, enormous, giant, gigantic, huge, immense, massive, monumental, mountainous, prodigious
man *noun* 1 MALE, chap (*informal*), dude (*informal*), gentleman, guy (*informal*)
2 HUMAN, human being, individual, person, soul
3 MANKIND, Homo sapiens, humanity, humankind, human race, people
4 MANSERVANT, attendant, retainer, servant, valet
▷ *verb* 5 STAFF, crew, garrison, occupy, people
manacle *noun* 1 HANDCUFF, bond, chain, fetter, iron, shackle
▷ *verb* 2 HANDCUFF, bind, chain, fetter, put in chains, shackle
manage *verb* 1 ADMINISTER, be in charge *or* be in charge of, command, conduct, direct, handle, run, supervise
2 SUCCEED, accomplish, arrange, contrive, effect, engineer
3 HANDLE, control, manipulate, operate, use
4 COPE, carry on, get by (*informal*), make do, muddle through, survive
manageable *adjective* DOCILE, amenable, compliant, easy, submissive
management *noun* 1 DIRECTORS, administration, board, employers, executive *or* executives
2 ADMINISTRATION, command, control, direction, handling, operation, running, supervision

noun 1 power of human effort 2 available number of workers > **man'slaugh•ter** [-slaw-tər] *noun* culpable homicide without malice aforethought

man•a•cle [MAN-ə-kəl] *noun* 1 fetter, handcuff ▷ *verb transitive* **-cled, -cling** 2 shackle

man•age [MAN-ij] *verb transitive* **-aged, -ag•ing** 1 be in charge of, administer 2 succeed in doing 3 control 4 handle, cope with 5 conduct, carry on 6 persuade > **man'age•a•ble** *adjective* > **man'age•ment** *noun* 1 those who manage, as board of directors, etc. 2 administration 3 skillful use of means 4 conduct > **man'ag•er** *noun* 1 one in charge of business, institution, actor, etc. 2 one who manages efficiently > **man•a•ge'ri•al** *adjective*

man•a•tee [MAN-ə-tee] *noun* large, plant-eating aquatic mammal

man•da•rin [MAN-də-rin] *noun* 1 *hist.* Chinese high-ranking bureaucrat 2 any high government official 3 Chinese variety of orange

man•date [MAN-dayt] *noun* 1 command of, or commission to act for, another 2 commission from United Nations to govern a territory 3 instruction from electorate to representative or government > **man'dat•ed** *adjective* committed to a mandate > **man'da•tor•y** [-də-tor-ee] *noun* holder of a mandate > **man'da•to•ry** *adjective* compulsory

man•di•ble [MAN-də-bəl] *noun* 1 lower jawbone 2 either part of bird's beak > **man•dib'u•lar** *adjective* of, like mandible

man•do•lin [MAN-dl-in] *noun* stringed musical instrument

man•drel [MAN-drəl] *noun* 1 axis on which material is supported in a lathe 2 spindle around which metal is forged

man'drill *noun* large blue-faced baboon

mane [mayn] *noun* long hair on neck of horse, lion, etc.

ma•neu•ver [mə-NOO-vər] *noun* 1 contrived, complicated, perhaps deceptive plan or action 2 skillful management ▷ *verb* 3 employ stratagems, work adroitly 4 (cause to) perform maneuvers

man•ga•nese [MANG-gə-neez] *noun* 1 metallic element 2 black oxide of this

mange [maynj] *noun* skin disease of dogs, etc. > **man'gy** *adjective* **-gi•er, -gi•est** scruffy, shabby

man•ger [MAYN-jər] *noun* eating trough in stable

man•gle[1] [MANG-gəl] *noun* 1 machine for pressing clothes, etc. to remove water ▷ *verb transitive* **-gled, -gling** 2 press in mangle

man•gle[2] *verb transitive* **-gled, -gling** mutilate, spoil, hack

man•go [MANG-goh] *noun, plural* **-goes** 1 tropical fruit 2 tree bearing it

man•grove [MANG-grohv] *noun* tropical tree that grows on muddy banks of estuaries

ma•ni•a [MAY-nee-ə] *noun* 1 madness 2 prevailing craze > **ma'ni•ac, ma•ni'a•cal, man'ic** *adjective* affected by mania > **maniac** *noun* (*informal*) 1 mad person 2 wild enthusiast

man•i•cure [MAN-i-kyuur] *noun* 1 treatment and care of fingernails and hands ▷ *verb transitive* **-cured, -cur•ing** 2 apply such treatment > **man'i•cur•ist** *noun* one who does this professionally

man•i•fest [MAN-ə-fest] *adjective* 1 clearly revealed, visible, undoubted ▷ *verb transitive* 2 make manifest ▷ *noun* 3 list of cargo for customs > **man•i•fes•ta'tion** *noun* > **man'i•fest•ly** *adverb* clearly > **man•i•fes'to** *noun, plural* **-toes** declaration of policy by political party, government, or movement

man•i•fold [MAN-ə-fohld] *adjective* 1 numerous and varied ▷ *noun* 2 in internal combustion engine, pipe with several outlets

ma•nip•u•late [mə-NIP-yə-layt] *verb transitive*

DICTIONARY

m

THESAURUS

manager *noun* SUPERVISOR, administrator, boss (*informal*), director, executive, governor, head, organizer

mandate *noun* COMMAND, commission, decree, directive, edict, instruction, order

mandatory *adjective* COMPULSORY, binding, obligatory, required, requisite

maneuver *noun* 1 STRATAGEM, dodge, intrigue, machination, ploy, ruse, scheme, subterfuge, tactic, trick
2 MOVEMENT, exercise, operation
▷ *verb* 3 MANIPULATE, contrive, engineer, machinate, pull strings, scheme, wangle (*informal*)
4 MOVE, deploy, exercise

manfully *adverb* BRAVELY, boldly, courageously, determinedly, gallantly, hard, resolutely, stoutly, valiantly

mangle *verb* CRUSH, deform, destroy, disfigure, distort, mutilate, ruin, spoil, tear, wreck

mangy *adjective* DIRTY, moth-eaten, scuzzy (*slang*), seedy, shabby, shoddy, squalid

manhandle *verb* ROUGH UP, knock about *or* knock around, maul, paw (*informal*)

manhood *noun* MANLINESS, masculinity, virility

mania *noun* 1 MADNESS, delirium, dementia, derangement, insanity, lunacy
2 OBSESSION, craze, fad (*informal*), fetish, fixation, passion, preoccupation, thing (*informal*)

maniac *noun* 1 MADMAN *or* MADWOMAN, lunatic, psycho (*slang*), psychopath
2 FANATIC, enthusiast, fan, fiend (*informal*), freak (*informal*)

manifest *adjective* 1 OBVIOUS, apparent, blatant, clear, conspicuous, evident, glaring, noticeable, palpable, patent
▷ *verb* 2 DISPLAY, demonstrate, exhibit, expose, express, reveal, show

manifestation *noun* DISPLAY, demonstration, exhibition, expression, indication, mark, show, sign, symptom

manifold *adjective* NUMEROUS, assorted, copious, diverse, many, multifarious, multiple, varied, various

manipulate *verb* 1 WORK, handle, operate, use
2 INFLUENCE, control, direct, engineer, maneuver

mankind *noun* PEOPLE, Homo sapiens, humanity, humankind, human race, man

manliness *noun* VIRILITY, boldness, bravery, courage, fearlessness, masculinity, valor, vigor

manly *adjective* VIRILE, bold, brave, courageous, fearless, manful, masculine, strapping, strong, vigorous

man-made *adjective* ARTIFICIAL, ersatz, manufactured, mock, synthetic

-lat•ed, -lat•ing 1 handle 2 deal with skillfully 3 manage 4 falsify > ma•nip•u•la'tion *noun* 1 act of manipulating, working by hand 2 skilled use of hands > ma•nip'u•la•tive *adjective*

man•na [MAN-ə] *noun* 1 food of Israelites in the wilderness 2 unexpected benefit

man•ne•quin [MAN-i-kin] *noun* 1 person who models clothes, esp. at fashion shows 2 clothing dummy

man•ner [MAN-ər] *noun* 1 way thing happens or is done 2 sort, kind 3 custom 4 style > **man•ners** social behavior > **man'ner•ism** *noun* person's distinctive habit, trait > **man'ner•ly** *adjective* polite

man•or [MAN-ər] *noun* main house of estate or plantation > **ma•no'ri•al** *adjective*

man•sard [MAN-sahrd] *noun* roof with break in its slope, lower part being steeper than upper

man•sion [MAN-shən] *noun* large house

man•tel [MAN-tl] *noun* 1 structure around fireplace 2 mantelpiece > **man'tel•piece, man'tel•shelf** *noun* shelf at top of mantel

man•til•la [man-TIL-ə] *noun* in Spain, (lace) scarf worn as headdress

man'tis *noun, plural* **-tis•es** genus of insects including the stick insects and leaf insects

man•tle [MAN-tl] *noun* 1 loose cloak 2 covering 3 incandescent fireproof network hood around gas jet ▷ *verb transitive* **-tled, -tling** 4 cover 5 conceal > **man•tle•piece** *noun* mantel

man•tra [MAN-trə] *noun* word or phrase repeated as object of concentration in meditation

man•u•al [MAN-yoo-əl] *adjective* 1 of, or done with, the hands 2 by human labor, not automatic ▷ *noun* 3 handbook 4 textbook 5 organ keyboard

man•u•fac•ture [man-yə-FAK-chər] *verb transitive* **-tured, -tur•ing** 1 process, make (materials) into finished articles 2 produce (articles) 3 invent, concoct ▷ *noun* 4 making of articles, materials, esp. in large quantities 5 anything produced from raw materials > **man•u•fac'tur•er** *noun*

ma•nure [mə-NUUR] *verb transitive* **-nured, -nur•ing** 1 enrich land ▷ *noun* 2 dung, chemical fertilizer (used to enrich land)

man•u•script [MAN-yə-skript] *noun* 1 book, document, written by hand 2 copy for printing ▷ *adjective* 3 handwritten or typed

man•y [MEN-ee] *adjective* **more, most** 1 numerous ▷ *noun, pronoun* 2 large number

Ma•o•ri [MAH-aw-ree] *noun* 1 member of New Zealand aboriginal population 2 their language

map *noun* 1 flat representation of Earth or some part of it, or of the heavens ▷ *verb transitive* **mapped, map•ping** 2 make a map of 3 (with *out*) plan

ma•ple [MAY-pəl] *noun* tree with broad leaves, a variety of which (**sugar maple**) yields sugar

ma•quis [mah-KEE] *noun* 1 scrubby undergrowth of Mediterranean countries 2 name adopted by French resistance movement in WWII

mar [mahr] *verb transitive* **marred, mar•ring** spoil, impair

mar•a•bou [MAR-ə-boo] *noun* 1 kind of stork 2 its soft white lower tail feathers, formerly used to trim hats, etc. 3 kind of silk

ma•rac•a [mə-RAH-kə] *noun* percussion instrument of gourd containing dried seeds, etc.

mar•a•schi•no [mar-ə-SKEE-noh] *noun* liqueur made from cherries

mar•a•thon [MAR-ə-thon] *noun* 1 long-distance race 2 endurance contest

ma•raud [mə-RAWD] *verb* 1 make raid for plunder 2 pillage > **ma•raud'er** *noun*

mar•ble [MAHR-bəl] *noun* 1 kind of limestone capable of taking polish 2 slab of, sculpture in this 3 small ball used in children's game > **mar'bled** *adjective* 1 having mottled appearance, like marble 2 (of beef) streaked with fat

march [mahrch] *verb intransitive* 1 walk with military step 2 go, progress ▷ *verb transitive* 3 cause to march ▷ *noun* 4 action of marching 5 distance marched in day 6 tune to accompany marching

DICTIONARY • THESAURUS

manner *noun* 1 BEHAVIOR, air, aspect, bearing, conduct, demeanor
2 STYLE, custom, fashion, method, mode, way
3 TYPE, brand, category, form, kind, sort, variety

mannered *adjective* AFFECTED, artificial, pretentious, stilted

mannerism *noun* HABIT, characteristic, foible, idiosyncrasy, peculiarity, quirk, trait, trick

manners *plural noun* 1 BEHAVIOR, conduct, demeanor
2 POLITENESS, courtesy, decorum, etiquette, p's and q's, refinement

mansion *noun* RESIDENCE, hall, manor, seat, villa

mantle *noun* 1 CLOAK, cape, hood, shawl, wrap
2 COVERING, blanket, canopy, curtain, pall, screen, shroud, veil

manual *adjective* 1 HAND-OPERATED, human, physical
▷ *noun* 2 HANDBOOK, bible, instructions

manufacture *verb* 1 MAKE, assemble, build, construct, create, mass-produce, produce, put together, turn out
2 CONCOCT, cook up (*informal*), devise, fabricate, invent, make up, think up, trump up
▷ *noun* 3 MAKING, assembly, construction, creation, production

manufacturer *noun* MAKER, builder, constructor, creator, industrialist, producer

manure *noun* COMPOST, droppings, dung, excrement, fertilizer, muck, ordure

many *adjective* 1 NUMEROUS, abundant, countless, innumerable, manifold, myriad, umpteen (*informal*), various
▷ *noun* 2 A LOT, heaps (*informal*), lots (*informal*), plenty, scores

mar *verb* SPOIL, blemish, damage, detract from, disfigure, hurt, impair, ruin, scar, stain, taint, tarnish

maraud *verb* RAID, forage, loot, pillage, plunder, ransack, ravage

marauder *noun* RAIDER, bandit, buccaneer, outlaw, plunderer

march *verb* 1 WALK, file, pace, parade, stride, strut
▷ *noun* 2 WALK, routemarch, trek
3 PROGRESS, advance, development, evolution, progression

mar•chion•ess [MAHR-shə-nis] *noun* wife, widow of marquis
Mar•di Gras [MAHR-dee grah] *noun* 1 festival of Shrove Tuesday 2 revelry celebrating this
mare [mair] *noun* female horse > **mare's-nest** *noun* supposed discovery that proves worthless
mar•ga•rine [MAHR-jər-in] *noun* butter substitute made from vegetable fats
mar•gin [MAHR-jin] *noun* 1 border, edge 2 space around printed page 3 amount allowed beyond what is necessary > **mar'gin•al** *adjective*
mar•i•gold [MAR-i-gohld] *noun* plant with yellow flowers
ma•ri•jua•na [mar-ə-WAH-nə] *noun* dried flowers and leaves of hemp plant, used as narcotic
ma•ri•na [mə-REE-nə] *noun* mooring facility for yachts and pleasure boats
mar•i•nade [mar-ə-NAYD] *noun* seasoned, flavored liquid used to soak fish, meat, etc. before cooking > **mar'i•nate** *verb transitive* **-nat•ed, -nat•ing**
ma•rine [mə-REEN] *adjective* 1 of the sea or shipping 2 used at, found in sea ▷ *noun* 3 shipping, fleet 4 soldier trained for land or sea combat > **mar'i•ner** *noun* sailor
mar•i•on•ette [mar-ee-ə-NET] *noun* puppet worked with strings
mar•i•tal [MAR-i-tl] *adjective* relating to marriage
mar•i•time [MAR-i-tīm] *adjective* 1 connected with seafaring 2 naval 3 bordering on the sea
mar•jo•ram [MAHR-jər-əm] *noun* aromatic herb
mark[1] [mahrk] *noun* 1 line, dot, scar, etc. 2 sign, token 3 inscription 4 letter, number showing evaluation of schoolwork, etc. 5 indication 6 target ▷ *verb transitive* 7 make a mark on 8 be distinguishing mark of 9 indicate 10 notice 11 watch 12 assess, e.g. examination paper ▷ *verb intransitive* 13 take notice > **mark'er** *noun* 1 one who, that which marks 2 counter used at card playing, etc. 3 (*slang*) an IOU > **marks'man** *noun* skilled shot
mark[2] *noun* former German monetary unit
mar•ket [MAHR-kit] *noun* 1 assembly, place for buying and selling 2 demand for goods 3 center for trade ▷ *verb transitive* 4 offer or produce for sale > **mar'ket•a•ble** *adjective*
mar•ma•lade [MAHR-mə-layd] *noun* preserve usually made of oranges, lemons, etc.
mar•mo•re•al [mahr-MOR-ee-əl] *adjective* of or like marble
ma•roon[1] [mə-ROON] *noun* 1 brownish-red 2 firework ▷ *adjective* 3 of the color
ma•roon[2] *verb transitive* 1 leave (person) on deserted island or coast 2 isolate, cut off by any means
mar•quee [mahr-KEE] *noun* 1 rooflike shelter with open sides 2 rooflike projection above theater, etc. displaying name of play, etc. being performed
mar•quis [MAHR-kwis] *noun* nobleman of rank below duke
mar•row [MAR-oh] *noun* 1 fatty substance inside bones 2 vital part
mar•ry [MAR-ee] *verb* **-ried, -ry•ing** 1 join as husband and wife 2 unite closely > **mar•riage** [MAR-ij] *noun* 1 state of being married 2 wedding > **mar'riage•a•ble** *adjective*
Mars [mahrz] *noun* 1 Roman god of war 2 planet nearest but one to Earth > **Mar•tian** [MAHR-shən] *noun* 1 supposed inhabitant of Mars ▷ *adjective* 2 of Mars
marsh [mahrsh] *noun* low-lying wet land > **marsh'y** *adjective* **marsh•i•er, marsh•i•est**
mar•shal [MAHR-shəl] *noun* 1 high officer of state 2 law enforcement officer ▷ *verb transitive*

DICTIONARY

m

THESAURUS

margin *noun* EDGE, border, boundary, brink, perimeter, periphery, rim, side, verge
marginal *adjective* 1 BORDERLINE, bordering, on the edge, peripheral
2 INSIGNIFICANT, minimal, minor, negligible, slight, small
marijuana *noun* CANNABIS, dope (*slang*), grass (*slang*), hemp, pot (*slang*)
marine *adjective* NAUTICAL, maritime, naval, seafaring, seagoing
mariner *noun* SAILOR, salt, sea dog, seafarer, seaman
marital *adjective* MATRIMONIAL, conjugal, connubial, nuptial
maritime *adjective* 1 NAUTICAL, marine, naval, oceanic, seafaring
2 COASTAL, littoral, seaside
mark *noun* 1 SPOT, blemish, blot, line, scar, scratch, smudge, stain, streak
2 SIGN, badge, device, emblem, flag, hallmark, label, symbol, token
3 CRITERION, measure, norm, standard, yardstick
4 TARGET, aim, goal, object, objective, purpose
▷ *verb* 5 SCAR, blemish, blot, scratch, smudge, stain, streak
6 CHARACTERIZE, brand, flag, identify, label, stamp
7 DISTINGUISH, denote, exemplify, illustrate, show
8 OBSERVE, attend, mind, note, notice, pay attention, pay heed, watch
9 GRADE, appraise, assess, correct, evaluate
marked *adjective* NOTICEABLE, blatant, clear, conspicuous, decided, distinct, obvious, patent, prominent, pronounced, striking
markedly *adverb* NOTICEABLY, clearly, considerably, conspicuously, decidedly, distinctly, obviously, strikingly
market *noun* 1 FAIR, bazaar, mart
▷ *verb* 2 SELL, retail, vend
marketable *adjective* SOUGHT AFTER, in demand, salable, wanted
marksman *or* **markswoman** *noun* SHARPSHOOTER, crack shot (*informal*), good shot
maroon *verb* ABANDON, desert, leave, leave high and dry (*informal*), strand
marriage *noun* WEDDING, match, matrimony, nuptials, wedlock
marry *verb* 1 WED, get hitched (*slang*), tie the knot (*informal*)
2 UNITE, ally, bond, join, knit, link, merge, unify, yoke
marsh *noun* SWAMP, bog, fen, morass, quagmire, slough
marshal *verb* 1 ARRANGE, align, array, deploy, draw up, group, line up, order, organize
2 CONDUCT, escort, guide, lead, shepherd, usher

-shaled, -shal•ing 3 arrange in due order 4 conduct with ceremony **field marshal** in some nations, military officer of the highest rank
marsh'mal•low [MAHRSH-mal-oh] *noun* spongy candy orig. made from root of **marsh mallow**, shrubby plant growing near marshes
mar•su•pi•al [mahr-SOO-pee-əl] *noun* animal that carries its young in pouch, e.g. kangaroo ▷ *adjective*
mar•ten [MAHR-tn] *noun* 1 weasel-like animal 2 its fur
mar•tial [MAHR-shəl] *adjective* 1 relating to war 2 warlike, brave **court martial** *see* **court** > **martial law** law enforced by military authorities in times of danger or emergency
mar'tin *noun* species of swallow
mar•ti•net [mahr-tn-ET] *noun* strict disciplinarian
mar•ti•ni [mahr-TEE-nee] *noun, plural* **-nis** cocktail containing gin and vermouth
mar•tyr [MAHR-tər] *noun* 1 one put to death for not renouncing beliefs 2 one who suffers in some cause 3 one in constant suffering ▷ *verb transitive* 4 make martyr of > **mar'tyr•dom** [-dəm] *noun*
mar•vel [MAHR-vəl] *verb intransitive* **-veled, -vel•ing** 1 wonder ▷ *noun* 2 wonderful thing > **mar'vel•ous** *adjective* 1 amazing 2 wonderful
mar•zi•pan [MAHR-zə-pan] *noun* paste of almonds, sugar, etc. used in candies, cakes, etc.
mas•car•a [ma-SKAIR-ə] *noun* cosmetic for darkening eyelashes and eyebrows
mas•cot [MAS-kot] *noun* animal, person or thing supposed to bring luck
mas•cu•line [MAS-kyə-lin] *adjective* 1 relating to males 2 manly 3 of the grammatical gender to which names of males belong
mash *noun* 1 grain, meal mixed with warm water 2 warm food for horses, etc. ▷ *verb transitive* 3 make into a mash 4 crush into soft mass or pulp
mask *noun* 1 covering for face 2 *surgery* covering for nose and mouth 3 disguise, pretense ▷ *verb transitive* 4 cover with mask 5 hide, disguise
mas•och•ism [MAS-ə-kiz-əm] *noun* abnormal condition in which pleasure (esp. sexual) is derived from pain, humiliation, etc. > **mas'och•ist** *noun* > **mas•och•is'tic** *adjective*
ma•son [MAY-sən] *noun* 1 worker in stone 2 (**Ma•son**) Freemason > **Ma•son'ic** *adjective* of Freemasonry > **ma'son•ry** *noun* 1 stonework 2 (**Ma'son•ry**) Freemasonry
masque [mask] *noun hist.* form of theatrical performance > **mas•quer•ade'** *noun* 1 masked ball ▷ *verb intransitive* **-ad•ed, -ad•ing** 2 appear in disguise
Mass *noun* service of the Eucharist
mass *noun* 1 quantity of matter 2 dense collection of this 3 large quantity or number ▷ *verb* 4 form into a mass > **mas'sive** *adjective* large and heavy > **mass-pro•duce'** *verb transitive* **-duced, -duc•ing** produce standardized articles in large quantities > **mass production** manufacturing of standardized goods in large quantities **the masses** the common people
mas•sa•cre [MAS-ə-kər] *noun* 1 indiscriminate, large-scale killing, esp. of unresisting people ▷ *verb transitive* **-cred, -cring** 2 kill indiscriminately
mas•sage [mə-SAHZH] *noun* 1 rubbing and kneading of muscles, etc. as curative treatment ▷ *verb transitive* **-saged, -sag•ing** 2 apply this treatment to > **mas•seur'** [-SUR], *(fem)* **mass•euse** [-SOOS] *noun* one who practices massage
mast *noun* 1 pole for supporting ship's sails 2 tall upright support for aerial, etc.
mas•tec•to•my [ma-STEK-tə-mee] *noun, plural* **-mies** surgical removal of a breast
mas•ter [MAS-tər] *noun* 1 one in control 2

DICTIONARY • THESAURUS

marshy *adjective* SWAMPY, boggy, quaggy, waterlogged, wet
martial *adjective* MILITARY, bellicose, belligerent, warlike
martinet *noun* DISCIPLINARIAN, stickler
martyrdom *noun* PERSECUTION, ordeal, suffering
marvel *verb* 1 WONDER, be amazed, be awed, gape
▷ *noun* 2 WONDER, miracle, phenomenon, portent, prodigy
marvelous *adjective* 1 AMAZING, astonishing, astounding, breathtaking, brilliant, extraordinary, miraculous, phenomenal, prodigious, spectacular, stupendous
2 EXCELLENT, fabulous (*informal*), fantastic (*informal*), great (*informal*), splendid, superb, terrific (*informal*), wonderful
masculine *adjective* MALE, manlike, manly, mannish, virile
mask *noun* 1 DISGUISE, camouflage, cover, façade, front, guise, screen, veil
▷ *verb* 2 DISGUISE, camouflage, cloak, conceal, cover, hide, obscure, screen, veil
masquerade *noun* 1 MASKED BALL, fancy dress party, revel
2 PRETENSE, cloak, cover-up, deception, disguise, mask, pose, screen, subterfuge
▷ *verb* 3 POSE, disguise, dissemble, dissimulate, impersonate, pass oneself off, pretend *or* pretend to be
mass *noun* 1 PIECE, block, chunk, hunk, lump
2 LOT, bunch, collection, heap, load, pile, quantity, stack
3 SIZE, bulk, greatness, magnitude
▷ *adjective* 4 LARGE-SCALE, extensive, general, indiscriminate, wholesale, widespread
▷ *verb* 5 GATHER, accumulate, assemble, collect, congregate, rally, swarm, throng
massacre *noun* 1 SLAUGHTER, annihilation, blood bath, butchery, carnage, extermination, holocaust, murder
▷ *verb* 2 SLAUGHTER, butcher, cut to pieces, exterminate, kill, mow down, murder, wipe out
massage *noun* 1 RUB-DOWN, manipulation
▷ *verb* 2 RUB DOWN, knead, manipulate
massive *adjective* HUGE, big, colossal, enormous, gigantic, hefty, immense, mammoth, monumental, whopping (*informal*)
master *noun* 1 RULER, boss (*informal*), chief, commander, controller, director, governor, lord, manager
2 EXPERT, ace (*informal*), doyen, genius, maestro, past master, virtuoso, wizard
3 TEACHER, guide, guru, instructor, tutor
▷ *adjective* 4 MAIN, chief, foremost, leading, predominant, prime, principal

employer 3 head of household 4 owner 5 document, etc. from which copies are made 6 captain of merchant ship 7 expert 8 great artist 9 teacher ▷ *verb transitive* 10 overcome 11 acquire knowledge of or skill in > **mas'ter•ful** *adjective* imperious, domineering > **mas'ter•ly** *adjective* showing great competence > **mas'ter•y** *noun* 1 full understanding (of) 2 expertise 3 authority 4 victory > **master key** one that opens many different locks > **mas'ter•mind** *verb transitive* plan, direct ▷ *noun* > **mas'ter•piece** *noun* outstanding work

mas•tic [MAS-tik] *noun* 1 gum obtained from certain trees 2 pasty substance

mas•ti•cate [MAS-ti-kayt] *verb transitive* **-cat•ed, -cat•ing** chew > **mas•ti•ca'tion** *noun*

mas'tiff *noun* large dog

mas'toid *adjective* 1 nipple-shaped ▷ *noun* 2 prominence on bone behind human ear > **mas•toid•i'tis** *noun* inflammation of this area

mas•tur•bate [MAS-tər-bayt] *verb* **-bat•ed, -bat•ing** stimulate (one's own) genital organs > **mas•tur•ba'tion** *noun*

mat[1] *noun* 1 small rug 2 piece of fabric to protect another surface or to wipe feet on, etc. 3 thick tangled mass ▷ *verb* **mat•ted, mat•ting** 4 form into such mass **go to the mat** struggle unyieldingly

mat[2] *see* **matte**

mat•a•dor [MAT-ə-dor] *noun* bullfighter who slays bulls in bullfights

match[1] [mach] *noun* 1 contest, game 2 equal 3 person, thing exactly corresponding to another 4 marriage 5 person regarded as eligible for marriage ▷ *verb transitive* 6 get something corresponding to (color, pattern, etc.) 7 oppose, put in competition (with) 8 arrange marriage for 9 join (in marriage) ▷ *verb intransitive* 10 correspond > **match'less** *adjective* unequaled > **match'mak•er** *noun* one who schemes to bring about a marriage

match[2] *noun* 1 small stick with head that ignites when rubbed 2 fuse > **match'box** *noun*

mate[1] [mayt] *noun* 1 husband, wife 2 one of pair 3 officer in merchant ship ▷ *verb* **mat•ed, mat•ing** 4 marry 5 pair

mate[2] *noun, verb transitive* **mat•ed, mat•ing** *chess* checkmate

ma•te•ri•al [mə-TEER-ee-əl] *noun* 1 substance from which thing is made 2 cloth, fabric ▷ *adjective* 3 of matter or body 4 affecting physical well-being 5 unspiritual 6 important, essential > **ma•te'ri•al•ism** *noun* 1 excessive interest in, desire for money and possessions 2 doctrine that nothing but matter exists, denying independent existence of spirit > **ma•te•ri•al•is'tic** *adjective* > **ma•te'ri•al•ize** *verb intransitive* **-ized, -iz•ing** 1 come into existence or view ▷ *verb transitive* **-ized, -iz•ing** 2 make material > **ma•te'ri•al•ly** *adverb* appreciably

ma•ter•nal [mə-TUR-nl] *adjective* 1 motherly 2 of a mother 3 related through mother > **ma•ter'ni•ty** *noun* motherhood

math•e•mat•ics [math-ə-MAT-iks] *noun* science of numbers, quantities and shapes > **math•e•mat'i•cal** *adjective* > **math•e•ma•ti'cian** [-TI-shən] *noun*

mat•i•née [mat-n-AY] *noun* afternoon performance in theater

ma•tri•arch [MAY-tree-ahrk] *noun* mother as head and ruler of family > **ma'tri•ar•chy** *noun, plural* **-chies** society with government by women and descent reckoned in female line

mat•ri•cide [MA-tri-sīd] *noun* 1 the crime of killing one's mother 2 one who does this

ma•tric•u•late [mə-TRIK-yə-layt] *verb* **-lat•ed, -lat•ing** enroll, be enrolled as degree candidate in a college or university > **ma•tric•u•la'tion** *noun*

mat•ri•mo•ny [MA-trə-moh-nee] *noun*

DICTIONARY

m

THESAURUS

▷ *verb* 5 LEARN, get the hang of (*informal*), grasp 6 OVERCOME, conquer, defeat, tame, triumph over, vanquish

masterful *adjective* 1 SKILLFUL, adroit, consummate, expert, fine, first-rate, masterly, superlative, supreme, world-class 2 DOMINEERING, arrogant, bossy (*informal*), high-handed, imperious, overbearing, overweening

masterly *adjective* SKILLFUL, adroit, consummate, crack (*slang*), expert, first-rate, masterful, supreme, world-class

mastermind *verb* 1 PLAN, conceive, devise, direct, manage, organize ▷ *noun* 2 ORGANIZER, architect, brain *or* brains (*informal*), director, engineer, manager, planner

masterpiece *noun* CLASSIC, jewel, magnum opus, pièce de résistance (*French*), tour de force (*French*)

mastery *noun* 1 EXPERTISE, finesse, know-how (*informal*), proficiency, prowess, skill, virtuosity 2 CONTROL, ascendancy, command, domination, superiority, supremacy, upper hand, whip hand

match *noun* 1 GAME, bout, competition, contest, head-to-head, test, trial 2 EQUAL, counterpart, peer, rival 3 MARRIAGE, alliance, pairing, partnership ▷ *verb* 4 CORRESPOND, accord, agree, fit, go with, harmonize, tally 5 RIVAL, compare, compete, emulate, equal, measure up to

matching *adjective* IDENTICAL, coordinating, corresponding, equivalent, like, twin

matchless *adjective* UNEQUALED, incomparable, inimitable, superlative, supreme, unmatched, unparalleled, unrivaled, unsurpassed

mate *noun* 1 PARTNER, husband *or* wife, spouse 2 COLLEAGUE, associate, companion 3 ASSISTANT, helper, subordinate ▷ *verb* 4 PAIR, breed, couple

material *noun* 1 SUBSTANCE, matter, stuff 2 INFORMATION, data, evidence, facts, notes 3 CLOTH, fabric ▷ *adjective* 4 PHYSICAL, bodily, concrete, corporeal, palpable, substantial, tangible 5 IMPORTANT, essential, meaningful, momentous, serious, significant, vital, weighty 6 RELEVANT, applicable, apposite, apropos, germane, pertinent

materialize *verb* OCCUR, appear, come about, come to pass, happen, take shape, turn up

materially *adverb* SIGNIFICANTLY, essentially, gravely, greatly, much, seriously, substantially

maternal *adjective* MOTHERLY

maternity *noun* MOTHERHOOD, motherliness

matrimonial *adjective* MARITAL, conjugal, connubial, nuptial

marriage > **mat•ri•mo'ni•al** *adjective*
ma•trix [MAY-triks] *noun, plural* **-tri•ces** [-tri-seez] 1 substance, situation in which something originates, takes form, or is enclosed 2 mold for casting 3 *math.* rectangular array of elements set out in rows and columns
ma•tron [MAY-trən] *noun* 1 married woman esp. of established social position 2 woman who superintends domestic arrangements of public institution, boarding school, etc. 3 woman guard in prison, etc. > **ma'tron•ly** *adjective* sedate
Matt. Matthew
matte [mat] *adjective* of photographic print, dull, lusterless, not shiny
mat•ter [MAT-ər] *noun* 1 substance of which thing is made 2 physical or bodily substance 3 affair, business 4 cause of trouble 5 substance of book, etc. ▷ *verb intransitive* 6 be of importance, signify
mat•tock [MAT-ək] *noun* tool like pick with ends of blades flattened for cutting, hoeing
mat•tress [MA-tris] *noun* stuffed flat case, often with springs, or foam rubber pad, used as part of bed **air mattress** inflatable mattress usu. of rubbery material
ma•ture [mə-CHUUR] *adjective* **-tur•er, -tur•est** 1 ripe, completely developed 2 grown-up ▷ *verb* **-tured, -tur•ing** 3 bring, come to maturity ▷ *verb intransitive* 4 (of bond, etc.) come due > **mat•u•ra'tion** *noun* process of maturing > **ma•tu'ri•ty** *noun* state of being mature
maud•lin [MAWD-lin] *adjective* weakly or tearfully sentimental
maul [mawl] *verb transitive* 1 handle roughly 2 beat or bruise ▷ *noun* 3 heavy wooden hammer
maulstick *noun see* **mahlstick**
mau•so•le•um [maw-sə-LEE-əm] *noun* stately building as a tomb
mauve [mawv] *adjective, noun* (of) pale purple color
mav•er•ick [MAV-ər-ik] *noun* 1 unbranded steer, strayed cow 2 independent, unorthodox person
maw *noun* stomach, crop
mawk•ish [MAW-kish] *adjective* 1 weakly sentimental, maudlin 2 sickening
max•im [MAK-sim] *noun* 1 general truth, proverb 2 rule of conduct, principle
max•i•mum [MAK-sə-məm] *noun* 1 greatest size or number 2 highest point ▷ *adjective* 3 greatest > **max'i•mize** *verb transitive* **-mized, -miz•ing**
may *verb, past tense* **might** used as an auxiliary to express possibility, permission, opportunity, etc. > **may'be** *adverb* 1 perhaps 2 possibly
May'day *noun* international radiotelephone distress signal
may•fly [MAY-flī] *noun* short-lived flying insect, found near water
may'hem *noun* 1 in law, depriving person by violence of limb, member or organ, or causing mutilation of body 2 any violent destruction 3 confusion
may•on•naise [may-ə-NAYZ] *noun* creamy sauce of egg yolks, etc., esp. for salads
may•or [MAY-ər] *noun* head of municipality > **may'or•al** *adjective* > **may'or•al•ty** [-əl-tee] *noun* (time of) office of mayor
may•pole [MAY-pohl] *noun* pole set up for dancing around on **May Day** to celebrate spring
maze [mayz] *noun* 1 labyrinth 2 network of paths, lines 3 state of confusion
ma•zur•ka [mə-ZUR-kə] *noun* 1 lively Polish dance like polka 2 music for it
MC *noun* master of ceremonies
me [mee] *pronoun objective case singular of first personal pronoun* **I** > **me'-time** *noun* time a person has to himself or herself, in which to do something enjoyable
me•a cul•pa [ME-ah KUUL-pah] *Lat.* my fault
mead•ow [MED-oh] *noun* tract of grassland
mea•ger [MEE-gər] *adjective* lean, thin, scanty, insufficient

DICTIONARY • THESAURUS

matrimony *noun* MARRIAGE, nuptials, wedding ceremony, wedlock
matted *adjective* TANGLED, knotted, tousled, uncombed
matter *noun* 1 SUBSTANCE, body, material, stuff 2 SITUATION, affair, business, concern, event, incident, proceeding, question, subject, topic 3 PROBLEM, complication, difficulty, distress, trouble, worry
▷ *verb* 4 BE IMPORTANT, carry weight, count, make a difference, signify
matter-of-fact *adjective* UNSENTIMENTAL, deadpan, down-to-earth, emotionless, mundane, plain, prosaic, sober, unimaginative
mature *adjective* 1 GROWN-UP, adult, full-grown, fully fledged, mellow, of age, ready, ripe, seasoned
▷ *verb* 2 DEVELOP, age, bloom, blossom, come of age, grow up, mellow, ripen
maturity *noun* ADULTHOOD, experience, manhood *or* womanhood, ripeness, wisdom
maudlin *adjective* SENTIMENTAL, mawkish, overemotional, slushy (*informal*), tearful, weepy (*informal*)
maul *verb* 1 ILL-TREAT, abuse, manhandle, molest, paw
2 TEAR, batter, claw, lacerate, mangle
maverick *noun* 1 REBEL, dissenter, eccentric, heretic, iconoclast, individualist, nonconformist, protester, radical
▷ *adjective* 2 REBEL, dissenting, eccentric, heretical, iconoclastic, individualistic, nonconformist, radical
mawkish *adjective* SENTIMENTAL, emotional, maudlin, schmaltzy (*slang*), slushy (*informal*)
maxim *noun* SAYING, adage, aphorism, axiom, dictum, motto, proverb, rule
maximum *noun* 1 TOP, ceiling, height, peak, pinnacle, summit, upper limit, utmost, zenith
▷ *adjective* 2 GREATEST, highest, most, paramount, supreme, topmost, utmost
maybe *adverb* PERHAPS, perchance (*archaic*), possibly
mayhem *noun* CHAOS, commotion, confusion, destruction, disorder, fracas, havoc, trouble, violence
maze *noun* 1 LABYRINTH
2 WEB, confusion, imbroglio, tangle
meadow *noun* FIELD, grassland, lea (*poetic*), pasture
meager *adjective* INSUBSTANTIAL, inadequate, lousy (*slang*), measly, paltry, poor, puny, scanty,

meal¹ [meel] *noun* 1 occasion when food is served and eaten 2 the food
meal² *noun* grain ground to powder > **meal'y** *adjective* **meal•i•er, meal•i•est** > **mealy-mouthed** [-mowthd] *adjective* euphemistic, insincere in what one says
mean¹ [meen] *verb* **meant** [ment], **mean•ing** 1 intend 2 signify 3 have a meaning 4 have the intention of behaving > **mean'ing** *noun* 1 sense, significance ▷ *adjective* 2 expressive > **mean'ing•ful** [-fəl] *adjective* of great meaning or significance > **mean'ing•less** *adjective*
mean² *adjective* **-er, -est** 1 ungenerous, petty 2 miserly, niggardly 3 unpleasant 4 callous 5 shabby 6 ashamed > **mean'ness** *noun*
mean³ *noun* 1 thing that is intermediate 2 middle point ▷ *adjective* 3 intermediate in time, quality, etc. 4 average > **means** *plural noun* 1 that by which thing is done 2 money 3 resources > **means test** inquiry into person's means to decide eligibility for pension, grant, etc. > **mean'time, mean'while** *adverb, noun* (during) time between one happening and another **by all means** certainly **by no means** not at all
me•an•der [mee-AN-dər] *verb intransitive* 1 flow windingly 2 wander aimlessly
mea•sles [MEE-zəlz] *noun* infectious disease producing rash of red spots > **mea'sly** *adjective* **-sli•er, -sli•est** (*informal*) 1 poor, wretched, stingy 2 of measles
meas•ure [MEZH-ər] *noun* 1 size, quantity 2 vessel, rod, line, etc. for ascertaining size or quantity 3 unit of size or quantity 4 course, plan of action 5 law 6 poetical rhythm 7 musical time 8 *poet.* tune 9 (*obsolete*) dance ▷ *verb transitive* **-ured, -ur•ing** 10 ascertain size, quantity of 11 be (so much) in size or quantity 12 indicate measurement of 13 estimate 14 bring into competition (against) > **meas'ur•a•ble** *adjective* > **meas'ured** *adjective* 1 determined by measure 2 steady 3 rhythmical 4 carefully considered > **meas'ure•ment** *noun* 1 measuring 2 size > **meas'ure•ments** dimensions
meat [meet] *noun* 1 animal flesh as food 2 food > **meat'y** *adjective* **meat•i•er, meat•i•est** 1 (tasting) of, like meat 2 brawny 3 full of import or interest
Mec•ca [MEK-ə] *noun* 1 holy city of Islam 2 (**mec•ca**) place that attracts visitors
me•chan•ic [mə-KAN-ik] *noun* 1 one employed in working with machinery 2 skilled worker > **me•chan•ics** scientific theory of motion > **me•chan'i•cal** *adjective* 1 concerned with machines or operation of them 2 worked, produced (as though) by machine 3 acting without thought > **me•chan'i•cal•ly** *adverb*
mech•an•ism [MEK-ə-niz-əm] *noun* 1 structure

slight, small
meal *noun* (*informal*) FEAST, feed, repast, spread (*informal*)
mean¹ *verb* 1 SIGNIFY, convey, denote, express, imply, indicate, represent, spell, stand for, symbolize
2 INTEND, aim, aspire, design, desire, plan, set out, want, wish
mean² *adjective* 1 MISERLY, mercenary, niggardly, parsimonious, penny-pinching, stingy, tight-fisted, ungenerous
2 DESPICABLE, callous, contemptible, hard-hearted, lousy (*slang*), petty, scuzzy (*slang*), shabby, shameful, sordid, vile
mean³ *noun* 1 AVERAGE, balance, compromise, happy medium, middle, midpoint, norm
▷ *adjective* 2 AVERAGE, middle, standard
meander *verb* 1 WIND, snake, turn, zigzag
2 WANDER, ramble, stroll
▷ *noun* 3 CURVE, bend, coil, loop, turn, twist
meaning *noun* SENSE, connotation, drift, gist, message, significance, substance
meaningful *adjective* SIGNIFICANT, important, material, purposeful, relevant, useful, valid, worthwhile
meaningless *adjective* POINTLESS, empty, futile, inane, inconsequential, insignificant, senseless, useless, vain, worthless
meanness *noun* 1 MISERLINESS, niggardliness, parsimony, selfishness, stinginess
2 PETTINESS, disgracefulness, ignobility, narrow-mindedness, shabbiness, shamefulness
means *plural noun* 1 METHOD, agency, instrument, medium, mode, process, way
2 MONEY, affluence, capital, fortune, funds, income, resources, wealth, wherewithal
3 ▷ **by all means** CERTAINLY, definitely, doubtlessly, of course, surely
4 ▷ **by no means** IN NO WAY, definitely not, not in the least, on no account
meantime *or* **meanwhile** *adverb* AT THE SAME TIME, concurrently, in the interim, simultaneously
measly *adjective* MEAGER, miserable, paltry, pathetic, pitiful, poor, puny, scanty, skimpy
measurable *adjective* QUANTIFIABLE, assessable, perceptible, significant
measure *noun* 1 QUANTITY, allotment, allowance, amount, portion, quota, ration, share
2 GAUGE, meter, rule, scale, yardstick
3 ACTION, act, deed, expedient, maneuver, means, procedure, step
4 LAW, act, bill, resolution, statute
5 RHYTHM, beat, cadence, meter, verse
▷ *verb* 6 QUANTIFY, assess, calculate, calibrate, compute, determine, evaluate, gauge, weigh
measured *adjective* 1 STEADY, dignified, even, leisurely, regular, sedate, slow, solemn, stately, unhurried
2 CONSIDERED, calculated, deliberate, reasoned, sober, studied, well-thought-out
measurement *noun* CALCULATION, assessment, calibration, computation, evaluation, mensuration, valuation
measure up to *verb* FULFILL THE EXPECTATIONS, be equal to, be suitable, come up to scratch (*informal*), fit the bill *or* fill the bill, make the grade (*informal*)
meat *noun* FLESH
meaty *adjective* 1 BRAWNY, beefy (*informal*), burly, heavily built, heavy, muscular, solid, strapping, sturdy
2 INTERESTING, meaningful, profound, rich, significant, substantial
mechanical *adjective* 1 AUTOMATIC, automated
2 UNTHINKING, automatic, cursory, impersonal, instinctive, involuntary, perfunctory, routine, unfeeling

of machine 2 piece of machinery > **mech'a•nize** *verb transitive* **-nized, -niz•ing** 1 equip with machinery 2 make mechanical, automatic 3 *military* equip with armored vehicles

med•al [MED-l] *noun* piece of metal with inscription, etc. used as reward or memento > **me•dal'lion** [mə-DAL-yən] *noun* 1 large medal 2 various things like this in decorative work > **med'al•ist** *noun* 1 winner of a medal 2 maker of medals

med•dle [MED-l] *verb intransitive* **-dled, -dling** interfere, busy oneself with unnecessarily > **med'dle•some** [-səm] *adjective*

me•di•a [MEE-dee-ə] *noun* 1 *pl. of* **medium** 2 used esp. of the mass media, radio, TV, etc. > **media event** event staged for or exploited by mass media

mediaeval *see* **medieval**

me•di•al [MEE-dee-əl] *adjective* 1 in the middle 2 pert. to a mean or average > **me'di•an** *adjective, noun* middle (point or line)

me•di•ate [MEE-dee-ayt] *verb intransitive* **-at•ed, -at•ing** 1 intervene to reconcile ▷ *verb transitive* **-at•ed, -at•ing** 2 bring about by mediation ▷ *adjective* 3 depending on mediation > **me•di•a'tion** *noun* 1 intervention on behalf of another 2 act of going between

med•i•cine [MED-i-sin] *noun* 1 drug or remedy for treating disease 2 science of preventing, diagnosing, alleviating, or curing disease > **med'i•cal** [-kəl] *adjective* > **me•dic'a•ment** *noun* remedy > **med'i•cate** [-kayt] *verb transitive* **-cat•ed, -cat•ing** treat, impregnate with medicinal substances > **med•i•ca'tion** *noun* > **me•dic'i•nal** [-DIS-ə-nəl] *adjective* curative

me•di•e•val [mee-dee-EE-vəl] *adjective* of Middle Ages > **me•di•e'val•ist** *noun* student of the Middle Ages

me•di•o•cre [mee-dee-OH-kər] *adjective* 1 neither bad nor good, ordinary, middling 2 second-rate > **me•di•oc'ri•ty** [-OK-rə-tee] *noun*

med•i•tate [MED-i-tayt] *verb intransitive* **-tat•ed, -tat•ing** 1 be occupied in thought 2 reflect deeply on spiritual matters 3 engage in transcendental meditation ▷ *verb transitive* **-tat•ed, -tat•ing** 4 think about 5 plan > **med•i•ta'tion** [-TAY-shən] *noun* 1 thought 2 absorption in thought 3 religious contemplation > **med'i•ta•tive** *adjective* 1 thoughtful 2 reflective

me•di•um [MEE-dee-əm] *adjective* 1 between two qualities, degrees, etc., average ▷ *noun, plural* **-di•a** *or* **-di•ums** 2 middle quality, degree 3 intermediate substance conveying force 4 means, agency of communicating news, etc. to public, as radio, newspapers, etc. 5 person through whom communication can supposedly be held with spirit world 6 surroundings 7 environment

med•ley [MED-lee] *noun, plural* **-leys** miscellaneous mixture

meds [medz] *plural noun* medicinal substances

Me•du•sa [mə-DOO-sə] *noun, plural* **-sas** *mythology* Gorgon whose head turned beholders into stone

meek *adjective* **-er, -est** submissive, humble > **meek'ly** *adverb* > **meek'ness** *noun*

meer•schaum [MEER-shəm] *noun* 1 white substance like clay 2 tobacco pipe bowl of this

meet *verb transitive* **met, meet•ing** 1 come face to face come face to face with, encounter 2 satisfy 3 pay 4 converge at specified point 5 assemble 6 come into contact ▷ *noun* 7 meeting, esp. for sports > **meeting** *noun* 1 assembly 2 encounter

meg•a•bit [MEG-ə-bit] *noun computing* 1 1,048,576 bits 2 (loosely) one million bits

mechanism *noun* 1 MACHINE, apparatus, appliance, contrivance, device, instrument, tool 2 PROCESS, agency, means, method, operation, procedure, system, technique

meddle *verb* INTERFERE, butt in, intervene, intrude, pry, tamper

meddlesome *adjective* INTERFERING, intrusive, meddling, mischievous, officious, prying

mediate *verb* INTERVENE, arbitrate, conciliate, intercede, reconcile, referee, step in (*informal*), umpire

mediation *noun* ARBITRATION, conciliation, intercession, intervention, reconciliation

mediator *noun* NEGOTIATOR, arbiter, arbitrator, go-between, honest broker, intermediary, middleman, peacemaker, referee, umpire

medicinal *adjective* THERAPEUTIC, curative, healing, medical, remedial, restorative

medicine *noun* REMEDY, cure, drug, medicament, medication, nostrum

mediocre *adjective* SECOND-RATE, average, indifferent, inferior, middling, ordinary, passable, pedestrian, so-so (*informal*), undistinguished

mediocrity *noun* INSIGNIFICANCE, indifference, inferiority, ordinariness, unimportance

meditate *verb* 1 REFLECT, cogitate, consider, contemplate, deliberate, muse, ponder, ruminate, think
2 PLAN, have in mind, intend, purpose, scheme

meditation *noun* REFLECTION, cogitation, contemplation, musing, pondering, rumination, study, thought

medium *adjective* 1 MIDDLE, average, fair, intermediate, mean, median, mediocre, middling, midway
▷ *noun* 2 MIDDLE, average, center, compromise, mean, midpoint
3 MEANS, agency, channel, instrument, mode, organ, vehicle, way
4 ENVIRONMENT, atmosphere, conditions, milieu, setting, surroundings
5 SPIRITUALIST

medley *noun* MIXTURE, assortment, farrago, jumble, mélange (*French*), miscellany, mishmash, mixed bag (*informal*), potpourri

meek *adjective* SUBMISSIVE, acquiescent, compliant, deferential, docile, gentle, humble, mild, modest, timid, unassuming, unpretentious

meekness *noun* SUBMISSIVENESS, acquiescence, compliance, deference, docility, gentleness, humility, mildness, modesty, timidity

meet *verb* 1 ENCOUNTER, bump into, chance on, come across, confront, contact, find, happen on, run across, run into
2 CONVERGE, come together, connect, cross, intersect, join, link up, touch
3 SATISFY, answer, come up to, comply with, discharge, fulfill, match, measure up to

meg•a•byte [MEG-ə-bīt] *noun computing* 1 1,048,576 bytes 2 (loosely) one million bytes
meg•a•lith [MEG-ə-lith] *noun* great stone > **meg•a•lith'ic** *adjective*
meg•a•lo•ma'ni•a [meg-ə-loh-MAY-nee-ə] *noun* desire for, delusions of grandeur, power, etc.
meg•a•pix•el [MEG-ə-piks-əl] *noun* one million pixels
meg•a•ton [MEG-ə-tun] *noun* 1 one million tons 2 explosive power equal to that of million tons of TNT
meg'ohm *noun electricity* one million ohms
mel•an•chol•y [MEL-ən-kol-ee] *noun* 1 sadness, dejection, gloom ▷ *adjective* 2 gloomy, dejected > **mel•an•cho'li•a** [-KOH-lee-ə] *noun former name for* **depression**
mé•lange [may-LAHNZH] *noun* mixture
mel•a•nin [MEL-ə-nin] *noun* dark pigment found in hair, skin, etc. of man
me•lee [MAY-lay] *noun* 1 confused fight among several people 2 confusion 3 turmoil
mel•io•rate [MEEL-yə-rayt] *verb* **-rat•ed, -rat•ing** improve > **mel•io•ra'tion** *noun* > **mel'io•rism** *noun* doctrine that the world can be improved by human effort
mel•lif•lu•ous [mə-LIF-loo-əs] *adjective* (of sound, voice) smooth, sweet
mel•low [MEL-oh] *adjective* **-er, -est** 1 ripe 2 softened by age, experience 3 soft, not harsh 4 genial, gay ▷ *verb* 5 make, become mellow
mel•o•dra•ma [MEL-ə-dram-ə] *noun* 1 play full of sensational and startling situations, often highly emotional 2 overly dramatic behavior, emotion > **mel•o•dra•mat'ic** [-drə-MAT-ik] *adjective*
mel•o•dy [MEL-ə-dee] *noun, plural* **-dies** 1 series of musical notes that make tune 2 sweet sound > **me•lo•di•ous** [mə-LOH-dee-əs] *adjective* 1 pleasing to the ear 2 tuneful
mel•on [MEL-ən] *noun* large, fleshy, juicy fruit
melt *verb* **melt•ed, melt•ed** *or* **mol•ten, melt•ing** 1 (cause to) become liquid by heat 2 dissolve 3 soften 4 waste away 5 blend (into) 6 disappear > **melting** *adjective* 1 softening 2 languishing 3 tender > **melt'down** *noun* in nuclear reactor, melting of fuel rods, with possible release of radiation
mem•ber [MEM-bər] *noun* 1 any of individuals making up body or society 2 limb 3 any part of complex whole
mem•brane [MEM-brayn] *noun* thin flexible tissue in plant or animal body
me•men•to [mə-MEN-toh] *noun, plural* **-tos** *or* **-toes** thing serving to remind, souvenir
mem•oir [MEM-wahr] *noun* 1 autobiography, personal history, biography 2 record of events
mem•o•ry [MEM-ə-ree] *noun, plural* **-ries** 1 faculty of recollecting, recalling to mind 2 recollection 3 thing remembered 4 length of time one can remember 5 commemoration 6 part or faculty of computer that stores information > **me•mo'ri•al** *adjective* 1 of, preserving memory ▷ *noun* 2 thing, esp. a monument, that serves to keep in memory > **mem'or•a•ble** *adjective* worthy of remembrance, noteworthy > **mem•o•ran'dum** *noun, plural* **-dums** *or* **-da** 1 note to help the memory, etc. 2 informal letter 3 note of contract > **me•mo'ri•al•ize** *verb transitive* **-ized, -iz•ing** commemorate > **mem'o•rize** *verb transitive* **-ized, -iz•ing** commit to memory > **memory stick** transportable data storage device

DICTIONARY

m

THESAURUS

4 GATHER, assemble, collect, come together, congregate, convene, muster
5 EXPERIENCE, bear, encounter, endure, face, go through, suffer, undergo
meeting *noun* 1 ENCOUNTER, assignation, confrontation, engagement, introduction, rendezvous, tryst
2 CONFERENCE, assembly, conclave, congress, convention, gathering, get-together (*informal*), reunion, session
melancholy *noun* 1 SADNESS, dejection, depression, despondency, gloom, low spirits, misery, sorrow, unhappiness
▷ *adjective* 2 SAD, depressed, despondent, dispirited, downhearted, gloomy, glum, miserable, mournful, sorrowful
melee *or* **mêlée** *noun* FIGHT, brawl, fracas, free-for-all (*informal*), rumpus, scrimmage, scuffle, skirmish, tussle
mellifluous *adjective* SWEET, dulcet, euphonious, honeyed, silvery, smooth, soft, soothing, sweet-sounding
mellow *adjective* 1 SOFT, delicate, full-flavored, mature, rich, ripe, sweet
▷ *verb* 2 MATURE, develop, improve, ripen, season, soften, sweeten
melodious *adjective* TUNEFUL, dulcet, euphonious, harmonious, melodic, musical, sweet-sounding
melodramatic *adjective* SENSATIONAL, blood-and-thunder, extravagant, histrionic, overdramatic, overemotional, theatrical
melody *noun* 1 TUNE, air, music, song, strain, theme
2 TUNEFULNESS, euphony, harmony, melodiousness, musicality
melt *verb* 1 DISSOLVE, fuse, liquefy, soften, thaw
2 (*often with away*) DISAPPEAR, disperse, dissolve, evanesce, evaporate, fade, vanish
3 SOFTEN, disarm, mollify, relax
member *noun* 1 REPRESENTATIVE, associate, fellow
2 LIMB, appendage, arm, extremity, leg, part
membership *noun* 1 MEMBERS, associates, body, fellows
2 PARTICIPATION, belonging, enrollment, fellowship
memento *noun* SOUVENIR, keepsake, memorial, relic, remembrance, reminder, token, trophy
memoir *noun* ACCOUNT, biography, essay, journal, life, monograph, narrative, record
memoirs *plural noun* AUTOBIOGRAPHY, diary, experiences, journals, life story, memories, recollections, reminiscences
memorable *adjective* NOTEWORTHY, celebrated, famous, historic, momentous, notable, remarkable, significant, striking, unforgettable
memorandum *noun* NOTE, communication, jotting, memo, message, minute, reminder
memorial *noun* 1 MONUMENT, memento, plaque, record, remembrance, souvenir
▷ *adjective* 2 COMMEMORATIVE, monumental
memorize *verb* REMEMBER, commit to memory, learn, learn by heart, learn by rote

men•ace [MEN-is] *noun* 1 threat ▷ *verb transitive* **-aced, -ac•ing** 2 threaten, endanger
mé•nage [may-NAHZH] *noun* persons of a household > **ménage à trois** [ah TWAH] arrangement in which three persons, e.g. two men and one woman, share sexual relations while occupying same household
me•nag•er•ie [mə-NAJ-ə-ree] *noun* exhibition, collection of wild animals
mend *verb transitive* 1 repair, patch 2 reform, correct, put right ▷ *verb intransitive* 3 improve, esp. in health ▷ *noun* 4 repaired breakage, hole **on the mend** regaining health
men•da•cious [men-DAY-shəs] *adjective* untruthful > **men•dac'i•ty** [-DAS-i-tee] *noun* (tendency to) untruthfulness
men•di•cant [MEN-di-kənt] *adjective* 1 begging ▷ *noun* 2 beggar > **men'di•can•cy** *noun* begging
me•ni•al [MEE-nee-əl] *adjective* 1 of work requiring little skill 2 of household duties or servants 3 servile ▷ *noun* 4 servant 5 servile person
men•in•gi•tis [men-in-JĪ-tis] *noun* inflammation of the membranes of the brain
me•nis•cus [mə-NIS-kəs] *noun* 1 curved surface of liquid 2 curved lens
men•o•pause [MEN-ə-pawz] *noun* final cessation of menstruation
men•stru•a•tion [men-stroo-AY-shən] *noun* approximately monthly discharge of blood and cellular debris from womb of nonpregnant woman > **men'stru•al** *adjective* > **men'stru•ate** *verb intransitive* **-at•ed, -at•ing**
men•su•ra•tion [men-shə-RAY-shən] *noun* measuring, esp. of areas
men•tal [MEN-təl] *adjective* 1 of, done by the mind 2 (*informal*) slightly mad > **men•tal'i•ty** *noun* state or quality of mind
men•thol [MEN-thawl] *noun* organic compound found in peppermint, used medicinally
men•tion [MEN-shən] *verb transitive* 1 refer to briefly, speak of ▷ *noun* 2 acknowledgment 3 reference to or remark about (person or thing) > **men'tion•a•ble** *adjective* fit or suitable to be mentioned
men'tor *noun* wise, trusted adviser, guide, teacher
men•u [MEN-yoo] *noun* 1 list of dishes to be served, or from which to order 2 *computing* list of options available to user
mer•can•tile [MUR-kən-tīl] *adjective* of, engaged in trade, commerce
mer•ce•nar•y [MUR-sə-ner-ee] *adjective* 1 influenced by greed 2 working merely for reward ▷ *noun* **-nar•ies** 3 hired soldier
mer•chant [MUR-chənt] *noun* 1 one engaged in trade 2 storekeeper > **mer'chan•dise** *noun* merchant's wares > **mer'chant•man** [-mən] *noun* trading ship > **merchant navy** ships engaged in a nation's commerce
mer•cu•ry [MUR-kyə-ree] *noun* 1 silvery metal, liquid at ordinary temperature, quicksilver 2 (**Mer•cu•ry**) Roman god of eloquence, messenger of the gods, etc. 3 planet nearest to sun > **mer•cu'ri•al** [-KYOO-ree-əl] *adjective* 1 relating to, containing mercury 2 lively, changeable
mer•cy [MUR-see] *noun, plural* **-cies** refraining from infliction of suffering by one who has right, power to inflict it, compassion > **mer'ci•ful** [-fəl] *adjective* > **mer'ci•less** [-lis] *adjective*

DICTIONARY • THESAURUS

memory *noun* 1 RECALL, recollection, remembrance, reminiscence, retention
2 COMMEMORATION, honor, remembrance
menace *noun* 1 THREAT, intimidation, warning
2 (*informal*) NUISANCE, annoyance, pest, plague, troublemaker
▷ *verb* 3 THREATEN, bully, frighten, intimidate, loom, lour *or* lower, terrorize
menacing *adjective* THREATENING, forbidding, frightening, intimidating, looming, louring *or* lowering, ominous
mend *verb* 1 REPAIR, darn, fix, patch, refit, renew, renovate, restore, retouch
2 IMPROVE, ameliorate, amend, correct, emend, rectify, reform, revise
3 HEAL, convalesce, get better, recover, recuperate
▷ *noun* 4 REPAIR, darn, patch, stitch
5 ▷ **on the mend** CONVALESCENT, getting better, improving, recovering, recuperating
mendacious *adjective* LYING, deceitful, deceptive, dishonest, duplicitous, fallacious, false, fraudulent, insincere, untruthful
menial *adjective* 1 UNSKILLED, boring, dull, humdrum, low-status, routine
▷ *noun* 2 SERVANT, attendant, drudge, flunky, lackey, underling
mental *adjective* 1 INTELLECTUAL, cerebral
2 (*informal*) INSANE, deranged, disturbed, mad, mentally ill, psychotic, unbalanced, unstable
mentality *noun* ATTITUDE, cast of mind, character, disposition, make-up, outlook, personality, psychology
mentally *adverb* IN THE MIND, in one's head, intellectually, inwardly, psychologically
mention *verb* 1 REFER TO, bring up, declare, disclose, divulge, intimate, point out, reveal, state, touch upon
▷ *noun* 2 ACKNOWLEDGMENT, citation, recognition, tribute
3 REFERENCE, allusion, indication, observation, remark
mentor *noun* GUIDE, adviser, coach, counselor, guru, instructor, teacher, tutor
menu *noun* BILL OF FARE, carte du jour (*French*)
mercantile *adjective* COMMERCIAL, trading
mercenary *adjective* 1 GREEDY, acquisitive, avaricious, grasping, money-grubbing (*informal*), sordid, venal
▷ *noun* 2 HIRELING, soldier of fortune
merchandise *noun* GOODS, commodities, produce, products, stock, wares
merchant *noun* TRADESMAN, broker, dealer, purveyor, retailer, salesman, seller, shopkeeper, supplier, trader, trafficker, vendor, wholesaler
merciful *adjective* COMPASSIONATE, clement, forgiving, generous, gracious, humane, kind, lenient, sparing, sympathetic, tender-hearted
merciless *adjective* CRUEL, barbarous, callous, hard-hearted, harsh, heartless, pitiless, ruthless, unforgiving
mercurial *adjective* LIVELY, active, capricious, changeable, impulsive, irrepressible, mobile, quicksilver, spirited, sprightly, unpredictable, volatile
mercy *noun* 1 COMPASSION, clemency,

mere [meer] *adjective, superlative* **mer•est** 1 only 2 not more than 3 nothing but > **mere'ly** *adverb*
mer•e•tri•cious [mer-i-TRISH-əs] *adjective* 1 superficially or garishly attractive 2 insincere
merge [murj] *verb* **merged, merg•ing** (cause to) lose identity or be absorbed > **mer'ger** *noun* 1 combination of business firms into one 2 absorption into something greater
me•rid•i•an [mə-RID-ee-ən] *noun* 1 circle of Earth passing through poles 2 imaginary circle in sky passing through celestial poles 3 highest point reached by star, etc. 4 period of greatest splendor ▷ *adjective* 5 of meridian 6 at peak of something
me•ringue [mə-RANG] *noun* 1 baked mixture of white of eggs and sugar 2 cake of this
mer'it *noun* 1 excellence, worth 2 quality of deserving reward ▷ *verb transitive* 3 deserve > **mer'its** *plural noun* excellence > **mer•i•to'ri•ous** *adjective* deserving praise
mer•maid [MUR-mayd] *noun* imaginary sea creature with upper part of woman and lower part of fish
mer•ry [MER-ee] *adjective* **-ri•er, -ri•est** joyous, cheerful > **mer'ri•ly** *adverb* > **mer'ri•ment** *noun*
mesh *noun* 1 (one of the open spaces of, or wires, etc. forming) network, net ▷ *verb* 2 entangle, become entangled 3 (of gears) engage ▷ *verb intransitive* 4 coordinate (with)
mes•mer•ism [MEZ-mə-riz-əm] *noun former term for* **hypnotism** > **mes'mer•ize** *verb transitive* **-ized, -iz•ing** 1 hypnotize 2 fascinate, hold spellbound
me•son [MEE-zon] *noun* elementary atomic particle
mess *noun* 1 untidy confusion 2 trouble, difficulty 3 place where military personnel group regularly eat together ▷ *verb intransitive* 4 make mess 5 putter (about) 6 *military* eat in a mess **mess up** 7 make dirty 8 botch 9 spoil > **mess'y** *adjective* **mess•i•er, mess•i•est**
mes•sage [MES-ij] *noun* 1 communication sent 2 meaning, moral > **mes'sen•ger** *noun* bearer of message
Mes•si•ah [mi-SĪ-ə] *noun* 1 Jews' promised deliverer 2 Christ > **mes•si•an'ic** [mes-ee-AN-ik] *adjective*
Messrs [MES-ərz] *pl. of* **Mr**
met *pt./pp. of* **meet**
meta- *combining form* change: *metamorphose; metathesis*
me•tab•o•lism [mə-TAB-ə-liz-əm] *noun* chemical process of living body > **met•a•bol'ic** *adjective* > **me•tab'o•lize** *verb transitive* **-lized, -liz•ing**
met•a•da•ta [MET-ə-day-tə] *noun* information that is held as a description of stored data
met•al [MET-l] *noun* 1 mineral substance, opaque, fusible and malleable, capable of conducting heat and electricity 2 object made of metal > **me•tal'lic** *adjective* > **met'al•lur•gist** *noun* > **met'al•lur•gy** *noun* scientific study of extracting, refining metals, and their structure and properties
met•a•mor•pho•sis [met-ə-MOR-fə-sis] *noun, plural* **-ses** change of shape, character, etc. > **met•a•mor'phic** *adjective* (esp. of rocks) changed in texture, structure by heat, pressure, etc. > **met•a•mor'phose** [-fohz] *verb transitive* **-phosed, -phos•ing** transform
met•a•phor [MET-ə-for] *noun* 1 figure of speech in which term is transferred to something it does not literally apply to 2 instance of this > **met•a•phor'i•cal** *adjective* figurative
met•a•phys•ics [met-ə-FIZ-iks] *noun* branch of philosophy concerned with being and knowing
me•tath•e•sis [mə-TATH-ə-sis] *noun, plural* **-ses** [-seez] transposition, esp. of letters in word, e.g.

DICTIONARY

m

THESAURUS

forbearance, forgiveness, grace, kindness, leniency, pity
2 BLESSING, boon, godsend
mere *adjective* SIMPLE, bare, common, nothing more than, plain, pure, sheer
meretricious *adjective* TRASHY, flashy, garish, gaudy, gimcrack, showy, tawdry, tinsel
merge *verb* COMBINE, amalgamate, blend, coalesce, converge, fuse, join, meet, mingle, mix, unite
merger *noun* UNION, amalgamation, coalition, combination, consolidation, fusion, incorporation
merit *noun* 1 WORTH, advantage, asset, excellence, goodness, integrity, quality, strong point, talent, value, virtue
▷ *verb* 2 DESERVE, be entitled to, be worthy of, earn, have a right to, rate, warrant
meritorious *adjective* PRAISEWORTHY, admirable, commendable, creditable, deserving, excellent, good, laudable, virtuous, worthy
merriment *noun* FUN, amusement, festivity, glee, hilarity, jollity, joviality, laughter, mirth, revelry
merry *adjective* CHEERFUL, blithe, carefree, convivial, festive, happy, jolly, joyous
mesh *noun* 1 NET, netting, network, tracery, web
▷ *verb* 2 ENGAGE, combine, connect, coordinate, dovetail, harmonize, interlock, knit
mesmerize *verb* ENTRANCE, captivate, enthrall, fascinate, grip, hold spellbound, hypnotize
mess *noun* 1 DISORDER, chaos, clutter, confusion, disarray, disorganization, jumble, litter, shambles, untidiness
2 DIFFICULTY, dilemma, fix (*informal*), hot water, jam (*informal*), muddle, pickle (*informal*), plight, predicament, tight spot
▷ *verb* 3 (*often with up*) DIRTY, clutter, disarrange, dishevel, muddle, pollute, scramble
4 (*often with with*) INTERFERE, meddle, play, tamper, tinker
message *noun* 1 COMMUNICATION, bulletin, communiqué, dispatch, letter, memorandum, note, tidings, word
2 POINT, idea, import, meaning, moral, purport, theme
messenger *noun* COURIER, carrier, delivery boy, emissary, envoy, errand-boy, go-between, herald, runner
messy *adjective* UNTIDY, chaotic, cluttered, confused, dirty, disheveled, disordered, disorganized, muddled, scuzzy (*slang*), shambolic, sloppy (*informal*)
metamorphosis *noun* TRANSFORMATION, alteration, change, conversion, mutation, transmutation
metaphor *noun* FIGURE OF SPEECH, allegory, analogy, image, symbol, trope

Old English *bridd* gives modern *bird*

mete [meet] *verb transitive* **met•ed, met•ing** measure **mete out** 1 distribute 2 allot as punishment

me•te•or [MEE-tee-ər] *noun* small, fast-moving celestial body, visible as streak of incandescence if it enters Earth's atmosphere > **me•te•or'ic** *adjective* 1 of, like meteor 2 brilliant but short-lived > **me'te•or•ite** *noun* fallen meteor

me•te•or•ol•o•gy [mee-tee-ə-ROL-ə-jee] *noun* study of Earth's atmosphere, esp. for weather forecasting

me•ter[1] [MEE-tər] *noun* 1 unit of length in decimal system 2 SI unit of length 3 rhythm of poem > **met'ric** *adjective* of system of weights and measures in which meter is a unit > **met'ri•cal** *adjective* of measurement of poetic meter

meter[2] *noun* 1 that which measures 2 instrument for recording consumption of gas, electricity, etc.

meth•ane [METH-ayn] *noun* inflammable gas, compound of carbon and hydrogen

meth•od [METH-əd] *noun* 1 way, manner 2 technique 3 orderliness, system > **me•thod'i•cal** *adjective* orderly > **meth•od•ol'o•gy** *noun, plural* **-gies** particular method or procedure

Meth•od•ist [METH-ə-dist] *noun* member of any of the churches originated by Wesley and his followers ▷ *adjective* > **Meth'od•ism** *noun*

me•tic•u•lous [mə-TIK-yə-ləs] *adjective* (over)particular about details

mé•tier [MAY-tyay] *noun* 1 profession, vocation 2 one's forte

me•ton•y•my [mi-TON-ə-mee] *noun* figure of speech in which thing is replaced by another associated with it, e.g. *the Oval Office* for *the president*

met•ro•nome [ME-trə-nohm] *noun* instrument that marks musical time by means of ticking pendulum

me•trop•o•lis [mi-TROP-ə-lis] *noun, plural* **-lis•es** chief city of a country, region > **met•ro•pol'i•tan** *adjective* 1 of metropolis ▷ *noun* 2 bishop with authority over other bishops of an ecclesiastical province

met•tle [MET-l] *noun* courage, spirit > **met'tle•some** [-səm] *adjective* high-spirited

mew [myoo] *noun* 1 cry of cat ▷ *verb intransitive* 2 utter this cry

mez•za•nine [MEZ-ə-neen] *noun* 1 in a theater, lowest balcony or forward part of balcony 2 in a building, low story between two other stories, esp. between first and second stories

mez•zo-so•pran•o [MET-soh-sə-PRAN-oh] *noun, plural* **-pran•os** voice, singer between soprano and contralto

Mg *chem.* magnesium

mi [mee] *noun* third sol-fa note

mi•as•ma [mī-AZ-mə] *noun, plural* **-mas** unwholesome or foreboding atmosphere

mi•ca [MĪ-kə] *noun* mineral found as glittering scales, plates

mi•crobe [MĪ-krohb] *noun* 1 minute organism 2 disease germ > **mi•cro'bi•al** *adjective*

mi•cro•chip [MĪ-kroh-chip] *noun* small wafer of silicon, etc. containing electronic circuits, chip

mi•cro•com•put•er [MĪ-kroh-kəm-pyoo-tər] *noun* computer having a central processing unit contained in one or more silicon chips

mi•cro•cosm [MĪ-krə-koz-əm] *noun* 1 miniature representation, model, etc. of some larger system 2 human beings, society as epitome of universe

mi•cro•fi•ber [MĪ-krə-fī-bər] *noun* very fine synthetic yarn

mi•cro•fiche [MĪ-krə-feesh] *noun* microfilm in sheet form

mi•cro•film [MĪ-krə-film] *noun* miniaturized recording of manuscript, book on roll of film

mi•crom•e•ter [mī-KROM-i-tər] *noun* instrument for measuring very small distances or angles

mi•cron [MĪ-kron] *noun* unit of length, one millionth of a meter

mi•cro•or•gan•ism [mī-kroh-OR-gə-niz-əm] *noun* organism of microscopic size

mi•cro•pay•ment [mī-kroh-PAY-mənt] *noun* system by which a user pays a small fee to access a specific area of a website

mi•cro•phone [MĪ-krə-fohn] *noun* instrument for amplifying, transmitting sounds

mi•cro•proc•es•sor [MĪ-kroh-pros-es-ər] *noun* integrated circuit acting as central processing unit in small computer

mi•cro•scope [MĪ-krə-skohp] *noun* instrument by which very small body is magnified and made visible > **mi•cro•scop'ic** [-SKOP-ik] *adjective* 1 of microscope 2 very small > **mi•cros'co•py** [-KROS-kə-pee] *noun* use of microscope

mi•cro•site [MĪ-kroh-sīt] *noun* website, often temporary, intended for a specific limited purpose

mi•cro•wave [MĪ-kroh-wayv] *noun* 1 electromagnetic wave with wavelength of a few centimeters, used in radar, cooking, etc. 2 microwave oven

mid *adjective* intermediate, in the middle of > **mid'day** *noun* noon > **mid'night** *noun* twelve o'clock at night > **mid'ship•man** [-mən] *noun*

DICTIONARY • THESAURUS

metaphorical *adjective* FIGURATIVE, allegorical, emblematic, symbolic

mete *verb* DISTRIBUTE, administer, apportion, assign, deal, dispense, portion

meteoric *adjective* SPECTACULAR, brilliant, dazzling, fast, overnight, rapid, speedy, sudden, swift

method *noun* 1 MANNER, approach, mode, modus operandi, procedure, process, routine, style, system, technique, way
2 ORDERLINESS, order, organization, pattern, planning, purpose, regularity, system

methodical *adjective* ORDERLY, businesslike, deliberate, disciplined, meticulous, organized, precise, regular, structured, systematic

meticulous *adjective* THOROUGH, exact, fastidious, fussy, painstaking, particular, precise, punctilious, scrupulous, strict

mettle *noun* COURAGE, bravery, fortitude, gallantry, life, nerve, pluck, resolution, spirit, valor, vigor

microbe *noun* MICROORGANISM, bacillus, bacterium, bug (*informal*), germ, virus

microscopic *adjective* TINY, imperceptible, infinitesimal, invisible, minuscule, minute, negligible

student, e.g. at U.S. Naval Academy, training for commission as naval officer > **mid'sum'mer** *noun* 1 middle of summer 2 summer solstice > **mid'way** *adjective, adverb* halfway > **mid'win'ter** *noun*

mid•dle [MID-l] *adjective* 1 equidistant from two extremes 2 medium, intermediate ▷ *noun* 3 middle point or part > **mid'dling** *adjective* 1 mediocre 2 moderate ▷ *adverb* **Middle Ages** period from about 1000 AD to the 15th century > **middle class** 1 social class of business, professional people, etc. 2 middle economic class > **mid'dle-class** *adjective* > **mid'dle•man** *noun* business person between producer and consumer

midge [mij] *noun* gnat or similar insect

midg•et [MIJ-it] *noun* very small person or thing

mid'riff *noun* middle part of body

midst *preposition* 1 in the middle of ▷ *noun* 2 middle **in the midst of** surrounded by, among

mid•wife [MID-wīf] *noun* trained person who assists at childbirth > **mid•wife'ry** [-WĪF-ə-ree] *noun* art, practice of this

mien [meen] *noun* person's bearing, demeanor or appearance

might[1] [mīt] *see* **may**

might[2] *noun* power, strength > **might'i•ly** *adverb* 1 strongly 2 powerfully > **might'y** *adjective* **might•i•er, might•i•est** 1 of great power 2 strong 3 valiant 4 important ▷ *adverb* 5 (*informal*) very

mi•graine [MĪ-grayn] *noun* severe headache, oft. with nausea and other symptoms

mi•grate [MĪ-grayt] *verb intransitive* **-grat•ed, -grat•ing** move from one place to another > **mi'grant** [-grənt] *noun, adjective* > **mi•gra'tion** *noun* 1 act of passing from one place, condition to another 2 number migrating together > **mi'gra•to•ry** [-grə-TOR-ee] *adjective* 1 of, capable of migration 2 (of animals) changing from one place to another according to season

mild [mīld] *adjective* **-er, -est** 1 not strongly flavored 2 gentle, merciful 3 calm or temperate > **mild'ly** *adverb* > **mild'ness** *noun*

mil•dew [MIL-doo] *noun* 1 destructive fungus on plants or things exposed to damp ▷ *verb* 2 become tainted, affect with mildew

mile [mīl] *noun* measure of length, 1760 yards (1.609 km) > **mile'age** *noun* 1 distance in miles 2 traveling expenses per mile 3 miles traveled (per gallon of gasoline) > **mile'stone** *noun* 1 stone marker showing distance 2 significant event, achievement

mi•lieu [mil-YUU] *noun* environment, condition in life

mil•i•tar•y [MIL-i-ter-ee] *adjective* 1 of, for, soldiers, armies or war ▷ *noun* 2 armed services > **mil'i•tan•cy** [-tən-see] *noun* > **mil'i•tant** *adjective* 1 aggressive, vigorous in support of cause 2 prepared, willing to fight > **mil'i•ta•rism** [-tə-riz-əm] *noun* enthusiasm for military force and methods > **mil'i•ta•rize** *verb transitive* **-rized, -riz•ing** convert to military use > **mi•li'tia** [-LISH-ə] *noun* military force of citizens serving full time only in emergencies

mil•i•tate [MIL-i-tayt] *verb intransitive* **-tat•ed, -tat•ing** (esp. with *against*) have strong influence, effect on

milk *noun* 1 white fluid with which mammals

midday *noun* NOON, noonday, twelve o'clock

middle *adjective* 1 CENTRAL, halfway, intermediate, intervening, mean, median, medium, mid
▷ *noun* 2 CENTER, focus, halfway point, heart, midpoint, midsection, midst

middle-class *adjective* BOURGEOIS, conventional, traditional

middling *adjective* 1 MEDIOCRE, indifferent, so-so (*informal*), tolerable, unexceptional, unremarkable
2 MODERATE, adequate, all right, average, fair, medium, modest, O.K. *or* okay (*informal*), ordinary, passable, serviceable

midget *noun* DWARF, pygmy *or* pigmy, shrimp (*informal*), Tom Thumb

midnight *noun* TWELVE O'CLOCK, dead of night, middle of the night, the witching hour

midst *noun* ▷ **in the midst of** AMONG, amidst, during, in the middle of, in the thick of, surrounded by

midway *adjective*
▷ *adverb* HALFWAY, betwixt and between, in the middle

might *noun* 1 POWER, energy, force, strength, vigor
2 ▷ **with might and main** FORCEFULLY, lustily, manfully, mightily, vigorously

mightily *adverb* 1 VERY, decidedly, exceedingly, extremely, greatly, highly, hugely, intensely, much
2 POWERFULLY, energetically, forcefully, lustily, manfully, strongly, vigorously

mighty *adjective* POWERFUL, forceful, lusty, robust, strapping, strong, sturdy, vigorous

migrant *noun* 1 WANDERER, drifter, emigrant, immigrant, itinerant, nomad, rover, traveler
▷ *adjective* 2 TRAVELING, drifting, immigrant, itinerant, migratory, nomadic, roving, shifting, transient, vagrant, wandering

migrate *verb* MOVE, emigrate, journey, roam, rove, travel, trek, voyage, wander

migration *noun* WANDERING, emigration, journey, movement, roving, travel, trek, voyage

migratory *adjective* NOMADIC, itinerant, migrant, peripatetic, roving, transient

mild *adjective* 1 GENTLE, calm, docile, easy-going, equable, meek, peaceable, placid
2 BLAND, smooth
3 CALM, balmy, moderate, temperate, tranquil, warm

mildness *noun* GENTLENESS, calmness, clemency, docility, moderation, placidity, tranquillity, warmth

milieu *noun* SURROUNDINGS, background, element, environment, locale, location, scene, setting

militant *adjective* AGGRESSIVE, active, assertive, combative, vigorous

military *adjective* 1 WARLIKE, armed, martial, soldierly
▷ *noun* 2 ARMED FORCES, army, forces, services

militate *verb* ▷ **militate against** COUNTERACT, be detrimental to, conflict with, counter, oppose, resist, tell against, weigh against

milk *verb* EXPLOIT, extract, pump, take

feed their young **2** fluid in some plants ▷ *verb transitive* **3** draw milk from **> milk'y** *adjective* **milk•i•er, milk•i•est** **1** containing, like milk **2** (of liquids) opaque, clouded **> milk'sop** *noun* **1** weak, effeminate fellow **2** milquetoast **> milk teeth** first set of teeth in young mammals **> Milky Way** luminous band of stars, etc. stretching across sky, the galaxy

mill *noun* **1** factory **2** machine for grinding, pulverizing grain, paper, etc. ▷ *verb transitive* **3** put through mill **4** cut fine grooves across edges of (e.g. coins) ▷ *verb intransitive* **5** move in confused manner, as cattle or crowds of people **> mill'er** *noun* **> mill'stone** *noun* **1** flat circular stone for grinding **2** heavy emotional or mental burden

mil•len•ni•um [mi-LEN-ee-əm] *noun, plural* **-ni•a** [-nee-ə] **1** period of a thousand years during which some claim Christ is to reign on earth **2** period of a thousand years **3** period of peace, happiness **> millennium bug** *noun computers* software problem arising from the change in date at the start of the 21st century

mil•let [MIL-it] *noun* a cereal grass

milli- *combining form* **1** thousandth: *milligram* **2** thousandth part of a gram

mil•li•bar [MIL-ə-bahr] *noun* unit of atmospheric pressure

mil•li•ner [MIL-ə-nər] *noun* maker of, dealer in women's hats, ribbons, etc. **> mil'li•ner•y** *noun* milliner's goods or work

mil•lion [MIL-yən] *noun* 1000 thousands **> mil•lion•aire'** *noun* **1** owner of a million dollars, etc. or more **2** very rich person **> mil'lionth** *adjective, noun*

mil•li•pede [MIL-ə-peed] *noun* small arthropod, like centipede, with jointed body and many pairs of legs

milque•toast [MILK-tohst] *noun* ineffectual person esp. one easily dominated

milt *noun* spawn of male fish

mime [mīm] *noun* **1** acting without the use of words **2** actor who does this ▷ *verb* **mimed, mim•ing** **3** act in mime

mim•ic [MIM-ik] *verb transitive* **-icked, -ick•ing** **1** imitate (person, manner, etc.) esp. for satirical effect ▷ *noun* **2** one who, or animal that does this, or is adept at it ▷ *adjective* **> mim'ic•ry** *noun, plural* **-ries** mimicking

min•a•ret [min-ə-RET] *noun* tall slender tower of mosque

mince [mins] *verb transitive* **minced, minc•ing** **1** cut, chop very small **2** soften or moderate (words, etc.) ▷ *verb intransitive* **minced, minc•ing** **3** walk, speak in affected manner ▷ *noun* **4** something minced **5** mincemeat **> minc'ing** *adjective* affected in manner **> mince'meat** *noun* mixture of minced apples, currants, spices, sometimes meat, etc. **> mince pie** pie containing mincemeat or mince

mind [mīnd] *noun* **1** thinking faculties as distinguished from the body, intellectual faculties **2** memory, attention **3** intention **4** taste **5** sanity ▷ *verb transitive* **6** take offense at **7** care for **8** attend to **9** be cautious, careful about (something) **10** be concerned, troubled about ▷ *verb intransitive* **11** be careful **12** heed **> mind'ful** [fəl] *adjective* **1** heedful **2** keeping in memory **> mind'less** [-lis] *adjective* stupid, careless **> mind candy** something that is entertaining or enjoyable but lacks depth or significance

mine¹ [mīn] *pronoun* belonging to me

mine² *noun* **1** deep hole for digging out coal, metals, etc. **2** in war, hidden deposit of explosive to blow up ship, etc. **3** land mine **4** profitable source ▷ *verb transitive* **mined, min•ing** **5** dig from mine **6** make mine in or under **7** place explosive mines in, on ▷ *verb intransitive* **mined, min•ing** **8** make, work in mine **> mi'ner** *noun* one who works in a mine **> mine'field** *noun* area of land or sea containing mines **> mine'lay•er** *noun* ship for laying mines **> mine'sweep•er** *noun* ship, helicopter for clearing away mines

min•er•al [MIN-ər-əl] *noun* **1** naturally occurring inorganic substance, esp. as obtained by mining ▷ *adjective* **2** of, containing, or like minerals **> min•er•al'o•gy** *noun* science of minerals **> mineral water** water containing some mineral, esp. natural or artificial kinds for drinking

---

advantage of

mill *noun* **1** FACTORY, foundry, plant, works
2 GRINDER, crusher
▷ *verb* **3** GRIND, crush, grate, pound, powder
4 SWARM, crowd, throng

millstone *noun* **1** GRINDSTONE, quernstone
2 BURDEN, affliction, albatross, encumbrance, load, weight

mime *verb* ACT OUT, gesture, represent, simulate

mimic *verb* **1** IMITATE, ape, caricature, do (*informal*), impersonate, parody
▷ *noun* **2** IMITATOR, caricaturist, copycat (*informal*), impersonator, impressionist

mimicry *noun* IMITATION, burlesque, caricature, impersonation, mimicking, mockery, parody

mince *verb* **1** CUT, chop, crumble, grind, hash
2 (*words*) TONE DOWN, moderate, soften, spare, weaken

mincing *adjective* AFFECTED, camp (*informal*), dainty, effeminate, foppish, precious, pretentious, sissy

mind *noun* **1** INTELLIGENCE, brain *or* brains (*informal*), gray matter (*informal*), intellect, reason, sense, understanding, wits
2 MEMORY, recollection, remembrance
3 INTENTION, desire, disposition, fancy, inclination, leaning, notion, urge, wish
4 SANITY, judgment, marbles (*informal*), mental balance, rationality, reason, senses, wits
5 ▷ **make up one's mind** DECIDE, choose, determine, resolve
▷ *verb* **6** TAKE OFFENSE, be affronted, be bothered, care, disapprove, dislike, object, resent
7 PAY ATTENTION, heed, listen to, mark, note, obey, observe, pay heed to, take heed
8 GUARD, attend to, keep an eye on, look after, take care of, tend, watch
9 BE CAREFUL, be cautious, be on guard *or* be on one's guard, be wary, take care, watch

mindful *adjective* AWARE, alert, alive to, careful, conscious, heedful, wary, watchful

mindless *adjective* STUPID, foolish, idiotic, inane, moronic (*offensive*), thoughtless, unthinking, witless

min•e•stro•ne [min-ə-STROH-nee] *noun* type of vegetable soup containing pasta

min•gle [MING-gəl] *verb* **-gled, -gling** mix, blend, unite, merge

min•i [MIN-ee] *noun* 1 something small or miniature 2 short skirt 3 small computer ▷ *adjective*

min•i•a•ture [MIN-ee-ə-chər] *noun* 1 small painted portrait 2 anything on small scale ▷ *adjective* 3 small-scale, minute

min•i•bus [MIN-ee-bus] *noun* small bus for about fifteen passengers

min•im [MIN-əm] *noun* 1 unit of fluid measure, one-sixtieth of a dram 2 *mus.* note half the length of semibreve

min•i•mize [MIN-ə-mīz] *verb transitive* **-mized, -miz•ing** bring to, estimate at smallest possible amount > **min'i•mal** [-məl] *adjective* > **min'i•mum** [-məm] *noun, plural* **-mums** 1 lowest size or quantity ▷ *adjective* 2 least possible

min•ion [MIN-yən] *noun* 1 favorite 2 servile follower

min•is•ter [MIN-ə-stər] *noun* 1 person in charge of government department 2 diplomatic representative 3 clergyman ▷ *verb intransitive* 4 attend to needs of, take care of > **min•is•te'ri•al** [-STEER-ee-əl] *adjective* > **min•is•tra'tion** *noun* rendering help, esp. to sick > **min'is•try** *noun, plural* **-tries** 1 office of clergyman 2 body of ministers forming government 3 act of ministering > **minister without portfolio** minister of state not in charge of specific department

mink [mingk] *noun* 1 variety of weasel 2 its (brown) fur

min•now [MIN-oh] *noun* small freshwater fish

mi•nor [MĪ-nər] *adjective* 1 lesser 2 under age ▷ *noun* 3 person below age of legal majority 4 scale in music > **mi•nor•i•ty** [mi-NOR-i-tee] *noun* 1 lesser number 2 smaller party voting together 3 ethical or religious group in a minority in any country 4 state of being a minor

Min•o•taur [MIN-ə-tor] *noun* fabled monster, half bull, half man

min•strel [MIN-strəl] *noun* medieval singer, musician, poet > **min•strels** performers in minstrel show > **minstrel show** formerly, an entertainment of songs and jokes provided by white performers with blackened faces

mint[1] *noun* 1 place where money is coined ▷ *verb transitive* 2 coin, invent

mint[2] *noun* aromatic plant

min•u•et [min-yoo-ET] *noun* 1 stately dance 2 music for it

mi•nus [MĪ-nəs] *preposition, adjective* 1 less, with the deduction of, deprived of 2 lacking 3 negative ▷ *noun* 4 the sign (-) denoting subtraction

mi•nus•cule [MIN-iss-skyool] *adjective* very small

mi•nute[1] [mī-NOOT] *adjective* **-nut•er, -nut•est** 1 very small 2 precise > **mi•nute'ly** *adverb* > **mi•nu•ti•ae** [mi-NOO-shee-ee] *plural noun* trifles, precise details

min•ute[2] [MIN-it] *noun* 1 60th part of hour or degree 2 moment 3 memorandum > **min•utes** record of proceedings of meeting, etc.

minx [mingks] *noun* bold, flirtatious girl

mir•a•cle [MIR-ə-kəl] *noun* 1 supernatural event 2 marvel > **mi•rac'u•lous** *adjective* > **miracle play** drama (esp. medieval) based on

DICTIONARY

m

THESAURUS

mine *noun* 1 PIT, colliery, deposit, excavation, shaft
2 SOURCE, abundance, fund, hoard, reserve, stock, store, supply, treasury, wealth
▷ *verb* 3 DIG UP, dig for, excavate, extract, hew, quarry, unearth

mingle *verb* 1 MIX, blend, combine, intermingle, interweave, join, merge, unite
2 ASSOCIATE, consort, fraternize, hang about *or* hang around, hobnob, rub shoulders (*informal*), socialize

miniature *adjective* SMALL, diminutive, little, minuscule, minute, scaled-down, tiny, toy

minimal *adjective* MINIMUM, least, least possible, nominal, slightest, smallest, token

minimize *verb* 1 REDUCE, curtail, decrease, diminish, miniaturize, prune, shrink
2 PLAY DOWN, belittle, decry, deprecate, discount, disparage, make light of *or* make little of, underrate

minimum *adjective* 1 LEAST, least possible, lowest, minimal, slightest, smallest
▷ *noun* 2 LEAST, lowest, nadir

minion *noun* FOLLOWER, flunky, hanger-on, henchman, hireling, lackey, underling, yes man

minister *noun* 1 CLERGYMAN, cleric, parson, pastor, preacher, priest, rector, vicar
▷ *verb* 2 ATTEND, administer, cater to, pander to, serve, take care of, tend

ministry *noun* 1 DEPARTMENT, bureau, council, office, quango
2 THE PRIESTHOOD, holy orders, the church

minor *adjective* SMALL, inconsequential, insignificant, lesser, petty, slight, trivial, unimportant
▷ *noun* UNDERAGE PERSON, adolescent, child, juvenile, teenager, youngster (*informal*), youth

minstrel *noun* MUSICIAN, bard, singer, songstress, troubadour

mint *verb* MAKE, cast, coin, produce, punch, stamp, strike

minuscule *adjective* TINY, diminutive, infinitesimal, little, microscopic, miniature, minute

minute[1] *noun* MOMENT, flash, instant, jiffy (*informal*), second, trice

minute[2] *adjective* 1 SMALL, diminutive, infinitesimal, little, microscopic, miniature, minuscule, tiny
2 PRECISE, close, critical, detailed, exact, exhaustive, meticulous, painstaking, punctilious

minutes *plural noun* RECORD, memorandum, notes, proceedings, transactions, transcript

minutiae *plural noun* DETAILS, finer points, ins and outs, niceties, particulars, subtleties, trifles, trivia

minx *noun* FLIRT, coquette, hussy

miracle *noun* WONDER, marvel, phenomenon, prodigy

miraculous *adjective* WONDERFUL, amazing, astonishing, astounding, extraordinary, incredible, phenomenal, prodigious, unaccountable, unbelievable

sacred subject
mi•rage [mi-RAHZH] *noun* deceptive image in atmosphere, e.g. of lake in desert
mire [mīr] *noun* 1 swampy ground, mud ▷ *verb transitive* **mired, mir•ing** 2 stick in, dirty with mud 3 entangle, involve
mir•ror [MIR-ər] *noun* 1 glass or polished surface reflecting images ▷ *verb transitive* 2 reflect
mirth [murth] *noun* merriment, gaiety > **mirth'ful** *adjective*
MIS management information system(s)
mis- *prefix* wrong(ly), bad(ly)
mis•an•thrope [MIS-ən-throhp] *noun* hater of mankind > **mis•an•throp'ic** *adjective*
mis•ap•pro•pri•ate [mis-ə-PROH-pree-ayt] *verb transitive* **-at•ed, -at•ing** 1 put to dishonest use 2 embezzle
mis•be•have' *verb* behave badly > **mis•be•hav'iour** *noun*
mis•cal'cu•late *verb transitive* calculate or judge wrongly > **mis•cal•cu•la'tion** *noun*
mis•car•ry [mis-KA-ree] *verb intransitive* **-ried, -ry•ing** 1 bring forth young prematurely 2 go wrong, fail > **mis•car'riage** [-KA-rij] *noun*
mis•cast' *verb* **-cast, -cast•ing** 1 distribute acting parts wrongly 2 assign to unsuitable role
mis•cel•la•ne•ous [mis-ə-LAY-nee-əs] *adjective* mixed, assorted > **mis'cel•la•ny** *noun, plural* **-nies** 1 collection of assorted writings in one book 2 medley
mis•chief [MIS-chif] *noun* 1 annoying behavior 2 inclination to tease, disturb 3 harm 4 source of harm or annoyance > **mis'chie•vous** [-chi-vəs] *adjective* 1 of a child, full of pranks 2 disposed to mischief 3 having harmful effect
mis•ci•ble [MIS-ə-bəl] *adjective* capable of mixing
mis•con•cep•tion [mis-kən-SEP-shən] *noun* wrong idea, belief
mis•con'duct *noun* immoral or unethical behaviour
mis•cre•ant [MIS-kree-ənt] *noun* wicked person, evildoer, villain
mis'deed *noun* wrongful act
mis•de•mean•or [mis-di-MEE-nər] *noun* 1 in law, offense less grave than a felony 2 minor offense
mi•ser [MĪ-zər] *noun* 1 hoarder of money 2 stingy person > **mi'ser•ly** *adjective* 1 avaricious 2 niggardly
mis•er•a•ble [MIZ-ər-ə-bəl] *adjective* 1 very unhappy, wretched 2 causing misery 3 worthless 4 squalid > **mis'er•y** *noun, plural* **-er•ies** 1 great unhappiness 2 distress 3 poverty

DICTIONARY • THESAURUS

mirage *noun* ILLUSION, hallucination, optical illusion
mire *noun* 1 SWAMP, bog, marsh, morass, quagmire
2 MUD, dirt, muck, ooze, slime
mirror *noun* 1 LOOKING-GLASS, glass, reflector ▷ *verb* 2 REFLECT, copy, echo, emulate, follow
mirth *noun* MERRIMENT, amusement, cheerfulness, fun, gaiety, glee, hilarity, jollity, joviality, laughter, revelry
mirthful *adjective* MERRY, blithe, cheerful, cheery, festive, happy, jolly, jovial, light-hearted, playful, sportive
misadventure *noun* MISFORTUNE, accident, bad luck, calamity, catastrophe, debacle, disaster, mishap, reverse, setback
misanthropic *adjective* ANTISOCIAL, cynical, malevolent, unfriendly
misapprehend *verb* MISUNDERSTAND, misconstrue, misinterpret, misread, mistake
misapprehension *noun* MISUNDERSTANDING, delusion, error, fallacy, misconception, misinterpretation, mistake
misappropriate *verb* STEAL, embezzle, misspend, misuse, peculate, pocket
misbehave *verb* ACT UP, be disobedient, make a fuss, make trouble, make waves
miscalculate *verb* MISJUDGE, blunder, err, overestimate, overrate, slip up, underestimate, underrate
miscarriage *noun* FAILURE, breakdown, error, mishap, perversion
miscarry *verb* FAIL, come to grief, fall through, go awry, go wrong, misfire
miscellaneous *adjective* MIXED, assorted, diverse, jumbled, motley, sundry, varied, various
miscellany *noun* ASSORTMENT, anthology, collection, jumble, medley, mélange (*French*), mixed bag, mixture, potpourri, variety
mischance *noun* MISFORTUNE, accident, calamity, disaster, misadventure, mishap
mischief *noun* 1 TROUBLE, impishness, misbehavior, monkey business (*informal*), naughtiness, shenanigans (*informal*), waywardness
2 HARM, damage, evil, hurt, injury, misfortune, trouble
mischievous *adjective* 1 NAUGHTY, impish, playful, puckish, rascally, roguish, sportive, troublesome, wayward
2 MALICIOUS, damaging, destructive, evil, harmful, hurtful, spiteful, vicious, wicked
misconception *noun* DELUSION, error, fallacy, misapprehension, misunderstanding
misconduct *noun* IMMORALITY, impropriety, malpractice, mismanagement, wrongdoing
miscreant *noun* WRONGDOER, criminal, rascal, reprobate, rogue, scoundrel, sinner, vagabond, villain
misdeed *noun* OFFENSE, crime, fault, misconduct, misdemeanor, sin, transgression, wrong
misdemeanor *noun* OFFENSE, fault, infringement, misdeed, peccadillo, transgression
miser *noun* SKINFLINT, cheapskate (*informal*), niggard, penny-pincher (*informal*), Scrooge
miserable *adjective* 1 UNHAPPY, dejected, depressed, despondent, disconsolate, forlorn, gloomy, sorrowful, woebegone, wretched
2 SQUALID, deplorable, lamentable, shameful, sordid, sorry, wretched
miserly *adjective* MEAN, avaricious, grasping, niggardly, parsimonious, penny-pinching (*informal*), stingy, tightfisted, ungenerous
misery *noun* UNHAPPINESS, anguish, depression, desolation, despair, distress, gloom, grief, sorrow, suffering, torment, woe
misfire *verb* FAIL, fall through, go wrong, miscarry

mis'fit *noun* esp. person not suited to surroundings or work
mis•for'tune *noun* (piece of) bad luck
mis•giv'ing *noun* (*often plural*) feeling of fear, doubt, etc.
mis•guid•ed [mis-GĪ-did] *adjective* foolish, unreasonable
mis'hap *noun* minor accident
mis•in•form' *verb transitive* give incorrect information to > **mis•in•for•ma'tion** *noun*
mis•judge' *verb* judge wrongly or unfairly > **mis•judg'ment** *noun*
mis•lay' *verb transitive* **-laid, -lay•ing** 1 put in place that cannot later be remembered 2 place wrongly
mis•lead [mis-LEED] *verb transitive* **-led, -lead•ing** 1 give false information to 2 lead astray > **misleading** *adjective* deceptive
mis•man'age *verb transitive* organize or run (something) badly > **mis•man'age•ment** *noun*
mis•no•mer [mis-NOH-mər] *noun* 1 wrong name or term 2 use of this
mi•sog•y•ny [mi-SOJ-ə-nee] *noun* hatred of women > **mi•sog'y•nist** *noun*
mis•place' *verb transitive* 1 mislay 2 put in the wrong place 3 give (trust or affection) inappropriately
mis'print *noun* printing error ▷ *verb transitive*
mis•pro•nounce' *verb* pronounce (a word) wrongly > **mis•pro•nun•ci•a'tion** *noun*
miss *verb transitive* 1 fail to hit, reach, find, catch, or notice 2 be late for 3 omit 4 notice or regret absence of 5 avoid ▷ *verb intransitive* (of engine) misfire ▷ *noun* 6 fact, instance of missing > **miss'ing** *adjective* 1 lost 2 absent
mis•sal [MIS-əl] *noun* book containing prayers, etc. of the Mass
mis•shap'en [mis-SHAY-pən] *adjective* badly shaped, deformed
mis•sile [MIS-əl] *noun* that which may be thrown, shot, homed to damage, destroy **guided missile** *see* **guide**
mis•sion [MISH-ən] *noun* 1 specific task or duty 2 calling in life 3 delegation 4 sending or being sent on some service 5 those sent > **mis'sion•ar•y** *noun, plural* **-ar•ies** one sent to a place, society to spread religion ▷ *adjective*
mis•sive [MIS-iv] *noun* letter
mis•spell' *verb* spell (a word) wrongly
mis•spent' *adjective* wasted or misused
mist *noun* water vapor in fine drops > **mist'y** *adjective* **mist•i•er, mist•i•est** 1 full of mist 2 dim 3 obscure
mis•take [mi-STAYK] *noun* 1 error, blunder ▷ *verb transitive* **-took** [-TUUK], **-tak•en, -tak•ing** 2 fail to understand 3 form wrong opinion

DICTIONARY

m

THESAURUS

misfit *noun* NONCONFORMIST, eccentric, fish out of water (*informal*), oddball (*informal*), square peg or square peg in a round hole (*informal*)
misfortune *noun* 1 BAD LUCK, adversity, hard luck, ill luck, infelicity
2 MISHAP, affliction, calamity, disaster, reverse, setback, tragedy, tribulation, trouble
misgiving *noun* UNEASE, anxiety, apprehension, distrust, doubt, qualm, reservation, suspicion, trepidation, uncertainty, worry
misguided *adjective* UNWISE, deluded, erroneous, ill-advised, imprudent, injudicious, misplaced, mistaken, unwarranted
mishandle *verb* MISMANAGE, botch, bungle, make a mess of, mess up (*informal*), muff
mishap *noun* ACCIDENT, calamity, misadventure, mischance, misfortune
misinform *verb* MISLEAD, deceive, misdirect, misguide
misinterpret *verb* MISUNDERSTAND, distort, misapprehend, misconceive, misconstrue, misjudge, misread, misrepresent, mistake
misjudge *verb* MISCALCULATE, overestimate, overrate, underestimate, underrate
mislay *verb* LOSE, lose track of, misplace
mislead *verb* DECEIVE, delude, fool, hoodwink, misdirect, misguide, misinform
misleading *adjective* CONFUSING, ambiguous, deceptive, disingenuous, evasive, false
mismanage *verb* MISHANDLE, botch, bungle, make a mess of, mess up, misconduct, misdirect, misgovern
misplace *verb* LOSE, lose track of, mislay
misprint *noun* MISTAKE, corrigendum, erratum, literal, typo (*informal*)
misquote *verb* MISREPRESENT, falsify, twist
misrepresent *verb* DISTORT, disguise, falsify, misinterpret
misrule *noun* DISORDER, anarchy, chaos, confusion, lawlessness, turmoil
miss¹ *verb* 1 OMIT, leave out, let go, overlook, pass over, skip
2 AVOID, escape, evade
3 LONG FOR, pine for, yearn for
▷ *noun* 4 MISTAKE, blunder, error, failure, omission, oversight
misshapen *adjective* DEFORMED, contorted, crooked, distorted, grotesque, malformed, twisted, warped
missile *noun* ROCKET, projectile, weapon
missing *adjective* ABSENT, astray, lacking, left out, lost, mislaid, misplaced, unaccounted-for
mission *noun* TASK, assignment, commission, duty, errand, job, quest, undertaking, vocation
missionary *noun* EVANGELIST, apostle, preacher
missive *noun* LETTER, communication, dispatch, epistle, memorandum, message, note, report
misspent *adjective* WASTED, dissipated, imprudent, profitless, squandered
mist *noun* FOG, cloud, film, haze, smog, spray, steam, vapor
mistake *noun* 1 ERROR, blunder, erratum, fault, faux pas, miscalculation, oversight, slip
▷ *verb* 2 MISUNDERSTAND, misapprehend, misconstrue, misinterpret, misjudge, misread
3 CONFUSE WITH, mix up with, take for
mistaken *adjective* WRONG, erroneous, false, faulty, inaccurate, incorrect, misguided, unsound, wide of the mark
mistakenly *adverb* INCORRECTLY, by mistake, erroneously, fallaciously, falsely, inaccurately, misguidedly, wrongly
mistimed *adjective* INOPPORTUNE, badly timed, ill-timed, untimely
mistreat *verb* ABUSE, harm, ill-treat, injure, knock about *or* knock around, maltreat, manhandle, misuse, molest
mistress *noun* LOVER, concubine, girlfriend, kept woman, paramour
mistrust *verb* 1 DOUBT, be wary of, distrust, fear,

about **4** take (person or thing) for another ▷ *verb intransitive* **-took** [-TUUK], **-tak•en, -tak•ing** **5** be in error

mis•ter [MIS-tər] *noun the full form of* **Mr**

mis•tle•toe [MIS-əl-toh] *noun* evergreen parasitic plant with white berries that grows on trees

mis•tress [MIS-tris] *noun* **1** object of man's illicit love **2** woman with mastery or control **3** woman owner **4** woman teacher **5** (*obsolete*) title given to married woman

mis•un•der•stand' *verb* fail to understand properly > **mis•un•der•stand'ing** *noun*

mis•use' *noun* **1** incorrect, improper, or careless use ▷ *verb transitive* **2** use wrongly **3** treat badly

mite [mīt] *noun* **1** very small insect **2** anything very small **3** small contribution but all one can afford

mi•ter [MĪ-tər] *noun* **1** bishop's headdress **2** joint between two pieces of wood, etc. meeting at right angles ▷ *verb transitive* **3** join with, shape for a miter joint **4** put miter on

mit•i•gate [MIT-i-gayt] *verb transitive* **-gat•ed, -gat•ing** make less severe > **mit•i•ga'tion** *noun*

mitt *noun* **1** baseball player's glove esp. for catcher, first baseman **2** (*slang*) hand

mit•ten [MIT-n] *noun* glove with two compartments, one for thumb and one for fingers

mix [miks] *verb transitive* **1** put together, combine, blend, mingle ▷ *verb intransitive* **2** be mixed **3** associate > **mixed** *adjective* composed of different elements, races, sexes, etc. > **mix'er** *noun* **1** one who, that which mixes **2** informal party intended to help guests meet one another > **mix'ture** [-chər] *noun* > **mixed-up** *adjective* **1** confused **2** emotionally unstable > **mix-up** *noun* **1** confused situation **2** a fight

mks units metric system of units based on the meter, kilogram and second

MMS Multimedia Messaging Service: method of transmitting graphics, video, or sound files and text messages over wireless networks

Mn *chem.* manganese

mne•mon•ic [ni-MON-ik] *adjective* **1** helping the memory ▷ *noun* **2** something intended to help the memory

Mo *chem.* molybdenum

moan [mohn] *noun* **1** low murmur, usually of pain ▷ *verb* **2** utter with moan, lament

moat [moht] *noun* **1** deep wide ditch esp. around castle ▷ *verb transitive* **2** surround with moat

mob *noun* **1** disorderly crowd of people **2** mixed assembly ▷ *verb transitive* **mobbed, mob•bing** **3** attack in mob **4** crowd around boisterously

mo•bile [MOH-bəl] *adjective* **1** capable of movement **2** easily moved or changed ▷ *noun* [moh-BEEL] **3** hanging structure of card, plastic, etc. designed to move in air currents > **mo•bil'i•ty** *noun* > **mobile home** large trailer, connected to utilities at a trailer park, etc., used as a residence > **mobile phone** *another name for* **cell phone**

mo•bi•lize [MOH-bə-līz] *verb* **-lized, -liz•ing** **1** (of armed services) prepare for military service ▷ *verb transitive* **2** organize for a purpose > **mo•bi•li•za'tion** [-ZAY-shən] *noun* in war time, calling up of men and women for active service

moc•ca•sin [MOK-ə-sin] *noun* Native American soft shoe, usu. of deerskin

mo•cha [MOH-kə] *noun* **1** type of strong, dark coffee **2** this flavor

mock [mok] *verb transitive* **1** make fun of,

suspect
▷ *noun* **2** SUSPICION, distrust, doubt, misgiving, skepticism, uncertainty, wariness

mistrustful *adjective* SUSPICIOUS, chary, cynical, distrustful, doubtful, fearful, hesitant, skeptical, uncertain, wary

misty *adjective* FOGGY, blurred, cloudy, dim, hazy, indistinct, murky, obscure, opaque, overcast

misunderstand *verb* MISINTERPRET, be at cross-purposes, get the wrong end of the stick, misapprehend, misconstrue, misjudge, misread, mistake

misunderstanding *noun* MISTAKE, error, misconception, misinterpretation, misjudgment, mix-up

misuse *noun* **1** WASTE, abuse, desecration, misapplication, squandering
▷ *verb* **2** WASTE, abuse, desecrate, misapply, prostitute, squander

mitigate *verb* EASE, extenuate, lessen, lighten, moderate, soften, subdue, temper

mitigation *noun* RELIEF, alleviation, diminution, extenuation, moderation, remission

mix *verb* **1** COMBINE, blend, cross, fuse, intermingle, interweave, join, jumble, merge, mingle
2 SOCIALIZE, associate, consort, fraternize, hang out (*informal*), hobnob, mingle
▷ *noun* **3** MIXTURE, alloy, amalgam, assortment, blend, combination, compound, fusion, medley

mixed *adjective* **1** COMBINED, amalgamated, blended, composite, compound, joint, mingled, united
2 VARIED, assorted, cosmopolitan, diverse, heterogeneous, miscellaneous, motley

mixed-up *adjective* CONFUSED, at sea, bewildered, distraught, disturbed, maladjusted, muddled, perplexed, puzzled, upset

mixture *noun* BLEND, amalgam, assortment, brew, compound, fusion, jumble, medley, mix, potpourri, variety

mix-up *noun* CONFUSION, mess, mistake, misunderstanding, muddle, tangle

mix up *verb* **1** COMBINE, blend, mix
2 CONFUSE, confound, muddle

moan *noun* **1** GROAN, lament, sigh, sob, wail, whine
2 (*informal*) GRUMBLE, complaint, gripe (*informal*), grouch (*informal*), grouse, protest, whine
▷ *verb* **3** GROAN, lament, sigh, sob, whine
4 (*informal*) GRUMBLE, bleat, carp, complain, groan, grouse, whine

mob *noun* **1** CROWD, drove, flock, horde, host, mass, multitude, pack, swarm, throng
2 (*slang*) GANG, crew (*informal*), group, lot, set
▷ *verb* **3** SURROUND, crowd around, jostle, set upon, swarm around

mobile *adjective* MOVABLE, itinerant, moving, peripatetic, portable, traveling, wandering

mobilize *verb* PREPARE, activate, call to arms, call up, get ready *or* make ready, marshal, organize, rally, ready

ridicule 2 mimic ▷ *verb intransitive* 3 scoff ▷ *noun* 4 act of mocking 5 laughingstock ▷ *adjective* 6 sham, imitation > **mock'er•y** *noun, plural* **-er•ies** 1 derision 2 travesty > **mocking bird** N Amer. bird that imitates songs of others > **mock-up** *noun* scale model

mode [mohd] *noun* 1 method, manner 2 prevailing fashion

mod•el [MOD-l] *noun* 1 miniature representation 2 pattern 3 person or thing worthy of imitation 4 person employed by artist to pose, or by dress designer to display clothing ▷ *verb transitive* **-eled, -el•ing** 5 make model of 6 mold 7 display (clothing) for dress designer

mo•dem [MOH-dem] *noun* device for connecting two computers via a telephone line

mod•er•ate [MOD-ər-it] *adjective* 1 not going to extremes, temperate, medium ▷ *noun* 2 person of moderate views ▷ *verb* [-ayt] 3 make, become less violent or excessive 4 preside over meeting, etc. > **mod'er•a•tor** *noun* 1 mediator 2 president of Presbyterian body 3 arbitrator 4 person presiding over panel discussion

mod•ern [MOD-ərn] *adjective* 1 of present or recent times 2 in, of current fashion ▷ *noun* 3 person living in modern times > **mod'ern•ism** *noun* (support of) modern tendencies, thoughts, etc. > **mod•ern•i•za'tion** [-ZAY-shən] *noun* > **mod'ern•ize** [-īz] *verb transitive* **-ized, -iz•ing** bring up to date

mod•est [MOD-ist] *adjective* 1 not overrating one's qualities or achievements 2 shy 3 moderate, not excessive 4 decorous, decent > **mod'es•ty** *noun*

mod•i•cum [MOD-i-kəm] *noun* small quantity

mod•i•fy [MOD-ə-fī] *verb* **-fied, -fy•ing** (*mainly transitive*) 1 change slightly 2 tone down > **mod•i•fi•ca'tion** *noun* > **mod'i•fi•er** [-fī-ər] *noun* esp. word qualifying another

mod•u•late [MOJ-ə-layt] *verb transitive* **-lat•ed, -lat•ing** 1 regulate 2 vary in tone ▷ *verb intransitive* **-lat•ed, -lat•ing** 3 change key of music > **mod•u•la'tion** *noun* 1 modulating 2 *electronics* superimposing signals onto high-frequency carrier

mod•ule [MOJ-ool] *noun* (detachable) unit, section, component with specific function

mo•dus op•e•ran•di [MOH-dəs op-ə-RAN-dee] *Lat.* method of operating, tackling task

mo•gul [MOH-gəl] *noun* 1 important or powerful person 2 bump in ski slope

mo•hair [MOH-hair] *noun* 1 fine cloth of goat hair 2 hair of Angora goat

mo•hel [MOH-əl] *noun* in Jewish tradition, person who performs rite of circumcision

moi•e•ty [MOI-i-tee] *noun, plural* **-ties** a half

moist *adjective* **-er, -est** damp, slightly wet > **moist'en** [MOI-sən] *verb* > **mois'ture** [-chər] *noun* liquid, esp. diffused or in drops

mock *verb* 1 LAUGH AT, deride, jeer, make fun of, poke fun at, ridicule, scoff, scorn, sneer, taunt, tease
2 MIMIC, ape, caricature, imitate, lampoon, parody, satirize
▷ *adjective* 3 IMITATION, artificial, dummy, fake, false, feigned, phoney *or* phony (*informal*), pretended, sham, spurious

mockery *noun* 1 DERISION, contempt, disdain, disrespect, insults, jeering, ridicule, scoffing, scorn
2 FARCE, disappointment, joke, letdown

mocking *adjective* SCORNFUL, contemptuous, derisive, disdainful, disrespectful, sarcastic, sardonic, satirical, scoffing

mode *noun* 1 METHOD, form, manner, procedure, process, style, system, technique, way
2 FASHION, craze, look, rage, style, trend, vogue

model *noun* 1 REPRESENTATION, copy, dummy, facsimile, image, imitation, miniature, mock-up, replica
2 PATTERN, archetype, example, ideal, original, paradigm, paragon, prototype, standard
3 SITTER, poser, subject
▷ *verb* 4 SHAPE, carve, design, fashion, form, mold, sculpt
5 SHOW OFF, display, sport (*informal*), wear

moderate *adjective* 1 MILD, controlled, gentle, limited, middle-of-the-road, modest, reasonable, restrained, steady
2 AVERAGE, fair, indifferent, mediocre, middling, ordinary, passable, so-so (*informal*), unexceptional
▷ *verb* 3 REGULATE, control, curb, ease, modulate, restrain, soften, subdue, temper, tone down

moderately *adverb* REASONABLY, fairly, passably, quite, rather, slightly, somewhat, tolerably

moderation *noun* RESTRAINT, fairness, reasonableness, temperance

modern *adjective* CURRENT, contemporary, fresh, new, newfangled, novel, present-day, recent, up-to-date

modernity *noun* NOVELTY, currency, freshness, innovation, newness

modernize *verb* UPDATE, make over, rejuvenate, remake, remodel, renew, renovate, revamp

modest *adjective* 1 UNPRETENTIOUS, bashful, coy, demure, diffident, reserved, reticent, retiring, self-effacing, shy
2 MODERATE, fair, limited, middling, ordinary, small, unexceptional

modesty *noun* RESERVE, bashfulness, coyness, demureness, diffidence, humility, reticence, shyness, timidity

modicum *noun* LITTLE, bit, crumb, drop, fragment, scrap, shred, touch

modification *noun* CHANGE, adjustment, alteration, qualification, refinement, revision, variation

modify *verb* 1 CHANGE, adapt, adjust, alter, convert, reform, remodel, revise, rework
2 TONE DOWN, ease, lessen, lower, moderate, qualify, restrain, soften, temper

modish *adjective* FASHIONABLE, chic, contemporary, cool (*informal*), current, in, phat (*slang*), smart, stylish, trendy (*informal*), up-to-the-minute, voguish

modulate *verb* ADJUST, attune, balance, regulate, tune, vary

mogul *noun* TYCOON, baron, big cheese (*informal*), big shot (*informal*), magnate, V.I.P.

moist *adjective* DAMP, clammy, dewy, humid, soggy, wet

moisten *verb* DAMPEN, damp, moisturize, soak, water, wet

mo•lar [MOH-lər] *adjective* 1 (of teeth) for grinding ▷ *noun* 2 molar tooth
mo•las•ses [mə-LAS-iz] *noun* thick brown syrup, byproduct of process of sugar refining
mold[1] [mohld] *noun* 1 hollow object in which metal, etc. is cast 2 pattern for shaping 3 character 4 shape, form ▷ *verb transitive* 5 shape or pattern > **mold'ing** *noun* 1 molded object 2 ornamental edging 3 decoration
mold[2] *noun* fungoid growth caused by dampness > **mold'y** *adjective* **mold•i•er, mold•i•est** stale, musty
mold[3] *noun* loose soil rich in organic matter > **mold'er** *verb intransitive* decay or cause to decay into dust
mole[1] [mohl] *noun* small dark protuberant spot on the skin
mole[2] *noun* 1 small burrowing animal 2 spy, informer
mole[3] *noun* SI unit of amount of substance
mol•e•cule [MOL-ə-kyool] *noun* 1 simplest freely existing chemical unit, composed of two or more atoms 2 very small particle > **mo•lec'u•lar** *adjective* of, inherent in molecules
mo•lest [mə-LEST] *verb transitive* 1 pester, interfere with so as to annoy or injure 2 make indecent sexual advances esp. to a child
mol•li•fy [MOL-ə-fī] *verb transitive* **-fied, -fy•ing** calm down, placate, soften > **mol•li•fi•ca'tion** *noun*
mol•lusk [MOL-əsk] *noun* soft-bodied, usu. hard-shelled animal, e.g. snail, oyster
molt [mohlt] *verb* 1 cast or shed fur, feathers, etc. ▷ *noun* 2 molting
molten *see* **melt**
mo•lyb•de•num [mə-LIB-də-nəm] *noun* silver-white metallic element
mo•ment [MOH-mənt] *noun* 1 very short space of time 2 (present) point in time > **mo•men•tar'i•ly** *adverb* > **mo'men•tar•y** *adjective* lasting only a moment
mo•men•tous [moh-MEN-təs] *adjective* of great importance
mo•men•tum [moh-MEN-təm] *noun* 1 force of a moving body 2 impetus gained from motion
mon•arch [MON-ərk] *noun* sovereign ruler of a country > **mo•nar'chi•cal** *adjective* > **mon'ar•chist** *noun* supporter of monarchy > **mon'ar•chy** *noun, plural* **-chies** 1 nation ruled by sovereign 2 monarch's rule
mon•as•ter•y [MON-ə-ster-ee] *noun, plural* **-ter•ies** house occupied by members of religious order > **mo•nas•tic** [mə-NAS-tik] *adjective* 1 relating to monks, nuns, or monasteries ▷ *noun* 2 monk, recluse
mon•ey [MUN-ee] *noun, plural* **-eys** *or* **-ies** banknotes, coin, etc., used as medium of exchange > **mon•e•ta•rism** [MON-ə-tə-riz-əm] *noun* theory that inflation is caused by increase in money supply > **mon'e•ta•rist** *noun, adjective* > **mon'e•tar•y** *adjective* > **mon•eyed, mon•ied** [MUN-eed] *adjective* rich
mon•gol•ism [MONG-gə-liz-əm] *noun a former and non-medical name for* **Down syndrome**
mon•goose [MON-goos] *noun, plural* **-goos•es** small animal of Asia and Africa noted for killing snakes
mon•grel [MONG-grəl] *noun* 1 animal, esp. dog, of mixed breed 2 hybrid ▷ *adjective*
mon•i•tor [MON-i-tər] *noun* 1 person or device that checks, controls, warns or keeps record of something 2 pupil assisting teacher with conduct of class 3 television set used in a studio for checking program being transmitted 4 *computing* cathode ray tube with screen for viewing data 5 type of large lizard ▷ *verb transitive* 6 watch, check on > **mon'i•to•ry** [-tor-ee] *adjective* giving warning
monk [munk] *noun* one of a religious community of men living apart under vows

moisture *noun* DAMPNESS, dew, liquid, water, wetness
mold[1] *noun* 1 CAST, pattern, shape
2 DESIGN, build, construction, fashion, form, format, kind, pattern, shape, style
3 NATURE, caliber, character, kind, quality, sort, stamp, type
▷ *verb* 4 SHAPE, construct, create, fashion, forge, form, make, model, sculpt, work
5 INFLUENCE, affect, control, direct, form, make, shape
mold[2] *noun* FUNGUS, blight, mildew, mustiness
moldy *adjective* STALE, bad, blighted, decaying, fusty, mildewed, musty, rotten
molecule *noun* PARTICLE, jot, speck
molest *verb* 1 ANNOY, badger, beset, bother, disturb, harass, persecute, pester, plague, torment, worry
2 ABUSE, attack, harm, hurt, ill-treat, interfere with, maltreat
mollify *verb* PACIFY, appease, calm, conciliate, de-stress, placate, quiet, soothe, sweeten
moment *noun* 1 INSTANT, flash, jiffy (*informal*), second, split second, trice, twinkling
2 TIME, juncture, point, stage
momentarily *adverb* BRIEFLY, for a moment, temporarily
momentary *adjective* SHORT-LIVED, brief, fleeting, passing, short, temporary, transitory
momentous *adjective* SIGNIFICANT, critical, crucial, fateful, historic, important, pivotal, vital, weighty
momentum *noun* IMPETUS, drive, energy, force, power, propulsion, push, strength, thrust
monarch *noun* RULER, emperor *or* empress, king, potentate, prince *or* princess, queen, sovereign
monarchy *noun* 1 SOVEREIGNTY, autocracy, kingship, monocracy, royalism
2 KINGDOM, empire, principality, realm
monastery *noun* ABBEY, cloister, convent, friary, nunnery, priory
monastic *adjective* MONKISH, ascetic, cloistered, contemplative, hermit-like, reclusive, secluded, sequestered, withdrawn
monetary *adjective* FINANCIAL, budgetary, capital, cash, fiscal, pecuniary
money *noun* CASH, capital, coin, currency, hard cash, legal tender, riches, silver, wealth
mongrel *noun* 1 HYBRID, cross, crossbreed, half-breed
▷ *adjective* 2 HYBRID, crossbred
monitor *noun* 1 WATCHDOG, guide, invigilator, supervisor
▷ *verb* 2 CHECK, follow, keep an eye on, keep tabs on, keep track of, observe, stalk, survey, watch

> **monk'ish** *adjective*
mon•key [MUN-kee] *noun, plural* **-keys** 1 long-tailed primate 2 mischievous child ▷ *verb intransitive* **-keyed, -key•ing** 3 meddle, fool (with) > **monkey wrench** one with adjustable jaw
mono- *combining form* single: *monosyllabic*
mon•o•chrome [MON-ə-krohm] *noun* 1 representation in one color ▷ *adjective* 2 of one color > **mon•o•chro•mat'ic** *adjective*
mon•o•cle [MON-ə-kəl] *noun* single eyeglass
mo•noc•u•lar [mə-NOK-yə-lər] *adjective* one-eyed
mo•nog•a•my [mə-NOG-ə-mee] *noun* custom of being married to one person at a time > **mo•nog'a•mous** *adjective*
mon•o•gram [MON-ə-gram] *noun* design of one or more letters interwoven
mon•o•graph [MON-ə-graf] *noun* short scholarly book on single subject
mon•o•lith [MON-ə-lith] *noun* monument consisting of single standing stone > **mon•o•lith'ic** *adjective* 1 of or like a monolith 2 massive, inflexible
mon•o•logue [MON-ə-lawg] *noun* 1 dramatic composition with only one speaker 2 long speech by one person
mon•o•ma•ni•a [mon-ə-MAY-nee-ə] *noun* excessive preoccupation with one thing
mo•nop•o•ly [mə-NOP-ə-lee] *noun, plural* **-lies** exclusive control of commerce, privilege, etc. > **mo•nop'o•lize** *verb transitive* **-lized, -liz•ing** claim, take exclusive possession of
mon•o•rail [MON-ə-rayl] *noun* railway with cars running on or suspended from single rail
mon•o•the•ism [MON-ə-thee-iz•əm] *noun* belief in only one God
mon•o•tone [MON-ə-tohn] *noun* continuing on one note > **mo•not•o•nous** [mə-NOT-n-əs] *adjective* lacking in variety, dull, wearisome > **mo•not'o•ny** *noun*
mon•soon' *noun* 1 seasonal wind of SE Asia 2 very heavy rainfall season
mon•ster [MON-stər] *noun* 1 fantastic imaginary beast 2 misshapen animal or plant 3 very wicked person 4 huge person, animal or thing ▷ *adjective* 5 huge > **mon•stros'i•ty** *noun* 1 monstrous being 2 deformity 3 distortion > **mon'strous** [-strəs] *adjective* 1 of, like monster 2 unnatural 3 enormous 4 horrible
mon•tage [mon-TAHZH] *noun* 1 elements of two or more pictures imposed upon a single background to give a unified effect 2 method of editing a film
month [munth] *noun* 1 one of twelve periods into which the year is divided 2 period of moon's revolution around Earth > **month'ly** *adjective* 1 happening or payable once a month ▷ *adverb* 2 once a month ▷ *noun* 3 magazine published every month
mon•u•ment [MON-yə-mənt] *noun* anything that commemorates, esp. a building or statue > **mon•u•ment'al** [-MEN-tl] *adjective* 1 vast, lasting 2 of or serving as monument
mooch *verb intransitive (slang)* 1 borrow without intending to repay 2 beg
mood[1] *noun* state of mind and feelings > **mood'y** *adjective* **mood•i•er, mood•i•est** 1 gloomy, pensive 2 changeable in mood
mood[2] *noun grammar* form indicating function of verb
moon *noun* 1 satellite that takes lunar month to revolve around Earth 2 any secondary planet ▷ *verb intransitive* 3 go about dreamily > **moon'light** *noun* > **moon'shine** *noun (informal)* 1 whiskey, esp. corn liquor, illicitly distilled 2 nonsense 3 moonlight > **moon'stone** *noun* transparent semiprecious stone
moor[1] *noun* tract of open uncultivated land, often hilly and overgrown with heath

DICTIONARY

m

THESAURUS

monk *noun* FRIAR, brother
monkey *noun* 1 SIMIAN, primate
2 RASCAL, devil, imp, rogue, scamp
▷ *verb* 3 FOOL, meddle, mess, play, tinker
monolithic *adjective* HUGE, colossal, impenetrable, intractable, massive, monumental, solid
monologue *noun* SPEECH, harangue, lecture, sermon, soliloquy
monopolize *verb* CONTROL, corner the market in, dominate, hog (*slang*), keep to oneself, take over
monotonous *adjective* TEDIOUS, boring, dull, humdrum, mind-numbing, repetitive, tiresome, unchanging, wearisome
monotony *noun* TEDIUM, boredom, monotonousness, repetitiveness, routine, sameness, tediousness
monster *noun* 1 BRUTE, beast, demon, devil, fiend, villain
2 FREAK, monstrosity, mutant
3 GIANT, colossus, mammoth, titan
▷ *adjective* 4 HUGE, colossal, enormous, gigantic, immense, mammoth, massive, stupendous, tremendous
monstrosity *noun* EYESORE, freak, horror, monster
monstrous *adjective* 1 UNNATURAL, fiendish, freakish, frightful, grotesque, gruesome, hideous, horrible
2 OUTRAGEOUS, diabolical, disgraceful, foul, inhuman, intolerable, scandalous, shocking
3 HUGE, colossal, enormous, immense, mammoth, massive, prodigious, stupendous, tremendous
monument *noun* MEMORIAL, cairn, cenotaph, commemoration, gravestone, headstone, marker, mausoleum, shrine, tombstone
monumental *adjective* 1 IMPORTANT, awesome, enormous, epoch-making, historic, majestic, memorable, significant, unforgettable
2 (*informal*) IMMENSE, colossal, great, massive, staggering
mood *noun* STATE OF MIND, disposition, frame of mind, humor, spirit, temper
moody *adjective* 1 SULLEN, gloomy, glum, ill-tempered, irritable, morose, sad, sulky, temperamental, touchy
2 CHANGEABLE, capricious, erratic, fickle, flighty, impulsive, mercurial, temperamental, unpredictable, volatile
moon *noun* 1 SATELLITE
▷ *verb* 2 IDLE, daydream, languish, mope, waste time
moor[1] *noun* MOORLAND, heath
moor[2] *verb* TIE UP, anchor, berth, dock, lash,

moor² *verb* secure (ship) with chains or ropes > **moor'ings** *plural noun* 1 ropes, etc. for mooring 2 something providing stability, security

moose [moos] *noun* N Amer. deer with large antlers

moot *adjective* 1 that is open to argument, debatable 2 purely academic

mop *noun* 1 bundle of yarn, cloth, etc. on end of stick, used for cleaning 2 tangle (of hair, etc.) ▷ *verb transitive* **mopped, mop•ping** 3 clean, wipe with mop or other absorbent material

mope [mohp] *verb intransitive* **moped, mop•ing** be gloomy, apathetic

mo•ped [MOH-ped] *noun* light motorized bicycle

mo•raine [mə-RAYN] *noun* accumulated mass of debris, earth, stones, etc., deposited by glacier

mor•al [MOR-əl] *adjective* 1 pert. to right and wrong conduct 2 of good conduct ▷ *noun* 3 practical lesson, e.g. of fable > **mor•als** habits with respect to right and wrong, esp. in matters of sex > **mor'al•ist** *noun* teacher of morality > **mo•ral•i•ty** [mə-RAL-ə-tee] *noun* 1 good moral conduct 2 moral goodness or badness 3 kind of medieval drama, containing moral lesson > **mor'al•ize** *verb intransitive* **-ized, -iz•ing** 1 write, think about moral aspect of things ▷ *verb transitive* **-ized, -iz•ing** 2 interpret morally **moral victory** triumph that is psychological rather than practical

mo•rale [mə-RAL] *noun* degree of confidence, hope of person or group

mo•rass [mə-RAS] *noun* 1 marsh 2 mess

mor•a•to•ri•um [mor-ə-TOR-ee-əm] *noun, plural* **-ri•ums** 1 act authorizing postponement of payments, etc. 2 delay

mor'bid *adjective* 1 unduly interested in death 2 gruesome 3 diseased

mor•dant [MOR-dnt] *adjective* 1 biting 2 corrosive 3 scathing ▷ *noun* 4 substance that fixes dyes

more [mor] *adjective* 1 greater in quantity or number 2 *comp. of* **many** or **much** ▷ *adverb* 3 to a greater extent 4 in addition ▷ *pronoun* 5 greater or additional amount or number > **more•o'ver** *adverb* besides, further

mor•ga•nat•ic marriage [mor-gə-NAT-ik] marriage of king or prince in which wife does not share husband's rank or possessions and children do not inherit from father

morgue [morg] *noun* 1 mortuary 2 newspaper reference file or file room

mor•i•bund [MOR-ə-bund] *adjective* 1 dying 2 stagnant

Mor•mon [MOR-mən] *noun* member of religious sect founded in U.S.

morn'ing *noun* early part of day until noon > **morning-after pill** woman's contraceptive pill for use within hours after sexual intercourse > **morning glory** plant with trumpet-shaped flowers that close in late afternoon

mo•roc•co [mə-ROK-oh] *noun* goatskin leather

mo•ron [MOR-on] *noun* 1 (formerly) person with low intelligence quotient 2 (*informal*) fool > **mo•ron'ic** *adjective*

mo•rose [mə-ROHS] *adjective* sullen, moody

morph [morf] *verb* cause or undergo change of shape or appearance via computer graphic effects

mor•phine [MOR-feen] *noun* narcotic extract of opium used to induce sleep and relieve pain

mor•phol•o•gy [mor-FOL-ə-jee] *noun* 1 science of structure of organisms 2 form and structure of words of a language

Morse [mors] *noun* system of telegraphic signaling in which letters of alphabet are represented by combinations of dots and dashes, or short and long flashes

make fast, secure

moot *adjective* 1 DEBATABLE, arguable, contestable, controversial, disputable, doubtful, undecided, unresolved, unsettled ▷ *verb* 2 BRING UP, broach, propose, put forward, suggest

mop *noun* 1 SQUEEGEE, sponge, swab 2 MANE, shock, tangle, thatch

mope *verb* BROOD, fret, languish, moon, pine, pout, sulk

mop up *verb* CLEAN UP, soak up, sponge, swab, wash, wipe

moral *adjective* 1 GOOD, decent, ethical, high-minded, honorable, just, noble, principled, right, virtuous ▷ *noun* 2 LESSON, meaning, message, point, significance

morale *noun* CONFIDENCE, esprit de corps, heart, self-esteem, spirit

morality *noun* 1 INTEGRITY, decency, goodness, honesty, justice, righteousness, virtue 2 STANDARDS, conduct, ethics, manners, morals, mores, philosophy, principles

morals *plural noun* MORALITY, behavior, conduct, ethics, habits, integrity, manners, mores, principles, scruples, standards

morass *noun* 1 MARSH, bog, fen, quagmire, slough, swamp 2 MESS, confusion, mix-up, muddle, tangle

moratorium *noun* POSTPONEMENT, freeze, halt, standstill, suspension

morbid *adjective* 1 UNWHOLESOME, ghoulish, gloomy, melancholy, sick, somber, unhealthy 2 GRUESOME, dreadful, ghastly, grisly, hideous, horrid, macabre

mordant *adjective* SARCASTIC, biting, caustic, cutting, incisive, pungent, scathing, stinging, trenchant

more *adjective* 1 EXTRA, added, additional, further, new, other, supplementary ▷ *adverb* 2 TO A GREATER EXTENT, better, further, longer

moreover *adverb* FURTHERMORE, additionally, also, as well, besides, further, in addition, too

morgue *noun* MORTUARY

moribund *adjective* DECLINING, on its last legs, stagnant, waning, weak

morning *noun* DAWN, a.m., break of day, daybreak, forenoon, morn (*poetic*), sunrise

moron *noun* FOOL, blockhead, cretin (*offensive*), dork (*slang*), dunce, dunderhead, halfwit, idiot, imbecile, oaf, schmuck (*slang*)

moronic *adjective* IDIOTIC, cretinous (*offensive*), foolish, halfwitted, imbecilic, mindless, stupid, unintelligent

morose *adjective* SULLEN, depressed, dour, gloomy, glum, ill-tempered, moody, sour, sulky, surly, taciturn

mor•sel [MOR-səl] *noun* fragment, small piece
mor•tal [MOR-tl] *adjective* 1 subject to death 2 causing death ▷ *noun* 3 mortal creature > **mor•tal'i•ty** *noun* 1 state of being mortal 2 great loss of life 3 death rate > **mor'tal•ly** *adverb* 1 fatally 2 deeply, intensely
mor•tar [MOR-tər] *noun* 1 mixture of lime, sand and water for holding bricks and stones together 2 small cannon firing over short range 3 vessel in which substances are pounded > **mor'tar•board** [-bord] *noun* square academic cap
mort•gage [MOR-gij] *noun* 1 conveyance of property as security for debt with provision that property be reconveyed on payment within agreed time ▷ *verb transitive* **-gaged, -gag•ing** 2 convey by mortgage 3 pledge as security > **mort•ga•gee'** *noun* person to whom property is mortgaged > **mort'ga•gor, mort'ga•ger** *noun* person who mortgages property
mor•ti•fy [MOR-tə-fī] *verb* **-fied, -fy•ing** 1 humiliate 2 subdue by self-denial 3 (of flesh) be affected with gangrene > **mor•ti•fi•ca'tion** [-fi-KAY-shən] *noun*
mor•tise [MOR-tis] *noun* 1 hole in piece of wood, etc. to receive the tongue (tenon) and end of another piece ▷ *verb transitive* **-tised, -tis•ing** 2 make mortise in 3 fasten by mortise and tenon
mor•tu•ar•y [MOR-choo-er-ee] *noun, plural* **-ar•ies** 1 funeral parlor ▷ *adjective* 2 of, for burial 3 pert. to death
mo•sa•ic [moh-ZAY-ik] *noun* 1 picture or pattern of small bits of colored stone, glass, etc. 2 this process of decoration
Mo•sa•ic [moh-ZAY-ik] *adjective* of Moses
mosh *verb intransitive* dance violently and frantically with others in group at rock concert ▷ *noun*
Moslem *noun see* **Muslim**
mosque [mosk] *noun* Muslim temple
mos•qui•to [mə-SKEE-toh] *noun, plural* **-toes** *or* **-tos** any of various kinds of flying, biting insects
moss [maws] *noun* small plant growing in masses on moist surfaces > **moss'y** *adjective* **moss•i•er, moss•i•est** covered with moss
most [mohst] *adjective* 1 greatest in size, number, or degree 2 *sup. of* **much** or **many** ▷ *noun* 3 greatest number, amount, or degree ▷ *adverb* 4 in the greatest degree 5 *abbrev of* **almost** > **most'ly** *adverb* for the most part, generally, on the whole
mo•tel [moh-TEL] *noun* roadside hotel with accommodation for motorists and their vehicles
mo•tet [moh-TET] *noun* short sacred vocal composition
moth [mawth] *noun* 1 usu. nocturnal insect like butterfly 2 its grub > **moth'ball** *noun* 1 small ball of camphor or naphthalene to repel moths from stored clothing, etc. ▷ *verb transitive* 2 put in mothballs 3 store, postpone, etc. > **moth'eat•en** *adjective* 1 eaten, damaged by grub of moth 2 decayed, scruffy
moth•er [MUTH-ər] *noun* 1 female parent 2 head of religious community of women ▷ *adjective* 3 natural, native, inborn ▷ *verb transitive* 4 act as mother to > **moth'er•hood** [-huud] *noun* > **moth'er•ly** *adjective* > **mother-in-law** *noun* mother of one's wife or husband > **mother of pearl** iridescent lining of certain shells
mo•tif [moh-TEEF] *noun* 1 dominating theme 2 recurring design
mo•tion [MOH-shən] *noun* 1 process or action or way of moving 2 proposal in meeting 3 application to judge ▷ *verb transitive* 4 direct by sign > **mo'tion•less** [-lis] *adjective* still, immobile
mo•tive [MOH-tiv] *noun* 1 that which makes

DICTIONARY

m

THESAURUS

morsel *noun* PIECE, bit, bite, crumb, mouthful, part, scrap, soupçon (*French*), taste, tidbit
mortal *adjective* 1 HUMAN, ephemeral, impermanent, passing, temporal, transient, worldly
2 FATAL, deadly, death-dealing, destructive, killing, lethal, murderous, terminal
▷ *noun* 3 HUMAN BEING, being, earthling, human, individual, man, person, woman
mortality *noun* 1 HUMANITY, impermanence, transience
2 KILLING, bloodshed, carnage, death, destruction, fatality
mortification *noun* 1 HUMILIATION, annoyance, chagrin, discomfiture, embarrassment, shame, vexation
2 DISCIPLINE, abasement, chastening, control, denial, subjugation
3 (*medical*) GANGRENE, corruption, festering
mortified *adjective* HUMILIATED, ashamed, chagrined, chastened, crushed, deflated, embarrassed, humbled, shamed
mortify *verb* 1 HUMILIATE, chagrin, chasten, crush, deflate, embarrass, humble, shame
2 DISCIPLINE, abase, chasten, control, deny, subdue
3 (*Of flesh*) PUTREFY, deaden, die, fester
mortuary *noun* MORGUE, funeral parlour
mostly *adverb* GENERALLY, as a rule, chiefly, largely, mainly, on the whole, predominantly, primarily, principally, usually
moth-eaten *adjective* DECAYED, decrepit, dilapidated, ragged, shabby, tattered, threadbare, worn-out
mother *noun* 1 PARENT, dam, ma (*informal*), mama *or* mamma (*old-fashioned informal*), mater (*old-fashioned informal, chiefly Brit*), mom (*informal*), mommy (*informal*), old lady (*informal*)
▷ *adjective* 2 NATIVE, inborn, innate, natural
▷ *verb* 3 NURTURE, care for, cherish, nurse, protect, raise, rear, tend
motherly *adjective* MATERNAL, affectionate, caring, comforting, loving, protective, sheltering
motif *noun* 1 THEME, concept, idea, leitmotif, subject
2 DESIGN, decoration, ornament, shape
motion *noun* 1 MOVEMENT, flow, locomotion, mobility, move, progress, travel
2 PROPOSAL, proposition, recommendation, submission, suggestion
▷ *verb* 3 GESTURE, beckon, direct, gesticulate, nod, signal, wave
motionless *adjective* STILL, fixed, frozen, immobile, paralyzed, standing, static, stationary, stock-still, transfixed, unmoving
motivate *verb* INSPIRE, arouse, cause, drive, induce, move, persuade, prompt, stimulate, stir

person act in particular way 2 inner impulse ▷ *adjective* 3 causing motion > **mo'ti•vate** *verb transitive* **-vat•ed, -vat•ing** 1 instigate 2 incite > **mo•ti•va'tion** [-VAY-shən] *noun*

mot•ley [MOT-lee] *adjective* 1 miscellaneous, varied 2 multicolored

mo•to•cross [MOH-toh-kraws] *noun* motorcycle race over rough course

mo•tor [MOH-tər] *noun* 1 that which imparts movement 2 machine to supply motive power 3 automobile ▷ *verb intransitive* 4 travel by automobile > **mo'tor•ist** *noun* user of automobile > **mo'tor•ize** *verb transitive* **-ized, -iz•ing** equip with motor > **motor home** large motor vehicle with living quarters, used for recreational travel

mot•tle [MOT-l] *verb transitive* **-tled, -tling** 1 mark with blotches, variegate ▷ *noun* 2 arrangement of blotches 3 blotch on surface

mot•to [MOT-oh] *noun, plural* **-toes** 1 saying adopted as rule of conduct 2 short inscribed sentence 3 word or sentence on badge or banner

mound [mownd] *noun* 1 heap of earth or stones 2 small hill

mount [mownt] *verb intransitive* 1 rise 2 increase 3 get on horseback ▷ *verb transitive* 4 get up on 5 frame (picture) 6 fix, set up 7 provide with horse ▷ *noun* 8 that on which thing is supported or fitted 9 horse 10 hill

moun•tain [MOWN-tn] *noun* 1 hill of great size 2 surplus > **moun•tain•eer'** *noun* one who lives among or climbs mountains > **moun'tain•ous** *adjective* very high, rugged > **mountain bike** bicycle with straight handlebars and broad, thick tires, for cycling over rough terrain

moun•te•bank [MOWN-tə-bangk] *noun* charlatan, fake

Moun•tie [MOWN-tee] *noun (informal)* member of Royal Canadian Mounted Police

mourn [morn] *verb* feel, show sorrow (for) > **mourn'er** *noun* > **mourn'ful** [-fəl] *adjective* 1 sad 2 dismal > **mourn'ful•ly** *adverb* > **mourn'ing** *noun* 1 grieving 2 conventional signs of grief for death 3 clothes of mourner

mouse [mows] *noun, plural* **mice** [mīs] 1 small rodent 2 *computing* hand-operated device for moving the cursor, clicking on icons, etc. without keying ▷ *verb intransitive* 3 catch, hunt mice 4 prowl > **mous'er** *noun* cat used for catching mice > **mous'y** *adjective* **mous•i•er, mous•i•est** 1 like mouse, esp. in color 2 meek, shy

mousse [moos] *noun* sweet dessert of flavored cream whipped and frozen

moustache *see* **mustache**

mouth [mowth] *noun* 1 opening in head for eating, speaking, etc. 2 opening into anything hollow 3 outfall of river 4 entrance to harbor, etc. ▷ *verb transitive* [mowth] 5 declaim, esp. in public 6 form (words) with lips without speaking 7 take, move in mouth > **mouth'piece** *noun* 1 end of anything placed between lips, e.g. pipe 2 spokesman

move [moov] *verb transitive* **moved, mov•ing** 1 change position of 2 stir emotions of 3 incite 4 propose for consideration ▷ *verb intransitive* **moved, mov•ing** 5 change places 6 change one's dwelling, etc. 7 take action ▷ *noun* 8 a moving 9 motion toward some goal

motivation *noun* INCENTIVE, incitement, inducement, inspiration, motive, reason, spur, stimulus

motive *noun* REASON, ground *or* grounds, incentive, inducement, inspiration, object, purpose, rationale, stimulus

motley *adjective* 1 MISCELLANEOUS, assorted, disparate, heterogeneous, mixed, varied
2 MULTICOLORED, checkered, variegated

mottled *adjective* BLOTCHY, dappled, flecked, piebald, speckled, spotted, stippled, streaked

motto *noun* SAYING, adage, dictum, maxim, precept, proverb, rule, slogan, watchword

mound *noun* 1 HEAP, drift, pile, rick, stack
2 HILL, bank, dune, embankment, hillock, knoll, rise

mount *verb* 1 CLIMB, ascend, clamber up, go up, scale
2 BESTRIDE, climb onto, jump on
3 INCREASE, accumulate, build, escalate, grow, intensify, multiply, pile up, swell
▷ *noun* 4 BACKING, base, frame, setting, stand, support
5 HORSE, steed (*archaic* or *literary*)

mountain *noun* 1 PEAK, alp, fell (*Brit*), mount
2 HEAP, abundance, mass, mound, pile, stack, ton

mountainous *adjective* 1 HIGH, alpine, highland, rocky, soaring, steep, towering, upland
2 HUGE, daunting, enormous, gigantic, great, immense, mammoth, mighty, monumental

mourn *verb* GRIEVE, bemoan, bewail, deplore, lament, rue, wail, weep

mournful *adjective* 1 SAD, melancholy, piteous, plaintive, sorrowful, tragic, unhappy, woeful
2 DISMAL, disconsolate, downcast, gloomy, grieving, heavy-hearted, lugubrious, miserable, rueful, somber

mourning *noun* 1 GRIEVING, bereavement, grief, lamentation, weeping, woe
2 BLACK, sackcloth and ashes, widow's weeds

mouth *noun* 1 LIPS, jaws, maw
2 OPENING, aperture, door, entrance, gateway, inlet, orifice

mouthful *noun* TASTE, bit, bite, little, morsel, sample, spoonful, swallow

mouthpiece *noun* SPOKESPERSON, agent, delegate, representative, spokesman *or* spokeswoman

movable *adjective* PORTABLE, detachable, mobile, transferable, transportable

> **mov'a•ble** *adjective, noun* > **move'ment** *noun* 1 process, action of moving 2 moving parts of machine 3 division of piece of music
mov•ie [MOOV-ee] *noun* (*informal*) cinema film
mow [moh] *verb* **mowed, mowed** *or* **mown, mow•ing** cut (grass, etc.) > **mow'er** *noun* person or machine that mows
MP3, Mpeg-1 la•yer3 *noun computing* Motion Picture Expert Group-1, Audio Layer-3: digital compression format used to reduce audio files to a fraction of their original size without loss of sound quality
Mr mister
Mrs title of married woman
Ms title used instead of Miss or Mrs.
Mt *chem.* meitnerium
much *adjective* **more, most** 1 existing in quantity ▷ *noun* 2 large amount 3 a great deal 4 important matter ▷ *adverb* 5 in a great degree 6 nearly
mu•ci•lage [MYOO-sə-lij] *noun* gum, glue
muck [muk] *noun* 1 horse, cattle dung 2 unclean refuse 3 insulting remarks ▷ *verb transitive* 4 make dirty > **muck'y** *adjective* **muck•i•er, muck•i•est** 1 dirty 2 messy 3 unpleasant > **muck out** *verb* remove muck from > **muck up** *verb* (*informal*) ruin, bungle, confuse
mu•cus [MYOO-kəs] *noun* viscid fluid secreted by mucous membrane > **mu'cous** [-kəs] *adjective* 1 resembling mucus 2 secreting mucus 3 slimy > **mucous membrane** lining of canals and cavities of the body
mud *noun* 1 wet and soft earth 2 (*informal*) slander > **mud'dy** *adjective* **-di•er, -di•est**
mud•dle [MUD-əl] *verb transitive* **-dled, -dling** 1 (esp. with *up*) confuse 2 bewilder 3 mismanage ▷ *noun* 4 confusion 5 tangle
mu•ez•zin [myoo-EZ-in] *noun* crier who summons Muslims to prayer
muff[1] *noun* tube-shaped covering to keep the hands warm
muff[2] *verb transitive* miss, bungle, fail in
muf'fin *noun* cup-shaped quick bread
muf•fle [MUF-əl] *verb transitive* **-fled, -fling** wrap up, esp. to deaden sound > **muf'fler** [-lər] *noun* 1 on motor vehicles, device for accomplishing this 2 scarf
muf•ti [MUF-tee] *noun* plain clothes as distinguished from uniform, e.g. of soldier
mug[1] *noun* drinking cup
mug[2] *noun* 1 (*slang*) face 2 (*slang*) ruffian, criminal ▷ *verb transitive* **mugged, mug•ging** 3 rob violently > **mug'ger** [-ər] *noun*
mug•gy [MUG-ee] *adjective* **-gi•er, -gi•est** damp and stifling
Mu•ham•mad, Mo•ham•med [muu-HAM-əd] *noun* prophet and founder of Islam > **Mu•ham•mad•an** *adjective, noun* Muslim
mu•lat•to [mə-LAT-oh] *adjective, noun, plural* **-oes** (child) of one white and one black parent
mul•ber•ry [MUL-ber-ee] *noun, plural* **-ries** 1 tree whose leaves are used to feed silkworms 2 its purplish fruit
mulch *noun* 1 straw, leaves, etc., spread as protection for roots of plants ▷ *verb transitive* 2 protect thus
mule [myool] *noun* 1 animal that is cross between female horse and male donkey 2 hybrid 3 spinning machine 4 small locomotive 5 slipper > **mul'ish** *adjective*

DICTIONARY

m

THESAURUS

move *verb* 1 GO, advance, budge, proceed, progress, shift, stir
2 CHANGE, shift, switch, transfer, transpose
3 LEAVE, migrate, pack one's bags (*informal*), quit, relocate, remove
4 DRIVE, activate, operate, propel, shift, start, turn
5 TOUCH, affect, excite, impress
6 INCITE, cause, induce, influence, inspire, motivate, persuade, prompt, rouse
7 PROPOSE, advocate, put forward, recommend, suggest, urge
▷ *noun* 8 ACTION, maneuver, measure, ploy, step, stratagem, stroke, turn
9 TRANSFER, relocation, removal, shift
movement *noun* 1 MOTION, action, activity, change, development, flow, maneuver, progress, stirring
2 GROUP, campaign, crusade, drive, faction, front, grouping, organization, party
3 WORKINGS, action, machinery, mechanism, works
4 (*music*) SECTION, division, part, passage
movie *noun* FILM, feature, flick (*slang*), picture
moving *adjective* 1 EMOTIONAL, affecting, inspiring, pathetic, persuasive, poignant, stirring, touching
2 MOBILE, movable, portable, running, unfixed
mow *verb* CUT, crop, scythe, shear, trim
mow down *verb* MASSACRE, butcher, cut down, cut to pieces, shoot down, slaughter
much *adjective* 1 GREAT, abundant, a lot of, ample, considerable, copious, plenty of, sizable *or* sizeable, substantial
▷ *noun* 2 A LOT, a good deal, a great deal, heaps (*informal*), lots (*informal*), plenty
▷ *adverb* 3 GREATLY, a great deal, a lot, considerably, decidedly, exceedingly
muck *noun* 1 MANURE, dung, ordure
2 DIRT, filth, mire, mud, ooze, slime, sludge
mucky *adjective* DIRTY, begrimed, filthy, grimy, messy, muddy, scuzzy (*slang*)
mud *noun* DIRT, clay, mire, ooze, silt, slime, sludge
muddle *verb* 1 JUMBLE, disarrange, disorder, disorganize, mess, scramble, spoil, tangle
2 CONFUSE, befuddle, bewilder, confound, daze, disorient, perplex, stupefy
▷ *noun* 3 CONFUSION, chaos, disarray, disorder, disorganization, jumble, mess, mix-up, predicament, tangle
muddy *adjective* 1 DIRTY, bespattered, grimy, mucky, mud-caked, scuzzy (*slang*), soiled
2 BOGGY, marshy, quaggy, swampy
muffle *verb* 1 WRAP UP, cloak, cover, envelop, shroud, swaddle, swathe
2 DEADEN, muzzle, quieten, silence, soften, stifle, suppress
muffled *adjective* INDISTINCT, faint, muted, stifled, strangled, subdued, suppressed
mug[1] *noun* CUP, beaker, flagon, pot, tankard
mug[2] *noun* FACE, countenance, features, visage 1 FOOL, dork (*slang*), schmuck (*slang*), sucker (*slang*)
▷ *verb* 2 ATTACK, assault, beat up, rob, set about *or* set upon
muggy *adjective* HUMID, clammy, close, moist,

obstinate
mull *verb transitive* 1 heat (wine) with sugar and spices 2 think (over), ponder
mul•lah [MUL-ə] *noun* Muslim theologian
mul•let[1] [MUL-it] *noun* edible sea fish
mul•let[2] *noun* haircut in which the hair is short at the top and sides and long at the back
mul•lion [MUL-yən] *noun* upright dividing bar in window
multi-, mult- *combining form* many: *multiracial; multistory*
mul•ti•far•i•ous [mul-tə-FAIR-ee-əs] *adjective* of various kinds or parts
mul•ti•ple [MUL-tə-pəl] *adjective* 1 having many parts ▷ *noun* 2 quantity that contains another an exact number of times > **mul•ti•pli•cand'** *noun math.* number to be multiplied > **mul•ti•pli•ca'tion** *noun* > **mul•ti•plic'i•ty** [-PLIS-i-tee] *noun* variety, greatness in number > **mul'ti•ply** [-plī] *verb* **-plied, -ply•ing** 1 (cause to) increase in number, quantity, or degree ▷ *verb transitive* 2 combine (two numbers or quantities) by multiplication 3 increase in number by reproduction
mul•ti•plex [MUL-tə-pleks] *adjective telecommunications* capable of transmitting numerous messages over same wire or channel
mul•ti•tude [MUL-ti-tood] *noun* 1 great number 2 great crowd 3 populace > **mul•ti•tu'di•nous** *adjective* very numerous
mum *adjective* silent **mum's the word** keep silent
mum•ble [MUM-bəl] *verb* **-bled, -bling** speak indistinctly, mutter
mum•my [MUM-ee] *noun, plural* **-mies** embalmed body > **mum'mi•fy** *verb transitive* **-fied, -fy•ing**
mumps *noun* infectious disease marked by swelling in the glands of the neck
munch *verb* 1 chew noisily and vigorously 2 crunch
mun•dane [mun-DAYN] *adjective* 1 ordinary, everyday 2 belonging to this world, earthly
mu•nic•i•pal [myuu-NIS-ə-pəl] *adjective* belonging to affairs of city or town > **mu•nic•i•pal'i•ty** *noun, plural* **-ties** 1 city or town with local self-government 2 its governing body
mu•nif•i•cent [myoo-NIF-ə-sənt] *adjective* very generous > **mu•nif'i•cence** *noun* bounty
mu•ni•tions [myoo-NISH-ənz] *plural noun* military stores
mu•ral [MYUUR-əl] *noun* 1 painting on a wall ▷ *adjective* 2 of or on a wall
mur•der [MUR-dər] *noun* 1 unlawful premeditated killing of human being ▷ *verb transitive* 2 kill thus > **mur'der•ous** *adjective*
murk *noun* thick darkness > **murk'y** *adjective* **murk•i•er, murk•i•est** gloomy
mur•mur [MUR-mər] *noun* 1 low, indistinct sound ▷ *verb intransitive* 2 make such a sound 3 complain ▷ *verb transitive* 4 utter in a low voice
mus•cle [MUS-əl] *noun* 1 part of body that produces movement by contracting 2 system of muscles > **mus'cu•lar** [-kyə-lər] *adjective* 1 with well-developed muscles 2 strong 3 of, like muscle > **mus'cle•bound** *adjective* with muscles stiff through overdevelopment > **muscular dystrophy** disease with wasting of muscles **muscle in** (*informal*) force one's way into > **muscle shirt** (*informal*) shirt that leaves full arm exposed
muse [myooz] *verb intransitive* **mused, mus•ing** 1 ponder 2 consider meditatively 3 be lost in thought
Muse [myooz] *noun* one of the nine goddesses inspiring learning and the arts
mu•seum [myoo-ZEE-əm] *noun* place housing collection of natural, artistic, historical or scientific objects
mush[1] *noun* 1 soft pulpy mass 2 cloying

oppressive, sticky, stuffy, sultry
mull *verb* PONDER, consider, contemplate, deliberate, meditate, reflect on, ruminate, think over, weigh
multifarious *adjective* DIVERSE, different, legion, manifold, many, miscellaneous, multiple, numerous, sundry, varied
multiple *adjective* MANY, manifold, multitudinous, numerous, several, sundry, various
multiply *verb* 1 INCREASE, build up, expand, extend, proliferate, spread
2 REPRODUCE, breed, propagate
multitude *noun* MASS, army, crowd, horde, host, mob, myriad, swarm, throng
munch *verb* CHEW, champ, chomp, crunch
mundane *adjective* 1 ORDINARY, banal, commonplace, day-to-day, everyday, humdrum, prosaic, routine, workaday
2 EARTHLY, mortal, secular, temporal, terrestrial, worldly
municipal *adjective* CIVIC, public, urban
municipality *noun* TOWN, borough, city, district, township
munificence *noun* GENEROSITY, beneficence, benevolence, bounty, largesse *or* largess, liberality, magnanimousness, philanthropy
munificent *adjective* GENEROUS, beneficent, benevolent, bountiful, lavish, liberal, magnanimous, open-handed, philanthropic, unstinting
murder *noun* 1 KILLING, assassination, bloodshed, butchery, carnage, homicide, manslaughter, massacre, slaying
▷ *verb* 2 KILL, assassinate, bump off (*slang*), butcher, eliminate (*slang*), massacre, slaughter, slay
murderer *noun* KILLER, assassin, butcher, cut-throat, hit man (*slang*), homicide, slaughterer, slayer
murderous *adjective* DEADLY, bloodthirsty, brutal, cruel, cut-throat, ferocious, lethal, savage
murky *adjective* DARK, cloudy, dim, dull, gloomy, gray, misty, overcast
murmur *verb* 1 MUMBLE, mutter, whisper
2 GRUMBLE, complain, moan (*informal*)
▷ *noun* 3 DRONE, buzzing, humming, purr, rumble, whisper
muscle *noun* 1 TENDON, sinew
2 STRENGTH, brawn, clout (*informal*), forcefulness, might, power, stamina, weight
muscular *adjective* STRONG, athletic, powerful, robust, sinewy, strapping, sturdy, vigorous
muse *verb* PONDER, brood, cogitate, consider, contemplate, deliberate, meditate, mull over,

sentimentality > **mush'y** *adjective* **mush•i•er, mush•i•est**
mush² *verb intransitive* 1 travel over snow with dog team and sled ▷ *verb transitive* 2 spur on (sled) dogs ▷ *interjection* 3 go!
mush'room *noun* 1 fungoid growth, typically with stem and cap structure, some species edible ▷ *verb intransitive* 2 shoot up rapidly 3 expand > **mushroom cloud** large cloud resembling mushroom, esp. from nuclear explosion
mu•sic [MYOO-zik] *noun* 1 art form using melodious and harmonious combination of notes 2 laws of this 3 composition in this art > **mu'si•cal** *adjective* 1 of, like music 2 interested in, or with instinct for, music 3 pleasant to ear ▷ *noun* 4 play, motion picture in which music plays essential part > **mu•si'cian** *noun* > **mu•si•col'o•gist** [-jist] *noun* > **mu•si•col'o•gy** *noun* scientific study of music > **musical comedy** light dramatic entertainment of songs, dances, etc.
musk *noun* 1 scent obtained from gland of **musk deer** 2 various plants with similar scent > **musk'y** *adjective* **musk•i•er, musk•i•est** > **musk ox** ox of Arctic Amer. > **musk'rat** *noun* 1 N Amer. rodent found near water 2 its fur
mus•ket [MUS-kit] *noun hist.* infantryman's gun > **mus•ket•eer'** *noun*
Mus•lim [MUZ-lim] *noun* 1 follower of religion of Islam ▷ *adjective* 2 of religion, culture, etc. of Islam
mus•lin [MUZ-lin] *noun* fine cotton fabric
mus•sel [MUS-əl] *noun* bivalve shellfish
must¹ *verb auxiliary* 1 be obliged to, or certain to ▷ *noun* 2 something one must do
must² *noun* 1 newly-pressed grape juice 2 unfermented wine
mus•tache, mous•tache [MUS-tash] *noun* hair on the upper lip
mus'tang *noun* wild horse
mus•tard [MUS-tərd] *noun* 1 powder made from the seeds of a plant, used in paste as a condiment 2 the plant > **mustard gas** poisonous gas causing blistering, lung damage, etc.
mus•ter [MUS-tər] *verb* 1 assemble ▷ *noun* 2 assembly, esp. for exercise, inspection
mus•ty [MUS-tee] *adjective* **-ti•er, -ti•est** moldy, stale > **must** *noun* > **mus'ti•ness** *noun*
mu•tate [MYOO-tayt] *verb* **-tat•ed, -tat•ing** (cause to) undergo mutation > **mu'ta•ble** [-tə-bəl] *adjective* liable to change > **mu'tant** [-tənt] *noun* mutated animal, plant, etc. > **mu•ta'tion** [-TAY-shən] *noun* change, esp. genetic change causing divergence from kind or racial type > **mu•ta'tive** *adjective*
mute [myoot] *adjective* **mut•er, mut•est** 1 dumb 2 silent ▷ *noun* 3 person incapable of speech 4 *mus.* contrivance to soften tone of instruments > **mut'ed** *adjective* 1 (of sound) muffled 2 (of light) subdued
mu•ti•late [MYOOT-l-ayt] *verb transitive* **-lat•ed, -lat•ing** 1 deprive of a limb or other part 2 damage 3 deface > **mu•ti•la'tion** *noun*
mu•ti•ny [MYOOT-n-ee] *noun, plural* **-nies** 1 rebellion against authority, esp. against officers of disciplined body ▷ *verb intransitive* **-nied, -ny•ing** 2 commit mutiny > **mu•ti•neer'** *noun* > **mu'tin•ous** *adjective* rebellious
mutt *noun* (*informal*) (mongrel) dog
mut•ter [MUT-ər] *verb intransitive* 1 speak with mouth nearly closed, indistinctly 2 grumble ▷ *verb transitive* 3 utter in such tones ▷ *noun* (act of) muttering
mut•ton [MUT-ən] *noun* flesh of sheep used as food > **mut•ton•chops** *plural noun* side whiskers broad at jaw, narrow at temples > **mut'ton•head** [-hed] *noun* (*informal*) slow-witted person
mu•tu•al [MYOO-choo-əl] *adjective* 1 done, possessed, etc., by each of two with respect to the other 2 reciprocal 3 common to both or all > **mu•tu•al'i•ty** *noun* > **mutual fund** investment company selling shares to public with repurchase on request
muz•zle [MUZ-əl] *noun* 1 mouth and nose of

DICTIONARY

m

THESAURUS

reflect, ruminate
mushy *adjective* 1 SOFT, pulpy, semi-solid, slushy, squashy, squelchy
2 (*informal*) SENTIMENTAL, maudlin, mawkish, saccharine, schmaltzy (*slang*), sloppy (*informal*), slushy (*informal*)
musical *adjective* MELODIOUS, dulcet, euphonious, harmonious, lyrical, melodic, sweet-sounding, tuneful
must¹ *noun* NECESSITY, essential, fundamental, imperative, prerequisite, requirement, requisite, sine qua non (*Latin*)
muster *verb* 1 ASSEMBLE, call together, convene, gather, marshal, mobilize, rally, summon
▷ *noun* 2 ASSEMBLY, collection, congregation, convention, gathering, meeting, rally, roundup
musty *adjective* STALE, airless, dank, funky (*slang*), fusty, mildewed, moldy, old, smelly, stuffy
mutability *noun* CHANGE, alteration, evolution, metamorphosis, transition, variation, vicissitude
mutable *adjective* CHANGEABLE, adaptable, alterable, fickle, inconsistent, inconstant, unsettled, unstable, variable, volatile
mutation *noun* CHANGE, alteration, evolution, metamorphosis, modification, transfiguration, transformation, variation
mute *adjective* SILENT, dumb, mum, speechless, unspoken, voiceless, wordless
mutilate *verb* 1 MAIM, amputate, cut up, damage, disfigure, dismember, injure, lacerate, mangle
2 DISTORT, adulterate, bowdlerize, censor, cut, damage, expurgate
mutinous *adjective* REBELLIOUS, disobedient, insubordinate, insurgent, refractory, riotous, subversive, unmanageable, unruly
mutiny *noun* 1 REBELLION, disobedience, insubordination, insurrection, revolt, revolution, riot, uprising
▷ *verb* 2 REBEL, disobey, resist, revolt, rise up
mutter *verb* GRUMBLE, complain, grouse, mumble, murmur, rumble
mutual *adjective* SHARED, common, interchangeable, joint, reciprocal, requited, returned
muzzle *noun* 1 JAWS, mouth, nose, snout
2 GAG, guard
▷ *verb* 3 SUPPRESS, censor, curb, gag, restrain,

animal **2** cover for these to prevent biting **3** open end of gun ▷ *verb transitive* **-zled, -zling** **4** put muzzle on **5** silence, gag
my [mī] *adjective* belonging to me > **my•self** *pronoun* *emphatic or reflexive form of* **I** or **me**
my•col•o•gy [mī-KOL-ə-jee] *noun* science of fungi
my•o•pi•a [mī-OH-pee-ə] *noun* **1** nearsightedness **2** obtuseness > **my•op'ic** *adjective*
myr•i•ad [MIR-ee-əd] *adjective* **1** innumerable ▷ *noun* **2** large indefinite number
myrrh [mur] *noun* aromatic gum, formerly used as incense
mys•ter•y [MIS-tə-ree] *noun, plural* **-teries** **1** obscure or secret thing **2** anything strange or inexplicable **3** religious rite **4** in Middle Ages, biblical play > **mys•te'ri•ous** [-TEER-ree-əs] *adjective*
mys•tic [MIS-tik] *noun* **1** one who seeks divine, spiritual knowledge, esp. by prayer, contemplation, etc. ▷ *adjective* **2** of hidden meaning, esp. in religious sense > **mys'ti•cal** *adjective* > **mys'ti•cism** [-siz-əm] *noun*
mys•ti•fy [MIS-tə-fī] *verb transitive* **-fied, -fy•ing** bewilder, puzzle > **mys•ti•fi•ca'tion** [-KAY-shən] *noun*
mys•tique [mi-STEEK] *noun* aura of mystery, power, etc.
myth [mith] *noun* **1** tale with supernatural characters or events **2** invented story **3** imaginary person or object > **myth'i•cal** *adjective* > **myth•o•log'i•cal** [-LOJ-ə-kəl] *adjective* > **my•thol'o•gy** *noun, plural* **-gies** **1** myths collectively **2** study of them

DICTIONARY • THESAURUS

silence, stifle
myopic *adjective* SHORT-SIGHTED, near-sighted
myriad *adjective* **1** INNUMERABLE, countless, immeasurable, incalculable, multitudinous, untold
▷ *noun* **2** MULTITUDE, army, horde, host, swarm
mysterious *adjective* STRANGE, arcane, enigmatic, inexplicable, inscrutable, mystifying, perplexing, puzzling, secret, uncanny, unfathomable, weird
mystery *noun* PUZZLE, conundrum, enigma, problem, question, riddle, secret, teaser
mystic *or* **mystical** *adjective* SUPERNATURAL, inscrutable, metaphysical, mysterious, occult, otherworldly, paranormal, preternatural, transcendental
mystify *verb* PUZZLE, baffle, bewilder, confound, confuse, flummox, nonplus, perplex, stump
mystique *noun* FASCINATION, awe, charisma, charm, glamour, magic, spell
myth *noun* **1** LEGEND, allegory, fable, fairy story, fiction, folk tale, saga, story, urban legend *or* urban myth
2 ILLUSION, delusion, fancy, fantasy, figment, imagination, superstition, tall tale (*informal*)
mythical *adjective* **1** LEGENDARY, fabled, fabulous, fairy-tale, mythological
2 IMAGINARY, fabricated, fantasy, fictitious, invented, made-up, make-believe, nonexistent, pretended, unreal, untrue
mythological *adjective* LEGENDARY, fabulous, mythic, mythical, traditional
mythology *noun* LEGEND, folklore, lore, tradition

Nn

N 1 *chem.* nitrogen 2 *physics* newton
Na *chem.* sodium
na•bob [NAY-bob] *noun* wealthy, powerful person
na•cre [NAY-kər] *noun* mother-of-pearl
na•dir [NAY-dər] *noun* 1 point opposite the zenith 2 lowest point
nag[1] *verb* **nagged, nag•ging** 1 scold or annoy constantly 2 cause pain to constantly ▷ *noun* 3 nagging 4 one who nags
nag[2] *noun* 1 old horse 2 (*slang*) any horse 3 small horse for riding
nai•ad [NAY-ad] *noun* water nymph
nail [nayl] *noun* 1 horny shield at ends of fingers, toes 2 claw 3 small metal spike for fastening wood, etc. ▷ *verb transitive* 4 fasten with nails 5 (*informal*) catch **hit the nail on the head** do or say the right thing
na•ive [nah-EEV] *adjective* simple, unaffected, ingenuous > **na•ive•té** [-eev-TAY] *noun*
nak•ed [NAY-kid] *adjective* 1 without clothes 2 exposed, bare 3 undisguised > **naked eye** the eye unassisted by any optical instrument
name [naym] *noun* 1 word by which person, thing, etc. is denoted 2 reputation 3 title 4 credit 5 family 6 famous person ▷ *verb transitive* **named, nam•ing** 7 give name to 8 call by name 9 entitle 10 appoint 11 mention

DICTIONARY

n

THESAURUS

nadir *noun* BOTTOM, depths, lowest point, minimum, rock bottom
nag[1] *verb* 1 SCOLD, annoy, badger, harass, hassle (*informal*), henpeck, irritate, pester, plague, upbraid, worry
▷ *noun* 2 SCOLD, harpy, shrew, tartar, virago
nag[2] *noun* HORSE, hack
nagging *adjective* IRRITATING, persistent, scolding, shrewish, worrying
nail *verb* FASTEN, attach, fix, hammer, join, pin, secure, tack
naive *adjective* 1 GULLIBLE, callow, credulous, green, unsuspicious, wet behind the ears (*informal*)
2 INNOCENT, artless, guileless, ingenuous, open, simple, trusting, unsophisticated, unworldly
naivety *or* **naïveté** *noun* 1 GULLIBILITY, callowness, credulity
2 INNOCENCE, artlessness, guilelessness, inexperience, ingenuousness, naturalness, openness, simplicity
naked *adjective* NUDE, bare, exposed, in one's birthday suit (*informal*), stripped, unclothed, undressed, without a stitch on (*informal*)
nakedness *noun* NUDITY, bareness, undress
name *noun* 1 TITLE, designation, epithet, handle (*slang*), moniker *or* monicker (*slang*), nickname, sobriquet, term
2 FAME, distinction, eminence, esteem, honor, note, praise, renown, repute
▷ *verb* 3 CALL, baptize, christen, dub, entitle, label, style, term
4 NOMINATE, appoint, choose, designate, select, specify
named *adjective* 1 CALLED, baptized, christened, dubbed, entitled, known as, labeled, styled, termed
2 NOMINATED, appointed, chosen, designated, mentioned, picked, selected, singled out, specified

12 specify > **name'less** [-lis] *adjective* 1 without a name 2 indescribable 3 too dreadful to be mentioned 4 obscure > **name'ly** *adverb* that is to say > **name'sake** *noun* 1 person named after another 2 person with same name as another **name and shame** make public the name of (a wrongdoer) in order to bring public condemnation on him or her

nap[1] *verb intransitive* **napped, nap•ping** 1 take short sleep, esp. in daytime ▷ *noun* 2 short sleep

nap[2] *noun* downy surface on cloth made by projecting fibers

na•palm [NAY-pahm] *noun* jellied gasoline, highly incendiary, used in bombs, etc.

nape [nayp] *noun* back of neck

naph•tha [NAF-thə] *noun* inflammable oil distilled from coal, etc. > **naph'tha•lene** [-leen] *noun* white crystalline product distilled from coal tar, used in disinfectants, mothballs, etc.

nap'kin *noun* cloth, paper for wiping fingers or lips at table

nar•cis•sus [nahr-SIS-əs] *noun, plural* **nar•cis•sus** genus of bulbous plants including daffodil, jonquil, esp. one with white flowers > **nar'cis•sism** *noun* abnormal love and admiration of oneself > **nar'cis•sist** *noun*

nar•cot•ic [nahr-KOT-ik] *noun* any of a group of drugs, including morphine and opium, producing numbness and stupor, used medicinally but addictive ▷ *adjective*

nar•rate [NAR-ayt] *verb transitive* **-rat•ed, -rat•ing** relate, recount, tell (story) > **nar•ra'tion** *noun* > **nar'ra•tive** [-rə-tiv] *noun* 1 account, story ▷ *adjective* 2 relating > **nar'ra•tor** [-ray-tər] *noun*

nar•row [NAR-oh] *adjective* **-er, -est** 1 of little breadth, or width esp. in comparison to length 2 limited 3 barely adequate or successful ▷ *verb* 4 make, become narrow > **nar'rows** *plural noun* narrow part of straits > **nar'row•ness** *noun* > **narrow-minded** *adjective* 1 illiberal 2 bigoted > **narrow-mindedness** *noun* prejudice, bigotry

na•sal [NAY-zəl] *adjective* 1 of nose ▷ *noun* 2 sound partly produced in nose > **na'sal•ly** *adverb*

nas•cent [NAYS-ənt] *adjective* 1 just coming into existence 2 springing up

nas•tur•tium [na-STUR-shəm] *noun* garden plant with red or orange flowers

nas•ty [NAS-tee] *adjective* **-ti•er, -ti•est** foul, disagreeable, unpleasant > **nas'ti•ly** *adverb* > **nas'ti•ness** *noun*

na•tal [NAYT-l] *adjective* of birth

na•tion [NAY-shən] *noun* people or race organized as a country > **na'tion•al** [NASH-ə-nl] *adjective* 1 belonging or pert. to a nation 2 public, general ▷ *noun* 3 member of a nation > **na'tion•al•ism** *noun* 1 loyalty, devotion to one's country 2 movement for independence of country, people, ruled by another > **na•tion•al'i•ty** *noun, plural* **-ties** 1 national quality or feeling 2 fact of belonging to particular nation 3 member of this > **na'tion•al•ize** *verb transitive* **-ized, -iz•ing** convert (private industry, resources, etc.) to government control

na•tive [NAY-tiv] *adjective* 1 inborn 2 born in particular place 3 found in pure state 4 that was place of one's birth ▷ *noun* 5 one born in a

nameless *adjective* 1 ANONYMOUS, unnamed, untitled
2 UNKNOWN, incognito, obscure, undistinguished, unheard-of, unsung
3 HORRIBLE, abominable, indescribable, unmentionable, unspeakable, unutterable

namely *adverb* SPECIFICALLY, to wit, viz.

nap[1] *noun* 1 SLEEP, catnap, forty winks (*informal*), rest, siesta
▷ *verb* 2 SLEEP, catnap, doze, drop off (*informal*), nod off (*informal*), rest, snooze (*informal*)

nap[2] *noun* WEAVE, down, fiber, grain, pile

napkin *noun* CLOTH, linen, wipe

narcissism *noun* EGOTISM, self-love, vanity

narcotic *noun* 1 DRUG, analgesic, anesthetic, anodyne, opiate, painkiller, sedative, tranquilizer
▷ *adjective* 2 SEDATIVE, analgesic, calming, hypnotic, painkilling, soporific

narrate *verb* TELL, chronicle, describe, detail, recite, recount, relate, report

narration *noun* TELLING, description, explanation, reading, recital, relation

narrative *noun* STORY, account, blog (*informal*), chronicle, history, report, statement, tale, weblog

narrator *noun* STORYTELLER, author, chronicler, commentator, reporter, writer

narrow *adjective* 1 THIN, attenuated, fine, slender, slim, spare, tapering
2 LIMITED, close, confined, constricted, contracted, meager, restricted, tight
3 INSULAR, dogmatic, illiberal, intolerant, narrow-minded, partial, prejudiced, small-minded
▷ *verb* 4 TIGHTEN, constrict, limit, reduce

narrowly *adverb* JUST, barely, by the skin of one's teeth, only just, scarcely

narrow-minded *adjective* INTOLERANT, bigoted, hidebound, illiberal, opinionated, parochial, prejudiced, provincial, small-minded

nastiness *noun* UNPLEASANTNESS, malice, meanness, spitefulness

nasty *adjective* 1 OBJECTIONABLE, disagreeable, loathsome, obnoxious, offensive, unpleasant, vile
2 SPITEFUL, despicable, disagreeable, distasteful, lousy (*slang*), malicious, mean, scuzzy (*slang*), unpleasant, vicious, vile
3 PAINFUL, bad, critical, dangerous, serious, severe

nation *noun* COUNTRY, people, race, realm, society, state, tribe

national *adjective* 1 NATIONWIDE, countrywide, public, widespread
▷ *noun* 2 CITIZEN, inhabitant, native, resident, subject

nationalism *noun* PATRIOTISM, allegiance, chauvinism, jingoism, loyalty

nationality *noun* RACE, birth, nation

nationwide *adjective* NATIONAL, countrywide, general, widespread

native *adjective* 1 LOCAL, domestic, home, indigenous
2 INBORN, congenital, hereditary, inbred, ingrained, innate, instinctive, intrinsic, natural
▷ *noun* 3 INHABITANT, aborigine, citizen, countryman, dweller, national, resident

place 6 member of indigenous people of a country 7 species of plant, animal, etc. originating in a place > **Native American** *noun* 1 person descended from the original inhabitants of the American continent ▷ *adjective* 2 of Native Americans

na•tiv•i•ty [nə-TIV-i-tee] *noun, plural* **-ties** 1 birth 2 time, circumstances of birth 3 (**Na•tiv•i•ty**) birth of Christ

nat•ter [NAT-ər] *verb intransitive* talk idly

nat•ty [NAT-ee] *adjective* **ti•er, -ti•est** 1 neat and smart 2 spruce > **nat'ti•ly** *adverb*

na•ture [NAY-chər] *noun* 1 innate or essential qualities of person or thing 2 class, sort 3 life force 4 (**Na•ture**) power underlying all phenomena in material world 5 material world as a whole 6 natural unspoiled scenery or countryside, and plants and animals in it 7 disposition 8 temperament > **nat•u•ral** [NACH-ər-əl] *adjective* 1 of, according to, occurring in, provided by, nature 2 inborn 3 normal 4 unaffected 5 illegitimate ▷ *noun* 6 something, somebody well suited for something 7 *mus.* symbol used to remove effect of sharp or flat preceding it > **nat'u•ral•ist** *noun* student of natural history > **nat•u•ral•is'tic** *adjective* of or imitating nature in effect or characteristics > **nat'u•ral•ize** *verb transitive* **-ized, -iz•ing** 1 admit to citizenship 2 accustom to different climate or environment > **nat'u•ral•ly** *adverb* 1 of or according to nature 2 by nature 3 of course > **natural history** study of animals and plants

naught [nawt] *noun* 1 nothing 2 nought

naugh•ty [NAW-tee] *adjective* **-ti•er, -ti•est** 1 disobedient, not behaving well 2 mildly indecent, tasteless > **naugh'ti•ly** *adverb*

nau•se•a [NAW-zee-ə] *noun* feeling that precedes vomiting > **nau'se•ate** *verb transitive* **-at•ed, -at•ing** sicken > **nau'seous** [NAW-shəs], **nau'se•at•ing** *adjective* 1 disgusting 2 causing nausea

nau•ti•cal [NAW-ti-kəl] *adjective* 1 of seamen or ships 2 marine > **nautical mile** 6080.20 feet (1853.25 meters)

nau•ti•lus [NAWT-l-əs] *noun, plural* **-lus•es** univalvular shellfish

naval *see* **navy**

nave [nayv] *noun* main part of church

na•vel [NAY-vəl] *noun* umbilicus, small scar, depression in middle of abdomen where umbilical cord was attached

nav•i•gate [NAV-i-gayt] *verb* **-gat•ed, -gat•ing** 1 plan, direct, plot path or position of ship, etc. 2 travel > **nav'i•ga•ble** *adjective* > **nav•i•ga'tion** *noun* 1 science of directing course of seagoing vessel, or of aircraft in flight 2 shipping > **nav'i•ga•tor** *noun* one who navigates

na•vy [NAY-vee] *noun, plural* **-vies** 1 fleet 2 warships of country with their crews and organization ▷ *adjective* 3 navy-blue > **na'val** *adjective* of the navy > **navy-blue** *adjective* very dark blue

Na•zi [NAHT-see] *noun* 1 member of the National Socialist political party in Germany, 1919—45 2 one who thinks, acts, like a Nazi ▷ *adjective*

Nb *chem.* niobium

Nd *chem.* neodymium

Ne *chem.* neon

Ne•an•der•thal [nee-AN-dər-thawl] *adjective* 1 of a type of primitive man 2 (**ne•an•der•thal**) primitive

neap [neep] *adjective* low > **neap tide** the low tide at the first and third quarters of the moon

near [neer] *preposition* 1 close to ▷ *adverb* **-er, -est** 2 at or to a short distance ▷ *adjective* **-er, -est** 3 close at hand 4 closely related 5 narrow, so as barely to escape 6 stingy 7 (of

natty *adjective* SMART, dapper, elegant, fashionable, neat, phat (*slang*), snazzy (*informal*), spruce, stylish, trim

natural *adjective* 1 NORMAL, common, everyday, legitimate, logical, ordinary, regular, typical, usual
2 UNAFFECTED, genuine, ingenuous, open, real, simple, spontaneous, unpretentious, unsophisticated
3 INNATE, characteristic, essential, inborn, inherent, instinctive, intuitive, native
4 PURE, organic, plain, unrefined, whole

naturalist *noun* BIOLOGIST, botanist, ecologist, zoologist

naturalistic *adjective* REALISTIC, lifelike, true-to-life

naturally *adverb* 1 OF COURSE, certainly
2 GENUINELY, normally, simply, spontaneously, typically, unaffectedly, unpretentiously

nature *noun* 1 CREATION, cosmos, earth, environment, universe, world
2 MAKE-UP, character, complexion, constitution, essence
3 KIND, category, description, sort, species, style, type, variety
4 TEMPERAMENT, disposition, humor, mood, outlook, temper

naughty *adjective* 1 DISOBEDIENT, bad, impish, misbehaved, mischievous, refractory, wayward, wicked, worthless
2 OBSCENE, improper, lewd, ribald, risqué, smutty, vulgar

nausea *noun* SICKNESS, biliousness, queasiness, retching, squeamishness, vomiting

nauseate *verb* SICKEN, disgust, offend, repel, repulse, revolt, turn one's stomach

nauseous *adjective* SICKENING, abhorrent, disgusting, distasteful, nauseating, offensive, repugnant, repulsive, revolting, scuzzy (*slang*)

nautical *adjective* MARITIME, marine, naval

naval *adjective* NAUTICAL, marine, maritime

navigable *adjective* 1 PASSABLE, clear, negotiable, unobstructed
2 SAILABLE, controllable, dirigible

navigate *verb* SAIL, drive, guide, handle, maneuver, pilot, steer, voyage

navigation *noun* SAILING, helmsmanship, seamanship, voyaging

navigator *noun* PILOT, mariner, seaman

navy *noun* FLEET, armada, flotilla

near *adjective* 1 CLOSE, adjacent, adjoining, nearby, neighboring
2 FORTHCOMING, approaching, imminent, impending, in the offing, looming, nigh, upcoming

vehicles, horses, etc.) at driver's left ▷ *verb* 8 approach > **near'by** *adjective* adjacent > **near'ly** *adverb* 1 closely 2 almost

neat [neet] *adjective* **-er, -est** 1 tidy, orderly 2 efficient 3 precise, deft 4 cleverly worded 5 undiluted 6 simple and elegant > **neat'ly** *adverb*

neb•u•la [NEB-yə-lə] *noun, plural* **-lae** [-lee] *astronomy* diffuse cloud of particles, gases > **neb'u•lous** *adjective* 1 cloudy 2 vague, indistinct

nec•es•sar•y [NES-ə-ser-ee] *adjective* 1 needful, requisite, that must be done 2 unavoidable, inevitable > **nec'es•sar•i•ly** *adverb* > **ne•ces'si•tate** *verb transitive* **-tat•ed, -tat•ing** make necessary > **ne•ces'si•tous** *adjective* poor, needy, destitute > **ne•ces'si•ty** *noun, plural* **-ties** 1 something needed, requisite 2 constraining power or state of affairs 3 compulsion 4 poverty

neck [nek] *noun* 1 part of body joining head to shoulders 2 narrower part of a bottle, etc. 3 narrow piece of anything between wider parts ▷ *verb intransitive* 4 (*informal*) embrace, cuddle > **neck'lace** [-lis] *noun* ornament around the neck

nec•ro•man•cy [NEK-rə-man-see] *noun* magic, esp. by communication with dead > **nec'ro•man•cer** *noun* wizard

ne•crop•o•lis [nə-KROP-ə-lis] *noun, plural* **-lis•es** cemetery

nec•tar [NEK-tər] *noun* 1 honey of flowers 2 drink of the gods

nec•tar•ine [nek-tə-REEN] *noun* variety of peach

nee [nay] *adjective* indicating maiden name of married woman

need *verb transitive* 1 want, require ▷ *noun* 2 (state, instance of) want 3 requirement 4 necessity 5 poverty > **need'ful** *adjective* necessary, requisite > **need'less** *adjective* unnecessary > **needs** *adverb* (with *must*) necessarily > **need'y** *adjective* **need•i•er, need•i•est** poor, in want

nee•dle [NEE-dl] *noun* **-dled, -dling** 1 pointed pin with an eye and no head, for sewing 2 long, pointed pin for knitting 3 pointer of gauge, dial 4 magnetized bar of compass 5 stylus for record player 6 leaf of fir, pine, etc. 7 obelisk 8 hypodermic syringe ▷ *verb transitive* 9 (*informal*) goad, provoke > **nee'dle•craft, nee'dle•work** *noun* embroidery, sewing

ne•far•i•ous [ni-FAIR-ee-əs] *adjective* wicked > **ne•far'i•ous•ness** *noun*

ne•gate [ni-GAYT] *verb transitive* **-gat•ed, -gat•ing** deny, nullify > **ne•ga'tion** *noun* contradiction, denial

---

nearby *adjective* NEIGHBORING, adjacent, adjoining, convenient, handy

nearly *adverb* ALMOST, approximately, as good as, just about, practically, roughly, virtually, well-nigh

nearness *noun* CLOSENESS, accessibility, availability, handiness, proximity, vicinity

near-sighted *adjective* SHORT-SIGHTED, myopic

neat *adjective* 1 TIDY, orderly, shipshape, smart, spick-and-span, spruce, systematic, trim 2 ELEGANT, adept, adroit, deft, dexterous, efficient, graceful, nimble, skillful, stylish 3 (*alcoholic drinks*) STRAIGHT, pure, undiluted, unmixed

neatly *adverb* 1 TIDILY, daintily, fastidiously, methodically, smartly, sprucely, systematically 2 ELEGANTLY, adeptly, adroitly, deftly, dexterously, efficiently, expertly, gracefully, nimbly, skillfully

neatness *noun* 1 TIDINESS, daintiness, orderliness, smartness, spruceness, trimness 2 ELEGANCE, adroitness, deftness, dexterity, efficiency, grace, nimbleness, skill, style

nebulous *adjective* VAGUE, confused, dim, hazy, imprecise, indefinite, indistinct, shadowy, uncertain, unclear

necessarily *adverb* CERTAINLY, automatically, compulsorily, incontrovertibly, inevitably, inexorably, naturally, of necessity, undoubtedly

necessary *adjective* 1 NEEDED, compulsory, essential, imperative, indispensable, mandatory, obligatory, required, requisite, vital 2 CERTAIN, fated, inescapable, inevitable, inexorable, unavoidable

necessitate *verb* COMPEL, call for, coerce, constrain, demand, force, impel, oblige, require

necessities *plural noun* ESSENTIALS, exigencies, fundamentals, needs, requirements

necessity *noun* 1 INEVITABILITY, compulsion, inexorableness, obligation 2 NEED, desideratum, essential, fundamental, prerequisite, requirement, requisite, sine qua non (*Latin*)

necromancy *noun* MAGIC, black magic, divination, enchantment, sorcery, witchcraft, wizardry

necropolis *noun* CEMETERY, burial ground, churchyard, graveyard

need *verb* 1 REQUIRE, call for, demand, entail, lack, miss, necessitate, want ▷ *noun* 2 POVERTY, deprivation, destitution, inadequacy, insufficiency, lack, paucity, penury, shortage 3 REQUIREMENT, demand, desideratum, essential, requisite 4 EMERGENCY, exigency, necessity, obligation, urgency, want

needed *adjective* NECESSARY, called for, desired, lacked, required, wanted

needful *adjective* NECESSARY, essential, indispensable, needed, required, requisite, stipulated, vital

needle *verb* IRRITATE, annoy, get on one's nerves (*informal*), goad, harass, nag, pester, provoke, rile, taunt

needless *adjective* UNNECESSARY, gratuitous, groundless, pointless, redundant, superfluous, uncalled-for, unwanted, useless

needlework *noun* EMBROIDERY, needlecraft, sewing, stitching, tailoring

needy *adjective* POOR, deprived, destitute, disadvantaged, impoverished, penniless, poverty-stricken, underprivileged

nefarious *adjective* WICKED, criminal, depraved, evil, foul, heinous, infernal, villainous

negate *verb* 1 INVALIDATE, annul, cancel, countermand, neutralize, nullify, obviate, reverse, wipe out 2 DENY, contradict, disallow, disprove, gainsay (*archaic or literary*), oppose, rebut, refute

neg•a•tive [NEG-ə-tiv] *adjective* 1 expressing denial or refusal 2 lacking enthusiasm, energy, interest 3 not positive 4 of electrical charge having the same polarity as the charge of an electron ▷ *noun* 5 negative word or statement 6 *photography* picture made by action of light on chemicals in which lights and shades are reversed

ne•glect [ni-GLEKT] *verb transitive* 1 disregard, take no care of 2 fail to do 3 omit through carelessness ▷ *noun* 4 fact of neglecting or being neglected > **ne•glect'ful** *adjective*

neg•li•gee [NEG-li-zhay] *noun* woman's light, gauzy nightgown or dressing gown

neg•li•gence [NEG-li-jəns] *noun* 1 neglect 2 carelessness > **neg'li•gent** *adjective* > **neg'li•gi•ble** *adjective* 1 able to be disregarded 2 very small or unimportant

ne•go•ti•ate [ni-GOH-shee-ayt] *verb intransitive* **-at•ed, -at•ing** 1 discuss with view to mutual settlement ▷ *verb transitive* **-at•ed, -at•ing** 2 arrange by conference 3 transfer (bill, check, etc.) 4 get over, past, around (obstacle) > **ne•go'ti•a•ble** [-shə-bəl] *adjective* > **ne•go•ti•a'tion** [-shee-AY-shən] *noun* 1 dealing with another on business 2 discussion 3 transference (of bill, check, etc.)

Ne•gro [NEE-groh] *noun, plural* **-groes** (*often offensive*) dark-skinned person of African ancestry ▷ *adjective*

neigh [nay] *noun* 1 cry of horse ▷ *verb intransitive* 2 utter this cry

neigh•bor [NAY-bər] *noun* one who lives near another > **neigh'bor•hood** *noun* 1 district 2 people of a district 3 region around about > **neigh'bor•ing** *adjective* situated nearby > **neigh'bor•ly** *adjective* 1 as or befitting a good or friendly neighbor 2 friendly 3 helpful

nei•ther [NEE-thər] *adjective, pronoun* 1 not the one or the other ▷ *adverb* 2 not on the one hand 3 not either ▷ *conjunction* 4 nor yet

nem•e•sis [NEM-ə-sis] *noun, plural* **-ses** [-seez] 1 retribution 2 (**Nem•e•sis**) the goddess of vengeance

neo- *combining form* new, later, revived in modified form, based upon: *neoclassicism*

neo•con•ser•va•tism [nee-oh-kən-SUR-və-tiz-əm] *noun* conservative tendency among supporters of the political left that has become characterized by its support of hawkish foreign policies

Ne•o•lith•ic [nee-ə-LITH-ik] *adjective* of the later Stone Age

ne•ol•o•gism [nee-OL-ə-jiz-əm] *noun* newly coined word or phrase

ne•on [NEE-on] *noun* one of the inert constituent gases of the atmosphere, used in illuminated signs and lights

ne•o•phyte [NEE-ə-fīt] *noun* 1 new convert 2 beginner, novice

neph•ew [NEF-yoo] *noun* brother's or sister's son

ne•phri•tis [nə-FRĪ-tis] *noun* inflammation of kidneys > **ne•phro•sis** [-FROH-sis] *noun* degenerative disease of kidneys

nep•o•tism [NEP-ə-tiz-əm] *noun* undue favoritism toward one's relations

Nep•tune [NEP-toon] *noun* 1 god of the sea 2 planet second farthest from sun

nep•tu•ni•um [nep-TOO-nee-əm] *noun* synthetic metallic element

nerd [nurd] *noun* (*slang*) boring person obsessed

DICTIONARY

n

THESAURUS

negation *noun* 1 CANCELLATION, neutralization, nullification
2 DENIAL, contradiction, converse, disavowal, inverse, opposite, rejection, renunciation, reverse

negative *adjective* 1 CONTRADICTORY, contrary, denying, dissenting, opposing, refusing, rejecting, resisting
2 PESSIMISTIC, cynical, gloomy, jaundiced, uncooperative, unenthusiastic, unwilling
▷ *noun* 3 CONTRADICTION, denial, refusal

neglect *verb* 1 DISREGARD, blow off (*slang*), disdain, ignore, overlook, rebuff, scorn, slight, spurn
2 FORGET, be remiss, evade, omit, pass over, shirk, skimp
▷ *noun* 3 DISREGARD, disdain, inattention, indifference
4 NEGLIGENCE, carelessness, dereliction, failure, laxity, oversight, slackness

neglected *adjective* 1 ABANDONED, derelict, overgrown
2 DISREGARDED, unappreciated, underestimated, undervalued

neglectful *adjective* CARELESS, heedless, inattentive, indifferent, lax, negligent, remiss, thoughtless, uncaring

negligence *noun* CARELESSNESS, dereliction, disregard, inattention, indifference, laxity, neglect, slackness, thoughtlessness

negligent *adjective* CARELESS, forgetful, heedless, inattentive, neglectful, remiss, slack, slapdash, thoughtless, unthinking

negligible *adjective* INSIGNIFICANT, imperceptible, inconsequential, minor, minute, small, trifling, trivial, unimportant

negotiable *adjective* DEBATABLE, variable

negotiate *verb* 1 DEAL, arrange, bargain, conciliate, debate, discuss, haggle, mediate, transact, work out
2 GET ROUND, clear, cross, get over, get past, pass, surmount

negotiation *noun* BARGAINING, arbitration, debate, diplomacy, discussion, haggling, mediation, transaction, wheeling and dealing (*informal*)

negotiator *noun* MEDIATOR, ambassador, delegate, diplomat, honest broker, intermediary, moderator

neighborhood *noun* DISTRICT, community, environs, locale, locality, quarter, region, vicinity

neighboring *adjective* NEARBY, adjacent, adjoining, bordering, connecting, near, next, surrounding

neighborly *adjective* HELPFUL, considerate, friendly, harmonious, hospitable, kind, obliging, sociable

nemesis *noun* RETRIBUTION, destiny, destruction, fate, vengeance

nepotism *noun* FAVORITISM, bias, partiality, patronage, preferential treatment

nerd *noun* BORE, doofus (*slang*), dork (*slang*), drip (*informal*), dweeb (*slang*), egghead (*informal*), geek

with a particular subject

nerve [nurv] *noun* 1 sinew, tendon 2 fiber or bundle of fibers conveying feeling, impulses to motion, etc. to and from brain and other parts of body 3 assurance 4 coolness in danger 5 audacity > **nerves** irritability, unusual sensitiveness to fear, annoyance, etc. > **nerve'less** [-lis] *adjective* 1 without nerves 2 useless 3 weak 4 paralyzed > **nerv'ous** [-əs] *adjective* 1 excitable 2 timid, apprehensive, worried 3 of the nerves > **nerv'y** [-ee] *adjective* **nerv•i•er, nerv•i•est** 1 nervous, jumpy, irritable 2 on edge > **nervous breakdown** condition of mental, emotional disturbance, disability

nest *noun* 1 place in which bird lays and hatches its eggs 2 animal's breeding place 3 snug retreat ▷ *verb intransitive* 4 make, have a nest > **nest egg** (fund of) money in reserve

nes•tle [NES-əl] *verb intransitive* **-tled, -tling** settle comfortably, usu. pressing in or close to something

nest'ling *noun* bird too young to leave nest

net[1] *noun* 1 openwork fabric of meshes of cord, etc. 2 piece of it used to catch fish, etc. 3 (**Net**) *short for* **Internet** ▷ *verb transitive* **net•ted, net•ting** 4 cover with, or catch in, net 5 catch, ensnare > **netting** *noun* string or wire net > **net'ball** *noun tennis* return shot that hits top of net and remains in play > **net•i•quette** [NET-i-kit] *noun* informal code of behaviour on the Internet

net[2] *adjective* 1 left after all deductions 2 free from deduction ▷ *verb transitive* **net•ted, net•ting** 3 gain, yield as clear profit

neth•er [NETH-ər] *adjective* lower

ne•tsu•ke [NET-skee] *noun* carved wooden or ivory toggle or button worn in Japan

net•tle [NET-l] *noun* 1 plant with stinging hairs on the leaves ▷ *verb transitive* **-tled, -tling** 2 irritate, provoke

net•work [NET-wurk] *noun* 1 system of intersecting lines, roads, etc. 2 interconnecting group of people or things 3 in broadcasting, group of stations connected to transmit same programs simultaneously 4 *computing* system of interconnected computers

neu•ral [NUUR-əl] *adjective* of the nerves

neu•ral•gia [nuu-RAL-jə] *noun* pain in, along nerves, esp. of face and head > **neu•ral'gic** [-jik] *adjective*

neu•ri•tis [nuu-RĪ-tis] *noun* inflammation of nerves

neu•rol•o•gy [nuu-ROL-ə-jee] *noun* science, study of nerves > **neu•rol'o•gist** *noun*

neu•ro•sis [nuu-ROH-sis] *noun, plural* **-ses** [-seez] relatively mild mental disorder > **neu•rot'ic** *adjective* 1 suffering from nervous disorder 2 abnormally sensitive ▷ *noun* 3 neurotic person

neu•ter [NOO-tər] *adjective* 1 neither masculine nor feminine ▷ *noun* 2 neuter word 3 neuter gender ▷ *verb transitive* 4 castrate, spay (domestic animals)

neu•tral [NOO-trəl] *adjective* 1 taking neither side in war, dispute, etc. 2 without marked qualities 3 belonging to neither of two classes ▷ *noun* 4 neutral nation or a citizen of one 5 neutral gear > **neu•tral'i•ty** *noun* > **neu'tral•ize** *verb transitive* **-ized, -iz•ing** 1 make ineffective 2

(*slang*), goober (*informal*)

nerve *noun* 1 BRAVERY, courage, daring, fearlessness, grit, guts (*informal*), pluck, resolution, will
2 IMPUDENCE, audacity, boldness, brazenness, cheek (*informal*), impertinence, insolence, temerity
▷ *verb* 3 ▷ **nerve oneself** BRACE ONESELF, fortify oneself, steel oneself

nerveless *adjective* CALM, composed, controlled, cool, impassive, imperturbable, self-possessed, unemotional

nerve-racking *adjective* TENSE, difficult, distressing, frightening, harrowing, stressful, trying, worrying

nerves *plural noun* TENSION, anxiety, butterflies *or* butterflies in one's stomach (*informal*), cold feet (*informal*), fretfulness, nervousness, strain, stress, worry

nervous *adjective* APPREHENSIVE, anxious, edgy, fearful, jumpy, on edge, tense, uneasy, uptight (*informal*), wired (*slang*), worried

nervousness *noun* ANXIETY, agitation, disquiet, excitability, fluster, tension, touchiness, worry

nervy *adjective* ANXIOUS, agitated, fidgety, jittery (*informal*), jumpy, nervous, on edge, tense, twitchy (*informal*), wired (*slang*)

nest *noun* REFUGE, den, haunt, hideaway, retreat

nest egg *noun* RESERVE, cache, deposit, fall-back, fund *or* funds, savings, store

nestle *verb* SNUGGLE, cuddle, curl up, huddle, nuzzle

nestling *noun* CHICK, fledgling

net[1] *noun* 1 MESH, lattice, netting, network, openwork, tracery, web
▷ *verb* 2 CATCH, bag, capture, enmesh, ensnare, entangle, trap

net[2] *adjective* 1 FINAL, after taxes, clear, take-home
▷ *verb* 2 EARN, accumulate, bring in, clear, gain, make, realize, reap

nether *adjective* LOWER, below, beneath, bottom, inferior, under, underground

nettled *adjective* IRRITATED, annoyed, exasperated, galled, harassed, incensed, peeved, put out, riled, vexed

network *noun* SYSTEM, arrangement, complex, grid, labyrinth, lattice, maze, organization, structure, web

neurosis *noun* OBSESSION, abnormality, affliction, derangement, instability, maladjustment, mental illness, phobia

neurotic *adjective* UNSTABLE, abnormal, compulsive, disturbed, maladjusted, manic, nervous, obsessive, unhealthy

neuter *verb* CASTRATE, doctor (*informal*), emasculate, fix (*informal*), geld, spay

neutral *adjective* 1 UNBIASED, disinterested, even-handed, impartial, nonaligned, nonpartisan, uncommitted, uninvolved, unprejudiced
2 INDETERMINATE, dull, indistinct, intermediate, undefined

neutrality *noun* IMPARTIALITY, detachment, nonalignment, noninterference, noninvolvement, nonpartisanship

neutralize *verb* COUNTERACT, cancel, compensate for, counterbalance, frustrate, negate, nullify,

counterbalance > **neutral gear** in vehicle, position of gears that leaves transmission disengaged

neu•tron [NOO-tron] *noun* electrically neutral particle of the nucleus of an atom > **neutron bomb** nuclear bomb designed to destroy people but not buildings

nev•er [NEV-ər] *adverb* at no time > **nev'er•the•less'** *adverb* for all that, notwithstanding

ne•vus [NEE-vəs] *noun* **1** congenital mark on skin **2** birthmark, mole

new [noo] *adjective* **-er, -est 1** not existing before, fresh **2** that has lately come into some state or existence **3** unfamiliar, strange ▷ *adverb* **4** newly > **new'ly** *adverb* recently, fresh > **new'ness** *noun* > **New Age** cultural movement originating in the 1980s, characterized by such things as alternative medicine, astrology, and meditation > **new'com•er** *noun* recent arrival > **new'fang'led** [-FANG-əld] *adjective* of new fashion

new•el [NOO-əl] *noun* **1** central pillar of winding staircase **2** post at top or bottom of staircase rail

news [nooz] *noun* **1** report of recent happenings, tidings **2** interesting fact not previously known > **news'cast** *noun* news broadcast > **news'deal•er** *noun* shopkeeper who sells newspapers and magazines > **news'flash** *noun* brief news item, oft. interrupting radio, TV program > **news'group** *noun* electronic discussion group on the Internet that is devoted to a specific topic > **news'pa•per** *noun* periodical publication containing news, advertisements, etc. > **news'print** *noun* paper of the kind used for newspapers, etc. > **news'reel** *noun* motion picture giving news > **news'room** *noun* room where news is received and prepared for publication or broadcast > **news'wor•thy** [-wur-thee] *adjective* **-thi•er, -thi•est** sufficiently interesting or important to be reported as news

newt [noot] *noun* small, tailed amphibious creature

new•ton [NOOT-n] *noun* SI unit of force

next [nekst] *adjective, adverb* **1** nearest **2** immediately following > **next of kin** nearest relative(s)

nex•us [NEK-səs] *noun, plural* **nexus 1** tie **2** connection, link

Ni *chem.* nickel

nib•ble [NIB-əl] *verb* **-bled, -bling 1** take little bites of ▷ *noun* **2** little bite

nice [nīs] *adjective* **nic•er, nic•est 1** pleasant **2** friendly, kind **3** attractive **4** subtle, fine **5** careful, exact **6** difficult to decide > **nice'ly** *adverb* > **ni'ce•ty** *noun, plural* **-ties 1** minute distinction or detail **2** subtlety **3** precision

niche [nich] *noun* **1** recess in wall **2** suitable place in life, public estimation, etc.

nick [nik] *verb transitive* **1** make notch in, indent **2** (*slang*) steal ▷ *noun* **3** notch **4** exact point of time **in the nick of time** at the last possible moment

nick•el [NIK-əl] *noun* **1** silver-white metal much used in alloys and plating **2** five-cent piece

nick•name [NIK-naym] *noun* familiar name added to or replacing an ordinary name

nic•o•tine [NIK-ə-teen] *noun* poisonous oily liquid in tobacco

niece [nees] *noun* brother's or sister's daughter

nif•ty [NIFT-ee] *adjective* **-tier, -tiest** (*informal*)

DICTIONARY

n

THESAURUS

---

offset, undo

never *adverb* AT NO TIME, not at all, on no account, under no circumstances

nevertheless *adverb* NONETHELESS, but, even so, though *or* even though, however, notwithstanding, regardless, still, yet

new *adjective* **1** MODERN, contemporary, current, fresh, ground-breaking, latest, novel, original, recent, state-of-the-art, unfamiliar, up-to-date **2** CHANGED, altered, improved, modernized, redesigned, renewed, restored **3** EXTRA, added, more, supplementary

newcomer *noun* NOVICE, arrival, beginner, Johnny-come-lately (*informal*), new kid in town (*informal*), parvenu

newfangled *adjective* NEW, contemporary, cool (*informal*), fashionable, gimmicky, modern, novel, phat (*slang*), recent, state-of-the-art

newly *adverb* RECENTLY, anew, freshly, just, lately, latterly

newness *noun* NOVELTY, freshness, innovation, oddity, originality, strangeness, unfamiliarity, uniqueness

news *noun* INFORMATION, bulletin, communiqué, exposé, gossip, hearsay, intelligence, latest (*informal*), report, revelation, rumor, story

newsworthy *adjective* INTERESTING, important, notable, noteworthy, remarkable, significant, stimulating

next *adjective* **1** FOLLOWING, consequent, ensuing, later, subsequent, succeeding **2** NEAREST, adjacent, adjoining, closest, neighboring ▷ *adverb* **3** AFTERWARDS, following, later, subsequently, thereafter

nibble *verb* **1** BITE, eat, gnaw, munch, nip, peck, pick at ▷ *noun* **2** SNACK, bite, crumb, morsel, peck, soupçon (*French*), taste, tidbit

nice *adjective* **1** PLEASANT, agreeable, attractive, charming, delightful, good, pleasurable **2** KIND, courteous, friendly, likable *or* likeable, polite, well-mannered **3** NEAT, dainty, fine, tidy, trim **4** SUBTLE, careful, delicate, fastidious, fine, meticulous, precise, strict

nicely *adverb* **1** PLEASANTLY, acceptably, agreeably, attractively, charmingly, delightfully, pleasurably, well **2** KINDLY, amiably, commendably, courteously, politely **3** NEATLY, daintily, finely, tidily, trimly

nicety *noun* SUBTLETY, daintiness, delicacy, discrimination, distinction, nuance, refinement

niche *noun* **1** ALCOVE, corner, hollow, nook, opening, recess **2** POSITION, calling, pigeonhole (*informal*), place, slot (*informal*), vocation

nick *verb* **1** CUT, chip, dent, mark, notch, scar, score, scratch, snick ▷ *noun* **2** CUT, chip, dent, mark, notch, scar, scratch

nickname *noun* PET NAME, diminutive, epithet,

neat or smart
nig•gard [NIG-ərd] *noun* mean, stingy person > **nig'gard•ly** *adjective, adverb* > **nig'gard•li•ness** *noun*
nig•gle [NIG-əl] *verb intransitive* **-gled, -gling** 1 find fault continually 2 annoy > **niggling** *adjective* 1 petty 2 irritating and persistent
nigh [nī] *adjective, adverb, preposition* (*literary*) near
night [nīt] *noun* 1 time of darkness between sunset and sunrise 2 end of daylight 3 dark > **night'ie** *noun* (*informal*) nightgown > **night'ly** *adjective* 1 happening, done every night 2 of the night ▷ *adverb* 3 every night 4 by night > **night'cap** *noun* 1 cap worn in bed 2 (*informal*) late-night (alcoholic) drink > **night'club** *noun* establishment for dancing, music, etc. open until early morning > **night'gown** *noun* woman's or child's loose gown worn in bed > **night'in•gale** *noun* small Old World bird that sings usu. at night > **night'mare** [-mair] *noun* 1 very bad dream 2 terrifying experience > **night'time** *noun*
ni•hil•ism [NĪ-ə-liz-əm] *noun* 1 rejection of all religious and moral principles 2 opposition to all constituted authority, or government > **ni'hil•ist** *noun* > **ni•hil•ist'ic** *adjective*
nim•ble [NIM-bəl] *adjective* **-bler, -blest** agile, active, quick, dexterous > **nim'bly** *adverb*
nim•bus [NIM-bəs] *noun, plural* **-bi** [-bī] **-bus•es** 1 rain or storm cloud 2 cloud of glory, halo
nine [nīn] *adjective, noun* cardinal number next above eight > **ninth** *adjective* > **ninth'ly** *adverb* > **nine•teen'** *adjective, noun* nine more than ten > **nine•teenth'** *adjective* > **nine'ty** *adjective, noun* nine tens > **nine'ti•eth** *adjective* > **nine'pins** *noun* game where wooden pins are set up to be knocked down by rolling ball, skittles
nip *verb* **nipped, nip•ping** 1 pinch sharply 2 detach by pinching, bite 3 check growth (of plants) thus 4 (*informal*) steal 5 (*informal*) beat (opponent) by close margin 6 hurry ▷ *noun* 7 pinch 8 check to growth 9 sharp coldness of weather 10 small alcoholic drink > **nip'per** *noun* 1 thing (e.g. crab's claw) that nips 2 (*informal*) small boy > **nip'pers** pincers > **nip'py** *adjective* **-pi•er, -pi•est** (*informal*) 1 cold 2 quick
nip•ple [NIP-əl] *noun* 1 point of a breast, teat 2 anything like this
nir•va•na [nir-VAH-nə] *noun* 1 *Buddhism* absolute blessedness 2 *Hinduism* merging of individual in supreme spirit
nit *noun* egg of louse or other parasite > **nit'pick•ing** *adjective* (*informal*) overconcerned with detail, esp. to find fault > **nit'pick** *verb* 1 show such overconcern 2 criticize over petty faults > **nit'wit** *noun* (*informal*) fool > **nit•ty-grit•ty** *noun* (*slang*) basic facts, details
ni•tro•gen [NĪ-trə-jən] *noun* one of the gases making up the air > **ni'trate** *noun* compound of nitric acid and an alkali > **ni'tric** *adjective* > **ni'trous** *adjective* > **ni•trog'e•nous** [-TROJ-ə-nəs] *adjective* of, containing nitrogen > **ni•tro•glyc'er•in** [-troh-GLIS-ə-rin] *noun* explosive liquid
No *chem.* nobelium
no [noh] *adjective* 1 not any, not a 2 not at all ▷ *adverb* 3 expresses negative reply to question or request ▷ *noun, plural* **noes** 4 refusal 5 denial 6 negative vote or voter > **no one** nobody > **no-go** *adjective* (*slang*) 1 not operating 2 canceled > **no man's land** 1 waste or unclaimed land 2 contested land between two opposing forces > **no way** (*informal*) absolutely not
no•bel•i•um [noh-BEL-ee-əm] *noun* synthetic element produced from curium
no•ble [NOH-bəl] *adjective* **-bler, -blest** 1 of the nobility 2 showing, having high moral qualities 3 impressive, excellent ▷ *noun* 4 member of the nobility > **no•bil'i•ty** *noun* 1 in some countries, class holding special rank, usu.

label, moniker *or* monicker (*slang*), sobriquet
nifty *adjective* NEAT, attractive, chic, deft, pleasing, smart, stylish
niggard *noun* MISER, cheapskate (*informal*), Scrooge, skinflint
niggardly *adjective* STINGY, avaricious, frugal, grudging, mean, miserly, parsimonious, tightfisted, ungenerous
niggle *verb* 1 WORRY, annoy, irritate, rankle 2 CRITICIZE, carp, cavil, find fault, fuss
niggling *adjective* 1 PERSISTENT, gnawing, irritating, troubling, worrying 2 PETTY, finicky, fussy, nit-picking (*informal*), pettifogging, picky (*informal*), quibbling
night *noun* DARKNESS, dark, night-time
nightfall *noun* EVENING, dusk, sundown, sunset, twilight
nightly *adjective* 1 NOCTURNAL, night-time ▷ *adverb* 2 EVERY NIGHT, each night, night after night, nights (*informal*)
nightmare *noun* 1 BAD DREAM, hallucination 2 ORDEAL, horror, torment, trial, tribulation
nil *noun* NOTHING, love, naught, none, zero
nimble *adjective* AGILE, brisk, deft, dexterous, lively, quick, sprightly, spry, swift
nimbly *adverb* QUICKLY, briskly, deftly, dexterously, easily, readily, smartly, spryly, swiftly
nip[1] *verb* PINCH, bite, squeeze, tweak
nip[2] *noun* DRAM, draft, drop, mouthful, shot (*informal*), sip, snifter (*informal*)
nippy *adjective* CHILLY, biting, sharp, stinging
nirvana *noun* PARADISE, bliss, joy, peace, serenity, tranquillity
nit-picking *adjective* FUSSY, captious, carping, finicky, hairsplitting, pedantic, pettifogging, quibbling
nitty-gritty *noun* BASICS, brass tacks (*informal*), core, crux, essentials, fundamentals, gist, substance
nitwit *noun* (*informal*) FOOL, dimwit (*informal*), doofus (*slang*), dork (*slang*), dummy (*slang*), halfwit, oaf, schmuck (*slang*), simpleton
no *interjection* 1 NEVER, nay, not at all, no way ▷ *noun* 2 REFUSAL, denial, negation
nobility *noun* 1 INTEGRITY, honor, incorruptibility, uprightness, virtue 2 ARISTOCRACY, elite, lords, nobles, patricians, peerage, upper class
noble *adjective* 1 WORTHY, generous, honorable, magnanimous, upright, virtuous 2 ARISTOCRATIC, blue-blooded, highborn, lordly, patrician, titled 3 GREAT, dignified, distinguished, grand, imposing, impressive, lofty, splendid, stately ▷ *noun* 4 LORD, aristocrat, nobleman, peer

hereditary 2 being noble > **no'bly** *adverb*
no•bod•y [NOH-bod-ee] *pronoun* 1 no person 2 no one ▷ *noun, plural* **-bod•ies** 3 person of no importance
noc•tur•nal [nok-TUR-nl] *adjective* 1 of, in, by, night 2 active by night
noc•turne [NOK-turn] *noun* dreamy piece of music
nod *verb* **nod•ded, nod•ding** 1 bow head slightly and quickly in assent, command, etc. 2 let head droop with sleep ▷ *noun* 3 act of nodding **nodding acquaintance** slight knowledge of person or subject **give the nod to** (*informal*) express approval of > **nod off** fall asleep
node [nohd] *noun* 1 knot or knob 2 point at which curve crosses itself > **no'dal** [-əl] *adjective*
nod•ule [NOJ-ool] *noun* 1 little knot 2 rounded irregular mineral mass
No•el [noh-EL] *noun* 1 Christmas 2 (**no•el**) Christmas carol
nog *noun* 1 drink made with beaten eggs 2 eggnog 3 peg, block
nog•gin [NOG-ən] *noun* 1 small amount of liquor 2 small mug 3 (*informal*) head
noise [noyz] *noun* 1 any sound, esp. disturbing one 2 clamor, din 3 loud outcry 4 talk or interest ▷ *verb transitive* 5 rumor > **noise'less** [-lis] *adjective* without noise, quiet, silent > **nois'i•ly** *adverb* > **nois'y** *adjective* **nois•i•er, nois•i•est** 1 making much noise 2 clamorous
noi•some [NOI-səm] *adjective* 1 disgusting 2 noxious
no•mad [NOH-mad] *noun* 1 member of tribe with no fixed dwelling place 2 wanderer > **no•mad'ic** *adjective*
nom de plume [nom də PLOOM] *Fr.* 1 writer's assumed name 2 pen name 3 pseudonym
no•men•cla•ture [NOH-mən-klay-chər] *noun* terminology of particular science, etc.
nom•i•nal [NOM-ə-nəl] *adjective* 1 in name only 2 (of fee, etc.) small, insignificant 3 of a name or names > **nom'i•nal•ly** *adverb* 1 in name only 2 not really
nom•i•nate [NOM-ə-nayt] *verb transitive* **-nat•ed, -nat•ing** 1 propose as candidate 2 appoint to office > **nom•i•na'tion** *noun* > **nom'i•na•tive** [-nə-tiv] *adjective, noun* (of) case of nouns, pronouns when subject of verb > **nom•i•nee'** *noun* candidate
non- *prefix* 1 (indicating) negation: *nonexistent* 2 (indicating) refusal or failure: *noncooperation* 3 (indicating) exclusion from a specified class: *nonfiction* 4 (indicating) lack or absence: *nonevent*
non•a•ge•nar•i•an [non-ə-jə-NAIR-ee-ən] *adjective* 1 aged between ninety and ninety-nine ▷ *noun* 2 person of such age
non•ag•gres'sion *noun* policy of not attacking other countries
non•al•co•hol'ic *adjective* containing no alcohol
nonce [nons] *noun* **for the nonce** 1 for the occasion only 2 for the present
non•cha•lant [non-shə-LAHNT] *adjective* casually unconcerned, indifferent, cool > **non'cha•lance** *noun*
non•com•bat•ant [non-kəm-BAT-nt] *noun* 1 civilian during war 2 member of army who does not fight, e.g. chaplain
non•com•mit•tal [non-kə-MIT-l] *adjective* avoiding definite preference or pledge
non com•pos men•tis [NON KOM-pohs MEN-tis] *Lat.* of unsound mind
non•con•duc'tor *noun* substance that is a poor conductor of heat, electricity, or sound
non•con•trib'u•to•ry *adjective* denoting a pension scheme for employees, the premiums of which are paid entirely by the employer
non•de•script [non-di-SKRIPT] *adjective* lacking distinctive characteristics, indeterminate

DICTIONARY

n

THESAURUS

nobody *pronoun* 1 NO-ONE
▷ *noun* 2 NONENTITY, cipher, lightweight (*informal*), menial
nocturnal *adjective* NIGHTLY, night-time
nod *verb* 1 ACKNOWLEDGE, bow, gesture, indicate, signal
2 SLEEP, doze, drowse, nap
▷ *noun* 3 GESTURE, acknowledgment, greeting, indication, sign, signal
noggin *noun* 1 CUP, dram, mug, nip, tot
2 (*informal*) HEAD, block (*informal*), noodle (*slang*), nut (*slang*)
no go *adjective* IMPOSSIBLE, futile, hopeless, vain
noise *noun* SOUND, clamor, commotion, din, hubbub, racket, row, uproar
noiseless *adjective* SILENT, hushed, inaudible, mute, quiet, soundless, still
noisome *adjective* 1 POISONOUS, bad, harmful, pernicious, pestilential, unhealthy, unwholesome
2 OFFENSIVE, disgusting, fetid, foul, funky (*slang*), malodorous, noxious, putrid, smelly, stinking
noisy *adjective* LOUD, boisterous, cacophonous, clamorous, deafening, ear-splitting, strident, tumultuous, uproarious, vociferous
nomad *noun* WANDERER, drifter, itinerant, migrant, rambler, rover, vagabond
nomadic *adjective* WANDERING, itinerant, migrant, peripatetic, roaming, roving, traveling, vagrant
nom de plume *noun* PSEUDONYM, alias, assumed name, nom de guerre, pen name
nomenclature *noun* TERMINOLOGY, classification, codification, phraseology, taxonomy, vocabulary
nominal *adjective* 1 SO-CALLED, formal, ostensible, professed, puppet, purported, supposed, theoretical, titular
2 SMALL, inconsiderable, insignificant, minimal, symbolic, token, trifling, trivial
nominate *verb* NAME, appoint, assign, choose, designate, elect, propose, recommend, select, suggest
nomination *noun* CHOICE, appointment, designation, election, proposal, recommendation, selection, suggestion
nominee *noun* CANDIDATE, aspirant, contestant, entrant, protégé, runner
nonaligned *adjective* NEUTRAL, impartial, uncommitted, undecided
nonchalance *noun* INDIFFERENCE, calm, composure, equanimity, imperturbability, sang-froid, self-possession, unconcern
nonchalant *adjective* CASUAL, blasé, calm, careless, indifferent, insouciant, laid-back (*informal*), offhand, unconcerned, unperturbed
noncombatant *noun* CIVILIAN, neutral,

none [nun] *pronoun* 1 no one, not any ▷ *adjective* 2 no ▷ *adverb* 3 in no way > **none•the•less'** *adverb* despite that, however
non•en•ti•ty [non-EN-ti-tee] *noun, plural* **-ties** 1 insignificant person, thing 2 nonexistent thing
non•e•vent' *noun* disappointing or insignificant occurrence
non•exist'ent *adjective* not existing, imaginary > **nonexistence** *noun*
non•fic'tion *noun* writing that deals with facts or real events
non•in•ter•ven'tion *noun* refusal to intervene in the affairs of others
non•pa•reil [non-pə-REL] *adjective* 1 unequaled, matchless ▷ *noun* 2 person or thing unequaled or unrivaled 3 small bead of colored sugar used to decorate cakes, etc. 4 flat round piece of chocolate covered with this sugar
non•pay'ment *noun* failure to pay money owed
non•plus' *verb transitive* **-plussed, -plus•sing** disconcert, confound, or bewilder completely
non•prof•it *adjective* not run with the intention of making a profit
non•sense [NON-sens] *noun* 1 lack of sense 2 absurd language 3 absurdity 4 silly conduct > **non•sen'si•cal** *adjective* 1 ridiculous 2 meaningless 3 without sense
non se•qui•tur [non SEK-wi-tər] *Lat.* statement with little or no relation to what preceded it
non•smok'er *noun* person who does not smoke > **non-smok'ing, no-smok'ing** *adjective* denoting an area in which smoking is forbidden
non•stand'ard *adjective* denoting language that is not regarded as correct by educated native speakers
non•start'er *noun* person or idea that has little chance of success
non•stick' *adjective* coated with a substance that food will not stick to when cooked
non•stop' *adjective, adverb* without a stop
non•tox'ic *adjective* not poisonous
non•vi'o•lent *adjective* using peaceful methods to bring about change > **non•vi'o•lence** *noun*
noo•dle[1] [NOOD-l] *noun* strip of pasta served in soup, etc.
noodle[2] *noun* 1 simpleton, fool 2 (*slang*) the head
nook [nuuk] *noun* sheltered corner, retreat
noon *noun* midday, twelve o'clock > **noon'day** *noun* noon > **noon'tide** *noun* the time about noon
noose [noos] *noun* 1 running loop 2 snare ▷ *verb transitive* **noosed, noos•ing** 3 catch, ensnare in noose, lasso
nor *conjunction* and not
Nor•dic [NOR-dik] *adjective* pert. to peoples of Germanic stock, e.g. Scandinavians
norm *noun* 1 average level of achievement 2 rule or authoritative standard 3 model 4 standard type or pattern > **nor'mal** *adjective* 1 ordinary 2 usual 3 conforming to type ▷ *noun geom.* 4 perpendicular > **nor'mal•ly** *adverb*
north *noun* 1 direction to the right of person facing the sunset 2 part of the world, of country, etc. toward this point ▷ *adverb* 3 toward or in the north ▷ *adjective* 4 to, from, or in the north > **north•er•ly** [NOR-*th*ər-lee] *adjective* 1 (of wind) from the north ▷ *noun* 2 a

DICTIONARY • THESAURUS

nonbelligerent
noncommittal *adjective* EVASIVE, cautious, circumspect, equivocal, guarded, neutral, politic, temporizing, tentative, vague, wary
non compos mentis *adjective* INSANE, crazy, deranged, mentally ill, unbalanced, unhinged
nonconformist *noun* MAVERICK, dissenter, eccentric, heretic, iconoclast, individualist, protester, radical, rebel
nonconformity *noun* DISSENT, eccentricity, heresy, heterodoxy
nondescript *adjective* ORDINARY, commonplace, dull, featureless, undistinguished, unexceptional, unremarkable
none *pronoun* NOT ANY, nil, nobody, no-one, nothing, not one, zero
nonentity *noun* NOBODY, cipher, lightweight (*informal*), mediocrity, small fry
nonessential *adjective* UNNECESSARY, dispensable, expendable, extraneous, inessential, peripheral, superfluous, unimportant
nonetheless *adverb* NEVERTHELESS, despite that, even so, however, in spite of that, yet
nonevent *noun* FLOP (*informal*), disappointment, dud (*informal*), failure, fiasco, washout
nonexistent *adjective* IMAGINARY, chimerical, fictional, hypothetical, illusory, legendary, mythical, unreal
nonsense *noun* RUBBISH, balderdash, claptrap (*informal*), drivel, gibberish, hot air (*informal*), stupidity, tripe (*informal*), twaddle
nonsensical *adjective* SENSELESS, absurd, crazy, foolish, inane, incomprehensible, irrational, meaningless, ridiculous, silly
nonstarter *noun* DEAD LOSS, dud (*informal*), lemon (*informal*), loser, no-hoper (*informal*), turkey (*informal*), washout (*informal*)
nonstop *adjective* 1 CONTINUOUS, constant, endless, incessant, interminable, relentless, twenty-four-seven (*slang*), unbroken, uninterrupted
▷ *adverb* 2 CONTINUOUSLY, ceaselessly, constantly, endlessly, incessantly, interminably, perpetually, relentlessly, twenty-four-seven (*slang*), unremittingly
noodle *noun* (*slang*) HEAD, common sense, gut feeling (*informal*), intuition, sense
nook *noun* NICHE, alcove, corner, cubbyhole, hideout, opening, recess, retreat
noon *noun* MIDDAY, high noon, noonday, noontide, twelve noon
norm *noun* STANDARD, average, benchmark, criterion, par, pattern, rule, yardstick
normal *adjective* 1 USUAL, average, common, conventional, natural, ordinary, regular, routine, standard, typical
2 SANE, rational, reasonable, well-adjusted
normality *noun* 1 REGULARITY, conventionality, naturalness
2 SANITY, balance, rationality, reason
normally *adverb* USUALLY, as a rule, commonly, generally, habitually, ordinarily, regularly, typically
north *adjective* 1 NORTHERN, Arctic, boreal, northerly, polar
▷ *adverb* 2 NORTHWARD *or* NORTHWARDS, northerly

wind from the north > **north'ern** *adjective* > **north'ern•er** *noun* person from the north > **north•ward** [NORTH-wərd] *adjective* > **north'ward** *or* **north'wards** *adverb*

nose [nohz] *noun* 1 organ of smell, used also in breathing 2 any projection resembling a nose, as prow of ship, aircraft, etc. ▷ *verb* **nosed, nos•ing** 3 (cause to) move forward slowly and carefully ▷ *verb transitive* 4 touch with nose 5 smell, sniff ▷ *verb intransitive* 6 smell 7 pry > **nos•y** *adjective* **nos•i•er, nos•i•est** inquisitive > **nose'dive** *noun* 1 downward sweep of aircraft 2 any sudden sharp fall > **nose'gay** *noun* bunch of flowers

nos•tal•gia [no-STAL-jə] *noun* 1 longing for return of past events 2 homesickness > **nos•tal'gic** *adjective*

nos•tril [NOS-trəl] *noun* one of the two external openings of the nose

nos•trum [NOS-trəm] *noun* 1 quack medicine 2 secret remedy

not *adverb* expressing negation, refusal, denial

no•ta be•ne [NOH-tah BE-ne] *Lat.* note well

no•ta•ble [NOH-tə-bəl] *adjective* 1 worthy of note, remarkable ▷ *noun* 2 person of distinction > **no•ta•bil'i•ty** *noun, plural* **-ties** 1 prominence 2 an eminent person > **no'ta•bly** *adverb*

no•ta•tion [noh-TAY-shən] *noun* 1 representation of numbers, quantities, by symbols 2 set of such symbols

notch [noch] *noun* 1 V-shaped cut or indentation 2 (*informal*) step, grade ▷ *verb transitive* 3 make notches in

note [noht] *noun* 1 brief comment or record 2 short letter 3 promissory note 4 symbol for musical sound 5 single tone 6 sign 7 indication, hint 8 fame 9 notice 10 regard > **notes** 1 brief jottings written down for future reference ▷ *verb transitive* **not•ed, not•ing** 2 observe, record 3 heed > **noted** *adjective* 1 well-known 2 celebrated > **note'book** *noun* small book with blank pages for writing > **note'wor•thy** [-wur-thee] *adjective* worth noting, remarkable

noth•ing [NUTH-ing] *noun* 1 no thing, not anything, nought ▷ *adverb* 2 not at all, in no way

no•tice [NOH-tis] *noun* 1 observation 2 attention, consideration 3 warning, intimation, announcement 4 advance notification of intention to end a contract, etc., as of employment 5 review ▷ *verb transitive* **-ticed, -tic•ing** 6 observe, mention 7 give attention to > **no'tice•a•ble** *adjective* 1 conspicuous 2 attracting attention 3 appreciable

no•ti•fy [NOH-tə-fī] *verb transitive* **-fied, -fy•ing** 1 report 2 give notice of or to > **no•ti•fi•ca'tion** [-KAY-shən] *noun*

no•tion [NOH-shən] *noun* 1 concept 2 opinion 3 whim > **no•tions** small items e.g. buttons, thread for sale in store > **no'tion•al** *adjective*

DICTIONARY

n

THESAURUS

nose *noun* 1 SNOUT, beak, bill, honker (*slang*), proboscis
▷ *verb* 2 EASE FORWARD, nudge, nuzzle, push, shove
3 PRY, meddle, snoop (*informal*)

nosegay *noun* POSY, bouquet

nostalgia *noun* REMINISCENCE, homesickness, longing, pining, regretfulness, remembrance, wistfulness, yearning

nostalgic *adjective* SENTIMENTAL, emotional, homesick, longing, maudlin, regretful, wistful

nostrum *noun* MEDICINE, cure, drug, elixir, panacea, potion, remedy, treatment

nosy *adjective* INQUISITIVE, curious, eavesdropping, interfering, intrusive, meddlesome, prying, snooping (*informal*)

notability *noun* FAME, celebrity, distinction, eminence, esteem, renown

notable *adjective* 1 REMARKABLE, conspicuous, extraordinary, memorable, noteworthy, outstanding, rare, striking, uncommon, unusual
▷ *noun* 2 CELEBRITY, big name, dignitary, personage, V.I.P.

notably *adverb* PARTICULARLY, especially, outstandingly, strikingly

notation *noun* SIGNS, characters, code, script, symbols, system

notch *noun* 1 CUT, cleft, incision, indentation, mark, nick, score
2 (*informal*) LEVEL, degree, grade, step
▷ *verb* 3 CUT, indent, mark, nick, score, scratch

notch up *verb* REGISTER, achieve, gain, make, score

note *noun* 1 MESSAGE, comment, communication, epistle, jotting, letter, memo, memorandum, minute, remark, reminder
2 SYMBOL, indication, mark, sign, token
▷ *verb* 3 SEE, notice, observe, perceive
4 MARK, denote, designate, indicate, record, register
5 MENTION, remark

notebook *noun* JOTTER, diary, exercise book, journal, notepad

noted *adjective* FAMOUS, acclaimed, celebrated, distinguished, eminent, illustrious, notable, prominent, renowned, well-known

noteworthy *adjective* REMARKABLE, exceptional, extraordinary, important, notable, outstanding, significant, unusual

nothing *noun* NOUGHT, emptiness, nada (*informal*), nil, nothingness, nullity, void, zero

nothingness *noun* 1 OBLIVION, nonbeing, nonexistence, nullity
2 INSIGNIFICANCE, unimportance, worthlessness

notice *noun* 1 OBSERVATION, cognizance, consideration, heed, interest, note, regard
2 ATTENTION, civility, respect
3 ANNOUNCEMENT, advice, communication, instruction, intimation, news, notification, order, warning
▷ *verb* 4 OBSERVE, detect, discern, distinguish, mark, note, perceive, see, spot

noticeable *adjective* OBVIOUS, appreciable, clear, conspicuous, evident, manifest, perceptible, plain, striking

notification *noun* ANNOUNCEMENT, advice, declaration, information, intelligence, message, notice, statement, warning

notify *verb* INFORM, advise, alert, announce, declare, make known, publish, tell, warn

notion *noun* 1 IDEA, belief, concept, impression, inkling, opinion, sentiment, view
2 WHIM, caprice, desire, fancy, impulse,

speculative, imaginary, abstract
no•to•ri•ous [noh-TOR-ee-əs] *adjective* 1 known for something bad 2 well-known > **no•to•ri'e•ty** [-tə-RĪ-i-tee] *noun* discreditable publicity
not•with•stand'ing *preposition* 1 in spite of ▷ *adverb* 2 all the same ▷ *conjunction* 3 although
nou•gat [NOO-gət] *noun* chewy candy containing nuts, fruit, etc.
nought [nawt] *noun* 1 nothing 2 figure 0
noun [nown] *noun* word used as name of person, idea, or thing, substantive
nour•ish [NUR-ish] *verb transitive* 1 feed 2 nurture 3 tend 4 encourage
nou•velle cui•sine [noo-vel kwee-ZEEN] Fr. style of preparing and presenting food with light sauces and unusual combinations of flavors
no•va [NOH-və] *noun, plural* **-vas** star that suddenly becomes brighter then loses brightness through months or years
nov•el[1] [NOV-əl] *noun* fictitious tale in book form > **nov'el•ist** *noun* writer of novels
novel[2] *adjective* 1 new, recent 2 strange > **nov'el•ty** *noun, plural* **-ties** 1 newness 2 something new or unusual 3 small ornament, trinket
no•ve•na [noh-VEE-nə] *noun* R.C. *Church* prayers, services usu. extending over nine days
nov•ice [NOV-is] *noun* 1 one new to anything 2 beginner 3 candidate for admission to religious order > **no•vi•ti•ate** [noh-VISH-ee-it] *noun* 1 probationary period 2 part of religious house for novices 3 novice
now *adverb* 1 at the present time 2 immediately 3 (oft. with *just*) recently ▷ *conjunction* 4 seeing that, since > **now'a•days** *adverb* in these times, at present
no•where [NOH-hwair] *adverb* not in any place or state
no•wise [NOH-wīz] *adverb* not in any manner or degree
nox•ious [NOK-shəs] *adjective* poisonous, harmful
noz•zle [NOZ-əl] *noun* pointed spout, esp. at end of hose
Np *chem.* neptunium
NT New Testament
nu•ance [NOO-ahns] *noun* delicate shade of difference, in color, tone of voice, etc.
nub *noun* 1 small lump 2 main point (of story, etc.)
nu•bile [NOO-bil] *adjective* marriageable > **nu•bil'i•ty** *noun*
nu•cle•us [NOO-klee-əs] *noun, plural* **-cle•i** [-klee-ī] 1 center, kernel 2 beginning meant to receive additions 3 core of the atom > **nu'cle•ar** [-klee-ər] *adjective* of, pert. to atomic nucleus > **nuclear energy** energy released by nuclear fission > **nuclear fission** disintegration of the atom > **nuclear reaction** change in structure and energy content of atomic nucleus by interaction with another nucleus, particle > **nuclear reactor** *see* **reactor** > **nuclear winter** period of extremely low temperatures and little light after nuclear war
nude [nood] *noun* 1 state of being naked 2 (picture, statue, etc. of) naked person ▷ *adjective* 3 naked > **nud'ism** *noun* practice of nudity > **nud'ist** *noun* > **nu'di•ty** *noun*
nudge [nuj] *verb transitive* **nudged, nudg•ing** 1 touch slightly esp. with elbow to gain someone's attention, prod someone into action ▷ *noun* 2 such touch
nu•ga•to•ry [NOO-gə-tor-ee] *adjective* 1 trifling 2 futile
nug•get [NUG-it] *noun* 1 rough lump of native gold 2 anything of significance, value

inclination, wish
notional *adjective* SPECULATIVE, abstract, conceptual, hypothetical, imaginary, theoretical, unreal
notoriety *noun* SCANDAL, dishonor, disrepute, infamy, obloquy, opprobrium
notorious *adjective* INFAMOUS, dishonorable, disreputable, opprobrious, scandalous
notoriously *adverb* INFAMOUSLY, dishonorably, disreputably, opprobriously, scandalously
notwithstanding *preposition* DESPITE, in spite of
nought *noun* ZERO, nil, nothing
nourish *verb* 1 FEED, nurse, nurture, supply, sustain, tend
2 ENCOURAGE, comfort, cultivate, foster, maintain, promote, support
nourishing *adjective* NUTRITIOUS, beneficial, nutritive, wholesome
nourishment *noun* FOOD, nutriment, nutrition, sustenance
novel[1] *noun* STORY, fiction, narrative, romance, tale
novel[2] *adjective* NEW, different, fresh, innovative, original, strange, uncommon, unfamiliar, unusual
novelty *noun* 1 NEWNESS, freshness, innovation, oddity, originality, strangeness, surprise, unfamiliarity, uniqueness
2 GIMMICK, curiosity, gadget
3 KNICK-KNACK, bauble, memento, souvenir, trifle, trinket
novice *noun* BEGINNER, amateur, apprentice, learner, newcomer, probationer, pupil, trainee
now *adverb* 1 NOWADAYS, anymore, at the moment
2 IMMEDIATELY, at once, instantly, promptly, straightaway
3 ▷ **now and then, now and again** OCCASIONALLY, from time to time, infrequently, intermittently, on and off, sometimes, sporadically
nowadays *adverb* NOW, anymore, at the moment, in this day and age, today
noxious *adjective* HARMFUL, deadly, destructive, foul, hurtful, injurious, poisonous, unhealthy, unwholesome
nuance *noun* SUBTLETY, degree, distinction, gradation, nicety, refinement, shade, tinge
nubile *adjective* MARRIAGEABLE, ripe (*informal*)
nucleus *noun* CENTER, basis, core, focus, heart, kernel, nub, pivot
nude *adjective* NAKED, bare, disrobed, in one's birthday suit, stark-naked, stripped, unclad, unclothed, undressed, without a stitch on (*informal*)
nudge *verb* PUSH, bump, dig, elbow, jog, poke, prod, shove, touch
nudity *noun* NAKEDNESS, bareness, deshabille, nudism, undress
nugget *noun* LUMP, chunk, clump, hunk,

nui•sance [NOO-səns] *noun* something or someone harmful, offensive, annoying or disagreeable
null *adjective* of no effect, void > **nul'li•fy** [-fī] *verb transitive* **-fied, -fy•ing** 1 cancel 2 make useless or ineffective > **nul'li•ty** *noun* state of being null and void
Num. Numbers
numb [num] *adjective* **-er, -est** 1 deprived of feeling, esp. by cold ▷ *verb transitive* 2 make numb 3 deaden
num•ber [NUM-bər] *noun* 1 sum or aggregate 2 word or symbol saying how many 3 single issue of a journal, etc., issued in regular series 4 classification as to singular or plural 5 song, piece of music 6 performance 7 company, collection 8 identifying number, as of particular house, telephone, etc. 9 (*informal*) measure, correct estimation of ▷ *verb transitive* 10 count 11 class, reckon 12 give a number to 13 amount to > **num'ber•less** *adjective* countless > **number crunching** (*informal*) large-scale processing of numerical data
nu•mer•al [NOO-mər-əl] *noun* sign or word denoting a number > **nu'mer•ate** *verb transitive* **-at•ed, -at•ing** count > **nu•mer•a'tion** *noun* > **nu'mer•a•tor** *noun* top part of fraction, figure showing how many of the fractional units are taken > **nu•mer'i•cal** *adjective* of, in respect of, number or numbers > **nu'mer•ous** [-əs] *adjective* many
nu-met•al [noo-MET-l] *noun* type of rock music featuring sounds typical of heavy metal but also influenced by rap and hip-hop
nu•mis•mat•ic [noo-miz-MAT-ik] *adjective* of coins > **nu•mis•mat'ics** *noun* the study of coins > **nu•mis'ma•tist** [-mə-tist] *noun*
nun *noun* woman living (in convent) under religious vows > **nun'ner•y** *noun, plural* **-ies** convent of nuns
nun•cu•pa•tive [NUNG-kyə-pay-tiv] *adjective* 1 of a will, oral 2 not written
nup•tial [NUP-shəl] *adjective* of, relating to marriage > **nup'tials** *plural noun* 1 marriage 2 wedding ceremony
nurse [nurs] *noun* 1 person trained for care of sick or injured 2 woman tending another's child ▷ *verb transitive* **nursed, nurs•ing** 3 act as nurse to 4 suckle 5 pay special attention to 6 harbor (grudge, etc.) > **nurs'er•y** *noun, plural* **-er•ies** 1 room for children 2 rearing place for plants > **nurs'er•y•man** [-mən] *noun* one who raises plants for sale > **nursing home** institution for housing and caring for the aged or chronically ill
nur•ture [NUR-chər] *noun* 1 bringing up 2 education 3 rearing 4 nourishment ▷ *verb transitive* **-tured, -tur•ing** 5 bring up 6 educate
nut *noun* 1 fruit consisting of hard shell and kernel 2 hollow metal collar into which a screw fits 3 (*slang*) the head 4 (*slang*) eccentric or crazy person ▷ *verb intransitive* **nut•ted, nut•ting** 5 gather nuts > **nut'ty** *adjective* **-ti•er, -ti•est** 1 of, like nut 2 pleasant to taste and bite 3 (*slang*) insane, crazy 4 eccentric > **nuts** *adjective* (*slang*) insane > **nut'hatch** *noun* small songbird > **nut'meg** *noun* aromatic seed of Indian tree
nu•tri•ent [NOO-tree-ənt] *adjective* 1 nourishing ▷ *noun* 2 something nutritious
nu•tri•ment [NOO-trə-mənt] *noun* nourishing food > **nu•tri'tion** [-TRISH-ən] *noun* 1 food 2 act of nourishing 3 study of this process > **nu•tri'tion•ist** *noun* one trained in nutrition > **nu•tri'tious, nu'tri•tive** *adjective* 1 nourishing 2 promoting growth

mass, piece
nuisance *noun* PROBLEM, annoyance, bother, drag (*informal*), hassle (*informal*), inconvenience, irritation, pain in the neck, pest, trouble
null *adjective*
▷ **null and void** INVALID, inoperative, useless, valueless, void, worthless
nullify *verb* CANCEL, counteract, invalidate, negate, neutralize, obviate, render null and void, veto
nullity *noun* NONEXISTENCE, invalidity, powerlessness, uselessness, worthlessness
numb *adjective* 1 UNFEELING, benumbed, dead, deadened, frozen, immobilized, insensitive, paralyzed, torpid
▷ *verb* 2 DEADEN, benumb, dull, freeze, immobilize, paralyze
number *noun* 1 NUMERAL, character, digit, figure, integer
2 QUANTITY, aggregate, amount, collection, crowd, horde, multitude, throng
3 ISSUE, copy, edition, imprint, printing
▷ *verb* 4 COUNT, account, add, calculate, compute, enumerate, include, reckon, total
numberless *adjective* INFINITE, countless, endless, innumerable, multitudinous, myriad, unnumbered, untold
numbness *noun* DEADNESS, dullness, insensitivity, paralysis, torpor
numeral *noun* NUMBER, digit, figure, integer
numerous *adjective* MANY, abundant, copious, plentiful, profuse, several, thick on the ground
nunnery *noun* CONVENT, abbey, cloister, house
nuptial *adjective* MARITAL, bridal, conjugal, connubial, matrimonial
nuptials *plural noun* WEDDING, marriage, matrimony
nurse *verb* 1 LOOK AFTER, care for, minister to, tend, treat
2 BREAST-FEED, feed, nourish, nurture, suckle, wet-nurse
3 FOSTER, cherish, cultivate, encourage, harbor, preserve, promote, succor, support
nursery *noun* CRECHE, kindergarten, playgroup
nurture *noun* 1 DEVELOPMENT, discipline, education, instruction, rearing, training, upbringing
▷ *verb* 2 DEVELOP, bring up, discipline, educate, instruct, rear, school, train
nut *noun* 1 (*slang*) MADMAN, crank (*informal*), lunatic, maniac, nutcase (*slang*), psycho (*slang*)
2 (*slang*) HEAD, brain, mind, reason, senses
nutrition *noun* FOOD, nourishment, nutriment, sustenance
nutritious *adjective* NOURISHING, beneficial, health-giving, invigorating, nutritive, strengthening, wholesome
nuts *adjective* (*informal*) INSANE, deranged, disturbed, mad, mentally ill, psychotic, unbalanced, unstable

nuz•zle [NUZ-əl] *verb intransitive* **-zled, -zling 1** burrow, press with nose **2** nestle

ny•lon [NĪ-lon] *noun* synthetic material used for fabrics, bristles, ropes, etc. > **ny•lons** stockings made of this

nymph [nimf] *noun* legendary semidivine maiden of sea, woods, mountains, etc.

nym•pho•ma•ni•a [nim-fə-MAY-nee-ə] *noun* abnormally intense sexual desire in women > **nym•pho•ma'ni•ac** *noun*

nuzzle *verb* SNUGGLE, burrow, cuddle, fondle, nestle, pet

nymph *noun* SYLPH, dryad, girl, maiden, naiad

O *chem.* oxygen

oaf [ohf] *noun* 1 lout 2 dolt

oak [ohk] *noun* common, deciduous forest tree > **oak'en** [-in] *adjective* of oak

oa•kum [OH-kəm] *noun* loose fiber, used for caulking, got by unraveling old rope

oar [or] *noun* 1 wooden lever with broad blade worked by the hands to propel boat 2 oarsman ▷ *verb* 3 row > **oars•man** [ORZ-mən] *noun, plural* **-men** > **oars'manship** *noun* skill in rowing

o•a•sis [oh-AY-sis] *noun, plural* **-ses** [-seez] 1 fertile spot in desert 2 place serving as pleasant change from routine

oat [oht] *noun* *(usually plural)* 1 grain of cereal grass 2 the plant > **oat'en** [-in] *adjective* > **oat'meal** [-meel] *noun*

oath [ohth] *noun, plural* **oaths** [ohthz] 1 confirmation of truth of statement by naming something sacred 2 curse

ob•bli•ga•to [ob-li-GAH-toh] *adjective, noun, plural* **-tos** *or* **-ti** [-tee] 1 (in musical score) essential 2 essential part of a musical score

ob•du•rate [OB-duu-rit] *adjective* stubborn, unyielding > **ob'du•ra•cy** [-rə-see] *noun*

o•be•di•ence [oh-BEE-dee-əns] *noun* submission to authority > **o•be'di•ent** *adjective* 1 willing to obey 2 compliant 3 dutiful

o•bei•sance [oh-BAY-səns] *noun* 1 deference 2 a bow or curtsy

ob•e•lisk [OB-ə-lisk] *noun* tapering rectangular stone column, with pyramidal apex

o•bese [oh-BEES] *adjective* very fat, corpulent > **o•be'si•ty** *noun*

o•bey [oh-BAY] *verb transitive* 1 do the bidding of 2 act in accordance with ▷ *verb intransitive* 3 do as ordered 4 submit to authority

ob•fus•cate [OB-fə-skayt] *verb transitive* **-cat•ed, -cat•ing** 1 perplex 2 darken 3 make obscure

DICTIONARY **O** THESAURUS

---

oaf *noun* IDIOT, blockhead, clod, dolt, dork (*slang*), dunce, fool, goon, lout, moron (*offensive*), schmuck (*slang*)

oafish *adjective* MORONIC (*offensive*), dense, dim-witted (*informal*), doltish, dumb (*informal*), loutish, stupid, thick

oath *noun* 1 PROMISE, affirmation, avowal, bond, pledge, vow, word
2 SWEARWORD, blasphemy, curse, expletive, profanity

obdurate *adjective* STUBBORN, dogged, hard-hearted, immovable, implacable, inflexible, obstinate, pig-headed, unyielding

obedience *noun* RESPECT, acquiescence, compliance, docility, observance, reverence, submissiveness, subservience

obedient *adjective* RESPECTFUL, acquiescent, biddable, compliant, deferential, docile, dutiful, submissive, subservient, well-trained

obelisk *noun* COLUMN, monolith, monument, needle, pillar, shaft

obese *adjective* FAT, corpulent, gross, heavy, overweight, paunchy, plump, portly, rotund, stout, tubby

obesity *noun* FATNESS, bulk, corpulence, grossness, portliness, stoutness, tubbiness

obey *verb* CARRY OUT, abide by, act upon, adhere to, comply, conform, follow, heed, keep, observe

obfuscate *verb* CONFUSE, befog, cloud, darken, muddy the waters, obscure, perplex

o•bit•u•ar•y [oh-BICH-oo-er-ee] *noun, plural* **-ar•ies** 1 notice, record of death 2 biographical sketch of deceased person, esp. in newspaper (*also* **ob'it**)
ob•ject[1] [OB-jikt] *noun* 1 material thing 2 that to which feeling or action is directed 3 end or aim 4 *grammar* word dependent on verb or preposition > **object lesson** lesson with practical and concrete illustration **no object** not an obstacle or hindrance
ob•ject[2] [əb-JEKT] *verb transitive* 1 state in opposition ▷ *verb intransitive* 2 feel dislike or reluctance to something > **ob•jec'tion** *noun* > **ob•jec'tion•a•ble** *adjective* 1 disagreeable 2 justly liable to objection
ob•jec•tive [əb-JEK-tiv] *adjective* 1 external to the mind 2 impartial ▷ *noun* 3 thing or place aimed at > **ob•jec•tiv'i•ty** [ob-jek-TIV-] *noun*
ob•jur•gate [OB-jər-gayt] *verb transitive* **-gat•ed, -gat•ing** scold, reprove > **ob•jur•ga'tion** *noun*
ob•late [OB-layt] *adjective* of a sphere, flattened at the poles
o•blige [ə-BLĪJ] *verb transitive* **o•bliged, o•blig•ing** 1 bind morally or legally to do service to 2 compel > **ob'li•gate** *verb transitive* **-gat•ed, -gat•ing** 1 bind esp. by legal contract 2 put under obligation > **ob•li•ga'tion** *noun* 1 binding duty, promise 2 debt of gratitude > **o•blig'a•to•ry** *adjective* 1 required 2 binding > **o•blig'ing** *adjective* ready to serve others, civil, helpful, courteous
o•blique [ə-BLEEK] *adjective* 1 slanting 2 indirect > **o•blique'ly** *adverb* > **o•bliq'ui•ty** [-BLIK-wi-tee] *noun, plural* **-ties** 1 slant 2 dishonesty > **oblique angle** one not a right angle
ob•lit•er•ate [ə-BLIT-ə-rayt] *verb transitive* **-at•ed, -at•ing** blot out, efface, destroy completely
ob•liv•i•on [ə-BLIV-ee-ən] *noun* forgetting or being forgotten > **ob•liv'i•ous** *adjective* 1 forgetful 2 unaware
ob•long [OB-lawng] *adjective* 1 rectangular, with adjacent sides unequal ▷ *noun* 2 oblong figure
ob•lo•quy [OB-lə-kwee] *noun, plural* **-quies** 1 reproach, abuse 2 disgrace 3 detraction
ob•nox•ious [əb-NOK-shəs] *adjective* offensive, disliked, odious
o•boe [OH-boh] *noun* woodwind instrument > **o'bo•ist** *noun*
ob•scene [əb-SEEN] *adjective* indecent, lewd, repulsive > **ob•scen'i•ty** [-SEN-i-tee] *noun*
ob•scure [əb-SKYUUR] *adjective* **-scur•er, -scur•est** 1 unclear, indistinct 2 unexplained

DICTIONARY • THESAURUS

---

object[1] *noun* 1 THING, article, body, entity, item, phenomenon
2 TARGET, focus, recipient, victim
3 PURPOSE, aim, design, end, goal, idea, intention, objective, point
object[2] *verb* PROTEST, argue against, demur, draw the line *or* draw the line at something, expostulate, oppose, take exception
objection *noun* PROTEST, counter-argument, demur, doubt, opposition, remonstrance, scruple
objectionable *adjective* UNPLEASANT, deplorable, disagreeable, intolerable, obnoxious, offensive, regrettable, repugnant, unseemly
objective *noun* 1 PURPOSE, aim, ambition, end, goal, intention, mark, object, target
▷ *adjective* 2 UNBIASED, detached, disinterested, dispassionate, even-handed, fair, impartial, open-minded, unprejudiced
objectively *adverb* IMPARTIALLY, disinterestedly, dispassionately, even-handedly, with an open mind
objectivity *noun* IMPARTIALITY, detachment, disinterestedness, dispassion
obligation *noun* DUTY, accountability, burden, charge, compulsion, liability, requirement, responsibility
obligatory *adjective* COMPULSORY, binding, de rigueur (*French*), essential, imperative, mandatory, necessary, required, requisite, unavoidable
oblige *verb* 1 COMPEL, bind, constrain, force, impel, make, necessitate, require
2 INDULGE, accommodate, benefit, gratify, please
obliged *adjective* 1 GRATEFUL, appreciative, beholden, indebted, in (someone's) debt, thankful
2 BOUND, compelled, forced, required
obliging *adjective* COOPERATIVE, accommodating, agreeable, considerate, good-natured, helpful, kind, polite, willing
oblique *adjective* 1 SLANTING, angled, aslant, sloping, tilted
2 INDIRECT, backhanded, circuitous, implied, roundabout, sidelong
obliterate *verb* DESTROY, annihilate, blot out, efface, eradicate, erase, expunge, extirpate, root out, wipe out
obliteration *noun* ANNIHILATION, elimination, eradication, extirpation, wiping out
oblivion *noun* 1 NEGLECT, abeyance, disregard, forgetfulness
2 UNCONSCIOUSNESS, insensibility, obliviousness, unawareness
oblivious *adjective* UNAWARE, forgetful, heedless, ignorant, insensible, neglectful, negligent, regardless, unconcerned, unconscious, unmindful
obloquy *noun* 1 ABUSE, aspersion, attack, blame, censure, criticism, invective, reproach, slander, vilification
2 DISCREDIT, disgrace, dishonor, humiliation, ignominy, infamy, shame, stigma
obnoxious *adjective* OFFENSIVE, disagreeable, insufferable, loathsome, nasty, nauseating, objectionable, odious, repulsive, revolting, scuzzy (*slang*), unpleasant
obscene *adjective* 1 INDECENT, dirty, filthy, immoral, improper, lewd, offensive, pornographic, salacious, scuzzy (*slang*), X-rated
2 SICKENING, atrocious, disgusting, evil, heinous, loathsome, outrageous, shocking, vile, wicked
obscenity *noun* 1 INDECENCY, coarseness, dirtiness, impropriety, lewdness, licentiousness, pornography, smut
2 SWEARWORD, four-letter word, profanity, vulgarism
3 OUTRAGE, abomination, affront, atrocity, blight, evil, offense, wrong
obscure *adjective* 1 VAGUE, ambiguous, arcane,

3 dark, dim 4 humble ▷ *verb transitive* **-scured, -scur•ing** 5 make unintelligible 6 dim 7 conceal > **ob•scu'rant** [-SKYUUR-ənt] *noun* one who opposes enlightenment or reform > **ob•scu'rant•ism** *noun* > **ob•scu'ri•ty** *noun* 1 indistinctness 2 lack of intelligibility 3 darkness 4 obscure, esp. unrecognized, place or position

ob•se•quies [OB-si-kweez] *plural noun* funeral rites

ob•se•qui•ous [əb-SEE-kwee-əs] *adjective* servile, fawning

ob•serve [əb-ZURV] *verb transitive* **-served, -serv•ing** 1 notice, remark 2 watch 3 note systematically 4 keep, follow ▷ *verb intransitive* **-served, -serv•ing** 5 make a remark > **ob•serv'a•ble** *adjective* > **ob•serv'ance** [-əns] *noun* 1 paying attention 2 keeping > **ob•serv'ant** *adjective* 1 quick to notice 2 careful in observing > **ob•ser•va'tion** *noun* 1 action, habit of observing 2 noticing 3 remark > **ob•serv'a•to•ry** [-və-tor-ee] *noun, plural* **-ries** place for watching stars, etc.

ob•sess [əb-SES] *verb transitive* haunt, fill the mind > **ob•ses'sion** [-SESH-ən] *noun* 1 fixed idea 2 domination of the mind by one idea > **ob•ses'sive** *adjective*

ob•sid•i•an [əb-SID-ee-ən] *noun* fused volcanic rock, forming hard, dark, natural glass

ob•so•lete [ob-sə-LEET] *adjective* disused, out of date > **ob•so•les'cent** [-LES-ənt] *adjective* going out of use

ob•sta•cle [OB-stə-kəl] *noun* 1 hindrance 2 impediment, barrier, obstruction

ob•stet•rics [əb-STE-triks] *noun* branch of medicine concerned with childbirth and care of women before and after childbirth > **ob•stet'ric** *adjective* > **ob•ste•tri'cian** [-shən] *noun*

ob•sti•nate [OB-stə-nit] *adjective* 1 stubborn 2 self-willed 3 unyielding 4 hard to overcome or cure > **ob'sti•na•cy** *noun*

ob•strep•er•ous [əb-STREP-ər-əs] *adjective* unruly, noisy, boisterous

ob•struct [əb-STRUKT] *verb transitive* 1 block up 2 hinder 3 impede > **ob•struc'tion** *noun* > **ob•struc'tion•ist** *noun* one who deliberately opposes transaction of business

ob•tain [əb-TAYN] *verb transitive* 1 get 2 acquire 3 procure by effort ▷ *verb intransitive* 4 be customary > **ob•tain'a•ble** *adjective* procurable

ob•trude [əb-TROOD] *verb transitive* **-trud•ed, -trud•ing** thrust forward unduly > **ob•tru'sion** [-TROO-zhən] *noun* > **ob•tru'sive** *adjective* forward, pushing

DICTIONARY **O** THESAURUS

confusing, cryptic, enigmatic, esoteric, mysterious, opaque, recondite
2 INDISTINCT, blurred, cloudy, dim, faint, gloomy, murky, shadowy
3 LITTLE-KNOWN, humble, lowly, out-of-the-way, remote, undistinguished, unheard-of, unknown
▷ *verb* 4 CONCEAL, cover, disguise, hide, obfuscate, screen, veil

obscurity *noun* 1 DARKNESS, dimness, dusk, gloom, haze, shadows
2 INSIGNIFICANCE, lowliness, unimportance

obsequious *adjective* SYCOPHANTIC, cringing, deferential, fawning, flattering, grovelling, ingratiating, servile, submissive, unctuous

observable *adjective* NOTICEABLE, apparent, detectable, discernible, evident, obvious, perceptible, recognizable, visible

observance *noun* HONORING, carrying out, compliance, fulfillment, performance

observant *adjective* ATTENTIVE, alert, eagle-eyed, perceptive, quick, sharp-eyed, vigilant, watchful, wide-awake

observation *noun* 1 STUDY, examination, inspection, monitoring, review, scrutiny, surveillance, watching
2 REMARK, comment, note, opinion, pronouncement, reflection, thought, utterance

observe *verb* 1 SEE, detect, discern, discover, note, notice, perceive, spot, witness
2 WATCH, check, keep an eye on (*informal*), keep track of, look at, monitor, scrutinize, study, survey, view
3 REMARK, comment, mention, note, opine, say, state
4 HONOR, abide by, adhere to, comply, conform to, follow, heed, keep, obey, respect

observer *noun* SPECTATOR, beholder, bystander, eyewitness, fly on the wall, looker-on, onlooker, viewer, watcher, witness

obsessed *adjective* PREOCCUPIED, dominated, gripped, haunted, hung up on (*slang*), infatuated, troubled

obsession *noun* PREOCCUPATION, complex, fetish, fixation, hang-up (*informal*), infatuation, mania, phobia, thing (*informal*)

obsessive *adjective* COMPULSIVE, besetting, consuming, gripping, haunting

obsolescent *adjective* WANING, ageing, declining, dying out, on the wane, on the way out, past its prime

obsolete *adjective* EXTINCT, antiquated, archaic, discarded, disused, old, old-fashioned, outmoded, out of date, passé

obstacle *noun* DIFFICULTY, bar, barrier, block, hindrance, hitch, hurdle, impediment, obstruction, snag, stumbling block

obstinacy *noun* STUBBORNNESS, doggedness, inflexibility, intransigence, obduracy, persistence, pig-headedness, tenacity, willfulness

obstinate *adjective* STUBBORN, determined, dogged, inflexible, intractable, intransigent, pig-headed, refractory, self-willed, strong-minded, willful

obstreperous *adjective* UNRULY, disorderly, loud, noisy, riotous, rowdy, turbulent, unmanageable, wild

obstruct *verb* BLOCK, bar, barricade, check, hamper, hinder, impede, restrict, stop, thwart

obstruction *noun* OBSTACLE, bar, barricade, barrier, blockage, difficulty, hindrance, impediment

obstructive *adjective* UNCOOPERATIVE, awkward, blocking, delaying, hindering, restrictive, stalling, unhelpful

obtain *verb* 1 GET, achieve, acquire, attain, earn, gain, land, procure, secure
2 EXIST, be in force, be prevalent, be the case, hold, prevail

obtainable *adjective* AVAILABLE, achievable, attainable, on tap (*informal*), to be had

obtrusive *adjective* NOTICEABLE, blatant, obvious,

ob•tuse [əb-TOOS] *adjective* 1 dull of perception 2 stupid 3 greater than right angle 4 not pointed
ob•verse [OB-vurs] *noun* 1 a fact, idea, etc. that is the complement of another 2 side of coin, medal, etc. that has the principal design ▷ *adjective* [ob-VURS]
ob•vi•ate [OB-vee-ayt] *verb transitive* **-at•ed, -at•ing** remove, make unnecessary
ob•vi•ous [OB-vee-əs] *adjective* 1 clear, evident 2 wanting in subtlety
oc•ca•sion [ə-KAY-zhən] *noun* 1 time when thing happens 2 reason, need 3 opportunity 4 special event ▷ *verb transitive* 5 cause > **oc•ca'sion•al** *adjective* 1 happening, found now and then 2 produced for some special event: *occasional music* > **oc•ca'sion•al•ly** *adverb* sometimes, now and then
Oc•ci•dent [OK-si-dənt] *noun* the West > **oc•ci•dent'al** *adjective*
oc•ci•put [OK-sə-put] *noun* back of head > **oc•cip'i•tal** *adjective*
oc•clude [ə-KLOOD] *verb transitive* **-clud•ed, -clud•ing** shut in or out > **oc•clu'sion** [-zhən] *noun* > **oc•clu'sive** *adjective* serving to occlude
oc•cult [ə-KULT] *adjective* 1 secret, mysterious 2 supernatural ▷ *noun* 3 esoteric knowledge ▷ *verb transitive* 4 hide from view > **oc•cul•ta•tion** [ok-əl-TAY-shən] *noun* eclipse > **oc'cult•ism** *noun* study of supernatural
oc•cu•py [OK-yə-pī] *verb transitive* **-pied, -py•ing** 1 inhabit, fill 2 employ 3 take possession of > **oc'cu•pan•cy** *noun* 1 fact of occupying 2 residing > **oc'cu•pant** *noun* tenant > **oc•cu•pa'tion** *noun* 1 employment 2 pursuit 3 fact of occupying 4 seizure > **oc•cu•pa'tion•al** *adjective* 1 pert. to occupation, esp. of diseases arising from a particular occupation 2 pert. to use of occupations, e.g. craft, hobbies, etc. as means of rehabilitation
oc•cur [ə-KUR] *verb intransitive* **-curred, -cur•ring** 1 happen 2 come to mind > **oc•cur'rence** *noun* happening
o•cean [OH-shən] *noun* 1 great body of water 2 large division of this 3 the sea > **o•ce•an'ic** [-shee-AN-ik] *adjective* > **o•cea•nol•o•gy** [oh-shə-NOL-ə-jee] *noun* branch of science that relates to ocean
oc•e•lot [OS-ə-lot] *noun* American leopardlike cat
o•cher [OH-kər] *noun* 1 various earths used as yellow or brown pigments 2 this color, from yellow to brown
o'clock [ə-KLOK] *adverb* by the clock
oct-, octa-, octo- *combining form* eight: *octagon; octopus*
oc•ta•gon [OK-tə-gon] *noun* plane figure with eight angles > **oc•tag'o•nal** *adjective*
oc•tane [OK-tayn] *noun* ingredient of gasoline > **octane number** measure of ability of gasoline to reduce engine knock
oc•tave [OK-tiv] *noun mus.* 1 eighth note above or below given note 2 this space
oc•ta•vo [ok-TAY-voh] *noun, plural* **-vos** book in which each sheet is folded three times forming eight leaves
oc•tet [ok-TET] *noun* 1 group of eight 2 music for eight instruments or singers
oc•to•ge•nar•i•an [ok-tə-jə-NAIR-ee-ən] *noun* person aged between eighty and ninety ▷ *adjective*
oc•to•pus [OK-tə-pəs] *noun* mollusk with eight

---

prominent, protruding, protuberant, sticking out
obtuse *adjective* SLOW, dense, dull, stolid, stupid, thick, uncomprehending
obviate *verb* PRECLUDE, avert, prevent, remove
obvious *adjective* EVIDENT, apparent, clear, conspicuous, distinct, indisputable, manifest, noticeable, plain, self-evident, undeniable, unmistakable
obviously *adverb* CLEARLY, manifestly, of course, palpably, patently, plainly, undeniably, unmistakably, unquestionably, without doubt
occasion *noun* 1 TIME, chance, moment, opening, opportunity, window
2 EVENT, affair, celebration, experience, happening, occurrence
3 REASON, call, cause, excuse, ground *or* grounds, justification, motive, prompting, provocation
▷ *verb* 4 CAUSE, bring about, engender, generate, give rise to, induce, inspire, lead to, produce, prompt, provoke
occasional *adjective* INFREQUENT, incidental, intermittent, irregular, odd, rare, sporadic, uncommon
occasionally *adverb* SOMETIMES, at times, from time to time, irregularly, now and again, once in a while, periodically
occult *adjective* SUPERNATURAL, arcane, esoteric, magical, mysterious, mystical
occupancy *noun* TENURE, possession, residence, tenancy, use
occupant *noun* INHABITANT, incumbent, indweller, inmate, lessee, occupier, resident, tenant
occupation *noun* 1 PROFESSION, business, calling, employment, job, line *or* line of work, pursuit, trade, vocation, walk of life
2 POSSESSION, control, holding, occupancy, residence, tenancy, tenure
3 INVASION, conquest, seizure, subjugation
occupied *adjective* 1 BUSY, employed, engaged, working
2 IN USE, engaged, full, taken, unavailable
3 INHABITED, lived-in, peopled, settled, tenanted
occupy *verb* 1 (*often passive*) TAKE UP, divert, employ, engage, engross, involve, monopolize, preoccupy, tie up
2 LIVE IN, dwell in, inhabit, own, possess, reside in
3 FILL, cover, permeate, pervade, take up
4 INVADE, capture, overrun, seize, take over
occur *verb* 1 HAPPEN, befall, come about, crop up (*informal*), take place, turn up (*informal*)
2 EXIST, appear, be found, be present, develop, manifest itself, show itself
3 ▷ **occur to** COME TO MIND, cross one's mind, dawn on, enter one's head, spring to mind, strike one, suggest itself
occurrence *noun* 1 INCIDENT, adventure, affair, circumstance, episode, event, happening, instance
2 EXISTENCE, appearance, development, manifestation, materialization

arms covered with suckers > **oc'to•pod** *noun, adjective* (mollusk) with eight feet
oc•tu•ple [ok-TUU-pəl] *adjective* 1 eight times as many or as much 2 eightfold
oc•u•lar [OK-yə-lər] *adjective* of eye or sight
OD [oh-DEE] *noun* 1 overdose esp. of dangerous drug 2 person who has taken overdose ▷ *verb* **-ed, -ing** 3 take, die of, overdose
odd *adjective* **-er, -est** 1 strange, queer 2 incidental, random 3 that is one in addition when the rest have been divided into equal groups 4 not even 5 not part of a set > **odds** *plural noun* 1 advantage conceded in betting 2 likelihood > **odd'i•ty** *noun, plural* **-ties** 1 odd person or thing 2 quality of being odd > **odd'ments** [-mənts] *plural noun* 1 remnants 2 trifles > **odds and ends** odd fragments or scraps
ode [ohd] *noun* lyric poem on particular subject
o•di•um [OH-dee-əm] *noun* hatred, widespread dislike > **o'di•ous** *adjective* hateful, repulsive
o•dor [OH-dər] *noun* smell > **o•dor•if•er•ous** [oh-də-RIF-ər-əs] *adjective* spreading an odor > **o'dor•ize** *verb transitive* **-ized, -iz•ing** fill with scent > **o'dor•ous** *adjective* 1 fragrant 2 scented > **o'dor•less** [-lis] *adjective*
od•ys•sey [OD-ə-see] *noun, plural* **-seys** any long adventurous journey
of [əv] *preposition* denotes removal, separation, ownership, attribute, material, quality
off [awf] *adverb* 1 away ▷ *preposition* 2 away from ▷ *adjective* 3 not operative 4 canceled or postponed 5 bad, sour, etc. 6 distant 7 of horses, vehicles, etc., to driver's right > **off-color** *adjective* 1 slightly ill 2 risqué > **off•hand'** *adjective, adverb* 1 without previous thought 2 curt > **off•line'** *adjective* 1 (of a computer) not directly controlled by a central processor 2 not connected to or done via the Internet ▷ *adverb* > **off-mes'sage** *adjective* not following the official line, not saying what is expected > **off-road** *adjective* (of a motor vehicle) designed for use away from public roads > **off'set** *noun* 1 that which counterbalances, compensates 2 method of printing > **off•set'** *verb transitive* > **off'spring** *noun* children, issue **in the offing** likely to happen soon
of•fal [AW-fəl] *noun* 1 edible entrails of animal 2 refuse
of•fend [ə-FEND] *verb transitive* 1 hurt feelings of, displease ▷ *verb intransitive* 2 do wrong > **of•fense'** *noun* 1 wrong 2 crime 3 insult 4 *sports, military* attacking team, force > **of•fen'sive** *adjective* 1 causing displeasure 2 aggressive ▷ *noun* 3 position or movement of attack
of•fer [AW-fər] *verb transitive* 1 present for acceptance or refusal 2 tender 3 propose

DICTIONARY **O** THESAURUS

---

odd *adjective* 1 UNUSUAL, bizarre, extraordinary, freakish, irregular, peculiar, rare, remarkable, singular, strange
2 OCCASIONAL, casual, incidental, irregular, periodic, random, sundry, various
3 SPARE, leftover, remaining, solitary, surplus, unmatched, unpaired
oddity *noun* 1 IRREGULARITY, abnormality, anomaly, eccentricity, freak, idiosyncrasy, peculiarity, quirk
2 MISFIT, crank (*informal*), maverick, oddball (*informal*)
oddment *noun* LEFTOVER, bit, fag end, fragment, off cut, remnant, scrap, snippet
odds *plural noun* 1 PROBABILITY, chances, likelihood
2 ▷ **at odds** IN CONFLICT, at daggers drawn, at loggerheads, at sixes and sevens, at variance, out of line
odds and ends *plural noun* SCRAPS, bits, bits and pieces, debris, oddments, remnants
odious *adjective* OFFENSIVE, detestable, horrid, loathsome, obnoxious, repulsive, revolting, scuzzy (*slang*), unpleasant
odor *noun* SMELL, aroma, bouquet, essence, fragrance, perfume, redolence, scent, stench
odyssey *noun* JOURNEY, crusade, pilgrimage, quest, trek, voyage
off *adverb* 1 AWAY, apart, aside, elsewhere, out ▷ *adjective* 2 UNAVAILABLE, canceled, finished, gone, postponed
offbeat *adjective* UNUSUAL, eccentric, left-field (*informal*), novel, outré, strange, unconventional, unorthodox, way-out (*informal*)
off color *adjective* ILL, out of sorts, peaky, poorly (*informal*), queasy, run down, sick, under the weather (*informal*), unwell
offend *verb* INSULT, affront, annoy, displease, hurt (someone's) feelings, outrage, slight, snub, upset, wound
offended *adjective* RESENTFUL, affronted, disgruntled, displeased, outraged, piqued, put out (*informal*), smarting, stung, upset
offender *noun* CRIMINAL, crook, culprit, delinquent, lawbreaker, miscreant, perp (*informal*), sinner, transgressor, villain, wrongdoer
offense *noun* 1 CRIME, fault, misdeed, misdemeanor, sin, transgression, trespass, wrongdoing
2 SNUB, affront, hurt, indignity, injustice, insult, outrage, slight
3 ANNOYANCE, anger, displeasure, indignation, pique, resentment, umbrage, wrath
offensive *adjective* 1 INSULTING, abusive, discourteous, disrespectful, impertinent, insolent, objectionable, rude
2 DISAGREEABLE, disgusting, nauseating, obnoxious, odious, repellent, revolting, unpleasant, vile
3 AGGRESSIVE, attacking, invading
▷ *noun* 4 ATTACK, campaign, drive, onslaught, push (*informal*)
offer *verb* 1 BID, proffer, tender
2 PROVIDE, afford, furnish, present
3 PROPOSE, advance, submit, suggest
4 VOLUNTEER, come forward, offer one's services
▷ *noun* 5 BID, proposal, proposition, submission, suggestion, tender
offering *noun* DONATION, contribution, gift, hand-out, present, sacrifice, subscription
offhand *adjective* 1 CASUAL, aloof, brusque, careless, curt, glib
▷ *adverb* 2 IMPROMPTU, ad lib, extempore, off the cuff (*informal*)
office *noun* POST, function, occupation, place, responsibility, role, situation
officer *noun* OFFICIAL, agent, appointee, executive, functionary, office-holder, representative

4 attempt ▷ *verb intransitive* 5 present itself ▷ *noun* 6 offering, bid > **of'fer•er, of'fer•or** *noun* > **of'fer•to•ry** *noun, plural* **-ies** 1 offering of the bread and wine at the Eucharist 2 collection in church service

of•fice [AW-fis] *noun* 1 room(s), building, in which business, clerical work, etc. is done 2 commercial or professional organization 3 official position 4 service 5 duty 6 form of worship > **of•fic•es** 1 task 2 service > **of'fi•cer** *noun* 1 one in command in army, navy, etc. 2 official

of•fi•cial [ə-FISH-əl] *adjective* 1 with, by, authority ▷ *noun* 2 one holding office, esp. in public body > **of•fi'cial•dom** [-dəm] *noun* officials collectively, or their attitudes, work, usu. in contemptuous sense

of•fi•ci•ate [ə-FISH-ee-ayt] *verb intransitive* **-at•ed, -at•ing** 1 perform duties of office 2 perform ceremony

of•fi•cious [ə-FISH-əs] *adjective* 1 objectionably persistent in offering service 2 interfering

of•ten [AW-fən] *adverb* many times, frequently > **oft** *adverb* (*poetic*) often

o•gle [OH-gəl] *verb* **o•gled, o•gling** 1 stare, look (at) amorously ▷ *noun* 2 this look > **o'gler** *noun*

o•gre [OH-gər] *noun folklore* 1 man-eating giant 2 monster

ohm *noun* unit of electrical resistance > **ohm'me•ter** [-ee-tər] *noun*

oil *noun* 1 any of a number of viscous liquids with smooth, sticky feel and wide variety of uses 2 petroleum 3 any of variety of petroleum derivatives, esp. as fuel or lubricant ▷ *verb transitive* 4 lubricate with oil 5 apply oil to > **oil'y** *adjective* **oil•i•er, oil•i•est** > **oil'skin** *noun* cloth treated with oil to make it waterproof > **oiled** (*slang*) drunk

oint•ment [OINT-mənt] *noun* greasy preparation for healing or beautifying the skin

OK, o•kay [oh-kay] *adjective, adverb* (*informal*) 1 all right ▷ *noun, plural* **OK's** 2 approval ▷ *verb transitive* **OK'd, OK'ing** 3 approve

o•ka•pi [oh-KAH-pee] *noun, plural* **-pis** Afr. animal like short-necked giraffe

old [ohld] *adjective* **old•er, old•est** *or* **eld•er eld•est** 1 aged, having lived or existed long 2 belonging to earlier period > **old-fash'ioned** [-FASH-ənd] *adjective* 1 in style of earlier period, out of date 2 fond of old ways > **old maid** (*offensive*) 1 elderly spinster 2 fussy person

o•le•ag•i•nous [oh-lee-AJ-ə-nəs] *adjective* 1 oily, producing oil 2 unctuous, fawning

ol•fac•to•ry [ohl-FAK-tə-ree] *adjective* of smelling

ol•i•gar•chy [OL-i-gahr-kee] *noun, plural* **-chies** government by a few > **ol•i•gar'chic** *adjective*

ol•ive [OL-iv] *noun* 1 evergreen tree 2 its oil-yielding fruit 3 its wood, color ▷ *adjective* 4 grayish-green

O•lym•pi•ad [ə-LIM-pee-ad] *noun* 1 four-year period between Olympic games 2 celebration of modern Olympic games

om•buds•man [OM-bədz-mən] *noun, plural* **-men** 1 official who investigates citizens' complaints against government 2 person appointed to perform analogous function in a business

o•me•ga [oh-MAY-gə] *noun* 1 last letter of Greek alphabet 2 end

om•e•let [OM-lit] *noun* dish of eggs beaten up and cooked in melted butter with other ingredients and seasoning

o•men [OH-mən] *noun* prophetic object or happening > **om•i•nous** [OM-ə-nəs] *adjective* boding evil, threatening

o•mit [oh-MIT] *verb transitive* **o•mit•ted, o•mit•ting** 1 leave out, neglect 2 leave undone > **o•mis'sion** [-MISH-ən] *noun*

DICTIONARY • THESAURUS

official *adjective* 1 AUTHORIZED, accredited, authentic, certified, formal, legitimate, licensed, proper, sanctioned
▷ *noun* 2 OFFICER, agent, bureaucrat, executive, functionary, office bearer, representative

officiate *verb* PRESIDE, chair, conduct, manage, oversee, serve, superintend

officious *adjective* INTERFERING, dictatorial, intrusive, meddlesome, obtrusive, overzealous, pushy (*informal*), self-important

offing *noun*
▷ **in the offing** IN PROSPECT, imminent, on the horizon, upcoming

offset *verb* CANCEL OUT, balance out, compensate for, counteract, counterbalance, make up for, neutralize

offshoot *noun* BY-PRODUCT, adjunct, appendage, development, spin-off

offspring *noun* 1 CHILD, descendant, heir, scion, successor
2 CHILDREN, brood, descendants, family, heirs, issue, progeny, young

often *adverb* FREQUENTLY, generally, repeatedly, time and again

ogle *verb* LEER, eye up (*informal*)

ogre *noun* MONSTER, bogeyman, bugbear, demon, devil, giant, specter

oil *verb* LUBRICATE, grease

oily *adjective* GREASY, fatty, oleaginous

ointment *noun* LOTION, balm, cream, embrocation, emollient, liniment, salve, unguent

O.K. *or* **okay** *interjection* 1 ALL RIGHT, agreed, right, roger, very good, very well, yes
▷ *adjective* 2 ALL RIGHT, acceptable, adequate, fine, good, in order, permitted, satisfactory, up to scratch (*informal*)
▷ *verb* 3 APPROVE, agree to, authorize, endorse, give the green light, rubber-stamp (*informal*), sanction
▷ *noun* 4 APPROVAL, agreement, assent, authorization, consent, go-ahead (*informal*), green light, permission, sanction, say-so (*informal*), seal of approval

old *adjective* 1 SENILE, aged, ancient, decrepit, elderly, mature, venerable
2 ANTIQUE, antediluvian, antiquated, dated, obsolete, timeworn
3 FORMER, earlier, erstwhile, one-time, previous

old-fashioned *adjective* OUT OF DATE, behind the times, dated, obsolescent, obsolete, old hat, outdated, outmoded, passé, unfashionable

omen *noun* SIGN, foreboding, indication, portent, premonition, presage, warning

ominous *adjective* SINISTER, fateful, foreboding, inauspicious, portentous, threatening, unpromising, unpropitious

omission *noun* EXCLUSION, failure, lack, neglect,

omni- *combining form* all: *omnipresent*
om•ni•bus [OM-nə-bəs] *noun* 1 bus 2 book containing several works ▷ *adjective* 3 serving, containing several objects or subjects
om•ni•di•rec•tion•al *adjective* [om-nə-di-REK-shə-nl] in radio, denotes transmission, reception in all directions
om•nip•o•tent [om-NIP-ə-tənt] *adjective* all-powerful > **om•nip'o•tence** *noun*
om•ni•pres•ent [om-nə-PREZ-ənt] *adjective* present everywhere > **om•ni•pres'ence** *noun*
om•nis•cient [om-NISH-ənt] *adjective* knowing everything > **om•nis'cience** *noun*
om•niv•o•rous [om-NIV-ər-əs] *adjective* 1 devouring all foods 2 not selective e.g. in reading
on *preposition* 1 above and touching, at, near, toward, etc. 2 attached to 3 concerning 4 performed upon 5 during 6 taking regularly ▷ *adjective* 7 operating 8 taking place ▷ *adverb* 9 so as to be on 10 forward 11 continuously, etc. 12 in progress > **on•line'** *adjective* 1 (of a computer) directly controlled by a central processor 2 connected to, or done via, the Internet ▷ *adverb* > **on-mes'sage** *adjective* following the official line, saying what is expected
o•nan•ism [OH-nə-niz-əm] *noun* masturbation
once [wuns] *adverb* 1 one time 2 formerly 3 ever > **once'-o•ver** *noun* (*informal*) quick examination **at once** 1 immediately 2 simultaneously
on•co•gene [ONG-kə-jeen] *noun* any of several genes that when abnormally activated can cause cancer > **on•co•gen'ic** *adjective*
on•col•o•gy [ong-KOL-ə-jee] *noun* 1 branch of medicine dealing with tumors 2 study of cancer
one [wun] *adjective* 1 lowest cardinal number 2 single 3 united 4 only, without others 5 identical ▷ *noun* 6 number or figure 1 7 unity 8 single specimen ▷ *pronoun* 9 particular but not stated person 10 any person > **one'ness** *noun* 1 unity 2 uniformity 3 singleness > **one•self'** *pronoun* > **one'-sid'ed** *adjective* 1 partial 2 uneven > **one-way** *adjective* denotes system of traffic circulation in one direction only
on•er•ous [ON-ər-əs] *adjective* burdensome
on•ion [UN-yən] *noun* edible bulb of pungent flavor **know one's onions** (*slang*) know one's field, etc. thoroughly
on•ly [OHN-lee] *adjective* 1 being the one specimen ▷ *adverb* 2 solely, merely, exclusively ▷ *conjunction* 3 but then, excepting that
on•o•mas•tics [on-ə-MAS-tiks] *noun* study of proper names
on•o•mat•o•poe•ia [on-ə-mat-ə-PEE-ə] *noun* formation of a word by using sounds that resemble or suggest the object or action to be named > **on•o•mat•o•poe'ic, on•o•mat•o•po•et'ic** *adjective*
on•set *noun* 1 violent attack 2 assault 3 beginning
on•slaught [ON-slawt] *noun* attack
on•to [ON-too] *preposition* 1 on top of 2 aware of
on•tog•e•ny [on-TOJ-ə-nee] *noun* development of an individual organism
on•tol•o•gy [on-TOL-ə-jee] *noun* science of being or reality
o•nus [OH-nəs] *noun, plural* **-nus•es** responsibility, burden
on•ward [ON-wərd] *adjective* 1 advanced or advancing ▷ *adverb* 2 in advance, ahead, forward > **on'wards** *adverb*
on•yx [ON-iks] *noun* variety of chalcedony
ooze [ooz] *verb intransitive* **oozed, ooz•ing** 1 pass slowly out, exude (moisture) ▷ *noun* 2 sluggish flow 3 wet mud, slime
o•pal [OH pəl] *noun* glassy gemstone displaying variegated colors > **o•pal•es'cent** *adjective*
o•paque [oh-PAYK] *adjective* not allowing the passage of light, not transparent > **o•pac'i•ty** [-PAS-i-tee] *noun*
op. cit. [op sit] in the work cited
o•pen [OH-pən] *adjective* 1 not shut or blocked up 2 without lid or door 3 bare 4 undisguised 5 not enclosed, covered or exclusive 6 spread out, accessible 7 frank, sincere ▷ *verb transitive* 8 set open, uncover, give access to 9 disclose, lay bare 10 begin 11 make a hole in ▷ *verb intransitive* 12 become open 13 begin ▷ *noun* 14 clear space, unenclosed country 15 *sports* competition in which all may enter > **o'pen•ing**

oversight
omit *verb* LEAVE OUT, drop, eliminate, exclude, forget, neglect, overlook, pass over, skip
omnipotence *noun* SUPREMACY, invincibility, mastery
omnipotent *adjective* ALMIGHTY, all-powerful, supreme
omniscient *adjective* ALL-KNOWING, all-wise
once *adverb* 1 FORMERLY, at one time, long ago, once upon a time, previously
2 ▷ **at once a** IMMEDIATELY, directly, forthwith, instantly, now, right away, straight away, this minute *or* this very minute **b** SIMULTANEOUSLY, at the same time, together
oncoming *adjective* APPROACHING, advancing, forthcoming, looming, onrushing
onerous *adjective* DIFFICULT, burdensome, demanding, exacting, hard, heavy, laborious, oppressive, taxing
one-sided *adjective* BIASED, lopsided, partial, partisan, prejudiced, unfair, unjust
ongoing *adjective* EVOLVING, continuous, developing, progressing, unfinished, unfolding
onlooker *noun* OBSERVER, bystander, eyewitness, looker-on, spectator, viewer, watcher, witness
only *adjective* 1 SOLE, exclusive, individual, lone, single, solitary, unique
▷ *adverb* 2 MERELY, barely, just, purely, simply
onset *noun* BEGINNING, inception, outbreak, start
onslaught *noun* ATTACK, assault, blitz, charge, offensive, onrush, onset
onus *noun* BURDEN, liability, load, obligation, responsibility, task
onward *or* **onwards** *adverb* AHEAD, beyond, forth, forward, in front, on
ooze[1] *verb* SEEP, drain, dribble, drip, escape, filter, leak
ooze[2] *noun* MUD, alluvium, mire, silt, slime, sludge
opaque *adjective* CLOUDY, dim, dull, filmy, hazy, impenetrable, muddy, murky

noun 1 hole, gap 2 beginning 3 opportunity ▷ *adjective* 4 first 5 initial > **o'pen•ly** *adverb* without concealment > **o'pen•hand'ed** *adjective* generous > **o'pen-heart'ed** *adjective* frank, magnanimous > **o'pen-mind'ed** *adjective* unprejudiced > **open source** intellectual property, esp. computer source code, that is made freely available to the general public > **o'pen•work** *noun* pattern with interstices

op•er•a [OP-ər-ə] *noun* musical drama > **op•er•at'ic** *adjective* of opera > **op•er•et'ta** *noun* light, comic opera

op•er•a•tion [op-ə-RAY-shən] *noun* 1 working, way things work 2 scope 3 act of surgery 4 military action > **op'er•ate** *verb transitive* **-at•ed, -at•ing** 1 cause to function 2 effect ▷ *verb intransitive* **-at•ed, -at•ing** 3 work 4 produce an effect 5 perform act of surgery 6 exert power > **op•er•a'tion•al** *adjective* 1 of operation(s) 2 working > **op'er•a•tive** [-ə-tiv] *adjective* 1 working ▷ *noun* 2 worker, esp. with a special skill 3 secret agent

o•phid•i•an [oh-FID-ee-ən] *adjective, noun* (reptile) of the order including snakes

oph•thal•mic [of-THAL-mik] *adjective* of eyes > **oph•thal•mol'o•gist** [-jist] *noun* > **oph•thal•mol'o•gy** *noun* study of eye and its diseases > **oph•thal'mo•scope** [-skohp] *noun* instrument for examining interior of eye

opiate *see* **opium**

o•pin•ion [ə-PIN-yən] *noun* 1 what one thinks about something 2 belief, judgment > **o•pine** [oh-PĪN] *verb transitive* **o•pined, o•pin•ing** 1 think 2 utter opinion > **o•pin'ion•at•ed** *adjective* 1 stubborn in one's opinions 2 dogmatic

o•pi•um [OH-pee-əm] *noun* sedative-narcotic drug made from poppy > **o'pi•ate** [-it] *noun* 1 drug containing opium 2 narcotic ▷ *adjective* 3 inducing sleep 4 soothing

o•pos•sum [ə-POS-əm] *noun* small American marsupial animal, possum

op•po•nent [ə-POH-nənt] *noun* adversary, antagonist

op•por•tune [op-ər-TOON] *adjective* seasonable, well-timed > **op•por•tun'ism** *noun* policy of doing what is expedient at the time regardless of principle > **op•por•tun'ist** *noun, adjective* > **op•por•tu'ni•ty** *noun, plural* **-ties** 1 favorable time or condition 2 good chance

op•pose [ə-POHZ] *verb transitive* **-posed, -pos•ing** 1 resist, withstand 2 contrast 3 set against > **op•po•site** [OP-ə-zit] *adjective* 1 contrary 2 facing 3 diametrically different 4 adverse ▷ *noun* 5 the contrary ▷ *preposition, adverb* 6 facing 7 on the other side > **op•po•si'tion** [-ZISH-ən] *noun* 1 antithesis 2 resistance 3

DICTIONARY • THESAURUS

open *adjective* 1 UNFASTENED, agape, ajar, gaping, uncovered, unfolded, unfurled, unlocked, yawning
2 ACCESSIBLE, available, free, public, unoccupied, unrestricted, vacant
3 UNRESOLVED, arguable, debatable, moot, undecided, unsettled
4 FRANK, candid, guileless, honest, sincere, transparent
▷ *verb* 5 START, begin, commence, inaugurate, initiate, kick off (*informal*), launch, set in motion
6 UNFASTEN, unblock, uncork, uncover, undo, unlock, untie, unwrap
7 UNFOLD, expand, spread *or* spread out, unfurl, unroll

open-air *adjective* OUTDOOR, alfresco

open-handed *adjective* GENEROUS, bountiful, free, lavish, liberal, munificent, unstinting

opening *noun* 1 HOLE, aperture, chink, cleft, crack, fissure, gap, orifice, perforation, slot, space
2 OPPORTUNITY, chance, occasion, vacancy
3 BEGINNING, commencement, dawn, inception, initiation, launch, outset, start
▷ *adjective* 4 FIRST, beginning, inaugural, initial, introductory, maiden, primary

openly *adverb* CANDIDLY, forthrightly, frankly, overtly, plainly, unhesitatingly, unreservedly

open-minded *adjective* TOLERANT, broad-minded, impartial, liberal, reasonable, receptive, unbiased, undogmatic, unprejudiced

operate *verb* 1 WORK, act, function, go, perform, run
2 HANDLE, be in charge of, manage, maneuver, use, work

operation *noun* PROCEDURE, action, course, exercise, motion, movement, performance, process

operational *adjective* WORKING, functional, going, operative, prepared, ready, up and running, usable, viable, workable

operative *adjective* 1 IN FORCE, active, effective, functioning, in operation, operational
▷ *noun* 2 WORKER, artisan, employee, laborer

operator *noun* WORKER, conductor, driver, handler, mechanic, operative, practitioner, technician

opinion *noun* BELIEF, assessment, feeling, idea, impression, judgment, point of view, sentiment, theory, view

opinionated *adjective* DOGMATIC, bigoted, cocksure, doctrinaire, overbearing, pig-headed, prejudiced, single-minded

opponent *noun* COMPETITOR, adversary, antagonist, challenger, contestant, enemy, foe, rival

opportune *adjective* TIMELY, advantageous, appropriate, apt, auspicious, convenient, favorable, fitting, suitable, well-timed

opportunism *noun* EXPEDIENCY, exploitation, pragmatism, unscrupulousness

opportunity *noun* CHANCE, moment, occasion, opening, scope, time

oppose *verb* FIGHT, block, combat, counter, defy, resist, take issue with, take on, thwart, withstand

opposed *adjective* AVERSE, antagonistic, clashing, conflicting, contrary, dissentient, hostile

opposing *adjective* HOSTILE, conflicting, contrary, enemy, incompatible, opposite, rival

opposite *adjective* 1 FACING, fronting
2 DIFFERENT, antithetical, conflicting, contrary, contrasted, reverse, unlike
▷ *noun* 3 REVERSE, antithesis, contradiction, contrary, converse, inverse

opposition *noun* 1 HOSTILITY, antagonism, competition, disapproval, obstruction, prevention, resistance, unfriendliness
2 OPPONENT, antagonist, competition, foe, other

obstruction 4 hostility 5 group opposing another 6 party opposing that in power
op•press [ə-PRES] *verb transitive* 1 govern with tyranny 2 weigh down > **op•pres'sion** [-PRESH-ən] *noun* 1 act of oppressing 2 severity 3 misery > **op•pres'sive** *adjective* 1 tyrannical 2 hard to bear 3 heavy 4 hot and tiring (of weather) > **op•pres'sor** [-ər] *noun*
op•pro•bri•um [ə-PROH-bree-əm] *noun* disgrace > **op•pro'bri•ous** *adjective* 1 reproachful 2 shameful 3 abusive
opt *verb intransitive* make a choice > **op'ta•tive** [OP-tə-tiv] *adjective* expressing wish or desire
op•tic [OP-tik] *adjective* 1 of eye or sight ▷ *noun* 2 eye > **optics** *noun* science of sight and light > **op'ti•cal** *adjective* > **optical character reader** device for scanning magnetically coded data on labels, cans, etc. > **op•ti'cian** [-TISH-ən] *noun* maker of, dealer in eyeglasses, contact lenses
op•ti•mism [OP-tə-miz-əm] *noun* 1 disposition to look on the bright side 2 doctrine that good must prevail in the end 3 belief that the world is the best possible world > **op'ti•mist** *noun* > **op•ti•mis'tic** *adjective*
op•ti•mum [OP-tə-məm] *adjective, noun* the best, the most favorable
op•tion [OP-shən] *noun* 1 choice 2 preference 3 thing chosen 4 in business, purchased privilege of either buying or selling things at specified price within specified time > **op'tion•al** *adjective* leaving to choice
op•tom•e•trist [op-TOM-i-trist] *noun* person qualified in testing eyesight, prescribing corrective lenses, etc. > **op•tom'e•try** *noun*
op•u•lent [OP-yə-lənt] *adjective* 1 rich 2 copious > **op'u•lence** *noun* riches, wealth
o•pus [OH-pəs] *noun, plural* **o•pus•es** *or* **op•er•a** [OHP-ə-rə] 1 work 2 musical composition: *Grieg's opus 53*
or *conjunction* 1 introduces alternatives 2 if not
or•a•cle [OR-ə-kəl] *noun* 1 divine utterance, prophecy, oft. ambiguous, given at shrine of god 2 the shrine 3 wise or mysterious adviser > **o•rac•u•lar** [aw-RAK-yə-lər] *adjective* 1 of oracle 2 prophetic 3 authoritative 4 ambiguous
o•ral [OR-əl] *adjective* 1 spoken 2 by mouth ▷ *noun* 3 spoken examination > **o'ral•ly** *adverb*
or•ange [OR-inj] *noun* 1 bright reddish-yellow round fruit 2 tree bearing it 3 fruit's color
o•rang•u•tan [aw-RANG-uu-tan] *noun* large E. Indian ape
or•a•tor [OR-ə-tər] *noun* 1 maker of speech 2 skillful speaker > **o•ra'tion** [aw-RAY-shən] *noun* formal speech > **or•a•tor'i•cal** *adjective* of orator or oration > **or'a•to•ry** *noun* 1 speeches 2 eloquence 3 small private chapel
or•a•to•ri•o [or-ə-TOR-ee-oh] *noun, plural* **-ri•os** semidramatic composition of sacred music
orb *noun* 1 globe, sphere 2 eye, eyeball
or'bit *noun* 1 track of planet, satellite, comet, etc., around another heavenly body 2 field of influence, sphere 3 eye socket ▷ *verb* 4 move in, or put into, an orbit
or•chard [OR-chərd] *noun* 1 area for cultivation of fruit trees 2 the trees
or•ches•tra [OR-kə-strə] *noun* 1 band of musicians 2 place for such band in theater, etc. > **or•ches'tral** *adjective* > **or'ches•trate** *verb transitive* **-trat•ed, -trat•ing** 1 compose or arrange music for orchestra 2 organize, arrange
or•chid [OR-kid] *noun* genus of various flowering plants
or•dain [or-DAYN] *verb transitive* 1 admit to religious ministry 2 confer holy orders upon 3 decree, enact 4 destine > **or•di•na'tion** *noun*

DICTIONARY

O

THESAURUS

side, rival
oppress *verb* 1 DEPRESS, afflict, burden, dispirit, harass, sadden, torment, vex
2 PERSECUTE, abuse, maltreat, subdue, subjugate, suppress, wrong
oppressed *adjective* DOWNTRODDEN, abused, browbeaten, disadvantaged, harassed, maltreated, tyrannized, underprivileged
oppression *noun* PERSECUTION, abuse, brutality, cruelty, injury, injustice, maltreatment, subjection, tyranny
oppressive *adjective* 1 TYRANNICAL, brutal, cruel, despotic, harsh, inhuman, repressive, severe, unjust
2 SULTRY, airless, close, muggy, stifling, stuffy
oppressor *noun* PERSECUTOR, autocrat, bully, despot, scourge, slave-driver, tormentor, tyrant
opt *verb* (*often with for*) CHOOSE, decide *or* decide on, elect, go for, plump for, prefer
optimistic *adjective* HOPEFUL, buoyant, cheerful, confident, encouraged, expectant, positive, rosy, sanguine
optimum *adjective* IDEAL, best, highest, optimal, peak, perfect, superlative
option *noun* CHOICE, alternative, preference, selection
optional *adjective* VOLUNTARY, discretionary, elective, extra, open, possible
opulence *noun* 1 WEALTH, affluence, luxuriance, luxury, plenty, prosperity, riches
2 ABUNDANCE, copiousness, cornucopia, fullness, profusion, richness, superabundance
opulent *adjective* 1 RICH, affluent, lavish, luxurious, moneyed, prosperous, sumptuous, wealthy, well-off, well-to-do
2 ABUNDANT, copious, lavish, luxuriant, plentiful, profuse, prolific
opus *noun* WORK, brainchild, composition, creation, oeuvre (*French*), piece, production
oracle *noun* 1 PROPHECY, divination, prediction, prognostication, revelation
2 PUNDIT, adviser, authority, guru, mastermind, mentor, wizard
oral *adjective* SPOKEN, verbal, vocal
oration *noun* SPEECH, address, discourse, harangue, homily, lecture
orator *noun* PUBLIC SPEAKER, declaimer, lecturer, rhetorician, speaker
oratorical *adjective* RHETORICAL, bombastic, declamatory, eloquent, grandiloquent, high-flown, magniloquent, sonorous
oratory *noun* ELOQUENCE, declamation, elocution, grandiloquence, public speaking, rhetoric, speech-making
orb *noun* SPHERE, ball, circle, globe, ring
orbit *noun* 1 PATH, circle, course, cycle, revolution, rotation, trajectory
2 SPHERE OF INFLUENCE, ambit, compass, domain, influence, range, reach, scope, sweep
▷ *verb* 3 CIRCLE, circumnavigate, encircle,

or•deal [or-DEEL] *noun* 1 severe, trying experience 2 *hist.* form of trial by which accused underwent severe physical test
or•der [OR-dər] *noun* 1 regular or proper arrangement or condition 2 sequence 3 peaceful condition of society 4 rank, class 5 group 6 command 7 request for something to be supplied 8 mode of procedure 9 instruction 10 monastic society ▷ *verb transitive* 11 command 12 request (something) to be supplied or made 13 arrange > **or'der•li•ness** *noun* > **or'der•ly** *adjective* 1 tidy 2 methodical 3 well-behaved ▷ *noun* 4 hospital attendant 5 soldier performing chores for officer > **or•di•nal** [OR-dn-əl] *adjective* 1 showing position in a series ▷ *noun* 2 ordinal number
or•di•nance [OR-dn-əns] *noun* 1 decree, rule 2 rite, ceremony
or•di•nar•y [OR-dn-er-ee] *adjective* 1 usual, normal 2 common 3 plain 4 commonplace ▷ *noun* 5 average condition > **or'di•nar•i•ly** *adverb*
ord•nance [ORD-nəns] *noun* 1 big guns, artillery 2 military stores
or•dure [OR-jər] *noun* 1 dung 2 filth
ore [or] *noun* naturally occurring mineral that yields metal
o•reg•a•no [ə-REG-ə-noh] *noun* herb, variety of marjoram
org Internet domain name for an organization, usually a non-profit-making organization
or•gan [OR-gən] *noun* 1 musical wind instrument of pipes and stops, played by keys 2 member of animal or plant carrying out particular function 3 means of action 4 medium of information, esp. newspaper > **or•gan'ic** *adjective* 1 of, derived from, living organisms 2 of bodily organs 3 affecting bodily organs 4 having vital organs 5 *chem.* of compounds formed from carbon 6 grown with fertilizers derived from animal or vegetable matter 7 organized, systematic > **or•gan'i•cal•ly** *adverb* > **or'gan•ist** *noun* organ player
or•gan•ize [OR-gə-nīz] *verb transitive* **-nized, -niz•ing** 1 give definite structure 2 get up, arrange 3 put into working order 4 unite in a society > **or'gan•ism** *noun* 1 organized body or system 2 plant, animal > **or•gan•i•za'tion** *noun* 1 act of organizing 2 body of people 3 society
or•gasm [OR-gaz-əm] *noun* sexual climax
or•gy [OR-jee] *noun, plural* **-gies** 1 drunken or licentious revel, debauch 2 act of immoderation, overindulgence
o•ri•el [OR-ee-əl] *noun* 1 projecting part of an upper room with a window 2 the window
o•ri•ent [OR-ee-ənt] *noun* 1 (**O•ri•ent**) East 2 luster of best pearls ▷ *adjective* 3 rising 4 (**O•ri•ent**) Eastern ▷ *verb transitive* [OR-ee-ent] 5 place so as to face east or other known direction 6 take bearings 7 determine one's position > **o•ri•en'tal** *adjective* 1 of, or from, the East ▷ *noun* 2 (*often offensive*) person from the East or of Eastern descent > **o•ri•en'tal•ist** *noun* expert in Eastern languages and history

revolve around
orchestrate *verb* 1 SCORE, arrange
2 ORGANIZE, arrange, coordinate, put together, set up, stage-manage
ordain *verb* 1 APPOINT, anoint, consecrate, invest, nominate
2 ORDER, decree, demand, dictate, fix, lay down, legislate, prescribe, rule, will
ordeal *noun* HARDSHIP, agony, anguish, baptism of fire, nightmare, suffering, test, torture, trial, tribulation *or* tribulations
order *noun* 1 INSTRUCTION, command, decree, dictate, direction, directive, injunction, law, mandate, regulation, rule
2 SEQUENCE, arrangement, array, grouping, layout, line-up, progression, series, structure
3 TIDINESS, method, neatness, orderliness, organization, pattern, regularity, symmetry, system
4 DISCIPLINE, calm, control, law, law and order, peace, quiet, tranquillity
5 REQUEST, application, booking, commission, requisition, reservation
6 CLASS, caste, grade, position, rank, status
7 KIND, class, family, genre, ilk, sort, type
8 SOCIETY, association, brotherhood, community, company, fraternity, guild, organization
▷ *verb* 9 INSTRUCT, bid, charge, command, decree, demand, direct, require
10 REQUEST, apply for, book, reserve, send away for
11 ARRANGE, catalog, classify, group, marshal, organize, sort out, systematize
orderly *adjective* 1 WELL-ORGANIZED, businesslike, in order, methodical, neat, regular, scientific, shipshape, systematic, tidy
2 WELL-BEHAVED, controlled, disciplined, law-abiding, peaceable, quiet, restrained
ordinarily *adverb* USUALLY, as a rule, commonly, customarily, generally, habitually, in general, normally
ordinary *adjective* 1 USUAL, common, conventional, everyday, normal, regular, routine, standard, stock, typical
2 COMMONPLACE, banal, humble, humdrum, modest, mundane, plain, unremarkable, workaday
organ *noun* 1 PART, element, structure, unit
2 MOUTHPIECE, forum, medium, vehicle, voice
organic *adjective* 1 NATURAL, animate, biological, live, living
2 SYSTEMATIC, integrated, methodical, ordered, organized, structured
organism *noun* CREATURE, animal, being, body, entity, structure
organization *noun* 1 GROUP, association, body, company, confederation, corporation, institution, outfit (*informal*), syndicate
2 MANAGEMENT, construction, coordination, direction, organizing, planning, running, structuring
3 ARRANGEMENT, chemistry, composition, format, make-up, pattern, structure, unity
organize *verb* ARRANGE, classify, coordinate, group, marshal, put together, run, set up, systematize, take care of
orgy *noun* 1 REVEL, bacchanalia, carousal, debauch, revelry, Saturnalia
2 SPREE, binge (*informal*), bout, excess, indulgence, overindulgence, splurge, surfeit
orient *verb* FAMILIARIZE, acclimatize, adapt,

> **o•ri•en•ta'tion** *noun*
or•i•fice [OR-ə-fis] *noun* opening, mouth of a cavity, e.g. pipe
o•ri•ga•mi [or-i-GAH-mee] *noun* Japanese art of paper folding
or•i•gin [OR-i-jin] *noun* **1** beginning **2** source **3** parentage
o•rig•i•nal [ə-RIJ-ə-nl] *adjective* **1** primitive, earliest **2** new, not copied or derived **3** thinking or acting for oneself **4** eccentric ▷ *noun* **5** pattern, thing from which another is copied **6** unconventional or strange person > **o•rig•i•nal'i•ty** *noun* power of producing something individual to oneself > **o•rig'i•nal•ly** *adverb* **1** at first **2** in the beginning
o•rig•i•nate [ə-RIJ-ə-nayt] *verb* **-nat•ed, -nat•ing** come or bring into existence, begin > **o•rig'i•na•tor** [-tər] *noun*
o•ri•ole [OR-ee-ohl] *noun* any of several thrushlike birds
O•ri•on [ə-RĪ-ən] *noun* bright constellation
or•i•son [OR-ə-zən] *noun* prayer
or•mo•lu [OR-mə-loo] *noun* **1** gilded bronze **2** gold-colored alloy **3** articles of these
or•na•ment [OR-nə-mənt] *noun* **1** any object used to adorn or decorate **2** decoration ▷ *verb transitive* [-ment] **3** adorn > **or•na•ment'al** *adjective* > **or•na•men•ta'tion** *noun*
or•nate [or-NAYT] *adjective* highly decorated or elaborate
or•ni•thol•o•gy [or-nə-THOL-ə-jee] *noun* science of birds > **or•ni•thol'o•gist** *noun*
o•ro•tund [OR-ə-tund] *adjective* **1** full, clear, and musical **2** pompous
or•phan [OR-fən] *noun* child bereaved of one or both parents > **or'phan•age** [-fə-nij] *noun* institution for care of orphans
ortho- *combining form* right, correct
or•tho•dox [OR-thə-doks] *adjective* **1** holding accepted views **2** conventional > **or'tho•dox•y** *noun*
or•thog•ra•phy [or-THOG-rə-fee] *noun* correct spelling
or•tho•pe•dic [or-thə-PEE-dik] *adjective* for curing deformity, disorder of bones > **or•tho•pe'dics** *noun* medical specialty dealing with this > **or•tho•pe'dist** *noun*
Os *chem.* osmium
os•cil•late [OS-ə-layt] *verb intransitive* **-lat•ed, -lat•ing** **1** swing to and fro **2** waver **3** fluctuate (regularly) > **os•cil•la'tion** *noun* > **os'cil•la•tor** *noun* > **os'cil•la•to•ry** *adjective* > **os•cil'lo•scope** *noun* electronic instrument producing visible representation of rapidly changing quantity
os•mi•um [OZ-mee-əm] *noun* heaviest known of metallic elements
os•mos•is [oz-MOH-sis] *noun* percolation of fluids through porous partitions > **os•mot'ic** *adjective*
os•se•ous [OS-ee-əs] *adjective* **1** of, like bone **2** bony > **os•si•fi•ca'tion** *noun* > **os'si•fy** [-fī] *verb* **-fied, -fy•ing** **1** turn into bone **2** grow rigid
os•ten•si•ble [o-STEN-sə-bəl] *adjective* **1** apparent **2** professed > **os•ten'si•bly** *adverb*
os•ten•ta•tion [os-ten-TAY-shən] *noun* show, pretentious display > **os•ten•ta'tious** *adjective* **1** given to display **2** showing off

DICTIONARY **O** THESAURUS

adjust, align, get one's bearings, orientate
orientation *noun* **1** POSITION, bearings, direction, location **2** FAMILIARIZATION, acclimatization, adaptation, adjustment, assimilation, introduction, settling in
orifice *noun* OPENING, aperture, cleft, hole, mouth, pore, rent, vent
origin *noun* **1** ROOT, base, basis, derivation, fount, fountainhead, source, wellspring **2** BEGINNING, birth, creation, emergence, foundation, genesis, inception, launch, start
original *adjective* **1** FIRST, earliest, initial, introductory, opening, primary, starting **2** NEW, fresh, ground-breaking, innovative, novel, seminal, unprecedented, unusual **3** CREATIVE, fertile, imaginative, ingenious, inventive, resourceful ▷ *noun* **4** PROTOTYPE, archetype, master, model, paradigm, pattern, precedent, standard
originality *noun* NOVELTY, creativity, freshness, imagination, ingenuity, innovation, inventiveness, newness, unorthodoxy
originally *adverb* INITIALLY, at first, first, in the beginning, to begin with
originate *verb* **1** BEGIN, arise, come, derive, emerge, result, rise, spring, start, stem **2** INTRODUCE, bring about, create, formulate, generate, institute, launch, pioneer
originator *noun* CREATOR, architect, author, father *or* mother, founder, inventor, maker, pioneer
ornament *noun* **1** DECORATION, accessory, adornment, bauble, embellishment, festoon, knick-knack, trimming, trinket ▷ *verb* **2** DECORATE, adorn, beautify, embellish, festoon, grace, prettify
ornamental *adjective* DECORATIVE, attractive, beautifying, embellishing, for show, showy
ornamentation *noun* DECORATION, adornment, elaboration, embellishment, embroidery, frills, ornateness
ornate *adjective* ELABORATE, baroque, busy, decorated, fancy, florid, fussy, ornamented, overelaborate, rococo
orthodox *adjective* ESTABLISHED, accepted, approved, conventional, customary, official, received, traditional, well-established
orthodoxy *noun* CONFORMITY, authority, conventionality, received wisdom, traditionalism
oscillate *verb* FLUCTUATE, seesaw, sway, swing, vacillate, vary, vibrate, waver
oscillation *noun* SWING, fluctuation, instability, vacillation, variation, wavering
ossify *verb* HARDEN, fossilize, solidify, stiffen
ostensible *adjective* APPARENT, outward, pretended, professed, purported, seeming, so-called, superficial, supposed
ostensibly *adverb* APPARENTLY, on the face of it, professedly, seemingly, supposedly
ostentation *noun* DISPLAY, affectation, exhibitionism, flamboyance, flashiness, flaunting, parade, pomp, pretentiousness, show, showing off (*informal*)
ostentatious *adjective* PRETENTIOUS, brash, conspicuous, flamboyant, flashy, gaudy, loud, obtrusive, showy

os•te•op•a•thy [os-tee-OP-ə-thee] *noun* art of treating disease by removing structural derangement by manipulation, esp. of spine > **os'te•o•path** *noun* one skilled in this art
os•tra•cize [OS-trə-sīz] *verb transitive* **-cized, -ciz•ing** exclude, banish from society, exile > **os'tra•cism** [-siz-əm] *noun* social boycotting
os'trich *noun* large swift-running flightless Afr. bird
oth•er [UTH-ər] *adjective* **1** not this **2** not the same **3** alternative, different ▷ *pronoun* **4** other person or thing > **oth'er•wise** *adverb* **1** differently **2** in another way ▷ *conjunction* **3** else, if not
o•ti•ose [OH-shee-ohs, OH-tee-ohs] *adjective* **1** superfluous **2** useless
o•ti•tis [oh-TĪ-tis] *noun* inflammation of the ear
ot•ter [OT-ər] *noun* furry aquatic fish-eating animal
Ot•to•man [OT-ə-mən] *adjective* **1** Turkish ▷ *noun* **2** Turk **3** (**ot•to•man**) cushioned, backless seat **4** (**ot•to•man**) cushioned footstool
ought [awt] *verb auxiliary* **1** expressing duty or obligation or advisability **2** be bound
Oui•ja [WEE-jə] *noun* ® board with letters and symbols used to obtain messages at seances
ounce [owns] *noun* a weight, sixteenth of avoirdupois pound (28.349 grams), twelfth of troy pound (31.103 grams)
our [OW-ər] *adjective* belonging to us > **ours** *pronoun* thing(s) belonging to us > **our•selves'** *pronoun emphatic or reflexive form of* **we**
oust [owst] *verb transitive* put out, expel
out [owt] *adverb* **1** from within, away **2** wrong **3** on strike ▷ *adjective* **4** not worth considering **5** not allowed **6** unfashionable **7** unconscious **8** not in use, operation, etc. **9** at an end **10** not burning **11** *baseball* failed to get on base ▷ *verb transitive* **12** (*informal*) name (public figure) as being homosexual > **out'er** *adjective* away from the inside > **out'er•most** [-mohst] *adjective* on extreme outside > **out'ing** *noun* pleasure excursion > **out'ward** [-wurd] *adjective, adverb* > **out'wards** [-wurdz] *adverb*
out- *prefix* beyond, in excess: *outclass; outdistance; outsize*
out•bal•ance [owt-BAL-əns] *verb transitive* **-anced, -anc•ing 1** outweigh **2** exceed in weight
out•board [OWT-bord] *adjective* of boat's engine, mounted on, outside stern
out•break [OWT-brayk] *noun* sudden occurrence, esp. of disease or strife
out•burst [OWT-burst] *noun* bursting out, esp. of violent emotion
out•cast [OWT-kast] *noun* someone rejected ▷ *adjective*
out•class [owt-KLAS] *verb transitive* excel, surpass
out•come [OWT-kum] *noun* result
out•crop [OWT-krop] *noun* **1** *geology* rock coming out of stratum to the surface ▷ *verb intransitive* [owt-KROP], **-cropped, -crop•ping 2** come out to the surface
out•doors [owt-DORZ] *adverb* in the open air > **out'door** *adjective*
out•fit [OWT-fit] *noun* **1** equipment **2** clothes and accessories **3** (*informal*) group or association regarded as a unit > **out'fit•ter** *noun* one who supplies clothing and accessories
out•flank [owt-FLANGK] *verb transitive* **1** to get beyond the flank (of enemy army) **2** circumvent **3** outmaneuver
out•go•ing [OWT-goh-ing] *adjective* **1** departing **2** friendly, sociable
out•grow [owt-GROH] *verb transitive* **-grew, -grown, -grow•ing 1** become too large or too old

ostracism *noun* EXCLUSION, banishment, exile, isolation, rejection
ostracize *verb* EXCLUDE, banish, cast out, cold-shoulder, exile, give (someone) the cold shoulder, reject, shun
other *adjective* **1** ADDITIONAL, added, alternative, auxiliary, extra, further, more, spare, supplementary
2 DIFFERENT, contrasting, dissimilar, distinct, diverse, separate, unrelated, variant
otherwise *conjunction* **1** OR ELSE, if not, or then ▷ *adverb* **2** DIFFERENTLY, any other way, contrarily
ounce *noun* SHRED, atom, crumb, drop, grain, scrap, speck, trace
oust *verb* EXPEL, depose, dislodge, displace, dispossess, eject, throw out, topple, turn out, unseat
out *adjective* **1** AWAY, abroad, absent, elsewhere, gone, not at home, outside
2 EXTINGUISHED, at an end, dead, ended, exhausted, expired, finished, used up
outbreak *noun* ERUPTION, burst, epidemic, explosion, flare-up, outburst, rash, upsurge
outburst *noun* OUTPOURING, eruption, explosion, flare-up, outbreak, paroxysm, spasm, surge
outcast *noun* PARIAH, castaway, exile, leper, persona non grata (*Latin*), refugee, vagabond, wretch
outclass *verb* SURPASS, eclipse, excel, leave standing (*informal*), outdo, outshine, outstrip, overshadow, run rings around (*informal*)
outcome *noun* RESULT, conclusion, consequence, end, issue, payoff (*informal*), upshot
outcry *noun* PROTEST, clamor, commotion, complaint, hue and cry, hullaballoo, outburst, uproar
outdated *adjective* OLD-FASHIONED, antiquated, archaic, obsolete, outmoded, out of date, passé, unfashionable
outdo *verb* SURPASS, beat, best, eclipse, exceed, get the better of, outclass, outmaneuver, overcome, top, transcend
outdoor *adjective* OPEN-AIR, alfresco, out-of-door *or* out-of-doors, outside
outer *adjective* EXTERNAL, exposed, exterior, outlying, outside, outward, peripheral, surface
outfit *noun* **1** COSTUME, clothes, ensemble, garb, get-up (*informal*), kit, suit
2 GROUP, company, crew, organization, setup (*informal*), squad, team, unit
outgoing *adjective* **1** LEAVING, departing, former, retiring, withdrawing
2 SOCIABLE, approachable, communicative, expansive, extrovert, friendly, gregarious, open, warm
outgoings *plural noun* EXPENSES, costs, expenditure, outlay, overheads
outing *noun* TRIP, excursion, expedition, jaunt, spin (*informal*)

for **2** surpass in growth
out•house [OWT-hows] *noun* **1** outdoor toilet **2** shed, etc. near main building
out•land•ish [owt-LAN-dish] *adjective* queer, extravagantly strange
out•law [OWT-law] *noun* **1** one beyond protection of the law **2** exile, bandit ▷ *verb transitive* **3** make (someone) an outlaw **4** ban
out•lay [OWT-lay] *noun* expenditure
out•let [OWT-let] *noun* **1** opening, vent **2** means of release or escape **3** market for product or service
out•line [OWT-līn] *noun* **1** rough sketch **2** general plan **3** lines enclosing visible figure ▷ *verb transitive* **-lined, lin•ing 4** sketch **5** summarize
out•look [OWT-luuk] *noun* **1** point of view **2** probable outcome **3** view
out•ly•ing [OWT-lī-ing] *adjective* distant, remote
out•mod•ed [owt-MOH-did] *adjective* no longer fashionable or accepted
out•pa•tient [OWT-pay-shənt] *noun* patient treated but not kept at hospital
out•put [OWT-puut] *noun* **1** quantity produced **2** *computing* data produced ▷ *verb transitive* **3** *computing* produce (data) at the end of a process
out•rage [OWT-rayj] *noun* **1** violation of others' rights **2** gross or violent offense or indignity **3** anger arising from this ▷ *verb transitive* **-raged, rag•ing 4** offend grossly **5** insult **6** injure, violate > **out•ra'geous** [-RAY-jəs] *adjective*
ou•tré [oo-TRAY] *adjective* **1** extravagantly odd **2** bizarre
out•rig•ger [OWT-rig-ər] *noun* **1** frame, esp. with float attached, outside boat's gunwale **2** frame on rowing boat's side with rowlock **3** boat with one
out•right [OWT-rīt] *adjective* **1** undisputed **2** downright **3** positive ▷ *adverb* [owt-rīt] **4** completely **5** once for all **6** openly
out•set [OWT-set] *noun* beginning
out•side [OWT-sīd] *noun* **1** exterior ▷ *adverb* [owt-SĪD] **2** not inside **3** in the open air ▷ *adjective* [owt-SĪD] **4** on exterior **5** remote, unlikely **6** greatest possible, probable > **out•sid'er** *noun* **1** person outside specific group **2** contestant thought unlikely to win
out•skirts [OWT-skurts] *plural noun* outer areas, districts, esp. of city
out•spok•en [OWT-SPOH-kən] *adjective* frank, candid

DICTIONARY **O** THESAURUS

outlandish *adjective* STRANGE, bizarre, exotic, fantastic, far-out (*slang*), freakish, outré, preposterous, unheard-of, weird
outlaw *noun* **1** BANDIT, desperado, fugitive, highwayman, marauder, outcast, robber ▷ *verb* **2** FORBID, ban, bar, disallow, exclude, prohibit, proscribe
outlay *noun* EXPENDITURE, cost, expenses, investment, outgoings, spending
outlet *noun* **1** RELEASE, avenue, channel, duct, exit, opening, vent
2 SHOP, market, store
outline *noun* **1** SUMMARY, recapitulation, résumé, rundown, synopsis, thumbnail sketch
2 SHAPE, configuration, contour, delineation, figure, form, profile, silhouette
▷ *verb* **3** SUMMARIZE, adumbrate, delineate, draft, plan, rough out, sketch *or* sketch in, trace
outlive *verb* SURVIVE, outlast
outlook *noun* **1** ATTITUDE, angle, frame of mind, perspective, point of view, slant, standpoint, viewpoint
2 PROSPECT, expectations, forecast, future
outlying *adjective* REMOTE, distant, far-flung, out-of-the-way, peripheral, provincial
outmoded *adjective* OLD-FASHIONED, anachronistic, antiquated, archaic, obsolete, out-of-date, outworn, passé, unfashionable
out-of-date *adjective* OLD-FASHIONED, antiquated, dated, expired, invalid, lapsed, obsolete, outmoded, outworn, passé
outpouring *noun* STREAM, cascade, effusion, flow, spate, spurt, torrent
output *noun* PRODUCTION, achievement, manufacture, productivity, yield
outrage *noun* **1** VIOLATION, abuse, affront, desecration, indignity, insult, offense, sacrilege, violence
2 INDIGNATION, anger, fury, hurt, resentment, shock, wrath
▷ *verb* **3** OFFEND, affront, incense, infuriate, madden, scandalize, shock
outrageous *adjective* **1** OFFENSIVE, atrocious, disgraceful, flagrant, heinous, iniquitous, nefarious, unspeakable, villainous, wicked
2 SHOCKING, exorbitant, extravagant, immoderate, preposterous, scandalous, steep (*informal*), unreasonable
outré *adjective* ECCENTRIC, bizarre, fantastic, freakish, odd, off-the-wall (*slang*), outlandish, unconventional, weird
outright *adjective* **1** ABSOLUTE, complete, out-and-out, perfect, thorough, thoroughgoing, total, unconditional, unmitigated, unqualified
2 DIRECT, definite, flat, straightforward, unequivocal, unqualified
▷ *adverb* **3** ABSOLUTELY, completely, openly, overtly, straightforwardly, thoroughly, to the full
outset *noun* BEGINNING, commencement, inauguration, inception, kickoff (*informal*), onset, opening, start
outshine *verb* OVERSHADOW, eclipse, leave in the shade *or* put in the shade, outclass, outdo, outstrip, surpass, transcend, upstage
outside *adjective* **1** EXTERNAL, exterior, extraneous, outer, outward
2 (*chance*) UNLIKELY, distant, faint, marginal, remote, slight, slim, small
▷ *noun* **3** SURFACE, exterior, façade, face, front, skin, topside
outsider *noun* INTERLOPER, incomer, intruder, newcomer, odd man out, stranger
outsize *adjective* EXTRA-LARGE, giant, gigantic, huge, jumbo (*informal*), mammoth, monster, oversized, supersize
outskirts *plural noun* EDGE, boundary, environs, periphery, suburbia, suburbs
outspoken *adjective* FORTHRIGHT, abrupt, blunt, explicit, frank, open, plain-spoken, unceremonious, unequivocal
outstanding *adjective* **1** EXCELLENT, cool (*informal*), exceptional, great, important, impressive, phat (*slang*), special, superior,

out•stand•ing [owt-STAN-ding] *adjective* 1 excellent 2 remarkable 3 unsettled, unpaid
out•strip [owt-STRIP] *verb transitive* **-stripped, -strip•ping** outrun, surpass
out•wit [owt-WIT] *verb transitive* **-wit•ted, -wit•ting** get the better of by cunning
o•val [OH-vəl] *adjective* 1 egg-shaped, elliptical ▷ *noun* 2 something of this shape
o•va•ry [OH-və-ree] *noun, plural* **-ries** female egg-producing organ > **o•var'i•an** [-VAIR-ee-ən] *adjective*
o•va•tion [oh-VAY-shən] *noun* enthusiastic burst of applause
ov•en [UV-ən] *noun* heated chamber for baking in
o•ver [OH-vər] *adverb* 1 above, above and beyond, going beyond, in excess, too much, past, finished, in repetition, across, downward, etc. ▷ *preposition* 2 above 3 on, upon 4 more than, in excess of, along, etc. ▷ *adjective* 5 upper, outer
over- *prefix* 1 too much: *overeat* 2 above: *overlord* 3 on top: *overshoe*
o•ver•all [OH-vər-awl] *adjective, adverb* 1 in total ▷ *noun* 2 coat-shaped protective garment > **o•ver•alls** protective garment consisting of trousers with a part extending up over the chest
o•ver•awe' *verb transitive* affect (someone) with an overpowering sense of awe
o•ver•bal'ance *verb* lose balance
o•ver•bear•ing [oh-vər-BAIR-ing] *adjective* domineering
o•ver•blown [OH-vər-BLOHN] *adjective* excessive, bombastic
o•ver•board [OH-vər-bord] *adverb* from a vessel into the water
o•ver•cast [OH-vər-KAST] *adjective* covered over, esp. by clouds
o'ver•coat *noun* heavy coat
o•ver•come [oh-vər-KUM] *verb transitive* **-came, -come, -com•ing** 1 conquer 2 surmount 3 make powerless
o•ver•crowd' *verb transitive* fill with more people or things than is desirable > **ov•er•crowd'ing** *noun*
o•ver•do' *verb transitive* 1 do to excess 2 exaggerate (something)
o'ver•dose *noun* 1 excessive dose of a drug ▷ *verb* 2 take an overdose
o•ver•draft [OH-vər-draft] *noun* withdrawal of money in excess of credit balance on bank account
o•ver•due' *adjective* still due after the time allowed

DICTIONARY • THESAURUS

superlative
2 UNPAID, due, payable, pending, remaining, uncollected, unsettled
outstrip *verb* SURPASS, better, eclipse, exceed, excel, outdistance, outdo, overtake, transcend
outward *adjective* APPARENT, noticeable, observable, obvious, ostensible, perceptible, surface, visible
outwardly *adverb* OSTENSIBLY, apparently, externally, on the face of it, on the surface, seemingly, superficially, to all intents and purposes
outweigh *verb* OVERRIDE, cancel *or* cancel out, compensate for, eclipse, prevail over, take precedence over, tip the scales
outwit *verb* OUTTHINK, cheat, dupe, fool, get the better of, outfox, outmaneuver, outsmart (*informal*), swindle
outworn *adjective* OUTDATED, antiquated, discredited, disused, hackneyed, obsolete, outmoded, out-of-date, threadbare, worn-out
oval *adjective* ELLIPTICAL, egg-shaped, ovoid
ovation *noun* APPLAUSE, acclaim, acclamation, big hand, cheers, clapping, plaudits, tribute
over *preposition* 1 ON, above, on top of, upon
2 EXCEEDING, above, in excess of, more than
▷ *adverb* 3 ABOVE, aloft, on high, overhead
4 EXTRA, beyond, in addition, in excess, left over
▷ *adjective* 5 FINISHED, bygone, closed, completed, concluded, done *or* done with, ended, gone, past
overact *verb* EXAGGERATE, ham *or* ham up (*informal*), overdo, overplay
overall *adjective* 1 TOTAL, all-embracing, blanket, complete, comprehensive, general, global, inclusive
▷ *adverb* 2 IN GENERAL, on the whole
overawe *verb* INTIMIDATE, abash, alarm, daunt, frighten, scare, terrify
overbalance *verb* OVERTURN, capsize, keel over, slip, tip over, topple over, tumble, turn turtle
overbearing *adjective* ARROGANT, bossy (*informal*), dictatorial, domineering, haughty, high-handed, imperious, supercilious, superior
overblown *adjective* EXCESSIVE, disproportionate, immoderate, inflated, overdone, over the top, undue
overcast *adjective* CLOUDY, dismal, dreary, dull, gray, leaden, louring *or* lowering, murky
overcharge *verb* CHEAT, fleece, rip off (*slang*), short-change, sting (*informal*), surcharge
overcome *verb* 1 CONQUER, beat, defeat, master, overpower, overwhelm, prevail, subdue, subjugate, surmount, triumph over, vanquish
▷ *adjective* 2 AFFECTED, at a loss for words, bowled over (*informal*), overwhelmed, speechless, swept off one's feet
overconfident *adjective* BRASH, cocksure, foolhardy, overweening, presumptuous
overcrowded *adjective* CONGESTED, bursting at the seams, choked, jam-packed, overloaded, overpopulated, packed *or* packed out, swarming
overdo *verb* 1 EXAGGERATE, belabor, gild the lily, go overboard (*informal*), overindulge, overreach, overstate
2 ▷ **overdo it** OVERWORK, bite off more than one can chew, burn the candle at both ends (*informal*), overload, strain oneself *or* overstrain oneself, wear oneself out
overdone *adjective* 1 EXCESSIVE, exaggerated, fulsome, immoderate, inordinate, overelaborate, too much, undue, unnecessary
2 OVERCOOKED, burnt, charred, dried up, spoiled
overdue *adjective* LATE, behindhand, behind schedule, belated, owing, tardy, unpunctual
overeat *verb* OVERINDULGE, binge (*informal*), gorge, gormandize, guzzle, pig out (*slang*), stuff oneself
overemphasize *verb* OVERSTRESS, belabor, blow up out of all proportion, make a mountain out of a molehill (*informal*), overdramatize

o•ver•flow' *verb* 1 flow over 2 be filled beyond capacity ▷ *noun* 3 something that overflows 4 outlet for excess liquid 5 excess amount
o•ver•haul [oh-vər-HAWL] *verb transitive* 1 examine and set in order, repair 2 overtake ▷ *noun* [OH-vər-hawl] 3 thorough examination, esp. for repairs
o•ver•head [OH-vər-hed] *adjective* 1 over one's head, above ▷ *noun* 2 expense of running a business, over and above cost of manufacturing and of raw materials ▷ *adverb* [OH-vər-HED] 3 aloft, above
o•ver•kill [OH-vər-kil] *noun* capacity, advantage greater than required
o•ver•lap' *verb* 1 share part of the same space or period of time (as) ▷ *noun* 2 area overlapping
o•ver•look [oh-vər-LUUK] *verb transitive* 1 fail to notice 2 disregard 3 look over
o•ver•pow'er *verb* 1 subdue or overcome (someone) 2 make helpless or ineffective > **o•ver•pow'er•ing** *adjective*
o•ver•re•act' *verb intransitive* react more strongly than is necessary
o•ver•ride [oh-vər-RĪD] *verb transitive* **-rode, -rid•den, -rid•ing** 1 set aside, disregard 2 cancel 3 trample down
o•ver•rule' *verb transitive* 1 reverse the decision of (a person with less power) 2 reverse (someone else's decision)
o•ver•run' *verb* 1 conquer rapidly 2 spread over (a place) rapidly 3 extend beyond a set limit
o•ver•seas [OH-vər-SEEZ] *adjective* 1 foreign ▷ *adjective, adverb* [oh-vər-SEEZ] 2 to, from place over the sea
o•ver•se•er [OH-vər-see-ər] *noun* supervisor > **o•ver•see'** *verb transitive* **-saw, -seen, -see•ing** supervise
o•ver•shoot' *verb* go beyond (a mark or target)
o•ver•sight [OH-vər-sīt] *noun* 1 failure to notice 2 mistake 3 supervision
o•vert [oh-VURT] *adjective* open, unconcealed > **o•vert'ly** *adverb*
o•ver•take [oh-vər-TAYK] *verb transitive* **-took, -tak•en, -tak•ing** 1 move past (vehicle, person) traveling in same direction 2 come up with in pursuit 3 catch up
o•ver•tax [oh-vər-TAKS] *verb transitive* 1 tax too heavily 2 impose too great a strain on
o•ver•throw [oh-vər-THROH] *verb transitive* **-threw, -thrown, -throw•ing** 1 upset, overturn 2 defeat ▷ *noun* [OH-vər-throh] ruin 3 defeat 4 fall
o•ver•tone [OH-vər-tohn] *noun* additional meaning, nuance
o•ver•ture [OH-vər-chər] *noun* 1 *mus.* orchestral introduction 2 opening of

---

overflow *verb* 1 SPILL, brim over, bubble over, pour over, run over, well over
▷ *noun* 2 SURPLUS, overabundance, spilling over
overhang *verb* PROJECT, extend, jut, loom, protrude, stick out
overhaul *verb* 1 REPAIR, check, do up (*informal*), examine, inspect, recondition, refurbish, restore, service
2 OVERTAKE, catch up with, get ahead of, pass
▷ *noun* 3 CHECKUP, check, examination, inspection, reconditioning, service
overhead *adverb* 1 ABOVE, aloft, in the sky, on high, skyward, up above, upward
▷ *adjective* 2 AERIAL, overhanging, upper
overheads *plural noun* RUNNING COSTS, operating costs
overindulgence *noun* EXCESS, immoderation, intemperance, overeating, surfeit
overjoyed *adjective* DELIGHTED, elated, euphoric, jubilant, on cloud nine (*informal*), over the moon (*informal*), thrilled
overload *verb* OVERBURDEN, burden, encumber, oppress, overtax, saddle *or* saddle with, strain, weigh down
overlook *verb* 1 FORGET, disregard, miss, neglect, omit, pass
2 IGNORE, condone, disregard, excuse, forgive, make allowances for, pardon, turn a blind eye to, wink at
3 HAVE A VIEW OF, look over *or* look out on
overpower *verb* OVERWHELM, conquer, crush, defeat, master, overcome, overthrow, quell, subdue, subjugate, vanquish
overpowering *adjective* IRRESISTIBLE, forceful, invincible, irrefutable, overwhelming, powerful, strong
overrate *verb* OVERESTIMATE, exaggerate, overvalue
override *verb* OVERRULE, annul, cancel, countermand, nullify, outweigh, supersede
overriding *adjective* ULTIMATE, dominant, paramount, predominant, primary, supreme
overrule *verb* REVERSE, alter, annul, cancel, countermand, override, overturn, repeal, rescind, veto
overrun *verb* 1 INVADE, occupy, overwhelm, rout
2 INFEST, choke, inundate, permeate, ravage, spread over, swarm over
3 EXCEED, go beyond, overshoot, run over *or* run on
overseer *noun* SUPERVISOR, boss (*informal*), chief, foreman, master, superintendent
overshadow *verb* 1 OUTSHINE, dominate, dwarf, eclipse, leave in the shade *or* put in the shade, surpass, tower above
2 SPOIL, blight, mar, put a damper on, ruin, temper
oversight *noun* MISTAKE, blunder, carelessness, error, fault, lapse, neglect, omission, slip
overt *adjective* OPEN, blatant, manifest, observable, obvious, plain, public, unconcealed, undisguised
overtake *verb* 1 PASS, catch up with, get past, leave behind, outdistance, outdo, outstrip, overhaul
2 BEFALL, engulf, happen, hit, overwhelm, strike
overthrow *verb* 1 DEFEAT, bring down, conquer, depose, dethrone, oust, overcome, overpower, topple, unseat, vanquish
▷ *noun* 2 DOWNFALL, defeat, destruction, dethronement, fall, ousting, undoing, unseating
overtone *noun* CONNOTATION, hint, implication, innuendo, intimation, nuance, sense, suggestion, undercurrent
overture *noun* 1 (*music*) INTRODUCTION, opening, prelude
2 ▷ **overtures** APPROACH, advance, invitation, offer, proposal, proposition

negotiations **3** formal offer
o•ver•ween•ing [OH-vər-WEE-ning] *adjective* thinking too much of oneself
o•ver•whelm [oh-vər-HWELM] *verb transitive* **1** crush **2** submerge, engulf > **o•ver•whelm'ing** *adjective* **1** decisive **2** irresistible
o•ver•wrought [OH-vər-RAWT] *adjective* **1** overexcited **2** too elaborate
o•vip•a•rous [oh-VIP-ər-əs] *adjective* laying eggs
ov•ule [OV-yool] *noun* unfertilized seed > **ov'u•late** [-yə-layt] *verb intransitive* **-lat•ed, -lat•ing** produce, discharge (egg) from ovary
o•vum [OH-vəm] *noun, plural* **o•va** [OH-və] female egg cell, in which development of fetus takes place
owe [oh] *verb transitive* **owed, ow•ing** be bound to repay, be indebted for > **owing** *adjective* owed, due **owing to** caused by, as result of
owl *noun* night bird of prey > **owl'ish** *adjective* resembling an owl
own [ohn] *adjective* **1** emphasizes possession ▷ *verb transitive* **2** possess **3** acknowledge ▷ *verb intransitive* **4** to confess > **own'er•ship** *noun* possession
ox [oks] *noun, plural* **ox•en** **1** large cloven-footed and usu. horned farm animal **2** bull or cow > **ox'bow** [-boh] *noun* **1** U-shaped harness collar of ox **2** bow-shaped bend in river
ox•ide [OK-sīd] *noun* compound of oxygen and another element > **ox'i•dize** *verb* **-dized, -diz•ing** (cause to) combine with oxide, rust
ox•y•gen [OK-si-jən] *noun* gas in atmosphere essential to life, combustion, etc. > **ox'y•gen•ate** *verb transitive* **-at•ed, -at•ing** combine or treat with oxygen
ox•y•mo•ron [ok-si-MOR-on] *noun* figure of speech in which two ideas of opposite meaning are combined to form an expressive phrase or epithet, such as *cruel kindness*
oys•ter [OI-stər] *noun* edible bivalve mollusk or shellfish
o•zone [OH-zohn] *noun* form of oxygen with pungent odor > **ozone layer** layer of upper atmosphere with concentration of ozone

DICTIONARY • THESAURUS

overturn *verb* **1** TIP OVER, capsize, keel over, overbalance, topple, upend, upturn
2 OVERTHROW, bring down, depose, destroy, unseat
overweight *adjective* FAT, bulky, chubby, chunky, corpulent, heavy, hefty, obese, plump, portly, stout, tubby (*informal*)
overwhelm *verb* **1** DEVASTATE, bowl over (*informal*), knock (someone) for six (*informal*), overcome, stagger, sweep (someone) off his feet *or* sweep (someone) off her feet, take (someone's) breath away
2 DESTROY, crush, cut to pieces, massacre, overpower, overrun, rout
overwhelming *adjective* DEVASTATING, breathtaking, crushing, irresistible, overpowering, shattering, stunning, towering
overwork *verb* **1** STRAIN, burn the midnight oil, sweat (*informal*), work one's fingers to the bone
2 OVERUSE, exhaust, exploit, fatigue, oppress, wear out, weary
overwrought *adjective* AGITATED, distracted, excited, frantic, keyed up, on edge, overexcited, tense, uptight (*informal*), wired (*slang*)
owe *verb* BE IN DEBT, be in arrears, be obligated *or* be indebted
owing *adjective* UNPAID, due, outstanding, overdue, owed, payable, unsettled
owing to *preposition* BECAUSE OF, as a result of, on account of
own *adjective* **1** PERSONAL, individual, particular, private
▷ *pronoun* **2** ▷ **hold one's own** COMPETE, keep going, keep one's end up, keep one's head above water
3 ▷ **on one's own** ALONE, by oneself, independently, singly, unaided, unassisted, under one's own steam
▷ *verb* **4** POSSESS, be in possession of, enjoy, have, hold, keep, retain
5 ACKNOWLEDGE, admit, allow, concede, confess, grant, recognize
6 ▷ **own up** CONFESS, admit, come clean, make a clean breast, tell the truth
owner *noun* POSSESSOR, holder, landlord *or* landlady, proprietor
ownership *noun* POSSESSION, dominion, title

Pp

P *chem.* phosphorus
Pa *chem.* protactinium
PAC Political Action Committee: political organization formed to raise money for the campaigns of political candidates likely to advance the organization's interests
pace [pays] *noun* 1 step 2 its length 3 rate of movement 4 walk, gait ▷ *verb* **paced, pac•ing** 5 *verb intransitive* 6 step ▷ *verb transitive* 7 set speed for 8 cross, measure with steps > **pac'er** *noun* 1 one who sets the pace for another 2 horse used for pacing in harness racing > **pace'mak•er** *noun* esp. electronic device surgically implanted in those with heart disease
pa•chin•ko [pə-CHING-koh] *noun* Japanese pinball machine
pach•y•derm [PAK-i-durm] *noun* thick-skinned animal, such as an elephant > **pach•y•der'ma•tous** [-mə-təs] *adjective* thick-skinned, stolid
pac•i•fy [PAS-ə-fī] *verb transitive* **-fied, -fy•ing** 1 calm 2 establish peace > **pa•cif'ic** *adjective* 1 peaceable 2 calm, tranquil > **pa'ci•fi•er** ring or nipple for baby to suck or chew > **pac'i•fism** *noun* > **pac'i•fist** *noun* 1 advocate of abolition of war 2 one who refuses to help in war
pack [pak] *noun* 1 bundle 2 band of animals 3 large set of people or things 4 set of, container for, retail commodities 5 set of playing cards 6 mass of floating ice ▷ *verb transitive* 7 put together in suitcase, etc. 8 make into a bundle 9 press tightly together, cram 10 fill with things 11 fill (meeting, etc.) with one's own supporters 12 order off > **pack'age** [-ij] *noun* 1 parcel 2 set of items offered together ▷ *verb transitive* **-aged, -ag•ing** > **pack'et** [-it] *noun* 1 small parcel 2 small container (and contents) 3 (*informal*) large sum of money 4 small mail,

DICTIONARY

P

THESAURUS

pace *noun* 1 STEP, gait, stride, tread, walk
2 SPEED, rate, tempo, velocity
▷ *verb* 3 STRIDE, march, patrol, pound
4 ▷ **pace out** MEASURE, count, mark out, step
pacifist *noun* PEACE LOVER, conscientious objector, dove
pacify *verb* CALM, allay, appease, assuage, de-stress, mollify, placate, propitiate, soothe
pack *verb* 1 PACKAGE, bundle, load, store, stow
2 CRAM, compress, crowd, fill, jam, press, ram, stuff
3 ▷ **pack off** SEND AWAY, dismiss, send packing (*informal*)
▷ *noun* 4 BUNDLE, back pack, burden, kitbag, knapsack, load, parcel, rucksack
5 PACKET, package
6 GROUP, band, bunch, company, crowd, flock, gang, herd, mob, troop
package *noun* 1 PARCEL, box, carton, container, packet
2 UNIT, combination, whole
▷ *verb* 3 PACK, box, parcel *or* parcel up, wrap
packed *adjective* FULL, chock-a-block, chock-full, crammed, crowded, filled, jammed, jam-packed
packet *noun* 1 PACKAGE, bag, carton, container, parcel
pack up *verb* 1 PUT AWAY, store
2 (*informal*) STOP, finish, give up, pack it in (*informal*)
3 BREAK DOWN, conk out (*informal*), fail

passenger, freight boat > **pack'horse** *noun* horse for carrying goods > **pack ice** loose floating ice that has been compacted together
pact [pakt] *noun* covenant, agreement, compact
pad[1] *noun* 1 piece of soft material used as a cushion, protection, etc. 2 block of sheets of paper 3 foot or sole of various animals 4 place for launching rockets 5 (*slang*) residence ▷ *verb transitive* **pad•ded, pad•ding** 6 make soft, fill in, protect, etc., with pad or padding 7 add to dishonestly > **padding** *noun* 1 material used for stuffing 2 literary matter put in simply to increase quantity
pad[2] *verb intransitive* **pad•ded, pad•ding** 1 walk with soft step 2 travel slowly ▷ *noun* 3 sound of soft footstep
pad•dle[1] [PAD-əl] *noun* 1 short oar with broad blade at one or each end ▷ *verb* **-dled, -dling** 2 move by, or with, paddles 3 row gently > **paddle wheel** wheel with crosswise blades striking water successively to propel ship
paddle[2] *verb transitive* **-dled, -dling** 1 walk with bare feet in shallow water ▷ *noun* 2 such a walk
pad•dock [PAD-ək] *noun* small grass field or enclosure
pad•dy [PAD-ee] *noun, plural* **-dies** rice growing or in the husk > **paddy field** field where rice is grown
pad•lock [PAD-lok] *noun* 1 detachable lock with hinged hoop to go through staple or ring ▷ *verb transitive* 2 fasten thus
pae•an [PEE-ən] *noun* song of triumph or thanksgiving
pa•gan [PAY-gən] *adjective, noun* heathen > **pa'gan•ism** *noun*
page[1] [payj] *noun* 1 one side of leaf of book, etc. 2 screenful of information from a website or teletext service
page[2] *noun* 1 boy servant 2 attendant ▷ *verb transitive* **paged, pag•ing** 3 summon (a person), by bleeper or loudspeaker, in order to pass on a message > **page'boy** *noun* hair style with hair rolled under usu. at shoulder length
pag•eant [PAJ-ənt] *noun* 1 show of persons in costume in procession, dramatic scenes, etc., usu. illustrating history 2 brilliant show > **pag'eant•ry** *noun, plural* **-ies**
pag•i•nate [PAJ-ə-nate] *verb transitive* **-nat•ed, -nat•ing** number pages of > **pag•i•na'tion** *noun*
pa•go•da [pə-GOH-də] *noun* pyramidal temple or tower of Chinese or Indian type
paid [payd] *pt. of* **pay.** > **paid-up** *adjective* paid in full
pail [payl] *noun* bucket > **pail'ful** [-fəl] *noun, plural* **-fuls**
pain [payn] *noun* 1 bodily or mental suffering 2 penalty or punishment ▷ *verb transitive* 3 inflict pain upon > **pains** *plural noun* trouble, exertion > **pain'ful** [-fəl] *adjective* > **pain'less** [-lis] *adjective* > **pain'kill•er** *noun* drug, as aspirin, that reduces pain > **pains'tak•ing** *adjective* diligent, careful
paint [paynt] *noun* 1 coloring matter spread on a surface with brushes, roller, spray gun, etc. ▷ *verb transitive* 2 portray, color, coat, or make picture of, with paint 3 apply makeup 4 describe > **paint'er** *noun* > **paint'ing** *noun* picture in paint
paint•er [PAYN-tər] *noun* line at bow of boat for tying it up
pair *noun* 1 set of two, esp. existing or generally used together ▷ *verb* 2 arrange in twos 3 group or be grouped in twos
pais•ley [PAYZ-lee] *noun, plural* **-leys** pattern of small curving shapes

pact *noun* AGREEMENT, alliance, bargain, covenant, deal, treaty, understanding
pad[1] *noun* 1 CUSHION, buffer, protection, stuffing, wad
2 NOTEPAD, block, jotter, writing pad
3 PAW, foot, sole
4 (*slang, dated*) HOME, apartment, flat, place
▷ *verb* 5 PACK, cushion, fill, protect, stuff
6 ▷ **pad out** LENGTHEN, elaborate, fill out, flesh out, protract, spin out, stretch
pad[2] *verb* SNEAK, creep, go barefoot, steal
padding *noun* 1 FILLING, packing, stuffing, wadding
2 WORDINESS, hot air (*informal*), verbiage, verbosity
paddle[1] *noun* 1 OAR, scull
▷ *verb* 2 ROW, propel, pull, scull
paddle[2] *verb* 1 WADE, slop, splash *or* splash about
2 DABBLE, stir
pagan *adjective* 1 HEATHEN, idolatrous, infidel, polytheistic
▷ *noun* 2 HEATHEN, idolater, infidel, polytheist
page[1] *noun* FOLIO, leaf, sheet, side
page[2] *noun* 1 ATTENDANT, pageboy, servant, squire
▷ *verb* 2 CALL, send for, summon
pageant *noun* SHOW, display, parade, procession, spectacle, tableau
pageantry *noun* SPECTACLE, display, grandeur, parade, pomp, show, splendor, theatricality
pain *noun* 1 HURT, ache, discomfort, irritation, pang, soreness, tenderness, throb, twinge
2 SUFFERING, agony, anguish, distress, heartache, misery, torment, torture
▷ *verb* 3 HURT, smart, sting, throb
4 DISTRESS, agonize, cut to the quick, grieve, hurt, sadden, torment, torture
pained *adjective* DISTRESSED, aggrieved, hurt, injured, offended, upset, wounded
painful *adjective* 1 DISTRESSING, disagreeable, distasteful, grievous, unpleasant
2 SORE, aching, agonizing, smarting, tender
3 DIFFICULT, arduous, hard, laborious, troublesome, trying
painfully *adverb* DISTRESSINGLY, clearly, dreadfully, sadly, unfortunately
painkiller *noun* ANALGESIC, anesthetic, anodyne, drug
painless *adjective* SIMPLE, easy, effortless, fast, quick
pains *plural noun* TROUBLE, bother, care, diligence, effort
painstaking *adjective* THOROUGH, assiduous, careful, conscientious, diligent, meticulous, scrupulous
paint *noun* 1 COLORING, color, dye, pigment, stain, tint
▷ *verb* 2 DEPICT, draw, picture, portray, represent, sketch
3 COAT, apply, color, cover, daub
pair *noun* 1 COUPLE, brace, duo, twins
▷ *verb* 2 COUPLE, bracket, join, match *or* match up, team, twin

pa•ja•mas [pə-JAH-məz] *plural noun* sleeping suit of loose-fitting trousers and jacket
pal *noun* (*informal*) friend
pal•ace [PAL-is] *noun* 1 residence of king, bishop, etc. 2 stately mansion > **pa•la•tial** [pə-LAY-shəl] *adjective* 1 like a palace 2 magnificent > **pal•a•tine** [PAL-ə-tīn] *adjective* with royal privileges
pal•ate [PAL-it] *noun* 1 roof of mouth 2 sense of taste > **pal'at•a•ble** *adjective* agreeable to eat > **pal'a•tal** [-təl] *adjective* 1 of the palate 2 made by placing tongue against palate
palatial, palatine *see* palace
pa•lav•er [pə-LAV-ər] *noun* 1 fuss 2 conference, discussion
pale[1] [payl] *adjective* **pal•er, pal•est** 1 wan, dim, whitish ▷ *verb intransitive* **paled, pal•ing** whiten 2 lose superiority or importance
pale[2] *noun* stake, boundary > **pal'ing** *noun* upright stakes making up fence **beyond the pale** beyond limits of propriety, safety, etc.
pa•le•o•lith•ic [pay-lee-ə-LITH-ik] *adjective* of the old Stone Age
pa•le•on•tol•o•gy [pay-lee-ən-TOL-ə-jee] *noun* study of past geological periods and fossils
pal•ette [PAL-it] *noun* artist's flat board for mixing colors on
pal•i•mo•ny [PAL-ə-moh-nee] *noun* alimony awarded to partner in broken romantic relationship
pal•in•drome [PAL-in-drohm] *noun* word, verse or sentence that is the same when read backward or forward
pal•i•sade [pal-ə-SAYD] *noun* 1 fence of stakes ▷ *verb transitive* **-sad•ed, -sad•ing** 2 to enclose or protect with one > **pal•i•sades** *plural noun* line of cliffs
pall[1] [pawl] *noun* 1 cloth spread over a coffin 2 depressing, oppressive atmosphere > **pall'bear•er** *noun* one carrying, attending coffin at funeral
pall[2] *verb intransitive* 1 become tasteless or tiresome 2 cloy
pal•let[1] [PAL-it] *noun* 1 straw mattress 2 small bed
pallet[2] *noun* portable platform for storing and moving goods
pal•li•ate [PAL-ee-ayt] *verb transitive* **-at•ed, -at•ing** 1 relieve without curing 2 excuse > **pal'li•a•tive** [-ə-tiv] *adjective* 1 giving temporary or partial relief ▷ *noun* 2 that which excuses, mitigates or alleviates
pal•lid [PAL-id] *adjective* pale, wan, colorless > **pal'lor** [-ər] *noun* paleness
palm [pahm] *noun* 1 inner surface of hand 2 tropical tree 3 leaf of the tree as symbol of victory ▷ *verb transitive* 4 conceal in palm of hand 5 pass off by trickery > **palm'is•try** *noun* fortune telling from lines on palm of hand > **palm'y** *adjective* **palm•i•er, palm•i•est** flourishing, successful > **Palm Sunday** Sunday before Easter > **palm'top** *adjective* 1 (of a computer) small enough to be held in the hand ▷ *noun* 2 such a computer
pal•o•mi•no [pal-ə-MEE-noh] *noun, plural* **-nos** golden horse with white mane and tail
pal•pa•ble [PAL-pə-bəl] *adjective* 1 obvious 2 certain 3 that can be touched or felt > **pal'pa•bly** *adverb*
pal•pate [PAL-payt] *verb transitive* **-pat•ed, -pat•ing** *med.* examine by touch
pal•pi•tate [PAL-pi-tayt] *verb intransitive* **-tat•ed, -tat•ing** 1 throb 2 pulsate violently > **pal•pi•ta'tion** *noun* 1 throbbing 2 violent, irregular beating of heart
pal•sy [PAWL-zee] *noun, plural* **-sies** paralysis, esp. with tremors > **pal'sied** *adjective* affected with palsy
pal•try [PAWL-tree] *adjective* **-tri•er, -tri•est** worthless, contemptible, trifling
pam•pas [PAM-pəz] *plural noun* vast grassy treeless plains in South America
pam•per [PAM-pər] *verb transitive* overindulge, spoil by coddling
pam•phlet [PAM-flit] *noun* thin unbound book usu. on some topical subject > **pam•phlet•eer'** *noun* writer of these
pan[1] *noun* 1 broad, shallow vessel 2 depression in ground, esp. where salt forms ▷ *verb transitive* **panned, pan•ning** 3 wash gold ore in pan 4 (*informal*) criticize harshly > **pan out** *verb intransitive* (*informal*) result, esp. successfully

DICTIONARY

P

THESAURUS

pal *noun* (*informal*) FRIEND, buddy (*informal*), chum (*informal*), companion, comrade, crony, homeboy (*slang*), homegirl (*slang*)
palatable *adjective* DELICIOUS, appetizing, luscious, mouthwatering, tasty, yummy (*informal*)
palate *noun* TASTE, appetite, stomach
palatial *adjective* MAGNIFICENT, grand, imposing, majestic, opulent, regal, splendid, stately
palaver *noun* FUSS, big deal (*informal*), performance (*informal*), rigmarole, song and dance (*informal*), to-do
pale[1] *adjective* 1 WHITE, ashen, bleached, colorless, faded, light, pallid, pasty, wan ▷ *verb* 2 BECOME PALE, blanch, go white, lose color, whiten
pall[1] *noun* 1 CLOUD, mantle, shadow, shroud, veil 2 GLOOM, check, damp, damper
pall[2] *verb* BECOME BORING, become dull, become tedious, cloy, jade, sicken, tire, weary
pallid *adjective* PALE, anemic, ashen, colorless, pasty, wan
pallor *noun* PALENESS, lack of color, pallidness, wanness, whiteness
palm off *verb* FOB OFF, foist off, pass off
palpable *adjective* OBVIOUS, clear, conspicuous, evident, manifest, plain, unmistakable, visible
palpitate *verb* BEAT, flutter, pound, pulsate, throb, tremble
paltry *adjective* INSIGNIFICANT, contemptible, despicable, inconsiderable, lousy (*slang*), meager, mean, measly, minor, miserable, petty, poor, puny, scuzzy (*slang*), slight, small, trifling, trivial, unimportant, worthless
pamper *verb* SPOIL, cater to, coddle, cosset, indulge, overindulge, pet
pamphlet *noun* BOOKLET, brochure, circular, leaflet, tract
pan[1] *noun* 1 POT, container, saucepan ▷ *verb* 2 SIFT OUT, look for, search for 3 (*informal*) CRITICIZE, censure, knock (*informal*), slam (*slang*)
pan[2] *verb* MOVE, follow, sweep, track

pan² *verb* **panned, pan•ning** move motion picture or TV camera slowly while shooting to cover scene, follow moving object, etc.
pan-, pant-, panto- *combining form* all: *panacea; pan-American*
pan•a•ce•a [pan-ə-SEE-ə] *noun* universal remedy, cure for all ills
pa•nache [pə-NASH] *noun* dashing style
pan•cake [PAN-kayk] *noun* 1 thin cake of batter fried in pan 2 flat cake or stick of compressed makeup ▷ *verb intransitive* **-caked, -cak•ing** 3 *aviation* make flat landing by dropping in a level position
pan•chro•mat•ic [pan-kroh-MAT-ik] *adjective photography* sensitive to light of all colors
pan•cre•as [PAN-kree-əs] *noun* digestive gland behind stomach > **pan•cre•at'ic** *adjective*
pan•da [PAN-də] *noun* large black and white bearlike mammal of China
pan•dem•ic [pan-DEM-ik] *adjective* (of disease) occurring over wide area
pan•de•mo•ni•um [pan-də-MOH-nee-əm] *noun* scene of din and uproar
pan•der [PAN-dər] *verb* 1 (esp. with *to*) give gratification to (weakness or desires) ▷ *noun* 2 pimp
pane [payn] *noun* single piece of glass in a window or door
pan•e•gyr•ic [pan-ə-JIR-ik] *noun* speech of praise > **pan•e•gyr'i•cal** *adjective* laudatory > **pan•e•gyr'ist** *noun*
pan•el [PAN-l] *noun* 1 compartment of surface, usu. raised or sunk, for example in a door 2 any distinct section of something 3 strip of material inserted in garment 4 group of persons as team in quiz game, etc. 5 list of jurors, doctors, etc. 6 thin board with picture on it ▷ *verb transitive* **-eled, -el•ing** 7 adorn with panels > **paneling** *noun* paneled work > **pan'el•ist** *noun* member of panel
pang *noun* 1 sudden pain, sharp twinge 2 compunction
pan•ic [PAN-ik] *noun* 1 sudden and infectious fear 2 extreme fright 3 unreasoning terror ▷ *adjective* 4 of fear, etc. ▷ *verb* **-icked, -ick•ing** 5 feel or cause to feel panic > **pan'ick•y** *adjective* 1 inclined to panic 2 nervous > **panic button** button or switch that operates safety device, for use in emergency > **panic room** secure room within a house, to which a person can flee if someone breaks in > **panic-stricken, panic-struck** *adjective* panicky
pan•o•ply [PAN-ə-plee] *noun, plural* **-plies** complete, magnificent array > **pan'o•plied** *adjective*
pan•o•ram•a [pan-ə-RAM-ə] *noun* 1 wide or complete view 2 picture arranged around spectators or unrolled before them > **pan•o•ram'ic** *adjective*
pan•sy [PAN-zee] *noun, plural* **-sies** 1 flower, species of violet 2 (*slang, offensive*) effeminate man
pant *verb intransitive* 1 gasp for breath 2 yearn 3 long 4 throb ▷ *noun* 5 gasp
pan•ta•loon [PAN-tl-oon] *noun* in pantomime, foolish old man who is the butt of clown > **pan•ta•loons** (*obsolete*) baggy trousers
pan•the•ism [PAN-thee-iz-əm] *noun* identification of God with the universe > **pan•the•is'tic** *adjective* > **pan'the•on** [-thee-ən] *noun* temple of all gods
pan•ther [PAN-thər] *noun* 1 cougar 2 puma 3 variety of leopard
pant•ies [PAN-teez] *plural noun* women's undergarment
pan•to•mime [PAN-tə-mīm] *noun* dramatic entertainment without speech
pan•try [PAN-tree] *noun, plural* **-tries** [-treez] room for storing food or utensils
pants *plural noun* 1 trousers 2 undergarment for lower trunk
pant•y•hose [PAN-tee-hohz] *plural noun* women's one-piece garment combining stockings and panties
pant•y•waist [PAN-tee-wayst] *noun* (*informal, offensive*) effeminate man
pap *noun* 1 soft food for infants, invalids, etc. 2 pulp, mash 3 idea, book, etc. lacking substance
pa•pa•cy [PAY-pə-see] *noun, plural* **-cies** 1 office of Pope 2 papal system > **pa'pal** *adjective* of, relating to, the Pope > **pa'pist** *noun, adjective* (*offensive*) Roman Catholic
pa•pa•raz•zo [pah-pə-RAHT-soh] *noun, plural* **-raz•zi** [-RAHT-see] freelance photographer specializing in candid shots of celebrities
pa•pa•ya [pə-PAH-yə] *noun* 1 tree bearing melon-shaped fruit 2 its fruit
pa•per [PAY-pər] *noun* 1 material made by pressing pulp of rags, straw, wood, etc., into thin, flat sheets 2 printed sheet of paper 3 newspaper 4 article, essay ▷ *verb transitive* 5 cover, decorate with paper > **pa•pers** *plural noun*

panacea *noun* CURE-ALL, nostrum, universal cure
panache *noun* STYLE, dash, élan, flamboyance
pandemonium *noun* UPROAR, bedlam, chaos, confusion, din, hullabaloo, racket, rumpus, turmoil
pander *verb*
▷ **pander to** INDULGE, cater to, gratify, play up to (*informal*), please, satisfy
pang *noun* TWINGE, ache, pain, prick, spasm, stab, sting
panic *noun* 1 FEAR, alarm, fright, hysteria, scare, terror
▷ *verb* 2 GO TO PIECES, become hysterical, lose one's nerve
3 ALARM, scare, unnerve
panic-stricken *adjective* FRIGHTENED, frightened out of one's wits, hysterical, in a cold sweat (*informal*), panicky, scared, scared stiff, terrified
panoply *noun* ARRAY, attire, dress, garb, regalia, trappings
panorama *noun* VIEW, prospect, vista
panoramic *adjective* WIDE, comprehensive, extensive, overall, sweeping
pant *verb* PUFF, blow, breathe, gasp, heave, wheeze
pants *plural noun* TROUSERS, slacks
paper *noun* 1 NEWSPAPER, daily, gazette, journal
2 ESSAY, article, dissertation, report, treatise
3 ▷ **papers a** DOCUMENTS, certificates, deeds, records **b** LETTERS, archive, diaries, documents, dossier, file, records
▷ *verb* 4 WALLPAPER, hang

documents, etc. > **paper over** (try to) conceal (differences, etc.) in order to preserve friendship, etc.

pa•pier-mâ•ché [PAY-pər mə-SHAY] *noun* pulp from rags or paper mixed with size, shaped by molding and dried hard

pa•poose [pa-POOS] *noun* Native American child

pap•ri•ka [pa-PREE-kə] *noun* (powdered seasoning prepared from) type of red pepper

pa•py•rus [pə-PĪ-rəs] *noun, plural* **-py•ri** [-PĪ-rī] 1 species of reed 2 (manuscript written on) kind of paper made from this plant

par [pahr] *noun* 1 equality of value or standing 2 face value (of stocks and bonds) 3 *golf* estimated standard score ▷ *verb transitive* **parred, par•ring** 4 *golf* make par on hole or round > **par'i•ty** *noun* 1 equality 2 analogy

para-, par-, pa- *combining form* beside, beyond: *paradigm; parallel; parody*

par•a•ble [PA-rə-bəl] *noun* allegory, story with a moral lesson

pa•rab•o•la [pə-RAB-ə-lə] *noun* section of cone cut by plane parallel to the cone's side

par•a•chute [PA-rə-shoot] *noun* 1 apparatus extending like umbrella used to retard the descent of a falling body ▷ *verb* **-chut•ed, -chut•ing** 2 land or cause to land by parachute > **par'a•chut•ist** *noun* **golden parachute** employment contract for key employee of company guaranteeing substantial severance pay, etc. if company is sold

pa•rade [pə-RAYD] *noun* 1 display 2 muster of troops 3 parade ground ▷ *verb* **-rad•ed, -rad•ing** 4 march 5 display

par•a•digm [PA-rə-dīm] *noun* 1 example 2 model > **par•a•dig•mat'ic** [-dig-MAT-ik] *adjective*

par•a•dise [PA-rə-dīs] *noun* 1 heaven 2 state of bliss 3 (**Par•a•dise**) Garden of Eden

par•a•dox [PA-rə-doks] *noun* statement that seems absurd or self-contradictory but may be true > **par•a•dox'i•cal** *adjective*

par•af•fin [PA-rə-fin] *noun* waxlike or liquid hydrocarbon mixture used as fuel, solvent, in candles, etc.

par•a•gon [PA-rə-gon] *noun* pattern or model of excellence

par•a•graph [PA-rə-graf] *noun* 1 section of chapter or book 2 short notice, as in newspaper ▷ *verb transitive* 3 arrange in paragraphs

par•a•keet [PA-rə-keet] *noun* small parrot

par•al•lax [PA-rə-laks] *noun* apparent difference in object's position or direction as viewed from different points

par•al•lel [PA-rə-lel] *adjective* 1 continuously at equal distances 2 precisely corresponding ▷ *noun* 3 line equidistant from another at all points 4 thing exactly like another 5 comparison 6 line of latitude ▷ *verb transitive* **-leled, -lel•ing** 7 represent as similar, compare > **par'al•lel•ism** *noun* > **par•al•lel'o•gram** [-ə-gram] *noun* four-sided plane figure with opposite sides parallel

pa•ral•y•sis [pə-RAL-ə-sis] *noun, plural* **-ses** [-seez] incapacity to move or feel, due to damage to nervous system > **par•a•lyze** [PA-rə-līz] *verb transitive* **-lyzed, -lyz•ing** 1 affect with paralysis 2 cripple 3 make useless or ineffectual > **par•a•lyt'ic** [-LIT-ik] *adjective, noun* (person) affected with paralysis **infantile paralysis** poliomyelitis

par•a•med•i•cal [pa-rə-MED-i-kəl] *adjective* of persons working in various capacities in support of medical profession > **par•a•med'ic** *noun*

pa•ram•e•ter [pə-RAM-i-tər] *noun* 1 measurable characteristic 2 any constant limiting factor

par•a•mil•i•tar•y [pa-rə-MIL-i-ter-ee] *adjective* of civilian group organized on military lines or in support of the military

par•a•mount [PA-rə-mownt] *adjective* supreme, eminent, preeminent, chief

par•a•mour [PA-rə-moor] *noun* (*old-fashioned*) lover, esp. of a person married to someone else

par•a•noi•a [pa-rə-NOI-ə] *noun* mental disease with delusions of fame, grandeur, persecution > **par•a•noi'ac** *adjective, noun* > **par'a•noid** *adjective* 1 of paranoia 2 (*informal*) exhibiting fear of persecution, etc. ▷ *noun*

par•a•pet [PA-rə-pit] *noun* low wall, railing along edge of balcony, bridge, etc.

par•a•pher•na•lia [pa-rə-fər-NAYL-yə] *plural noun* 1 personal belongings 2 odds and ends of equipment

DICTIONARY P THESAURUS

par *noun* AVERAGE, level, mean, norm, standard, usual

parable *noun* LESSON, allegory, fable, moral tale, story

parade *noun* 1 PROCESSION, array, cavalcade, march, pageant
2 SHOW, display, spectacle
▷ *verb* 3 FLAUNT, display, exhibit, show off (*informal*)
4 MARCH, process

paradigm *noun* MODEL, example, ideal, pattern

paradise *noun* 1 HEAVEN, Elysian fields, Happy Valley, Promised Land
2 BLISS, delight, felicity, heaven, utopia

paradox *noun* CONTRADICTION, anomaly, enigma, oddity, puzzle

paradoxical *adjective* CONTRADICTORY, baffling, confounding, enigmatic, puzzling

paragon *noun* MODEL, epitome, exemplar, ideal, nonpareil, pattern, quintessence

paragraph *noun* SECTION, clause, item, part, passage, subdivision

parallel *adjective* 1 EQUIDISTANT, alongside, side by side
2 MATCHING, analogous, corresponding, like, resembling, similar
▷ *noun* 3 EQUIVALENT, analogue, counterpart, equal, match, twin
4 SIMILARITY, analogy, comparison, likeness, resemblance

paralysis *noun* 1 IMMOBILITY, palsy
2 STANDSTILL, breakdown, halt, stoppage

paralytic *adjective* PARALYZED, challenged, crippled, disabled, incapacitated, lame, palsied

paralyze *verb* 1 DISABLE, cripple, incapacitate, lame
2 IMMOBILIZE, freeze, halt, numb, petrify, stun

parameter *noun* LIMIT, framework, limitation, restriction, specification

paramount *adjective* PRINCIPAL, cardinal, chief, first, foremost, main, primary, prime, supreme

paranoid *adjective* 1 MENTALLY ILL, deluded,

par•a•phrase [PA-rə-frayz] *noun* 1 expression of meaning of passage in other words 2 free translation ▷ *verb transitive* **-phrased, -phras•ing** 3 put into other words

par•a•ple•gi•a [pa-rə-PLEE-jee-ə] *noun* paralysis of lower half of body > **par•a•ple'gic** *noun, adjective*

par•a•psy•chol•o•gy [pa-rə-sī-KOL-ə-jee] *noun* study of subjects pert. to extrasensory perception, e.g. telepathy

par•a•site [PA-rə-sīt] *noun* 1 animal or plant living in or on another 2 self-interested hanger-on > **par•a•sit'ic** [-SIT-ik] *adjective* of the nature of, living as, parasite > **par'a•sit•ism** [-si-tiz-əm] *noun* > **par•a•si•tol'o•gy** *noun* study of animal and vegetable parasites, esp. as causes of disease

par•a•sol [PA-rə-sawl] *noun* lightweight umbrella used as sunshade

par•a•troop•er [PA-rə-troo-pər] *noun* soldier trained to descend from airplane by parachute

par•a•ty•phoid [pa-rə-TĪ-foid] *noun* an infectious disease similar to but distinct from typhoid fever

par•boil [PAHR-boil] *verb transitive* boil until partly cooked

par•cel [PAHR-səl] *noun* 1 packet of goods, esp. one enclosed in paper 2 quantity dealt with at one time 3 tract of land ▷ *verb transitive* **-celed, -cel•ing** 4 wrap up 5 divide into, distribute in, parts

parch [pahrch] *verb* 1 dry by heating 2 make, become hot and dry 3 scorch 4 roast slightly

parch•ment [PAHRCH-mənt] *noun* 1 sheep, goat, calf skin prepared for writing 2 manuscript of this

par•don [PAHR-dn] *verb transitive* 1 forgive, excuse ▷ *noun* 2 forgiveness 3 release from punishment > **par'don•a•ble** *adjective*

pare [pair] *verb transitive* **pared, par•ing** 1 trim, cut edge or surface of 2 decrease bit by bit > **par'ing** *noun* piece pared off, rind

par•e•gor•ic [pa-ri-GOR-ik] *noun* tincture of opium used to stop diarrhea

par•ent [PAIR-ənt] *noun* father or mother > **par'ent•age** *noun* descent, extraction > **pa•rent•al** [pə-REN-tl] *adjective* > **par'ent•hood** [-huud] *noun*

pa•ren•the•sis [pə-REN-thə-sis] *noun* word, phrase, etc. inserted in passage independently of grammatical sequence and usu. marked off by brackets, dashes, or commas > **pa•ren'the•ses** [-seez] *plural noun* round brackets, ( ) > **par•en•thet'ic•al** *adjective*

pa•ri•ah [pə-RĪ-ə] *noun* social outcast

par•ish [PA-rish] *noun* 1 district under one clergyman 2 subdivision of county > **pa•rish'ion•er** *noun* member, inhabitant of parish

parity *see* par

park [pahrk] *noun* 1 large area of land in natural state preserved for recreational use 2 field or stadium for sporting events 3 large enclosed piece of ground, usu. with grass or woodland, attached to country house or for public use 4 space in camp for military supplies ▷ *verb transitive* 5 leave for a short time 6 maneuver (automobile, etc) into a suitable space 7 (*informal*) engage in caressing and kissing in parked automobile

par•ka [PAHR-kə] *noun* warm waterproof coat with hood

par•lance [PAHR-ləns] *noun* 1 way of speaking, conversation 2 idiom

par•ley [PAHR-lee] *noun, plural* **-leys** 1 meeting between leaders or representatives of opposing forces to discuss terms ▷ *verb intransitive* **-leyed, -ley•ing** 2 hold discussion about terms

par•lia•ment [PAHR-lə-mənt] *noun* legislature of some countries > **par•lia•men•tar'i•an** [-TAIR-ee-ən] *noun* expert in rules and procedures of a legislature or other formal organization

par•lor [PAHR-lər] *noun* 1 sitting room, room for receiving company in small house 2 place for milking cows 3 room or building as

---

disturbed, manic, neurotic, paranoiac, psychotic 2 (*informal*) SUSPICIOUS, fearful, nervous, wired (*slang*), worried

paraphernalia *noun* EQUIPMENT, apparatus, baggage, belongings, effects, gear, stuff, tackle, things, trappings

paraphrase *noun* 1 REWORDING, rephrasing, restatement
▷ *verb* 2 REWORD, express in other words *or* express in one's own words, rephrase, restate

parasite *noun* SPONGER (*informal*), bloodsucker (*informal*), hanger-on, leech, scrounger (*informal*)

parasitic *or* **parasitical** *adjective* SCROUNGING (*informal*), bloodsucking (*informal*), sponging (*informal*)

parcel *noun* 1 PACKAGE, bundle, pack
▷ *verb* 2 (*often with up*) WRAP, do up, pack, package, tie up

parch *verb* DRY UP, dehydrate, desiccate, evaporate, shrivel, wither

parched *adjective* DRIED OUT *or* DRIED UP, arid, dehydrated, dry, thirsty

pardon *verb* 1 FORGIVE, absolve, acquit, excuse, exonerate, let off (*informal*), overlook
▷ *noun* 2 FORGIVENESS, absolution, acquittal, amnesty, exoneration

pardonable *adjective* FORGIVABLE, excusable, minor, understandable, venial

pare *verb* 1 PEEL, clip, cut, shave, skin, trim 2 CUT BACK, crop, cut, decrease, dock, reduce

parent *noun* FATHER *or* MOTHER, procreator, progenitor, sire

parentage *noun* FAMILY, ancestry, birth, descent, lineage, pedigree, stock

pariah *noun* OUTCAST, exile, undesirable, untouchable

parish *noun* COMMUNITY, church, congregation, flock

parity *noun* EQUALITY, consistency, equivalence, uniformity, unity

park *noun* PARKLAND, estate, garden, grounds, woodland

parlance *noun* LANGUAGE, idiom, jargon, phraseology, speech, talk, tongue

parliament *noun* ASSEMBLY, congress, convention, council, legislature, senate

parliamentary *adjective* GOVERNMENTAL, law-making, legislative

parlor *noun* (*old-fashioned*) SITTING ROOM, drawing room, front room, living room, lounge

business premises, esp. undertaker, hairdresser, etc.
Par•me•san [PAHR-mə-zahn] *noun* hard dry Italian cheese for grating
pa•ro•chi•al [pə-ROH-kee-əl] *adjective* 1 narrow, provincial 2 of a parish > **pa•ro'chi•al•ism** *noun*
par•o•dy [PA-rə-dee] *noun, plural* **-dies** 1 composition in which author's style is made fun of by imitation 2 travesty ▷ *verb transitive* **-died, -dy•ing** 3 write parody of > **par'o•dist** *noun*
pa•role [pə-ROHL] *noun* 1 early freeing of prisoner on condition of good behavior 2 word of honor ▷ *verb transitive* **-roled, rol•ing** 3 place on parole
par•ox•ysm [PA-rək-siz-əm] *noun* sudden violent attack of pain, rage, laughter
par•quet [pahr-KAY] *noun* 1 flooring of wooden blocks arranged in pattern ▷ *verb transitive* **-queted** [-KAYD], **-quet•ing** [-KAY-ing] 2 lay a parquet
par•ri•cide [PA-rə-sīd] *noun* murder or murderer of a parent
par•rot [PA-rət] *noun* 1 bird with short hooked beak, some varieties of which can imitate speaking 2 unintelligent imitator ▷ *verb transitive* 3 imitate or repeat without understanding
par•ry [PA-ree] *verb transitive* **-ried, -ry•ing** 1 ward off, turn aside ▷ *noun, plural* **-ries** 2 act of parrying, esp. in fencing
parse [pahrs] *verb transitive* **parsed, pars•ing** describe (word), analyze (sentence) in terms of grammar
par•si•mo•ny [PAHR-sə-moh-nee] *noun* 1 stinginess 2 undue economy > **par•si•mo'ni•ous** *adjective* sparing
pars•ley [PAHR-slee] *noun* herb used for seasoning, garnish, etc.
pars•nip [PAHR-snip] *noun* edible whitish root vegetable
par•son [PAHR-sən] *noun* 1 clergyman of parish or church 2 clergyman > **par'son•age** *noun* parson's house
part [pahrt] *noun* 1 portion, section, share 2 division 3 actor's role 4 duty ▷ *verb* 5 divide 6 separate > **parts** *plural noun* region > **part'ing** *noun* 1 division between sections of hair on head 2 separation 3 leave-taking > **part'ly** *adverb* in part > **part song** song for several voices singing in harmony
par•take [pahr-TAYK] *verb* **-took, -tak•en, -tak•ing** 1 take or have share in 2 take food or drink
par•tial [PAHR-shəl] *adjective* 1 not general or complete 2 prejudiced 3 fond of > **par'tial•ly** *adverb* partly > **par•ti•al•i•ty** [pahr-shee-AL-i-tee] *noun* 1 favoritism 2 fondness for
par•tic•i•pate [pahr-TIS-ə-payt] *verb* **-pat•ed, -pat•ing** 1 share in 2 take part in > **par•tic'i•pant** *noun* > **par•tic'i•pa•to•ry** *adjective*
par•ti•ci•ple [PAHR-tə-sip-əl] *noun* adjective made by inflection from verb and keeping verb's relation to dependent words > **par•ti•cip'i•al** *adjective*
par•ti•cle [PAHR-ti-kəl] *noun* 1 minute portion of matter 2 least possible amount 3 minor part of speech in grammar, prefix, suffix

DICTIONARY

P

THESAURUS

parochial *adjective* PROVINCIAL, insular, limited, narrow, narrow-minded, petty, small-minded
parody *noun* SATIRE (*informal*), burlesque, caricature, skit, spoof (*informal*)
▷ *verb* SATIRIZE (*informal*), burlesque, caricature
paroxysm *noun* OUTBURST, attack, convulsion, fit, seizure, spasm
parrot *verb* REPEAT, copy, echo, imitate, mimic
parry *verb* 1 WARD OFF, block, deflect, rebuff, repel, repulse
2 EVADE, avoid, dodge, sidestep
parsimonious *adjective* MEAN, close, frugal, miserly, niggardly, penny-pinching (*informal*), stingy, tightfisted
parson *noun* CLERGYMAN, churchman, cleric, minister, pastor, preacher, priest, vicar
part *noun* 1 PIECE, bit, fraction, fragment, portion, scrap, section, share
2 COMPONENT, branch, constituent, division, member, unit
3 (*theatre*) ROLE, character, lines
4 SIDE, behalf, cause, concern, interest
5 (*often plural*) REGION, area, district, neighborhood, quarter, vicinity
6 ▷ **in good part** GOOD-NATUREDLY, cheerfully, well, without offense
7 ▷ **in part** PARTLY, a little, in some measure, partially, somewhat
▷ *verb* 8 DIVIDE, break, come apart, detach, rend, separate, sever, split, tear
9 SEPARATE, depart, go, go away, leave, split up, withdraw
partake *verb* 1 ▷ **partake of** CONSUME, chow down (*slang*), eat, take
2 ▷ **partake in** PARTICIPATE IN, engage in, share in, take part in
partial *adjective* 1 INCOMPLETE, imperfect, uncompleted, unfinished
2 BIASED, discriminatory, one-sided, partisan, prejudiced, unfair, unjust
partiality *noun* 1 BIAS, favoritism, preference, prejudice
2 LIKING, fondness, inclination, love, penchant, predilection, taste, weakness
partially *adverb* PARTLY, fractionally, incompletely, in part, not wholly, somewhat
participant *noun* PARTICIPATOR, contributor, member, player, stakeholder
participate *verb* TAKE PART, be involved in, join in, partake, perform, share
participation *noun* TAKING PART, contribution, involvement, joining in, partaking, sharing in
particle *noun* BIT, grain, iota, jot, mite, piece, scrap, shred, speck
particular *adjective* 1 SPECIFIC, distinct, exact, peculiar, precise, special
2 SPECIAL, especial, exceptional, marked, notable, noteworthy, remarkable, singular, uncommon, unusual
3 FUSSY, choosy (*informal*), demanding, fastidious, finicky, picky (*informal*)
▷ *noun* 4 (*usually plural*) DETAIL, circumstance, fact, feature, item, specification
5 ▷ **in particular** ESPECIALLY, distinctly, exactly, particularly, specifically
particularly *adverb* 1 ESPECIALLY, exceptionally, notably, singularly, uncommonly, unusually
2 SPECIFICALLY, distinctly, especially, explicitly,

par•ti-col•ored [PAHR-tee-kul-ərd] *adjective* differently colored in different parts, variegated
par•tic•u•lar [pahr-TIK-yə-lər] *adjective* 1 relating to one, not general 2 distinct 3 minute 4 very exact 5 fastidious ▷ *noun* 6 detail, item > **par•tic•u•lars** 1 detailed account 2 items of information > **par•tic'u•lar•ize** *verb transitive* **-ized, -iz•ing** mention in detail > **par•tic'u•lar•ly** *adverb*
par•ti•san [PAHR-tə-zən] *noun* 1 adherent of a party 2 guerrilla, member of resistance movement ▷ *adjective* 3 adhering to faction 4 prejudiced
par•ti•tion [pahr-TISH-ən] *noun* 1 division 2 interior dividing wall ▷ *verb transitive* 3 divide, cut into sections
part•ner [PAHRT-nər] *noun* 1 ally or companion 2 member of a partnership 3 one who dances with another 4 a husband or wife 5 *sport* one who plays with another against opponents ▷ *verb transitive* 6 be a partner of > **part'ner•ship** *noun* association of persons for business, etc.
par•tridge [PAHR-trij] *noun, plural* **-tridg•es** game bird of the grouse family
par•tu•ri•tion [pahr-tyuu-RISH-ən] *noun* 1 act of bringing forth young 2 childbirth
par•ty [PAHR-tee] *noun, plural* **-ties** 1 social assembly 2 group of persons traveling or working together 3 group of persons united in opinion 4 side 5 person ▷ *adjective* 6 of, belonging to, a party or faction > **party line** 1 telephone line serving two or more subscribers 2 policies of political party > **party wall** common wall separating adjoining premises
par•ve•nu [PAHR-və-noo] *noun* 1 one newly risen into position of notice, power, wealth 2 upstart
Pas•cal [PAS-kal] *noun* high-level computer programming language developed as a teaching language
pas•chal [PAS-kəl] *adjective* of Passover or Easter
pass *verb transitive* 1 go by, beyond, through, etc. 2 exceed 3 be accepted by 4 undergo successfully 5 spend 6 transfer 7 exchange 8 disregard 9 bring into force, sanction a legislative bill, etc. ▷ *verb intransitive* 10 go 11 be transferred from one state or person to another 12 elapse 13 undergo examination successfully 14 be taken as member of religious or racial group other than one's own ▷ *noun* 15 way, esp. a narrow and difficult way 16 permit, license, authorization 17 successful result from test 18 condition 19 *sports* transfer of ball by kick or throw > **pass'a•ble** *adjective* (just) acceptable > **pass'ing** *adjective* 1 transitory 2 cursory, casual > **pass off** present (something) under false pretenses > **pass up** ignore, neglect, reject
pas•sage [PAS-ij] *noun* 1 channel, opening 2 way through, corridor 3 part of book, etc. 4 journey, voyage, fare 5 enactment of rule, law by legislature, etc. 6 conversation, dispute 7 incident
pas•sé [pa-SAY] *adjective* 1 out-of-date 2 past the prime

expressly, in particular
parting *noun* 1 GOING, farewell, good-bye
2 DIVISION, breaking, rift, rupture, separation, split
partisan *noun* 1 SUPPORTER, adherent, devotee, upholder
2 UNDERGROUND FIGHTER, guerrilla, resistance fighter
▷ *adjective* 3 PREJUDICED, biased, interested, one-sided, partial, sectarian
partition *noun* 1 SCREEN, barrier, wall
2 DIVISION, segregation, separation
3 ALLOTMENT, apportionment, distribution
▷ *verb* 4 SEPARATE, divide, screen
partly *adverb* PARTIALLY, slightly, somewhat
partner *noun* 1 SPOUSE, consort, husband *or* wife, mate, significant other (*informal*)
2 COMPANION, ally, associate, colleague, comrade, helper, mate
partnership *noun* COMPANY, alliance, cooperative, firm, house, society, union
party *noun* 1 GET-TOGETHER (*informal*), celebration, festivity, function, gathering, reception, social gathering
2 GROUP, band, company, crew, gang, squad, team, unit
3 FACTION, camp, clique, coterie, league, set, side
4 PERSON, individual, someone
pass *verb* 1 GO BY *or* GO PAST, elapse, go, lapse, move, proceed, run
2 QUALIFY, do, get through, graduate, succeed
3 SPEND, fill, occupy, while away
4 GIVE, convey, deliver, hand, send, transfer
5 APPROVE, accept, decree, enact, legislate, ordain, ratify
6 EXCEED, beat, go beyond, outdo, outstrip, surpass
7 END, blow over, cease, go
▷ *noun* 8 GAP, canyon, gorge, ravine, route
9 LICENSE, authorization, passport, permit, ticket, warrant
passable *adjective* ADEQUATE, acceptable, all right, average, fair, mediocre, so-so (*informal*), tolerable
passage *noun* 1 WAY, alley, avenue, channel, course, path, road, route
2 CORRIDOR, hall, lobby, vestibule
3 EXTRACT, excerpt, piece, quotation, reading, section, text
4 JOURNEY, crossing, trek, trip, voyage
5 SAFE-CONDUCT, freedom, permission, right
passageway *noun* CORRIDOR, aisle, alley, hall, hallway, lane, passage
pass away *verb* (*euphemistic*) DIE, expire, kick the bucket (*slang*), pass on, pass over, shuffle off this mortal coil, snuff it (*informal*)
passé *adjective* OUT-OF-DATE, dated, obsolete, old-fashioned, old hat, outdated, outmoded, unfashionable
passenger *noun* TRAVELER, fare, rider
passer-by *noun* BYSTANDER, onlooker, witness
passing *adjective* 1 MOMENTARY, brief, ephemeral, fleeting, short-lived, temporary, transient, transitory
2 SUPERFICIAL, casual, cursory, glancing, quick, short
passion *noun* 1 LOVE, ardor, desire, infatuation, lust
2 EMOTION, ardor, excitement, feeling, fervor, fire, heat, intensity, warmth, zeal
3 RAGE, anger, fit, frenzy, fury, outburst,

pas•sen•ger [PAS-ən-jər] *noun* traveler, esp. by public conveyance

pas•ser•ine [PAS-ər-in] *adjective* of the order of perching birds

pas'sim *Lat.* everywhere, throughout

pas•sion [PASH-ən] *noun* 1 ardent desire, esp. sexual 2 any strongly felt emotion 3 suffering (esp. that of Christ) > **pas'sion•ate** [-it] *adjective* (easily) moved by strong emotions

pas•sive [PAS-iv] *adjective* 1 unresisting 2 submissive 3 inactive 4 denoting grammatical voice of verb in which the subject receives the action > **pas•siv'i•ty** *noun* > **passive-aggressive** *adjective* relating to a personality that harbors aggressive emotions while behaving in a passive manner > **passive smoking** involuntary inhalation of smoke from other's cigarettes

Pass•o•ver [PAS-oh-vər] *noun* Jewish spring festival commemorating exodus of Jews from Egypt

pass'port *noun* official document granting permission to pass, travel abroad, etc.

pass•word [PAS-wurd] *noun* 1 word, phrase, to distinguish friend from enemy 2 countersign

past *adjective* 1 ended 2 gone by 3 elapsed ▷ *noun* 4 bygone times ▷ *adverb* 5 by 6 along ▷ *preposition* 7 beyond 8 after

pas•ta [PAH-stə] *noun* type of food, such as spaghetti, that is made in different shapes from flour and water

paste [payst] *noun* 1 soft composition, as toothpaste 2 soft plastic mixture or adhesive 3 fine glass to imitate gems ▷ *verb transitive* **past•ed, past•ing** 4 fasten with paste > **past•y** *adjective* **past•i•er, past•i•est** 1 like paste 2 white 3 sickly

pas•tel [pa-STEL] *noun* 1 colored crayon 2 art of drawing with crayons 3 pale, delicate color ▷ *adjective* 4 delicately tinted

pas•teur•ize [PAS-chə-rīz] *verb transitive* **-ized, -iz•ing** sterilize by heat > **pas•teur•i•za'tion** *noun*

pas•tiche [pa-STEESH] *noun* 1 literary, musical, artistic work composed of parts borrowed from other works and loosely connected together 2 work imitating another's style

pas•tille [pa-STEEL] *noun* 1 lozenge 2 aromatic substance burned as deodorant or fumigator

pas•time [PAS-tīm] *noun* 1 that which makes time pass agreeably 2 recreation

pas•tor [PAS-tər] *noun* 1 priest or minister in charge of a church > **pas'to•ral** *adjective* 1 of, or like, shepherd's or rural life 2 of office of pastor ▷ *noun* 3 poem describing rural life

pas•try [PAY-stree] *noun, plural* **-tries** article of food made chiefly of flour, shortening and water

pas•ture [PAS-chər] *noun* 1 grass for food of cattle 2 ground on which cattle graze ▷ *verb* **-tured, -tur•ing** 3 (cause to) graze > **pas'tur•age** *noun* (right to) pasture

pat[1] *verb transitive* **pat•ted, pat•ting** 1 tap ▷ *noun* 2 light, quick blow 3 small mass, as of butter, beaten into shape

pat[2] *adverb* 1 exactly 2 fluently 3 opportunely 4 glib 5 exactly right

patch [pach] *noun* 1 piece of cloth sewn on garment 2 spot 3 plot of ground 4 protecting pad for the eye 5 small contrasting area 6 short period ▷ *verb transitive* 7 mend 8 repair clumsily > **patch'y** *adjective* **patch•i•er, patch•i•est** 1 of uneven quality 2 full of patches > **patch'work** *noun* 1 work composed of pieces sewn together 2 jumble

patch•ou•li [pə-CHOO-lee] *noun* 1 Indian herb 2 perfume from it

pate [payt] *noun* 1 head 2 top of head

pâ•té [pah-TAY] *noun* spread of finely chopped liver, etc. > **pâté de foie gras** [də-fwah-GRAH] one made of goose liver

pa•tel•la [pə-TEL-ə] *noun, plural* **-las** kneecap > **pa•tel'lar** *adjective*

pat•ent [PAT-nt] *noun* 1 document securing to

DICTIONARY P THESAURUS

paroxysm, storm
4 MANIA, bug (*informal*), craving, craze, enthusiasm, fascination, obsession

passionate *adjective* 1 LOVING, amorous, ardent, erotic, hot, lustful
2 EMOTIONAL, ardent, eager, fervent, fierce, heartfelt, impassioned, intense, strong

passive *adjective* SUBMISSIVE, compliant, docile, inactive, quiescent, receptive

pass off *verb* FAKE, counterfeit, make a pretense of, palm off

pass out *verb* FAINT, become unconscious, black out (*informal*), lose consciousness

pass over *verb* DISREGARD, ignore, overlook, take no notice of

pass up *verb* MISS, abstain, decline, forgo, let slip, neglect

password *noun* SIGNAL, key word, watchword

past *adjective* 1 FORMER, ancient, bygone, early, olden, previous
2 OVER, done, ended, finished, gone
▷ *noun* 3 BACKGROUND, history, life, past life
4 ▷ **the past** FORMER TIMES, days gone by, long ago, olden days
▷ *preposition* 5 AFTER, beyond, later than
6 BEYOND, across, by, over

paste *noun* 1 ADHESIVE, cement, glue, gum
▷ *verb* 2 STICK, cement, glue, gum

pastel *adjective* PALE, delicate, light, muted, soft

pastiche *noun* MEDLEY, blend, mélange (*French*), miscellany, mixture

pastime *noun* ACTIVITY, amusement, diversion, entertainment, game, hobby, recreation

pastor *noun* CLERGYMAN, churchman, ecclesiastic, minister, parson, priest, rector, vicar

pastoral *adjective* 1 RUSTIC, bucolic, country, rural
2 ECCLESIASTICAL, clerical, ministerial, priestly

pasture *noun* GRASSLAND, grass, grazing, meadow

pasty *adjective* PALE, anemic, pallid, sickly, wan

pat[1] *verb* 1 STROKE, caress, fondle, pet, tap, touch
▷ *noun* 2 STROKE, clap, tap

patch *noun* 1 REINFORCEMENT
2 SPOT, bit, scrap, shred, small piece
3 PLOT, area, ground, land, tract
▷ *verb* 4 MEND, cover, reinforce, repair, sew up

patchwork *noun* MIXTURE, jumble, medley, pastiche

patchy *adjective* UNEVEN, erratic, fitful, irregular, sketchy, spotty, variable

patent *noun* 1 COPYRIGHT, license
▷ *adjective* 2 OBVIOUS, apparent, clear, evident,

person or organization exclusive right to invention ▷ *adjective* 2 open 3 evident 4 manifest 5 open to public perusal: *letters patent* ▷ *verb transitive* 6 secure a patent > **pat•ent•ee'** *noun* 1 one who has a patent > **pat'ent•ly** *adverb* obviously > **patent leather** (imitation) leather processed to give hard, glossy surface
pa•ter•fa•mil•i•as [pah-tər-fə-MIL-ee-əs] *noun, plural* **-ases** father of a family
pa•ter•nal [pə-TUR-nl] *adjective* 1 fatherly 2 of a father 3 related through a father > **pa•ter'nal•ism** *noun* authority exercised in a way that limits individual responsibility > **pa•ter•nal•is'tic** *adjective* > **pa•ter'ni•ty** *noun* 1 relation of a father to his offspring 2 fatherhood
pa•ter•nos•ter [PAY-tər-NOS-tər] *noun* 1 Lord's Prayer 2 beads of rosary
path *noun, plural* **paths** [pathz] 1 way or track 2 course of action > **path'name** *noun* name of an electronic file or directory together with its position relative to other directories traced back to its source
pa•thet•ic [pə-THET-ik] *adjective* 1 affecting or moving tender emotions 2 distressingly inadequate > **pa•thet'i•cal•ly** *adverb*
path•o•gen•ic [path-ə-JEN-ik] *adjective* producing disease > **path'o•gen** *noun* disease-producing agent, e.g. virus
pa•thol•o•gy [pə-THOL-ə-jee] *noun* science of diseases > **path•o•log'i•cal** [-LOJ-i-kəl] *adjective* 1 of the science of disease 2 due to disease 3 compulsively motivated > **pa•thol'o•gist** *noun*
pa•thos [PAY-thos] *noun* power of exciting tender emotions
pa•tient [PAY-shənt] *adjective* 1 bearing trials calmly ▷ *noun* 2 person under medical treatment > **pa'tience** *noun* 1 quality of enduring 2 card game for one player
pat•i•na [pə-TEE-nə] *noun* 1 fine layer on a surface 2 sheen of age on woodwork
pat•i•o [PAT-ee-oh] *noun, plural* **-ios** (usu. paved) area adjoining house for lounging, etc.
pat•ois [PA-twah] *noun* regional dialect
pa•tri•arch [PAY-tree-ahrk] *noun* father and founder of family, esp. Biblical > **pa•tri•ar'chal** *adjective* venerable
pa•tri•cian [pə-TRISH-ən] *noun* 1 noble of ancient Rome 2 one of noble birth ▷ *adjective* 3 of noble birth
pat•ri•cide [PA-trə-sīd] *noun* murder or murderer of father
pat•ri•mo•ny [PA-trə-moh-nee] *noun, plural* **-nies** property inherited from ancestors
pa•tri•ot [PAY-tree-ət] *noun* one who loves own country and maintains its interests > **pa'tri•ot•ism** *noun* [-ə-tiz-əm] love of, loyalty to one's country > **pa•tri•ot'ic** [-OT-ik] *adjective* inspired by love of one's country
pa•trol [pə-TROHL] *noun* 1 regular circuit by guard 2 person, small group patrolling 3 unit of Boy Scouts or Girl Scouts ▷ *verb* **-trolled, -trol•ling** 4 go around on guard, or reconnoitering
pa•tron [PAY-trən] *noun* 1 one who sponsors or aids artists, charities, etc. 2 protector 3 regular customer 4 guardian saint 5 one who has disposition of benefice, etc. > **pa'tron•age** *noun* support given by, or position of, a patron > **pa'tron•ize** *verb transitive* **-ized, -iz•ing** 1 assume air of superiority toward 2 frequent as customer 3 encourage
pat•ro•nym•ic [pa-trə-NIM-ik] *noun* name derived from that of parent or an ancestor
pat•ter [PAT-ər] *verb intransitive* 1 make noise, as sound of quick, short steps 2 tap in quick

DICTIONARY • THESAURUS

glaring, manifest
paternal *adjective* FATHERLY, concerned, protective, solicitous
paternity *noun* 1 FATHERHOOD
2 PARENTAGE, descent, extraction, family, lineage
path *noun* 1 WAY, footpath, road, track, trail
2 COURSE, direction, road, route, way
pathetic *adjective* SAD, affecting, distressing, heart-rending, moving, pitiable, plaintive, poignant, tender, touching
pathos *noun* SADNESS, pitifulness, plaintiveness, poignancy
patience *noun* 1 FORBEARANCE, calmness, restraint, serenity, sufferance, tolerance
2 ENDURANCE, constancy, fortitude, long-suffering, perseverance, resignation, stoicism, submission
patient *adjective* 1 LONG-SUFFERING, calm, enduring, persevering, philosophical, resigned, stoical, submissive, uncomplaining
2 FORBEARING, even-tempered, forgiving, indulgent, lenient, mild, tolerant, understanding
▷ *noun* 3 SICK PERSON, case, invalid, sufferer
patriot *noun* NATIONALIST, chauvinist, loyalist
patriotic *adjective* NATIONALISTIC, chauvinistic, jingoistic, loyal
patriotism *noun* NATIONALISM, jingoism
patrol *noun* 1 POLICING, guarding, protecting, vigilance, watching
2 GUARD, patrolman, sentinel, watch, watchman
▷ *verb* 3 POLICE, guard, inspect, keep guard, keep watch, safeguard
patron *noun* 1 SUPPORTER, backer, benefactor, champion, friend, helper, philanthropist
2 CUSTOMER, buyer, client, frequenter, habitué, shopper
patronage *noun* 1 SUPPORT, aid, assistance, backing, help, promotion, sponsorship
2 CUSTOM, business, clientele, commerce, trade, trading, traffic
patronize *verb* 1 TALK DOWN TO, look down on
2 BE A CUSTOMER OF *or* BE A CLIENT OF, do business with, frequent, shop at
3 SUPPORT, back, fund, help, maintain, promote, sponsor
patronizing *adjective* CONDESCENDING, disdainful, gracious, haughty, snobbish, supercilious, superior
patter[1] *verb* 1 TAP, beat, pat, pitter-patter
2 WALK LIGHTLY, scurry, scuttle, skip, trip
▷ *noun* 3 TAPPING, pattering, pitter-patter
patter[2] *noun* 1 SPIEL (*informal*), line, pitch
2 CHATTER, gabble, jabber, nattering, prattle
3 JARGON, argot, cant, lingo (*informal*), patois, slang, vernacular
▷ *verb* 4 CHATTER, jabber, prate, rattle on, spout (*informal*)

succession 3 pray, talk rapidly ▷ *noun* 4 quick succession of taps 5 (*informal*) glib, rapid speech

pat•tern [PAT-ərn] *noun* 1 arrangement of repeated parts 2 design 3 shape to direct cutting of cloth, etc. 4 model 5 specimen ▷ *verb transitive* 6 (with *on* or *after*) model 7 decorate with pattern

pat•ty [PAT-ee] *noun, plural* **-ties** 1 a little pie 2 thin round piece of meat, candy, etc.

pau•ci•ty [PAW-si-tee] *noun* 1 scarcity 2 smallness of quantity 3 fewness

paunch [pawnch] *noun* 1 belly 2 potbelly

pau•per [PAW-pər] *noun* poor person, esp. formerly, one supported by the public > **pau'per•ism** *noun* 1 destitution 2 extreme poverty > **pau'per•ize** *verb transitive* **-ized, -iz•ing** reduce to pauperism

pause [pawz] *verb intransitive* **paused, paus•ing** 1 cease for a time ▷ *noun* 2 stop or rest

pave [payv] *verb transitive* **paved, pav•ing** form surface with stone or brick > **pave'ment** [-mənt] *noun* 1 paved floor, footpath 2 material for paving **pave the way for** 3 lead up to 4 facilitate entrance of

pa•vil•ion [pə-VIL-yən] *noun* 1 clubhouse on playing field, etc. 2 building for housing exhibition, etc. 3 large ornate tent

paw *noun* 1 foot of animal ▷ *verb* 2 scrape with forefoot 3 handle roughly 4 stroke with the hands

pawn¹ *verb transitive* 1 deposit (article) as security for money borrowed ▷ *noun* 2 article deposited > **pawn'bro•ker** *noun* lender of money on goods pledged

pawn² *noun* 1 piece in chess 2 any person used as a mere tool

pay *verb transitive* **paid, pay•ing** 1 give money, etc., for goods or services rendered 2 compensate 3 give or bestow 4 be profitable to 5 (with *out*) release bit by bit, as rope ▷ *verb intransitive* **paid, pay•ing** 6 be remunerative 7 be profitable 8 (with *out*) spend ▷ *noun* 9 wages 10 paid employment > **pay'a•ble** *adjective* 1 justly due 2 profitable > **pay•ee'** *noun* person to whom money is paid or due > **pay'ment** [-mənt] *noun* discharge of debt > **pay'load** *noun* 1 part of cargo earning revenue 2 explosive power of missile, etc. > **paying guest** boarder, lodger, esp. in private house > **pay television** programs provided for viewers who pay monthly or per-program fees

Pb *chem.* lead

pc 1 politically correct 2 personal computer

Pd *chem.* palladium

PDF Portable Document Format: a format in which electronic documents may be viewed

pea [pee] *noun* 1 fruit, growing in pods, of climbing plant 2 the plant > **pea-green** *adjective* of shade of green like color of green peas > **pea green** this color > **pea soup** 1 thick soup made of green peas 2 (*informal*) thick fog

peace [pees] *noun* 1 freedom from war 2 harmony 3 quietness of mind 4 calm 5 repose > **peace'a•ble** *adjective* disposed to peace > **peace'a•bly** *adverb* > **peace'ful** *adjective* 1 free from war, tumult 2 mild 3 undisturbed

peach [peech] *noun* 1 stone fruit of delicate flavor 2 (*informal*) person or thing very pleasant

---

pattern *noun* 1 DESIGN, arrangement, decoration, device, figure, motif
2 ORDER, method, plan, sequence, system
3 PLAN, design, diagram, guide, original, stencil, template
▷ *verb* 4 MODEL, copy, follow, form, imitate, mold, style

paucity *noun* (*formal*) SCARCITY, dearth, deficiency, lack, rarity, scantiness, shortage, sparseness

paunch *noun* BELLY, pot, potbelly, spare tire (*slang*)

pauper *noun* DOWN-AND-OUT, bankrupt, beggar, mendicant, poor person

pause *verb* 1 STOP BRIEFLY, break, cease, delay, halt, have a breather (*informal*), interrupt, rest, take a break, wait
▷ *noun* 2 STOP, break, breather (*informal*), cessation, gap, halt, interlude, intermission, interval, lull, respite, rest, stoppage

pave *verb* COVER, concrete, floor, surface, tile

paw *verb* MANHANDLE, grab, handle roughly, maul, molest

pawn¹ *verb* HOCK (*informal*), deposit, mortgage, pledge

pawn² *noun* TOOL, cat's-paw, instrument, plaything, puppet, stooge (*slang*)

pay *verb* 1 REIMBURSE, compensate, give, recompense, remit, remunerate, requite, reward, settle
2 GIVE, bestow, extend, grant, hand out, present
3 BENEFIT, be worthwhile, repay
4 BE PROFITABLE, make a return, make money
5 YIELD, bring in, produce, return
▷ *noun* 6 WAGES, allowance, earnings, fee, income, payment, recompense, reimbursement, remuneration, reward, salary, stipend

payable *adjective* DUE, outstanding, owed, owing

pay back *verb* 1 REPAY, refund, reimburse, settle up, square
2 GET EVEN WITH (*informal*), hit back, retaliate

payment *noun* 1 PAYING, discharge, remittance, settlement
2 REMITTANCE, advance, deposit, installment, premium
3 WAGE, fee, hire, remuneration, reward

pay off *verb* 1 SETTLE, clear, discharge, pay in full, square
2 SUCCEED, be effective, work

pay out *verb* SPEND, disburse, expend, fork out *or* fork over fork up (*slang*), shell out (*informal*)

peace *noun* 1 STILLNESS, calm, calmness, hush, quiet, repose, rest, silence, tranquillity
2 SERENITY, calm, composure, contentment, repose
3 HARMONY, accord, agreement, concord
4 TRUCE, armistice, treaty

peaceable *adjective* PEACE-LOVING, conciliatory, friendly, gentle, mild, peaceful, unwarlike

peaceful *adjective* 1 AT PEACE, amicable, friendly, harmonious, nonviolent
2 CALM, placid, quiet, restful, serene, still, tranquil, undisturbed
3 PEACE-LOVING, conciliatory, peaceable, unwarlike

peacemaker *noun* MEDIATOR, arbitrator, conciliator, pacifier

3 pinkish-yellow color > **peach'y** *adjective* **peach•i•er, peach•i•est** 1 like peach 2 (*informal*) fine, excellent

pea•cock [PEE-kok] *noun* male of bird with fanlike tail, brilliantly colored > **pea'hen** *noun feminine* > **pea'fowl** *noun* peacock or peahen

peak [peek] *noun* 1 pointed end of anything, esp. hill's sharp top 2 point of greatest development, etc. 3 sharp increase 4 projecting piece on front of cap ▷ *verb* 5 (cause to) form, reach peaks > **peaked** *adjective* like, having a peak > **peak•ed** [PEE-kid] sickly, wan, drawn

peal [peel] *noun* 1 loud sound or succession of loud sounds 2 changes rung on set of bells 3 chime ▷ *verb intransitive* 4 sound loudly

pea•nut [PEE-nut] *noun* 1 pea-shaped nut that ripens underground 2 the plant > **pea•nuts** (*informal*) trifling amount of money

pear [pair] *noun* 1 tree yielding sweet, juicy fruit 2 the fruit > **pear-shaped** *adjective* shaped like a pear, heavier at the bottom than the top

pearl [purl] *noun* hard, lustrous structure found in several mollusks, esp. pearl oyster and used as jewel > **pearl'y** *adjective* **pearl•i•er, pearl•i•est** like pearls

peas•ant [PEZ-ənt] *noun* 1 in certain countries, member of low social class, esp. in rural district 2 boorish person > **peas'ant•ry** *noun* peasants collectively

peat [peet] *noun* 1 decomposed vegetable substance found in bogs 2 turf of it used for fuel > **peat moss** dried peat, used as mulch, etc.

peb•ble [PEB-əl] *noun* 1 small roundish stone 2 pale, transparent rock crystal 3 grainy, irregular surface ▷ *verb transitive* **-bled, -bling** 4 pave, cover with pebbles

pe•can [pi-KAHN] *noun* 1 North American tree, species of hickory, allied to walnut 2 its edible nut

pec•ca•dil•lo [pek-ə-DIL-oh] *noun, plural* **-loes** 1 slight offense 2 petty crime

pec•ca•ry [PEK-ə-ree] *noun, plural* **-ries** vicious American animal allied to pig

peck[1] [pek] *noun* 1 fourth part of bushel, equal to 8.81 liters 2 great deal

peck[2] *verb* 1 pick, strike with or as with beak 2 nibble ▷ *noun* 3 quick kiss > **peck'ish** *adjective* (*informal*) irritable

pecs [peks] *plural noun* (*informal*) pectoral muscles

pec•tin [PEK-tin] *noun* gelatinizing substance obtained from ripe fruits > **pec'tic** *adjective* 1 congealing 2 denoting pectin

pec•to•ral [PEK-tər-əl] *adjective* 1 of the breast ▷ *noun* 2 pectoral part of organ 3 breastplate

pec•u•late [PEK-yə-layt] *verb* **-lat•ed, -lat•ing** 1 embezzle 2 steal > **pec•u•la'tion** *noun*

pe•cu•liar [pi-KYOOL-yər] *adjective* 1 strange 2 particular 3 belonging to > **pe•cu•li•ar'i•ty** *noun* 1 oddity 2 characteristic 3 distinguishing feature

pe•cu•ni•ar•y [pi-KYOO-nee-er-ee] *adjective* relating to, or consisting of, money

ped•a•gogue [PED-ə-gog] *noun* 1 schoolmaster 2 pedant > **ped•a•gog'ic** [-GOJ-ik] *adjective*

ped•al [PED-l] *noun* 1 something to transmit motion from foot 2 foot lever to modify tone or swell of musical instrument 3 *mus.* note, usu. bass, held through successive harmonies ▷ *adjective* 4 of a foot ▷ *verb* **-daled, -dal•ing** 5 propel bicycle, etc. by using its pedals 6 use pedal

ped•ant [PED-ənt] *noun* one who overvalues, or insists on, petty details of book learning, grammatical rules, etc. > **pe•dan'tic** *adjective* > **ped'ant•ry** *noun, plural* **-tries**

ped•dle [PED-l] *verb transitive* **-dled, -dling** go around selling goods > **ped'dler, ped'lar** *noun*

ped•er•ast [PED-ə-rast] *noun* man who has homosexual relations with boy > **ped'er•as•ty** *noun*

ped•es•tal [PED-ə-stl] *noun* base of column, pillar **put on a pedestal** idealize

pe•des•tri•an [pə-DES-tree-ən] *noun* 1 one who goes on foot 2 walker ▷ *adjective* 3 going on foot 4 commonplace 5 dull, uninspiring

pe•di•at•rics [pee-dee-A-triks] *noun* branch of medicine dealing with diseases and disorders of children > **pe•di•a•tri'cian** [-ə-TRISH-ən] *noun*

ped•i•cel [PED-ə-səl] *noun* small, short stalk of leaf, flower or fruit

peak *noun* 1 POINT, apex, brow, crest, pinnacle, summit, tip, top
2 HIGH POINT, acme, climax, crown, culmination, zenith
▷ *verb* 3 CULMINATE, climax, come to a head

peal *noun* 1 RING, blast, chime, clang, clap, crash, reverberation, roar, rumble
▷ *verb* 2 RING, chime, crash, resound, roar, rumble

peasant *noun* RUSTIC, countryman

peccadillo *noun* MISDEED, error, indiscretion, lapse, misdemeanor, slip

peck *verb*
▷ *noun* PICK, dig, hit, jab, poke, prick, strike, tap

peculiar *adjective* 1 ODD, abnormal, bizarre, curious, eccentric, extraordinary, freakish, funny, offbeat, outlandish, outré, quaint, queer, singular, strange, uncommon, unconventional, unusual, weird
2 SPECIFIC, characteristic, distinctive, particular, special, unique

peculiarity *noun* 1 ECCENTRICITY, abnormality, foible, idiosyncrasy, mannerism, oddity, quirk
2 CHARACTERISTIC, attribute, feature, mark, particularity, property, quality, trait

pedagogue *noun* TEACHER, instructor, master *or* mistress, schoolmaster *or* schoolmistress

pedant *noun* HAIRSPLITTER, nit-picker (*informal*), quibbler

pedantic *adjective* HAIRSPLITTING, academic, bookish, donnish, formal, fussy, nit-picking (*informal*), particular, precise, punctilious

pedantry *noun* HAIRSPLITTING, punctiliousness, quibbling

peddle *verb* SELL, hawk, market, push (*informal*), trade

peddler *noun* SELLER, door-to-door salesman, hawker, huckster, vendor

pedestal *noun* SUPPORT, base, foot, mounting, plinth, stand

pedestrian *noun* 1 WALKER, foot-traveler
▷ *adjective* 2 DULL, banal, boring, commonplace, humdrum, mediocre, mundane, ordinary, prosaic, uninspired

ped•i•cure [PED-i-kyoor] *noun* medical or cosmetic treatment of feet
ped'i•gree *noun* 1 register of ancestors 2 genealogy
ped•i•ment [PED-ə-mənt] *noun* triangular part over Greek portico, etc. > **ped•i•men'tal** [-MEN-tl] *adjective*
pedlar *see* **peddle**
pe•dom•e•ter [pə-DOM-i-tər] *noun* instrument that measures the distance walked
pe•dun•cle [pi-DUNG-kəl] *noun* 1 flower stalk 2 stalklike structure
peek *verb intransitive, noun* peep, glance
peel *verb transitive* 1 strip off skin, rind or any form of covering ▷ *verb intransitive* 2 come off, as skin, rind ▷ *noun* 3 rind, skin > **peeled** *adjective* (*informal*) of eyes, watchful > **peel'ings** *plural noun* parings
peep[1] *verb intransitive* 1 look slyly or quickly ▷ *noun* 2 such a look
peep[2] *verb intransitive* 1 cry, as chick 2 chirp ▷ *noun* 3 such a cry
peer[1] *noun* 1 nobleman 2 one of the same rank, ability, etc. > **peer'age** [-ij] *noun* 1 body of peers 2 rank of peer > **peer'ess** *noun feminine* > **peer'less** [-lis] *adjective* without match or equal
peer[2] *verb intransitive* look closely and intently
peeved [peevd] *adjective* sulky, irritated > **peeve** *verb transitive* **peeved, peev•ing** 1 annoy 2 vex
pee'vish *adjective* 1 fretful 2 irritable > **pee'vish•ly** *adverb* > **pee'vish•ness** [-nis] *noun* annoyance
peg *noun* 1 nail or pin for joining, fastening, marking, etc. 2 (mark of) level, standard, etc. ▷ *verb* **pegged, peg•ging** 3 fasten with pegs 4 stabilize (prices) 5 (*informal*) throw 6 (with *away*) persevere **take down a peg** humble (someone)
peign•oir [pain-WAHR] *noun* woman's dressing gown, jacket, wrapper
pe•jo•ra•tive [pi-JOR-ə-tiv] *adjective* (of words, etc.) with unpleasant, disparaging connotation
Pe•king•ese [pee-kə-NEEZ] *noun* small Chinese dog
pe•lag•ic [pə-LAJ-ik] *adjective* of the deep sea
pel•i•can [PEL-i-kən] *noun* large, fish-eating waterfowl with large pouch beneath its bill
pel•let [PEL-it] *noun* little ball, pill
pell-mell *adverb* in utter confusion, headlong
pel•lu•cid [pə-LOO-sid] *adjective* 1 translucent 2 clear
pelt[1] *verb transitive* 1 strike with missiles ▷ *verb intransitive* 2 throw missiles 3 rush 4 fall persistently, as rain
pelt[2] *noun* raw hide or skin
pel'vis *noun, plural* **-vis•es** bony cavity at base of human trunk > **pel'vic** *adjective* pert. to pelvis
pen[1] *noun* 1 instrument for writing ▷ *verb transitive* **penned, pen•ning** 2 compose 3 write > **pen name** author's pseudonym > **pen pal** person with whom one corresponds, usu. someone whom one has never met
pen[2] *noun* 1 small enclosure, as for sheep ▷ *verb transitive* **penned, pen•ning** 2 put, keep in enclosure
pen[3] *noun* female swan
pe•nal [PEEN-l] *adjective* of, incurring, inflicting, punishment > **pe'nal•ize** *verb transitive* **-ized, -iz•ing** 1 impose penalty on 2 handicap > **pen'al•ty** *noun, plural* **-ties** 1 punishment for crime or offense 2 forfeit 3 *sports* handicap or disadvantage imposed for infringement of rule, etc.
pen•ance [PEN-əns] *noun* 1 suffering submitted to as expression of penitence 2 repentance
pen•chant [PEN-chənt] *noun* inclination, decided taste
pen•cil [PEN-səl] *noun* 1 instrument as of

---

pedigree *noun* 1 LINEAGE, ancestry, blood, breed, descent, extraction, family, family tree, genealogy, line, race, stock ▷ *adjective* 2 PUREBRED, full-blooded, thoroughbred
peek *verb* 1 GLANCE, look, peep ▷ *noun* 2 GLANCE, glimpse, look, look-see (*slang*), peep
peel *verb* 1 SKIN, flake off, pare, scale, strip off ▷ *noun* 2 SKIN, peeling, rind
peep[1] *verb* 1 PEEK, look, sneak a look, steal a look ▷ *noun* 2 LOOK, glimpse, look-see (*slang*), peek
peep[2] *verb* ▷ *noun* TWEET, cheep, chirp, squeak
peephole *noun* SPYHOLE, aperture, chink, crack, hole, opening
peer[1] *noun* 1 NOBLE, aristocrat, lord, nobleman 2 EQUAL, compeer, fellow, like
peer[2] *verb* SQUINT, gaze, inspect, peep, scan, snoop, spy
peerage *noun* ARISTOCRACY, lords and ladies, nobility, peers
peerless *adjective* UNEQUALED, beyond compare, excellent, incomparable, matchless, outstanding, unmatched, unparalleled, unrivaled
peevish *adjective* IRRITABLE, cantankerous, childish, churlish, cross, crotchety, fractious, fretful, grumpy, petulant, querulous, snappy, sulky, sullen, surly
peg *verb* FASTEN, attach, fix, join, secure
pejorative *adjective* DEROGATORY, deprecatory, depreciatory, disparaging, negative, uncomplimentary, unpleasant
pelt[1] *verb* 1 THROW, batter, bombard, cast, hurl, pepper, shower, sling, strike 2 RUSH, belt (*slang*), charge, dash, hurry, run fast, shoot, speed, tear 3 POUR, bucket down (*informal*), rain cats and dogs (*informal*), rain hard, teem
pelt[2] *noun* COAT, fell, hide, skin
pen[1] *verb* WRITE, compose, draft, draw up, jot down
pen[2] *noun* 1 ENCLOSURE, cage, coop, fold, hutch, pound, sty ▷ *verb* 2 ENCLOSE, cage, confine, coop up, fence in, hedge, shut up *or* shut in
penal *adjective* DISCIPLINARY, corrective, punitive
penalize *verb* PUNISH, discipline, handicap, impose a penalty on
penalty *noun* PUNISHMENT, fine, forfeit, handicap, price
penance *noun* ATONEMENT, penalty, reparation, sackcloth and ashes
penchant *noun* LIKING, bent, bias, fondness, inclination, leaning, partiality, predilection, proclivity, propensity, taste, tendency

graphite, for writing, etc. **2** *optics* narrow beam of light ▷ *verb transitive* **-ciled, -cil•ing 3** paint or draw **4** mark with pencil

pend•ant [PEN-dənt] *noun* hanging ornament > **pend'ent** *adjective* **1** suspended **2** hanging **3** projecting

pend'ing *preposition* **1** during, until ▷ *adjective* **2** awaiting settlement **3** undecided **4** imminent

pen•du•lous [PEN-jə-ləs] *adjective* hanging, swinging > **pen'du•lum** [-ləm] *noun* suspended weight swinging to and fro, esp. as regulator for clock

pen•e•trate [PEN-i-trayt] *verb transitive* **-trat•ed, trat•ing 1** enter into **2** pierce **3** arrive at the meaning of > **pen•e•tra•bil'i•ty** *noun* quality of being penetrable > **pen'e•tra•ble** [-trə-bəl] *adjective* capable of being entered or pierced > **penetrating** *adjective* **1** sharp **2** easily heard **3** subtle **4** quick to understand > **pen•e•tra'tion** *noun* insight, acuteness > **pen'e•tra•tive** [-tray-tiv] *adjective* **1** piercing **2** discerning

pen•guin [PENG-gwin] *noun* flightless, short-legged swimming bird

pen•i•cil•lin [pen-ə-SIL-in] *noun* antibiotic drug effective against a wide range of diseases, infections

pen•in•su•la [pə-NINS-yə-lə] *noun* portion of land nearly surrounded by water > **pen•in'su•lar** *adjective*

pe•nis [PEE-nis] *noun, plural* **-nis•es** male organ of copulation (and of urination) in man and many mammals

pen•i•tent [PEN-i-tənt] *adjective* **1** affected by sense of guilt ▷ *noun* **2** one that repents of sin > **pen'i•tence** *noun* **1** sorrow for sin **2** repentance > **pen•i•ten'tial** [-TEN-shəl] *adjective* of, or expressing, penitence > **pen•i•ten'tia•ry** [-TEN-shə-ree] *adjective* **1** relating to penance, or to the rules of penance ▷ *noun, plural* **-ries 2** prison

pen•nant [PEN-ənt] *noun* long narrow flag

pen•non [PEN-ən] *noun* small pointed or swallow-tailed flag

pen•ny [PEN-ee] *noun, plural* **-nies 1** coin, 100th part of dollar **2** similar coin of other countries > **pen'ni•less** [-lis] *adjective* **1** having no money **2** poor **a pretty penny** (*informal*) considerable amount of money

pe•nol•o•gy [pee-NOL-ə-jee] *noun* study of punishment and prevention of crime

pen•sion [PEN-shən] *noun* **1** regular payment to old people, retired public officials, workers, etc. ▷ *verb transitive* **2** grant pension to > **pen'sion•er** *noun*

pen•sive [PEN-siv] *adjective* **1** thoughtful with sadness **2** wistful

pent *adjective* shut up, kept in > **pent-up** *adjective* not released, repressed

pen•ta•gon [PEN-tə-gon] *noun* plane figure having five angles > **pen•tag'o•nal** [-TAG-ə-nl] *adjective*

pen•tam•e•ter [pen-TAM-i-tər] *noun* verse of five metrical feet

Pen•ta•teuch [PEN-tə-tyook] *noun* first five books of Old Testament

pen•tath•lon [pen-TATH-lən] *noun* athletic contest of five events

Pen•te•cost [PEN-ti-kawst] *noun* Christian festival of seventh Sunday after Easter

pent•house [PENT-hows] *noun, plural* **-hous•es** [-howz-iz] apartment or other structure on top, or top floor, of building

pen•tode [PEN-tohd] *noun electronics* five-electrode vacuum tube, having anode, cathode and three grids

pe•nult [PEE-nult] *noun* last syllable but one of word > **pen•ul•ti•mate** [pi-NUL-tə-mit] *adjective* next before the last

pe•num•bra [pi-NUM-brə] *noun* **1** imperfect shadow **2** in an eclipse, the partially shadowed region that surrounds the full shadow

pen•u•ry [PEN-yə-ree] *noun* **1** extreme poverty **2** extreme scarcity > **pe•nu•ri•ous** [pə-NUUR-ee-əs] *adjective* **1** niggardly, stingy **2** poor, scanty

peo•ple [PEE-pəl] *plural noun* **1** persons generally **2** community, nation **3** race **4** family ▷ *verb transitive* **-pled, -pling 5** stock with inhabitants **6** populate

pep *noun* (*informal*) **1** vigor **2** energy **3**

pending *adjective* UNDECIDED, awaiting, imminent, impending, in the balance, undetermined, unsettled

penetrate *verb* **1** PIERCE, bore, enter, go through, prick, stab
2 GRASP, comprehend, decipher, fathom, figure out (*informal*), get to the bottom of, work out

penetrating *adjective* **1** SHARP, carrying, harsh, piercing, shrill
2 PERCEPTIVE, acute, astute, incisive, intelligent, keen, perspicacious, quick, sharp, sharp-witted, shrewd

penetration *noun* **1** PIERCING, entrance, entry, incision, puncturing
2 PERCEPTION, acuteness, astuteness, insight, keenness, sharpness, shrewdness

penitence *noun* REPENTANCE, compunction, contrition, regret, remorse, shame, sorrow

penitent *adjective* REPENTANT, abject, apologetic, conscience-stricken, contrite, regretful, remorseful, sorry

pen name *noun* PSEUDONYM, nom de plume

pennant *noun* FLAG, banner, ensign, pennon, streamer

penniless *adjective* POOR, broke (*informal*), destitute, dirt-poor (*informal*), down and out, down on one's luck (*informal*), flat broke (*informal*), impecunious, impoverished, indigent, penurious, poverty-stricken

pension *noun* ALLOWANCE, annuity, benefit, superannuation

pensive *adjective* THOUGHTFUL, contemplative, dreamy, meditative, musing, preoccupied, reflective, sad, serious, solemn, wistful

pent-up *adjective* SUPPRESSED, bottled up, curbed, held back, inhibited, repressed, smothered, stifled

penury *noun* POVERTY, beggary, destitution, indigence, need, privation, want

people *plural noun* **1** PERSONS, humanity, mankind, men and women, mortals
2 NATION, citizens, community, folk, inhabitants, population, public
3 FAMILY, clan, race, tribe
▷ *verb* **4** INHABIT, colonize, occupy, populate, settle

enthusiasm ▷ *verb transitive* **pepped, pep•ping** 4 impart energy to 5 speed up
pep•per [PEP-ər] *noun* 1 fruit of climbing plant that yields pungent aromatic spice 2 various slightly pungent vegetables, e.g. capsicum ▷ *verb transitive* 3 season with pepper 4 sprinkle, dot 5 pelt with missiles > **pep'per•y** *adjective* 1 having the qualities of pepper 2 irritable > **pep'per•corn** *noun* 1 dried pepper berry 2 something trifling > **pep'per•mint** *noun* 1 plant noted for aromatic pungent liquor distilled from it 2 a candy flavored with this
pep•tic [PEP-tik] *adjective* relating to digestion or digestive juices
per [pər] *preposition* 1 for each 2 by 3 in the manner of
per-, par-, pel-, pil- *prefix* through, thoroughly: *perfect; pellucid*
per•am•bu•late [pər-AM-byə-layt] *verb transitive* **-lat•ed, -lat•ing** 1 walk through or over 2 traverse ▷ *verb intransitive* **-lat•ed, -lat•ing** 3 walk about > **per•am'bu•la•tor** *noun* baby carriage
per an•num [pər AN-əm] *Lat.* by the year
per•cale [pər-KAYL] *noun* woven cotton used esp. for sheets
per cap•i•ta [pər KAP-i-tə] *Lat.* for each person
per•ceive [pər-SEEV] *verb transitive* **-ceived, -ceiv•ing** 1 obtain knowledge of through senses 2 observe 3 understand > **per•ceiv'a•ble** *adjective* > **per•cep'ti•ble** *adjective* discernible, recognizable > **per•cep'tion** *noun* 1 faculty of perceiving 2 intuitive judgment > **per•cep'tive** *adjective*
per•cent•age [pər-SEN-tij] *noun* proportion or rate per hundred > **per cent** in each hundred
perception *noun see* **perceive**
perch¹ [purch] *noun* freshwater fish
perch² *noun* 1 resting place, as for bird ▷ *verb transitive* 2 place, as on perch ▷ *verb intransitive* 3 alight, settle on fixed body 4 roost 5 balance on
per•cip•i•ent [pər-SIP-ee-ənt] *adjective* 1 having faculty of perception 2 perceiving ▷ *noun* 3 one who perceives
per•co•late [PUR-kə-layt] *verb* **-lat•ed, -lat•ing** 1 pass through fine mesh as liquid 2 permeate 3 filter > **per'co•la•tor** *noun* coffeepot with filter
per•cus•sion [pər-KUSH-ən] *noun* 1 collision 2 impact 3 vibratory shock > **percussion instrument** musical instrument played by being struck, such as drums or cymbals
per di•em [pər DEE-əm] *Lat.* 1 by the day 2 for each day
per•di•tion [pər-DISH-ən] *noun* spiritual ruin
per•e•gri•nate [PER-i-grə-nayt] *verb intransitive* **-nat•ed, -nat•ing** 1 travel about 2 roam
per•e•grine [PER-i-grin] *noun* type of falcon
per•emp•to•ry [pə-REMP-tə-ree] *adjective* 1 authoritative, imperious 2 forbidding debate 3 decisive
per•en•ni•al [pə-REN-ee-əl] *adjective* 1 lasting through the years 2 perpetual, unfailing ▷ *noun* 3 plant lasting more than two years
per•fect [PUR-fikt] *adjective* 1 complete 2 finished 3 whole 4 unspoiled 5 faultless 6 correct, precise 7 excellent 8 of highest quality ▷ *noun* 9 tense denoting a complete act ▷ *verb transitive* [pər-FEKT] 10 improve 11 finish 12 make skillful > **per•fect'i•ble** *adjective* capable of becoming perfect > **per•fec'tion** [-FEK-shən] *noun* 1 state of being perfect 2 faultlessness > **per'fect•ly** *adverb*
per•fi•dy [PUR-fi-dee] *noun, plural* **-dies** treachery, disloyalty > **per•fid'i•ous** *adjective*
per•fo•rate [PUR-fə-rayt] *verb transitive* **-rat•ed, -rat•ing** make hole(s) in, penetrate > **per•fo•ra'tion** *noun* hole(s) through thing

pepper *noun* 1 SEASONING, flavor, spice ▷ *verb* 2 SPRINKLE, dot, fleck, spatter, speck 3 PELT, bombard, shower
perceive *verb* 1 SEE, behold, discern, discover, espy, make out, note, notice, observe, recognize, spot
2 UNDERSTAND, comprehend, gather, grasp, learn, realize, see
perceptible *adjective* VISIBLE, apparent, appreciable, clear, detectable, discernible, evident, noticeable, observable, obvious, recognizable, tangible
perception *noun* UNDERSTANDING, awareness, conception, consciousness, feeling, grasp, idea, impression, notion, sensation, sense
perceptive *adjective* OBSERVANT, acute, alert, astute, aware, percipient, perspicacious, quick, sharp
perch *noun* 1 RESTING PLACE, branch, pole, post ▷ *verb* 2 SIT, alight, balance, land, rest, roost, settle
percussion *noun* IMPACT, blow, bump, clash, collision, crash, knock, smash, thump
peremptory *adjective* 1 IMPERATIVE, absolute, binding, compelling, decisive, final, obligatory
2 IMPERIOUS, authoritative, bossy (*informal*), dictatorial, dogmatic, domineering, overbearing
perennial *adjective* LASTING, abiding, constant, continual, enduring, incessant, persistent, recurrent, twenty-four-seven (*slang*)
perfect *adjective* 1 COMPLETE, absolute, consummate, entire, finished, full, sheer, unmitigated, utter, whole
2 FAULTLESS, flawless, immaculate, impeccable, pure, spotless, unblemished
3 EXCELLENT, ideal, splendid, sublime, superb, superlative, supreme
4 EXACT, accurate, correct, faithful, precise, true, unerring
▷ *verb* 5 IMPROVE, develop, polish, refine
6 ACCOMPLISH, achieve, carry out, complete, finish, fulfill, perform
perfection *noun* 1 COMPLETENESS, maturity
2 PURITY, integrity, perfectness, wholeness
3 EXCELLENCE, exquisiteness, sublimity, superiority
4 EXACTNESS, faultlessness, precision
perfectionist *noun* STICKLER, precisionist, purist
perfectly *adverb* 1 COMPLETELY, absolutely, altogether, fully, quite, thoroughly, totally, utterly, wholly
2 FLAWLESSLY, faultlessly, ideally, impeccably, superbly, supremely, wonderfully
perfidious *adjective* (*literary*) TREACHEROUS, disloyal, double-dealing, traitorous, two-faced, unfaithful
perforate *verb* PIERCE, bore, drill, penetrate, punch, puncture

per•force [pər-FORS] *adverb* of necessity
per•form [pər-FORM] *verb transitive* 1 bring to completion 2 accomplish 3 fulfill 4 represent on stage ▷ *verb intransitive* 5 function 6 act part 7 play, as on musical instrument
> **per•for'mance** [-məns] *noun*
per•fume [PUR-fyoom] *noun* 1 agreeable scent 2 fragrance ▷ *verb transitive* **-fumed, -fum•ing** 3 imbue with an agreeable odor 4 scent
> **per•fum'er** *noun*
per•func•to•ry [pər-FUNGK-tə-ree] *adjective* 1 superficial 2 hasty 3 done indifferently
per•go•la [PUR-gə-lə] *noun* 1 area covered by plants growing on trellis 2 the trellis
per•haps [pər-HAPS] *adverb* possibly
peri- *prefix* round: *perimeter; period; periphrasis*
per•i•car•di•um [per-i-KAHR-dee-əm] *noun, plural* **-di•a** [-dee-ə] membrane enclosing the heart > **per•i•car•di'tis** *noun* inflammation of this
per•i•he•li•on [per-ə-HEE-lee-ən] *noun, plural* **-li•a** [-lee-ə] point in orbit of planet or comet nearest to sun
per•il [PER-əl] *noun* 1 danger 2 exposure to injury > **per'il•ous** *adjective* full of peril, hazardous
pe•rim•e•ter [pə-RIM-i-tər] *noun* 1 outer boundary of an area 2 length of this
pe•ri•od [PEER-ee-əd] *noun* 1 particular portion of time 2 a series of years 3 single occurrence of menstruation 4 cycle 5 conclusion 6 full stop (.) at the end of a sentence 7 complete sentence ▷ *adjective* 8 of furniture, dress, play, etc., belonging to particular time in history
> **pe•ri•od'ic** *adjective* recurring at regular intervals > **pe•ri•od'i•cal** *adjective, noun* 1 (of) publication issued at regular intervals ▷ *adjective* 2 of a period 3 periodic > **pe•ri•o•dic'i•ty** [-DIS-i-tee] *noun*
per•i•pa•tet•ic [per-ə-pə-TET-ik] *adjective* 1 itinerant 2 walking, traveling about
pe•riph•er•y [pə-RIF-ə-ree] *noun, plural* **-er•ies** 1 circumference 2 surface, outside > **pe•riph'er•al** [-ə-rəl] *adjective* 1 minor, unimportant 2 of periphery
pe•riph•ra•sis [pə-RIF-rə-sis] *noun, plural* **-ses** [-seez] roundabout speech or phrase; circumlocution > **per•i•phras'tic** *adjective*
per•i•scope [PER-ə-skohp] *noun* instrument used esp. in submarines, for giving view of objects on different level
per'ish *verb intransitive* 1 die, waste away 2 decay, rot > **per'ish•a•ble** *adjective* 1 that will not last long ▷ *plural noun* 2 perishable food
per•i•to•ne•um [per-i-tn-EE-əm] *noun, plural* **-ne•ums** *or* **-to•ne•a** [-EE-ə] membrane lining internal surface of abdomen > **per•i•to•ni'tis** [-NĪ-tis] *noun* inflammation of it
per•i•wink•le [PER-i-wing-kəl] *noun* 1 myrtle 2 small edible shellfish
per•jure [PUR-jər] *verb transitive* **-jured, -jur•ing** 1 be guilty of perjury > **per'ju•ry** *noun, plural* **-ries** 1 crime of false testimony under oath 2 false swearing
perk•y [PUR-kee] *adjective* **perk•i•er, perk•i•est** lively, cheerful, jaunty, gay > **perk up** make, become cheerful
per•ma•frost [PUR-mə-frawst] *noun* permanently frozen ground
per•ma•nent [PUR-mə-nənt] *adjective* 1 continuing in same state 2 lasting
> **per'ma•nence, per'ma•nen•cy** *noun* fixedness
> **permanent wave** *noun* (treatment of hair producing) long-lasting style
per•me•ate [PUR-mee-ayt] *verb transitive* **-at•ed, -at•ing** 1 pervade, saturate 2 pass through

perform *verb* 1 CARRY OUT, accomplish, achieve, complete, discharge, do, execute, fulfill, pull off, work
2 PRESENT, act, enact, play, produce, put on, represent, stage
performance *noun* 1 CARRYING OUT, accomplishment, achievement, act, completion, execution, fulfillment, work
2 PRESENTATION, acting, appearance, exhibition, gig (*informal*), play, portrayal, production, show
performer *noun* ARTISTE, actor *or* actress, player, Thespian, trouper
perfume *noun* FRAGRANCE, aroma, bouquet, odor, scent, smell
perfunctory *adjective* OFFHAND, cursory, heedless, indifferent, mechanical, routine, sketchy, superficial
perhaps *adverb* MAYBE, conceivably, feasibly, it may be, perchance (*archaic*), possibly
peril *noun* DANGER, hazard, jeopardy, menace, risk, uncertainty
perilous *adjective* DANGEROUS, hazardous, precarious, risky, threatening, unsafe
perimeter *noun* BOUNDARY, ambit, border, bounds, circumference, confines, edge, limit, margin, periphery
period *noun* TIME, interval, season, space, span, spell, stretch, term, while
periodic *adjective* RECURRENT, cyclical, intermittent, occasional, regular, repeated
periodical *noun* PUBLICATION, journal, magazine, monthly, paper, quarterly, weekly
peripheral *adjective* 1 INCIDENTAL, inessential, irrelevant, marginal, minor, secondary, unimportant
2 OUTERMOST, exterior, external, outer, outside
perish *verb* 1 DIE, be killed, expire, lose one's life, pass away
2 BE DESTROYED, collapse, decline, disappear, fall, vanish
3 ROT, decay, decompose, disintegrate, molder, waste
perishable *adjective* SHORT-LIVED, decaying, decomposable
perjure *verb* ▷ **perjure oneself** (*criminal law*) COMMIT PERJURY, bear false witness, forswear, give false testimony, lie under oath, swear falsely
perjury *noun* LYING UNDER OATH, bearing false witness, false statement, forswearing, giving false testimony
perk *noun* (*informal*) BONUS, benefit, extra, fringe benefit, perquisite, plus
permanence *noun* CONTINUITY, constancy, continuance, durability, endurance, finality, indestructibility, perpetuity, stability
permanent *adjective* LASTING, abiding, constant, enduring, eternal, everlasting, immutable, perpetual, persistent, stable, steadfast, twenty-four-seven (*slang*), unchanging

pores of > **per'me•a•ble** [-ə-bəl] *adjective* admitting of passage of fluids
per•mit [pər-MIT] *verb transitive* **-mit•ted, -mit•ting** 1 allow 2 give leave to ▷ *noun* [PUR-mit] 3 license to do something 4 written permission > **permis'si•ble** *adjective* allowable > **per•mis'sion** *noun* 1 authorization 2 leave, liberty > **per•mis'sive** *adjective* (too) tolerant, lenient, esp. as parent
per•mute [pər-MYOOT] *verb transitive* **-mut•ed, -mut•ing** interchange > **per•mu•ta•tion** [pur-myuu-TAY-shən] *noun* 1 mutual transference 2 *math.* arrangement of a number of quantities in every possible order
per•ni•cious [pər-NISH-əs] *adjective* 1 wicked or mischievous 2 extremely hurtful 3 having quality of destroying or injuring
per•o•ra•tion [per-ə-RAY-shən] *noun* concluding part of oration
per•ox•ide [pə-ROK-sīd] *noun* 1 oxide of a given base containing greatest quantity of oxygen 2 *short for* **hydrogen peroxide**
perp [purp] *noun* (*informal*) person who has committed a crime
per•pen•di•cu•lar [pur-pən-DIK-yə-lər] *adjective* 1 at right angles to the plane of the horizon 2 at right angles to given line or surface 3 exactly upright ▷ *noun* 4 line falling at right angles on another line or plane
per•pe•trate [PUR-pi-trayt] *verb transitive* **-trat•ed, -trat•ing** perform or be responsible for (something bad)
per•pet•u•al [pər-PECH-oo-əl] *adjective* 1 continuous 2 lasting for ever > **per•pet'u•ate** *verb transitive* **at•ed, -at•ing** 1 make perpetual 2 not to allow to be forgotten > **per•pet•u•a'tion** *noun* > **per•pe•tu•i•ty** [pur-pi-TOO-i-tee] *noun*
per•plex [pər-PLEKS] *verb transitive* 1 puzzle 2 bewilder 3 make difficult to understand > **per•plex'i•ty** *noun, plural* **-ties** puzzled or tangled state
per•qui•site [PUR-kwi-zit] *noun* 1 any incidental benefit from a certain type of employment 2 casual payment in addition to salary 3 something due as a privilege
per se [pur SAY] *Lat.* by or in itself
per•se•cute [PUR-si-kyoot] *verb transitive* **-cut•ed, -cut•ing** 1 oppress because of race, religion, etc. 2 subject to persistent ill-treatment > **per•se•cu'tion** *noun*
per•se•vere [pur-sə-VEER] *verb intransitive* **-vered, -ver•ing** persist, maintain effort > **per•se•ver'ance** [-əns] *noun* persistence
per•si•flage [PUR-sə-flahzh] *noun* 1 idle talk 2 frivolous style of treating subject
per•sim•mon [pər-SIM-ən] *noun* 1 American tree 2 its hard wood 3 its fruit
per•sist [pər-SIST] *verb intransitive* continue in spite of obstacles or objections > **per•sist'ence** [-əns] *noun* > **per•sist'en•cy** *noun* > **per•sist'ent** *adjective* 1 persisting 2 steady 3 persevering 4 lasting
per•snick•et•y [pər-SNIK-i-tee] *adjective* (*informal*) 1 fussy 2 fastidious about trifles 3 snobbishly aloof 4 requiring great care
per•son [PUR-sən] *noun* 1 individual (human)

DICTIONARY P THESAURUS

permeate *verb* PERVADE, charge, fill, imbue, impregnate, infiltrate, penetrate, saturate, spread through
permissible *adjective* PERMITTED, acceptable, allowable, all right, authorized, lawful, legal, legitimate, O.K. *or* okay (*informal*)
permission *noun* AUTHORIZATION, allowance, approval, assent, consent, dispensation, go-ahead (*informal*), green light, leave, liberty, license, sanction
permissive *adjective* TOLERANT, easy-going, forbearing, free, indulgent, lax, lenient, liberal
permit *verb* 1 ALLOW, authorize, consent, enable, entitle, give leave *or* give permission, give the green light to, grant, let, license, sanction ▷ *noun* 2 LICENSE, authorization, pass, passport, permission, warrant
permutation *noun* TRANSFORMATION, alteration, change, transposition
pernicious *adjective* WICKED, bad, damaging, dangerous, deadly, destructive, detrimental, evil, fatal, harmful, hurtful, malign, poisonous
perpendicular *adjective* UPRIGHT, at right angles to, on end, plumb, straight, vertical
perpetrate *verb* COMMIT, carry out, do, enact, execute, perform, wreak
perpetual *adjective* 1 EVERLASTING, endless, eternal, infinite, lasting, never-ending, perennial, permanent, unchanging, unending 2 CONTINUAL, constant, continuous, endless, incessant, interminable, never-ending, persistent, recurrent, repeated, twenty-four-seven (*slang*)
perpetuate *verb* MAINTAIN, immortalize, keep going, preserve
perplex *verb* PUZZLE, baffle, bewilder, confound, confuse, mystify, stump
perplexing *adjective* PUZZLING, baffling, bewildering, complex, complicated, confusing, difficult, enigmatic, hard, inexplicable, mystifying
perplexity *noun* 1 PUZZLEMENT, bafflement, bewilderment, confusion, incomprehension, mystification 2 PUZZLE, difficulty, fix (*informal*), mystery, paradox
perquisite *noun* (*formal*) BONUS, benefit, dividend, extra, perk (*informal*), plus
persecute *verb* 1 VICTIMIZE, afflict, ill-treat, maltreat, oppress, torment, torture 2 HARASS, annoy, badger, bother, hassle (*informal*), pester, tease
perseverance *noun* PERSISTENCE, determination, diligence, doggedness, endurance, pertinacity, resolution, tenacity
persevere *verb* KEEP GOING, carry on, continue, go on, hang on, persist, remain, stick at *or* stick to
persist *verb* 1 CONTINUE, carry on, keep up, last, linger, remain 2 PERSEVERE, continue, insist, stand firm
persistence *noun* DETERMINATION, doggedness, endurance, grit, perseverance, pertinacity, resolution, tenacity, tirelessness
persistent *adjective* 1 CONTINUOUS, constant, continual, endless, incessant, never-ending, perpetual, repeated, twenty-four-seven (*slang*) 2 DETERMINED, dogged, obdurate, obstinate, persevering, pertinacious, steadfast, steady, stubborn, tenacious, tireless, unflagging

being 2 body of human being 3 *grammar* classification, or one of the classes, of pronouns and verb forms according to the person speaking, spoken to, or spoken of > **per•so•na** [pər-SOH-nə] *noun, plural* **-nas** assumed character > **per'son•a•ble** *adjective* good-looking > **per'son•age** [-ij] *noun* notable person > **per'son•al** *adjective* 1 individual, private, or one's own 2 of, relating to grammatical person > **per•son•al'i•ty** *noun, plural* **-ties** 1 distinctive character 2 a celebrity > **per'son•al•ly** *adverb* in person > **per'son•ate** *verb transitive* **-at•ed, -at•ing** pass oneself off as > **personal computer** small computer used for word processing, e-mail, computer games, etc. > **personal property** *law* all property except land and interests in land that pass to heir > **personal stereo** very small portable cassette player with headphones > **per'son•hood** *noun* condition of being a person who is an individual with inalienable rights

per•son•i•fy [pər-SON-ə-fī] *verb transitive* **-fied, -fy•ing** 1 represent as person 2 typify > **per•son•i•fi•ca'tion** *noun*

per•son•nel [pur-sə-NEL] *noun* staff employed in a service or institution

per•spec•tive [pər-SPEK-tiv] *noun* 1 mental view 2 art of drawing on flat surface to give effect of solidity and relative distances and sizes 3 drawing in perspective

per•spi•ca•cious [pur-spi-KAY-shəs] *adjective* having quick mental insight > **per•spi•cac'i•ty** [-KAS-i-tee] *noun*

per•spic•u•ous [pər-SPIK-yoo-əs] *adjective* 1 clearly expressed 2 lucid 3 plain 4 obvious > **per•spi•cu'i•ty** *noun*

per•spire [pər-SPĪR] *verb* **-spired, -spir•ing** sweat > **per•spi•ra'tion** [-spi-RAY-shən] *noun* 1 sweating 2 sweat

per•suade [pər-SWAYD] *verb transitive* **-suad•ed, -suad•ing** 1 bring (one to do something) by argument, charm, etc. 2 convince > **per•sua'sion** [-SWAY-zhən] *noun* 1 art, act of persuading 2 way of thinking or belief > **per•sua'sive** *adjective*

pert *adjective* **-er, -est** forward, saucy

per•tain [pər-TAYN] *verb intransitive* 1 belong, relate, have reference (to) 2 concern

per•ti•na•cious [pur-tn-AY-shəs] *adjective* obstinate, persistent > **per•ti•nac'i•ty** [-AS-i-tee] *noun* doggedness, resolution

per•ti•nent [PUR-tn-ənt] *adjective* to the point > **per'ti•nence** *noun* relevance

per•turb [pər-TURB] *verb transitive* 1 disturb greatly 2 alarm > **per•tur•ba'tion** *noun* 1 disturbance 2 agitation of mind

pe•ruse [pə-ROOZ] *verb transitive* **-rused, -rus•ing** examine, read, esp. in slow and careful, or leisurely, manner > **pe•rus'al** *noun*

per•vade [pər-VAYD] *verb transitive* **-vad•ed,**

DICTIONARY • THESAURUS

person *noun* 1 INDIVIDUAL, being, body, human, soul
2 ▷ **in person** PERSONALLY, bodily, in the flesh, oneself

personable *adjective* PLEASANT, agreeable, amiable, attractive, charming, good-looking, handsome, likable *or* likeable, nice

personage *noun* PERSONALITY, big shot (*informal*), celebrity, dignitary, luminary, megastar (*informal*), notable, public figure, somebody, V.I.P.

personal *adjective* 1 PRIVATE, exclusive, individual, intimate, own, particular, peculiar, special
2 OFFENSIVE, derogatory, disparaging, insulting, nasty

personality *noun* 1 NATURE, character, disposition, identity, individuality, make-up, temperament
2 CELEBRITY, famous name, household name, megastar (*informal*), notable, personage, star

personally *adverb* 1 BY ONESELF, alone, independently, on one's own, solely
2 IN ONE'S OPINION, for one's part, from one's own viewpoint, in one's books, in one's own view
3 INDIVIDUALLY, individualistically, privately, specially, subjectively

personification *noun* EMBODIMENT, epitome, image, incarnation, portrayal, representation

personify *verb* EMBODY, epitomize, exemplify, represent, symbolize, typify

personnel *noun* EMPLOYEES, helpers, human resources, people, staff, workers, workforce

perspective *noun* 1 OUTLOOK, angle, attitude, context, frame of reference
2 OBJECTIVITY, proportion, relation, relative importance, relativity

perspicacious *adjective* PERCEPTIVE, acute, alert, astute, discerning, keen, percipient, sharp, shrewd

perspiration *noun* SWEAT, moisture, wetness

perspire *verb* SWEAT, exude, glow, pour with sweat, secrete, swelter

persuade *verb* 1 TALK INTO, coax, entice, impel, incite, induce, influence, sway, urge, win over
2 CONVINCE, cause to believe, satisfy

persuasion *noun* 1 URGING, cajolery, enticement, inducement, wheedling
2 PERSUASIVENESS, cogency, force, potency, power
3 CREED, belief, conviction, credo, faith, opinion, tenet, views
4 FACTION, camp, denomination, party, school, school of thought, side

persuasive *adjective* CONVINCING, cogent, compelling, credible, effective, eloquent, forceful, influential, plausible, sound, telling, valid, weighty

pert *adjective* IMPUDENT, bold, cheeky, forward, impertinent, insolent, sassy (*informal*), saucy

pertain *verb* RELATE, apply, befit, belong, be relevant, concern, refer, regard

pertinent *adjective* RELEVANT, applicable, apposite, appropriate, apt, fit, fitting, germane, material, proper, to the point

pertness *noun* IMPUDENCE, audacity, cheek (*informal*), cheekiness, effrontery, forwardness, front, impertinence, insolence, sauciness

perturb *verb* DISTURB, agitate, bother, disconcert, faze, fluster, ruffle, trouble, unsettle, vex, worry

perturbed *adjective* DISTURBED, agitated, anxious, disconcerted, flustered, shaken, troubled, uncomfortable, uneasy, worried

peruse *verb* READ, browse, check, examine, inspect, scan, scrutinize, study

-vad•ing 1 spread through 2 be rife among
> **per•va'sive** *adjective*
per•vert [pər-VURT] *verb transitive* 1 turn to wrong use 2 lead astray ▷ *noun* [PUR-vərt] 3 one who shows unhealthy abnormality, esp. in sexual matters > **per•verse** [pər-VURS] *adjective* 1 obstinately or unreasonably wrong 2 self-willed 3 headstrong 4 wayward > **per•ver'sion** [-VUR-zhən] *noun*
pes•sa•ry [PES-ə-ree] *noun, plural* **-ries** 1 instrument used to support mouth and neck of uterus 2 appliance to prevent conception 3 medicated suppository
pes•si•mism [PES-ə-miz-əm] *noun* 1 tendency to see the worst side of things 2 theory that everything turns to evil > **pes'si•mist** *noun* > **pes•si•mis'tic** *adjective*
pest *noun* 1 troublesome or harmful thing, person or insect 2 plague > **pest'i•cide** [-sīd] *noun* chemical for killing pests, esp. insects > **pes•tif'er•ous** [-ər-əs] *adjective* 1 troublesome 2 bringing plague
pes•ter [PES-tər] *verb transitive* 1 trouble or vex persistently 2 harass
pes•ti•lence [PES-tl-əns] *noun* epidemic disease, esp. bubonic plague > **pes'ti•lent** *adjective* 1 troublesome 2 deadly > **pes•ti•len'tial** [-LEN-shəl] *adjective*
pes•tle [PES-əl] *noun* instrument with which things are pounded in a mortar
Pet. Peter
pet *noun* 1 animal or person kept or regarded with affection ▷ *verb transitive* **pet•ted, pet•ting** 2 make pet of 3 (*informal*) hug, embrace, fondle
pet•al [PET-l] *noun* white or colored leaflike part of flower > **pet'aled** *adjective*
pe•tard [pi-TAHRD] *noun* formerly, an explosive device **hoist by one's own petard** ruined, destroyed by plot one intended for another
pe•ter [PEE-tər] *verb intransitive* **peter out** (*informal*) disappear, lose power gradually
pe•tit [PET-ee] *adjective law* small, petty
pe•tite [pə-TEET] *adjective* small, dainty
pe•ti•tion [pə-TISH-ən] *noun* 1 entreaty, request, esp.one presented to a governing body or person ▷ *verb transitive* 2 present petition to > **pe•ti'tion•er** *noun*
pet•rel [PE-trəl] *noun* sea bird
pet•ri•fy [PE-trə-fī] *verb transitive* **-fied, -fy•ing** 1 turn to stone 2 make motionless with fear 3 make dumb with amazement > **pet•ri•fac'tion** *noun*
pe•tro•le•um [pə-TROH-lee-əm] *noun* unrefined oil
pet•ti•coat [PET-ee-koht] *noun* women's undergarment worn under skirts, dresses, etc.
pet•ti•fog•ger [PET-ee-fog-ər] *noun* 1 quibbler 2 unethical lawyer 3 one given to mean

DICTIONARY

P

THESAURUS

pervade *verb* SPREAD THROUGH, charge, fill, imbue, infuse, penetrate, permeate, suffuse
pervasive *adjective* WIDESPREAD, common, extensive, general, omnipresent, prevalent, rife, ubiquitous, universal
perverse *adjective* 1 ABNORMAL, contrary, deviant, disobedient, improper, rebellious, refractory, troublesome, unhealthy
2 WILLFUL, contrary, dogged, headstrong, intractable, intransigent, obdurate, wrong-headed
3 STUBBORN, contrary, mulish, obstinate, pig-headed, stiff-necked, wayward
4 ILL-NATURED, churlish, cross, fractious, ill tempered, peevish, surly
perversion *noun* 1 DEVIATION, aberration, abnormality, debauchery, depravity, immorality, kink (*informal*), kinkiness (*slang*), unnaturalness, vice
2 DISTORTION, corruption, falsification, misinterpretation, misrepresentation, twisting
perversity *noun* CONTRARINESS, contradictoriness, intransigence, obduracy, refractoriness, waywardness, wrong-headedness
pervert *verb* 1 DISTORT, abuse, falsify, garble, misrepresent, misuse, twist, warp
2 CORRUPT, debase, debauch, degrade, deprave, lead astray
▷ *noun* 3 DEVIANT, degenerate, sicko (*informal*), weirdo *or* weirdie (*informal*)
perverted *adjective* UNNATURAL, abnormal, corrupt, debased, debauched, depraved, deviant, kinky (*slang*), sick, twisted, unhealthy, warped
pessimism *noun* GLOOMINESS, dejection, depression, despair, despondency, distrust, gloom, hopelessness, melancholy
pessimist *noun* WET BLANKET (*informal*), cynic, defeatist, killjoy, prophet of doom, worrier
pessimistic *adjective* GLOOMY, bleak, cynical, dark, dejected, depressed, despairing, despondent, glum, hopeless, morose
pest *noun* 1 NUISANCE, annoyance, bane, bother, drag (*informal*), irritation, pain (*informal*), thorn in one's flesh, trial, vexation
2 INFECTION, blight, bug, epidemic, pestilence, plague, scourge
pester *verb* ANNOY, badger, bedevil, bother, bug (*informal*), harass, harry, hassle (*informal*), nag, plague, torment
pestilence *noun* PLAGUE, epidemic, visitation
pestilent *adjective* 1 ANNOYING, bothersome, irksome, irritating, tiresome, vexing
2 HARMFUL, detrimental, evil, injurious, pernicious
3 CONTAMINATED, catching, contagious, diseased, disease-ridden, infected, infectious
pestilential *adjective* DEADLY, dangerous, destructive, detrimental, harmful, hazardous, injurious, pernicious
pet[1] *noun* 1 FAVORITE, darling, jewel, treasure
▷ *adjective* 2 FAVORITE, cherished, dearest, dear to one's heart
▷ *verb* 3 PAMPER, baby, coddle, cosset, spoil
4 FONDLE, caress, pat, stroke
5 CUDDLE, kiss, make out, neck (*informal*), smooch (*informal*)
peter out *verb* DIE OUT, dwindle, ebb, fade, fail, run out, stop, taper off, wane
petite *adjective* SMALL, dainty, delicate, elfin, little, slight
petition *noun* 1 APPEAL, entreaty, plea, prayer, request, solicitation, suit, supplication
▷ *verb* 2 APPEAL, adjure, ask, beg, beseech, entreat, plead, pray, solicit, supplicate
petrify *verb* 1 TERRIFY, horrify, immobilize, paralyze, stun, stupefy, transfix
2 FOSSILIZE, calcify, harden, turn to stone

dealing in small matters
pet•ty [PET-ee] *adjective* **-ti•er, -ti•est** 1 unimportant, trivial 2 small-minded, mean 3 on a small scale > **petty cash** cash kept by firm to pay minor incidental expenses > **petty officer** noncommissioned officer in Navy
pet•u•lant [PECH-ə-lənt] *adjective* 1 given to small fits of temper 2 peevish > **pet'u•lance** *noun* peevishness
pe•tu•nia [pi-TOON-yə] *noun* plant with funnel-shaped purple or white flowers
pew [pyoo] *noun* 1 fixed seat in church 2 (*informal*) chair, seat
pew•ter [PYOO-tər] *noun* 1 alloy of tin and lead 2 utensil of this
pha•lanx [FAY-langks] *noun, plural* **-lanx•es** body of soldiers, etc. formed in close array
phal•lus [FAL-əs] *noun, plural* **-lus•es** 1 penis 2 symbol of it used in primitive rites > **phal'lic** *adjective*
phan•tas•ma•go•ri•a [fan-taz-mə-GOR-ee-ə] *noun* 1 crowd of dim or unreal figures 2 exhibition of illusions
phan•tom [FAN-təm] *noun* 1 apparition 2 specter, ghost 3 fancied vision
Phar•aoh [FAIR-oh] *noun* title of ancient Egyptian kings
phar•i•see [FA-rə-see] *noun* 1 sanctimonious person 2 hypocrite > **phar•i•sa'ic** [-SAY-ik] *adjective*
phar•ma•ceu•tic [fahr-mə-SOO-tik] *adjective* of pharmacy > **phar•ma•ceu'ti•cal** *adjective* > **phar'ma•cist** *noun* person qualified to dispense drugs > **phar•ma•col'o•gy** [-KOL-ə-jee] *noun* study of drugs > **phar•ma•co•poe'ia** [-kə-PEE-ə] *noun* official book with directions for use of drugs > **phar'ma•cy** [-mə-see] *noun* 1 preparation and dispensing of drugs 2 drugstore
pharm•ing [FAHRM-ing] *noun* practice of growing genetically-modified animals or plants in order to develop drugs and medicines
phar•ynx [FA-ringks] *noun, plural* **pha•ryn•ges** [fə-RIN-jeez] cavity forming back part of mouth and terminating in gullet > **pha•ryn'ge•al** *adjective*
phase [fayz] *noun* 1 any distinct or characteristic period or stage in a development or chain of events ▷ *verb transitive* **phased, phas•ing** 2 arrange, execute in stages or to coincide with something else
pheas•ant [FEZ-ənt] *noun* game bird with bright plumage
phe•no•bar•bi•tal [fee-noh-BAHR-bi-tawl] *noun* drug inducing sleep
phe•nom•e•non [fi-NOM-ə-non] *noun, plural* **-na** [-nə] 1 anything appearing or observed 2 remarkable person or thing > **phe•nom'e•nal** *adjective* 1 relating to phenomena 2 remarkable 3 recognizable or evidenced by senses
Phil. Philippians
phil- *combining form* loving: *philanthropy; philosophy*
phi•lan•der [fi-LAN-dər] *verb intransitive* (of man) flirt with, make love to, women, esp. with no intention of marrying them > **phi•lan'der•er** *noun*
phi•lan•thro•py [fi-LAN-thrə-pee] *noun, plural* **-pies** 1 practice of doing good to people 2 love of mankind 3 a philanthropic organization > **phi•lan•throp'ic** *adjective* 1 loving mankind 2 benevolent > **phi•lan'thro•pist** *noun*
phi•lat•e•ly [fi-LAT-l-ee] *noun* stamp collecting > **phi•lat'e•list** *noun*
phil•is•tine [FIL-ə-steen] *noun* ignorant, smug person ▷ *adjective*
phi•lol•o•gy [fi-LOL-ə-jee] *noun* science of structure and development of languages > **phi•lol'o•gist** *noun*
phi•los•o•phy [fi-LOS-ə-fee] *noun* 1 pursuit of wisdom 2 study of realities and general principles 3 system of theories on nature of things or on conduct 4 calmness of mind > **phi•los'o•pher** *noun* one who studies, possesses, or originates philosophy

petty *adjective* 1 TRIVIAL, contemptible, inconsiderable, insignificant, little, lousy (*slang*), measly (*informal*), negligible, paltry, slight, small, trifling, unimportant
2 SMALL-MINDED, mean, mean-minded, shabby, spiteful, ungenerous
petulance *noun* SULKINESS, bad temper, ill humor, irritability, peevishness, pique, sullenness
petulant *adjective* SULKY, bad-tempered, huffy, ill-humored, moody, peevish, sullen
phantom *noun* 1 SPECTER, apparition, ghost, phantasm, shade (*literary*), spirit, spook (*informal*), wraith
2 ILLUSION, figment of the imagination, hallucination, vision
phase *noun* STAGE, chapter, development, juncture, period, point, position, step, time
phase out *verb* WIND DOWN, close, ease off, eliminate, pull out, remove, run down, terminate, wind up, withdraw
phenomenal *adjective* EXTRAORDINARY, exceptional, fantastic, marvelous, miraculous, outstanding, prodigious, remarkable, unusual
phenomenon *noun* 1 OCCURRENCE, circumstance, episode, event, fact, happening, incident
2 WONDER, exception, marvel, miracle, prodigy, rarity, sensation
philanderer *noun* WOMANIZER (*informal*), Casanova, Don Juan, flirt, gigolo, ladies' man, playboy, stud (*slang*), wolf (*informal*)
philanthropic *adjective* HUMANITARIAN, beneficent, benevolent, charitable, humane, kind, kind-hearted, munificent, public-spirited
philanthropist *noun* HUMANITARIAN, benefactor, contributor, donor, giver, patron
philanthropy *noun* HUMANITARIANISM, almsgiving, beneficence, benevolence, brotherly love, charitableness, charity, generosity, kind-heartedness
philistine *noun* 1 BOOR, barbarian, ignoramus, lout, lowbrow, vulgarian, yahoo
▷ *adjective* 2 UNCULTURED, boorish, ignorant, lowbrow, tasteless, uncultivated, uneducated, unrefined
philosopher *noun* THINKER, logician, metaphysician, sage, theorist, wise man
philosophical *adjective* 1 WISE, abstract, logical, rational, sagacious, theoretical, thoughtful
2 STOICAL, calm, collected, composed, cool,

> **phil•o•soph'i•cal** *adjective* 1 of, like philosophy 2 wise, learned 3 calm, stoical
> **phi•los'o•phize** [-fīz] *verb intransitive* **-phized, -phiz•ing** 1 reason like philosopher 2 theorize 3 moralize
phle•bi•tis [flə-BĪ-tis] *noun* inflammation of a vein
phlegm [flem] *noun* 1 viscid substance formed 2 by mucous membrane and ejected by coughing, etc. 3 apathy, sluggishness
> **phleg•mat•ic** [fleg-MAT-ik] *adjective* 1 not easily agitated 2 composed
pho•bi•a [FOH-bee-ə] *noun* 1 fear or aversion 2 unreasoning dislike
phoe•nix [FEE-niks] *noun* 1 legendary bird 2 unique thing
phone [fohn] *noun, verb* (*informal*) telephone
> **phone card** prepaid card used to pay for telephone calls > **phone tag** repeated unsuccessful attempts to contact by telephone
pho•net•ic [fə-NET-ik] *adjective* of, or relating to, vocal sounds > **pho•net'ics** *noun* science of vocal sounds > **pho•ne•ti•cian** [foh-ni-TISH-ən] *noun*
phono- *combining form* sound: *phonology*
pho•no•graph [FOH-nə-graf] *noun* instrument recording and reproducing sounds, record player
pho•ny [FOH-nee] (*informal*) ▷ *adjective* **-ni•er, -ni•est** 1 not genuine 2 insincere ▷ *noun, plural* **pho'nies** 3 phony person or thing
phos•pho•rus [FOS-fər-əs] *noun* toxic, flammable, nonmetallic element that appears luminous in the dark > **phos•phate** [FOS-fayt] *noun* compound of phosphorus
> **phos•pho•res'cence** *noun* faint glow in the dark
pho•to [FOH-toh] *noun* (*informal*) *short for* **photograph.** > **photo finish** photo taken at end of race to show placing of contestants
photo- *combining form* light: *photometer; photosynthesis*
pho•to•cop•y [FOH-toh-kop-ee] *noun, plural* **-cop•ies** photographic reproduction ▷ *verb transitive* **-cop•ied, -cop•y•ing**
pho•to•e•lec•tron [foh-toh-i-LEK-tron] *noun* electron liberated from metallic surface by action of beam of light
pho•to•gen•ic [foh-tə-JEN-ik] *adjective* capable of being photographed attractively
pho•to•graph [FOH-tə-graf] *noun* 1 picture made by chemical action of light on sensitive film ▷ *verb transitive* 2 take photograph of
> **pho•tog'ra•pher** [-rə-fər] *noun*
pho•to•syn•the•sis [foh-tə-SIN-thə-sis] *noun* process by which green plant uses sun's energy to build up carbohydrate reserves
phrase [frayz] *noun* 1 group of words 2 pithy expression 3 mode of expression ▷ *verb transitive* **phrased, phras•ing** 4 express in words
> **phra•se•ol•o•gy** [fray-zee-OL-ə-jee] *noun* manner of expression, choice of words
> **phras•al verb** [-əl] phrase consisting of verb and preposition, often with meaning different to the individual parts, such as *take in* meaning *deceive*
phre•nol•o•gy [frə-NOL-ə-jee] *noun* (formerly) study of skull's shape; theory that character and mental powers are indicated by shape of skull
> **phre•nol'o•gist** *noun*
phy•lac•ter•y [fi-LAK-tə-ree] *noun, plural* **-ter•ies** leather case containing religious texts worn by Jewish men during weekday morning prayers
phys•ic [FIZ-ik] *noun* medicine, esp. cathartic
> **phys•ics** science of properties of matter and energy > **phys'i•cal** *adjective* 1 bodily, as opposed to mental or moral 2 material 3 of physics of body > **phy•si'cian** *noun* medical doctor
> **phys'i•cist** *noun* one skilled in, or student of, physics
phys•i•og•no•my [fiz-ee-OG-nə-mee] *noun, plural* **-mies** 1 judging character by face 2 face 3 outward appearance of something
phys•i•ol•o•gy [fiz-ee-OL-ə-jee] *noun* science of normal function of living things
> **phy•si•ol'o•gist** *noun*
phys•i•o•ther•a•py [fiz-ee-oh-THER-ə-pee] *noun* therapeutic use of physical means, as massage, etc. > **phys•i•o•ther'a•pist** *noun*

DICTIONARY **P** THESAURUS

serene, tranquil, unruffled
philosophy *noun* 1 THOUGHT, knowledge, logic, metaphysics, rationalism, reasoning, thinking, wisdom
2 OUTLOOK, beliefs, convictions, doctrine, ideology, principles, tenets, thinking, values, viewpoint, world view
3 STOICISM, calmness, composure, equanimity, self-possession, serenity
phlegmatic *adjective* UNEMOTIONAL, apathetic, impassive, indifferent, placid, stoical, stolid, undemonstrative, unfeeling
phobia *noun* TERROR, aversion, detestation, dread, fear, hatred, horror, loathing, repulsion, revulsion, thing (*informal*)
phone *noun* 1 TELEPHONE, blower (*informal*), cell, cell phone, horn (*informal*)
2 CALL
▷ *verb* 3 CALL, get on the blower (*informal*), get on the horn (*informal*), give someone a call, make a call, telephone
phony (*informal*) *adjective* 1 FAKE, bogus, counterfeit, ersatz, false, imitation, pseudo (*informal*), sham
▷ *noun* 2 FAKE, counterfeit, forgery, fraud, impostor, pseud (*informal*), sham
photograph *noun* 1 PICTURE, photo (*informal*), print, shot, snap (*informal*), snapshot, transparency
▷ *verb* 2 TAKE A PICTURE OF, film, record, shoot, snap (*informal*), take (someone's) picture
photographic *adjective* 1 LIFELIKE, graphic, natural, pictorial, realistic, visual, vivid
2 (*memory*) ACCURATE, exact, faithful, precise, retentive
phrase *noun* 1 EXPRESSION, group of words, idiom, remark, saying
▷ *verb* 2 EXPRESS, put, put into words, say, voice, word
phraseology *noun* WORDING, choice of words, expression, idiom, language, parlance, phrase, phrasing, speech, style, syntax
physical *adjective* 1 BODILY, corporal, corporeal, earthly, fleshly, incarnate, mortal
2 MATERIAL, natural, palpable, real, solid, substantial, tangible
physician *noun* DOCTOR, doc (*informal*), doctor of medicine, general practitioner, G.P., M.D., medic

phy•sique [fi-ZEEK] *noun* bodily structure, constitution and development

pi [pī] *noun math.* ratio of circumference of circle to its diameter, approx. 3.141592

pi•an•o [pee-AN-oh] *noun, plural* **-an•os** musical instrument with strings that are struck by hammers worked by keyboard (*also* **pianofor'te**) > **pi•an•ist** [pee-AN-ist] *noun* performer on piano

pi•az•za [pee-AZ-ə] *noun* 1 square, marketplace 2 veranda

pi•ca [PĪ-kə] *noun* 1 printing type of 6 lines to the inch 2 size of type, 12 point 3 typewriter type size (10 letters to inch)

pi•ca•dor [PIK-ə-dor] *noun* mounted bullfighter with lance

pic•a•resque [pik-ə-RESK] *adjective* of fiction, esp. episodic and dealing with the adventures of rogues

pic•co•lo [PIK-ə-loh] *noun, plural* **-los** small flute

pick[1] [pik] *verb transitive* 1 choose, select carefully 2 pluck, gather 3 peck at 4 pierce with something pointed 5 find occasion for ▷ *noun* 6 act of picking 7 choicest part > **pick'ings** *plural noun* 1 gleanings 2 odds and ends of profit > **pick-me-up** *noun* (*informal*) stimulating drink, tonic > **pick'pock•et** *noun* one who steals from another's pocket > **pick'up** *noun* device for conversion of mechanical energy into electric signals, as in record player, etc. > **pickup truck** small truck with open body > **pick on** find fault with > **pick up** 1 raise, lift 2 collect 3 improve, get better 4 accelerate

pick[2] *noun* tool with curved steel crossbar and wooden shaft, for breaking up hard ground or masonry > **pick'ax** *noun* pick

pick•er•el [PIK-ər-əl] *noun* small pike

pick•et [PIK-it] *noun* 1 prong, pointed stake 2 person, esp. striker, posted outside building, etc. to prevent use of facility, deter would-be workers during strike ▷ *verb transitive* 3 post as picket 4 beset with pickets 5 tether to peg > **picket fence** fence of pickets > **picket line** line of pickets

pick•le [PIK-əl] *noun* 1 food, esp. cucumber, preserved in brine, vinegar, etc. 2 liquid used for preserving 3 (*informal*) awkward situation ▷ *verb transitive* **-led, -ling** 4 preserve in pickle > **pick•les** *plural noun* pickled vegetables > **pickled** *adjective* (*slang*) drunk

pic•nic [PIK-nik] *noun* 1 pleasure outing including meal out of doors ▷ *verb intransitive* **-nicked, -nick•ing** 2 take part in picnic

Pict [pikt] *noun* member of ancient people of NE Scotland

pic•ture [PIK-chər] *noun* 1 drawing or painting 2 mental image 3 beautiful or picturesque object ▷ *verb transitive* **-tured, -tur•ing** 4 represent in, or as in, a picture > **pic•tures** *plural noun* (*informal*) movies > **pic•to'ri•al** *adjective* 1 of, in, with, painting or pictures 2 graphic > **pic•tur•esque** [pik-chə-RESK] *adjective* 1 such as would be effective in picture 2 striking, vivid > **picture messaging** practice of sending and receiving photographs by cell phone > **picture phone** cell phone that can take, send, and receive photographs

pidg•in [PIJ-ən] *noun* language, not a mother tongue, made up of elements of two or more other languages

---

(*informal*), medical practitioner

physique *noun* BUILD, body, constitution, figure, form, frame, shape, structure

pick *verb* 1 SELECT, choose, decide upon, elect, fix upon, hand-pick, opt for, settle upon, single out
2 GATHER, collect, harvest, pluck, pull
3 NIBBLE, have no appetite, peck at, play with *or* toy with, push the food round the plate
4 PROVOKE, incite, instigate, start
5 OPEN, break into, break open, crack, force
▷ *noun* 6 CHOICE, decision, option, preference, selection
7 THE BEST, crème de la crème (*French*), elect, elite, the cream

picket *noun* 1 PROTESTER, demonstrator, picketer
2 LOOKOUT, guard, patrol, sentinel, sentry, watch
3 STAKE, pale, paling, post, stanchion, upright
▷ *verb* 4 BLOCKADE, boycott, demonstrate

pickle *noun* 1 (*informal*) PREDICAMENT, bind (*informal*), difficulty, dilemma, fix (*informal*), hot water (*informal*), jam (*informal*), quandary, scrape (*informal*), tight spot
▷ *verb* 2 PRESERVE, marinade, steep

pick-me-up *noun* (*informal*) TONIC, bracer (*informal*), refreshment, restorative, shot in the arm (*informal*), stimulant

pick on *verb* TORMENT, badger, bait, bully, goad, hector, tease

pick out *verb* IDENTIFY, discriminate, distinguish, make out, perceive, recognize, tell apart

pick up *verb* 1 LIFT, gather, grasp, raise, take up, uplift
2 OBTAIN, buy, come across, find, purchase
3 RECOVER, be on the mend, get better, improve, mend, rally, take a turn for the better, turn the corner
4 LEARN, acquire, get the hang of (*informal*), master
5 COLLECT, call for, get

pick-up *noun* IMPROVEMENT, change for the better, rally, recovery, revival, rise, strengthening, upswing, upturn

picnic *noun* EXCURSION, outdoor meal, outing

pictorial *adjective* GRAPHIC, illustrated, picturesque, representational, scenic

picture *noun* 1 REPRESENTATION, drawing, engraving, illustration, image, likeness, painting, photograph, portrait, print, sketch
2 DESCRIPTION, account, depiction, image, impression, report
3 DOUBLE, carbon copy, copy, dead ringer (*slang*), duplicate, image, likeness, lookalike, replica, spitting image (*informal*), twin
4 PERSONIFICATION, embodiment, epitome, essence
5 FILM, flick (*slang*), motion picture, movie
▷ *verb* 6 IMAGINE, conceive of, envision, see, visualize
7 REPRESENT, depict, draw, illustrate, paint, photograph, show, sketch

picturesque *adjective* 1 PRETTY, attractive, beautiful, charming, quaint, scenic, striking
2 VIVID, colorful, graphic

pie [pī] *noun* baked dish of fruit, meat, etc., usu. with pastry crust
pie•bald [PĪ-bawld] *adjective* 1 irregularly marked with black and white 2 motley ▷ *noun* 3 piebald horse or other animal
piece [pees] *noun* 1 bit, part, fragment 2 single object 3 literary or musical composition, etc. 4 small object used in checkers, chess, etc. 5 firearm ▷ *verb transitive* **pieced, piec•ing** 6 mend, put together > **piece'meal** *adverb* by, in, or into pieces, a bit at a time > **piece'work** *noun* work paid for according to quantity produced
pièce de ré•sis•tance [pyes də ray-zee-STAHNS] Fr. most impressive item
pied [pīd] *adjective* 1 piebald 2 variegated
pie-eyed [PĪ-īd] *adjective* (*slang*) drunk
pier [peer] *noun* 1 structure running into sea as landing stage 2 piece of solid upright masonry as foundation for building, etc.
pierce [peers] *verb transitive* **pierced, pierc•ing** 1 make hole in 2 make a way through > **piercing** *adjective* 1 keen 2 penetrating
pi•e•ty [PĪ-i-tee] *noun, plural* **-ties** 1 godliness 2 devoutness, goodness 3 dutifulness
pig *noun* 1 wild or domesticated mammal killed for pork, ham, bacon 2 (*informal*) greedy, dirty person 3 (*offensive slang*) policeman 4 oblong mass of smelted metal ▷ *verb intransitive* **pigged, pig•ging** 5 of sow, produce litter > **pig'gish** *adjective* 1 dirty 2 greedy 3 stubborn > **pig'head•ed** *adjective* obstinate > **pig'skin** *noun* 1 (leather made from) the skin of a pig 2 (*informal*) a football > **pig'tail** *noun* braid of hair hanging from back of head
pi•geon [PIJ-ən] *noun* 1 bird of many varieties, often trained to carry messages 2 (*slang*) dupe > **pi'geon•hole** [-hohl] *noun* 1 compartment for papers in desk, etc. ▷ *verb transitive* **-holed, -hol•ing** 2 defer 3 classify > **pi'geon-toed** [-tohd] *adjective* with feet, toes turned inward
pig•ment [PIG-mənt] *noun* coloring matter, paint or dye
pigmy *see* **pygmy**
pike[1] [pīk] *noun* various types of large, predatory freshwater fish
pike[2] *noun* spear formerly used by infantry
pi•laf [PEE-lahf] *noun* Middle Eastern dish of steamed rice with spices, sometimes with meat or fowl, etc.
pi•las•ter [pi-LAS-tər] *noun* square column, usu. set in wall
pile[1] [pīl] *noun* 1 heap 2 great mass of building ▷ *verb transitive* **piled, pil•ing** 3 heap (up), stack load ▷ *verb intransitive* **piled, pil•ing** 4 (with *in* or *out*) move in a group **atomic pile** nuclear reactor
pile[2] *noun* beam driven into the ground, esp. as foundation for building in water or wet ground > **pile driver** *noun* 1 machine for driving down piles 2 person who operates this machine
pile[3] *noun* 1 nap of cloth, esp. of velvet, carpet, etc. 2 down
piles [pīlz] *plural noun* tumors of veins of rectum, hemorrhoids
pil•fer [PIL-fər] *verb* steal in small quantities > **pil'fer•age** [-ij] *noun* > **pil'fer•er** *noun*
pil'grim *noun* 1 one who journeys to sacred place 2 wanderer, wayfarer > **pil'grim•age** [-ij] *noun*
pill *noun* 1 small ball of medicine swallowed whole 2 anything disagreeable that has to be endured **the pill** oral contraceptive > **pill'box** *noun* 1 small box for pills 2 small concrete fort
pil•lage [PIL-ij] *verb* **-laged, -lag•ing** 1 plunder,

DICTIONARY

P

THESAURUS

piebald *adjective* PIED, black and white, brindled, dappled, flecked, mottled, speckled, spotted
piece *noun* 1 BIT, chunk, fragment, morsel, part, portion, quantity, segment, slice
2 WORK, article, composition, creation, item, study, work of art
piecemeal *adverb* BIT BY BIT, by degrees, gradually, little by little
pier *noun* 1 JETTY, landing place, promenade, quay, wharf
2 PILLAR, buttress, column, pile, post, support, upright
pierce *verb* PENETRATE, bore, drill, enter, perforate, prick, puncture, spike, stab, stick into
piercing *adjective* 1 (*sound*) PENETRATING, ear-splitting, high-pitched, loud, sharp, shrill
2 KEEN, alert, penetrating, perceptive, perspicacious, quick-witted, sharp, shrewd
3 (*wind, etc.*) COLD, arctic, biting, bitter, freezing, nippy, wintry
4 SHARP, acute, agonizing, excruciating, intense, painful, severe, stabbing
piety *noun* HOLINESS, faith, godliness, piousness, religion, reverence
pig *noun* 1 HOG, boar, porker, sow, swine
2 (*informal*) SLOB (*slang*), boor, brute, glutton, hog (*informal*), swine
pigeonhole *noun* 1 COMPARTMENT, cubbyhole, locker, niche, place, section
▷ *verb* 2 CLASSIFY, categorize, characterize, compartmentalize, label, slot (*informal*)
3 PUT OFF, defer, postpone, shelve
pig-headed *adjective* STUBBORN, contrary, inflexible, mulish, obstinate, self-willed, stiff-necked, unyielding
pigment *noun* COLOR, coloring, dye, paint, stain, tincture, tint
pile[1] *noun* 1 HEAP, accumulation, collection, hoard, mass, mound, mountain, stack
2 (*often plural*)
3 BUILDING, edifice, erection, structure
▷ *verb* 4 COLLECT, accumulate, amass, assemble, gather, heap, hoard, stack
5 CROWD, crush, flock, flood, jam, pack, rush, stream
pile[2] *noun* FOUNDATION, beam, column, pillar, post, support, upright
pile[3] *noun* NAP, down, fiber, fur, hair, plush
pile-up *noun* (*informal*) COLLISION, accident, crash, multiple collision, smash, smash-up (*informal*)
pilfer *verb* STEAL, appropriate, embezzle, filch, lift (*informal*), pinch (*informal*), purloin, swipe (*slang*), take
pilgrim *noun* TRAVELER, wanderer, wayfarer
pilgrimage *noun* JOURNEY, excursion, expedition, mission, tour, trip
pill *noun* 1 TABLET, capsule, pellet
2 ▷ **the pill** ORAL CONTRACEPTIVE
pillage *verb* 1 PLUNDER, despoil, loot, maraud, raid, ransack, ravage, sack
▷ *noun* 2 PLUNDER, marauding, robbery, sack, spoliation

ravage, sack ▷ *noun* 2 seizure of goods, esp. in war 3 plunder

pil•lar [PIL-ər] *noun* 1 slender, upright structure, column 2 prominent supporter

pil•lo•ry [PIL-ə-ree] *noun, plural* **-ries** 1 frame with holes for head and hands in which offender was confined and exposed to public abuse and ridicule ▷ *verb transitive* **-ried, -ry•ing** 2 expose to ridicule and abuse 3 set in pillory

pil•low [PIL-oh] *noun* 1 cushion for the head, esp. in bed ▷ *verb transitive* 2 lay on, or as on, pillow

pi•lot [PĪ-lət] *noun* 1 person qualified to fly an aircraft or spacecraft 2 one qualified to take charge of ship entering or leaving harbor, or where knowledge of local water is needed 3 steersman 4 guide ▷ *adjective* 5 experimental and preliminary ▷ *verb transitive* 6 act as pilot to 7 steer > **pilot light** small auxiliary flame lighting main one in gas appliance, etc.

pi•mi•en•to [pi-MYEN-toh] *noun, plural* **-tos** (fruit of the) sweet red pepper (*also* **pi•men'to**)

pimp *noun* 1 one who solicits for prostitute ▷ *verb intransitive* 2 act as pimp

pim•ple [PIM-pəl] *noun* small pus-filled spot on the skin > **pim'ply** *adjective* **-pli•er, -li•est**

pin *noun* 1 short thin piece of stiff wire with point and head, for fastening 2 wooden or metal peg or rivet ▷ *verb transitive* **pinned, pin•ning** 3 fasten with pin 4 seize and hold fast > **pin'ball** *noun* table game, where small ball is shot through various hazards > **pin money** trivial sum > **pin'point** *verb transitive* mark exactly

pin•a•fore [PIN-ə-for] *noun* 1 child's apron 2 woman's dress with a bib top

pince-nez [PANS-nay] *noun, plural* **pince-nez** eyeglasses kept on nose by spring

pin•cers [PIN-sərz] *plural noun* 1 tool for gripping, composed of two limbs crossed and pivoted 2 claws of lobster, etc. > **pincers movement** military maneuver in which both flanks of a force are attacked simultaneously

pinch *verb transitive* 1 nip, squeeze 2 stint 3 (*slang*) steal 4 (*slang*) arrest ▷ *noun* 5 nip 6 as much as can be taken up between finger and thumb 7 stress 8 emergency > **pinch'bar** *noun* crowbar

pine[1] [pīn] *noun* 1 evergreen coniferous tree 2 its wood

pine[2] *verb intransitive* **pined, pin•ing** 1 yearn 2 waste away with grief, etc.

pin•e•al [PIN-ee-əl] *adjective* shaped like pine cone > **pineal gland** small cone-shaped gland situated at base of brain

pine•ap•ple [PĪ-nap-əl] *noun* 1 tropical plant with spiny leaves bearing large edible fruit 2 the fruit 3 (*slang*) a bomb

ping *verb intransitive* 1 produce brief ringing sound 2 of engine, knock

pin•guid [PING-gwid] *adjective* 1 oily 2 fat

pin•ion[1] [PIN-yən] *noun* 1 bird's wing ▷ *verb transitive* 2 disable or confine by binding wings, arms, etc.

pinion[2] *noun* small cogwheel

pink [pingk] *noun* 1 pale red color 2 garden plant 3 best condition, fitness ▷ *adjective* 4 of color pink ▷ *verb transitive* 5 pierce 6 finish edge (of fabric) with perforations or scallops

pin•na•cle [PIN-ə-kəl] *noun* 1 highest pitch or point 2 mountain peak 3 pointed turret on buttress or roof

pint [pīnt] *noun* liquid measure, one eighth of gallon (.568 liter)

pin•tle [PIN-tl] *noun* pivot pin

pin'up *noun* picture of sexually attractive person, esp. (partly) naked

pi•o•neer [pī-ə-NEER] *noun* 1 explorer 2 early settler 3 originator 4 one of advance party preparing road, etc. for troops ▷ *verb intransitive* 5 act as pioneer or leader

pi•ous [PĪ-əs] *adjective* 1 devout 2 righteous

pip[1] *noun* 1 seed in fruit 2 (*informal*) something or someone outstanding

pip[2] *noun* 1 spot on playing cards, dice, or dominoes 2 (*informal*) metal insigne on officer's shoulder showing rank

pip[3] *noun* disease of poultry

DICTIONARY • THESAURUS

pillar *noun* 1 SUPPORT, column, pier, post, prop, shaft, stanchion, upright
2 SUPPORTER, follower, mainstay, upholder

pillory *verb* RIDICULE, brand, denounce, stigmatize

pilot *noun* 1 AIRMAN, aviator, flyer
2 HELMSMAN, navigator, steersman
▷ *adjective* 3 TRIAL, experimental, model, test
▷ *verb* 4 FLY, conduct, direct, drive, guide, handle, navigate, operate, steer

pimple *noun* SPOT, boil, pustule, zit (*slang*)

pin *verb* 1 FASTEN, affix, attach, fix, join, secure
2 HOLD FAST, fix, hold down, immobilize, pinion

pinch *verb* 1 SQUEEZE, compress, grasp, nip, press
2 HURT, cramp, crush, pain
3 (*informal*) STEAL, filch, lift (*informal*), pilfer, purloin, swipe (*slang*)
▷ *noun* 4 SQUEEZE, nip
5 DASH, bit, jot, mite, soupçon (*French*), speck
6 HARDSHIP, crisis, difficulty, emergency, necessity, plight, predicament, strait

pinched *adjective* THIN, drawn, gaunt, haggard, peaky, worn

pin down *verb* 1 FORCE, compel, constrain, make, press, pressurize
2 DETERMINE, identify, locate, name, pinpoint, specify

pine *verb* 1 (*often with for*) LONG, ache, crave, desire, eat one's heart out over, hanker, hunger for, thirst for, wish for, yearn for
2 WASTE, decline, fade, languish, sicken

pinion *verb* IMMOBILIZE, bind, chain, fasten, fetter, manacle, shackle, tie

pink[1] *adjective* ROSY, flushed, reddish, rose, roseate, salmon

pinnacle *noun* PEAK, apex, crest, crown, height, summit, top, vertex, zenith

pinpoint *verb* IDENTIFY, define, distinguish, locate

pioneer *noun* 1 SETTLER, colonist, explorer
2 FOUNDER, developer, innovator, leader, trailblazer
▷ *verb* 3 DEVELOP, create, discover, establish, initiate, instigate, institute, invent, originate, show the way, start

pious *adjective* RELIGIOUS, devout, God-fearing,

pipe [pīp] *noun* 1 tube of metal or other material 2 tube with small bowl at end for smoking tobacco 3 musical instrument, whistle ▷ *verb* **piped, pip•ing** 4 play on pipe 5 utter in shrill tone 6 convey by pipe 7 ornament with a piping or fancy edging > **pipes** *plural noun* bagpipes > **pip'er** *noun* player on pipe or bagpipes > **piping** *noun* 1 system of pipes 2 fancy edging or trimming on clothes 3 act or art of playing on pipe, esp. bagpipes > **pipe down** (*informal*) 1 stop making noise 2 stop talking > **pipe dream** fanciful, impossible plan, etc. > **pipe'line** *noun* 1 long pipe for transporting oil, water, etc. 2 means of communications > **pipe up** (*informal*) 1 assert oneself by speaking 2 speak louder **in the pipeline** 3 yet to come 4 in process of completion, etc.

pi•pette [pī-PET] *noun* slender glass tube to transfer fluids from one vessel to another

pip'pin *noun* kind of apple

pi•quant [PEE-kənt] *adjective* 1 pungent 2 stimulating > **pi'quan•cy** *noun*

pique [peek] *noun* 1 feeling of injury, baffled curiosity or resentment ▷ *verb transitive* **piqued, piqu•ing** 2 hurt pride of 3 irritate 4 stimulate

pi•qué [pi-KAY] *noun* stiff ribbed cotton fabric

pi•ra•nha [pi-RAHN-yə] *noun, plural* **-nhas** small voracious freshwater fish of tropical Amer.

pi•rate [PI-rət] *noun* 1 sea robber 2 publisher, etc., who infringes copyright ▷ *noun, adjective* 3 (person) broadcasting illegally ▷ *verb transitive* **-rat•ed, -rat•ing** 4 use or reproduce (artistic work, etc.) illicitly > **pi'ra•cy** [-see] *noun, plural* **-cies**

pir•ou•ette [pir-oo-ET] *noun* 1 spinning around on the toe ▷ *verb intransitive* **-et•ted, -et•ting** 2 do this

pissed [pist] *adjective* (*slang*) angry, annoyed, or disappointed

pis•tach•i•o [pi-STASH-ee-oh] *noun, plural* **-i•os** 1 small hard-shelled, sweet-tasting nut 2 tree producing it

pis•til [PIS-tl] *noun* seed-bearing organ of flower

pis•tol [PIS-tl] *noun* 1 small firearm for one hand ▷ *verb transitive* **-toled, -tol•ing** 2 shoot with pistol

pis•ton [PIS-tən] *noun* in internal combustion engine, steam engine, etc., cylindrical part propelled to and fro in hollow cylinder by pressure of gas, etc. to convert reciprocating motion to rotation

pit *noun* 1 deep hole in ground 2 mine or its shaft 3 depression 4 enclosure where cocks are set to fight 5 servicing, refueling area on automobile racetrack ▷ *verb transitive* **pit•ted, pit•ting** 6 set to fight, match 7 mark with small dents or scars > **pit'fall** *noun* 1 any hidden danger 2 covered pit for trapping animals or people

pitch[1] [pich] *verb transitive* 1 cast or throw 2 set up 3 set the key of (a tune) ▷ *verb intransitive* 4 fall headlong 5 of ship, plunge lengthwise ▷ *noun* 6 act of pitching 7 degree, height, intensity 8 slope 9 distance propeller advances during one revolution 10 distance between threads of screw, teeth of saw, etc. 11 acuteness of tone 12 *baseball* ball delivered by pitcher to batter 13 (*informal*) persuasive sales talk > **pitch'er** *noun baseball* player who delivers ball to batter > **pitch'fork** *noun* 1 fork for lifting hay, etc. ▷ *verb transitive* 2 throw with, as with, pitchfork > **pitch'out** *noun baseball* pitch thrown intentionally beyond batter's reach to improve catcher's chance of putting out base runner attempting to steal

pitch[2] *noun* 1 dark sticky substance obtained from tar or turpentine ▷ *verb transitive* 2 coat with this > **pitch'y** *adjective* **pitch•i•er, pitch•i•est** 1 covered with pitch 2 black as pitch > **pitch-black, pitch-dark** *adjective* very dark

pitch•blende [PICH-blend] *noun* mineral composed largely of uranium oxide, yielding radium

---

godly, holy, reverent, righteous, saintly

pipe *noun* 1 TUBE, conduit, duct, hose, line, main, passage, pipeline
▷ *verb* 2 WHISTLE, cheep, peep, play, sing, sound, warble
3 CONVEY, channel, conduct

pipe down *verb* (*informal*) BE QUIET, hold one's tongue, hush, quieten down, shush, shut one's mouth, shut up (*informal*)

pipeline *noun* TUBE, conduit, duct, passage, pipe

piquant *adjective* 1 SPICY, biting, pungent, savory, sharp, tangy, tart, zesty
2 INTERESTING, lively, provocative, scintillating, sparkling, stimulating

pique *noun* 1 RESENTMENT, annoyance, displeasure, huff, hurt feelings, irritation, offense, umbrage, wounded pride
▷ *verb* 2 DISPLEASE, affront, annoy, get (*informal*), irk, irritate, nettle, offend, rile, sting
3 AROUSE, excite, rouse, spur, stimulate, stir, whet

piracy *noun* ROBBERY, buccaneering, freebooting, stealing, theft

pirate *noun* 1 BUCCANEER, corsair, freebooter, marauder, raider
2 PLAGIARIST, infringer, plagiarizer
▷ *verb* 3 COPY, appropriate, plagiarize, poach, reproduce, steal

pit *noun* 1 HOLE, abyss, cavity, chasm, crater, dent, depression, hollow
▷ *verb* 2 SCAR, dent, indent, mark, pockmark

pitch *verb* 1 THROW, cast, chuck (*informal*), fling, heave, hurl, lob (*informal*), sling, toss
2 SET UP, erect, put up, raise, settle
3 FALL, dive, drop, topple, tumble
4 TOSS, lurch, plunge, roll
▷ *noun* 5 SPORTS FIELD, field of play, ground, park
6 LEVEL, degree, height, highest point, point, summit
7 SLOPE, angle, dip, gradient, incline, tilt
8 TONE, modulation, sound, timbre
9 SALES TALK, patter, spiel (*informal*)

pitch-black *adjective* JET-BLACK, dark, inky, pitch-dark, unlit

pitch in *verb* HELP, chip in (*informal*), contribute, cooperate, do one's bit, join in, lend a hand, participate

piteous *adjective* PATHETIC, affecting, distressing, harrowing, heartbreaking, heart-rending, moving, pitiable, pitiful, plaintive, poignant, sad

pitch•er [PICH-ər] *noun* 1 large jug 2 *see also* pitch
pith *noun* 1 tissue in stems and branches of certain plants 2 essential substance, most important part > **pith'i•ly** *adverb* > **pith'y** *adjective* **pith•i•er, pith•i•est** 1 terse, cogent, concise 2 consisting of pith
pi•ton [PEE-ton] *noun* metal spike used in mountain climbing
pit•tance [PIT-ns] *noun* 1 small allowance 2 inadequate wages
pi•tu•i•tar•y [pi-TOO-i-ter-ee] *adjective* of, pert. to, the endocrine gland at base of brain
pit•y [PIT-ee] *noun, plural* **pit•ies** 1 sympathy, sorrow for others' suffering 2 regrettable fact ▷ *verb transitive* **pit•ied, pit•y•ing** 3 feel pity for > **pit'e•ous** *adjective* 1 deserving pity 2 sad, wretched > **pit'i•a•ble** *adjective* > **pit'i•ful** [-i-fəl] *adjective* 1 woeful 2 contemptible > **pit'i•less** [-i-lis] *adjective* 1 feeling no pity 2 hard, merciless
piv•ot [PIV-ət] *noun* 1 shaft or pin on which thing turns ▷ *verb transitive* 2 furnish with pivot ▷ *verb intransitive* 3 hinge on one > **piv'ot•al** [-ət-əl] *adjective* 1 of, acting as, pivot 2 of crucial importance
pix•el [PIKS-əl] *noun* any of a number of very small picture elements that make up a picture, as on a visual display unit
pix•ie [PIK-see] *noun* 1 fairy 2 mischievous person
pi•zazz [pə-ZAZ] *noun* (*informal*) sparkle, vitality, glamour
piz•za [PEET-sə] *noun* dish of baked disk of dough covered with cheese and tomato sauce and wide variety of garnishes > **piz•ze•ri'a** [-REE-ə] *noun* place selling pizzas
piz•zi•ca•to [pit-si-KAH-toh] *adjective mus.* played by plucking string of violin, etc., with finger
plac•ard [PLAK-ahrd] *noun* 1 paper or card with notice on one side for posting up or carrying, poster ▷ *verb transitive* 2 post placards on 3 advertise, display on placards
pla•cate [PLAY-klayt] *verb transitive* **-cat•ed, -cat•ing** conciliate, pacify, appease > **pla•ca•to'ry** [-kə-tor-ee] *adjective*
place [plays] *noun* 1 locality, spot 2 position 3 stead 4 duty 5 town, village, residence, buildings 6 office, employment 7 seat, space ▷ *verb transitive* **placed, plac•ing** 8 put in particular place 9 set 10 identify 11 make (order, bet, etc.)
pla•ce•bo [plə-SEE-boh] *noun, plural* **-bos** sugar pill, etc. given to unsuspecting patient as active drug
pla•cen•ta [plə-SEN-tə] *noun, plural* **-tas** 1 organ formed in uterus during pregnancy, providing nutrients for fetus 2 afterbirth
plac•id [PLAS-id] *adjective* 1 calm 2 equable > **pla•cid•i•ty** [plə-SID-i-tee] *noun* mildness, quiet
pla•gia•rism [PLAY-jə-riz-əm] *noun* taking ideas, passages, etc. from an author and presenting them, unacknowledged, as one's own > **pla'gia•rize** [-rīz] *verb* **-rized, -riz•ing** > **pla'gia•rist** *noun*
plague [playg] *noun* 1 highly contagious

DICTIONARY • THESAURUS

pitfall *noun* DANGER, catch, difficulty, drawback, hazard, peril, snag, trap
pith *noun* ESSENCE, core, crux, gist, heart, kernel, nub, point, quintessence, salient point
pithy *adjective* SUCCINCT, brief, cogent, concise, epigrammatic, laconic, pointed, short, terse, to the point, trenchant
pitiful *adjective* 1 PATHETIC, distressing, grievous, harrowing, heartbreaking, heart-rending, piteous, pitiable, sad, wretched
2 CONTEMPTIBLE, abject, base, lousy (*slang*), low, mean, miserable, paltry, shabby, sorry
pitiless *adjective* MERCILESS, callous, cold-blooded, cold-hearted, cruel, hardhearted, heartless, implacable, relentless, ruthless, unmerciful
pittance *noun* PEANUTS (*slang*), chicken feed (*slang*), drop, mite, slave wages, trifle
pity *noun* 1 COMPASSION, charity, clemency, fellow feeling, forbearance, kindness, mercy, sympathy
2 SHAME, bummer (*slang*), crying shame, misfortune, sin
▷ *verb* 3 FEEL SORRY FOR, bleed for, feel for, grieve for, have compassion for, sympathize with, weep for
pivot *noun* 1 AXIS, axle, fulcrum, spindle, swivel
2 HUB, center, heart, hinge, kingpin
▷ *verb* 3 TURN, revolve, rotate, spin, swivel, twirl
4 RELY, be contingent, depend, hang, hinge
pivotal *adjective* CRUCIAL, central, critical, decisive, vital
pixie *noun* ELF, brownie, fairy, sprite
placard *noun* NOTICE, advertisement, bill, poster
placate *verb* CALM, appease, assuage, conciliate, humor, mollify, pacify, propitiate, soothe
place *noun* 1 SPOT, area, location, point, position, site, venue, whereabouts
2 REGION, district, locale, locality, neighborhood, quarter, vicinity
3 POSITION, grade, rank, station, status
4 SPACE, accommodation, room
5 HOME, abode, domicile, dwelling, house, pad (*slang, dated*), property, residence
6 DUTY, affair, charge, concern, function, prerogative, responsibility, right, role
7 JOB, appointment, employment, position, post
8 ▷ **take place** HAPPEN, come about, go on, occur, transpire (*informal*)
▷ *verb* 9 PUT, deposit, install, lay, locate, position, rest, set, situate, stand, station, stick (*informal*)
10 CLASSIFY, arrange, class, grade, group, order, rank, sort
11 IDENTIFY, know, put one's finger on, recognize, remember
12 ASSIGN, allocate, appoint, charge, entrust, give
placid *adjective* CALM, collected, composed, equable, even-tempered, imperturbable, serene, tranquil, unexcitable, unruffled, untroubled
plagiarism *noun* COPYING, borrowing, infringement, piracy, theft
plagiarize *verb* COPY, borrow, lift (*informal*), pirate, steal
plague *noun* 1 DISEASE, epidemic, infection, pestilence

disease, esp. bubonic plague 2 nuisance 3 affliction ▷ *verb transitive* **plagued, pla•guing** 4 trouble, annoy

plaid [plad] *noun* 1 checked or tartan pattern 2 fabric made of this

plain [playn] *adjective* **-er, -est** 1 flat, level 2 unobstructed, not intricate 3 clear, obvious 4 easily understood 5 simple 6 ordinary 7 without decoration 8 not beautiful ▷ *noun* 9 tract of level country ▷ *adverb* 10 clearly > **plain'ly** [-lee] *adverb* > **plain'ness** [-nis] *noun* > **plain clothes** civilian dress, as opposed to uniform > **plain dealing** directness and honesty in transactions > **plain sailing** unobstructed course of action > **plain speaking** frankness, candor

plain•tiff [PLAYN-tif] *noun law* one who sues in court

plain•tive [PLAYN-tiv] *adjective* sad, mournful, melancholy

plait [playt] *noun* 1 braid of hair, straw, etc. ▷ *verb transitive* 2 form or weave into braids

plan *noun* 1 scheme 2 way of proceeding 3 project, design 4 drawing of horizontal section 5 diagram, map ▷ *verb transitive* **planned, plan•ning** 6 make plan of 7 arrange beforehand

planch•et [PLAN-chit] *noun* 1 flat sheet of metal 2 disk of metal from which coin is stamped

plan•chette [plan-SHET] *noun* small board used in spiritualism

plane[1] [playn] *noun* 1 smooth surface 2 a level 3 carpenter's tool for smoothing wood ▷ *verb transitive* **planed, plan•ing** 4 make smooth with one ▷ *adjective* 5 perfectly flat or level > **plan'er** *noun* planing machine

plane[2] *verb* **planed, plan•ing** 1 of airplane, glide 2 of boat, rise and partly skim over water ▷ *noun* 3 wing of airplane 4 airplane

plan•et [PLAN-it] *noun* heavenly body revolving around the sun > **plan'e•tar•y** [-i-ter-ee] *adjective* of, like, planets

plan•e•tar•i•um [plan-i-TAIR-ee-əm] *noun* 1 an apparatus that shows the movement of sun, moon, stars and planets by projecting lights on the inside of a dome 2 building in which the apparatus is housed

plan•gent [PLAN-jənt] *adjective* resounding

plank [plangk] *noun* 1 long flat piece of sawn timber ▷ *verb transitive* 2 cover with planks

plank•ton [PLANGK-tən] *noun* minute animal and vegetable organisms floating in ocean

plant *noun* 1 living organism feeding on inorganic substances and without power of locomotion 2 such an organism that is smaller than tree or shrub 3 equipment or machinery needed for manufacture 4 building and equipment for manufacturing purposes 5 complete equipment used for heating, air conditioning, etc. ▷ *verb transitive* 6 set in ground, to grow 7 support, establish 8 stock with plants 9 (*slang*) hide, esp. to deceive or observe > **plant'er** *noun* 1 one who plants 2 ornamental pot or stand for house plants

plan•tain[1] [PLAN-tin] *noun* low-growing weed with broad leaves

plantain[2] *noun* 1 tropical plant like banana 2 its fruit

plan•ta•tion [plan-TAY-shən] *noun* 1 estate or large farm for cultivation of tobacco, cotton, etc. 2 wood of planted trees 3 formerly, colony

plaque [plak] *noun* 1 ornamental plate, tablet 2 plate of clasp or brooch 3 filmy deposit on surfaces of teeth, conducive to decay

plas•ma [PLAZ-mə] *noun* clear, fluid portion of blood

plas•ter [PLAS-tər] *noun* 1 mixture of lime, sand, etc. for coating walls, etc. 2 piece of fabric spread with medicinal or adhesive substance ▷ *verb transitive* 3 apply plaster to 4 apply like plaster 5 (*informal*) defeat soundly > **plas'tered** *adjective* (*slang*) drunk

plas•tic [PLAS-tik] *noun* 1 any of a group of

DICTIONARY

P

THESAURUS

2 AFFLICTION, bane, blight, curse, evil, scourge, torment
▷ *verb* 3 PESTER, annoy, badger, bother, harass, harry, hassle (*informal*), tease, torment, torture, trouble, vex

plain *adjective* 1 CLEAR, comprehensible, distinct, evident, manifest, obvious, overt, patent, unambiguous, understandable, unmistakable, visible
2 HONEST, blunt, candid, direct, downright, forthright, frank, open, outspoken, straightforward, upfront (*informal*)
3 UNADORNED, austere, bare, basic, severe, simple, Spartan, stark, unembellished, unfussy, unornamented
4 UGLY, dumpy (*informal*), frowzy, homely (*United States*), ill-favored, no oil painting (*informal*), not beautiful, unattractive, unlovely, unprepossessing
5 ORDINARY, common, commonplace, everyday, simple, unaffected, unpretentious
▷ *noun* 6 FLATLAND, grassland, plateau, prairie, steppe, veld

plain-spoken *adjective* BLUNT, candid, direct, downright, forthright, frank, outspoken

plaintive *adjective* SORROWFUL, heart-rending, mournful, pathetic, piteous, pitiful, sad

plan *noun* 1 SCHEME, design, method, plot, program, proposal, strategy, suggestion, system
2 DIAGRAM, blueprint, chart, drawing, layout, map, representation, road map, sketch
▷ *verb* 3 DEVISE, arrange, contrive, design, draft, formulate, organize, outline, plot, scheme, think out
4 INTEND, aim, mean, propose, purpose

plane *noun* 1 AIRPLANE, aircraft, jet
2 FLAT SURFACE, level surface
3 LEVEL, condition, degree, position
▷ *adjective* 4 LEVEL, even, flat, horizontal, regular, smooth
▷ *verb* 5 SKIM, glide, sail, skate

plant *noun* 1 VEGETABLE, bush, flower, herb, shrub, weed
2 FACTORY, foundry, mill, shop, works, yard
3 MACHINERY, apparatus, equipment, gear
▷ *verb* 4 SOW, put in the ground, scatter, seed, transplant
5 PLACE, establish, fix, found, insert, put, set

plaster *noun* 1 MORTAR, gypsum, plaster of Paris, stucco
2 BANDAGE, adhesive plaster, dressing, Elastoplast ®, sticking plaster

synthetic products derived from casein, cellulose, etc. that can be readily molded into any form and are extremely durable ▷ *adjective* 2 made of plastic 3 easily molded, pliant 4 capable of being molded 5 produced by molding > **plas•tic•i•ty** [pla-STIS-i-tee] *noun* ability to be molded > **plastic surgery** repair or reconstruction of missing or malformed parts of the body for medical or cosmetic reasons

plate [playt] *noun* 1 shallow round dish 2 flat thin sheet of metal, glass, etc. 3 household utensils of gold or silver 4 device for printing 5 illustration in book 6 set of false teeth, part of this that adheres to roof of mouth ▷ *verb transitive* **plat•ed, plat•ing** 7 cover with thin coating of gold, silver, or other metal > **plate'ful** [-fəl] *noun, plural* **-fuls** > **plat'er** *noun* 1 person who plates 2 inferior race horse > **plate glass** kind of thick glass used for mirrors, windows, etc. > **plate tec•ton'ics** *geology* study of structure of Earth's crust, esp. movement of layers of rocks

pla•teau [pla-TOH] *noun, plural* **-teaus** [-TOHZ] 1 tract of level high land, tableland 2 period of stability

plat•en [PLAT-n] *noun printing* 1 plate by which paper is pressed against type 2 roller in typewriter

plat•form *noun* 1 raised level surface or floor, stage 2 raised area in station from which passengers board trains 3 political program

plat•i•num [PLAT-n-əm] *noun* white heavy malleable metal

plat•i•tude [PLAT-i-tood] *noun* commonplace remark > **plat•i•tu'di•nous** *adjective*

Pla•ton•ic [plə-TON-ik] *adjective* 1 of Plato or his philosophy 2 (**pla•ton•ic**) (of love) purely spiritual, friendly

pla•toon [plə-TOON] *noun* two or more squads of soldiers employed as unit

plat•ter [PLAT-ər] *noun* flat dish

plat•y•pus [PLAT-i-pəs] *noun, plural* **-pus•es** small Australian egg-laying amphibious mammal, with dense fur, webbed feet and ducklike bill (*also* **duckbilled platypus**)

plau•dit [PLAW-dit] *noun* act of applause, handclapping

plau•si•ble [PLAW-zə-bəl] *adjective* 1 apparently fair or reasonable 2 fair-spoken > **plau•si•bil'i•ty** *noun*

play *verb intransitive* 1 amuse oneself 2 take part in game 3 behave carelessly 4 act a part on the stage 5 perform on musical instrument 6 move with light or irregular motion, flicker, etc. ▷ *verb transitive* 7 contend with in game 8 take part in (game) 9 trifle 10 act the part of 11 perform (music) 12 perform on (instrument) 13 use, work (instrument) ▷ *noun* 14 dramatic piece or performance 15 sport 16 amusement 17 manner of action or conduct 18 activity 19 brisk or free movement 20 gambling > **play'boy** *noun* rich man who lives only for pleasure > **play'ful** [-fəl] *adjective* lively > **play'group** [-groop] *noun* group of young children playing regularly under adult supervision > **play'house** *noun* 1 theater 2 small house for children to play in > **playing card** one of set of usu. 52 cards used in card games > **playing field** extensive piece of ground for open-air games > **play'thing** *noun* toy > **play'wright** [-rīt] *noun* author of

DICTIONARY • THESAURUS

▷ *verb* 3 COVER, coat, daub, overlay, smear, spread

plastic *adjective* 1 MANAGEABLE, docile, malleable, pliable, receptive, responsive, tractable
2 PLIANT, ductile, flexible, moldable, pliable, soft, supple

plate *noun* 1 PLATTER, dish, trencher (*archaic*)
2 HELPING, course, dish, portion, serving
3 LAYER, panel, sheet, slab
4 ILLUSTRATION, lithograph, print
▷ *verb* 5 COAT, cover, gild, laminate, overlay

plateau *noun* 1 UPLAND, highland, table, tableland
2 LEVELLING OFF, level, stability, stage

platform *noun* 1 STAGE, dais, podium, rostrum, stand
2 POLICY, manifesto, objective *or* objectives, party line, principle, program

platitude *noun* CLICHÉ, banality, commonplace, truism

platoon *noun* SQUAD, company, group, outfit (*informal*), patrol, squadron, team

platter *noun* PLATE, dish, salver, tray, trencher (*archaic*)

plaudits *plural noun* APPROVAL, acclaim, acclamation, applause, approbation, praise

plausible *adjective* 1 REASONABLE, believable, conceivable, credible, likely, persuasive, possible, probable, tenable
2 GLIB, smooth, smooth-talking, smooth-tongued, specious

play *verb* 1 AMUSE ONESELF, entertain oneself, fool, have fun, revel, romp, sport, trifle
2 COMPETE, challenge, contend against, participate, take on, take part
3 ACT, act the part of, perform, portray, represent
▷ *noun* 4 DRAMA, comedy, dramatic piece, farce, pantomime, piece, show, stage show, tragedy
5 AMUSEMENT, diversion, entertainment, fun, game, pastime, recreation, sport
6 FUN, humor, jest, joking, lark (*informal*), prank, sport
7 SPACE, elbowroom, latitude, leeway, margin, room, scope

playboy *noun* WOMANIZER, ladies' man, philanderer, rake, roué

play down *verb* MINIMIZE, gloss over, make light of, make little of, underplay, underrate

player *noun* 1 SPORTSMAN *or* SPORTSWOMAN, competitor, contestant, participant
2 MUSICIAN, artist, instrumentalist, performer, virtuoso
3 PERFORMER, actor *or* actress, entertainer, Thespian, trouper

playful *adjective* LIVELY, frisky, impish, merry, mischievous, spirited, sportive, sprightly, vivacious

playmate *noun* FRIEND, chum (*informal*), companion, comrade, pal (*informal*), playfellow

play on, play upon *verb* TAKE ADVANTAGE OF, abuse, capitalize on, exploit, impose on, trade on

plays
pla•za [PLAH-zə] *noun* 1 open space or square 2 complex of retail stores, etc.
plea [plee] *noun* 1 entreaty 2 statement of prisoner or defendant 3 excuse > **plead** *verb* **plead•ed** *or* **pled, plead•ing** 1 make earnest appeal 2 address court of law 3 bring forward as excuse or plea > **plea bargaining** procedure in which defendant agrees to plead guilty in return for leniency in sentencing, etc.
please [pleez] *verb transitive* **pleased, pleas•ing** 1 be agreeable to 2 gratify 3 delight ▷ *verb intransitive* **pleased, pleas•ing** 4 like 5 be willing ▷ *adverb* 6 word of request > **pleas'ant** [PLEZ-ənt] *adjective* pleasing, agreeable > **pleas'ant•ry** [-ən-tree] *noun, plural* **-ries** joke, humor > **pleas•ur•a•ble** [PLEZH-ər-ə-bəl] *adjective* giving pleasure > **pleas'ure** *noun* 1 enjoyment 2 satisfaction, will, choice
pleat [pleet] *noun* 1 any of various types of fold made by doubling material back on itself ▷ *verb intransitive* 2 make, gather into pleats
plebe [pleeb] *noun* at US military and naval academies, member of first-year class
ple•be•ian [pli-BEE-ən] *adjective* 1 belonging to the common people 2 low or rough ▷ *noun* 3 one of the common people
pleb•i•scite [PLEB-ə-sīt] *noun* decision by direct voting of the electorate
plec•trum [PLEK-trəm] *noun, plural* **-trums** small implement for plucking strings of guitar, etc.
pledge [plej] *noun* 1 promise 2 thing given over as security 3 toast ▷ *verb transitive* **pledged, pledg•ing** 4 promise formally 5 bind or secure by pledge 6 give over as security
Pleis•to•cene [PLĪ-stə-seen] *adjective geology* of the glacial period of formation
ple•na•ry [PLEE-nə-ree] *adjective* 1 complete, without limitations, absolute 2 of meeting, etc., with all members present
plen•i•po•ten•ti•ar•y [plen-ə-pə-TEN-shee-er-ee] *adjective, noun* (envoy) having full powers
plen•i•tude [PLEN-i-tood] *noun* completeness, abundance, entirety
plen•ty *noun, plural* **-ties** 1 abundance 2 quite enough > **plen'te•ous** [-tee-əs] *adjective* 1 ample 2 rich 3 copious > **plen'ti•ful** [-ti-fəl] *adjective* abundant
ple•num [PLEE-nəm] *noun, plural* **-nums** 1 space as considered to be full of matter (opposed to vacuum) 2 condition of fullness 3 space above ceiling, etc. for storing heated or cooled air
ple•o•nasm [PLEE-ə-naz-əm] *noun* use of more words than necessary > **ple•o•nas'tic** [-NAS-tik] *adjective* redundant
pleth•o•ra [PLETH-ər-ə] *noun* oversupply > **ple•thor•ic** [ple-THOR-ik] *adjective*
pleu•ri•sy [PLUUR-ə-see] *noun* inflammation of the pleura > **pleura** *noun* membrane lining the chest and covering the lungs
plex•us [PLEK-səs] *noun, plural* **-us•es** network of nerves, or fibers
pli•a•ble [PLĪ-ə-bəl] *adjective* easily bent or influenced > **pli•a•bil'i•ty** *noun* > **pli'an•cy** [-ən-see] *noun* > **pli'ant** *adjective* pliable
pli•ers [PLĪ-ərz] *plural noun* tool with hinged arms and jaws for gripping
plight[1] [plīt] *noun* 1 distressing state 2 predicament
plight[2] *verb transitive* promise, engage oneself to

---

plaything *noun* TOY, amusement, game, pastime, trifle
play up *verb* EMPHASIZE, accentuate, highlight, stress, underline
plea *noun* 1 APPEAL, entreaty, intercession, petition, prayer, request, suit, supplication 2 EXCUSE, defense, explanation, justification
plead *verb* APPEAL, ask, beg, beseech, entreat, implore, petition, request
pleasant *adjective* 1 PLEASING, agreeable, amusing, delightful, enjoyable, fine, lovely, nice, pleasurable 2 NICE, affable, agreeable, amiable, charming, congenial, engaging, friendly, genial, likable *or* likeable
pleasantry *noun* JOKE, badinage, banter, jest, quip, witticism
please *verb* DELIGHT, amuse, entertain, gladden, gratify, humor, indulge, satisfy, suit
pleased *adjective* HAPPY, contented, delighted, euphoric, glad, gratified, over the moon (*informal*), satisfied, thrilled
pleasing *adjective* ENJOYABLE, agreeable, charming, delightful, engaging, gratifying, likable *or* likeable, pleasurable, satisfying
pleasurable *adjective* ENJOYABLE, agreeable, delightful, fun, good, lovely, nice, pleasant
pleasure *noun* HAPPINESS, amusement, bliss, delectation, delight, enjoyment, gladness, gratification, joy, satisfaction
plebeian *adjective* 1 COMMON, base, coarse, low, lower-class, proletarian, uncultivated, unrefined, vulgar, working-class ▷ *noun* 2 COMMONER, common man, man in the street, pleb, proletarian
pledge *noun* 1 PROMISE, assurance, covenant, oath, undertaking, vow, warrant, word 2 GUARANTEE, bail, collateral, deposit, pawn, security, surety ▷ *verb* 3 PROMISE, contract, engage, give one's oath, give one's word, swear, vow
plentiful *adjective* ABUNDANT, ample, bountiful, copious, generous, lavish, liberal, overflowing, plenteous, profuse
plenty *noun* 1 LOTS (*informal*), abundance, enough, great deal, heap *or* heaps (*informal*), masses, pile *or* piles (*informal*), plethora, quantity, stack *or* stacks 2 ABUNDANCE, affluence, copiousness, fertility, fruitfulness, plenitude, profusion, prosperity, wealth
plethora *noun* EXCESS, glut, overabundance, profusion, superabundance, surfeit, surplus
pliable *adjective* 1 FLEXIBLE, bendable, bendy, malleable, plastic, pliant, supple 2 IMPRESSIONABLE, adaptable, compliant, docile, easily led, pliant, receptive, responsive, susceptible, tractable
pliant *adjective* 1 FLEXIBLE, bendable, bendy, plastic, pliable, supple 2 IMPRESSIONABLE, biddable, compliant, easily led, pliable, susceptible, tractable
plight[1] *noun* DIFFICULTY, condition, jam (*informal*), predicament, scrape (*informal*),

Plim•soll line [PLIM-səl] mark on ships indicating maximum displacement permitted when loaded
Pli•o•cene [PLĪ-ə-seen] *noun geology* the most recent tertiary deposits
plod *verb intransitive* **plod•ded, plod•ding** walk or work doggedly
plop *noun* 1 sound of object falling into water ▷ *verb intransitive* **plopped, plop•ping** 2 fall with, as though with, such a sound 3 make the sound
plot[1] *noun* 1 secret plan, conspiracy 2 essence of story, play, etc. ▷ *verb* **plot•ted, plot•ting** 3 devise secretly 4 mark position of 5 make map of 6 conspire
plot[2] *noun* small piece of land
plov•er [PLUV-ər] *noun* one of various shore birds, typically with round head, straight bill and long pointed wings
plow *noun* 1 implement for turning up soil 2 similar implement for clearing snow, etc. ▷ *verb transitive* 3 turn up with plow, furrow ▷ *verb intransitive* 4 work at slowly > **plow'share** [-shair] *noun* blade of plow **plow under** 1 bury beneath soil by plowing 2 overwhelm
ploy [ploi] *noun* 1 stratagem 2 occupation 3 prank
pluck [pluk] *verb transitive* 1 pull, pick off 2 strip from 3 sound strings of (guitar, etc.) with fingers, plectrum ▷ *noun* 4 courage 5 sudden pull or tug > **pluck'y** *adjective* **pluck•i•er, pluck•i•est** courageous
plug *noun* 1 thing fitting into and filling a hole 2 *electricity* device connecting appliance to electricity supply 3 tobacco pressed hard 4 (*informal*) recommendation, advertisement 5 (*slang*) worn-out horse ▷ *verb transitive* **plugged, plug•ging** 6 stop with plug 7 (*informal*) advertise anything by constant repetition 8 (*slang*) punch 9 (*slang*) shoot **plug away** work hard > **plug in** connect (electrical appliance) with power source by means of plug
plum *noun* 1 stone fruit 2 tree bearing it 3 choicest part, piece, position, etc. 4 dark reddish-purple color ▷ *adjective* 5 choice 6 plum-colored
plumage *see* **plume**
plumb [plum] *noun* 1 ball of lead attached to string used for sounding, finding the perpendicular, etc. ▷ *adjective* 2 perpendicular ▷ *adverb* 3 perpendicularly 4 exactly 5 (*informal*) downright 6 honestly ▷ *verb transitive* 7 set exactly upright 8 find depth of 9 reach, undergo 10 equip with, connect to plumbing system > **plumb'er** [PLUM-ər] *noun* worker who attends to water and sewage systems > **plumb'ing** *noun* 1 trade of plumber 2 system of water and sewage pipes > **plumb'line** *noun* cord with plumb attached
plume [ploom] *noun* 1 feather 2 ornament of feathers, etc. ▷ *verb transitive* **plumed, plum•ing** 3 furnish with plumes 4 pride oneself > **plum•age** [PLOO-mij] *noun* bird's feathers collectively
plum•met [PLUM-it] *verb intransitive* 1 plunge headlong ▷ *noun* 2 plumbline
plump[1] *adjective* **-er, -est** 1 of rounded form, moderately fat, chubby ▷ *verb* 2 make, become plump
plump[2] *verb intransitive* 1 sit, fall abruptly 2 (with *for*) support enthusiastically ▷ *verb transitive* 3 drop, throw abruptly ▷ *adverb* 4 suddenly 5 heavily 6 directly
plun•der [PLUN-dər] *verb transitive* 1 take by force 2 rob systematically ▷ *verb intransitive* 3 rob ▷ *noun* 4 pillage 5 booty, spoils
plunge [plunj] *verb transitive* **plunged, plung•ing** 1 put forcibly (into) ▷ *verb intransitive* **plunged, plung•ing** 2 throw oneself (into) 3 enter, rush with violence 4 descend very suddenly ▷ *noun*

situation, spot (*informal*), state, trouble
plod *verb* 1 TRUDGE, clump, drag, lumber, tramp, tread
2 SLOG, grind (*informal*), labor, persevere, plow through, soldier on, toil
plot[1] *noun* 1 PLAN, cabal, conspiracy, intrigue, machination, scheme, stratagem
2 STORY, action, narrative, outline, scenario, story line, subject, theme
▷ *verb* 3 PLAN, collude, conspire, contrive, intrigue, machinate, maneuver, scheme
4 DEVISE, conceive, concoct, contrive, cook up (*informal*), design, hatch, lay
5 CHART, calculate, locate, map, mark, outline
plot[2] *noun* PATCH, allotment, area, ground, lot, parcel, tract
plow *verb* 1 TURN OVER, cultivate, dig, till
2 (*usually with through*) FORCE, cut, drive, plunge, press, push, wade
ploy *noun* TACTIC, device, dodge, maneuver, move, ruse, scheme, stratagem, trick, wile
pluck *verb* 1 PULL OUT *or* PULL OFF, collect, draw, gather, harvest, pick
2 TUG, catch, clutch, jerk, pull at, snatch, tweak, yank
3 STRUM, finger, pick, twang
▷ *noun* 4 COURAGE, backbone, boldness, bravery, grit, guts (*informal*), nerve
plucky *adjective* COURAGEOUS, bold, brave, daring, game, gutsy (*slang*), intrepid
plug *noun* 1 STOPPER, bung, cork, spigot
2 (*informal*) MENTION, advertisement, hype, publicity, push
▷ *verb* 3 SEAL, block, bung, close, cork, fill, pack, stop, stopper, stop up, stuff
4 (*informal*) MENTION, advertise, build up, hype, promote, publicize, push
5 ▷ **plug away**
plum *adjective* CHOICE, best, first-class, prize
plumb *verb* 1 DELVE, explore, fathom, gauge, go into, penetrate, probe, unravel
▷ *noun* 2 WEIGHT, lead, plumb bob, plummet
▷ *adverb* 3 EXACTLY, bang, precisely, slap
plume *noun* FEATHER, crest, pinion, quill
plummet *verb* PLUNGE, crash, descend, dive, drop down, fall, nose-dive, tumble
plump[1] *adjective* CHUBBY, corpulent, dumpy, fat, roly-poly, rotund, round, stout, tubby
plunder *verb* 1 LOOT, pillage, raid, ransack, rifle, rob, sack, strip
▷ *noun* 2 LOOT, booty, ill-gotten gains, pillage, prize, spoils, swag (*slang*)
plunge *verb* 1 THROW, cast, pitch
2 HURTLE, career, charge, dash, jump, rush, tear
3 DESCEND, dip, dive, drop, fall, nose-dive, plummet, sink, tumble

5 dive > **plung'er** *noun* rubber suction cap with handle to unblock drains **take the plunge** (*informal*) 1 embark on risky enterprise 2 get married
plunk *verb* 1 pluck (string of banjo, etc.) 2 drop, fall suddenly and heavily ▷ *noun*
plu•ral [PLUUR-əl] *adjective* 1 of, denoting more than one person or thing ▷ *noun* 2 word in its plural form > **plu'ral•ism** *noun* 1 holding of more than one office at a time 2 coexistence of different social groups, etc., in one society > **plu•ral'i•ty** *noun, plural* **-ties** 1 of three or more candidates, etc. 2 largest share of votes
plus *preposition* 1 with addition of ▷ *adjective* 2 to be added 3 positive ▷ *noun* 4 sign (+) denoting addition 5 advantage
plush *noun* 1 fabric with long nap, long-piled velvet ▷ *adjective* **-er, -est** 2 luxurious
Plu•to [PLOO-toh] *noun* 1 Greek god of the underworld 2 farthest planet from the sun
plu•toc•ra•cy [ploo-TOK-rə-see] *noun, plural* **-cies** 1 government by the rich 2 state ruled thus 3 wealthy class > **plu'to•crat** [-tə-krat] *noun* wealthy person
plu•to•ni•um [ploo-TOH-nee-əm] *noun* radioactive metallic element used esp. in nuclear reactors and weapons
ply[1] [plī] *verb* **plied, ply•ing** 1 wield 2 work at 3 supply pressingly 4 urge 5 keep busy 6 go to and fro, run regularly
ply[2] *noun* 1 fold or thickness 2 strand of yarn > **ply'wood** [-wuud] *noun* board of thin layers of wood glued together with grains at right angles
Pm *chem.* promethium
pneu•mat•ic [nuu-MAT-ik] *adjective* of, worked by, inflated with wind or air
pneu•mo•nia [nuu-MOHN-yə] *noun* inflammation of the lungs
Po *chem.* polonium
poach[1] [pohch] *verb transitive* 1 take (game) illegally 2 trample, make swampy or soft ▷ *verb intransitive* 3 trespass for this purpose 4 encroach > **poach'er** *noun*
poach[2] *verb transitive* simmer (eggs, fish, etc.) gently in water, etc. > **poach'er** *noun*
pock [pok] *noun* pustule, as in smallpox, etc. > **pock'marked** *adjective*
pock•et [POK-it] *noun* 1 small bag inserted in garment 2 cavity filled with ore, etc. 3 socket, cavity, pouch or hollow 4 mass of water or air differing from that surrounding it 5 isolated group or area ▷ *verb transitive* 6 put into one's pocket 7 appropriate, steal ▷ *adjective* 8 small > **pocket money** 1 small, regular allowance given to children by parents 2 allowance for small, occasional expenses > **pocket veto** indirect veto of bill by president, governor, who retains bill unsigned until legislative adjournment
pod *noun* 1 long seed vessel, as of peas, beans, etc. ▷ *verb intransitive* **pod•ded, pod•ding** 2 form pods ▷ *verb transitive* **pod•ded, pod•ding** 3 shell
po•di•um [POH-dee-əm] *noun* small raised platform
po•em [POH-əm] *noun* imaginative composition in rhythmic lines > **po'et** [-it] *noun* writer of poems > **po'et•ry** *noun* art or work of poet, verse > **po'e•sy** [-ə-see] *noun* poetry > **po•et'ic** [-ET-ik] *adjective* > **po•et'i•cal•ly** *adverb* > **po'et•as•ter** [-as-tər] *noun* would-be or inferior poet
po•grom [pə-GRUM] *noun* organized persecution and massacre, esp. of Jews
poign•ant [POIN-yənt] *adjective* 1 moving 2 biting, stinging 3 vivid 4 pungent > **poign'an•cy** *noun, plural* **-cies**
poin•set•ti•a [poin-SET-ee-ə] *noun* orig. American shrub, widely cultivated for its clusters of scarlet leaves, resembling petals
point *noun* 1 dot, mark 2 punctuation mark 3 item, detail 4 unit of value 5 position, degree, stage 6 moment 7 gist of an argument 8 purpose 9 striking or effective part or quality

DICTIONARY

P

THESAURUS

▷ *noun* 4 DIVE, descent, drop, fall, jump
plus *preposition* 1 AND, added to, coupled with, with
▷ *adjective* 2 ADDITIONAL, added, add-on, extra, supplementary
▷ *noun* 3 ADVANTAGE, asset, benefit, bonus, extra, gain, good point
plush *adjective* LUXURIOUS, deluxe, lavish, luxury, opulent, rich, sumptuous
ply[1] *verb* 1 WORK AT, carry on, exercise, follow, practice, pursue
2 USE, employ, handle, manipulate, wield
poach *verb* ENCROACH, appropriate, infringe, intrude, trespass
pocket *noun* 1 POUCH, bag, compartment, receptacle, sack
▷ *verb* 2 STEAL, appropriate, filch, lift (*informal*), pilfer, purloin, take
▷ *adjective* 3 SMALL, abridged, compact, concise, little, miniature, portable
pod *noun, verb* SHELL, hull, husk, shuck
podium *noun* PLATFORM, dais, rostrum, stage
poem *noun* VERSE, lyric, ode, rhyme, song, sonnet
poet *noun* BARD, lyricist, rhymer, versifier
poetic *adjective* LYRICAL, elegiac, lyric, metrical
poetry *noun* VERSE, poems, rhyme, rhyming
poignancy *noun* 1 SADNESS, emotion, feeling, pathos, sentiment, tenderness
2 SHARPNESS, bitterness, intensity, keenness
poignant *adjective* MOVING, bitter, distressing, heart-rending, intense, painful, pathetic, sad, touching
point *noun* 1 ESSENCE, crux, drift, gist, heart, import, meaning, nub, pith, question, subject, thrust
2 AIM, end, goal, intent, intention, motive, object, objective, purpose, reason
3 ITEM, aspect, detail, feature, particular
4 CHARACTERISTIC, aspect, attribute, quality, respect, trait
5 PLACE, location, position, site, spot, stage
6 FULL STOP, dot, mark, period, stop
7 END, apex, prong, sharp end, spike, spur, summit, tip, top
8 HEADLAND, cape, head, promontory
9 STAGE, circumstance, condition, degree, extent, position
10 MOMENT, instant, juncture, time, very minute
11 UNIT, score, tally
▷ *verb* 12 INDICATE, call attention to, denote, designate, direct, show, signify

10 essential object or thing **11** sharp end **12** single unit in scoring **13** headland **14** one of direction marks of compass **15** fine kind of lace **16** act of pointing **17** printing unit, one-twelfth of a pica ▷ *verb intransitive* **18** show direction or position by extending finger **19** direct attention **20** (of dog) indicate position of game by standing facing it ▷ *verb transitive* **21** aim, direct **22** sharpen **23** fill up joints with mortar **24** give value to (words, etc.) > **points** *plural noun* electrical contacts in distributor of engine > **point'ed** *adjective* **1** sharp **2** direct, telling > **point'er** *noun* **1** index **2** indicating rod, etc., used for pointing **3** indication **4** dog trained to point > **point'less** [-lis] *adjective* **1** blunt **2** futile, irrelevant > **point-blank** *adjective* **1** aimed horizontally **2** plain, blunt ▷ *adverb* **3** with level aim (there being no necessity to elevate for distance) **4** at short range

poise [poiz] *noun* **1** composure **2** self-possession **3** balance, equilibrium, carriage (of body, etc.) ▷ *verb* **poised, pois•ing 4** (cause to be) balanced or suspended ▷ *verb transitive* **5** hold in readiness

poi•son [POI-zən] *noun* **1** substance that kills or injures when introduced into living organism ▷ *verb transitive* **2** give poison to **3** infect **4** pervert, spoil > **poi'son•ous** *adjective* > **poison-pen letter** malicious anonymous letter

poke¹ [pohk] *verb transitive* **poked, pok•ing 1** push, thrust with finger, stick, etc. **2** thrust forward ▷ *verb intransitive* **poked, pok•ing 3** make thrusts **4** pry ▷ *noun* **5** act of poking > **pok'er** *noun* metal rod for poking fire > **pok'y** *adjective* **pok•i•er, pok•i•est** small, confined, cramped

poke² *noun* **pig in a poke** something bought, etc. without previous inspection

pok•er [POHK-ər] *noun* card game > **poker face 1** expressionless face **2** person with this

polar *adjective see* **pole²**

Po•lar•oid [POH-lə-roid] *noun* ® **1** type of plastic that polarizes light **2** camera that develops print very quickly inside itself

pole¹ [pohl] *noun* **1** long rounded piece of wood, etc. ▷ *verb transitive* **poled, pol•ing 2** propel with pole

pole² *noun* **1** each of the ends of axis of Earth or celestial sphere **2** each of opposite ends of magnet, electric battery, etc. > **po•lar** [POH-lər] *adjective* **1** pert. to the N and S pole, or to magnetic poles **2** directly opposite in tendency, character, etc. > **po•lar'i•ty** *noun* > **po•lar•i•za'tion** [-ZAY-shən] *noun* > **po'lar•ize** *verb transitive* **-rized, -riz•ing 1** give polarity to **2** affect light in order to restrict vibration of its waves to certain directions > **polar bear** white Arctic bear > **poles apart** having completely opposite interests, etc.

po•lem•ic [pə-LEM-ik] *adjective* **1** controversial ▷ *noun* **2** argument > **po•lem'i•cal** *adjective* > **po•lem'i•cize** [-sīz] *verb transitive* **-cized, -ciz•ing**

po•lice [pə-LEES] *noun* **1** the civil force that maintains public order ▷ *verb transitive* **-liced, -lic•ing 2** keep in order > **police officer** member of police force

pol•i•cy¹ [POL-ə-see] *noun, plural* **-cies 1** course of action adopted, esp. in state affairs **2** prudence

policy² *noun, plural* **-cies** insurance contract

po•li•o [poh-lee-oh] *noun* (*also* **po•li•o•my•e•li•tis**) disease of spinal cord characterized by fever and possibly paralysis

pol'ish *verb transitive* **1** make smooth and glossy

DICTIONARY • THESAURUS

13 AIM, direct, level, train

point-blank *adjective* **1** DIRECT, blunt, downright, explicit, express, plain ▷ *adverb* **2** DIRECTLY, bluntly, candidly, explicitly, forthrightly, frankly, openly, plainly, straight

pointed *adjective* **1** SHARP, acute, barbed, edged **2** CUTTING, acute, biting, incisive, keen, penetrating, pertinent, sharp, telling

pointer *noun* **1** HINT, advice, caution, information, recommendation, suggestion, tip **2** INDICATOR, guide, hand, needle

pointless *adjective* SENSELESS, absurd, aimless, fruitless, futile, inane, irrelevant, meaningless, silly, stupid, useless

point out *verb* MENTION, allude to, bring up, identify, indicate, show, specify

poise *noun* COMPOSURE, aplomb, assurance, calmness, cool (*slang*), dignity, presence, sang-froid, self-possession

poised *adjective* **1** READY, all set, prepared, standing by, waiting **2** COMPOSED, calm, collected, dignified, self-confident, self-possessed, together (*informal*)

poison *noun* **1** TOXIN, bane, venom ▷ *verb* **2** MURDER, give (someone) poison, kill **3** CONTAMINATE, infect, pollute **4** CORRUPT, defile, deprave, pervert, subvert, taint, undermine, warp

poisonous *adjective* **1** TOXIC, deadly, fatal, lethal, mortal, noxious, venomous, virulent **2** EVIL, baleful, corrupting, malicious, noxious, pernicious

poke *verb* **1** JAB, dig, nudge, prod, push, shove, stab, stick, thrust ▷ *noun* **2** JAB, dig, nudge, prod, thrust

poky *adjective* SMALL, confined, cramped, narrow, tiny

pole *noun* ROD, bar, mast, post, shaft, spar, staff, stick

police *noun* **1** THE LAW (*informal*), boys in blue (*informal*), constabulary, fuzz (*slang*), police force ▷ *verb* **2** CONTROL, guard, patrol, protect, regulate, watch

policeman *noun* COP (*slang*), constable, copper (*slang*), fuzz (*slang*), officer

policy *noun* PROCEDURE, action, approach, code, course, custom, plan, practice, rule, scheme

polish *verb* **1** SHINE, brighten, buff, burnish, rub, smooth, wax **2** PERFECT, brush up, enhance, finish, improve, refine, touch up ▷ *noun* **3** VARNISH, wax **4** SHEEN, brightness, finish, glaze, gloss, luster **5** STYLE, breeding, class (*informal*), elegance, finesse, finish, grace, refinement

polished *adjective* **1** ACCOMPLISHED, adept, expert, fine, masterly, professional, skillful, superlative **2** SHINING, bright, burnished, gleaming, glossy, smooth **3** ELEGANT, cultivated, polite, refined, sophisticated, well-bred

2 refine ▷ *noun* 3 shine 4 polishing 5 substance for polishing 6 refinement
po•lite [pə-LĪT] *adjective* **-lit•er, -lit•est** 1 showing regard for others in manners, speech, etc. 2 refined, cultured > **po•lite'ness** *noun* courtesy
pol•i•tic [POL-i-tik] *adjective* wise, shrewd, expedient, cunning > **pol'i•tics** *noun* 1 art of government 2 political affairs or life > **po•lit'i•cal** *adjective* of the state or its affairs > **pol•i•ti'cian** [-TISH-ən] *noun* one engaged in politics > **pol'i•ty** *noun, plural* **-ties** 1 form of government 2 organized state 3 civil government > **politically correct** (esp. of language) intended to avoid any implied prejudice
pol•ka [POHL-kə] *noun, plural* **-kas** 1 lively 19th-century dance 2 music for it > **polka dot** one of pattern of bold spots on fabric, etc.
poll [pohl] *noun* 1 voting 2 counting of votes 3 number of votes recorded 4 canvassing of sample of population to determine general opinion 5 (top of) head ▷ *verb transitive* 6 receive (votes) 7 take votes of 8 lop, shear 9 cut horns from animals ▷ *verb intransitive* 10 vote > **polls** *plural noun* place where votes are cast > **polled** *adjective* hornless > **poll'ster** *noun* one who conducts polls > **poll tax** (esp. formerly) tax on each person
pol•lard [POL-ərd] *noun* 1 hornless animal of normally horned variety 2 tree on which a close head of young branches has been made by polling ▷ *verb transitive* 3 make a pollard of
pol•len [POL-ən] *noun* fertilizing dust of flower > **pol'li•nate** *verb transitive* **-nat•ed, -nat•ing**
pol•lute [pə-LOOT] *verb transitive* **-lut•ed, -lut•ing** 1 make foul 2 corrupt 3 desecrate > **pol•lu'tant** [-tənt] *noun* > **pol•lu'tion** *noun*
po•lo [POH-loh] *noun* game like hockey played by teams of 4 players on horseback **water polo** game played similarly by swimmers seven to a side
pol•o•naise [pol-ə-NAYZ] *noun* 1 Polish dance 2 music for it
pol•ter•geist [POHL-tər-gīst] *noun* noisy mischievous spirit
poly- *combining form* many: *polysyllabic*
pol•y•an•dry [POL-ee-an-dree] *noun* polygamy in which woman has more than one husband > **pol•y•an'drous** *adjective*
pol•y•chrome [POL-ee-krohm] *adjective* 1 many colored ▷ *noun* 2 work of art in many colors > **pol•y•chro•mat'ic** *adjective*
pol•y•es•ter [POL-ee-es-tər] *noun* any of large class of synthetic materials used as plastics, textile fibers, etc.
pol•y•eth•yl•ene [pol-ee-ETH-ə-leen] *noun* tough thermoplastic material
po•lyg•a•my [pə-LIG-ə-mee] *noun* custom of being married to several persons at a time > **po•lyg'a•mist** *noun*
pol•y•glot [POL-ee-glot] *adjective* 1 speaking, writing in several languages ▷ *noun* 2 person who speaks, reads, and writes in many languages
pol•y•gon [POL-ee-gon] *noun* figure with many angles or sides
po•lyg•y•ny [pə-LIJ-ə-nee] *noun* polygamy in which one man has more than one wife
pol•y•he•dron [pol-ee-HEE-drən] *noun* solid figure contained by many faces
pol•y•math [POL-ee-math] *noun* learned person
pol•y•mer [POL-ə-mər] *noun* compound, as polystyrene, that has large molecules formed from repeated units > **po•lym•er•i•za•tion** [pə-lim-ər-ə-ZAY-shən] *noun* > **po•lym'er•ize** [-LIM-ər-īz] *verb transitive* **-ized, -iz•ing**
pol•yp [POL-ip] *noun* 1 sea anemone, or allied animal 2 tumor with branched roots
pol•y•sty•rene [pol-ee-STĪ-reen] *noun* synthetic material used esp. as white rigid foam for packing, etc.
pol•y•tech•nic [pol-ee-TEK-nik] *noun* college dealing mainly with technical subjects ▷ *adjective*
pol•y•the•ism [POL-ee-thee-iz-əm] *noun* belief in many gods > **pol•y•the•is'tic** *adjective*
pol•y•un•sat•u•rat•ed [pol-ee-un-SACH-ə-ray-tid] *adjective* of group of fats that do not form cholesterol in blood
pol•y•u•re•thane [pol-ee-YUUR-ə-thayn] *noun* class of synthetic materials, often in foam or flexible form
po•made [po-MAYD] *noun* scented ointment for hair
po•me•gran•ate [POM-ə-gran-it] *noun* 1 tree 2 its fruit with thick rind containing many seeds in red pulp
pom•mel [PUM-əl] *noun* 1 front of saddle 2 knob of sword hilt ▷ *verb transitive* **-meled, -mel•ing** 3 pummel
pomp *noun* splendid display or ceremony
pom'pom *noun* tuft of ribbon, wool, feathers, etc., decorating hat, shoe, etc.

DICTIONARY **P** THESAURUS

polite *adjective* 1 MANNERLY, civil, complaisant, courteous, gracious, respectful, well-behaved, well-mannered
2 REFINED, civilized, cultured, elegant, genteel, polished, sophisticated, well-bred
politeness *noun* COURTESY, civility, courteousness, decency, etiquette, mannerliness
politic *adjective* WISE, advisable, diplomatic, expedient, judicious, prudent, sensible
political *adjective* GOVERNMENTAL, parliamentary, policy-making
politician *noun* STATESMAN, bureaucrat, congressman, legislator, office bearer, public servant, representative
politics *noun* STATESMANSHIP, affairs of state, civics, government, political science
poll *noun* 1 CANVASS, ballot, census, count, sampling, survey
2 VOTE, figures, returns, tally, voting
▷ *verb* 3 TALLY, register
4 QUESTION, ballot, canvass, interview, sample, survey
pollute *verb* 1 CONTAMINATE, dirty, foul, infect, poison, soil, spoil, stain, taint
2 DEFILE, corrupt, debase, debauch, deprave, desecrate, dishonor, profane, sully
pollution *noun* CONTAMINATION, corruption, defilement, dirtying, foulness, impurity, taint, uncleanness
pomp *noun* 1 CEREMONY, flourish, grandeur, magnificence, pageant, pageantry, splendor, state

pomp•ous [POM-pəs] *adjective* 1 self-important 2 ostentatious 3 of language, inflated, stilted > **pom•pos'i•ty** *noun, plural* **-ties**
pon•cho [PON-choh] *noun, plural* **-chos** loose circular cloak with hole for head
pond *noun* small body, pool or lake of still water
pon•der [PON-dər] *verb* 1 muse, meditate, think over 2 consider, deliberate on
pon•der•ous [PON-dər-əs] *adjective* 1 heavy, unwieldy 2 boring > **pon'der•a•ble** *adjective* able to be evaluated or weighed
pon'tiff *noun* 1 Pope 2 high priest 3 bishop > **pon•tif'i•cal** *adjective* > **pon•tif'i•cate** [-kit] *noun* dignity or office of pontiff > **pon•tif'i•cate** [-kayt] *verb intransitive* **-cat•ed, -cat•ing** 1 speak bombastically 2 act as pontiff
pon•toon' *noun* flat-bottomed boat or metal drum for use in supporting temporary bridge
po•ny [POH-nee] *noun, plural* **-nies** 1 horse of small breed 2 small horse 3 very small glass > **po'ny•tail** *noun* long hair tied in one bunch at back of head
poo•dle [POOD-l] *noun* pet dog with long curly hair often clipped fancifully
pool[1] *noun* 1 small body of still water 2 deep place in river or stream 3 puddle 4 swimming pool
pool[2] *noun* 1 common fund or resources 2 group of people, e.g. typists, any of whom can work for any of several employers 3 collective stakes in various games 4 cartel 5 variety of billiards ▷ *verb transitive* 6 put in common fund
poop[1] *noun* ship's stern
poop[2] *verb transitive* (*slang*) exhaust (someone) **poop out** (*slang*) 1 fail in something 2 cease functioning
poop[3] *noun* (*children's slang*) 1 excrement ▷ *verb intransitive* 2 defecate
poop[4] *noun* (*slang*) pertinent information
poor [puur] *adjective* **-er, -est** 1 having little money 2 unproductive 3 inadequate, insignificant 4 needy 5 miserable, pitiable 6 feeble 7 not fertile > **poor'ly** *adverb, adjective* not in good health
pop[1] *verb intransitive* **popped, pop•ping** 1 make small explosive sound 2 (*informal*) 3 go or come unexpectedly or suddenly ▷ *verb transitive* **popped, pop•ping** 4 cause to make small explosive sound 5 put or place suddenly ▷ *noun* 6 small explosive sound 7 (*informal*) nonalcoholic soda > **pop'corn** *noun* 1 any kind of corn with kernels that puff up when roasted 2 the roasted product > **pop-up** *adjective* 1 (of an appliance) characterized by or having a mechanism that pops up 2 (of a book) having pages that rise when opened to simulate a three-dimensional form 3 (of a menu on a computer screen, etc.) suddenly appearing when an option is selected ▷ *noun* 4 something that appears over or above the open window on a computer screen > **pop up** to appear suddenly
pop[2] *noun* (*informal*) 1 father 2 old man
pop[3] *noun* 1 music of general appeal, esp. to young people ▷ *adjective* 2 *short for* **popular**
Pope [pohp] *noun* bishop of Rome and head of R.C. Church
pop•lar [POP-lər] *noun* tree noted for its slender tallness
pop'lin *noun* corded fabric usu. of cotton
pop•pa•dom [POP-ə-dəm] *noun* thin, round, crisp Indian bread
pop•py [POP-ee] *noun, plural* **-pies** bright-flowered plant yielding opium
pop•u•lace [POP-yə-ləs] *noun* 1 the common people 2 the masses
pop•u•lar [POP-yə-lər] *adjective* 1 finding general favor 2 of, by the people > **pop•u•lar'i•ty** *noun* state or quality of being

DICTIONARY • THESAURUS

2 SHOW, display, grandiosity, ostentation
pomposity *noun* SELF-IMPORTANCE, affectation, airs, grandiosity, pompousness, portentousness, pretension, pretentiousness
pompous *adjective* 1 SELF-IMPORTANT, arrogant, grandiose, ostentatious, pretentious, puffed up, showy
2 GRANDILOQUENT, boastful, bombastic, high-flown, inflated
pond *noun* POOL, duck pond, fish pond, millpond, small lake, tarn
ponder *verb* THINK, brood, cogitate, consider, contemplate, deliberate, meditate, mull over, muse, reflect, ruminate
ponderous *adjective* 1 DULL, heavy, long-winded, pedantic, tedious
2 UNWIELDY, bulky, cumbersome, heavy, huge, massive, weighty
3 CLUMSY, awkward, heavy-footed, lumbering
pontificate *verb* EXPOUND, hold forth, lay down the law, preach, pronounce, sound off
pool[1] *noun* 1 POND, lake, mere, puddle, tarn
2 SWIMMING POOL, swimming bath
pool[2] *noun* 1 SYNDICATE, collective, consortium, group, team, trust
2 KITTY, bank, funds, jackpot, pot
▷ *verb* 3 COMBINE, amalgamate, join forces, league, merge, put together, share
poor *adjective* 1 IMPOVERISHED, broke (*informal*), destitute, down and out, down on one's luck (*informal*), hard up (*informal*), impecunious, indigent, needy, on the breadline, penniless, penurious, poverty-stricken, short
2 INADEQUATE, deficient, incomplete, insufficient, lacking, lousy (*slang*), meager, measly, scant, scanty, skimpy
3 INFERIOR, below par, lousy (*slang*), low-grade, mediocre, rotten (*informal*), rubbishy, second-rate, substandard, unsatisfactory
4 UNFORTUNATE, hapless, ill-fated, luckless, pitiable, unhappy, unlucky, wretched
poorly *adverb* 1 BADLY, inadequately, incompetently, inexpertly, insufficiently, unsatisfactorily, unsuccessfully
pop *verb* 1 BURST, bang, crack, explode, go off, snap
2 PUT, insert, push, shove, slip, stick, thrust, tuck
▷ *noun* 3 BANG, burst, crack, explosion, noise, report
pope *noun* HOLY FATHER, Bishop of Rome, pontiff, Vicar of Christ
populace *noun* PEOPLE, general public, hoi polloi, masses, mob, multitude
popular *adjective* 1 WELL-LIKED, accepted, approved, cool (*informal*), fashionable, favorite, in (*informal*), in demand, in favor, liked, phat (*slang*), sought-after

generally liked > **pop'u•lar•ize** *verb transitive* **-ized, -iz•ing** make popular
pop•u•late [POP-yə-layt] *verb transitive* **-lat•ed, -lat•ing** fill with inhabitants > **pop•u•la'tion** [-LAY-shən] *noun* 1 inhabitants 2 their number > **pop'u•lous** [-ləs] *adjective* thickly populated or inhabited
pop•u•list [POP-yə-list] *adjective* claiming to represent the whole of the people ▷ *noun* > **pop'u•lism** [-liz-əm] *noun*
por•ce•lain [POR-sə-lin] *noun* fine earthenware, china
porch *noun* 1 covered approach to entrance of building 2 veranda
por•cine [POR-sin] *adjective* of, like a pig
por•cu•pine [POR-kyə-pīn] *noun* rodent covered with long, pointed quills
pore[1] [por] *verb intransitive* **pored, por•ing** 1 fix eye or mind upon 2 study closely
pore[2] *noun* minute opening, esp. in skin > **po•ros•i•ty** [pə-ROS-i-tee] *noun* > **por•ous** [POR-əs] *adjective* 1 allowing liquid to soak through 2 full of pores
pork *noun* pig's flesh as food > **pork'er** *noun* pig raised for food > **pork'y** *adjective* **pork•i•er, pork•i•est** fleshy, fat
porn, por'no *noun (informal) short for* pornography
por•nog•ra•phy [por-NOG-rə-fee] *noun* indecent literature, films, etc. > **por•nog'ra•pher** *noun* > **por•no•graph'ic** *adjective*
por•phy•ry [POR-fə-ree] *noun, plural* **-ries** reddish stone with embedded crystals
por•poise [POR-pəs] *noun* blunt-nosed sea mammal like dolphin
por•ridge [POR-ij] *noun* soft food of oatmeal, etc. boiled in water
port[1] *noun* 1 harbor, haven 2 town with harbor
port[2] *noun* 1 larboard or left side of ship ▷ *verb transitive* 2 turn to left side of a ship
port[3] *noun* strong sweet, usu. red, fortified wine from Portugal
port[4] *noun* opening in side of ship > **port'hole** *noun* small opening or window in side of ship
port[5] *verb transitive military* 1 carry rifle, etc. diagonally across body ▷ *noun* 2 this position
port•a•ble [POR-tə-bəl] *noun, adjective* (something) easily carried
por•tage [POR-tij] *noun* (cost of) transport
por•tal [POR-tl] *noun* 1 large doorway or imposing gate 2 *computing* Internet site providing links to other sites > **portal-to-portal pay** payment to worker that includes pay for all time spent on employer's premises
port•cul•lis [port-KUL-is] *noun* defense grating to raise or lower in front of castle gateway
por•tend' *verb transitive* 1 foretell 2 be an omen of > **por'tent** *noun* 1 omen, warning 2 marvel > **por•ten'tous** [-təs] *adjective* 1 ominous 2 threatening 3 pompous
por•ter [POR-tər] *noun* 1 person employed to carry luggage 2 doorkeeper
port•fo•li•o [port-FOH-lee-oh] *noun, plural* **-li•os** 1 flat portable case for loose papers 2 office of minister of state, member of cabinet
por•ti•co [POR-ti-koh] *noun, plural* **-coes** *or* **-cos** 1 colonnade 2 covered walk
por•tiere [por-TYAIR] *noun* heavy door curtain
por•tion [POR-shən] *noun* 1 part, share, helping 2 destiny, lot ▷ *verb transitive* 3 divide into shares
port•ly [PORT lee] *adjective* **-li•er, -li•est** bulky, stout
port•man•teau [port-MAN-toh] *noun, plural* **-teaus** leather suitcase, esp. one opening into two compartments > **portmanteau word** word made by putting together parts of other words, such as *motel* from *motor* and *hotel*

DICTIONARY

P

THESAURUS

2 COMMON, conventional, current, general, prevailing, prevalent, universal
popularity *noun* FAVOR, acceptance, acclaim, approval, currency, esteem, regard, vogue
popularize *verb* MAKE POPULAR, disseminate, give currency to, give mass appeal, make available to all, spread, universalize
popularly *adverb* GENERALLY, commonly, conventionally, customarily, ordinarily, traditionally, universally, usually, widely
populate *verb* INHABIT, colonize, live in, occupy, settle
population *noun* INHABITANTS, community, denizens, folk, natives, people, residents, society
populous *adjective* POPULATED, crowded, heavily populated, overpopulated, packed, swarming, teeming
pore[1] *verb*
▷ **pore over** STUDY, examine, peruse, ponder, read, scrutinize
pore[2] *noun* OPENING, hole, orifice, outlet
pornographic *adjective* OBSCENE, blue, dirty, filthy, indecent, lewd, salacious, scuzzy (*slang*), smutty, X-rated
pornography *noun* OBSCENITY, dirt, filth, indecency, porn (*informal*), smut
porous *adjective* PERMEABLE, absorbent, absorptive, penetrable, spongy
port *noun* HARBOR, anchorage, haven, seaport
portable *adjective* LIGHT, compact, convenient, easily carried, handy, manageable, movable
portend *verb* FORETELL, augur, betoken, bode, foreshadow, herald, indicate, predict, prognosticate, promise, warn of
portent *noun* OMEN, augury, forewarning, indication, prognostication, sign, warning
portentous *adjective* 1 SIGNIFICANT, crucial, fateful, important, menacing, momentous, ominous
2 POMPOUS, ponderous, self-important, solemn
porter[1] *noun* BAGGAGE ATTENDANT, bearer, carrier
porter[2] *noun* DOORMAN, caretaker, concierge, gatekeeper, janitor
portion *noun* 1 PART, bit, fragment, morsel, piece, scrap, section, segment
2 SHARE, allocation, allotment, allowance, lot, measure, quantity, quota, ration
3 HELPING, piece, serving
4 DESTINY, fate, fortune, lot, luck
▷ *verb* 5 ▷ **portion out** DIVIDE, allocate, allot, apportion, deal, distribute, dole out, share out
portly *adjective* STOUT, burly, corpulent, fat, fleshy, heavy, large, plump

por•tray' *verb transitive* make pictures of, describe > **por'trait** [-trit] *noun* likeness of (face of) person > **por'trai•ture** [-tri-chər] *noun* > **por•tray'al** [-əl] *noun* act of portraying
pose [pohz] *verb transitive* **posed, pos•ing** 1 place in attitude 2 put forward ▷ *verb intransitive* **posed, pos•ing** 3 assume attitude, affect or pretend to be a certain character ▷ *noun* 4 attitude, esp. one assumed for effect > **po•seur** [poh-ZUR] *noun* one who assumes affected attitude to create impression
pos•er [POH-zər] *noun* puzzling question
posh *adjective* (*informal*) smart, elegant, stylish
pos•it [POZ-it] *verb transitive* lay down as principle
po•si•tion [pə-ZISH-ən] *noun* 1 place 2 situation 3 location, attitude 4 status 5 state of affairs 6 employment 7 strategic point ▷ *verb transitive* 8 place in position
pos•i•tive [POZ-i-tiv] *adjective* 1 certain 2 sure 3 definite, absolute, unquestionable 4 utter 5 downright 6 confident 7 not negative 8 greater than zero 9 *electricity* having deficiency of electrons ▷ *noun* 10 something positive 11 *photography* print in which lights and shadows are not reversed > **pos'i•tiv•ism** *noun* philosophy recognizing only matters of fact and experience > **pos'i•tiv•ist** *noun* believer in this
pos•i•tron [POZ-i-tron] *noun* positive electron
pos•se [POS-ee] *noun* body of armed people, esp. for maintaining law and order
pos•sess [pə-ZES] *verb transitive* 1 own 2 (of evil spirit, etc.) have mastery of > **pos•ses'sion** *noun* 1 act of possessing 2 thing possessed 3 ownership > **pos•ses'sive** *adjective* 1 of, indicating possession 2 with excessive desire to possess, control ▷ *noun* 3 possessive case in grammar > **pos•ses'sor** *noun* owner
pos•si•ble [POS-ə-bəl] *adjective* 1 that can, or may, be, exist, happen or be done 2 worthy of consideration ▷ *noun* 3 possible candidate > **pos•si•bil'i•ty** *noun, plural* **-ties** > **pos'si•bly** *adverb* perhaps
pos•sum [POS-əm] *noun* opossum **play possum** pretend to be dead, asleep, etc. to deceive opponent
post[1] [pohst] *noun* 1 upright pole of timber or metal fixed firmly, usu. to support or mark something ▷ *verb transitive* 2 display 3 stick up (on notice board, etc.) 4 *computing* make (e-mail) publicly available > **post'er** *noun* 1 large advertising bill 2 one who posts bills > **poster**

portrait *noun* 1 PICTURE, image, likeness, painting, photograph, representation
2 DESCRIPTION, characterization, depiction, portrayal, profile, thumbnail sketch
portray *verb* 1 REPRESENT, depict, draw, figure, illustrate, paint, picture, sketch
2 DESCRIBE, characterize, depict, put in words
3 PLAY, act the part of, represent
portrayal *noun* REPRESENTATION, characterization, depiction, interpretation, performance, picture
pose *verb* 1 POSITION, model, sit
2 PUT ON AIRS, posture, show off (*informal*)
3 ▷ **pose as** IMPERSONATE, masquerade as, pass oneself off as, pretend to be, profess to be
▷ *noun* 4 POSTURE, attitude, bearing, position, stance
5 ACT, affectation, air, façade, front, mannerism, posturing, pretense
poser *noun* PUZZLE, enigma, problem, question, riddle
posit *verb* PUT FORWARD, advance, assume, postulate, presume, propound, state
position *noun* 1 PLACE, area, bearings, locale, location, point, post, situation, spot, station, whereabouts
2 POSTURE, arrangement, attitude, pose, stance
3 ATTITUDE, belief, opinion, outlook, point of view, slant, stance, view, viewpoint
4 STATUS, importance, place, prestige, rank, reputation, standing, station, stature
5 JOB, duty, employment, occupation, office, place, post, role, situation
▷ *verb* 6 PLACE, arrange, lay out, locate, put, set, stand
positive *adjective* 1 CERTAIN, assured, confident, convinced, sure
2 DEFINITE, absolute, categorical, certain, clear, conclusive, decisive, explicit, express, firm, real
3 HELPFUL, beneficial, constructive, practical, productive, progressive, useful
positively *adverb* DEFINITELY, absolutely, assuredly, categorically, certainly, emphatically, firmly, surely, unequivocally, unquestionably
possess *verb* 1 HAVE, enjoy, hold, own
2 CONTROL, acquire, dominate, hold, occupy, seize, take over
possessed *adjective* CRAZED, berserk, demented, frenzied, obsessed, raving
possession *noun* 1 OWNERSHIP, control, custody, hold, occupation, tenure, title
2 ▷ **possessions** PROPERTY, assets, belongings, chattels, effects, estate, things
possessive *adjective* JEALOUS, controlling, covetous, dominating, domineering, overprotective, selfish
possibility *noun* 1 FEASIBILITY, likelihood, potentiality, practicability, workableness
2 LIKELIHOOD, chance, hope, liability, odds, probability, prospect, risk
3 (*often plural*) POTENTIAL, capabilities, potentiality, promise, prospects, talent
possible *adjective* 1 CONCEIVABLE, credible, hypothetical, imaginable, likely, potential
2 LIKELY, hopeful, potential, probable, promising
3 FEASIBLE, attainable, doable, practicable, realizable, viable, workable
possibly *adverb* PERHAPS, maybe, perchance (*archaic*)
post[1] *noun* 1 ▷ **keep someone posted** NOTIFY, advise, brief, fill in on (*informal*), inform, report to
post[2] *noun* 1 SUPPORT, column, picket, pillar, pole, shaft, stake, upright
▷ *verb* 2 PUT UP, affix, display, pin up
post[3] *noun* 1 JOB, appointment, assignment, employment, office, place, position, situation
2 STATION, beat, place, position
▷ *verb* 3 STATION, assign, place, position, put, situate
poster *noun* NOTICE, advertisement, announcement, bill, placard, public notice, sticker

paints, colors flat paints suited for posters
post[2] *noun* 1 mail 2 collection or delivery of this 3 office 4 situation 5 point, station, place of duty 6 place where soldier is stationed 7 place held by body of troops 8 fort ▷ *verb transitive* 9 put into mailbox 10 supply with latest information 11 station (soldiers, etc.) in particular spot 12 transfer (entries) to ledger ▷ *adverb* 13 with haste > **post•age** [POH-stij] *noun* charge for carrying letter > **post'al** [-əl] *adjective* > **postal money order** written order, available at post office, for payment of sum of money > **post'card** *noun* stamped card sent by mail > **post'man** [-mən] *noun, plural* **-men** postal employee who collects or delivers mail > **post'mark** *noun* official mark with name of office, etc. stamped on letters > **post'mas•ter** *noun* official in charge of post office > **post'mis•tress** [-tris] *noun feminine* > **post office** place where postal business is conducted
post- *prefix* after, behind, later than: *postwar*
post•date [pohst-DAYT] *verb transitive* **-dat•ed, -dat•ing** give date later than actual date
poste res•tante [pohst re-STAHNT] Fr. direction on mail to indicate that post office should keep traveler's letters till called for
pos•te•ri•or [po-STEER-ee-ər] *adjective* 1 later, hinder ▷ *noun* 2 the buttocks
pos•ter•i•ty [po-STER-i-tee] *noun* 1 later generations 2 descendants
post•grad•u•ate [pohst-GRAJ-oo-it] *adjective* carried on after graduation ▷ *noun*
post•hu•mous [POS-chə-məs] *adjective* 1 occurring after death 2 born after father's death 3 published after author's death > **post'hu•mous•ly** *adverb*
post•mor•tem [pohst-MOR-təm] *noun* 1 medical examination of dead body 2 evaluation after event, etc. ends ▷ *adjective* 3 taking place after death
post•par•tum [pohst-PAHR-təm] *adjective* occurring after childbirth
post•pone [pohs-POHN] *verb transitive* **-poned, -pon•ing** put off to later time, defer
post•pran•di•al [pohst-PRAN-dee-əl] *adjective* after a meal, esp. dinner
post-rock [pohst-ROK] *noun* type of music that often varies from traditional rock in terms of form and instrumentation
post•script [POHST-skript] *noun* addition to letter, book, etc.
pos•tu•lant [POS-chə-lənt] *noun* candidate for admission to religious order
pos•tu•late [POS-chə-layt] *verb transitive* **-lat•ed, -lat•ing** 1 take for granted 2 lay down as self-evident 3 stipulate ▷ *noun* [-lit] 4 proposition assumed without proof 5 prerequisite
pos•ture [POS-chər] *noun* 1 attitude, position of body ▷ *verb* **-tured, -tur•ing** 2 pose
po•sy [POH-zee] *noun, plural* **-sies** 1 flower 2 bunch of flowers
pot *noun* 1 round vessel 2 cooking vessel 3 trap, esp. for crabs, lobsters 4 (*slang*) marijuana 5 (*informal*) a lot ▷ *verb transitive* **pot•ted, pot•ting** 6 put into, preserve in pot > **potted** *adjective* 1 cooked, preserved, in a pot 2 (*slang*) drunk > **pot'hole** *noun* 1 pitlike cavity in rocks, usu. limestone, produced by faulting and water action 2 hole worn in road > **pot'luck** *noun* whatever is to be had (to eat) > **pot'sherd** [-shurd] *noun* broken fragment of pottery > **pot shot** easy or random shot
po•ta•ble [POH-tə-bəl] *adjective* drinkable > **po•ta'tion** [-TAY-shən] *noun* 1 drink 2 drinking
pot'ash *noun* 1 alkali used in soap, etc. 2 crude potassium carbonate
po•tas•si•um [pə-TAS-ee-əm] *noun* white metallic element
po•ta•to [pə-TAY-toh] *noun, plural* **-toes** plant with tubers grown for food **hot potato** topic, etc. too threatening to bring up **sweet potato** 1 trailing plant 2 its edible sweetish tubers
po•tent [POHT-nt] *adjective* 1 powerful, influential 2 (of male) capable of sexual intercourse > **po'ten•cy** *noun* 1 physical or moral power 2 efficacy
po•ten•tate [POHT-n-tayt] *noun* ruler
po•ten•tial [pə-TEN-shəl] *adjective* 1 latent, that may or might but does not now exist or act ▷ *noun* 2 possibility 3 amount of potential energy 4 *electricity* level of electric pressure > **po•ten•ti•al'i•ty** [-shee-AL-i-tee] *noun*
po•tion [POH-shən] *noun* dose of medicine or poison
pot•pour•ri [poh-puu-REE] *noun* 1 mixture of rose petals, spices, etc. 2 musical, literary medley
pot•tage [POT-ij] *noun* soup or stew
pot•ter [POT-ər] *noun* maker of earthenware vessels > **pot'ter•y** *noun, plural* **-ter•ies** 1 earthenware 2 where it is made 3 art of making it
pouch [powch] *noun* 1 small bag 2 pocket

DICTIONARY

P

THESAURUS

posterity *noun* 1 FUTURE, succeeding generations
2 DESCENDANTS, children, family, heirs, issue, offspring, progeny
postpone *verb* PUT OFF, adjourn, defer, delay, put back, put on the back burner (*informal*), shelve, suspend
postponement *noun* DELAY, adjournment, deferment, deferral, stay, suspension
postscript *noun* P.S., addition, afterthought, supplement
postulate *verb* PRESUPPOSE, assume, hypothesize, posit, propose, suppose, take for granted, theorize
posture *noun* 1 BEARING, attitude, carriage, disposition, set, stance
▷ *verb* 2 SHOW OFF (*informal*), affect, pose, put on airs
pot[1] *noun* CONTAINER, bowl, pan, vessel
potency *noun* POWER, effectiveness, force, influence, might, strength
potent *adjective* 1 POWERFUL, authoritative, commanding, dominant, dynamic, influential
2 STRONG, forceful, mighty, powerful, vigorous
potential *adjective* 1 POSSIBLE, dormant, future, hidden, inherent, latent, likely, promising
▷ *noun* 2 ABILITY, aptitude, capability, capacity, possibility, potentiality, power, wherewithal
potion *noun* CONCOCTION, brew, dose, draft, elixir, mixture, philtre
pottery *noun* CERAMICS, earthenware, stoneware, terracotta

▷ *verb transitive* 3 put into one
poul•tice [POHL-tis] *noun* soft composition of cloth, bread, etc., applied hot to sore or inflamed parts of the body
poul•try [POHL-tree] *noun* domestic fowl collectively
pounce[1] [powns] *verb intransitive* **pounced, pounc•ing** 1 spring upon suddenly, swoop (upon) ▷ *noun* 2 swoop or sudden descent
pounce[2] *noun* fine powder used to prevent ink from spreading on unsized paper or in pattern making
pound[1] [pownd] *verb transitive* 1 beat, thump 2 crush to pieces or powder 3 walk, run heavily
pound[2] *noun* 1 unit of troy weight 2 unit of avoirdupois weight equal to 0.453 kg 3 monetary unit in United Kingdom
pound[3] *noun* 1 enclosure for stray animals or officially removed vehicles 2 confined space
pound•al [POWN-dl] *noun* a unit of force in the foot-pound-second system
pour [por] *verb intransitive* 1 come out in a stream, crowd, etc. 2 flow freely 3 rain heavily ▷ *verb transitive* 4 give out thus 5 cause to run out
pout [powt] *verb* 1 thrust out (lips), look sulky ▷ *noun* 2 act of pouting > **pout'er** *noun* pigeon with power of inflating its crop
pov•er•ty [POV-ər-tee] *noun* 1 state of being poor 2 poorness 3 lack of means 4 scarcity
pow•der [POW-dər] *noun* 1 solid matter in fine dry particles 2 medicine in this form 3 gunpowder 4 face powder, etc. ▷ *verb transitive* 5 apply powder to 6 reduce to powder > **pow'der•y** *adjective*
pow•er [POW-ər] *noun* 1 ability to do or act 2 strength 3 authority 4 control 5 person or thing having authority 6 mechanical energy 7 electricity supply 8 rate of doing work 9 product from continuous multiplication of number by itself > **pow'ered** *adjective* having or operated by mechanical or electrical power > **pow'er•ful** [-fəl] *adjective* > **pow'er•less** [-lis] *adjective* > **pow'er•house, power station** *noun* installation for generating and distributing electric power
pow'wow *noun* 1 conference ▷ *verb intransitive* 2 confer
pox [poks] *noun* 1 one of several diseases marked by pustular eruptions of skin 2 (*informal*) syphilis
Pr *chem.* praseodymium
prac•ti•cal [PRAK-ti-kəl] *adjective* 1 given to action rather than theory 2 relating to action or real existence 3 useful 4 in effect though not in name 5 virtual > **prac'ti•cal•ly** *adverb* > **prac'ti•ca•ble** [-kə-bəl] *adjective* that can be done, used, etc. > **prac•ti'tion•er** *noun* one engaged in a profession
prac•tice [PRAK-tis] *verb transitive* **-ticed, -tic•ing** 1 do repeatedly, work at to gain skill 2 do habitually 3 put into action ▷ *verb intransitive* **-ticed, -tic•ing** 4 exercise oneself 5 exercise profession > **practice** *noun* 1 habit 2 mastery or

pouch *noun* BAG, container, pocket, purse, sack
pounce *verb* 1 SPRING, attack, fall upon, jump, leap at, strike, swoop
▷ *noun* 2 SPRING, assault, attack, bound, jump, leap, swoop
pound[1] *verb* 1 BEAT, batter, belabor, clobber (*slang*), hammer, pummel, strike, thrash, thump
2 CRUSH, powder, pulverize
3 PULSATE, beat, palpitate, pulse, throb
4 STOMP (*informal*), march, thunder, tramp
pound[2] *noun* ENCLOSURE, compound, pen, yard
pour *verb* 1 FLOW, course, emit, gush, run, rush, spew, spout, stream
2 LET FLOW, decant, spill, splash
3 RAIN, bucket down (*informal*), pelt *or* pelt down, teem
4 STREAM, crowd, swarm, teem, throng
pout *verb* 1 SULK, glower, look petulant, pull a long face
▷ *noun* 2 SULLEN LOOK, glower, long face
poverty *noun* 1 PENNILESSNESS, beggary, destitution, hardship, indigence, insolvency, need, penury, privation, want
2 SCARCITY, dearth, deficiency, insufficiency, lack, paucity, shortage
poverty-stricken *adjective* PENNILESS, broke (*informal*), destitute, down and out, down on one's luck (*informal*), flat broke (*informal*), impecunious, impoverished, indigent, poor
powder *noun* 1 DUST, fine grains, loose particles, talc
▷ *verb* 2 DUST, cover, dredge, scatter, sprinkle, strew
powdery *adjective* FINE, crumbly, dry, dusty, grainy, granular
power *noun* 1 ABILITY, capability, capacity, competence, competency, faculty, potential
2 CONTROL, ascendancy, authority, command, dominance, domination, dominion, influence, mastery, rule
3 AUTHORITY, authorization, license, prerogative, privilege, right, warrant
4 STRENGTH, brawn, energy, force, forcefulness, intensity, might, muscle, potency, vigor
powerful *adjective* 1 CONTROLLING, authoritative, commanding, dominant, influential, prevailing
2 STRONG, energetic, mighty, potent, strapping, sturdy, vigorous
3 PERSUASIVE, cogent, compelling, convincing, effectual, forceful, impressive, striking, telling, weighty
powerless *adjective* 1 DEFENSELESS, dependent, ineffective, subject, tied, unarmed, vulnerable
2 HELPLESS, challenged, debilitated, disabled, feeble, frail, impotent, incapable, incapacitated, ineffectual, weak
practicability *noun* FEASIBILITY, advantage, possibility, practicality, use, usefulness, viability
practicable *adjective* FEASIBLE, achievable, attainable, doable, possible, viable
practical *adjective* 1 FUNCTIONAL, applied, empirical, experimental, factual, pragmatic, realistic, utilitarian
2 SENSIBLE, businesslike, down-to-earth, hard-headed, matter-of-fact, ordinary, realistic
3 FEASIBLE, doable, practicable, serviceable, useful, workable
4 SKILLED, accomplished, efficient, experienced, proficient
practically *adverb* 1 ALMOST, all but, basically, essentially, fundamentally, in effect, just about, nearly, very nearly, virtually, well-nigh

skill **3** exercise of art or profession **4** action, not theory

prag•mat•ic [prag-MAT-ik] *adjective* **1** concerned with practical consequence **2** of the affairs of state > **prag'ma•tism** [-mə-tiz-əm] *noun* > **prag'ma•tist** *noun*

prair•ie [PRAIR-ee] *noun* large mostly treeless tract of grassland > **prairie dog** small Amer. rodent allied to marmot > **prairie oyster** **1** as remedy for hangover, a drink of raw egg usu. with seasonings **2** as food, testis of a calf

praise [prayz] *noun* **1** commendation **2** fact, state of being praised ▷ *verb transitive* **praised, prais•ing** **3** express approval, admiration of **4** speak well of **5** glorify > **praise'wor•thy** [-wur-thee] *adjective*

pra•line [PRAH-leen] *noun* candy made of nuts with caramel covering

prance [prans] *verb intransitive* **pranced, pranc•ing** **1** swagger **2** caper **3** walk with bounds ▷ *noun* **4** prancing

pran•di•al [PRAN-dee-əl] *adjective* of a meal, esp. dinner

prank [prangk] *noun* mischievous trick or escapade, frolic

pra•se•o•dym•i•um [pray-zee-oh-DIM-ee-əm] *noun* rare-earth chemical element

prate [prayt] *verb intransitive* **prat•ed, prat•ing** **1** talk idly, chatter ▷ *noun* **2** idle chatter

prat•tle [PRAT-l] *verb intransitive* **-tled, -tling** **1** talk like child ▷ *noun* **2** trifling, childish talk > **prat'tler** *noun* babbler

prawn *noun* edible sea crustacean like a shrimp

pray *verb transitive* **1** ask earnestly **2** entreat ▷ *verb intransitive* **3** offer prayers, esp. to God > **prayer** [prair] *noun* **1** action, practice of praying to God **2** earnest entreaty > **pray'er** *noun* one who prays

pre- *prefix* before, beforehand: *prenatal; prerecord; preshrunk*

preach [preech] *verb intransitive* **1** deliver sermon **2** give moral, religious advice ▷ *verb transitive* **3** set forth in religious discourse **4** advocate > **preach'er** *noun*

pre•am•ble [PREE-am-bəl] *noun* introductory part of document, story, etc.

pre•car•i•ous [pri-KAIR-ee-əs] *adjective* insecure, unstable, perilous

pre•cau•tion [pri-KAW-shən] *noun* **1** previous care to prevent evil or secure good **2** preventive measure > **pre•cau'tion•ar•y** *adjective*

pre•cede [pri-SEED] *verb* **-ced•ed, -ced•ing** go, come before in rank, order, time, etc. > **prec•e•dence** [PRES-i-dəns] *noun* priority in position, rank, time, etc. > **prec'e•dent** *noun* previous case or occurrence taken as rule

pre•cept [PREE-sept] *noun* rule for conduct, maxim > **pre•cep'tor** *noun* instructor

pre•ces•sion [pree-SESH-ən] *noun* **1** act of preceding **2** motion of spinning body, in which

DICTIONARY

P

THESAURUS

---

2 SENSIBLY, clearly, matter-of-factly, rationally, realistically, reasonably

practice *noun* **1** CUSTOM, habit, method, mode, routine, rule, system, tradition, usage, way, wont
2 REHEARSAL, drill, exercise, preparation, repetition, study, training
3 PROFESSION, business, career, vocation, work
4 USE, action, application, exercise, experience, operation
▷ *verb* **5** REHEARSE, drill, exercise, go over, go through, prepare, repeat, study, train
6 DO, apply, carry out, follow, observe, perform
7 WORK AT, carry on, engage in, pursue

practiced *adjective* SKILLED, able, accomplished, experienced, expert, proficient, seasoned, trained, versed

pragmatic *adjective* PRACTICAL, businesslike, down-to-earth, hard-headed, realistic, sensible, utilitarian

praise *verb* **1** APPROVE, acclaim, admire, applaud, cheer, compliment, congratulate, eulogize, extol, honor, laud
2 GIVE THANKS TO, adore, bless, exalt, glorify, worship
▷ *noun* **3** APPROVAL, acclaim, acclamation, approbation, commendation, compliment, congratulation, eulogy, kudos, plaudit, tribute
4 THANKS, adoration, glory, homage, kudos, worship

praiseworthy *adjective* CREDITABLE, admirable, commendable, laudable, meritorious, worthy

prance *verb* **1** DANCE, caper, cavort, frisk, gambol, romp, skip
2 STRUT, parade, show off (*informal*), stalk, swagger

prank *noun* TRICK, antic, escapade, jape, lark (*informal*), practical joke

pray *verb* **1** SAY ONE'S PRAYERS, offer a prayer, recite the rosary
2 BEG, adjure, ask, beseech, entreat, implore, petition, plead, request, solicit

prayer *noun* **1** ORISON, devotion, invocation, litany, supplication
2 PLEA, appeal, entreaty, petition, request, supplication

preach *verb* **1** DELIVER A SERMON, address, evangelize
2 LECTURE, advocate, exhort, moralize, sermonize

preacher *noun* CLERGYMAN, evangelist, minister, missionary, parson

preamble *noun* INTRODUCTION, foreword, opening statement *or* opening remarks, preface, prelude

precarious *adjective* DANGEROUS, hazardous, insecure, perilous, risky, shaky, tricky, unreliable, unsafe, unsure

precaution *noun* **1** SAFEGUARD, insurance, protection, provision, safety measure
2 FORETHOUGHT, care, caution, providence, prudence, wariness

precede *verb* GO BEFORE, antedate, come first, head, introduce, lead, preface

precedence *noun* PRIORITY, antecedence, pre-eminence, primacy, rank, seniority, superiority, supremacy

precedent *noun* INSTANCE, antecedent, example, model, paradigm, pattern, prototype, standard

preceding *adjective* PREVIOUS, above, aforementioned, aforesaid, earlier, foregoing, former, past, prior

precept *noun* RULE, canon, command, commandment, decree, instruction, law, order, principle, regulation, statute

the axis of rotation sweeps out a cone
pre•cinct [PREE-singkt] *noun* 1 enclosed, limited area 2 administrative area of city, esp. of police, board of elections > **pre•cincts** environs > **precinct house** police station
pre•cious [PRE-shəs] *adjective* 1 beloved, cherished 2 of great value, highly valued 3 rare > **pre•ci•os•i•ty** [presh-ee-OS-i-tee] *noun* overrefinement in art or literature > **prec'ious•ly** *adverb*
prec•i•pice [PRES-ə-pis] *noun* very steep cliff or rockface > **pre•cip'i•tous** *adjective* sheer
pre•cip•i•tant [prə-SIP-i-tənt] *adjective* 1 hasty, rash 2 abrupt > **pre•cip'i•tance, pre•cip'i•tan•cy** *noun*
pre•cip•i•tate [pri-SIP-i-tayt] *verb transitive* **-tat•ed, -tat•ing** 1 hasten happening of 2 throw headlong 3 *chem.* cause to be deposited in solid form from solution ▷ *adjective* [-i-tit] 4 too sudden 5 rash, impetuous ▷ *noun* [-i-tit] 6 substance chemically precipitated > **pre•cip'i•tate•ly** [-tit-lee] *adverb* > **pre•cip•i•ta•tion** [-TAY-shən] *noun* esp. rain, snow, etc.
pré•cis [PRAY-see] *noun, plural* **pré•cis** [PRAY-seez] abstract, summary
pre•cise [pri-SĪS] *adjective* 1 definite 2 particular 3 exact, strictly worded 4 careful in observance 5 punctilious, formal > **pre•cise'ly** *adverb* > **pre•ci•sion** [-SIZH-ən] *noun* accuracy
pre•clude [pri-KLOOD] *verb transitive* **-clud•ed, -clud•ing** 1 prevent from happening 2 shut out
pre•co•cious [pri-KOH-shəs] *adjective* developed, matured early or too soon > **pre•coc'i•ty** [-KOS-i-tee], **pre•co'cious•ness** [-KOH-shəs-nis] *noun*
pre•con•ceive [pree-kən-SEEV] *verb transitive* **-ceived, -ceiv•ing** form an idea beforehand > **pre•con•cep'tion** [-SEP-shən] *noun*
pre•con•di•tion [pree-kən-DISH-ən] *noun* necessary or required condition
pre•cur•sor [pri-KUR-sər] *noun* forerunner > **pre•cur'sive** *adjective* > **pre•cur'so•ry** *adjective*
pred•a•to•ry [PRED-ə-tor-ee] *adjective* 1 hunting, killing other animals, etc. for food 2 plundering > **pred'a•tor** *noun* predatory animal
pred•e•ces•sor [PRED-ə-ses-ər] *noun* 1 one who precedes another in an office 2 ancestor
pre•des•tine [pri-DES-tin] *verb transitive* **-tined, -tin•ing** decree beforehand, foreordain > **pre•des•ti•na'tion** *noun*
pre•dic•a•ment [pri-DIK-ə-mənt] *noun* perplexing, embarrassing or difficult situation
pred•i•cate [PRED-i-kayt] *verb transitive* **-cat•ed, -cat•ing** 1 affirm, assert 2 base (on or upon) ▷ *noun* [-kit] 3 that which is predicated 4 *grammar* statement made about a subject
pre•dict [pri-DIKT] *verb transitive* foretell, prophesy > **pre•dict'a•ble** *adjective*
pre•di•lec•tion [pred-l-EK-shən] *noun* preference, liking, partiality
pre•dis•pose [pree-dis-POHZ] *verb transitive*

DICTIONARY • THESAURUS

---

precinct *noun* 1 ENCLOSURE, confine, limit
2 AREA, district, quarter, section, sector, zone
precious *adjective* 1 VALUABLE, costly, dear, expensive, fine, invaluable, priceless, prized
2 LOVED, adored, beloved, cherished, darling, dear, prized, treasured
3 AFFECTED, artificial, overnice, overrefined
precipice *noun* CLIFF, bluff, crag, height, rock face
precipitate *verb* 1 QUICKEN, accelerate, advance, bring on, expedite, hasten, hurry, speed up, trigger
2 THROW, cast, fling, hurl, launch, let fly
▷ *adjective* 3 HASTY, heedless, impetuous, impulsive, precipitous, rash, reckless
4 SWIFT, breakneck, headlong, rapid, rushing
5 SUDDEN, abrupt, brief, quick, unexpected, without warning
precipitous *adjective* 1 SHEER, abrupt, dizzy, high, perpendicular, steep
2 HASTY, heedless, hurried, precipitate, rash, reckless
précis *noun* 1 SUMMARY, abridgment, outline, résumé, synopsis
▷ *verb* 2 SUMMARIZE, abridge, outline, shorten, sum up
precise *adjective* 1 EXACT, absolute, accurate, correct, definite, explicit, express, particular, specific, strict
2 STRICT, careful, exact, fastidious, finicky, formal, meticulous, particular, punctilious, rigid, scrupulous, stiff
precisely *adverb* EXACTLY, absolutely, accurately, correctly, just so, plumb (*informal*), smack (*informal*), square, squarely, strictly
precision *noun* EXACTNESS, accuracy, care, meticulousness, particularity, preciseness
preclude *verb* PREVENT, check, debar, exclude, forestall, inhibit, obviate, prohibit, rule out, stop
precocious *adjective* ADVANCED, ahead, bright, developed, forward, quick, smart
preconceived *adjective* PRESUMED, forejudged, prejudged, presupposed
preconception *noun* PRECONCEIVED IDEA *or* PRECONCEIVED NOTION, bias, notion, predisposition, prejudice, presupposition
precursor *noun* 1 HERALD, forerunner, harbinger, vanguard
2 FORERUNNER, antecedent, forebear, predecessor
predatory *adjective* HUNTING, carnivorous, predacious, raptorial
predecessor *noun* 1 PREVIOUS JOB HOLDER, antecedent, forerunner, precursor
2 ANCESTOR, antecedent, forebear, forefather
predestination *noun* FATE, destiny, foreordainment, foreordination, predetermination
predestined *adjective* FATED, doomed, meant, preordained
predetermined *adjective* PREARRANGED, agreed, fixed, preplanned, set
predicament *noun* FIX (*informal*), dilemma, jam (*informal*), mess, pinch, plight, quandary, scrape (*informal*), situation, spot (*informal*)
predict *verb* FORETELL, augur, divine, forecast, portend, prophesy
predictable *adjective* LIKELY, anticipated, certain, expected, foreseeable, reliable, sure
prediction *noun* PROPHECY, augury, divination, forecast, prognosis, prognostication
predilection *noun* LIKING, bias, fondness, inclination, leaning, love, partiality, penchant,

-posed, -pos•ing 1 incline, influence someone (toward) 2 make susceptible (to)
pre•dom•i•nate [pri-DOM-ə-nayt] *verb intransitive* **-nat•ed, -nat•ing** be main or controlling element > **pre•dom'i•nance** [-nəns] *noun* > **pre•dom'i•nant** *adjective* chief
pre•em•i•nent [pree-EM-ə-nənt] *adjective* excelling all others, outstanding > **pre•em'i•nence** *noun*
pre•empt [pree-EMPT] *verb transitive* acquire in advance or act in advance of or to exclusion of others > **pre•emp'tive** *adjective*
preen *verb transitive* 1 trim (feathers) with beak, plume 2 smarten oneself
pre•fab•ri•cate [pree-FAB-ri-kayt] *verb transitive* **-cat•ed, -cat•ing** manufacture buildings, etc. in shaped sections, for rapid assembly on the site > **pre'fab** *noun* building so made
pref•ace [PREF-is] *noun* 1 introduction to book, etc. ▷ *verb transitive* **-faced, -fac•ing** 2 introduce > **pref'a•to•ry** *adjective*
pre•fect [PREE-fekt] *noun* person put in authority > **pre•fec•ture** [PREE-fek-chər] *noun* office, residence, jurisdiction of a prefect
pre•fer [pri-FUR] *verb transitive* **-ferred, -fer•ring** 1 like better 2 promote > **pref•er•a•ble** [PREF-ər-ə-bəl] *adjective* more desirable > **pref'er•a•bly** *adverb* > **pref'er•ence** [-əns] *noun* > **pref•er•en'tial** [-EN-shəl] *adjective* giving, receiving preference
pre•fix [PREE-fiks] *noun* 1 preposition or particle put at beginning of word or title ▷ *verb transitive* 2 put as introduction 3 put before word to make compound
preg•nant [PREG-nənt] *adjective* 1 carrying fetus in womb 2 full of meaning, significance 3 inventive > **preg'nan•cy** *noun*
pre•hen•sile [pri-HEN-sil] *adjective* capable of grasping
pre•his•tor•ic [pree-hi-STOR-ik] *adjective* before period in which written history begins > **pre•his'to•ry** *noun*
prej•u•dice [PREJ-ə-dis] *noun* 1 preconceived opinion 2 bias, partiality 3 damage or injury likely to happen to person or person's rights as a result of others' action or judgment ▷ *verb transitive* **-diced, -dic•ing** 4 influence 5 bias 6 injure > **prej•u•di'cial** [-DISH-əl] *adjective* 1 injurious 2 disadvantageous
prel•ate [PREL-it] *noun* bishop or other church dignitary of equal or higher rank > **prel'a•cy** [-ə-see] *noun* prelate's office
pre•lim•i•nar•y [pri-LIM-ə-ner-ee] *adjective* 1 preparatory, introductory ▷ *noun, plural* **-ies** 2 introductory, preparatory statement, action
prel•ude [PRAY-lood] *noun* 1 *mus.* introductory movement 2 performance, event, etc. serving as introduction ▷ *verb* **-ud•ed, -ud•ing** 3 serve as prelude, introduce

DICTIONARY **P** THESAURUS

preference, propensity, taste, weakness
predispose *verb* INCLINE, affect, bias, dispose, influence, lead, prejudice, prompt
predisposed *adjective* INCLINED, given, liable, minded, ready, subject, susceptible, willing
predominant *adjective* MAIN, ascendant, chief, dominant, leading, paramount, prevailing, prevalent, prime, principal
predominantly *adverb* MAINLY, chiefly, for the most part, generally, largely, mostly, primarily, principally
predominate *verb* PREVAIL, be most noticeable, carry weight, hold sway, outweigh, overrule, overshadow
pre-eminence *noun* SUPERIORITY, distinction, excellence, predominance, prestige, prominence, renown, supremacy
pre-eminent *adjective* OUTSTANDING, chief, distinguished, excellent, foremost, incomparable, matchless, predominant, renowned, superior, supreme
pre-empt *verb* ANTICIPATE, appropriate, assume, usurp
preen *verb* 1 (*of a bird*) CLEAN, plume
2 SMARTEN, dress up, spruce up, titivate
3 ▷ **preen oneself** **preen oneself on** PRIDE ONESELF, congratulate oneself
preface *noun* 1 INTRODUCTION, foreword, preamble, preliminary, prelude, prologue
▷ *verb* 2 INTRODUCE, begin, open, prefix
prefer *verb* LIKE BETTER, be partial to, choose, desire, fancy, favor, go for, incline towards, opt for, pick
preferable *adjective* BETTER, best, chosen, favored, more desirable, superior
preferably *adverb* RATHER, by choice, first, in preference *or* for preference, sooner
preference *noun* 1 FIRST CHOICE, choice, desire, favorite, option, partiality, pick, predilection, selection
2 PRIORITY, favored treatment, favoritism, first place, precedence
preferential *adjective* PRIVILEGED, advantageous, better, favored, special
preferment *noun* PROMOTION, advancement, elevation, exaltation, rise, upgrading
pregnant *adjective* 1 EXPECTANT, big with child *or* heavy with child, expecting (*informal*), with child
2 MEANINGFUL, charged, eloquent, expressive, loaded, pointed, significant, telling, weighty
prehistoric *adjective* EARLIEST, early, primeval, primitive, primordial
prejudge *verb* JUMP TO CONCLUSIONS, anticipate, presume, presuppose
prejudice *noun* 1 BIAS, partiality, preconceived notion, preconception, prejudgment
2 DISCRIMINATION, bigotry, chauvinism, injustice, intolerance, narrow-mindedness, unfairness
▷ *verb* 3 BIAS, color, distort, influence, poison, predispose, slant
4 HARM, damage, hinder, hurt, impair, injure, mar, spoil, undermine
prejudiced *adjective* BIASED, bigoted, influenced, intolerant, narrow-minded, one-sided, opinionated, unfair
prejudicial *adjective* HARMFUL, damaging, deleterious, detrimental, disadvantageous, hurtful, injurious, unfavorable
preliminary *adjective* 1 FIRST, initial, introductory, opening, pilot, prefatory, preparatory, prior, test, trial
▷ *noun* 2 INTRODUCTION, beginning, opening, overture, preamble, preface, prelude, start
prelude *noun* INTRODUCTION, beginning, foreword, overture, preamble, preface, prologue, start

pre•mar•i•tal [pree-MA-ri-təl] *adjective* occurring before marriage
pre•ma•ture [pree-mə-CHUUR] *adjective* happening, done before proper time
pre•med•i•tate [pri-MED-i-tayt] *verb transitive* **-tat•ed, -tat•ing** consider, plan beforehand > **pre•med•i•ta'tion** *noun*
pre•mier [pri-MEER] *noun* 1 prime minister ▷ *adjective* 2 chief, foremost 3 first > **pre•mier'ship** *noun* 1 office of premier
pre•miere [pri-MEER] *noun* 1 first performance of a play, film, etc. ▷ *verb intransitive* **-miered, -mier•ing** 2 have first performance
prem•ise [PREM-is] *noun* 1 *logic* proposition from which inference is drawn > **prem•is•es** house, building with its belongings > **premise** *verb transitive* **-mised, -mis•ing** state by way of introduction
pre•mi•um [PREE-mee-əm] *noun* 1 prize, bonus 2 sum paid for insurance 3 excess over nominal value 4 great value or regard
pre•mo•ni•tion [pree-mə-NISH-ən] *noun* presentiment, foreboding > **pre•mon•i•to•ry** [pri-MON-i-tor-ee] *adjective*
pre•na•tal [pree-NAYT-l] *adjective* occurring before birth
pre•oc•cu•py [pree-OK-yə-pī] *verb transitive* **-pied, -py•ing** occupy to the exclusion of other things > **pre•oc•cu•pa'tion** *noun* mental concentration or absorption
prep [prep] *noun* preppy
pre•pare [pri-PAIR] *verb transitive* **-pared, -par•ing** 1 make ready 2 make ▷ *verb intransitive* **-pared, -par•ing** 3 get ready > **prep•a•ra'tion** *noun* 1 making ready beforehand 2 something that is prepared, as a medicine 3 at school, (time spent) preparing work for lesson > **pre•par'a•to•ry** [-PA-rə-tor-ee] *adjective* 1 serving to prepare 2 introductory > **pre•par'ed•ness** [-id-nis] *noun* state of being prepared > **preparatory school** private school preparing students for college
pre•pay [pree-PAY] *verb transitive* **-paid, -pay•ing** pay or pay for beforehand > **pre•paid'** *adjective*
pre•pon•der•ate [pri-PON-də-rayt] *verb intransitive* **-at•ed, -at•ing** be of greater weight or power > **pre•pon'der•ance** [-əns] *noun* superiority of power, numbers, etc.
prep•o•si•tion [prep-ə-ZISH-ən] *noun* word marking relation between noun or pronoun and other words > **prep•o•si'tion•al** *adjective*
pre•pos•sess [pree-pə-ZES] *verb transitive* 1 impress, esp. favorably, beforehand 2 possess beforehand > **pre•pos•sess'ing** *adjective* inviting favorable opinion, attractive, winning
pre•pos•ter•ous [pri-POS-tər-əs] *adjective* utterly absurd, foolish
prep•py, prep•pie [PRE-pee] *noun* **-ies** (*informal*) (person who behaves like) student or former student of preparatory school ▷ *adjective*
pre•puce [PRE-pyoos] *noun* retractable fold of skin covering tip of penis, foreskin
pre•req•ui•site [pri-REK-wə-zit] *noun, adjective* (something) required as prior condition
pre•rog•a•tive [pri-ROG-ə-tiv] *noun* 1 peculiar power or right, esp. as vested in ruler ▷ *adjective* 2 privileged
pres•age [PRES-ij] *noun* 1 omen, indication of something to come ▷ *verb transitive* **-aged, -ag•ing** 2 foretell

DICTIONARY • THESAURUS

premature *adjective* 1 EARLY, forward, unseasonable, untimely
2 HASTY, ill-timed, overhasty, rash, too soon, untimely
premeditated *adjective* PLANNED, calculated, conscious, considered, deliberate, intentional, willful
premeditation *noun* PLANNING, design, forethought, intention, plotting, prearrangement, predetermination, purpose
premier *noun* 1 HEAD OF GOVERNMENT, chancellor, chief minister, chief officer, prime minister
▷ *adjective* 2 CHIEF, alpha male, first, foremost, head, highest, leading, main, primary, prime, principal
premiere *noun* FIRST NIGHT, debut, opening
premise *noun* ASSUMPTION, argument, assertion, hypothesis, postulation, presupposition, proposition, supposition
premises *plural noun* BUILDING, establishment, place, property, site
premium *noun* 1 BONUS, bounty, fee, perk (*informal*), perquisite, prize, reward
2 ▷ **at a premium** IN GREAT DEMAND, hard to come by, in short supply, rare, scarce
premonition *noun* FEELING, foreboding, hunch, idea, intuition, presentiment, suspicion
preoccupation *noun* 1 OBSESSION, bee in one's bonnet, fixation
2 ABSORPTION, absent-mindedness, abstraction, daydreaming, engrossment, immersion, reverie, woolgathering
preoccupied *adjective* ABSORBED, absent-minded, distracted, engrossed, immersed, lost in, oblivious, rapt, wrapped up
preparation *noun* 1 GROUNDWORK, getting ready, preparing
2 (*often plural*) ARRANGEMENT, measure, plan, provision
3 MIXTURE, compound, concoction, medicine
preparatory *adjective* INTRODUCTORY, opening, prefatory, preliminary, primary
prepare *verb* MAKE READY *or* GET READY, adapt, adjust, arrange, practice, prime, train, warm up
prepared *adjective* 1 READY, arranged, in order, in readiness, primed, set
2 WILLING, disposed, inclined
preponderance *noun* PREDOMINANCE, dominance, domination, extensiveness, greater numbers, greater part, lion's share, mass, prevalence, supremacy
prepossessing *adjective* ATTRACTIVE, appealing, charming, engaging, fetching, good-looking, handsome, likable *or* likeable, pleasing
preposterous *adjective* RIDICULOUS, absurd, crazy, incredible, insane, laughable, ludicrous, nonsensical, out of the question, outrageous, unthinkable
prerequisite *noun* 1 REQUIREMENT, condition, essential, must, necessity, precondition, qualification, requisite, sine qua non (*Latin*)
▷ *adjective* 2 REQUIRED, essential, indispensable, mandatory, necessary, obligatory, requisite, vital
prerogative *noun* RIGHT, advantage, due, exemption, immunity, liberty, privilege

pres•by•o•pi•a [prez-bee-OH-pee-ə] *noun* progressively diminishing ability of the eye to focus, esp. on near objects, farsightedness
pres•by•ter [PREZ-bi-tər] *noun* 1 elder in early Christian church 2 priest 3 member of a presbytery > **Pres•by•te'ri•an** *adjective, noun* (member) of Protestant church governed by lay elders > **pres'by•ter•y** *noun* 1 church court composed of all ministers within a certain district and one or two ruling elders from each church 2 R.C. *Church* rectory
pre•science [PRESH-əns] *noun* foreknowledge > **pres'cient** *adjective*
pre•scribe [pri-SKRĪB] *verb* **-scribed, -scrib•ing** 1 set out rules for 2 order 3 ordain 4 order use of (medicine) > **pre•scrip'tion** *noun* 1 prescribing 2 thing prescribed 3 written statement of it > **pre•scrip'tive** *adjective*
pres•ent[1] [PREZ-ənt] *adjective* 1 that is here 2 now existing or happening ▷ *noun* 3 present time or tense > **pres'ence** *noun* 1 being present 2 appearance, bearing > **pres'ent•ly** *adverb* 1 soon 2 at present
present[2] [pri-ZENT] *verb transitive* 1 introduce formally 2 show 3 give 4 offer 5 point, aim > **pres'ent** *noun* gift > **pre•sent'a•ble** *adjective* fit to be seen > **pres•en•ta'tion** [-TAY-shən] *noun* > **pre•sent'er** *noun* person who presents, esp. an award
pre•sen•ti•ment [pri-ZEN-tə-mənt] *noun* sense of something (esp. evil) about to happen
pre•serve [pri-ZURV] *verb transitive* **-served, -serv•ing** 1 keep from harm, injury or decay 2 maintain 3 pickle, can ▷ *noun* 4 special area 5 that which is preserved, as fruit, etc. 6 place where game is kept for private fishing, shooting > **pre•serves** preserved vegetables, fruit, etc. > **pres•er•va'tion** *noun* > **pre•serv'a•tive** *noun* 1 chemical put into perishable foods, drinks, etc. to keep them from going bad ▷ *adjective* 2 tending to preserve 3 having quality of preserving
pre•side [pri-ZĪD] *verb intransitive* **-sid•ed, -sid•ing** 1 be chairperson 2 superintend > **pres'i•dent** [-dənt] *noun* head of organization, company, republic, etc. > **pres'i•den•cy** *noun, plural* **-cies** > **pres•i•den'tial** [-DEN-shəl] *adjective*
press[1] *verb transitive* 1 subject to push or squeeze 2 smooth by pressure or heat 3 urge steadily, earnestly ▷ *verb intransitive* 4 bring weight to bear 5 throng 6 hasten ▷ *noun* 7 a pressing 8 machine for pressing, esp. printing machine 9 printing house 10 its work or art 11 newspapers collectively 12 reporters, journalists 13 crowd 14 stress > **press'ing** *adjective* 1 urgent 2 persistent > **press agent** person employed to advertise and secure publicity for any person, enterprise, etc. > **press'man** [-mən] *noun* printer who attends to the press
press[2] *verb transitive* force to serve esp. in navy or army > **press gang** formerly, body of men employed to press men into naval service
pres•sure [PRESH-ər] *noun* 1 act of pressing 2 influence 3 authority 4 difficulties 5 *physics*

DICTIONARY **P** THESAURUS

presage *verb* PORTEND, augur, betoken, bode, foreshadow, foretoken, signify
prescience *noun* FORESIGHT, clairvoyance, foreknowledge, precognition, second sight
prescribe *verb* ORDER, decree, dictate, direct, lay down, ordain, recommend, rule, set, specify, stipulate
prescription *noun* 1 INSTRUCTION, direction, formula, recipe
2 MEDICINE, drug, mixture, preparation, remedy
presence *noun* 1 BEING, attendance, existence, inhabitance, occupancy, residence
2 PERSONALITY, air, appearance, aspect, aura, bearing, carriage, demeanor, poise, self-assurance
presence of mind *noun* LEVEL-HEADEDNESS, calmness, composure, cool (*slang*), coolness, self-possession, wits
present[1] *adjective* 1 HERE, at hand, near, nearby, ready, there
2 CURRENT, contemporary, existent, existing, immediate, present-day
▷ *noun* 3 ▷ **the present** NOW, here and now, the present moment, the time being, today
4 ▷ **at present** JUST NOW, at the moment, now, right now
5 ▷ **for the present** FOR NOW, for the moment, for the time being, in the meantime, temporarily
present[2] *noun* 1 GIFT, boon, donation, endowment, grant, gratuity, hand-out, offering
▷ *verb* 2 INTRODUCE, acquaint with, make known
3 PUT ON, display, exhibit, give, show, stage
4 GIVE, award, bestow, confer, grant, hand out, hand over
presentable *adjective* DECENT, acceptable, becoming, fit to be seen, O.K. *or* okay (*informal*), passable, respectable, satisfactory, suitable
presentation *noun* 1 GIVING, award, bestowal, conferral, donation, offering
2 PRODUCTION, demonstration, display, exhibition, performance, show
presently *adverb* SOON, anon (*archaic*), before long, by and by, shortly
preservation *noun* PROTECTION, conservation, maintenance, safeguarding, safekeeping, safety, salvation, support
preserve *verb* 1 SAVE, care for, conserve, defend, keep, protect, safeguard, shelter, shield
2 MAINTAIN, continue, keep, keep up, perpetuate, sustain, uphold
▷ *noun* 3 AREA, domain, field, realm, sphere
preside *verb* RUN, administer, chair, conduct, control, direct, govern, head, lead, manage, officiate
press *verb* 1 FORCE DOWN, compress, crush, depress, jam, mash, push, squeeze
2 HUG, clasp, crush, embrace, fold in one's arms, hold close, squeeze
3 SMOOTH, flatten, iron
4 URGE, beg, entreat, exhort, implore, petition, plead, pressurize
5 CROWD, flock, gather, herd, push, seethe, surge, swarm, throng
▷ *noun* 6 ▷ **the press a** NEWSPAPERS, Fleet Street, fourth estate, news media, the papers **b** JOURNALISTS, columnists, correspondents, newsmen, pressmen, reporters
pressing *adjective* URGENT, crucial, high-priority, imperative, important, importunate, serious, vital

thrust per unit area > **pres•sur•i•za'tion** [-ZAY-shən] *noun* in aircraft, maintenance of normal atmospheric pressure at high altitudes > **pres'sur•ize** *verb transitive* **-ized, -iz•ing** > **pressure cooker** reinforced pot that cooks food rapidly by steam under pressure > **pressure group** organized group that exerts influence on policies, public opinion, etc.

pres•ti•dig•i•ta•tion [pres-ti-dij-i-TAY-shən] *noun* sleight of hand > **pres•ti•dig'i•ta•tor** *noun*

pres•tige [pre-STEEZH] *noun* 1 reputation 2 influence depending on it > **pres•tig'i•ous** [-STIJ-əs] *adjective*

pres•to [PRES-toh] *adverb mus.* quickly

pre•stressed [PREE-strest] *adjective* (of concrete) containing stretched steel cables for strengthening

pre•sume [pri-ZOOM] *verb transitive* **-sumed, -sum•ing** 1 take for granted ▷ *verb intransitive* **-sumed, -sum•ing** 2 take liberties > **pre•sum'a•bly** *adverb* 1 probably 2 doubtlessly > **pre•sump'tion** [-ZUM-shən] *noun* 1 forward, arrogant opinion or conduct 2 strong probability > **pre•sump'tive** *adjective* that may be assumed as true or valid until contrary is proved > **pre•sump'tu•ous** [-shoo-əs] *adjective* forward, impudent, taking liberties

pre•sup•pose [pree-sə-POHZ] *verb transitive* **-posed, -pos•ing** assume or take for granted beforehand > **pre•sup•po•si'tion** [-ZI-shən] *noun* previous supposition

pre•tend [pri-TEND] *verb transitive* 1 claim or allege (something untrue) 2 make believe, as in play ▷ *verb intransitive* 3 lay claim (to) > **pre•tense'** *noun* 1 simulation 2 pretext > **pre•tend'er** *noun* claimant (to throne) > **pre•ten'sion** *noun* > **pre•ten'tious** [-shəs] *adjective* 1 making claim to special merit or importance 2 given to outward show

pre•ter•nat•u•ral [pre-tər-NACH-ər-əl] *adjective* 1 out of ordinary way of nature 2 abnormal, supernatural

pre•text [PREE-tekst] *noun* 1 excuse 2 pretense

pret•ty [PRIT-ee] *adjective* **-ti•er, -ti•est** 1 having beauty that is attractive rather than imposing 2 charming, etc. ▷ *adverb* 3 fairly, moderately > **pret'ti•ness** [-nis] *noun*

pret•zel [PRET-səl] *noun* crisp, dry biscuit usu. shaped as knot or stick

pre•vail [pri-VAYL] *verb intransitive* 1 gain mastery 2 triumph 3 be in fashion, generally established > **pre•vail'ing** *adjective* 1 widespread 2 predominant > **prev'a•lence** [-ləns] *noun* > **prev'a•lent** [-lənt] *adjective* extensively existing, rife

pre•var•i•cate [pri-VA-ri-kayt] *verb intransitive* **-cat•ed, -cat•ing** 1 make evasive or misleading statements 2 lie > **pre•var'i•ca•tor** *noun*

DICTIONARY • THESAURUS

pressure *noun* 1 FORCE, compressing, compression, crushing, squeezing, weight
2 POWER, coercion, compulsion, constraint, force, influence, sway
3 STRESS, burden, demands, hassle (*informal*), heat, load, strain, urgency

prestige *noun* STATUS, credit, distinction, eminence, fame, honor, importance, kudos, renown, reputation, standing

prestigious *adjective* CELEBRATED, eminent, esteemed, great, illustrious, important, notable, prominent, renowned, respected

presumably *adverb* IT WOULD SEEM, apparently, in all likelihood, in all probability, on the face of it, probably, seemingly

presume *verb* 1 BELIEVE, assume, conjecture, guess (*informal*), infer, postulate, suppose, surmise, take for granted, think
2 DARE, go so far, make so bold, take the liberty, venture

presumption *noun* 1 CHEEK (*informal*), audacity, boldness, effrontery, gall (*informal*), impudence, insolence, nerve (*informal*)
2 PROBABILITY, basis, chance, likelihood

presumptuous *adjective* PUSHY (*informal*), audacious, bold, forward, insolent, overconfident, too big for one's boots

presuppose *verb* PRESUME, assume, imply, posit, postulate, take as read, take for granted

presupposition *noun* ASSUMPTION, belief, preconception, premise, presumption, supposition

pretend *verb* 1 FEIGN, affect, allege, assume, fake, falsify, impersonate, profess, sham, simulate
2 MAKE BELIEVE, act, imagine, make up, suppose

pretended *adjective* FEIGNED, bogus, counterfeit, fake, false, phoney *or* phony (*informal*), pretend (*informal*), pseudo (*informal*), sham, so-called

pretender *noun* CLAIMANT, aspirant

pretense *noun* 1 DECEPTION, acting, charade, deceit, falsehood, feigning, sham, simulation, trickery
2 SHOW, affectation, artifice, display, façade, veneer

pretension *noun* 1 CLAIM, aspiration, assumption, demand, pretense, profession
2 AFFECTATION, airs, conceit, ostentation, pretentiousness, self-importance, show, snobbery, vanity

pretentious *adjective* AFFECTED, conceited, grandiloquent, grandiose, high-flown, inflated, mannered, ostentatious, pompous, puffed up, showy, snobbish

pretext *noun* GUISE, cloak, cover, excuse, ploy, pretense, ruse, show

pretty *adjective* 1 ATTRACTIVE, beautiful, bonny, charming, comely, fair, good-looking, lovely ▷ *adverb* 2 FAIRLY, kind of (*informal*), moderately, quite, rather, reasonably, somewhat

prevail *verb* 1 WIN, be victorious, overcome, overrule, succeed, triumph
2 BE WIDESPREAD, abound, be current, be prevalent, exist generally, predominate

prevailing *adjective* 1 WIDESPREAD, common, cool (*informal*), current, customary, established, fashionable, general, in vogue, ordinary, phat (*slang*), popular, prevalent, usual
2 PREDOMINATING, dominant, main, principal, ruling

prevalence *noun* COMMONNESS, currency, frequency, popularity, universality

prevalent *adjective* COMMON, current, customary, established, frequent, general, popular, universal, usual, widespread

prevaricate *verb* EVADE, beat about the bush, cavil, deceive, dodge, equivocate, hedge

pre•vent [pri-VENT] *verb transitive* stop, hinder > **pre•vent'a•ble** *adjective* > **pre•ven'tion** [-shən] *noun* > **pre•ven'tive** *adjective, noun*
pre•view [PREE-vyoo] *noun* 1 advance showing 2 a showing of scenes from a forthcoming film, etc.
pre•vi•ous [PREE-vee-əs] *adjective* 1 earlier 2 preceding 3 happening before > **pre'vi•ous•ly** *adverb* before
prey [pray] *noun* 1 animal hunted and killed by carnivorous animals 2 victim ▷ *verb intransitive* 3 seize for food 4 treat as prey 5 (with *upon*) afflict, obsess
price [prīs] *noun* 1 amount, etc. for which thing is bought or sold 2 cost 3 value 4 reward 5 odds in betting ▷ *verb transitive* **priced, pric•ing** 6 fix, ask price for > **price'less** [-lis] *adjective* 1 invaluable 2 very funny > **pric'ey** [-ee] *adjective* **pric•i•er, pric•i•est** expensive
prick [prik] *verb transitive* 1 pierce slightly with sharp point 2 cause to feel mental pain 3 mark by prick 4 erect (ears) ▷ *noun* 5 slight hole made by pricking 6 pricking or being pricked 7 sting 8 remorse 9 that which pricks 10 sharp point > **prick'le** *noun* 1 thorn, spike ▷ *verb intransitive* **-kled, -kling** 2 feel tingling or pricking sensation > **prick'ly** *adjective* **-li•er, -li•est** > **prickly heat** inflammation of skin with stinging pains
pride [prīd] *noun* 1 too high an opinion of oneself 2 worthy self-esteem 3 feeling of elation or great satisfaction 4 something causing this 5 group (of lions) ▷ *verb reflexive* **prid•ed, prid•ing** 6 take pride
priest [preest] *noun* official minister of religion, member of clergy > **priest'ess** *noun feminine* > **priest'hood** [-huud] *noun* > **priest'ly** *adjective* **-li•er, -li•est**
prig *noun* self-righteous person who professes superior culture, morality, etc. > **prig'gish** *adjective*
prim *adjective* **prim•mer, prim•mest** very restrained, formally prudish
pri•ma•cy [PRĪ-me-see] *noun* 1 state of being first in rank, grade, etc. 2 *office of* **primate**[1]
pri•ma don•na [pree-mə DON-ə] *noun, plural* **donnas** 1 principal female singer in opera 2 temperamental person
pri•ma fa•ci•e [PRĪ-mə FAY-shee] *Lat.* 1 at first sight 2 obvious
pri•mal [PRĪ-məl] *adjective* 1 of earliest age 2 first, original > **pri•ma'ri•ly** *adverb* > **pri'ma•ry** *adjective* 1 chief 2 of the first stage, decision, etc. 3 elementary
pri•mate[1] [PRĪ-mit] *noun* archbishop
primate[2] [PRĪ-mayt] *noun* one of order of mammals including monkeys and man
prime[1] [prīm] *adjective* 1 fundamental 2

DICTIONARY

P

THESAURUS

prevent *verb* STOP, avert, avoid, foil, forestall, frustrate, hamper, hinder, impede, inhibit, obstruct, obviate, preclude, thwart
prevention *noun* ELIMINATION, avoidance, deterrence, precaution, safeguard, thwarting
preventive *adjective* 1 HINDERING, hampering, impeding, obstructive
2 PROTECTIVE, counteractive, deterrent, precautionary
▷ *noun* 3 HINDRANCE, block, impediment, obstacle, obstruction
4 PROTECTION, deterrent, prevention, remedy, safeguard, shield
preview *noun* ADVANCE SHOWING, foretaste, sneak preview, taster, trailer
previous *adjective* EARLIER, erstwhile, foregoing, former, past, preceding, prior
previously *adverb* BEFORE, beforehand, earlier, formerly, hitherto, in the past, once
prey *noun* 1 QUARRY, game, kill
2 VICTIM, dupe, fall guy (*informal*), mug (*Brit slang*), target
price *noun* 1 COST, amount, charge, damage (*informal*), estimate, expense, fee, figure, rate, value, worth
2 CONSEQUENCES, cost, penalty, toll
▷ *verb* 3 EVALUATE, assess, cost, estimate, rate, value
priceless *adjective* 1 VALUABLE, costly, dear, expensive, invaluable, precious
2 (*informal*) HILARIOUS, amusing, comic, droll, funny, rib-tickling, side-splitting
pricey *adjective* EXPENSIVE, costly, dear, high-priced, steep (*informal*)
prick *verb* 1 PIERCE, jab, lance, perforate, punch, puncture, stab
2 STING, bite, itch, prickle, smart, tingle
▷ *noun* 3 PUNCTURE, hole, perforation, pinhole, wound
prickle *noun* 1 SPIKE, barb, needle, point, spine, spur, thorn
▷ *verb* 2 TINGLE, itch, smart, sting
3 PRICK, jab, stick
prickly *adjective* 1 SPINY, barbed, bristly, thorny
2 ITCHY, crawling, scratchy, sharp, smarting, stinging, tingling
pride *noun* 1 SATISFACTION, delight, gratification, joy, pleasure
2 SELF-RESPECT, dignity, honor, self-esteem, self-worth
3 CONCEIT, arrogance, egotism, hubris, pretension, pretentiousness, self-importance, self-love, superciliousness, vanity
4 GEM, jewel, pride and joy, treasure
priest *noun* CLERGYMAN, cleric, curate, divine, ecclesiastic, father, minister, pastor, vicar
prig *noun* GOODY-GOODY (*informal*), prude, puritan, stuffed shirt (*informal*)
priggish *adjective* SELF-RIGHTEOUS, goody-goody (*informal*), holier-than-thou, prim, prudish, puritanical
prim *adjective* PRUDISH, demure, fastidious, fussy, priggish, prissy (*informal*), proper, puritanical, strait-laced
prima donna *noun* DIVA, leading lady, star
primarily *adverb* 1 CHIEFLY, above all, essentially, fundamentally, generally, largely, mainly, mostly, principally
2 AT FIRST, at the start *or* from the start, first and foremost, initially, in the beginning, in the first place, originally
primary *adjective* 1 CHIEF, cardinal, cutting-edge, first, greatest, highest, main, paramount, prime, principal
2 ELEMENTARY, introductory, rudimentary, simple
prime *adjective* 1 MAIN, chief, leading, predominant, pre-eminent, primary, principal

original 3 chief 4 best ▷ *noun* 5 first, best part of anything 6 youth 7 full health and vigor ▷ *verb transitive* **primed, prim•ing** 8 prepare (gun, engine, pump, etc.) for use 9 fill up, e.g. with information > **prime minister** leader of parliamentary government

prime² *verb transitive* **primed, prim•ing** prepare for paint with preliminary coating of oil, etc. > **prim'er** [PRĪM-ər] *noun* paint, etc. for priming

prim•er [PRIM-ər] *noun* elementary schoolbook or manual

pri•me•val [prī-MEE-vəl] *adjective* of the earliest age of the world

prim•i•tive [PRIM-i-tiv] *adjective* 1 of an early undeveloped kind, ancient 2 crude, rough

pri•mo•gen•i•ture [prī-mə-JEN-i-chər] *noun* rule by which real estate passes to the first born son > **pri•mo•gen'i•tor** *noun* 1 earliest ancestor 2 forefather

pri•mor•di•al [pri-MOR-dee-əl] *adjective* existing at or from the beginning

prince [prins] *noun* 1 son or (in some countries) grandson of king or queen 2 ruler, chief > **prin'cess** *noun feminine* > **prince'ly** *adjective* **-li•er, -li•est** 1 generous, lavish 2 stately 3 magnificent

prin•ci•pal [PRIN-sə-pəl] *adjective* 1 chief in importance ▷ *noun* 2 person for whom another is agent 3 head of institution, esp. school 4 sum of money lent and yielding interest 5 chief actor > **prin•ci•pal'i•ty** *noun* territory, dignity of prince

prin•ci•ple [PRIN-sə-pəl] *noun* 1 moral rule 2 settled reason of action 3 uprightness 4 fundamental truth or element

print *verb transitive* 1 reproduce (words, pictures, etc., by pressing inked plates, type, blocks, etc. to paper, etc.) 2 produce thus 3 write in imitation of this 4 impress 5 *photography* produce pictures from negatives 6 stamp (fabric) with colored design ▷ *noun* 7 printed matter 8 printed lettering 9 written imitation of printed type 10 photograph 11 impression, mark left on surface by thing that has pressed against it 12 printed cotton fabric > **print'er** *noun* person or device engaged in printing > **printed circuit** electronic circuit with wiring printed on an insulating base > **print'out** *noun* printed information from computer, teleprinter, etc.

pri•or [PRĪ-ər] *adjective* 1 earlier ▷ *noun* 2 chief of religious house or order > **pri'or•ess** *noun feminine* > **pri•or'i•ty** *noun, plural* **-ties** 1 precedence 2 something given special attention > **pri'o•ry** *noun, plural* **-ries** monastery, convent under prior, prioress **prior to** before, earlier

prise [prīz] *verb transitive* **prised, pris•ing** 1 force open by levering 2 obtain (information, etc.) with difficulty

prism [PRIZ-əm] *noun* transparent solid usu. with triangular ends and rectangular sides, used to disperse light into spectrum or refract it in optical instruments, etc. > **pris•mat'ic** *adjective* 1 of prism shape 2 (of color) such as is produced by refraction through prism, rainbowlike, brilliant

pris•on [PRIZ-ən] *noun* jail > **pris'on•er** *noun* 1 one kept in prison 2 captive

pris•sy [PRIS-ee] *adjective* **-si•er, -si•est** fussy, prim

pris•tine [pris-TEEN] *adjective* original, primitive, unspoiled, good

pri•vate [PRĪ-vit] *adjective* 1 secret, not public 2 reserved for, or belonging to, or concerning, an

---

2 BEST, choice, excellent, first-class, first-rate, highest, quality, select, top
▷ *noun* 3 PEAK, bloom, flower, height, heyday, zenith
▷ *verb* 4 INFORM, brief, clue in (*informal*), fill in (*informal*), notify, tell
5 PREPARE, coach, get ready, make ready, train

primeval *adjective* EARLIEST, ancient, early, first, old, prehistoric, primal, primitive, primordial

primitive *adjective* 1 EARLY, earliest, elementary, first, original, primary, primeval, primordial
2 CRUDE, rough, rudimentary, simple, unrefined

prince *noun* RULER, lord, monarch, sovereign

princely *adjective* 1 REGAL, imperial, majestic, noble, royal, sovereign
2 GENEROUS, bounteous, gracious, lavish, liberal, munificent, open-handed, rich

principal *adjective* 1 MAIN, cardinal, chief, cutting-edge, essential, first, foremost, key, leading, paramount, pre-eminent, primary, prime
▷ *noun* 2 HEAD (*informal*), dean, headmaster *or* headmistress, superintendent
3 STAR, alpha male, lead, leader
4 CAPITAL, assets, money

principally *adverb* MAINLY, above all, chiefly, especially, largely, mostly, predominantly, primarily

principle *noun* 1 RULE, canon, criterion, doctrine, dogma, fundamental, law, maxim, precept, standard, truth
2 MORALS, conscience, integrity, probity, scruples, sense of honor
3 ▷ **in principle** IN THEORY, ideally, theoretically

print *verb* 1 PUBLISH, engrave, impress, imprint, issue, mark, stamp
▷ *noun* 2 PUBLICATION, book, magazine, newspaper, newsprint, periodical, printed matter
3 REPRODUCTION, copy, engraving, photo (*informal*), photograph, picture

prior *adjective* 1 EARLIER, foregoing, former, preceding, pre-existent, pre-existing, previous
2 ▷ **prior to** BEFORE, earlier than, preceding, previous to

priority *noun* PRECEDENCE, pre-eminence, preference, rank, right of way, seniority

priory *noun* MONASTERY, abbey, convent, nunnery, religious house

prison *noun* JAIL, clink (*slang*), confinement, cooler (*slang*), dungeon, lockup, penitentiary, slammer (*slang*)

prisoner *noun* 1 CONVICT, con (*slang*), jailbird, lag (*slang*)
2 CAPTIVE, detainee, hostage, internee

prissy *adjective* PRIM, old-maidish (*informal*), prim and proper, prudish, strait-laced

pristine *adjective* NEW, immaculate, pure, uncorrupted, undefiled, unspoiled, unsullied, untouched, virginal

privacy *noun* SECLUSION, isolation, retirement, retreat, solitude

individual only 3 personal 4 secluded 5 denoting soldier or marine of lowest rank 6 not controlled by government ▷ *noun* 7 private soldier or marine > **pri'va•cy** [-vi-see] *noun* > **pri•va•tize** *verb transitive* **-tized, -tiz•ing** transfer from government or public ownership to private enterprise

pri•va•tion [prī-VAY-shən] *noun* 1 want of comforts or necessities 2 hardship 3 act of depriving > **priv•a•tive** [PRIV-ə-tiv] *adjective* of privation or negation

priv•et [PRIV-it] *noun* bushy shrub used for hedges

priv•i•lege [PRIV-ə-lij] *noun* 1 advantage or favor that only a few obtain 2 right, advantage belonging to person or class > **priv'i•leged** *adjective* enjoying special right or immunity

priv•y [PRIV-ee] *adjective* 1 admitted to knowledge of secret ▷ *noun, plural* **priv•ies** 2 outhouse 3 *law* person having interest in an action

prize[1] [prīz] *noun* 1 reward given for success in competition 2 thing striven for 3 thing won ▷ *adjective* 4 winning or likely to win a prize ▷ *verb transitive* **prized, priz•ing** 5 value highly > **prize'fight** *noun* boxing match for money

prize[2] *noun* ship, property captured in (naval) warfare

pro[1] [proh] *adjective, adverb* in favor of

pro[2] *noun* 1 professional ▷ *adjective* 2 professional

pro- *prefix* for, instead of, before, in front: *proconsul; pronoun; project*

pro•ac•tive [proh-AK-tiv] *adjective* taking the initiative and acting in advance, rather than simply reacting to circumstances and events

prob•a•ble [PROB-ə-bəl] *adjective* likely > **prob•a•bil'i•ty** *noun* 1 likelihood 2 anything that has appearance of truth > **prob'a•bly** *adverb*

pro•bate [PROH-bayt] *noun* 1 proving of authenticity of will 2 certificate of this > **probate court** court with power over administration of estates of dead persons

pro•ba•tion [proh-BAY-shən] *noun* 1 system of releasing lawbreakers, but placing them under supervision for stated period 2 testing of candidate before admission to full membership

probe [prohb] *verb transitive* **probed, prob•ing** 1 search into, examine, question closely ▷ *noun* 2 that which probes, or is used to probe 3 thorough inquiry

pro•bi•ty [PROH-bi-tee] *noun* honesty, uprightness, integrity

prob•lem [PROB-ləm] *noun* 1 matter, etc. difficult to deal with or solve 2 question set for solution 3 puzzle > **prob•le•mat'ic** *adjective* 1 questionable 2 uncertain 3 disputable

pro•bos•cis [proh-BOS-is] *noun, plural* **-cis•es** 1 trunk or long snout 2 (*informal*) nose, esp. prominent one

pro•ceed [prə-SEED] *verb intransitive* 1 go forward, continue 2 be carried on 3 take legal action > **pro•ceeds** [PROH-seedz] *plural noun* amount of money or profit received > **pro•ce'dur•al** [-SEE-jər-əl] *adjective* > **pro•ce'dure** *noun* 1 act, manner of proceeding 2 conduct > **pro•ceed'ing** *noun* 1 act or course of action 2 transaction > **pro•ceed'ings** 1 minutes of meeting 2 methods of prosecuting charge, claim, etc.

proc•ess [PROS-es] *noun* 1 series of actions or changes 2 method of operation 3 state of

DICTIONARY

P

THESAURUS

private *adjective* 1 EXCLUSIVE, individual, intimate, own, personal, reserved, special 2 SECRET, clandestine, confidential, covert, hush-hush (*informal*), off the record, unofficial 3 SECLUDED, concealed, isolated, secret, separate, sequestered, solitary

privilege *noun* RIGHT, advantage, claim, concession, due, entitlement, freedom, liberty, prerogative

privileged *adjective* SPECIAL, advantaged, elite, entitled, favored, honored

privy *adjective* 1 ▷ **privy to** INFORMED OF, apprised of, aware of, cognizant of, in on, in the know about (*informal*), wise to (*slang*) ▷ *noun* 2 LAVATORY, latrine, outside toilet

prize[1] *noun* 1 REWARD, accolade, award, honor, trophy 2 WINNINGS, haul, jackpot, purse, stakes ▷ *adjective* 3 CHAMPION, award-winning, best, first-rate, outstanding, top, winning

prize[2] *verb* VALUE, cherish, esteem, hold dear, treasure

probability *noun* LIKELIHOOD, chance *or* chances, expectation, liability, likeliness, odds, prospect

probable *adjective* LIKELY, apparent, credible, feasible, plausible, possible, presumable, reasonable

probably *adverb* LIKELY, doubtless, maybe, most likely, perchance (*archaic*), perhaps, possibly, presumably

probation *noun* TRIAL PERIOD, apprenticeship, trial

probe *verb* 1 EXAMINE, explore, go into, investigate, look into, scrutinize, search 2 EXPLORE, feel around, poke, prod ▷ *noun* 3 EXAMINATION, detection, exploration, inquiry, investigation, scrutiny, study

problem *noun* 1 DIFFICULTY, complication, dilemma, dispute, predicament, quandary, trouble 2 PUZZLE, conundrum, enigma, poser, question, riddle

problematic *adjective* TRICKY, debatable, doubtful, dubious, problematical, puzzling

procedure *noun* METHOD, action, conduct, course, custom, modus operandi, policy, practice, process, routine, strategy, system

proceed *verb* 1 GO ON, carry on, continue, go ahead, move on, press on, progress 2 ARISE, come, derive, emanate, flow, issue, originate, result, spring, stem

proceeding *noun* 1 ACTION, act, deed, measure, move, procedure, process, step 2 ▷ **proceedings** BUSINESS, account, affairs, archives, doings, minutes, records, report, transactions

proceeds *plural noun* INCOME, earnings, gain, products, profit, returns, revenue, takings, yield

process *noun* 1 PROCEDURE, action, course, manner, means, measure, method, operation, performance, practice, system 2 DEVELOPMENT, advance, evolution, growth, movement, progress, progression ▷ *verb* 3 HANDLE, deal with, fulfill

going on 4 action of law 5 outgrowth ▷ *verb transitive* 6 handle, treat, prepare by special method of manufacture, etc. > **pro•ces•sion** [prə-SESH-ən] *noun* 1 regular, orderly progress 2 line of persons in formal order > **pro•ces'sion•al** *adjective* > **proc'es•sor** *noun* 1 person or device that processes 2 *computing same as* **central processing unit**

pro•claim [proh-KLAYM] *verb transitive* announce publicly, declare > **proc•la•ma'tion** [prok-lə-MAY-shən] *noun*

pro•cliv•i•ty [proh-KLIV-i-tee] *noun, plural* **-ties** inclination, tendency

pro•cras•ti•nate [proh-KRAS-tə-nayt] *verb intransitive* **-nat•ed, -nat•ing** delay > **pro•cras•ti•na'tion** *noun* > **pro•cras'ti•na•tor** *noun*

pro•cre•ate [PROH-kree-ayt] *verb transitive* **-at•ed, -at•ing** produce offspring, generate > **pro•cre•a'tion** *noun*

Pro•crus•te•an [proh-KRUS-tee-ən] *adjective* compelling uniformity by violence

proc•tol•o•gy [prok-TOL-ə-jee] *noun* medical specialty dealing with diseases of anus and rectum

proc•tor [PROK-tər] *noun* 1 person appointed to supervise students during examinations 2 university official with administrative, esp. disciplinary, duties

pro•cure [prə-KYUUR] *verb transitive* **-cured, -cur•ing** 1 obtain, acquire 2 provide 3 bring about ▷ *verb intransitive* **-cured, -cur•ing** 4 act as pimp > **pro•cure'ment** *noun* > **pro•cur'er** *noun* 1 one who procures 2 pimp > **pro•cur'ess** *noun feminine*

prod *verb transitive* **prod•ded, prod•ding** 1 poke with something pointed 2 stimulate to action ▷ *noun* 3 prodding 4 goad 5 pointed instrument

prod•i•gal [PROD-i-gəl] *adjective* 1 wasteful 2 extravagant ▷ *noun* 3 spendthrift > **prod•i•gal'i•ty** *noun* reckless extravagance

prod•i•gy [PROD-i-jee] *noun, plural* **-gies** 1 person esp. precocious child with some marvelous gift 2 thing causing wonder > **pro•di•gious** [prə-DIJ-əs] *adjective* 1 very great, immense 2 extraordinary > **pro•di'gious•ly** *adverb*

pro•duce [prə-DOOS] *verb transitive* **-duced, -duc•ing** 1 bring into existence 2 yield 3 make 4 bring forward 5 manufacture 6 exhibit 7 present on stage, film, TV 8 *geometry* extend in length ▷ *noun* [PROD-oos] 9 that which is yielded or made, esp. vegetables > **pro•duc'er** *noun* person who produces, esp. play, film, etc. > **prod'uct** [-əkt] *noun* 1 result of process of manufacture 2 number resulting from multiplication > **pro•duc'tion** *noun* 1 producing 2 things produced > **pro•duc'tive** *adjective* 1 fertile 2 creative 3 efficient > **pro•duc•tiv'i•ty** *noun*

pro•fam•i•ly [proh-FAM-ə-lee] *adjective* 1 antiabortion 2 pro-life

pro•fane [prə-FAYN] *adjective* 1 irreverent, blasphemous 2 not sacred ▷ *verb transitive* **-faned, -fan•ing** 3 pollute, desecrate > **prof•a•na•tion** [prof-ə-NAY-shən] *noun* > **pro•fan•i•ty** [prə-FAN-i-tee] *noun* profane talk or behavior, blasphemy

procession *noun* PARADE, cavalcade, cortege, file, march, train

proclaim *verb* DECLARE, advertise, announce, circulate, herald, indicate, make known, profess, publish

proclamation *noun* DECLARATION, announcement, decree, edict, notice, notification, pronouncement, publication

procrastinate *verb* DELAY, dally, drag one's feet (*informal*), gain time, play for time, postpone, put off, stall, temporize

procure *verb* OBTAIN, acquire, buy, come by, find, gain, get, pick up, purchase, score (*slang*), secure, win

prod *verb* 1 POKE, dig, drive, jab, nudge, push, shove
2 PROMPT, egg on, goad, impel, incite, motivate, move, rouse, spur, stimulate, urge
▷ *noun* 3 POKE, dig, jab, nudge, push, shove
4 PROMPT, cue, reminder, signal, stimulus

prodigal *adjective* EXTRAVAGANT, excessive, immoderate, improvident, profligate, reckless, spendthrift, wasteful

prodigious *adjective* 1 HUGE, colossal, enormous, giant, gigantic, immense, massive, monstrous, vast
2 WONDERFUL, amazing, exceptional, extraordinary, fabulous, fantastic (*informal*), marvelous, phenomenal, remarkable, staggering

prodigy *noun* 1 GENIUS, mastermind, talent, whizz (*informal*), wizard
2 WONDER, marvel, miracle, phenomenon, sensation

produce *verb* 1 CAUSE, bring about, effect, generate, give rise to
2 BRING FORTH, bear, beget, breed, deliver
3 SHOW, advance, demonstrate, exhibit, offer, present
4 MAKE, compose, construct, create, develop, fabricate, invent, manufacture
5 PRESENT, direct, do, exhibit, mount, put on, show, stage
▷ *noun* 6 FRUIT AND VEGETABLES, crop, greengrocery, harvest, product, yield

producer *noun* 1 DIRECTOR, impresario
2 MAKER, farmer, grower, manufacturer

product *noun* 1 GOODS, artefact, commodity, creation, invention, merchandise, produce, work
2 RESULT, consequence, effect, outcome, upshot

production *noun* 1 PRODUCING, construction, creation, fabrication, formation, making, manufacture, manufacturing
2 PRESENTATION, direction, management, staging

productive *adjective* 1 FERTILE, creative, fecund, fruitful, inventive, plentiful, prolific, rich
2 USEFUL, advantageous, beneficial, constructive, effective, profitable, rewarding, valuable, win-win (*informal*), worthwhile

productivity *noun* OUTPUT, production, work rate, yield

profane *adjective* 1 SACRILEGIOUS, disrespectful, godless, impious, impure, irreligious, irreverent, sinful, ungodly, wicked
2 CRUDE, blasphemous, coarse, filthy, foul, obscene, vulgar
▷ *verb* 3 DESECRATE, commit sacrilege, debase, defile, violate

pro•fess [prə-FES] *verb transitive* 1 affirm belief in 2 confess publicly 3 assert 4 claim, pretend > **pro•fess'ed•ly** *adverb* avowedly > **pro•fes'sion** *noun* 1 calling or occupation, esp. learned, scientific or artistic 2 a professing 3 vow of religious faith on entering religious order > **pro•fes'sion•al** *adjective* 1 engaged in a profession 2 engaged in a game or sport for money ▷ *noun* 3 member of profession 4 paid player > **pro•fes'sor** *noun* teacher of highest rank in college or university > **pro•fes•so'ri•al** *adjective*
proffer *verb transitive, noun* offer
pro•fi•cient [prə-FISH-ənt] *adjective* 1 skilled 2 expert > **pro•fi'cien•cy** *noun*
pro•file [PROH-fīl] *noun* 1 outline, esp. of face, as seen from side 2 brief biographical sketch
prof'it *noun* 1 money gained 2 benefit obtained ▷ *verb* 3 benefit > **prof'it•a•ble** *adjective* yielding profit > **prof•it•eer'** *noun* 1 one who makes excessive profits at the expense of the public ▷ *verb intransitive* 2 do this
prof•li•gate [PROF-li-git] *adjective* 1 dissolute 2 reckless, wasteful ▷ *noun* 3 dissolute person > **prof'li•ga•cy** [-li-gi-see] *noun*
pro for•ma [proh FOR-mə] *Lat.* 1 prescribing a set form 2 for the sake of form
pro•found [prə-FOWND] *adjective* **-er, -est** 1 very learned 2 deep > **pro•fun'di•ty** *noun*
pro•fuse [prə-FYOOS] *adjective* abundant, prodigal > **pro•fu•sion** [-FYOO-zhən] *noun*
prog•e•ny [PROJ-ə-nee] *noun* children > **pro•gen•i•tor** [proh-JEN-i-tər] *noun* ancestor
pro•ges•ter•one [proh-JES-tə-rohn] *noun* hormone that prepares uterus for pregnancy and prevents further ovulation
prog•na•thous [prog-NAY-thəs] *adjective* with projecting lower jaw
prog•no•sis [prog-NOH-sis] *noun, plural* **-ses** [-seez] 1 art of foretelling course of disease by symptoms 2 forecast > **prog•nos'tic** *adjective* 1 of, serving as prognosis ▷ *noun* > **prog•nos'ti•cate** *verb transitive* **-cat•ed, -cat•ing** foretell
pro•gram [PROH-gram] *noun* 1 plan, detailed notes of intended proceedings 2 broadcast on radio or television 3 detailed instructions for a computer ▷ *verb transitive* **-grammed, -gram•ming** 4 feed program into (computer) 5 arrange detailed instructions for computer > **pro'gram•mer** *noun*
prog'ress *noun* 1 onward movement 2 development ▷ *verb intransitive* [prə-GRES] 3 go forward 4 improve > **pro•gres'sion** *noun* 1 moving forward 2 advance, improvement 3

DICTIONARY **P** THESAURUS

profanity *noun* 1 SACRILEGE, blasphemy, impiety, profaneness
2 SWEARING, curse, cursing, irreverence, obscenity
profess *verb* 1 CLAIM, allege, fake, feign, make out, pretend, purport
2 STATE, admit, affirm, announce, assert, avow, confess, declare, proclaim, vouch
professed *adjective* 1 SUPPOSED, alleged, ostensible, pretended, purported, self-styled, so-called, would-be
2 DECLARED, avowed, confessed, confirmed, proclaimed, self-acknowledged, self-confessed
profession *noun* 1 OCCUPATION, business, calling, career, employment, office, position, sphere, vocation
2 DECLARATION, affirmation, assertion, avowal, claim, confession, statement
professional *adjective* 1 EXPERT, adept, competent, efficient, experienced, masterly, proficient, qualified, skilled
▷ *noun* 2 EXPERT, adept, maestro, master, past master, pro (*slang*), specialist, virtuoso
professor *noun* TEACHER, don (*Brit*), fellow (*Brit*), prof (*informal*)
proficiency *noun* SKILL, ability, aptitude, competence, dexterity, expertise, knack, know-how (*informal*), mastery
proficient *adjective* SKILLED, able, accomplished, adept, capable, competent, efficient, expert, gifted, masterly, skillful
profile *noun* 1 OUTLINE, contour, drawing, figure, form, side view, silhouette, sketch
2 BIOGRAPHY, characterization, sketch, thumbnail sketch, vignette
profit *noun* 1 (*often plural*) EARNINGS, gain, proceeds, receipts, return, revenue, takings, yield
2 BENEFIT, advancement, advantage, gain, good, use, value
▷ *verb* 3 BENEFIT, be of advantage to, gain, help, improve, promote, serve
4 MAKE MONEY, earn, gain
profitable *adjective* 1 MONEY-MAKING, commercial, cost-effective, fruitful, lucrative, paying, remunerative, worthwhile
2 BENEFICIAL, advantageous, fruitful, productive, rewarding, useful, valuable, win-win (*informal*), worthwhile
profiteer *noun* 1 RACKETEER, exploiter
▷ *verb* 2 RACKETEER, exploit, make a quick buck (*slang*)
profligate *adjective* 1 EXTRAVAGANT, immoderate, improvident, prodigal, reckless, spendthrift, wasteful
2 DEPRAVED, debauched, degenerate, dissolute, immoral, licentious, shameless, wanton, wicked, wild
▷ *noun* 3 SPENDTHRIFT, squanderer, waster, wastrel
4 DEGENERATE, debauchee, libertine, rake, reprobate, roué
profound *adjective* 1 WISE, abstruse, deep, learned, penetrating, philosophical, sagacious, sage
2 INTENSE, acute, deeply felt, extreme, great, heartfelt, keen
profuse *adjective* PLENTIFUL, abundant, ample, bountiful, copious, luxuriant, overflowing, prolific
profusion *noun* ABUNDANCE, bounty, excess, extravagance, glut, plethora, quantity, surplus, wealth
progeny *noun* CHILDREN, descendants, family, issue, lineage, offspring, posterity, race, stock, young
prognosis *noun* FORECAST, diagnosis, prediction, prognostication, projection
program *noun* 1 SCHEDULE, agenda, curriculum, line-up, list, listing, order of events, plan, syllabus, timetable
2 SHOW, broadcast, performance, presentation,

increase or decrease of numbers or magnitudes according to fixed law 4 *mus.* regular succession of chords > **pro•gres'sive** *adjective* 1 progressing by degrees 2 favoring political or social reform
pro•hi•bit [proh-HIB-it] *verb transitive* forbid > **pro•hi•bi'tion** *noun* 1 act of forbidding 2 interdict 3 interdiction of supply and consumption of alcoholic drinks > **pro•hib'i•tive** *adjective* 1 tending to forbid or exclude 2 (of prices) very high
pro•ject [PROJ-ekt] *noun* 1 plan, scheme 2 design ▷ *verb transitive* [prə-JEKT] 3 plan 4 throw 5 cause to appear on distant background ▷ *verb intransitive* [prə-JEKT] 6 stick out, protrude > **pro•jec'tile** [-JEK-til] *noun* 1 heavy missile, esp. shell or ball ▷ *adjective* 2 for throwing > **pro•jec'tion** *noun* > **pro•jec'tion•ist** *noun* operator of film projector > **pro•jec'tor** *noun* 1 apparatus for projecting photographic images, films, slides on screen 2 one that forms scheme or design
pro•lapse [proh-LAPS] *noun* 1 falling, slipping down of part of body from normal position ▷ *verb intransitive* 2 fall or slip down in this way
pro•le•tar•i•at [proh-li-TAIR-ee-ət] *noun* lowest class of community, working class > **pro•le•tar'i•an** *adjective, noun*
pro-life *adjective* see **profamily**
pro•lif•er•ate [prə-LIF-ə-rayt] *verb* **-at•ed, -at•ing** grow or reproduce rapidly > **pro•lif•er•a'tion** *noun*
pro•li•fic [prə-LIF-ik] *adjective* 1 fruitful 2 producing much
pro•lix [proh-LIKS] *adjective* wordy, long-winded > **pro•lix'i•ty** *noun*
pro•logue [PROH-lawg] *noun* preface, esp. speech before a play
pro•long [prə-LAWNG] *verb transitive* 1 lengthen 2 protract
prom *noun* school or college dance, esp. at end of school year
prom•e•nade [prom-ə-NAYD] *noun* 1 leisurely walk 2 place made or used for this ▷ *verb intransitive* **-nad•ed, -nad•ing** 3 take leisurely walk 4 go up and down
prom•i•nent [PROM-ə-nənt] *adjective* 1 sticking out 2 conspicuous 3 distinguished > **prom'i•nence** *noun*
pro•mis•cu•ous [prə-MIS-kyoo-əs] *adjective* 1 indiscriminate, esp. in sexual relations 2 mixed without distinction > **prom•is•cu'i•ty** [-KYOO-ə-tee] *noun*
prom•ise [PROM-is] *verb transitive* **-mised, -mis•ing** 1 give assurance ▷ *verb intransitive* **-mised, -mis•ing** 2 be likely to ▷ *noun* 3 undertaking to do or not to do something 4 potential > **prom'is•ing** *adjective* showing good

DICTIONARY • THESAURUS

---

production
progress *noun* 1 DEVELOPMENT, advance, breakthrough, gain, growth, headway, improvement
2 MOVEMENT, advance, course, passage, way
3 ▷ **in progress** GOING ON, being done, happening, occurring, proceeding, taking place, under way
▷ *verb* 4 DEVELOP, advance, gain, grow, improve
5 MOVE ON, advance, continue, go forward, make headway, proceed, travel
progression *noun* 1 PROGRESS, advance, advancement, furtherance, gain, headway, movement forward
2 SEQUENCE, chain, course, cycle, series, string, succession
progressive *adjective* 1 ENLIGHTENED, advanced, avant-garde, forward-looking, liberal, modern, radical, reformist, revolutionary
2 GROWING, advancing, continuing, developing, increasing, ongoing
prohibit *verb* 1 FORBID, ban, debar, disallow, outlaw, proscribe, veto
2 PREVENT, hamper, hinder, impede, restrict, stop
prohibition *noun* 1 PREVENTION, constraint, exclusion, obstruction, restriction
2 BAN, bar, boycott, embargo, injunction, interdict, proscription, veto
prohibitive *adjective* EXORBITANT, excessive, extortionate, steep (*informal*)
project *noun* 1 SCHEME, activity, assignment, enterprise, job, occupation, plan, task, undertaking, venture, work
▷ *verb* 2 FORECAST, calculate, estimate, extrapolate, gauge, predict, reckon
3 STICK OUT, bulge, extend, jut, overhang, protrude, stand out
projectile *noun* MISSILE, bullet, rocket, shell
projection *noun* 1 PROTRUSION, bulge, ledge, overhang, protuberance, ridge, shelf
2 FORECAST, calculation, computation, estimate, estimation, extrapolation, reckoning
proletarian *adjective* 1 WORKING-CLASS, common, plebeian
▷ *noun* 2 WORKER, commoner, man of the people, pleb, plebeian
proletariat *noun* WORKING CLASS, commoners, hoi polloi, laboring classes, lower classes, plebs, the common people, the masses
proliferate *verb* INCREASE, breed, expand, grow rapidly, multiply
proliferation *noun* MULTIPLICATION, expansion, increase, spread
prolific *adjective* PRODUCTIVE, abundant, copious, fecund, fertile, fruitful, luxuriant, profuse
prologue *noun* INTRODUCTION, foreword, preamble, preface, preliminary, prelude
prolong *verb* LENGTHEN, continue, delay, drag out, draw out, extend, perpetuate, protract, spin out, stretch
promenade *noun* 1 WALKWAY, esplanade, parade, prom
2 STROLL, constitutional, saunter, turn, walk
▷ *verb* 3 STROLL, perambulate, saunter, take a walk, walk
prominence *noun* 1 CONSPICUOUSNESS, markedness
2 FAME, celebrity, distinction, eminence, importance, name, prestige, reputation
prominent *adjective* 1 NOTICEABLE, conspicuous, eye-catching, obtrusive, obvious, outstanding, pronounced
2 FAMOUS, distinguished, eminent, foremost, important, leading, main, notable, renowned, top, well-known
promiscuity *noun* LICENTIOUSNESS, debauchery, immorality, looseness, permissiveness,

signs, hopeful > **prom'is•so•ry** *adjective* containing promise > **promissory note** written promise to pay sum to person named, at specified time

prom•on•to•ry [PROM-ən-tor-ee] *noun, plural* **-ries** point of high land jutting out into the sea, headland

pro•mote [prə-MOHT] *verb transitive* **-mot•ed, -mot•ing** 1 help forward 2 move up to higher rank or position 3 work for 4 encourage sale of > **pro•mot'er** *noun* > **pro•mo'tion** *noun* 1 advancement 2 preferment

prompt *adjective* **-er, -est** 1 done at once 2 acting with alacrity 3 punctual 4 ready ▷ *verb* 5 urge, suggest 6 help out (actor or speaker) by reading or suggesting next words > **prompt'er** *noun* > **prompt'ness** [-nis] *noun* > **prompt'ly** *adverb*

prom•ul•gate [PROM-əl-gayt] *verb transitive* **-gat•ed, -gat•ing** proclaim, publish > **prom•ul•ga'tion** *noun*

prone [prohn] *adjective* 1 lying face downward 2 inclined (to) > **prone'ness** [-nis] *noun*

prong *noun* one tine of fork or similar instrument

pro•noun [PROH-nown] *noun* word used to replace noun > **pro•nom'i•nal** *adjective* pert. to, like pronoun

pro•nounce [prə-NOWNS] *verb transitive* **-nounced, -nounc•ing** 1 utter formally 2 form with organs of speech 3 speak distinctly 4 declare ▷ *verb intransitive* **-nounced, -nounc•ing** 5 give opinion or decision > **pro•nounce'able** *adjective* > **pro•nounced'** *adjective* strongly marked, decided > **pro•nounce'ment** *noun* declaration > **pro•nun•ci•a'tion** *noun* 1 way word, etc. is pronounced 2 articulation

pron•to [PRON-toh] *adverb* (*informal*) at once, immediately, quickly

proof *noun* 1 evidence 2 thing that proves 3 test, demonstration 4 trial impression from type or engraved plate 5 *photography* print from a negative 6 standard of strength of alcoholic drink ▷ *adjective* 7 giving impenetrable defense against 8 of proven strength > **proof'read** [-reed] *verb* **-read, -read•ing** read and correct proofs > **proof'read•er** *noun*

prop[1] *verb transitive* **propped, prop•ping** 1 support, sustain, hold up ▷ *noun* 2 pole, beam, etc. 3 used as support

prop[2] *noun short for* **propeller**

prop[3] *noun short for* **property** (sense 3)

prop•a•gan•da [prop-ə-GAN-də] *noun* organized dissemination of information to assist or damage political cause, etc. > **prop•a•gan'dist** *noun* > **prop•a•gan'dize** [-dīz] *verb transitive* **-dized, -diz•ing**

prop•a•gate [pro-pə-gayt] *verb transitive* **-gat•ed, -gat•ing** 1 reproduce, breed, spread by sowing, breeding, etc. 2 transmit ▷ *verb intransitive* **-gat•ed, -gat•ing** 3 breed, multiply

DICTIONARY

P

THESAURUS

promiscuousness, wantonness

promiscuous *adjective* LICENTIOUS, abandoned, debauched, fast, immoral, libertine, loose, wanton, wild

promise *verb* 1 GUARANTEE, assure, contract, give an undertaking, give one's word, pledge, swear, take an oath, undertake, vow, warrant
2 SEEM LIKELY, augur, betoken, indicate, look like, show signs of, suggest
▷ *noun* 3 GUARANTEE, assurance, bond, commitment, oath, pledge, undertaking, vow, word
4 POTENTIAL, ability, aptitude, capability, capacity, flair, talent

promising *adjective* 1 ENCOURAGING, auspicious, bright, favorable, hopeful, likely, propitious, reassuring, rosy
2 TALENTED, able, gifted, rising

promontory *noun* POINT, cape, foreland, head, headland

promote *verb* 1 HELP, advance, aid, assist, back, boost, encourage, forward, foster, support
2 RAISE, elevate, exalt, upgrade
3 ADVERTISE, hype, plug (*informal*), publicize, push, sell

promotion *noun* 1 RISE, advancement, elevation, exaltation, honor, move up, preferment, upgrading
2 PUBLICITY, advertising, plugging (*informal*)
3 ENCOURAGEMENT, advancement, boosting, furtherance, support

prompt *verb* 1 CAUSE, elicit, give rise to, occasion, provoke
2 REMIND, assist, cue, help out
▷ *adjective* 3 IMMEDIATE, early, instant, quick, rapid, speedy, swift, timely
▷ *adverb* 4 (*informal*) EXACTLY, on the dot, promptly, punctually, sharp

promptly *adverb* IMMEDIATELY, at once, directly, on the dot, on time, punctually, quickly, speedily, swiftly

promptness *noun* SWIFTNESS, briskness, eagerness, haste, punctuality, quickness, speed, willingness

promulgate *verb* MAKE KNOWN, broadcast, circulate, communicate, disseminate, make public, proclaim, promote, publish, spread

prone *adjective* 1 LIABLE, apt, bent, disposed, given, inclined, likely, predisposed, subject, susceptible, tending
2 FACE DOWN, flat, horizontal, prostrate, recumbent

prong *noun* POINT, spike, tine

pronounce *verb* 1 SAY, accent, articulate, enunciate, sound, speak
2 DECLARE, affirm, announce, decree, deliver, proclaim

pronounced *adjective* NOTICEABLE, conspicuous, decided, definite, distinct, evident, marked, obvious, striking

pronouncement *noun* ANNOUNCEMENT, declaration, decree, dictum, edict, judgment, proclamation, statement

pronunciation *noun* INTONATION, accent, articulation, diction, enunciation, inflection, speech, stress

proof *noun* 1 EVIDENCE, authentication, confirmation, corroboration, demonstration, substantiation, testimony, verification
▷ *adjective* 2 IMPERVIOUS, impenetrable, repellent, resistant, strong

prop *verb* 1 SUPPORT, bolster, brace, buttress, hold up, stay, sustain, uphold
▷ *noun* 2 SUPPORT, brace, buttress, mainstay, stanchion, stay

propaganda *noun* INFORMATION, advertising,

> **prop•a•ga'tion** *noun*
pro•pane [PROH-payn] *noun* colorless, flammable gas from petroleum
pro•pel [prə-PEL] *verb transitive* **-pelled, -pel•ling** cause to move forward > **pro•pel'lant, pro•pel'lent** *noun* something causing propulsion, such as rocket fuel > **pro•pel'ler** *noun* revolving shaft with blades for driving ship or aircraft > **pro•pul'sion** *noun* act of, means of, driving forward > **pro•pul'sive, pro•pul'so•ry** *adjective* 1 tending, having power to propel 2 urging on
pro•pen•si•ty [prə-PEN-si-tee] *noun, plural* **-ties** 1 inclination or bent 2 tendency 3 disposition
prop•er [PROP-ər] *adjective* 1 appropriate 2 correct 3 conforming to etiquette, decorous 4 strict 5 (of noun) denoting individual person or place
prop•er•ty [PROP-ər-tee] *noun, plural* **-ties** 1 that which is owned 2 estate whether in lands, goods, or money 3 quality, attribute of something 4 article used on stage in play, etc.
proph•et [PROF-it] *noun* 1 inspired teacher or revealer of divine will 2 foreteller of future > **proph'e•cy** [-ə-see] *noun, plural* **-cies** prediction, prophetic utterance > **proph'e•sy** [-ə-sī] *verb* **-sied, -sy•ing** 1 foretell, predict 2 make predictions > **pro•phet'ic** *adjective* > **pro•phet'i•cal•ly** *adverb*
pro•phy•lac•tic [prof-ə-LAK-tik] *noun, adjective* 1 (something) done or used to ward off disease 2 condom > **pro•phy•lax'is** *noun*
pro•pin•qui•ty [proh-PING-kwi-tee] *noun* nearness, proximity, close kinship
pro•pi•ti•ate [prə-PISH-ee-ayt] *verb transitive* **-at•ed, -at•ing** appease, gain favor of > **pro•pi'ti•a•to•ry** *adjective* > **pro•pi'tious** *adjective* favorable, auspicious
pro•po•nent [prə-POH-nənt] *noun* one who advocates something
pro•por•tion [prə-POR-shən] *noun* 1 relative size or number 2 comparison 3 due relation between connected things or parts 4 share 5 relation ▷ *verb transitive* 6 arrange proportions of > **pro•por•tions** *plural noun* dimensions > **pro•por'tion•al, pro•por'tion•ate** *adjective* 1 having a due proportion 2 corresponding in size, number, etc. > **pro•por'tion•al•ly** *adverb*
pro•pose [prə-POHZ] *verb transitive* **-posed, -pos•ing** 1 put forward for consideration 2 nominate 3 intend ▷ *verb intransitive* **-posed, -pos•ing** 4 offer marriage > **pro•pos'al** *noun* > **prop•o•si'tion** *noun* 1 offer 2 statement, assertion 3 theorem 4 suggestion of terms 5 thing to be dealt with 6 proposal of illicit sexual relations
pro•pound [prə-POWND] *verb transitive* put forward for consideration or solution
pro•pri•e•tor [prə-PRĪ-i-tər] *noun* owner > **pro•pri'e•tar•y** [-ter-ee] *adjective* 1 belonging to owner 2 made by firm with exclusive rights of manufacture
pro•pri•e•ty [prə-PRĪ-itee] *noun, plural* **-ties** properness, correct conduct, fitness

DICTIONARY • THESAURUS

disinformation, hype, promotion, publicity
propagate *verb* 1 SPREAD, broadcast, circulate, disseminate, promote, promulgate, publish, transmit
2 REPRODUCE, beget, breed, engender, generate, increase, multiply, procreate, produce
propel *verb* DRIVE, force, impel, launch, push, send, shoot, shove, thrust
propensity *noun* TENDENCY, bent, disposition, inclination, liability, penchant, predisposition, proclivity
proper *adjective* 1 SUITABLE, appropriate, apt, becoming, befitting, fit, fitting, right
2 CORRECT, accepted, conventional, established, formal, orthodox, precise, right
3 POLITE, decent, decorous, genteel, gentlemanly, ladylike, mannerly, respectable, seemly
properly *adverb* 1 SUITABLY, appropriately, aptly, fittingly, rightly
2 CORRECTLY, accurately
3 POLITELY, decently, respectably
property *noun* 1 POSSESSIONS, assets, belongings, capital, effects, estate, goods, holdings, riches, wealth
2 LAND, estate, freehold, holding, real estate
3 QUALITY, attribute, characteristic, feature, hallmark, trait
prophecy *noun* PREDICTION, augury, divination, forecast, prognostication, second sight, soothsaying
prophesy *verb* PREDICT, augur, divine, forecast, foresee, foretell, prognosticate
prophet *noun* SOOTHSAYER, diviner, forecaster, oracle, prophesier, seer, sibyl
prophetic *adjective* PREDICTIVE, oracular, prescient, prognostic, sibylline
propitious *adjective* FAVORABLE, auspicious, bright, encouraging, fortunate, happy, lucky, promising
proportion *noun* 1 RELATIVE AMOUNT, ratio, relationship
2 BALANCE, congruity, correspondence, harmony, symmetry
3 PART, amount, division, fraction, percentage, quota, segment, share
4 ▷ **proportions** DIMENSIONS, capacity, expanse, extent, size, volume
proportional *or* **proportionate** *adjective* BALANCED, commensurate, compatible, consistent, corresponding, equitable, even, in proportion
proposal *noun* SUGGESTION, bid, offer, plan, presentation, program, project, recommendation, scheme
propose *verb* 1 PUT FORWARD, advance, present, submit, suggest
2 NOMINATE, name, present, recommend
3 INTEND, aim, design, have in mind, mean, plan, scheme
4 OFFER MARRIAGE, ask for someone's hand *or* ask for someone's hand in marriage, pop the question (*informal*)
proposition *noun* 1 PROPOSAL, plan, recommendation, scheme, suggestion
▷ *verb* 2 MAKE A PASS AT, accost, make an improper suggestion, solicit
propound *verb* PUT FORWARD, advance, postulate, present, propose, submit, suggest
proprietor *or* **proprietress** *noun* OWNER, landlord *or* landlady, titleholder
propriety *noun* 1 CORRECTNESS, aptness, fitness,

propulsion *see* propel
pro ra•ta [proh RAY-tə] *Lat.* in proportion
pro•sa•ic [proh-ZAY-ik] *adjective* commonplace, unromantic
pro•sce•ni•um [proh-SEE-nee-əm] *noun, plural* **-ni•a** [-nee-ə] arch or opening framing stage
pro•scribe [proh-SKRĪB] *verb transitive* **-scribed, -scrib•ing** outlaw, condemn > **pro•scrip'tion** *noun*
prose [prohz] *noun* speech or writing not verse > **pros'y** *adjective* **pros•i•er, pros•i•est** tedious, dull
pros•e•cute [PROS-i-kyoot] *verb transitive* **-cut•ed, -cut•ing** carry on, bring legal proceedings against > **pros•e•cu'tion** *noun* > **pros'e•cu•tor** *noun*
pros•e•lyte [PROS-ə-līt] *noun* convert > **pros'e•lyt•ize** [li-tīz] *verb transitive* **-ized, -iz•ing**
pros•o•dy [PROS-ə-dee] *noun* system, study of versification > **pros'o•dist** *noun*
pros•pect [PROS-pekt] *noun* 1 expectation, chance for success 2 view, outlook 3 likely customer or subscriber 4 mental view ▷ *verb* 5 explore, esp. for gold > **pro•spec'tive** *adjective* 1 anticipated 2 future > **pros•pec'tor** *noun* > **pro•spec•tus** [prə-SPEK-təs] *noun, plural* **-tus•es** document describing company, school, etc.
pros•per [PROS-pər] *verb intransitive* do well > **pros•per'i•ty** *noun, plural* **-ties** good fortune, well-being > **pros'per•ous** *adjective* 1 doing well, successful 2 flourishing, rich, well-off
pros•tate [PROS-tayt] *noun* gland accessory to male generative organs
pros•the•sis [pros-THEE-sis] *noun, plural* **-ses** [-seez] (replacement of part of body with) artificial substitute
pros•ti•tute [PROS-ti-toot] *noun* 1 one who offers sexual intercourse in return for payment ▷ *verb transitive* **-tut•ed, -tut•ing** 2 make a prostitute of 3 put to unworthy use > **pros•ti•tu'tion** *noun*
pros•trate [PROS-trayt] *adjective* 1 lying flat 2 crushed, submissive, overcome ▷ *verb transitive* **-trat•ed, -trat•ing** 3 throw flat on ground 4 reduce to exhaustion > **pros•tra'tion** *noun*
pro•tag•o•nist [proh-TAG-ə-nist] *noun* 1 leading character 2 principal actor 3 champion of a cause
pro•te•an [PROH-tee-ən] *adjective* 1 variable 2 versatile
pro•tect [prə-TEKT] *verb transitive* defend, guard, keep from harm > **pro•tec'tion** *noun* > **pro•tec'tion•ist** *noun* one who advocates protecting industries by taxing competing imports > **pro•tec'tive** *adjective* > **pro•tec'tor** *noun* 1 one who protects 2 regent > **pro•tec'tor•ate** [-tər-it] *noun* 1 relation of country to territory it protects and controls 2 such territory 3 office, period of protector of a country
pro•té•gé [PROH-tə-zhay] *noun* one under another's care, protection or patronage > **pro•té•gée** *noun feminine*
pro•tein [PROH-teen] *noun* any of kinds of organic compounds that form most essential part of food of living creatures
pro•test [PROH-test] *noun* 1 declaration or

DICTIONARY

P

THESAURUS

rightness, seemliness
2 DECORUM, courtesy, decency, etiquette, manners, politeness, respectability, seemliness
propulsion *noun* DRIVE, impetus, impulse, propelling force, push, thrust
prosaic *adjective* DULL, boring, everyday, humdrum, matter-of-fact, mundane, ordinary, pedestrian, routine, trite, unimaginative
proscribe *verb* 1 PROHIBIT, ban, embargo, forbid, interdict
2 OUTLAW, banish, deport, exclude, exile, expatriate, expel, ostracize
prosecute *verb* (*law*) PUT ON TRIAL, arraign, bring to trial, indict, litigate, sue, take to court, try
prospect *noun* 1 EXPECTATION, anticipation, future, hope, odds, outlook, probability, promise
2 (*sometimes plural*) LIKELIHOOD, chance, possibility
3 VIEW, landscape, outlook, scene, sight, spectacle, vista
▷ *verb* 4 LOOK FOR, search for, seek
prospective *adjective* FUTURE, anticipated, coming, destined, expected, forthcoming, imminent, intended, likely, possible, potential
prospectus *noun* CATALOG, list, outline, program, syllabus, synopsis
prosper *verb* SUCCEED, advance, do well, flourish, get on, progress, thrive
prosperity *noun* SUCCESS, affluence, fortune, good fortune, luxury, plenty, prosperousness, riches, wealth
prosperous *adjective* 1 WEALTHY, affluent, moneyed, rich, well-heeled (*informal*), well-off, well-to-do
2 SUCCESSFUL, booming, doing well, flourishing, fortunate, lucky, thriving
prostitute *noun* 1 WHORE, call girl, fallen woman, harlot, ho (*slang*), hooker (*slang*), loose woman, streetwalker, strumpet, tart (*informal*), trollop
▷ *verb* 2 CHEAPEN, debase, degrade, demean, devalue, misapply, pervert, profane
prostrate *adjective* 1 PRONE, flat, horizontal
2 EXHAUSTED, dejected, depressed, desolate, drained, inconsolable, overcome, spent, worn out
▷ *verb* 3 EXHAUST, drain, fatigue, sap, tire, wear out, weary
4 ▷ **prostrate oneself** BOW DOWN TO, abase oneself, fall at (someone's) feet, grovel, kiss ass (*slang*), kneel, kowtow
protagonist *noun* 1 SUPPORTER, advocate, champion, exponent
2 LEADING CHARACTER, central character, hero *or* heroine, principal
protect *verb* KEEP SAFE, defend, guard, look after, preserve, safeguard, save, screen, shelter, shield, stick up for (*informal*), support, watch over
protection *noun* 1 SAFETY, aegis, care, custody, defense, protecting, safeguard, safekeeping, security
2 SAFEGUARD, barrier, buffer, cover, guard, screen, shelter, shield
protective *adjective* PROTECTING, defensive, fatherly, maternal, motherly, paternal, vigilant, watchful
protector *noun* DEFENDER, bodyguard, champion, guard, guardian, patron
protest *noun* 1 OBJECTION, complaint, dissent,

demonstration of objection ▷ *verb intransitive* [prə-TEST] **2** object **3** make declaration against **4** assert formally > **prot•es•ta•tion** [prot-ə-STAY-shən] *noun* strong declaration

Prot•es•tant [PROT-ə-stənt] *adjective* **1** belonging to any branch of the Western Christian Church outside the Roman Catholic Church ▷ *noun* **2** member of such church > **Prot'es•tant•ism** *noun*

proto-, prot- *combining form* first: *prototype*

pro•to•col [PROH-tə-kawl] *noun* **1** diplomatic etiquette **2** draft of terms signed by parties as basis of formal treaty **3** *computers.* standardized format for exchanging data, esp. between different computer systems

pro•ton [PROH-ton] *noun* positively charged particle in nucleus of atom

pro•to•plasm [PROH-tə-plaz-əm] *noun* substance that is living matter of all animal and plant cells

pro•to•type [PROH-tə-tīp] *noun* **1** original, or model, after which thing is copied **2** pattern

pro•to•zo•an [proh-tə-ZOH-ən] *noun* minute animal of lowest and simplest class

pro•tract [proh-TRAKT] *verb transitive* **1** lengthen **2** prolong **3** delay **4** draw to scale > **pro•tract'ed** *adjective* **1** long drawn out **2** tedious > **pro•trac'tor** *noun* instrument for measuring angles on paper

pro•trude [proh-TROOD] *verb* **-trud•ed, -trud•ing** stick out, project > **pro•tru'sion** [-*zhən*] *noun* > **pro•tru'sive** [-siv] *adjective* thrusting forward

pro•tu•ber•ant [proh-TOO-bər-ənt] *adjective* bulging out > **pro•tu'ber•ance** [-əns] *noun* bulge, swelling

proud [prowd] *adjective* **-er, -est** **1** feeling or displaying pride **2** arrogant **3** gratified **4** noble **5** self-respecting **6** stately > **proud'ly** *adverb* > **proud flesh** flesh growing around healing wound

Prov. Proverbs

prove [proov] *verb transitive* **proved, proved** *or* **prov•en, prov•ing** **1** establish validity of **2** demonstrate, test ▷ *verb intransitive* **proved, proved** *or* **prov•en, prov•ing** **3** turn out (to be, etc.) **4** (of dough) rise in warm place before baking > **proven** *adjective* proved

prov•e•nance [PROV-ə-nəns] *noun* place of origin, source

prov•en•der [PROV-ən-dər] *noun* fodder

prov•erb [PROV-ərb] *noun* short, pithy, traditional saying in common use > **pro•ver'bi•al** [prə-VUR-bee-əl] *adjective*

pro•vide [prə-VĪD] *verb intransitive* **-vid•ed, -vid•ing** **1** make preparation ▷ *verb transitive* **-vid•ed, -vid•ing** **2** supply, equip, prepare, furnish, give > **pro•vid'er** *noun* **1** provided that **2** on condition that

prov•i•dent [PROV-i-dənt] *adjective* **1** thrifty **2** showing foresight > **prov'i•dence** *noun* **1** kindly care of God or nature **2** foresight **3** economy > **prov•i•den'tial** [-DEN-shəl] *adjective* strikingly fortunate, lucky

prov•ince [PROV-əns] *noun* **1** division of a country, district **2** sphere of action

outcry, protestation, remonstrance ▷ *verb* **2** OBJECT, complain, cry out, demonstrate, demur, disagree, disapprove, express disapproval, oppose, remonstrate
3 ASSERT, affirm, attest, avow, declare, insist, maintain, profess

protestation *noun* DECLARATION, affirmation, avowal, profession, vow

protester *noun* DEMONSTRATOR, agitator, rebel

protocol *noun* CODE OF BEHAVIOR, conventions, customs, decorum, etiquette, manners, propriety

prototype *noun* ORIGINAL, example, first, model, pattern, standard, type

protracted *adjective* EXTENDED, dragged out, drawn-out, long-drawn-out, prolonged, spun out

protrude *verb* STICK OUT, bulge, come through, extend, jut, obtrude, project, stand out

protrusion *noun* PROJECTION, bulge, bump, lump, outgrowth, protuberance

protuberance *noun* BULGE, bump, excrescence, hump, knob, lump, outgrowth, process, prominence, protrusion, swelling

proud *adjective* **1** SATISFIED, content, glad, gratified, pleased, well-pleased
2 CONCEITED, arrogant, boastful, disdainful, haughty, imperious, lordly, overbearing, self-satisfied, snobbish, supercilious

prove *verb* **1** VERIFY, authenticate, confirm, demonstrate, determine, establish, justify, show, substantiate
2 TEST, analyze, assay, check, examine, try
3 TURN OUT, come out, end up, result

proven *adjective* ESTABLISHED, attested, confirmed, definite, proved, reliable, tested, verified

proverb *noun* SAYING, adage, dictum, maxim, saw

proverbial *adjective* CONVENTIONAL, acknowledged, axiomatic, current, famed, famous, legendary, notorious, traditional, typical, well-known

provide *verb* **1** SUPPLY, cater, equip, furnish, outfit, purvey, stock up
2 GIVE, add, afford, bring, impart, lend, present, produce, render, serve, yield
3 ▷ **provide for, provide against** TAKE PRECAUTIONS, anticipate, forearm, plan ahead, plan for, prepare for
4 ▷ **provide for** SUPPORT, care for, keep, maintain, sustain, take care of

providence *noun* FATE, destiny, fortune

provident *adjective* **1** THRIFTY, economical, frugal, prudent
2 FORESIGHTED, careful, cautious, discreet, far-seeing, forearmed, shrewd, vigilant, well-prepared, wise

providential *adjective* LUCKY, fortuitous, fortunate, happy, heaven-sent, opportune, timely

provider *noun* **1** SUPPLIER, donor, giver, source
2 BREADWINNER, earner, supporter, wage earner

providing *or* **provided** *conjunction* ON CONDITION THAT, as long as, given

province *noun* **1** REGION, colony, department, district, division, domain, patch, section, zone
2 AREA, business, capacity, concern, duty, field, function, line, responsibility, role, sphere

> **prov•inc•es** any part of country outside capital or largest cities > **pro•vin'cial** [prə-VIN-shəl] *adjective* 1 of a province 2 unsophisticated 3 narrow in outlook ▷ *noun* 4 unsophisticated person 5 inhabitant of province > **pro•vin'cial•ism** *noun* 1 narrowness of outlook 2 lack of refinement 3 idiom peculiar to district

pro•vi•sion [prə-VIZH-ən] *noun* 1 a providing, esp. for the future 2 thing provided 3 *law* article of instrument or statute ▷ *verb transitive* 4 supply with food > **pro•vi•sions** *plural noun* food > **pro•vi'sion•al** *adjective* 1 temporary 2 conditional

pro•vi•so [prə-VĪ-zoh] *noun, plural* **-sos** *or* **-soes** condition

pro•vo•ca•teur [prə-vok-ə-TUR] *noun* 1 one who causes dissension, makes trouble 2 agitator 3 *see* **agent provocateur**

pro•voke [prə-VOHK] *verb transitive* **-voked, -vok•ing** 1 irritate 2 incense 3 arouse 4 excite 5 cause > **prov•o•ca'tion** [-ə-KAY-shən] *noun* > **pro•voc'a•tive** [-VOK-ə-tiv] *adjective*

pro•vost [PROH-vohst] *noun* 1 one who superintends or presides 2 high administrative officer of university > **provost marshal** head of military police

prow [rhymes with **cow**] *noun* bow of vessel

prow•ess [PROW-is] *noun* 1 skill 2 bravery, fighting capacity

prowl *verb intransitive* roam stealthily, esp. in search of prey or booty ▷ *noun* > **prowl'er** *noun* **on the prowl** 1 searching stealthily 2 seeking sexual partner

prox•i•mate [PROK-sə-mit] *adjective* nearest, next, immediate > **prox•im'i•ty** *noun*

prox•y [PROK-see] *noun, plural* **prox•ies** 1 authorized agent or substitute 2 writing authorizing one to act as this

prude [prood] *noun* one who affects excessive modesty or propriety > **prud'er•y** *noun, plural* **-er•ies** > **prud'ish** *adjective*

pru•dent [PROOD-nt] *adjective* 1 careful, discreet 2 sensible > **pru'dence** *noun* 1 habit of acting with careful deliberation 2 wisdom applied to practice > **pru•den'tial** *adjective*

prune[1] [proon] *noun* dried plum

prune[2] *verb transitive* **pruned, prun•ing** 1 cut out dead parts, excessive branches, etc. 2 shorten, reduce

pru•ri•ent [PRUUR-ee-ənt] *adjective* 1 given to, springing from lewd thoughts 2 having unhealthy curiosity or desire > **pru'ri•ence** *noun*

pry [prī] *verb intransitive* **pried, pry•ing** 1 make furtive or impertinent inquiries 2 look curiously 3 force open

Ps. Psalm(s)

psalm [sahm] *noun* 1 sacred song 2 (**Psalm**) any of the sacred songs making up the Book of Psalms in the Bible > **psalm'ist** *noun* writer of psalms > **psal•mo•dy** [SAHM-ə-dee] *noun* art, act of singing sacred music > **psal•ter** [SAWL-tər] *noun* 1 book of psalms 2 (**Psal•ter**) copy of the Psalms as separate book > **psal'ter•y** [-tə-ree] *noun, plural* **-ter•ies** obsolete stringed instrument like lyre

pseu•do [SOO-doh] *adjective* sham, fake

pseudo- *combining form* false, sham: *pseudo-Gothic; pseudoscience*

pseu•do•nym [SOOD-n-im] *noun* 1 false, fictitious name 2 pen name

psit•ta•co•sis [sit-ə-KOH-sis] *noun* dangerous

DICTIONARY

P

THESAURUS

provincial *adjective* 1 RURAL, country, hick (*informal*), homespun, local, rustic 2 NARROW-MINDED, insular, inward-looking, limited, narrow, parochial, small-minded, small-town, unsophisticated ▷ *noun* 3 YOKEL, country cousin, hayseed, hick (*informal*), rustic

provision *noun* 1 SUPPLYING, catering, equipping, furnishing, providing 2 CONDITION, clause, demand, proviso, requirement, rider, stipulation, term

provisional *adjective* 1 TEMPORARY, interim 2 CONDITIONAL, contingent, limited, qualified, tentative

provisions *plural noun* FOOD, comestibles, eatables, edibles, fare, foodstuff, rations, stores, supplies, victuals

proviso *noun* CONDITION, clause, qualification, requirement, rider, stipulation

provocation *noun* 1 CAUSE, grounds, incitement, motivation, reason, stimulus 2 OFFENSE, affront, annoyance, challenge, dare, grievance, indignity, injury, insult, taunt

provocative *adjective* OFFENSIVE, annoying, galling, goading, insulting, provoking, stimulating

provoke *verb* 1 ANGER, aggravate (*informal*), annoy, enrage, hassle (*informal*), incense, infuriate, irk, irritate, madden, rile 2 CAUSE, bring about, elicit, evoke, incite, induce, occasion, produce, promote, prompt, rouse, stir

prowess *noun* 1 SKILL, accomplishment, adeptness, aptitude, excellence, expertise, genius, mastery, talent 2 BRAVERY, courage, daring, fearlessness, heroism, mettle, valiance, valor

prowl *verb* MOVE STEALTHILY, skulk, slink, sneak, stalk, steal

proximity *noun* NEARNESS, closeness

proxy *noun* REPRESENTATIVE, agent, delegate, deputy, factor, substitute

prudence *noun* COMMON SENSE, care, caution, discretion, good sense, judgment, vigilance, wariness, wisdom

prudent *adjective* 1 SENSIBLE, careful, cautious, discerning, discreet, judicious, politic, shrewd, vigilant, wary, wise 2 THRIFTY, canny, careful, economical, far-sighted, frugal, provident, sparing

prudish *adjective* PRIM, old-maidish (*informal*), overmodest, priggish, prissy (*informal*), proper, puritanical, starchy (*informal*), strait-laced, stuffy, Victorian

prune *verb* CUT, clip, dock, reduce, shape, shorten, snip, trim

pry *verb* BE INQUISITIVE, be nosy (*informal*), interfere, intrude, meddle, poke, snoop (*informal*)

prying *adjective* INQUISITIVE, curious, interfering, meddlesome, meddling, nosy (*informal*), snooping (*informal*), spying

psalm *noun* HYMN, chant

pseudo- *adjective* FALSE, artificial, fake, imitation, mock, phoney *or* phony (*informal*),

infectious disease, germ of which is carried by parrots
psy•che [SĪ-kee] *noun* human mind or soul
psych•e•del•ic [sī-ki-DEL-ik] *adjective* 1 of or causing hallucinations 2 like intense colors, etc. experienced during hallucinations
psy•chic [SĪ-kik] *adjective* 1 sensitive to phenomena lying outside range of normal experience 2 of soul or mind 3 that appears to be outside region of physical law
> **psy•chi•a•try** [si-KĪ-ə-tree] *noun* medical treatment of mental diseases > **psy•chi•a•trist** *noun* > **psy•cho•a•nal'y•sis** [sī-koh-] *noun* method of studying and treating mental disorders > **psy•cho•an'a•lyst** *noun*
> **psy•cho•log•i•cal** [sī-kə-LOJ-i-kəl] *adjective* 1 of psychology 2 of the mind > **psy•chol'o•gist** *noun* > **psy•chol'o•gy** *noun* 1 study of mind 2 person's mental makeup > **psy•chom'e•try** *noun* 1 measurement, testing of psychological processes 2 supposed ability to divine unknown persons' qualities by handling object used or worn by them > **psy'cho•path** *noun* person afflicted with severe mental disorder causing him or her to commit antisocial, often violent acts > **psy•cho•path'ic** *adjective* > **psy•cho'sis** *noun, plural* **-ses** [-seez] severe mental disorder in which person's contact with reality becomes distorted > **psy•cho'tic** *adjective, noun*
> **psy•cho•so•mat'ic** [-sə-MAT-ik] *adjective* of physical disorders thought to have psychological causes > **psy•cho•ther'a•py** *noun* treatment of disease by psychological, not physical, means
psych up [sīk] *verb transitive* prepare (oneself or another) psychologically for action, performance, etc.
Pt *chem.* platinum
ptar•mi•gan [TAHR-mi-gən] *noun* bird of grouse family that turns white in winter
PT boat small, fast naval vessel used primarily for torpedoing enemy shipping
pter•o•dac•tyl [ter-ə-DAK-til] *noun* extinct flying reptile with large batlike wings
pto•maine [TOH-mayn] *noun* any of kinds of poisonous alkaloid found in decaying matter
Pu *chem.* plutonium
pu•ber•ty [PYOO-bər-tee] *noun* sexual maturity
pubic [PYOO-bik] *adjective* of the lower abdomen
pub•lic [PUB-lik] *adjective* 1 of or concerning the public as a whole 2 not private 3 open to general observation or knowledge 4 accessible to all 5 serving the people ▷ *noun* 6 the community or its members > **pub'lic•ly** *adverb* 1 public relations 2 promotion of good relations of an organization or business with the general public > **public school** local elementary school > **public service** government employment > **public spirit** interest in and devotion to welfare of community
pub•li•cist [PUB-lə-sist] *noun* 1 press agent 2 writer on public concerns > **pub•lic'i•ty** *noun* 1 process of attracting public attention 2 attention thus gained > **pub'li•cize** *verb transitive* **-cized, -ciz•ing** 1 give publicity to 2 bring to public notice
pub'lish *verb transitive* 1 prepare and issue for sale (books, music, etc.) 2 make generally known 3 proclaim > **pub•li•ca'tion** [-KAY-shən] *noun* > **pub'lish•er** *noun*
puce [pyoos] *adjective, noun* purplish-brown (color)
puck[1] [puk] *noun* hard rubber disk used instead of ball in ice hockey
puck[2] *noun* mischievous sprite > **puck'ish** *adjective*
puck•er [PUK-ər] *verb* 1 gather into wrinkles ▷ *noun* 2 crease, fold
pud•ding [PUUD-ing] *noun* thick, cooked dessert, often made from flour, milk, eggs, flavoring, etc.
pud•dle [PUD-l] *noun* 1 small pool of water 2 rough cement for lining walls of canals, etc. ▷ *verb transitive* **-dled, -dling** 3 line with puddle

DICTIONARY • THESAURUS

pretended, sham, spurious
pseudonym *noun* FALSE NAME, alias, assumed name, incognito, nom de plume, pen name
psyche *noun* SOUL, anima, individuality, mind, personality, self, spirit
psychiatrist *noun* PSYCHOTHERAPIST, analyst, headshrinker (*slang*), psychoanalyst, psychologist, shrink (*slang*), therapist
psychic *adjective* 1 SUPERNATURAL, mystic, occult 2 MENTAL, psychological, spiritual
psychological *adjective* 1 MENTAL, cerebral, intellectual
2 IMAGINARY, all in the mind, irrational, psychosomatic, unreal
psychology *noun* 1 BEHAVIORISM, science of mind, study of personality
2 WAY OF THINKING, attitude, mental make-up, mental processes, thought processes, what makes one tick
psychopath *noun* MADMAN, headcase (*informal*), lunatic, maniac, nutcase (*slang*), psychotic, sociopath
psychotic *adjective* MAD, certifiable, demented, deranged, insane, loony (*informal*), lunatic, non compos mentis (*Latin*), unbalanced
puberty *noun* ADOLESCENCE, pubescence, teens
public *adjective* 1 GENERAL, civic, common, national, popular, social, state, universal, widespread
2 COMMUNAL, accessible, open, unrestricted
3 WELL-KNOWN, important, prominent, respected
4 PLAIN, acknowledged, known, obvious, open, overt, patent
▷ *noun* 5 PEOPLE, citizens, community, electorate, everyone, nation, populace, society
publication *noun* 1 PAMPHLET, brochure, issue, leaflet, magazine, newspaper, periodical, title
2 ANNOUNCEMENT, broadcasting, declaration, disclosure, notification, proclamation, publishing, reporting
publicity *noun* ADVERTISING, attention, boost, hype, plug (*informal*), press, promotion
publicize *verb* ADVERTISE, hype, make known, play up, plug (*informal*), promote, push
public-spirited *adjective* ALTRUISTIC, charitable, humanitarian, philanthropic, unselfish
publish *verb* 1 PUT OUT, issue, print, produce
2 ANNOUNCE, advertise, broadcast, circulate, disclose, divulge, proclaim, publicize, reveal, spread
pucker *verb* 1 WRINKLE, contract, crease, draw together, gather, knit, purse, screw up, tighten ▷ *noun* 2 WRINKLE, crease, fold

4 make muddy > **puddling** *noun* method of converting pig iron to wrought iron by oxidizing the carbon

pu•den•dum [pyoo-DEN-dəm] *noun, plural* **-da** [-də] 1 external genital organs, esp. of a woman 2 vulva

pu•er•ile [PYOO-ər-il] *adjective* 1 childish 2 foolish 3 trivial

puff *noun* 1 short blast of breath, wind, etc. 2 its sound 3 type of pastry 4 laudatory review or advertisement ▷ *verb intransitive* 5 blow abruptly 6 breathe hard ▷ *verb transitive* 7 send out in a puff 8 blow out, inflate 9 advertise 10 smoke hard > **puff'y** *adjective* **puff•i•er, puff•i•est** 1 short-winded 2 swollen > **puff'ball** *noun* ball-shaped fungus

puf'fin *noun* sea bird with large brightly-colored beak

pug *noun* 1 small snub-nosed dog 2 (*slang*) boxer > **pug nose** snub nose

pu•gi•list [PYOO-jə-list] *noun* boxer > **pu'gi•lism** *noun* > **pu•gi•lis'tic** *adjective*

pug•na•cious [pug-NAY-shəs] *adjective* given to fighting > **pug•nac'i•ty** [-NAS-i-tee] *noun*

puke [pyook] (*slang*) ▷ *verb intransitive* **puked, puk•ing** 1 vomit ▷ *noun* 2 vomit

pul•chri•tude [PUL-kri-tood] *noun* beauty > **pul•chri•tu'di•nous** *adjective*

pull [puul] *verb transitive* 1 exert force on object to move it toward source of force 2 strain or stretch 3 tear 4 propel by rowing ▷ *noun* 5 act of pulling 6 force exerted by it 7 drink of liquor 8 (*informal*) power, influence > **pull in** (of train) arrive 1 attract 2 (*slang*) arrest > **pull off** (*informal*) carry through to successful issue > **pull out** 1 withdraw 2 extract 3 (of train) depart 4 (of car, etc.) move away from side of road or move out to overtake > **pull over** (of car, etc.) drive to side of road and stop **pull someone's leg** make fun of > **pull up** 1 tear up 2 recover lost ground 3 improve 4 come to a stop 5 halt 6 reprimand

pul•let [PUUL-it] *noun* young hen

pul•ley [PUUL-ee] *noun, plural* **-leys** wheel with groove in rim for cord, used to raise weights by downward pull

Pull•man [PUUL-mən] ® *noun, plural* **-mans** railroad sleeping car or parlor car

pull•o•ver [PUUL-oh-vər] *noun* sweater without fastening, to be pulled over head

pul•mo•nar•y [PUUL-mə-ner-ee] *adjective* of lungs

pulp *noun* 1 soft, moist, vegetable or animal matter 2 flesh of fruit 3 any soft soggy mass ▷ *verb transitive* 4 reduce to pulp

pul•pit [PUUL-pit] *noun* (enclosed) platform for preacher, minister, rabbi, etc.

pul•sar [PUL-sahr] *noun* small dense star emitting radio waves

pulse [puls] *noun* 1 movement of blood in arteries corresponding to heartbeat, discernible to touch, for example in the wrist 2 any regular beat or vibration > **pul•sate** [PUL-sayt] *verb intransitive* **-sat•ed, -sat•ing** throb, quiver > **pul•sa'tion** [-SAY-shən] *noun*

pul•ver•ize [PUL-və-rīz] *verb transitive* **-ized, -iz•ing** 1 reduce to powder 2 smash or demolish

pu•ma [PYOO-mə] *noun* large Amer. feline carnivore, cougar

pum•ice [PUM-is] *noun* light porous variety of lava

pum•mel [PUM-əl] *verb transitive* **-meled, -mel•ing** strike repeatedly with fists

pump[1] *noun* 1 appliance in which piston and handle are used for raising water, or putting in or taking out air or liquid, etc. ▷ *verb transitive* 2 raise, put in, take out, etc. with pump 3 empty by means of a pump 4 extract information from ▷ *verb intransitive* 5 work pump 6 work like pump > **pump iron** lift weights as exercise

pump[2] *noun* light shoe

pump'kin *noun* any of varieties of gourd, eaten esp. as vegetable, in pie

pun *noun* 1 play on words ▷ *verb intransitive* **punned, pun•ning** 2 make one > **pun'ster** [-stər]

DICTIONARY

P

THESAURUS

---

puerile *adjective* CHILDISH, babyish, foolish, immature, juvenile, silly, trivial

puff *noun* 1 BLAST, breath, draft, gust, whiff
2 SMOKE, drag (*slang*), pull
▷ *verb* 3 BLOW, breathe, exhale, gasp, gulp, pant, wheeze
4 SMOKE, drag (*slang*), draw, inhale, pull at *or* pull on, suck
5 (*usually with up*) SWELL, bloat, dilate, distend, expand, inflate

puffy *adjective* SWOLLEN, bloated, distended, enlarged, puffed up

pugilist *noun* BOXER, fighter, prizefighter

pugnacious *adjective* AGGRESSIVE, belligerent, combative, hot-tempered, quarrelsome

pull *verb* 1 DRAW, drag, haul, jerk, tow, trail, tug, yank
2 STRAIN, dislocate, rip, sprain, stretch, tear, wrench
3 EXTRACT, draw out, gather, pick, pluck, remove, take out, uproot
▷ *noun* 4 TUG, jerk, twitch, yank
5 PUFF, drag (*slang*), inhalation
6 (*informal*) INFLUENCE, clout (*informal*), muscle, power, weight

pull down *verb* DEMOLISH, bulldoze, destroy, raze, remove

pull off *verb* SUCCEED, accomplish, carry out, do the trick, manage

pull out *verb* WITHDRAW, depart, evacuate, leave, quit, retreat

pull through *verb* SURVIVE, get better, rally, recover

pulp *noun* 1 PASTE, mash, mush
2 FLESH, soft part
▷ *verb* 3 CRUSH, mash, pulverize, squash
▷ *adjective* 4 CHEAP, lurid, rubbishy, trashy

pulsate *verb* THROB, beat, palpitate, pound, pulse, quiver, thump

pulse *noun* 1 BEAT, beating, pulsation, rhythm, throb, throbbing, vibration
▷ *verb* 2 BEAT, pulsate, throb, vibrate

pulverize *verb* 1 CRUSH, granulate, grind, mill, pound
2 DEFEAT, annihilate, crush, demolish, destroy, flatten, smash, wreck

pummel *verb* BEAT, batter, hammer, pound, punch, strike, thump

pump *verb* 1 (*often with into*) DRIVE, force, inject, pour, push, send, supply

noun
punch¹ *noun* 1 tool for perforating or stamping 2 blow with fist 3 vigor ▷ *verb transitive* 4 stamp, perforate with punch 5 strike with fist **pull punches** 6 punch lightly 7 (*informal*) lessen, withhold, criticism > **punch-drunk** *adjective* (*informal*) dazed, as by repeated blows
punch² *noun* drink of spirits or wine with fruit juice, spice, etc.
punc•til•i•ous [pungk-TIL-ee-əs] *adjective* 1 making much of details of etiquette 2 very exact, particular > **punc•til'i•ous•ness** [-nis] *noun*
punc•tu•al [PUNGK-choo-əl] *adjective* in good time, not late, prompt > **punc•tu•al'i•ty** *noun*
punc•tu•ate [PUNGK-choo-ayt] *verb transitive* **-at•ed, -at•ing** 1 put in punctuation marks 2 interrupt at intervals 3 emphasize > **punc•tu•a'tion** *noun* marks, such as commas and colons, put in writing to assist in making sense clear
punc•ture [PUNGK-chər] *noun* 1 small hole made by sharp object, esp. in tire 2 act of puncturing ▷ *verb transitive* **-tured, -tur•ing** 3 prick hole in, perforate
pun'dit *noun* self-appointed expert
pun•gent [PUN-jənt] *adjective* 1 biting 2 irritant 3 piercing 4 tart 5 caustic > **pun'gen•cy** *noun*
pun'ish *verb transitive* 1 cause to suffer for offense 2 inflict penalty on 3 use or treat roughly > **pun'ish•a•ble** *adjective* > **pun'ish•ment** *noun* > **pu'ni•tive** [PYOO-ni-tiv] *adjective* inflicting or intending to inflict punishment
punk *adjective, noun* 1 inferior, rotten, worthless (person or thing) 2 petty (hoodlum) 3 (of) style of rock music
punt¹ *noun* 1 flat-bottomed square-ended boat, propelled by pushing with pole ▷ *verb transitive* 2 propel thus
punt² *verb transitive* *football* 1 kick ball before it touches ground, when let fall from hands ▷ *noun* 2 such a kick
punt³ *verb intransitive* gamble, bet > **punt'er** *noun* 1 one who punts 2 gambler
pu•ny [PYOO-nee] *adjective* **-ni•er, -ni•est** small and feeble
pup *noun* young of certain animals, such as dogs and seals
pu•pa [PYOO-pə] *noun, plural* **-pas** stage between larva and adult in metamorphosis of insect, chrysalis > **pu'pal** *adjective*
pu•pil [PYOO-pəl] *noun* 1 person being taught 2 opening in iris of eye
pup•pet [PUP-it] *noun* small doll or figure of person, etc. controlled by operator's hand > **pup•pet•eer'** *noun* > **puppet show** show with puppets worked by hidden performer
pup•py [PUP-ee] *noun, plural* **-pies** young dog
pur•chase [PUR-chəs] *verb transitive* **-chased, -chas•ing** 1 buy ▷ *noun* 2 buying 3 what is bought 4 leverage, grip
pur•dah [PUR-də] *noun* 1 Muslim, Hindu custom of keeping women in seclusion 2 screen, veil to achieve this
pure [pyuur] *adjective* **pur•er, pur•est** 1 unmixed, untainted 2 simple 3 spotless 4 faultless 5 innocent 6 concerned with theory

DICTIONARY • THESAURUS

2 INTERROGATE, cross-examine, probe, quiz
pun *noun* PLAY ON WORDS, double entendre, quip, witticism
punch¹ *verb* 1 HIT, belt (*informal*), bop (*informal*), box, pummel, smash, sock (*slang*), strike ▷ *noun* 2 BLOW, bop (*informal*), hit, jab, sock (*slang*), wallop (*informal*)
3 (*informal*) EFFECTIVENESS, bite, drive, forcefulness, impact, verve, vigor
punch² *verb* PIERCE, bore, cut, drill, perforate, prick, puncture, stamp
punctilious *adjective* PARTICULAR, exact, finicky, formal, fussy, meticulous, nice, precise, proper, strict
punctual *adjective* ON TIME, exact, on the dot, precise, prompt, timely
punctuality *noun* PROMPTNESS, promptitude, readiness
punctuate *verb* 1 INTERRUPT, break, intersperse, pepper, sprinkle
2 EMPHASIZE, accentuate, stress, underline
puncture *noun* 1 HOLE, break, cut, damage, leak, nick, opening, slit
2 FLAT TIRE, flat
▷ *verb* 3 PIERCE, bore, cut, nick, penetrate, perforate, prick, rupture
pungent *adjective* STRONG, acrid, bitter, hot, peppery, piquant, sharp, sour, spicy, tart
punish *verb* DISCIPLINE, castigate, chasten, chastise, correct, penalize, sentence
punishable *adjective* CULPABLE, blameworthy, criminal, indictable
punishing *adjective* HARD, arduous, backbreaking, exhausting, grueling, strenuous, taxing, tiring, wearing
punishment *noun* PENALTY, chastening, chastisement, correction, discipline, penance, retribution
punitive *adjective* RETALIATORY, in reprisal, retaliative
punt *verb* 1 BET, back, gamble, lay, stake, wager ▷ *noun* 2 BET, gamble, stake, wager
puny *adjective* FEEBLE, frail, little, sickly, stunted, tiny, weak
pupil *noun* LEARNER, beginner, disciple, novice, schoolboy *or* schoolgirl, student
puppet *noun* 1 MARIONETTE, doll, ventriloquist's dummy
2 PAWN, cat's-paw, instrument, mouthpiece, stooge, tool
purchase *verb* 1 BUY, acquire, come by, gain, get, obtain, pay for, pick up, score (*slang*) ▷ *noun* 2 BUY, acquisition, asset, gain, investment, possession, property
3 GRIP, foothold, hold, leverage, support
pure *adjective* 1 UNMIXED, authentic, flawless, genuine, natural, neat, real, simple, straight, unalloyed
2 CLEAN, germ-free, sanitary, spotless, squeaky-clean, sterilized, uncontaminated, unpolluted, untainted, wholesome
3 INNOCENT, blameless, chaste, impeccable, modest, uncorrupted, unsullied, virginal, virtuous
4 COMPLETE, absolute, outright, sheer, thorough, unmitigated, unqualified, utter

only > **pure'ly** *adverb* > **pu•ri•fi•ca'tion** *noun* > **pu'ri•fy** *verb transitive* **-fied, -fy•ing** make, become pure, clear or clean > **pur'ism** *noun* excessive insistence on correctness of language > **pur'ist** *noun* > **pu'ri•ty** *noun* state of being pure

pu•rée [pyuu-RAY] *noun* pulp, soup, of cooked fruit or vegetables put through sieve, etc. ▷ *verb transitive* **-réed, -rée•ing**

pur•ga•to•ry [PUR-gə-tor-ee] *noun* **-ries** place or state of torment, pain or distress, esp. temporary

purge [purj] *verb transitive* **purged, purg•ing** 1 make clean, purify 2 remove, get rid of 3 clear out ▷ *noun* 4 act, process of purging 5 removal of undesirable members from political party, army, etc. > **pur'ga•tive** [-gə-tiv] *adjective, noun*

Pu•ri•tan [PYUUR-i-tn] *noun* 1 *hist.* member of extreme Protestant party 2 (**pu•ri•tan**) person of extreme strictness in morals or religion > **pu•ri•tan'i•cal** *adjective* 1 strict in the observance of religious and moral duties 2 overscrupulous > **pu'ri•tan•ism** *noun*

purl *noun* 1 stitch that forms ridge in knitting ▷ *verb intransitive* 2 knit in purl

pur•loin [pər-LOIN] *verb transitive* 1 steal 2 pilfer

pur•ple [PUR-pəl] *noun, adjective* **-pler, -plest** (of) color between crimson and violet

pur•port [pər-PORT] *verb transitive* 1 claim to be (true, etc.) 2 signify, imply ▷ *noun* [PUR-port] 3 meaning 4 apparent meaning 5 significance

pur•pose [PUR-pəs] *noun* 1 reason, object 2 design 3 aim, intention ▷ *verb transitive* **-posed, -pos•ing** 4 intend > **pur'pose•ly** *adverb* **on purpose** intentionally

purr *noun* 1 pleased noise that cat makes ▷ *verb intransitive* 2 utter this

purse [purs] *noun* 1 small bag for money 2 handbag 3 resources 4 money as prize ▷ *verb transitive* **pursed, purs•ing** 5 pucker in wrinkles ▷ *verb intransitive* **pursed, purs•ing** 6 become wrinkled and drawn in > **purs'er** *noun* ship's officer who keeps accounts

pur•sue [pər-SOO] *verb transitive* **-sued, -su•ing** 1 run after 2 chase 3 aim at 4 engage in 5 continue 6 follow ▷ *verb intransitive* **-sued, -su•ing** 7 go in pursuit 8 continue > **pur•su'ance** [-əns] *noun* carrying out > **pur•su'ant** [-ənt] *adverb* accordingly > **pur•su'er** *noun* > **pur•suit'** [-SOOT] *noun* 1 running after, attempt to catch 2 occupation

purulent *adjective* *see* **pus**

pur•vey [pər-VAY] *verb transitive* supply (provisions) > **pur•vey'or** *noun*

pur•view [PUR-vyoo] *noun* scope, range

pus *noun* yellowish matter produced by suppuration > **pu•ru•lence** [PYUUR-ə-ləns] *noun* > **pu'ru•lent** *adjective* 1 forming, discharging pus 2 septic

push [puush] *verb transitive* 1 move, try to move

DICTIONARY

P

THESAURUS

purely *adverb* ABSOLUTELY, completely, entirely, exclusively, just, merely, only, simply, solely, wholly

purge *verb* 1 GET RID OF, do away with, eradicate, expel, exterminate, remove, wipe out ▷ *noun* 2 REMOVAL, ejection, elimination, eradication, expulsion

purify *verb* 1 CLEAN, clarify, cleanse, decontaminate, disinfect, refine, sanitize, wash 2 ABSOLVE, cleanse, redeem, sanctify

purist *noun* STICKLER, formalist, pedant

puritan *noun* 1 MORALIST, fanatic, prude, rigorist, zealot ▷ *adjective* 2 STRICT, ascetic, austere, moralistic, narrow-minded, prudish, severe, strait-laced

puritanical *adjective* STRICT, ascetic, austere, narrow-minded, proper, prudish, puritan, severe, strait-laced

purity *noun* 1 CLEANNESS, cleanliness, faultlessness, immaculateness, pureness, wholesomeness
2 INNOCENCE, chasteness, chastity, decency, honesty, integrity, virginity, virtue, virtuousness

purloin *verb* STEAL, appropriate, filch, pilfer, pinch (*informal*), swipe (*slang*), thieve

purport *verb* 1 CLAIM, allege, assert, profess ▷ *noun* 2 SIGNIFICANCE, drift, gist, idea, implication, import, meaning

purpose *noun* 1 REASON, aim, idea, intention, object, point
2 AIM, ambition, desire, end, goal, hope, intention, object, plan, wish
3 DETERMINATION, firmness, persistence, resolution, resolve, single-mindedness, tenacity, will
4 ▷ **on purpose** DELIBERATELY, designedly, intentionally, knowingly, purposely

purposeless *adjective* POINTLESS, aimless, empty, motiveless, needless, senseless, uncalled-for, unnecessary

purposely *adverb* DELIBERATELY, consciously, expressly, intentionally, knowingly, on purpose, with intent

purse *noun* 1 POUCH, money-bag, wallet
2 MONEY, exchequer, funds, means, resources, treasury, wealth
▷ *verb* 3 PUCKER, contract, pout, press together, tighten

pursue *verb* 1 FOLLOW, chase, dog, hound, hunt, hunt down, run after, shadow, stalk, tail (*informal*), track
2 TRY FOR, aim for, desire, seek, strive for, work towards
3 ENGAGE IN, carry on, conduct, perform, practice
4 CONTINUE, carry on, keep on, maintain, persevere in, persist in, proceed

pursuit *noun* 1 PURSUING, chase, hunt, quest, search, seeking, trailing
2 OCCUPATION, activity, hobby, interest, line, pastime, pleasure

purvey *verb* SUPPLY, cater, deal in, furnish, provide, sell, trade in

push *verb* 1 SHOVE, depress, drive, press, propel, ram, thrust
2 MAKE ONE'S WAY *or* FORCE ONE'S WAY, elbow, jostle, move, shoulder, shove, squeeze, thrust
3 URGE, encourage, hurry, impel, incite, persuade, press, spur
▷ *noun* 4 SHOVE, butt, nudge, thrust
5 DRIVE, ambition, dynamism, energy, enterprise, go (*informal*), initiative, vigor, vitality
6 ▷ **the push**

pushed *adjective* (*often with for*) SHORT OF, hurried, pressed, rushed, under pressure

pushover *noun* 1 PIECE OF CAKE (*informal*), breeze

away by pressure 2 drive or impel 3 (*slang*) sell (esp. narcotic drugs) illegally ▷ *verb intransitive* 4 make thrust 5 advance with steady effort ▷ *noun* 6 thrust 7 persevering self-assertion 8 big military advance > **push'er** *noun* > **push'y** *adjective* **push•i•er, push•i•est** given to pushing oneself

pu•sil•lan•i•mous [pyoo-sə-LAN-ə-məs] *adjective* cowardly > **pu•sil•la•nim'i•ty** [-lə-NIM-ə-tee] *noun*

puss [puus], **pus'sy** *noun, plural* **-ses, -sies** (*informal*) cat

puss•y•foot [PUUS-ee-fuut] *verb intransitive* 1 move stealthily 2 act indecisively, procrastinate

pus•tule [PUS-chuul] *noun* pimple containing pus

put [puut] *verb transitive* **put, put•ting** 1 place 2 set 3 express 4 throw (esp. shot) ▷ *noun* 5 throw > **put across** express, carry out successfully > **put off** 1 postpone 2 disconcert 3 repel > **put up** 1 erect 2 accommodate 3 nominate

pu•ta•tive [PYOO-tə-tiv] *adjective* reputed, supposed

pu•trid [PYOO-trid] *adjective* 1 decomposed 2 rotten > **pu'tre•fy** [-trə-fī] *verb* **-fied, -fy•ing** make or become rotten > **pu•tre•fac'tion** *noun* > **pu•tres'cent** [-ənt] *adjective* becoming rotten

putsch [puuch] *noun* surprise attempt to overthrow the existing power, political revolt

putt [put] *verb transitive* strike (golf ball) along ground in direction of hole > **putt'er** *noun* 1 golf club for putting 2 person who putts

put•ter [PUT-ər] *verb intransitive* work, act in feeble, unsystematic way

put•ty [PUT-ee] *noun, plural* **-ties** 1 paste of ground chalk and oil as used by glaziers ▷ *verb transitive* **-tied, -ty•ing** 2 fix, fill with putty

puz•zle [PUZ-əl] *verb* **-zled, -zling** 1 perplex or be perplexed ▷ *noun* 2 bewildering, perplexing question, problem or toy > **puz'zle•ment** *noun*

pyg•my, pig•my [PIG-mee] *noun, plural* **-mies** 1 abnormally undersized person 2 (**Pyg•my**) member of one of dwarf peoples of Equatorial Africa ▷ *adjective* 3 undersized

py•lon [PĪ-lon] *noun* 1 post, tower, esp. for guiding aviators 2 steel tower for supporting power lines

py•or•rhe•a [pī-ə-REE-ə] *noun* inflammation of the gums with discharge of pus and loosening of teeth

pyr•a•mid [PIR-ə-mid] *noun* 1 solid figure with sloping sides meeting at apex 2 structure of this shape, esp. ancient Egyptian 3 group of persons or things arranged, organized, like pyramid > **py•ram'i•dal** *adjective*

pyre [pīr] *noun* pile of wood for burning a dead body

py•ri•tes [pī-RĪ-teez] *noun, plural* **py•ri•tes** sulfide of a metal, esp. iron pyrites

py•ro•ma•ni•ac [pī-rə-MAY-nee-ak] *noun* person with uncontrollable desire to set things

DICTIONARY • THESAURUS

(*informal*), child's play (*informal*), cinch (*slang*), picnic (*informal*), plain sailing, walkover (*informal*)
2 SUCKER (*slang*), easy game (*informal*), easy mark *or* soft mark (*informal*), mug (*Brit slang*), walkover (*informal*)

pushy *adjective* FORCEFUL, ambitious, assertive, bold, brash, bumptious, obtrusive, presumptuous, self-assertive

pussyfoot *verb* HEDGE, beat about the bush, be noncommittal, equivocate, hum and haw, prevaricate, sit on the fence

put *verb* 1 PLACE, deposit, lay, position, rest, set, settle, situate
2 EXPRESS, phrase, state, utter, word
3 THROW, cast, fling, heave, hurl, lob, pitch, toss

put across, put over *verb* COMMUNICATE, convey, explain, get across, make clear, make oneself understood

put aside, put by *verb* SAVE, deposit, lay by, stockpile, store

put away *verb* 1 SAVE, deposit, keep, put by
2 COMMIT, certify, institutionalize, lock up
3 CONSUME, devour, eat up, gobble, wolf down
4 PUT BACK, replace, tidy away

put down *verb* 1 RECORD, enter, set down, take down, write down
2 STAMP OUT, crush, quash, quell, repress, suppress
3 (*usually with to*) ATTRIBUTE, ascribe, impute, set down
4 PUT TO SLEEP, destroy, do away with, put out of its misery
5 (*slang*) HUMILIATE, disparage, mortify, shame, slight, snub

put forward *verb* RECOMMEND, advance, nominate, propose, submit, suggest, tender

put off *verb* 1 POSTPONE, defer, delay, hold over, put on the back burner (*informal*)
2 DISCONCERT, confuse, discomfit, dismay, faze, nonplus, perturb, throw (*informal*), unsettle
3 DISCOURAGE, dishearten, dissuade

put on *verb* 1 DON, change into, dress, get dressed in, slip into
2 FAKE, affect, assume, feign, pretend, sham, simulate
3 PRESENT, do, mount, produce, show, stage
4 ADD, gain, increase by

put out *verb* 1 ANNOY, anger, exasperate, irk, irritate, nettle, vex
2 EXTINGUISH, blow out, douse, quench
3 INCONVENIENCE, bother, discomfit, discommode, impose upon, incommode, trouble

putrid *adjective* ROTTEN, bad, decayed, decomposed, putrefied, rancid, rotting, spoiled

putter *verb* MESS AROUND, dabble, dawdle, monkey around (*informal*), tinker

put up *verb* 1 ERECT, build, construct, fabricate, raise
2 ACCOMMODATE, board, house, lodge, take in
3 RECOMMEND, nominate, offer, present, propose, put forward, submit
4 ▷ **put up with** STAND, abide, bear, endure, stand for, swallow, take, tolerate

puzzle *verb* 1 PERPLEX, baffle, bewilder, confound, confuse, mystify, stump
▷ *noun* 2 PROBLEM, conundrum, enigma, mystery, paradox, poser, question, riddle

puzzled *adjective* PERPLEXED, at a loss, at sea, baffled, bewildered, confused, lost, mystified

puzzlement *noun* PERPLEXITY, bafflement, bewilderment, confusion, doubt, mystification

puzzling *adjective* PERPLEXING, abstruse, baffling, bewildering, enigmatic, incomprehensible, involved, mystifying

on fire

py•rom•e•ter [pī-ROM-i-tər] *noun* instrument for measuring very high temperature

py•ro•tech•nics [pī-rə-TEK-niks] *noun* manufacture, display of fireworks

Pyr•rhic victory [PIR-ik] one won at too high cost

py•thon [PĪ-thon] *noun* large nonpoisonous snake that crushes its prey

pyx [piks] *noun* vessel in which consecrated Host is preserved

Qq

Q.E.D. which was to be shown or proved
qua [kway] *preposition* in the capacity of
quack [kwak] *noun* 1 harsh cry of duck 2 pretender to medical or other skill ▷ *verb intransitive* 3 (of duck) utter cry
quadr-, quadri- *combining form* four: *quadrilateral*
quad•ran•gle [KWOD-rang-gəl] *noun* 1 four-sided figure 2 four-sided courtyard in a building > **quad•ran'gu•lar** [-gyə-lər] *adjective*
quad•rant [KWOD-rənt] *noun* 1 quarter of circle 2 instrument for taking angular measurements > **quad•rat'ic** *adjective* of equation, involving square of unknown quantity
quad•ra•phon•ic [kwod-rə-FON-ik] *adjective* of a sound system using four independent speakers
quad•ri•lat•er•al [kwod-rə-LAT-ər-əl] *adjective* 1 four-sided ▷ *noun* 2 four-sided figure
quad•rille [kwo-DRIL] *noun* 1 square dance 2 music played for it
quad•ril•lion [kwo-DRIL-yən] *noun* cardinal number of 1 followed by 15 zeros
quad•ru•man•ous [kwo-DROO-mə-nəs] *adjective* of apes, etc. having four feet that can be used as hands
quad•ru•ped [KWOD-ruu-ped] *noun* four-footed animal
quad•ru•ple [kwo-DROO-pəl] *adjective* 1 fourfold ▷ *verb* **-pled, -pling** 2 make, become four times as much > **quad•ru'pli•cate** [-kit] *adjective* fourfold
quad•ru•plet [kwo-DRUP-lit] *noun* one of four offspring born at one birth
quaff [kwof] *verb* drink heartily or in one swallow
quag•mire [KWAG-mīr] *noun* bog, swamp
quail[1] [kwayl] *noun* small bird of partridge family
quail[2] *verb intransitive* 1 flinch 2 cower
quaint [kwaynt] *adjective* **-er, -est** 1 interestingly old-fashioned or odd 2 curious 3 whimsical > **quaint'ness** [-nis] *noun*
quake [kwayk] *verb intransitive* **quaked, quak•ing** shake, tremble
Quak•er [KWAY-kər] *noun* member of Christian sect, the **Society of Friends**
qual•i•fy [KWOL-ə-fī] *verb* **-fied, -fy•ing** 1 make oneself competent 2 moderate 3 limit 4 make

DICTIONARY • THESAURUS

quack *noun* CHARLATAN, fake, fraud, humbug, impostor, mountebank, phoney *or* phony (*informal*), pretender
quaff *verb* DRINK, down, gulp, imbibe, swallow, swig (*informal*)
quagmire *noun* BOG, fen, marsh, mire, morass, quicksand, slough, swamp
quail *verb* SHRINK, blanch, blench, cower, cringe, falter, flinch, have cold feet (*informal*), recoil, shudder
quaint *adjective* 1 UNUSUAL, bizarre, curious, droll, eccentric, fanciful, odd, old-fashioned, peculiar, queer, singular, strange 2 OLD-FASHIONED, antiquated, old-world, picturesque
quake *verb* SHAKE, move, quiver, rock, shiver, shudder, tremble, vibrate
qualification *noun* 1 ATTRIBUTE, ability, aptitude, capability, eligibility, fitness, quality, skill, suitability

competent 5 ascribe quality to 6 describe
> **qual•i•fi•ca'tion** *noun* 1 thing that qualifies, attribute 2 restriction 3 qualifying
qual•i•ty [KWOL-i-tee] *noun, plural* **-ties** 1 attribute, characteristic, property 2 degree of excellence 3 rank > **qual'i•ta•tive** *adjective* depending on quality
qualm [kwahm] *noun* 1 misgiving 2 sudden feeling of sickness, nausea
quan•da•ry [KWAN-dree] *noun, plural* **-ries** state of perplexity, puzzling situation, dilemma
quan•ti•ty [KWON-ti-tee] *noun, plural* **-ties** 1 size, number, amount 2 specified or considerable amount > **quan'ti•fy** [-fī] *verb transitive* **-fied, -fy•ing** discover, express quantity of > **quan'ti•ta•tive** *adjective* > **quan'tum** [-təm] *noun, plural* **-ta** [-tə] desired or required amount > **quantum leap, quantum jump** (*informal*) sudden large change, increase, or advance > **quantum theory** theory that in radiation, energy of electrons is discharged not continuously but in discrete units, or quanta
quar•an•tine [KWOR-ən-teen] *noun* 1 isolation to prevent spreading of infection ▷ *verb transitive* **-tined, -tin•ing** 2 put, keep in quarantine
quark [kwork] *noun physics* any of several hypothetical particles thought to be fundamental units of matter
quar•rel [KWOR-əl] *noun* 1 angry dispute 2 argument ▷ *verb intransitive* **-reled, -rel•ing** 3 argue 4 find fault with > **quar'rel•some** [-səm] *adjective*
quar•ry[1] [KWOR-ee] *noun, plural* **-ries** 1 object of hunt or pursuit 2 prey
quarry[2] *noun, plural* **-ries** 1 excavation where stone, etc. is obtained from ground for building, etc. ▷ *verb* **-ried, -ry•ing** 2 get from quarry
quart [kwort] *noun* liquid measure, quarter of gallon or 2 pints (0.964 liter)
quar•ter [KWOR-tər] *noun* 1 fourth part 2 25 cents 3 region, district 4 mercy ▷ *verb transitive* 5 divide into quarters 6 lodge > **quar•ters** *plural noun* lodgings > **quar'ter•ly** *adjective* 1 happening, due, etc. each quarter of year ▷ *noun, plural* **-lies** 2 quarterly periodical > **quar•tet'** *noun* 1 group of four musicians 2 music for four performers > **quar'to** *noun, plural* **-tos** 1 size of book in which sheets are folded into four leaves ▷ *adjective* 2 of this size > **quar'ter•deck** *noun* after part of upper deck used esp. for official, ceremonial purposes > **quarter horse** small, powerful breed of horse bred for short races > **quar'ter•mas•ter** *noun* officer responsible for quarters, clothing, etc.
quartz [kworts] *noun* stone of pure crystalline silica > **quartz'ite** [-īt] *noun* quartz rock > **quartz timepiece** watch or clock operated by a vibrating quartz crystal
qua•sar [KWAY-zahr] *noun* extremely distant starlike object emitting powerful radio waves
quash [kwosh] *verb transitive* 1 annul 2 reject 3 subdue forcibly
quasi- [KWAY-zī] *combining form* seemingly, resembling but not actually being: *quasi-scientific*
quat•er•nar•y [KWOT-ər-ner-ee] *adjective* 1 of the number four 2 having four parts 3 (**Quat•er•nar•y**) *geology* of most recent period after Tertiary
quat•rain [KWO-trayn] *noun* four-line stanza, esp. rhymed alternately
qua•ver [KWAY-vər] *verb transitive* 1 say or sing in quavering tones ▷ *verb intransitive* 2 tremble, shake, vibrate ▷ *noun* 3 musical note half length of crotchet 4 quavering trill
quay [kee] *noun* 1 solid, fixed landing stage 2 wharf

DICTIONARY

q

THESAURUS

2 CONDITION, caveat, limitation, modification, proviso, requirement, reservation, rider, stipulation
qualified *adjective* 1 CAPABLE, able, adept, competent, efficient, experienced, expert, fit, practiced, proficient, skillful, trained
2 RESTRICTED, bounded, conditional, confined, contingent, limited, modified, provisional, reserved
qualify *verb* 1 CERTIFY, empower, equip, fit, permit, prepare, ready, train
2 MODERATE, diminish, ease, lessen, limit, reduce, regulate, restrain, restrict, soften, temper
quality *noun* 1 EXCELLENCE, caliber, distinction, grade, merit, position, rank, standing, status
2 CHARACTERISTIC, aspect, attribute, condition, feature, mark, property, trait
3 NATURE, character, kind, make, sort
qualm *noun* MISGIVING, anxiety, apprehension, compunction, disquiet, doubt, hesitation, scruple, twinge of conscience *or* pang of conscience, uneasiness
quandary *noun* DIFFICULTY, Catch-22, dilemma, impasse, plight, predicament, puzzle, strait
quantity *noun* 1 AMOUNT, lot, number, part, sum, total
2 SIZE, bulk, capacity, extent, length, magnitude, mass, measure, volume
quarrel *noun* 1 DISAGREEMENT, argument, brawl, breach, contention, controversy, dispute, dissension, feud, fight, row, squabble, tiff
▷ *verb* 2 DISAGREE, argue, bicker, brawl, clash, differ, dispute, fall out (*informal*), fight, row, squabble
quarrelsome *adjective* ARGUMENTATIVE, belligerent, combative, contentious, disputatious, pugnacious
quarry *noun* PREY, aim, game, goal, objective, prize, victim
quarter *noun* 1 DISTRICT, area, locality, neighborhood, part, place, province, region, side, zone
2 MERCY, clemency, compassion, forgiveness, leniency, pity
▷ *verb* 3 ACCOMMODATE, billet, board, house, lodge, place, post, station
quarters *plural noun* LODGINGS, abode, barracks, billet, chambers, dwelling, habitation, residence, rooms
quash *verb* 1 ANNUL, cancel, invalidate, overrule, overthrow, rescind, reverse, revoke
2 SUPPRESS, beat, crush, overthrow, put down, quell, repress, squash, subdue
quasi- *adjective* PSEUDO-, apparent, seeming, semi-, so-called, would-be
quaver *verb* 1 TREMBLE, flicker, flutter, quake, quiver, shake, vibrate, waver
▷ *noun* 2 TREMBLING, quiver, shake, tremble, tremor, vibration

quea•sy [KWEE-zee] *adjective* **-si•er, -si•est** inclined to, or causing, sickness
queen [kween] *noun* 1 king's wife 2 female ruler 3 piece in chess 4 fertile female bee, wasp, etc. 5 playing card with picture of a queen, ranking between king and jack 6 (*slang, offensive*) male homosexual > **queen'ly** *adjective* **-li•er, -li•est**
queer [kweer] *adjective* **-er, -est** 1 odd, strange 2 (*slang, usually offensive*) homosexual ▷ *noun* 3 (*slang, usually offensive*) homosexual ▷ *verb transitive* 4 spoil 5 interfere with
quell [kwel] *verb transitive* 1 crush, put down 2 allay 3 pacify
quench [kwench] *verb transitive* 1 slake 2 extinguish, put out, suppress
quer•u•lous [KWER-ə-ləs] *adjective* fretful, peevish, whining
que•ry [KWEER-ee] *noun, plural* **-ries** 1 question 2 mark of interrogation ▷ *verb transitive* **-ried, -ry•ing** 3 question, ask
quest [kwest] *noun, verb intransitive* search
ques•tion [KWES-chən] *noun* 1 sentence seeking for answer 2 that which is asked 3 interrogation 4 inquiry 5 problem 6 point for debate 7 debate, strife ▷ *verb transitive* 8 ask questions of, interrogate 9 dispute 10 doubt > **ques'tion•a•ble** *adjective* doubtful, esp. not clearly true or honest > **ques•tion•naire'** *noun* list of questions drawn up for formal answer
queue [kyoo] *noun* 1 line of waiting persons, vehicles 2 sequence of computer tasks awaiting action ▷ *verb intransitive* **queued, queu•ing** 3 (with *up*) wait in line 4 arrange computer tasks in queue
quib•ble [KWIB-əl] *noun* 1 trivial objection ▷ *verb* **-bled, -bling** 2 make this
quiche [keesh] *noun* open pielike dish of cheese, etc. on light pastry shell
quick [kwik] *adjective* **-er, -est** 1 rapid, swift 2 keen 3 brisk 4 hasty ▷ *noun* 5 part of body sensitive to pain 6 sensitive flesh **the quick** (*obsolete*) living people ▷ *adverb* 7 rapidly > **quick'en** *verb* make, become faster or more lively > **quick'ie** *noun* (*informal*) a quick drink, etc. > **quick'ly** *adverb* > **quick'sand** *noun* loose wet sand easily yielding to pressure and engulfing persons, animals, etc. > **quick'silver** *noun* mercury > **quick-tempered** *adjective* irascible
quid pro quo [KWID proh KWOH] *Lat.* something given in exchange
qui•es•cent [kwee-ES-ənt] *adjective* 1 at rest, inactive, inert 2 silent > **qui•es'cence** *noun*
qui•et [KWĪ-it] *adjective* **-er, -est** 1 with little or no motion or noise 2 undisturbed 3 not showy or obtrusive ▷ *noun* 4 state of peacefulness,

---

DICTIONARY • THESAURUS

queasy *adjective* 1 SICK, bilious, green around the gills (*informal*), ill, nauseated, off color, squeamish, upset
2 UNEASY, anxious, fidgety, ill at ease, restless, troubled, uncertain, worried
queen *noun* 1 SOVEREIGN, consort, monarch, ruler
2 IDEAL, mistress, model, star
queer *adjective* 1 STRANGE, abnormal, curious, droll, extraordinary, funny, odd, peculiar, uncommon, unusual, weird
2 FAINT, dizzy, giddy, light-headed, queasy
quell *verb* 1 SUPPRESS, conquer, crush, defeat, overcome, overpower, put down, quash, subdue, vanquish
2 ASSUAGE, allay, appease, calm, mollify, pacify, quiet, soothe
quench *verb* 1 SATISFY, allay, appease, sate, satiate, slake
2 PUT OUT, crush, douse, extinguish, smother, stifle, suppress
querulous *adjective* COMPLAINING, captious, carping, critical, discontented, dissatisfied, fault-finding, grumbling, peevish, whining
query *noun* 1 QUESTION, doubt, inquiry, objection, problem, suspicion
▷ *verb* 2 DOUBT, challenge, disbelieve, dispute, distrust, mistrust, suspect
3 ASK, inquire *or* enquire, question
quest *noun* SEARCH, adventure, crusade, enterprise, expedition, hunt, journey, mission
question *noun* 1 ISSUE, motion, point, point at issue, proposal, proposition, subject, theme, topic
2 DIFFICULTY, argument, contention, controversy, dispute, doubt, problem, query
3 ▷ **in question** UNDER DISCUSSION, at issue, in doubt, open to debate
4 ▷ **out of the question** IMPOSSIBLE, inconceivable, unthinkable
▷ *verb* 5 ASK, cross-examine, examine, inquire, interrogate, interview, probe, quiz
6 DISPUTE, challenge, disbelieve, doubt, mistrust, oppose, query, suspect
questionable *adjective* DUBIOUS, controversial, debatable, doubtful, iffy (*informal*), moot, suspect, suspicious
queue *noun* LINE, chain, file, sequence, series, string, train
quibble *verb* 1 SPLIT HAIRS, carp, cavil
▷ *noun* 2 OBJECTION, cavil, complaint, criticism, nicety, niggle
quick *adjective* 1 FAST, brisk, express, fleet, hasty, rapid, speedy, swift
2 BRIEF, cursory, hasty, hurried, perfunctory
3 SUDDEN, prompt
4 INTELLIGENT, acute, alert, astute, bright (*informal*), clever, perceptive, quick-witted, sharp, shrewd, smart
5 DEFT, adept, adroit, dexterous, skillful
6 EXCITABLE, irascible, irritable, passionate, testy, touchy
quicken *verb* 1 SPEED, accelerate, expedite, hasten, hurry, impel, precipitate
2 INVIGORATE, arouse, energize, excite, incite, inspire, revive, stimulate, vitalize
quickly *adverb* SWIFTLY, abruptly, apace, briskly, fast, hastily, hurriedly, promptly, pronto (*informal*), rapidly, soon, speedily
quick-tempered *adjective* HOT-TEMPERED, choleric, fiery, irascible, irritable, quarrelsome, testy
quick-witted *adjective* CLEVER, alert, astute, bright (*informal*), keen, perceptive, sharp, shrewd, smart
quiet *adjective* 1 SILENT, hushed, inaudible, low, noiseless, peaceful, soft, soundless
2 CALM, mild, peaceful, placid, restful, serene, smooth, tranquil
3 UNDISTURBED, isolated, private, secluded,

absence of noise or disturbance ▷ *verb* 5 make, become quiet > **qui'et•ly** *adverb* > **qui'e•tude** *noun*
quill [kwil] *noun* 1 large feather 2 hollow stem of this 3 pen, plectrum made from feather 4 spine of porcupine
quilt [kwilt] *noun* 1 padded coverlet ▷ *verb transitive* 2 stitch (two pieces of cloth) with pad between
quince [kwins] *noun* 1 acid pear-shaped fruit 2 tree bearing it
qui•nine [KWĪ-nīn] *noun* bitter drug made from bark of tree, used to treat fever, and as mixer
quin•quen•ni•al [kwin-KWEN-ee-əl] *adjective* occurring once in, or lasting, five years
quin•sy [KWIN-zee] *noun* inflammation of throat or tonsils
quint [kwint] *noun short for* **quintuplet**
quin•tes•sence [kwin-TES-əns] *noun* 1 purest form, essential feature 2 embodiment > **quin•tes•sen'tial** [-tə-SEN-shəl] *adjective*
quin•tet [kwin-TET] *noun* 1 set of five singers or players 2 composition for five voices or instruments
quin•tu•plet [kwin-TUP-lit] *noun* one of five offspring born at one birth
quip [kwip] *noun, verb* **quipped, quip•ping** (utter) witty saying
quire [kwīr] *noun* 24 sheets of writing paper
quirk [kwurk] *noun* 1 individual peculiarity of character 2 unexpected twist or turn
quis•ling [KWIZ-ling] *noun* traitor who aids occupying enemy force
quit [kwit] *verb* **quit** *or* **quit•ted, quit•ting** 1 stop doing a thing 2 depart 3 leave, go away from 4 cease from ▷ *adjective* 5 free, rid > **quits** *adjective* on equal or even terms by repayment, etc. > **quit'tance** [KWIT-ns] *noun* 1 discharge 2 receipt > **quit'ter** *noun* one lacking perseverance
quite [kwīt] *adverb* 1 wholly, completely 2 very considerably 3 somewhat, rather ▷ *interjection* 4 exactly, just so
quiv•er[1] [KWIV-ər] *verb intransitive* 1 shake or tremble ▷ *noun* 2 quivering 3 vibration
quiver[2] *noun* carrying case for arrows
quix•ot•ic [kwik-SOT-ik] *adjective* unrealistically and impractically optimistic, idealistic, chivalrous
quiz [kwiz] *noun, plural* **quiz•zes** 1 entertainment in which general or specific knowledge of players is tested by questions 2 examination, interrogation ▷ *verb transitive* **quizzed, quiz•zing** 3 question, interrogate > **quiz'zi•cal** *adjective* 1 questioning 2 mocking
quoit [kwoit] *noun* ring for throwing at peg as a game > **quoits** the game in which quoits are tossed at a stake in the ground in attempts to encircle it
quo•rum [KWOR-əm] *noun* least number that must be present in meeting to make its transactions valid
quo•ta [KWOH-tə] *noun* 1 share to be contributed or received 2 specified number, quantity, that may be imported or admitted
quote [kwoht] *verb transitive* **quot•ed, quot•ing** 1 copy or repeat passages from 2 refer to, esp. to confirm view 3 state price for > **quot'a•ble** *adjective* > **quo•ta'tion** *noun*
quoth [kwohth] *verb* (*obsolete*) said
quo•tid•i•an [kwoh-TID-ee-ən] *adjective* 1 daily 2 everyday, commonplace
quo•tient [KWOH-shənt] *noun* number resulting from dividing one number by another
q.v. which see: used to refer a reader to another item in the same book

DICTIONARY

q

THESAURUS

sequestered, unfrequented
4 RESERVED, gentle, meek, mild, retiring, sedate, shy
▷ *noun* 5 PEACE, calmness, ease, quietness, repose, rest, serenity, silence, stillness, tranquillity
quieten *verb* 1 SILENCE, compose, hush, muffle, mute, quell, quiet, stifle, still, stop, subdue
2 SOOTHE, allay, appease, blunt, calm, deaden, dull
quietly *adverb* 1 SILENTLY, in an undertone, inaudibly, in silence, mutely, noiselessly, softly
2 CALMLY, mildly, patiently, placidly, serenely
quietness *noun* PEACE, calm, hush, quiet, silence, stillness, tranquillity
quilt *noun* BEDSPREAD, continental quilt, counterpane, coverlet, duvet, eiderdown
quintessence *noun* ESSENCE, distillation, soul, spirit
quintessential *adjective* ULTIMATE, archetypal, definitive, prototypical, typical
quip *noun* JOKE, gibe, jest, pleasantry, retort, riposte, sally, wisecrack (*informal*), witticism
quirk *noun* PECULIARITY, aberration, characteristic, eccentricity, foible, habit, idiosyncrasy, kink, mannerism, oddity, trait
quirky *adjective* ODD, eccentric, idiosyncratic, offbeat, peculiar, unusual
quit *verb* 1 STOP, abandon, cease, discontinue, drop, end, give up, halt
2 RESIGN, abdicate, go, leave, pull out, retire, step down (*informal*)
3 DEPART, go, leave, pull out
quite *adverb* 1 SOMEWHAT, fairly, moderately, rather, reasonably, relatively
2 ABSOLUTELY, completely, entirely, fully, perfectly, totally, wholly
3 TRULY, in fact, in reality, in truth, really
quiver *verb* 1 SHAKE, oscillate, quake, quaver, shiver, shudder, tremble, vibrate
▷ *noun* 2 SHAKE, oscillation, shiver, shudder, tremble, tremor, vibration
quixotic *adjective* UNREALISTIC, dreamy, fanciful, idealistic, impractical, romantic
quiz *noun* 1 EXAMINATION, investigation, questioning, test
▷ *verb* 2 QUESTION, ask, examine, interrogate, investigate
quizzical *adjective* MOCKING, arch, questioning, sardonic, teasing
quota *noun* SHARE, allowance, assignment, part, portion, ration, slice
quotation *noun* 1 PASSAGE, citation, excerpt, extract, quote (*informal*), reference
2 (*commerce*) ESTIMATE, charge, cost, figure, price, quote (*informal*), rate, tender
quote *verb* REPEAT, cite, detail, instance, name, recall, recite, recollect, refer to

Rr

Ra *chem.* radium
rab•bet [RAB-it] *noun* 1 recess, groove cut into piece of timber to join with matching piece ▷ *verb transitive* **-bet•ed, -bet•ing** 2 cut rabbet in
rab•bi [RAB-ī] *noun, plural* **-bis** Jewish learned man, spiritual leader, teacher > **rab•bin'i•cal** *adjective*
rab'bit *noun* 1 small burrowing rodent like hare ▷ *verb intransitive* 2 hunt rabbits > **rabbit punch** 1 sharp blow to back of neck 2 *see* **rarebit**
rab•ble [RAB-əl] *noun* 1 crowd of vulgar, noisy people 2 mob
rab'id *adjective* 1 relating to or having rabies 2 furious 3 mad 4 fanatical
ra•bies [RAY-beez] *noun* acute infectious viral disease transmitted by dogs, etc.
rac•coon [ra-KOON] *noun* small N Amer. mammal
race[1] [rays] *noun* 1 contest of speed, as in running, swimming, etc. 2 contest, rivalry 3 strong current of water, esp. leading to water wheel ▷ *verb transitive* **raced, rac•ing** 4 cause to run rapidly ▷ *verb intransitive* **raced, rac•ing** 5 run swiftly 6 of engine, pedal, etc., to move rapidly and erratically, esp. on removal of resistance > **rac•es** *plural noun* meeting for horse racing > **rac'er** *noun* person, vehicle, animal that races
race[2] *noun* 1 group of people of common ancestry with distinguishing physical features (skin color, etc.) 2 species 3 type > **ra•cial** [RAY-shəl] *adjective* > **rac'ism** *noun* 1 belief in innate superiority of particular race 2 antagonism toward members of different race based on this belief > **rac'ist** *adjective, noun*
rack[1] [rak] *noun* 1 framework for displaying or holding baggage, books, hats, bottles, etc. 2 *mechanics* straight bar with teeth on its edge, to work with pinion 3 instrument of torture by stretching ▷ *verb transitive* 4 stretch on rack or wheel 5 torture 6 stretch, strain > **rack'ing** *adjective* agonizing (pain)
rack[2] *noun* **rack and ruin** destruction
rack[3] *noun* neck or rib section of mutton, lamb, pork
rack•et[1] [RAK-it] *noun* 1 loud noise, uproar 2 occupation by which money is made illegally > **rack•et•eer** [rak-i-TEER] *noun* one making illegal profits > **rack'et•y** *adjective* noisy
racket[2], rac•quet [RAK-it] *noun* bat used in

---

rabble *noun* MOB, canaille, crowd, herd, horde, swarm, throng
rabid *adjective* 1 FANATICAL, extreme, fervent, irrational, narrow-minded, zealous 2 MAD, hydrophobic
race[1] *noun* 1 CONTEST, chase, competition, dash, pursuit, rivalry ▷ *verb* 2 RUN, career, compete, contest, dart, dash, fly, gallop, hurry, speed, tear, zoom
race[2] *noun* PEOPLE, blood, folk, nation, stock, tribe, type
racial *adjective* ETHNIC, ethnological, folk, genealogical, genetic, national, tribal
rack *noun* 1 FRAME, framework, stand, structure ▷ *verb* 2 TORTURE, afflict, agonize, crucify, harrow, oppress, pain, torment
racket *noun* 1 NOISE, clamor, din, disturbance, fuss, outcry, pandemonium, row

tennis, etc. > **rackets** ball game played in paved, walled court

rac•on•teur [rak-ən-TUR] *noun* skilled storyteller

racquet *see* **racket²**

rac•y [RAY-see] *adjective* **rac•i•er, rac•i•est** 1 spirited 2 lively 3 having strong flavor 4 spicy 5 piquant > **rac'i•ly** *adverb* > **rac'i•ness** *noun*

ra•dar [RAY-dahr] *noun* device for finding range and direction by ultrahigh frequency point-to-point radio waves, which reflect back to their source and reveal position and nature of objects sought

radial *see* **radius**

ra•di•ate [RAY-dee-ayt] *verb* **-at•ed, -at•ing** 1 emit, be emitted in rays 2 spread out from center > **ra'di•ance** [-əns] *noun* 1 brightness 2 splendor > **ra'di•ant** [-ənt] *adjective* 1 beaming 2 shining 3 emitting rays > **ra•di•a'tion** *noun* 1 transmission of heat, light, etc. from one body to another 2 particles, rays, emitted in nuclear decay 3 act of radiating > **ra'di•a•tor** *noun* 1 that which radiates, esp. heating apparatus for rooms 2 cooling apparatus of automobile engine

rad•i•cal [RAD-i-kəl] *adjective* 1 fundamental, thorough 2 extreme 3 of root ▷ *noun* 4 person of extreme (political) views 5 number expressed as root of another 6 group of atoms of several elements that remain unchanged in a series of chemical compounds

ra•di•o [RAY-dee-oh] *noun, plural* **-di•os** 1 use of electromagnetic waves for broadcasting, communication, etc. 2 device for receiving, amplifying radio signals 3 broadcasting, content of radio program ▷ *verb transitive* **-di•oed, -di•o•ing** 4 transmit message, etc. by radio

radio- *combining form* of rays, of radiation, of radium: *radiology*

ra•di•o•ac•tive [ray-dee-oh-AK-tiv] *adjective* emitting invisible rays that penetrate matter > **ra•di•o•ac•tiv'i•ty** *noun*

ra•di•o•gra•phy [ray-dee-OG-rə-fee] *noun* production of image on film or plate by radiation

ra•di•ol•o•gy [ray-dee-OL-ə-jee] *noun* science of use of rays in medicine > **ra•di•ol'o•gist** *noun*

ra•di•o•ther•a•py [ray-dee-oh-THER-ə-pee] *noun* diagnosis and treatment of disease by x-rays

rad'ish *noun* pungent root vegetable

ra•di•um [RAY-dee-əm] *noun* radioactive metallic element

ra•di•us [RAY-dee-əs] *noun, plural* **-di•i** [-dee-ī] 1 straight line from center to circumference of circle 2 outer of two bones in forearm > **ra'di•al** [-əl] *adjective* 1 arranged like radii of circle 2 of ray or rays 3 of radius

ra•dome [RAY-dohm] *noun* dome-shaped housing for radar

ra•don [RAY-don] *noun* radioactive gaseous element

raf•fi•a [RAF-fee-ə] *noun* prepared palm fiber for making mats, etc.

raff'ish *adjective* disreputable

raf•fle [RAF-əl] *noun* 1 lottery in which an article is assigned by lot to one of those buying tickets ▷ *verb transitive* **-fled, -fling** 2 dispose of by raffle

raft *noun* floating structure of logs, planks, etc.

raf•ter [RAF-tər] *noun* one of the main beams of a roof

raft•ing [RAF-ting] *noun* sport of traveling on rivers by raft > **raft•er** *noun* participant in this

rag¹ *noun* 1 fragment of cloth 2 torn piece 3 (*informal*) newspaper, etc., esp. one considered worthless 4 piece of ragtime music > **rags** tattered clothing > **rag•ged** [RAG-id] *adjective* 1 shaggy 2 torn 3 clothed in torn clothes 4 lacking smoothness > **rag'bag** *noun* confused assortment > **rag'time** *noun* style of jazz piano music

rag² *verb transitive* **ragged, rag•ging** 1 tease 2 torment 3 play practical jokes on

rag•a•muf•fin [RAG-ə-muf-in] *noun* ragged, dirty person or child

rage [rayj] *noun* 1 violent anger or passion 2 fury 3 aggressive behavior associated with a certain activity, e.g., road rage ▷ *verb intransitive* **raged, rag•ing** 4 speak, act with fury 5 proceed violently and without check (as storm, battle, etc.) 6 be widely and violently prevalent **all the rage** very popular

DICTIONARY

r

THESAURUS

2 FRAUD, scheme

racy *adjective* 1 RISQUÉ, bawdy, blue, naughty, smutty, suggestive
2 LIVELY, animated, energetic, entertaining, exciting, sparkling, spirited

radiance *noun* 1 HAPPINESS, delight, gaiety, joy, pleasure, rapture, warmth
2 BRIGHTNESS, brilliance, glare, gleam, glow, light, luster, shine

radiant *adjective* 1 HAPPY, blissful, delighted, ecstatic, glowing, joyful, joyous, on cloud nine (*informal*), rapturous
2 BRIGHT, brilliant, gleaming, glittering, glowing, luminous, lustrous, shining

radiate *verb* 1 SPREAD OUT, branch out, diverge, issue
2 EMIT, diffuse, give off *or* give out, pour, scatter, send out, shed, spread

radical *adjective* 1 FUNDAMENTAL, basic, deep-seated, innate, natural, profound
2 EXTREME, complete, drastic, entire, extremist, fanatical, severe, sweeping, thorough
▷ *noun* 3 EXTREMIST, fanatic, militant, revolutionary

raffle *noun* DRAW, lottery, sweep, sweepstake

ragamuffin *noun* URCHIN, guttersnipe

rage *noun* 1 FURY, anger, frenzy, ire, madness, passion, rampage, wrath
▷ *verb* 2 BE FURIOUS, blow one's top, blow up (*informal*), fly off the handle (*informal*), fume, go ballistic (*slang*), go up the wall (*slang*), see red, seethe, storm, wig out (*slang*) ▷ **all the rage** IN FASHION, fashionable, du jour (*French*), the latest thing, trendy, voguish, culty

ragged *adjective* 1 TATTERED, in rags, in tatters, shabby, tatty, threadbare, torn, unkempt
2 ROUGH, jagged, rugged, serrated, uneven, unfinished

raging *adjective* FURIOUS, beside oneself, enraged, fuming, incensed, infuriated, mad, raving, seething

rags *plural noun* TATTERS, castoffs, old clothes,

rag•lan [RAG-lən] *adjective* of sleeves that continue to the neck so that there are no shoulder seams
ra•gout [ra-GOO] *noun* highly seasoned stew of meat and vegetables
raid [rayd] *noun* 1 rush, attack 2 foray ▷ *verb transitive* 3 make raid on
rail[1] [rayl] *noun* 1 horizontal bar, esp. as part of fence, track, etc. 2 (*slang*) line of cocaine for sniffing > **rail'ing** *noun* fence, barrier made of rails supported by posts > **rail'head** [-hed] *noun* farthest point to which railway line extends > **rail'road, rail'way** *noun* 1 track of steel rails on which trains run 2 company operating railroad
rail[2] *verb intransitive* 1 utter abuse 2 scoff 3 scold 4 reproach > **rail'ler•y** [-ə-ree] *noun, plural* **-ler•ies** banter
rail[3] *noun* any of various marsh birds
rai•ment [RAY-mənt] *noun* clothing
rain [rayn] *noun* 1 moisture falling in drops from clouds 2 fall of such drops ▷ *verb intransitive* 3 fall as rain ▷ *verb transitive* 4 pour down like rain > **rain'y** *adjective* **rain•i•er, rain•i•est** > **rain'bow** [-boh] *noun* arch of prismatic colors in sky > **rain'coat** *noun* light water-resistant overcoat
raise [rayz] *verb transitive* **raised, rais•ing** 1 lift up 2 set up 3 build 4 increase 5 elevate 6 promote 7 heighten, as pitch of voice 8 breed into existence 9 levy, collect 10 end (siege) **raise Cain** [KAYN] be riotous, angry, etc.
rai•sin [RAY-zin] *noun* dried grape
rai•son d'ê•tre [RAY-zohn DE-trə] Fr. reason or justification for existence
raj [rahj] *noun* rule, sway, esp. in India > **ra'jah** *noun* Indian prince or ruler
rake[1] [rayk] *noun* 1 tool with long handle and crosspiece with teeth for gathering hay, leaves, etc. ▷ *verb transitive* **raked, rak•ing** 2 gather, smooth with rake 3 sweep, search over 4 sweep with shot > **rake-off** *noun* monetary commission, esp. illegal
rake[2] *noun* dissolute or dissipated man
rake[3] *noun* 1 slope, esp. backward, of ship's funnel, etc. ▷ *verb* **raked, rak•ing** 2 incline from perpendicular > **rak'ish** *adjective* appearing dashing or speedy
ral•ly [RAL-ee] *verb* **-lied, -ly•ing** 1 bring together, esp. what has been scattered, as routed army or dispersed troops 2 come together 3 regain health or strength, revive ▷ *noun* 4 act of rallying 5 assembly, esp. outdoor, of any organization 6 *tennis* lively exchange of strokes
ram *noun* 1 male sheep 2 hydraulic machine 3 battering engine ▷ *verb transitive* **rammed, ram•ming** 4 force, drive 5 strike against with force 6 stuff 7 strike with ram
RAM [ram] *computing* random-access memory (as on a hard disk)
ram•ble [RAM-bəl] *verb intransitive* **-bled, -bling** 1 walk without definite route 2 wander 3 talk incoherently 4 spread in random fashion ▷ *noun* 5 rambling walk > **ram'bler** *noun* 1 climbing rose 2 one who rambles
ram•e•kin [RAM-i-kin] *noun* 1 small fireproof dish 2 food baked in it
ram•i•fy [RAM-ə-fī] *verb* **-fied, -fy•ing** 1 spread in branches, subdivide 2 become complex > **ram•i•fi•ca'tion** *noun* 1 branch, subdivision 2 process of branching out 3 consequence
ra•mose [RAY-məs] *adjective* branching
ramp *noun* gradual slope joining two level surfaces
ram•page [ram-PAYJ] *verb intransitive* **-paged,**

DICTIONARY • THESAURUS

tattered clothing
raid *noun* 1 ATTACK, foray, incursion, inroad, invasion, sally, sortie
▷ *verb* 2 ATTACK, assault, foray, invade, pillage, plunder, sack
raider *noun* ATTACKER, invader, marauder, plunderer, robber, thief
railing *noun* FENCE, balustrade, barrier, paling, rails
rain *noun* 1 RAINFALL, cloudburst, deluge, downpour, drizzle, fall, raindrops, showers, torrent
▷ *verb* 2 POUR, bucket down (*informal*), come down in buckets (*informal*), drizzle, pelt *or* pelt down, rain cats and dogs, teem
3 FALL, deposit, drop, shower, sprinkle
rainy *adjective* WET, damp, drizzly, showery
raise *verb* 1 LIFT, build, elevate, erect, heave, hoist, rear, uplift
2 INCREASE, advance, amplify, boost, enhance, enlarge, heighten, inflate, intensify, magnify, strengthen
3 COLLECT, assemble, form, gather, mass, obtain, rally, recruit
4 CAUSE, create, engender, occasion, originate, produce, provoke, start
5 BRING UP, develop, nurture, rear
6 SUGGEST, advance, broach, introduce, moot, put forward
rake[1] *verb* 1 GATHER, collect, remove
2 SEARCH, comb, scour, scrutinize
rake[2] *noun* LIBERTINE, debauchee, lecher, playboy, roué
rakish *adjective* DASHING, dapper, debonair, devil-may-care, jaunty, raffish
rally[1] *noun* 1 GATHERING, assembly, congress, convention, meeting
2 RECOVERY, improvement, recuperation, revival
▷ *verb* 3 REASSEMBLE, regroup, reorganize, unite
4 GATHER, assemble, collect, convene, marshal, muster, round up, unite
5 RECOVER, get better, improve, recuperate, revive
ram *verb* 1 HIT, butt, crash, dash, drive, force, impact, smash
2 CRAM, crowd, force, jam, stuff, thrust
ramble *verb* 1 WALK, range, roam, rove, saunter, stray, stroll, wander
2 BABBLE
▷ *noun* 3 WALK, hike, roaming, roving, saunter, stroll, tour
rambler *noun* WALKER, hiker, rover, wanderer, wayfarer
rambling *adjective* LONG-WINDED, circuitous, digressive, disconnected, discursive, disjointed, incoherent, wordy
ramification *noun*
▷ **ramifications** CONSEQUENCES, developments, results, sequel, upshot
ramp *noun* SLOPE, gradient, incline, rise
rampage *verb* 1 GO BERSERK, rage, run amok, run riot, storm

-**pag•ing** 1 dash about violently ▷ *noun* [RAM-payj] 2 angry or destructive behavior > **ram•pa'geous** [-jəs] *adjective*
ramp•ant [RAM-pənt] *adjective* 1 violent 2 rife 3 rearing
ram•part [RAM-pahrt] *noun* mound, wall for defense
ram•shack•le [RAM-shak-əl] *adjective* tumble-down, rickety, makeshift
ran *pt. of* **run**
ranch *noun* 1 cattle farm ▷ *verb intransitive* 2 manage one > **ranch'er** *noun*
ran•cid [RAN-sid] *adjective* smelling or tasting offensive, like stale fat
ran•cor [RANG-kər] *noun* bitter, inveterate hate > **ran'cor•ous** *adjective* 1 malignant 2 virulent
ran•dom [RAN-dəm] *adjective* made or done by chance, without plan **at random** haphazard(ly)
rang *pt. of* **ring²**
range [raynj] *noun* 1 limits 2 row 3 scope, sphere 4 distance missile can travel 5 distance of mark shot at 6 place for shooting practice or rocket testing 7 rank 8 kitchen stove ▷ *verb transitive* **ranged, rang•ing** 9 set in row 10 classify 11 roam ▷ *verb intransitive* **ranged, rang•ing** 12 extend 13 roam 14 pass from one point to another 15 fluctuate (as prices) > **rang'er** *noun* official in charge of or patrolling park, etc. > **rang'y** *adjective* **rang•i•er, rang•i•est** 1 with long, slender limbs 2 spacious > **range'find•er** *noun* instrument for finding distance away of given object
rank¹ [rangk] *noun* 1 row, line 2 order 3 social class 4 status 5 relative place or position ▷ *verb transitive* 6 draw up in rank, classify ▷ *verb intransitive* 7 have rank, place 8 have certain distinctions **the ranks** common soldiers > **rank and file** (esp. in labor unions) great mass or majority of people
rank² *adjective* **-er, -est** 1 growing too thickly, coarse 2 offensively strong 3 rancid 4 vile 5 flagrant > **rank'ly** *adverb*
ran•kle [RANG-kəl] *verb intransitive* **-kled, -kling** fester, continue to cause anger, resentment or bitterness
ran•sack [RAN-sak] *verb transitive* 1 search thoroughly 2 pillage, plunder
ran•som [RAN-səm] *noun* 1 release from captivity by payment 2 amount paid ▷ *verb transitive* 3 pay ransom for
rant *verb intransitive* 1 rave in violent, high-sounding language ▷ *noun* 2 noisy, boisterous speech 3 wild gaiety
rap¹ *noun* 1 smart slight blow 2 rhythmic monologue performed to music ▷ *verb* **rapped, rap•ping** 3 give rap to 4 utter abruptly 5 perform rhythmic monologue to music > **rap'per** *noun* 1 singer of rap 2 person or thing that raps **take the rap** (*slang*) take blame, suffer punishment (for), whether guilty or not
rap² *noun* **not care a rap** not care at all
ra•pa•cious [rə-PAY-shəs] *adjective* 1 greedy 2 grasping > **ra•pac'i•ty** [-PAS-i-tee] *noun*
rape [rayp] *verb transitive* **raped, rap•ing** 1 force (person) to submit unwillingly to sexual intercourse ▷ *noun* 2 act of raping 3 any violation or abuse > **rap'ist** *noun*
rap'id *adjective* quick, swift > **rapids** *plural noun* part of river with fast, turbulent current > **ra•pid'i•ty** *noun*

DICTIONARY

r

THESAURUS

▷ *noun* 2 ▷ **on the rampage** BERSERK, amok, out of control, raging, riotous, violent, wild
rampant *adjective* 1 WIDESPREAD, prevalent, profuse, rife, spreading like wildfire, unchecked, uncontrolled, unrestrained
2 (*heraldry*) UPRIGHT, erect, rearing, standing
rampart *noun* DEFENSE, bastion, bulwark, fence, fortification, wall
ramshackle *adjective* RICKETY, crumbling, decrepit, derelict, flimsy, shaky, tumbledown, unsafe, unsteady
rancid *adjective* ROTTEN, bad, fetid, foul, putrid, rank, sour, stale, strong-smelling, tainted
rancor *noun* HATRED, animosity, bad blood, bitterness, hate, ill feeling, ill will
random *adjective* 1 CHANCE, accidental, adventitious, casual, fortuitous, haphazard, hit or miss, incidental
2 ▷ **at random** HAPHAZARDLY, arbitrarily, by chance, randomly, unsystematically, willy-nilly
range *noun* 1 LIMITS, area, bounds, orbit, province, radius, reach, scope, sphere
2 SERIES, assortment, collection, gamut, lot, selection, variety
▷ *verb* 3 VARY, extend, reach, run, stretch
4 ROAM, ramble, rove, traverse, wander
rangy *adjective* LONG-LIMBED, gangling, lanky, leggy, long-legged
rank¹ *noun* 1 STATUS, caste, class, degree, division, grade, level, order, position, sort, type
2 ROW, column, file, group, line, range, series, tier
▷ *verb* 3 ARRANGE, align, array, dispose, line up, order, sort
rank² *adjective* 1 ABSOLUTE, arrant, blatant, complete, downright, flagrant, gross, sheer, thorough, total, utter
2 FOUL, bad, disgusting, funky (*slang*), noisome, noxious, offensive, rancid, revolting, smelly, stinking
3 ABUNDANT, dense, lush, luxuriant, profuse
rank and file *noun* GENERAL PUBLIC, majority, mass, masses
rankle *verb* ANNOY, anger, gall, get on one's nerves (*informal*), irk, irritate, rile
ransack *verb* 1 SEARCH, comb, explore, go through, rummage, scour, turn inside out
2 PLUNDER, loot, pillage, raid, strip
ransom *noun* PAYMENT, money, payoff, price
rant *verb* SHOUT, cry, declaim, rave, roar, yell
rap *verb* 1 HIT, crack, knock, strike, tap
▷ *noun* 2 BLOW, clout (*informal*), crack, knock, tap
3 (*slang*) PUNISHMENT, blame, responsibility
rapacious *adjective* GREEDY, avaricious, grasping, insatiable, predatory, preying, voracious
rape *verb* 1 SEXUALLY ASSAULT, abuse, force, outrage, ravish, violate
▷ *noun* 2 SEXUAL ASSAULT, outrage, ravishment, violation
3 DESECRATION, abuse, defilement, violation
rapid *adjective* QUICK, brisk, express, fast, hasty, hurried, prompt, speedy, swift
rapidity *noun* SPEED, alacrity, briskness, fleetness, haste, hurry, promptness, quickness, rush, swiftness, velocity
rapidly *adverb* QUICKLY, briskly, fast, hastily,

ra•pi•er [RAY-pee-ər] *noun* fine-bladed sword for thrusting only
rap•ine [RAP-in] *noun* plunder
rap•port [ra-POR] *noun* harmony, agreement
rap•proche•ment [rap-rohsh-MAHN] *noun* reestablishment of friendly relations, esp. between nations
rapt *adjective* engrossed, spellbound > **rap'ture** [-chər] *noun* ecstasy > **rap'tur•ous** *adjective*
rare[1] [rair] *adjective* **rar•er, rar•est** 1 uncommon 2 infrequent 3 of uncommon quality 4 of atmosphere, having low density, thin > **rare'ly** *adverb* seldom > **rar'i•ty** *noun, plural* **-ties** 1 anything rare 2 rareness
rare[2] *adjective* **rar•er, rar•est** (of meat) lightly cooked
rare•bit [RAIR-bit] *noun* *see* **Welsh rabbit**
rar•e•fy [RAIR-ə-fī] *verb* **-fied, -fy•ing** 1 make, become thin, rare, or less dense 2 refine
rar•ing [RAIR-ing] *adjective* (*informal*) enthusiastically willing, ready
ras•cal [RAS-kəl] *noun* 1 rogue 2 naughty (young) person > **ras•cal'i•ty** [-KAL-i-tee] *noun* roguery, baseness > **ras'cal•ly** [-kəl-ee] *adjective*
rash[1] *adjective* **-er, -est** hasty, reckless, incautious
rash[2] *noun* 1 skin eruption 2 outbreak, series of (unpleasant) occurrences
rash•er [RASH-ər] *noun* 1 serving of bacon, usu. three or four slices 2 thin slice of bacon or ham
rasp *noun* 1 harsh, grating noise 2 coarse file ▷ *verb* 3 scrape with rasp 4 make scraping noise 5 speak in grating voice 6 grate upon 7 irritate
rasp•ber•ry [RAZ-ber-ee] *noun* 1 red, juicy edible berry 2 plant which bears it 3 (*informal*) spluttering noise with tongue and lips to show contempt
Ras•ta•far•i•an [ras-tə-FAIR-ee-ən] *noun, adjective* (member) of Jamaican cult regarding Haile Selassie, late emperor of Ethiopia, as the messiah
rat *noun* 1 small rodent 2 (*slang*) contemptible person, esp. deserter, informer, etc. ▷ *verb intransitive* **rat•ted, rat•ting** 3 (*slang*) inform (on), betray, desert, abandon 4 hunt rats > **rat'ty** *adjective* **-ti•er, -ti•est** (*slang*) mean, ill-tempered, irritable > **rat race** continual hectic competitive activity > **rat'trap** *noun* 1 device for catching rats 2 dilapidated dwelling
ratch•et [RACH-it] *noun* set of teeth on bar or wheel allowing motion in one direction only
rate[1] [rayt] *noun* 1 proportion between two things 2 charge 3 degree of speed, etc. ▷ *verb transitive* **rat•ed, rat•ing** 4 value 5 estimate value of > **rat'a•ble** *adjective* that can be rated or appraised
rate[2] *verb transitive* **rat•ed, rat•ing** scold, chide
rath•er [RATH-ər] *adverb* 1 to some extent 2 preferably 3 more willingly
rat•i•fy [RAT-ə-fī] *verb transitive* **-fied, -fy•ing** confirm > **rat•i•fi•ca'tion** [-fi-KAY-shən] *noun*
rat•ing [RAY-ting] *noun* 1 credit standing 2 fixing a rate 3 classification, esp. of ship, enlisted member of armed forces 4 angry rebuke
ra•tio [RAY-shoh] *noun, plural* **-tios** 1 proportion 2 quantitative relation
ra•ti•oc•i•nate [rash-ee-OS-ə-nayt] *verb intransitive* **-nat•ed, -nat•ing** reason > **ra•ti•oc•i•na'tion** [-NAY-shən] *noun*
ra•tion [RASH-ən] *noun* 1 fixed allowance of food, etc. ▷ *verb transitive* 2 supply with, limit to certain amount
ra•tion•al [RASH-ə-nl] *adjective* 1 reasonable,

DICTIONARY • THESAURUS

hurriedly, in haste, promptly, pronto (*informal*), speedily, swiftly
rapport *noun* BOND, affinity, empathy, harmony, link, relationship, sympathy, tie, understanding
rapprochement *noun* RECONCILIATION, detente, reunion
rapt *adjective* SPELLBOUND, absorbed, engrossed, enthralled, entranced, fascinated, gripped
rapture *noun* ECSTASY, bliss, delight, euphoria, joy, rhapsody, seventh heaven, transport
rapturous *adjective* ECSTATIC, blissful, euphoric, in seventh heaven, joyful, overjoyed, over the moon (*informal*), transported
rare[1] *adjective* 1 UNCOMMON, few, infrequent, scarce, singular, sparse, strange, unusual 2 SUPERB, choice, excellent, fine, great, peerless, superlative
rarefied *adjective* EXALTED, elevated, high, lofty, noble, spiritual, sublime
rarely *adverb* SELDOM, hardly, hardly ever, infrequently
raring *adjective*
▷ **raring to** EAGER TO, desperate to, enthusiastic to, impatient to, keen to, longing to, ready to
rarity *noun* 1 CURIO, collector's item, find, gem, treasure 2 UNCOMMONNESS, infrequency, scarcity, shortage, sparseness, strangeness, unusualness
rascal *noun* ROGUE, devil, good-for-nothing, imp, scamp, scoundrel, villain
rash[1] *adjective* RECKLESS, careless, foolhardy, hasty, heedless, ill-advised, impetuous, imprudent, impulsive, incautious
rash[2] *noun* 1 OUTBREAK, eruption 2 SPATE, flood, outbreak, plague, series, wave
rashness *noun* RECKLESSNESS, carelessness, foolhardiness, hastiness, heedlessness, indiscretion, thoughtlessness
rate[1] *noun* 1 SPEED, pace, tempo, velocity 2 DEGREE, proportion, ratio, scale, standard 3 CHARGE, cost, fee, figure, price 4 ▷ **at any rate** IN ANY CASE, anyhow, anyway, at all events ▷ *verb* 5 EVALUATE, consider, count, estimate, grade, measure, rank, reckon, value 6 DESERVE, be entitled to, be worthy of, merit
rather *adverb* 1 TO SOME EXTENT, a little, fairly, moderately, quite, relatively, somewhat, to some degree 2 PREFERABLY, more readily, more willingly, sooner
ratify *verb* APPROVE, affirm, authorize, confirm, endorse, establish, sanction, uphold
rating *noun* POSITION, class, degree, grade, order, placing, rank, rate, status
ratio *noun* PROPORTION, fraction, percentage, rate, relation
ration *noun* 1 ALLOWANCE, allotment, helping, measure, part, portion, quota, share ▷ *verb* 2 LIMIT, budget, control, restrict
rational *adjective* SANE, intelligent, logical, lucid, realistic, reasonable, sensible, sound, wise

sensible **2** capable of thinking, reasoning ▸ **ra•tion•ale'** [-NAL] *noun* reasons given for actions, etc. ▸ **ra'tion•al•ism** *noun* philosophy that regards reason as only guide or authority ▸ **ra•tion•al'i•ty** *noun* ▸ **ra•tion•al•i•za'tion** *noun* ▸ **ra'tion•al•ize** *verb transitive* **-ized, -iz•ing** **1** justify by plausible reasoning **2** reorganize to improve efficiency, etc.

rat•tan [ra-TAN] *noun* **1** climbing palm with jointed stems **2** cane of this oft. used for furniture

rat•tle [RAT-l] *verb intransitive* **-tled, -tling** **1** give out succession of short sharp sounds **2** clatter ▹ *verb transitive* **-tled, -tling** **3** shake briskly causing a sharp clatter of sounds **4** confuse, fluster ▹ *noun* **5** such sound **6** instrument for making it **7** set of horny rings in rattlesnake's tail ▸ **rat'tle•snake** *noun* poisonous snake

rau•cous [RAW-kəs] *adjective* **1** hoarse **2** harsh

raun•chy [RAWN-chee] *adjective* **-chi•er, -chi•est** (*informal*) **1** earthy, vulgar, sexy **2** slovenly

rav•age [RAV-ij] *verb transitive* **-aged, -ag•ing** **1** lay waste, plunder ▹ *noun* **2** destruction

rave [rayv] *verb intransitive* **raved, rav•ing** talk wildly in delirium or enthusiastically ▹ *noun*

rav•el [RAV-əl] *verb transitive* **-eled, -el•ing** **1** entangle **2** fray out **3** disentangle

ra•ven[1] [RAY-vən] *noun* **1** black bird like crow ▹ *adjective* **2** shiny black

raven[2] *verb* seek prey, plunder ▸ **rav•en•ous** [RAV-ə-nəs] *adjective* very hungry

ra•vine [rə-VEEN] *noun* narrow steep-sided valley worn by stream, gorge

ra•vi•o•li [rav-ee-OH-lee] *plural noun* small, thin pieces of dough filled with highly seasoned, chopped meat and cooked

rav'ish *verb transitive* **1** enrapture **2** commit rape upon ▸ **rav'ish•ing** *adjective* lovely, entrancing

raw *adjective* **-er, -est** **1** uncooked **2** not manufactured or refined **3** skinned **4** inexperienced, unpracticed, as recruits **5** sensitive **6** chilly ▸ **raw deal** unfair or dishonest treatment ▸ **raw'hide** *noun* **1** untanned hide **2** whip of this

ray[1] *noun* **1** single line or narrow beam of light, heat, etc. **2** any of set of radiating lines ▹ *verb intransitive* **3** come out in rays **4** radiate

ray[2] *noun* marine fish, often very large, with winglike pectoral fins and whiplike tail

ray'on *noun* (fabric of) synthetic fiber

raze [rayz] *verb transitive* **razed, raz•ing** **1** destroy completely **2** wipe out, delete **3** level

ra•zor [RAY-zər] *noun* sharp instrument for shaving or for cutting hair

Rb *chem.* rubidium

re[1] [ray] *noun* second sol-fa note

re[2] *preposition* with reference to, concerning

Re *chem.* rhenium

re- *prefix* again: *re-enter; retrial*

reach [reech] *verb transitive* **1** arrive at **2** extend **3** succeed in touching **4** attain to ▹ *verb intransitive* **5** stretch out hand **6** extend ▹ *noun* **7** act of reaching **8** power of touching **9** grasp, scope **10** range **11** straight stretch of river between two bends

re•act [ree-AKT] *verb intransitive* act in return, opposition or toward former state ▸ **re•ac'tance** [-əns] *noun electricity* resistance in coil, apart from ohmic resistance, due to current reacting on itself ▸ **re•ac'tion** [-AK-shən] *noun* **1** any action resisting another **2** counter or backward tendency **3** response **4** chemical or nuclear change, combination or decomposition ▸ **re•ac'tion•ar•y** *noun, adjective, plural* **-ar•ies** (person) opposed to change, esp. in politics, etc. ▸ **re•ac'tive** *adjective* chemically active ▸ **re•ac'tor** *noun* apparatus in which nuclear reaction is maintained and controlled to produce nuclear energy

read [reed] *verb transitive* **read** [red], **read•ing** **1** look at and understand written or printed matter **2** learn by reading **3** interpret mentally

DICTIONARY **r** THESAURUS

---

rationale *noun* REASON, grounds, logic, motivation, philosophy, principle, raison d'être (*French*), theory

rationalize *verb* JUSTIFY, account for, excuse, vindicate

rattle *verb* **1** CLATTER, bang, jangle **2** SHAKE, bounce, jar, jolt, vibrate **3** (*informal*) FLUSTER, disconcert, disturb, faze, perturb, shake, upset

raucous *adjective* HARSH, grating, hoarse, loud, noisy, rough, strident

raunchy *adjective* (*slang*) SEXY, coarse, earthy, lusty, sexual, steamy (*informal*)

ravage *verb* **1** DESTROY, demolish, despoil, devastate, lay waste, ransack, ruin, spoil ▹ *noun* **2** ▹ **ravages** DAMAGE, destruction, devastation, havoc, ruin, ruination, spoliation

rave *verb* **1** RANT, babble, be delirious, go mad (*informal*), rage, roar **2** ENTHUSE, be excited about (*informal*), be wild about (*informal*), gush, praise

ravenous *adjective* STARVING, famished, starved

ravine *noun* CANYON, defile, gorge, gulch, gully, pass

raving *adjective* MAD, crazed, crazy, delirious, hysterical, insane, irrational, wild

ravish *verb* **1** ENCHANT, captivate, charm, delight, enrapture, entrance, fascinate, spellbind **2** RAPE, abuse, force, sexually assault, violate

ravishing *adjective* ENCHANTING, beautiful, bewitching, charming, entrancing, gorgeous, lovely

raw *adjective* **1** UNCOOKED, fresh, natural **2** UNREFINED, basic, coarse, crude, natural, rough, unfinished, unprocessed **3** INEXPERIENCED, callow, green, immature, new **4** CHILLY, biting, bitter, cold, freezing, piercing

ray *noun* BEAM, bar, flash, gleam, shaft

raze *verb* DESTROY, demolish, flatten, knock down, level, pull down, ruin

re[2] *preposition* CONCERNING, about, apropos, regarding, with reference to, with regard to

reach *verb* **1** ARRIVE AT, attain, get to, make **2** TOUCH, contact, extend to, grasp, stretch to **3** CONTACT, communicate with, get hold of, get in touch with, get through to ▹ *noun* **4** RANGE, capacity, distance, extension, extent, grasp, influence, power, scope, stretch

react *verb* **1** RESPOND, answer, reply **2** ACT, behave, function, operate, proceed, work

reaction *noun* **1** RESPONSE, answer, reply **2** RECOIL, counteraction **3** CONSERVATISM, the right

4 read and utter 5 interpret 6 study 7 understand any indicating instrument 8 (of instrument) register ▷ *verb intransitive* **read** [red], **read•ing** 9 be occupied in reading 10 find mentioned in reading > **read'a•ble** *adjective* that can be read, or read with pleasure > **read'er** *noun* 1 one who reads 2 university professor's assistant 3 school textbook 4 one who reads manuscripts submitted to publisher

re•ad•just' *verb* adapt to a new situation > **re•ad•just'ment** *noun*

re•ad•mit' *verb transitive* **-mitting, -mitted** let (person, country, etc.) back in to a place or organization

read•y [RED-ee] *adjective* **read•i•er, read•i•est** 1 prepared for use or action 2 willing, prompt > **read'i•ly** *adverb* 1 promptly 2 willingly > **read'i•ness** [-nis] *noun*

re•a•gent [ree-AY-jənt] *noun* chemical substance that reacts with another and is used to detect presence of the other

re•al [REE-əl] *adjective* 1 existing in fact 2 happening 3 actual 4 genuine 5 (of property) consisting of land and houses > **re'al•ism** *noun* 1 regarding things as they are 2 artistic treatment with this outlook > **re•al•is'tic** *adjective* > **re•al'i•ty** *noun* real existence > **re'al•ly** *adverb* > **re'al•ty** *noun* real estate > **real estate** landed property

re•al•ize [REE-ə-līz] *verb transitive* **-ized, -iz•ing** 1 apprehend, grasp significance of 2 make real 3 convert into money > **re•al•i•za'tion** *noun*

realm [relm] *noun* kingdom, province, domain, sphere

ream¹ [reem] *noun* twenty quires or 500 sheets of paper > **reams** large quantity of written matter

ream² *verb transitive* enlarge, bevel out, as hole in metal > **ream'er** *noun* tool for this

reap [reep] *verb* 1 cut and gather harvest 2 receive as fruit of previous activity > **reap'er** *noun*

re•ap•pear' *verb intransitive* appear again > **re•ap•pear'ance** *noun*

rear¹ [reer] *noun* 1 back part 2 part of army, procession, etc. behind others > **rear admiral** lowest flag rank in certain navies > **rear'guard** *noun* troops protecting rear of army > **rear'most** [-mohst] *adjective*

rear² *verb transitive* 1 care for and educate (children) 2 breed 3 erect ▷ *verb intransitive* 4 rise, esp. on hind feet

re•arm' *verb* 1 arm again ▷ *verb transitive* 2 equip (army, nation, etc.) with better weapons > **re•ar'ma•ment** *noun*

re•ar•range' *verb transitive* organize differently, alter > **re•ar•range'ment** *noun*

rea•son [REE-zən] *noun* 1 ground, motive 2 faculty of thinking 3 sanity 4 sensible or logical thought or view ▷ *verb intransitive* 5 think logically in forming conclusions ▷ *verb*

DICTIONARY • THESAURUS

reactionary *adjective* 1 CONSERVATIVE, right-wing
▷ *noun* 2 CONSERVATIVE, die-hard, right-winger

read *verb* 1 LOOK AT, peruse, pore over, scan, study
2 INTERPRET, comprehend, construe, decipher, discover, see, understand
3 REGISTER, display, indicate, record, show

readable *adjective* 1 ENJOYABLE, entertaining, enthralling, gripping, interesting
2 LEGIBLE, clear, comprehensible, decipherable

readily *adverb* 1 WILLINGLY, eagerly, freely, gladly, promptly, quickly
2 EASILY, effortlessly, quickly, smoothly, speedily, unhesitatingly

readiness *noun* 1 WILLINGNESS, eagerness, keenness
2 EASE, adroitness, dexterity, facility, promptness

reading *noun* 1 PERUSAL, examination, inspection, scrutiny, study
2 RECITAL, lesson, performance, sermon
3 INTERPRETATION, grasp, impression, version
4 LEARNING, education, erudition, knowledge, scholarship

ready *adjective* 1 PREPARED, arranged, fit, organized, primed, ripe, set
2 WILLING, agreeable, disposed, eager, glad, happy, inclined, keen, prone
3 PROMPT, alert, bright, clever, intelligent, keen, perceptive, quick, sharp, smart
4 AVAILABLE, accessible, convenient, handy, near, present

real *adjective* GENUINE, actual, authentic, factual, rightful, sincere, true, unfeigned, valid

realistic *adjective* 1 PRACTICAL, common-sense, down-to-earth, level-headed, matter-of-fact, real, sensible
2 LIFELIKE, authentic, faithful, genuine, natural, true, true to life

reality *noun* TRUTH, actuality, fact, realism, validity, verity

realization *noun* 1 AWARENESS, cognizance, comprehension, conception, grasp, perception, recognition, understanding
2 ACHIEVEMENT, accomplishment, fulfillment

realize *verb* 1 BECOME AWARE OF, comprehend, get the message, grasp, take in, understand
2 ACHIEVE, accomplish, carry out *or* carry through, complete, do, effect, fulfill, perform

really *adverb* TRULY, actually, certainly, genuinely, in actuality, indeed, in fact, positively, surely

realm *noun* 1 KINGDOM, country, domain, dominion, empire, land
2 SPHERE, area, branch, department, field, province, territory, world

reap *verb* 1 COLLECT, bring in, cut, garner, gather, harvest
2 OBTAIN, acquire, derive, gain, get

rear¹ *noun* 1 BACK, end, rearguard, stern, tail, tail end
▷ *adjective* 2 BACK, following, hind, last

rear² *verb* 1 BRING UP, breed, educate, foster, nurture, raise, train
2 RISE, loom, soar, tower

reason *noun* 1 CAUSE, aim, goal, grounds, incentive, intention, motive, object, purpose
2 SENSE *or* SENSES, intellect, judgment, logic, mind, rationality, sanity, soundness, understanding
▷ *verb* 3 DEDUCE, conclude, infer, make out, think, work out
4 ▷ **reason with** PERSUADE, bring round (*informal*), prevail upon, talk into *or* talk out of, urge, win over

transitive 6 (usu. with *with*) persuade by logical argument into doing, etc. > **rea'son•a•ble** *adjective* 1 sensible, not excessive 2 suitable 3 logical
re•as•sure [ree-ə-SHUUR] *verb transitive* **-sured, -sur•ing** restore confidence to
re•bate [REE-bayt] *noun* 1 discount, refund ▷ *verb transitive* **-bat•ed, -bat•ing** 2 deduct
re•bel [ri-BEL] *verb intransitive* **-belled, -bel•ling** 1 revolt, resist lawful authority, take arms against ruling power ▷ *noun* [REB-əl] 2 one who rebels 3 insurgent ▷ *adjective* [REB-əl] 4 in rebellion > **re•bel•lion** [ri-BEL-yən] *noun* organized open resistance to authority, revolt > **re•bel'lious** *adjective*
re•birth' *noun* revival or renaissance > **re•born'** *adjective* active again after a period of inactivity
re•boot' *verb* to shut down and then restart (a computer system)
re•bound [ri-BOWND] *verb intransitive* 1 spring back 2 misfire, esp. so as to hurt perpetrator (of plan, deed, etc.) ▷ *noun* [REE-bownd] 3 act of springing back or recoiling 4 return
re•buff [ri-BUF] *noun* 1 blunt refusal 2 check ▷ *verb transitive* 3 repulse, snub
re•build' *verb transitive* **-build'ing, -built** 1 build (building, town) again, after severe damage 2 develop (business, relationship, etc.) again after destruction or damage
re•buke [ri-BYOOK] *verb transitive* **-buked, -buk•ing** reprove, reprimand, find fault with ▷ *noun*
re•bus [REE-bəs] *noun, plural* **-bus•es** riddle in which names of things, etc. are represented by pictures standing for syllables, etc.
re•but [ri-BUT] *verb transitive* **-but•ted, -but•ting** refute, disprove > **re•but'tal** *noun*
re•cal•ci•trant [ri-KAL-si-trənt] *adjective, noun* willfully disobedient (person)
re•call [ri-KAWL] *verb transitive* 1 recollect, remember 2 call, summon, order back 3 annul, cancel 4 revive, restore ▷ *noun* [REE-kawl] 5 summons to return 6 ability to remember
re•cant [ri-KANT] *verb transitive* withdraw statement, opinion, etc. > **re•can•ta'tion** *noun*
re•ca•pit•u•late [ree-kə-PICH-ə-layt] *verb transitive* **-lat•ed, -lat•ing** 1 state again briefly 2 repeat
re•cap'ture *verb transitive* 1 experience again 2 capture again
re•cede [ri-SEED] *verb intransitive* **-ced•ed, -ced•ing** 1 go back 2 become distant 3 slope backward 4 begin balding
re•ceipt [ri-SEET] *noun* 1 written acknowledgment of money received 2 receiving or being received ▷ *verb transitive* 3 acknowledge payment of in writing
re•ceive [ri-SEEV] *verb transitive* **-ceived, -ceiv•ing** 1 take, accept, get 2 experience 3 greet (guests) > **re•ceiv'a•ble** *adjective* > **re•ceiv'er** *noun* 1 official appointed to receive money 2 fence, one who takes stolen goods knowing them to have been stolen 3 equipment in telephone, radio or TV that converts electrical signals into sound, light

DICTIONARY r THESAURUS

reasonable *adjective* 1 SENSIBLE, logical, plausible, practical, sane, sober, sound, tenable, wise
2 MODERATE, equitable, fair, fit, just, modest, O.K. *or* okay (*informal*), proper, right
reasoned *adjective* SENSIBLE, clear, logical, well-thought-out
reasoning *noun* THINKING, analysis, logic, thought
reassure *verb* ENCOURAGE, comfort, hearten, put one's mind at rest *or* set one's mind at rest, restore confidence to
rebate *noun* REFUND, allowance, bonus, deduction, discount, reduction
rebel *verb* 1 REVOLT, mutiny, resist, rise up
2 DEFY, disobey, dissent
▷ *noun* 3 REVOLUTIONARY, insurgent, revolutionist, secessionist
4 NONCONFORMIST, apostate, dissenter, heretic, schismatic
▷ *adjective* 5 REBELLIOUS, insurgent, insurrectionary, revolutionary
rebellion *noun* 1 RESISTANCE, mutiny, revolt, revolution, rising, uprising
2 NONCONFORMITY, defiance, heresy, schism
rebellious *adjective* 1 REVOLUTIONARY, disloyal, disobedient, disorderly, insurgent, mutinous, rebel, seditious, unruly
2 DEFIANT, difficult, refractory, resistant, unmanageable
rebound *verb* 1 BOUNCE, recoil, ricochet
2 MISFIRE, backfire, boomerang, recoil
rebuff *verb* 1 REJECT, cold-shoulder, cut, knock back (*slang*), refuse, repulse, slight, snub, spurn, turn down
▷ *noun* 2 REJECTION, cold shoulder, kick in the teeth (*slang*), knock-back (*slang*), refusal, repulse, slap in the face (*informal*), slight, snub
rebuke *verb* 1 SCOLD, admonish, castigate, censure, chide, reprimand, reprove, tell off (*informal*)
▷ *noun* 2 SCOLDING, admonition, censure, reprimand, row, telling-off (*informal*)
rebut *verb* DISPROVE, confute, invalidate, negate, overturn, prove wrong, refute
rebuttal *noun* DISPROOF, confutation, invalidation, negation, refutation
recalcitrant *adjective* DISOBEDIENT, defiant, insubordinate, refractory, unmanageable, unruly, wayward, willful
recall *verb* 1 RECOLLECT, bring to mind *or* call to mind, evoke, remember
2 ANNUL, cancel, countermand, repeal, retract, revoke, withdraw
▷ *noun* 3 RECOLLECTION, memory, remembrance
4 ANNULMENT, cancellation, repeal, rescindment, retraction, withdrawal
recant *verb* WITHDRAW, disclaim, forswear, renege, repudiate, retract, revoke, take back
recapitulate *verb* REPEAT, outline, recap (*informal*), recount, restate, summarize
recede *verb* FALL BACK, abate, ebb, regress, retire, retreat, return, subside, withdraw
receipt *noun* 1 SALES SLIP, counterfoil, proof of purchase
2 RECEIVING, acceptance, delivery, reception
receive *verb* 1 GET, accept, acquire, be given, collect, obtain, pick up, take
2 EXPERIENCE, bear, encounter, suffer, sustain, undergo

re•cent [REE-sənt] *adjective* 1 that has lately happened 2 new > **re'cent•ly** *adverb*
re•cep•ta•cle [ri-SEP-tə-kəl] *noun* vessel, place or space, to contain anything
re•cep•tion [ri-SEP-shən] *noun* 1 receiving 2 manner of receiving 3 welcome 4 formal party 5 in broadcasting, quality of signals received > **re•cep'tion•ist** *noun* person who receives guests, clients, etc.
re•cep•tive [ri-SEP-tiv] *adjective* able, quick, willing to receive new ideas, suggestions, etc. > **re•cep•tiv'i•ty** *noun*
re•cess [REE-ses] *noun* 1 niche, alcove 2 hollow 3 secret, hidden place 4 remission or suspension of business 5 vacation, holiday
re•ces•sion [ri-SESH-ən] *noun* 1 period of reduction in economic activity 2 act of receding > **re•ces'sive** *adjective* receding
re•ces•sion•al [ri-SESH-ə-nl] *noun* hymn sung while clergy retire
re•cher•ché [rə-SHAIR-shay] *adjective* 1 of studied elegance 2 exquisite 3 choice
re•cid•i•vist [ri-SID-ə-vist] *noun* one who relapses into crime
rec•i•pe [RES-ə-pee] *noun* 1 directions for cooking a dish 2 prescription 3 expedient
re•cip•i•ent [ri-SIP-ee-ənt] *adjective* 1 that can or does receive ▷ *noun* 2 one who, that which receives
re•cip•ro•cal [ri-SIP-rə-kəl] *adjective* 1 complementary 2 mutual 3 moving backward and forward 4 alternating > **re•cip'ro•cate** [-rə-kayt] *verb transitive* **-cat•ed, -cat•ing** 1 give and receive mutually 2 return ▷ *verb intransitive* **-cat•ed, -cat•ing** 3 move backward and forward > **re•ci•proc•i•ty** [res-ə-PROS-i-tee] *noun*
re•cite [ri-SĪT] *verb transitive* **-cit•ed, -cit•ing** repeat aloud, esp. to audience > **re•cit'al** [-əl] *noun* 1 musical performance, usu. by one person 2 act of reciting 3 narration of facts, etc. 4 story 5 public entertainment of recitations, etc. > **rec•i•ta'tion** *noun* 1 recital, usu. from memory, of poetry or prose 2 recountal > **rec•i•ta•tive** [res-i-tə-TEEV] *noun* musical declamation
reck•less [REK-lis] *adjective* heedless, incautious
reck•on [REK-ən] *verb* 1 count 2 include 3 consider 4 (*informal*) think, deem 5 make calculations
re•claim [ri-KLAYM] *verb transitive* 1 make fit for cultivation 2 bring back 3 reform 4 demand the return of > **rec•la•ma'tion** *noun*
re•cline [ri-KLĪN] *verb intransitive* **-clined, -clin•ing** sit or lie back on one's side
rec•luse [REK-loos] *noun* 1 hermit ▷ *adjective* [ri-KLOOS] 2 living in seclusion, shut off from the world > **re•clu'sive** *adjective*
rec•og•nize [REK-əg-nīz] *verb transitive* **-nized, -niz•ing** 1 know again 2 treat as valid 3 notice, show appreciation of > **rec•og•ni'tion** *noun* > **rec•og•niz'a•ble** *adjective* > **re•cog•ni•zance** [ri-KOG-nə-zəns] *noun* 1 avowal 2 bond by which person undertakes before court to observe some condition 3 (*obsolete*) recognition
re•coil [ri-KOIL] *verb intransitive* 1 draw back in horror, etc. 2 go wrong so as to hurt the

DICTIONARY • THESAURUS

3 GREET, accommodate, admit, entertain, meet, welcome
recent *adjective* NEW, current, fresh, late, modern, novel, present-day, up-to-date
recently *adverb* NEWLY, currently, freshly, lately, latterly, not long ago, of late
receptacle *noun* CONTAINER, holder, repository
reception *noun* 1 PARTY, function, levee, soirée
2 WELCOME, acknowledgment, greeting, reaction, response, treatment
receptive *adjective* OPEN, amenable, interested, open-minded, open to suggestions, susceptible, sympathetic
recess *noun* 1 ALCOVE, bay, corner, hollow, niche, nook
2 BREAK, holiday, intermission, interval, respite, rest, vacation
recession *noun* DEPRESSION, decline, drop, slump
recipe *noun* 1 DIRECTIONS, ingredients, instructions
2 METHOD, formula, prescription, procedure, process, technique
reciprocal *adjective* MUTUAL, alternate, complementary, correlative, corresponding, equivalent, exchanged, interchangeable
reciprocate *verb* RETURN, exchange, reply, requite, respond, swap, trade
recital *noun* 1 PERFORMANCE, rehearsal, rendering
2 RECITATION, account, narrative, reading, relation, statement, telling
recitation *noun* RECITAL, lecture, passage, performance, piece, reading
recite *verb* REPEAT, declaim, deliver, narrate, perform, speak
reckless *adjective* CARELESS, hasty, headlong, heedless, imprudent, mindless, precipitate, rash, thoughtless, wild
reckon *verb* 1 THINK, assume, believe, guess (*informal*), imagine, suppose
2 CONSIDER, account, count, deem, esteem, judge, rate, regard
3 COUNT, add up, calculate, compute, figure, number, tally, total
reckoning *noun* 1 COUNT, addition, calculation, estimate
2 BILL, account, charge, due, score
reclaim *verb* REGAIN, recapture, recover, redeem, reform, retrieve, salvage
recline *verb* LEAN, lie *or* lie down, loll, lounge, repose, rest, sprawl
recluse *noun* HERMIT, anchoress, anchorite, monk, solitary
reclusive *adjective* SOLITARY, hermit-like, isolated, retiring, withdrawn
recognition *noun* 1 IDENTIFICATION, discovery, recollection, remembrance
2 ACCEPTANCE, admission, allowance, confession
3 APPRECIATION, notice, respect
recognize *verb* 1 IDENTIFY, know, notice, place, recall, recollect, remember, spot
2 ACCEPT, acknowledge, admit, allow, concede, grant
3 APPRECIATE, notice, respect
recoil *verb* 1 JERK BACK, kick, react, rebound, spring back
2 DRAW BACK, falter, quail, shrink
3 BACKFIRE, boomerang, misfire, rebound

perpetrator 3 rebound (esp. of gun when fired) ▷ *noun* [REE-koil] 4 backward spring 5 retreat 6 recoiling

rec•ol•lect [rek-ə-LEKT] *verb transitive* call back to mind, remember

rec•om•mend [rek-ə-MEND] *verb transitive* 1 advise, counsel 2 praise, commend 3 make acceptable > **rec•om•men•da'tion** *noun*

rec•om•pense [REK-əm-pens] *verb transitive* **-pensed, -pens•ing** 1 reward 2 compensate, make up for ▷ *noun* 3 compensation 4 reward 5 requital

rec•on•cile [REK-ən-sīl] *verb transitive* **-ciled, -cil•ing** 1 bring back into friendship 2 adjust, settle, harmonize > **rec•on•cil'a•ble** *adjective* > **rec•on•cil•i•a'tion** *noun*

rec•on•dite [REK-ən-dīt] *adjective* obscure, abstruse, little known

re•con•di•tion [ree-kən-DISH-ən] *verb transitive* restore to good condition, working order

re•con•noi•ter [ree-kə-NOI-tər] *verb transitive* 1 make preliminary survey of 2 survey position of enemy ▷ *verb intransitive* 3 make reconnaissance > **re•con•nais•sance** [ri-KON-ə-səns] *noun* 1 examination or survey for military or engineering purposes 2 scouting

re•con•sid'er *verb* think about again, consider changing

re•con•sti•tute [ree-KON-sti-toot] *verb transitive* **-tut•ed, -tut•ing** restore (food) to former state esp. by addition of water to a concentrate

re•con•struct' *verb* 1 rebuild 2 use evidence to re-create > **re•con•struc'tion** *noun*

re•cord [REK-ərd] *noun* 1 being recorded 2 document or other thing that records 3 disk with indentations that phonograph transforms into sound 4 best recorded achievement 5 known facts about person's past ▷ *verb* [ri-KORD] 6 preserve (sound, TV programs, etc.) on plastic disk, magnetic tape, etc. for reproduction on playback device ▷ *verb transitive* 7 put in writing 8 register > **re•cord'er** *noun* 1 one who, that which records 2 type of flute > **re•cord'ing** *noun* 1 process of making records from sound 2 something recorded, e.g. radio or TV program > **record player** instrument for reproducing sound on disks **off the record** not for publication

re•count [ri-KOWNT] *verb transitive* tell in detail

re•coup [ri-KOOP] *verb transitive* 1 recompense, compensate 2 recover what has been expended or lost

re•course [REE-kors] *noun* 1 (resorting to) source of help 2 *law* right of action or appeal

re•cov•er [ri-KUV-ər] *verb transitive* 1 regain, get back ▷ *verb intransitive* 2 get back health > **re•cov'er•y** *noun, plural* **-er•ies**

re•cre•ate' *verb* make happen or exist again

rec•re•a•tion [rek-ree-AY-shən] *noun* agreeable or refreshing occupation, relaxation,

DICTIONARY

r

THESAURUS

▷ *noun* 4 REACTION, backlash, kick, rebound, repercussion

recollect *verb* REMEMBER, place, recall, summon up

recollection *noun* MEMORY, impression, recall, remembrance, reminiscence

recommend *verb* 1 ADVISE, advance, advocate, counsel, prescribe, propose, put forward, suggest
2 PRAISE, approve, commend, endorse

recommendation *noun* 1 ADVICE, counsel, proposal, suggestion
2 PRAISE, advocacy, approval, commendation, endorsement, reference, sanction, testimonial

recompense *verb* 1 REWARD, pay, remunerate
2 COMPENSATE, make up for, pay for, redress, reimburse, repay, requite
▷ *noun* 3 COMPENSATION, amends, damages, payment, remuneration, reparation, repayment, requital, restitution
4 REWARD, payment, return, wages

reconcile *verb* 1 RESOLVE, adjust, compose, put to rights, rectify, settle, square
2 REUNITE, appease, conciliate, make peace between, propitiate
3 ACCEPT, put up with (*informal*), resign oneself, submit, yield

reconciliation *noun* REUNION, conciliation, pacification, reconcilement

recondite *adjective* OBSCURE, arcane, concealed, dark, deep, difficult, hidden, mysterious, occult, profound, secret

recondition *verb* RESTORE, do up (*informal*), overhaul, remodel, renew, renovate, repair, revamp

reconnaissance *noun* INSPECTION, exploration, investigation, observation, scan, survey

reconnoiter *verb* INSPECT, case (*slang*), explore, investigate, observe, scan, spy out, survey

reconsider *verb* RETHINK, reassess, review, revise, think again

reconstruct *verb* 1 REBUILD, recreate, regenerate, remake, remodel, renovate, restore
2 DEDUCE, build up, piece together

record *noun* 1 DOCUMENT, account, blog (*informal*), chronicle, diary, entry, file, journal, log, register, report, weblog
2 EVIDENCE, documentation, testimony, trace, witness
3 DISC, album, LP, single, vinyl
4 BACKGROUND, career, history, performance
5 ▷ **off the record** CONFIDENTIAL, not for publication, private, unofficial
▷ *verb* 6 WRITE DOWN, chronicle, document, enter, log, minute, note, register, set down, take down
7 TAPE, make a recording of, tape-record, video, video tape
8 REGISTER, give evidence of, indicate, say, show

recorder *noun* CHRONICLER, archivist, clerk, diarist, historian, scribe

recording *noun* RECORD, disc, tape, video

recount *verb* TELL, depict, describe, narrate, recite, relate, repeat, report

recoup *verb* 1 REGAIN, recover, retrieve, win back
2 COMPENSATE, make up for, refund, reimburse, remunerate, repay, requite

recourse *noun* OPTION, alternative, choice, expedient, remedy, resort, resource, way out

recover *verb* 1 GET BETTER, convalesce, get well, heal, improve, mend, rally, recuperate, revive
2 REGAIN, get back, recapture, reclaim, redeem, repossess, restore, retrieve

recovery *noun* 1 IMPROVEMENT, convalescence, healing, mending, recuperation, revival
2 RETRIEVAL, reclamation, repossession, restoration

amusement > **rec•re•a'tion•al** *adjective* > **recreational vehicle** large vanlike vehicle equipped to be lived in

re•crim•i•nate [ri-KRIM-ə-nayt] *verb intransitive* **-nat•ed, -nat•ing** make countercharge or mutual accusation > **re•crim•i•na'tion** *noun* mutual abuse and blame

re•cru•desce [ree-kroo-DES] *verb intransitive* **-desced, -desc•ing** break out again > **re•cru•des'cent** *adjective*

re•cruit [ri-KROOT] *noun* 1 newly-enlisted soldier 2 one newly joining society, etc. ▷ *verb transitive* 3 enlist fresh soldiers, etc.

rec•tan•gle [REK-tang-gəl] *noun* oblong four-sided figure with four right angles > **rec•tang'u•lar** *adjective* shaped thus

rec•ti•fy *verb transitive* **-fied, -fy•ing** put right, correct, remedy, purify > **rec•ti•fi•ca'tion** *noun* 1 act of setting right 2 *electricity* conversion of alternating current into direct current > **rec'ti•fi•er** [-fī-ər] *noun* person or thing that rectifies

rec•ti•lin•e•ar [rek-tl-IN-ee-ər] *adjective* 1 in straight line 2 characterized by straight lines

rec•ti•tude [REK-ti-tood] *noun* 1 moral uprightness 2 honesty of purpose

rec•to [REK-toh] *noun, plural* **-tos** right-hand page of book, front of leaf

rec•tor [REK-tər] *noun* 1 member of clergy with care of parish 2 head of certain institutions, chiefly academic > **rec'to•ry** *noun* rector's house

rec•tum [REK-təm] *noun* final section of large intestine > **rec'tal** [-tl] *adjective*

re•cum•bent [ri-KUM-bənt] *adjective* lying down > **re•cum'ben•cy** *noun*

re•cu•per•ate [ri-KOO-pər-ayt] *verb* **-at•ed, -at•ing** 1 restore, be restored from illness, losses, etc. 2 convalesce > **re•cu•per•a'tion** *noun*

re•cur [ri-KUR] *verb intransitive* **-curred, -cur•ring** 1 happen again 2 return again and again 3 go or come back in mind > **re•cur'rence** [-əns] *noun* repetition > **re•cur'rent** [-ənt] *adjective*

re•cy•cle [ree-SĪ-kəl] *verb transitive* **-cled, -cling** 1 reprocess a manufactured substance for use again 2 reuse

red *adjective* 1 of color varying from crimson to orange and seen in blood, rubies, glowing fire, etc. ▷ *noun* 2 the color 3 communist > **red'den** *verb* 1 make red 2 become red 3 flush > **red'dish** *adjective* > **red-blood•ed** [-blud-id] *adjective* 1 vigorous 2 virile > **red'coat** *noun* in American Revolution, a British soldier > **red flag** danger signal > **red-hand'ed** *adjective* (caught) in the act > **red herring** topic introduced to divert attention from main issue > **red-hot** 1 red with heat 2 creating excitement > **red state** US state with a majority of Republican voters > **red tape** excessive adherence to official rules > **red'wood** [-wuud] *noun* giant coniferous tree of California **in the red** 1 operating at loss 2 in debt **see red** (*informal*) be very angry

re•deem [ri-DEEM] *verb transitive* 1 buy back 2 set free 3 free from sin 4 make up for > **re•demp'tion** [-DEM-shən] *noun* > **re•deem'a•ble** *adjective* **The Re•deem•er** Jesus Christ

re•de•vel'op *verb* rebuild or renovate (an area or building) > **re•de•vel'op•ment** *noun*

red•o•lent [RED-l-ənt] *adjective* 1 smelling strongly, fragrant 2 reminiscent (of) > **red'o•lence** *noun*

re•dou•ble [ree-DUB-əl] *verb* **-bled, -bling** 1 increase, multiply, intensify 2 double a second time

re•doubt [ri-DOWT] *noun* detached outwork in fortifications

re•doubt•a•ble [ri-DOWT-ə-bəl] *adjective* dreaded, formidable

DICTIONARY • THESAURUS

recreation *noun* PASTIME, amusement, diversion, enjoyment, entertainment, fun, hobby, leisure activity, play, relaxation, sport

recrimination *noun* BICKERING, counterattack, mutual accusation, quarrel, squabbling

recruit *verb* 1 ENLIST, draft, enroll, levy, mobilize, muster, raise
2 WIN *or* WIN OVER, engage, obtain, procure
▷ *noun* 3 BEGINNER, apprentice, convert, helper, initiate, learner, novice, trainee

rectify *verb* CORRECT, adjust, emend, fix, improve, redress, remedy, repair, right

rectitude *noun* MORALITY, decency, goodness, honesty, honor, integrity, principle, probity, virtue

recuperate *verb* RECOVER, convalesce, get better, improve, mend

recur *verb* HAPPEN AGAIN, come again, persist, reappear, repeat, return, revert

recurrent *adjective* PERIODIC, continued, frequent, habitual, recurring

recycle *verb* REPROCESS, reclaim, reuse, salvage, save

red *adjective* 1 CRIMSON, carmine, cherry, coral, ruby, scarlet, vermilion
2 (*hair*) CHESTNUT, carroty, flame-colored, reddish, sandy, titian
3 FLUSHED, blushing, embarrassed, florid, shamefaced
▷ *noun* 4 ▷ **in the red** (*informal*) IN DEBT, in arrears, insolvent, overdrawn
5 ▷ **see red** (*informal*) LOSE ONE'S TEMPER, blow one's top, crack up (*informal*), fly off the handle (*informal*), go ballistic (*slang*), go mad (*informal*)

red-blooded *adjective* (*informal*) VIGOROUS, lusty, robust, strong, virile

redden *verb* FLUSH, blush, color *or* color up, crimson, go red

redeem *verb* 1 MAKE UP FOR, atone for, compensate for, make amends for
2 REINSTATE, absolve, restore to favor
3 SAVE, deliver, emancipate, free, liberate, ransom
4 BUY BACK, reclaim, recover, regain, repurchase, retrieve

redemption *noun* 1 COMPENSATION, amends, atonement, reparation
2 SALVATION, deliverance, emancipation, liberation, release, rescue
3 REPURCHASE, reclamation, recovery, repossession, retrieval

red-handed *adjective* IN THE ACT, flagrante delicto *or* in flagrante delicto

redolent *adjective* 1 REMINISCENT, evocative, suggestive
2 SCENTED, aromatic, fragrant, odorous, perfumed, sweet-smelling

redoubtable *adjective* FORMIDABLE, fearful,

re•dound [ri-DOWND] *verb transitive* 1 contribute (to) 2 recoil
re•dress [ri-DRES] *verb transitive* 1 set right 2 make amends for ▷ *noun* [REE-dres] 3 compensation, amends
re•duce [ri-DOOS] *verb transitive* **-duced, -duc•ing** 1 bring down, lower 2 lessen, weaken 3 bring by force or necessity to some state or action 4 slim 5 simplify 6 dilute 7 *chem.* separate substance from others with which it is combined > **re•duc'i•ble** *adjective* > **re•duc'tion** [-DUK-shən] *noun* > **reducing agent** substance used to deoxidize or lessen density of another substance
re•dun•dant [ri-DUN-dənt] *adjective* superfluous > **re•dun'dan•cy** *noun*
re•ech'o *verb* **-ech•o•ing, -ech•oed** echo over and over again, resound
reed *noun* 1 various marsh or water plants 2 tall straight stem of one 3 *mus.* vibrating cane or metal strip of certain wind instruments > **reed'y** *adjective* **reed•i•er, reed•i•est** 1 full of reeds 2 like reed instrument, harsh and thin in tone
reef *noun* 1 ridge of rock or coral near surface of sea 2 vein of ore 3 part of sail that can be rolled up to reduce area ▷ *verb transitive* 4 take in a reef of > **reef'er** *noun* 1 sailor's close-fitting jacket 2 *(slang)* marijuana cigarette
reek *noun* 1 strong (unpleasant) smell ▷ *verb intransitive* 2 emit fumes 3 smell
reel *noun* 1 spool on which film is wound 2 *motion pictures* portion of film 3 winding apparatus 4 bobbin 5 thread wound on this 6 lively dance 7 music for it 8 act of staggering ▷ *verb transitive* 9 wind on reel 10 draw (in) by means of reel ▷ *verb intransitive* 11 stagger, sway, rock > **reel off** recite, write fluently, quickly
re•fec•to•ry [ri-FEK-tə-ree] *noun, plural* **-ries** dining room in monastery, college, etc. > **re•fec'tion** *noun* a meal
re•fer [ri-FUR] *verb intransitive* **-ferred, -fer•ring** 1 relate (to), allude ▷ *verb transitive* **-ferred, -fer•ring** 2 send to for information 3 trace, ascribe to 4 submit for decision > **re•fer'ral** *noun* act, instance of referring > **ref•er•ee'** *noun* 1 arbitrator 2 person willing to whom scientific paper, etc. is sent for judgment of its quality, etc. 3 umpire ▷ *verb* **-eed, -ee•ing** 4 act as referee > **ref'er•ence** [-ins] *noun* 1 act of referring 2 citation or direction in book 3 appeal to judgment of another 4 testimonial 5 one to whom inquiries as to character, etc. may be made > **ref•er•en'dum** *noun, plural* **-da** [-də] submitting of question to electorate
re•fill' *verb* 1 fill again ▷ *noun* 2 second or subsequent filling 3 replacement supply of something in a permanent container
re•fine [ri-FĪN] *verb transitive* **-fined, -fin•ing** purify > **re•fine'ment** *noun* 1 subtlety 2 improvement, elaboration 3 fineness of feeling, taste or manners > **re•fin'er•y** *noun, plural* **-er•ies** place for refining sugar, oil, etc.
re•fla•tion [ri-FLAY-shən] *noun* (steps taken to produce) increase in economic activity of country, etc.
re•flect [ri-FLEKT] *verb transitive* 1 throw back, esp. rays of light 2 cast (discredit, etc.) upon ▷ *verb intransitive* 3 meditate > **re•flec'tion** [-FLEK-shən] *noun* 1 act of reflecting 2 return of rays of heat, light, or waves of sound, from surface 3 image of object given back by mirror, etc. 4

fearsome, mighty, powerful, strong
redress *verb* 1 MAKE AMENDS FOR, compensate for, make up for
2 PUT RIGHT, adjust, balance, correct, even up, rectify, regulate
▷ *noun* 3 AMENDS, atonement, compensation, payment, recompense, reparation
reduce *verb* 1 LESSEN, abate, curtail, cut down, decrease, diminish, lower, moderate, shorten, weaken
2 DEGRADE, break, bring low, downgrade, humble
redundant *adjective* SUPERFLUOUS, extra, inessential, supernumerary, surplus, unnecessary, unwanted
reek *verb* 1 STINK, smell
▷ *noun* 2 STINK, fetor, odor, smell, stench
reel *verb* 1 STAGGER, lurch, pitch, rock, roll, sway
2 WHIRL, revolve, spin, swirl
refer *verb* 1 ALLUDE, bring up, cite, mention, speak of
2 RELATE, apply, belong, be relevant to, concern, pertain
3 CONSULT, apply, go, look up, turn to
4 DIRECT, guide, point, send
referee *noun* 1 UMPIRE, adjudicator, arbiter, arbitrator, judge, ref (*informal*)
▷ *verb* 2 UMPIRE, adjudicate, arbitrate, judge, mediate
reference *noun* 1 CITATION, allusion, mention, note, quotation
2 TESTIMONIAL, character, credentials, endorsement, recommendation
3 RELEVANCE, applicability, bearing, connection, relation
referendum *noun* PUBLIC VOTE, plebiscite, popular vote
refine *verb* 1 PURIFY, clarify, cleanse, distill, filter, process
2 IMPROVE, hone, perfect, polish
refined *adjective* 1 CULTURED, civilized, cultivated, elegant, polished, polite, well-bred
2 PURE, clarified, clean, distilled, filtered, processed, purified
3 DISCERNING, delicate, discriminating, fastidious, fine, precise, sensitive
refinement *noun* 1 SOPHISTICATION, breeding, civility, courtesy, cultivation, culture, discrimination, gentility, good breeding, polish, taste
2 SUBTLETY, fine point, nicety, nuance
3 PURIFICATION, clarification, cleansing, distillation, filtering, processing
reflect *verb* 1 THROW BACK, echo, mirror, reproduce, return
2 SHOW, demonstrate, display, indicate, manifest, reveal
3 THINK, cogitate, consider, meditate, muse, ponder, ruminate, wonder
reflection *noun* 1 IMAGE, echo, mirror image
2 THOUGHT, cogitation, consideration, contemplation, idea, meditation, musing, observation, opinion, thinking

conscious thought **5** meditation **6** expression of thought > **re•flec'tive** *adjective* **1** meditative, quiet, contemplative **2** throwing back images > **re•flec'tor** *noun* polished surface for reflecting light, etc.

re•flex [REE-fleks] *noun* **1** reflex action **2** reflected image **3** reflected light, color, etc. ▷ *adjective* **4** (of muscular action) involuntary **5** reflected **6** bent back > **re•flex•ive** [ri-FLEK-siv] *adjective grammar* describes verb denoting agent's action on self > **reflex action** involuntary response to (nerve) stimulation

re•form [ri-FORM] *verb* **1** improve **2** abandon evil practices **3** reconstruct ▷ *noun* **4** improvement > **ref•or•ma•tion** [ref-ər-MAY-shən] *noun* > **re•form'a•to•ry** *noun, plural* **-ries** institution for reforming juvenile offenders

re•fract [ri-FRAKT] *verb intransitive* change course of light, etc. passing from one medium to another > **re•frac'tion** *noun*

re•frac•to•ry [ri-FRAK-tə-ree] *adjective* **1** unmanageable **2** difficult to treat or work **3** *med.* resistant to treatment **4** resistant to heat

re•frain[1] [ri-FRAYN] *verb intransitive* abstain (from)

re•frain[2] *noun* **1** phrase or verse repeated regularly esp. in song or poem **2** chorus

re•fran•gi•ble [ri-FRAN-jə-bəl] *adjective* that can be refracted

re•fresh [ri-FRESH] *verb transitive* **1** give freshness to **2** revive **3** renew **4** brighten **5** provide with refreshment > **re•fresh'er** *noun* that which refreshes > **re•fresh'ment** *noun* **1** that which refreshes, esp. food, drink **2** restorative

re•frig•er•ate [ri-FRIJ-ə-rayt] *verb transitive* **-at•ed, -at•ing** **1** freeze **2** cool > **re•frig'er•ant** *noun* refrigerating substance ▷ *adjective* > **re•frig'er•a•tor** *noun* apparatus in which foods, drinks are kept cool

ref•uge [REF-yooj] *noun* shelter, protection, retreat, sanctuary > **ref•u•gee** [ref-yuu-JEE] *noun* one who seeks refuge, esp. in foreign country

re•ful•gent [ri-FUL-jənt] *adjective* shining, radiant > **re•ful'gence** *noun* > **re•ful'gen•cy** *noun* splendor

re•fund [ri-FUND] *verb transitive* **1** pay back ▷ *noun* [REE-fund] **2** return of money **3** amount returned

re•fur•bish [ree-FUR-bish] *verb transitive* furbish, furnish or brighten anew

re•fuse[1] [ri-FYOOZ] *verb* **-fused, -fus•ing** decline, deny, reject > **re•fus'al** *noun* **1** denial of anything demanded or offered **2** option

ref•use[2] [REF-yoos] *noun* rubbish, useless matter

re•fute [ri-FYOOT] *verb transitive* **-fut•ed, -fut•ing** disprove > **re•fut'a•ble** *adjective* > **ref•u•ta•tion** [ref-yuu-TAY-shən] *noun*

re•gal [REE-gəl] *adjective* of, like a king > **re•ga•li•a** [ri-GAY-lee-ə] *plural noun* **1** insignia of royalty, as used at coronation, etc. **2** emblems of high office, an order, etc. > **re•gal•i•ty** [ri-GAL-i-tee] *noun, plural* **-ties**

re•gale [ri-GAYL] *verb transitive* **-galed, -gal•ing** **1** give pleasure to **2** feast

re•gard [ri-GAHRD] *verb transitive* **1** look at **2** consider **3** relate to **4** heed ▷ *noun* **5** look **6** attention **7** particular respect **8** esteem

DICTIONARY • THESAURUS

reflective *adjective* THOUGHTFUL, contemplative, meditative, pensive

reform *noun* **1** IMPROVEMENT, amendment, betterment, rehabilitation
▷ *verb* **2** IMPROVE, amend, correct, mend, rectify, restore
3 MEND ONE'S WAYS, clean up one's act (*informal*), go straight (*informal*), shape up (*informal*), turn over a new leaf

refractory *adjective* UNMANAGEABLE, difficult, disobedient, headstrong, high-maintenance, intractable, uncontrollable, unruly, willful

refrain[1] *verb* STOP, abstain, avoid, cease, desist, forbear, leave off, renounce

refrain[2] *noun* CHORUS, melody, tune

refresh *verb* **1** REVIVE, brace, enliven, freshen, reinvigorate, revitalize, stimulate
2 STIMULATE, jog, prompt, renew

refreshing *adjective* **1** STIMULATING, bracing, fresh, invigorating
2 NEW, novel, original

refreshment *noun* ▷ **refreshments** FOOD AND DRINK, drinks, snacks, tidbits

refrigerate *verb* COOL, chill, freeze, keep cold

refuge *noun* SHELTER, asylum, haven, hideout, protection, retreat, sanctuary

refugee *noun* EXILE, displaced person, émigré, escapee

refund *verb* **1** REPAY, pay back, reimburse, restore, return
▷ *noun* **2** REPAYMENT, reimbursement, return

refurbish *verb* RENOVATE, clean up, do up (*informal*), mend, overhaul, repair, restore, revamp

refusal *noun* DENIAL, knock-back (*slang*), rebuff, rejection

refuse[1] *verb* REJECT, decline, deny, say no, spurn, turn down, withhold

refuse[2] *noun* RUBBISH, garbage, junk (*informal*), litter, trash, waste

refute *verb* DISPROVE, discredit, negate, overthrow, prove false, rebut

regain *verb* **1** RECOVER, get back, recapture, recoup, retrieve, take back, win back
2 GET BACK TO, reach again, return to

regal *adjective* ROYAL, kingly *or* queenly, magnificent, majestic, noble, princely

regale *verb* ENTERTAIN, amuse, delight, divert

regalia *plural noun* EMBLEMS, accouterments, decorations, finery, paraphernalia, trappings

regard *verb* **1** CONSIDER, believe, deem, esteem, judge, rate, see, suppose, think, view
2 LOOK AT, behold, check out (*informal*), eye, gaze at, observe, scrutinize, view, watch
3 HEED, attend, listen to, mind, pay attention to, take notice of
4 ▷ **as regards** CONCERNING, pertaining to, regarding, relating to
▷ *noun* **5** HEED, attention, interest, mind, notice
6 RESPECT, care, concern, consideration, esteem, thought
7 LOOK, gaze, glance, scrutiny, stare

regarding *preposition* CONCERNING, about, as regards, in regard to *or* with regard to, on the subject of, re, respecting, with reference to

> **re•gards** expression of good will > **re•gard'ful** *adjective* heedful, careful > **re•gard'less** *adjective* 1 heedless ▷ *adverb* 2 in spite of everything

re•gat•ta [ri-GAT-ə] *noun* meeting for yacht or boat races

re•gen•er•ate [ri-JEN-ə-rayt] *verb* **-at•ed, -at•ing** 1 cause spiritual rebirth 2 reform morally 3 reproduce, re-create 4 reorganize ▷ *adjective* [-ə-rit] 5 born anew > **re•gen•er•a'tion** *noun* > **re•gen'er•a•tive** *adjective*

re•gent [REE-jənt] *noun* 1 ruler of kingdom during absence, minority, etc., of its monarch ▷ *adjective* 2 ruling > **re'gen•cy** *noun* status, (period of) office of regent

reg•gae [REG-ay] *noun* style of popular West Indian music with strong beat

reg•i•cide [REJ-ə-sīd] *noun* 1 one who kills a king 2 this crime

re•gime [rə-ZHEEM] *noun* system of government, administration > **regime change** transition from one political regime to another, esp. through concerted political or military action

reg•i•men [REJ-ə-mən] *noun* 1 prescribed system of diet, etc. 2 rule

reg•i•ment [REJ-ə-mənt] *noun* 1 organized body of troops as unit of army ▷ *verb transitive* [REJ-ə-ment] 2 discipline, organize rigidly or too strictly > **reg•i•men'tal** *adjective* of regiment

re•gion [REE-jən] *noun* 1 area, district 2 stretch of country 3 part of the body 4 sphere, realm 5 administrative division of a country > **re'gion•al** *adjective*

reg•is•ter [REJ-ə-stər] *noun* 1 list 2 catalogue 3 roll 4 device for registering 5 written record 6 range of voice or instrument ▷ *verb* 7 show, be shown on meter, face, etc. ▷ *verb transitive* 8 enter in register 9 record 10 show 11 set down in writing 12 *printing, photography* cause to correspond precisely > **reg'is•trar** [-trahr] *noun* keeper of a register esp. in college or university > **reg•is•tra'tion** *noun* > **reg'is•try** *noun, plural* **-tries** 1 registering 2 place where registers are kept, esp. of births, marriages, deaths

re•gorge [ri-GORJ] *verb* **-gorged, -gorg•ing** vomit up

re•gress [ri-GRES] *verb intransitive* return, revert to former place, condition, etc. ▷ *noun* > **re•gres'sion** [-shən] *noun* 1 act of returning 2 retrogression > **re•gres'sive** *adjective* falling back

re•gret [ri-GRET] *verb transitive* **-gret•ted, -gret•ting** 1 feel sorry, distressed for loss of or on account of ▷ *noun* 2 sorrow, distress for thing done or left undone or lost > **re•gret'ful** *adjective* > **re•gret'ta•ble** *adjective*

reg•u•lar [REG-yə-lər] *adjective* 1 normal 2 habitual 3 done, occurring, according to rule 4 periodical 5 straight, level 6 living under rule 7 belonging to standing army ▷ *noun* 8 regular soldier 9 regular customer > **reg•u•lar'i•ty** *noun* > **reg'u•lar•ize** *verb transitive* **-ized, -iz•ing**

reg•u•late [REG-yə-layt] *verb transitive* **-lat•ed, -lat•ing** 1 adjust 2 arrange 3 direct 4 govern 5 put under rule > **reg•u•la'tion** *noun* > **reg'u•la•tor** *noun* contrivance to produce uniformity of motion, as flywheel, governor, etc.

re•gur•gi•tate [ri-GUR-ji-tayt] *verb* 1 vomit 2 bring back (swallowed food) into mouth

re•ha•bil•i•tate [ree-hə-BIL-i-tayt] *verb transitive* **-tat•ed, -tat•ing** 1 help (person) to readjust to society after a period of illness, imprisonment, etc. 2 restore to reputation or former position 3 make fit again 4 reinstate

re•hash [ree-HASH] *verb transitive* 1 rework, reuse ▷ *noun* [REE-hash] 2 old materials presented in new form

DICTIONARY r THESAURUS

---

regardless *adjective* 1 HEEDLESS, inconsiderate, indifferent, neglectful, negligent, rash, reckless, unmindful
▷ *adverb* 2 ANYWAY, in any case, in spite of everything, nevertheless

regards *plural noun* GOOD WISHES, best wishes, compliments, greetings, respects

regenerate *verb* RENEW, breathe new life into, invigorate, reawaken, reinvigorate, rejuvenate, restore, revive

regime *noun* GOVERNMENT, leadership, management, reign, rule, system

regimented *adjective* CONTROLLED, disciplined, ordered, organized, regulated, systematized

region *noun* AREA, district, locality, part, place, quarter, section, sector, territory, tract, zone

regional *adjective* LOCAL, district, parochial, provincial, zonal

register *noun* 1 LIST, archives, catalog, chronicle, diary, file, log, record, roll, roster
▷ *verb* 2 RECORD, catalog, chronicle, enlist, enroll, enter, list, note
3 SHOW, display, exhibit, express, indicate, manifest, mark, reveal

regress *verb* REVERT, backslide, degenerate, deteriorate, fall away *or* fall off, go back, lapse, relapse, return

regret *verb* 1 FEEL SORRY ABOUT, bemoan, bewail, deplore, grieve, lament, miss, mourn, repent, rue
▷ *noun* 2 SORROW, bitterness, compunction, contrition, penitence, remorse, repentance, ruefulness

regretful *adjective* SORRY, apologetic, contrite, penitent, remorseful, repentant, rueful, sad, sorrowful

regrettable *adjective* UNFORTUNATE, disappointing, distressing, lamentable, sad, shameful

regular *adjective* 1 NORMAL, common, customary, habitual, ordinary, routine, typical, usual
2 EVEN, balanced, flat, level, smooth, straight, symmetrical, uniform
3 SYSTEMATIC, consistent, constant, even, fixed, ordered, set, stated, steady, uniform

regulate *verb* 1 CONTROL, direct, govern, guide, handle, manage, rule, run, supervise
2 ADJUST, balance, fit, moderate, modulate, tune

regulation *noun* 1 RULE, decree, dictate, edict, law, order, precept, statute
2 CONTROL, direction, government, management, supervision
3 ADJUSTMENT, modulation, tuning

regurgitate *verb* VOMIT, barf (*slang*), disgorge, puke (*slang*), spew *or* spew out spew up, throw up (*informal*)

rehabilitate *verb* 1 REINTEGRATE, adjust

re•hearse [ri-HURS] *verb transitive* **-hearsed, -hears•ing** 1 practice (play, etc.) 2 repeat aloud 3 say over again 4 train, drill > **re•hears'al** *noun*

reign [rayn] *noun* 1 period of sovereign's rule ▷ *verb intransitive* 2 be ruler 3 be supreme

re•im•burse [ree-im-BURS] *verb transitive* 1 **-bursed, -burs•ing** 2 refund 3 pay back > **re•im•burse'ment** *noun*

rein [rayn] *noun* 1 narrow strap attached to bit to guide horse 2 instrument for governing ▷ *verb transitive* 3 check, manage with reins 4 control **give free rein to** remove restraints

re•in•car•na•tion [ree-in-kahr-NAY-shən] *noun* 1 rebirth of soul in successive bodies 2 one of series of such transmigrations > **re•in•car'nate** [-KAHR-nayt] *verb transitive* **-nat•ed, -nat•ing**

rein•deer [RAYN-deer] *noun* deer, with large branched antlers, that lives in the arctic regions

re•in•force [ree-in-FORS] *verb transitive* **-forced, -forc•ing** 1 strengthen with new support, material, force 2 strengthen with additional troops, ships, etc. > **re•in•force'ment** *noun* > **reinforced concrete** concrete strengthened internally by steel bars

re•in•state [ree-in-STAYT] *verb transitive* **-stat•ed, -stat•ing** replace, restore, reestablish

re•it•er•ate [ree-IT-ə-rayt] *verb transitive* **-at•ed, -at•ing** repeat again and again > **re•it•er•a'tion** *noun* repetition > **re•it'er•a•tive** [-ər-ə-tiv] *adjective*

re•ject [ri-JEKT] *verb transitive* 1 refuse to accept 2 put aside 3 discard 4 renounce ▷ *noun* [REE-jekt] 5 person or thing rejected as not up to standard > **re•jec'tion** *noun* refusal

re•joice [ri-JOIS] *verb* **-joiced, -joic•ing** 1 make or be joyful, merry 2 gladden 3 exult

re•join [ree-JOIN] *verb transitive* 1 reply 2 join again > **re•join•der** [ri-JOIN-dər] *noun* answer, retort

re•ju•ve•nate [ri-JOO-və-nayt] *verb transitive* **-nat•ed, -nat•ing** restore to youth > **re•ju•ve•na'tion** *noun* > **re•ju•ve•nes•cence** [ri-joo-və-NES-əns] *noun* process of growing young again

re•lapse [ri-LAPS] *verb intransitive* **-lapsed, -laps•ing** 1 fall back into evil, illness, etc. ▷ *noun* [REE-laps] 2 return of bad habits, illness, etc.

re•late [ri-LAYT] *verb transitive* **-lat•ed, -lat•ing** 1 narrate, recount 2 establish relation between 3 have reference or relation to ▷ *verb intransitive* **-lat•ed, -lat•ing** 4 (with *to*) form sympathetic relationship

re•la•tion [ri-LAY-shən] *noun* 1 relative quality

2 REDEEM, clear, reform, restore, save

rehash *verb* 1 REWORK, refashion, rejig (*informal*), reuse, rewrite
▷ *noun* 2 REWORKING, new version, rearrangement, rewrite

rehearsal *noun* PRACTICE, drill, preparation, rehearsing, run-through

rehearse *verb* PRACTICE, drill, go over, prepare, recite, repeat, run through, train

reign *noun* 1 RULE, command, control, dominion, monarchy, power
▷ *verb* 2 RULE, be in power, command, govern, influence
3 BE SUPREME, hold sway, predominate, prevail

reimburse *verb* PAY BACK, compensate, recompense, refund, remunerate, repay, return

rein *verb* 1 CONTROL, check, curb, halt, hold back, limit, restrain, restrict
▷ *noun* 2 CONTROL, brake, bridle, check, curb, harness, hold, restraint

reincarnation *noun* REBIRTH, transmigration of souls

reinforce *verb* SUPPORT, bolster, emphasize, fortify, prop, strengthen, stress, supplement, toughen

reinforcement *noun* 1 STRENGTHENING, augmentation, fortification, increase
2 SUPPORT, brace, buttress, prop, stay
3 ▷ **reinforcements** RESERVES, additional troops *or* fresh troops, auxiliaries, support

reinstate *verb* RESTORE, recall, re-establish, replace, return

reiterate *verb* REPEAT, do again, restate, say again

reject *verb* 1 DENY, decline, disallow, exclude, renounce, repudiate, veto
2 REBUFF, jilt, refuse, repulse, say no to, spurn, turn down
3 DISCARD, eliminate, jettison, scrap, throw away *or* throw out
▷ *noun* 4 CASTOFF, discard, failure, second

rejection *noun* 1 DENIAL, dismissal, exclusion, renunciation, repudiation, thumbs down, veto
2 REBUFF, brushoff (*slang*), kick in the teeth (*slang*), knock-back (*slang*), refusal

rejig *verb* REARRANGE, alter, juggle, manipulate, reorganize, tweak

rejoice *verb* BE GLAD, be happy, be overjoyed, celebrate, exult, glory

rejoicing *noun* HAPPINESS, celebration, elation, exultation, gladness, joy, jubilation, merrymaking

rejoin *verb* REPLY, answer, respond, retort, riposte

rejoinder *noun* REPLY, answer, comeback (*informal*), response, retort, riposte

rejuvenate *verb* REVITALIZE, breathe new life into, refresh, regenerate, reinvigorate, renew, restore

relapse *verb* 1 LAPSE, backslide, degenerate, fail, regress, revert, slip back
2 WORSEN, deteriorate, fade, fail, sicken, sink, weaken
▷ *noun* 3 LAPSE, backsliding, regression, retrogression
4 WORSENING, deterioration, turn for the worse, weakening

relate *verb* 1 CONNECT, associate, correlate, couple, join, link
2 CONCERN, apply, be relevant to, have to do with, pertain, refer
3 TELL, describe, detail, narrate, recite, recount, report

related *adjective* 1 AKIN, kindred
2 ASSOCIATED, affiliated, akin, connected, interconnected, joint, linked

relation *noun* 1 CONNECTION, bearing, bond, comparison, correlation, link
2 RELATIVE, kin, kinsman *or* kinswoman
3 KINSHIP, affinity, kindred

relations *plural noun* 1 DEALINGS, affairs, connections, contact, interaction, intercourse,

or condition 2 connection by blood or marriage 3 connection between things 4 act of relating 5 narrative > **re•la'tion•ship** *noun* > **rel•a•tive** [REL-ə-tiv] *adjective* 1 dependent on relation to something else, not absolute 2 having reference or relation (to) ▷ *noun* 3 one connected by blood or marriage 4 relative word or thing > **rel•a•tiv'i•ty** *noun* 1 state of being relative 2 subject of two theories of Albert Einstein, dealing with relationships of space, time and motion, and acceleration and gravity

re•lax [ri-LAKS] *verb transitive* 1 make loose or slack ▷ *verb intransitive* 2 become loosened or slack 3 ease up from effort or attention 4 become more friendly, less strict > **re•lax•a'tion** [ree-] *noun* 1 relaxing recreation 2 alleviation 3 abatement

re•lay [REE-lay] *noun* 1 fresh set of people or animals relieving others 2 *electricity* device for making or breaking local circuit ▷ *verb transitive* **-layed, -laying** 3 pass on, as message > **relay race** race between teams of which each runner races part of distance

re•lease [ri-LEES] *verb transitive* **-leased, -leas•ing** 1 give up, surrender, set free 2 permit public showing of (movie, etc.) ▷ *noun* 3 setting free 4 releasing 5 written discharge 6 permission to show publicly 7 film, record, etc. newly issued

rel•e•gate [REL-i-gayt] *verb transitive* **-gat•ed, -gat•ing** 1 banish, consign 2 demote > **re•le•ga'tion** *noun*

re•lent [ri-LENT] *verb intransitive* give up harsh intention, become less severe > **re•lent'less** [-lis] *adjective* 1 pitiless 2 merciless

rel•e•vant [REL-ə-vənt] *adjective* having to do with the matter in hand, to the point > **rel'e•vance** *noun*

reliable, reliance *see* **rely**

rel•ic [REL-ik] *noun* 1 thing remaining, esp. as memorial of saint 2 memento > **rel•ics** remains, traces

re•lief [ri-LEEF] *noun* 1 alleviation, end of pain, distress, etc. 2 money, food given to victims of disaster, poverty, etc. 3 release from duty 4 one who relieves another 5 freeing of besieged city, etc. 6 projection of carved design from surface 7 distinctness, prominence > **re•lieve** [ri-LEEV] *verb transitive* **-lieved, -liev•ing** bring or give relief to > **relief map** map showing elevations and depressions of country in relief

re•li•gion [ri-LIJ-ən] *noun* system of belief in, worship of a supernatural power or god > **re•li'gious** *adjective* 1 pert. to religion 2 pious 3 conscientious > **re•li'gious•ly** *adverb* 1 in religious manner 2 scrupulously 3 conscientiously

re•lin•quish [ri-LING-kwish] *verb transitive* give up, abandon

rel•i•quar•y [REL-i-kwer-ee] *noun, plural* **-quar•ies** case or shrine for holy relics

rel•ish [REL-ish] *verb* 1 enjoy, like ▷ *noun* 2 liking, gusto 3 appetizing savory food, such as pickle 4 taste or flavor

re•luc•tant [ri-LUK-tənt] *adjective* unwilling,

relationship
2 FAMILY, clan, kin, kindred, kinsfolk, kinsmen, relatives, tribe

relationship *noun* 1 ASSOCIATION, affinity, bond, connection, kinship, rapport
2 AFFAIR, liaison
3 CONNECTION, correlation, link, parallel, similarity, tie-up

relative *adjective* 1 DEPENDENT, allied, associated, comparative, contingent, corresponding, proportionate, related
2 RELEVANT, applicable, apposite, appropriate, apropos, germane, pertinent
▷ *noun* 3 RELATION, kinsman *or* kinswoman, member of one's family *or* member of the family

relatively *adverb* COMPARATIVELY, rather, somewhat

relax *verb* 1 BE AT EASE *or* FEEL AT EASE, calm, chill out (*slang*), de-stress, lighten up (*slang*), rest, take it easy, unwind
2 LESSEN, abate, ease, ebb, let up, loosen, lower, moderate, reduce, relieve, slacken, weaken

relaxation *noun* LEISURE, enjoyment, fun, pleasure, recreation, rest

relaxed *adjective* EASY-GOING, casual, comfortable, easy, free and easy, homey, informal, laid-back (*informal*), leisurely

relay *noun* 1 SHIFT, relief, turn
2 MESSAGE, dispatch, transmission
▷ *verb* 3 PASS ON, broadcast, carry, communicate, send, spread, transmit

release *verb* 1 SET FREE, discharge, drop, extricate, free, liberate, loose, unbridle, undo, unfasten
2 ACQUIT, absolve, exonerate, let go, let off
3 ISSUE, circulate, distribute, launch, make known, make public, publish, put out
▷ *noun* 4 LIBERATION, deliverance, discharge, emancipation, freedom, liberty
5 ACQUITTAL, absolution, exemption, exoneration
6 ISSUE, proclamation, publication

relegate *verb* DEMOTE, downgrade

relent *verb* BE MERCIFUL, capitulate, change one's mind, come round, have pity, show mercy, soften, yield

relentless *adjective* 1 UNREMITTING, incessant, nonstop, persistent, unrelenting, unrelieved
2 MERCILESS, cruel, fierce, implacable, pitiless, remorseless, ruthless, unrelenting

relevant *adjective* SIGNIFICANT, apposite, appropriate, apt, fitting, germane, pertinent, related, to the point

reliable *adjective* DEPENDABLE, faithful, safe, sound, staunch, sure, true, trustworthy

reliance *noun* TRUST, belief, confidence, dependence, faith

relic *noun* REMNANT, fragment, keepsake, memento, souvenir, trace, vestige

relief *noun* 1 EASE, comfort, cure, deliverance, mitigation, release, remedy, solace
2 REST, break, breather (*informal*), relaxation, respite
3 AID, assistance, help, succor, support

relieve *verb* 1 EASE, alleviate, assuage, calm, comfort, console, cure, mitigate, relax, soften, soothe
2 HELP, aid, assist, succor, support, sustain

religious *adjective* 1 DEVOUT, devotional, faithful, godly, holy, pious, sacred, spiritual
2 CONSCIENTIOUS, faithful, meticulous, punctilious, rigid, scrupulous

loath, disinclined > **re•luc'tance** *noun*
re•ly [ri-LĪ] *verb intransitive* **-lied, -ly•ing** 1 depend (on) 2 trust > **re•li•a•bil'i•ty** *noun* > **re•li'a•ble** *adjective* trustworthy, dependable > **re•li•ance** [ri-LĪ-əns] *noun* 1 trust 2 confidence 3 dependence > **re•li'ant** [-ənt] *adjective* 1 confident 2 trustful
re•main [ri-MAYN] *verb intransitive* 1 stay, be left behind 2 continue 3 abide 4 last > **remains** *plural noun* 1 relics, esp. of ancient buildings 2 dead body > **re•main'der** *noun* 1 rest, what is left after subtraction ▷ *verb transitive* 2 offer (end of consignment of goods, material, etc.) at reduced prices
re•mand [ri-MAND] *verb transitive* send back, esp. into custody
re•mark [ri-MAHRK] *verb intransitive* 1 make casual comment (on) ▷ *verb transitive* 2 comment, observe 3 say 4 take notice of ▷ *noun* 5 observation, comment > **re•mark'a•ble** *adjective* noteworthy, unusual > **re•mark'a•bly** *adverb* 1 exceedingly 2 unusually
re•mar'ry *verb* **-ry•ing, -ried** marry again following a divorce or the death of one's previous husband or wife
rem•e•dy [REM-i-dee] *noun, plural* **-dies** means of curing, counteracting or relieving disease, trouble, etc. ▷ *verb transitive* **-died, -dy•ing** put right > **re•me'di•a•ble** *adjective* > **re•me'di•al** *adjective* designed, intended to correct specific disability, handicap, etc. > **re•me•di•a'tion** *noun*
re•mem•ber [ri-MEM-bər] *verb transitive* 1 retain in, recall to memory ▷ *verb intransitive* 2 have in mind > **re•mem'brance** [-brəns] *noun* 1 memory 2 token 3 souvenir 4 reminiscence
re•mind [ri-MĪND] *verb transitive* 1 cause to remember 2 put in mind (of) > **re•mind'er** *noun*
rem•i•nisce [rem-ə-NIS] *verb intransitive* **-nisced, -nisc•ing** talk, write of past times, experiences, etc. > **rem•i•nis'cence** *noun* 1 remembering 2 thing recollected > **rem•i•nis'cenc•es** memoirs > **rem•i•nis'cent** *adjective* reminding or suggestive (of)
re•miss [ri-MIS] *adjective* negligent, careless
re•mit [ri-MIT] *verb* **-mit•ted, -mit•ting** 1 send money for goods, services, etc., esp. by mail 2 refrain from exacting 3 give up 4 restore, return 5 slacken 6 forgive (sin, etc.) ▷ *noun* 7 *law* transfer of court record to another court > **re•mis'sion** *noun* 1 abatement 2 reduction in length of prison term 3 pardon, forgiveness > **re•mit'tance** *noun* 1 sending of money 2 money sent
rem•nant [REM-nənt] *noun* 1 fragment or small piece remaining 2 oddment
re•mon•strate [ri-MON-strayt] *verb intransitive* **-strat•ed, -strat•ing** protest, reason with, argue > **re•mon'strance** [-strəns] *noun*
re•morse [ri-MORS] *noun* regret and repentance > **re•morse'ful** [-fəl] *adjective* > **re•morse'less** [-lis]

---

relinquish *verb* GIVE UP, abandon, abdicate, cede, drop, forsake, leave, let go, renounce, surrender
relish *verb* 1 ENJOY, delight in, fancy, like, revel in, savor
▷ *noun* 2 ENJOYMENT, fancy, fondness, gusto, liking, love, partiality, penchant, predilection, taste
3 CONDIMENT, sauce, seasoning
4 FLAVOR, piquancy, smack, spice, tang, taste, trace
reluctance *noun* UNWILLINGNESS, aversion, disinclination, dislike, distaste, loathing, repugnance
reluctant *adjective* UNWILLING, disinclined, hesitant, loath, unenthusiastic
rely *verb* DEPEND, bank, bet, count, trust
remain *verb* 1 CONTINUE, abide, dwell, endure, go on, last, persist, stand, stay, survive
2 STAY BEHIND, be left, delay, linger, wait
remainder *noun* REST, balance, excess, leavings, remains, remnant, residue, surplus
remaining *adjective* LEFT-OVER, lingering, outstanding, persisting, surviving, unfinished
remains *plural noun* 1 REMNANTS, debris, dregs, leavings, leftovers, relics, residue, rest
2 BODY, cadaver, carcass, corpse
remark *verb* 1 COMMENT, declare, mention, observe, pass comment, reflect, say, state
2 NOTICE, espy, make out, mark, note, observe, perceive, see
▷ *noun* 3 COMMENT, observation, reflection, statement, utterance
remarkable *adjective* EXTRAORDINARY, notable, outstanding, rare, singular, striking, surprising, uncommon, unusual, wonderful
remedy *noun* 1 CURE, medicine, nostrum, treatment
▷ *verb* 2 PUT RIGHT, correct, fix, rectify, set to rights
remember *verb* 1 RECALL, call to mind, commemorate, look back *or* look back on, recollect, reminisce, think back
2 BEAR IN MIND, keep in mind
remembrance *noun* 1 MEMORY, recall, recollection, reminiscence, thought
2 SOUVENIR, commemoration, keepsake, memento, memorial, monument, reminder, token
remind *verb* CALL TO MIND, jog one's memory, make (someone) remember, prompt
reminisce *verb* RECALL, hark back, look back, recollect, remember, think back
reminiscence *noun* RECOLLECTION, anecdote, memoir, memory, recall, remembrance
reminiscent *adjective* SUGGESTIVE, evocative, similar
remiss *adjective* CARELESS, forgetful, heedless, lax, neglectful, negligent, thoughtless
remission *noun* 1 PARDON, absolution, amnesty, discharge, exemption, release, reprieve
2 LESSENING, abatement, alleviation, ebb, lull, relaxation, respite
remit *verb* 1 SEND, dispatch, forward, mail, post, transmit
2 CANCEL, halt, repeal, rescind, stop
3 POSTPONE, defer, delay, put off, shelve, suspend
▷ *noun* 4 INSTRUCTIONS, brief, guidelines, orders
remittance *noun* PAYMENT, allowance, fee
remnant *noun* REMAINDER, end, fragment, leftovers, remains, residue, rest, trace, vestige
remonstrate *verb* ARGUE, dispute, dissent, object, protest, take issue
remorse *noun* REGRET, anguish, compunction, contrition, grief, guilt, penitence, repentance, shame, sorrow

adjective pitiless
re•mote [ri-MOHT] *adjective* **-mot•er, -mot•est** 1 far away, distant 2 aloof 3 slight > **re•mote'ly** *adverb* > **remote control** control of apparatus from a distance by electrical device
re•move [ri-MOOV] *verb transitive* **-moved, -mov•ing** 1 take away or off 2 transfer 3 withdraw ▷ *verb intransitive* **-moved, -mov•ing** 4 go away, change residence ▷ *noun* 5 degree of difference > **re•mov•a•ble** *adjective* > **re•mov'al** *noun*
re•mu•ner•ate [ri-MYOO-nə-rayt] *verb transitive* reward, pay > **re•mu•ner•a'tion** *noun* > **re•mu'ner•a•tive** *adjective*
ren•ais•sance [REN-ə-sahns] *noun* revival, rebirth, esp. revival of learning in 14th to 16th centuries
re•nal [REEN-l] *adjective* of the kidneys
re•nas•cent [ri-NAS-ənt] *adjective* springing up again into being
rend *verb* **rent, rend•ing** 1 tear, wrench apart 2 burst, break, split
ren•der [REN-dər] *verb transitive* 1 submit, present 2 give in return, deliver up 3 cause to become 4 portray, represent 5 melt down 6 cover with plaster
ren•dez•vous [RAHN-de-voo] *noun, plural* **rendezvous** [-vooz] 1 meeting place 2 appointment 3 haunt 4 assignation ▷ *verb intransitive* **-voused** [-vood], **-vous•ing** [-voo-ing] 5 meet, come together
ren•di•tion [ren-DISH-ən] *noun* 1 performance 2 translation
ren•e•gade [REN-i-gayd] *noun* 1 deserter 2 outlaw 3 rebel ▷ *adjective*
re•nege [ri-NIG] *verb intransitive* **-neged, -neg•ing** 1 (usu. with *on*) go back on (promise, etc.) 2 in cards, break rule
re•new [ri-NOO] *verb transitive* 1 begin again 2 reaffirm 3 make valid again 4 make new 5 revive 6 restore to former state 7 replenish ▷ *verb intransitive* 8 be made new 9 grow again > **re•new•a•bil'i•ty** *noun* quality of being renewable > **re•new'a•ble** *adjective* > **re•new'al** *noun* 1 revival, restoration 2 regeneration
ren•net [REN-it] *noun* 1 lining membrane of calf's fourth stomach 2 preparation from this membrane for curdling milk
re•nounce [ri-NOWNS] *verb transitive* **-nounced, -nounc•ing** 1 give up, cast off, disown 2 abjure 3 resign, as title or claim > **re•nun•ci•a'tion** *noun*
ren•o•vate [REN-ə-vayt] *verb transitive* restore, repair, renew, do up > **ren•o•va'tion** *noun*
re•nown [ri-NOWN] *noun* fame
rent¹ *noun* 1 payment for use of land, buildings, machines, etc. ▷ *verb transitive* 2 hold by lease 3 hire 4 let > **rent•al** [RENT-əl] *noun* sum

---

remorseful *adjective* REGRETFUL, apologetic, ashamed, conscience-stricken, contrite, guilty, penitent, repentant, sorry
remorseless *adjective* 1 PITILESS, callous, cruel, inhumane, merciless, ruthless
2 RELENTLESS, inexorable
remote *adjective* 1 DISTANT, far, inaccessible, in the middle of nowhere, isolated, out-of-the-way, secluded
2 ALOOF, abstracted, cold, detached, distant, reserved, standoffish, uncommunicative, withdrawn
3 SLIGHT, doubtful, dubious, faint, outside, slender, slim, small, unlikely
removal *noun* 1 TAKING AWAY *or* TAKING OFF taking out, dislodgment, ejection, elimination, eradication, extraction, uprooting, withdrawal
2 DISMISSAL, expulsion
3 MOVE, departure, relocation, transfer
remove *verb* 1 TAKE AWAY *or* TAKE OFF take out, abolish, delete, detach, displace, eject, eliminate, erase, excise, extract, get rid of, wipe from the face of the earth, withdraw
2 DISMISS, depose, dethrone, discharge, expel, oust, throw out
3 MOVE, depart, flit (*Scottish & N English dialect*), relocate
remunerate *verb* PAY, compensate, recompense, reimburse, repay, requite, reward
remuneration *noun* PAYMENT, earnings, fee, income, pay, return, reward, salary, stipend, wages
remunerative *adjective* PROFITABLE, economic, lucrative, moneymaking, paying, rewarding, worthwhile
renaissance *or* **renascence** *noun* REBIRTH, reappearance, reawakening, renewal, restoration, resurgence, revival
rend *verb* TEAR, rip, rupture, separate, wrench
render *verb* 1 MAKE, cause to become, leave
2 PROVIDE, furnish, give, hand out, pay, present, submit, supply, tender
3 PORTRAY, act, depict, do, give, perform, play, represent
rendezvous *noun* 1 APPOINTMENT, assignation, date, engagement, meeting, tryst
2 MEETING PLACE, gathering point, venue
▷ *verb* 3 MEET, assemble, come together, gather, join up
rendition *noun* 1 PERFORMANCE, arrangement, interpretation, portrayal, presentation, reading, rendering, version
2 TRANSLATION, interpretation, reading, transcription, version
renegade *noun* 1 DESERTER, apostate, defector, traitor, turncoat
▷ *adjective* 2 REBELLIOUS, apostate, disloyal, traitorous, unfaithful
renege *verb* BREAK ONE'S WORD, back out, break a promise, default, go back
renew *verb* 1 RECOMMENCE, continue, extend, reaffirm, recreate, reopen, repeat, resume
2 RESTORE, mend, modernize, overhaul, refit, refurbish, renovate, repair
3 REPLACE, refresh, replenish, restock
renounce *verb* GIVE UP, abjure, deny, disown, forsake, forswear, quit, recant, relinquish, waive
renovate *verb* RESTORE, do up (*informal*), modernize, overhaul, recondition, refit, refurbish, renew, repair
renown *noun* FAME, distinction, eminence, note, reputation, repute
renowned *adjective* FAMOUS, celebrated, distinguished, eminent, esteemed, notable, noted, well-known
rent¹ *verb* 1 HIRE, charter, lease, let
▷ *noun* 2 HIRE, fee, lease, payment, rental
rent² *noun* TEAR, gash, hole, opening, rip, slash,

payable as rent
rent² *noun* 1 tear 2 fissure 3 *pt./pp. of* **rend**
renunciation *see* **renounce**
rep¹ *noun* fabric with corded surface for upholstery, etc.
rep² *adjective, noun short for* **repertory theater**
rep³ *noun short for* **representative**
re•paid [ri-PAYD] *pt./pp. of* **repay**
re•pair¹ [ri-PAIR] *verb transitive* 1 make whole, sound again 2 mend 3 patch 4 restore ▷ *noun* > **re•pair'a•ble** *adjective* > **rep•a•ra•tion** [rep-ə-RAY-shən] *noun* 1 repairing 2 amends, compensation
repair² *verb intransitive* resort (to), go
rep•ar•tee [rep-ər-TEE] *noun* 1 witty retort 2 interchange of retorts
re•past [ri-PAST] *noun* a meal
re•pa•tri•ate [ri-PAY-tree-ayt] *verb transitive* **-at•ed, -at•ing** send (someone) back to own country
re•pay [ri-PAY] *verb transitive* **-paid, -pay•ing** 1 pay back, refund 2 make return for > **re•pay'ment** *noun*
re•peal [ri-PEEL] *verb transitive* 1 revoke, annul, cancel ▷ *noun* 2 act of repealing
re•peat [ri-PEET] *verb transitive* 1 say, do again 2 reproduce 3 recur ▷ *verb intransitive* 4 recur 5 of food, be tasted repeatedly for some time after being eaten ▷ *noun* 6 act, instance of repeating, esp. TV show broadcast again > **re•peat'ed•ly** *adverb* 1 again and again 2 frequently > **re•peat'er** *noun* 1 firearm that can be discharged many times without reloading 2 watch that strikes hours > **rep•e•ti•tion** [rep-i-TISH-ən] *noun* 1 act of repeating 2 thing repeated 3 piece learned by heart and repeated > **rep•e•ti'tious** *adjective* repeated unnecessarily > **re•pet'i•tive** *adjective* repeated
re•pel [ri-PEL] *verb transitive* **-pelled, -pel•ling** 1 drive back, ward off, refuse 2 be repulsive to > **re•pel'lent** [-ənt] *adjective* 1 distasteful 2 resisting water, etc. ▷ *noun* 3 that which repels, esp. chemical to repel insects
re•pent [ri-PENT] *verb intransitive* 1 wish one had not done something 2 feel regret for deed or omission ▷ *verb transitive* 3 feel regret for > **re•pent'ance** [-əns] *noun* contrition > **re•pent'ant** [-ənt] *adjective*
re•per•cus•sion [ree-pər-KUSH-ən] *noun* 1 indirect effect, oft. unpleasant 2 recoil 3 echo
rep•er•to•ry [REP-ər-tor-ee] *noun, plural* **-ries** 1 repertoire, collection 2 store > **rep'er•toire** [-twahr] *noun* stock of plays, songs, etc. that performer or company can give > **repertory theater** theater with permanent company producing succession of plays
repetition, repetitious, repetitive *see* **repeat**
re•pine [ri-PĪN] *verb intransitive* **-pined, -pin•ing** fret, complain
re•place [ri-PLAYS] *verb transitive* **-placed, -plac•ing** 1 substitute for 2 put back
re•play [REE-play] *noun* 1 (*also* **instant replay**) immediate reshowing on TV of incident in sport, esp. in slow motion 2 replaying of a match ▷ *verb transitive* [ree-PLAY]
re•plen•ish [ri-PLEN-ish] *verb transitive* fill up again > **re•plen'ish•ment** *noun*
re•plete [ri-PLEET] *adjective* filled, gorged

DICTIONARY • THESAURUS

slit, split
renunciation *noun* GIVING UP, abandonment, abdication, abjuration, denial, disavowal, forswearing, rejection, relinquishment, repudiation
reorganize *verb* REARRANGE, reshuffle, restructure
repair¹ *verb* 1 MEND, fix, heal, patch, patch up, renovate, restore
▷ *noun* 2 MEND, darn, overhaul, patch, restoration
reparation *noun* COMPENSATION, atonement, damages, recompense, restitution, satisfaction
repartee *noun* WIT, badinage, banter, riposte, wittiness, wordplay
repast *noun* MEAL, food
repay *verb* 1 PAY BACK, compensate, recompense, refund, reimburse, requite, return, square
2 GET EVEN WITH (*informal*), avenge, hit back, reciprocate, retaliate, revenge
repeal *verb* 1 ABOLISH, annul, cancel, invalidate, nullify, recall, reverse, revoke
▷ *noun* 2 ABOLITION, annulment, cancellation, invalidation, rescindment
repeat *verb* 1 REITERATE, echo, replay, reproduce, rerun, reshow, restate, retell
▷ *noun* 2 REPETITION, echo, reiteration, replay, rerun, reshowing
repeatedly *adverb* OVER AND OVER, frequently, many times, often
repel *verb* 1 DISGUST, gross out (*slang*), nauseate, offend, revolt, sicken
2 DRIVE OFF, fight, hold off, parry, rebuff, repulse, resist, ward off
repellent *adjective* 1 DISGUSTING, abhorrent, hateful, horrid, loathsome, nauseating, noxious, offensive, repugnant, repulsive, revolting, scuzzy (*slang*), sickening
2 PROOF, impermeable, repelling, resistant
repent *verb* REGRET, be sorry, feel remorse, rue
repentance *noun* REGRET, compunction, contrition, grief, guilt, penitence, remorse
repentant *adjective* REGRETFUL, contrite, penitent, remorseful, rueful, sorry
repercussion *noun* ▷ **repercussions** CONSEQUENCES, backlash, result, sequel, side effects
repertoire *noun* RANGE, collection, list, repertory, stock, store, supply
repetition *noun* REPEATING, echo, recurrence, reiteration, renewal, replication, restatement, tautology
repetitious *adjective* LONG-WINDED, prolix, tautological, tedious, verbose, wordy
repetitive *adjective* MONOTONOUS, boring, dull, mechanical, recurrent, tedious, unchanging, unvaried
rephrase *verb* REWORD, paraphrase, put differently
repine *verb* COMPLAIN, fret, grumble, moan
replace *verb* TAKE THE PLACE OF, follow, oust, substitute, succeed, supersede, supplant, take over from
replacement *noun* SUCCESSOR, double, proxy, stand-in, substitute, surrogate, understudy
replenish *verb* REFILL, fill, provide, reload, replace, restore, top up
replete *adjective* FULL, crammed, filled, full up,

rep•li•ca [REP-li-kə] *noun* 1 exact copy 2 facsimile, duplicate > **rep•li•cate** [REP-li-kayt] *verb transitive* **-cat•ed, -cat•ing** make, be a copy of > **rep•li•ca'tion** *noun* > **rep'li•ca•ble** *adjective*
re•ply [ri-PLĪ] *verb* **-plied, -ply•ing** 1 answer or respond ▷ *noun, plural* **-lies** 2 answer or response
re•port [ri-PORT] *noun* 1 account, statement 2 written statement of child's progress at school 3 rumor 4 repute 5 bang ▷ *verb transitive* 6 announce, relate 7 make, give account of 8 take down in writing 9 complain about ▷ *verb intransitive* 10 make report 11 act as reporter 12 present oneself (to) > **re•port'er** *noun* one who reports, esp. for newspaper
re•pose [ri-POHZ] *noun* 1 peace 2 composure 3 sleep ▷ *verb intransitive* **-posed, -pos•ing** 4 rest ▷ *verb transitive* **-posed, -pos•ing** 5 lay to rest 6 place 7 rely, lean (on) > **re•pos'i•tor•y** [-POZ-i-tor-ee] *noun, plural* **-tor•ies** 1 place where valuables are deposited for safekeeping 2 store
rep•re•hend [rep-ri-HEND] *verb transitive* find fault with > **rep•re•hen'si•ble** *adjective* 1 deserving censure 2 unworthy > **rep•re•hen'sion** *noun* censure
rep•re•sent [rep-ri-ZENT] *verb transitive* 1 stand for 2 deputize for 3 act, play 4 symbolize 5 make out to be 6 call up by description or portrait > **rep•re•sen•ta'tion** *noun* > **rep•re•sent'a•tive** *noun* 1 one chosen to stand for group 2 (traveling) salesman ▷ *adjective* 3 typical
re•press [ri-PRES] *verb transitive* keep down or under, quell, check > **re•pres'sion** [-PRESH-ən] *noun* restraint > **re•pres'sive** *adjective*
re•prieve [ri-PREEV] *verb transitive* **-prieved, -priev•ing** 1 suspend execution of (condemned person) 2 give temporary relief (to) ▷ *noun* 3 postponement or cancelation of punishment 4 respite 5 last-minute intervention
rep•ri•mand [REP-rə-mand] *noun* 1 sharp rebuke ▷ *verb transitive* 2 rebuke sharply
re•print' *verb transitive* 1 print further copies of (a book) ▷ *noun* 2 reprinted copy
re•pris•al [ri-PRĪ-zəl] *noun* retaliation
re•proach [ri-PROHCH] *verb transitive* 1 blame, rebuke ▷ *noun* 2 scolding, upbraiding 3 expression of this 4 thing bringing discredit > **re•proach'ful** [-fəl] *adjective*
rep•ro•bate [REP-rə-bayt] *adjective* 1 depraved 2 rejected by God ▷ *noun* 3 depraved or disreputable person ▷ *verb transitive* **-bat•ed, -bat•ing** 4 disapprove of, reject
re•pro•duce [ree-prə-DOOS] *verb transitive* **-duced, -duc•ing** 1 produce copy of 2 bring

DICTIONARY **r** THESAURUS

glutted, gorged, stuffed
replica *noun* DUPLICATE, carbon copy (*informal*), copy, facsimile, imitation, model, reproduction
replicate *verb* COPY, duplicate, mimic, recreate, reduplicate, reproduce
reply *verb* 1 ANSWER, counter, reciprocate, rejoin, respond, retaliate, retort
▷ *noun* 2 ANSWER, counter, counterattack, reaction, rejoinder, response, retaliation, retort, riposte
report *verb* 1 COMMUNICATE, broadcast, cover, describe, detail, inform of, narrate, pass on, recount, relate, state, tell
2 PRESENT ONESELF, appear, arrive, come, turn up
▷ *noun* 3 ACCOUNT, communication, description, narrative, news, record, statement, word
4 ARTICLE, piece, story, write-up
5 RUMOR, buzz, gossip, hearsay, talk
6 BANG, blast, boom, crack, detonation, discharge, explosion, noise, sound
reporter *noun* JOURNALIST, correspondent, hack (*derogatory*), pressman, writer
repose *noun* 1 PEACE, ease, quietness, relaxation, respite, rest, stillness, tranquillity
2 COMPOSURE, calmness, poise, self-possession
3 SLEEP, slumber
▷ *verb* 4 REST, lie, lie down, recline, rest upon
repository *noun* STORE, depository, storehouse, treasury, vault
reprehensible *adjective* BLAMEWORTHY, bad, culpable, disgraceful, shameful, unworthy
represent *verb* 1 STAND FOR, act for, betoken, mean, serve as, speak for, symbolize
2 SYMBOLIZE, embody, epitomize, exemplify, personify, typify
3 PORTRAY, denote, depict, describe, illustrate, outline, picture, show
representation *noun* PORTRAYAL, account, depiction, description, illustration, image, likeness, model, picture, portrait
representative *noun* 1 DELEGATE, agent, deputy, member, proxy, spokesman *or* spokeswoman
2 SALESMAN, agent, commercial traveler, rep
▷ *adjective* 3 TYPICAL, archetypal, characteristic, exemplary, symbolic
repress *verb* 1 INHIBIT, bottle up, check, control, curb, hold back, restrain, stifle, suppress
2 SUBDUE, quell, subjugate
repression *noun* SUBJUGATION, constraint, control, despotism, domination, restraint, suppression, tyranny
repressive *adjective* OPPRESSIVE, absolute, authoritarian, despotic, dictatorial, tyrannical
reprieve *verb* 1 GRANT A STAY OF EXECUTION TO, let off the hook (*slang*), pardon
2 RELIEVE, abate, allay, alleviate, mitigate, palliate
▷ *noun* 3 STAY OF EXECUTION, amnesty, deferment, pardon, postponement, remission
4 RELIEF, alleviation, mitigation, palliation, respite
reprimand *verb* 1 BLAME, censure, rap over the knuckles, rebuke, scold
▷ *noun* 2 BLAME, censure, rebuke, reproach, reproof, talking-to (*informal*)
reprisal *noun* RETALIATION, retribution, revenge, vengeance
reproach *noun* 1 BLAME, censure, condemnation, disapproval, opprobrium, rebuke
▷ *verb* 2 BLAME, censure, condemn, criticize, lambast *or* lambaste, rebuke, reprimand, scold, upbraid
reproachful *adjective* CRITICAL, censorious, condemnatory, disapproving, fault-finding, reproving
reprobate *noun* 1 SCOUNDREL, bad egg (*old-fashioned informal*), degenerate, evildoer, miscreant, profligate, rake, rascal, villain
▷ *adjective* 2 DEPRAVED, abandoned, bad, base, corrupt, degenerate, dissolute, immoral, sinful, wicked

new individuals into existence 3 re-create, produce anew ▷ *verb intransitive* **-duced, -duc•ing** 4 propagate 5 generate > **re•pro•duc'i•ble** *adjective* > **re•pro•duc'tion** *noun* 1 process of reproducing 2 that which is reproduced 3 facsimile, as of painting, etc. > **re•pro•duc'tive** *adjective*

re•prove [ri-PROOV] *verb transitive* **-proved, -prov•ing** censure, rebuke > **re•proof'** *noun*

rep•tile [REP-til, REP-tīl] *noun* cold-blooded, air breathing vertebrate with horny scales or plates, as snake, tortoise, etc. > **rep•til'i•an** *adjective*

re•pub•lic [ri-PUB-lik] *noun* country without monarch in which supremacy of people or their elected representatives is formally acknowledged > **re•pub'li•can** *adjective, noun*

re•pu•di•ate [ri-PYOO-dee-ayt] *verb transitive* **-at•ed, -at•ing** 1 reject authority or validity of 2 cast off, disown > **re•pu•di•a'tion** *noun*

re•pug•nant [ri-PUG-nənt] *adjective* 1 offensive 2 distasteful 3 contrary > **re•pug'nance** *noun* 1 dislike, aversion 2 incompatibility

re•pulse [ri-PULS] *verb transitive* **-pulsed, -puls•ing** 1 drive back 2 rebuff 3 repel ▷ *noun* 4 driving back, rejection, rebuff > **re•pul'sion** [-shən] *noun* 1 distaste, aversion 2 *physics* force separating two objects > **re•pul'sive** *adjective* loathsome, disgusting

re•pute [ri-PYOOT] *verb transitive* **-put•ed, -put•ing** 1 reckon, consider ▷ *noun* 2 reputation, credit > **rep'u•ta•ble** *adjective* 1 of good repute 2 respectable > **rep•u•ta'tion** *noun* 1 estimation in which person is held 2 character 3 good name

re•quest [ri-KWEST] *noun* 1 asking 2 thing asked for ▷ *verb transitive* 3 ask

Req•ui•em [REK-wee-əm] *noun* 1 Mass for the dead 2 (**req•ui•em**) music for this

re•quire [ri-KWĪR] *verb transitive* **-quired, -quir•ing** 1 want, need 2 demand > **re•quire'ment** *noun* 1 essential condition 2 specific need 3 want

req•ui•site [REK-wə-zit] *adjective* 1 necessary 2 essential ▷ *noun*

req•ui•si•tion [rek-wə-ZISH-ən] *noun* 1 formal demand, such as for materials or supplies ▷ *verb transitive* 2 demand (supplies) 3 press into service

re•quite [ri-KWĪT] *verb transitive* **-quit•ed, -quit•ing** repay

re•scind [ri-SIND] *verb transitive* cancel, annul > **re•scis'sion** [-SIZH-ən] *noun*

res•cue [RES-kyoo] *verb transitive* **-cued, -cu•ing** save, deliver, extricate ▷ *noun* > **res'cu•er** *noun*

re•search [ri-SURCH] *noun* 1 investigation, esp. scientific study to discover facts ▷ *verb* 2 carry out investigations (on, into)

re•sem•ble [ri-ZEM-bəl] *verb transitive* **-bled,**

DICTIONARY • THESAURUS

reproduce *verb* 1 COPY, duplicate, echo, imitate, match, mirror, recreate, repeat, replicate 2 BREED, multiply, procreate, propagate, spawn

reproduction *noun* 1 BREEDING, generation, increase, multiplication 2 COPY, duplicate, facsimile, imitation, picture, print, replica

reproof *noun* REBUKE, blame, censure, condemnation, criticism, reprimand, scolding

reprove *verb* REBUKE, berate, blame, censure, condemn, reprimand, scold, tell off (*informal*)

repudiate *verb* REJECT, deny, disavow, disclaim, disown, renounce

repugnance *noun* DISTASTE, abhorrence, aversion, disgust, dislike, hatred, loathing

repugnant *adjective* DISTASTEFUL, abhorrent, disgusting, loathsome, nauseating, offensive, repellent, revolting, sickening, vile

repulse *verb* 1 DRIVE BACK, beat off, fight off, rebuff, repel, ward off 2 REBUFF, refuse, reject, snub, spurn, turn down

repulsion *noun* DISTASTE, abhorrence, aversion, detestation, disgust, hatred, loathing, repugnance, revulsion

repulsive *adjective* DISGUSTING, abhorrent, foul, loathsome, nauseating, repellent, revolting, scuzzy (*slang*), sickening, vile

reputable *adjective* RESPECTABLE, creditable, excellent, good, honorable, reliable, trustworthy, well-thought-of, worthy

reputation *noun* ESTIMATION, character, esteem, name, renown, repute, standing, stature

repute *noun* REPUTATION, celebrity, distinction, eminence, fame, name, renown, standing, stature

reputed *adjective* SUPPOSED, alleged, believed, considered, deemed, estimated, held, reckoned, regarded

reputedly *adverb* SUPPOSEDLY, allegedly, apparently, seemingly

request *verb* 1 ASK *or* ASK FOR, appeal for, demand, desire, entreat, invite, seek, solicit ▷ *noun* 2 ASKING, appeal, call, demand, desire, entreaty, suit

require *verb* 1 NEED, crave, desire, lack, miss, want, wish 2 DEMAND, ask, bid, call upon, command, compel, exact, insist upon, oblige, order

required *adjective* NEEDED, called for, essential, necessary, obligatory, requisite

requirement *noun* NECESSITY, demand, essential, lack, must, need, prerequisite, stipulation, want

requisite *adjective* 1 NECESSARY, called for, essential, indispensable, needed, needful, obligatory, required ▷ *noun* 2 NECESSITY, condition, essential, must, need, prerequisite, requirement

requisition *verb* 1 DEMAND, call for, request ▷ *noun* 2 DEMAND, call, request, summons

requital *noun* RETURN, repayment

requite *verb* RETURN, get even, give in return, pay (someone) back in his own coin *or* pay (someone) back in her own coin, reciprocate, repay, respond, retaliate

rescind *verb* ANNUL, cancel, countermand, declare null and void, invalidate, repeal, set aside

rescue *verb* 1 SAVE, deliver, get out, liberate, recover, redeem, release, salvage ▷ *noun* 2 LIBERATION, deliverance, recovery, redemption, release, salvage, salvation, saving

research *noun* 1 INVESTIGATION, analysis, examination, exploration, probe, study ▷ *verb* 2 INVESTIGATE, analyze, examine, explore, probe, study

resemblance *noun* SIMILARITY, correspondence, kinship, likeness, parallel, sameness, similitude

-bling 1 be like 2 look like > **re•sem'blance** *noun*
re•sent [ri-ZENT] *verb transitive* 1 show, feel indignation at 2 retain bitterness about > **re•sent'ful** [-fəl] *adjective* > **re•sent'ment** [-mənt] *noun*
re•serve [ri-ZURV] *verb transitive* **-served, -serv•ing** 1 hold back, set aside, keep for future use ▷ *noun* 2 (*also plural*) something, esp. money, troops, etc. kept for emergencies 3 (*also* **reservation**) area of land reserved for particular purpose or for use by particular group of people, etc. 4 reticence, concealment of feelings or friendliness > **re•ser•va'tion** *noun* 1 reserving 2 thing reserved 3 doubt 4 exception or limitation > **reserved** *adjective* not showing feelings, lacking cordiality > **re•serv'ist** *noun* one serving in reserve
res•er•voir [REZ-ər-vwahr] *noun* 1 enclosed area for storage of water, esp. for community supplies 2 receptacle for liquid, gas, etc. 3 place where anything is kept in store
re•shuf'fle *noun* 1 reorganization ▷ *verb* 2 reorganize
re•side [ri-ZĪD] *verb intransitive* **-sid•ed, -sid•ing** dwell permanently > **res•i•dence** [REZ-i-dəns] *noun* 1 home 2 house > **res'i•den•cy** *noun* 1 dwelling 2 position or period of medical resident > **res'i•dent** [-dənt] *adjective, noun* > **res•i•den'tial** *adjective* 1 (of part of town) consisting mainly of residences 2 of, connected with residence 3 providing living accommodation > **resident** physician in residence at hospital and serving on staff to obtain advanced training
res•i•due [REZ-i-doo] *noun* what is left, remainder > **re•sid'u•al** [ri-ZIJ-oo-əl] *adjective* > **residuals** *plural noun* additional payments to performers for reruns of film, TV programs, etc. in which they appear
re•sign [ri-ZĪN] *verb transitive* 1 give up ▷ *verb intransitive* 2 give up office, employment, etc. 3 reconcile (oneself) to > **res•ig•na'tion** [-ig-NAY-shən] *noun* 1 resigning 2 being resigned, submission > **re•signed'** [-ZĪND] *adjective* content to endure
re•sil•ient [ri-ZIL-yənt] *adjective* 1 capable of returning to normal after stretching, etc., elastic 2 (of person) recovering quickly from shock, etc. > **re•sil'ience, re•sil'ien•cy** *noun*
res•in [REZ-in] *noun* sticky substance formed in and oozing from plants, esp. firs and pines > **res'in•ous** [-nəs] *adjective* of, like resin
re•sist [ri-ZIST] *verb* withstand, oppose > **re•sist'ance** [-əns] *noun* 1 act of resisting 2 opposition 3 hindrance 4 *electricity* opposition offered by circuit to passage of current through it > **re•sist'ant** [-ənt] *adjective* > **re•sist'i•ble** *adjective* > **re•sis•tiv'i•ty** *noun* measure of electrical resistance > **re•sist'or** *noun* component of electrical circuit producing resistance

DICTIONARY

r

THESAURUS

resemble *verb* BE LIKE, bear a resemblance to, be similar to, look like, mirror, parallel
resent *verb* BE BITTER ABOUT, begrudge, grudge, object to, take exception to, take offense at
resentful *adjective* BITTER, angry, embittered, grudging, indignant, miffed (*informal*), offended, piqued, ticked off (*informal*)
resentment *noun* BITTERNESS, animosity, bad blood, grudge, ill feeling, ill will, indignation, pique, rancor, umbrage
reservation *noun* 1 DOUBT, hesitancy, scruple 2 CONDITION, proviso, qualification, rider, stipulation 3 RESERVE, preserve, sanctuary, territory
reserve *verb* 1 KEEP, hoard, hold, put by, retain, save, set aside, stockpile, store 2 BOOK, engage, prearrange, secure ▷ *noun* 3 STORE, cache, fund, hoard, reservoir, savings, stock, supply 4 RESERVATION, park, preserve, sanctuary, tract 5 SHYNESS, constraint, reservation, restraint, reticence, secretiveness, silence, taciturnity ▷ *adjective* 6 SUBSTITUTE, auxiliary, extra, fall-back, secondary, spare
reserved *adjective* 1 UNCOMMUNICATIVE, restrained, reticent, retiring, secretive, shy, silent, standoffish, taciturn, undemonstrative 2 SET ASIDE, booked, engaged, held, kept, restricted, retained, spoken for, taken
reservoir *noun* 1 LAKE, basin, pond, tank 2 STORE, pool, reserves, source, stock, supply
reshuffle *noun* 1 REORGANIZATION, change, rearrangement, redistribution, regrouping, restructuring, revision ▷ *verb* 2 REORGANIZE, change around, rearrange, redistribute, regroup, restructure, revise
reside *verb* LIVE, abide, dwell, inhabit, lodge, stay
residence *noun* HOME, abode, domicile, dwelling, flat, habitation, house, lodging, place
resident *noun* INHABITANT, citizen, local, lodger, occupant, occupier, tenant
residual *adjective* REMAINING, leftover, unconsumed, unused, vestigial
residue *noun* REMAINDER, dregs, excess, extra, leftovers, remains, remnant, rest, surplus
resign *verb* 1 QUIT, abdicate, give in one's notice, leave, step down (*informal*), vacate 2 GIVE UP, abandon, forgo, forsake, relinquish, renounce, surrender, yield 3 ▷ **resign oneself** ACCEPT, acquiesce, give in, submit, succumb, yield
resignation *noun* 1 LEAVING, abandonment, abdication, departure 2 ENDURANCE, acceptance, acquiescence, compliance, nonresistance, passivity, patience, submission, sufferance
resigned *adjective* STOICAL, compliant, long-suffering, patient, subdued, unresisting
resilient *adjective* 1 TOUGH, buoyant, hardy, irrepressible, strong 2 FLEXIBLE, elastic, plastic, pliable, rubbery, springy, supple
resist *verb* 1 OPPOSE, battle, combat, defy, hinder, stand up to 2 REFRAIN FROM, abstain from, avoid, forbear, forgo, keep from 3 WITHSTAND, be proof against
resistance *noun* FIGHTING, battle, defiance, fight, hindrance, impediment, obstruction, opposition, struggle
resistant *adjective* 1 IMPERVIOUS, hard, proof against, strong, tough, unaffected by 2 OPPOSED, antagonistic, hostile, intractable, intransigent, unwilling

DICTIONARY

res•o•lute [REZ-ə-loot] *adjective* determined > **res•o•lu'tion** *noun* 1 resolving 2 firmness 3 purpose or thing resolved upon 4 decision or vote of assembly

re•solve [ri-ZOLV] *verb transitive* **-solved, -solv•ing** 1 make up one's mind 2 decide with effort of will 3 form by resolution of vote 4 separate component parts of 5 make clear ▷ *noun* 6 resolution 7 fixed purpose

res•o•nance [REZ-ə-nəns] *noun* 1 echoing, esp. in deep tone 2 sound produced by body vibrating in sympathy with neighboring source of sound > **res'o•nant** [-nənt] *adjective* > **res'o•nate** *verb intransitive, verb transitive* **-nat•ed, -nat•ing**

re•sort [ri-ZORT] *verb intransitive* 1 have recourse 2 frequent ▷ *noun* 3 place for vacations 4 recourse 5 frequented place 6 haunt

re•sound [ri-ZOWND] *verb intransitive* echo, ring, go on sounding > **re•sound'ing** *adjective* 1 echoing 2 thorough

re•source [ri-ZORS, ri-SORS] *noun* 1 capability, ingenuity 2 that to which one resorts for support 3 expedient > **re•sourc•es** 1 source of economic wealth 2 supply that can be drawn on 3 means of support, funds > **re•source'ful** [-fəl] *adjective*

re•spect [ri-SPEKT] *noun* 1 deference, esteem 2 point or aspect 3 reference, relation ▷ *verb transitive* 4 treat with esteem 5 show consideration for > **re•spect•a•bil'i•ty** *noun* > **re•spect'a•ble** *adjective* 1 worthy of respect, decent 2 fairly good > **re•spect'ful** *adjective* > **re•spect'ing** *preposition* concerning > **re•spect'ive** *adjective* 1 relating separately to each of those in question 2 several, separate

res•pi•ra•tion [res-pə-RAY-shən] *noun* breathing > **res'pi•ra•tor** *noun* apparatus worn over mouth and breathed through as protection against dust, poison gas, etc. or to provide artificial respiration > **res'pi•ra•to•ry** [-rə-tor-ee] *adjective*

res•pite [RES-pit] *noun* 1 pause 2 interval 3 suspension of labor 4 delay 5 reprieve

re•splend•ent [ri-SPLEN-dənt] *adjective* 1 brilliant, splendid 2 shining > **re•splend'en•cy** [-ən-see] *noun*

re•spond [ri-SPOND] *verb intransitive* 1 answer 2 act in answer to stimulus 3 react > **re•spond'ent** *adjective* 1 replying ▷ *noun* 2 one who answers 3 defendant > **re•sponse'** *noun* answer > **re•spon'sive** *adjective* readily reacting to some influence

re•spon•si•ble [ri-SPON-sə-bəl] *adjective* 1 liable to answer for 2 accountable 3 dependable 4 involving responsibility 5 of good credit or

---

THESAURUS

resolute *adjective* DETERMINED, dogged, firm, fixed, immovable, inflexible, set, steadfast, strong-willed, tenacious, unshakable, unwavering

resolution *noun* 1 DETERMINATION, doggedness, firmness, perseverance, purpose, resoluteness, resolve, steadfastness, tenacity, willpower
2 DECISION, aim, declaration, determination, intent, intention, purpose, resolve

resolve *verb* 1 DECIDE, agree, conclude, determine, fix, intend, purpose
2 BREAK DOWN, analyze, reduce, separate
3 WORK OUT, answer, clear up, crack, fathom
▷ *noun* 4 DETERMINATION, firmness, resoluteness, resolution, steadfastness, willpower
5 DECISION, intention, objective, purpose, resolution

resonant *adjective* ECHOING, booming, resounding, reverberating, ringing, sonorous

resort *verb* 1 ▷ **resort to** USE, employ, fall back on, have recourse to, turn to, utilize
▷ *noun* 2 HOLIDAY CENTER, haunt, retreat, spot, tourist center
3 RECOURSE, reference

resound *verb* ECHO, re-echo, resonate, reverberate, ring

resounding *adjective* ECHOING, booming, full, powerful, resonant, reverberating, ringing, sonorous

resource *noun* 1 INGENUITY, ability, capability, cleverness, initiative, inventiveness
2 MEANS, course, device, expedient, resort

resourceful *adjective* INGENIOUS, able, bright, capable, clever, creative, inventive

resources *plural noun* RESERVES, assets, capital, funds, holdings, money, riches, supplies, wealth

respect *noun* 1 REGARD, admiration, consideration, deference, esteem, estimation, honor, recognition
2 POINT, aspect, characteristic, detail, feature, matter, particular, sense, way
3 RELATION, bearing, connection, reference, regard
▷ *verb* 4 THINK HIGHLY OF, admire, defer to, esteem, have a good opinion of *or* have a high opinion of, honor, look up to, value
5 SHOW CONSIDERATION FOR, abide by, adhere to, comply with, follow, heed, honor, obey, observe

respectable *adjective* 1 HONORABLE, decent, estimable, good, honest, reputable, upright, worthy
2 REASONABLE, ample, appreciable, considerable, decent, fair, sizable *or* sizeable, substantial

respectful *adjective* POLITE, civil, courteous, deferential, mannerly, reverent, well-mannered

respective *adjective* SPECIFIC, individual, own, particular, relevant

respite *noun* PAUSE, break, cessation, halt, interval, lull, recess, relief, rest

resplendent *adjective* BRILLIANT, bright, dazzling, glorious, radiant, shining, splendid

respond *verb* ANSWER, counter, react, reciprocate, rejoin, reply, retort, return

response *noun* ANSWER, counterattack, feedback, reaction, rejoinder, reply, retort, return

responsibility *noun* 1 AUTHORITY, importance, power
2 FAULT, blame, culpability, guilt
3 DUTY, care, charge, liability, obligation, onus
4 LEVEL-HEADEDNESS, conscientiousness, dependability, rationality, sensibleness, trustworthiness

responsible *adjective* 1 IN CHARGE, in authority, in control
2 TO BLAME, at fault, culpable, guilty
3 ACCOUNTABLE, answerable, liable
4 SENSIBLE, dependable, level-headed, rational,

position > **re•spon•si•bil'i•ty** *noun* 1 state of being answerable 2 duty 3 charge 4 obligation

rest[1] *noun* 1 repose 2 freedom from exertion, etc. 3 that on which anything rests or leans 4 pause, esp. in music 5 support ▷ *verb intransitive* 6 take rest 7 be supported ▷ *verb transitive* 8 give rest to 9 place on support > **rest'ful** [-fəl] *adjective* > **rest'less** [-lis] *adjective* 1 offering no rest 2 uneasy, impatient > **rest home** residential establishment providing care for aged, convalescent, etc.

rest[2] *noun* 1 remainder 2 others ▷ *verb intransitive* 3 remain 4 continue to be

res•tau•rant [RES-tər-ənt] *noun* commercial establishment serving food > **res•tau•ra•teur'** [-ə-TUR] *noun* keeper of one

res•ti•tu•tion [res-ti-TOO-shən] *noun* 1 giving back or making up 2 reparation, compensation

res•tive [RES-tiv] *adjective* 1 restless 2 resisting control, impatient

re•store [ri-STOR] *verb transitive* **-stored, -stor•ing** 1 build up again, repair, renew 2 reestablish 3 give back > **res•to•ra'tion** *noun* > **re•stor'a•tive** *adjective* 1 restoring ▷ *noun* 2 medicine to strengthen, etc. > **re•stor'er** *noun*

re•strain [ri-STRAYN] *verb transitive* 1 check, hold back 2 prevent 3 confine > **re•straint'** *noun* restraining, control, esp. self-control > **restraining order** order issued by a civil court to a potential abuser to keep away from another specified person

re•strict [ri-STRIKT] *verb transitive* limit, bound > **re•stric'tion** *noun* 1 limitation 2 restraint 3 rule > **re•stric'tive** *adjective* > **re•stric'ted** *adjective* denying residence, membership to persons of certain races, ethnic groups, etc.

re•sult [ri-ZULT] *verb intransitive* 1 follow as consequence 2 happen 3 end ▷ *noun* 4 effect, outcome > **re•sult'ant** [-ZUL-tnt] *adjective* arising as result

re•sume [ri-ZOOM] *verb transitive* **-sumed, -sum•ing** begin again > **ré•su•mé** [REZ-uu-may] *noun* 1 summary, abstract 2 brief statement of one's qualifications for employment, public office, etc. > **re•sump'tion** [-shən] *noun* 1 resuming 2 fresh start

re•sur•gence [ri-SUR-jəns] *noun* rising again > **re•sur'gent** *adjective*

res•ur•rect [rez-ə-REKT] *verb transitive* 1 restore to life, resuscitate 2 use once more (something discarded, etc.) > **res•ur•rec'tion** *noun* 1 rising again (esp. from dead) 2 revival

re•sus•ci•tate [ri-SUS-i-tayt] *verb transitive*

DICTIONARY **r** THESAURUS

---

reliable, trustworthy

responsive *adjective* SENSITIVE, alive, impressionable, open, reactive, receptive, susceptible

rest[1] *noun* 1 REPOSE, calm, inactivity, leisure, relaxation, relief, stillness, tranquillity
2 PAUSE, break, cessation, halt, interlude, intermission, interval, lull, respite, stop
3 SUPPORT, base, holder, prop, stand
▷ *verb* 4 RELAX, be at ease, de-stress, put one's feet up, sit down, take it easy
5 BE SUPPORTED, lean, lie, prop, recline, repose, sit

rest[2] *noun* REMAINDER, balance, excess, others, remains, remnants, residue, surplus

restaurant *noun* BISTRO, café, cafeteria, diner, eatery, tearoom

restful *adjective* RELAXING, calm, calming, peaceful, quiet, relaxed, serene, soothing, tranquil

restitution *noun* COMPENSATION, amends, recompense, reparation, requital

restive *adjective* RESTLESS, edgy, fidgety, impatient, jumpy, nervous, on edge, wired (*slang*)

restless *adjective* 1 MOVING, nomadic, roving, transient, unsettled, unstable, wandering
2 UNSETTLED, antsy (*slang*), edgy, fidgeting, fidgety, jumpy, nervous, on edge, restive, wired (*slang*)

restlessness *noun* 1 MOVEMENT, activity, bustle, unrest, unsettledness
2 RESTIVENESS, edginess, jitters (*informal*), jumpiness, nervousness

restoration *noun* 1 REPAIR, reconstruction, renewal, renovation, revitalization, revival
2 REINSTATEMENT, re-establishment, replacement, restitution, return

restore *verb* 1 REPAIR, fix, mend, rebuild, recondition, reconstruct, refurbish, renew, renovate
2 REVIVE, build up, refresh, revitalize, strengthen
3 RETURN, bring back, give back, hand back, recover, reinstate, replace, send back
4 REINSTATE, reintroduce

restrain *verb* HOLD BACK, check, constrain, contain, control, curb, curtail, hamper, hinder, inhibit, restrict

restrained *adjective* CONTROLLED, calm, mild, moderate, self-controlled, undemonstrative

restraint *noun* 1 SELF-CONTROL, control, inhibition, moderation, self-discipline, self-possession, self-restraint
2 LIMITATION, ban, check, curb, embargo, interdict, limit, rein

restrict *verb* LIMIT, bound, confine, contain, hamper, handicap, inhibit, regulate, restrain

restriction *noun* LIMITATION, confinement, control, curb, handicap, inhibition, regulation, restraint, rule

result *noun* 1 CONSEQUENCE, effect, end, end result, outcome, product, sequel, upshot
▷ *verb* 2 HAPPEN, appear, arise, derive, develop, ensue, follow, issue, spring
3 ▷ **result in** END IN, culminate in, finish with

resume *verb* BEGIN AGAIN, carry on, continue, go on, proceed, reopen, restart

résumé *noun* SUMMARY, précis, recapitulation, rundown, synopsis

resumption *noun* CONTINUATION, carrying on, re-establishment, renewal, reopening, restart, resurgence

resurgence *noun* REVIVAL, rebirth, re-emergence, renaissance, resumption, resurrection, return

resurrect *verb* REVIVE, bring back, reintroduce, renew

resurrection *noun* REVIVAL, reappearance, rebirth, renaissance, renewal, restoration, resurgence, return

resuscitate *verb* REVIVE, bring round, resurrect,

-tat•ed, -tat•ing revive to life, consciousness
re•tail [REE-tayl] *noun* 1 sale in small quantities ▷ *adverb* 2 at retail ▷ *verb* 3 sell, be sold, retail 4 recount
re•tain [ri-TAYN] *verb transitive* 1 keep 2 engage services of > **re•tain'er** *noun* fee to retain professional adviser, esp. lawyer > **re•ten'tion** [-shən] *noun* > **re•ten'tive** *adjective* capable of retaining, remembering
re•tal•i•ate [ri-TAL-ee-ayt] *verb* **-at•ed, at•ing** 1 repay in kind 2 revenge > **re•tal•i•a'tion** *noun* > **re•tal'i•a•to•ry** *adjective*
re•tard [ri-TAHRD] *verb transitive* 1 make slow or late 2 keep back 3 impede development of > **re•tard'ed** *adjective* underdeveloped, esp. mentally > **re•tar•da'tion** *noun*
retch [rech] *verb intransitive* try to vomit
ret•i•cent [RET-ə-sənt] *adjective* 1 reserved in speech 2 uncommunicative > **ret'i•cence** *noun*
ret•i•na [RET-n-ə] *noun, plural* **-nas** light-sensitive membrane at back of eye > **ret'i•nal** *adjective* > **ret•i•ni'tis** [-NĪ-tis] *noun* inflammation of retina
ret•i•nue [RET-n-yoo] *noun* band of followers or attendants
re•tire [ri-TĪR] *verb intransitive* **-tired, -tir•ing** 1 give up office or work 2 go away 3 withdraw 4 go to bed ▷ *verb transitive* **-tired, -tir•ing** 5 cause to retire > **retired** *adjective* that has retired from office, etc. > **re•tire'ment** [-mənt] *noun* > **re•tir'ing** *adjective* unobtrusive, shy
re•tort [ri-TORT] *verb transitive* 1 reply 2 repay in kind, retaliate 3 hurl back (charge, etc.) ▷ *verb intransitive* 4 reply with countercharge ▷ *noun* 5 vigorous reply or repartee 6 vessel with bent neck used for distilling
re•touch [ree-TUCH] *verb transitive* touch up, improve by new touches, esp. of paint, etc.
re•trace [ri-TRAYS] *verb transitive* **-traced, -trac•ing** go back over (a route, etc.) again
re•tract [ri-TRAKT] *verb* draw back, recant > **re•tract'a•ble** *adjective* > **re•trac'tion** *noun* drawing or taking back, esp. of statement, etc. > **re•trac'tor** *noun* 1 muscle 2 surgical instrument
re•tread [ree-TRED] *verb transitive* 1 restore tread to worn rubber tire ▷ *noun* [REE-tred] 2 retreaded tire 3 (*slang*) person returned to work after dismissal 4 person training for new type of work 5 (*informal*) reworked old idea, etc.
re•treat [ri-TREET] *verb intransitive* 1 move back from any position 2 retire ▷ *noun* 3 act of, or military signal for, retiring, withdrawal 4 place to which anyone retires esp. for meditation 5 refuge 6 sunset call on bugle
re•trench [ri-TRENCH] *verb transitive* 1 reduce expenditure, esp. by dismissing staff 2 cut down
ret•ri•bu•tion [re-trə-BYOO-shən] *noun* 1 recompense, esp. for evil deeds 2 vengeance
re•trieve [ri-TREEV] *verb transitive* **-trieved, -triev•ing** 1 fetch back again 2 restore 3 rescue from ruin 4 recover, esp. information from computer 5 regain > **re•triev'al** *noun* > **re•triev'er** *noun* dog trained to retrieve game
ret•ro•ac•tive [re-troh-AK-tiv] *adjective* applying or referring to the past
ret•ro•grade [RE-trə-grayd] *adjective* 1 going backward, reverting 2 reactionary > **ret•ro•gres'sion** [-GRE-shən] *noun* > **ret•ro•gres'sive** *adjective*
ret•ro•spect [RE-trə-spekt] *noun* looking back,

DICTIONARY • THESAURUS

revitalize, save
retain *verb* 1 KEEP, hold, hold back, maintain, preserve, reserve, save
2 HIRE, commission, employ, engage, pay, reserve
retainer *noun* 1 FEE, advance, deposit
2 SERVANT, attendant, domestic
retaliate *verb* PAY (SOMEONE) BACK, get even with (*informal*), hit back, reciprocate, strike back, take revenge
retaliation *noun* REVENGE, an eye for an eye, counterblow, reciprocation, repayment, reprisal, requital, vengeance
retard *verb* SLOW DOWN, arrest, check, delay, handicap, hinder, hold back *or* hold up, impede, set back
retch *verb* GAG, barf (*slang*), heave, puke (*slang*), regurgitate, spew, throw up (*informal*), vomit
reticence *noun* SILENCE, quietness, reserve, taciturnity
reticent *adjective* UNCOMMUNICATIVE, close-lipped, quiet, reserved, silent, taciturn, tight-lipped, unforthcoming
retinue *noun* ATTENDANTS, aides, entourage, escort, followers, servants
retire *verb* 1 STOP WORKING, give up work
2 WITHDRAW, depart, exit, go away, leave
3 GO TO BED, hit the hay (*slang*), hit the sack (*slang*), turn in (*informal*)
retirement *noun* WITHDRAWAL, privacy, retreat, seclusion, solitude
retiring *adjective* SHY, bashful, quiet, reserved, self-effacing, timid, unassertive, unassuming
retort *verb* 1 REPLY, answer, come back with, counter, respond, return, riposte
▷ *noun* 2 REPLY, answer, comeback (*informal*), rejoinder, response, riposte
retract *verb* 1 WITHDRAW, deny, disavow, disclaim, eat one's words, recant, renege, renounce, revoke, take back
2 DRAW IN, pull back, pull in, sheathe
retreat *verb* 1 WITHDRAW, back away, back off, depart, draw back, fall back, go back, leave, pull back
▷ *noun* 2 WITHDRAWAL, departure, evacuation, flight, retirement
3 REFUGE, haven, hideaway, sanctuary, seclusion, shelter
retrench *verb* CUT BACK, economize, make economies, save, tighten one's belt
retrenchment *noun* CUTBACK, cost-cutting, cut, economy, tightening one's belt
retribution *noun* PUNISHMENT, justice, Nemesis, reckoning, reprisal, retaliation, revenge, vengeance
retrieve *verb* GET BACK, recapture, recoup, recover, redeem, regain, restore, save, win back
retrograde *adjective* DECLINING, backward, degenerative, deteriorating, downward, regressive, retrogressive, worsening
retrogress *verb* DECLINE, backslide, deteriorate, go back, go downhill (*informal*), regress, relapse, worsen
retrospect *noun* HINDSIGHT, re-examination,

survey of past > **ret•ro•spec'tion** [-SPEK-shən] *noun* > **ret•ro•spec'tive** *adjective*
re•trous•sé [ri-troo-SAY] *adjective* of nose, turned upward
re•turn [ri-TURN] *verb intransitive* 1 go, come back ▷ *verb transitive* 2 give, send back 3 report officially 4 elect ▷ *noun* 5 returning, being returned 6 profit 7 official report esp. tax return
re•un•ion [ree-YOON-yən] *noun* gathering of people who have been apart > **re•u•nite'** *verb* bring or come together again after a separation
Rev. Revelations
rev *noun* (*informal*) 1 revolution (of engine) ▷ *verb* **revved, rev•ving** 2 (oft. with *up*) increase speed of revolution (of engine)
re•val•ue [ree-VAL-yoo] *verb* **-ued, -u•ing** adjust exchange value of currency upward
re•vamp [ree-VAMP] *verb transitive* renovate, restore
re•veal [ri-VEEL] *verb transitive* 1 make known 2 show > **rev•e•la'tion** *noun*
rev•eil•le [REV-ə-lee] *noun* morning bugle call, etc. to waken soldiers
rev•el [REV-əl] *verb intransitive* **-eled, -el•ing** 1 take pleasure (in) 2 make merry ▷ *noun* 3 (*usually plural*) merrymaking > **rev'el•ry** *noun* festivity
re•venge [ri-VENJ] *noun* 1 retaliation for wrong done 2 act that satisfies this 3 desire for this ▷ *verb transitive* **-venged, -veng•ing** 4 avenge 5 make retaliation for ▷ *verb reflexive* **-venged, -veng•ing** 6 avenge oneself > **re•venge'ful** [-fəl] *adjective* 1 vindictive 2 resentful
rev•e•nue [REV-ən-yoo] *noun* income, esp. of nation, as taxes, etc.
re•ver•ber•ate [ri-VUR-bə-rayt] *verb* **-at•ed, -at•ing** echo, resound, throw back (sound, etc.)
re•vere [ri-VEER] *verb transitive* **-vered, -ver•ing** hold in great regard or religious respect > **rev'er•ence** [-əns] *noun* 1 revering 2 awe mingled with respect and esteem 3 veneration > **rev'er•end** [-ənd] *adjective* (esp. as prefix to clergyman's name) worthy of reverence > **rev'er•ent** [-ənt] *adjective* showing reverence > **rev•er•en'tial** *adjective* marked by reverence
rev•er•ie [REV-ə-ree] *noun* daydream, absent-minded state
re•verse [ri-VURS] *verb* **-versed, -vers•ing** 1 (of vehicle) (cause to) move backward ▷ *verb transitive* 2 turn upside down or other way round 3 change completely ▷ *noun* 4 opposite, contrary 5 side opposite, obverse 6 defeat 7 reverse gear ▷ *adjective* 8 opposite, contrary > **re•ver'sal** [-səl] *noun* > **re•vers'i•ble** *adjective* > **reverse gear** mechanism enabling vehicle to move backward
re•vert [ri-VURT] *verb intransitive* 1 return to former state 2 come back to subject 3 refer to a second time 4 turn backward > **re•ver'sion** [-VUR-zhən] *noun* (of property) rightful passing to owner or designated heir, etc.
re•vet•ment [ri-VET-mənt] *noun* facing of stone, sandbags, etc. for wall
re•view [ri-VYOO] *verb transitive* 1 examine 2 look back on 3 reconsider 4 hold, make, write review of ▷ *noun* 5 general survey 6 critical notice of book, etc. 7 periodical with critical

review
return *verb* 1 COME BACK, go back, reappear, rebound, recur, retreat, revert, turn back
2 PUT BACK, re-establish, reinstate, replace, restore
3 GIVE BACK, pay back, recompense, refund, reimburse, repay
4 REPLY, answer, respond, retort
5 ELECT, choose, vote in
▷ *noun* 6 RESTORATION, re-establishment, reinstatement
7 REAPPEARANCE, recurrence
8 RETREAT, rebound, recoil
9 PROFIT, gain, income, interest, proceeds, revenue, takings, yield
10 REPORT, account, form, list, statement, summary
11 REPLY, answer, comeback (*informal*), rejoinder, response, retort
revamp *verb* RENOVATE, do up (*informal*), overhaul, recondition, refurbish, restore
reveal *verb* 1 MAKE KNOWN, announce, disclose, divulge, give away, impart, let out, let slip, make public, proclaim, tell
2 SHOW, display, exhibit, manifest, uncover, unearth, unmask, unveil
revel *verb* 1 CELEBRATE, carouse, live it up (*informal*), make merry
2 ▷ **revel in** ENJOY, delight in, indulge in, lap up, luxuriate in, relish, take pleasure in, thrive on
▷ *noun* 3 (*often plural*) MERRYMAKING, carousal, celebration, festivity, party, spree
revelation *noun* DISCLOSURE, exhibition, exposé, exposure, news, proclamation, publication, uncovering, unearthing, unveiling
reveller *noun* CAROUSER, merrymaker, partygoer
revelry *noun* FESTIVITY, carousal, celebration, fun, jollity, merrymaking, party, spree
revenge *noun* 1 RETALIATION, an eye for an eye, reprisal, retribution, vengeance
▷ *verb* 2 AVENGE, get even, hit back, repay, retaliate, take revenge for
revenue *noun* INCOME, gain, proceeds, profits, receipts, returns, takings, yield
reverberate *verb* ECHO, re-echo, resound, ring, vibrate
revere *verb* BE IN AWE OF, exalt, honor, look up to, respect, reverence, venerate, worship
reverence *noun* AWE, admiration, high esteem, honor, respect, veneration, worship
reverent *adjective* RESPECTFUL, awed, deferential, humble, reverential
reverie *noun* DAYDREAM, abstraction, brown study, woolgathering
reverse *verb* 1 TURN ROUND, invert, transpose, turn back, turn over, turn upside down, upend
2 CHANGE, annul, cancel, countermand, invalidate, overrule, overthrow, overturn, quash, repeal, rescind, revoke, undo
3 GO BACKWARDS, back, back up, move backwards, retreat
▷ *noun* 4 OPPOSITE, contrary, converse, inverse
5 BACK, other side, rear, underside, wrong side
6 MISFORTUNE, adversity, affliction, blow, disappointment, failure, hardship, misadventure, mishap, reversal, setback
▷ *adjective* 7 OPPOSITE, contrary, converse

articles 8 inspection of troops 9 revue
> **re•view'er** *noun* writer of reviews
re•vile [ri-VĪL] *verb transitive* **-viled, -vil•ing** be viciously scornful of, abuse
re•vise [ri-VĪZ] *verb transitive* **-vised, -vis•ing** 1 look over and correct 2 change, alter > **re•vi'sion** [-zhən] *noun* 1 reexamination for purpose of correcting 2 act of revising 3 revised copy
> **re•vi'sion•ism** *noun* departure from generally accepted theory, interpretation > **re•vi'sion•ist** *adjective, noun*
re•vive [ri-VĪV] *verb* **-vived, -viv•ing** bring, come back to life, vigor, use, etc. > **re•viv'al** [-vəl] *noun* reviving, esp. of religious fervor
> **re•viv'al•ist** *noun* organizer of religious revival
re•voke [ri-VOHK] *verb transitive* **-voked, -vok•ing** 1 take back, withdraw 2 cancel
> **rev'o•ca•ble** [-ə-kə-bəl] *adjective* > **rev•o•ca'tion** *noun* repeal
re•volt [ri-VOHLT] *noun* 1 rebellion ▷ *verb intransitive* 2 rise in rebellion 3 feel disgust ▷ *verb transitive* 4 affect with disgust > **re•volt'ing** *adjective* disgusting, horrible
re•volve [ri-VOLV] *verb intransitive* **-volved, -volv•ing** 1 turn around, rotate 2 be centered on ▷ *verb transitive* **-volved, -volv•ing** 3 rotate
> **rev•o•lu'tion** *noun* 1 violent overthrow of government 2 great change 3 complete rotation, turning or spinning around
> **rev•o•lu'tion•ar•y** *adjective, noun*
> **rev•o•lu'tion•ize** *verb transitive* **-ized, -iz•ing** 1 change considerably 2 bring about revolution in
re•volv•er [ri-VOL-vər] *noun* repeating pistol with revolving cylinder
re•vue, re•view [ri-VYOO] *noun* theatrical entertainment with topical sketches and songs
re•vul•sion [ri-VUL-shən] *noun* 1 sudden violent change of feeling 2 marked repugnance or abhorrence
re•ward [ri-WORD] *verb transitive* pay, make return for service, conduct, etc. ▷ *noun*
> **re•ward'ing** *adjective* giving personal satisfaction, worthwhile
re•wind' *verb* run (tape or film) back to an earlier point in order to replay
Rf *chem.* rutherfordium
Rh *chem.* rhodium
rhap•so•dy [RAP-sə-dee] *noun, plural* **-dies** enthusiastic or high-flown (musical) composition or utterance > **rhap•sod'ic** *adjective*
> **rhap'so•dize** [-sə-dīz] *verb* **-dized, -diz•ing**
rhe•o•stat [REE-ə-stat] *noun* instrument for regulating the value of the resistance in an electric circuit
rhe•sus [REE-səs] *noun* small, long-tailed monkey of S Asia > **rhesus factor, Rh factor** feature distinguishing different types of human blood
rhet•o•ric [RET-ər-ik] *noun* 1 art of effective speaking or writing 2 artificial or exaggerated language > **rhe•tor•i•cal** [ri-TOR-i-kəl] *adjective*

revert *verb* RETURN, come back, go back, resume
review *noun* 1 CRITIQUE, commentary, criticism, evaluation, judgment, notice
2 MAGAZINE, journal, periodical
3 SURVEY, analysis, examination, scrutiny, study
4 (*military*) INSPECTION, march past, parade
▷ *verb* 5 ASSESS, criticize, evaluate, judge, study
6 RECONSIDER, reassess, re-evaluate, re-examine, rethink, revise, think over
7 LOOK BACK ON, recall, recollect, reflect on, remember
8 INSPECT, examine
9 STUDY, cram (*informal*), revise (*chiefly Brit*)
reviewer *noun* CRITIC, commentator, judge
revile *verb* MALIGN, abuse, bad-mouth (*slang*), denigrate, knock (*informal*), reproach, run down, vilify
revise *verb* CHANGE, alter, amend, correct, edit, emend, redo, review, rework, update
revision *noun* CHANGE, amendment, correction, emendation, updating
revival *noun* RENEWAL, reawakening, rebirth, renaissance, resurgence, resurrection, revitalization
revive *verb* REVITALIZE, awaken, bring round, come round, invigorate, reanimate, recover, refresh, rekindle, renew, restore
revoke *verb* CANCEL, annul, countermand, disclaim, invalidate, negate, nullify, obviate, quash, repeal, rescind, retract, reverse, set aside, withdraw
revolt *noun* 1 UPRISING, insurgency, insurrection, mutiny, rebellion, revolution, rising
▷ *verb* 2 REBEL, mutiny, resist, rise
3 DISGUST, gross out (*slang*), make one's flesh creep, nauseate, repel, repulse, sicken, turn one's stomach
revolting *adjective* DISGUSTING, foul, horrible, horrid, nauseating, repellent, repugnant, repulsive, scuzzy (*slang*), sickening, yucky *or* yukky (*slang*)
revolution *noun* 1 REVOLT, coup, insurgency, mutiny, rebellion, rising, uprising
2 TRANSFORMATION, innovation, reformation, sea change, shift, upheaval
3 ROTATION, circle, circuit, cycle, lap, orbit, spin, turn
revolutionary *adjective* 1 REBEL, extremist, insurgent, radical, subversive
2 NEW, different, drastic, ground-breaking, innovative, novel, progressive, radical
▷ *noun* 3 REBEL, insurgent, revolutionist
revolutionize *verb* TRANSFORM, modernize, reform
revolve *verb* ROTATE, circle, go round, orbit, spin, turn, twist, wheel, whirl
revulsion *noun* DISGUST, abhorrence, detestation, loathing, repugnance, repulsion
reward *noun* 1 PAYMENT, bonus, bounty, premium, prize, recompense, repayment, return, wages
2 PUNISHMENT, just deserts, retribution
▷ *verb* 3 PAY, compensate, recompense, remunerate, repay
rewarding *adjective* WORTHWHILE, beneficial, enriching, fruitful, fulfilling, productive, profitable, satisfying, valuable
rhapsodize *verb* ENTHUSE, go into ecstasies, gush, rave (*informal*)
rhetoric *noun* 1 ORATORY, eloquence
2 HYPERBOLE, bombast, grandiloquence, magniloquence, verbosity, wordiness

(of question) not requiring an answer
> **rhet•o•ri'cian** [-RISH-ən] *noun*

rheu•ma•tism [ROO-mə-tiz-əm] *noun* painful inflammation of joints or muscles
> **rheu•mat•ic** [ruu-MAT-ik] *adjective, noun*
> **rheu•ma•toid** [ROO-mə-toid] *adjective* of, like rheumatism

Rh factor *see* **rhesus**

rhi•no•cer•os [rī-NOS-ər-əs] *noun, plural* **-os•es** large thick-skinned animal with one or two horns on nose

rho•di•um [ROH-dee-əm] *noun* hard metal like platinum

rhom•bus [ROM-bəs] *noun, plural* **-bus•es** *or* **-bi** [-bī] equilateral but not right-angled parallelogram, diamond-shaped figure

rhu•barb [ROO-bahrb] *noun* 1 garden plant of which the fleshy stalks are cooked and used as fruit 2 laxative from root of allied Chinese plant 3 (*slang*) argument, fight

rhyme [rīm] *noun* 1 identity of sounds at ends of lines of verse, or in words 2 word or syllable identical in sound to another 3 verse marked by rhyme ▷ *verb transitive* **rhymed, rhym•ing** 4 make rhymes

rhythm [RITH-əm] *noun* measured beat or flow, esp. of words, music, etc. > **rhyth'mic** *adjective* > **rhyth'mi•cal•ly** *adverb*

rib[1] *noun* 1 one of curved bones springing from spine and forming framework of upper part of body 2 cut of meat including rib(s) 3 curved timber of framework of boat 4 raised series of rows in knitting, etc. ▷ *verb transitive* **ribbed, rib•bing** 5 furnish, mark with ribs 6 knit to form a rib pattern > **rib'bing** *noun*

rib[2] *verb transitive* **ribbed, rib•bing** (*informal*) tease, ridicule > **rib'bing** *noun*

rib•ald [RIB-əld] *adjective* 1 irreverent, scurrilous 2 indecent ▷ *noun* 3 ribald person > **rib'ald•ry** *noun* vulgar, indecent talk

rib•bon [RIB-ən] *noun* 1 narrow band of fabric used for trimming, tying, etc. 2 long strip or line of anything > **ribbon development** building of houses, etc. along main road leading out of town, etc.

ri•bo•fla•vin [RĪ-boh-flay-vin] *noun* form of vitamin B

rice [rīs] *noun* 1 cereal plant 2 its seeds as food > **rice paper** fine (edible) Chinese paper

rich *adjective* **-er, -est** 1 wealthy 2 fertile 3 abounding 4 valuable 5 (of food) containing much fat or sugar 6 mellow 7 amusing ▷ *noun* 8 the wealthy classes > **rich•es** [RICH-iz] *plural noun* wealth > **rich'ly** *adverb*

rick•ets [RIK-its] *noun* disease of children marked by softening of bones, bow legs, etc., caused by vitamin D deficiency > **rick'et•y** *adjective* **-et•i•er, -et•i•est** 1 shaky, insecure, unstable 2 suffering from rickets

rick•shaw [RIK-shaw] *noun* light two-wheeled man-drawn Asian vehicle

ric•o•chet [rik-ə-SHAY] *verb intransitive* **-cheted** [-SHAYD], **-chet•ing** [-SHAY-ing] 1 (of bullet) rebound or be deflected by solid surface or water ▷ *noun* 2 bullet or shot to which this happens

rid *verb transitive* **rid** *or* **rid•ded, rid•ding** 1 clear, relieve of 2 free 3 deliver > **rid•dance** [RID-ns] *noun* 1 clearance 2 act of ridding 3 deliverance 4 relief

rid•den [RID-n] 1 *pp of* **ride.** ▷ *adjective* 2 afflicted or affected by the thing specified: *disease-ridden*

rid•dle[1] [RID-l] *noun* 1 question made puzzling to test one's ingenuity 2 enigma 3 puzzling thing, person ▷ *verb intransitive* **-dled, -dling** 4 speak in, make riddles

rid•dle[2] *verb transitive* **-dled, -dling** pierce with many holes **riddled with** full of, esp. holes

ride [rīd] *verb* **rode, rid•den, rid•ing** 1 sit on and control or propel (horse, bicycle, etc.) 2 be carried on or across ▷ *verb intransitive* 3 go on horseback or in vehicle 4 lie at anchor ▷ *verb transitive* 5 travel over ▷ *noun* 6 journey on horse, etc., or in any vehicle > **rid'er** *noun* 1 one who rides 2 supplementary clause 3 addition to a document

ridge [rij] *noun* 1 long narrow hill 2 long, narrow elevation on surface 3 line of meeting of two sloping surfaces ▷ *verb transitive* **ridged, ridg•ing** 4 form into ridges

DICTIONARY

r

THESAURUS

---

rhetorical *adjective* ORATORICAL, bombastic, declamatory, grandiloquent, high-flown, magniloquent, verbose

rhyme *noun* 1 POETRY, ode, poem, song, verse ▷ *verb* 2 SOUND LIKE, harmonize

rhythm *noun* BEAT, accent, cadence, lilt, meter, pulse, swing, tempo, time

rhythmic *or* **rhythmical** *adjective* CADENCED, lilting, metrical, musical, periodic, pulsating, throbbing

ribald *adjective* RUDE, bawdy, blue, broad, coarse, earthy, naughty, obscene, racy, smutty, vulgar

rich *adjective* 1 WEALTHY, affluent, loaded (*slang*), moneyed, prosperous, well-heeled (*informal*), well-off, well-to-do
2 WELL-STOCKED, full, productive, well-supplied
3 ABUNDANT, abounding, ample, copious, fertile, fruitful, lush, luxurious, plentiful, productive, prolific
4 FULL-BODIED, creamy, fatty, luscious, succulent, sweet, tasty

riches *plural noun* WEALTH, affluence, assets, fortune, plenty, resources, substance, treasure

richly *adverb* 1 ELABORATELY, elegantly, expensively, exquisitely, gorgeously, lavishly, luxuriously, opulently, splendidly, sumptuously
2 FULLY, amply, appropriately, properly, suitably, thoroughly, well

rickety *adjective* SHAKY, insecure, precarious, ramshackle, tottering, unsound, unsteady, wobbly

rid *verb* 1 FREE, clear, deliver, disburden, disencumber, make free, purge, relieve, unburden
2 ▷ **get rid of** DISPOSE OF, dump, eject, eliminate, expel, remove, throw away *or* throw out

riddle[1] *noun* PUZZLE, conundrum, enigma, mystery, poser, problem

riddled *adjective* FILLED, damaged, infested, permeated, pervaded, spoilt

ride *verb* 1 CONTROL, handle, manage
2 TRAVEL, be carried, go, move
▷ *noun* 3 TRIP, drive, jaunt, journey, lift, outing

ri•dic•u•lous [ri-DIK-yə-ləs] *adjective* deserving to be laughed at, absurd, foolish > **rid•i•cule** [RID-i-kyool] *noun* 1 treatment of person or thing as ridiculous ▷ *verb transitive* **-culed, -cul•ing** 2 laugh at, deride

rife [rīf] *adjective* prevalent, common

rif•fle [RIF-əl] *verb* **-fled, -fling** flick through (pages, etc.) quickly

riff'raff *noun* rabble, disreputable people

ri•fle [RĪ-fəl] *verb transitive* **-fled, -fling** 1 search and rob 2 ransack 3 make spiral grooves in (gun barrel, etc.) ▷ *noun* 4 firearm with long barrel > **rifling** *noun* 1 arrangement of grooves in gun barrel 2 pillaging

rift *noun* crack, split, cleft

rig *verb transitive* **rigged, rig•ging** 1 provide (ship) with spars, ropes, etc. 2 equip 3 set up, esp. as makeshift 4 arrange in dishonest way ▷ *noun* 5 way ship's masts and sails are arranged 6 apparatus for drilling for oil and gas 7 tractor-trailer truck 8 style of dress > **rigging** *noun* 1 ship's spars and ropes 2 lifting tackle

right [rīt] *adjective* 1 just 2 in accordance with truth and duty 3 true 4 correct 5 proper 6 of side that faces east when front is turned to north 7 *politics* (*also* **right wing**) conservative or reactionary 8 straight 9 upright 10 of outer or more finished side of fabric ▷ *verb transitive* 11 bring back to vertical position 12 do justice to ▷ *verb intransitive* 13 come back to vertical position ▷ *noun* 14 claim, title, etc. allowed or due 15 what is right, just or due 16 conservative political party 17 punch, blow with right hand ▷ *adverb* 18 straight 19 properly 20 very 21 on or to right side > **right'ful** [-fəl] *adjective* > **right'ly** *adverb* 1 right angle 2 angle of 90 degrees > **right of way** *law* 1 right to pass over someone's land 2 path used 3 right to driver to proceed

right•eous [RĪ-chəs] *adjective* 1 just, upright 2 godly 3 virtuous 4 good 5 honest

rig•id [RIJ-id] *adjective* 1 inflexible 2 harsh, stiff > **ri•gid'i•ty** *noun*

rig•ma•role [RIG-mə-rohl] *noun* 1 meaningless string of words 2 long, complicated procedure

rig•or[1] [RIG-ər] *noun* sudden coldness attended by shivering > **rigor mor'tis** stiffening of body after death

rigor[2] *noun* 1 harshness, severity, strictness 2 hardship > **rig'or•ous** *adjective* stern, harsh, severe

rile [rīl] *verb transitive* **riled, ril•ing** (*informal*) anger, annoy

rill *noun* small stream

rim *noun* 1 edge, border, margin 2 outer ring of wheel ▷ *verb transitive* **rimmed, rim•ming** 3 furnish with rim 4 coat or encrust 5 *basketball, golf* of ball, go around basket, hole, and not drop in > **rimmed** *adjective* bordered, edged > **rim'less** *adjective*

rime [rīm] *noun* hoarfrost > **rim'y** *adjective* **rim•i•er, rim•i•est**

DICTIONARY • THESAURUS

---

ridicule *noun* 1 MOCKERY, chaff, derision, gibe, jeer, laughter, raillery, scorn
▷ *verb* 2 LAUGH AT, chaff, deride, jeer, make fun of, mock, poke fun at, sneer

ridiculous *adjective* LAUGHABLE, absurd, comical, farcical, funny, ludicrous, risible, silly, stupid

rife *adjective* WIDESPREAD, common, frequent, general, prevalent, rampant, ubiquitous, universal

riffraff *noun* RABBLE, dregs of society (*slang*), hoi polloi, scum of the earth (*slang*)

rifle *verb* RANSACK, burgle, go through, loot, pillage, plunder, rob, sack, strip

rift *noun* 1 BREACH, disagreement, division, falling out (*informal*), quarrel, separation, split
2 SPLIT, break, cleft, crack, crevice, fault, fissure, flaw, gap, opening

rig *verb* 1 FIX (*informal*), arrange, engineer, gerrymander, manipulate, tamper with
2 EQUIP, fit out, furnish, outfit, supply
▷ *noun* 3 APPARATUS, equipment, fittings, fixtures, gear, tackle

right *adjective* 1 JUST, equitable, ethical, fair, good, honest, lawful, moral, proper
2 CORRECT, accurate, exact, factual, genuine, precise, true, valid
3 PROPER, appropriate, becoming, desirable, done, fit, fitting, seemly, suitable
▷ *adverb* 4 CORRECTLY, accurately, exactly, genuinely, precisely, truly
5 PROPERLY, appropriately, aptly, fittingly, suitably
6 STRAIGHT, directly, promptly, quickly, straightaway
7 EXACTLY, precisely, squarely
▷ *noun* 8 CLAIM, authority, business, due, freedom, liberty, license, permission, power, prerogative, privilege
▷ *verb* 9 RECTIFY, correct, fix, put right, redress, settle, sort out, straighten

right away *adverb* IMMEDIATELY, at once, directly, forthwith, instantly, now, pronto (*informal*), straightaway

righteous *adjective* VIRTUOUS, ethical, fair, good, honest, honorable, just, moral, pure, upright

righteousness *noun* VIRTUE, goodness, honesty, honor, integrity, justice, morality, probity, purity, rectitude, uprightness

rightful *adjective* LAWFUL, due, just, legal, legitimate, proper, real, true, valid

rigid *adjective* 1 STRICT, exact, fixed, inflexible, rigorous, set, stringent, unbending, uncompromising
2 STIFF, inflexible, unyielding

rigmarole *noun* PROCEDURE, bother, fuss, hassle (*informal*), nonsense, palaver

rigor *noun* 1 STRICTNESS, harshness, inflexibility, rigidity, sternness, stringency
2 HARDSHIP, ordeal, privation, suffering, trial

rigorous *adjective* STRICT, demanding, exacting, hard, harsh, inflexible, severe, stern, stringent, tough

rig-out *noun* OUTFIT, costume, dress, garb, gear (*informal*), get-up (*informal*), togs

rig out *verb* 1 DRESS, array, attire, clothe, costume
2 EQUIP, fit, furnish, outfit

rig up *verb* SET UP, arrange, assemble, build, construct, erect, fix up, improvise, put together, put up

rile *verb* ANGER, aggravate (*informal*), annoy, get one's back up *or* put one's back up, irk, irritate

rim *noun* EDGE, border, brim, brink, lip, margin, verge

rind [rīnd] *noun* outer coating of fruits, etc.
ring[1] *noun* 1 circle of gold, etc., esp. for finger 2 any circular band, coil, rim, etc. 3 circle of persons 4 enclosed area, esp. roped-in square for boxing ▷ *verb transitive* **ringed, ring•ing** 5 put ring round 6 mark (bird, etc.) with ring > **ring'er** *noun* 1 one who rings bells 2 (*slang*) student, athlete, racehorse, etc. participating in examination, sporting event, etc. under false pretenses or fraudulently in place of another **dead ringer** (*slang*) person, thing apparently identical to another > **ring'lead•er** [-leed-ər] *noun* instigator of mutiny, riot, etc > **ring'let** [-lit] *noun* curly lock of hair > **ring'worm** [-wurm] *noun* fungal skin disease in circular patches
ring[2] *verb intransitive* **rang, rung, ring•ing** 1 give out clear resonant sound, as bell 2 resound 3 cause (bell) to sound 4 telephone ▷ *noun* 5 a ringing 6 telephone call > **ring'tone** *noun* tune played by a cell phone when it receives a call
rink [ringk] *noun* 1 sheet of ice for skating or hockey 2 floor for roller skating
rinse [rins] *verb transitive* **rinsed, rins•ing** 1 remove soap (from washed clothes, hair, etc.) by applying clean water 2 wash lightly ▷ *noun* 3 a rinsing 4 liquid to tint hair
ri•ot [RĪ-ət] *noun* 1 tumult, disorder 2 loud revelry 3 disorderly, unrestrained disturbance 4 profusion ▷ *verb intransitive* 5 make, engage in riot > **ri'ot•ous** *adjective* unruly, rebellious, wanton
R.I.P. rest in peace
rip[1] *verb transitive* **ripped, rip•ping** 1 cut, tear away, slash, rend ▷ *noun* 2 rent, tear > **rip'cord** *noun* cord pulled to open parachute > **rip'saw** *noun* saw with coarse teeth (used for cutting wood along grain) > **rip off** (*slang*) steal, cheat, overcharge > **rip'off** *noun* (*slang*) act of stealing, overcharging, etc.
rip[2] *noun* strong current, esp. one moving away from the shore
ri•par•i•an [ri-PAIR-ee-ən] *adjective* of, on banks of river
ripe [rīp] *adjective* **rip•er, rip•est** 1 ready to be reaped, eaten, etc. 2 matured 3 (of judgment, etc.) sound > **rip'en** *verb* 1 grow ripe 2 mature
ri•poste [ri-POHST] *noun* 1 verbal retort 2 counterstroke 3 *fencing* quick lunge after parry
rip•ple [RIP-əl] *noun* 1 slight wave, ruffling of surface 2 anything like this 3 sound like ripples of water ▷ *verb intransitive* **-pled, -pling** 4 flow, form into little waves 5 (of sounds) rise and fall gently ▷ *verb transitive* **-pled, -pling** 6 form ripples on
rise [rīz] *verb intransitive* **rose, ris•en, ris•ing** 1 get up 2 move upward 3 appear above horizon 4 reach higher level 5 increase in value or price 6 rebel 7 adjourn 8 have its source ▷ *noun* 9 rising 10 upslope 11 increase, esp. of prices > **ris'er** *noun* 1 one who rises, esp. from bed 2 vertical part of stair step > **rising** *noun* 1 revolt ▷ *adjective* 2 increasing in rank, maturity
ris•i•ble [RIS-ə-bəl] *adjective* 1 inclined to laugh 2 laughable > **ris•i•bil'i•ty** *noun, plural* **-ties**
risk *noun* 1 chance of disaster or loss ▷ *verb transitive* 2 venture 3 put in jeopardy 4 take chance of > **risk'y** *adjective* **risk•i•er, risk•i•est** 1 dangerous 2 hazardous
ri•sot•to [ri-SAW-toh] *noun* dish of rice cooked

DICTIONARY

r

THESAURUS

rind *noun* SKIN, crust, husk, outer layer, peel
ring[1] *verb* 1 CHIME, clang, peal, reverberate, sound, toll
2 PHONE, buzz (*informal*), call, telephone
▷ *noun* 3 CHIME, knell, peal
4 CALL, buzz (*informal*), phone call
ring[2] *noun* 1 CIRCLE, band, circuit, halo, hoop, loop, round
2 ARENA, circus, enclosure, rink
3 GANG, association, band, cartel, circle, group, mob, syndicate
▷ *verb* 4 ENCIRCLE, enclose, gird, girdle, surround
rinse *verb* 1 WASH, bathe, clean, cleanse, dip, splash
▷ *noun* 2 WASH, bath, dip, splash
riot *noun* 1 DISTURBANCE, anarchy, confusion, disorder, lawlessness, strife, tumult, turbulence, turmoil, upheaval
2 REVELRY, carousal, festivity, frolic, high jinks, merrymaking
3 PROFUSION, display, extravaganza, show, splash
4 ▷ **run riot a** RAMPAGE, be out of control, go wild **b** GROW PROFUSELY, spread like wildfire
▷ *verb* 5 RAMPAGE, go on the rampage, run riot
riotous *adjective* 1 UNRESTRAINED, boisterous, loud, noisy, uproarious, wild
2 UNRULY, anarchic, disorderly, lawless, rebellious, rowdy, ungovernable, violent
rip *verb* 1 TEAR, burst, claw, cut, gash, lacerate, rend, slash, slit, split
▷ *noun* 2 TEAR, cut, gash, hole, laceration, rent, slash, slit, split
ripe *adjective* 1 MATURE, mellow, ready, ripened, seasoned
2 SUITABLE, auspicious, favorable, ideal, opportune, right, timely
ripen *verb* MATURE, burgeon, develop, grow ripe, season
rip-off *noun* SWINDLE, cheat, con (*informal*), con trick (*informal*), fraud, scam (*slang*), theft
rip off *verb* (*slang*) SWINDLE, cheat, con (*informal*), defraud, fleece, rob
riposte *noun* 1 RETORT, answer, comeback (*informal*), rejoinder, reply, response, sally
▷ *verb* 2 RETORT, answer, come back, reply, respond
rise *verb* 1 GET UP, arise, get to one's feet, stand up
2 GO UP, ascend, climb
3 ADVANCE, get on, progress, prosper
4 GET STEEPER, ascend, go uphill, slope upwards
5 INCREASE, go up, grow, intensify, mount
6 REBEL, mutiny, revolt
7 ORIGINATE, happen, issue, occur, spring
▷ *noun* 8 INCREASE, upsurge, upswing, upturn
9 ADVANCEMENT, climb, progress, promotion
10 UPWARD SLOPE, ascent, elevation, incline
11 ▷ **give rise to** CAUSE, bring about, effect, produce, result in
risk *noun* 1 DANGER, chance, gamble, hazard, jeopardy, peril, pitfall, possibility
▷ *verb* 2 DARE, chance, endanger, gamble, hazard, imperil, jeopardize, venture
risky *adjective* DANGEROUS, chancy (*informal*),

in stock with various other ingredients
ris•qué [ri-SKAY] *adjective* suggestive of indecency
rite [rīt] *noun* formal practice or custom, esp. religious > **rit•u•al** [RICH-oo-əl] *noun* 1 prescribed order or book of rites 2 regular, stereotyped action or behavior ▷ *adjective* 3 concerning rites > **rit'u•al•ism** *noun* practice of ritual
ri•val [RĪ-vəl] *noun* 1 one that competes with another for favor, success, etc. ▷ *verb transitive* **-valed, -val•ing** 2 vie with ▷ *adjective* 3 in position of rival > **ri'val•ry** *noun* keen competition
riv•er [RIV-ər] *noun* 1 large natural stream of water 2 copious flow
riv•et [RIV-it] *noun* 1 bolt for fastening metal plates, the end being put through holes and then beaten flat ▷ *verb transitive* **-et•ed, -et•ing** 2 fasten with rivets 3 cause to be fixed or held firmly, esp. in surprise, horror, etc. > **riv'et•er** *noun*
riv•u•let [RIV-yə-lit] *noun* small stream
Rn *chem.* radon
roach [rohch] *noun* 1 cockroach 2 (*slang*) butt of marijuana cigarette
road [rohd] *noun* 1 track, way prepared for passengers, vehicles, etc. 2 direction, way 3 street > **road'block** *noun* barricade across road to stop traffic for inspection, etc. > **road hog** selfish, aggressive driver > **road map** 1 map intended for drivers, showing roads, distances, etc. in a country or area 2 plan or guide for future actions > **road'run•ner** *noun* large cuckoo of W US, Mexico, C Amer. able to run quickly > **road'side** *noun, adjective* > **road'ster** *noun* (*obsolete*) touring car > **road warrior** (*informal*) frequent business traveler > **road'work** [-wurk] *noun* 1 repairs to road 2 running, jogging along country roads as exercise for boxers > **road'worth•y** [-wur-thee] *adjective* (of vehicle) mechanically sound
roam [rohm] *verb* wander about, rove > **roam'er** *noun*
roan [rohn] *adjective* 1 (of horses) having coat in which main color is thickly interspersed with another, esp. bay, sorrel or chestnut mixed with white or gray ▷ *noun* 2 roan horse
roar [ror] *verb* 1 make or utter loud deep hoarse sound as of lion, thunder, voice in anger, etc. ▷ *noun* 2 such a sound > **roar'ing** *adjective* 1 brisk and profitable ▷ *adverb* 2 noisily
roast [rohst] *verb* 1 bake, cook in closed oven 2 cook by exposure to open fire 3 make, be very hot ▷ *noun* 4 piece of meat for roasting 5 (*informal*) roasting ▷ *adjective* 6 roasted > **roast'ing** *noun* 1 severe criticism, scolding 2 session of good-natured scolding by way of tribute to honored person
rob *verb transitive* **robbed, rob•bing** 1 plunder, steal from 2 pillage, defraud > **rob'ber** *noun* > **rob'ber•y** *noun, plural* **-ber•ies**
robe [rohb] *noun* 1 long outer garment, often denoting rank or office ▷ *verb transitive* **robed, rob•ing** 2 dress ▷ *verb intransitive* **robed, rob•ing** 3 put on robes, vestments
rob'in *noun* large thrush with red breast > **robin's-egg blue** pale green to light blue
ro•bot [ROH-bət] *noun* 1 automated machine, esp. performing functions in human manner 2 person of machine-like efficiency > **ro•bot•ics** [roh-BOT-iks] *noun* science of designing and using robots
ro•bust [roh-BUST] *adjective* sturdy, strong > **ro•bust'ness** [-nis] *noun*
roc [rok] *noun* monstrous bird of Arabian mythology
rock[1] [rok] *noun* 1 stone 2 large rugged mass of stone 3 (*slang*) diamond, gem > **rock'er•y** *noun, plural* **-er•ies** mound or grotto of stones or rocks for plants in a garden > **rock'y** *adjective* **rock•i•er, rock•i•est** 1 having many rocks 2 rugged,

DICTIONARY • THESAURUS

hazardous, perilous, uncertain, unsafe
risqué *adjective* SUGGESTIVE, bawdy, blue, improper, indelicate, naughty, racy, ribald
rite *noun* CEREMONY, custom, observance, practice, procedure, ritual
ritual *noun* 1 CEREMONY, observance, rite
2 CUSTOM, convention, habit, practice, procedure, protocol, routine, tradition
▷ *adjective* 3 CEREMONIAL, conventional, customary, habitual, routine
rival *noun* 1 OPPONENT, adversary, competitor, contender, contestant
▷ *adjective* 2 COMPETING, conflicting, opposing
▷ *verb* 3 EQUAL, be a match for, come up to, compare with, compete, match
rivalry *noun* COMPETITION, conflict, contention, contest, opposition
river *noun* 1 STREAM, brook, creek, tributary, waterway
2 FLOW, flood, rush, spate, torrent
riveting *adjective* ENTHRALLING, absorbing, captivating, engrossing, fascinating, gripping, hypnotic, spellbinding
road *noun* WAY, course, highway, lane, motorway, path, pathway, roadway, route, track
roam *verb* WANDER, prowl, ramble, range, rove, stray, travel, walk
roar *verb* 1 CRY, bawl, bay, bellow, howl, shout, yell
2 GUFFAW, hoot, laugh heartily, split one's sides (*informal*)
▷ *noun* 3 CRY, bellow, howl, outcry, shout, yell
4 GUFFAW, hoot
rob *verb* STEAL FROM, burgle, cheat, con (*informal*), defraud, deprive, dispossess, hold up, loot, mug (*informal*), pillage, plunder, raid, rip off (*slang*)
robber *noun* THIEF, bandit, burglar, cheat, con man (*informal*), fraud, looter, mugger (*informal*), plunderer, raider, stealer
robbery *noun* THEFT, burglary, hold-up, larceny, mugging (*informal*), pillage, plunder, raid, rip-off (*slang*), stealing, stick-up (*slang*), swindle
robe *noun* 1 GOWN, costume, habit
▷ *verb* 2 CLOTHE, dress, garb
robot *noun* MACHINE, android, automaton, mechanical man
robust *adjective* STRONG, fit, hale, hardy, healthy, muscular, powerful, stout, strapping, sturdy, tough, vigorous
rock[1] *noun* STONE, boulder
rock[2] *verb* 1 SWAY, lurch, pitch, reel, roll, swing, toss
2 SHOCK, astonish, astound, shake, stagger, stun, surprise

presenting difficulty > **rock bottom** lowest possible level **between a rock and a hard place** between equally unattractive alternatives
rock² *verb* 1 (cause to) sway to and fro ▷ *noun* 2 style of pop music derived from rock-'n'-roll > **rock'er** *noun* curved piece of wood, etc. on which thing may rock > **rocking chair** chair allowing the sitter to rock backwards and forwards > **rock-'n-'roll** *noun* popular dance rhythm **rock the boat** (*informal*) disrupt smooth routine of company, etc. **off one's rocker** (*slang*) insane
rock•et [ROK-it] *noun* 1 self-propelling device powered by burning of explosive contents (used as firework, for display, signaling, line carrying, weapon, etc.) 2 vehicle propelled by rocket engine, as weapon or carrying spacecraft ▷ *verb intransitive* 3 move fast, esp. upward, as rocket > **rock'et•ry** *noun*
ro•co•co [rə-KOH-koh] *adjective* 1 of furniture, architecture, etc. having much conventional decoration in style of early 18th cent. work in France 2 tastelessly florid
rod *noun* 1 slender straight bar, stick 2 cane 3 old unit of length equal to 5.5 yards
rode *pt. of* **ride**
ro•dent [ROHD-nt] *noun* animal with teeth specialized for gnawing, such as a rat or squirrel
ro•de•o [ROH-dee-oh] *noun* display of skills, competition, with bareback riding, cattle handling techniques, etc.
roe [roh] *noun* mass of eggs in fish
roent•gen [RENT-gən] *noun* measuring unit of radiation dose
rogue [rohg] *noun* 1 rascal, knave, scoundrel 2 mischief-loving person or child 3 wild beast of savage temper, living apart from herd > **ro'guish** *adjective* > **rogue state** sovereign political power that conducts its policy in a dangerously unpredictable way, disregarding international law
rois•ter [ROI-stər] *verb intransitive* be noisy, boisterous, bragging > **roist'er•er** *noun* reveler
role, rôle [rohl] *noun* 1 actor's part 2 specific task or function
roll [rohl] *verb* 1 move by turning over and over ▷ *verb transitive* 2 wind around 3 smooth out with roller ▷ *verb intransitive* 4 move, sweep along 5 undulate 6 of ship, swing from side to side 7 of aircraft, turn about a line from nose to tail in flight ▷ *noun* 8 act of lying down and turning over and over or from side to side 9 piece of paper, etc. rolled up 10 any object thus shaped, e.g. jelly roll 11 list, catalogue 12 bread baked into small oval or round 13 continuous sound, as of drums, thunder, etc. > **roll'er** *noun* 1 cylinder of wood, stone, metal, etc. used for pressing, crushing, smoothing, supporting thing to be moved, winding thing on, etc. 2 long wave of sea > **roll call** act, time of calling over list of names, as in schools or army > **roller bearings** bearings of hardened steel rollers > **Roll'er•blade** *noun* ® roller skate with the wheels set in a straight line, mounted on a boot > **roller coaster** 1 small gravity railroad in amusement park with steep ascents and descents for frightening riders 2 any experience with similar ups and downs > **roller skate** skate with wheels instead of runner > **roller towel** loop of towel on roller > **rolling pin** cylindrical roller for pastry or dough > **rolling stock** locomotives, freight cars, etc. of railroad > **roll top** *noun* 1 in desk, flexible lid sliding in grooves 2 such a desk > **roll up** 1 appear, turn up 2 increase, accumulate
rol•lick•ing [ROL-i-king] *adjective* boisterously jovial and merry
ro•ly-po•ly [ROH-lee-poh-lee] *adjective* 1 round, plump ▷ *noun* 2 round, plump person or thing
ROM [rom] *computing* read-only memory (permanently recorded on a computer chip)
Rom. Romans
Ro•man [ROH-mən] *adjective* of Rome or Roman Catholic Church > **Roman Catholic** member of Roman Catholic Church > **Roman Catholic Church** the Christian church that acknowledges supremacy of the Pope > **Roman numerals** letters I, V, X, L, C, D, M used to represent numbers in manner of Romans > **roman type** plain upright letters, ordinary style of printing
roman á clef [roh-mah-na-KLAY] *noun, plural* **romans á clef** [roh-mah-na-KLAY] *Fr.* novel that disguises real events and people
ro•mance [roh-MANS] *noun* 1 love affair, esp. intense and happy one 2 mysterious or exciting quality 3 tale of chivalry 4 tale with scenes remote from ordinary life 5 literature like this 6 picturesque falsehood ▷ *verb intransitive* **-manced, -manc•ing** 7 exaggerate, fantasize ▷ *verb transitive* **-manced, -manc•ing** (*informal*) 8 woo, court > **Romance language** any of vernacular languages of certain countries, developed from Latin, as French, Spanish, etc. > **ro•man'tic** *adjective* 1 characterized by romance

DICTIONARY

r

THESAURUS

rocky¹ *adjective* ROUGH, craggy, rugged, stony
rocky² *adjective* UNSTABLE, rickety, shaky, unsteady, wobbly
rod *noun* STICK, bar, baton, cane, pole, shaft, staff, wand
rogue *noun* SCOUNDREL, crook (*informal*), fraud, rascal, scamp, villain
role *noun* 1 JOB, capacity, duty, function, part, position, post, task
2 PART, character, portrayal, representation
roll *verb* 1 TURN, go round, revolve, rotate, spin, swivel, trundle, twirl, wheel, whirl
2 WIND, bind, enfold, envelop, furl, swathe, wrap
3 FLOW, run, undulate
4 LEVEL, even, flatten, press, smooth
5 TUMBLE, lurch, reel, rock, sway, toss
▷ *noun* 6 TURN, cycle, reel, revolution, rotation, spin, twirl, wheel, whirl
7 REGISTER, census, index, list, record
8 RUMBLE, boom, reverberation, roar, thunder
rollicking *adjective* BOISTEROUS, carefree, devil-may-care, exuberant, hearty, jaunty, lively, playful
roly-poly *adjective* PLUMP, buxom, chubby, fat, rounded, tubby
romance *noun* 1 LOVE AFFAIR, affair, amour, attachment, liaison, relationship
2 EXCITEMENT, charm, color, fascination, glamour, mystery
3 STORY, fairy tale, fantasy, legend, love story, melodrama, tale

2 of or dealing with love 3 of literature, etc., preferring passion and imagination to proportion and finish ▷ *noun* > **ro•man'ti•cism** [-ti-sizm] *noun* > **ro•man'ti•cize** *verb intransitive* **-cized, -ciz•ing**

Ro•man•esque [rohm-ən-NESK] *adjective, noun* (in) style of round-arched vaulted architecture of period between Classical and Gothic

romp *verb intransitive* 1 run, play wildly, joyfully ▷ *noun* 2 spell of romping 3 easy victory > **romp'ers** [-ərz] *plural noun* child's loose one-piece garment **romp home** win easily

ron•deau [ron-DOH] *noun, plural* **-deaux** [-DOHZ] short poem with opening words used as refrain > **ron•del'** *noun* extended rondeau > **ron•de•let** [ron-dl-ET] *noun* short rondeau

ron•do [RON-doh] *noun, plural* **-dos** piece of music with leading theme to which return is continually made

roof *noun, plural* **roofs** 1 outside upper covering of building 2 top, covering part of anything ▷ *verb transitive* 3 put roof on, over

rook¹ [ruuk] *noun* 1 bird of crow family ▷ *verb transitive* 2 swindle, cheat > **rook'er•y** *noun, plural* **-er•ies** colony of rooks

rook² *noun* chess piece shaped like a castle

rook•ie [RUUK-ee] *noun* 1 recruit, esp. in army 2 *sports* professional athlete playing in first season

room *noun* 1 space 2 space enough 3 division of house 4 scope, opportunity > **rooms** lodgings > **room'y** *adjective* **room•i•er, room•i•est** spacious

roost *noun* 1 perch for poultry ▷ *verb intransitive* 2 perch > **roost'er** *noun* 1 male of domestic fowl 2 cock

root¹ *noun* 1 part of plant that grows down into earth and conveys nourishment to plant 2 plant with edible root, such as a carrot 3 vital part 4 (*also* **roots**) source, origin, original cause of anything 5 *anatomy* embedded portion of tooth, nail, hair, etc. 6 primitive word from which other words are derived 7 factor of a quantity that, when multiplied by itself the number of times indicated, gives the quantity ▷ *verb* 8 (cause to) take root 9 pull by roots 10 dig, burrow

root² *verb intransitive* 1 cheer 2 applaud 3 encourage > **root'er** *noun*

rope [rohp] *noun* 1 thick cord ▷ *verb transitive* **roped, rop•ing** 2 secure, mark off with rope > **rope in** (*informal*) entice, lure by deception

ro•sa•ry [ROH-zə-ree] *noun, plural* **-ries** 1 series of prayers 2 string of beads for counting these prayers as they are recited 3 rose garden, bed of roses

rose¹ [rohz] *noun* 1 shrub, climbing plant usu. with prickly stems and fragrant flowers 2 the flower 3 perforated flat nozzle for hose, watering can, etc. 4 pink color ▷ *adjective* 5 of this color > **ro•se•ate** [ROH-zee-it] *adjective* rose-colored, rosy > **ro•sette** [roh-ZET] *noun* 1 rose-shaped bunch of ribbon 2 rose-shaped architectural ornament > **ros'y** *adjective* **ros•i•er, ros•i•est** 1 flushed 2 hopeful, promising > **rose-colored** *adjective* 1 having color of rose 2 unwarrantably optimistic > **rose window** circular window with series of mullions branching from center > **rose of Sharon** [SHAR-ən] low, spreading small tree or shrub with white, purplish or red flowers

rose² *pt. of* **rise**

ro•sé [roh-ZAY] *noun* pink wine

rose•mar•y [ROHZ-mair-ee] *noun* 1 evergreen fragrant flowering shrub 2 its leaves and flowers used as seasoning

Ro•si•cru•cian [roh-zi-KROO-shən] *noun* member of secret order devoted to occult law ▷ *adjective* > **Ro•si•cru'cian•ism** *noun*

ros•in [ROZ-in] *noun* resin esp. used for rubbing on bows of violins, etc.

ros•ter [ROS-tər] *noun* list or plan showing turns of duty

ros•trum [ROS-trəm] *noun, plural* **-tra** [-trə] **-trums** 1 platform, stage, pulpit 2 beak or bill of a bird

rot *verb* **rot•ted, rot•ting** 1 decompose naturally 2 corrupt ▷ *noun* 3 decay, putrefaction 4 any

romantic *adjective* 1 LOVING, amorous, fond, passionate, sentimental, tender
2 IDEALISTIC, dreamy, impractical, starry-eyed, unrealistic
3 EXCITING, colorful, fascinating, glamorous, mysterious
▷ *noun* 4 IDEALIST, dreamer, sentimentalist

romp *verb* 1 FROLIC, caper, cavort, frisk, gambol, have fun, sport
2 WIN EASILY, walk it (*informal*), win by a mile (*informal*), win hands down
▷ *noun* 3 FROLIC, caper, lark (*informal*)

room *noun* 1 CHAMBER, apartment, office
2 SPACE, area, capacity, expanse, extent, leeway, margin, range, scope
3 OPPORTUNITY, chance, occasion, scope

roomy *adjective* SPACIOUS, ample, broad, capacious, commodious, extensive, generous, large, sizable *or* sizeable, wide

root¹ *noun* 1 STEM, rhizome, tuber
2 SOURCE, base, bottom, cause, core, foundation, heart, nucleus, origin, seat, seed
3 ▷ **roots** SENSE OF BELONGING, birthplace, cradle, family, heritage, home, origins
▷ *verb* 4 ESTABLISH, anchor, fasten, fix, ground, implant, moor, set, stick

root² *verb* DIG, burrow, ferret

rooted *adjective* DEEP-SEATED, confirmed, deep, deeply felt, entrenched, established, firm, fixed, ingrained

root out *verb* GET RID OF, abolish, do away with, eliminate, eradicate, exterminate, extirpate, remove, weed out

rope *noun* 1 CORD, cable, hawser, line, strand
2 ▷ **know the ropes** BE EXPERIENCED, be an old hand, be knowledgeable

rope in *verb* PERSUADE, engage, enlist, inveigle, involve, talk into

roster *noun* ROTA, agenda, catalog, list, register, roll, schedule, table

rostrum *noun* STAGE, dais, platform, podium, stand

rosy *adjective* 1 PINK, red
2 GLOWING, blooming, healthy-looking, radiant, ruddy
3 PROMISING, auspicious, bright, cheerful, encouraging, favorable, hopeful, optimistic

rot *verb* 1 DECAY, crumble, decompose,

disease producing decomposition of tissue **5** nonsense > **rot'ten** *adjective* **1** decomposed, putrid **2** corrupt

ro•ta•ry [ROH-tə-ree] *adjective* **1** (of movement) circular **2** operated by rotary movement > **ro•tate** [ROH-tayt] *verb* **-tat•ed, -tat•ing** (cause to) move around center or on pivot > **ro•ta'tion** *noun* **1** rotating **2** regular succession > **Rotary Club** one of international association of businessmen's clubs > **Ro•tar'i•an** *noun* member of such

rote [roht] *noun* habitual, mechanical repetition **by rote** by memory

ro•tis•ser•ie [roh-TIS-ə-ree] *noun* (electrically driven) rotating spit for cooking meat

ro•tor [ROH-tər] *noun* rotating portion of a dynamo motor or turbine

rotten *see* **rot**

ro•tund [roh-TUND] *adjective* **1** round **2** plump **3** sonorous > **ro•tun'di•ty** *noun*

rouble *see* **ruble**

rou•é [roo-AY] *noun* **1** dissolute or dissipated man **2** rake

rouge [roozh] *noun* **1** red powder, cream used to color cheeks ▷ *verb* **rouged, roug•ing** **2** color with rouge

rough [ruf] *adjective* **-er, -est** **1** not smooth, of irregular surface **2** violent, stormy, boisterous **3** rude **4** uncivil **5** lacking refinement **6** approximate **7** in preliminary form ▷ *verb transitive* **8** make rough **9** plan out approximately **10** (with *it*) live without usual comforts, etc. ▷ *noun* **11** rough condition or area **12** sketch **diamond in the rough** excellent, valuable but unsophisticated person > **rough'en** [-n] *verb transitive* > **rough•age** [RUF-ij] *noun* unassimilated portion of food promoting proper intestinal action > **rough'house** [-hows] *noun, verb* **-housed, -hous•ing** fight, row

rou•lette [roo-LET] *noun* game of chance played with revolving dishlike wheel and ball

round [rownd] *adjective* **-er, -est** **1** spherical, cylindrical, circular, curved **2** full, complete **3** roughly correct **4** large, considerable **5** plump **6** unqualified, positive ▷ *adverb* **7** with circular or circuitous course ▷ *noun* **8** thing round in shape **9** recurrent duties **10** stage in competition **11** customary course, as of postman **12** game (of golf) **13** one of several periods in boxing match, etc. **14** cartridge for firearm **15** rung **16** movement in circle ▷ *preposition* **17** about **18** on all sides of ▷ *verb* **19** make, become round ▷ *verb transitive* **20** move around > **round'ers** *noun* British ball game resembling baseball > **round'ly** *adverb* **1** plainly **2** thoroughly > **round•a•bout'** *adjective* not straightforward > **round robin** sports tournament in which all contestants play one another > **round up** **1** drive (cattle) together **2** collect and arrest criminals

roun•de•lay [ROWN-dl-ay] *noun* simple song with refrain

rouse [rowz] *verb transitive* **roused, rous•ing** **1** wake up, stir up, excite to action **2** cause to rise

DICTIONARY

r

THESAURUS

deteriorate, go bad, molder, perish, putrefy, spoil
2 DETERIORATE, decline, waste away
▷ *noun* **3** DECAY, blight, canker, corruption, decomposition, mold, putrefaction

rotary *adjective* REVOLVING, rotating, spinning, turning

rotate *verb* **1** REVOLVE, go round, gyrate, pivot, reel, spin, swivel, turn, wheel
2 TAKE TURNS, alternate, switch

rotation *noun* **1** REVOLUTION, orbit, reel, spin, spinning, turn, turning, wheel
2 SEQUENCE, alternation, cycle, succession, switching

rotten *adjective* **1** DECAYING, bad, corrupt, crumbling, decomposing, festering, funky (*slang*), moldy, perished, putrescent, rank, smelly, sour, stinking
2 CORRUPT, crooked (*informal*), dishonest, dishonorable, immoral, perfidious
3 (*informal*) DESPICABLE, base, contemptible, dirty, lousy (*slang*), mean, nasty, scuzzy (*slang*)

rotund *adjective* **1** ROUND, globular, rounded, spherical
2 PLUMP, chubby, corpulent, fat, fleshy, portly, stout, tubby

rough *adjective* **1** UNEVEN, broken, bumpy, craggy, irregular, jagged, rocky, stony
2 UNGRACIOUS, blunt, brusque, coarse, impolite, rude, unceremonious, uncivil, uncouth, unmannerly
3 APPROXIMATE, estimated, general, imprecise, inexact, sketchy, vague
4 STORMY, choppy, squally, turbulent, wild
5 NASTY, cruel, hard, harsh, tough, unfeeling, unpleasant, violent
6 BASIC, crude, imperfect, incomplete, rudimentary, sketchy, unfinished, unpolished, unrefined
7 UNPLEASANT, arduous, hard, tough, uncomfortable
▷ *verb* **8** ▷ **rough out** OUTLINE, draft, plan, sketch
▷ *noun* **9** OUTLINE, draft, mock-up, preliminary sketch

rough-and-ready *adjective* MAKESHIFT, crude, improvised, provisional, sketchy, stopgap, unpolished, unrefined

round *adjective* **1** SPHERICAL, circular, curved, cylindrical, globular, rotund, rounded
2 PLUMP, ample, fleshy, full, full-fleshed, rotund
▷ *verb* **3** GO ROUND, bypass, circle, encircle, flank, skirt, turn
▷ *noun* **4** SPHERE, ball, band, circle, disc, globe, orb, ring
5 STAGE, division, lap, level, period, session, turn
6 SERIES, cycle, sequence, session, succession
7 COURSE, beat, circuit, routine, schedule, series, tour

roundabout *adjective* INDIRECT, circuitous, devious, discursive, evasive, oblique, tortuous

round off *verb* COMPLETE, close, conclude, finish off

roundup *noun* GATHERING, assembly, collection, herding, marshalling, muster, rally

round up *verb* GATHER, collect, drive, group, herd, marshal, muster, rally

rouse *verb* **1** WAKE UP, awaken, call, rise, wake
2 EXCITE, agitate, anger, animate, incite, inflame, move, provoke, stimulate, stir

rousing *adjective* LIVELY, exciting, inspiring,

▷ *verb intransitive* **roused, rous•ing** 3 waken > **roust•a•bout** [ROWST-ə-bowt] *noun* laborer working in circus, oil rig, etc.

rout [rowt] *noun* 1 overwhelming defeat, disorderly retreat 2 noisy rabble ▷ *verb transitive* 3 scatter and put to flight

route [root] *noun* road, chosen way **go the route** (*informal*) 1 see through to the end 2 *baseball* pitch complete game

rou•tine [roo-TEEN] *noun* 1 regularity of procedure, unvarying round 2 regular course ▷ *adjective* 3 ordinary, regular

roux [roo] *noun* fat and flour cooked together as thickener for sauces

rove [rohv] *verb* **roved, rov•ing** 1 wander, roam > **rov'er** *noun* 1 one who roves 2 pirate

row[1] [roh] *noun* 1 number of things in a straight line 2 rank 3 file 4 line

row[2] *verb* 1 propel boat by oars ▷ *noun* 2 spell of rowing > **row'boat** *noun*

row[3] [rhymes with **cow**] *noun* 1 dispute 2 disturbance ▷ *verb intransitive* 3 quarrel noisily

row•dy [ROW-dee] *adjective* **-di•er, -di•est** 1 disorderly, noisy and rough ▷ *noun* 2 person like this

roy•al [ROI-əl] *adjective* 1 of, worthy of, befitting, patronized by, king or queen 2 splendid > **roy'al•ist** *noun* supporter of monarchy > **roy'al•ty** *noun* 1 royal dignity or power 2 royal persons 3 payment to owner of land for right to work minerals, or to inventor for use of invention 4 payment to author depending on sales

Ru *chem.* ruthenium

rub *verb transitive* **rubbed, rub•bing** 1 apply pressure to with circular or backward and forward movement 2 clean, polish, dry, thus 3 pass hand over 4 abrade, chafe 5 remove by friction ▷ *verb intransitive* **rubbed, rub•bing** 6 come into contact accompanied by friction 7 become frayed or worn by friction ▷ *noun* 8 rubbing 9 impediment

rub•ber[1] [RUB-ər] *noun* 1 coagulated sap of rough, elastic consistency, of certain tropical trees 2 piece of rubber, etc. used for erasing 3 thing for rubbing 4 person who rubs 5 (*slang*) condom ▷ *adjective* 6 of rubber > **rub'ber•ize** *verb transitive* **-ized, -iz•ing** coat, impregnate, treat with rubber > **rub'ber•y** *adjective* > **rub'ber•neck** *verb* gawk at > **rubber stamp** 1 device for imprinting dates, etc. 2 automatic authorization

rubber[2] *noun* 1 series of odd number of games or contests at various games, such as bridge 2 two out of three games won > **rubber match** deciding contest between tied opponents

rub•bish [RUB-ish] *noun* 1 refuse, waste material, garbage 2 anything worthless 3 trash, nonsense > **rub'bish•y** *adjective* valueless

rub•ble [RUB-əl] *noun* 1 fragments of stone, etc. 2 builders' rubbish

ru•bel•la [roo-BEL-ə] *noun* mild contagious viral disease, German measles

ru•bi•cund [ROO-bi-kund] *adjective* ruddy

ru•ble, rou•ble [ROO-bəl] *noun* unit of currency of Russia and Belarus

ru•bric [ROO-brik] *noun* 1 title, heading 2 direction in liturgy 3 instruction

ru•by [ROO-bee] *noun* **-bies** 1 precious red gem 2 its color ▷ *adjective* 3 of this color

ruck•sack [RUK-sak] *noun* pack carried on back, knapsack

ruck•us [RUK-əs] *noun* uproar, disturbance

rud•der [RUD-ər] *noun* flat piece hinged to boat's stern or rear of aircraft to steer by

rud•dy [RUD-ee] *adjective* **-di•er, -di•est** 1 of fresh or healthy red color 2 rosy 3 florid

rude [rood] *adjective* 1 impolite 2 coarse 3 vulgar 4 primitive 5 roughly made 6 uneducated 7 sudden, violent > **rude'ly** *adverb*

---

moving, spirited, stimulating, stirring

rout *noun* 1 DEFEAT, beating, debacle, drubbing, overthrow, thrashing
▷ *verb* 2 DEFEAT, beat, conquer, crush, destroy, drub, overthrow, thrash, trounce, wipe the floor with (*informal*)

route *noun* WAY, beat, circuit, course, direction, itinerary, journey, path, road

routine *noun* 1 PROCEDURE, custom, method, order, pattern, practice, program
▷ *adjective* 2 USUAL, customary, everyday, habitual, normal, ordinary, standard, typical
3 BORING, dull, humdrum, predictable, tedious, tiresome

rove *verb* WANDER, drift, ramble, range, roam, stray, traipse (*informal*)

row[1] *noun* LINE, bank, column, file, range, series, string

row[2] *noun* 1 DISPUTE, brawl, quarrel, squabble, tiff, trouble
2 DISTURBANCE, commotion, noise, racket, rumpus, tumult, uproar
▷ *verb* 3 QUARREL, argue, dispute, fight, squabble, wrangle

rowdy *adjective* 1 DISORDERLY, loud, noisy, rough, unruly, wild
▷ *noun* 2 HOOLIGAN, lout, ruffian

royal *adjective* 1 REGAL, imperial, kingly, princely, queenly, sovereign
2 SPLENDID, grand, impressive, magnificent, majestic, stately

rub *verb* 1 POLISH, clean, scour, shine, wipe
2 CHAFE, abrade, fray, grate, scrape
▷ *noun* 3 POLISH, shine, stroke, wipe
4 MASSAGE, caress, kneading

rubbish *noun* 1 WASTE, garbage, junk (*informal*), litter, lumber, refuse, scrap, trash
2 NONSENSE, claptrap (*informal*), garbage, hogwash, hot air (*informal*), trash, tripe (*informal*)

rub out *verb* ERASE, cancel, delete, efface, obliterate, remove, wipe out

ruckus *noun* (*informal*) UPROAR, commotion, disturbance, fracas, fuss, hoopla, trouble

ruddy *adjective* ROSY, blooming, fresh, glowing, healthy, radiant, red, reddish, rosy-cheeked

rude *adjective* 1 IMPOLITE, abusive, cheeky, discourteous, disrespectful, ill-mannered, impertinent, impudent, insolent, insulting, uncivil, unmannerly
2 VULGAR, boorish, brutish, coarse, graceless, loutish, oafish, rough, uncivilized, uncouth, uncultured
3 UNPLEASANT, abrupt, harsh, sharp, startling, sudden
4 ROUGHLY-MADE, artless, crude, inartistic, inelegant, makeshift, primitive, raw, rough,

> **rude'ness** *noun*
ru•di•ments [ROO-də-mənts] *plural noun* elements, first principles > **ru•di•men'ta•ry** *adjective*
rue¹ [roo] *verb* **rued, ru•ing** 1 grieve for 2 regret 3 deplore 4 repent ▷ *noun* 5 sorrow 6 repentance > **rue'ful** [-fəl] *adjective* 1 sorry 2 regretful 3 dejected 4 deplorable
rue² *noun* plant with evergreen bitter leaves
ruff¹ *noun* 1 starched and frilled collar 2 natural collar of feathers, fur, etc. on some birds and animals 3 type of shore bird > **ruf'fle** *verb transitive* **-fled, -fling** 1 rumple, disorder 2 annoy, put out 3 frill, pleat ▷ *noun* 4 frilled trimming
ruff² *noun, verb cards* trump
ruf•fi•an [RUF-ee-ən] *noun* violent, lawless person
rug *noun* 1 small, oft. shaggy or thick-piled floor mat 2 thick woolen wrap, coverlet 3 (*slang*) toupee, hairpiece > **rug'rat** *noun* (*informal*) small child
rug•by [RUG-bee] *noun* form of football with two teams of 15 players
rug•ged [RUG-id] *adjective* 1 rough 2 broken 3 unpolished 4 harsh, austere
ru•in [ROO-in] *noun* 1 decay, destruction 2 downfall 3 fallen or broken state 4 loss of wealth, position, etc. ▷ *verb transitive* 5 reduce to ruins 6 bring to decay or destruction 7 spoil 8 impoverish > **ru•ins** *plural noun* ruined buildings, etc. > **ru•in•a'tion** *noun* > **ru'in•ous** *adjective* causing or characterized by ruin or destruction
rule [rool] *noun* 1 principle 2 precept 3 authority 4 government 5 what is usual 6 control 7 measuring stick ▷ *verb transitive* **ruled, rul•ing** 8 govern 9 decide 10 mark with straight lines 11 draw (line) > **rul'er** *noun* 1 one who governs 2 stick for measuring or ruling lines
rum *noun* liquor distilled from sugar cane
rum•ba [RUM-bə] *noun, plural* **-bas** 1 rhythmic dance, orig. Cuban 2 music for it
rum•ble [RUM-bəl] *verb intransitive* **-bled, -bling** 1 make noise as of distant thunder, heavy vehicle, etc. 2 (*slang*) engage in gang street fight ▷ *noun* 3 noise like thunder, etc. 4 gang street fight
ru•mi•nate [ROO-mə-nayt] *verb intransitive* **-nat•ed, -nat•ing** 1 chew cud 2 ponder over 3 meditate > **ru'mi•nant** [-nənt] *adjective, noun* cud-chewing (animal) > **ru•mi•na'tion** [-NAY-shən] *noun* quiet meditation and reflection > **ru'mi•na•tive** [-mə-nə-tiv] *adjective*
rum•mage [RUM-ij] *verb* **-maged, -mag•ing** search thoroughly ▷ *noun* > **rummage sale** sale of miscellaneous, usu. secondhand, items
rum•my¹ [RUM-ee] *noun* card game
rum•my² [RUM-ee] *noun, plural* **-mies** (*slang*) drunkard
ru•mor [ROO-mər] *noun* 1 hearsay, common talk, unproved statement ▷ *verb transitive* 2 put

---

simple
rudimentary *adjective* BASIC, early, elementary, fundamental, initial, primitive, undeveloped
rudiments *plural noun* BASICS, beginnings, elements, essentials, foundation, fundamentals
rue *verb* REGRET, be sorry for, kick oneself for, lament, mourn, repent
rueful *adjective* REGRETFUL, contrite, mournful, penitent, remorseful, repentant, sorrowful, sorry
ruffian *noun* THUG, brute, bully, hoodlum, hooligan, tough
ruffle *verb* 1 DISARRANGE, dishevel, disorder, mess up, rumple, tousle
2 ANNOY, agitate, fluster, irritate, nettle, peeve (*informal*), tick off, upset
rugged *adjective* 1 ROUGH, broken, bumpy, craggy, difficult, irregular, jagged, ragged, rocky, uneven
2 STRONG-FEATURED, rough-hewn, weather-beaten
3 TOUGH, brawny, burly, husky (*informal*), muscular, robust, strong, sturdy, well-built
ruin *verb* 1 DESTROY, crush, defeat, demolish, devastate, lay waste, smash, wreck
2 BANKRUPT, impoverish, pauperize
3 SPOIL, blow (*slang*), botch, damage, make a mess of, mess up, screw up (*informal*)
▷ *noun* 4 DESTRUCTION, breakdown, collapse, defeat, devastation, downfall, fall, undoing, wreck
5 DISREPAIR, decay, disintegration, ruination, wreckage
6 BANKRUPTCY, destitution, insolvency
ruinous *adjective* 1 DEVASTATING, calamitous, catastrophic, destructive, dire, disastrous, shattering
2 EXTRAVAGANT, crippling, immoderate, wasteful
rule *noun* 1 REGULATION, axiom, canon, decree, direction, guideline, law, maxim, precept, principle, tenet
2 CUSTOM, convention, habit, practice, procedure, routine, tradition
3 GOVERNMENT, authority, command, control, dominion, jurisdiction, mastery, power, regime, reign
4 ▷ **as a rule** USUALLY, generally, mainly, normally, on the whole, ordinarily
▷ *verb* 5 GOVERN, be in authority, be in power, command, control, direct, reign
6 BE PREVALENT, be customary, predominate, preponderate, prevail
7 DECREE, decide, judge, pronounce, settle
rule out *verb* EXCLUDE, ban, debar, dismiss, disqualify, eliminate, leave out, preclude, prohibit, reject
ruler *noun* 1 GOVERNOR, alpha male, commander, controller, head of state, king *or* queen, leader, lord, monarch, potentate, sovereign
2 MEASURE, rule, yardstick
ruling *noun* 1 DECISION, adjudication, decree, judgment, pronouncement, verdict
▷ *adjective* 2 GOVERNING, commanding, controlling, reigning
3 PREDOMINANT, chief, dominant, main, pre-eminent, preponderant, prevailing, principal
ruminate *verb* PONDER, cogitate, consider, contemplate, deliberate, mull over, muse, reflect, think, turn over in one's mind
rummage *verb* SEARCH, delve, forage, hunt, ransack, root
rumor *noun* STORY, buzz, dirt (*slang*), gossip,

out as, by way of, rumor
rump *noun* 1 tail end 2 buttocks
rum•ple [RUM-pəl] *verb, noun* **-pled, -pling** crease, wrinkle
rum•pus [RUM-pəs] *noun, plural* **-us•es** 1 disturbance 2 noise and confusion
run *verb intransitive* **ran, run, run•ning** 1 move with more rapid gait than walking 2 go quickly 3 flow 4 flee 5 compete in race, contest, election 6 revolve 7 continue 8 function 9 travel according to schedule 10 fuse 11 melt 12 spread over 13 have certain meaning ▷ *verb transitive* **ran, run, run•ning** 14 cross by running 15 expose oneself (to risk, etc.) 16 cause to run 17 (of newspaper) print, publish 18 transport and dispose of (smuggled goods) 19 manage 20 operate ▷ *noun* 21 act, spell of running 22 rush 23 tendency, course 24 period 25 sequence 26 heavy demand 27 enclosure for domestic poultry, animals 28 ride in car 29 series of unraveled stitches, ladder 30 score of one at baseball 31 steep snow-covered course for skiing > **run'ner** *noun* 1 racer 2 messenger 3 curved piece of wood on which sleigh slides 4 any similar appliance 5 slender stem of plant running along ground forming new roots at intervals 6 strip of cloth, carpet > **running** *adjective* 1 continuous 2 consecutive 3 flowing 4 discharging 5 effortless 6 entered for race 7 used for running ▷ *noun* 8 act of moving or flowing quickly 9 management > **run'ny** *adjective* **-ni•er, -ni•est** tending to flow or exude moisture > **run'down** *noun* summary > **run-down** *adjective* exhausted > **run down** 1 stop working 2 reduce 3 exhaust 4 denigrate > **run'way** *noun* level stretch where aircraft take off and land **in the running** having fair chance in competition
rung[1] *noun* crossbar or spoke, esp. in ladder
rung[2] *pp of* **ring**[2]
runt *noun* 1 small animal, below usual size of species 2 (*offensive*) undersized person
ru•pee [roo-PEE] *noun* monetary unit of India and Pakistan
rup•ture [RUP-chər] *noun* 1 breaking, breach 2 hernia ▷ *verb* **-tured, tur•ing** 3 break 4 burst, sever
ru•ral [RUUR-əl] *adjective* 1 of the country 2 rustic

hearsay, news, report, talk, whisper, word
rump *noun* BUTTOCKS, backside (*informal*), bottom, buns (*slang*), butt (*informal*), derrière (*euphemistic*), hindquarters, posterior, rear, rear end, seat
rumpus *noun* COMMOTION, disturbance, furor, fuss, hue and cry, noise, row, uproar
run *verb* 1 RACE, bolt, dash, gallop, hurry, jog, lope, rush, scurry, sprint
2 FLEE, beat a retreat, beat it (*slang*), bolt, escape, make a run for it, take flight, take off (*informal*), take to one's heels
3 MOVE, course, glide, go, pass, roll, skim
4 WORK, function, go, operate, perform
5 MANAGE, administer, be in charge of, control, direct, handle, head, lead, operate
6 CONTINUE, extend, go, proceed, reach, stretch
7 FLOW, discharge, go, gush, leak, pour, spill, spout, stream
8 MELT, dissolve, go soft, liquefy
9 PUBLISH, display, feature, print
10 COMPETE, be a candidate, contend, put oneself up for, stand, take part
11 SMUGGLE, bootleg, traffic in
▷ *noun* 12 RACE, dash, gallop, jog, rush, sprint, spurt
13 RIDE, drive, excursion, jaunt, outing, spin (*informal*), trip
14 SEQUENCE, course, period, season, series, spell, stretch, string
15 ENCLOSURE, coop, pen
16 ▷ **in the long run** EVENTUALLY, in the end, ultimately
run across *verb* MEET, bump into, come across, encounter, run into
runaway *noun* 1 FUGITIVE, deserter, escapee, refugee, truant
▷ *adjective* 2 ESCAPED, fleeing, fugitive, loose, wild
run away *verb* FLEE, abscond, bolt, escape, fly the coop (*informal*), make a run for it, scram (*informal*), take to one's heels
run-down *adjective* 1 EXHAUSTED, below par, debilitated, drained, enervated, unhealthy, weak, weary, worn-out
2 DILAPIDATED, broken-down, decrepit, ramshackle, seedy, shabby, worn-out
run down *verb* 1 CRITICIZE, bad-mouth (*slang*), belittle, decry, denigrate, disparage, knock (*informal*)
2 REDUCE, curtail, cut, cut back, decrease, downsize, trim
3 KNOCK DOWN, hit, knock over, run into, run over
4 WEAKEN, debilitate, exhaust
run into *verb* 1 MEET, bump into, come across *or* come upon, encounter, run across
2 HIT, collide with, strike
runner *noun* 1 ATHLETE, jogger, sprinter
2 MESSENGER, courier, dispatch bearer, errand boy
running *adjective* 1 CONTINUOUS, constant, incessant, perpetual, twenty-four-seven (*slang*), unbroken, uninterrupted
2 FLOWING, moving, streaming
▷ *noun* 3 MANAGEMENT, administration, control, direction, leadership, organization, supervision
4 WORKING, functioning, maintenance, operation, performance
runny *adjective* FLOWING, fluid, liquefied, liquid, melted, watery
run off *verb* FLEE, bolt, escape, fly the coop (*informal*), make off, run away, take flight, take to one's heels
run out *verb* BE USED UP, be exhausted, dry up, end, fail, finish, give out
run over *verb* 1 KNOCK DOWN, hit, knock over, run down
2 GO THROUGH, check, go over, rehearse, run through
run through *verb* REHEARSE, go over, practise, read, run over
rupture *noun* 1 BREAK, breach, burst, crack, fissure, rent, split, tear
▷ *verb* 2 BREAK, burst, crack, separate, sever, split, tear
rural *adjective* RUSTIC, agricultural, country, pastoral, sylvan

ruse [rooz] *noun* stratagem, trick
rush[1] *verb transitive* 1 impel, carry along violently and rapidly 2 take by sudden assault ▷ *verb intransitive* 3 cause to hurry 4 move violently or rapidly ▷ *noun* 5 rushing, charge 6 hurry 7 eager demand for 8 heavy current (of air, water, etc.) ▷ *adjective* 9 done with speed 10 characterized by speed > **rush hour** period at beginning and end of day when many people are traveling to and from work
rush[2] *noun* 1 marsh plant with slender pithy stem 2 the stems as material for baskets
rusk *noun* kind of sweet raised bread esp. used for feeding babies
rus•set [RUS-it] *adjective* 1 reddish-brown ▷ *noun* 2 the color 3 apple with skin of this color
rust *noun* 1 reddish-brown coating formed on iron by oxidation 2 disease of plants ▷ *verb* 3 contract, affect with rust > **rust'y** *adjective* **rust•i•er, rust•i•est** 1 coated with rust, of rust color 2 out of practice > **rust'proof** *adjective*
rus•tic [RUS-tik] *adjective* 1 of, or as of, country people 2 rural 3 of rough manufacture 4 made of untrimmed tree limbs ▷ *noun* 5 country person, peasant > **rus'ti•cate** *verb transitive* **-cat•ed, -cat•ing** 1 send to, house in, country ▷ *verb intransitive* **-cat•ed, -cat•ing** 2 live a country life
rus•tle[1] [RUS-əl] *verb intransitive* **-tled, -tling** 1 make sound as of blown dead leaves, etc. ▷ *noun* 2 this sound
rustle[2] *verb transitive* **-tled, -tling** steal (cattle) > **rus'tler** *noun* cattle thief
rut[1] *noun* 1 furrow made by wheel 2 settled habit or way of living 3 groove > **rut'ty** *adjective* **-ti•er, -ti•est**
rut[2] *noun* 1 periodic sexual excitement among animals ▷ *verb intransitive* **rut•ted, rut•ting** 2 be under influence of this
ruth•less [ROOTH-lis] *adjective* pitiless, merciless
RV *noun* recreational vehicle
rye [rī] *noun* 1 grain used for forage and bread 2 plant bearing it 3 whisky made from rye

---

ruse *noun* TRICK, device, dodge, hoax, maneuver, ploy, stratagem, subterfuge
rush *verb* 1 HURRY, bolt, career, dash, fly, hasten, race, run, shoot, speed, tear
2 PUSH, hurry, hustle, press
3 ATTACK, charge, storm
▷ *noun* 4 HURRY, charge, dash, haste, race, scramble, stampede, surge
5 ATTACK, assault, charge, onslaught
▷ *adjective* 6 HASTY, fast, hurried, quick, rapid, swift, urgent
rust *noun* 1 CORROSION, oxidation
2 MILDEW, blight, mold, must, rot
▷ *verb* 3 CORRODE, oxidize
rustic *adjective* 1 RURAL, country, pastoral, sylvan
2 UNCOUTH, awkward, coarse, crude, rough
▷ *noun* 3 YOKEL, boor, bumpkin, clod, clodhopper (*informal*), hick (*informal*), hillbilly, peasant, redneck (*slang*)
rustle *verb* 1 CRACKLE, crinkle, whisper
▷ *noun* 2 CRACKLE, crinkling, rustling, whisper
rusty *adjective* 1 CORRODED, oxidized, rust-covered, rusted
2 REDDISH, chestnut, coppery, reddish-brown, russet, rust-colored
3 OUT OF PRACTICE, stale, unpracticed, weak
rut *noun* 1 GROOVE, furrow, indentation, track, trough, wheel mark
2 HABIT, dead end, pattern, routine, system
ruthless *adjective* MERCILESS, brutal, callous, cruel, harsh, heartless, pitiless, relentless, remorseless
rutted *adjective* GROOVED, cut, furrowed, gouged, holed, indented, marked, scored

Ss

S *chem.* sulfur
Sab•bath [SAB-əth] *noun* **1** Saturday, devoted to worship and rest from work in Judaism and certain Christian churches **2** Sunday, observed by Christians as day of worship and rest
> **sab•bat•i•cal** [sə-BAT-ə-kəl] *adjective, noun* (denoting) leave granted to university staff, etc. for study
sa•ber [SAY-bər] *noun* **1** curved cavalry sword **2** fencing sword having two cutting edges and blunt point
sa•ble [SAY-bəl] *noun* **1** small weasellike animal of cold regions **2** its fur **3** black ▷ *adjective* **4** black
sab•o•tage [SAB-ə-tahzh] *noun* intentional damage done to roads, machines, etc., esp. secretly in war ▷ *verb* **-taged, -tag•ing**
> **sab•o•teur** [sab-ə-TUR] *noun*
sac [sak] *noun* pouchlike structure in an animal or vegetable body
sac•cha•rin [SAK-ər-in] *noun* artificial sweetener > **sac'cha•rine** [-in] *adjective* excessively sweet
sac•er•do•tal [sas-ər-DOHT-l] *adjective* of priests
sa•chet [sa-SHAY] *noun* small envelope or bag, esp. one holding scented powder
sack [sak] *noun* **1** large bag, orig. of coarse material **2** pillaging **3** (*slang*) dismissal **4** (*slang*) bed ▷ *verb transitive* **5** pillage (captured town) **6** (*slang*) fire (person) from a job
> **sack'ing** *noun* material for sacks > **sack•cloth** [SAK-klawth] *noun* coarse fabric used for sacks and worn as sign of mourning
sac•ra•ment [SAK-rə-mənt] *noun* one of certain ceremonies of Christian church esp. Eucharist
> **sac•ra•men'tal** *adjective*
sa•cred [SAY-krid] *adjective* **1** dedicated, regarded as holy **2** set apart, reserved **3** inviolable **4** connected with, intended for religious use
sac•ri•fice [SAK-rə-fīs] *noun* **1** giving something up for sake of something else **2** act of giving up **3** thing so given up **4** making of offering to a god **5** thing offered ▷ *verb transitive* **-ficed, -fic•ing 6** offer as sacrifice **7** give up **8** sell at very cheap price > **sac•ri•fi'cial** [-FISH-l] *adjective*
sac•ri•lege [SAK-rə-lij] *noun* misuse,

---

sabotage *noun* **1** DAMAGE, destruction, disruption, subversion, wrecking
▷ *verb* **2** DAMAGE, destroy, disable, disrupt, incapacitate, subvert, vandalize, wreck
saccharine *adjective* OVERSWEET, cloying, honeyed, nauseating, sickly, sugary, syrupy
sack¹ *noun* **1** ▷ **the sack** DISMISSAL, discharge, the ax (*informal*), the boot (*slang*)
▷ *verb* **2** DISMISS, ax (*informal*), discharge, fire (*informal*)
sack² *noun* **1** PLUNDERING, looting, pillage
▷ *verb* **2** PLUNDER, loot, pillage, raid, rob, ruin, strip
sacred *adjective* **1** HOLY, blessed, divine, hallowed, revered, sanctified
2 RELIGIOUS, ecclesiastical, holy
3 INVIOLABLE, protected, sacrosanct
sacrifice *noun* **1** SURRENDER, loss, renunciation
2 OFFERING, oblation
▷ *verb* **3** GIVE UP, forego, forfeit, let go, lose, say

desecration of something sacred > **sac•ri•leg'ious** [-LEEJ-əs] *adjective* 1 profane 2 desecrating
sac•ro•sanct [SAK-roh-sangkt] *adjective* 1 preserved by religious fear against desecration or violence 2 inviolable
sac•rum [SAK-rəm] *noun, plural* **sac•ra** [SAK-rə] five vertebrae forming compound bone at base of spinal column
sad *adjective* **sad•der, sad•dest** 1 sorrowful 2 unsatisfactory, deplorable > **sad•den** [SAD-n] *verb transitive* make sad
sad•dle [SAD-l] *noun* 1 rider's seat to fasten on horse, bicycle, etc. 2 anything resembling a saddle 3 cut of mutton, venison, etc. for roasting 4 ridge of hill ▷ *verb transitive* **-dled, -dling** 5 put saddle on 6 lay burden, responsibility on
sa•dism [SAY-diz-əm] *noun* form of (sexual) perversion marked by love of inflicting pain > **sa'dist** *noun* > **sa•dis•tic** [sə-DIS-tik] *adjective*
sa•fa•ri [sə-FAH-ree] *noun* (party making) overland (hunting) journey, esp. in Africa > **safari park** park where lions, etc. may be viewed by public from automobiles
safe [sayf] *adjective* **saf•er, saf•est** 1 secure, protected 2 uninjured, out of danger 3 not involving risk 4 trustworthy 5 sure, reliable 6 cautious ▷ *noun* 7 strong lockable container 8 structure for storing meat, etc. > **safe'ly** *adverb* > **safe'ty** *noun* > **safe-conduct** [KON-dukt] *noun* a permit to pass somewhere > **safe'guard** [-GAHRD] *noun* 1 protection ▷ *verb transitive* 2 protect > **safety glass** glass resistant to fragmenting when broken
saf•fron [SAF-rən] *noun* 1 crocus 2 orange colored flavoring obtained from it 3 the color ▷ *adjective* 4 orange
sag *verb intransitive* **sagged, sagging** 1 sink in middle 2 hang sideways 3 curve downward under pressure 4 give way 5 tire 6 (of clothes) hang loosely ▷ *noun* 7 droop
sa•ga [SAH-gə] *noun* 1 legend of Norse heroes 2 any long (heroic) story
sa•ga•cious [sə-GAY-shəs] *adjective* wise > **sa•gac'i•ty** [-GAS-i-tee] *noun*
sage[1] [sayj] *noun* 1 very wise person ▷ *adjective* **sag•er, sag•est** 2 wise
sage[2] *noun* aromatic herb
said [sed] *pt./pp. of* **say**
sail [sayl] *noun* 1 piece of fabric stretched to catch wind for propelling ship, etc. 2 act of sailing 3 journey upon the water 4 ships collectively 5 arm of windmill ▷ *verb intransitive* 6 travel by water 7 move smoothly 8 begin voyage ▷ *verb transitive* 9 navigate > **sail'or** *noun* 1 seaman 2 one who sails > **sail'board** [-bord] *noun* craft used for windsurfing like surfboard with mast and single sail
saint [saynt] *noun* 1 (title of) person formally recognized (esp. by R.C. Church) after death, as having gained by holy deeds a special place in heaven 2 exceptionally good person > **saint'ed** [-id] *adjective* 1 canonized 2 sacred > **saint'li•ness** [-nis] *noun* holiness > **saint'ly** *adjective*
sake[1] [sayk] *noun* 1 cause, account 2 end, purpose **for the sake of** 3 on behalf of 4 to please or benefit
sa•ke[2] [SAH-kee] *noun* Japanese alcoholic drink made of fermented rice
sa•laam [sə-LAHM] *noun* 1 bow of salutation, mark of respect in East ▷ *verb transitive* 2 salute
salable *adjective see* **sale**
sa•la•cious [sə-LAY-shəs] *adjective* excessively

good-bye to, surrender
4 OFFER, immolate, offer up
sacrilege *noun* DESECRATION, blasphemy, heresy, impiety, irreverence, profanation, violation
sacrilegious *adjective* PROFANE, blasphemous, desecrating, impious, irreligious, irreverent
sacrosanct *adjective* INVIOLABLE, hallowed, inviolate, sacred, sanctified, set apart, untouchable
sad *adjective* 1 UNHAPPY, blue, dejected, depressed, doleful, down, low, low-spirited, melancholy, mournful, woebegone
2 TRAGIC, depressing, dismal, grievous, harrowing, heart-rending, moving, pathetic, pitiful, poignant, upsetting
3 DEPLORABLE, bad, lamentable, sorry, wretched
sadden *verb* UPSET, deject, depress, distress, grieve, make sad
saddle *verb* BURDEN, encumber, load
sadistic *adjective* CRUEL, barbarous, brutal, ruthless, vicious
sadness *noun* UNHAPPINESS, dejection, depression, despondency, grief, melancholy, misery, poignancy, sorrow, the blues
safe *adjective* 1 SECURE, impregnable, in safe hands, out of danger, out of harm's way, protected, safe and sound
2 UNHARMED, all right, intact, O.K. *or* okay (*informal*), undamaged, unhurt, unscathed
3 RISK-FREE, certain, impregnable, secure, sound
▷ *noun* 4 STRONGBOX, coffer, deposit box, repository, safe-deposit box, vault
safeguard *verb* 1 PROTECT, defend, guard, look after, preserve
▷ *noun* 2 PROTECTION, defense, guard, security
safely *adverb* IN SAFETY, in one piece, safe and sound, with impunity, without risk
safety *noun* 1 SECURITY, impregnability, protection
2 SHELTER, cover, refuge, sanctuary
sag *verb* 1 SINK, bag, dip, droop, fall, give way, hang loosely, slump
2 TIRE, droop, flag, wane, weaken, wilt
saga *noun* TALE, epic, legend, narrative, story, yarn
sage *noun* 1 WISE MAN, elder, guru, master, philosopher
▷ *adjective* 2 WISE, judicious, sagacious, sapient, sensible
sail *verb* 1 EMBARK, set sail
2 GLIDE, drift, float, fly, skim, soar, sweep, wing
3 PILOT, steer
sailor *noun* MARINER, marine, sea dog, seafarer, seaman
saintly *adjective* VIRTUOUS, godly, holy, pious, religious, righteous, saintlike
sake *noun* 1 BENEFIT, account, behalf, good, interest, welfare
2 PURPOSE, aim, end, motive, objective, reason
salacious *adjective* LASCIVIOUS, carnal, erotic, lecherous, lewd, libidinous, lustful

concerned with sex, lewd
sal•ad [SAL-əd] *noun* mixed vegetables, or fruit, used as food without cooking, oft. combined with fish, meat, etc. ▷ *adjective* > **salad days** period of youthful inexperience > **salad dressing** oil, vinegar, herbs, etc. mixed together as sauce for salad
sal•a•man•der [SAL-ə-man-dər] *noun* 1 variety of lizard 2 portable space heater
sa•la•mi [sə-LAH-mee] *noun* variety of highly-spiced sausage
sal•a•ry [SAL-ə-ree] *noun, plural* **-ries** fixed regular payment to persons employed usu. in nonmanual work > **sal'a•ried** *adjective*
sale [sayl] *noun* 1 selling 2 selling of goods at unusually low prices 3 auction > **sal'a•ble** *adjective* capable of being sold > **sales'per•son** *noun* 1 one who sells goods, etc. in store 2 one traveling to sell goods, esp. as representative of firm > **sales'man•ship** *noun* art of selling or presenting goods in most effective way
sa•li•ent [SAY-lee-ənt] *adjective* 1 prominent, noticeable 2 jutting out ▷ *noun* 3 salient angle, esp. in fortification or line of battle
sa•line [SAY-leen] *adjective* 1 containing, consisting of a chemical salt, esp. common salt 2 salty > **sa•lin•i•ty** [sə-LIN-i-tee] *noun*
sa•li•va [sə-LĪ-və] *noun* liquid that forms in mouth, spittle > **sal•i•var•y** [SAL-ə-ver-ee] *adjective* > **sal'i•vate** *verb* **-vat•ed, -vat•ing**
sal•low [SAL-oh] *adjective* of unhealthy pale or yellowish color
sal•ly [SAL-ee] *noun, plural* **-lies** 1 rushing out, esp. by troops 2 outburst 3 witty remark ▷ *verb intransitive* **-lied, -ly•ing** 4 rush 5 set out
salm•on [SAM-ən] *noun* 1 large silvery fish with orange-pink flesh valued as food 2 color of its flesh ▷ *adjective* 3 of this color
sal•mo•nel•la [sal-mə-NEL-ə] *noun, plural* **-lae** [-lee] bacteria causing disease (esp. food poisoning)
sa•lon [sə-LON] *noun* 1 (reception room for) guests in fashionable household 2 commercial premises of hairdressers, beauticians, etc.
sa•loon [sə-LOON] *noun* 1 principal cabin or sitting room in passenger ship 2 bar 3 public room for specified use, e.g. billiards
salt [sawlt] *noun* 1 white powdery or granular crystalline substance consisting mainly of sodium chloride, used to season or preserve food 2 chemical compound of acid and metal 3 wit ▷ *verb transitive* 4 season, sprinkle with, spread, preserve with salt > **salt'y** *adjective* **salt•i•er, salt•i•est** of, like salt **old salt** sailor > **salt'cel•lar** [-sel-ər] *noun* salt shaker > **salt lick** deposit, block of salt licked by game, cattle, etc. > **salt pan** *noun* depression encrusted with salt after partial draining away of water > **salt•pe•ter** [sawlt-PEE-tər] *noun* potassium nitrate used in gunpowder **with a pinch of salt** allowing for exaggeration **worth one's salt** efficient
sa•lu•bri•ous [sə-LOO-bree-əs] *adjective* favorable to health, beneficial
Sa•lu•ki [sə-LOO-kee] *noun* tall hound with silky coat
sal•u•tar•y [SAL-yə-ter-ee] *adjective* wholesome, resulting in good
sa•lute [sə-LOOT] *verb transitive* **-lut•ed, -lut•ing** 1 greet with words or sign 2 acknowledge with praise ▷ *verb intransitive* **-lut•ed, -lut•ing** 3 perform military salute ▷ *noun* 4 word, sign by which one greets another 5 motion of arm as mark of respect to superior, etc. in military usage 6 firing of guns as military greeting of honor > **sal•u•ta'tion** [-yə-TAY-shən] *noun*
sal•vage [SAL-vij] *noun* 1 act of saving ship or other property from danger of loss 2 property so saved ▷ *verb transitive* **-vaged, -vag•ing**
sal•va•tion [sal-VAY-shən] *noun* fact or state of being saved, esp. of soul
salve [sav] *noun* 1 healing ointment ▷ *verb transitive* **salved, salv•ing** 2 anoint with such, soothe
sal•ver [SAL-vər] *noun* (silver) tray for presentation of food, letters, etc.
sal•vo [SAL-voh] *noun, plural* **-vos** *or* **-voes** simultaneous discharge of guns, etc.
Sam. Samuel
Sa•mar•i•tan [sə-MAR-i-tn] *noun* 1 native of ancient Samaria 2 (**sa•mar•i•tan**) benevolent person
sam•ba [SAM-bə] *noun* 1 dance of S Amer. origin 2 music for it
same [saym] *adjective* 1 identical, not different, unchanged 2 uniform 3 just mentioned previously > **same'ness** [-nis] *noun* 1 similarity 2 monotony
sam•o•var [SAM-ə-vahr] *noun* Russian tea urn
Sam•o•yed [sam-ə-YED] *noun* dog with thick white coat and tightly curled tail
sam'pan *noun* small oriental boat
sam•ple [SAM-pəl] *noun* 1 specimen ▷ *verb transitive* **-pled, -pling** 2 take, give sample of 3

---

salary *noun* PAY, earnings, income, wage, wages
sale *noun* 1 SELLING, deal, disposal, marketing, transaction
2 ▷ **for sale** AVAILABLE, obtainable, on the market
salient *adjective* PROMINENT, conspicuous, important, noticeable, outstanding, pronounced, striking
sallow *adjective* WAN, anemic, pale, pallid, pasty, sickly, unhealthy, yellowish
salt *noun* 1 SEASONING, flavor, relish, savor, taste
2 ▷ **with a grain of salt with a pinch of salt** SKEPTICALLY, cynically, disbelievingly, suspiciously, with reservations
▷ *adjective* 3 SALTY, brackish, briny, saline
salty *adjective* SALT, brackish, briny, saline
salubrious *adjective* HEALTHY, beneficial, good for one, health-giving, wholesome
salutary *adjective* BENEFICIAL, advantageous, good for one, profitable, useful, valuable
salute *noun* 1 GREETING, address, recognition, salutation
▷ *verb* 2 GREET, acknowledge, address, hail, welcome
3 HONOR, acknowledge, pay tribute to *or* pay homage to, recognize
salvage *verb* SAVE, recover, redeem, rescue, retrieve
salvation *noun* SAVING, deliverance, escape, preservation, redemption, rescue
salve *noun* OINTMENT, balm, cream, emollient, lotion

try 4 test 5 select 6 use part of (old sound recording) in new recording > **sam'pler** *noun* beginner's exercise in embroidery > **sampling** *noun* 1 the taking of samples 2 sample

sam•u•rai [SAM-uu-rī] *noun, plural* **samurai** member of ancient Japanese warrior caste

san•a•to•ri•um [san-ə-TOR-ee-əm] *noun, plural* **-ri•ums** *or* **-ri•a** [-ree-ə] 1 hospital, esp. for chronically ill 2 health resort

sanc•ti•fy [SANGK-tə-fī] *verb transitive* **-fied, -fying** 1 set apart as holy 2 free from sin > **sanc•ti•fi•ca'tion** *noun* > **sanc'ti•ty** *noun, plural* **-ti•ties** 1 saintliness 2 sacredness 3 inviolability > **sanc'tu•ar•y** [-choo-er-ee] *noun, plural* **-ar•ies** 1 holy place 2 part of church nearest altar 3 place of special holiness in synagogue 4 place where fugitive was safe from arrest or violence 5 place protected by law where animals, etc. can live without interference > **sanc•tum** [SANGK-təm] *noun* 1 sacred place or shrine 2 person's private room > **sanctum sanc•to•rum** [sangk-TOR-əm] *noun* 1 holy of holies in Temple in Jerusalem 2 sanctum

sanc•ti•mo•ni•ous [sangk-tə-MOH-nee-əs] *adjective* making a show of piety, holiness > **sanc•ti•mo'ni•ous•ness** *noun*

sanc•tion [SANGK-shən] *noun* 1 permission, authorization 2 penalty for breaking law ▷ *verb transitive* 3 allow, authorize, permit > **sanc•tions** *plural noun* boycott or other coercive measure esp. by one country against another regarded as having violated a law, right, etc.

sand *noun* 1 substance consisting of small grains of rock or mineral, esp. on beach or in desert ▷ *verb transitive* 2 polish, smooth with sandpaper 3 cover, mix with sand > **sands** *plural noun* stretches or banks of this, usually forming seashore > **sand'er** *noun* (power) tool for smoothing surfaces > **sand'y** *adjective* **sand•i•er, sand•i•est** 1 like sand 2 sand-colored 3 consisting of, covered with sand > **sand'bag** *noun* 1 bag filled with sand or soil, used as protection against gunfire, floodwater, etc. and as weapon ▷ *verb transitive* **-bagged, -bag•ging** 2 beat, hit with sandbag 3 (*informal*) in football, tackle passer as if from ambush > **sand'blast** *noun* jet of sand blown from a nozzle under pressure for cleaning, grinding, etc. ▷ *verb transitive* > **sand'pa•per** *noun* paper with sand stuck on it for scraping or polishing wood, etc. > **sand'pit, sand'box** *noun* quantity of sand for children to play in > **sand'stone** *noun* rock composed of sand

san•dal [SAN-dl] *noun* shoe consisting of sole attached by straps

sand'wich *noun* 1 two slices of bread with meat or other food between 2 anything resembling this ▷ *verb transitive* 3 insert between two other things

sane [sayn] *adjective* **san•er, san•est** 1 of sound mind 2 sensible, rational > **san•i•ty** [SAN-i-tee] *noun*

sang *pt. of* **sing**

sang-froid [sahn-FRWAH] *noun Fr.* 1 composure 2 indifference 3 self-possession

san•guine [SANG-gwin] *adjective* 1 cheerful, confident 2 ruddy in complexion > **san•gui•nar•y** [SANG-gwə-ner-ee] *adjective* 1 accompanied by bloodshed 2 bloodthirsty

san•i•tar•y [SAN-i-ter-ee] *adjective* helping protection of health against dirt, etc. > **san•i•ta'tion** *noun* measures, apparatus for preservation of public health

sank *pt. of* **sink**

San'skrit *noun* ancient language of India

sap[1] *noun* 1 moisture that circulates in plants 2 energy ▷ *verb* **sapped, sap•ping** 3 drain off sap > **sap'ling** *noun* young tree

sap[2] *verb* **sapped, sap•ping** 1 undermine 2 destroy insidiously 3 weaken ▷ *noun* 4 trench dug in order to approach or undermine enemy position > **sap'per** [-pər] *noun* soldier doing this

sap[3] *noun* (*slang*) foolish, gullible person

sa•pi•ent [SAY-pee-ənt] *adjective* (*usually ironical*) 1 wise 2 discerning 3 shrewd 4 knowing > **sa'pi•ence** *noun*

Sap•phic [SAF-ik] *adjective* 1 of Sappho, a Grecian poet 2 denoting a kind of verse ▷ *noun* 3 Sapphic verse > **sap'phism** [SAF-iz-əm] *noun* lesbianism

sap•phire [SAF-īr] *noun* 1 (usu. blue) precious

DICTIONARY S THESAURUS

---

same *adjective* 1 AFOREMENTIONED, aforesaid 2 IDENTICAL, alike, corresponding, duplicate, equal, twin
3 UNCHANGED, changeless, consistent, constant, invariable, unaltered, unvarying

sample *noun* 1 SPECIMEN, example, instance, model, pattern
▷ *verb* 2 TEST, experience, inspect, taste, try
▷ *adjective* 3 TEST, representative, specimen, trial

sanctify *verb* CONSECRATE, cleanse, hallow

sanctimonious *adjective* HOLIER-THAN-THOU, hypocritical, pious, self-righteous, smug

sanction *noun* 1 PERMISSION, approval, authority, authorization, backing, O.K. *or* okay (*informal*), stamp of approval *or* seal of approval
2 (*often plural*) BAN, boycott, coercive measures, embargo, penalty
▷ *verb* 3 PERMIT, allow, approve, authorize, endorse

sanctity *noun* 1 SACREDNESS, inviolability
2 HOLINESS, godliness, goodness, grace, piety, righteousness

sanctuary *noun* 1 SHRINE, altar, church, temple
2 PROTECTION, asylum, haven, refuge, retreat, shelter
3 RESERVE, conservation area, national park, nature reserve

sane *adjective* 1 RATIONAL, all there (*informal*), compos mentis (*Latin*), in one's right mind, mentally sound, of sound mind
2 SENSIBLE, balanced, judicious, level-headed, reasonable, sound

sanguine *adjective* CHEERFUL, buoyant, confident, hopeful, optimistic

sanitary *adjective* HYGIENIC, clean, germ-free, healthy, wholesome

sanity *noun* 1 MENTAL HEALTH, normality, rationality, reason, saneness
2 GOOD SENSE, common sense, level-headedness, rationality, sense

sap[1] *noun* 1 VITAL FLUID, essence, lifeblood
2 (*informal & slang*) FOOL, dork (*slang*), idiot, jerk (*slang*), ninny, schmuck (*slang*), simpleton

sap[2] *verb* WEAKEN, deplete, drain, exhaust,

stone **2** deep blue ▷ *adjective*
sar•a•band [SAR-ə-band] *noun* **1** slow, stately Spanish dance **2** music for it
sar•casm [SAHR-kaz-əm] *noun* **1** bitter or wounding ironic remark **2** such remarks **3** taunt **4** sneer **5** irony **6** use of such expressions > **sar•cas'tic** [-KAS-tik] *adjective* > **sar•cas'ti•cal•ly** *adverb*
sar•coph•a•gous [sahr-KOF-ə-gəs] *adjective* carnivorous
sar•coph•a•gus [sahr-KOF-ə-gəs] *noun, plural* **-gi** [-jī] stone coffin
sar•dine [sahr-DEEN] *noun* small fish of herring family, usu. preserved in oil
sar•don•ic [sahr-DON-ik] *adjective* characterized by irony, mockery or derision
sar•don•yx [sahr-DON-iks] *noun* gemstone, variety of chalcedony
sar•gas•sum [sahr-GAS-əm], **sar•gas•so** [-GAS-oh] *noun* gulfweed, type of floating seaweed
sa•ri [SAHR-ee] *noun, plural* **-ris** Hindu woman's robe
sa•rong [sə-RAWNG] *noun* skirtlike garment worn in Asian and Pacific countries
sar•sa•pa•ril•la [sas-pə-RIL-ə] *noun* (flavor of) drink like root beer orig. made from root of plant
sar•to•ri•al [sahr-TOR-ee-əl] *adjective* of tailor, tailoring, or men's clothes
sash[1] *noun* decorative belt, ribbon, wound around the body
sash[2] *noun* window frame opened by moving up and down in grooves
sas•sa•fras [SAS-ə-fras] *noun* tree of laurel family with aromatic bark used medicinally
sat *pt./pp. of* **sit**
Sa•tan [SAYT-n] *noun* the devil > **sa•tan'ic** [sə-TAN-ik], **sa•tan'i•cal** *adjective* devilish, fiendish
satch•el [SACH-əl] *noun* small bag, oft. with shoulder strap
sate [sayt] *verb transitive* **sat•ed, sat•ing** satisfy a desire or appetite fully or excessively
sat•el•lite [SAT-l-īt] *noun* **1** celestial body or manmade projectile orbiting planet **2** person, country, etc. dependent on another
sa•ti•ate [SAY-shee-ayt] *verb transitive* **-at•ed, at•ing** **1** satisfy to the full **2** surfeit > **sa•ti•a'tion** *noun* > **sa•ti•e•ty** [sə-TĪ-i-tee] *noun* feeling of having had too much
sat•in [SAT-n] *noun* fabric (of silk, nylon, etc.) with glossy surface on one side > **sat'in•y** *adjective* of, like satin
sat•ire [SAT-īr] *noun* **1** composition in which vice, folly or foolish person is held up to ridicule **2** use of ridicule or sarcasm to expose vice and folly > **sa•tir•i•cal** [sə-TIR-i-kəl] *adjective* **1** of nature of satire **2** sarcastic **3** bitter > **sat'i•rist** *noun* > **sat'i•rize** *verb transitive* **-rized, -riz•ing** **1** make object of satire **2** censure thus
sat•is•fy [SAT-is-fī] *verb transitive* **-fied, -fy•ing** **1** content, meet wishes of **2** pay **3** fulfill, supply adequately **4** convince > **sat•is•fac'tion** *noun* > **sat•is•fac'to•ry** *adjective*
sa•trap [SAY-trap] *noun* **1** provincial governor in ancient Persia **2** subordinate ruler, oft. despotic
sat•u•rate [SACH-ə-rayt] *verb transitive* **-rat•ed, -rat•ing** **1** soak thoroughly **2** cause to absorb maximum amount **3** *chem.* cause substance to combine to its full capacity with another **4** shell or bomb heavily > **sat•u•ra'tion** *noun* act, result of saturating
Sat•urn [SAT-ərn] *noun* **1** Roman god **2** one of planets > **sat•ur•nine** [SAT-ər-nīn] *adjective* **1** gloomy **2** sluggish in temperament, dull, morose > **Sat•ur•na'li•a** [-NAY-lee-ə] *noun, plural* **-li•as** **1** ancient festival of Saturn **2** (**sat•ur•na'li•a**) noisy revelry, orgy
sa•tyr [SAY-tər] *noun* **1** woodland deity, part man, part goat **2** lustful man
sauce [saws] *noun* **1** liquid added to food to enhance flavor **2** (*informal*) impudence **3** (*slang*) whiskey ▷ *verb transitive* **sauced, sauc•ing** **4** add sauce to **5** (*informal*) be cheeky, impudent to > **sau'ci•ly** *adverb* > **sau'cy** *adjective* **-ci•er, -ci•est** impudent > **sauce'pan** *noun* cooking pot with long handle
sau•cer [SAW-sər] *noun* **1** curved plate put under cup **2** shallow depression
sau•er•kraut [SOW-ər-krowt] *noun* German dish of finely shredded and pickled cabbage

DICTIONARY • THESAURUS

undermine
sarcasm *noun* IRONY, bitterness, cynicism, derision, mockery, satire
sarcastic *adjective* IRONIC, acid, biting, caustic, cutting, cynical, mocking, sardonic, satirical
sardonic *adjective* MOCKING, cynical, derisive, dry, ironic, sarcastic, sneering, wry
Satan *noun* THE DEVIL, Beelzebub, Lord of the Flies, Lucifer, Mephistopheles, Prince of Darkness, The Evil One
satanic *adjective* EVIL, black, demonic, devilish, diabolic, fiendish, hellish, infernal, wicked
satiate *verb* **1** GLUT, cloy, gorge, jade, nauseate, overfill, stuff, surfeit
2 SATISFY, sate, slake
satire *noun* MOCKERY, burlesque, caricature, irony, lampoon, parody, ridicule, spoof (*informal*)
satirical *adjective* MOCKING, biting, caustic, cutting, incisive, ironic
satirize *verb* RIDICULE, burlesque, deride, lampoon, parody, pillory
satisfaction *noun* **1** CONTENTMENT, comfort, content, enjoyment, happiness, pleasure, pride, repletion, satiety
2 FULFILLMENT, achievement, assuaging, gratification
satisfactory *adjective* ADEQUATE, acceptable, all right, average, fair, good enough, passable, sufficient
satisfy *verb* **1** CONTENT, assuage, gratify, indulge, pacify, pander to, please, quench, sate, slake
2 FULFILL, answer, do, meet, serve, suffice
3 PERSUADE, assure, convince, reassure
saturate *verb* SOAK, drench, imbue, souse, steep, suffuse, waterlog, wet through
saturated *adjective* SOAKED, drenched, dripping, soaking *or* soaking wet, sodden, sopping *or* sopping wet, waterlogged, wet through
saturnine *adjective* GLOOMY, dour, glum, grave, morose, somber
saucy *adjective* **1** IMPUDENT, cheeky (*informal*), forward, impertinent, insolent, pert, presumptuous, rude

sau•na [SAW-nə] *noun* steam bath, orig. Finnish
saun•ter [SAWN-tər] *verb intransitive* 1 walk in leisurely manner, stroll ▷ *noun* 2 leisurely walk or stroll
sau•ri•an [SOR-ee-ən] *noun* one of the order of reptiles including the alligator, lizard, etc.
sau•sage [SAW-sij] *noun* chopped seasoned meat enclosed in thin tube of animal intestine or synthetic material > **sausage meat** meat prepared for this
sau•té [soh-TAY] *adjective* 1 cooked or browned in pan with little butter, oil, etc. ▷ *verb transitive* **-téed, -té•ing** 2 cook in this way
Sau•ternes [soh-TURN] *noun* 1 sweet white wine from S Bordeaux, France 2 (**sau•ternes**) similar wine made elsewhere
sav•age [SAV-ij] *adjective* 1 wild 2 ferocious 3 brutal 4 uncivilized, primitive ▷ *noun* 5 member of savage tribe, barbarian ▷ *verb transitive* **-aged, -ag•ing** 6 attack ferociously > **sav'age•ry** *noun*
sa•van•na, sa•van•nah (sə-VAN-ə) ▷ *noun* extensive open grassy plain
sa•vant [sa-VAHNT] *noun* person of learning
save [sayv] *verb transitive* **saved, sav•ing** 1 rescue, preserve 2 protect 3 secure 4 keep for future, lay by 5 prevent need of 6 spare 7 except 8 *computing* keep (data) by moving to location for storage ▷ *verb intransitive* **saved, sav•ing** 9 lay by money ▷ *preposition* 10 except ▷ *conjunction* 11 but > **saving** *adjective* 1 frugal 2 thrifty 3 delivering from sin 4 excepting 5 compensating ▷ *preposition* 6 except ▷ *noun* 7 economy > **savings** money, earnings put by for future use
sav•ior [SAYV-yər] *noun* 1 person who rescues another 2 (**Sav•ior**) Christ
sa•voir-faire [sav-wahr-FAIR] *noun* Fr. ability to do, say, the right thing in any situation
sa•vor [SAY-vər] *noun* 1 characteristic taste 2 flavor 3 odor 4 distinctive quality ▷ *verb intransitive* 5 have particular smell or taste 6 have suggestion (of) ▷ *verb transitive* 7 give flavor to 8 have flavor of 9 enjoy, appreciate > **sa'vor•y** *adjective* 1 attractive to taste or smell 2 not sweet
sa•vor•y [SAY-və-ree] *noun, plural* **-vor-ies** aromatic herb used in cooking
sav•vy [SAV-ee] *verb transitive* **-vied, -vy•ing** (*informal*) 1 understand ▷ *noun* 2 wits, intelligence
saw[1] *noun* 1 tool for cutting wood, etc. by tearing it with toothed edge ▷ *verb* **sawed, sawed** *or* **sawn, saw•ing** 2 cut with saw 3 make movements of sawing > **saw'dust** *noun* fine wood fragments made in sawing > **saw'mill** *noun* mill where timber is sawed by machine into planks, etc.
saw[2] *pt. of* **see**
saw[3] *noun* wise saying, proverb
sax•i•frage [SAK-sə-frij] *noun* alpine or rock plant
Sax•on [SAK-sən] *noun* member of West Germanic people who settled widely in Europe in the early Middle Ages ▷ *adjective*
sax•o•phone [SAK-sə-fohn] *noun* keyed wind instrument
say *verb transitive* **said** [sed], **say•ing, says** [sez] 1 speak 2 pronounce 3 state 4 express 5 take as example or as near enough 6 form and deliver opinion ▷ *noun* 7 what one has to say 8 chance of saying it 9 share in decision > **saying** *noun* maxim, proverb
Sb *chem.* antimony
Sc *chem.* scandium
scab [skab] *noun* 1 crust formed over wound 2 skin disease 3 disease of plants 4 strikebreaker > **scab'by** *adjective* **-bi•er, -bi•est**
scab•bard [SKAB-ərd] *noun* sheath for sword or dagger
scab•rous [SKAYB-rəs] *adjective* 1 having rough surface 2 thorny 3 indecent 4 risky

DICTIONARY

S

THESAURUS

2 JAUNTY, dashing, gay, perky
saunter *verb* 1 STROLL, amble, meander, mosey (*informal*), ramble, roam, wander
▷ *noun* 2 STROLL, airing, amble, ramble, turn, walk
savage *adjective* 1 WILD, feral, undomesticated, untamed
2 UNCULTIVATED, rough, rugged, uncivilized
3 CRUEL, barbarous, bestial, bloodthirsty, brutal, ferocious, fierce, harsh, ruthless, sadistic, vicious
4 PRIMITIVE, rude, unspoilt
▷ *noun* 5 LOUT, boor, yahoo
▷ *verb* 6 ATTACK, lacerate, mangle, maul
savagery *noun* CRUELTY, barbarity, brutality, ferocity, ruthlessness, viciousness
save *verb* 1 RESCUE, deliver, free, liberate, recover, redeem, salvage
2 PROTECT, conserve, guard, keep safe, look after, preserve, safeguard
3 KEEP, collect, gather, hoard, hold, husband, lay by, put by, reserve, set aside, store
saving *noun* 1 ECONOMY, bargain, discount, reduction
▷ *adjective* 2 REDEEMING, compensatory, extenuating
savings *plural noun* NEST EGG, fund, reserves, resources, store
savior *noun* RESCUER, defender, deliverer, liberator, preserver, protector, redeemer
Savior *noun* CHRIST, Jesus, Messiah, Redeemer
savoir-faire *noun* SOCIAL KNOW-HOW (*informal*), diplomacy, discretion, finesse, poise, social graces, tact, urbanity, worldliness
savor *verb* 1 ENJOY, appreciate, delight in, luxuriate in, relish, revel in
2 (*often with of*) SUGGEST, be suggestive, show signs, smack
▷ *noun* 3 FLAVOR, piquancy, relish, smack, smell, tang, taste
savory *adjective* SPICY, appetizing, full-flavored, luscious, mouthwatering, palatable, piquant, rich, tasty
say *verb* 1 SPEAK, affirm, announce, assert, declare, maintain, mention, pronounce, remark, state, utter, voice
2 SUPPOSE, assume, conjecture, estimate, guess, imagine, presume, surmise
3 EXPRESS, communicate, convey, imply
▷ *noun* 4 CHANCE TO SPEAK, voice, vote
5 INFLUENCE, authority, clout (*informal*), power, weight
saying *noun* PROVERB, adage, aphorism, axiom, dictum, maxim

scaf•fold [SKAF-əld] *noun* 1 temporary platform for workmen 2 gallows > **scaf'fold•ing** *noun* (material for building) scaffold

sca•lar [SKAY-lər] *noun* variable quantity, e.g. time, having magnitude but no direction ▷ *adjective*

scald [skawld] *verb transitive* 1 burn with hot liquid or steam 2 clean, sterilize with boiling water 3 heat (liquid) almost to boiling point ▷ *noun* 4 injury by scalding

scale[1] [skayl] *noun* 1 one of the thin, overlapping plates covering fishes and reptiles 2 thin flake 3 incrustation that forms in boilers, etc. ▷ *verb transitive* **scaled, scal•ing** 4 remove scales from ▷ *verb intransitive* **scaled, scal•ing** 5 come off in scales > **scal'y** *adjective* **scal•i•er, scal•i•est** resembling or covered in scales > **scale insect** plant pest covered by waxy secretion

scale[2] *noun* 1 (*chiefly in plural*) weighing instrument ▷ *verb transitive* **scaled, scal•ing** 2 weigh in scales 3 have weight of

scale[3] *noun* 1 graduated table or sequence of marks at regular intervals used as reference or for fixing standards, as in making measurements, in music, etc. 2 ratio of size between a thing and a model or map of it 3 (relative) degree, extent ▷ *verb transitive* **scaled, scal•ing** 4 climb ▷ *adjective* 5 proportionate > **scale up** *verb* increase proportionately in size > **scale down** *verb* decrease proportionately in size

sca•lene [SKAY-leen] *adjective* (of triangle) with three unequal sides

scal•lop [SKOL-əp] *noun* 1 edible shellfish 2 edging in small curves like edge of scallop shell ▷ *verb transitive* 3 shape like scallop shell 4 cook in scallop shell or dish like one

scalp [skalp] *noun* 1 skin and hair of top of head ▷ *verb transitive* 2 cut off scalp of

scal•pel [SKAL-pəl] *noun* small surgical knife

scam [skam] *noun* (*informal*) a dishonest scheme

scamp [skamp] *noun* 1 mischievous person or child ▷ *verb* 2 do or make hastily or carelessly

scamp•er [SKAM-pər] *verb intransitive* 1 run about 2 run hastily from place to place ▷ *noun*

scam•pi [SKAM-pee] *noun, plural* **scampi** 1 large shrimp 2 dish of these sautéed in oil or butter and garlic

scan [skan] *verb* **scanned, scan•ning** 1 look at carefully, scrutinize 2 measure or read (verse) by metrical feet 3 examine, search by systematically varying the direction of a radar or sonar beam 4 glance over quickly 5 (of verse) conform to metrical rules ▷ *noun* 6 scanning > **scan'ner** *noun* device, esp. electronic, that scans > **scan'sion** [-shən] *noun*

scan•dal [SKAN-dl] *noun* 1 action, event generally considered disgraceful 2 malicious gossip > **scan'dal•ize** *verb transitive* **-ized, -iz•ing** shock > **scan'dal•ous** [-dl-əs] *adjective* outrageous, disgraceful

scant [skant] *adjective* **-er, -est** barely sufficient or not sufficient > **scant'i•ly** *adverb* > **scant'y** *adjective* **scant•i•er, scant•i•est** > **scant•ies** [SKAN-teez] *noun* very brief underpants

scape•goat [SKAYP-goht] *noun* person bearing blame due to others > **scape'grace** [-grays] *noun* 1 rascal 2 unscrupulous person

scap•u•la [SKAP-yə-lə] *noun, plural* **-las** shoulder blade > **scap'u•lar** [-lər] *adjective* 1 of scapula ▷ *noun* 2 loose sleeveless monastic garment

scar [skar] *noun* 1 mark left by healed wound, burn or sore 2 change resulting from emotional distress ▷ *verb* **scarred, scar•ring** 3 mark, heal with scar

scar•ab [SKA-rəb] *noun* 1 sacred beetle of ancient Egypt 2 gem cut in shape of this

scarce [skairs] *adjective* 1 hard to find 2 existing or available in insufficient quantity 3 uncommon > **scarce'ly** *adverb* 1 only just 2 not quite 3 definitely or probably not > **scar'ci•ty** [-si-tee] *noun*

scare [skair] *verb transitive* **scared, scar•ing** 1

DICTIONARY • THESAURUS

scale[1] *noun* FLAKE, lamina, layer, plate

scale[2] *noun* 1 GRADUATION, gradation, hierarchy, ladder, progression, ranking, sequence, series, steps
2 RATIO, proportion
3 DEGREE, extent, range, reach, scope
▷ *verb* 4 CLIMB, ascend, clamber, escalade, mount, surmount
5 ADJUST, proportion, regulate

scam *verb* (*slang*) 1 CHEAT, cook the books (*informal*), diddle (*informal*), fix, swindle, wangle (*informal*)
▷ *noun* 2 (*slang*) FRAUD, fix, racket (*slang*), swindle

scamp *noun* RASCAL, devil, imp, monkey, rogue, scallywag (*informal*)

scamper *verb* RUN, dart, dash, hasten, hurry, romp, scoot, scurry, scuttle

scan *verb* 1 GLANCE OVER, check, check out (*informal*), examine, eye, look through, run one's eye over, run over, skim
2 SCRUTINIZE, investigate, scour, search, survey, sweep

scandal *noun* 1 CRIME, disgrace, embarrassment, offense, sin, wrongdoing
2 SHAME, defamation, discredit, disgrace, dishonor, ignominy, infamy, opprobrium, stigma
3 GOSSIP, aspersion, dirt, rumors, slander, talk, tattle

scandalize *verb* SHOCK, affront, appall, horrify, offend, outrage

scandalous *adjective* 1 SHOCKING, disgraceful, disreputable, infamous, outrageous, shameful, unseemly
2 SLANDEROUS, defamatory, libelous, scurrilous, untrue

scant *adjective* MEAGER, barely sufficient, little, minimal, sparse

scanty *adjective* MEAGER, bare, deficient, inadequate, insufficient, lousy (*slang*), poor, scant, short, skimpy, sparse, thin

scapegoat *noun* WHIPPING BOY, fall guy (*informal*)

scar *noun* 1 MARK, blemish, injury, wound
▷ *verb* 2 MARK, damage, disfigure

scarce *adjective* RARE, few, few and far between, infrequent, in short supply, insufficient, uncommon

scarcely *adverb* 1 HARDLY, barely
2 DEFINITELY NOT, hardly

scarcity *noun* SHORTAGE, dearth, deficiency, insufficiency, lack, paucity, rareness, want

frighten ▷ *noun* 2 fright, sudden panic > **scar'y** *adjective* **scar•i•er, scar•i•est** > **scare'crow** [-kroh] *noun* 1 thing set up to frighten birds from crops 2 badly dressed or miserable looking person > **scare•mon•ger** [-mung-gər] *noun* one who spreads alarming rumors

scarf[1] [skarf] *noun, plural* **scarfs** *or* **scarves** long narrow strip, large piece of material to put around neck, head, etc.

scarf[2] *noun, plural* **scarfs** 1 part cut away from each of two pieces of timber to be jointed longitudinally 2 joint so made ▷ *verb transitive* 3 cut or join in this way

scar•i•fy [SKA-rə-fī] *verb transitive* **-fied, -fy•ing** 1 scratch, cut slightly all over 2 lacerate 3 stir surface soil of 4 criticize mercilessly

scar•let [SKAHR-lit] *noun* 1 a brilliant red color 2 cloth or clothing of this color ▷ *adjective* 3 of this color 4 immoral, esp. unchaste > **scarlet fever** infectious fever with scarlet rash

scarp [skahrp] *noun* 1 steep slope 2 inside slope of ditch in fortifications

scath•ing [SKAY*th*-ing] *adjective* 1 harshly critical 2 cutting 3 damaging

scat•ter [SKAT-ər] *verb transitive* 1 throw in various directions 2 put here and there 3 sprinkle ▷ *verb intransitive* 4 disperse ▷ *noun* > **scat'ter•brain** [-brayn] *noun* silly, careless person

scav•enge [SKAV-inj] *verb* **-enged, -eng•ing** 1 search for (anything usable) usu. among discarded material > **scav'en•ger** *noun* 1 person who scavenges 2 animal, bird that feeds on refuse

scene [seen] *noun* 1 place of action of novel, play, etc. 2 place of any action 3 subdivision of play 4 view 5 episode 6 display of strong emotion > **scen'er•y** *noun, plural* **-er•ies** 1 natural features of area 2 constructions of wood, canvas, etc. used on stage to represent a place where action is happening > **sce'nic** *adjective* 1 picturesque 2 of or on the stage > **sce•nar•i•o** [si-NAIR-ee-oh] *noun, plural* **-i•os** summary of plot (of play, etc.) or plan

scent [sent] *noun* 1 distinctive smell, esp. pleasant one 2 trail, clue 3 perfume ▷ *verb transitive* 4 detect or track (by smell) 5 suspect, sense 6 fill with fragrance

scep•ter [SEP-tər] *noun* 1 ornamental staff as symbol of royal power 2 royal dignity

sched•ule [SKEJ-uul] *noun* 1 plan of procedure for a project 2 list 3 timetable ▷ *verb transitive* **-uled, -ul•ing** 4 enter in schedule 5 plan to occur at certain time **on schedule** on time

sche•ma [SKEE-mə] *noun, plural* **-ma•ta** [-mə-tə] **-mas** overall plan or diagram > **sche•mat'ic** *adjective* presented as plan or diagram > **sche'ma•tize** [-tīz] *verb* **-tized, -tiz•ing**

scheme [skeem] *noun* 1 plan, design 2 project 3 outline ▷ *verb* **schemed, schem•ing** 4 devise, plan, esp. in underhand manner > **schem'er** *noun*

scher•zo [SKERT-soh] *noun mus.* light playful composition

schism [SIZ-əm] *noun* (group resulting from) division in political party, church, etc. > **schis•mat'ic** *noun, adjective*

schist [shist] *noun* crystalline rock that splits into layers

schiz•o•phre•ni•a [skit-sə-FREE-nee-ə] *noun* mental disorder involving deterioration of, confusion about personality > **schiz•o•phren'ic** [-FREN-ik] *adjective, noun* > **schiz'oid** [-soid] *adjective* relating to schizophrenia

schmaltz [shmahlts] *noun* excessive sentimentality > **schmaltz'y** *adjective*

DICTIONARY

S

THESAURUS

---

scare *verb* 1 FRIGHTEN, alarm, dismay, intimidate, panic, shock, startle, terrify ▷ *noun* 2 FRIGHT, panic, shock, start, terror

scared *adjective* FRIGHTENED, fearful, panicky, panic-stricken, petrified, shaken, startled, terrified

scary *adjective* FRIGHTENING, alarming, chilling, creepy (*informal*), horrifying, spine-chilling, spooky (*informal*), terrifying

scathing *adjective* CRITICAL, biting, caustic, cutting, harsh, sarcastic, scornful, trenchant, withering

scatter *verb* 1 THROW ABOUT, diffuse, disseminate, fling, shower, spread, sprinkle, strew
2 DISPERSE, disband, dispel, dissipate

scatterbrain *noun* FEATHERBRAIN, butterfly, flibbertigibbet

scenario *noun* STORY LINE, outline, résumé, summary, synopsis

scene *noun* 1 SITE, area, locality, place, position, setting, spot
2 SETTING, backdrop, background, location, set
3 SHOW, display, drama, exhibition, pageant, picture, sight, spectacle
4 ACT, division, episode, part
5 VIEW, landscape, panorama, prospect, vista
6 FUSS, commotion, exhibition, performance, row, tantrum, to-do
7 (*informal*) WORLD, arena, business, environment

scenery *noun* 1 LANDSCAPE, surroundings, terrain, view, vista
2 (*theatre*) SET, backdrop, flats, setting, stage set

scenic *adjective* PICTURESQUE, beautiful, panoramic, spectacular, striking

scent *noun* 1 FRAGRANCE, aroma, bouquet, odor, perfume, smell
2 TRAIL, spoor, track
▷ *verb* 3 DETECT, discern, nose out, sense, smell, sniff

scented *adjective* FRAGRANT, aromatic, odoriferous, perfumed, sweet-smelling

schedule *noun* 1 PLAN, agenda, calendar, catalog, inventory, list, program, timetable
▷ *verb* 2 PLAN, appoint, arrange, book, organize, program

scheme *noun* 1 PLAN, program, project, proposal, road map, strategy, system, tactics
2 DIAGRAM, blueprint, chart, draft, layout, outline, pattern
3 PLOT, conspiracy, intrigue, maneuver, ploy, ruse, stratagem, subterfuge
▷ *verb* 4 PLAN, lay plans, project, work out
5 PLOT, collude, conspire, intrigue, machinate, maneuver

scheming *adjective* CALCULATING, artful, conniving, cunning, sly, tricky, underhand, wily

schism *noun* DIVISION, breach, break, rift, rupture, separation, split

schmaltz•i•er, schmaltz•i•est
schnapps [shnops] *noun* 1 spirit distilled from potatoes 2 any strong spirit
schnit•zel [SHNIT-səl] *noun* thin slice of meat, esp. veal
scholar *noun see* **school¹**
school¹ [skool] *noun* 1 institution for teaching children or for giving instruction in any subject 2 buildings of such institution 3 group of thinkers, writers, artists, etc. with principles or methods in common ▷ *verb transitive* 4 educate 5 bring under control, train > **school bus** vehicle used to transport children to or from school or on school-related activities > **school'man** *noun* medieval philosopher > **schol'ar** [SKOL-ər] *noun* 1 learned person 2 one taught in school 3 one quick to learn > **schol'ar•ly** *adjective* learned, erudite > **schol'ar•ship** *noun* 1 learning 2 prize, grant to student for payment of school or college fees > **scho•las•tic** [skə-LAS-tik] *adjective* 1 of schools or scholars, or education 2 pedantic
school² *noun* large number (of fish, whales, etc.)
schoon•er [SKOO-nər] *noun* 1 fore-and-aft rigged vessel with two or more masts 2 tall glass
schot•tische [SHOT-ish] *noun* 1 kind of dance 2 music for this
sci•at•i•ca [sī-AT-i-kə] *noun* 1 neuralgia of hip and thigh 2 pain in sciatic nerve > **sci•at'ic** *adjective* 1 of the hip 2 of sciatica
sci•ence [SĪ-əns] *noun* 1 systematic study and knowledge of natural or physical phenomena 2 any branch of study concerned with observed material facts > **sci•en•tif'ic** *adjective* 1 of the principles of science 2 systematic > **sci•en•tif'i•cal•ly** *adverb* > **sci'en•tist** *noun* one versed in natural sciences > **science fiction** stories set in the future making imaginative use of scientific knowledge
scim•i•tar [SIM-i-tər] *noun* oriental curved sword
scin•til•late [SIN-tl-ayt] *verb intransitive* **-lat•ed, -lat•ing** 1 sparkle 2 be animated, witty, clever > **scin•til•la'tion** *noun*
sci•on [SĪ-ən] *noun* 1 descendant, heir 2 slip for grafting
scis•sors [SIZ-ərs] *plural noun* cutting instrument with two crossed pivoted blades
scle•ro•sis [skli-ROH-sis] *noun, plural* **-ses** [-seez] a hardening of bodily organs, tissues, etc. > **scle•rot'ic** [-ROT-ik] *adjective*
scoff [skof] *verb transitive* 1 express derision for ▷ *noun* 2 derision 3 mocking words > **scoff'er** *noun*
scold [skohld] *verb* 1 find fault 2 reprimand, be angry with ▷ *noun* 3 someone who does this > **scold'ing** *noun*
sconce [skons] *noun* bracket candlestick on wall
scone [skohn] *noun* small plain biscuit baked on griddle or in oven
scoop [skoop] *noun* 1 small shovel-like tool for ladling, hollowing out, etc. 2 (*informal*) exclusive news item 3 (*informal*) information ▷ *verb transitive* 4 ladle out 5 hollow out, rake in with scoop 6 make sudden profit 7 beat (rival newspaper, etc.)
scoot [skoot] *verb intransitive* (*informal*) move off quickly > **scoot'er** *noun* 1 child's vehicle propelled by pushing on ground with one foot 2 light motorcycle (*also* **motor scooter**)
scope [skohp] *noun* 1 range of activity or application 2 room, opportunity
scorch [skorch] *verb* 1 burn, be burned, on surface 2 parch 3 shrivel 4 wither ▷ *noun* 5 slight burn > **scorch'er** *noun* (*informal*) very hot day
score [skor] *noun* 1 points gained in game,

scholar *noun* 1 INTELLECTUAL, academic, savant 2 STUDENT, disciple, learner, pupil, schoolboy *or* schoolgirl
scholarly *adjective* LEARNED, academic, bookish, erudite, intellectual, lettered, scholastic
scholarship *noun* 1 LEARNING, book-learning, education, erudition, knowledge 2 BURSARY, fellowship
scholastic *adjective* LEARNED, academic, lettered, scholarly
school *noun* 1 ACADEMY, college, faculty, institute, institution, seminary 2 GROUP, adherents, circle, denomination, devotees, disciples, faction, followers, set ▷ *verb* 3 TRAIN, coach, discipline, drill, educate, instruct, tutor
schooling *noun* 1 TEACHING, education, tuition 2 TRAINING, coaching, drill, instruction
science *noun* 1 DISCIPLINE, body of knowledge, branch of knowledge 2 SKILL, art, technique
scientific *adjective* SYSTEMATIC, accurate, controlled, exact, mathematical, precise
scientist *noun* INVENTOR, technophile
scintillating *adjective* BRILLIANT, animated, bright, dazzling, exciting, glittering, lively, sparkling, stimulating
scoff¹ *verb* SCORN, belittle, deride, despise, jeer, knock (*informal*), laugh at, mock, pooh-pooh, ridicule, sneer
scoff² *verb* GOBBLE *or* GOBBLE UP, bolt, devour, gorge oneself on, gulp down, guzzle, wolf
scold *verb* 1 REPRIMAND, berate, castigate, censure, chew out (*slang*), find fault with, lecture, rebuke, reproach, reprove, tell off (*informal*), upbraid
scolding *noun* REBUKE, lecture, row, telling-off (*informal*)
scoop *noun* 1 LADLE, dipper, spoon 2 EXCLUSIVE, exposé, revelation, sensation ▷ *verb* 3 (*often with up*) LIFT, gather up, pick up, take up 4 (*often with out*) HOLLOW, bail, dig, empty, excavate, gouge, shovel
scope *noun* 1 OPPORTUNITY, freedom, latitude, liberty, room, space 2 RANGE, area, capacity, orbit, outlook, reach, span, sphere
scorch *verb* BURN, parch, roast, sear, shrivel, singe, wither
scorching *adjective* BURNING, baking, boiling, fiery, flaming, red-hot, roasting, searing
score *noun* 1 POINTS, grade, mark, outcome, record, result, total 2 GROUNDS, basis, cause, ground, reason 3 GRIEVANCE, grudge, injury, injustice, wrong 4 ▷ **scores** LOTS, hundreds, masses, millions, multitudes, myriads, swarms

competition **2** group of 20 **3** musical notation **4** mark or notch, esp. to keep tally **5** reason, account **6** grievance ▷ *verb transitive* **scored, scor•ing** **7** gain points in game **8** mark **9** cross out **10** arrange music (for) ▷ *verb intransitive* **scored, scor•ing** **11** keep tally of points **12** succeed > **scores** *plural noun* lots

scorn [skorn] *noun* **1** contempt, derision ▷ *verb transitive* **2** despise > **scorn'ful** [-fəl] *adjective* derisive > **scorn'ful•ly** *adverb*

scor•pi•on [SKOR-pee-ən] *noun* small lobster-shaped animal with sting at end of jointed tail

Scot [skot] *noun* native of Scotland > **Scot'tish** *adjective* > **Scotch** *noun* whisky distilled in Scotland > **Scots** *adjective* **1** Scottish ▷ *noun* **2** English dialect spoken in Scotland > **Scots'man** [-mən], **Scots'wom•an** *noun*

scotch [skoch] *verb transitive* put an end to

scot-free [skot-free] *adjective* without harm or loss

scoun•drel [SKOWN-drəl] *noun* villain, blackguard > **scoun'drel•ly** *adjective*

scour[1] [skowr] *verb transitive* **1** clean, polish by rubbing **2** clear or flush out

scour[2] *verb* move rapidly along or over (territory) in search of something

scourge [skurj] *noun* **1** whip, lash **2** severe affliction **3** pest **4** calamity ▷ *verb transitive* **scourged, scourg•ing** **5** flog **6** punish severely

scout [skowt] *noun* **1** one sent out to reconnoiter **2** (**Scout**) member of organization for young people which aims to develop character and responsibility ▷ *verb intransitive* **3** go out, act as scout **4** reconnoiter

> **scout'mas•ter** *noun* leader of troop of Boy Scouts

scow [skow] *noun* unpowered barge

scowl [skowl] *verb intransitive* **1** frown gloomily or sullenly ▷ *noun* **2** angry or gloomy expression

scrab•ble [SKRAB-əl] *verb* **-bled, -bling** **1** scrape at with hands, claws in disorderly manner ▷ *noun* **2** (**Scrab•ble**) ® board game in which words are formed by letter tiles

scrag [skrag] *noun* **1** lean person or animal **2** lean end of a neck of mutton > **scrag'gy** *adjective* **-gi•er, -gi•est** thin, bony

scrag•gly [SKRAG-lee] *adjective* **-gli•er, -gli•est** untidy

scram[1] [skram] *verb* **scrammed, scram•ming** (*informal*) go away hastily, get out

scram[2] *noun* emergency shutdown of nuclear reactor ▷ *verb* **scrammed, scram•ming**

scram•ble [SKRAM-bəl] *verb intransitive* **-bled, -bling** **1** move along or up by crawling, climbing, etc. **2** struggle with others (for) **3** (of aircraft, aircrew) take off hurriedly ▷ *verb transitive* **-bled, -bling** **4** mix up **5** cook (eggs) beaten up with milk **6** render (speech) unintelligible by electronic device ▷ *noun* **7** scrambling **8** rough climb **9** disorderly proceeding **10** emergency takeoff of military aircraft

scrap [skrap] *noun* **1** small piece or fragment **2** leftover material **3** (*informal*) fight ▷ *verb* **scrapped, scrap•ping** **4** break up, discard as useless **5** fight > **scrap'py** *adjective* **-pi•er, -pi•est** **1** unequal in quality **2** badly finished

DICTIONARY

S

THESAURUS

▷ *verb* **5** GAIN, achieve, chalk up (*informal*), make, notch up (*informal*), win
6 KEEP COUNT, count, record, register, tally
7 CUT, deface, gouge, graze, mark, scrape, scratch, slash
8 (*with out or through*) CROSS OUT, cancel, delete, obliterate, strike out
9 (*music*) ARRANGE, adapt, orchestrate, set

scorn *noun* **1** CONTEMPT, derision, disdain, disparagement, mockery, sarcasm
▷ *verb* **2** DESPISE, be above, deride, disdain, flout, reject, scoff at, slight, spurn

scornful *adjective* CONTEMPTUOUS, derisive, disdainful, haughty, jeering, mocking, sarcastic, sardonic, scathing, scoffing, sneering

scoundrel *noun* ROGUE, bastard (*offensive*), good-for-nothing, heel (*slang*), miscreant, rascal, reprobate, scamp, swine, villain

scour[1] *verb* RUB, abrade, buff, clean, polish, scrub, wash

scour[2] *verb* SEARCH, beat, comb, hunt, ransack

scourge *noun* **1** AFFLICTION, bane, curse, infliction, misfortune, pest, plague, terror, torment
2 WHIP, cat, lash, strap, switch, thong
▷ *verb* **3** AFFLICT, curse, plague, terrorize, torment
4 WHIP, beat, cane, flog, horsewhip, lash, thrash

scout *noun* **1** VANGUARD, advance guard, lookout, outrider, precursor, reconnoiterer
▷ *verb* **2** RECONNOITER, investigate, observe, probe, spy, survey, watch

scowl *verb* **1** GLOWER, frown, lour *or* lower
▷ *noun* **2** GLOWER, black look, dirty look, frown

scrabble *verb* SCRAPE, claw, scramble, scratch

scraggy *adjective* SCRAWNY, angular, bony, lean, skinny

scram *verb* GO AWAY, abscond, beat it (*slang*), clear off (*informal*), get lost (*informal*), leave, make oneself scarce (*informal*), make tracks, vamoose (*slang*)

scramble *verb* **1** STRUGGLE, climb, crawl, scrabble, swarm
2 STRIVE, contend, jostle, push, run, rush, vie
▷ *noun* **3** CLIMB, trek
4 STRUGGLE, commotion, competition, confusion, melee *or* mêlée, race, rush, tussle

scrap[1] *noun* **1** PIECE, bit, crumb, fragment, grain, morsel, part, particle, portion, sliver, snippet
2 WASTE, junk, off cuts
3 ▷ **scraps** LEFTOVERS, bits, leavings, remains
▷ *verb* **4** DISCARD, abandon, ditch (*slang*), drop, jettison, throw away *or* throw out, write off

scrap[2] (*informal*) *noun* **1** FIGHT, argument, battle, disagreement, dispute, quarrel, row, squabble, wrangle
▷ *verb* **2** FIGHT, argue, row, squabble, wrangle

scrape *verb* **1** GRAZE, bark, rub, scratch, scuff, skin
2 RUB, clean, erase, remove, scour
3 GRATE, grind, rasp, scratch, squeak
4 SCRIMP, pinch, save, skimp, stint
5 ▷ **scrape through** GET BY (*informal*), just make it, struggle
▷ *noun* **6** (*informal*) PREDICAMENT, awkward situation, difficulty, dilemma, fix (*informal*),

> **scrap'book** [-buuk] *noun* book in which newspaper clippings, etc. are kept

scrape [skrayp] *verb transitive* **scraped, scrap•ing** 1 rub with something sharp 2 clean, smooth thus 3 grate 4 scratch 5 rub with harsh noise ▷ *noun* 6 act, sound of scraping 7 awkward situation, esp. as result of escapade > **scrap'er** *noun* 1 instrument for scraping 2 contrivance on which mud, etc. is scraped from shoes

scratch [skrach] *verb transitive* 1 score, make narrow surface wound with claws, nails, or anything pointed 2 make marks on with pointed instruments 3 scrape (skin) with nails to relieve itching 4 remove, withdraw from list, race, etc. ▷ *verb intransitive* 5 use claws or nails, esp. to relieve itching ▷ *noun* 6 wound, mark or sound made by scratching 7 line or starting point ▷ *adjective* 8 got together at short notice 9 impromptu 10 *golf* without any allowance > **scratch'y** *adjective* **scratch•i•er, scratch•i•est** > **scratch hit** *baseball* weak hit barely enabling batter to reach first base

scrawl [skrawl] *verb transitive* 1 write, draw untidily ▷ *noun* 2 thing scrawled 3 careless writing

scrawn•y [SKRAW-nee] *adjective* **scrawn•i•er, scrawn•i•est** thin, bony

scream [skreem] *verb intransitive* 1 utter piercing cry, esp. of fear, pain, etc. 2 be very obvious ▷ *verb transitive* 3 utter in a scream ▷ *noun* 4 shrill, piercing cry 5 (*informal*) very funny person or thing

scree [skree] *noun* 1 loose shifting stones 2 slope covered with these

screech [skreech] *verb intransitive, noun* scream

screed [skreed] *noun* 1 long (tedious) letter, passage or speech 2 thin layer of cement 3 in masonry, board used to make level

screen [skreen] *noun* 1 device to shelter from heat, light, draft, observation, etc. 2 anything used for such purpose 3 mesh over doors, windows to keep out insects 4 white or silvered surface on which photographic images are projected 5 windscreen 6 wooden or stone partition in church ▷ *verb transitive* 7 shelter, hide 8 protect from detection 9 show (film) 10 scrutinize 11 examine (group of people) for presence of disease, weapons, etc. 12 examine for political motives 13 *electricity* protect from stray electric or magnetic fields > **screen saver** *computing* software that produces changing images on a monitor when the computer is operating but idle **the screen** motion pictures generally

screw [skroo] *noun* 1 (nail-like device or cylinder with) spiral thread cut to engage similar thread or to bore into material (wood, etc.) to pin or fasten 2 anything resembling a screw in shape, esp. in spiral form 3 propeller 4 twist ▷ *verb transitive* 5 fasten with screw 6 twist around 7 extort > **screw'y** *adjective* **screw•i•er, screw•i•est** (*slang*) crazy, eccentric > **screw'driv•er** *noun* 1 tool for turning screws 2 drink of vodka and orange juice > **screw up** (*slang*) bungle, distort

scrib•ble [SKRIB-əl] *verb* **-bled, -bling** 1 write, draw carelessly 2 make meaningless marks with pen or pencil ▷ *noun* 3 something scribbled

scribe [skrīb] *noun* 1 writer 2 copyist ▷ *verb* **scribed, scrib•ing** 3 scratch a line with pointed instrument

scrim•mage [SKRIM-ij] *noun* 1 scuffle 2 *football* a play ▷ *verb* **-maged, -mag•ing** 3 engage in scrimmage

scrimp [skrimp] *verb transitive* 1 make too small or short 2 treat meanly > **scrimp'y** *adjective* **scrimp•i•er, scrimp•i•est**

scrip [skrip] *noun* 1 written certificate esp. of holding fractional share of stock 2 paper certificates issued in place of money

script [skript] *noun* (system or style of)

mess, plight, tight spot

scrapheap *noun*
▷ **on the scrapheap** DISCARDED, ditched (*slang*), jettisoned, put out to pasture (*informal*), redundant

scrappy *adjective* FRAGMENTARY, bitty, disjointed, incomplete, piecemeal, sketchy, thrown together

scratch *verb* 1 MARK, claw, cut, damage, etch, grate, graze, lacerate, score, scrape
2 WITHDRAW, abolish, call off, cancel, delete, eliminate, erase, pull out
▷ *noun* 3 MARK, blemish, claw mark, gash, graze, laceration, scrape
4 ▷ **up to scratch** ADEQUATE, acceptable, satisfactory, sufficient, up to standard
▷ *adjective* 5 IMPROVISED, impromptu, rough-and-ready

scrawl *verb* SCRIBBLE, doodle, squiggle, writing

scrawny *adjective* THIN, bony, gaunt, lean, scraggy, skin-and-bones (*informal*), skinny, undernourished

scream *verb* 1 CRY, bawl, screech, shriek, yell
▷ *noun* 2 CRY, howl, screech, shriek, yell, yelp

screech *noun*
▷ *verb* CRY, scream, shriek

screen *noun* 1 COVER, awning, canopy, cloak, guard, partition, room divider, shade, shelter, shield
2 MESH, net
▷ *verb* 3 COVER, cloak, conceal, hide, mask, shade, veil
4 PROTECT, defend, guard, shelter, shield
5 VET, evaluate, examine, filter, gauge, scan, sift, sort
6 BROADCAST, present, put on, show

screw *verb* 1 TURN, tighten, twist
2 (*informal*) (*often with out of*) EXTORT, extract, wrest, wring

screw up *verb* 1 (*informal*) BUNGLE, botch, make a mess of (*slang*), mess up, mishandle, spoil
2 DISTORT, contort, pucker, wrinkle

screwy *adjective* CRAZY, crackpot (*informal*), eccentric, loopy (*informal*), nutty (*slang*), odd, off-the-wall (*slang*), out to lunch (*informal*), weird

scribble *verb* SCRAWL, dash off, jot, write

scribe *noun* COPYIST, amanuensis, writer

scrimp *verb* ECONOMIZE, be frugal, save, scrape, skimp, stint, tighten one's belt

script *noun* 1 TEXT, book, copy, dialogue, libretto, lines, words
2 HANDWRITING, calligraphy, penmanship, writing

Scripture *noun* THE BIBLE, Holy Bible, Holy

handwriting **1** written characters **2** written text of film, play, radio or television program ▷ *verb transitive* **3** write a script
scrip•ture [SKRIP-chər] *noun* **1** sacred writings **2** (**Scrip•ture**) the Bible > **scrip'tur•al** *adjective*
scrof•u•la [SKROF-yə-lə] *noun* tuberculosis of lymphatic glands, esp. of neck > **scrof'u•lous** [-ləs] *adjective*
scroll [skrohl] *noun* **1** roll of parchment or paper **2** list **3** ornament shaped thus ▷ *verb* **4** *computers.* move (text) up or down on a VDU screen
scro•tum [SKROH-təm] *noun, plural* **-tums** pouch containing testicles
scrounge [skrownj] *verb* **scrounged, scroung•ing** get without cost, by begging > **scroung'er** *noun*
scrub[1] [skrub] *verb transitive* **scrubbed, scrub•bing** **1** clean with hard brush and water **2** scour **3** (*slang*) cancel, get rid of ▷ *noun* **4** scrubbing
scrub[2] *noun* **1** stunted trees **2** brushwood > **scrub'by** *adjective* **-bi•er, -bi•est** **1** covered with scrub **2** stunted **3** shabby
scruff [skruf] *noun* nape (of neck)
scrum [skrum] *noun rugby* restarting of play in which opposing packs of forwards push against each other to gain possession of the ball
scrunch [skrunch] *verb* **1** crumple or crunch or be crumpled or crunched ▷ *noun* **2** act or sound of scrunching > **scrun'chie** [SKRUNCH-ee] *noun* loop of elastic covered loosely with fabric, used to hold the hair in a ponytail
scru•ple [SKROO-pəl] *noun* **1** doubt or hesitation about what is morally right **2** weight of 20 grains ▷ *verb intransitive* **-pled, -pling** **3** hesitate > **scru'pu•lous** [-pyə-ləs] *adjective* **1** extremely conscientious **2** thorough, attentive to small points
scru•ti•ny [SKROOT-n-ee] *noun, plural* **-nies** **1** close examination **2** critical investigation **3** searching look > **scru'ti•nize** *verb transitive* **-nized, -niz•ing** examine closely
scu•ba [SKOO-bə] *noun, adjective* (relating to) self-contained underwater breathing apparatus
scud [skud] *verb intransitive* **scud•ded, scud•ding** **1** run fast **2** run before wind
scuff [skuf] *verb intransitive* **1** drag, scrape with feet in walking ▷ *verb transitive* **2** scrape with feet **3** scratch (something) by scraping ▷ *noun* **4** act, sound of scuffing > **scuffs** thong sandals > **scuffed** *adjective* (of shoes) scraped or slightly grazed
scuf•fle [SKUF-əl] *verb intransitive* **-fled, -fling** **1** fight in disorderly manner **2** shuffle ▷ *noun*
scull [skul] *noun* **1** oar used in stern of boat **2** short oar used in pairs ▷ *verb* **3** propel, move by means of scull(s)
scul•ler•y [SKUL-ə-ree] *noun, plural* **-ler•ies** place for washing dishes, etc. > **scul•lion** [SKUL-yən] *noun* **1** despicable person **2** kitchen servant doing menial work
sculp•ture [SKULP-chər] *noun* **1** art of forming figures in relief or solid **2** product of this art ▷ *verb transitive* **-tured, -tur•ing** **3** represent by sculpture > **sculpt** *verb* > **sculp'tur•al** *adjective* with qualities proper to sculpture > **sculp•tor, sculp'tress** [-tris] *noun*
scum [skum] *noun* **1** froth or other floating matter on liquid **2** waste part of anything **3** vile person(s) or thing(s) > **scum'my** *adjective* **-mi•er, -mi•est**
scup•per [SKUP-ər] *noun* hole in ship's side level with deck to carry off water
scurf [skurf] *noun* flaky matter on scalp, dandruff > **scurf'y** *adjective* **scurf•i•er, scurf•i•est**
scur•ril•ous [SKUR-ə-ləs] *adjective* coarse, indecently abusive > **scur•ril•i•ty** [skə-RIL-i-tee] *noun, plural* **-ties**
scur•ry [SKUR-ee] *verb intransitive* **-ried, -ry•ing** **1** run hastily ▷ *noun, plural* **-ries** **2** bustling haste **3** flurry
scur•vy [SKUR-vee] *noun* **1** disease caused by lack of vitamin C ▷ *adjective* **-vi•er, -vi•est** **2** afflicted with the disease **3** mean, contemptible
scut•tle[1] [SKUT-l] *noun* fireside container for coal
scuttle[2] *verb intransitive* **-tled, -tling** **1** rush away **2** run hurriedly ▷ *noun*
scuttle[3] *verb transitive* **-tled, -tling** **1** make hole in ship to sink it **2** abandon, cause to be abandoned
scut•work [SKUT-wurk] *noun* (*informal*) menial work
scythe [sīth] *noun* **1** manual implement with long curved blade for cutting grass, grain ▷ *verb transitive* **scythed, scyth•ing** **2** cut with scythe
Se *chem.* selenium
sea [see] *noun* **1** mass of salt water covering greater part of Earth **2** broad tract of this **3**

Scripture, Holy Writ, The Good Book, The Gospels, The Scriptures
scrounge *verb* (*informal*) CADGE, beg, bum (*informal*), freeload (*slang*), sponge (*informal*)
scrounger *adjective* CADGER, freeloader (*slang*), parasite, sponger (*informal*)
scrub *verb* SCOUR, clean, cleanse, rub
scruple *noun* **1** MISGIVING, compunction, doubt, hesitation, qualm, reluctance, second thoughts, uneasiness
▷ *verb* **2** HAVE MISGIVINGS ABOUT, demur, doubt, have qualms about, hesitate, think twice about
scrupulous *adjective* **1** MORAL, conscientious, honorable, principled, upright
2 CAREFUL, exact, fastidious, meticulous, precise, punctilious, rigorous, strict
scrutinize *verb* EXAMINE, explore, inspect, investigate, peruse, pore over, probe, scan, search, study
scrutiny *noun* EXAMINATION, analysis, exploration, inspection, investigation, perusal, search, study
scuffle *verb* **1** FIGHT, clash, grapple, jostle, struggle, tussle
▷ *noun* **2** FIGHT, brawl, commotion, disturbance, fray, scrimmage, skirmish, tussle
sculpture *verb* SCULPT, carve, chisel, fashion, form, hew, model, mold, shape
scum *noun* **1** IMPURITIES, dross, film, froth
2 RABBLE, dregs of society, riffraff, trash
scurrilous *adjective* SLANDEROUS, abusive, defamatory, insulting, scandalous, vituperative
scurry *verb* **1** HURRY, dart, dash, race, scamper, scoot, scuttle, sprint
▷ *noun* **2** FLURRY, scampering, whirl
scuttle *verb* RUN, bustle, hasten, hurry, rush,

waves **4** swell **5** large quantity **6** vast expanse > **sea'board** [-bord] *noun* coast > **sea'far•ing** [-fair-ing] *adjective* occupied in sea voyages > **sea horse** fish with bony plated body and horselike head > **sea lion** kind of large seal > **sea'man** [-mən] *noun* sailor > **sea'sick•ness** *noun* nausea caused by motion of ship > **sea'sick** *adjective* > **sea urchin** marine animal, echinus > **sea'weed** *noun* plant growing in sea > **sea'wor•thy** [-wurth-ee] *adjective* **-thi•er, -thi•est** in fit condition to put to sea

seal[1] [seel] *noun* **1** piece of metal or stone engraved with device for impression on wax, etc. **2** impression thus made (on letters, etc.) **3** device, material preventing passage of water, air, oil, etc. (*also* **seal'er**) ▷ *verb transitive* **4** affix seal to ratify, authorize **5** mark with stamp as evidence of some quality **6** keep close or secret **7** settle **8** make watertight, airtight, etc.

seal[2] *noun* **1** amphibious furred carnivorous mammal with flippers as limbs ▷ *verb intransitive* **2** hunt seals > **seal'er** *noun* person or ship engaged in sealing > **seal'skin** *noun* skin, fur of seals

seam [seem] *noun* **1** line of junction of two edges, e.g. of two pieces of cloth, or two planks **2** thin layer, stratum ▷ *verb transitive* **3** mark with furrows or wrinkles > **seam'less** [-lis] *adjective* > **seam'y** *adjective* **seam•i•er, seam•i•est** **1** sordid **2** marked with seams > **seam'stress** [-stris] *noun* sewing woman

sé•ance [SAY-ahns] *noun* meeting at which spiritualists attempt to communicate with the dead

sear [seer] *verb transitive* **1** scorch, brand with hot iron **2** deaden

search [surch] *verb* **1** look over or through to find something **2** probe into, examine ▷ *noun* **3** act of searching **4** quest > **search'ing** *adjective* **1** keen **2** thorough **3** severe > **search engine** *computing* Internet service enabling users to search for items of interest online > **search'light** *noun* powerful electric light with concentrated beam

sea•son [SEE-zən] *noun* **1** one of four divisions of year associated with type of weather and stage of agriculture **2** period during which thing happens, grows, is active, etc. **3** proper time ▷ *verb transitive* **4** flavor with salt, herbs, etc. **5** make reliable or ready for use **6** make experienced > **sea'son•a•ble** *adjective* **1** appropriate for the season **2** opportune **3** fit > **sea'son•al** [-əl] *adjective* depending on, varying with seasons > **sea'son•ing** *noun* flavoring **in season** (of an animal) in heat > **season ticket** one for series of events within a certain time

seat [seet] *noun* **1** thing for sitting on **2** buttocks **3** base **4** right to sit (e.g. in legislature, etc.) **5** place where something is located, centered **6** locality of disease, trouble, etc. **7** country house ▷ *verb transitive* **8** make to sit **9** provide sitting accommodation for **10** install firmly

se•ba•ceous [si-BAY-shəs] *adjective* **1** of, pert. to fat **2** secreting fat, oil

se•cant [SEE-kant] *noun math.* **1** (secant of an angle) reciprocal of its cosine **2** line that intersects a curve

se•cede [si-SEED] *verb intransitive* **-ced•ed, -ced•ing** withdraw formally from federation, union, etc. > **se•ces'sion** [-SESH-ən] *noun*

se•clude [si-KLOOD] *verb transitive* **-clud•ed, -clud•ing** guard from, remove from sight, view, contact with others > **secluded** *adjective* **1** remote **2** private > **se•clu'sion** [-KLOO-zhən] *noun*

sec•ond [SEK-ənd] *adjective* **1** next after first **2** alternate, additional **3** of lower quality ▷ *noun* **4** person or thing coming second **5** attendant

DICTIONARY • THESAURUS

scamper, scoot, scurry

sea *noun* **1** OCEAN, main, the deep, the waves **2** EXPANSE, abundance, mass, multitude, plethora, profusion **3** ▷ **at sea** BEWILDERED, baffled, confused, lost, mystified, puzzled

seafaring *adjective* NAUTICAL, marine, maritime, naval

seal *noun* **1** AUTHENTICATION, confirmation, imprimatur, insignia, ratification, stamp ▷ *verb* **2** CLOSE, bung, enclose, fasten, plug, shut, stop, stopper, stop up **3** AUTHENTICATE, confirm, ratify, stamp, validate **4** SETTLE, clinch, conclude, consummate, finalize **5** ▷ **seal off** ISOLATE, put out of bounds, quarantine, segregate

seam *noun* **1** JOINT, closure **2** LAYER, lode, stratum, vein **3** RIDGE, furrow, line, wrinkle

sear *verb* SCORCH, burn, sizzle

search *verb* **1** LOOK, comb, examine, explore, hunt, inspect, investigate, ransack, scour, scrutinize ▷ *noun* **2** LOOK, examination, exploration, hunt, inspection, investigation, pursuit, quest

searching *adjective* KEEN, close, intent, penetrating, piercing, probing, quizzical, sharp

season *noun* **1** PERIOD, spell, term, time ▷ *verb* **2** FLAVOR, enliven, pep up, salt, spice

seasonable *adjective* APPROPRIATE, convenient, fit, opportune, providential, suitable, timely, well-timed

seasoned *adjective* EXPERIENCED, hardened, practiced, time-served, veteran

seasoning *noun* FLAVORING, condiment, dressing, relish, salt and pepper, sauce, spice

seat *noun* **1** CHAIR, bench, pew, settle, stall, stool **2** CENTER, capital, heart, hub, place, site, situation, source **3** RESIDENCE, abode, ancestral hall, house, mansion **4** MEMBERSHIP, chair, constituency, incumbency, place ▷ *verb* **5** SIT, fix, install, locate, place, set, settle **6** HOLD, accommodate, cater for, contain, sit, take

seating *noun* ACCOMMODATION, chairs, places, room, seats

secede *verb* WITHDRAW, break with, leave, pull out, quit, resign, split from

secluded *adjective* PRIVATE, cloistered, cut off, isolated, lonely, out-of-the-way, sheltered, solitary

seclusion *noun* PRIVACY, isolation, shelter, solitude

second[1] *adjective* **1** NEXT, following, subsequent, succeeding

6 sixtieth part of minute 7 SI unit of time 8 moment ▷ *verb transitive* 9 support 10 support (motion in meeting) so that discussion may be in order > **sec•onds** *plural noun* inferior goods > **sec•ond•hand'** *adjective* 1 bought after use by another 2 not original > **second sight** faculty of seeing events before they occur

sec•ond•ar•y [SEK-ən-der-ee] *adjective* 1 subsidiary, of less importance 2 developed from, or dependent on, something else 3 *education* after primary stage > **sec'ond•ar•i•ly** *adverb*

se•cret [SEE-krit] *adjective* 1 kept, meant to be kept from knowledge of others 2 hidden 3 private ▷ *noun* 4 thing kept secret > **se'cre•cy** [-krə-see] *noun, plural* **-cies** keeping or being kept secret > **se'cre•tive** *adjective* 1 given to having secrets 2 uncommunicative 3 reticent > **se'cre•tive•ness** [-tiv-nis] *noun*

sec•re•tar•y [SEK-ri-ter-ee] *noun, plural* **-tar•ies** 1 one employed by individual or organization to deal with papers and correspondence, keep records, prepare business, etc. 2 member of presidential cabinet > **sec•re•tar'i•al** [-TAIR-ee-əl] *adjective* > **sec•re•tar'i•at** [-ət] *noun* 1 body of secretaries 2 building occupied by secretarial staff

se•crete [si-KREET] *verb transitive* **-cret•ed, -cret•ing** 1 hide 2 conceal 3 (of gland, etc.) collect and supply particular substance in body > **se•cre'tion** *noun*

sect [sekt] *noun* 1 group of people (within religious body, etc.) with common interest 2 faction > **sec•tar'i•an** [-TAIR-ee-ən] *adjective* 1 of a sect 2 narrow-minded

sec•tion [SEK-shən] *noun* 1 part cut off 2 division 3 portion 4 distinct part of city, country, people, etc. 5 cutting 6 drawing of anything as if cut through > **sec'tion•al** *adjective*

sec•tor [SEK-tər] *noun* 1 part or subdivision 2 part of circle enclosed by two radii and the arc they cut off

sec•u•lar [SEK-yə-lər] *adjective* 1 worldly 2 lay, not religious 3 not monastic 4 lasting for, or occurring once in, an age 5 centuries old > **sec'u•lar•ism** *noun* > **sec'u•lar•ist** *noun* one who believes that religion should have no place in civil affairs > **sec•u•lar•i•za'tion** *noun* > **sec'u•lar•ize** *verb transitive* **-ized, -iz•ing** transfer from religious to lay possession or use

se•cure [si-KYOOR] *adjective* **-cur•er, -cur•est** 1 safe 2 free from fear, anxiety 3 firmly fixed 4 certain 5 sure, confident ▷ *verb transitive* **-cured, -cur•ing** 6 gain possession of 7 make safe 8 free (creditor) from risk of loss 9 make firm > **se•cur'i•ty** *noun, plural* **-ties** state of safety 1

---

2 ADDITIONAL, alternative, extra, further, other
3 INFERIOR, lesser, lower, secondary, subordinate
▷ *noun* 4 SUPPORTER, assistant, backer, helper
▷ *verb* 5 SUPPORT, approve, assist, back, endorse, go along with

second² *noun* MOMENT, flash, instant, jiffy (*informal*), minute, sec (*informal*), trice

secondary *adjective* 1 SUBORDINATE, inferior, lesser, lower, minor, unimportant
2 RESULTANT, contingent, derived, indirect
3 BACKUP, auxiliary, fall-back, reserve, subsidiary, supporting

second-class *adjective* INFERIOR, indifferent, mediocre, second-best, second-rate, undistinguished, uninspiring

second-hand *adjective* 1 USED, hand-me-down (*informal*), nearly new
▷ *adverb* 2 INDIRECTLY

second in command *noun* DEPUTY, number two, right-hand man

secondly *adverb* NEXT, in the second place, second

second-rate *adjective* INFERIOR, low-grade, low-quality, mediocre, poor, rubbishy, shoddy, substandard, tacky (*informal*), tawdry, two-bit (*slang*)

secrecy *noun* 1 MYSTERY, concealment, confidentiality, privacy, silence
2 SECRETIVENESS, clandestineness, covertness, furtiveness, stealth

secret *adjective* 1 CONCEALED, close, disguised, furtive, hidden, undercover, underground, undisclosed, unknown, unrevealed
2 STEALTHY, secretive, sly, underhand
3 MYSTERIOUS, abstruse, arcane, clandestine, cryptic, occult
▷ *noun* 4 MYSTERY, code, enigma, key
5 ▷ **in secret** SECRETLY, slyly, surreptitiously

secrete *verb* 1 GIVE OFF, emanate, emit, exude
2 HIDE, cache, conceal, harbor, stash (*informal*), stow

secretive *adjective* RETICENT, close, deep, reserved, tight-lipped, uncommunicative

secretly *adverb* IN SECRET, clandestinely, covertly, furtively, privately, quietly, stealthily, surreptitiously

sect *noun* GROUP, camp, denomination, division, faction, party, schism

sectarian *adjective* 1 NARROW-MINDED, bigoted, doctrinaire, dogmatic, factional, fanatical, limited, parochial, partisan
▷ *noun* 2 BIGOT, dogmatist, extremist, fanatic, partisan, zealot

section *noun* 1 PART, division, fraction, installment, passage, piece, portion, segment, slice
2 DISTRICT, area, region, sector, zone

sector *noun* PART, area, district, division, quarter, region, zone

secular *adjective* WORLDLY, civil, earthly, lay, nonspiritual, temporal

secure *adjective* 1 SAFE, immune, protected, unassailable
2 SURE, assured, certain, confident, easy, reassured
3 FIXED, fast, fastened, firm, immovable, stable, steady
▷ *verb* 4 OBTAIN, acquire, gain, get, procure, score (*slang*)
5 FASTEN, attach, bolt, chain, fix, lock, make fast, tie up

security *noun* 1 PRECAUTIONS, defense, protection, safeguards, safety measures
2 SAFETY, care, custody, refuge, safekeeping, sanctuary
3 SURENESS, assurance, certainty, confidence, conviction, positiveness, reliance
4 PLEDGE, collateral, gage, guarantee, hostage, insurance, pawn, surety

protection 2 that which secures 3 assurance 4 anything given as bond, caution or pledge 5 one who becomes surety for another
se•dan [si-DAN] *noun* enclosed automobile body with two or four doors > **sedan chair** *hist.* closed chair for one person, carried on poles by bearers
se•date[1] [si-DAYT] *adjective* calm, collected, serious
sedate[2] *verb transitive* **-dat•ed, -dat•ing** make calm by sedative > **se•da'tion** *noun* > **sed'a•tive** *adjective* 1 having soothing or calming effect ▷ *noun* 2 sedative drug
sed•en•ta•ry [SED-n-ter-ee] *adjective* 1 done sitting down 2 sitting much
Se•der [SAY-dər] *noun* ritual for the first or first two nights of Passover
sed•i•ment [SED-ə-mənt] *noun* 1 matter that settles to the bottom of liquid 2 dregs, lees > **sed•i•men'ta•ry** *adjective*
se•di•tion [si-DISH-ən] *noun* speech or action threatening authority of a state > **se•di'tious** [-shəs] *adjective*
se•duce [SI-doos] *verb transitive* **-duced, -duc•ing** 1 persuade to commit some (wrong) deed, esp. sexual intercourse 2 tempt 3 attract > **se•duc'er, se•duc'tress** *noun* > **se•duc'tion** [-DUK-shən] *noun* > **se•duc'tive** *adjective* 1 alluring 2 winning
sed•u•lous [SEJ-ə-ləs] *adjective* 1 diligent 2 industrious 3 persevering, persistent > **se•du•li•ty** [si-DOO-li-tee] *noun*
see[1] *verb* **saw, seen, see•ing** 1 perceive with eyes or mentally 2 observe 3 watch 4 find out 5 reflect 6 come to know 7 interview 8 make sure 9 accompany 10 perceive 11 consider 12 understand > **seeing** *conjunction* 1 since 2 in view of the fact that
see[2] *noun* diocese, office, or jurisdiction of bishop
seed *noun* 1 reproductive germs of plants 2 one grain of this 3 such grains saved or used for sowing 4 origin 5 sperm 6 offspring ▷ *verb transitive* 7 sow with seed 8 arrange draw for tennis or other tournament, so that best players do not meet in early rounds ▷ *verb intransitive* 9 produce seed > **seed'ling** *noun* young plant raised from seed > **seed'y** *adjective* **seed•i•er, seed•i•est** 1 shabby 2 gone to seed 3 unwell, ill
seek *verb* **sought** [sawt], **seek•ing** 1 make search or inquiry for 2 search
seem *verb intransitive* 1 appear (to be or to do) 2 look 3 appear to one's judgment > **seem'ing** *adjective* apparent but not real > **seem'ing•ly** *adverb*
seem•ly [SEEM-lee] *adjective* **-li•er, -li•est** becoming and proper > **seem'li•ness** [-nis] *noun*
seen *pp of* **see**[1]
seep *verb intransitive* trickle through slowly, as water, ooze
seer *noun* prophet
seer•suck•er [SEER-suk-ər] *noun* light cotton fabric with slightly crinkled surface
see'saw *noun* 1 game in which children sit at opposite ends of plank supported in middle and swing up and down 2 plank used for this ▷ *verb*

DICTIONARY • THESAURUS

sedate *adjective* CALM, collected, composed, cool, dignified, serene, tranquil
sedative *adjective* 1 CALMING, anodyne, relaxing, soothing, tranquilizing
▷ *noun* 2 TRANQUILIZER, anodyne, downer *or* down (*slang*)
sedentary *adjective* INACTIVE, desk, desk-bound, seated, sitting
sediment *noun* DREGS, deposit, grounds, lees, residue
sedition *noun* RABBLE-ROUSING, agitation, incitement to riot, subversion
seditious *adjective* REVOLUTIONARY, dissident, mutinous, rebellious, refractory, subversive
seduce *verb* 1 CORRUPT, debauch, deflower, deprave, dishonor
2 TEMPT, beguile, deceive, entice, inveigle, lead astray, lure, mislead
seduction *noun* 1 CORRUPTION
2 TEMPTATION, enticement, lure, snare
seductive *adjective* ALLURING, attractive, bewitching, enticing, inviting, provocative, tempting
seductress *noun* TEMPTRESS, enchantress, femme fatale (*French*), siren, succubus, vamp (*informal*)
see[1] *verb* 1 PERCEIVE, behold, catch sight of, discern, distinguish, espy, glimpse, look, make out, notice, observe, sight, spot, witness
2 UNDERSTAND, appreciate, comprehend, fathom, feel, follow, get, grasp, realize
3 FIND OUT, ascertain, determine, discover, learn
4 MAKE SURE, ensure, guarantee, make certain, see to it
5 CONSIDER, decide, deliberate, reflect, think over
6 VISIT, confer with, consult, interview, receive, speak to
7 GO OUT WITH, court, date (*informal*), go steady with (*informal*)
8 ACCOMPANY, escort, lead, show, usher, walk
seed *noun* 1 GRAIN, egg, embryo, germ, kernel, ovum, pip, spore
2 ORIGIN, beginning, germ, nucleus, source, start
3 OFFSPRING, children, descendants, issue, progeny
4 ▷ **go to seed, run to seed** DECLINE, decay, degenerate, deteriorate, go downhill (*informal*), go to pot, let oneself go
seedy (*informal*) *adjective* SHABBY, dilapidated, dirty, grubby, mangy, run-down, scuzzy (*slang*), sleazy, squalid, tatty
seeing *conjunction* SINCE, as, inasmuch as, in view of the fact that
seek *verb* 1 LOOK FOR, be after, follow, hunt, pursue, search for, stalk
2 TRY, aim, aspire to, attempt, endeavor, essay, strive
seem *verb* APPEAR, assume, give the impression, look
seemly *adjective* FITTING, appropriate, becoming, correct, decent, decorous, fit, proper, suitable
seep *verb* OOZE, exude, leak, permeate, soak, trickle, well
seer *noun* PROPHET, sibyl, soothsayer
seesaw *verb* ALTERNATE, fluctuate, oscillate, swing

intransitive 3 move up and down
seethe [seeth] *verb intransitive* **seethed, seeth•ing** 1 boil, foam 2 be very agitated 3 be in constant movement (as large crowd, etc.)
seg•ment [SEG-mənt] *noun* 1 piece cut off 2 section ▷ *verb* [SEG-ment] 3 to divide into segments > **seg•men•ta'tion** *noun*
seg•re•gate [SEG-ri-gayt] *verb transitive* **-gat•ed, -gat•ing** 1 set apart from rest 2 dissociate 3 separate 4 isolate > **seg•re•ga'tion** *noun*
se•gue [SAY-gway] *verb intransitive* **-gued, -gue•ing** 1 proceed from one section or piece of music to another without break 2 make a transition smoothly e.g. from one topic of conversation to another ▷ *noun*
seis•mic [SĪZ-mik] *adjective* pert. to earthquakes > **seis'mo•graph** [-mə-graf] *noun* instrument to record earthquakes > **seis•mo•log'ic•al** *adjective* pert. to seismology > **seis•mol'o•gist** [-MOL-ə-jist] *noun* one versed in seismology > **seis•mol'o•gy** *noun* science concerned with study of earthquakes
seize [seez] *verb transitive* **seized, seiz•ing** 1 grasp 2 lay hold of 3 capture ▷ *verb intransitive* **seized, seiz•ing** 4 in machine, of bearing or piston, to stick tightly through overheating > **seiz•ure** [SEE-zhər] *noun* 1 act of taking, esp. by legal writ, as goods 2 sudden onset of disease
sel•dom [SEL-dəm] *adverb* not often, rarely
se•lect [si-LEKT] *verb transitive* 1 pick out, choose ▷ *adjective* 2 choice, picked 3 exclusive > **se•lec'tion** *noun* > **se•lec'tive** *adjective* > **se•lec•tiv'i•ty** *noun*
se•le•ni•um [si-LEE-nee-əm] *noun* nonmetallic element with photoelectric properties
sel•e•nog•ra•phy [sel-ə-NOG-rə-fee] *noun* study of surface of moon
self *pronoun, plural* **selves** 1 used reflexively or to express emphasis ▷ *adjective* 2 (of color, etc.) same throughout, uniform ▷ *noun* 3 one's own person or individuality > **self'ish** *adjective* 1 concerned unduly over personal profit or pleasure 2 lacking consideration for others 3 greedy > **self'ish•ly** *adverb* > **self'less** [-lis] *adjective* 1 having no regard for self 2 unselfish
self- *prefix* 1 of oneself or itself 2 by, to, in, due to, for, or from the self 3 automatic(ally) > **self-ad•dressed'** *adjective* addressed to the sender > **self-as•sured'** *adjective* confident > **self-cen'tered** *adjective* totally preoccupied with one's own concerns > **self-con'fi•dent** *adjective* > **self-con•tained'** 1 containing everything needed, complete 2 (of an apartment) having its own facilities > **self-con•trol'** *noun* ability to control one's feelings and reactions > **self-de•fense'** *noun* defending of oneself or one's property > **self-em•ployed'** *adjective* earning a living from one's own business > **self-ev'i•dent** *adjective* obvious without proof > **self-help'** *noun* 1 use of one's own abilities to solve problems 2 practice of solving one's problems within a group of people with similar problems > **self-in•dul'gent** *adjective* tending to indulge one's desires > **self-in'ter•est** *adjective* one's own advantage > **self-rais'ing** *adjective* (of flour) containing a raising agent > **self-sat'is•fied** *adjective* conceited
self-con'scious [-KON-shəs] *adjective* 1 unduly

DICTIONARY

S

THESAURUS

seethe *verb* 1 BE FURIOUS, be livid, fume, go ballistic (*slang*), rage, see red (*informal*), simmer
2 BOIL, bubble, fizz, foam, froth
see through *verb* 1 BE UNDECEIVED BY, be wise to (*informal*), fathom, not fall for, penetrate
2 ▷ **see (something) through** PERSEVERE *or* PERSEVERE WITH, keep at, persist, stick out (*informal*)
3 ▷ **see (someone) through** HELP OUT, stick by, support
segment *noun* SECTION, bit, division, part, piece, portion, slice, wedge
segregate *verb* SET APART, discriminate against, dissociate, isolate, separate
segregation *noun* SEPARATION, apartheid, discrimination, isolation
seize *verb* 1 GRAB, catch up, clutch, grasp, grip, lay hands on, snatch, take
2 CONFISCATE, appropriate, commandeer, impound, take possession of
3 CAPTURE, apprehend, arrest, catch, take captive
seizure *noun* 1 ATTACK, convulsion, fit, paroxysm, spasm
2 CAPTURE, apprehension, arrest
3 TAKING, annexation, commandeering, confiscation, grabbing
seldom *adverb* RARELY, hardly ever, infrequently, not often
select *verb* 1 CHOOSE, opt for, pick, single out
▷ *adjective* 2 CHOICE, excellent, first-class, hand-picked, special, superior, top-notch (*informal*)
3 EXCLUSIVE, cliquish, elite, privileged
selection *noun* 1 CHOICE, choosing, option, pick, preference
2 RANGE, assortment, choice, collection, medley, variety
selective *adjective* PARTICULAR, careful, discerning, discriminating
self-assurance *noun* CONFIDENCE, assertiveness, positiveness, self-confidence, self-possession
self-centered *adjective* SELFISH, egotistic, narcissistic, self-seeking
self-confidence *noun* SELF-ASSURANCE, aplomb, confidence, nerve, poise
self-confident *adjective* SELF-ASSURED, assured, confident, poised, sure of oneself
self-conscious *adjective* EMBARRASSED, awkward, bashful, diffident, ill at ease, insecure, nervous, uncomfortable, wired (*slang*)
self-control *noun* WILLPOWER, restraint, self-discipline, self-restraint
self-esteem *noun* SELF-RESPECT, confidence, faith in oneself, pride, self-assurance, self-regard
self-evident *adjective* OBVIOUS, clear, incontrovertible, inescapable, undeniable
self-important *adjective* CONCEITED, bigheaded, cocky, full of oneself, pompous, swollen-headed
self-indulgence *noun* INTEMPERANCE, excess, extravagance
selfish *adjective* SELF-CENTERED, egoistic, egoistical, egotistic, egotistical, greedy, self-interested, ungenerous
selfless *adjective* UNSELFISH, altruistic, generous, self-denying, self-sacrificing
self-possessed *adjective* SELF-ASSURED, collected, confident, cool, poised, unruffled

aware of oneself **2** conscious of one's acts or states
self-de•ter•mi•na•tion [-di-tur-mə-NAY-shən] *noun* the right of person or nation to decide for itself
self-made [-mayd] *adjective* having achieved wealth, status, etc. by one's own efforts
self-pos•sessed [-pə-ZEST] *adjective* calm, composed > **self-pos•ses'sion** [-pə-ZESH-ən] *noun*
self-re•spect' [-ri-SPEKT] *noun* proper sense of one's own dignity and integrity
self-right'eous [-RĪ-chəs] *adjective* smugly sure of one's own virtue
self•same [-saym] *adjective* very same
self-seek'ing *adjective, noun* (having) preoccupation with one's own interests
self-serv'ice [-SUR-vis] *adjective, noun* (of) the serving of oneself in a store or restaurant
self-suf•fi'cient [-sə-FISH-ənt] *adjective* **1** sufficient in itself **2** relying on one's own powers
self-will' *noun* **1** obstinacy **2** willfulness > **self-willed'** *adjective* headstrong
sell *verb* **sold, sell•ing** **1** hand over for a price **2** stock, have for sale **3** make someone accept **4** find purchasers **5** (*informal*) betray, cheat ▷ *noun* **6** (*informal*) hoax > **sell'er** *noun* > **sell'out** *noun* **1** disposing of completely by selling **2** betrayal
selt•zer [SELT-sər], **selt•zer water** *noun* effervescent (mineral) water
sel•vage [SEL-vij] *noun* finished, unfraying edge of cloth
se•man•tic [si-MAN-tik] *adjective* relating to meaning of words or symbols > **se•man'tics** *noun* study of linguistic meaning
sem•a•phore [SEM-ə-for] *noun* **1** post with movable arms for signaling **2** system of signaling by human or mechanical arms
sem•blance [SEM-bləns] *noun* (false) appearance; image, likeness
se•men [SEE-mən] *noun* **1** fluid carrying sperm of male animals **2** sperm
se•mes•ter [si-MES-tər] *noun* (half-year) session of academic year in many universities, colleges
sem•i [SEM-ī] *noun* (*informal*) semitrailer
semi- *combining form* half, partly, not completely: *semicircle*
sem•i•breve [SEM-ee-breev] *noun* musical note half the length of a breve
sem•i•cir•cle [SEM-i-sur-kəl] *noun* half of circle > **sem•i•cir'cu•lar** [-SUR-kyə-lər] *adjective*
sem•i•co•lon [SEM-i-koh-lən] *noun* punctuation mark (;)
sem•i•con•duc•tor [sem-i-kən-DUK-tər] *noun* *physics* substance with an electrical conductivity that increases with temperature or voltage
sem•i•de•tached [sem-ee-di-TACHT] *adjective, noun* (of) house joined to another on one side only
sem•i•fi•nal [sem-ee-FĪN-l] *noun* match, round, etc. before final
sem•i•nal [SEM-ə-nl] *adjective* **1** capable of developing **2** influential, important **3** rudimentary **4** of semen or seed
sem•i•nar [SEM-ə-nahr] *noun* meeting of group (of students) for discussion
sem•i•nar•y [SEM-ə-ner-ee] *noun, plural* **-nar•ies** college for priests > **sem•i•nar'i•an** *noun* student at seminary
sem•i•pre•cious [sem-ee-PRESH-əs] *adjective* (of gemstones) having less value than precious stones
sem•i•skilled [sem-ee-SKILD] *adjective* partly skilled, trained but not for specialized work
Sem•ite [SEM-īt] *noun* **1** member of ancient and modern peoples including Jews and Arabs **2** Jew > **Se•mit•ic** [sə-MIT-ik] *adjective* **1** denoting a Semite **2** Jewish
sem•i•tone [SEM-ee-tohn] *noun* musical half tone
sem•i•trail•er [SEM-i-tray-lər] *noun* trailer used for hauling freight, having wheels at back but supported by towing vehicle in front
sem•o•li•na [sem-ə-LEE-nə] *noun* milled product of durum wheat, used for pasta, etc.
sen•ate [SEN-it] *noun* **1** upper legislative body of country **2** upper council of university, etc. > **sen'a•tor** [-ə-tər] *noun* > **sen•a•to'ri•al** [-TOR-ee-əl] *adjective*
send *verb transitive* **sent, send•ing** **1** cause to go or be conveyed **2** dispatch **3** transmit (by radio)
se•nile [SEE-nīl] *adjective* showing weakness of

---

self-reliant *adjective* INDEPENDENT, self-sufficient, self-supporting
self-respect *noun* PRIDE, dignity, morale, self-esteem
self-restraint *noun* SELF-CONTROL, self-command, self-discipline, willpower
self-righteous *adjective* SANCTIMONIOUS, complacent, holier-than-thou, priggish, self-satisfied, smug, superior
self-sacrifice *noun* SELFLESSNESS, altruism, generosity, self-denial
self-satisfied *adjective* SMUG, complacent, pleased with oneself, self-congratulatory
self-seeking *adjective* SELFISH, careerist, looking out for number one (*informal*), out for what one can get, self-interested, self-serving
sell *verb* **1** TRADE, barter, exchange
2 DEAL IN, handle, market, peddle, retail, stock, trade in, traffic in
seller *noun* DEALER, agent, merchant, purveyor, retailer, salesman *or* saleswoman, supplier, vendor
selling *noun* DEALING, business, trading, traffic
sell out *verb* **1** DISPOSE OF, be out of stock of, get rid of, run out of
2 (*informal*) BETRAY, double-cross (*informal*), sell down the river (*informal*), stab in the back
semblance *noun* APPEARANCE, aspect, façade, mask, pretense, resemblance, show, veneer
seminal *adjective* INFLUENTIAL, formative, ground-breaking, important, innovative, original
send *verb* **1** CONVEY, direct, dispatch, forward, remit, transmit
2 PROPEL, cast, fire, fling, hurl, let fly, shoot
send for *verb* SUMMON, call for, order, request
sendoff *noun* FAREWELL, departure, leave-taking, start, valediction
senile *adjective* DODDERING, decrepit, doting, in one's dotage

old age > **se•nil•i•ty** [si-NIL-i-tee] *noun*
sen•ior [SEEN-yər] *adjective* 1 superior in rank or standing 2 older ▷ *noun* 3 superior 4 elder person > **sen•ior'i•ty** [-YOR-i-tee] *noun*
se•ñor [sayn-YOR] *noun Sp.* title of respect, like Mr. > **se•ñor'a** *noun* Mrs. > **se•ño•ri'ta** [-REE-tə] *noun* Miss
sen•sa•tion [sen-SAY-shən] *noun* 1 operation of sense, feeling, awareness 2 excited feeling, state of excitement 3 exciting event 4 strong impression 5 commotion > **sen•sa'tion•al** *adjective* 1 producing great excitement 2 melodramatic 3 of perception by senses > **sen•sa'tion•al•ism** *noun* 1 use of sensational language, etc. to arouse intense emotional excitement 2 doctrine that sensations are basis of all knowledge
sense [sens] *noun* 1 any of bodily faculties of perception or feeling 2 sensitiveness of any or all of these faculties 3 ability to perceive, mental alertness 4 consciousness 5 meaning 6 coherence, intelligible meaning 7 sound practical judgment ▷ *verb transitive* **sensed, sens•ing** 8 perceive 9 understand > **sense'less** [-lis] *adjective*
sen•si•ble [SEN-sə-bəl] *adjective* 1 reasonable, wise 2 perceptible by senses 3 aware, mindful 4 considerable, appreciable > **sen•si•bil'i•ty** *noun* ability to feel esp. emotional or moral feelings > **sen'si•bly** *adverb*
sen•si•tive [SEN-si-tiv] *adjective* 1 open to, acutely affected by, external impressions 2 easily affected or altered 3 easily upset by criticism 4 responsive to slight changes > **sen•si•tiv'i•ty** *noun* > **sen'si•tize** [-tīz] *verb transitive* **-tized, -tiz•ing** make sensitive, esp. make (photographic film, etc.) sensitive to light
sen•sor [SEN-sər] *noun* device that responds to stimulus
sen•so•ry [SEN-sə-ree] *adjective* relating to organs, operation, of senses
sen•su•al [SEN-shoo-əl] *adjective* 1 of senses only and not of mind 2 given to pursuit of pleasures of sense 3 self-indulgent 4 licentious > **sen'su•al•ist** *noun*
sen•su•ous [SEN-shoo-əs] *adjective* stimulating, or apprehended by, senses esp. in aesthetic manner
sent *pt./pp. of* **send**
sen•tence [SEN-tns] *noun* 1 combination of words that is complete as expressing a thought 2 judgment passed on criminal by court or judge ▷ *verb transitive* **-tenced, -tenc•ing** 3 pass sentence on, condemn > **sen•ten'tial** [-TEN-shəl] *adjective* 1 of sentence > **sen•ten'tious** [-shəs] *adjective* 1 full of axioms and maxims 2 pithy 3 pompously moralizing > **sen•ten'tious•ness** *noun*
sen•tient [SEN-shənt] *adjective* 1 capable of feeling 2 feeling 3 thinking > **sen'tience** *noun*
sen•ti•ment [SEN-tə-mənt] *noun* 1 tendency to be moved by feeling rather than reason 2 verbal expression of feeling 3 mental feeling, emotion 4 opinion > **sen•ti•men'tal** *adjective* 1 given to indulgence in sentiment and in its

senility *noun* DOTAGE, decrepitude, infirmity, loss of one's faculties, senile dementia
senior *adjective* 1 HIGHER RANKING, superior
2 OLDER, elder
senior citizen *noun* PENSIONER, old fogey (*slang*), old person *or* elderly person, retired person
seniority *noun* SUPERIORITY, precedence, priority, rank
sensation *noun* 1 FEELING, awareness, consciousness, impression, perception, sense
2 EXCITEMENT, commotion, furor, stir, thrill
sensational *adjective* 1 DRAMATIC, amazing, astounding, awesome, exciting, melodramatic, shock-horror (*facetious*), shocking, thrilling
2 EXCELLENT, awesome (*informal*), cool (*informal*), fabulous (*informal*), impressive, marvelous, mind-blowing (*informal*), out of this world (*informal*), phat (*slang*), superb
sense *noun* 1 FACULTY, feeling, sensation
2 FEELING, atmosphere, aura, awareness, consciousness, impression, perception
3 (*sometimes plural*) INTELLIGENCE, brains (*informal*), cleverness, common sense, judgment, reason, sagacity, sanity, sharpness, understanding, wisdom, wit *or* wits
4 MEANING, drift, gist, implication, import, significance
▷ *verb* 5 PERCEIVE, be aware of, discern, feel, get the impression, pick up, realize, understand
senseless *adjective* 1 STUPID, asinine, bonkers (*informal*), crazy, daft (*informal*), foolish, idiotic, illogical, inane, irrational, mad, mindless, nonsensical, pointless, ridiculous, silly
2 UNCONSCIOUS, insensible, out, out cold, stunned
sensibility *noun* 1 (*often plural*) FEELINGS, emotions, moral sense, sentiments, susceptibilities
2 SENSITIVITY, responsiveness, sensitiveness, susceptibility
sensible *adjective* 1 WISE, canny, down-to-earth, intelligent, judicious, practical, prudent, rational, realistic, sage, sane, shrewd, sound
2 (*usually with of*) AWARE, conscious, mindful, sensitive to
sensitive *adjective* 1 EASILY HURT, delicate, tender
2 SUSCEPTIBLE, easily affected, impressionable, responsive, touchy-feely (*informal*)
3 TOUCHY, easily offended, easily upset, thin-skinned
4 RESPONSIVE, acute, fine, keen, precise
sensitivity *noun* SENSITIVENESS, delicacy, receptiveness, responsiveness, susceptibility
sensual *adjective* 1 PHYSICAL, animal, bodily, carnal, fleshly, luxurious, voluptuous
2 EROTIC, lascivious, lecherous, lewd, lustful, raunchy (*slang*), sexual
sensuality *noun* EROTICISM, carnality, lasciviousness, lecherousness, lewdness, sexiness (*informal*), voluptuousness
sensuous *adjective* PLEASURABLE, gratifying, hedonistic, sybaritic
sentence *noun* 1 PUNISHMENT, condemnation, decision, decree, judgment, order, ruling, verdict
▷ *verb* 2 CONDEMN, doom, penalize
sententious *adjective* POMPOUS, canting, judgmental, moralistic, preachifying (*informal*), sanctimonious
sentient *adjective* FEELING, conscious, living, sensitive

expression 2 weak 3 sloppy
> **sen•ti•men•tal'i•ty** *noun*

sen•ti•nel [SEN-tn-l] *noun* sentry

sen•try [SEN-tree] *noun, plural* **-tries** soldier on watch

se•pal [SEE-pəl] *noun* leaf or division of the calyx of a flower

sep•a•rate [SEP-ə-rayt] *verb transitive* **-rat•ed, -rat•ing** 1 part 2 divide 3 sever 4 put apart 5 occupy place between ▷ *verb intransitive* **-rat•ed, -rat•ing** 6 withdraw, become parted from ▷ *adjective* [SEP-ər-it] 7 disconnected, apart, distinct, individual > **sep'a•ra•ble** *adjective* > **sep•a•ra'tion** [-RAY-shən] *noun* 1 disconnection 2 *law* living apart of married people without divorce > **sep'a•ra•tor** *noun* 1 that which separates 2 apparatus for separating cream from milk

se•pi•a [SEE-pee-ə] *noun* 1 reddish-brown pigment made from a fluid secreted by the cuttlefish ▷ *adjective* 2 of this color

sep'sis *noun* presence of pus-forming bacteria in body

sep•ten•ni•al [sep-TEN-ee-əl] *adjective* lasting, occurring every seven years

sep•tet' *noun* 1 music for seven instruments or voices 2 group of seven performers

sep•tic [SEP-tik] *adjective* 1 of, caused by, sepsis 2 (of wound) infected > **sep•ti•ce'mi•a** [-SEE-mee-ə] *noun* blood poisoning

sep•tu•a•ge•nar•i•an [sep-choo-ə-jə-NAIR-ee-ən] *adjective* aged between seventy and eighty ▷ *noun*

sep•ul•cher [SEP-əl-kər] *noun* 1 tomb 2 burial vault > **se•pul•chral** [sə-PUL-krəl] *adjective* 1 of burial, or the grave 2 mournful 3 gloomy > **sep'ul•ture** [-əl-chər] *noun* burial

se•quel [SEE-kwəl] *noun* 1 consequence 2 continuation, e.g. of story

se•quence [SEE-kwəns] *noun* 1 arrangement of things in successive order 2 section, episode of motion picture > **se•quen•tial** [si-KWEN-shəl] *adjective*

se•ques•ter [si-KWES-tər] *verb transitive* 1 separate 2 seclude 3 put aside > **se•ques'trate** [-KWES-trayt] *verb transitive* **-trat•ed, -trat•ing** 1 confiscate 2 divert or appropriate income of property to satisfy claims against its owner > **se•ques•tra'tion** [-TRAY-shən] *noun*

se•quin [SEE-kwin] *noun* 1 small ornamental metal disk or spangle on dresses, etc. 2 orig. Venetian gold coin

se•quoi•a [si-KWOI-ə] *noun* giant Californian coniferous tree

se•ragl•io [si-RAL-yoh] *noun, plural* **-ragl•ios** harem, palace, of Turkish sultan

ser•aph [SER-əf] *noun, plural* **-a•phim** [-ə-fim] member of highest order of angels

ser•e•nade [ser-ə-NAYD] *noun* 1 sentimental piece of music or song of type addressed to woman by lover esp. at evening ▷ *verb* **-nad•ed, -nad•ing** 2 sing serenade (to someone)

ser•en•dip•i•ty [ser-ən-DIP-i-tee] *noun* faculty of making fortunate discoveries by accident

se•rene [sə-REEN] *adjective* 1 calm, tranquil 2 unclouded 3 quiet, placid > **se•ren'i•ty** [-REN-i-tee] *noun*

serf [surf] *noun* one of class of medieval laborers bound to, and transferred with, land > **serf'dom** [-dəm] *noun*

serge [surj] *noun* strong hard-wearing twilled worsted fabric

ser•geant [SAHR-jənt] *noun* noncommissioned officer in Army, Marine Corps, police department > **sergeant major** 1 noncommissioned Army officer serving as chief administrative assistant 2 noncommissioned officer ranking above first sergeant in Marine Corps > **sergeant at arms** legislative, organizational officer assigned to keep order, etc.

se•ries [SEER-eez] *noun, plural* **series** 1 sequence 2 succession, set (e.g. of radio, TV programs with same characters, setting, but different

sentiment *noun* 1 EMOTION, sensibility, tenderness
2 (*often plural*) FEELING, attitude, belief, idea, judgment, opinion, view
3 SENTIMENTALITY, emotionalism, mawkishness, romanticism

sentimental *adjective* ROMANTIC, emotional, maudlin, nostalgic, overemotional, schmaltzy (*slang*), slushy (*informal*), soft-hearted, touching, weepy (*informal*)

sentimentality *noun* ROMANTICISM, corniness (*slang*), emotionalism, mawkishness, nostalgia, schmaltz (*slang*)

sentinel *noun* GUARD, lookout, sentry, watch, watchman

separable *adjective* DISTINGUISHABLE, detachable, divisible

separate *verb* 1 DIVIDE, come apart, come away, detach, disconnect, disjoin, remove, sever, split, sunder
2 PART, break up, disunite, diverge, divorce, estrange, part company, split up
3 ISOLATE, segregate, single out
▷ *adjective* 4 UNCONNECTED, detached, disconnected, divided, divorced, isolated, unattached
5 INDIVIDUAL, alone, apart, distinct, particular, single, solitary

separated *adjective* DISCONNECTED, apart, disassociated, disunited, divided, parted, separate, sundered

separately *adverb* INDIVIDUALLY, alone, apart, severally, singly

separation *noun* 1 DIVISION, break, disconnection, dissociation, disunion, gap
2 SPLIT-UP, break-up, divorce, parting, rift, split

septic *adjective* INFECTED, festering, poisoned, putrefying, putrid, suppurating

sepulcher *noun* TOMB, burial place, grave, mausoleum, vault

sequel *noun* 1 FOLLOW-UP, continuation, development
2 CONSEQUENCE, conclusion, end, outcome, result, upshot

sequence *noun* SUCCESSION, arrangement, chain, course, cycle, order, progression, series

serene *adjective* CALM, composed, peaceful, tranquil, unruffled, untroubled

serenity *noun* CALMNESS, calm, composure, peace, peacefulness, quietness, stillness, tranquillity

series *noun* SEQUENCE, chain, course, order,

stories) > **se•ri•al** [SEER-ee-əl] *noun* 1 story or play produced in successive episodes or installments 2 periodical publication ▷ *adjective* > **se'ri•al•ize** *verb* **-ized, -iz•ing** publish, present as serial > **serial killer** murderer who commits series of murders in same pattern oft. in same locality

ser'if *noun* small line finishing off stroke of letter

se•ri•ous [SEER-ee-əs] *adjective* 1 thoughtful, solemn 2 earnest, sincere 3 of importance 4 giving cause for concern

ser•mon [SUR-mən] *noun* 1 discourse of religious instruction or exhortation spoken or read from pulpit 2 any similar discourse > **ser'mon•ize** *verb intransitive* **-ized, -iz•ing** 1 talk like preacher 2 compose sermons

ser•pent [SUR-pənt] *noun* snake > **serp'en•tine** [-teen] *adjective* like, shaped like, serpent

ser•rate [SER-ayt], **ser•rat•ed** [SER-ay-tid] *adjective* having notched, sawlike edge > **ser•ra'tion** *noun*

se•rum [SEER-əm] *noun, plural* **-rums** watery animal fluid, esp. thin part of blood as used-for inoculation or vaccination

serve [surv] *verb* **served, serv•ing** (*mainly transitive*) 1 work for, under, another 2 attend (to customers) in store, etc. 3 provide 4 help to (food, etc.) 5 present (food, etc.) in particular way 6 provide with regular supply of 7 be member of military unit 8 pay homage to 9 spend time doing 10 be useful, suitable enough 11 *tennis etc* put (ball) into play ▷ *noun tennis, etc* 12 act of serving ball > **ser'vant** [-vənt] *noun* personal or domestic attendant > **ser'ver** [-vər] *noun* 1 person who serves 2 *computing* computer or program that supplies data to other machines on a network > **serv'ice** [-vis] *noun* 1 the act of serving, helping, assisting 2 system organized to provide for needs of public 3 maintenance of vehicle 4 use 5 readiness, availability for use 6 set of dishes, etc. 7 form, session, of public worship ▷ *verb transitive* **-iced, -ic•ing** 8 overhaul > **serv'ic•es** *plural noun* armed forces > **serv'ice•a•ble** *adjective* 1 in working order, usable 2 durable > **service road** narrow road giving access to houses, stores, etc. > **service station** place supplying fuel, oil, maintenance for motor vehicles

ser•vile [SUR-vil] *adjective* 1 slavish, without independence 2 cringing 3 fawning 4 menial > **ser•vil'i•ty** *noun*

ser•vi•tude [SUR-vi-tood] *noun* bondage, slavery

ser•vo•mech•an•ism [SUR-voh-mek-ə-niz-əm] *noun* electronic device for converting small mechanical, hydraulic or other type of force into larger, esp. in steering mechanisms

ses•a•me [SES-ə-mee] *noun* plant with seeds used as herbs and for making oil

ses•sion [SESH-ən] *noun* 1 meeting of court, etc. 2 assembly 3 continuous series of such meetings 4 any period devoted to an activity 5 school or university term: *summer session*

set *verb* **set, set•ting** (*mainly transitive*) 1 put or place in specified position or condition 2 cause to sit 3 fix, point, put up 4 make ready 5 become firm or fixed 6 establish 7 prescribe,

DICTIONARY **S** THESAURUS

---

progression, run, set, string, succession, train

serious *adjective* 1 SEVERE, acute, critical, dangerous
2 IMPORTANT, crucial, fateful, grim, momentous, no laughing matter, pressing, significant, urgent, worrying
3 SOLEMN, grave, humorless, sober, unsmiling
4 SINCERE, earnest, genuine, honest, in earnest

seriously *adverb* 1 GRAVELY, acutely, badly, critically, dangerously, severely
2 SINCERELY, gravely, in earnest

seriousness *noun* 1 IMPORTANCE, gravity, significance, urgency
2 SOLEMNITY, earnestness, gravitas, gravity

sermon *noun* 1 HOMILY, address
2 LECTURE, harangue, talking-to (*informal*)

servant *noun* ATTENDANT, domestic, help, maid, retainer, slave

serve *verb* 1 WORK FOR, aid, assist, attend to, help, minister to, wait on
2 PERFORM, act, complete, discharge, do, fulfill
3 PROVIDE, deliver, dish up, present, set out, supply
4 BE ADEQUATE, answer the purpose, be acceptable, do, function as, satisfy, suffice, suit

service *noun* 1 HELP, assistance, avail, benefit, use, usefulness
2 WORK, business, duty, employment, labor, office
3 OVERHAUL, check, maintenance
4 CEREMONY, observance, rite, worship
▷ *verb* 5 OVERHAUL, check, fine tune, go over, maintain, tune *or* tune up

serviceable *adjective* USEFUL, beneficial, functional, helpful, operative, practical, profitable, usable, utilitarian

servile *adjective* SUBSERVIENT, abject, fawning, groveling, obsequious, sycophantic, toadying

serving *noun* PORTION, helping

session *noun* MEETING, assembly, conference, congress, discussion, hearing, period, sitting

set[1] *verb* 1 PUT, deposit, lay, locate, place, plant, position, rest, seat, situate, station, stick
2 PREPARE, arrange, lay, make ready, spread
3 HARDEN, cake, congeal, crystallize, solidify, stiffen, thicken
4 ARRANGE, appoint, decide *or* decide upon, determine, establish, fix, fix up, resolve, schedule, settle, specify
5 ASSIGN, allot, decree, impose, ordain, prescribe, specify
6 GO DOWN, decline, dip, disappear, sink, subside, vanish
▷ *noun* 7 POSITION, attitude, bearing, carriage, posture
8 SCENERY, scene, setting, stage set
▷ *adjective* 9 FIXED, agreed, appointed, arranged, decided, definite, established, prearranged, predetermined, scheduled, settled
10 INFLEXIBLE, hard and fast, immovable, rigid, stubborn
11 CONVENTIONAL, stereotyped, stock, traditional, unspontaneous
12 ▷ **set on, set upon** DETERMINED, bent, intent, resolute

set[2] *noun* 1 SERIES, assortment, batch, collection, compendium
2 GROUP, band, circle, clique, company, coterie,

allot **8** put to music **9** of hair, arrange while wet, so that it dries in position **10** of sun, go down **11** have direction ▷ *adjective* **12** fixed, established **13** deliberate **14** formal, arranged beforehand **15** unvarying ▷ *noun* **16** act or state of being set **17** bearing, posture **18** *radio, tv* complete apparatus for reception or transmission **19** *theater, films* **20** organized settings and equipment to form ensemble of scene **21** number of things, persons associated as being similar, complementary or used together **22** *math.* group of numbers, objects, etc. with at least one common property > **set'back** *noun* anything that hinders or impedes > **set'up** *noun* **1** position **2** organization > **set up 1** establish **2** (*informal*) treat, as to drinks **3** (*informal*) frame, entrap **4** (*informal*) lure into embarrassing, dangerous, situation > **set shot** *basketball* shot at basket taken from standing position and relatively distant from basket

set•tee' *noun* couch

set•ter [SET-ər] *noun* various breeds of gun dog

set•ting [SET-ing] *noun* **1** background **2** surroundings **3** scenery and other stage accessories **4** act of fixing **5** decorative metalwork holding precious stone, etc. in position **6** tableware and cutlery for (single place at) table **7** descending below horizon of sun **8** music for song

set•tle [SET-l] *verb transitive* **-tled, -tling 1** arrange, put in order **2** establish, make firm or secure or quiet **3** decide upon **4** end (dispute, etc.) **5** pay **6** bestow (property) by legal deed ▷ *verb intransitive* **-tled, -tling 7** come to rest **8** subside **9** become clear **10** take up residence **11** subside, sink to bottom **12** come to agreement > **set'tle•ment** [-mənt] *noun* **1** act of settling **2** place newly inhabited **3** money bestowed legally **4** subsidence (of building) > **set•tler** [SET-lər] *noun* colonist

sev•en [SEV-ən] *adjective, noun* cardinal number, next after six > **sev'enth** *adjective* the ordinal number > **sev'en•teen'** *adjective, noun* ten and seven > **sev'en•ty** *adjective, noun, plural* **-ties** ten times seven

sev•er [SEV-ər] *verb* **1** separate, divide **2** cut off > **sev•er•ance** [-əns] *noun* > **severance pay** compensation paid by a firm to an employee for loss of employment

sev•er•al [SEV-ər-əl] *adjective* **1** some, a few **2** separate **3** individual **4** various **5** different ▷ *pronoun* **6** indefinite small number > **sev'er•al•ly** *adverb* **1** apart from others **2** singly

se•vere [sə-VEER] *adjective* **-ver•er, -ver•est 1** strict **2** rigorous **3** hard to do **4** harsh **5** austere **6** extreme > **se•ver'i•ty** [-VER-i-tee] *noun*

sew [soh] *verb* **sewed, sewn** *or* **sewed, sew•ing 1** join with needle and thread **2** make by sewing

sew•age [SOO-ij] *noun* refuse, waste matter, excrement conveyed in sewer > **sew'er** *noun* underground drain to remove waste water and refuse > **sew'er•age** *noun* **1** arrangement of sewers **2** sewage

sex [seks] *noun* **1** state of being male or female **2** males or females collectively **3** sexual intercourse ▷ *adjective* **4** concerning sex ▷ *verb transitive* **5** ascertain sex of > **sex'ism** *noun* discrimination on basis of sex > **sex'ist** *noun, adjective* > **sex•u•al** [SEK-shoo-əl] *adjective* > **sex'y** *adjective* **sex•i•er, sex•i•est** > **sexual intercourse** act of procreation in which male's penis is

crowd, faction, gang

setback *noun* HOLD-UP, blow, check, defeat, disappointment, hitch, misfortune, reverse

set back *verb* HOLD UP, delay, hinder, impede, retard, slow

set off *verb* **1** LEAVE, depart, embark, start out
2 DETONATE, explode, ignite

setting *noun* BACKGROUND, backdrop, context, location, scene, scenery, set, site, surroundings

settle *verb* **1** PUT IN ORDER, adjust, order, regulate, straighten out, work out
2 LAND, alight, come to rest, descend, light
3 MOVE TO, dwell, inhabit, live, make one's home, put down roots, reside, set up home, take up residence
4 COLONIZE, people, pioneer, populate
5 CALM, lull, pacify, quell, quiet, quieten, reassure, relax, relieve, soothe
6 PAY, clear, discharge, square *or* square up
7 (*often with on* or *upon*) DECIDE, agree, confirm, determine, establish, fix
8 RESOLVE, clear up, decide, put an end to, reconcile

settlement *noun* **1** AGREEMENT, arrangement, conclusion, confirmation, establishment, working out
2 PAYMENT, clearing, discharge
3 COLONY, community, encampment, outpost

settler *noun* COLONIST, colonizer, frontiersman, immigrant, pioneer

setup *noun* ARRANGEMENT, conditions, organization, regime, structure, system

set up *verb* **1** BUILD, assemble, construct, erect, put together, put up, raise
2 ESTABLISH, arrange, begin, found, initiate, institute, organize, prearrange, prepare

sever *verb* **1** CUT, cut in two, detach, disconnect, disjoin, divide, part, separate, split
2 BREAK OFF, dissociate, put an end to, terminate

several *adjective* SOME, different, diverse, manifold, many, sundry, various

severe *adjective* **1** STRICT, austere, cruel, drastic, hard, harsh, oppressive, rigid, unbending
2 GRIM, forbidding, grave, serious, stern, tight-lipped, unsmiling
3 INTENSE, acute, extreme, fierce
4 PLAIN, austere, classic, homely, restrained, simple, Spartan, unadorned, unembellished, unfussy

severely *adverb* **1** STRICTLY, harshly, sharply, sternly
2 SERIOUSLY, acutely, badly, extremely, gravely

severity *noun* STRICTNESS, hardness, harshness, severeness, sternness, toughness

sex *noun* **1** GENDER
2 INTERCOURSE *or* SEXUAL INTERCOURSE, coition, coitus, copulation, fornication, lovemaking, sexual relations

sexual *adjective* **1** CARNAL, erotic, intimate, sensual, sexy
2 REPRODUCTIVE, genital, procreative, sex

inserted into female's vagina
sex•a•ge•nar•i•an [sek-sə-jə-NAIR-ee-ən] *adjective, noun* (person) sixty to seventy years old
sex•tant [SEK-stənt] *noun* navigator's instrument for measuring elevations of heavenly body, etc.
sex•tet [seks-TET] *noun* (composition for) six singers or players; group of six
sex•ton [SEK-stən] *noun* 1 official who takes care of church building and its contents and sometimes assists in burial of dead 2 official who takes care of synagogue and sometimes assists cantor in conducting services
Sg *chem.* seaborgium
shab•by [SHAB-ee] *adjective* **-bi•er, -bi•est** 1 faded, worn, ragged 2 poorly dressed 3 mean, dishonorable 4 stingy > **shab'bi•ly** *adverb* > **shab'bi•ness** [-nis] *noun*
shack [shak] *noun* rough hut > **shack up** *or* **shack up with** (*slang*) live (with) esp. as husband and wife without being legally married
shack•le [SHAK-əl] *noun* 1 metal ring or fastening for prisoner's wrist or ankle 2 anything that confines ▷ *verb transitive* **-led, -ling** 3 fasten with shackles 4 hamper
shade [shayd] *noun* 1 partial darkness 2 shelter, place sheltered from light, heat, etc. 3 darker part of anything 4 depth of color 5 tinge 6 ghost 7 screen 8 anything used to screen 9 window blind ▷ *verb transitive* **shad•ed, shad•ing** 10 screen from light, darken 11 represent shades in drawing > **shades** *plural noun* (*slang*) sunglasses > **shad'y** *adjective* **shad•i•er, shad•i•est** 1 shielded from sun 2 dim 3 dubious 4 dishonest 5 dishonorable
shad•ow [SHAD-oh] *noun* 1 dark figure projected by anything that intercepts rays of light 2 patch of shade 3 slight trace 4 indistinct image 5 gloom 6 inseparable companion ▷ *verb transitive* 7 cast shadow over 8 follow and watch closely > **shad'ow•y** *adjective*
shaft *noun* 1 straight rod, stem, handle 2 arrow 3 ray, beam (of light) 4 revolving rod for transmitting power 5 one of the bars between which horse is harnessed 6 entrance boring of mine
shag[1] *noun* 1 matted wool or hair 2 long-napped cloth 3 coarse shredded tobacco > **shag'gy** *adjective* **-gi•er, -gi•est** 1 covered with rough hair or wool 2 tousled 3 unkempt
shag[2] *verb transitive* **shagged, shag•ging** 1 chase after 2 *baseball* in practice, chase and catch fly balls
shah *noun* formerly, ruler of Iran
shake [shayk] *verb* **shook** [shuuk], **shak•en** 1 (cause to) move with quick vibrations 2 tremble 3 grasp the hand (of another) in greeting 4 upset 5 wave, brandish ▷ *noun* 6 act of shaking 7 vibration 8 jolt 9 (*informal*) short period of time, jiffy > **shak'i•ly** *adverb* > **shak'y** *adjective* **shak•i•er, shak•i•est** unsteady, insecure
shale [shayl] *noun* flaky, sedimentary rock
shall [shal] *verb, past tense* **should** used as an auxiliary to make the future tense or to indicate intention, obligation, or inevitability
shal•lot [SHAL-ət] *noun* kind of small onion
shal•low [SHAL-oh] *adjective* **-er, -est** 1 not deep

sexual intercourse *noun* COPULATION, carnal knowledge, coition, coitus, sex, union
sexuality *noun* DESIRE, carnality, eroticism, lust, sensuality, sexiness (*informal*)
sexy *adjective* EROTIC, arousing, naughty, provocative, seductive, sensual, sensuous, suggestive, titillating
shabby *adjective* 1 TATTY, dilapidated, mean, ragged, run-down, seedy, tattered, threadbare, worn
2 MEAN, cheap, contemptible, despicable, dirty, dishonorable, lousy (*slang*), low, rotten (*informal*), scurvy, scuzzy (*slang*)
shack *noun* HUT, cabin, shanty
shackle *noun* 1 (*often plural*) FETTER, bond, chain, iron, leg-iron, manacle
▷ *verb* 2 FETTER, bind, chain, manacle, put in irons
shade *noun* 1 DIMNESS, dusk, gloom, gloominess, semidarkness, shadow
2 SCREEN, blind, canopy, cover, covering, curtain, shield, veil
3 COLOR, hue, tinge, tint, tone
4 DASH, hint, suggestion, trace
5 (*literary*) GHOST, apparition, phantom, specter, spirit
6 ▷ **put into the shade** OUTSHINE, eclipse, outclass, overshadow
▷ *verb* 7 COVER, conceal, hide, obscure, protect, screen, shield, veil
8 DARKEN, cloud, dim, shadow
shadow *noun* 1 DIMNESS, cover, darkness, dusk, gloom, shade
2 TRACE, hint, suggestion, suspicion
3 CLOUD, blight, gloom, sadness
▷ *verb* 4 SHADE, darken, overhang, screen, shield
5 FOLLOW, stalk, tail (*informal*), trail
shadowy *adjective* 1 DARK, dim, dusky, gloomy, murky, shaded, shady
2 VAGUE, dim, dreamlike, faint, ghostly, nebulous, phantom, spectral, unsubstantial
shady *adjective* 1 SHADED, cool, dim
2 (*informal*) CROOKED, disreputable, dubious, questionable, shifty, suspect, suspicious, unethical
shaft *noun* 1 HANDLE, pole, rod, shank, stem
2 RAY, beam, gleam
shaggy *adjective* UNKEMPT, hairy, hirsute, long-haired, rough, tousled, unshorn
shake *verb* 1 VIBRATE, bump, jar, jolt, quake, rock, shiver, totter, tremble
2 WAVE, brandish, flourish
3 UPSET, distress, disturb, frighten, rattle (*informal*), shock, unnerve
▷ *noun* 4 VIBRATION, agitation, convulsion, jerk, jolt, quaking, shiver, shudder, trembling, tremor
shake up *verb* 1 STIR *or* STIR UP, agitate, churn *or* churn up, mix
2 UPSET, disturb, shock, unsettle
shaky *adjective* 1 UNSTEADY, faltering, precarious, quivery, rickety, trembling, unstable, weak
2 UNCERTAIN, dubious, iffy (*informal*), questionable, suspect
shallow *adjective* 1 SUPERFICIAL, empty, slight, surface, trivial

2 having little depth of water 3 superficial 4 not sincere ▷ *noun* 5 shallow place
sham *adjective, noun* 1 imitation, counterfeit ▷ *verb* **shammed, sham•ming** 2 pretend, feign
sham•ble [SHAM-bəl] *verb intransitive* **-bled, -bling** walk in shuffling, awkward way
sham•bles [SHAM-bəlz] *noun* messy, disorderly thing or place
shame [shaym] *noun* 1 emotion caused by consciousness of guilt or dishonor in one's conduct or state 2 cause of disgrace 3 ignominy 4 pity, hard luck ▷ *verb transitive* **shamed, sham•ing** 5 cause to feel shame 6 disgrace 7 force by shame (into) > **shame'ful** [-fəl] *adjective* disgraceful > **shame•less** [-lis] *adjective* 1 with no sense of shame 2 indecent > **shame'faced** [-faysd] *adjective* ashamed
sham•poo' *noun* 1 various preparations of liquid soap for washing hair, carpets, etc. 2 this process ▷ *verb transitive* **-pooed, -poo•ing** 3 use shampoo to wash
sham•rock [SHAM-rok] *noun* cloverlike plant with three leaves on each stem, esp. as Irish emblem
shang•hai [SHANG-hī] *verb transitive* **-haied, -hai•ing** force, trick someone to do something
shank *noun* 1 lower leg 2 shinbone 3 stem of thing **shank of the evening** best or main part of the evening
shan'tung *noun* soft, natural Chinese silk
shan•ty[1] [SHAN-tee] *noun, plural* **-ties** 1 temporary wooden building 2 crude dwelling
shanty[2] *see* **chantey**
shape [shayp] *noun* 1 external form or appearance, esp. of a woman 2 mold, pattern 3 condition, esp. of physical fitness ▷ *verb transitive* **shaped, shap•ing** 4 form, mold, fashion, make ▷ *verb intransitive* **shaped, shap•ing** 5 develop > **shape'less** [-lis] *adjective* > **shape'ly** *adjective* **-li•er, -li•est** well-proportioned
shard [shahrd] *noun* broken fragment, esp. of earthenware
share[1] [shair] *noun* 1 portion 2 quota 3 lot 4 unit of ownership in corporation ▷ *verb* **shared, shar•ing** 5 give, take a share 6 join with others in doing, using, something > **share'hold•er** *noun*
share[2] *noun* blade of plow
shark [shahrk] *noun* 1 large sometimes predatory sea fish 2 person who cheats others 3 (*informal*) person of great ability in cards, etc.
sharp [shahrp] *adjective* **-er, -est** 1 having keen cutting edge or fine point 2 keen 3 not gradual or gentle 4 brisk 5 clever 6 harsh 7 dealing cleverly but unfairly 8 shrill 9 strongly marked, esp. in outline ▷ *adverb* 10 promptly ▷ *noun* 11 *mus.* note half a tone above natural pitch 12 cheat, swindler (*also* **sharp'er**) > **sharp'en** *verb transitive* make sharp > **sharp'shoot•er** *noun* marksman
shat•ter [SHAT-ər] *verb* 1 break in pieces 2 ruin (plans, etc.) 3 disturb (person) greatly
shave [shayv] *verb* **shaved, shaved** *or* **shav•en, shav•ing** 1 cut close, esp. hair of face or head 2 pare away 3 graze 4 reduce ▷ *noun* 5 shaving > **shav'ings** *plural noun* parings **close shave**

DICTIONARY • THESAURUS

2 UNINTELLIGENT, foolish, frivolous, ignorant, puerile, simple
sham *noun* 1 PHONEY *or* PHONY (*informal*), counterfeit, forgery, fraud, hoax, humbug, imitation, impostor, pretense
▷ *adjective* 2 FALSE, artificial, bogus, counterfeit, feigned, imitation, mock, phoney *or* phony (*informal*), pretended, simulated
▷ *verb* 3 FAKE, affect, assume, feign, pretend, put on, simulate
shambles *noun* CHAOS, confusion, disarray, disorder, havoc, madhouse, mess, muddle
shame *noun* 1 EMBARRASSMENT, abashment, humiliation, ignominy, mortification
2 DISGRACE, blot, discredit, dishonor, disrepute, infamy, reproach, scandal, smear
▷ *verb* 3 EMBARRASS, abash, disgrace, humble, humiliate, mortify
4 DISHONOR, blot, debase, defile, degrade, smear, stain
shamefaced *adjective* EMBARRASSED, abashed, ashamed, humiliated, mortified, red-faced, sheepish
shameful *adjective* 1 EMBARRASSING, humiliating, mortifying
2 DISGRACEFUL, base, dishonorable, low, mean, outrageous, scandalous, wicked
shameless *adjective* BRAZEN, audacious, barefaced, flagrant, hardened, insolent, unabashed, unashamed
shanty *noun* SHACK, cabin, hut, shed
shape *noun* 1 FORM, build, configuration, contours, figure, lines, outline, profile, silhouette
2 PATTERN, frame, model, mold
3 CONDITION, fettle, health, state, trim
▷ *verb* 4 FORM, create, fashion, make, model, mold, produce
5 DEVELOP, adapt, devise, frame, modify, plan
shapeless *adjective* FORMLESS, amorphous, irregular, misshapen, unstructured
shapely *adjective* WELL-FORMED, curvaceous, elegant, graceful, neat, trim, well-proportioned
share *noun* 1 PART, allotment, allowance, contribution, due, lot, portion, quota, ration, whack (*informal*)
▷ *verb* 2 DIVIDE, assign, distribute, partake, participate, receive, split
sharp *adjective* 1 KEEN, acute, jagged, pointed, serrated, spiky
2 SUDDEN, abrupt, distinct, extreme, marked
3 CLEAR, crisp, distinct, well-defined
4 QUICK-WITTED, alert, astute, bright, clever, discerning, knowing, penetrating, perceptive, quick
5 DISHONEST, artful, crafty, cunning, sly, unscrupulous, wily
6 CUTTING, barbed, biting, bitter, caustic, harsh, hurtful
7 SOUR, acid, acrid, hot, piquant, pungent, tart
8 ACUTE, intense, painful, piercing, severe, shooting, stabbing
▷ *adverb* 9 PROMPTLY, exactly, on the dot, on time, precisely, punctually
sharpen *verb* WHET, edge, grind, hone
shatter *verb* 1 SMASH, break, burst, crack, crush, pulverize
2 DESTROY, demolish, ruin, torpedo, wreck
shattered *adjective* (*informal*) DEVASTATED, blown away, crushed

narrow escape
shawl *noun* piece of fabric to cover woman's shoulders or head
she [shee] *pronoun* 3rd person singular feminine pronoun
sheaf [sheef] *noun, plural* **sheaves** 1 bundle, esp. corn 2 loose leaves of paper
shear [sheer] *verb transitive* **sheared, sheared** *or* **shorn, shear•ing** 1 clip hair, wool from 2 cut through 3 trim (e.g. hedge) 4 fracture > **shears** *plural noun* 1 large pair of scissors 2 mechanical shearing, cutting instrument
sheath [sheeth] *noun, plural* **sheaths** [sheethz] 1 close-fitting cover, esp. for knife or sword 2 scabbard 3 condom > **sheathe** [sheeth] *verb transitive* **sheathed, sheath•ing** put into sheath
she•bang [shə-BANG] *noun* (*informal*) situation, matter, esp. whole shebang
shed[1] *noun* roofed shelter used for storage or as workshop
shed[2] *verb transitive* **shed, shed•ding** 1 (cause to) pour forth (e.g. tears, blood) 2 cast off
sheen *noun* gloss
sheep *noun* ruminant animal bred for wool and meat > **sheep'ish** *adjective* embarrassed, shy > **sheep-dip** *noun* solution in which sheep are immersed to kill vermin and germs in fleece > **sheep'dog** *noun* dog of various breeds orig. for herding sheep > **sheep'skin** *noun* 1 skin of sheep (with fleece) used for clothing, rug or without fleece for parchment 2 (*informal*) diploma
sheer[1] *adjective* **-er, -est** 1 perpendicular 2 of material, very fine, transparent 3 absolute, unmitigated
sheer[2] *verb intransitive* 1 deviate from course 2 swerve 3 turn aside
sheet[1] *noun* 1 large piece of cotton, etc. to cover bed 2 broad piece of any thin material 3 large expanse ▷ *verb transitive* 4 cover with sheet
sheet[2] *noun* rope fastened in corner of sail > **sheet anchor** large anchor for emergency
sheik [shayk, sheek] *noun* Arab chief
shek•el [SHEK-əl] *noun* monetary unit of Israel > **shek•els** (*informal*) money
shelf *noun, plural* **shelves** 1 board fixed horizontally (on wall, etc.) for holding things 2 ledge
shell *noun* 1 hard outer case (esp. of egg, nut, etc.) 2 husk 3 explosive projectile 4 outer part of structure left when interior is removed ▷ *verb transitive* 5 take shell from 6 take out of shell 7 fire at with shells > **racing shell** long light racing boat for rowing by crew of one or more > **shell'fish** *noun* 1 mollusk 2 crustacean > **shell shock** battle fatigue, nervous disorder caused by bursting of shells or bombs > **shell out** (*informal*) pay up
shel•lac [shə-LAK] *noun* 1 varnish ▷ *verb transitive* **-lacked, -lack•ing** 2 coat with shellac
shel•ter [SHEL-tər] *noun* 1 place, structure giving protection 2 protection 3 refuge 4 haven ▷ *verb transitive* 5 give protection to 6 screen ▷ *verb intransitive* 7 take shelter
shelve [shelv] *verb transitive* **shelved, shelv•ing** 1 put on a shelf 2 put off 3 cease to employ 4 defer indefinitely ▷ *verb intransitive* **shelved, shelv•ing** 5 slope gradually
she•nan•i•gans [shə-NAN-i-gənz] *plural noun* (*informal*) 1 frolicking 2 playing tricks, etc.
shep•herd [SHEP-ərd] *noun* 1 person who tends sheep ▷ *verb transitive* 2 guide, watch over > **shep'herd•ess** [-is] *noun feminine*
sher•bet [SHUR-bit] *noun* frozen fruit-flavored dessert like ices but with gelatin, etc. added
sher'iff *noun* law enforcement officer
Sher•pa [SHUR-pə] *noun, plural* **-pas** *or* **-pa** member of a Tibetan people
sher•ry [SHER-ee] *noun, plural* **-ries** fortified wine from S Spain
shib•bo•leth [SHIB-ə-lith] *noun* 1 custom, word, etc. distinguishing people of particular class or group 2 test word, pet phrase of sect or party
shield [sheeld] *noun* 1 piece of armor carried on arm 2 any protection used to stop blows, missiles, etc. 3 any protective device 4 sports trophy ▷ *verb transitive* 5 cover, protect
shift *verb* (cause to) move, change position ▷ *noun* 1 relay of workers 2 time of their working 3 evasion 4 expedient 5 removal 6 woman's underskirt or dress > **shift'i•ness** [-nis] *noun* > **shift'less** [-lis] *adjective* lacking in

shave *verb* TRIM, crop, pare, shear
shed[1] *noun* HUT, outhouse, shack
shed[2] *verb* 1 GIVE OUT, cast, drop, emit, give, radiate, scatter, shower, spill
2 CAST OFF, discard, moult, slough
sheen *noun* SHINE, brightness, gleam, gloss, luster, polish
sheepish *adjective* EMBARRASSED, abashed, ashamed, mortified, self-conscious, shamefaced
sheer *adjective* 1 TOTAL, absolute, complete, downright, out-and-out, pure, unmitigated, utter
2 STEEP, abrupt, precipitous
3 FINE, diaphanous, gauzy, gossamer, see-through, thin, transparent
sheet *noun* 1 COAT, film, lamina, layer, overlay, stratum, surface, veneer
2 PIECE, panel, plate, slab
3 EXPANSE, area, blanket, covering, stretch, sweep
shell *noun* 1 CASE, husk, pod
2 FRAME, framework, hull, structure
▷ *verb* 3 BOMB, attack, blitz, bombard, strafe
shell out *verb* PAY OUT, fork out (*slang*), give, hand over
shelter *noun* 1 PROTECTION, cover, defense, guard, screen
2 SAFETY, asylum, haven, refuge, retreat, sanctuary, security
▷ *verb* 3 PROTECT, cover, defend, guard, harbor, hide, safeguard, shield
4 TAKE SHELTER, hide, seek refuge
sheltered *adjective* PROTECTED, cloistered, isolated, quiet, screened, secluded, shaded, shielded
shelve *verb* POSTPONE, defer, freeze, put aside, put on ice, put on the back burner (*informal*), suspend, take a rain check on (*informal*)
shepherd *verb* GUIDE, conduct, herd, steer, usher
shield *noun* 1 PROTECTION, cover, defense, guard, safeguard, screen, shelter
▷ *verb* 2 PROTECT, cover, defend, guard, safeguard, screen, shelter
shift *verb* 1 MOVE, budge, displace, move around,

resource or character > **shift'y** *adjective* **shift•i•er, shift•i•est** evasive, of dubious character
shil•le•lagh [shə-LAY-lə] *noun* (in Ireland) cudgel
shil'ling *noun* 1 former Brit coin, now 5 pence 2 monetary unit in various countries
shil•ly-shal•ly [SHIL-ee-shal-ee] *verb intransitive* **-lied, -ly•ing** 1 waver ▷ *noun* 2 wavering, indecision
shim•mer [SHIM-ər] *verb intransitive* 1 shine with quivering light ▷ *noun* 2 such light 3 glimmer
shin *noun* 1 front of lower leg ▷ *verb* **shinned, shin•ning** 2 climb with arms and legs > **shin'bone** [-bohn] *noun* tibia
shin'dig *noun* (*informal*) elaborate party, dance, etc.
shine [shīn] *verb* **shone, shin•ing** 1 give out, reflect light 2 perform very well, excel 3 cause to shine by polishing ▷ *noun* 4 brightness, luster 5 polishing > **shin'y** *adjective* **shin•i•er, shin•i•est**
shin•gle[1] [SHIN-gəl] *noun* 1 wooden roof and wall tile ▷ *verb transitive* **-gled, -gling** 2 cover with shingles
shingle[2] *noun* mass of pebbles
shin•gles [SHIN-gəlz] *noun* disease causing inflammation along a nerve
Shin•to [SHIN-toh] *noun* native Japanese religion > **Shin'to•ism** *noun*
ship *noun* 1 large seagoing vessel ▷ *verb* **shipped, ship•ping** 2 put on or send (esp. by ship) 3 embark 4 take employment on ship > **ship'ment** [-mənt] *noun* 1 act of shipping 2 goods shipped > **shipping** *noun* 1 freight transport business 2 ships collectively > **ship'shape** [-shayp] *adjective* orderly, trim > **ship'wreck** [-rek] *noun* 1 destruction of a ship through storm, collision, etc. ▷ *verb transitive* 2 cause to undergo shipwreck > **ship'yard** *noun* place for building and repair of ships > **ship out** 1 leave by ship 2 (*informal*) quit, resign, be fired
shirk [shurk] *verb transitive* evade, try to avoid (duty, etc.)
shirr [shur] *verb transitive* 1 gather (fabric) into parallel rows ▷ *noun* 2 series of gathered rows decorating a dress, blouse, etc. (*also* **shir'ring**)
shirt [shurt] *noun* garment for upper part of body
shiv *noun* (*slang*) knife
shiv•er[1] [SHIV-ər] *verb intransitive* 1 tremble, usu. with cold or fear 2 shudder 3 vibrate ▷ *noun* 4 act, state, of shivering
shiver[2] *verb* 1 splinter, break in pieces ▷ *noun* 2 splinter
shoal [shohl] *noun* 1 stretch of shallow water 2 sandbank or bar ▷ *verb* 3 make, become, shallow
shock[1] [shok] *verb transitive* 1 horrify, scandalize ▷ *noun* 2 violent or damaging blow 3 emotional disturbance 4 state of weakness, illness, caused by physical or mental shock 5 paralytic stroke 6 collision 7 effect on sensory nerves of electric discharge > **shock'er** *noun* person or thing that shocks or distresses > **shock absorber** device (esp. in automobiles) to absorb shocks
shock[2] *noun* group of corn sheaves placed together
shock[3] *noun* 1 mass of hair ▷ *adjective* 2 shaggy > **shock'head•ed** [-hed-id] *adjective*
shod•dy [SHOD-ee] *adjective* **-di•er, -di•est** worthless, trashy, second-rate, of poor material
shoe [shoo] *noun, plural* **shoes** 1 covering for foot, not enclosing ankle 2 metal rim or curved bar put on horse's hoof 3 various protective plates or undercoverings ▷ *verb transitive* **shod** *or* **shoed, shod** *or* **shoed, shoe•ing** 4 protect, furnish with shoe or shoes > **shoe'string** *adjective, noun* very small (amount of money, etc.)
shone *pt./pp. of* **shine**
shoo *interjection* 1 go away! ▷ *verb transitive* **shooed, shoo•ing** 2 drive away > **shoo'-in** *noun* (*informal*) 1 person or thing certain to win or succeed 2 match or contest that is easy to win
shook [shuuk] *pt. of* **shake**

DICTIONARY • THESAURUS

rearrange, relocate, reposition
▷ *noun* 2 MOVE, displacement, rearrangement, shifting
shiftless *adjective* LAZY, aimless, good-for-nothing, idle, lackadaisical, slothful, unambitious, unenterprising
shifty *adjective* UNTRUSTWORTHY, deceitful, devious, evasive, furtive, slippery, sly, tricky, underhand
shimmer *verb* 1 GLEAM, glisten, scintillate, twinkle
▷ *noun* 2 GLEAM, iridescence
shine *verb* 1 GLEAM, beam, flash, glare, glisten, glitter, glow, radiate, sparkle, twinkle
2 POLISH, brush, buff, burnish
3 STAND OUT, be conspicuous, excel
▷ *noun* 4 BRIGHTNESS, glare, gleam, light, radiance, shimmer, sparkle
5 POLISH, gloss, luster, sheen
shining *adjective* BRIGHT, beaming, brilliant, gleaming, glistening, luminous, radiant, shimmering, sparkling
shiny *adjective* BRIGHT, gleaming, glistening, glossy, lustrous, polished
ship *noun* VESSEL, boat, craft
shipshape *adjective* TIDY, neat, orderly, spick-and-span, trim, well-ordered, well-organized
shirk *verb* DODGE, avoid, evade, get out of, slack
shirker *noun* SLACKER, clock-watcher, dodger, idler
shiver[1] *verb* 1 TREMBLE, quake, quiver, shake, shudder
▷ *noun* 2 TREMBLING, flutter, quiver, shudder, tremor
shiver[2] *verb* SPLINTER, break, crack, fragment, shatter, smash, smash to smithereens
shivery *adjective* SHAKING, chilled, chilly, cold, quaking, quivery, shaky
shock *verb* 1 HORRIFY, appall, disgust, nauseate, revolt, scandalize, sicken
2 ASTOUND, jolt, shake, stagger, stun, stupefy
▷ *noun* 3 IMPACT, blow, clash, collision
4 UPSET, blow, bombshell, distress, disturbance, stupefaction, stupor, trauma
shocking *adjective* DREADFUL, appalling, atrocious, disgraceful, disgusting, ghastly, horrifying, nauseating, outrageous, revolting, scandalous, sickening
shoddy *adjective* INFERIOR, poor, rubbishy, second-rate, slipshod, tawdry, trashy

shoot *verb* **shot, shoot•ing** 1 hit, wound, kill with missile fired from weapon 2 discharge weapon 3 send, slide, push rapidly 4 photograph, film 5 hunt 6 sprout ▷ *noun* 7 young branch, sprout 8 shooting competition 9 hunting expedition
shop *noun* 1 store, place for retail sale of goods and services 2 workshop, factory ▷ *verb intransitive* **shopped, shop•ping** 3 visit stores to buy or examine > **shop'lift•er** *noun* one who steals from store > **shop stew'ard** [STOO-ərd] labor union representative of workers in factory, etc. **talk shop** talk of one's business, etc. at unsuitable moments
shore[1] [shor] *noun* edge of sea or lake
shore[2] *verb transitive* **shored, shor•ing** prop (up)
shorn *pp of* **shear**
short *adjective* **-er, -est** 1 not long 2 not tall 3 brief, hasty 4 not reaching quantity or standard required 5 wanting, lacking 6 abrupt, rude 7 *stock exchange* not in possession of stock shares when selling them ▷ *adverb* 8 suddenly, abruptly 9 without reaching end ▷ *noun* 10 short film > **shorts** short trousers > **short'age** [-ij] *noun* deficiency > **short'en** *verb* > **short'ly** *adverb* 1 soon 2 briefly > **short'bread** [-bred] *noun* butter cookie > **short'cake** [-kayk] 1 cake made of butter, flour and sugar 2 dessert of biscuit dough with fruit topping > **short circuit** *electricity* connection, often accidental, of low resistance between two parts of circuit > **short'com•ing** [-kum-ing] *noun* 1 failing 2 defect > **short'hand** *noun* method of rapid writing by signs or contractions > **short'-hand•ed** *adjective* lacking the usual or necessary number of workers, helpers > **short list** selected list of candidates (esp. for job) from which final selection will be made > **short shrift** summary treatment > **short ton** ton (2000 lbs.) > **short wave** radio wave of frequency greater than 1600 kHz
short•en•ing [SHORT-ning] *noun* 1 fat used to make cake, etc. rich and crumbly 2 *pr. p. of* **shorten**
shot *noun* 1 act of shooting 2 missile 3 lead in small pellets 4 marksman, shooter 5 try, attempt 6 photograph 7 short film sequence 8 dose 9 hypodermic injection ▷ *adjective* 10 woven so that color is different, according to angle of light 11 *pt./pp. of* **shoot**
should [shuud] *verb* past tense of **shall** used as an auxiliary to make the subjunctive mood or to indicate obligation or possibility
shoul•der [SHOHL-dər] *noun* 1 part of body to which arm or foreleg is attached 2 anything resembling shoulder 3 side of road ▷ *verb transitive* 4 undertake 5 bear (burden) 6 accept (responsibility) 7 put on one's shoulder ▷ *verb intransitive* 8 make way by pushing > **shoulder blade** [blayd] shoulder bone
shout [showt] *noun* 1 loud cry ▷ *verb* 2 utter (cry, etc.) with loud voice
shove [shuv] *verb transitive* **shoved, shov•ing** 1 push ▷ *noun* 2 push > **shove off** (*informal*) go away
shovel [SHUV-əl] *noun* 1 instrument for scooping, lifting earth, etc. ▷ *verb transitive* **-eled, -el•ing** 2 lift, move (as) with shovel
show [shoh] *verb* **showed, shown, show•ing** 1 expose to view 2 point out 3 display 4 exhibit

DICTIONARY

S

THESAURUS

shoot *verb* 1 HIT, blast (*slang*), bring down, kill, open fire, plug (*slang*)
2 FIRE, discharge, emit, fling, hurl, launch, project, propel
3 SPEED, bolt, charge, dart, dash, fly, hurtle, race, rush, streak, tear
▷ *noun* 4 BRANCH, bud, offshoot, sprig, sprout
shop *noun* STORE, boutique, emporium, hypermarket, supermarket
shore *noun* BEACH, coast, sands, seashore, strand (*poetic*)
shore up *verb* SUPPORT, brace, buttress, hold, prop, reinforce, strengthen, underpin
short *adjective* 1 CONCISE, brief, compressed, laconic, pithy, succinct, summary, terse
2 SMALL, diminutive, dumpy, little, petite, squat
3 BRIEF, fleeting, momentary
4 (*often with of*) LACKING, deficient, limited, low *or* low on, scant, scarce, wanting
5 ABRUPT, brusque, curt, discourteous, impolite, sharp, terse, uncivil
▷ *adverb* 6 ABRUPTLY, suddenly, without warning
shortage *noun* DEFICIENCY, dearth, insufficiency, lack, paucity, scarcity, want
shortcoming *noun* FAILING, defect, fault, flaw, imperfection, weakness
shorten *verb* CUT, abbreviate, abridge, curtail, decrease, diminish, lessen, reduce
shortly *adverb* SOON, before long, in a little while, presently
short-sighted *adjective* 1 NEAR-SIGHTED, myopic
2 UNTHINKING, ill-advised, ill-considered, impolitic, impractical, improvident, imprudent, injudicious
short-tempered *adjective* QUICK-TEMPERED, hot-tempered, impatient, irascible, testy
shot *noun* 1 THROW, discharge, lob, pot shot
2 PELLET, ball, bullet, lead, projectile, slug
3 MARKSMAN, shooter
4 (*slang*) ATTEMPT, effort, endeavor, go (*informal*), stab (*informal*), try, turn
shoulder *verb* 1 BEAR, accept, assume, be responsible for, carry, take on
2 PUSH, elbow, jostle, press, shove
shout *noun* 1 CRY, bellow, call, roar, scream, yell
▷ *verb* 2 CRY *or* CRY OUT, bawl, bellow, call *or* call out, holler (*informal*), roar, scream, yell
shout down *verb* SILENCE, drown, drown out, overwhelm
shove *verb* PUSH, drive, elbow, impel, jostle, press, propel, thrust
shovel *verb* MOVE, dredge, heap, ladle, load, scoop, toss
shove off *verb* GO AWAY, clear off (*informal*), depart, leave, push off (*informal*), scram (*informal*)
show *verb* 1 BE VISIBLE, appear
2 DISPLAY, exhibit, present
3 PROVE, clarify, demonstrate, elucidate, point out
4 INSTRUCT, demonstrate, explain, teach
5 DISPLAY, indicate, manifest, register, reveal
6 GUIDE, accompany, attend, conduct, escort, lead
▷ *noun* 7 ENTERTAINMENT, presentation, production

5 explain 6 prove 7 guide 8 accord (favor, etc.) 9 appear 10 be noticeable ▷ *noun* 11 display, exhibition 12 spectacle 13 theatrical or other entertainment 14 indication 15 competitive event 16 ostentation 17 semblance 18 pretense > **show'i•ly** *adverb* > **show'y** *adjective* **show•i•er, show•i•est** 1 gaudy 2 ostentatious > **show'down** *noun* 1 confrontation 2 final test > **show jump•ing** horse-riding competition to demonstrate skill in jumping obstacles > **show'man** [-mən] *noun, plural* **-men** 1 organizer of theatrical events, circuses, etc. 2 one skilled at presenting anything in effective way > **show off** 1 exhibit to invite admiration 2 behave in this way > **show-off** *noun* > **show up** 1 reveal 2 expose 3 embarrass 4 arrive

show•er [SHOW-ər] *noun* 1 short fall of rain 2 anything coming down like rain 3 kind of bath in which person stands while being sprayed with water 4 party to present gifts to a person, as a prospective bride ▷ *verb transitive* 5 bestow liberally ▷ *verb intransitive* 6 take bath in shower > **show'er•y** *adjective*

shrank *pt. of* **shrink**

shrap•nel [SHRAP-nəl] *noun* 1 shell filled with pellets that scatter on bursting 2 shell splinters

shred *noun* 1 fragment, torn strip 2 small amount ▷ *verb transitive* **shred** *or* **shred•ded, shred•ding** 3 cut, tear to shreds

shrew [shroo] *noun* 1 animal like mouse 2 bad-tempered woman 3 scold > **shrew'ish** *adjective* nagging

shrewd [shrood] *adjective* **-er, -est** 1 astute, intelligent 2 crafty > **shrewd'ness** [-nis] *noun*

shriek [shreek] *noun* 1 shrill cry 2 piercing scream ▷ *verb* 3 screech

shrike [shrīk] *noun* bird of prey with heavy hooked bill

shrill *adjective* 1 piercing, sharp in tone ▷ *verb* 2 utter in such tone > **shril'ly** *adverb*

shrimp *noun* 1 (*plural* **shrimp** *or* **shrimps**) small edible crustacean 2 (*plural* **shrimps**) (*informal*) undersized person ▷ *verb intransitive* 3 go catching shrimps

shrine [shrīn] *noun* place (building, tomb, alcove) of worship, usu. associated with saint

shrink [shreenk] *verb* **shrank** *or* **shrunk, shrunk** *or* **shrunk•en, shrink•ing** 1 become smaller 2 retire, flinch, recoil 3 make smaller ▷ *noun* (*slang*) 4 psychiatrist, psychotherapist > **shrink'age** [-ij] *noun*

shrive [shrīv] *verb transitive* **shrove** *or* **shrived, shriv•en** *or* **shrived, shriv•ing** give absolution to > **shrift** *noun* (*obsolete*) 1 confession 2 absolution

shriv•el [SHRIV-əl] *verb intransitive* **-eled, -el•ing** shrink and wither

shroud [shrowd] *noun* 1 sheet, wrapping, for corpse 2 anything that covers, envelops like shroud ▷ *verb transitive* 3 put shroud on 4 screen, veil 5 wrap up > **shrouds** *plural noun* set of ropes to masthead

Shrove Tuesday [shrohv] day before Ash Wednesday

shrub *noun* 1 bushy plant 2 drink of fruit juices, etc. oft. with alcohol > **shrub'ber•y** [-ər-ee] *noun, plural* **-ber•ies** 1 planting of shrubs 2 shrubs collectively

shrug *verb* **shrugged, shrug•ging** 1 raise shoulders, as sign of indifference, ignorance, etc. 2 move (shoulders) thus 3 (with *off*) dismiss as unimportant ▷ *noun* 4 shrugging

shrunk, shrunken *pp of* **shrink**

shuck [shuk] *noun* 1 shell, husk, pod ▷ *verb transitive* 2 remove husks, etc. from > **shucks** *interjection* (*informal*) used as mild expression of regret

shud•der [SHUD-ər] *verb intransitive* 1 shake, tremble violently, esp. with horror ▷ *noun* 2 shuddering, tremor

shuf•fle [SHUF-əl] *verb intransitive* **-fled, -fling** 1 move feet without lifting them 2 dance like this 3 act evasively ▷ *verb transitive* 4 mix

---

8 EXHIBITION, array, display, fair, pageant, parade, sight, spectacle
9 PRETENSE, affectation, air, appearance, display, illusion, parade, pose

showdown *noun* CONFRONTATION, clash, face-off (*slang*)

shower *noun* 1 DELUGE, barrage, stream, torrent, volley
▷ *verb* 2 INUNDATE, deluge, heap, lavish, pour, rain

showman *noun* PERFORMER, entertainer

show-off *noun* EXHIBITIONIST, boaster, braggart, poseur

show off *verb* 1 EXHIBIT, demonstrate, display, flaunt, parade
2 BOAST, blow one's own trumpet, brag, swagger

show up *verb* 1 STAND OUT, appear, be conspicuous, be visible
2 REVEAL, expose, highlight, lay bare
3 (*informal*) EMBARRASS, let down, mortify, put to shame
4 ARRIVE, appear, come, turn up

showy *adjective* 1 OSTENTATIOUS, brash, flamboyant, flash (*informal*), flashy, over the top (*informal*)
2 GAUDY, garish, loud

shred *noun* 1 STRIP, bit, fragment, piece, scrap, sliver, tatter
2 PARTICLE, atom, grain, iota, jot, scrap, trace

shrew *noun* NAG, harpy, harridan, scold, spitfire, vixen

shrewd *adjective* CLEVER, astute, calculating, canny, crafty, cunning, intelligent, keen, perceptive, perspicacious, sharp, smart

shrewdness *noun* ASTUTENESS, canniness, discernment, judgment, perspicacity, quick wits, sharpness, smartness

shriek *verb, noun* CRY, scream, screech, squeal, yell

shrill *adjective* PIERCING, high, penetrating, sharp

shrink *verb* 1 DECREASE, contract, diminish, dwindle, grow smaller, lessen, narrow, shorten
2 RECOIL, cower, cringe, draw back, flinch, quail

shrivel *verb* WITHER, dehydrate, desiccate, shrink, wilt, wizen

shroud *noun* 1 WINDING SHEET, grave clothes
2 COVERING, mantle, pall, screen, veil
▷ *verb* 3 CONCEAL, blanket, cloak, cover, envelop, hide, screen, veil

shudder *verb* 1 SHIVER, convulse, quake, quiver, shake, tremble
▷ *noun* 2 SHIVER, quiver, spasm, tremor

shuffle *verb* 1 SCUFFLE, drag, scrape, shamble

(cards) 5 (with *off*) evade, pass to another ▷ *noun* 6 shuffling 7 rearrangement
shun *verb transitive* **shunned, shun•ning** 1 avoid 2 keep away from
shunt *verb transitive* 1 push aside 2 divert 3 move (train) from one line to another
shut *verb* **shut, shut•ting** 1 close 2 bar 3 forbid entrance to > **shut'ter** [-ər] *noun* 1 movable window screen, usu. hinged to frame 2 device in camera admitting light as required to film or plate > **shut down** close or stop factory, machine, etc.
shut•tle [SHUT-l] *noun* 1 instrument that threads weft between threads of warp in weaving 2 similar appliance in sewing machine 3 plane, bus, etc. traveling to and fro over short distance ▷ *verb* **-tled, -tling** 4 (cause to) move back and forth > **shut'tle•cock** *noun* small, light cone with cork stub and fan of feathers used as a ball in badminton
shy[1] [shī] *adjective* **shy•er** *or* **shi•er, shy•est** *or* **shi•est** 1 awkward in company 2 timid, bashful 3 reluctant 4 scarce, lacking (esp. in card games, not having enough money for bet, etc.) ▷ *verb intransitive* **shied, shy•ing** 5 start back in fear 6 show sudden reluctance ▷ *noun, plural* **shies** 7 start of fear by horse > **shy'ly** *adverb* > **shy'ness** [-nis] *noun*
shy[2] *verb transitive, noun* **shied, shy•ing** throw
shy•ster [SHĪ-stər] *noun* (*informal*) dishonest, deceitful person, esp. unprofessional lawyer
SI *Fr.* Système International (d'Unités), international system of units of measurement based on units of ten
Si *chem.* silicon
Si•a•mese cat [SĪ-ə-MEEZ] breed of cat with blue eyes
Siamese twins *nontechnical name for* **conjoined twins**
sib•i•lant [SIB-ə-lənt] *adjective* 1 hissing ▷ *noun* 2 speech sound with hissing effect
sib'ling *noun* person's brother or sister ▷ *adjective*
sib•yl [SIB-əl] *noun* woman endowed with spirit of prophecy > **sib'yl•line** [-een] *adjective* occult
sic [sik] *Lat.* thus: oft. used to call attention to a quoted mistake
sick [sik] *adjective* **-er, -est** 1 inclined to vomit, vomiting 2 not well or healthy, physically or mentally 3 macabre, sadistic, morbid 4 bored, tired 5 disgusted > **sick'en** [-ən] *verb* 1 make, become, sick 2 disgust 3 nauseate > **sick'ly** *adjective* 1 unhealthy, weakly 2 inducing nausea > **sick'ness** [-nis] *noun* > **sick bay** place set aside for treating sick people, esp. aboard ships
sick•le [SIK-əl] *noun* reaping hook
side [sīd] *noun* 1 one of the surfaces of object, esp. upright inner or outer surface 2 either surface of thing having only two 3 part of body that is to right or left 4 region nearer or farther than, or right or left of, dividing line, etc. 5 region 6 aspect or part 7 one of two parties or sets of opponents 8 sect, faction 9 line of descent traced through one parent ▷ *adjective* 10 at, in, the side 11 subordinate, incidental ▷ *verb intransitive* **sid•ed, sid•ing** 12 (usu. with *with*) take up cause of > **siding** *noun* short line of rails on which trains or wagons are shunted from main line > **side'board** [-bord] *noun* piece of furniture for holding dishes, etc. in dining room > **side'burns** [-burnz] *plural noun* man's side whiskers > **side'car** *noun* 1 small car attached to side of motorcycle 2 cocktail made with brandy, orange liqueur and lemon juice > **side'kick** *noun* 1 pal 2 assistant > **side'light** [-līt] *noun* 1 esp. either of two lights on vessel for use at night 2 item of incidental information > **side'line** *noun* 1 *sports* boundary of playing area 2 subsidiary interest or activity > **side'long** [-lawng] *adjective* 1 lateral, not directly forward ▷ *adverb* 2 obliquely > **side'man** *noun, plural* **-men**

2 REARRANGE, disarrange, disorder, jumble, mix
shun *verb* AVOID, keep away from, steer clear of
shut *verb* CLOSE, fasten, seal, secure, slam
shut down *verb* 1 STOP, halt, switch off 2 CLOSE, shut up
shut out *verb* EXCLUDE, bar, debar, keep out, lock out
shuttle *verb* GO BACK AND FORTH, alternate, commute, go to and fro
shut up *verb* 1 (*informal*) BE QUIET, fall silent, gag, hold one's tongue, hush, silence 2 CONFINE, cage, coop up, immure, imprison, incarcerate
shy[1] *adjective* 1 TIMID, bashful, coy, diffident, retiring, self-conscious, self-effacing, shrinking 2 CAUTIOUS, chary, distrustful, hesitant, suspicious, wary ▷ *verb* 3 (*sometimes with off or away*) RECOIL, balk, draw back, flinch, start
shy[2] *verb* THROW, cast, fling, hurl, pitch, sling, toss
shyness *noun* TIMIDNESS, bashfulness, diffidence, lack of confidence, self-consciousness, timidity, timorousness
sick *adjective* 1 NAUSEOUS, ill, nauseated, queasy 2 UNWELL, ailing, diseased, indisposed, poorly (*informal*), under the weather (*informal*) 3 (*informal*) MORBID, black, ghoulish, macabre, sadistic 4 ▷ **sick of** TIRED, bored, fed up, jaded, weary
sicken *verb* 1 DISGUST, gross out (*slang*), nauseate, repel, revolt, turn one's stomach 2 FALL ILL, ail, take sick
sickening *adjective* DISGUSTING, distasteful, foul, gross (*slang*), loathsome, nauseating, noisome, offensive, repulsive, revolting, scuzzy (*slang*), stomach-turning (*informal*), vile, yucky *or* yukky (*slang*)
sickly *adjective* 1 UNHEALTHY, ailing, delicate, faint, feeble, infirm, pallid, peaky, wan, weak 2 NAUSEATING, cloying, mawkish
sickness *noun* 1 ILLNESS, affliction, ailment, bug (*informal*), complaint, disease, disorder, malady 2 NAUSEA, queasiness, vomiting
side *noun* 1 BORDER, boundary, division, edge, limit, margin, perimeter, rim, sector, verge 2 PART, aspect, face, facet, flank, hand, surface, view 3 PARTY, camp, cause, faction, sect, team 4 POINT OF VIEW, angle, opinion, position, slant, stand, standpoint, viewpoint ▷ *adjective* 5 SUBORDINATE, ancillary, incidental, lesser, marginal, minor, secondary, subsidiary ▷ *verb* 6 (*usually with with*) SUPPORT, ally with, favor, go along with, take the part of
sidelong *adjective* SIDEWAYS, covert, indirect,

instrumentalist in band > **side'track** *verb* deviate from main topic ▷ *noun* > **side'walk** *noun* footpath beside road > **side'ways** [-wayz] *adverb* 1 to or from the side 2 laterally
si•de•re•al [sī-DEER-ee-əl] *adjective* relating to, fixed by, stars
si•dle [SĪD-l] *verb intransitive* **-dled, -dling** 1 move in furtive or stealthy manner 2 move sideways
SIDS Sudden Infant Death Syndrome, unexplained death of baby while asleep
siege [seej] *noun* besieging of town or fortified place
si•en•na [see-EN-ə] *noun* (pigment of) brownish-yellow color
si•er•ra [see-ER-ə] *noun* range of mountains with jagged peaks
si•es•ta [see-ES-tə] *noun* rest, sleep in afternoon
sieve [siv] *noun* 1 device with network or perforated bottom for sifting ▷ *verb* **sieved, siev•ing** 2 sift 3 strain
sift *verb transitive* 1 separate (e.g. with sieve) coarser portion from finer 2 examine closely > **sift'er** *noun*
sigh [sī] *verb, noun* (utter) long audible breath **sigh for** yearn for, grieve for
sight [sīt] *noun* 1 faculty of seeing 2 seeing 3 thing seen 4 view 5 glimpse 6 device for guiding eye 7 spectacle 8 (*informal*) pitiful or ridiculous or unusual object 9 (*informal*) large number, great deal ▷ *verb transitive* 10 catch sight of 11 adjust sights of gun, etc. **sight for sore eyes** (*informal*) person or thing one is glad to see > **sight'less** [-lis] *adjective* > **sight-read** [-reed] *verb* **-read** [-red], **-read•ing** [-reed-ing] play, sing music without previous preparation > **sight'see** *verb* visit (place) to look at interesting sights
sign [sīn] *noun* 1 mark, gesture, etc. to convey some meaning 2 (board, placard, bearing) notice, warning, etc. 3 symbol 4 omen 5 evidence ▷ *verb transitive* 6 put one's signature to 7 ratify ▷ *verb intransitive* 8 make sign or gesture 9 affix signature 10 use symbols of sign language > **sign language** gestures used for communicating with deaf people
sig•nal [SIG-nəl] *noun* 1 sign to convey order or information, esp. on railroads 2 that which in first place impels any action 3 sequence of electrical impulses or radio waves transmitted or received ▷ *adjective* 4 remarkable, striking ▷ *verb* **-naled, -nal•ing** 5 make signals to 6 give orders, etc. by signals > **sig'nal•ize** *verb transitive* **-ized, -iz•ing** make notable
sig•na•to•ry [SIG-nə-tor-ee] *noun, plural* **-ries** one of those who sign agreements, treaties
sig•na•ture [SIG-nə-chər] *noun* 1 person's name written by self 2 act of writing it > **signature tune** theme song
sig•net [SIG-nit] *noun* small seal
sig•nif•i•cant [sig-NIF-i-kənt] *adjective* 1 revealing 2 designed to make something known 3 important > **sig•nif'i•cance** [-kəns] *noun* 1 import, weight 2 meaning > **sig•ni•fi•ca'tion** *noun* meaning
sig•ni•fy [SIG-nə-fī] *verb* **-fied, -fy•ing** 1 mean 2 indicate 3 denote 4 imply 5 be of importance
si•gnor [SEEN-yor] *noun* Italian title of respect, like Mr. > **si•gno•ra** [sin-YOR-ə] *noun* Mrs. > **si•gno•ri'na** [seen-yə-REEN-ə] *noun* Miss
Sikh [seek] *noun* member of Hindu religious sect
si•lage [SĪ-lij] *noun* fodder crop harvested while green and stored in state of partial fermentation
si•lence [SĪ-ləns] *noun* 1 absence of noise 2 refraining from speech ▷ *verb transitive* **-lenced, -lenc•ing** 3 make silent 4 put a stop to > **si'lenc•er** *noun* device to reduce noise of firearm > **si'lent** *adjective*

DICTIONARY • THESAURUS

oblique
sidestep *verb* AVOID, circumvent, dodge, duck (*informal*), evade, skirt
sidetrack *verb* DIVERT, deflect, distract
sideways *adverb* 1 OBLIQUELY, edgeways, laterally, sidelong, to the side ▷ *adjective* 2 OBLIQUE, sidelong
sidle *verb* EDGE, creep, inch, slink, sneak, steal
siesta *noun* NAP, catnap, doze, forty winks (*informal*), sleep, snooze (*informal*)
sieve *noun* 1 STRAINER, colander ▷ *verb* 2 SIFT, separate, strain
sift *verb* 1 SIEVE, filter, separate 2 EXAMINE, analyze, go through, investigate, research, scrutinize, work over
sight *noun* 1 VISION, eye, eyes, eyesight, seeing 2 VIEW, appearance, perception, range of vision, visibility 3 SPECTACLE, display, exhibition, pageant, scene, show, vista 4 EYESORE, mess, monstrosity 5 ▷ **catch sight of** SPOT, espy, glimpse ▷ *verb* 6 SPOT, behold, discern, distinguish, make out, observe, perceive, see
sign *noun* 1 INDICATION, clue, evidence, hint, mark, proof, signal, symptom, token 2 NOTICE, board, placard, warning 3 SYMBOL, badge, device, emblem, logo, mark 4 OMEN, augury, auspice, foreboding, portent, warning ▷ *verb* 5 AUTOGRAPH, endorse, initial, inscribe 6 GESTURE, beckon, gesticulate, indicate, signal
signal *noun* 1 SIGN, beacon, cue, gesture, indication, mark, token ▷ *verb* 2 GESTURE, beckon, gesticulate, indicate, motion, sign, wave
significance *noun* 1 IMPORTANCE, consequence, moment, relevance, weight 2 MEANING, force, implication *or* implications, import, message, point, purport, sense
significant *adjective* 1 IMPORTANT, critical, material, momentous, noteworthy, serious, vital, weighty 2 MEANINGFUL, eloquent, expressive, indicative, suggestive
signify *verb* 1 INDICATE, be a sign of, betoken, connote, denote, imply, intimate, mean, portend, suggest 2 MATTER, be important, carry weight, count
silence *noun* 1 QUIET, calm, hush, lull, peace, stillness 2 MUTENESS, dumbness, reticence, taciturnity ▷ *verb* 3 QUIETEN, cut off, cut short, deaden, gag, muffle, quiet, stifle, still, suppress
silent *adjective* 1 QUIET, hushed, muted, noiseless, soundless, still 2 MUTE, dumb, speechless, taciturn, voiceless, wordless

sil•hou•ette [sil-oo-ET] *noun* 1 outline of object seen against light background 2 profile portrait in black ▷ *verb transitive* **-et•ted, -et•ting** 3 show in or as if in silhouette
sil•i•ca [SIL-i-kə] *noun* naturally occurring dioxide of silicon > **si•li•ceous** [sə-LEE-shəs] *adjective* > **si•li•co•sis** [si-li-KOH-sis] *noun* lung disease caused by inhaling silica dust over a long period
sil•i•con [SIL-i-kən] *noun* brittle metalloid element found in sand, clay, stone, widely used in chemistry, industry > **sil'i•cone** [-kohn] *noun* large class of synthetic substances, related to silicon and used in chemistry, industry, medicine
silk *noun* 1 fiber made by larvae (**silkworms**) of a certain moth 2 thread, fabric made from this > **silk'en** *adjective* 1 made of, like silk 2 soft 3 smooth 4 dressed in silk > **silk'i•ness** [-nis] *noun*
sill *noun* 1 ledge beneath window 2 bottom part of door or window frame
sil•ly [SIL-ee] *adjective* **-li•er, -li•est** 1 foolish 2 trivial 3 feebleminded > **sil'li•ness** [-nis] *noun*
si•lo [SĪ-loh] *noun, plural* **-los** 1 pit, tower for storing fodder or grain 2 underground missile launching site
silt *noun* 1 mud deposited by water ▷ *verb* 2 fill, be choked with silt > **sil•ta'tion** *noun*
sil•ver [SIL-vər] *noun* 1 white precious metal 2 things made of it 3 silver coins 4 cutlery ▷ *adjective* 5 made of silver 6 resembling silver or its color 7 having pale luster, as moon 8 soft, melodious, as sound 9 bright ▷ *verb transitive* 10 coat with silver > **sil'ver•y** *adjective* > **silver birch** tree having silvery white peeling bark > **silver wedding** 25th wedding anniversary
sim•i•an [SIM-ee-ən] *adjective* of, like apes
sim•i•lar [SIM-ə-lər] *adjective* resembling, like > **sim•i•lar'i•ty** *noun* 1 likeness 2 close resemblance
sim•i•le [SIM-ə-lee] *noun* comparison of one thing with another, using *as* or *like*, esp. in poetry
si•mil•i•tude [si-MIL-i-tood] *noun* 1 outward appearance, likeness 2 guise
sim•mer [SIM-ər] *verb* 1 keep or be just bubbling or just below boiling point 2 to be in state of suppressed anger or laughter
sim•per [SIM-pər] *verb intransitive* smile, utter in silly or affected way ▷ *noun*
sim•ple [SIM-pəl] *adjective* **-pler, -plest** 1 not complicated 2 plain 3 not combined or complex 4 ordinary, mere 5 guileless 6 stupid > **sim'ple•ton** [-tən] *noun* foolish person > **sim•plic'i•ty** [-PLIS-ə-tee] *noun, plural* **-ties** simpleness, clearness, artlessness > **sim•pli•fi•ca'tion** *noun* > **sim'pli•fy** *verb transitive* **-fied, -fy•ing** make simple, plain or easy > **sim•plis'tic** *adjective* extremely simple, naive > **sim'ply** *adverb* > **simple fraction** one in which both the numerator and the denominator are whole numbers
sim•u•late [SIM-yə-layt] *verb transitive* **-lat•ed, -lat•ing** 1 make pretense of 2 reproduce, copy, esp. conditions of particular situation > **sim•u•la'tion** *noun* > **sim'u•la•tor** *noun*
si•mul•ta•ne•ous [sī-məl-TAY-nee-əs] *adjective* occurring at the same time > **si•mul•ta•ne'i•ty** [-tə-NEE-i-tee] *noun* > **simulta'ne•ous•ly** *adverb*

silently *adjective* QUIETLY, inaudibly, in silence, mutely, noiselessly, soundlessly, without a sound, wordlessly
silhouette *noun* 1 OUTLINE, form, profile, shape ▷ *verb* 2 OUTLINE, etch, stand out
silky *adjective* SMOOTH, silken, sleek, velvety
silly *adjective* FOOLISH, absurd, asinine, fatuous, idiotic, inane, ridiculous, senseless, stupid, unwise
silt *noun* 1 SEDIMENT, alluvium, deposit, ooze, sludge
▷ *verb* 2 ▷ **silt up** CLOG, choke, congest
similar *adjective* ALIKE, analogous, close, comparable, like, resembling
similarity *noun* RESEMBLANCE, affinity, agreement, analogy, closeness, comparability, correspondence, likeness, sameness
simmer *verb* FUME, be angry, rage, seethe, smolder
simmer down *verb* CALM DOWN, control oneself, cool off *or* cool down, de-stress
simper *verb* SMILE COYLY, smile affectedly, smirk
simple *adjective* 1 EASY, clear, intelligible, lucid, plain, straightforward, uncomplicated, understandable, uninvolved
2 PLAIN, classic, natural, unembellished, unfussy
3 PURE, elementary, unalloyed, uncombined, unmixed
4 ARTLESS, childlike, guileless, ingenuous, innocent, naive, natural, sincere, unaffected, unsophisticated
5 HONEST, bald, basic, direct, frank, naked, plain, sincere, stark
6 HUMBLE, dumpy (*informal*), homely, modest, unpretentious
7 FEEBLE-MINDED, foolish, half-witted, moronic (*offensive*), slow, stupid
simple-minded *adjective* FEEBLE-MINDED, backward, dim-witted, foolish, idiot, idiotic, moronic (*offensive*), retarded, simple, stupid
simpleton *noun* HALFWIT, doofus (*slang*), dork (*slang*), dullard, fool, idiot, imbecile (*informal*), moron (*offensive*), schmuck (*slang*)
simplicity *noun* 1 EASE, clarity, clearness, straightforwardness
2 PLAINNESS, lack of adornment, purity, restraint
3 ARTLESSNESS, candor, directness, innocence, naivety, openness
simplify *verb* MAKE SIMPLER, abridge, disentangle, dumb down, reduce to essentials, streamline
simply *adverb* 1 PLAINLY, clearly, directly, easily, intelligibly, naturally, straightforwardly, unpretentiously
2 JUST, merely, only, purely, solely
3 TOTALLY, absolutely, completely, really, utterly, wholly
simulate *verb* PRETEND, act, affect, feign, put on, sham
simultaneous *adjective* COINCIDING, at the same time, coincident, concurrent, contemporaneous, synchronous
simultaneously *adverb* AT THE SAME TIME, concurrently, together

sin *noun* 1 transgression of divine or moral law, esp. committed consciously 2 offense against principle or standard ▷ *verb intransitive* **sinned, sin•ning** 3 commit sin > **sin'ful** [-fəl] *adjective* 1 of nature of sin 2 guilty of sin > **sin'ful•ly** *adverb*
since [sins] *preposition* 1 during or throughout period of time after ▷ *conjunction* 2 from time when 3 because ▷ *adverb* 4 from that time
sin•cere [sin-SEER] *adjective* 1 not hypocritical, actually moved by or feeling apparent emotions 2 true, genuine 3 unaffected > **sin•cere'ly** *adverb* > **sin•cer'i•ty** [-SER-i-tee] *noun*
sine [sīn] *noun* mathematical function, esp. ratio of length of hypotenuse to opposite side in right triangle
si•ne•cure [SĪ-ni-kyuur] *noun* office with pay but minimal duties
si•ne di•e [SĪ-nee DĪ-ee] *Lat.* with no date, indefinitely postponed
si•ne qua non [SĪ-nee kway non] *Lat.* essential condition or requirement
sin•ew [SIN-yoo] *noun* tough, fibrous cord joining muscle to bone > **sin•ews** muscles, strength > **sin'ew•y** *adjective* 1 stringy 2 muscular
sing *verb* **sang, sung, sing•ing** 1 utter musical sounds 2 hum, whistle, ring 3 utter (words) with musical modulation 4 celebrate in song or poetry > **sing'song** [-sawng] *adjective* monotonously regular in tone, rhythm
singe [sinj] *verb transitive* **singed, singe•ing** 1 burn surface of ▷ *noun* 2 act or effect of singeing
sin•gle [SING-gəl] *adjective* 1 one only 2 alone, separate 3 unmarried 4 for one 5 formed of only one part, fold, etc. 6 wholehearted, straightforward ▷ *noun* 7 single thing 8 phonograph record with one short item on each side 9 *baseball* one-base hit ▷ *verb transitive* **-gled, -gling** 10 pick (out) 11 make single > **sin'gly** *adverb* > **single file** persons, things arranged in one line > **single-hand•ed** *adjective* without assistance > **singles bar** bar or club that is social meeting place esp. for single people
sin•gu•lar [SING-gyə-lər] *adjective* 1 remarkable 2 unusual 3 unique 4 denoting one person or thing > **sin•gu•lar'i•ty** *noun, plural* **-ties** something unusual > **sin'gu•lar•ly** [-lər-lee] *adverb* 1 particularly 2 peculiarly
sin•is•ter [SIN-ə-stər] *adjective* 1 threatening 2 evil-looking 3 wicked 4 unlucky 5 *heraldry* on bearer's left-hand side > **sin'is•trous** [-trəs] *adjective* ill-omened
sink [singk] *verb* **sank** *or* **sunk, sunk** *or* **sunk•en, sink•ing** 1 become submerged (in water) 2 drop, give way 3 decline in value, health, etc. 4 penetrate (into) 5 cause to sink 6 make by digging out 7 invest ▷ *noun* 8 receptacle with pipe for carrying away waste water 9 cesspool 10 place of corruption, vice > **sink'er** *noun* weight for fishing line > **sink'hole** [-hohl] *noun* 1 low land where drainage collects 2 cavity formed in rock by water > **sinking fund** money set aside at intervals for payment of particular liability at fixed date
Sino- *combining form* Chinese, of China: *Sino-American relations*
sin•u•ous [SIN-yoo-əs] *adjective* curving, devious, lithe > **sin•u•os'i•ty** [-OS-i-tee] *noun, plural* **-ties**
si•nus [SĪ-nəs] *noun, plural* **-nus•es** cavity, esp. air passages in bones of skull > **si•nus•i'tis** [-SĪ-tis] *noun* inflammation of sinus
sip *verb* **sipped, sip•ping** drink in very small

sin *noun* 1 WRONGDOING, crime, error, evil, guilt, iniquity, misdeed, offense, transgression ▷ *verb* 2 TRANSGRESS, err, fall, go astray, lapse, offend
sincere *adjective* HONEST, candid, earnest, frank, genuine, guileless, heartfelt, real, serious, true, unaffected
sincerely *adverb* HONESTLY, earnestly, genuinely, in earnest, seriously, truly, wholeheartedly
sincerity *noun* HONESTY, candor, frankness, genuineness, seriousness, truth
sinecure *noun* SOFT JOB (*informal*), gravy train (*slang*), money for jam *or* money for old rope (*informal*), soft option
sinful *adjective* GUILTY, bad, corrupt, criminal, erring, immoral, iniquitous, wicked
sing *verb* 1 WARBLE, carol, chant, chirp, croon, pipe, trill, yodel
2 HUM, buzz, purr, whine
singe *verb* BURN, char, scorch, sear
singer *noun* VOCALIST, balladeer, cantor, chorister, crooner, minstrel, soloist
single *adjective* 1 ONE, distinct, individual, lone, only, separate, sole, solitary
2 INDIVIDUAL, exclusive, separate, undivided, unshared
3 SIMPLE, unblended, unmixed
4 UNMARRIED, free, unattached, unwed
▷ *verb* 5 (*usually with out*) PICK, choose, distinguish, fix on, pick on *or* pick out, select, separate, set apart
single-handed *adverb* UNAIDED, alone, by oneself, independently, on one's own, solo, unassisted, without help
single-minded *adjective* DETERMINED, dedicated, dogged, fixed, unswerving
singly *adverb* ONE BY ONE, individually, one at a time, separately
singular *adjective* 1 SINGLE, individual, separate, sole
2 REMARKABLE, eminent, exceptional, notable, noteworthy, outstanding
3 UNUSUAL, curious, eccentric, extraordinary, odd, peculiar, queer, strange
singularly *adverb* REMARKABLY, especially, exceptionally, notably, outstandingly, particularly, uncommonly, unusually
sinister *adjective* THREATENING, dire, disquieting, evil, malign, menacing, ominous
sink *verb* 1 DESCEND, dip, drop, fall, founder, go down, go under, lower, plunge, submerge, subside
2 FALL, abate, collapse, drop, lapse, slip, subside
3 DECLINE, decay, deteriorate, diminish, dwindle, fade, fail, flag, lessen, weaken, worsen
4 DIG, bore, drill, drive, excavate
5 STOOP, be reduced to, lower oneself
sink in *verb* BE UNDERSTOOD, get through to, penetrate, register (*informal*)
sinner *noun* WRONGDOER, evildoer, malefactor, miscreant, offender, transgressor
sip *verb* 1 DRINK, sample, sup, taste

portions ▷ *noun*

si•phon [SĪ-fən] *noun* 1 device, esp. bent tube, that uses atmospheric or gaseous pressure to draw liquid from container ▷ *verb* 2 draw off thus 3 draw off in small amounts

sir [sur] *noun* 1 polite term of address for a man 2 (**Sir**) title of knight or baronet

sire [sīr] *noun* 1 male parent, esp. of horse or domestic animal 2 term of address to king ▷ *verb* **sired, sir•ing** 3 beget

si•ren [SĪ-rən] *noun* 1 device making loud wailing noise, esp. giving warning of danger 2 legendary sea nymph who lured sailors to destruction 3 alluring woman

sir•loin [SUR-loin] *noun* prime cut of loin of beef

si•sal [SĪ-səl] *noun* (fiber of) plant used in making ropes

sis•sy [SIS-ee] *adjective, noun, plural* **-sies** 1 weak, cowardly (person) 2 effeminate boy or man

sis•ter [SIS-tər] *noun* 1 daughter of same parents 2 woman fellow member esp. of religious body ▷ *adjective* 3 closely related, similar > **sis'ter•hood** [-huud] *noun* 1 relation of sister 2 order, band of women > **sis'ter•ly** *adjective* > **sister-in-law** *noun* 1 sister of husband or wife 2 brother's wife

sit *verb* **sat, sit•ting** (*mainly intransitive*) 1 adopt posture or rest on buttocks, thighs 2 perch 3 incubate 4 pose for portrait 5 occupy official position 6 hold session 7 remain 8 take examination 9 keep watch over baby, etc. > **sit in** protest by refusing to move from place > **sit-in** *noun* such protest

si•tar [si-TAHR] *noun* stringed musical instrument, esp. of India > **si•tar'ist** *noun*

site [sīt] *noun* 1 place, location 2 space for, with, a building 3 *same as* **website.** > **site map** plan of a website showing its contents and where it can be viewed

sit•u•ate [SICH-oo-ayt] *verb* **-at•ed, -at•ing** 1 place, locate > **sit•u•a'tion** *noun* 1 place, position 2 state of affairs 3 employment, post

six [siks] *adjective, noun* cardinal number one more than five > **sixth** *adjective* 1 ordinal number ▷ *noun* 2 sixth part > **six'teen'** *noun, adjective* six and ten > **six'ty** *noun, adjective, plural* **-ties** six times ten

size¹ [sīz] *noun* 1 bigness, dimensions 2 one of series of standard measurements of clothes, etc. 3 (*informal*) state of affairs ▷ *verb transitive* **sized, siz•ing** 4 arrange according to size > **siz'a•ble, size'a•ble** *adjective* quite large > **size up** (*informal*) assess (person, situation, etc.)

size² *noun* 1 gluelike sealer, filler ▷ *verb transitive* **sized, siz•ing** 2 coat, treat with size

siz•zle [SIZ-l] *verb, noun* **-zled, -zling** (make) hissing, spluttering sound as of frying > **siz'zler** [-lər] *noun* (*informal*) hot day

skate¹ [skayt] *noun* 1 steel blade attached to boot, for gliding over ice ▷ *verb intransitive* **skat•ed, skat•ing** 2 glide as on skates > **skat'er** *noun* > **skate'board** *noun* small board mounted on roller-skate wheels

skate² *noun* large marine ray

ske•dad•dle [ski-DAD-l] *verb intransitive* **-dled, -dling** (*informal*) 1 flee 2 run away hurriedly

skeet *noun* shooting sport with clay target propelled from trap to simulate flying bird

skein [skayn] *noun* 1 quantity of yarn, wool, etc. in loose knot 2 flight of wildfowl

skel•e•ton [SKEL-i-tn] *noun* 1 bones of animal 2 bones separated from flesh and preserved in their natural position 3 very thin person 4 outline, draft, framework 5 nucleus ▷ *adjective* 6 reduced to a minimum 7 drawn in outline 8 not in detail > **skel'e•tal** [-təl] *adjective* > **skeleton key** key filed down so as to open many different locks

skep•tic [SKEP-tik] *noun* 1 one who maintains doubt or disbelief 2 agnostic 3 unbeliever > **skep'ti•cal** [-kəl] *adjective* > **skep'ti•cism** [-siz-əm] *noun*

sketch [skech] *noun* 1 rough drawing 2 brief account 3 essay 4 short humorous play ▷ *verb* 5 make sketch (of) > **sketch'y** *adjective* **sketch•i•er, sketch•i•est** 1 omitting detail 2 incomplete 3 inadequate

skew [skyoo] *verb intransitive* 1 move obliquely ▷ *adjective* 2 slanting 3 crooked

skew•er [SKYOO-ər] *noun* 1 pin to fasten (meat)

DICTIONARY

S

THESAURUS

▷ *noun* 2 SWALLOW, drop, taste, thimbleful

sissy *noun* 1 WIMP (*informal*), coward, mama's boy, softie (*informal*), weakling
▷ *adjective* 2 WIMPISH *or* WIMPY (*informal*), cowardly, effeminate, feeble, soft (*informal*), unmanly, weak

sit *verb* 1 REST, perch, settle
2 CONVENE, assemble, deliberate, meet, officiate, preside

site *noun* 1 LOCATION, place, plot, position, setting, spot
▷ *verb* 2 LOCATE, install, place, position, set, situate

situation *noun* 1 STATE OF AFFAIRS, case, circumstances, condition, plight, state
2 LOCATION, place, position, setting, site, spot
3 STATUS, rank, station
4 JOB, employment, office, place, position, post

sizable *or* **sizeable** *adjective* LARGE, considerable, decent, goodly, largish, respectable, substantial, supersize

size *noun* DIMENSIONS, amount, bulk, extent, immensity, magnitude, mass, proportions, range, volume

size up *verb* ASSESS, appraise, evaluate, take stock of

sizzle *verb* HISS, crackle, frizzle, fry, spit

skedaddle *verb* (*slang*) RUN AWAY, abscond, beat it (*slang*), clear off (*informal*), disappear, flee, run for it, scram (*informal*), take to one's heels

skeleton *noun* FRAMEWORK, bare bones, draft, frame, outline, sketch, structure

skeptic *noun* DOUBTER, cynic, disbeliever, doubting Thomas

skeptical *adjective* DOUBTFUL, cynical, disbelieving, dubious, incredulous, mistrustful, unconvinced

skepticism *noun* DOUBT, cynicism, disbelief, incredulity, unbelief

sketch *noun* 1 DRAWING, delineation, design, draft, outline, plan
▷ *verb* 2 DRAW, delineate, depict, draft, outline, represent, rough out

sketchy *adjective* INCOMPLETE, cursory, inadequate, perfunctory, rough, scrappy, skimpy, superficial

together ▷ *verb* 2 pierce or fasten (as though) with skewer

ski [skee] *noun, plural* **skis** 1 long runner fastened to boot for sliding over snow or water ▷ *verb* **skied, ski•ing** 2 slide on skis 3 go skiing

skid *verb* **skid•ded, skid•ding** 1 slide (sideways), esp. vehicle out of control with wheels not rotating ▷ *noun* 2 instance of this 3 device to facilitate sliding, e.g. in moving heavy objects > **skid•dy** *adjective* **-di•er, -di•est**

skiff *noun* small boat

skill *noun* 1 practical ability, cleverness, dexterity > **skilled** *adjective* 1 having, requiring knowledge, united with readiness and dexterity > **skill'ful** [-fəl] *adjective* 1 expert, masterly 2 adroit

skil•let [SKIL-it] *noun* small frying pan

skim *verb* **skimmed, skim•ming** 1 remove floating matter from surface of liquid 2 glide over lightly and rapidly 3 read thus 4 move thus > **skim milk, skimmed milk** milk from which cream has been removed

skimp *verb transitive* 1 give short measure 2 do thing imperfectly > **skimp'y** *adjective* **skimp•i•er, skimp•i•est** 1 meager 2 scanty

skin *noun* 1 outer covering of vertebrate body, lower animal or fruit 2 animal skin used as material or container 3 film on surface of cooling liquid, etc. 4 complexion ▷ *verb transitive* **skinned, skin•ning** 5 remove skin of > **skin'ny** *adjective* **-ni•er, -ni•est** thin > **skin-deep** *adjective* 1 superficial 2 slight > **skin diving** underwater swimming using breathing apparatus > **skin'flint** *noun* miser, niggard > **skin graft** transplant of piece of healthy skin to wound to form new skin > **skin•tight** [-tīt] *adjective* fitting close to skin

skip[1] *verb* **skipped, skip•ping** 1 leap lightly 2 jump a rope as it is swung under one 3 pass over, omit ▷ *noun* 4 act of skipping

skip[2] *noun* large bucket, container for transporting people, materials in mines, etc.

skip•per [SKIP-ər] *noun* 1 captain of ship, plane or team ▷ *verb transitive* 2 captain

skirl [skurl] *noun* sound of bagpipes

skir•mish [SKUR-mish] *noun* 1 fight between small parties, small battle ▷ *verb intransitive* 2 fight briefly or irregularly

skirt [skurt] *noun* 1 woman's garment hanging from waist 2 lower part of woman's dress, coat, etc. 3 outlying part 4 (*slang, offensive*) woman ▷ *verb intransitive* 5 border 6 go around > **skirt'ing** *noun* material for women's skirts

skit *noun* short satirical piece, esp. theatrical sketch

skit'tish *adjective* frisky, frivolous

skit•tle [SKIT-l] *noun* bottle-shaped object used as a target in some games > **skit•tles** game in which players try to knock over skittles by rolling a ball at them

skoal [skohl] *interjection* (as a toast) to your health

skul•dug•ger•y [skul-DUG-ə-ree] *noun, plural* **-ger•ies** trickery

skulk *verb intransitive* 1 sneak out of the way 2 lurk > **skulk'er** *noun*

skull *noun* bony case that encloses brain > **skull'cap** *noun* close-fitting cap

skunk *noun* 1 small N Amer. animal that emits evil-smelling fluid 2 (*informal*) mean person

sky [skī] *noun, plural* **skies** 1 apparently dome-shaped expanse extending upward from the horizon 2 outer space 3 heavenly regions ▷ *verb transitive* **skied, sky•ing** 4 (*informal*) hit, throw (ball) high > **sky'div•ing** *noun* parachute jumping with delayed opening of parachute > **sky'light** [-līt] *noun* window in roof or ceiling > **sky'scrap•er** [-skrayp-ər] *noun* very tall building

slab *noun* thick, broad piece

slack [slak] *adjective* 1 loose 2 sluggish 3 careless, negligent 4 not busy ▷ *noun* 5 loose part, as of rope ▷ *verb intransitive* 6 be idle or lazy > **slack'en** *verb* 1 become looser 2 become slower, abate

slacks [slaks] *plural noun* informal trousers worn

DICTIONARY • THESAURUS

---

skill *noun* EXPERTISE, ability, art, cleverness, competence, craft, dexterity, facility, knack, proficiency, skillfulness, talent, technique

skilled *adjective* EXPERT, able, masterly, professional, proficient, skillful

skillful *adjective* EXPERT, able, adept, adroit, clever, competent, dexterous, masterly, practiced, professional, proficient, skilled

skim *verb* 1 SEPARATE, cream
2 GLIDE, coast, float, fly, sail, soar
3 (*usually with through*) SCAN, glance, run one's eye over

skimp *verb* STINT, be mean with, be sparing with, cut corners, scamp, scrimp

skin *noun* 1 HIDE, fell, pelt
2 COATING, casing, crust, film, husk, outside, peel, rind
▷ *verb* 3 PEEL, flay, scrape

skin alive *verb* (*informal*) ATTACK, assail, assault, let have it (*informal*), let loose on (*informal*)

skinflint *noun* MISER, niggard, penny-pincher (*informal*), Scrooge

skinny *adjective* THIN, emaciated, lean, scrawny, undernourished

skip *verb* 1 HOP, bob, bounce, caper, dance, flit, frisk, gambol, prance, trip
2 PASS OVER, eschew, give (something) a miss, leave out, miss out, omit

skirmish *noun* 1 FIGHT, battle, brush, clash, conflict, encounter, fracas, scrap (*informal*)
▷ *verb* 2 FIGHT, clash, collide

skirt *verb* 1 BORDER, edge, flank
2 (*often with around* or *round*) AVOID, circumvent, evade, steer clear of

skit *noun* 1 PARODY, burlesque, sketch, spoof (*informal*)
2 PLAY, comedy, drama, performance

skittish *adjective* LIVELY, excitable, fidgety, highly strung, jumpy, nervous, restive, wired (*slang*)

skulk *verb* LURK, creep, prowl, slink, sneak

sky *noun* HEAVENS, firmament

slab *noun* PIECE, chunk, lump, portion, slice, wedge

slack *adjective* 1 LOOSE, baggy, lax, limp, relaxed
2 NEGLIGENT, idle, inactive, lax, lazy, neglectful, remiss, slapdash, slipshod
3 SLOW, dull, inactive, quiet, slow-moving, sluggish
▷ *noun* 4 ROOM, excess, give (*informal*), leeway
▷ *verb* 5 SHIRK, dodge, idle

slacken *verb* (*often with off*) LESSEN, abate,

by men or women
slag *noun* refuse of smelted metal
slain *pp of* **slay**
slake [slayk] *verb transitive* **slaked, slak•ing** 1 satisfy (thirst, desire, etc.) 2 combine (lime) with water to produce calcium hydroxide
sla•lom [SLAH-ləm] *noun, verb* race over winding course in skiing, automobile racing, etc.
slam *verb* **slammed, slam•ming** 1 shut noisily 2 bang 3 hit 4 dash down 5 (*informal*) criticize harshly ▷ *noun* 6 (noise of) this action > **slam dunk** *noun* 1 *basketball.* forceful downward basket 2 (*informal*) clearcut success ▷ *verb transitive* **slam-dunked', slam-dunk'ing** *basketball.* 3 shoot (ball) in a slam dunk **grand slam** 4 *cards* winning of all tricks 5 *sports* winning of selected group of major tournaments in one year
slan•der [SLAN-dər] *noun* 1 false or malicious statement about person ▷ *verb* 2 utter such statement > **slan'der•ous** *adjective*
slang *noun* words, etc. or meanings of these used very informally for novelty or vividness or for the sake of unconventionality
slant *verb* 1 slope 2 put at angle 3 write, present (news, etc.) with bias ▷ *noun* 4 slope 5 point of view 6 idea ▷ *adjective* 7 sloping, oblique > **slant'wise** [-wīz] *adverb*
slap *noun* 1 blow with open hand or flat instrument ▷ *verb transitive* **slapped, slap•ping** 2 strike thus 3 put on, down carelessly or messily > **slap'dash** *adjective* careless and abrupt > **slap'stick** *noun* broad boisterous comedy
slash *verb transitive* 1 gash 2 lash 3 cut, slit 4 criticize unmercifully ▷ *noun* 5 gash 6 cutting stroke 7 sloping punctuation mark, either / or \
slat *noun* narrow strip of wood or metal as in window blinds, etc.
slate [slayt] *noun* 1 kind of stone that splits easily in flat sheets 2 piece of this for covering roof or, formerly, for writing on ▷ *verb transitive* **slat•ed, slat•ing** 3 cover with slates
slath•er [SLATH-ər] *noun* (*informal*) 1 generous amount ▷ *verb transitive* **-ered, -er•ing** (*informal*) 2 spread, apply thickly
slat•tern [SLAT-ərn] *noun* 1 slut > **slatt'ern•ly** *adjective* 1 slovenly, untidy
slaugh•ter [SLAW-tər] *noun* 1 killing ▷ *verb transitive* 2 kill > **slaugh'ter•ous** *adjective* > **slaugh'ter•house** [-hows] *noun* place for butchering animals for food
slave [slayv] *noun* 1 captive, person without freedom or personal rights 2 one dominated by another or by a habit, etc. ▷ *verb intransitive* **slaved, slav•ing** 3 work like slave > **slav'er** *noun* person, ship engaged in slave traffic > **slav'er•y** *noun* > **slav'ish** *adjective* servile
slav•er [SLAV-ər] *verb intransitive* 1 dribble saliva from mouth 2 fawn ▷ *noun* 3 saliva running from mouth
slay *verb transitive* **slew, slain, slay•ing** 1 kill 2 (*informal*) impress, esp. by being very funny > **slay'er** *noun* killer
slea•zy [SLEE-zee] *adjective* **-zi•er, -zi•est** sordid > **sleaze** [sleez] *noun* (*slang*) 1 sordidness 2 contemptible person
sled *noun* 1 carriage on runners for sliding on snow 2 toboggan ▷ *verb* **sled•ded, sled•ding**
sledge [slej] *noun* 1 sledgehammer 2 sled
sledge•ham•mer [SLEJ-ham-ər] *noun* heavy hammer with long handle
sleek *adjective* **-er, -est** glossy, smooth, shiny
sleep *noun* 1 unconscious state regularly occurring in humans and animals 2 slumber, repose 3 (*informal*) dried particles oft. found in corners of eyes after sleeping ▷ *verb* **slept, sleep•ing** 4 take rest in sleep, slumber 5 accommodate for sleeping > **sleep'er** *noun* 1 one who sleeps 2 railroad sleeping car 3 (*informal*)

decrease, diminish, drop off, moderate, reduce, relax
slacker *noun* IDLER, couch potato (*slang*), dodger, loafer, shirker
slake *verb* SATISFY, assuage, quench, sate
slam *verb* BANG, crash, dash, fling, hurl, smash, throw
slander *noun* 1 DEFAMATION, calumny, libel, scandal, smear
▷ *verb* 2 DEFAME, blacken (someone's) name, libel, malign, smear
slanderous *adjective* DEFAMATORY, damaging, libelous, malicious
slant *verb* 1 SLOPE, bend, bevel, cant, heel, incline, lean, list, tilt
2 BIAS, angle, color, distort, twist
▷ *noun* 3 SLOPE, camber, gradient, incline, tilt
4 BIAS, angle, emphasis, one-sidedness, point of view, prejudice
slanting *adjective* SLOPING, angled, at an angle, bent, diagonal, inclined, oblique, tilted, tilting
slap *noun* 1 SMACK, blow, cuff, spank
▷ *verb* 2 SMACK, clap, cuff, paddle, spank
slapdash *adjective* CARELESS, clumsy, hasty, hurried, messy, slipshod, sloppy (*informal*)
slash *verb* 1 CUT, gash, hack, lacerate, rend, rip, score, slit
2 REDUCE, cut, drop, lower
▷ *noun* 3 CUT, gash, incision, laceration, rent, rip, slit
slaughter *verb* 1 MURDER, butcher, kill, massacre, slay
▷ *noun* 2 MURDER, bloodshed, butchery, carnage, killing, massacre, slaying
slaughterhouse *noun* ABATTOIR
slave *noun* 1 SERVANT, drudge, serf, vassal
▷ *verb* 2 TOIL, drudge, slog
slavery *noun* ENSLAVEMENT, bondage, captivity, servitude, subjugation
slavish *adjective* 1 SERVILE, abject, base, cringing, fawning, grovelling, obsequious, submissive, sycophantic
2 IMITATIVE, second-hand, unimaginative, unoriginal
slay *verb* KILL, butcher, massacre, mow down, murder, slaughter
sleaze *noun* CORRUPTION, bribery, dishonesty, extortion, fraud, unscrupulousness, venality
sleazy *adjective* SORDID, disreputable, low, run-down, scuzzy (*slang*), seedy, squalid
sleek *adjective* GLOSSY, lustrous, shiny, smooth
sleep *noun* 1 SLUMBER *or* SLUMBERS, doze, forty winks (*informal*), hibernation, nap, siesta, snooze (*informal*)
▷ *verb* 2 SLUMBER, catnap, doze, drowse, hibernate, snooze (*informal*), take a nap

person, firm, etc. that succeeds unexpectedly > **sleep'i•ly** *adverb* > **sleep'i•ness** [-nis] *noun* > **sleep'less** [-lis] *adjective* > **sleep'y** *adjective* **sleep•i•er, sleep•i•est** > **sleeping sickness** Afr. disease spread by tsetse fly > **sleep'o•ver** *noun* instance of spending the night at another person's home

sleet *noun* rain and snow or hail falling together

sleeve [sleev] *noun* 1 part of garment that covers arm 2 case surrounding shaft 3 phonograph record cover ▷ *verb transitive* **sleeved, sleev•ing** 4 furnish with sleeves > **sleeved** *adjective* > **sleeve'less** [-lis] *adjective* **have up one's sleeve** have something prepared secretly for emergency or as trick

sleigh [slay] *noun* sled

sleight [slīt] *noun* 1 dexterity 2 trickery 3 deviousness > **sleight of hand** 1 (manual dexterity in) conjuring, juggling 2 legerdemain

slen•der [SLEN-dər] *adjective* 1 slim, slight 2 feeble

slept *pt./pp. of* **sleep**

sleuth [slooth] *noun* 1 detective 2 bloodhound ▷ *verb transitive* 3 track

slew[1] [sloo] *pt. of* **slay**

slew[2] *verb* swing around

slew[3] *noun* (*informal*) large number or quantity

slice [slīs] *noun* 1 thin flat piece cut off 2 share 3 spatula 4 slice of pizza ▷ *verb transitive* **sliced, slic•ing** 5 cut into slices 6 cut cleanly 7 hit with bat, club, etc. at angle

slick [slik] *adjective* 1 smooth 2 smooth-tongued 3 flattering 4 superficially attractive 5 sly ▷ *verb transitive* 6 make glossy, smooth ▷ *noun* 7 slippery area 8 patch of oil on water

slide [slīd] *verb* **slid, slid** *or* **slid•den, slid•ing** 1 slip smoothly along 2 glide, as over ice 3 pass imperceptibly 4 deteriorate morally ▷ *noun* 5 sliding 6 surface, track for sliding 7 sliding part of mechanism 8 piece of glass holding object to be viewed under microscope 9 photographic transparency > **slide rule** mathematical instrument of two parts, one of which slides upon the other, for rapid calculations > **sliding scale** schedule for automatically varying one thing (e.g. wages) according to fluctuations of another (e.g. cost of living)

slight [slīt] *adjective* 1 small, trifling 2 not substantial, fragile 3 slim, slender ▷ *verb transitive* 4 disregard 5 neglect ▷ *noun* 6 indifference 7 act of discourtesy

slim *adjective* **slim•mer, slim•mest** 1 thin 2 slight ▷ *verb* **slimmed, slim•ming** 3 reduce person's weight by diet and exercise > **slim'ness** *noun* > **slim'line** *adjective* 1 appearing slim 2 pert. to slimness

slime [slīm] *noun* greasy, thick, liquid mud or similar substance > **slim'y** *adjective* **slim•i•er, slim•i•est** 1 like slime 2 fawning

sling *noun* 1 strap, loop with string attached at each end for hurling stone 2 bandage for supporting wounded limb 3 rope, belt, etc. for hoisting, carrying weights ▷ *verb transitive* **slung, sling•ing** 4 throw 5 hoist, swing by rope

slink *verb intransitive* **slunk, slink•ing** move stealthily, sneak > **slink'y** *adjective* **slink•i•er, slink•i•est** 1 sinuously graceful 2 (of clothes, etc.) figure-hugging

slip[1] *verb* **slipped, slip•ping** 1 (cause to) move smoothly, easily, quietly 2 pass out of (mind, etc.) 3 (of motor vehicle clutch) engage partially, fail ▷ *verb intransitive* 4 lose balance by sliding 5 fall from person's grasp 6 (usu. with *up*) make mistake 7 decline in health, morals ▷ *verb transitive* 8 put on or take off easily, quickly 9 let go (anchor, etc.) 10 dislocate (bone) ▷ *noun* 11 act or occasion of slipping 12 mistake 13 petticoat 14 small piece of paper 15 plant cutting 16 launching slope on which ships are built 17 covering for pillow 18 small child > **slip'shod** *adjective* slovenly, careless

sleepless *adjective* WAKEFUL, insomniac, restless

sleepy *adjective* DROWSY, dull, heavy, inactive, lethargic, sluggish

slender *adjective* 1 SLIM, lean, narrow, slight, willowy
2 FAINT, poor, remote, slight, slim, tenuous, thin
3 MEAGER, little, scant, scanty, small

sleuth *noun* DETECTIVE, gumshoe (*slang*), private eye (*informal*), investigator *or* private investigator

slice *noun* 1 SHARE, cut, helping, portion, segment, sliver, wedge
▷ *verb* 2 CUT, carve, divide, sever

slick *adjective* 1 GLIB, plausible, polished, smooth, specious
2 SKILLFUL, adroit, deft, dexterous, polished, professional
▷ *verb* 3 SMOOTH, plaster down, sleek

slide *verb* SLIP, coast, glide, skim, slither

slight *adjective* 1 SMALL, feeble, insignificant, meager, measly, minor, paltry, scanty, trifling, trivial, unimportant
2 SLIM, delicate, feeble, fragile, lightly-built, small, spare
▷ *verb* 3 SNUB, affront, blow off (*slang*), disdain, ignore, insult, scorn
▷ *noun* 4 SNUB, affront, insult, neglect, rebuff, slap in the face (*informal*), cold shoulder *or* the cold shoulder

slightly *adverb* A LITTLE, somewhat

slim *adjective* 1 SLENDER, lean, narrow, slight, svelte, thin, trim
2 SLIGHT, faint, poor, remote, slender
▷ *verb* 3 LOSE WEIGHT, diet, reduce

slimy *adjective* 1 VISCOUS, clammy, glutinous, oozy
2 OBSEQUIOUS, creeping, grovelling, oily, servile, smarmy (*Brit informal*), unctuous

sling *verb* 1 THROW, cast, chuck (*informal*), fling, heave, hurl, lob (*informal*), shy, toss
2 HANG, dangle, suspend

slink *verb* CREEP, prowl, skulk, slip, sneak, steal

slinky *adjective* FIGURE-HUGGING, clinging, close-fitting, skintight

slip[1] *verb* 1 FALL, skid
2 SLIDE, glide, skate, slither
3 SNEAK, conceal, creep, hide, steal
4 (*sometimes with up*) MAKE A MISTAKE, blunder, err, miscalculate
5 ▷ **let slip** GIVE AWAY, disclose, divulge, leak, reveal
▷ *noun* 6 MISTAKE, blunder, error, failure, fault, lapse, omission, oversight
7 ▷ **give (someone) the slip** ESCAPE FROM,

> **slip'stream** *noun aviation* stream of air driven astern by engine
slip² *noun* clay mixed with water to creamy consistency, used for decorating ceramic ware
slip•per [SLIP-ər] *noun* light shoe for indoor use > **slip'pered** *adjective*
slip•per•y [SLIP-ə-ree] *adjective* 1 so smooth as to cause slipping or to be difficult to hold or catch 2 changeable 3 unreliable 4 crafty 5 wily
slit *verb transitive* **slit, slit•ting** 1 make long straight cut in 2 cut in strips ▷ *noun*
slith•er [SLITH-ər] *verb intransitive* slide unsteadily (down slope, etc.)
sliv•er [SLIV-ər] *noun* 1 thin small piece torn off something 2 splinter
slob *noun* slovenly, coarse person
slob•ber [SLOB-ər] *verb* 1 slaver 2 be weakly and excessively demonstrative ▷ *noun* 3 running saliva 4 maudlin speech
sloe [sloh] *noun* blue-black, sour fruit of blackthorn > **sloe-eyed** *adjective* 1 dark-eyed 2 slanty-eyed > **sloe gin** [jin] liqueur of sloes steeped in gin
slog *verb* **slogged, slog•ging** 1 hit vigorously, esp. in boxing 2 work or study with dogged determination 3 move, work with difficulty ▷ *noun*
slo•gan [SLOH-gən] *noun* distinctive phrase (in advertising, etc.)
sloop *noun* 1 small one-masted vessel 2 *hist.* small warship
slop *verb* **slopped, slop•ping** 1 spill 2 splash ▷ *noun* 3 spilled liquid 4 watery food 5 dirty liquid > **slops** liquid refuse > **slop'py** *adjective* **-pi•er, -pi•est** 1 careless, untidy 2 sentimental 3 wet, muddy
slope [slohp] *verb transitive* **sloped, slop•ing** 1 place slanting ▷ *verb intransitive* **sloped, slop•ing** 2 lie in, follow an inclined course 3 go furtively ▷ *noun* 4 slant 5 upward, downward inclination
slosh *noun* 1 watery mud, etc. ▷ *verb* 2 splash > **sloshed** *adjective* (*slang*) drunk
slot *noun* 1 narrow hole or depression 2 slit for coins ▷ *verb transitive* **slot•ted, slot•ting** 3 put in slot 4 sort 5 place in series, organization > **slot machine** automatic machine worked by insertion of coin
sloth [slawth] *noun* 1 sluggish S Amer. animal 2 sluggishness > **sloth'ful** [-fəl] *adjective* lazy, idle
slouch [slowch] *verb intransitive* 1 walk, sit, etc. in lazy or ungainly, drooping manner ▷ *noun, adjective* 2 (of hat) with wide, flexible brim
slough¹ [rhymes with **cow**] *noun* bog
slough² [sluf] *noun* 1 skin shed by snake ▷ *verb* 2 shed (skin) 3 drop off
slov•en [SLUV-ən] *noun* dirty, untidy person > **slov'en•ly** *adjective* **-li•er, -li•est** 1 untidy 2 careless 3 disorderly ▷ *adverb*
slow [sloh] *adjective* **-er, -est** 1 lasting a long time 2 moving at low speed 3 behind the true time 4 dull ▷ *verb* 5 slacken speed (of) > **slow motion** motion picture showing movement greatly slowed down > **slow'poke** [-pohk] *noun* person slow in moving, acting, deciding, etc.
sludge [sluj] *noun* 1 slush, ooze 2 sewage

DICTIONARY S THESAURUS

dodge, elude, evade, get away from, lose (someone)
slippery *adjective* 1 SMOOTH, glassy, greasy, icy, slippy (*informal/dialect*), unsafe
2 DEVIOUS, crafty, cunning, dishonest, evasive, shifty, tricky, untrustworthy
slipshod *adjective* CARELESS, casual, slapdash, sloppy (*informal*), slovenly, untidy
slit *noun* 1 CUT, gash, incision, opening, rent, split, tear
▷ *verb* 2 CUT *or* CUT OPEN, gash, knife, lance, pierce, rip, slash
slither *verb* SLIDE, glide, slink, slip, snake, undulate
sliver *noun* SHRED, fragment, paring, shaving, splinter
slobber *verb* DROOL, dribble, drivel, salivate, slaver
slobbish *adjective* MESSY, slovenly, unclean, unkempt, untidy
slog *verb* 1 WORK, labor, plod, plow through, slave, toil
2 TRUDGE, tramp, trek
3 HIT, punch, slug, sock (*slang*), strike, thump, wallop (*informal*)
▷ *noun* 4 LABOR, effort, exertion, struggle
5 TRUDGE, hike, tramp, trek
slogan *noun* CATCH PHRASE, catchword, motto
slop *verb* 1 SPILL, overflow, slosh (*informal*), splash
▷ *noun* 2 (*informal*) FOOD, grub (*slang*), mess (*slang*)
slope *noun* 1 INCLINATION, gradient, incline, ramp, rise, slant, tilt
▷ *verb* 2 SLANT, drop away, fall, incline, lean, rise, tilt
3 ▷ **slope off** SLINK AWAY, creep away, slip away
sloping *adjective* SLANTING, inclined, leaning, oblique
sloppy *adjective* 1 CARELESS, messy, slipshod, slovenly, untidy
2 SENTIMENTAL, gushing, mawkish, slushy (*informal*)
slot *noun* 1 OPENING, aperture, groove, hole, slit, vent
2 (*informal*) PLACE, opening, position, space, time, vacancy
▷ *verb* 3 FIT IN, fit, insert
sloth *noun* LAZINESS, idleness, inactivity, inertia, slackness, sluggishness, torpor
slothful *adjective* LAZY, idle, inactive, indolent, workshy
slouch *verb* SLUMP, droop, loll, stoop
slovenly *adjective* CARELESS, disorderly, negligent, slack, slapdash, slipshod, sloppy (*informal*), untidy
slow *adjective* 1 PROLONGED, gradual, lingering, long-drawn-out, protracted
2 UNHURRIED, dawdling, lackadaisical, laggard, lazy, leisurely, ponderous, sluggish
3 LATE, backward, behind, delayed, tardy
4 STUPID, braindead (*informal*), dense, dim, dull-witted, obtuse, retarded, thick
▷ *verb* 5 (*often with up or down*) REDUCE SPEED, brake, decelerate, handicap, hold up, retard, slacken *or* slacken off
slowly *adverb* GRADUALLY, leisurely, unhurriedly
sludge *noun* SEDIMENT, mire, muck, mud, ooze,

slug[1] *noun* 1 land snail with no shell 2 bullet > **slug'gard** [-ərd] *noun* lazy, idle person > **slug'gish** *adjective* 1 slow 2 lazy, inert 3 not functioning well > **slug'gish•ness** *noun*

slug[2] *verb* **slugged, slug•ging** 1 hit, slog ▷ *noun* (*informal*) 2 heavy blow 3 shot of whiskey > **slug'ger** *noun* hard-hitting boxer, baseball batter

sluice [sloos] *noun* 1 gate, door to control flow of water ▷ *verb transitive* **sluiced, sluic•ing** 2 pour water over, through

slum *noun* 1 squalid street or neighborhood ▷ *verb intransitive* **slummed, slum•ming** 2 visit slums > **slum'lord** *noun* landlord who owns buildings in slums and neglects them

slum•ber [SLUM-bər] *verb intransitive, noun* sleep > **slum'ber•er** *noun*

slump *verb* 1 fall heavily 2 relax ungracefully 3 decline suddenly in value, volume or esteem ▷ *noun* 4 sudden decline 5 (of prices, etc.) sharp fall 6 depression

slung *pt./pp. of* **sling**

slunk *pt./pp. of* **slink**

slur *verb transitive* **slurred, slur•ring** 1 pass over lightly 2 run together (words, musical notes) 3 disparage ▷ *noun* 4 slight, stigma 5 *mus.* curved line above or below notes to be slurred

slurp *verb* eat, drink noisily

slur•ry [SLUR-ee] *noun, plural* **-ries** muddy liquid mixture as cement, mud, etc.

slush *noun* 1 watery, muddy substance 2 excessive sentimentality > **slush'y** *adjective* **slush•i•er, slush•i•est** > **slush fund** fund for financing bribery, corruption

slut *noun* (*offensive*) promiscuous woman > **slut'tish** *adjective*

sly [slī] *adjective* **sly•er** *or* **sli•er, sly•est** *or* **sli•est** 1 cunning, wily, knowing 2 secret, deceitful > **sly'ly, sli'ly** *adverb* > **sly'ness** [-nis] *noun*

Sm *chem.* samarium

smack[1] [smak] *noun* 1 taste, flavor 2 (*slang*) heroin ▷ *verb intransitive* 3 taste (of) 4 suggest

smack[2] *verb transitive* 1 slap 2 open and close (lips) with loud sound ▷ *noun* 3 smacking slap 4 crack 5 such sound 6 loud kiss ▷ *adverb* (*informal*) 7 squarely 8 directly > **smack'dab'** *adverb* (*informal*) smack

smack[3] *noun* small sailing vessel, usu. for fishing

small [smawl] *adjective* **-er, -est** 1 little, unimportant 2 petty 3 short 4 weak 5 mean ▷ *noun* 6 small slender part esp. of the back > **small hours** hours just after midnight > **small-mind•ed** [-mīnd-id] *adjective* 1 having narrow views 2 petty > **small'pox** *noun* contagious disease > **small talk** light, polite conversation

smarm•y [SMAHR-mee] *adjective* **smarm•i•er, smarm•i•est** 1 unpleasantly suave 2 fawning

smart [smahrt] *adjective* **-er, -est** 1 astute 2 brisk 3 clever, witty 4 impertinent 5 trim, well dressed 6 fashionable 7 causing stinging pain ▷ *verb* 8 feel, cause pain ▷ *noun* 9 sharp pain > **smart'en** *verb transitive* > **smart'ly** *adverb* > **smart'ness** [-nis] *noun* > **smart al'eck** conceited person, know-it-all > **smart ass** (*slang, offensive*) smart aleck > **smart card** plastic card with integrated circuit capable of storing and processing data, used for identification, bank and store transactions, etc. > **smart'phone** *noun* combination of cell phone and handheld computer

smash *verb transitive* 1 break violently 2 strike hard 3 ruin 4 destroy ▷ *verb intransitive* 5 break 6 dash violently against ▷ *noun* 7 heavy blow 8 collision (of vehicles, etc.) 9 total financial failure 10 (*informal*) popular success > **smashed** *adjective* (*slang*) very drunk or affected by drugs > **smash'er** *noun* attractive person, thing

residue, silt, slime

sluggish *adjective* INACTIVE, dull, heavy, indolent, inert, lethargic, slothful, slow, torpid

slum *noun* HOVEL, ghetto

slumber *verb* SLEEP, doze, drowse, nap, snooze (*informal*)

slump *verb* 1 FALL, collapse, crash, plunge, sink, slip
2 SAG, droop, hunch, loll, slouch
▷ *noun* 3 FALL, collapse, crash, decline, downturn, drop, reverse, trough
4 RECESSION, depression

slur *noun* INSULT, affront, aspersion, calumny, innuendo, insinuation, smear, stain

slut *noun* (*offensive*) TART, ho (*slang*), trollop, whore

sly *adjective* 1 CUNNING, artful, clever, crafty, devious, scheming, secret, shifty, stealthy, subtle, underhand, wily
2 ROGUISH, arch, impish, knowing, mischievous
▷ *noun* 3 ▷ **on the sly** SECRETLY, covertly, on the quiet, privately, surreptitiously

smack *verb* 1 SLAP, clap, cuff, hit, paddle, spank, strike
▷ *noun* 2 SLAP, blow
▷ *adverb* 3 (*informal*) DIRECTLY, exactly, precisely, right, slap (*informal*), squarely, straight

small *adjective* 1 LITTLE, diminutive, mini, miniature, minute, petite, pygmy *or* pigmy, teeny, teeny-weeny, tiny, undersized, wee
2 UNIMPORTANT, insignificant, minor, negligible, paltry, petty, trifling, trivial
3 PETTY, base, mean, narrow
4 MODEST, humble, unpretentious

small-minded *adjective* PETTY, bigoted, intolerant, mean, narrow-minded, ungenerous

small-time *adjective* MINOR, insignificant, of no account, petty, unimportant

smarmy *adjective* (*Brit informal*) OBSEQUIOUS, crawling, ingratiating, servile, smooth, suave, sycophantic, toadying, unctuous

smart *adjective* 1 CLEVER, acute, astute, bright, canny, ingenious, intelligent, keen, quick, sharp, shrewd
2 BRISK, lively, quick, vigorous
▷ *verb* 3 STING, burn, hurt
▷ *noun* 4 STING, pain, soreness

smart aleck *noun* (*informal*) KNOW-ALL (*informal*), smarty pants (*informal*), wise guy (*informal*)

smarten *verb* TIDY, groom, put in order, put to rights, spruce up

smash *verb* 1 BREAK, crush, demolish, pulverize, shatter
2 COLLIDE, crash
3 DESTROY, lay waste, ruin, trash (*slang*), wreck
▷ *noun* 4 DESTRUCTION, collapse, downfall, failure, ruin
5 COLLISION, accident, crash

smat•ter•ing [SMAT-ər-ing] *noun* slight superficial knowledge
smear [smeer] *verb transitive* 1 rub with grease, etc. 2 smudge, spread with dirt, grease, etc. ▷ *noun* 3 mark made thus 4 sample of secretion for medical examination 5 slander
smell *verb* **smelled** *or* **smelt, smell'ing** 1 perceive by nose 2 suspect 3 give out odor 4 use nose ▷ *noun* 5 faculty of perceiving odors by nose 6 anything detected by sense of smell > **smell'y** *adjective* **smell•i•er, smell•i•est** with strong (unpleasant) smell
smelt[1] *verb transitive* extract metal from ore > **smelt'er** *noun*
smelt[2] *noun* fish of salmon family
smid•gen [SMIJ-ən] *noun* very small amount
smile [smīl] *noun* 1 curving or parting of lips in pleased or amused expression ▷ *verb* **smiled, smil•ing** 2 wear, assume a smile 3 approve, favor
smirch [smurch] *verb transitive* 1 dirty, sully 2 disgrace, discredit ▷ *noun* 3 stain 4 disgrace
smirk [smurk] *noun* smile expressing scorn, smugness ▷ *verb*
smite [smīt] *verb transitive* **smote, smit'ten** *or* **smit, smit'ing** 1 strike 2 attack 3 afflict 4 affect, esp. with love or fear
smith *noun* worker in iron, gold, etc. > **smith'y** *noun, plural* **smith•ies** 1 blacksmith's workshop 2 blacksmith
smith•er•eens [SMITH-ər-eenz] *plural noun* small bits
smock [smok] *noun* 1 loose outer garment ▷ *verb transitive* 2 gather by sewing in honeycomb pattern > **smock'ing** *noun*
smog *noun* mixture of smoke and fog
smoke [smohk] *noun* 1 cloudy mass of suspended particles that rises from fire or anything burning 2 spell of tobacco smoking ▷ *verb intransitive* **smoked, smok•ing** 3 give off smoke 4 inhale and expel tobacco smoke ▷ *verb transitive* **smoked, smok•ing** 5 use (tobacco) by smoking 6 expose to smoke (esp. in curing fish, etc.) > **smok'er** *noun* 1 one who smokes 2 informal party
smol•der [SMOHL-dər] *verb intransitive* 1 burn slowly without flame 2 (of feelings) exist in suppressed state
smooch *verb, noun* (*informal*) kiss, cuddle
smooth [smooth] *adjective* 1 not rough, even of surface or texture 2 sinuous 3 flowing 4 calm, soft, soothing 5 suave, plausible 6 free from jolts ▷ *verb transitive* 7 make smooth 8 quiet > **smooth'ly** *adverb*
smor•gas•bord [SMOR-gəs-bord] *noun* buffet meal of assorted dishes
smote *pt. of* **smite**
smoth•er [SMUTH-ər] *verb* 1 suffocate 2 envelop 3 suppress ▷ *verb intransitive* 4 be suffocated
SMS Short Message Server, system for sending messages of no more than 160 characters to a cell phone
smudge [smuj] *verb* **smudged, smudg•ing** make smear, stain, dirty mark (on) ▷ *noun*
smug *adjective* **smug•ger, smug•ger** self-satisfied, complacent > **smug'ly** *adverb*
smug•gle [SMUG-əl] *verb transitive* **-gled, -gling** 1 import, export without paying customs duties 2 conceal, take secretly > **smug'gler** *noun*
smut *noun* 1 piece of soot, particle of dirt 2 lewd or obscene talk, etc. 3 disease of grain ▷ *verb transitive* **smut•ted, smut•ting** 4 blacken, smudge > **smut'ty** *adjective* **-ti•er, -ti•est** 1 soiled with smut, soot 2 obscene, lewd
Sn *chem.* tin
snack [snak] *noun* 1 light portion of food eaten hastily between meals ▷ *verb intransitive* 2 eat thus > **snack bar** lunchroom at which light meals are served
snag *noun* 1 difficulty 2 sharp protuberance 3 hole, loop in fabric caused by sharp object 4 obstacle (e.g. tree branch, etc. in river bed) ▷ *verb transitive* **snagged, snag'ging** 5 catch, damage on snag
snail [snayl] *noun* 1 slow-moving mollusk with

smattering *noun* MODICUM, bit, rudiments
smear *verb* 1 SPREAD OVER, bedaub, coat, cover, daub, rub on
2 DIRTY, smudge, soil, stain, sully
3 SLANDER, besmirch, blacken, malign
▷ *noun* 4 SMUDGE, blot, blotch, daub, splotch, streak
5 SLANDER, calumny, defamation, libel
smell *verb* 1 SNIFF, scent
2 STINK, reek
▷ *noun* 3 ODOR, aroma, bouquet, fragrance, perfume, scent
4 STINK, fetor, stench
smelly *adjective* STINKING, fetid, foul, foul-smelling, funky (*slang*), malodorous, noisome, reeking
smirk *noun* SMUG LOOK, simper
smitten *adjective* 1 AFFLICTED, laid low, plagued, struck
2 INFATUATED, beguiled, bewitched, captivated, charmed, enamored
smolder *verb* SEETHE, boil, fume, rage, simmer
smooth *adjective* 1 EVEN, flat, flush, horizontal, level, plane
2 SLEEK, glossy, polished, shiny, silky, soft, velvety
3 EASY, effortless, well-ordered
4 FLOWING, regular, rhythmic, steady, uniform
5 SUAVE, facile, glib, persuasive, slick, smarmy (*Brit informal*), unctuous, urbane
6 MELLOW, agreeable, mild, pleasant
▷ *verb* 7 FLATTEN, iron, level, plane, press
8 CALM, appease, assuage, ease, mitigate, mollify, soften
smother *verb* 1 SUFFOCATE, choke, stifle, strangle
2 SUPPRESS, conceal, hide, muffle, repress, stifle
smudge *verb* 1 SMEAR, daub, dirty, mark, smirch
▷ *noun* 2 SMEAR, blemish, blot
smug *adjective* SELF-SATISFIED, complacent, conceited, superior
smuggler *noun* TRAFFICKER, bootlegger, runner
smutty *adjective* OBSCENE, bawdy, blue, coarse, crude, dirty, indecent, indelicate, suggestive, vulgar
snack *noun* LIGHT MEAL, bite, refreshment *or* refreshments
snag *noun* 1 DIFFICULTY, catch, complication, disadvantage, downside, drawback, hitch, obstacle, problem

shell **2** slow, sluggish person > **snail'like** *adjective* > **snail mail** *noun* (*informal*) **1** conventional mail, as opposed to e-mail **2** the conventional postal system > **snail-mail** *verb transitive* send by the conventional postal system, rather than by e-mail

snake [snayk] *noun* **1** long scaly limbless reptile, serpent ▷ *verb* **snaked, snak•ing 2** move like snake > **snak'y** *adjective* **snak•i•er, snak•i•est** twisted or winding **snake in the grass** hidden enemy

snap *verb* **snapped, snap•ping 1** break suddenly **2** make cracking sound **3** bite (at) suddenly **4** speak suddenly, angrily ▷ *noun* **5** act of snapping **6** fastener **7** snapshot **8** (*informal*) easy task **9** brief period, esp. of cold weather ▷ *adjective* **10** sudden, unplanned, arranged quickly > **snap'py** *adjective* **-pi•er, -pi•est 1** irritable **2** (*informal*) quick **3** (*informal*) well-dressed, fashionable > **snap'drag•on** *noun* plant with flowers that can be opened like a mouth > **snap'shot** *noun* informal photograph

snare [snair] *noun* (noose used as) trap ▷ *verb transitive* **snared, snar•ing** catch with one

snarl [snahrl] *noun* **1** growl of angry dog **2** tangle, knot ▷ *verb intransitive* **3** utter snarl **4** grumble

snatch [snach] *verb* **1** make quick grab or bite (at) **2** seize, catch ▷ *noun* **3** grab **4** fragment **5** short spell

sneak [sneek] *verb intransitive* **sneaked, sneak•ing 1** slink **2** move about furtively **3** act in mean, underhand manner ▷ *noun* **4** mean, treacherous person > **sneak'ing** *adjective* secret but persistent > **sneak pre'view** unannounced showing of movie before general release

sneak•ers [SNEEK-ərz] *plural noun* flexible, informal sports shoes

sneer *noun* scornful, contemptuous expression or remark ▷ *verb*

sneeze [sneez] *verb intransitive* **sneezed, sneez•ing** emit breath through nose with sudden involuntary spasm and noise ▷ *noun*

snick•er [SNIK-ər] *noun* sly, disrespectful laugh, esp. partly stifled ▷ *verb*

snide [snīd] *adjective* **snid•er, snid•est** malicious, supercilious

sniff *verb intransitive* **1** inhale through nose with sharp hiss **2** (with *at*) express disapproval, etc. by sniffing ▷ *verb transitive* **3** take up through nose, smell ▷ *noun* > **sniffle** *verb intransitive* **-fled, -fling 1** sniff noisily through nose, esp. when suffering from a cold in the head **2** snuffle

snig•ger [SNIG-ər] *noun* snicker

snip *verb transitive* **snipped, snip•ping 1** cut, cut bits off ▷ *noun* **2** act, sound of snipping **3** bit cut off **4** (*informal*) small, insignificant, impertinent person > **snip•pet** [SNIP-it] *noun* shred, fragment, clipping > **snips** *plural noun* tool for cutting

snipe [snīp] *noun* **1** wading bird ▷ *verb* **sniped, snip•ing 2** shoot at enemy from cover **3** (with *at*) criticize, attack (person) slyly > **snip'er** *noun*

snit *noun* irritated state of mind

snitch [snich] *verb transitive* (*informal*) **1** steal ▷ *verb intransitive* **2** inform ▷ *noun* **3** informer

sniv•el [SNIV-əl] *verb intransitive* **-eled, -el•ing 1** sniffle to show distress **2** whine

snob *noun* one who pretentiously judges others by social rank, etc. > **snob'ber•y** *noun* > **snob'bish** *adjective* of or like a snob

snook•er [SNUUK-ər] *noun* **1** game like pool played with 21 balls ▷ *verb transitive* **2** leave (opponent) in unfavorable position **3** place

DICTIONARY • THESAURUS

▷ *verb* **2** CATCH, rip, tear

snap *verb* **1** BREAK, crack, separate
2 CRACKLE, click, pop
3 BITE AT, bite, nip, snatch
4 SPEAK SHARPLY, bark, jump down (someone's) throat (*informal*), lash out at
▷ *noun* **5** CRACKLE, pop
6 BITE, grab, nip
▷ *adjective* **7** INSTANT, immediate, spur-of-the-moment, sudden

snappy *adjective* **1** IRRITABLE, cross, edgy, testy, touchy
2 SMART, chic, cool (*informal*), dapper, fashionable, phat (*slang*), stylish

snap up *verb* SEIZE, grab, pounce upon, take advantage of

snare *noun* **1** TRAP, gin, net, noose, wire
▷ *verb* **2** TRAP, catch, entrap, net, seize, wire

snarl *verb* (*often with up*) TANGLE, entangle, entwine, muddle, ravel

snarl-up *noun* TANGLE, confusion, entanglement, muddle

snatch *verb* **1** SEIZE, clutch, grab, grasp, grip
▷ *noun* **2** BIT, fragment, part, piece, snippet

sneak *verb* **1** SLINK, lurk, pad, skulk, slip, steal
2 SLIP, smuggle, spirit
▷ *noun* **3** INFORMER, telltale

sneaking *adjective* **1** NAGGING, persistent, uncomfortable, worrying
2 SECRET, hidden, private, undivulged, unexpressed, unvoiced

sneaky *adjective* SLY, deceitful, devious, dishonest, double-dealing, down and dirty (*informal*), furtive, low, mean, shifty, untrustworthy

sneer *noun* **1** SCORN, derision, gibe, jeer, mockery, ridicule
▷ *verb* **2** SCORN, deride, disdain, jeer, laugh, mock, ridicule

snide *adjective* NASTY, cynical, disparaging, hurtful, ill-natured, malicious, sarcastic, scornful, sneering, spiteful

sniff *verb* INHALE, breathe, smell

snigger *noun*
▷ *verb* LAUGH, giggle, snicker, titter

snip *verb* **1** CUT, clip, crop, dock, shave, trim
▷ *noun* **2** BIT, clipping, fragment, piece, scrap, shred

snipe *verb* CRITICIZE, carp, denigrate, disparage, jeer, knock (*informal*), put down

snippet *noun* PIECE, fragment, part, scrap, shred

snitch *verb* **1** (*informal*) INFORM ON, grass on (*Brit slang*), tattle on, tell on (*informal*), tell tales
▷ *noun* **2** INFORMER, tattletale, telltale

snivel *verb* WHINE, cry, moan, sniffle, whimper

snob *noun* ELITIST, highbrow, prig

snobbery *noun* ARROGANCE, airs, pretension, pride, snobbishness

snobbish *adjective* SUPERIOR, arrogant, patronizing, pretentious, snooty (*informal*), stuck-up (*informal*)

(someone) in difficult situation **4** (*slang*) cheat
snoop *verb* **1** pry, meddle **2** peer into ▷ *noun* **3** one who acts thus **4** snooping
snoot•y [SNOOT-ee] *adjective* **snoot•i•er, snoot•i•est** (*informal*) haughty
snooze [snooz] *verb intransitive* **snoozed, snooz•ing** **1** take short sleep ▷ *noun* **2** nap
snore [snor] *verb intransitive* **snored, snor•ing** breathe noisily when asleep ▷ *noun*
snor•kel [SNOR-kəl] *noun* **1** tube for breathing underwater ▷ *verb intransitive* **2** swim, fish using this
snort *verb intransitive* **1** make (contemptuous) noise by driving breath through nostrils **2** (*slang*) inhale drug ▷ *noun* **3** noise of snorting **4** (*slang*) shot of liquor **5** (*slang*) amount of drug inhaled
snot *noun* (*vulgar*) mucus from nose > **snot•ty** [-tee] *adjective* **-ti•er, -ti•est** (*informal*) arrogant
snout [snowt] *noun* animal's nose
snow [snoh] *noun* **1** frozen vapor that falls in flakes **2** (*slang*) cocaine ▷ *verb* **3** fall, sprinkle as snow **4** let fall, throw down like snow **5** cover with snow **6** (*slang*) overwhelm **7** (*slang*) deceive > **snow'y** *adjective* **snow•i•er, snow•i•est** **1** of, like snow **2** covered with snow **3** very white > **snow'ball** *noun* **1** snow pressed into hard ball for throwing ▷ *verb* **2** increase rapidly **3** play, fight with snowballs > **snow blind•ness** temporary blindness due to brightness of snow > **snow'board** *noun* board like surfboard for descending ski slopes > **snow'drift** *noun* bank of deep snow > **snow fence** fence for erecting in winter beside exposed road > **snow job** (*slang*) attempt to deceive by flattery or exaggeration > **snow line** elevation above which snow does not melt > **snow'shoes** [-shooz] *plural noun* shoes like rackets for traveling on snow **snow under** **1** cover and block with snow **2** overwhelm
snub *verb transitive* **snubbed, snub•bing** **1** insult (esp. by ignoring) intentionally ▷ *noun, adjective* **2** short and blunt > **snub-nosed** *adjective*
snuff[1] *noun* powdered tobacco for inhaling through nose **up to snuff** (*informal*) up to a standard
snuff[2] *verb* extinguish (esp. candle, etc.)
snuf•fle [SNUF-əl] *verb intransitive* **-fled, -fling** breathe noisily, with difficulty
snug *adjective* **-ger, -gest** warm, comfortable > **snug'gle** *verb* **-gled, -gling** lie close to for warmth or affection > **snug'ly** *adverb*
so[1] [soh] *adverb* **1** to such an extent **2** in such a manner **3** very **4** the case being such **5** accordingly ▷ *conjunction* **6** therefore **7** in order that **8** with the result that ▷ *interjection* **9** well! > **so-called** *adjective* called by but doubtfully deserving that name > **so long** (*informal*) goodbye
so[2] *see* **sol**
soak [sohk] *verb* **1** steep **2** absorb **3** drench **4** lie in liquid **5** (*slang*) overcharge (customer) ▷ *noun* **6** soaking **7** (*slang*) habitual drunkard
soap [sohp] *noun* **1** compound of alkali and oil used in washing ▷ *verb transitive* **2** apply soap to > **soap'y** *adjective* **soap•i•er, soap•i•est** > **soap opera** radio or TV serial of domestic life
soar [sor] *verb intransitive* **1** fly high **2** increase, rise (in price, etc.)
sob *verb intransitive* **sobbed, sob•bing** **1** catch breath, esp. in weeping ▷ *noun* **2** sobbing > **sob story** tale of personal distress told to arouse sympathy
so•ber [SOH-bər] *adjective* **-ber-er, -ber-est** **1** not drunk **2** temperate **3** subdued **4** dull, plain **5** solemn ▷ *verb* **6** make, become sober > **so•bri•e•ty** [sə-BRĪ-i-tee] *noun* state of being sober
so•bri•quet [SOH-brə-kay] *noun* **1** nickname **2** assumed name
soc•cer [SOK-ər] *noun* ball game played with feet and spherical ball
so•cia•ble [SOH-shə-bəl] *adjective* **1** friendly **2** convivial > **so•cia•bil'i•ty** *noun*
so•cial [SOH-shəl] *adjective* **1** living in communities **2** relating to society **3** sociable ▷ *noun* **4** informal gathering > **so'cial•ite** *noun* **1** member of fashionable society > **so'cial•ize** *verb* **-ized, -iz•ing** > **so'cial•ly** *adverb* > **social security**

DICTIONARY

S

THESAURUS

snoop *verb* PRY, interfere, poke one's nose in (*informal*), spy
snooper *noun* NOSY ROSY (*informal*), busybody, meddler, snoop (*informal*)
snooze *verb* **1** DOZE, catnap, nap, take forty winks (*informal*)
▷ *noun* **2** DOZE, catnap, forty winks (*informal*), nap, siesta
snub *verb* **1** PUT DOWN, avoid, blow off (*slang*), cold-shoulder, cut (*informal*), humiliate, ignore, rebuff, slight
▷ *noun* **2** INSULT, affront, put-down, slap in the face
snug *adjective* COZY, comfortable, comfy (*informal*), homey, warm
snuggle *verb* NESTLE, cuddle, nuzzle
soak *verb* **1** WET, bathe, damp, drench, immerse, moisten, saturate, steep
2 PENETRATE, permeate, seep
3 ▷ **soak up** ABSORB, assimilate
soaking *adjective* SOAKED, drenched, dripping, saturated, sodden, sopping, streaming, wet through, wringing wet
soar *verb* **1** ASCEND, fly, mount, rise, wing
2 RISE, climb, escalate, rocket, shoot up
sob *verb* CRY, howl, shed tears, weep
sober *adjective* **1** ABSTINENT, abstemious, moderate, temperate
2 SERIOUS, composed, cool, grave, level-headed, rational, reasonable, sedate, solemn, staid, steady
3 PLAIN, dark, drab, dumpy (*informal*), frowzy, homely, quiet, somber, subdued
sobriety *noun* **1** ABSTINENCE, abstemiousness, moderation, nonindulgence, soberness, temperance
2 SERIOUSNESS, gravity, level-headedness, solemnity, staidness, steadiness
so-called *adjective* ALLEGED, pretended, professed, self-styled, supposed
sociable *adjective* FRIENDLY, affable, companionable, convivial, cordial, genial, gregarious, outgoing, social, warm
social *adjective* **1** COMMUNAL, collective, common, community, general, group, public
▷ *noun* **2** GET-TOGETHER (*informal*), gathering, party
socialize *verb* MIX, fraternize, get about *or* get

government-sponsored provision for the disabled, unemployed, aged, etc. > **social work** work to improve welfare of others
so•cial•ism [SOH-shə-liz-əm] *noun* political system that advocates public ownership of means of production, distribution and exchange > **so'cial•ist** *noun, adjective*
so•ci•e•ty [sə-SĪ-i-tee] *noun, plural* **-ties** 1 living associated with others 2 those so living 3 companionship 4 company 5 association 6 club 7 fashionable people collectively
so•ci•ol•o•gy [soh-see-OL-ə-jee] *noun* study of societies
sock[1] [sok] *noun* cloth covering for foot
sock[2] *verb transitive* 1 hit ▷ *noun* 2 blow
sock•et [SOK-it] *noun* hole or recess for something to fit into
So•crat•ic [sə-KRAT-ik] *adjective* of, like Greek philosopher Socrates
sod *noun* lump of earth with grass
so•da [SOH-də] *noun* 1 compound of sodium 2 soda water > **soda water** water charged with carbon dioxide
sod•den [SOD-n] *adjective* 1 soaked 2 drunk 3 heavy and lumpy
so•di•um [SOD-dee-əm] *noun* metallic alkaline element > **sodium bicarbonate** white crystalline soluble compound (*also* **bicarbonate of soda**)
sod•om•y [SOD-ə-mee] *noun* anal intercourse > **sod'om•ite** *noun*
so•fa [SOH-fə] *noun* upholstered couch with back and arms, for two or more people
soft [sawft] *adjective* **-er, -est** 1 yielding easily to pressure, not hard 2 mild 3 easy 4 subdued 5 quiet, gentle 6 (too) lenient 7 oversentimental 8 foolish, stupid 9 (of water) containing few mineral salts 10 (of drugs) not liable to cause addiction > **soft'en** [SAWF-ən] *verb* 1 make, become soft or softer 2 mollify 3 lighten 4 mitigate 5 make less loud > **soft'ly** *adverb* gently, quietly > **soft'ball** *noun* (ball used in) variation of baseball using larger, softer ball > **soft drink** one that is nonalcoholic > **soft goods** nondurable goods, e.g. curtains, rugs > **soft soap** (*informal*) flattery > **soft'ware** *noun* programs used with a computer > **soft'wood** [-wuud] *noun* wood of coniferous tree
sog•gy [SOG-ee] *adjective* **-gi•er, -gi•est** 1 soaked with liquid 2 damp and heavy
soil[1] *noun* 1 earth, ground 2 country, territory
soil[2] *verb* 1 make, become dirty 2 tarnish, defile ▷ *noun* 3 dirt 4 sewage 5 stain
soir•ee [swah-RAY] *noun* private evening party esp. with music
so•journ [SOH-jurn] *verb intransitive* 1 stay for a time ▷ *noun* 2 short stay > **so'journ•er** *noun*
sol, so *noun* fifth sol-fa note
sol•ace [SOL-is] *noun, verb transitive* **-aced, -ac•ing** comfort in distress
sol•ar [SOH-lər] *adjective* of the sun > **solar plex'us** network of nerves at pit of stomach
so•lar•i•um [sə-LAIR-ee-əm] *noun, plural* **-i•ums** room built mainly of glass to give exposure to sun
sold *pt./pp. of* **sell**
sol•der [SOD-ər] *noun* 1 easily-melted alloy used for joining metal ▷ *verb transitive* 2 join with it > **soldering iron** tool for melting and applying solder
sol•dier [SOHL-jər] *noun* 1 one serving in army ▷ *verb intransitive* 2 serve in army 3 (*informal*) loaf 4 (with *on*) persist doggedly > **sol'dier•ly** *adjective*
sole[1] [sohl] *adjective* 1 one and only, unique 2 solitary > **sole'ly** *adverb* 1 alone 2 only 3 entirely
sole[2] *noun* 1 underside of foot 2 underpart of shoe, etc. ▷ *verb transitive* **soled, sol•ing** 3 fit with sole
sole[3] *noun* small edible flatfish
sol•e•cism [SOL-ə-siz-əm] *noun* breach of grammar or etiquette

DICTIONARY • THESAURUS

around, go out
society *noun* 1 MANKIND, civilization, humanity, people, the community, the public
2 ORGANIZATION, association, circle, club, fellowship, group, guild, institute, league, order, union
3 UPPER CLASSES, beau monde, elite, gentry, high society
4 COMPANIONSHIP, company, fellowship, friendship
sodden *adjective* SOAKED, drenched, saturated, soggy, sopping, waterlogged
sofa *noun* COUCH, chaise longue, divan, settee
soft *adjective* 1 PLIABLE, bendable, elastic, flexible, malleable, moldable, plastic, supple
2 YIELDING, elastic, gelatinous, pulpy, spongy, squashy
3 VELVETY, downy, feathery, fleecy, silky, smooth
4 QUIET, dulcet, gentle, murmured, muted, soft-toned
5 PALE, bland, light, mellow, pastel, subdued
6 DIM, dimmed, faint, restful
7 MILD, balmy, temperate
8 LENIENT, easy-going, indulgent, lax, overindulgent, permissive, spineless
9 OUT OF CONDITION, effeminate, flabby, flaccid, limp, weak
10 (*informal*) EASY, comfortable, undemanding
11 KIND, compassionate, gentle, sensitive, sentimental, tenderhearted, touchy-feely (*informal*)
soften *verb* LESSEN, allay, appease, cushion, ease, mitigate, moderate, mollify, still, subdue, temper
softhearted *adjective* KIND, charitable, compassionate, sentimental, sympathetic, tender, tenderhearted, warm-hearted
soggy *adjective* SODDEN, dripping, moist, saturated, soaked, sopping, waterlogged
soil[1] *noun* 1 EARTH, clay, dirt, dust, ground
2 LAND, country
soil[2] *verb* DIRTY, befoul, besmirch, defile, foul, pollute, spot, stain, sully, tarnish
solace *noun* 1 COMFORT, consolation, relief
▷ *verb* 2 COMFORT, console
soldier *noun* FIGHTER, man-at-arms, serviceman, trooper, warrior
sole *adjective* ONLY, alone, exclusive, individual, one, single, solitary
solely *adverb* ONLY, alone, completely, entirely, exclusively, merely

sol•emn [SOL-əm] *adjective* 1 serious 2 formal 3 impressive > **sol'emn•ly** *adverb* > **so•lem•ni•ty** [sə-LEM-ni-tee] *noun* > **sol•em•nize** [SOL-əm-nīz] *verb transitive* **-nized, -niz•ing** 1 celebrate, perform 2 make solemn

so•le•noid [SOH-lə-noid] *noun* coil of wire as part of electrical apparatus

sol-fa [sohl-FAH] *noun mus.* system of syllables sol, fa, etc. sung in scale

so•lic•it [sə-LIS-it] *verb transitive* 1 request 2 accost 3 urge 4 entice > **so•lic•i•ta'tion** *noun* > **so•lic'i•tor** *noun* one who solicits > **so•lic'i•tous** *adjective* 1 anxious 2 eager 3 earnest > **so•lic'i•tude** *noun*

sol'id *adjective* 1 not hollow 2 compact 3 composed of one substance 4 firm 5 massive 6 reliable, sound ▷ *noun* 7 body of three dimensions 8 substance not liquid or gas > **sol•i•dar'i•ty** *noun* 1 unity of interests 2 united condition > **so•lid'i•fy** *verb* **-fied, -fy•ing** 1 make, become solid or firm 2 harden > **so•lid'i•ty** *noun*

so•lil•o•quy [sə-LIL-ə-kwee] *noun, plural* **-quies** (esp. in drama) thoughts spoken by person while alone > **so•lil'o•quize** *verb intransitive* **-quized, -quiz•ing**

sol•ip•sism [SOL-ip-siz-əm] *noun* doctrine that self is the only thing known to exist > **sol'ip•sist** *noun*

sol•i•tar•y [SOL-i-ter-ee] *adjective* 1 alone, single ▷ *noun* 2 hermit > **sol'i•taire** *noun* 1 game for one person played with cards or with pegs set in board 2 single precious stone set by itself > **sol'i•tude** *noun* 1 state of being alone 2 loneliness

so•lo [SOH-loh] *noun, plural* **-los** 1 music for one performer ▷ *adjective* 2 not concerted 3 unaccompanied, alone 4 piloting airplane alone > **so'lo•ist** *noun*

sol•stice [SOL-stis] *noun* either shortest (winter) or longest (summer) day of year

solve [solv] *verb transitive* **solved, solv•ing** 1 work out, explain 2 find answer to > **sol•u•bil•i•ty** [sol-yə-BIL-i-tee] *noun* > **sol'u•ble** *adjective* 1 capable of being dissolved in liquid 2 able to be solved or explained > **so•lu•tion** [sə-LOO-shən] *noun* 1 answer to problem 2 dissolving 3 liquid with something dissolved in it > **solv'a•ble** *adjective* > **sol'ven•cy** [-vən-see] *noun* > **sol'vent** *adjective* 1 able to meet financial obligations ▷ *noun* 2 liquid with power of dissolving

som•ber [SOM-bər] *adjective* dark, gloomy

som•bre•ro [som-BRAIR-oh] *noun, plural* **-bre•ros** wide-brimmed hat worn in Mexico, Spain, etc.

some [sum] *adjective* 1 denoting an indefinite number, amount or extent 2 one or other 3 amount of 4 certain 5 approximately ▷ *pronoun* 6 portion, quantity > **some'bod•y** *noun* 1 some person 2 important person > **some'how** *adverb* by some means unknown > **some'thing** *noun* 1 thing not clearly defined 2 indefinite amount, quantity or degree > **-something** *combining form* (person) of an age above a given figure: *thirtysomething* > **some'time** *adverb* 1 formerly 2 at some (past or future) time ▷ *adjective* 3 former > **some'times** *adverb* 1 occasionally 2 now and then > **some'what** [-hwot] *adverb* to some extent, rather > **some'where** [-hwair] *adverb*

som•er•sault [SUM-ər-sawlt] *noun* tumbling head over heels

som•nam•bu•list [som-NAM-byə-list] *noun* sleepwalker > **som•nam'bu•lism** *noun*

som•no•lent [SOM-nə-lənt] *adjective* 1 drowsy 2 causing sleep > **som'no•lence** *noun*

son [sun] *noun* male child > **son-in-law** *noun* daughter's husband

so•nar [SOH-nahr] *noun* device like echo sounder

so•na•ta [sə-NAH-tə] *noun* piece of music in several movements > **son•a•ti•na** [son-ə-TEE-nə]

DICTIONARY S THESAURUS

solemn *adjective* 1 FORMAL, ceremonial, dignified, grand, grave, momentous, stately
2 SERIOUS, earnest, grave, sedate, sober, staid

solemnity *noun* 1 SERIOUSNESS, earnestness, gravity
2 FORMALITY, grandeur, impressiveness, momentousness

solicitous *adjective* CONCERNED, anxious, attentive, careful

solicitude *noun* CONCERN, anxiety, attentiveness, care, consideration, regard

solid *adjective* 1 FIRM, compact, concrete, dense, hard
2 STRONG, stable, sturdy, substantial, unshakable
3 SOUND, genuine, good, pure, real, reliable
4 RELIABLE, dependable, trusty, upright, upstanding, worthy

solidarity *noun* UNITY, accord, cohesion, concordance, like-mindedness, team spirit, unanimity, unification

solidify *verb* HARDEN, cake, coagulate, cohere, congeal, jell, set

solitary *adjective* 1 UNSOCIABLE, cloistered, isolated, reclusive, unsocial
2 SINGLE, alone, lone, sole
3 LONELY, companionless, friendless, lonesome
4 ISOLATED, hidden, out-of-the-way, remote, unfrequented

solitude *noun* ISOLATION, loneliness, privacy, retirement, seclusion

solution *noun* 1 ANSWER, explanation, key, result
2 (*chemistry*) MIXTURE, blend, compound, mix, solvent

solve *verb* ANSWER, clear up, crack, decipher, disentangle, get to the bottom of, resolve, unravel, work out

somber *adjective* 1 DARK, dim, drab, dull, gloomy, sober
2 GLOOMY, dismal, doleful, grave, joyless, lugubrious, mournful, sad, sober

somebody *noun* CELEBRITY, dignitary, household name, luminary, megastar (*informal*), name, notable, personage, star

someday *adverb* EVENTUALLY, one day, one of these days *or* one of these fine days, sooner or later

somehow *adverb* ONE WAY OR ANOTHER, by fair means or foul, by hook or crook *or* by hook or by crook, by some means or other, come hell or high water (*informal*), come what may

sometimes *adverb* OCCASIONALLY, at times, now and then

noun short sonata

son et lumière [saw-nay-luu-MYAIR] Fr. entertainment staged at night at famous place, building, giving dramatic history of it with lighting and sound effects

song [sawng] *noun* 1 singing 2 poem, etc. for singing > **song'ster** *noun* 1 singer 2 songbird > **song'stress** [-stris] *noun feminine*

sonic [SON-ik] *adjective* pert. to sound waves > **sonic boom** explosive sound caused by aircraft traveling at supersonic speed

son•net [SON-it] *noun* fourteen-line poem with definite rhyme scheme > **son•net•eer** [son-i-TEER] *noun* writer of this

so•no•rous [sə-NOR-ees, SAHN-ər-us] *adjective* giving out (deep) sound, resonant > **so•nor'i•ty** *noun*

soon *adverb* 1 in a short time 2 before long 3 early, quickly

soot [suut] *noun* black powdery substance formed by burning of coal, etc. > **soot'y** *adjective* **soot•i•er, soot•i•est** of, like soot

sooth *noun* truth > **sooth'say•er** *noun* 1 one who foretells future 2 diviner

soothe [sooth] *verb transitive* **soothed, sooth•ing** 1 make calm, tranquil 2 relieve (pain, etc.)

sop *noun* 1 piece of bread, etc. soaked in liquid 2 concession, bribe ▷ *verb transitive* **sopped, sop•ping** 3 steep in water, etc. 4 soak (up) > **sopping** *adjective* completely soaked

soph•ist [SOF-ist] *noun* fallacious reasoner, quibbler > **soph'ism** [-izm] *noun* specious argument > **soph'ist•ry** *noun*

so•phis•ti•cate [sə-FIS-ti-kayt] *verb transitive* **-cat•ed, -cat•ing** 1 make artificial, spoil, falsify, corrupt ▷ *noun* [-kit] 2 sophisticated person > **sophisticated** *adjective* 1 having refined or cultured tastes, habits 2 worldly wise 3 superficially clever 4 complex > **so•phis•ti•ca'tion** *noun*

soph•o•more [SOF-ə-mor] *noun* student in second year at high school or college > **soph•o•mor'ic** intellectually pretentious

sop•o•rif•ic [sop-ə-RIF-ik] *adjective* causing sleep (esp. by drugs)

so•pran•o [sə-PRAN-oh] *noun, plural* **-pran•os** 1 highest voice in women and boys 2 singer with this voice 3 musical part for it

sor•bet [sor-BAY] *noun* sherbet

sor•cer•er [SOR-sər-ər] *noun* magician > **sor'cer•ess** [-ris] *noun feminine* > **sor'cer•y** *noun, plural* **-ies** witchcraft, magic

sor'did *adjective* 1 mean, squalid 2 ignoble, base > **sor'did•ly** *adverb* > **sor'did•ness** [-nis] *noun*

sore [sor] *adjective* **sor•er, sor•est** 1 painful 2 causing annoyance 3 severe 4 distressed 5 annoyed ▷ *adverb* (*obsolete*) 6 grievously, intensely ▷ *noun* 7 sore place, ulcer, boil, etc. > **sore'ly** *adverb* 1 grievously 2 greatly

sor•ghum [SOR-gəm] *noun* kind of grass cultivated for grain

sor•rel [SOR-əl] *noun* 1 plant 2 reddish-brown color 3 horse of this color ▷ *adjective* 4 of this color

sor•row [SOR-oh] *noun* 1 pain of mind, grief, sadness ▷ *verb intransitive* 2 grieve > **sor'row•ful** [-fəl] *adjective*

sor•ry [SOR-ee] *adjective* **-ri•er, -ri•est** 1 feeling pity or regret 2 distressed 3 miserable, wretched 4 mean, poor > **sor'ri•ly** *adverb*

sort *noun* 1 kind or class ▷ *verb transitive* 2 classify > **sort'er** *noun*

sor•tie [SOR-tee] *noun* sally by besieged forces

SOS *noun* 1 international code signal of distress

DICTIONARY • THESAURUS

song *noun* BALLAD, air, anthem, carol, chant, chorus, ditty, hymn, number, psalm, tune

soon *adverb* BEFORE LONG, in the near future, shortly

soothe *verb* 1 CALM, allay, appease, de-stress, hush, lull, mollify, pacify, quiet, still 2 RELIEVE, alleviate, assuage, ease

soothing *adjective* CALMING, emollient, palliative, relaxing, restful

soothsayer *noun* PROPHET, diviner, fortune-teller, seer, sibyl

sophisticated *adjective* 1 CULTURED, cosmopolitan, cultivated, refined, urbane, worldly 2 COMPLEX, advanced, complicated, delicate, elaborate, intricate, refined, subtle

sophistication *noun* SAVOIR-FAIRE, finesse, poise, urbanity, worldliness, worldly wisdom

soporific *adjective* 1 SLEEP-INDUCING, sedative, somnolent, tranquilizing ▷ *noun* 2 SEDATIVE, narcotic, opiate, tranquilizer

sorcerer *noun* MAGICIAN, enchanter, necromancer, warlock, witch, wizard

sorcery *noun* BLACK MAGIC, black art, enchantment, magic, necromancy, witchcraft, wizardry

sordid *adjective* 1 DIRTY, filthy, foul, mean, scuzzy (*slang*), seedy, sleazy, squalid, unclean 2 BASE, debauched, degenerate, low, shabby, shameful, vicious, vile 3 MERCENARY, avaricious, covetous, grasping, selfish

sore *adjective* 1 PAINFUL, angry, burning, inflamed, irritated, raw, sensitive, smarting, tender 2 ANNOYING, severe, sharp, troublesome 3 ANNOYED, aggrieved, angry, cross, hurt, irked, irritated, pained, resentful, stung, upset 4 URGENT, acute, critical, desperate, dire, extreme, pressing

sorrow *noun* 1 GRIEF, anguish, distress, heartache, heartbreak, misery, mourning, regret, sadness, unhappiness, woe 2 AFFLICTION, hardship, misfortune, trial, tribulation, trouble, woe ▷ *verb* 3 GRIEVE, agonize, bemoan, be sad, bewail, lament, mourn

sorrowful *adjective* SAD, dejected, dismal, doleful, grieving, miserable, mournful, sorry, unhappy, woebegone, woeful, wretched

sorry *adjective* 1 REGRETFUL, apologetic, conscience-stricken, contrite, penitent, remorseful, repentant, shamefaced 2 SYMPATHETIC, commiserative, compassionate, full of pity, moved 3 WRETCHED, deplorable, mean, miserable, pathetic, pitiful, poor, sad

sort *noun* 1 KIND, brand, category, class, ilk, make, nature, order, quality, style, type, variety ▷ *verb* 2 ARRANGE, categorize, classify, divide, grade, group, order, put in order, rank

sort out *verb* 1 RESOLVE, clarify, clear up

2 call for help
so-so [SOH-soh] *adjective* 1 mediocre ▷ *adverb* 2 tolerably
sot *noun* habitual drunkard
sot•to vo•ce [SOT-oh VOH-chee] It. in an undertone
souf•flé [soo-FLAY] *noun* 1 dish of eggs beaten to froth, flavored and baked 2 dessert like this of various ingredients
sough [rhymes with **cow**] *noun* low murmuring sound as of wind in trees
sought [sawt] *pt./pp. of* **seek**
soul [sohl] *noun* 1 spiritual and immortal part of human being 2 example, pattern 3 person 4 (*also* **soul music**) type of Black music combining urban blues with jazz, pop, etc. > **soul'ful** [-fəl] *adjective* full of emotion or sentiment > **soul'less** [-lis] *adjective* 1 mechanical 2 lacking sensitivity or nobility 3 heartless, cruel
sound[1] [sownd] *noun* 1 what is heard 2 noise ▷ *verb intransitive* 3 make a sound 4 seem 5 give impression of ▷ *verb transitive* 6 cause to sound 7 utter > **sound barrier** hypothetical barrier to flight at speed of sound waves > **sound bite** short pithy statement extracted from a longer speech for use esp. in television or radio news reports > **sound track** recorded sound accompaniment of motion picture, etc.
sound[2] *adjective* **-er, -est** 1 in good condition 2 solid 3 of good judgment 4 legal 5 solvent 6 thorough 7 effective 8 watertight 9 deep > **sound'ly** *adverb* thoroughly
sound[3] *verb transitive* 1 find depth of, as water 2 ascertain views of 3 probe > **sound'ings** *plural noun* measurements taken by sounding
sound[4] *noun* 1 channel 2 strait
soup [soop] *noun* liquid food made by boiling or simmering meat, vegetables, etc. > **soup'y** *adjective* **soup•i•er, soup•i•est** 1 like soup 2 murky 3 sentimental
sour [sowr] *adjective* 1 acid 2 gone bad 3 rancid 4 peevish 5 disagreeable ▷ *verb* 6 make, become sour > **sour'ness** [-nis] *noun* > **sour'puss** [-puus] *noun* (*informal*) sullen, sour-faced person
source [sors] *noun* 1 origin, starting point 2 spring
souse [rhymes with **louse**] *verb* **soused, sous•ing** 1 plunge, drench 2 pickle ▷ *noun* 3 sousing 4 brine for pickling 5 (*slang*) drunkard > **soused** *adjective* (*slang*) drunk
south [sowth] *noun* 1 cardinal point opposite north 2 region, part of country, etc. lying to that side ▷ *adjective, adverb* 3 (that is) toward south > **south'ward** [-wərd] *adjective, adverb* > **south'wards** [-wərdz] *adverb* > **south•er•ly** [SUTH-ər-lee] *adjective* 1 toward south ▷ *noun, plural* **-lies** 2 wind from the south > **south•ern** [SUTH-ərn] *adjective* in south > **south•west•er** [sowth-WES-tər] *noun* wind, storm from the southwest
sou•ve•nir [soo-və-NEER] *noun* keepsake, memento
sov•er•eign [SOV-rin] *noun* 1 king, queen 2 former British gold coin worth 20 shillings ▷ *adjective* 3 supreme 4 efficacious > **sov'er•eign•ty** *noun, plural* **-ties** 1 supreme power and right to exercise it 2 dominion 3 independent state
so•vi•et [SOH-vee-et] *noun* 1 formerly, elected council at various levels of government in USSR 2 (**So•vi•et**) official or citizen of the former USSR ▷ *adjective* 3 of the former USSR
sow[1] [soh] *verb intransitive* **sowed, sown** *or* **sowed, sow•ing** 1 scatter, plant seed ▷ *verb transitive* **sowed, sown** *or* **sowed, sow•ing** 2 scatter, deposit (seed) 3 spread abroad
sow[2] [rhymes with **cow**] *noun* female adult pig
soy•bean [SOI-been] *noun* edible bean used as livestock feed, meat substitute, etc.
soy sauce [SOI saws] sauce made by fermenting soybeans in brine
spa [spah] *noun* 1 medicinal spring 2 place, resort with one
space [spays] *noun* 1 extent 2 room 3 period 4 empty place 5 area 6 expanse 7 region beyond Earth's atmosphere ▷ *verb transitive* **spaced, spac•ing** 8 place at intervals > **spa'cious** [-shəs] *adjective* roomy, extensive > **space'craft,**

DICTIONARY

S

THESAURUS

2 ORGANIZE, tidy up
soul *noun* 1 SPIRIT, essence, life, vital force
2 PERSONIFICATION, embodiment, epitome, essence, quintessence, type
3 PERSON, being, body, creature, individual, man *or* woman
sound[1] *noun* 1 NOISE, din, report, reverberation, tone
2 IMPRESSION, drift, idea, look
▷ *verb* 3 RESOUND, echo, reverberate
4 SEEM, appear, look
5 PRONOUNCE, announce, articulate, declare, express, utter
sound[2] *adjective* 1 PERFECT, fit, healthy, intact, solid, unhurt, unimpaired, uninjured, whole
2 SENSIBLE, correct, logical, proper, prudent, rational, reasonable, right, trustworthy, valid, well-founded, wise
3 DEEP, unbroken, undisturbed, untroubled
sound[3] *verb* FATHOM, plumb, probe
sound out *verb* PROBE, canvass, pump, question, see how the land lies
sour *adjective* 1 SHARP, acetic, acid, bitter, pungent, tart
2 GONE OFF, curdled, gone bad, turned
3 ILL-NATURED, acrimonious, disagreeable, embittered, ill-tempered, peevish, tart, ungenerous, waspish
source *noun* 1 ORIGIN, author, beginning, cause, derivation, fount, originator
2 INFORMANT, authority
souvenir *noun* KEEPSAKE, memento, reminder
sovereign *noun* 1 MONARCH, chief, emperor *or* empress, king *or* queen, potentate, prince, ruler
▷ *adjective* 2 SUPREME, absolute, imperial, kingly *or* queenly, principal, royal, ruling
3 EXCELLENT, effectual, efficacious, efficient
sovereignty *noun* SUPREME POWER, domination, kingship, primacy, supremacy
sow *verb* SCATTER, implant, plant, seed
space *noun* 1 ROOM, capacity, elbowroom, expanse, extent, leeway, margin, play, scope
2 GAP, blank, distance, interval, omission
3 TIME, duration, interval, period, span, while
spacious *adjective* ROOMY, ample, broad, capacious, commodious, expansive, extensive,

space'ship *noun* vehicle for travel beyond Earth's atmosphere > **space shuttle** vehicle for repeated space flights > **space'suit** *noun* sealed, pressurized suit worn by astronaut

spade[1] [spayd] *noun* tool for digging > **spade•work** [SPAYD-wurk] *noun* arduous preparatory work

spade[2] *noun* leaf-shaped black symbol on playing card

spa•ghet•ti [spə-GET-ee] *noun* pasta in form of long strings

spake [spayk] *(obsolete) pt. of* **speak**

spam *computers. (slang)* ▷ *verb* **spams, spamming, spammed** 1 send unsolicited text messages simultaneously to many cell phones ▷ *noun* 2 unsolicited e-mail or text messages sent in this way

span *noun* 1 space from thumb to little finger as measure 2 extent, space 3 stretch of arch, etc. ▷ *verb transitive* **spanned, span•ning** 4 stretch over 5 measure with hand

span•gle [SPANG-gəl] *noun* 1 small shiny metallic ornament ▷ *verb transitive* **-gled, -gling** 2 decorate with spangles

span•iel [SPAN-yəl] *noun* breed of dog with long ears and silky hair

spank [spangk] *verb transitive* slap with flat of hand, etc. esp. on buttocks ▷ *noun* > **spank'ing** *noun* 1 series of spanks ▷ *adjective* 2 quick, lively 3 large, fine

spar[1] [spahr] *noun* pole, beam, esp. as part of ship's rigging

spar[2] *verb intransitive* **sparred, spar•ring** 1 box 2 dispute, esp. in fun ▷ *noun* 3 sparring

spar[3] *noun* various kinds of crystalline mineral

spare [spair] *verb transitive* **spared, spar•ing** 1 leave unhurt 2 show mercy 3 abstain from using 4 do without 5 give away ▷ *adjective* 6 additional 7 in reserve 8 thin 9 lean 10 scanty ▷ *noun* 11 spare part (for machine) > **sparing** *adjective* economical, careful

spark [spahrk] *noun* 1 small glowing or burning particle 2 flash of light produced by electrical discharge 3 vivacity, humor 4 trace 5 in internal-combustion engines, electric spark (in spark plug) that ignites explosive mixture in cylinder ▷ *verb* 6 emit sparks 7 kindle, excite 8 *(obsolete)* woo

spar•kle [SPAHR-kəl] *verb intransitive* **-kled, -kling** 1 glitter 2 effervesce 3 scintillate ▷ *noun* 4 small spark 5 glitter 6 flash 7 lustre > **sparkling** *adjective* 1 flashing 2 glittering 3 brilliant 4 lively 5 (of wines) effervescent

spar•row [SPA-roh] *noun* small finch

sparse [spahrs] *adjective* **spars•er, spars•est** thinly scattered

spar•tan [SPAHR-tn] *adjective* 1 hardy 2 austere 3 frugal 4 undaunted

spasm [SPAZ-əm] *noun* 1 sudden convulsive (muscular) contraction 2 sudden burst of activity, etc. > **spas•mod•ic** [spaz-MOD-ik] *adjective* occurring in spasms

spas•tic [SPAS-tik] *noun* 1 *(often considered offensive)* person who has cerebral palsy ▷ *adjective* 2 affected by involuntary muscle contractions: *spastic colon* 3 *(often considered offensive)* suffering from cerebral palsy

spat[1] *pt. of* **spit**[1]

spat[2] *noun* short gaiter

spat[3] *noun* 1 slight quarrel ▷ *verb intransitive* **spat•ted, spat•ting** 2 quarrel

spate [spayt] *noun* 1 rush, outpouring 2 flood

spa•tial [SPAY-shəl] *adjective* of, in space

spat•ter [SPAT-ər] *verb transitive* 1 splash, cast drops over ▷ *verb intransitive* 2 be scattered in drops ▷ *noun* 3 slight splash 4 sprinkling

spat•u•la [SPACH-ə-lə] *noun* utensil with broad, flat blade for various purposes

spav'in [SPA-vin] *noun* injury to, growth on horse's leg > **spav'ined** *adjective* lame, decrepit

spawn *noun* 1 eggs of fish, frog, etc. ▷ *verb intransitive* (of fish or frog) cast eggs 2 produce in great numbers

spay *verb transitive* remove ovaries from (animal)

speak [speek] *verb* **spoke, spo•ken, speak•ing** 1 utter words 2 converse 3 deliver discourse 4

huge, large, sizable *or* sizeable

spadework *noun* PREPARATION, donkey-work, groundwork, labor

span *noun* 1 EXTENT, amount, distance, length, reach, spread, stretch
2 PERIOD, duration, spell, term
▷ *verb* 3 EXTEND ACROSS, bridge, cover, cross, link, traverse

spank *verb* SMACK, cuff, paddle, slap

spar *verb* ARGUE, bicker, row, scrap *(informal)*, squabble, wrangle

spare *adjective* 1 EXTRA, additional, free, leftover, odd, over, superfluous, surplus, unoccupied, unused, unwanted
2 THIN, gaunt, lean, meager, wiry
▷ *verb* 3 HAVE MERCY ON, be merciful to, go easy on *(informal)*, leave, let off *(informal)*, pardon, save from
4 AFFORD, do without, give, grant, let (someone) have, manage without, part with

spare time *noun* LEISURE, free time, odd moments

sparing *adjective* ECONOMICAL, careful, frugal, prudent, saving, thrifty

spark *noun* 1 FLICKER, flare, flash, gleam, glint
2 TRACE, atom, hint, jot, scrap, vestige
▷ *verb* 3 *(often with off)* START, inspire, precipitate, provoke, set off, stimulate, trigger *or* trigger off

sparkle *verb* 1 GLITTER, dance, flash, gleam, glint, glisten, scintillate, shimmer, shine, twinkle
▷ *noun* 2 GLITTER, brilliance, flash, flicker, gleam, glint, twinkle
3 VIVACITY, dash, élan, life, spirit, vitality

sparse *adjective* SCATTERED, few and far between, meager, scanty, scarce

spartan *adjective* AUSTERE, ascetic, disciplined, frugal, plain, rigorous, self-denying, severe, strict

spasm *noun* 1 CONVULSION, contraction, paroxysm, twitch
2 BURST, eruption, fit, frenzy, outburst, seizure

spasmodic *adjective* SPORADIC, convulsive, erratic, fitful, intermittent, irregular, jerky

spate *noun* FLOOD, deluge, flow, outpouring, rush, torrent

speak *verb* 1 TALK, articulate, converse, express, pronounce, say, state, tell, utter
2 LECTURE, address, declaim, discourse, hold

utter 5 pronounce 6 express 7 communicate in > **speak'er** *noun* 1 one who speaks 2 one who specializes in speechmaking 3 (**Speak'er**) official chairman of US House of Representatives, other legislative bodies 4 loudspeaker > **speak'er•phone** *noun* telephone including an external microphone and loudspeaker, allowing several people to participate in a call

spear [speer] *noun* 1 long pointed weapon 2 slender shoot, as of asparagus ▷ *verb transitive* 3 transfix, pierce, wound with spear > **spear'head** [-hed] *noun* leading force in attack, campaign ▷ *verb transitive*

spear•mint [SPEER-mint] *noun* type of mint

spec [spek] *noun* **on spec** (*informal*) as a risk or gamble

spe•cial [SPESH-əl] *adjective* 1 beyond the usual 2 particular, individual 3 distinct 4 limited > **spe'cial•ist** *noun* one who devotes self to special subject or branch of subject > **spe'cial•ty** *noun, plural* **-ties** special product, skill, characteristic, etc. > **spe'cial•ize** *verb intransitive* **-ized, -iz•ing** 1 be specialist 2 be adapted to special function or environment ▷ *verb transitive* **-ized, -iz•ing** 3 make special

spe•cie [SPEE-shee] *noun* coined, as distinct from paper, money

spe•cies [SPEE-sheez] *noun, plural* **species** 1 sort, kind, esp. animals, etc. 2 class 3 subdivision

spe•cif•ic [spə-SIF-ik] *adjective* 1 definite 2 exact in detail 3 characteristic of a thing or kind > **spe•cif'i•cal•ly** *adverb* > **spec'i•fy** *verb transitive* **-fied, -fy•ing** state definitely or in detail > **spec•i•fi•ca'tion** [-KAY-shən] *noun* detailed description of something to be made, done > **specific gravity** ratio of density of substance to that of water

spec•i•men [SPES-ə-mən] *noun* 1 part typifying whole 2 individual example

spe•cious [SPEE-shəs] *adjective* deceptively plausible, but false > **spe'cious•ly** *adverb* > **spe'cious•ness** [-nis] *noun*

speck [spek] *noun* 1 small spot, particle ▷ *verb transitive* 2 spot > **speck•le** [SPEK-l] *noun, verb transitive* **-led, -ling** speck

spec•ta•cle [SPEK-tə-kəl] *noun* 1 show 2 thing exhibited 3 ridiculous sight > **spectacles** *plural noun* eyeglasses > **spec•tac'u•lar** *adjective* 1 impressive 2 showy 3 grand 4 magnificent ▷ *noun* 5 lavishly produced performance > **spec•ta•tor** [SPEK-tay-tər] *noun* one who looks on

spec•ter [SPEK-tər] *noun* 1 ghost 2 image of something unpleasant > **spec•tral** [-trəl] *adjective* ghostly

spec•trum [SPEK-trəm] *noun, plural* **-tra** [-trə] 1 band of colors into which beam of light can be decomposed e.g. by prism 2 range (of e.g. opinions, occupations) > **spec'tro•scope** [-trə-skohp] *noun* instrument for producing, examining physical spectra

spec•u•late [SPEK-yə-layt] *verb intransitive* **-lat•ed, -lat•ing** 1 guess, conjecture 2 engage in (risky) commercial transactions > **spec•u•la'tion** *noun* > **spec'u•la•tive** [-lə-tiv] *adjective* given to, characterized by speculation > **spec'u•la•tor** *noun*

spec•u•lum [SPEK-yə-ləm] *noun, plural* **-lums** 1 mirror 2 reflector of polished metal, esp. in reflecting telescopes

speech *noun* 1 act, faculty of speaking 2 words,

---

forth

speaker *noun* LECTURER, orator, public speaker, spokesman *or* spokeswoman, spokesperson

speak out, speak up *verb* SPEAK ONE'S MIND, have one's say, make one's position plain, voice one's opinions

spearhead *verb* LEAD, head, initiate, launch, pioneer, set in motion, set off

special *adjective* 1 EXCEPTIONAL, extraordinary, important, memorable, significant, uncommon, unique, unusual
2 PARTICULAR, appropriate, distinctive, individual, precise, specific

specialist *noun* EXPERT, authority, buff (*informal*), connoisseur, consultant, master, professional

speciality *noun* FORTE, bag (*slang, dated*), métier, pièce de résistance (*French*), specialty

species *noun* KIND, breed, category, class, group, sort, type, variety

specific *adjective* 1 PARTICULAR, characteristic, distinguishing, special
2 DEFINITE, clear-cut, exact, explicit, express, precise, unequivocal

specification *noun* REQUIREMENT, condition, detail, particular, qualification, stipulation

specify *verb* STATE, define, designate, detail, indicate, mention, name, stipulate

specimen *noun* SAMPLE, example, exemplification, instance, model, pattern, representative, type

speck *noun* 1 MARK, blemish, dot, fleck, mote, speckle, spot, stain
2 PARTICLE, atom, bit, grain, iota, jot, mite, shred

speckled *adjective* FLECKED, dappled, dotted, mottled, spotted, sprinkled

spectacle *noun* 1 SIGHT, curiosity, marvel, phenomenon, scene, wonder
2 SHOW, display, event, exhibition, extravaganza, pageant, performance

spectacular *adjective* 1 IMPRESSIVE, cool (*informal*), dazzling, dramatic, grand, magnificent, phat (*slang*), sensational, splendid, striking, stunning (*informal*)
▷ *noun* 2 SHOW, display, spectacle

spectator *noun* ONLOOKER, bystander, looker-on, observer, viewer, watcher

specter *noun* GHOST, apparition, phantom, spirit, vision, wraith

speculate *verb* 1 CONJECTURE, consider, guess, hypothesize, suppose, surmise, theorize, wonder
2 GAMBLE, hazard, risk, venture

speculation *noun* 1 GUESSWORK, conjecture, hypothesis, opinion, supposition, surmise, theory
2 GAMBLE, hazard, risk

speculative *adjective* HYPOTHETICAL, academic, conjectural, notional, suppositional, theoretical

speech *noun* 1 COMMUNICATION, conversation, dialogue, discussion, talk
2 TALK, address, discourse, homily, lecture, oration, spiel (*informal*)
3 LANGUAGE, articulation, dialect, diction, enunciation, idiom, jargon, parlance, tongue

language **3** conversation **4** discourse **5** (formal) talk given before audience > **speech'i•fy** *verb intransitive* **-fied, -fy•ing** make speech, esp. long and tedious one > **speech'less** [-lis] *adjective* **1** mute **2** at a loss for words

speed *noun* **1** swiftness **2** rate of progress **3** degree of sensitivity of photographic film **4** (*slang*) amphetamine ▷ *verb* **sped** *or* **speed•ed, speed•ing 5** move quickly **6** drive vehicle at high speed **7** further **8** expedite > **speed'ing** *noun* driving (vehicle) at high speed, esp. over legal limit > **speed'i•ly** *adverb* > **speed'y** *adjective* **speed•i•er, speed•i•est 1** quick **2** rapid **3** nimble **4** prompt > **speed'boat** *noun* light fast motorboat > **speed•om'e•ter** [-OM-ə-tər] *noun* instrument to show speed of vehicle > **speed'way** *noun* track for automobile or motorcycle racing

spe•le•ol•o•gy [spee-lee-OL-ə-jee] *noun* study, exploring of caves > **spe•le•ol'o•gist** *noun*

spell[1] *verb transitive* **spelled** *or* **spelt, spell•ing 1** give letters of in order **2** read letter by letter **3** indicate, result in > **spelling** *noun* > **spell'check•er** *noun computing* program that finds words in a document that are not recognized as being correctly spelled > **spell out** make explicit

spell[2] *noun* **1** magic formula **2** enchantment > **spell'bound** [-bownd] *adjective* **1** enchanted **2** entranced

spell[3] *noun* (short) period of time, work

spend *verb transitive* **spent, spend•ing 1** pay out **2** pass (time) on activity, etc. **3** use up completely > **spend'thrift** *noun* wasteful person

sperm [spurm] *noun* **1** male reproductive cell **2** semen > **sper•mat'ic** *adjective* of sperm > **sperm'i•cide** [-sīd] *noun* drug, etc. that kills sperm

sper•ma•cet•i [spur-mə-SET-ee] *noun* white, waxy substance obtained from oil from head of sperm whale > **sperm whale** large, toothed whale

spew [spyoo] *verb* **1** vomit **2** gush

sphag•num [SFAG-nəm] *noun* moss that grows in bogs

sphere [sfeer] *noun* **1** ball, globe **2** range **3** field of action **4** status **5** position **6** province > **spher•i•cal** [SFER-i-kəl] *adjective*

sphinc•ter [SFINGK-tər] *noun* ring of muscle surrounding opening of hollow bodily organ

sphinx [sfingks] *noun, plural* **-es 1** figure in Egypt with lion's body and human head **2** (**Sphinx**) the great statue of this near the pyramids of Giza **3** monster, half woman, half lion **4** enigmatic person

spice [spīs] *noun* **1** aromatic or pungent vegetable substance **2** spices collectively **3** anything that adds flavor, relish, piquancy, interest, etc. ▷ *verb transitive* **spiced, spic•ing 4** season with spices, flavor > **spic'y** *adjective* **spic•i•er, spic•i•est 1** flavored with spices **2** slightly indecent, risqué

spick-and-span [SPIK-ən-SPAN] *adjective* **1** spotlessly clean **2** neat, smart, new-looking

spi•der [SPĪ-dər] *noun* small eight-legged creature that spins web to catch prey > **spi'der•y** *adjective*

spiel [speel] *noun* (*informal*) **1** glib (sales) talk ▷ *verb intransitive* **2** deliver spiel, recite > **spiel'er** *noun*

spig•ot [SPIG-ət] *noun* **1** peg or plug **2** faucet

spike [spīk] *noun* **1** sharp point **2** sharp pointed object **3** long flower cluster with flowers attached directly to the stalk ▷ *verb transitive* **spiked, spik•ing 4** pierce, fasten with spike **5** render ineffective **6** add alcohol to (drink)

spill *verb* **spilled** *or* **spilt, spill•ing 1** (cause to) pour from, flow over, fall out, esp. unintentionally **2** upset **3** be lost or wasted ▷ *noun* **4** spillway **5** spillage > **spill'age** [-ij] *noun* amount spilled > **spill'way** *noun* passageway through which excess water spills

DICTIONARY • THESAURUS

speechless *adjective* **1** MUTE, dumb, inarticulate, silent, wordless
2 ASTOUNDED, aghast, amazed, dazed, shocked

speed *noun* **1** SWIFTNESS, haste, hurry, pace, quickness, rapidity, rush, velocity
▷ *verb* **2** RACE, career, gallop, hasten, hurry, make haste, rush, tear, zoom
3 HELP, advance, aid, assist, boost, expedite, facilitate

speed up *verb* ACCELERATE, gather momentum, increase the tempo

speedy *adjective* QUICK, express, fast, hasty, headlong, hurried, immediate, precipitate, prompt, rapid, swift

spell[1] *verb* INDICATE, augur, imply, mean, point to, portend, signify

spell[2] *noun* **1** INCANTATION, charm
2 FASCINATION, allure, bewitchment, enchantment, glamour, magic

spell[3] *noun* PERIOD, bout, course, interval, season, stretch, term, time

spellbound *adjective* ENTRANCED, bewitched, captivated, charmed, enthralled, fascinated, gripped, mesmerized, rapt

spend *verb* **1** PAY OUT, disburse, expend, fork out (*slang*)
2 PASS, fill, occupy, while away
3 USE UP, consume, dissipate, drain, empty, exhaust, run through, squander, waste

spendthrift *noun* **1** SQUANDERER, big spender, profligate, spender, waster
▷ *adjective* **2** WASTEFUL, extravagant, improvident, prodigal, profligate

spew *verb* VOMIT, barf (*slang*), disgorge, puke (*slang*), regurgitate, throw up (*informal*)

sphere *noun* **1** BALL, circle, globe, globule, orb
2 FIELD, capacity, department, domain, function, patch, province, realm, scope, territory, turf (*slang*)

spherical *adjective* ROUND, globe-shaped, globular, rotund

spice *noun* **1** SEASONING, relish, savor
2 EXCITEMENT, color, pep, piquancy, zest, zing (*informal*)

spicy *adjective* **1** HOT, aromatic, piquant, savory, seasoned
2 (*informal*) SCANDALOUS, hot (*informal*), indelicate, racy, ribald, risqué, suggestive, titillating

spike *noun* **1** POINT, barb, prong, spine
▷ *verb* **2** IMPALE, spear, spit, stick

spill *verb* **1** POUR, discharge, disgorge, overflow, slop over
▷ *noun* **2** FALL, tumble

spin *verb* **spun, spin•ning** 1 (cause to) revolve rapidly 2 whirl 3 twist into thread 4 prolong 5 tell (a story) 6 fish with lure ▷ *noun* 7 spinning 8 (of aircraft) descent in dive with continued rotation 9 rapid run or ride 10 *politics* interpretation (of event, speech, etc.) to gain partisan advantage > **spinning** *noun* act, process of drawing out and twisting into threads, as wool, cotton, flax, etc. > **spinning wheel** household machine with large wheel turned by treadle for spinning wool, etc. into thread > **spin doctor** (*informal*) person who provides a favourable slant to a news item or policy on behalf of a political personality or party > **spin-dry** *verb transitive* **-dried, -dry•ing** spin clothes in (washing) machine to remove excess water > **spin machine** group of people acting together to present news or information in a way that creates a particular impression

spin•ach [SPIN-ich] *noun* dark green leafy vegetable

spin•dle [SPIN-dl] *noun* rod, axis for spinning > **spin'dly** *adjective* **-dli•er, -dli•est** 1 long and slender 2 attenuated

spin'drift *noun* spray blown along surface of sea

spine [spīn] *noun* 1 backbone 2 thin spike, esp. on fish, etc. 3 ridge 4 back of book > **spi'nal** [-əl] *adjective* > **spine'less** [-lis] *adjective* 1 lacking spine 2 cowardly

spin•et [SPIN-it] *noun* 1 small piano 2 small harpsichord

spin•na•ker [SPIN-ə-kər] *noun* large yacht sail

spin•ster [SPIN-stər] *noun* unmarried woman

spi•ral [SPĪ-rəl] *noun* 1 continuous curve drawn at ever increasing distance from fixed point 2 anything resembling this 3 *football* kick or pass turning on longer axis ▷ *verb* **-raled, -ral•ing** 4 of e.g. football or inflation, (cause to) take spiral course ▷ *adjective*

spire [spīr] *noun* 1 pointed part of steeple 2 pointed stem of plant

spir'it *noun* 1 life principle animating body 2 disposition 3 liveliness 4 courage 5 frame of mind 6 essential character or meaning 7 soul 8 ghost 9 liquid got by distillation, alcohol ▷ *verb transitive* 10 carry away mysteriously > **spir'its** *plural noun* 1 emotional state 2 strong alcoholic drink e.g. whiskey > **spir'it•ed** [-id] *adjective* lively > **spir'it•less** [-lis] *adjective* listless, apathetic > **spir•it•u•al** [-choo-əl] *adjective* 1 given to, interested in things of the spirit ▷ *noun* 2 religious song, hymn > **spir'it•u•al•ism** *noun* belief that spirits of the dead communicate with the living > **spir'it•u•al•ist** *noun* > **spir'it•u•ous** *adjective* alcoholic > **spirit level** glass tube containing bubble in liquid, used to check horizontal, vertical surfaces

spirt *noun see* **spurt**

spit[1] *verb* **spit** *or* **spat, spit•ting** 1 eject saliva 2 eject from mouth ▷ *noun* 3 spitting, saliva > **spit•tle** [SPIT-l] *noun* saliva > **spit'ball** *noun* 1 illegal pitch of baseball moistened with saliva by pitcher 2 ball of chewed paper used as missile > **spit•toon'** *noun* vessel to spit into > **spit'fire** *noun* person, esp. woman or girl, with fiery temper

spit[2] *noun* 1 sharp rod to put through meat for roasting 2 sandy point projecting into the sea ▷ *verb transitive* **spit•ted, spit•ting** 3 thrust through

spite [spīt] *noun* 1 malice ▷ *verb transitive* **spit•ed, spit•ing** 2 thwart spitefully > **spite'ful** [-fəl] *adjective* > **in spite of** *preposition* 1 regardless of 2 notwithstanding

splash *verb* 1 scatter liquid about or on, over something 2 print, display prominently ▷ *noun* 3 sound of this 4 patch, esp. of color 5 (effect of) extravagant display 6 small amount

splat *noun* wet, slapping sound

splat•ter [SPLAT-ər] *verb, noun* spatter

splay *adjective* 1 spread out 2 slanting 3 turned

DICTIONARY

S

THESAURUS

spin *verb* 1 REVOLVE, gyrate, pirouette, reel, rotate, turn, twirl, whirl
2 REEL, swim, whirl
▷ *noun* 3 REVOLUTION, gyration, roll, whirl
4 (*informal*) DRIVE, joy ride (*informal*), ride

spine *noun* 1 BACKBONE, spinal column, vertebrae, vertebral column
2 BARB, needle, quill, ray, spike, spur

spine-chilling *adjective* FRIGHTENING, bloodcurdling, eerie, horrifying, scary (*informal*), spooky (*informal*), terrifying

spineless *adjective* WEAK, cowardly, faint-hearted, feeble, gutless (*informal*), lily-livered, soft, weak-kneed (*informal*)

spin out *verb* PROLONG, amplify, delay, drag out, draw out, extend, lengthen

spiral *noun* 1 COIL, corkscrew, helix, whorl
▷ *adjective* 2 COILED, helical, whorled, winding

spirit *noun* 1 LIFE FORCE, life, soul, vital spark
2 FEELING, atmosphere, gist, tenor, tone
3 TEMPERAMENT, attitude, character, disposition, outlook, temper
4 LIVELINESS, animation, brio, energy, enthusiasm, fire, force, life, mettle, vigor, zest
5 COURAGE, backbone, gameness, grit, guts (*informal*), spunk (*informal*)
6 ESSENCE, intention, meaning, purport, purpose, sense, substance
7 GHOST, apparition, phantom, specter
8 ▷ **spirits** MOOD, feelings, frame of mind, morale
▷ *verb* 9 (*with away or off*) REMOVE, abduct, abstract, carry, purloin, seize, steal, whisk

spirited *adjective* LIVELY, active, animated, energetic, feisty (*informal*), mettlesome, vivacious

spiritual *adjective* SACRED, devotional, divine, holy, religious

spit *verb* 1 EJECT, expectorate, splutter, throw out
▷ *noun* 2 SALIVA, dribble, drool, slaver, spittle

spite *noun* 1 MALICE, animosity, hatred, ill will, malevolence, spitefulness, spleen, venom
2 ▷ **in spite of** DESPITE, though *or* even though, notwithstanding, regardless of
▷ *verb* 3 HURT, annoy, harm, injure, vex

spiteful *adjective* MALICIOUS, bitchy (*informal*), ill-natured, malevolent, nasty, vindictive

splash *verb* 1 SCATTER, shower, slop, spatter, spray, sprinkle, wet
2 PUBLICIZE, broadcast, tout, trumpet
▷ *noun* 3 DASH, burst, patch, spattering, touch
4 (*informal*) DISPLAY, effect, impact, sensation, stir

splash out *verb* (*informal*) SPEND, be extravagant,

outward ▷ *verb transitive* 4 spread out 5 twist outward ▷ *noun* 6 slanted surface > **splay'foot•ed** [-fuut-id] *adjective* flat and broad (of foot)

spleen *noun* 1 organ in the abdomen 2 anger 3 irritable or morose temper > **sple•net•ic** [splə-NET-ik] *adjective*

splen'did *adjective* magnificent, brilliant, excellent > **splen'did•ly** *adverb* > **splen'dor** [-dər] *noun*

splice [splīs] *verb transitive* **spliced, splic•ing** 1 join by interweaving strands 2 join (wood) by overlapping 3 (*informal*) join in marriage ▷ *noun* 4 spliced joint

spline [splīn] *noun* narrow groove, ridge, strip, esp. joining wood, etc.

splint *noun* rigid support for broken limb, etc.

splin•ter [SPLIN-tər] *noun* 1 thin fragment ▷ *verb intransitive* 2 break into fragments, shiver > **splinter group** group that separates from main party, organization, oft. after disagreement

split *verb* **split, split'ting** 1 break asunder 2 separate 3 divide 4 (*slang*) depart ▷ *noun* 5 crack, fissure 6 dessert of fruit, usu. banana, and ice cream

splotch [sploch] *noun, verb* splash, daub > **splotch'y** *adjective* **splotch•i•er, splotch•i•est**

splurge [splurj] *verb* **splurged, splurg•ing** spend money extravagantly ▷ *noun*

splut•ter [SPLUT-ər] *verb* 1 make hissing, spitting sounds 2 utter incoherently with spitting sounds ▷ *noun*

spoil *verb* **spoiled** *or* **spoilt, spoil•ing** 1 damage, injure 2 damage manners or behavior of (esp. child) by indulgence 3 pillage 4 go bad ▷ *noun* 5 booty 6 waste material, esp. in mining (*also* **spoil'age**) > **spoil'er** *noun* slowing device on aircraft wing, etc. **spoiling for** eager for

spoke[1] [spohk] *pt. of* **speak** > **spokes'per•son, spokes'wo•man, spokes'man** *noun* one deputed to speak for others

spoke[2] *noun* radial bar of a wheel

spoken *pp of* **speak**

spo•li•a•tion [spoh-lee-AY-shən] *noun* 1 act of spoiling 2 robbery 3 destruction > **spo'li•ate** [-ayt] *verb* **-at•ed, -at•ing** despoil, plunder, pillage

spon'dee *noun* metrical foot consisting of two long syllables

sponge [spunj] *noun* 1 marine animal 2 its skeleton, or a synthetic substance like it, used to absorb liquids 3 type of light cake ▷ *verb transitive* **sponged, spong•ing** 4 wipe with sponge ▷ *verb intransitive* **sponged, spong•ing** 5 live meanly at expense of others 6 cadge > **spong'er** *noun* (*slang*) one who cadges, or lives at expense of others > **spon'gy** *adjective* **-gi•er, -gi•est** 1 spongelike 2 wet and soft

spon•sor [SPON-sər] *noun* 1 one promoting, advertising something 2 one who agrees to give money to a charity on completion of specified activity by another 3 one taking responsibility (esp. for welfare of child at baptism, i.e. godparent) 4 guarantor ▷ *verb transitive* 5 act as sponsor > **spon'sor•ship** *noun*

spon•ta•ne•ous [spon-TAY-nee-əs] *adjective* 1 voluntary 2 natural 3 not forced 4 produced without external force > **spon•ta•ne'i•ty** [-tə-NEE-i-tee] *noun*

spoof *noun* 1 mild satirical mockery 2 trick, hoax ▷ *verb*

spook *noun* 1 ghost ▷ *verb transitive* 2 haunt > **spook'y** *adjective* **spook•i•er, spook•i•est**

spool *noun* reel, bobbin

spoon *noun* 1 implement with shallow bowl at end of handle for carrying food to mouth, etc. ▷ *verb transitive* 2 lift with spoon > **spoon'ful** [-fəl] *noun, plural* **-fuls** [-fəlz] > **spoon'fed** *adjective* 1 fed (as if) with spoon 2 pampered

spoon•er•ism [SPOO-nə-riz-əm] *noun* amusing transposition of initial consonants, such as *half-warmed fish* for *half-formed wish*

spoor [spuur] *noun* 1 trail of wild animals ▷ *verb* 2 follow spoor

DICTIONARY • THESAURUS

---

spare no expense, splurge

splendid *adjective* 1 fantastic (*informal*), first-class, glorious, great (*informal*) MARVELOUS, wonderful
2 MAGNIFICENT, cool (*informal*), costly, gorgeous, impressive, lavish, luxurious, ornate, phat (*slang*), resplendent, rich, sumptuous, superb

splendor *noun* MAGNIFICENCE, brightness, brilliance, display, glory, grandeur, pomp, richness, show, spectacle, sumptuousness

splinter *noun* 1 SLIVER, chip, flake, fragment ▷ *verb* 2 SHATTER, disintegrate, fracture, split

split *verb* 1 BREAK, burst, come apart, come undone, crack, give way, open, rend, rip
2 SEPARATE, branch, cleave, disband, disunite, diverge, fork, part
3 SHARE OUT, allocate, allot, apportion, distribute, divide, halve, partition
▷ *noun* 4 CRACK, breach, division, fissure, gap, rent, rip, separation, slit, tear
5 DIVISION, breach, break-up, discord, dissension, estrangement, rift, rupture, schism
▷ *adjective* 6 DIVIDED, broken, cleft, cracked, fractured, ruptured

split up *verb* SEPARATE, break up, divorce, part

spoil *verb* 1 RUIN, damage, destroy, disfigure, harm, impair, injure, mar, mess up, trash (*slang*), wreck
2 OVERINDULGE, coddle, cosset, indulge, pamper
3 GO BAD, addle, curdle, decay, decompose, rot, turn

spoils *plural noun* BOOTY, loot, plunder, prey, swag (*slang*), treasure

spoilsport *noun* KILLJOY, damper, misery (*informal*), sourpuss, wet blanket (*informal*)

spoken *adjective* SAID, expressed, oral, told, unwritten, uttered, verbal, viva voce, voiced

spokesperson *noun* SPEAKER, mouthpiece, official, spin doctor (*informal*), spokesman *or* spokeswoman, voice

spongy *adjective* POROUS, absorbent

sponsor *noun* 1 BACKER, patron, promoter ▷ *verb* 2 BACK, finance, fund, patronize, promote, subsidize

spontaneous *adjective* UNPLANNED, impromptu, impulsive, instinctive, natural, unprompted, voluntary, willing

spoof *noun* (*informal*) PARODY, burlesque, caricature, mockery, satire

spooky *adjective* EERIE, chilling, creepy (*informal*), frightening, scary (*informal*), spine-chilling, uncanny, unearthly, weird

spo•rad•ic [spə-RAD-ik] *adjective* 1 intermittent 2 scattered, single > **spo•rad'i•cal•ly** *adverb*
spore [spor] *noun* minute reproductive organism of some plants and protozoans
sport *noun* 1 game, activity for pleasure, competition, exercise 2 enjoyment 3 mockery 4 cheerful person, good loser ▷ *verb transitive* 5 wear (esp. ostentatiously) ▷ *verb intransitive* 6 frolic 7 play (sport) > **sport'ing** *adjective* 1 of sport 2 behaving with fairness, generosity > **sport'ive** *adjective* playful > **sports car** fast (open) car > **sports jacket** man's casual jacket > **sports'man** [-mən] *noun, plural* **-men** 1 one who engages in sport 2 good loser > **sports'man•ship** *noun* > **sport utility vehicle** powerful four-wheel drive vehicle for rough terrain
spot *noun* 1 small mark, stain 2 blemish 3 pimple 4 place 5 (difficult) situation ▷ *verb transitive* **spot•ted, spot•ting** 6 mark with spots 7 detect 8 observe 9 blemish > **spot'less** [-lis] *adjective* 1 unblemished 2 pure > **spot'less•ly** *adverb* > **spot'ty** *adjective* **-ti•er, -ti•est** 1 with spots 2 uneven > **spot check** random examination > **spot'light** *noun* 1 powerful light illuminating small area 2 center of attention
spouse [spows] *noun* husband or wife > **spous•al** [SPOWZ-əl] *noun, adjective* (of) marriage
spout [spowt] *verb* 1 pour out 2 (*informal*) speechify ▷ *noun* 3 projecting tube or lip for pouring liquids 4 copious discharge
sprain *noun, verb transitive* wrench or twist (of muscle, etc.)
sprang *pt. of* **spring**
sprat *noun* small sea fish
sprawl *verb intransitive* 1 lie or sit about awkwardly 2 spread in rambling, unplanned way ▷ *noun* 3 sprawling
spray[1] *noun* (device for producing) fine drops of liquid ▷ *verb transitive* sprinkle with shower of fine drops
spray[2] *noun* 1 branch, twig with buds, flowers, etc. 2 floral ornament, brooch, etc. like this
spread [spred] *verb* **spread, spread'ing** 1 extend 2 stretch out 3 open out 4 scatter 5 distribute 6 unfold 7 cover ▷ *noun* 8 extent 9 increase 10 ample meal 11 food that can be spread on bread, etc. > **spread'-ea•gle** *adjective* with arms and legs outstretched > **spread'sheet** *noun* computer program for manipulating figures
spree *noun* 1 session of overindulgence 2 romp
sprig *noun* 1 small twig 2 ornamental design like this 3 small headless nail
spright•ly [SPRĪT-lee] *adjective* **-li•er, -li•est** lively, brisk > **spright'li•ness** [-nis] *noun*
spring *verb* **sprang, sprung, spring•ing** 1 leap 2 shoot up or forth 3 come into being 4 appear 5 grow 6 become bent or split 7 produce unexpectedly 8 set off (trap) ▷ *noun* 9 leap 10 recoil 11 piece of coiled or bent metal with much resilience 12 flow of water from earth 13 first season of year > **spring'y** *adjective* **spring•i•er, spring•i•est** elastic > **spring'board** [-bord] *noun* 1 flexible board for diving 2 anything that supplies impetus for action
sprin•kle [SPRING-kəl] *verb transitive* **-kled, -kling**

DICTIONARY

S

THESAURUS

sporadic *adjective* INTERMITTENT, irregular, occasional, scattered, spasmodic
sport *noun* 1 GAME, amusement, diversion, exercise, pastime, play, recreation
2 FUN, badinage, banter, jest, joking, teasing
▷ *verb* 3 (*old-fashioned, informal*) WEAR, display, exhibit, show off
sporting *adjective* FAIR, game (*informal*), sportsmanlike
sporty *adjective* ATHLETIC, energetic, outdoor
spot *noun* 1 MARK, blemish, blot, blotch, scar, smudge, speck, speckle, stain
2 PLACE, location, point, position, scene, site
3 (*informal*) PREDICAMENT, difficulty, hot water (*informal*), mess, plight, quandary, tight spot, trouble
▷ *verb* 4 SEE, catch a glimpse of, catch sight of, detect, discern, espy, make out, observe, recognize, sight
5 MARK, dirty, fleck, mottle, smirch, soil, spatter, speckle, splodge, splotch, stain
spotless *adjective* CLEAN, flawless, gleaming, immaculate, impeccable, pure, shining, unblemished, unstained, unsullied, untarnished
spotlight *noun* 1 ATTENTION, fame, limelight, public eye
▷ *verb* 2 HIGHLIGHT, accentuate, draw attention to
spotted *adjective* SPECKLED, dappled, dotted, flecked, mottled
spouse *noun* PARTNER, consort, husband *or* wife, mate, significant other (*informal*)
spout *verb* STREAM, discharge, gush, shoot, spray, spurt, surge
sprawl *verb* LOLL, flop, lounge, slouch, slump
spray[1] *noun* 1 DROPLETS, drizzle, fine mist
2 AEROSOL, atomizer, sprinkler
▷ *verb* 3 SCATTER, diffuse, shower, sprinkle
spray[2] *noun* SPRIG, branch, corsage, floral arrangement
spread *verb* 1 OPEN *or* OPEN OUT, broaden, dilate, expand, extend, sprawl, stretch, unfold, unroll, widen
2 PROLIFERATE, escalate, multiply
3 CIRCULATE, broadcast, disseminate, make known, propagate
▷ *noun* 4 INCREASE, advance, development, dispersal, dissemination, expansion, proliferation
5 EXTENT, span, stretch, sweep
spree *noun* BINGE (*informal*), bacchanalia, carousal, fling, orgy, revel
sprightly *adjective* LIVELY, active, agile, brisk, energetic, nimble, spirited, spry, vivacious
spring *verb* 1 JUMP, bounce, bound, leap, vault
2 (*often with from*) ORIGINATE, arise, come, derive, descend, issue, proceed, start, stem
3 (*often with up*) APPEAR, develop, mushroom, shoot up
▷ *noun* 4 JUMP, bound, leap, vault
5 ELASTICITY, bounce, buoyancy, flexibility, resilience
springy *adjective* ELASTIC, bouncy, buoyant, flexible, resilient, rubbery
sprinkle *verb* SCATTER, dredge, dust, pepper, powder, shower, spray, strew

scatter small drops on, strew > **sprin'kler** *noun* > **sprinkling** *noun* small amount or number
sprint *verb transitive* 1 run short distance at great speed ▷ *noun* 2 such run, race > **sprint'er** *noun* one who sprints
sprit *noun* small spar set diagonally across a fore-and-aft sail in order to extend it
sprite [sprī] *noun* fairy, elf
sprock•et [SPROK-it] *noun* 1 projection on wheel or capstan for engaging chain 2 wheel with these
sprout [sprowt] *verb intransitive* 1 put forth shoots, spring up ▷ *noun* 2 shoot > **Brus'sels sprout** [-səlz] kind of miniature cabbage
spruce[1] [sproos] *noun* variety of fir
spruce[2] *adjective* **spruc•er, spruc•est** 1 neat in dress ▷ *verb* **spruced, spruc•ing** 2 (with *up*) make (oneself) spruce
sprung *pp of* **spring**
spry [sprī] *adjective* **spry•er** *or* **spri•er, spry•est** *or* **spri•est** nimble, vigorous
spud *noun* (*informal*) potato
spume [spyoom] *noun, verb intransitive* **spumed, spum•ing** foam, froth
spun *pt./pp. of* **spin**
spunk *noun* courage, spirit
spur *noun* 1 pricking instrument attached to horseman's heel 2 incitement 3 stimulus 4 projection on rooster's leg 5 projecting mountain range 6 branch (road, etc.) ▷ *verb transitive* **spurred, spur•ring** 7 equip with spurs 8 urge on
spu•ri•ous [SPYUUR-ee-əs] *adjective* not genuine
spurn *verb transitive* reject with scorn, thrust aside
spurt *verb* 1 send, come out in jet 2 rush suddenly ▷ *noun* 3 jet 4 short sudden effort, esp. in race
sput•nik [SPUUT-nik] *noun* one of series of Russian satellites
sput•ter [SPUT-ər] *verb* splutter
spu•tum [SPYOO-təm] *noun, plural* **-ta** [-tə] spittle
spy [spī] *noun, plural* **spies** 1 one who watches (esp. in rival countries, companies, etc.) and reports secretly ▷ *verb* **spied, spy•ing** 2 act as spy 3 catch sight of > **spy'glass** *noun* small telescope > **spy'ware** *noun* software secretly installed in a computer via the Internet to gather and transmit information about the user
squab•ble [SKWOB-əl] *verb intransitive* **-bled, -bling** engage in petty, noisy quarrel, bicker ▷ *noun*
squad [skwod] *noun* small party, esp. of soldiers or police > **squad car** police patrol automobile (*also* **patrol car**) > **squad•ron** [-rən] *noun* division of an air force, fleet, or cavalry regiment
squal•id [SKWOL-id] *adjective* mean and dirty > **squal'or** [-ər] *noun*
squall [skwawl] *noun* 1 harsh cry 2 sudden gust of wind 3 short storm ▷ *verb intransitive* 4 yell
squan•der [SKWON-dər] *verb transitive* spend wastefully, dissipate
square [skwair] *noun* 1 equilateral rectangle 2 area of this shape 3 in town, open space (of this shape) 4 product of a number multiplied by itself 5 instrument for drawing right angles 6 (*slang*) person behind the times ▷ *adjective* 7 square in form 8 honest 9 straight, even 10 level, equal 11 denoting a measure of area 12 (*informal*) straightforward, honest 13 (*slang*) ignorant of current trends in dress, music, etc., conservative ▷ *verb* **squared, squar•ing** 14 *verb transitive* 15 make square 16 find square of 17 pay ▷ *verb intransitive* 18 fit, suit > **square'ly** *adverb* > **square off** get ready to dispute or fight > **square root** number that, multiplied by itself, gives number of which it is factor
squash [skwosh] *verb transitive* 1 crush flat 2 pulp 3 suppress 4 humiliate (person) ▷ *noun* 5 act of squashing 6 (*also* **squash racquets**) game

sprinkling *noun* SCATTERING, dash, dusting, few, handful, sprinkle
sprint *verb* RACE, dart, dash, shoot, tear
sprite *noun* SPIRIT, brownie, elf, fairy, goblin, imp, pixie
sprout *verb* GROW, bud, develop, shoot, spring
spruce *adjective* SMART, dapper, neat, trim, well-groomed, well turned out
spruce up *verb* SMARTEN UP, tidy, titivate
spry *adjective* ACTIVE, agile, nimble, sprightly, supple
spur *noun* 1 STIMULUS, impetus, impulse, incentive, incitement, inducement, motive
2 GOAD, prick
3 ▷ **on the spur of the moment** ON IMPULSE, impromptu, impulsively, on the spot, without planning
▷ *verb* 4 INCITE, animate, drive, goad, impel, prick, prod, prompt, stimulate, urge
spurious *adjective* FALSE, artificial, bogus, fake, phoney *or* phony (*informal*), pretended, sham, specious, unauthentic
spurn *verb* REJECT, despise, disdain, rebuff, repulse, scorn, slight, snub
spurt *verb* 1 GUSH, burst, erupt, shoot, squirt, surge
▷ *noun* 2 BURST, fit, rush, spate, surge
spy *noun* 1 UNDERCOVER AGENT, mole
▷ *verb* 2 CATCH SIGHT OF, espy, glimpse, notice, observe, spot
squabble *verb* 1 QUARREL, argue, bicker, dispute, fight, row, wrangle
▷ *noun* 2 QUARREL, argument, disagreement, dispute, fight, row, tiff
squad *noun* TEAM, band, company, crew, force, gang, group, troop
squalid *adjective* DIRTY, filthy, scuzzy (*slang*), seedy, sleazy, slummy, sordid, unclean
squalor *noun* FILTH, foulness, sleaziness, squalidness
squander *verb* WASTE, blow (*slang*), expend, fritter away, misspend, misuse, spend
square *adjective* 1 HONEST, above board, ethical, fair, genuine, kosher (*informal*), straight
2 (*informal*) UNCOOL, dorky (*slang*), nerdy, unhip
▷ *verb* 3 EVEN UP, adjust, align, level
4 (*sometimes with up*) PAY OFF, settle
5 (*often with with*) AGREE, correspond, fit, match, reconcile, tally
squash *verb* 1 CRUSH, compress, distort, flatten, mash, press, pulp, smash
2 SUPPRESS, annihilate, crush, humiliate, quell, silence
squashy *adjective* SOFT, mushy, pulpy, spongy,

played with rackets and soft balls in walled court **7** plant bearing gourds used as a vegetable

squat [skwot] *verb intransitive* **squat•ted** *or* **squat, squat•ting 1** sit on heels **2** act as squatter ▷ *adjective* **squat•ter, squat•test** short and thick > **squatter** *noun* one who settles on land or occupies house without permission

squaw [skwaw] *noun* **1** (*offensive*) Native American woman **2** (*slang*) wife

squawk [skwawk] *noun* **1** short harsh cry, esp. of bird ▷ *verb* **2** utter this

squeak [skweek] *verb, noun* (make) short shrill sound

squeal [skweel] *noun* **1** long piercing squeak ▷ *verb intransitive* **2** make one **3** (*slang*) turn informer, supply information (about another) > **squeal'er** *noun*

squeam•ish [SKWEEM-ish] *adjective* **1** easily nauseated **2** easily shocked **3** overscrupulous

squee•gee [SKWEE-jee] *noun* **1** tool with rubber blade for clearing water (from glass, etc., spreading wet paper, etc.) ▷ *verb transitive* **-geed, -gee•ing 2** press, smooth with a squeegee

squeeze [skweez] *verb transitive* **squeezed, squeez•ing 1** press **2** wring **3** force **4** hug **5** subject to extortion ▷ *noun* **6** act of squeezing **7** period of hardship, difficulty caused by financial weakness

squelch [skwelch] *verb transitive* **1** squash **2** silence with crushing rebuke, etc. ▷ *verb intransitive* **3** make, walk with wet sucking sound, as in walking through mud ▷ *noun*

squib [skwib] *noun* **1** small (faulty) firework **2** short piece of writing **3** short news story

squid [skwid] *noun* type of cuttlefish

squig•gle [SKWIG-əl] *noun* **1** wavy, wriggling mark ▷ *verb intransitive* **-gled, -gling 2** wriggle **3** draw squiggle

squint [skwint] *verb intransitive* **1** look with eyes partially closed **2** have the eyes turned in different directions **3** glance sideways **4** look askance ▷ *noun* **5** partially closed eyes **6** crossed eyes **7** (*informal*) a glance

squire [skwīr] *noun* country gentleman

squirm [skwurm] *verb intransitive* **1** wriggle **2** be embarrassed ▷ *noun*

squir•rel [SKWUR-əl] *noun* **1** small graceful bushy-tailed tree animal ▷ *verb transitive* **-reled, -rel•ing 2** store or hide (possession) for future use

squirt [skwurt] *verb* (of liquid) force, be forced through narrow opening ▷ *noun* **1** jet **2** (*informal*) short or insignificant person **3** (*informal*) (impudent) youngster

squish [skwish] *verb, noun* (make) soft splashing sound

Sr *chem.* strontium

stab *verb* **stabbed, stab•bing 1** pierce, strike (at) with pointed weapon ▷ *noun* **2** blow, wound so inflicted **3** sudden unpleasant sensation **4** attempt

sta•bil•ize [STAY-bə-līz] *verb transitive* **-ized, -iz•ing** make steady, restore to equilibrium, esp. of money values, prices and wages > **sta•bi•li•za'tion** *noun* > **sta'bi•liz•er** *noun* device to maintain equilibrium of ship, aircraft, etc.

sta•ble[1] [STAY-bəl] *noun* **1** building for horses **2** racehorses of particular owner, establishment **3** such establishment ▷ *verb transitive* **-bled, -bling 4** put into, lodge in, a stable

stable[2] *adjective* **-bler, -blest 1** firmly fixed **2** steadfast, resolute > **sta•bil•i•ty** [stə-BIL-ə-tee] *noun* **1** steadiness **2** ability to resist change of any kind > **sta'bly** *adverb*

stac•ca•to [stə-KAH-toh] *adjective, adverb* **1** *mus.* with notes sharply separated **2** abrupt

stack [stak] *noun* **1** ordered pile, heap **2** chimney ▷ *verb transitive* **3** pile in stack **4** control aircraft waiting to land so that they fly safely at different altitudes

sta•di•um [STAY-dee-əm] *noun, plural* **-di•ums** open-air or covered arena for athletics, etc.

staff[1] *noun, plural* **staffs 1** body of officers or workers **2** personnel **3** pole ▷ *verb transitive* **4** employ personnel **5** supply with personnel

staff[2] *noun, plural* **staffs** *or* **staves** five lines on which music is written

stag *noun* **1** adult male deer ▷ *adjective* **2** for men only: *stag party*

stage [stayj] *noun* **1** period, division of development **2** raised floor or platform **3** (platform of) theater **4** scene of action **5** stopping place of stagecoach, etc. on road,

---

yielding

squawk *verb* CRY, hoot, screech

squeak *verb* BEEP, pipe, squeal

squeal *noun*
▷ *verb* SCREAM, screech, shriek, wail, yell

squeamish *adjective* **1** DELICATE, fastidious, prudish, strait-laced
2 SICK, nauseous, queasy

squeeze *verb* **1** PRESS, clutch, compress, crush, grip, pinch, squash, wring
2 CRAM, crowd, force, jam, pack, press, ram, stuff
3 HUG, clasp, cuddle, embrace, enfold
4 EXTORT, milk, pressurize, wrest
▷ *noun* **5** HUG, clasp, embrace
6 CRUSH, congestion, crowd, jam, press, squash

squirm *verb* WRIGGLE, twist, writhe

squirt *noun* (*informal*) CHILD, baby, boy, girl, infant, kid (*informal*), minor, toddler, tot, whippersnapper (*old-fashioned*), youngster

stab *verb* **1** PIERCE, impale, jab, knife, spear, stick, thrust, transfix, wound
▷ *noun* **2** WOUND, gash, incision, jab, puncture, thrust
3 TWINGE, ache, pang, prick
4 ▷ **make a stab at, have a stab at** (*informal*) ATTEMPT, endeavor, have a go, try

stability *noun* FIRMNESS, solidity, soundness, steadiness, strength

stable *adjective* **1** FIRM, constant, established, fast, fixed, immovable, lasting, permanent, secure, sound, strong
2 STEADY, reliable, staunch, steadfast, sure

stack *noun* **1** PILE, heap, load, mass, mound, mountain
▷ *verb* **2** PILE, accumulate, amass, assemble, heap up, load

staff *noun* **1** WORKERS, employees, personnel, team, workforce
2 STICK, cane, crook, pole, rod, scepter, stave, wand

stage *noun* POINT, division, juncture, lap, leg,

S DICTIONARY THESAURUS

distance between two of them 6 separate unit of space rocket, which can usu. be jettisoned ▷ *verb transitive* **staged, stag•ing** 7 put (play) on stage 8 arrange, bring about > **stag'y** *adjective* **stag•i•er, stag•i•est** 1 theatrical **by easy stages** 2 unhurriedly 3 gradually > **stage whisper** loud whisper intended to be heard by audience

stag•ger [STAG-ər] *verb intransitive* 1 walk unsteadily ▷ *verb transitive* 2 astound 3 arrange in overlapping or alternating positions, times 4 distribute over a period ▷ *noun* 5 act of staggering > **stag'gers** *noun* 1 form of vertigo 2 disease of horses > **stag'ger•ing** *adjective* astounding

stag•nate [STAG-nayt] *verb intransitive* **-nat•ed, -nat•ing** cease to flow or develop > **stag•na'tion** *noun* > **stag'nant** [-nənt] *adjective* 1 sluggish 2 not flowing 3 foul, impure

staid [stayd] *adjective* of sober and quiet character, sedate > **staid'ly** *adverb* > **staid'ness** [-nis] *noun*

stain [stayn] *verb* 1 spot, mark 2 apply liquid coloring to (wood, etc.) 3 bring disgrace upon ▷ *noun* > **stain'less** *adjective* > **stainless steel** rustless steel alloy

stairs [stairz] *plural noun* set of steps, esp. as part of house > **stair'case, stair'way** *noun* 1 structure enclosing stairs 2 stairs > **stair'well** *noun* vertical opening enclosing staircase

stake [stayk] *noun* 1 sharpened stick or post 2 money wagered or contended for ▷ *verb transitive* **staked, stak•ing** 3 secure, mark out with stakes 4 wager, risk

sta•lac•tite [stə-LAK-tīt] *noun* lime deposit like icicle on roof of cave

sta•lag•mite [stə-LAG-mīt] *noun* lime deposit like pillar on floor of cave

stale [stayl] *adjective* **stal•er, stal•est** 1 old, lacking freshness 2 hackneyed 3 lacking energy, interest through monotony > **stale'mate** *noun* 1 *chess* draw through one player being unable to move 2 deadlock, impasse

stalk[1] [stawk] *noun* 1 plant's stem 2 anything like this

stalk[2] *verb* 1 follow, approach stealthily 2 walk in stiff and stately manner 3 pursue persistently and, sometimes, attack (a person with whom one is obsessed) ▷ *noun* 4 stalking > **stalk'er** *noun* > **stalk'ing-horse** *noun* pretext

stall [stawl] *noun* 1 compartment in stable, etc. 2 booth for display and sale of goods 3 seat in choir or chancel of church 4 slowdown ▷ *verb* 5 put in stall 6 stick fast 7 (motor engine) unintentionally stop 8 (aircraft) lose flying speed 9 delay 10 hinder

stal•lion [STAL-yən] *noun* uncastrated male horse, esp. for breeding

stal•wart [STAWL-wərt] *adjective* 1 strong, brave 2 staunch ▷ *noun* 3 stalwart person

sta•men [STAY-mən] *noun* male organ of a flowering plant

stam•i•na [STAM-ə-nə] *noun* power of endurance, vitality

stam•mer [STAM-ər] *verb* 1 speak, say with repetition of syllables, stutter ▷ *noun* 2 habit of so speaking > **stam'mer•er** *noun*

stamp *verb intransitive* 1 put down foot with force ▷ *verb transitive* 2 impress mark on 3 affix postage stamp 4 fix in memory 5 reveal, characterize ▷ *noun* 6 stamping with foot 7 imprinted mark 8 appliance for marking 9 piece of gummed paper printed with device as evidence of postage, etc. 10 character

stam•pede [stam-PEED] *noun* 1 sudden frightened rush, esp. of herd of cattle, crowd ▷ *verb* **-ped•ed, -ped•ing** 2 cause, take part in stampede

stance [stans] *noun* 1 manner, position of standing 2 attitude 3 point of view

stanch [stawnch] *verb transitive* stop flow (of blood) from

stan•chion [STAN-shən] *noun* 1 upright bar, support ▷ *verb transitive* 2 make secure with stanchion

stand *verb* **stood** [stuud], **stand•ing** 1 have, take, set in upright position 2 remain 3 be

DICTIONARY • THESAURUS

level, period, phase, step

stagger *verb* 1 TOTTER, lurch, reel, sway, wobble 2 ASTOUND, amaze, astonish, confound, overwhelm, shake, shock, stun, stupefy 3 OVERLAP, alternate, step

stagnant *adjective* STALE, quiet, sluggish, still

stagnate *verb* VEGETATE, decay, decline, idle, languish, rot, rust

staid *adjective* SEDATE, calm, composed, grave, serious, sober, solemn, steady

stain *verb* 1 MARK, blemish, blot, dirty, discolor, smirch, soil, spot, tinge ▷ *noun* 2 MARK, blemish, blot, discoloration, smirch, spot 3 STIGMA, disgrace, dishonor, shame, slur

stake[1] *noun* POLE, pale, paling, palisade, picket, post, stick

stake[2] *noun* 1 BET, ante, pledge, wager 2 INTEREST, concern, investment, involvement, share ▷ *verb* 3 BET, chance, gamble, hazard, risk, venture, wager

stale *adjective* 1 OLD, decayed, dry, flat, fusty, hard, musty, sour 2 UNORIGINAL, banal, hackneyed, overused, stereotyped, threadbare, trite, worn-out

stalk *verb* PURSUE, follow, haunt, hunt, shadow, track

stall *verb* PLAY FOR TIME, hedge, temporize

stalwart *adjective* STRONG, staunch, stout, strapping, sturdy

stamina *noun* STAYING POWER, endurance, energy, force, power, resilience, strength

stammer *verb* STUTTER, falter, hesitate, pause, stumble

stamp *noun* 1 IMPRINT, brand, earmark, hallmark, mark, signature ▷ *verb* 2 TRAMPLE, crush 3 IDENTIFY, brand, categorize, label, mark, reveal, show to be 4 IMPRINT, impress, mark, print

stampede *noun* RUSH, charge, flight, rout

stamp out *verb* ELIMINATE, crush, destroy, eradicate, put down, quell, scotch, suppress

stance *noun* 1 ATTITUDE, position, stand, standpoint, viewpoint 2 POSTURE, bearing, carriage, deportment

stand *verb* 1 BE UPRIGHT, be erect, be vertical, rise 2 PUT, mount, place, position, set

situated 4 remain firm or stationary 5 cease to move 6 endure 7 adhere to principles 8 offer oneself as a candidate 9 be symbol, etc. of 10 provide free treat to ▷ *noun* 11 holding firm 12 position 13 halt 14 something on which thing can be placed 15 structure from which spectators watch sport, etc. 16 stop made by traveling entertainer, etc.: *one-night stand* > **standing** *noun* 1 reputation, status 2 duration ▷ *adjective* 3 erect 4 permanent, lasting 5 stagnant 6 performed from stationary position: *standing jump* > **stand'by** [-bī] *noun, plural* **-bys** [-bīz] someone, something that can be relied on > **stand in** act as substitute (for) > **stand-in** *noun* substitute > **stand over** 1 watch closely 2 postpone

stand•ard [STAN-dərd] *noun* 1 accepted example of something against which others are judged 2 degree, quality 3 flag 4 weight or measure to which others must conform 5 post ▷ *adjective* 6 usual, regular 7 average 8 of recognized authority, competence 9 accepted as correct > **stand'ard•ize** *verb transitive* **-ized, -iz•ing** regulate by a standard

stand•off [STAND-awf] *noun* (objectionable) aloofness 1 *sports* a tie ▷ *adjective* 2 (objectionably) aloof 3 reserved

stand'point *noun* 1 point of view, opinion 2 mental attitude

stank *pt. of* **stink**

stan•nous [STAN-əs] *adjective* of, containing tin

stan•za [STAN-zə] *noun, plural* **-zas** group of lines of verse

sta•ple [STAY-pəl] *noun* 1 U-shaped piece of metal with pointed ends to drive into wood for use as ring 2 paper fastener 3 main product 4 fiber 5 pile of wool, etc. ▷ *adjective* 6 principal 7 regularly produced or made for market ▷ *verb transitive* **-pled, -pling** 8 fasten with staple 9 sort, classify (wool, etc.) according to length of fibre > **sta'pler** *noun* small device for fastening papers together

star [stahr] *noun* 1 celestial body, seen as twinkling point of light 2 asterisk 3 celebrated player, actor 4 medal, jewel, etc. of apparent shape of star ▷ *verb* **starred, star•ring** 5 adorn with stars 6 mark (with asterisk) 7 feature as star performer 8 play leading role in film, etc. ▷ *adjective* 9 leading, most important, famous > **star'ry** *adjective* **-ri•er, -ri•est** covered with stars > **star'dom** [-dəm] *noun* > **star'fish** *noun* small star-shaped sea creature

star•board [STAHR-bərd] *noun* 1 right-hand side of ship, looking forward ▷ *adjective* 2 of, on this side

starch *noun* 1 substance forming the main food element in bread, potatoes, etc., and used mixed with water, for stiffening laundered fabrics 2 (*informal*) boldness 3 vigor 4 energy ▷ *verb transitive* 5 stiffen thus > **starch'y** *adjective* **starch•i•er, starch•i•est** 1 containing starch 2 stiff 3 formal 4 prim

stare [stair] *verb intransitive* **stared, star•ing** 1 look fixedly at 2 gaze with eyes wide open 3 be obvious or visible to ▷ *noun* 4 staring, fixed gaze > **stare down** 1 abash by staring at 2 defeat by staring

stark [stahrk] *adjective* **-er, -est** 1 blunt, bare 2 desolate 3 absolute ▷ *adverb* 4 completely

start [stahrt] *verb transitive* 1 begin 2 set going ▷ *verb intransitive* 3 begin, esp. journey 4 make sudden movement ▷ *noun* 5 beginning 6

DICTIONARY

S

THESAURUS

---

3 EXIST, be valid, continue, hold, obtain, prevail, remain
4 TOLERATE, abide, allow, bear, brook, countenance, deal with (*slang*), endure, handle, put up with (*informal*), stomach, take
▷ *noun* 5 STALL, booth, table
6 POSITION, attitude, determination, opinion, stance
7 SUPPORT, base, bracket, dais, platform, rack, stage, tripod

standard *noun* 1 BENCHMARK, average, criterion, gauge, grade, guideline, measure, model, norm, yardstick
2 (*often plural*) PRINCIPLES, ethics, ideals, morals
3 FLAG, banner, ensign
▷ *adjective* 4 USUAL, average, basic, customary, normal, orthodox, regular, typical
5 ACCEPTED, approved, authoritative, definitive, established, official, recognized

standardize *verb* BRING INTO LINE, institutionalize, regiment

stand by *verb* 1 BE PREPARED, wait
2 SUPPORT, back, be loyal to, champion, take (someone's) part

stand for *verb* 1 REPRESENT, betoken, denote, indicate, mean, signify, symbolize
2 (*informal*) TOLERATE, bear, brook, endure, put up with

stand-in *noun* SUBSTITUTE, deputy, locum, replacement, reserve, stopgap, surrogate, understudy

stand in for *verb* BE A SUBSTITUTE FOR, cover for, deputize for, represent, take the place of

standing *adjective* 1 PERMANENT, fixed, lasting, regular
2 UPRIGHT, erect, vertical
▷ *noun* 3 STATUS, eminence, footing, position, rank, reputation, repute
4 DURATION, continuance, existence

standoffish *adjective* RESERVED, aloof, cold, distant, haughty, remote, unapproachable, unsociable

stand out *verb* BE CONSPICUOUS, be distinct, be obvious, be prominent

standpoint *noun* POINT OF VIEW, angle, position, stance, viewpoint

stand up for *verb* SUPPORT, champion, defend, stick up for (*informal*), uphold

staple *adjective* PRINCIPAL, basic, chief, fundamental, key, main, predominant

star *noun* 1 HEAVENLY BODY
2 CELEBRITY, big name, luminary, main attraction, megastar (*informal*), name, superstar (*informal*)
▷ *adjective* 3 LEADING, brilliant, celebrated, major, prominent, well-known

stare *verb* GAZE, eyeball (*slang*), gape, gawk, goggle, look, watch

stark *adjective* 1 HARSH, austere, bare, barren, bleak, grim, hard, homely, plain, severe
2 ABSOLUTE, blunt, downright, out-and-out, pure, sheer, unmitigated, utter
▷ *adverb* 3 ABSOLUTELY, altogether, completely, entirely, quite, utterly, wholly

abrupt movement **7** advantage of a lead in a race > **start'er** *noun* **1** electric motor starting car engine **2** competitor in, supervisor of, start of race
star•tle [STAHR-tl] *verb transitive* **-tled, -tling** give a fright to
starve [stahrv] *verb* **starved, starv•ing** (cause to) suffer or die from hunger > **star•va'tion** [-VAY-shən] *noun*
stash *verb transitive* **1** put away, store, hide ▷ *noun* **2** anything stashed **3** place for this **4** (*slang*) supply of illicit drugs
state [stayt] *noun* **1** condition **2** place, situation **3** politically organized people e.g. any of the fifty states of the USA **4** government **5** rank **6** pomp ▷ *verb transitive* **stat•ed, stat•ing** **7** express in words > **stated** *adjective* **1** fixed **2** regular **3** settled > **state'ly** *adjective* **-li•er, -li•est** dignified, lofty > **state'ment** [-mənt] *noun* **1** expression in words **2** account > **state'room** [-ruum] *noun* private cabin on ship > **states'man** [-mən] *noun, plural* **-men** respected political leader > **states'man•ship** *noun* statesman's art
stat•ic [STAT-ik] *adjective* **1** motionless, inactive **2** pert. to bodies at rest, or in equilibrium ▷ *noun* **3** electrical interference in radio reception > **stat'i•cal•ly** *adverb*
sta•tion [STAY-shən] *noun* **1** place where thing stops or is placed **2** stopping place for railroad trains, buses **3** local office for police force, fire department, etc. **4** place equipped for radio or television transmission **5** post **6** status **7** position in life ▷ *verb transitive* **8** put in position > **sta'tion•ar•y** [-er-ee] *adjective* **1** not moving, fixed **2** not changing
sta•tion•er [STAY-shən-ər] *noun* dealer in writing materials, etc. > **sta'tion•er•y** *noun*
sta•tis•tic [stə-TIS-tik] *noun* numerical fact collected and classified systematically > **sta•tis•tics** *noun* science of classifying and interpreting numerical information > **sta•tis'ti•cal** [-kəl] *adjective* > **stat•is•ti•cian** [stat-i-STISH-ən] *noun* one who compiles and studies statistics
stat•ue [STACH-oo] *noun* solid carved or cast image of person, animal, etc. > **stat'u•ar•y** [-er-ee] *noun* statues collectively > **stat•u•esque'** [-esk] *adjective* **1** like statue **2** dignified
stat•ure [STACH-ər] *noun* **1** bodily height **2** greatness
sta•tus [STAY-təs] *noun* **1** position, rank **2** prestige **3** relation to others > **status quo** [kwoh] existing state of affairs
stat•ute [STACH-oot] *noun* written law > **stat'u•to•ry** [-ə-tor-ee] *adjective* enacted, defined or authorized by statute
staunch [stawnch] *adjective* **-er, -est** trustworthy, loyal
stave [stayv] *noun* **1** one of the pieces forming barrel **2** verse, stanza **3** *mus.* staff ▷ *verb transitive* **staved** *or* **stove, stav•ing** **4** break hole in **5** ward (off)
stay[1] *verb* **stayed, stay•ing** **1** remain **2** sojourn **3** pause **4** wait **5** endure **6** stop **7** hinder **8** postpone ▷ *noun* **9** remaining, sojourning **10** check **11** restraint **12** deterrent **13** postponement
stay[2] *noun* support, prop, rope supporting mast, etc. > **stays** formerly, laced corsets
stead [sted] *noun* place **in stead** in place (of) **in good stead** of service
stead•y [STED-ee] *adjective* **stead•i•er, stead•i•est** **1** firm **2** regular **3** temperate **4**

start *verb* **1** BEGIN, appear, arise, commence, issue, originate
2 SET ABOUT, embark upon, make a beginning, take the first step
3 SET IN MOTION, activate, get going, initiate, instigate, kick-start, open, originate, trigger
4 JUMP, flinch, jerk, recoil, shy
5 ESTABLISH, begin, create, found, inaugurate, initiate, institute, launch, pioneer, set up
▷ *noun* **6** BEGINNING, birth, dawn, foundation, inception, initiation, onset, opening, outset
7 ADVANTAGE, edge, head start, lead
8 JUMP, convulsion, spasm
startle *verb* SURPRISE, frighten, make (someone) jump, scare, shock
starving *adjective* HUNGRY, famished, ravenous, starved
state *noun* **1** CONDITION, circumstances, position, predicament, shape, situation
2 FRAME OF MIND, attitude, humor, mood, spirits
3 COUNTRY, commonwealth, federation, government, kingdom, land, nation, republic, territory
4 CEREMONY, display, glory, grandeur, majesty, pomp, splendor, style
▷ *verb* **5** EXPRESS, affirm, articulate, assert, declare, expound, present, say, specify, utter, voice
stately *adjective* GRAND, august, dignified, lofty, majestic, noble, regal, royal
statement *noun* ACCOUNT, announcement, communication, communiqué, declaration, proclamation, report
state-of-the-art *adjective* LATEST, newest, up-to-date, up-to-the-minute
static *adjective* STATIONARY, fixed, immobile, motionless, still, unmoving
station *noun* **1** HEADQUARTERS, base, depot
2 PLACE, location, position, post, seat, situation
3 POSITION, post, rank, situation, standing, status
▷ *verb* **4** ASSIGN, establish, install, locate, post, set
stationary *adjective* MOTIONLESS, fixed, parked, standing, static, stock-still, unmoving
statuesque *adjective* WELL-PROPORTIONED, imposing, Junoesque
stature *noun* IMPORTANCE, eminence, prestige, prominence, rank, standing
status *noun* POSITION, condition, consequence, eminence, grade, prestige, rank, standing
staunch *adjective* LOYAL, faithful, firm, sound, stalwart, steadfast, true, trusty
stay[1] *verb* **1** REMAIN, abide, continue, halt, linger, loiter, pause, stop, tarry, wait
▷ *noun* **2** VISIT, holiday, sojourn, stop, stopover
3 POSTPONEMENT, deferment, delay, halt, stopping, suspension
steadfast *adjective* FIRM, faithful, fast, fixed, intent, loyal, resolute, stalwart, staunch, steady, unswerving, unwavering

industrious 5 reliable ▷ *verb transitive* **stead•ied, stead•y•ing** 6 make steady > **stead'i•ly** *adverb* > **stead'i•ness** [-nis] *noun* > **stead'fast** [-fəst] *adjective* firm, fixed, unyielding > **stead'fast•ly** *adverb*

steak [stayk] *noun* 1 slice of meat, esp. beef 2 slice of fish

steal [steel] *verb* **stole, sto•len, steal•ing** 1 rob 2 move silently 3 take without right or leave

stealth [stelth] *noun* secret or underhanded procedure, behavior > **stealth'i•ly** *adverb* > **stealth'y** *adjective* **stealth•i•er, stealth•i•est**

steam [steem] *noun* 1 vapor of boiling water 2 (*informal*) power, energy ▷ *verb intransitive* 3 give off steam 4 rise in vapor 5 move by steam power ▷ *verb transitive* 6 cook or treat with steam > **steam'er** *noun* 1 steam-propelled ship 2 vessel for cooking or treating with steam > **steam engine** engine worked or propelled by steam > **steam'roll•er** *noun* 1 large roller, orig. moved by steam, for leveling road surfaces, etc. 2 any great power used to crush opposition ▷ *verb transitive* 3 crush

steed *noun poet.* horse

steel *noun* 1 hard and malleable metal made by mixing carbon in iron 2 tool, weapon of steel ▷ *verb transitive* 3 harden > **steel'y** *adjective* **steel•i•er, steel•i•est**

steep[1] *adjective* **-er, -est** 1 rising, sloping abruptly 2 precipitous 3 (of prices) very high or exorbitant 4 unreasonable > **steep'en** *verb* > **steep'ly** *adverb* > **steep'ness** *noun*

steep[2] *verb* 1 soak, saturate ▷ *noun* 2 act or process of steeping 3 the liquid used

stee•ple [STEE-pəl] *noun* church tower with spire > **stee'ple•chase** *noun* 1 horse race with ditches and fences to jump 2 foot race with hurdles, etc. to jump > **stee'ple•jack** *noun* one who builds, repairs chimneys, steeples, etc.

steer[1] *verb transitive* 1 guide, direct course of vessel, motor vehicle, etc. ▷ *verb intransitive* 2 direct one's course > **steer'age** [-ij] *noun* formerly, cheapest accommodation on ship > **steer'ing wheel** wheel turned by the driver of a vehicle in order to steer it

steer[2] *noun* castrated bull

stein [stīn] *noun* earthenware beer mug

ste•le [STEE-lee] *noun* ancient carved stone pillar or slab

stel•lar [STEL-ər] *adjective* of stars

stem[1] *noun* 1 stalk, trunk 2 long slender part, as in tobacco pipe 3 part of word to which inflections are added 4 foremost part of ship > **stem cell** *histology.* undifferentiated embryonic cell that gives rise to specialized cells, such as blood, bone, etc

stem[2] *verb transitive* **stemmed, stem•ming** check, stop, dam up

stench *noun* evil smell

sten•cil [STEN-səl] *noun* 1 thin sheet pierced with pattern which is brushed over with paint or ink, leaving pattern on surface under it 2 the pattern 3 the plate 4 pattern made ▷ *verb transitive* **-ciled, -cil•ing**

ste•nog•ra•phy [stə-NOG-rə-fee] *noun* shorthand writing > **sten•og'ra•pher** *noun* > **sten•o•graph'ic** *adjective*

stent *noun* surgical implant to keep an artery open

sten•to•ri•an [sten-TOR-ee-ən] *adjective* (of voice) very loud

step *verb* **stepped, step•ping** 1 move and set down foot 2 proceed (in this way) 3 measure in paces ▷ *noun* 4 act of stepping 5 sound made by stepping 6 mark made by foot 7 manner of walking 8 series of foot movements forming part of dance 9 gait 10 pace 11 measure, act, stage in proceeding 12 board, rung, etc. to put foot on 13 degree in scale 14 mast socket 15 promotion > **steps** portable ladder with hinged prop attached, stepladder > **step'lad•der** *noun* four-legged ladder having broad flat steps

step•child [STEP-chīld] *noun, plural* **-child•ren** [-CHIL-drən] 1 child of husband or wife by former marriage 2 person, organization, idea, etc. treated improperly > **step'broth•er** *noun* > **step'fa•ther** *noun* > **step'moth•er** *noun* > **step'sis•ter** *noun*

steppe [step] *noun* extensive treeless plain in European and Asiatic Russia

stere [steer] *noun* cubic meter

ster•e•o•phon•ic [ster-ee-ə-FON-ik] *adjective* (of sound) giving effect of coming from many

steady *adjective* 1 FIRM, fixed, safe, stable
2 SENSIBLE, balanced, calm, dependable, equable, level-headed, reliable, sober
3 CONTINUOUS, ceaseless, consistent, constant, incessant, nonstop, persistent, regular, twenty-four-seven (*slang*), unbroken, uninterrupted
▷ *verb* 4 STABILIZE, balance, brace, secure, support

steal *verb* 1 TAKE, appropriate, embezzle, filch, lift (*informal*), misappropriate, pilfer, pinch (*informal*), purloin, thieve
2 SNEAK, creep, slink, slip, tiptoe

stealth *noun* SECRECY, furtiveness, slyness, sneakiness, stealthiness, surreptitiousness, unobtrusiveness

stealthy *adjective* SECRET, furtive, secretive, sneaking, surreptitious

steep[1] *adjective* 1 SHEER, abrupt, precipitous
2 HIGH, exorbitant, extortionate, extreme, overpriced, unreasonable

steep[2] *verb* 1 SOAK, drench, immerse, macerate, marinate (*cookery*), moisten, souse, submerge
2 SATURATE, fill, imbue, infuse, permeate, pervade, suffuse

steer *verb* DIRECT, conduct, control, guide, handle, pilot

stem[1] *noun* 1 STALK, axis, branch, shoot, trunk
▷ *verb* 2 ▷ **stem from** ORIGINATE IN, arise from, be caused by, derive from

stem[2] *verb* STOP, check, curb, dam, hold back, staunch

stench *noun* STINK, foul smell, reek, whiff

step *noun* 1 FOOTSTEP, footfall, footprint, pace, print, stride, track
2 STAGE, move, phase, point
3 ACTION, act, deed, expedient, means, measure, move
4 DEGREE, level, rank
▷ *verb* 5 WALK, move, pace, tread

step in *verb* INTERVENE, become involved, take action

step up *verb* INCREASE, intensify, raise

directions > **ster'e•o** *adjective, noun* (of, for) stereophonic record player, etc.
ster•e•o•scop•ic [ster-ee-ə-SKOP-ik] *adjective* having three-dimensional effect
ster•e•o•type [STER-ee-ə-tīp] *noun* 1 metal plate for printing cast from type 2 something (monotonously) familiar, conventional, predictable ▷ *verb transitive* **-typed, -typ•ing** 3 make stereotype of
ster•ile [STER-əl] *adjective* 1 unable to produce fruit, crops, young, etc. 2 free from (harmful) germs > **ste•ril•i•ty** [stə-RIL-ə-tee] *noun* > **ster•i•li•za'tion** *noun* process or act of making sterile > **ster'i•lize** *verb transitive* **-lized, -liz•ing** render sterile
ster•ling [STUR-ling] *adjective* 1 genuine, true 2 of solid worth, dependable 3 in British money ▷ *noun* 4 British money
stern[1] [sturn] *adjective* severe, strict > **stern'ly** *adverb* > **stern'ness** [-nis] *noun*
stern[2] *noun* rear part of ship
ster•num [STUR-nəm] *noun* the breast bone
ster•to•rous [STUR-tər-əs] *adjective* with sound of heavy breathing, hoarse snoring
stet *Lat.* let it stand (proofreader's direction to cancel alteration previously made)
steth•o•scope [STETH-ə-skohp] *noun* instrument for listening to action of heart, lungs, etc.
Stet•son [STET-sən] *noun* ® type of broad-brimmed felt hat esp. cowboy hat
ste•ve•dore [STEE-vi-dor] *noun* one who loads or unloads ships
stew [stoo] *noun* 1 food cooked slowly in closed vessel 2 state of excitement, agitation or worry ▷ *verb* 3 cook by stewing 4 worry **stew in one's own juice** suffer consequences of one's own actions
stew•ard [STOO-ərd] *noun* 1 one who manages another's property 2 official managing race meeting, assembly, etc. 3 attendant on ship's or aircraft's passengers > **stew'ard•ess** [-is] *noun feminine*
stick [stik] *noun* 1 long, thin piece of wood 2 anything shaped like a stick 3 (*informal*) uninteresting person ▷ *verb transitive* **stuck, stick•ing** 4 pierce, stab 5 place, fasten, as by pins, glue 6 protrude 7 bewilder 8 (*informal*) impose disagreeable responsibility on (someone) ▷ *verb intransitive* **stuck, stick•ing** 9 adhere 10 come to stop, jam 11 remain 12 be fastened 13 protrude > **stick'er** *noun* adhesive label: *bumper sticker* > **stick'y** *adjective* **stick•i•er, stick•i•est** 1 covered with, like adhesive substance 2 (of weather) warm, humid 3 (*informal*) difficult, unpleasant > **stick shift** automobile transmission with manually operated shift lever
stick•ler [STIK-lər] *noun* person who insists on something
stiff *adjective* **-er, -est** 1 not easily bent or moved 2 rigid 3 awkward 4 difficult 5 thick, not fluid 6 formal 7 stubborn 8 unnatural 9 strong or fresh, as breeze 10 (*informal*) excessive ▷ *noun* 11 (*slang*) corpse 12 (*slang*) a drunk ▷ *verb transitive* 13 (*slang*) fail to tip (waiter, etc.) > **stiff'en** [-in] *verb* > **stiff'ly** *adverb* > **stiff-necked** [-nekt] *adjective* 1 obstinate, stubborn 2 haughty
sti•fle [STĪF-əl] *verb transitive* **-fled, -fling** smother, suppress
stig•ma [STIG-mə] *noun, plural* **-mas** *or* **-ma•ta** [-MAH-tə] distinguishing mark esp. of disgrace > **stig'ma•tize** *verb transitive* **-tized, -tiz•ing** mark with stigma
sti•let•to [sti-LET-oh] *noun, plural* **-tos** *or* **-toes** 1 small dagger 2 small boring tool ▷ *adjective* 3 thin, pointed like a stiletto
still[1] *adjective* **-er, -est** 1 motionless, noiseless, at

---

stereotype *noun* 1 FORMULA, pattern ▷ *verb* 2 CATEGORIZE, pigeonhole, standardize, typecast
sterile *adjective* 1 GERM-FREE, aseptic, disinfected, sterilized
2 BARREN, bare, dry, empty, fruitless, unfruitful, unproductive
sterilize *verb* DISINFECT, fumigate, purify
sterling *adjective* EXCELLENT, fine, genuine, sound, superlative, true
stern *adjective* SEVERE, austere, forbidding, grim, hard, harsh, inflexible, rigid, serious, strict
stick[1] *noun* 1 CANE, baton, crook, pole, rod, staff, twig
2 (*Brit slang*) ABUSE, criticism, flak (*informal*)
stick[2] *verb* 1 POKE, dig, jab, penetrate, pierce, prod, puncture, spear, stab, thrust, transfix
2 FASTEN, adhere, affix, attach, bind, bond, cling, fix, glue, hold, join, paste, weld
3 (*with out, up etc.*) PROTRUDE, bulge, extend, jut, obtrude, poke, project, show
4 PUT, deposit, lay, place, set
5 STAY, linger, persist, remain
6 (*slang*) TOLERATE, abide, stand, stomach, take
7 ▷ **stick up for** DEFEND, champion, stand up for, support
stickler *noun* PERFECTIONIST, fanatic, fusspot (*informal*), purist
sticky *adjective* 1 TACKY, adhesive, clinging, gluey, glutinous, gooey (*informal*), gummy, viscid, viscous
2 (*informal*) DIFFICULT, awkward, delicate, embarrassing, nasty, tricky, unpleasant
3 HUMID, clammy, close, muggy, oppressive, sultry, sweltering
stiff *adjective* 1 INFLEXIBLE, firm, hard, inelastic, rigid, solid, taut, tense, tight, unbending, unyielding
2 AWKWARD, clumsy, graceless, inelegant, jerky (*informal*), ungainly, ungraceful
3 DIFFICULT, arduous, exacting, hard, tough
4 SEVERE, drastic, extreme, hard, harsh, heavy, strict
5 UNRELAXED, artifical, constrained, forced, formal, stilted, unnatural
stiffen *verb* 1 BRACE, reinforce, tauten, tense
2 SET, congeal, crystallize, harden, jell, solidify, thicken
stifle *verb* 1 SUPPRESS, check, hush, repress, restrain, silence, smother, stop
2 SUFFOCATE, asphyxiate, choke, smother, strangle
stigma *noun* DISGRACE, dishonor, shame, slur, smirch, stain
still[1] *adjective* 1 MOTIONLESS, calm, peaceful, restful, serene, stationary, tranquil, undisturbed
2 SILENT, hushed, quiet
▷ *verb* 3 QUIETEN, allay, calm, hush, lull, pacify,

rest ▷ *verb transitive* 2 quiet ▷ *adverb* 3 to this time 4 yet 5 even ▷ *noun* 6 photograph esp. of motion picture scene > **still'born** *adjective* born dead > **still life** a painting of inanimate objects

still² *noun* apparatus for distilling

stilt *noun* 1 pole with footrests for walking raised from ground 2 long post supporting building, etc. > **stilt'ed** [-id] *adjective* stiff in manner, pompous

stim•u•lus [STIM-yə-ləs] *noun, plural* **-li** [-lī] 1 something that rouses to activity 2 incentive > **stim'u•lant** [-lənt] *noun* drug, etc. acting as a stimulus > **stim'u•late** *verb transitive* **-lat•ed, -lat•ing** rouse up, spur > **stim'u•lat•ing** *adjective* acting as stimulus > **stim•u•la'tion** *noun* > **stim'u•la•tive** [-lə-tiv] *adjective*

sting *verb* **stung, sting•ing** 1 thrust sting into 2 cause sharp pain to 3 (*slang*) cheat, take advantage of, esp. by overcharging 4 feel sharp pain ▷ *noun* (wound, pain, caused by) sharp pointed organ, often poisonous, of certain insects and animals 5 (*slang*) illegal operation conducted by police, etc. to collect evidence against criminals

stin•gy [STIN-jee] *adjective* **-gi•er, -gi•est** 1 mean 2 avaricious 3 niggardly > **stin'gi•ness** [-nis] *noun*

stink *verb intransitive* **stank** *or* **stunk, stunk, stink•ing** 1 give out strongly offensive smell 2 (*informal*) be markedly inferior ▷ *noun* 3 such smell, stench 4 (*informal*) fuss, bother 5 scandal

stint *verb transitive* 1 be frugal, miserly to (someone) or with (something) ▷ *noun* 2 allotted amount of work or time 3 limitation, restriction

sti•pend [STĪ-pend] *noun* payment, esp. scholarship or fellowship allowance given to student > **sti•pen'di•ar•y** [-dee-er-ee] *adjective* receiving stipend

stip•ple [STIP-əl] *verb transitive* **-pled, -pling** 1 engrave, paint in dots ▷ *noun* 2 this process

stip•u•late [STIP-yə-layt] *verb intransitive* **-lat•ed, -lat•ing** specify in making a bargain > **stip•u•la'tion** *noun* 1 proviso 2 condition

stir [stur] *verb* **stirred, stir•ring** 1 (begin to) move 2 rouse 3 cause trouble 4 set, keep in motion 5 excite ▷ *noun* 6 commotion, disturbance

stir•rup [STUR-əp] *noun* metal loop hung from strap for supporting foot of rider on horse

stitch [stich] *noun* 1 movement of needle in sewing, etc. 2 its result in the work 3 sharp pain in side 4 least fragment (of clothing) ▷ *verb* 5 sew

stock [stok] *noun* 1 goods, material stored, esp. for sale or later use 2 reserve, fund 3 shares in, or capital of, company, etc. 4 standing, reputation 5 farm animals (livestock) 6 plant, stem from which cuttings are taken 7 handle of gun, tool, etc. 8 liquid broth produced by boiling meat, etc. 9 flowering plant 10 lineage ▷ *adjective* 11 kept in stock 12 standard, hackneyed ▷ *verb transitive* 13 keep, store 14 supply with livestock, fish, etc. > **stocks** *plural noun* 1 *hist.* frame to secure feet, hands (of offender) 2 frame to support ship during construction > **stock'y** *adjective* **stock•i•er, stock•i•est** thickset > **stock'brok•er** [-brohk-ər] *noun* agent for buying, selling stocks and bonds > **stock car** ordinary automobile strengthened and modified for a form of racing in which automobiles often collide > **stock ex•change** institution for buying and selling shares > **stock'pile** *verb* acquire and store large quantity of (something) > **stock-still** *adjective* motionless > **stock'tak•ing** *noun* examination, counting and valuing of goods in a store, etc. **put stock in** believe, trust

stock•ade [sto-KAYD] *noun* enclosure of stakes, barrier

stock•ing [STOK-ing] *noun* close-fitting covering for leg and foot

stodg•y [STOJ-ee] *adjective* **stodg•i•er, stodg•i•est** heavy, dull

sto•gy [STOH-gee] *noun, plural* **-gies** cheap cigar

---

quiet, settle, silence, soothe ▷ *conjunction* 4 HOWEVER, but, nevertheless, notwithstanding, yet

stilted *adjective* STIFF, constrained, forced, unnatural, wooden

stimulant *noun* PICK-ME-UP (*informal*), restorative, tonic, upper (*slang*)

stimulate *verb* AROUSE, encourage, fire, impel, incite, prompt, provoke, rouse, spur

stimulating *adjective* EXCITING, exhilarating, inspiring, provocative, rousing, stirring

stimulus *noun* INCENTIVE, encouragement, goad, impetus, incitement, inducement, spur

sting *verb* 1 HURT, burn, pain, smart, tingle, wound
2 (*informal*) CHEAT, defraud, fleece, overcharge, rip off (*slang*), swindle

stingy *adjective* MEAN, miserly, niggardly, parsimonious, penny-pinching (*informal*), tightfisted, ungenerous

stink *noun* 1 STENCH, fetor, foul smell ▷ *verb* 2 REEK

stint *verb* 1 BE MEAN, be frugal, be sparing, hold back, skimp on
▷ *noun* 2 SHARE, period, quota, shift, spell, stretch, term, time, turn

stipulate *verb* SPECIFY, agree, contract, covenant, insist upon, require, settle

stipulation *noun* SPECIFICATION, agreement, clause, condition, precondition, proviso, qualification, requirement

stir *verb* 1 MIX, agitate, beat, shake
2 STIMULATE, arouse, awaken, excite, incite, provoke, rouse, spur
▷ *noun* 3 COMMOTION, activity, bustle, disorder, disturbance, excitement, flurry, fuss

stock *noun* 1 GOODS, array, choice, commodities, merchandise, range, selection, variety, wares
2 SUPPLY, fund, hoard, reserve, stockpile, store
3 PROPERTY, assets, capital, funds, investment
4 LIVESTOCK, beasts, cattle, domestic animals
▷ *adjective* 5 STANDARD, conventional, customary, ordinary, regular, routine, usual
6 HACKNEYED, banal, overused, trite
▷ *verb* 7 SELL, deal in, handle, keep, supply, trade in
8 PROVIDE WITH, equip, fit out, furnish, supply
9 ▷ **stock up** STORE *or* STORE UP, accumulate, amass, gather, hoard, lay in, put away, save

stocky *adjective* THICKSET, chunky, dumpy, solid,

sto•ic [STOH-ik] *adjective* 1 capable of much self-control, great endurance without complaint ▷ *noun* 2 stoical person > **sto'i•cal** [-kəl] *adjective*
stoke [stohk] *verb* **stoked, stok•ing** feed, tend fire or furnace > **stok'er** *noun*
stole[1] [stohl] *pt. of* **steal**
stole[2] *noun* long scarf or shawl
sto•len [stohl-ən] *pp of* **steal**
stol'id *adjective* 1 hard to excite 2 heavy, slow, apathetic
stom•ach [STUM-ək] *noun* 1 sac forming chief digestive organ in any animal 2 appetite 3 desire, inclination ▷ *verb transitive* 4 put up with
stomp *verb intransitive* put down foot with force
stone [stohn] *noun* 1 (piece of) rock 2 gem 3 hard seed of fruit 4 hard deposit formed in kidneys, bladder 5 British unit of weight, 14 lbs. ▷ *verb transitive* **stoned, ston•ing** 6 throw stones at 7 free (fruit) from stones > **stoned** *adjective* (*slang*) stupefied by alcohol or drugs > **ston'i•ly** *adverb* > **ston'y** *adjective* **ston•i•er, ston•i•est** 1 of, like stone 2 hard 3 cold > **stone-broke** [-brohk] *adjective* with no money left > **stone-dead** *adjective* completely dead > **stone-deaf** *adjective* completely deaf > **stone'wall** *verb* 1 stall 2 evade 3 filibuster > **stone'ware** [-wair] *noun* heavy common pottery
stood [stuud] *pt./pp. of* **stand**
stooge [stooj] *noun* 1 performer always the butt of another's jokes 2 anyone taken advantage of by another
stool *noun* 1 backless chair 2 excrement
stoop[1] *verb intransitive* 1 lean forward or down, bend 2 swoop 3 abase, degrade oneself ▷ *noun* 4 stooping carriage of the body
stoop[2] *noun* steps or small porch in front of house
stop *verb* **stopped, stop•ping** 1 check, bring to halt 2 prevent 3 interrupt 4 suspend 5 desist from 6 fill up an opening 7 cease, come to a halt 8 stay ▷ *noun* 9 stopping or becoming stopped 10 any device for altering or regulating pitch 11 set of pipes in organ having tones of a distinct quality > **stop'page** [-ij] *noun* > **stop'per** [-ər] *noun* plug for closing bottle, etc. > **stop'gap** *noun* temporary substitute > **stop'off, stop'o•ver** *noun* short break in journey > **stop'watch** *noun* one that can be stopped for exact timing e.g. of race **pull out all the stops** use all available means
store [stor] *verb transitive* **stored, stor•ing** 1 stock, furnish, keep 2 *computing* enter or retain (data) ▷ *noun* 3 retail store 4 abundance 5 stock 6 place for keeping goods 7 warehouse > **stores** stocks of goods, provisions > **stor'age** *noun* **in store** 1 in readiness 2 imminent
stork *noun* large wading bird
storm *noun* 1 violent weather with wind, rain, hail, sand, snow, etc. 2 assault on fortress 3 violent outbreak, discharge ▷ *verb transitive* 4 assault 5 take by storm ▷ *verb intransitive* 6 rage > **storm'y** *adjective* **storm•i•er, storm•i•est** 1 like storm 2 (emotionally) violent
sto•ry[1] [STOR-ee] *noun, plural* **-ries** 1 (book, piece of prose, etc.) telling about events, happenings 2 lie
story[2] *noun, plural* **-ries** horizontal division of a building
stoup [stoop] *noun* small basin for holy water
stout [stowt] *adjective* **-er, -est** 1 fat 2 sturdy, resolute ▷ *noun* 3 kind of beer > **stout'ly** *adverb*

stubby, sturdy
stodgy *adjective* 1 HEAVY, filling, leaden, starchy 2 DULL, boring, heavy going, staid, stuffy, tedious, unexciting
stoical *adjective* RESIGNED, dispassionate, impassive, long-suffering, philosophical, phlegmatic, stoic, stolid
stoicism *noun* RESIGNATION, acceptance, forbearance, fortitude, impassivity, long-suffering, patience, stolidity
stolid *adjective* APATHETIC, dull, lumpish, unemotional, wooden
stomach *noun* 1 BELLY, abdomen, gut (*informal*), pot, tummy (*informal*)
2 INCLINATION, appetite, desire, relish, taste
▷ *verb* 3 BEAR, abide, endure, swallow, take, tolerate
stony *adjective* COLD, blank, chilly, expressionless, hard, hostile, icy, unresponsive
stoop *verb* 1 BEND, bow, crouch, duck, hunch, lean
2 ▷ **stoop to** SINK TO, descend to, lower oneself by, resort to
▷ *noun* 3 SLOUCH, bad posture, round-shoulderedness
stop *verb* 1 HALT, cease, conclude, cut short, desist, discontinue, end, finish, pause, put an end to, quit, refrain, shut down, terminate
2 PREVENT, arrest, forestall, hinder, hold back, impede, repress, restrain
3 PLUG, block, obstruct, seal, staunch, stem
4 STAY, lodge, rest
▷ *noun* 5 END, cessation, finish, halt, standstill
6 STAY, break, rest
7 STATION, depot, terminus
stopgap *noun* MAKESHIFT, improvisation, resort, substitute
stoppage *noun* STOPPING, arrest, close, closure, cutoff, halt, hindrance, shutdown, standstill
store *verb* 1 PUT BY, deposit, garner, hoard, keep, put aside, reserve, save, stockpile
▷ *noun* 2 SHOP, market, mart, outlet
3 SUPPLY, accumulation, cache, fund, hoard, quantity, reserve, stock, stockpile
4 REPOSITORY, depository, storeroom, warehouse
storm *noun* 1 TEMPEST, blizzard, gale, hurricane, squall
2 OUTBURST, agitation, commotion, disturbance, furor, outbreak, outcry, row, rumpus, strife, tumult, turmoil
▷ *verb* 3 ATTACK, assail, assault, charge, rush
4 RAGE, bluster, rant, rave, thunder
5 RUSH, flounce, fly, stamp
stormy *adjective* WILD, blustery, inclement, raging, rough, squally, turbulent, windy
story *noun* 1 TALE, account, anecdote, history, legend, narrative, romance, yarn
2 REPORT, article, feature, news, news item, scoop
stout *adjective* 1 FAT, big, bulky, burly, corpulent, fleshy, heavy, overweight, plump, portly, rotund, tubby
2 STRONG, able-bodied, brawny, muscular,

> **stout'ness** [-nis] *noun*
stove[1] [stohv] *noun* apparatus for cooking, heating, etc.
stove[2] *pt./pp. of* **stave**
stow [stoh] *verb transitive* pack away > **stow'age** [-ij] *noun* > **stow'a•way** *noun* one who hides in ship to obtain free passage
strad•dle [STRAD-l] *verb transitive* **-dled, -dling** 1 bestride ▷ *verb intransitive* **-dled, -dling** 2 spread legs wide ▷ *noun*
strafe [strayf] *verb transitive* **strafed, straf•ing** attack (esp. with bullets, rockets) from air
strag•gle [STRAG-əl] *verb intransitive* **-gled, -gling** stray, get dispersed, linger > **strag'gler** *noun*
straight [strayt] *adjective* **-er, -est** 1 without bend 2 honest 3 level 4 in order 5 (of whiskey) undiluted, neat 6 expressionless 7 (of drama, actor, etc.) serious 8 (*slang*) heterosexual ▷ *noun* 9 straight condition or part ▷ *adverb* 10 direct > **straight'en** [-in] *verb* > **straight'a•way** *adverb* immediately > **straight•for'ward** [-wərd] *adjective* 1 open, frank 2 simple 3 honest
strain[1] [strayn] *verb transitive* 1 stretch tightly 2 stretch to full or to excess 3 filter ▷ *verb intransitive* 4 make great effort ▷ *noun* 5 stretching force 6 violent effort 7 injury from being strained 8 burst of music or poetry 9 great demand 10 (condition caused by) overwork, worry, etc. 11 tone of speaking or writing > **strain'er** [-ər] *noun* filter, sieve
strain[2] *noun* 1 breed or race 2 type (esp. in biology) 3 trace, streak
strait [strayt] *noun* 1 channel of water connecting two larger areas of water ▷ *adjective* 2 narrow 3 strict > **straits** *plural noun* position of difficulty or distress > **strait'en** [-in] *verb transitive* 1 make strait, narrow 2 press with poverty > **strait'jack•et** *noun* jacket to confine arms of violent person > **strait-laced** [-laysd] *adjective* 1 austere, strict 2 puritanical
strand[1] *verb* 1 run aground 2 leave, be left in difficulties or helpless
strand[2] *noun* one single string or wire of rope, etc.
strange [straynj] *adjective* **strang•er, strang•est** 1 odd 2 queer 3 unaccustomed 4 foreign 5 uncommon 6 wonderful 7 singular > **stran'ger** *noun* 1 unknown person 2 foreigner 3 one unaccustomed (to) > **strange'ness** [-nis] *noun*
stran•gle [STRANG-gəl] *verb transitive* **-gled, -gling** 1 kill by squeezing windpipe 2 suppress > **stran•gu•la'tion** [-yə-LAY-shən] *noun* strangling
strap *noun* 1 strip, esp. of leather ▷ *verb transitive* **strapped, strap•ping** 2 fasten, beat with strap > **strap'ping** *adjective* tall and powerful > **strap'hang•er** *noun* in bus, subway car, one who has to stand, steadying self with strap provided for this purpose

robust, stalwart, strapping, sturdy
3 BRAVE, bold, courageous, fearless, gallant, intrepid, plucky, resolute, valiant
stow *verb* PACK, bundle, load, put away, stash (*informal*), store
straight *adjective* 1 DIRECT, near, short
2 LEVEL, aligned, even, horizontal, right, smooth, square, true
3 UPRIGHT, erect, plumb, vertical
4 HONEST, above board, accurate, fair, honorable, just, law-abiding, trustworthy, upright
5 FRANK, blunt, bold, candid, forthright, honest, outright, plain, straightforward
6 SUCCESSIVE, consecutive, continuous, nonstop, running, solid
7 UNDILUTED, neat, pure, unadulterated, unmixed
8 ORDERLY, arranged, in order, neat, organized, shipshape, tidy
9 (*slang*) CONVENTIONAL, bourgeois, conservative
▷ *adverb* 10 DIRECTLY, at once, immediately, instantly
straight away *adverb* IMMEDIATELY, at once, directly, instantly, now, right away
straighten *verb* NEATEN, arrange, order, put in order, tidy *or* tidy up
straightforward *adjective* 1 HONEST, candid, direct, forthright, genuine, open, sincere, truthful, upfront (*informal*)
2 EASY, elementary, routine, simple, uncomplicated
strain[1] *verb* 1 STRETCH, distend, draw tight, tauten, tighten
2 OVEREXERT, injure, overtax, overwork, pull, sprain, tax, tear, twist, wrench
3 STRIVE, bend over backwards (*informal*), endeavor, give it one's best shot (*informal*), go for it (*informal*), knock oneself out (*informal*), labor, struggle
4 SIEVE, filter, purify, sift
▷ *noun* 5 STRESS, anxiety, burden, pressure, tension
6 EXERTION, effort, force, struggle
7 INJURY, pull, sprain, wrench
strain[2] *noun* 1 BREED, ancestry, blood, descent, extraction, family, lineage, race
2 TRACE, streak, suggestion, tendency
strained *adjective* 1 FORCED, artificial, false, put on, unnatural
2 TENSE, awkward, difficult, embarrassed, stiff, uneasy
strait *noun* 1 (*often plural*) CHANNEL, narrows, sound
2 ▷ **straits** DIFFICULTY, dilemma, extremity, hardship, plight, predicament
strait-laced *adjective* STRICT, moralistic, narrow-minded, prim, proper, prudish, puritanical
strand *noun* FILAMENT, fiber, string, thread
stranded *adjective* 1 BEACHED, aground, ashore, grounded, marooned, shipwrecked
2 HELPLESS, abandoned, high and dry
strange *adjective* 1 ODD, abnormal, bizarre, curious, extraordinary, peculiar, queer, uncommon, weird, wonderful
2 UNFAMILIAR, alien, exotic, foreign, new, novel, unknown, untried
stranger *noun* NEWCOMER, alien, foreigner, guest, incomer, outlander, visitor
strangle *verb* 1 THROTTLE, asphyxiate, choke, strangulate
2 SUPPRESS, inhibit, repress, stifle
strap *noun* 1 BELT, thong, tie
▷ *verb* 2 FASTEN, bind, buckle, lash, secure, tie
strapping *adjective* WELL-BUILT, big, brawny, husky (*informal*), powerful, robust, sturdy

strat•a•gem [STRAT-ə-jəm] *noun* plan, trick > **strat'e•gy** *noun, plural* **-gies** 1 art of war 2 overall plan > **strat'e•gist** *noun* > **stra•te•gic** [strə-TEE-jik] *adjective*

strat•o•sphere [STRAT-ə-sfeer] *noun* upper part of the atmosphere from approx. 11 km to 50 km above Earth's surface

stra•tum [STRAY-təm] *noun, plural* **stra•ta** [-tə] 1 layer, esp. of rock 2 class in society > **strat'i•fy** *verb* **-fied, -fy•ing** form, deposit in layers > **strat•i•fi•ca'tion** *noun*

straw *noun* 1 stalks of grain 2 single stalk 3 long, narrow tube used to suck up liquid > **straw'ber•ry** *noun* 1 creeping plant producing a red, juicy fruit 2 the fruit

stray *verb intransitive* 1 wander 2 digress 3 get lost ▷ *adjective* 4 strayed 5 occasional, scattered ▷ *noun* 6 stray animal

streak [streek] *noun* 1 long line or band 2 element, trace ▷ *verb transitive* 3 mark with streaks ▷ *verb intransitive* 4 move fast 5 run naked in public > **streak'y** *adjective* **streak•i•er, streak•i•est** 1 having streaks 2 striped

stream [streem] *noun* 1 flowing body of water or other liquid 2 steady flow ▷ *verb intransitive* 3 flow 4 run with liquid 5 float, wave in the air ▷ *verb transitive* 6 discharge, send in stream > **stream'er** [-ər] *noun* (paper) ribbon, narrow flag

stream•lined [STREEM-līnd] *adjective* (of train, plane, etc.) built so as to offer least resistance to air

street *noun* road in town, etc. usu. lined with houses > **street'car** *noun* vehicle (esp. electrically driven and for public transport) running usu. on rails laid on roadway > **street'walk•er** *noun* prostitute > **street'wise, street'smart** *adjective* (*informal*) adept at surviving in urban, oft. criminal, environment

strength [strengkth] *noun* 1 quality of being strong 2 power 3 capacity for exertion or endurance 4 vehemence 5 force 6 full or necessary number of people > **strength'en** *verb* make stronger, reinforce **on the strength of** 1 relying on 2 because of

stren•u•ous [STREN-yoo-əs] *adjective* 1 energetic 2 earnest

strep•to•coc•cus [strep-tə-KOK-əs] *noun, plural* **-coc•ci** [-KOK-sī] genus of bacteria

strep•to•my•cin [strep-tə-MĪ-sin] *noun* antibiotic drug

stress *noun* 1 emphasis 2 strain 3 impelling force 4 effort 5 tension ▷ *verb transitive* 6 emphasize 7 accent 8 put mechanical stress on

stretch [strech] *verb transitive* 1 extend 2 exert to utmost 3 tighten, pull out 4 reach out ▷ *verb intransitive* 5 reach 6 have elasticity ▷ *noun* 7 stretching, being stretched, expanse 8 spell > **stretch'er** *noun* 1 person, thing that stretches 2 appliance on which disabled person is carried 3 bar linking legs of chair

strew [stroo] *verb transitive* **strewed, strewn** *or* **strewed, strew•ing** scatter over surface, spread

stri•ate [STRĪ-ayt] *verb transitive* **-at•ed, -at•ing** 1 mark with streaks 2 score > **stri•a'tion** *noun* > **striated** *adjective* streaked, furrowed, grooved

strick•en [STRIK-ən] *adjective* 1 seriously affected by disease, grief, famine 2 afflicted 3 *pp of* **strike**

strict [strikt] *adjective* **-er, -est** 1 stern, not lax or indulgent 2 defined 3 without exception

stric•ture [STRIK-chər] *noun* 1 critical remark 2 constriction

stride [strīd] *verb intransitive* **strode, strid•den, strid•ing** 1 walk with long steps ▷ *noun* 2 single step 3 its length 4 regular pace **hit one's stride** reach the level at which one consistently functions best

stri•dent [STRĪD-nt] *adjective* 1 harsh in tone 2

DICTIONARY • THESAURUS

stratagem *noun* TRICK, device, dodge, maneuver, plan, ploy, ruse, scheme, subterfuge

strategic *adjective* 1 TACTICAL, calculated, deliberate, diplomatic, planned, politic
2 CRUCIAL, cardinal, critical, decisive, important, key, vital

strategy *noun* PLAN, approach, policy, procedure, scheme

stray *verb* 1 WANDER, drift, err, go astray
2 DIGRESS, deviate, diverge, get off the point
▷ *adjective* 3 LOST, abandoned, homeless, roaming, vagrant
4 RANDOM, accidental, chance

streak *noun* 1 BAND, layer, line, slash, strip, stripe, stroke, vein
2 TRACE, dash, element, strain, touch, vein
▷ *verb* 3 SPEED, dart, flash, fly, hurtle, sprint, tear, whizz (*informal*), zoom

stream *noun* 1 RIVER, bayou, beck, brook, rivulet, tributary
2 FLOW, course, current, drift, run, rush, surge, tide, torrent
▷ *verb* 3 FLOW, cascade, course, flood, gush, issue, pour, run, spill, spout

streamlined *adjective* EFFICIENT, organized, rationalized, slick, smooth-running

street *noun* ROAD, avenue, boulevard, lane, parkway, roadway, row, terrace

strength *noun* 1 MIGHT, brawn, courage, fortitude, muscle, robustness, stamina, sturdiness, toughness
2 INTENSITY, effectiveness, efficacy, force, potency, power, vigor
3 ADVANTAGE, asset, strong point

strengthen *verb* 1 FORTIFY, brace up, consolidate, harden, invigorate, restore, stiffen, toughen
2 REINFORCE, augment, bolster, brace, build up, buttress, harden, intensify, support

strenuous *adjective* DEMANDING, arduous, hard, laborious, taxing, tough, uphill

stress *noun* 1 STRAIN, anxiety, burden, pressure, tension, trauma, worry
2 EMPHASIS, force, significance, weight
3 ACCENT, accentuation, beat, emphasis
▷ *verb* 4 EMPHASIZE, accentuate, dwell on, underline

stretch *verb* 1 EXTEND, cover, put forth, reach, spread, unroll
2 PULL, distend, draw out, elongate, expand, strain, tighten
▷ *noun* 3 EXPANSE, area, distance, extent, spread, tract
4 PERIOD, space, spell, stint, term, time

strict *adjective* 1 SEVERE, authoritarian, firm, harsh, stern, stringent

loud **3** urgent
strife [strīf] *noun* **1** conflict **2** quarreling
strike [strīk] *verb* **struck, struck** *or* **strick•en, strik•ing 1** hit (against) **2** ignite **3** (of snake) bite **4** arrive at, come upon **5** of plants (cause to) take root **6** attack **7** hook (fish) **8** sound (time) as bell in clock, etc. **9** *baseball* swing and miss a pitch, etc. ▷ *verb transitive* **10** affect **11** enter mind of **12** discover (gold, oil, etc.) **13** dismantle, remove **14** make (coin) ▷ *verb intransitive* **15** cease work as protest or to make demands ▷ *noun* **16** act of striking > **strik'er** *noun* > **striking** *adjective* noteworthy, impressive **strike it rich** meet unexpected financial success > **strike off** remove > **strike out 1** fail in a venture **2** *baseball* make three strikes
string *noun* **1** (length of) thin cord or other material **2** strand, row **3** series **4** fiber in plants ▷ *verb transitive* **strung, string•ing 5** provide with, thread on string **6** form in line, series > **strings** *plural noun* conditions > **stringed** *adjective* (of musical instruments) furnished with strings > **string'y** *adjective* **string•i•er, string•i•est 1** like string **2** fibrous
strin•gent [STRIN-jənt] *adjective* strict, rigid, binding > **strin'gen•cy** *noun* severity
strip *verb* **stripped, strip•ping 1** lay bare, take covering off **2** dismantle **3** deprive (of) **4** undress ▷ *noun* **5** long, narrow piece > **strip'per** *noun* person who performs a striptease > **strip'tease** [-teez] *noun* nightclub or theater act in which stripper undresses in time to music
stripe [strīp] *noun* **1** narrow mark, band **2** chevron as symbol of military rank **3** style, kind
strip'ling *noun* a youth
strive [strīv] *verb intransitive* **strove** *or* **strived, striv•en** *or* **strived, striv•ing** try hard, struggle, contend
strobe [strohb] *noun* apparatus that produces high-intensity flashing light
strode [strohd] *pt. of* **stride**
stroke [strohk] *noun* **1** blow **2** sudden action, occurrence **3** apoplexy **4** mark of pen, pencil, brush, etc. **5** chime of clock **6** completed movement in series **7** act, manner of striking (ball, etc.) **8** style, method of swimming **9** rower sitting nearest stern setting the rate **10** act of stroking ▷ *verb transitive* **stroked, strok•ing 11** set time in rowing **12** pass hand lightly over
stroll [strohl] *verb intransitive* walk in leisurely or idle manner ▷ *noun*
strong [strawng] *adjective* **-er, -est 1** powerful, robust, healthy **2** difficult to break **3** noticeable **4** intense **5** emphatic **6** not diluted **7** having a certain number > **strong'hold** [-hohld] *noun* fortress
stron•ti•um [STRON-shee-əm] *noun* silvery-white chemical element > **strontium 90** radioactive isotope of strontium present in fallout of nuclear explosions
strop *noun* **1** leather for sharpening razors ▷ *verb transitive* **stropped, strop•ping 2** sharpen on one
strove [strohv] *pt. of* **strive**
struck *pt./pp. of* **strike**
struc•ture [STRUK-chər] *noun* **1** (arrangement of parts in) construction, building, etc. **2** form **3** organization ▷ *verb transitive* **-tured, -tur•ing 4** give structure to > **struc'tur•al** [-chər-əl] *adjective*
strug•gle [STRUG-əl] *verb intransitive* **-gled, -gling 1** contend **2** fight **3** proceed, work, move with difficulty and effort ▷ *noun*
strum *verb* **strummed, strum•ming** strike notes of guitar, etc.
strum•pet [STRUM-pit] *noun* **1** promiscuous

---

2 EXACT, accurate, close, faithful, meticulous, precise, scrupulous, true
3 ABSOLUTE, total, utter
strident *adjective* HARSH, discordant, grating, jarring, raucous, screeching, shrill
strife *noun* CONFLICT, battle, clash, discord, dissension, friction, quarrel
strike *verb* **1** WALK OUT, down tools, mutiny, revolt
2 HIT, beat, clobber (*slang*), clout (*informal*), cuff, hammer, knock, punch, slap, smack, thump, wallop (*informal*)
3 COLLIDE WITH, bump into, hit, run into
4 ATTACK, assail, assault, hit
5 OCCUR TO, come to, dawn on *or* dawn upon, hit, register (*informal*)
striking *adjective* IMPRESSIVE, conspicuous, cool (*informal*), dramatic, noticeable, outstanding, phat (*slang*)
string *noun* **1** CORD, fiber, twine
2 SERIES, chain, file, line, procession, row, sequence, succession
stringent *adjective* STRICT, inflexible, rigid, rigorous, severe, tight, tough
stringy *adjective* FIBROUS, gristly, sinewy, tough
strip[1] *verb* **1** UNDRESS, disrobe, unclothe
2 PLUNDER, despoil, divest, empty, loot, pillage, ransack, rob, sack
strip[2] *noun* PIECE, band, belt, shred
strive *verb* TRY, attempt, bend over backwards (*informal*), break one's neck (*informal*), do one's best, give it one's best shot (*informal*), go all out (*informal*), knock oneself out (*informal*), labor, make an all-out effort (*informal*), struggle, toil
stroke *verb* **1** CARESS, fondle, pet, rub
▷ *noun* **2** APOPLEXY, attack, collapse, fit, seizure
3 BLOW, hit, knock, pat, rap, thump
stroll *verb* **1** WALK, amble, promenade, ramble, saunter
▷ *noun* **2** WALK, breath of air, constitutional, promenade, ramble, turn
strong *adjective* **1** POWERFUL, athletic, brawny, burly, hardy, lusty, muscular, robust, strapping, sturdy, tough
2 DURABLE, hard-wearing, heavy-duty, sturdy, substantial, well-built
3 PERSUASIVE, compelling, convincing, effective, potent, sound, telling, weighty, well-founded
4 INTENSE, acute, deep, fervent, fervid, fierce, firm, keen, vehement, violent, zealous
5 EXTREME, drastic, forceful, severe
6 BRIGHT, bold, brilliant, dazzling
stronghold *noun* FORTRESS, bastion, bulwark, castle, citadel, fort
structure *noun* **1** BUILDING, construction, edifice, erection
2 ARRANGEMENT, configuration, construction, design, form, formation, make-up, organization
▷ *verb* **3** ARRANGE, assemble, build up, design, organize, shape

woman **2** prostitute

strung *pt./pp. of* **string**

strut *verb intransitive* **strut•ted, strut•ting 1** walk affectedly or pompously ▷ *noun* **2** brace **3** rigid support, usu. set obliquely **4** strutting gait

strych•nine [STRIK-nin] *noun* poison obtained from nux vomica seeds

stub *noun* **1** remnant of anything, e.g. pencil, cigarette, etc. **2** retained portion of check, etc. ▷ *verb transitive* **stubbed, stub•bing 3** strike (e.g. toes) against fixed object **4** extinguish by pressing against surface > **stub'by** *adjective* **-bi•er, -bi•est** short, broad

stub•ble [STUB-əl] *noun* **1** stumps of cut grain, etc. after cutting **2** short growth of beard

stub•born [STUB-ərn] *adjective* unyielding, obstinate > **stub'born•ness** [-nis] *noun*

stuc•co [STUK-oh] *noun, plural* **-coes** *or* **-cos 1** plaster ▷ *verb transitive* **-coed, -co•ing 2** apply stucco to (wall)

stuck *pt./pp. of* **stick**

stud[1] *noun* **1** nail with large head **2** type of button **3** vertical wall support ▷ *verb transitive* **stud'ded, stud'ding 4** set with studs > **stud'ding** *noun*

stud[2] *noun* **1** stallion, set of horses, kept for breeding **2** (*slang*) man known for sexual prowess > **stud'book** [-buuk] *noun* book giving pedigree of noted or thoroughbred animals, esp. horses > **stud farm** establishment where horses are kept for breeding

stu•di•o [STOO-dee-oh] *noun, plural* **-di•os 1** workroom of artist, photographer, etc. **2** building, room where motion pictures, TV or radio shows are made, broadcast **3** apartment of one main room

stud•y [STUD-ee] *verb* **stud•ied, stud•y•ing 1** be engaged in learning **2** make study of **3** try constantly to do **4** consider **5** scrutinize > **stud•ies** *plural noun* **6** effort to acquire knowledge **7** subject of this **8** room to study in **9** book, report, etc. produced as result of study **10** sketch > **stu•dent** [STOOD-nt] *noun* one who studies, esp. at college, etc. > **studied** *adjective* carefully designed, premeditated > **stu•di•ous** [STOO-dee-əs] *adjective* **1** fond of study **2** thoughtful **3** painstaking **4** deliberate > **stu'di•ous•ly** *adverb*

stuff *verb* **1** pack, cram, fill (completely) **2** eat large amount **3** fill with seasoned mixture **4** fill (animal's skin) with material to preserve lifelike form ▷ *noun* **5** material, fabric **6** any substance > **stuff'ing** *noun* material for stuffing, esp. seasoned mixture for inserting in poultry, etc. before cooking > **stuff'y** *adjective* **stuff•i•er, stuff•i•est 1** lacking fresh air **2** dull, conventional > **stuffed shirt** pompous person

stul•ti•fy [STUL-tə-fī] *verb transitive* **-fied, -fy•ing** make ineffectual > **stul•ti•fi•ca'tion** *noun*

stum•ble [STUM-bəl] *verb intransitive* **-bled, -bling 1** trip and nearly fall **2** falter ▷ *noun* > **stumbling block** obstacle

stump *noun* **1** remnant of tree, tooth, etc., when main part has been cut away **2** part of leg or arm remaining after amputation ▷ *verb transitive* **3** confuse, puzzle ▷ *verb intransitive* **4** walk heavily, noisily > **stump'y** *adjective* **stump•i•er, stump•i•est** short and thickset

stun *verb transitive* **stunned, stun•ning 1** knock senseless **2** amaze

DICTIONARY • THESAURUS

---

struggle *verb* **1** STRIVE, exert oneself, give it one's best shot (*informal*), go all out (*informal*), knock oneself out (*informal*), labor, make an all-out effort (*informal*), strain, toil, work
2 FIGHT, battle, compete, contend, grapple, wrestle
▷ *noun* **3** EFFORT, exertion, labor, pains, scramble, toil, work
4 FIGHT, battle, brush, clash, combat, conflict, contest, tussle

strut *verb* SWAGGER, parade, peacock, prance

stub *noun* **1** BUTT, end, remainder, remnant, stump, tail, tail end
2 COUNTERFOIL

stubborn *adjective* OBSTINATE, dogged, headstrong, inflexible, intractable, obdurate, persistent, pig-headed, recalcitrant, tenacious, unyielding

stubby *adjective* STOCKY, chunky, dumpy, short, squat, thickset

stuck *adjective* **1** FASTENED, cemented, fast, fixed, glued, joined
2 (*informal*) BAFFLED, beaten, stumped

stuck-up *adjective* SNOBBISH, arrogant, bigheaded (*informal*), conceited, haughty, proud, snooty (*informal*)

stud *verb* ORNAMENT, bejewel, dot, spangle, spot

student *noun* LEARNER, apprentice, disciple, pupil, scholar, trainee, undergraduate

studied *adjective* PLANNED, conscious, deliberate, intentional, premeditated

studio *noun* WORKSHOP, atelier

studious *adjective* SCHOLARLY, academic, assiduous, bookish, diligent, hard-working, intellectual

study *verb* **1** CONTEMPLATE, consider, examine, go into, ponder, pore over, read
2 LEARN, cram (*informal*), read up, review
3 EXAMINE, analyze, investigate, look into, research, scrutinize, survey
▷ *noun* **4** LEARNING, application, lessons, reading, research, school work
5 EXAMINATION, analysis, consideration, contemplation, inquiry, inspection, investigation, review, scrutiny, survey

stuff *noun* **1** THINGS, belongings, effects, equipment, gear, kit, objects, paraphernalia, possessions, tackle
2 SUBSTANCE, essence, matter
3 MATERIAL, cloth, fabric, textile
▷ *verb* **4** CRAM, crowd, fill, force, jam, pack, push, ram, shove, squeeze

stuffing *noun* FILLING, packing, wadding

stuffy *adjective* **1** AIRLESS, close, frowsty, heavy, muggy, oppressive, stale, stifling, sultry, unventilated
2 (*informal*) STAID, dreary, dull, pompous, priggish, prim, stodgy

stumble *verb* **1** TRIP, fall, falter, lurch, reel, slip, stagger
2 (*with across* or *on* or *upon*) DISCOVER, chance upon, come across, find

stump *verb* BAFFLE, bewilder, confuse, flummox, mystify, nonplus, perplex, puzzle

stumpy *adjective* STOCKY, dumpy, short, squat, stubby, thickset

stung *pt./pp. of* **sting**
stunk *pp of* **stink**
stunt[1] *verb transitive* 1 check growth of, dwarf > **stunt'ed** *adjective* 1 underdeveloped 2 undersized
stunt[2] *noun* 1 feat of dexterity or daring 2 anything spectacular, usually done to gain publicity
stu•pe•fy [STOO-pə-fī] *verb transitive* **-fied, -fy•ing** 1 make insensitive, lethargic 2 astound > **stu•pe•fac'tion** *noun*
stu•pen•dous [stoo-PEN-dəs] *adjective* 1 astonishing 2 amazing 3 huge
stu•pid [STOO-pid] *adjective* **-er, -est** 1 slow-witted 2 silly 3 in a stupor > **stu•pid'i•ty** *noun, plural* **-ties**
stu•por [STOO-pər] *noun* 1 dazed state 2 insensibility > **stu'por•ous** *adjective*
stur•dy [STUR-dee] *adjective* **-di•er, -di•est** 1 robust, strongly built 2 vigorous > **stur'di•ly** *adverb*
stur•geon [STUR-jən] *noun* fish yielding caviar
stut•ter [STUT-ər] *verb* 1 speak with difficulty 2 stammer ▷ *noun*
sty[1] [stī] *noun, plural* **sties** 1 place to keep pigs in 2 hovel, dirty place
sty[2] *noun, plural* **sties** inflammation on edge of eyelid
Styg•i•an [STIJ-ee-ən] *adjective* 1 of river Styx in Hades 2 gloomy 3 infernal
style [stīl] *noun* 1 manner of writing, doing, etc. 2 designation 3 sort 4 elegance, refinement 5 superior manner, quality 6 design ▷ *verb transitive* **styled, styl•ing** 7 shape, design 8 adapt 9 designate > **styl'ish** *adjective* fashionable > **styl'ist** *noun* 1 one cultivating style in literary or other execution 2 designer 3 hairdresser > **styl•is'tic** *adjective* > **styl'ize** *verb transitive* **-ized, -iz•ing** give conventional stylistic form to
sty•lus [STĪ-ləs] *noun, plural* **-lus•es** 1 writing instrument 2 (in record player) tiny point running in groove of record
sty•mie [STĪ-mee] *verb transitive* **-mied, -my•ing** hinder, thwart
styp•tic [STIP-tik] *adjective, noun* (designating) a substance that stops bleeding
suave [swahv] *adjective* **suav•er, suav•est** smoothly polite, affable, bland > **suav'i•ty** *noun*
sub 1 submarine 2 submarine sandwich 3 substitute ▷ *verb intransitive* **subbed, sub•bing** (*informal*) 4 serve as substitute
sub- *prefix* under, less than, in lower position, subordinate, forming subdivision, etc.: *subaquatic; subheading; subnormal; subsoil*
sub•com•mit•tee [SUB-kə-mit-ee] *noun* section of committee functioning separately from main body
sub•con•scious [sub-KON-shəs] *adjective* 1 acting, existing without one's awareness ▷ *noun* 2 *psychology* that part of the human mind unknown, or only partly known to possessor
sub•cu•ta•ne•ous [sub-kyoo-TAY-nee-əs] *adjective* under the skin
sub•di•vide [sub-di-VĪD] *verb transitive* **-vid•ed, -vid•ing** divide again > **sub'di•vi•sion** [-vizh-ən] *noun*
sub•due [səb-DOO] *verb* **-dued, -du•ing** 1 overcome > **subdued'** *adjective* 1 cowed, quiet 2

---

stun *verb* OVERCOME, astonish, astound, bewilder, confound, confuse, overpower, shock, stagger, stupefy
stunning *adjective* WONDERFUL, beautiful, cool (*informal*), dazzling, gorgeous, impressive, lovely, marvelous, phat (*slang*), sensational (*informal*), spectacular, striking
stunt *noun* FEAT, act, deed, exploit, trick
stunted *adjective* UNDERSIZED, diminutive, little, small, tiny
stupefy *verb* ASTOUND, amaze, daze, dumbfound, shock, stagger, stun
stupendous *adjective* 1 WONDERFUL, amazing, astounding, breathtaking, marvelous, overwhelming, sensational (*informal*), staggering, superb
2 HUGE, colossal, enormous, gigantic, mega (*slang*), vast
stupid *adjective* 1 UNINTELLIGENT, brainless, dense, dim, dumb (*informal*), half-witted, moronic (*offensive*), obtuse, simple, simple-minded, slow, slow-witted, thick
2 FOOLISH, asinine, bonkers (*informal*), daft (*informal*), idiotic, imbecilic, inane, nonsensical, pointless, rash, senseless, unintelligent
3 DAZED, groggy, insensate, semiconscious, stunned, stupefied
stupidity *noun* 1 LACK OF INTELLIGENCE, brainlessness, denseness, dimness, dullness, imbecility, obtuseness, slowness, thickness
2 FOOLISHNESS, absurdity, fatuousness, folly, idiocy, inanity, lunacy, madness, silliness
stupor *noun* DAZE, coma, insensibility, stupefaction, unconsciousness
sturdy *adjective* 1 ROBUST, athletic, brawny, hardy, lusty, muscular, powerful
2 WELL-BUILT, durable, solid, substantial, well-made
stutter *verb* STAMMER, falter, hesitate, stumble
style *noun* 1 DESIGN, cut, form, manner
2 MANNER, approach, method, mode, technique, way
3 ELEGANCE, chic, élan, flair, panache, polish, smartness, sophistication, taste
4 TYPE, category, genre, kind, sort, variety
5 FASHION, mode, rage, trend, vogue
6 LUXURY, affluence, comfort, ease, elegance, grandeur
▷ *verb* 7 DESIGN, adapt, arrange, cut, fashion, shape, tailor
8 CALL, designate, dub, entitle, label, name, term
stylish *adjective* SMART, chic, cool (*informal*), dressy (*informal*), fashionable, modish, phat (*slang*), trendy (*informal*), voguish
suave *adjective* SMOOTH, charming, courteous, debonair, polite, sophisticated, urbane
subconscious *adjective* HIDDEN, inner, intuitive, latent, repressed, subliminal
subdue *verb* 1 OVERCOME, break, conquer, control, crush, defeat, master, overpower, quell, tame, vanquish
2 MODERATE, mellow, quieten down, soften, suppress, tone down
subdued *adjective* 1 QUIET, chastened, crestfallen, dejected, downcast, down in the mouth, sad, serious
2 SOFT, dim, hushed, muted, quiet, subtle,

(of light) not bright or intense
subject [SUB-jikt] *noun* 1 theme, topic 2 that about which something is predicated 3 conscious self 4 one under power of another ▷ *adjective* 5 owing allegiance 6 subordinate 7 dependent 8 liable (to) ▷ *verb transitive* [səb-JEKT] 9 cause to undergo 10 make liable 11 subdue > **sub•jec'tion** [-JEK-shən] *noun* act of bringing, or state of being, under control > **sub•ject'ive** *adjective* 1 based on personal feelings, not impartial 2 of the self 3 existing in the mind 4 displaying artist's individuality > **sub•jec•tiv'i•ty** *noun*
sub ju•di•ce [sub JOO-di-see] *Lat.* under judicial consideration
sub•ju•gate [SUB-jə-gayt] *verb transitive* **-gat•ed, -gat•ing** 1 force to submit 2 conquer > **sub•ju•ga'tion** *noun*
sub•junc•tive [səb-JUNGK-tiv] *noun* 1 mood used mainly in subordinate clauses expressing wish, possibility ▷ *adjective* 2 in, of, that mood
sub•let' *verb transitive* **-let, -let•ting** (of tenant) let to another all or part of what tenant has rented
sub•li•mate [SUB-lə-mayt] *verb transitive* **-mat•ed, -mat•ing** 1 *psychology* direct energy (esp. sexual) into activities considered more socially acceptable 2 refine ▷ *noun* [-mit] 3 *chem.* material obtained when substance is sublimed > **sub•li•ma'tion** *noun* 1 *psychology* unconscious diversion of sexual impulses towards new aim and activities 2 *chem.* process in which a solid changes directly into a vapor
sub•lime [sə-BLĪM] *adjective* 1 elevated 2 eminent 3 majestic 4 inspiring awe 5 exalted ▷ *verb* **-limed, -lim•ing** 6 *chem.* change or cause to change from solid to vapor > **sub•lime'ly** *adverb*
sub•lim•i•nal [sub-LIM-ə-nl] *adjective* resulting from processes of which the individual is not aware
sub•ma•rine [sub-mə-REEN] *noun* 1 ship that can travel below surface of sea and remain submerged for long periods ▷ *adjective* 2 below surface of sea > **submarine sandwich** overstuffed sandwich of meats, cheese, etc. in long loaf of Italian bread
sub•merge [səb-MURJ] *verb* **-merged, -merg•ing** place, go under water > **sub•mer'sion** [-MUR-zhən] *noun*
sub•mit [səb-MIT] *verb* **-mit•ted, -mit•ting** 1 surrender 2 put forward for consideration 3 surrender 4 defer > **sub•mis'sion** [-MISH-ən] *noun* > **sub•mis'sive** *adjective* meek, obedient
sub•or•di•nate [sə-BOR-dn-it] *adjective* 1 of lower rank or less importance ▷ *noun* 2 inferior 3 one under order of another ▷ *verb transitive* [-dn-ayt], **-nat•ed, -nat•ing** make, treat as subordinate > **sub•or•di•na'tion** [-NAY-shən] *noun*
sub•orn [sə-BORN] *verb transitive* bribe to do evil > **sub•or•na•tion** [sub-or-NAY-shən] *noun*
sub•poe•na [sə-PEE-nə] *noun* 1 writ requiring attendance at court of law ▷ *verb transitive* **-naed, -na•ing** 2 summon by such order
sub•scribe [səb-SKRĪB] *verb transitive* **-scribed, -scrib•ing** 1 pay, promise to pay (contribution) 2 write one's name at end of document > **sub•scrip'tion** *noun* 1 subscribing 2 money paid
sub•se•quent [SUB-si-kwənt] *adjective* later, following or coming after in time
sub•ser•vi•ent [səb-SUR-vee-ənt] *adjective* submissive, servile > **sub•ser'vi•ence** *noun*
sub•side [səb-SĪD] *verb intransitive* **-sid•ed, -sid•ing** 1 abate, come to an end 2 sink 3 settle 4 collapse > **sub•sid'ence** *noun*
sub•sid•i•ar•y [səb-SID-ee-er-ee] *adjective* 1 supplementing 2 secondary 3 auxiliary ▷ *noun, plural* **-ar•ies**

DICTIONARY • THESAURUS

toned down, unobtrusive
subject *noun* 1 TOPIC, affair, business, issue, matter, object, point, question, substance, theme
2 CITIZEN, national, subordinate
▷ *adjective* 3 SUBORDINATE, dependent, inferior, obedient, satellite
4 ▷ **subject to** **a** LIABLE TO, exposed to, in danger of, open to, prone to, susceptible to, vulnerable to **b** CONDITIONAL ON, contingent on, dependent on
▷ *verb* 5 PUT THROUGH, expose, lay open, submit, treat
subjective *adjective* PERSONAL, biased, nonobjective, prejudiced
subjugate *verb* CONQUER, enslave, master, overcome, overpower, quell, subdue, suppress, vanquish
sublime *adjective* NOBLE, elevated, exalted, glorious, grand, great, high, lofty
submerge *verb* IMMERSE, deluge, dip, duck, engulf, flood, inundate, overflow, overwhelm, plunge, sink, swamp
submission *noun* 1 SURRENDER, assent, capitulation, giving in, yielding
2 PRESENTATION, entry, handing in, tendering
3 MEEKNESS, compliance, deference, docility, obedience, passivity, resignation
submissive *adjective* MEEK, accommodating, acquiescent, amenable, compliant, docile, obedient, passive, pliant, tractable, unresisting, yielding
submit *verb* 1 SURRENDER, accede, agree, capitulate, comply, endure, give in, succumb, tolerate, yield
2 PUT FORWARD, hand in, present, proffer, table, tender
subordinate *adjective* 1 LESSER, dependent, inferior, junior, lower, minor, secondary, subject
▷ *noun* 2 INFERIOR, aide, assistant, attendant, junior, second
subordination *noun* INFERIORITY, inferior status *or* secondary status, servitude, subjection
subscribe *verb* 1 DONATE, contribute, give
2 SUPPORT, advocate, endorse
subscription *noun* 1 MEMBERSHIP FEE, annual payment, dues
2 DONATION, contribution, gift
subsequent *adjective* FOLLOWING, after, ensuing, later, succeeding, successive
subsequently *adverb* LATER, afterwards
subservient *adjective* SERVILE, abject, deferential, obsequious, slavish, submissive, sycophantic
subside *verb* 1 DECREASE, abate, diminish, ease, ebb, lessen, quieten, slacken, wane

sub•si•dize [SUB-si-dīz] *verb transitive* **-dized, -diz•ing** 1 help financially 2 pay grant to > **sub'si•dy** [-dee] *noun, plural* **-dies** money granted
sub•sist [səb-SIST] *verb intransitive* exist, sustain life > **sub•sist'ence** [-əns] *noun* 1 the means by which one supports life 2 livelihood
sub•son•ic [sub-SON-ik] *adjective* concerning speeds less than that of sound
sub•stance [SUB-stəns] *noun* 1 matter 2 particular kind of matter 3 chief part, essence 4 wealth > **sub•stan•tial** [səb-STAN-shəl] *adjective* 1 considerable 2 of real value 3 solid, big, important 4 really existing > **sub•stan'ti•ate** [-shee-ayt] *verb transitive* **-at•ed, -at•ing** bring evidence for, confirm, prove > **sub•stan•ti•a'tion** *noun* > **sub'stan•tive** [-stən-tiv] *adjective* 1 having independent existence 2 real, fixed ▷ *noun* 3 noun
sub•sti•tute [SUB-sti-toot] *verb* **-tut•ed, -tut•ing** 1 put, serve in exchange (for) ▷ *noun* 2 thing, person put in place of another 3 deputy > **sub•sti•tu'tion** *noun*
sub•sume [səb-SOOM] *verb transitive* **-sumed, -sum•ing** incorporate (idea, case, etc.) under comprehensive heading, classification
sub•tend [səb-TEND] *verb transitive* be opposite to and delimit
sub•ter•fuge [SUB-tər-fyooj] *noun* trick, lying excuse used to evade something
sub•ter•ra•ne•an [sub-tə-RAY-nee-ən] *adjective* 1 underground 2 in concealment
sub•ti•tle [SUB-tīt-l] *noun* 1 secondary title of book 2 written translation of film dialogue, superimposed on film
sub•tle [SUT-l] *adjective* **-tler, -tlest** 1 not immediately obvious 2 ingenious, acute 3 crafty 4 intricate 5 delicate 6 making fine distinctions > **sub'tle•ty** [-tee] *noun, plural* **-ties**
sub•tract [səb-TRAKT] *verb transitive* take away, deduct > **sub•trac'tion** [-TRAK-shən] *noun*
sub•trop•i•cal [sub-TROP-i-kəl] *adjective* of regions bordering on the tropics
sub'urb *noun* residential area on outskirts of city > **sub•ur•ban** [sə-BUR-bən] *adjective* > **sub•ur'bi•a** [-bee-ə] *noun* suburbs of a city
sub•ven•tion [səb-VEN-shən] *noun* subsidy
sub•vert [səb-VURT] *verb transitive* 1 overthrow 2 corrupt > **sub•ver'sion** [-zhən] *noun* > **sub•ver'sive** [-siv] *adjective*
sub'way *noun* 1 underground passage 2 underground railroad
suc•ceed [sək-SEED] *verb intransitive* 1 accomplish purpose 2 turn out satisfactorily 3 follow ▷ *verb transitive* 4 follow, take place of > **suc•cess'** *noun* 1 favorable accomplishment, attainment, issue or outcome 2 successful person or thing > **suc•cess'ful** [-fəl] *adjective* > **suc•ces'sion** [-SESH-ən] *noun* 1 following 2 series 3 succeeding > **suc•ces'sive** *adjective* 1 following in order 2 consecutive > **suc•ces'sor** [-ər] *noun*
suc•cinct [sək-SINGKT] *adjective* terse, concise > **succinct'ly** *adverb* > **suc•cinct'ness** [-nis] *noun*
suc•cor [SUK-ər] *verb transitive, noun* help in distress
suc•cu•bus [SUK-yə-bəs] *noun, plural* **-bi** [-bī] female demon fabled to have sexual intercourse

2 SINK, cave in, collapse, drop, lower, settle
subsidence *noun* 1 SINKING, settling
2 DECREASE, abatement, easing off, lessening, slackening
subsidiary *adjective* LESSER, ancillary, auxiliary, minor, secondary, subordinate, supplementary
subsidize *verb* FUND, finance, promote, sponsor, support
subsidy *noun* AID, allowance, assistance, grant, help, support
substance *noun* 1 MATERIAL, body, fabric, stuff
2 MEANING, essence, gist, import, main point, significance
3 REALITY, actuality, concreteness
4 WEALTH, assets, estate, means, property, resources
substantial *adjective* BIG, ample, considerable, important, large, significant, sizable *or* sizeable, supersize
substantiate *verb* SUPPORT, authenticate, confirm, establish, prove, verify
substitute *verb* 1 REPLACE, change, exchange, interchange, swap, switch
▷ *noun* 2 REPLACEMENT, agent, deputy, locum, proxy, reserve, sub, surrogate
▷ *adjective* 3 REPLACEMENT, alternative, fall-back, proxy, reserve, second, surrogate
substitution *noun* REPLACEMENT, change, exchange, swap, switch
subterfuge *noun* TRICK, deception, dodge, maneuver, ploy, ruse, stratagem
subtle *adjective* 1 SOPHISTICATED, delicate, refined
2 FAINT, delicate, implied, slight, understated
3 CRAFTY, artful, cunning, devious, ingenious, shrewd, sly, wily
subtlety *noun* 1 SOPHISTICATION, delicacy, refinement
2 CUNNING, artfulness, cleverness, craftiness, deviousness, ingenuity, slyness, wiliness
subtract *verb* TAKE AWAY, deduct, diminish, remove, take from, take off
subversive *adjective* 1 SEDITIOUS, riotous, treasonous
▷ *noun* 2 DISSIDENT, fifth columnist, saboteur, terrorist, traitor
subvert *verb* OVERTURN, sabotage, undermine
succeed *verb* 1 MAKE IT (*informal*), be successful, flourish, make good, make the grade (*informal*), prosper, thrive, triumph, work
2 FOLLOW, come next, ensue, result
success *noun* 1 LUCK, fame, fortune, happiness, prosperity, triumph
2 HIT (*informal*), celebrity, megastar (*informal*), sensation, smash (*informal*), star, superstar, winner
successful *adjective* THRIVING, booming, flourishing, fortunate, fruitful, lucky, profitable, prosperous, rewarding, top, victorious
successfully *adverb* WELL, favorably, victoriously, with flying colors
succession *noun* 1 SERIES, chain, course, cycle, order, progression, run, sequence, train
2 TAKING OVER, accession, assumption, inheritance
successive *adjective* CONSECUTIVE, following, in succession
succinct *adjective* BRIEF, compact, concise,

with sleeping men
suc•cu•lent [SUK-yə-lənt] *adjective* 1 juicy, full of juice 2 (of plant) having thick, fleshy leaves ▷ *noun* 3 such plant > **suc'cu•lence** [-lins] *noun*
suc•cumb [sə-KUM] *verb intransitive* 1 yield, give way 2 die
such *adjective* 1 of the kind or degree mentioned 2 so great, so much 3 so made, etc. 4 of the same kind > **such'like** *adjective* 1 such ▷ *pronoun* 2 other such things
suck [suk] *verb transitive* 1 draw into mouth 2 hold (dissolve) in mouth 3 draw in ▷ *noun* 4 sucking > **suck'er** *noun* 1 person, thing that sucks 2 organ, appliance that adheres by suction 3 shoot coming from root or base of stem of plant 4 (*informal*) person easily deceived or taken in
suck•le [SUK-əl] *verb* **-led, -ling** feed from the breast > **suck'ling** *noun* unweaned infant
suc•tion [SUK-shən] *noun* 1 drawing or sucking of air or fluid 2 force produced by difference in pressure
sud•den [SUD-n] *adjective* 1 done, occurring unexpectedly 2 abrupt, hurried > **sud'den•ness** [-dən-is] *noun*
su•dor•if•ic [soo-də-RIF-ik] *adjective* 1 causing perspiration ▷ *noun* 2 medicine that produces sweat
suds [sudz] *plural noun* 1 froth of soap and water, lather 2 (*slang*) beer
sue [soo] *verb transitive* **sued, su•ing** 1 prosecute 2 seek justice from ▷ *verb intransitive* **sued, su•ing** 3 make application or entreaty 4 beseech
suede [swayd] *noun* leather with soft, velvety finish
su•et [SOO-it] *noun* hard animal fat from sheep, cow, etc.
suf•fer [SUF-ər] *verb* 1 undergo, endure, experience (pain, etc.) 2 allow > **suf'fer•a•ble** *adjective* > **suf'fer•ance** [-əns] *noun* toleration
suf•fice [sə-FĪS] *verb* **-ficed, -fic•ing** be adequate, satisfactory (for) > **suf•fi•cien•cy** [sə-FISH-ən-see] *noun* adequate amount > **suf•fi'cient** *adjective* enough, adequate
suf•fix [SUF-iks] *noun* 1 letter or word added to end of word ▷ *verb transitive* 2 add, annex to the end
suf•fo•cate [SUF-ə-kayt] *verb* **-cat•ed, -cat•ing** 1 kill, be killed by deprivation of oxygen 2 smother
suf•frage [SUF-rij] *noun* vote or right of voting > **suf'fra•gist** *noun* one claiming a right of voting > **suf•fra•gette'** *noun feminine*
suf•fuse [sə-FYOOZ] *verb transitive* **-fused, -fus•ing** well up and spread over > **suf•fu'sion** [-FYOO-zhən] *noun*
sug•ar [SHUUG-ər] *noun* 1 sweet crystalline vegetable substance ▷ *verb transitive* 2 sweeten, make pleasant (with sugar) > **sug'ar•y** *adjective* > **sugar cane** plant from whose juice sugar is obtained > **sugar daddy** (*informal*) wealthy (elderly) man who pays for (esp. sexual) favors of younger woman
sug•gest [səg-JEST] *verb transitive* 1 propose 2 call up the idea of > **sug•gest'i•ble** *adjective* easily influenced > **sug•gest'ion** [-chən] *noun* 1 hint 2 proposal 3 insinuation of impression, belief, etc., into mind > **sug•gest'ive** *adjective* containing, open to suggestion, esp. of something indecent
su•i•cide [SOO-ə-sīd] *noun* (act of) one who takes own life > **su•i•cid'al** [-əl] *adjective*
suit [soot] *noun* 1 set of clothing 2 garment worn for particular event, purpose 3 one of four sets in pack of cards 4 action at law ▷ *verb* 5 make, be fit or appropriate for 6 be acceptable to (someone) > **suit'a•ble** *adjective* 1 fitting, proper, convenient 2 becoming > **suit'a•bly** *adverb* > **suit'case** [-kays] *noun* flat rectangular traveling case
suite [sweet] *noun* 1 matched set esp. furniture 2 set of rooms
suit•or [SOOT-ər] *noun* 1 wooer 2 one who sues 3 petitioner
sul•fate [SUL-fayt] *noun* salt formed by sulfuric

DICTIONARY • THESAURUS

laconic, pithy, terse
succor *noun* 1 HELP, aid, assistance
▷ *verb* 2 HELP, aid, assist
succulent *adjective* JUICY, luscious, lush, moist
succumb *verb* 1 SURRENDER, capitulate, give in, submit, yield
2 DIE, fall
sucker *noun* (*slang*) FOOL, dork (*slang*), dupe, mug (*Brit slang*), pushover (*slang*), schmuck (*slang*), victim
sudden *adjective* QUICK, abrupt, hasty, hurried, rapid, rash, swift, unexpected
suddenly *adverb* ABRUPTLY, all of a sudden, unexpectedly
sue *verb* (*law*) TAKE (SOMEONE) TO COURT, charge, indict, prosecute, summon
suffer *verb* 1 UNDERGO, bear, endure, experience, go through, sustain
2 TOLERATE, put up with (*informal*)
suffering *noun* PAIN, agony, anguish, discomfort, distress, hardship, misery, ordeal, torment
suffice *verb* BE ENOUGH, be adequate, be sufficient, do, meet requirements, serve
sufficient *adjective* ADEQUATE, enough, satisfactory
suffocate *verb* CHOKE, asphyxiate, smother, stifle
suggest *verb* 1 RECOMMEND, advise, advocate, prescribe, propose
2 BRING TO MIND, evoke
3 HINT, imply, indicate, intimate
suggestion *noun* 1 RECOMMENDATION, motion, plan, proposal, proposition
2 HINT, breath, indication, intimation, trace, whisper
suggestive *adjective* SMUTTY, bawdy, blue, indelicate, provocative, racy, ribald, risqué, rude
suit *noun* 1 OUTFIT, clothing, costume, dress, ensemble, habit
2 LAWSUIT, action, case, cause, proceeding, prosecution, trial
▷ *verb* 3 BE ACCEPTABLE TO, do, gratify, please, satisfy
4 BEFIT, agree, become, go with, harmonize, match, tally
suitability *noun* APPROPRIATENESS, aptness, fitness, rightness
suitable *adjective* APPROPRIATE, apt, becoming, befitting, fit, fitting, proper, right, satisfactory
suite *noun* ROOMS, apartment

acid in combination with any base
sul•fon•a•mides [sul-FON-ə-mīdz] *noun* group of drugs used as internal germicides in treatment of many bacterial diseases
sul•fur [SUL-fər] *noun* pale yellow nonmetallic element > **sul•fur•ic** [sul-FYUUR-ik] *adjective*
sulk *verb intransitive* 1 be silent, resentful, esp. to draw attention to oneself ▷ *noun* 2 this mood > **sulk'y** *adjective* **sulk•i•er, sulk•i•est**
sul•len [SUL-ən] *adjective* 1 unwilling to talk or be sociable, morose 2 dismal 3 dull
sul•ly [SUL-ee] *verb transitive* **-lied, -ly•ing** stain, tarnish, disgrace
sul•tan [SUL-tn] *noun* ruler of Muslim country > **sul•tan'a** *noun* 1 sultan's wife or concubine 2 kind of raisin
sul•try [SUL-tree] *adjective* **-tri•er, -tri•est** 1 (of weather) hot, humid 2 (of person) looking sensual
sum *noun* 1 amount, total 2 problem in arithmetic ▷ *verb* **summed, sum•ming** 3 add up 4 make summary of main parts
sum•ma•ry [SUM-ə-ree] *noun, plural* **-ries** 1 abridgment or statement of chief points of longer document, speech, etc. 2 abstract ▷ *adjective* 3 done quickly > **sum•mar•i•ly** [sə-MAIR-ə-lee] *adverb* 1 speedily 2 abruptly > **sum'ma•rize** [-ə-rīz] *verb transitive* **-rized, -riz•ing** 1 make summary of 2 present briefly and concisely
sum•mer [SUM-ər] *noun* 1 second, warmest season ▷ *verb intransitive* 2 pass the summer > **sum'mer•y** *adjective*
sum'mit *noun* top, peak > **summit conference** meeting of heads of governments > **sum'mit•ry** [-mi-tree] *noun* practice, art of holding summit conferences
sum•mon [SUM-ən] *verb transitive* 1 demand attendance of 2 call on 3 bid witness appear in court 4 gather up (energies, etc.) > **sum'mons** *noun* 1 call 2 authoritative demand
sump *noun* place or receptacle (esp. as oil reservoir in engine) where fluid collects
sump•tu•ous [SUMP-choo-əs] *adjective* 1 lavish, magnificent 2 costly > **sump'tu•ous•ness** [-nis] *noun* > **sump'tu•ar•y** [-er-ee] *adjective* pert. to or regulating expenditure
sun *noun* 1 luminous body around which Earth and other planets revolve 2 its rays ▷ *verb* **sunned, sun•ning** 3 expose (self) to sun's rays > **sun'ny** *adjective* **-ni•er, -ni•est** 1 like the sun 2 warm 3 cheerful > **sun'bath•ing** [-bay*th*-ing] *noun* exposure of whole or part of body to sun's rays > **sun'beam** [-beem] *noun* ray of sun > **sun'burn** *noun* inflammation of skin due to excessive exposure to sun > **sun'down** *noun* sunset > **sun'spot** *noun* dark patch appearing temporarily on sun's surface > **sun'stroke** [-strohk] *noun* illness caused by prolonged exposure to intensely hot sun > **sun'tan** *noun* coloring of skin by exposure to sun
sun•dae [SUN-day] *noun* ice cream topped with fruit, etc.
sun•der [SUN-dər] *verb transitive* separate, sever
sun•dry [SUN-dree] *adjective* several, various > **sun'dries** *plural noun* odd items not mentioned in detail
sung *pp of* **sing**
sunk, sunk'en [-in] *pp of* **sink**
sup *verb* **supped, sup•ping** 1 take by sips 2 take supper ▷ *noun* 3 mouthful of liquid
su•per [SOO-pər] *adjective* 1 very good ▷ *noun* 2 *short for* **superintendent**
super- *prefix* above, greater, exceeding(ly): *superhuman; superman; supertanker*
su•per•a•ble [SOO-pər-ə-bəl] *adjective* 1 capable of being overcome 2 surmountable
su•per•an•nu•ate [soo-pər-AN-yoo-ayt] *verb transitive* **-at•ed, -at•ing** 1 pension off 2 discharge or dismiss as too old
su•perb [suu-PURB] *adjective* splendid, grand, impressive
su•per•charge [SOO-pər-chahrj] *verb transitive* **-charged, -charg•ing** charge, fill to excess > **su'per•charg•er** *noun* (internal-combustion engine) device to ensure complete filling of cylinder with explosive mixture when running at high speed
su•per•cil•i•ous [soo-pər-SIL-ee-əs] *adjective* displaying arrogant pride, scorn, indifference

DICTIONARY **S** THESAURUS

suitor *noun* (*old-fashioned*) ADMIRER, beau (*old-fashioned*), young man
sulk *verb* BE SULLEN, be in a huff, pout
sulky *adjective* HUFFY, cross, disgruntled, in the sulks, moody, petulant, querulous, resentful, sullen
sullen *adjective* MOROSE, cross, dour, glowering, moody, sour, surly, unsociable
sully *verb* DEFILE, besmirch, disgrace, dishonor, smirch, stain, tarnish
sultry *adjective* 1 HUMID, close, hot, muggy, oppressive, sticky, stifling 2 SEDUCTIVE, provocative, sensual, sexy (*informal*)
sum *noun* TOTAL, aggregate, amount, tally, whole
summarize *verb* SUM UP, abridge, condense, encapsulate, epitomize, précis
summary *noun* SYNOPSIS, abridgment, outline, précis, résumé, review, rundown
summit *noun* PEAK, acme, apex, head, height, pinnacle, top, zenith
summon *verb* 1 SEND FOR, bid, call, invite 2 (*often with up*) GATHER, draw on, muster
sumptuous *adjective* LUXURIOUS, gorgeous, grand, lavish, opulent, splendid, superb
sum up *verb* SUMMARIZE, put in a nutshell, recapitulate, review
sunburned *adjective* TANNED, bronzed, brown, burnt, peeling, red
sundry *adjective* VARIOUS, assorted, different, miscellaneous, several, some
sunken *adjective* 1 HOLLOW, drawn, haggard 2 LOWER, buried, recessed, submerged
sunny *adjective* 1 BRIGHT, clear, fine, radiant, summery, sunlit, unclouded 2 CHEERFUL, buoyant, cheery, happy, joyful, light-hearted
sunrise *noun* DAWN, break of day, cockcrow, daybreak
sunset *noun* NIGHTFALL, close of day *or* close of the day, dusk, eventide
super *adjective* (*informal*) EXCELLENT, glorious, magnificent, marvelous, outstanding, sensational (*informal*), superb, terrific (*informal*), wonderful
superb *adjective* SPLENDID, excellent, exquisite,

> **su•per•cil'i•ous•ness** [-nis] *noun*
su•per•fi•cial [soo-pər-FISH-əl] *adjective* 1 of or on surface 2 not careful or thorough 3 without depth, shallow
su•per•flu•ous [suu-PUR-floo-əs] *adjective* 1 extra, unnecessary 2 excessive 3 left over > **su•per•flu'i•ty** [-FLOO-i-tee] *noun, plural* **-ties** 1 superabundance 2 unnecessary amount
su•per•high•way [soo-pər-HĪ-way] *noun* broad multilane highway for travel at high speeds
su•per•in•tend [soo-pər-in-TEND] *verb* 1 have charge of 2 overlook 3 supervise > **su•per•in•tend'ent** *noun* esp. person in charge of building maintenance
su•pe•ri•or [sə-PEER-ee-ər] *adjective* 1 greater in quality or quantity 2 upper, higher in position, rank or quality 3 showing consciousness of being so > **su•pe•ri•or'i•ty** *noun* quality of being higher, greater, or more excellent
su•per•la•tive [sə-PUR-lə-tiv] *adjective* 1 of, in highest degree or quality 2 surpassing 3 *grammar* denoting form of adjective, adverb meaning *most* ▷ *noun* 4 *grammar* superlative degree of adjective or adverb
su•per•mar•ket [SOO-pər-mahr-kit] *noun* large self-service store selling chiefly food and household goods
su•per•mod•el [SOO-pər-mod-l] *noun* famous and highly-paid fashion model
su•per•nal [suu-PUR-nl] *adjective* celestial
su•per•nat•u•ral [soo-pər-NACH-ər-əl] *adjective* 1 being beyond the powers or laws of nature 2 miraculous ▷ *noun* 3 being, place, etc. of miraculous powers
su•per•nu•mer•ar•y [soo-pər-NOO-mə-rer-ee] *adjective* 1 in excess of normal number, extra ▷ *noun, plural* **-ar•ies** 2 extra person or thing
su•per•script [SOO-pər-skript] *noun, adjective* (character) printed, written above the line
su•per•sede [soo-pər-SEED] *verb transitive* **-sed•ed, -sed•ing** 1 take the place of 2 set aside, discard, supplant
su•per•size [SOO-pər-sīz] *adjective* 1 larger than standard size ▷ *verb transitive* 2 increase the size of
su•per•son•ic [soo-pər-SON-ik] *adjective* denoting speed greater than that of sound
su•per•sti•tion [soo-pər-STISH-ən] *noun* religion, opinion or practice based on belief in luck or magic > **su•per•sti'tious** [-STI-shəs] *adjective*
su•per•vene [soo-pər-VEEN] *verb intransitive* **-vened, -ven•ing** happen, as an interruption or change > **su•per•ven'tion** [-shən] *noun*
su•per•vise [SOO-pər-vīz] *verb transitive* **-vised, -vis•ing** 1 oversee 2 direct 3 inspect and control 4 superintend > **su•per•vi'sion** [-VIZH-ən] *noun* > **su'per•vis•or** *noun*
su•pine [soo-PĪN] *adjective* 1 lying on back with face upward 2 indolent ▷ *noun* [SOO-pīn] 3 Latin verbal noun
sup•per [SUP-ər] *noun* (light) evening meal
sup•plant [sə-PLANT] *verb transitive* 1 take the place of, esp. unfairly 2 oust
sup•ple [SUP-əl] *adjective* **-pler, -plest** 1 pliable 2 flexible 3 compliant > **sup•ply** [SUP-lee] *adverb*
sup•ple•ment [SUP-lə-mənt] *noun* 1 thing added to fill up, supply deficiency, esp. extra part added to book, etc. 2 additional number of periodical, usu. on special subject 3 separate, often illustrated section published periodically with newspaper ▷ *verb transitive* 4 add to 5 supply deficiency > **sup•ple•men'ta•ry** [-tə-ree] *adjective* additional
sup•pli•ant [SUP-lee-ənt] *adjective* 1 petitioning ▷ *noun* 2 petitioner
sup•pli•cate [SUP-li-kayt] *verb* **-cat•ed, -cat•ing**

fine, first-rate, grand, magnificent, marvelous, superior, superlative, world-class
supercilious *adjective* SCORNFUL, arrogant, contemptuous, disdainful, haughty, lofty, snooty (*informal*), stuck-up (*informal*)
superficial *adjective* 1 HASTY, casual, cursory, desultory, hurried, perfunctory, sketchy, slapdash
2 SHALLOW, empty-headed, frivolous, silly, trivial
3 SURFACE, exterior, external, on the surface, slight
superfluous *adjective* EXCESS, extra, left over, redundant, remaining, spare, supernumerary, surplus
superhuman *adjective* 1 HEROIC, phenomenal, prodigious
2 SUPERNATURAL, paranormal
superintendence *noun* SUPERVISION, charge, control, direction, government, management
superintendent *noun* SUPERVISOR, chief, controller, director, governor, inspector, manager, overseer
superior *adjective* 1 BETTER, grander, greater, higher, surpassing, unrivaled
2 SUPERCILIOUS, condescending, disdainful, haughty, lofty, lordly, patronizing, pretentious, snobbish
3 FIRST-CLASS, choice, deluxe, excellent, exceptional, exclusive, first-rate
▷ *noun* 4 BOSS (*informal*), chief, director, manager, principal, senior, supervisor
superiority *noun* SUPREMACY, advantage, ascendancy, excellence, lead, predominance
superlative *adjective* OUTSTANDING, excellent, supreme, unparalleled, unrivaled, unsurpassed
supernatural *adjective* PARANORMAL, ghostly, hidden, miraculous, mystic, occult, psychic, spectral, uncanny, unearthly
supersede *verb* REPLACE, displace, oust, supplant, take the place of, usurp
supervise *verb* OVERSEE, control, direct, handle, look after, manage, run, superintend
supervision *noun* SUPERINTENDENCE, care, charge, control, direction, guidance, management
supervisor *noun* BOSS (*informal*), administrator, chief, foreman, inspector, manager, overseer
supplant *verb* REPLACE, displace, oust, supersede, take the place of
supple *adjective* FLEXIBLE, limber, lissom *or* lissome, lithe, pliable, pliant
supplement *noun* 1 ADDITION, add-on, appendix, extra, insert, postscript, pull-out
▷ *verb* 2 ADD, augment, complement, extend, reinforce
supplementary *adjective* ADDITIONAL, add-on, ancillary, auxiliary, extra, secondary

beg humbly, entreat > **sup'pli•cant** [-pli-kənt] *noun* > **sup•pli•ca'tion** [-KAY-shən] *noun* > **sup'pli•ca•to•ry** [-kə-tor-ee] *adjective*
sup•ply [sə-PLĪ] *verb transitive* **-plied, -ply•ing** 1 furnish 2 make available 3 provide ▷ *noun, plural* **-plies** 4 supplying, substitute 5 stock, store
sup•port [sə-PORT] *verb transitive* 1 hold up 2 sustain 3 assist ▷ *noun* 4 supporting, being supported 5 means of support > **sup•port'a•ble** *adjective* > **sup•port'er** *noun* adherent > **sup•port'ing** *adjective* (of motion picture, etc. role) less important > **sup•port'ive** *adjective*
sup•pose [sə-POHZ] *verb transitive* **-posed, -pos•ing** 1 assume as theory 2 take for granted 3 accept as likely 4 (in passive) be expected, obliged 5 ought > **sup•posed'** *adjective* > **sup•pos•ed•ly** [sə-POH-zid-lee] *adverb* > **sup•po•si'tion** [-ZISH-ən] *noun* 1 assumption 2 belief without proof 3 conjecture > **sup•po•si'tious** *adjective* > **sup•pos•i•ti•tious** [sə-poz-i-TISH-əs] *adjective* 1 sham 2 spurious 3 counterfeit
sup•pos•i•to•ry [sə-POZ-i-tor-ee] *noun, plural* **-ries** medication (in capsule) for insertion in orifice of body
sup•press [sə-PRES] *verb transitive* 1 put down, restrain 2 crush, stifle 3 keep or withdraw from publication > **sup•pres'sion** [-PRESH-ən] *noun*
sup•pu•rate [SUP-yə-rayt] *verb intransitive* **-rat•ed, -rat•ing** fester, form pus > **sup•pu•ra'tion** [-shən] *noun*
supra- *prefix* above, over: *supranational*
su•preme [sə-PREEM] *adjective* 1 highest in authority or rank 2 utmost > **su•prem•a•cy** [-PREM-ə-see] *noun* position of being supreme
sur•cease [sur-SEES] *verb intransitive* **-ceased, -ceas•ing** 1 cease, desist ▷ *noun* 2 cessation
sur•charge [SUR-chahrj] *noun* 1 additional charge ▷ *verb transitive* [sur-CHAHRJ], **-charged, -charg•ing** 2 make additional charge
sure [shuur] *adjective* 1 certain 2 trustworthy 3 without doubt ▷ *adverb* (*informal*) 4 certainly > **sure'ly** *adverb* > **sur•e•ty** [SHUUR-i-tee] *noun, plural* **-ties** 1 one who takes responsibility for another's obligations 2 security against damage, etc. 3 certainty
surf *noun* 1 waves breaking on shore ▷ *verb* 2 swim in, ride surf 3 move quickly through a medium such as the World Wide Web > **surf'ing** *noun* this sport > **surf'er** *noun* one who (often) goes surfing > **surf'board** *noun* board used in surfing
sur•face [SUR-fis] *noun* 1 outside face of body 2 exterior 3 plane 4 top, visible side 5 superficial appearance, outward impression ▷ *adjective* 6 involving the surface only 7 going no deeper than surface ▷ *verb* **-faced, -fac•ing** 8 (cause to) come to surface 9 put a surface on
sur•feit [SUR-fit] *noun* 1 excess 2 disgust caused by excess ▷ *verb* 3 feed to excess 4 provide anything in excess
surge [surj] *noun* 1 wave 2 sudden increase 3 *electricity* sudden rush of current in circuit ▷ *verb intransitive* **surged, surg•ing** 4 move in large

DICTIONARY

S

THESAURUS

supplication *noun* PLEA, appeal, entreaty, petition, prayer, request
supply *verb* 1 PROVIDE, contribute, endow, equip, furnish, give, grant, produce, stock, yield ▷ *noun* 2 STORE, cache, fund, hoard, quantity, reserve, source, stock 3 (*usually plural*) PROVISIONS, equipment, food, materials, necessities, rations, stores
support *verb* 1 BEAR, brace, buttress, carry, hold, prop, reinforce, sustain 2 PROVIDE FOR, finance, fund, keep, look after, maintain, sustain 3 HELP, aid, assist, back, champion, defend, second, side with 4 BEAR OUT, confirm, corroborate, substantiate, verify ▷ *noun* 5 HELP, aid, assistance, backing, encouragement, loyalty 6 PROP, brace, foundation, pillar, post 7 SUPPORTER, backer, mainstay, prop, second, tower of strength 8 UPKEEP, keep, maintenance, subsistence, sustenance
supporter *noun* FOLLOWER, adherent, advocate, champion, fan, friend, helper, patron, sponsor, well-wisher
supportive *adjective* HELPFUL, encouraging, sympathetic, understanding
suppose *verb* 1 PRESUME, assume, conjecture, expect, guess (*informal*), imagine, think 2 IMAGINE, conjecture, consider, hypothesize, postulate, pretend
supposed *adjective* 1 PRESUMED, accepted, alleged, assumed, professed 2 (*usually with to*) MEANT, expected, obliged, required
supposedly *adverb* ALLEGEDLY, hypothetically, ostensibly, presumably, theoretically
supposition *noun* GUESS, conjecture, hypothesis, presumption, speculation, surmise, theory
suppress *verb* 1 STOP, check, conquer, crush, overpower, put an end to, quash, quell, subdue 2 RESTRAIN, conceal, contain, curb, hold in *or* hold back, repress, silence, smother, stifle
suppression *noun* ELIMINATION, check, crushing, quashing, smothering
supremacy *noun* DOMINATION, mastery, predominance, primacy, sovereignty, supreme power, sway
supreme *adjective* HIGHEST, chief, foremost, greatest, head, leading, paramount, pre-eminent, prime, principal, top, ultimate
sure *adjective* 1 CERTAIN, assured, confident, convinced, decided, definite, positive 2 RELIABLE, accurate, dependable, foolproof, infallible, undeniable, undoubted, unerring, unfailing 3 INEVITABLE, assured, bound, guaranteed, inescapable
surely *adverb* UNDOUBTEDLY, certainly, definitely, doubtlessly, indubitably, unquestionably, without doubt
surface *noun* 1 OUTSIDE, covering, exterior, face, side, top, veneer ▷ *verb* 2 APPEAR, arise, come to light, come up, crop up (*informal*), emerge, materialize, transpire
surfeit *noun* EXCESS, glut, plethora, superfluity
surge *noun* 1 RUSH, flood, flow, gush, outpouring 2 WAVE, billow, roller, swell

waves **5** swell, billow **6** rise precipitately
sur•geon [SUR-jən] *noun* physician who performs operations > **sur'ger•y** *noun* medical treatment by operation > **sur'gi•cal** [-kəl] *adjective*
sur•ly [SUR-lee] *adjective* **-li•er, -li•est** **1** gloomily morose **2** ill-natured **3** cross and rude > **sur'li•ness** [-nis] *noun*
sur•mise [sər-MĪZ] *verb, noun* **-mised, -mis•ing** guess, conjecture
sur•mount [sər-MOWNT] *verb transitive* get over, overcome > **sur•mount'a•ble** *adjective*
sur•name [SUR-naym] *noun* family name
sur•pass [sər-PAS] *verb transitive* **1** go beyond **2** excel **3** outstrip > **sur•pass'a•ble** *adjective* > **sur•pass'ing** *adjective* **1** excellent **2** exceeding others
sur•plice [SUR-plis] *noun* loose white vestment worn by clergy and choir members
sur'plus *noun* what remains over in excess
sur•prise [sər-PRĪZ] *verb transitive* **-prised, -pris•ing** **1** cause surprise to **2** astonish **3** take, come upon unexpectedly **4** startle (someone) into action thus ▷ *noun* **5** what takes unawares **6** something unexpected **7** emotion aroused by being taken unawares
sur•re•al•ism [sə-REE-ə-liz-əm] *noun* movement in art and literature emphasizing expression of the unconscious > **sur•re'al** *adjective* > **sur•re'al•ist** *noun, adjective*
sur•ren•der [sə-REN-dər] *verb transitive* **1** hand over, give up ▷ *verb intransitive* **2** yield **3** cease resistance **4** capitulate ▷ *noun* **5** act of surrendering
sur•rep•ti•tious [sur-əp-TISH-əs] *adjective* **1** done secretly or stealthily **2** furtive
sur•ro•gate [SUR-ə-gayt, SUR-ə-git] *noun* **1** deputy, esp. of bishop **2** substitute **3** judicial officer supervising probate of wills > **surrogate mother** woman who bears child on behalf of childless woman
sur•round [sə-ROWND] *verb transitive* **1** be, come all around, encompass **2** encircle **3** hem in ▷ *noun* **4** border, edging > **sur•round'ings** *plural noun* conditions, scenery, etc. around a person, place, environment
sur•tax [SUR-taks] *noun* additional tax
sur•veil•lance [sər-VAY-ləns] *noun* close watch, supervision > **sur•veil'lant** *adjective, noun*
sur•vey [sər-VAY] *verb transitive* **1** view, scrutinize **2** inspect, examine **3** measure, map (land) ▷ *noun* [SUR-vay] *plural* **-veys** **4** a surveying **5** inspection **6** report incorporating results of survey > **sur•vey'or** *noun*
sur•vive [sər-VĪV] *verb transitive* **-vived, -viv•ing** **1** outlive **2** come through alive ▷ *verb intransitive* **-vived, -viv•ing** **3** continue to live or exist > **sur•viv'al** [-əl] *noun* continuation of existence of persons, things, etc. > **sur•viv'or** [-ər] *noun* **1** one left alive when others have died **2** one who continues to function despite setbacks
sus•cep•ti•ble [sə-SEP-tə-bəl] *adjective* **1** yielding readily (to) **2** capable (of) **3** impressionable > **sus•cep•ti•bil'i•ty** *noun*
sus•pect [sə-SPEKT] *verb transitive* **1** doubt innocence of **2** have impression of existence or presence of **3** be inclined to believe that **4** mistrust ▷ *adjective* [SUS-pekt] **5** of suspected character ▷ *noun* [SUS-pekt] **6** suspected person
sus•pend [sə-SPEND] *verb transitive* **1** hang up **2** cause to cease for a time **3** debar from an office

DICTIONARY • THESAURUS

▷ *verb* **3** RUSH, gush, heave, rise, roll
surly *adjective* ILL-TEMPERED, churlish, cross, grouchy (*informal*), morose, sulky, sullen, uncivil, ungracious
surmise *verb* **1** GUESS, conjecture, imagine, presume, speculate, suppose
▷ *noun* **2** GUESS, assumption, conjecture, presumption, speculation, supposition
surpass *verb* OUTDO, beat, eclipse, exceed, excel, outshine, outstrip, transcend
surpassing *adjective* SUPREME, exceptional, extraordinary, incomparable, matchless, outstanding, unrivaled
surplus *noun* **1** EXCESS, balance, remainder, residue, surfeit
▷ *adjective* **2** EXCESS, extra, odd, remaining, spare, superfluous
surprise *noun* **1** SHOCK, bombshell, eye-opener (*informal*), jolt, revelation
2 AMAZEMENT, astonishment, incredulity, wonder
▷ *verb* **3** AMAZE, astonish, stagger, stun, take aback
4 CATCH UNAWARES *or* CATCH OFF-GUARD, discover, spring upon, startle
surprised *adjective* AMAZED, astonished, speechless, taken by surprise, thunderstruck
surprising *adjective* AMAZING, astonishing, extraordinary, incredible, remarkable, staggering, unexpected, unusual
surrender *verb* **1** GIVE IN, capitulate, give way, submit, succumb, yield
2 GIVE UP, abandon, cede, concede, part with, relinquish, renounce, waive, yield
▷ *noun* **3** SUBMISSION, capitulation, relinquishment, renunciation, resignation
surreptitious *adjective* SECRET, covert, furtive, sly, stealthy, underhand
surrogate *noun* SUBSTITUTE, proxy, representative, stand-in
surround *verb* ENCLOSE, encircle, encompass, envelop, hem in, ring
surroundings *plural noun* ENVIRONMENT, background, location, milieu, setting
surveillance *noun* OBSERVATION, inspection, scrutiny, supervision, watch
survey *verb* **1** LOOK OVER, contemplate, examine, inspect, observe, scan, scrutinize, view
2 ESTIMATE, appraise, assess, measure, plan, plot, size up
▷ *noun* **3** EXAMINATION, inspection, scrutiny
4 STUDY, inquiry, review
survive *verb* REMAIN ALIVE, endure, last, live on, outlast, outlive
susceptible *adjective* **1** (*usually with to*) LIABLE, disposed, given, inclined, prone, subject, vulnerable
2 IMPRESSIONABLE, receptive, responsive, sensitive, suggestible
suspect *verb* **1** BELIEVE, consider, feel, guess, speculate, suppose
2 DISTRUST, doubt, mistrust
▷ *adjective* **3** DUBIOUS, doubtful, iffy (*informal*), questionable

or privilege 4 keep inoperative 5 sustain in fluid > **sus•pend'ers** *plural noun* straps for supporting trousers, etc.

sus•pense [sə-SPENS] *noun* 1 state of uncertainty, esp. while awaiting news, an event, etc. 2 anxiety, worry > **sus•pen'sion** [-shən] *noun* 1 state of being suspended 2 springs on axle of body of vehicle > **sus•pen'so•ry** [-sə-ree] *adjective*

sus•pi•cion [sə-SPISH-ən] *noun* 1 suspecting, being suspected 2 slight trace > **sus•pi'cious** *adjective*

sus•tain [sə-STAYN] *verb transitive* 1 keep, hold up 2 endure 3 keep alive 4 confirm > **sus•tain'a•ble** *adjective* > **sus'te•nance** [-nəns] *noun* food

su•ture [SOO-chər] *noun* 1 act of sewing 2 sewing up of a wound 3 material used for this 4 a joining of the bones of the skull ▷ *verb transitive* **-tured, -tur•ing** 5 join by suture

SUV sport utility vehicle

su•ze•rain [SOO-zə-rin] *noun* 1 sovereign with rights over autonomous state 2 feudal lord > **su'ze•rain•ty** [-tee] *noun*

svelte [svelt] *adjective* **svelt•er, svelt•est** 1 lightly built, slender 2 sophisticated

swab [swob] *noun* 1 mop 2 pad of surgical cotton, etc. for cleaning, taking specimen, etc. 3 (*slang*) sailor, low or unmannerly fellow ▷ *verb transitive* **swabbed, swab'bing** 4 clean with swab

swad•dle [SWOD-l] *verb transitive* **-dled, -dling** swathe > **swaddling clothes** *hist.* long strips of cloth for wrapping infant

swag *noun* (*slang*) stolen property

swag•ger [SWAG-ər] *verb intransitive* 1 strut 2 boast ▷ *noun* 3 strutting gait 4 boastful, overconfident manner

swain [swayn] *noun* rustic lover

swal•low[1] [SWOL-oh] *verb transitive* 1 cause, allow to pass down gullet 2 engulf 3 suppress, keep back 4 believe gullibly ▷ *noun* 5 act of swallowing

swallow[2] *noun* migratory bird with forked tail and skimming manner of flight

swam *pt. of* **swim**

swamp [swomp] *noun* 1 bog ▷ *verb transitive* 2 entangle in swamp 3 overwhelm 4 flood > **swamp'y** *adjective* **swamp•i•er, swamp•i•est**

swan [swon] *noun* large, web-footed water bird with graceful curved neck > **swan song** 1 fabled song of a swan before death 2 last act, etc. before death

swank [swangk] *verb intransitive* 1 swagger 2 show off ▷ *noun* 3 smartness 4 style > **swank'y** *adjective* **swank•i•er, swank•i•est** 1 smart 2 showy

swap [swop] *noun, verb* **swapped, swap•ping** 1 exchange 2 barter

swarm [sworm] *noun* 1 large cluster of insects 2 vast crowd ▷ *verb intransitive* (of bees) be on the move in swarm 3 gather in large numbers

swarth•y [SWOR-*thee*] *adjective* **swarth•i•er, swarth•i•est** of dark complexion

swash•buck•ler [SWOSH-buk-lər] *noun* swaggering daredevil person > **swash'buck•ling** *adjective*

swas•ti•ka [SWOS-ti-kə] *noun* form of cross with arms bent at right angles, used as emblem by Nazis

swat [swot] *verb transitive* **swat•ted, swat•ting** 1 hit smartly 2 kill, esp. insects

swath [swoth] *noun* 1 line of grass or grain cut and thrown together by scythe or mower 2 whole sweep of scythe or mower

swathe [swo*th*] *verb transitive* **swathed, swath•ing** cover with wraps or bandages

sway *verb* 1 swing unsteadily 2 (cause to) vacillate in opinion, etc. 3 influence opinion, etc. ▷ *noun* 4 control 5 power 6 swaying motion

swear [swair] *verb transitive* **swore, sworn, swear•ing** 1 promise on oath 2 cause to take an oath ▷ *verb intransitive* **swore, sworn,**

---

suspend *verb* 1 HANG, attach, dangle
2 POSTPONE, cease, cut short, defer, discontinue, interrupt, put off, shelve

suspense *noun* UNCERTAINTY, anxiety, apprehension, doubt, expectation, insecurity, irresolution, tension

suspension *noun* POSTPONEMENT, abeyance, break, breaking off, deferment, discontinuation, interruption

suspicion *noun* 1 DISTRUST, doubt, dubiety, misgiving, mistrust, qualm, skepticism, wariness
2 IDEA, guess, hunch, impression, notion
3 TRACE, hint, shade, soupçon (*French*), streak, suggestion, tinge, touch

suspicious *adjective* 1 DISTRUSTFUL, doubtful, skeptical, unbelieving, wary
2 SUSPECT, doubtful, dubious, fishy (*informal*), questionable

sustain *verb* 1 MAINTAIN, continue, keep up, prolong, protract
2 KEEP ALIVE, aid, assist, help, nourish
3 WITHSTAND, bear, endure, experience, feel, suffer, undergo
4 SUPPORT, bear, uphold

sustained *adjective* CONTINUOUS, constant, nonstop, perpetual, prolonged, steady, twenty-four-seven (*slang*), unremitting

swagger *verb* SHOW OFF (*informal*), boast, brag, parade

swallow *verb* GULP, chow down (*slang*), consume, devour, drink, eat, swig (*informal*)

swamp *noun* 1 BOG, fen, marsh, mire, morass, quagmire, slough
▷ *verb* 2 FLOOD, capsize, engulf, inundate, sink, submerge
3 OVERWHELM, flood, inundate, overload

swarm *noun* 1 MULTITUDE, army, crowd, flock, herd, horde, host, mass, throng
▷ *verb* 2 CROWD, flock, mass, stream, throng
3 TEEM, abound, bristle, crawl

swarthy *adjective* DARK-SKINNED, black, brown, dark, dark-complexioned, dusky

swashbuckling *adjective* DASHING, bold, daredevil, flamboyant

swathe *verb* WRAP, bundle up, cloak, drape, envelop, shroud

sway *verb* 1 LEAN, bend, rock, roll, swing
2 INFLUENCE, affect, guide, induce, persuade
▷ *noun* 3 POWER, authority, clout (*informal*), control, influence

swear *verb* 1 CURSE, be foul-mouthed,

swear•ing 3 declare 4 use profanity
sweat [swet] *noun* 1 moisture oozing from, forming on skin, esp. in humans ▷ *verb* **sweat** *or* **sweat•ed, sweat•ing** 2 (cause to) exude sweat 3 toil 4 employ at wrongfully low wages 5 worry 6 wait anxiously > **sweat'y** *adjective* **sweat•i•er, sweat•i•est** > **sweat'shirt** [-shurt] *noun* long-sleeved cotton pullover
sweat•er [SWET-ər] *noun* knitted pullover or cardigan with or without sleeves
sweep *verb intransitive* **swept, sweep•ing** 1 effect cleaning with broom 2 pass quickly or magnificently 3 extend in continuous curve ▷ *verb transitive* **swept, sweep•ing** 4 clean with broom 5 carry impetuously ▷ *noun* 6 act of cleaning with broom 7 sweeping motion 8 wide curve 9 range 10 long oar 11 one who cleans chimneys > **sweeping** *adjective* 1 wide-ranging 2 without limitations, reservations > **sweep'stakes** *noun* 1 gamble in which winner takes stakes contributed by all 2 type of lottery 3 risky venture promising great return
sweet *adjective* **-er, -est** 1 tasting like sugar 2 agreeable 3 kind, charming 4 fresh, fragrant 5 in good condition 6 tuneful 7 gentle, dear, beloved ▷ *noun* 8 small piece of sweet food 9 something pleasant > **sweets** cake, etc. containing much sugar > **sweet'en** [-in] *verb* > **sweet'en•er** [-ən-ər] *noun* > **sweet'bread** [-bred] *noun* animal's pancreas used as food > **sweet'heart** *noun* lover > **sweetheart contract** collusive contract between labor union and company benefiting latter > **sweet'meat** *noun* sweetened delicacy e.g. small cake, candy > **sweet potato** 1 trailing plant 2 its edible, sweetish, starchy tubers > **sweet talk** (*informal*) flattery > **sweet-talk** *verb* (*informal*) coax, flatter
swell *verb* **swelled, swol•len** [SWOHL-ən] **swelled, swel•ling** 1 expand ▷ *verb intransitive* 2 be greatly filled with pride, emotion ▷ *noun* 3 act of swelling or being swollen 4 wave of sea 5 mechanism in organ to vary volume of sound 6 (*informal*) person of high social standing ▷ *adjective* (*informal*) 7 stylish, socially prominent 8 fine
swel•ter [SWEL-tər] *verb intransitive* be oppressed with heat
swept *pt./pp. of* **sweep**
swerve [swurv] *verb intransitive* **swerved, swerv•ing** 1 swing around, change direction during motion 2 turn aside (from duty, etc.) ▷ *noun* 3 swerving
swift *adjective* **-er, -est** 1 rapid, quick, ready ▷ *noun* 2 bird like a swallow
swig *noun* (*informal*) 1 large swallow of drink ▷ *verb* **swigged, swig•ging** (*informal*) 2 drink thus
swill *verb* 1 drink greedily 2 feed (pigs) with swill ▷ *noun* 3 liquid or wet pig food 4 greedy drinking 5 kitchen refuse 6 drivel
swim *verb intransitive* **swam, swum, swim•ming** 1 support and move oneself in water 2 float 3 be flooded 4 have feeling of dizziness ▷ *verb transitive* **swam, swum, swim•ming** 5 cross by swimming 6 compete in by swimming ▷ *noun* 7 spell of swimming > **swim'ming•ly** *adverb* successfully, effortlessly
swin•dle [SWIN-dl] *noun, verb* **-dled, -dling** cheat > **swind'ler** [-lər] *noun* > **swind'ling** *noun*
swine [swīn] *noun, plural* **swine** 1 pig 2 contemptible person > **swin'ish** *adjective*
swing *verb* **swung, swing•ing** 1 (cause to) move to and fro 2 (cause to) pivot, turn 3 hang 4 arrange, play music with (jazz) rhythm ▷ *verb*

DICTIONARY • THESAURUS

blaspheme
2 DECLARE, affirm, assert, attest, promise, testify, vow
swearing *noun* BAD LANGUAGE, blasphemy, cursing, foul language, profanity
swearword *noun* OATH, curse, expletive, four-letter word, obscenity, profanity
sweat *noun* 1 PERSPIRATION
2 (*informal*) LABOR, chore, drudgery, toil
3 (*informal*) WORRY, agitation, anxiety, distress, panic, strain
▷ *verb* 4 PERSPIRE, glow
5 (*informal*) WORRY, agonize, fret, suffer, torture oneself
sweaty *adjective* PERSPIRING, clammy, sticky
sweep *verb* 1 CLEAR, brush, clean, remove
2 SAIL, fly, glide, pass, skim, tear, zoom
▷ *noun* 3 ARC, bend, curve, move, stroke, swing
4 EXTENT, range, scope, stretch
sweeping *adjective* 1 WIDE-RANGING, all-embracing, all-inclusive, broad, comprehensive, extensive, global, wide
2 INDISCRIMINATE, blanket, exaggerated, overstated, unqualified, wholesale
sweet *adjective* 1 SUGARY, cloying, saccharine
2 CHARMING, agreeable, appealing, cute, delightful, engaging, kind, likable *or* likeable, lovable, winning
3 MELODIOUS, dulcet, harmonious, mellow, musical
4 FRAGRANT, aromatic, clean, fresh, pure
▷ *noun* 5 (*usually plural*) CONFECTIONERY, bonbon
sweeten *verb* 1 SUGAR
2 MOLLIFY, appease, pacify, soothe
sweetheart *noun* LOVER, beloved, boyfriend *or* girlfriend, darling, dear, love
swell *verb* 1 EXPAND, balloon, bloat, bulge, dilate, distend, enlarge, grow, increase, rise
▷ *noun* 2 WAVE, billow, surge
swelling *noun* ENLARGEMENT, bulge, bump, distension, inflammation, lump, protuberance
sweltering *adjective* HOT, boiling, burning, oppressive, scorching, stifling
swerve *verb* VEER, bend, deflect, deviate, diverge, stray, swing, turn, turn aside
swift *adjective* QUICK, fast, hurried, prompt, rapid, speedy
swiftly *adverb* QUICKLY, fast, hurriedly, promptly, rapidly, speedily
swiftness *noun* SPEED, promptness, quickness, rapidity, speediness, velocity
swindle *verb* 1 CHEAT, con, defraud, fleece, rip (someone) off (*slang*), sting (*informal*), trick
▷ *noun* 2 FRAUD, con trick (*informal*), deception, racket, rip-off (*slang*), scam (*slang*)
swindler *noun* CHEAT, con man (*informal*), fraud, rogue, shark, trickster
swing *verb* 1 SWAY, oscillate, rock, veer, wave
2 (*usually with round*) TURN, curve, pivot, rotate, swivel
3 HANG, dangle, suspend
▷ *noun* 4 SWAYING, oscillation

intransitive 5 be hanged 6 hit out (at) ▷ *noun* 7 act, instance of swinging 8 seat hung to swing on 9 fluctuation (esp. e.g. in voting pattern) > **swing'er** *noun* (*slang*) person regarded as modern and lively or sexually promiscuous

swipe [swīp] *verb* **swiped, swip•ing** 1 strike with wide, sweeping or glancing blow 2 (*informal*) steal 3 pass (a plastic card, such as a credit card) through a machine which electronically reads information on the card

swirl [swurl] *verb* (cause to) move with eddying motion ▷ *noun* such motion

swish *verb* (cause to) move with audible hissing sound ▷ *noun* 1 the sound 2 (*slang*) effeminate homosexual male ▷ *adjective* 3 (*slang*) effeminate

switch [swich] *noun* 1 mechanism to complete or interrupt electric circuit, etc. 2 abrupt change 3 flexible stick or twig 4 tufted end of animal's tail 5 type of women's hairpiece ▷ *verb intransitive* 6 shift, change 7 swing ▷ *verb transitive* 8 affect (current, etc.) with switch 9 change abruptly 10 strike with switch > **switch'back** *noun* road, railway with steep rises and descents > **switch'board** [-bord] *noun* installation for establishing or varying connections in telephone and electric circuits

swiv•el [SWIV-əl] *noun* 1 mechanism of two parts that can revolve the one on the other ▷ *verb* **-eled, -el•ing** 2 turn (on swivel)

swollen [SWOH-lən] *pp of* **swell**

swoon *verb intransitive, noun* faint

swoop *verb intransitive* 1 dive, as hawk ▷ *noun* 2 act of swooping 3 sudden attack

sword [sord] *noun* weapon with long blade for cutting or thrusting

swore *verb pt. of* **swear**

sworn *verb* 1 *pp of* **swear.** ▷ *adjective* 2 bound by or as if by an oath: *sworn enemies*

swum *pp of* **swim**

swung *pt./pp. of* **swing**

syb•a•rite [SIB-ə-rīt] *noun* lover of luxury > **syb•a•rit'ic** [-RIT-ik] *adjective*

syc•o•phant [SIK-ə-fənt] *noun* one using flattery to gain favors > **syc•o•phan'tic** [-FAN-tik] *adjective* > **syc'o•phan•cy** [-fən-see] *noun*

syl•la•ble [SIL-ə-bəl] *noun* division of word as unit for pronunciation > **syl•lab'ic** *adjective* > **syl•lab'i•fy** *verb transitive* **-fied, -fy•ing**

syl•la•bus [SIL-ə-bəs] *noun, plural* **-bus•es, -bi** [-bī] 1 outline of a course of study 2 list of subjects studied in course

syl•lo•gism [SIL-ə-jiz-əm] *noun* form of logical reasoning consisting of two premises and conclusion > **syl•lo•gis'tic** *adjective*

sylph [silf] *noun* 1 slender, graceful woman 2 sprite

syl•van [SIL-vən] *adjective* of forests, trees

sym- *see* **syn-**

sym•bi•o•sis [sim-bee-OH-sis] *noun, plural* **-ses** [-seez] 1 living together of two organisms of different kinds, esp. to their mutual benefit 2 similar relationship involving people, etc. > **sym•bi•ot'ic** [-OT-ik] *adjective*

sym•bol [SIM-bəl] *noun* 1 sign 2 thing representing or typifying something > **sym•bol'ic** *adjective* > **sym•bol'i•cal•ly** *adverb* > **sym'bol•ism** *noun* 1 use of, representation by symbols 2 movement in art holding that work of art should express idea in symbolic form > **sym'bol•ist** *noun, adjective* > **sym'bol•ize** *verb transitive* **-ized, -iz•ing**

sym•me•try [SIM-ə-tree] *noun, plural* **-tries** 1 proportion between parts 2 balance of arrangement between two sides 3 order > **sym•met'ri•cal** *adjective* 1 having due proportion in its parts 2 harmonious 3 regular

sym•pa•thy [SIM-pə-thee] *noun, plural* **-thies** 1 feeling for another in pain, etc. 2 compassion, pity 3 sharing of emotion, interest, desire, etc. 4 fellow feeling > **sym•pa•thet'ic** *adjective* > **sym'pa•thize** [-thīz] *verb intransitive* **-thized, -thiz•ing**

sym•pho•ny [SIM-fə-nee] *noun, plural* **-nies** 1 composition for full orchestra 2 harmony of sounds > **sym•phon'ic** [-FON-ik] *adjective*

---

swipe *verb* 1 HIT, lash out at, slap, strike, wallop (*informal*)
2 (*slang*) STEAL, appropriate, filch, lift (*informal*), pinch (*informal*), purloin
▷ *noun* 3 BLOW, clout (*informal*), cuff, slap, smack, wallop (*informal*)

swirl *verb* WHIRL, churn, eddy, spin, twist

switch *noun* 1 CHANGE, reversal, shift
2 EXCHANGE, substitution, swap
▷ *verb* 3 CHANGE, deflect, deviate, divert, shift
4 EXCHANGE, substitute, swap

swivel *verb* TURN, pivot, revolve, rotate, spin

swollen *adjective* ENLARGED, bloated, distended, inflamed, puffed up

swoop *verb* 1 POUNCE, descend, dive, rush, stoop, sweep
▷ *noun* 2 POUNCE, descent, drop, lunge, plunge, rush, stoop, sweep

swop *verb* EXCHANGE, barter, interchange, switch, trade

sycophant *noun* CRAWLER, brown-noser (*slang*), fawner, flatterer, toady, yes man

sycophantic *adjective* OBSEQUIOUS, crawling, fawning, flattering, grovelling, ingratiating, servile, slimy, smarmy (*Brit informal*), toadying, unctuous

syllabus *noun* COURSE OF STUDY, curriculum

symbol *noun* SIGN, badge, emblem, figure, icon, image, logo, mark, representation, token

symbolic *adjective* REPRESENTATIVE, allegorical, emblematic, figurative

symbolize *verb* REPRESENT, denote, mean, personify, signify, stand for, typify

symmetrical *adjective* BALANCED, in proportion, regular

symmetry *noun* BALANCE, evenness, order, proportion, regularity

sympathetic *adjective* 1 CARING, compassionate, concerned, interested, kind, pitying, supportive, understanding, warm
2 LIKE-MINDED, agreeable, companionable, compatible, congenial, friendly

sympathize *verb* 1 FEEL FOR, commiserate, condole, pity
2 AGREE, side with, understand

sympathizer *noun* SUPPORTER, partisan, well-wisher

sympathy *noun* 1 COMPASSION, commiseration, pity, understanding
2 AGREEMENT, affinity, fellow feeling, rapport

> **sym•pho'ni•ous** [-FOH-nee-əs] *adjective* harmonious

sym•po•si•um [sim-POH-zee-əm] *noun, plural* **-si•a** [-zee-ə] **1** conference, meeting **2** discussion, writings on a given topic

symp•tom [SIMP-təm] *noun* **1** change in body indicating its state of health or disease **2** sign, token > **symp•to•mat'ic** *adjective*

syn-, sym- *prefix* with, together, alike: *synchronize; syncopate*

syn•a•gogue [SIN-ə-gog] *noun* (place of worship of) Jewish congregation

syn•chro•nize [SING-krə-nīz] *verb transitive* **-nized, -niz•ing 1** make agree in time ▷ *verb intransitive* **-nized, -niz•ing 2** happen at same time > **syn•chro•ni•za'tion** *noun* > **syn'chro•nous** [-nis] *adjective* simultaneous

syn•co•pate [SING-kə-payt] *verb transitive* **-pat•ed, -pat•ing** accentuate weak beat in bar of music > **syn•co•pa'tion** *noun*

syn•di•cate [SIN-di-kit] *noun* **1** body of people, delegates associated for some enterprise ▷ *verb* [-kayt], **-cat•ed, -cat•ing 2** form syndicate ▷ *verb transitive* **3** publish in many newspapers at the same time

syn•drome [SIN-drohm] *noun* **1** combination of several symptoms in disease **2** symptom, set of symptoms or characteristics

syn•ec•do•che [si-NEK-də-kee] *noun* figure of speech by which whole of thing is put for part or part for whole, such as *sail* for *ship*

syn•er•gy [SIN-ər-jee] *noun* potential ability for people or groups to be more successful working together than on their own

syn•od [SIN-əd] *noun* **1** church council **2** convention

syn•o•nym [SIN-ə-nim] *noun* word with (nearly) same meaning as another > **syn•on•y•mous** [si-NON-ə-məs] *adjective*

syn•op•sis [si-NOP-sis] *noun, plural* **-ses** [-seez] summary, outline > **syn•op'tic** *adjective* **1** of, like synopsis **2** having same viewpoint

syn•tax [SIN-taks] *noun* part of grammar treating of arrangement of words in sentence > **syn•tac'tic** *adjective*

syn•the•sis [SIN-thə-sis] *noun, plural* **-ses** [-seez] putting together, combination > **syn'the•size** *verb* **-sized, -siz•ing** make artificially > **syn'the•siz•er** [-sīz-ər] *noun* electronic keyboard instrument capable of reproducing a wide range of musical sounds > **syn•thet'ic** *adjective* **1** artificial **2** of synthesis

syph•i•lis [SIF-ə-lis] *noun* contagious venereal disease > **syph•i•lit'ic** *adjective*

sy•ringe [sə-RINJ] *noun* **1** instrument for drawing in liquid by piston and forcing it out in fine stream or spray **2** squirt ▷ *verb transitive* **-ringed, -ring•ing 3** spray, cleanse with syringe

syr•up [SIR-əp] *noun* **1** thick solution obtained in process of refining sugar, molasses, etc. **2** any liquid like this, esp. in consistency > **syr'up•y** *adjective*

sys•tem [SIS-təm] *noun* **1** complex whole, organization **2** method **3** classification > **sys•tem•at'ic** *adjective* methodical > **sys'tem•a•tize** [-tīz] *verb transitive* **-tized, -tiz•ing 1** reduce to system **2** arrange methodically > **sys•tem'ic** *adjective* affecting entire body or organism

sys•to•le [SIS-tə-lee] *noun* contraction of heart and arteries for expelling blood and carrying on circulation > **sys•tol•ic** [sis-TOL-ik] *adjective* **1** contracting **2** of systole

DICTIONARY • THESAURUS

symptom *noun* SIGN, expression, indication, mark, token, warning

symptomatic *adjective* INDICATIVE, characteristic, suggestive

synthetic *adjective* ARTIFICIAL, fake, man-made

system *noun* **1** METHOD, practice, procedure, routine, technique **2** ARRANGEMENT, classification, organization, scheme, structure

systematic *adjective* METHODICAL, efficient, orderly, organized

T *chem.* tritium **to a T** precisely, to a nicety
Ta *chem.* tantalum
tab *noun* tag, label, short strap **keep tabs on** (*informal*) keep watchful eye on
tab•er•na•cle [TAB-ər-nak-əl] *noun* 1 portable shrine of Israelites 2 receptacle containing reserved Eucharist 3 place of worship
ta•ble [TAY-bəl] *noun* 1 piece of furniture consisting of flat board supported by legs 2 food 3 set of facts, figures arranged in lines or columns ▷ *verb transitive* **-bled, -bling** 4 lay on table 5 lay aside (motion, etc.) for possible but unlikely consideration in future > **ta'ble•land** *noun* plateau, high flat area > **ta'ble•spoon** *noun* spoon used for serving food, etc. **under the table** 1 secretly 2 as bribe 3 drunk
tab•leau [ta-BLOH] *noun, plural* **-leaux** *or* **-leaus** [-BLOHZ] 1 group of persons, silent and motionless, arranged to represent some scene 2 dramatic scene
ta•ble d'hôte [TAH-bəl DOHT] *noun, plural* **ta•bles d'hôte** [TAH-bəl DOHT] Fr. meal, with limited choice of dishes, at a fixed price
tab•let [TAB-lit] *noun* 1 pill of compressed powdered medicinal substance 2 writing pad 3 slab of stone, wood, etc., esp. used formerly for writing on
tab'loid *noun* (illustrated) popular small-sized newspaper usu. with terse, sensational headlines
ta•boo [tə-BOO] *adjective* 1 forbidden or disapproved of ▷ *noun, plural* **-boos** 2 prohibition resulting from social conventions, etc. 3 thing prohibited ▷ *verb transitive* **-booed, -boo•ing** 4 place under taboo
tab•u•lar [TAB-yə-lər] *adjective* shaped, arranged like a table > **tab•u•late** [-layt] *verb transitive* **-lat•ed, -lat•ing** arrange (figures, facts, etc.) in tables
tacho- *combining form* speed: *tachometer*
ta•chom•e•ter [ta-KOM-i-tər] *noun* device for measuring speed, esp. of revolving shaft (e.g. in automobile) and hence revolutions per minute
tac•it [TAS-it] *adjective* 1 implied but not spoken 2 silent > **tac'it•ly** *adverb* > **tac'i•turn** *adjective* 1 talking little 2 habitually silent
tack[1] [tak] *noun* 1 small nail 2 long loose stitch 3 *nautical* course of ship obliquely to windward

---

table *noun* 1 COUNTER, bench, board, stand 2 LIST, catalog, chart, diagram, record, register, roll, schedule, tabulation
▷ *verb* 3 SUBMIT, enter, move, propose, put forward, suggest
tableau *noun* PICTURE, representation, scene, spectacle
taboo *noun* 1 PROHIBITION, anathema, ban, interdict, proscription, restriction
▷ *adjective* 2 FORBIDDEN, anathema, banned, outlawed, prohibited, proscribed, unacceptable, unmentionable
tacit *adjective* IMPLIED, implicit, inferred, undeclared, understood, unexpressed, unspoken, unstated
taciturn *adjective* UNCOMMUNICATIVE, quiet, reserved, reticent, silent, tight-lipped, unforthcoming, withdrawn
tack[1] *noun* 1 NAIL, drawing pin, pin
▷ *verb* 2 FASTEN, affix, attach, fix, nail, pin

4 course, direction ▷ *verb transitive* 5 nail with tacks 6 stitch lightly 7 append, attach 8 sail to windward
tack² *noun* riding harness for horses
tack•le [TAK-əl] *noun* 1 equipment, apparatus, esp. for fishing 2 lifting appliances with ropes 3 *football* lineman between guard and end ▷ *verb transitive* **-led, -ling** 4 take in hand 5 grip, grapple with 6 undertake to cope with, master, etc. 7 *football* seize, bring down (ball-carrier)
tack•y [TAK-ee] *adjective* **tack•i•er, tack•i•est** 1 sticky 2 not quite dry 3 dowdy, shabby > **tack'i•ness** [-nis] *noun*
ta•co [TAK-oh] *noun* **-cos** usu. fried tortilla folded or wrapped round filling
tact [takt] *noun* 1 skill in dealing with people or situations 2 delicate perception of the feelings of others > **tact'ful** [-fəl] *adjective* > **tact'less** [-lis] *adjective*
tac•tics [TAK-tiks] *noun* 1 art of handling troops, ships in battle 2 adroit management of a situation 3 plans for this > **tac•ti•cal** [TAK-ti-kəl] *adjective* > **tac•ti'cian** [-TISH-ən] *noun*
tac•tile [TAK-til] *adjective* of, relating to the sense of touch
tad•pole [TAD-pohl] *noun* immature frog, in its first state before gills and tail are absorbed
taf•fe•ta [TAF-i-tə] *noun* smooth, stiff fabric of silk, nylon, etc.
taf•fy [TAF-ee] *noun, plural* **-fies** candy of molasses and sugar
tag¹ *noun* 1 label identifying or showing price of (something) 2 ragged, hanging end 3 pointed end of shoelace, etc. 4 trite saying or quotation 5 any appendage ▷ *verb transitive* **tagged, tag•ging** 6 append, add (on) 7 trail (along) behind
tag² *noun* 1 children's game where one being chased becomes the chaser upon being touched ▷ *verb transitive* **tagged, tag•ging** 2 touch > **tag wrestling** wrestling match for teams of two, where one partner may replace the other upon being touched on hand
tail [tayl] *noun* 1 flexible prolongation of animal's spine 2 lower or inferior part of anything 3 appendage 4 rear part of aircraft 5 (*informal*) person employed to follow another ▷ *verb transitive* 6 remove tail of 7 (*informal*) follow closely, trail > **tails** *plural noun* 1 reverse side of coin 2 tail coat > **tail'ings** *plural noun* waste left over from some (e.g. industrial) process > **tail'less** [-lis] *adjective* > **tail'board** [-bord] *noun* removable or hinged rear board on truck, etc. > **tail end** last part > **tail'light** *noun* light carried at rear of vehicle > **tail'spin** *noun* 1 spinning dive of aircraft 2 sudden (e.g. emotional, financial) collapse > **tail'wind** *noun* wind coming from behind > **tail off** diminish gradually, dwindle **turn tail** run away
tai•lor [TAY-lər] *noun* maker of outer clothing, esp. for men > **tailor-made** *adjective* 1 made by tailor 2 well-fitting 3 appropriate
taint [taynt] *verb* 1 affect or be affected by pollution, corruption, etc. ▷ *noun* 2 defect, flaw 3 infection, contamination
take [tayk] *verb transitive* **took** [tuuk], **tak•en, tak•ing** 1 grasp, get hold of 2 get 3 receive, assume 4 adopt 5 accept 6 understand 7 consider 8 carry, conduct 9 use 10 capture 11 consume 12 subtract 13 require ▷ *verb intransitive* **took** [tuuk], **tak•en, tak•ing** 14 be effective 15 please 16 go ▷ *noun* 17 *motion pictures* (recording of) scene, sequence photographed without interruption 18 (*informal*) earnings, receipts > **tak'ing** *adjective* charming

3 STITCH, baste
4 ▷ **tack on** APPEND, add, attach, tag
tack² *noun* COURSE, approach, direction, heading, line, method, path, plan, procedure, way
tackle *verb* 1 DEAL WITH, attempt, come to grips with *or* get to grips with, embark upon, get stuck into (*informal*), set about, undertake
2 CONFRONT, challenge, grab, grasp, halt, intercept, seize, stop
▷ *noun* 3 CHALLENGE, block
4 EQUIPMENT, accouterments, apparatus, gear, paraphernalia, tools, trappings
tacky¹ *adjective* STICKY, adhesive, gluey, gummy, wet
tacky² *adjective* (*informal*) VULGAR, cheap, off-color, scuzzy (*slang*), seedy, shabby, shoddy, sleazy, tasteless, tatty
tact *noun* DIPLOMACY, consideration, delicacy, discretion, sensitivity, thoughtfulness, understanding
tactful *adjective* DIPLOMATIC, considerate, delicate, discreet, polite, politic, sensitive, thoughtful, understanding
tactic *noun* 1 POLICY, approach, maneuver, method, move, ploy, scheme, stratagem
2 ▷ **tactics** STRATEGY, campaigning, generalship, maneuvers, plans
tactical *adjective* STRATEGIC, cunning, diplomatic, shrewd, smart
tactician *noun* STRATEGIST, general, mastermind, planner
tactless *adjective* INSENSITIVE, impolite, impolitic, inconsiderate, indelicate, indiscreet, thoughtless, undiplomatic, unsubtle
tag *noun* 1 LABEL, flap, identification, mark, marker, note, slip, tab, ticket
▷ *verb* 2 LABEL, mark
3 (*with along* or *on*) ACCOMPANY, attend, follow, shadow, stalk, tail (*informal*), trail
tail *noun* 1 EXTREMITY, appendage, end, rear end, tailpiece
2 ▷ **turn tail** RUN AWAY, cut and run, flee, retreat, run off, take to one's heels
▷ *verb* 3 (*informal*) FOLLOW, shadow, stalk, track, trail
tailor *noun* 1 OUTFITTER, clothier, costumier, couturier, dressmaker, seamstress
▷ *verb* 2 ADAPT, adjust, alter, customize, fashion, modify, mold, shape, style
taint *verb* 1 SPOIL, blemish, contaminate, corrupt, damage, defile, pollute, ruin, stain, sully, tarnish
▷ *noun* 2 STAIN, black mark, blemish, blot, defect, demerit, fault, flaw, spot
take *verb* 1 CAPTURE, acquire, catch, get, grasp, grip, obtain, secure, seize
2 ACCOMPANY, bring, conduct, convoy, escort, guide, lead, usher
3 CARRY, bear, bring, convey, ferry, fetch, haul,

> **take'off** *noun* 1 instant at which aircraft becomes airborne 2 commencement of flight > **take after** resemble in face or character > **take down** 1 write down 2 dismantle 3 humiliate > **take in** 1 understand 2 make (garment, etc.) smaller 3 deceive **take in vain** 4 blaspheme 5 be facetious > **take off** 1 (of aircraft) leave ground 2 (*informal*) go away 3 (*informal*) mimic > **take to** become fond of

tal•cum pow'der [TAL-kəm] powder, usu. scented, to absorb body moisture, deodorize, etc.

tale [tayl] *noun* 1 story, narrative, report 2 fictitious story

tal•ent [TAL-ənt] *noun* 1 natural ability or power 2 ancient weight or money > **tal'ent•ed** [-id] *adjective* gifted

tal•is•man [TAL-is-mən] *noun, plural* **-mans** 1 object supposed to have magic power 2 amulet > **tal•is•man'ic** [-MAN-ik] *adjective*

talk [tawk] *verb intransitive* 1 express, exchange ideas, etc. in words ▷ *verb transitive* 2 express in speech, utter 3 discuss ▷ *noun* 4 speech, lecture 5 conversation 6 rumor > **talk'a•tive** *adjective* fond of talking > **talking-to** *noun, plural* **-tos** reproof > **talk show** TV or radio program in which guests are interviewed informally

tall [tawl] *adjective* 1 high 2 of great stature > **tall story** unlikely and probably untrue tale

tal•low [TAL-oh] *noun* 1 melted and clarified animal fat ▷ *verb transitive* 2 smear with this

tal•ly [TAL-ee] *verb intransitive* **-lied, -ly•ing** 1 correspond one with the other 2 keep record ▷ *noun, plural* **-lies** 3 record, account, total number

Tal•mud [TAHL-muud] *noun* body of Jewish law > **Tal•mud'ic** [-MUUD-ik] *adjective*

tal•on [TAL-ən] *noun* claw

tam•bou•rine [tam-bə-REEN] *noun* flat half-drum with jingling disks of metal attached

tame [taym] *adjective* **tam•er, tam•est** 1 not wild, domesticated 2 subdued 3 uninteresting ▷ *verb transitive* 4 make tame > **tame'ly** *adverb* 1 in a tame manner 2 without resisting

tamp *verb transitive* pack, force down by repeated blows

tam•per [TAM-pər] *verb intransitive* 1 interfere (with) improperly 2 meddle

tam'pon *noun* plug of lint, cotton, etc. inserted in wound, body cavity, to stop flow of blood, absorb secretions, etc.

tan *noun, adjective* **tan•ner, tan•nest** 1 (of) brown color of skin after long exposure to rays of sun, etc. ▷ *verb* **tanned, tan•ning** 2 (cause to) go brown 3 (of animal hide) convert to leather by chemical treatment > **tan'ner** *noun* > **tan'ner•y** *noun* place where hides are tanned > **tan'nic**

---

transport

4 STEAL, appropriate, misappropriate, pinch (*informal*), pocket, purloin

5 REQUIRE, call for, demand, necessitate, need

6 TOLERATE, abide, bear, endure, put up with (*informal*), stand, stomach, withstand

7 HAVE ROOM FOR, accept, accommodate, contain, hold

8 SUBTRACT, deduct, eliminate, remove

9 ASSUME, believe, consider, perceive, presume, regard, understand

take in *verb* 1 UNDERSTAND, absorb, assimilate, comprehend, digest, get the hang of (*informal*), grasp

2 DECEIVE, cheat, con (*informal*), dupe, fool, hoodwink, mislead, swindle, trick

takeoff *noun* 1 DEPARTURE, launch, liftoff

take off *verb* 1 REMOVE, discard, peel off, strip off

2 LIFT OFF, take to the air

3 (*informal*) DEPART, abscond, decamp, disappear, go, leave, slope off

takeover *noun* MERGER, coup, incorporation

take up *verb* 1 OCCUPY, absorb, consume, cover, extend over, fill, use up

2 START, adopt, become involved in, engage in

taking *adjective* 1 CHARMING, attractive, beguiling, captivating, enchanting, engaging, fetching (*informal*), likable *or* likeable, prepossessing

▷ *noun* 2 ▷ **takings** REVENUE, earnings, income, proceeds, profits, receipts, returns, take

tale *noun* STORY, account, anecdote, fable, legend, narrative, saga, yarn (*informal*)

talent *noun* ABILITY, aptitude, capacity, flair, genius, gift, knack

talented *adjective* GIFTED, able, brilliant

talisman *noun* CHARM, amulet, fetish, lucky charm, mascot

talk *verb* 1 SPEAK, chat, chatter, chew the fat (*slang*), communicate, converse, gossip, natter, utter

2 NEGOTIATE, confabulate, confer, parley

3 INFORM, blab, give the game away, let the cat out of the bag, tell all

▷ *noun* 4 SPEECH, address, discourse, disquisition, lecture, oration, sermon

talkative *adjective* LOQUACIOUS, chatty, effusive, garrulous, gossipy, long-winded, mouthy, verbose, voluble, wordy

talker *noun* SPEAKER, chatterbox, conversationalist, lecturer, orator

talking-to *noun* REPRIMAND, criticism, lecture, rebuke, reproach, reproof, scolding, telling-off (*informal*)

tall *adjective* 1 HIGH, big, elevated, giant, lanky, lofty, soaring, towering

2 (with *tale*) (*informal*) IMPLAUSIBLE, absurd, cock-and-bull (*informal*), exaggerated, far-fetched, incredible, preposterous, unbelievable

3 (with *order*) DIFFICULT, demanding, hard, unreasonable, well-nigh impossible

tally *verb* 1 CORRESPOND, accord, agree, coincide, concur, conform, fit, harmonize, match, square

▷ *noun* 2 RECORD, count, mark, reckoning, running total, score, total

tame *adjective* 1 DOMESTICATED, amenable, broken, disciplined, docile, gentle, obedient, tractable

2 SUBMISSIVE, compliant, docile, manageable, meek, obedient, subdued, unresisting

3 UNINTERESTING, bland, boring, dull, humdrum, insipid, unexciting, uninspiring, vapid

▷ *verb* 4 DOMESTICATE, break in, house-train, train

5 DISCIPLINE, bring to heel, conquer, humble, master, subdue, subjugate, suppress

tamper *verb* INTERFERE, alter, fiddle (*informal*), fool about (*informal*), meddle, mess about, tinker

adjective > **tan'nin** *noun* vegetable substance used as tanning agent > **tan'bark** *noun* bark of certain trees, yielding tannin

tang *noun* 1 strong pungent taste or smell 2 trace, hint 3 spike, barb > **tang'y** *adjective* **tang•i•er, tang•i•est**

tan•gent [TAN-jənt] *noun* 1 line that touches a curve without cutting 2 divergent course ▷ *adjective* 3 touching, meeting without cutting > **tan•gen'tial** [-JEN-shəl] *adjective* > **tan•gen'tial•ly** *adverb*

tan•ge•rine [tan-jə-REEN] *noun* 1 citrus tree 2 its fruit, a variety of orange

tan•gi•ble [TAN-jə-bəl] *adjective* 1 that can be touched 2 definite 3 palpable 4 concrete

tan•gle [TANG-gəl] *noun* 1 confused mass or situation ▷ *verb transitive* **-gled, -gling** 2 twist together in muddle 3 contend (with)

tan•go [TANG-goh] *noun, plural* **-gos** dance of S Amer. origin

tank *noun* 1 storage vessel for liquids or gas 2 armored motor vehicle moving on tracks 3 cistern 4 reservoir > **tank'er** *noun* ship, truck, etc. for carrying liquid in bulk

tan•kard [TANG-kərd] *noun* 1 large drinking cup of metal or glass 2 its contents, esp. beer

tannin *see* tan

tan•ta•lize [TAN-tə-līz] *verb transitive* **-lized, -liz•ing** 1 torment by appearing to offer something desired 2 tease

tan•ta•mount [TAN-tə-mownt] *adjective* 1 equivalent in value or signification 2 equal, amounting (to)

tan•trum [TAN-trəm] *noun* childish outburst of temper

tap[1] *verb* **tapped, tap•ping** 1 strike lightly but with some noise ▷ *noun* 2 slight blow, rap

tap[2] *noun* 1 valve with handle to regulate or stop flow of fluid in pipe, etc. 2 stopper, plug permitting liquid to be drawn from cask, etc. 3 steel tool for forming internal screw threads ▷ *verb transitive* **tapped, tap•ping** 4 put tap in 5 draw off with or as with tap 6 make secret connection to telephone wire to overhear conversation on it 7 make connection for supply of electricity at intermediate point in supply line 8 form internal threads in

tape [tayp] *noun* 1 narrow long strip of fabric, paper, etc. 2 magnetic recording of music, data, etc. ▷ *verb transitive* **taped, tap•ing** 3 record (speech, music, etc.) > **tape deck** device for playing magnetic tape recordings > **tape measure** tape of fabric, metal marked off in centimeters, inches, etc. > **tape recorder** apparatus for recording sound on magnetized tape and playing it back > **tape'worm** [-wurm] *noun* long flat worm parasitic in animals and people

ta•per [TAY-pər] *verb intransitive* 1 become gradually thinner toward one end ▷ *noun* 2 thin candle 3 long wick covered with wax 4 a narrowing

tap•es•try [TAP-ə-stree] *noun, plural* **-tries** fabric decorated with designs in colors woven by needles > **tap'es•tried** *adjective*

tap•i•o•ca [tap-ee-OH-kə] *noun* beadlike starch made from cassava root, used esp. in puddings, as thickener, etc.

ta•pir [TAY-pər] *noun* American animal with elongated snout, allied to pig

tap'root *noun* large single root growing straight down

tar[1] [tahr] *noun* 1 thick black liquid distilled from coal, etc. ▷ *verb transitive* **tarred, tar•ring** 2 coat, treat (as though) with tar **tarred with same brush** (made to appear) guilty of same misdeeds

tar[2] *noun* (*informal*) sailor

tar•an•tel•la [ta-rən-TEL-ə] *noun* 1 lively Italian dance 2 music for it

ta•ran•tu•la [tə-RAN-chuu-lə] *noun, plural* **-las** any of various large (poisonous) hairy spiders

tar•dy [TAHR-dee] *adjective* **-di•er, -di•est** slow, late > **tar'di•ly** *adverb*

tare [tair] *noun* 1 weight of wrapping, container for goods 2 unladen weight of vehicle

tar•get [TAHR-git] *noun* 1 mark to aim at in shooting 2 thing aimed at 3 object of criticism 4 butt

tar•iff [TA-rif] *noun* 1 tax levied on imports, etc. 2 list of charges 3 bill

tarn [tahrn] *noun* small mountain lake

tar•nish [TAHR-nish] *verb* 1 (cause to) become stained, lose shine or become dimmed or sullied ▷ *noun* 2 discoloration, blemish

---

THESAURUS • DICTIONARY

tangible *adjective* DEFINITE, actual, concrete, material, palpable, perceptible, positive, real

tangle *noun* 1 KNOT, coil, entanglement, jungle, twist, web
2 CONFUSION, complication, entanglement, fix (*informal*), imbroglio, jam, mess, mix-up
▷ *verb* 3 TWIST, coil, entangle, interweave, knot, mat, mesh, ravel
4 (*often with with*) COME INTO CONFLICT, come up against, contend, contest, cross swords, dispute, lock horns

tangled *adjective* 1 TWISTED, entangled, jumbled, knotted, matted, messy, snarled, tousled
2 COMPLICATED, complex, confused, convoluted, involved, knotty, messy, mixed-up

tangy *adjective* SHARP, piquant, pungent, spicy, tart

tantalize *verb* TORMENT, frustrate, lead on, taunt, tease, torture

tantamount *adjective* EQUIVALENT, commensurate, equal, synonymous

tantrum *noun* OUTBURST, fit, flare-up, hysterics, temper

tap[1] *verb* 1 KNOCK, beat, drum, pat, rap, strike, touch
▷ *noun* 2 KNOCK, pat, rap, touch

tap[2] *noun* 1 VALVE, stopcock
2 ▷ **on tap a** (*informal*) AVAILABLE, at hand, in reserve, on hand, ready **b** ON DRAFT
▷ *verb* 3 LISTEN IN ON, bug (*informal*), eavesdrop on
4 DRAW OFF, bleed, drain, siphon off

tape *noun* 1 STRIP, band, ribbon
▷ *verb* 2 RECORD, tape-record, video
3 BIND, seal, secure, stick, wrap

taper *verb* 1 NARROW, come to a point, thin
2 ▷ **taper off** LESSEN, decrease, die away, dwindle, fade, reduce, subside, wane, wind down

target *noun* 1 GOAL, aim, ambition, end, intention, mark, object, objective
2 VICTIM, butt, scapegoat

ta•ro [TAHR-oh] *noun, plural* **-ros** 1 plant of Pacific islands now cultivated widely 2 its edible tuber

ta•rot [TA-roh] *noun* one of special pack of cards now used mainly in fortunetelling

tar•pau•lin [tahr-PAW-lin] *noun* (sheet of) heavy hard-wearing waterproof fabric

tar•ry *verb intransitive* **-ried, -ry•ing** 1 linger, delay 2 stay behind

tart[1] [tahrt] *noun* 1 small pie filled with fruit, jam, etc. 2 (*slang*) promiscuous woman 3 prostitute

tart[2] *adjective* **-er, -est** 1 sour 2 sharp 3 bitter

tar•tan [TAHR-tn] *noun* 1 woolen cloth woven in pattern of colored checks, esp. in colors, patterns associated with Scottish clans 2 such pattern

tar•tar[1] [TAHR-tər] *noun* 1 crust deposited on teeth 2 deposit formed during fermentation of wine

tartar[2] *noun* 1 ill-tempered person, difficult to deal with 2 (**Tartar**) member of group of peoples including Mongols and Turks

task *noun* 1 piece of work (esp. unpleasant or difficult) set or undertaken ▷ *verb transitive* 2 assign task to 3 exact > **task force** 1 naval or military unit dispatched to carry out specific undertaking 2 any similar group in government, industry > **task'mas•ter** *noun* (stern) overseer **take to task** reprove

tas•sel [TAS-əl] *noun* 1 ornament of fringed knot of threads, etc. 2 tuft > **tas'seled** *adjective*

taste [tayst] *noun* 1 sense by which flavor, quality of substance is detected by the tongue 2 this act or sensation 3 (brief) experience of something 4 small amount 5 preference, liking 6 power of discerning, judging 7 discretion, delicacy ▷ *verb* **tast•ed, tast•ing** 8 observe or distinguish the taste of a substance 9 take small amount into mouth 10 experience ▷ *verb intransitive* 11 have specific flavor > **taste'ful** [-fəl] *adjective* 1 in good style 2 with, showing good taste > **taste'less** [-lis] *adjective* > **tast'y** *adjective* **tast•i•er, tast•i•est** pleasantly or highly flavored > **taste bud** small organ of taste on tongue

tat *verb* **tat•ted, tat•ting** make tatting > **tatting** *noun* type of handmade lace

tat•ter [TAT-ər] *verb* 1 make or become ragged, worn to shreds ▷ *noun* 2 ragged piece

tat•tle *verb intransitive, noun, verb* **-tled, -tling** gossip, chatter

tat•too[1] [ta-TOO] *noun, plural* **-toos** 1 beat of drum and bugle call 2 military spectacle or pageant

tattoo[2] *verb transitive* **-tooed, -too•ing** 1 mark skin in patterns, etc. by pricking and filling punctures with indelible colored inks ▷ *noun, plural* **-toos** 2 mark so made

tat•ty [TAT-ee] *adjective* **-ti•er, -ti•est** shabby, worn out

taught [tawt] *pt./pp. of* **teach**

taunt [tawnt] *verb transitive* 1 provoke, deride with insulting words, etc. ▷ *noun* 2 instance of this 3 words used for this

taut [tawt] *adjective* **-er, -est** 1 drawn tight 2 under strain

tau•tol•o•gy [taw-TOL-ə-gee] *noun, plural* **-gies** needless repetition of same thing in other words in same sentence > **tau•to•log'i•cal** [-tə-LOJ-ə-kəl] *adjective*

tav•ern [TAV-ərn] *noun* 1 bar 2 inn

taw•dry [TAW-dree] *adjective* **-dri•er, -dri•est** showy, but cheap and without taste, flashy > **taw'dri•ness** [-nis] *noun*

taw•ny [TAW-nee] *adjective, noun* **-ni•er, -ni•est** (of) light (yellowish) brown

tax [taks] *noun* 1 compulsory payments by wage

DICTIONARY **t** THESAURUS

tariff *noun* 1 TAX, duty, excise, levy, toll

tarnish *verb* 1 STAIN, blacken, blemish, blot, darken, discolor, sully, taint
▷ *noun* 2 STAIN, blemish, blot, discoloration, spot, taint

tart[1] *noun* PIE, pastry, tartlet

tart[2] *adjective* SHARP, acid, bitter, piquant, pungent, sour, tangy, vinegary

tart[3] *noun* SLUT, call girl, floozy (*slang*), ho (*slang*), prostitute, trollop, whore

task *noun* 1 JOB, assignment, chore, duty, enterprise, exercise, mission, undertaking
2 ▷ **take to task** CRITICIZE, blame, censure, reprimand, reproach, reprove, scold, tell off (*informal*), upbraid

taste *noun* 1 FLAVOR, relish, savor, smack, tang
2 BIT, bite, dash, morsel, mouthful, sample, soupçon (*French*), spoonful, tidbit
3 LIKING, appetite, fancy, fondness, inclination, partiality, penchant, predilection, preference
4 REFINEMENT, appreciation, discernment, discrimination, elegance, judgment, sophistication, style
▷ *verb* 5 DISTINGUISH, differentiate, discern, perceive
6 SAMPLE, savor, sip, test, try
7 HAVE A FLAVOR OF, savor of, smack of
8 EXPERIENCE, encounter, know, meet with, partake of, undergo

tasteful *adjective* REFINED, artistic, cultivated, cultured, discriminating, elegant, exquisite, in good taste, polished, stylish

tasteless *adjective* 1 INSIPID, bland, boring, dull, flat, flavorless, mild, thin, weak
2 VULGAR, crass, crude, gaudy, gross, inelegant, off-color, tacky (*informal*), tawdry

tasty *adjective* DELICIOUS, appetizing, delectable, full-flavored, luscious, palatable, savory, toothsome, yummy (*informal*)

tatters *noun* ▷ **in tatters** RAGGED, down at heel, in rags, in shreds, ripped, tattered, threadbare, torn

tatty *adjective* RAGGED, bedraggled, dilapidated, down at heel, neglected, run-down, shabby, threadbare, worn

taunt *verb* 1 TEASE, deride, insult, jeer, mock, provoke, ridicule, torment
▷ *noun* 2 JEER, derision, dig, gibe, insult, provocation, ridicule, sarcasm, teasing

taut *adjective* TIGHT, flexed, rigid, strained, stressed, stretched, tense

tavern *noun* INN, alehouse (*archaic*), bar, hostelry, public house

tawdry *adjective* VULGAR, cheap, flashy, gaudy, gimcrack, tacky (*informal*), tasteless, tatty, tinselly

tax *noun* 1 CHARGE, duty, excise, levy, tariff, tithe, toll

earners, companies, etc. imposed by government to raise revenue **2** heavy demand on something ▷ *verb transitive* **3** impose tax on **4** strain **5** accuse, blame > **tax'a•ble** *adjective* > **tax•a'tion** *noun* levying of taxes > **tax'pay•er** *noun* > **tax return** statement supplied to authorities of personal income and tax due

tax•i [TAK-see] *noun, plural* **tax•is** **1** (*also* **tax'i•cab**) motor vehicle for hire with driver ▷ *verb intransitive* **tax•ied, tax•i•ing** *or* **tax•y•ing** **2** (of aircraft) run along ground under its own power **3** ride in taxi

tax•i•der•my [TAK-si-dur-mee] *noun* art of stuffing, mounting animal skins to give them lifelike appearance > **tax'i•der•mist** *noun*

tax•on•o•my [tak-SON-ə-mee] *noun* science, practice of classification, esp. of biological organisms

Tb *chem.* terbium

T-bone steak loin steak with T-shaped bone

Tc *chem.* technetium

te *see* **Ti**

Te *chem.* tellurium

tea [tee] *noun* **1** dried leaves of plant cultivated esp. in (sub)tropical Asia **2** infusion of it as beverage **3** various herbal beverages **4** tea, cakes, etc. as light afternoon meal **5** (*slang*) marijuana > **tea bag** small porous bag of paper containing tea leaves > **tea'spoon** *noun* small spoon for stirring tea, etc.

teach [teech] *verb* **taught** [tawt], **teach•ing** **1** instruct **2** educate **3** train **4** impart knowledge of **5** act as teacher > **teach'er** *noun*

teak [teek] *noun* **1** East Indian tree **2** very hard wood obtained from it

teal [teel] *noun* **1** type of small duck **2** greenish-blue color

team [teem] *noun* **1** set of animals, players of game, etc. associated in activity ▷ *verb intransitive* **2** (usu. with *up*) (cause to) make a team > **team'ster** *noun* driver of truck or team of draft animals > **team spirit** subordination of individual desire for good of team > **team'work** *noun* cooperative work by team acting as unit

tear[1] [teer] *noun* drop of fluid appearing in and falling from eye > **tear'ful** [-fəl] *adjective* **1** inclined to weep **2** involving tears > **tear gas** irritant gas causing abnormal watering of eyes, and temporary blindness > **tear•jerk•er** [TEER-jur-kər] *noun* (*informal*) excessively sentimental story, moving picture, etc.

tear[2] [tair] *verb* **tore, torn, tear•ing** **1** pull apart, rend **2** become torn **3** rush ▷ *noun* **4** hole, cut or split

tease [teez] *verb transitive* **teased, teas•ing** **1** tantalize, torment, irritate, bait **2** pull apart fibers of ▷ *noun* **3** one who teases

teat [teet] *noun* **1** nipple of female breast **2** rubber nipple of baby's feeding bottle

tech•ni•cal [TEK-ni-kəl] *adjective* **1** of, specializing in industrial, practical or mechanical arts and applied sciences **2** skilled in practical and mechanical arts **3** belonging to particular art or science **4** according to letter of the law > **tech•ni•cal'i•ty** *noun* **1** point of procedure **2** state of being technical > **tech•ni'cian** [-NISH-ən] *noun* one skilled in technique of an art > **tech•nique** [tek-NEEK] *noun* **1** method of performance in an art **2** skill required for mastery of subject > **technical college** higher educational institution specializing in mechanical and industrial arts and applied science, etc. > **technical knockout** *boxing* termination of bout by referee who judges that one boxer is not fit to continue

tech•noc•ra•cy [tek-NOK-rə-see] *noun* **1** government by technical experts **2** example of this > **tech'no•crat** [-nə-krat] *noun*

tech•nol•o•gy [tek-NOL-ə-gee] *noun, plural* **-gies** **1** application of practical, mechanical sciences to industry, commerce **2** technical methods, skills, knowledge > **tech•no•log'i•cal** *adjective*

tec•ton•ic [tek-TON-ik] *adjective* **1** of construction or building **2** *geology* pert. to (forces or condition of) structure of Earth's crust > **tec•ton'ics** *noun* art, science of building

te•di•ous [TEE-dee-əs] *adjective* causing fatigue or boredom, monotonous > **te'di•um** [-əm] *noun*

▷ *verb* **2** CHARGE, assess, rate **3** STRAIN, burden, exhaust, load, stretch, test, try, weaken, weary

taxing *adjective* DEMANDING, exacting, exhausting, onerous, punishing, sapping, stressful, tiring, tough, trying

teach *verb* INSTRUCT, coach, drill, educate, enlighten, guide, inform, show, train, tutor

teacher *noun* INSTRUCTOR, coach, educator, guide, lecturer, master *or* mistress, mentor, schoolteacher, trainer, tutor

team *noun* **1** GROUP, band, body, bunch, company, gang, line-up, set, side, squad ▷ *verb* **2** (*often with up*) JOIN, band together, cooperate, couple, get together, link, unite, work together

teamwork *noun* COOPERATION, collaboration, coordination, esprit de corps, fellowship, harmony, unity

tear *verb* **1** RIP, claw, lacerate, mangle, mutilate, pull apart, rend, rupture, scratch, shred, split **2** RUSH, bolt, charge, dash, fly, hurry, race, run, speed, sprint, zoom ▷ *noun* **3** HOLE, laceration, rent, rip, rupture, scratch, split

tearful *adjective* WEEPING, blubbering, crying, in tears, lachrymose, sobbing, weepy (*informal*), whimpering

tears *plural noun* **1** CRYING, blubbering, sobbing, wailing, weeping **2** ▷ **in tears** CRYING, blubbering, distressed, sobbing, weeping

tease *verb* MOCK, goad, lead on, provoke, pull someone's leg (*informal*), tantalize, taunt, torment

technical *adjective* SCIENTIFIC, hi-tech *or* high-tech, skilled, specialist, specialized, technological

technique *noun* **1** METHOD, approach, manner, means, mode, procedure, style, system, way **2** SKILL, artistry, craft, craftsmanship, execution, performance, proficiency, touch

tedious *adjective* BORING, drab, dreary, dull, humdrum, irksome, laborious, mind-numbing, monotonous, tiresome, wearisome

tedium *noun* BOREDOM, drabness, dreariness, dullness, monotony, routine, sameness, tediousness

monotony

tee *noun golf* 1 slightly raised ground from which first stroke of hole is made 2 small peg supporting ball for this stroke > **tee off** 1 make first stroke of hole in golf 2 (*slang*) scold 3 (*slang*) irritate

teem *verb intransitive* 1 abound with 2 swarm 3 be prolific 4 pour, rain heavily

teens [teenz] *plural noun* years of life from 13 to 19 > **teen'age** *adjective* > **teen'ag•er** *noun* person in teens

teepee *noun see* **tepee**

tee•ter [TEE-tər] *verb intransitive* 1 seesaw or make similar movements 2 vacillate

teeth *pl. of* **tooth**

teethe [teeth] *verb intransitive* **teethed, teeth•ing** (of baby) grow first teeth > **teething ring** ring on which baby can bite

tee•to•tal [tee-TOHT-l] *adjective* pledged to abstain from alcohol > **tee•to'tal•er** *noun*

tele- *combining form* 1 at a distance, and from far off: *telecommunications* 2 by telephone: *telebanking* 3 of or involving television: *telecast*

tel•e•cast [TEL-i-kast] *verb, noun* **-cast** *or* **-cast•ed, -cast•ing** (broadcast) TV program

tel•e•com•mu•ni•ca•tions [tel-i-kə-myoo-ni-KAY-shənz] *noun* science and technology of communications by telephony, radio, TV, etc.

tel•e•gram [TEL-i-gram] *noun* message sent by telegraph

tel•e•graph [TEL-i-graf] *noun* 1 electrical apparatus for transmitting messages to a distance 2 any signaling device for transmitting messages ▷ *verb* 3 communicate by telegraph > **tel•e•graph'ic** *adjective* > **te•leg'ra•pher** *noun* one who works telegraph > **te•leg'ra•phy** *noun* 1 science of telegraph 2 use of telegraph

tel•e•mar•ket•ing [tel-ə-MAHR-ki-ting] *noun* selling or advertising by telephone, television

tel•e•ol•o•gy [tel-ee-OL-ə-jee] *noun* 1 doctrine of final causes 2 belief that things happen because of the purpose or design that will be fulfilled by them

te•lep•a•thy [tə-LEP-ə-thee] *noun* action of one mind on another at a distance > **tel•e•path'ic** [-ə-PATH-ik] *adjective*

tel•e•phone [tel-ə-FOHN] *noun* 1 apparatus for communicating sound to hearer at a distance ▷ *verb* **-phoned, -phon•ing** 2 communicate, speak by telephone > **tel•e•phon'ic** [-FON-ik] *adjective* > **te•leph•o•ny** [tə-LEF-ə-nee] *noun*

tel•e•pho•to [TEL-ə-foh-toh] *adjective* (of lens) producing magnified image of distant object

Tel•e•Promp•Ter [TEL-ə-promp-tər] *noun* ® off-camera device to enable TV performer to refer to magnified script out of sight of the cameras

tel•e•scope [TEL-ə-skohp] *noun* 1 optical instrument for magnifying images of distant objects ▷ *verb* **-scoped, -scop•ing** 2 slide or drive together, esp. parts designed to fit one inside the other 3 make smaller, shorter > **tel•e•scop'ic** [-SKOP-ik] *adjective*

tel•e•text [TEL-i-tekst] *noun* electronic system that shows information, news, graphics on subscribers' TV screens

tel•e•vi•sion [TEL-ə-vizh-ən] *noun* 1 system of producing on screen images of distant objects, events, etc. by electromagnetic radiation 2 device for receiving this transmission and converting it to optical images 3 programs, etc. viewed on TV set > **tel'e•vise** [-vīz] *verb transitive* **-vised, -vis•ing** 1 transmit by TV 2 make, produce as TV program

tel•e•work•ing [TEL-i-wurk-ing] *noun* use of home computers, telephones, etc., to enable a person to work from home while maintaining contact with colleagues or customers > **tel'e•work•er** *noun*

tell *verb transitive* **told, tel•ling** 1 let know 2 order, direct 3 narrate, make known 4 discern 5 distinguish 6 count ▷ *verb intransitive* **told, tel•ling** 7 give account 8 be of weight, importance 9 reveal secrets > **tel'ler** *noun* 1 narrator 2 bank cashier > **telling** *adjective* effective, striking > **tell'tale** *noun* 1 sneak 2 automatic indicator ▷ *adjective* 3 revealing

tel•lu•ri•um [te-LUUR-ee-əm] *noun* nonmetallic bluish-white element > **tel•lu'ric** *adjective*

tem•blor [TEM-blər] *noun* earthquake

te•mer•i•ty [tə-MER-i-tee] *noun* boldness, audacity

temp *noun* (*informal*) one employed on

teeming[1] *adjective* FULL, abundant, alive, brimming, bristling, bursting, crawling, overflowing, swarming, thick

teeming[2] *adjective* POURING, pelting, raining cats and dogs (*informal*)

teenager *noun* YOUTH, adolescent, boy, girl, juvenile, minor

teeter *verb* WOBBLE, rock, seesaw, stagger, sway, totter, waver

teetotaler *noun* ABSTAINER, nondrinker

telepathy *noun* MIND-READING, E.S.P., sixth sense

telephone *noun* 1 PHONE, cell, cell phone, handset, line
▷ *verb* 2 CALL, dial, phone

telescope *noun* 1 GLASS, spyglass
▷ *verb* 2 SHORTEN, abbreviate, abridge, compress, condense, contract, shrink

television *noun* TV, small screen (*informal*), the tube (*slang*)

tell *verb* 1 INFORM, announce, communicate, disclose, divulge, express, make known, notify, proclaim, reveal, state
2 INSTRUCT, bid, call upon, command, direct, order, require, summon
3 DESCRIBE, chronicle, depict, narrate, portray, recount, relate, report
4 DISTINGUISH, differentiate, discern, discriminate, identify
5 CARRY WEIGHT, count, have effect *or* take effect, make its presence felt, register, take its toll, weigh

telling *adjective* EFFECTIVE, considerable, decisive, forceful, impressive, influential, marked, powerful, significant, striking

telling-off *noun* REPRIMAND, criticism, lecture, rebuke, reproach, reproof, scolding, talking-to

tell off *verb* REPRIMAND, berate, censure, chide, lecture, rebuke, reproach, scold

temerity *noun* BOLDNESS, audacity, chutzpah (*informal*), effrontery, front, impudence, nerve (*informal*), rashness, recklessness

temporary basis
tem•per [TEM-pər] *noun* 1 frame of mind 2 anger, oft. noisy 3 mental constitution 4 degree of hardness of steel, etc. ▷ *verb transitive* 5 restrain, qualify, moderate 6 harden 7 bring to proper condition
tem•per•a [TEM-pər-ə] *noun* 1 emulsion used as painting medium ▷ *noun* 2 painting made with this
tem•per•a•ment [TEM-pər-ə-mənt] *noun* 1 natural disposition 2 emotional mood 3 mental constitution > **tem•per•a•men'tal** *adjective* 1 given to extremes of temperament, moody 2 of, occasioned by temperament
tem•per•ate [TEM-pər-it] *adjective* 1 not extreme 2 showing, practicing moderation > **tem'per•ance** [-əns] *noun* 1 moderation 2 abstinence, esp. from alcohol
tem•per•a•ture [TEM-pər-ə-chər] *noun* 1 degree of heat or coldness 2 (*informal*) (abnormally) high body temperature
tem•pest [TEM-pist] *noun* violent storm > **tem•pes•tu•ous** [tem-PES-choo-əs] *adjective* 1 turbulent 2 violent, stormy
tem•plate [TEM-plit] *noun* mold, pattern to help shape something accurately
tem•ple¹ [TEM-pəl] *noun* 1 building for worship 2 shrine
temple² *noun* flat part on either side of forehead
tem•po [TEM-poh] *noun, plural* **-pos** rate, rhythm, esp. in music
tem•po•ral [TEM-pə-rəl] *adjective* 1 of time 2 of this life or world, secular
tem•po•rar•y [TEM-pə-rer-ee] *adjective* 1 lasting, used only for a time ▷ *noun, plural* **-ies** 2 person employed on temporary basis > **tem•po•rar'i•ly** *adverb*
tem•po•rize [TEM-pə-rīz] *verb intransitive* **-ized, -iz•ing** 1 use evasive action 2 hedge 3 gain time by negotiation, etc. 4 conform to circumstances > **tem'po•riz•er** *noun*
tempt *verb transitive* 1 try to persuade, entice, esp. to something wrong or unwise 2 dispose, cause to be inclined to > **temp•ta'tion** [-TAY-shən] *noun* 1 act of tempting 2 thing that tempts > **tempt'er, tempt'ress** *noun* > **tempt'ing** *adjective* attractive, inviting
ten *noun, adjective* cardinal number next after nine > **tenth** *adjective, noun* ordinal number
ten•a•ble [TEN-ə-bəl] *adjective* able to be held, defended, maintained
te•na•cious [tə-NAY-shəs] *adjective* 1 holding fast 2 retentive 3 stubborn > **te•nac'i•ty** [-NAS-i-tee] *noun*
ten•ant [TEN-ənt] *noun* one who holds lands, house, etc. on rent or lease > **ten'an•cy** *noun, plural* **-cies**
tend¹ *verb intransitive* 1 be inclined 2 be conducive 3 make in direction of > **ten'den•cy** [-dən-see] *noun, plural* **-cies** inclination, bent

DICTIONARY • THESAURUS

temper *noun* 1 RAGE, bad mood, fury, passion, tantrum
2 IRRITABILITY, hot-headedness, irascibility, passion, petulance, resentment, surliness
3 SELF-CONTROL, calmness, composure, cool (*slang*), equanimity
4 FRAME OF MIND, constitution, disposition, humor, mind, mood, nature, temperament
▷ *verb* 5 MODERATE, assuage, lessen, mitigate, mollify, restrain, soften, soothe, tone down
6 STRENGTHEN, anneal, harden, toughen
temperament *noun* 1 NATURE, bent, character, constitution, disposition, humor, make-up, outlook, personality, temper
2 EXCITABILITY, anger, hot-headedness, moodiness, petulance, volatility
temperamental *adjective* 1 MOODY, capricious, emotional, excitable, highly strung, hypersensitive, irritable, sensitive, touchy, volatile
2 UNRELIABLE, erratic, inconsistent, inconstant, unpredictable
temperance *noun* 1 MODERATION, continence, discretion, forbearance, restraint, self-control, self-discipline, self-restraint
2 TEETOTALISM, abstemiousness, abstinence, sobriety
temperate *adjective* 1 MILD, calm, cool, fair, gentle, moderate, pleasant
2 SELF-RESTRAINED, calm, composed, dispassionate, even-tempered, mild, moderate, reasonable, self-controlled, sensible
tempest *noun* GALE, cyclone, hurricane, squall, storm, tornado, typhoon
tempestuous *adjective* 1 STORMY, blustery, gusty, inclement, raging, squally, turbulent, windy
2 VIOLENT, boisterous, emotional, furious, heated, intense, passionate, stormy, turbulent, wild
temple *noun* SHRINE, church, place of worship, sanctuary
temporarily *adverb* BRIEFLY, fleetingly, for the time being, momentarily, pro tem
temporary *adjective* IMPERMANENT, brief, ephemeral, fleeting, interim, momentary, provisional, short-lived, transitory
tempt *verb* ENTICE, allure, attract, coax, invite, lead on, lure, seduce, tantalize
temptation *noun* ENTICEMENT, allurement, inducement, lure, pull, seduction, tantalization
tempting *adjective* ENTICING, alluring, appetizing, attractive, inviting, mouthwatering, seductive, tantalizing
tenable *adjective* SOUND, arguable, believable, defensible, justifiable, plausible, rational, reasonable, viable
tenacious *adjective* 1 FIRM, clinging, forceful, immovable, iron, strong, tight, unshakable
2 STUBBORN, adamant, determined, dogged, obdurate, obstinate, persistent, resolute, steadfast, unswerving, unyielding
tenacity *noun* PERSEVERANCE, application, determination, doggedness, obduracy, persistence, resolve, steadfastness, stubbornness
tenancy *noun* LEASE, occupancy, possession, renting, residence
tenant *noun* LEASEHOLDER, inhabitant, lessee, occupant, occupier, renter, resident
tend¹ *verb* 1 BE INCLINED, be apt, be liable, gravitate, have a tendency, incline, lean
2 GO, aim, bear, head, lead, make for, point
tend² *verb* TAKE CARE OF, attend, cultivate, keep, look after, maintain, manage, nurture, watch over
tendency *noun* INCLINATION, disposition, leaning, liability, proclivity, proneness,

> **ten•den'tious** [-DEN-shəs] *adjective* 1 having, showing tendency or bias 2 controversial
tend² *verb transitive* take care of, watch over
> **tend'er** *noun* 1 small boat carried by yacht or ship 2 carriage for fuel and water attached to steam locomotive 3 one who tends: *bartender*
ten•der¹ [TEN-dər] *adjective* 1 not tough or hard 2 easily injured 3 gentle, loving, affectionate 4 delicate, soft > **ten'der•ness** [-nis] *noun*
> **ten'der•ize** *verb transitive* **-ized, -iz•ing** soften (meat) by pounding or by treating (it) with substance made for this purpose > **ten'der•foot** [-fuut] *noun, plural* **-feet** *or* **-foots** newcomer, esp. to ranch, etc.
tender² *verb transitive* 1 offer ▷ *verb intransitive* 2 make offer or estimate ▷ *noun* 3 offer 4 offer or estimate for contract to undertake specific work 5 what may legally be offered in payment
ten•don [TEN-dən] *noun* sinew attaching muscle to bone, etc. > **ten•di•ni'tis** [-NĪ-tis] *noun* inflammation of tendon
ten'dril *noun* 1 slender curling stem by which climbing plant clings to anything 2 curl, as of hair
ten•e•ment [TEN-ə-mənt] *noun* run-down apartment house, esp. in slum
ten•et [TEN-it] *noun* doctrine, belief
ten'nis *noun* game in which ball is struck with racket by players on opposite sides of net, lawn tennis > **tennis elbow** strained muscle as a result of playing tennis
ten•on [TEN-ən] *noun* tongue put on end of piece of wood, etc., to fit into a mortise
ten•or [TEN-ər] *noun* 1 male voice between alto and bass 2 music for, singer with this 3 general course, meaning
tense¹ [tens] *noun* modification of verb to show time of action
tense² *adjective* **tens•er, tens•est** 1 stretched tight 2 strained 3 taut 4 emotionally strained ▷ *verb* **tensed, tens•ing** 5 make, become tense
> **ten'sile** [-səl] *adjective* 1 of, relating to tension 2 capable of being stretched > **ten'sion** [-shən] *noun* 1 stretching 2 strain when stretched 3 emotional strain or excitement 4 hostility, suspense 5 *electricity* voltage
tent *noun* portable shelter of canvas, etc.
ten•ta•cle [TEN-tə-kəl] *noun* elongated, flexible organ of some animals (e.g. octopus) used for grasping, feeding, etc.
ten•ta•tive [TEN-tə-tiv] *adjective* 1 done as a trial 2 experimental, cautious
ten•ter•hooks [TEN-tər-huuks] *plural noun* **on tenterhooks** in anxious suspense
ten•u•ous [TEN-yoo-əs] *adjective* 1 flimsy, uncertain 2 thin, fine, slender
ten•ure [TEN-yər] *noun* (length of time of) possession, holding of office, position, etc.
te•pee, tee•pee [TEE-pee] *noun* N Amer. Indian cone-shaped tent of animal skins
tep'id *adjective* 1 moderately warm, lukewarm 2 half-hearted
te•qui•la [tə-KEE-lə] *noun* Mexican alcoholic liquor
tera- *combining form* denoting one million million (10^{12}): *terameter*
ter•bi•um [TUR-bee-əm] *noun* rare metallic element
ter•cen•ten•ar•y [tur-sen-TEN-ə-ree] *adjective, noun, plural* **-nar•ies** (of) three-hundredth anniversary
term [turm] *noun* 1 word, expression 2 limited period of time 3 period during which courts sit, schools are open, etc. 4 limit, end ▷ *verb transitive* 5 name, designate > **terms** *plural noun* 1 conditions 2 mutual relationship
ter•mi•nal [TUR-mə-nl] *adjective* 1 at, forming an end 2 pert. to, forming a terminus 3 (of disease) ending in death ▷ *noun* 4 terminal part or structure 5 extremity 6 point where current enters, leaves electrical device (e.g. battery) 7 device permitting operation of

propensity, susceptibility
tender¹ *adjective* 1 GENTLE, affectionate, caring, compassionate, considerate, kind, loving, sympathetic, tenderhearted, warm-hearted
2 VULNERABLE, immature, impressionable, inexperienced, raw, sensitive, young, youthful
3 SENSITIVE, bruised, inflamed, painful, raw, sore
tender² *verb* 1 OFFER, give, hand in, present, proffer, propose, put forward, submit, volunteer
▷ *noun* 2 OFFER, bid, estimate, proposal, submission
3 ▷ **legal tender** CURRENCY, money, cash
tenderness *noun* 1 GENTLENESS, affection, care, compassion, consideration, kindness, love, sentimentality, sympathy, warmth
2 SORENESS, inflammation, pain, sensitivity
tense *adjective* 1 NERVOUS, anxious, apprehensive, edgy, jumpy, keyed up, on edge, on tenterhooks, strained, uptight (*informal*), wired (*slang*)
2 STRESSFUL, exciting, nerve-racking, worrying
3 TIGHT, rigid, strained, stretched, taut
▷ *verb* 4 TIGHTEN, brace, flex, strain, stretch
tension *noun* 1 SUSPENSE, anxiety, apprehension, hostility, nervousness, pressure, strain, stress, unease
2 TIGHTNESS, pressure, rigidity, stiffness, stress, stretching, tautness
tentative *adjective* 1 EXPERIMENTAL, conjectural, indefinite, provisional, speculative, unconfirmed, unsettled
2 HESITANT, cautious, diffident, doubtful, faltering, timid, uncertain, undecided, unsure
tenuous *adjective* SLIGHT, doubtful, dubious, flimsy, insubstantial, nebulous, shaky, sketchy, weak
tepid *adjective* 1 LUKEWARM, warmish
2 HALF-HEARTED, apathetic, cool, indifferent, lukewarm, unenthusiastic
term *noun* 1 WORD, expression, name, phrase, title
2 PERIOD, duration, interval, season, span, spell, time, while
▷ *verb* 3 CALL, designate, dub, entitle, label, name, style
terminal *adjective* 1 DEADLY, fatal, incurable, killing, lethal, mortal
2 FINAL, concluding, extreme, last, ultimate, utmost
▷ *noun* 3 TERMINUS, depot, end of the line, station
terminate *verb* END, abort, cease, close, complete, conclude, discontinue, finish, stop

computer at some distance from it

ter•mi•nate [TUR-mə-nayt] *verb* **-nat•ed, -nat•ing** bring, come to an end > **ter•mi•na'tion** [-shən] *noun*

ter•mi•nol•o•gy [tur-mə-NOL-ə-jee] *noun, plural* **-gies** 1 set of technical terms or vocabulary 2 study of terms

ter•mi•nus [TUR-mə-nəs] *noun, plural* **-ni** [-nī] 1 finishing point 2 farthest limit 3 railroad station, bus station, etc. at end of long-distance line

ter•mite [TUR-mīt] *noun* insect, some species of which feed on and damage wood (*also* **white ant**)

ter•race [TER-əs] *noun* 1 raised level place 2 level cut out of hill 3 row, street of houses built as one block ▷ *verb transitive* **-raced, -rac•ing** 4 form into, furnish with terrace

ter•ra cot•ta [TER-ə KOT-ə] 1 hard unglazed pottery 2 its color, a brownish-red

ter•ra fir•ma [FUR-mə] *Lat.* 1 firm ground 2 dry land

ter•rain [tə-RAYN] *noun* area of ground, esp. with reference to its physical character

ter•ra•pin [TER-ə-pin] *noun* type of aquatic tortoise

ter•rar•i•um [tə-RAIR-ee-əm] *noun, plural* **-i•ums** enclosed container in which small plants, animals are kept

ter•raz•zo [tə-RAZ-oh] *noun* floor, wall finish of chips of stone set in mortar and polished

ter•res•tri•al [tə-RES-tree-əl] *adjective* 1 of the earth 2 of, living on land

ter•ri•ble [TER-ə-bəl] *adjective* 1 serious 2 dreadful, frightful 3 excessive 4 causing fear > **ter'ri•bly** *adverb*

ter•ri•er [TER-ee-ər] *noun* small dog of various breeds, orig. for following quarry into burrow

ter•rif•ic [tə-RIF-ik] *adjective* 1 very great 2 (*informal*) good, excellent 3 terrible, awe-inspiring

ter•ri•fy [TER-ə-fī] *verb transitive* **-fied, -fy•ing** fill with fear, dread

ter•ri•to•ry [TER-i-tor-ee] *noun, plural* **-ries** 1 region 2 geographical area under control of a political unit, esp. a sovereign state 3 area of knowledge > **ter•ri•to'ri•al** *adjective*

ter•ror [TER-ər] *noun* 1 great fear 2 (*informal*) troublesome person or thing > **ter'ror•ism** *noun* 1 use of violence, intimidation to achieve ends 2 state of terror > **ter'ror•ist** *noun, adjective* > **ter'ror•ize** *verb transitive* **-ized, -iz•ing** force, oppress by fear, violence

terse [turs] *adjective* **ters•er, ters•est** 1 expressed in few words, concise 2 abrupt

ter•ti•ar•y [TUR-shee-er-ee] *adjective* 1 third in degree, order, etc. ▷ *noun* 2 (**Ter•ti•ar•y**) geological period before Quaternary

tes•sel•late [TES-ə-layt] *verb transitive* **-lat•ed, -lat•ing** 1 make, pave, inlay with mosaic of small tiles 2 (of identical shapes) fit together exactly > **tes'ser•a** [-ər-ə] *noun, plural* **-ae** [-ee] stone used in mosaic

test *verb transitive* 1 try, put to the proof 2 carry out test(s) on ▷ *noun* 3 (critical) examination 4 means of trial > **test'ing** *adjective* difficult > **test case** lawsuit viewed as means of establishing precedent > **test tube** narrow cylindrical glass vessel used in scientific experiments > **test-tube baby** baby conceived in artificial womb

tes•ta•ment [TES-tə-mənt] *noun* 1 *law* will 2 declaration 3 (**Tes•ta•ment**) one of the two main divisions of the Bible > **tes•ta•men'ta•ry** *adjective*

tes•tate [TES-tayt] *adjective* having left a valid will > **tes'ta•cy** *noun* [-tə-see] state of being testate > **tes'ta•tor** [-tay-tər], (*fem.*) **tes•ta•trix** [te-STAY-triks] *noun* maker of will

tes•ti•cle [TES-ti-kəl] *noun* either of two male

termination *noun* ENDING, abortion, cessation, completion, conclusion, discontinuation, end, finish

terminology *noun* LANGUAGE, jargon, nomenclature, phraseology, terms, vocabulary

terminus *noun* END OF THE LINE, depot, garage, last stop, station

terms *plural noun* 1 CONDITIONS, particulars, provisions, provisos, qualifications, specifications, stipulations
2 RELATIONSHIP, footing, relations, standing, status

terrain *noun* GROUND, country, going, land, landscape, topography

terrestrial *adjective* EARTHLY, global, worldly

terrible *adjective* 1 SERIOUS, dangerous, desperate, extreme, severe
2 BAD, abysmal, awful, dire, dreadful, poor, rotten (*informal*)
3 FEARFUL, dreadful, frightful, horrendous, horrible, horrifying, monstrous, shocking, terrifying

terribly *adverb* EXTREMELY, awfully (*informal*), decidedly, desperately, exceedingly, seriously, thoroughly, very

terrific *adjective* 1 GREAT, enormous, fearful, gigantic, huge, intense, tremendous
2 (*informal*) EXCELLENT, amazing, brilliant, fantastic (*informal*), magnificent, marvelous, outstanding, sensational (*informal*), stupendous, superb, wonderful

terrified *adjective* FRIGHTENED, alarmed, appalled, horrified, horror-struck, panic-stricken, petrified, scared

terrify *verb* FRIGHTEN, alarm, appall, horrify, make one's hair stand on end, scare, shock, terrorize

territory *noun* DISTRICT, area, country, domain, land, patch, province, region, zone

terror *noun* 1 FEAR, alarm, anxiety, dread, fright, horror, panic, shock
2 SCOURGE, bogeyman, bugbear, devil, fiend, monster

terrorize *verb* OPPRESS, browbeat, bully, coerce, intimidate, menace, threaten

terse *adjective* 1 CONCISE, brief, condensed, laconic, monosyllabic, pithy, short, succinct
2 CURT, abrupt, brusque, short, snappy

test *verb* 1 CHECK, analyze, assess, examine, experiment, investigate, put to the test, research, try out
▷ *noun* 2 EXAMINATION, acid test, analysis, assessment, check, evaluation, investigation, research, trial

testament *noun* 1 PROOF, demonstration, evidence, testimony, tribute, witness
2 WILL, last wishes

testify *verb* BEAR WITNESS, affirm, assert, attest,

reproductive glands
tes•ti•fy [TES-tə-fī] *verb* **-fied, -fy•ing** 1 declare 2 bear witness (to)
tes•ti•mo•ny [TES-tə-moh-nee] *noun, plural* **-nies** 1 affirmation 2 evidence > **tes•ti•mo'ni•al** [-əl] *noun* 1 certificate of character, ability, etc. 2 gift, reception, etc. by organization or person expressing regard for recipient ▷ *adjective*
tes•tis *noun, plural* **-tes** [-teez] testicle
tes'ty *adjective* **-ti•er, -ti•est** irritable, short-tempered > **tes'ti•ly** *adverb*
tet•a•nus [TET-n-əs] *noun* acute infectious disease producing muscular spasms, contractions (*also* **lockjaw**)
tête-à-tête [TAYT-ə-TAYT] *noun, plural* **tête-à-têtes** [-tayts] *Fr.* private conversation
teth•er [TETH-ər] *noun* 1 rope or chain for fastening (grazing) animal ▷ *verb transitive* 2 tie up with rope **be at the end of one's tether** have reached limit of one's endurance
Teu•ton•ic [too-TON-ik] *adjective* 1 German 2 of ancient Teutons
text [tekst] *noun* 1 (actual words of) book, passage, etc. 2 passage of Scriptures, etc., esp. as subject of discourse ▷ *verb* 3 send text message (to) > **tex'tu•al** [-choo-əl] *adjective* of, in a text > **text'book** *noun* book of instruction on particular subject > **text message** message, usu. in form of coded abbreviations, sent from cell phone to cell phone
tex•tile [TEKS-tīl] *noun* 1 any fabric or cloth, esp. woven ▷ *adjective* 2 of (the making of) fabrics
tex•ture [TEKS-chər] *noun* 1 character, structure 2 consistency
Th *chem.* thorium
tha•lid•o•mide [thə-LID-ə-mīd] *noun* drug formerly used as sedative, but found to cause abnormalities in developing fetus
thal•li•um [THAL-ee-əm] *noun* highly toxic metallic element > **thal'lic** *adjective*
than [than] *conjunction* introduces second part of comparison
thank [thangk] *verb transitive* 1 express gratitude to 2 say thanks 3 hold responsible > **thanks** *plural noun* words of gratitude > **thank'ful** [-fəl] *adjective* grateful, appreciative > **thank'less** [-lis] *adjective* 1 having, bringing no thanks 2 unprofitable > **Thanks•giv'ing Day** public holiday in US, Canada
that [that] *adjective, pronoun* 1 used to refer to something already mentioned or familiar, or further away ▷ *conjunction* 2 used to introduce a clause ▷ *pronoun* 3 used to introduce a relative clause
thatch [thach] *noun* 1 reeds, straw, etc. used as roofing material ▷ *verb transitive* 2 to roof (a house) with reeds, straw, etc. > **thatch'er** *noun*
thaw *verb* 1 melt 2 (cause to) unfreeze 3 defrost 4 become warmer, or more genial ▷ *noun* 5 a melting (of frost, etc.)
the [*thə, thee*] *adjective* the definite article
the•a•ter [THEE-ə-tər] *noun* 1 place where plays, etc. are performed 2 drama, dramatic works generally 3 large room with (tiered) seats, used for lectures, etc. 4 surgical operating room > **the•at'ri•cal** *adjective* 1 of, for the theater 2 exaggerated, affected
thee [*thee*] *pronoun* (*obsolete*) *objective and dative of* **thou**
theft *noun* stealing
their [*thair*] *adjective* of or associated with them > **theirs** *pronoun* (thing or person) belonging to them
the•ism [THEE-iz-əm] *noun* belief in creation of universe by one god > **the'ist** *noun*
them [*them*] *pronoun* refers to people or things other than the speaker or those addressed > **themselves** *pronoun emphatic and reflexive form of* **they** OR THEM
theme [theem] *noun* 1 main idea or topic of conversation, book, etc. 2 subject of composition 3 recurring melody in music > **the•mat•ic** [thə-MAT-ik] *adjective* > **theme park** leisure area designed around one subject > **theme song** one associated with particular program, person, etc.
then [*then*] *adverb* 1 at that time 2 next 3 that being so
thence [*thens*] *adverb* (*obsolete*) from that place, point of reasoning, etc.
the•oc•ra•cy [thee-OK-rə-see] *noun, plural* **-cies**

---

certify, corroborate, state, swear, vouch
testimonial *noun* TRIBUTE, commendation, endorsement, recommendation, reference
testimony *noun* 1 EVIDENCE, affidavit, deposition, statement, submission
2 PROOF, corroboration, demonstration, evidence, indication, manifestation, support, verification
testing *adjective* DIFFICULT, arduous, challenging, demanding, exacting, rigorous, searching, strenuous, taxing, tough
tether *noun* 1 ROPE, chain, fetter, halter, lead, leash
2 ▷ **at the end of one's tether** EXASPERATED, at one's wits' end, exhausted
▷ *verb* 3 TIE, bind, chain, fasten, fetter, secure
text *noun* 1 CONTENTS, body
2 WORDS, wording
texture *noun* FEEL, consistency, grain, structure, surface, tissue
thank *verb* SAY THANK YOU, show one's appreciation
thankful *adjective* GRATEFUL, appreciative, beholden, indebted, obliged, pleased, relieved
thankless *adjective* UNREWARDING, fruitless, unappreciated, unprofitable, unrequited
thanks *plural noun* 1 GRATITUDE, acknowledgment, appreciation, credit, gratefulness, kudos, recognition
2 ▷ **thanks to** BECAUSE OF, as a result of, due to, owing to, through
thaw *verb* MELT, defrost, dissolve, liquefy, soften, unfreeze, warm
theatrical *adjective* 1 DRAMATIC, Thespian
2 EXAGGERATED, affected, dramatic, histrionic, mannered, melodramatic, ostentatious, showy, stagy
theft *noun* STEALING, embezzlement, fraud, larceny, pilfering, purloining, robbery, thieving
theme *noun* 1 SUBJECT, idea, keynote, subject matter, topic
2 MOTIF, leitmotif
theological *adjective* RELIGIOUS, doctrinal, ecclesiastical

government by a deity or a priesthood
> **the•o•crat'ic** [-ə-KRAT-ik] *adjective*
the•od•o•lite [thee-OD-l-īt] *noun* surveying instrument for measuring angles
the•ol•o•gy [thee-OL-ə-jee] *noun, plural* **-gies** systematic study of religion(s) and religious belief(s) > **the•o•lo•gian** [thee-ə-LOH-jən] *noun*
the•o•rem [THEE-ər-əm, THEER-əm] *noun* proposition that can be demonstrated by argument
the•o•ry [THEE-ə-ree] *noun, plural* **-ries** 1 supposition to account for something 2 system of rules and principles 3 rules and reasoning, etc. as distinguished from practice
> **the•o•ret'i•cal** *adjective* 1 based on theory 2 speculative, as opposed to practical > **the'o•rize** *verb intransitive* **-rized, -riz•ing** form theories, speculate
the•os•o•phy [thee-OS-ə-fee] *noun* any of various religious, philosophical systems claiming possibility of intuitive insight into divine nature
ther•a•py [THER-ə-pee] *noun, plural* **-pies** healing treatment > **ther•a•peu'tic** [-PYOO-tik] *adjective* 1 of healing 2 serving to improve or maintain health > **ther•a•peu'tics** *noun* art of healing > **ther'a•pist** *noun* esp. psychotherapist
there [thair] *adverb* 1 in that place 2 to that point > **there•by'** *adverb* by that means
> **there'fore** *adverb* in consequence, that being so
> **there'up•on** *conjunction* at that point, immediately afterward
therm [thurm] *noun* unit of measurement of heat > **ther'mal** [-əl] *adjective* 1 of, pert. to heat 2 hot, warm (esp. of a spring, etc.)
therm•i•on [THURM-ī-ən] *noun* ion emitted by incandescent body > **therm•i•on•ic** [thur-mee-ON-ik] *adjective* pert. to thermion
thermo- *combining form* related to, caused by or producing heat
ther•mo•dy•nam•ics [thur-moh-dī-NAM-iks] *noun* the science that deals with the interrelationship and interconversion of different forms of energy
ther•mom•e•ter [thə-MOM-ə-tər] *noun* instrument to measure temperature
> **ther•mo•met•ric** [thur-mə-MET-rik] *adjective*
ther•mo•nu•cle•ar [thur-moh-NOO-klee-ər] *adjective* involving nuclear fusion
ther•mo•plas•tic [thur-mə-PLAS-tik] *noun* plastic that retains its properties after being melted and solidified ▷ *adjective*
ther•mos [THUR-məs] *noun* double-walled flask with vacuum between walls, for keeping contents of inner flask at temperature at which they were inserted
ther•mo•stat [THUR-mə-stat] *noun* apparatus for automatically regulating temperature
> **ther•mo•stat'ic** *adjective*
the•sau•rus [thi-SOR-əs] *noun* 1 book containing lists of synonyms and antonyms 2 dictionary of selected words, topics
these [theez] *pl. of* **this**
the•sis [THEE-sis] *noun, plural* **-ses** [-seez] 1 written work submitted for degree, diploma 2 theory maintained in argument
thes•pi•an [THES-pee-ən] *adjective* 1 theatrical ▷ *noun* 2 actor, actress
they [thay] *pronoun* the third person plural pronoun
thick [thik] *adjective* **-er, -est** 1 having great thickness, not thin 2 dense, crowded 3 viscous 4 (of voice) throaty 5 (*informal*) stupid, insensitive 6 (*informal*) friendly ▷ *noun* 7 busiest, most intense part > **thick•en** [THIK-ən] *verb* 1 make, become thick 2 become more involved, complicated > **thick'ly** *adverb*
> **thick'ness** [-nis] *noun* 1 dimensions of anything measured through it, at right angles to length and breadth 2 state of being thick 3 layer > **thick•et** [THIK-it] *noun* thick growth of small trees > **thick'set** *adjective* 1 sturdy and solid of body 2 set closely together
thief [theef] *noun, plural* **thieves** one who steals
> **thieve** [theev] *verb* **thieved, thiev•ing** steal
> **thiev'ish** *adjective*
thigh [thī] *noun* upper part of leg
thim•ble [THIM-bəl] *noun* cap protecting end of finger when sewing
thin *adjective* **thin•ner, thin•nest** 1 of little thickness 2 slim 3 lean 4 of little density 5 sparse 6 fine 7 loose, not close-packed 8

DICTIONARY • THESAURUS

---

theoretical *adjective* ABSTRACT, academic, conjectural, hypothetical, notional, speculative
theorize *verb* SPECULATE, conjecture, formulate, guess, hypothesize, project, propound, suppose
theory *noun* SUPPOSITION, assumption, conjecture, hypothesis, presumption, speculation, surmise, thesis
therapeutic *adjective* BENEFICIAL, corrective, curative, good, healing, remedial, restorative, salutary
therapist *noun* HEALER, physician
therapy *noun* REMEDY, cure, healing, treatment
therefore *adverb* CONSEQUENTLY, accordingly, as a result, ergo, hence, so, then, thence, thus
thesis *noun* 1 DISSERTATION, essay, monograph, paper, treatise
2 PROPOSITION, contention, hypothesis, idea, opinion, proposal, theory, view
thick *adjective* 1 WIDE, broad, bulky, fat, solid, substantial
2 DENSE, close, compact, concentrated, condensed, heavy, impenetrable, opaque
3 (*informal*) FRIENDLY, close, devoted, familiar, inseparable, intimate, pally (*informal*)
4 FULL, brimming, bristling, bursting, covered, crawling, packed, swarming, teeming
5 ▷ **a bit thick** UNFAIR, unjust, unreasonable
thicken *verb* SET, clot, coagulate, condense, congeal, jell
thicket *noun* WOOD, brake, coppice, copse, covert, grove
thickset *adjective* WELL-BUILT, bulky, burly, heavy, muscular, stocky, strong, sturdy
thief *noun* ROBBER, burglar, embezzler, housebreaker, pickpocket, pilferer, plunderer, shoplifter, stealer
thieve *verb* STEAL, filch, pilfer, pinch (*informal*), purloin, rob, swipe (*slang*)
thin *adjective* 1 NARROW, attenuated, fine
2 SLIM, bony, emaciated, lean, scrawny, skeletal, skinny, slender, slight, spare, spindly
3 MEAGER, deficient, scanty, scarce, scattered, skimpy, sparse, wispy
4 DELICATE, diaphanous, filmy, fine, flimsy,

(*informal*) unlikely ▷ *verb* **thinned, thin•ning** 9 make, become thin > **thin'ness** [-nis] *noun*
thine [thīn] *pronoun, adjective* (*obsolete*) belonging to thee
thing *noun* 1 material object 2 any possible object of thought
think [thingk] *verb intransitive* **thought** [thawt], **think•ing** 1 have one's mind at work 2 reflect, meditate 3 reason 4 deliberate 5 imagine 6 hold opinion ▷ *verb transitive* **thought** [thawt], **think•ing** 7 conceive, consider in the mind 8 believe 9 esteem > **think'a•ble** *adjective* able to be conceived, considered, possible, feasible > **thinking** *adjective* reflecting > **think tank** group of experts studying specific problems
third [thurd] *adjective* 1 ordinal number corresponding to three ▷ *noun* 2 third part > **third degree** violent interrogation > **third party** *law* person involved by chance or only incidentally in legal proceedings, etc. > **third rail** 1 rail through which electrical current is supplied to an electric vehicle 2 issue that is avoided by politicians because of its controversial nature > **Third World** developing countries of Africa, Asia, Latin Amer.
thirst [thurst] *noun* 1 desire to drink 2 feeling caused by lack of drink 3 craving 4 yearning ▷ *verb* 5 feel lack of drink > **thirst'y** *adjective* **thirst•i•er, thirst•i•est**
thir•teen [thur-TEEN] *adjective, noun* three plus ten > **thir'ty** *noun, adjective, plural* **-ties** three times ten
this [this] *adjective, pronoun* 1 used to refer to a thing or person nearby, just mentioned, or about to be mentioned ▷ *adjective* 2 used to refer to the present time: *this morning*
this•tle [THIS-əl] *noun* prickly plant with dense flower heads
thong [thawng] *noun* 1 narrow strip of leather, strap 2 type of light sandal
thor•ax [THOR-aks] *noun* part of body between neck and belly > **tho•rac•ic** [thaw-RAS-ik] *adjective*
tho•ri•um [THOR-ee-əm] *noun* radioactive metallic element
thorn *noun* 1 prickle on plant 2 spine 3 bush noted for its thorns 4 anything that causes trouble or annoyance > **thorn'y** *adjective* **thorn•i•er, thorn•i•est**
thor•ough [THUR-oh] *adjective* 1 careful, methodical 2 complete, entire > **thor'ough•ly** *adverb* > **thor'ough•bred** *adjective* 1 of pure breed ▷ *noun* 2 purebred animal, esp. horse > **thor'ough•fare** [-fair] *noun* 1 road or passage open at both ends 2 right of way
those [thohz] *adjective, pronoun pl. of* **that**
thou [thow] *pronoun, plural* **ye** *or* **you** (*obsolete*) the second person singular pronoun
though [thoh] *conjunction* 1 in spite of the fact that, even if ▷ *adverb* 2 nevertheless
thought [thawt] *noun* 1 process of thinking 2 what one thinks 3 product of thinking 4 meditation 5 *pt./pp. of* **think** > **thought'ful** [-fəl] *adjective* 1 considerate 2 showing careful

DICTIONARY **t** THESAURUS

gossamer, sheer, unsubstantial
5 UNCONVINCING, feeble, flimsy, inadequate, lame, lousy (*slang*), poor, superficial, weak
thing *noun* 1 OBJECT, article, being, body, entity, something, substance
2 (*informal*) OBSESSION, bee in one's bonnet, fetish, fixation, hang-up (*informal*), mania, phobia, preoccupation
3 ▷ **things** POSSESSIONS, belongings, effects, equipment, gear, luggage, stuff
think *verb* 1 BELIEVE, consider, deem, estimate, imagine, judge, reckon, regard, suppose
2 PONDER, cerebrate, cogitate, contemplate, deliberate, meditate, muse, reason, reflect, ruminate
thinker *noun* PHILOSOPHER, brain (*informal*), intellect (*informal*), mastermind, sage, theorist, wise man
thinking *noun* 1 REASONING, conjecture, idea, judgment, opinion, position, theory, view ▷ *adjective* 2 THOUGHTFUL, contemplative, intelligent, meditative, philosophical, rational, reasoning, reflective
think up *verb* DEVISE, come up with, concoct, contrive, create, dream up, invent, visualize
thirst *noun* 1 THIRSTINESS, drought, dryness
2 CRAVING, appetite, desire, hankering, keenness, longing, passion, yearning
thirsty *adjective* 1 PARCHED, arid, dehydrated, dry
2 EAGER, avid, craving, desirous, greedy, hungry, longing, yearning
thorn *noun* PRICKLE, barb, spike, spine
thorny *adjective* PRICKLY, barbed, bristly, pointed, sharp, spiky, spiny
thorough *adjective* 1 CAREFUL, assiduous, conscientious, efficient, exhaustive, full, in-depth, intensive, meticulous, painstaking, sweeping
2 COMPLETE, absolute, out-and-out, outright, perfect, total, unmitigated, unqualified, utter
thoroughbred *adjective* PUREBRED, pedigree
thoroughfare *noun* ROAD, avenue, highway, passage, passageway, street, way
thoroughly *adverb* 1 CAREFULLY, assiduously, conscientiously, efficiently, exhaustively, from top to bottom, fully, intensively, meticulously, painstakingly, scrupulously
2 COMPLETELY, absolutely, downright, perfectly, quite, totally, to the hilt, utterly
though *conjunction* 1 ALTHOUGH, even if, even though, notwithstanding, while
▷ *adverb* 2 NEVERTHELESS, for all that, however, nonetheless, notwithstanding, still, yet
thought *noun* 1 THINKING, brainwork, cogitation, consideration, deliberation, meditation, musing, reflection, rumination
2 IDEA, concept, judgment, notion, opinion, view
3 CONSIDERATION, attention, heed, regard, scrutiny, study
4 INTENTION, aim, design, idea, notion, object, plan, purpose
5 EXPECTATION, anticipation, aspiration, hope, prospect
thoughtful *adjective* 1 CONSIDERATE, attentive, caring, helpful, kind, kindly, solicitous, unselfish
2 WELL-THOUGHT-OUT, astute, canny, prudent
3 REFLECTIVE, contemplative, deliberative, meditative, pensive, ruminative, serious, studious

thought **3** engaged in meditation **4** attentive > **thought'less** [-lis] *adjective* inconsiderate, careless, heedless

thou•sand [THOW-zənd] *noun, adjective* cardinal number, ten hundred

thrall [thrawl] *noun* **1** slavery **2** slave, bondsman > **thrall'dom** [-dəm] *noun* bondage

thrash *verb transitive* **1** beat, whip soundly **2** defeat soundly **3** thresh ▷ *verb intransitive* **4** move, plunge (esp. arms, legs) in wild manner > **thrash out** **1** argue about from every angle **2** solve by exhaustive discussion

thread [thred] *noun* **1** fine cord **2** yarn **3** ridge cut spirally on screw **4** theme, meaning ▷ *verb transitive* **5** put thread into **6** fit film, magnetic tape, etc. into machine **7** put on thread **8** pick (one's way, etc.) > **thread'bare** [-bair] *adjective* **1** worn, with nap rubbed off **2** meager **3** shabby

threat [thret] *noun* **1** declaration of intention to harm, injure, etc. **2** person or thing regarded as dangerous > **threat•en** [THRET-n] *verb transitive* **1** utter threats against **2** menace

three *noun, adjective* cardinal number, one more than two > **three-ply** [-plī] *adjective* having three layers (as wood) or strands (as wool) > **three'some** [-səm] *noun* group of three > **three-di•men'sion•al, 3-D** *adjective* **1** having three dimensions **2** simulating the effect of depth

thresh *verb* **1** beat, rub (wheat, etc.) to separate grain from husks and straw **2** thrash

thresh•old [THRESH-ohld] *noun* **1** bar of stone or wood forming bottom of doorway **2** entrance **3** starting point **4** point at which a stimulus is perceived, or produces a response

threw [throo] *pt. of* **throw**

thrice [thrīs] *adverb* three times

thrift *noun* **1** saving, economy **2** savings organization **3** genus of plant, sea pink > **thrift'y** *adjective* **thrift•i•er, thrift•i•est** economical, frugal, sparing

thrill *noun* **1** sudden sensation of excitement and pleasure ▷ *verb* (cause to) feel a thrill **2** vibrate, tremble > **thrill'er** *noun* book, motion picture, etc. with story of mystery, suspense > **thrill'ing** *adjective* exciting

thrive [thrīv] *verb intransitive* **thrived** *or* **throve** [throhv], **thrived** *or* **thriv•en, thriv•ing** **1** grow well **2** flourish, prosper

throat [throht] *noun* **1** front of neck **2** either or both of passages through it > **throat'y** *adjective* **throat•i•er, throat•i•est** (of voice) hoarse

throb *verb intransitive* **throbbed, throb•bing** **1** beat, quiver strongly, pulsate ▷ *noun* **2** pulsation, beat **3** vibration

throes [throhz] *plural noun* condition of violent pangs, pain, etc. **in the throes of** in the process of

throm•bo•sis [throm-BOH-sis] *noun* formation of clot of coagulated blood in blood vessel or heart

throne [throhn] *noun* **1** ceremonial seat, powers and duties of king or queen ▷ *verb transitive* **throned, thron•ing** **2** place on throne, declare king, etc.

throng [thrawng] *noun, verb* crowd

DICTIONARY • THESAURUS

thoughtless *adjective* INCONSIDERATE, impolite, insensitive, rude, selfish, tactless, uncaring, undiplomatic, unkind

thrash *verb* **1** BEAT, belt (*informal*), cane, flog, paddle (*United States & Canadian*), scourge, spank, whip
2 DEFEAT, beat, crush, run rings around (*informal*), slaughter (*informal*), trounce, wipe the floor with (*informal*)
3 THRESH, flail, jerk, toss and turn, writhe

thrashing *noun* **1** BEATING, belting (*informal*), flogging, punishment, whipping
2 DEFEAT, beating, hammering (*informal*), trouncing

thrash out *verb* SETTLE, argue out, debate, discuss, have out, resolve, solve, talk over

thread *noun* **1** STRAND, fiber, filament, line, string, yarn
2 THEME, direction, drift, plot, story line, train of thought
▷ *verb* **3** PASS, ease, pick *or* pick one's way, squeeze through

threadbare *adjective* **1** SHABBY, down at heel, frayed, old, ragged, tattered, tatty, worn
2 HACKNEYED, commonplace, conventional, familiar, overused, stale, stereotyped, tired, trite, well-worn

threat *noun* **1** WARNING, foreboding, foreshadowing, omen, portent, presage, writing on the wall
2 DANGER, hazard, menace, peril, risk

threaten *verb* **1** INTIMIDATE, browbeat, bully, lean on (*slang*), menace, pressurize, terrorize
2 ENDANGER, imperil, jeopardize, put at risk, put in jeopardy, put on the line
3 FORESHADOW, forebode, impend, portend, presage

threatening *adjective* **1** MENACING, bullying, intimidatory
2 OMINOUS, forbidding, grim, inauspicious, sinister

threshold *noun* **1** ENTRANCE, door, doorstep, doorway
2 START, beginning, brink, dawn, inception, opening, outset, verge
3 MINIMUM, lower limit

thrift *noun* FRUGALITY, carefulness, economy, parsimony, prudence, saving, thriftiness

thrifty *adjective* ECONOMICAL, careful, frugal, parsimonious, provident, prudent, saving, sparing

thrill *noun* **1** PLEASURE, buzz (*slang*), kick (*informal*), stimulation, tingle, titillation
▷ *verb* **2** EXCITE, arouse, electrify, move, stimulate, stir, titillate

thrilling *adjective* EXCITING, electrifying, gripping, riveting, rousing, sensational, stimulating, stirring

thrive *verb* PROSPER, boom, develop, do well, flourish, get on, grow, increase, succeed

thriving *adjective* PROSPEROUS, blooming, booming, burgeoning, flourishing, healthy, successful, well

throb *verb* **1** PULSATE, beat, palpitate, pound, pulse, thump, vibrate
▷ *noun* **2** PULSE, beat, palpitation, pounding, pulsating, thump, thumping, vibration

throng *noun* **1** CROWD, crush, horde, host, mass, mob, multitude, pack, swarm
▷ *verb* **2** CROWD, congregate, converge, flock,

throt•tle [THROT-l] *noun* 1 device controlling amount of fuel entering engine and thereby its speed ▷ *verb transitive* **-tled, -tling** 2 strangle 3 suppress 4 restrict (flow of liquid, etc.)
through [throo] *preposition* 1 from end to end, from side to side of 2 between the sides of 3 in consequence of 4 by means or fault of ▷ *adverb* 5 from end to end 6 to the end ▷ *adjective* 7 completed 8 finished 9 continuous 10 (of transport, traffic) not stopping > **through•out'** [-OWT] *adverb, preposition* in every part (of) > **through'put** [-puut] *noun* quantity of material processed, esp. by computer > **through train** train that travels whole (unbroken) length of long journey **carry through** accomplish
throve [throhv] *pt. of* **thrive**
throw [throh] *verb transitive* **threw** [throo], **thrown, throw•ing** 1 fling, cast 2 move, put abruptly, carelessly 3 give, hold (party, etc.) 4 cause to fall 5 shape on potter's wheel 6 move (switch, lever, etc.) 7 (*informal*) baffle, disconcert ▷ *noun* 8 act or distance of throwing > **throw'back** *noun* 1 one who, that which reverts to character of an ancestor 2 this process
thrush[1] *noun* songbird
thrush[2] *noun* 1 fungal disease of mouth, esp. in infants 2 foot disease of horses
thrust *verb* **thrust, thrust•ing** 1 push, drive 2 stab 3 push one's way ▷ *noun* 4 lunge, stab with pointed weapon, etc. 5 cutting remark 6 propulsive force or power
thud *noun* 1 dull heavy sound ▷ *verb intransitive* **thud•ded, thud•ding** 2 make thud
thug *noun* brutal, violent person
thumb [thum] *noun* 1 first, shortest, thickest finger of hand ▷ *verb transitive* 2 handle, dirty with thumb 3 make hitchhiker's signal to get ride 4 flick through (pages of book, etc.)
thump *noun* 1 dull heavy blow 2 sound of one ▷ *verb transitive* 3 strike heavily
thun•der [THUN-dər] *noun* 1 loud noise accompanying lightning ▷ *verb intransitive* 2 rumble with thunder 3 make noise like thunder ▷ *verb transitive* 4 utter loudly > **thun'der•ous** [-əs] *adjective* > **thun'der•bolt** [-bohlt], **thun'der•clap** *noun* 1 lightning flash followed by peal of thunder 2 anything totally unexpected and unpleasant > **thun'der•struck** *adjective* amazed
thus [thus] *adverb* 1 in this way 2 therefore
thwack [thwak] *verb transitive, noun* whack
thwart [thwort] *verb transitive* 1 foil, frustrate, baffle ▷ *adverb* 2 (*obsolete*) across ▷ *noun* 3 seat across a boat
thy [thī] *adjective* (*obsolete*) belonging to thee > **thy•self'** *pronoun emphasized form of* **thou**
thyme [tīm] *noun* aromatic herb
thy•mus [THĪ-məs] *noun* small ductless gland in upper part of chest
thy•roid gland [THĪ-roid] endocrine gland controlling body growth, situated (in people) at base of neck
ti, te [tee] *noun* seventh sol-fa note
Ti *chem.* titanium
ti•ar•a [tee-AR-ə] *noun* woman's jeweled head ornament, coronet
tib•i•a [TIB-ee-ə] *noun, plural* **-i•as** thicker inner bone of lower leg
tic [tik] *noun* spasmodic twitch in muscles, esp. of face
tick[1] [tik] *noun* 1 slight tapping sound, as of watch movement 2 small mark (✓) ▷ *verb transitive* 3 mark with tick ▷ *verb intransitive* 4 make the sound > **tick•er tape** continuous paper ribbon > **tick off** 1 mark off 2 reprimand 3 make angry > **tick over** 1 (of engine) idle 2 continue to function smoothly
tick[2] *noun* small insect-like parasite living on

DICTIONARY **t** THESAURUS

mill around, pack, swarm around
throttle *verb* STRANGLE, choke, garrotte, strangulate
through *preposition* 1 BETWEEN, by, past
2 BECAUSE OF, by means of, by way of, using, via
3 DURING, in, throughout
▷ *adjective* 4 FINISHED, completed, done, ended
▷ *adverb* 5 ▷ **through and through** COMPLETELY, altogether, entirely, fully, thoroughly, totally, utterly, wholly
throughout *adverb* EVERYWHERE, all over, from start to finish, right through
throw *verb* 1 HURL, cast, chuck (*informal*), fling, launch, lob (*informal*), pitch, send, sling, toss
2 (*informal*) CONFUSE, astonish, baffle, confound, disconcert, dumbfound, faze
▷ *noun* 3 TOSS, fling, heave, lob (*informal*), pitch, sling
throwaway *adjective* CASUAL, careless, offhand, passing, understated
throw away *verb* DISCARD, dispense with, dispose of, ditch (*slang*), dump (*informal*), get rid of, jettison, reject, scrap, throw out, chuck (*informal*), bin (*informal*)
thrust *verb* 1 PUSH, drive, force, jam, plunge, bin (*informal*), propel, ram, shove
▷ *noun* 2 PUSH, drive, lunge, poke, prod, shove, stab
3 MOMENTUM, impetus
thud *noun, verb* THUMP, clunk, crash, knock, smack
thug *noun* RUFFIAN, bruiser (*informal*), bully boy, gangster, hooligan, tough
thump *noun* 1 CRASH, bang, clunk, thud, thwack
2 BLOW, clout (*informal*), knock, punch, rap, smack, wallop (*informal*), whack
▷ *verb* 3 STRIKE, beat, clobber (*slang*), clout (*informal*), hit, knock, pound, punch, smack, wallop (*informal*), whack
thunder *noun* 1 RUMBLE, boom, crash, explosion
▷ *verb* 2 RUMBLE, boom, crash, peal, resound, reverberate, roar
3 SHOUT, bark, bellow, roar, yell
thunderous *adjective* LOUD, booming, deafening, ear-splitting, noisy, resounding, roaring, tumultuous
thunderstruck *adjective* AMAZED, astonished, astounded, dumbfounded, flabbergasted (*informal*), open-mouthed, shocked, staggered, stunned, taken aback
thus *adverb* 1 THEREFORE, accordingly, consequently, ergo, for this reason, hence, on that account, so, then
2 IN THIS WAY, as follows, like this, so
thwart *verb* FRUSTRATE, foil, hinder, obstruct, outwit, prevent, snooker, stymie
tick[1] *noun* 1 MITE, bug, insect
2 TAPPING, clicking, ticktock

and sucking blood of warm-blooded animals
tick³ *noun* mattress case > **tick'ing** *noun* strong material for mattress covers
tick•et [TIK-it] *noun* 1 card, paper entitling holder to admission, travel, etc. 2 list of candidates of one party for election ▷ *verb transitive* 3 attach label to 4 issue tickets to
tick•le [TIK-əl] *verb transitive* **-led, -ling** 1 touch, stroke, poke (person, part of body, etc.) to produce laughter, etc. 2 please, amuse ▷ *verb intransitive* **-led, -ling** 3 be irritated, itch ▷ *noun* 4 act, instance of this > **tick'lish** *adjective* 1 sensitive to tickling 2 requiring care or tact
tid'bit *noun* 1 tasty morsel of food 2 pleasing scrap (of scandal, etc.)
tide [tīd] *noun* 1 rise and fall of sea happening twice each lunar day 2 stream 3 season, time > **tid'al** [-əl] *adjective* of, like tide > **tidal wave** great wave, esp. produced by earthquake > **tide over** help someone for a while, esp. by loan, etc.
ti•dings [TĪ-dingz] *plural noun* news
ti•dy [TĪ-dee] *adjective* **-di•er, -di•est** 1 orderly, neat 2 of fair size ▷ *verb transitive* **-died, -dy•ing** 3 put in order
tie [tī] *verb* **tied, ty•ing** 1 equal (score of) ▷ *verb transitive* 2 fasten, bind, secure 3 restrict ▷ *noun* 4 that with which anything is bound 5 restriction, restraint 6 long, narrow piece of material worn knotted around neck 7 bond 8 connecting link 9 drawn game, contest 10 match, game in eliminating competition > **tie'-dye•ing** *noun* way of dyeing cloth in patterns by tying sections tightly so they will not absorb dye
tier [teer] *noun* row, rank, layer
tiff *noun* petty quarrel
ti•ger [TI-gər] *noun* large carnivorous feline animal
tight [tīt] *adjective* **-er, -est** 1 taut, tense 2 closely fitting 3 secure, firm 4 not allowing passage of water, etc. 5 cramped 6 (*informal*) mean, stingy 7 (*slang*) drunk > **tights** *plural noun* one-piece clinging garment covering body from waist to feet > **tight'en** [-ən] *verb* > **tight'rope** *noun* rope stretched taut above the ground, on which acrobats perform
tile [tīl] *noun* 1 flat piece of ceramic, plastic, etc. 2 material used for roofs, walls, floors, fireplaces, etc. ▷ *verb transitive* **tiled, til•ing** 3 cover with tiles
till¹ *preposition* 1 up to the time of ▷ *conjunction* 2 to the time that
till² *verb transitive* cultivate > **till'er** *noun*
till³ *noun* 1 drawer for money in store 2 cash register
til•ler [TIL-ər] *noun* lever to move rudder of boat
tilt *verb* 1 incline, slope, slant 2 tip up ▷ *verb intransitive* 3 take part in medieval combat with lances 4 thrust, aim (at) ▷ *noun* 5 slope, incline 6 *hist.* combat for mounted men with lances, joust
tim•ber [TIM-bər] *noun* 1 wood for building, etc. 2 trees suitable for the sawmill > **tim'bered** *adjective* 1 made of wood 2 covered with trees > **timber line** geographical limit beyond which trees will not grow
tim•bre [TAM-bər] *noun* quality of musical sound, or sound of human voice
time [tīm] *noun* 1 existence as a succession of states 2 hour 3 duration 4 period 5 point in duration 6 opportunity 7 occasion 8 leisure 9 tempo ▷ *verb transitive* **timed, tim•ing** 10 choose time for 11 note time taken by > **time'ly** *adjective* at opportune or appropriate time > **tim'er** [-ər] *noun* person, device for recording or indicating time > **time bomb** 1 bomb containing a timing mechanism that determines when it will explode 2 situation which, if allowed to continue, will develop into a serious problem > **time frame** period of time within which certain events are scheduled to occur > **time-**

---

tick² *noun* CREDIT, account
ticket *noun* 1 VOUCHER, card, certificate, coupon, pass, slip, token
2 LABEL, card, docket, marker, slip, sticker, tab, tag
tidbit *noun* DELICACY, dainty, morsel, snack, treat
tide *noun* 1 CURRENT, ebb, flow, stream, tideway, undertow
2 TENDENCY, direction, drift, movement, trend
tidy *adjective* 1 NEAT, clean, methodical, orderly, shipshape, spruce, well-kept, well-ordered
2 (*informal*) CONSIDERABLE, ample, generous, goodly, handsome, healthy, large, sizable *or* sizeable, substantial
▷ *verb* 3 NEATEN, clean, groom, order, spruce up, straighten
tie *verb* 1 FASTEN, attach, bind, connect, join, knot, link, secure, tether
2 RESTRICT, bind, confine, hamper, hinder, limit, restrain
3 DRAW, equal, match
▷ *noun* 4 BOND, affiliation, allegiance, commitment, connection, liaison, relationship
5 FASTENING, bond, cord, fetter, knot, ligature, link
6 DRAW, dead heat, deadlock, gridlock, stalemate
tier *noun* ROW, bank, layer, level, line, rank, story, stratum
tight *adjective* 1 STRETCHED, close, constricted, cramped, narrow, rigid, snug, taut
2 (*informal*) MISERLY, grasping, mean, niggardly, parsimonious, stingy, tightfisted
3 CLOSE, even, evenly-balanced, well-matched
tighten *verb* SQUEEZE, close, constrict, narrow
till¹ *verb* CULTIVATE, dig, plow, work
till² *noun* CASH REGISTER, cash box
tilt *verb* 1 SLANT, heel, incline, lean, list, slope, tip
▷ *noun* 2 SLOPE, angle, inclination, incline, list, pitch, slant
3 (*medieval history*) JOUST, combat, duel, fight, lists, tournament
4 ▷ **full tilt, at full tilt** FULL SPEED, for dear life, headlong
timber *noun* WOOD, beams, boards, logs, planks, trees
timbre *noun* TONE, color, resonance, ring
time *noun* 1 PERIOD, duration, interval, season, space, span, spell, stretch, term
2 OCCASION, instance, juncture, point, stage
3 (*music*) TEMPO, beat, measure, rhythm
▷ *verb* 4 SCHEDULE, set
timeless *adjective* ETERNAL, ageless, changeless, enduring, everlasting, immortal, lasting,

honored [-on-ərd] *adjective* respectable because old > **time-lag** *noun* period of time between cause and effect > **time'piece** [-pees] *noun* watch, clock > **time share** *noun* system of part ownership of vacation property for specified period each year > **time'ta•ble** *noun* plan showing hours of work, times of arrival and departure, etc. **Greenwich Mean Time** [GREN-ich] world standard time, time as settled by passage of sun over the meridian at Greenwich, England

tim'id *adjective* 1 easily frightened 2 lacking self-confidence > **ti•mid'i•ty** *noun* > **tim'or•ous** [-ər-əs] *adjective* 1 timid 2 indicating fear

tim•pa•ni [TIM-pə-nee] *plural noun* set of kettledrums > **tim'pa•nist** *noun*

tin *noun* 1 malleable metal ▷ *verb transitive* **tinned, tin•ning** 2 coat with tin > **tin'ny** *adjective* **-ni•er, -ni•est** 1 (of sound) thin, metallic 2 cheap, shoddy

tinc•ture [TINGK-chər] *noun* 1 solution of medicinal substance in alcohol 2 color, stain ▷ *verb transitive* **-tured, -tur•ing** 3 color, tint

tin•der [TIN-dər] *noun* dry easily-burning material used to start fire

tine [tīn] *noun* tooth, spike of fork, antler, etc.

tinge [tinj] *noun* 1 slight trace, flavor ▷ *verb transitive* **tinged, tinge•ing** 2 color, flavor slightly

tin•gle [TING-gəl] *verb intransitive* **-gled, -gling** feel thrill or pricking sensation ▷ *noun*

tin•ker [TING-kər] *noun* 1 formerly, traveling mender of pots and pans ▷ *verb intransitive* 2 fiddle, meddle (e.g. with machinery) oft. inexpertly

tin•kle [TING-kəl] *verb* **-kled, -kling** 1 (cause to) give out series of light sounds like small bell ▷ *noun* 2 this sound or action

tin•sel [TIN-səl] *noun* 1 glittering metallic substance for decoration 2 anything sham and showy

tint *noun* 1 color 2 shade of color 3 tinge ▷ *verb transitive* 4 dye, give tint to

ti•ny [TĪ-nee] *adjective* **-ni•er, -ni•est** very small, minute

tip¹ *noun* 1 slender or pointed end of anything 2 piece of metal, leather, etc. protecting an extremity ▷ *verb transitive* **tipped, tip•ping** 3 put a tip on

tip² *noun* 1 small present of money given for service rendered 2 helpful piece of information 3 warning, hint ▷ *verb transitive* **tipped, tip•ping** 4 give tip to > **tip'ster** [-stər] *noun* one who sells tips about races, etc.

tip³ *verb transitive* **tipped, tip•ping** 1 tilt, upset 2 touch lightly ▷ *verb intransitive* **tipped, tip•ping** 3 topple over

tip•ple [TIP-əl] *verb* **-pled, -pling** 1 drink (liquor) habitually, esp. in small quantities ▷ *noun* 2 drink of liquor > **tip'pler** [-lər] *noun*

tip•sy *adjective* **-si•er, -si•est** drunk, partly drunk

tip•toe *verb intransitive* **-toed, -to•ing** 1 walk on ball of foot and toes 2 walk softly

ti•rade [TĪ-rayd] *noun* long speech, generally vigorous and hostile, denunciation

tire¹ [tīr] *verb transitive* **tired, tir•ing** 1 reduce energy of, esp. by exertion 2 bore 3 irritate ▷ *verb intransitive* **tired, tir•ing** 4 become tired, wearied, bored > **tire'some** [-səm] *adjective* wearisome, irritating, tedious

tire² *noun* (inflated) rubber or synthetic rubber ring over rim of road vehicle

tis•sue [TISH-oo] *noun* 1 substance of animal

permanent

timely *adjective* OPPORTUNE, appropriate, convenient, judicious, propitious, seasonable, suitable, well-timed

timetable *noun* SCHEDULE, agenda, calendar, curriculum, diary, list, program

timid *adjective* FEARFUL, apprehensive, bashful, coy, diffident, faint-hearted, shrinking, shy, timorous

timorous *adjective* TIMID, apprehensive, bashful, coy, diffident, faint-hearted, fearful, shrinking, shy

tinge *noun* 1 TINT, color, shade
2 BIT, dash, drop, smattering, sprinkling, suggestion, touch, trace
▷ *verb* 3 TINT, color, imbue, suffuse

tingle *verb* 1 PRICKLE, have goose pimples, itch, sting, tickle
▷ *noun* 2 QUIVER, goose pimples, itch, pins and needles (*informal*), prickling, shiver, thrill

tinker *verb* MEDDLE, dabble, fiddle (*informal*), mess about, play, potter

tint *noun* 1 SHADE, color, hue, tone
2 DYE, rinse, tincture, tinge, wash
▷ *verb* 3 DYE, color

tiny *adjective* SMALL, diminutive, infinitesimal, little, microscopic, miniature, minute, negligible, petite, slight

tip¹ *noun* 1 END, extremity, head, peak, pinnacle, point, summit, top
▷ *verb* 2 CAP, crown, finish, surmount, top

tip² *noun* 1 GRATUITY, gift
2 HINT, clue, pointer, suggestion, warning
▷ *verb* 3 REWARD, remunerate
4 ADVISE, caution, forewarn, suggest, warn

tip³ *verb* 1 TILT, incline, lean, list, slant
2 DUMP, empty, pour out, unload
▷ *noun* 3 DUMP, refuse heap, rubbish heap

tipple *verb* 1 DRINK, imbibe, indulge (*informal*), quaff, swig, tope
▷ *noun* 2 ALCOHOL, booze (*informal*), drink, liquor

tipsy *adjective* DRUNK, fuzzy, happy, mellow, three sheets to the wind

tirade *noun* OUTBURST, diatribe, fulmination, harangue, invective, lecture

tire *verb* 1 FATIGUE, drain, exhaust, wear out, weary
2 BORE, exasperate, irk, irritate, weary

tired *adjective* 1 EXHAUSTED, drained, drowsy, fatigued, flagging, jaded, sleepy, weary, worn out
2 BORED, fed up, sick, weary
3 HACKNEYED, clichéd, corny (*slang*), old, outworn, stale, threadbare, trite, well-worn

tireless *adjective* ENERGETIC, indefatigable, industrious, resolute, unflagging, untiring, vigorous

tiresome *adjective* BORING, dull, irksome, irritating, tedious, trying, vexatious, wearing, wearisome

tiring *adjective* EXHAUSTING, arduous, demanding, exacting, laborious, strenuous,

body, plant, etc. **2** fine, soft paper, esp. used as handkerchief, etc. **3** fine woven fabric **4** interconnection e.g. of lies
tit¹ *noun* any of various small songbirds
tit² *noun* (*slang*) female breast
ti•tan•ic [tī-TAN-ik] *adjective* huge, epic
ti•ta•ni•um [tī-TAY-nee-əm] *noun* rare metal of great strength and rust-resisting qualities
tit for tat blow for blow, retaliation
tithe [tīth] *noun* **1** esp. formerly, one tenth part of agricultural produce paid for the upkeep of the clergy or as tax ▷ *verb transitive* **tithed, tith•ing** **2** exact tithes from ▷ *verb intransitive* **tithed, tith•ing** **3** give, pay tithe
ti•tian [TISH-ən] *adjective* (of hair) reddish-gold, auburn
tit•il•late [TIT-l-ayt] *verb transitive* **-lat•ed, -lat•ing** tickle, stimulate agreeably
ti•tle [TĪT-l] *noun* **1** name of book **2** heading **3** name **4** appellation denoting rank **5** legal right or document proving it **6** *sports* championship > **title deed** legal document as proof of ownership
tit•ter [TIT-ər] *verb intransitive* **1** laugh in suppressed way ▷ *noun* **2** such laugh
tit•tle [TIT-l] *noun* whit, detail
tit•tle-tat•tle [TIT-l-tat-l] *noun, verb intransitive* **-tled, -tling** gossip
tit•u•lar [TICH-ə-lər] *adjective* **1** pert. to title **2** nominal **3** held by virtue of a title
tiz•zy [TIZ-ee] *noun, plural* **-zies** (*slang*) state of confusion, anxiety
Tl *chem.* thallium
Tm *chem.* thulium
to *preposition* **1** toward, in the direction of **2** as far as **3** used to introduce a comparison, ratio, indirect object, infinitive, etc. ▷ *adverb* **4** to the required or normal state or position
toad [tohd] *noun* animal like frog > **toad'y** *noun, plural* **toad•ies** **1** obsequious flatterer, sycophant ▷ *verb intransitive* **toad•ied, toad•y•ing** **2** do this > **toad'stool** *noun* fungus like mushroom, but usu. poisonous
toast [tohst] *noun* **1** slice of bread crisped and browned on both sides by heat **2** tribute, proposal of health, success, etc. made by company of people and marked by drinking together **3** one toasted ▷ *verb transitive* **4** crisp and brown (as bread) **5** drink toast to **6** dry or warm at fire > **toast'er** *noun* electrical device for toasting bread
to•bac•co [tə-BAK-oh] *noun, plural* **-cos** *or* **-coes** **1** plant with leaves used for smoking **2** the prepared leaves
to•bog•gan [tə-BOG-ən] *noun* **1** sled for sliding down slope of snow ▷ *verb intransitive* **2** slide on one
toc•ca•ta [tə-KAH-tə] *noun* rapid piece of music for keyboard instrument
toc•sin [TOK-sin] *noun* alarm signal, bell
to•day [tə-DAY] *noun* **1** this day ▷ *adverb* **2** on this day **3** nowadays
tod•dle [TOD-l] *verb intransitive* **-dled, -dling** **1** walk with unsteady short steps ▷ *noun* **2** toddling > **tod'dler** [-lər] *noun* **1** child beginning to walk
tod•dy [TOD-ee] *noun, plural* **-dies** sweetened mixture of alcoholic liquor, hot water, etc.
to-do [tə-DOO] *noun, plural* **-dos** (*informal*) fuss, commotion
toe [toh] *noun* **1** digit of foot **2** anything resembling toe in shape or position ▷ *verb transitive* **toed, toe•ing** **3** reach, touch with toe **toe the line** conform
tof•fee [TAW-fee] *noun* brittle candy made of sugar and butter, etc.
to•ga [TOH-gə] *noun, plural* **-gas** loose outer garment worn by ancient Romans
to•geth•er [tə-GETH-ər] *adverb* **1** in company, simultaneously ▷ *adjective* **2** (*slang*) (well) organized
tog•gle [TOG-əl] *noun* **1** small wooden, metal peg fixed crosswise on cord, wire, etc. and used for fastening as button **2** any similar device
togs [togz] *plural noun* clothes
toil *noun* **1** heavy work or task ▷ *verb intransitive* **2** labor > **toil'worn** *adjective* **1** weary with toil **2** hard and lined
toi•let [TOI-lit] *noun* **1** lavatory **2** ceramic toilet bowl **3** process of washing, dressing **4** articles

tough, wearing
titillate *verb* EXCITE, arouse, interest, stimulate, tantalize, tease, thrill
titillating *adjective* EXCITING, arousing, interesting, lurid, provocative, stimulating, suggestive, teasing
title *noun* **1** NAME, designation, handle (*slang*), moniker *or* monicker (*slang*), term
2 CHAMPIONSHIP, crown
3 OWNERSHIP, claim, entitlement, prerogative, privilege, right
titter *verb* LAUGH, chortle (*informal*), chuckle, giggle, snigger
tizzy *noun* (*informal*) PANIC, agitation, commotion, fluster, state (*informal*), sweat (*informal*)
toady *noun* **1** SYCOPHANT, brown-noser (*slang*), creep (*slang*), flatterer, flunkey, hanger-on, lackey, minion, scuzzbucket (*slang*), yes man
▷ *verb* **2** FLATTER, brown-nose (*slang*), fawn on, grovel, kiss ass (*slang*), kowtow to, pander to, suck up to (*informal*)
toast¹ *verb* WARM, brown, grill, heat, roast
toast² *noun* **1** TRIBUTE, compliment, health, pledge, salutation, salute
2 FAVORITE, darling, hero *or* heroine
▷ *verb* **3** DRINK TO, drink the health of *or* drink to the health of, salute
together *adverb* **1** COLLECTIVELY, as one, hand in glove, in concert, in unison, jointly, mutually, shoulder to shoulder, side by side
2 AT THE SAME TIME, at one fell swoop, concurrently, contemporaneously, simultaneously
▷ *adjective* **3** (*informal*) WELL-ORGANIZED, composed, well-adjusted, well-balanced
toil *noun* **1** HARD WORK, application, drudgery, effort, elbow grease (*informal*), exertion, slog, sweat
▷ *verb* **2** WORK, drudge, labor, slave, slog, strive, struggle, sweat (*informal*), work one's fingers to the bone
toilet *noun* LAVATORY, bathroom, convenience, gents (*Brit informal*), ladies' room, latrine, privy, urinal, water closet, W.C.

used for this
to•ken [TOH-kən] *noun* 1 sign or object used as evidence 2 symbol 3 disk used as money ▷ *adjective* 4 nominal, slight
told [tohld] *pt./pp. of* **tell**
tol•er•ate [TOL-ər-ayt] *verb transitive* **-at•ed, -at•ing** 1 put up with 2 permit > **tol'er•a•ble** *adjective* 1 bearable 2 fair, moderate > **tol'er•ance** [-əns] *noun* (degree of) ability to endure stress, pain, radiation, etc. > **tol'er•ant** [-ənt] *adjective* 1 disinclined to interfere with others' ways or opinions 2 forbearing 3 broad-minded
toll[1] [tohl] *verb transitive* 1 make (bell) ring slowly at regular intervals 2 announce death thus ▷ *verb intransitive* 3 ring thus ▷ *noun* 4 tolling sound
toll[2] *noun* 1 tax, esp. for the use of bridge or road 2 loss, damage incurred through accident, disaster, etc.
tom *noun* male of some animals, esp. cat
tom•a•hawk [TOM-ə-hawk] *noun* 1 formerly, fighting ax of N Amer. Indians ▷ *verb transitive* 2 strike, kill with one
to•ma•to [tə-MAY-toh] *noun, plural* **-toes** 1 plant with red fruit 2 the fruit, used in salads, etc.
tomb [toom] *noun* 1 grave 2 monument over one > **tomb'stone** *noun* gravestone
tom•boy [TOM-boi] *noun* girl who acts, dresses in boyish way
tome [tohm] *noun* large book or volume
tom•fool•er•y [tom-FOO-lə-ree] *noun, plural* **-er•ies** nonsense, silly behavior
to•mog•ra•phy [tə-MOG-rə-fee] *noun* technique used to obtain an X-ray photograph of a plane section of the human body or some other object
to•mor•row [tə-MOR-oh] *adverb, noun* (on) the day after today
tom-tom *noun* drum associated with N Amer. Indians or with Asia
ton [tun] *noun* 1 measure of weight equal to 2000 pounds or 907 kilograms (short ton) 2 measure of weight equal to 2240 pounds or 1016 kilograms (long ton) > **ton•nage** [TUN-ij] *noun* 1 carrying capacity 2 charge per ton 3 ships collectively
tone [tohn] *noun* 1 quality of musical sound 2 quality of voice, color, etc. 3 general character, style 4 healthy condition ▷ *verb transitive* **toned, ton•ing** 5 give tone to 6 blend, harmonize (with) > **ton'er** [-ər] *noun* substance that modifies color or composition > **ton'al** [-əl] *adjective* > **to•nal'i•ty** *noun, plural* **-ties** > **tone poem** orchestral work based on story, legend, etc.
tongs [tongz] *plural noun* large pincers, esp. for handling coal, sugar
tongue [tung] *noun* 1 muscular organ inside mouth, used for speech, taste, etc. 2 various things shaped like this 3 language, speech, voice
ton•ic [TON-ik] *noun* 1 medicine to improve bodily tone or condition 2 *mus.* keynote 3 *mus.* first note of scale ▷ *adjective* 4 invigorating, restorative 5 of tone > **tonic** *or* **tonic water** mineral water oft. containing quinine
to•night [tə-NĪT] *noun* 1 this night 2 the coming night ▷ *adverb* 3 on this night
ton•sil [TON-səl] *noun* gland in throat > **ton•sil•li'tis** [-LĪ-tis] *noun* inflammation of tonsils > **ton•sil•lec•to•my** [-sə-LEK-tə-mee] *noun, plural* **-mies** surgical removal of tonsil(s)
ton•sure [TON-shər] *noun* 1 shaving of part of head as religious or monastic practice 2 part shaved ▷ *verb transitive* **-sured, -sur•ing** 3 shave thus
too *adverb* 1 also, in addition 2 in excess, overmuch
took [tuuk] *pt. of* **take**
tool *noun* 1 implement or appliance for mechanical operations 2 servile helper 3

DICTIONARY **t** THESAURUS

token *noun* 1 SYMBOL, badge, expression, indication, mark, note, representation, sign ▷ *adjective* 2 NOMINAL, hollow, minimal, perfunctory, superficial, symbolic
tolerable *adjective* 1 BEARABLE, acceptable, allowable, endurable, sufferable, supportable 2 FAIR, acceptable, adequate, all right, average, O.K. *or* okay (*informal*), passable
tolerance *noun* 1 BROAD-MINDEDNESS, forbearance, indulgence, open-mindedness, permissiveness 2 ENDURANCE, fortitude, hardiness, resilience, resistance, stamina, staying power, toughness
tolerant *adjective* BROAD-MINDED, catholic, forbearing, liberal, long-suffering, open-minded, understanding, unprejudiced
tolerate *verb* ALLOW, accept, brook, condone, endure, permit, put up with (*informal*), stand, stomach, take
toleration *noun* ACCEPTANCE, allowance, endurance, indulgence, permissiveness, sanction
toll[1] *verb* 1 RING, chime, clang, knell, peal, sound, strike ▷ *noun* 2 RINGING, chime, clang, knell, peal
toll[2] *noun* 1 CHARGE, duty, fee, levy, payment, tariff, tax 2 DAMAGE, cost, loss, penalty
tomb *noun* GRAVE, catacomb, crypt, mausoleum, sarcophagus, sepulcher, vault
tombstone *noun* GRAVESTONE, headstone, marker, memorial, monument
tomfoolery *noun* FOOLISHNESS, buffoonery, clowning, fooling around (*informal*), horseplay, shenanigans (*informal*), silliness, skylarking (*informal*), stupidity
ton *noun* (*often plural*) (*informal*) A LOT, great deal, ocean, quantity, stacks
tone *noun* 1 PITCH, inflection, intonation, modulation, timbre 2 CHARACTER, air, attitude, feel, manner, mood, spirit, style, temper 3 COLOR, hue, shade, tinge, tint ▷ *verb* 4 HARMONIZE, blend, go well with, match, suit
tone down *verb* MODERATE, play down, reduce, restrain, soften, subdue, temper
tongue *noun* LANGUAGE, dialect, parlance, speech
tonic *noun* STIMULANT, boost, pick-me-up (*informal*), restorative, shot in the arm (*informal*)
too *adverb* 1 ALSO, as well, besides, further, in addition, likewise, moreover, to boot 2 EXCESSIVELY, extremely, immoderately,

means to an end ▷ *verb transitive* 4 work on with tool, esp. chisel stone 5 indent design on leather book cover, etc. > **tool'ing** *noun* 1 decorative work 2 setting up, etc. of tools, esp. for machine operation > **tool'bar** *noun* row of buttons displayed on a computer screen, allowing the user to select various functions
tooth *noun, plural* **teeth** 1 bonelike projection in gums of upper and lower jaws of vertebrates 2 various pointed things like this 3 prong, cog
top[1] *noun* 1 highest part, summit 2 highest rank 3 first in merit 4 garment for upper part of body 5 lid, stopper of bottle, etc. ▷ *verb transitive* **topped, top'ping** 6 cut off, pass, reach, surpass top 7 provide top for > **top'less** [-lis] *adjective* (of costume, woman) with no covering for breasts > **top'most** [-mohst] *adjective* 1 supreme 2 highest > **top dressing** layer of fertilizer spread on the surface of land > **top hat** man's hat with tall cylindrical crown > **top-heavy** *adjective* 1 unbalanced 2 with top too heavy for base > **top•notch** *adjective* excellent, first-class > **top-secret** *adjective* needing highest level of secrecy, security > **top'soil** *noun* 1 surface layer of soil 2 more fertile soil spread on lawns, etc.
top[2] *noun* toy that spins on tapering point or ball bearing
to•paz [TOH-paz] *noun* precious stone of various colors
to•pee [toh-PEE] *noun* lightweight hat made of pith
to•pi•ar•y [TOH-pee-er-ee] *adjective* (of shrubs) shaped by cutting or pruning, made ornamental by trimming or training ▷ *noun*
top•ic [TOP-ik] *noun* subject of discourse, conversation, etc. > **top'i•cal** [-ik-əl] *adjective* 1 up-to-date, having news value 2 of topic
to•pog•ra•phy [tə-POG-rə-fee] *noun, plural* **-phies** (description of) surface features of a place > **to•pog'ra•pher** *noun*
top•ple [TOP-əl] *verb* **-pled, -ling** (cause to) fall over, collapse
top•sy-tur•vy [TOP-see-TUR-vee] *adjective, adverb* upside down, in confusion
tor *noun* high, rocky hill
To•rah [TOH-rə] *noun* parchment on which is written the Pentateuch
torch *noun* 1 portable hand light containing electric battery and bulb 2 burning brand, etc. 3 any apparatus burning with hot flame, e.g. for welding > **torch'bear•er** [-bair-ər] *noun*
tore *pt. of* **tear[2]**
tor•e•a•dor [TOR-ee-ə-dor] *noun* bullfighter
tor•ment' *verb* 1 torture in body or mind 2 afflict 3 tease ▷ *noun* [TOR-ment] 4 suffering, torture, agony of body or mind
torn *pp of* **tear[2]**
tor•na•do [tor-NAY-doh] *noun, plural* **-does** 1 whirlwind 2 violent storm
tor•pe•do [tor-PEE-doh] *noun, plural* **-does** 1 cylindrical self-propelled underwater missile with explosive warhead, fired esp. from submarine ▷ *verb transitive* **-doed, -do•ing** 2 strike, sink with, as with, torpedo
tor'pid *adjective* sluggish, apathetic > **tor•por** [TOR-pər] *noun* torpid state
torque [tork] *noun* 1 collar, similar ornament of twisted gold or other metal 2 *mechanics* rotating or twisting force
tor•rent [TOR-ənt] *noun* 1 a rushing stream 2 downpour > **tor•ren•tial** [tə-REN-shəl] *adjective* 1 resembling a torrent 2 overwhelming
tor•rid [TOR-id] *adjective* 1 parched, dried with heat 2 highly emotional > **Torrid Zone** land between tropics
tor•sion [TOR-shən] *noun* twist, twisting
tor•so [TOR-soh] *noun, plural* **-sos** 1 (statue of) body without head or limbs 2 trunk
tort *noun law* private or civil wrong
tor•til•la [tor-TEE-yə] *noun, plural* **-til•las** thin Mexican pancake
tor•toise [TOR-təs] *noun* four-footed reptile covered with shell of horny plates > **tor'toise•shell** *noun* mottled brown shell of hawksbill turtle used commercially ▷ *adjective*
tor•tu•ous [TOR-choo-əs] *adjective* 1 winding, twisting 2 involved, not straightforward

inordinately, overly, unduly, unreasonably, very
tool *noun* 1 IMPLEMENT, appliance, contraption, contrivance, device, gadget, instrument, machine, utensil
2 PUPPET, cat's-paw, creature, flunkey, hireling, lackey, minion, pawn, stooge (*slang*)
top *noun* 1 PEAK, apex, crest, crown, culmination, head, height, pinnacle, summit, zenith
2 FIRST PLACE, head, lead
3 LID, cap, cover, stopper
▷ *adjective* 4 LEADING, best, chief, elite, finest, first, foremost, head, highest, pre-eminent, principal, uppermost
▷ *verb* 5 COVER, cap, crown, finish, garnish
6 LEAD, be first, head
7 SURPASS, beat, best, better, eclipse, exceed, excel, outstrip, transcend
topic *noun* SUBJECT, issue, matter, point, question, subject matter, theme
topical *adjective* CURRENT, contemporary, newsworthy, popular, up-to-date, up-to-the-minute
topmost *adjective* HIGHEST, dominant, foremost, leading, paramount, principal, supreme, top, uppermost
topple *verb* 1 FALL OVER, collapse, fall, keel over, overbalance, overturn, totter, tumble
2 OVERTHROW, bring down, bring low, oust, overturn, unseat
topsy-turvy *adjective* CONFUSED, chaotic, disorderly, disorganized, inside-out, jumbled, messy, mixed-up, upside-down
torment *verb* 1 TORTURE, crucify, distress, rack
2 TEASE, annoy, bother, harass, hassle (*informal*), irritate, nag, pester, vex
▷ *noun* 3 SUFFERING, agony, anguish, distress, hell, misery, pain, torture
torn *adjective* 1 CUT, lacerated, ragged, rent, ripped, slit, split
2 UNDECIDED, in two minds (*informal*), irresolute, uncertain, unsure, vacillating, wavering
tornado *noun* WHIRLWIND, cyclone, gale, hurricane, squall, storm, tempest, typhoon
torpor *noun* INACTIVITY, apathy, drowsiness, indolence, laziness, lethargy, listlessness, sloth, sluggishness
torrent *noun* STREAM, cascade, deluge,

tor•ture [TOR-chər] *noun* 1 infliction of severe pain ▷ *verb transitive* **-tured, -tur•ing** 2 subject to torture > **tor'tur•er** *noun*
toss [taws] *verb transitive* 1 throw up, about ▷ *verb intransitive* 2 be thrown, fling oneself about ▷ *noun* 3 act of tossing
tot[1] *noun* very small child
tot[2] *verb* **tot•ted, tot•ting** 1 (with *up*) add up 2 amount to
to•tal [TOHT-l] *noun* 1 whole amount 2 sum, aggregate ▷ *adjective* 3 complete, entire, full, absolute ▷ *verb* **-taled, -tal•ing** 4 amount to 5 add up > **to•tal'i•ty** *noun, plural* **-ties** > **to•tal•i•za•tor** [TOHT-l-ə-zay-tər] *noun* machine to operate system of betting at racetrack in which money is paid out to winners in proportion to their bets
to•tal•i•tar•i•an [toh-tal-i-TAIR-ee-ən] *adjective* of dictatorial, one-party government
tote[1] [toht] *noun short for* **totalizator**
tote[2] *verb transitive* **tot•ed, tot•ing** haul, carry
to•tem [TOH-təm] *noun* tribal badge or emblem > **totem pole** post carved, painted with totems, esp. by Native Americans
tot•ter [TOT-ər] *verb intransitive* 1 walk unsteadily 2 begin to fall
touch [tuch] *noun* 1 sense by which qualities of object, etc. are perceived by touching 2 characteristic manner or ability 3 touching 4 slight blow, stroke, contact, amount, etc. ▷ *verb transitive* 5 come into contact with 6 put hand on 7 reach 8 affect emotions of 9 deal with, handle 10 eat, drink 11 (*slang*) (try to) borrow from ▷ *verb intransitive* 12 be in contact 13 (with *on*) refer to > **touch'ing** *adjective* 1 emotionally moving ▷ *preposition* 2 concerning > **touch'y** *adjective* **touch•i•er, touch•i•est** easily offended, sensitive > **touch'down** *noun* 1 *football* crossing of goal line with football 2 act of, moment of, landing of aircraft > **touch'stone** *noun* criterion > **touch and go** precarious (situation) **touch base** make contact, renew communication
tou•ché [too-SHAY] *interjection* acknowledgment that blow (orig. in fencing), remark, etc. has been successful
tough [tuf] *adjective* **-er, -est** 1 strong, resilient, not brittle 2 sturdy 3 able to bear hardship, strain 4 difficult 5 needing effort to chew 6 rough 7 uncivilized 8 violent 9 unlucky, unfair ▷ *noun* 10 rough, violent person > **tough'en** [-ən] *verb* > **tough'ness** [-nis] *noun*
tou•pee [too-PAY] *noun* man's hairpiece, wig
tour [toor] *noun* 1 traveling around 2 journey to one place after another 3 excursion ▷ *verb* 4 make tour (of) > **tour'ism** *noun* 1 tourist travel 2 this as an industry > **tour'ist** *noun* one who

DICTIONARY **t** THESAURUS

---

downpour, flood, flow, rush, spate, tide
torrid *adjective* 1 ARID, dried, parched, scorched
2 PASSIONATE, ardent, fervent, intense, steamy (*informal*)
tortuous *adjective* 1 WINDING, circuitous, convoluted, indirect, mazy, meandering, serpentine, sinuous, twisting, twisty
2 COMPLICATED, ambiguous, convoluted, devious, indirect, involved, roundabout, tricky
torture *verb* 1 TORMENT, afflict, crucify, distress, persecute, put on the rack, rack
▷ *noun* 2 AGONY, anguish, distress, pain, persecution, suffering, torment
toss *verb* 1 THROW, cast, fling, flip, hurl, launch, lob (*informal*), pitch, sling
2 THRASH, rock, roll, shake, wriggle, writhe
▷ *noun* 3 THROW, lob (*informal*), pitch
tot *noun* INFANT, baby, child, mite, toddler
total *noun* 1 WHOLE, aggregate, entirety, full amount, sum, totality
▷ *adjective* 2 COMPLETE, absolute, comprehensive, entire, full, gross, thoroughgoing, undivided, utter, whole
▷ *verb* 3 AMOUNT TO, come to, mount up to, reach
4 ADD UP, reckon, tot up
totalitarian *adjective* DICTATORIAL, authoritarian, despotic, oppressive, tyrannous, undemocratic
totality *noun* WHOLE, aggregate, entirety, sum, total
totally *adverb* COMPLETELY, absolutely, comprehensively, entirely, fully, one hundred per cent, thoroughly, utterly, wholly
totter *verb* STAGGER, falter, lurch, reel, stumble, sway
touch *verb* 1 HANDLE, brush, caress, contact, feel, finger, fondle, stroke, tap
2 MEET, abut, adjoin, be in contact, border, contact, graze, impinge upon
3 AFFECT, disturb, impress, influence, inspire, move, stir
4 EAT, chow down (*slang*), consume, drink, partake of
5 MATCH, compare with, equal, hold a candle to (*informal*), parallel, rival
6 ▷ **touch on** REFER TO, allude to, bring in, cover, deal with, mention, speak of
▷ *noun* 7 FEELING, handling, physical contact
8 TAP, brush, contact, pat, stroke
9 BIT, dash, drop, jot, small amount, smattering, soupçon (*French*), spot, trace
10 STYLE, manner, method, technique, trademark, way
touch and go *adjective* RISKY, close, critical, near, nerve-racking, precarious
touching *adjective* MOVING, affecting, emotive, pathetic, pitiable, poignant, sad, stirring
touchstone *noun* STANDARD, criterion, gauge, measure, norm, par, yardstick
touchy *adjective* OVERSENSITIVE, irascible, irritable, querulous, quick tempered, testy, tetchy, thin-skinned
tough *adjective* 1 RESILIENT, durable, hard, inflexible, leathery, resistant, rugged, solid, strong, sturdy
2 STRONG, hardy, seasoned, stout, strapping, sturdy, vigorous
3 ROUGH, hard-boiled, pugnacious, ruthless, violent
4 STRICT, firm, hard, merciless, resolute, severe, stern, unbending
5 DIFFICULT, arduous, exacting, hard, laborious, strenuous, troublesome, uphill
6 (*informal*) UNLUCKY, lamentable, regrettable, unfortunate
tour *noun* 1 JOURNEY, excursion, expedition, jaunt, outing, trip
▷ *verb* 2 VISIT, explore, go round, journey, sightsee, travel through

travels for pleasure

tour de force [toor də FORS] *Fr.* brilliant stroke, achievement

tour•ma•line [TUUR-mə-lin] *noun* crystalline mineral used for optical instruments and as gem

tour•na•ment [TUUR-nə-mənt] *noun* competition, contest usu. with several stages to decide overall winner > **tour•ney** [TUUR-nee] *noun, plural* **-neys** tournament

tour•ni•quet [TUR-ni-kit] *noun* bandage, surgical instrument to constrict artery and stop bleeding

tou•sle [TOW-zəl] *verb transitive* **-sled, -sling** 1 tangle, ruffle 2 treat roughly

tout [towt] *verb intransitive* 1 solicit trade (usu. in undesirable fashion) 2 obtain and sell information about racehorses, etc. ▷ *noun* 3 one who touts

tow[1] [toh] *verb transitive* 1 drag along behind, esp. at end of rope ▷ *noun* 2 towing or being towed 3 vessel, vehicle in tow > **tow'path** *noun* path beside canal, river, orig. for towing

tow[2] *noun* fiber of hemp, flax > **tow-head•ed** [-hed-id] *adjective* with pale-colored, or rumpled hair

to•ward [tord], **to•wards** [tords] *preposition* 1 in direction of 2 with regard to 3 as contribution to

tow•el [TOW-əl] *noun* cloth for wiping off moisture after washing > **tow'el•ing** *noun* material used for making towels

tow•er [TOW-ər] *noun* 1 tall strong structure often forming part of church or other large building 2 fortress ▷ *verb intransitive* 3 stand very high 4 loom (over)

town *noun* collection of dwellings, etc. larger than village and smaller than city > **town'ship** *noun* small town > **towns'peo•ple** *noun*

tox•ic [TOK-sik] *adjective* 1 poisonous 2 due to poison > **tox•e•mi•a** [tok-SEEM-ee-ə] *noun* blood poisoning > **tox•ic'i•ty** [-IS-i-tee] *noun* strength of a poison > **tox•i•col•o•gy** [tok-si-KOL-ə-jee] *noun* study of poisons > **tox'in** *noun* poison of bacterial origin

toy [toi] *noun* 1 something designed to be played with 2 (miniature) replica ▷ *adjective* 3 very small ▷ *verb intransitive* 4 act idly, trifle

trace[1] [trays] *noun* 1 track left by anything 2 indication 3 minute quantity ▷ *verb transitive* **traced, trac•ing** 4 follow course, track of 5 find out 6 make plan of 7 draw or copy exactly, esp. using tracing paper > **trace element** chemical element occurring in very small quantity in soil, etc. > **tracer** *noun* bullet or shell that leaves visible trail so that aim can be checked > **tracing paper** transparent paper placed over drawing, map, etc. to enable exact copy to be taken

trace[2] *noun* chain, strap by which horse pulls vehicle **kick over the traces** become defiant, independent

tra•che•a [TRAY-kee-ə] *noun, plural* **-che•as** windpipe > **tra'che•al** [-əl] *adjective* > **tra•che•ot'o•my** [-OT-ə-mee] *noun, plural* **-mies** surgical incision into trachea

tra•cho•ma [trə-KOH-mə] *noun* contagious viral disease of eye

track [trak] *noun* 1 mark, line of marks, left by passage of anything 2 path 3 rough road 4 course 5 railroad line 6 distance between two road wheels on one axle 7 circular jointed metal band driven by wheels as on tank, bulldozer, etc. 8 course for running or racing 9 separate section on phonograph record 10 class, division of schoolchildren grouped together because of similar ability ▷ *verb transitive* 11 follow trail or path of 12 find thus > **track record** past accomplishments of person, company, etc.

tract[1] [trakt] *noun* 1 wide expanse, area 2 *anatomy* system of organs, etc. with particular function

tract[2] *noun* treatise or pamphlet, esp. religious one > **trac'tate** [-tayt] *noun* short tract

trac•ta•ble [TRAK-tə-bəl] *adjective* easy to manage, docile, amenable

trac•tion [TRAK-shən] *noun* action of drawing,

DICTIONARY • THESAURUS

tourist *noun* TRAVELER, excursionist, globetrotter, holiday-maker, sightseer, tripper, voyager

tournament *noun* COMPETITION, contest, event, meeting, series

tow *verb* DRAG, draw, haul, lug, pull, tug

towards *preposition* 1 IN THE DIRECTION OF, en route for, for, on the way to, to
2 REGARDING, about, concerning, for, with regard to, with respect to

tower *noun* COLUMN, belfry, obelisk, pillar, skyscraper, steeple, turret

towering *adjective* HIGH, colossal, elevated, imposing, impressive, lofty, magnificent, soaring, tall

toxic *adjective* POISONOUS, deadly, harmful, lethal, noxious, pernicious, pestilential, septic

toy *noun* 1 PLAYTHIIING, doll, game
▷ *verb* 2 PLAY, amuse oneself, dally, fiddle (*informal*), fool *or* fool about fool around, trifle

trace *verb* 1 FIND, detect, discover, ferret out, hunt down, track, unearth
2 COPY, draw, outline, sketch
▷ *noun* 3 TRACK, footmark, footprint, footstep, path, spoor, trail
4 BIT, drop, hint, shadow, suggestion, suspicion, tinge, touch, whiff
5 INDICATION, evidence, mark, record, remnant, sign, survival, vestige

track *noun* 1 PATH, course, line, orbit, pathway, road, trajectory, way
2 TRAIL, footmark, footprint, footstep, mark, path, spoor, trace, wake
3 LINE, permanent way, rails
▷ *verb* 4 FOLLOW, chase, hunt down, pursue, shadow, stalk, tail (*informal*), trace, trail

track down *verb* FIND, dig up, discover, hunt down, run to earth *or* run to ground, sniff out, trace, unearth

tract[1] *noun* AREA, district, expanse, extent, plot, region, stretch, territory

tract[2] *noun* TREATISE, booklet, dissertation, essay, homily, monograph, pamphlet

tractable *adjective* MANAGEABLE, amenable, biddable, compliant, docile, obedient, submissive, tame, willing, yielding

traction *noun* GRIP, friction, pull, purchase, resistance pulling > **traction engine** locomotive running on surfaces other than tracks

trac•tor [TRAK-tər] *noun* motor vehicle for hauling, pulling, etc.

trade [trayd] *noun* 1 commerce, business 2 buying and selling 3 any profitable pursuit 4 those engaged in trade ▷ *verb* **trad•ed, trad•ing** 5 engage in trade 6 buy and sell 7 barter > **trade-in** *noun* used article given in part payment for new > **trade'mark, trade'name** *noun* distinctive mark (secured by legal registration) on maker's goods > **trades'man** [-mən] *noun, plural* **-men** 1 person engaged in trade 2 skilled worker > **trade union** society of workers for protection of their interests > **trade wind** wind blowing constantly toward equator in certain parts of globe

tra•di•tion [trə-DISH-ən] *noun* 1 unwritten body of beliefs, facts, etc. handed down from generation to generation 2 custom, practice of long standing 3 process of handing down

tra•duce [trə-DOOS] *verb transitive* **-duced, -duc•ing** slander

traf•fic [TRAF-ik] *noun* 1 vehicles passing to and fro in street, town, etc. 2 (illicit) trade ▷ *verb intransitive* **-ficked, -fick•ing** 3 trade, esp. in illicit goods, e.g. drugs > **traf'fick•er** *noun* trader > **traffic lights** set of colored lights at road junctions, etc. to control flow of traffic

trag•e•dy [TRAJ-i-dee] *noun, plural* **-dies** 1 sad or calamitous event 2 dramatic, literary work dealing with serious, sad topic and with ending marked by (inevitable) disaster > **tra•ge•di•an** [trə-JEE-dee-ən] *noun* actor in, writer of tragedies > **trag'ic** *adjective* 1 of, in manner of tragedy 2 disastrous 3 appalling > **trag'i•cal•ly** *adverb*

trail [trayl] *verb transitive* 1 drag behind one ▷ *verb intransitive* 2 be drawn behind 3 hang, grow loosely ▷ *noun* 4 track or trace 5 thing that trails 6 rough ill-defined track in wild country > **trail'er** *noun* 1 vehicle towed by another vehicle 2 trailing plant 3 *motion pictures* advertisement of forthcoming film > **trailer park** site for parking mobile homes, usu. providing facilities for trailer residents > **trailer trash** (*offensive*) poor person or people living in trailer parks

train [trayn] *verb transitive* 1 educate, instruct, exercise 2 cause to grow in particular way 3 aim (gun, etc.) ▷ *verb intransitive* 4 follow course of training, esp. to achieve physical fitness for athletics ▷ *noun* 5 line of railroad vehicles joined to locomotive 6 succession, esp. of thoughts, events, etc. 7 procession of animals, vehicles, etc. traveling together 8 trailing part of dress 9 body of attendants > **train•ee'** *noun* one training to be skilled worker, esp. in industry

traipse [trayps] *verb intransitive* **traipsed, traips•ing** (*informal*) walk wearily

trait [trayt] *noun* characteristic feature

trai•tor [TRAY-tər] *noun* one who betrays or is guilty of treason > **trai'tor•ous** [-əs] *adjective* 1 disloyal 2 guilty of treachery

tra•jec•to•ry [trə-JEK-tə-ree] *noun, plural* **-ries** line of flight, (curved) path of projectile

tram•mel [TRAM-əl] *noun* 1 anything that restrains or holds captive 2 type of compasses ▷ *verb transitive* **-meled, -mel•ing** 3 restrain 4 hinder

tramp *verb intransitive* 1 travel on foot, esp. as vagabond or for pleasure 2 walk heavily ▷ *noun* 3 homeless person who travels about on foot 4 walk 5 tramping 6 vessel that takes cargo wherever shippers desire

tram•ple [TRAM-pəl] *verb transitive* **-pled, -pling** tread on and crush under foot

DICTIONARY **t** THESAURUS

---

trade *noun* 1 COMMERCE, barter, business, dealing, exchange, traffic, transactions, truck
2 JOB, business, craft, employment, line of work, métier, occupation, profession
▷ *verb* 3 DEAL, bargain, do business, have dealings, peddle, traffic, transact, truck
4 EXCHANGE, barter, swap, switch

trader *noun* DEALER, merchant, purveyor, seller, supplier

tradesman *noun* 1 CRAFTSMAN, artisan, journeyman, workman
2 SHOPKEEPER, dealer, merchant, purveyor, retailer, seller, supplier, vendor

tradition *noun* CUSTOM, convention, folklore, habit, institution, lore, ritual

traditional *adjective* CUSTOMARY, accustomed, conventional, established, old, time-honored, usual

traffic *noun* 1 TRANSPORT, freight, transportation, vehicles
2 TRADE, business, commerce, dealings, exchange, peddling, truck
▷ *verb* 3 TRADE, bargain, deal, do business, exchange, have dealings, peddle

tragedy *noun* DISASTER, adversity, calamity, catastrophe, misfortune

tragic *adjective* DISASTROUS, appalling, calamitous, catastrophic, deadly, dire, dreadful, miserable, pathetic, sad, unfortunate

trail *noun* 1 PATH, footpath, road, route, track, way
2 TRACKS, footprints, marks, path, scent, spoor, trace, wake
▷ *verb* 3 DRAG, dangle, draw, haul, pull, tow
4 LAG, dawdle, follow, hang back, linger, loiter, straggle, traipse (*informal*)
5 FOLLOW, chase, hunt, pursue, shadow, stalk, tail (*informal*), trace, track

train *verb* 1 INSTRUCT, coach, drill, educate, guide, prepare, school, teach, tutor
2 EXERCISE, prepare, work out
3 AIM, direct, focus, level, point
▷ *noun* 4 SEQUENCE, chain, progression, series, set, string, succession

trainer *noun* COACH, handler

training *noun* 1 INSTRUCTION, coaching, discipline, education, grounding, schooling, teaching, tuition
2 EXERCISE, practice, preparation, working out

traipse *verb* TRUDGE, drag oneself, footslog, slouch, trail, tramp

trait *noun* CHARACTERISTIC, attribute, feature, idiosyncrasy, mannerism, peculiarity, quality, quirk

traitor *noun* BETRAYER, apostate, back-stabber, defector, deserter, Judas, quisling, rebel, renegade, turncoat

trajectory *noun* PATH, course, flight path, line,

tram•po•line [tram-pə-LEEN] *noun* tough canvas sheet stretched horizontally with elastic cords, etc. to frame, for gymnastic, acrobatic use
trance [trans] *noun* 1 unconscious or dazed state 2 state of ecstasy or total absorption
tran•quil [TRANG-kwil] *adjective* 1 calm, quiet 2 serene > **tran•quil'li•ty** *noun* > **tran'quil•ize** *verb transitive* **-ized, -iz•ing** make calm > **tran'quil•iz•er** *noun* drug that induces calm, tranquil state
trans- *prefix* 1 across, through, beyond: *transnational* 2 changing thoroughly: *transliterate*
trans•act [tran-SAKT] *verb transitive* 1 carry through 2 negotiate 3 conduct (affair, etc.) > **trans•ac'tion** *noun* 1 performing of any business 2 that which is performed 3 single sale or purchase > **trans•ac'tions** 1 proceedings 2 reports of a society
trans•ceiv•er [tran-SEE-vər] *noun* combined radio transmitter and receiver
tran•scend [tran-SEND] *verb transitive* 1 rise above 2 exceed, surpass > **tran•scend'ent** *adjective* > **tran•scen•den'tal** *adjective* 1 surpassing experience 2 supernatural 3 abstruse > **transcendental meditation** process seeking to induce detachment from problems, etc. by system of meditation
tran•scribe [tran-SKRĪB] *verb transitive* **-scribed, -scrib•ing** 1 copy out 2 record for later broadcast 3 arrange (music) for different instrument > **tran'script** *noun* copy
tran'sept *noun* 1 transverse part of cruciform church 2 either of its arms
trans•fer [trans-FUR] *verb transitive* **-ferred, -fer•ring** 1 move, send from one person, place, etc. to another ▷ *noun* [TRANS-fur] 2 removal of person or thing from one place to another 3 design that can be transferred from one surface to another by pressure, heat, etc. > **trans•fer'a•ble** *adjective* > **trans•fer'ence** *noun* transfer
trans•fig•ure [trans-FIG-yər] *verb transitive* **-ured, -ur•ing** alter appearance of
trans•fix [trans-FIKS] *verb transitive* 1 astound, stun 2 pierce
trans•form' *verb transitive* change shape, character of > **trans•for•ma'tion** *noun* > **trans•form'er** *noun* *electricity* apparatus for changing voltage of alternating current
trans•fuse [trans-FYOOZ] *verb transitive* **-fused, -fus•ing** convey from one vessel to another, esp. blood from healthy person to one injured or ill > **trans•fu'sion** [-FYOO-zhən] *noun*
trans•gress [trans-GRES] *verb transitive* 1 break (law) 2 sin > **trans•gres'sion** [-GRESH-ən] *noun* > **trans•gres'sor** *noun*
tran•sient [TRAN-shənt] *adjective* fleeting, not permanent > **tran'sience** *noun*
tran•sis•tor [tran-ZIS-tər] *noun* 1 *electronics* small semiconducting device used to amplify electric currents 2 (*informal*) portable radio using transistors
tran'sit *noun, verb* **-sit•ed, -sit•ing** (make) passage, crossing > **tran•si'tion** [-ZISH-ən] *noun* change from one state to another > **tran•si'tion•al** *adjective* > **tran'si•tive** *adjective* (of verb) requiring direct object > **tran'si•to•ry** *adjective* not lasting long, transient

DICTIONARY • THESAURUS

route, track
tramp *verb* 1 HIKE, footslog, march, ramble, roam, rove, slog, trek, walk
2 TRUDGE, plod, stump, toil, traipse (*informal*)
▷ *noun* 3 VAGRANT, derelict, down-and-out, drifter
4 HIKE, march, ramble, slog, trek
5 TREAD, footfall, footstep, stamp
trample *verb* CRUSH, flatten, run over, squash, stamp, tread, walk over
trance *noun* DAZE, abstraction, dream, rapture, reverie, stupor, unconsciousness
tranquil *adjective* CALM, peaceful, placid, quiet, restful, sedate, serene, still, undisturbed
tranquilize *verb* CALM, lull, pacify, quell, quiet, relax, sedate, settle one's nerves, soothe
tranquilizer *noun* SEDATIVE, barbiturate, bromide, downer (*slang*), opiate
tranquillity *noun* CALM, hush, peace, placidity, quiet, repose, rest, serenity, stillness
transaction *noun* DEAL, bargain, business, enterprise, negotiation, undertaking
transcend *verb* SURPASS, eclipse, exceed, excel, go beyond, outdo, outstrip, rise above
transcendent *adjective* UNPARALLELED, consummate, incomparable, matchless, pre-eminent, sublime, unequaled, unrivaled
transcribe *verb* WRITE OUT, copy out, reproduce, take down, transfer
transcript *noun* COPY, duplicate, manuscript, record, reproduction, transcription
transfer *verb* 1 MOVE, change, convey, hand over, pass on, relocate, shift, transplant, transport, transpose
▷ *noun* 2 MOVE, change, handover, relocation, shift, transference, translation, transmission, transposition
transfix *verb* 1 STUN, engross, fascinate, hold, hypnotize, mesmerize, paralyze
2 PIERCE, impale, puncture, run through, skewer, spear
transform *verb* CHANGE, alter, convert, remodel, revolutionize, transmute
transformation *noun* CHANGE, alteration, conversion, metamorphosis, revolution, sea change, transmutation
transgress *verb* OFFEND, break the law, contravene, disobey, encroach, infringe, sin, trespass, violate
transgression *noun* OFFENSE, contravention, crime, encroachment, infraction, infringement, misdeed, misdemeanor, sin, trespass, violation, wrongdoing
transgressor *noun* OFFENDER, criminal, culprit, lawbreaker, miscreant, sinner, perp (*informal*), trespasser, villain, wrongdoer
transient *adjective* TEMPORARY, brief, ephemeral, fleeting, impermanent, momentary, passing, short-lived, transitory
transit *noun* MOVEMENT, carriage, conveyance, crossing, passage, transfer, transport, transportation
transition *noun* CHANGE, alteration, conversion, development, metamorphosis, passing, progression, shift, transmutation
transitional *adjective* CHANGING, developmental, fluid, intermediate, passing, provisional, temporary, unsettled

trans•late [trans-LAYT] *verb transitive* **-lat•ed, -lat•ing** 1 turn from one language into another 2 interpret > **trans•la'tion** *noun* > **trans•la'tor** *noun*
trans•lit•er•ate [trans-LIT-ər-ayt] *verb transitive* **-at•ed, -at•ing** write in the letters of another alphabet > **trans•lit•er•a'tion** *noun*
trans•lu•cent [trans-LOO-sənt] *adjective* letting light pass through, semitransparent > **trans•lu'cence** *noun*
trans•mi•grate [trans-MĪ-grayt] *verb intransitive* **-grat•ed, -grat•ing** (of soul) pass into another body > **trans•mi•gra'tion** *noun*
trans•mit [trans-MIT] *verb transitive* **-mit•ted, -mit•ting** 1 send, cause to pass to another place, person, etc. 2 communicate 3 send out (signals) by means of radio waves 4 broadcast (radio, television program) > **trans•mis'sion** *noun* 1 transference 2 gear by which power is communicated from engine to road wheels > **trans•mit'tal** *noun* transmission
trans•mog•ri•fy [trans-MOG-rə-fī] *verb transitive* **-fied, -fy•ing** (*informal*) change completely esp. into bizarre form
trans•mute [trans-MYOOT] *verb transitive* **-mut•ed, -mut•ing** change in form, properties, or nature > **trans•mu•ta'tion** *noun*
tran•som [TRAN-səm] *noun* 1 window above door 2 crosspiece separating the door and window
trans•par•ent [trans-PA-rənt] *adjective* 1 letting light pass without distortion 2 that can be seen through distinctly 3 obvious > **trans•par'en•cy** *noun, plural* **-cies** 1 quality of being transparent 2 photographic slide 3 picture made visible by light behind it
tran•spire [tran-SPĪR] *verb intransitive* **-spired, -spir•ing** 1 become known 2 (*informal*) happen 3 (of plants) give off water vapor through leaves > **tran•spi•ra'tion** *noun*
trans•plant [trans-PLANT] *verb transitive* 1 move and plant again in another place 2 transfer organ surgically from one body to another ▷ *noun* [TRANS-plant] 3 surgical transplanting of organ 4 anything transplanted > **trans•plan•ta'tion** *noun*
trans•port [trans-PORT] *verb transitive* 1 convey from one place to another 2 enrapture ▷ *noun* [TRANS-port] 3 means of conveyance 4 ships, aircraft, etc. used in transporting supplies, troops, etc. 5 a ship, etc. so used
trans•pose [trans-POHZ] *verb transitive* **-posed, -pos•ing** 1 change order of 2 interchange 3 put music into different key > **trans•po•si'tion** [-pə-ZISH-ən] *noun*
tran•sub•stan•ti•a•tion *noun* [tran-səb-stan-shee-AY-shən] doctrine that substance of bread and wine changes into substance of Christ's body when consecrated in Eucharist
trans•verse [trans-VURS] *adjective* 1 lying across 2 at right angles
trans•ves•tite [trans-VES-tīt] *noun* person seeking sexual pleasure by wearing clothes normally worn by opposite sex
trap *noun* 1 snare, device for catching game, etc. 2 anything planned to deceive, betray, etc. 3 arrangement of pipes to prevent escape of gas 4 movable opening, esp. through ceiling, etc. 5 (*slang*) mouth ▷ *verb transitive* **trapped, trap•ping** 6 catch, ensnare > **trap'per** *noun* one who traps animals for their fur > **trap'door** *noun* door in floor or roof
tra•peze [tra-PEEZ] *noun* horizontal bar suspended from two ropes for use in gymnastics, acrobatic exhibitions, etc. > **trapeze artist** one who performs on trapeze
trap•e•zoid [TRAP-ə-zoid] *noun* quadrilateral with two parallel sides
trap•pings [TRAP-ingz] *plural noun* equipment, ornaments

---

transitory *adjective* SHORT-LIVED, brief, ephemeral, fleeting, impermanent, momentary, passing, short, temporary, transient
translate *verb* INTERPRET, construe, convert, decipher, decode, paraphrase, render
translation *noun* INTERPRETATION, decoding, paraphrase, rendering, rendition, version
transmission *noun* 1 TRANSFER, conveyance, dissemination, sending, shipment, spread, transference
2 BROADCASTING, dissemination, putting out, relaying, sending, showing
3 PROGRAM, broadcast, show
transmit *verb* 1 PASS ON, bear, carry, convey, disseminate, hand on, impart, send, spread, transfer
2 BROADCAST, disseminate, radio, relay, send out
transparency *noun* 1 CLARITY, clearness, limpidity, pellucidness, translucence
2 PHOTOGRAPH, slide
transparent *adjective* 1 CLEAR, crystalline, diaphanous, limpid, lucid, see-through, sheer, translucent
2 PLAIN, evident, explicit, manifest, obvious, patent, recognizable, unambiguous, undisguised
transpire *verb* 1 EMERGE, become known, come out, come to light
2 (*informal*) HAPPEN, arise, befall, chance, come about, occur, take place
transplant *verb* TRANSFER, displace, relocate, remove, resettle, shift, uproot
transport *verb* 1 CONVEY, bear, bring, carry, haul, move, take, transfer
2 EXILE, banish, deport
3 ENRAPTURE, captivate, delight, enchant, entrance, move, ravish
▷ *noun* 4 VEHICLE, conveyance, transportation
5 TRANSFERENCE, conveyance, shipment, transportation
6 ECSTASY, bliss, delight, enchantment, euphoria, heaven, rapture, ravishment
transpose *verb* INTERCHANGE, alter, change, exchange, move, reorder, shift, substitute, swap, switch, transfer
trap *noun* 1 SNARE, ambush, gin, net, noose, pitfall
2 TRICK, ambush, deception, ruse, stratagem, subterfuge, wile
▷ *verb* 3 CATCH, corner, enmesh, ensnare, entrap, snare, take
4 TRICK, ambush, beguile, deceive, dupe, ensnare, inveigle
trappings *plural noun* ACCESSORIES, accouterments, equipment, finery, furnishings, gear, panoply, paraphernalia, things, trimmings

trash *noun* 1 rubbish 2 nonsense > **trash'y** *adjective* **trash•i•er, trash•i•est** worthless, cheap
trau•ma [TROW-mə, TRAW-mə] *noun* 1 nervous shock 2 injury > **trau•mat'ic** *adjective* of, causing, caused by trauma
tra•vail [trə-VAYL] *verb intransitive, noun* labor, toil
trav•el [TRAV-əl] *verb* **-eled, -el•ing** 1 go, move from one place to another ▷ *noun* 2 act of traveling, esp. as tourist 3 *machinery* distance component is allowed to move > **trav•els** (account of) traveling > **trav'el•er** *noun* > **trav•e•logue** [TRAV-ə-log] *noun* film, etc. about travels
trav•erse [trə-VURS] *verb transitive* **-ersed, -ers•ing** 1 cross, go through or over 2 (of gun) move laterally ▷ *noun* [TRA-vurs] 3 anything set across 4 partition 5 *mountaineering* face, steep slope to be crossed from side to side ▷ *adjective* 6 being, lying across
trav•es•ty [TRAV-ə-stee] *noun, plural* **-ties** 1 farcical, grotesque imitation 2 mockery ▷ *verb transitive* **-tied, -ty•ing** 3 make, be a travesty of
trawl *noun* 1 net dragged at deep levels behind special boat, to catch fish, shrimp, etc. ▷ *verb intransitive* 2 fish with one > **trawl'er** *noun* trawling vessel
tray *noun* 1 flat board, usu. with rim, for carrying things 2 any similar utensil
treach•er•y [TRECH-ə-ree] *noun, plural* **-er•ies** deceit, betrayal > **treach'er•ous** [-rəs] *adjective* 1 disloyal 2 unreliable, dangerous
trea•cle [TREE-kəl] *noun* 1 cloying sentimentally 2 *Brit* molasses
tread [tred] *verb* **trod, trod•den** *or* **trod, tread•ing** 1 set foot on 2 trample 3 oppress 4 walk ▷ *noun* 5 treading 6 fashion of walking 7 upper surface of step 8 part of motor vehicle tire in contact with ground > **tread'mill** *noun* dreary routine, etc.
trea•dle [TRED-l] *noun* lever worked by foot to turn wheel
trea•son [TREE-zən] *noun* 1 violation by citizen of allegiance to country or ruler 2 treachery 3 disloyalty > **trea'son•a•ble** *adjective* constituting treason > **trea'son•ous** *adjective*
treas•ure [TREZH-ər] *noun* 1 riches 2 stored wealth or valuables ▷ *verb transitive* **-ured, -ur•ing** 3 prize, cherish 4 store up > **treas'ur•er** *noun* official in charge of funds > **treas'ur•y** *noun, plural* **-ur•ies** 1 place for treasure 2 government department in charge of finance > **treasure-trove** [-trohv] *noun* treasure found hidden (with no evidence of ownership)
treat (treet) *noun* 1 pleasure, entertainment given ▷ *verb transitive* 2 deal with, act toward 3 give medical treatment to 4 (with *of*) discourse on 5 entertain, esp. with food or drink ▷ *verb intransitive* 6 negotiate > **treat'ment** [-mənt] *noun* 1 method of counteracting a disease 2 act or mode of treating 3 manner of handling an artistic medium
trea•tise [TREE-tis] *noun* book discussing a subject, formal essay

DICTIONARY • THESAURUS

trash *noun* 1 NONSENSE, drivel, hogwash, moonshine, rot, rubbish, tripe (*informal*), twaddle
2 LITTER, dross, garbage, junk (*informal*), refuse, rubbish, waste
▷ *verb* 3 DESTROY, defeat, demolish, put paid to, ruin, torpedo, trounce, wreck
trashy *adjective* WORTHLESS, cheap, inferior, rubbishy, shabby, shoddy, tawdry
trauma *noun* SUFFERING, agony, anguish, hurt, ordeal, pain, shock, torture
traumatic *adjective* SHOCKING, agonizing, damaging, disturbing, hurtful, injurious, painful, scarring, upsetting, wounding
travel *verb* 1 GO, journey, move, progress, roam, tour, trek, voyage, wander
▷ *noun* 2 (*usually plural*) WANDERING, excursion, expedition, globetrotting, journey, tour, trip, voyage
traveler *noun* WANDERER, explorer, globetrotter, gypsy, holiday-maker, tourist, voyager, wayfarer
traveling *adjective* MOBILE, itinerant, migrant, nomadic, peripatetic, roaming, roving, touring, wandering, wayfaring
traverse *verb* CROSS, go over, span, travel over
travesty *noun* 1 MOCKERY, burlesque, caricature, distortion, lampoon, parody, perversion
▷ *verb* 2 MOCK, burlesque, caricature, distort, lampoon, make a mockery of, parody, ridicule
treacherous *adjective* 1 DISLOYAL, deceitful, double dealing, duplicitous, faithless, false, perfidious, traitorous, unfaithful, untrustworthy
2 DANGEROUS, deceptive, hazardous, icy, perilous, precarious, risky, slippery, unreliable, unsafe, unstable
treachery *noun* BETRAYAL, back-stabbing (*informal*), disloyalty, double-dealing, duplicity, faithlessness, infidelity, perfidy, treason
tread *verb* 1 STEP, hike, march, pace, stamp, stride, walk
2 TRAMPLE, crush underfoot, squash
▷ *noun* 3 STEP, footfall, footstep, gait, pace, stride, walk
treason *noun* DISLOYALTY, back-stabbing (*informal*), duplicity, lese-majesty, mutiny, perfidy, sedition, traitorousness, treachery
treasonable *adjective* DISLOYAL, mutinous, perfidious, seditious, subversive, traitorous, treacherous
treasure *noun* 1 RICHES, cash, fortune, gold, jewels, money, valuables, wealth
2 DARLING, apple of one's eye, gem, jewel, nonpareil, paragon, pride and joy
▷ *verb* 3 PRIZE, adore, cherish, esteem, hold dear, idolize, love, revere, value
treasury *noun* STOREHOUSE, bank, cache, hoard, repository, store, vault
treat *verb* 1 HANDLE, act towards, behave towards, consider, deal with, look upon, manage, regard, use
2 ATTEND TO, care for, nurse
3 ENTERTAIN, lay on, provide, regale, stand (*informal*)
▷ *noun* 4 ENTERTAINMENT, banquet, celebration, feast, gift, party, refreshment
5 PLEASURE, delight, enjoyment, fun, joy, satisfaction, surprise, thrill
treatise *noun* ESSAY, dissertation, monograph, pamphlet, paper, study, thesis, tract, work
treatment *noun* 1 CARE, cure, healing, medication, medicine, remedy, surgery, therapy
2 HANDLING, action, behavior, conduct, dealing,

trea•ty [TREE-tee] *noun, plural* **-ties** signed contract between nations, etc.
tre•ble [TREB-l] *adjective* 1 threefold, triple 2 *mus.* high-pitched ▷ *noun* 3 soprano voice 4 part of music for it 5 singer with such voice ▷ *verb* **-bled, -bling** 6 increase threefold > **tre'bly** [-blee] *adverb*
tree *noun* 1 large perennial plant with woody trunk 2 beam 3 anything (e.g. genealogical chart) resembling tree, or tree's structure ▷ *verb transitive* **treed, tree•ing** 4 force, drive up tree 5 plant with trees
tre•foil [TREE-foil] *noun* 1 plant with three-lobed leaf, clover 2 carved ornament like this
trek *verb intransitive, noun* **trekked, trek•king** (make) long difficult journey
trel•lis [TREL-is] *noun* 1 lattice or grating of light bars fixed crosswise ▷ *verb transitive* 2 screen, supply with one
trem•ble [TREM-bəl] *verb intransitive* **-bled, -bling** 1 quiver, shake 2 feel fear, anxiety ▷ *noun* 3 involuntary shaking 4 quiver 5 tremor
tre•men•dous [tri-MEN-dəs] *adjective* 1 vast, immense 2 exciting, unusual 3 excellent
trem•o•lo [TREM-ə-loh] *noun, plural* **-los** quivering or vibrating effect in singing or playing
trem•or [TREM-ər] *noun* 1 quiver 2 shaking 3 minor earthquake
trem•u•lous [TREM-yə-ləs] *adjective* 1 quivering slightly 2 fearful, agitated
trench *noun* 1 long narrow ditch, esp. as shelter in war ▷ *verb transitive* 2 cut grooves or ditches in > **trench coat** double-breasted waterproof overcoat
trench•ant [TRENCH-ənt] *adjective* cutting, incisive, biting
trend *noun* direction, tendency, inclination, drift > **trend'y** *noun, adjective* **trend•i•er, trend•i•est** consciously fashionable (person) > **trend'i•ness** [-nis] *noun*
tre•pan [tri-PAN] *noun* instrument for cutting circular pieces, esp. from skull ▷ *verb transitive* **-panned, -pan•ning**
trep•i•da•tion [trep-i-DAY-shən] *noun* fear, anxiety
tres•pass [TRES-pəs] *verb intransitive* 1 intrude (on) property, etc. of another 2 transgress, sin ▷ *noun* 3 wrongful entering on another's land 4 wrongdoing
tress *noun* long lock of hair
tres•tle [TRES-l] *noun* 1 board fixed on pairs of spreading legs and used as support 2 structural member of bridge
tri- *combining form* 1 three or thrice: *trilingual* 2 occurring every three: *triweekly*
tri•ad [TRĪ-ad] *noun* 1 group of three 2 *chem.* element, radical with valence of three
tri•al [TRĪ-əl] *noun* 1 act of trying, testing 2 experimental examination 3 *law* conduct of case before judge, jury 4 thing, person that strains endurance or patience
tri•an•gle [TRĪ-ang-gəl] *noun* 1 figure with three angles 2 percussion musical instrument > **tri•an'gu•lar** [-lər] *adjective*
tribe [trīb] *noun* subdivision of race of people > **trib'al** [-əl] *adjective*
trib•u•la•tion [trib-yə-LAY-shən] *noun* 1 misery, trouble, affliction, distress 2 cause of this
tri•bu•nal [trī-BYOON-l] *noun* 1 law court 2 body appointed to inquire into and decide specific matter 3 place, seat of judgment
trib•u•tar•y [TRIB-yə-ter-ee] *noun, plural* **-tar•ies** 1 stream flowing into another ▷ *adjective* 2 auxiliary 3 contributory 4 paying tribute
trib•ute [TRIB-yoot] *noun* 1 sign of honor or recognition 2 tax paid by one country to another as sign of subjugation
trice [trīs] *noun* moment **in a trice** instantly

---

management, manipulation
treaty *noun* PACT, agreement, alliance, compact, concordat, contract, convention, covenant, entente
trek *noun* 1 JOURNEY, expedition, hike, march, odyssey, safari, slog, tramp
▷ *verb* 2 JOURNEY, footslog, hike, march, rove, slog, traipse (*informal*), tramp, trudge
tremble *verb* 1 SHAKE, quake, quiver, shiver, shudder, totter, vibrate, wobble
▷ *noun* 2 SHAKE, quake, quiver, shiver, shudder, tremor, vibration, wobble
tremendous *adjective* 1 HUGE, colossal, enormous, formidable, gigantic, great, immense, stupendous, terrific
2 (*informal*) EXCELLENT, amazing, brilliant, exceptional, extraordinary, fantastic (*informal*), great, marvelous, sensational (*informal*), wonderful
tremor *noun* 1 SHAKE, quaking, quaver, quiver, shiver, trembling, wobble
2 EARTHQUAKE, quake (*informal*), shock
trench *noun* DITCH, channel, drain, excavation, furrow, gutter, trough
trenchant *adjective* 1 INCISIVE, acerbic, caustic, cutting, penetrating, pointed, pungent, scathing
2 EFFECTIVE, energetic, forceful, potent, powerful, strong, vigorous
trend *noun* 1 TENDENCY, bias, current, direction, drift, flow, inclination, leaning
2 FASHION, craze, fad (*informal*), mode, rage, style, thing, vogue
trendy *adjective* (*informal*) FASHIONABLE, cool (*informal*), in fashion, in vogue, modish, phat (*slang*), stylish, voguish, with it (*informal*)
trepidation *noun* ANXIETY, alarm, apprehension, consternation, disquiet, dread, fear, nervousness, uneasiness, worry
trespass *verb* 1 INTRUDE, encroach, infringe, invade, obtrude
▷ *noun* 2 INTRUSION, encroachment, infringement, invasion, unlawful entry
trespasser *noun* INTRUDER, interloper, invader, poacher
trial *noun* 1 HEARING, litigation, tribunal
2 TEST, audition, dry run (*informal*), experiment, probation, test-run
3 HARDSHIP, adversity, affliction, distress, ordeal, suffering, tribulation, trouble
tribe *noun* RACE, clan, family, people
tribunal *noun* HEARING, court, trial
tribute *noun* 1 ACCOLADE, commendation, compliment, eulogy, panegyric, recognition, testimonial
2 TAX, charge, homage, payment, ransom

tri•chi•na [tri-KĪ-nə] *noun, plural* **-nae** [-nee] minute parasitic worm > **trich•i•no•sis** *noun* [tri-kə-NOH-sis] disease caused by this
trick [trik] *noun* 1 deception 2 prank 3 mannerism 4 illusion 5 feat of skill or cunning 6 knack 7 cards played in one round 8 spell of duty 9 (*slang*) prostitute's customer, sexual act ▷ *verb transitive* 10 cheat 11 hoax 12 deceive > **trick'ster** *noun* > **trick'y** *adjective* **trick•i•er, trick•i•est** 1 difficult, needing careful handling 2 crafty
trick•le [TRIK-l] *verb* **-led, -ling** (cause to) run, flow, move in thin stream or drops
tri•col•or [TRĪ-kul-ər] *adjective* 1 three-colored ▷ *noun* 2 tricolor flag
tri•cy•cle [TRĪ-si-kəl] *noun* child's three-wheeled bike
tri•dent [TRĪD-nt] *noun* three-pronged fork or spear
tri•en•ni•al [trī-EN-ee-əl] *adjective* happening every, or lasting, three years
tri•fle [TRĪ-fəl] *noun* 1 insignificant thing or matter 2 small amount ▷ *verb intransitive* **-fled, -fling** 3 toy (with) 4 act, speak idly > **tri'fler** [-flər] *noun*
trig•ger [TRIG-ər] *noun* catch that releases spring esp. to fire gun ▷ *verb transitive* (oft. with *off*) start, set in action, etc. > **trigger-happy** *adjective* tending to irresponsible, ill-considered behavior, esp. in use of firearms
trig•o•nom•et•ry [trig-ə-NOM-i-tree] *noun* branch of mathematics dealing with relations of sides and angles of triangles > **trig•o•no•met'ric** [-nə-MET-rik] *adjective*
tri•lat•er•al [trī-LAT-ər-əl] *adjective* having three sides
trill *verb intransitive* 1 sing with quavering voice 2 sing lightly 3 warble ▷ *noun* 4 such singing or sound
tril•lion [TRIL-yən] *noun* number 1 followed by 12 zeroes
tril•o•gy [TRIL-ə-jee] *noun, plural* **-gies** series of three related (literary) works
trim *adjective* **trim•mer, trim•mest** 1 neat, smart 2 slender 3 in good order ▷ *verb transitive* **trimmed, trim•ming** 4 shorten slightly by cutting 5 prune 6 decorate 7 adjust 8 put in good order 9 adjust balance of (ship, aircraft) ▷ *noun* 10 decoration 11 order, state of being trim 12 haircut that neatens existing style 13 upholstery, accessories in automobile 14 edging material, as inside woodwork around doors, windows, etc. > **trimming** *noun* 1 (*often plural*) decoration, addition 2 (*informal*) a defeat > **trimmings** garnish to main dish
tri•ma•ran [TRĪ-mə-ran] *noun* three-hulled vessel
trin•i•ty [TRIN-i-tee] *noun* 1 the state of being threefold 2 (**Trin•i•ty**) the three persons of the Godhead > **trin•i•tar'i•an** [-TAIR-ee-ən] *noun, adjective*
trin•ket [TRING-kit] *noun* small ornament, trifle
tri•o [TREE-oh] *noun, plural* **tri•os** 1 group of three 2 music for three parts
tri•ode [TRĪ-ohd] *noun electronics* three-electrode vacuum tube
trip *noun* 1 (short) journey for pleasure 2 stumble 3 switch 4 (*slang*) hallucinatory experience caused by drug ▷ *verb* **tripped, trip•ping** 5 (cause to) stumble 6 (cause to) make false step, mistake ▷ *verb intransitive* 7 run

trick *noun* 1 DECEPTION, fraud, hoax, maneuver, ploy, ruse, stratagem, subterfuge, swindle, trap, wile
2 JOKE, antic, jape, practical joke, prank, stunt
3 SECRET, hang (*informal*), knack, know-how (*informal*), skill, technique
4 MANNERISM, characteristic, foible, habit, idiosyncrasy, peculiarity, practice, quirk, trait
▷ *verb* 5 DECEIVE, cheat, con (*informal*), dupe, fool, hoodwink, kid (*informal*), mislead, swindle, take in (*informal*), trap
trickery *noun* DECEPTION, cheating, chicanery, deceit, dishonesty, guile, monkey business (*informal*)
trickle *verb* 1 DRIBBLE, drip, drop, exude, ooze, run, seep, stream
▷ *noun* 2 DRIBBLE, drip, seepage
tricky *adjective* 1 DIFFICULT, complicated, delicate, knotty, problematic, risky, thorny, ticklish
2 CRAFTY, artful, cunning, deceitful, devious, scheming, slippery, sly, wily
trifle *noun* 1 KNICK-KNACK, bagatelle, bauble, plaything, toy
▷ *verb* 2 TOY, dally, mess about, play
trifling *adjective* INSIGNIFICANT, measly, negligible, paltry, trivial, unimportant, worthless
trigger *verb* SET OFF, activate, cause, generate, produce, prompt, provoke, set in motion, spark off, start
trim *adjective* 1 NEAT, dapper, shipshape, smart, spruce, tidy, well-groomed
2 SLENDER, fit, shapely, sleek, slim, streamlined, svelte, willowy
▷ *verb* 3 CUT, clip, crop, even up, pare, prune, shave, tidy
4 DECORATE, adorn, array, beautify, deck out, dress, embellish, ornament
▷ *noun* 5 DECORATION, adornment, border, edging, embellishment, frill, ornamentation, piping, trimming
6 CONDITION, fettle, fitness, health, shape (*informal*), state
7 CUT, clipping, crop, pruning, shave, shearing, tidying up
trimming *noun* 1 DECORATION, adornment, border, edging, embellishment, frill, ornamentation, piping
2 ▷ **trimmings** EXTRAS, accessories, accompaniments, frills, ornaments, paraphernalia, trappings
trinity *noun* THREESOME, triad, trio, triumvirate
trinket *noun* ORNAMENT, bagatelle, bauble, knick-knack, toy, trifle
trio *noun* THREESOME, triad, trilogy, trinity, triumvirate
trip *noun* 1 JOURNEY, errand, excursion, expedition, foray, jaunt, outing, run, tour, voyage
2 STUMBLE, fall, misstep, slip
▷ *verb* 3 STUMBLE, fall, lose one's footing, misstep, slip, tumble
4 CATCH OUT, trap

lightly **8** skip **9** dance **10** (*slang*) take hallucinatory drugs ▷ *verb transitive* **11** operate (switch)
tri•par•tite [trī-PAHR-tīt] *adjective* having, divided into three parts
tripe [trīp] *noun* **1** stomach of cow, etc. prepared for food **2** (*slang*) nonsense
tri•ple [TRIP-əl] *adjective* **1** threefold ▷ *verb* **-pled, -pling 2** treble **3** hit triple ▷ *noun* **4** *baseball* three-base hit > **trip•let** [TRIP-lit] *noun* **1** three of a kind **2** one of three offspring born at one birth > **trip'lex** *adjective* **1** threefold **2** (of apartment) having three floors > **trip'ly** [-lee] *adverb*
trip•li•cate [TRIP-li-kit] *adjective* **1** threefold ▷ *noun* **2** state of being triplicate **3** one of set of three copies ▷ *verb transitive* [-kayt], **-cat•ed, -cat•ing 4** make threefold
tri•pod [TRĪ-pod] *noun* stool, stand, etc. with three feet
trip•tych [TRIP-tik] *noun* carving, set of pictures (esp. altarpiece) on three panels hinged side by side
trite [trīt] *adjective* hackneyed, banal
trit•i•um [TRIT-ee-əm] *noun* radioactive isotope of hydrogen
tri•umph [TRĪ-əmf] *noun* **1** great success **2** victory **3** exultation ▷ *verb intransitive* **4** achieve great success or victory **5** prevail **6** exult > **tri•um'phal** [-UMF-əl] *adjective* > **tri•um'phant** [-fənt] *adjective* victorious
tri•um•vi•rate [trī-UM-vər-it] *noun* joint rule by three persons
triv•et [TRIV-it] *noun* metal bracket or stand for pot or kettle
triv•i•a [TRIV-ee-ə] *plural noun* petty, unimportant things, details > **triv'i•al** *adjective* **1** of little consequence **2** commonplace > **triv•i•al'i•ty** *noun, plural* **-ties**
tro•chee [TROH-kee] *noun* in verse, foot of two syllables, first long and second short > **tro•cha'ic** [-KAY-ik] *adjective*
trod *pt./pp. of* **tread.** > **trod'den** [TROD-ən] *pp of* **tread**
trog•lo•dyte [TROG-lə-dīt] *noun* cave dweller
Tro•jan [TROH-jən] *adjective, noun* **1** (inhabitant) of ancient Troy **2** steadfast or persevering (person)
troll[1] [trohl] *verb transitive* fish for by dragging baited hook or lure through water
troll[2] *noun* supernatural being in Scandinavian mythology and folklore
trol•ley [TROL-ee] *noun, plural* **-leys 1** small wheeled table for food and drink **2** wheeled cart for moving goods, etc. **3** streetcar
trol•lop [TROL-əp] *noun* promiscuous or slovenly woman
trom•bone [trom-BOHN] *noun* deep-toned brass wind instrument with sliding tube > **trom•bon'ist** *noun*
troop *noun* **1** group or crowd of persons or animals **2** unit of cavalry ▷ *verb intransitive* **3** move in a troop, flock > **troops** *plural noun* soldiers > **troop'er** *noun* **1** cavalry soldier **2** state police officer
trope [trohp] *noun* figure of speech
tro•phy [TROH-fee] *noun, plural* **-phies 1** prize, award, as shield, cup **2** memorial of victory, hunt, etc. ▷ *adjective* **3** (*informal*) regraded as highly desirable symbol of wealth or success: *a trophy wife*
trop•ic [TROP-ik] *noun* **1** either of two lines of latitude at 23½°N (**tropic of Cancer**) or 23½°S (**tropic of Capricorn**) > **trop•ics** area of Earth's surface between these lines > **trop'i•cal** [-kəl] *adjective* **1** pert. to, within tropics **2** (of climate) very hot
trot *verb intransitive* **trot•ted, trot•ting 1** (of horse) move at medium pace, lifting feet in diagonal pairs **2** (of person) run easily with short strides ▷ *noun* **3** trotting, jog > **trot'ter** *noun* **1** horse trained to trot in race **2** foot of certain animals, esp. pig
troth [trawth] *noun* fidelity, truth
trou•ba•dour [TROO-bə-dor] *noun* one of school of early poets and singers
trou•ble [TRUB-əl] *noun* **1** state or cause of mental distress, pain, inconvenience, etc. **2**

DICTIONARY **t** THESAURUS

5 SKIP, dance, gambol, hop
triple *adjective* 1 THREEFOLD, three-way, tripartite
▷ *verb* 2 TREBLE, increase threefold
trite *adjective* UNORIGINAL, banal, clichéd, commonplace, hackneyed, stale, stereotyped, threadbare, tired
triumph *noun* 1 JOY, elation, exultation, happiness, jubilation, pride, rejoicing
2 SUCCESS, accomplishment, achievement, attainment, conquest, coup, feat, victory
▷ *verb* 3 (*often with over*) WIN, overcome, prevail, prosper, succeed, vanquish
4 REJOICE, celebrate, crow, exult, gloat, glory, revel
triumphant *adjective* VICTORIOUS, celebratory, conquering, elated, exultant, jubilant, proud, successful, winning
trivia *plural noun* MINUTIAE, details, trifles, trivialities
trivial *adjective* UNIMPORTANT, incidental, inconsequential, insignificant, meaningless, minor, petty, small, trifling, worthless
triviality *noun* INSIGNIFICANCE, meaninglessness, pettiness, unimportance, worthlessness
trivialize *verb* UNDERVALUE, belittle, laugh off, make light of, minimize, play down, scoff at, underestimate, underplay
troop *noun* 1 GROUP, band, body, company, crowd, horde, multitude, squad, team, unit
2 ▷ **troops** SOLDIERS, armed forces, army, men, servicemen, soldiery
▷ *verb* 3 FLOCK, march, stream, swarm, throng, traipse (*informal*)
trophy *noun* PRIZE, award, booty, cup, laurels, memento, souvenir, spoils
tropical *adjective* HOT, steamy, stifling, sultry, sweltering, torrid
trot *verb* 1 RUN, canter, jog, lope, scamper
▷ *noun* 2 RUN, canter, jog, lope
trouble *noun* 1 DISTRESS, anxiety, disquiet, grief, misfortune, pain, sorrow, torment, woe, worry
2 DISEASE, ailment, complaint, defect, disorder, failure, illness, malfunction
3 DISORDER, agitation, bother (*informal*), commotion, discord, disturbance, strife, tumult, unrest

care, effort ▷ *verb transitive* **-bled, -bling** 3 be trouble to ▷ *verb intransitive* **-bled, -bling** 4 be inconvenienced, concerned (about) 5 be agitated 6 take pains, exert oneself > **trou'ble•some** [-səm] *adjective*

trough [trawf] *noun* 1 long open vessel, esp. for animals' food or water 2 hollow between two waves 3 *meteorology* area of low pressure

trounce [trowns] *verb transitive* **trounced, trounc•ing** beat thoroughly, thrash

troupe [troop] *noun* company of performers > **troup'er** *noun*

trou•sers [TROW-zərz] *plural noun* two-legged outer garment with legs reaching to the ankles

trous•seau [TROO-soh] *noun, plural* **-seaux** [-sohz] bride's outfit of clothing

trout [trowt] *noun* freshwater sport and food fish

trow•el [TROW-əl] *noun* 1 small tool like spade for spreading mortar, lifting plants, etc. ▷ *verb transitive* **-eled, -el•ing** 2 work with or as if with trowel

troy weight [troi] system of weights used for gold, silver and gems

tru•ant [TROO-ənt] *noun* one absent without leave, esp. child so absenting self from school ▷ *adjective* > **tru'an•cy** [-ən-see] *noun, plural* **-cies**

truce [troos] *noun* 1 temporary cessation of fighting 2 respite, lull

truck[1] [truk] *noun* wheeled (motor) vehicle for moving goods

truck[2] *noun* **have no truck with** refuse to be involved with

truck•le [TRUK-əl] *verb intransitive* **-led, -ling** yield weakly (to)

truc•u•lent [TRUK-yə-lənt] *adjective* aggressive, defiant > **truc•u•lence** [-ləns] *noun*

trudge [truj] *verb intransitive* **trudged, trudg•ing** 1 walk laboriously ▷ *noun* 2 laborious or wearisome walk

true [troo] *adjective* **tru•er, tru•est** 1 in accordance with facts 2 faithful 3 exact, correct 4 genuine > **tru•ism** [TROO-iz-əm] *noun* self-evident truth > **tru'ly** *adverb* 1 exactly 2 really 3 sincerely > **truth** [trooth] *noun* 1 state of being true 2 something that is true > **truth'ful** [-fəl] *adjective* 1 accustomed to speak the truth 2 accurate, exact

truf•fle [TRUF-əl] *noun* 1 edible fungus growing underground 2 candy resembling this

truism [TROO-iz-əm] *noun* *see* **true**

trump *noun* 1 card of suit temporarily ranking above others ▷ *verb transitive* 2 take trick with a trump > **trump up** concoct, fabricate

trump•er•y [TRUM-pə-ree] *adjective* 1 showy but worthless ▷ *noun, plural* **-er•ies** 2 worthless finery 3 trash 4 worthless stuff

trum•pet [TRUM-pit] *noun* 1 metal wind instrument like horn ▷ *verb intransitive* 2 blow trumpet 3 make sound like one, as elephant ▷ *verb transitive* 4 proclaim, make widely known

trun•cate [TRUNG-kayt] *verb transitive* **-cat•ed, -cat•ing** cut short

trun•cheon [TRUN-chən] *noun* 1 police officer's club 2 staff of office or authority 3 baton

trun•dle [TRUN-dəl] *verb transitive* **-dled, -dling** roll, as a thing on little wheels

trunk *noun* 1 main stem of tree 2 person's body without or excluding head and limbs 3 box for clothes, etc. 4 elephant's proboscis > **trunks** man's bathing suit > **trunk line** main line of railroad, telephone, etc.

truss *verb transitive* 1 fasten up, tie up ▷ *noun* 2 support 3 medical device of belt, etc. to hold

4 EFFORT, care, exertion, inconvenience, labor, pains, thought, work
▷ *verb* 5 WORRY, bother, disconcert, distress, disturb, pain, perturb, plague, sadden, upset
6 TAKE PAINS, exert oneself, make an effort, take the time
7 INCONVENIENCE, bother, burden, disturb, impose upon, incommode, put out

troublesome *adjective* 1 WORRYING, annoying, demanding, difficult, inconvenient, irksome, high-maintenance, taxing, tricky, trying, vexatious
2 DISORDERLY, rebellious, rowdy, turbulent, uncooperative, undisciplined, unruly, violent

trough *noun* 1 MANGER, water trough
2 CHANNEL, canal, depression, ditch, duct, furrow, gully, gutter, trench

trounce *verb* THRASH, beat, crush, drub, hammer (*informal*), rout, slaughter (*informal*), wipe the floor with (*informal*)

troupe *noun* COMPANY, band, cast

truancy *noun* ABSENCE, absence without leave, malingering, shirking

truant *noun* ABSENTEE, malingerer, runaway, shirker

truce *noun* CEASEFIRE, armistice, cessation, let-up (*informal*), lull, moratorium, peace, respite

truculent *adjective* HOSTILE, aggressive, bellicose, belligerent, defiant, ill-tempered, obstreperous, pugnacious

trudge *verb* 1 PLOD, footslog, lumber, slog, stump, traipse (*informal*), tramp, trek
▷ *noun* 2 HIKE, footslog, march, slog, traipse (*informal*), tramp, trek

true *adjective* 1 CORRECT, accurate, authentic, factual, genuine, precise, real, right, truthful, veracious
2 FAITHFUL, dedicated, devoted, dutiful, loyal, reliable, staunch, steady, trustworthy
3 EXACT, accurate, on target, perfect, precise, unerring

truism *noun* CLICHÉ, axiom, bromide, commonplace, platitude

truly *adverb* 1 CORRECTLY, authentically, exactly, factually, genuinely, legitimately, precisely, rightly, truthfully
2 FAITHFULLY, devotedly, dutifully, loyally, sincerely, staunchly, steadily
3 REALLY, extremely, greatly, indeed, of course, very

trumpet *noun* 1 HORN, bugle, clarion
▷ *verb* 2 PROCLAIM, advertise, announce, broadcast, shout from the rooftops, tout (*informal*)

trump up *verb* FABRICATE, concoct, contrive, cook up (*informal*), create, fake, invent, make up

truncate *verb* SHORTEN, abbreviate, curtail, cut short, dock, lop, pare, prune, trim

truncheon *noun* CLUB, baton, cudgel, staff

trunk *noun* 1 STEM, bole, stalk
2 CHEST, box, case, casket, coffer, crate
3 BODY, torso

hernia in place 4 pack, bundle 5 cluster of flowers at end of single stalk

trust *noun* 1 confidence 2 firm belief 3 reliance 4 combination of producers to reduce competition and keep up prices 5 care, responsibility 6 property held for another ▷ *verb transitive* 7 rely on 8 believe in 9 expect, hope 10 consign for care > **trust•ee'** *noun* 1 one legally holding property on another's behalf 2 trusty > **trust•ee'ship** *noun* > **trust'ful** [-fəl] *adjective* 1 inclined to trust 2 credulous > **trust'wor•thy** [-wur-*thee*] *adjective* 1 reliable 2 dependable 3 honest 4 safe > **trust'y** *adjective* **trust•i•er, trust•i•est** 1 faithful 2 reliable ▷ *noun, plural* **trust•ies** 3 trustworthy convict with special privileges

truth [trooth] *see* **true**

try [trī] *verb intransitive* **tried, try•ing** 1 attempt, endeavor ▷ *verb transitive* **tried, try•ing** 2 attempt 3 test 4 make demands upon 5 investigate (case) 6 examine (person) in court of law 7 purify or refine (as metals) ▷ *noun, plural* **tries** 8 attempt, effort > **tried** *adjective* 1 proved 2 afflicted > **trying** *adjective* 1 upsetting, annoying 2 difficult

tryst [trist] *noun* 1 appointment to meet 2 place appointed

tsar [zahr] *see* **Czar**

tset•se [TSET-see] *noun* Afr. bloodsucking fly whose bite transmits various diseases to man and animals

T-shirt [TEE-shurt] *noun* informal (short-sleeved) undershirt, sweater usu. of cotton

T square *noun* T-shaped ruler for drawing parallel lines, right angles, etc.

tsu•na•mi [tsuu-NAH-mee] *noun* tidal wave, usu. caused by an earthquake under the sea

tub *noun* 1 open wooden vessel like bottom half of barrel 2 small round container 3 bath 4 (*informal*) short, fat person 5 old, slow ship, etc.

tu•ba [TOO-bə] *noun, plural* **-bas** valved brass wind instrument of low pitch

tube [toob] *noun* 1 long, narrow, hollow cylinder 2 flexible cylinder with cap to hold liquids, pastes > **tu'bu•lar** [-byə-lər] *adjective* like tube

tu•ber [TOO-bər] *noun* fleshy underground stem of some plants, e.g. potato > **tu'ber•ous** [-əs] *adjective*

tu•ber•cle [TOO-bər-kəl] *noun* 1 any small rounded nodule on skin, etc. 2 small lesion of tissue, esp. produced by tuberculosis > **tu•ber•cu•lar** *adjective* (tuu-BUR-kyə-lər) > **tu•ber'cu•lin** *noun* extraction from bacillus used to test for and treat tuberculosis > **tu•ber•cu•lo'sis** *noun* communicable disease, esp. of lungs

tuck [tuk] *verb transitive* 1 push, fold into small space 2 gather, stitch in folds 3 draw, roll together ▷ *noun* 4 stitched fold > **tuck'er** *noun* 1 strip of linen or lace formerly worn across bosom by women ▷ *verb transitive* (*informal*) 2 weary 3 tire

tu•fa [TOO-fə] *noun* porous rock formed as deposit from springs, etc.

tuf•fet [TUF-it] *noun* (*obsolete*) small mound or seat

tuft *noun* bunch of feathers, threads, etc.

tug *verb transitive* **tugged, tug•ging** 1 pull hard or violently 2 haul 3 jerk forward ▷ *noun* 4 violent pull 5 ship used to tow other vessels > **tug of war** 1 contest in which two teams pull against one another on a rope 2 hard-fought contest for supremacy

tu•i•tion [too-ISH-ən] *noun* 1 teaching, instruction 2 fee for instruction

tu•lip [TOO-lip] *noun* plant with bright cup-shaped flowers

tulle [tool] *noun* kind of fine thin silk or lace

tum•ble [TUM-bəl] *verb* **-bled, -bling** 1 (cause to) fall or roll, twist, etc. (esp. in play) 2 rumple, disturb ▷ *noun* 3 fall 4 somersault > **tum'bler** *noun* 1 stemless drinking glass 2 acrobat 3 spring catch in lock > **tum'ble-down** *adjective* dilapidated > **tumble to** (*informal*)

DICTIONARY

t

THESAURUS

4 SNOUT, proboscis

truss *verb* 1 TIE, bind, fasten, make fast, secure, strap, tether
▷ *noun* 2 (*medical*) SUPPORT, bandage
3 JOIST, beam, brace, buttress, prop, stanchion, stay, strut, support

trust *verb* 1 BELIEVE IN, bank on, count on, depend on, have faith in, rely upon
2 CONSIGN, assign, commit, confide, delegate, entrust, give
3 EXPECT, assume, hope, presume, suppose, surmise
▷ *noun* 4 CONFIDENCE, assurance, belief, certainty, conviction, credence, credit, expectation, faith, reliance

trustful *or* **trusting** *adjective* UNWARY, credulous, gullible, naive, unsuspecting, unsuspicious

trustworthy *adjective* HONEST, dependable, honorable, principled, reliable, reputable, responsible, staunch, steadfast, trusty

trusty *adjective* FAITHFUL, dependable, reliable, solid, staunch, steady, strong, trustworthy

truth *noun* TRUTHFULNESS, accuracy, exactness, fact, genuineness, legitimacy, precision, reality, validity, veracity

truthful *adjective* HONEST, candid, frank, precise, sincere, straight, true, trustworthy

try *verb* 1 ATTEMPT, aim, endeavor, have a go, make an effort, seek, strive, struggle
2 TEST, appraise, check out, evaluate, examine, investigate, put to the test, sample, taste
▷ *noun* 3 ATTEMPT, crack (*informal*), effort, go (*informal*), shot (*informal*), stab (*informal*), whack (*informal*)

trying *adjective* ANNOYING, bothersome, difficult, exasperating, hard, high-maintenance, stressful, taxing, tiresome, tough, wearisome

tubby *adjective* FAT, chubby, corpulent, obese, overweight, plump, portly, stout

tuck *verb* 1 PUSH, fold, gather, insert
▷ *noun* 2 FOLD, gather, pinch, pleat

tuft *noun* CLUMP, bunch, cluster, collection, knot, tussock

tug *verb* 1 PULL, jerk, wrench, yank
▷ *noun* 2 PULL, jerk, yank

tuition *noun* TRAINING, education, instruction, lessons, schooling, teaching, tutelage, tutoring

tumble *verb* 1 FALL, drop, flop, plummet, stumble, topple
▷ *noun* 2 FALL, drop, plunge, spill, stumble, trip

tumbledown *adjective* DILAPIDATED, crumbling,

realize, understand
tu•me•fy [TOO-mə-fī] *verb* **-fied, -fy•ing** (cause to) swell > **tu•mes•cence** [too-MES-əns] *noun* > **tu•mes'cent** [-ənt] *adjective* (becoming) swollen
tu•mor [TOO-mər] *noun* abnormal growth in or on body
tu•mult [TOO-məlt] *noun* violent uproar, commotion > **tu•mult'u•ous** [-MUL-choo-əs] *adjective*
tu•na [TOO-nə] *noun* large marine food and game fish
tun•dra [TUN-drə] *noun* vast treeless zone between ice cap and timber line of N America and Eurasia
tune [toon] *noun* 1 melody 2 quality of being in pitch 3 adjustment of musical instrument 4 concord 5 frame of mind ▷ *verb transitive* **tuned, tun•ing** 6 put in tune 7 adjust machine to obtain most efficient running 8 adjust radio circuit > **tune'ful** [-fəl] *adjective* > **tun'er** [-ər] *noun* > **tune in** adjust (radio, TV) to receive (a station, program)
tung•sten [TUNG-stən] *noun* grayish-white metal, used in lamp filaments, some steels, etc.
tu•nic [TOO-nik] *noun* 1 close-fitting jacket forming part of uniform 2 loose hip-length or knee-length garment
tun•nel [TUN-l] *noun* 1 underground passage, esp. as track for railroad line 2 burrow of a mole, etc. ▷ *verb* **-neled, -nel•ing** 3 make tunnel (through)
tur•ban [TUR-bən] *noun* 1 in certain countries, man's headdress, made by coiling length of cloth around head or a cap 2 woman's hat like this
tur'bid *adjective* 1 muddy, not clear 2 disturbed > **tur•bid'i•ty** *noun*
tur•bine [TUR-bin] *noun* rotary engine driven by steam, gas, water or air playing on blades
turbo- *combining form* of, relating to, or driven by a turbine
tur•bu•lent [TUR-byə-lənt] *adjective* 1 in commotion 2 swirling 3 riotous > **tur'bu•lence** [-ləns] *noun* esp. instability of atmosphere causing gusty air currents, etc.
tu•reen [tuu-REEN] *noun* serving dish for soup
turf *noun, plural* **turfs** 1 short grass with earth bound to it by matted roots 2 grass, esp. as lawn 3 (*slang*) claimed territory of gang ▷ *verb transitive* 4 lay with turf
tur•gid [TUR-jid] *adjective* 1 swollen, inflated 2 bombastic > **tur•gid'i•ty** *noun*
tur•key [TUR-kee] *noun* 1 large bird reared for food 2 (*slang*) loser, naive person 3 (*slang*) a flop
Turk•ish [TUR-kish] *adjective* of, pert. to Turkey, the Turks > **Turkish bath** steam bath > **Turkish delight** gelatin candy flavored and coated with powdered sugar
tur'moil *noun* confusion and bustle, commotion
turn *verb* 1 move around, rotate 2 change, reverse, alter position or direction (of) 3 (oft. with *into*) change in nature, character, etc. ▷ *verb transitive* 4 make, shape on lathe ▷ *noun* 5 act of turning 6 inclination, etc. 7 period, spell 8 turning 9 short walk 10 (part of) rotation 11 performance > **turn'ing** *noun* road, path leading off main route > **turn'coat** [-koht] *noun* one who forsakes own party or principles > **turn'out** *noun* 1 number of people appearing for some purpose, occasion 2 way in which person is dressed, equipped > **turn'o•ver** *noun* 1

DICTIONARY • THESAURUS

decrepit, ramshackle, rickety, ruined
tumor *noun* GROWTH, cancer, carcinoma (*pathology*), lump, sarcoma (*medical*), swelling
tumult *noun* COMMOTION, clamor, din, hubbub, pandemonium, riot, row, turmoil, upheaval, uproar
tumultuous *adjective* WILD, boisterous, excited, noisy, riotous, rowdy, turbulent, unruly, uproarious, wired (*slang*)
tune *noun* 1 MELODY, air, song, strain, theme
2 PITCH, concord, consonance, euphony, harmony
▷ *verb* 3 ADJUST, adapt, attune, harmonize, pitch, regulate
tuneful *adjective* MELODIOUS, catchy, euphonious, harmonious, mellifluous, melodic, musical, pleasant
tuneless *adjective* DISCORDANT, atonal, cacophonous, dissonant, harsh, unmusical
tunnel *noun* 1 PASSAGE, burrow, channel, hole, passageway, shaft, subway, underpass
▷ *verb* 2 DIG, burrow, excavate, mine, scoop out
turbulence *noun* CONFUSION, agitation, commotion, disorder, instability, tumult, turmoil, unrest, upheaval
turbulent *adjective* AGITATED, blustery, choppy, foaming, furious, raging, rough, tempestuous, tumultuous
turf *noun* 1 GRASS, sod, sward
2 ▷ **the turf** HORSE-RACING, racing, the flat
turmoil *noun* CONFUSION, agitation, chaos, commotion, disarray, disorder, tumult, upheaval, uproar
turn *verb* 1 CHANGE COURSE, move, shift, swerve, switch, veer, wheel
2 ROTATE, circle, go round, gyrate, pivot, revolve, roll, spin, twist, whirl
3 CHANGE, alter, convert, mold, mutate, remodel, shape, transform
4 SHAPE, fashion, frame, make, mold
5 GO BAD, curdle, sour, spoil, taint
▷ *noun* 6 ROTATION, circle, cycle, gyration, revolution, spin, twist, whirl
7 SHIFT, departure, deviation
8 OPPORTUNITY, chance, crack (*informal*), go, stint, time, try
9 DIRECTION, drift, heading, tendency, trend
10 DEED, act, action, favor, gesture, service
turncoat *noun* TRAITOR, apostate, backslider, defector, deserter, renegade
turn down *verb* 1 LOWER, lessen, muffle, mute, quieten, soften
2 REFUSE, decline, rebuff, reject, repudiate, spurn
turn in *verb* 1 GO TO BED, go to sleep, hit the sack (*slang*)
2 HAND IN, deliver, give up, hand over, return, submit, surrender, tender
turning *noun* JUNCTION, bend, crossroads, curve, side road, turn, turn-off
turning point *noun* CROSSROADS, change, crisis, crux, moment of truth
turn off *verb* STOP, cut out, put out, shut down, switch off, turn out, unplug

total sales made by business over certain period 2 rate at which employees leave and are replaced 3 small pastry 4 *football, basketball* loss of ball to opponents through mistake > **turn'pike** *noun* 1 *hist.* (gate across) road where toll was paid 2 highway > **turn'stile** *noun* revolving gate for controlling admission of people > **turn'ta•ble** *noun* revolving platform > **turn down** refuse > **turn up** 1 appear 2 be found 3 increase (flow, volume)

tur'nip *noun* plant with globular root used as food

tur•pen•tine [TUR-pən-tīn] *noun* 1 resin obtained from certain trees 2 oil made from this > **turps** *noun* short for turpentine

tur•pi•tude [TUR-pi-tood] *noun* depravity

tur•quoise [TUR-kwoiz] *noun* 1 bluish-green precious stone 2 this color

tur•ret [TUR-it] *noun* 1 small tower 2 revolving armored tower for guns on warship, tank, etc.

tur•tle [TUR-tl] *noun* (esp. sea) tortoise

tusk *noun* long pointed side tooth of an elephant, walrus, etc.

tus•sle [TUS-əl] *noun, verb* **-sled, -sling** fight, wrestle, struggle

tu•te•lage [TOOT-l-ij] *noun* act, office of tutor or guardian > **tu'te•lar•y** [-ler-ee] *adjective*

tu•tor [TOO-tər] *noun* 1 one teaching individuals or small groups ▷ *verb* 2 teach thus > **tu•to'ri•al** [-TOR-ee-əl] *noun* period of instruction with tutor

tu•tu [TOO-too] *noun, plural* **-tus** short, stiff skirt worn by ballerinas

tux•e•do [tuk-SEE-doh] *noun, plural* **-dos** dinner jacket

TV television > **TV dinner** frozen meal in tray for heating before serving > **TV game** game played on TV screen using special attachment

twad•dle [TWOD-l] *noun* silly talk

twain [twayn] *noun* two **in twain** asunder

twang *noun* 1 vibrating metallic sound 2 nasal speech ▷ *verb* 3 (cause to) make such sounds

tweak [tweek] *verb transitive* pinch and twist or pull ▷ *noun*

tweed *noun* rough-surfaced cloth used for clothing > **tweeds** suit of tweed

tween *noun* child of about 8 to 12 years of age

tweet *noun, verb intransitive* chirp > **tweet'er** *noun* small loudspeaker reproducing high-frequency sounds

tweez•ers [TWEE-zərz] *plural noun* small forceps or tongs

twelve [twelv] *noun, adjective* cardinal number two more than ten > **twelfth** *adjective* the ordinal number ▷ *noun*

twen•ty [TWEN-tee] *noun, adjective, plural* **-ties** cardinal number, twice ten > **twen'ti•eth** [-tee-ith] *adjective* the ordinal number ▷ *noun* > **twenty-four-seven, 24/7** *adjective, adverb* (*informal*) all the time

twerp [twurp] *noun* (*slang*) silly person

twice [twīs] *adverb* two times

twid•dle [TWID-l] *verb* **-dled, -dling** 1 fiddle 2 twist

twig *noun* small branch, shoot

twi•light [TWĪ-līt] *noun* soft light after sunset

twill *noun* fabric woven so as to have surface of parallel ridges

twin *noun* 1 one of pair, esp. of two children born together ▷ *adjective* 2 being a twin ▷ *verb* **twinned, twin•ning** 3 pair, be paired

twine [twīn] *verb* **twined, twin•ing** 1 twist, coil around ▷ *noun* 2 string, cord

twinge [twinj] *noun* 1 momentary sharp, shooting pain 2 qualm

twin•kle [TWING-kəl] *verb intransitive* **-kled, -kling** 1 shine with dancing or quivering light, sparkle ▷ *noun* 2 twinkling 3 flash 4 gleam of amusement in eyes > **twinkling** *noun* very brief time

twirl [twurl] *verb transitive* 1 turn or twist round quickly 2 whirl 3 twiddle

twist *verb* 1 make, become spiral, by turning with one end fast 2 distort, change 3 wind

---

turn on *verb* 1 START, activate, ignite, kick-start, start up, switch on
2 ATTACK, assail, assault, fall on, round on
3 (*informal*) EXCITE, arouse, attract, please, stimulate, thrill, titillate

turnout *noun* ATTENDANCE, assembly, audience, congregation, crowd, gate, number, throng

turnover *noun* 1 OUTPUT, business, productivity
2 MOVEMENT, change, coming and going

turn up *verb* 1 ARRIVE, appear, attend, come, put in an appearance, show one's face, show up (*informal*)
2 FIND, dig up, disclose, discover, expose, reveal, unearth
3 COME TO LIGHT, crop up (*informal*), pop up
4 INCREASE, amplify, boost, enhance, intensify, raise

tussle *noun* 1 FIGHT, battle, brawl, conflict, contest, scrap (*informal*), scuffle, struggle
▷ *verb* 2 FIGHT, battle, grapple, scrap (*informal*), scuffle, struggle, vie, wrestle

tutor *noun* 1 TEACHER, coach, educator, guardian, guide, guru, instructor, lecturer, mentor
▷ *verb* 2 TEACH, coach, drill, educate, guide, instruct, school, train

twaddle *noun* NONSENSE, claptrap (*informal*), drivel, garbage (*informal*), gobbledegook (*informal*), poppycock (*informal*), rubbish

tweak *verb, noun* TWIST, jerk, pinch, pull, squeeze

twig *noun* BRANCH, shoot, spray, sprig, stick

twilight *noun* DUSK, dimness, evening, gloaming (*poetic*), gloom, half-light, sundown, sunset

twin *noun* 1 DOUBLE, clone, counterpart, duplicate, fellow, likeness, lookalike, match, mate
▷ *verb* 2 PAIR, couple, join, link, match, yoke

twine *noun* 1 STRING, cord, yarn
▷ *verb* 2 COIL, bend, curl, encircle, loop, spiral, twist, wind

twinge *noun* PAIN, pang, prick, spasm, stab, stitch

twinkle *verb* 1 SPARKLE, blink, flash, flicker, gleam, glint, glisten, glitter, shimmer, shine
▷ *noun* 2 FLICKER, flash, gleam, glimmer, shimmer, spark, sparkle

twirl *verb* 1 TURN, pirouette, pivot, revolve, rotate, spin, twist, wheel, whirl, wind
▷ *noun* 2 TURN, pirouette, revolution, rotation, spin, twist, wheel, whirl

twist *verb* 1 WIND, coil, curl, screw, spin, swivel,

▷ *noun* **4** thing twisted **> twist'er** *noun* **1** person or thing that twists **2** (*informal*) tornado, whirlwind **> twist'y** *adjective* **twist•i•er, twist•i•est**

twit *noun* (*informal*) **1** foolish person ▷ *verb transitive* **twit•ted, twit•ting** **2** taunt

twitch [twich] *verb* **1** give momentary sharp pull or jerk (to) ▷ *noun* **2** such pull or jerk **3** spasmodic jerk, spasm

twit•ter [TWIT-ər] *verb intransitive* **1** giggle **2** talk idly **3** (of birds) utter succession of tremulous sounds ▷ *noun* **4** such succession of notes

two [too] *noun, adjective* cardinal number, one more than one **> two'fold** *adjective, adverb* **> two-faced** *adjective* **1** double-dealing, deceitful **2** with two faces **> two-stroke** [-strohk] *adjective* (of internal-combustion engine) making one explosion to every two strokes of piston

ty•coon [tī-KOON] *noun* powerful, influential businessperson

tyke [tīk] *noun* **1** small, cheeky child **2** small (mongrel) dog

tympani *see* **timpani**

type [tīp] *noun* **1** class **2** sort **3** model **4** pattern **5** characteristic build **6** specimen **7** block bearing letter used for printing **8** such pieces collectively ▷ *verb transitive* **typed, typ•ing** **9** print with typewriter **10** typify **11** classify **> type'script** *noun* typewritten document or copy **> type'writ•er** *noun* keyed writing machine **> typ'ist** *noun* one who operates typewriter **> ty'po** *noun, plural* **ty•pos** (*informal*) error in typing, printing

ty•phoid [TĪ-foid] *noun* acute infectious disease, affecting esp. intestines ▷ *adjective* **> ty•phus** [TĪ-fəs] *noun* infectious disease

ty•phoon [tī-FOON] *noun* violent tropical storm or cyclone

typ•i•cal [TIP-i-kəl] *adjective* **1** true to type **2** characteristic **> typ'i•cal•ly** *adverb*

typ•i•fy [TIP-i-fī] *verb transitive* **-fied, -fy•ing** serve as type or model of

ty•pog•ra•phy [tī-POG-rə-fee] *noun* **1** art of printing **2** style of printing **> ty•po•graph'i•cal** *adjective* **> ty•pog'ra•pher** [-POG-rə-fər] *noun*

ty•rant [TĪ-rənt] *noun* **1** oppressive or cruel ruler **2** one who forces own will on others cruelly and arbitrarily **> ty•ran•ni•cal** [ti-RAN-i-kəl] *adjective* **1** despotic **2** ruthless **> tyr•an•nize** [TIR-ə-nīz] *verb* **-nized, -niz•ing** exert ruthless or tyrannical authority (over) **> tyr'an•nous** [-ə-nəs] *adjective* **> tyr'an•ny** *noun* despotism

ty•ro [tī-roh] *noun, plural* **-ros** novice, beginner

DICTIONARY • THESAURUS

---

wrap, wring
2 DISTORT, contort, screw up
▷ *noun* **3** WIND, coil, curl, spin, swivel
4 DEVELOPMENT, change, revelation, slant, surprise, turn, variation
5 CURVE, arc, bend, meander, turn, undulation, zigzag
6 DISTORTION, defect, deformation, flaw, imperfection, kink, warp

twitch *verb* **1** JERK, flutter, jump, squirm ▷ *noun* **2** SPASM, flutter, jerk, jump, tic

two-faced *adjective* HYPOCRITICAL, deceitful, dissembling, duplicitous, false, insincere, treacherous, untrustworthy

tycoon *noun* MAGNATE, baron, capitalist, fat cat (*slang*), financier, industrialist, mogul, plutocrat

type *noun* CATEGORY, class, genre, group, kind, order, sort, species, style, variety

typhoon *noun* STORM, cyclone, squall, tempest, tornado

typical *adjective* CHARACTERISTIC, archetypal, average, classic, model, normal, orthodox, representative, standard, stock, usual

typify *verb* SYMBOLIZE, characterize, embody, epitomize, exemplify, illustrate, personify, represent, sum up

tyrannical *adjective* OPPRESSIVE, authoritarian, autocratic, cruel, despotic, dictatorial, domineering, high-handed, imperious, overbearing, tyrannous

tyranny *noun* OPPRESSION, absolutism, authoritarianism, autocracy, cruelty, despotism, dictatorship, high-handedness, imperiousness

tyrant *noun* DICTATOR, absolutist, authoritarian, autocrat, bully, despot, martinet, oppressor, slave-driver

Uu

U *chem.* uranium
u•biq•ui•tous [yoo-BIK-wi-təs] *adjective* **1** everywhere at once **2** omnipresent
> **u•biq'ui•ty** *noun*
ud•der [UD-ər] *noun* milk-secreting organ of cow, etc.
ug•ly [UG-lee] *adjective* **-li•er, -li•est** **1** unpleasing, repulsive to the sight, hideous **2** ill-omened **3** threatening > **ug'li•ness** [-nis] *noun*
u•kase [yoo-KAYS] *noun* an arbitrary command
u•ku•le•le [yoo-kə-LAY-lee] *noun* small four-stringed guitar, esp. of Hawaii
ul•cer [UL-sər] *noun* open sore on skin, mucous membrane that is slow to heal > **ul'cer•ate** *verb* **-at•ed, -at•ed** make, form ulcer(s)
> **ul•cer•a'tion** *noun*
ul•lage [UL-ij] *noun* quantity by which a container falls short of being full
ul•na [UL-nə] *noun, plural* **-nae** [-nee] longer of two bones of forearm
ul•te•ri•or [ul-TEER-ee-ər] *adjective* **1** lying beneath, beyond what is revealed or evident (e.g. motives) **2** situated beyond
ul•ti•mate [UL-tə-mit] *adjective* **1** last **2** highest **3** most significant **4** fundamental
> **ul•ti•ma'tum** [-MAY-təm] *noun, plural* **-tums** *or* **-ta** [-tə] **1** final proposition **2** final terms offered
ultra- *prefix* beyond, excessively: *ultramodern*
ul'tra•high frequency [UL-trə-hī] (band of) radio waves of very short wavelength
ul•tra•ma•rine [ul-trə-mə-REEN] *noun* blue pigment
ul•tra•son•ic [ul-trə-SON-ik] *adjective* of sound waves beyond the range of human ear
ul•tra•vi•o•let [ul-trə-VĪ-ə-lit] *adjective* of electromagnetic radiation (e.g. of sun, etc.) beyond limit of visibility at violet end of spectrum
um•bel [UM-bəl] *noun* umbrella-like flower cluster with stalks springing from central point
> **um•bel•lif'er•ous** [-LIF-ər-əs] *adjective* bearing umbel(s)
um•ber [UM-bər] *noun* dark brown pigment
um•bil•i•cal [um-BIL-i-kəl] *adjective* of (region of) navel > **umbilical cord** **1** cordlike structure connecting fetus with placenta of mother **2** cord joining astronaut to spacecraft, etc.
um•brage [UM-brij] *noun* offense, resentment
um•brel•la [um-BREL-ə] *noun* **1** folding circular cover of nylon, etc. on stick, carried in hand to

---

ubiquitous *adjective* EVERYWHERE, ever-present, omnipresent, pervasive, universal
ugly *adjective* **1** UNATTRACTIVE, dumpy (*informal*), frowzy, hideous, homely (*United States*), ill-favored, plain, unlovely, unprepossessing, unsightly
2 UNPLEASANT, disagreeable, distasteful, horrid, objectionable, shocking, terrible
3 OMINOUS, baleful, dangerous, menacing, sinister
ulcer *noun* SORE, abscess, boil, gumboil, peptic ulcer, pustule
ulterior *adjective* HIDDEN, concealed, covert, secret, undisclosed
ultimate *adjective* **1** FINAL, end, last
2 SUPREME, extreme, greatest, highest,

protect against rain, heat of sun **2** anything shaped or functioning like an umbrella

um•pire [UM-pīr] *noun* **1** person chosen to decide question, or to decide disputes and enforce rules in a game ▷ *verb* **-pired, -pir•ing** **2** act as umpire (in)

un- *prefix* **1** not: *unidentified* **2** denoting reversal of an action: *untie* **3** denoting removal from: *unthrone*

un•ac•count•a•ble [un-ə-KOWNT-ə-bəl] *adjective* that cannot be explained

u•nan•i•mous [yoo-NAN-ə-məs] *adjective* **1** in complete agreement **2** agreed by all > **u•na•nim•i•ty** [yoo-nə-NIM-ə-tee] *noun*

un•as•sum•ing [un-ə-SOO-ming] *adjective* not pretentious, modest

un•a•vail•ing [un-ə-VAY-ling] *adjective* useless, futile

un•a•ware [un-ə-WAIR] *adjective* not aware, uninformed > **un•a•wares'** [-WAIRZ] *adverb* **1** without previous warning **2** unexpectedly

un•bear'a•ble *adjective* not able to be endured

un•bos•om [un-BUUZ-əm] *verb transitive* tell or reveal (one's secrets, etc.)

DICTIONARY • THESAURUS

paramount, superlative, utmost

ultimately *adverb* FINALLY, after all, at last, eventually, in due time, in the end, sooner or later

umpire *noun* **1** REFEREE, arbiter, arbitrator, judge
▷ *verb* **2** REFEREE, adjudicate, arbitrate, judge

unabashed *adjective* UNEMBARRASSED, blatant, bold, brazen

unable *adjective* INCAPABLE, impotent, ineffectual, powerless, unfit, unqualified

unabridged *adjective* UNCUT, complete, full-length, unexpurgated, whole

unacceptable *adjective* UNSATISFACTORY, displeasing, objectionable

unaccompanied *adjective* **1** ALONE, by oneself, lone, on one's own, solo, unescorted
2 (*music*) A CAPPELLA

unaccountable *adjective* **1** INEXPLICABLE, baffling, mysterious, odd, puzzling, unexplainable, unfathomable
2 NOT ANSWERABLE, exempt, not responsible

unaccustomed *adjective* **1** UNFAMILIAR, new, strange, unwonted
2 ▷ **unaccustomed to** NOT USED TO, inexperienced at, unfamiliar with, unused to

unaffected[1] *adjective* NATURAL, artless, genuine, plain, simple, sincere, unpretentious

unaffected[2] *adjective* IMPERVIOUS, proof, unmoved, unresponsive, untouched

unafraid *adjective* FEARLESS, daring, dauntless, intrepid

unalterable *adjective* UNCHANGEABLE, fixed, immutable, permanent

unanimity *noun* AGREEMENT, accord, assent, concord, concurrence, consensus, harmony, like-mindedness, unison

unanimous *adjective* AGREED, common, concerted, harmonious, in agreement, like-minded, united

unanimously *adverb* WITHOUT EXCEPTION, as one, in concert, of one mind, with one accord

unanswerable *adjective* CONCLUSIVE, absolute, incontestable, incontrovertible, indisputable

unanswered *adjective* UNRESOLVED, disputed, open, undecided

unappetizing *adjective* UNPLEASANT, distasteful, repulsive, scuzzy (*slang*), unappealing, unattractive, unpalatable

unapproachable *adjective* **1** UNFRIENDLY, aloof, chilly, cool, distant, remote, reserved, standoffish
2 INACCESSIBLE, out of reach, remote

unarmed *adjective* DEFENSELESS, exposed, helpless, open, unprotected, weak

unassailable *adjective* IMPREGNABLE, invincible, invulnerable, secure

unassuming *adjective* MODEST, humble, quiet, reserved, retiring, self-effacing, unassertive, unobtrusive, unpretentious

unattached *adjective* **1** FREE, independent
2 SINGLE, available, not spoken for, unengaged, unmarried

unattended *adjective* **1** ABANDONED, unguarded, unwatched
2 ALONE, on one's own, unaccompanied

unauthorized *adjective* ILLEGAL, unlawful, unofficial, unsanctioned

unavoidable *adjective* INEVITABLE, certain, fated, inescapable

unaware *adjective* IGNORANT, oblivious, unconscious, uninformed, unknowing

unawares *adverb* **1** BY SURPRISE, off guard, suddenly, unexpectedly
2 UNKNOWINGLY, accidentally, by accident, inadvertently, unwittingly

unbalanced *adjective* **1** BIASED, one-sided, partial, partisan, prejudiced, unfair
2 SHAKY, lopsided, uneven, unstable, wobbly
3 DERANGED, crazy, demented, disturbed, eccentric, insane, irrational, mad, non compos mentis (*Latin*), not all there, unhinged, unstable

unbearable *adjective* INTOLERABLE, insufferable, too much (*informal*), unacceptable

unbeatable *adjective* INVINCIBLE, indomitable

unbeaten *adjective* UNDEFEATED, triumphant, victorious

unbecoming *adjective* **1** UNSIGHTLY, unattractive, unbefitting, unflattering, unsuitable
2 UNSEEMLY, discreditable, improper, offensive

unbelievable *adjective* INCREDIBLE, astonishing, far-fetched, implausible, impossible, improbable, inconceivable, preposterous, unconvincing, unimaginable

unbending *adjective* INFLEXIBLE, firm, intractable, resolute, rigid, severe, strict, stubborn, tough, uncompromising

unbiased *adjective* FAIR, disinterested, equitable, impartial, just, neutral, objective, unprejudiced

unblemished *adjective* SPOTLESS, flawless, immaculate, impeccable, perfect, pure, untarnished

unborn *adjective* EXPECTED, awaited, embryonic, fetal

unbreakable *adjective* INDESTRUCTIBLE, durable, lasting, rugged, strong

unbridled *adjective* UNRESTRAINED, excessive, intemperate, licentious, riotous, unchecked, unruly, wanton

unbroken *adjective* **1** INTACT, complete, entire, whole
2 CONTINUOUS, constant, incessant, twenty-

un•can•ny [un-KAN-ee] *adjective* 1 weird, mysterious 2 extraordinary
un•cer'tain *adjective* 1 not able to be accurately known or predicted 2 not able to be depended upon 3 changeable
un•cle [UNG-kəl] *noun* 1 brother of father or mother 2 husband of aunt
un•com'fort•a•ble *adjective* 1 not physically relaxed 2 anxious or uneasy
un•com'mon *adjective* 1 not happening or encountered often 2 in excess of what is normal
un•com•pli•men•ta•ry [un-kom-plə-MEN-tə-ree] *adjective* 1 not complimentary 2 insulting, derogatory
un•con•di'tion•al *adjective* without conditions or limitations
un•con•scion•a•ble [un-KON-shə-nə-bəl] *adjective* 1 unscrupulous, unprincipled 2 excessive
un•con•scious [un-KON-shəs] *adjective* 1 insensible 2 not aware 3 not knowing 4 of thoughts, memories, etc. of which one is not normally aware ▷ *noun* 5 these thoughts > **un•con'scious•ness** [-nis] *noun*
un•couth [un-KOOTH] *adjective* 1 clumsy, boorish 2 without ease or polish
unc•tion [UNGK-shən] *noun* 1 anointing 2 excessive politeness 3 soothing words or thoughts > **unc'tu•ous** [-choo-əs] *adjective* 1

four-seven (*slang*), uninterrupted
unburden *verb* CONFESS, confide, disclose, get (something) off one's chest (*informal*), reveal
uncalled-for *adjective* UNJUSTIFIED, gratuitous, needless, undeserved, unnecessary, unwarranted
uncanny *adjective* 1 WEIRD, mysterious, strange, supernatural, unearthly, unnatural
2 EXTRAORDINARY, astounding, exceptional, incredible, miraculous, remarkable, unusual
unceasing *adjective* CONTINUAL, constant, continuous, endless, incessant, nonstop, perpetual, twenty-four-seven (*slang*)
uncertain *adjective* 1 UNPREDICTABLE, doubtful, indefinite, questionable, risky, speculative
2 UNSURE, dubious, hazy, irresolute, unclear, unconfirmed, undecided, vague
uncertainty *noun* DOUBT, ambiguity, confusion, dubiety, hesitancy, indecision, unpredictability
unchangeable *adjective* UNALTERABLE, constant, fixed, immutable, invariable, irreversible, permanent, stable
unchanging *adjective* CONSTANT, continuing, enduring, eternal, immutable, lasting, permanent, perpetual, twenty-four-seven (*slang*), unvarying
uncharitable *adjective* UNKIND, cruel, hardhearted, unfeeling, ungenerous
uncharted *adjective* UNEXPLORED, strange, undiscovered, unfamiliar, unknown
uncivil *adjective* IMPOLITE, bad-mannered, discourteous, ill-mannered, rude, unmannerly
uncivilized *adjective* 1 PRIMITIVE, barbarian, savage, wild
2 UNCOUTH, boorish, coarse, philistine, uncultivated, uneducated
unclean *adjective* DIRTY, corrupt, defiled, evil, filthy, foul, impure, polluted, scuzzy (*slang*), soiled, stained
unclear *adjective* 1 INDISTINCT, blurred, dim, faint, fuzzy, hazy, obscure, shadowy, undefined, vague
2 DOUBTFUL, ambiguous, indefinite, indeterminate, vague
uncomfortable *adjective* 1 AWKWARD, cramped, painful, rough
2 UNEASY, awkward, discomfited, disturbed, embarrassed, troubled
uncommitted *adjective* UNINVOLVED, floating, free, neutral, nonaligned, not involved, unattached
uncommon *adjective* 1 RARE, infrequent, novel, odd, peculiar, queer, scarce, strange, unusual
2 EXTRAORDINARY, distinctive, exceptional, notable, outstanding, remarkable, special
uncommonly *adverb* 1 RARELY, hardly ever, infrequently, occasionally, seldom
2 EXCEPTIONALLY, particularly, very
uncommunicative *adjective* RETICENT, close, reserved, secretive, silent, taciturn, tight-lipped, unforthcoming
uncompromising *adjective* INFLEXIBLE, firm, inexorable, intransigent, rigid, strict, tough, unbending
unconcern *noun* INDIFFERENCE, aloofness, apathy, detachment, lack of interest, nonchalance
unconcerned *adjective* INDIFFERENT, aloof, apathetic, cool, detached, dispassionate, distant, uninterested, unmoved
unconditional *adjective* ABSOLUTE, complete, entire, full, outright, positive, total, unlimited, unqualified, unreserved
unconnected *adjective* 1 SEPARATE, detached, divided
2 MEANINGLESS, disjointed, illogical, incoherent, irrelevant
unconscious *adjective* 1 SENSELESS, insensible, knocked out, out, out cold, stunned
2 UNAWARE, ignorant, oblivious, unknowing
3 UNINTENTIONAL, accidental, inadvertent, unwitting
uncontrollable *adjective* WILD, frantic, furious, mad, strong, unruly, violent
uncontrolled *adjective* UNRESTRAINED, rampant, riotous, unbridled, unchecked, undisciplined
unconventional *adjective* UNUSUAL, eccentric, individual, irregular, nonconformist, odd, offbeat, original, outré, unorthodox
unconvincing *adjective* IMPLAUSIBLE, dubious, feeble, flimsy, improbable, lame, questionable, suspect, thin, unlikely, weak
uncooperative *adjective* UNHELPFUL, awkward, difficult, disobliging, high-maintenance, obstructive
uncoordinated *adjective* CLUMSY, awkward, bungling, graceless, lumbering, maladroit, ungainly, ungraceful
uncouth *adjective* COARSE, boorish, crude, graceless, ill-mannered, loutish, oafish, rough, rude, vulgar
uncover *verb* 1 REVEAL, disclose, divulge, expose, make known
2 OPEN, bare, show, strip, unwrap
uncritical *adjective* UNDISCRIMINATING, indiscriminate, undiscerning

slippery, greasy **2** oily in manner, gushing
un•de•cid'ed *adjective* **1** not having made up one's mind **2** (of an issue or problem) not agreed or decided upon
un•der [UN-dər] *preposition* **1** below, beneath **2** bound by, included in **3** less than **4** subjected to **5** known by **6** in the time of ▷ *adverb* **7** in lower place or condition ▷ *adjective* **8** lower
under- *prefix* beneath, below, lower: *underground*
un•der•car•riage [UN-dər-ka-rij] *noun* landing gear of vehicle esp. aircraft
un•der•charge [un-dər-CHAHRJ] *verb transitive* **-charged, -charg•ing** **1** charge less than proper amount ▷ *noun* [UN-dər-chahrj] **2** too low a charge
un•der•class [UN-dər-klas] *noun* the most economically disadvantaged people, such as the long-term unemployed
un•der•coat [UN-dər-koht] *noun* coat of paint applied before top coat
un•der•dog [un-dər-dawg] *noun* person or team in a weak or underprivileged position
un•der•go [un-dər-GOH] *verb transitive* **-went, -gone, -go•ing** experience, endure, sustain
un•der•grad•u•ate [un-dər-GRAJ-oo-it] *noun* student at college who has not received degree
un•der•ground [UN-dər-grownd] *adjective* **1** under the ground **2** secret ▷ *adverb* **3** secretly ▷ *noun* **4** secret but organized resistance to government in power **5** subway
un•der•hand [UN-dər-hand] *adjective* **1** secret, sly **2** *sports* (of softball pitch, etc.) with hand swung below shoulder level
un•der•lie [un-dər-LĪ] *verb transitive* **-lay, -lain, -ly•ing** be situated under, lie beneath
un•der•line [UN-dər-līn] *verb transitive* **-lined, -lin•ing** **1** put line under **2** emphasize
un•der•ling [UN-dər-ling] *noun* subordinate
un•der•mine [un-dər-MĪN] *verb transitive* **-mined, -min•ing** **1** wear away base, support of **2** weaken insidiously
un•der•neath [un-dər-NEETH] *adverb, preposition* **1** under or beneath ▷ *adjective, noun* **2** lower (part or surface)
un•der•pass [UN-dər-pas] *noun* section of road passing under another road, railroad line, etc.
un•der•stand [un-dər-STAND] *verb* **-stood** [-stuud], **-stand•ing** **1** know and comprehend **2** realize ▷ *verb transitive* **3** infer **4** take for granted > **un•der•stand'a•ble** *adjective* > **un•der•stand'ing** *noun* **1** intelligence **2** opinion **3** agreement ▷ *adjective* **4** sympathetic
un•der•stud•y [UN-dər-stud-ee] *noun, plural* **-stud•ies** **1** one prepared to take over theatrical part from performer if necessary ▷ *verb transitive* **-stud•ied, -stud•y•ing** **2** work as understudy to (performer)
un•der•take [un-dər-TAYK] *verb transitive* **-took** [-tuuk], **-tak•en, -tak•ing** **1** make oneself responsible for **2** enter upon **3** promise > **un'der•tak•er** *noun* one who arranges funerals > **un'der•tak•ing** *noun* **1** that which is

DICTIONARY • THESAURUS

undecided *adjective* **1** UNSURE, dithering, hesitant, in two minds, irresolute, torn, uncertain
2 UNSETTLED, debatable, iffy (*informal*), indefinite, moot, open, unconcluded, undetermined
undefined *adjective* **1** UNSPECIFIED, imprecise, inexact, unclear
2 INDISTINCT, formless, indefinite, vague
undeniable *adjective* CERTAIN, clear, incontrovertible, indisputable, obvious, sure, unquestionable
under *preposition* **1** BELOW, beneath, underneath
2 SUBJECT TO, governed by, secondary to, subordinate to
▷ *adverb* **3** BELOW, beneath, down, lower
underclothes *plural noun* UNDERWEAR, lingerie, undergarments, undies (*informal*)
undercover *adjective* SECRET, concealed, covert, hidden, private
undercurrent *noun* **1** UNDERTOW, riptide
2 UNDERTONE, atmosphere, feeling, hint, overtone, sense, suggestion, tendency, tinge, vibes (*slang*)
underdog *noun* OUTSIDER, little fellow (*informal*)
underestimate *verb* UNDERRATE, belittle, minimize, miscalculate, undervalue
undergo *verb* EXPERIENCE, bear, endure, go through, stand, suffer, sustain
underground *adjective* **1** SUBTERRANEAN, buried, covered
2 SECRET, clandestine, covert, hidden
▷ *noun* **3** ▷ **the underground** THE RESISTANCE, partisans
undergrowth *noun* SCRUB, bracken, briars, brush, underbrush
underhand *or* **underhanded** *adjective* SLY, crafty, deceitful, devious, dishonest, down and dirty (*informal*), furtive, secret, sneaky, stealthy
underline *verb* **1** UNDERSCORE, mark
2 EMPHASIZE, accentuate, highlight, stress
underlying *adjective* FUNDAMENTAL, basic, elementary, intrinsic, primary, prime
undermine *verb* WEAKEN, disable, sabotage, sap, subvert
underprivileged *adjective* DISADVANTAGED, deprived, destitute, impoverished, needy, poor
underrate *verb* UNDERESTIMATE, belittle, discount, undervalue
undersized *adjective* STUNTED, dwarfish, miniature, pygmy *or* pigmy, small
understand *verb* **1** COMPREHEND, conceive, fathom, follow, get, grasp, perceive, realize, see, take in
2 BELIEVE, assume, gather, presume, suppose, think
understandable *adjective* REASONABLE, justifiable, legitimate, natural, to be expected
understanding *noun* **1** PERCEPTION, appreciation, awareness, comprehension, discernment, grasp, insight, judgment, knowledge, sense
2 INTERPRETATION, belief, idea, judgment, notion, opinion, perception, view
3 AGREEMENT, accord, pact
▷ *adjective* **4** SYMPATHETIC, compassionate, considerate, kind, patient, sensitive, tolerant
understood *adjective* **1** IMPLIED, implicit, inferred, tacit, unspoken, unstated
2 ASSUMED, accepted, taken for granted
understudy *noun* STAND-IN, replacement, reserve, substitute
undertake *verb* AGREE, bargain, contract, engage, guarantee, pledge, promise

undertaken 2 project 3 guarantee
un•der•tone [UN-dər-tohn] *noun* 1 quiet, dropped tone of voice 2 underlying tone or suggestion
un•der•tow [UN-dər-toh] *noun* 1 backwash of wave 2 current beneath surface moving in different direction from surface current
un•der•wear [UN-dər-wair] *noun* (*also* **un'der•clothes**) garments worn next to skin
un•der•world [UN-dər-wurld] *noun* 1 criminals and their associates 2 *mythology* abode of the dead
un•der•write [un-dər-RĪT] *verb transitive* **-wrote, -writ•ten, -writ•ing** 1 agree to pay 2 accept liability in insurance policy > **un'der•writ•er** *noun* agent for insurance or stock issue
un•do [un-DOO] *verb transitive* **-did, -done, -do•ing** 1 untie, unfasten 2 reverse 3 cause downfall of > **un•do'ing** *noun* > **un•done** *adjective* [un-DUN] 1 ruined 2 not performed
un•du•late [UN-jə-layt] *verb* **-lat•ed, -lat•ing** move up and down like waves > **un•du•la'tion** *noun*
un•earth [un-URTH] *verb transitive* 1 dig up 2 discover
un•eas•y [un-EE-zee] *adjective* **-eas•i•er, -eas•i•est** 1 anxious 2 uncomfortable > **un•eas'i•ness** [-nis] *noun*
un•em•ployed [un-im-PLOID] *adjective* having no paid employment, out of work

DICTIONARY **U** THESAURUS

undertaking *noun* 1 TASK, affair, attempt, business, effort, endeavor, enterprise, operation, project, venture
2 PROMISE, assurance, commitment, pledge, vow, word
undertone *noun* 1 MURMUR, whisper
2 UNDERCURRENT, hint, suggestion, tinge, touch, trace
undervalue *verb* UNDERRATE, depreciate, hold cheap, minimize, misjudge, underestimate
underwater *adjective* SUBMERGED, submarine, sunken
under way *adjective* BEGUN, going on, in progress, started
underwear *noun* UNDERCLOTHES, lingerie, undergarments, underthings, undies (*informal*)
underweight *adjective* SKINNY, emaciated, half-starved, puny, skin and bone (*informal*), undernourished, undersized
underworld *noun* 1 CRIMINALS, gangland (*informal*), gangsters, organized crime
2 NETHER WORLD, Hades, nether regions
underwrite *verb* 1 FINANCE, back, fund, guarantee, insure, sponsor, subsidize
2 SIGN, endorse, initial
undesirable *adjective* OBJECTIONABLE, disagreeable, distasteful, unacceptable, unattractive, unsuitable, unwanted, unwelcome
undeveloped *adjective* POTENTIAL, immature, latent
undignified *adjective* UNSEEMLY, improper, indecorous, inelegant, unbecoming, unsuitable
undisciplined *adjective* UNCONTROLLED, obstreperous, unrestrained, unruly, wayward, wild, willful
undisguised *adjective* OBVIOUS, blatant, evident, explicit, open, overt, patent, unconcealed
undisputed *adjective* ACKNOWLEDGED, accepted, certain, indisputable, recognized, unchallenged, undeniable, undoubted
undistinguished *adjective* ORDINARY, everyday, mediocre, unexceptional, unimpressive, unremarkable
undisturbed *adjective* 1 QUIET, tranquil
2 CALM, collected, composed, placid, sedate, serene, tranquil, unfazed (*informal*), unperturbed, untroubled
undivided *adjective* COMPLETE, entire, exclusive, full, solid, thorough, undistracted, united, whole
undo *verb* 1 OPEN, disentangle, loose, unbutton, unfasten, untie
2 REVERSE, annul, cancel, invalidate, neutralize, offset
3 RUIN, defeat, destroy, overturn, quash, shatter, subvert, undermine, upset, wreck
undoing *noun* DOWNFALL, collapse, defeat, disgrace, overthrow, reversal, ruin, shame
undone *adjective* UNFINISHED, left, neglected, omitted, unfulfilled, unperformed
undoubted *adjective* CERTAIN, acknowledged, definite, indisputable, indubitable, sure, undisputed, unquestioned
undoubtedly *adverb* CERTAINLY, assuredly, definitely, doubtless, surely, without doubt
undress *verb* 1 STRIP, disrobe, shed, take off one's clothes
▷ *noun* 2 NAKEDNESS, nudity
undue *adjective* EXCESSIVE, extreme, improper, needless, uncalled-for, unnecessary, unwarranted
unduly *adverb* EXCESSIVELY, overly, unnecessarily, unreasonably
undying *adjective* ETERNAL, constant, deathless, everlasting, infinite, permanent, perpetual, twenty-four-seven (*slang*), unending
unearth *verb* 1 DISCOVER, expose, find, reveal, uncover
2 DIG UP, dredge up, excavate, exhume
unearthly *adjective* EERIE, ghostly, phantom, spectral, spooky (*informal*), strange, supernatural, uncanny, weird
uneasiness *noun* ANXIETY, disquiet, doubt, misgiving, qualms, trepidation, worry
uneasy *adjective* 1 ANXIOUS, disturbed, edgy, nervous, on edge, perturbed, troubled, twitchy (*informal*), uncomfortable, wired (*slang*), worried
2 AWKWARD, insecure, precarious, shaky, strained, tense, uncomfortable
uneconomic *adjective* UNPROFITABLE, loss-making, nonpaying
uneducated *adjective* 1 IGNORANT, illiterate, unlettered, unschooled, untaught
2 LOWBROW, uncultivated, uncultured
unemotional *adjective* IMPASSIVE, apathetic, cold, cool, phlegmatic, reserved, undemonstrative, unexcitable
unemployed *adjective* OUT OF WORK, idle, jobless, laid off, redundant
unending *adjective* PERPETUAL, continual, endless, eternal, everlasting, interminable, unceasing
unendurable *adjective* UNBEARABLE, insufferable, insupportable, intolerable
unenthusiastic *adjective* INDIFFERENT, apathetic, half-hearted, nonchalant

> **un•em•ploy'ment** [-mənt] *noun*
un•e•quiv'o•cal *adjective* completely clear in meaning
un•err•ing [un-ER-ing] *adjective* 1 not missing the mark 2 consistently accurate
un•fail'ing *adjective* continuous or reliable
un•fair' *adjective* not right, fair, or just
un•fit' *adjective* 1 unqualified or unsuitable 2 in poor physical condition
un•fold' *verb* 1 open or spread out from a folded state 2 reveal or be revealed
un•for•get'ta•ble *adjective* impossible to forget, memorable
un•for'tu•nate *adjective* 1 unlucky, unsuccessful, or unhappy 2 regrettable or unsuitable ▷ *noun* 3 unlucky person
un•gain•ly [un-GAYN-lee] *adjective* **-li•er, -li•est** awkward, clumsy > **un•gain'li•ness** [-nis] *noun*
un•guent [UNG-gwənt] *noun* ointment
un•hap'py *adjective* 1 sad or depressed 2

unenviable *adjective* UNPLEASANT, disagreeable, uncomfortable, undesirable
unequal *adjective* 1 DIFFERENT, differing, disparate, dissimilar, unlike, unmatched, varying
2 DISPROPORTIONATE, asymmetrical, ill-matched, irregular, unbalanced, uneven
unequaled *adjective* INCOMPARABLE, matchless, paramount, peerless, supreme, unparalleled, unrivaled
unequivocal *adjective* CLEAR, absolute, certain, definite, explicit, incontrovertible, indubitable, manifest, plain, unambiguous
unerring *adjective* ACCURATE, exact, infallible, perfect, sure, unfailing
unethical *adjective* DISHONEST, disreputable, illegal, immoral, improper, shady (*informal*), unprincipled, unscrupulous, wrong
uneven *adjective* 1 ROUGH, bumpy
2 VARIABLE, broken, fitful, irregular, jerky, patchy, spasmodic
3 UNBALANCED, lopsided, odd
4 UNEQUAL, ill-matched, unfair
uneventful *adjective* HUMDRUM, boring, dull, ho-hum (*informal*), monotonous, routine, tedious, unexciting
unexceptional *adjective* ORDINARY, commonplace, conventional, mediocre, normal, pedestrian, undistinguished, unremarkable
unexpected *adjective* UNFORESEEN, abrupt, chance, fortuitous, sudden, surprising, unanticipated, unlooked-for, unpredictable
unfailing *adjective* 1 CONTINUOUS, boundless, endless, persistent, unflagging
2 RELIABLE, certain, dependable, faithful, loyal, staunch, sure, true
unfair *adjective* 1 BIASED, bigoted, one-sided, partial, partisan, prejudiced, unjust
2 UNSCRUPULOUS, dishonest, unethical, unsporting, wrongful
unfaithful *adjective* 1 FAITHLESS, adulterous, two-timing (*informal*), untrue
2 DISLOYAL, deceitful, faithless, false, traitorous, treacherous, untrustworthy
unfamiliar *adjective* STRANGE, alien, different, new, novel, unknown, unusual
unfashionable *adjective* PASSÉ, antiquated, dated, dumpy (*informal*), frowzy, homely (*United States*), obsolete, old-fashioned, old hat
unfasten *verb* UNDO, detach, let go, loosen, open, separate, unlace, untie
unfathomable *adjective* 1 BAFFLING, deep, impenetrable, incomprehensible, indecipherable, inexplicable, profound
2 IMMEASURABLE, bottomless, unmeasured
unfavorable *adjective* 1 ADVERSE, contrary, inauspicious, unfortunate, unlucky, unpropitious
2 HOSTILE, inimical, negative, unfriendly
unfeeling *adjective* 1 HARDHEARTED, apathetic, callous, cold, cruel, heartless, insensitive, pitiless, uncaring
2 NUMB, insensate, insensible
unfinished *adjective* 1 INCOMPLETE, half-done, uncompleted, undone
2 ROUGH, bare, crude, natural, raw, unrefined
unfit *adjective* 1 INCAPABLE, inadequate, incompetent, lousy (*slang*), no good, unqualified, useless
2 UNSUITABLE, inadequate, ineffective, unsuited, useless
3 OUT OF SHAPE, feeble, flabby, in poor condition, unhealthy
unflappable *adjective* IMPERTURBABLE, calm, collected, composed, cool, impassive, level-headed, self-possessed
unflattering *adjective* 1 BLUNT, candid, critical, honest
2 UNATTRACTIVE, dumpy (*informal*), frowzy, homely (*United States*), plain, unbecoming
unflinching *adjective* DETERMINED, firm, immovable, resolute, staunch, steadfast, steady, unfaltering
unfold *verb* 1 OPEN, expand, spread out, undo, unfurl, unravel, unroll, unwrap
2 REVEAL, disclose, divulge, make known, present, show, uncover
unforeseen *adjective* UNEXPECTED, accidental, sudden, surprising, unanticipated, unpredicted
unforgettable *adjective* MEMORABLE, exceptional, impressive, notable
unforgivable *adjective* INEXCUSABLE, deplorable, disgraceful, shameful, unpardonable
unfortunate *adjective* 1 DISASTROUS, adverse, calamitous, ill-fated
2 UNLUCKY, cursed, doomed, hapless, unhappy, unsuccessful, wretched
3 REGRETTABLE, deplorable, lamentable, unsuitable
unfounded *adjective* GROUNDLESS, baseless, false, idle, spurious, unjustified
unfriendly *adjective* 1 HOSTILE, aloof, chilly, cold, distant, uncongenial, unsociable
2 UNFAVORABLE, alien, hostile, inhospitable
ungainly *adjective* AWKWARD, clumsy, inelegant, lumbering, ungraceful
ungodly *adjective* 1 UNREASONABLE, dreadful, intolerable, outrageous, unearthly
2 WICKED, corrupt, depraved, godless, immoral, impious, irreligious, profane, sinful
ungracious *adjective* BAD-MANNERED, churlish, discourteous, impolite, rude, uncivil, unmannerly
ungrateful *adjective* UNAPPRECIATIVE, unmindful, unthankful
unguarded *adjective* 1 UNPROTECTED,

unfortunate or wretched
un•health'y *adjective* 1 likely to cause poor health 2 not fit or well 3 morbid, unnatural
uni- *combining form* one: *unicorn; uniform*
u•ni•corn [YOO-ni-korn] *noun* mythical horselike animal with single long horn
u•ni•form [YOO-ni-form] *noun* 1 identifying clothes worn by members of same group e.g. soldiers, nurses, etc. ▷ *adjective* 2 not changing, unvarying 3 regular, consistent 4 conforming to same standard or rule > **u•ni•form'i•ty** *noun* sameness > **u'ni•form•ly** *adverb*
u•ni•fy [YOO-nə-fī] *verb* **-fied, -fy•ing** make or become one > **u•ni•fi•ca'tion** [-KAY-shən] *noun*
u•ni•lat•er•al [yoo-nə-LAT-ər-əl] *adjective* 1 one-sided 2 (of contract) binding one party only
un•ion [YOON-yən] *noun* 1 joining into one 2 state of being joined 3 result of being joined 4 federation, combination of states, etc. 5 labor union, trade union > **un'ion•ize** *verb* **-ized, -iz•ing** organize (workers) into labor union
u•nique [yoo-NEEK] *adjective* 1 being only one of its kind 2 unparalleled
u•ni•son [YOO-nə-sən] *noun* 1 *mus.* singing, etc. of same note as others 2 agreement, harmony, concord
u•nit [YOO-nit] *noun* 1 single thing or person 2 standard quantity 3 group of people or things with one purpose
u•nite [yoo-NĪT] *verb transitive* **u•nit•ed,**

DICTIONARY

U

THESAURUS

defenseless, undefended, vulnerable
2 CARELESS, heedless, ill-considered, imprudent, incautious, rash, thoughtless, unthinking, unwary
unhappiness *noun* SADNESS, blues, dejection, depression, despondency, gloom, heartache, low spirits, melancholy, misery, sorrow, wretchedness
unhappy *adjective* 1 SAD, blue, dejected, depressed, despondent, downcast, melancholy, miserable, mournful, sorrowful
2 UNLUCKY, cursed, hapless, ill-fated, unfortunate, wretched
unharmed *adjective* UNHURT, intact, safe, sound, undamaged, unscathed, whole
unhealthy *adjective* 1 HARMFUL, detrimental, insalubrious, insanitary, unwholesome
2 SICK, ailing, delicate, feeble, frail, infirm, invalid, sickly, unwell
unheard-of *adjective* 1 UNPRECEDENTED, inconceivable, new, novel, singular, unique
2 SHOCKING, disgraceful, outrageous, preposterous
3 OBSCURE, unfamiliar, unknown
unhesitating *adjective* 1 INSTANT, immediate, prompt, ready
2 WHOLEHEARTED, resolute, unfaltering, unquestioning, unreserved
unholy *adjective* EVIL, corrupt, profane, sinful, ungodly, wicked
unhurried *adjective* LEISURELY, easy, sedate, slow
unidentified *adjective* UNNAMED, anonymous, nameless, unfamiliar, unrecognized
unification *noun* UNION, alliance, amalgamation, coalescence, coalition, confederation, federation, uniting
uniform *noun* 1 OUTFIT, costume, dress, garb, habit, livery, regalia, suit
▷ *adjective* 2 UNVARYING, consistent, constant, even, regular, smooth, unchanging
3 ALIKE, equal, like, on a level playing field (*informal*), same, similar
uniformity *noun* 1 REGULARITY, constancy, evenness, invariability, sameness, similarity
2 MONOTONY, dullness, flatness, sameness, tedium
unify *verb* UNITE, amalgamate, combine, confederate, consolidate, join, merge
unimaginable *adjective* INCONCEIVABLE, fantastic, impossible, incredible, unbelievable
unimaginative *adjective* UNORIGINAL, banal, derivative, dull, hackneyed, ordinary, pedestrian, predictable, prosaic, uncreative, uninspired
unimportant *adjective* INSIGNIFICANT, inconsequential, irrelevant, minor, paltry, petty, trifling, trivial, worthless
uninhabited *adjective* DESERTED, barren, desolate, empty, unpopulated, vacant
uninhibited *adjective* 1 UNSELFCONSCIOUS, free, liberated, natural, open, relaxed, spontaneous, unrepressed, unreserved
2 UNRESTRAINED, free, unbridled, unchecked, unconstrained, uncontrolled, unrestricted
uninspired *adjective* UNIMAGINATIVE, banal, dull, humdrum, ordinary, prosaic, unexciting, unoriginal
unintelligent *adjective* STUPID, braindead (*informal*), brainless, dense, dull, foolish, obtuse, slow, thick
unintelligible *adjective* INCOMPREHENSIBLE, inarticulate, incoherent, indistinct, jumbled, meaningless, muddled
unintentional *adjective* ACCIDENTAL, casual, inadvertent, involuntary, unconscious, unintended
uninterested *adjective* INDIFFERENT, apathetic, blasé, bored, listless, unconcerned
uninteresting *adjective* BORING, drab, dreary, dry, dull, flat, humdrum, monotonous, tedious, unexciting
uninterrupted *adjective* CONTINUOUS, constant, nonstop, steady, sustained, unbroken
union *noun* 1 JOINING, amalgamation, blend, combination, conjunction, fusion, mixture, uniting
2 ALLIANCE, association, coalition, confederacy, federation, league
3 AGREEMENT, accord, concord, harmony, unanimity, unison, unity
unique *adjective* 1 SINGLE, lone, only, solitary
2 UNPARALLELED, incomparable, inimitable, matchless, unequaled, unmatched, unrivaled
unison *noun* AGREEMENT, accord, accordance, concert, concord, harmony, unity
unit *noun* 1 ITEM, entity, whole
2 PART, component, constituent, element, member, section, segment
3 SECTION, detachment, group
4 MEASURE, measurement, quantity
unite *verb* 1 JOIN, amalgamate, blend, combine, couple, fuse, link, merge, unify
2 COOPERATE, ally, band, join forces, pool
united *adjective* 1 COMBINED, affiliated, allied, banded together, collective, concerted, pooled, unified

u•nit•ing 1 join into one, connect 2 associate 3 cause to adhere ▷ *verb intransitive* **u•nit•ed, u•nit•ing** 4 become one 5 combine > **u'ni•ty** [-nə-tee] *noun* 1 state of being one 2 harmony 3 agreement, uniformity 4 combination of separate parts into connected whole 5 *mathematics* the number one

u•ni•verse [YOO-nə-vurs] *noun* 1 all existing things considered as constituting systematic whole 2 the world > **u•ni•ver'sal** [-səl] *adjective* 1 relating to all things or all people 2 applying to all members of a community > **u•ni•ver•sal'i•ty** [-SAL-ə-tee] *noun*

u•ni•ver•si•ty [yoo-nə-VUR-si-tee] *noun, plural* **-ties** educational institution for research, study, examination and award of degrees in various branches of learning

un•kempt' *adjective* of rough or uncared-for appearance

un•less' *conjunction* if not, except

un•men'tion•a•ble *adjective* unsuitable as a topic of conversation

un•moved' *adjective* not affected by emotion, indifferent

un•or'tho•dox *adjective* 1 (of ideas, methods, etc.) unconventional and not generally accepted

DICTIONARY • THESAURUS

2 IN AGREEMENT, agreed, of one mind, of the same opinion, unanimous

unity *noun* 1 WHOLENESS, entity, integrity, oneness, singleness, union
2 AGREEMENT, accord, assent, concord, consensus, harmony, solidarity, unison

universal *adjective* WIDESPREAD, common, general, total, unlimited, whole, worldwide

universally *adverb* EVERYWHERE, always, invariably, without exception

universe *noun* COSMOS, creation, macrocosm, nature

unjust *adjective* UNFAIR, biased, one-sided, partial, partisan, prejudiced, wrong, wrongful

unjustifiable *adjective* INEXCUSABLE, indefensible, outrageous, unacceptable, unforgivable, unpardonable, wrong

unkempt *adjective* 1 UNCOMBED, shaggy, tousled
2 UNTIDY, disheveled, disordered, messy, slovenly, ungroomed

unkind *adjective* CRUEL, harsh, malicious, mean, nasty, spiteful, uncharitable, unfeeling, unfriendly, unsympathetic

unknown *adjective* 1 HIDDEN, concealed, dark, mysterious, secret, unrevealed
2 STRANGE, alien, new
3 UNIDENTIFIED, anonymous, nameless, uncharted, undiscovered, unexplored, unnamed
4 OBSCURE, humble, unfamiliar

unlawful *adjective* ILLEGAL, banned, criminal, forbidden, illicit, outlawed, prohibited

unleash *verb* RELEASE, free, let go, let loose

unlike *adjective* DIFFERENT, dissimilar, distinct, diverse, not alike, opposite, unequal

unlikely *adjective* 1 IMPROBABLE, doubtful, faint, remote, slight
2 UNBELIEVABLE, implausible, incredible, questionable

unlimited *adjective* 1 INFINITE, boundless, countless, endless, extensive, great, immense, limitless, unbounded, vast
2 COMPLETE, absolute, full, total, unqualified, unrestricted

unload *verb* EMPTY, discharge, dump, lighten, relieve, unpack

unlock *verb* OPEN, release, undo, unfasten, unlatch

unlooked-for *adjective* UNEXPECTED, chance, fortuitous, surprising, unanticipated, unforeseen, unpredicted

unloved *adjective* NEGLECTED, forsaken, loveless, rejected, spurned, unpopular, unwanted

unlucky *adjective* 1 UNFORTUNATE, cursed, hapless, luckless, miserable, unhappy, wretched
2 ILL-FATED, doomed, inauspicious, ominous, unfavorable

unmarried *adjective* SINGLE, bachelor, maiden, unattached, unwed

unmask *verb* REVEAL, disclose, discover, expose, lay bare, uncover

unmentionable *adjective* TABOO, forbidden, indecent, obscene, scandalous, shameful, shocking, unspeakable

unmerciful *adjective* MERCILESS, brutal, cruel, hard, implacable, pitiless, remorseless, ruthless

unmistakable *adjective* CLEAR, certain, distinct, evident, manifest, obvious, plain, sure, unambiguous

unmitigated *adjective* 1 UNRELIEVED, intense, persistent, unalleviated, unbroken, undiminished
2 COMPLETE, absolute, arrant, downright, outright, sheer, thorough, utter

unmoved *adjective* UNAFFECTED, cold, impassive, indifferent, unimpressed, unresponsive, untouched

unnatural *adjective* 1 STRANGE, extraordinary, freakish, outlandish, queer
2 ABNORMAL, anomalous, irregular, odd, perverse, perverted, unusual
3 FALSE, affected, artificial, feigned, forced, insincere, phoney *or* phony (*informal*), stiff, stilted

unnecessary *adjective* NEEDLESS, expendable, inessential, redundant, superfluous, unneeded, unrequired

unnerve *verb* INTIMIDATE, demoralize, discourage, dishearten, dismay, faze, fluster, frighten, psych out (*informal*), rattle (*informal*), shake, upset

unnoticed *adjective* UNOBSERVED, disregarded, ignored, neglected, overlooked, unheeded, unperceived, unrecognized, unseen

unobtrusive *adjective* INCONSPICUOUS, low-key, modest, quiet, restrained, retiring, self-effacing, unassuming

unoccupied *adjective* EMPTY, uninhabited, vacant

unofficial *adjective* UNAUTHORIZED, informal, private, unconfirmed

unorthodox *adjective* UNCONVENTIONAL, abnormal, irregular, off-the-wall (*slang*), unusual

unpaid *adjective* 1 VOLUNTARY, honorary, unsalaried
2 OWING, due, outstanding, overdue, payable, unsettled

unpalatable *adjective* UNPLEASANT, disagreeable, distasteful, horrid, offensive, repugnant, unappetizing, unsavory

unparalleled *adjective* UNEQUALED,

2 (of a person) having unusual opinions or methods

un•pleas'ant *adjective* not pleasant or agreeable

un•rav•el [un-RAV-əl] *verb transitive* **-eled, -el•ing** undo, untangle

un•re•mit•ting [un-ri-MIT-ing] *adjective* never slackening or stopping

un•re•quit'ed *adjective* not returned: *unrequited love*

un•roll' *verb* open out or unwind (something rolled or coiled) or (of something rolled or coiled) become opened out or unwound

un•ru•ly [un-ROO-lee] *adjective* **-li•er, -li•est** badly behaved, ungovernable, disorderly

un•sa•vor•y [un-SAY-və-ree] *adjective* distasteful, disagreeable

un•sight•ly [un-SĪT-lee] *adjective* ugly

un•suit'a•ble *adjective* not right or appropriate for a particular purpose

un•ten•a•ble [un-TEN-ə-bəl] *adjective* (of

DICTIONARY

U

THESAURUS

incomparable, matchless, superlative, unique, unmatched, unprecedented, unsurpassed

unpardonable *adjective* UNFORGIVABLE, deplorable, disgraceful, indefensible, inexcusable

unperturbed *adjective* CALM, as cool as a cucumber, composed, cool, placid, unfazed (*informal*), unruffled, untroubled, unworried

unpleasant *adjective* NASTY, bad, disagreeable, displeasing, distasteful, horrid, objectionable

unpopular *adjective* DISLIKED, rejected, shunned, unwanted, unwelcome

unprecedented *adjective* EXTRAORDINARY, abnormal, new, novel, original, remarkable, singular, unheard-of

unpredictable *adjective* INCONSTANT, chance, changeable, doubtful, erratic, random, unforeseeable, unreliable, variable

unprejudiced *adjective* IMPARTIAL, balanced, fair, just, objective, open-minded, unbiased

unprepared *adjective* 1 TAKEN OFF GUARD, surprised, unaware, unready
2 IMPROVISED, ad-lib, off the cuff (*informal*), spontaneous

unpretentious *adjective* MODEST, dumpy (*informal*), homely, humble, plain, simple, straightforward, unaffected, unassuming, unostentatious

unprincipled *adjective* DISHONEST, amoral, crooked, devious, immoral, underhand, unethical, unscrupulous

unproductive *adjective* 1 USELESS, fruitless, futile, idle, ineffective, unprofitable, unrewarding, vain
2 BARREN, fruitless, sterile

unprofessional *adjective* 1 UNETHICAL, improper, lax, negligent, unprincipled
2 AMATEURISH, incompetent, inefficient, inexpert

unprotected *adjective* VULNERABLE, defenseless, helpless, open, undefended

unqualified *adjective* 1 UNFIT, ill-equipped, incapable, incompetent, ineligible, unprepared
2 TOTAL, absolute, complete, downright, outright, thorough, utter

unquestionable *adjective* CERTAIN, absolute, clear, conclusive, definite, incontrovertible, indisputable, sure, undeniable, unequivocal, unmistakable

unravel *verb* 1 UNDO, disentangle, free, separate, untangle, unwind
2 SOLVE, explain, figure out (*informal*), resolve, work out

unreal *adjective* 1 IMAGINARY, dreamlike, fabulous, fanciful, illusory, make-believe, visionary
2 INSUBSTANTIAL, immaterial, intangible, nebulous
3 FAKE, artificial, false, insincere, mock, pretended, sham

unrealistic *adjective* IMPRACTICAL, impracticable, improbable, romantic, unworkable

unreasonable *adjective* 1 EXCESSIVE, extortionate, immoderate, undue, unfair, unjust, unwarranted
2 BIASED, blinkered, opinionated

unrelated *adjective* 1 DIFFERENT, unconnected, unlike
2 IRRELEVANT, extraneous, inapplicable, inappropriate, unconnected

unreliable *adjective* 1 UNDEPENDABLE, irresponsible, treacherous, untrustworthy
2 UNCERTAIN, deceptive, fallible, false, implausible, inaccurate, unsound

unrepentant *adjective* IMPENITENT, abandoned, callous, hardened, incorrigible, shameless, unremorseful

unreserved *adjective* 1 TOTAL, absolute, complete, entire, full, unlimited, wholehearted
2 OPEN, demonstrative, extrovert, free, outgoing, uninhibited, unrestrained

unresolved *adjective* UNDECIDED, doubtful, moot, unanswered, undetermined, unsettled, unsolved, vague

unrest *noun* DISCONTENT, agitation, discord, dissension, protest, rebellion, sedition, strife

unrestrained *adjective* UNCONTROLLED, abandoned, free, immoderate, intemperate, unbounded, unbridled, unchecked, uninhibited

unrestricted *adjective* 1 UNLIMITED, absolute, free, open, unbounded, unregulated
2 OPEN, public

unrivaled *adjective* UNPARALLELED, beyond compare, incomparable, matchless, supreme, unequaled, unmatched, unsurpassed

unruly *adjective* UNCONTROLLABLE, disobedient, mutinous, rebellious, wayward, wild, willful

unsafe *adjective* DANGEROUS, hazardous, insecure, perilous, risky, unreliable

unsatisfactory *adjective* UNACCEPTABLE, deficient, disappointing, inadequate, insufficient, lousy (*slang*), not good enough, not up to scratch (*informal*), poor

unsavory *adjective* 1 UNPLEASANT, distasteful, nasty, obnoxious, offensive, repellent, repulsive, revolting, scuzzy (*slang*)
2 UNAPPETIZING, nauseating, sickening, unpalatable

unscathed *adjective* UNHARMED, safe, unhurt, uninjured, unmarked, whole

unscrupulous *adjective* UNPRINCIPLED, corrupt, dishonest, dishonorable, immoral, improper, unethical

unseat *verb* 1 THROW, unhorse, unsaddle
2 DEPOSE, dethrone, displace, oust, overthrow, remove

DICTIONARY • THESAURUS

theories, etc.) incapable of being maintained, defended
un•think•a•ble [un-THING-kə-bəl] *adjective* 1 out of the question 2 inconceivable 3 unreasonable
un•til' *conjunction* 1 up to the time that ▷ *preposition* 2 in or throughout the period before
un•to [UN-too] *preposition* to
un•touched [un-TUCHT] *adjective* 1 not touched 2 not harmed > **un•touch'a•ble** *adjective* 1 not able to be touched ▷ *noun* 2 esp. formerly, non-caste Hindu, forbidden to be touched by one of caste
un•to•ward [un-TORD] *adjective* awkward, inconvenient
un•tram•meled [un-TRAM-əld] *adjective* not confined, not constrained
un•u'su•al *adjective* uncommon or extraordinary
un•wield•y [un-WEEL-dee] *adjective* **-wield•i•er,**

---

unseemly *adjective* IMPROPER, inappropriate, indecorous, unbecoming, undignified, unsuitable
unseen *adjective* UNOBSERVED, concealed, hidden, invisible, obscure, undetected, unnoticed
unselfish *adjective* GENEROUS, altruistic, kind, magnanimous, noble, selfless, self-sacrificing
unsettle *verb* DISTURB, agitate, bother, confuse, disconcert, faze, fluster, perturb, ruffle, trouble, upset
unsettled *adjective* 1 UNSTABLE, disorderly, insecure, shaky, unsteady
2 RESTLESS, agitated, anxious, confused, disturbed, flustered, restive, shaken, tense, wired (*slang*)
3 CHANGING, inconstant, uncertain, variable
unshakable *adjective* FIRM, absolute, fixed, immovable, staunch, steadfast, sure, unswerving, unwavering
unsightly *adjective* UGLY, disagreeable, dumpy (*informal*), hideous, homely (*United States*), horrid, repulsive, scuzzy (*slang*), unattractive
unskilled *adjective* UNPROFESSIONAL, amateurish, inexperienced, unqualified, untrained
unsociable *adjective* UNFRIENDLY, chilly, cold, distant, hostile, retiring, unforthcoming, withdrawn
unsolicited *adjective* UNREQUESTED, gratuitous, unasked for, uncalled-for, uninvited, unsought
unsophisticated *adjective* 1 NATURAL, artless, childlike, guileless, ingenuous, unaffected
2 SIMPLE, dumpy (*informal*), frowzy, homely (*United States*), plain, uncomplicated, unrefined, unspecialized
unsound *adjective* 1 UNHEALTHY, ailing, defective, diseased, ill, unbalanced, unstable, unwell, weak
2 UNRELIABLE, defective, fallacious, false, flawed, illogical, shaky, specious, weak
unspeakable *adjective* 1 INDESCRIBABLE, inconceivable, unbelievable, unimaginable
2 DREADFUL, abominable, appalling, awful, heinous, horrible, monstrous, shocking
unspoiled *or* **unspoilt** *adjective* 1 PERFECT, intact, preserved, unchanged, undamaged, untouched
2 NATURAL, artless, innocent, unaffected
unspoken *adjective* TACIT, implicit, implied, understood, unexpressed, unstated
unstable *adjective* 1 INSECURE, precarious, shaky, tottering, unsettled, unsteady, wobbly
2 CHANGEABLE, fitful, fluctuating, inconstant, unpredictable, variable, volatile
3 UNPREDICTABLE, capricious, changeable, erratic, inconsistent, irrational, temperamental
unsteady *adjective* 1 UNSTABLE, infirm, insecure, precarious, shaky, unsafe, wobbly
2 CHANGEABLE, erratic, inconstant, temperamental, unsettled, volatile
unsuccessful *adjective* 1 USELESS, failed, fruitless, futile, unavailing, unproductive, vain
2 UNLUCKY, hapless, luckless, unfortunate
unsuitable *adjective* INAPPROPRIATE, improper, inapposite, inapt, ineligible, unacceptable, unbecoming, unfit, unfitting, unseemly
unsure *adjective* 1 UNCONFIDENT, insecure, unassured
2 DOUBTFUL, distrustful, dubious, hesitant, mistrustful, skeptical, suspicious, unconvinced
unsuspecting *adjective* TRUSTING, credulous, gullible, trustful, unwary
unswerving *adjective* CONSTANT, firm, resolute, single-minded, staunch, steadfast, steady, true, unwavering
unsympathetic *adjective* HARD, callous, cold, cruel, harsh, heartless, insensitive, unfeeling, unkind, unmoved
untangle *verb* DISENTANGLE, extricate, unravel, unsnarl
untenable *adjective* UNSUSTAINABLE, groundless, illogical, indefensible, insupportable, shaky, unsound, weak
unthinkable *adjective* 1 IMPOSSIBLE, absurd, out of the question, unreasonable
2 INCONCEIVABLE, implausible, incredible, unimaginable
untidy *adjective* MESSY, chaotic, cluttered, disarrayed, disordered, jumbled, littered, muddled, shambolic, unkempt
untie *verb* UNDO, free, loosen, release, unbind, unfasten, unknot, unlace
untimely *adjective* 1 EARLY, premature
2 ILL-TIMED, awkward, inappropriate, inconvenient, inopportune, mistimed
untiring *adjective* TIRELESS, constant, determined, dogged, persevering, steady, unflagging, unremitting
untold *adjective* 1 INDESCRIBABLE, inexpressible, undreamed of, unimaginable, unthinkable, unutterable
2 COUNTLESS, incalculable, innumerable, myriad, numberless, uncountable
untouched *adjective* UNHARMED, intact, undamaged, unhurt, uninjured, unscathed
untoward *adjective* 1 ANNOYING, awkward, inconvenient, irritating, troublesome, unfortunate
2 UNLUCKY, adverse, inauspicious, inopportune, unfavorable
untrained *adjective* AMATEUR, green, inexperienced, raw, uneducated, unqualified, unschooled, unskilled, untaught
untroubled *adjective* UNDISTURBED, calm, cool, peaceful, placid, tranquil, unfazed (*informal*), unperturbed, unworried

-**wield•i•est** 1 awkward, big, heavy to handle 2 clumsy
un•wit'ting *adjective* 1 not knowing 2 not intentional
un•wrap' *verb* remove the wrapping from (something)
up *preposition* 1 from lower to higher position 2 along ▷ *adverb* 3 in or to higher position, source, activity, etc. 4 indicating completion > **up'ward** *adjective, adverb* > **up'wards** *adverb* 1 up against 2 confronted with
up- *combining form* up, upper, upwards: *uproot; upgrade*
up•braid [up-BRAYD] *verb transitive* scold, reproach
up'bring•ing *noun* rearing and education of children
up•date [up-DAYT] *verb transitive* **-dat•ed, -dat•ing** bring up to date ▷ *noun*
up•front [up-frunt] *adjective* 1 (*informal*) open, frank ▷ *adjective, adverb* 2 (*informal*) (of money) paid out at beginning of business arrangement
up•grade [up-GRAYD] *verb transitive* **-grad•ed, -grad•ing** 1 promote to higher position 2 improve
up•heav•al [up-HEE-vəl] *noun* sudden or violent disturbance
up•hold [up-HOHLD] *verb transitive* **-held, -hold•ing** maintain, support, etc.
up•hol•ster [up-HOHL-stər] *verb transitive* fit springs, padding and coverings on chairs, etc. > **up•hol'ster•er** *noun* one who does this work > **up•hol'ster•y** *noun*
up'keep *noun* act, process or cost of keeping something in good repair
up•lift' *verb transitive* 1 raise aloft ▷ *noun* [UP-lift]

DICTIONARY

U

THESAURUS

untrue *adjective* 1 FALSE, deceptive, dishonest, erroneous, inaccurate, incorrect, lying, mistaken, wrong
2 UNFAITHFUL, deceitful, disloyal, faithless, false, inconstant, treacherous, untrustworthy
untrustworthy *adjective* UNRELIABLE, deceitful, devious, dishonest, disloyal, false, slippery, treacherous, tricky
untruth *noun* LIE, deceit, falsehood, fib, story, white lie
untruthful *adjective* DISHONEST, deceitful, deceptive, false, lying, mendacious
unusual *adjective* EXTRAORDINARY, curious, different, exceptional, odd, queer, rare, remarkable, singular, strange, uncommon, unconventional
unveil *verb* REVEAL, disclose, divulge, expose, make known, uncover
unwanted *adjective* UNDESIRED, outcast, rejected, uninvited, unneeded, unsolicited, unwelcome
unwarranted *adjective* UNNECESSARY, gratuitous, groundless, indefensible, inexcusable, uncalled-for, unjustified, unprovoked
unwavering *adjective* STEADY, consistent, determined, immovable, resolute, staunch, steadfast, unshakable, unswerving
unwelcome *adjective* 1 UNWANTED, excluded, rejected, unacceptable, undesirable
2 DISAGREEABLE, displeasing, distasteful, undesirable, unpleasant
unwell *adjective* ILL, ailing, sick, sickly, under the weather (*informal*), unhealthy
unwholesome *adjective* 1 HARMFUL, deleterious, noxious, poisonous, unhealthy
2 WICKED, bad, corrupting, degrading, demoralizing, evil, immoral
unwieldy *adjective* 1 AWKWARD, cumbersome, inconvenient, unmanageable
2 BULKY, clumsy, hefty, massive, ponderous
unwilling *adjective* RELUCTANT, averse, disinclined, grudging, indisposed, loath, resistant, unenthusiastic
unwind *verb* 1 UNRAVEL, slacken, uncoil, undo, unroll, untwine, untwist
2 RELAX, de-stress, loosen up, take it easy, wind down
unwise *adjective* FOOLISH, foolhardy, improvident, imprudent, inadvisable, injudicious, rash, reckless, senseless, silly, stupid
unwitting *adjective* 1 UNINTENTIONAL, accidental, chance, inadvertent, involuntary, unplanned
2 UNKNOWING, ignorant, innocent, unaware, unconscious, unsuspecting
unworldly *adjective* 1 SPIRITUAL, metaphysical, nonmaterialistic
2 NAIVE, idealistic, innocent, unsophisticated
unworthy *adjective* 1 UNDESERVING, not fit for, not good enough
2 DISHONORABLE, base, contemptible, degrading, discreditable, disgraceful, disreputable, ignoble, lousy (*slang*), shameful
3 ▷ **unworthy of** UNBEFITTING, beneath, inappropriate, unbecoming, unfitting, unseemly, unsuitable
unwritten *adjective* 1 ORAL, vocal
2 CUSTOMARY, accepted, tacit, understood
unyielding *adjective* FIRM, adamant, immovable, inflexible, obdurate, obstinate, resolute, rigid, stiff-necked, stubborn, tough, uncompromising
upbeat *adjective* CHEERFUL, cheery, encouraging, hopeful, optimistic, positive
upbraid *verb* SCOLD, admonish, berate, rebuke, reprimand, reproach, reprove
upbringing *noun* EDUCATION, breeding, raising, rearing, training
update *verb* REVISE, amend, bring up to date, modernize, renew
upgrade *verb* PROMOTE, advance, better, elevate, enhance, improve, raise
upheaval *noun* DISTURBANCE, disorder, disruption, revolution, turmoil
uphill *adjective* 1 ASCENDING, climbing, mounting, rising
2 ARDUOUS, difficult, exhausting, grueling, hard, laborious, strenuous, taxing, tough
uphold *verb* SUPPORT, advocate, aid, back, champion, defend, endorse, maintain, promote, sustain
upkeep *noun* 1 MAINTENANCE, keep, repair, running, subsistence
2 OVERHEADS, expenditure, expenses, running costs
uplift *verb* 1 RAISE, elevate, hoist, lift up
2 IMPROVE, advance, better, edify, inspire, raise, refine
▷ *noun* 3 IMPROVEMENT, advancement, edification, enhancement, enlightenment,

2 a lifting up 3 mental, social or emotional improvement
up•load *verb transitive computers.* transfer data from a single computer to a server or host
up•on [ə-PON] *preposition* on
up•per [UP-ər] *adjective* 1 higher, situated above 2 *comp. of* **up.** ▷ *noun* 3 upper part of boot or shoe > **up'per•cut** *noun* short-arm upward blow > **up'per•most** [-mohst] *adjective sup. of* **up**
up•right [UP-rīt] *adjective* 1 erect 2 honest, just ▷ *adverb* 3 vertically ▷ *noun* 4 thing standing upright, e.g. post in framework
up•ris•ing [UP-rī-zing] *noun* rebellion, revolt
up•roar [UP-ror] *noun* tumult, disturbance > **up•roar'i•ous** [-ee-əs] *adjective* rowdy
up•set' *verb transitive* **-set, -set•ting** 1 overturn 2 distress 3 disrupt 4 make ill ▷ *noun* [UP-set] 5 unexpected defeat 6 confusion 7 trouble 8 overturning
up'shot *noun* outcome, end
up•stage [up-stayj] *adjective* 1 of back of stage ▷ *verb transitive* **-staged, -stag•ing** 2 draw attention away from another to oneself
up•start [UP-stahrt] *noun* one suddenly raised to wealth, power, etc.
up•tight [up-tīt] *adjective* (*slang*) 1 displaying tense nervousness, irritability 2 repressed
u•ra•ni•um [yuu-RAY-nee-əm] *noun* white radioactive metallic element, used as chief source of nuclear energy
U•ra•nus [YUUR-ə-nəs] *noun* 1 Greek god, personification of sky 2 seventh planet from the sun
ur•ban [UR-bən] *adjective* 1 relating to town or city 2 describing modern pop music of African-American origin, such as hip-hop > **ur•ban•ize** *verb transitive* **-ized, -iz•ing** change countryside to residential or industrial area
ur•bane [ur-BAIN] *adjective* elegant, sophisticated > **ur•ban'i•ty** [-BAN-i-tee] *noun*
ur'chin *noun* mischievous, unkempt child
u•re•a [yuu-REE-ə] *noun* substance occurring in urine
u•re•thra [yuu-REE-thrə] *noun* canal conveying urine from bladder out of body
urge [urj] *verb transitive* **urged, urg•ing** 1 exhort earnestly 2 entreat 3 drive on ▷ *noun* 4 strong desire > **ur'gen•cy** [-jən-see] *noun, plural* **-cies** > **ur'gent** [-jənt] *adjective* 1 pressing 2 needing attention at once > **ur'gent•ly** *adverb*

enrichment, refinement
upmarket *adjective* (*informal*) UPPER-CLASS, classy (*informal*), grand, high-class, luxurious, smart, stylish, swanky (*informal*)
upper *adjective* 1 HIGHER, high, loftier, top, topmost
2 SUPERIOR, eminent, greater, important
upper-class *adjective* ARISTOCRATIC, blue-blooded, highborn, high-class, noble, patrician
upper hand *noun* CONTROL, advantage, ascendancy, edge, mastery, supremacy
uppermost *adjective* 1 TOP, highest, loftiest, topmost
2 SUPREME, chief, dominant, foremost, greatest, leading, main, principal
uppity *adjective* (*informal*) CONCEITED, bumptious, cocky, full of oneself, impertinent, self-important
upright *adjective* 1 VERTICAL, erect, perpendicular, straight
2 HONEST, conscientious, ethical, good, honorable, just, principled, righteous, virtuous
uprising *noun* REBELLION, disturbance, insurgence, insurrection, mutiny, revolt, revolution, rising
uproar *noun* COMMOTION, din, furor, mayhem, noise, outcry, pandemonium, racket, riot, turmoil
uproarious *adjective* 1 HILARIOUS, hysterical, rib-tickling, rip-roaring (*informal*), side-splitting, very funny
2 LOUD, boisterous, rollicking, unrestrained
uproot *verb* 1 PULL UP, dig up, rip up, root out, weed out
2 DISPLACE, exile
upset *adjective* 1 SICK, ill, queasy
2 DISTRESSED, agitated, bothered, dismayed, disturbed, grieved, hurt, put out, troubled, worried
3 DISORDERED, chaotic, confused, disarrayed, in disarray, muddled
4 OVERTURNED, capsized, spilled, upside down
▷ *verb* 5 TIP OVER, capsize, knock over, overturn, spill
6 MESS UP, change, disorder, disorganize, disturb, spoil
7 DISTRESS, agitate, bother, disconcert, disturb, faze, fluster, grieve, perturb, ruffle, trouble
▷ *noun* 8 REVERSAL, defeat, shake-up (*informal*)
9 ILLNESS, bug (*informal*), complaint, disorder, malady, sickness
10 DISTRESS, agitation, bother, disturbance, shock, trouble, worry
upshot *noun* RESULT, culmination, end, end result, finale, outcome, sequel
upside down *adjective* 1 INVERTED, backward, overturned, upturned
2 CONFUSED, chaotic, disordered, muddled, topsy-turvy
upstanding *adjective* HONEST, ethical, good, honorable, incorruptible, moral, principled, upright
upstart *noun* SOCIAL CLIMBER, arriviste, nouveau riche (*French*), parvenu
uptight *adjective* (*informal*) TENSE, anxious, edgy, on edge, uneasy, wired (*slang*)
up-to-date *adjective* MODERN, cool (*informal*), current, fashionable, in vogue, phat (*slang*), stylish, trendy (*informal*), up-to-the-minute
upturn *noun* RISE, advancement, improvement, increase, recovery, revival, upsurge, upswing
urban *adjective* CIVIC, city, metropolitan, municipal, town
urbane *adjective* SOPHISTICATED, courteous, cultivated, cultured, debonair, polished, refined, smooth, suave, well-bred
urchin *noun* RAGAMUFFIN, brat, gamin, waif
urge *noun* 1 IMPULSE, compulsion, desire, drive, itch, longing, thirst, wish, yearning
▷ *verb* 2 BEG, beseech, entreat, exhort, implore, plead
3 ADVOCATE, advise, counsel, recommend, support
4 DRIVE, compel, force, goad, impel, incite, induce, press, push, spur
urgency *noun* IMPORTANCE, extremity, gravity,

u•rine [YUUR-in] *noun* fluid excreted by kidneys to bladder and passed as waste from body > **u'ric** *adjective* > **u•ri•nal** [YUUR-ə-nl] *noun* (place with) sanitary fitting used by men for urination > **ur•i•nar•y** *adjective* > **u'ri•nate** *verb intransitive* **-nat•ed, -nat•ing** discharge urine
URL *computers.* uniform resource locator: standardized address of a location on the Internet
urn *noun* 1 vessel like vase, esp. for ashes of the dead 2 large container with tap for making and dispensing tea, coffee, etc.
ur•sine [UR-sin] *adjective* of, like a bear
us *pronoun plural the objective case of the pronoun* **we**
USB port *noun computers.* type of serial port for connecting peripheral devices in a computing system
use [yooz] *verb transitive* **used, us•ing** 1 employ, avail oneself of 2 exercise 3 exploit 4 consume ▷ *noun* [yoos] 5 employment, application to a purpose 6 need to employ 7 serviceableness 8 profit 9 habit > **us•a•ble** [YOO-zə-bəl] *adjective* fit for use > **us•age** [YOOS-ij] *noun* 1 act of using 2 custom 3 customary way of using > **used** [yoozd] *adjective* secondhand, not new > **use•ful** [YOOS-fəl] *adjective* 1 of use 2 helpful 3 serviceable > **use'ful•ness** [-nis] *noun* > **use'less•ness** [-lis-nis] *noun* > **used to** [yoost] *adjective* 1 accustomed to ▷ *verb transitive* 2 did so formerly > **us'er** *noun* > **us•er friendly** [YOO-zər] (of computer, etc.) easily understood and operated > **us'er•name** *noun* 1 computer account name that, with a password, allows access to a computer system 2 part of an e mail address before the @ symbol
ush•er [USH-ər] *noun* 1 doorkeeper, one showing people to seats, etc. ▷ *verb transitive* 2 introduce, announce 3 inaugurate
u•su•al [YOO-zhoo-əl] *adjective* habitual, ordinary > **u'su•al•ly** *adverb* 1 as a rule 2 generally, commonly
u•surp [yoo-SURP] *verb transitive* seize wrongfully > **u•sur•pa•tion** [yoo-sər-PAY-shən] *noun* violent or unlawful seizing of power > **u•surp'er** *noun*
u•su•ry [YOO-zhə-ree] *noun* 1 lending of money at excessive interest 2 such interest > **u'su•rer** *noun* money lender > **u•su'ri•ous** [-ZHUUR-ee-əs] *adjective*
u•ten•sil [yoo-TEN-səl] *noun* vessel, implement, esp. in domestic use
u•ter•us [YOO-tər-əs] *noun, plural* **-us•es** womb > **u•ter•ine** [-tər-in] *adjective*
u•til•i•ty [yoo-TIL-i-tee] *noun, plural* **-ties** 1 usefulness 2 benefit 3 useful thing 4 a public service, such as electricity ▷ *adjective* 5 made for practical purposes > **u•til•i•tar'i•an** [-TAIR-ee-ən] *adjective* useful rather than beautiful > **u•til•i•tar'i•an•ism** *noun* doctrine that morality of actions is to be tested by their utility, esp. that the greatest good of the greatest number should be the sole end of public action > **u•ti•li•za'tion** [-ZAY-shən] *noun* > **u'ti•lize** *verb transitive* **-lized, -liz•ing** make use of
ut•most [UT-mohst] *adjective* 1 to the highest degree 2 extreme, furthest ▷ *noun* 3 greatest possible amount
u•to•pi•a [yoo-TOH-pee-ə] *noun* imaginary state with perfect political and social conditions, or constitution > **u•to'pi•an** [-pee-ən] *adjective* ideally perfect but impracticable
ut•ter[1] [UT-ər] *verb transitive* 1 express, emit audibly, say 2 put in circulation (forged bills,

DICTIONARY

U

THESAURUS

hurry, necessity, need, pressure, seriousness
urgent *adjective* CRUCIAL, compelling, critical, immediate, imperative, important, pressing
usable *adjective* SERVICEABLE, available, current, functional, practical, utilizable, valid, working
usage *noun* 1 USE, control, employment, handling, management, operation, running 2 PRACTICE, convention, custom, habit, method, mode, procedure, regime, routine
use *verb* 1 EMPLOY, apply, exercise, exert, operate, practice, utilize, work 2 TAKE ADVANTAGE OF, exploit, manipulate 3 CONSUME, exhaust, expend, run through, spend ▷ *noun* 4 USAGE, application, employment, exercise, handling, operation, practice, service 5 GOOD, advantage, avail, benefit, help, point, profit, service, usefulness, value 6 PURPOSE, end, object, reason
used *adjective* SECOND-HAND, cast-off, nearly new, shopsoiled
used to *adjective* ACCUSTOMED TO, familiar with
useful *adjective* HELPFUL, advantageous, beneficial, effective, fruitful, practical, profitable, serviceable, valuable, win-win (*informal*), worthwhile
usefulness *noun* HELPFULNESS, benefit, convenience, effectiveness, efficacy, practicality, use, utility, value, worth
useless *adjective* 1 WORTHLESS, fruitless, futile, impractical, ineffectual, pointless, unproductive, vain, valueless 2 (*informal*) INEPT, hopeless, incompetent, ineffectual, no good
use up *verb* CONSUME, absorb, drain, exhaust, finish, run through
usher *noun* 1 ATTENDANT, doorkeeper, doorman, escort, guide ▷ *verb* 2 ESCORT, conduct, direct, guide, lead
usual *adjective* NORMAL, common, customary, everyday, general, habitual, ordinary, regular, routine, standard, typical
usually *adverb* NORMALLY, as a rule, commonly, generally, habitually, mainly, mostly, on the whole
usurp *verb* SEIZE, appropriate, assume, commandeer, take, take over, wrest
utility *noun* USEFULNESS, benefit, convenience, efficacy, practicality, serviceableness
utilize *verb* USE, avail oneself of, employ, make use of, put to use, take advantage of, turn to account
utmost *adjective* 1 GREATEST, chief, highest, maximum, paramount, pre-eminent, supreme 2 FARTHEST, extreme, final, last ▷ *noun* 3 GREATEST, best, hardest, highest
Utopia *noun* PARADISE, bliss, Eden, Garden of Eden, heaven, Shangri-la
Utopian *adjective* PERFECT, dream, fantasy, ideal, idealistic, imaginary, romantic, visionary
utter[1] *verb* EXPRESS, articulate, pronounce, say, speak, voice

counterfeit coin) > **ut'ter•ance** [-əns] *noun* 1 act of speaking 2 expression in words 3 spoken words

utter[2] *adjective* complete, total, absolute > **ut'ter•ly** *adverb*

ut•ter•most [UT-ər-mohst] *adjective* 1 farthest out 2 utmost ▷ *noun* 3 highest degree

u•vu•la [YOO-vyə-lə] *noun, plural* **-las** *or* **-lae** [-lee] pendent fleshy part of soft palate > **u'vu•lar** [-lər] *adjective*

ux•o•ri•ous [uk-SOR-ee-əs] *adjective* excessively fond of one's wife

utter[2] *adjective* ABSOLUTE, complete, downright, outright, sheer, thorough, total, unmitigated

utterance *noun* SPEECH, announcement, declaration, expression, remark, statement, words

utterly *adverb* TOTALLY, absolutely, completely, entirely, extremely, fully, perfectly, thoroughly

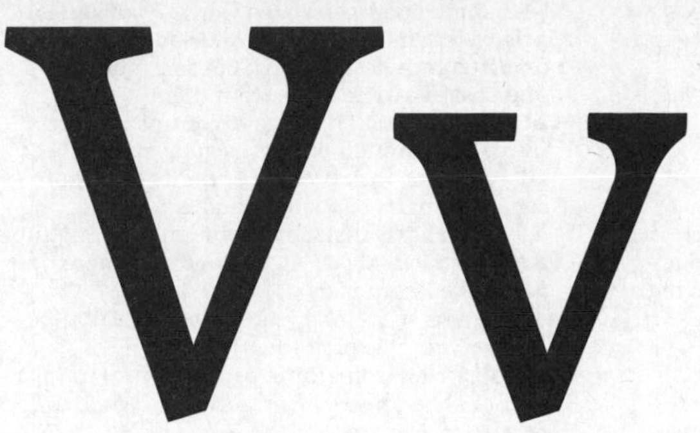

V *chem.* vanadium

va•cant [VAY-kənt] *adjective* 1 without thought, empty 2 unoccupied > **va'can•cy** [-kən-see] *noun, plural* **-cies** 1 state of being unoccupied 2 unfilled position, accommodation, etc.

va•cate [VAY-kayt] *verb transitive* **-cat•ed, -cat•ing** quit, leave empty > **va•ca'tion** [-KAY-shən] *noun* 1 act of vacating 2 holidays 3 time when schools and courts, etc. are closed

vac•ci•nate [VAK-sə-nayt] *verb transitive* **-nat•ed, -nat•ing** inoculate with vaccine as protection against a specific disease > **vac•ci•na'tion** *noun* > **vac•cine** [vak-SEEN] *noun* any substance used for inoculation against disease

vac•il•late [VAS-ə-layt] *verb intransitive* **-lat•ed, -lat•ing** 1 fluctuate in opinion 2 waver 3 move to and fro > **vac•il•la'tion** *noun* 1 indecision 2 wavering 3 unsteadiness

vac•u•um [VAK-yoom] *noun, plural* **-u•ums** 1 place, region containing no matter and from which all or most air, gas has been removed ▷ *verb* 2 clean with vacuum cleaner > **va•cu•i•ty** [va-KYOO-i-tee] *noun* > **vac•u•ous** [VA-kyoo-əs] *adjective* 1 vacant 2 expressionless 3 unintelligent > **vacuum cleaner** apparatus for removing dust by suction > **vac'uum-packed** *adjective* contained in packaging from which air has been removed

vag•a•bond [VAG-ə-bond] *noun* 1 person with no fixed home 2 wandering beggar or thief ▷ *adjective* 3 like a vagabond

va•gar•y [VAY-gə-ree] *noun, plural* **-gar•ies** 1 something unusual, erratic 2 whim

va•gi•na [və-JĪ-nə] *noun, plural* **-nas** passage from womb to exterior > **vag•i•nal** [VAJ-ə-nl] *adjective*

va•grant [VAY-grənt] *noun* 1 vagabond, tramp ▷ *adjective* 2 wandering, esp. without purpose > **va'gran•cy** *noun, plural* **-cies**

vague [vayg] *adjective* **va•guer** [-gər], **va•guest** [-gəst] 1 indefinite or uncertain 2 indistinct 3 not clearly expressed 4 absent-minded

vain [vayn] *adjective* **-er, -est** 1 conceited 2 worthless, useless 3 unavailing 4 foolish

vacancy *noun* JOB, opening, opportunity, position, post, situation

vacant *adjective* 1 UNOCCUPIED, available, empty, free, idle, unfilled, untenanted, void 2 VAGUE, absent-minded, abstracted, blank, dreamy, idle, inane, vacuous

vacate *verb* LEAVE, evacuate, quit

vacuous *adjective* UNINTELLIGENT, blank, inane, stupid, uncomprehending, vacant

vacuum *noun* EMPTINESS, gap, nothingness, space, vacuity, void

vagabond *noun* BEGGAR, down-and-out, itinerant, rover, tramp, vagrant

vagrant *noun* 1 TRAMP, drifter, hobo, itinerant, rolling stone, wanderer ▷ *adjective* 2 ITINERANT, nomadic, roaming, rootless, roving, unsettled, vagabond

vague *adjective* UNCLEAR, equivocal, hazy, ill-defined, imprecise, indefinite, indeterminate, indistinct, loose, nebulous, uncertain, unspecified

vain *adjective* 1 PROUD, arrogant, conceited, egotistical, narcissistic, self-important, swaggering

> **vain'ly** *adverb*
vain•glo•ry [VAYN-glor-ee] *noun* boastfulness, vanity > **vain•glo'ri•ous** *adjective*
val•ance [VAL-əns] *noun* short curtain around base of bed, etc.
vale [vayl] *noun poet.* valley
val•e•dic•tion [val-i-DIK-shən] *noun* farewell > **val•e•dic•to'ri•an** [-TOR-ee-ən] *noun* > **val•e•dic'to•ry** [-DIK-tə-ree] *noun* farewell address ▷ *adjective*
va•lence [VAY-ləns], **va•len•cy** [-lən-see] *noun chem.* combining power of element or atom
val•en•tine [VAL-ən-tīn] *noun* (one receiving) card, gift, expressing affection, on Saint Valentine's Day, Feb. 14th
val•et [va-LAY] *noun* gentleman's personal servant
val•e•tu•di•nar•y [val-i-TOOD-n-er-ee] *adjective* 1 sickly 2 infirm > **val•e•tu•di•nar'i•an** [-NAIR-ee-ən] *noun* person obliged or disposed to live the life of an invalid
Val•hal•la [val-HAL-ə] *noun norse mythology* place of immortality for heroes slain in battle
val•iant [VAL-yənt] *adjective* brave, courageous
val'id *adjective* 1 sound 2 capable of being justified 3 of binding force in law > **va•lid•i•ty** [və-LID-i-tee] *noun* 1 soundness 2 power to convince 3 legal force > **val'i•date** *verb transitive* **-dat•ed, -dat•ing** make valid
va•lise [və-LEES] *noun* traveling bag
Val•kyr•ie [val-KEER-ee, VAL-ker-ee] *noun* one of the Norse war goddesses who chose the slain and guided them to Valhalla
val•ley [VAL-ee] *noun, plural* **-leys** 1 low area between hills 2 river basin
val•or [VAL-ər] *noun* bravery > **val'or•ous** [-əs] *adjective*
val•ue [VAL-yoo] *noun* 1 worth 2 utility 3 equivalent 4 importance ▷ *verb transitive* **-ued, -u•ing** 5 estimate value of 6 hold in respect 7 prize > **val•ues** *plural noun* principles, standards > **val'u•a•ble** [-ə-bəl] *adjective* 1 precious 2 worthy 3 capable of being valued ▷ *noun* (*usually plural*) 4 valuable thing > **val•u•a'tion** [-AY-shən] *noun* estimated worth > **val'ue•less** [-lis] *adjective* worthless > **value added tax** tax on difference between cost of basic materials and cost of article made from them
valve [valv] *noun* 1 device to control passage of fluid, etc. through pipe 2 *anatomy* part of body allowing one-way passage of fluids 3 any of separable parts of shell of mollusk 4 *mus.* device on brass instrument for lengthening tube
va•moose [va-MOOS] *verb* **-moosed, -moos•ing** (*slang*) depart quickly
vamp[1] *noun* 1 woman who deliberately allures men ▷ *verb* 2 exploit (man) as vamp
vamp[2] *noun* 1 something patched up 2 front part of shoe upper ▷ *verb transitive* 3 patch up, rework 4 *jazz* improvise
vam•pire [VAM-pīr] *noun* (in folklore) corpse that rises from dead to drink blood of the living > **vampire bat** one that sucks blood of animals
van[1] *noun* 1 large covered truck, esp. for furniture 2 smaller such vehicle for camping, etc.
van[2] *noun short for* **vanguard**
va•na•di•um [və-NAY-dee-əm] *noun* metallic element used in manufacture of hard steel
van•dal [VAN-dl] *noun* one who wantonly and deliberately damages or destroys > **van'dal•ism** *noun* > **van'dal•ize** *verb transitive* **-ized, -iz•ing**
vane [vayn] *noun* 1 weather vane 2 blade of propeller 3 fin on bomb, etc. 4 sight on quadrant
van•guard [VAN-gahrd] *noun* leading, foremost group, position, etc.
va•nil•la [və-NIL-ə] *noun* 1 tropical climbing orchid 2 its seed(pod) 3 essence of this for flavoring
van'ish *verb intransitive* 1 disappear 2 fade away
van•i•ty [VAN-i-tee] *noun, plural* **-ties** 1 excessive pride or conceit 2 ostentation
van•quish [VANG-kwish] *verb transitive* 1 subdue

2 FUTILE, abortive, fruitless, idle, pointless, senseless, unavailing, unprofitable, useless, worthless
▷ *noun* 3 ▷ **in vain** TO NO AVAIL, fruitless *or* fruitlessly, ineffectual *or* ineffectually, unsuccessful *or* unsuccessfully, useless *or* uselessly, vain *or* vainly
valiant *adjective* BRAVE, bold, courageous, fearless, gallant, heroic, intrepid, lion-hearted
valid *adjective* 1 LOGICAL, cogent, convincing, good, sound, telling, well-founded, well-grounded
2 LEGAL, authentic, bona fide, genuine, lawful, legitimate, official
validate *verb* CONFIRM, authenticate, authorize, certify, corroborate, endorse, ratify, substantiate
validity *noun* 1 SOUNDNESS, cogency, force, power, strength, weight
2 LEGALITY, authority, lawfulness, legitimacy, right
valley *noun* HOLLOW, dale, dell, depression, glen, vale
valor *noun* BRAVERY, boldness, courage, fearlessness, gallantry, heroism, intrepidity, spirit
valuable *adjective* 1 PRECIOUS, costly, dear, expensive, high-priced
2 USEFUL, beneficial, helpful, important, prized, profitable, worthwhile
▷ *noun* 3 ▷ **valuables** TREASURES, heirlooms
value *noun* 1 IMPORTANCE, advantage, benefit, desirability, merit, profit, usefulness, utility, worth
2 COST, market price, rate
3 ▷ **values** PRINCIPLES, ethics, standards *or* moral standards
▷ *verb* 4 EVALUATE, appraise, assess, estimate, price, rate, set at
5 RESPECT, appreciate, cherish, esteem, hold dear, prize, regard highly, treasure
vandal *noun* HOOLIGAN, delinquent, rowdy
vanguard *noun* FORERUNNERS, cutting edge, forefront, front line, leaders, spearhead, trailblazers, trendsetters, van
vanish *verb* DISAPPEAR, dissolve, evanesce, evaporate, fade *or* fade away, melt *or* melt away
vanity *noun* PRIDE, arrogance, conceit, conceitedness, egotism, narcissism
vanquish *verb* (*literary*) DEFEAT, beat, conquer, crush, master, overcome, overpower, overwhelm, triumph over

in battle 2 conquer, overcome
vap'id *adjective* flat, dull, insipid > **va•pid•i•ty** [və-PID-i-tee] *noun*
va•por [VAY-pər] *noun* 1 gaseous form of a substance more familiar as liquid or solid 2 steam, mist 3 invisible moisture in air > **va'por•ize** [-pə-rīz] *verb* **-ized, -iz•ing** convert into, pass off in, vapor
var'i•a•ble *see* **vary**
var•i•cose [VAR-i-kohs] *adjective* of vein, swollen, twisted
var•i•e•gate [VA-ree-i-gayt] *verb transitive* **-gat•ed, -gat•ing** diversify by patches of different colors > **var'i•e•gat•ed** *adjective* streaked, spotted, dappled
va•ri•e•ty [və-RĪ-i-tee] *noun, plural* **-ties** 1 state of being varied or various 2 diversity 3 varied assortment 4 sort or kind
var•i•o•rum [va-ree-OR-əm] *adjective, noun* (edition) with notes by various commentators
var•i•ous [VA-ree-əs] *adjective* manifold, diverse, of several kinds
var•nish [VAHR-nish] *noun* 1 resinous solution put on a surface to make it hard and shiny ▷ *verb transitive* 2 apply varnish to
var•y [VAIR-ee] *verb* **var•ied, var•y•ing** (cause to) change, diversify, differ, deviate > **var•i•a•bil'i•ty** *noun* > **var'i•a•ble** *adjective* 1 changeable 2 unsteady or fickle ▷ *noun* 3 something subject to variation > **var'i•ance** [-əns] *noun* state of discord, discrepancy > **var'i•ant** [-ənt] *adjective* 1 different ▷ *noun* 2 difference in form 3 alternative form or reading > **var•i•a'tion** [-AY-shən] *noun* 1 alteration 2 extent to which thing varies 3 modification > **var'ied** *adjective* 1 diverse 2 modified 3 variegated
vas *noun, plural* **va•sa** [VA-sə] vessel, tube carrying bodily fluid
vas•cu•lar [VAS-kyə-lər] *adjective* of, with vessels for conveying sap, blood, etc.
vase [vayz] *noun* vessel, jar as ornament or for holding flowers
vas•ec•to•my [va-SEK-tə-mee] *noun, plural* **-mies** contraceptive measure of surgical removal of part of vas bearing sperm from testicle
vas•sal [VAS-əl] *noun* 1 holder of land by feudal tenure 2 dependent
vast *adjective* **-er, -est** very large > **vast'ly** [-lee] *adverb* > **vast'ness** [-nis] *noun*
vat *noun* large tub, tank
Vat•i•can [VAT-i-kən] *noun* 1 Pope's palace 2 papal authority
vaude•ville [VAWD-vil] *noun* theatrical entertainment with songs, juggling acts, dance
vault[1] [vawlt] *noun* 1 arched roof 2 arched apartment 3 cellar 4 burial chamber 5 place for storing valuables ▷ *verb transitive* 6 build with arched roof
vault[2] *verb* 1 spring, jump over with the hands resting on something ▷ *noun* 2 such jump > **vaulting horse** padded apparatus for support of hands in gymnastics
vaunt [vawnt] *verb, noun* boast > **vaunt'ed** [-id] *adjective* excessively praised
VDU visual display unit, monitor
veal [veel] *noun* calf flesh as food
vec•tor [VEK-tər] *noun* 1 quantity (e.g. force) having both magnitude and direction 2 disease-carrying organism, esp. insect 3 compass direction, course
veer *verb intransitive* 1 change direction 2 change one's mind
veg•e•ta•ble [VEJ-tə-bəl] *noun* 1 plant, esp. edible one 2 (*informal*) person who has lost use of mental and physical faculties 3 dull person ▷ *adjective* 4 of, from, concerned with plants
veg•e•tar•i•an [vej-i-TAIR-ee-ən] *noun* one who does not eat meat ▷ *adjective* > **veg•e•tar'i•an•ism** *noun*
veg•e•tate [VEJ-i-tayt] *verb intransitive* **-tat•ed, -tat•ing** 1 (of plants) grow, develop 2 (of person) live dull, unproductive life > **veg•e•ta'tion** *noun* 1 plants collectively 2 plants growing in a place 3 process of plant growth > **veg'e•ta•tive** [-tay tiv] *adjective*
ve•he•ment [VEE-ə-mənt] *adjective* 1 marked by intensity of feeling 2 vigorous 3 forcible

---

vapid *adjective* DULL, bland, boring, flat, insipid, tame, uninspiring, uninteresting, weak, wishy-washy (*informal*)
vapor *noun* MIST, exhalation, fog, haze, steam
variable *adjective* CHANGEABLE, flexible, fluctuating, inconstant, mutable, shifting, temperamental, uneven, unstable, unsteady
variance *noun* ▷ **at variance** IN DISAGREEMENT, at loggerheads, at odds, conflicting, out of line
variant *adjective* 1 DIFFERENT, alternative, divergent, modified
▷ *noun* 2 VARIATION, alternative, development, modification
variation *noun* DIFFERENCE, change, departure, deviation, diversity, innovation, modification, novelty, variety
varied *adjective* DIFFERENT, assorted, diverse, heterogeneous, miscellaneous, mixed, motley, sundry, various
variety *noun* 1 DIVERSITY, change, difference, discrepancy, diversification, multifariousness, variation
2 RANGE, array, assortment, collection, cross section, medley, miscellany, mixture
3 TYPE, brand, breed, category, class, kind, sort, species, strain
various *adjective* DIFFERENT, assorted, disparate, distinct, diverse, miscellaneous, several, sundry, varied
varnish *noun, verb* POLISH, glaze, gloss, lacquer
vary *verb* CHANGE, alter, differ, disagree, diverge, fluctuate
vast *adjective* HUGE, boundless, colossal, enormous, gigantic, great, immense, massive, monumental, wide
vault[1] *noun* 1 STRONGROOM, depository, repository
2 CRYPT, catacomb, cellar, charnel house, mausoleum, tomb, undercroft
vault[2] *verb* JUMP, bound, clear, hurdle, leap, spring
vaulted *adjective* ARCHED, cavernous, domed
veer *verb* SWERVE, change course, change direction, sheer, shift, turn
vegetate *verb* STAGNATE, deteriorate, go to seed, idle, languish, loaf
vehemence *noun* FORCEFULNESS, ardor, emphasis, energy, fervor, force, intensity,

> **ve'he•mence** [-məns] *noun*

ve•hi•cle [VEE-i-kəl] *noun* **1** means of conveying **2** means of expression **3** medium > **ve•hic'u•lar** [-HIK-yə-lər] *adjective*

veil [vayl] *noun* **1** light material to cover face or head **2** mask, cover ▷ *verb transitive* **3** cover with, or as with, veil > **veiled** *adjective* disguised **take the veil** become a nun

vein [vayn] *noun* **1** tube in body taking blood to heart **2** rib of leaf or insect's wing **3** fissure in rock filled with ore **4** streak **5** distinctive trait, strain, etc. **6** mood ▷ *verb transitive* **7** mark with streaks > **ve•nous** [VEE-nəs] *adjective* of veins

veld, veldt [velt] *noun* elevated grassland in S Afr.

vel•lum [VEL-əm] *noun* **1** parchment of calf skin used for manuscripts or bindings **2** paper resembling this

ve•loc•i•ty [və-LOS-i-tee] *noun, plural* **-ties** **1** rate of motion in given direction, esp. of inanimate things **2** speed

ve•lour [və-LUUR] *noun* fabric with velvety finish

ve•lum [VEE-ləm] *noun, plural* **-la** [-lə] *zoology* **1** membranous covering or organ **2** soft palate

vel•vet [VEL-vit] *noun* silk or cotton fabric with thick, short pile > **vel•vet•een'** *noun* cotton fabric resembling velvet > **vel'vet•y** *adjective* **1** of, like velvet **2** soft and smooth

ve•nal [VEEN-l] *adjective* **1** guilty of taking, prepared to take, bribes **2** corrupt > **ve•nal'i•ty** *noun*

vend *verb transitive* sell > **ven•dor** [VEN-dər] *noun* > **vending machine** one that automatically dispenses goods when money is inserted

ven•det•ta [ven-DET-ə] *noun* bitter, prolonged feud

ve•neer [və-NEER] *noun* **1** thin layer of fine wood **2** superficial appearance ▷ *verb transitive* **3** cover with veneer

ven•er•a•ble [VEN-ər-ə-bəl] *adjective* worthy of reverence > **ven•er•ate** [VEN-ə-rayt] *verb transitive* **-at•ed, -at•ing** look up to, respect, revere

> **ven•er•a'tion** *noun*

ve•ne•re•al [və-NEER-ee-əl] *adjective* **1** (of disease) transmitted by sexual intercourse **2** infected with venereal disease **3** of, relating to genitals or sexual intercourse

ven•er•y [VEN-ə-ree] *noun* (*obsolete*) pursuit of sexual gratification

Ve•ne•tian [və-NEE-shən] *adjective* **1** of Venice, port in NE Italy ▷ *noun* **2** native or inhabitant of Venice > **Venetian blind** window blind made of thin horizontal slats that turn to let in more or less light

ven•geance [VEN-jəns] *noun* **1** revenge **2** retribution for wrong done > **venge'ful** [-fəl] *adjective*

ve•ni•al [VEE-nee-əl] *adjective* pardonable

ven•i•son [VEN-ə-sən] *noun* flesh of deer as food

ven•om [VEN-əm] *noun* **1** poison **2** spite > **ven'om•ous** [-əs] *adjective* poisonous

venous [VEE-nəs] *see* **vein**

vent[1] *noun* **1** small hole or outlet ▷ *verb transitive* **2** give outlet to **3** utter **4** pour forth

vent[2] *noun* vertical slit in garment esp. at back of jacket

ven•ti•late [VEN-tl-ayt] *verb transitive* **-lat•ed, -lat•ing** **1** supply with fresh air **2** bring into discussion > **ven'ti•la•tor** *noun*

ven•tral [VEN-trəl] *adjective* abdominal

ven•tri•cle [VEN-tri-kəl] *noun* cavity, hollow in body, esp. in heart or brain > **ven•tric'u•lar** [-TRIK-yə-lər] *adjective*

ven•tril•o•quist [ven-TRIL-ə-kwist] *noun* one who can so speak that the sounds seem to come from some other person or place > **ven•tril'o•quism** *noun*

ven•ture [VEN-chər] *verb transitive* **-tured, -tur•ing** **1** expose to hazard **2** risk ▷ *verb intransitive* **-tured, -tur•ing** **3** dare **4** have courage to do something or go somewhere ▷ *noun* **5** risky undertaking **6** speculative commercial undertaking > **ven'ture•some** [-səm] *adjective*

DICTIONARY • THESAURUS

passion, vigor

vehement *adjective* STRONG, ardent, emphatic, fervent, fierce, forceful, impassioned, intense, passionate, powerful

vehicle *noun* **1** TRANSPORT, conveyance, transportation
2 MEDIUM, apparatus, channel, means, mechanism, organ

veil *noun* **1** COVER, blind, cloak, curtain, disguise, film, mask, screen, shroud
▷ *verb* **2** COVER, cloak, conceal, disguise, hide, mask, obscure, screen, shield

veiled *adjective* DISGUISED, concealed, covert, hinted at, implied, masked, suppressed

vein *noun* **1** BLOOD VESSEL
2 SEAM, course, current, lode, stratum, streak, stripe
3 MOOD, mode, note, style, temper, tenor, tone

velocity *noun* SPEED, pace, quickness, rapidity, swiftness

velvety *adjective* SMOOTH, delicate, downy, soft

vendetta *noun* FEUD, bad blood, quarrel

veneer *noun* MASK, appearance, façade, front, guise, pretense, semblance, show

venerable *adjective* RESPECTED, august, esteemed, honored, revered, sage, wise, worshipped

venerate *verb* RESPECT, adore, esteem, honor, look up to, revere, reverence, worship

vengeance *noun* REVENGE, reprisal, retaliation, retribution

venom *noun* **1** MALICE, acrimony, bitterness, hate, rancor, spite, spleen, virulence
2 POISON, bane, toxin

venomous *adjective* **1** MALICIOUS, hostile, malignant, rancorous, savage, spiteful, vicious, vindictive
2 POISONOUS, mephitic, noxious, toxic, virulent

vent *noun* **1** OUTLET, aperture, duct, opening, orifice
▷ *verb* **2** EXPRESS, air, discharge, emit, give vent to, pour out, release, utter, voice

venture *noun* **1** UNDERTAKING, adventure, endeavor, enterprise, gamble, hazard, project, risk
▷ *verb* **2** RISK, chance, hazard, speculate, stake, wager
3 DARE, hazard, make bold, presume, take the liberty, volunteer

ven•ue [VEN-yoo] *noun* 1 *law* district in which case is tried 2 meeting place 3 location
Ve•nus [VEE-nəs] *noun* 1 Roman goddess of love 2 planet between Earth and Mercury > **Venus's flytrap** insect-eating plant
ve•ra•cious [və-RAY-shəs] *adjective* 1 truthful 2 true > **ve•rac'i•ty** [-RAS-i-tee] *noun*
ve•ran•da, ve•ran•dah [və-RAN-də] *noun* open or partly enclosed porch on outside of house
verb [vurb] *noun* part of speech used to express action or being > **ver•bal** [VUR-bəl] *adjective* 1 of, by, or relating to words spoken rather than written 2 of, like a verb > **ver'bal•ize** *verb* **-ized, -iz•ing** put into words, speak > **ver'bal•ly** *adverb* > **ver•ba•tim** [vər-BAY-tim] *adverb, adjective* word for word, literal
ver•bi•age [VUR-bee-ij] *noun* excess of words > **ver•bose** [vər-BOHS] *adjective* wordy, long-winded > **ver•bos'i•ty** [-BOS-i-tee] *noun*
ver•dant [VUR-dnt] *adjective* green and fresh > **ver•dure** [-jər] *noun* 1 greenery 2 freshness
ver•dict [VUR-dikt] *noun* 1 decision of a jury 2 opinion reached after examination of facts
ver•di•gris [VUR-di-grees] *noun* green film on copper
verdure [VUR-jər] *see* **verdant**
verge [vurj] *noun* 1 edge 2 brink ▷ *verb intransitive* **verged, verg•ing** 3 come close to 4 be on the border of
ver•i•fy [VER-i-fī] *verb transitive* **-fied, -fy•ing** 1 prove, confirm truth of 2 test accuracy of > **ver'i•fi•a•ble** *adjective*
ver•i•si•mil•i•tude [ver-ə-si-MIL-i-tood] *noun* 1 appearance of truth 2 likelihood
ver•i•ta•ble [VER-i-tə-bəl] *adjective* actual, true, genuine > **ver'i•ta•bly** *adverb*
ver•i•ty [VER-i-tee] *noun, plural* **-ties** 1 truth 2 reality 3 true assertion
ver•mi•cide [VUR-mə-sīd] *noun* substance to destroy worms > **ver'mi•form** *adjective* shaped like a worm: *vermiform appendix*
ver•mil•ion [vər-MIL-yən] *adjective, noun* (of) bright red color or pigment
ver•min [VUR-min] *plural noun* injurious animals, parasites, etc.
ver•mouth [vər-MOOTH] *noun* wine flavored with aromatic herbs, etc.
ver•nac•u•lar [vər-NAK-yə-lər] *noun* 1 commonly spoken language or dialect of particular country or place ▷ *adjective* 2 of vernacular 3 native
ver•nal [VUR-nl] *adjective* of spring
ver•ni•er [VUR-nee-ər] *noun* sliding scale for obtaining fractional parts of subdivision of graduated scale
ver•sa•tile [VUR-sə-tl] *adjective* 1 capable of or adapted to many different uses, skills, etc. 2 liable to change > **ver•sa•til'i•ty** *noun*
verse [vurs] *noun* 1 stanza or short subdivision of poem or the Bible 2 poetry 3 line of poetry > **ver•si•fy** [VUR-sə-fī] *verb* **-fied, -fy•ing** turn into verse > **ver•si•fi•ca'tion** *noun* > **versed in** skilled
ver•sion [VUR-*zh*ən] *noun* 1 description from certain point of view 2 translation 3 adaptation
ver•so [VUR-soh] *noun* back of sheet of printed paper, left-hand page
ver•sus [VUR-səs] *preposition* against
ver•te•bra [VUR-tə-brə] *noun, plural* **-brae** [-bree] single section of backbone > **ver'te•bral** [-brəl] *adjective* of the spine > **ver'te•brate** [-brit] *noun* animal with backbone ▷ *adjective*
ver•tex [VUR-teks] *noun, plural* **-ti•ces** [-tə-seez] summit
ver•ti•cal [VUR-ti-kəl] *adjective* 1 at right angles to the horizon 2 upright 3 overhead
ver•ti•go [VUR-ti-goh] *noun, plural* **-goes** giddiness > **ver•tig•i•nous** [vər-TIJ-ə-nəs] *adjective* dizzy
verve [vurv] *noun* 1 enthusiasm 2 spirit 3 energy, vigor
ver•y [VER-ee] *adjective* 1 exact, ideal 2 same 3 complete 4 actual ▷ *adverb* 5 extremely, to great extent
ves•i•cle [VES-i-kəl] *noun* small blister, bubble, or cavity > **ve•sic•u•lar** [və-SIK-yə-lər] *adjective*
ves•pers [VES-pərz] *plural noun* 1 evening church service 2 evensong

DICTIONARY

V

THESAURUS

4 GO, embark on, plunge into, set out
verbal *adjective* SPOKEN, oral, unwritten, word-of-mouth
verbatim *adverb* EXACTLY, precisely, to the letter, word for word
verbose *adjective* LONG-WINDED, circumlocutory, diffuse, periphrastic, prolix, tautological, windy, wordy
verbosity *noun* LONG-WINDEDNESS, loquaciousness, prolixity, verboseness, wordiness
verdant *adjective* GREEN, flourishing, fresh, grassy, leafy, lush
verdict *noun* DECISION, adjudication, conclusion, finding, judgment, opinion, sentence
verge *noun* 1 BORDER, boundary, brim, brink, edge, limit, margin, threshold
▷ *verb* 2 ▷ **verge on** BORDER, approach, come near
verification *noun* PROOF, authentication, confirmation, corroboration, substantiation, validation
verify *verb* CHECK, authenticate, bear out, confirm, corroborate, prove, substantiate, support, validate
vernacular *noun* DIALECT, idiom, parlance, patois, speech
versatile *adjective* ADAPTABLE, adjustable, all purpose, all-round, flexible, multifaceted, resourceful, variable
versed *adjective* KNOWLEDGEABLE, acquainted, conversant, experienced, familiar, practiced, proficient, seasoned, well informed
version *noun* 1 FORM, design, model, style, variant
2 ACCOUNT, adaptation, interpretation, portrayal, rendering
vertical *adjective* UPRIGHT, erect, on end, perpendicular
vertigo *noun* DIZZINESS, giddiness, light-headedness
verve *noun* ENTHUSIASM, animation, energy, gusto, liveliness, sparkle, spirit, vitality
very *adverb* 1 EXTREMELY, acutely, decidedly, deeply, exceedingly, greatly, highly, profoundly, uncommonly, unusually

ves•sel [VES-əl] *noun* 1 any object used as a container, esp. for liquids 2 ship, large boat 3 tubular structure conveying liquids (e.g. blood) in body

vest *noun* 1 sleeveless garment worn under jacket or coat ▷ *verb transitive* 2 place 3 bestow 4 confer 5 clothe > **vest'ment** [-mənt] *noun* robe or official garment > **vested interest** strong personal interest in particular state of affairs

ves•tal [VES-tl] *adjective* pure, chaste

ves•ti•bule [VES-tə-byool] *noun* entrance hall, lobby

ves•tige [VES-tij] *noun* small trace, amount > **ves•tig'i•al** [-TIJ-ee-əl] *adjective*

ves•try [VES-tree] *noun, plural* **-tries** room in church for keeping vestments, holding meetings, etc.

vet *noun* 1 *short for* **veteran** 2 *short for* **veterinarian** ▷ *verb transitive* **vet•ted, vet•ting** 3 examine 4 check

vet•er•an [VET-ər-ən] *noun* 1 one who has served a long time, esp. in fighting services ▷ *adjective* 2 long-serving

vet•er•i•nar•i•an [vet-ər-ə-NAIR-ee-ən] *noun* one qualified to treat animal ailments > **vet'er•i•nar•y** [-ner-ee] *adjective* 1 of, concerning the health of animals ▷ *noun* 2 veterinarian

ve•to [VEE-toh] *noun, plural* **-toes** 1 power of rejecting piece of legislation, or preventing it from coming into effect 2 any prohibition ▷ *verb transitive* **-toed, -to•ing** 3 enforce veto against 4 forbid with authority

vex [veks] *verb transitive* 1 annoy 2 distress > **vex•a'tion** *noun* 1 cause of irritation 2 state of distress > **vex•a'tious** *adjective* > **vexed** *adjective* 1 cross 2 annoyed 3 much discussed

vi•a [VĪ-ə] *adverb* by way of

vi•a•ble [VĪ-ə-bəl] *adjective* 1 practicable 2 able to live and grow independently > **vi•a•bil'i•ty** *noun*

vi•a•duct [VĪ-ə-dukt] *noun* bridge over valley for a road or railroad

Vi•ag•ra [vī-AG-rə] *noun* ® drug used to treat impotence in men

vi•al [VĪ-əl] *noun* small bottle for medicine, etc.

vi•ands [VĪ-əndz] *plural noun* food esp. delicacies

vi•bra•harp [VĪ-brə-hahrp] *noun* musical instrument like xylophone, but with electronic resonators, that produces a gentle vibrato (*also* **vi'bra•phone**)

vi•brate [VĪ-brayt] *verb* **-brat•ed, -brat•ing** 1 (cause to) move to and fro rapidly and continuously 2 give off (light or sound) by vibration ▷ *verb intransitive* 3 oscillate 4 quiver > **vibes** *plural noun* (*informal*) 1 emotional reactions between people 2 atmosphere of a place > **vi'brant** [-brənt] *adjective* 1 throbbing 2 vibrating 3 appearing vigorous, lively > **vi•bra'tion** *noun* a vibrating > **vi•bra•to** [vi-BRAH-toh] *noun, plural* **-os** vibrating effect in music

vic•ar [VIK-ər] *noun* member of clergy in charge of parish > **vic'ar•age** [-ij] *noun* vicar's house > **vi•car•i•al** [vī-KAIR-ee-əl] *adjective* of vicar

vi•car•i•ous [vī-KAIR-ee-əs] *adjective* 1 obtained, enjoyed or undergone through sympathetic experience of another's experiences 2 suffered, done, etc. as substitute for another

vice [vīs] *noun* 1 evil or immoral habit or practice 2 criminal immorality esp. prostitution 3 fault, imperfection

vice- *combining form* in place of, second to: *vice-chairman; viceroy*

vice•roy [VĪS-roi] *noun* ruler acting for king in province or dependency > **vice•re•gal** *adjective*

vi•ce ver•sa [VĪ-sə VUR-sə] *Lat.* conversely, the other way round

vi•cin•i•ty [vi-SIN-i-tee] *noun, plural* **-ties** neighborhood

vi•cious [VISH-əs] *adjective* 1 wicked, cruel 2 ferocious, dangerous 3 leading to vice

vi•cis•si•tude [vi-SIS-i-tood] *noun* change of fortune > **vi•cis•si•tudes** ups and downs of fortune

▷ *adjective* 2 EXACT, precise, selfsame

vessel *noun* 1 SHIP, boat, craft 2 CONTAINER, pot, receptacle, utensil

vest *verb* (*with in* or *with*) PLACE, bestow, confer, consign, endow, entrust, invest, settle

vestibule *noun* HALL, anteroom, foyer, lobby, porch, portico

vestige *noun* TRACE, glimmer, indication, remnant, scrap, suspicion

vet *verb* CHECK, appraise, examine, investigate, review, scrutinize

veteran *noun* 1 OLD HAND, old stager, past master, warhorse (*informal*) ▷ *adjective* 2 LONG-SERVING, battle-scarred, old, seasoned

veto *noun* 1 BAN, boycott, embargo, interdict, prohibition ▷ *verb* 2 BAN, boycott, disallow, forbid, prohibit, reject, rule out, turn down

vex *verb* ANNOY, bother, distress, exasperate, irritate, plague, trouble, upset, worry

vexation *noun* 1 ANNOYANCE, chagrin, displeasure, dissatisfaction, exasperation, frustration, irritation, pique 2 PROBLEM, bother, difficulty, hassle (*informal*), headache (*informal*), nuisance, trouble, worry

viable *adjective* WORKABLE, applicable, feasible, operable, practicable, usable

vibrant *adjective* ENERGETIC, alive, animated, dynamic, sparkling, spirited, vigorous, vivacious, vivid

vibrate *verb* SHAKE, fluctuate, oscillate, pulsate, quiver, reverberate, shudder, throb, tremble

vibration *noun* TREMOR, oscillation, pulsation, quiver, reverberation, shake, shudder, throbbing, trembling

vicarious *adjective* INDIRECT, delegated, substituted, surrogate

vice *noun* 1 WICKEDNESS, corruption, depravity, evil, immorality, iniquity, sin, turpitude 2 FAULT, blemish, defect, failing, imperfection, shortcoming, weakness

vice versa *adverb* CONVERSELY, contrariwise, in reverse, the other way round

vicinity *noun* NEIGHBORHOOD, area, district, environs, locality, neck of the woods (*informal*), proximity

vicious *adjective* 1 VIOLENT, barbarous, cruel, ferocious, savage, wicked 2 MALICIOUS, cruel, mean, spiteful, venomous,

vic•tim [VIK-tim] *noun* 1 person or thing killed, injured, etc. as result of another's deed, or accident, circumstances, etc. 2 person cheated 3 sacrifice > **vic•tim•i•za'tion** [-ZAY-shən] *noun* > **vic'ti•mize** *verb transitive* **-mized, -miz•ing** 1 punish unfairly 2 make victim of

vic•tor [VIK-tər] *noun* 1 conqueror 2 winner > **vic•to•ri•ous** [vik-TOR-ee-əs] *adjective* 1 winning 2 triumphant > **vic'to•ry** [-tə-ree] *noun, plural* **-ries** winning of battle, etc.

vict•ual [VIT-l] *noun* (*usually in plural*) 1 food ▷ *verb* **-ualed, -ual•ing** 2 supply with or obtain food

vi•cu•na [vī-KOO-nə] *noun* 1 S American animal like llama 2 fine, light cloth made from its wool

vi•de [VĪ-dee] *Lat.* see **vide in•fra** [IN-frə] see below **vide su•pra** [SOO-prə] see above

vi•de•li•cet [vi-DEL-ə-sit] *Lat.* namely

vid•e•o [VID-ee-oh] *adjective* 1 relating to or used in transmission or production of TV image ▷ *noun* 2 apparatus for recording TV programs 3 film, etc. on videocassette for viewing on this apparatus > **video call** call made via a camera phone, allowing the participants to see each other as they talk > **videocassette** cassette containing video tape > **videocassette recorder** tape recorder for vision and sound signals, used for recording and playing back TV programs and films on cassette > **video game** any of various games played on video screen using electronic control > **videotape** magnetic tape on which to record TV program > **videotape recorder** tape recorder for signals for TV broadcast > **vid'e•o•tex** *noun* means of providing written or graphical representation of computerized information on TV screen for information retrieval, shopping at home, etc.

vie [vī] *verb intransitive* **vied, vy•ing** (foll by *with* or *for*) contend, compete against or for someone, something

view [vyoo] *noun* 1 survey by eyes or mind 2 range of vision 3 picture 4 scene 5 opinion 6 purpose ▷ *verb transitive* 7 look at 8 survey 9 consider > **view'er** *noun* 1 one who views 2 one who watches TV 3 optical device to assist viewing of photographic slides > **viewfinder** *noun* device on camera enabling user to see what will be included in photograph > **viewpoint** *noun* 1 way of regarding a subject 2 position commanding view of landscape

vig•il [VIJ-əl] *noun* 1 a keeping awake, watch 2 eve of church festival > **vig'i•lance** [-ləns] *noun* > **vig'i•lant** [-lənt] *adjective* watchful, alert

vig•i•lan•te [vij-ə-LAN-tee] *noun* one (esp. as member of group) who unofficially takes on duty of enforcing law

vi•gnette [vin-YET] *noun* 1 short literary essay, sketch 2 photograph or portrait with the background shaded off

vig•or [VIG-ər] *noun* 1 force, strength 2 energy, activity > **vig'or•ous** [-əs] *adjective* 1 strong 2 energetic 3 flourishing

Vi•king [VĪ-king] *noun* medieval Scandinavian seafarer, raider, settler

vile [vīl] *adjective* **vil•er, vil•est** 1 very wicked, shameful 2 disgusting 3 despicable > **vil•i•fy** [VIL-ə-fī] *verb transitive* **-fied, -fy•ing** 1 speak ill of 2 slander > **vil•i•fi•ca'tion** [-fi-KAY-shən] *noun*

vil•la [VIL-ə] *noun* large, luxurious country house

vil•lage [VIL-ij] *noun* small group of houses in country area

vil•lain [VIL-ən] *noun* 1 wicked person 2 (*informal*) mischievous person > **vil'lain•ous** [-əs] *adjective* 1 wicked 2 vile > **vil'lain•y** *noun, plural* **-lain•ies**

vim *noun* force, energy

vin•ai•grette [vin-ə-GRET] *noun* 1 small bottle of smelling salts 2 type of salad dressing ▷ *adjective* 3 (of food) served with vinaigrette

vin•di•cate [VIN-di-kayt] *verb transitive* **-cat•ed, -cat•ing** 1 clear of charges 2 justify 3 establish

DICTIONARY

V

THESAURUS

vindictive

victim *noun* CASUALTY, fatality, martyr, sacrifice, scapegoat, sufferer

victimize *verb* PERSECUTE, discriminate against, pick on

victor *noun* WINNER, champion, conqueror, prizewinner, vanquisher

victorious *adjective* WINNING, champion, conquering, first, prizewinning, successful, triumphant, vanquishing

victory *noun* WIN, conquest, success, triumph

vie *verb* COMPETE, contend, strive, struggle

view *noun* 1 (*sometimes plural*) OPINION, attitude, belief, conviction, feeling, impression, point of view, sentiment
2 SCENE, landscape, outlook, panorama, perspective, picture, prospect, spectacle, vista
3 VISION, sight
▷ *verb* 4 REGARD, consider, deem, look on

viewer *noun* WATCHER, observer, onlooker, spectator

vigilance *noun* WATCHFULNESS, alertness, attentiveness, carefulness, caution, circumspection, observance

vigilant *adjective* WATCHFUL, alert, attentive, careful, cautious, circumspect, on one's guard, on the lookout, wakeful

vigor *noun* ENERGY, animation, dynamism, forcefulness, gusto, liveliness, power, spirit, strength, verve, vitality

vigorous *adjective* ENERGETIC, active, dynamic, forceful, lively, lusty, powerful, spirited, strenuous, strong

vigorously *adverb* ENERGETICALLY, forcefully, hard, lustily, strenuously, strongly

vile *adjective* 1 WICKED, corrupt, degenerate, depraved, evil, nefarious, perverted
2 DISGUSTING, foul, horrid, nasty, nauseating, offensive, repugnant, repulsive, revolting, scuzzy (*slang*), sickening

vilify *verb* MALIGN, abuse, berate, denigrate, disparage, revile, slander, smear

villain *noun* 1 EVILDOER, criminal, miscreant, reprobate, rogue, scoundrel, wretch
2 ANTIHERO, baddy (*informal*)

villainous *adjective* WICKED, bad, cruel, degenerate, depraved, evil, fiendish, nefarious, vicious, vile

villainy *noun* WICKEDNESS, delinquency, depravity, devilry, iniquity, turpitude, vice

vindicate *verb* 1 CLEAR, absolve, acquit, exculpate, exonerate, rehabilitate

the truth or merit of > **vin•di•ca'tion** *noun*
vin•dic•tive [vin-DIK-tiv] *adjective* 1 revengeful 2 inspired by resentment
vine [vīn] *noun* climbing plant bearing grapes > **vine•yard** [VIN-yərd] *noun* plantation of vines > **vin'tage** [-tij] *noun* 1 gathering of the grapes 2 the yield 3 wine of particular year 4 time of origin ▷ *adjective* 5 best and most typical > **vint'ner** [-nər] *noun* dealer in wine
vin•e•gar [VIN-i-gər] *noun* acid liquid obtained from wine and other alcoholic liquors > **vin'e•gar•y** *adjective* 1 like vinegar 2 sour 3 bad-tempered
vi•nyl [VĪn-l] *noun* plastic material with variety of domestic and industrial uses
vi•ol [VĪ-əl] *noun* early stringed instrument preceding violin
vi•o•la[1] [vee-OH-lə] *noun* large violin with lower range
vi•o•la[2] [vī-OH-lə] *noun* single-colored variety of pansy
vi•o•late [VĪ-ə-layt] *verb transitive* **-lat•ed, -lat•ing** 1 break (law, agreement, etc.), infringe 2 rape 3 outrage, desecrate > **vi'o•la•ble** [-lə-bəl] *adjective* > **vi•o•la'tion** [-LAY-shən] *noun*
vi•o•lent [VĪ-ə-lənt] *adjective* 1 marked by, due to, extreme force, passion or fierceness 2 of great force 3 intense > **vi'o•lence** [-lins] *noun*
vi•o•let [VĪ-ə-lit] *noun* 1 plant with small bluish-purple or white flowers 2 the flower 3 bluish-purple color ▷ *adjective* 4 of this color
vi•o•lin [vī-ə-LIN] *noun* small four-stringed musical instrument > **vi•o•lin'ist** *noun* > **vi•o•lon•cel•lo** [vee-ə-lən-CHEL-oh] *noun see* **cello**
VIP very important person
vi•per [VĪ-pər] *noun* venomous snake
vi•ra•go [vi-RAH-goh] *noun, plural* **-goes** *or* **-gos** abusive woman
vir•gin [VUR-jin] *noun* 1 one who has not had sexual intercourse ▷ *adjective* 2 without experience of sexual intercourse 3 unsullied, fresh 4 (of land) untilled > **vir•gin•al** [VUR-jə-nl] *adjective* 1 of, like virgin ▷ *noun* 2 type of spinet > **vir•gin'i•ty** *noun*
vir•ile [VIR-əl] *adjective* 1 (of male) capable of copulation or procreation 2 strong, forceful > **vi•ril'i•ty** [-RIL-i-tee] *noun*
virology [vī-ROL-ə-jee] *see* **virus**
vir•tu•al [VUR-choo-əl] *adjective* so in effect, though not in appearance or name > **vir'tu•al•ly** *adverb* practically, almost > **virtual reality** computer-generated environment that seems real to the user
vir•tue [VUR-choo] *noun* 1 moral goodness 2 good quality 3 merit 4 inherent power > **vir'tu•ous** [-əs] *adjective* 1 morally good 2 chaste
vir•tu•o•so [vur-choo-OH-soh] *noun, plural* **-sos** *or* **-si** [-see] one with special skill, esp. in a fine art > **vir•tu•os'i•ty** *noun* great technical skill, esp. in a fine art as music
vir•u•lent [VIR-yə-lənt] *adjective* 1 very infectious, poisonous, etc. 2 malicious
vi•rus [VĪ-rəs] *noun* 1 any of various submicroscopic organisms, some causing disease 2 *computing* program that propagates itself, via disks and electronic networks, to cause disruption > **vi•rol'o•gy** *noun* study of viruses
vi•sa [VEEZ-ə] *noun, plural* **-sas** endorsement on passport permitting the bearer to travel into country of issuing government > **visa** *verb transitive* **-saed, -sa•ing** approve visa for (someone)
vis•age [VIZ-ij] *noun* face
vis-à-vis [vee-zə-VEE] *Fr.* 1 in relation to, regarding 2 opposite to
vis•cer•a [VIS-ər-ə] *plural noun* large internal organs of body, esp. of abdomen > **visc'er•al** [-əl] *adjective*
vis•cid [VIS-id] *adjective* sticky, of a consistency like molasses > **vis•cid'i•ty** *noun*
vis•cous [VIS-kəs] *adjective* thick and sticky

DICTIONARY • THESAURUS

2 JUSTIFY, defend, excuse
vindication *noun* 1 EXONERATION, exculpation, rehabilitation
2 JUSTIFICATION, defense, excuse
vindictive *adjective* VENGEFUL, implacable, malicious, resentful, revengeful, spiteful, unforgiving, unrelenting
vintage *adjective* BEST, choice, classic, prime, select, superior
violate *verb* 1 BREAK, contravene, disobey, disregard, encroach upon, infringe, transgress
2 DESECRATE, abuse, befoul, defile, dishonor, pollute, profane
3 RAPE, abuse, assault, debauch, ravish
violation *noun* 1 INFRINGEMENT, abuse, breach, contravention, encroachment, infraction, transgression, trespass
2 DESECRATION, defilement, profanation, sacrilege, spoliation
violence *noun* 1 FORCE, bloodshed, brutality, cruelty, ferocity, fighting, savagery, terrorism
2 INTENSITY, abandon, fervor, force, severity, vehemence
violent *adjective* DESTRUCTIVE, brutal, cruel, hot-headed, murderous, riotous, savage, uncontrollable, unrestrained, vicious
V.I.P. *noun* CELEBRITY, big name, luminary, somebody, star
virgin *noun* 1 MAIDEN, girl
▷ *adjective* 2 PURE, chaste, immaculate, uncorrupted, undefiled, vestal, virginal
virginity *noun* CHASTITY, maidenhood
virile *adjective* MANLY, lusty, macho, manlike, masculine, red-blooded, strong, vigorous
virility *noun* MASCULINITY, machismo, manhood, vigor
virtual *adjective* PRACTICAL, essential, in all but name
virtually *adverb* PRACTICALLY, almost, as good as, in all but name, in effect, in essence, nearly
virtue *noun* 1 GOODNESS, incorruptibility, integrity, morality, probity, rectitude, righteousness, uprightness, worth
2 MERIT, advantage, asset, attribute, credit, good point, plus (*informal*), strength
virtuosity *noun* MASTERY, brilliance, craft, expertise, flair, panache, polish, skill
virtuoso *noun* MASTER, artist, genius, maestro, magician
virtuous *adjective* GOOD, ethical, honorable, incorruptible, moral, praiseworthy, righteous, upright, worthy

> **vis•cos'i•ty** *noun, plural* **-ties**
vise [vīs] *noun* appliance with screw jaw for holding things while working on them
vis•i•ble [VIZ-ə-bəl] *adjective* that can be seen > **vis•i•bil'i•ty** *noun* degree of clarity of atmosphere, esp. for navigation > **vis'i•bly** *adverb*
vi•sion [VIZH-ən] *noun* 1 sight 2 insight 3 dream 4 phantom 5 imagination > **vi'sion•ar•y** [-er-ee] *adjective* 1 marked by vision 2 impractical ▷ *noun, plural* **-ar•ies** 3 mystic 4 impractical person
vis•it [VIZ-it] *verb* 1 go, come and see, stay temporarily with (someone) ▷ *noun* 2 stay 3 call at person's home, etc. 4 official call > **vis•it•a'tion** [-ə-TAY-shən] *noun* 1 formal visit or inspection 2 affliction or plague > **vis'i•tor** *noun*
vi•sor [VĪ-zər] *noun* 1 front part of helmet made to move up and down before the face 2 eyeshade, esp. on car 3 peak on cap
vis•ta [VIS-tə] *noun* view, esp. distant view
vis•u•al [VIZH-oo-əl] *adjective* 1 of sight 2 visible > **vis'u•al•ize** *verb transitive* **-ized, -iz•ing** form mental image of > **vis•u•al•i•za'tion** *noun*
vi•tal [VĪT-l] *adjective* 1 necessary to, affecting life 2 lively, animated 3 essential 4 highly important > **vi'tals** *plural noun* vital organs of body > **vi•tal'i•ty** *noun* life, vigor > **vi'tal•ize** [-tə-līz] *verb transitive* **-ized, -iz•ing** 1 give life to 2 lend vigor to > **vi'tal•ly** *adverb*
vi•ta•min [VĪ-tə-min] *noun* any of group of substances occurring in foodstuffs and essential to health
vi•ti•ate [VISH-ee-ayt] *verb transitive* **-at•ed, -at•ing** 1 spoil 2 deprive of efficacy 3 invalidate > **vi•ti•a'tion** *noun*
vit•re•ous [VI-tree-əs] *adjective* 1 of glass 2 glassy > **vit•ri•fy** [VI-trə-fī] *verb* **-fied, -fy•ing** convert into glass, or glassy substance > **vit•ri•fi•ca'tion** *noun*
vit•ri•ol [VI-tree-əl] *noun* 1 sulfuric acid 2 caustic speech > **vit•ri•ol'ic** *adjective*
vi•tu•per•ate [vī-TOO-pə-rayt] *verb transitive* **-at•ed, -at•ing** abuse in words, revile > **vi•tu'per•a•tive** *adjective*
vi•va•cious [vi-VAY-shəs] *adjective* lively, gay, sprightly > **vi•vac'i•ty** [-VAS-i-tee] *noun*
vi•va vo•ce [VĪ-və VOH-see] *Lat. adjective, adverb* 1 by word of mouth ▷ *noun* 2 in European universities, oral examination
viv'id *adjective* 1 bright, intense 2 clear 3 lively, animated 4 graphic > **viv'id•ly** *adverb*
viv•i•fy [VIV-ə-fī] *verb transitive* **-fied, -fy•ing** animate, inspire
vi•vip•a•rous [vī-VIP-ər-əs] *adjective* bringing forth young alive
viv•i•sec•tion [viv-ə-SEK-shən] *noun* dissection of, or operating on, living animals > **viv•i•sec'tion•ist** *noun*
vix•en [VIK-sən] *noun* 1 female fox 2 spiteful woman > **vix'en•ish** *adjective*
viz. *short for* **videlicet**
vi•zier [vi-ZEER] *noun* (formerly) high official in some Muslim countries
vo•cab•u•lar•y [voh-KAB-yə-ler-ee] *noun, plural* **-lar•ies** 1 list of words, usu. in alphabetical order 2 stock of words used in particular language, etc.
vo•cal [VOH-kəl] *adjective* 1 of, with, or giving out voice 2 outspoken, articulate ▷ *noun* 3 piece of popular music that is sung > **vo'cal•ist** *noun* singer > **vo'cal•ize** *verb transitive* **-ized, -iz•ing** utter with voice
vo•ca•tion [voh-KAY-shən] *noun* (urge,

DICTIONARY

V

THESAURUS

virulent *adjective* POISONOUS, deadly, lethal, pernicious, toxic, venomous
viscous *adjective* THICK, gelatinous, sticky, syrupy
visible *adjective* APPARENT, clear, discernible, evident, in view, manifest, observable, perceptible, unconcealed
vision *noun* 1 SIGHT, eyesight, perception, seeing, view
2 IMAGE, concept, conception, daydream, dream, fantasy, idea, ideal
3 HALLUCINATION, apparition, chimera, delusion, illusion, mirage, revelation
4 FORESIGHT, discernment, farsightedness, imagination, insight, intuition, penetration, prescience
visionary *adjective* 1 PROPHETIC, mystical
2 IMPRACTICAL, idealistic, quixotic, romantic, speculative, starry-eyed, unrealistic, unworkable, utopian
▷ *noun* 3 PROPHET, mystic, seer
visit *verb* 1 CALL ON, drop in on (*informal*), look (someone) up, stay with, stop by
▷ *noun* 2 CALL, sojourn, stay, stop
visitation *noun* 1 INSPECTION, examination, visit
2 CATASTROPHE, blight, calamity, cataclysm, disaster, ordeal, punishment, scourge
visitor *noun* GUEST, caller, company
vista *noun* VIEW, panorama, perspective, prospect
visual *adjective* 1 OPTICAL, ocular, optic
2 OBSERVABLE, discernible, perceptible, visible
visualize *verb* PICTURE, conceive of, envisage, imagine
vital *adjective* 1 ESSENTIAL, basic, fundamental, imperative, indispensable, necessary, requisite
2 IMPORTANT, critical, crucial, decisive, key, life-or-death, significant, urgent
3 LIVELY, animated, dynamic, energetic, spirited, vibrant, vigorous, vivacious, zestful
vitality *noun* ENERGY, animation, exuberance, life, liveliness, strength, vigor, vivacity
vitriolic *adjective* BITTER, acerbic, caustic, envenomed, sardonic, scathing, venomous, virulent, withering
vivacious *adjective* LIVELY, bubbling, ebullient, high-spirited, sparkling, spirited, sprightly, upbeat (*informal*), vital
vivacity *noun* LIVELINESS, animation, ebullience, energy, gaiety, high spirits, sparkle, spirit, sprightliness
vivid *adjective* 1 BRIGHT, brilliant, clear, colorful, glowing, intense, rich
2 LIFELIKE, dramatic, graphic, memorable, powerful, realistic, stirring, telling, true to life
vocabulary *noun* WORDS, dictionary, glossary, language, lexicon
vocal *adjective* 1 SPOKEN, oral, said, uttered, voiced
2 OUTSPOKEN, articulate, eloquent, expressive, forthright, frank, plain-spoken, strident, vociferous

inclination, predisposition to) particular career, profession, etc. > **vo•ca'tion•al** [-əl] *adjective*

voc•a•tive [VOK-ə-tiv] *noun* in some languages, case of nouns used in addressing a person

vo•cif•er•ate [voh-SIF-ə-rayt] *verb* **-at•ed, -at•ing** exclaim, cry out > **vo•cif'er•ous** [-əs] *adjective* shouting, noisy

vod•ka [VOD-kə] *noun* Russian spirit distilled from grain, potatoes, etc.

vogue [vohg] *noun* 1 fashion, style 2 popularity

voice [vois] *noun* 1 sound given out by person in speaking, singing, etc. 2 quality of the sound 3 expressed opinion 4 (right to) share in discussion 5 verbal forms proper to relation of subject and action ▷ *verb transitive* **voiced, voic•ing** 6 give utterance to, express > **voice'less** [-lis] *adjective* > **voice mail** electronic system for recording and storage of telephone messages, which can then be checked later or accessed remotely

void *adjective* 1 empty 2 destitute 3 not legally binding ▷ *noun* 4 empty space ▷ *verb transitive* 5 make ineffectual or invalid 6 empty out

vol•a•tile [VOL-ə-tl] *adjective* 1 evaporating quickly 2 lively 3 fickle, changeable > **vol•a•til'i•ty** *noun* > **vol'a•ti•lize** *verb* **-lized, -liz•ing** (cause to) evaporate

vol•ca•no [vol-KAY-noh] *noun, plural* **-noes, -nos** 1 hole in Earth's crust through which lava, ashes, smoke, etc. are discharged 2 mountain so formed > **vol•can'ic** *adjective* > **vol•can•ol'o•gy** [-kə-NOL-ə-jee] *noun* study of volcanoes and volcanic phenomena, vulcanology

vole [vohl] *noun* small rodent

vo•li•tion [voh-LISH-ən] *noun* 1 act, power of willing 2 exercise of the will

vol•ley [VOL-ee] *noun, plural* **-leys** 1 simultaneous discharge of weapons or missiles 2 rush of oaths, questions, etc. 3 *tennis* flight, return of moving ball before it touches ground ▷ *verb* **-leyed, -ley•ing** 4 discharge 5 utter 6 fly, strike, etc. in volley > **vol'ley•ball** *noun* team game where large ball is hit by hand over high net

volt [vohlt] *noun* unit of electric potential > **volt'age** [-ij] *noun* electric potential difference expressed in volts > **volt'me•ter** *noun*

volte-face [vohlt-FAHS] *noun, plural* **volte-face** *Fr.* complete reversal of opinion or direction

vol•u•ble [VOL-yə-bəl] *adjective* talking easily, readily and at length > **vol'u•bly** *adverb* > **vol•u•bil'i•ty** *noun*

vol•ume [VOL-yəm] *noun* 1 space occupied 2 bulk, mass 3 amount 4 power, fullness of voice or sound 5 control on radio, etc. for adjusting this 6 book 7 part of book bound in one cover > **vol•u•met'ric** *adjective* pert. to measurement by volume > **vo•lu•mi•nous** [və-LOO-mə-nəs] *adjective* bulky, copious

vol•un•tar•y [VOL-ən-ter-ee] *adjective* 1 having, done by free will 2 done without payment 3 supported by freewill contributions 4 spontaneous ▷ *noun, plural* **-tar•ies** 5 organ solo in church service > **vol•un•tar'i•ly** *adverb* > **vol•un•teer'** *noun* 1 one who offers service, joins force, etc. of own free will ▷ *verb* 2 offer oneself or one's services

vol•up•tu•ous [və-LUP-choo-əs] *adjective* of, contributing to pleasures of the senses > **vol•up'tu•ar•y** [-er-ee] *noun, plural* **-ar•ies** one given to luxury and sensual pleasures

vo•lute [və-LOOT] *noun* spiral or twisting turn, form or object

vom•it *verb* 1 eject (contents of stomach) through mouth ▷ *noun* 2 matter vomited

voo'doo *noun, plural* **-doos** 1 practice of black magic, esp. in W Indies, witchcraft ▷ *verb transitive* **-dooed, -doo•ing** 2 affect by voodoo

vo•ra•cious [vaw-RAY-shəs] *adjective* greedy, ravenous > **vo•rac'i•ty** [-RAS-i-tee] *noun*

vor•tex [VOR-teks] *noun, plural* **-ti•ces** [-tə-seez] 1

vocation *noun* PROFESSION, calling, career, job, mission, pursuit, trade

vociferous *adjective* NOISY, clamorous, loud, outspoken, strident, uproarious, vehement, vocal

vogue *noun* 1 FASHION, craze, custom, mode, style, trend, way
2 ▷ **in vogue** POPULAR, accepted, current, in favor, prevalent, in use, trendy

voice *noun* 1 SOUND, articulation, tone, utterance
2 SAY, view, vote, will, wish
▷ *verb* 3 EXPRESS, air, articulate, declare, enunciate, utter

void *noun* 1 EMPTINESS, blankness, gap, lack, space, vacuity, vacuum
▷ *adjective* 2 INVALID, ineffective, inoperative, null and void, useless, vain, worthless
3 EMPTY, bare, free, tenantless, unfilled, unoccupied, vacant
▷ *verb* 4 INVALIDATE, cancel, nullify, rescind
5 EMPTY, drain, evacuate

volatile *adjective* 1 CHANGEABLE, explosive, inconstant, unsettled, unstable, unsteady, variable
2 TEMPERAMENTAL, erratic, fickle, mercurial, up and down (*informal*)

volition *noun* FREE WILL, choice, choosing, discretion, preference, will

volley *noun* BARRAGE, blast, bombardment, burst, cannonade, fusillade, hail, salvo, shower

voluble *adjective* TALKATIVE, articulate, fluent, forthcoming, glib, loquacious

volume *noun* 1 CAPACITY, compass, dimensions
2 AMOUNT, aggregate, body, bulk, mass, quantity, total
3 BOOK, publication, title, tome, treatise

voluminous *adjective* LARGE, ample, capacious, cavernous, roomy, vast

voluntarily *adverb* WILLINGLY, by choice, freely, off one's own bat, of one's own accord

voluntary *adjective* UNFORCED, discretionary, free, optional, spontaneous, willing

volunteer *verb* OFFER, step forward

voluptuous *adjective* 1 BUXOM, ample, curvaceous (*informal*), enticing, seductive, shapely
2 SENSUAL, epicurean, hedonistic, licentious, luxurious, self-indulgent, sybaritic

vomit *verb* RETCH, barf (*slang*), disgorge, emit, heave, regurgitate, spew out *or* spew up, throw up (*informal*)

voracious *adjective* 1 GLUTTONOUS, greedy, hungry, insatiable, omnivorous, ravenous

whirlpool 2 whirling mass or motion
vo•ta•ry [VOH-tə-ree] *noun, plural* **-ta•ries** one vowed to service or pursuit > **vo'tive** [-tiv] *adjective* given, consecrated by vow
vote [voht] *noun* 1 formal expression of choice 2 individual pronouncement 3 right to give it, in question or election 4 result of voting 5 that which is given or allowed by vote ▷ *verb* **vot•ed, vot•ing** 6 express, declare opinion, choice, preference, etc. by vote 7 authorize, enact, etc. by vote
vouch [vowch] *verb intransitive* (usu. with *for*) guarantee, make oneself responsible for > **vouch'er** *noun* 1 document proving correctness of item in accounts, or to establish facts 2 ticket as substitute for cash > **vouch•safe'** [-SAYF] *verb transitive* **-safed, -saf•ing** agree, condescend to grant or do something
vow *noun* 1 solemn promise, esp. religious one ▷ *verb transitive* 2 promise, threaten by vow
vow•el [VOW-əl] *noun* 1 any speech sound pronounced without stoppage or friction of the breath 2 letter standing for such sound: *a, e, i, o, u*
voy•age [VOI-ij] *noun* 1 journey, esp. long one, by sea or air ▷ *verb intransitive* **-aged, -ag•ing** 2 make voyage > **voy'ag•er** *noun*
vo•yeur [vwah-YUR] *noun* one obtaining sexual pleasure by watching sexual activities of others
vul•can•ize [VUL-kə-nīz] *verb transitive* **-ized, -iz•ing** treat (rubber) with sulfur at high temperature to increase its durability > **vul'can•ite** *noun* rubber so hardened > **vul•can•i•za'tion** *noun* > **vul•can•ol'o•gy** *see* **volcanology**
vul•gar [VUL-gər] *adjective* 1 offending against good taste 2 coarse 3 common > **vul•gar'i•an** [-GAIR-ee-ən] *noun* vulgar (rich) person > **vul'gar•ism** *noun* coarse, obscene word, phrase > **vul•gar'i•ty** *noun, plural* **-ties** > **vul•gar•i•za'tion** [-gə-ri-ZAY-shən] *noun* > **vul'gar•ize** *verb transitive* **-ized, -iz•ing** make vulgar or too common
Vul•gate [VUL-gayt] *noun* fourth-century Latin version of the Bible
vul•ner•a•ble [VUL-nər-ə-bəl] *adjective* 1 capable of being physically or emotionally wounded or hurt 2 exposed, open to attack, persuasion, etc.
vul•pine [VUL-pin] *adjective* 1 of foxes 2 foxy
vul•ture [VUL-chər] *noun* large bird that feeds on carrion > **vul'tur•ous** [-əs] *adjective* 1 of vulture 2 rapacious
vul•va [VUL-və] *noun, plural* **-vas** external genitals of human female
vy•ing [VĪ-ing] *pr. p. of* **vie**

DICTIONARY

V

THESAURUS

2 AVID, hungry, insatiable, rapacious, uncontrolled, unquenchable
vortex *noun* WHIRLPOOL, eddy, maelstrom
vote *noun* 1 POLL, ballot, franchise, plebiscite, referendum, show of hands
▷ *verb* 2 ELECT, cast one's vote, opt
voucher *noun* TICKET, coupon, token
vouch for *verb* 1 GUARANTEE, answer for, certify, give assurance of, stand witness, swear to
2 CONFIRM, affirm, assert, attest to, support, uphold
vow *noun* 1 PROMISE, oath, pledge
▷ *verb* 2 PROMISE, affirm, pledge, swear
voyage *noun* JOURNEY, crossing, cruise, passage, trip
vulgar *adjective* CRUDE, coarse, common, impolite, indecent, off-color, ribald, risqué, rude, tasteless, uncouth, unrefined
vulgarity *noun* CRUDENESS, bad taste, coarseness, indelicacy, ribaldry, rudeness, tastelessness
vulnerable *adjective* 1 WEAK, sensitive, susceptible, tender, thin-skinned
2 EXPOSED, accessible, assailable, defenseless, unprotected, wide open

Ww

W *chem.* tungsten
wack•y [WAK-ee] *adjective* **wack•i•er, wack•i•est** (*informal*) eccentric or funny > **wack'i•ness** [-nis] *noun*
wad [wod] *noun* 1 small pad of fibrous material 2 thick roll of paper money 3 sum of money ▷ *verb transitive* **wad•ded, wad•ding** 4 line, pad, stuff, etc. with wad > **wadding** *noun* stuffing
wad•dle [WOD-l] *verb intransitive* **-dled, -dling** 1 walk like duck ▷ *noun* 2 this gait
wade [wayd] *verb intransitive* **wad•ed, wad•ing** 1 walk through something that hampers movement, esp. water 2 proceed with difficulty > **wad'er** *noun* 1 person or bird that wades > **wad'ers** 1 angler's high waterproof boots
wa•di [WO-dee] *noun, plural* **-dis** in the East, watercourse that is dry except in wet season
wa•fer [WAY-fər] *noun* 1 thin, crisp biscuit 2 thin slice of anything 3 thin disk of unleavened bread used in the Eucharist
waf•fle[1] [WOF-əl] *noun* kind of batter cake with gridlike design
waf•fle[2] (*informal*) ▷ *verb intransitive* **-fled, -fling** 1 speak, write in vague wordy manner ▷ *noun* 2 vague speech, etc. 3 nonsense
waft [wahft] *verb transitive* 1 convey smoothly through air or water ▷ *noun* 2 breath of wind 3 odor, whiff
wag *verb* **wagged, wag•ging** 1 (cause to) move rapidly from side to side ▷ *noun* 2 instance of wagging 3 humorous, witty person > **wag'gish** *adjective*
wage [wayj] *noun* 1 (*often plural*) payment for work done ▷ *verb transitive* **waged, wag•ing** 2 carry on
wa•ger [WAY-jər] *noun, verb transitive* bet
wag•on [WAG-ən] *noun* four-wheeled vehicle for heavy loads **off the wagon** (*slang*) drinking alcoholic beverages again **on the wagon** (*slang*) abstaining from alcoholic beverages
waif [wayf] *noun* homeless person, esp. child
wail [wayl] *verb* 1 cry out, lament ▷ *noun* 2

DICTIONARY • THESAURUS

wacky *adjective* (*informal*) FOOLISH, absurd, asinine, crackpot (*informal*), crazy, idiotic, silly, stupid, witless
wad *noun* MASS, bundle, hunk, roll
waddle *verb* SHUFFLE, sway, toddle, totter, wobble
wade *verb* 1 WALK THROUGH, ford, paddle, splash 2 ▷ **wade through** PLOW THROUGH, drudge at, labor at, peg away at, toil at, work one's way through
waft *verb* CARRY, bear, convey, drift, float, transport
wag[1] *verb* 1 WAVE, bob, nod, quiver, shake, stir, vibrate, wiggle ▷ *noun* 2 WAVE, bob, nod, quiver, shake, vibration, wiggle
wage *noun* 1 *also* **wages** PAYMENT, allowance, emolument, fee, pay, recompense, remuneration, reward, stipend ▷ *verb* 2 ENGAGE IN, carry on, conduct, practice, proceed with, prosecute, pursue, undertake
wager *noun* 1 BET, gamble ▷ *verb* 2 BET, chance, gamble, lay, pledge, risk, speculate, stake, venture
waif *noun* STRAY, foundling, orphan
wail *verb* 1 CRY, bawl, grieve, howl, lament,

mournful cry

wain•scot [WAYN-skət] *noun* 1 wooden lining of walls of room ▷ *verb transitive* **-scot•ed, -scot•ting** 2 line thus

waist [wayst] *noun* 1 part of body between hips and ribs 2 various narrow central parts > **waist•coat** [WES-kət] *noun* *Brit* vest > **waist'line** *noun* line, size of waist (of person, garment)

wait [wayt] *verb* 1 stay in one place, remain inactive in expectation (of something) 2 be prepared (for something) 3 delay ▷ *verb intransitive* 4 serve in restaurant, etc. ▷ *noun* 5 act or period of waiting > **wait'er** *noun* 1 attendant serving diners at hotel, restaurant, etc. 2 one who waits > **wait•ress** [WAY-tris] *noun feminine*

waive [wayv] *verb transitive* **waived, waiv•ing** 1 forgo 2 not to insist on > **waiv'er** *noun* (written statement of) this act

wake[1] [wayk] *verb* **waked** *or* **woke, waked** *or* **wok•en, wak•ing** 1 rouse from sleep 2 stir up ▷ *noun* 3 vigil 4 watch beside corpse > **wak•en** [WAY-kən] *verb* wake > **wake•ful** [-fəl] *adjective*

wake[2] *noun* track or path left by anything that has passed, as track of turbulent water behind ship

walk [wawk] *verb* 1 (cause, assist to) move, travel on foot at ordinary pace ▷ *verb transitive* 2 cross, pass through by walking 3 escort, conduct by walking ▷ *noun* 4 act, instance of walking 5 path or other place or route for walking 6 manner of walking 7 occupation, career > **walk'er** *noun* 1 one who walks 2 framework of metal for support while walking > **walk•ie-talk•ie** [WAW-kee-TAW-kee] *noun* portable radio set containing both transmission and receiver units > **walking stick** stick, cane carried while walking > **Walk•man** [WAWK-man] *noun* ® small portable cassette player, radio, etc. equipped with headphones > **walk'out** *noun* 1 strike 2 act of leaving as a protest > **walk'o•ver** *noun* unopposed or easy victory

wall [wawl] *noun* 1 structure of brick, stone, etc. serving as fence, side of building, etc. 2 surface of one 3 anything resembling this ▷ *verb transitive* 4 enclose with wall 5 block up with wall > **wall'flow•er** *noun* 1 garden flower, often growing on walls 2 at dance, person who remains seated for lack of partner > **wall'pa•per** *noun* paper, usu. patterned, to cover interior walls

wal•la•by [WOL-ə-bee] *noun, plural* **-bies** Aust. marsupial similar to and smaller than kangaroo

wal•let [WOL-it] *noun* small folding case, esp. for paper money, documents, etc.

wall•eyed [WAWL-īd] *adjective* 1 having eyes turned outward in squint 2 having eyes with pale irises

wal•lop [WOL-əp] (*informal*) 1 *verb transitive* beat soundly 2 strike hard ▷ *noun* 3 stroke or blow > **wal'lop•er** *noun* (*informal*) one who wallops > **wal'lop•ing** (*informal*) ▷ *noun* 1 thrashing ▷ *adjective, adverb* 2 very, great(ly)

wal•low [WOL-oh] *verb intransitive* 1 roll (in liquid or mud) 2 revel (in) ▷ *noun*

wal•nut [WAWL-nut] *noun* 1 large nut with crinkled shell splitting easily into two halves 2 the tree 3 its wood

wal•rus [WAWL-rəs] *noun* large sea mammal with long tusks

waltz [wawlts] *noun* 1 ballroom dance 2 music for it ▷ *verb*

wam•pum [WOM-pəm] *noun* beads made of shells, formerly used by N American Indians as money and for ornament

wan [won] *adjective* **wan•ner, wan•nest** pale, sickly complexioned, pallid

wand [wond] *noun* stick, usu. straight and slender, esp. as carried by magician, etc.

DICTIONARY

W

THESAURUS

weep, yowl
▷ *noun* 2 CRY, complaint, howl, lament, moan, weeping, yowl

wait *verb* 1 REMAIN, hang fire, hold back, linger, pause, rest, stay, tarry
▷ *noun* 2 DELAY, halt, hold-up, interval, pause, rest, stay

waiter *or* **waitress** *noun* ATTENDANT, server, steward *or* stewardess

wait on, wait upon *verb* SERVE, attend, minister to, tend

waive *verb* SET ASIDE, abandon, dispense with, forgo, give up, relinquish, remit, renounce

wake[1] *verb* 1 AWAKEN, arise, awake, bestir, come to, get up, rouse, stir
2 ACTIVATE, animate, arouse, excite, fire, galvanize, kindle, provoke, stimulate, stir up
▷ *noun* 3 VIGIL, deathwatch, funeral, watch

wake[2] *noun* SLIPSTREAM, aftermath, backwash, path, track, trail, train, wash, waves

wakeful *adjective* 1 SLEEPLESS, insomniac, restless
2 WATCHFUL, alert, alive, attentive, observant, on guard, vigilant, wary

waken *verb* AWAKEN, activate, arouse, awake, rouse, stir

walk *verb* 1 GO, amble, hike, march, move, pace, step, stride, stroll
2 ESCORT, accompany, convoy, take
▷ *noun* 3 STROLL, hike, march, promenade, ramble, saunter, trek, trudge
4 GAIT, carriage, step
5 PATH, alley, avenue, esplanade, footpath, lane, promenade, trail
6 ▷ **walk of life** PROFESSION, calling, career, field, line, trade, vocation

walker *noun* PEDESTRIAN, hiker, rambler, wayfarer

walkout *noun* STRIKE, industrial action, protest, stoppage

walkover *noun* PUSHOVER (*slang*), breeze (*informal*), cakewalk (*informal*), child's play (*informal*), picnic (*informal*), piece of cake (*informal*)

wall *noun* 1 PARTITION, enclosure, screen
2 BARRIER, fence, hedge, impediment, obstacle, obstruction

wallet *noun* HOLDER, case, pocketbook, pouch, purse

wallop *verb* 1 HIT, batter, beat, clobber (*slang*), pound, pummel, strike, thrash, thump, whack
▷ *noun* 2 BLOW, bash, punch, slug, smack, thump, thwack, whack

wallow *verb* 1 REVEL, bask, delight, glory, luxuriate, relish, take pleasure
2 ROLL ABOUT, splash around

wan *adjective* PALE, anemic, ashen, pallid, pasty,

wan•der [WON-dər] *verb* 1 roam, ramble ▷ *verb intransitive* 2 go astray, deviate ▷ *noun* > **wan'der•er** *noun* > **wand'er•lust** *noun* irrepressible urge to wander or travel
wane [wayn] *verb intransitive, noun* **waned, wan•ing** 1 decline 2 (of moon) decrease in size
wan•gle [WANG-gəl] *verb transitive* **-gled, -gling** (*informal*) manipulate, manage in skillful way
want [wont] *verb* 1 desire 2 lack ▷ *noun* 3 desire 4 need 5 deficiency > **want'ed** [-id] *adjective* being sought, esp. by the police > **want'ing** *adjective* 1 lacking 2 below standard
wan•ton [WON-tən] *adjective* 1 dissolute 2 without motive, thoughtless 3 unrestrained ▷ *noun* 4 wanton person
war [wor] *noun* 1 fighting between nations 2 state of hostility 3 conflict, contest ▷ *verb intransitive* **warred, war•ring** 4 make war > **war'like** *adjective* 1 of, for war 2 fond of war > **war•ri•or** [WOR-ee-ər] *noun* fighter > **war cry** 1 cry used by attacking troops in war 2 distinctive word, phrase used by political party, etc. > **war'fare** [-fair] *noun* hostilities > **war'head** [-hed] *noun* part of missile, etc. containing explosives > **war•mon•ger** [WOR-mung-gər] *noun* one fostering, encouraging war > **war'ship** *noun* vessel armed, armored for naval warfare
war•ble [WOR-bəl] *verb intransitive* **-bled, -bling** sing with trills > **war•bler** [-blər] *noun* 1 person or bird that warbles 2 any of various kinds of small songbirds
ward [word] *noun* 1 division of city, hospital, etc. 2 minor under care of guardian 3 guardianship 4 curved bar in lock, groove in key that prevents incorrectly cut key opening lock > **ward'room** *noun* officers' mess on warship > **ward off** avert, repel
war•den [WOR-dn] *noun* person, officer in charge of prison
ward•robe [WOR-drohb] *noun* 1 piece of furniture for hanging clothes in 2 person's supply of clothes 3 costumes of theatrical company
ware [wair] *noun* 1 goods 2 articles collectively > **wares** 1 goods for sale 2 commodities 3 merchandise > **ware'house** *noun* 1 storehouse for goods prior to distribution and sale ▷ *verb transitive* 2 store for future shipment or use
war•lock [WOR-lok] *noun* wizard, sorcerer
warm [worm] *adjective* 1 moderately hot 2 serving to maintain heat 3 affectionate 4 ardent 5 earnest 6 hearty 7 (of color) having yellow or red for a basis ▷ *verb* 8 make, become warm > **warm'ly** *adverb* > **warmth** *noun* 1 mild heat 2 cordiality 3 vehemence, anger
warn [worn] *verb transitive* 1 put on guard 2

DICTIONARY • THESAURUS

sickly, washed out, white
wand *noun* STICK, baton, rod
wander *verb* 1 ROAM, drift, meander, ramble, range, rove, stray, stroll
2 DEVIATE, depart, digress, diverge, err, go astray, swerve, veer
▷ *noun* 3 EXCURSION, cruise, meander, ramble
wanderer *noun* TRAVELER, drifter, gypsy, nomad, rambler, rover, vagabond, voyager
wandering *adjective* NOMADIC, itinerant, migratory, peripatetic, rootless, roving, traveling, vagrant, wayfaring
wane *verb* 1 DECLINE, decrease, diminish, dwindle, ebb, fade, fail, lessen, subside, taper off, weaken
▷ *noun* 2 ▷ **on the wane** DECLINING, dwindling, ebbing, fading, obsolescent, on the decline, tapering off, weakening
wangle *verb* CONTRIVE, arrange, engineer, fix (*informal*), maneuver, manipulate, pull off
want *verb* 1 DESIRE, covet, crave, hanker after, hope for, hunger for, long for, thirst for, wish, yearn for
2 NEED, call for, demand, lack, miss, require
▷ *noun* 3 WISH, appetite, craving, desire, longing, need, requirement, yearning
4 LACK, absence, dearth, deficiency, famine, insufficiency, paucity, scarcity, shortage
5 POVERTY, destitution, neediness, penury, privation
wanting *adjective* 1 LACKING, absent, incomplete, missing, short, shy
2 INADEQUATE, defective, deficient, faulty, imperfect, lousy (*slang*), poor, substandard, unsound
wanton *adjective* 1 UNPROVOKED, arbitrary, gratuitous, groundless, motiveless, needless, senseless, uncalled-for, unjustifiable, willful
2 PROMISCUOUS, dissipated, dissolute, immoral, lecherous, libidinous, loose, lustful, shameless, unchaste
war *noun* 1 FIGHTING, battle, combat, conflict, enmity, hostilities, struggle, warfare
▷ *verb* 2 FIGHT, battle, campaign against, clash, combat, take up arms, wage war
warble *verb* SING, chirp, trill, twitter
ward *noun* 1 ROOM, apartment, cubicle
2 DISTRICT, area, division, precinct, quarter, zone
3 DEPENDANT, charge, minor, protégé, pupil
warden *noun* KEEPER, administrator, caretaker, curator, custodian, guardian, ranger, superintendent
ward off *verb* REPEL, avert, avoid, deflect, fend off, parry, stave off
wardrobe *noun* 1 CLOTHES CUPBOARD, closet
2 CLOTHES, apparel, attire
warehouse *noun* STORE, depository, depot, stockroom, storehouse
wares *plural noun* GOODS, commodities, merchandise, produce, products, stock, stuff
warfare *noun* WAR, arms, battle, combat, conflict, fighting, hostilities
warily *adverb* CAUTIOUSLY, carefully, charily, circumspectly, distrustfully, gingerly, suspiciously, vigilantly, watchfully, with care
warlike *adjective* BELLIGERENT, aggressive, bellicose, bloodthirsty, hawkish, hostile, martial, warmongering
warlock *noun* MAGICIAN, conjurer, enchanter, sorcerer, wizard
warm *adjective* 1 HEATED, balmy, lukewarm, pleasant, sunny, tepid, thermal
2 AFFECTIONATE, amorous, cordial, friendly, hospitable, kindly, loving, tender
▷ *verb* 3 HEAT, heat up, melt, thaw, warm up
warmonger *noun* HAWK, belligerent, militarist, saber-rattler
warmth *noun* 1 HEAT, hotness, warmness
2 AFFECTION, amorousness, cordiality,

caution, admonish 3 give advance information to 4 notify authoritatively > **warn'ing** *noun* 1 hint of harm, etc. 2 admonition 3 advance notice of
warp [worp] *verb* 1 (cause to) twist (out of shape) 2 pervert or be perverted ▷ *noun* 3 state, condition of being warped 4 lengthwise threads on loom
war•rant [WOR-ənt] *noun* 1 authority 2 document giving authority ▷ *verb transitive* 3 guarantee 4 authorize, justify > **war•ran•tee'** *noun* person given warranty > **war'ran•tor** [-tər] *noun* person, company giving warranty > **war'ran•ty** [-tee] *noun, plural* **-ties** 1 guarantee of quality of goods 2 security > **warrant officer** officer in certain armed services holding rank between commissioned and noncommissioned officer
war•ren [WOR-ən] *noun* (burrows inhabited by) colony of rabbits
warrior [WOR-ee-ər] *noun see* **war**
wart [wort] *noun* small hard growth on skin > **wart hog** kind of African wild pig
war•y [WAIR-ee] *adjective* **war•i•er, war•i•est** watchful, cautious, alert > **war'i•ly** *adverb*
was [wuz, woz] *verb first and third person sing pt. of* **be**
wash [wosh] *verb* 1 clean (oneself, clothes, etc.) esp. with water, soap, etc. ▷ *verb intransitive* 2 be washable 3 (*informal*) be able to be proved true ▷ *verb transitive* 4 move, be moved by water 5 flow, sweep over, against ▷ *noun* 6 act of washing 7 clothes washed at one time 8 sweep of water, esp. set up by moving ship 9 thin coat of color > **wash'a•ble** *adjective* capable of being washed without damage, etc. > **wash'er** *noun* 1 one who, that which, washes 2 ring put under a nut > **wash'ing** *noun* clothes to be washed > **wash'y** *adjective* **wash•i•er, wash•i•est** 1 dilute 2 watery 3 insipid > **wash'out** *noun* 1 rainout 2 (*informal*) complete failure
wasp [wosp] *noun* striped stinging insect resembling bee > **wasp'ish** *adjective* irritable, snappish > **wasp waist** very small waist
waste [wayst] *verb transitive* **wast•ed, wast•ing** 1 expend uselessly, use extravagantly 2 fail to take advantage of 3 lay desolate ▷ *verb intransitive* **wast•ed, wast•ing** 4 dwindle 5 pine away ▷ *noun* 6 act of wasting 7 what is wasted 8 desert ▷ *adjective* 9 worthless, useless 10 desert 11 wasted > **wast•age** [WAY-stij] *noun* 1 loss by use or decay 2 losses as result of wastefulness > **waste'ful** [-fəl] *adjective* extravagant > **waste'ful•ness** [-nis] *noun* > **waste product** 1 discarded material in manufacturing process 2 excreted urine, feces > **wast•rel** [WAY-strəl] *noun* wasteful person, spendthrift
watch [woch] *verb transitive* 1 observe closely 2 guard ▷ *verb intransitive* 3 wait expectantly (for) 4 be on watch ▷ *noun* 5 portable timepiece for wrist, pocket, etc. 6 state of being on the lookout 7 guard 8 spell of duty > **watch'ful** [-fəl] *adjective* > **watch'mak•er** *noun* one skilled in making and repairing watches > **watch'man** [-mən] *noun, plural* **-men** person guarding building, etc., esp. at night > **watch'word** [-wurd] *noun* 1 password 2 rallying cry

heartiness, kindliness, love, tenderness
warn *verb* NOTIFY, advise, alert, apprise, caution, forewarn, give notice, inform, make (someone) aware, tip off
warning *noun* CAUTION, advice, alarm, alert, notification, omen, sign, tip-off
warp *verb* 1 TWIST, bend, contort, deform, distort
▷ *noun* 2 TWIST, bend, contortion, distortion, kink
warrant *noun* 1 AUTHORIZATION, authority, license, permission, permit, sanction
▷ *verb* 2 CALL FOR, demand, deserve, excuse, justify, license, necessitate, permit, require, sanction
3 GUARANTEE, affirm, attest, certify, declare, pledge, vouch for
warranty *noun* GUARANTEE, assurance, bond, certificate, contract, covenant, pledge
warrior *noun* SOLDIER, combatant, fighter, gladiator, man-at-arms
wary *adjective* CAUTIOUS, alert, careful, chary, circumspect, distrustful, guarded, suspicious, vigilant, watchful
wash *verb* 1 CLEAN, bathe, cleanse, launder, rinse, scrub
2 SWEEP AWAY, bear away, carry off, move
3 (*informal*) BE PLAUSIBLE, bear scrutiny, be convincing, carry weight, hold up, hold water, stand up, stick
▷ *noun* 4 CLEANING, cleansing, laundering, rinse, scrub
5 COAT, coating, film, layer, overlay
6 SWELL, surge, wave
washout *noun* FAILURE, disappointment, disaster, dud (*informal*), fiasco, flop (*informal*)
waste *verb* 1 MISUSE, blow (*slang*), dissipate, fritter away, lavish, squander, throw away
2 ▷ **waste away** DECLINE, atrophy, crumble, decay, dwindle, fade, wane, wear out, wither
▷ *noun* 3 MISUSE, dissipation, extravagance, frittering away, prodigality, squandering, wastefulness
4 RUBBISH, debris, dross, garbage, leftovers, litter, refuse, scrap, trash
5 ▷ **wastes** DESERT, wasteland, wilderness
▷ *adjective* 6 UNWANTED, leftover, superfluous, supernumerary, unused, useless, worthless
7 UNCULTIVATED, bare, barren, desolate, empty, uninhabited, unproductive, wild
wasteful *adjective* EXTRAVAGANT, lavish, prodigal, profligate, spendthrift, thriftless, uneconomical
waster *noun* IDLER, couch potato (*slang*), good-for-nothing, loafer, shirker, wastrel
watch *verb* 1 LOOK AT, contemplate, eye, observe, regard, see, view
2 GUARD, keep, look after, mind, protect, superintend, take care of, tend
▷ *noun* 3 WRISTWATCH, chronometer, timepiece
4 LOOKOUT, observation, surveillance, vigil
watchdog *noun* 1 GUARD DOG
2 GUARDIAN, custodian, monitor, protector, scrutineer
watchful *adjective* ALERT, attentive, observant, on the lookout, suspicious, vigilant, wary, wide awake
watchman *noun* GUARD, caretaker, custodian, security guard

wa•ter [WAW-tər] *noun* 1 transparent, colorless, odorless, tasteless liquid, substance of rain, river, etc. 2 body of water 3 river 4 lake 5 sea 6 tear 7 urine ▷ *verb transitive* 8 put water on or into 9 irrigate or provide with water ▷ *verb intransitive* 10 salivate 11 (of eyes) fill with tears 12 take in or obtain water > **wa'ter•y** *adjective* > **water buffalo** oxlike Asian animal > **water closet** [KLOZ-it] toilet > **wa'ter•col•or** *noun* 1 pigment mixed with water 2 painting in this > **wa'ter•course** *noun* stream > **wa'ter•cress** *noun* plant growing in clear ponds and streams > **wa'ter•fall** *noun* perpendicular descent of waters of river, stream > **wa'ter•logged** *adjective* saturated, filled with water > **wa'ter•mark** *noun* faint translucent design stamped on substance of sheet of paper > **wa'ter•proof** *adjective* 1 not letting water through ▷ *verb* 2 make waterproof > **wa'ter•shed** *noun* 1 area drained by a river 2 important division between conditions, phases > **water-ski•ing** *noun* sport of riding over water on ski towed by speedboat > **water sports** various sports, as swimming, windsurfing, that take place in or on water > **water•tight** [-tīt] *adjective* 1 so fitted as to prevent water entering or escaping 2 with no loopholes or weak points

watt [wot] *noun* unit of electric power > **watt'age** [-ij] *noun* electric power expressed in watts

wat•tle [WOT-l] *noun* fleshy pendent lobe on head or neck of certain birds, e.g. turkey

wave [wayv] *verb* **waved, wav•ing** 1 move to and fro, as hand in greeting or farewell 2 signal by waving 3 give, take shape of waves (as hair, etc.) ▷ *noun* 4 ridge and trough on water, etc. 5 act, gesture of waving 6 vibration, as in radio waves, of electric and magnetic forces alternating in direction 7 prolonged spell of something 8 upsurge 9 wavelike shapes in the hair, etc. > **wav'y** [-ee] *adjective* **wav•i•er, wav•i•est** > **wave'length** *noun* distance between same points of two successive sound waves

wav•er [WAY-vər] *verb intransitive* 1 hesitate, be irresolute 2 be, become unsteady

wax[1] [waks] *noun* 1 yellow, soft, pliable material made by bees 2 this or similar substance used for sealing, making candles, etc. 3 waxy secretion of ear ▷ *verb transitive* **waxed, wax•ing** 4 put wax on > **wax'y** [-ee] *adjective* **wax•i•er, wax•i•est** like wax > **wax'wing** *noun* small songbird > **wax'work** [-wurk] *noun* lifelike figure, esp. of famous person, reproduced in wax

wax[2] *verb intransitive* **waxed, wax•ing** grow, increase

way *noun* 1 manner 2 method, means 3 track 4 direction 5 path 6 passage 7 course 8 route 9 progress 10 state or condition > **way'far•er** [-fair-ər] *noun* traveler, esp. on foot > **way'lay** *verb transitive* **-laid, -lay•ing** lie in wait for and accost, attack > **way'side** *noun* side or edge of a road ▷ *adjective* > **way'ward** [-wərd] *adjective* capricious, perverse, willful > **way'ward•ness** [-nis] *noun*

we [wee] *pronoun* first person plural pronoun

weak [week] *adjective* **-er, -est** 1 lacking strength 2 feeble 3 fragile 4 defenseless 5 easily influenced 6 faint > **weak•en** [WEE-kən] *verb* > **weak'ling** *noun* feeble creature > **weak'ly** *adjective* 1 weak 2 sickly ▷ *adverb*

wealth [welth] *noun* 1 riches 2 abundance > **wealth'y** *adjective* **wealth•i•er, wealth•i•est**

DICTIONARY • THESAURUS

watchword *noun* MOTTO, battle cry, byword, catch phrase, catchword, maxim, rallying cry, slogan

water *noun* 1 LIQUID, H_2O
▷ *verb* 2 MOISTEN, dampen, douse, drench, hose, irrigate, soak, spray

water down *verb* DILUTE, thin, water, weaken

waterfall *noun* CASCADE, cataract, fall

watertight *adjective* 1 WATERPROOF
2 FOOLPROOF, airtight, flawless, impregnable, sound, unassailable

watery *adjective* 1 WET, aqueous, damp, fluid, liquid, moist, soggy
2 DILUTED, runny, thin, washy, watered-down, weak

wave *verb* 1 SIGNAL, beckon, direct, gesticulate, gesture, indicate, sign
2 FLAP, brandish, flourish, flutter, oscillate, shake, stir, swing, wag
▷ *noun* 3 RIPPLE, billow, breaker, ridge, roller, swell, undulation
4 OUTBREAK, flood, rash, rush, stream, surge, upsurge

waver *verb* 1 HESITATE, dither, falter, fluctuate, hum and haw, seesaw, vacillate
2 TREMBLE, flicker, quiver, shake, totter, wobble

wax *verb* INCREASE, develop, enlarge, expand, grow, magnify, swell

way *noun* 1 METHOD, fashion, manner, means, mode, procedure, process, system, technique
2 STYLE, custom, habit, manner, nature, personality, practice, wont
3 ROUTE, channel, course, direction, path, pathway, road, track, trail
4 JOURNEY, approach, march, passage
5 DISTANCE, length, stretch

wayfarer *noun* TRAVELER, gypsy, itinerant, nomad, rover, voyager, wanderer

wayward *adjective* ERRATIC, capricious, inconstant, ungovernable, unmanageable, unpredictable, unruly

weak *adjective* 1 FEEBLE, debilitated, effete, fragile, frail, infirm, puny, sickly, unsteady
2 UNSAFE, defenseless, exposed, helpless, unguarded, unprotected, vulnerable
3 UNCONVINCING, feeble, flimsy, hollow, lame, pathetic, unsatisfactory
4 TASTELESS, diluted, insipid, runny, thin, watery

weaken *verb* 1 LESSEN, diminish, dwindle, fade, flag, lower, moderate, reduce, sap, undermine, wane
2 DILUTE, thin out, water down

weakling *noun* SISSY, baby (*informal*), drip (*informal*), wimp (*informal*)

weakness *noun* 1 FRAILTY, decrepitude, feebleness, fragility, infirmity, powerlessness, vulnerability
2 FAILING, blemish, defect, deficiency, fault, flaw, imperfection, lack, shortcoming
3 LIKING, fondness, inclination, partiality, passion, penchant, soft spot

wean [ween] *verb transitive* 1 accustom to food other than mother's milk 2 win over, coax away from
weap•on [WEP-ən] *noun* 1 implement to fight with 2 anything used to get the better of an opponent > **weap'on•ry** [-ree] *noun*
wear [wair] *verb transitive* **wore, worn, wear•ing** 1 have on the body 2 show 3 produce (hole, etc.) by rubbing, etc. 4 harass or weaken ▷ *verb intransitive* **wore, worn, wear•ing** 5 last 6 become impaired by use 7 (of time) pass slowly ▷ *noun* 8 act of wearing 9 things to wear 10 damage caused by use 11 ability to resist effects of constant use
wea•ry [WEER-ee] *adjective* **-ri•er, -ri•est** 1 tired, exhausted, jaded 2 tiring 3 tedious ▷ *verb* **-ried, -ry•ing** 4 make, become weary > **wea'ri•ness** [-ree-nis] *noun* > **wea'ri•some** [-ree-səm] *adjective* causing weariness
wea•sel [WEE-zəl] *noun* small carnivorous mammal with long body and short legs
weath•er [WETH-ər] *noun* 1 day-to-day meteorological conditions, esp. temperature, cloudiness, etc. of a place ▷ *adjective* 2 toward the wind ▷ *verb transitive* 3 affect by weather 4 endure 5 resist 6 come safely through 7 sail to windward of > **weath'er•vane** [-vain] *noun* rotating vane to show which way wind blows
weave [weev] *verb transitive* **wove** *or* **weaved, wo•ven** *or* **wove, weav•ing** 1 form into texture or fabric by interlacing, esp. on loom 2 fashion, construct ▷ *verb intransitive* **wove** *or* **weaved, wo•ven** *or* **wove, weav•ing** 3 become woven 4 make one's way, esp. with side to side motion > **weav'er** [-ər] *noun*
web *noun* 1 woven fabric 2 net spun by spider 3 membrane between toes of waterfowl, frogs, etc. **the Web** *short for* **World Wide Web.** > **web address** *another name for* **URL.** > **web'bing** *noun* strong fabric woven in strips > **web'cam** *noun* camera that transmits images over the Internet > **web'cast** *noun* broadcast of an event over the Internet > **web'log** *noun* person's online journal > **web'mail** *noun* system of electronic mail that allows account holders to access their mail via an Internet site > **web'site** *noun* group of pages on the World Wide Web with a single address
web•er [WEB-ər] *noun* SI unit of magnetic flux
wed *verb transitive* **wed•ded, wed•ding** 1 marry 2 unite closely > **wedding** *noun* act of marrying, nuptial ceremony > **wed'lock** *noun* marriage
wedge [wej] *noun* 1 piece of wood, metal, etc., thick at one end, tapering to a thin edge ▷ *verb transitive* **wedged, wedg•ing** 2 fasten, split with wedge 3 stick by compression or crowding
weed *noun* 1 plant growing where undesired 2 (*informal*) tobacco 3 (*slang*) marijuana 4 thin, sickly person, animal ▷ *verb transitive* 5 clear of weeds > **weed'y** *adjective* **weed•i•er, weed•i•est** 1 full of weeds 2 thin, weakly > **weed out** remove, eliminate what is unwanted
weeds [weedz] *plural noun* (*obsolete*) (widow's) mourning clothes
week *noun* 1 period of seven days, esp. one beginning on Sunday and ending on Saturday 2 hours, days of work in seven-day period > **week'ly** *adjective, adverb* 1 happening, done, published, etc. once a week ▷ *noun* 2 newspaper or magazine published once a week > **week'day** *noun* any day of week except Sunday and usu. Saturday > **week'end** *noun* (at least) Saturday and Sunday, esp. considered as rest period
weep *verb* **wept, weep•ing** 1 shed tears (for) 2 grieve > **weep'y** *adjective* **weep•i•er, weep•i•est** > **weeping willow** willow with drooping

wealth *noun* 1 RICHES, affluence, capital, fortune, money, opulence, prosperity
2 PLENTY, abundance, copiousness, cornucopia, fullness, profusion, richness
wealthy *adjective* RICH, affluent, flush (*informal*), moneyed, opulent, prosperous, well-heeled (*informal*), well-off, well-to-do
wear *verb* 1 BE DRESSED IN, don, have on, put on, sport (*informal*)
2 SHOW, display, exhibit
3 DETERIORATE, abrade, corrode, erode, fray, grind, rub
▷ *noun* 4 CLOTHES, apparel, attire, costume, dress, garb, garments, gear (*informal*), things
5 DAMAGE, abrasion, attrition, corrosion, deterioration, erosion, wear and tear
weariness *noun* TIREDNESS, drowsiness, exhaustion, fatigue, languor, lassitude, lethargy, listlessness
wearing *adjective* TIRESOME, exasperating, fatiguing, irksome, oppressive, trying, wearisome
wearisome *adjective* TEDIOUS, annoying, boring, exhausting, fatiguing, irksome, oppressive, tiresome, troublesome, trying, wearing
wear off *verb* SUBSIDE, decrease, diminish, disappear, dwindle, fade, peter out, wane
weary *adjective* 1 TIRED, done in (*informal*), drained, drowsy, exhausted, fatigued, flagging, jaded, sleepy, worn out
2 TIRING, arduous, laborious, tiresome, wearisome
▷ *verb* 3 TIRE, drain, enervate, fatigue, sap, take it out of (*informal*), tax, tire out, wear out
weather *noun* 1 CLIMATE, conditions
▷ *verb* 2 WITHSTAND, brave, come through, endure, overcome, resist, ride out, stand, survive
weave *verb* 1 KNIT, braid, entwine, interlace, intertwine, plait
2 CREATE, build, construct, contrive, fabricate, make up, put together, spin
3 ZIGZAG, crisscross, wind
web *noun* 1 SPIDER'S WEB, cobweb
2 NETWORK, lattice, tangle
wed *verb* 1 MARRY, get married, take the plunge (*informal*), tie the knot (*informal*)
2 UNITE, ally, blend, combine, interweave, join, link, merge
wedding *noun* MARRIAGE, nuptials, wedlock
wedge *noun* 1 BLOCK, chunk, lump
▷ *verb* 2 SQUEEZE, cram, crowd, force, jam, lodge, pack, ram, stuff, thrust
wedlock *noun* MARRIAGE, matrimony
weed out *verb* ELIMINATE, dispense with, eradicate, get rid of, remove, root out, uproot
weedy *adjective* WEAK, feeble, frail, ineffectual, puny, skinny, thin
weep *verb* CRY, blubber, lament, mourn, shed tears, snivel, sob, whimper
weepy *adjective* (*informal*) SENTIMENTAL,

branches
wee•vil [WEE-vəl] *noun* small beetle harmful to cotton, etc.
weft *noun* cross threads in weaving, woof
weigh [way] *verb transitive* 1 find weight of 2 consider 3 raise (anchor) ▷ *verb intransitive* 4 have weight 5 be burdensome > **weight** *noun* 1 measure of the heaviness of an object 2 quality of heaviness 3 heavy mass 4 object of known mass for weighing 5 unit of measurement of weight 6 importance, influence ▷ *verb transitive* 7 add weight to > **weight'y** *adjective* **weight•i•er, weight•i•est** 1 heavy 2 onerous 3 important 4 momentous
weir [weer] *noun* 1 small dam in river or stream 2 fence or net in stream, etc. for catching fish
weird [weerd] *adjective* **-er, -est** 1 unearthly, uncanny 2 strange, bizarre
wel•come [WEL-kəm] *adjective* 1 received gladly 2 freely permitted ▷ *noun, interjection* 3 kindly greeting ▷ *verb transitive* **-comed, -com•ing** 4 greet with pleasure 5 receive gladly
weld *verb transitive* 1 unite metal by softening with heat 2 unite closely ▷ *noun* 3 welded joint > **weld'er** *noun* 1 person who welds 2 machine used in welding > **weld'ment** [-mənt] *noun* welded assembly
wel•fare [WEL-fair] *noun* well-being > **welfare state** system in which the government takes responsibility for the social, economic, etc. security of its citizens
well¹ *adverb* 1 in good manner or degree 2 suitably 3 intimately 4 fully 5 favorably, kindly 6 to a considerable degree ▷ *adjective* **bet•ter, best** 7 in good health 8 suitable ▷ *interjection* 9 exclamation of surprise, interrogation, etc. > **well-being** *noun* state of being well, happy, or prosperous > **well-disposed** *adjective* inclined to be friendly, kindly (toward) > **well-mannered** *adjective* having good manners > **well-off** *adjective* fairly rich > **well-read** [-red] *adjective* having read much > **well-spoken** *adjective* speaking fluently, graciously, aptly > **well-to-do** *adjective* moderately wealthy
well² *noun* 1 hole sunk into the earth to reach water, gas, oil, etc. 2 spring 3 any shaft like a well ▷ *verb intransitive* 4 spring, gush
Welsh *adjective* 1 of Wales ▷ *noun* 2 language, people of Wales > **Welsh rabbit, Welsh rarebit** dish of melted cheese, beer, spices on toast
welsh *verb intransitive* (*informal*) fail to pay debt or fulfill obligation (*also* **welch**) > **welsh'er** [-ər], **welch•er** [WELCH-ər] *noun*
welt *noun* 1 raised, strengthened seam 2 weal ▷ *verb transitive* 3 provide with welt 4 thrash
wel•ter [WEL-tər] *verb intransitive* 1 roll or tumble ▷ *noun* 2 turmoil, disorder
wel•ter•weight [WEL-tər-wayt] *noun boxing* 1 weight between light and middle 2 boxer of this weight
wen *noun* cyst, esp. on scalp
wench *noun* (*obsolete or facetious*) young woman
wend *verb* go, travel
went *pt. of* **go**
wept *pt./pp. of* **weep**
were [wur] *past indicative, plural and subjunctive sing and pl. of* **be**
were•wolf [WAIR-wuulf] *noun, plural* **-wolves** (in

overemotional, schmaltzy (*slang*), slushy (*informal*)
weigh *verb* 1 HAVE A WEIGHT OF, tip the scales at (*informal*)
2 CONSIDER, contemplate, deliberate upon, evaluate, examine, meditate upon, ponder, reflect upon, think over
3 MATTER, carry weight, count
weight *noun* 1 HEAVINESS, load, mass, poundage, tonnage
2 IMPORTANCE, authority, consequence, impact, import, influence, power, value
▷ *verb* 3 LOAD, freight
4 BIAS, load, slant, unbalance
weighty *adjective* 1 IMPORTANT, consequential, crucial, grave, momentous, portentous, serious, significant, solemn
2 HEAVY, burdensome, cumbersome, hefty (*informal*), massive, ponderous
weird *adjective* STRANGE, bizarre, creepy (*informal*), eerie, freakish, mysterious, odd, queer, spooky (*informal*), unnatural
welcome *verb* 1 GREET, embrace, hail, meet, receive
▷ *noun* 2 GREETING, acceptance, hospitality, reception, salutation
▷ *adjective* 3 ACCEPTABLE, agreeable, appreciated, delightful, desirable, gratifying, pleasant, refreshing
4 FREE, under no obligation
weld *verb* JOIN, bind, bond, connect, fuse, link, solder, unite
welfare *noun* 1 WELLBEING, advantage, benefit, good, happiness, health, interest, prosperity
2 BENEFIT, allowance, gift, grant, handout
well¹ *adverb* 1 SATISFACTORILY, agreeably, nicely, pleasantly, smoothly, splendidly, successfully
2 SKILLFULLY, ably, adeptly, adequately, admirably, correctly, efficiently, expertly, proficiently, properly
3 PROSPEROUSLY, comfortably
4 SUITABLY, fairly, fittingly, justly, properly, rightly
5 INTIMATELY, deeply, fully, profoundly, thoroughly
6 FAVORABLY, approvingly, glowingly, highly, kindly, warmly
7 CONSIDERABLY, abundantly, amply, fully, greatly, heartily, highly, substantially, thoroughly, very much
▷ *adjective* 8 HEALTHY, fit, in fine fettle, sound
9 SATISFACTORY, agreeable, fine, pleasing, proper, right, thriving
well² *noun* 1 HOLE, bore, pit, shaft
▷ *verb* 2 FLOW, gush, jet, pour, spout, spring, spurt, surge
well-known *adjective* FAMOUS, celebrated, familiar, noted, popular, renowned
well-off *adjective* RICH, affluent, comfortable (*informal*), moneyed, prosperous, wealthy, well-heeled (*informal*), well-to-do
well-to-do *adjective* RICH, affluent, comfortable (*informal*), moneyed, prosperous, wealthy, well-heeled (*informal*), well-off
well-worn *adjective* STALE, banal, commonplace, hackneyed, overused, stereotyped, trite
welt *noun* MARK, contusion, streak, stripe, wale, weal

folklore) human being turned into wolf

west *noun* 1 part of sky where sun sets 2 part of country, etc. lying to this side 3 occident ▷ *adjective* 4 that is toward or in this region ▷ *adverb* 5 to the west > **west'er•ly** [-ər-lee] *adjective* > **west'ward** [-wərd] *adjective, adverb* > **west'ward** *or* **west'wards** *adverb* toward the west > **west'ern** [-ərn] *adjective* 1 of, in the west ▷ *noun* 2 film, story, etc. about cowboys or frontiersmen in western US **go west** (*informal*) die

wet *adjective* **wet•ter, wet•test** 1 having water or other liquid on a surface or being soaked in it 2 rainy 3 not yet dry (paint, ink, etc.) ▷ *verb transitive* **wet** *or* **wet•ted, wet•ting** 4 make wet ▷ *noun* 5 moisture, rain > **wet blanket** one depressing spirits of others > **wet'land** [-lənd] *noun* area of swamp or marsh > **wet nurse** woman suckling another's child > **wet suit** close-fitting rubber suit worn by divers, etc.

whack [hwak] *verb transitive* 1 strike with sharp resounding blow ▷ *noun* 2 such blow 3 (*slang*) share 4 (*informal*) attempt > **whack'ing** *adjective* (*informal*) big, enormous

whale [hwayl] *noun* large fish-shaped sea mammal > **whal'er** *noun* person, ship employed in hunting whales > **whale'bone** *noun* horny elastic substance from projections of upper jaw of certain whales > **whal'ing** *noun* **a whale of a time** (*informal*) very enjoyable time

wharf [hworf] *noun* platform at harbor, on river, etc. for loading and unloading ships

what [hwut, hwot] *pronoun* 1 which thing 2 that which 3 request for statement to be repeated ▷ *adjective* 4 which 5 as much as 6 how great, surprising, etc. ▷ *interjection* 7 exclamation of surprise, anger, etc. > **what•ev'er** *pronoun* 1 anything which 2 of what kind it may be > **what'not** *noun* 1 small stand with shelves 2 something, anything of same kind

wheat [hweet] *noun* cereal plant with thick four-sided seed spikes of which bread is chiefly made > **wheat'en** [-ən] *adjective* > **wheat germ** [-jurm] embryo of wheat kernel

whee•dle [HWEED-l] *verb* **-dled, -dling** coax, cajole

wheel [hweel] *noun* 1 circular frame or disk (with spokes) revolving on axle 2 anything like a wheel in shape or function 3 act of turning 4 steering wheel ▷ *verb* (cause to) turn as if on axis 5 (cause to) move on or as if on wheels 6 (cause to) change course, esp. in opposite direction > **wheel'bar•row** [-ba-roh] *noun* barrow with one wheel > **wheel'base** [-bays] *noun* distance between front and rear hubs of vehicle > **wheel'chair** *noun* chair mounted on large wheels, used by people who cannot walk

wheeze [hweez] *verb intransitive* **wheezed, wheez•ing** 1 breathe with difficulty and whistling noise ▷ *noun* 2 this sound 3 story, etc. told too often > **wheez'y** [-ee] *adjective* **wheez•i•er, wheez•i•est**

whelp [hwelp] *noun* 1 pup, cub ▷ *verb* 2 produce whelps

when [hwen] *adverb* 1 at what time ▷ *conjunction* 2 at the time that 3 although 4 since ▷ *pronoun* 5 at which (time) > **when•ev'er** *adverb, conjunction* at whatever time

whence [hwens] *adverb, conjunction* (*obsolete*) 1 from what place or source 2 how

where [hwair] *adverb, conjunction* 1 at what place 2 at or to the place in which > **where'a•bouts** *adverb, conjunction* 1 in what, which place ▷ *noun* 2 present position > **where•as'** *conjunction* 1 considering that 2 while, on the contrary > **where•by'** [-BĪ] *conjunction* by which > **where'fore** *adverb* (*obsolete*) 1 why ▷ *conjunction* 2 consequently > **where•up•on'** *conjunction* at which point > **wher•ev'er** *adverb* at whatever place > **where'with•al** [-with-awl] *noun* necessary funds, resources, etc.

whet [hwet] *verb transitive* **whet•ted, whetting** 1 sharpen 2 stimulate > **whet'stone** *noun* stone for sharpening tools

wheth•er [HWETH-ər] *conjunction* introduces the first of two alternatives, of which the second may be expressed or implied

whey [hway] *noun* watery part of milk left after separation of curd in cheese making

which [hwich] *adjective* 1 used in requests for a selection from alternatives ▷ *pronoun* 2 which person or thing 3 the thing *who* > **which•ev'er** *pronoun*

whiff [hwif] *noun* 1 brief smell or suggestion of 2 puff of air ▷ *verb* 3 smell

while [hwīl] *conjunction* 1 in the time that 2 in

DICTIONARY

W

THESAURUS

welter *noun* JUMBLE, confusion, mess, muddle, tangle, web

wet *adjective* 1 DAMP, dank, moist, saturated, soaking, sodden, soggy, sopping, waterlogged, watery
2 RAINY, drizzling, pouring, raining, showery, teeming
▷ *noun* 3 RAIN, drizzle
4 MOISTURE, condensation, damp, dampness, humidity, liquid, water, wetness
▷ *verb* 5 MOISTEN, dampen, douse, irrigate, saturate, soak, spray, water

whack *verb* 1 STRIKE, bang, belt (*informal*), clobber (*slang*), hit, smack, thrash, thump, thwack, wallop (*informal*)
▷ *noun* 2 BLOW, bang, belt (*informal*), hit, smack, stroke, thump, thwack, wallop (*informal*)
3 (*informal*) SHARE, bit, cut (*informal*), part, portion, quota
4 (*informal*) ATTEMPT, bash (*informal*), crack (*informal*), go (*informal*), shot (*informal*), stab (*informal*), try, turn

wharf *noun* DOCK, jetty, landing stage, pier, quay

wheedle *verb* COAX, cajole, entice, inveigle, persuade

wheel *noun* 1 CIRCLE, gyration, pivot, revolution, rotation, spin, turn
▷ *verb* 2 TURN, gyrate, pirouette, revolve, rotate, spin, swing, swivel, twirl, whirl

wheeze *verb* 1 GASP, cough, hiss, rasp, whistle
▷ *noun* 2 GASP, cough, hiss, rasp, whistle
3 (*Brit slang*) TRICK, idea, plan, ploy, ruse, scheme, stunt

whereabouts *noun* POSITION, location, site, situation

wherewithal *noun* RESOURCES, capital, funds, means, money, supplies

whet *verb* 1 (*someone's appetite*) STIMULATE, arouse, awaken, enhance, excite, kindle, quicken, rouse, stir

spite of the fact that, although 3 whereas ▷ *verb transitive* **whiled, whil•ing** 4 pass (time, usu. idly) ▷ *noun* 5 period of time

whim [hwim] *noun* sudden, passing fancy > **whim'si•cal** [-zi-kəl] *adjective* 1 fanciful 2 full of whims > **whim•si•cal'i•ty** [-zi-KAL-i-tee] *noun, plural* **-ties** > **whim'sy** [-zee] *noun, plural* **-sies** 1 whim 2 caprice

whim•per [HWIM-pər] *verb intransitive* 1 cry or whine softly 2 complain in this way ▷ *noun* 3 such cry or complaint

whine [hwīn] *noun* 1 high-pitched plaintive cry 2 peevish complaint ▷ *verb intransitive* **whined, whin•ing** 3 utter this

whin•ny [HWIN-ee] *verb intransitive* **-nied, -ny•ing** neigh softly ▷ *noun*

whip [hwip] *verb transitive* **whipped, whip•ping** 1 strike with whip 2 thrash 3 beat (cream, eggs) to a froth 4 lash 5 pull, remove, quickly ▷ *verb intransitive* **whipped, whip•ping** 6 dart ▷ *noun* 7 lash attached to handle for urging or punishing 8 one who enforces attendance, voting, etc. of political party 9 elastic quality permitting bending in mast, fishing rod, etc. 10 whipped dessert > **whip'lash** *noun* injury to neck as result of sudden jerking of unsupported head > **whipping boy** scapegoat

whip•pet [HWIP-it] *noun* racing dog like small greyhound

whir [hwur] *verb* **whirred, whir•ring** 1 (cause to) fly, spin, etc. with buzzing or whizzing sound 2 bustle ▷ *noun* 3 this sound

whirl [hwurl] *verb* 1 swing rapidly around 2 move rapidly in a circular course 3 drive at high speed ▷ *noun* 4 whirling movement 5 confusion, bustle, giddiness > **whirl'pool** *noun* circular current, eddy > **whirl'wind** *noun* wind whirling around while moving forward ▷ *adjective*

whisk [hwisk] *verb* 1 brush, sweep, beat lightly 2 move, remove, quickly 3 beat to a froth ▷ *noun* 4 light brush 5 eggbeating implement

whisk•er [HWIS-kər] *noun* 1 any of the long stiff hairs at side of mouth of cat or other animal 2 any of hairs on a man's face **by a whisker** only just

whis•key [HWIS-kee] *noun, plural* **-keys** alcoholic liquor distilled from fermented cereals > **whis'ky** *noun, plural* **-kies** Scotch or Canadian whiskey

whis•per [HWIS-pər] *verb* 1 speak in soft, hushed tones, without vibration of vocal cords 2 rustle ▷ *noun* 3 such speech 4 trace or suspicion 5 rustle

whist [hwist] *noun* card game

whis•tle [HWIS-əl] *verb intransitive* **-tled, -tling** 1 produce shrill sound by forcing breath through rounded, nearly closed lips 2 make such a sound ▷ *verb transitive* **-tled, -tling** 3 utter, summon, etc. by whistle ▷ *noun* 4 such sound 5 any similar sound 6 instrument to make it > **whis•tler** [HWIS-lər] *noun* > **whistle-blower** *noun* person who informs on or puts stop to something

whit [hwit] *noun* **not a whit** not the slightest amount

white [hwīt] *adjective* **whit•er, whit•est** 1 of the color of snow 2 pale 3 light in color 4 having a light-colored skin ▷ *noun* 5 color of snow 6 white pigment 7 white part 8 clear fluid round yolk of egg 9 Caucasian person > **whi'ten** [-ən] *verb* > **white ant** termite > **white-collar** *adjective* denoting nonmanual salaried workers > **white elephant** useless, unwanted, gift or possession > **white flag** white banner or cloth used as signal of surrender or truce > **white hope** one (formerly, a white person) expected to bring honor or glory to his group, team, etc. > **white lie** minor, unimportant lie > **white paper** government report on matter recently investigated > **white slave** woman, child forced or enticed away for purposes of prostitution > **white'wash** [-wosh] *noun* 1 substance for whitening walls, etc. ▷ *verb transitive* 2 apply this 3 cover up, gloss over, suppress

whith•er [HWITH-ər] *adverb* 1 to what place 2 to which

whit•tle [HWIT-l] *verb transitive* **-tled, -tling** 1 cut, carve with knife 2 pare away **whittle down**

DICTIONARY • THESAURUS

2 SHARPEN, hone

whiff *noun* SMELL, aroma, hint, odor, scent, sniff

whim *noun* IMPULSE, caprice, fancy, notion, urge

whimper *verb* 1 CRY, moan, snivel, sob, weep, whine
▷ *noun* 2 SOB, moan, snivel, whine

whimsical *adjective* FANCIFUL, curious, eccentric, freakish, funny, odd, playful, quaint, unusual

whine *noun* 1 CRY, moan, sob, wail, whimper
2 COMPLAINT, gripe (*informal*), grouch (*informal*), grouse, grumble, moan

whip *noun* 1 LASH, birch, cane, cat-o'-nine-tails, crop, scourge
▷ *verb* 2 LASH, beat, birch, cane, flagellate, flog, paddle (*United States & Canadian*), scourge, spank, strap, thrash
3 (*informal*) DASH, dart, dive, fly, rush, shoot, tear, whisk
4 BEAT, whisk
5 INCITE, agitate, drive, foment, goad, spur, stir, work up

whirl *verb* 1 SPIN, pirouette, revolve, roll, rotate, swirl, turn, twirl, twist
2 FEEL DIZZY, reel, spin
▷ *noun* 3 REVOLUTION, pirouette, roll, rotation, spin, swirl, turn, twirl, twist
4 BUSTLE, flurry, merry-go-round, round, series, succession
5 CONFUSION, daze, dither, giddiness, spin

whirlwind *noun* 1 TORNADO, waterspout
▷ *adjective* 2 RAPID, hasty, quick, short, speedy, swift

whisk *verb* 1 FLICK, brush, sweep, whip
2 BEAT, fluff up, whip
▷ *noun* 3 FLICK, brush, sweep, whip
4 BEATER

whisper *verb* 1 MURMUR, breathe
2 RUSTLE, hiss, sigh, swish
▷ *noun* 3 MURMUR, undertone
4 RUSTLE, hiss, sigh, swish

white *adjective* PALE, ashen, pallid, pasty, wan

white-collar *adjective* CLERICAL, nonmanual, professional, salaried

whiten *verb* PALE, blanch, bleach, fade

whitewash *noun* 1 COVER-UP, camouflage, concealment, deception
▷ *verb* 2 COVER UP, camouflage, conceal, gloss over, suppress

reduce gradually, wear (away)

whiz [hwiz] *noun* 1 loud hissing sound 2 (*informal*) person skillful at something ▷ *verb* **whizzed, whiz•zing** 3 move with such sound, or make it 4 (*informal*) move quickly **take a whizz** (*informal*) urinate

who [hoo] *pronoun* relative and interrogative pronoun, always referring to persons > **who•dun'it** *noun* (*informal*) detective story > **who•ev'er** *pronoun* who, any one or every one that

whole [hohl] *adjective* 1 complete 2 containing all elements or parts 3 entire 4 not defective or imperfect 5 healthy ▷ *noun* 6 complete thing or system > **whol'ly** *adverb* > **whole•heart'ed** [-HART-id] *adjective* 1 sincere 2 enthusiastic > **whole'sale** [-sayl] *noun* 1 sale of goods in large quantities to retailers ▷ *adjective* 2 dealing by wholesale 3 extensive ▷ *verb transitive* **-saled, -sal•ing** > **whole'sal•er** *noun* > **whole'some** [-səm] *adjective* producing good effect, physically or morally > **whole•wheat** *adjective* of, pert. to flour that contains the complete wheat kernel **on the whole** 1 taking everything into consideration 2 in general

whom [hoom] *pronoun objective case of* **who**

whoop [hwuup] *noun* shout or cry expressing excitement, etc.

whoop•ee [HWUUP-ee] *noun* (*informal*) gay, riotous time **make whoopee** 1 participate in wild noisy party 2 go on spree

whoop•ing cough [HUUP-ing] infectious disease of mucous membrane lining air passages, marked by convulsive coughing with loud whoop or indrawing of breath

whop•per [HWOP-ər] *noun* (*informal*) 1 anything unusually large 2 monstrous lie > **whop'ping** *adjective*

whore [hor] *noun* prostitute

whorl [hwurl] *noun* 1 ring of leaves or petals 2 turn of spiral 3 anything forming part of circular pattern, e.g. lines of human fingerprint

whose [hooz] *pronoun* of whom or of which

why [hwī] *adverb* for what cause or reason

wick [wik] *noun* strip of thread feeding flame of lamp or candle with oil, grease, etc.

wick•ed [WIK-id] *adjective* 1 evil, sinful 2 very bad 3 mischievous > **wick'ed•ness** [-nis] *noun*

wick•er [WIK-ər] *noun* woven cane, etc. basketwork (*also* **wick•er•work**)

wick•et [WIK-it] *noun* 1 small window, gate 2 *croquet* wire arch

wide [wīd] *adjective* **wid•er, wid•est** 1 having a great extent from side to side, broad 2 having considerable distance between 3 spacious 4 liberal 5 vast 6 far from the mark 7 opened fully ▷ *adverb* 8 to the full extent 9 far from the intended target > **wi•den** [WĪD-n] *verb* > **width** *noun* breadth > **wide'spread** [-spred] *adjective* extending over a wide area

wid•ow [WID-oh] *noun* 1 woman whose husband is dead and who has not married again ▷ *verb transitive* 2 make a widow of > **wid'ow•er** *noun* man whose wife is dead and who has not married again > **wid'ow•hood** [-huud] *noun*

wield [weeld] *verb transitive* 1 hold and use 2 brandish 3 manage

wife [wīf] *noun, plural* **wives** a man's partner in marriage, married woman > **wife'ly** *adjective*

Wi-Fi [WĪ-fī] *noun* system of wireless access to the Internet

wig *noun* artificial hair > **wigged** *adjective*

DICTIONARY

W

THESAURUS

whittle *verb* 1 CARVE, cut, hew, pare, shape, shave, trim
2 ▷ **whittle down, whittle away** REDUCE, consume, eat away, erode, wear away

whole *adjective* 1 COMPLETE, entire, full, total, unabridged, uncut, undivided
2 UNDAMAGED, in one piece, intact, unbroken, unharmed, unscathed, untouched
▷ *noun* 3 TOTALITY, ensemble, entirety
4 ▷ **on the whole** a ALL IN ALL, all things considered, by and large b GENERALLY, as a rule, in general, in the main, mostly, predominantly

wholehearted *adjective* SINCERE, committed, dedicated, determined, devoted, enthusiastic, unstinting, zealous

wholesale *adjective* 1 EXTENSIVE, broad, comprehensive, far-reaching, indiscriminate, mass, sweeping, wide-ranging
▷ *adverb* 2 EXTENSIVELY, comprehensively, indiscriminately

wholesome *adjective* 1 BENEFICIAL, good, healthy, nourishing, nutritious, salubrious
2 MORAL, decent, edifying, improving, respectable

wholly *adverb* COMPLETELY, altogether, entirely, fully, in every respect, perfectly, thoroughly, totally, utterly

whopper *noun* 1 GIANT, colossus, crackerjack (*informal*), jumbo (*informal*), leviathan, mammoth, monster
2 BIG LIE, fabrication, falsehood, tall tale (*informal*), untruth

whopping *adjective* GIGANTIC, big, enormous, giant, great, huge, mammoth, massive

whore *noun* PROSTITUTE, call girl, ho (*slang*), streetwalker, tart (*informal*)

wicked *adjective* 1 BAD, corrupt, depraved, devilish, evil, fiendish, immoral, sinful, vicious, villainous
2 MISCHIEVOUS, impish, incorrigible, naughty, rascally, roguish

wide *adjective* 1 BROAD, expansive, extensive, far-reaching, immense, large, sweeping, vast
2 SPACIOUS, baggy, capacious, commodious, full, loose, roomy
3 EXPANDED, dilated, distended, outspread, outstretched
4 DISTANT, off course, off target, remote
▷ *adverb* 5 FULLY, completely
6 OFF TARGET, astray, off course, off the mark, out

widen *verb* BROADEN, dilate, enlarge, expand, extend, spread, stretch

widespread *adjective* COMMON, broad, extensive, far-reaching, general, pervasive, popular, universal

width *noun* BREADTH, compass, diameter, extent, girth, scope, span, thickness

wield *verb* 1 BRANDISH, employ, flourish, handle, manage, manipulate, ply, swing, use
2 (*power*) EXERT, exercise, have, maintain, possess

wife *noun* SPOUSE, better half (*humorous*), bride,

wig•gle [WIG-əl] *verb* **-gled, -gling** (cause to) move jerkily from side to side ▷ *noun* > **wiggle room** scope for freedom of action or thought
wig•wam [WIG-wom] *noun* Native American's tent
wild [wīld] *adjective* **-er, -est** 1 not tamed or domesticated 2 not cultivated 3 savage 4 stormy 5 uncontrolled 6 random 7 excited 8 rash 9 frantic 10 (of party, etc.) rowdy, unrestrained > **wild'ly** *adverb* > **wild'ness** [-nis] *noun* > **wild'cat** *noun* 1 any of various undomesticated feline animals 2 wild, savage person ▷ *adjective* 3 unsound, irresponsible 4 sudden, unofficial, unauthorized > **wildcat strike** strike called without sanction of labor union > **wild-goose chase** futile pursuit > **wild'life** *noun* wild animals and plants collectively
wil•der•ness [WIL-dər-nis] *noun* 1 desert, waste place 2 state of desolation or confusion
wild•fire [WĪLD-fīr] *noun* 1 raging, uncontrollable fire 2 anything spreading, moving fast
wile [wīl] *noun* trick > **wil'y** *adjective* **wil•i•er, wil•i•est** crafty, sly
will *verb auxiliary, past tense* **would** [wuud] 1 forms moods and tenses indicating intention or conditional result ▷ *verb intransitive* 2 have a wish ▷ *verb transitive* 3 wish 4 intend 5 leave as legacy ▷ *noun* 6 faculty of deciding what one will do 7 purpose 8 volition 9 determination 10 wish 11 directions written for disposal of property after death > **will'ing** *adjective* 1 ready 2 given cheerfully > **will'ing•ly** *adverb* > **will'ing•ness** [-nis] *noun* > **will'pow•er** *noun* ability to control oneself, one's actions, impulses
will•ful [WIL-fəl] *adjective* 1 obstinate, self-willed 2 intentional > **will'ful•ness** [-nis] *noun*
will-o'-the-wisp [WIL-ə-*thə*-WISP] *noun* 1 brief pale flame or phosphorescence sometimes seen over marshes 2 elusive person or hope
wil•low [WIL-oh] *noun* 1 tree, such as **weeping willow**, with long thin flexible branches 2 its wood > **wil'low•y** *adjective* lithe, slender, supple
wil•ly-nil•ly [WIL-ee-NIL-ee] *adverb, adjective* (occurring) whether desired or not
wilt *verb* (cause to) become limp, drooping or lose strength, etc.
wimp *noun* (*informal*) feeble, ineffective person
wim•ple [WIM-pəl] *noun* garment worn by nun, around face
win *verb intransitive* **won, win•ning** 1 be successful, victorious ▷ *verb transitive* **won, win•ning** 2 get by labor or effort 3 reach 4 lure 5 be successful in 6 gain the support, consent, etc. of ▷ *noun* 7 victory, esp. in games > **winning** *adjective* charming > **winnings** *plural noun* sum won in game, betting, etc. > **win-win**

DICTIONARY • THESAURUS

---

mate, partner
wiggle *verb, noun* flutter JERK, jiggle, oscillate, shake, shimmy, squirm, twitch, wag, wave, writhe
wild *adjective* 1 UNTAMED, feral, ferocious, fierce, savage, unbroken, undomesticated
2 UNCULTIVATED, free, natural
3 UNCIVILIZED, barbaric, barbarous, brutish, ferocious, fierce, primitive, savage
4 UNCONTROLLED, disorderly, riotous, rowdy, turbulent, undisciplined, unfettered, unmanageable, unrestrained, unruly, wayward
5 STORMY, blustery, choppy, raging, rough, tempestuous, violent
6 EXCITED, crazy (*informal*), enthusiastic, hysterical, raving, wired (*slang*)
▷ *noun* 7 ▷ **wilds** WILDERNESS, back of beyond (*informal*), desert, middle of nowhere (*informal*), wasteland
wilderness *noun* DESERT, jungle, wasteland, wilds
wiles *plural noun* TRICKERY, artfulness, chicanery, craftiness, cunning, guile, slyness
will *noun* 1 DETERMINATION, purpose, resolution, resolve, willpower
2 WISH, desire, fancy, inclination, mind, preference, volition
3 TESTAMENT, last wishes
▷ *verb* 4 WISH, desire, prefer, see fit, want
5 BEQUEATH, confer, give, leave, pass on, transfer
willful *adjective* 1 OBSTINATE, determined, headstrong, inflexible, intransigent, obdurate, perverse, pig-headed, stubborn, uncompromising
2 INTENTIONAL, conscious, deliberate, intended, purposeful, voluntary
willing *adjective* READY, agreeable, amenable, compliant, consenting, game (*informal*), inclined, prepared
willingly *adverb* READILY, by choice, cheerfully, eagerly, freely, gladly, happily, of one's own accord, voluntarily
willingness *noun* INCLINATION, agreement, consent, volition, will, wish
willowy *adjective* SLENDER, graceful, lithe, slim, supple, svelte, sylphlike
willpower *noun* SELF-CONTROL, determination, drive, grit, resolution, resolve, self-discipline, single-mindedness
wilt *verb* 1 DROOP, sag, shrivel, wither
2 WEAKEN, fade, flag, languish, wane
wily *adjective* CUNNING, artful, astute, crafty, guileful, sharp, shrewd, sly, tricky
wimp *noun* (*informal*) WEAKLING, coward, drip (*informal*), loser (*slang*), mouse, sissy, softy *or* softie
wimpy *adjective* (*informal*) FEEBLE, effete, ineffectual, soft, spineless, timorous, weak, weedy (*informal*)
win *verb* 1 TRIUMPH, come first, conquer, overcome, prevail, succeed, sweep the board
2 GAIN, achieve, acquire, attain, earn, get, land, obtain, procure, secure
▷ *noun* 3 VICTORY, conquest, success, triumph
wince *verb* 1 FLINCH, blench, cower, cringe, draw back, quail, recoil, shrink, start
▷ *noun* 2 FLINCH, cringe, start
wind[1] *noun* 1 AIR, blast, breeze, draft, gust, zephyr
2 BREATH, puff, respiration
3 FLATULENCE, gas
4 TALK, babble, blather, bluster, boasting, hot air, humbug
5 ▷ **get wind of** HEAR ABOUT, get an inkling of,

adjective guaranteeing a favourable outcome for everyone involved

wince [wins] *verb intransitive* **winced, winc•ing** 1 flinch, draw back, as from pain, etc. ▷ *noun* 2 this act

winch *noun* 1 machine for hoisting or hauling using cable wound around drum ▷ *verb transitive* 2 move (something) by using a winch

wind[1] *noun* 1 air in motion 2 breath 3 flatulence 4 idle talk 5 hint or suggestion 6 scent borne by air ▷ *verb transitive* **wind•ed, wind•ing** 7 render short of breath, esp. by blow, etc. 8 get the scent of > **wind•ward** [-wərd] *noun* side against which wind is blowing > **wind'y** *adjective* **wind•i•er, wind•i•est** 1 exposed to wind 2 flatulent 3 talking too much > **wind'fall** *noun* 1 unexpected good luck 2 fallen fruit > **wind instrument** musical instrument played by blowing or air pressure > **wind'mill** *noun* wind-driven apparatus with fanlike sails for raising water, crushing grain, etc. > **wind'pipe** *noun* passage from throat to lungs > **wind'shield** [-sheeld] *noun* protective sheet of glass, etc. in front of driver or pilot > **wind'sock** *noun* cone of material flown on mast at airfield to indicate wind direction > **wind'surf•ing** *noun* sport of sailing standing up on sailboard holding special boom to control sail

wind[2] [wīnd] *verb intransitive* **wound** [wownd], **wind•ing** 1 twine 2 meander ▷ *verb transitive* **wound** [wownd], **wind•ing** 3 twist around, coil 4 wrap 5 make ready for working by tightening spring ▷ *noun* 6 act of winding 7 single turn of something wound 8 a turn, curve

wind•lass [WIND-ləs] *noun* winch, esp. simple one worked by a crank

win•dow [WIN-doh] *noun* 1 hole in wall (with glass) to admit light, air, etc. 2 anything similar in appearance or function 3 area for display of goods behind glass of store front > **window dressing** 1 arrangement of goods in a shop window 2 deceptive display

wine [wīn] *noun* fermented juice of grape, etc. > **wine'press** *noun* apparatus for extracting juice from grape

wing *noun* 1 feathered limb a bird uses in flying 2 one of organs of flight of insect or some animals 3 main lifting surface of aircraft 4 lateral extension 5 side portion of building projecting from main central portion 6 one of sides of a stage 7 flank corps of army on either side 8 part of car body that surrounds wheels 9 administrative, tactical unit of air force 10 faction esp. of political party > **wings** 1 insignia worn by qualified aircraft pilot 2 sides of stage ▷ *verb intransitive* 3 fly 4 move, go very fast ▷ *verb transitive* 5 disable, wound slightly > **wing'span** *noun* distance between the wing tips of an aircraft, bird, or insect

wink [wingk] *verb* 1 close and open (an eye) rapidly, esp. to indicate friendliness or as signal 2 twinkle ▷ *noun* 3 act of winking

win•now [WIN-oh] *verb transitive* 1 blow free of chaff 2 sift, examine

win•some [WIN-səm] *adjective* charming, winning > **win'some•ly** *adverb*

win•ter [WIN-tər] *noun* 1 the coldest season ▷ *verb intransitive* 2 pass, spend the winter > **win'try** *adjective* **-tri•er, -tri•est** 1 of, like winter 2 cold

wipe [wīp] *verb transitive* **wiped, wip•ing** 1 rub so as to clean ▷ *noun* 2 wiping > **wi'per** *noun* 1 one that wipes 2 automatic wiping apparatus (esp. windshield wiper) > **wipe out** 1 erase 2 annihilate 3 (*informal*) kill 4 (*slang*) beat decisively > **wiped-out** *adjective* (*slang*) 1 exhausted 2 intoxicated > **wipe'out** *noun* (*informal*) 1 murder 2 decisive defeat

wire [wīr] *noun* 1 metal drawn into thin, flexible strand 2 something made of wire, e.g. fence 3 telegram ▷ *verb transitive* **wired, wir•ing** 4 provide, fasten with wire 5 send by telegraph > **wired** *adjective* (*slang*) 1 excited or nervous 2 using computers and the Internet to send and receive information > **wiring** *noun* system of wires > **wir'y** *adjective* **wir•i•er, wir•i•est** 1 like wire 2 lean and tough > **wire-haired** *adjective* (of various breeds of dog) with short stiff hair

wire•less [WĪR-lis] *noun* 1 *obs. term for* **radio** or RADIO SET ▷ *adjective* 2 not requiring wires

DICTIONARY

W

THESAURUS

notice, hear tell of, learn of, find out about

wind[2] *verb* 1 COIL, curl, encircle, loop, reel, roll, spiral, twist
2 MEANDER, bend, curve, ramble, snake, turn, twist, zigzag

windfall *noun* GODSEND, bonanza, find, jackpot, manna from heaven

wind up *verb* 1 END, close, conclude, finalize, finish, settle, terminate, wrap up
2 END UP, be left, finish up

windy *adjective* BREEZY, blowy, blustery, gusty, squally, stormy, wild, windswept

wing *noun* 1 FACTION, arm, branch, group, section
▷ *verb* 2 FLY, glide, soar
3 WOUND, clip, hit

wink *verb* 1 BLINK, bat, flutter
2 TWINKLE, flash, gleam, glimmer, sparkle
▷ *noun* 3 BLINK, flutter

winner *noun* VICTOR, champ (*informal*), champion, conqueror, master

winning *adjective* 1 VICTORIOUS, conquering, successful, triumphant
2 CHARMING, alluring, attractive, cute, disarming, enchanting, endearing, engaging, likable *or* likeable, pleasing

winnings *plural noun* SPOILS, gains, prize, proceeds, profits, takings

winnow *verb* SEPARATE, divide, select, sift, sort out

win over *verb* CONVINCE, bring round *or* talk round, convert, influence, persuade, prevail upon, sway

wintry *adjective* COLD, chilly, freezing, frosty, frozen, icy, snowy

wipe *verb* 1 CLEAN, brush, mop, rub, sponge, swab
2 ERASE, remove
▷ *noun* 3 RUB, brush

wipe out *verb* DESTROY, annihilate, eradicate, erase, expunge, exterminate, massacre, obliterate

wiry *adjective* LEAN, sinewy, strong, tough

wise[1] [wīz] *adjective* 1 having intelligence and knowledge 2 sensible > **wis•dom** [WIZ-dəm] *noun* (accumulated) knowledge, learning 1 erudition > **wise'ly** *adverb* > **wise'a•cre** *noun* one who wishes to seem wise > **wisdom tooth** third molar usually cut about 20th year

wise[2] *noun* (*obsolete*) manner

wise•crack [WĪZ-krak] *noun* (*informal*) flippant (would-be) clever remark

wish *verb intransitive* 1 have a desire ▷ *verb transitive* 2 desire ▷ *noun* 3 desire 4 thing desired > **wish'ful** [-fəl] *adjective* 1 desirous 2 too optimistic > **wish'bone** *noun* V-shaped bone above breastbone of fowl

wisp *noun* 1 light, delicate streak, as of smoke 2 twisted handful, usu. of straw, etc. 3 stray lock of hair > **wisp'y** *adjective* **wisp•i•er, wisp•i•est**

wist•ful [WIST-fəl] *adjective* 1 longing, yearning 2 sadly pensive > **wist'ful•ly** *adverb*

wit *noun* 1 ingenuity in connecting amusingly incongruous ideas 2 person gifted with this power 3 sense 4 intellect 5 understanding 6 ingenuity 7 humor > **wit'ti•cism** [-ti-sizm] *noun* witty remark > **wit'ti•ly** *adverb* > **wit'ting•ly** *adverb* 1 on purpose 2 knowingly > **wit'less** [-lis] *adjective* foolish > **wit'ty** *adjective* **-ti•er, -ti•est**

witch [wich] *noun* 1 person, usu. female, believed to practice, practicing, or professing to practice (black) magic, sorcery 2 ugly, wicked woman 3 fascinating woman > **witch'craft** *noun* > **witch doctor** in certain societies, person appearing to cure or cause injury, disease by magic

with [with] *preposition* 1 in company or possession of 2 against 3 in relation to 4 through 5 by means of > **with•al** [with-AWL] *adverb* also, likewise > **with•in'** *preposition, adverb* in, inside > **with•out'** *preposition* 1 lacking 2 (*obsolete*) outside

with•draw [with-DRAW] *verb* **-drew, -drawn, -draw•ing** draw back or out > **with•draw'al** *noun* > **with•drawn'** *adjective* reserved, unsociable

with•er [WITH-ər] *verb* (cause to) wilt, dry up, decline > **with'er•ing** *adjective* (of glance, etc.) scornful

with•ers [WITH-ərz] *plural noun* ridge between a horse's shoulder blades

with•hold [with-HOHLD] *verb transitive* **-held, -hold•ing** 1 restrain 2 keep back 3 refrain from giving

with•stand' *verb transitive* **-stood** [-stuud], **-stand•ing** oppose, resist, esp. successfully

wit•ness [WIT-nis] *noun* 1 one who sees something 2 testimony 3 one who gives testimony ▷ *verb intransitive* 4 give testimony ▷ *verb transitive* 5 see 6 attest 7 see and sign as having seen

wiz•ard [WIZ-ərd] *noun* 1 sorcerer, magician 2 conjurer > **wiz'ard•ry** *noun*

wiz•ened [WIZ-ənd] *adjective* shriveled, wrinkled

WMD weapon(s) of mass destruction: nuclear, chemical, or biological weapons that can cause death or injury on a large scale

wob•ble [WOB-əl] *verb intransitive* **-bled, -bling** 1 move unsteadily 2 sway ▷ *noun* 3 an unsteady

wisdom *noun* UNDERSTANDING, discernment, enlightenment, erudition, insight, intelligence, judgment, knowledge, learning, sense

wise *adjective* SENSIBLE, clever, discerning, enlightened, erudite, intelligent, judicious, perceptive, prudent, sage

wisecrack *noun* (*informal*) 1 JOKE, jest, jibe, quip, witticism
▷ *verb* 2 JOKE, jest, jibe, quip

wish *verb* 1 WANT, aspire, crave, desire, hanker, hope, long, yearn
▷ *noun* 2 DESIRE, aspiration, hope, intention, urge, want, whim, will

wispy *adjective* THIN, attenuated, delicate, fine, flimsy, fragile, frail

wistful *adjective* MELANCHOLY, contemplative, dreamy, longing, meditative, pensive, reflective, thoughtful

wit *noun* 1 HUMOR, badinage, banter, drollery, jocularity, raillery, repartee, wordplay
2 HUMORIST, card (*informal*), comedian, joker, wag
3 CLEVERNESS, acumen, brains, common sense, ingenuity, intellect, sense, wisdom

witch *noun* ENCHANTRESS, crone, hag, magician, sorceress

witchcraft *noun* MAGIC, enchantment, necromancy, occultism, sorcery, the black art, voodoo, wizardry

withdraw *verb* REMOVE, draw back, extract, pull out, take away, take off

withdrawal *noun* REMOVAL, extraction

withdrawn *adjective* UNCOMMUNICATIVE, distant, introverted, reserved, retiring, shy, taciturn, unforthcoming

wither *verb* WILT, decay, decline, disintegrate, fade, perish, shrivel, waste

withering *adjective* SCORNFUL, devastating, humiliating, hurtful, mortifying, snubbing

withhold *verb* KEEP BACK, conceal, hide, hold back, refuse, reserve, retain, suppress

withstand *verb* RESIST, bear, cope with, endure, hold off, oppose, stand up to, suffer, tolerate

witless *adjective* FOOLISH, halfwitted, idiotic, inane, moronic (*offensive*), senseless, silly, stupid

witness *noun* 1 OBSERVER, beholder, bystander, eyewitness, looker-on, onlooker, spectator, viewer, watcher
2 TESTIFIER, corroborator
▷ *verb* 3 SEE, note, notice, observe, perceive, view, watch
4 SIGN, countersign, endorse

wits *plural noun* INTELLIGENCE, acumen, brains (*informal*), cleverness, comprehension, faculties, ingenuity, reason, sense, understanding

witticism *noun* QUIP, bon mot, one-liner (*slang*), pun, riposte

witty *adjective* HUMOROUS, amusing, clever, droll, funny, piquant, sparkling, waggish, whimsical

wizard *noun* MAGICIAN, conjurer, magus, necromancer, occultist, shaman, sorcerer, warlock, witch

wizardry *noun* MAGIC, sorcery, voodoo, witchcraft

wizened *adjective* WRINKLED, dried up, gnarled, lined, shriveled, shrunken, withered

wobble *verb* 1 SHAKE, rock, sway, teeter, totter, tremble
▷ *noun* 2 UNSTEADINESS, shake, tremble, tremor

movement > **wob'bly** *adjective* **-bli•er, -bli•est**
woe [woh] *noun* grief > **woe•be•gone** [WOH-bi-gawn] *adjective* looking sorrowful > **woe'ful** [-fəl] *adjective* 1 sorrowful 2 pitiful 3 wretched > **woe'ful•ly** *adverb*
wolf [wuulf] *noun, plural* **wolves** 1 wild predatory doglike animal of northern countries 2 (*informal*) man who habitually tries to seduce women ▷ *verb transitive* 3 eat ravenously > **wolf whistle** whistle by man expressing admiration for a woman **cry wolf** raise false alarm
wolf•ram [WUUL-frəm] *noun* tungsten
wol•ver•ine [wuul-və-REEN] *noun* carnivorous mammal inhabiting northern regions
wom•an [WUUM-ən] *noun, plural* **wom•en** [WIM-in] 1 adult human female 2 women collectively > **wom'an•hood** [-huud] *noun* > **wom'an•ish** *adjective* effeminate > **wom'an•ize** *verb intransitive* **-ized, -iz•ing** (of man) indulge in many casual affairs with women > **wom'an•kind** [-kīnd] *noun* > **wom'an•ly** *adjective* of, proper to woman > **women's liberation** movement for removal of attitudes, practices that preserve social, economic, etc. inequalities between women and men (*also* **women's lib**)
womb [woom] *noun* female organ of conception and gestation, uterus
won [wun] *pt./pp. of* **win**
won•der [WUN-dər] *noun* 1 emotion excited by amazing or unusual thing 2 marvel, miracle ▷ *verb intransitive* 3 be curious about 4 feel amazement > **won'der•ful** [-fəl] *adjective* 1 remarkable 2 very fine > **won'der•ment** [-mənt] *noun* surprise > **won'drous** [-drəs] *adjective* 1 inspiring wonder 2 strange
wont [wawnt] *noun* 1 custom ▷ *adjective* 2 accustomed > **wont'ed** [-id] *adjective* habitual, established
woo *verb transitive* court, seek to marry > **woo'er** [-ər] *noun* suitor
wood [wuud] *noun* 1 substance of trees, timber 2 firewood 3 tract of land with growing trees > **wood'ed** [-id] *adjective* having (many) trees > **wood'en** [-n] *adjective* 1 made of wood 2 obstinate 3 without expression > **wood'y** *adjective* > **wood'chuck** *noun* American burrowing rodent > **wood'cut** *noun* 1 engraving on wood 2 impression from this > **wood'land** [-lənd] *noun* woods, forest > **wood'peck•er** *noun* bird that searches tree trunks for insects > **wood'wind** *adjective, noun* (of) wind instruments of orchestra, orig. made of wood
woof [wuuf] *noun* the threads that cross the warp in weaving
woof•er [WUUF-ər] *noun* loudspeaker for reproducing low-frequency sounds
wool [wuul] *noun* 1 soft hair of sheep, goat, etc. 2 yarn spun from this > **wool'en** [-in] *adjective* > **wool'ly** *adjective* **-li•er, -li•est** 1 of wool 2 vague, muddled ▷ *noun* 3 [-eez] (*often plural*) knitted woolen garment, esp. warm undergarment > **wool'gath•er•ing** *noun* daydreaming
word [wurd] *noun* 1 unit of speech or writing regarded by users of a language as the smallest separate meaningful unit 2 term 3 message 4 brief remark 5 information 6 promise 7 command ▷ *verb transitive* 8 express in words, esp. in particular way > **word'ing** *noun* choice and arrangement of words > **word'y** *adjective* **word•i•er, word•i•est** using more words than necessary, verbose > **word processor** keyboard, microprocessor and monitor for electronic organization and storage of written text
wore *pt. of* **wear**
work [wurk] *noun* 1 labor 2 employment 3 occupation 4 task 5 toil 6 something made or accomplished 7 production of art or science 8

DICTIONARY **W** THESAURUS

wobbly *adjective* UNSTEADY, rickety, shaky, teetering, tottering, uneven
woe *noun* GRIEF, agony, anguish, distress, gloom, misery, sadness, sorrow, unhappiness, wretchedness
woeful *adjective* 1 SAD, deplorable, dismal, distressing, grievous, lamentable, miserable, pathetic, tragic, wretched
2 PITIFUL, abysmal, appalling, bad, deplorable, dreadful, feeble, pathetic, poor, sorry
woman *noun* LADY, female, girl
womanizer *noun* PHILANDERER, Casanova, Don Juan, lecher, seducer
womanly *adjective* FEMININE, female, ladylike, matronly, motherly, tender, warm
wonder *verb* 1 THINK, conjecture, meditate, ponder, puzzle, query, question, speculate
2 BE AMAZED, be astonished, gape, marvel, stare
▷ *noun* 3 PHENOMENON, curiosity, marvel, miracle, prodigy, rarity, sight, spectacle
4 AMAZEMENT, admiration, astonishment, awe, bewilderment, fascination, surprise, wonderment
wonderful *adjective* 1 EXCELLENT, brilliant, fabulous (*informal*), fantastic (*informal*), great (*informal*), magnificent, marvelous, outstanding, superb, terrific (*informal*), tremendous
2 REMARKABLE, amazing, astonishing, extraordinary, incredible, miraculous, phenomenal, staggering, startling, unheard-of
woo *verb* COURT, cultivate, pursue
wood *noun* 1 TIMBER
2 WOODLAND, coppice, copse, forest, grove, thicket
wooded *adjective* TREE-COVERED, forested, sylvan (*poetic*), timbered, tree-clad
wooden *adjective* 1 WOODY, ligneous, timber
2 EXPRESSIONLESS, deadpan, lifeless, unresponsive
wool *noun* FLEECE, hair, yarn
woolly *adjective* 1 FLEECY, hairy, shaggy, woollen
2 VAGUE, confused, hazy, ill-defined, indefinite, indistinct, muddled, unclear
word *noun* 1 TERM, expression, name
2 CHAT, confab (*informal*), consultation, discussion, talk, tête-à-tête
3 REMARK, comment, utterance
4 MESSAGE, communiqué, dispatch, information, intelligence, news, notice, report
5 PROMISE, assurance, guarantee, oath, pledge, vow
6 COMMAND, bidding, decree, mandate, order
▷ *verb* 7 EXPRESS, couch, phrase, put, say, state, utter
wording *noun* PHRASEOLOGY, language, phrasing, terminology, words
wordy *adjective* LONG-WINDED, diffuse, prolix, rambling, verbose, windy

book **9** needlework > **works** **1** factory **2** total of person's deeds, writings, etc. **3** (*informal*) everything, full or extreme treatment **4** mechanism of clock, etc. ▷ *verb transitive* **5** cause to operate **6** make, shape ▷ *verb intransitive* **7** apply effort **8** labor **9** operate **10** be engaged in trade, profession, etc. **11** turn out successfully **12** ferment > **work'a•ble** *adjective* > **work•a•hol•ic** [wur-kə-HAW-lik] *noun* person addicted to work > **work•ing class** social class consisting of wage earners, esp. manual > **working-class** *adjective* > **work•man** [WURK-mən] *noun, plural* **-men** **1** manual worker **2** male worker > **work'man•ship** *noun* **1** skill of workman **2** way thing is finished **3** style > **work'shop** *noun* **1** place where things are made **2** discussion group, seminar

world [wurld] *noun* **1** the universe **2** Earth **3** sphere of existence **4** mankind, people generally **5** society > **world'ly** *adjective* **1** earthly **2** mundane **3** absorbed in the pursuit of material gain, advantage **4** carnal > **World Wide Web** global computer network sharing graphics, etc., via the Internet

worm [wurm] *noun* **1** small limbless creeping snakelike creature **2** anything resembling worm in shape or movement **3** gear wheel with teeth forming part of screw threads **4** (*informal*) weak, despised person **5** *computing* type of virus > **worms** **1** (disorder caused by) infestation of worms, esp. in intestines ▷ *verb intransitive* **2** crawl ▷ *verb transitive* **3** work (oneself) in insidiously **4** extract (secret) craftily **5** rid of worms > **worm'-eaten** *adjective* **1** full of holes gnawed by worms **2** old, antiquated > **worm'y** *adjective* **worm•i•er, worm•i•est**

worm•wood [WURM-wuud] *noun* **1** bitter herb **2** bitterness

worn *pp of* **wear**

wor•ry [WUR-ee] *verb intransitive* **-ried, -ry•ing** **1** be (unduly) concerned ▷ *verb transitive* **-ried, -ry•ing** **2** trouble, pester, harass **3** (of dog) seize, shake with teeth ▷ *noun, plural* **-ries** **4** (cause of) anxiety, concern > **wor'ri•er** *noun*

worse [wurs] *adjective, adverb comp. of* **bad, badly.** ▷ *noun* > **worst** *adjective, adverb sup. of* **bad, badly.** ▷ *noun* > **wors'en** [-in] *verb* **1** make, grow worse **2** impair **3** deteriorate

wor•ship [WUR-ship] *verb transitive* **-shiped, -ship•ing** **1** show religious devotion to **2** adore **3** love and admire ▷ *noun* **4** act of worshiping > **wor'ship•er** *noun*

wor•sted [WUUS-tid] *noun* **1** woolen yarn ▷ *adjective* **2** made of woolen yarn **3** spun from wool

worth [wurth] *adjective* **1** having or deserving to

DICTIONARY • THESAURUS

work *noun* **1** EFFORT, drudgery, elbow grease (*facetious*), exertion, industry, labor, sweat, toil
2 EMPLOYMENT, business, duty, job, livelihood, occupation, profession, trade
3 TASK, assignment, chore, commission, duty, job, stint, undertaking
4 CREATION, achievement, composition, handiwork, opus, piece, production
▷ *verb* **5** LABOR, drudge, exert oneself, peg away, slave, slog *or* slog away, sweat, toil
6 BE EMPLOYED, be in work
7 OPERATE, control, drive, handle, manage, manipulate, move, use
8 FUNCTION, go, operate, run
9 CULTIVATE, dig, farm, till
10 MANIPULATE, fashion, form, knead, mold, shape

workable *adjective* VIABLE, doable, feasible, possible, practicable, practical

worker *noun* EMPLOYEE, artisan, craftsman, hand, laborer, tradesman, workman

working *adjective* **1** EMPLOYED, active, in work
2 FUNCTIONING, going, operative, running

workman *noun* LABORER, artisan, craftsman, employee, hand, journeyman, mechanic, operative, tradesman, worker

workmanship *noun* SKILL, artistry, craftsmanship, expertise, handiwork, technique

work out *verb* **1** SOLVE, calculate, figure out, find out
2 HAPPEN, develop, evolve, result, turn out
3 EXERCISE, practice, train, warm up

works *plural noun* **1** FACTORY, mill, plant, workshop
2 WRITINGS, canon, oeuvre (*French*), output
3 MECHANISM, action, machinery, movement, parts, workings

workshop *noun* STUDIO, factory, mill, plant, workroom

world *noun* **1** EARTH, globe
2 MANKIND, everybody, everyone, humanity, humankind, man, the public
3 SPHERE, area, domain, environment, field, realm

worldly *adjective* **1** EARTHLY, physical, profane, secular, temporal, terrestrial
2 MATERIALISTIC, grasping, greedy, selfish
3 WORLDLY-WISE, blasé, cosmopolitan, experienced, knowing, sophisticated, urbane

worldwide *adjective* GLOBAL, general, international, omnipresent, pandemic, ubiquitous, universal

worn *adjective* RAGGED, frayed, shabby, tattered, tatty, the worse for wear, threadbare

worn-out *adjective* **1** RUN-DOWN, on its last legs, ragged, shabby, threadbare, used-up, useless, worn
2 EXHAUSTED, dead-tired, done in (*informal*), fatigued, ready to drop, spent, tired out, weary

worried *adjective* ANXIOUS, afraid, apprehensive, concerned, fearful, frightened, nervous, perturbed, tense, troubled, uneasy, wired (*slang*)

worry *verb* **1** BE ANXIOUS, agonize, brood, fret
2 TROUBLE, annoy, bother, disturb, perturb, pester, unsettle, upset, vex
▷ *noun* **3** ANXIETY, apprehension, concern, fear, misgiving, trepidation, trouble, unease
4 PROBLEM, bother, care, hassle (*informal*), trouble

worsen *verb* **1** AGGRAVATE, damage, exacerbate
2 DETERIORATE, decay, decline, degenerate, get worse, go downhill (*informal*), sink

worship *verb* **1** PRAISE, adore, exalt, glorify, honor, pray to, revere, venerate
2 LOVE, adore, idolize, put on a pedestal
▷ *noun* **3** PRAISE, adoration, adulation, devotion, glory, honor, kudos, regard, respect, reverence

worth *noun* **1** VALUE, cost, price, rate, valuation
2 EXCELLENCE, goodness, importance, merit, quality, usefulness, value, worthiness

have value specified **2** meriting ▷ *noun* **3** excellence **4** merit, value **5** virtue **6** usefulness **7** price **8** quantity to be had for a given sum > **wor•thy** [WUR-*thee*] *adjective* **-thi•er, -thi•est** **1** virtuous **2** meriting ▷ *noun* **3** one of eminent worth **4** celebrity > **wor'thi•ness** [-*thee*-nis] *noun* > **worth•less** [WURTH-lis] *adjective* useless > **worth•while** [wurth-hwīl] *adjective* worth the time, effort, etc. involved

would [wuud] *verb auxiliary* **1** expressing wish, intention, probability **2** *pt. of* **will** > **would-be** [WUUD-bee] *adjective* wishing, pretending to be

wound[1] [woond] *noun* **1** injury, hurt from cut, stab, etc. ▷ *verb transitive* **2** inflict wound on, injure **3** pain

wound[2] [rhymes with **sound**] *pt./pp. of* **wind**[2]

wove [wohv] *pt. of* **weave.** > **wo'ven** *pp of* **weave**

wow *interjection* **1** of astonishment ▷ *noun* (*informal*) **2** object of astonishment, admiration, etc. **3** variation, distortion in pitch in record player, etc.

wraith [rayth] *noun* **1** apparition of a person seen shortly before or after death **2** specter

wran•gle [RANG-gəl] *verb intransitive* **-gled, -gling** **1** quarrel (noisily) **2** dispute **3** herd cattle ▷ *noun* **4** noisy quarrel **5** dispute > **wran'gler** [-glər] *noun* **1** cowboy **2** disputant

wrap [rap] *verb* **wrapped, wrap•ping** **1** cover, esp. by putting something around **2** put around ▷ *noun* **3** sandwich made by wrapping filling in a tortilla, etc. > **wrap'per** *noun* **1** loose garment **2** covering > **wrapping** *noun* material used to wrap

wrath [rath] *noun* anger > **wrath'ful** [-fəl] *adjective* > **wrath'ful•ly** *adverb*

wreak [reek] *verb transitive* **1** inflict (vengeance) **2** cause

wreath [reeth] *noun* something twisted into ring form, esp. band of flowers, etc. as memorial or tribute on grave, etc. > **wreathe** [reeth] *verb transitive* **wreathed, wreath•ing** **1** form into wreath **2** surround **3** wind around

wreck [rek] *noun* **1** destruction of ship **2** wrecked ship **3** ruin **4** something ruined ▷ *verb transitive* **5** cause the wreck of > **wreck'age** [-ij] *noun* > **wreck'er** *noun* **1** person or thing that destroys, ruins **2** vehicle for towing disabled, wrecked, etc. automobiles, a tow truck

wren [ren] *noun* kind of small songbird

wrench [rench] *verb transitive* **1** twist **2** distort **3** seize forcibly **4** sprain ▷ *noun* **5** violent twist **6** tool for twisting or turning **7** tool for gripping nut or bolt head **8** sudden pain caused esp. by parting

wrest [rest] *verb transitive* **1** take by force **2** twist violently

wres•tle [RES-əl] *verb intransitive* **-tled, -tling** **1** fight (esp. as sport) by grappling and trying to throw down **2** strive (with) **3** struggle ▷ *noun* > **wrest'ler** [-lər] *noun*

wretch [rech] *noun* **1** despicable person **2** miserable creature > **wretch'ed** [-id] *adjective* **-ed•er, -ed•est** **1** miserable, unhappy **2** worthless > **wretch'ed•ly** *adverb* > **wretch'ed•ness** [-nis] *noun*

wrig•gle [RIG-əl] *verb* **-gled, -gling** **1** move with twisting action, as worm **2** squirm ▷ *noun* **3** this action

wring [ring] *verb transitive* **wrung, wring•ing** **1** twist **2** extort **3** pain **4** squeeze out

worthless *adjective* **1** USELESS, ineffectual, rubbishy, unimportant, valueless
2 GOOD-FOR-NOTHING, contemptible, despicable, lousy (*slang*), scuzzy (*slang*), vile

worthwhile *adjective* USEFUL, beneficial, constructive, expedient, helpful, productive, profitable, valuable

worthy *adjective* PRAISEWORTHY, admirable, creditable, deserving, laudable, meritorious, valuable, virtuous, worthwhile

would-be *adjective* BUDDING, self-appointed, self-styled, unfulfilled, wannabe (*informal*)

wound *noun* **1** INJURY, cut, gash, hurt, laceration, lesion, trauma (*pathology*)
2 INSULT, offense, slight
▷ *verb* **3** INJURE, cut, gash, hurt, lacerate, pierce, wing
4 OFFEND, annoy, cut (someone) to the quick, hurt, mortify, sting

wrangle *verb* **1** ARGUE, bicker, contend, disagree, dispute, fight, quarrel, row, squabble
▷ *noun* **2** ARGUMENT, altercation, bickering, dispute, quarrel, row, squabble, tiff

wrap *verb* **1** COVER, bind, bundle up, encase, enclose, enfold, pack, package, shroud, swathe
▷ *noun* **2** CLOAK, cape, mantle, shawl, stole

wrapper *noun* COVER, case, envelope, jacket, packaging, wrapping

wrap up *verb* **1** GIFTWRAP, bundle up, pack, package
2 (*informal*) END, conclude, finish off, polish off, round off, terminate, wind up

wrath *noun* ANGER, displeasure, fury, indignation, ire, rage, resentment, temper

wreath *noun* GARLAND, band, chaplet, crown, festoon, ring

wreck *verb* **1** DESTROY, break, demolish, devastate, ruin, shatter, smash, spoil
▷ *noun* **2** SHIPWRECK, hulk

wreckage *noun* REMAINS, debris, fragments, pieces, rubble, ruin

wrench *verb* **1** TWIST, force, jerk, pull, rip, tear, tug, yank
2 SPRAIN, rick, strain
▷ *noun* **3** TWIST, jerk, pull, rip, tug, yank
4 SPRAIN, strain, twist
5 BLOW, pang, shock, upheaval
6 SPANNER, adjustable spanner

wrest *verb* SEIZE, extract, force, take, win, wrench

wrestle *verb* FIGHT, battle, combat, grapple, scuffle, struggle, tussle

wretch *noun* SCOUNDREL, good-for-nothing, miscreant, rascal, rogue, swine, worm

wretched *adjective* **1** UNHAPPY, dejected, depressed, disconsolate, downcast, forlorn, hapless, miserable, woebegone
2 WORTHLESS, inferior, miserable, paltry, pathetic, poor, sorry

wriggle *verb* **1** TWIST, jerk, jiggle, squirm, turn, wiggle, writhe
2 CRAWL, slink, snake, worm, zigzag
▷ *noun* **3** TWIST, jerk, jiggle, squirm, turn, wiggle ▷ **wriggle out of** MANEUVER, dodge, extricate oneself, worm out of

wring *verb* TWIST, extract, force, screw, squeeze

wrin•kle [RING-kəl] *noun* **1** slight ridge or furrow on surface **2** crease in the skin **3** fold **4** pucker **5** (*informal*) (useful) trick, hint ▷ *verb* **-kled, -kling 6** make, become wrinkled, pucker
wrist [rist] *noun* joint between hand and arm > **wrist'let** [-lit] *noun* band worn on wrist
writ [rit] *noun* written command from law court or other authority
write [rīt] *verb intransitive* **wrote, writ•ten, writ•ing 1** mark paper, etc. with the symbols that are used to represent words or sounds **2** compose **3** send a letter ▷ *verb transitive* **wrote, writ•ten, writ•ing 4** set down in words **5** compose **6** communicate in writing > **writ'er** *noun* **1** one who writes **2** author > **write-off** *noun* **1** cancellation from accounts as loss **2** (*informal*) person or thing considered hopeless > **write-up** *noun* written (published) account of something
writhe [rīth] *verb* **writhed, writh•ing 1** twist, squirm in or as in pain, etc. ▷ *verb intransitive* **2** be acutely embarrassed, etc.
wrong [rawng] *adjective* **1** not right or good **2** not suitable **3** wicked **4** incorrect **5** mistaken **6** not functioning properly ▷ *noun* **7** that which is wrong **8** harm **9** evil ▷ *verb transitive* **10** do wrong to **11** think badly of without justification > **wrong'do•er** [-doo-ər] *noun* one who acts immorally or illegally > **wrong'ful** [-fəl] *adjective* > **wrong'ful•ly** *adverb*
wrote [roht] *pt. of* **write**
wrought [rawt] *adjective* (of metals) shaped by hammering or beating > **wrought iron** pure form of iron used esp. in decorative railings, etc.
wrung *pt./pp. of* **wring**
wry [rī] *adjective* **wri•er, wri•est 1** turned to one side, contorted, askew **2** sardonic, dryly humorous
wuss [woos] *noun, plural* **-us•ses** (*slang*) feeble person
WWW World Wide Web

DICTIONARY • THESAURUS

wrinkle¹ *noun* **1** CREASE, corrugation, crinkle, crow's-foot, crumple, fold, furrow, line ▷ *verb* **2** CREASE, corrugate, crumple, fold, furrow, gather, pucker, rumple
writ *noun* SUMMONS, court order, decree, document
write *verb* RECORD, draft, draw up, inscribe, jot down, pen, scribble, set down
writer *noun* AUTHOR, hack, novelist, penpusher, scribbler, scribe, wordsmith
writhe *verb* SQUIRM, jerk, struggle, thrash, thresh, toss, twist, wiggle, wriggle
writing *noun* **1** SCRIPT, calligraphy, hand, handwriting, penmanship, scrawl, scribble **2** DOCUMENT, book, composition, opus, publication, work
wrong *adjective* **1** INCORRECT, erroneous, fallacious, false, inaccurate, mistaken, untrue, wide of the mark **2** BAD, criminal, dishonest, evil, illegal, immoral, sinful, unjust, unlawful, wicked, wrongful **3** INAPPROPRIATE, incongruous, incorrect, unacceptable, unbecoming, undesirable, unseemly, unsuitable **4** DEFECTIVE, amiss, askew, awry, faulty ▷ *adverb* **5** INCORRECTLY, badly, erroneously, inaccurately, mistakenly, wrongly **6** AMISS, askew, astray, awry ▷ *noun* **7** OFFENSE, crime, error, injury, injustice, misdeed, sin, transgression, wickedness ▷ *verb* **8** MISTREAT, abuse, cheat, dishonor, harm, hurt, malign, oppress, take advantage of
wrongdoer *noun* OFFENDER, criminal, culprit, delinquent, evildoer, lawbreaker, miscreant, perp (*informal*), sinner, villain
wrongful *adjective* IMPROPER, criminal, evil, illegal, illegitimate, immoral, unethical, unjust, unlawful, wicked
wry *adjective* **1** IRONIC, droll, dry, mocking, sarcastic, sardonic **2** CONTORTED, crooked, twisted, uneven

Xx

X 1 Christ 2 Christian 3 cross 4 Roman numeral, 10 5 mark indicating something wrong, a choice, a kiss, signature, etc. ▷ *noun* 6 unknown, mysterious person, factor
Xe *chem.* xenon
xe•non [ZEE-non] *noun* colorless, odorless gas occurring in very small quantities in air
xen•o•pho•bi•a [zen-ə-FOH-bee-ə] *noun* dislike, hatred, fear, of strangers or aliens
> **xen•o•pho'bic** *adjective*
xe•rog•ra•phy [zi-ROG-rə-fee] *noun* photocopying process
Xmas [EKS-məs] *noun* (*informal*) Christmas
x-rays [EKS-rayz] *plural noun* radiation of very short wavelengths, capable of penetrating solid bodies, and printing on photographic plate shadow picture of objects not permeable by rays
> **x-ray** *verb* photograph by x-rays
xy•li•tol [ZĪ-lə-tol] *noun* artificial sweetener produced from xylose and used esp. in chewing gum
xy•lo•carp [ZĪ-lə-kahrp] *noun* hard, woody fruit
> **xy•lo•carp'ous** *adjective* having fruit that becomes hard or woody
xy•lo•graph [ZĪ-lə-graf] *noun* 1 wood engraving 2 impression from wood block
xy•loid [ZĪ-loid] *adjective* 1 pert. to wood 2 woody, ligneous
xy•lo•phone [ZĪ-lə-fohn] *noun* musical instrument of wooden bars that sound when struck

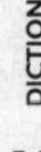

X

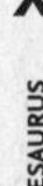

Xmas *noun* CHRISTMAS, festive season, Noel, Yule, Yuletide
X-rated *adjective* PORNOGRAPHIC, adult, dirty, graphic, hardcore (*slang*), obscene, scuzzy (*slang*)
X-rays *plural noun* RÖNTGEN RAYS (*old-fashioned*)

Yy

Y *chem.* yttrium
Y2K *noun* (*informal*) name for AD 2000 (esp. referring to the millennium bug)
yacht [yot] *noun* vessel propelled by sail or power, used for racing, pleasure, etc.
> **yachts•man** [YOTS-mən] *noun, plural* **-men**
ya•hoo [YAH-hoo] *noun, plural* **-hoos** crude, coarse person
Yah•weh [YAH-we] *noun* Jehovah, God
yak *noun* shaggy-haired, long-horned ox of Central Asia
yam *noun* large edible tuber, sweet potato
yank [yangk] *verb* 1 jerk, tug 2 pull quickly ▷ *noun* 3 quick tug
Yank [yangk], **Yank'ee** *adjective, noun* (*informal*) American
yap *verb intransitive* **yapped, yap•ping** 1 bark (as small dog) 2 (*slang*) talk shrilly, idly ▷ *noun* 3 a bark 4 (*slang*) the mouth
yard[1] [yahrd] *noun* 1 unit of length, 3 feet (36 inches, 0.9144 meter) 2 spar slung across ship's mast to extend sails > **yard'stick** *noun* 1 36-inch ruler 2 formula or standard of measurement or comparison > **yard'age** [-ij] *noun* 1 measurement of distance in yards 2 length in yards
yard[2] *noun* piece of enclosed ground adjoining building and used for some specific purpose, as garden, storage, holding livestock, etc.
> **yard'age** *noun* 1 use of yard 2 charge made for this
yar•mul•ke [YAHR-məl-kə] *noun* skullcap worn by Jewish men and boys, esp. in synagogue
yarn [yahrn] *noun* 1 spun thread 2 (*informal*) long involved story
yash•mak [yahsh-MAHK] *noun* face veil worn by Muslim women
yaw *verb intransitive* 1 of aircraft, etc., turn about vertical axis 2 deviate temporarily from course
yawl *noun* two-masted sailing vessel
yawn *verb intransitive* 1 open mouth wide, esp. in sleepiness 2 gape ▷ *noun* 3 a yawning
yaws [yawz] *noun* contagious tropical skin disease
Yb *chem.* ytterbium
ye [yee] *pronoun* (*obsolete*) you
yea [yay] *interjection* 1 yes ▷ *noun* 2 affirmative vote
year [yeer] *noun* 1 time taken by one revolution of Earth around sun, about 365 days 2 twelve months > **year'ling** *noun* animal one year old
> **year'ly** *adverb* 1 every year, once a year

---

yank *verb, noun* PULL, hitch, jerk, snatch, tug, wrench
yardstick *noun* STANDARD, benchmark, criterion, gauge, measure, par, touchstone
yarn *noun* 1 THREAD, fiber
2 (*old-fashioned, informal*) STORY, anecdote, cock-and-bull story (*informal*), fable, tale, tall tale (*informal*)
yawning *adjective* GAPING, cavernous, vast, wide
yearly *adjective* 1 ANNUAL
▷ *adverb* 2 ANNUALLY, every year, once a year, per annum

▷ *adjective* 2 happening, etc. once a year

yearn [yurn] *verb intransitive* 1 feel longing, desire 2 be filled with pity, tenderness > **yearn'ing** *noun*

yeast [yeest] *noun* substance used as fermenting, leavening agent, esp. in brewing and in baking bread > **yeast'y** *adjective* **yeast•i•er, yeast•i•est** 1 of, like yeast 2 frothy, fermenting 3 (of time) characterized by excitement, change, etc.

yell *verb* 1 cry out in loud shrill tone 2 speak in this way ▷ *noun* 3 loud shrill cry 4 a cheer, shout

yel•low [YEL-oh] *adjective* **-er, -est** 1 of the color of lemons, gold, etc. 2 (*informal*) cowardly ▷ *noun* 3 this color > **yel'low•bel•ly** *noun, plural* **-lies** (*slang*) coward > **yellow fever** acute infectious disease of (sub)tropical climates > **yellow jacket** 1 type of wasp 2 (*slang*) yellow capsule of phenobarbital

yelp *verb intransitive, noun* (produce) quick, shrill cry

yen[1] *noun* Japanese monetary unit

yen[2] *noun* (*informal*) longing, craving

yeo•man [YOH-mən] *noun, plural* **-men** 1 petty officer in U.S. Navy having mainly clerical duties 2 *Brit hist.* farmer cultivating own land ▷ *adjective* 3 performed in valiant, thorough manner

yes *interjection* 1 affirms or consents, gives an affirmative answer ▷ *noun, plural* **yes•ses** 2 affirmative reply > **yes-man** *noun, plural* **-men** weak person willing to agree to anything

yes•ter•day [YES-tər-day] *noun* 1 day before today 2 recent time ▷ *adverb, adjective*

yet *adverb* 1 now, still, besides, hitherto 2 nevertheless ▷ *conjunction* 3 but, at the same time, nevertheless

yet•i [YET-ee] *noun see* **abominable snowman**

yew [yoo] *noun* 1 evergreen tree with dark leaves 2 its wood

Yid•dish [YID-ish] *adjective, noun* (of, in) language used by many Jews in or from Europe, orig. a form of German written in Hebrew letters, with words from Hebrew and many other languages

yield [yeeld] *verb transitive* 1 give or return as food 2 produce 3 provide 4 concede 5 give up, surrender ▷ *verb intransitive* 6 produce 7 submit 8 comply 9 surrender, give way ▷ *noun* 10 amount produced, return, profit, result

yo•del [YOHD-l] *verb intransitive* **-deled, -del•ing** 1 warble in falsetto tone ▷ *noun* 2 falsetto warbling as practiced by Swiss mountaineers

yo•ga [YOH-gə] *noun* Hindu philosophical system aiming at spiritual, mental and physical well-being by means of certain physical and mental exercises > **yo'gi** [-gee] *noun, plural* **-gis** one who practices yoga

yo•gurt [YOH-gərt] *noun* thick, custard-like preparation of curdled milk

yoke [yohk] *noun* 1 wooden bar put across the necks of two animals to hold them together and to which plow, etc. can be attached 2 various objects like a yoke in shape or use 3 fitted part of garment, esp. around neck, shoulders 4 bond or tie 5 domination ▷ *verb transitive* **yoked, yok•ing** 6 put a yoke on, couple, unite

yo•kel [YOH-kəl] *noun* (*offensive*) person who lives in the country and is usu. simple and old-fashioned

yolk [yohk] *noun* 1 yellow central part of egg 2 oily secretion of skin of sheep

yon *adjective* (*obsolete or dialect*) that or those over there > **yon•der** [YON-dər] *adjective* 1 yon ▷ *adverb* 2 over there, in that direction

yore [yor] *noun poet.* the distant past

York•shire pudding [YORK-shər] baked batter eaten with roast beef

you [yoo] *pronoun* referring to person(s) addressed, or to unspecified person(s)

young [yung] *adjective* **-er, -est** 1 not far advanced in growth, life or existence 2 not yet old 3 immature 4 junior 5 recently formed 6 vigorous ▷ *noun* 7 offspring > **young'ster** [-stər] *noun* child

your [yuur] *adjective* 1 of, belonging to, or associated with you 2 of, belonging to, or associated with an unspecified person or people in general > **yours** *pronoun* something belonging to you > **your•self** *pronoun, plural* **-selves**

youth [yooth] *noun* 1 state or time of being

DICTIONARY

Y

THESAURUS

yearn *verb* LONG, ache, covet, crave, desire, hanker, hunger, itch

yell *verb* 1 SCREAM, bawl, holler (*informal*), howl, screech, shout, shriek, squeal
▷ *noun* 2 SCREAM, cry, howl, screech, shriek, whoop

yell at *verb* (*informal*) CRITICIZE, censure, rebuke, scold, tear into (*informal*)

yelp *verb* CRY, yap, yowl

yen *noun* LONGING, ache, craving, desire, hankering, hunger, itch, passion, thirst, yearning

yes man *noun* SYCOPHANT, brown-noser (*slang*), minion, timeserver, toady

yet *conjunction* 1 NEVERTHELESS, however, notwithstanding, still
▷ *adverb* 2 SO FAR, as yet, thus far, until now, up to now
3 STILL, besides, in addition, into the bargain, to boot
4 NOW, just now, right now, so soon

yield *verb* 1 PRODUCE, bear, bring forth, earn, generate, give, net, provide, return, supply
2 SURRENDER, bow, capitulate, give in, relinquish, resign, submit, succumb
▷ *noun* 3 PROFIT, crop, earnings, harvest, income, output, produce, return, revenue, takings

yielding *adjective* 1 SUBMISSIVE, accommodating, acquiescent, biddable, compliant, docile, flexible, obedient, pliant
2 SOFT, elastic, pliable, spongy, springy, supple, unresisting

yoke *verb* BURDEN, encumber, land, load, saddle

yokel *noun* PEASANT, bumpkin *or* country bumpkin, countryman, hick (*informal, chiefly United States & Canadian*), hillbilly, redneck (*slang*), rustic

young *adjective* 1 IMMATURE, adolescent, callow, green, infant, junior, juvenile, little, youthful
2 NEW, early, fledgling, recent, undeveloped
▷ *plural noun* 3 OFFSPRING, babies, brood, family, issue, litter, progeny

youngster *noun* YOUTH, boy, girl, juvenile, kid

young **2** state before adult age **3** young man **4** young people > **youth'ful** [-fəl] *adjective*

yowl *verb, noun* (produce) mournful cry

yo-yo [YOH-yoh] *noun, plural* **-yos** toy consisting of a spool attached to a string, by which it can be spun out and reeled in while attached to the finger

yuc•ca [YUK-ə] *noun* tropical plant with stiff lancelike leaves

Yule [yool] *noun* the Christmas festival or season

yup•pie [YUP-ee] *noun* young urban professional ▷ *adjective*

(*informal*), lad, lass, teenager

youth *noun* **1** IMMATURITY, adolescence, boyhood, girlhood, salad days
2 BOY, adolescent, kid (*informal*), lad, stripling, teenager, young man, youngster

youthful *adjective* YOUNG, boyish, childish, fresh-faced, girlish, immature, inexperienced, juvenile, rosy-cheeked

Zz

za•ba•glio•ne [zah-bəl-YOH-nee] *noun* Italian custardlike dessert of whipped and heated egg yolks, sugar and Marsala wine
za•ny [ZAY-nee] *adjective* **-ni•er, -ni•est** 1 comical, funny in unusual way ▷ *noun, plural* **-nies** 2 eccentric person 3 silly person
zap (*informal*) ▷ *verb transitive* **zapped, zap•ping** 1 attack, kill or destroy 2 *computing* clear from screen, erase 3 change (TV channels) rapidly by remote control 4 skip over or delete sound of (commercials)
zeal [zeel] *noun* 1 fervor 2 keenness, enthusiasm > **zeal•ot** [ZEL-ət] *noun* 1 fanatic 2 enthusiast > **zeal'ous** [-əs] *adjective* 1 ardent 2 enthusiastic 3 earnest > **zeal'ous•ly** *adverb*
ze•bra [ZEE-brə] *noun, plural* **-bras** striped Afr. animal like a horse
ze•bu [ZEE-byoo] *noun* humped Indian ox or cow
Zen *noun* Japanese school teaching contemplation, meditation
ze•nith [ZEE-nith] *noun* 1 point of the heavens directly above an observer 2 point opposite nadir 3 summit, peak 4 climax
zeph•yr [ZEF-ər] *noun* soft, gentle breeze
zep•pe•lin [ZEP-ə-lin] *noun* large, cylindrical, rigid airship
ze•ro [ZEER-oh] *noun, plural* **-ros, -roes** 1 nothing 2 figure 0 3 point on graduated instrument from which positive and negative quantities are reckoned 4 the lowest point ▷ *verb transitive* **-roed, -ro•ing** 5 reduce to zero 6 adjust (instrument, etc.) to zero
zest *noun* 1 enjoyment 2 excitement, interest, flavor 3 peel of orange or lemon > **zest'ful** [-fəl] *adjective*
zig'zag *noun* 1 line or course characterized by sharp turns in alternating directions ▷ *verb intransitive* **-zagged, -zag•ging** 2 move along in zigzag course
zinc [zingk] *noun* bluish-white metallic element with wide variety of uses, esp. in alloys like brass
zin•ni•a [ZIN-ee-ə] *noun* plant with daisylike, brightly colored flowers
Zi•on [ZĪ-ən] *noun* 1 hill on which Jerusalem stands 2 modern Jewish nation 3 Israel 4 *Christian Church* heaven > **Zi'on•ism** *noun* movement to found, support Jewish homeland in what now is state of Israel > **Zi'on•ist** *noun, adjective*

---

zany *adjective* COMICAL, clownish, crazy, eccentric, goofy (*informal*), wacky (*slang*)
zeal *noun* ENTHUSIASM, ardor, eagerness, fanaticism, fervor, gusto, keenness, passion, spirit, verve, zest
zealot *noun* FANATIC, bigot, enthusiast, extremist, militant
zealous *adjective* ENTHUSIASTIC, ardent, devoted, eager, fanatical, fervent, impassioned, keen, passionate
zenith *noun* HEIGHT, acme, apex, apogee, climax, crest, high point, peak, pinnacle, summit, top
zero *noun* 1 NOTHING, nada (*informal*), nil, nought, zilch (*informal*)
2 BOTTOM, nadir, rock bottom
zest *noun* 1 ENJOYMENT, appetite, gusto, keenness, relish, zeal
2 FLAVOR, charm, interest, piquancy, pungency,

zip *noun* 1 short whizzing sound 2 energy, vigor ▷ *verb* **zipped, zip•ping** 3 move with zip
zip code [kohd] system of numbers used to aid sorting of mail (*also* **ZIP code**)
zip•per [ZIP-ər] *noun* 1 device for fastening with two rows of flexible metal or plastic teeth, interlocked and opened by a sliding clip ▷ *verb transitive* 2 fasten with zipper
zir•con [ZUR-kon] *noun* mineral used as gemstone and in industry
zith•er [ZITH-ər] *noun* flat stringed instrument
Zn *chem.* zinc
zo•di•ac [ZOH-dee-ak] *noun* imaginary belt of the heavens along which the sun, moon, and chief planets appear to move, divided crosswise into twelve equal areas, called **signs of the zodiac**, each named after a constellation > **zo•di•a•cal** [zoh-DĪ-ə-kəl] *adjective*
zom•bie [ZOM-bee] *noun* 1 person appearing lifeless, apathetic, etc. 2 corpse supposedly brought to life by supernatural spirit
zone [zohn] *noun* 1 region with particular characteristics or use 2 any of the five belts into which tropics and arctic and antarctic circles divide Earth
zoo *noun* place where wild animals are kept, studied, bred and exhibited
zo•og•ra•phy [zoh-OG-rə-fee] *noun* descriptive zoology > **zo•og'ra•pher, zo•og'ra•phist** *noun* > **zo•o•graph'i•cal** *adjective*
zo•ol•o•gy [zoh-OL-ə-jee] *noun* 1 scientific study of animals 2 characteristics of particular animals or of fauna of particular area > **zo•o•log'i•cal** *adjective* > **zo•ol'o•gist** *noun*
zoom *verb* 1 (cause to) make loud buzzing, humming sound 2 (cause to) go fast or rise, increase sharply ▷ *verb intransitive* 3 (of camera) use lens of adjustable focal length to make subject appear to move closer or farther away > **zoom lens** lens used in this way
zo•o•phyte [ZOH-ə-fīt] *noun* animal resembling a plant, such as a sea anemone > **zo•o•phyt'ic** [-FIT-ik] *adjective*
Zr *chem.* zirconium
zuc•chi•ni [zoo-KEEN-ee] *noun, plural* **-ni** *or* **-nis** green-skinned summer squash
Zu•lu [ZOO-loo] *noun* member, language of S Afr. Bantu tribes
zy•gote [ZĪ-goht] *noun* fertilized egg cell
zy•mot•ic [zī-MOT-ik] *adjective* 1 of, or caused by fermentation 2 of, caused by infection

DICTIONARY • THESAURUS

relish, spice, tang, taste
zip *noun* 1 (*informal*) ENERGY, drive, gusto, liveliness, verve, vigor, zest
▷ *verb* 2 SPEED, flash, fly, shoot, whizz (*informal*), zoom
zone *noun* AREA, belt, district, region, section, sector, sphere
zoom *verb* SPEED, dash, flash, fly, hurtle, pelt, rush, shoot, whizz (*informal*)

Microsoft® Office Professional 2007 – the basics and beyond

Technology is an essential feature of 21st century life. Whether one wishes to write a letter, complete a tax return, or deliver that all-important presentation at work, it is now almost unimaginable that a computer will not be switched on at some stage of these processes.

As information technology advances apace, one must be sure to keep up with new developments (or risk becoming obsolete). To help you negotiate the ever-changing world of software, Collins Dictionaries and Microsoft® have joined forces to provide you with a guide to Microsoft® Office Professional 2007.

This supplement gives you a clear insight into the basics (and beyond) of the newest version of Office Professional 2007 and its core applications with which you are already familiar.

Office Professional 2007 uses a new common interface (called Fluent) with commands and features organized around what the user wants to do, so that things are where you want them, when you need them.

This improved functionality addresses all of your everyday requirements and more, whether you wish to publish to a blog using Word 2007, or guard against spam and phishing emails using Outlook 2007. Providing not only security and flexibility of use with other applications, Office Professional 2007 also includes a wide selection of Themes and Galleries to give your documents a strong visual focus and professional look.

The following sections deal with Word 2007, Excel 2007, Outlook 2007, and Powerpoint 2007 in turn. Features and functionality of the different applications are discussed alongside illustrative examples of their use.

Find out more about Microsoft® Office 2007 at

http://www.microsoft.com.

1 • Microsoft® Office Word 2007

The Fluent user interface and Ribbon in Word 2007

The main new feature of Office Word 2007 is the new Fluent interface and Ribbon. Its command tabs replace the old toolbars and menus and create an uncluttered, practical, context-sensitive way of working with Word 2007 that enables you to find what you want, when you need it, more easily.

Other new features of the Word 2007 window are:

• the Office Button (used mainly to open files, create new files, publish, print, and close files, and exit Word 2007)

• the Quick Access Toolbar, located by default next to the Office Button:

• the view controls (at the bottom of the window), enabling you to quickly see which view you are using, and to easily switch between different types of view:

• the Zoom control, enabling you to easily zoom in and out without actually changing the document's style or the size of fonts used:

Most of Word 2007's command tabs are designed to be handy for tasks associated with typical stages in the process of creating a document. For example, the Home tab is the most useful one for typing and editing, choosing styles and fonts, copying and pasting, and picking paragraph and list formats. It is the tab that encapsulates most of what we need when doing our usual work on a document.

A quick look at each of the main tabs:

• ***The Home tab*** includes commands relating to the Clipboard, font selections, paragraph settings, styles, and editing.

• ***The Insert tab*** is used to add pages, tables, illustrations, links, headers and footers, text objects, and symbols to your document.

• ***The Page Layout tab*** contains the commands for working with themes, page backgrounds, and paragraph spacing in your document. Additionally, you may choose page setup options and arrange the order of elements on your page.

• ***The References tab*** includes special elements to use when you create longer or more complete documents. On this tab, you'll find what you need to create a table of contents, footnotes, citations and bibliographies, captions, an index, and a table of authorities.

• ***The Mailings tab*** is a new addition in the Word 2007 interface. Here you can find everything you need for creating, previewing, and producing a mail merge project.

• ***The Review tab*** has all the commands you need for checking your document and sharing it with others for review. There are tools for spelling, a thesaurus, and more commands for adding comments, tracking and working with changes, comparing versions, and protecting the document.

• ***The View tab*** is where you'll find all the options for displaying your document in different ways: from basic document views, to a set of display tools for adding rulers and gridlines, to options for working with multiple documents in multiple windows.

Templates and Themes

Templates enable to you to quickly and easily produce professional-looking documents of all types including brochures, calendars, contracts, forms, invoices, memos, newsletters, and time sheets.

Using a template allows you to reuse a particular format, saving time on retyping and reformatting every time you start a new document.

To start a new document from a template, click on the Office Button and select New:

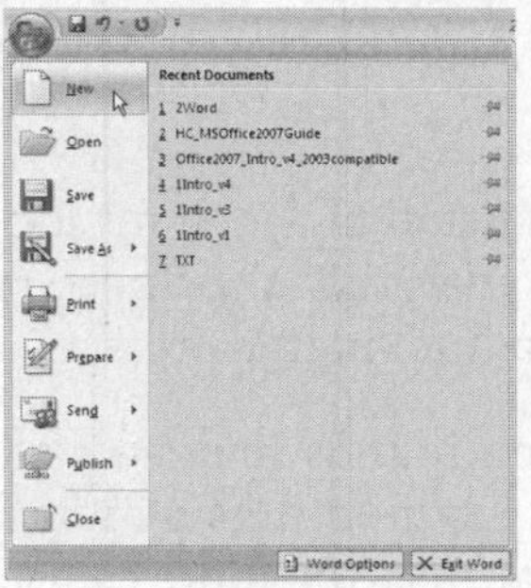

You can use your own templates (based on existing documents) or a blank template:

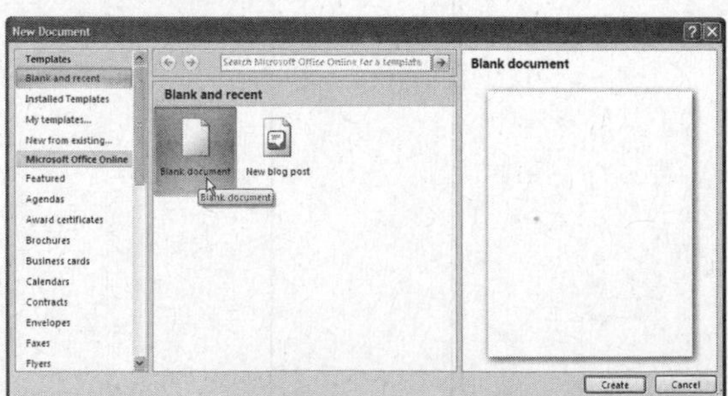

Alternatively, choose from one of the installed templates:

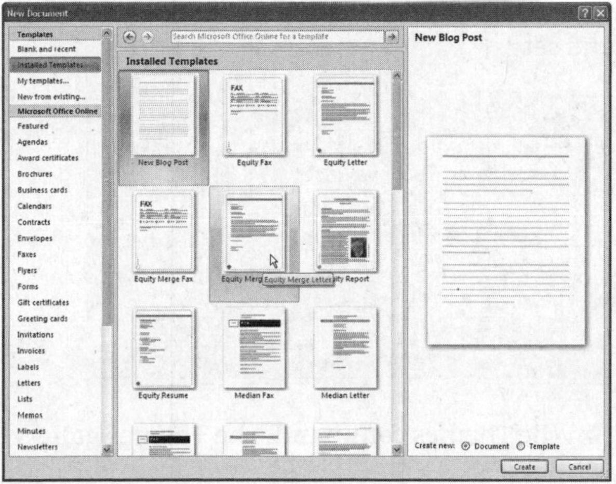

In addition you can choose from a large number online – from within the same New Document window without having to open a browser window separately.

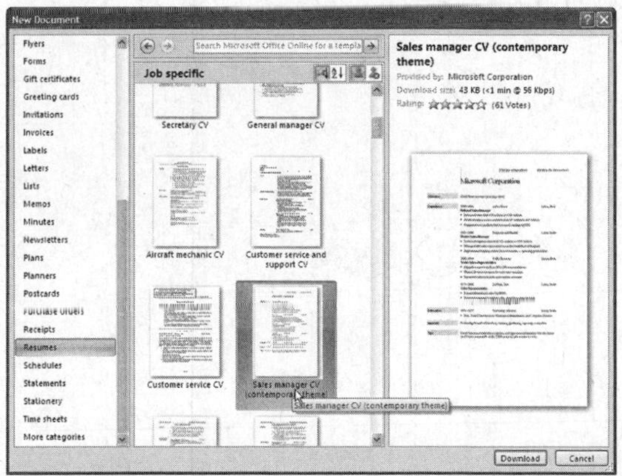

A document theme is a set of formatting choices that includes theme colors, theme fonts, and theme effects. For example, you might want to give your document a modern theme if you are designing a brochure for your IT consultancy, or an old-fashioned theme if you are designing a newsletter for your second-hand books business.

You can choose a different theme for a current document by going to the Page Layout tab and clicking on Themes in the Themes command set:

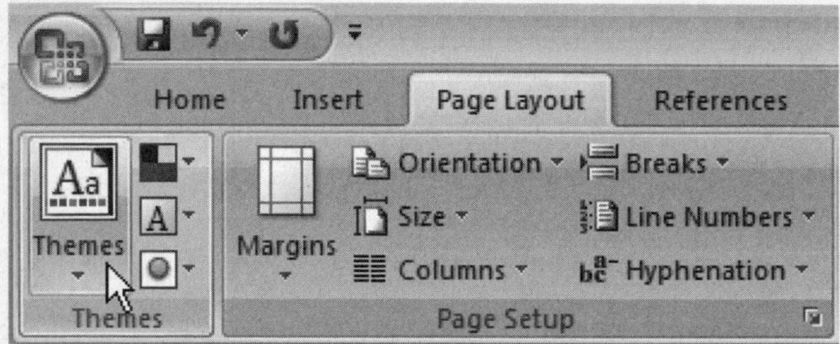

When you click on the Themes command, the Themes gallery opens:

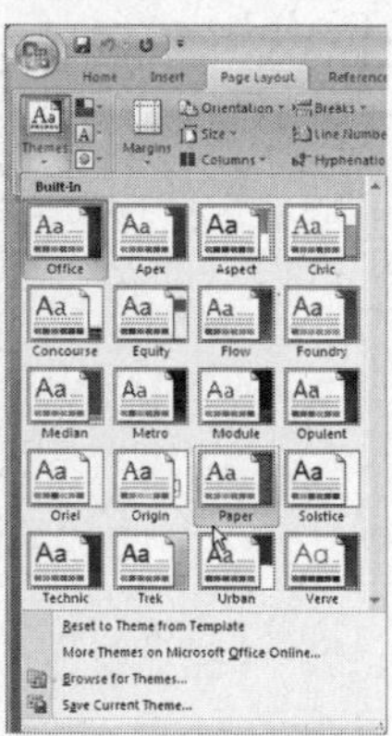

The individual theme options within the gallery show sample typefaces and colors to convey quickly the effect of each.

Cover pages

These are preset title pages with fields for title, subtitle, author, date, etc., depending on the type of cover page chosen. They are found in the Pages command set under the Insert tab in the Ribbon. The examples are picked from a gallery and follow the Document Theme.

Open the gallery by clicking on the Cover Page command. Hovering over the command with the mouse will bring up the SuperTooltip description:

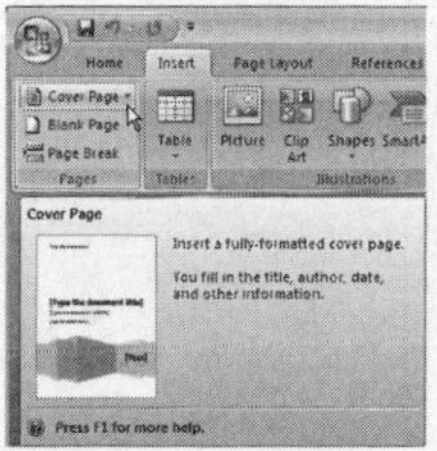

A mouse click brings up the gallery of Cover Page choices:

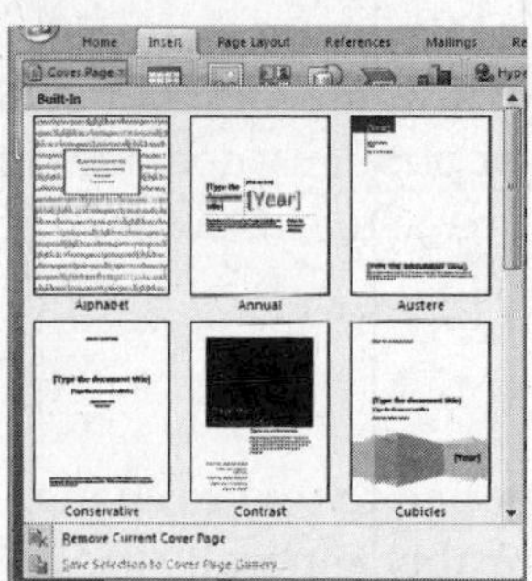

When you click on a cover page of your choice in the gallery, it is added at the beginning of your current document. You can click in the text boxes to add your own text to the page.

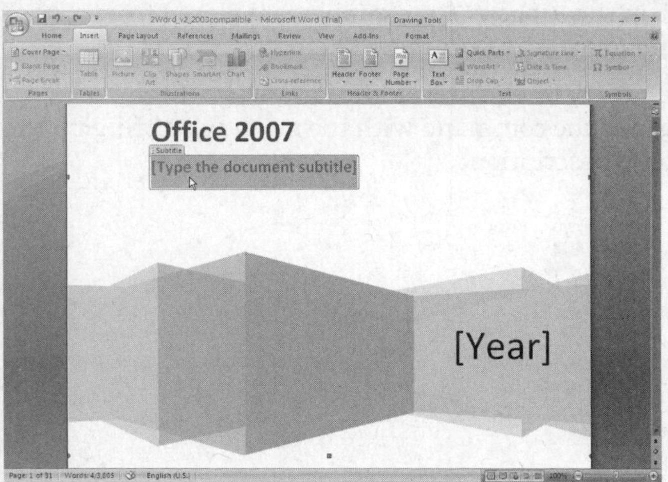

You can customize any cover page you select by, for example, adding your logo and changing the color scheme and font style to fit your existing business stationery or publicity documents. You can then save the customized cover page to the Cover Page gallery to use it again with other documents.

Applying Quick Styles

A style is a set of format instructions applied to text to change its format details. For example, you probably generally use one font and font size for your main headings, and another font or (at least) font size for your sub-headings. The main body text will require something different again.

The Quick Styles feature enables you to preview a number of styles before you select the one you want to apply.

To preview styles, you need to be in the Print Layout view. Either select some text or click to position the cursor in your document at the point you want to apply the new style; then let the mouse pointer hover over the style you'd like to preview in the Styles command set. To see additional styles, click the More button in the lower-right corner of the style examples, and a gallery of further style options appears:

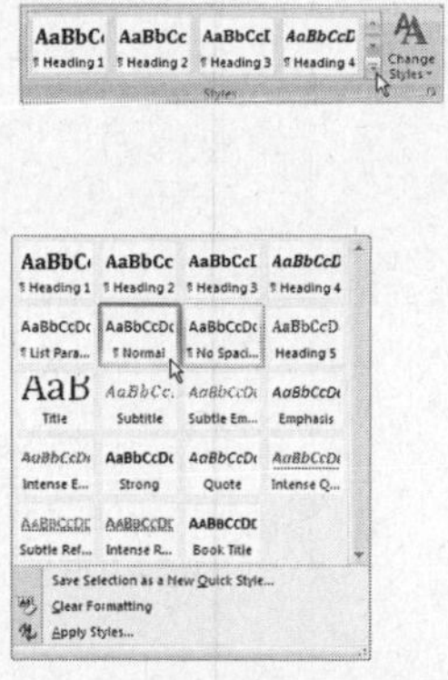

Preview a style by pointing to it in the Styles command set or gallery, and click to apply the style of your choice.

Inserting and editing tables

To insert a table, go to the Insert tab and use the Tables command set:

When you click on the Tables command, a dialog box opens that lets you choose the number of columns and rows for your table:

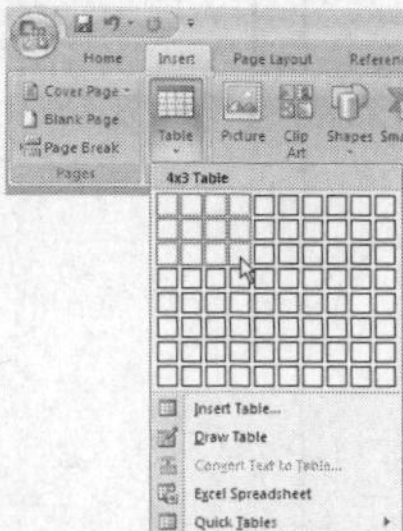

To insert a new column, first decide where you would like it to go. Then right-click in any cell of the column next to where the new column is to be inserted. In the pop-up menu, choose Insert (or press the I key) and then either Insert Columns to the Left or Insert Columns to the Right in the submenu (or press the L or R keys):

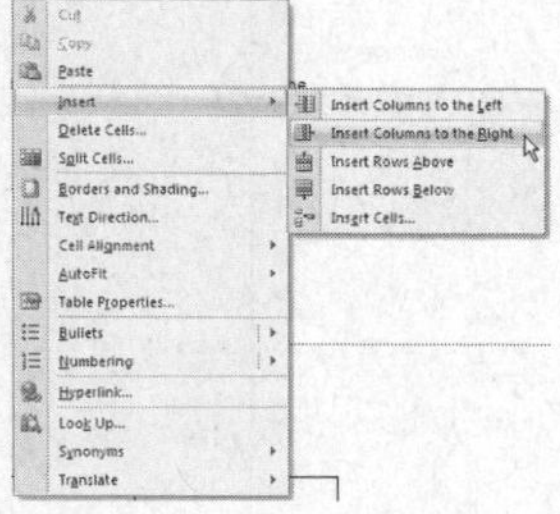

A new column is then inserted to the left or right of the column you right-clicked.

To insert multiple columns, first select a number of existing columns in the table by dragging over them with the mouse. If you want two new columns, select two existing columns, three for three, and so on. Once the desired number of columns is selected, right-click and choose Insert from the popup menu, and then choose where you'd like the new columns to be inserted (left or right of the selected columns), as before.

To add rows, right-click on the row next to where you'd like to add a row and select Insert again, but this time choose either Insert Rows Above or Insert Rows Below.

To delete cells, columns, or rows, right-click on the cell(s), column(s), or row(s) you'd like to delete and choose Delete Cells.

Make your choice in the dialog box that appears and press OK to confirm:

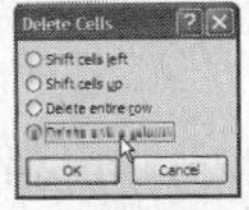

Tab Tip for Tables: When the cursor is inside a cell, the Tab key will move the cursor to the *next* cell if it is empty, or select the contents of the next cell if it is not empty. Similarly, Shift+Tab will move the cursor to the *previous* cell or select its contents. If the cursor is in the last cell of the last row, pressing Tab will insert a new row at the bottom of the table and move the cursor there, ready to start typing or pasting.

SmartArt graphics

SmartArt graphics are preformatted graphic elements (Venn diagrams, flow charts, etc.) that size text to fit within them and change font, color, etc. to match changes in Document Theme.

Choose SmartArt from the Insert tab to start the process; then select one of the four basic layout styles (Process, Hierarchy,

Cycle, and Relationship) to find the diagram type that is right for your document. Each diagram style offers several style possibilities.

SmartArt graphics enable you to create sophisticated diagrams quickly by customizing them with pictures and descriptive text.

Collaborating on files and comparing documents

Reviewing is an important stage in producing documents of many kinds. The information here applies to Microsoft® Office Excel 2007 Worksheets and Microsoft® Office PowerPoint 2007 presentations as well as to Word documents.

Adding comments

When working with others on a document, you may sometimes want to add comments. To make a comment, use the Review Tab and click on New Comment:

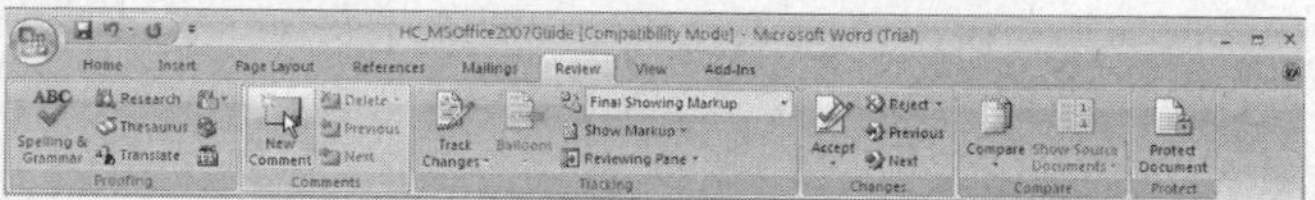

The Reviewing Pane will then open (if it is not open already) and you can start typing your comment:

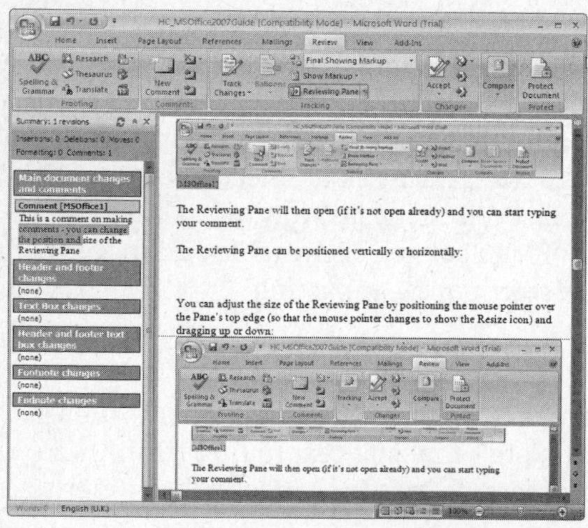

The Reviewing Pane can be positioned vertically or horizontally:

You can adjust the size of the Reviewing Pane by positioning the mouse pointer over the Pane's top edge when horizontal, or right edge when vertical (so that the mouse pointer changes to show the Resize icon) and dragging up and down (or left and right):

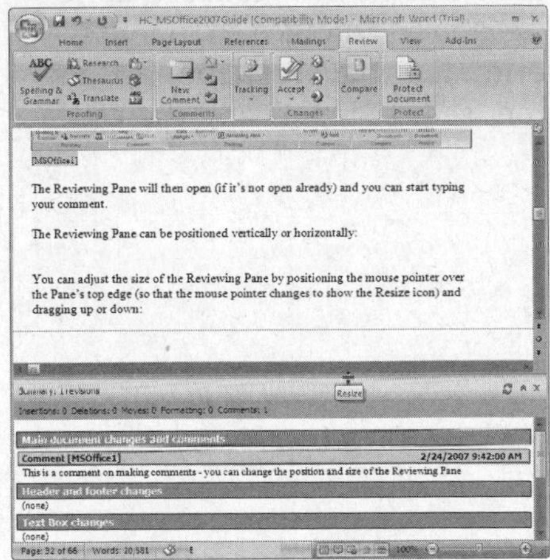

To close the Pane, click on the cross in its top-right corner. To open it again, click on Reviewing Pane in the Tracking command set under the Review tab.

Track Changes

There are times when you will want to track the changes made to a document used only by yourself, however the Track Changes facility is usually used to track the edits made by different people. When you turn on Track Changes, any changes you make are highlighted and key facts (such as the person making the change and when they made it) are recorded. Before you turn Track Changes on, make sure that Word 2007 knows who you are:

Telling Word 2007 who you are

When you first install it, Microsoft® Office Professional 2007 will attempt to determine your identity from information already on your computer or from a previous installation. If you share a computer with someone else, install on a brand new machine, or have inherited a computer from someone else, this information may need to be changed so that it's accurate. To inspect the information that Word 2007 already has, click on the Office Button, select Prepare and then click on Properties.

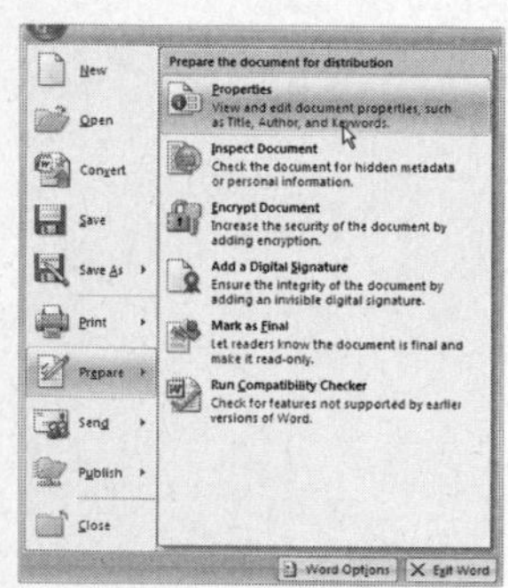

You can then view or edit your information:

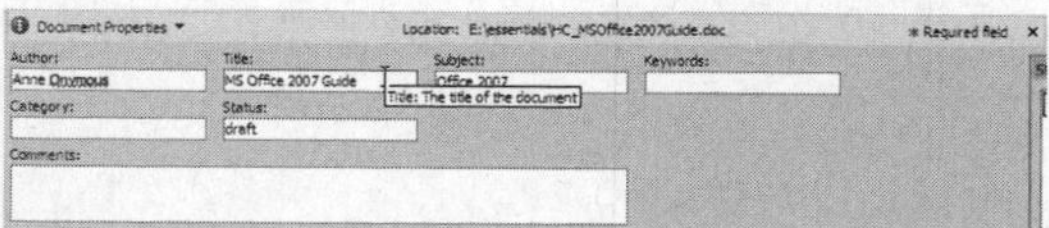

When you have finished, close the window.

Before creating new comments or implementing Track Changes, you can check that Word 2007 knows who you are by clicking on Track Changes (or pressing Ctrl+Shift+E) and selecting Change User Name (or pressing U):

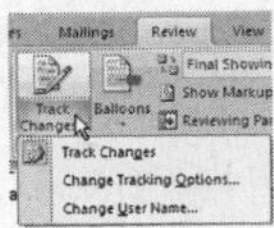

This opens the Word 2007 Options dialog box which is also useful for:

• switching between users when both are working on the same document and using the same computer

• setting other popular options, such as suspending/activating the Quick Format toolbar, or the Developer's tab, etc., or some of the many other options accessible via the Word 2007 Options dialog box:

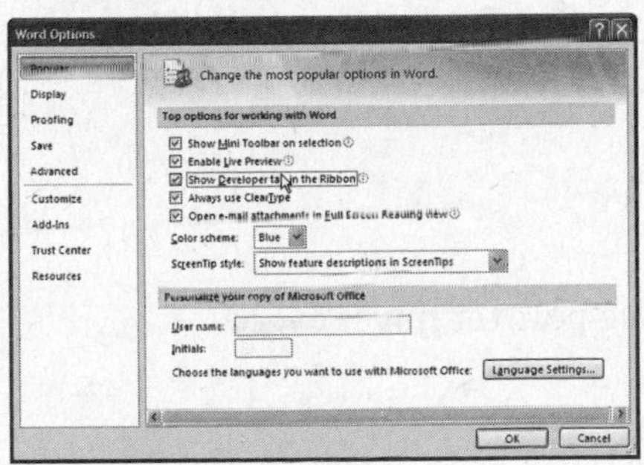

You can also open the Word 2007 Options dialog box by clicking on the Office Button, then clicking on the Word 2007 Options button (or press I while the Office menu is open):

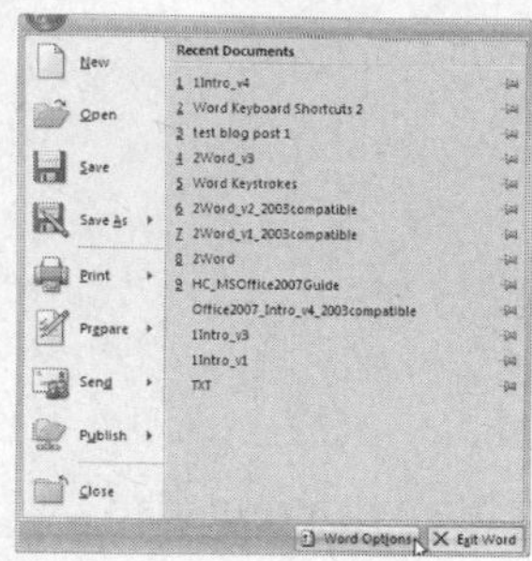

As long as Word 2007 knows who users are, they can use Track Changes to monitor who has changed what (and when) in the process of working collaboratively on a document.

Such changes are highlighted by color-coding of text, vertical lines in the margin, and strike-through text for deletions:

When you have been wc
different file names, Wo
~~to say how to do this.~~

In addition, letting the mouse pointer hover over a

highlighted change will show you a SuperTooltip with details:

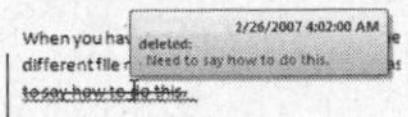

Track Changes in Print Layout view, showing formatting changes in the markup column at the right-hand side, without using the Reviewing Pane:

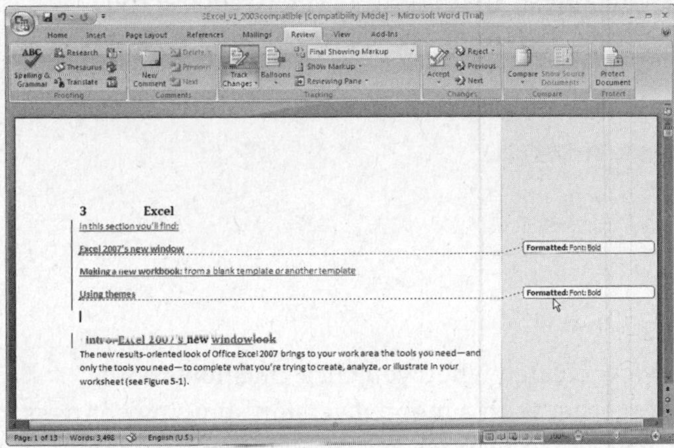

Track Changes in the same view, but using the Reviewing Pane:

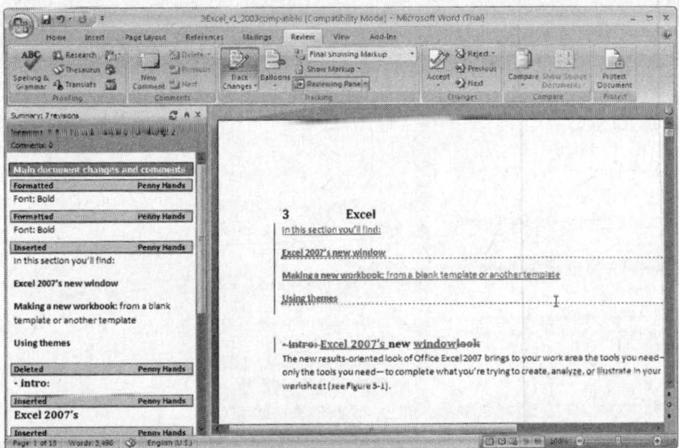

Document comparison

When you have multiple versions of a document with different file names, Word 2007 makes it very easy for you to compare the versions and highlight differences. Click on Compare in the Compare group, under the Review tab:

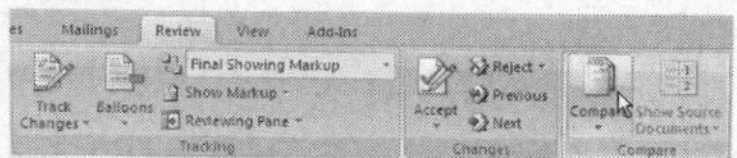

A dialog box will appear that prompts you to choose the original and revised documents that you wish to compare:

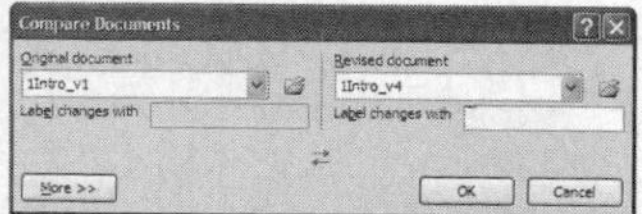

The new window created when you click OK shows both documents, together with a merged version showing changes in a similar way to that of Track Changes, but without the need for Track Changes to be turned on:

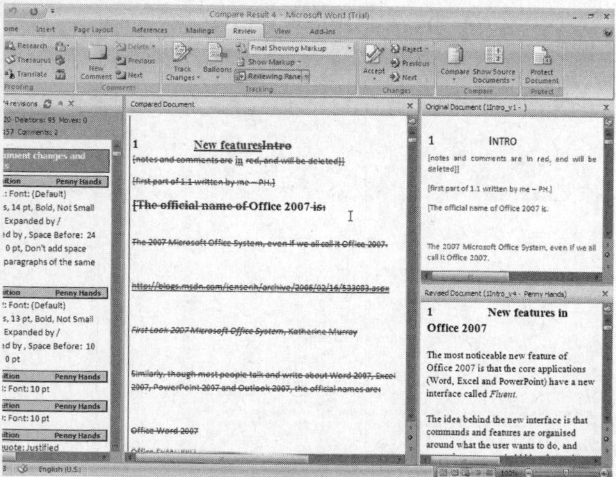

This enables you to review the merged version and the original and revised versions of the document at the same time.

Blogging from Word

Word 2007 makes it easy to post directly to a blog, giving you the advantages of using spelling and grammar tools, SmartArt, easy insertion of graphics and photos, etc.

To do this, choose the Blog template when creating a new document and then create your post:

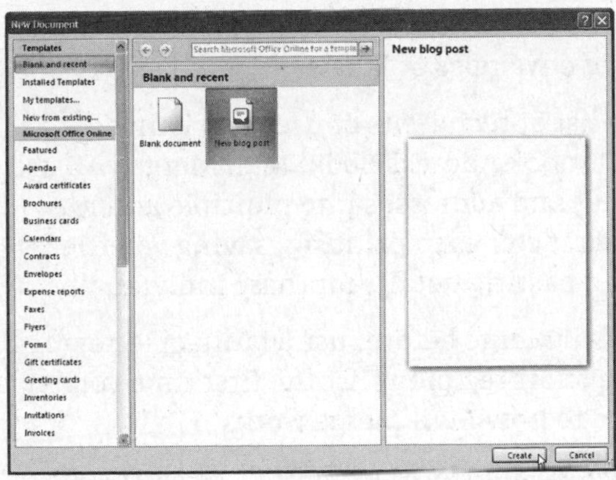

The first time you try to publish a post, Word 2007 will prompt you for your blog's location and your log-in details. If you do not already have a compatible blog, Word 2007 will provide you with information on suitable blogs and how to register.

The blog template's Ribbon is simpler, with only three main tabs, Blog, Insert, and Add-Ins:

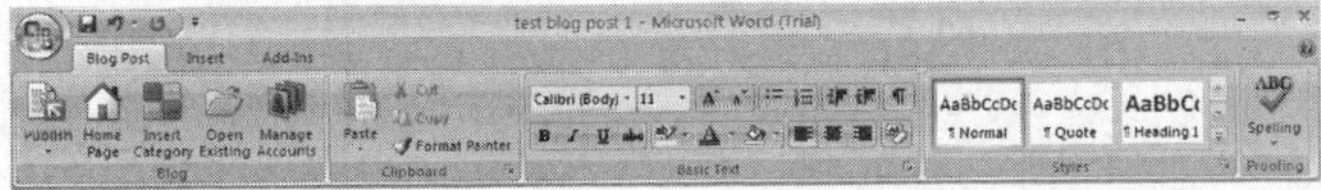

Just as when working with a regular Word 2007 document, clicking on a graphic object will make the Format tab (with Picture Styles and Arrange groups, etc.) appear:

If you manage to publish your post successfully, Word records the fact across the top of the Word version of your post.

The Mailings Tab and Mail Merge

The Mailings tab enables you to create, preview, organize, and print a letter (or possibly email a newsletter, etc.) destined for multiple recipients, quickly and efficiently. It also lets you control the printing of envelopes or labels.

You can create a new list of recipients or use an existing list, such as one in your Outlook Address Book. Mail Merge will use the list to insert names and addresses into multiple letters/ envelopes/labels when it comes to printing, saving you the trouble of copying and pasting details for these individually.

If you haven't used Mail Merge before, use a built-in letter (or other) template and a short recipient list the first time you try it out, just to get used to how Mail Merge works.

Click Start Mail Merge, under the Mailings tab, to start the process and, unless you are already familiar with all the required steps, choose the Mail Merge wizard:

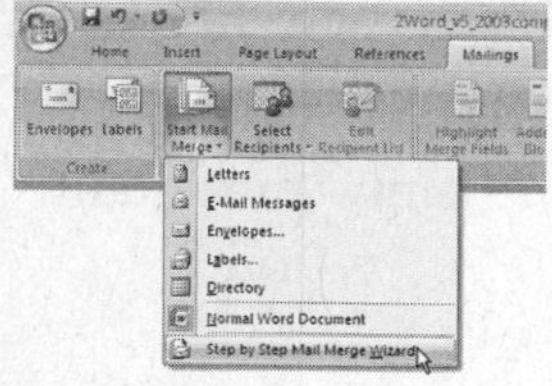

The wizard guides you through all the necessary steps in the process, from choosing the sort of document that you want to send to printing or emailing:

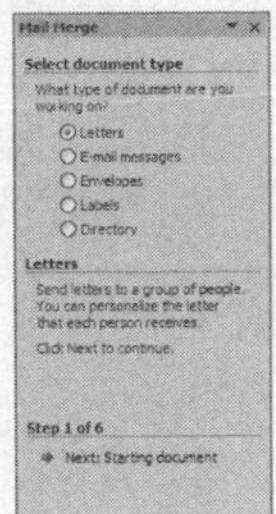

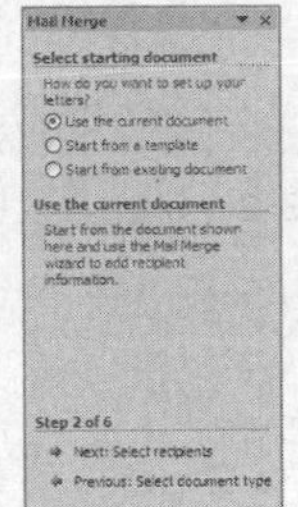

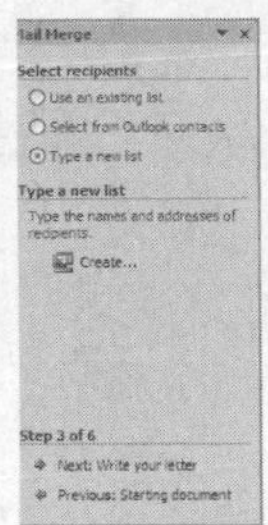

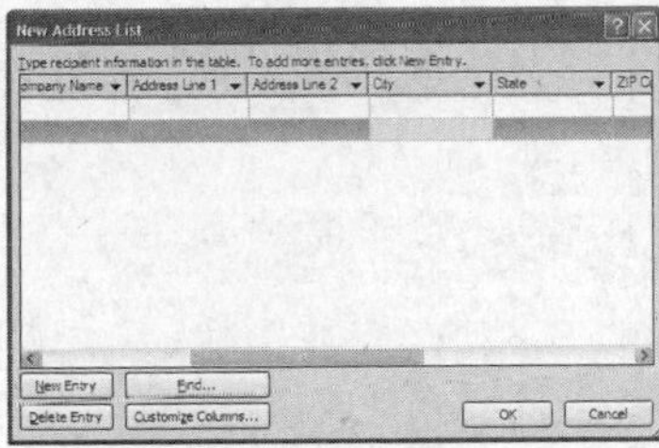

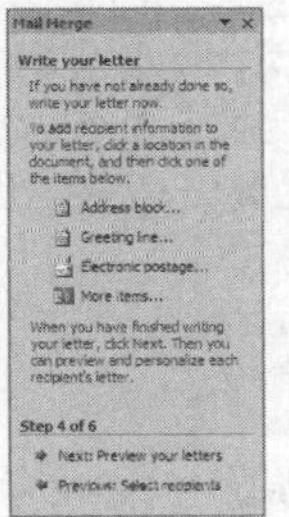

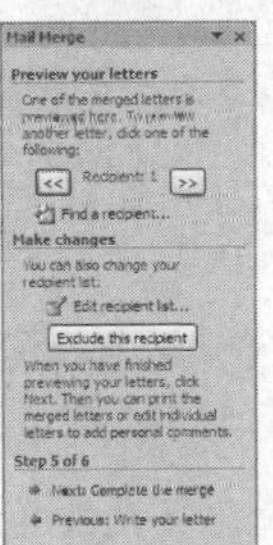

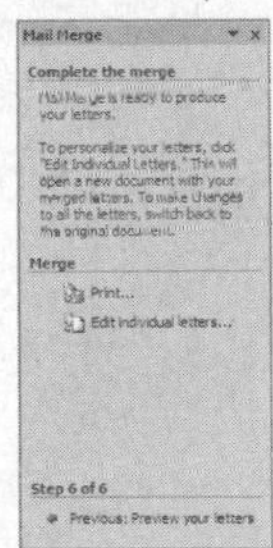

Keyboard shortcuts for Word 2007

You can use all of the keyboard shortcuts for formatting that worked in previous versions of Word 2007.

Shortcut	Command
Ctrl+B	makes selection bold
Ctrl+I	makes selection italic
Ctrl+U	makes selection underlined
Ctrl+Shift+A	Upper case
Ctrl+Alt+1	Heading 1 style
Ctrl+Alt+2	Heading 2 style
Ctrl+Alt+3	Heading 3 style
Ctrl+Shift+N	Normal style
Ctrl+E	Align center
Ctrl+J	Justify
Ctrl+L	Align left
Ctrl+R	Align right
Ctrl+Backspace	Deletes from cursor position to the beginning of a word (if cursor is in the space after a word, the whole of the previous word is deleted)
Ctrl+Delete	Deletes from cursor position to the end of a word (if cursor is in the space before a word, the whole of the following word is deleted)
Shift+Home	Selects from current cursor position to the beginning of a line
Shift+Home, Delete	Deletes from current cursor position to the beginning of a line
Shift+Home, Ctrl+X	Cuts from current cursor position to the beginning of a line
Shift+End	Selects from current cursor position to the end of a line
Shift+ End, Delete	Deletes from current cursor position to the end of a line

Quick Tips

Formatting

Formatting options such as Bold, Italic, Font color, Align to left or right, Bullets and Numbering, and Styles are found in the Home tab. For further options, click on the dialog launcher in the bottom right-hand corner of any command set.

Quick formatting is available via the Mini Toolbar that pops up when text is selected:

Calibri
11
When you select text, the Mini Toolbar pops up to help you format it without having to

Saving

To save, go to the Office menu and click on Save (or press S) or press Ctrl+S (without opening the menu). To save the document under a new name, click on the Office Button and choose Save As or simply press F12 at any time.

Lists

To apply bullets and numbering styles, use the new Bullet Library and Numbering Library. To do this, click on the small down-arrow in the Bullets or Numbering options in the Home tab. This will display all available options.

Inserting symbols and special characters

To find symbols and other non-standard characters that are not on the keyboard, go to the Insert tab and click on the Symbol command in the Symbols command set.

Find and Replace

Go to the Home tab and click on Find to carry out a simple search for an item, or Replace to find an item and replace it with another. Alternatively, press Ctrl+F to open the Find & Replace dialog box.

Footnotes and endnotes

To add a footnote or an endnote, go to the References tab and click on Insert Footnote or Insert Endnote.

2 • Microsoft® Office Excel® 2007

Microsoft® Office Excel® 2007's new window

As with other major Office Professional 2007 system applications, Office Excel 2007's new Fluent user interface is designed to help you be more productive by organizing many commonly-used commands under tabs in the Ribbon, as well as under contextual tabs when carrying out specific operations (such as printing) or when particular objects in your worksheet are selected.

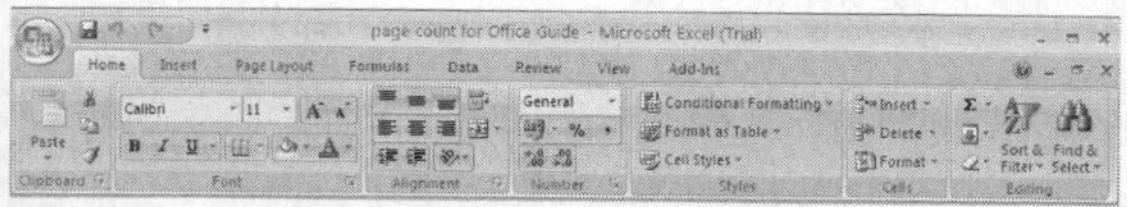

The Home tab includes the commands that you need to work with the Clipboard: choose and change fonts, control the alignment of cell content, select number formats, choose cell style and format, and edit, sort, and search your data.

The Insert tab houses the commands for the objects you add to your worksheets, for example: tables, charts, illustrations, links, and various kinds of text items such as column or row labels.

The Page Layout tab offers all things related to setting up the worksheet, including choosing themes, selecting page setup options, controlling the scaling of individual objects, selecting worksheet options, and arranging items on the sheet.

The Formulas tab includes the Function Wizard, the Function Library, the commands you need for creating and working with named cells, commands for formula auditing, and calculation options.

The Data tab offers commands for getting external data, managing the connections to external links, sorting and filtering your data, removing duplicates, validating and consolidating your data, and grouping and ungrouping cells.

The Review tab includes options to proof, comment on, share, and protect the sheet.

The View tab provides commands for choosing different

workbook views, hiding and redisplaying worksheet elements (gridlines, the ruler, the formula bar, and more), magnifying or reducing the display, and working with the worksheet window.

Excel 2007 is much more powerful than previous versions. It can handle worksheets with enormous amounts of data, more than 16,000 columns and more than 1,000,000 rows. It also has enhanced formatting and charting abilities and in this section you can see some of the features that can help you to create professional-looking worksheets.

Templates, themes, and cell styles

When you make a new workbook by clicking the Office Button and choosing New from the Office menu, the New Workbook window offers you a comprehensive list of template categories to choose from:

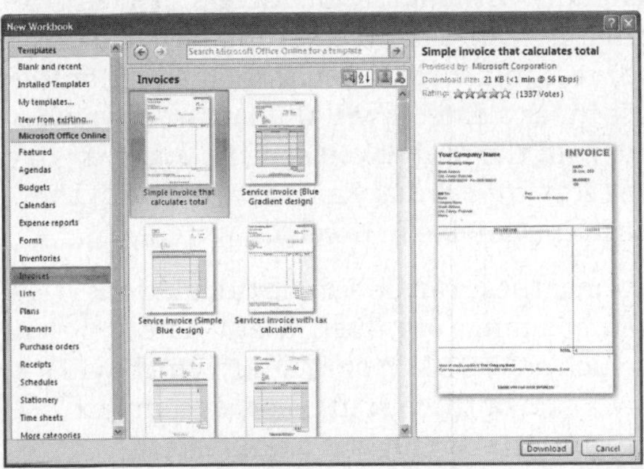

Think of templates as starter documents that already have a theme and use fonts, colors, and other attributes (e.g. types of border and shading) that look good together. Naturally, many templates also already have useful built-in functions (such as for today's date) and formulas for particular ranges of cells, and, even if a template is not exactly what you need, you can often find something that approximates what you would like and adapt it for your own purposes.

The New Workbook window makes it very easy for you to browse template categories online as well as installed templates. If you find an online template that you'd like to use, click the Download button and after an automated validation check a new workbook is created, based on the template.

If you'd rather start your new workbook from scratch, you can choose the blank template from the New Workbook menu (or Crl+N as a shortcut).

Entering data and navigating

Click on any cell to start entering data into it. Data can be text, numbers, or formulas.

Text: could be titles, descriptions, labels such as "year", "month", "income", etc., or could be text and number combinations (which still count as text) such as "Q1 Sales", "2006 accounts", etc.

Numbers: these are always whole or decimal positive or negative values, generally without any characters such as dollar signs. You can use slashes between numbers to create dates that Excel 2007 recognizes when you format a cell, or the column or range it is in, as a date. It will then turn the value you enter into a date with the format you specify, e.g. 2/27/07 could be displayed as 2/27/07; February 27, 2007, or one of the many other date formats available in Excel.

Formulas and functions: these can be simple calculations, such as adding together a range of values, useful date-sensitive functions such as =TODAY() or =YEAR() which will always display today's date or the current year, or complex calculations involving multiple ranges of data, tests of whether certain conditions are true, and much more.

When you've finished entering data into a cell, you can confirm the fact by pressing:

• Enter (which takes you to the next cell down, ready to enter more data there)

• Arrow key (taking you to the cell immediately above, below, left, or right of the current cell, depending upon which arrow key you press)

• Tab (taking you to the next cell to the right, in the same row as the current cell)

• Shift+Tab (taking you to the cell immediately to the left)

Alternatively (unless the current cell has a formula that you've been editing) you can use the mouse and click on any other cell. Cells with formulas that involve other cells or a range are sensitive (until you confirm that you've finished editing them) to clicking in other cells, assuming that you want that cell to be included in the formula. Rather than click in another cell, you can confirm a formula by using the keyboard, as above, or by clicking the tick that represents Enter in the formula bar:

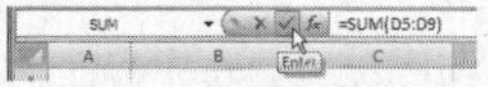

Using AutoFill to enter data

You can use AutoFill to enter data that follows any sort of pattern. Try entering data into the first two cells of the range you'd like to use AutoFill on (or even only the first cell if the progression is an obvious one such as 1 to 10 or Jan to Dec), then drag over the two cells to select them and position the mouse pointer over the bottom-right corner of the second cell (where you'll see a small square) so that it changes into a smaller, solid black, cross-shaped mouse pointer. This is known as the fill handle. Click on the fill handle and drag it outside the selection over the rest of the range (Excel 2007 gives you a preview of the result in a tool tip) and release the mouse button to confirm:

	A	B	C
10			
11	item	ex TAX price	price with TAX
12	bg 24	32.5	
13	xk 345	125.95	
14	d32	8.75	
15	amx-64	25	
16	cat 35 t1	29.99	
17	cat 35 t2	39.99	
18	cat 35 t3		
19	cat 35 t4		
20	cat 35 t5		

	A	B	C
10			
11	item	ex TAX price	price with TAX
12	bg 24	32.5	
13	xk 345	125.95	
14	d32	8.75	
15	amx-64	25	
16	cat 35 t1	29.99	
17	cat 35 t2	39.99	
18	cat 35 t3		
19	cat 35 t4		
20	cat 35 t5		69.99
21			

	A	B	C
10			
11	item	ex TAX price	price with TAX
12	bg 24	32.5	
13	xk 345	125.95	
14	d32	8.75	
15	amx-64	25	
16	cat 35 t1	29.99	
17	cat 35 t2	39.99	
18	cat 35 t3	49.99	
19	cat 35 t4	59.99	
20	cat 35 t5	69.99	
21			

Formatting

You can apply predesigned formats to selected cells or ranges by clicking Cell Styles, in the Styles group under the Home command tab, and choosing the type of formatting from the gallery that appears.

The Cell Styles gallery also contains options for different types of number format, such as currency and percentage.

Tip: You can create formats for your own cell styles and add them to the gallery.

- apply the format that you want to a specific cell
- click Cell Styles in the Styles group under the Home command tab
- choose New Cell Style in the Cell Styles gallery
- review the information in the Style dialog box and click Format if you need to make any changes
- type a name for the style in the Style Name field, then click OK to save the style

The new style that you created appears at the top of the gallery in the Custom category. If you ever want to delete your custom style from the gallery, right-click on it within the gallery and select Delete.

Formulas and functions

Formulas perform calculations on the contents of one or more cells.

For example, to add cell A1 and cell C9 together and show the result in cell D3, you could click on D3 and type:

=A1+C9

Order of precedence

Excel 2007 observes an order of precedence in formulas: multiply, divide, add, subtract.

This means that it will multiply elements in a formula before it divides, and will then do any adding or subtracting required. This is an essential basic fact to be remembered and understood in order to avoid confusing results in complex formulas. For example:

Formula	What it means
=A10-D4*E4	multiply the value in D4 by that in E4 and subtract the result from the value in A10

e.g. if A10 is 5, D4 is 2 and E4 is 3, the result is -1

Using parentheses

If you'd actually like to subtract D4 from A10 and multiply the result by E4, you should use one of these formulas instead:

=(A10-D4)*E4 or =E4*(A10-D4)

e.g. if A10 is 5, D4 is 2 and E4 is 3, the result is 9

To work out the sales tax (at 12.5%) that should be applied to an item with an untaxed price in cell E7, you could use this formula: =E7*12.5%

To calculate the price including sales tax, you could use this formula:
= E7*12.5%+ E7

But it's probably as easy to just multiply by 1.125 in a basic, quick calculation:
= E7*1.125

Absolute references: using $

If, however, you want to see what prices would be with different rates of sales tax, you could put the rate of sales tax in a cell of its own (say D5) and reference that in your formula: =E7*D5+E7

By putting the value in one cell, and basing all formulas for individual calculations on the value of that single cell, you can type different values for the rate of tax in just that cell and see the effects in all the calculations based on it. For this to work, the reference to the cell in each of the individual formulas must be an absolute reference (one that doesn't change when copied from a cell and pasted elsewhere) rather than a conventional one (which is relative, and does change when pasted).

The dollar signs make the reference absolute (people also refer to the reference being "anchored") so that if, for example, you put your formula in F7, to calculate the price including tax of an item with an untaxed price in E7, and have a range of other untaxed prices in column E from E8 to E15, you can copy and paste (or autofill) the formula all the way down column F without the D5 reference changing:

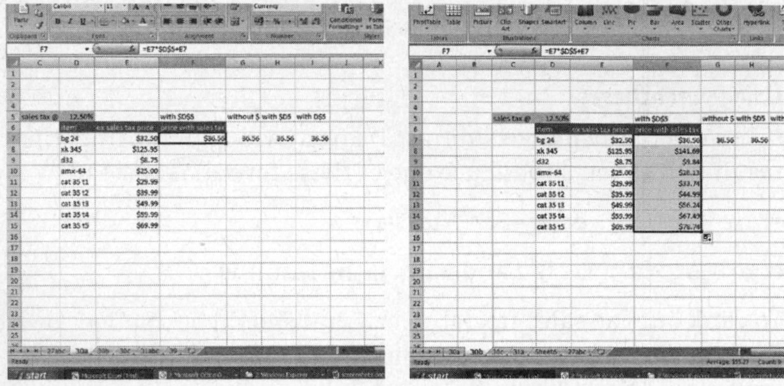

The formula in cell F15 would therefore be =E15*D5+E15, whereas if you copied and pasted =E15*D5+E15 to the same range, F8:F15, it would be =E15*D13+E15 in F15. Here's an example of that faulty formula used in column F:

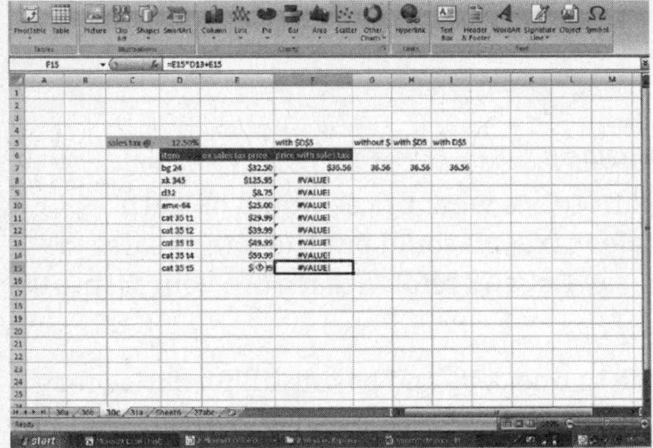

The lack of the dollar sign causes the D5 reference to change from cell to cell in the range, in the same way as the E7 reference. This would mean that only one calculation (the one in row 7) would work. All the other formulas in the range would fail due to an empty reference, because the cells D6:D13 do not have a percentage to use in the calculation.

By using $ to create an absolute reference to D5 in all the formulas in the range F7:F15, you can change the tax value in just one cell (D5) and see the effect of the change on the prices of all of your products.

Using AutoFill to add formulas to a range

Rather than using copy and paste, it's often easier to use AutoFill to fill a range with formulas. Type the formula into the first cell in the range and then drag the fill handle to fill the range:

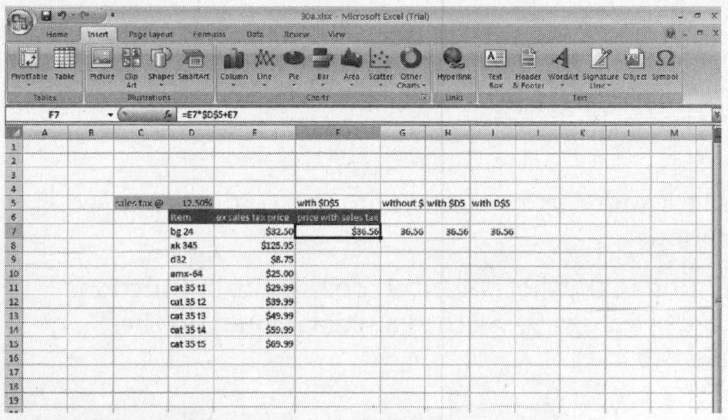

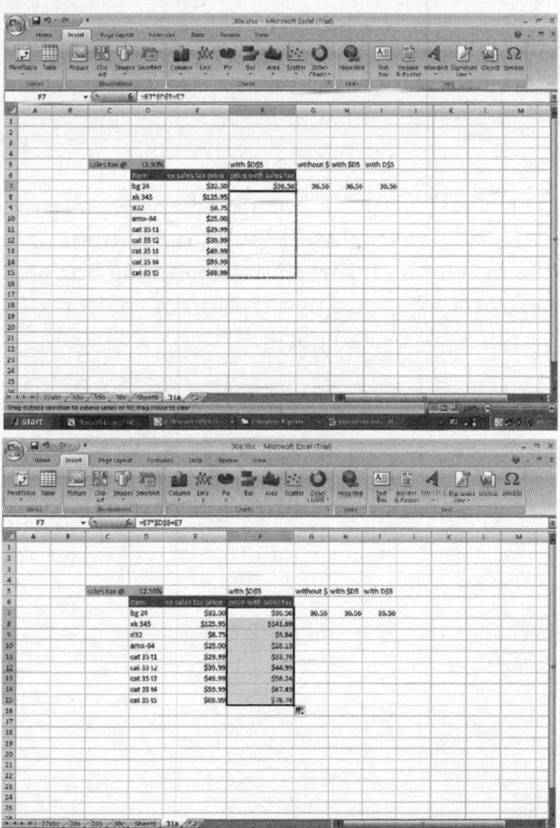

Functions are very useful, such as for automatically adding a range of cells (AutoSum), displaying the current year, etc.

AutoSum is probably the most used function. To use it, click in the cell where you would like the total of a range of values to appear and then click on the AutoSum command in the Function Library, within the Formulas tab:

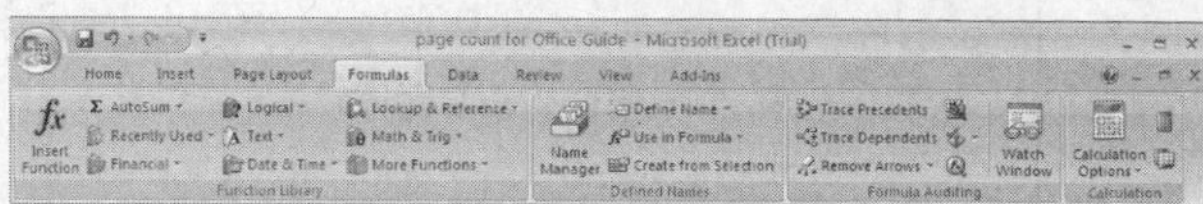

Click on the More arrow on the AutoSum command to see more options.

You can find many more of Excel 2007's built-in functions, organized by category, via the Function Library in the Formulas tab:

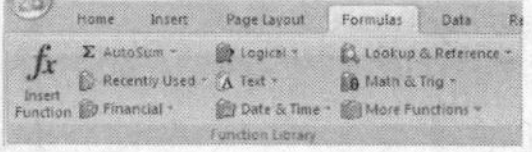

Alternatively, you can click on the Insert Function symbol in the formula bar. This opens the Insert Function dialog box and you can search for a function, type a description of the sort of function you need, or browse by category:

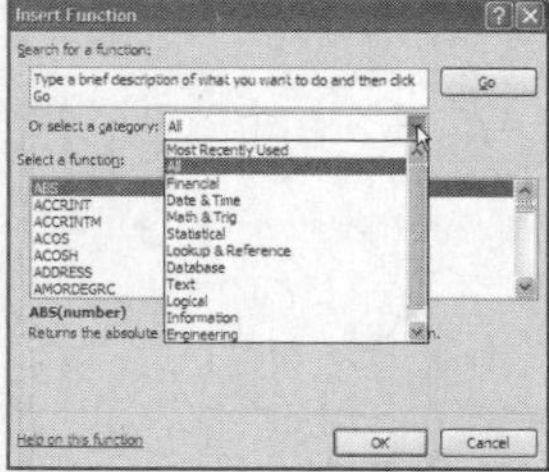

When you select a function, a useful description is provided of its use. If you think a function might be what you want, but you're still unsure what it does, you can select it in the Insert Function window and click on the Help on this function link in the bottom-left corner.

Another way to access functions, if a cell already has a function that you would like to change, is to click within the cell with the function (as though to start editing it) and then click on the down arrow next to the current function in the name box in the formula bar:

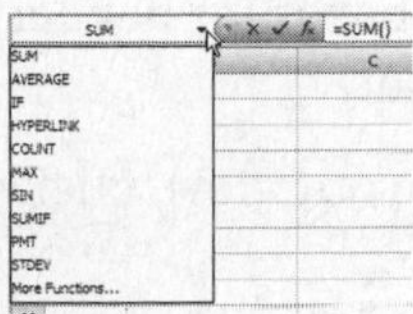

Page Layout view and printing

Page Layout view (new in Excel 2007) lets you see, while you're working on it, how your worksheet should look when it is printed. Page Layout view is not just a preview — everything is fully editable.

You can switch to Page Layout view either by clicking the View tab and selecting Page Layout View or by clicking Page Layout in the Quick Views control in the bottom-right of the window:

You can use the Zoom control to zoom out and view multiple pages in Page Layout view:

Headers and footers

You can insert and edit headers and footers by clicking on Header & Footer under the Insert tab. Alternatively, simply go to the Print Layout view. This always displays boxes for header and footer, even if you haven't yet created either.

To create or edit your header/footer in Print Layout view, click inside the header or footer box:

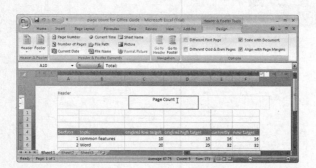

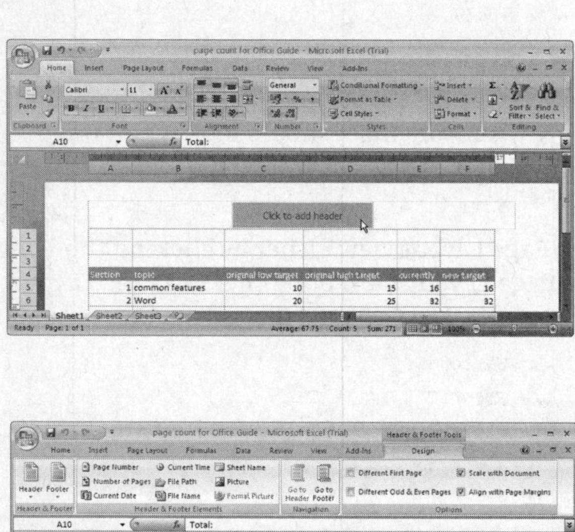

As soon as you click inside the header or footer box, the Design contextual tab appears on the Ribbon, with relevant Header & Footer tools:

The Header and Footer commands under the Design tab showing the context-sensitive Header & Footer tools (these tools only appear when you click within a header or footer box) provide suggestions for ready-made headers and footers, using elements such as author name, document name, date, page number, file name and location, etc.

Charts

Charts help you to illustrate, in a colorful and understandable way, what the information in your sheet's data means.

Start by selecting the data range(s) you want to chart. Then click the Insert tab and choose the chart type you want to create:

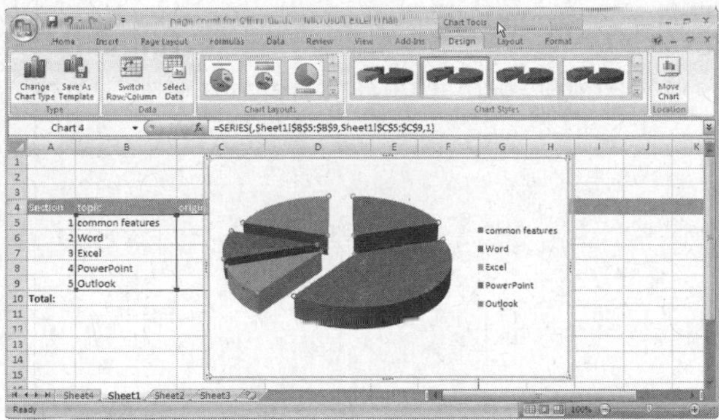

The chart appears on your worksheet, and the Chart Tools contextual tab offers three full sets of options for customizing your charts:

• The Design tab gives you choices for selecting the chart type, data source, and arrangement; and the Quick Layout, Quick Styles, and the Move Chart command:

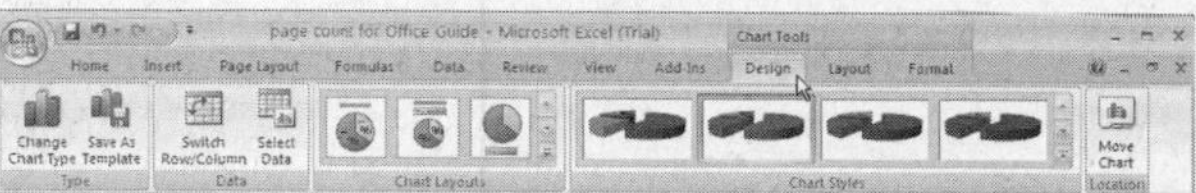

• The Layout tab in Chart Tools enables you to enter chart properties, choose Office Shapes, add or edit chart elements, and make choices related to 3-D charts:

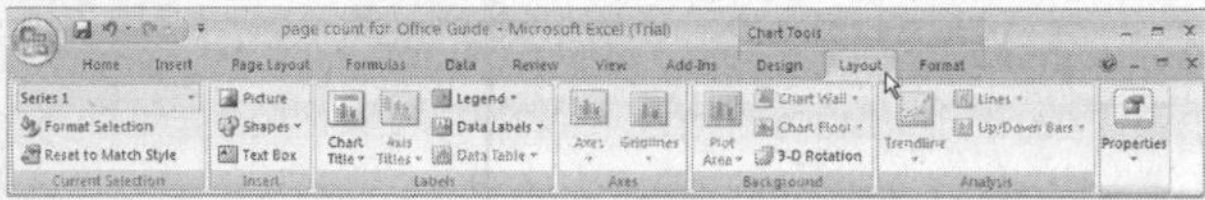

• The Format tab lets you select different chart elements and add styles to the chart shape, such as 3-D edges, shadows, bevel, etc:

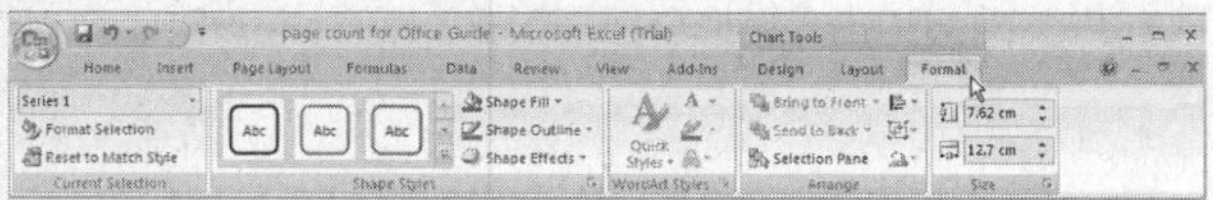

You could, for example, click on the Shape Effects command within Shape Styles in the Format tab to give your chart a new look:

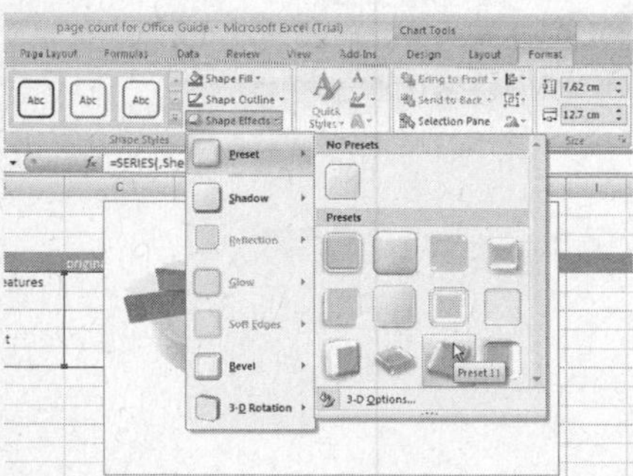

Shapes, WordArt and SmartArt

Shapes (the lines, rectangles, block arrows, etc., that used to be situated in the Drawing toolbar) now have their own space within the Insert tab. To see the expanded collection of shapes, click the Shapes command in the Illustrations group:

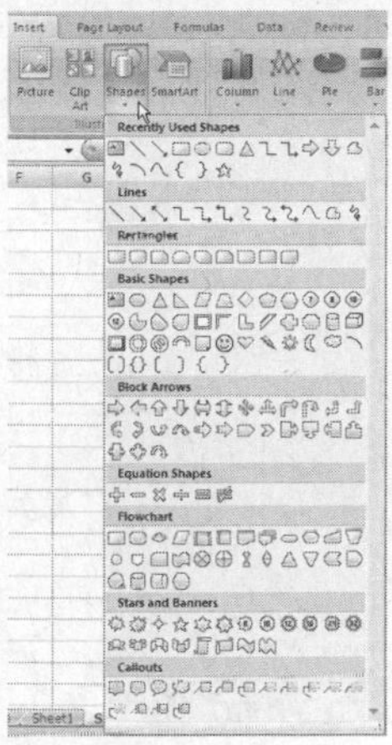

WordArt is now accessible via the Text group of the Insert tab. When you choose the WordArt command, a gallery of styles appears. Click the one that you want and the WordArt item is placed on your worksheet. Click the item to replace it with your own text:

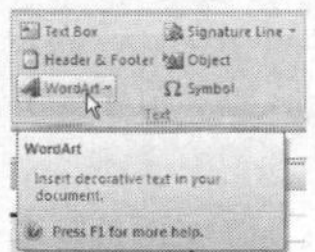

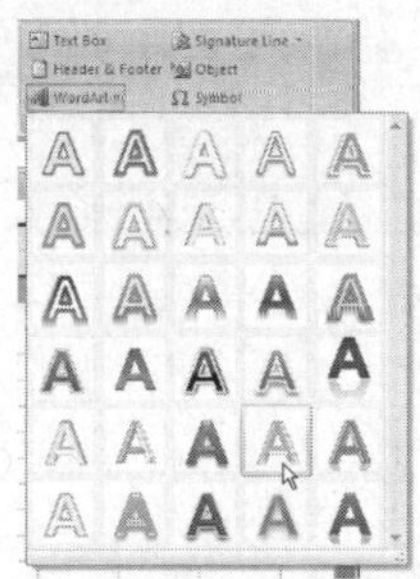

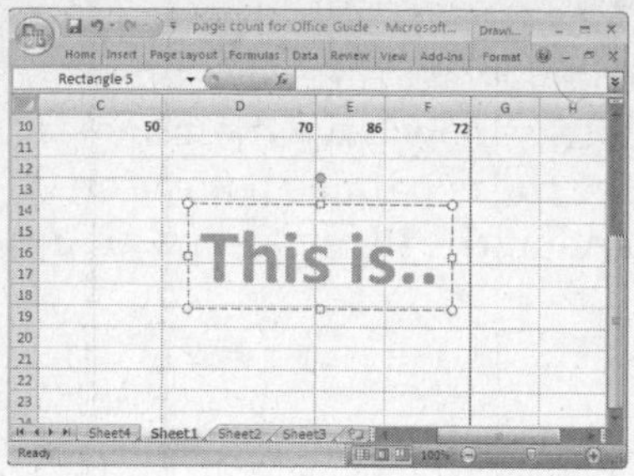

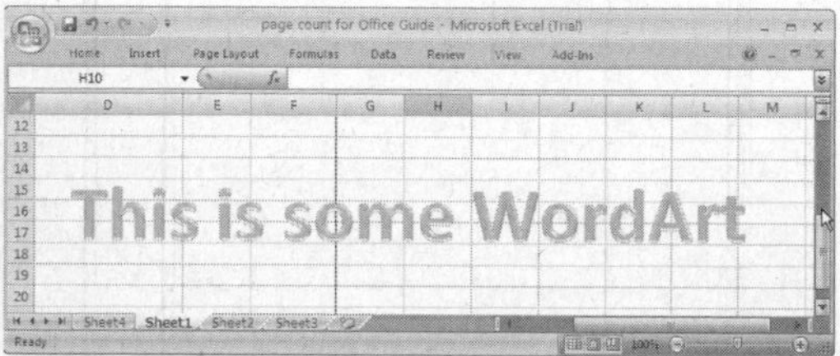

To create SmartArt graphics, open the Insert tab and click SmartArt in the Illustrations command set. Then select the diagram type that you want to create, choose the style that you prefer, and click OK:

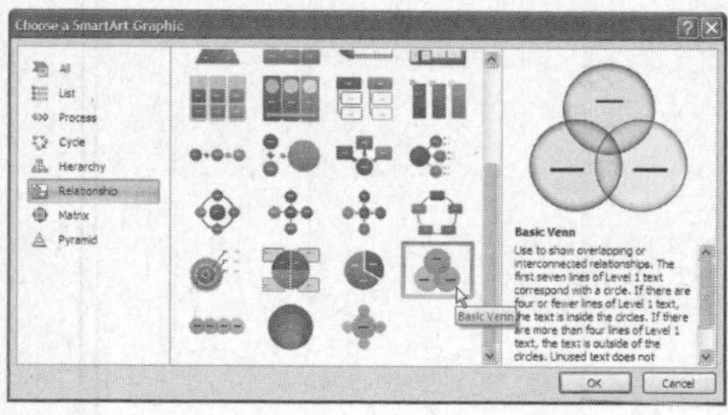

Conditional Formatting and Data Visualizations

Conditional formatting lets you apply specific formatting to cells according to the value of a cell or the value of a formula. For example, you could color code a set of test results according to whether marks were higher than a particular value or not, and so label fails as red and passes as green:

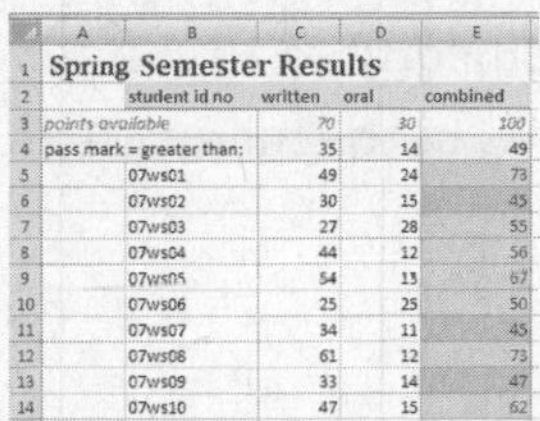

	A	B	C	D	E
1	Spring Semester Results				
2		student id no	written	oral	combined
3	points available		70	30	100
4	pass mark = greater than:		35	14	49
5		07ws01	49	24	73
6		07ws02	30	15	45
7		07ws03	27	28	55
8		07ws04	44	12	56
9		07ws05	54	13	67
10		07ws06	25	25	50
11		07ws07	34	11	45
12		07ws08	61	12	73
13		07ws09	33	14	47
14		07ws10	47	15	62

To do this, select the range of cells to which you'd like to apply the conditional formatting. Then in the Sheet tab, click Conditional Formatting.

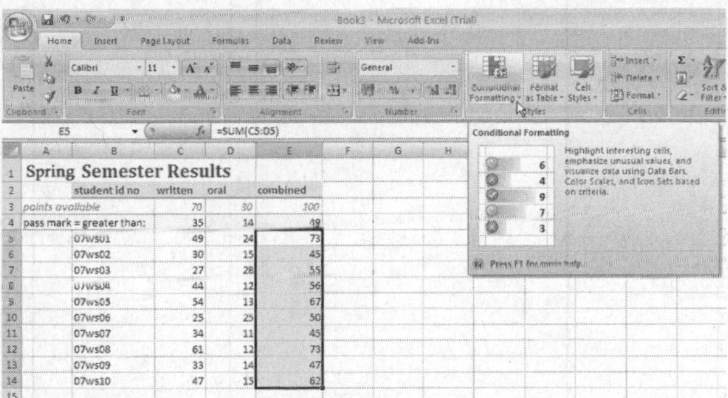

The menu that appears offers two different sets of rules (Highlight Cell Rules and Top/Bottom Rules) that you can apply to your data.

To automatically highlight the cells with a value over 49 (and so label the pass marks in the test results) you need to identify all of the marks in your range that get more than the value in the cell E4 (as 49 or less is a fail). When you point to Highlight Cells Rules such an option becomes obvious in the menu that appears:

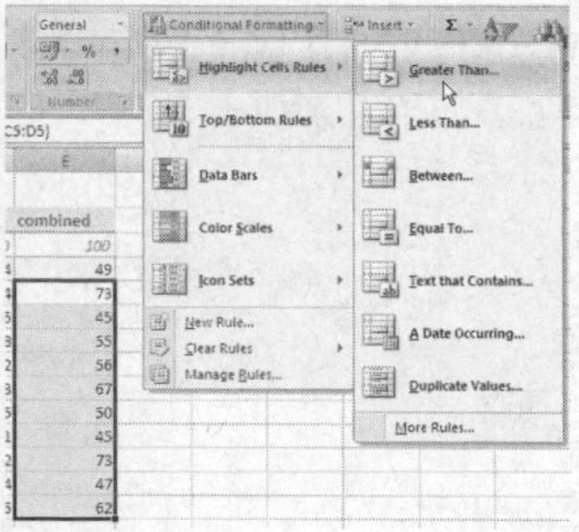

Click on the Greater Than option and then enter the cell reference of the fail mark with an equal sign at the beginning (or just type in 49 if the mark is fixed) and choose a highlighting method (e.g. Green Fill with Dark Green Text) in the dialog box.

As soon as you type a value you can preview the effect of the highlighting. Finally, click OK to save the change and apply the rule you've chosen.

The automatic highlighting appears:

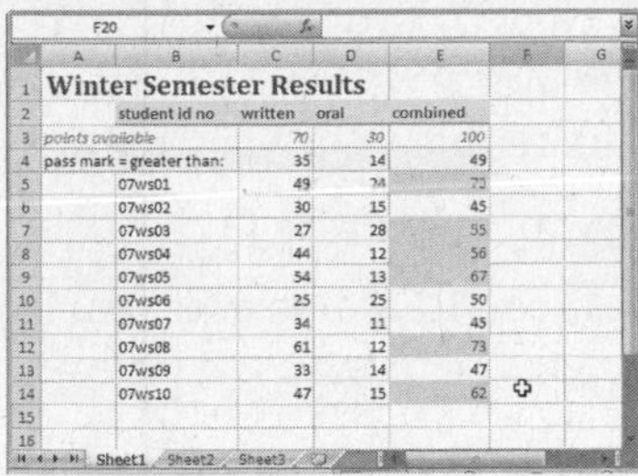

To give the other marks a colored background, select the whole range and fill it with a color of your choice using the Fill Color tool:

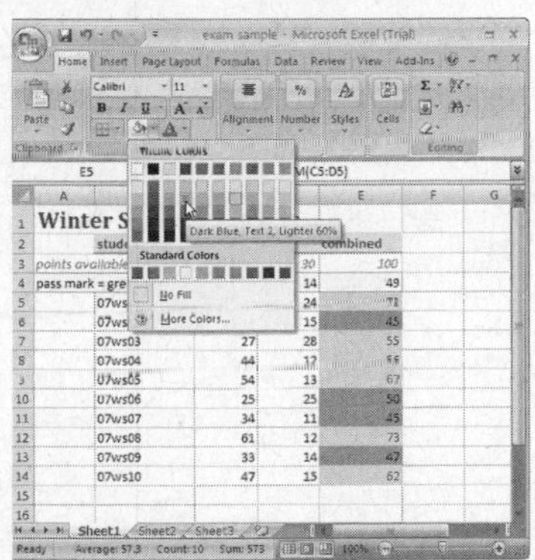

Keyboard shortcuts for Excel 2007

Arrow keys	Go one cell up, down, left, or right
Tab	Go one cell to the right
Shift+Tab	Go one cell to the left
Ctrl+arrow key	Go to the edge of the current data region
Ctrl+Home	Go to the beginning of the worksheet

Ctrl+Home	Go to the last occupied cell of the worksheet
Ctrl +Spacebar	Select the entire column
Shift + Spacebar	Select the entire row
Shift +F11	Insert a new worksheet
Ctrl +Page Down	Move to the next sheet in a workbook
Ctrl + Page Up	Move to the previous sheet in a workbook
Shift + Ctrl + Page Down	Select the current and next sheet
Shift + Ctrl + Page Up	Select the current and previous sheet
Alt +E, M	Move or copy the current sheet
Alt+E, L	Delete the current sheet

3 • Microsoft® Office Outlook® 2007

Office Outlook 2007's new features

Office Outlook 2007's main window doesn't share the same new Fluent interface that Microsoft Office Word 2007, Microsoft Office Excel 2007, and Microsoft Office PowerPoint 2007 all have, and its menus (File, Edit, View, Go, Tools, Actions, and Help) and navigation pane should be familiar to anyone who has used earlier versions.

The new Fluent interface is present in some of Office Outlook 2007's windows, such as the New Message window:

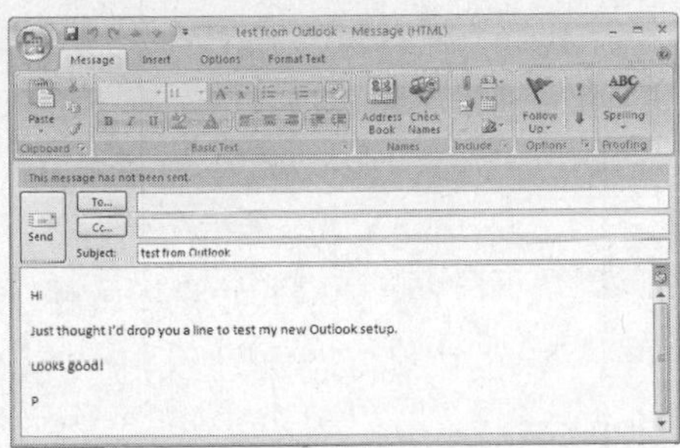

Here are a few of the new features present in the main Outlook 2007 window:

- Search box at the top of the Inbox column
- RSS Feeds folder in the Mail Folders navigation pane
- To-Do Bar along the right side of the window
- Attachment Preview enables you to preview the contents of attachments without opening them

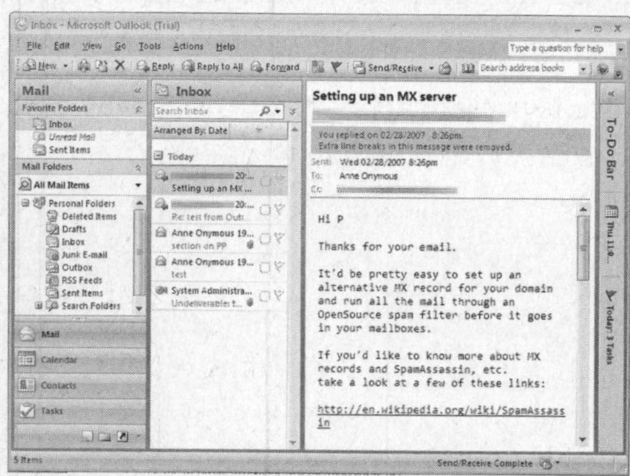

Managing time and organizing tasks

Use the To-Do Bar to organize tasks and appointments. It expands when you click on it and shows a calendar, appointments, and tasks.

The To-Do Bar is always visible, whether you're working in Mail, Calendar, Contacts, or Tasks.

An item is added to the To-Do Bar automatically whenever you flag an email message or contact, or when you drag a message to the To-Do Bar.

Adding tasks to your calendar

Because the Daily Task List displays your tasks in the To-Do Bar according to the day on which they are due, you can easily drag them to your Calendar and then allocate time to complete them. Using the Daily Task List you can also modify the date of tasks by dragging them from one day to another, and the To-Do Bar will update the lists accordingly.

Tasks from the Daily Task List in the To-Do Bar are displayed automatically in the Calendar module:

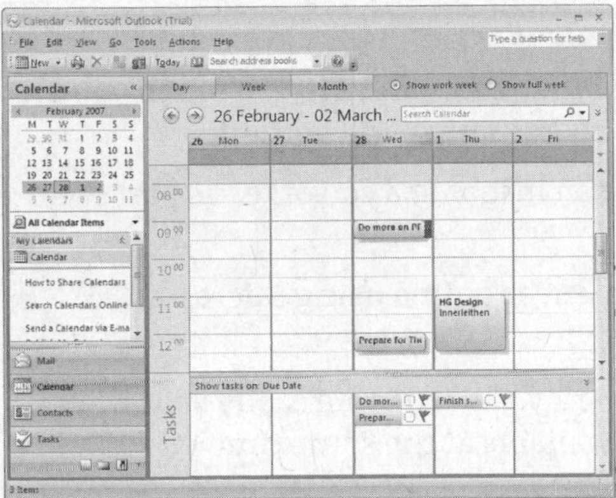

Tasks remain active on your To-Do Bar and also in your Daily Task List and Calendar until you mark them as completed. If you don't manage to complete a task on your Daily Task List, it is automatically carried over to the next day.

Applying color labels to tasks, appointments, messages, and contacts

You can apply a color category to any item that you create in Outlook 2007 so that it stands out visually, no matter which view you are using. For example, if you want an appointment that you just created to be easy to spot on your Calendar, you can assign a color to it using the Categorize control in the user interface. When the Appointment window is open, click the Categorize button and choose the color you want from the displayed list.

Sharing and comparing calendars

Outlook 2007 has new features that can help you when you are arranging meetings and coordinating with others:

• You can send a calendar snapshot to a coworker as part of an email message

• You can publish your calendar online using Microsoft® Office Online Hosting Services

• You can use calendar overlay view to more easily spot when owners of calendars are available at the same time

Sending a calendar via email

To send your calendar to others by email, click Send A Calendar Via E-Mail in the Calendar navigation pane.

A new message window opens automatically, and you can use the dialog box to choose the Date Range and how much Detail you want to show (e.g. just when you are available, the subject lines of calendar entries, or full details of all entries).

Publishing a calendar on the web

To publish your calendar on the web, click on the Publish My Calendar link in the Calendar navigation bar. In the Publish Calendar To Microsoft Office Online dialog box, you specify the following items:

• Choose the time span for the calendar you want to display

• Select the level of detail to show (Availability only, Limited details, or Full details)

• Set permissions to determine who has access to your calendar

• Choose whether the calendar will be uploaded only once or

automatically as updated

After you publish the calendar online, you are given the option of sharing it with others. After you enter the email addresses of others you want to receive your calendar information, the web address of your calendar is sent, along with instructions on how others can access it.

Tip: Microsoft Office Online has a number of calendars you can download. Click Browse Calendars Online to look for calendar templates.

Taking control of the Inbox

Outlook 2007 includes a number of new features that can save you time and effort, from setting up email accounts to filtering junk mail.

Find what you need faster

A new search box is available in all views (Mail, Calendar, Contacts, and Tasks). Just type the word or phrase that you want to find.

Attachment Previews

The new ability to preview attachments saves you from opening them in their parent applications (Word 2007, Excel 2007, etc.) just to view them. To preview an attachment, click the attachment, and the file displays in the body of the email message.

If the sender is not on your Safe Senders list, you might see a message before the preview appears, warning you of a potential security risk. If you trust the sender, click Preview File to continue the process.

Making emails Action Items

You can use the enhanced flagging feature to identify an important message as one which you will need to act on immediately. When you add the flag, the item is automatically added to the To-Do Bar.

Flagging Action Items for others

When other Outlook 2007 users receive a message that you have flagged, it is added to their To-Do Bars as a task with a specific response date.

Setting up new email accounts

A new automated account setup feature asks for your email account name and password, and then does the rest.

Getting RSS news feeds

RSS is a great way of being notified of new content on any websites you choose, as long as they have RSS. You can receive RSS news feeds directly in your Outlook 2007 Inbox.

To use the RSS feature in Office Outlook 2007, double-click the RSS Feeds folder in your Personal Folders in the Mail navigation pane. A window appears telling you how to get started.

Improved junk mail filter

Office Outlook 2007 includes an enhanced Junk E-Mail Filter that catches incoming messages that could be junk mail — or its more dangerous counterpart, a phishing message — and then intercepts and eliminates it for you. When a message arrives that Office Outlook 2007 suspects might be a phishing message, a notification alerts you, and images and links in the message are disabled until you approve them.

When a message arrives that the filter thinks is spam, it puts it in the Junk folder. You should check this folder from time to time to see if there are any false positives, i.e. genuine messages falsely identified as junk.

You should identify such messages as not being spam by clicking on them and then choosing: Actions, Junk E-mail, Mark as Not Junk, or press Ctrl+Alt+J after selecting the message.

Blocking a sender

If you decide that you don't want to see mail from a particular sender and would like it to be put in the Junk folder as soon as it arrives, you can add the sender to a list of blocked senders.

There are a number of ways to do this, but the easiest way to block an individual sender is to click a message from that sender, choose Actions, Junk E-mail, and then click on Add Sender to Blocked Senders.

Adding people to the Safe Senders list

You can add the email addresses of people whom you trust to the Safe Senders list to make sure that messages they send to you are never inadvertently filtered off as junk.

The easiest way to do this is to click on a message that the person has already sent to you, choose Actions, Junk E-mail, and then click on either of these commands:

- Add Sender to Safe Senders List
- Add Sender's Domain (@example.com) to Safe Senders List

You'd choose the second if you trusted everyone using a particular company's or organization's domain, but you should not do it for any domain that spammers might use.

Postmarking

A new feature in Office Outlook 2007 automatically adds postmarks to messages that you send. The postmark includes the list of recipients and the time when you sent the message, which is what makes the postmark valid as an identification of that unique message. Spammers send thousands of emails out at one time from the same computer, which makes a unique postmark impossible. This makes it possible for the email program of the person receiving the postmarked email to be sure that the message really is from you and so is not likely to be spam.

Creating email signatures

Email signatures are optional, but can be helpful to recipients. They are added to the end of a message, and usually tell people a little more about the sender, and can include full name, company name, mailing address, web address, phone numbers, etc.

You might have different signatures for different types of email, depending on the information which you wanted to share or the impression that you wanted to convey.

You can create or edit a signature by going to Tools, Options and clicking the Mail Format tab, and then choosing Signatures. Click New to display the New Signature dialog box, type a descriptive name for your new signature, and click OK. You can then type the signature in the Edit area and click Save (and then OK) when done:

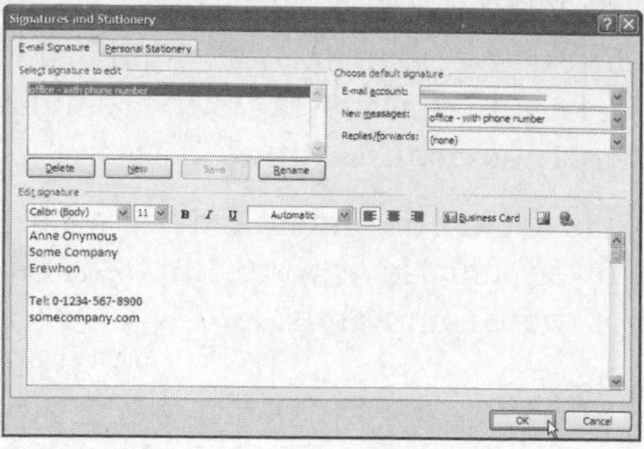

Creating electronic business cards

To share your contact information with others as an Electronic Business Card, first create your card. In the New Contact window, click Business Card in the Write tab to customize the default card that is created for a new contact. You can add photos and other special design elements.

To send electronic business cards to others via email or attach your business card to your outgoing messages, choose Options from the Tools menu and click the Mail Format tab in the Options dialog box. Click Signatures to display the Signatures and Stationery dialog box, then click Business Card in the Edit Signature area to display the Insert Business Card dialog box so that you can select the card that you want to attach.

Creating new mail messages

Click on New or press Ctrl+N. Edit your message, check that the To and Subject fields are filled in, and then click Send. If you want to Save the message before sending, perhaps so that you can work on it again later, click on Save or press Ctrl+S. If you close a message that you've saved, you can find it in your draft folder.

When done editing, click Send.

Replying

To reply to a message, select or open the message and click on Reply (or press Ctrl+R).

Forwarding

To forward a message, select or open the message and click on Forward (or press Ctrl+F).

Attaching a file

To Attach a file to a message which you are editing, click on Attach in the Include group, under the Message tab in the New Message window.

Then browse for the file, select it, and click on Insert.

Sending to multiple recipients

To send mail to multiple recipients, type their addresses (or add them from your Contacts) in the To, Cc, or Bcc fields in the New Message window, with each address separated by a comma. The Cc field is for sending copies, and people in the To field see who the copies are sent to. Any addresses in the Bcc field stay hidden from everyone.

Creating distribution lists

When you regularly send messages to the same group of people, it's easier to create a distribution list with all of their addresses to save you the trouble of entering them all every time that you send a message. To do this, choose Actions, New Distribution List, or press Ctrl+Shift+L.

In the form that pops up, type a name for the list, add people's addresses (either by hand or from your Contacts) and then click Save & Close.

To send a message to all of the recipients in the list, type the list's name in the To field of a new message.

Keyboard shortcuts

Ctrl+N	Creates a new message when working in Mail, a new appointment when working in Calendar, a new contact when working in Contacts, and a new Task when working in Tasks
Ctrl+R	Reply
Ctrl+F	Forward
Ctrl+S	Save a message, appointment, etc. that you are currently editing
Ctrl+P	Print
Ctrl+J	Marks a selected message that's not currently in the Junk folder as junk
Ctrl+Alt+J	Marks a selected message in the Junk folder as not being junk
Ctrl+Shift+L	Create a distribution list

4 • Microsoft® Office PowerPoint® 2007

PowerPoint 2007's new window

The command tabs in the new Fluent interface correspond to the main things that you do when you create a presentation:

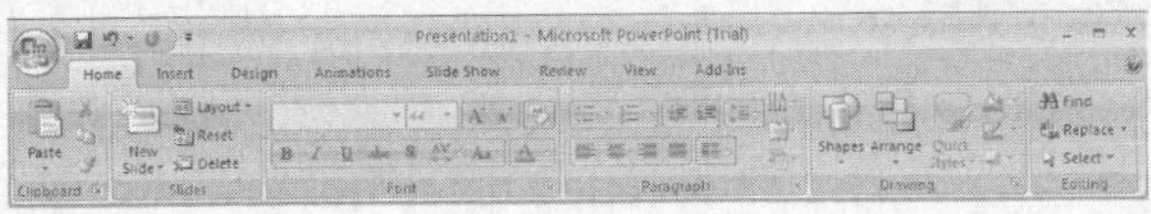

- ***The Home tab*** contains commands which you are likely to use when you are creating and working with slides. You'll find commands for adding and deleting slides, choosing slide layouts, making font and paragraph choices, adding WordArt, and finding and replacing text.

- ***The Insert tab*** lets you add tables, pictures, diagrams, charts, Office shapes, links, text objects, and media clips.

- ***The Design tab*** has commands to set the page orientation, choose a presentation theme, design the slide background, and arrange objects on the slide.

- ***The Animations tab*** lets you choose animations and add sound, transitions, and timing selections.

- ***The Slide Show tab*** has commands for setting up, rehearsing, and displaying a slide show. It also has commands for recording narration, setting up dual monitors, and changing display resolution.

- ***The Review tab*** offers the spelling checker and thesaurus, and provides translation and research tools. You'll also find commands for working with comments.

- ***The View tab*** provides a number of different options for the way in which you view your presentation. Choose among the traditional PowerPoint views, add gridlines and the ruler, make color and grayscale changes, and work with presentation windows.

Tip: The Zoom slider in the bottom-right corner of the window is a helpful tool when you want to zoom in or out on a specific item in your presentation. In Normal view, use the Fit Slide To Current Window tool, to the right of the Zoom slider, to maximize the current slide within the size of the display window.

Starting a new presentation

To start a new presentation from a blank template, press Ctrl+N. To get more choices, click on the Office button and then select New, or press N.

In the New Presentation window that then opens you can:

• Browse through collections of templates by choosing from the template categories in the panel on the left side of the window

• Create a new presentation from scratch by clicking Blank Presentation

• Choose one of your own customized templates by clicking My Templates

• Build a new presentation based on one that you already have by clicking New From Existing

• Get tips, ideas, and additional presentation templates from Microsoft Office Online

You can create your presentation by adding text and/or other elements to your slide and by creating new slides.

You can create new slides by clicking on the New Slide command in the Slides group of the Home tab, or by using the Outline mode in the navigation pane down the left-hand side of the PowerPoint window.

Clicking the down arrow of the New Slide command opens a gallery of Office Themes to choose from.

Using Outline mode will be familiar to anyone who has used earlier versions of PowerPoint:

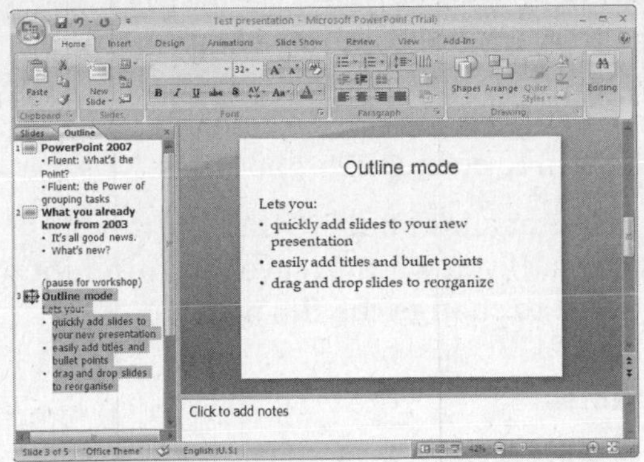

When working in Outline mode, typing a title for a slide and then pressing Enter will create a new slide. This makes it easy to quickly create all of your slides with appropriate titles. You can also use Outline mode to include text content within slides without having to type anything in the main pane — just stay in the outline and use the Enter and Tab keys to organize slides and add basic content to them.

The Tab key indents (or "demotes") elements in Outline mode (as does Alt+Shift+Right Arrow). Indented elements will appear, by default, as bullet points within the slides in the outline that are their "parents" (you can easily remove or restyle bullets within individual slides using the Bullets command in the Paragraph group under the Home tab). To "promote" any paragraph or point in your outline, use Shift+Tab (or Alt+Shift+Left Arrow). A promoted bullet point will move up in the hierarchy it's in, i.e. if it's already a main bullet point it will become a slide in its own right, with any associated sub-points becoming main points on that slide.

You can change the order of slides by dragging and dropping them, whether in Slides or Outline mode, or use Alt+Shift+Up Arrow or Alt+Shift+Down Arrow to move selected slides up or down.

Tip: To share PowerPoint 2007 files with users working with PowerPoint 2003, you can save your presentation in the PowerPoint 97–2003 format. Alternatively, users of versions of Office prior to Office 2007 can download a free file converter that enables them to open Office 2007 files. To save a presentation, press Ctrl+S or click on the Office Button and choose Save (or Save As, if you want to save in a different format or location, or want to change the file name).

Themes and color schemes

Whether you start with a predesigned template or a blank template, you can use themes and styles in the Design tab, and the Themes gallery lets you preview options and get a good idea of their effect before you select them.

You can apply a selected theme to selected slides or set a theme as your default presentation theme if you right-click on a Theme:

- in the Themes command set (under the Design tab), or
- in the Theme gallery that opens when you click on the More button in the Themes command set

You can easily modify themes and save them to the Themes gallery for later reuse, which is helpful if you have specific corporate colors that you'd like to use in your business presentations. To do this, first modify the slide and then click the Save Current Theme command at the bottom of the Themes gallery.

Choosing a New Color Scheme

When you select a color theme in PowerPoint 2007, the selection changes the background, all tables, text, and objects to match a consistent, coordinated, and cohesive set of colors.

The Colors command is in the Themes command set in the Design tab. Click the Colors down arrow to display the gallery of choices. Point to a new color selection to get a preview of how it will affect the current presentation, and click to apply it.

Background Styles and Slide Master Layouts

The Background Styles command, in the Background group

under the Design tab, provides a collection of background styles which you can apply to the current slide or to all of the slides in your presentation.

You can make additional choices for the background of your slides by clicking the Format Background command in the Background Styles gallery.

The Format Background dialog box that appears enables you to choose a picture or texture for the background, change colors and gradients for fills, etc.:

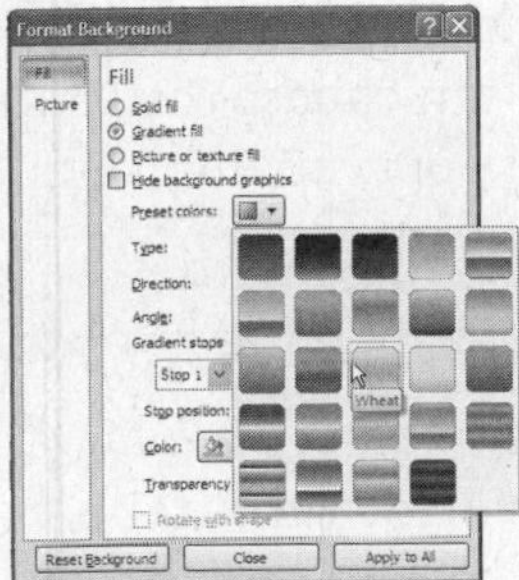

Custom Slide Master Layouts

In PowerPoint 2007, you can create custom slide master layouts. You can put placeholders (elements in position ready to be filled with media objects, text, etc.) on your custom slide master layout using Insert Placeholder in the Master Layout command tab of the Slide Master tab.

The Slide Master tab and the Insert Placeholder command become available when you select the SlideMaster command in the View tab.

Formatting text

Formatting text in PowerPoint is very similar to formatting text in Word. The Home tab has font and paragraph command sets, and the Mini Toolbar becomes available whenever text is selected or whenever you right-click on text:

In addition, text can be formatted via the Themes group under the Design tab. For example, you can choose the Fonts command to preview changes in a gallery of available fonts.

Tip: The Format Painter is a useful tool for copying the formatting already applied to any text and applying it to other bits of text.

To use the Format Painter, position the cursor within the word, line, or paragraph using the format that you'd like to copy and then double click the Format Painter command in the Home tab (or in the Mini Toolbar). You can then click on other words or drag over text elements (whole lines or paragraphs) to apply the same formatting to them. When done, click the Format Painter command again.

Text can also be modified via the WordArt Styles command set under the Format tab that appears whenever you click on or select text:

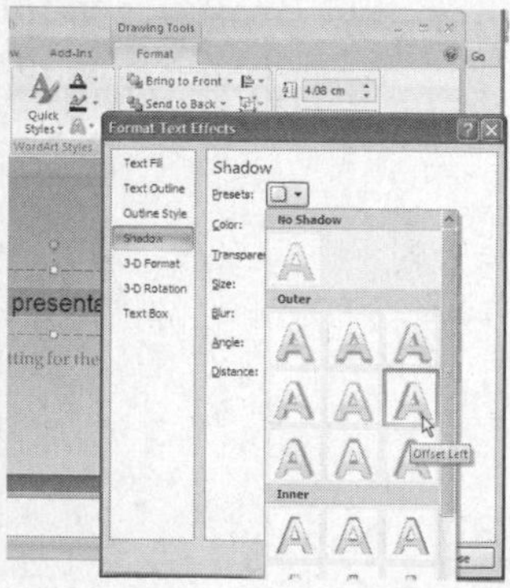

Shapes

Shapes are available from either the Drawing group under the Home tab, or the Illustrations group of the Insert tab (or from the Insert Shapes group of the Format tab, when available):

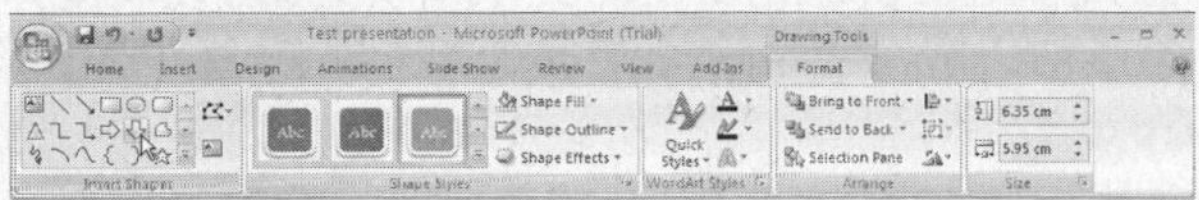

When you click on the Shapes command, a gallery appears for you to choose a shape from.

Once you've added a shape to your slide (or whenever such an object is selected), the Format tab appears, with a number of tools that enable you to work with the selected shape:

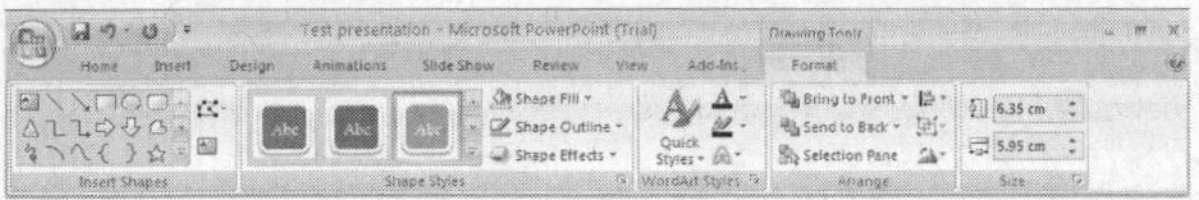

The Quick Styles command enables you to choose the lighting, color, style, and shadow of the shape and you can use WordArt Quick Styles to control the look of any text that you add to the shape. The Arrange and Size command sets give you options for the size and position of the object.

You can click on and drag the handles on a shape's placeholder (the small circles, squares, and diamonds on the outline that surrounds it when it's selected) to rotate, stretch, or resize it.

Diagram Tools

The SmartArt diagramming tool enables you to create flexible, customizable diagrams:

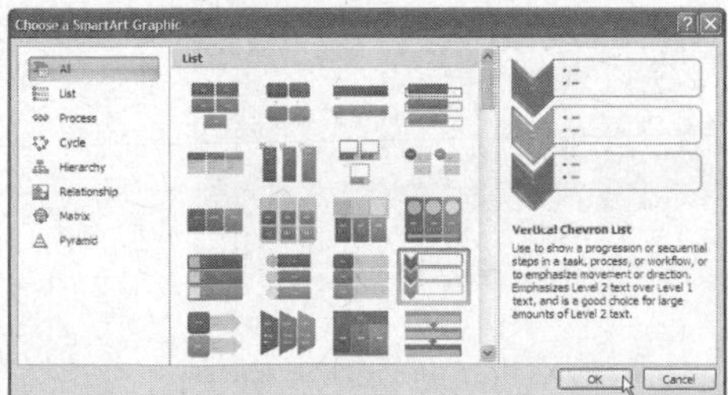

You can add diagrams to your slides by clicking the Insert tab and choosing SmartArt, or by clicking on the Insert SmartArt Graphic prompt on any new slide that has prompts for content.

Similarly, you can use the prompts on such new slides to add tables, charts, images you already have available as files, clip art, or media clips.

You can also easily convert text into a SmartArt diagram. Right-click the content area of a slide that has relevant text in it, hover over Convert to SmartArt, and then select the diagram type of your choice:

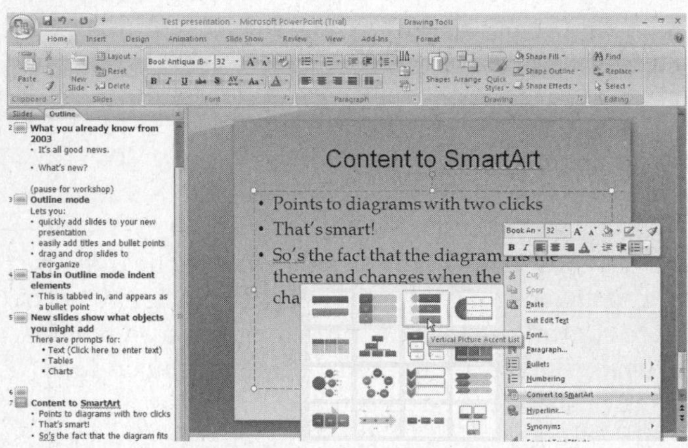

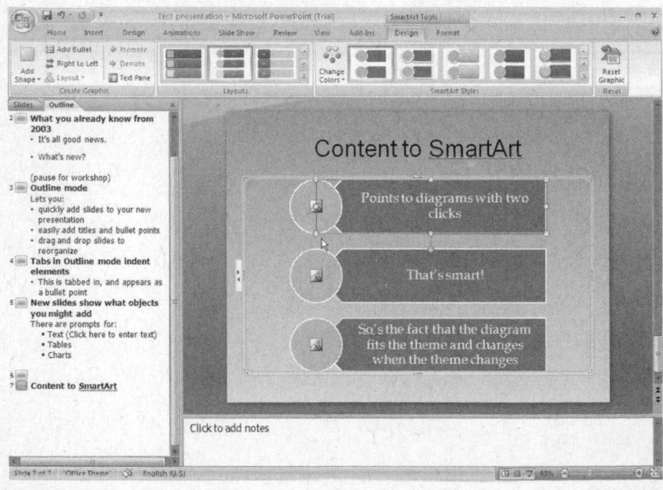

Transitions

Slide transitions are used to create a short pause between slides that helps to maintain the audience's interest and helps you to control the pace of your presentation. Beware of employing too much variety in transition effects within a single presentation, however. The use of different types of transitions can be distracting for your audience, who may go away remembering more about your transitions than your message. It may be tempting to pick a handful or more transitions from the nearly 60 offered by PowerPoint 2007, but it's much better to use just one or two transition effects so that audiences are not distracted from you, your presentation, and your message.

To create transitions, select a slide and click on the Animation tab, if it isn't already active. In the Transition to This Slide command set, click on the transitions already displayed in the Transition Scheme command, or click on its More button to display the gallery. Let the mouse pointer hover over an option to preview its effect and click to apply:

You can choose a sound effect from the same command set, as well as the speed.

If you'd like to apply the same transition to the whole presentation, click on the Apply to All command. When transitions are applied to a slide, a star appears on it in the navigation pane (in Slides mode, not Outline Mode) so that you can easily see if any slides are missing a transition. Finally, set whether you want the trigger for moving from one slide to the next to be a mouse click or a set period of time:

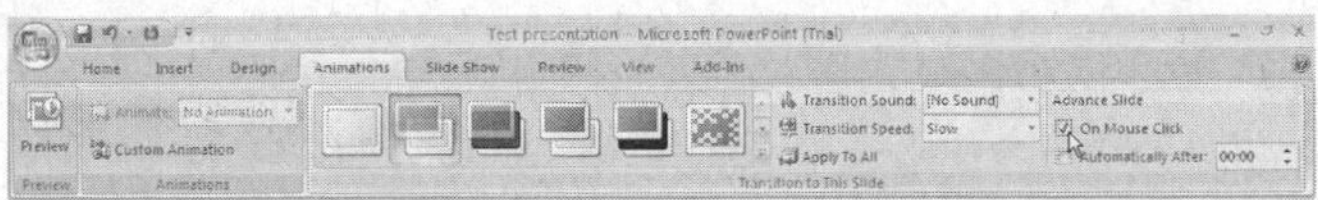

Animations

Animations should enhance your content, rather than distract from its message. It's also important to match animations

to your audience. For a young, creative audience, greater use of animation may be more appropriate than for a formal presentation to a board, for example.

A popular use of animation is to make bullet points appear one at a time, controlled by a click from the presenter. This is an effective strategy because it:

• Gives you control of the display of items in your presentation

• Prevents the audience from being distracted by points you're not talking about

• Enables you to hide surprize points until you are ready to reveal them

• Allows you to put emphasis on individual bullets

To create individual bullet animations, choose a slide with the bullets you'd like to animate and click the placeholder that contains them. In the Animations command set (under the Animation tab) click on the Custom Animation command:

The Custom Animation pane will display. Next, click Add Effect and choose the effect that you'd like to apply.

The effect is initially applied to all bullets. Click the expand Contents button and click the first bullet. To make the effect appear only when you click the mouse, click on the Change button and select Entrance, and then click the effect you want (again, possibly, if it's the same effect you chose earlier for all bullets). Next select the On Click option in the Start list for that button:

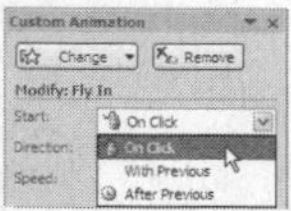

This will delay its appearance until you click with the mouse during the presentation.

Set the effects you want for the button in the Direction and Speed lists, also:

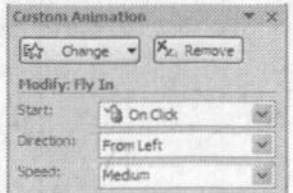

Do the same for the other bullets, making sure that they are numbered in the Start list in the order in which you would like them to appear. To preview the effect, click the Slide Show tab and then the From Current Slide command in the Start Slide Show command set:

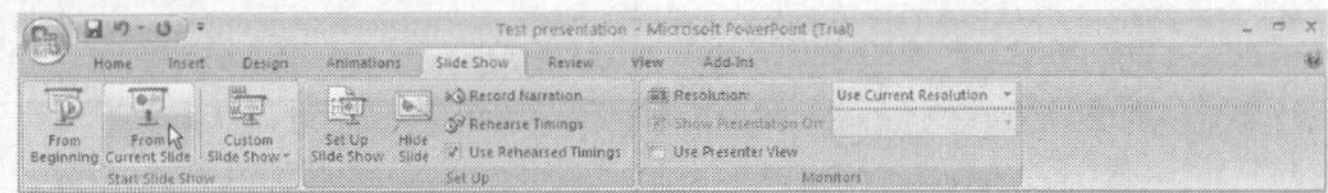

To leave the slide show and return to the PowerPoint window, press the Escape key.

Tips for PowerPoint presentations

The slides

- Match your presentation to your audience (see Animations, for example).
- Try to reflect any company color scheme or style in your presentation.
- Try to make slides consistent. Avoid using multiple typefaces and colors. Ensure that elements on every slide (such as the company logo) are always in the same place, so as not to distract your audience from the content. At the same time, try not to use the same layout on every slide, as this may become monotonous. So, for example, the first slide might be title only, the next, title and text, the following one, text and graphics, then diagram or table, etc., and so on.

• Resist the temptation to use fancy fonts. They can be difficult to read, especially from a distance.

• The font size you use will depend on the size of your screen and your audience's distance from it, but as a general rule, go for at least 20 point size.

• Make sure there is sufficient contrast between the font color and the background color. Yellow on white, for example, is nearly always a bad idea.

• Do not include too much information on each slide. As a general rule, 1–5 items is optimal (where a bullet point counts as one item).

You

• Try not to feel tied to a screen, or use a desk or lectern as a safety barrier. Move about freely and engage your audience.

• Ensure that you make eye contact with every part of your audience and, if appropriate, encourage them to answer questions and offer opinions during the presentation, rather that just at the end.

• Remember that you and your message are the main focus. The slides are there to support you.

• Practice your talk beforehand, and if possible videotape yourself. Reviewing the video will help to improve your technique; refined technique and well-rehearsed presentations help to build your confidence.